Main Cities
of Europe

2013

Contents

Dear reader,

Welcome to the 32th edition of the 'Main Cities of Europe' guide.

This guide is aimed primarily at the international business traveller who regularly journeys throughout Europe but it is equally ideal for those wishing to discover the delights of some of Europe's most romantic and culturally stimulating cities for a weekend break or special occasion.

Entry in the MICHELIN Guide is completely free of charge and it continues to be compiled by our professionally trained teams of full-time inspectors from across Europe who make their assessments anonymously in order to ensure complete impartiality and independence. Their mission is to check the quality and consistency of the amenities and services provided by the hotels and restaurants throughout the year and our listings are updated annually in order to ensure the most up-to-date information.

Most of the establishments featured have been hand-picked from our other national guides and therefore our European selection is, effectively, a best-of-the-best listing.

In addition to the user-friendly layout, the guide contains key thematic words which succinctly convey the style of the establishment; practical and cultural information on each country and each city; suggestions on when to go, what to see and what to eat.

Thank you for your support and please continue to send us your comments. We hope you will enjoy travelling with the 'Main Cities of Europe' guide 2013.

Consult the MICHELIN Guide at:
www.ViaMichelin.com
and write to us at:
themichelinguide-europe@uk.michelin.com

Classification & Awards

The MICHELIN Guide selection lists the best hotels and restaurants in each category of comfort and price. The establishments we choose are classified according to their levels of comfort and, within each category, are listed in order of preference.

🏨🏨🏨	XXXXX	Luxury in the traditional style
🏨🏨🏨	XXXX	Top class comfort
🏨🏨🏨	XXX	Very comfortable
🏨🏨	XX	Comfortable
🏨	X	Quite comfortable
🏠		Other recommended accommodation
without rest.		This hotel has no restaurant
with rm		This restaurant also offers accommodation

🍺	Pubs serving good food
♀/	Tapas bars

THE AWARDS

To help you make the best choice, some exceptional establishments have been given an award in this year's Guide. They are marked ✿ or ⊛.

THE BEST CUISINE

Michelin stars are awarded to establishments serving cuisine, of whatever style, which is of the highest quality. The cuisine is judged on the quality of ingredients, the skill in their preparation, the combination of flavours, the levels of creativity, the value for money and the consistency of culinary standards.

For every restaurant awarded a star we include 3 specialities that are typical of their cooking style. These specific dishes may not always be available.

✿✿✿ **Exceptional cuisine, worth a special journey**
One always eats extremely well here, sometimes superbly.

✿✿ **Excellent cooking, worth a detour**

✿ **A very good restaurant in its category**

RISING STARS

In certain years, "Rising Stars" are awarded to establishments which have the potential to become "one star", once the consistency of their cooking has been confirmed over a period of time. In this way we can share with you those restaurants that will be, in our opinion, the "Rising stars" of future gastronomy.

GOOD FOOD AT MODERATE PRICES

☺ **Bib Gourmand**
Establishments offering good quality cuisine at reasonable prices (the actual price limit varies from country to country according to the relative costs).

PLEASANT HOTELS AND RESTAURANTS

Symbols shown in red indicate particularly pleasant or restful establishments: the character of the building, its décor, the setting, the welcome and services offered may all contribute to this special appeal.

🏠 to 🏨🏨🏨🏨 **Pleasant hotels**
ⵝ to ⵝⵝⵝⵝⵝ **Pleasant restaurants**

OTHER SPECIAL FEATURES

As well as the categories and awards given to the establishment, Michelin inspectors also make special note of other criteria which can be important when choosing an establishment.

LOCATION

If you are looking for a particularly restful establishment, or one with a special view, look out for the following symbols:

🦢 🦢 **Quiet hotel / Very quiet hotel**
⟨ ⟨ **Interesting view / Exceptional view**

WINE LIST

If you are looking for an establishment with an excellent wine list, look out for the following symbol:

🍇 **Particularly interesting wine list**
This symbol might cover the list presented by a sommelier in a luxury restaurant or that of a simple restaurant where the owner has a passion for wine. The two lists will offer something exceptional but very different, so beware of comparing them by each other's standards.

Facilities & Services

30 rm	Number of rooms
AC	Air conditioning (in all or part of the establishment)
⧸	Establishment with areas reserved for non-smokers
♿	Establishment at least partly accessible to those of restricted mobility
🍽	Meals served in garden or on terrace
📞	Broadband Internet access in bedrooms
📶	Wireless Internet access in bedrooms
Spa	Wellness centre: an extensive facility for relaxation and well-being
♨ ⅃	Sauna – Exercise room
⊿ ⊠	Swimming pool: outdoor or indoor
⚘ ⊞	Park – Garden
✖	Tennis court
♟	Equipped conference room
⊡	Private dining rooms
☕	Restaurant offering lower priced pre and/or post theatre menus
🏵	Restaurant offering vegetarian menus (London)
⊶ 🚗	Valet parking – Garage
P P	Car park – Enclosed parking
Ⓜ	Nearest metro station
March-April	Dates when open, as indicated by the hotelier
AE Ⓓ	Credit cards accepted by the establishment:
⊕ *VISA*	American Express – Diners Club – MasterCard – Visa
⊿	Credit cards not accepted

Prices

The prices are given in the currency of the country in question. Valid for 2013 the rates shown should only vary if the cost of living changes to any great extent.

SERVICE AND TAXES

Except in Greece, Hungary, Poland and Spain, prices shown are inclusive, that is to say service and V.A.T. included. In the U.K. and Ireland, s = service included. In Italy, when not included, a percentage for service is shown after the meal prices, eg. (16 %).

MEALS

Meals 40/56	Set meal prices
Carte	'à la carte' meal prices
b.i.	House wine included

HOTEL

86 rm -♦ 650/750	Lowest and highest price for a comfortable single
♦♦ 750/890	and for a double room
28 rm ⌁ - **♦** 100 **♦♦** 180	Prices include breakfast
⌁ 20	Price of breakfast (where not included in rate)

Plan key

- ● Hotels
- ● Restaurants

SIGHTS

▬	Place of interest	🏛	Interesting place of worship

ROADS

▭	Motorway	❶	Junctions: complete
▭	Dual carriageway	❶	Junctions: limited
▭	Pedestrian street	🚉	Station and railway

VARIOUS SIGNS

🛈	Tourist Information Centre	✈	Airport
⬜⬜	Mosque	⊞	Hospital
▦▦	Synagogue	✉	Covered market
♣♣	Ruins	▭	Public buildings:
▬	Garden, Park, Wood	H	Town Hall
🚌	Coach station	R	Town Hall (Germany)
Ⓜ	Metro station	M	Museum
		U	University

11

The Michelin Adventure

It all started with rubber balls! This was the product made by a small company based in Clermont-Ferrand that André and Edouard Michelin inherited, back in 1880. The brothers quickly saw the potential for a new means of transport and their first success was the invention of detachable pneumatic tyres for bicycles. However, the automobile was to provide the greatest scope for their creative talents. Throughout the 20th century, Michelin never ceased developing and creating ever more reliable and high-performance tyres, not only for vehicles ranging from trucks to F1 but also for underground transit systems and aeroplanes.

From early on, Michelin provided its customers with tools and services to facilitate mobility and make travelling a more pleasurable and more frequent experience. As early as 1900, the Michelin Guide supplied motorists with a host of useful information related to vehicle maintenance, accommodation and restaurants, and was to become a benchmark for good food. At the same time, the Travel Information Bureau offered travellers personalised tips and itineraries.

The publication of the first collection of roadmaps, in 1910, was an instant hit! In 1926, the first regional guide to France was published, devoted to the principal sites of Brittany, and before long each region of France had its own Green Guide. The collection was later extended to more far-flung destinations, including New York in 1968 and Taiwan in 2011.

In the 21st century, with the growth of digital technology, the challenge for Michelin maps and guides is to continue to develop alongside the company's tyre activities. Now, as before, Michelin is committed to improving the mobility of travellers.

MICHELIN TODAY

WORLD NUMBER ONE TYRE MANUFACTURER
- 69 production sites in 18 countries
- 115,000 employees from all cultures and on every continent
- 6,000 people employed in research and development

Moving
for a world

Moving forward means developing tyres with better road grip and shorter braking distances, whatever the state of the road.

CORRECT TYRE PRESSURE

RIGHT PRESSURE

- Safety
- Longevity
- Optimum fuel consumption

-0,5 bar

- Durability reduced by 20% (- 8,000 km)

-1 bar

- Risk of blowouts
- Increased fuel consumption
- Longer braking distances on wet surfaces

forward together
where mobility is safer

It also involves helping motorists take care of their safety and their tyres. To do so, Michelin organises "Fill Up With Air" campaigns all over the world to remind us that correct tyre pressure is vital.

WEAR

DETECTING TYRE WEAR

MICHELIN tyres are equipped with tread wear indicators, which are small blocks of rubber molded into the base of the main grooves at a height of 1.6 mm. When tread depth is the same level as indicators, the tyres are worn and need replacing.

Tyres are the only point of contact between vehicle and the road, a worn tyre can be dangerous on wet surfaces.

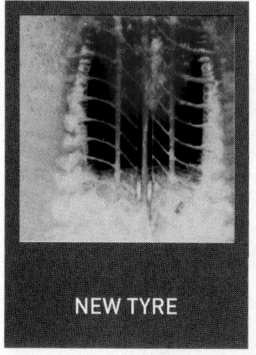

NEW TYRE

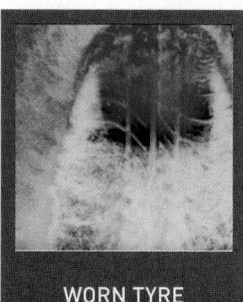

WORN TYRE
(1,6 mm tread)

The photo shows the actual contact zone on wet surfaces.

Moving forward
means sustainable mobility

By 2050, Michelin aims to cut the quantity of raw materials used in its tyre manufacturing process by half and to have developed renewable energy in its facilities. The design of MICHELIN tyres has already saved billions of litres of fuel and, by extension, billions of tonnes of CO2.

Similarly, Michelin prints its maps and guides on paper produced from sustainably managed forests and is diversifying its publishing media by offering digital solutions to make travelling easier, more fuel efficient and more enjoyable!

The group's whole-hearted commitment to eco-design on a daily basis is demonstrated by ISO 14001 certification.

Like you, Michelin is committed to preserving our planet.

Chat with Bibendum

Go to
www.michelin.com/corporate/fr
Find out more about Michelin's
history and the latest news.

QUIZ

Michelin develops tyres for all types of vehicles. See if you can match the right tyre with the right vehicle…

Solution : A-6 / B-4 / C-2 / D-1 / E-3 / F-7 / G-5

Selection by country

AUSTRIA
ÖSTERREICH

VIENNA ●

● Salzburg

→ **AREA:**
83 853 km²
(32 376 sq mi).

→ **POPULATION:**
8 219 743 inhabitants.
Density = 98 per km².

→ **CAPITAL:**
Vienna.

→ **CURRENCY:**
Euro (€).

→ **GOVERNMENT:**
Parliamentary republic and federal
state (since 1955). Member of
European Union since 1995.

→ **LANGUAGE:**
German.

→ **PUBLIC HOLIDAYS:**
New Years' Day (1 Jan); Epiphany
(6 Jan); Easter Monday (late Mar/
Apr); Labor Day (1 May); Ascension
Day (May); Whit Monday (late May/
June); Corpus Christi (late May/
June); Assumption of the Virgin
Mary (15 Aug); National Day
(26 Oct); All Saints' Day (1 Nov);
Immaculate Conception
(8 Dec); Christmas Day (25 Dec);
St Stephen's Day (26 Dec).

→ **LOCAL TIME:**
GMT+1 hour in winter and GMT+2
hours in summer.

→ **CLIMATE:**
Temperate continental with cold
winters - high snow levels - and
warm summers (Vienna: January
0°C; July 20°C).

→ **EMERGENCY:**
Police: ℘ **133**;
Medical Assistance: ℘ **144**;
Fire Brigade: ℘ **122.**
(Dialling **112** within any EU country
will redirect your call and contact
the emergency services.)

→ **ELECTRICITY:**
230 volts AC, 50Hz; 2 round pin
sockets.

→ **FORMALITIES:**
Travellers from the European Union
(EU), Switzerland, Iceland and the
main countries of North and South
America need a national identity
card or passport (America: passport
required) to visit Austria for less
than three months (tourism or
business purpose).
For visitors from other countries a
visa may be required, in addition
to a passport, especially for those
wishing to stay for longer than
three months. We advise you to
check with your embassy before
travelling.

VIENNA
WIEN

Population: 1 731 236

ReSeandra/Fotolia.com

Beethoven, Brahms, Mozart, Haydn, Strauss...not a bad list of former residents, by any stretch of the imagination. One and all, they succumbed to the opulent aura of Vienna, a city where an appreciation of the arts is as conspicuous as its famed cakes. Sumptuous architecture and a refined air reflect the city's historic position as the seat of the powerful Habsburg dynasty and former epicentre of the Austro-Hungarian Empire. Despite its grand image, Vienna has propelled itself into the 21C with a handful of innovative hotspots, most notably the MuseumsQuartier cultural complex, a stone's throw from the mighty Hofburg Imperial Palace. This is not a big city, although its vivid image gives that impression. The compact centre teems with elegant shops, fashionable coffee-houses and grand avenues, and the empire's awesome 19C remnants keep visitors' eyes fixed forever upwards. Many towns and cities are defined by their ring roads, but Vienna can boast a truly upmarket version: the Ringstrasse, a showpiece boulevard that cradles the inner city and the riches that lie therein. Just outside, to the southwest are the districts of Neubau and Spittelberg, both of which have taken on a quirky, modernistic feel. To the east lies Prater, the green lung of Vienna and further out lies the suburban area enhanced by the grandeur of the Schönbrunn palace.

VIENNA IN...

➜ **ONE DAY**
A tram ride round the Ringstrasse, St Stephen's Cathedral, a section of the Hofburg Palace, cakes in a café.

➜ **TWO DAYS**
MuseumsQuartier, Spittelberg, Hundertwasserhaus, Prater.

➜ **THREE DAYS**
A day at the Belvedere, a night at the opera.

PRACTICAL INFORMATION

ARRIVAL-DEPARTURE

✈ Wien-Schwechat Airport is 19km from the city centre.

The City Airport Express train to Wien Mitte takes 16min and leaves every 30min. A taxi will take around 30min.

GETTING AROUND

The city's buses, trams and metro are renowned for their impressive efficiency. You can purchase Rover tickets for 24hr or 72hr. There are around eighty bus routes in the city. Night buses run every half-hour; trams run every 5-10min and there are timetables at every stop. The Vienna Card, which allows unlimited travel on the whole of the city's public transport network for 72hr and offers a discount to sights, cafes, restaurants and shops, can be bought from the Tourist Office, at your hotel or from ticket offices of the Vienna Transport Authority.

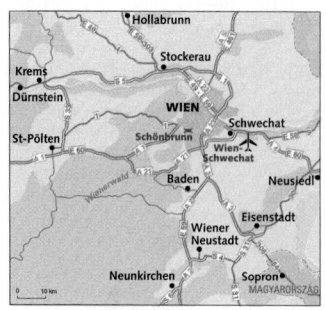

CALENDAR HIGHLIGHTS

January
New Year's Day Concert at the Musik-verein.

February
Opera Ball.

April
City Festival.

May
The Vienna Festival, International Music Festival.

July
Jazz Festival.

September
Literature Festival.

October
Viennale Film Festival.

November
Wien Modern Festival.

EATING OUT

Vienna is the spiritual home of the café and Austrians drink nearly twice as much coffee as beer. It is also a city with a sweet tooth: cream cakes enhance the window displays of most eateries and is there a visitor to Vienna who hasn't succumbed to the sponge of the Sachertorte? Viennese food is essentially the food of Bohemia, which means that meat has a strong presence on the plate. Expect beef, veal and pork, alongside potatoes, dumplings or cabbage - be sure to try traditional boiled beef and the ubiquitous Wiener schnitzel (deep-fried breaded veal). Also worth experiencing are the Heurigen, traditional Austrian wine taverns which are found in Grinzing, Heiligenstadt, Neustift and Nussdorf. You'll find plenty of snug cafés and bars too. If you want to snack, the place to go is Naschmarkt, Vienna's best market, where the stalls spill over into the vibrant little restaurants. When it comes to tipping, if you're in the more relaxed, local pubs and wine taverns, just round up the bill, otherwise add on ten per cent.

Palais Coburg Residenz 🚗 🈂 🈁 🖾 🕭 🗚 rm, 🛜 🗼 🚘

Coburgbastei 4 ⊠ 1010 – Ⓜ *Stubentor* 🔳 🆚 🔒 🔟
– ℰ (01) 51 81 80 – www.palais-coburg.com **E2**
35 suites 🖴 *–* ♦670/2700 € ♦♦670/2700 €
Rest *Gourmet Restaurant Silvio Nickol* ❀ ❀ – see restaurant listing
Rest *Basteigarten – ℰ (01) 51 81 88 70 –* Menu 53/68 € – Carte 37/88 € 🈯
♦ **Grand Luxury** ♦ **Historic** ♦ **Modern** ♦
Established in 1840 this magnificent building presents its guests with an impressive structure. Guests, who are housed in maisonettes or comfortable, luxurious suites, receive excellent service. This restaurant consists of a light and airy garden pavilion, a wine bar and a pretty bastion garden.

Imperial 🈂 🕭 🈁 🗚 🛜 🗼 🔳 🆚 🔒 🔟

Kärntner Ring 16 ⊠ 1015 – Ⓜ *Karlsplatz – ℰ (01) 50 11 00*
– www.imperialvienna.com **E3**
138 rm *–* ♦359/919 € ♦♦359/919 €, 🖴 39 € – 31 suites
Rest *Imperial – ℰ (01) 50 11 03 56 (dinner only) (booking advisable)*
Carte 51/84 €
Rest *Café Imperial – ℰ (01) 50 11 03 89 –* Carte 22/59 €
♦ **Palace** ♦ **Grand Luxury** ♦ **Historic** ♦
This grand hotel was opened in 1873 to celebrate Vienna's World Expo, and still promises all the majesty of the Austrian Empire in its splendid interior. The lobby is stylish, the dining rooms magnificent, and the rooms and suites lavish and elegant. Don't miss the fascinating 'Course of History'. The restaurant is decidedly upmarket and the Café Imperial is a classic Vienna coffee house.

Sacher 🕭 🈂 🕭 🗚 🛜 🗼 🚘 🔳 🆚 🔒 🔟

Philharmonikerstr. 4 ⊠ 1010 – Ⓜ *Karlsplatz – ℰ (01) 51 45 60 – www.sacher.com*
149 rm *–* ♦480/840 € ♦♦480/840 €, 🖴 35 € – 16 suites **D3**
Rest *Anna Sacher* – see restaurant listing
Rest *Rote Bar – ℰ (01) 51 45 68 41 –* Menu 58/86 € – Carte 48/79 €
♦ **Grand Luxury** ♦ **Classic** ♦ **Personalised** ♦
The rooms in this hotel dating back to 1876 are elegant and classic. They are also modern and equipped with all the latest technology. Even after extensive restoration work the traditional feel is still here, as is the attentive service. The suites and rooms on the top floor enjoy a wonderful roof terrace. The Rote Bar serves traditional fare including, of course, the famous Austrian sachertorte.

Grand Hotel 🈂 🕭 🕭 🗚 🛜 🗼 🚘 🔳 🆚 🔒

Kärntner Ring 9 ⊠ 1010 – Ⓜ *Karlsplatz – ℰ (01) 51 58 00*
– www.grandhotelwien.com **E3**
205 rm *–* ♦390/490 € ♦♦440/540 €, 🖴 32 € – 11 suites
Rest *Le Ciel*
Rest *Unkai* – see restaurant listing
Rest *Grand Café – ℰ (01) 5 15 80 91 20 –* Menu 32 € – Carte 30/54 €
♦ **Grand Luxury** ♦ **Classic** ♦
A truly classic grand hotel in a historical setting with a suitably imposing lobby. It offers elegant and sumptuously furnished rooms. Try the spacious corner suites. Don't miss the house speciality of Guglhupf: a delicious ring-shaped cake. The restaurant serves traditional cuisine best enjoyed on the pavement terrace.

The Ritz-Carlton 🈂 🕭 🕭 🈁 🗚 🛜 🗼 🚘 🔳 🆚 🔒 🔟

Schubertring 5 ⊠ 1010 – Ⓜ *Karlsplatz – ℰ (01) 3 11 88*
– www.ritzcarlton.com/vienna **E3**
202 rm *–* ♦325/550 € ♦♦325/550 €, 🖴 24 € – 20 suites
Rest *Dstrikt –* Carte 40/62 €
♦ **Business** ♦ **Grand Luxury** ♦ **Modern** ♦
The combination of historic setting and elegant modern interior is always appealing. Add the Ritz-Carlton's excellent service, a magnificent Guerlain Spa and first-class business facilities and it is even better. For a little extra exclusivity, book a room on the Club Floor, which has its own Club Lounge. And don't forget to try out the Atmosphere Rooftop Lounge & Bar!

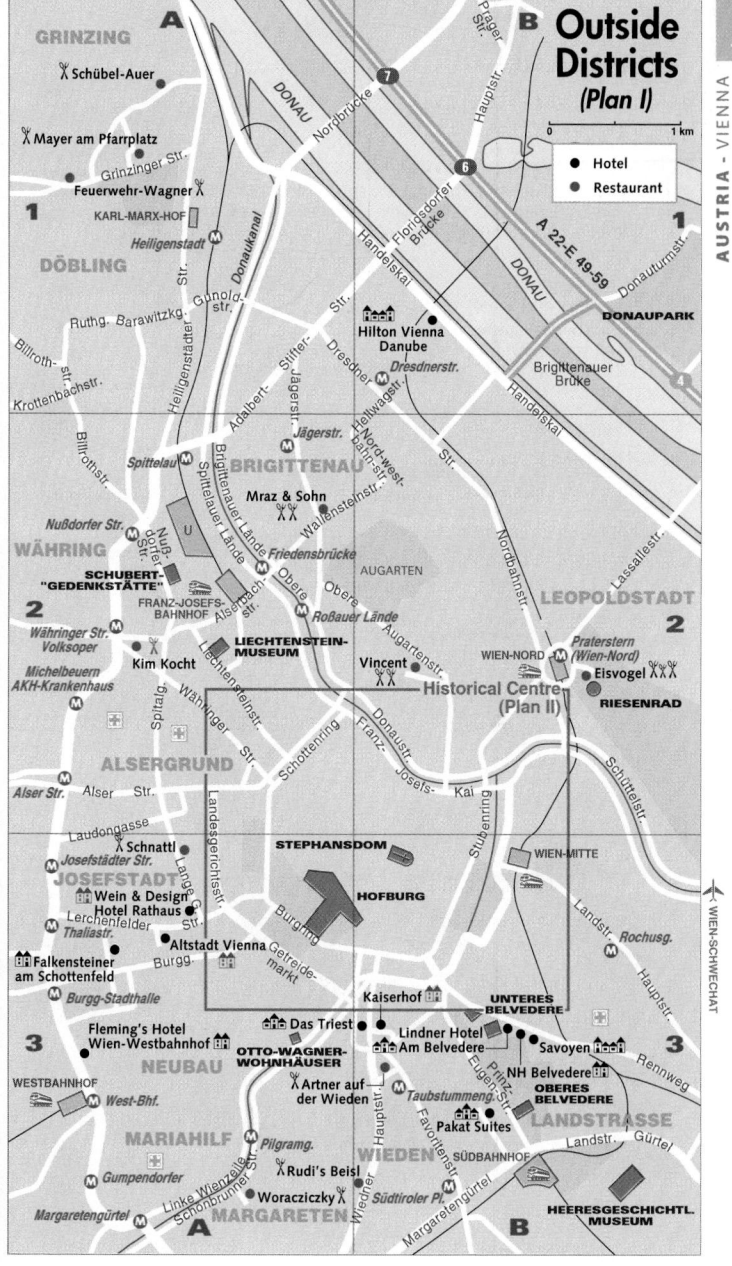

Outside Districts
(Plan I)

0   1 km

● Hotel
● Restaurant

GRINZING

Schübel-Auer

Mayer am Pfarrplatz

Feuerwehr-Wagner

KARL-MARX-HOF

Heiligenstadt

DÖBLING

Ruthg.   Barawitzkg.

Billroth-str.

Krottenbächstr.

Spittelau

Nußdorfer Str.

WÄHRING

SCHUBERT-
"GEDENKSTÄTTE"

FRANZ-JOSEFS-
BAHNHOF

Währinger Str.
Volksoper

Kim Kocht

Michelbeuern
AKH-Krankenhaus

ALSERGRUND

Alser Str.   Alser   Str.

Laudongasse

Schnattl
Josefstädter Str.

JOSEFSTADT

Wein & Design
Hotel Rathaus
Lerchenfelder
Thaliastr.

Altstadt Vienna

Falkensteiner
am Schottenfeld

Burgg.-Stadthalle

Fleming's Hotel
Wien-Westbahnhof

WESTBAHNHOF

West-Bhf.

NEUBAU

OTTO-WAGNER-
WOHNHÄUSER

MARIAHILF

Gumpendorfer

Margaretengürtel

DONAU

Nordbrücke

Grinzinger Str.

Heiligenstädter   Str.

Gunold.
str.

Donaukanal

BRIGITTENAU

Mraz & Sohn

Spittelauer Lände

Nußdorfer Str.

Friedensbrücke

Obere

Roßauer Lände

Obere Lände

AUGARTEN

Augartenstr.

LIECHTENSTEIN-
MUSEUM

Vincent

Historical Centre
(Plan II)

STEPHANSDOM

HOFBURG

Burgring

Getreide-
markt

Kaiserhof

Das Triest

Lindner Hotel
Am Belvedere

Artner auf
der Wieden

Taubstummeng.

WIEDEN

Pilgramg.

Rudi's Beisl

Woraczizcky

Südtiroler Pl.

MARGARETEN

Linke Wienzeile

Schönbrunner

Prager
Str.

Hauptstr.

Floridsdorfer
Brücke

Handelskai

A 22-E 49-59

DONAU

Donauturmstr.

DONAUPARK

Brigittenauer
Brücke

Handelskai

Lassallestr.

LEOPOLDSTADT

Praterstern
(Wien-Nord)

WIEN-NORD

Eisvogel

RIESENRAD

Schüttelstr.

WIEN-MITTE

Landstr.   Rochusg.

Stubenring

UNTERES
BELVEDERE

Savoyen

NH Belvedere

OBERES
BELVEDERE

LANDSTRASSE

Rennweg

Hauptstr.

Gürtel

SÜDBAHNHOF

Pakat Suites

Landstr.

HEERESGESCHICHTL.
MUSEUM

Margaretengürtel

Hilton Vienna
Danube

Dresdnerstr.

Jägerstr.

Nordwest-
bahn-Str.

Hellwagstr.

Nordbahnstr.

Dresdner
Str.

Stifter-
str.

Adalbert-
str.

Jägerstr.

WIEN-SCHWECHAT

25

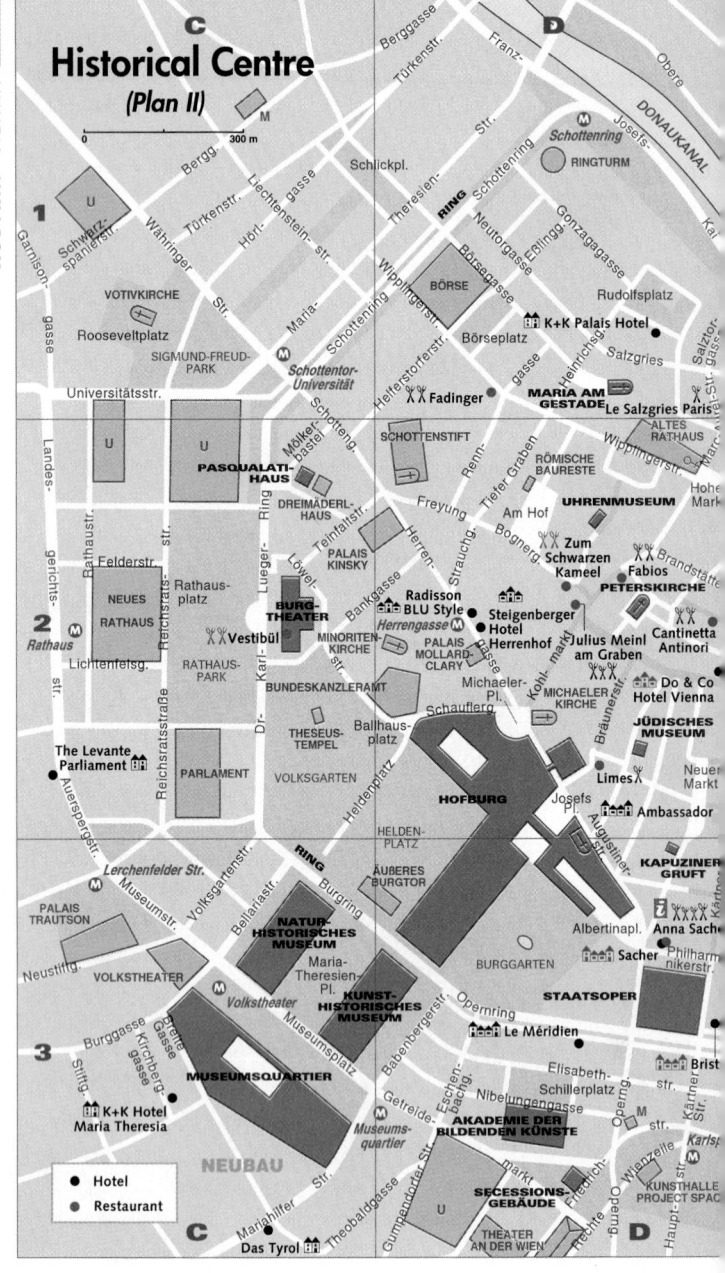

Historical Centre
(Plan II)

0   300 m

- Hotel
- Restaurant

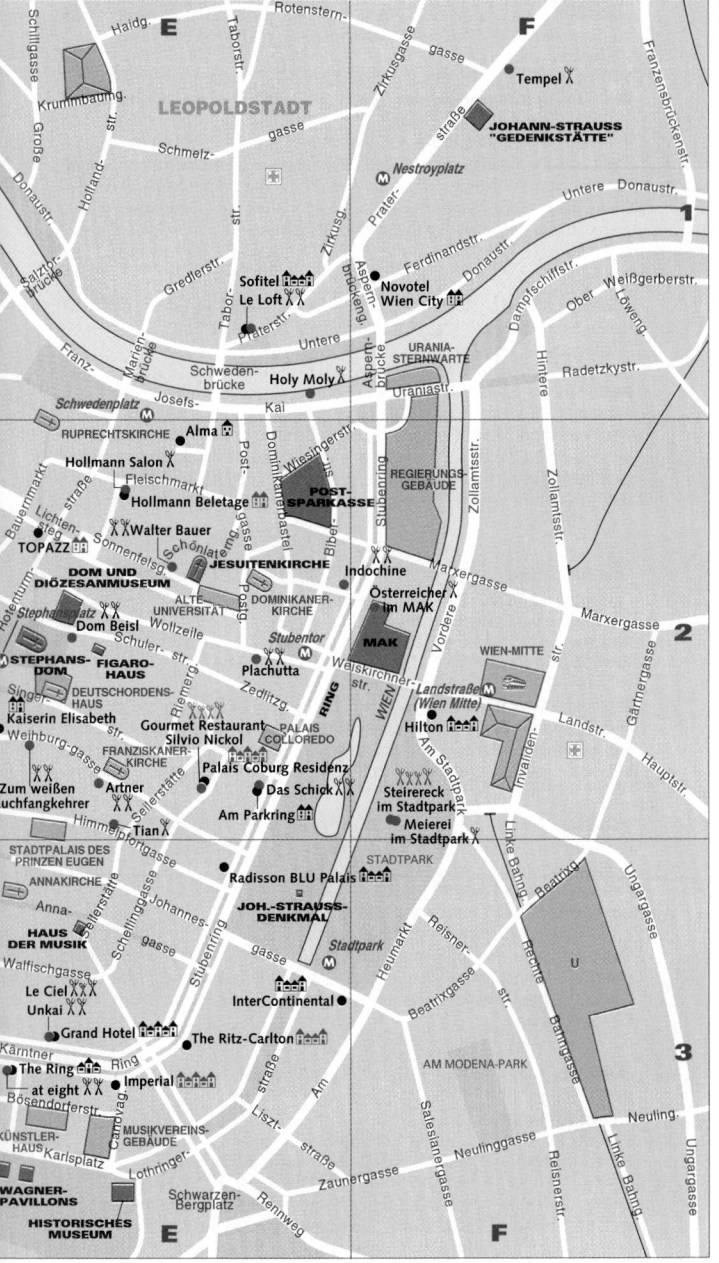

Bristol
🏠 ƒ�is ṡ 🅰 🛜 Ⅲ 🆅🅸🆂🅰 🆇🆇 🅰🅴 ⓪

Kärntner Ring 1 ✉ *1010 –* Ⓜ *Karlsplatz –* ☎ *(01) 51 51 60*
– www.bristolwien.at   **D3**
140 rm – 🛏245/800 € 🛏🛏275/800 €, ⊡ 35 € – 10 suites
Rest *Das Restaurant bei der Oper* – ☎ *(01) 51 51 65 46* – Menu 48/68 €
– Carte 33/68 €
◆ Luxury ◆ Traditional ◆ Classic ◆
This traditional hotel is run with dedication and Viennese charm. It has a number of lovely old lounges, which underscore the historical setting. The Opera Suites facing the Staatsoper really do live up to their name, while the Prince of Wales Suite is genuinely stately. Siegfried Kröpfl serves classic cuisine at restaurant.

Savoyen
ƒ�is 🐾 ṡ 🅰 ☏ 🆂🅰 🚗 🆅🅸🆂🅰 🆇🆇 🅰🅴 ⓪

Rennweg 16 ✉ *1030 –* Ⓜ *Karlsplatz –* ☎ *(01) 20 63 30*
– www.austria-trend.at/sav   *Plan I* **B3**
309 rm – 🛏128/300 € 🛏🛏128/300 €, ⊡ 22 € – 43 suites
Rest – Menu 29/41 € – Carte 30/50 €
◆ Luxury ◆ Contemporary ◆
This hotel is housed in the most imposing building of the former government printing works. It boasts an impressive atrium-style lobby and good conference facilities (including the largest venue in Vienna at 1 100m^2), providing modern-style in a historic setting. The rooms on the seventh and eighth floors have balconies. The restaurant serves international cuisine.

Le Méridien
🏠 ƒ�is 🐾 ▢ ṡ 🅰 🛜 🆂🅰 🆅🅸🆂🅰 🆇🆇 🅰🅴 ⓪

Opernring 13 ✉ *1010 –* Ⓜ *Karlsplatz –* ☎ *(01) 58 89 00*
– www.lemeridienvienna.com   **D3**
294 rm – 🛏185/419 € 🛏🛏185/419 €, ⊡ 29 € – 17 suites
Rest *Shambala* – ☎ *(01) 5 88 90 70 00* – Carte 29/64 €
◆ Chain hotel ◆ Design ◆
Behind its classic façade, this hotel features modern design, a host of art works and a special lighting concept. See and be seen in the Moet Champagne Bar, which serves choice snacks and, of course, champagne! The bar also boasts a DJ from breakfast to dinner.

Sofitel
◁ ƒ�is ⊛ ṡ 🅰 🛜 🆂🅰 🚗 🆅🅸🆂🅰 🆇🆇 🅰🅴 ⓪

Praterstr. 1 ✉ *1020 –* Ⓜ *Schwedenplatz –* ☎ *(01) 90 61 60*
– www.sofitel-vienna-stephansdom.com   **E1**
182 rm – 🛏200/420 € 🛏🛏200/420 €, ⊡ 32 € – 25 suites
Rest *Le Loft* – see restaurant listing
◆ Luxury ◆ Business ◆ Design ◆
This hotel is the work of French architect Jean Nouvel. It offers a harmonious blend of ultramodern urban style both inside and out. Its minimalist design has lots of glass, classic whites, greys and blacks – not to mention a unique view of Vienna.

Hilton
◁ 🏠 ƒ�is 🐾 ṡ 🅰 🛜 🆂🅰 🚗 🆅🅸🆂🅰 🆇🆇 🅰🅴 ⓪

Am Stadtpark 1 ✉ *1030 –* Ⓜ *Landstraße –* ☎ *(01) 71 70 00*
– www.hiltonaustria.com   **F2**
579 rm ⊡ – 🛏179/519 € 🛏🛏199/539 € – 23 suites
Rest *S' PARKS* – ☎ *(01) 71 70 01 21 20* – Carte 32/58 €
◆ Chain hotel ◆ Luxury ◆ Contemporary ◆
A large conference hotel with a central location offering an atrium-style lobby and modern rooms. The executive rooms and suites on the 10th to 15th floors offer superior accommodation, while the 12th floor houses the Executive Lounge. The roof has a lovely terrace with wonderful views. Fish market buffet on Fridays and brunch on Sundays.

AUSTRIA - VIENNA

 InterContinental

Johannesgasse 28 ⊠ *1037 –* **Ⓜ** *Stadtpark – ℰ (01) 71 12 20*
– www.vienna.intercontinental.com   **E3**
459 rm – ♦179/399 € ♦♦179/399 €, ⌼ 32 € – 15 suites
Rest *– (dinner only)* Carte 31/69 €
♦ Chain hotel ♦ Business ♦ Classic ♦
This business hotel close to the Stadtpark has a tasteful, elegant lobby and
extensive conference facilities. If you are looking for that little something extra,
try the 140m² Presidential Suite on the 12th floor with its wonderful views over
the city. The culinary delights on offer include a champagne lunch on Sundays
(from September to May).

 Radisson BLU Palais

Parkring 16 ⊠ *1010 –* **Ⓜ** *Stadtpark – ℰ (01) 51 51 70*
– www.radissonblu.com/palaishotel-vienna   **E3**
247 rm – ♦179/199 € ♦♦179/199 €, ⌼ 28 € – 9 suites   **Rest** – Carte 40/80 €
♦ Chain hotel ♦ Luxury ♦ Classic ♦
The decor in both the two residential buildings, Leitenberger and Donners-
marck, and in the Le Siècle restaurant is stylish. Everything fits perfectly with
the historic setting. Try the flotation tanks, which are the speciality of the Ven-
dome Spa. Located opposite the Stadtpark.

 Ambassador

Kärntner Str. 22 ⊠ *1010 –* **Ⓜ** *Stephansdom – ℰ (01) 96 16 10*
– www.ambassador.at   **D2**
89 rm – ♦262/480 € ♦♦332/602 €, ⌼ 25 € – 4 suites
Rest *– (closed Saturday lunch and Sunday lunch)* Carte 29/48 €
♦ Townhouse ♦ Classic ♦
The Ambassador is one of the city's most venerable institutions. The style is
resolutely traditional, although never at the expense of modern comfort. It has
marble columns in the atrium lobby and most of the rooms feature antique furniture. The themed rooms are dedicated to famous celebrities.

 The Ring

Kärntner Ring 8 ⊠ *1010 –* **Ⓜ** *Karlsplatz – ℰ (01) 22 12 20 – www.theringhotel.com*
68 rm – ♦330/450 € ♦♦380/500 €, ⌼ 31 € – 1 suite   **E3**
Rest *at eight* – see restaurant listing
♦ Townhouse ♦ Modern ♦ Contemporary ♦
This modern, well-run business hotel is housed in a historic townhouse. It has a
luxurious touch and a pleasant, informal atmosphere. The heritage protected lift
is not to be missed.

 Do & Co Hotel Vienna

Stephansplatz 12 (6 th floor) ⊠ *1010 –* **Ⓜ** *Stephansplatz – ℰ (01) 2 41 88*
– www.doco.com   **D2**
43 rm – ♦245/380 € ♦♦245/380 €, ⌼ 29 € – 2 suites   **Rest** – Carte 35/60 €
♦ Business ♦ Design ♦ Stylish ♦
This fashionable, highly individual designer hotel sits right opposite St Stephen's Cathedral. The rooms are modern, functional yet comfortable, and the
smokers' bar is one of the places to be seen in Vienna. The show kitchen on
the seventh floor serves southeast Asian cuisine accompanied by great views
from both the restaurant and terrace.

Steigenberger Hotel Herrenhof

Herrengasse 10 ⊠ *1010 –* **Ⓜ** *Herrengasse*
– ℰ (01) 53 40 40 – www.steigenberger.com/wien   **D2**
196 rm – ♦175/295 € ♦♦175/295 €, ⌼ 28 €
Rest *– (closed 2 weeks early August and Saturday lunch, Sunday)*
Menu 50/75 € – Carte 35/65 €
♦ Townhouse ♦ Historic ♦ Contemporary ♦
This hotel is housed in a former boarding school with a grand 1913 façade. It
offers contemporary rooms that appeal to business guests and holidaymakers
alike. The restaurant, decorated with striking splashes of purple, serves Viennese
cuisine alongside international dishes.

Radisson BLU Style   Ⅰ₅ 🏠 ⅙ 𝔸ℂ rm, 🛜 🚗 𝚅𝙸𝚂𝙰 ⓪ 𝙰𝙴 ⓪

Herrengasse 12 ✉ 1010 – Ⓜ Herrengasse – ℰ (01) 22 78 00
– www.radissonblu.com/stylehotel-vienna   **D2**
78 rm ☷ – ♦188/395 € ♦♦211/395 €
Rest *Sapori – (closed July-August, Saturday-Sunday and Bank Holidays)*
Carte 28/44 €

♦ Townhouse ♦ Historic ♦ Design ♦

Cosmopolitan-style and high quality materials right up into the eaves characterise this former bank building. Even the old vault doors in the gym have been
retained! If you like international cuisine, try the Sapori restaurant.

Das Triest   🏠 Ⅰ₅ 🏠 ⅙ rest, 𝔸ℂ 🛜 🚗 𝚅𝙸𝚂𝙰 ⓪ 𝙰𝙴 ⓪

Wiedner Hauptstr. 12 ✉ 1040 – Ⓜ Karlsplatz – ℰ (01) 58 91 80
– www.dastriest.at   *Plan I* **B3**
72 rm ☷ – ♦232 € ♦♦299/393 € – 2 suites
Rest *Collio – ℰ (01) 58 91 81 33 (closed 1-6 January, 5-18 August, Satur-*
day lunch, Sunday and Bank Holidays) Menu 45/50 € (dinner)
– Carte 29/53 €

♦ Business ♦ Design ♦

The clean-cut lines of this designer hotel, with its homely rooms, are the work of
Sir Terence Conran. The hotel is a former post station on the Vienna-Trieste run.
This modern restaurant serves Italian cuisine in an attractive interior courtyard.

Lindner Hotel Am Belvedere   Ⅰ₅ 🏠 ⅙ 𝔸ℂ 🛜 🏊 🚗

Rennweg 12 ✉ 1030 – Ⓜ Karlsplatz – ℰ (01)   𝚅𝙸𝚂𝙰 ⓪ 𝙰𝙴 ⓪
79 47 70 – www.lindnerhotels.at   *Plan I* **B3**
219 rm – ♦89/199 € ♦♦109/219 €, ☷ 21 € – 1 suite
Rest *TASTE IT! – ℰ (01) 74 97 70 (closed Sunday)* Menu 17 € (lunch)/57 €
– Carte 30/50 €
Rest *Heuriger Am Belvedere – (Monday to Saturday dinner only)*
Carte 26/35 €

♦ Business ♦ Modern ♦

This hotel offers a perfect blend of contemporary style, quality and technology.
If you like your privacy, try one of the individual saunas in the wellness suite. The
leisure area on the seventh floor offers great views of the Belvedere Castle. The
restaurant 'Taste it!' serves international and Euro-Asian fusion cuisine. The
modern yet rustic 'Heurigen Am Belvedere' serves regional fare.

TOPAZZ *without rest*   ⅙ 𝔸ℂ 🛜 🏊 𝚅𝙸𝚂𝙰 ⓪ 𝙰𝙴 ⓪

Lichtensteg 3 ✉ 1010 – Ⓜ Stephansplatz – ℰ (01) 5 32 22 50
– www.hoteltopazz.com   **E2**
32 rm – ♦208/378 € ♦♦208/378 €, ☷ 25 €

♦ Business ♦ Luxury ♦ Design ♦

The façade at Topazz looks as if it has been set with precious stones. The interior
is equally exclusive, boasting an elegant design and muted colour scheme, as
well as a 'Privileged Club Service', which meets the very highest standards. The
latter includes a special bed system, free mini-bar and revitalised Grander water,
an à-la-carte breakfast with homemade specialities, free afternoon drinks in the
salon, and much more.

The Levante Parliament   🏠 Ⅰ₅ 🏠 𝔸ℂ 🛜 🏊 🚗

Auerspergstr. 9 ✉ 1080 – Ⓜ Rathaus – ℰ (01)   𝚅𝙸𝚂𝙰 ⓪ 𝙰𝙴 ⓪
22 82 80 – www.thelevante.com   **C2**
67 rm ☷ – ♦150/290 € ♦♦175/335 €
Rest *nemtoi – (closed Sunday and Bank Holidays)* Carte 24/45 €

♦ Townhouse ♦ Design ♦ Modern ♦

Glassworks by Ioan Nemtoi and original photographs by Curt Themessl blend
beautifully into this stylish, urban boutique hotel. It offers good service, a great
location and modern rooms. Relax in the comfortable lounge in the interior
courtyard or enjoy the international cuisine served in the restaurant.

AUSTRIA - VIENNA

Kaiserhof without rest 🔥 🐾 AC 🛜 ⚡ 🚗 VISA ⬤⬤ AE ⓪

Frankenberggasse 10 ✉ *1040* – ⓜ *Karlsplatz* – ℰ *(01) 5 05 17 01 89*
– www.hotel-kaiserhof.at   *Plan I* **B3**
74 rm ☶ – †125/175 € ††159/209 € – 3 suites
◆ Traditional ◆ Art Deco ◆ Modern ◆
Remarkable friendly service, Viennese charm, and a tasteful juxtaposition of
modern and classic features characterise this beautiful 1896 hotel. There is a
lovely breakfast room with a buffet service. Snack menu in the bar.

Hotel Rathaus - Wein & Design without rest AC 🛜 ⚡

Lange Gasse 13 ✉ *1080* – ⓜ *Rathaus* – ℰ *(01)*   VISA ⬤⬤ AE ⓪
4 00 11 22 – *www.hotel-rathaus-wien.at*
– Closed 23-26 December   *Plan I* **A3**
40 rm – †120/150 € ††160/210 €, ☶ 17 € – 1 suite
◆ Townhouse ◆ Historic ◆ Design ◆
The atmosphere at this hotel is immediately relaxing and homely thanks first
and foremost to the wonderful service. The building itself also has its charms
with its historical façade and modern interior. Breakfast is an impressively generous buffet, which can be enjoyed in the pretty interior courtyard. There is also a
wine bar with a selection of some 450 Austrian wines.

Hollmann Beletage 🐾 AC 🛜 ⚡ VISA ⬤⬤ AE ⓪

Köllnerhofgasse 6 (2nd floor) ✉ *1010* – ⓜ *Stephansplatz* – ℰ *(01)*
9 61 19 60 – *www.hollmann-beletage.at*   **E2**
26 rm ☶ – †150/200 € ††150/220 € – 1 suite
Rest *Hollmann Salon* – see restaurant listing
◆ Townhouse ◆ Design ◆ Modern ◆
An upmarket boutique hotel, the Hollmann Beletage combines ornate mid-19C
architecture and a friendly, modern atmosphere. It offers a leafy terrace in the
interior courtyard, a small cinema (complete with popcorn machine), afternoon
cakes and patisseries for residents... and an iPad for the length of your stay!
Don't miss the 93m². Séparée Suite complete with its own hammam.

Kaiserin Elisabeth without rest AC 🛜 ⚡ VISA ⬤⬤ AE ⓪

Weihburggasse 3 ✉ *1010* – ⓜ *Stephansplatz* – ℰ *(01) 51 52 60*
www.kaiserinelisabeth.at   **E2**
63 rm ☶ – †126/138 € ††195/220 €
◆ Traditional ◆ Classic ◆
This hotel has been welcoming guests for over 200 years. This long history is
reflected in the classic decor, which includes paintings by Elisabeth and Kaiser
Franz in the stylish lobby. The superior rooms are particularly comfortable. Why
not try some of the delicious Kaiserschmarrn for breakfast?

Novotel Wien City 🏖 🔥 🐾 ⚜ AC 🛜 ⚡ 🚗 VISA ⬤⬤ AE ⓪

Aspernbrückengasse 1 ✉ *1020* – ⓜ *Nestroyplatz* – ℰ *(01) 9 03 03*
– www.novotel.com   **F1**
124 rm – †119/243 € ††119/243 €, ☶ 17 € – 2 suites
Rest – Carte 21/48 €
◆ Chain hotel ◆ Modern ◆
This modern business hotel is located right on the Aspern bridge. It offers seminar facilities and some executive rooms complete with French-style balcony terraces and great views on the top floor. The '5 Senses' restaurant offers a convenient 'Quick Lunch Menu'.

K+K Hotel Maria Theresia without rest 🐾 AC 🛜 ⚡ 🚗

Kirchberggasse 6 ✉ *1070* – ⓜ *Volkstheater*   VISA ⬤⬤ AE ⓪
– ℰ (01) 5 21 23 – www.kkhotels.com   **C3**
132 rm ☶ – †150/250 € ††175/290 €
◆ Business ◆ Functional ◆
Located in arty Spittelberg, this hotel offers functional rooms. Ask for one with a
view over the city. The spacious lobby has a bar that serves a small menu.

AUSTRIA - VIENNA

Falkensteiner Am Schottenfeld without rest   🕸 AC 🤝 ⚙

Schottenfeldgasse 74 ✉ *1070*   🚗 VISA 🌐 AE ①
– ⓜ *Burggasse Stadthalle* – ℰ *(01) 5 26 51 81*
– *www.schottenfeld.falkensteiner.com*   *Plan I* **A3**
144 rm – ♦99/210 € ♦♦99/230 €, ⌑ 17 € – 1 suite
♦ Business ♦ Functional ♦
This hotel offers good service for business guests but is also popular with holidaymakers due to its contemporary feel. Fans of the loft-style should book one
of the deluxe rooms in a former factory building in the interior courtyard.

Altstadt Vienna without rest   AC 🤝 ⚙ VISA 🌐 AE ①

Kirchengasse 41 ✉ *1070* – ⓜ *Volkstheater* – ℰ *(01) 5 22 66 66*
– *www.altstadt.at*   *Plan I* **A3**
45 rm ⌑ – ♦125/175 € ♦♦145/185 € – 9 suites
♦ Historic ♦ Design ♦ Personalised ♦
From the outside you would never guess the tasteful and individual mix of art,
design and charm behind the façade of this pretty Viennese patrician house.
Every room is different.

Das Tyrol without rest   🕸 AC 🤝 🚗 VISA 🌐 AE ①

Mariahilfer Str. 15 ✉ *1060* – ⓜ *Museumsquartier* – ℰ *(01) 5 87 54 15*
– *www.das-tyrol.at*   **C3**
30 rm ⌑ – ♦109/229 € ♦♦149/299 €
♦ Townhouse ♦ Personalised ♦
This hotel is housed in a beautifully restored corner building. It offers attractive
and modern guestrooms, an excellent breakfast, and a small sauna decorated in
gold tones. Contemporary art hangs on the walls throughout the hotel.

Am Parkring   ≤ AC 🤝 ⚙ 🚗 VISA 🌐 AE ①

Parkring 12 ✉ *1010* – ⓜ *Stubentor* – ℰ *(01) 51 48 00*
– *www.schick-hotels.com*   **E2**
58 rm ⌑ – ♦114/196 € ♦♦160/292 € – 8 suites
Rest *Das Schick* – see restaurant listing
♦ Business ♦ Functional ♦
This hotel is located opposite the Stadtpark and on the upper floors of Vienna's
high-rise Gartenbauhochhaus. It offers modern rooms with great views over
Vienna, some of which have balconies. Be sure to ask for a room on the 13th
floor.

Fleming's Hotel Wien-Westbahnhof   ♨ 🕸 ♿ AC 🤝 ⚙

Neubaugürtel 26 ✉ *1070* – ⓜ *West-Bahnhof*   VISA 🌐 AE ①
– ℰ *(01) 22 73 70* – *www.flemings-hotels.com*   *Plan I* **A3**
173 rm ⌑ – ♦89/359 € ♦♦105/375 € – 2 suites   **Rest** – Carte 25/51 €
♦ Business ♦ Contemporary ♦
The business hotel close to the west railway station has been maintained in a
thoroughly modern style. All the rooms possess glassed-in bathrooms. Restaurant with a brasserie-style atmosphere.

NH Belvedere without rest   ♨ 🕸 AC 🤝 ⚙ VISA 🌐 AE ①

Rennweg 12a ✉ *1030* – ⓜ *Karlsplatz* – ℰ *(01) 2 06 11*
– *www.nh-hotels.com*   *Plan I* **B3**
114 rm – ♦99/280 € ♦♦99/280 €, ⌑ 17 €
♦ Chain hotel ♦ Functional ♦
This hotel in the classicist building of the former State Printing Office offers
modern rooms, some with views over the Botanical Gardens. Bistro with snacks.

K+K Palais Hotel without rest   AC 🤝 VISA 🌐 AE ①

Rudolfsplatz 11 ✉ *1010* – ⓜ *Schwedenplatz* – ℰ *(01) 5 33 13 53*
– *www.kkhotels.com*   **D1**
66 rm ⌑ – ♦150/250 € ♦♦175/290 €
♦ Traditional ♦ Contemporary ♦ Cosy ♦
A pleasant city hotel with a magnificent historical façade. It has an interior that is
comfortably decorated in clean lines and warm colours. The rooms facing the
Rudolfsplatz are particularly good.

AUSTRIA - VIENNA

🏠 **Alma** without rest   AC 📶 🚗 VISA ⓪ AE ⓪
Hafnersteig 7 ⊠ 1010 – Ⓜ Schwedenplatz – ℰ (01) 5 33 29 61
– www.hotel-alma.com   E2
26 rm ⌂ – †91/134 € ††134/182 €
♦ Business ♦ Townhouse ♦ Modern ♦
This thoroughly modern hotel is located in a narrow side street and has convenient parking just 3min away. It offers deluxe rooms with whirlpools, a small terrace with a Jacuzzi, and a wonderful view over Vienna from the roof. Water, tea and coffee are free all day.

XXXX **Steirereck im Stadtpark** (Heinz Reitbauer)   🌿 ⭐ AC ⟷
🕸🕸 *Am Heumarkt 2a ⊠ 1030 – Ⓜ Stadtpark*   VISA ⓪ AE ⓪
– ℰ (01) 7 13 31 68 – www.steirereck.at
– Closed Saturday-Sunday and Bank Holidays   F2
Rest – *(booking essential)* Menu 65 € (lunch)/128 € – Carte 70/100 € 🍴
Rest *Meierei im Stadtpark* 🌿 – see restaurant listing
♦ Creative ♦ Design ♦ Formal ♦
Creative and full of contrasts, the dishes served up at Steirereck by Heinz Reitbauer are of the very highest quality. One of Austria's greatest chefs, Reitbauer sets great store by regional and seasonal produce. The light, airy and elegant setting could hardly be more fitting. Ditto his charming partner who is in charge front-of-house. To cap it all the homemade bread is a dream!
➔ Saibling im Bienenwachs mit gelber Rübe, Pollen & Rahm. Gebratene Taube mit Petersilie, Amaranth, Hirse & Sesam. Java Kaffee mit gelben Datteln, Zwetschken & Zimtblüten.

XXXX **Gourmet Restaurant Silvio Nickol** – Hotel Palais Coburg Residenz
🕸🕸 *Coburgbastei 4 ⊠ 1010 – Ⓜ Stubentor*   🌿 ⭐ AC ⟷ VISA ⓪ AE ⓪
– ℰ (01) 51 81 88 00 – www.palais-coburg.com
– Closed 19 February-2 March, 4-26 August and Sunday-Monday
Rest – *(dinner only) (booking advisable)* Menu 137/168 €   E2
– Carte 119/147 € 🍴
♦ Modern ♦ Elegant ♦ Luxury ♦
A truly upmarket restaurant experience awaits beneath the lovingly restored vaulted ceiling of this restaurant. It offers exquisite table settings and the choice of Silvio Nickol's 'Chef's Menu' or a seasonal alternative (for example, 'Colourful Autumn'). There is also a unique selection of over 5 000 wines! Two 'chef's tables' offer live CCTV coverage of work in the kitchen.
➔ "Wald" - Entenleber, Tannenwipfel, Moos. "Vogelfrei" - Rote Rübe, Perlhuhn, Walnuss. "Marmorkuchen" - Schokolade, Pistazie, Kiwi.

XXXX **Anna Sacher** – Hotel Sacher   ⭐ AC VISA ⓪ AE ⓪
Philharmonikerstr. 4 ⊠ 1010 – Ⓜ Karlsplatz – ℰ (01) 51 45 68 40
– www.sacher.com
– Closed July-August and Monday   D3
Rest – *(bookings advisable at dinner)* Menu 64/86 € – Carte 59/79 €
♦ Classic ♦ Luxury ♦
Sumptuously decorated in green and beautiful wood, the decor at this restaurant features original art works by Anton Faistauer. The cuisine is contemporary-classic with a reasonably priced two-course lunch.

XXX **Le Ciel** – Grand Hotel   🌿 ⭐ AC ⟷ VISA ⓪ AE
Kärntner Ring 9 (7th floor) ⊠ 1010 – Ⓜ Karlsplatz – ℰ (01) 5 15 80 91 00
– www.leciel.at
– Closed Sunday   E3
Rest – Menu 53/73 € – Carte 51/88 €
♦ Classic ♦ Elegant ♦
Le Ciel is an elegant restaurant on the seventh-floor with spacious dining rooms, elegant table service and a beautiful roof terrace. Exciting cuisine with a fair priced lunch menu.

Eisvogel

Riesenradplatz 5 (Prater) ✉ *1022 –* Ⓜ *Praterstern –* ☎ *(01) 9 08 11 87*
– www.stadtgasthaus-eisvogel.at *Plan I* **B2**
Rest *– (bookings advisable at dinner)* Menu 41/67 € – Carte 30/49 €
♦ Austrian ♦ Elegant ♦
This area close to the Big Wheel at the Prater amusement park is full of life
– why not treat yourself to an aperitif in the cocktail carriage (by reservation
only)? The flavoursome classic Austrian fare on offer in the restaurant contains
some contemporary Mediterranean touches.

Julius Meinl am Graben

Graben 19 (1st floor) ✉ *1010 –* Ⓜ *Stephansplatz*
– ☎ *(01) 5 32 33 34 60 00 – www.meinlamgraben.at*
– Closed 1-21 August, Sunday and Bank Holidays **D2**
Rest *– (booking essential)* Menu 47/93 € – Carte 60/73 € 🏶
♦ Classic ♦ Formal ♦
This restaurant and its sister delicatessen come to life early in the morning.
They serve ambitious cuisine using the finest quality ingredients from break-
fast through to dinner. This comes with a view over Vienna's pedestrian
zone.

Walter Bauer

Sonnenfelsgasse 17 ✉ *1010 –* Ⓜ *Stubentor –* ☎ *(01) 5 12 98 71*
– Closed 1-5 April, 22 July-16 August, Saturday-Monday lunch and Bank
Holidays **E2**
Rest *– (booking advisable)* Menu 79 € – Carte 47/68 € 🏶
♦ Classic ♦ Cosy ♦ Family ♦
This restaurant set in a narrow alleyway in the old town positively exudes Vien-
nese family charm. This is due in no small part to Walter Bauer who runs the
restaurant with great dedication and commitment. The food offers a modern
take on culinary classics. It is accompanied by an excellent list of wines from
Austria, France and Italy.
→ Gänseleberparfait mit Brioche. Geschmorter Ochsenschlepp mit Kartof-
felpüree. Variation von Sorbets und Eis.

Vestibül

Universitätsring 2 (at Burgtheater) ✉ *1010 –* Ⓜ *Herrengasse*
– ☎ *(01) 5 32 49 99 – www.vestibuel.at*
– Closed 1 week early January, 28 July-18 August, Saturday lunch, Sunday
and Bank Holidays **C2**
Rest *–* Menu 33 € (lunch)/59 € – Carte 28/68 € 🏶
♦ International ♦ Classic ♦ Brasserie ♦
Even though Christian Domschitz uses exclusively organic Austrian ingredients
in his cuisine, there is no substituting the lobster in his Szegediner lobster with
cabbage. Whatever else you eat here, don't miss this! The inimitable location in
the charming historical setting of Vienna's celebrated Burgtheater is equally striking. Good wines served by the magnum.

Mraz & Sohn

Wallensteinstr. 59 ✉ *1200 –* Ⓜ *Friedensbrücke –* ☎ *(01) 3 30 45 94*
– www.mraz-sohn.at
– Closed 25 March-2 April, 12-30 August, 24 December-7 January, Saturday
- Sunday and Bank Holidays *Plan I* **A2**
Rest *– (booking advisable)* Menu 45/99 € – Carte 66/84 € 🏶
♦ Individual ♦ Fashionable ♦
You can really sense the younger generation at work here. Markus Mraz cooks
with his son Lukas who has introduced a modern note into the restaurant. His
creative dishes blend perfectly with the smart grey interior, making for a com-
plete eating experience.
→ Gänseleber upside down - Joghurt - Holler. US Cote de Boeuf - Burrata
- Pfefferoni - Erdäpfel cremig & kugelig. Saturnpfirsich - Cottagecheese
- Brombeeren - Puffreis.

AUSTRIA - VIENNA

XX **Indochine**   🏠 ⟷ VISA ⓞⓞ AE ⓞ

Stubenring 18 ⊠ *1010* – ⓜ *Stubentor* – *℘ (01) 5 13 76 60*
– *www.indochine.at*
– *Closed Saturday lunch*   E2
Rest – Menu 32 € (lunch)/68 € – Carte 39/71 €
♦ Vietnamese ♦ Exotic ♦ Cosy ♦

The elegant, minimalist-style interior offers a gentle hint of southeast Asia. While the culinary style of chef Wini Brugger (with his many years' experience of Asian cuisine) is more clearly marked with an accent on Vietnamese/French cuisine.

XX **Artner**   🏠 AC VISA ⓞⓞ

Franziskanerplatz 5 ⊠ *1010* – ⓜ *Stephansplatz* – *℘ (01) 5 03 50 34*
– *www.artner.co.at*
– *Closed Sunday and Bank Holidays*   E2
Rest – Carte 36/55 €
♦ Modern ♦ Trendy ♦

Housed in an old printing shop close to the Franciscan Church, this restaurant offers a concise menu of brasserie fare. On your way downstairs to the smoking area with its lovely barrel vaulting admire the glass-fronted wine cabinets.

XX **Zum weißen Rauchfangkehrer**   AC VISA ⓞⓞ

Weihburggasse 4 ⊠ *1010* – ⓜ *Stephansplatz* – *℘ (01) 5 12 34 71*
– *www.weisser-rauchfangkehrer.at*
– *Closed Sunday*   E2
Rest – *(booking advisable)* Menu 32/37 € – Carte 32/55 € ⅏
♦ Regional/country ♦ Traditional ♦ Formal ♦

This restaurant serves Viennese cuisine including seasonal dishes, such as duo of Schneebergland duck and specials like calf's head brawn. These are served throughout the day in comfortable, traditional dining rooms. There is also a wide range of wines and digestifs.

XX **Fabios**   🏠 AC VISA ⓞⓞ AE ⓞ

Tuchlauben 6 ⊠ *1010* – ⓜ *Stephansplatz* – *℘ (01) 5 32 22 22*
– *www.fabios.at*
– *Closed Sunday*   D2
Rest – *(booking essential)* Carte 46/70 €
♦ Italian ♦ Trendy ♦

The Italian food served in this trendy city restaurant is as modern and minimalist as the interior design. Both the food and decor are well worth a visit. Chef Joachim Gradwohl has already made his reputation in the kitchen – try his ravioli!

XX **Zum Schwarzen Kameel**   🏠 AC ⟷ VISA ⓞⓞ AE ⓞ

Bognergasse 5 ⊠ *1010* – ⓜ *Herrengasse* – *℘ (01) 5 33 81 25*
– *www.kameel.at*
– *Closed Sunday and Bank Holidays*   D2
Rest – *(booking essential)* Menu 36 € (lunch)/90 € – Carte 48/82 € ⅏
♦ Traditional ♦ Friendly ♦ Cosy ♦

One of Vienna's oldest restaurants (established in 1618), it was fitted out in the much admired Vienna Art Nouveau-style in 1901/02. From the outside you can see into the sparkling kitchens where the chefs prepare international and regional cuisine. The restaurant's own delicatessen and patisserie are great for gifts.

XX **Vincent**   AC ⟷ VISA ⓞⓞ AE ⓞ

Große Pfarrgasse 7 ⊠ *1020* – ⓜ *Nestroyplatz* – *℘ (01) 2 14 15 16*
– *www.restaurant-vincent.at*
– *Closed end July-mid August and Sunday-Monday*   *Plan I* **B2**
Rest – Menu 48 € (Vegetarian)/110 € – Carte 49/66 € ⅏
♦ International ♦ Individual ♦

At this restaurant you must first decide which of the three dining rooms to sit in, and then whether to eat Austrian or international food. This is no easy matter when it is all prepared with consummate skill by Peter Zinter.

AUSTRIA - VIENNA

XX **Le Loft** – Hotel Sofitel ⇐ 🐾 AC VISA ⚫⚫ AE ⓪
Praterstr. 1 (18th floor) ✉ *1020 –* Ⓜ *Schwedenplatz –* 𝒞 *(01) 90 61 60*
– www.sofitel-vienna-stephansdom.com   E1
Rest – Menu 30 € (lunch)/98 € – Carte 61/126 €
♦ French ♦ Design ♦ Fashionable ♦
This restaurant will really take your breath away. It is set in an airy, high-ceilinged
room on the 18th floor with glazed walls all around and an enormous view! There
is nothing quite like it for an evening meal as the sun goes down over the rooftops of Vienna.

XX **Das Schick** – Hotel Am Parkring ⇐ AC VISA ⚫⚫ AE ⓪
Parkring 12 ✉ *1010 –* Ⓜ *Stubentor –* 𝒞 *(01) 51 48 04 17*
– www.schick-hotels.com
– Closed Saturday-Sunday   E2
Rest – Carte 31/48 €
♦ International ♦ Fashionable ♦ Elegant ♦
This modern restaurant is located on the 12th floor with lovely views. The ser-
vice is very friendly and the food largely seasonal.

XX **Dom Beisl**   🖼 VISA ⚫⚫ AE ⓪
✿
Schulerstr. 4 ✉ *1010 –* Ⓜ *Stephansplatz –* 𝒞 *(01) 5 12 03 02*
– www.dombeisl.at
– Closed over Christmas and Saturday-Sunday   E2
Rest – Menu 20/43 € – Carte 21/58 € 🏵
♦ International ♦ Friendly ♦ Traditional ♦
If you decide to eat at Harald Riedl's Dom Beisl, try to book a table on the terrace
– it is the ideal setting to enjoy the chef's classic yet modern cuisine. There is an
extensive wine list, plus a more concise lunchtime menu that comprises of a
selection of Viennese specialities. This friendly, informal restaurant has already
started to make a name for itself in the city.
→ Gebackenes Parmesanei mit eingelegtem Muskatkürbis und Sot l'y
laisse. Confierter Bauch vom Durocschwein mit Speckwirsing und Grieskno-
del. Variation von der Valrhona-Schokolade mit eingelegten Zwetschken.

XX **at eight** – The Ring   🖼 🐾 AC VISA ⚫⚫ AE
Kärntner Ring 8 ✉ *1010 –* Ⓜ *Karlsplatz –* 𝒞 *(01) 2 21 22 38 30*
– www.theringhotel.com   E3
Rest – Menu 41/58 € – Carte 39/52 €
♦ Classic ♦ Fashionable ♦
Simple, modern lines set the tone at this restaurant where the chairs are
dressed with covers and the tables with runners in the evenings. The seasonal,
classic but contemporary cuisine is accompanied by primarily Viennese wines.
The terrace looks out onto the Ring.

XX **Cantinetta Antinori**   🖼 AC VISA ⚫⚫ AE ⓪
Jasomirgottstr. 3 ✉ *1010 –* Ⓜ *Stephansplatz –* 𝒞 *(01) 5 33 77 22*
– www.antinori.it   D2
Rest – (booking advisable) Carte 38/58 €
♦ Italian ♦ Bistro ♦
The Viennese offshoot of the original Florentine restaurant serves primarily Tuscan cuisine, including succulent braised rabbit. It has a lively but stylish atmosphere. There is a wide selection of high quality Antinori wines (available by
the glass).

XX **Fadinger**   VISA ⚫⚫ ⓪
Wipplingerstr. 29 ✉ *1010 –* Ⓜ *Schottentor-Universität –* 𝒞 *(01) 5 33 43 41*
– www.fadinger.at
– Closed Saturday lunch, Sunday and Bank Holidays   D1
Rest – (booking advisable) Menu 20 € (lunch)/58 € – Carte 26/57 €
♦ International ♦ Friendly ♦
Located close to the stock exchange, this friendly restaurant is known for its
lively, exuberant atmosphere. The cuisine is Austrian based but also offers a
range of international dishes. Good wine selection.

AUSTRIA - VIENNA

XX **Plachutta**

Wollzeile 38 ✉ *1010* – Ⓜ *Stubentor* – ℰ *(01) 5 12 15 77* – *www.plachutta.at*
Rest – *(booking advisable)* Carte 27/49 € **E2**
♦ Regional/country ♦ Traditional ♦ Inn ♦
For years, the Plachutta family has been committed to Viennese tradition. They serve beef in many forms in the green panelled dining room or on the large terrace.

XX **Unkai** – Grand Hotel

Kärntner Ring 9 (7th floor) ✉ *1010* – Ⓜ *Karlsplatz* – ℰ *(01) 5 15 80 91 10*
– www.grandhotelwien.com
– Closed Monday lunch **E3**
Rest – Menu 38/130 € – Carte 28/77 €
♦ Japanese ♦ Minimalist ♦
Unkai is a pleasantly bright and modern restaurant offering authentic teppanyaki dishes. These are served in both low Japanese-style and more conventional European tables. The Unkai Sushi Bar in the basement serves sushi brunches on Saturdays, Sundays and public holidays.

X **Kim kocht**

Lustkandlgasse 4 ✉ *1090* – Ⓜ *Währinger Str. - Volksoper* – ℰ *(01) 3 19 02 42* – *www.kimkocht.at*
– Closed 22 December-6 January, 1-25 August, Saturday-Monday
Rest – *(booking essential)* Menu 17 € (lunch)/70 € *Plan I* **A2**
♦ Asian ♦ Design ♦ Family ♦
It is great fun watching Soyhi'Kim and her team at work in the kitchen – they seem to enjoy it so much! A range of different cuisines fuse with southeast Asian here, and the chef herself presents the menu at your table. Three-course meals are served from 6pm to 8pm, followed by four- and five-course meals after 8pm. Small menu at lunchtimes.

X **Tian**

Himmelpfortegasse 23 ✉ *1010* – Ⓜ *Stephansplatz* – ℰ *(01) 8 90 46 65*
– www.tian-vienna.com
– Closed 1-20 January, Sunday and Bank Holidays **E2**
Rest – Menu 34/87 € – Carte 31/71 €
♦ Vegetarian ♦ Elegant ♦ Fashionable ♦
Tian is unusual for the simple fact that it serves excellent, exclusively vegetarian cuisine that is beautifully presented, environmentally sustainable and made largely from ingredients produced in the restaurant's own garden. With dishes such as the excellent Venere risotto and tomato ravioli, the lack of meat is really no hardship. The setting – a beautifully restored room with high, stuccoed ceilings – is equally stylish. This ideally located restaurant also boasts a basement bar.

X **Limes**

Bräunerstr. 11 ✉ *1010* – Ⓜ *Herrengasse* – ℰ *(01) 90 58 00*
– www.restaurant-limes.at **D2**
Rest – Carte 26/48 €
♦ Mediterranean ♦ Fashionable ♦ Friendly ♦
Limes (formerly Novelli) has a modern-style restaurant meets bar concept in line with the latest fashion. The kitchen serves up Mediterranean fare including dishes such as fillet of sea bass with ratatouille, herbs and a lemon cream sauce. This friendly restaurant close to the Hofburg and St Stephen's Cathedral is now open all day.

X **Schnattl**

Lange Gasse 40 ✉ *1080* – Ⓜ *Rathaus* – ℰ *(01) 4 05 34 00* – *www.schnattl.com*
– Closed 2 weeks after Easter, 2 weeks end August, Saturday-Sunday and Bank Holidays *Plan I* **A3**
Rest – Menu 33/56 € – Carte 35/56 €
♦ Regional ♦ Cosy ♦
This friendly, personally-run restaurant is set a little out of the way but remains popular with regulars and theatregoers. They appreciate the classic cuisine and warm, friendly atmosphere.

Artner auf der Wieden   🛖 VISA ⓭ ①

Floragasse 6 ✉ *1040 –* Ⓜ *Taubstummengasse – 𝒞 (01) 5 03 50 33*
– www.artner.co.at
– Closed Saturday lunch, Sunday lunch and Bank Holidays lunch
Rest *– Carte 28/55 €*   *Plan I* **B3**
♦ Regional ♦ Fashionable ♦ Minimalist ♦

This is a great place to sample real Viennese cooking including Wiener Schnitzel
and the delicious 'kaiserschmarrn' dessert. Dishes from the the charcoal grill are
also available. You may like to join the busy business diners to sample the excellent value lunchtime menu.

Meierei im Stadtpark – Restaurant Steirereck   🛖 ⅋ 🅰🅚

Am Heumarkt 2a ✉ *1030 –* Ⓜ *Stadtpark*   VISA ⓭ 🅰🅴 ①
– 𝒞 (01) 7 13 31 68 – www.steirereck.at
– Closed Bank Holidays   **F2**
Rest *– Carte 27/45 €*
♦ Regional ♦ Friendly ♦

The Steirereck's pleasantly light and airy diary and cheese bar is fitted out entirely in white with splashes of light green. The menu has a regional slant and
naturally includes a selection of local pastries.

Österreicher im MAK   🛖 VISA ⓭ 🅰🅴 ①

Stubenring 5 (at Museum MAK) ✉ *1010 –* Ⓜ *Stubentor*
– 𝒞 (01) 7 14 01 21 – www.oesterreicherimmak.at   **F2**
Rest *– Carte 23/43 €*
♦ Austrian ♦ Minimalist ♦

This restaurant is located in the historic building that houses the Museum for
Applied and Contemporary Arts. It serves regional food in a simple, modern setting. Don't miss the beef goulash with bread dumplings. Lovely restaurant garden.

Tempel   🛖 VISA ⓭ 🅰🅴 ①

Praterstr. 56 ✉ *1020 –* Ⓜ *Nestroyplatz – 𝒞 (01) 2 14 01 79*
– www.restaurant-tempel.at
– Closed 23 December-10 January and Saturday lunch, Sunday-Monday
Rest *– Menu 16 € (lunch)/49 € – Carte 25/44 €*   **F1**
♦ Regional ♦ Bistro ♦

You may have to search for the slightly concealed entrance to the interior courtyard and lovely terrace of this restaurant. It leads to this bright, friendly establishment serving flavoursome, contemporary Mediterranean cuisine. Good
value lunchtime menu.

Hollmann Salon – Hotel Hollmann Beletage   🛖 ⟳

Grashofgasse 3 (at Heiligenkreuzerhof) ✉ *1010*   VISA ⓭ 🅰🅴 ①
– Ⓜ *Stephansplatz – 𝒞 (01) 9 61 19 60 40 – www.hollmann-salon.at*
– Closed 1 week early January, 27-30 December, Sunday and Bank Holidays
Rest *– Menu 38/48 € – Carte 31/50 €*   **E2**
♦ Regional ♦ Rustic ♦

This restaurant serves regional dishes in the Heiligenkreuzerhof, a beautiful
Baroque interior courtyard in the old town. There is a special lunch concept:
for your business lunch you pay whatever you consider it is worth.

Le Salzgries Paris   🛖 🅰🅚 VISA ⓭ 🅰🅴 ①

Marc-Aurel-Str. 6 ✉ *1010 –* Ⓜ *Schwedenplatz – 𝒞 (01) 5 33 40 30*
– www.le-salzgries.at
– Closed 1-7 January, 24 March-1 April Sunday-Monday and Bank Holidays
Rest *– Menu 22 € (lunch)/63 € – Carte 33/66 €*   **D1**
♦ French ♦ Brasserie ♦ Fashionable ♦

The exterior of this restaurant boasts all the charm of a typical Viennese townhouse, while the interior features a modern, brasserie-style atmosphere. It has
all the classic French dishes on the menu and for sale: oysters, lobster (in season) and tinned vintage sardines.

Holy Moly

Am Donaukanal (at Badeschiff Wien) ✉ *1010 –* Ⓜ *Schwedenplatz – ✆ (0699) 15 13 07 50 – www.badeschiff.at – Closed 1 week early February, Sunday and Bank Holidays* **E1**

Rest – *(dinner only) (booking advisable)* Menu 34/51 € – Carte 31/40 €

♦ Classic ♦ Trendy ♦ Bistro ♦

In the evenings the Danube Canal between Urania and the Schwedenplatz is bathed in bright lights. It is here that Christian Petz and his team invite you to the Holy Moly. The Fest.Land.Bar serves 'suppitos' (simple, five-ingredient soups) in an informal atmosphere at lunchtimes, as well as selected dishes from the contemporary restaurant menu in the evenings. There is also a sundeck and the Laderaum Club.

OUTER DISTRICTS

Plan I

Park Royal Palace Vienna

Schlossalle 8 (by Mariahilfer Straße **C3***)* ✉ *1140 – ✆ (01) 8 91 10 – www.austria-trend.at/prw*

233 rm – †89/300 € ††89/300 €, ☕ 19 € – 21 suites

Rest ***Regio*** – Carte 24/38 €

♦ Conference hotel ♦ Functional ♦

The first thing to strike you on entering this conference hotel is the large atrium-style lobby. It has a decor of modern straight lines and muted colours. The spacious suites offer the best views of Schöllbrunn Castle. The hotel also offers direct access to Vienna's Museum of Technology, which serves as an occasional venue for events.

Hilton Vienna-Danube

Handelskai 269 ✉ *1020 –* Ⓜ *Dresdnerstr. – ✆ (01) 72 77 77 21 20 – www.hiltonaustria.at* **B1**

367 rm – †189/260 € ††189/260 €, ☕ 23 € **Rest** – Carte 24/54 €

♦ Chain hotel ♦ Contemporary ♦

The rooms in this former warehouse building are spacious, elegant and modern and offer views over the Danube or the city. There are executive rooms on the sixth and seventh floors, and the Executive Lounge on the eighth. The Waterfront restaurant and terrace also provide river views, while the Pier 269 bar is ideal for an enjoyable evening drink.

Kahlenberg Suite Hotel

Am Kahlenberg 2 (by Heiligenstädter Straße **A1***)* ✉ *1190 – ✆ (01) 32 81 50 09 00 – www.kahlenberg.eu*

20 rm ☕ – †149/199 € ††189/239 €

Rest – *(closed November-early March: Monday-Wednesday)* Carte 17/54 €

♦ Conference hotel ♦ Modern ♦

Its location is on Vienna's local mountain. The amazing views, as well as the spacious, high quality, very modern rooms with panoramic windows, makes this a very unique hotel. This restaurant with a simple, elegant style has a wonderful terrace.

Courtyard by Marriott Wien Messe

Trabrennstr. 4 (by Handelskai **B2***)* ✉ *1020 –* Ⓜ *Praterstern – ✆ (01) 7 27 30 – www.courtyard-wien-messe.at*

251 rm – †111/211 € ††111/211 €, ☕ 19 € – 7 suites

Rest – Carte 26/40 €

♦ Conference hotel ♦ Contemporary ♦ Modern ♦

Located in Exhibition Hall D, the Courtyard is ideal for business travellers. The rooms are designed along clean, simple lines and are comfortable yet functional. The hotel also offers modern conference facilities. The Grü Bistro serves a weekly specials menu including: 'Grü Wood, Meadow, Mountain and Lake', (Austrian) 'Grü Classics' and 'Grü goes to America'.

Pakat Suites [5] [AC] 🛜 🏋 🚗 [VISA] 🐠 [AE] ①

Mommsengasse 5 ☒ *1040* – **Ⓜ** *Südtiroler Platz* – ℰ *(01) 50 46 69 00*
– www.pakatsuites.com **B3**
52 rm – ✦109/350 € ✦✦109/400 €, ☲ 16 €
Rest *Diverso* – *(closed Saturday-Sunday and Bank Holidays)*
Carte 38/54 €

✦ Business ✦ Design ✦

This comfortable boutique hotel is located in the embassy quarter. It offers a
simple, modern style from the lobby through to the spacious rooms and the
pretty interior courtyard. The modern Italian restaurant with its good value
lunchtime menu stands diagonally across from the hotel on the other side of
the road.

 Landhaus Fuhrgassl-Huber without rest   🚗 🏠 [AC] 🛜 🚗

Rathstr. 24 (by Krottenbachstr.) ☒ *1190*   [VISA] 🐠 [AE] ①
– ℰ (01) 4 40 30 33 – www.fuhrgassl-huber.at
38 rm ☲ – ✦77/85 € ✦✦115/138 €

✦ Family ✦ Country house ✦ Cosy ✦

This family-run hotel is located in Vienna's Heuriger quarter. It offers comfortable, country house-style rooms with lovely parquet floors. In summer guests
often prefer to enjoy the generous breakfast buffet outside in the charming
interior courtyard.

 roomz Vienna   🛜 [5] [] [AC] (📞) [VISA] 🐠 [AE] ①

Paragonstr. 1 (by Landstr. Gürtel **B3**) ☒ *1110* – ℰ *(01) 7 43 17 77*
– www.roomz-vienna.com
152 rm – ✦59/145 € ✦✦69/155 €, ☲ 15 €   **Rest** – Carte 19/31 €

✦ Business ✦ Design ✦

This well-run and practically equipped hotel has a young, colourful design. The
underground station is a 10min journey from the Dom. Handy, nearby underground car park. The lobby with its open restaurant is also fashionable.

XX **Eckel**   🏠 ⇔ [VISA] 🐠 [AE] ①

Sieveringer Str. 46 (by Billrothstraße **A1**) ☒ *1190* – ℰ *(01) 3 20 32 18*
– www.restauranteckel.at
– Closed 4-19 August, 23 December-22 January and Sunday-Monday
Rest – Carte 29/55 €

✦ Regional ✦ Family ✦ Traditional ✦

Visitors to the comfortable dining rooms at Eckel appreciate the traditional service, and the equally traditional fare (including lobster and trout). In summer the
wonderful garden is particularly popular.

X **Kutschker 44**   🏠 [VISA] 🐠 [AE] ①

Kutschkergasse 44 (by Währinger Straße **A2**) ☒ *1180* – ℰ *(01) 4 70 20 47*
– www.kutschker44.at
*– Closed 1-7 January, 29 March-1 April, 28 July-19 August, Sunday - Monday
and Bank Holidays*
Rest – *(Tuesday-Friday dinner only)* Menu 32/42 € – Carte 20/56 €

✦ International ✦ Fashionable ✦

A feature of this modern restaurant is the show kitchen in the bar, where you
can watch your choice being prepared. Choose from the contemporary, seasonal menu and enjoy the informal atmosphere.

X **Freyenstein**   🏠 ⇔ [VISA] 🐠
(☺)
Thimiggasse 11 (by Währinger Straße **A2**) ☒ *1180* – ℰ *(0664) 4 39 08 37*
– www.freyenstein.at
– Closed 3 weeks February, 1 week during Easter and Sunday-Monday
Rest – *(dinner only) (booking advisable)* Menu 43/47 €

✦ Modern ✦ Family ✦ Individual ✦

It is worth making the trip out of town to Freyenstein where the friendly and
informal atmosphere is catching. This is much appreciated by diners, as is the
seasonal cuisine. This is served in the form of a daily changing five-course
menu (choice of two dishes per course).

Woracziczky

Spengergasse 52 ✉ 1050 – Ⓜ Pilgramgasse – ✆ (0699) 11 22 95 30 – www.woracziczky.at – Closed 24 December-15 January, 3 weeks end August, Saturday-Sunday and Bank Holidays **A3**

Rest – Menu 35 € – Carte 20/43 €

♦ Regional/country ♦ Neighbourhood ♦ Family ♦

The chef reserves a warm personal welcome for diners in this friendly, pleasantly informal inn (pronounced 'Vorashitkzy'). It is particularly popular for its casual atmosphere and local Viennese cuisine.

Rudi's Beisl

Wiedner Hauptstr. 88 ✉ 1050 – Ⓜ Taubstummengasse – ✆ (01) 5 44 51 02 – www.rudisbeisl.at – Closed Saturday-Sunday and Bank Holidays **B3**

Rest – *(booking advisable)* Carte 16/43 €

♦ Regional ♦ Simple ♦

Everyone in Vienna seems to meet up in the smoking room at Rudi's Beisl. The friendly chef often manages to have a personal word with guests. He is usually busy in the kitchen preparing a wide range of traditional dishes including: schnitzel, goulash, boiled beef and pancakes.

Schübel-Auer

Kahlenberger Str. 22 (Döbling) ✉ 1190 – ✆ (01) 3 70 22 22 – www.schuebel-auer.at – Closed 21 July-5 August, 26 October-4 November, 22-31 December and Sunday-Monday **A1**

Rest – *(open from 4 pm)* Carte 9/22 €

♦ Regional ♦ Wine bar ♦ Cosy ♦

Built in 1642 as a winegrower's house with a functioning mill, this carefully renovated building and its secluded interior courtyard, is a lovingly furnished restaurant.

Feuerwehr-Wagner

Grinzingerstr. 53 (Heiligenstadt) ✉ 1190 – ✆ (01) 3 20 24 42 – www.feuerwehrwagner.at **A1**

Rest – *(open from 4 pm)* Carte 14/33 €

♦ Regional ♦ Wine bar ♦ Rustic ♦

This typical, traditional Austrian wine tavern is greatly appreciated by regulars. Find a cosy, rustic decor with dark wood and simple tables. The terraced garden is particularly nice.

Mayer am Pfarrplatz

Pfarrplatz 2 (Heiligenstadt) ✉ 1190 – ✆ (01) 3 70 12 87 – www.pfarrplatz.at **A1**

Rest – *(open Monday–Saturday from 4 pm, April-October: Saturday open from 12 am)* Carte 16/31 €

♦ Regional ♦ Wine bar ♦ Rustic ♦

A textbook traditional Austrian wine tavern: rustic furnishings, traditional Viennese folk music, and an attractive courtyard terrace. Of note: Beethoven lived here in 1817.

AT THE AIRPORT

NH Vienna Airport

rest,

Einfahrtsstr. 1 (at Airport) ✉ 1300 – ✆ (01) 70 15 10 – www.nh-hotels.com

499 rm – †119/349 € ††119/349 €, ☕ 19 € **Rest** – Carte 32/65 €

♦ Business ♦ Modern ♦ Personalised ♦

The lobby, bar and restaurant areas are spacious, the rooms are well-equipped, and the hotel enjoys a convenient location close to the arrivals hall. All in all an ideal destination for the business traveller. The restaurant serves upmarket international cuisine alongside Austrian classics.

SALZBURG

SALZBURG

Population: 148 521

Gérald Schléwitz/Fotolia.com

Small but perfectly formed, Salzburg is a chocolate-box treasure, gift-wrapped in stunning Alpine surroundings. It's immortalised as the birthplace and inspiration of one of classical music's greatest stars, and shows itself off as northern Europe's grandest exhibitor of baroque style. Little wonder that in summer its population rockets, as the sound of music wafts from hotel rooms and festival hall windows during rehearsals for the Festspiele. In quieter times of the year, Salzburgers enjoy a leisurely and relaxed pace of life. Their love of music and the arts is renowned; and they enjoy the outdoors, too, making the most of the mountains and lakes, and the paths which run along the river Salzach and zig-zag through the woods and the grounds of Hellbrunn. The dramatic natural setting of Salzburg means you're never likely to get lost. Rising above the left bank (the Old Town) is the Mönchsberg Mountain and its fortress, the Festung Hohensalzburg, while the right bank (the New Town, this being a relative term) is guarded by the even taller Kapuzinerberg. In the New Town stands the Mozart family home, while the graceful gardens of the Schloss Mirabell draw the right bank crowds. The Altstadt (Old Town) is a UNESCO World Heritage Site and its star turn is its Cathedral. To the east is the quiet Nonntal area overlooked by the Nuns' Mountain.

SALZBURG IN...

→ **ONE DAY**
Festung Hohensalzburg, Museum der Moderne, Cathedral, Residenzplatz.

→ **TWO DAYS**
Mozart's birthplace, Nonntal, Kapuzinerberg, Mirabell Gardens, concert at Mozarteum.

→ **THREE DAYS**
Mozart's residence, Hangar 7, Hellbrunn Palace, concert at Landestheater.

PRACTICAL INFORMATION

ARRIVAL-DEPARTURE

⏏ Wolfgang Amadeus Mozart Airport is just west of the centre.

🚆 The Hauptbahnhof (railway station) is centrally located on the right bank and is served by trains from all Europe's major locations.

Bus no.2 connects the airport with the Hauptbahnhof.

GETTING AROUND

Salzburg boasts a very efficient bus system. There are two main bus departure points on the left bank (Mozartsteg Bridge and Hanuschplatz) and two on the right (Hauptbahnhof and Mirabellplatz). You can buy tickets in three ways: in blocks of five singles; for a day's duration; or for a week. If you take your sightseeing seriously, then get a Salzburg Card for free travel on public transport and reduced admission to many tourist attractions; choose a card for 24, 48 or 72 hours.

CALENDAR HIGHLIGHTS

February
Mozartwoche (Mozart Week).

March
Osterfestspiele (Easter Festival).

May
Pfingstfestspiele (Whitsun Festival).

June
Sommerszene (Performance Festival).

August
Festspiele (Salzburg Festival).

October
Kulturtage (Cultural Days).

EATING OUT

Salzburg's cuisine takes much of its influence from the days of the Austro-Hungarian Empire, with Bavarian elements added to the mix. Over the centuries it was characterised by substantial pastry and egg dishes to fill the stomachs of local salt mine workers; it's still hearty and meaty and is typified by dumplings and broths. In the city's top restaurants, a regional emphasis is still very important but the cooking has a lighter, more modern touch. Beyond the city are picturesque inns and tranquil beer gardens, many idyllically set by lakes. Do try the dumplings: Pinzgauer Nocken are made of potato pastry and filled with minced pork; another favourite is Gröstl, a filling meal of 'leftovers', including potatoes, dumplings, sausages and smoked meat roasted in a pan. If you want a snack, then Jausen is for you – cold meals with bread and sausage, cheese, dumplings, bacon etc, followed by an Obstler, made from distilled fruit. Salzburg's sweet tooth is evident in the Salzburger Nockerl, a rich soufflé omelette made with fruit and soft meringue.

43

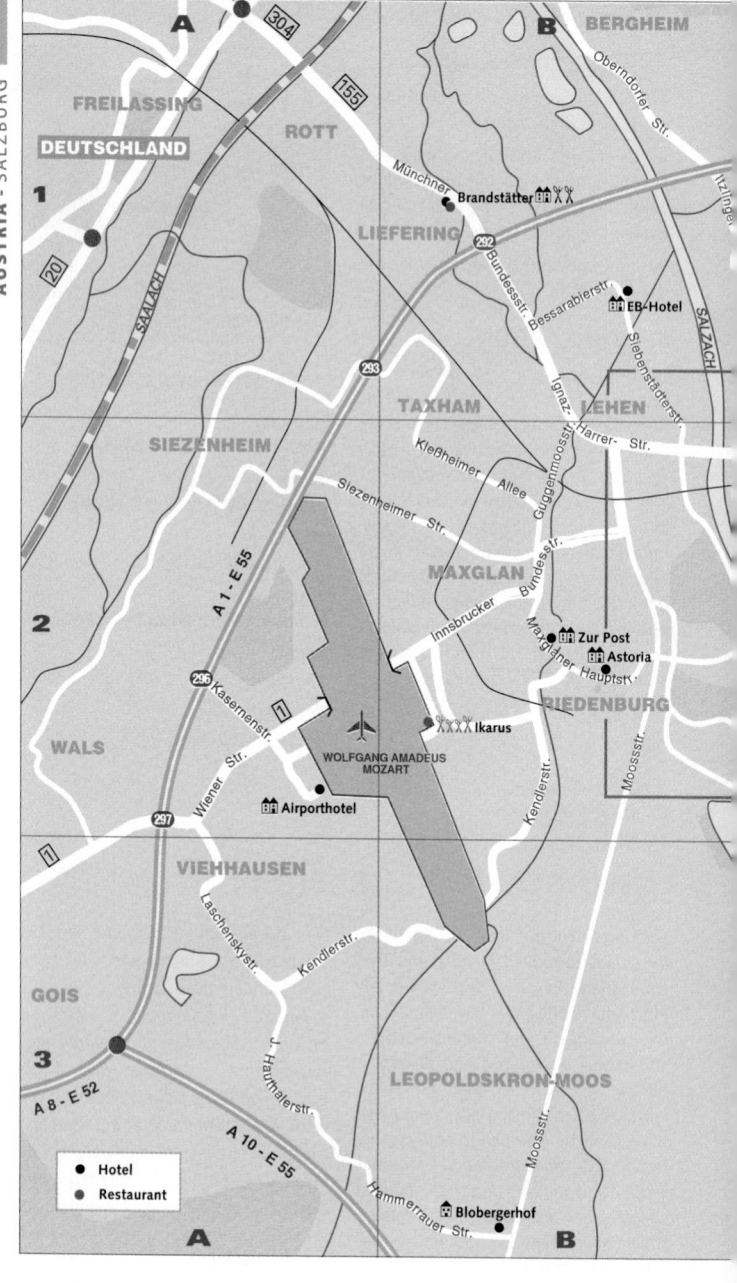

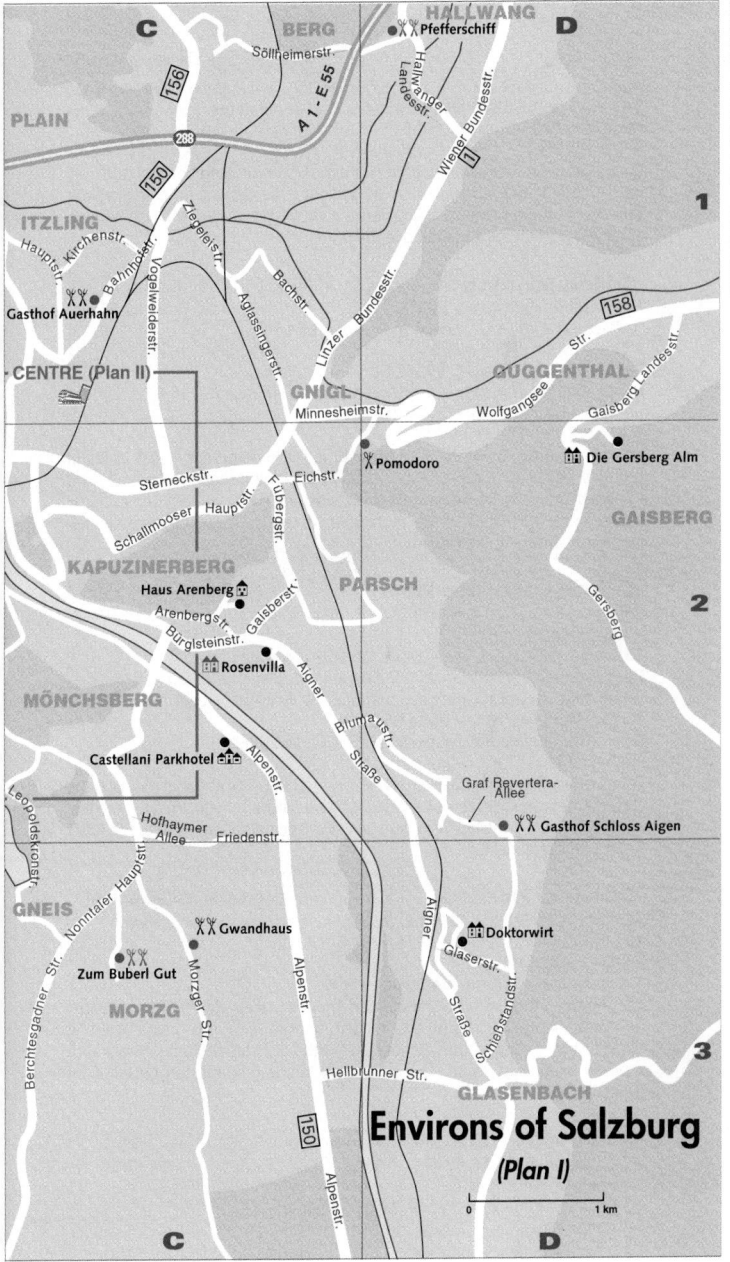

Environs of Salzburg
(Plan I)

0   1 km

AUSTRIA - SALZBURG

Sheraton 🛬 ⅃♨ 🏚 ⅊ 🅰🅲 🛜 🔏 🚗 🆅🆂🅰 💳 🅰🅴 🄾

Auerspergstr. 4 ✉ 5020 – 𝒞 (0662) 88 99 90 – www.sheratonsalzburg.at
166 rm – ♦165/380 € ♦♦180/430 €, � 30 € – 8 suites   **E1**
Rest *Mirabell* – Carte 35/60 €
♦ Chain hotel ♦ Functional ♦

This smart hotel with comfortably furnished rooms is situated between the Congress Centre and Mirabell Gardens. A highlight is the elegant, modern Sky Suite on seventh-floor. Mirabell offers classic cuisine and a garden-facing terrace. Small regional dishes are offered in the bistro.

Schloss Mönchstein 🦢 ⪡ 🚙 🐒 🛬 ⅃♨ 🌐 🏚 ⅊ rest, 🅰🅲 🛜

Mönchsberg Park 26 ✉ 5020   ⅊ 🅿 🆅🆂🅰 💳 🅰🅴 🄾
– 𝒞 (0662) 8 48 55 50 – www.monchstein.at
– Closed 28 January-4 March   **E1**
24 rm ⊠ – ♦276/468 € ♦♦345/585 € – 3 suites
Rest – *(closed Tuesday, except festival period)* Menu 59/110 €
– Carte 41/75 €
♦ Historic ♦ Personalised ♦

This small castle dating back to the 14C is set in three and a half acres of grounds. The elegant rooms and beautifully appointed modern spa are set off to perfection by the stunning views over Salzburg. The restaurant serves classic cuisine using the highest quality ingredients, as well as a good wine list. The terrace has a view over the city.

Crowne Plaza - The Pitter 🛬 ⅃♨ 🏚 ⅊ 🅰🅲 🛜 ⅊ 🚗

Rainerstr. 6 ✉ 5020 – 𝒞 (0662) 88 97 80   🆅🆂🅰 💳 🅰🅴 🄾
– www.imlauer.com   **F1**
199 rm – ♦79/199 € ♦♦99/249 €, ⊠ 18 € – 4 suites
Rest *Imlauer* – 𝒞 (0662) 88 97 87 04 *(closed 2 weeks February, 2 weeks July, 2 weeks September and Sunday-Monday, except festival period)* Menu 45/78 € – Carte 35/58 €
Rest *Pitter-Keller* – Auerspergstr. 23 – Carte 20/42 €
♦ Chain hotel ♦ Functional ♦

This centrally located hotel was built in 1864. It offers comfortable rooms in the classic American style, as well as the exclusive Salzburg Suite. Imlauer, the elegant, Swiss pine-panelled restaurant serves classic traditional cuisine. The Pitter Keller offers regional fare.

Castellani Parkhotel 🛬 ⅃♨ ⅊ 🅰🅲 🛜 ⅊ 🅿 🚗 🆅🆂🅰 💳 🅰🅴 🄾

Alpenstr. 6 ✉ 5020 – 𝒞 (0662) 2 06 00 – www.hotel-castellani.com
151 rm ⊠ – ♦102/192 € ♦♦142/232 € – 4 suites   *Plan I* **C2**
Rest – Carte 23/46 €
♦ Business ♦ Classic ♦ Modern ♦

The theme at the Castellani Parkhotel is 'modern meets classic'. The combination of listed mansion house and modern annexe really is a great success. It offers lovely, timeless rooms, junior suites with balconies and a restaurant with a pretty interior courtyard. The old rectory in the grounds can be hired for events.

Wolf-Dietrich Altstadthotel without rest 🏚 🖻 🛜

Wolf-Dietrich-Str. 7 ✉ 5020 – 𝒞 (0662) 87 12 75   🆅🆂🅰 💳 🅰🅴 🄾
– www.wolf-dietrich.at   **F1**
40 rm ⊠ – ♦80/130 € ♦♦110/245 € – 4 suites
♦ Townhouse ♦ Cosy ♦

This city hotel offers tasteful rooms, four lavishly decorated themed suites, and an attractive terrace. It also has a pretty spa area that offers relaxing massages by appointment.

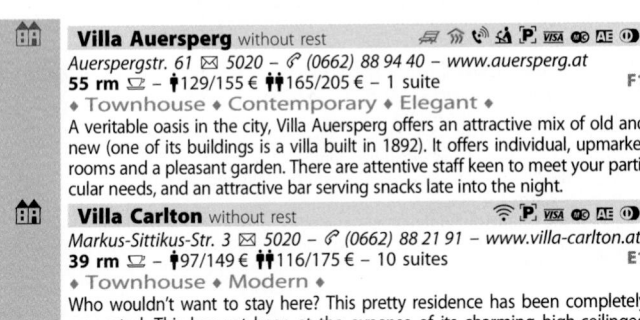

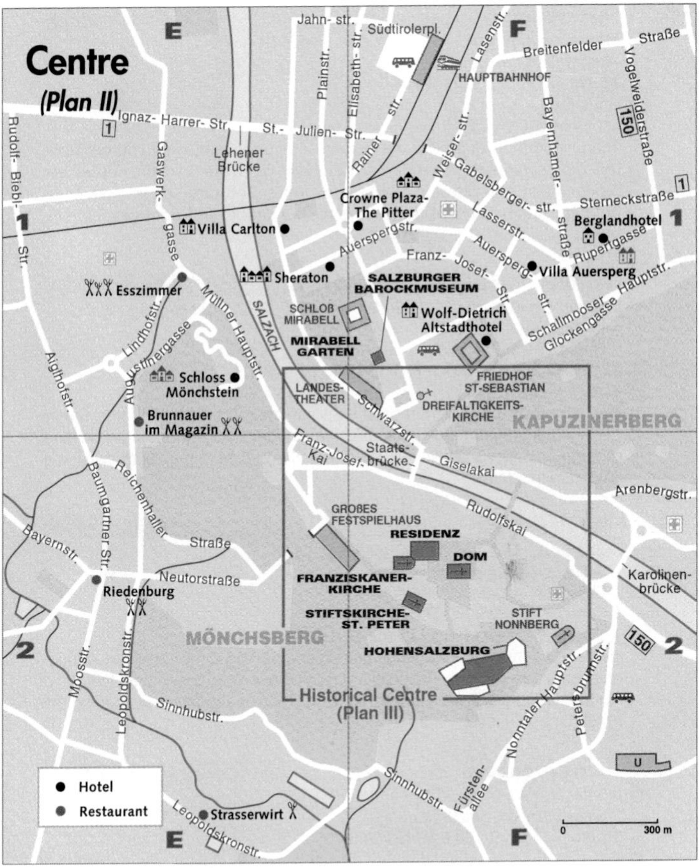
Centre
(Plan II)
E
F
1
2
Jahn- str.
Südtirolerpl.
Lasenstr.
Breitenfelder
Straße
Vogelweiderstraße
150
HAUPTBAHNHOF
Plainstr.
Elisabeth- str.
Ignaz- Harrer- Str.
St.- Julien- Str.
Lehener Brücke
Rainer str.
Weiser- str.
Bayerhamer- straße
Gabelsberger- str.
Sterneckstraße
Rudolf- Biebl- Str.
Gaswerk- gasse
Crowne Plaza- The Pitter
Villa Carlton
Auerspergstr.
Lasserstr.
Berglandhotel
Rupertgasse
Franz- Josef- Str.
Auersperg- str.
Villa Auersperg
Sheraton
SALZBURGER BAROCKMUSEUM
Esszimmer
Müllner Hauptstr.
SCHLOß MIRABELL
SALZACH
Wolf-Dietrich Altstadthotel
Schallmooser Hauptstr.
Glockengasse
Lindhofstr.
Augustinergasse
MIRABELL GARTEN
Aiglhofstr.
Schloss Mönchstein
LANDES- THEATER
Schwarzstr.
FRIEDHOF ST-SEBASTIAN
DREIFALTIGKEITS- KIRCHE
KAPUZINERBERG
Brunnauer im Magazin
Franz-Josef- Kai
Staats- brücke
Giselakai
Reichenhaller Straße
Baumgartner Str.
Arenbergstr.
GROßES FESTSPIELHAUS
RESIDENZ
Rudolfskai
Bayernstr.
DOM
Neutorstraße
Karolinen- brücke
FRANZISKANER- KIRCHE
Riedenburg
STIFTSKIRCHE- ST. PETER
STIFT NONNBERG
MÖNCHSBERG
HOHENSALZBURG
Moosstr.
Leopoldskronstr.
Historical Centre (Plan III)
Nonntaler Hauptstr.
Petersbrunnstr.
Sinnhubstr.
Fürsten- allee
U
Hotel
Restaurant
Strasserwirt
Leopoldskronstr.
0
300 m

Villa Auersperg without rest

Auerspergstr. 61 ✉ *5020 – 𝒞 (0662) 88 94 40 – www.auersperg.at*

55 rm ☕ – ♦129/155 € ♦♦165/205 € – 1 suite **F1**

♦ Townhouse ♦ Contemporary ♦ Elegant ♦

A veritable oasis in the city, Villa Auersperg offers an attractive mix of old and new (one of its buildings is a villa built in 1892). It offers individual, upmarket rooms and a pleasant garden. There are attentive staff keen to meet your particular needs, and an attractive bar serving snacks late into the night.

Villa Carlton without rest

Markus-Sittikus-Str. 3 ✉ *5020 – 𝒞 (0662) 88 21 91 – www.villa-carlton.at*

39 rm ☕ – ♦97/149 € ♦♦116/175 € – 10 suites **E1**

♦ Townhouse ♦ Modern ♦

Who wouldn't want to stay here? This pretty residence has been completely renovated. This has not been at the expense of its charming high-ceilinged rooms, which now come in a variety of styles. These are all modern and include country house, elegant, traditional and pop art.

Astoria without rest 🛜 P VISA ⓪ AE ⓪

Maxglaner Hauptstr. 7 ✉ *5020* – ℰ *(0662) 83 42 77*
– *www.salzburgastoria.com*   *Plan I* **B2**
28 rm ⊒ – ♦68/110 € ♦♦88/160 €
– 3 suites
♦ Family ♦ Functional ♦ Modern ♦
There is nothing quite like the individual, personal welcome you get from
the Illinger family. Everything is beautifully cared for and the rooms are
modern and decorated in warm earth tones. The café serves pastries to
hotel guests throughout the day, as well as snacks and drinks in the evenings.

Zur Post without rest (with guesthouses) 🛜 ☏ P VISA ⓪ AE ⓪

Maxglaner Hauptstr. 45 ✉ *5020* – ℰ *(0662) 8 32 33 90*
– *www.hotelzurpost.info*
– *Closed 22 - 26 December*   *Plan I* **B2**
37 rm ⊒ – ♦69/134 € ♦♦86/158 €
♦ Inn ♦ Functional ♦
You will enjoy the lovely rooms, excellent breakfast and dedicated family
management at Zur Post. The hotel's main building and the Georg and Renate
guesthouses offer a classic feel. While the Villa Ceconi, some 200m away, is a
little more modern.

Berglandhotel without rest 🛜 P VISA ⓪ AE ⓪

Rupertgasse 15 ✉ *5020* – ℰ *(0662) 87 23 18*
– *www.berglandhotel.at*
– *Closed 18-28 December*   **F1**
18 rm ⊒ – ♦70/90 € ♦♦90/139 €
♦ Family ♦ Personalised ♦ Functional ♦
The rooms at this hotel are either modern or rustic and some have parquet flooring or antique furniture. The breakfast room is warm and cosy thanks to its tiled
wood-burning stove and modern red decor. There is a small terrace behind the
hotel.

Haus Arenberg without rest

Blumensteinstr. 8 ✉ *5020* – ℰ *(0662) 64 00 97*
– *www.arenberg-salzburg.at*   *Plan I* **C2**
16 rm ⊒ – ♦79/108 € ♦♦129/165 €
♦ Family ♦ Cosy ♦
This pleasant hotel with its own parking enjoys a quiet location within walking
distance of the city centre. Enjoy the view at breakfast on the terrace looking
out onto the pretty garden or browse through the books in the library. Charming chef.

Esszimmer (Andreas Kaiblinger)

Müllner Hauptstr. 33 ✉ *5020* – ℰ *(0662) 87 08 99*
– *www.esszimmer.at*
– *Closed 1 week early January, 2 weeks July-August and Sunday–Monday,
except August and December: Sunday*   **E1**
Rest – *(booking advisable)* Menu 64 € (Vegetarian)/105 €
– Carte 63/95 €
♦ Classic ♦ Fashionable ♦ Elegant ♦
As soon as you enter Esszimmer you can see through the small windows into
the kitchen. Here the chefs are hard at work preparing the restaurant's four
menus (including vegetarian and fish options). The restaurant itself is spacious,
fresh and decorated in a Mediterranean style. There is a small terrace in the rear
courtyard.
➔ Geräuchertes Rinderherz mit Langostinotatar. Zander mit Fenchelkraut
und Blutwurst. Dunkle Schokoladenblätter mit Ziegenkäse und Kürbis.

AUSTRIA - SALZBURG

XX **Gasthof Auerhahn** with rm 🛐 🛜 🏠 **P** 💳 ⊚ 🄰🄴 ⓪

☺ *Bahnhofstr. 15 (by Plainstraße* **A1**) ✉ *5020 – 𝒞 (0662) 45 10 52*
– www.auerhahn-salzburg.at
– Closed 1 week January, 3 weeks July, 1 week October Plan I **C1**
13 rm 🛏 – ♦50/55 € ♦♦80/88 €
Rest – *(closed Sunday dinner-Monday, except festival period)* Menu 29 €
(Vegetarian)/49 € – Carte 24/46 €
♦ Regional ♦ Friendly ♦ Cosy ♦
If you have a sweet tooth, don't miss the delicious topfenknödel (curd cheese dumplings) on offer here. Along with the other, predominantly regional, dishes on the menu they ensure that the restaurant is always full. Many guests prefer to stay the night, and the rooms, although not enormous, are cheerful and well cared for.

XX **Brunnauer im Magazin** 🛐 🏠 💳 ⊚ 🄰🄴 ⓪

Augustinergasse 13 a ✉ *5020 – 𝒞 (0662) 84 15 84 21*
– www.magazin.co.at
– Closed 1-13 January, Sunday and Bank Holidays, except festival period
Rest – *(booking advisable)* Menu 57/79 € – Carte 45/71 € **E1**
♦ Classic ♦ Fashionable ♦ Minimalist ♦
Brunnauer combines classic cuisine, a wine shop and delicatessen – Magazin – and an events venue with style and success. It is located in a former quarry, which was originally opened to supply stone for the construction of the castle. Manager and chef Richard Brunnauer, no stranger to Salzburg, serves fresh contemporary cuisine alongside classics such as Wiener Schnitzel and chateaubriand steak.

X **Strasserwirt** 🛐 **P** 💳 ⊚ ⓪

Leopoldskronstr. 39 ✉ *5020 – 𝒞 (0662) 82 63 91*
– www.zumstrasserwirt.at
– Closed 14-24 January, 29 September-3 October and Monday, October-April :
Monday-Tuesday **E2**
Rest – Carte 22/49 €
♦ Regional ♦
This guesthouse from 1856 houses a classically decorated restaurant with high quality cherry wood-panelling and a conservatory on the terrace. It serves a regional city menu.

X **Pomodoro** 🛐 **P** 💳 ⊚ ⓪

Eichstr. 54 ✉ *5020 – 𝒞 (0662) 64 04 38*
– Closed August and Monday-Wednesday Plan I **D2**
Rest – *(bookings advisable at dinner)* Carte 27/39 €
♦ Italian ♦ Family ♦ Rustic ♦
A little unprepossessing at first glance, this restaurant delights its many regulars with its authentic Italian cuisine. It is run by a charming couple: Giovanni Tomassetti in the kitchen and Brigitte Lercher front of house.

HISTORICAL CENTRE Plan III

🏛 **Sacher** 🛐 🧖 🛜 👶 🅰 🛜 🧖 🚗 💳 ⊚ 🄰🄴 ⓪

Schwarzstr. 5 ✉ *5020 – 𝒞 (0662) 88 97 70 – www.sacher.com*
113 rm – ♦226/336 € ♦♦241/651 €, 🛏 32 € – 5 suites **G1**
Rest *Zirbelzimmer* – Menu 42 € (lunch)/63 € – Carte 38/75 €
Rest *Salzachgrill* – Carte 34/48 €
♦ Traditional ♦ Historic ♦ Classic ♦
This grand hotel on the banks of the river Salzach is luxurious and elegant. Enjoy the beautiful rooms and individual suites. Some of the rooms are astonishing with their special view of the river. The specialty of the café is Viennese Sacher torte. The Zirbelzimmer is elegantly rustic. This Salzach grill restaurant has a glorious terrace on the Salzach.

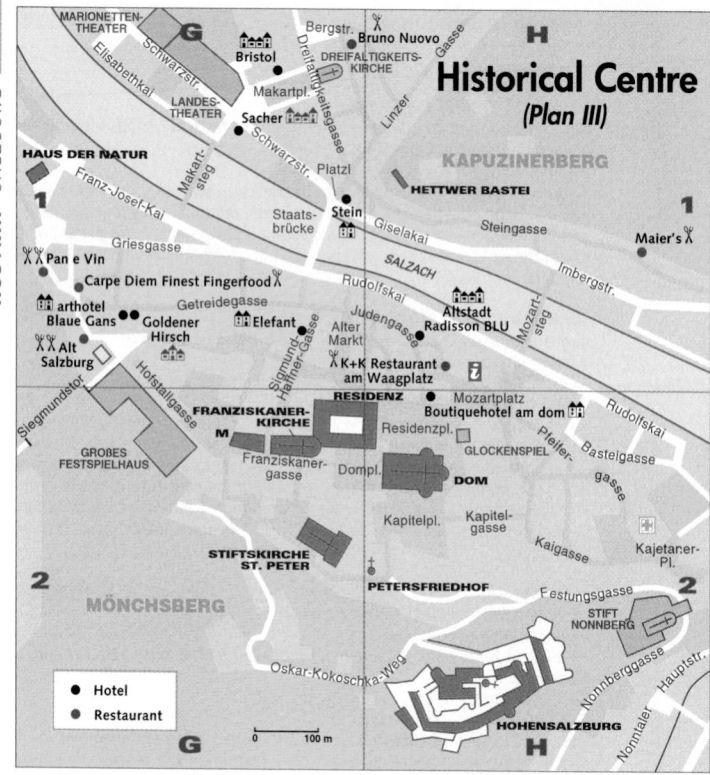

Historical Centre
(Plan III)

Bristol   AC 🛜 ♨ VISA ⨂ ①

Makartplatz 4 ⊠ 5020 – ℰ (0662) 87 35 57 – www.bristol-salzburg.at
– Closed February   G1
60 rm ⌂ – ♦165/355 € ♦♦225/480 € – 9 suites
Rest – *(closed Sunday, except festival period)* Carte 28/75 €
♦ Traditional ♦ Classic ♦

The stylish, tasteful decor in the lovely, high-ceilinged rooms hint at the history of
this hotel, built in 1619 and run as a hotel since 1892. All the rooms are individually designed with stucco work, crystal chandeliers, antiques, sumptuous fabrics and paintings. The restaurant serves classic cuisine with traditional influences.

Altstadt Radisson BLU   ♨ AC rest, 🛜 ♨ VISA ⨂ AE ①

Rudolfskai 28 (Judengasse 15) ⊠ 5020 – ℰ (0662) 8 48 57 10
– www.austria-trend.at/hotel-altstadt-salzburg   H1
62 rm – ♦108/480 € ♦♦216/480 €, ⌂ 26 € – 13 suites
Rest – Carte 30/44 €
♦ Townhouse ♦ Personalised ♦

Behind historical walls, not far from Mozartplatz, find the beautiful rooms of this
hotel with their classic, elegant style. The executive room and suites are spacious. This international restaurant has a conservatory on the Salzach river, and
a terrace in the interior court.

Goldener Hirsch

Getreidegasse 37 ✉ 5020 – ✆ (0662) 8 08 40 – www.goldenerhirsch.com
70 rm – †195/570 € ††215/570 €, ☕ 32 € – 5 suites **G1**
Rest – Carte 39/79 €

♦ Townhouse ♦ Historic ♦ Personalised ♦

Staying in this patrician house, which dates back to 1407, you are literally surrounded by history. The rustic wooden furniture in the guestrooms does nothing to detract from the homely feel, on the contrary, the traditional charm adds to the atmosphere. The restaurant offers international cuisine with classic and Austrian influences. The Herz is a little more rustic in style.

Elefant

Sigmund-Haffner-Gasse 4 ✉ 5020 – ✆ (0662) 84 33 97 – www.bestwestern-ce.com/elefant **G1**
31 rm ☕ – †89/126 € ††109/226 €
Rest – *(closed Sunday, except December and festival period)*
Carte 19/47 €

♦ Townhouse ♦ Classic ♦ Contemporary ♦

This 700 year-old hotel is located in the centre of Salzburg. It is in a narrow side street close to the famous Getreidegasse shopping street. It features a tasteful contemporary interior and a traditional-style restaurant.

arthotel Blaue Gans

Getreidegasse 41 ✉ 5020 – ✆ (0662) 8 42 49 10 – www.blauegans.at
35 rm ☕ – †135/179 € ††179/265 € – 3 suites **G1**
Rest – *(closed Sunday, except festival period)* Carte 29/51 €

♦ Townhouse ♦ Modern ♦ Personalised ♦

This 650 year-old Salzburg guesthouse is right in the centre of the city. It houses bright, modern rooms including the special, chic 'Artelierzimmer', as well as displaying contemporary art. Pleasant, bright restaurant with attractive vaulted ceiling and a nice terrace.

Stein without rest

Giselakai 3 ✉ 5020 – ✆ (0662) 8 74 34 60 – www.hotelstein.at
56 rm ☕ – †85/157 € ††97/209 € – 6 suites **G1**

♦ Townhouse ♦ Modern ♦

This historic guesthouse dating back to 1399 offers modern rooms and facilities. Located close to the Staats bridge, its roof terrace has become one of Salzburg's major attractions. As a guest you will be able to enjoy the view over breakfast.

Boutiquehotel am Dom without rest

Goldgasse 17 ✉ 5020 – ✆ (0662) 84 27 65 – www.hotelamdom.at
15 rm – †90/160 € ††140/280 €, ☕ 9 € **H2**

♦ Historic ♦ Design ♦ Contemporary ♦

You would never imagine that this small hidden house full of nooks and crannies would conceal such large rooms. As well as space they also offer smart, modern design and beautifully appointed bathrooms. Everything is immaculate! The most convenient parking is in the underground car park in the old town.

Pan e Vin

Gstättengasse 1 (1st floor) ✉ 5020 – ✆ (0662) 84 46 66 – www.panevin.at – Closed 2 weeks early September **G1**
Rest – *(closed Sunday, except festival period)* Menu 48/78 € – Carte 31/72 €
Rest *Trattoria* – *✆ (0662) 84 46 66 14 (closed Sunday - Monday, except festival period)* Carte 27/50 €

♦ Mediterranean ♦ Cosy ♦

Mediterranean flavoured cuisine awaits guests in this 600 year-old building comfortably decorated in warm tones. The wine menu offers a good international selection. On the ground floor, the Trattoria serves pure Italian cuisine with a starter buffet.

AUSTRIA - SALZBURG

XX Alt Salzburg

Bürgerspitalgasse 2 ⊠ *5020 –* ℰ *(0662) 84 14 76*
– www.altsalzburg.at
– Closed 24 February-10 March, Sunday-Monday lunch, except festival period
Rest – *(bookings advisable at dinner)* Menu 43/58 €   **G1**
– Carte 27/58 €
♦ Regional ♦ Traditional ♦

The Kögl family has been running this charming, tasteful and elegant restaurant for many years. It is located in the former servants' quarters of the Bürgerspital. Father and daughter work together in the kitchen to produce the largely regional fare.

X Carpe Diem Finest Fingerfood

Getreidegasse 50 (1st floor) ⊠ *5020 –* ℰ *(0662) 84 88 00*
– www.carpediem.com
– Closed 2 weeks February and Sunday, except festival period   **G1**
Rest – Menu 68/98 € (dinner) – Carte 51/79 €
♦ International ♦ Fashionable ♦ Design ♦

No one strolling along Salzburg's main shopping street will fail to notice this restaurant. Entering through the lounge-cum-terrace (perfect for a drink) you come upon the fashionable ground floor bar. This serves sophisticated finger food in 'cones', which also feature on the modern, international menu in the informal restaurant upstairs.
➜ Flusskrebse mit Pastinaken, Paprika und Thaispargel. Taube mit Mangold, Roten Rüben und Steinpilze. Rücken vom Black Angus mit Senferde und Kürbiskraut.

X K+K Restaurant am Waagplatz

Waagplatz 2 (1st floor) ⊠ *5020 –* ℰ *(0662) 84 21 56*
– www.kkhotels.com/waagplatz   **H1**
Rest – *(booking advisable)* Menu 65/72 € – Carte 21/47 €
♦ Regional ♦ Rustic ♦

The comfortable dining rooms at this restaurant have become a real Salzburg institution. Their old wooden interiors beloved by the regulars. The regional fare on offer is the same wherever you sit. Although the slightly faster service on the ground floor will suit busy shoppers and tourists.

X Maier's

Steingasse 61 ⊠ *5020 –* ℰ *(0662) 87 93 79 – www.maiers-salzburg.at*
– Closed 2 weeks May-June, 2 weeks September-October, Sunday-Monday and Bank Holidays   **H1**
Rest – *(dinner only) (booking advisable)* Carte 30/46 €
♦ International ♦ Friendly ♦ Cosy ♦

Maier's is a popular eatery, set a little out of the way in a historical old alleyway. It serves international dishes such as guinea fowl with red wine risotto and various beef cuts. Choose from the blackboard and dine at the small, prettily laid tables. The friendly new husband and wife team of chefs also look after front of house.

X Bruno Nuovo

Priesterhausgasse 20 ⊠ *5020 –* ℰ *(0662) 87 08 11*
– www.brunonuovo.at
– Closed 1 week September, Sunday and Bank Holidays, except festival period
Rest – Menu 14 € (lunch)/60 € – Carte 44/66 €   **G1**
♦ Regional ♦ Family ♦

At Bruno Nuovo the Plotegher family serves tasty, seasonal food. There is a simpler menu at lunchtimes when the evening menu is available by reservation only. Why not take a stroll in the nearby Mirabell Gardens before or after your meal.

AUSTRIA - SALZBURG

Die Gersberg Alm   ⅌ ≼ 🚗 🏠 ♨ ✕ ⅌ rest, 📶 ♨ P

Gersberg 37 ⊠ 5020 – ℰ (0662) 64 12 57   VISA ⓪ AE ①

– www.gersbergalm.at   **D2**

44 rm � – †95/125 € ††139/295 € – 4 suites

Rest – *(booking advisable)* Carte 28/50 €

♦ Inn ♦ Rustic ♦

This isolated mountain guesthouse dating back to 1832 has kept its friendly, rustic charm. This is also reflected in the cosy restaurant, which serves seasonal cuisine. The guestrooms also have a rustic charm, although there are a number of elegant, modern rooms. The garden offers an idyllic country setting for breakfast, afternoon coffee or a snack.

Doktorwirt   🚗 🏠 ♨ 🏊 ⌧ ⅌ rest, 📞 ♨ P VISA ⓪ AE ①

Glaser Str. 9 ⊠ 5026 – ℰ (0662) 62 29 73 – www.doktorwirt.at

– Closed 3 weeks February, mid October-end November   **D3**

41 rm ⊠ – †75/98 € ††115/185 €

Rest – *(closed Sunday dinner-Monday, festival period: Monday)* Menu 31/39 € – Carte 15/45 € ⅋

♦ Inn ♦ Rustic ♦ Cosy ♦

The Schnöll family run this cosy 12C tavern. There is a spacious spa area and a lovely garden, as well as beautiful tower rooms with small bay windows. Regional cuisine is served in very comfortable rooms or on the terraces in front and behind the building. There is a wine cellar.

Rosenvilla *without rest*   📶 P VISA ⓪ AE ①

Höfelgasse 4 ⊠ 5020 – ℰ (0662) 62 17 65 – www.rosenvilla.com

– Closed 10-25 February   **C2**

15 rm ⊠ – †79/114 € ††135/177 €

♦ Family ♦ Modern ♦ Cosy ♦

Stefanie Fleischhaker is a born hostess! Though the individual rooms may be a little small, this is more than made up for by the great service, tasteful decor and lovely terrace (where you can eat breakfast in summer).

Brandstätter   🚗 🏠 ⌧ 📶 ♨ P VISA ⓪

Münchner Bundesstr. 69 ⊠ 5020 – ℰ (0662) 43 45 35

– www.hotel-brandstaetter.com

– Closed 23-26 December   **B1**

35 rm ⊠ – †85/140 € ††120/195 €

Rest *Brandstätter* 🍴 – see restaurant listing

♦ Family ♦ Cosy ♦

Don't be put off by the hotel's proximity to the main street and the motorway – this is more than compensated for by the hospitality of the Brandstätter family and their staff. Some of the lovely country house-style rooms face out onto the garden.

EB-Hotel *without rest*   📶 ♨ P VISA ⓪ AE

Aribonenstr. 20 ⊠ 5020 – ℰ (0662) 23 06 48 – www.ebhotel.at

– Closed 2-6 January, 21-26 December   **B1**

15 rm ⊠ – †68/98 € ††116/166 €

♦ Business ♦ Modern ♦ Functional ♦

This friendly hotel has a characteristic orange façade. It offers immaculately kept, contemporary yet comfortable guestrooms, including a number of quiet rooms to the rear. Good breakfast, plus a bus stop nearby.

Airporthotel   🏊 🏠 ⌧ ⅌ rm, 🄺 rm, 📶 ♨ P 🚗 VISA ⓪ AE ①

Dr.-Matthias-Laireiter-Str. 9 ⊠ 5020 Salzburg-Loig – ℰ (0662) 85 00 20

– www.airporthotel.at   **A2**

36 rm ⊠ – †95/155 € ††125/185 €   **Rest** – *(dinner for residents only)*

♦ Inn ♦ Cosy ♦

This hotel is across from the airport, and consists of two connected hotel buildings, which are typical of the region. Functional rooms, some with air-conditioning.

Blobergerhof

🛋 🏠 🛜 **P** 💳 ⊚

Hammerauerstr. 4 ✉ *5020 – ☎ (0662) 83 02 27 – www.blobergerhof.at*
– Closed 23-26 Dezember   **B3**
21 rm 🛏 – ♦65/70 € ♦♦80/105 €
Rest – *(closed 1 week June, 2 weeks mid November and Sunday) (dinner for residents only)* Carte 16/40 €
♦ Inn ♦ Cosy ♦
The Keuschnigg family offers everything you need when you are on the road. Find comfortable rooms (book one in the more spacious 'superior' category), a good breakfast with homemade jam, warm, friendly service and parking right outside the door. Some rooms have a view of the Untersberg and others have balconies.

Ikarus

← 🏠 🛴 📶 ⟷ **P** 💳 ⊚ 🄰🄴 ⓪

Wilhelm-Spazier-Str. 7a (Hangar-7, 1st floor) ✉ *5020 – ☎ (0662) 21 97*
– www.hangar-7.com
– closed 23 December-4 January   **B2**
Rest – *(booking essential)* Menu 150 € – Carte 40/114 €
♦ Creative ♦ Fashionable ♦ Elegant ♦
Guest cooks from around the world each spend a month in the kitchens of this striking glass restaurant. This results in a great range of culinary offerings. The regulars here are particularly partial to head chef Roland Trettl's set Ikarus menu, while others prefer the finger food served in the bar. In summer grilled meats are served in the outdoor lounge.

Zum Buberl Gut

🏠 ⟷ **P** 💳 ⊚

Gneiser Str. 31 ✉ *5020 – ☎ (0662) 82 68 66*
– Closed 1 week early July, 1 week early September and Tuesday, festival period: Tuesday lunch   **C3**
Rest – *(booking advisable)* Menu 22 € (lunch) – Carte 45/69 €
♦ Italian ♦ Cosy ♦ Rustic ♦
This restaurant is in the really lovely setting of a 17C manor house. It serves Italian food in an elegant yet comfortable atmosphere. If you visit in summer, don't miss the chance to eat out on the pretty, leafy terrace.

Brandstätter - Hotel Brandstätter

🛋 🏠 **P** 💳 ⊚

Münchner Bundesstr. 69 ✉ *5020 – ☎ (0662) 43 45 35*
– www.hotel-brandstaetter.com
– closed 23 - 26 December and Sunday, except festival period and Advent
Rest – *(booking advisable)* Carte 31/68 €   **B1**
♦ Regional ♦ Cosy ♦
Your hosts here clearly have an affinity with the region as is shown in their cooking. This includes traditional dishes such as veal goulash with dumplings. All the dining rooms are comfortable but the Swiss pine room with its tiled oven has a particular charm.

Gwandhaus

← 🏠 🛴 📶 ⟷ **P** 💳 ⊚ 🄰🄴 ⓪

Morzger Str. 31 ✉ *5020 – ☎ (0662) 46 96 64 56 – www.gwandhaus.com*
Rest – *(booking advisable)* Menu 33/47 € – Carte 22/50 €   **C3**
♦ International ♦ Classic ♦
While they are putting the finishing touches to your traditional Dirndl outfit in the famous dress shop, take your time over breakfast, coffee and cakes, lunch or dinner in the adjoining restaurant. Don't forget the terrace with its lovely view.

Gasthof Schloss Aigen

🏠 ⟷ **P** 💳 ⊚ 🄰🄴 ⓪

Schwarzenbergpromenade 37 ✉ *5026 – ☎ (0662) 62 12 84*
– www.schloss-aigen.at
– Closed 10-20 February and Monday-Wednesday lunch   **D2**
Rest – Menu 40/53 € – Carte 27/62 €
♦ Regional ♦ Inn ♦ Friendly ♦
In this former manor guesthouse with its tasteful, rustically furnished rooms, beef dishes are a speciality. A romantic terrace has been laid out under the chestnut trees of the interior courtyard.

AT **ELIXHAUSEN** North: 7,5 km by Vogelweiderstraße C1

🏨 **Gmachl** 🛋 🏠 🗲🐧 🌀 🏊 🔳 ⅙ 🕸 rm, 🕻 🗝 P 🚗 🚗 🚗 🚗 🚗

Dorfstr. 14 ⊠ 5161 – ℰ (0662) 48 02 12 – www.gmachl.com
73 rm 🖭 – 🛏114/184 € 🛏🛏192/294 € – 7 suites
Rest – Menu 39/74 € – Carte 24/61 €
♦ Country house ♦ Family ♦ Cosy ♦
Stay at this country hotel if you want to escape the hustle and bustle of the city
but remain within easy travelling distance of Salzburg. It has been run by the
Hirnböck-Gmachl family since 1334. The spa in the cloistered courtyard offers
a wonderful panoramic view. The comfortable dining rooms serve sausages
and meat prepared in the hotel's own butchery.

AT **HALLWANG**

🍴🍴 **Pfefferschiff** (Jürgen Vigne) 🏠 P 🚗 🚗 🚗
🟢 *Söllheim 3 ⊠ 5300 – ℰ (0662) 66 12 42 – www.pfefferschiff.at*
– Closed 2 weeks February-March, 2 weeks end July and Sunday-Monday,
except festival period
Rest – *(Tuesday - Friday dinner only) (booking essential)* Menu 68/84 €
– Carte 55/84 € 🕸
♦ Classic ♦ Elegant ♦ Cosy ♦
The picture could hardly be more perfect: a historic country rectory, comfor-
table dining rooms with wooden floors, as well as lovingly chosen fabrics and
pictures. A wonderful setting for the restaurant's excellent food, which is seaso-
nal, creative and classically based. The friendly waitresses are in traditional dress.
→ Gänseleber mit Wachauer Marille. Renke mit schwarzem Trüffel und
Salatherzen. "Mehr im Hemd" à la Jürgen Vigne.

AT **HOF BEI SALZBURG** North-East: 18 km by Wolfgangsee Straße D1

🏨 **Schloss Fuschl** 🛥 ⪦ 🛋 🏠 🗲🐧 🌀 🏊 🔳 🖼 ⅙ rm, 🕸 🛜 🗝 P
Schloss Str. 19 ⊠ 5322 Hof bei Salzburg 🚗 🚗 🚗 🚗 🚗
– ℰ (06229) 2 25 30 – www.schlossfuschlsalzburg.com
110 rm 🖭 – 🛏310/450 € 🛏🛏360/500 € – 19 suites
Rest *Schloss Restaurant* – Carte 53/76 €
♦ Luxury ♦ Classic ♦
This idyllic hotel on a small peninsula projecting into the lake didn't stay a secret
for long. It is here that the famous 'Sissi' films starring Romy Schneider were
filmed in the 1950s. There is a bathing beach with a jetty (and a restaurant for
guests in the summer), motorboats for trips out and a fish farm, where the catch
is smoked in the hotel. The bar serves snacks throughout the day.

BELGIUM
BELGIQUE - BELGIË

Antwerp

BRUSSELS

→ **AREA:**
30 528 km² (11 781 sq mi)

→ **POPULATION:**
11 076 847 inhabitants: nearly 55% Flemish, 33% Walloons and about 10% foreigners. Density = 363 per km².

→ **CAPITAL:**
Brussels.

→ **CURRENCY:**
Euro (€).

→ **GOVERNMENT:**
Constitutional parliamentary monarchy (since 1830) and a federal state (since 1994). Member of European Union since 1957 (one of the 6 founding countries).

→ **LANGUAGES:**
French (Wallonia), Flemish (Flanders), German (Eastern cantons); most Belgians also speak English.

→ **PUBLIC HOLIDAYS:**
New Year's Day (1 Jan); Easter Monday (late Mar/Apr); Labor Day (1 May); Ascension Day (May); Whit Monday (late May/June); Independence Day (21 July); Assumption of the Virgin Mary (15 Aug); All Saints' Day (1 Nov); Armistice Day 1918 (11 Nov); Christmas Day (25 Dec); Boxing Day (26 Dec).

→ **LOCAL TIME:**
GMT+1 hour in winter and GMT+2 hours in summer.

→ **CLIMATE:**
Temperate maritime with cool winters and mild summers (Brussels: January 2°C; July 18°C); more continental towards the Ardennes. Rainfall evenly distributed throughout the year.

→ **EMERGENCY:**
Police ℘ **101**; Medical Assistance and Fire Brigade ℘ **100**. (Dialling **112** within any EU country will redirect your call and contact the emergency services.

→ **ELECTRICITY:**
230 volts AC, 50Hz; 2 round pin sockets.

→ **FORMALITIES:**
Travellers from the European Union (EU), Switzerland, Iceland and the main countries of North and South America need a national identity card or passport (America: passport required) to visit Belgium for less than three months (tourism or business purpose). For visitors from other countries a visa may be required, in addition to a passport, especially for those wishing to stay for longer than three months. We advise you to check with your embassy before travelling.

57

BRUSSELS
BRUXELLES/BRUSSEL

Population: 1 136 920

Guitain/Fotolia.com

There aren't many cities where you can use a 16C century map and accurately navigate your way around; or where there are enough restaurants to dine somewhere different every day for five years; or where you'll find a museum dedicated to the comic strip – but then every city isn't Brussels. It was tagged a 'grey' capital because of its EU associations but those who've spent time here know it to be, by contrast, a buzzing town. It's the home of art nouveau, it features a wonderful maze of medieval alleys and places to eat, and it's warm and friendly, with an outgoing, cosmopolitan feel – due in no small part to its turbulent history, which has seen it under frequent occupation. Generally speaking, the Bruxellois believe that you shouldn't take things too seriously: they have a soft spot for puppets and Tintin, street music and majorettes; and they do their laundry in communal places like the Wash Club.

The area where all visitors wend is the Lower Town and the Grand Place but the northwest and southern quarters (Ste-Catherine and The Marolles) are also of particular interest. To the east, higher up an escarpment, lies the Upper Town – this is the traditional home of the aristocracy and encircles the landmark Parc de Bruxelles. Two suburbs of interest are St Gilles, to the southwest, and Ixelles, to the southeast, where trendy bars and art nouveau are the order of the day.

BRUSSELS IN...

→ ONE DAY
Grand Place, Place Ste-Catherine, Musées Royaux des Beaux-Arts.

→ TWO DAYS
Marolles, Place du Grand Sablon, Musical Instrument Museum, concert at Palais des Beaux-Arts.

→ THREE DAYS
Parc du Cinquantenaire, Horta's house, tour St Gilles and Ixelles.

PRACTICAL INFORMATION

ARRIVAL-DEPARTURE

✈ Brussels Zaventem Airport is 14km northeast.

The Airport City Express train runs every 20min and takes 25min.

Eurostar - Brussels Midi Train Station is 2km southwest.
Take Metro Lines 4, 55 or 56.

GETTING AROUND

Buses, trams and metro all run efficiently. You can buy 1, 5 or 10 trip cards and one or three day travel cards. These are available from metro stations, travel authority offices (STIB/MIVB), tourist information centres and newsagents. Remember to stamp your ticket before each journey; orange machines are on every metro station concourse and on every tram and bus. Single tickets are valid for an hour and you can hop on and off all forms of public transport. (Roving inspectors impose heavy on-the-spot fines for anyone caught without a valid ticket.)

EATING OUT

CALENDAR HIGHLIGHTS

January
Brussels Festival.

February
Palais des Beaux-Arts Antiques Fair, International Comic Strip and Cartoon Festival, Brussels Book Fair.

March-April
Ars Musica.

May
Kunsten Festival des Arts, Queen Elisabeth Music Contest.

July
Ommegang (Renaissance Procession).

July-August
Brussels Summer Festival.

July-September
Drive-In Movies at the Esplanade du Cinquantenaire.

August
Fiesta Latina.

September
Lucky Town Festival.

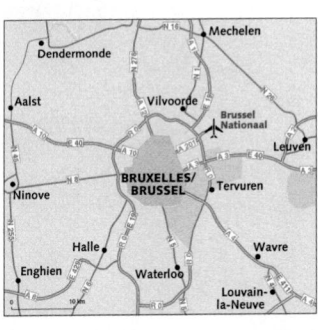

As long as your appetite hasn't been sated at the chocolatiers, or with a cone of frites from a street stall, you'll relish the dining experience in Brussels. As long as you stay off the main tourist drag (i.e. Rue des Bouchers), you're guaranteed somewhere good to eat within a short strolling distance. There are lots of places to enjoy Belgian dishes such as moules frites, Ostend lobster, eels with green herbs, or waterzooi (chicken or fish stew with vegetables). Wherever you're eating, at whatever price range, food is invariably well cooked and often bursting with innovative touches. As a rule of thumb, the Lower Town has the best places, with the Ste-Catherine quarter's fish and seafood establishments the pick of the bunch; you'll also find a mini Chinatown here. Because of the city's cosmopolitan character there are dozens of international restaurants - ranging from French and Italian to more unusual Moroccan, Tunisian and Congolese destinations. Belgium beers are famous the world over and are served in specially designed glasses.

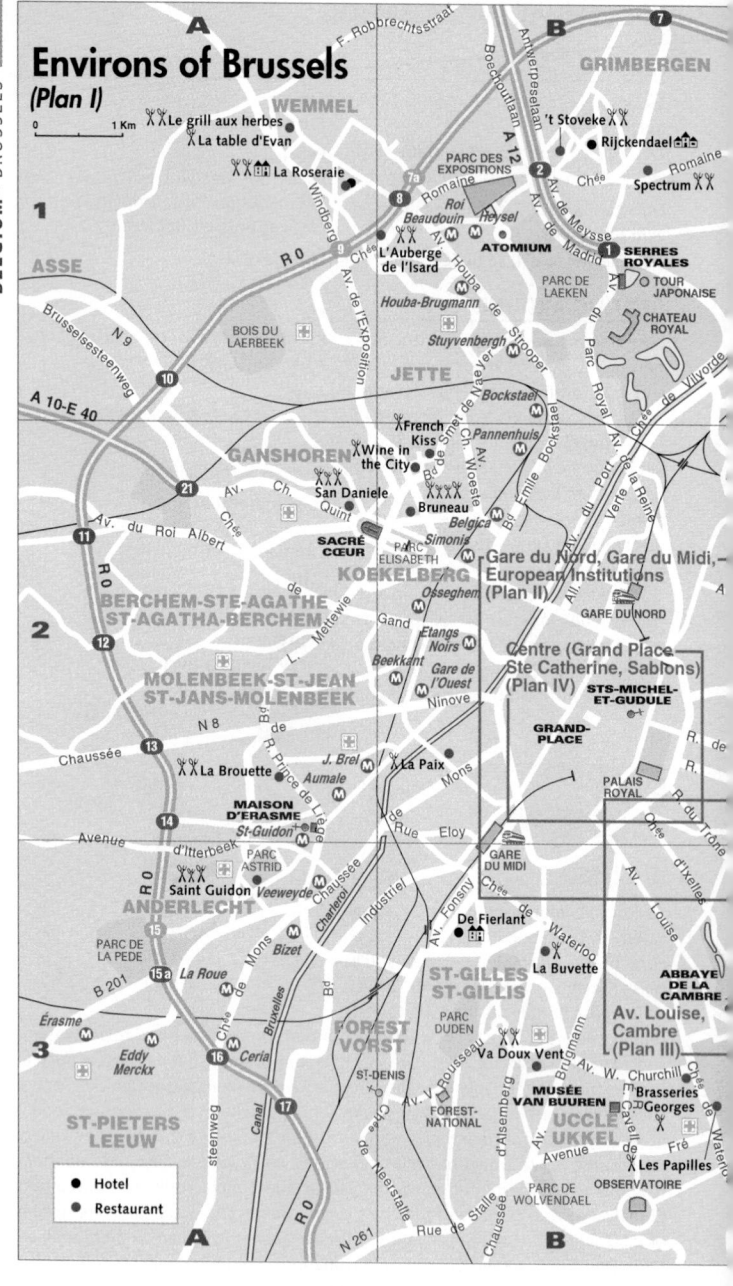

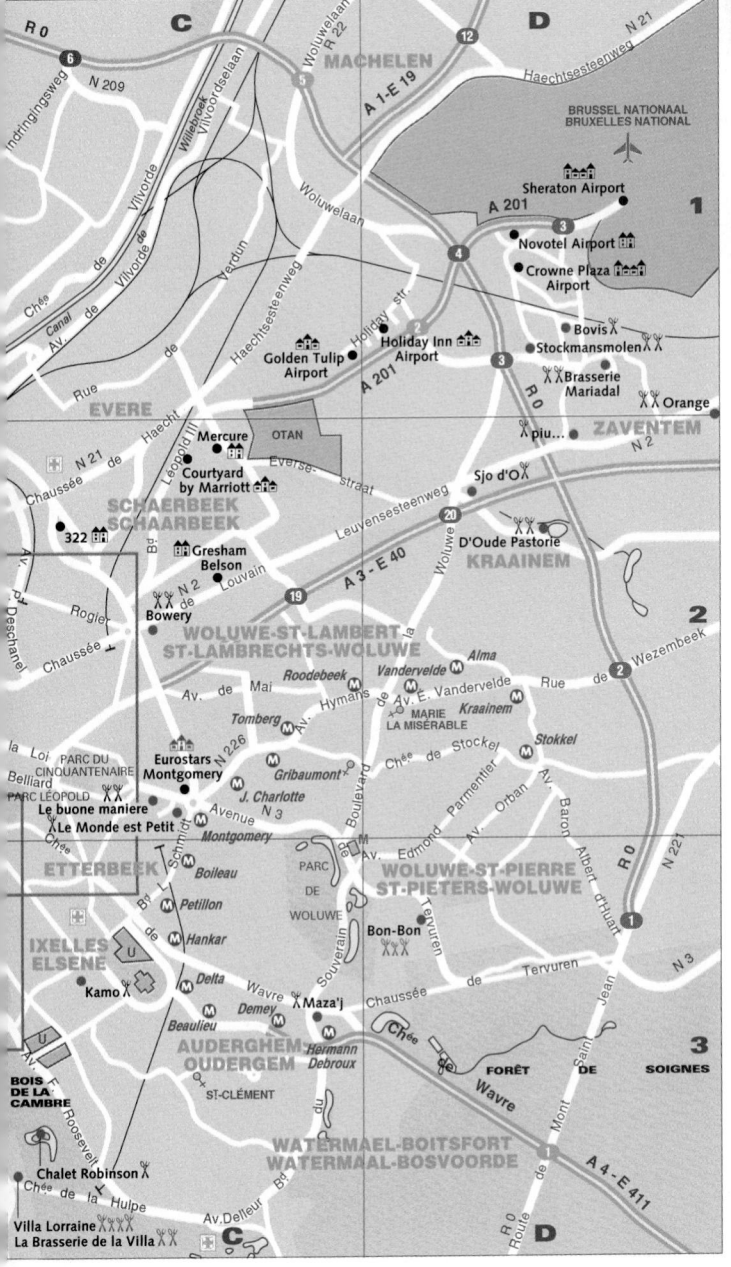

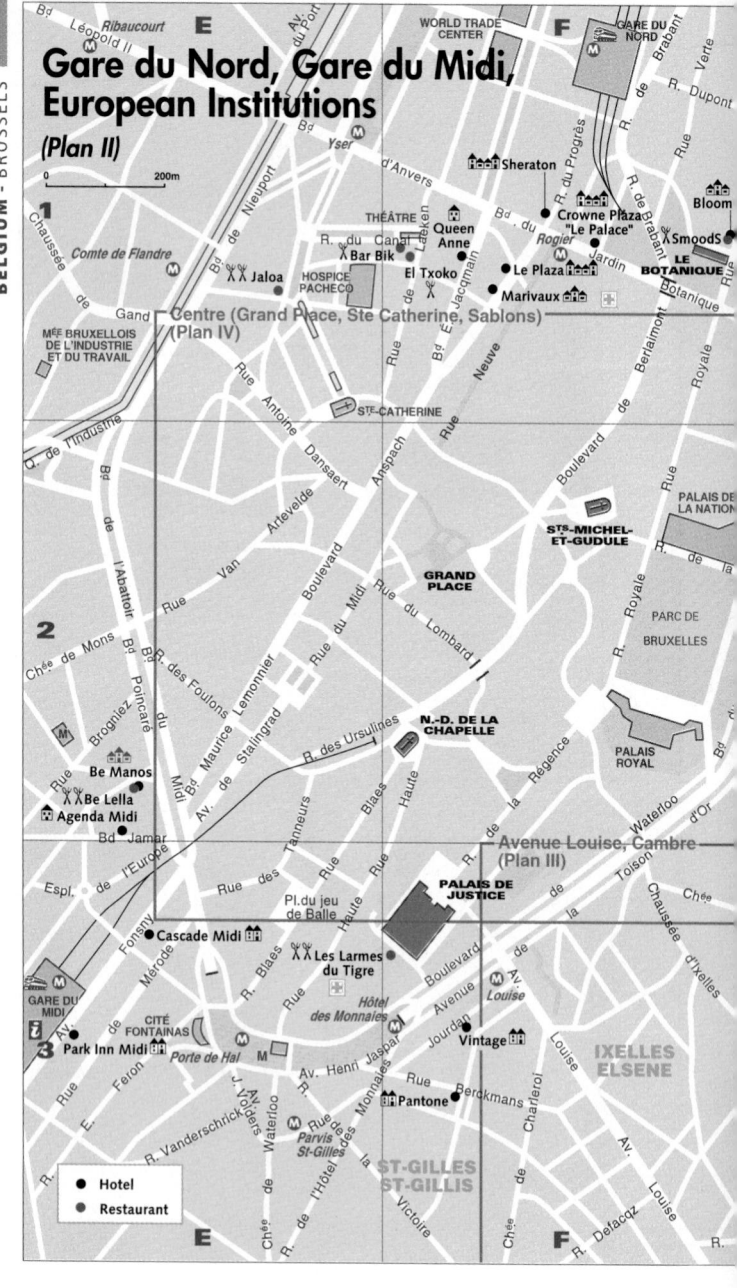

Gare du Nord, Gare du Midi, European Institutions

(Plan II)

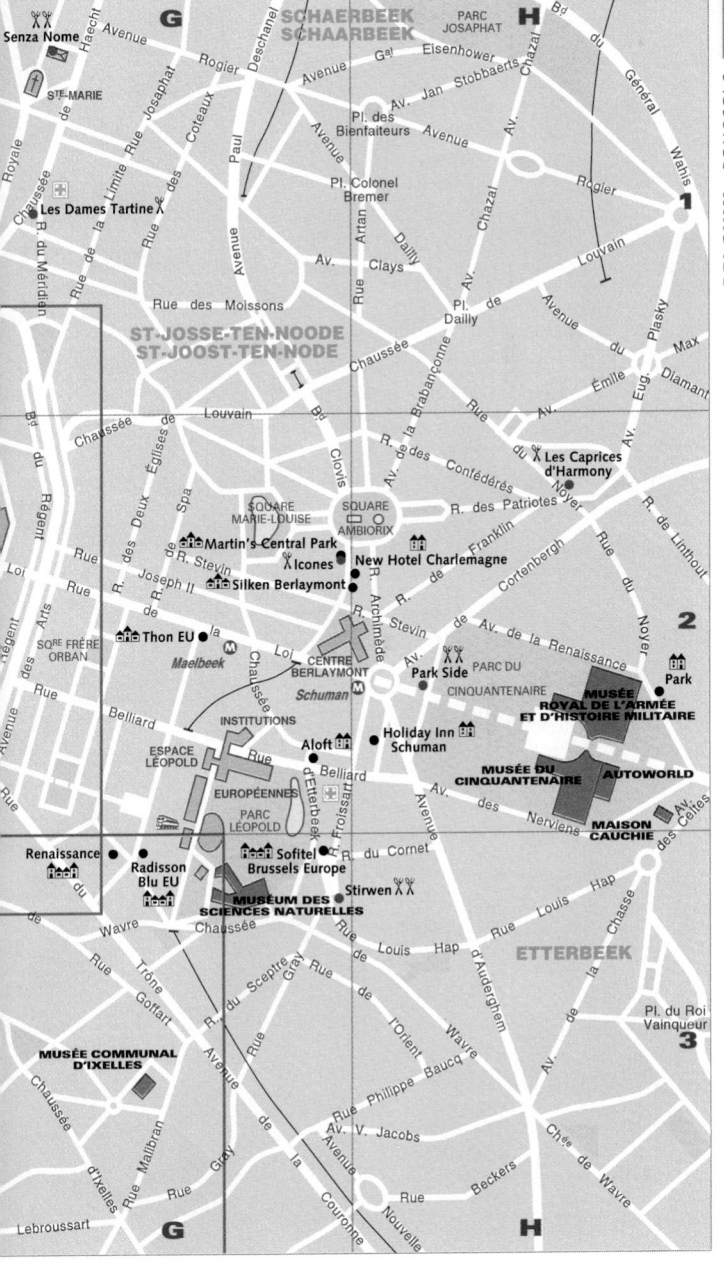

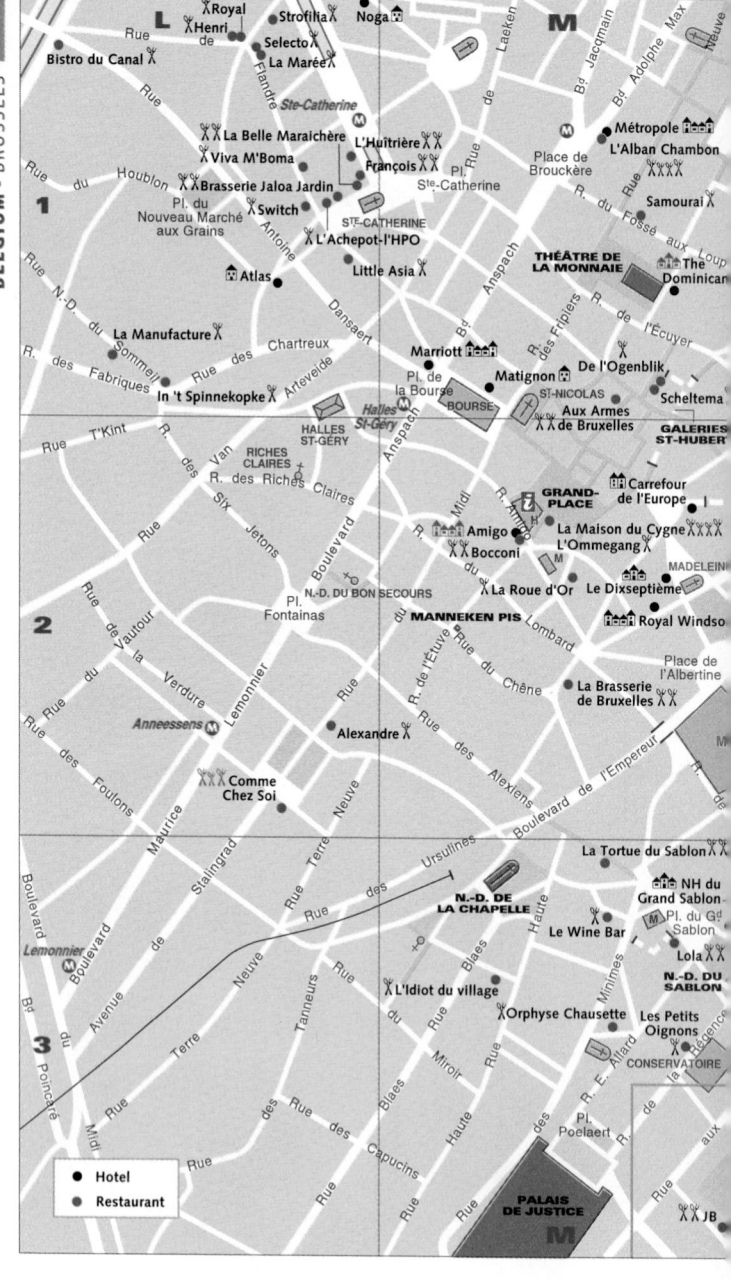

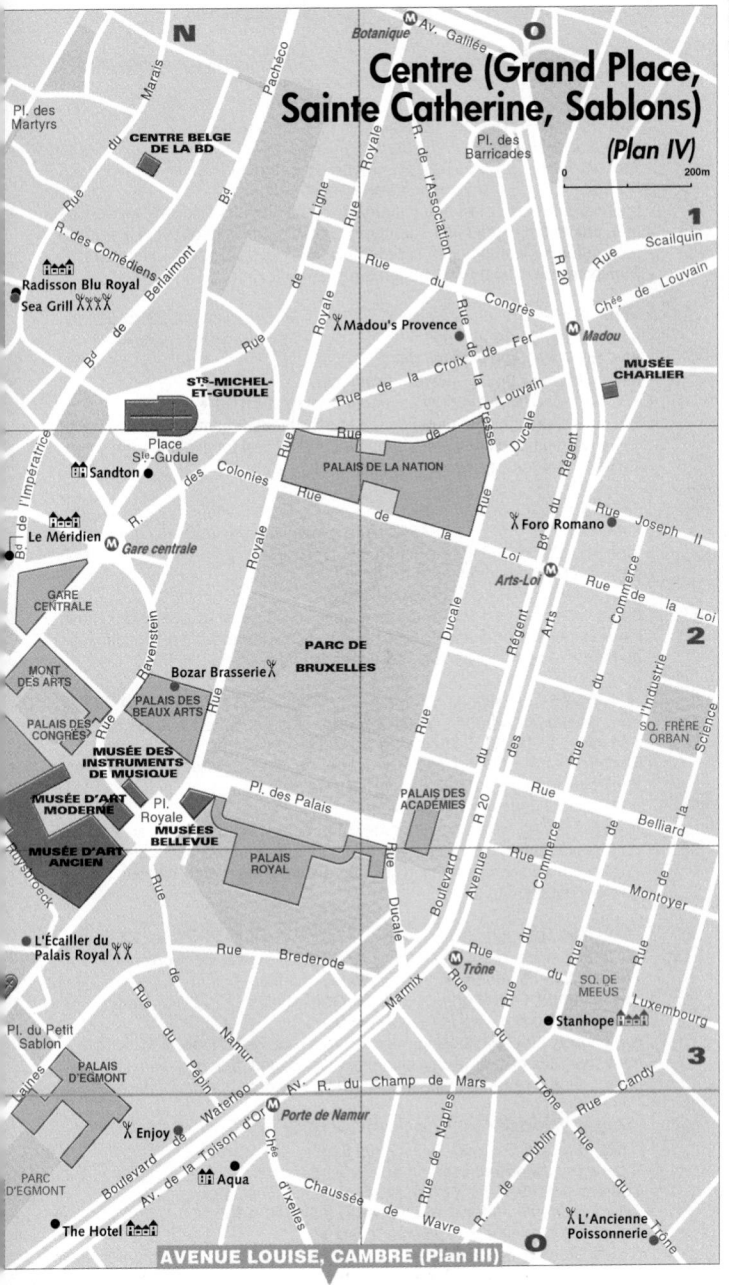

Centre (Grand Place, Sainte Catherine, Sablons)
(Plan IV)

0   200m

Pl. des Martyrs

CENTRE BELGE DE LA BD

Botanique

Av. Galilée

Pl. des Barricades

Pachéco

Marais

Bd

Rue

R. des Comédiens

Berlaimont

Ligne

Rue

Royale

R. de l'Association

Rue

du

Congrès

Rue

Scailquin

Chée de Louvain

Radisson Blu Royal
Sea Grill

Rue

de

Royale

Rue

Madou's Provence

de la Croix de Fer

M Madou

STS-MICHEL-ET-GUDULE

Rue

de la

Passe

Louvain

Ducale

MUSÉE CHARLIER

Place Ste-Gudule

Sandton

des

Colonies

Rue

de

la

Régent

Rue

Joseph II

Bd de l'Impératrice

Le Méridien M Gare centrale

R.

Royale

Rue

PALAIS DE LA NATION

Rue

Loi

Foro Romano

Rue

Joseph II

GARE CENTRALE

Ravenstein

Arts-Loi M

Arts-Loi

Rue

Commerce

de la Loi

MONT DES ARTS

Bozar Brasserie

PARC DE BRUXELLES

Ducale

Régent

des

Arts

Rue

de l'Industrie

PALAIS DES CONGRÈS

PALAIS DES BEAUX ARTS

du

SQ. FRÈRE ORBAN

Science

MUSÉE DES INSTRUMENTS DE MUSIQUE

Rue

MUSÉE D'ART MODERNE

Pl. des Palais

PALAIS DES ACADÉMIES

R. 20

Rue

Belliard

Pl. Royale

MUSÉES BELLEVUE

de

la

de

MUSÉE D'ART ANCIEN

Rue

PALAIS ROYAL

Ducale

Boulevard

Avenue

Commerce

Rue

de

Montoyer

Ruysbroeck

L'Écailler du Palais Royal

Rue

de

Brederode

Marnix

Rue

Trône M

du

Rue

Rue

SQ. DE MEEUS

Luxembourg

Stanhope

Pl. du Petit Sablon

PALAIS D'EGMONT

Rue

du

Pépin

Namur

Av. R. du Champ de Mars

Rue

de

Naples

Trône

Rue

Candy

Enjoy

de

Chée

Waterloo

Av. de la Toison d'Or

d'Ixelles

Porte de Namur

Rue

de

Dublin

Rue

du

Trône

PARC D'EGMONT

Aqua

Laines

Boulevard

Chaussée

de

Wavre

The Hotel

L'Ancienne Poissonnerie

AVENUE LOUISE, CAMBRE (Plan III)

Radisson Blu Royal

r. Fossé-aux-Loups 47 ✉ *1000* – ✆ *02 219 28 28*
– *www.radissonblu.com/royalhotel-brussels* **N1**
269 rm – 🛉95/175 € 🛉🛉105/185 €, ☕ 29 € – 12 suites
Rest *Sea Grill* ✿✿ – see restaurant listing
Rest *Atrium* – ✆ *02 227 31 70* – Menu 38 € (lunch) – Carte 30/48 €
◆ Palace ◆ Chain hotel ◆ Personalised ◆

Impressive modern glass atrium, remains of the city's fortifications, and extremely comfortable suites and guestrooms. Bar with comic book decor. Breakfast room adorned with wooden railway sleepers. A contemporary style brasserie illuminated by natural light through the glass roof.

The Hotel

bd de Waterloo 38 ✉ *1000* – ✆ *02 504 11 11* – *www.thehotel.be*
433 rm – 🛉90/400 € 🛉🛉90/400 €, ☕ 25 € **N3**
Rest – Menu 29/62 € – Carte approx. 55 €
◆ Chain hotel ◆ Grand Luxury ◆ Functional ◆

Enjoy the breathtaking view of Brussels and the hidden charms of the city in this well-preserved district. This establishment is also ideal for exploring the shops along Avenue Louise. Shopaholics take note!

Amigo

r. Amigo 1 ✉ *1000* – ✆ *02 547 47 47* – *www.roccofortehotels.com*
154 rm – 🛉199/660 € 🛉🛉199/660 € – 19 suites **M2**
Rest *Bocconi* – see restaurant listing
◆ Grand Luxury ◆ Personalised ◆

A real institution, and one of the best hotels in Brussels! Its assets? Its central location (behind the Grand Place), luxurious rooms, impeccable service and refined charm. You may even run into a celebrity here.

Le Plaza

bd A. Max 118 ✉ *1000* – ✆ *02 278 01 00* – *www.leplaza-brussels.be*
184 rm – 🛉120/495 € 🛉🛉140/495 €, ☕ 29 € – 6 suites *Plan II* **F1**
Rest *Brasserie l'Esterel* – *(closed school holidays, Saturday, Sunday and Bank Holidays)* Menu 39 € (lunch) – Carte 50/65 €
◆ Palace ◆ Personalised ◆

A 1930s building imitating the George V hotel in Paris. Classic public areas, large cosy guestrooms and a superb Baroque theatre used for receptions and events. An elegant bar and restaurant beneath an attractive dome painted with a trompe l'œil sky.

Métropole

pl. de Brouckère 31 ✉ *1000* – ✆ *02 217 23 00* – *www.metropolehotel.com*
283 rm ☕ – 🛉140/489 € 🛉🛉140/539 € – 5 suites **M1**
Rest *L'Alban Chambon* – see restaurant listing
◆ Grand Luxury ◆ Personalised ◆

A 19C luxury hotel overlooking Place de Brouckère. Period lobby and lounges, a retro-style lounge bar with columns, a piano and frescoes, and luxurious bedrooms and suites. Breakfast is served to a backdrop of colonial decor.

Royal Windsor

r. Duquesnoy 5 ✉ *1000* – ✆ *02 505 55 55*
– *www.royalwindsorbrussels.com* **M2**
260 rm – 🛉109/525 € 🛉🛉109/525 €, ☕ 30 € – 7 suites
Rest *Chutney's* – Menu 16 € (lunch) – Carte 40/65 €
◆ Grand Luxury ◆ Personalised ◆

Luxury, comfort and refinement are the hallmarks of this hotel, which has undergone recent refurbishment. Superb service. A varied choice of traditional dishes, bistro cuisine and Belgian specialities.

Marriott   ♨ 🕥 🔥 🎱 📶 🚭 🚲 🅥🅢🅐 ⓪ 🅐🅔

r. A. Orts 7 (opposite stock exchange) ⊠ 1000 – ℰ 0 2 516 90 90
– www.marriottbrussels.com   **M1**
214 rm – ♦99/399 € ♦♦99/399 €, ⊊ 25 € – 5 suites
Rest *Midtown Grill* – Carte approx. 35 €
♦ Luxury ♦ Personalised ♦
A famous piece of local folklore (The Marriage of Mademoiselle Beulemans) was
conceived behind the 1900 façade adjoining the Stock Exchange. Chic public
areas and bedrooms boasting every creature comfort. A brasserie with an
open kitchen serving grilled dishes and American-style cuisine. Lunch buffet.

 Le Méridien   ♨ 🔥 rm, 🎱 📶 🚭 🅥🅢🅐 ⓪ 🅐🅔 ⓪

Carrefour de l'Europe 3 ⊠ 1000 – ℰ 0 2 548 42 11
– www.lemeridien.com/brussels   **N2**
223 rm – ♦149/450 € ♦♦149/450 €, ⊊ 29 € – 1 suite
Rest *L'Épicerie* – Menu 38 € (lunch) – Carte approx. 50 €
♦ Luxury ♦ Personalised ♦
Built in the 1990s opposite the central station, the Méridien's curved façade is
palatial in style. Elegant lobby, varying categories of guestroom, and excellent
seminar facilities. The focus in the traditional dining room is on refined cuisine,
including a few typically Belgian dishes. Brunch on Sundays.

 The Dominican   ♨ 🕥 🔥 🎱 📶 🚭 🅥🅢🅐 ⓪ 🅐🅔 ⓪

r. Léopold 9 ⊠ 1000 – ℰ 0 2 203 08 08 – www.thedominican.be
147 rm – ♦450 € ♦♦477 €, ⊊ 27 € – 3 suites   **M1**
Rest *The Grand Lounge* – Menu 26 € (lunch), 30/60 € – Carte 35/58 €
♦ Luxury ♦ Business ♦ Personalised ♦
A designer-inspired luxury hotel on the site of a former Dominican convent.
Open spaces, elegant furniture and modern comforts which benefit from maximum attention to detail. The Grand Lounge takes full advantage of the natural
light from the patio. A modern menu and non-stop service, including the popular "after-work" drinks on Thursdays.

 Le Dixseptième without rest   🎱 📶 🚭 🅥🅢🅐 ⓪ 🅐🅔 ⓪

r. Madeleine 25 ⊠ 1000 – ℰ 0 2 517 17 17 – www.ledixseptieme.be
22 rm ⊊ – ♦140/300 € ♦♦180/400 € – 2 suites   **M2**
♦ Luxury ♦ Stylish ♦
This townhouse dating from the 17C was once the official residence of the Spanish ambassador in the city. Elegant lounges, attractive inner courtyard, and
guestrooms embellished with furniture of varying styles.

 NH du Grand Sablon   🔥 🎱 📶 🚭 🚭 🚲 🅥🅢🅐 ⓪ 🅐🅔 ⓪

r. Bodenbroek 2 ⊠ 1000 – ℰ 0 2 518 11 00 – www.nh-hotels.com
195 rm – ♦89/180 € ♦♦109/200 €, ⊊ 25 € – 1 suite   **M3**
Rest – (closed Sunday and Bank Holidays) Menu 17 € (lunch), 30 € bi/
60 € bi – Carte 44/56 €
♦ Chain hotel ♦ Business ♦ Personalised ♦
This establishment is well located in the antiques district, close to the city's prestigious royal museums. There is a marble adorned lobby, comfortable guestrooms, and facilities for business meetings. The hotel's restaurant specialises in
Italian cuisine.

Marivaux   🎱 📶 🚭 🚲 🅥🅢🅐 ⓪ 🅐🅔 ⓪

bd Adolphe Max 98 ⊠ 1000 – ℰ 0 2 227 03 00 – www.hotelmarivaux.be
96 rm ⊊ – ♦89/325 € ♦♦89/345 €   *Plan II* **F1**
Rest – (closed Saturday lunch and Sunday) Menu 10 € (lunch)/25 €
– Carte 32/43 €
♦ Business ♦ Functional ♦ Modern ♦
This hotel occupies several adjoining houses in the city centre. Revamped public areas, plus a conference centre which has taken over the old Marivaux
cinema. New guestrooms and a gastronomic restaurant are also planned. Brasserie cuisine served amid a contemporary decor.

Carrefour de l'Europe without rest 🏧 🛜 ⅏ 🆚 💳 🆎 ①

r. Marché-aux-Herbes 110 ✉ *1000 –* ℰ *0 2 504 94 00*
– www.carrefourhotel.be   **M2**
59 rm ⚏ – ♦129/339 € ♦♦149/359 € – 6 suites
♦ Business ♦ Functional ♦
This hotel built a decade or so ago is situated between the Grand Place and
the central train station on the edge of the Ilot Sacré. Reasonably sized, functional guestrooms which are brighter in appearance following their upgrade
in 2009.

Sandton without rest 🐾 ᴕ 🛜 ⅏ 🚗 🆚 💳 🆎 ①

r. Paroissiens 15 ✉ *1000 –* ℰ *0 2 274 08 10 – www.sandton.eu*
67 rm – ♦89/400 € ♦♦89/400 €, ⚏ 20 € – 3 suites   **N2**
♦ Business ♦ Modern ♦
If location is your prime criteria, this hotel, located only 5min from the station
and bang in the heart of the city, is perfect. The rooms are brand new and well
looked after, and all have reasonable rates.

Atlas without rest 🐾 ᴕ 🛜 ⅏ 🚗 🆚 💳 🆎 ①

r. Vieux Marché-aux-Grains 30 ✉ *1000 –* ℰ *0 2 502 60 06*
– www.atlas.be   **L1**
88 rm ⚏ – ♦79/230 € ♦♦90/260 €
♦ Family ♦ Functional ♦
This extensively modernised 18C townhouse is situated in a lively part of the
city renowned for its Belgian fashion boutiques. The majority of the hotel's
rooms overlook the courtyard.

Noga without rest 🛜 🚗 🆚 💳 🆎 ①

r. Béguinage 38 ✉ *1000 –* ℰ *0 2 218 67 63 – www.nogahotel.com*
19 rm ⚏ – ♦75/115 € ♦♦85/135 €   **L1**
♦ Family ♦ Classic ♦
This welcoming mansion located in a quiet part of the city offers a cosy lounge,
nautically themed bar, and comfortable, traditional guestrooms. Portraits of the
Belgian royal family line the stairwell.

Queen Anne without rest 🛜 🆚 💳 🆎 ①

bd E. Jacqmain 110 ✉ *1000 –* ℰ *0 2 217 16 00 – www.queen-anne.be*
60 rm ⚏ – ♦60/200 € ♦♦70/250 €   *Plan II* **F1**
♦ Family ♦ Modern ♦
Recognisable by its glass-fronted façade, this hotel is located close to the city
centre. Guestrooms and apartments offering a bright minimalist feel and discreet designer touches.

Matignon without rest 🛜 🆚 💳 🆎

r. Bourse 10 ✉ *1000 –* ℰ *0 2 511 08 88 – www.hotelmatignon.be*
37 rm ⚏ – ♦95/150 € ♦♦115/150 €   **M1**
♦ Family ♦ Functional ♦
This hotel close to the city's stock exchange has been run by the same family for
two decades. Well-maintained guestrooms, including nine junior suites.

XXX Sea Grill (Yves Mattagne) – Hôtel Radisson Blu Royal ᴕ 🏧 ⇔ 🍽
🌸🌸

r. Fossé-aux-Loups 47 ✉ *1000 –* ℰ *0 2 212 08 00*
– www.seagrill.be   🆚 💳 🆎
– closed 8-14 April, 9-12 May, 22 July-18 August, 1-6 January, Bank Holidays,
Saturday and Sunday   **N1**
Rest – Menu 65 € (lunch), 120/185 € – Carte 110/174 € ❀
♦ Fish and seafood ♦ Elegant ♦
The menu varies according to the catch of the day. The sea supplies the treasu-
res and the crew steers the ship with flying colours! A challenging, first-rate per-
formance with some prestigious wines in the hold for an unforgettable crossing.
It has secluded tables that are ideal for business lunches.
➜ Langoustine et foie gras aux carottes, piment, caramel et cacahouètes.
Turbot rôti à l'arête, béarnaise à l'eau d'huîtres, raviolis d'algues et chloro-
phylle d'estragon. Citron de Menton, nougat et granité au mojito.

XXXX **La Maison du Cygne** 🔲 ⬄ 🍴 **P** VISA ⮂ AE ⓘ

r. Charles Buls 2 (1st Floor) ✉ *1000 –* ☎ *0 2 511 82 44*
– www.lamaisonducygne.be
– closed 3 weeks August, Christmas-New Year, Saturday lunch and Sunday
Rest – Menu 45 € (lunch)/65 € – Carte 71/91 €   M2
Rest *L'Ommegang* – see restaurant listing
♦ Traditional ♦ Elegant ♦
This prestigious 17C building on the Grand Place was once home to the city's butchers' guild. Varied traditional cuisine and an opulent decor.

XXXX **Bruneau** (Jean-Pierre Bruneau) 🍴 🔲 ⬄ 🍴 (dinner)
🍀

av. Broustin 75 ✉ *1083 –* ☎ *0 2 421 70 70*   VISA ⮂ AE ⓘ
– www.bruneau.be
– closed mid June-mid July, 3-12 January, Bank Holiday Thursdays, Tuesday and Wednesday   Plan I **B2**
Rest – Menu 40 € (lunch), 55/95 € – Carte 86/195 € ❀
♦ Classic ♦ Elegant ♦
A renowned restaurant offering a perfect balance between the traditional and the innovative, while at the same time showcasing regional cuisine. Impressive wine list. Outdoor terrace for summer dining.
→ Carpaccio de langoustines à la crème au raifort et caviar. Turbot au fenouil et curry rouge à l'huile d'olive citronnée. Sablé au fondant de chocolat noir.

XXXX **L'Alban Chambon** – Hôtel Métropole 🔲 ⬄ 🍴 VISA ⮂ AE ⓘ

pl. de Brouckère 31 ✉ *1000 –* ☎ *0 2 217 23 00 – www.albanchambon.com*
– closed July-August, Saturday lunch, Sunday, Monday and Bank Holidays
Rest – Menu 30 € (lunch), 68/110 €   M1
♦ Classic ♦ Elegant ♦ Luxury ♦
The name of the Métropole's restaurant pays homage to its architect. Classic cuisine in an old Baroque-style ballroom.

XXX **Comme Chez Soi** (Lionel Rigolet) 🔲 ⬄ 🍴 VISA ⮂ AE ⓘ
🍀🍀

pl. Rouppe 23 ✉ *1000 –* ☎ *0 2 512 29 21 – www.commechezsoi.be*
– closed 2 and 3 April, 1st May, 14 July-12 August, 29 October, 23 December-7 January, 12 February, Wednesday lunch, Sunday and Monday   L2
Rest – (pre-book) Menu 55 € (lunch), 89/151 € – Carte 91/311 €
♦ Traditional ♦ Formal ♦
This Brussels institution was founded in 1926. The menu features specialities that have held their own over four generations, complemented by new creations by Lionel Rigolet. It has all the comfort of a bistro, Horta-inspired decor and comfortable tables in the kitchen itself, from where you can watch the chefs in action.
→ Daurade royale, bouillon de petits gris à l'estragon et au curry. Pigeon au jus léger épicé au miel et fondue de lentins de chêne. Croquant au chocolat, ganache de caramel à la fleur de sel et riz soufflé, écume à la liqueur de café.

XXX **San Daniele** (Franco Spinelli) 🔲 ⬄ VISA ⮂ AE ⓘ
🍀

av. Charles-Quint 6 ✉ *1083 –* ☎ *0 2 426 79 23 – www.san-daniele.be*
– closed mid July-mid August, Bank Holidays, Sunday and Monday
Rest – Menu 38 € (lunch)/85 € – Carte 54/95 € ❀   Plan I **A2**
♦ Italian ♦ Elegant ♦
An attractive dining room serving typical Italian cuisine accompanied by an enticing Italian wine list. Friendly, attentive service from the Spinelli family.
→ Tartare de thon et citron confit au foie gras, pesto de roquette et croquant de parmesan. Turbot en croûte de tomate confite, écume de beurre au basilic. Raviolis à la crème de tonka et sorbet au pamplemousse rose.

XXX **Bocconi** – Hôtel Amigo ♿ 🔲 ⬄ 🍴 VISA ⮂ AE ⓘ

r. Amigo 1 ✉ *1000 –* ☎ *0 2 547 47 15 – www.ristorantebocconi.com*
Rest – Menu 19/55 € – Carte 38/71 €   M2
♦ Italian ♦ Brasserie ♦ Elegant ♦
This renowned Italian restaurant occupies a luxury hotel near the Grand Place. Modern brasserie-style decor provides the backdrop for enticing Italian cuisine.

XX **L'Écailler du Palais Royal** ⁣ AC VISA ⁣⁣ AE ⁣⁣

r. Bodenbroek 18 ⊠ 1000 – ℰ 02 512 87 51 – www.lecaillerdupalaisroyal.be
– closed August, late December, Bank Holidays and Sunday **N3**
Rest – Menu 55 € (lunch) – Carte 68/156 €
♦ Fish and seafood ♦ Cosy ♦

An elegant and cosy oyster bar frequented by diplomats and top business executives for the past 40 years. Choose from banquette seating and a convivial counter-bar downstairs or round tables upstairs. Refined fish and seafood.

XX **Aux Armes de Bruxelles** ⁣ AC ⇔ VISA ⁣⁣ AE

r. Bouchers 13 ⊠ 1000 – ℰ 02 511 55 50
– www.auxarmesdebruxelles.com **M1**
Rest – Menu 35/85 € bi – Carte 30/69 €
♦ Traditional ♦ Brasserie ♦

This veritable Brussels institution in the Ilot Sacré district has been honouring Belgian culinary traditions since 1921. Contrasting dining rooms and a lively atmosphere.

XX **La Brasserie de Bruxelles** ⁣ AC VISA ⁣⁣ AE
☺

pl. de la Vieille Halle aux Blés 39 ⊠ 1000 – ℰ 02 513 98 12
– www.labrasseriedebruxelles.be
– closed 15 July-1 August, 1-15 January and Monday **M2**
Rest – (open until 11pm) Menu 22 € (lunch)/35 € – Carte 36/63 €
♦ Traditional ♦ Brasserie ♦ Formal ♦

Fancy a glimpse of the local life of Brussels? Head for the Brasserie de Bruxelles and immerse yourself in the city's ambience on the picturesque Vieille-Halles-aux-Blés square, and savour the unpretentious, authentic flavours of the capital.

XX **La Belle Maraîchère** ⁣ AC ⇔ P VISA ⁣⁣ AE ⁣⁣
☺

pl. Ste-Catherine 11 ⊠ 1000 – ℰ 02 512 97 59 – www.labellemaraichere.com
– closed late July-early August, 2 weeks at carnival, Wednesday and Thursday
Rest – (booking advisable) Menu 36/58 € – Carte 49/104 € **L1**
♦ Fish and seafood ♦ Bistro ♦

This welcoming, family-run restaurant is a popular choice for locals with charmingly nostalgic decor in the dining room. Enticing traditional cuisine, including fish, seafood and game depending on the season, as well as high quality sauces. Attractive set menus.

XX **JB** ⁣ AC ⇔ VISA ⁣⁣ AE ⁣⁣
☺

r. Grand Cerf 24 ⊠ 1000 – ℰ 02 512 04 84 – www.restaurantjb.be
– closed August, Bank Holidays, Saturday lunch and Sunday **M3**
Rest – Menu 25/44 € – Carte 51/66 €
♦ Classic ♦ Friendly ♦ Family ♦

A family affair founded in 1979. The owner is also a sauce chef with many strings to his bow; he offers refined dishes at affordable prices. The restaurant has Lloyd Loom chairs, an Italian chandelier and yellow patina on the walls.

XX **Lola** ⁣ AC VISA ⁣⁣ AE

pl. du Grand Sablon 33 ⊠ 1000 – ℰ 02 514 24 60 – www.restolola.be
– closed first 2 weeks August **M3**
Rest – (open until 11.30pm) Carte 39/74 €
♦ Italian ♦ Brasserie ♦

Friendly brasserie with a contemporary decor serving Italian dishes based on the freshest ingredients. The pleasant counter is perfect for a meal on the hoof.

XX **Jaloa** (Gaëtan Colin) ⁣ AC ⇔ ⇨ VISA ⁣⁣ AE ⁣⁣
✤

quai aux Barques 4 ⊠ 1000 – ℰ 02 513 19 92 – www.jaloa.com
– closed 4-17 August, 6-12 November, 21-27 February, Sunday and Monday
Rest – (set menu only) Menu 45 € (lunch), 65/105 € *Plan II* **E1**
♦ Innovative ♦ Fashionable ♦

This restaurant is housed in one of the oldest buildings in "Vismet" (17C). The innovative food – served in a single set menu – is in stark contrast with the historical setting.

➜ Tomate mozzarella et homard. Turbot rôti aux champignons des bois, textures de betterave rouge. Feuilleté de mangue à la crème brûlée.

XX **L'Huîtrière** 🛖 ↻ 𝗩𝗜𝗦𝗔 ⦾ 𝗔𝗘 ⓞ

quai aux Briques 20 ✉ 1000 – 𝒞 0 2 512 08 66 – www.lhuitriere.be
Rest – Menu 17 € (lunch), 25/47 € – Carte 37/78 €   **L1**
♦ Fish and seafood ♦ Inn ♦ Rustic ♦
Fish and seafood are to the fore here, to a backdrop of old Brussels, including wood panelling and Bruegel-inspired murals. Popular with celebrities, although the star turn here is the house speciality: lobster with sea urchin butter.

XX **Les Larmes du Tigre** 🛖 ↻ 𝗩𝗜𝗦𝗔 ⦾ 𝗔𝗘 ⓞ

r. Wynants 21 ✉ 1000 – 𝒞 0 2 512 18 77 – www.leslarmesdutigre.be
– closed Saturday lunch and Monday   *Plan II* **F3**
Rest – Menu 13 € (lunch), 27 € bi/38 € – Carte 34/45 €
♦ Thai ♦ Exotic ♦
A real voyage for the taste buds! They have been serving authentic Thai food here for 25 years, and the enjoyment for money ratio is excellent. Buffet at lunch and Sunday evenings.

XX **La Tortue du Sablon** 🛖 𝗩𝗜𝗦𝗔 ⦾ 𝗔𝗘 ⓞ

r. Rollebeek 31 ✉ 1000 – 𝒞 0 2 513 10 62 – www.latortue.be
– closed Thursday   **M3**
Rest – Menu 25 € (lunch), 36/79 € – Carte 54/80 €
♦ Classic ♦ Friendly ♦
After a stroll through the Sablon neighbourhood, home to the capital's antique dealers, where better to build up your strength than with a meal here? Fine ingredients take pride of place on the classical menu, including truffles in season. You won't be disappointed!

XX **Brasserie Jaloa Jardin** 🛖 𝗔𝗖 ↻ 𝗩𝗜𝗦𝗔 ⦾ 𝗔𝗘 ⓞ

pl. Ste-Catherine 5 ✉ 1000 – 𝒞 0 2 512 18 31 – www.jaloa.com
– closed 15-24 August   **L1**
Rest – Menu 22 € (lunch), 49/79 € bi – Carte 41/64 €
♦ Traditional ♦ Friendly ♦ Design ♦
Typical Belgian brasserie fare is served in two bright and elegant dining rooms or on the charming and secluded courtyard terrace.

XX **François** 🛖 𝗔𝗖 ↻ 🛋 𝗩𝗜𝗦𝗔 ⦾ 𝗔𝗘 ⓞ

quai aux Briques 2 ✉ 1000 – 𝒞 0 2 511 60 89
– www.restaurantfrancois.be
– closed 18 August-10 September, Sunday and Monday   **L1**
Rest – Menu 27 € (lunch), 35/42 € – Carte 44/105 €
♦ Fish and seafood ♦ Brasserie ♦
Fish and seafood take pride of place in this restaurant run by the same family since the 1930s. Maritime-inspired decor including photos from the past. Fishmonger's next door.

X **La Manufacture** 🛖 ↻ 🛋 𝗩𝗜𝗦𝗔 ⦾ 𝗔𝗘

r. Notre-Dame du Sommeil 12 ✉ 1000 – 𝒞 0 2 502 25 25
– www.manufacture.be
– closed Saturday lunch and Sunday   **L1**
Rest – *(open until 11pm)* Menu 16 € (lunch), 35/70 € bi – Carte 34/53 €
♦ Modern ♦ Brasserie ♦ Trendy ♦
Metals, wood, leather and granite provide the decor in this lively, trendy brasserie in the former workshop of a famous Belgian luggage maker. Contemporary cuisine.

X **Bozar Brasserie** 🛖 ↻ 𝗩𝗜𝗦𝗔 ⦾ 𝗔𝗘

r. Baron Horta 3 ✉ 1000 – 𝒞 0 2 503 00 00 – www.bozarbrasserie.be
– closed Sunday and Monday   **N2**
Rest – Menu 23 € (lunch), 33/37 € – Carte 40/76 €
♦ Traditional ♦ Friendly ♦
If you know the chef at La Paix - the "benefactress" of this restaurant - you'll recognise her touch right away. Refinement and presentation are the strongpoints of the original brasserie food here. An establishment that's well worth a try!

BELGIUM - BRUSSELS

Alexandre (Alexandre Dionisio)

r. Midi 164 ⊠ 1000 – 𝒞 0 2 502 40 55 – www.alexandre-restaurant.be
– closed first 2 weeks April, 29 July-23 August, 1 week at All Saints' day, first 2
weeks January, Saturday, Sunday and Monday **L2**
Rest – (booking essential) Menu 35 € (lunch), 75/130 € – Carte 57/115 €
♦ Innovative ♦ Bistro ♦ Minimalist ♦

One of the finalists of a television show in 2010, this young chef has not ceased
to sparkle ever since. His cuisine, based on fine produce, is both appetising and
intelligent. It is poised between modernity and classicism, and has given him a
well-earned place in Brussels' limelight.

➔ Joue de bœuf aux pommes caramélisées et morilles. Sole aux légumes
de saison et sauce à la sarriette. Dame blanche.

L'Ommegang – Rest La Maison du Cygne

Grand'Place 9 ⊠ 1000 – 𝒞 0 2 511 82 44
– www.brasseriedelommegang.be
– closed 3 weeks August, Christmas-New Year, Saturday lunch and Sunday
Rest – Carte 34/60 € **M2**
♦ Traditional ♦ Rustic ♦

You will enjoy the classic, copious Belgian cuisine served at this brasserie, which
is the little sister of the famous Maison du Cygne. It is surrounded by the
ambience of "the most beautiful square in the world", as Victor Hugo once
said. The affable staff display typical Brussels humour.

De l'Ogenblik

Galerie des Princes 1 ⊠ 1000 – 𝒞 0 2 511 61 51 – www.ogenblik.be
– closed 1-15 August, lunch on Bank Holidays and Sunday **M1**
Rest – (open until midnight) Menu 51/58 € – Carte 48/70 €
♦ Traditional ♦ Bistro ♦

This restaurant popular with the city's business crowd has the appearance of an
old café. Traditional cuisine including typical bistro dishes. The same chef has
been working here since 1975.

Scheltema

r. Dominicains 7 ⊠ 1000 – 𝒞 0 2 512 20 84 – www.scheltema.be
– closed 24 and 25 December and Sunday **M1**
Rest – (open until 11.30pm) Menu 18 € (lunch), 29/39 € – Carte 42/90 €
♦ Fish and seafood ♦ Brasserie ♦

An attractive old brasserie located in the city's Ilot Sacré district. Traditional
dishes and daily specials with fish and seafood specialities. A lively atmosphere
and a pleasant retro-style wooden decor.

La Roue d'Or

r. Chapeliers 26 ⊠ 1000 – 𝒞 0 2 514 25 54
– closed 15 July-13 August **M2**
Rest – (open until 11.30pm) Menu 15 € (lunch) – Carte 42/55 €
♦ Traditional ♦ Brasserie ♦

This typical old Brussels café with a friendly atmosphere mixes traditional brasserie-style dishes with a handful of Belgian specialities. Decor includes Magritte-
style murals and a superb clock in the dining room.

Samourai

r. Fossé-aux-Loups 28 ⊠ 1000 – 𝒞 0 2 217 56 39
– www.samourai-restaurant.be
– closed 1-21 August, 24 December-6 January, Sunday and Monday
Rest – Menu 27 € (lunch), 69/110 € – Carte 52/80 € **M1**
♦ Japanese ♦ Exotic ♦ Minimalist ♦

A Japanese restaurant which opened in 1975 near the Théâtre de la Monnaie.
Dining rooms on three floors with a Japanese decorative theme. Top-notch cuisine based around quality products and adapted to Western tastes.

Little Asia   AC ⇔ VISA ⦿ AE

r. Ste-Catherine 8 ⊠ 1000 – ☏ 0 2 502 88 36 – www.littleasia.be
– closed last 2 weeks July, Wednesday, Sunday and Bank Holidays
Rest – (open until 11pm) Menu 25 € (lunch), 40/60 €   **L1**
– Carte 38/80 €
♦ Vietnamese ♦ Fashionable ♦
A restaurant known for its well-prepared Vietnamese specialities, modern decor
and smiling waitresses, overseen by a charming female owner.

Royal   ⋒ ⇔ VISA ⦿ AE

r. Flandre 103 ⊠ 1000 – ☏ 0 2 217 85 00 – www.royalbrasseriebrussels.be
Rest – (open until 11.30pm) Menu 25 € (lunch)/38 € – Carte   **L1**
approx. 40 €
♦ Traditional ♦ Fashionable ♦ Musical ♦
An exceedingly fashionable establishment, ideal for an evening in town. The
service is hip (in sailor's t-shirts) and diligent, to the satisfaction of the numerous
patrons who come (back) for the great brasserie classics.

Selecto   VISA ⦿ AE

r. Flandre 95 ⊠ 1000 – ☏ 0 2 511 40 95 – www.le-selecto.com
– closed Sunday and Monday   **L1**
Rest – Menu 18 € (lunch), 33/39 € – Carte approx. 50 €
♦ Traditional ♦ Fashionable ♦ Bistro ♦
In the heart of the lively Ste-Catherine neighbourhood, the Selecto leads Belgium's vanguard of bistronomic (bistro + gastronomic) culture. Good food, a
great atmosphere and reasonable prices!

Viva M'Boma   ⋒ AC ⇔ VISA ⦿

r. Flandre 17 ⊠ 1000 – ☏ 0 2 512 15 93
– closed first week April, 1-15 August, first week January, Wednesday, Sunday
and Bank Holidays   **L1**
Rest – Carte 27/41 €
♦ Traditional ♦ Family ♦
This elegant canteen-style restaurant has closely packed tables and tiled walls
reminiscent of a Parisian métro station. It is popular with fans of offal and old
Brussels specialities (cow's udder, choesels (sweetbreads), marrowbone, ox cheek).

Henri   VISA ⦿ AE

r. Flandre 113 ⊠ 1000 – ☏ 0 2 218 00 08 – www.restohenri.be
– closed 20 July-12 August, Saturday lunch, Sunday and Monday
Rest – Menu 15 € (lunch) – Carte 36/59 € 🕭   **L1**
♦ Traditional ♦ Brasserie ♦ Friendly ♦
Who would not dream of having such a brasserie just down the street? Henri
has been delighting the locals of this Flemish-speaking neighbourhood with
its good food. It is an ideal marriage between flawlessly prepared French dishes
and a laidback ambience. The minute you leave, you will want to return, just like
the many regulars.

La Marée   ⋒ AC ⇔ VISA ⦿ AE

r. Flandre 99 ⊠ 1000 – ☏ 0 2 511 00 40 – www.lamaree-sa.com
– closed 20 June-15 July, Christmas, New Year, Sunday and Monday
Rest – Carte 23/71 €   **L1**
♦ Fish and seafood ♦ Bistro ♦
A convivial restaurant with simple decor and uncomplicated cuisine, with an
emphasis on fish and seafood and Portuguese dishes (on request). Open kitchen and summer terrace.

L'Idiot du village   VISA ⦿ AE

r. Notre Seigneur 19 ⊠ 1000 – ☏ 0 2 502 55 82 – www.lidiotduvillage.be
– closed 20 July-16 August, 23 December-3 January, Saturday and Sunday
Rest – (open until 11pm) Menu 17 € (lunch) – Carte 40/65 €   **M3**
♦ Classic ♦ Bistro ♦
A neighbourhood restaurant with friendly staff, charmingly kitsch decor, an intimate ambience, and bistro-style cuisine with a contemporary flourish based
around fresh ingredients. Very popular with locals.

BELGIUM - BRUSSELS

In 't Spinnekopke

pl. du Jardin aux Fleurs 1 ⊠ *1000* – ℰ *0 2 511 86 95*
– *www.spinnekopke.be*
– *closed Saturday lunch and Sunday* **L1**
Rest – *(open until 11pm)* Menu 15 € (lunch) – Carte 30/55 €
♦ **Traditional** ♦ **Bistro** ♦
A charming inn so typical of Brussels, with a bistro-style ambience and a menu that pays homage to the traditions of Belgian brasseries. Terrace on the square.

Bar Bik

quai aux Pierres de Taille 3 ⊠ *1000* – ℰ *0 2 219 75 00*
– *closed late December-early January, Saturday, Sunday and Bank Holidays*
Rest – *(booking advisable)* Carte 28/58 € *Plan II* **F1**
♦ **Traditional** ♦ **Friendly** ♦ **Minimalist** ♦
The Bar Bik (Brussels International Kitchen) features a slate menu with dishes from near and far. Friendly, laidback atmosphere and a minimalist decor.

Madou's Provence

r. Presse 23 ⊠ *1000* – ℰ *0 2 217 38 31* – *www.madousprovence.be*
– *closed Easter week, 21 July-15 August, Monday dinner, Saturday, Sunday and Bank Holidays* **O1**
Rest – Menu 28 € (lunch), 36/45 € – Carte 42/56 €
♦ **Provençal** ♦ **Bistro** ♦
The mild climate and art de vivre of Provençal France come together here in your plate. The chef takes a new look at Mediterranean classics, inventing recipes such as crème brûlée flavoured with lavender or smoked salmon with gaspacho.

El Txoko

r. Laeken 122 ⊠ *1000* – ℰ *0 2 203 10 22* – *www.eltxoko.be*
– *closed Bank Holidays, Monday dinner, Tuesday dinner, Saturday lunch and Sunday* *Plan II* **F1**
Rest – Menu 14 € (lunch)/30 € bi – Carte 23/43 €
♦ **Spanish** ♦ **Fashionable** ♦ **Tapas bar** ♦
This excellent Basque tapas bar has a minimalist interior and is located in a trendy area. Assortment of *pintxos* and an appealing and varied array of Spanish wines. The nearby KVS (Théâtre Royal Flamand) draws in a culture loving crowd but everyone is welcome!

L'Achepot - l'HPO

pl. Ste-Catherine 1 ⊠ *1000* – ℰ *0 2 511 62 21*
– *closed 1 week at Easter, last 2 weeks July, Sunday and Monday*
Rest – Menu 16 € (lunch) – Carte 34/55 € **L1**
♦ **Classic** ♦ **Bistro** ♦
An elegant and welcoming neo-bistro on the lively Place Sainte-Catherine. The menu board highlights a mix of local and southern French dishes.

Switch

r. Flandre 6 ⊠ *1000* – ℰ *0 2 503 14 80* – *www.switchrestofood.be*
– *closed Monday lunch, Saturday lunch and Sunday* **L1**
Rest – Menu 35/75 € bi – Carte 41/62 €
♦ **Traditional** ♦ **Bistro** ♦
Marc Boutsen switched from a career as a food critic to that of a restaurateur. His original idea at Switch is that you compose your own meal with two or three dishes from the menu. Unbeatable value for money.

Strofilia

r. Marché-aux-Porcs 11 ⊠ *1000* – ℰ *0 2 512 32 93* – *www.strofilia.be*
– *closed 21 July-15 August, Saturday lunch and Sunday* **L1**
Rest – *(open until 11.30pm)* Menu 13 € (lunch)/25 € – Carte approx. 40 €
♦ **Greek** ♦ **Trendy** ♦
Located close to the trendy Dansaert district, this typical "ouzeri" serves guests in its large loft-style dining rooms and vaulted cellar. A choice of Greek mezze, main courses and wines. The name comes from the attractive grape press on display ("strofilia" in Greek).

X **Enjoy**   AC ⇄ VISA ©© AE

bd de Waterloo 22 ✉ *1000* – ☎ *02 641 57 90* – *www.enjoybrussels.be*
– *closed Sunday and Bank Holidays*   **N3**
Rest – Carte 34/64 €
♦ Modern ♦ Brasserie ♦
For those who can't choose between lunch and a BMW. This contemporary
brasserie is housed in the showroom of the famous car manufacturer.

X **Les Petits Oignons**   ⛲ ⇄ VISA ©© AE

r. Régence 25 ✉ *1000* – ☎ *02 511 76 15* – *www.lespetitsoignons.be*
Rest – *(open until 11pm)* Menu 35/50 € – Carte 36/57 €   **M3**
♦ Classic ♦ Brasserie ♦
People love this brasserie with its nostalgic decor and food that combines gene-
rosity and expertise. They flock here from all over the neighbourhood, delighted
to be given the royal treatment!

X **Orphyse Chaussette**   ⛲ VISA ©© AE

r. Charles Hanssens 5 ✉ *1000* – ☎ *02 502 75 81*
– *closed 7-15 April, 21 July-15 August, 23 December-1 January, Sunday,*
Monday and Bank Holidays   **M3**
Rest – Menu 15 € bi (lunch), 42/49 € – Carte 43/63 €
♦ Traditional ♦ Wine bar ♦ Neighbourhood ♦
Trompe-l'œil library, crystal chandelier and old tiling: this restaurant in the Sab-
lon area may be small, but it has plenty of charm! Tasty cooking from the South
of France.

X **Bistro du Canal**   ⛲ VISA ©© AE

r. Antoine Dansaert 208 ✉ *1000* – ☎ *02 511 03 60*
– *www.bistroducanal.be*
– *closed 21 July-15 August, Saturday and Sunday*   **L1**
Rest – Menu 15 € (lunch) – Carte 27/35 €
♦ Traditional ♦ Bistro ♦ Friendly ♦
Those who appreciate France's wine, food, language and culture will love this
friendly, open-plan bistro, as much for its wholesome dishes, as well as its reasonable prices.

X **Le Wine Bar**   VISA ©©

r. Pigeons 9 ✉ *1000* – ☎ *02 503 62 50* – *www.winebarsablon.be*
– *closed mid July-mid August, Christmas-New Year, Bank Holiday Mondays and*
Sunday   **M3**
Rest – *(dinner only until 11pm)* Carte 24/48 € 🏠
♦ Traditional ♦ Wine bar ♦ Bistro ♦
Are you a fan of dishes that draw on local specialities, redolent of the *terroir*? If
so, don't miss Le Wine Bar! Known only to insiders, this restaurant installed in a
vaulted cellar offers hearty cuisine and a good choice of wines.

QUARTIER LOUISE-CAMBRE   *Plan III*

🏨🏨🏨 **Conrad**   ᵇ ⊕ 🐾 🗒 ⅄ AC 🛜 ⅄ ⊅ ⌂ VISA ©© AE ⓪

av. Louise 71 ✉ *1050* – ☎ *02 542 42 42* – *www.conradbrussels.com*
253 rm – ♦198/450 € ♦♦198/599 €, � 38 € – 14 suites   **J1**
Rest *Café Wiltcher's* – ☎ *02 542 48 50* – Menu 55 € (lunch)
– Carte 53/82 €
♦ Chain hotel ♦ Grand Luxury ♦ Personalised ♦
The Conrad offers modern luxury within the walls of an historic building dating
from 1918. Attractive and stylish guestrooms, excellent leisure and spa options,
as well as extensive conference facilities.

BELGIUM - BRUSSELS

Bristol Stephanie   🔥 🏠 🔥 rest, 🅰️ 🛜 🧖 🍽 🚗 VISA ⓪ 🅰️ ①

av. Louise 91 ✉ *1050* – 🕿 *0 2 543 33 11*
– *www.thonhotels.com/bristolstephanie*   **J1**
140 rm – 🛏180/425 € 🛏🛏200/450 €, ☕ 25 € – 2 suites
Rest – *(closed lunch Saturday and Sunday)* Menu 19 € (lunch)/35 €
– Carte approx. 43 €
◆ Luxury ◆ Business ◆ Personalised ◆
A luxury hotel with attractive guestrooms (49 of which have been renovated) spread between two interconnecting buildings. Superb, Norwegian-style suites. A modern brasserie with the typical decor of a leading hotel.

Sofitel Le Louise   🔥 🔥 🅰️ 🛜 🧖 VISA ⓪ 🅰️ ①

av. de la Toison d'Or 40 ✉ *1050* – 🕿 *0 2 514 22 00* – *www.sofitel.com*
159 rm – 🛏430/530 € 🛏🛏430/530 €, ☕ 29 € – 10 suites   **J1**
Rest *Crystal Lounge* – see restaurant listing
◆ Chain hotel ◆ Business ◆ Modern ◆
An escalator skirting an unusual lace mural leads to the chandelier crowned lobby of this hotel. It has been refurbished by interior designer Antoine Pinto and has attractive guestrooms. This restaurant has an ever-changing ambience and is a must for dedicated gourmets. Find an attractive menu, sophisticated decor, as well as the cocktail bar with a display of Val Saint-Lambert crystal carafes.

Le Châtelain   🕳 🏠 🔥 🔥 🅰️ 🛜 🧖 🍽 🚗 VISA ⓪ 🅰️ ①

r. Châtelain 17 ✉ *1000* – 🕿 *0 2 646 00 55* – *www.le-chatelain.com*
91 rm – 🛏85/350 € 🛏🛏100/450 €, ☕ 25 € – 16 suites   **J2**
Rest – *(closed Friday and Saturday) (dinner only)* Carte 36/44 €
◆ Luxury ◆ Business ◆ Personalised ◆
An opulent hotel offering well-appointed large guestrooms with an Internet connection, satellite TV and air-conditioning. Meeting rooms and a fitness centre. Belgian and French gastronomy influenced by Asian cuisine is to the fore in Le Châtelain restaurant.

Warwick Barsey   🏠 🔥 🅰️ 🛜 🧖 🍽 🚗 VISA ⓪ 🅰️

av. Louise 381 ✉ *1050* – 🕿 *0 2 649 98 00* – *www.warwickbarsey.com*
94 rm – 🛏99/450 € 🛏🛏99/450 €, ☕ 29 € – 5 suites   **K3**
Rest *Barsey* – Menu 17 € (lunch), 34/95 € – Carte 45/72 €
◆ Luxury ◆ Business ◆ Stylish ◆
A magnificent Second Empire hotel near the Bois de la Cambre, with spacious and luxurious rooms. A favourite with artists and filmmakers!

Manos Premier   🚗 🔥 🏠 🅰️ 🛜 🧖 🚗 VISA ⓪ 🅰️ ①

chaussée de Charleroi 102 ✉ *1060* – 🕿 *0 2 537 96 82*
– *www.manoshotel.com*   **J2**
47 rm – 🛏109/449 € 🛏🛏129/499 €, ☕ 20 € – 3 suites
Rest *Kolya* – see restaurant listing
◆ Luxury ◆ Business ◆ Stylish ◆
The Manos Premier has the grace of a late-19C townhouse with its rich Louis XV and Louis XVI furnishings. If possible, book a room overlooking the garden. Authentic oriental hammam in the basement. Stylish restaurant, veranda and lounge bar. Chic and elegant decor, plus a charming patio.

Manos Stéphanie *without rest*   🛜 🚗 VISA ⓪ 🅰️ ①

chaussée de Charleroi 28 ✉ *1060* – 🕿 *0 2 539 02 50*
– *www.manoshotel.com*   **J1**
55 rm – 🛏99/249 € 🛏🛏129/299 €, ☕ 20 €
◆ Luxury ◆ Stylish ◆
A townhouse with warm, classically styled guestrooms with a contemporary feel and light wood furnishings. Cupola above the breakfast room.

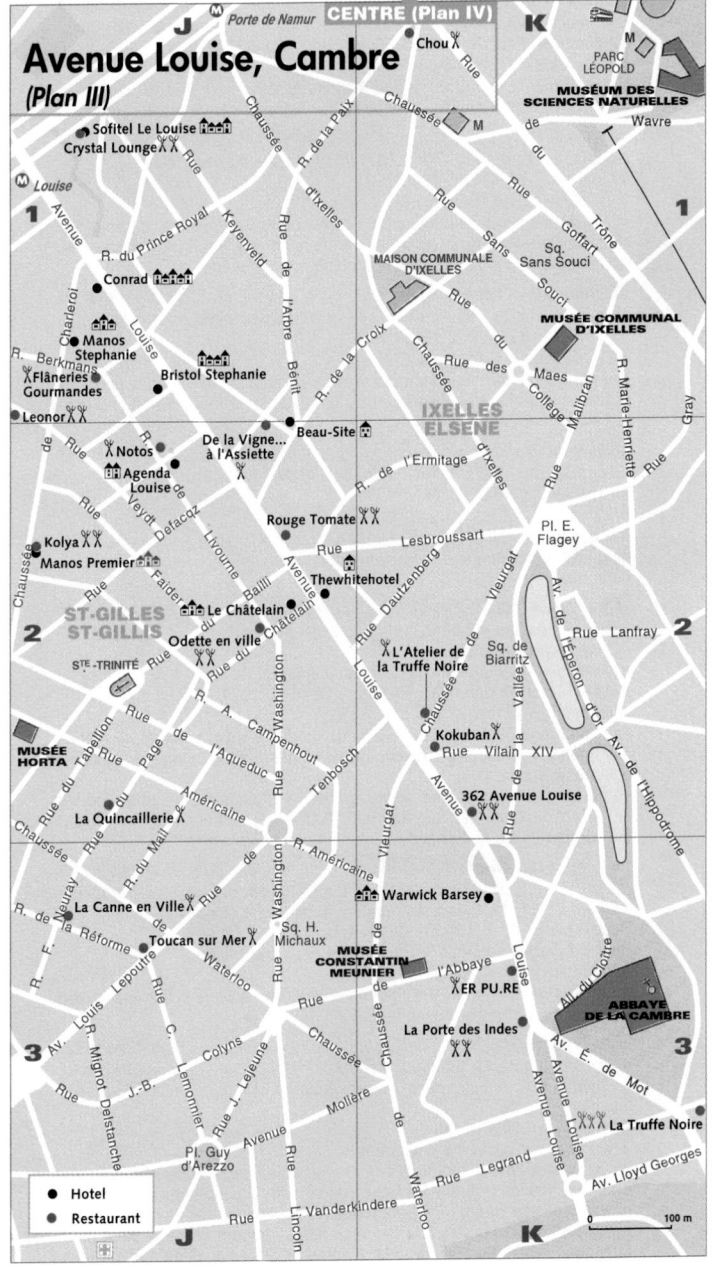

Avenue Louise, Cambre
(Plan III)

CENTRE (Plan IV)

Porte de Namur

Chou

PARC LÉOPOLD

MUSÉUM DES
SCIENCES NATURELLES

Sofitel Le Louise
Crystal Lounge

Louise

Conrad

Manos
Stephanie

Bristol Stephanie

Flâneries
Gourmandes

Leonor

De la Vigne...
à l'Assiette

Notos

Agenda
Louise

Beau-Site

MAISON COMMUNALE
D'IXELLES

MUSÉE COMMUNAL
D'IXELLES

IXELLES
ELSENE

Rouge Tomate

Kolya

Manos Premier

Le Châtelain

Thewhitehotel

Odette en ville

STE-TRINITÉ

ST-GILLES
ST-GILLIS

L'Atelier de
la Truffe Noire

Pl. E.
Flagey

Lesbroussart

Sq. de
Biarritz

Rue Lanfray

MUSÉE
HORTA

La Quincaillerie

Kokuban

362 Avenue Louise

La Canne en Ville

Toucan sur Mer

Warwick Barsey

Sq. H.
Michaux

MUSÉE
CONSTANTIN
MEUNIER

ER PU.RE

La Porte des Indes

ABBAYE
DE LA CAMBRE

La Truffe Noire

Av. Lloyd Georges

Pl. Guy
d'Arezzo

● Hotel
● Restaurant

0   100 m

BELGIUM - BRUSSELS

77

Agenda Louise without rest 🄰🄲 📶 🚗 🆅🅸🆂🅰 ⓒⓞ 🄰🄴 ⓞ
r. Florence 6 ⊠ 1000 – 𝒞 02 539 00 31 – www.hotel-agenda.com
37 rm ☲ – ✝75/145 € ✝✝95/160 €   J2
♦ Business ♦ Family ♦ Functional ♦
Spacious modern guestrooms and friendly, attentive staff are the main selling
points of this hotel near the Avenue Louise. Buffet breakfast. Small garden.

Aqua without rest 🛏 ♿ 🄰🄲 📶 🏋 🚗 🆅🅸🆂🅰 ⓒⓞ 🄰🄴 ⓞ
r. Stassart 43 ⊠ 1050 – 𝒞 02 213 01 01 – www.aqua-hotel.be
97 rm ☲ – ✝75/245 € ✝✝80/250 €   Plan IV **N3**
♦ Business ♦ Modern ♦
Minimalist decor embellished with a blue wood "wave" sculpture, created by
contemporary artist Arne Quinze. It offers pared-down rooms with walls painted
white and blue and parquet flooring. A calm environment.

Thewhitehotel without rest 🄰🄲 📶 🏋 🚗 🆅🅸🆂🅰 ⓒⓞ 🄰🄴
av. Louise 212 ⊠ 1050 – 𝒞 02 644 29 29 – www.thewhitehotel.be
53 rm ☲ – ✝85/185 € ✝✝85/185 €   J2
♦ Business ♦ Family ♦ Design ♦
This designer hotel has a name that says it all! In addition to the white decor, the
hotel displays works by Belgian artists and designers. Obliging staff and large,
immaculate guestrooms.

Beau-Site without rest 📶 🆅🅸🆂🅰 ⓒⓞ 🄰🄴 ⓞ
r. Longue Haie 76 ⊠ 1000 – 𝒞 02 640 88 89 – www.beausitebrussels.com
38 rm ☲ – ✝60/149 € ✝✝65/159 €   J1-2
♦ Family ♦ Classic ♦
A sober, functional, but friendly family-run hotel occupying a small corner building just 100m from one of Brussels' most select streets. Reasonably spacious
bedrooms.

🍴🍴🍴 Le Chalet de la Forêt (Pascal Devalkeneer) 🏡 ⇄ 🅿
🕸🕸 Drève de Lorraine 43 ⊠ 1180 – 𝒞 02 374 54 16   🆅🅸🆂🅰 ⓒⓞ 🄰🄴 ⓞ
– www.lechaletdelaforet.be
– closed first week January, Saturday and Sunday
Rest – Menu 45 € (lunch), 79/98 € – Carte 90/127 € ⅋
♦ Classic ♦ Formal ♦
Tasty and creative classic meals are meticulously served in a refined, contemporary interior, or outside, on the edge of the Sonian Forest. Lounge-veranda with
a fireplace.
➔ Oursins et langoustines servis en coque, mousseline de petits pois et
émulsion de crustacés. Ris de veau clouté à la truffe noire, gnocchis et
tian de bettes. Soufflé chaud et sabayon à la kriek.

🍴🍴🍴 Villa Lorraine 🏡 🄰🄲 ⇄ ➡ 🅿 🆅🅸🆂🅰 ⓒⓞ 🄰🄴 ⓞ
av. du Vivier d'Oie 75 ⊠ 1000 – 𝒞 02 374 31 63 – www.villalorraine.be
– closed 21 July-19 August, 1-7 January, Sunday and Monday   Plan I **C3**
Rest – Menu 48 € (lunch), 95/195 € bi – Carte 91/134 € ⅋
Rest La Brasserie de la Villa🏡 – see restaurant listing
♦ Traditional ♦ Elegant ♦
An institution opened in 1953 on the edge of the Bois de la Cambre. Superb
setting for a gastronomic experience.

🍴🍴🍴 La Truffe Noire 🏡 🄰🄲 ⇄ ➡ 🆅🅸🆂🅰 ⓒⓞ 🄰🄴
🕸 bd de la Cambre 12 ⊠ 1000 – 𝒞 02 640 44 22 – www.truffenoire.com
– closed 1 week at Easter, first 2 weeks August, Christmas-New Year, Saturday
lunch and Sunday   K3
Rest – Menu 50 € bi (lunch), 175/225 € – Carte 82/139 € ⅋
♦ Italian ♦ Luxury ♦ Elegant ♦
As you might expect, The Black Truffle serves the famous Tuber Melanosporum
in all manner of dishes. An elegant decor with a patio-terrace. Charismatic
owner. Splendid choice of wines... some at staggering prices!
➔ Carpaccio aux truffes à la façon de Luigi, préparé en salle. Saint-pierre
farci aux truffes et son coulis à la périgourdine. Soufflé chaud aux noisettes
grillées et sabayon à la vanille.

XX **Odette en ville** with rm   🏠 AC rm, 🛜 ☕ VISA 🎴 AE

r. Châtelain 25 ✉ *1050 – ℰ 0 2 640 26 26 – www.chez-odette.com*
– *closed late July-early August*   **J2**
8 rm – ♦250/425 € ♦♦250/425 €, ☲ 25 €
Rest – Menu 22 € (lunch)/28 € – Carte approx. 50 €
♦ Modern ♦ Trendy ♦
The place to be and be seen! Here, you will rub shoulders with a mixed clientele
in a trendy atmosphere. Quality cuisine and conscientious, professional service.
This discreetly luxurious hotel with monochrome decor has a cosy lounge with
a well-stocked library and designer guestrooms.

XX **La Porte des Indes**   AC ⇔ VISA 🎴 AE

av. Louise 455 ✉ *1050 – ℰ 0 2 647 86 51 – www.laportedesindes.com*
– *closed 25 December, 1 January and Sunday lunch*   **K3**
Rest – Menu 19 € (lunch), 43/58 € – Carte 28/57 €
♦ Indian ♦ Exotic ♦
Enjoy the classic dishes of Indian and Thai cuisine amid the authentic, evocative
and colourful decor of La Porte des Indes.

XX **Crystal Lounge** – Hôtel Sofitel Le Louise   ♿ AC ☕ VISA 🎴 AE ①

av. de la Toison d'Or 40 ✉ *1050 – ℰ 0 2 549 61 44*
– *www.crystallounge.be*   **J1**
Rest – Menu 25 € (lunch) – Carte 52/85 €
♦ Modern ♦ Trendy ♦
An elegant decor, an appetising menu, and a cocktail bar with Val St Lambert
crystal carafes, all in a 'foody' atmosphere. DJ from Thursday to Saturday.

XX **Kolya** – Hôtel Manos Premier   🚗 AC ⇔ ☕ (dinner) VISA 🎴 AE ①

chaussée de Charleroi 102 ✉ *1060 – ℰ 0 2 533 18 30 – www.kolya.be*
– *closed Saturday lunch and Sunday*   **J2**
Rest – Menu 18 € (lunch)/35 € – Carte 48/67 €
♦ Classic ♦ Cosy ♦
Enjoy contemporary French cuisine with a Mediterranean accent in the refined
setting at Kolya. The veranda and patio are amazing, and the dining room is just
as nice.

XX **La Brasserie de la Villa** – Rest Villa Lorraine   🏠 AC ☕ **P.**
🙂
av. du Vivier d'Oie 75 ✉ *1000 – ℰ 0 2 374 31 63*   VISA 🎴 AE ①
– *www.villalorraine.be*
– *closed 21 July-19 August, 1-7 January and Sunday*   *Plan I* **C3**
Rest – Menu 35 € – Carte 31/65 €
♦ Classic ♦ Elegant ♦
The little sister of the Villa Lorraine where you can soak up the atmosphere of
that prestigious establishment at more affordable prices. Classic brasserie
dishes and appetising light meals.

XX **Rouge Tomate**   🏠 ⇔ VISA 🎴 AE

av. Louise 190 ✉ *1050 – ℰ 0 2 647 70 44 – www.rougetomate.com*
– *closed 22 December-3 January and lunch Saturday and Sunday*
Rest – Menu 29 € (lunch), 44/75 € bi – Carte 53/76 €   **J2**
♦ Modern ♦ Minimalist ♦
A healthy mind in a healthy body – such could be the motto of this minimalist
restaurant. The recipes are all designed with the help of nutritionists, so tuck in
without fear of blushing tomato red!

XX **362 Avenue Louise**   🏠 AC ⇔ VISA 🎴 AE

av. Louise 362 ✉ *1000 – ℰ 0 2 648 30 48 – www.362avenuelouise.be*
– *closed 1-20 August, Saturday lunch, Sunday and Monday*   **K2**
Rest – Menu 25/30 € – Carte approx. 65 €
♦ Modern ♦ Fashionable ♦
This restaurant, located at 362 Avenue Louise as its name suggests, serves flavoursome, up-to-the-minute cuisine with choice produce, ingredients and careful presentation. Enjoy dishes like tuna with sesame seeds, mango foie gras, etc.

BELGIUM - BRUSSELS

XX **Leonor** 🛱 AC ⇔ VISA ❤

r. Saint-Bernard 1 ⊠ 1060 – ℰ 0 2 544 02 08 – www.leonor.be
– closed August, Saturday lunch, Sunday and Monday **J1**
Rest – Menu 15 € (lunch), 36/65 € – Carte 35/65 €
♦ Spanish ♦ Brasserie ♦

The chef has brought a whiff of Spain to this neighbourhood, without forgoing contemporary creations. Try prawns in garlic, tapas, soft boiled eggs at low temperature or salmon on an aniseed mousse – all of which in a brasserie ambience.

X **Brasseries Georges** 🛱 AC ⊐♞ VISA ❤ AE ①

av. Winston Churchill 259 ⊠ 1180 – ℰ 0 2 347 21 00
– www.brasseriesgeorges.be *Plan I* **B3**
Rest – (open until 00.30am) Menu 10 € (lunch), 16/96 € bi
– Carte 30/101 €
♦ Traditional ♦ Brasserie ♦

One of the greatest oyster bar/brasseries in Brussels, decorated in Parisian style. A short counter menu at lunchtime. Friendly atmosphere and service with a handy car parking service.

X **Chalet Robinson** ≼ ᴆ 🛱 AC ⇔ VISA ❤ AE

Sentier de l'Embarcadère 1 ⊠ 1000 – ℰ 0 2 372 92 92
– www.chaletrobinson.be
– closed Monday and Tuesday January-15 March *Plan I* **C3**
Rest – (open until 11pm) Menu 12 € (lunch), 27/44 € – Carte 32/55 €
♦ Traditional ♦ Fashionable ♦ Brasserie ♦

This large chalet on a little island in the Bois de la Cambre is a unique place, full of nostalgia. Classic interior design and food at accessible prices. Small boats can be rented. Venue for events.

X **Notos** 🛱 ⇔ VISA ❤ AE

r. Livourne 154 ⊠ 1000 – ℰ 0 2 513 29 59 – www.notos.be
– closed last week July-2 weeks August, 1 week late December, Monday lunch and Sunday **J2**
Rest – Menu 19 € (lunch), 45/70 € – Carte 53/66 €
♦ Greek ♦ Minimalist ♦

A 'new generation' Greek restaurant located in what used to be a garage. Restrained contemporary setting, authentic Greek dishes with a modern touch, and a good selection of Hellenic wines.

X **L'Atelier de la Truffe Noire** 🛱 AC VISA ❤ AE ①

av. Louise 300 ⊠ 1050 – ℰ 0 2 640 54 55
– www.atelier.truffenoire.com
– closed 30 July-19 August, first week January, Monday dinner and Sunday
Rest – Menu 35 € (lunch), 47/95 € – Carte 37/73 € **K2**
♦ Italian ♦ Bistro ♦

This chic eatery serving Italian and world cuisine is a tea-room, trattoria and bistro rolled into one. Perfect for a quick coffee and pastry, a lunch or a relaxed dinner which might even include a dish flavoured by the eponymous truffle.

X **De la Vigne... à l'Assiette** AC VISA ❤ AE

r. Longue Haie 51 ⊠ 1000 – ℰ 0 2 647 68 03
– closed 20 July-10 August, 25 December-1 January, Saturday lunch, Sunday and Monday **J2**
Rest – Menu 16 € (lunch), 25/40 € – Carte 39/52 € ❦
♦ Modern ♦ Bistro ♦

This 'gastro bistro' serves unusual, hearty cuisine washed down with a choice of reasonably priced world wines. Professional and knowledgeable staff.

Secret de Grands Chefs

The oldest Wine House in Champagne: Aÿ 1584

www.champagne-gosset.com

horizon-bleu.com

Kamo (Kamo Tomoyasu)   VISA ⓒⓢ AE

av. des Saisons 123 ⊠ 1050 – ℰ 0 2 648 78 48
– closed Saturday, Sunday and Bank Holidays   *Plan I* **C3**
Rest – *(booking essential)* Menu 15 € (lunch)/45 € – Carte 32/83 €

♦ Japanese ♦ Trendy ♦

A slice of Tokyo in Ixelles: the classics of Japanese cuisine and remarkable suggestions with bold flavours are served in a pared-down setting with a trendy atmosphere. Sit at the counter to admire the skills of the two chefs at work. Good lunch *bento*.

➔ Fruits de mer vinaigrés. Joue de porc braisée aux légumes japonais, gambas frites en aigre-doux. Mousse au sésame noir, crème brûlée au thé matcha.

La Quincaillerie   ⌂ AC ⇔ ⇱ P VISA ⓒⓢ AE ⓪

r. Page 45 ⊠ 1050 – ℰ 0 2 533 98 33 – www.quincaillerie.be
– closed lunch on Bank Holidays except 11 November and Sunday lunch
Rest – *(open until midnight)* Menu 14 € (lunch)/29 €   **J2**
– Carte 38/60 €

♦ Traditional ♦ Brasserie ♦

Shiny and majestic brasserie occupying a former Art Deco hardware store. Daily specials and fresh oysters. Very professional service. Doorman.

La Canne en Ville   ⌂ ⇔ VISA ⓒⓢ AE

r. Réforme 22 ⊠ 1050 – ℰ 0 2 347 29 26 – www.lacanneenville.be
– closed 22 December-14 January, Saturday dinner in July-August, Saturday lunch and Sunday   **J3**
Rest – Menu 16 € (lunch)/70 € bi – Carte 45/57 €

♦ Traditional ♦ Family ♦

It will soon be the twentieth anniversary for this peaceful and welcoming bistrot, where the tiling proves it once was a butcher's shop. Cuisine based on market offerings.

Flâneries Gourmandes   VISA ⓒⓢ AE

r. Berckmans 2 ⊠ 1060 – ℰ 0 2 537 32 20
– closed 20 July-14 August, Saturday lunch, Sunday, Monday and Bank Holidays   **J1**
Rest – Menu 26 € (lunch)/65 € – Carte 57/72 €

♦ Traditional ♦ Bistro ♦

In the mood for a gourmet stroll? Then check out the slogan of this gastro-bistro ("you'll stay for dessert"). Tasting menu in the evenings and weekends. "Natural" wines.

ER PU.RE   ⌂ ⇥

av. Louise 423 ⊠ 1050 – ℰ 0 2 808 08 58 – www.erpure.be
– closed 27 July-19 August, 4-20 January, Saturday and Sunday   **K3**
Rest – Menu 17 € (lunch), 35/95 € – Carte 59/88 €

♦ Creative ♦ Friendly ♦

A desire to stand out has ever been a hallmark of the establishments that line the smart, trendy Avenue Louise. The chef of this restaurant showcases cuisine based on tea and cigar flavours. A daring and inventive concept, which is made to measure for a clientele in search of originality!

Kokuban   VISA ⓒⓢ

r. Vilain XIV 53 ⊠ 1000 – ℰ 0 2 611 06 22 – www.kokuban.be
– closed Sunday   **K2**
Rest – Carte 17/36 €

♦ Japanese ♦ Minimalist ♦

Japanese classics served in a minimalist decor are the secret of success at the Kokuban. Thanks to its authenticity, rich flavours and moderate prices, the establishment has conquered both the hearts of the local inhabitants, as well as those of the Japanese expats who claim to feel at home here – what more can we say?

BELGIUM - BRUSSELS

BELGIUM - BRUSSELS

✗ **Toucan sur Mer** 🛜 *VISA* 💳 AE ①

av. Louis Lepoutre 17 ✉ *1050* – ✆ *0 2 340 07 40*
– www.toucanbrasserie.com **J3**
Rest – *(open until 11pm) (booking advisable)* Menu 16 € (lunch), 39/54 €
– Carte 38/54 €

♦ Fish and seafood ♦ Bistro ♦

The impeccable quality and freshness of the fish and seafood of the Toucan sur Mer are more than comparable with seafood restaurants on the coast. We will take a bet that this pleasant bistro will appeal to seafood lovers. However, it shouldn't be confused with another Toucan restaurant in the vicinity, run by the same owners.

✗ **Maza'j** 🛜 *VISA* 💳 AE

😊 *bd du Souverain 145* ✉ *1160* – ✆ *0 2 675 55 10* – *www.mazaj.be*
– closed Saturday lunch and Sunday *Plan I* **C3**
Rest – Menu 30 € (lunch), 35/45 € – Carte 29/54 €

♦ Lebanese ♦ Friendly ♦

If you feel like exploring a new culinary horizon, why not book a table at Maza'j? Don't be misled by the bright contemporary interior, this establishment is the champion of traditional Lebanese cuisine and culture. All the dishes are laid on the table for everyone to sample, in a friendly, relaxed atmosphere.

✗ **Les Papilles** 🛜 *VISA* 💳 AE

chausée de Waterloo 782 ✉ *1180* – ✆ *0 2 374 69 66* – *www.lespapilles.be*
– closed Saturday lunch and Sunday *Plan I* **B3**
Rest – Menu 18 € (lunch)/35 € – Carte approx. 40 €

♦ Classic ♦ Wine bar ♦

Your taste buds will definitely start tingling when you enter this delightful establishment. It specialises in distinctive and characteristic brasserie fare. Before sitting down for your meal, pick yourself a bottle of wine directly from the shelves. Friendly and relaxed.

EUROPEAN INSTITUTIONS *Plan II*

🏨 **Renaissance** ⅃🐾🗔 ♿ 🅰🅒 🛜 ⚙ 🚐 *VISA* 💳 AE ①

r. Parnasse 19 ✉ *1050* – ✆ *0 2 505 29 29* – *www.renaissancebrussels.com*
256 rm – 💲79/500 € 💲💲79/500 €, ⚌ 25 € – 6 suites **G3**
Rest – Menu 25 € – Carte approx. 45 €

♦ Chain hotel ♦ Business ♦ Modern ♦

A modern chain hotel adjoining the European institutions district. Well-appointed bedrooms, studios in the annexe, conference rooms, business facilities, and a 'health academy'. Traditional cuisine and a three-course lunch menu provided at this brasserie.

🏨 **Radisson Blu EU** ⅃🐾 ♿ rm, 🅰🅒 🛜 ⚙ 🚐 *VISA* 💳 AE ①

r. Idalie 35 ✉ *1050* – ✆ *0 2 626 81 11*
– www.radissonblu.com/euhotel-brussels **G3**
145 rm – 💲149/529 € 💲💲149/529 €, ⚌ 19 € – 4 suites
Rest – *(dinner only in July-August)* Carte 28/51 €

♦ Chain hotel ♦ Business ♦ Modern ♦

A new, ultra-contemporary hotel offering three types of rooms: Fresh, Chic and Fashion. Popular with a business clientele and European civil servants. Classic, modern cuisine served at your table or at the large, designer bar. Trendy, contemporary decor.

🏨 **Sofitel Brussels Europe** ⅃ ♿ 🅰🅒 🛜 ⚙ 🚐 *VISA* 💳 AE ①

pl. Jourdan 1 ✉ *1040* – ✆ *0 2 235 51 00* – *www.sofitel-brussels-europe.com*
138 rm – 💲180/530 € 💲💲180/530 €, ⚌ 29 € – 11 suites **G3**
Rest – Menu 30 € (lunch)/39 € – Carte 47/61 €

♦ Palace ♦ Business ♦ Design ♦

A modern luxury hotel overlooking a busy square at the heart of the European institutions district. Glass hall-atrium, leisure facilities, and fully equipped rooms, junior suites and suites. This smart restaurant has a relaxed feel and trendy decor.

Stanhope
🛎 🎋 🕸 ⚐ AC 📶 ⤾ 🚗 VISA ⬥ AE ⓪

r. Commerce 9 ⊠ *1000* – ℰ *0 2 506 91 11* – *www.stanhope.be*
125 rm – †75/365 € ††75/365 €, ⊡ 29 € – 9 suites   *Plan IV* **O3**
Rest *Brighton* – ℰ *0 2 506 90 35 (closed Saturday and Sunday)*
Menu 42 € (lunch) – Carte 55/75 €
♦ Grand Luxury ♦ Traditional ♦ Stylish ♦
The splendours of the Victorian era are brought to life in this British-style town-house. It offers varying categories of rooms, including superb suites and duplexes. Elegant and classic dining room in line with the menu. Pretty courtyard-terrace.

Eurostars Montgomery
🎋 🕸 AC ⚐ 🚐 🚗 VISA ⬥ AE ⓪

av. de Tervuren 134 ⊠ *1150* – ℰ *0 2 741 85 11*
– *www.eurostarsmontgomery.com*   *Plan I* **C2**
61 rm – †99/650 € ††99/650 €, ⊡ 20 € – 2 suites
Rest – *(closed late July-late August, Saturday and Sunday)* Menu 24 € (lunch) – Carte approx. 50 €
♦ Chain hotel ♦ Business ♦ Classic ♦
An elegant and intimate business hotel facing the Square Montgomery. Early-20C façade, guestrooms of varying styles, penthouses, lounge-library, English bar, fitness room and sauna. A cosy restaurant serving international cuisine adapted to a business clientele.

Silken Berlaymont
🎋 🕸 ⚐ AC ⚐ 🚐 🚗 VISA ⬥ AE ⓪

bd Charlemagne 11 ⊠ *1000* – ℰ *0 2 231 09 09*
– *www.hotelsilkenberlaymont.com*   **G-H2**
212 rm – †79/395 € ††79/395 €, ⊡ 27 € – 2 suites
Rest *L'Objectif* – *(closed lunch Saturday and Sunday)* Menu 16 € (lunch), 33/54 € bi – Carte 38/56 €
♦ Business ♦ Modern ♦
A hotel with functional but comfortable rooms; those to the rear are generally quieter. Interior decor based on the theme of contemporary photography. Enjoy varied cuisine in this restaurant's contemporary setting.

Martin's Central Park
🎋 🕸 AC ⚐ 🚐 🚗 VISA ⬥ AE ⓪

bd Charlemagne 80 ⊠ *1000* – ℰ *0 2 230 85 55* – *www.martinshotels.com*
97 rm ⊡ – †69/450 € ††79/460 € – 3 suites   **G2**
Rest *Icones* – see restaurant listing
♦ Chain hotel ♦ Modern ♦
A modern hotel near the Berlaymont building with three categories of guest-rooms and excellent business and seminar facilities. Designer public areas adorned with snapshots of Hollywood stars. Trendy brasserie with a decor and special effects inspired by the world of film. Lounge bar.

Thon EU
🎋 ⚐ rm, AC ⚐ 🚐 🚗 VISA ⬥ AE ⓪

r. Loi 75 ⊠ *1040* – ℰ *0 2 204 39 11* – *www.thonhotels.be*   **G2**
405 rm – †90/382 € ††90/382 €, ⊡ 25 € – 14 suites
Rest – Menu 21 € (lunch)/28 € – Carte approx. 47 €
♦ Business ♦ Modern ♦
Brightly coloured, well-proportioned and comfortable rooms. This hotel, part of the Thon chain, is popular with Eurocrats and others.

Park *without rest*
🚐 🕸 ⚐ ⚐ VISA ⬥ AE ⓪

av. de l'Yser 21 ⊠ *1040* – ℰ *0 2 735 74 00* – *www.parkhotelbrussels.be*
54 rm ⊡ – †117/400 € ††139/425 €   **H2**
♦ Traditional ♦ Classic ♦
This intimate hotel comprising of two impressive mansions dating from 1903 face the Parc du Cinquantenaire. Traditional breakfast room overlooking an attractive town garden.

BELGIUM - BRUSSELS

Holiday Inn Schuman without rest
r. Breydel 20 ✉ 1040 – ✆ 0 2 280 40 00
– www.holidayinn.com/brusselschuman **H2**
59 rm – 🚹49/449 € 🚹🚹49/449 €, ☕ 15 €
♦ Chain hotel ♦ Business ♦ Classic ♦
An unbeatable location in the heart of the European quarter, with facilities that are popular with members of parliament, civil servants and businesspeople.

Aloft without rest
pl. Jean Rey ✉ 1040 – ✆ 0 2 800 08 88
– www.aloftbrussels.com **G2**
150 rm – 🚹65/450 € 🚹🚹65/450 €, ☕ 10 €
♦ Business ♦ Modern ♦
On the doorstep of Europe's institutions, a loft spirit and design reign throughout this hotel. The spacious, comfortable and practical rooms are equally popular with business travellers and civil servants.

New Hotel Charlemagne without rest
bd Charlemagne 25 ✉ 1000 – ✆ 0 2 230 21 35
– www.new-hotel.com **H2**
68 rm – 🚹95/350 € 🚹🚹106/350 €, ☕ 22 €
♦ Business ♦ Family ♦ Functional ♦
Located between the Square Ambiorix and the Berlaymont complex, this small, comfortable hotel is popular with European politicians and civil servants. The renovated guestrooms are perhaps preferable.

Bon-Bon (Christophe Hardiquest)
av. de Tervuren 453 ✉ 1150 – ✆ 0 2 346 66 15
– www.bon-bon.be
– closed first week April, 21 July-13 August, first week January, Bank Holidays, Monday lunch, Saturday and Sunday *Plan I* **D3**
Rest – Menu 50 € (lunch), 72/145 € – Carte 62/117 €
♦ Innovative ♦ Elegant ♦
Bon-Bon has moved, but its name is still well deserved! The chef creates refined dishes with top quality ingredients. The popular surprise menu always boasts lots of new finds.
➔ Foie gras cuit en tuile d'argile. Turbot grillé au vin jaune et poivre du Sichuan. Cappuccino cèpe-café.

Stirwen
chaussée St-Pierre 15 ✉ 1040 – ✆ 0 2 640 85 41 – www.stirwen.be
– closed August, 2 weeks December, Saturday and Sunday **G3**
Rest – *(lunch only except Thursday)* Menu 35 € (lunch), 50/85 € bi – Carte 54/77 €
♦ Classic ♦ Retro ♦
A restaurant with a plush, elegant feel enhanced by attractive Belle Époque-style wood decor. Traditional cuisine, include specialities from around France. Popular with diplomats.

Le buone maniere
av. de Tervuren 59 ✉ 1040 – ✆ 0 2 762 61 05
– www.buonemaniere.be
– closed 10-20 August, Saturday lunch and Sunday *Plan I* **C2**
Rest – Menu 40 € (lunch)/60 € – Carte 52/75 €
♦ Italian ♦ Elegant ♦
Le buone maniere occupies a mansion along a busy road. Authentic Italian-Mediterranean cuisine served to a backdrop of contemporary decor or on the front terrace.

XX **Park Side**   🏠 ⚙ Ⓐ ⇩ 💳 ⓥ 🅰

av. de la Joyeuse Entrée 24 ✉ *1040 –* ☎ *0 2 238 08 08 – www.restoparkside.be*
– closed Saturday lunch   **H2**
Rest – Carte 31/56 €
♦ Traditional ♦ Fashionable ♦ Design ♦
English speakers will get the reference right away, since this establishment
abuts the Jubilee Park (parc du Cinquantenaire). A great location for an equally
attractive and chic decor with an ultra-modern design – the main ceiling light in
particular attracts a lot of stares! New-style brasserie specialities on the à la carte
menu.

X   **L'Ancienne Poissonnerie**   Ⓐ 💳 ⓥ 🅰

r. Trône 65 ✉ *1050 –* ☎ *0 2 502 75 05 – www.anciennepoissonnerie.be*
– closed 1-16 August, Saturday lunch and Sunday   *Plan IV* **O3**
Rest – Carte 32/51 €
♦ Italian ♦ Minimalist ♦
A designer influenced, family-run Italian restaurant in a former Art Nouveau fishmonger's. Open kitchen, and period decor including the façade and painted
wall tiles. No menu.

X   **Chou**   🏠 💳 ⓥ 🅰

pl. de Londres 4 ✉ *1050 –* ☎ *0 2 511 92 38 – www.restaurantchou.eu*
– closed late July-early August, Saturday and Sunday   *Plan III* **K1**
Rest – Menu 20 € bi (lunch), 45/95 € – Carte 57/76 €
♦ Classic ♦ Trendy ♦
At the Chou restaurant (the nickname of the French owner) the elegant decor is
enhanced by soft lighting. The decor includes old casting moulds which act as
tables, a sloping dresser, a red plexiglass floor above the wine cellar, and a kitchen that opens out on to the dining room.

X   **Foro Romano**   ⇩ 💳 ⓥ

r. Joseph II 19 ✉ *1000 –* ☎ *0 2 280 15 14 – www.fororomano.be*
– closed Monday dinner, Saturday except first day of the month and Sunday
Rest – *(open until 11.30pm)* Carte 37/59 €   *Plan IV* **O2**
♦ Italian ♦ Neighbourhood ♦
The enoteca offers hearty Italian cuisine, created with its international clientele
firmly in mind, and gets very busy at lunchtime. Eat in the dining room or at the
counter.

X   **Icones** – Hôtel Martin's Central Park   ⚙ Ⓐ 💳 ⓥ 🅰 Ⓞ

bd Charlemagne 80 ✉ *1000 –* ☎ *0 2 230 85 55 – www.martinshotels.com*
– closed 20 July-25 August and lunch Saturday and Sunday   **G2**
Rest – Menu 23 € (lunch), 35/60 € bi – Carte 36/60 €
♦ International ♦ Fashionable ♦ Brasserie ♦
Eat under the gaze of iconic film stars at this fashionable restaurant. The inter-
national fare attracts a clientele of Eurocrats.

X   **Les Caprices d'Harmony**   ⇩ 💳 ⓥ 🅰 Ⓞ

r. Noyer 236 ✉ *1030 –* ☎ *0 2 733 14 02*
– closed Monday dinner, Saturday lunch, Sunday and Bank Holidays
Rest – Menu 15 € (lunch) – Carte 23/38 €   **H2**
♦ Classic ♦ Brasserie ♦
The understated decor of dark brown hues is perfectly in keeping with the classic menu. The owner is also the chef; his two specialities are onglet à l'échalote
and sole meunière.

X   **Le Monde est Petit**   🏠 ⇩ 💳 ⓥ 🅰

r. Bataves 65 ✉ *1040 –* ☎ *0 2 732 44 34 – www.lemondeestpetit.be*
*– closed last week July-first 2 weeks August, 1 week late December, Saturday
and Sunday*   *Plan I* **C2**
Rest – Menu 18 € (lunch) – Carte 42/64 €
♦ Modern ♦ Cosy ♦ Fashionable ♦
The atmosphere at this establishment is really enjoyable, and the regulars are
there to prove it. The chef has opted for a rather limited menu in order to
focus on contemporary dishes with international touches.

BELGIUM - BRUSSELS

Sheraton

pl. Rogier 3 ⊠ *1210 – ℰ 0 2 224 31 11 – www.sheratonbrussels.com*
480 rm 🖵 – ✝119/399 € ✝✝134/414 € – 6 suites   F1
Rest – *(closed Saturday dinner and Sunday)* Menu 29 € (lunch)/35 €
– Carte 29/58 €

♦ Chain hotel ♦ Business ♦ Modern ♦

Imposing tower hotel with superb facilities for a mainly international business
and conference clientele. Spacious standard and club rooms, as well as numerous suites. Attractive contemporary bar. Traditional cuisine in this hotel restaurant facing Place Rogier. Lunch buffet.

Crowne Plaza "Le Palace"

r. Gineste 3 ⊠ *1210 – ℰ 0 2 203 62 00 – www.crowneplazabrussels.com*
346 rm – ✝75/250 € ✝✝75/250 €, 🖵 28 € – 8 suites   F1
Rest – *(closed lunch Saturday and Sunday)* Menu 21 € (lunch) – Carte
approx. 45 €

♦ Chain hotel ♦ Business ♦ Classic ♦

This Belle Époque palace, which celebrated its centenary in 2008, has redisco-
vered its former glory. Impressively elegant public areas, a brand-new bar,
neo-retro-style guestrooms and new suites. Cosmopolitan cuisine to a backdrop
of chic and trendy decor.

Bloom!

r. Royale 250 ⊠ *1210 – ℰ 0 2 220 66 11 – www.hotelbloom.com*
305 rm – ✝65/300 € ✝✝65/300 €, 🖵 25 € – 4 suites   F1
Rest *SmoodS* – see restaurant listing

♦ Business ♦ Design ♦ Personalised ♦

This fashionable business hotel has made quite an impression with its breathtaking design. Bright, art-inspired bedrooms, each embellished with a modern
fresco. Meeting rooms, fitness area, sauna and hammam. Contemporary cuisine
is served in a trendy ambience.

322 without rest

av. Lambermont 322 ⊠ *1030 – ℰ 0 2 242 55 95*
– www.lambermonthotels.com   Plan I **C2**
45 rm – ✝79/275 € ✝✝89/280 €, 🖵 18 €

♦ Business ♦ Family ♦ Modern ♦

This family-run hotel looks deceptively like a residential block. Minimalist, functional rooms. Guests are invited to leave their mark on the walls of the breakfast
room.

Senza Nome (Giovanni Bruno)

r. Royale Ste-Marie 22 ⊠ *1030 – ℰ 0 2 223 16 17 – www.senzanome.be*
*– closed mid July-mid August, Christmas-New Year, Saturday, Sunday and Bank
Holidays*   G1
Rest – Menu 70/95 € – Carte 62/78 € 🏵

♦ Italian ♦ Bistro ♦ Fashionable ♦

The best of Italian cuisine and wine are on offer in this restaurant near the Halles
de Schaerbeek. Welcoming decor and popular with politicians and celebrities.
Bookings essential for lunch and dinner.

➔ Mozzarella burratina, huile d'olive au basilic et sorbet à la tomate.
Agneau en croûte d'herbes et sauce parfumée à la grappa. Mousse de mascarpone au chocolat noir.

Bowery

chaussée de Louvain 650 ⊠ *1030 – ℰ 0 2 325 12 90 – www.bowery.be*
*– closed 20 July-19 August, 26 October-3 November, 23 December-1 January,
Saturday and Sunday*   Plan I **C2**
Rest – Menu 24 € (lunch), 65/85 € – Carte 65/79 €

♦ Traditional ♦ Fashionable ♦ Design ♦

A trendy restaurant in the buildings of a design company: now that's original!
Ensconced in his kitchens, chef Benjamin Laborie concocts traditional recipes
– and adds a contemporary touch. Fine food, in an equally fine setting.

✗ **SmoodS** – Hôtel Bloom!   🕭 AC 🔄 VISA ◎ AE ⓞ

r. Royale 250 ⊠ 1210 – 𝒞 0 2 220 66 66 – www.smoods.net
– closed Saturday lunch and Sunday   **F1**
Rest – Menu 19 € (lunch), 35/45 € – Carte 25/53 €
♦ Modern ♦ Fashionable ♦
Are you in a 'flower power' or a 'safari' mood? Have a seat in one of the 'mood islands', depending on how you are feeling at that moment. The food is adaptable too – ranging from snacks to copious meals – so there is something for everyone.

✗ **Les Dames Tartine**   VISA ◎ AE ⓞ

chaussée de Haecht 58 ⊠ 1210 – 𝒞 0 2 218 45 49
– closed first 3 weeks August, Saturday lunch, Sunday and Monday
Rest – Menu 20 € (lunch), 35/46 € – Carte 44/51 €   **G1**
♦ Traditional ♦ Rustic ♦ Family ♦
Two women run this restaurant with great panache. Excellent seasonal cuisine, an intimate atmosphere and an impressive wine list.

GARE DU MIDI   *Plan I*

Be Manos   🕭 ⌂ AC 🛜 🛁 🖙 VISA ◎ AE ⓞ

Square de l'Aviation 23 ⊠ 1070 – 𝒞 0 2 520 65 65 – www.bemanos.com
59 rm – †119/449 € ††129/499 €, ⊡ 20 € – 1 suite   Plan II **E2**
Rest Be Lella – see restaurant listing
♦ Luxury ♦ Design ♦
Ultra trendy and high on design, superlatives barely do justice to this hotel opened in 2007 in a fashionable district of Anderlecht. Attractive terraces and a spa. This very trendy restaurant serves both Belgian and Brussels specialities.

De Fierlant without rest   🛜 P VISA ◎ AE

r. De Fierlant 67 ⊠ 1190 – 𝒞 0 2 538 60 70 – www.hoteldefierlant.be
41 rm ⊡ – †66/99 € ††69/109 €   **B3**
♦ Family ♦ Functional ♦
The De Fierlant is located between the Midi TGV train station and the Forest-National concert hall. Well-maintained guestrooms, modern (buffet) breakfast area, lounge and bar.

Park Inn Midi   🕭 🕭 AC 🛜 🛁 🖙 VISA ◎ AE ⓞ

pl. Marcel Broodthaers 3 ⊠ 1060 – 𝒞 0 2 535 14 00
– www.parkinn.com/hotel-brussels   Plan II **E3**
142 rm ⊡ – †99/309 € ††114/324 €
Rest – Menu 15 € (lunch)/30 € – Carte 35/58 €
♦ Business ♦ Functional ♦
Next to Brussels South (Midi) station, this establishment offers practical, well-kept rooms that are perfect for business travellers.

Cascade Midi without rest   🕭 AC 🛜 🖙 VISA ◎ AE

av. Fonsny 5 ⊠ 1060 – 𝒞 0 2 533 10 90 – www.cascadehotel.be
93 rm – †70/335 € ††70/335 €, ⊡ 15 €   Plan II **E3**
♦ Business ♦ Functional ♦
This hotel enjoys a choice location opposite the Brussels South (Midi) railway station. The rooms are practical and well soundproofed – so it is ideal for a stopover on your way to or from – the South!

Vintage without rest   🕭 🛜 VISA ◎ AE

r. Dejoncker 45 ⊠ 1060 – 𝒞 0 2 533 99 80 – www.vintagehotel.be
30 rm ⊡ – †90/290 € ††90/290 €   Plan II **F3**
♦ Family ♦ Retro ♦
Furnished with 1960s fixtures and fittings, complete with psychedelic wallpaper – fans of Sixties memorabilia will love the Vintage. What's more, the hotel is well located, just off the smart, trendy Avenue Louise.

Agenda Midi without rest 🏧 📶 📧 ⊕⊕ 📇 ⓘ

bd Jamar 11 ✉ 1060 – ✆ 0 2 520 00 10 – www.hotel-agenda.com
35 rm ☑ – ♦89/149€ ♦♦99/165€   Plan II **E2**
◆ Business ◆ Traditional ◆ Functional ◆

The Agenda Midi occupies a building just a stone's throw from the Midi TGV station. Bright, well-maintained guestrooms with those to the rear perhaps preferable. Business corner and buffet breakfast.

Pantone without rest 📶 ⚴ 📧 ⊕⊕ 📇

pl. Loix 1 ✉ 1060 – ✆ 0 2 541 48 98 – www.pantonehotel.com
61 rm – ♦59/350€ ♦♦59/350€, ☑ 15€   Plan II **F3**
◆ Family ◆ Design ◆ Minimalist ◆

Pantone is something of a household name in the field of colour charts, of which it is one of the world's leading manufacturers. Accordingly, the hotel's motto 'Live in colour, dream in colour' is brought to technicolour life in this design interior.

XXX Saint Guidon 🏧 ⇦⇨ 🅿 📧 ⊕⊕

av. Théo Verbeeck 2 ✉ 1070 – ✆ 0 2 520 55 36 – www.saint-guidon.be
– closed 21 June-21 July, Christmas-New Year, Saturday, Sunday and Club's
home match days   **A3**
Rest – (lunch only) Menu 35€ (lunch), 45/63€ bi – Carte 45/92€
◆ Classic ◆ Elegant ◆

This popular restaurant is located inside the RSC Anderlecht football stadium with views of the pitch. Refined, traditional cuisine served by an attentive and professional staff.

XX Va Doux Vent (Stefan Jacobs et Romain Mouton) 🏧 ⇦⇨ ⌂♟

r. Carmélites 93 ✉ 1180 – ✆ 0 2 346 65 05   📧 ⊕⊕ 📇
– www.vadouxvent.be
– closed 1 week at Easter, last 2 weeks July-first week August, late December,
Saturday lunch, Sunday, Monday and Bank Holidyas   **B3**
Rest – Menu 35€ (lunch), 49/69€ – Carte 55/69€
◆ Classic ◆ Bistro ◆

This 'dream team' has barely started and they are already a success. The two chefs met at the Brussels Sea Grill and their sommelier partner used to work at Comme Chez Soi. The original and refined contemporary cuisine features spices such as vadouvan.
➜ Foie gras de canard poché, salade fine de lentille et de topinambour. Volaille patte jaune, chutney de tomate au xérès et légumes du sud. Pain perdu brioché aux condiments de betteraves rouges.

XX La Brouette 🏠 🏧 📧 ⊕⊕ 📇 ⓘ

bd Prince de Liège 61 ✉ 1070 – ✆ 0 2 522 51 69 – www.labrouette.be
– closed 1 week at Easter, 2 August-3 September, 15 and 16 September, 4-6
January, 5-10 February, Saturday lunch, Sunday dinner and Monday
Rest – Menu 30€ (lunch), 35/50€ – Carte 50/63€ ⅋⅋   **A2**
◆ Classic ◆ Friendly ◆

Herman Dedapper isn't afraid of thinking outside the box. Omnipresent in the dining room, he always wore his chef's hat until passing it onto his right hand man. He is still the owner, and nowadays also the sommelier! Don't miss the 'Brouette' menu, which you can put together yourself.

XX Be Lella – Hôtel Be Manos 🏧 ⇦⇨ 📧 ⊕⊕ 📇 ⓘ

Square de l'Aviation 23 ✉ 1070 – ✆ 0 2 520 65 65 – www.bemanos.com
– closed Saturday lunch and Sunday   Plan II **E2**
Rest – (open until 11pm) Menu 18€ (lunch), 35/75€ – Carte 49/66€
◆ Modern ◆ Fashionable ◆ Design ◆

This trendy, ultra-modern restaurant features a decidedly eclectic and international menu. Dishes include, sole meunière, ostrich fillet, brie pastries and scampi kebabs. Be… a food lover!

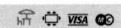

BELGIUM - BRUSSELS

✗ **La Paix** (David Martin) ⇆ 🆚 ⓪ AE
✿

r. Ropsy-Chaudron 49 (opposite abattoirs) ✉ 1070 – 𝒞 0 2 523 09 58
– www.lapaix.eu
– closed July, Christmas-New Year, Saturday and Sunday **B2**
Rest – (lunch only except Friday) Menu 55/85 € – Carte 56/80 €
♦ Traditional ♦ Brasserie ♦

In an establishment that was formerly a café frequented by butchers, the French chef explores and reinvents bistro cuisine in a typical Brussels ambience. Diners have a view over the kitchens, where the meat is cooked in a wood-fired oven.
➜ Mille oreilles de cochon cuites au saké, tête de cochon aux aromates. Volaille rôtie au foin en deux services. Pain perdu à la vanille Bourbon.

✗ **La Buvette** 🎐 ⇆ 🆚 ⓪

chaussée d'Alsemberg 108 ✉ 1060 – 𝒞 0 2 534 13 03 – www.la-buvette.be
– closed 4-26 August, 21 December-7 January, Saturday, Sunday, Monday and after 20.30pm **B3**
Rest – (dinner only except Thursday and Friday) Menu 30 € (lunch)/45 €
♦ Classic ♦ Bistro ♦ Retro ♦

This simply appointed restaurant, formerly a butcher's, has foregone starched tablecloths and plush armchairs for vintage formica furniture. Who cares though – what counts is what is on the plate! Good food lovers will appreciate the flavoursome cuisine in touch with contemporary tastes in this modern-day 'watering hole'.

ATOMIUM QUARTER  Plan I

 Rijckendael ⇘ ᛚ 🎐 🄰 rm,�🛜 🕴 🄿 🖼 🆚 ⓪ AE ⓞ

Luitberg 1 ✉ 1853 Strombeek-Bever – 𝒞 0 2 267 41 24 – www.rijckendael.be
49 rm ⬚ – †75/185 € ††95/215 € **B1**
Rest – (closed Sunday dinner and Friday) Menu 20 € (lunch)/44 €
– Carte 32/67 €
♦ Business ♦ Functional ♦

This modern-style hotel is located in a residential district with easy access to the Atomium and Heysel stadium. Functional guestrooms. Private car park. Restaurant with rustic charm in an old farmhouse dating from 1857. Classic, traditional cuisine.

🏠 **La Roseraie**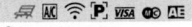

De Limburg Stirumlaan 213 ✉ 1780 Wemmel – 𝒞 0 2 456 99 10
– www.laroseraie.be **A1**
8 rm ⬚ – †107/220 € ††130/300 € – 1 suite
Rest La Roseraie – see restaurant listing
♦ Family ♦ Personàlised ♦ Functional ♦

La Roseraie is a friendly, family-run hotel occupying a 1930s building. Meticulous guestrooms decorated according to different themes, such as African, Japanese, Roman, etc. A contemporary restaurant decorated in bright tones, with a unique piano lobster tank!

✗✗ **'t Stoveke** (Daniel Antuna) 🎐 ⇆ 🆚 ⓪
✿

Jetsestraat 52 ✉ 1853 Strombeek-Bever – 𝒞 0 2 267 67 25 – www.tstoveke.be
– closed August, late December-early January, Saturday lunch, Sunday dinner, Tuesday and Wednesday **B1**
Rest – (number of covers limited, pre-book) Menu 32 € (lunch), 60/103 € bi – Carte 65/85 €
♦ Modern ♦ Elegant ♦

The chef of 't Stoveke follows in the footsteps of some of the best-known chefs in the world, including Escoffier, but has added his own personal touch. This has ensured that his cuisine remains resolutely up to date. The dishes reveal an explosion of flavours that are as much a delight to the eye as to the palate.
➜ Homard cuit à basse température à la saladelle, sauce au champagne et au corail. Turbot à la plancha aux graines de moutarde et petits navets glacés, sauce bordelaise et jus de carottes. Parfait à la fraise, crumble d'amandes, glace à la fève tonka et spaghettis de framboise.

XX ⊕ **L'Auberge de l'Isard** 🍴 ♿ **P** 𝚟𝚒𝚜𝚊 ⓞⓞ ⒜Ⓔ

Romeinsesteenweg 964 ✉ *1780 Wemmel* – ✆ *0 2 479 85 64*
– *www.isard.be*
– *closed 1 week at Easter school holidays, last week July-first 2 weeks August,
dinner on Bank Holidays, Sunday dinner and Monday* **A-B1**
Rest – Menu 25 € (lunch), 35/65 € bi – Carte 46/69 €
♦ Traditional ♦ Formal ♦
This restaurant is located between the ring road and Heysel Stadium. It has a
modern dining room with round tables and comfortable armchairs, as well as
a pergola on the terrace. Contemporary à la carte menu. The affordable, flexible
lunch and set menus mean you can eat well even on a budget.

XX **Le gril aux herbes** 🍴 **P** 𝚟𝚒𝚜𝚊 ⓞⓞ ⒜Ⓔ

Brusselsesteenweg 21 ✉ *1780 Wemmel* – ✆ *0 2 460 52 39*
– *www.evanrestaurants.be*
– *closed Saturday lunch and Sunday* **A1**
Rest – Menu 35 € (lunch), 50/110 € – Carte 41/77 €
Rest *La table d'Evan* – see restaurant listing
♦ Classic ♦ Trendy ♦
Gastronomic! The chef cooks up fine contemporary dishes using simple,
authentic ingredients (snails, beefsteak tomatoes) on a traditional base. And
the lovely neo-Baroque decor adds a really nice touch.

XX **La Roseraie** – Hôtel La Roseraie 🚗 𝔸ℂ **P** 𝚟𝚒𝚜𝚊 ⓞⓞ ⒜Ⓔ

De Limburg Stirumlaan 213 ✉ *1780 Wemmel* – ✆ *0 2 456 99 10*
– *www.laroseraie.be*
– *closed Saturday lunch, Sunday dinner and Monday* **A1**
Rest – Menu 19 € (lunch), 38/55 € – Carte 48/67 €
♦ Traditional ♦ Elegant ♦
In the mood for fish or shellfish? Head for La Roseraie, an elegant restaurant on
the road to the Heysel and the Atomium. Nice specimens in the piano lobster
tank!

XX **Spectrum** 🍴 𝚟𝚒𝚜𝚊 ⓞⓞ ⒜Ⓔ

Romeinsesteenweg 220 (Koningslo) ✉ *1800 Vilvoorde* – ✆ *0 2 267 00 45*
– *closed Monday dinner, Saturday lunch and Sunday* **B1**
Rest – Menu 34/58 € bi – Carte 36/54 €
♦ Classic ♦ Friendly ♦
Good food lovers pay heed! The Spectrum offers one of the best value for
money deals in the region of Brussels. Generous, traditional dishes.

X ⊕ **French Kiss** 🍴 𝔸ℂ 𝚟𝚒𝚜𝚊 ⓞⓞ ⒜Ⓔ

r. Léopold Ier 470 ✉ *1090* – ✆ *0 2 425 22 93*
– *www.restaurantfrenchkiss.com*
– *closed 30 July-18 August, 24 and 31 December and Monday* **B2**
Rest – Menu 26 € (lunch)/36 € – Carte 34/58 € 🦞
♦ Meats and grills ♦ Friendly ♦
A pleasant restaurant renowned for its excellent grilled dishes and impressive
wine list. Dining area with a low ceiling and bright paintings adding colour to
the brick walls.

X **La table d'Evan** – Rest Le grill aux herbes 🍴 **P** 𝚟𝚒𝚜𝚊 ⓞⓞ ⒜Ⓔ

Brusselsesteenweg 21 ✉ *1780 Wemmel* – ✆ *0 2 460 52 39*
– *www.evanrestaurants.be*
– *closed Sunday and Monday* **A1**
Rest – Menu 35 € (lunch), 49/60 € – Carte 39/61 €
♦ Classic ♦ Trendy ♦ Tapas bar ♦
Refined tapas are the latest invention of creative and imaginative chef Evan. A
great idea, which is perfect for a bit of a change.

✗ **Wine in the City**   🏠 🏧 VISA ⬤⬤ AE ⓪

*pl. Reine Astrid 34 ✉ 1090 – ☏ 0 2 420 09 20 – www.wineinthecity.be
– closed Sunday and Monday*   **B2**
Rest – *(lunch only except Friday) (booking essential)* Menu 35/100 € bi
– Carte 22/43 € 🍴

♦ Traditional ♦ Wine bar ♦

Paradise for wine lovers. This wine bar-cum-restaurant seeks to regale epicureans with tasty bistro cuisine and a setting worthy of some of the most prestigious wine cellars. All the more so as it isn't just for show!

BELGIUM - BRUSSELS

AIRPORT & NATO   *Plan I*

🏨 **Sheraton Airport**   ᵻᵹ & rm, 🏧 rm, 🛜 🧖 🅿 🚗 VISA ⬤⬤ AE ⓪

*Brussels National airport ✉ 1930 Zaventem – ☏ 0 2 710 80 00
– www.sheratonbrusselsairport.com*   **D1**
294 rm – †139/399 € ††154/414 €
Rest – *(open until 11pm)* Carte 42/61 €

♦ Business ♦ Modern ♦

This comfortable chain hotel is part of the airport terminal. Redesigned lounges and public areas, and bright, contemporary bedrooms. Popular with business travellers. A full range of guest services. Restaurant offering an international menu from Belgian ingredients.

🏨 **Crowne Plaza Airport**   � 🕭 🏠 ᵻᵹ 🧖 & 🏧 🕻 🧖 🚗 🅿

Da Vincilaan 4 ✉ 1831 Diegem – ☏ 0 2 416 33 33   VISA ⬤⬤ AE ⓪
– www.crowneplaza.com/cpbrusselsarpt   **D1**
312 rm – †179/289 € ††179/289 €, � 22 € – 3 suites
Rest – Menu 25 € (lunch)/45 € – Carte 45/57 €

♦ Chain hotel ♦ Business ♦ Modern ♦

This upmarket chain hotel is located in a business district close to the airport. Central atrium, well-appointed guestrooms, a full range of conference facilities, fitness room and sauna. Club floor with a private lounge. A restaurant with an adjoining lounge bar. Buffet lunch midweek. Terrace overlooking a public park.

🏨 **Holiday Inn Airport**   ᵻᵹ 🧖 🗔 🍽 & 🏧 🛜 🧖 🅿 VISA ⬤⬤ AE ⓪

Holidaystraat 7 ✉ 1831 Diegem – ☏ 0 2 720 58 65 – www.skoj.be
310 rm – †70/300 € ††70/300 €, ⊿ 23 €   **D1**
Rest – Carte 27/52 €

♦ Chain hotel ♦ Business ♦ Modern ♦

A 1970s hotel near the airport that has just embarked on an extensive programme of modernisation. Extensive leisure and business facilities. Contemporary in style, with traditional à la carte choices and buffet menus.

🏨 **Golden Tulip Airport**   ᵻᵹ 🏊 🏧 🛜 🧖 🚗 🅿 VISA ⬤⬤ AE ⓪

*Bessenveldstraat 15 ✉ 1831 Diegem – ☏ 0 2 713 66 66
– www.goldentulipbrusselsairport.be*   **C1**
125 rm – †79/340 € ††79/340 €, ⊿ 20 €   **Rest** – Carte 35/60 €

♦ Chain hotel ♦ Business ♦ Stylish ♦

Quiet, cosy guestrooms, seven meeting rooms and a variety of leisure facilities are on offer in this hotel along the motorway, just 4km from Zaventem airport. A friendly bar and restaurant with the feel of an upmarket brasserie.

🏨 **Courtyard by Marriott**   ᵻᵹ 🧖 & 🏧 🛜 🧖 🚗 VISA ⬤⬤ AE ⓪

*av. des Olympiades 6 ✉ 1140 – ☏ 0 2 337 08 08
– www.courtyardbrussels.com*   **C2**
188 rm – †69/600 € ††69/600 €, ⊿ 24 € – 3 suites
Rest – *(closed Sunday lunch, Friday dinner and Saturday)* Menu 16 € bi (lunch)/35 € – Carte 30/50 €

♦ Chain hotel ♦ Business ♦ Modern ♦

This hotel, part of a chain, was opened in 2004 half way between the airport and the town centre. Light and modern spaces, a pleasant lounge and good conference facilities, as well as classic-modern style rooms. Traditional cuisine served in this brasserie style restaurant. Business lunch is a good deal.

Gresham Belson without rest

chaussée de Louvain 805 ✉ 1140 – ✆ 0 2 708 31 00 – www.greshambelsonhotel.com C2

136 rm – 60/250 € 80/270 €, ☕ 23 €

♦ Chain hotel ♦ Business ♦ Modern ♦

You will get as easily to the centre of town as to the airport (Zaventem) from this chain hotel with its two room categories. Fitness space.

Novotel Airport

Leonardo Da Vincilaan 25 ✉ 1831 Diegem – ✆ 0 2 725 30 50 – www.novotel.com D1

209 rm – 89/260 € 99/270 €, ☕ 20 €

Rest – *(open until 11.30pm)* Carte approx. 45 €

♦ Chain hotel ♦ Business ♦ Functional ♦

Convenient for stopover or business travellers, this Novotel is being gradually upgraded in line with the rest of the chain. Outdoor pool, fitness centre and meeting rooms. Modern brasserie with buffet menus (except weekends).

Mercure

av. Jules Bordet 74 ✉ 1140 – ✆ 0 2 726 73 35 – www.mercure.com

113 rm – 79/250 € 79/250 €, ☕ 20 € – 7 suites C2

Rest – *(closed Sunday lunch, Friday dinner and Saturday)* Menu 24 € (lunch) – Carte 38/48 €

♦ Chain hotel ♦ Business ♦ Modern ♦

A step away from NATO and 5 m from Zaventem's runways, this is an Accor group classic - rooms up to the hotel name's standards, and seminar rooms. Restaurant with a sober decor brightened up with comic-book references.

Orange

Leuvensesteenweg 614 ✉ 1930 Nossegem – ✆ 0 2 757 05 59 – www.orangerestaurant.be – closed Monday dinner, Saturday lunch and Sunday D1

Rest – Menu 25 € (lunch)/35 € – Carte 34/60 €

♦ Traditional ♦ Friendly ♦

A modern take on good old brasserie cooking, served in an inviting setting: terracotta and chocolate tones, banquettes with fake crocodile-skin upholstery, and designer lighting. Pretty terrace surrounded by greenery.

D'Oude Pastorie

Pastoorkesweg 1 ✉ 1950 Kraainem – ✆ 0 2 720 63 46 – www.doudepastorie-jaloa.com – closed 3-18 September, Monday and Tuesday D2

Rest – Menu 22 € (lunch), 34/55 € – Carte 41/66 €

♦ Traditional ♦ Romantic ♦ Friendly ♦

The gardens of Jourdain Castle represent a genuine haven of tranquillity, including a superb terrace by a large water feature. The menu will appeal to fans of classical fare, but those with more adventurous tastes will probably want to taste some of the more unusual dishes, such as chicken moambe, a Congolese speciality.

Stockmansmolen

H. Henneaulaan 164 ✉ 1930 Zaventem – ✆ 0 2 725 34 34 – www.stockmansmolen.be – closed Saturday lunch and Sunday dinner D1

Rest – Menu 45/79 € bi – Carte 54/58 €

♦ Classic ♦ Friendly ♦

This 13C watermill is now home to a restaurant on the ground floor and to a banquet hall upstairs. The decor sports a compromise between old and new, while the cuisine is firmly rooted in classical traditions.

XX
Brasserie Mariadal

Kouterweg 2 (communal park) ⊠ 1930 Zaventem – ✆ 0 2 720 59 30
– www.brasseriemariadal.be **D1**
Rest – Menu 19 € (lunch), 35/53 € bi – Carte 29/60 €
♦ Traditional ♦ Brasserie ♦
This modern brasserie occupies an attractive manor house in a public park with a lake. Find an uncluttered, stylish decor, an orangerie, reception rooms and play area. A good value for money menu.

X
piu...

Leuvensesteenweg 491 ⊠ 1930 Zaventem – ✆ 0 2 720 60 96
– www.piu-zaventem.be
– closed Saturday lunch and Sunday **D2**
Rest – Menu 35 € – Carte approx. 48 €
♦ Italian ♦ Brasserie ♦
Art Deco brasserie-style. Tasty Italian cooking placing the onus on vegetables; in season, shellfish feature on the menu. Large terrace at the back.

X
Sjo d'O

Statieplaats 3 ⊠ 1950 Kraainem – ✆ 0 2 306 40 50
– closed Saturday and Sunday **D2**
Rest – Menu 20 € (lunch)/30 €
♦ Traditional ♦ Family ♦
Sjo d'O? An original name for a classic repertory featuring excellent ingredients at attractive prices. You can even treat yourself to a bottle of champagne!

X
Bovis

Heldenplein 16 ⊠ 1930 Zaventem – ✆ 0 2 308 83 43
– www.bovis-zaventem.be
– closed Saturday lunch, Sunday and Bank Holidays **D1**
Rest – *(booking essential at lunch)* Carte 44/80 €
♦ Meats and grills ♦ Friendly ♦
The baseline of this restaurant is 'simply meat', where it uses only the very best quality and ensures that each carcass is aged until it reaches perfect maturity. All is served with handcut chips that are fried in beef fat, along with equally authentic wines.

ANTWERP
ANVERS – ANTWERPEN

Population: 507 001

Nimbus/Fotolia.com

Antwerp calls itself the pocketsize metropolis, and with good reason. Although it's Europe's second largest port, it still retains a compact intimacy, defined by bustling squares and narrow streets. It's a place with many facets, not least its marked link to Rubens, the diamond trade and, in later years, the fashion collective The Antwerp Six.

The city's centre teems with ornate gabled guildhouses, and in summer, open-air cafés line the area beneath the towering cathedral, giving the place a festive, almost bohemian air. It's a fantastic place to shop: besides clothing boutiques, there are antiques emporiums and diamond stores – to say nothing of the chocolate shops with their appealing window displays. Bold regeneration projects have transformed the skyline and the waterfront's decrepit warehouses have started new lives as ritzy storerooms of 21C commerce. The nightlife here is the best in Belgium, while the beer is savoured the way others might treat a vintage wine. The Old Town is defined by Grote Markt, Groenplaats and The Meir shopping street – these are a kind of dividing line between Antwerp's north and south. North of the centre is Het Eilandje, the hip former warehouse area; to the east is the Diamond District. Antique and bric-a-brac shops are in abundance in the 'designer heart' Het Zuid, south of the centre, which is also home to the best museums and art galleries.

ANTWERP IN...

→ ONE DAY
Grote Markt, Our Lady's Cathedral, MoMu, Het Zuid.

→ TWO DAYS
Rubens' House, Royal Museum of Fine Arts, a stroll to the Left Bank via the Sint-Anna tunnel.

→ THREE DAYS
Het Eilandje and MAS, a river trip, Kloosterstraat, Nationalestraat.

PRACTICAL INFORMATION

ARRIVAL-DEPARTURE

 Brussels Zaventem Airport is 40km south. The SN Brussels Airlines shuttle bus to Central Station takes 45min.

 Antwerp Deurne Airport is 7km southeast. Bus Number 16 goes to to Pelikaanstraat.

Inter-city trains run to Antwerpen-Central and Antwerpen-Berchem Stations.

GETTING AROUND

Antwerp has an efficient network of buses, trams and premetro (trams which run underground at some stage of their journey). Invest in a Dagpas Stad - a city day pass - which gives unlimited travel on the whole of the city's public transport system; it's obtainable on board buses and trams and from De Lijn kiosks. On many occasions you'll find it quicker to walk around, as this is a compact city ideal for pedestrians. If you'd rather get about by bike, head to Tourism Antwerp on Grote Markt for more information.

EATING OUT

CALENDAR HIGHLIGHTS

March
Eurantica Antwerp Antiques Festival.

May
Sinksefoor Funfair.

May – September
Free carillon concerts on Monday nights.

June
Beer Passion Weekend.

Summer
Antwerp Beach.

July
Festival of Flanders, International Summer Festival.

August
Rubens Market.

September
Laundry Day, Open Monument Day.

The menus of Flanders are heavily influenced by the lush meadows, the canals swarming with eels and the proximity of the North Sea – but the eating culture in Antwerp offers more than just seafood. With its centuries old connection to more exotic climes, there's no shortage of fragrant spices such as cinnamon in their dishes, especially in the rich stews so beloved by the locals. If you want to eat with the chic, hang around the Het Eilandje dockside or the rejuvenated ancient warehouses south of Grote Markt. For early risers, the grand cafés are a popular port of call, ideal for a slow coffee and a trawl through the papers. Overall the city boasts the same tempting Belgian specialities as Brussels (stewed eel in chervil sauce; mussels; dishes containing rabbit; beef stew and chicory), but also with a focus on more contemporary cuisine. Don't miss out on the local chocolate (shaped like a hand in keeping with the legend which gave Antwerp its name), and be sure to try their keuninkske beer, served in a glass designed like an open bowl.

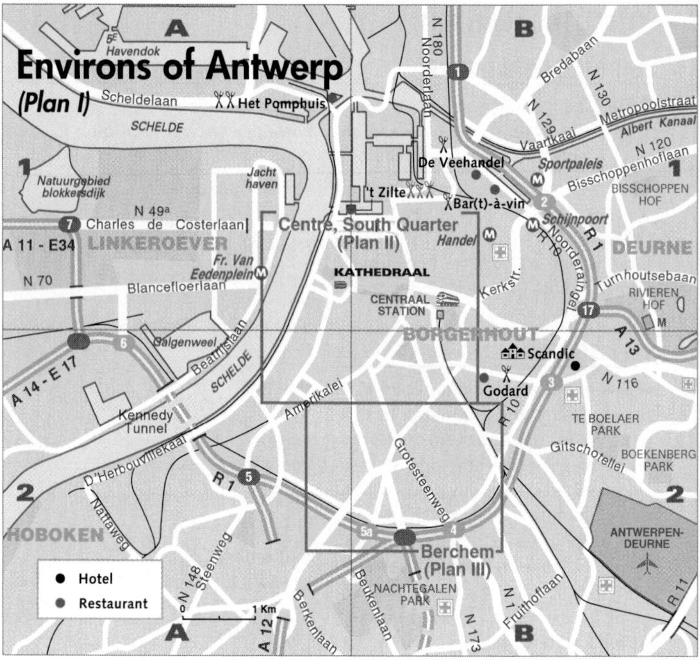

Environs of Antwerp
(Plan I)

Map of Antwerp environs showing locations including Havendok, Scheldelaan, Het Pomphuis, Natuurgebied blokkersdijk, Jacht haven, De Veehandel, 't Zilte, Bar(t)-à-vin, Sportpaleis, Bisschoppenhoflaan, BISSCHOPPEN HOF, DEURNE, RIVIEREN HOF, Centre South Quarter (Plan II), KATHEDRAAL, CENTRAAL STATION, BORGERHOUT, Scandic, Godard, TE BOELAER PARK, BOEKENBERG PARK, Berchem (Plan III), NACHTEGALEN PARK, ANTWERPEN-DEURNE, HOBOKEN, LINKEROEVER, Kennedy Tunnel, and various road references N 180, N 130, N 129, N 120, N 49a, N 70, N 116, N 173, A 11 - E34, A 14 - E 17, A 12, A 13, R 1, R 11

- ● Hotel
- ● Restaurant

0 ——— 1 Km

CENTRE (Old Town and Main Station)   *Plan II*

Hilton   ⠀ 🍴 🛁 & 🅰️ 🛜 🛋 🚗 *VISA* ❶ 🅰️ ⓪

Groenplaats 32 – ℰ 03 204 12 12 – www.antwerp.hilton.com
210 rm – 👤159/429 € 👥👥159/429 €, ⌕ 25 € – 12 suites   **D2**
Rest *Brasserie Terrace Café* – see restaurant listing
♦ Chain hotel ♦ Luxury ♦ Stylish ♦
A luxury hotel established in 1994 within the walls of the superb, early-20C Grand Bazar building. Sumptuous Belle Époque ballroom. Suites facing the city, standard guestrooms overlooking the courtyard. Views of the cathedral and busy Groenplaats from the Terrace Café's veranda.

Radisson Blu Astrid   ⟨ 🍴 🛁 🔲 & rm, 🅰️ 🛜 🛋 🚗
Koningin Astridplein 7 ⊠ 2018 – ℰ 03 203 12 34   *VISA* ❶ 🅰️ ⓪
– www.radissonblu.com/astridhotel-antwerp   **F2**
247 rm ⌕ – 👤129/279 € 👥👥129/279 € – 3 suites
Rest – Menu 27 € (lunch)/32 € – Carte 34/52 €
♦ Chain hotel ♦ Luxury ♦ Stylish ♦
This modern, elegant hotel caters admirably for guests in the city on business or for pleasure. The Aquatopia oceanarium inside the hotel is home to 10,000 fish and reptiles. This bright and trendy canteen-style brasserie has a distinctly urban atmosphere.

Radisson Blu Park Lane

Van Eycklei 34 ✉ *2018* – ☎ *0 3 285 85 85*
– www.radissonblu.com/parklanehotel-antwerp
VISA ◉◉ AE
E3
161 rm – †89/259 € ††89/259 €, ⊊ 22 € – 13 suites
Rest – Menu 15 € (lunch), 28/35 € – Carte 35/51 €
♦ Chain hotel ♦ Business ♦ Stylish ♦

This luxury hotel is on a main road alongside a park. The bedrooms and suites are well appointed. It also offers a conference centre, lounge-bar, swimming pool, fitness room and sauna. The hotel's brasserie offers an international menu including pastas and pizzas. Valet parking.

De Witte Lelie *without rest*

Keizerstraat 16 – ☎ *0 3 226 19 66* – *www.dewittelelie.be*
D1
8 rm – †225/565 € ††295/565 €, ⊊ 25 € – 3 suites
♦ Luxury ♦ Stylish ♦

This historic abode fully justifies its reputation for poised sophistication and graceful hospitality. The 17C walls, tasteful decor down to the tiniest detail, and its precious peace and quiet in the city centre explain the appeal of this luxury boutique hotel.

Julien *without rest*

Korte Nieuwstraat 24 – ☎ *0 3 229 06 00* – *www.hotel-julien.com*
– closed last week July-first week August
D2
21 rm ⊊ – †165/295 € ††165/295 €
♦ Luxury ♦ Stylish ♦ Design ♦

Hidden behind its carriage entrance this hotel is a real gem. It boasts a warm welcome, cosy atmosphere and very refined Scandinavian-style rooms. Don't miss the spa built in the 16C cellar. From the roof terrace there is a breathtaking view of the cathedral.

't Sandt *without rest*

Zand 17 – ☎ *0 3 232 93 90* – *www.hotel-sandt.be*
C2
28 rm ⊊ – †150/230 € ††170/250 € – 1 suite
♦ Luxury ♦ Stylish ♦

This establishment is in an attractive building with a fine Rococo façade near the banks of the Escaut. It offers attentive service, bedrooms full of character, meeting rooms, a patio and a roof terrace.

Theater

Arenbergstraat 30 – ☎ *0 3 203 54 10* – *www.vhv-hotels.be*
E2
122 rm – †110/220 € ††130/240 €, ⊊ 20 € – 5 suites
Rest – *(closed 14 July-17 August and 21 December-2 January) (dinner only)* Menu 18/55 € – Carte 34/43 €
♦ Business ♦ Classic ♦

This modern hotel enjoys a strategic location between a theatre, museums and designer boutiques – ideal for a business trip or a weekend in the city! International menu at the restaurant.

Les Nuits

Lange Gasthuisstraat 12 – ☎ *0 3 225 02 04* – *www.hotellesnuits.be*
24 rm – †139/179 € ††139/179 €, ⊊ 19 €
D2
Rest – *(closed Sunday and Bank Holidays)* Carte 46/59 €
♦ Luxury ♦ Cosy ♦ Modern ♦

A chic hotel above the Flamant stores. Rooms decorated with natural materials in the elegant style of this famous interior design brand. Refined brasserie fare is served at the Flamant Dining restaurant. A hip place in a hip town!

Hyllit *without rest*

De Keyserlei 28 (access via Appelmansstraat) ✉ *2018* – ☎ *0 3 202 68 00*
– www.hyllit.com
E2
197 rm – †120/190 € ††120/215 €, ⊊ 20 € – 3 suites
♦ Business ♦ Stylish ♦

This hotel on a busy shopping street has obliging staff. There are large and well-appointed rooms, suites and junior suites, as well as an extensive breakfast buffet, meeting rooms, lounge and leisure facilities.

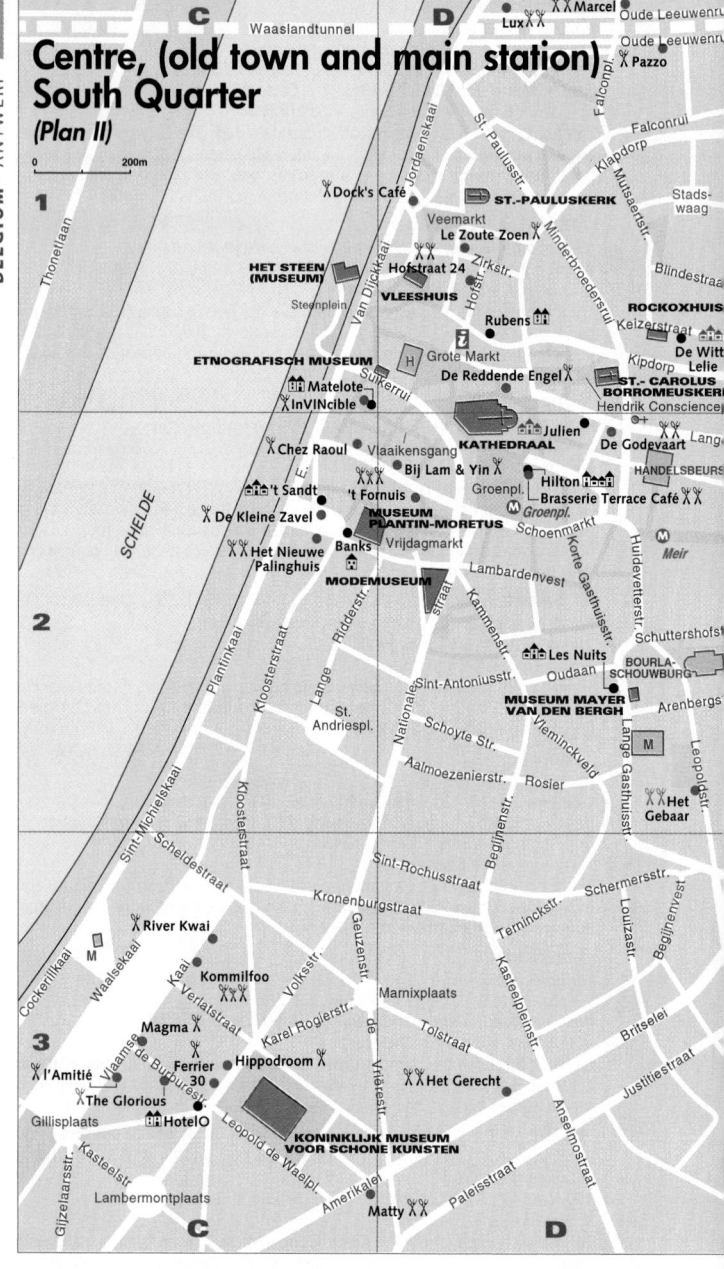

Centre, (old town and main station) South Quarter

(Plan II)

0   200m

Waaslandtunnel

✗✗ Marcel
Lux ✗ ✗   Oude Leeuwenr.
                                 Oude Leeuwenr.
                    ✗ Pazzo

Falconpl.

Falconrui

St.-Paulusstr.

Jordaenskaai

Klapdorp

St.-Paulusstr.

✗ Dock's Café

Minderbroedersr.

Musastr.

Stads-
waag

ST.-PAULUSKERK

Veemarkt

Le Zoute Zoen

✗✗ Hofstraat 24

Zirkstr.

Blindestraa

HET STEEN
(MUSEUM)

Van Dijckkaai

VLEESHUIS

Hofstr.

ROCKOXHUIS

Keizerstraat

Steenplein

Rubens 🏛

De Witt
Lelie

Kipdorp

ETNOGRAFISCH MUSEUM

🏛

H Grote Markt

Suikerrui

ST.- CAROLUS
BORROMEUSKERK

🏛 Matelote

De Reddende Engel ✗

Hendrik Conscience

✗ InVINcible

🏛 Julien

De Godevaart ✗✗

Lang

✗ Chez Raoul

Vlaaikensgang

KATHEDRAAL

HANDELSBEURS

🏛🏛 't Sandt

Bij Lam & Yin ✗
✗✗✗

Hilton 🏨🏨

Groenpl.

Brasserie Terrace Café ✗✗

Huidevettersstr.

M Meir

✗ De Kleine Zavel

't Fornuis

Groenpl.

Schoenmarkt

Korte Gasthuisstr.

SCHELDE

✗✗ Het Nieuwe
Palinghuis

Banks 🏦

Vrijdagmarkt

MUSEUM
PLANTIN-MORETUS

Schuttershofs

Schoytestraat

MODEMUSEUM

Kammenstr.

Lambardenvest

Plantinkaai

Kloosterstraat

Lange
Ridderstr.

Sint-Antoniusstr.

🏛🏛 Les Nuits

BOURLA-
SCHOUWBURG

Arenbergs

Leopold

St.
Andriespl.

Nationalestr.

MUSEUM MAYER
VAN DEN BERGH

Vleminckveld

Lange Gasthuisstr.

M

Sint-Michelskaai

Scheldestraat

Schoyte Str.

Aalmoezenierstr.

Rosier

✗✗ Het
Gebaar

Sint-Rochusstraat

Begijnenstr.

Kronenburgstraat

Geuzenstr.

Schermersstr.

Terninckstr.

Louizastr.

Begijnenvest

✗ River Kwai

M

Kommilfoo
✗✗✗

Waaslekaai

Kaai

Verlatstraat

Volksstr.

Marnixplaats

Kasteelpleinstr.

Britselei

Justitiestraat

Magma ✗

Karel Rogierstr.

de Vrièrestr.

Tolstraat

✗ l'Amitié

Ferrier
30 ✗

Hippodroom ✗

✗✗ Het Gerecht

Vlaamse de Burgerstr.

✗ The Glorious

Gillisplaats

🏛🏛 HotelO

Leopold de Waelpl.

KONINKLIJK MUSEUM
VOOR SCHONE KUNSTEN

Anselmostraat

Cockerillkaai

Kasteelstr.

Gijzelaarsstr.

Lambermontplaats

Amerikalei

Paleisstraat

Matty ✗✗

C   D

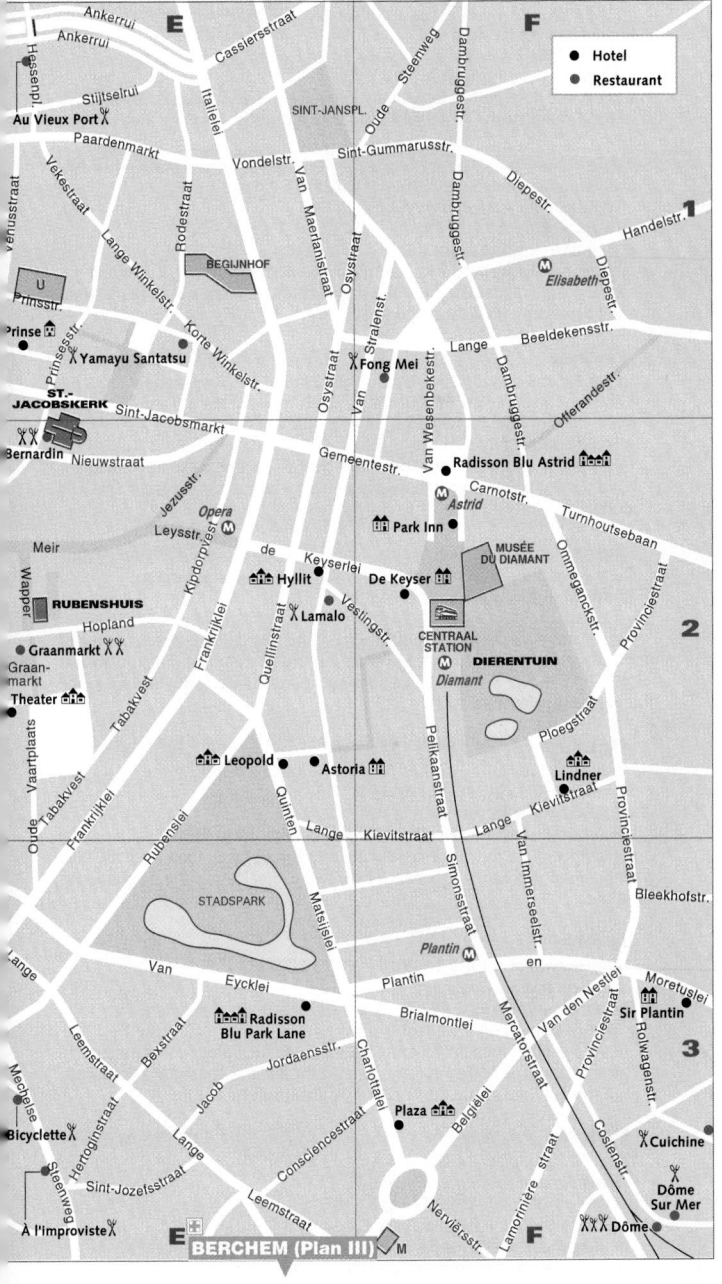

Ankerrui
Ankerrui
Hessenpl.
Au Vieux Port
Stijtselrui
Paardenmarkt
Cassierssstraat
Italielei
SINT-JANSPL.
Oude Steenweg
Dambruggestr.
Hotel
Restaurant

Venusstraat
Vekestraat
Lange Winkelstr.
Rodestraat
Vondelstr.
Van Maerlantstraat
Sint-Gummarusstr.
Diepestr.
Handelstr.
Prinsstr.
Prinsesstr.
Prinse
BEGIJNHOF
Korte Winkelstr.
Osystraat
Van Stralenst.
Elisabeth
Diepestr.
Yamayu Santatsu
Fong Mei
Lange
Beeldekensstr.
ST.-JACOBSKERK
Sint-Jacobsmarkt
Bernardin
Nieuwstraat
Jezusstr.
Gemeentestr.
Van Wesenbekestr.
Dambruggestr.
Offerandestr.
Radisson Blu Astrid
Carnotstr.
Turnhoutsebaan

Opera
Leysstr.
Kipdorpvest
Astrid
Park Inn
Meir
Wapper
RUBENSHUIS
Hopland
de
Keyserlei
Frankrijklei
Quellinstraat
Vestingstr.
Hyllit
De Keyser
Lamalo
MUSÉE DU DIAMANT
Ommeganckstr.
Provinciestraat
Graanmarkt
Graan-markt
Theater
Tabaksvest
CENTRAAL STATION
DIERENTUIN
Diamant
Ploegstraat
Vaartplaats
Oude Tabakslei
Frankrijklei
Leopold
Astoria
Lindner
Kievitstraat
Provinciestraat
Rubenslei
Quinten
Matsijslei
Lange Kievitstraat
Lange
Pelikaanstraat
Simonsstraat
Van Immerseelstr.
Bleekhofstr.
Lange
STADSPARK
Van
Eycklei
Plantin
Plantin
en
Moretuslei
Sir Plantin
Rolwagenstr.
Leemstraat
Bexstraat
Radisson Blu Park Lane
Jordaensstr.
Jacob
Brialmontlei
Mercatorstraat
Van den Nestlei
Provinciestraat
Mechelse
Hertoginstraat
Lange
Charlottalei
Plaza
Belgiëlei
Bicyclette
Sint-Jozefsstraat
Conciencestraat
Lamorinièrestraat
Cuichine
Nerviërsstr.
Coslensstr.
Dôme Sur Mer
À l'improviste
Leemstraat
BERCHEM (Plan III)
Dôme

BELGIUM - ANTWERP

99

Plaza without rest 🔲 🛜 🛗 🚗 VISA 💳 AE ⓪
Charlottalei 49 ✉ *2018 – ℰ 0 3 287 28 70 – www.plaza.be* **F3**
81 rm – 🛏89/299 € 🛏🛏99/399 €, ☕ 16 €
♦ Business ♦ Stylish ♦
A family-run hotel perfect for a good night's sleep. Spacious bedrooms and cosy suites, a lounge with Chesterfield chairs, plus a pleasant breakfast area and bar.

Leopold without rest 🔲 🛜 🛗 🚗 VISA 💳 AE ⓪
Quinten Matsijslei 25 ✉ *2018 – ℰ 0 3 231 15 15*
– www.leopoldhotels.com/antwerp **E2**
126 rm – 🛏99/139 € 🛏🛏99/139 €, ☕ 12 € – 1 suite
♦ Business ♦ Design ♦
This chain boutique hotel is located opposite a park near the city's diamond district. There is a modern decor with plenty of character in the hotel's public areas and guestrooms. Conference rooms available.

Lindner 🛗 🐾 ♿ rm, 🔲 rm, 🛜 🚗 VISA 💳 AE ⓪
Lange Kievitstraat 125 ✉ *2018 – ℰ 0 3 227 77 00 – www.lindnerhotels.be*
173 rm – 🛏109/179 € 🛏🛏109/179 €, ☕ 18 € – 4 suites **F2**
Rest – Menu 25 € (lunch)/33 € – Carte approx. 42 €
♦ Business ♦ Modern ♦
This modern, almost futuristic hotel was cleverly built near the new station. A good starting point for your trip, whether it is for business or pleasure. Spacious rooms.

Rubens without rest 🐾 🔲 🛜 🚗 VISA 💳 AE
Oude Beurs 29 – ℰ 0 3 222 48 48 – www.hotelrubensantwerp.be
35 rm ☕ – 🛏120/230 € 🛏🛏120/230 € – 1 suite **D1**
♦ Family ♦ Classic ♦
The Rubens occupies a stately building near the Grand Place, in which some of the guestrooms have a terrace overlooking the garden. Welcoming breakfast room and lounge, as well as a colonnaded courtyard filled with flowers. Peace and quiet guaranteed.

Matelote without rest 🔲 🛜 VISA 💳 AE
Haarstraat 11a – ℰ 0 3 201 88 00 – www.hotel-matelote.be **C1**
10 rm – 🛏90/130 € 🛏🛏110/190 €, ☕ 12 €
♦ Luxury ♦ Modern ♦
A very well-located hotel a stone's throw from the Grand Place. The decidedly contemporary decor fits in marvellously with the perfectly preserved 16C building. An original luxury experience in Antwerp. Breakfast at the neighbouring restaurant.

Astoria without rest 🔲 🛜 🚗 VISA 💳 AE ⓪
Korte Herentalsestraat 5 ✉ *2018 – ℰ 0 3 227 31 30*
– www.astoria-antwerp.com **E2**
66 rm ☕ – 🛏69/109 € 🛏🛏79/129 €
♦ Business ♦ Functional ♦
The Astoria offers modern, functional guestrooms (including two with a terrace-balcony), and fully equipped apartments in the annexe. These are a good base for a short or long stay in the city. Close to the diamond district.

Park Inn without rest 🛗 🔲 🛜 VISA 💳 AE ⓪
Koningin Astridplein 14 ✉ *2018 – ℰ 0 3 202 31 70*
– www.parkinn.com/hotel-antwerpen **F2**
59 rm – 🛏99/149 € 🛏🛏99/149 €, ☕ 16 €
♦ Chain hotel ♦ Business ♦ Design ♦
This new chain hotel is handily located in the area around the main railway station. A contemporary feel extends to the bedrooms, the best of which overlook Place Reine Astrid.

Sir Plantin without rest   🚻 📶 🛜 🚗 🆚 💳 🅰🅴

Plantin en Moretuslei 136 ✉ 2018 – ℰ 03 271 07 00
– www.sirplantin-antwerp.com   **F3**
176 rm – ∮69/249 € ∮∮69/249 €, 🍽 15 €
♦ Business ♦ Modern ♦
A new hotel perfect for soaking up the atmosphere in the hip Antwerp neighbourhood of Zurenborg. The design is stunning, with a particularly unusual decor and colours. Ideal for trend followers.

De Keyser without rest   🆎 🛜 🏋 🆚 💳 🅰🅴 🅾

De Keyserlei 66 ✉ 2018 – ℰ 03 206 74 60 – www.vhv-hotels.be
120 rm 🍽 – ∮110/190 € ∮∮130/290 € – 3 suites   **F2**
♦ Business ♦ Modern ♦
This hotel has an excellent central location between the railway station and shopping district. Modern guestrooms and public areas, a choice of meeting rooms, a trendy bar, as well as a swimming pool and relaxation centre.

Prinse without rest   🏊 🚻 🛜 🏋 🚗 🆚 💳 🅰🅴 🅾

Keizerstraat 63 – ℰ 03 226 40 50 – www.hotelprinse.be
– closed 23-27 December   **E1**
32 rm 🍽 – ∮115/120 € ∮∮140/150 € – 2 suites
♦ Business ♦ Classic ♦
A 16C townhouse blending charm and modernity. Enjoy the spacious rooms after a day of sightseeing in Antwerp. It has a peaceful atmosphere in its inner courtyards with well-pruned boxwood bushes.

Banks without rest   🆎 🛜 🆚 💳

Steenhouwersvest 55 – ℰ 03 232 40 02 – www.hotelbanks.com
68 rm – ∮80/150 € ∮∮90/200 €, 🍽 15 €   **C2**
♦ Business ♦ Functional ♦ Minimalist ♦
This hotel with an ultra-modern design exemplifies Antwerp hospitality – even if the owners are Dutch. Right near the city centre, it features streamlined rooms at reasonable prices. A welcome drink is offered at the reception, which is open until 8pm.

't Zilte (Viki Geunes)   ≤ 🚻 🆚 💳 🅰🅴
❀❀

Hanzestedenplaats 5 (9th floor of the MAS - Museum Aan de Stroom)
– ℰ 03 283 40 40 – www.tzilte.be
– closed 1 week at Easter, 2 weeks in July, 1 week at All Saints' day, late
December-early January, Monday lunch, Saturday and Sunday   Plan I **A-B1**
Rest – (booking advisable) Menu 65 € (lunch), 110/135 €
– Carte 90/165 €
♦ Creative ♦ Design ♦ Fashionable ♦
This establishment has moved to the top floor of the MAS, so the location is now at the same level as the food! The urban gastronomy here is indeed top flight, a magnificent blend of craftsmanship and creativity – in one of the loveliest spots in town overlooking the harbour.
➔ Langoustines au chou-fleur, caviar et crème aigre. Ris de veau à la carotte, yaourt et noix de kemiri. Chocolat et fruits de la passion, carotte et multivitamines.

't Fornuis (Johan Segers)   ✂ 🆚 💳 🅰🅴 🅾
❀

Reyndersstraat 24 – ℰ 03 233 62 70
– closed 22 July-16 August, late December, Bank Holidays, Saturday
and Sunday   **D2**
Rest – (pre-book) Carte 75/130 € 🍷
♦ Traditional ♦ Rustic ♦
Fine classic cuisine and quality wines are served in this rustic restaurant housed in an old building. The owner/chef introduces the menu in person. He has been running the show since 1976 and was awarded his first Michelin star in 1986. Miniature stoves exhibited downstairs.
➔ Tourteau entre deux tuiles aux épices. Barbue à la mousseline de pomme de terre et œuf poché. Crêpe caramélisée.

BELGIUM - ANTWERP

XXX **Dôme** (Julien Burlat)   `AC` `VISA` `OO` `AE` `O`
❋
Grote Hondstraat 2 ✉ 2018 – ℰ 0 3 239 90 03 – www.domeweb.be
– closed 2 weeks in August, 24 December-9 January, Saturday lunch, Sunday
and Monday   **F3**
Rest – *(bookings advisable at dinner)* Menu 41 € (lunch)/79 €
– Carte 80/97 € 🕸
♦ Traditional ♦ Elegant ♦
Chef Julien Burlat is obsessed with quality and constantly on the lookout for the finest ingredients. The menu changes according to his latest discoveries and feature dishes that are always authentic without being fussy. Organic and sulfite-free wines figure prominently on the excellent wine list.
➔ Cuisses de grenouilles à la réglisse et salade de jambon de bœuf ibérique. Jambon aux petits pois à la bergamote et boudin basque aux pickles maison. Tarte au chocolat maison, chantilly à la vanille.

XX **Het Nieuwe Palinghuis**   `AC` `VISA` `OO` `AE`
Sint-Jansvliet 14 – ℰ 0 3 231 74 45 – www.hetnieuwepalinghuis.be
– closed June, Monday and Tuesday   **C2**
Rest – Menu 39/130 € bi – Carte 49/111 €
♦ Fish and seafood ♦ Friendly ♦
Eel is king at this fish restaurant, only dethroned by Escaut lobster in season. The dining room and veranda are decorated with seascapes and old photographs of Antwerp. The perfect place to enjoy the pleasures of the North Sea.

XX **Hofstraat 24**   `⇔` `VISA` `OO` `AE`
Hofstraat 24 – ℰ 0 3 225 05 45 – www.hofstraat24.be
– closed 2 weeks at Easter, last week July-first 2 weeks August, 2 weeks at
Christmas, Wednesday and Sunday   **D1**
Rest – *(dinner only)* Carte 48/80 €
♦ Classic ♦ Cosy ♦
À la carte dishes (no menus) that are changed monthly are served beneath the restaurant's glass roof or in two pleasant rooms, one of which is a more intimate library. The owner-chef is at the helm in the kitchen.

XX **Het Pomphuis**   `⇐` `🏠` `⇔` `P` `VISA` `OO` `AE` `O`
Siberiastraat ✉ 2030 – ℰ 0 3 770 86 25 – www.hetpomphuis.be
– closed 24 December   *Plan I* **A1**
Rest – Menu 29 € (lunch)/47 € – Carte 48/70 €
♦ Classic ♦ Retro ♦
This extraordinary restaurant occupies a huge warehouse dating from 1920, where the decor includes three enormous bilge pumps. Enjoy the sophisticated, contemporary menu and views of the docks from the terrace.

XX **Het Gebaar** (Roger van Damme)   `VISA` `OO` `AE`
❋
Leopoldstraat 24 – ℰ 0 3 232 37 10 – www.hetgebaar.be
– closed Sunday, Monday and Bank Holidays   **D2**
Rest – *(lunch only) (booking advisable)* Menu 65 € – Carte 65/85 €
♦ Creative ♦ Cosy ♦
This restaurant is located in an elegant building on the edge of the botanical park. Luxury tea room cuisine, which the chef enriches with modern twists; mouthwatering desserts! Non-stop service until 6pm.
➔ Carpaccio de langoustines et salade de pomme et avocat. Pigeon et textures variées de potiron, perles de foie gras. Pannacotta à la vanille et fruits exotiques au chocolat blanc.

XX **Graanmarkt 13**   `🏠` `AC` `⇔` `VISA` `OO` `AE` `O`
Graanmarkt 13 – ℰ 0 3 337 79 91 – www.graanmarkt13.be
– closed first 3 weeks August, last week December, Sunday and Monday
Rest – Menu 29 € (lunch), 39/65 € – Carte 53/72 €   **E2**
♦ Traditional ♦ Minimalist ♦ Trendy ♦
This trendy, minimalist loft in the mezzanine of a bourgeois house lies in the heart of Antwerp, behind the Théâtre Bourla. Tasty and originally presented dishes.

XX **De Godevaart** 🏠 ♻ ⌨ (dinner) VISA ⓪ AE

Sint-Katelijnevest 23 – ℘ *0 3 231 89 94* – *www.degodevaart.be*
– *closed first week May, first 2 weeks September, second week*
January, Saturday lunch, Sunday and Monday D2
Rest – *(pre-book)* Menu 35 € (lunch), 65/115 € – Carte 57/91 €
♦ Creative ♦ Fashionable ♦
The cutting-edge gastronomy of this young, ambitious chef is well worth disco-
vering. The restaurant is set in an old house, which has retained part of its origi-
nal decor (stuccowork and fireplace). Valet parking in the evening.

XX **Bernardin** 🏠 ⌨ VISA ⓪

Sint-Jacobsstraat 17 – ℘ *0 3 213 07 00* – *www.restaurantbernardin.be*
– *closed 1 week at Easter, last 2 weeks August, 25 December-4 January,*
Saturday lunch, Sunday and Monday E2
Rest – Menu 30 € (lunch)/43 € – Carte 45/67 €
♦ Traditional ♦ Fashionable ♦
This 17C house has been renovated inside and out. Depending on the season
and the weather, choose between the modern, sober decor of the dining room
or the delightful courtyard in the shadow of St Jacob's church.

XX **Marcel** ♻ VISA ⓪ AE
☺
Van Schoonbekeplein 13 – ℘ *0 3 336 33 02* – *www.restaurantmarcel.be*
– *closed Saturday lunch and Sunday* D1
Rest – Menu 27 € (lunch), 35/65 € – Carte 41/79 €
♦ Classic ♦ Brasserie ♦ Retro ♦
Welcome to Marcel's – a vintage bistro with a distinctly French feel. The culinary
repertory mingles traditional recipes with touches of modernity, resulting in cui-
sine steeped in wholesome flavours. Terrace overlooking the MAS.

XX **Brasserie Terrace Café** – Hôtel Hilton ♿ AC ⌨ VISA ⓪ AE ①

Groenplaats 32 – ℘ *0 3 204 12 12* – *www.antwerp.hilton.com*
Rest – Menu 30 € – Carte 36/72 € D2
♦ Classic ♦ Brasserie ♦ Friendly ♦
Have a nice drink on the terrace while taking in the splendid view of the Grand
Place, then enjoy some of the classic Belgian and international dishes served
here.

XX **Lux** ≤ 🏠 ♻ ⌨ (lunch) VISA ⓪ AE ①

Adriaan Brouwerstraat 13 – ℘ *0 3 233 30 30* – *www.luxantwerp.com*
– *closed 1 January* D1
Rest – Menu 24 € (lunch)/35 € – Carte 35/59 €
♦ Classic ♦ Luxury ♦
This restaurant occupies the house of a former ship owner, and has a terrace
that overlooks the port. There is a profusion of marble (columns, fireplaces), a
wine and cocktail bar, à la carte options, plus an attractive lunch menu.

X **InVINcible** 🏠 AC VISA ⓪ AE ①
☺
Haarstraat 9 – ℘ *0 3 231 32 07* – *www.invincible.be*
– *closed last 2 weeks September, 1-9 January, Saturday and Sunday*
Rest – Menu 35/60 € 🍷 C1
♦ Traditional ♦ Trendy ♦ Fashionable ♦
Kenny and Wendy's restaurant really is InVINcible! The food, which is of French
inspiration, has the starring role. The vol-au-vent, for instance, plays off sweetbreads! All paired with excellent wines of course. The story always ends happily
with a cup of coffee – Kenny being a well-known barista.

X **Dock's Café** 🏠 AC ♻ ⌨ VISA ⓪ AE
☺
Jordaenskaai 7 – ℘ *0 3 226 63 30* – *www.docks.be*
– *closed Sunday* D1
Rest – *(open until 11pm)* Menu 18 € (lunch), 26/34 € – Carte 37/85 €
♦ Traditional ♦ Fashionable ♦ Brasserie ♦
Set in the post-industrial landscape of the docks, this brasserie encapsulates
contemporary taste: Jules Verne decor, trendy clientele and tasty "terre-mer"
cuisine (oyster bar). Booking advisable.

Chez Raoul 🕤 ⇔ ⊕

Vlasmarkt 21 – ℰ 03 213 09 77 – www.chezraoul.be
– closed last 3 weeks July, Tuesday and Wednesday **C2**
Rest – *(dinner only)* Menu 50 € – Carte 48/65 €
♦ Classic ♦ Bistro ♦

A pocket-sized restaurant with warm atmosphere to spare! The many regulars who come here love the daily suggestions on the blackboard and the seasonal menus. Fine selection of champagnes and liqueurs.

Le Zoute Zoen ⇔ 𝘝𝘐𝘚𝘈 ⊕ 𝘈𝘌

Zirkstraat 23 – ℰ 03 226 92 20
– closed Saturday lunch and Monday **D1**
Rest – Menu 18 € (lunch), 32/46 € – Carte 38/59 €
♦ Classic ♦ Bistro ♦

This is an intimate and cosy bistro. The culinary emphasis of its female chef is placed as much as possible on Belgian dishes and produce, including the set 'Zoenmenu'.

De Reddende Engel 🕤 ⇔ 𝘝𝘐𝘚𝘈 ⊕ 𝘈𝘌 ⓪

Torfburg 3 – ℰ 03 233 66 30 – www.de-reddende-engel.be
– closed mid August-mid September, 10-20 February, Saturday lunch, Tuesday and Wednesday **D1**
Rest – Menu 28/35 € – Carte 37/55 €
♦ Traditional ♦ Rustic ♦

Provence and Gascony come together in this rustic house near the cathedral. Enjoy dishes such as bouillabaisse from Marseille, brandade from Nîmes, duck liver from the Landes, cassoulet etc.

De Kleine Zavel 🕤 𝘈𝘒 𝘝𝘐𝘚𝘈 ⊕ 𝘈𝘌 ⓪

Stoofstraat 2 – ℰ 03 231 96 91 – www.kleinezavel.be
– Closed Saturday lunch and Monday **C2**
Rest – Menu 35/70 € – Carte 52/77 €
♦ Modern ♦ Bistro ♦

Don't be fooled by the vintage floor, retro counter, little bare tables, wine shelves and old wooden beer racks. The food served at this typical Antwerp bistro is as up-to-the-minute as it gets!

Bij Lam & Yin (Lap Yee Lam) 𝘈𝘒 𝘝𝘐𝘚𝘈 ⊕ 𝘈𝘌

Reynderstraat 17 – ℰ 03 232 88 38
– closed Easter school holidays, Monday and Tuesday **D2**
Rest – *(dinner only) (booking essential)* Carte approx. 45 €
♦ Chinese ♦ Minimalist ♦ Exotic ♦

This Chinese restaurant goes against the grain, challenging preconceived ideas about Asian cuisine. It has a minimalist decor and a small menu placing the onus on fresh ingredients, originality and flavour. Be sure to book a table!
→ Panier de dim-sum. Drunken chicken. Tartelette à la mousse de thé vert.

Dôme Sur Mer 🕤 𝘝𝘐𝘚𝘈 ⊕

Arendstraat 1 ✉ 2018 – ℰ 03 281 74 33 – www.domeweb.be
– closed 2 weeks early September, 24 December-10 January and Saturday lunch
Rest – Carte 36/71 € **F3**
♦ Fish and seafood ♦ Bistro ♦

This manor house has been transformed into a trendy seafood brasserie. It has a whitewashed decor punctuated by several bluish coloured aquariums full of goldfish.

Pazzo 𝘈𝘒 ⇔ 𝘝𝘐𝘚𝘈 ⊕ 𝘈𝘌 ⓪

Oude Leeuwenrui 12 – ℰ 03 232 86 82 – www.pazzo.be
– closed mid July-mid August, late December-early January, Saturday, Sunday and Bank Holidays **D1**
Rest – *(open until 11pm)* Carte 47/60 € 🍷
♦ Modern ♦ Friendly ♦ Fashionable ♦

This trendy brasserie with a lively atmosphere occupies a former warehouse near the docks. Enjoy Mediterranean- and Asian-inspired bistro cuisine with excellent wine recommendations from the owner-sommelier.

Lamalo

AC ⇔ VISA ⬤⬤ AE ⓪

Appelmansstraat 21 ⊠ 2018 – 𝒞 0 3 213 22 00 – www.lamalo.com
– closed first 2 weeks August, Jewish Holidays, Friday and Saturday
Rest – Carte 40/65 €   **E2**
♦ Traditional ♦ Cosy ♦
This restaurant in the city's diamond district is a popular haunt for Antwerp's Jewish community. Tasty Kosher cuisine with a Mediterranean twist. Bright and welcoming decor.

Fong Mei

AC VISA ⬤⬤

Van Arteveldestraat 65 ⊠ 2060 – 𝒞 0 3 225 06 54
– closed Thursday   **F1**
Rest – Menu 20 € (lunch) – Carte 18/29 €
♦ Chinese ♦ Exotic ♦
If you are looking for a Chinese restaurant that serves watered-down dishes to suit the Western palate, then go elsewhere! This establishment's dim sum are truly worthy of Asia, while the wok lobster, straight from the tank, is unforgettable.

Yamayu Santatsu

AC ⇔ VISA ⬤⬤ AE

Ossenmarkt 19 – 𝒞 0 3 234 09 49 – www.santatsu.be
– closed Sunday lunch and Monday   **E1**
Rest – Menu 23 € (lunch), 30/60 € – Carte 25/65 €
♦ Japanese ♦ Friendly ♦
A lively and authentic Japanese restaurant that only uses the best hand picked ingredients, and prepares sushi in full view of diners. Assorted à la carte options with four different menus for two people.

Cuichine

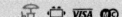 VISA ⬤⬤ AE

Draakstraat 13 ⊠ 2018 – 𝒞 0 3 289 92 45 – www.cuichine.be
– closed first 2 weeks September, Christmas-New Year, Saturday lunch and
Monday   **F3**
Rest – Menu 18 € (lunch)/35 € – Carte 35/56 €
♦ Chinese ♦ Friendly ♦
Two childhood friends whose parents ran Chinese restaurants created 'Cuichine' with the idea of serving up the kind of dishes they enjoyed at home. They have succeeded admirably with this no frills establishment that is original and refined! Reasonably priced à la carte dishes and very attractive surprise menu!

De Veehandel

 ⇔ VISA ⬤⬤

Lange Lobroekstraat 61 ⊠ 2060 – 𝒞 0 3 271 06 06
– www.de-veehandel.be
– closed Saturday lunch and Sunday   *Pan I* **B1**
Rest – Menu 45 € – Carte approx. 50 €
♦ Meats and grills ♦ Bistro ♦ Friendly ♦
Where can you find the best steaks in the city? Look no further than this old bistro with a profusion of wood decor near the city's abattoir. Limousin beef takes pride of place.

Godard

VISA ⬤⬤

Wolfstraat 35 ⊠ 2018 – 𝒞 0 3 283 68 21 – www.restaurantgodard.be
– closed Saturday lunch, Sunday and Monday   *Plan I* **B2**
Rest – *(booking advisable)* Menu 23 € (lunch)/35 € – Carte 43/60 €
♦ Classic ♦ Bistro ♦ Neighbourhood ♦
This new neighbourhood bistro is always packed! The recipe for their success? A charming welcome, modern setting, pleasant atmosphere and unpretentious food. Don't forget to book.

BELGIUM - ANTWERP

Bicyclette

☆ ♻ VISA ⦿

Mechelsesteenweg 76 ⊠ 2018 – ℰ 03 257 77 07
– www.brasseriebicyclette.be
– closed Saturday lunch, Sunday and Monday **E3**
Rest – Menu 15 € (lunch) – Carte 37/47 €
♦ Traditional ♦ Bistro ♦
If you are in the mood for simple, traditional fare that is tasty and well-prepared, this charmingly French bistro is the place for you.

À l'improviste

AC VISA ⦿

Mechelsesteenweg 112 ⊠ 2018 – ℰ 03 216 33 03 – www.alimproviste.be
– closed Saturday lunch, Sunday, Monday and Bank Holidays **E3**
Rest – *(number of covers limited, pre-book)* Menu 22 € (lunch), 35/60 € bi
♦ Modern ♦ Bistro ♦ Trendy ♦
Don't show up unexpectedly (à l'improviste) at this "culinary theatre" which is full every lunchtime. Interesting choices on the set daily menu, to a backdrop of modern decor, including an open kitchen.

Au Vieux Port

VISA ⦿ AE ⓪

Napelsstraat 130 – ℰ 03 290 77 11
– closed first 2 weeks August, 24 December-2 January, Saturday and Sunday
Rest – *(booking advisable)* Carte 46/70 € ⅏ **E1**
♦ Traditional ♦ Bistro ♦
This brasserie is worth keeping in mind for its simple, rustic and tasty cuisine, its gently nostalgic air, and its ritualised service (flambés and carving at guests' tables). Busy atmosphere at lunchtime.

Bar(t)-à-vin

VISA ⦿

Lange Slachterijstraat 3 ⊠ 2060 – ℰ 0 474 94 17 86 – www.bartavin.info
– closed Saturday, Sunday and Bank Holidays *Plan I* **B1**
Rest – Carte 39/53 €
♦ Traditional ♦ Bistro ♦
Bart, the proprietor, converted his wine bar into a bistro in this attractive former butcher shop. Everything has gone smoothly thanks to the food with a focus on ingredients, classic recipes and the limited but varied selections.

SOUTH QUARTER AND BERCHEM *Plan III*

Crowne Plaza

☆ ᛁ⤤ 🏠 ☒ ᵭ rest, AC 🛜 ⅏ P 🚗 VISA ⦿ AE ⓪

Gerard Le Grellelaan 10 ⊠ 2020 – ℰ 03 259 75 00
– www.crowneplaza-antwerpen.be **G1**
262 rm � – ♦99/189 € ♦♦99/189 €
Rest – Menu 40 € (lunch) – Carte 46/53 €
♦ Business ♦ Functional ♦
Located close to the ring road and a main road into the city. This huge chain hotel has 260 guestrooms on 16 floors, which are being renovated in stages. Numerous meeting rooms. A relaxed gastro-lounge in which to enjoy a meal or meet with friends or business colleagues.

Firean

♨ AC 🛜 🚗 VISA ⦿ AE ⓪

Karel Oomsstraat 6 ⊠ 2018 – ℰ 03 237 02 60 – www.hotelfirean.com
– closed 24 July-18 August and 24 December-10 January **G1**
12 rm – ♦150/160 € ♦♦150/160 €, � 16 €
Rest *Minerva* – see restaurant listing
♦ Luxury ♦ Personalised ♦
This property full of charm occupies an Art Deco-style building (1929). It features public rooms in the style of the period, a flower-filled patio, and personalised guestrooms with antique furnishings. Impeccable service.

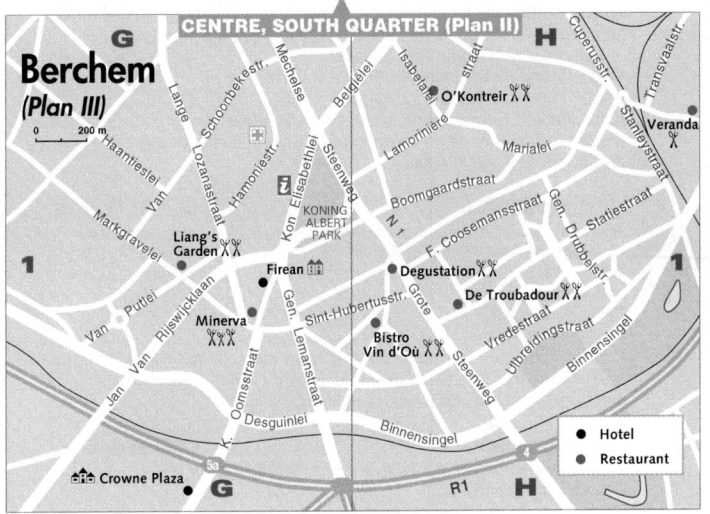

🛏️ HotelO 🛜 🛜 VISA ⓪ AE ①

Leopold de Waelplaats 34 – ℰ 03 292 65 10 – www.hotelhotelo.com
16 rm – ♦155/195 € ♦♦155/195 €, ☑ 16 €   *Plan II* **C3**
Rest – *(open until midnight)* Menu 15 € (lunch), 25/45 € bi
– Carte 30/50 €

◆ **Luxury** ◆ **Modern** ◆

A hotel just across from the Fine Arts Museum. It has an unusual architectural style that fits in well with this artistic neighbourhood in the southern part of town. There is an ultra-modern design in the rooms and bathrooms. Breakfast served in the brasserie.

🍴🍴🍴 Kommilfoo (Olivier de Vinck de Winnezeele) AC P VISA ⓪ AE ①
❀

Vlaamse Kaai 17 – ℰ 03 237 30 00 – www.restaurantkommilfoo.be
– *closed first 3 weeks July, Christmas, Saturday lunch, Sunday and Monday*
Rest – Menu 35 € (lunch), 60/90 € – Carte 72/95 €   *Plan II* **C3**

◆ **Creative** ◆ **Cosy** ◆

A comfortable, modern dining room is the setting for the culinary creations of this innovative chef who alternates ever-evolving recipes with molecular experimentation. Pyrenean goat is an ever-present dish on the menu here!
→ Langoustines en deux préparations : en carpaccio à l'avocat et au yuzu et rôties aux textures de fenouil. Côtes de chevreau rôties au boulgour épicé et épaule braisée. Rhubarbe confite aux textures de yaourt et betterave rouge.

🍴🍴🍴 Minerva – Hôtel Firean AC ⌖ VISA ⓪ AE ①

Karel Oomsstraat 36 ✉ 2018 – ℰ 03 216 00 55
– *www.restaurantminerva.be*
– *closed last week July-first 2 weeks August, late December-early January,*
Saturday and Sunday   **G1**
Rest – Menu 38 € (lunch)/60 € – Carte 58/101 €

◆ **Classic** ◆ **Elegant** ◆

Highly professional service and chic decor in the improbable setting of the ex Minerva garage, which has even retained its old car inspection pit. Modern take on classic dishes.

XX **Liang's Garden** 🔲 ⇄ 🅅🅸🆂🄰 ⓸ 🄰🄴

Markgravelei 141 ✉ 2018 – ✆ 0 3 237 22 22 – www.liangsgarden.be
– closed 15 July-11 August and Sunday **G1**
Rest – Menu 32 € (lunch), 45/95 € bi – Carte 34/82 €
♦ Chinese ♦ Exotic ♦ Luxury ♦
A stalwart of Chinese cuisine in the city! A spacious and elegant restaurant where the authentic menu covers specialities from Canton (dim sum), Peking (duck) and Szechuan (fondue).

XX **Bistro Vin d'Où** 🏠 🔲 ⇄ 🄿 🅅🅸🆂🄰 ⓸ 🄰🄴

Terlinckstraat 2 ✉ 2600 Berchem – ✆ 0 3 230 55 99 – www.vindou.be
– closed 1-14 April, 15 July-12 August, 28 October-3 November, 24 December-6 January, Monday dinner, Tuesday dinner, Wednesday dinner, Saturday lunch and Sunday **H1**
Rest – Carte 56/93 €
♦ Modern ♦ Brasserie ♦
This old house in a residential area has been transformed into a cosy bistro. Modern, artisanal-style cuisine, which only uses carefully selected high quality products. Attractive patio for summer dining.

XX **De Troubadour** 🔲 ⇄ 🄿 🅅🅸🆂🄰 ⓸ 🄰🄴 ⓞ

😊 *Driekoningenstraat 72 ✉ 2600 Berchem – ✆ 0 3 239 39 16*
– www.detroubadour.be
– closed first 3 weeks August, Sunday and Monday **H1**
Rest – Menu 23 € (lunch), 35/44 € – Carte 29/65 €
♦ Creative ♦ Trendy ♦ Friendly ♦
A modern, cosy dining room where the gregarious owner fosters a warm and friendly atmosphere. Classic, creative à la carte options, as well as appetising menus and daily specials announced at your table. Parking available (prior booking required).

XX **Het Gerecht** 🏠 ⇄ 🅅🅸🆂🄰 ⓸ 🄰🄴

Amerikalei 20 – ✆ 0 3 248 79 28 – www.hetgerecht.be
– closed Easter school holidays, 15 July-6 August, first week January, Wednesday dinner, Saturday lunch, Sunday and Monday *Plan II* **D3**
Rest – Menu 33 € (lunch)/49 € – Carte 53/73 €
♦ Classic ♦ Cosy ♦
A sure bet. The owner handles the cooking (up-to-the-minute cuisine) while his companion looks after the service. Stylish, rather cosy decor, with a courtyard terrace enclosed by brick walls.

XX **Matty** 🏠 ⇄ 🅅🅸🆂🄰 ⓸

Brederodestraat 23 ✉ 2018 – ✆ 0 3 293 54 41 – www.restaurantmatty.be
– closed first 3 weeks August, Saturday lunch, Sunday and Monday
Rest – *(booking advisable)* Menu 30 € (lunch)/53 € – Carte *Plan II* **C3**
approx. 65 €
♦ Classic ♦ Design ♦
Contemporary cuisine prepared by a chef who can be seen at work from one of the two dining rooms. Modern, startlingly white decor and an outdoor terrace for summer dining.

XX **Degustation** 🏠 ⇄ 🅅🅸🆂🄰 ⓸ 🄰🄴 ⓞ

Frederik de Merodeplein 6 ✉ 2600 Berchem – ✆ 0 495 63 04 97
– www.degustation-restaurant.be
– closed Saturday lunch, Sunday lunch, Monday and Tuesday **H1**
Rest – Menu 25 € (lunch), 35/55 € – Carte 50/65 €
♦ Classic ♦ Fashionable ♦
The menu boasts many delights, such as turbot with summer truffles and quinoa with sage. The chef selects the finest ingredients in preparing his flavourful dishes, which are offered at reasonable prices.

✗ ### The Glorious   🍴 AC VISA ⦿ AE

De Burburestraat 4a – ℰ 0 3 237 06 13 – www.theglorious.be
– closed 3 weeks June, Saturday and Sunday   Plan II **C3**
Rest – Menu 25 € (lunch), 35/75 € bi – Carte 51/76 € ⅏
♦ Traditional ♦ Wine bar ♦ Formal ♦
This former industrial warehouse has a carefully designed, trendy interior. It features an à la carte Wining & Dining concept.

The Glorious Inn ⌂   AC 🛜 VISA ⦿ AE

– closed 3 weeks June
3 rm ⌸ – ♦150/199 € ♦♦150/199 €
♦ Luxury ♦ Personalised ♦
Second-hand furniture makes for an original, contemporary interior decoration.
Delicious breakfast prepared by the owner.

✗ ### l'Amitié   🍴 VISA ⦿

Vlaamse Kaai 43 – ℰ 0 3 257 50 05 – www.lamitie.net
– closed 2 weeks June, Christmas-New Year, Saturday lunch, Sunday and
Monday   Plan II **C3**
Rest – Menu 25 € (lunch), 45/65 € – Carte 46/77 €
♦ Traditional ♦ Bistro ♦
This welcoming address, located in one of the city's liveliest districts, dedicates
itself to the concept of bistronomy (traditional dishes with an inventive twist).
On fine sunny days take advantage of the Mediterranean-style terrace.

✗ ### Hippodroom   🍴 VISA ⦿ AE

Leopold de Waelplaats 10 – ℰ 0 3 248 52 52 – www.hippodroom.be
– closed Saturday lunch and Sunday   Plan II **C3**
Rest – Menu 24 € (lunch)/35 € – Carte 43/66 €
♦ Traditional ♦ Trendy ♦
This brasserie mixes an arty atmosphere with trendy, imaginatively presented
cuisine in a mansion opposite the city's Fine Arts Museum. Outdoor terraces
on the street and to the rear.

✗ ### Ferrier 30   🍴 AC ⇄ VISA ⦿ AE

Leopold de Waelplaats 30 – ℰ 0 3 216 50 62 – www.ferrier-30.be
– closed Wednesday   Plan II **C3**
Rest – *(open until 11pm)* Carte 37/59 €
♦ Italian ♦ Design ♦
The best Italian restaurant of the area is doubtless Ferrier 30. The meat, fish and
pasta dishes (lasagne al ragu, taglioni con prosciutto) are all steeped in authentic Italian flavours. All of which are further enhanced by wines brought back by
the owner in person.

✗ ### River Kwai   🍴 AC ⇄ VISA ⦿ AE

Vlaamse Kaai 14 – ℰ 0 3 237 46 51 – www.riverkwai.be
– closed Wednesday   Plan II **C3**
Rest – *(dinner only except Thursday and Friday)* Menu 30 € (lunch), 44 €
bi/49 € bi – Carte 33/46 €
♦ Thai ♦ Exotic ♦
This reliable restaurant has been serving authentic Thai cuisine for the past 20
years. Find an attractive retro façade, dining rooms on separate floors with a
typical decor, an elegant lounge and a front terrace.

✗ ### Veranda   🍴 VISA ⦿

Guldenvliesstraat 60 ✉ 2600 Berchem – ℰ 0 3 218 55 95
– closed late December-early January, Saturday lunch, Sunday lunch, Monday
and Tuesday   **H1**
Rest – Menu 23 € (lunch)/45 €
♦ Creative ♦ Bistro ♦ Trendy ♦
Talented chef Davy Schellemans has kept his feet firmly planted on the ground
despite all the buzz around his discreetly elegant new establishment. There
aren't enough superlatives to describe his inventive, amazing and yet reasonably priced dishes.

BELGIUM - ANTWERP

Scandic ᴦᴓ 🕯 🔲 ᴋ rm, 🎬 🛜 ᴋᴀ 🅿 ᴠɪsᴀ ⓜ ᴀᴇ ⓞ

Luitenant Lippenslaan 66 ✉ *2140 Borgerhout –* 𝄐 *0 3 235 91 91*
– www.scandichotels.com/antwerpen **B2**
204 rm ⊡ – 🛉85/185 € 🛉🛉105/205 € **Rest** – Carte 29/51 €
♦ Chain hotel ♦ Functional ♦
This chain hotel has a number of advantages: easy access to the ring road and
centre of the city, a full range of creature comforts in its guestrooms, as well as
meeting and leisure facilities. A restaurant offering a classic international à la
carte menu. Bar with a terrace.

CZECH REPUBLIC
ČESKÁ REPUBLIKA

● PRAGUE

→ **AREA:**
78 864 km²
(30 449 sq mi).

→ **POPULATION:**
10 512 208 inhabitants.
Density = 133 per km².

→ **CAPITAL:**
Prague.

→ **CURRENCY:**
Czech crown (Kč).

→ **GOVERNMENT:**
Parliamentary republic (since 1993).
Member of European Union since
2004.

→ **LANGUAGE:**
Czech; also German and English.

→ **PUBLIC HOLIDAYS:**
New Year's Day (1 Jan); Easter
Monday (late Mar/Apr); Labor Day
(1 May); Liberation Day (8 May);
St Cyril and St Methodius Day
(5 July); Martyrdom of Jan Hus
(6 July); Czech Statehood Day
(28 Sept); Independence Day
(28 Oct); Freedom and Democracy
Day (17 Nov); Christmas Eve (24 Dec
– Half Day); Christmas Day (25 Dec);
2nd Day of Christmas (26 Dec).

→ **LOCAL TIME:**
GMT + 1 hour in winter and GMT
+ 2 hours in summer.

→ **CLIMATE:**
Temperate continental with
cold winters and warm summers
(Prague: January 0°C; July 20°C).

→ **EMERGENCY:**
Police ☎ **158**;
Medical Assistance ☎ **155**;
Fire Brigade ☎ **150**.
(Dialling **112** within any EU country
will redirect your call and contact
the emergency services.)

→ **ELECTRICITY:**
230 volts AC, 50Hz; 2 round pin
sockets.

→ **FORMALITIES:**
Travellers from the European Union
(EU), Switzerland, Iceland and the
main countries of North and South
America need a national identity
card or passport (America: passport
required) to visit Czech Republic
for less than three months (tourism
or business purpose). For visitors
from other countries a visa may be
required, in addition to a passport,
especially for those wishing to
stay for longer than three months.
We advise you to check with your
embassy before travelling.

PRAGUE
PRAHA

Population: 1 272 690

Courtyardpix/Fotolia.com

Prague's history stretches back to the Dark Ages. In the ninth century a princely seat comprising a simple walled-in compound was built where the castle now stands; in the tenth century the first bridge over the Vltava arrived; and by the 13C the enchanting cobbled alleyways below the castle were complete. But Prague has come of age and Europe's most perfectly preserved capital now proffers consumer choice as well as medieval marvels. Its state-of-the-art shopping malls and pulsing nightlife bear testament to its popularity with tourists – the iron glove of communism long since having given way to western consumerism. These days there are practically two versions of Prague: the lively, youthful, 'stag party capital', and the sedate, enchanting 'city of a hundred spires'.

The four main zones of Prague were originally independent towns in their own right. The river Vltava winds its way through their heart and is spanned by the iconic Charles Bridge. On the west side lie Hradčany – the castle quarter, built on a rock spur – and Mala Strana, Prague's most perfectly preserved district, located at the bottom of the castle hill. Over the river are Stare Město, the old town with its vibrant medieval square and outer boulevards, and Nove Město, the new town, which is the city's commercial heart and where you'll find Wenceslas Square and Prague's young partygoers.

PRAGUE IN...

→ **ONE DAY**
Old Town Square, the astronomical clock, Charles Bridge, Prague Castle, Petrin Hill.

→ **TWO DAYS**
Josefov, the National Theatre, Golden Lane.

→ **THREE DAYS**
Wenceslas Square, the National Museum, cross the bridge to look round Mala Strana.

PRACTICAL INFORMATION

ARRIVAL-DEPARTURE

 Vaclav Havel Airport (20km west). The shuttle bus leaves every 30min. Only use a taxi displaying an 'Airport Cars' sign. International trains stop at Hlavni nadraži.

GETTING AROUND

Trams and buses are frequent and run from early morning to past midnight; there's also a metro covering much of the city. All three are invariably cheap and a short-term season pass allows unlimited travel on bus, tram, metro and Petrin funicular. Be wary of taxis; although regulations specify rates, it's always best to use a designated rank and avoid flagging down a cab on the street.

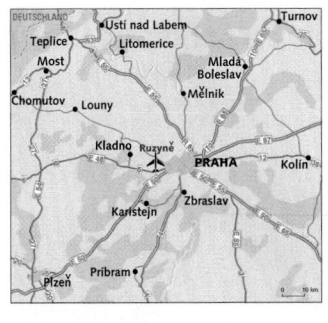

CALENDAR HIGHLIGHTS

January
Winter Festival.

May
Spring Festival, World Roma Festival.

June
Dance Prague, Many visit Kafka's burial place.

September
Autumn Festival.

December
Celebrate Christmas and New Year with various events in the Old Town Square.

EATING OUT

Since the late 1980s, Prague has undergone a bit of a foodie revolution. Global menus have become common currency and the heavy, traditional Czech cuisine is now often served – in the better establishments – with a creative flair and an international touch. Lunch is the main meal of the Czech day and many restaurants close well before midnight. Prague was and still is, to an extent, famous for its infinite variety of dumplings – these were the glutinous staple that saw locals through the long years of stark Communist rule. The favoured local

dish is still pork, pickled cabbage and dumplings, and those on a budget can also mix the likes of schnitzel, beer and ginger cake for a ridiculously cheap outlay. Lots of restaurants include a tip in your final bill, so check closely to make sure you don't tip twice. Czechs consume more beer than anyone else in the world and there are some excellent microbrewery tipples to be had; if you don't know where to start, the fittingly named 'Alcohol Bar' in Stare Město offers an amazing selection of beers.

Environs of Prague
(Plan I)

0   1 km

A

B

1

Podbabská

DEJVICE

BUBENEČ

U

Korunovační

Horoměřická

Evropská

Miladý

Horákové

nábřeží Edvard

VOKOVICE

Evropská

PRAŽSKÝ
HRAD

Křižovnická

7

STŘEŠOVICE

Karmelit-
ská

KARLŮV
MOST

BŘEVNOV

Patočkova

Masarykovo
nábřeží

BŘEVNOVSKÝ
KLÁŠTER

2

Po stadiony

Újezd

Rašínovo
nábřeží

Bělohorská

Prague Centre
(Plan II)

Kukulova

RUZYNĚ ✈

MOTOL

SMÍCHOV

KOŠÍŘE

Smíchovské
nádraží

M

Radlická

Radlická

M

RADLICE

Jinonice

M

5

Bucharova

JINONICE

Nové Butovice

Radlická

3

STODŮLKY

M

Húrka

Jeremiášova

● Hotel
● Restaurant

HLUBOČEPY

4

A

B

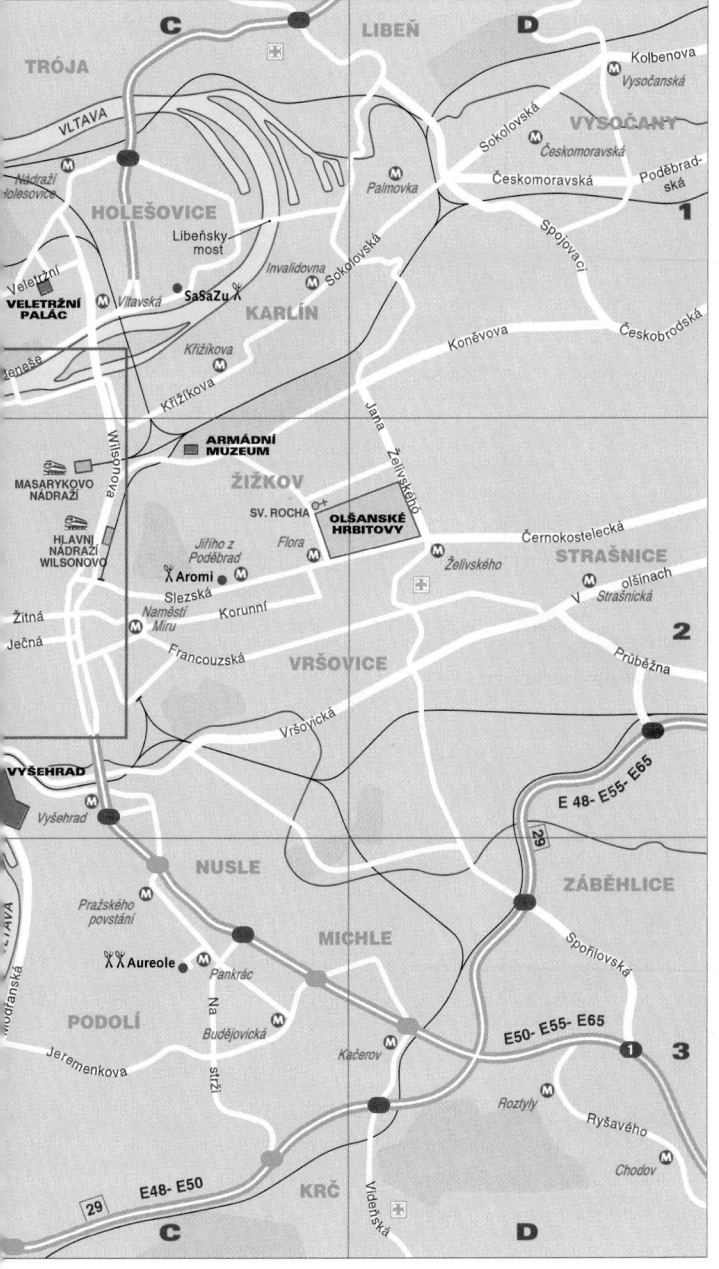

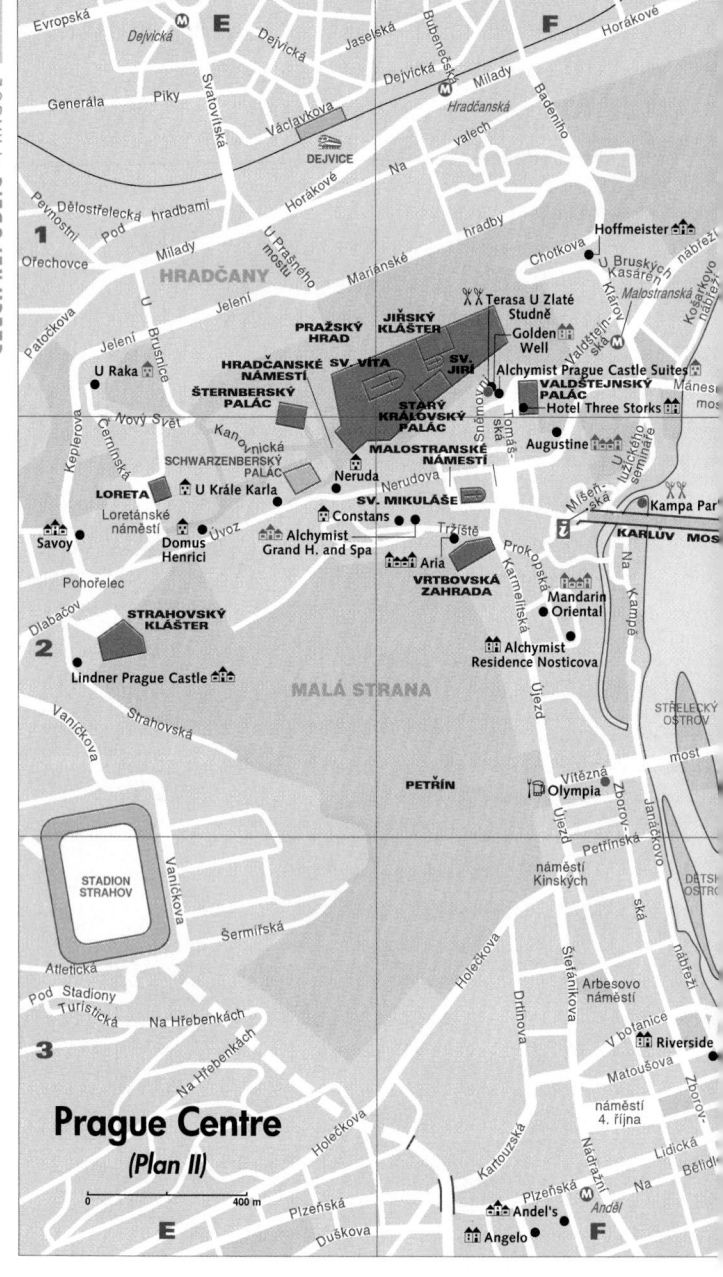

Evropská

Dejvická

Dejvická

Jaselská

Bubenečská

Horákové

Generála

Piky

Svatovítská

Václavkova

Dejvická

Milady

Hradčanská

Na valech

DEJVICE

Ořechovce

Pevnostní

Dělostřelecka

hradbami

Pod

Milady

U Prašného

Mariánské

hradby

Hoffmeister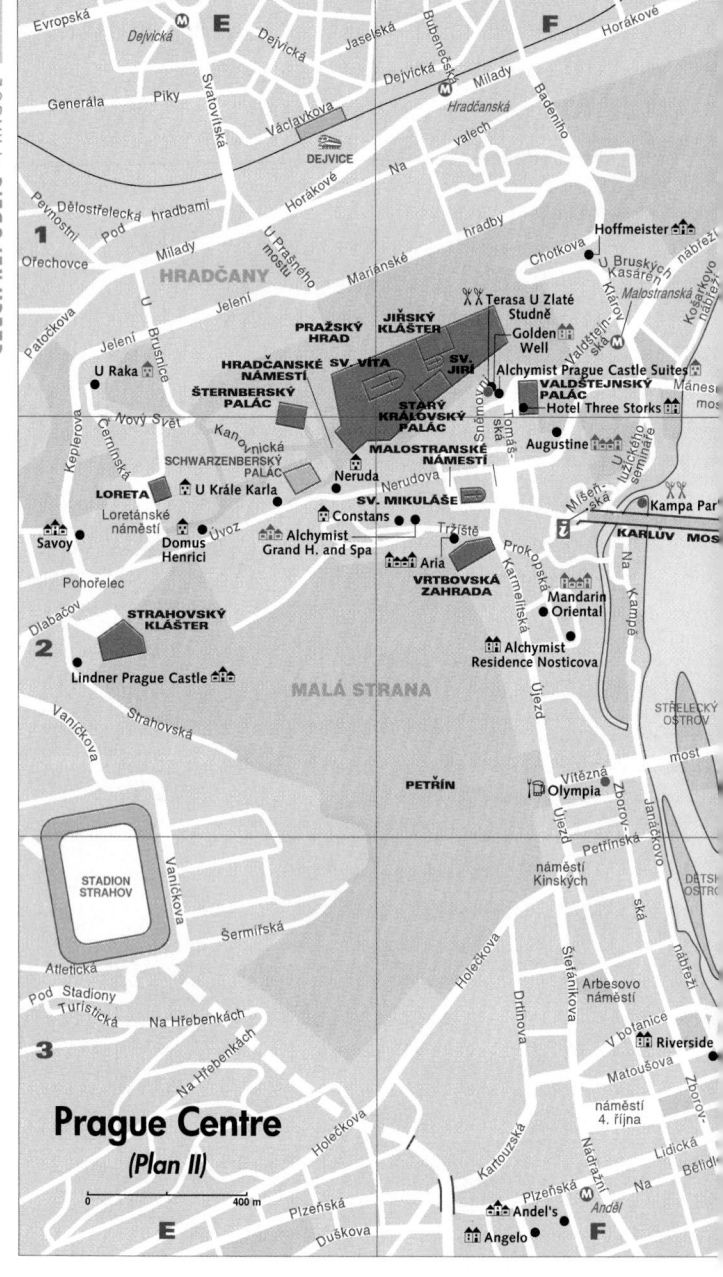

Chotkova

U Bruských Kasáren

Malostranska

Košařovo nábřeží

HRADČANY

Patočkova

Jelení

U

Brusnice

Jelení

U Raka 🏠

Černínská

Nový Svět

Keplerova

Kanovnická

PRAŽSKÝ HRAD

HRADČANSKÉ NÁMĚSTÍ

ŠTERNBERSKÝ PALÁC

JIŘSKÝ KLÁŠTER

SV. VÍTA

SV. JIŘÍ

Terasa U Zlaté Studně

Golden Well

Alchymist Prague Castle Suites

VALDŠTEJNSKÝ PALÁC

Valdštejn-ská

Mánes

mos

SCHWARZENBERSKÝ PALÁC

U Krále Karla 🏠

STARÝ KRÁLOVSKÝ PALÁC

Sněmovní

Hotel Three Storks

LORETA

Loretánské náměstí

Domus Henrici

Úvoz

Neruda

Nerudova

MALOSTRANSKÉ NÁMĚSTÍ

Tomáš-ská

SV. MIKULÁŠE

Augustine

Tržíště

Míšeň-ská

Tužického semináře

Kampa Par

Savoy

Constans

KARLŮV MOS

Pohořelec

Alchymist Grand H. and Spa

Aria

Prokopská

Karmelitská

Na Kampě

Diabačov

STRAHOVSKÝ KLÁŠTER

VRTBOVSKÁ ZAHRADA

Mandarin Oriental

Vaníčkova

Strahovská

Lindner Prague Castle

Alchymist Residence Nosticova

Újezd

MALÁ STRANA

STŘELECKÝ OSTROV

Vaníčkova

STADION STRAHOV

PETŘÍN

Olympia

Vítězná

Zborov-

most

Janáčkovo

Šermířská

Petřínská

náměstí Kinských

ská

DĚTSK OSTRO

Atletická

Pod Stadiony

Turistická

Na Hřebenkách

Holečkova

Štefánikova

Arbesovo náměstí

Drtinova

V botanice

Riverside

Matoušova

Zborov-

nábřeží

Na Hřebenkách

náměstí 4. října

Prague Centre

(Plan II)

0 —————— 400 m

Holečkova

Kartouzská

Nádražní

Andel's

Angelo

Anděl

Plzeňská

Lidická

Na

Bělidl

Plzeňská

Duškova

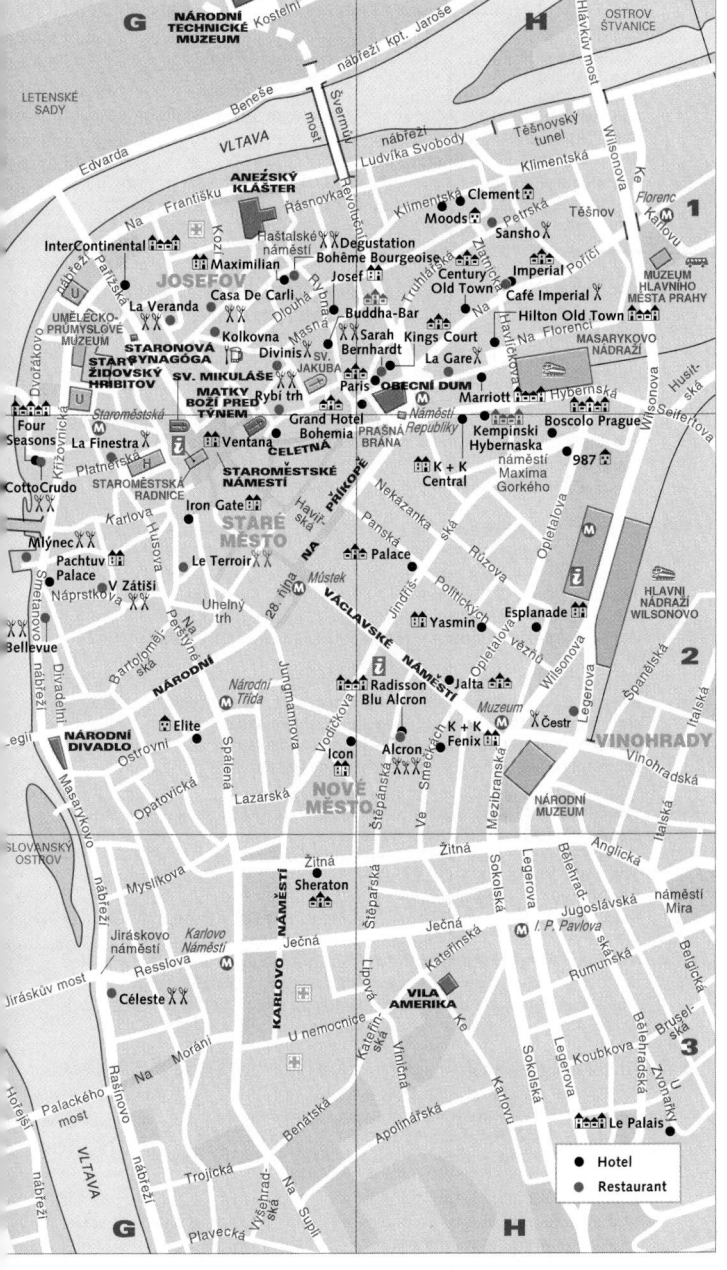

Hotel ●
Restaurant ●

CZECH REPUBLIC - PRAGUE

Four Seasons

Veleslavínova 1098/2A ⊠ 110 00 – **Ⓜ** Staroměstská – ✆ 221 427 000
– www.fourseasons.com/prague   **G2**
141 rm – 🛏7575/20942 CZK 🛏🛏7575/20942 CZK, ⊑ 750 CZK – 20 suites
Rest *CottoCrudo* – see restaurant listing
♦ Grand Luxury ♦ Modern ♦
Imposing riverside hotel made up of four buildings; each with its own distinct
character. Renaissance-style façade and charming, antique-furnished lobby. Elegant, well-kept bedrooms in varying sizes; ask for one with river and castle
views.

Boscolo Prague

Senovážné Nám. 13 ⊠ 110 00 – **Ⓜ** Náměsti Republiky – ✆ 224 593 111
– www.boscolohotels.com   **H2**
150 rm – 🛏3500/10000 CZK 🛏🛏3500/10000 CZK, ⊑ 635 CZK – 2 suites
Rest *Salon* – Menu 320 CZK – Carte 700/950 CZK
♦ Grand Luxury ♦ Stylish ♦
Impressive former bank with a stunning marble lobby, an ornate ceiling, neo-
Renaissance style pillars and a smart Roman spa and pool. Bedrooms are luxurious; those in the original building are the most spacious. The elegant, contemporary restaurant serves a mix of Czech and international dishes.

Kempinski Hybernská

Hybernská 12 ⊠ 110 00 – **Ⓜ** Náměsti Republiky – ✆ 226 226 111
– www.kempinski.com/prague   **H2**
13 rm – 🛏5572/10641 CZK 🛏🛏5572/10641 CZK – **62 suites** – 🛏🛏7532/
21000 CZK, ⊑ 657 CZK
Rest *Le Grill and Garden* – Menu 590/1350 CZK – Carte 560/1410 CZK
♦ Historic ♦ Stylish ♦
200 year old listed building with a delightful glass-topped atrium, a cosy bar,
inner courtyard and a formally planted rear garden. Contemporary international
art is displayed throughout. Well-equipped, stylish and comfortable bedrooms
include suites with their own private jacuzzis and terraces. Internationally influenced menu in cosy Le Grill and its charming Garden.

Radisson Blu Alcron

Štepánská 40 ⊠ 110 00 – **Ⓜ** Muzeum
– ✆ 222 820 000 – www.radissonblu.com/hotel-prague   **H2**
176 rm – 🛏3166/7793 CZK 🛏🛏3166/7793 CZK, ⊑ 633 CZK – 30 suites
Rest *Alcron* ✿ – see restaurant listing
Rest *La Rotonde* – ✆ 222 820 410 – Menu 690 CZK – Carte 670/1510 CZK
♦ Luxury ♦ Business ♦ Modern ♦
Imposing 1930s building with an executive lounge and warmly styled
bedrooms offering high levels of comfort and good facilities. Attentive service.
Brasserie-style restaurant with a summer terrace serves international and Czech
dishes.

InterContinental

Parižská 30 ⊠ 110 00 – **Ⓜ** Staroměstská
– ✆ 296 631 111 – www.intercontinental.com/prague   **G1**
344 rm – 🛏3722/6451 CZK 🛏🛏3722/6451 CZK, ⊑ 670 CZK – 28 suites
Rest *Zlatá Praha* – (closed first week January) (dinner only and Sunday
lunch) Menu 1290 CZK – Carte 810/1510 CZK
♦ Grand Luxury ♦ Modern ♦
Modern hotel with elegant bedrooms in hues of soft caramel and fresh apple;
most enjoy views of the river or the old part of the city. Well-equipped conference rooms and large leisure and well-being facility. International dishes and
impressive city views in smart 9th floor restaurant.

CZECH REPUBLIC - PRAGUE

 Le Palais

U Zvonarky 1 ✉ *120 00* – **Ⓜ** *I. P. Pavlova* – ☎ *234 634 111*
– www.palaishotel.cz **H3**
60 rm ☲ – †3324/5433 CZK ††4440/7194 CZK – 12 suites
Rest *Le Papillon* – Menu 850/1450 CZK – Carte 1010/1350 CZK
♦ Luxury ♦ Classic ♦

Late 19C mansion in a quiet location overlooking city. Stylish bedrooms with luxurious pink marble bathrooms and complimentary mini bars. Classically styled, spacious dining room with a delightful outlook from the terrace. Contemporary, seasonal, international cooking, featuring some modernised Czech dishes.

 Marriott

V Celnici 8 ✉ *110 00* – **Ⓜ** *Náměsti Republiky* – ☎ *222 888 888*
– www.marriottprague.com **H1**
265 rm – †3990/10830 CZK ††3990/10830 CZK, ☲ 764 CZK – 28 suites
Rest *Midtown Grill* – Menu 295 CZK (lunch) – Carte 635/1365 CZK
♦ Business ♦ Classic ♦

International hotel providing first class conference facilities and an excellent leisure club. Spacious, comfortable bedrooms are classically decorated in red and gold, and boast king-sized beds. Midtown Grill offers steaks and seafood.

 Hilton Old Town

V Celnici 7 ✉ *111 21* – **Ⓜ** *Náměsti Republiky* – ☎ *221 822 100*
– www.hiltonpragueoldtown.com **H1**
284 rm – †3000/7500 CZK ††3000/7500 CZK, ☲ 660 CZK – 19 suites
Rest *Zinc* – ☎ *221 822 300* – Carte 820/1810 CZK
♦ Business ♦ Modern ♦

Located in the heart of the city and boasting an art deco style lobby with white marble, mirrors and gold décor. Soft, contemporary colour schemes in well-equipped bedrooms. Zinc offers modern European cooking with Asian influences under a shimmering zinc ceiling.

Buddha-Bar

Jakubská 8 ✉ *110 00* – **Ⓜ** *Náměsti Republiky* – ☎ *221 776 300*
– www.buddhabarhotelprague.com **G1**
37 rm ☲ – †5563/9467 CZK ††5563/9467 CZK – 2 suites
Rest – Menu 310 CZK (lunch) – Carte 519/929 CZK
♦ Luxury ♦ Personalised ♦ Oriental ♦

Chic hotel in a historical building. Cosy, hi-tech red and gold bedrooms with bewitching Chinese lamps and huge black jacaranda beds featuring dragon designs; some have private terraces or mini Japanese gardens. Luxurious, intimately lit restaurant and bar with richly decorated chandeliers and a giant Buddha statue offers mostly Asian cuisine. Colourful Siddharta Café.

Sheraton

Zitna 8 ✉ *120 00* – **Ⓜ** *Karlovo Náměstí* – ☎ *225 999 999*
– www.sheratonprague.com **G3**
122 rm ☲ – †3200/7000 CZK ††4500/7000 CZK – 38 suites
Rest *Brasserie Délice* – Menu 390 CZK (lunch) – Carte 515/1130 CZK
♦ Townhouse ♦ Stylish ♦

Modern, boutique-style hotel composed of four 19C buildings. Comfortable bedrooms, some with balconies; ask for one of the newer rooms facing the back. Rooftop terrace affords impressive views. International dishes in Brasserie Délice.

 Palace

Panská 12 ✉ *111 21* – **Ⓜ** *Můstek* – ☎ *224 093 111* – *www.palacehotel.cz*
121 rm ☲ – †2964/7697 CZK ††3463/8196 CZK – 3 suites **H2**
Rest *Gourmet Club* – *(dinner only)* Carte 870/1371 CZK 🕸
♦ Traditional ♦ Classic ♦

Built in 1909 and still boasting its original Viennese art nouveau façade. Elegant interior: the spacious lobby features a wooden wall and bedrooms combine period furniture with modern facilities and services. Classic French dishes, intimate ambience and professional staff in Gourmet Club.

CZECH REPUBLIC - PRAGUE

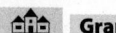

 Grand Hotel Bohemia   🕭 rest, 🎪 ♨ 🛜 🕭 🎪 📶 VISA 🆑 🆑 🆑

Králodvorská 4 ✉ *110 00* – Ⓜ *Náměstí Republiky* – 🕿 *234 608 111*
– www.grandhotelbohemia.cz   **H1**
77 rm 🖵 – 🛏3176/9773 CZK 🛏🛏3420/9773 CZK – 1 suite
Rest – Menu 450/650 CZK – Carte 660/1090 CZK
♦ Traditional ♦ Modern ♦
This classic 1920s hotel, with its splendid neo-baroque ballroom, is run by a friendly, professional team. Immaculately kept, contemporary bedrooms have a good level of facilities; compact bathrooms boast underfloor heating. Traditional Czech dishes are modernised in Franz Josef bistro.

🏨 **Imperial**   🕭 🛋 🎪 ♨ 🛜 🕭 🚗 VISA 🆑 🆑 🆑

Na Poříčí 15 ✉ *110 00* – Ⓜ *Náměsti Republiky* – 🕿 *246 011 600*
– www.hotel-imperial.cz   **H1**
125 rm 🖵 – 🛏3734/10133 CZK 🛏🛏3734/13028 CZK – 1 suite
Rest *Café Imperial* – see restaurant listing
♦ Business ♦ Retro ♦
This charming, historic hotel's listed façade dates from 1914 and its characterful interior features exquisite ceramic mosaics in an art deco style. Its well-kept, dark wood bedrooms combine retro styling with modern comforts.

🏨 **Paris**   🕭 🛋 🎪 ♨ 🛜 🕭 VISA 🆑 🆑 🆑

U obecního domu 1 ✉ *110 00* – Ⓜ *Náměsti Republiky* – 🕿 *222 195 195*
– www.hotel-paris.cz   **H1**
83 rm 🖵 – 🛏3418/6103 CZK 🛏🛏3418/6103 CZK – 3 suites
Rest *Sarah Bernhardt* – see restaurant listing
♦ Traditional ♦ Classic ♦
Charming art nouveau townhouse, its bright corridors hung with art. Well-equipped, characterful bedrooms are furnished in soft hues; the corner rooms are the largest. Bistro-style Café de Paris; more formal dining in Sarah Bernhardt.

🏨 **Kings Court**   🛜 🕭 🆑 🛋 🕭 ♨ 🛜 🎪 VISA 🆑 🆑 🆑

U Obecního domu 3 ✉ *110 00* – Ⓜ *Náměsti Republiky* – 🕿 *224 222 888*
– www.hotelkingscourt.cz   **H1**
131 rm 🖵 – 🛏2930/6103 CZK 🛏🛏2930/7324 CZK – 4 suites
Rest – Menu 366 CZK – Carte 781/1050 CZK
♦ Townhouse ♦ Stylish ♦
Former chamber of commerce located beneath the Obecni Dum; now a contemporary hotel with smart, well-equipped bedrooms and a basement spa zone. Original art nouveau windows feature. International menu and buffet breakfasts in café-restaurant with summer terrace.

🏨 **Jalta**   🛜 🕭 🆑 🎪 ♨ 🛜 🕭 VISA 🆑 🆑 🆑

Václavské Nám. 45 ✉ *110 00* – Ⓜ *Muzeum* – 🕿 *222 822 111*
– www.hoteljalta.com   **H2**
89 rm 🖵 – 🛏5865/7331 CZK 🛏🛏5865/7331 CZK – 5 suites
Rest *Como* – 🕿 *222 822 865* – Menu 180/250 CZK – Carte 655/1060 CZK
♦ Business ♦ Traditional ♦ Stylish ♦
Well-kept and well-situated hotel named after the historical Jalta conference, with a façade protected by UNESCO. Spacious, comfortable, well-equipped bedrooms boast art deco styling and balconies. Mediterranean and Czech cooking in trendy Como, complete with a charming terrace and live music at weekends.

🏨 **Century Old Town**   🛜 🆑 🎪 ♨ 🛜 VISA 🆑 🆑 🆑

Na Poříčí 7 ✉ *110 00* – Ⓜ *Náměsti Republiky* – 🕿 *221 800 800*
– www.hotelcenturyprague.com   **H1**
173 rm – 🛏1956/6165 CZK 🛏🛏2352/6561 CZK, 🖵 396 CZK – 1 suite
Rest – Carte 495/725 CZK
♦ Business ♦ Functional ♦
Modern hotel located in the former headquarters of the Workmen's Accident Insurance Institute – Kafka's place of work from 1908 to 1922. Well-maintained, contemporary bedrooms come with compact, functional bathrooms. The restuarant boasts a pleasant terrace; it is being redesigned in early 2013.

Josef without rest 　Ⅰ⑥ 🕸 🗚 ↳ 令 🛁 🚗 🆚 ⓔ 🅐🅔 ①

Rybná 20 ⊠ *110 00 –* ⓜ *Námĕsti Republiky –* 🕾 *221 700 111*
– www.hoteljosef.com　G1
109 rm ⊡ – †3219/10149 CZK ††3514/14940 CZK

◆ Townhouse ◆ Design ◆

Modern boutique hotel with a light-filled lobby and a delightful courtyard garden. Smart, design-led bedrooms, some featuring glass bathrooms; ask for a
room with a view on either the 7th or 8th floor. Superb buffet breakfasts.

Pachtuv Palace　≤ 🚗 Ⅰ⑥ 🗚 rm, ↳ 令 🆚 ⓔ 🅐🅔 ①

Karolíny Svetlé 34 ⊠ *110 00 –* ⓜ *Staromĕstská –* 🕾 *234 705 111*
– www.mamaison.com　G2
20 rm – †5939/8661 CZK ††5939/8661 CZK – **30 suites** – ††8167/
10890 CZK, ⊡ 495 CZK
Rest *Amade* – 🕾 *230 234 316* – Carte 540/870 CZK

◆ Traditional ◆ Cosy ◆

17C residence near the river; renovated in a baroque style, with an elegant
lobby and a pleasant courtyard terrace. Charming, well-equipped, antique-furnished bedrooms; ask for one with a river view. Fresh flowers decorate the
chic, bright restaurant. Modern, seasonal menu of Czech and international
dishes.

Yasmin　🕸 Ⅰ⑥ ᖾ 🗚 ↳ 令 🛁 🚗 🆚 ⓔ 🅐🅔 ①

Politických veznu 12/913 ⊠ *110 00 –* ⓜ *Muzeum –* 🕾 *234 100 100*
– www.hotel-yasmin.cz　H2
195 rm ⊡ – †2600/4160 CZK ††2600/4160 CZK – 1 suite
Rest – Menu 520/620 CZK – Carte 334/684 CZK

◆ Business ◆ Modern ◆

Chic hotel with contemporary styling; spacious, green-hued bedrooms come
with good mod cons and dark tiled bathrooms. The garden can be accessed
from Wenceslas Square. International and Asian dishes served in the trendy,
colourful restaurant, with its friendly atmosphere.

Maximilian without rest　ᖾ 🗚 ↳ 令 🛁 🚗 🆚 ⓔ 🅐🅔 ①

Haštalská 14 ⊠ *110 00 –* ⓜ *Námĕsti Republiky –* 🕾 *225 303 111*
– www.maximilianhotel.com　G1
70 rm ⊡ – †2237/5901 CZK ††2508/6466 CZK – 1 suite

◆ Business ◆ Modern ◆

Well-maintained, modern hotel in a quiet area, with a bright lobby and comfortable, contemporary bedrooms. Basement Thai massage spa. Good choice from
the breakfast buffet in the glass and steel winter garden.

K + K Central　Ⅰ⑥ 🕸 🗚 ↳ 令 🛁 🆚 ⓔ 🅐🅔 ①

Hybernská 10 ⊠ *110 00 –* ⓜ *Námĕsti Republiky –* 🕾 *225 022 000*
– www.kkhotels.com　H2
126 rm ⊡ – †3000/7750 CZK ††3500/8250 CZK – 1 suite
Rest – Menu 675 CZK – Carte 650/1050 CZK

◆ Business ◆ Modern ◆

Beautifully restored hotel in the centre of city, with a wonderful art nouveau
façade and well-kept, green and lilac hued bedrooms. Glass cube conference
room. Breakfast served in impressive former theatre. Light dishes in modern
bar/bistro.

Icon　🗚 ↳ 令 🆚 ⓔ 🅐🅔 ①

V Jáme 1263/6 ⊠ *110 00 –* ⓜ *Mûstek –* 🕾 *221 634 100*
– www.iconhotel.eu　G2
29 rm ⊡ – †2000/4000 CZK ††2000/4000 CZK – 2 suites
Rest – Menu 90 CZK (lunch) – Carte 290/630 CZK

◆ Business ◆ Modern ◆ Design ◆

Modern, centrally located hotel featuring contemporary Czech artwork. Stylish,
well-equipped bedrooms and superb Asian wellness centre; friendly, helpful
staff and a relaxed feel. Small purple basement bar and restaurant offer a large
international menu and a hip vibe. All-day breakfasts.

CZECH REPUBLIC - PRAGUE

Ventana without rest   ⒶⒸ ⅛ 📶 🆅🆂🅰 ⓄⓄ 🅰🅴 ⓄⓄ
Celetná 7 (Entrance from 2 Stuparska Street) ✉ *110 00*
– Ⓜ *Náměstí Republiky –* ✆ *221 776 600 – www.ventana-hotel.net*
27 rm � – **♦**2458/4425 CZK **♦♦**2950/12292 CZK – 2 suites   **G2**
♦ Traditional ♦ Classic ♦

Former residential house with an art deco façade, near the Old Town market. Spacious, well-kept bedrooms, in muted shades, are set over 4 floors; marble bathrooms are modern and well-equipped. Top floor loft rooms have a separate lounge.

Iron Gate   📶 ⒶⒸ ⅛ ⓒ 🆅🆂🅰 ⓄⓄ 🅰🅴 ⓄⓄ
Michalská 19 ✉ *110 00 –* Ⓜ *Staroměstská –* ✆ *225 777 777*
– www.irongate.cz   **G2**
12 rm – **♦**2500/9000 CZK **♦♦**2500/9000 CZK – **31 suites** ⊆ – **♦♦**4000/15000 CZK
Rest *Zelezná vrata – (dinner only)* Menu 738 CZK – Carte 860/1280 CZK
♦ Traditional ♦ Classic ♦

14C building hidden away down picturesque cobbled streets; now a luxury hotel, with wooden ceilings and original wall paintings. Functional bedrooms and a pleasant courtyard garden. Chic, comfortable, contemporary restaurant in the vaulted basement offers a mix of Italian and traditional Czech dishes.

K + K Fenix   🝗 🎍 🕭 ⒶⒸ ⅛ 📶 🆂🅰 🚗 🆅🆂🅰 ⓄⓄ 🅰🅴 ⓄⓄ
Ve Smeckách 30 ✉ *110 00 –* ⓂⓄ *Muzeum –* ✆ *225 012 000*
– www.kkhotels.com   **H2**
128 rm ⊆ – **♦**2500/7500 CZK **♦♦**3000/8000 CZK
Rest – Menu 675 CZK – Carte 650/1050 CZK
♦ Business ♦ Modern ♦

Located in an area busy with nightlife; an up-to-date interior behind a classic façade. Ask for one of the refurbished bedrooms, which are decorated in contemporary greys and greens. Light international dishes on offer in the modern bar-restaurant. Warm, contemporary breakfast room.

Esplanade   📶 ⒶⒸ ⅛ 📶 🆂🅰 🆅🆂🅰 ⓄⓄ 🅰🅴 ⓄⓄ
Washingtonova 1600-19 ✉ *110 00 –* ⓂⓄ *Muzeum –* ✆ *224 501 111*
– www.esplanade.cz   **H2**
74 rm ⊆ – **♦**2242/4733 CZK **♦♦**2491/7221 CZK
Rest – Menu 623 CZK – Carte 666/1087 CZK
♦ Traditional ♦ Classic ♦

Charming and atmospheric; this art nouveau building is something of an architectural gem. Original features abound; variously sized bedrooms are stylish, with a timeless elegance. International menu offered in friendly surroundings.

Clement without rest   ♿ ⒶⒸ ⅛ 📶 🆂🅰 🚗 🆅🆂🅰 ⓄⓄ 🅰🅴 ⓄⓄ
Klimentská 30 ✉ *110 00 –* ⓂⓄ *Náměsti Republiky –* ✆ *222 314 350*
– www.hotelclement.cz   **H1**
77 rm ⊆ – **♦**1586/6100 CZK **♦♦**1586/6100 CZK
♦ Business ♦ Functional ♦

Former office building not far from either the river or the city centre; now a modern hotel featuring clean, functional bedrooms in a contemporary style. Friendly, helpful staff.

987 without rest   ♿ ⒶⒸ ⅛ 📶 🆂🅰 ⓄⓄ 🅰🅴 ⓄⓄ
Senovážné Nám.15 ✉ *110 00 –* ⓂⓄ *Náměsti Republiky –* ✆ *255 737 100*
– www.987praguehotel.com   **H2**
74 rm ⊆ – **♦**2435/6088 CZK **♦♦**2435/6088 CZK – 6 suites
♦ Traditional ♦ Modern ♦

Centrally located, Spanish design hotel. Mix of compact bedrooms and duplex suites – set over 6 floors, they are well-equipped and feature modern designs and furnishings; sinks are located in the rooms. Colourful ground floor breakfast room.

Moods without rest 🎰 🛜 ⚐ VISA ⓪ AE ⓪
Klimentska 28 ✉ 110 00 – ⓜ *Náměsti Republiky –* ☏ *222 330 100*
– www.hotelmoods.com   **H1**
51 rm ☕ – **♦**2742/8725 CZK **♦♦**4238/10222 CZK
♦ Business ♦ Design ♦

The bright reception and trendy bar of this boutique hotel make interesting use of natural materials such as bamboo and moss. Colourful bedrooms feature dark wood floors, handmade Hästens beds and Apple technology. Well-equipped bathrooms.

Élite without rest 🎰 🎰 🛜 ⚐ 🚗 VISA ⓪ AE ⓪
Ostrovni 32 ✉ 11000 – ⓜ *Národní třída –* ☏ *211 156 500*
– www.hotelelite.cz   **G2**
78 rm ☕ – **♦**3683/5588 CZK **♦♦**4191/7112 CZK
♦ Townhouse ♦ Classic ♦

14C house in a peaceful central street, which marries the romantic charm of ancient architecture with the comforts of a modern hotel. Bedrooms vary in size; the 17C suite features a beautiful Renaissance-style ceiling. Relaxing terrace garden. Stylish restaurant serving Thai and Asian cuisine.

XXX Alcron – at Radisson Blu Alcron Hotel 🎰 ↳ P VISA ⓪ AE ⓪
☼ *Štepánská 40 ✉ 110 00 –* ⓜ *Muzeum –* ☏ *222 820 038 – www.alcron.cz*
– Closed 2 weeks July-August, Saturday and Sunday   **H2**
Rest – *(booking essential)* Menu 1500 CZK (dinner) – Carte 1030/1640 CZK
♦ Modern ♦ Intimate ♦

Intimate, semi-circular restaurant dominated by an art deco mural of dancing Manhattan couples by Tamara de Lempicka. Choice of hot and cold tasting dishes from an international menu; well-presented, creative and contemporary cooking uses top ingredients. Good choice of wines. Attentive, professional staff.
➔ Ceviche of scallops with cucumber, chilli and hazelnut. Beef with miso glaze and smoked potato purée. Elderflower blossom tart with candied lemon.

XX Degustation Bohême Bourgeoise (Oldřich Sahajdák) 🎰
☼ *Haštalská 18 ✉ 11000 –* ⓜ *Náměsti Republiky*   ↳ VISA ⓪ AE ⓪
– ☏ 222 311 234 – www.ladegustation.cz
– Closed 2 weeks July and 24 December,   **G1**
Rest – *(dinner only)* Menu 2150 CZK (lunch), 1000/3150 CZK 🍴
♦ Innovative ♦ Intimate ♦

Intimate, L-shaped restaurant in a historical building, with an elegant, dark wood interior, an open kitchen and a chef's table. Two tasting menus of modern European dishes make good use of quality regional produce; cooking is technically precise, innovative and flavourful. Charming, professional service.
➔ Oyster mushrooms with horseradish sauce and tapioca pearls. Poultry hearts and chicken liver with parsley oil. Rum gingerbread and egg yolk crème with marinated plums.

XX Le Terroir 🍴 🎰 ↳ VISA ⓪ AE ⓪
☺ *Vejvodova 1 (Entrance from Jilskà Street) ✉ 110 00 –* ⓜ *Můstek*
– ☏ 222 220 260 – www.leterroir.cz
– Closed Sunday-Monday   **G2**
Rest – Menu 1290 CZK, 1790/1620 CZK 🍴
♦ Innovative ♦ Rustic ♦ Elegant ♦

Characterful cellar restaurant with a vaulted ceiling, hidden away through a courtyard and down a winding staircase. Good value, fresh European cooking displays innovative touches; French and Italian produce features highly. Excellent fromagerie and impressive wine cave. Attentive, professional service.

CZECH REPUBLIC - PRAGUE

XX **Céleste** ≤ 🄰🄲 ♿ 🆅🅸🆂🄰 ⓪🄰 🄰🄴 ⓪

Rasínovo Nábr. 80 (Tancící dům, Dancing House) ✉ *120 00*
– ⓜ *Karlovo Náměstí* – ℰ *221 984 160* – *www.celesterestaurant.cz*
– *Closed 24 December, 1 January and Sunday* **G3**
Rest – *(booking essential at dinner)* Menu 690 CZK (lunch)
– Carte 985/1505 CZK
♦ French ♦ Elegant ♦ Minimalist ♦
Busy, modern restaurant located on the 7th floor of the Dancing House, with
superb views of the city and castle. Dark wood furnished dining room with
grey and purple hues. Creative, French-based cooking features contemporary
twists.

XX **Aureole** ≤ 🄶 🄰🄲 🆅🅸🆂🄰 ⓪🄰 🄰🄴 ⓪

City Tower, 27. p. (Hvězdova 1716/2b) ✉ *140 000* – ⓜ *Pankrác*
– ℰ *222 755 380* – *www.aureole.cz*
– *Closed 25-26 December and 1 January* *Plan I* **C3**
Rest – Menu 390/950 CZK – Carte 1000/1500 CZK
♦ International ♦ Design ♦ Trendy ♦
Hip 27th floor restaurant affording superb city and castle views. Moody red and
black dining room, chic cocktail bar and lounges, and a fantastic panoramic ter-
race. Refined, modern cooking cleverly blends East and West; try the sushi and
the udon noodles, or sample a range of dishes on the degustation menu.

XX **CottoCrudo** – Four Seasons Hotel ≤ 🄶 🄰🄲 🆅🅸🆂🄰 ⓪🄰 🄰🄴 ⓪

Veleslavínova 1098/2A ✉ *110 00* – ⓜ *Staroměstská* – ℰ *(221) 426 880*
– *www.cottocrudo.cz* **G2**
Rest – Menu 390 CZK (lunch) – Carte 850/1380 CZK
♦ Italian ♦ Fashionable ♦ Design ♦
Smart, all-day restaurant with a chic cocktail bar, an open-plan kitchen and a
fish counter; set in an elegant hotel. Freshly imported Italian meats and cheeses
on display. Unfussy dishes have deep, gutsy flavours and a refined edge.

XX **V Zátiši** 🄰🄲 ♿ 🆅🅸🆂🄰 ⓪🄰 🄰🄴 ⓪

Liliová 1, Betlémské Nám. ✉ *110 00* – ⓜ *Můstek* – ℰ *222 221 155*
– *www.zatisigroup.cz*
– *Closed 24 December* **G2**
Rest – *(booking essential at dinner)* Menu 1090 CZK – Carte 1035/
1185 CZK
♦ Modern ♦ Cosy ♦ Elegant ♦
Popular, modern, city centre restaurant with a name meaning 'timeless'. Tradi-
tional Czech dishes with some Asian influences. Friendly, attentive service.
Wines for sale to take away.

XX **Bellevue** ≤ 🄶 🄰🄲 ♿ 🆅🅸🆂🄰 ⓪🄰 🄰🄴 ⓪

Smetanovo Nábřeží 18 ✉ *110 00* – ⓜ *Staroměstská* – ℰ *222 221 443*
– *www.zatisigroup.cz*
– *Closed 25 December* **G2**
Rest – Menu 1190/1790 CZK
♦ International ♦ Formal ♦
Elegant 19C townhouse with a pleasant summer terrace and river views; con-
temporary interior decorated in a pastel palette, with neo-baroque lighting.
Fixed price, international menu.

XX **La Veranda** 🄰🄲 ♿ 🆅🅸🆂🄰 ⓪🄰 🄰🄴 ⓪

Elišky Krásnohorské 2 ✉ *110 00* – ⓜ *Staroměstská* – ℰ *224 814 733*
– *www.laveranda.cz*
– *Closed Sunday* **G1**
Rest – Menu 225 CZK (lunch) – Carte 430/1010 CZK
♦ Mediterranean ♦ Cosy ♦
Choose between the main restaurant, decorated in bright, sunny colours and
the more intimate downstairs room with its contemporary styling. Mediterra-
nean dishes. Friendly service.

CZECH REPUBLIC - PRAGUE

XX **Mlýnec** ⇐ 🏠 AC ↳ VISA ◐◑ AE ⓪

Novotného Lávka 9 ✉ *110 00* – ⓜ *Staroměstská* – ✆ *277 000 777*
– www.mlynec.cz
– Closed 24 December **G2**
Rest – Menu 650/1190 CZK – Carte 835/1235 CZK
♦ Modern ♦ Trendy ♦
Modern styling with paintings, antiques and crystal lighting. Well presented, contemporary European and Czech cuisine. Terrace views of Charles Bridge on fine summer evenings.

XX **Rybí trh** 🏠 AC ↳ VISA ◐◑ AE ⓪

Týnský dvůr 5 ✉ *110 00* – ⓜ *Náměsti Republiky* – ✆ *602 295 911*
– www.rybitrh.cz **G1**
Rest – Menu 490 CZK (lunch) – Carte 590/1710 CZK
♦ Fish and seafood ♦ Friendly ♦ Intimate ♦
Set in a picturesque spot in the city's heart, a seafood-based restaurant featuring aquariums, a fresh counter display and a pleasant terrace. The raw fish is presented at the table, accompanied by an explanation of how it is to be cooked.

XX **Sarah Bernhardt** – at Hotel Paris ↳ VISA ◐◑ AE ⓪

U obecniho domu 1 ✉ *110 00* – ⓜ *Náměsti Republiky* – ✆ *222 195 195*
– www.hotel-paris.cz **H1**
Rest – Menu 500/790 CZK – Carte 590/1030 CZK
♦ International ♦ Brasserie ♦ Retro ♦
High-ceilinged, art deco restaurant, named after the famous actress. Fine French and Czech cuisine with some international choices; keenly prepared dishes make good use of quality ingredients. Friendly, professional service.

XX **Casa De Carli** 🏠 AC ⇆ VISA ◐◑ ⓪

Vezenskská 5 ✉ *11 000* – ⓜ *Staromestská* – ✆ *224 816 688*
– www.casadecarli.com – Closed Sunday **G1**
Rest – Carte 505/825 CZK
♦ Italian ♦ Friendly ♦ Neighbourhood ♦
Friendly, family-run Italian restaurant with colourful Murano chandeliers, and tables on the cobbled street. Flavoursome classical cooking with seasonal ingredients imported from Italy; lovely home-baked breads and pastas; appealing meats.

X **Café Imperial** – at Hotel Imperial AC VISA ◐◑ AE ⓪

Na Porící 15 ✉ *110 00* – ⓜ *Náměsti Republiky* – ✆ *246 011 440*
– www.cafeimperial.cz **H1**
Rest – (booking essential) Carte 550/650 CZK
♦ International ♦ Brasserie ♦ Retro ♦
Popular, high-ceilinged restaurant with the feel of a Parisian brasserie, and a remarkable backdrop of colourfully tiled pillars and walls in an art deco style. Seasonal, international menu uses quality produce. Professional service.

X **La Finestra** AC ⇆ VISA ◐◑ AE ⓪

Platnérská 90/13 ✉ *110 00* – ⓜ *Staroměstská* – ✆ *222 325 325*
– www.lafinestra.cz **G2**
Rest – (booking essential) Menu 195 CZK (lunch) – Carte 935/1115 CZK 🍷
♦ Italian ♦ Rustic ♦ Cosy ♦
Vaulted restaurant located in the basement of a townhouse, with a cosy, rustic, red-brick interior. Italian menu with emphasis on fresh, good quality meat. Superb Italian wine list and friendly, professional staff.

X **Aromi** 🏠 ↳ VISA ◐◑ AE ⓪
😊

Mánesova 78/1442 ✉ *120 00* – ⓜ *Jiřiho z Poděbrad* – ✆ *222 713 222*
– www.aromi.cz *Plan I* **C2**
Rest – (booking essential at dinner) Menu 195 CZK (lunch)
– Carte 795/1115 CZK 🍷
♦ Italian ♦ Rustic ♦
Charming neighbourhood restaurant with a rustic interior, an open kitchen and a lively atmosphere. Open all day for fresh, tasty, simply prepared and great value Italian dishes; go for the daily specials. Excellent choice of Italian wines. Attentive, charming service.

CZECH REPUBLIC - PRAGUE

Divinis
`AC` `⇄` `VISA` `◐◐` `AE` `①`

Týnská 21 ⌧ 110 00 – ⓜ Staroměstská – ℰ 222 325 440 – www.divinis.cz
– Closed 24-25 December and Sunday **G1**
Rest *– (dinner only) (booking essential)* Carte 700/1070 CZK
♦ Italian ♦ Trendy ♦ Friendly ♦

Intimate, popular, candlelit restaurant with wooden décor, fresh flowers and a friendly, homely atmosphere. Imaginative, passionate kitchen offers a concise, sensibly priced menu of fresh, tasty, well-prepared Italian dishes. Relaxed, informed service.

Sansho
`⇧` `AC` `VISA` `◐◐` `①`

Petrská 25 ⌧ 110 00 – ⓜ Florenc – ℰ 222 317 425 – www.sansho.cz
– Closed 3 weeks Christmas-New Year, first two weeks August, Saturday lunch, Sunday and Monday **H1**
Rest *– (booking essential at dinner)* Menu 250/900 CZK
– Carte lunch 495/835 CZK
♦ Asian ♦ Friendly ♦

Homely restaurant serving eclectic Asian cuisine with an emphasis on the south-east. Passionate chef-patron sources the very best organic ingredients from small suppliers to produce well-crafted, unfussy, flavoursome dishes. Informal atmosphere, with communal tables in the front room. Dynamic, attentive service.

Cestr
`⇧` `VISA` `◐◐` `AE` `①`

Legerova 75/57 ⌧ 110 00 – ⓜ Muzeum – ℰ (222) 727 851 – www.ambi.cz
– Closed 24 December **H2**
Rest *–* Carte 367/929 CZK
♦ Meats and grills ♦ Friendly ♦ Design ♦

Bright, canteen-style restaurant with an open kitchen; the chefs deliver the food to the table. Named after a breed of cattle, its focus is on meat hung for 60+ days, then braised, spit-roasted or grilled; slow-braised ribs are a speciality.

La Gare
`⇧` `VISA` `◐◐` `①`

V Celnici 3 ⌧ 110 00 – ⓜ Náměsti Republiky – ℰ 222 313 712
– www.lagare.cz **H1**
Rest *–* Menu 95/265 CZK – Carte 319/724 CZK
♦ French ♦ Brasserie ♦ Friendly ♦

Lively French-style brasserie with beautiful vaulted arches and chandeliers, offering generous, tasty, homemade cuisine. Front terrace, good choice of French wines and friendly service. Adjoining deli serves cheese, pastries and the like.

Kolkovna
`⇧` `AC` `⇄` `VISA` `◐◐` `AE` `①`

V Kolkovne 8 ⌧ 110 00 – ⓜ Staroměstská – ℰ 224 819 701
– www.kolkovna-restaurant.cz **G1**
Rest *–* Carte 304/764 CZK
♦ Traditional ♦ Friendly ♦ Pub ♦

Popular pub/brasserie located in the Jewish Quarter, with a pavement terrace and a large beer counter at the entrance. Tasty, traditional Czech cooking comes in generous portions and is good value for money. Lively, friendly atmosphere.

ON THE LEFT BANK
Plan II

Mandarin Oriental
`⊞` `⇧` `♨` `◉` `⇩` `AC` `⇄` `⌘` `≋` `⌂`

Nebovidská 459/1 ⌧ 118 00 – ⓜ Malostranská `VISA` `◐◐` `AE` `①`
– ℰ 233 088 888 – www.mandarinoriental.com/prague **F2**
79 rm *–* ⴖ7196/10084 CZK ⴖⴖ7694/10581 CZK – 20 suites
Rest *Essensia* *–* Menu 747 CZK (lunch) – Carte 986/1559 CZK
♦ Luxury ♦ Stylish ♦

Peacefully located, 14C former monastery in a central quarter, now a charming, modern hotel. Warm, contemporary décor has an Asian edge; bedrooms are luxurious and well-equipped. Relax on the terraces or in the delightful spa in the old chapel. Essensia serves Asian and Czech dishes presented in a European style; service is professional.

CZECH REPUBLIC - PRAGUE

Augustine 🚗 🛎 Ⅰ♠ 🌐 🍴 ♿ rm, 🖼 ↳ 🛜 🏋 🅿 💳 ⑩ 🅰🅴 ⓞ
Letenská 12/33 ✉ *118 000* – **Ⓜ** *Malostranská* – ☎ *266 112 233*
– www.theaugustine.com   **F2**
90 rm ☲ – 🛏8775/11475 CZK 🛏🛏9275/11975 CZK – 11 suites
Rest *Lichfield* – Menu 650 CZK (lunch) – Carte 600/1920 CZK
♦ Historic ♦ Design ♦ Stylish ♦

Set over 7 buildings, including the 13C monastery after which it is named.
Variously sized bedrooms come in a cubist style, with good mod cons and
dark marble bathrooms. The 3-floored Tower Suite offers impressive views.
Two bars: one in the double-vaulted former refectory and one in the cellar.
International dishes in the chic brasserie with garden views.

Aria 🛎 Ⅰ♠ 🍴 ♿ 🖼 ↳ 🛜 🏋 🅿 🚬 💳 ⑩ 🅰🅴 ⓞ
Tržiště 9 ✉ *118 00* – **Ⓜ** *Malostranská* – ☎ *225 334 111*
– www.ariahotel.net   **F2**
44 rm ☲ – 🛏4200/7500 CZK 🛏🛏4200/7500 CZK – 7 suites
Rest *Coda* – Menu 590 CZK (lunch) – Carte 1105/1635 CZK
♦ Luxury ♦ Design ♦

Stylish hotel with a musical motif. Warmly decorated, variously sized bedrooms
are individually themed to different composers or styles of music. International
influences on the tasting menu in cosy, art deco Coda, which boasts a superb
rooftop terrace with a view to the castle, and live music at dinner.

Alchymist Grand H. and Spa 🛎 Ⅰ♠ 🌐 🍴 🗔 🖼 ↳ 🛜 🏋
Tržiště 19 ✉ *118 00* – **Ⓜ** *Malostranská*   💳 ⑩ 🅰🅴 ⓞ
– ☎ 257 286 011 – www.alchymisthotel.com   **F2**
39 rm ☲ – 🛏4990/9980 CZK 🛏🛏4990/9980 CZK – 7 suites
Rest *Aquarius* – ☎ *257 286 019* – Carte 835/2140 CZK
♦ Luxury ♦ Classic ♦

Charming, cosy 16C townhouse with carefully chosen décor and sumptuous
furniture. Bedrooms are in a neo-baroque or Renaissance style and feature
good-sized bathrooms. Impressive oriental spa. Aquarius offers contemporary
international cooking and features interesting Indian paintings, along with a
pleasant terrace.

Lindner Prague Castle 🚬 🛎 Ⅰ♠ 🍴 ♿ 🖼 ↳ 🕽 🏋 🚬
Strahovská 128 ✉ *118 00* – ☎ *226 080 000*   💳 ⑩ 🅰🅴 ⓞ
– www.lindnerhotels.cz   **E2**
135 rm – 🛏1679/2400 CZK 🛏🛏1679/2400 CZK, ☲ 365 CZK – 3 suites
Rest – Menu 390 CZK – Carte 400/875 CZK
♦ Business ♦ Historic ♦

Located in a UNESCO designated area behind the Strahov Monastery. Well-kept,
well-equipped bedrooms feature art deco paintings; the bedrooms in the 16C
building are the most spacious. Small, Zen-style massage area. International
dishes are offered in the warmly decorated restaurant and on the pleasant terrace.

Andel's Ⅰ♠ 🍴 ♿ 🖼 ↳ 🛜 🏋 🚬 💳 ⑩ 🅰🅴
Stroupežnického 21 ✉ *150 00* – **Ⓜ** *Anděl* – ☎ *296 889 688*
– www.andelshotel.com   **F3**
259 rm ☲ – 🛏2000/4875 CZK 🛏🛏2000/4875 CZK – 31 suites
Rest *Oscar's* – Carte 375/605 CZK
♦ Business ♦ Modern ♦

Stylish hotel in a business area near the Nový Smíchov shopping centre, with
good rail and road connections. Spacious, contemporary bedrooms and luxurious long stay apartments. Oscar's serves international cuisine in a modern setting.

Savoy 🛏 🐾 🍴 🅰️ rm, ⇆ 🤶 🚭 🍽️ 💳 ⓥ AE ⓞ

Keplerova 6 ✉ *118 00 –* ☎ *224 302 430*
– www.goldentulipsavoyprague.com   **E2**
59 rm 🛏 – ♦2750/6250 CZK ♦♦5250/8750 CZK – 2 suites
Rest *Hradcany – (closed Saturday and Sunday)* Menu 345/735 CZK
– Carte 700/1265 CZK
♦ Luxury ♦ Classic ♦

Former cinema complex located at the top of the hill; rebuilt as a classic hotel, with a relaxed atmosphere. Traditionally styled, brightly coloured bedrooms; opt for one of the spacious suites. The elegant restaurant serves international dishes and the roof is opened on beautiful summer evenings.

Hoffmeister 🍴 ♿ 🅰️ ⇆ 🤶 🚭 🍽️ 💳 ⓥ AE ⓞ

Pod Bruskou 7 ✉ *118 00 –* Ⓜ *Malostranská –* ☎ *251 017 111*
– www.hoffmeister.cz   **F1**
44 rm – ♦1600/2750 CZK ♦♦1875/3000 CZK, 🛏 375 CZK – 5 suites
Rest *Ada –* Menu 660/790 CZK – Carte 660/1000 CZK
♦ Traditional ♦ Classic ♦

Situated in a busy corner location, with well-equipped, variously sized, individually styled bedrooms; some featuring underfloor heated bathrooms. Unique steam bath in a cave. Elegant, modern Ada is decorated in pastel colours and hung with contemporary paintings. Menus display French and Czech influences.

Golden Well 🚲 ≤ 🅰️ ⇆ 🤶 💳 ⓥ AE ⓞ

U Zlaté Studne 166/4 ✉ *118 00 –* Ⓜ *Malostranská –* ☎ *257 011 213*
– www.goldenwell.cz   **F1**
17 rm – ♦4375/10875 CZK ♦♦4375/10875 CZK, 🛏 375 CZK – 2 suites
Rest *Terasa U Zlaté Studne –* see restaurant listing
♦ Historic ♦ Classic ♦

Charming, intimate hotel, situated in a quiet cobbled street close to Charles Bridge and the Royal Gardens. Cosy, antique-furnished bedrooms; most with a view over the city, some overlooking the castle. Pleasant heated roof terrace. Professional, friendly staff.

Alchymist Residence Nosticova without rest 🚲 🚗 🅰️

Nosticova 1, Malá Strana ✉ *118 00*   ⇆ 🤶 **P.** 💳 ⓥ AE ⓞ
– Ⓜ *Malostranská –* ☎ *257 312 513 – www.nosticova.com*   **F2**
13 rm 🛏 – ♦4550/9100 CZK ♦♦4550/9100 CZK – 3 suites
♦ Townhouse ♦ Classic ♦

17C building in a quiet street, with a splendid garden terrace. Spacious, high-ceilinged bedrooms are furnished with antiques and feature kitchenettes. Guests can use the spa at its sister hotel, the Alchymist Grand.

Riverside without rest ≤ 🅰️ ⇆ 🤶 🚭 💳 ⓥ AE ⓞ

Janáckovo Nábreži 15 ✉ *150 00 –* Ⓜ *Andĕl –* ☎ *225 994 611*
– www.mamaison.com   **F3**
77 rm – ♦2343/2880 CZK ♦♦2343/2880 CZK, 🛏 366 CZK – 3 suites
♦ Business ♦ Modern ♦

Charming, well-kept riverside hotel with a cosy bar and stylish, characterful bedrooms. The newer rooms are more modern, with spacious bathrooms; some have river views and the quieter ones look onto the courtyard. Good choice at breakfast.

Hotel Three Storks 🅰️ ⇆ 🤶 🚭 💳 ⓥ AE ⓞ

Tomášská 20 (Waldstejnska Square) ✉ *118 00 –* Ⓜ *Malostranská*
– ☎ *257 210 779 – www.hotelthreestorks.cz*   **F1**
20 rm 🛏 – ♦2880/6150 CZK ♦♦3125/6825 CZK
Rest – Carte 380/779 CZK
♦ Townhouse ♦ Modern ♦

Renovated 17C house with a white 19C façade. Choice of superior or deluxe bedrooms: all have luxury bathrooms; the latter are more spacious. Modern lobby bar and panoramic lift. Contemporary restaurant with clean, bright interior, serving mix of international and Czech dishes.

Angelo without rest ♿ 🗚 ⇄ 🛜 🏊 🅿 VISA ⑩ AE ①
Radlicka 1g ✉ *150 00 –* Ⓜ *Anděl –* 𝒞 *234 801 111*
– www.angelohotel.com **F3**
168 rm ⊡ – †1890/4750 CZK ††1890/4750 CZK
♦ Business ♦ Modern ♦
Jazz is the theme of this chic, brightly coloured hotel, with its red, yellow and black décor. Well-equipped, uniform bedrooms are set over 5 floors; executive suites are on the top two floors. Spacious, shower-only bathrooms. Quiet terrace.

Alchymist Prague Castle Suites without rest 🛎 🐾 🗚
Snemovni 8 ✉ *118 00 –* Ⓜ *Malostranká* 🛜 🏊 VISA ⑩ AE ①
– 𝒞 257 286 960 – www.alchymistpraguecastle.com **F1**
8 rm ⊡ – †4940/9880 CZK ††4940/9880 CZK
♦ Townhouse ♦ Personalised ♦ Stylish ♦
Impressive 15C house in a quiet square beneath the castle; the owner once lived here and has lovingly restored it. Guest areas are lavishly decorated with gilt furnishings. Bedrooms display a keen eye for detail and come with butler service. Cheese and wine served early evening; dinner is at the nearby hotel.

U Krále Karla 🛜 VISA ⑩ AE ①
Nerudova-Úvoz 4 ✉ *118 00 – 𝒞 257 531 211 – www.ukralekarla.cz*
19 rm ⊡ – †1369/3611 CZK ††1469/3710 CZK **E2**
Rest – Carte 399/748 CZK
♦ Historic ♦ Classic ♦
Quiet baroque townhouse close to the castle; formerly a Gothic-style home to a Benedictine order. Splendid staircase leads to traditional bedrooms featuring parquet floors and antique furnishings. Stunning stained glass ceiling on display in the hall. Small, homely bistro serves an international menu.

U Raka without rest ♨ 🗚 ⇄ 🛜 🅿 VISA ⑩ AE ①
Cernínská 10 ✉ *118 00 – 𝒞 220 511 100 – www.romantikhotel-uraka.cz*
6 rm ⊡ – †2074/2928 CZK ††2684/5856 CZK **E1**
♦ Family ♦ Cosy ♦
Cosy, rustic, family-run hotel; tucked away in a quiet neighbourhood. Warmly decorated, tidy bedrooms; ask for the luxury room with its own fireplace and garden terrace. Friendly, attentive staff. Fresh breakfast buffet served on typical Czech plates.

Neruda without rest 🐾 🗚 ⇄ 🛜 VISA ⑩ AE ①
Nerudova 44 ✉ *118 00 – 𝒞 257 535 557 – www.hotelneruda.cz*
42 rm ⊡ – †1869/4211 CZK ††1869/4211 CZK **E2**
♦ Townhouse ♦ Modern ♦
Named after a local Czech writer, whose poems decorate the walls. Cosy orange and brown coloured bedrooms in the original 14C building; more modern rooms in the newer building. Relax on the roof terrace overlooking the nearby castle.

Domus Henrici without rest ⇄ 🛜 VISA ⑩ AE ①
Loretánská 11 ✉ *118 00 – 𝒞 220 511 369 – www.hidden-places.com*
7 rm ⊡ – †1800/2600 CZK ††2250/3750 CZK – 1 suite **E2**
♦ Townhouse ♦ Minimalist ♦
Well-maintained, privately run townhouse perched on hill in a tranquil location close to castle. Spacious, comfy, antique-furnished bedrooms are set over 3 floors; some have jacuzzi baths. South-facing terrace offers a unique view of city.

Constans without rest 🗚 ⇄ 🛜 🏊 🛜 VISA ⑩ AE ①
Bretislavova 309 ✉ *110 00 –* Ⓜ *Malostranká – 𝒞 234 091 818*
– www.hotelconstans.cz **F2**
29 rm ⊡ – †1549/3393 CZK ††1549/3393 CZK – 2 suites
♦ Townhouse ♦ Classic ♦
A warm welcome awaits at this charming hotel: comprising three converted townhouses in a quiet street below the castle. Huge bedrooms boast period furniture and well-equipped marble bathrooms; some have balconies. Traditional breakfast room.

XX **Kampa Park**   ≼ 🛋 AC 🅷 VISA ⊙⊙ AE ⊙

Na Kampe 8b, Malá Strana ✉ *118 00 –* ⓜ *Malostranská – ☎ 296 826 102*
– www.kampagroup.com   **F2**
Rest *– (booking essential at dinner)* Carte 1135/1785 CZK
 ♦ International ♦ Fashionable ♦ Design ♦
Stunningly located at the water's edge by Charles Bridge, a popular, contemporary restaurant run by a charming and professional team. In winter, dine in the winter garden; in summer enjoy the view from the terrace. Fairly priced global menus – carefully prepared dishes use quality produce.

XX **Terasa U Zlaté Studne** – at Golden Well Hotel   ≼ 🛋 AC 🅷

U Zlaté Studne 4 ✉ *118 00 –* ⓜ *Malostranská*   VISA ⊙⊙ AE ⊙
– ☎ 257 533 322 – www.terasauzlatestudne.cz   **F1**
Rest – Menu 850/1400 CZK – Carte 890/2200 CZK
 ♦ Modern ♦ Cosy ♦
Enjoy magnificent views over the city from this professionally run, top floor restaurant and its heated terrace. Blue and gold décor, fine china and professional service. Well-presented, full-flavoured modern dishes use quality ingredients.

X **SaSaZu**   AC 🅿 VISA ⊙⊙ AE ⊙
🈯

Bubenské nábr. 306 ✉ *170 04 –* ⓜ *Vltavská – ☎ 284 097 455*
– www.sasazu.cz
– Closed 24-25 December   *Plan I* **C1**
Rest – Menu 690/850 CZK – Carte 440/980 CZK
 ♦ Asian ♦ Exotic ♦ Fashionable ♦
Funky, stylish, high-ceilinged restaurant and bar located within the Prague Market and decorated with unique statues and huge red lamps. Well-balanced, innovative Asian cooking; flavourful dishes are prepared with care in the open kitchen and offered at a reasonable price. Attentive, knowledgeable service.

🍴 **Olympia**   AC 🅷 VISA ⊙⊙ AE ⊙

Vítezná 7 ✉ *110 00 –* ⓜ *Národni Třída – ☎ 251 511 080*
– www.kolkovna.cz   **F2**
Rest – Menu 110 CZK (lunch) – Carte 235/760 CZK
 ♦ Traditional ♦ Retro ♦
Converted bank close to tramstop 22; now a lively, friendly, popular pub-owned brasserie, with beer on draught. Classical interior with huge windows. Traditional, international menu; try the tasty Czech dishes and the homemade sausages.

DENMARK
DANMARK

COPENHAGEN

→ **AREA:**
43 069 km² (16 629 sq mi) excluding the Faroe Islands and Greenland.

→ **POPULATION:**
5 587 085 inhabitants. Density = 130 per km².

→ **CAPITAL:**
Copenhagen.

→ **CURRENCY:**
Danish Krone (DKK).

→ **GOVERNMENT:**
Constitutional parliamentary (single chamber) monarchy (since 1849). Member of European Union since 1973.

→ **LANGUAGES:**
Danish; many Danes also understand and speak English.

→ **PUBLIC HOLIDAYS:**
New Year's Day (1 Jan); Maundy Thursday (late Mar/Apr); Good Friday (late Mar/Apr); Easter Monday (late Mar/Apr); Prayer Day (late Apr/May); Ascension Day (May); Whit Monday (late May/June); Constitution Day (5 June); Christmas Eve (24 Dec – Half Day); Christmas Day (25 Dec); 2nd Day of Christmas (26 Dec).

→ **LOCAL TIME:**
GMT +1 hour in winter and GMT + 2 hours in summer.

→ **CLIMATE:**
Temperate northern maritime with cold winters and mild summers (Copenhagen: January 1°C, July 18°C).

→ **EMERGENCY:**
Police, Medical Assistance and Fire Brigade ℰ **112**.

→ **ELECTRICITY:**
230 volts AC, 50Hz; 2 round pin sockets.

→ **FORMALITIES:**
Travellers from the European Union (EU), Switzerland, Norway, Iceland and the main countries of North and South America need a national identity card or passport (America: passport required) to visit Denmark for less than three months (tourism or business purpose). For visitors from other countries a visa may be required, in addition to a passport, especially for those wishing to stay for longer than three months. If you plan to visit Greenland or Faroe Islands while in Denmark, you must purchase a visa in advance in your own country. We advise you to check with your embassy before travelling.

COPENHAGEN
KØBENHAVN

Population: 542 832

HaPu99/Fotolia.com

Some cities overwhelm you, and give the impression that there's too much of them to take in. Not Copenhagen. Most of its key sights are neatly compressed within its central Slotsholmen 'island', an area that enjoyed its first golden age in the early seventeenth century in the reign of Christian IV, when it became a harbour of great consequence. It has canals on three sides and opposite the harbour is the area of Christianshavn, home of the legendary freewheeling 'free-town' community of Christiania. Further up from the centre are Nyhavn, the much-photographed canalside with brightly coloured buildings where the sightseeing cruises leave from, and the elegant Frederiksstaden, whose wide streets contain palaces and museums. West of the centre is where Copenhageners love to hang out: the Tivoli Gardens, a kind of magical fairyland. Slightly more down-to-earth are the western suburbs of Vesterbro and Nørrebro, which were run-down areas given a street credible spit and polish for the 21C, and are now two of the trendiest districts.

Once you've idled away some time in the Danish capital, you'll wonder why anyone might ever want to leave. With its waterfronts, quirky shops and cafés, the city presents a modern, user-friendly ambience – but it also boasts world class art collections, museums, and impressive parks, gardens and lakes, all of which bear the mark of an earlier time.

COPENHAGEN IN...

→ **ONE DAY**
Walk along Strøget, National Museum, Ny Carlsberg Glyptotek, Black Diamond, boat watching at Nyhavn.

→ **TWO DAYS**
Tivoli Gardens, Vesterbro, Opera House, Christiania.

→ **THREE DAYS**
Royal palaces at Frederiksstaden, train ride along the coast.

PRACTICAL INFORMATION

ARRIVAL-DEPARTURE

 Copenhagen Airport is located in Kastrup, 9km southeast of the city. The metro will take you to the centre in 15min. A taxi will take 25min.

GETTING AROUND

The metro is a triumph of sleek, smooth efficiency which runs 24 hours a day. If you want to see as much of the city as possible, get a Copenhagen Card, which gives free entry to all museums and galleries, as well as free bus, train and metro travel. They can be purchased from the main tourist office just across the road from the central railway station. Hiring a bicycle is a good way to see the city; it takes about two hours to circumnavigate the major attractions. It's also possible to see the city by kayak. Kajak Ole can get you paddling round the central harbour area for a very different perspective.

CALENDAR HIGHLIGHTS

February
Fashion Festival.

April
Queen Margrethe's birthday.

May
May Day Festival, Copenhagen Beer Festival, Latin American Festival.

June
Whitsun Carnival, St Hans Eve Festival, Roskilde Music Festival.

July
Jazz Festival.

August
Ballet Festival, Historic Grand Prix, Cooking Festival.

November/December
Tivoli's Special Christmas Market.

EATING OUT

Fresh regional ingredients have revolutionized the menus of Copenhagen's hip restaurants and its reputation for food just keeps getting bigger. The city's dining establishments manage to marry Danish dining traditions such as herring or frikkadeller meatballs with global influences to impressive effect. So impressive that in recent times the city has earned itself more Michelin stars, for its crisp and precise cooking, than any other in Scandinavia. Many good restaurants blend French methods and dishes with regional ingredients and innovative touches and there is a trend towards fixed price, no choice menus involving several courses, which means that dinner can be a pleasingly drawn-out affair, stretching over three or four hours. There's no need to tip, as it should be included in the cost of the meal. Danes, though, have a very good reputation as cheerful, helpful waiting staff, so you might feel like adding a bit extra. But be warned, many restaurants – and even hotels – charge between 2.5% and 5% for using a foreign credit card.

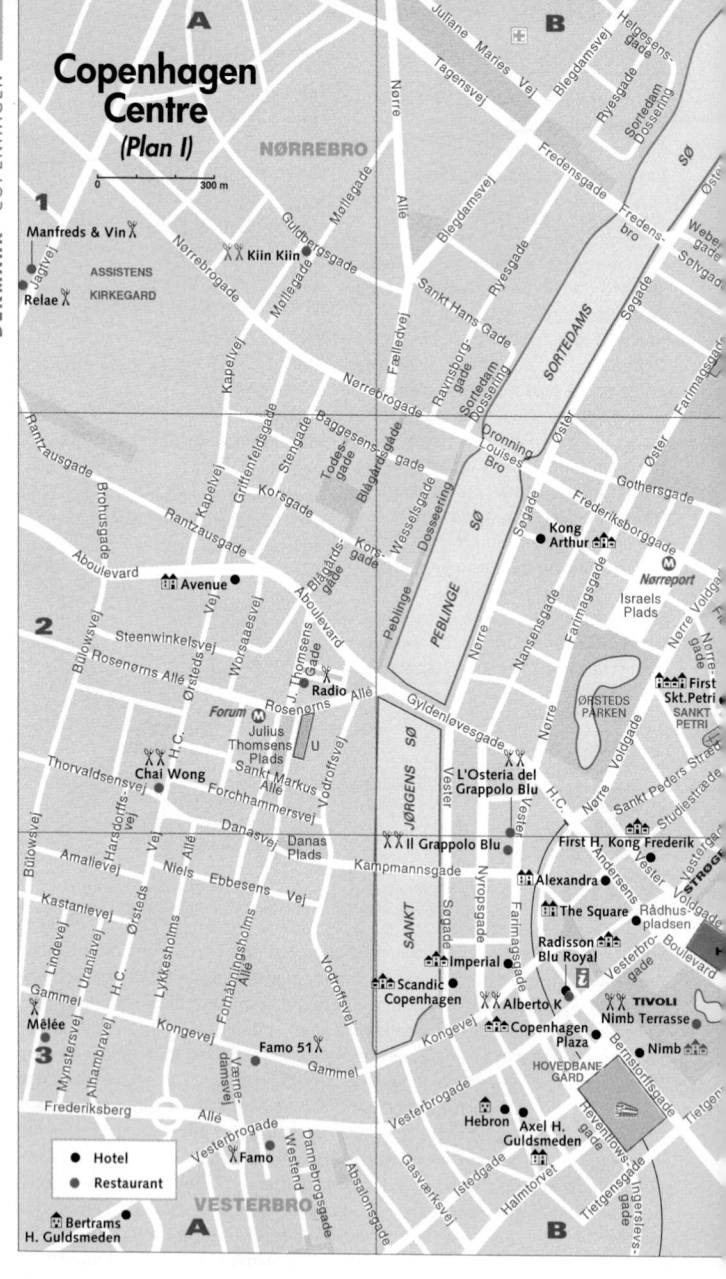

Copenhagen Centre
(Plan I)

NØRREBRO

Manfreds & Vin

ASSISTENS
KIRKEGARD

Relae

Kiin Kiin

Avenue

Radio

Forum

Chai Wong

Julius
Thomsens
Plads

Sankt Markus
Alle

Danas
Plads

Kong
Arthur

Nørreport

Israels
Plads

ØRSTEDS
PARKEN

First
Skt.Petri

SANKT
PETRI

L'Osteria del
Grappolo Blu

Il Grappolo Blu

First H. Kong Frederik

Alexandra

The Square

Radisson
Blu Royal

Imperial

Scandic
Copenhagen

Alberto K

Copenhagen
Plaza

Rådhus-
pladsen

Nimb Terrasse

TIVOLI

Nimb

HOVEDBANE
GÅRD

Mêlée

Famo 51

Hebron

Axel H.
Guldsmeden

Famo

VESTERBRO

Bertrams
H. Guldsmeden

● Hotel
● Restaurant

PEBLINGE

SORTEDAMS SØ

SANKT JØRGENS SØ

0   300 m

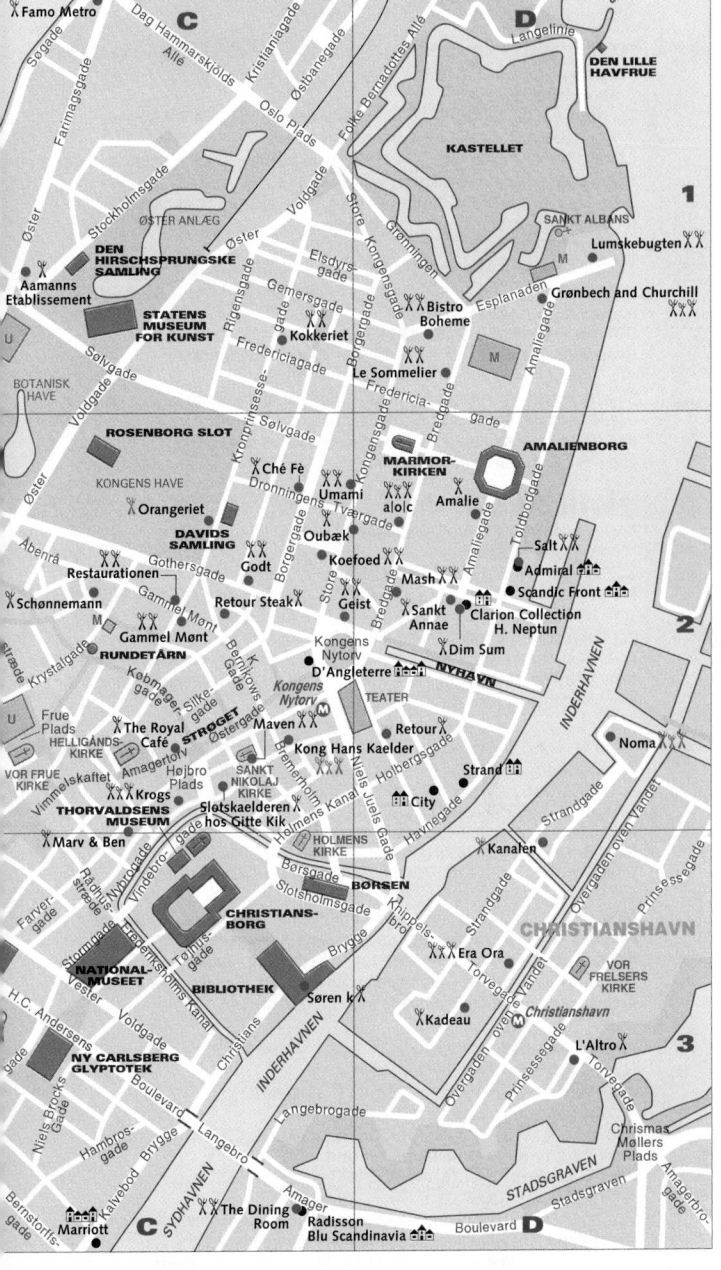

Famo Metro

Dag Hammarskjölds Allé

Kristianiagade

Østbanegade

DEN LILLE HAVFRUE

Langelinie

C

D

KASTELLET

1

Søgade

Farimagsgade

Øster

Stockholmsgade

Østerbrogade

Folke Bernadottes Allé

Oslo Plads

ØSTER ANLÆG

Øster

Voldgade

Store Kongensgade

Grønningen

SANKT ALBANS

Lumskebugten

DEN HIRSCHSPRUNGSKE SAMLING

Aamanns Etablissement

STATENS MUSEUM FOR KUNST

Rigensgade

Elsdyrsgade

Gemersgade

Bistro Boheme

Esplanaden

Grønbech and Churchill

Amaliegade

Fredericiagade

Kokkeriet

M

BOTANISK HAVE

U

Sølvgade

Voldgade

Le Sommelier

Fredericia-gade

M

Kronprinsesse-gade

Sølvgade

Kongensgade

Bredgade

ROSENBORG SLOT

Ché Fè

Umami

MARMOR-KIRKEN

AMALIENBORG

Øster

Åbenrå

KONGENS HAVE

Dronningens Tværgade

aloic

Amalie

Toldbodgade

Orangeriet

DAVIDS SAMLING

Oubæk

Koefoed

Amaliegade

Salt

Admiral

Gothersgade

Godt

Borgergade

Mash

Scandic Front

2

Restaurationen

Gammel Mønt

Retour Steak

Store

Geist

Sankt Annae

Clarion Collection H. Neptun

Schønnemann

M

Gammel Mønt

Kongens Nytorv

Bredgade

Dim Sum

RUNDETÅRN

Købmagergade

Silkegade

Kongens Nytorv

D'Angleterre

NYHAVN

INDERHAVNEN

U

Frue Plads

The Royal Café

Østergade

Maven

TEATER

Retour

Noma

HELLIGÅNDS-KIRKE

STRØGET

Bremerholm

Kong Hans Kaelder

Holbergsgade

VOR FRUE KIRKE

Amagertorv

Vimmelskaftet

Højbro Plads

SANKT NIKOLAJ KIRKE

Niels Juels Gade

Strand

City

Strandgade

Krogs

Slotskaelderen hos Gitte Kik

Havnegade

THORVALDSENS MUSEUM

Marv & Ben

Holmens Kanal

HOLMENS KIRKE

Kanalen

Rådhus-stræde

Nybrogade

Vindebro-gade

Børsgade

BØRSEN

Slotsholmsgade

Overgaden oven Vandet

Prinsessegade

CHRISTIANSHAVN

Farver-gade

Stormgade

Frederiksholms Kanal

CHRISTIANS-BORG

Tøjhus-gade

Knippels-bro

Brygge

Strandgade

VOR FRELSERS KIRKE

H.C. Andersens

Vester Voldgade

BIBLIOTEK

Søren k

Era Ora

Torvegade

Christianshavn

NATIONAL MUSEET

Christians

INDERHAVNEN

Kadeau

M

3

NY CARLSBERG GLYPTOTEK

Boulevard

Prinsessegade

L'Altro

Niels Brocks Gade

Hambros-gade

Langebro

Langebrogade

Amager Boulevard

Overgaden oven Vandet

Torvegade

Amagerbro-gade

Chrismas Møllers Plads

STADSGRAVEN

Stadsgraven

Bernstorffs-gade

Kalvebod Brygge

SYDHAVNEN

The Dining Room

Amager Boulevard

Radisson Blu Scandinavia

C

D

Marriott

135

DENMARK - COPENHAGEN

D'Angleterre without rest 🕭 🌐 🏠 🗔 🗚 🗘 🛜 🖏 🗚 💳 ⑳ 🅰🅴 ⓞ
Kongens Nytorv 34 ⊠ 1050 K – ⓜ *Kongens Nytorv – ℰ 33 12 00 95*
– www.dangleterre.dk   **C2**
85 rm – ♦3900/7900 DKK ♦♦3900/7900 DKK, � 250 DKK – 6 suites
♦ Traditional ♦ Historic ♦ Classic ♦

Landmark hotel dating back over 250 years, in a central location across from the
Opera House. Bedrooms come in various shapes and sizes; pay the extra for a
Royal Square view or stylish suite. Elegant restaurant and champagne bar. Due
to reopen mid-2013 following refurbishment.

Copenhagen Marriott ≼ 🕭 🕭 🗚 🗘 🖏 🖏 🗘 🛜 🖏 🅿
Kalvebod Brygge 5 ⊠ 1560 V – ℰ 88 33 99 00   💳 ⑳ 🅰🅴 ⓞ
– www.copenhagenmarriott.dk   **C3**
391 rm – ♦1499/3049 DKK ♦♦1499/3049 DKK, ⊠ 220 DKK – 10 suites
Rest *Midtown Grill* – ℰ 88 33 12 31 – Carte 620/880 DKK
♦ Luxury ♦ Business ♦ Modern ♦

Striking hotel with large, open-fired lounge-bar and floor to ceiling windows
overlooking the water. Bright, spacious bedrooms are handsomely appointed
and afford canal or city views. American grill offers steaks, chops and seafood,
and has a lively open kitchen.

First H. Skt. Petri 🕭 🖏 🖭 🗚 🛜 🖏 🖏 💳 ⑳ 🅰🅴 ⓞ
Krystalgade 22 ⊠ 1172 K – ⓜ *Nørreport – ℰ 33 45 91 00*
– www.firsthotels.com   **B2**
257 rm ⊠ – ♦1195/2695 DKK ♦♦1395/3295 DKK – 11 suites
Rest *Brasserie Petri* – Menu 445 DKK (dinner) – Carte 485/655 DKK
♦ Business ♦ Modern ♦

Centrally located former department store, close to St Peter's Church. Spacious
open-plan atrium with large, lively bar. White bedrooms boast stylish design
features by Per Arnoldi. Huge brasserie dining room with courtyard terrace; concise Mediterranean menu.

Nimb 🕭 🖭 rm, 🗚 🛜 🖏 💳 ⑳ 🅰🅴 ⓞ
Bernstorffsgade 5 ⊠ 1577 V – ⓜ *København Hovedbane Gård*
– ℰ 88 70 00 00 – www.nimb.dk   **B3**
13 rm ⊠ – ♦2200/6900 DKK ♦♦9000 DKK
Rest *Nimb Terrasse* – see restaurant listing
Rest *Brasserie* – ℰ 88 70 00 10 – Carte 305/385 DKK
Rest *Bar' n' Grill* – ℰ 88 70 00 60 (dinner only) Carte 340/730 DKK
♦ Luxury ♦ Design ♦

Moorish-style private residence built in 1909, situated beside the Tivoli Gardens.
First floor baronial lounge with stone fireplace; pleasant bar in former ballroom.
Sympathetically designed, well-equipped bedrooms – most overlook the gardens. Informal brasserie with 3 open kitchens offers popular weekend brunch;
lively bar and grill. Wine bar boasts over 1,700 bottles.

Radisson Blu Royal ≼ 🕭 🖏 🖏 🖭 🗚 🛜 🖏 🅿 🖘
Hammerichsgade 1 ⊠ 1611 V   💳 ⑳ 🅰🅴 ⓞ
– ⓜ *København Hovedbane Gård – ℰ 33 42 60 00*
– www.radissonblu.com   **B3**
258 rm – ♦1195/3195 DKK ♦♦1295/3295 DKK, ⊠ 195 DKK – 2 suites
Rest *Alberto K* – see restaurant listing
Rest *Café Royal* – Carte 393/480 DKK
♦ Business ♦ Design ♦

Vast hotel designed by Arne Jacobson. Large lobby with shops; extensive conference and fitness facilities. Scandinavian-style bedrooms: the largest are the
double-aspect corner rooms; 606 still has its original décor. Informal restaurant
boasts floor to ceiling windows.

Radisson Blu Scandinavia   ⟨ ┠ᗡ ⍉ ᖼ ₺ 🜨 ᇂ 🙪 P

Amager Boulevard 70 ⊠ *2300 S –* Ⓜ *Island Brygge*   VISA ⚊ AE ⓪
– 𝒸 33 96 50 00
– www.radissonblu.com/scandinaviahotel-copenhagen   **C3**
518 rm – 🛉995/2495 DKK 🛉🛉995/2495 DKK, ⚌ 185 DKK – 24 suites
Rest *The Dining Room* – see restaurant listing
Rest *Blue Elephant* – 𝒸 33 96 59 70 (closed Christmas, Easter and Sunday) (dinner only) Menu 495 DKK – Carte 305/505 DKK
Rest *Kyoto* – 𝒸 33 32 16 74 (closed Christmas and New Year)
(dinner only) Carte 270/700 DKK
 ◆ Business ◆ Personalised ◆
Modern tower block with a busy bar, shops and a casino. Fitness and conference rooms are on the first floor. Bedrooms come in six different themes, including 'Oriental' and 'High-Tech'; all have great views. Exotic décor in appealing Thai restaurant Blue Elephant. Wide-ranging Japanese menu in Kyoto.

Copenhagen Plaza   🅰️Ҝ ₺ 🜨 🙪 VISA ⚊ AE ⓪

Bernstorffsgade 4 ⊠ *1577 V –* Ⓜ *København Hovedbane Gård*
– 𝒸 33 14 92 62 – www.profilhotels.dk   **B3**
91 rm ⚌ – 🛉1095/2195 DKK 🛉🛉1195/2395 DKK – 2 suites
Rest – *(closed Sunday) (dinner only)* Carte 280/430 DKK
 ◆ Traditional ◆ Retro ◆
Located next to the railway station and Tivoli Gardens, an early 20C hotel commissioned by King Frederik VIII. Mix of charmingly old-fashioned and more contemporary bedrooms; some are being refurbished. Lovely library bar and welcoming, traditionally appointed restaurant with open kitchen.

Island   ⟨ 🥘 ┠ᗡ ᖼ 🅰️Ҝ ₺ 🜨 🙪 P VISA ⚊ AE ⓪

Kalvebod Brygge 53 (via Kalvebod Brygge C 3) ⊠ *1560 V –* 𝒸 *33 38 96 00*
– www.copenhagenisland.dk
325 rm – 🛉820/2125 DKK 🛉🛉890/4025 DKK, ⚌ 150 DKK
Rest *The Harbour* – Menu 265/315 DKK – Carte 605/725 DKK
 ◆ Business ◆ Modern ◆
Contemporary glass and steel hotel set just outside the city, on a man-made island in the harbour. Well-equipped bedrooms, some with balconies; choose a water over a city view. Allergy friendly rooms available. Multi-level lounge bar and restaurant serves a wide-ranging menu.

Admiral   ⟨ ᖼ ₺ 🜨 🙪 P VISA ⚊ AE ⓪

Toldbodgade 24-28 ⊠ *1253 K –* Ⓜ *Kongens Nytorv –* 𝒸 *33 74 14 14*
– www.admiralhotel.dk   **D2**
314 rm – 🛉1235/1725 DKK 🛉🛉1595/2025 DKK, ⚌ 140 DKK
– 52 suites
Rest *Salt* – see restaurant listing
 ◆ Business ◆ Modern ◆
Impressive 1787 former grain-drying warehouse with extensive conference facilities; a maritime theme runs throughout. Bedrooms boast vintage beams, bespoke wood furniture and harbour or city views.

Kong Arthur *without rest*   🌙 ᖼ ₺ 🜨 🙪 P VISA ⚊ AE ⓪

Nørre Søgade 11 ⊠ *1370 K –* Ⓜ *Nørreport –* 𝒸 *33 11 12 12*
– www.kongarthur.dk   **B2**
155 rm – 🛉950/2400 DKK 🛉🛉1100/4800 DKK, ⚌ 155 DKK
 ◆ Business ◆ Classic ◆
Four 1881 buildings set around a courtyard, in an elegant residential avenue close to Peblinge Lake. Vaulted breakfast room. Well-equipped bedrooms vary in size; the courtyard rooms are the quietest.

DENMARK - COPENHAGEN

First H. Kong Frederik
      ⇔ rm, 🛜 🖥 ⓥⓘⓢⓐ ⓜⓞ ⒶⒺ ⓘ

Vester Voldgade 25 ⊠ 1552 V – Ⓜ Vesterport – ℰ 33 12 59 02
– www.firsthotels.dk
                                            D2
109 rm – ♦795/2295 DKK ♦♦995/2995 DKK, ⊊ 135 DKK – 1 suite
Rest *Public House* – ℰ 70 26 23 20 (closed Sunday) (dinner only)
Menu 295 DKK – Carte 220/385 DKK
♦ Townhouse ♦ Personalised ♦
One hundred year old townhouse in the very centre of the city, 5min from Tivoli
Park. Intimate lobby in dark hues; cosy bedrooms with colourful feature walls,
set around a glass-roofed courtyard. Contemporary gastropub-style dining
room offers a concise menu.

Scandic Front
      🖪 🎖 rm, ⇔ rm, 🛜 🖥 ⓥⓘⓢⓐ ⓜⓞ ⒶⒺ ⓘ

Sankt Annae Plads 21 ⊠ 1250 K – Ⓜ Kongens Nytorv – ℰ 33 13 34 00
– www.scandichotels.com/front
                                            D2
129 rm ⊊ – ♦910/2590 DKK ♦♦1210/2990 DKK – 3 suites
Rest – Carte 271/465 DKK
♦ Business ♦ Modern ♦
Contemporary harbourside hotel with pleasant lobby-lounge, airy function
rooms and well-equipped fitness area. White-walled bedrooms boast design
furniture; some are duplex or have balconies and harbour views. Modern dining
room serves salads, tapas and grills.

Imperial
      🖪 🎖 ⇔ 🕻 🖥 🚗 ⓥⓘⓢⓐ ⓜⓞ ⒶⒺ ⓘ

Vester Farimagsgade 9 ⊠ 1606 V – Ⓜ Vesterport – ℰ 33 12 80 00
– www.imperialhotel.dk
                                            B3
287 rm – ♦890/2150 DKK ♦♦1030/2350 DKK, ⊊ 170 DKK – 1 suite
Rest – Carte 250/455 DKK
♦ Business ♦ Modern ♦
Spacious, modern hotel, centrally located on a wide city thoroughfare, close to
the train station. Smart, comfortable bedrooms are furnished in dark wood and
equipped with good technological extras. Contemporary restaurant features a
brightly coloured Italian theme wall and serves Italian dishes to match.

Scandic Copenhagen
      ≤ 🖪 🐎 🖪 🎖 ⇔ 🛜 🖥 🚗

Vester Søgade 6 ⊠ 1601 V
                                            ⓥⓘⓢⓐ ⓜⓞ ⒶⒺ ⓘ
– Ⓜ København Hovedbane Gård – ℰ 33 14 35 35 – www.scandichotels.com
– Closed Christmas
                                            B3
446 rm ⊊ – ♦2600 DKK ♦♦2750/3100 DKK – 40 suites
Rest – Menu 328 DKK (dinner) – Carte 253/395 DKK
♦ Business ♦ Conference hotel ♦ Design ♦
One of the city's tallest hotels, with a crisp, clean interior and state-of-the-art
events facilities. White 'trees' sprout from the floor in the unusual lobby. Stylish,
minimalist bedrooms feature striking murals; choose a lake or city view. Large
restaurant with central booths serves organic Scandic produce.

The Square without rest
      🎖 ⇔ 🛜 🖥 ⓥⓘⓢⓐ ⓜⓞ ⒶⒺ ⓘ

Rådhuspladsen 14 ⊠ 1550 V – Ⓜ København Hovedbane Gård
– ℰ 33 38 12 00 – www.thesquarecopenhagen.com
                                            B3
267 rm – ♦1000/1425 DKK ♦♦1200/2225 DKK, ⊊ 125 DKK
♦ Business ♦ Modern ♦
Set on the Town Hall square, close to the station and the Tivoli Gardens. Modern
lobby and bright 6th floor breakfast room. Fairly compact bedrooms with a
'square' theme in the décor; a few have balconies.

Avenue without rest
      ⇔ 🛜 🖥 🅿 ⓥⓘⓢⓐ ⓜⓞ ⒶⒺ ⓘ

Åboulevard 29 ⊠ 1960 C – Ⓜ Forum – ℰ 35 37 31 11 – www.avenuehotel.dk
– Closed 22 December-3 January
                                            A2
68 rm ⊊ – ♦1000/1400 DKK ♦♦1200/1800 DKK
♦ Business ♦ Modern ♦
Set within a building dating back to 1899, not far from the metro station. Pleasant lounge, relaxing bar and nice courtyard patio. Comfortable, well-maintained bedrooms with a bright, crisp style.

Axel H. Guldsmeden 🛖 ⇄ 🛜 🛁 VISA ⦾ AE ⓸

Helgolandsgade 11 ⊠ 1653V – **Ⓜ** *København Hovedbane Gård*
– ☏ 33 31 32 66 – www.hotelguldsmeden.com **B3**
129 rm – **♦**765/1265 DKK **♦♦**895/1475 DKK, ⌸ 165 DKK
Rest – Menu 295 DKK

♦ Business ♦ Oriental ♦

Stylish hotel with a charming courtyard and a uniquely styled interior. Exotic bedrooms boast furniture from Indonesia and other Asian knick-knacks: most have four-posters; some have small balconies. Relaxation area in the basement. Restaurant offers original, organic tapas.

Alexandra without rest ⇄ 🛜 VISA ⦾ AE ⓸

H.C. Andersens Boulevard 8 ⊠ 1553 V
*– **Ⓜ** København Hovedbane Gård*
– ☏ 33 74 44 44 – www.hotelalexandra.dk **B3**
61 rm – **♦**1245/1545 DKK **♦♦**1345/2545 DKK, ⌸ 99 DKK

♦ Traditional ♦ Personalised ♦

Classical hotel close to the city centre. Bedrooms are uniquely styled and there's an entire 'allergy friendly' floor; the 13 'Design' rooms are decorated by famous Danish designers.

Clarion Collection H. Neptun without rest ⇄ 🛜 🛁

Sankt Annae Plads 18-20 ⊠ 1250 K VISA ⦾ AE ⓸
*– **Ⓜ** Kongens Nytorv – ☏ 33 96 20 00*
– www.nordicchoicehotels.no **D2**
133 rm ⌸ – **♦**740/1740 DKK **♦♦**990/1990 DKK – 15 suites

♦ Business ♦ Functional ♦

Adjoining 1854 houses in a residential area of bustling Nyhavn. Bedrooms vary in size from tiny singles to large doubles, and boast classical Gustavian-style furniture. Courtyard breakfasts.

City without rest ⇄ 🛜 🛁 VISA ⦾ AE ⓸

Peder Skrams Gade 24 ⊠ 1054 K
*– **Ⓜ** Kongens Nytorv – ☏ 33 13 06 66*
– www.hotelcity.dk **D2**
81 rm ⌸ – **♦**700/1400 DKK **♦♦**900/1700 DKK

♦ Business ♦ Functional ♦

Modern hotel in a quiet street between the city and the docks. Designer furniture, including Jacobsen armchairs, features throughout. Bedrooms boast monochrome Jan Persson jazz photos. Cosy bar.

Strand without rest ⇄ 🛜 🛁 VISA ⦾ AE ⓸

Havnegade 37 ⊠ 1058 K – **Ⓜ** *Kongens Nytorv – ☏ 33 48 99 00*
– www.copenhagenstrand.dk
– Closed 20-26 December **D2**
172 rm – **♦**940/2090 DKK **♦♦**1040/2190 DKK, ⌸ 125 DKK – 2 suites

♦ Business ♦ Functional ♦

Centrally located hotel in a 19C former paper factory on the harbourside. Comfortable, functional bedrooms, in light maritime colours, are furnished in polished wood. Large basement lobby-lounge.

Bertrams H. Guldsmeden without rest ⇄ 🛜 🛁

Vesterbrogade 107 ⊠ 1620 V – ☏ 33 25 04 05 VISA ⦾ AE ⓸
– www.bertramshotel.com **A3**
46 rm – **♦**950/1495 DKK **♦♦**1190/2195 DKK, ⌸ 140 DKK

♦ Townhouse ♦ Personalised ♦

Younger sister to Axel H. Guldsmeden, with similarly styled Indonesian interior. Largest, most peaceful bedrooms overlook the courtyard; some boast four-posters or balconies. Good breakfasts.

🏠 **Hebron** without rest ⅙ 🛜 🏰 📼 💳 🟦 ⓪

Helgolandsgade 4 ✉ *1653 V* – Ⓜ *København Hovedbane Gård*
– ℰ *33 31 69 06* – *www.hebron.dk*
– *Closed 20 December-2 January*   **B3**
97 rm ⊡ – ♦650/1370 DKK ♦♦850/1570 DKK – 2 suites
♦ Traditional ♦ Functional ♦

This was one of the city's biggest hotels when it opened in 1899 and some original features still remain. Set close to the shops and gardens, it's simple, functional and ideal for short stays.

XXXX **Geranium** (Rasmus Kofoed) ≤ 🄰🄲 ⅙ 📼 💳 🟦
🕄🕄
Per Henrik Lings Allé 4 (8th Fl), Parken National Stadium (3 km via Dag Hammaraskjölds Allé C 1) ✉ *2100* – ℰ *69 96 00 20* – *www.geranium.dk*
– *Closed 2 weeks Christmas, Sunday-Tuesday and Wednesday lunch*
Rest – *(booking essential) (set menu only)* Menu 698/1298 DKK 🕃
♦ Innovative ♦ Design ♦ Elegant ♦

Take the lift up to the elegant lounge-bar for an aperitif then head for the spacious, modern dining room with its huge tables and slick styling. Interesting, innovative set menus; highly skilled cooking relies on local, organic and biodynamic produce. Views into the impressive kitchen and over the treetops.
→ Mackerel with burnt juniper and a horseradish and cucumber granité. Venison tartare and beetroot. Raspberries with flowers and fresh goat's cream.

XXX **Noma** (Rene Redzepi) ⅙ 🕄 📼 💳 🟦 ⓪
🕄🕄
Strandgade 93 ✉ *1401 K* – Ⓜ *Christianshavn* – ℰ *32 96 32 97*
– *www.noma.dk*
– *Closed last 3 weeks July, 22 December-6 January, Sunday and Monday*
Rest – *(booking essential) (set menu only)* Menu 1500 DKK 🕃   **D2**
♦ Innovative ♦ Design ♦

Stylish, understated restaurant in converted harbourside warehouse, with just 12 tables but over 65 staff. Highly skilled kitchen uses quality Nordic ingredients to produce unique, beautifully crafted dishes which stimulate the senses and create a memorable dining experience. Professional yet relaxed service.
→ Radish and carrot 'planted' in grass emulsion. Turbot roasted on the bone with sea vegetables. Grilled pear with green juniper and spruce.

XXX **Kong Hans Kaelder** ⅙ 📼 💳 🟦 ⓪
🕄
Vingårdsstraede 6 ✉ *1070 K* – Ⓜ *Kongens Nytorv* – ℰ *33 11 68 68*
– *www.konghans.dk*
– *Closed 3 weeks July-August, 2 weeks January, Easter, Sunday and bank holidays*
Rest – *(dinner only) (booking essential)* Menu 1150 DKK   **C2**
– Carte 870/1215 DKK
♦ Danish ♦ Elegant ♦

Well-established and enthusiastically run restaurant, in a vaulted Gothic cellar. Cooking is classically grounded with a modern edge; choice of concise à la carte or 9 course 'Innovation' menu. Well-kept Danish cheeses come with their own individual accompaniments.
→ Carpaccio of wild ox with caviar. Turbot and blanquette sauce with horseradish, dill oil and cockles. Passion fruit soufflé with passion fruit and caramel ice cream.

XXX **Mielcke & Hurtigkarl** 🕄 ⅙ 📼 💳 🟦 ⓪
Runddel 1 (2 km via Frederiksberg Allé A 3) ✉ *2000 C* – ℰ *38 34 84 36*
– *www.mhcph.com*
– *Closed 23 December-17 January, Tuesday-Wednesday October-March, Sunday and Monday*
Rest – *(dinner only and lunch April-September) (booking essential)*
Menu 550/850 DKK
♦ Innovative ♦ Elegant ♦

1744 orangery with a lovely summer terrace, set in Frederiksberg Gardens. Charming interior features walls painted with garden scenes and backing tracks of birdsong. Confident chef follows the seasons closely – ambitious, innovative dishes often display several elements.

XXX formel B (Kristian Møller)

Vesterbrogade 182-184, Frederiksberg (2 km via Vesterbrogade A 3)
✉ *1800 C – ℰ 33 25 10 66 – www.formel-b.dk*
– Closed 22 July-5 August and 23 December-7 January
Rest *– (dinner only) (booking essential)* Carte approx. 390 DKK
♦ Modern ♦ Fashionable ♦ Design ♦
Striking back-lit building with chic, split-level interior of polished marble and
stainless steel; sit by the window or above the glass-ceilinged wine cellar. Skilled
cooking of original, tasty, modern dishes. Confident young team and knowledgeable sommelier.
→ Langoustines with carrot purée. Turbot with parsley and garlic sauce,
braised veal tails. Sea buckthorn 'en surprise'.

XXX a|o|c

Dronningens Tvaergade 2 ✉ 1302 K – Ⓜ Kongens Nytorv – ℰ 33 11 11 45
– www.restaurantaoc.dk
– Closed July, Easter, Christmas, Sunday and Monday   **D2**
Rest *– (dinner only) (set menu only)* Menu 750/1200 DKK
♦ Modern ♦ Formal ♦
Large 17C vaulted cellar restaurant, owned and run by an experienced sommelier. 4, 5, 6 and 7 course set menus provide the full sensory experience, featuring
well-presented, very innovative combinations. Dishes are flavoursome and
arrive with a touch of theatre.
→ Langoustine baked in pine with cod crumble. Fillet of beef with beet-
root and smoked marrow. 'Birch Tree' ice cream, meringue and malt twigs.

XXX Grønbech & Churchill (Rasmus Grønbech)

Esplanden 48 / Amaliegade 49 ✉ 1256K – Ⓜ Kongens Nytorv
– ℰ 32213230 – www.gronbech-churchill.dk
– Closed 3 weeks summer, Easter, Christmas, Saturday lunch, Sunday and bank
holidays   **D1**
Rest – Menu 360/500 DKK
♦ Modern ♦ Elegant ♦ Neighbourhood ♦
Set in the basement of a lovely 19C building, this light, ultra-chic restaurant
offers crisp linen, fine china, minimalist styling and views of the chefs at work
in the designer kitchen. Three set menus offer cleanly and confidently prepared
dishes with bold flavours. Relaxed service courtesy of a young team.
→ Marinated brill, wild garlic, spring onions and chives. Braised lamb with
liquorice and malt. Plums with citrus herbs, frozen yoghurt and white chocolate.

XXX Era Ora

Overgaden neden Vandet 33B ✉ 1414 K – Ⓜ Christianshavn
– ℰ 32 54 06 93 – www.era-ora.dk
– Closed Christmas, 1 January, Easter and Sunday   **D3**
Rest *– (booking essential)* Menu 395/1300 DKK
♦ Italian ♦ Elegant ♦
Old warehouse dating back to the 1600s and set in a lovely canalside location.
Modern interior of glass and beaten copper. Well-stocked cellar features Tuscan
and Piedmont wines. Weekly set menu offers imported Italian produce in well-
executed dishes with personality.
→ Lobster sandwich and marrow mayonnaise. Variations of quail with smo-
ked aubergine. Almond semi-freddo with orange and ginger marmalade.

XXX Krogs

Gammel Strand 38 ✉ 1202 K – Ⓜ Kongens Nytorv – ℰ 33 15 89 15
– www.krogs.dk
– Closed 23 December-3 January and Sunday   **C2**
Rest *– (dinner only) (booking essential)* Menu 500 DKK – Carte 550/
850 DKK
♦ Fish and seafood ♦ Formal ♦
Characterful 18C house beside the canal, with a classical high-ceilinged dining
room. Fresh, locally caught fish is simply cooked, to produce classic Danish seafood dishes with a modern edge. Focus on French wines, particularly Burgundies.

XX **Kiin Kiin** (Lertchai Treetawatchaiwong) 🔲 ⑭ ⟳ 🈁 VISA ⑳ AE

🏵 *Guldbergsgade 21 ⊠ 2200 N – 𝒞 35 35 75 55 – www.kiin.dk*
– *Closed last 2 weeks July, Easter, Christmas and Sunday*　　**A1**
Rest – *(dinner only) (booking essential) (set menu only)* Menu 825 DKK
  ♦ Thai ♦ Exotic ♦

Charming restaurant whose name means 'come and eat'. Comfortable lounge for canapés; tasteful dining room with gold masks and fresh flowers. Set menu offers modern, personal interpretations of Thai dishes and features some unusual flavour combinations. Excellent service.
→ Marinated lobster in ginger. Green curry with chicken confit. Pandan ice cream with pistachio.

XX **Kokkeriet** ⑭ ⟳ VISA ⑳ AE ⓪

🏵 *Kronprinsessegade 64 ⊠ 1306 K – 𝒞 33 15 27 77 – www.kokkeriet.dk*
– *Closed 24-26 December, 15 July-5 August and Sunday*　　**C1**
Rest – *(dinner only) (booking essential) (set menu only)*
Menu 650/800 DKK
  ♦ Modern ♦ Intimate ♦ Design ♦

Discreet corner restaurant where a narrow, atmospheric room blends contemporary artwork and light fittings with a classic copper bar and formally set tables. Confidently executed, original cooking offers flavoursome, modern interpretations of classic Danish dishes. Smooth, unobtrusive service.
→ Seared mackerel, peas, carrots and ham. Veal with celeriac, apple and walnuts. Strawberries, frozen cream, sorrel and black pepper.

XX **Nimb Terrasse** 🈐 ⑭ ⟳ VISA ⑳ AE ⓪

Vesterbrogade 3 ⊠ 1630 V – ⓜ København Hovedbane Gård
– *𝒞 33 75 07 50 – www.nimb.dk*
– *Closed late September-mid April*　　**B3**
Rest – Menu 345 DKK (dinner) – Carte 365/495 DKK
  ♦ Modern ♦ Elegant ♦ Fashionable ♦

In the heart of the beautiful Tivoli Gardens, with a lovely terrace furnished in white. Spacious, light and airy interior, with a chic, contemporary feel. Interesting modern dishes present classical flavour combinations in original ways.

XX **Umami** 🔲 ⑭ ⟳ VISA ⑳ AE ⓪

Store Kongensgade 59 ⊠ 1264 K – ⓜ Kongens Nytorv – 𝒞 33 38 75 00
– *www.restaurantumami.dk*
– *Closed Easter Monday, Christmas-New Year and Sunday*　　**C/D2**
Rest – *(dinner only)* Menu 750 DKK – Carte 415/515 DKK
  ♦ Asian ♦ Fashionable ♦

Attractive, modern building with large cocktail bar and lounge on the ground floor. Elegant upper level boasts a stylish dining room and sushi counter. Japanese dishes have a European slant.

XX **Salt** – at Admiral Hotel ≤ 🈐 𝐏 VISA ⑳ AE ⓪

Toldbodgade 24-28 ⊠ 1253 K – ⓜ Kongens Nytorv – 𝒞 33 74 14 44
– *www.salt.dk*　　**D2**
Rest – Menu 385 DKK – Carte 415/545 DKK
  ♦ Modern ♦ Design ♦

Trendy hotel restaurant with a terrace, inspired by a French brasserie. Old wood beams and colourful, contemporary furniture blend together nicely. European cooking displays Scandinavian touches.

XX **Maven** 🈐 ⑭ ⟳ VISA ⑳ AE ⓪

Nikolaj Plads 10 ⊠ 1067K – ⓜ Kongens Nytorv – 𝒞 32201100
– *www.restaurantmaven.dk*
– *Closed 23-26 December and Sunday*　　**C2**
Rest – Menu 300 DKK (dinner) – Carte 300/419 DKK
  ♦ Traditional ♦ Friendly ♦ Intimate ♦

Warm, welcoming restaurant in an old church, boasting beamed ceilings, mullioned windows, antique wooden tables and a candlelit intimacy. Hearty, robust cooking mixes Danish classics with French and Italian dishes. Friendly young team.

DENMARK - COPENHAGEN

XX **Geist** 🛐 🗚 ⅍ 💳 ⚫⚫ 🗚 ⓪

Kongens Nytorv 8 ✉ 1050K – Ⓜ *Kongens Nytorv – ☎ 33133713*
– www.restaurantgeist.dk
– Closed Christmas **C2**
Rest *– (dinner only)* Carte 285/435 DKK
♦ Modern ♦ Design ♦ Trendy ♦

Lively restaurant with an open kitchen and a sexy, nightclub vibe, set in a striking red-brick property with floor to ceiling windows; in a superb spot overlooking the square. Cleverly crafted dishes display a light touch; 5 should suffice.

XX **Restaurationen** ⅍ 💳 ⚫⚫ 🗚 ⓪

Møntergade 19 ✉ 1116 K – Ⓜ *Kongens Nytorv – ☎ 33 14 94 95*
– www.restaurationen.com
– Closed July, August, 21 December-8 January, Easter, Sunday and Monday
Rest *– (dinner only)* Menu 485 DKK 🍷 **C2**
♦ Classic ♦ Formal ♦ Romantic ♦

Long-standing restaurant run by a well-known chef, who also owns the next door wine bar. The dining room displays some impressive pieces of vibrant modern art. Dishes use classic French techniques but feature some Danish influences.

XX **Sommelier** ⅍ ✧ 💳 ⚫⚫ 🗚 ⓪
☺

Bredgade 63-65 ✉ 1260 K – ☎ 33 11 45 15 – www.lesommelier.dk
– Closed 23 December-3 January **D1**
Rest *–* Menu 295/415 DKK *–* Carte 410/555 DKK 🍷
♦ French ♦ Brasserie ♦

Attractive French brasserie in the heart of the Old Town. The traditional main dining room and three private rooms boast simple wooden furniture and wine-themed posters. The carefully prepared, daily changing set menu uses quality ingredients and offers classic French dishes. Excellent wine list.

XX **Koefoed** 💳 ⚫⚫ 🗚 ⓪

Landgreven 3 (basement) ✉ 1301 K – Ⓜ *Kongens Nytorv – ☎ 56 48 22 24*
– www.restaurant-koefoed.dk
– Closed 22 December-6 January **C2**
Rest *– (booking essential at dinner)* Menu 225/495 DKK
– Carte 385/535 DKK
♦ Modern ♦ Intimate ♦

Intimate restaurant where everything from the produce to the glassware celebrates the island of Bornholm. Set menu and upscale smørrebrød at lunch; concise à la carte and tasting menu at dinner.

XX **Chai Wong** 🛐 🗚 ⅍ 💳 ⚫⚫ 🗚

Thorvaldsensvej 2 ✉ 1871 F – Ⓜ *Forum – ☎ 27 52 35 65*
– www.chaiwong.dk **A2**
Rest *–* Menu 175/475 DKK *–* Carte 215/405 DKK
♦ Asian ♦ Neighbourhood ♦ Individual ♦

Younger sister to Kiin Kiin, and similarly located in a residential area. Black and white interior with black tables, banquettes and cushioned stools. Menus are a fusion of Thai, Malaysian, Chinese and Japanese; desserts are a highlight.

XX **Gammel Mønt** ⅍ 💳 ⚫⚫ 🗚 ⓪

Gammel Mønt 41 ✉ 1117 K – Ⓜ *Kongens Nytorv – ☎ 33 15 10 60*
– www.gammel-moent.dk
– Closed July-15 August, 21 December-10 January, Saturday, Sunday and bank holidays **C2**
Rest *– (lunch only dinner Thursday-Friday)* Menu 375/600 DKK *–* Carte 305/860 DKK
♦ Traditional ♦ Cosy ♦

18C house with striking red façade. Simple basement room with communal tables; elegant, linen-laid restaurant above. Authentic, generous, seasonal cooking. Tasty herring and home-aged beef.

XX **The Dining Room** – at Radisson Blu Scandinavia Hotel   ≤ ⅙
Amager Boulevard 70, (25th Fl) ⊠ *2300 S*   **P** VISA ◉ AE ◉
– ◉ *Island Brygge –* ℰ *33 96 58 58 – www.thediningroom.dk*
– Closed Sunday, Monday and bank holidays   **C3**
Rest *– (dinner only)* Menu 345 DKK – Carte 385/605 DKK
♦ Modern ♦ Romantic ♦
Independently run hotel restaurant on the 25th floor of the Radisson Blu Scandinavia. Long, modern room boasts delightful city and sea views. Concise but appealing contemporary Danish menu.

XX **Lumskebugten**   ⛺ ⅙ ⇕ VISA ◉ ◉
Esplanaden 21 ⊠ *1263 K –* ℰ *33 15 60 29 – www.lumskebugten.dk*
– Closed 1 week Easter, 1 week Christmas, dinner Monday-Tuesday, Sunday and bank holidays   **D1**
Rest *–* Menu 400 DKK – Carte 255/535 DKK
♦ Traditional ♦ Cosy ♦ Retro ♦
19C quayside pavilion, where the Royal Family occasionally dine. Several small rooms adorned with maritime memorabilia and paintings. Local menus offer a wide selection of classical fish dishes.

XX **Il Grappolo Blu**   ⅙ VISA ◉ AE
Vester Farimagsgade 35 ⊠ *1606 –* ◉ *Vesterport –* ℰ *33 11 57 20*
– www.ilgrappoloblu.com
– Closed Easter, Christmas and Sunday   **B3**
Rest *– (booking essential) (set menu only)* Menu 445/888 DKK
♦ Italian ♦ Rustic ♦ Elegant ♦
Cosy, personally run restaurant with dark panelling and ornate carvings. Choose 10, 15 or 20 courses from the tasting menu. Well-prepared, authentic Italian dishes include appealing antipasti and tasty pastas. Booking is essential at lunch.

XX **Alberto K** – at Radisson Blu Royal Hotel   ≤ AC **P** VISA ◉ AE ◉
Hammerichsgade 1 ⊠ *1611 V –* ◉ *København Hovedbane Gård*
– ℰ *33 42 61 61 – www.alberto-k.dk*
– Closed 3 weeks summer, 24-26 December, 1-7 January and Sunday
Rest *– (dinner only) (set menu only)* Menu 675/800 DKK   **B3**
♦ Modern ♦ Design ♦
Located on the 20th floor of the Radisson Blu Royal hotel and boasting stunning panoramic views over the city. 1960s inspired Danish design interior. Contemporary European set 7 course dinner menu.

XX **Godt**   VISA ◉ ◉
Gothersgade 38 ⊠ *1123 K –* ◉ *Kongens Nytorv –* ℰ *33 15 21 22*
– www.restaurant-godt.dk
– Closed 1 week Easter, early July- early August, Christmas-New Year, Sunday, Monday and bank holidays   **C2**
Rest *– (dinner only) (set menu only)* Menu 600/680 DKK
♦ Classic ♦ Friendly ♦
Stylish restaurant seating just 20, with old WWII shells acting as unique candle holders. Traditional French and European 4 and 5 course daily menus, formed around the latest market produce.

XX **Bistro Boheme**   AC ⇕ VISA ◉ AE ◉
Esplanaden 8 ⊠ *1263 K –* ℰ *70 22 08 70 – www.bistroboheme.dk*
– Closed 23-26 December, Easter and Sunday   **D1**
Rest *–* Carte 345/585 DKK
♦ Classic ♦ Bistro ♦
Former florist and gallery near the Old Town. Airy, split-level interior with buzzy atmosphere. Unfussy, classical French menus display Danish overtones. Good choice of wines by the glass.

XX · ☺ | **Frederiks Have** 🍴 ⅃⅄ ⅦⅠⅪⅬ ⓄⓄ ⒶⒺ ⓪

Smallegade 41, (entrance on Virginiavej) (West : 1.5 km. via Gammel Kongevej A 3) ✉ *2000 F –* Ⓜ *Frederiksberg –* ✆ *38 88 33 35*
– www.frederikshave.dk
– Closed Easter, Christmas-New Year and Sunday
Rest – Menu 268/385 DKK – Carte 385/515 DKK
◆ Danish ◆ Neighbourhood ◆

Sweet neighbourhood restaurant with a large terrace, set just off the main street in a residential area. Choice of a set price menu or à la carte, each consisting of well-presented, modern Danish dishes with a classical base. Tasty sweet and sour combinations feature.

XX | **Mash** ㎇ ⟷ ⅦⅠⅪⅬ ⓄⓄ ⒶⒺ ⓪

Bredgade 20 ✉ *1260 K –* Ⓜ *Kongens Nytorv –* ✆ *33 13 93 00*
– www.mashsteak.dk
– Closed Saturday and Sunday lunch **D2**
Rest – *(booking essential at dinner)* Carte approx. 450 DKK 🍴
◆ Meats and grills ◆ Brasserie ◆

Smart, American-style steakhouse with a trendy bar, red leather booths and aged meats on display. Simple, classical steak dishes and some fish alternatives. Largely French and American wine list.

XX | **L' Osteria del Grappolo Blu** ⅦⅠⅪⅬ ⓄⓄ ⒶⒺ

Vester Farimagsgade 37 ✉ *1606 V –* Ⓜ *Vesterport –* ✆ *33 12 57 20*
– www.osteria.dk – Closed Easter, Christmas and Sunday **B2/3**
Rest – Carte 315/485 DKK
◆ Italian ◆ Friendly ◆

More informal counterpart to Il Grappolo Blu, with smart osteria styling. Authentic homemade dishes have their roots in southern Italy; bread and ice cream are made on the premises daily.

X · ☺ | **Orangeriet** ≼ 🍴 ⅃⅄ ⟷ ⅦⅠⅪⅬ ⓄⓄ ⒶⒺ ⓪

Kronprinsessegade 13, (Kongens Have) ✉ *1306 K –* Ⓜ *Kongens Nytorv –* ✆ *33 11 13 07 – www.restaurant-orangeriet.dk*
– Closed 1 week late October, first 2 weeks January and Sunday dinner
Rest – Menu 255/355 DKK – Carte 392/512 DKK **C2**
◆ Danish ◆ Romantic ◆ Friendly ◆

Set in a charming location, with a bright dining room and delightful terrace overlooking the King's Garden. Typical orangery style with white walls, simple design furniture and lush plants, including an orange tree. Appealing selection of unfussy, carefully executed Danish dishes. Relaxed, amiable service.

X · ☺ | **Kanalen** ≼ 🍴 ⅃⅄ ⟷ Ⓟ ⅦⅠⅪⅬ ⓄⓄ ⒶⒺ ⓪

Christianshavn-Wilders Plads 1-3 ✉ *1403 K –* Ⓜ *Christianshavn – ✆ 32 95 13 30 – www.restaurant-kanalen.dk*
– Closed Sunday and bank holidays **D3**
Rest – *(booking essential)* Menu 255/360 DKK – Carte 448/596 DKK
◆ Danish ◆ Bistro ◆ Cosy ◆

Former Harbour Police office with a lovely terrace, set in a delightful canalside location. Red façade masks a simple, informal dining room with numerous French windows facing the water. Tiny open kitchen prepares a well-balanced Danish menu with light French touches.

X · ⮑ | **Relæ** (Christian Puglisi) ⅃⅄ ⅦⅠⅪⅬ ⓄⓄ ⒶⒺ

Jægersborggade 41 ✉ *2200 N –* ✆ *36 96 66 09 – www.restaurant-relae.dk*
– Closed July, January, Sunday-Tuesday and bank holidays **A1**
Rest – *(dinner only) (booking essential)* Menu 375 DKK
◆ Modern ◆ Minimalist ◆ Fashionable ◆

Book well in advance for a table at this simply styled restaurant – or grab a seat at the counter to watch the talented team in the open kitchen. 2 daily set menus – one features meat and fish and one is vegetarian: unfussy, flavourful dishes and original combinations, with innovative use of vegetables.
➜ Lamb with shrimps and dill. Calves' sweetbread with cauliflower and basil. Corn, breadcrumbs and marjoram.

DENMARK - COPENHAGEN

Kadeau (Nicolai Nørregaard) ⚐ VISA ✪ AE

Wildersgade 10A ✉ *1408* – **M** *Christianshavn* – ℰ *33 25 22 23*
– *www.kadeau.dk*
– *Closed Easter, July, Christmas, Sunday and Monday*   **D3**
Rest – *(dinner only) (booking essential)* Menu 500/2000 DKK
♦ Modern ♦ Simple ♦ Individual ♦

Simple little restaurant showcasing cuisine and ingredients from Bornholm island, just to the east of the mainland, from where the passionate owners originate. Cooking is honest, original and interesting, with light, modern dishes featuring many texture variations and well-balanced, flavoursome combinations.
➔ Cod, cabbages, green strawberries and trout roe. Lamb with celeriac, verbena pear and smoked butter. Jerusalem artichoke and wild carrot buttermilk, browned butter and hazel.

Retour ⚐ VISA ✪ AE ⓞ

Tordenskjoldsgade 11 ✉ *1055* – **M** *Kongens Nytorv* – ℰ *33 33 83 30*
– *www.retour.dk*
– *Closed Christmas and Sunday*   **D2**
Rest – *(dinner only) (booking essential)* Carte 300/485 DKK
♦ French ♦ Bistro ♦ Cosy ♦

Busy, buzzy bistro hidden behind the theatre, with simple furnishings and tightly packed tables. Concise, classically based French menus display a few Danish touches. Expertly prepared dishes keep things satisfyingly straightforward, relying on good quality ingredients and showcasing their natural flavours.

Radio ⚐ VISA ✪ AE

Julius Thomsens Gade 12 ✉ *1632 V* – **M** *Forum* – ℰ *25102733*
– *www.restaurantradio.dk*
– *Closed 3 weeks summer, Christmas-New Year, Sunday and Monday*
Rest – *(dinner only and lunch Friday-Saturday) (booking*   **A2**
essential) (set menu only) Menu 300 DKK
♦ Modern ♦ Simple ♦ Neighbourhood ♦

Informal restaurant with an unfussy urban style, typified by wooden walls and cool anglepoise lighting. Oft-changing set menus feature full-flavoured, good value dishes, with organic produce from the chefs' own fields just outside the city.

M/S Amerika 🌤 ⚐ VISA ✪ AE

Dampfaergevej 8, Pakhus 12, Amerikakaj (3 km via Folke Bernadottes Allée C 1) ✉ *2100 K* – ℰ *35 26 90 30* – *www.msamerika.dk*
– *Closed Sunday and bank holidays*
Rest – Menu 275/295 DKK – Carte 395/485 DKK
♦ Danish ♦ Brasserie ♦

Characterful 19C warehouse on the quayside. Industrial, brasserie-style interior with an open kitchen, a friendly atmosphere and a popular terrace. The daily blackboard menu offers Danish brasserie dishes.

L'Altro 🄰🄺 ⚐ VISA ✪ AE ⓞ

Torvegade 62 ✉ *1400 K* – **M** *Christianshavn* – ℰ *32 54 54 06*
– *www.laltro.dk*
– *Closed Christmas,1 January, Easter and Sunday*   **D3**
Rest – *(dinner only) (booking essential) (set menu only)* Menu 380/450 DKK
♦ Italian ♦ Intimate ♦

Cosy restaurant with a warm, rustic style, that celebrates *la cucina de la casa* – the homely Italian spirit of 'mama's kitchen'. Regularly changing menus feature tasty family recipes from Umbria and Tuscany; appealing dishes rely on fresh, good quality ingredients.

DENMARK - COPENHAGEN

Marv & Ben ✗ 😊   ⅓ 🆅🅸🆂🅰 ⓐ 🅰🅴 ⓞ

Snaregade 4 ⊠ 1205K – ⓜ Kongens Nytorv – ℰ 33 91 01 91
– www.marvogben.dk
– Closed Christmas, Easter and Sunday   **C2/3**
Rest *– (booking advisable)* Menu 285 DKK
♦ Modern ♦ Friendly ♦ Bistro ♦

A simple, two-floored restaurant set down a cobbled street off the main tourist track. Styling is stark and modern, with the kitchen on display behind a glass wall. Gutsy, flavourful, well-crafted dishes, with the focus on produce from the chefs' own fields. Friendly service; sometimes by the chefs themselves.

Famo 51 ✗   ⅓ ⇔ 🆅🅸🆂🅰 ⓐ 🅰🅴

Gammel Kongevej 51 ⊠ 1610 V – ℰ 33 22 22 50 – www.famo.dk
– Closed Christmas-New Year and Sunday   **A3**
Rest *– (dinner only) (booking essential)* Menu 400 DKK
♦ Italian ♦ Minimalist ♦

Laid-back restaurant with an intimate, two-tabled cellar. Extensive daily set menu offers rustic Italian dishes and relies on seasonal ingredients. On Fridays they only offer fish and shellfish.

Kødbyens Fiskebar ✗ 😊   ⅓ 🅿 🆅🅸🆂🅰 ⓐ 🅰🅴 ⓞ

Den Hvide Kødby, Flæsketorvet 100 (1 km via Halmtorvet and Sønder Blvd B3) ⊠ 1711 V – ℰ 32 15 56 56 – www.fiskebaren.dk
– Closed 24-25 December
Rest *– (dinner only and lunch Saturday-Sunday)* Carte 250/475 DKK
♦ Fish and seafood ♦ Trendy ♦

Set in a former meat market, with a buzzy atmosphere and a trendy, industrial feel. Sit on wall-mounted banquettes or on high stools at the central aluminium bar. Concise menu features fresh, simply prepared seafood dishes, which are based around the latest catch.

Enomania ✗ 😊   ⅓ 🆅🅸🆂🅰 ⓐ 🅰🅴 ⓞ

Vesterbrogade 187 (2.5 km via Vesterbrogade A 3) ⊠ 1800 C
– ℰ 33 23 60 80 – www.enomania.dk
– Closed 13 July-5 August, 12-21 October, 21 December-6 January, 8-17 February, Easter, 17-21 April- Saturday-Monday and bank holidays
Rest *– (dinner only lunch Thursday-Friday) (booking essential)*
Menu 365 DKK – Carte 330/360 DKK 🍷
♦ Italian ♦ Wine bar ♦

Simple, bistro-style restaurant near Frederiksberg Park; its name meaning 'Wine Mania'. Wine cellar with a table for tasting; excellent list of over 600 bins, mostly from Piedmont and Burgundy. Straightforward, tasty Italian dishes from a daily 4 course set menu.

Mêlée ✗ 😊   ⅓ 🆅🅸🆂🅰 ⓐ 🅰🅴

Martensens Allé 16 ⊠ 1828 – ⓜ Frederiksberg – ℰ 35 13 11 34 – www.melee.dk
– Closed July, 1 week Easter, 1 week autumn, 2 weeks Christmas and Saturday-Monday   **A3**
Rest *– (dinner only) (booking essential)* Menu 360 DKK – Carte 285/385 DKK
♦ French ♦ Friendly ♦ Bistro ♦

Bustling neighbourhood bistro with a friendly atmosphere, run by an experienced team. Modern, country-style French cooking with Danish influences; expect bold flavours and generous portions. Concise menu with a daily blackboard special. French wines accompany.

Søren k ✗ 😊   ⧉ 🍴 🅰🅺 ⅓ 🆅🅸🆂🅰 ⓐ 🅰🅴 ⓞ

Søren Kierkegaards Plads 1 ⊠ 1221 K – ℰ 33 47 49 49 – www.soerenk.dk
– Closed Sunday and bank holidays   **C3**
Rest *–* Menu 280/340 DKK – Carte 340/440 DKK
♦ Modern ♦ Minimalist ♦

Located in the contemporary 'Black Diamond' building. Modern dining room with design furniture, floor to ceiling windows overlooking the quayside and a lovely terrace. Menu features Danish recipes, Scandinavian ingredients, French influences and modern touches.

Famo

🍴 ☺ ↳ VISA ⬤ AE

Saxogade 3 ✉ 1662 V – ℰ 33 23 22 50 – www.famo.dk
– Closed Christmas and New Year **A3**
Rest – *(dinner only) (booking essential) (set menu only)* Menu 370 DKK
♦ Italian ♦ Bistro ♦

Simple Italian restaurant set in a small street; its red and white walls hung with contemporary art. Extensive daily menus are presented orally; with a choice of eight antipasti, followed by tasty homemade pasta, generous main courses and authentic desserts.

Ché Fè

🍴 ↳ VISA ⬤ AE ⓪

Borgergade 17a ✉ 1300 K – ⓜ Kongens Nytorv – ℰ 33 11 17 21
– www.biotrattoria.dk
– Closed Easter, Christmas and 1 January **C2**
Rest – *(dinner only) (booking essential)* Carte 300/364 DKK
♦ Italian ♦ Simple ♦ Neighbourhood ♦

An unassuming façade conceals an appealing trattoria with pastel hues and coffee bean sack curtains. Menus offer authentic Italian classics, including home-made pastas; virtually all ingredients are imported from small, organic producers.

Aamanns Etablissement

🍴 ↳ VISA ⬤ AE

Øster Farimagsgade 12 ✉ 2100 Ø – ⓜ Nørreport – ℰ 35 55 33 10
– www.aamanns.dk
– Closed July, Christmas, Sunday dinner, Monday and Tuesday **C1**
Rest – *(booking advisable)* Menu 165/285 DKK – Carte 180/270 DKK
♦ Danish ♦ Bistro ♦

Cosy, contemporary restaurant with an informal atmosphere and a cheery team. Concise, seasonal menus blend classical techniques and traditional smørrebrød with more modern 'small plates'. 1-5 course dinner menus come with wine pairings.

Oubaek

🍴 ↳ VISA ⬤ AE ⓪

Store Kongensgade 52 ✉ 1264 K – ⓜ Kongens Nytorv – ℰ 33 32 32 09
– www.restaurantoubaek.dk
– Closed mid July-mid August, 23 December-3 January, Saturday lunch and Sunday **C/D2**
Rest – *(booking essential)* Menu 425 DKK – Carte 300/450 DKK
♦ French ♦ Friendly ♦

Unassuming modern restaurant with 18C wood floors and tables set beside the open kitchen and on a mezzanine. Unfussy, simply presented French dishes display a Danish touch; dinner consists of small 'taster' plates. Friendly team.

Dim Sum

🍴 ↳ VISA ⬤ AE

Sankt Annae Plads 16 ✉ 1250 K – ⓜ Kongens Nytorv – ℰ 35 35 60 05
– www.restaurantdimsum.dk
– Closed last 3 weeks July, Sunday and Monday **D2**
Rest – *(booking essential)* Menu 150/350 DKK – Carte 295/385 DKK
♦ Dim sum ♦ Fashionable ♦

Narrow restaurant with a large black counter overlooking the open kitchen. Contemporary Chinese cooking; the fixed price menu offers a good selection of dim sum. Well-paced service and a laid-back ambience.

Manfreds & Vin

🍴 ↳ VISA ⬤ AE

Jægersborggade 40 ✉ 2200N – ℰ 36 96 65 33 – www.manfreds.dk
– Closed Christmas and Monday **A1**
Rest – Menu 245 DKK – Carte 250/295 DKK 🍷
♦ Traditional ♦ Wine bar ♦ Neighbourhood ♦

Simple, rustic restaurant in an up-and-coming district; sit at hand-painted Formica tables or at the tall bar facing the open kitchen. Tasty seasonal sharing plates showcase top quality Danish produce. Relaxed yet attentive service.

✗ **Famo Metro**   AC ↳ VISA ⦿ AE ⓪

Øster Søgade 114 ⊠ 2100 Ø – 𝒸 35 55 66 30 – www.famo.dk
– Closed 24-26 December and Sunday   **C1**
Rest – Menu 350/400 DKK – Carte 410/445 DKK
♦ Italian ♦ Minimalist ♦
The 3rd in the Famo group. Modern dining room boasts floor to ceiling windows and water views. Second basement room has a rotisserie fireplace. Classical Italian dishes include homemade pastas.

✗ **Retour Steak**   ↳ VISA ⦿ AE ⓪

Ny Østergade 21 ⊠ 1101 K – Ⓜ Kongens Nytorv – 𝒸 33 16 17 19
– www.retoursteak.dk
– Closed Christmas   **C2**
Rest – *(booking essential)* Carte 275/465 DKK
♦ Meats and grills ♦ Bistro ♦ Friendly ♦
Little sister to Retour, with a relaxed, informal atmosphere, a stark white interior and contrasting black furnishings. A small menu offers simply prepared grills, good quality American rib-eye steaks and an affordable selection of wines.

SMØRREBRØD *The following list of simpler restaurants and cafés/bars specialise in Danish open sandwiches and are generally open from 10.00am to 4.00pm.*

✗ **Sankt Annae**   🏠 ↳ ✿ VISA ⦿ AE ⓪

Sankt Annae Plads 12 ⊠ 1250 K – Ⓜ Kongens Nytorv – 𝒸 33 12 54 97
– www.restaurantsanktannae.dk
– Closed 23 December-1 January, 28 March-1 April, Saturday and Sunday
Rest – *(lunch only) (booking essential)* Carte 185/385 DKK   **D2**
♦ Smørrebrød ♦ Cosy ♦
Attractive terraced building from 1837, with charming maritime décor. Seasonal à la carte and daily blackboard menu: prices can vary so check before ordering. The lobster salad and shrimps – fresh from the local fjords – are a hit.

✗ **Amalie**   ↳ VISA ⦿ AE ⓪

Amaliegade 11 ⊠ 1256 K – Ⓜ Kongens Nytorv – 𝒸 33 12 88 10
– www.restaurantamalie.dk
– Closed Easter, Christmas-New Year, Sunday and bank holidays   **D2**
Rest – *(lunch only) (booking essential)* Carte 206/332 DKK
♦ Smørrebrød ♦ Intimate ♦ Inn ♦
Charming 18C townhouse next to Amalienborg Palace. Two tiny, cosy rooms displaying old paintings and elegant porcelain. Authentic Danish menu, with a large choice of herring, salmon and salads.

✗ **Schønnemann**   ↳ VISA ⦿ AE ⓪

Hauser Plads 16 ⊠ 1127 K – Ⓜ Nørreport – 𝒸 33 12 07 85
– www.restaurantschonnemann.dk
– Closed 28 March-1 April, 15 July-5 August, 22 December-2 January, Sunday and bank holidays   **C2**
Rest – *(lunch only) (booking essential)* Menu 338/528 DKK – Carte 198/414 DKK
♦ Smørrebrød ♦ Rustic ♦
Opened in 1877 and still putting sand on the floor of the rustic basement room as it did in its early days. Choose from smørrebrød, open sandwiches and a large selection of herring and tartar dishes.

✗ **The Royal Cafe**   🏠 AC ↳ VISA ⦿ AE ⓪

Amagertorv 6 ⊠ 1160K – Ⓜ Kongens Nytorv – 𝒸 33 12 11 22
– www.theroyalcafe.dk – Closed 24 and 31 December   **C2**
Rest – *(lunch only)* Carte 215/350 DKK
♦ Smørrebrød ♦ Fashionable ♦
Funky eatery in the Royal Copenhagen china showroom, with a homemade pastry counter and a peaceful courtyard terrace. Sit at a communal table for breakfast, afternoon tea or unique 21C 'smushies' – smørrebrød crossed with sushi (Mon-Sat).

X **Slotskælderen hos Gitte Kik**　　　⇔ 𝚅𝙸𝚂𝙰 ⓒ 𝙰𝙴 ⓞ

Fortunstræ 4 ✉ *1065 K* – ⓜ *Kongens Nytorv* – 𝒞 *33 11 15 37*
– www.slotskaelderen.dk
– Closed July, Sunday, Monday and bank holidays　　　　**C2**
Rest *– (lunch only) (booking essential)* Carte 185/275 DKK
♦ Smørrebrød ♦ Family ♦

Family-run since 1910, an established restaurant which sets the benchmark for this type of cuisine. Rustic inner filled with portraits and city scenes. Around 50 choices of appealing smørrebrød.

ENVIRONS OF COPENHAGEN

AT NORDHAVN North : 3 km by Østbanegade and Road 2

XX **Paustian**　　　⇐ 🏠 ⇔ 🅿 𝚅𝙸𝚂𝙰 ⓒ 𝙰𝙴 ⓞ

Kalkbraenderiløbskaj 2 ✉ *2100* – 𝒞 *39 18 55 01*
– www.restaurantpaustian.dk
– Closed Christmas, Saturday dinner, Sunday and Monday
Rest *– (booking advisable)* Carte 279/380 DKK
♦ Danish ♦ Fashionable ♦ Design ♦

Smart, modern restaurant next to a furniture store of the same name, with an open kitchen and views over the marina. Tasty, traditional Danish cooking uses seasonal, local produce. Courtyard terrace with a charcoal grill for the summer.

AT SKOVSHOVED North : 10 km by Østbanegade and Road 2

🏨 **Skovshoved**　　　🛜 🏊 🅿 𝚅𝙸𝚂𝙰 ⓒ 𝙰𝙴 ⓞ
😊

Strandvejen 267 ✉ *2920* – ⓜ *Charlottenlund* – 𝒞 *39 64 00 28*
– www.skovshovedhotel.com
21 rm – †1225/1425 DKK ††1525/1725 DKK, � 155 DKK – 1 suite
Rest *– (closed 24-26 December and 1 January)* Menu 295/395 DKK
– Carte 255/555 DKK
♦ Inn ♦ Cosy ♦

Set in a charming village and dating back to the 1890s; after the original 1660 hotel burnt down. Modern lounge furnished with white sofas and armchairs. Cosy, Scandinavian-style bedrooms: some look out to sea and some boast balconies. Appealing Danish dishes at lunch; more creative options served in the evening.

AT KLAMPENBORG North : 13 km by Østanegade and Road 2

XX **Den Røde Cottage** (Anita Klemensen and Lars Thomsen)　　🏠
🍴

Strandvejen 550 ✉ *2930* – ⓜ *Klampenborg*　　⇔ ⇆ 𝚅𝙸𝚂𝙰 ⓒ 𝙰𝙴 ⓞ
– 𝒞 39 90 46 14 – www.cottagerne.dk
– Closed 23 December-11 February and Sunday October-April
Rest *– (dinner only) (booking essential)* Menu 500/800 DKK
♦ Danish ♦ Design ♦

Charming former Forestry Officer's house dating back to 1881 and built on the site of an old plantation. Small but romantic dining room is set with Royal Copenhagen porcelain; lovely terrace offers partial sea views. The talented team offer a monthly Nordic menu, which is informed by quality seasonal produce.
➙ Lobster with peas, mint and almonds. Quail with cherry and fennel. Strawberries, verbena and buttermilk.

X **Den Gule Cottage**　　　⇐ 🏠 𝚅𝙸𝚂𝙰 ⓒ 𝙰𝙴 ⓞ

Strandvejen 506 ✉ *2930* – ⓜ *Klampenborg* – 𝒞 *39 64 06 91*
– www.cottageerne.dk
– Closed 23 December-14 February and Monday-Wednesday 14 October-April
Rest *– (booking advisable)* Menu 325 DKK – Carte 275/375 DKK
♦ Danish ♦ Inn ♦ Minimalist ♦

Lovely 1844 cottage facing the beach; from the same team as Den Røde. Two tiny, simply decorated rooms and a large terrace with pleasant sea views. Unfussy menu of five main dishes, salads and cheese plates.

AT SØLLERØD   North : 20 km by Tagensvej (take the train to Holte then taxi)
- ⊠ 2840 Holte

Søllerød Kro   ⛲ ⇆ ✿ P VISA ⨋ AE ⓪

Søllerødvej 35 (at Sollerod North : 20 km by Tagensvej) ⊠ 2840
– ℰ 45 80 25 05 – www.soelleroed-kro.dk
– *Closed 11-20 February, Easter, Monday and Tuesday*
Rest – Menu 530/995 DKK – Carte 645/1050 DKK ♨

♦ Classic ♦ Inn ♦

Characterful 17C thatched inn with three small but stylish dining rooms and a delightful courtyard terrace. Superb wine list features plenty of Burgundy and champagne. Choose from an array of menus that offer light, refined dishes with fresh, sharp flavours.

➜ Baerii caviar 'en surprise'. Lobster with Jerusalem artichokes. Rhubarb with vanilla.

AT KASTRUP AIRPORT   Southeast : 10 km by Amager Boulevard

Hilton Copenhagen Airport   ⇐ ⅃ ⨁ ⅏ ◲ ⅗ ◳ ⇆ ⦡ ⛵

Ellehammersvej 20 ⊠ 2770   ⛟ VISA ⨋ AE ⓪
– ⓜ *København Lufthavn Kastrup* – ℰ 32 50 15 01
– *www.copenhagen.hilton.com*
381 rm – ▮1195/2595 DKK ▮▮1195/2595 DKK, ⬭ 195 DKK – 1 suite
Rest Hamlet – ℰ 32 44 53 53 *(closed Easter, Christmas, Saturday and Sunday) (dinner only)* Menu 395 DKK – Carte 465/710 DKK
Rest Horizon – *(closed Saturday lunch and Sunday dinner)* Menu 270/305 DKK – Carte 315/655 DKK

♦ Business ♦ Modern ♦

Smart business hotel accessed from the airport via a glass walkway. Spacious, well-maintained bedrooms with excellent sound-proofing and good views from the higher floors. Asian-inspired Ni'mat Spa. Nordic specialties served in Hamlet. Buffet meals in Horizon.

AT ØRESTAD   South : 6 km by Amager Boulevard and Amagerfaelledvej

---

Crowne Plaza Towers   ⇐ ⅃ ⅗ rm, ◳ ⇆ ⦡ ⛵ ⛟

Ørestads boulevard 114-118 ⊠ 2300 S   VISA ⨋ AE ⓪
– ⓜ *Ørestads* – ℰ 88 77 66 55 – www.cpcopenhagen.dk
363 rm – ▮995/2095 DKK ▮▮995/2095 DKK, ⬭ 175 DKK – 3 suites
Rest Storm – *(closed 31 December and Sunday dinner)* Carte 338/555 DKK

♦ Business ♦ Modern ♦

Modern tower block between the city and the airport, next to a huge shopping mall. Airy, minimalist lobby and bar. Spacious, contemporary bedrooms with bright furniture and good views. One of the world's greenest hotels. Restaurant offers Scandinavian cuisine.

FINLAND
SUOMI

→ **AREA:**
338 145 km² (130 558 sq mi).

→ **POPULATION:**
5 401 267 inhabitants.
Density = 16 per km².

→ **CAPITAL:** Helsinki.

→ **CURRENCY:** Euro (€).

→ **GOVERNMENT:**
Parliamentary republic (since 1917).
Member of European Union since 1995.

→ **LANGUAGES:**
Finnish (a Finno-Ugric language
related to Estonian) spoken by
92% of Finns, Swedish (6%) and
Sami (some 7 000 native speakers).
English is widely spoken.

→ **PUBLIC HOLIDAYS:**
New Years' Day (1 Jan); Epiphany
(6 Jan); Good Friday (late Mar/Apr);
Easter Monday (late Mar/Apr);
May Day (1 May); Ascension Day
(May); Epiphany (6 Jan); Midsummer
(mid June); All Saints' Day
(1 Nov); Independence Day (6 Dec);
Christmas Day (25 Dec); Boxing Day
(26 Dec).

→ **LOCAL TIME:**
GMT+2 hours in winter and GMT
+3 hours in summer.

→ **CLIMATE:**
Temperate continental with very
cold winters and mild summers
(Helsinki: January -7°C; July 17°C).
Midnight sun: for several weeks
around Midsummer, the sun never
sets in the north. Snow settles from
early Dec-Apr in the south and
centre of the country.
Northern Lights (Aurora Borealis)
visible in the north on clear, dark
nights; highest frequency in Feb-
Mar and Sep-Oct.

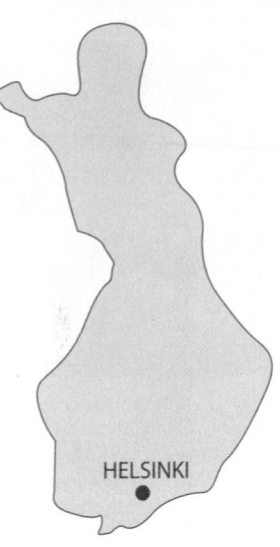

HELSINKI

→ **EMERGENCY:**
Police, Medical Assistance and Fire
Brigade: ☏ **112**

→ **ELECTRICITY:**
230 volts AC, 50Hz; 2 round pin
sockets.

→ **FORMALITIES:**
Travellers from the European Union
(EU), Switzerland, Iceland and the
main countries of North and South
America need a national identity
card or passport (America: passport
required) to visit Finland for less
than three months (tourism or
business purposes). For visitors
from other countries a visa may be
required, in addition to a passport,
especially for those wishing to
stay for longer than three months.
If you plan to visit Russia while in
Finland, you must purchase an
appropriate visa in advance in your
own country. We advise you to
check with your embassy before
travelling.

Helsinki
HELSINGFORS

Population: 602 200

Ph. Robic/MICHELIN

Cool, clean and chic, the 'Daughter of the Baltic' sits prettily on a peninsula, jutting out between the landmasses of its historical overlords, Sweden and Russia. Surrounded on three sides by water, Helsinki is a busy port, but that only tells a small part of the story: forests grow in abundance around here and trees reach down to the lapping shores. This is a striking city to look at: it was rebuilt in the 19C after a fire, and many of the buildings have a handsome neoclassical or art nouveau façade. Shoppers can browse the picturesque outdoor food and tourist markets stretching along the main harbour, where island-hopping ferries ply their trade.

In a country with over 200,000 lakes it would be pretty hard to escape a green sensibility, and the Finnish capital has made sure that concrete and stone have never taken priority over its distinctive features of trees, water and open space. There are bridges at every turn connecting the city's varied array of small islands, and a ten kilometre strip of parkland acts as a spine running vertically up from the centre. Renowned as a city of cool, it's somewhere that also revels in a hot nightlife and even hotter saunas – this is where they were invented. And if your blast of dry heat has left you wanting a refreshing dip, there's always a freezing lake close at hand.

HELSINKI IN...

→ ONE DAY
Harbour market place, Uspensky Cathedral, Lutheran Cathedral, Katajanokka, Mannerheimintie.

→ TWO DAYS
A ferry to Suomenlinna, Church in the Rock, the nightlife of Fredrikinkatu.

→ THREE DAYS
Central Park, the Sibelius monument, Esplanadi.

PRACTICAL INFORMATION

ARRIVAL-DEPARTURE

✈ Helsinki-Vantaa Airport is 19km north of the city.
A taxi will take 20-30min to the centre. Buses to the Central Bus Station take 40min.

GETTING AROUND

Getting across Helsinki is fast and easy: trams and buses whizz you round efficiently. A single ticket is cheap and good for any transfers you make within an hour; buy them from the driver, ticket machines, kiosks, metro stations or the ferry terminal. If you need to make several journeys during one day or several days, a day ticket is a good choice. You can choose a ticket valid for 1 to 7 days. The Helsinki Card is valid for one, two or three days with a sliding scale of prices, and allows you unlimited transport plus free admission to museums and attractions. There are regular ferries from the harbour to Suomenlinna; they sail a little less frequently to the other main islands.

CALENDAR HIGHLIGHTS

June
Helsinki Day (the city's birthday), Juhannus (midsummer).

June-July
Helsinki Cup (international youth football tournament).

August
Helsinki Festival.

October
Baltic Herring Festival.

December
Traditional Christmas Markets, Lucia Parade to the Lutheran Cathedral.

EATING OUT

Local - and we mean local - ingredients are very much to the fore in the kitchens of Helsinki's restaurants. Produce is sourced from the country's abundant lakes, forests and seas, so your menu will assuredly be laden with the likes of reindeer, smoked reindeer, reindeer's tongue, elk in aspic, lampreys, Arctic char, Baltic herring, snow grouse and cloudberries. Generally speaking, complicated, fussy preparations are overlooked for those that let the natural flavours shine through. In the autumn, markets are piled high with woodland mushrooms, often from Lapland, and chefs make the most of this bounty. Local alcoholic drinks include schnapps, vodka and liqueurs made from local berries, while lakka (made from cloudberries) and mesimarja (brambleberries) are definitely worth discovering – you may not find them in any other European city. You'd find coffee anywhere in Europe, but not to the same extent as here: Finns are among the world's biggest coffee drinkers. In the gastronomic restaurants, lunch is a simpler affair, often with limited choice.

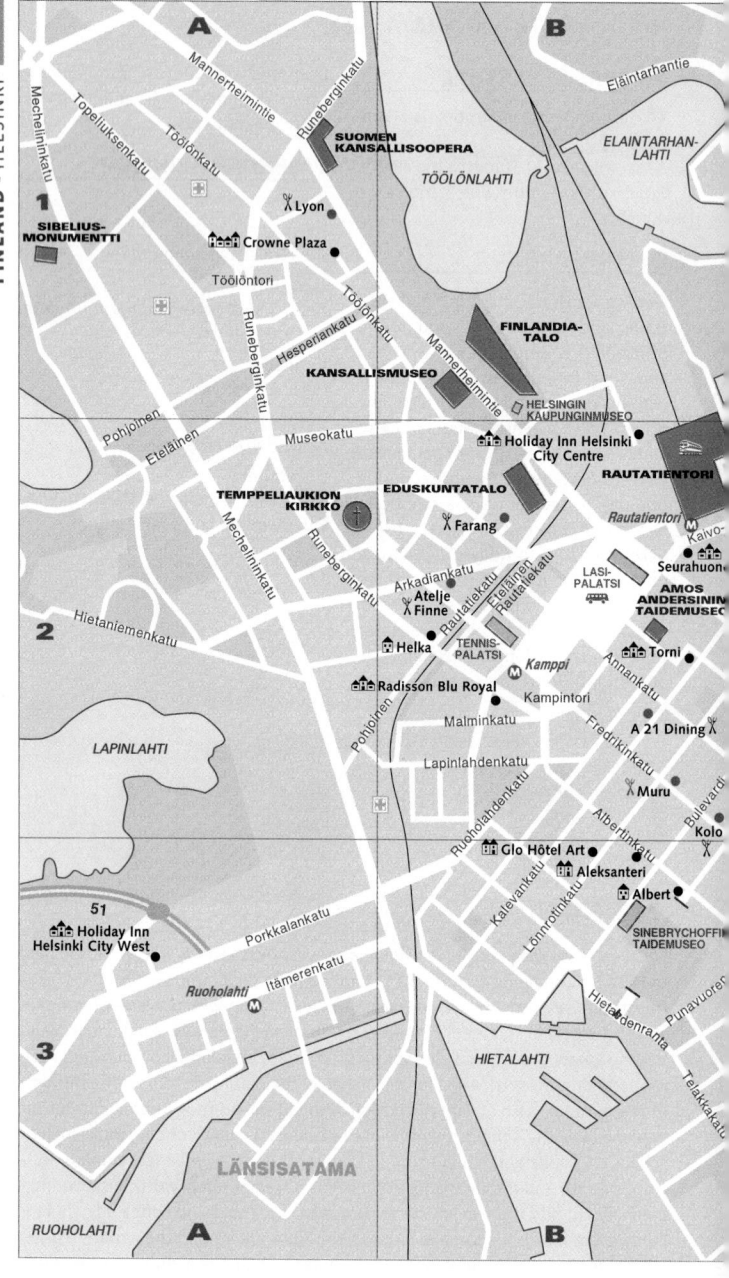

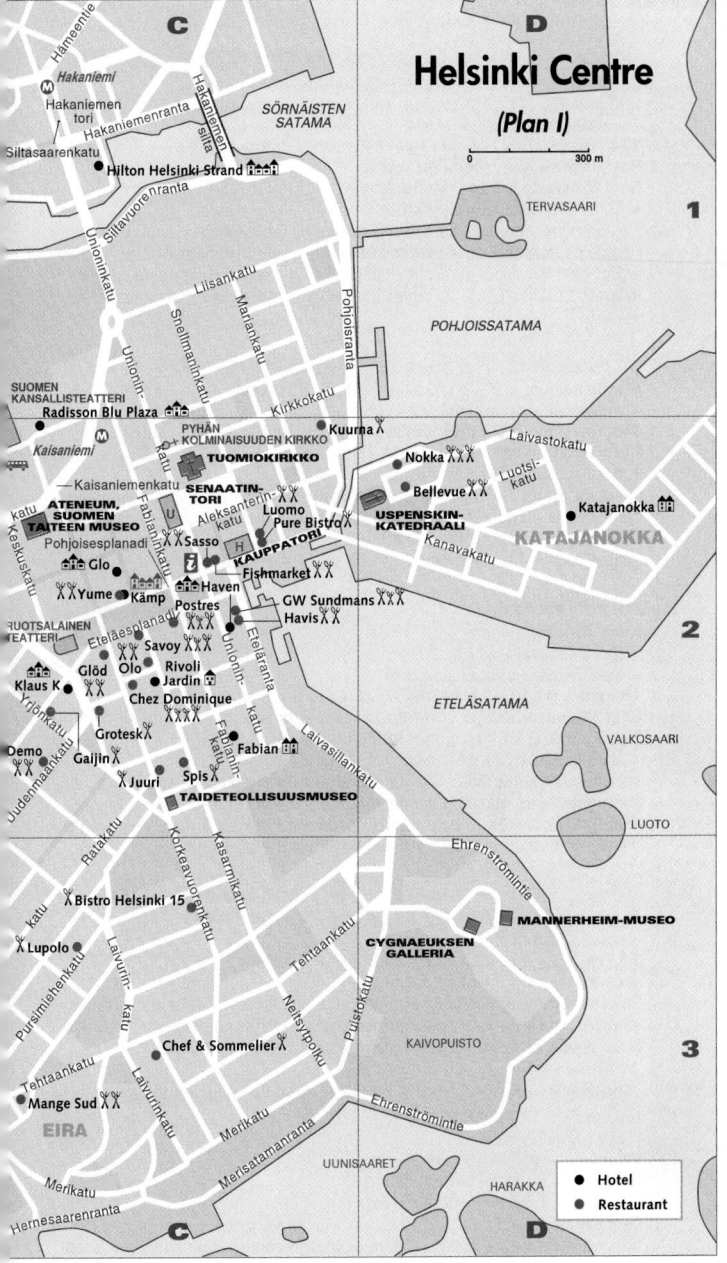

Helsinki Centre
(Plan I)

0   300 m

C

D

Hämeentie

Ⓜ Hakaniemi

Hakaniemen tori

Hakaniemenranta

SÖRNÄISTEN SATAMA

Hakaniemen silta

Siltasaarenkatu

● Hilton Helsinki Strand 🏨🏨

Siltavuorenranta

TERVASAARI

1

Unioninkatu

Liisankatu

Snellmaninkatu

Mariankatu

Pohjoisranta

POHJOISSATAMA

SUOMEN KANSALLISTEATTERI

● Radisson Blu Plaza 🏨🏨

Kirkkokatu

PYHÄN KOLMINAISUUDEN KIRKKO

Ⓜ Kaisaniemi

X Kuurna

Laivastokatu

● Nokka XXX

Luotsikatu

Kaisaniemenkatu

TUOMIOKIRKKO

SENAATIN-TORI

● Bellevue XX

● Katajanokka 🏨🏨

ATENEUM, SUOMEN TAITEEN MUSEO

Fabianinkatu

Aleksanterinkatu

Luomo

Pure Bistro X

USPENSKIN-KATEDRAALI

KATAJANOKKA

Keskuskatu

Pohjoisesplanadi

X Sasso

KAUPPATORI

Kanavakatu

● Glo 🏨🏨

XX Yume ● Kämp

Fishmarket XX

X Haven

Postres

GW Sundmans XXX

Ⓡ RUOTSALAINEN TEATTERI

Eteläesplanadi

Savoy XXX

Havis XX

Glöd ● Olo

Klaus K 🏨🏨

XX

Rivoli

Jardin 🏨

Unioninkatu

Eteläranta

ETELÄSATAMA

VALKOSAARI

Yrjönkatu

● Chez Dominique XXXX

Demo XX ●

Grotesk X

Gaijin X

X Juuri

Fabianinkatu

● Fabian 🏨🏨

LUOTO

Korkeavuorenkatu

Spis X

TAIDETEOLLISUUSMUSEO

Laivasillankatu

Ehrenströmintie

Ratakatu

Kasarmikatu

2

X Bistro Helsinki 15

X Lupolo ●

Laivurinkatu

Pursimiehenkatu

Tehtaankatu

Neitsytpolku

CYGNAEUKSEN GALLERIA

MANNERHEIM-MUSEO

Puistokatu

KAIVOPUISTO

3

Chef & Sommelier X

Tehtaankatu

Laivurinkatu

● Mange Sud XX

Merikatu

EIRA

Merisatamanranta

Ehrenströmintie

UUNISAARET

HARAKKA

Merikatu

Hernesaarenranta

● Hotel

● Restaurant

C

D

FINLAND - HELSINKI

157

FINLAND - HELSINKI

Kämp 🛱 Ⅰ₅ ⑩ ⋒ ₺ 🕮 ⇞ 🛜 🖴 🖙 🚗 VISA ⊙⊙ AE ①

Pohjoisesplanadi 29 ✉ 00100 – **Ⓜ** _Kaisaniemi_
_– ℰ (09) 576 111_
– www.hotelkamp.com **C2**
174 rm – 🛏179/475 € 🛏🛏179/475 €, � 29 € – 5 suites
Rest _Yume_ – see restaurant listing
Rest _Brasserie Kämp_ – Menu 37/55 € – Carte 15/25 €
◆ Grand Luxury ◆ Classic ◆
Luxurious 19C hotel with superb spa and fitness facility. Well-equipped, elegant bedrooms boast spacious marble bathrooms; suites are named after Finnish artists. Chic bar offers excellent champagne selection and tempting cocktails. Relaxed, bustling Brasserie serves an all-day international menu; Yume serves Asian cuisine.

Crowne Plaza Helsinki ⇞ Ⅰ₅ ⑩ ⋒ 🔲 ₺ 🕮 ⇞ 🛜 🖴 🚗

Mannerheimintie 50 ✉ 00260 – ℰ (09) 2521 0000 VISA ⊙⊙ AE ①
– www.crowneplaza-helsinki.fi **A1**
345 rm – 🛏157/333 € 🛏🛏172/333 €, ⊠ 25 € – 4 suites
Rest _Macu_ – Menu 42 € – Carte 28/50 €
◆ Business ◆ Modern ◆
Spacious hotel specialising in conferences. Comfortable, contemporary bedrooms boast good facilities and city or lake views; the higher the floor, the better the grade. Large basement fitness room, pool and spa. Pub serving classic bar food. Warm, welcoming Macu offers Mediterranean cuisine.

Hilton Helsinki Strand ⇞ Ⅰ₅ ⋒ 🔲 ₺ 🕮 ⇞ 🛜 🖴 🚗

John Stenbergin Ranta 4 ✉ 00530 VISA ⊙⊙ AE ①
_–_ **Ⓜ** _Hakaniemi – ℰ (09) 393 51_
– www.helsinki-strand.hilton.com **C1**
184 rm – 🛏129/340 € 🛏🛏149/375 €, ⊠ 25 € – 6 suites
Rest _Bridges_ – (closed Christmas, Easter, Saturday and Sunday lunch)
Menu 18/26 € – Carte dinner 40/58 €
◆ Business ◆ Chain hotel ◆ Functional ◆
Spacious waterfront hotel with classic '80s design, impressive atrium and 8th floor fitness and relaxation centre; take in city views from the sauna or pool. Smartly kept bedrooms boast marble bathrooms; ask for a room overlooking the water. Bridges offers international classics and local specialities.

Glo without rest Ⅰ₅ ⑩ ⋒ ₺ 🕮 ⇞ 🛜 VISA ⊙⊙ AE ①

Kluuvikatu 4 ✉ 00100 – **Ⓜ** _Kaisaniemi – ℰ (010) 3444 400_
– www.glohotels.fi **C2**
141 rm ⊠ – 🛏129/230 € 🛏🛏144/245 € – 3 suites
◆ Luxury ◆ Modern ◆ Design ◆
Stylish, centrally located hotel with good spa and fitness facilities and a complimentary bicycle service. Spacious bedrooms have a contemporary look and boast hi-tech extras. The bar has a lively atmosphere at weekends.

Haven ⇞ Ⅰ₅ ₺ 🕮 ⇞ 🛜 🖴 🚗 VISA ⊙⊙ AE ①

Unioninkatu 17 ✉ 00130 – ℰ (09) 681930
– www.hotelhaven.fi **C2**
77 rm ⊠ – 🛏139/325 € 🛏🛏169/355 €
Rest _Havis_ – see restaurant listing
◆ Luxury ◆ Townhouse ◆ Stylish ◆
Centrally located office block conversion, with an elegant, townhouse-style interior and water views. Stylish, modern bedrooms come in four types and boast top quality beds, fabrics and furniture; bathrooms feature marble units and TVs, along with Elemis spa toiletries and Egyptian cotton bathrobes.

Klaus K 🛏 🕭 🕭 🔅 🛂 💳 🃏 AE ⓪

Bulevardi 2 ✉ *00120* – Ⓜ *Rautatientori* – ✆ *(20) 770 4700*
– *www.klauskhotel.com*
– *Closed 23-27 December*   **C2**
137 rm ☕ – 🛏140/189 € 🛏🛏150/209 € – 2 suites
Rest *Toscanini* – ✆ *(20) 770 4713* – Menu 48 € *(dinner)*
– Carte 25/56 €
♦ Traditional ♦ Design ♦
Late 19C landmark building with great façade. Striking interior is designed to
reflect the epic themes of The Kalevala; the four styles of bedroom – Envy,
Desire, Passion and Mystical – reflect this. Stylish bar. Modern Tuscan cuisine in
lively Toscanini.

Radisson Blu Royal 🕭 🕭 🕭 🔅 🛂 🃏 💳 🃏 AE ⓪

Runeberginkatu 2 ✉ *00100* – Ⓜ *Kamppi* – ✆ *(020) 1234 701*
– *www.radissonblu.com/royalhotel-helsinki*   **B2**
255 rm ☕ – 🛏99/300 € 🛏🛏99/300 € – 7 suites
Rest *Grill it!* – Carte 30/57 €
♦ Business ♦ Modern ♦
Two-winged hotel close to the metro station. Spacious bedrooms boast
good-sized desks; the larger Business Class rooms offer more facilities, including bathrobes, Nespresso machines and complimentary breakfast. Pleasant,
high ceilinged bar. Good range of grilled specialities in the contemporary
restaurant.

Radisson Blu Plaza 🛏 🕭 🕭 🕭 🔅 rm, 🃏 🛂 🃏 💳 🃏 AE ⓪

Mikonkatu 23 ✉ *00100* – Ⓜ *Kaisaniemi* – ✆ *(20) 1234 703*
– *www.radissonblu.com/plazahotel-helsinki*   **C1/2**
301 rm ☕ – 🛏129/350 € 🛏🛏129/350 € – 1 suite
Rest *Kitzens* – *(closed Sunday lunch)* Menu 35/40 € – Carte 27/68 €
♦ Chain hotel ♦ Historic ♦ Functional ♦
Elegant, early 20C building– formerly a company HQ – set close to the station
and completed by a more modern wing. Bright, comfortable bedrooms have
up-to-date facilities. Contemporary bar. Kitzens offers five different types of cuisine listed on digital tablet menus.

Torni 🕭 🕭 🔅 🃏 🛂 💳 🃏 AE ⓪

Yrjönkatu 26 ✉ *00100* – Ⓜ *Rautatientori* – ✆ *(20) 1234 604*
– *www.sokoshoteltorni.fi*   **B2**
146 rm ☕ – 🛏95/250 € 🛏🛏115/270 € – 6 suites
Rest – *(closed Sunday)* Menu 41/59 € – Carte 36/62 €
♦ Business ♦ Stylish ♦
Charming, early 20C, city centre hotel boasting an 11 floor tower, great urban
views and a palpable sense of history. Warm, elegant décor with the choice of
'Art Deco', 'Functionalist' or 'Art Nouveau' themed bedrooms. Three different
bars, and a pleasant art deco restaurant offering various types of cuisine.

Seurahuone 🔅 🃏 🛂 💳 🃏 AE ⓪

Kaivokatu 12 ✉ *00100* – Ⓜ *Rautatientori* – ✆ *(09) 69 141*
– *www.hotelliseurahuone.fi*   **B2**
118 rm ☕ – 🛏95/189 € 🛏🛏105/209 €
Rest – *(closed Saturday lunch and Sunday)* Menu 46/59 €
– Carte dinner 36/62 €
♦ Historic ♦ Classic ♦
Early 20C hotel – one of the oldest in Finland – where a sympathetic renovation
has retained a pleasant period feel. Bedrooms display dark wood furniture and
Gustav Klimt prints. Traditional bar and an elegant, high-ceilinged restaurant
hung with chandeliers.

Holiday Inn Helsinki

Messuaukio 1 (near Pasila Railway Station)
(North : 5 km by Mannerheimintie, Nordenskiöldink, Savonkatu off Ratapihantie) ✉ 00520 – ℰ (09) 150 900 – www.holidayinn.com
– *Closed 24-30 December*
239 rm ☑ – †75/240 € ††95/265 € – 5 suites
Rest *Terra Nova* – *(closed lunch in summer)* Menu 18/44 € – Carte 36/54 €
♦ Business ♦ Modern ♦

Set just outside the city – but close to a station – in the Masscentrum Fair Centre, this chain hotel is popular for conferences. Bright, warm bedrooms offer varying levels of facilities. Welcoming Terra Nova serves international cuisine.

 Holiday Inn Helsinki City West

Sulhasenkuja 3 ✉ 00180 – **Ⓜ** *Ruoholahti*
– ℰ (09) 4152 1000 – www.restel.fi/holidayinn   **A3**
256 rm – †115/200 € ††130/215 €, ☑ 18 €
Rest *Fokka* – *(closed 23-25 December, Easter and lunch Saturday and Sunday)* Menu 9 € (weekday lunch)/36 € – Carte dinner 25/57 €
♦ Business ♦ Functional ♦

Sited in a business park well away from the city centre but close to a railway station. Modern bedrooms display touches of colour, pleasant furniture and excellent soundproofing; bathrooms are compact. Contemporary restaurant serves international cuisine.

 Holiday Inn Helsinki City Centre

Elielinaukio 5 ✉ 00100 – **Ⓜ** *Rautatientori*
– ℰ (09) 5425 5000 – www.finland.holidayinn.com   **B2**
174 rm ☑ – †135/310 € ††150/325 €
Rest *Verde* – *(closed lunch 17 June-11 August and dinner Christmas and Easter)* Menu 10/32 € – Carte dinner 23/57 €
♦ Chain hotel ♦ Functional ♦

Contemporary chain hotel located close to the post office, the station and the main shopping areas. Modern bedrooms boast good soundproofing, light wood furnishings and shower-only bathrooms; most have city views. Verde serves international and Finnish dishes.

 Fabian without rest

Fabiankatu 7 ✉ 00130 – **Ⓜ** *Kaisaniemi* – ℰ (09) 6128 2000
– www.hotelfabian.fi   **C2**
58 rm ☑ – †160 € ††185 €
♦ Townhouse ♦ Stylish ♦ Modern ♦

Charming and stylish boutique hotel in the heart of the city, opened in 2010 and sister to the Haven hotel. Modern, individually decorated bedrooms with wood floors and tiled bathrooms.

Katajanokka

Vyökatu 1 ✉ 00160 – ℰ (09) 686 450 – www.bwkatajanokka.fi
106 rm ☑ – †102/179 € ††112/295 €   **D2**
Rest *Jailbird* – Carte 32/55 €
♦ Historic ♦ Modern ♦

Pleasantly restored, late 19C former prison, with high ceilinged corridors and original staircases still in situ. Old cells are now comfortable, well-equipped bedrooms. Large cellar restaurant serves international cuisine and features a preserved prison cell.

Aleksanteri

Albertinkatu 34 ✉ 00180 – **Ⓜ** *Kamppi* – ℰ (20) 1234 643 – www.sokoshotels.fi
152 rm ☑ – †92/239 € ††107/314 €   **B3**
Rest *Fransmanni* – Menu 10/22 € – Carte 30/73 €
♦ Business ♦ Modern ♦

Two renovated buildings set by the Alexander Theatre. The 1920s building offers modern, comfortable well-equipped bedrooms, while the 1880s building boasts larger rooms and more characterful features. Restaurant serves French cuisine.

Pasila 🛏 ❀ ⅗ 🅰🅒 ⅔ 🛜 🏊 🅿 🚗 🆅🅸🆂🅰 ⓒⓞ 🅰🅴 ⓞ
Maistraatinportti 3 (North : 5 km by Mannerheimintie, Nordenskiöldink off Vetuvitie) ✉ 00240 – 𝒞 (20) 1234 613 – www.sokoshotels.fi
– *Closed 21 December-6 January*
178 rm 🖃 – ♦60/280 € ♦♦80/350 €
Rest *Sevilla* – Carte 17/48 €
♦ Business ♦ Modern ♦
Spacious hotel in a peaceful area close to the Hartwall Arena and Congress Centre; popular with business types during the week. Modern bedrooms display local decoration and furnishings. Spanish cuisine in Sevilla, with its Andalusian décor.

Glo Hôtel Art 🛏 ❀ rm, 🅰🅒 rm, 🛜 🏊 🚗 🆅🅸🆂🅰 ⓒⓞ 🅰🅴 ⓞ
Lönnrotinkatu 29 ✉ 00180 – 𝒞 (010) 3444 100 – www.hotelglo.fi/glo-art
171 rm 🖃 – ♦87/285 € ♦♦102/475 € **B3**
Rest – *(closed 6 December, 22-27 December, 1 January and Sunday)* *(dinner only)* Carte 29/48 €
♦ Townhouse ♦ Modern ♦
1903 art nouveau castle with modern extensions, set in the heart of the lively Design District and featuring its own art collection. The chic bedrooms were styled by Finnish designers. Facilities include a spa, bicycles and even painting equipment. A Nordic-based grill menu is served in the old cellars.

Rivoli Jardin *without rest* 🛏 ❀ 🅰🅒 ⅔ 🛜 🏊 🚗 🆅🅸🆂🅰 ⓒⓞ 🅰🅴 ⓞ
Kasarmikatu 40 ✉ 00130 – Ⓜ *Kaisaniemi* – 𝒞 (09) 681 500 – www.rivoli.fi
– *Closed Christmas* **C2**
55 rm 🖃 – ♦120/240 € ♦♦140/340 €
♦ Townhouse ♦ Classic ♦
Small city centre hotel with a pleasant breakfast room and functional, cosy, well-maintained bedrooms; the top floor rooms have terraces. A sauna and meeting room are hidden in the cellar.

Albert 🛏 ❀ 🅰🅒 ⅔ 🛜 🏊 🚗 🆅🅸🆂🅰 ⓒⓞ 🅰🅴 ⓞ
Albertinkatu 30 ✉ 00120 – Ⓜ *Kamppi* – 𝒞 (20) 1234 638 – www.sokoshotels.fi
– *Closed Christmas* **B3**
95 rm 🖃 – ♦82/239 € ♦♦97/294 €
Rest *Papa Albert* – *(closed Easter)* Carte 27/55 €
♦ Business ♦ Modern ♦
Late 19C building with welcoming lounge bar. Standard bedrooms are compact but well-equipped and are useful for business travellers; superior rooms are slightly larger. Contemporary Papa Albert offers an Italian menu.

Helka 🛏 ❀ 🅰🅒 ⅔ 🛜 🏊 🚗 🆅🅸🆂🅰 ⓒⓞ 🅰🅴 ⓞ
Pohjoinen Rautatiekatu 23 ✉ 00100 – Ⓜ *Kamppi* – 𝒞 (09) 613 580 – www.helka.fi
– *Closed 23-26 December* **B2**
146 rm 🖃 – ♦111/161 € ♦♦135/199 € – 3 suites
Rest *Helkan Keittiö* – Menu 10/39 € – Carte dinner 24/45 €
♦ Business ♦ Functional ♦
Early 20C building redesigned around the concept of 'nature'. Well-kept, contemporary bedrooms have white walls and huge photos of flora and fauna on the ceilings. In the restaurant, Finnish cuisine can be enjoyed among real tree trunks and large forest prints.

Chez Dominique *(Hans Valimaki)* 🅰🅒 ⅔ ✿ 🆅🅸🆂🅰 ⓒⓞ 🅰🅴 ⓞ
❀❀ *Rikhardinkatu 4* ✉ 00130 – Ⓜ *Rautatientori* – 𝒞 (09) 612 7393
– www.chezdominique.fi
– *Closed Easter, Christmas, Sunday, Monday and lunch Tuesday* **C2**
Rest – *(booking essential)* Menu 49/99 € – Carte dinner 128/148 € 🍸
♦ Innovative ♦ Elegant ♦
Graceful restaurant displaying neutral hues and retro furnishings. Skilled kitchen produces modern, well-balanced dishes, crafted from high quality produce. Complex, flavoursome combinations are presented in an innovative manner. Formal yet friendly service.
→ Seasonal vegetable salad, chlorophyll and buttermilk. Anjou pigeon, coco pastilla and pigeon jus. Sea buckthorn, chocolate and matcha tea.

FINLAND - HELSINKI

XXX G W Sundmans   ♿ ▣ ⇆ ⇌ VISA ◉◉ AE ①

Eteläranta 16 ⊠ 00130 – ℰ (09) 61285400 – www.royalravintolat.com
– Closed 22-30 December, Easter, Saturday lunch and Sunday   **C2**
Rest – Carte 53/87 €
♦ International ♦ Formal ♦

19C Russian Empire style building, with five elegant dining rooms; set opposite the Old Market Hall and formerly home to merchant ship captain Gustaf Wilhelm Sundman. Choose from 3, 5 or 7 courses and accompanying wines. Dishes are well-prepared, tasty, original, and presented in an appealing, modern manner.

XXX Savoy   ⇐ ⌂ ▣ ⇆ ⇌ VISA ◉◉ AE ①

Eteläesplanadi 14 (8th floor) ⊠ 00130 – Ⓜ Kaisaniemi
– ℰ (09) 6128 5300 – www.ravintolat.com/savoy
– Closed Easter, Christmas, midsummer, Saturday lunch and Sunday
Rest – Menu 65/109 € – Carte 77/94 € ⌂   **C2**
♦ Finnish ♦ Formal ♦

Opened in 1937, an elegant 8th floor restaurant with a pleasant art deco feel. Pleasant views from the enclosed summer roof terrace. Carefully sourced ingredients used in largely classical, Finnish dishes. Attentive service.

XXX Nokka   ⌂ ▣ ⇆ ⇌ VISA ◉◉ AE ①

Kanavaranta 7F ⊠ 00160 – ℰ (09) 6128 5600 – www.royalravintolat.com
– Closed Easter, Christmas, Saturday lunch and Sunday   **D2**
Rest – *(booking advisable)* Menu 49/63 € – Carte 43/67 € ⌂
♦ Modern ♦ Elegant ♦

Converted harbourside warehouse with exposed brick walls, an elegant bar, a wine cellar and a cookery school. The open kitchen prepares modern Finnish cuisine and relies on small farm producers.

XXX Postres (Samuli Wirgentius)   ▣ ⇆ VISA ◉◉ AE ①

⚙
Eteläesplanadi 8 ⊠ 00130 – Ⓜ Kaisaniemi – ℰ (09) 663 300 – www.postres.fi
– Closed 2 weeks July, 24 December-6 January, Sunday and Monday
Rest – Menu 32/62 €   **C2**
♦ Modern ♦ Design ♦ Intimate ♦

Contemporary, glass-fronted restaurant on the main esplanade, divided into two bright and stylish rooms. Classical Scandinavian cooking uses French techniques and modern, innovative touches to produce dishes that are full of flavour. Pleasant, polite service.
→ Smoked freshwater shrimps, fennel and horseradish snow. Grilled turbot with brown butter mayonnaise and celeriac. Strawberry sorbet with wild sorrel.

XX Olo (Pekka Terävä)   ▣ ⇆ ⇌ VISA ◉◉ AE ①

⚙
Kasarmikatu 44 ⊠ 00130 – Ⓜ Kaisaniemi – ℰ (10) 3206 250
– www.olo-restaurant.com – Closed July, Easter, midsummer,
Christmas, Saturday lunch, Monday dinner and Sunday   **C2**
Rest – *(booking advisable)* Menu 32/59 €
♦ Modern ♦ Elegant ♦

Attractive, comfortable and immaculately kept corner restaurant, with pleasant service from a young, efficient team. Elegant wine cellar and kitchen studio for private dining. Cooking is refined and unfussy with some modern touches, and dishes are prepared with confidence.
→ Salmon from Rörvik with mussels. Pork with forest mushrooms. Finnish apple with blueberries.

XX Luomo (Jouni Toivanen)   VISA ◉◉ AE ①

⚙
Katariinankatu 1 ⊠ 00170 – Ⓜ Kaisaniemi – ℰ (09) 1357287 – www.luomo.fi
– Closed 1 week January, Sunday and Monday   **C1**
Rest – *(dinner only) (booking essential) (set menu only)* Menu 59/99 €
♦ Innovative ♦ Intimate ♦ Neighbourhood ♦

Take the lift up to this minimalist, two-roomed restaurant with its bright spot-lights, and be sure to ask for a table overlooking the harbour. Modern 3, 5 or 7 course menus, with wines to match. Local ingredients feature in skilfully prepared, inventive dishes, which display influences from around the globe.
→ Lobster and rose. Halibut in Tokyo. Chocolate with ceps.

XX **Sasso** [AC] [icons] [VISA] [CO] [AE] [O]

Pohjoisesplanadi 17 ✉ *00170 –* Ⓜ *Kaisaniemi –* ☎ *(09) 1345 6240*
– www.sasso.fi
– Closed Easter, Christmas, Saturday lunch and Sunday   C2
Rest *– Menu 37/54 € – Carte dinner 48/57 €*
♦ Italian ♦ Fashionable ♦
Spacious harbourside restaurant decorated in contemporary brown hues, with
a stylish bar and lounge. Well-organised kitchen produces northern Italian
dishes, crafted from Scandinavian ingredients.

XX **Demo** (Tommi Tuominen) [icons] [VISA] [CO] [AE] [O]
ঃ
Uudenmaankatu 9-11 ✉ *00120 –* Ⓜ *Rautatientori –* ☎ *(09) 228 90 840*
– www.restaurantdemo.fi
– Closed Easter, Christmas, Sunday and Monday   C2
Rest *– (dinner only) (booking essential) Menu 62 €*
♦ Modern ♦ Intimate ♦
Atmospheric candlelit restaurant on a busy street, with neutral hues and a
relaxed, romantic feel; an established dining destination. Classical cooking
combines French and Finnish influences to produce robust and satisfying
dishes – opt for the recommended wines.
➜ Nettle soup with corn fed pork and king crab. Pigeon with foie gras and
cherry sauce. Vanilla soufflé with raspberry ice cream.

XX **Mange Sud** [AC] [icons] [VISA] [CO] [AE] [O]

Tehtaankatu 34 D2 ✉ *00150 –* ☎ *(020) 711 8350 – www.mangesud.fi*
– Closed 20-23 June, 24-26 December and Sunday   C3
Rest *– (dinner only and Saturday lunch) Menu 34/54 € – Carte 34/57 €*
♦ Mediterranean ♦ Neighbourhood ♦
Eye-catching red property in smart, southern residential area. Stylish dining
rooms; actors appear occasionally for some impromtu theatre. Confident coo-
king displays Mediterranean influences.

XX **FishMarket** [AC] [icons] [VISA] [CO] [AE] [O]

Pohjoisesplanadi 17 ✉ *00170 –* Ⓜ *Kaisaniemi –* ☎ *(09) 1345 6220*
– www.fishmarket.fi
– Closed Easter, Christmas and Sunday   C2
Rest *– (dinner only) Menu 50 € – Carte 50/80 €*
♦ Fish and seafood ♦ Elegant ♦
Several different dining areas set within the basement of a former pharmacy,
with elegant décor and bright, contemporary Scandinavian furnishings. The
daily catch is displayed at the bar.

XX **Yume** – at Kämp Hotel [icons] [AC] [icons] [VISA] [CO] [AE] [O]

Kluuvikatu 2 ✉ *00100 –* Ⓜ *Kaisaniemi –* ☎ *(09) 57611718*
– www.palacekamp.com
– Closed 22-24 June, 6 and 23-26 December, Sunday and bank holidays
Rest *– (dinner only) Menu 39 € – Carte 35/44 €*   C2
♦ Japanese ♦ Fashionable ♦
Contemporary restaurant in the Kämp Hotel, displaying seasonal décor and a
semi-open kitchen. Wide selection of Asian dishes includes Japanese hot
stone plates and dishes to share; many recipes have been adapted to suit European tastes.

XX **Alia** [icons] [icons] [icons] [P] [VISA] [CO] [AE] [O]

Mustikkamaankuja 1 (North : 3 km by Hämeentie) ✉ *00570*
– ☎ *(09) 66 00 66 – www.alia.fi*
– Closed Easter, Christmas and midsummer
Rest *– Menu 24/42 € – Carte 45/53 €*
♦ Finnish ♦ Rustic ♦
This country sister to Postres is housed within a traditional wooden building sur-
rounded by trees. Its interior is more modern and is divided into four rooms.
Expect classic Finnish and French dishes.

XX **Bellevue**   AC 🚫 ⇔ VISA ⓪ AE ①

Rahapajankatu 3 ✉ 00160 – **Ⓜ** *Kaisaniemi – ℰ (09) 179 560*
– www.restaurantbellevue.com
– Closed 22-26 December, Sunday and Monday   **D2**
Rest – Menu 28/60 € – Carte 43/106 €
◆ Russian ◆ Cosy ◆

Opened in 1917, this townhouse restaurant boasts several dining rooms adorned with paintings and knick-knacks. Russian cuisine proudly maintains tradition; waiters wear authentic costumes.

XX **Havis** – at Haven Hotel   🏠 AC 🚫 ⇔ VISA ⓪ AE ①

Eteläranta 16 ✉ 00130 – ℰ (09) 6128 5800
– www.royalravintolat.com/havis
– Closed 6 December, Easter and Sunday early September-1 May
Rest – Menu 35/49 € – Carte 50/64 €   **C2**
◆ Fish and seafood ◆ Elegant ◆

19C harbourside restaurant serving carefully crafted seafood dishes. Two rooms – one with an elegant vaulted ceiling and maritime knick-knacks, the other with a contemporary open kitchen and terrace.

XX **Glöd**   AC VISA ⓪ AE ①

Korkeavuorenkatu 34 ✉ 00130 – **Ⓜ** *Kaisaniemi – ℰ (50) 322 9885*
– www.glod.fi
– Closed Christmas, Sunday and bank holidays   **C2**
Rest – *(dinner only)* Menu 42 € – Carte 36/55 €
◆ International ◆ Exotic ◆ Fashionable ◆

It means 'glowing' in Swedish and, with its colourful, candlelit interior and easy-going vibe, Glöd certainly lives up to its name. Prime ingredients are cleverly combined to produce original, boldly flavoured dishes with global influences.

X **Spis**   VISA ⓪ AE ①

Kasarmikatu 26 ✉ 00130 – ℰ (045) 305 1211 – www.spis.fi
– Closed Sunday, Monday and bank holidays   **C2**
Rest – *(dinner only) (booking essential)* Carte 41/50 €
◆ Modern ◆ Bistro ◆

Intimate, unassuming restaurant seating just 18 and offering a warm welcome; the décor is simple yet trendy, with exposed brickwork and small tables. Cooking is creative and flavoursome, and features Nordic flavours in attractively presented, imaginative combinations – every plate and bowl is different.

X **Muru**   VISA ⓪ AE ①

Fredrikinkatu 41 ✉ 00120 – **Ⓜ** *Kamppi – ℰ (09) 42891213*
– www.murudining.fi
– Closed Easter, Christmas-New Year, midsummer, Sunday, Monday and bank holidays   **B2**
Rest – *(dinner only) (booking essential) (set menu only)* Menu 49 €
– Carte 45/49 € 🍷
◆ Modern ◆ Neighbourhood ◆ Trendy ◆

Four young owners have created a vibrant, welcoming spot run by a charming, chatty team. The cosy, rustic feel comes with a contemporary edge and the cooking is refined yet also gutsy. Quirky décor includes wine-themed lighting and a bar made from old wine boxes. Two sittings for dinner; booking is a must.

X **Grotesk**   🏠 AC 🚫 ⇔ VISA ⓪ AE ①

Ludviginkatu 10 ✉ 00130 – **Ⓜ** *Rautatientori – ℰ (10) 470 2100*
– www.grotesk.fi
– Closed Easter, Christmas, Saturday lunch and Sunday   **C2**
Rest – Menu 25/43 € – Carte 44/57 €
◆ Modern ◆ Fashionable ◆

Smart, buzzy restaurant with an open kitchen, stylish black and red décor, a canopy-covered patio, and a trendy lounge-bar which opens in the evening. Modern Finnish cooking is heartwarming and flavoursome; the lunch menu is limited.

FINLAND - HELSINKI

Solna 🛱 🕅 ↳ ⇄ VISA ⊕ AE ⓪

Solnantie 26 (Northwest : 5 km by Mannerheimintie, Tukholmankatu, Paciusgatan and Munkkiniemen puistotie, by tram N°4 alighting at Laaja Ladhden Aukio) ✉ 00330 – ☞ (09) 530 1411 – www.solna.fi
– Closed Easter, Christmas-New Year, Monday in July, Saturday lunch and Sunday
Rest – Menu 41/46 €
◆ Scandinavian ◆ Bistro ◆

Keenly run neighbourhood restaurant with contemporary bistro styling and a welcoming atmosphere. Concise, well-priced menus offer hearty, flavoursome dishes crafted from quality ingredients; lunch is limited. Friendly, efficient service.

Farang 🕅 ⇄ VISA ⊕ AE ⓪

Ainonkatu 3 (inside the Kunsthalle) ✉ 00100 – ⓜ *Kamppi*
– ☞ (10) 322 9380 – www.farang.fi
– Closed 23-26 December, Saturday lunch, Sunday and Monday   **B2**
Rest – Menu 28 € (lunch) – Carte 33/47 €
◆ Thai ◆ Trendy ◆ Minimalist ◆

The Kunsthalle exhibition venue also plays host to this stylish, modern restaurant, decorated in hues of red, black and grey. Black wood tables and chairs are separated by transparent curtains. Zesty, harmonious, vibrant dishes take their influence from South East Asia. Friendly, efficient service.

Chef & Sommelier ↳ VISA ⊕ AE ⓪

Huvilakatu 28A ✉ 00150 – ☞ (400) 959 440 – www.chefetsommelier.fi
– Closed 22-June-1 August, 10 days Christmas, 1 week February, Easter Sunday, Monday and bank holidays   **C3**
Rest – *(dinner only) (booking advisable)* Menu 44 €
◆ Modern ◆ Neighbourhood ◆

Cosy, simply decorated neighbourhood restaurant with a friendly atmosphere. The open kitchen uses carefully chosen organic and Fairtrade ingredients for its tasty Finnish cuisine; the 3-7 course set menus include a vegetarian option.

Gaijin 🕅 VISA ⊕ AE ⓪

Bulevardi 6 ✉ 00120 – ⓜ *Rautatientori* – ☞ (10) 3229386 – www.gaijin.fi
– Closed Christmas   **C2**
Rest – *(dinner only and lunch Tuesday-Friday) (booking advisable)* Menu 23/59 € – Carte approx. 40 €
◆ Asian ◆ Minimalist ◆ Trendy ◆

Sister restaurant to Farang, with authentic, contemporary décor, a buzzing atmosphere and attentive service. Its experienced young owners offer a modern take on Asian cooking, with bold flavours, skilled presentation and an emphasis on Japanese dishes. Choice of set, à la carte or tasting menus.

Pure Bistro 🛱 VISA ⊕ AE ⓪

Pohjoisesplanadi 9 ✉ 00170 – ☞ (50) 400 3372 – www.purebistro.fi
– Closed 24-25 December   **C2**
Rest – Menu 27/44 €
◆ Modern ◆ Friendly ◆

Modern bistro set below Luomo, with a light, airy feel, a bar and two summer terraces. Fresh, local ingredients feature on the concise, daily changing menu. Dishes are flavoursome, nicely balanced and represent good value.

Lyon 🕅 VISA ⊕ AE ⓪

Mannerheimintie 56 ✉ 00260 – ☞ (09) 408 131 – www.ravintolalyon.fi
– Closed July, Easter, Christmas, midsummer, Sunday, Monday and bank holidays   **A1**
Rest – *(dinner only)* Menu 59 € – Carte 54/74 €
◆ French ◆ Bistro ◆

Well-established, welcoming restaurant with a traditional bistro feel, set close to the Opera House. Wide-ranging menus offer seasonal French and vegetarian dishes crafted from good Finnish ingredients. Small French wine selection.

Ateljé Finne

Arkadiankatu 14 ⊠ 00100 – Ⓜ Kamppi – ℰ (09) 493 110
– www.ateljefinne.fi
– Closed Christmas, Sunday and Monday   **B2**
Rest – *(dinner only) (booking advisable)* Menu 42 € – Carte 42/67 €
♦ Modern ♦ Bistro ♦
Former studio of Finnish sculptor Gunnar Finne, who worked here from the
1920s until his death in 1952. Three small, bistro-style dining rooms decorated
with local art. Regional dishes are given contemporary and international twists.

Juuri

Korkeavuorenkatu 27 ⊠ 00130 – ℰ (09) 635 732 – www.juuri.fi
– Closed Christmas and midsummer   **C2**
Rest – Menu 35/45 € – Carte 37/50 €
♦ Finnish ♦ Bistro ♦
Small bistro with a traditional feel and friendly service, close to the Design
Museum. Classic Finnish cuisine and tapas-style starters; lunch menu is more
concise. Organic deli next door.

Kuurna

Merittullinkatu 6 ⊠ 00170 – Ⓜ Kaisaniemi – ℰ (09) 670 849
– www.kuurna.fi
– Closed Easter, Christmas and Sunday   **C2**
Rest – *(dinner only) (booking essential)* Menu 39/52 €
♦ Finnish ♦ Neighbourhood ♦
Small but very popular restaurant with a vaulted ceiling and seating for just
twenty. The weekly changing set menu offers three choices per course and
is supplemented by blackboard specials. Finnish cooking follows the seasons.

A21 Dining

Kalevankatu 17 ⊠ 00100 – Ⓜ Kamppi – ℰ (040) 1711117
– www.a21.fi
– Closed Christmas, Sunday, Monday and bank holidays   **B2**
Rest – *(dinner only) (set menu only)* Menu 49/79 €
♦ Modern ♦ Trendy ♦ Individual ♦
Fashionable spot known as much for its cocktails as for its food. Minimalist in
style, with all white decoration in the dining room and all black in the bar.
Understated, modern menu, with cocktails to match each dish.

Lupolo

Punavuorenkatu 3 ⊠ 00120 – ℰ (050) 5544050 – www.lupolo.fi
– Closed Sunday, lunch Monday and Saturday   **C3**
Rest – Menu 10 € (lunch) – Carte dinner 25/33 €
♦ Modern ♦ Bistro ♦ Neighbourhood ♦
Sultry bar-cum-diner just off the main tourist track and well worth seeking out.
Gutsy, flavoursome cooking is complemented by a selection of international
bottled beers. Service is smooth and relaxed. Sit on the high stools or ban-
quettes.

Bistro Helsinki 15

Korkeavuorenkatu 4B ⊠ 00150 – ℰ (09) 4242 7650
– www.bistrohelsinki.fi
– Closed July, Christmas, Easter, midsummer, Monday dinner, Sunday and bank
holidays   **C3**
Rest – Menu 35/41 € – Carte lunch approx. 34 €
♦ Italian ♦ Bistro ♦ Elegant ♦
Friendly neighbourhood restaurant with a narrow dining room and chrome bar.
Italian cooking has a modern edge and incorporates some Finnish touches;
simpler menu offered at lunch.

FINLAND - HELSINKI

✗ **Kolo** VISA ⊕⊙
Fredrikinkatu 37 ⊠ *00120 –* Ⓜ *Kamppi –* ℰ *(044) 0601661*
– www.ravintolakolo.fi
– Closed 19 July-20 August, 22 December-10 January and Sunday
Rest *– (booking essential at dinner)* Menu 43 € (dinner)   **B2**
– Carte 24/50 €
♦ **Modern** ♦ **Neighbourhood** ♦
Friendly, laid-back bistro that's a real hit with the locals; book ahead for dinner
and arrive early for lunch. Tasty, seasonal cooking with local ingredients show-
cased in unfussy combinations; simpler selection of dishes offered at lunch.

AT HELSINKI-VANTAA AIRPORT

 Hilton Helsinki Airport Ⅰƃ 🐾 ㄴ ᴬᶜ ↔ 🛜 ᶴᴬ 🅿
Lentàjànkuja 1 ⊠ *01530 –* ℰ *(09) 732 20*   VISA ⊕⊙ ᴬᴱ ⓪
– www.hilton.fi
330 rm – 🛉98/250 € 🛉🛉98/550 €, ⊑ 25 € – 5 suites
Rest *Gui – (closed Saturday and Sunday lunch)* Menu 46 € (dinner)
– Carte 36/62 €
♦ **Business** ♦ **Modern** ♦
Spacious glass hotel with a relaxed ambience and a large conference area; 3min
from the international terminal. Soundproofed bedrooms boast locally designed furniture, good facilities and large bathrooms; some have saunas. Contemporary restaurant serves Finnish and international dishes.

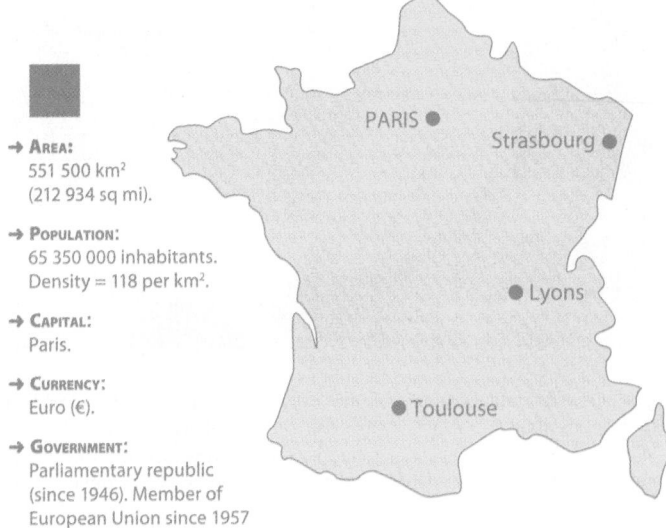

→ **AREA:**
551 500 km² (212 934 sq mi).

→ **POPULATION:**
65 350 000 inhabitants.
Density = 118 per km².

→ **CAPITAL:**
Paris.

→ **CURRENCY:**
Euro (€).

→ **GOVERNMENT:**
Parliamentary republic (since 1946). Member of European Union since 1957 (one of the 6 founding countries).

→ **LANGUAGE:**
French.

→ **PUBLIC HOLIDAYS:**
New Year's Day (1 Jan); Easter Monday (late Mar/Apr); Labor Day (1 May); Victory Day 1945 (8 May); Ascension Day (17 May); Whit Monday (late May/June); Bastille Day (14 July); Assumption of the Virgin Mary (15 Aug); All Saints' Day (1 Nov); Armistice Day 1918 (11 Nov); Christmas Day (25 Dec).

→ **LOCAL TIME:**
GMT+1 hour in winter and GMT +2 hours in summer.

→ **CLIMATE:**
Temperate with cool winters and warm summers (Paris: January 3°C; July 20°C). Mediterranean climate in the south (mild winters, hot and sunny summers, occasional strong wind called the mistral).

→ **EMERGENCY:**
Police ✆ **17**; Medical Assistance ✆ **15**; Fire Brigade ✆ **18**. (Dialling **112** within any EU country will redirect your call and contact the emergency services.)

→ **ELECTRICITY:**
230 volts AC, 50Hz; 2 round pin sockets.

→ **FORMALITIES:**
Travellers from the European Union (EU), Switzerland, Iceland and the main countries of North and South America need a national identity card or passport (America: passport required) to visit France for less than three months (tourism or business purpose). For visitors from other countries a visa may be required, in addition to a passport, especially for those wishing to stay for longer than three months. We advise you to check with your embassy before travelling.

PARIS
PARIS

Population 2 222 808

Cyrille Lips/Fotolia.com

The French capital is one of the truly great cities of the world, a metropolis that eternally satisfies the desires of its beguiled visitors. With its harmonious layout, typified by the grand geometric boulevards radiating from the Arc de Triomphe like the spokes of a wheel, Paris is designed to enrapture. Despite its ever-widening tentacles, most of the things worth seeing are contained within the city's ring road. Paris wouldn't be Paris sans its Left and Right Banks: the Right Bank comprises the north and west; the Left Bank takes in the city south of the Seine. A stroll along the Left Bank conjures images of Doisneau's magical monochrome photographs, while the narrow, cobbled streets of Montmartre vividly call up the colourful cool of Toulouse-Lautrec.

The Ile de la Cité is the nucleus around which the city grew and the oldest quarters around this site are the 1st, 2nd, 3rd, 4th arrondissements on the Right Bank and 5th and 6th on the Left Bank. Landmarks are universally known: the Eiffel Tower and the Arc de Triomphe to the west, the Sacré-Coeur to the north, Montparnasse Tower to the south, and, of course, Notre-Dame Cathedral in the middle. But Paris is not resting on its laurels. New buildings and new cultural sensations are never far away: Les Grands Travaux are forever in the wings, waiting to inspire.

PARIS IN...

→ **ONE DAY**
Eiffel Tower, Notre-Dame Cathedral, a café on Boulevard St Germain, Musée d'Orsay, Montmartre.

→ **TWO DAYS**
The Louvre, Musée du Quai Branly.

→ **THREE DAYS**
Canal Saint-Martin, Centre Pompidou, Picasso Museum and the Marais.

PRACTICAL INFORMATION

ARRIVAL-DEPARTURE

✈ Paris Charles de Gaulle Airport is 23km northeast of Paris. Air France Bus to Montparnasse or Porte Maillot runs every 15min.

✈ Orly Airport is 14km south. Air France Bus runs to Invalides or Montparnasse. Eurostar runs from Gare du Nord, on the Rue de Dunkerque.

GETTING AROUND

A single bus or metro ticket has a flat fare however far you travel; a carnet (book of ten) works out at good value. There are three travel cards: Paris Visite is a 1-day pass for three zones or a 5-day pass for five zones; Mobilis is a 1-day pass giving unlimited travel in either zones 1-2 or zones 1-5; Pass Navigo is a weekly or monthly pass (you'll need a photo). Or try the Velib, the bicycle system; pick up one of the 15,000 bikes at any of the 1,800 points, swipe a travel card to release your bike – then it's just you versus the Parisian traffic...

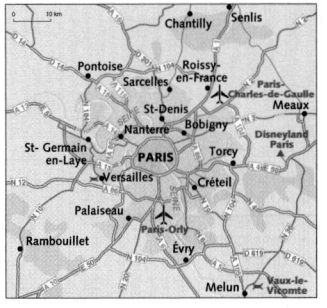

CALENDAR HIGHLIGHTS

February: Paris Fashion Week.

March: Salon du Livre Paris.

April: Banlieues Bleues.

May: La Nuit des Musées, Foire du Trône funfair.

June: French Open Tennis.

August: Paris Plages.

September: The Autumn Festival, Jazz à la Villette.

October: Nuit Blanche, International Contemporary Art Fair.

November: Great Wines Fair.

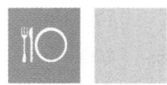

EATING OUT

Food plays such an important role in Gallic life that eating well is deemed a citizen's birth-right. Parisians are intensely knowledgeable about their food and wine - simply stroll around any part of the capital and you'll come across lavish looking shops offering perfectly presented treats. Restaurants, bistros and brasseries too can call on the best available bounty around: there are close to a hundred city-wide markets teeming with fresh produce. As Charles De Gaulle said: "How can you govern a country which has 246 varieties of cheese?" Whether you want to linger in a legendary café or dine in a grand salon, you'll find the choice is endless. The city's respect for its proud culinary heritage is palpable but it is not resting on its laurels. Just as other European cities with vibrant restaurant scenes have started to play catch-up, so have young chefs here taken up the cudgels. By breaking away from formulaic regimes and adopting more contemporary styles of cooking, they have ensured that the reputation of the city remains undimmed.

HOTELS FROM A TO Z

RESTAURANTS FROM A TO Z

OPEN SATURDAY AND SUNDAY

FRANCE – PARIS

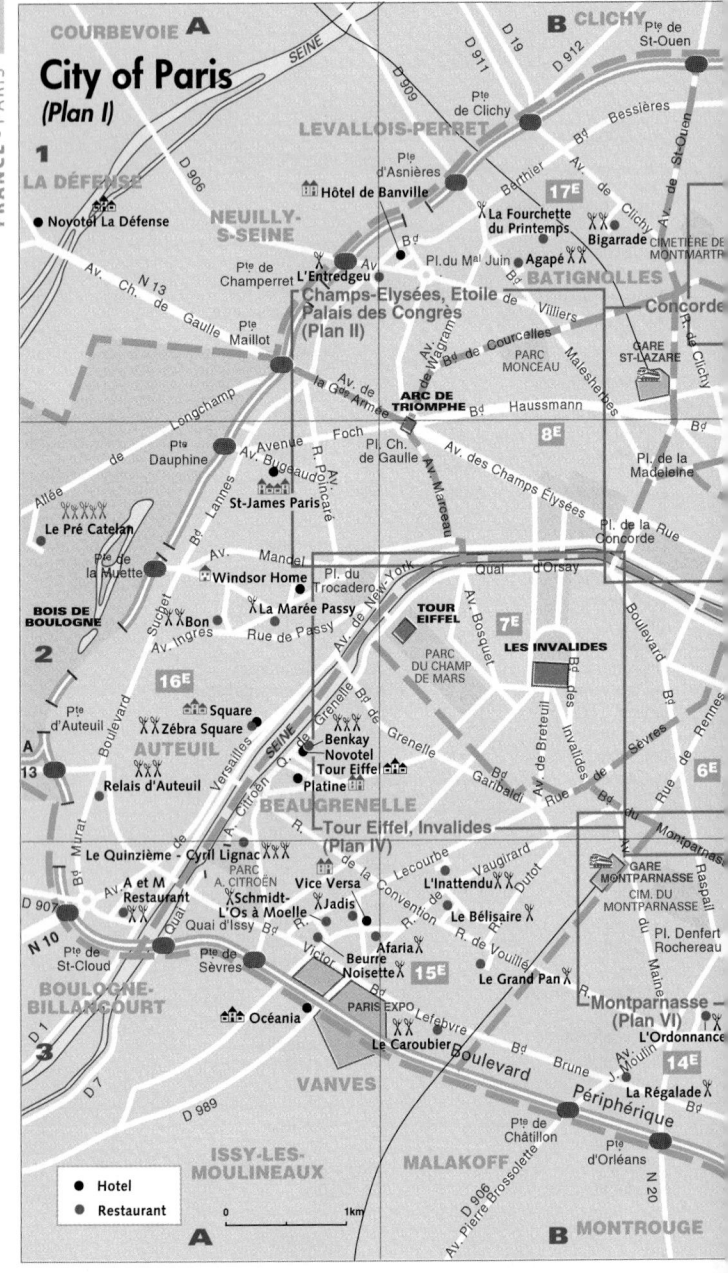

City of Paris
(Plan I)

- Hotel
- Restaurant

0   1km

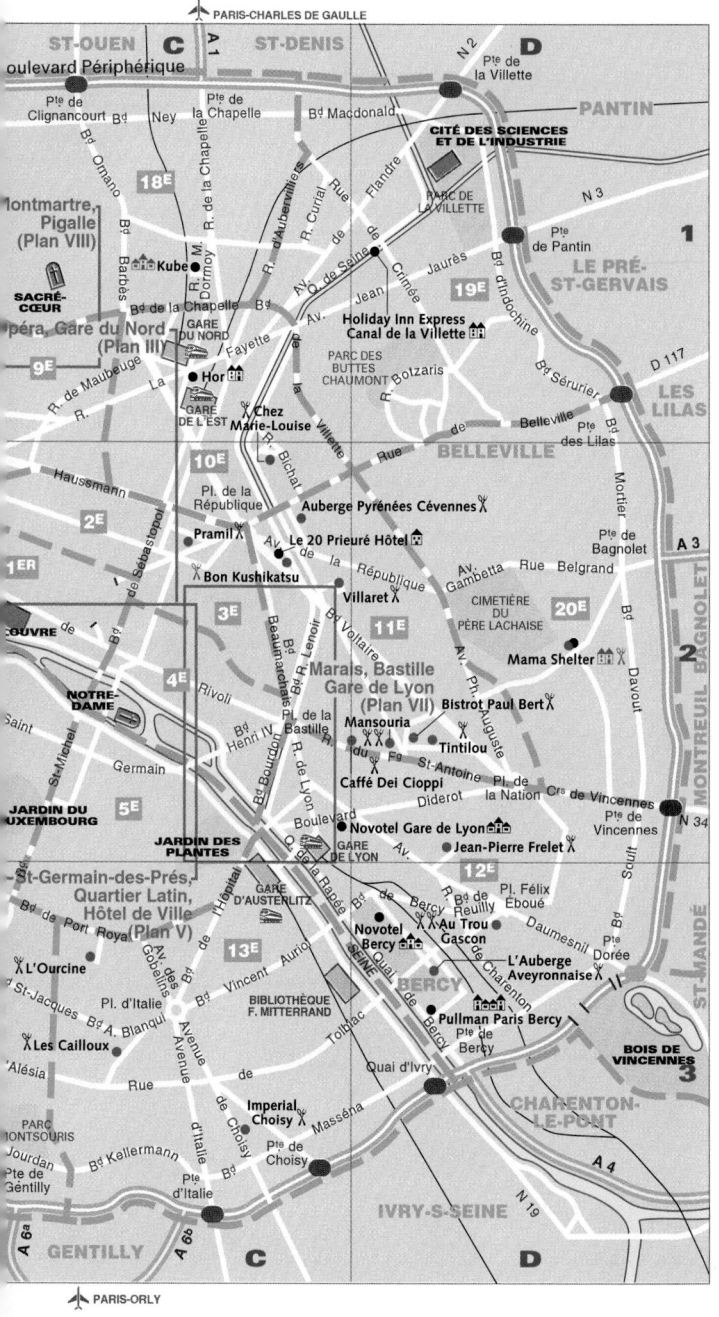

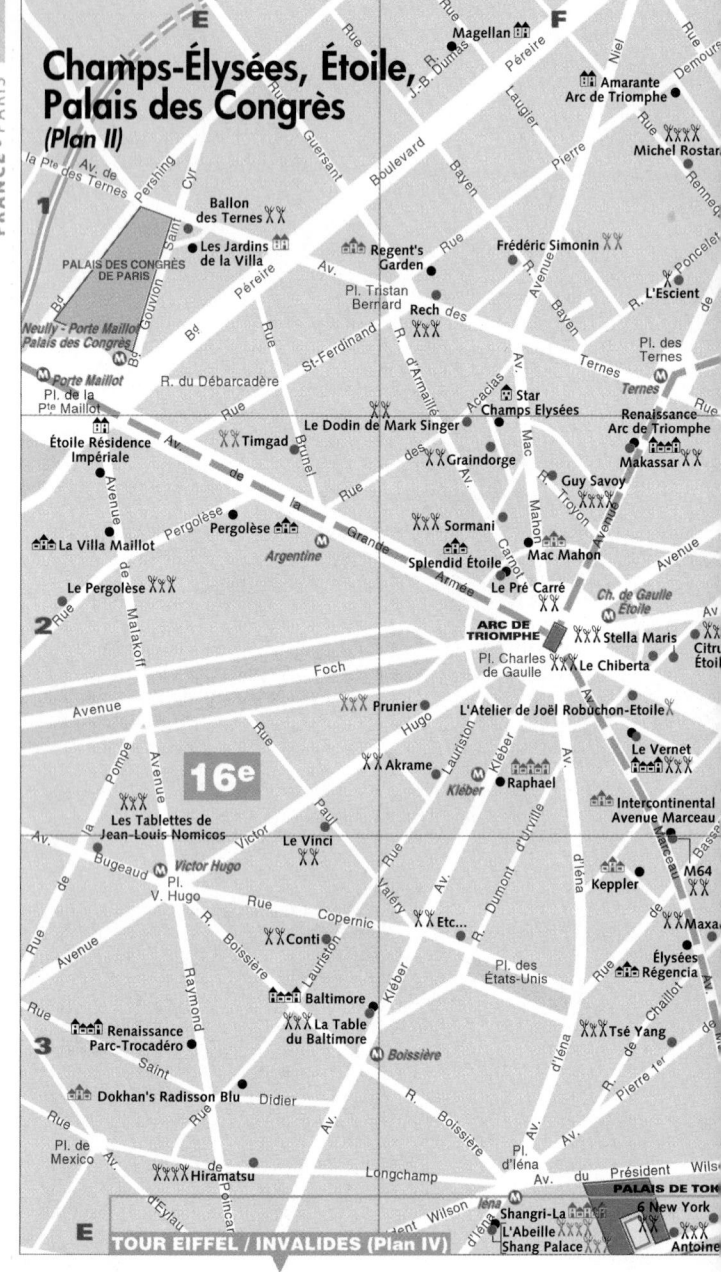

Champs-Élysées, Étoile, Palais des Congrès
(Plan II)

Magellan

Amarante
Arc de Triomphe

Michel Rostar

Ballon
des Ternes

Les Jardins
de la Villa

PALAIS DES CONGRÈS
DE PARIS

Neuilly - Porte Maillot
Palais des Congrès

Porte Maillot
Pl. de la
Pte Maillot

Regent's
Garden

Frédéric Simonin

L'Escient

Pl. Tristan
Bernard

Rech

Pl. des
Ternes

Étoile Résidence
Impériale

Le Dodin de Mark Singer

Timgad

Graindorge

Star
Champs Elysées

Renaissance
Arc de Triomphe

Makassar

La Villa Maillot

Pergolèse

Sormani

Guy Savoy

Le Pergolèse

Splendid Étoile

Mac Mahon

Le Pré Carré

Ch. de Gaulle
Étoile

Stella Maris

Citr
Étoil

ARC DE
TRIOMPHE

Pl. Charles
de Gaulle

Le Chiberta

Prunier

L'Atelier de Joël Robuchon-Etoile

Le Vernet

16e

Akrame

Kléber

Raphael

Intercontinental
Avenue Marceau

Les Tablettes de
Jean-Louis Nomicos

Le Vinci

Etc...

Keppler

M64

Maxa

Conti

Élysées
Régencia

Baltimore

Renaissance
Parc-Trocadéro

La Table
du Baltimore

Tsé Yang

Boissière

Dokhan's Radisson Blu

Didier

Pl. de
Mexico

Hiramatsu

Longchamp

Président Wils

PALAIS DE TOK

Shangri-La

6 New York

TOUR EIFFEL / INVALIDES (Plan IV)

L'Abeille
Shang Palace

Antoine

FRANCE - PARIS

180

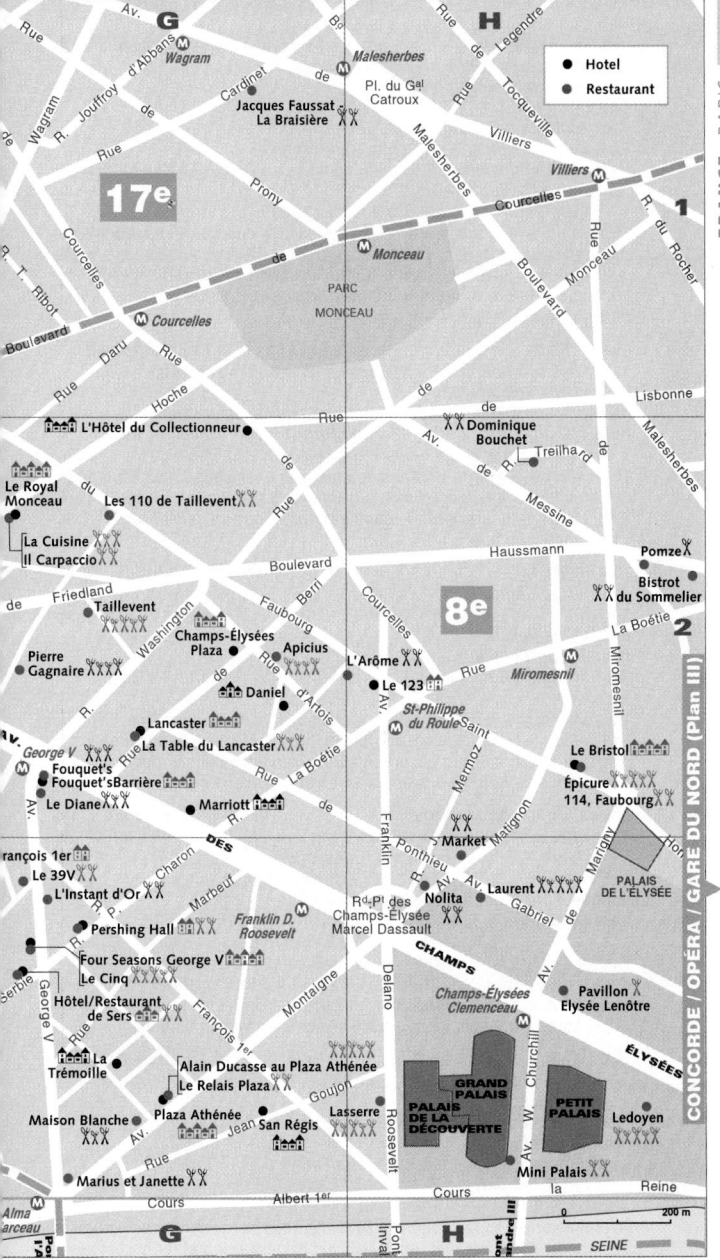

FRANCE - PARIS

Plaza Athénée

25 av. Montaigne (8th) – 🚇 Alma Marceau – 𝒞 01 53 67 66 65
– www.plaza-athenee-paris.com   G3
148 rm – ♦635/755 € ♦♦795/1025 €, ⚏ 75 € – 46 suites
Rest Alain Ducasse au Plaza Athénée ❀❀❀
Rest Le Relais Plaza – see restaurant listing
Rest La Cour Jardin – 𝒞 01 53 67 66 02 (open from mid-May to mid-September) Carte 80/140 €
◆ Palace ◆ Grand Luxury ◆ Classic ◆

This luxury Parisian hotel par excellence opened its doors in 1911. In addition to the classic and Art Deco styles of the guestrooms, the Plaza Athénée also boasts gilded fixtures and fittings, marble furnishings, and a luxurious Dior beauty centre. The essence of comfort! In summer enjoy classic dishes on the charming terrace of the Cour Jardin.

Le Bristol

112 r. Fg St-Honoré (8th) – 🚇 Miromesnil – 𝒞 01 53 43 43 00
– www.lebristolparis.com   H2
152 rm – ♦730/1850 € ♦♦730/1850 €, ⚏ 49 € – 36 suites
Rest Épicure ❀❀❀ **Rest 114, Faubourg** ❀ – see restaurant listing
◆ Palace ◆ Grand Luxury ◆ Stylish ◆

This luxury hotel, built in 1925 and boasting a new wing added in 2009, is arranged around a magnificent garden. Sumptuous guestrooms decorated in Louis XV or Louis XVI style, as well as a stunning swimming pool, reminiscent of a 19C yacht, on the top floor.

Shangri-La

10 av. d'Iéna (16th) ✉ 75116 – 🚇 Iéna – 𝒞 01 53 67 19 98 – www.shangri-la.com
54 rm – ♦550/1600 € ♦♦550/1600 €, ⚏ 48 € – 27 suites   F3
Rest L'Abeille ❀❀
Rest Shang Palace ❀ – see restaurant listing
Rest La Bauhinia – Menu 48 € (weekday lunch) – Carte 74/102 €
◆ Palace ◆ Historic ◆ Stylish ◆

The hallmark of this palatial hotel opened in 2011 is its fusion of French Empire and Asian styles. Occupying the former home of Prince Roland Bonaparte (1896), its classic architecture encompasses grandiose lounges, opulent luxury and dining options for every taste. A true sense of exclusivity!

Four Seasons George V

31 av. George-V (8th) – 🚇 George V
– 𝒞 01 49 52 70 00 – www.fourseasons.com/paris   G3
185 rm – ♦925/1550 € ♦♦925/1550 €, ⚏ 40 € – 59 suites
Rest Le Cinq ❀❀ – see restaurant listing
Rest La Galerie – 𝒞 01 49 52 70 06 – Carte 100/190 €
◆ Palace ◆ Grand Luxury ◆ Personalised ◆

This legendary luxury hotel, which opened in 1928, is decked out in 18C-style elegance and splendour. It offers luxurious, spacious guestrooms, beautiful works of art and a superb spa. Enjoy traditional cuisine at the Galerie restaurant, where tables are set out in the attractive inner courtyard in summer.

Le Royal Monceau

37 av. Hoche (8th) – 🚇 Charles de Gaulle-Etoile – 𝒞 01 42 99 88 00
– www.leroyalmonceau.com   G2
108 rm – ♦680/850 € ♦♦680/850 €, ⚏ 49 € – 41 suites
Rest La Cuisine ❀
Rest Il Carpaccio ❀ – see restaurant listing
Rest Le Grand Salon – (lunch only) Carte 60/80 €
◆ Palace ◆ Grand Luxury ◆ Design ◆

Refurbished from top to bottom in 2010, this hotel has been transformed into a 21C palace. The decor was designed by Philippe Starck and really confounds expectations. There is an art gallery, bookshop and high-tech cinema. At the cutting edge of modern interior design!

FRANCE - PARIS

 Raphael　　　　　　$\hat{L}$ & rm, $\overline{AC}$ $\widehat{\curvearrowright}$ $\hat{A}$ $\overline{VISA}$ $\overline{OO}$ $\overline{AE}$ ①

17 av. Kléber (16th) ⊠ *75116 –* Ⓜ *Kléber –* ℰ *01 53 64 32 00*
– www.raphael-hotel.com　　　　　　　　　　　　　　　　　**F2**
83 rm – †380/650 € ††650/950 €, ⊆ 40 €
– 37 suites
Rest *Raphael le Restaurant – (closed August, Saturday and Sunday)*
Carte 75/135 €
◆ Palace ◆ Stylish ◆
A magnificent hall with wood panelling, refined guestrooms, a fine dining restaurant and an elegant English style bar: such are the pleasures awaiting you at
Raphael... Opened in 1925 a stone's throw from the Arc de Triomphe, one of the
mythic hotels of Paris.

 Fouquet's Barrière　　　$\hat{L}$ ⑩ $\overline{\square}$ & $\overline{AC}$ $\widehat{\curvearrowright}$ $\hat{A}$ $\widehat{\curvearrowright}$ $\overline{VISA}$ $\overline{OO}$ $\overline{AE}$ ①

46 av. George-V (8th) – Ⓜ *George V –* ℰ *01 40 69 60 00*
– www.fouquets-barriere.com　　　　　　　　　　　　　　**G2**
50 rm – †640/770 € ††755/910 €, ⊆ 38 €
– 31 suites
Rest *Le Diane* ❀ *– see restaurant listing*
◆ Grand Luxury ◆ Modern ◆
This luxury hotel follows in the tradition of mythical Parisian brasseries. Founded
in 2006, its interior was designed by Jacques Garcia and blends French Empire-
style with Art Deco. There is plenty of mahogany, silk, and velvet combined with
high-tech facilities and a superb spa.

 Champs-Élysées Plaza　　$\hat{L}$ & rm, $\overline{AC}$ rm, $\widehat{\curvearrowright}$ $\overline{VISA}$ $\overline{OO}$ $\overline{AE}$ ①

35 r. de Berri (8th) – Ⓜ *George V –* ℰ *01 53 53 20 20*
– www.champselyseesplaza.com　　　　　　　　　　　　**G2**
25 rm – †490/810 € ††490/810 €, ⊆ 30 € *– 10 suites*
Rest *Le Keller – (closed 3 weeks in August and Bank Holidays)* Menu 46 €
– Carte 52/86 €
◆ Luxury ◆ Personalised ◆
With its elegance, space, harmony of colours, fusion of styles and attentive ser-
vice, this hotel is the epitome of opulent and cosy luxury. Fitness centre.

 Lancaster　　　　　　$\hat{L}$ $\overline{AC}$ $\widehat{\curvearrowright}$ $\hat{A}$ $\overline{VISA}$ $\overline{OO}$ $\overline{AE}$ ①

7 r. de Berri (8th) – Ⓜ *George V –* ℰ *01 40 76 40 76*
– www.hotel-lancaster.com　　　　　　　　　　　　　　**G2**
57 rm – †450/680 € ††560/760 €, ⊆ 40 €
– 14 suites
Rest *La Table du Lancaster* ❀ *– see restaurant listing*
◆ Luxury ◆ Classic ◆
Marlene Dietrich loved the discreet luxury of this property built in 1889 just a
stone's throw from the Champs-Élysées. Pleasant lobby and lounges filled with
antique furniture.

Renaissance Parc-Trocadéro　　$\otimes$ $\widehat{\curvearrowright}$ $\hat{L}$ $\overline{AC}$ $\widehat{\curvearrowright}$ $\hat{A}$ $\overline{\curvearrowright}$

55 av. R. Poincaré (16th) ⊠ *75116*　　　　　　　$\overline{VISA}$ $\overline{OO}$ $\overline{AE}$ ①
– Ⓜ *Victor Hugo –* ℰ *01 44 05 66 66*
– www.renaissanceleparctrocadero.com　　　　　　　　**E3**
122 rm – †299/899 € ††299/899 €, ⊆ 29 € *– 4 suites*
Rest *Le Relais du Parc –* ℰ *01 44 05 66 10 (closed 3 weeks in August,*
Saturday lunch and Sunday) Menu 35 € *(weekday lunch)*
– Carte 42/74 €
◆ Grand Luxury ◆ Chain hotel ◆ Elegant ◆
The hotel is well named as it was completely refurbished in the spring of 2011.
The French-style garden provided the inspiration for the contemporary decora-
tion in the guestrooms, which is in complete harmony with the Parisian archi-
tecture.

Marriott Champs-Élysées

70 av. des Champs-Élysées (8th)
– **M** *Franklin D. Roosevelt* – *℘ 01 53 93 55 00 – www.marriottchampselysees.com*
173 rm – †400/800 € ††500/1000 €, � 32 € – 19 suites   **G2**
Rest *Le Restaurant* – *℘ 01 53 93 55 44 (closed lunch Saturday and Sunday)* Carte 48/79 €
♦ Luxury ♦ Chain hotel ♦ Modern ♦

A beautiful Haussmann-style building along the Champs-Élysées. The spacious guestrooms, renovated in 2009, are the epitome of restrained contemporary elegance, with some boasting views of the city's famous avenue and others overlooking the atrium or interior courtyard. The menu in Le Restaurant is centred around traditional dishes and grilled meats.

L'Hôtel du Collectionneur

51 r. de Courcelles (8th) – **M** *Courcelles*
– *℘ 01 58 36 67 00 – www.hotelducollectionneur.com*   **G2**
418 rm – †300/790 € ††300/790 €, ⊻ 35 € – 52 suites
Rest *Safran* – *℘ 01 58 36 67 96* – Menu 49 € (dinner) – Carte approx. 55 €
♦ Luxury ♦ Chain hotel ♦ Functional ♦

Inspired by the cruise liners of the 1930s, this hotel has revived their luxurious and refined spirit, with its elegant Art Deco bedrooms designed by Jacques Garcia – those facing the patio are particularly quiet. Fitness centre. The brasserie-style menu at the Safran is adapted to international tastes.

Vernet

25 r. Vernet (8th) – **M** *Charles de Gaulle-Etoile* – *℘ 01 44 31 98 00*
– *www.hotelvernet.com*   **F2**
41 rm – †270/450 € ††290/490 €, ⊻ 30 € – 9 suites
Rest *Le Vernet* – see restaurant listing
♦ Luxury ♦ Classic ♦

Fine 1920s building in a little street near the Champs-Élysées. Elegant rooms mainly in traditional style, others have a more contemporary feel. A Parisian atmosphere reigns throughout.

Baltimore

88 bis av. Kléber (16th) ✉ *75116* – **M** *Boissière* – *℘ 01 44 34 54 54*
– *www.hotel-baltimore-paris.com*   **E3**
102 rm – †250/580 € ††250/580 €, ⊻ 26 € – 1 suite
Rest *La Table du Baltimore* – see restaurant listing
♦ Historic ♦ Personalised ♦

The contemporary decor of elegant furniture and trendy fabrics in the guestrooms contrasts with the building's 19C Haussmann architecture. The overall feel is warm and welcoming. The bar is worth a special mention and is appreciated by business travellers in particular.

La Trémoille

14 r. Trémoille (8th) – **M** *Alma Marceau* – *℘ 01 56 52 14 00*
– *www.hotel-tremoille.com*   **G3**
88 rm – †320/840 € ††320/840 €, ⊻ 28 € – 5 suites
Rest *Louis²* – *(closed Saturday, Sunday and Bank Holidays)* Carte 51/67 €
♦ Luxury ♦ Modern ♦

The showbiz crowd favours this hotel. The decor mixes the old with the contemporary, along with hi-tech fixtures and fittings, Portuguese marble and ceramics in the bathrooms. Contemporary cuisine in a lounge-style atmosphere.

Renaissance Arc de Triomphe

39 av. Wagram (17th) – **M** *Ternes*
– *℘ 01 55 37 55 37 – www.renaissancearcdetriomphe.fr*   **F2**
113 rm – †339/950 € ††339/950 €, ⊻ 30 € – 5 suites
Rest *Makassar* – see restaurant listing
♦ Luxury ♦ Chain hotel ♦ Design ♦

Occupying the site of the former Empire theatre, this hotel opened in 2009 was designed by Christian de Portzamparc. 1970s themed decor in the guestrooms and high-tech facilities.

FRANCE - PARIS

San Régis
🅰🅲 📶 🆅🅸🆂🅰 🆘 🅰🅴 ⓞ

12 r. J. Goujon (8th) – Ⓜ *Champs-Elysées Clemenceau* – ℰ 01 44 95 16 16
– *www.hotel-sanregis.fr*   **G3**
40 rm – 🛏430/790 € 🛏🛏590/790 €, ⬛ 30 € – 3 suites
Rest – *(closed August, Saturday and Sunday, except residents)*
Carte 52/74 €
◆ Luxury ◆ Stylish ◆

This townhouse dating from 1857 has been restored with great taste. Features
include a fine staircase adorned with stained glass and statues which leads to
delightful guestrooms, some classic in style, others more contemporary. The
hotel's exquisitely appointed classic restaurant occupies a luxurious and exclusive lounge-library.

Keppler without rest
🆑 🕉 ♿ 🅰🅲 📶 🕍 🆅🅸🆂🅰 🆘 🅰🅴 ⓞ

10 r. Keppler (16th) ✉ 75116 – Ⓜ *George V* – ℰ 01 47 20 65 05
– *www.keppler.fr*   **F3**
34 rm – 🛏250/370 € 🛏🛏300/500 €, ⬛ 22 € – 5 suites
◆ Luxury ◆ Personalised ◆ Cosy ◆

The Keppler's luxurious and refined decor bears the hallmark of Pierre-Yves
Rochon. There is a sense of magic pervading the lounges, library and guestrooms. A hammam, sauna and fitness room complete the picture at one of the
city's most elegant addresses.

Intercontinental Avenue Marceau
🆑 ♿ 🅰🅲 📶 🕍

64 av. Marceau (8th) – Ⓜ *George V*   🆅🅸🆂🅰 🆘 🅰🅴 ⓞ
– ℰ 01 44 43 36 36 – *www.ic-marceau.com*   **F2-3**
55 rm – 🛏250/1600 € 🛏🛏250/1600 €, ⬛ 30 €
Rest M64 – see restaurant listing
◆ Luxury ◆ Business ◆ Modern ◆

This luxury designer hotel is close to the Arc de Triomphe. The decor is a blend
of high technology, contemporary furnishings and replicas of Italian Renaissance frescoes and sketches.

Dokhan's Radisson Blu without rest
🅰🅲 📶 🛏 🆅🅸🆂🅰 🆘 🅰🅴 ⓞ

117 r. Lauriston (16th) ✉ 75116 – Ⓜ *Trocadéro* – ℰ 01 53 65 66 99
– *www.radissonblu.com/dokhanhotel-paristrocadero*   **E3**
41 rm – 🛏250/650 € 🛏🛏250/650 €, ⬛ 19 € – 4 suites
◆ Luxury ◆ Cosy ◆ Personalised ◆

In this beautiful Haussmann property, the neo-Classic decor couldn't be further
from contemporary functionality. The pale green, 18C wood-panelled champagne bar and richly decorated guestrooms in particular, are teeming with
decadent charm.

Hôtel de Sers
🆑 ♿ 🅰🅲 📶 🕍 🆅🅸🆂🅰 🆘 🅰🅴 ⓞ

41 av. Pierre 1er de Serbie (8th) – Ⓜ *George V* – ℰ 01 53 23 75 75
– *www.hoteldesers.com*   **G3**
45 rm – 🛏625/1050 € 🛏🛏625/1050 €, ⬛ 29 € – 7 suites
Rest Restaurant de Sers – see restaurant listing
◆ Luxury ◆ Modern ◆ Personalised ◆

The Marquis de Sers would fail to recognise his late-19C property! The mix of
styles is, however, a success. While the entrance hall has preserved its original
character, the guestrooms are resolutely contemporary. An elegant address.

Regent's Garden without rest
🚗 ♿ 🅰🅲 📶 🅿 🆅🅸🆂🅰 🆘 🅰🅴 ⓞ

6 r. P.-Demours (17th) – Ⓜ *Ternes* – ℰ 01 45 74 07 30
– *www.hotel-regents-paris.com*   **F1**
39 rm – 🛏250/520 € 🛏🛏250/520 €, ⬛ 22 € – 1 suite
◆ Traditional ◆ Modern ◆ Cosy ◆

This charming townhouse has been renovated in a contemporary style with the
guestrooms offering a blend of traditional and modern decor. Ecolabel certified.
Japanese garden.

FRANCE - PARIS

 Mac Mahon without rest   👌 🅰️🅲 🛜 🆅🆂🅰 ⓿ 🅰🅴 ⓪

3 av. Mac-Mahon (17th) – Ⓜ *Charles de Gaulle-Etoile –* ☎ *01 43 80 23 00*
– www.champselyseesmm.com   **F2**
40 rm – �199/1280 € ♟199/1280 €, � 25 €
♦ Luxury ♦ Design ♦
This Haussmann building is a stone's throw from the Arc de Triomphe. Completely refurbished in 2012, the hotel is a skilful blend of Empire-style and contemporary decoration. A perfect base for exploring all four corners of Paris.

 La Villa Maillot without rest   🦶 👌 🅰️🅲 🛜 🔏 🆅🆂🅰 ⓿ 🅰🅴 ⓪

143 av. Malakoff (opening scheduled in May after renovation) (16th)
✉ *75116 –* Ⓜ *Porte Maillot –* ☎ *01 53 64 52 52 – www.lavillamaillot.fr*
40 rm – ♟225/460 € ♟225/460 €, ⊒ 27 € – 2 suites   **E2**
♦ Business ♦ Personalised ♦
Situated near Porte Maillot, this hotel has well-soundproofed guestrooms decorated in soft colours. Breakfast is served in a glass conservatory. Sauna and hammam.

 Splendid Étoile   🅰️🅲 🛜 🔏 🆅🆂🅰 ⓿ 🅰🅴 ⓪

1bis av. Carnot (17th) – Ⓜ *Charles de Gaulle-Etoile –* ☎ *01 45 72 72 00*
– www.hsplendid.com   **F2**
55 rm – ♟230/390 € ♟245/410 €, ⊒ 25 € – 2 suites
Rest *Le Pré Carré* – see restaurant listing
♦ Traditional ♦ Personalised ♦
The Splendid Étoile is recognisable by its attractive stone façade and wrought-iron balconies. It offers large guestrooms (some with views of the Arc de Triomphe), which owe their character to the Louis XV inspired furniture and heavy drapes. Overall, a very pleasant, elegant style.

 Pergolèse without rest   🦶 🅰️🅲 🛜 🆅🆂🅰 ⓿ 🅰🅴 ⓪

3 r. Pergolèse (16th) ✉ *75116 –* Ⓜ *Argentine –* ☎ *01 53 64 04 04*
– www.pergolese.com   **E2**
40 rm – ♟149/348 € ♟149/540 €, ⊒ 18 €
♦ Business ♦ Modern ♦ Design ♦
Hidden behind a sober façade in this chic district is a hotel with a soothing interior design featuring whitewashed walls and light wood furniture. Tranquil, very well-maintained guestrooms with everything you could possibly need, from flat screen TVs to iPods docks. Cosy bar.

 Élysées Régencia without rest   🅰️🅲 🛜 🔏 🆅🆂🅰 ⓿ 🅰🅴 ⓪

41 av. Marceau (16th) ✉ *75116 –* Ⓜ *George V –* ☎ *01 47 20 42 65*
– www.regencia.com   **F3**
43 rm – ♟195/515 € ♟215/555 €, ⊒ 19 €
♦ Business ♦ Modern ♦
This hotel has spacious guestrooms decorated in bright, striking tones (blue, fuchsia and aniseed), along with two Provençal-style junior suites. After shopping along avenue Montaigne, relax to your heart's content in the deep red lounge.

 Daniel   🦶 rm, 🅰️🅲 🛜 🛋 🆅🆂🅰 ⓿ 🅰🅴 ⓪

8 r. Frédéric-Bastiat (8th) – Ⓜ *St-Philippe du Roule –* ☎ *01 42 56 17 00*
– www.hoteldanielparis.com   **G2**
22 rm – ♟350/590 € ♟420/590 €, ⊒ 24 € – 4 suites
Rest – *(closed August, Saturday and Sunday)* Menu 39 € (lunch), 55/74 €
– Carte 37/99 €
♦ Luxury ♦ Personalised ♦ Oriental ♦
The theme in the Daniel hotel is the world of travel, with an elegant and welcoming decor of Liberty prints and decorative objects from around the globe. Dishes bear the influence of the Mediterranean, as well as the local market.

Pershing Hall 🔥 AC 📶 🎴 VISA 💳 AE 🔵

49 r. Pierre Charron (8th) – Ⓜ *George V* – ☎ *01 58 36 58 00*
– www.pershinghall.com **G3**
20 rm – ♦590/690 € ♦♦590/690 €, ☒ 28 € – 6 suites
Rest *Pershing Hall* – see restaurant listing
♦ Luxury ♦ Modern ♦ Minimalist ♦
This townhouse was the residence of General Pershing during the Great War, it was then a veterans' club, and since 2001 it has been home to this luxury hotel styled by designer Andrée Putman. A veritable page in Parisian history with a chic and discreet ambience.

François 1er without rest AC 📶 🎴 VISA 💳 AE 🔵

7 r. Magellan (8th) – Ⓜ *George V* – ☎ *01 47 23 44 04*
– www.hotelfrancoispremier.com **G3**
38 rm – ♦250/490 € ♦♦270/490 €, ☒ 22 € – 2 suites
♦ Luxury ♦ Personalised ♦
Carrara marble, mouldings, curios, antique furniture and a plethora of paintings set the lavish decor created by French architect Pierre Yves Rochon. Substantial buffet breakfasts.

Les Jardins de la Villa without rest 🔥 🐾 ♿ AC 📶 🎴

5 r. Bélidor (17th) – Ⓜ *Porte Maillot* – ☎ *01 53 81 01 10* VISA 💳 AE
– www.jardinsdelavilla.com **E1**
33 rm – ♦250/480 € ♦♦250/600 €, ☒ 28 €
♦ Luxury ♦ Design ♦
Fashion addicts will be bowled over by this small hotel which is big on couture. With its black and shocking pink decor, the references to the world of fashion are numerous. Original, chic and comfortable.

Le 123 without rest AC 📶 VISA 💳 AE 🔵

123 r. du Faubourg-St-Honoré (8th) – Ⓜ *St-Philippe du Roule*
– ☎ 01 53 89 01 23 – www.astotel.com **H2**
41 rm – ♦199/560 € ♦♦199/560 €, ☒ 17 €
♦ Luxury ♦ Personalised ♦
The 123 is a fusion of varying styles, materials and colours. Haute-couture guest-rooms, which are the perfect base for a shopping trip in this highly fashionable district of the city.

Amarante Arc de Triomphe without rest ♿ AC 📶 🎴

25 r. Th.-de-Banville (17th) – Ⓜ *Pereire* VISA 💳 AE 🔵
– ☎ 01 47 63 76 69 – www.amarantearcdetriomphe.com **F1**
50 rm – ♦140/250 € ♦♦140/300 €, ☒ 20 €
♦ Chain hotel ♦ Classic ♦
A well-located hotel with elegant guestrooms inspired by the Directoire style, some of which overlook the patio. Popular with business and leisure travellers alike.

Étoile Résidence Impériale without rest AC 📶

155 av. de Malakoff (16th) ✉ *75116* VISA 💳 AE 🔵
– Ⓜ Porte Maillot – ☎ 01 45 00 23 45 – www.residenceimperiale.com
37 rm – ♦110/200 € ♦♦110/200 €, ☒ 15 € **E2**
♦ Townhouse ♦ Modern ♦ Cosy ♦
This hotel is located a stone's throw from the city's exhibition centre. It offers bedrooms that have been recently renovated in a pleasant, contemporary style. Every room is well soundproofed, ensuring a good night's sleep for every guest.

Magellan without rest 🐾 🚗 📶 VISA 💳 AE 🔵

17 r. J.-B. Dumas (17th) – Ⓜ *Porte de Champerret* – ☎ *01 45 72 44 51*
– www.hotelmagellan.com **F1**
72 rm – ♦118/168 € ♦♦173/193 €, ☒ 17 €
♦ Business ♦ Design ♦
The Magellan's charming guestrooms are gradually being refurbished in this building dating from 1900. The attractive garden, always a bonus in Paris, is used for breakfast in summer.

FRANCE - PARIS

Star Champs Élysées without rest   🔣 🛜 VISA ⓪ AE ⓪

18 r. de l'Arc-de-Triomphe (17th) – ⓜ Charles de Gaulle-Etoile
– ℰ 01 43 80 27 69 – www.hotelstarchampselysees.com   **F2**
62 rm – ✦100/250 € ✦✦110/250 €, 🖵 13 €
♦ Townhouse ♦ Modern ♦

This hotel is in a quiet street near the Place de l'Étoile and the Arc de Triomphe.
It offers guestrooms which, although small, are functional and well maintained.
The reception area with its medieval decoration makes for an original detail! A
good place that caters to both business travellers and tourists.

Le Cinq – Hôtel Four Seasons George V   🔣 ⇌ ⇌♈ VISA ⓪ AE ⓪

😃 😃 31 av. George V (8th) – ⓜ George V – ℰ 01 49 52 71 54
– www.fourseasons.com/paris   **G3**
Rest – Menu 95 € (lunch), 155/250 € – Carte 175/290 € 🏵
♦ Creative ♦ Luxury ♦

The superb dining room, a majestic evocation of the Grand Trianon, opens onto
a delightful interior garden. Impressive wine list and top-notch cuisine.
➜ Ventrèche de thon rouge de Méditerranée, tartare au caviar, gelée de
pomme verte, wasabi. Homard bleu cuit sur sel au goémon, ravioli vapeur
au fenouil sauvage. Fraisier minute, granité aux fraises, sorbet au caillé de
brebis à l'olive.

Ledoyen   🔣 ⇌ ⇌♈ P VISA ⓪ AE ⓪

😃 😃 😃 8 av. Dutuit (carré Champs-Élysées) (8th)
– ⓜ Champs-Elysées Clemenceau – ℰ 01 53 05 10 01
– Closed 27 July-18 August, Saturday, Sunday and Bank Holidays
Rest – Menu 98 € (lunch), 210/310 € bi – Carte 170/255 € 🏵   **H3**
♦ Creative ♦ Luxury ♦

This neo-Classical pavilion is located within the gardens of the Champs-Élysées.
Superb setting, luxurious decor and a remarkable dining experience. Christian
Le Squer champions cuisine that is unpretentious yet cooked to perfection. An
incomparable and intense pleasure for the senses.
➜ Grosses langoustines bretonnes, émulsion d'agrumes. Ris de veau en
brochette de bois de citronnelle rissolée, jus d'herbes. Croquant de pamplemousse cuit et cru.

Alain Ducasse au Plaza Athénée – Hôtel Plaza Athénée

😃 😃 😃 25 av. Montaigne (8th) – ⓜ Alma Marceau   🔣 ⇌♈ VISA ⓪ AE ⓪
– ℰ 01 53 67 65 00 – www.alain-ducasse.com
– Closed 2 to 26 August, Monday lunch, Tuesday lunch, Wednesday lunch,
Saturday and Sunday   **G3**
Rest – Menu 380 € – Carte 200/340 € 🏵
♦ Creative ♦ Luxury ♦

The sumptuous regency décor has been redone with a mind to design and
organza. Inventive dishes from a talented team coached by Ducasse and 1001
selected wines: the palatial life!
➜ Légumes et fruits. Homard et pomme de mer. Baba au rhum comme à
Monte-Carlo.

Épicure – Hôtel Bristol   🔣♈ 🔣 ⇌♈ VISA ⓪ AE ⓪

😃 😃 😃 112 r. Fg St-Honoré (8th) – ⓜ Miromesnil – ℰ 01 53 43 43 40
– www.lebristolparis.com   **H2**
Rest – Menu 130 € (lunch)/280 € – Carte 145/320 € 🏵
♦ Modern ♦ Luxury ♦ Intimate ♦

The Bristol's restaurant underwent a transformation in 2011. The bright dining
room overlooking the garden boasts a restrained, distinguished elegance in
which the glamour of the 18C shines forth. The virtuosity of Éric Fréchon's classic cuisine bears witness to his freedom of expression with regard to great tradition. He creates dishes that are fresh and endowed with the finest flavours!
➜ Macaronis à la truffe noire, artichaut et foie gras de canard gratinés au
vieux parmesan. Merlan de ligne en croûte de pain de mie, imprimé aux
amandes, tétragone mi-cuite relevée au curry. Précieux chocolat Nyangbo,
fine tuile croustillante.

XXXXX **Taillevent**   🔠 ⇔ ⊐⍩ 📷 🆅🅸🆂🅰 ⚫⚫ 🅰🅴 ⓪

❀❀ 15 r. Lamennais (8th) – ⓜ Charles de Gaulle-Etoile – ℰ 01 44 95 15 01
– www.taillevent.com
– Closed 27 July-26 August, Saturday, Sunday and Bank Holidays
Rest – (number of covers limited, pre-book) Menu 82 €   **G2**
(lunch)/195 € – Carte 145/250 € 🏵
♦ Classic ♦ Luxury ♦

Wainscoting and works of art adorn this former private residence dating from
the 19C. It was once home to the Duke of Morny, and is now a guardian of
French haute cuisine. Exquisite cuisine and magnificent wine list.
➜ Rémoulade de tourteau à l'aneth. Noix de ris de veau croustillante, jus à
l'oseille. Tarte renversée au chocolat et au café grillé.

XXXXX **Lasserre**   🔠 ⇔ ⊐⍩ 🆅🅸🆂🅰 ⚫⚫ 🅰🅴 ⓪

❀❀ 17 av. F.-D.-Roosevelt (8th) – ⓜ Franklin D. Roosevelt – ℰ 01 43 59 53 43
– www.restaurant-lasserre.com
– Closed August, Tuesday lunch, Wednesday lunch, Saturday lunch, Sunday and
Monday   **H3**
Rest – Menu 80 € (lunch)/195 € – Carte 143/245 €
♦ Classic ♦ Luxury ♦

Neo-Classical decor, columns, heavy fabrics and crystal chandeliers combine to
create a traditional ambience in this great Parisian institution, opened by René
Lasserre in 1942. Classic cuisine and stylish service.
➜ Langoustines en savoureux bouillon ginger-lime. Bar tomat 'o' girolles.
Vacherin à la verveine et cœur coulant à la framboise.

XXXXX **Laurent**   🔠 ⇔ ⊐⍩ 🆅🅸🆂🅰 ⚫⚫ 🅰🅴 ⓪

❀ 41 av. Gabriel (8th) – ⓜ Champs Elysées Clemenceau – ℰ 01 42 25 00 39
– www.le-laurent.com
– Closed 23 December-2 January, Saturday lunch, Sunday and Bank Holidays
Rest – Menu 88 € (weekdays)/170 € – Carte 145/225 € 🏵   **H3**
♦ Classic ♦ Luxury ♦

A stone's throw from the Champs Élysées, this former hunting lodge belonging
to Louis XIV with its elegant shaded terraces has a loyal following. Traditional
cuisine and a good wine list.
➜ Araignée de mer dans ses sucs en gelée, crème de fenouil. Flanchet de
veau de lait braisé, blettes à la moelle. Glace vanille minute.

XXXX **L'Abeille** – Hôtel Shangri-La   ₺ 🔠 ⊐⍩ 🆅🅸🆂🅰 ⚫⚫ 🅰🅴

❀❀ 10 av. d'Iéna (16th) ⊠ 75116 – ⓜ Iéna – ℰ 01 53 67 19 90
– www.shangri-la.com
– Closed 30 July-28 August, 22 to 30 December, Sunday and Monday
Rest – (dinner only) Menu 210 € – Carte 135/285 € 🏵   **F3**
♦ Classic ♦ Elegant ♦ Luxury ♦

The Shangri-La hotel's gastronomic French restaurant is named in honour of
Napoleon's emblem – the bee. Amid this extremely opulent decor, chef Philippe
Labbé conjures up highly ambitious classic cuisine. It is tinged with creativity
and showcases the very best ingredients.
➜ Cèpes de Corrèze au jus de sous bois, râpée de noisettes fraîches et de
pomme, crémeux de jaune d'œuf. Homard bleu de casier en deux services.
Mûres sauvages, feuilleté minute caramélisé.

XXXX **Apicius** (Jean-Pierre Vigato)   🔠 ⇔ ⊐⍩ 🅿 🆅🅸🆂🅰 ⚫⚫ 🅰🅴

❀❀ 20 r. d'Artois (8th) – ⓜ St-Philippe du Roule – ℰ 01 43 80 19 66
– www.restaurant-apicius.com
– Closed August, Saturday and Sunday
Rest – Menu 160/200 € – Carte 110/195 € 🏵   **G2**
♦ Classic ♦ Elegant ♦

Restaurant on the ground floor of a listed town house with a garden. There is a
succession of dining rooms in a chic mix of classic, rococo and modern styles.
Up-to-date cuisine; superb wine list.
➜ Les poissons bleus, maquereau, homard et crevettes aux algues. Pigeon
grillé, bettes braisées, persil craquant et sauce diable au beurre salé. Agrumes infusés à la cardamome et à la badiane, sorbet Campari.

FRANCE - PARIS

189

FRANCE - PARIS

XXXX   **Pierre Gagnaire**   🕭 🔃 ⇔ ⊐️ 𝘝𝘐𝘚𝘈 ⊚ 𝘈𝘌

❀❀❀   *6 r. Balzac (8th)* – 🚇 *George V* – 𝒞 *01 58 36 12 50*
– *www.pierregagnaire.com*
– *Closed August, Christmas Holidays, Saturday and Sunday*   **G2**
Rest – Menu 110 € (lunch)/280 € – Carte 285/380 € 🍷
♦ Creative ♦ Elegant ♦
The restaurant's chic and restrained contemporary decor is in complete contrast
to the renowned inventiveness of this famous chef.
→ Oreiller d'herbes de féra du lac Léman, berce et arroche rouge, lait caillé
de brebis au curry vert. Darne de turbot sauvage grillée, terminée à l'étouf-
fée au cerfeuil. Le grand dessert de Pierre Gagnaire.

XXXX   **Michel Rostang**   🔃 ⇔ ⊐️ 𝘝𝘐𝘚𝘈 ⊚ 𝘈𝘌 ⓪

❀❀   *20 r. Rennequin (17th)* – 🚇 *Ternes* – 𝒞 *01 47 63 40 77*
– *www.michelrostang.com*
– *Closed Monday except dinner from September-June, Saturday lunch and
Sunday*   **F1**
Rest – Menu 78 € (lunch), 169/198 € – Carte 140/225 € 🍷
♦ Classic ♦ Elegant ♦ Luxury ♦
Wood panelling, Robj statuettes, Lalique glass and Art Deco stained glass com-
bine to give this restaurant a luxurious and original look. Exquisite classic cuisine
and an equally outstanding wine list.
→ Escargots petits-gris, cannelloni de royale d'ail et persil, spaghettis noirs.
Noix de ris de veau croustillante aux écrevisses. Croquant de chocolat gua-
naja, crème des Pères Chartreux et noisettes en gelée de Chartreuse verte.

XXXX   **Guy Savoy**   🔃 ⇔ ⊐️ 𝘝𝘐𝘚𝘈 ⊚ 𝘈𝘌 ⓪

❀❀❀   *18 r. Troyon (17th)* – 🚇 *Charles de Gaulle-Etoile* – 𝒞 *01 43 80 40 61*
– *www.guysavoy.com*
– *Closed Christmas Holidays, Saturday lunch, Sunday and Monday*
Rest – Menu 315/490 € – Carte 170/300 € 🍷   **F2**
♦ Creative ♦ Trendy ♦
Glass, leather and wenge wood combine with African sculpture and works by
some of the greatest names in contemporary art to provide the setting for the
refined and inventive cuisine in this resolutely 21C restaurant.
→ Colours of caviar. Saumon "figé" sur la glace, consommé brûlant, perles
de citron. Boule noire.

XXXX   **Hiramatsu**   🔃 ⇔ ⊐️ (dinner) 𝘝𝘐𝘚𝘈 ⊚ 𝘈𝘌 ⓪

❀   *52 r. Longchamp (16th)* ✉ *75116* – 🚇 *Trocadéro* – 𝒞 *01 56 81 08 80*
– *www.hiramatsu.co.jp*
– *Closed August, 24 December-2 January, Saturday and Sunday*   **E3**
Rest – *(number of covers limited, pre-book)* Menu 48 € (lunch)/115 € 🍷
♦ Classic ♦ Elegant ♦ Luxury ♦
Despite its Japanese name, Hiramatsu honours French cuisine with both inven-
tiveness and talent. In this very elegant setting, high gastronomy is expressed in
the form of a single 'carte blanche' menu in the evening, which changes in line
with market availability.
→ Cuisine du marché.

XXX   **Shang Palace** – Hôtel Shangri-La   🕭 🔃 ⇔ ⊐️ 𝘝𝘐𝘚𝘈 ⊚ 𝘈𝘌

❀   *10 av. d'Iéna (16th)* ✉ *75116* – 🚇 *Iéna* – 𝒞 *01 53 67 19 92*
– *www.shangri-la.com*
– *Closed 15 July-21 August, Tuesday and Wednesday*   **F3**
Rest – Menu 58 € (weekday lunch), 70/98 € – Carte 60/100 €
♦ Chinese ♦ Exotic ♦
The Shang Palace occupies one of the basement floors at the Shangri-La hotel.
It gracefully recreates the decor of a luxury Chinese restaurant with its jade
columns, sculpted screens and crystal chandeliers. The menu pays homage to
the full flavours and authenticity of Cantonese gastronomy.
→ Crêpe de riz rouge aux crevettes. Canard laqué à la pékinoise en deux
services. Crème de mangue, pomélo et perles de sagou.

XXX **Prunier** 🛋 AC ♧ ⌗ VISA ⚏ AE ①

16 av. Victor-Hugo (16th) ✉ *75116 –* Ⓜ *Charles de Gaulle-Etoile*
– ✆ 01 44 17 35 85 – www.prunier.com
– Closed August, Saturday lunch, Sunday and Bank Holidays   F2
Rest – Menu 65 € (lunch), 90/150 € – Carte 68/168 €
♦ Fish and seafood ♦ Retro ♦ Luxury ♦
A culinary institution created in 1925 by the architect Boileau. It has a superb, listed Art Deco interior of black marble, mosaics and stained-glass windows. In addition to enjoying excellent fish and seafood, mark the occasion by tasting the "house" caviar from southwest France.

XXX **La Table du Lancaster** – Hôtel Lancaster   🛋 AC ♧ ⌗
ॐ
7 r. de Berri (8th) – Ⓜ *George V – ✆ 01 40 76 40 18*   VISA ⚏ AE ①
– www.hotel-lancaster.fr
– Closed Saturday lunch   G2
Rest – Menu 56 € bi (weekday lunch), 115/145 € – Carte 100/170 € ॐ
♦ Modern ♦
A hushed and elegant atmosphere; a terrace laid out in a plant-filled courtyard, away from prying eyes... La Table du Lancaster certainly provides a private and intimate setting. Come and savour the original and delicately flavoured dishes, which have a truly international feel.
➔ Grenouilles à la meunière, sauce persillée. Sole à la ciboulette (Troisgros brothers recipe, 1975). Soufflé.

XXX **La Cuisine** – Hôtel Le Royal Monceau   🛋 AC ⌗ VISA ⚏ AE ①
ॐ
37 av. Hoche (8th) – Ⓜ *Charles De Gaulle Etoile – ✆ 01 42 99 88 00*
– www.leroyalmonceau.com   G2
Rest – Menu 70 € (weekday lunch), 95/135 € – Carte 75/140 € ॐ
♦ Modern ♦ Design ♦
La Cuisine at the Royal Monceau has the exclusive atmosphere you would expect of such an establishment. This is combined with an intimate, arty feel (original photos, lithographs etc). The effect is reminiscent of a private parlour. French cuisine.
➔ Foie gras poêlé, figues fraîches et rôties, marmelade de châtaigne. Pavé de cabillaud confit à basse température, coquillages et chorizo, croquettes à l'ail. Tarte infiniment citron.

XXX **Le Diane** – Hôtel Fouquet's Barrière   🛋 & AC ⌗ VISA ⚏ AE ①
ॐ
46 av. George-V (8th) – Ⓜ *Georges V – ✆ 01 40 69 60 60*
– www.fouquets-barriere.com
– Closed 28 July-20 August, 1 to 7 January, Saturday lunch, Sunday and Monday   G2
Rest – Menu 65 € bi (lunch), 88/108 € – Carte 95/159 €
♦ Modern ♦ Luxury ♦
Tucked away inside the Hotel Fouquet's Barrière, Le Diane is the epitome of elegance and discretion. The dining area is housed in a rotunda, all done out in golden browns and opening onto a lovely patio. Beautifully prepared gourmet cuisine.
➔ Saumon mi-cuit, couteau et radis multicolores. Turbot de petit bateau, supions garnis de girolles et févettes, jus à la marjolaine. Soufflé au citron de Menton, sorbet mojito.

XXX **Le Vernet** – Hôtel Vernet   AC ⌗ VISA ⚏ AE
25 r. Vernet (8th) – Ⓜ *Charles de Gaulle-Etoile – ✆ 01 44 31 98 00*
– www.hotelvernet.com
– Closed August, 23 to 27 December, Monday dinner, Saturday and Sunday
Rest – Menu 125 € (dinner) – Carte 76/102 €   F2
♦ Modern ♦ Elegant ♦
The stunning dining room of the Hôtel Vernet is crowned by a large Eiffel designed glass canopy and embellished with pilasters and drapes. The perfect setting for a special occasion, where the refined cuisine encompasses a classic repertoire with new combinations of flavours.

FRANCE - PARIS

XXX ⚜ **Stella Maris** (Tateru Yoshino) 　AK ⟷ VISA ⊙⊙ AE ⓪

4 r. Arsène-Houssaye (8th) – Ⓜ *Charles de Gaulle-Etoile* – 𝒞 *01 42 89 16 22*
– *www.stellamaris-paris.com*
– *Closed Saturday lunch, Sunday and Bank Holidays* 　F2
Rest – Menu 68 € bi (lunch)/130 € – Carte 96/145 €
♦ Modern ♦ Elegant ♦
A brilliant Japanese chef who is fanatical about fine French cuisine has created a
classic menu at this refined restaurant near the Arc de Triomphe. Sleek decor
with Art Deco touches.
➔ Millefeuille de thon mariné et d'aubergine. Tête de veau en cocotte.
Kouign amann.

XXX **Fouquet's** 　🛱 ⟷ VISA ⊙⊙ AE ⓪

99 av. Champs-Élysées (8th) – Ⓜ *George V* – 𝒞 *01 40 69 60 50*
– *www.lucienbarriere.com* 　G2
Rest – Menu 78/125 € – Carte 92/138 €
♦ Classic ♦ Formal ♦
Since its creation in 1899, this mythical brasserie on "the world's most beautiful
avenue" has catered to the Paris jet set. It offers a lovely listed interior, a packed
terrace, and brasserie fare.

XXX **Maison Blanche** 　≤ 🛱 AK ⟷ VISA ⊙⊙ AE ⓪

15 av. Montaigne (8th) – Ⓜ *Alma Marceau* – 𝒞 *01 47 23 55 99*
– *www.maison-blanche.fr*
– *Closed 2 weeks in August, lunch Saturday and Sunday* 　G3
Rest – Menu 69/110 € – Carte 60/200 €
♦ Modern ♦ Elegant ♦
A modern, loft-style restaurant overlooking Paris from the top of the Théâtre
des Champs-Élysées. Contemporary cuisine with Mediterranean and Asian influ-
ences.

XXX **La Table du Baltimore** – Hôtel Baltimore 　AK ⟷ ⟷

1 r. Léo Delibes (16th) ✉ *75016* – Ⓜ *Boissière* 　VISA ⊙⊙ AE ⓪
– 𝒞 *01 44 34 54 34* – *www.hotel-baltimore-paris.com*
– *Closed August, Saturday, Sunday and Bank Holidays* 　E3
Rest – Menu 68 € (lunch), 78/95 € bi – Carte 74/89 €
♦ Modern ♦ Cosy ♦
The Hotel Baltimore is home to this chic restaurant boasting old wood panel-
ling, contemporary furniture and artwork. An elegant setting for cuisine in keep-
ing with the times.

XXX ⚜ **Le Chiberta** 　AK ⟷ ⟷ VISA ⊙⊙ AE ⓪

3 r. Arsène-Houssaye (8th) – Ⓜ *Charles de Gaulle-Etoile* – 𝒞 *01 53 53 42 00*
– *www.lechiberta.com*
– *Closed 2 weeks in August, Saturday lunch and Sunday* 　F2
Rest – Menu 60 € (weekdays), 100/155 € bi – Carte 88/123 €
♦ Creative ♦ Design ♦
Find a serene atmosphere, soft lighting and simple decor designed by J M Wil-
motte (dark colours and unusual wine bottle walls). This provides the setting for
inventive cuisine supervised by Guy Savoy.
➔ Autour du petit pois : œuf poché et tartine de pata negra. Filet de saint-
pierre en fine chapelure de tomate confite, orge perlé aux pignons de pin.
Terrine d'orange et de pamplemousse, tuile au thé earl grey.

XXX **Rech** 　🛱 AK VISA ⊙⊙ AE ⓪

62 av. des Ternes (17th) – Ⓜ *Ternes* – 𝒞 *01 45 72 29 47*
– *www.alain-ducasse.com*
– *Closed August, Sunday and Monday* 　F1
Rest – Menu 34 € (lunch) – Carte 72/93 €
♦ Fish and seafood ♦ Elegant ♦
A renowned Art Deco-style restaurant with an enticing list of house specialities:
shellfish, whole fish served for two people, Rech's own camembert and super-
sized éclairs.

XXX **Sormani**   AC ⇦ ⊏Ⴥ VISA ⓪ AE

4 r. Gén.-Lanrezac (17th) – Ⓜ *Charles de Gaulle-Etoile*
– ☎ 01 43 80 13 91
– *Closed August, Saturday, Sunday and Bank Holidays*   **F2**
Rest – Carte 80/180 € ⌘

♦ Italian ♦ Romantic ♦

Latin charm predominates in this restaurant near the Place de l'Etoile. Attractive
Baroque-style decor featuring a red colour scheme and Murano glass chandeliers. A "dolce vita" atmosphere in which to enjoy Italian cuisine.

XXX **Les Tablettes de Jean-Louis Nomicos**   AC ⊏Ⴥ VISA ⓪ AE
⍟
16 av. Bugeaud (16th) ✉ 75116 – Ⓜ *Victor Hugo* – ☎ 01 56 28 16 16
– *www.lestablettesjeanlouisnomicos.com*   **E3**
Rest – Menu 42 € (lunch), 80/145 €
– Carte 72/138 €

♦ Modern ♦ Elegant ♦

Having manned the kitchens at Lasserre, Jean-Louis Nomicos is now pursuing
his solo career on the premises formerly occupied by Joël Robuchon's La
Table. Savour his fine, Mediterranean inspired cuisine to a backdrop of original
and contemporary decor.
➜ Macaroni aux truffes noires et foie gras. Filets de rouget croustillants à
la marjolaine et aubergine fumée. Fraises des bois à l'eau de rose et granité
à la Chartreuse.

XXX **Antoine**   AC ⇦ ⊏Ⴥ VISA ⓪ AE
⍟
10 av. de New-York (16th) ✉ 75116 – Ⓜ *Alma Marceau*
– ☎ 01 40 70 19 28 – *www.antoine-paris.fr*
– *Closed 2 weeks in August*   **F3**
Rest – Menu 120 € (dinner) – Carte 85/120 €

♦ Fish and seafood ♦ Elegant ♦

With its direct links to Breton, Basque and Mediterranean ports, the Antoine ser-
ves the best fresh fish and seafood, prepared with great finesse and originality.
Contemporary decor.
➜ Finesse de coquillages juste tiédis, tartine au sarrasin et crevettes grises.
Bar de ligne grillé, cocotte de purée de ratte du Touquet. Tarte caramel-
chocolat, compote de poire pochée au thé fumé et sorbet poire.

XXX **Le Pergolèse** (Stéphane Gaborieau)   AC ⇦ ⊏Ⴥ VISA ⓪ AE
⍟
40 r. Pergolèse (16th) ✉ 75116 – Ⓜ *Porte Maillot* – ☎ 01 45 00 21 40
– *www.lepergolese.com*
– *Closed 3 weeks in August, 1 to 8 January, Saturday lunch and Sunday*
Rest – Menu 54 € bi (lunch)/95 € – Carte 77/137 €   **E2**

♦ Modern ♦ Elegant ♦

A successful reinterpretation of southern cuisine with a smattering of Japanese
touches by a chef awarded the 'Meilleur Ouvrier de France'. It is served in a
decor that is at once pared down and elegant.
➜ Moelleux de filets de sardine marinés, fondue de poivrons basquaise.
Sole meunière farcie d'une duxelles de champignons. Cannelloni en chocolat, mousse de marron et pomme au poivre de Sichuan.

XXX **Tsé Yang**   AC ⇦ VISA ⓪ AE

25 av. Pierre-1er-de-Serbie (16th) ✉ 75016 – Ⓜ *Iéna* – ☎ 01 47 20 70 22
– *www.tse-yang.fr*   **F3**
Rest – Menu 43/98 € – Carte 45/100 €

♦ Chinese ♦ Luxury ♦ Exotic ♦

Elegant dining rooms (gilded ceilings and dominant black colour scheme) provide the setting for traditional Chinese cuisine from Peking, Shanghai and
Sichuan. An exotic location in which guests will also appreciate the attentive
and stylish service.

FRANCE - PARIS

XXX **Citrus Étoile**   🚫 📶 🖥 📶 ⓥⓢⓐ ⓒⓞ ⒶⒺ

6 r. Arsène-Houssaye (8th) – ⓜ Charles de Gaulle-Étoile – ☎ 01 42 89 15 51
– www.citrusetoile.com
– Closed 23 December-4 January, Saturday, Sunday and Bank Holidays
Rest – Menu 69 € (lunch) – Carte 63/91 €   **F2**
♦ Modern ♦ Elegant ♦
Gilles Épié creates original cuisine that is inspired by his sound classic training
and rich experiences abroad (California). Elegant decor and delightful service.

XX **Le 39V** (Frédéric Vardon)   📶 🖥 (dinner) ⓥⓢⓐ ⓒⓞ ⒶⒺ
⁂ 39 av. George-V (6th floor) (entrance at 17 r. Quentin-Bauchart) (8th)
– ⓜ George V – ☎ 01 56 62 39 05 – www.le39v.com
– Closed August, Saturday and Sunday   **G3**
Rest – Menu 50 € (lunch), 95/145 € bi – Carte 57/116 €
♦ Modern ♦ Design ♦
The temperature is rising at 39, avenue George V! On the 6th floor of this
impressive Haussmann-style building overlooking the rooftops of Paris, diners
can enjoy the chef's refined cuisine in a stylish setting. Dishes are based around
a classic repertoire, top quality ingredients and fine flavours.
➜ Tourteau et araignée de mer décortiqués, macédoine de légumes et
émulsion d'une bisque. Saint-pierre de Bretagne, artichauts bouquet et
sucs persillés. Paris-brest, glace praliné-noisette.

XX **114, Faubourg** – Hôtel Bristol   📶 ⓥⓢⓐ ⓒⓞ ⒶⒺ ⓞ
⁂ 114 r. Fg St-Honoré (8th) – ⓜ Miromesnil – ☎ 01 53 43 44 44
– www.lebristolparis.com
– Closed 28 July-18 August, lunch Saturday and Sunday   **H2**
Rest – Carte 80/140 €
♦ Modern ♦ Elegant ♦
This chic brasserie within the premises of Le Bristol has a lavish interior with gilded columns, floral motifs and a grand staircase. Savour dishes from the menu
of fine brasserie classics cooked with care and lots of taste.
➜ Pâté de canard en croûte, légumes au vinaigre. Suprême de volaille fermière bio au tandoori, fraîcheur de concombre à la menthe. Millefeuille à la
vanille Bourbon, caramel au beurre demi-sel.

XX **Il Carpaccio** – Hôtel Le Royal Monceau   🍽 🚫 📶 ⇕ 🖥
⁂ 37 av. Hoche (8th) – ⓜ Charles de Gaulle-Etoile   ⓥⓢⓐ ⓒⓞ ⒶⒺ ⓞ
– ☎ 01 42 99 88 00 – www.leroyalmonceau.com
– Closed August, Sunday and Monday   **G2**
Rest – Menu 135/170 € bi – Carte 75/150 € 🏵
♦ Italian ♦ Elegant ♦
You reach the restaurant via a remarkable corridor decorated with thousands of
shells. The restaurant decor, reminiscent of a winter garden, is also delightful.
The menu is unapologetically simple and in the great tradition of Italian home
cooking.
➜ Carpaccio de bœuf aux champignons des bois. Pavé de turbot rôti à la
nage aux olives taggiasche, câpres et couteaux. Tiramisu.

XX **Le Relais Plaza** – Hôtel Plaza Athénée   📶 ⓥⓢⓐ ⓒⓞ ⒶⒺ ⓞ
25 av. Montaigne (8th) – ⓜ Alma Marceau – ☎ 01 53 67 64 00
– www.plaza-athenee-paris.com
– Closed August   **G3**
Rest – Menu 54 € – Carte 75/140 €
♦ Traditional ♦ Brasserie ♦ Luxury ♦
The chic, intimate 'local' for the nearby fashion houses. Timeless atmosphere
and beautiful 1930s decor inspired by the Normandie cruise ship. Classic, refined cuisine.

XX **Les 110 de Taillevent**   🅰️🅲 ⌧ 𝘝𝘐𝘚𝘈 🆎 ⓪

195 r. du Faubourg-St-Honoré (8th) – Ⓜ *Charles de Gaulle-Etoile*
– ℰ 01 40 74 20 20 – www.taillevent.com/les-110   **G2**
Rest – Menu 39 € – Carte 50/70 € 𝄢

♦ Traditional ♦ Elegant ♦ Brasserie ♦

Under the aegis of the prestigious Taillevent name, this ultra-chic brasserie puts
the onus on food and wine pairings. The concept is a success, with its remarkable choice of 110 wines by the glass, and nicely done traditional food (pâté
en croûte, bavette steak with a peppercorn sauce etc). Elegant and inviting
decor.

XX **Pershing Hall** – Hôtel Pershing Hall   🅰️🅲 𝘝𝘐𝘚𝘈 🆗 🆎 ⓪

49 r. Pierre Charron (8th) – Ⓜ *George V – ℰ 01 58 36 58 36*
– www.pershinghall.com   **G3**
Rest – Menu 45 € (weekday lunch) – Carte 70/100 €

♦ Modern ♦ Minimalist ♦

A contemporary atmosphere and hip cuisine – a fusion of French, Italian and
Asian influences – characterise this restaurant with its trendy decor. The courtyard facing the planted wall is particularly impressive, as is the fine choice of
champagnes.

XX **Restaurant de Sers** – Hôtel de Sers   🛋 🅰️🅲 ⇔ 𝘝𝘐𝘚𝘈 🆗 🆎 ⓪

41 av. Pierre 1er de Serbie (8th) – Ⓜ *George V – ℰ 01 53 23 75 13*
– www.hoteldesers.com   **G3**
Rest – Menu 57 € (weekday lunch)/125 € bi – Carte 66/107 €

♦ Modern ♦ Fashionable ♦

Minimalist elegance and a designer setting are the hallmarks of this restaurant
that showcases organic products. Some dishes are low-calorie for those keeping
an eye on their waistline. Pleasant terrace, as well as a private room for business
lunches.

XX **Mini Palais**   🛋 & 🅰️🅲 𝘝𝘐𝘚𝘈 🆗

Au Grand Palais - 3 av. Winston Churchill (8th)
– Ⓜ *Champs-Elysées Clemenceau – ℰ 01 42 56 42 42*
– www.minipalais.com   **H3**
Rest – Carte 33/69 €

♦ Modern ♦ Elegant ♦

Concealed within the Grand Palais, the Mini Palace is dedicated to the full pleasures of the palate, with a focus on generosity, abundance and the finest ingredients. The snack menu is available from midday to midnight. Tea room and an
exquisite terrace.

XX **Frédéric Simonin**   🅰️🅲 𝘝𝘐𝘚𝘈 🆗 🆎

❀ *25 r. Bayen (17th) –* Ⓜ *Ternes – ℰ 01 45 74 74 74*
– www.fredericsimonin.com
– Closed 4 to 28 August, Sunday and Monday   **F1**
Rest – Menu 39 € (lunch), 85/135 € – Carte 70/155 €

♦ Modern ♦ Cosy ♦ Elegant ♦

A white-and-black decor forms the backdrop to this chic restaurant opened in
2010 close to Place des Ternes. Fine, delicate cuisine from this chef with quite a
career behind him already.
➜ Le candele : gros macaronis farcis aux racines d'hiver et truffe noire,
beurre de foie gras. La côte de veau de Corrèze cuite en cocotte à la
sauge. Le payachoco : mousse légère au chocolat nyangbo, sorbet cacao
aux biscuits Oreo.

XX **Timgad**   🅰️🅲 ⌧ 𝘝𝘐𝘚𝘈 🆗 🆎

21 r. Brunel (17th) – Ⓜ *Argentine – ℰ 01 45 74 23 70 – www.timgad.fr*
Rest – Carte 45/80 €   **E2**

♦ Moroccan ♦ Exotic ♦ Elegant ♦

Experience the historic splendour of the city of Timgad in this elegant Moroccan
restaurant adorned with fine stuccowork. Fragrant North African cuisine, including couscous and tagines.

FRANCE - PARIS

L'Instant d'Or ✕✕ 🌼   AC ⇆ VISA ⓒⓞ AE

36 av. George-V (8th) – Ⓜ *George V* – ℰ *01 47 23 46 78 – www.linstantdor.com*
– Closed 30 July-27 August, Sunday and Monday   **G3**
Rest – Menu 36 € (lunch), 68/98 € – Carte 45/60 €

◆ Modern ◆ Design ◆ Luxury ◆

On avenue George V, this restaurant is in the heart of Paris' so-called "golden triangle". It promises fine gourmet moments, enhanced by the sunny influence of the South of France – the young chef is from Marseille. Precision, colour, technique and originality.

→ Filets de rouget sur une tartine au thym citron. Poitrine de caille fermière farcie, les cuisses confites et légumes de saison. Biscuit chaud au chocolat et parfait banane.

Marius et Janette ✕✕   🍴 AC 🖨 VISA ⓒⓞ AE

4 av. George V (8th) – Ⓜ *Alma Marceau* – ℰ *01 47 23 41 88*   **G3**
Rest – Menu 48 € (weekdays) – Carte 80/125 €

◆ Fish and seafood ◆ Formal ◆

This seafood restaurant's name recalls Marseille's Estaque district. It has an elegant nautical decor and a pleasant street terrace in summertime.

L'Arôme ✕✕ 🌼   AC 🖨 VISA ⓒⓞ AE

3 r. St-Philippe-du-Roule (8th) – Ⓜ *St-Philippe-du-Roule* – ℰ *01 42 25 55 98*
– www.larome.fr
– Closed 2 to 10 March, August, Saturday and Sunday   **G-H2**
Rest – Menu 89/149 € bi – Carte lunch approx. 85 €

◆ Modern ◆ Elegant ◆

Attractive restaurant run by Eric Martins (front of house) and Thomas Boullault (in the kitchen). Comfortable dining room with a warm atmosphere and open kitchen. Modern cuisine.

→ Carpaccio de veau de lait et salade de couteaux de mer, saint-florentin crémeux, cazette. Encornets et homard poêlés au saté, chou cœur de bœuf sauté au gingembre, cacahuètes. Fraisier léger, crème mascarpone à la vanille de Madagascar.

M64 – Hôtel Intercontinental Avenue Marceau ✕✕   🍴 & AC

64 av. Marceau (8th) – Ⓜ *George V*   VISA ⓒⓞ AE ①
– ℰ 01 44 43 36 50 – www.ic-marceau.com
– Closed Sunday dinner   **F2-3**
Rest – Menu 49 € (lunch) – Carte 70/85 €

◆ Modern ◆ Cosy ◆

Relax in the M64's lounge-style setting, where you can savour 'natural' cuisine based around spontaneity and, of course, the freshest produce. Guests can admire the chef's work in the open kitchen.

Conti ✕✕   AC VISA ⓒⓞ AE ①

72 r. Lauriston (16th) ✉ *75116* – Ⓜ *Boissière* – ℰ *01 47 27 74 67*
– www.leconti.fr
– Closed 4 to 26 August, 25 December-1 January, Saturday, Sunday and Bank Holidays   **E3**
Rest – Menu 35 € (lunch) – Carte 52/82 €

◆ Italian ◆ Intimate ◆ Cosy ◆

The intimate decor of this restaurant brings to mind a private club or an Italian theatre with its red velvet, crystal mirrors and chandeliers. The many regulars are drawn here by the excellent, classic Italian cuisine.

Maxan ✕✕   AC ⇆ VISA ⓒⓞ AE

3 r. Quentin-Bauchart (8th) – Ⓜ *George V* – ℰ *01 40 70 04 78*
– www.rest-maxan.com
– Closed 1 to 23 August, 24 December-3 January, Saturday lunch and Sunday
Rest – Menu 40 € – Carte 40/60 €   **F3**

◆ Modern ◆ Minimalist ◆

This restaurant boasts a truly original, contemporary decor by Pierre Pozzi that features paper artwork. The creative, well-presented cuisine is in keeping with the ambience. Tempting daily menu.

FRANCE - PARIS

XX **Nolita** `AC` `VISA` `OO` `AE`

1 av. Matignon (Motor Village - 2nd floor) (8th) – **M** *Franklin D. Roosevelt*
– ℰ 01 53 75 78 78 – www.nolita-ristorante.fr **H3**
Rest – Menu 39 € (dinner), 59/89 € – Carte 56/75 € ⅋

♦ Italian ♦ Design ♦

A chic restaurant inside the MotorVillage (the showroom of a major Italian car manufacturer). Authentic Italian cuisine with flavours to match.

XX **Market** `AC` `⊏♪` `VISA` `OO` `AE`

15 av. Matignon (8th) – **M** *Franklin D. Roosevelt* – ℰ *01 56 43 40 90*
– www.jean-georges.com **H3**
Rest – Carte 50/80 €

♦ Creative ♦ Design ♦

Polished concrete, linen, wood and ethnic touches set the scene for this chic, trendy bistro serving wonderful fusion cuisine supervised by New Yorker Jean-Georges Vongerichten.

XX **Dominique Bouchet** `AC` `⇔` `VISA` `OO` `AE`
ಬ
11 r. Treilhard (8th) – **M** *Miromesnil* – ℰ *01 45 61 09 46*
– www.dominique-bouchet.com
– Closed 10 August-2 September, Saturday and Sunday **H2**
Rest – *(pre-book)* Menu 105 € (dinner) – Carte 73/113 € ⅋

♦ Modern ♦ Bistro ♦ Trendy ♦

This is the kind of place you will want to recommend to all your friends. It has an intimate, contemporary atmosphere, attentive service, and beautifully prepared dishes based around fresh and tasty market ingredients.
➔ Jeunes légumes, œuf pané de brioche, foie gras et girolles. Gigot d'agneau de sept heures à la cuillère, fèves de cacao, pomme purée. Millefeuille aux pralins, noisettes légèrement caramélisées.

XX **etc...** `AC` `⊏♪` `VISA` `OO` `AE`
ಬ
2 r. La Pérouse (16th) ⊠ *75016* – **M** *Kléber* – ℰ *01 49 52 10 10*
– Closed 29 July-25 August, Saturday lunch and Sunday **F3**
Rest – Menu 90 € (dinner) – Carte approx. 75 €

♦ Modern ♦ Trendy ♦ Design ♦

This restaurant run by Christian Le Squer – the chef of the famous Ledoyen – is actually a chic, minimalist-style bistro that is both contemporary and convivial in style. It serves modern, high quality cuisine, as well as a concise menu that focuses on seasonal produce.
➔ Fantaisie voyageuse. Boudin maison version contemporaine. Caramel au goût de caramel glacé.

XX **Le Dodin de Mark Singer** `⇔` `VISA` `OO` `AE`
🖝
42 r. des Acacias (17th) – **M** *Charles de Gaulle-Etoile* – ℰ *01 43 80 28 54*
– www.ledodin.com
– Closed 2 weeks in August, Saturday lunch, Sunday and Monday
Rest – Menu 35 € – Carte 40/55 € **F2**

♦ Modern ♦ Fashionable ♦

An American who has been working in France for years, Mark Singer is first and foremost a chef without borders: his trademark is an assured grasp of classic techniques put to the service of original recipes. He has been running Le Dodin since the end of 2011, creating such winning combinations as scallop ceviche and kefir lemonade...

XX **Le Pré Carré** – Hôtel Splendid Étoile `AC` `VISA` `OO` `AE` `①`

1 bis av. Carnot (17th) – **M** *Charles de Gaulle-Etoile* – ℰ *01 46 22 57 35*
– www.restaurant-le-pre-carre.com
– Closed 3 weeks in August, 1 week Christmas Holidays, Saturday lunch and Sunday **F2**
Rest – Menu 38 € (dinner) – Carte 40/67 €

♦ Traditional ♦ Fashionable ♦

In the dining room, two mirrors facing each other reflect Le Pré Carré's infinite elegance and welcoming decor. Aromatic herbs and spices add a gentle touch to the gourmet cuisine, which is very much in keeping with the times.

FRANCE - PARIS

XX 🕸 **Jacques Faussat - La Braisière**　　　　AC ⇔ ⊐️ VISA ⓒⓞ AE

54 r. Cardinet (17th) – ⓜ *Malesherbes –* ℰ *01 47 63 40 37*
– www.jacquesfaussat.com
– Closed August, 24 December-2 January, Saturday except dinner from October-April, Sunday and Bank Holidays　　　　　　　　　　　　　**G1**
Rest – Menu 38 € (lunch)/110 € – Carte 62/74 € 🕸
♦ Traditional ♦
Comfortable, modern restaurant decorated in a tasteful restrained style. The menu is influenced by the cuisine of southwest France, and changes with the seasons and the chef's whims.
➙ Esturgeon de l'Adour mariné au citron vert et piquillos. Ris de veau à la fève tonka, marmelade de pomme et canneberge. Soufflé aux pêches de vigne.

XX **Makassar** – Hôtel Renaissance Arc de Triomphe　　🍴 ⅃ AC ⇔

39 av. Wagram (17th) – ⓜ *Ternes*　　　　　　　VISA ⓒⓞ AE ⓞ
– ℰ *01 55 37 55 57 – www.renaissancearcdetriomphe.fr*　　　　**F2**
Rest – Carte 45/65 €
♦ Creative ♦ Fashionable ♦
The decor of this restaurant (part of the Hôtel Renaissance) is inspired by Indonesia, as can be seen in the numerous discreet details on display. The cuisine is equally impressive with a menu that features many of the great classic French dishes alongside more exotic fare.

XX 🕸 **Agapé**　　　　　　　　　　　　AC ⊐️ VISA ⓒⓞ AE

51 r. Jouffroy-d'Abbans (17th) – ⓜ *Wagram –* ℰ *01 42 27 20 18*
– www.agape-paris.fr
– Closed 26 July-26 August, Saturday and Sunday　　　*Plan I* **B1**
Rest – Menu 35 € (lunch), 90/120 €
– Carte 88/130 € 🕸
♦ Modern ♦ Minimalist ♦
This smart restaurant, whose name means love in Greek, sports a minimalist decor. Concise, enticing menu. Extremely popular with gourmets.
➙ Noix de veau fumée au bois de hêtre, burrata et citron confit. Pêche des côtes bretonnes et légumes de saison. Chocolat grand cru, poivre sauvage et fruit de la passion.

XX 😊 **Graindorge**　　　　　　　　　　　　VISA ⓒⓞ AE

15 r. Arc-de-Triomphe (17th) – ⓜ *Charles de Gaulle-Étoile*
– ℰ *01 47 54 00 28 – www.le-graindorge.fr*
– Closed 1 to 15 August, Saturday lunch and Sunday　　　　　**F2**
Rest – Menu 35/45 € – Carte 44/58 €
♦ Flemish ♦ Retro ♦
Potjevlesch (potted meat), bintje farcie (stuffed potatoes), waterzoï (a stew with Ostend grey prawns) and kippers from Boulogne are just some of the hearty Northern dishes on offer in the Graindorge's attractive Art Deco setting, washed down with some delicious traditional beers.

XX **Bistrot du Sommelier**　　　　　　AC ⇔ VISA ⓒⓞ AE

97 bd Haussmann (8th) – ⓜ *St-Augustin –* ℰ *01 42 65 24 85*
– www.bistrotdusommelier.com
– Closed 27 July-25 August, 21 December-1 January, Saturday and Sunday
Rest – Menu 39 € (weekday lunch), 65 € bi/110 € bi　　　　**H2**
– Carte 50/77 € 🕸
♦ Traditional ♦ Bistro ♦
This bistro is run by Philippe Faure-Brac – winner of the 1992 world champion sommelier award. It offers market-based cuisine and a pleasant wine tasting cellar, which is the setting for weekly tasting events (Fridays).

Akrame

19 r. Lauriston (16th) ⊠ 75016 – Ⓜ Kléber – 𝒞 01 40 67 11 16 – www.akrame.com
– Closed August, 22 December-7 January, Saturday and Sunday **F2**
Rest – (pre-book) Menu 35 € (lunch), 60/80 €

♦ Modern ♦ Design ♦ Trendy ♦

A new address that is definitely on a roll. The young chef is developing a name for his modern, inventive and spontaneous cuisine. The trendy setting is a fitting backdrop for his surprise menus that change every month.

→ Foie gras poché, consommé de pomme de terre et hareng. Pigeon à l'hibiscus, crème de petits pois à l'oseille. Banane cacahouète en chaud-froid.

6 New York

6 av. de New York (16th) ⊠ 75016 – Ⓜ Alma Marceau – 𝒞 01 40 70 03 30
– www.6newyork.fr – Closed August, Saturday lunch and Sunday
Rest – Menu 35 € (lunch), 72/85 € bi – Carte 51/69 € **F3**

♦ Modern ♦ Design ♦

Although the name gives away the address – on Avenue de New York – the restaurant couldn't be further from a typical American restaurant. Well-defined, honest flavours and a respect for the seasons are behind cuisine in perfect harmony with the elegant and contemporary setting.

Le Vinci

23 r. P. Valéry (16th) ⊠ 75116 – Ⓜ Victor Hugo
– 𝒞 01 45 01 68 18 – Closed August, Saturday and Sunday **E2-3**
Rest – Menu 35 € (dinner) – Carte 56/78 €

♦ Italian ♦ Elegant ♦ Friendly ♦

The sympathetic interior design and friendly service make Le Vinci a very popular choice a stone's throw from the avenue Victor-Hugo. The impressive selection of pastas and risottos, as well as the à la carte meat and fish dishes vary according to the seasons.

Le Ballon des Ternes

103 av. Ternes (17th) – Ⓜ Porte Maillot – 𝒞 01 45 74 17 98
– www.leballondesternes.fr **E1**
Rest – Carte 45/70 €

♦ Traditional ♦ Retro ♦

No, you have not had a glass of wine too many! The table set upside down on the ceiling is part of the 1900 decor of this brasserie next to the Palais des Congrès.

L'Atelier de Joël Robuchon - Étoile

133 av. des Champs-Élysées (Publicis Drugstore basement) (8th)
– Ⓜ Charles de Gaulle-Étoile – 𝒞 01 47 23 75 75 – www.joel-robuchon.net
– Open from 11.30am to 3.30pm and 6.30pm to midnight. Reservations
possible for certain times only: please enquire. **A2**
Rest – Menu 40 € (lunch)/166 € – Carte 60/150 €

♦ Creative ♦ Design ♦ Minimalist ♦

This new restaurant run by the famous chef Joël Robuchon is situated just a stone's throw from the Arc de Triomphe. The "atelier" concept has proved popular – a long counter with stools, a red and black decor and delicate, simple dishes with a mix of French, Spanish and Asian influences.

→ Langoustine en papillote croustillante au basilic. Caille caramélisée au foie gras, pomme purée. Chocolat "tendance" et sa crème onctueuse au chocolat araguani, sorbet cacao.

Pavillon Elysée Lenôtre

10 av. des Champs-Elysées (8th) – Ⓜ Champs Elysées Clemenceau
– 𝒞 01 42 65 85 10 – www.lenotre.fr
– Closed 3 weeks in August, 19 February-18 March, Sunday except lunch from
April-October and Monday from November-March **H3**
Rest – Carte 48/66 €

♦ Modern ♦ Friendly ♦

Built for the 1900 Universal Exhibition, this pavilion exudes unpretentious elegance. Appealing lunch menu, best enjoyed in the sun on the lovely terrace. Boutique dedicated to the culinary arts and cookery school.

FRANCE - PARIS

FRANCE - PARIS

Pomze
〈AE〉 〈⇔〉 〈VISA〉 〈◎◎〉 〈AE〉

109 bd Haussmann (1st floor) (8th) – ⓜ St -Augustin – ℰ 01 42 65 65 83
– www.pomze.com – Closed 22 December-2 January, Saturday except
dinner from September-June and Sunday　　　　　　　　　　**H2**
Rest – Menu 33/50 € – Carte 45/63 €

♦ Modern ♦ Minimalist ♦ Brasserie ♦

The unusual concept behind Pomze is to take the humble apple as a starting
point for a culinary voyage! From the food shop (where you will find cider and
calvados) to the restaurant, the "forbidden fruit" provides the central theme.
Creative and intrepid dishes offer excellent value for money.

L'Escient
〈VISA〉 〈◎◎〉 〈AE〉

28 r. Poncelet (17th) – ⓜ Ternes – ℰ 09 66 92 49 13
– Closed 1 week in August, Monday dinner and Sunday　　　　　　**F1**
Rest – Menu 35/45 € – Carte approx. 43 €

♦ Modern ♦ Fashionable ♦

King prawns, taramasalata, daikon, lime and ginger; fresh cod, dried fig crust,
chorizo and lemon preserves etc. L'Escient offers a menu with plenty of original
associations and remains true to its name, always choosing these judiciously! A
very tasty fusion, in an understated decor.

L'Entredgeu
〈VISA〉 〈◎◎〉

83 r. Laugier (17th) – ⓜ Porte de Champerret – ℰ 01 40 54 97 24
– Closed 1 week early May, 3 weeks in August, 1 week Christmas Holidays,
Sunday and Monday　　　　　　　　　　　　　　　*Plan I* **AB1**
Rest – Menu 33/55 €

♦ Traditional ♦ Bistro ♦

Friendly service, a lively atmosphere, a decor that is reminiscent of southwest
France, and delicious seasonally based cuisine are the hallmarks of this restaurant with a tongue-twisting name.

CONCORDE – OPÉRA – BOURSE – GARE DU NORD　　　*Plan III*

Le Meurice
〈ḷ₆〉 〈📶〉 〈⅁〉 〈AE〉 〈🛜〉 〈ṣ⅄〉 〈VISA〉 〈◎◎〉 〈AE〉

228 r. Rivoli (1st) – ⓜ Tuileries – ℰ 01 44 58 10 10
– www.lemeurice.com　　　　　　　　　　　　　　　　　**J-K3**
120 rm – ✝550/1950 € ✝✝550/1950 €, ⌿ 54 € – 40 suites
Rest *Le Meurice* ❀❀❀
Rest *Le Dali* – see restaurant listing

♦ Palace ♦ Grand Luxury ♦ Historic ♦

This luxury hotel opposite the Tuileries was founded at the start of the 19C, making
it one of the first to be built in Paris. It has opulent guestrooms and a superb suite
on the top floor that has breathtaking panoramic views. The hotel now also bears
the contemporary touch of Philippe Starck. A truly fabulous place to stay.

Mandarin Oriental
〈ḷ₆〉 〈📶〉 〈▦〉 〈⅁〉 〈AE〉 〈🛜〉 〈ṣ⅄〉 〈VISA〉 〈◎◎〉 〈AE〉 〈⓪〉

251 r. St-Honoré (1st) – ⓜ Concorde – ℰ 01 70 98 78 88
– www.mandarinoriental.fr/paris/　　　　　　　　　　　　　**J3**
99 rm – ✝795/1345 € ✝✝795/1345 €, ⌿ 48 € – 39 suites
Rest *Sur Mesure par Thierry Marx* ❀❀
Rest *Camélia* – see restaurant listing

♦ Grand Luxury ♦ Elegant ♦ Personalised ♦

Among all the major new hotels in Paris, the opening of the Mandarin Oriental
in mid-2011 made quite an impact. Faithful to the principles of this Hong Kong
group, the property is the height of refinement. It combines French elegance
with the delicate touches of Asia and features sleek lines, lots of space and
peace and quiet. A capital address in the heart of the French capital!

Park Hyatt 🛜 ♨ 🆚 ♿ 🅰🅲 🛜 ♨ 🚗 🆚 📠 🅰🅴

5 r. de la Paix (2nd) – Ⓜ *Opéra* – ✆ *01 58 71 12 34*
– *www.paris.vendome.hyatt.fr* **K3**
156 rm – 🛏800/910 € 🛏🛏800/910 €, ☑ 37 € – 43 suites
Rest *Pur'* ❀ – see restaurant listing
Rest *Les Orchidées* – ✆ *01 58 71 10 60 (lunch only)* Carte 70/160 €
♦ Luxury ♦ Personalised ♦ Design ♦
Ed Tuttle designed his dream hotel, which stands on the famous rue de la Paix. It has a collection of contemporary art and French-style classicism with a subtle blend of Louis XVI-style and 1930s furnishings. There is a spa and high-tech equipment, as well as restaurants for all tastes. An authentic palace.

Intercontinental Le Grand ♨ 🆚 ♿ 🅰🅲 📞 ♨ 🚗

2 r. Scribe (9th) – Ⓜ *Opéra* – ✆ *01 40 07 32 32*
🆚 📠 🅰🅴 ①
– *www.paris.intercontinental.com* **K2**
442 rm – 🛏350/780 € 🛏🛏350/780 €, ☑ 39 € – 28 suites
Rest *Café de la Paix* – 12 bd des Capucines, ✆ *01 40 07 36 36*
– Menu 48 € (lunch)/79 € – Carte 64/118 €
♦ Historic ♦ Stylish ♦
Opened in 1862, this hotel celebrates its 150th anniversary in 2012. A true grand hotel typical of the 19C, the Intercontinental stands on the Place de l'Opéra in the heart of Haussmann's Paris. With its superbly decorated Café de la Paix, interior courtyard with a Proustian ambience and its Second Empire-style guestrooms, this is a real Parisian landmark.

Scribe ♨ 🆚 ♿ 🅰🅲 🛜 ♨ 🆚 📠 🅰🅴 ①

1 r. Scribe (9th) – Ⓜ *Opéra* – ✆ *01 44 71 24 24*
– *www.hotel-scribe-paris.com* **K2**
204 rm – 🛏315/800 € 🛏🛏315/800 €, ☑ 35 € – 9 suites
Rest *Le Lumière* ❀ – see restaurant listing
♦ Grand Luxury ♦ Personalised ♦
Fall under the charm of this chic, very Parisian hotel occupying a Haussmann-style building close to the Opéra, where the hushed atmosphere is almost secretive in feel. It was here, in 1895, that the Lumière brothers hosted their very first cinema screening. A legendary address with a discreet elegance all of its own.

Costes 🛜 ♨ 🖥 ♿ rm, 🅰🅲 🛜 🆚 📠 🅰🅴 ①

239 r. St-Honoré (1st) – Ⓜ *Concorde* – ✆ *01 42 44 50 00*
– *www.hotelcostes.com* **K3**
79 rm – 🛏400/800 € 🛏🛏400/800 €, ☑ 35 € – 3 suites
Rest – Carte 60/120 €
♦ Luxury ♦ Personalised ♦ Cosy ♦
This extremely chic and plush palace remains a firm favourite with the jet set. There are nooks and crannies everywhere, and it is furnished with squat armchairs and benches made from pear wood. The guestrooms are refined down to the smallest details: purple and gold colour scheme, monogrammed linen etc.

Le Burgundy ♨ 🆚 🐾 🖥 ♿ 🅰🅲 🛜 🆚 📠 🅰🅴 ①

6-8 r. Duphot (1st) – Ⓜ *Madeleine* – ✆ *01 42 60 34 12*
– *www.leburgundy.com* **J3**
51 rm – 🛏420/1250 € 🛏🛏420/1250 €, ☑ 44 € – 8 suites
Rest *Le Baudelaire* ❀ – see restaurant listing
♦ Grand Luxury ♦ Design ♦ Personalised ♦
In this luxury hotel, the wood panelling combines harmoniously with the coloured fabrics, designer furniture and contemporary art to provide a hushed, arty atmosphere.

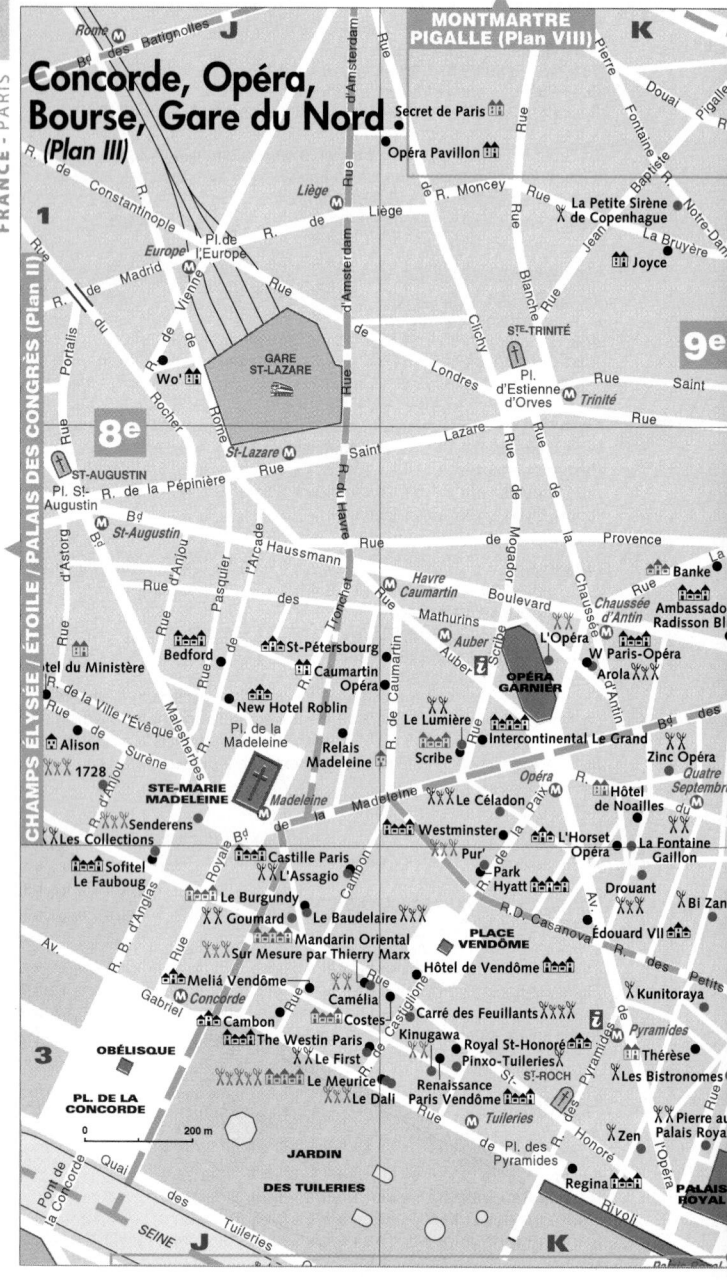

Concorde, Opéra, Bourse, Gare du Nord
(Plan III)

MONTMARTRE PIGALLE (Plan VIII)

Secret de Paris

Opéra Pavillon

La Petite Sirène de Copenhague

Joyce

Wo'

GARE ST-LAZARE

Pl. de l'Europe

St-Lazare

Pl. d'Estienne d'Orves

Trinité

STE-TRINITÉ

ST-AUGUSTIN

Pl. St-Augustin

St-Augustin

Hôtel du Ministère

Bedford

Alison

1728

Senderens

Les Collections

Sofitel Le Faubourg

St-Pétersbourg

Caumartin Opéra

New Hotel Roblin

Relais Madeleine

STE-MARIE MADELEINE

Castille Paris

L'Assagio

Le Burgundy

Goumard

Le Baudelaire

Mandarin Oriental

Sur Mesure par Thierry Marx

Meliá Vendôme

Cambon

Camélia

Costes

The Westin Paris

Le First

Le Meurice

Le Dali

OBÉLISQUE

PL. DE LA CONCORDE

0   200 m

JARDIN DES TUILERIES

SEINE

Banke

Ambassador Radisson Bl

W Paris-Opéra

Arola

L'Opéra

OPÉRA GARNIER

Le Lumière

Scribe

Intercontinental Le Grand

Zinc Opéra

Le Céladon

Hôtel de Noailles

Westminster

L'Horset Opéra

La Fontaine Gaillon

Pur'

Park Hyatt

Drouant

Bi Zan

Édouard VII

Kunitoraya

PLACE VENDÔME

Hôtel de Vendôme

Carré des Feuillants

Kinugawa

Royal St-Honoré

Pinxo-Tuileries

Renaissance Paris Vendôme

Tuileries

ST-ROCH

Thérèse

Les Bistronomes

Pierre au Palais Royal

Zen

Regina

PALAIS ROYAL

PL. DES PYRAMIDES

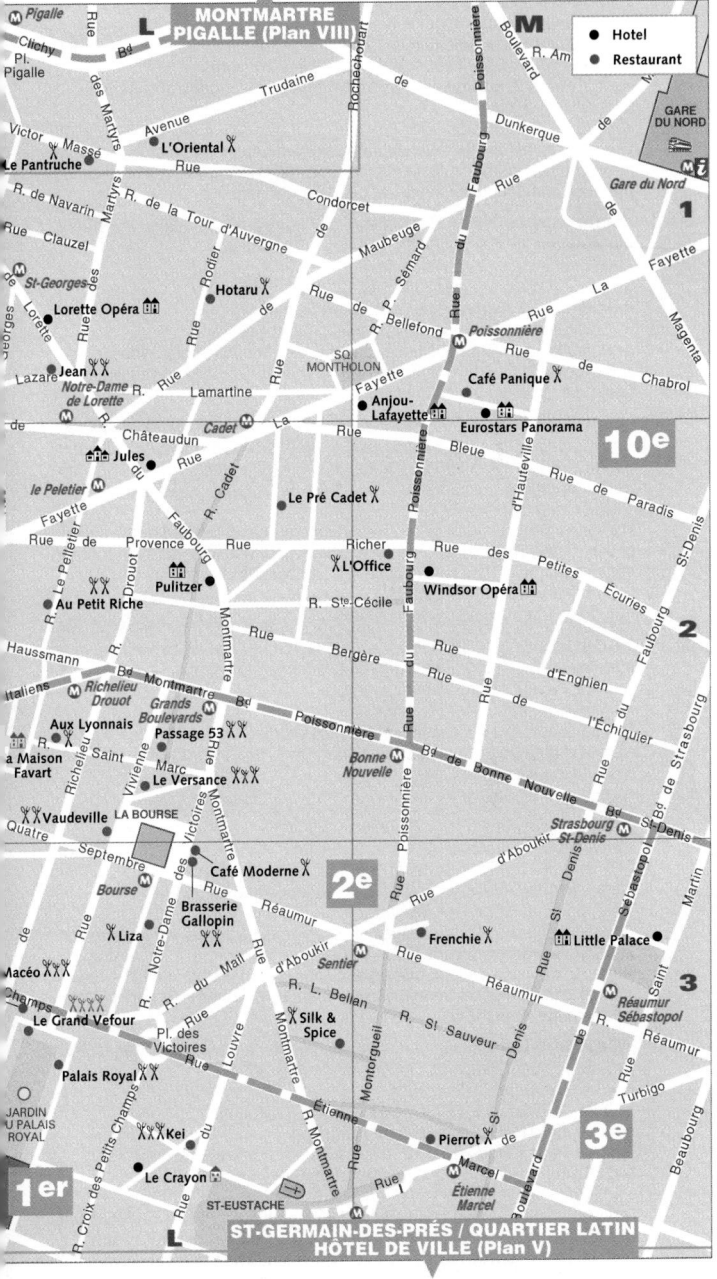

Hotel
Restaurant

MONTMARTRE
PIGALLE (Plan VIII)

Pigalle
Clichy
Pl. Pigalle
Rue des Martyrs
Victor Massé
Le Pantruche
L'Oriental
Avenue Trudaine
Rochechouart
Boulevard
Dunkerque
GARE DU NORD
R. Am
M
Poissonnière
de
Rue
Gare du Nord
R. de Navarin
Rue Clauzel
de St-Georges
Lorette
R. de la Tour d'Auvergne
Rue Condorcet
Maubeuge
P.
Rue du Faubourg
Rue
La Fayette
Magenta
Lorette Opéra
Hotaru
Rue Rodier
de
Bellefond
Poissonnière
Rue de Chabrol
Jean
Notre-Dame de Lorette
Lazare
R. Lamartine
SQ. MONTHOLON
Fayette
La
Rue
Café Panique
Rue
Châteaudun
Cadet
Anjou-Lafayette
Eurostars Panorama
Bleue
Rue d'Hauteville
10e
Jules
le Peletier
Rue Cadet
Le Pré Cadet
Rue de Paradis
Fayette
Le Peletier de
Rue Provence
Faubourg
Rue
Richer
Rue
L'Office
des
Petites
Rue
St-Denis
Pulitzer
R. Ste-Cécile
Windsor Opéra
Écuries
Faubourg
Au Petit Riche
Drouot
Montmartre
Bergère
Rue
2
Haussmann
Rue
d'Enghien
Italiens
Bd
Montmartre
Richelieu
Drouot
Grands
Boulevards
Poissonnière
Bd
Rue
de
l'Échiquier
Strasbourg
Aux Lyonnais
Passage 53
Saint
Marc
Bd de Bonne
Nouvelle
Bonne
Nouvelle
Rue de Strasbourg
a Maison Favart
R.
Richelieu
Vivienne
Le Versance
Vaudeville
LA BOURSE
Quatre
Septembre
Bourse
Notre-Dame des Victoires
Café Moderne
2e
Strasbourg St-Denis
Sébastopol
Bd St-Denis
Liza
Brasserie Gallopin
Rue Réaumur
Rue d'Aboukir
Frenchie
Little Palace
Martin
Macéo
Champs
R. du Mail
Sentier
R. L. Belian
Réaumur
3
Réaumur Sébastopol
Le Grand Vefour
Rue
Pl. des Victoires
Silk & Spice
R. St. Sauveur
Denis
Réaumur
Palais Royal
Louvre
Montmartre
Montorgueil
Rue
Turbigo
Beaubourg
JARDIN U PALAIS ROYAL
Kei
Étienne
R. Montmartre
Pierrot
de
3e
1er
Le Crayon
ST-EUSTACHE
Rue
Marcel
Étienne Marcel
Boulevard
Sébastopol
R. Croix des Petits Champs

ST-GERMAIN-DES-PRÉS / QUARTIER LATIN
HÔTEL DE VILLE (Plan V)

FRANCE - PARIS

Hôtel de Vendôme   🕭 rm, 🏧 rm, 🛜 🖴 VISA ©© AE ①

1 pl. Vendôme (1st) – 🔘 *Opéra* – 𝒞 01 55 04 55 00
– *www.hoteldevendome.com*   **K3**
19 rm – ♦300/865 € ♦♦390/865 €, ⌧ 35 € – 10 suites
Rest 1 Place Vendôme – *(closed 4 to 28 August, Sunday and Monday)*
(dinner only) Menu 90 €
♦ Luxury ♦ Palace ♦ Stylish ♦
The other hotel on Place Vendôme! Antique furniture and marble sit easily
alongside state-of-the-art facilities in this fine 18C building. A sense of elegance
pervades, and is found in the tiniest details. A real gem.

Renaissance Paris Vendôme   🕭 ◉ ◰ 🕭 🏧 🛜 VISA ©© AE

4 r. du Mont-Thabor (1st) – 🔘 *Tuileries* – 𝒞 01 40 20 72 00
– *www.renaissanceparisvendome.fr*   **K3**
89 rm – ♦350/929 € ♦♦350/929 €, ⌧ 29 € – 8 suites
Rest Pinxo - Tuileries – see restaurant listing
♦ Business ♦ Cosy ♦ Modern ♦
A 19C building transformed into a contemporary boutique hotel. Wood, honey
and chocolate tones: the rooms are elegant and really snug! And you will enjoy
lazing around in the pretty Chinese bar.

Castille Paris   🕭 🏧 🛜 🖴 VISA ©© AE

33 r. Cambon (1st) – 🔘 *Madeleine* – 𝒞 01 44 58 44 58 – *www.castille.com*
91 rm – ♦350/790 € ♦♦350/790 €, ⌧ 28 € – 17 suites   **J3**
Rest L'Assaggio – see restaurant listing
♦ Luxury ♦ Personalised ♦
The 'Opera Wing' boasts a splendid contemporary decor inspired by the beauty
of Venice. The 'Rivoli Wing' has a striking black and white colour scheme, intended as a tribute to the Chanel boutique next door. Whichever wing you stay in,
enjoy the allure of haute couture!

The Westin Paris   🕭 ◉ 🕭 🏧 🛜 🖴 VISA ©© AE ①

3 r. Castiglione (1st) – 🔘 *Tuileries* – 𝒞 01 44 77 11 11 – *www.thewestinparis.fr*
394 rm – ♦350/1200 € ♦♦350/1200 €, ⌧ 39 € – 34 suites   **J3**
Rest Le First – see restaurant listing
♦ Chain hotel ♦ Personalised ♦
This hotel built in 1878 combines old-world charm (Napoleon III lounges) and
elegant contemporary touches. Some guestrooms boast views across the Tuileries gardens. Pleasant spa.

Regina   🕮 🕭 rm, 🏧 🛜 🖴 VISA ©© AE ①

2 pl. des Pyramides (1st) – 🔘 *Tuileries* – 𝒞 01 42 60 31 10
– *www.regina-hotel.com*   **K3**
110 rm – ♦220/875 € ♦♦290/875 €, ⌧ 32 € – 10 suites
Rest – *(closed Saturday, Sunday and dinner)* Carte 47/56 €
♦ Historic ♦ Retro ♦ Classic ♦
This 1900s-style hotel has managed to preserve its traditional atmosphere and
Art Nouveau decor. Superb lobby and antique furniture in the guestrooms.
Those on the patio side are quieter, and some offer views of the Eiffel Tower.
Indulge in traditional cuisine in the dining room embellished with a pretty Majo-
relle fireplace, or in the flower-decked courtyard.

Westminster   🕭 🍸 🏧 🕻 🖴 🚗 VISA ©© AE ①

13 r. de la Paix (2nd) – 🔘 *Opéra* – 𝒞 01 42 61 57 46
– *www.hotelwestminster.com*   **K2**
85 rm – ♦230/550 € ♦♦230/550 €, ⌧ 30 € – 17 suites
Rest Le Céladon ❁ – see restaurant listing
Rest Le Petit Céladon – 𝒞 01 47 03 40 42 *(open weekends and closed
August and Christmas Holidays)* Menu 59 € bi
♦ Luxury ♦ Stylish ♦
Founded in 1809 – it has celebrated its 200th birthday! –, it was in 1846 that it
took the name of its most faithful client, the Duke of Westminster, who had a
taste for that distinctly French brand of refinement! The Céladon becomes the
Petit Céladon at the weekend, with a simplified menu and more relaxed service.

Ambassador Radisson Blu

16 bd Haussmann (9th) – Ⓜ *Richelieu Drouot* – ℰ *01 44 83 40 40*
– *www.radissonblu.com/ambassadorhotel-paris*   **K2**
290 rm – ♦290/850 € ♦♦310/880 €, � 29 € – 8 suites
Rest *16 Haussmann* – ℰ *01 48 00 06 38 (closed Saturday lunch, Sunday and Bank Holidays)* Menu 50 €
♦ Chain hotel ♦ Personalised ♦ Elegant ♦
This elegant and refined Art Deco-style hotel boasts painted wood panelling, crystal chandeliers and antique furnishings. Its guestrooms have been renovated in a cosy style, blending retro charm with a contemporary feel. The 16 Haussmann restaurant has a brasserie ambience.

W Paris Opéra

4 r. Meyerbeer (9th) – Ⓜ *Chaussée d'Antin* – ℰ *01 77 48 94 94*
– *www.wparisopera.fr*   **K2**
89 rm – ♦340/2000 € ♦♦380/2000 €, ⊆ 38 € – 2 suites
Rest *Arola* – see restaurant listing
♦ Chain hotel ♦ Luxury ♦ Personalised ♦
You would be hard-pushed to get any closer to the heart of Haussmann's Paris than in this fine 1870 building adjacent to the Opéra. This hotel, which opened in 2012, may plump for a "Paris-chic" decor, but it is in a resolutely designer vein. Luxury is combined with a laid-back attitude (for example, a circular bed and a view over the Palais Garnier). Very trendy and very enticing.

Bedford

17 r. de l'Arcade (8th) – Ⓜ *Madeleine* – ℰ *01 44 94 77 77*
– *www.hotel-bedford.com*   **J2**
135 rm – ♦180/266 € ♦♦226/312 €, ⊆ 20 € – 10 suites
Rest *Le Victoria* – *(closed August, Saturday, Sunday and Bank Holidays) (lunch only)* Menu 42 € – Carte 66/74 €
♦ Luxury ♦ Personalised ♦
This hotel founded in 1848 elegantly perpetuates classic hotel traditions with its pleasant, discreetly refined guestrooms. A comfortable, good value for money option given the district.

Sofitel le Faubourg

15 r. Boissy-d'Anglas (8th) – Ⓜ *Concorde* – ℰ *01 44 94 14 14* – *www.sofitel.com*
122 rm – ♦350/950 € ♦♦350/950 €, ⊆ 34 € – 25 suites   **J3**
Rest *Les Collections* – see restaurant listing
♦ Chain hotel ♦ Luxury ♦ Modern ♦
This elegant hotel occupies two 18C and 19C residences. It offers attractive suites that were renovated in a contemporary style in 2010, as well as elegant guestrooms. There is also a lounge crowned with a glass roof, a fitness centre and a hammam.

Banke

20 r. Lafayette (9th) – Ⓜ *Chaussée d'Antin* – ℰ *01 55 33 22 22*
– *www.derbyhotels.com*   **K2**
94 rm – ♦195/580 € ♦♦215/1265 €, ⊆ 29 €
Rest *Josefin* – Menu 29 € (weekday lunch) – Carte 39/69 €
♦ Luxury ♦ Design ♦
Situated in the heart of the Belle Epoque business district between the Bourse and the Opera, this former bank building was converted into a unique luxury hotel in 2009. The opulent lobby, crowned by a glass ceiling, is highly striking, while the guestrooms have a warm, welcoming feel.

New Hotel Roblin

6 r. Chauveau-Lagarde (8th) – Ⓜ *Madeleine* – ℰ *01 44 71 20 80*
– *www.new-hotel.com*   **J2**
77 rm – ♦380/560 € ♦♦380/680 €, ⊆ 22 €   **Rest** – Menu 37 €
♦ Luxury ♦ Business ♦ Cosy ♦
Do you prefer the bourgeois feel of the 16e arrondissement, the trendy Marais, the artists studios around Canal St Martin or the Left Bank atmosphere of St Germain? The rooms in this hotel are decorated along these themes. This brings the whole of Paris under one roof, within a stone's throw of Madeleine. A great success.

FRANCE - PARIS

 Cambon without rest   AC 🛜 VISA ⦾ AE ⓪

3 r. Cambon (1st) – Ⓜ Concorde – ℰ 01 44 58 93 93
– www.hotelcambon.com   **J3**
39 rm – 🛏300/380 € 🛏🛏380/850 €, ☑ 22 € – 1 suite
♦ Traditional ♦ Personalised ♦

This hotel between the Tuileries gardens and the Rue St-Honoré has a loyal following thanks to its friendly staff and pleasant guestrooms with their mix of contemporary furnishings and old paintings.

 Royal St-Honoré without rest   AC 🛜 VISA ⦾ AE ⓪

221 r. St-Honoré (1st) – Ⓜ Tuileries – ℰ 01 42 60 32 79
– www.hotel-royal-st-honore.com   **K3**
67 rm – 🛏200/490 € 🛏🛏200/490 €, ☑ 19 € – 5 suites
♦ Business ♦ Classic ♦ Functional ♦

On the site of the old Hôtel de Noailles, a plush 19C building with refined rooms. Breakfast is served in a Louis XVI decor and, in the evening, head for the cosy bar.

 Meliá Vendôme without rest   AC 🛜 🖧 VISA ⦾ AE ⓪

8 r. Cambon (1st) – Ⓜ Concorde – ℰ 01 44 77 54 00 – www.melia.com
82 rm – 🛏389/529 € 🛏🛏409/659 €, ☑ 28 € – 1 suite   **J3**
♦ Business ♦ Functional ♦ Cosy ♦

An elegant hotel with a hushed atmosphere and decorated in tones of red and gold. Romantic feel in the guestrooms, a lounge with a Belle-Époque glass roof, plus an attractive breakfast area.

 Édouard VII   🖧 AC 🛜 🖧 VISA ⦾ AE ⓪

39 av. de l'Opéra (2nd) – Ⓜ Opéra – ℰ 01 42 61 86 11
– www.edouard7hotel.com   **K3**
69 rm – 🛏460/1000 € 🛏🛏460/1000 €, ☑ 28 € – 12 suites
Rest Cuisine L'E 7 – ℰ 01 42 61 86 26 (closed August and Bank Holidays)
Menu 29 € – Carte 40/55 €
♦ Luxury ♦ Modern ♦ Cosy ♦

Shimmering fabrics and refined decor in the Couture rooms, while the mood in the Edouard VII rooms is more understated. The hotel exudes elegance and the suites are superb. Cosy bar and light meals in a very pleasant contemporary setting.

 L'Horset Opéra without rest   AC 🛜 VISA ⦾ AE ⓪

18 r. d'Antin (2nd) – Ⓜ Opéra – ℰ 01 44 71 87 00
– www.hotelhorsetopera.com   **K2-3**
54 rm ☑ – 🛏180/275 € 🛏🛏195/305 €
♦ Cosy ♦

The atmosphere inside this hotel a short distance from the Garnier Opera House is very hushed. The rooms are tastefully and classically decorated with matching wall hangings and fabrics, and warm wood panelling.

 Jules without rest   🖧 AC 🛜 🖧 VISA ⦾ AE ⓪

49 r. La Fayette (9th) – Ⓜ Le Peletier – ℰ 01 42 85 05 44
– www.hoteljules.com   **L2**
101 rm – 🛏150/500 € 🛏🛏180/1015 €, ☑ 18 €
♦ Business ♦ Personalised ♦

Fun yet chic, this hotel takes its inspiration from 1950s and 1960s decor. Guestrooms play the retro or contemporary card but always with elegance and pep! Colourful, vibrant and full of style!

 St-Pétersbourg without rest   AC 🛜 🖧 VISA ⦾ AE ⓪

33 r. Caumartin (9th) – Ⓜ Havre Caumartin – ℰ 01 42 66 60 38
– www.hotelsaintpetersbourg.com   **J2**
98 rm ☑ – 🛏145/192 € 🛏🛏166/249 €
♦ Traditional ♦ Classic ♦

A very traditional family-run hotel with a classic, slightly old-fashioned yet faultlessly maintained decor.

Hôtel du Ministère *without rest* ⓕⓖⓀ 🛜 ♨ ⓋⒾⓈⒶ ⓒⓞ ⒶⒺ
31 r. de Surène (8th) – Ⓜ *Madeleine* – ℰ *01 42 66 21 43*
– www.ministerehotel.com   **J2**
24 rm ☷ – †225/370 € ††255/655 €
◆ Elegant ◆ Personalised ◆
This hotel is a stone's throw from the French Home Office, the Palais de l'Élysée, and Faubourg St Honoré. The comfortable and very functional guestrooms pay tribute to the 1970s, which won't fail to please fans of the era, nor those who are feeling nostalgic. Charming service.

La Maison Favart *without rest* Ⓚ 🛜 ⓋⒾⓈⒶ ⓒⓞ ⒶⒺ
5 r. Marivaux (2nd) – Ⓜ *Richelieu Drouot* – ℰ *01 42 97 59 83*
– www.lamaisonfavart.com   **L2**
36 rm – †200/600 € ††200/600 €, ☷ 22 € – 1 suite
◆ Luxury ◆ Traditional ◆ Elegant ◆
The artist Goya stayed in this charming hotel of timeless appeal. The rooms to the front, facing the Opéra Comique, are the most pleasant.

Hôtel de Noailles *without rest* 🈸 Ⓚ 🛜 ♨ ⓋⒾⓈⒶ ⓒⓞ ⒶⒺ ⓞ
9 r. de la Michodière (2nd) – Ⓜ *Quatre Septembre* – ℰ *01 47 42 92 90*
– www.hotelnoailles.com   **K2**
56 rm – †195/325 € ††195/325 €, ☷ 18 € – 5 suites
◆ Modern ◆ Cosy ◆
Hip, contemporary elegance behind a pretty 1900 façade. Sleek, minimalist rooms, most of which open onto the patio (with a balcony on the 5th and 6th floors).

Secret de Paris *without rest* 🈸 Ⓚ 🛜 ♨ ⓋⒾⓈⒶ ⓒⓞ ⒶⒺ
2 r. de Parme (9th) – Ⓜ *Place de Clichy* – ℰ *01 53 16 33 33*
– www.hotelsecretdeparis.com   **K1**
29 rm – †186/500 € ††186/500 €, ☷ 18 €
◆ Historic ◆ Personalised ◆
The design concept in each bedroom is based around a famous Parisian monument, ranging from the Moulin Rouge to the Opéra Garnier. Enjoy comfort and high-tech facilities in a hotel that won't remain a secret for long!

Thérèse *without rest* Ⓚ 🛜 ⓋⒾⓈⒶ ⓒⓞ ⒶⒺ ⓞ
5 r. Thérèse (1st) – Ⓜ *Pyramides* – ℰ *01 42 96 10 01*
– www.hoteltherese.com   **K3**
43 rm – †165/360 € ††165/360 €, ☷ 15 €
◆ Townhouse ◆ Personalised ◆ Elegant ◆
A charming hotel with a cosy, personalised decor blending pastel tones and wood panelling. The rooms are snug and the lounge is very inviting!

Lorette Opéra *without rest* Ⓚ 🛜 ⓋⒾⓈⒶ ⓒⓞ ⒶⒺ ⓞ
36 r. Notre-Dame de Lorette (9th) – Ⓜ *St-Georges* – ℰ *01 42 85 18 81*
– www.astotel.com   **L1**
84 rm – †139/320 € ††139/320 €, ☷ 13 €
◆ Business ◆ Modern ◆
With its exposed beams and untreated parquet flooring the lobby of this hotel is a pleasant place to drop off your bags. Functional yet contemporary guestrooms of varying sizes.

Windsor Opéra *without rest* Ⓚ 🛜 ⓋⒾⓈⒶ ⓒⓞ ⒶⒺ ⓞ
10 r. G.-Laumain (10th) – Ⓜ *Bonne Nouvelle* – ℰ *01 48 00 98 98*
– www.hotelwindsor.com   **M2**
24 rm – †170/302 € ††180/302 €, ☷ 15 €
◆ Townhouse ◆ Modern ◆ Functional ◆
As soon as you enter the lobby, you will be impressed by the designer decor and superb collection of aeronautic exhibits on display (aircraft propellers, windows, engines etc). From here, you can head skywards to guestrooms that are modern and elegant.

Eurostars Panorama without rest

9 r. des Messageries (10th) – Ⓜ Poissonnière – ✆ 01 47 70 44 02 – www.eurostarshotels.com **M1**

43 rm – †95/550 € ††95/550 €, ☕ 10 €

◆ Business ◆ Modern ◆

This recent hotel stands in a quiet street near the Gare du Nord and Gare de l'Est railway stations. Although its façade is typical of the 19C, the guestrooms are contemporary and almost minimalist in style, with the occasional Parisian touch.

WO' without rest

10 r. de Stockholm (8th) – Ⓜ St-Lazare – ✆ 01 45 22 10 85 – www.hotelwo.com **J1**

30 rm – †100/290 € ††120/290 €, ☕ 13 €

◆ Townhouse ◆ Business ◆ Design ◆

WO' as in Wilson Opéra! In a quiet street, close to Gare St Lazare and the grands magasins, this hotel offers guestrooms which, although small, are designer and cosy. Some of them come with a balcony offering views over the city. It is like being in a cocoon, right in the heart of Paris. Competitive rates.

Little Palace without rest

4 r. Salomon-de-Caus (3rd) – Ⓜ Réaumur Sébastopol – ✆ 01 42 72 08 15 – www.littlepalacehotel.com **M3**

49 rm – †178/235 € ††198/273 €, ☕ 15 € – 4 suites

◆ Townhouse ◆ Personalised ◆ Elegant ◆

The charming Little Palace is a successful fusion of Belle Époque and contemporary styles. Welcoming guestrooms with those on the 6th and 7th floors (with a balcony and views of Paris) preferable.

Caumartin Opéra without rest

27 r. Caumartin (9th) – Ⓜ Havre Caumartin – ✆ 01 47 42 95 95 – www.astotel.com **J-K2**

40 rm – †165/320 € ††165/320 €, ☕ 13 €

◆ Minimalist ◆

This hotel has a trendy, colourful and pop-inspired decor. It also has the benefit of a convenient location in the heart of Paris' main shopping district, just a stone's throw from the department stores and the Opera.

Pulitzer without rest

23 r. du Faubourg-Montmartre (9th) – Ⓜ Grands Boulevards – ✆ 01 53 34 98 10 – www.hotelpulitzer.com **L2**

44 rm – †150/280 € ††160/280 €, ☕ 15 €

◆ Business ◆ Personalised ◆

The charm of a British library (comfy Chesterfield armchairs) and the contemporary elegance of industrial-style come together at this hotel. It is located in the heart of the city's theatres and department stores. This Pulitzer would be a worthy winner of a prize for originality.

Joyce without rest

29 r. La Bruyère (9th) – Ⓜ St-Georges – ✆ 01 55 07 00 01 – www.astotel.com **K1**

44 rm – †149/320 € ††149/320 €, ☕ 13 €

◆ Townhouse ◆ Design ◆ Personalised ◆

This stylish boutique hotel is full of character. Headboards, bookshelves, chandeliers and decorative wood panelling have all been drawn on the walls here, in the style of an architect's sketch. Enjoy breakfast beneath an attractive glazed ceiling.

Opéra Pavillon without rest

7 r. de Parme (9th) – Ⓜ Liège – ✆ 01 55 31 60 00 – www.pavillonparis.com **K1**

30 rm ☕ – †135/215 € ††155/335 €

◆ Business ◆ Cosy ◆

Located in a quiet street, this hotel has a restrained yet elegant decor and a hushed ambience. It has small but intimate rooms featuring wood furnishings and warm tones. The all-inclusive package of breakfast, teatime buffet and Wi-Fi is a particular plus.

Anjou Lafayette without rest 　　　　AC 🛜 VISA ◉◉ AE ①

4 r. Riboutté (9th) – ⓜ *Cadet* – ℘ *01 42 46 83 44*
– www.hotelanjoulafayette.com　　　　　　　　　　　　　　　**M1**
39 rm – ♦129/169 € ♦♦139/189 €, ⊑ 12 €

◆ Business ◆ Personalised ◆

This cosy, family-style hotel stands in a quiet street. It offers well-maintained, comfortable guestrooms with a warm, welcoming decor.

Relais Madeleine without rest 　　　& AC 🛜 VISA ◉◉ AE

11 bis r. Godot-de-Mauroy (9th) – ⓜ *Havre Caumartin* – ℘ *01 47 42 22 40*
– www.relaismadeleine.fr　　　　　　　　　　　　　　　　**J2**
23 rm – ♦185/280 € ♦♦230/350 €, ⊑ 15 €

◆ Luxury ◆ Personalised ◆ Classic ◆

Staying at this small hotel is a bit like spending time in a family home, but right in the centre of Paris! It has undeniable charm with carefully chosen furniture, sparkling colours and delightful fabrics. Not to mention the attentive service.

Le Crayon without rest 　　　　　AC ↩ 🛜 VISA ◉◉ AE

25 r. du Bouloi (1st) – ⓜ *Palais Royal* – ℘ *01 42 36 54 19*
– www.hotelcrayon.com　　　　　　　　　　　　　　　　　**L3**
26 rm – ♦149/347 € ♦♦149/347 €, ⊑ 12 €

◆ Townhouse ◆ Personalised ◆

This far from banal hotel is halfway between an artist's residence and a family home, featuring an explosive mix of colours, contrasts and vintage decor. Each bedroom is its own original creation, adorned with furniture tracked down personally by the hotel's designer.

Alison without rest 　　　　　　AC 🛜 VISA ◉◉ AE ①

21 r. de Surène (8th) – ⓜ *Madeleine* – ℘ *01 42 65 54 00*
– www.hotelalison.com　　　　　　　　　　　　　　　　　**J2**
34 rm – ♦103/182 € ♦♦127/202 €, ⊑ 11 €

◆ Family ◆ Functional ◆

This small hotel in a quiet street near the Théâtre de la Madeleine offers good value for money. Functional guestrooms offering high levels of comfort.

Le Meurice – Hôtel Le Meurice 　　　AC ⇔ ⊏ VISA ◉◉ AE

228 r. de Rivoli (1st) – ⓜ *Tuileries* – ℘ *01 44 58 10 55*
– www.lemeurice.com
– Closed 2 to 17 March, 27 July-26 August, Saturday, Sunday and Bank Holidays　　　　　　　　　　　　　　　　　　　　　　　　　**J-K3**
Rest – Menu 115 € (lunch)/280 € – Carte 200/350 € 🍃

◆ Creative ◆ Luxury ◆ Romantic ◆

The fabulous decor calls to mind the style of the 17C, and the State Apartments at Versailles. Head chef Yannick Alleno's cuisine reveals a brilliant alliance of classicism and inventiveness, where even the simplest ingredients are transformed into the most extravagant flavours. Service fit for a king!
→ Maquereau mariné au ponzu, huile de sésame, gelée à l'hibiscus, pétales de tomate au shiso. Vapeur de cabillaud à l'ail doux, chorizo, jus de kokotxas, coquillages et champignons. Meringue soufflée aux amandes, pêches macérées au lait d'amande.

Le Grand Véfour (Guy Martin) 　　　AC ⇔ ⊏ VISA ◉◉ AE ①

17 r. Beaujolais (1st) – ⓜ *Palais Royal* – ℘ *01 42 96 56 27*
– www.grand-vefour.com
– Closed 29 July-26 August, Saturday and Sunday　　　　　**L3**
Rest – Menu 96 € (lunch)/298 € – Carte 200/290 € 🍃

◆ Creative ◆ Luxury ◆

In the gardens of the Palais Royal, this luxurious Directoire-style restaurant has been a mecca for gourmets for over 200 years and is full of history! Inventive cuisine by Guy Martin.
→ Ravioles de foie gras, crème foisonnée truffée. Pigeon Prince Rainier III. Palet noisette et chocolat au lait, glace au caramel et prise de sel de Guérande.

FRANCE - PARIS

Carré des Feuillants (Alain Dutournier)

XXXX
£3 £3

14 r. de Castiglione (1st) – Ⓜ *Tuileries*
– ℰ *01 42 86 82 82 – www.carredesfeuillants.fr*
– Closed August, Saturday lunch and Sunday   **K3**
Rest – Menu 58 € (lunch), 155/200 € – Carte 135/170 € 🕸
♦ Modern ♦ Luxury ♦ Elegant ♦
Elegant and minimalist contemporary restaurant on the site of the old Feuillants convent. Modern menu with strong Gascony influences. Superb wines and Armagnacs.
➜ Écrevisses en infusion parfumée, huîtres spéciales d'Arcachon en ravioles de chair de Saint-Jacques. Lièvre mijoté au vin de Sauternes en prestigieuse royale avec truffe et foie gras. Miniclafoutis de cerises, crème glacée à l'infusion de verveine.

Sur Mesure par Thierry Marx – Hôtel Mandarin Oriental

XXX
£3 £3

251 r. St-Honoré (1st) – Ⓜ *Concorde*
– ℰ *01 70 98 73 00 – www.mandarinoriental.fr/paris/*
– Closed Sunday and Monday   **J3**
Rest – Menu 75 € (weekday lunch), 165/195 € 🕸
♦ Creative ♦ Design ♦ Elegant ♦
Precise 'tailor-made' (sur mesure) cuisine is the hallmark of Thierry Marx, who confirms his talent as a master culinary craftsman at the Mandarin Oriental's showcase restaurant. Every dish reveals his tireless scientific approach, which is sometimes teasing but always exacting. An experience in itself, aided by the stunning, immaculate and ethereal decor.
➜ Semi-pris de coquillages et longuet caviar. Bœuf charbon, réglisse, laque de petits pois, lard de Colonnata. Sweet bento et ylang-ylang.

Le Dali – Hôtel Le Meurice

XXX

228 r. Rivoli (1st) – Ⓜ *Tuileries –* ℰ *01 44 58 10 44 – www.lemeurice.com*
Rest – Carte 70/130 €   **J-K3**
♦ Modern ♦ Trendy ♦ Formal ♦
This, the 'second' restaurant of Le Meurice is also run by Yannick Alléno and pitches itself somewhere between upmarket canteen and plush restaurant. It has a beautiful classic decor with pilasters and mirrors, enhanced by a touch of surrealism (superb Dalí-style fresco by Ara Starck).

Senderens

XXX
£3 £3

9 pl. de la Madeleine (8th) – Ⓜ *Madeleine –* ℰ *01 42 65 22 90*
– www.senderens.fr
– Closed 3 to 26 August and Bank Holidays   **J2**
Rest – Menu 116/160 € bi – Carte 90/110 € 🕸
Rest *Bar le Passage –* ℰ *01 42 65 56 66* – Menu 36 € (lunch)/39 €
♦ Creative ♦ Design ♦
Formerly Lucas-Carton and now Senderens, this exclusive restaurant boasts a decor which fuses Art Nouveau wood with futuristic furnishings to create a relaxed ambience. The pleasures of the palate remain the priority here, as witnessed by the superbly creative and refined cuisine. The Bar le Passage has a lounge atmosphere and dishes inspired by the local markets.
➜ Mushroom burger de foie gras pur, larme de sésame noir. Cochon de lait de Burgos rôti, carottes fanes aux baies roses et avocat. Saint-honoré aux fraises mara des bois.

1728

XXX

8 r. d'Anjou (8th) – Ⓜ *Madeleine –* ℰ *01 40 17 04 77*
– www.1728-paris.com
– Closed 3 weeks in August, Sunday and Bank Holidays   **J2**
Rest – Carte 65/97 € 🕸
♦ Creative ♦ Romantic ♦
The 1728 occupies an 18C mansion house with romantic period lounges and serving a fusion of Eastern and Western cuisine. A journey through time and around the world.

XXX
ஐ
Pur' – Hôtel Park Hyatt ⬜ VISA ●● AE

5 r. de la Paix (2nd) – Ⓜ *Opéra –* ℰ *01 58 71 10 61*
– www.paris.vendome.hyatt.fr
– Closed August and lunch **K3**
Rest – Menu 100/250 € bi
– Carte 130/230 €
♦ Creative ♦ Fashionable ♦ Design ♦
Enjoy a sense of pure enjoyment as you dine in this restaurant. The highly elegant contemporary decor and creative dishes are carefully conjured by the chef using the finest ingredients. Attractive, delicious and refined.
➜ Fricassée de girolles "tête de clou", crumble de noisettes, mûres en pickles. Bœuf wagyu grillé, aubergines brûlées, pommes de terre fondantes. Fine tarte aux fraises des bois, Bloody Mary glacé et basilic.

XXX
ஐ
Le Céladon – Hôtel Westminster AC ⇧ ⬜ VISA ●● AE ⓪

15 r. Daunou (2nd) – Ⓜ *Opéra –* ℰ *01 42 61 77 42*
– www.leceladon.com
– Closed August, Saturday and Sunday **K2**
Rest – Menu 49 € (lunch)/64 € – Carte 80/120 €
♦ Modern ♦ Elegant ♦
A sophisticated decor that combines Regency-style furniture, old paintings and a collection of celadon vases. Contemporary-style cuisine with its roots in classic dishes.
➜ Girolles et cochon ibérique, pluma grillé et jambon en copeaux. Turbot sauvage cuit sur l'arête, gelée aux crevettes grises et thym citron. Pêche rôtie, chutney au romarin et brioche tiède.

XXX
Drouant 🔊 AC ⇧ ⬜ VISA ●● AE

16 pl. Gaillon (2nd) – Ⓜ *Quatre Septembre –* ℰ *01 42 65 15 16*
– www.drouant.com **K3**
Rest – Menu 45 € (lunch) – Carte 68/75 € 🍴
♦ Modern ♦ Elegant ♦
A legendary restaurant where the Prix Goncourt has been awarded since 1914. With Antoine Westermann at the helm, it serves traditional cuisine with a modern touch. Elegant, richly decorated interior.

XXX
ஐ
Le Baudelaire – Hôtel Le Burgundy AC ⬜ VISA ●● AE ⓪

6-8 r. Duphot (1st) – Ⓜ *Madeleine –* ℰ *01 42 60 34 12*
– www.lebaudelaire.com
– Closed Saturday lunch and Sunday **J3**
Rest – Menu 55 € (lunch)/145 € – Carte 75/140 €
♦ Modern ♦ Elegant ♦
Part of the luxury Hotel Burgundy, which opened in 2010, Le Baudelaire is very much a safe culinary bet. Run by a chef with an impressive CV, it offers delicate cuisine that blends together fine flavours.
➜ Terrine de foie gras de canard des Landes, figue de Solliès marinée. Turbot de petit bateau, haricots de Paimpol, pêche et tétragone. Chocolat grand cru d'Équateur, sablé fleur de sel et dentelle croustillante.

XXX
Arola – Hôtel W Paris Opéra ♿ AC ⬜ VISA ●● AE ⓪

4 r. Meyerbeer (1st floor) (9th) – Ⓜ *Chaussée d'Antin –* ℰ *01 77 48 94 94*
– www.restaurant-arola.fr **K2**
Rest – Menu 38 € (lunch)/70 €
– Carte 60/80 €
♦ Spanish ♦ Fashionable ♦ Design ♦
The Hotel W Paris Opéra, which opened in 2012, appealed to chef Sergi Arola to run its restaurant. In Madrid, he is a renowned figure of Spanish cooking. Here, he creates a "pica pica" menu: a take on tapas that is both inventive and fun. A concept perfectly in keeping with this chic new establishment.

XXX **Macéo** [AC] ⇔ [VISA] ⓸⓸

15 r. Petits-Champs (1st) – ⓶ *Bourse* – ☎ *01 42 97 53 85*
– *www.maceorestaurant.com*
– *Closed 3 to 26 August, Saturday lunch, Sunday and Bank Holidays*
Rest – Menu 36/58 € – Carte 52/76 € ❦   **L3**
♦ Modern ♦ Classic ♦

A Second Empire interior with mouldings, parquet flooring and beautiful mirrors is the setting for modern cuisine showcasing seasonal produce. Vegetarian
menu and international wine list.

XXX **Le Versance** [AC] [VISA] ⓸⓸ [AE]

16 r. Feydeau (2nd) – ⓶ *Bourse* – ☎ *01 45 08 00 08* – *www.leversance.fr*
– *Closed 22 July-20 August, 24 December-2 January, Saturday lunch, Sunday
and Monday*   **L2**
Rest – Menu 38 € bi (lunch) – Carte 57/75 €
♦ Modern ♦ Fashionable ♦

A sleek interior with a winning combination of exposed beams, stained-glass
windows and modern furniture. Equally as impressive is the globetrotting
chef's cuisine: think lobster curry, calf's sweetbread and spiced pears.

XXX **Kei** (Kei Kobayashi) [AC] [VISA] ⓸⓸ [AE]
🕸
5 r. du Coq-Héron (1st) – ⓶ *Louvre Rivoli* – ☎ *01 42 33 14 74*
– *www.restaurant-kei.fr*
– *Closed 5 to 26 August, Christmas Holidays, Sunday and Monday*
Rest – Menu 45 € (lunch), 100/125 €   **L3**
♦ Modern ♦ Elegant ♦ Minimalist ♦

Japanese-born Kei Kobayashi's discovery of French gastronomy on TV was a
revelation to him. So much so that as soon as he was old enough he headed
to France to train in some of the country's best restaurants. His career now
sees him branching out on his own. He offers fine cuisine that reflects his twin
influences and the passion for his work.
➜ Foie gras, gelée de raisin, amandes fraîches et pomme. Filet de rouget
au pamplemousse confit. Assiette chocolat, sorbet chocolat au lait.

XX **Camélia** – Hôtel Mandarin Oriental 🕮 ⚹ [AC] [VISA] ⓸⓸ [AE] ⓪

251 r. St-Honoré (1st) – ⓶ *Concorde* – ☎ *01 70 98 74 00*
– *www.mandarinoriental.fr/paris/*   **J3**
Rest – Carte 64/116 €
♦ Modern ♦ Elegant ♦ Design ♦

Keep it simple, concentrate on top quality produce full of flavour, take inspiration from classic French cuisine and add a touch of Asia. These are the aims of
Thierry Marx in this elegant, restful and minimalist-style restaurant.

XX **Kinugawa** [AC] ⊏🍴 (dinner) [VISA] ⓸⓸ [AE]

9 r. du Mont-Thabor (1st) – ⓶ *Tuileries* – ☎ *01 42 60 65 07*
– *www.kinugawa.fr*
– *Closed 23 December-1 January and Sunday*   **K3**
Rest – Menu 42 € (weekday lunch), 55/85 € – Carte 40/80 €
♦ Japanese ♦ Design ♦ Elegant ♦

Upstairs, fine Japanese food is served in typically minimalist surroundings: pure
lines and sober colours. Sushi bar downstairs.

XX **L'Opéra** 🕮 ⚹ [AC] [VISA] ⓸⓸ [AE]

pl. Jacques-Rouché - Palais Garnier (9th) – ⓶ *Opéra* – ☎ *01 42 68 86 80*
– *www.opera-restaurant.fr*   **K2**
Rest – Carte 50/75 €
♦ Modern ♦ Design ♦ Elegant ♦

This restaurant beneath the rotunda of Charles Garnier's Opera House is where
horse-drawn carriages would have once dropped off their passengers. The
decor makes an incredible leap from the 19C to avant-garde with a fashionable
feel on the ground floor and a more intimate ambience on the freestanding
mezzanine. Contemporary cuisine.

XX **La Fontaine Gaillon** 🛆 AC ⇔ ☐ VISA ⚫ AE

pl. Gaillon (2nd) – Ⓜ *Quatre Septembre –* ℰ *01 47 42 63 22*
– www.restaurant-la-fontaine-gaillon.com
– Closed 3 weeks in August, Saturday and Sunday **K2-3**
Rest – Menu 45 € (lunch) – Carte 60/90 €
♦ Fish and seafood ♦ Cosy ♦

Beautiful 17C townhouse supervised by Gérard Depardieu with a hushed setting and terrace around a fountain. Spotlight on seafood, accompanied by a pleasant selection of wines.

XX **Goumard** AC ⇔ ☐ VISA ⚫ AE ⓪

9 r. Duphot (1st) – Ⓜ *Madeleine –* ℰ *01 42 60 36 07 – www.goumard.com*
Rest – Menu 44/54 € bi – Carte 65/91 € **J3**
♦ Fish and seafood ♦ Cosy ♦

This restaurant dating back over a century has been given a new lease of life. Contemporary decor, a selection of meat dishes, plus a choice of seafood specialities (oysters at the bar). Open from midday to midnight.

XX **Le First** – Hôtel The Westin Paris 🛆 AC VISA ⚫ AE ⓪

234 r. de Rivoli (1st) – Ⓜ *Tuileries –* ℰ *01 44 77 10 40*
– www.lefirstrestaurant.com/fr/ **J3**
Rest – Menu 36 € (weekdays)/60 € bi – Carte 55/100 €
♦ Modern ♦ Elegant ♦ Retro ♦

Inside the Westin, this veritable boudoir has soft lighting designed by Jacques Garcia and is a stone's throw from the Tuileries. The cuisine puts a new spin on traditional dishes (young rabbit with sage). In summer, head for the peaceful terrace in the courtyard.

XX **Palais Royal** 🛆 AC ⇔ VISA ⚫ AE

110 Galerie de Valois - Jardin du Palais Royal (1st) – Ⓜ *Bourse*
– ℰ 01 40 20 00 27 – www.restaurantdupalaisroyal.com
– Closed Sunday **L3**
Rest – Carte 50/80 €
♦ Traditional ♦ Retro ♦

Beneath the windows of Colette's apartment, you can sample lovely traditional cuisine in an Art Deco-style interior. The terrace overlooks the gardens of the Palais Royal.

XX **Pierre au Palais Royal** AC VISA ⚫ AE

10 r. Richelieu (1st) – Ⓜ *Palais Royal –* ℰ *01 42 96 09 17*
– www.pierreaupalaisroyal.com
– Closed August, Saturday lunch and Sunday **K3**
Rest – Menu 39 € (lunch), 44/56 €
♦ Modern ♦ Neighbourhood ♦ Friendly ♦

This famous Parisian restaurant has changed its style over the years with its simple, chic dining room now decorated in black and white. The cuisine is inspired by southwest France, and presented with enthusiasm by the owner.

XX **Les Collections** – Hôtel Sofitel le Faubourg 🛆 AC VISA ⚫ AE ⓪

15 r. Boissy-d'Anglas (8th) – Ⓜ *Concorde –* ℰ *01 44 94 14 24*
– www.sofitel.com
– Closed lunch Saturday and Sunday **J3**
Rest – Carte 66/74 €
♦ Modern ♦ Friendly ♦

This highly fashionable restaurant appointed a new chef in 2011. Japanese in origin, with experience in a number of fine restaurants, he creates inventive dishes that are full of flavour. Try dishes such as poached monkfish tail, saffron broth and wild rice.

FRANCE - PARIS

XX **L'Assaggio** – Hôtel Castille Paris   🔈 AC ⇔ VISA ⚫ AE ①

37 r. Cambon (1st) – Ⓜ *Madeleine –* ☏ *01 44 58 45 67 – www.castille.com*
– Closed August, 24 to 30 December, Saturday and Sunday   **J3**
Rest – Carte 60/90 €
◆ Italian ◆ Mediterranean ◆

L'Assaggio means 'tasting' in Italian. Opening wide onto a patio painted with frescoes and adorned with a fountain, the setting is evocative of the Villa d'Este near Rome. Unmistakably Italian flavours with antipasti, pasta, risotto etc.

XX **Jean**   AC ⇔ VISA ⚫ AE ①
⁂
8 r. St-Lazare (9th) – Ⓜ *Notre-Dame de Lorette –* ☏ *01 48 78 62 73*
– www.restaurantjean.fr
– Closed 30 July-20 August, Saturday and Sunday   **L1**
Rest – Menu 48 € (lunch), 70/95 € – Carte 65/86 €
◆ Creative ◆ Elegant ◆ Cosy ◆

This restaurant is in the heart of the 9th arrondissement. It gives guests the illusion of having escaped to a charming property away from contemporary Paris with its painted beams and floral drapes. A new chef took the helm in late 2011 and continues the theme of fine dining with a focus on refinement and flavours.
➜ Anguille fumée et glacée au vinaigre de riz, caviar, pomme de terre fondante, tofu grillé et crème de raifort. Carré d'agneau, ballottine et côtelettes en croûte au piment d'Espelette. Baba au rhum, fruits frais et sorbet mûre.

XX **Le Lumière** – Hôtel Scribe   ⟁ AC ⇔ VISA ⚫ AE ①
⁂
1 r. Scribe (9th) – Ⓜ *Opéra –* ☏ *01 44 71 24 24*
– www.hotel-scribe-paris.com
– Closed Saturday and Sunday   **K2**
Rest – Menu 90 € – Carte 60/80 €
◆ Modern ◆ Cosy ◆ Formal ◆

The Lumière brothers presented their first film to the public in this very setting. The dining room, crowned by a superb glass roof, evokes the elegance of the Belle Epoque period. This image is continued in the kitchen, directed to perfection by a chef who embraces both vivacity and sparkle in his cooking. Simpler à la carte choices at weekends.
➜ Saumon sauvage mi-fumé en carpaccio, marinade au poivre du Sichuan, caviar de hareng. Turbot caramélisé au beurre salé, riz haenuki en maki, betterave fondante, fumet au sansho. Millefeuille déstructuré, mousse aérienne, crème glacée, chocolat noir et vanille de Tahiti.

XX **Au Petit Riche**   AC ⇔ VISA ⚫ AE ①

25 r. Le Peletier (9th) – Ⓜ *Richelieu Drouot –* ☏ *01 47 70 68 68*
– www.aupetitriche.com
– Closed weekends from mid July-late August and Bank Holidays
Rest – Menu 30/36 € bi – Carte 33/65 € 🍷   **L2**
◆ Traditional ◆ Bistro ◆

This place has preserved all the charm of a fashionable 19C bistro with its red velvet banquettes, engraved mirrors and elegantly laid tables. It is a veritable Paris institution. The cuisine is made up of dishes from the Touraine and a fine selection of Loire Valley wines.

XX **Passage 53** (Shinichi Sato)   AC VISA ⚫
⁂⁂
53 passage des Panoramas (2nd) – Ⓜ *Grands Boulevards*
– ☏ *01 42 33 04 35 – www.passage53.com*
– Closed 2 weeks in August, Sunday and Monday   **L2**
Rest – *(number of covers limited, pre-book)* Menu 60 € (weekday lunch)/ 120 €
◆ Creative ◆ Design ◆ Minimalist ◆

In an authentic covered passage, this restaurant has a minimalist decor and offers a fine panorama of contemporary cuisine. Using market-fresh produce, the young Japanese chef – trained at L'Astrance – turns out irrefutably precise compositions that are cooked to perfection.
➜ Menu dégustation surprise.

FRANCE - PARIS

Brasserie Gallopin

40 r. N.-D.-des-Victoires (2nd) – **Ⓜ** Bourse – ☏ 01 42 36 45 38
– www.brasseriegallopin.com   L3
Rest – Menu 25 € (lunch)/32 € – Carte 40/65 €
♦ Traditional ♦ Retro ♦

A real institution located opposite the Palais Brongniart, founded in 1876 by a certain Monsieur Gallopin. Once the haunt of Arletty and Raimu, now Parisians and tourists alike head here for the beautiful Victorian decor (mahogany panelling, Belle Époque glass partition etc) and the tasty classic dishes: tartare, rum baba, Paris-Brest pastry etc.

Vaudeville

29 r. Vivienne (2nd) – **Ⓜ** Bourse – ☏ 01 40 20 04 62
– www.vaudevilleparis.com   L2
Rest – Menu 33 € – Carte 36/71 €
♦ Traditional ♦

This large, quintessentially Parisian Art Deco brasserie is a favourite lunch haunt for journalists by day, and a popular post-theatre eatery by night.

Zinc Opéra

8 r. de Hanovre (2nd) – **Ⓜ** Opéra – ☏ 01 42 65 58 95
– www.restaurant-zinc.com
– Closed August, Saturday and Sunday   K2
Rest – Menu 30/35 € – Carte 35/55 €
♦ Modern ♦ Elegant ♦ Friendly ♦

The flavours call the tune at the recently opened Zinc Opéra! This chic and cosy bistro is run by a very competent team; the carefully prepared yet simple dishes let the ingredients do the talking. Confit de canard with fried potatoes, cherry clafoutis etc: classic dishes that are full of flavour.

Café Moderne

40 r. N.-D.-des-Victoires (2nd) – **Ⓜ** Bourse – ☏ 01 53 40 84 10
– Closed 1 to 24 August, Saturday and Sunday   L3
Rest – Menu 35/39 €
♦ Modern ♦ Elegant ♦ Fashionable ♦

This elegant, modern restaurant near the Bourse is packed at lunchtime and has an intimate ambience in the evening. It has a French-style decor and menu, as well as a chef who is passionate about seasonal produce.

Liza

14 r. de la Banque (2nd) – **Ⓜ** Bourse – ☏ 01 55 35 00 66
– www.restaurant-liza.com
– Closed Saturday lunch and Sunday dinner   L3
Rest – Carte 34/54 €
♦ Lebanese ♦ Exotic ♦ Elegant ♦

There's nothing clichéd about this Lebanese restaurant styled by Middle Eastern designers (lounge-style decor), where the focus is on fine, fragrant reinterpretations of traditional dishes.

Aux Lyonnais

32 r. St-Marc (2nd) – **Ⓜ** Richelieu Drouot – ☏ 01 42 96 65 04
– www.alain-ducasse.com
– Closed August, Saturday lunch, Sunday and Monday   L2
Rest – (pre-book) Menu 32 € (lunch) – Carte 41/57 €
♦ Lyonnaise ♦ Bistro ♦ Retro ♦

This bistro founded in 1890 serves delicious cuisine which explores the gastronomic history of the city. Deliciously retro decor, featuring a zinc counter, banquettes, bevelled mirrors and moulded fixtures and fittings.

Le Pantruche   VISA ⬤⬤

3 r. Victor-Massé (9th) – Ⓜ *Pigalle* – ℰ *01 48 78 55 60*
– *www.lepantruche.com*
– *Closed 3 weeks in August, 23 December-2 January, Saturday and Sunday*
Rest – *(number of covers limited, pre-book)* Menu 34 €   **L1**
♦ Traditional ♦ Bistro ♦

'Pantruche' is slang for Paris... An apt name for this bistro with a chic retro decor,
which happily cultivates a 1940s-1950s 'canaille' atmosphere. As for the food,
the chef and his small team put together lovely seasonal dishes in keeping
with current culinary trends.

Hotaru   VISA ⬤⬤

18 r. Rodier (9th) – Ⓜ *Notre-Dame de Lorette* – ℰ *01 48 78 33 74*
– *Closed 3 weeks in August, 20 December-3 January, Sunday and Monday*
Rest – Carte 20/49 €   **L1**
♦ Japanese ♦ Rustic ♦

A welcoming Japanese restaurant with a young chef who produces traditional,
family cuisine with an emphasis on fish. Enjoy sushi, maki and sashimi, as well as
a selection of cooked and fried dishes.

Café Panique   VISA ⬤⬤

12 r. des Messageries (10th) – Ⓜ *Poissonnière* – ℰ *01 47 70 06 84*
– *www.cafepanique.com*
– *Closed August, 1 week in February, Sunday, Bank Holidays and lunch*
Rest – Menu 35/45 € – Carte 42/55 €   **M1**
♦ Modern ♦ Intimate ♦

There is no panic in the kitchen of this contemporary loft-style restaurant, just a
healthy buzz of activity. Since 1992, chef Odile Guyader has created delightful
signature dishes here. These include fillet of beef with an emulsion of foie gras
and tiramisu with Carambar caramel.

La Petite Sirène de Copenhague   VISA ⬤⬤ AE

47 r. Notre Dame de Lorette (9th) – Ⓜ *St-Georges* – ℰ *01 45 26 66 66*
– *Closed August, 23 December-2 January, Saturday lunch, Sunday and Monday*
Rest – *(pre-book)* Menu 34 € (lunch)/38 € – Carte 48/77 €   **K1**
♦ Danish ♦ Exotic ♦

The Danish flag flying above the entrance provides a strong clue to the gourmet offerings inside. There is a daily menu chalked up on a slate board, as well
as a more expensive à la carte, from which guests can feast on Danish specialities such as herrings.

Les Bistronomes   VISA ⬤⬤

34 r. de Richelieu (1st) – Ⓜ *Palais Royal* – ℰ *01 42 60 59 66*
– *www.lesbistronomes.fr*
– *Closed 3 weeks in August, 1 week Christmas Holidays, Saturday lunch, Sunday
and Monday*   **K3**
Rest – Menu 35 € (lunch) – Carte 48/70 €
♦ Modern ♦ Bistro ♦

The reputation of this restaurant, which opened in early 2011, has spread
quickly amongst gourmet diners. Indeed, the quality of the food is difficult to
ignore with its blend of traditional French, contemporary and bistro styles.
Dishes such as cauliflower pannacotta, French-style pigeon and braised pineapple feature on the menu.

Kunitoraya   AC ⬤ VISA ⬤⬤

5 r. Villedo (1st) – Ⓜ *Pyramides* – ℰ *01 47 03 07 74* – *www.kunitoraya.com*
– *Closed 2 weeks in August, February Holidays, Sunday dinner and Monday*
Rest – Menu 26 € (weekday lunch), 50/90 €   **K3**
– Carte 45/60 €
♦ Japanese ♦ Retro ♦ Minimalist ♦

With its old zinc counter, mirrors and Métro-style tiling, Kunitoraya has the feel
of a late-night Parisian restaurant from the early 1900s. Refined Japanese cuisine
based around "udon", a thick homemade noodle made with wholemeal flour
imported from Japan.

FRANCE - PARIS

X **Pinxo - Tuileries** – Hôtel Renaissance Paris Vendôme   AC

9 r. d'Alger (1st) – Ⓜ *Tuileries* – ☏ *01 40 20 72 00*   VISA ⓸ AE
– www.pinxo.fr
– Closed August, Saturday lunch and Sunday   **K3**
Rest – Menu 29 € bi (lunch) – Carte 45/60 €
♦ Modern ♦ Fashionable ♦ Friendly ♦
The minimalist furniture, black-and-white colour scheme and open kitchen create an understated, stylish setting in which to share Alain Dutournier's creative dishes.

X **Zen**   🛖 AC VISA ⓸
☺
8 r. de L'Échelle (1st) – Ⓜ *Palais Royal* – ☏ *01 42 61 93 99*
– Closed 10 to 20 August   **K3**
Rest – Carte 20/52 €
♦ Japanese ♦ Minimalist ♦
Japanese restaurant serving an extensive, traditional menu against a contemporary, all-white decor with sleek curves and flashes of acid green.

X **Silk & Spice**   AC ⇔ VISA ⓸ AE

6 r. Mandar (2nd) – Ⓜ *Sentier* – ☏ *01 44 88 21 91* – *www.silkandspice.fr*
– Closed lunch Saturday and Sunday   **L3**
Rest – Menu 26/50 € – Carte 33/48 €
♦ Thai ♦ Exotic ♦
Hushed atmosphere and delicious Thai-inspired cuisine. The signature dishes here are king prawns and shrimps in a lemon grass reduction, and green beef curry.

X **Le Pré Cadet**   AC VISA ⓸ AE
☺
10 r. Saulnier (9th) – Ⓜ *Cadet* – ☏ *01 48 24 99 64*
– http://restaurant-leprecadet.e-monsite.com
– Closed 1 week in May, 3 weeks in August, 1 week in December, Saturday lunch, Sunday and Monday   **L2**
Rest – *(number of covers limited, pre-book)* Menu 30 € – Carte 36/57 €
♦ Traditional ♦ Friendly ♦ Bistro ♦
This small, friendly and welcoming restaurant is close to the Folies Bergère. It is known for its classic, traditional cuisine such as calf's head, the house speciality! The dining room is always packed.

X **L'Office**   AC VISA ⓸
☺
3 r. Richer (9th) – Ⓜ *Poissonnière* – ☏ *01 47 70 67 31*
– Closed 27 July-27 August, 23 December-4 January, Saturday and Sunday
Rest – *(number of covers limited, pre-book)* Menu 26 €   **M2**
(lunch)/33 €
♦ Modern ♦ Bistro ♦ Friendly ♦
A tiny bistro just a stone's throw from the Folies Bergère. Here, at tightly-packed tables, you tuck into dishes that vary with the seasons. The impressive cooking comes courtesy of a Japanese chef (who has clocked up plenty of experience in France), and is served with judiciously selected wines. Great value for money.

X **Pierrot**   🛖 AC ⇱ (dinner) VISA ⓸ AE

18 r. Étienne Marcel (2nd) – Ⓜ *Etienne Marcel* – ☏ *01 45 08 00 10*
– Closed Sunday   **M3**
Rest – Carte 40/55 €
♦ Traditional ♦ Bistro ♦
This friendly bistro run by two young people from the Aveyron serves meat from the Aubrac, house foie gras and herbed rack of lamb which is popular with regulars and visitors alike!

X **Bi Zan**   ⇔ VISA ⓸ AE

56 r. Ste-Anne (2nd) – Ⓜ *Quatre Septembre* – ☏ *01 42 96 67 76*
– Closed Sunday, Monday and Bank Holidays   **K3**
Rest – Menu 65 € bi/120 € bi – Carte dinner 68/135 €
♦ Japanese ♦ Minimalist ♦
Popular address (the name refers to a mountainous region of Japan) in minimalist style. Sushi counter, upstairs dining room and fine sake list.

✗ **Frenchie**

5 r. du Nil (2nd) – Ⓜ *Sentier* – ℰ *01 40 39 96 19*
– *www.frenchie-restaurant.com*
– *Closed 2 weeks in August, Christmas Holidays, Saturday, Sunday and lunch*
Rest – *(number of covers limited, pre-book)* Menu 45 € **M3**
◆ Modern ◆ Friendly ◆ Fashionable ◆
Near the Sentier metro station, this small, loft-style restaurant has exposed brickwork, stones and beams. It specialises in contemporary-style cuisine created by a young chef with international experience.

TOUR EIFFEL – INVALIDES   *Plan IV*

Sezz without rest

6 av. Frémiet (16th) ✉ *75016* – Ⓜ *Passy* – ℰ *01 56 75 26 26*
– *www.hotelsezz-paris.com* **N2**
19 rm – ♦282/570 € ♦♦282/570 €, ⚏ 30 € – 7 suites
◆ Luxury ◆ Design ◆
Behind the beautiful and elaborately sculpted façade of this building dating from 1913, the interior has adopted an ultra-design style. It features grey stone, original furniture, high-tech gadgetry and a sauna. Every guest is also assigned an individual assistant for the duration of his or her stay.

Mercure Suffren Tour Eiffel

20 r. Jean-Rey (15th) – Ⓜ *Bir-Hakeim*
– ℰ *01 45 78 50 00* – *www.mercure.com* **N2**
405 rm – ♦185/500 € ♦♦185/500 €, ⚏ 20 € **Rest** – Carte 31/59 €
◆ Chain hotel ◆ Business ◆ Functional ◆
This extensive Mercure, refurbished in a resolutely contemporary spirit, boasts a restaurant, meeting rooms and a fitness room open 24 hours a day. A particular selling point is the impressive view of the Eiffel Tower from the guestrooms on the upper floors.

Le Marquis without rest

15 r. Dupleix (15th) – Ⓜ *Dupleix* – ℰ *01 43 06 31 50*
– *www.lemarquisparis.com* **O2**
36 rm – ♦151/459 € ♦♦151/459 €, ⚏ 20 €
◆ Business ◆ Modern ◆ Personalised ◆
The noble name suits this refined hotel but that is as far as its affinity with the Ancien Régime goes – the decor is trendy and synonymous with comfort. It is a stone's throw from the rue du Commerce and the Champ de Mars.

Platine without rest

20 r. de l'Ingénieur-Robert-Keller (15th) – Ⓜ *Charles Michels*
– ℰ *01 45 71 15 15* – *www.platinehotel.fr* *Plan I* **A2**
46 rm – ♦149/459 € ♦♦149/459 €, ⚏ 12 €
◆ Townhouse ◆ Personalised ◆
Platine or platinum blonde – like Marilyn Monroe – to whom this hotel pays homage. The guestrooms are comfortable and well kept. Go for one of those with a round bed for optimum glamour and to channel your inner star! There is a pleasant relaxation suite in the basement.

Le Walt without rest

37 av. de la Motte-Picquet (7th) – Ⓜ *École Militaire* – ℰ *01 45 51 55 83*
– *www.lewaltparis.com* **P2**
25 rm – ♦305/375 € ♦♦305/375 €, ⚏ 16 €
◆ Business ◆ Personalised ◆ Elegant ◆
Le Walt is a haven of peace and quiet in the centre of Paris (not far from the Eiffel Tower and Les Invalides). It champions contemporary decor and originality in its design. Proof is provided by the reproductions of classical masterpieces acting as headboards.

FRANCE - PARIS

Duquesne Eiffel without rest   🛜 VISA ⦿ AE ⓘ

23 av. Duquesne (7th) – Ⓜ *École Militaire – 𝒞 01 44 42 09 09*
– www.hde.fr   **P2**
40 rm – 🛏140/250 € 🛏🛏140/250 €, � 13 €
♦ Business ♦ Cosy ♦
Not far from Invalides, this inviting hotel has contemporary, comfortable and
cosy guestrooms. From the fifth floor there is a superb view of the Eiffel Tower
and École Militaire.

Muguet without rest   AC 🛜 VISA ⦿ AE

11 r. Chevert (7th) – Ⓜ *École Militaire – 𝒞 01 47 05 05 93*
– www.hotelmuguet.com   **P2**
43 rm – 🛏110/155 € 🛏🛏125/195 €, ⊡ 13 €
♦ Family ♦ Classic ♦ Homely ♦
In a quiet street a stone's throw from Les Invalides, this hotel has been refurbished in a classic style. Attractively maintained guestrooms; those overlooking the
small flower-decked garden are generally quieter.

7 Eiffel without rest   ♿ AC 🛜 VISA ⦿ AE ⓘ

17 bis r. Amélie (7th) – Ⓜ *La Tour Maubourg – 𝒞 01 45 55 10 01*
– www.7eiffel.com   **P1**
32 rm – 🛏335/430 € 🛏🛏335/430 €, ⊡ 19 €
♦ Business ♦ Design ♦
The designer decor with its play of materials and transparency is very much of
the modern age. A hushed, comfortable atmosphere with lots of attention to
detail. Large rooftop terrace.

Bourgogne et Montana without rest   AC 🛜 VISA ⦿ AE ⓘ

3 r. de Bourgogne (7th) – Ⓜ *Assemblée Nationale – 𝒞 01 45 51 20 22*
– www.bourgogne-montana.com   **Q1**
27 rm ⊡ – 🛏330/430 € 🛏🛏330/430 € – 5 suites
♦ Family ♦ Business ♦ Personalised ♦
Elegance and beauty pervade this 18C hotel that mingles old with new. The top
floor rooms offer superb views over the Palais Bourbon (French parliament
house).

Hôtel de Varenne without rest   🌿 AC 🛜 VISA ⦿ AE

44 r. de Bourgogne (7th) – Ⓜ *Varenne – 𝒞 01 45 51 45 55*
– www.hoteldevarenne.com   **Q2**
25 rm – 🛏139/179 € 🛏🛏149/259 €, ⊡ 11 €
♦ Family ♦ Classic ♦
Located between the Rodin Museum and the National Assembly, this hotel is
nestled in an attractive and tranquil small courtyard. The overall feel is very classical (Louis XVI and Empire-style) – a look appreciated by the many tourists in
search of a true Parisian bolt hole.

Relais Bosquet without rest   AC 🛜 VISA ⦿ AE ⓘ

19 r. du Champ-de-Mars (7th) – Ⓜ *École Militaire – 𝒞 01 47 05 25 45*
– www.hotelrelaisbosquet.com   **P2**
40 rm – 🛏155/305 € 🛏🛏155/305 €, ⊡ 15 €
♦ Family ♦ Classic ♦ Functional ♦
This discreet hotel has an attractively decorated interior and classically styled
guestrooms in refreshing tones. Those overlooking the small courtyard to the
rear are quieter.

Cadran without rest   ♿ AC 🛜 VISA ⦿ AE ⓘ

10 r. du Champ-de-Mars (7th) – Ⓜ *École Militaire – 𝒞 01 40 62 67 00*
– www.cadranhotel.com   **P2**
41 rm – 🛏160/250 € 🛏🛏160/280 €, ⊡ 13 €
♦ Business ♦ Modern ♦
The clock face (cadran) theme is very much to the fore in the contemporary,
minimalist decor (clocks, alarm clocks etc) of this pleasant hotel. Two entrances,
one of which is via a chocolate shop!

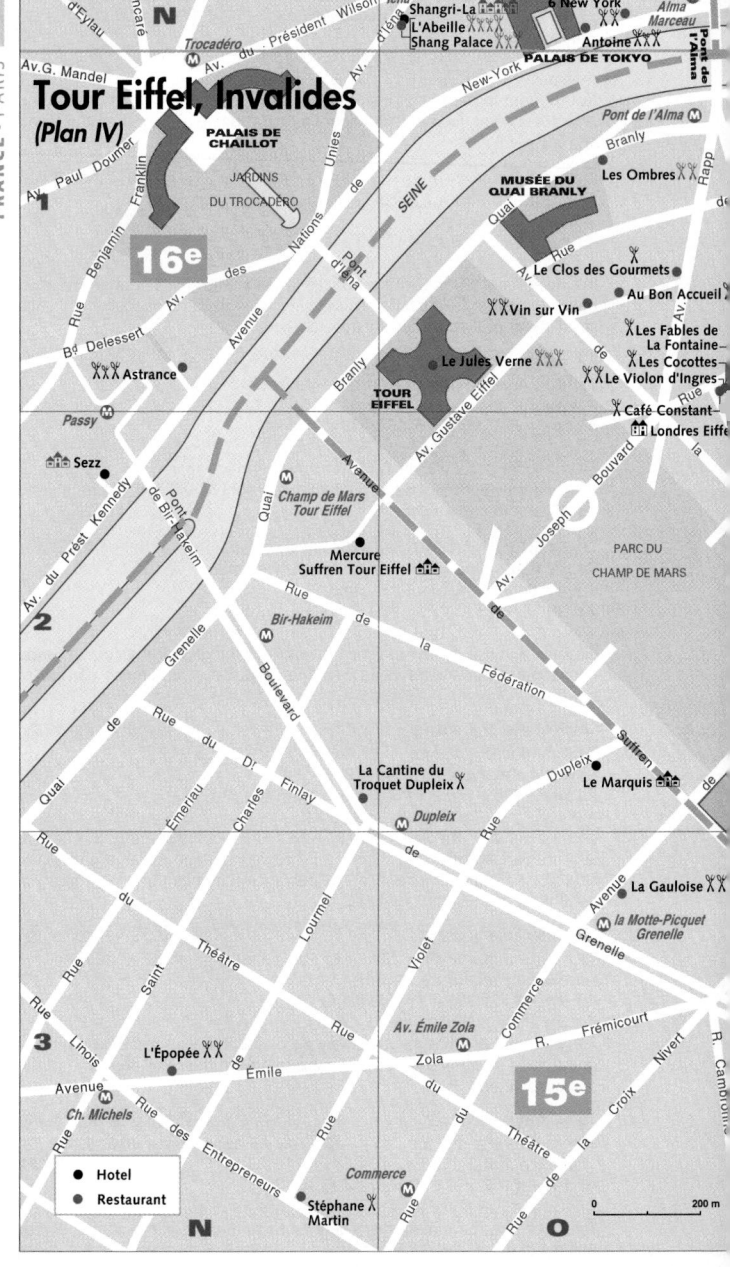

Tour Eiffel, Invalides
(Plan IV)

16e

15e

- ● Hotel
- ● Restaurant

0   200 m

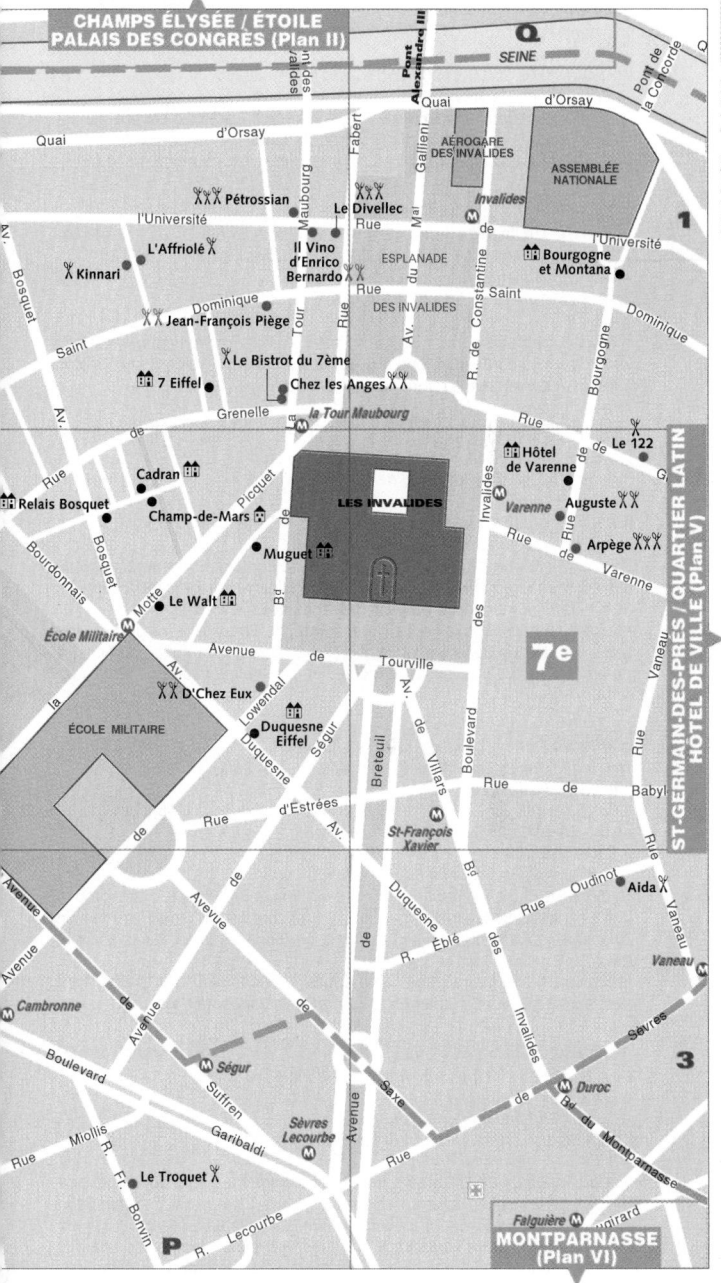

CHAMPS ÉLYSÉE / ÉTOILE
PALAIS DES CONGRÈS (Plan II)

Pont Alexandre III

SEINE

Quai

d'Orsay

AÉROGARE
DES INVALIDES

ASSEMBLÉE
NATIONALE

Quai

d'Orsay

Galliéni

Fabert

Maubourg

l'Université

XXX Pétrossian

Le Divellec

Invalides

de

1

L'Affriolé X

ESPLANADE

Bourgogne
et Montana

X Kinnari

Il Vino
d'Enrico
Bernardo

DES INVALIDES

Saint

l'Université

Dominique

Dominique

Jean-François Piège

Rue

du

R. de Constantine

Bourgogne

Saint

Av.

Bosquet

X Le Bistrot du 7ème

7 Eiffel

Chez les Anges XX

Rue

Grenelle

la Tour Maubourg

Le 122

Rue

de

ST-GERMAIN-DES-PRÉS / QUARTIER LATIN HÔTEL DE VILLE (Plan V)

Rue

Cadran

Hôtel
de Varenne

Relais Bosquet

Champ-de-Mars

LES INVALIDES

Invalides

Varenne

Auguste XX

Muguet

Arpège XXX

Rue

Picquet

Bosquet

Av.

Bourdonnais

Le Walt

de

Motte

de

Varenne

École Militaire

Avenue

de

des

7e

la

Tourville

ÉCOLE MILITAIRE

XX D'Chez Eux

Av.

de

Villars

Boulevard

Vaneau

Lowendal

Duquesne
Eiffel

Ségur

Breteuil

Rue

de

Babyl

Rue

d'Estrées

Av.

St-François
Xavier

Duquesne

Oudinot

Aida X

Vaneau

de

Avenue

Avenue

de

Éblé

R.

des

Invalides

Vaneau

Cambronne

Sèvres

Boulevard

Ségur

Saxe

de

Duroc

3

Suffren

Sèvres
Lecourbe

Bd. du Montparnasse

Rue

Miollis

Garibaldi

Avenue

Rue

Fr. Bonvin

Le Troquet X

Lecourbe

R.

P

Falguière

MONTPARNASSE
(Plan VI)

FRANCE - PARIS

Londres Eiffel without rest
⬛ 📶 VISA ⬤ AE ⓞ

1 r. Augereau (7th) – Ⓜ *École Militaire* – ℰ *01 45 51 63 02*
– *www.londres-eiffel.com*
O1-2
30 rm – ♦150/250 € ♦♦205/250 €, ⊡ 14 €
♦ Family ♦ Personalised ♦

A small cosy hotel characterised by delightful, carefully chosen fabrics (Liberty, toile de Jouy etc), and its friendly family atmosphere. An added bonus is its peace and quiet, despite its proximity to the bustling rue St-Dominique.

Champ de Mars without rest
📶 VISA ⬤

7 r. du Champ-de-Mars (7th) – Ⓜ *École Militaire* – ℰ *01 45 51 52 30*
– *www.hotelduchampdemars.com*
P2
25 rm – ♦100/120 € ♦♦120 €, ⊡ 9 €
♦ Cosy ♦

This small, reasonably priced family-run hotel has cosy and romantic rooms between the Champ-de-Mars and the Invalides. Attractive Liberty-style decor, which is at its best in the rooms already renovated.

Le Jules Verne
⟨ ⬛ 🍽 VISA ⬤ AE ⓞ
✿

2nd floor Eiffel Tower, private lift, South Pillar (7th)
– Ⓜ *Bir-Hakeim* – ℰ *01 45 55 61 44*
– *www.lejulesverne-paris.com*
O1
Rest – Menu 90 € (weekday lunch)/210 – Carte 165/205 € 🍷
♦ Modern ♦ Design ♦ Formal ♦

The designer decor on the second floor of the Eiffel Tower lives up to expectations, with a magical view as a bonus! French culinary heritage is the focus here, where classic dishes are accompanied by some excellent wines.
→ Saint-Jacques à la plancha, fine crème de chou-fleur et beurre noisette. Tournedos de bœuf et foie gras de canard, pommes soufflées et sauce Périgueux. L'écrou au chocolat et praliné croustillant, glace noisette.

Le Divellec (Jacques Le Divellec)
⬛ 🍽 VISA ⬤ AE ⓞ
✿

107 r. de l'Université (7th) – Ⓜ *Invalides* – ℰ *01 45 51 91 96*
– *www.le-divellec.com*
– *Closed 26 July-25 August, Christmas Holidays, Saturday and Sunday*
Rest – Menu 55 € (lunch), 67/160 €
P1
– Carte 110/200 €
♦ Fish and seafood ♦ Elegant ♦ Classic ♦

Enjoy a taste of the sea just a stone's throw from Les Invalides. To a backdrop of slightly antiquated decor, the chef's passion for cooking has remained intact (in 2012 he celebrated his 80th birthday) and he continues to set the standard in classic and delicious fish and seafood.
→ Cassolette de langoustines aux algues. Homard bleu à la presse servi avec son corail. Soufflé chaud à la rose et framboises fraîches.

Arpège (Alain Passard)
⬛ ⇔ VISA ⬤ AE ⓞ
✿✿✿

84 r. de Varenne (7th) – Ⓜ *Varenne* – ℰ *01 45 51 47 33*
– *www.alain-passard.com*
– *Closed Saturday and Sunday*
Rest – Menu 130 € (lunch)/350 € – Carte 190/270 €
Q2
♦ Creative ♦ Elegant ♦

Precious woods and a Lalique inspired decor provide the backdrop for the dazzling vegetable inspired cuisine of this culinary genius. He creates his astonishing dishes from organic produce grown in his three vegetable gardens!
→ Robes des champs arlequin et merguez légumière. Homard de Chausey au côtes-du-jura, pommes de terre fumées et chou croquant. Tarte aux pommes "bouquet de roses" et caramel au lait.

XXX

 සිසිසි **Astrance** (Pascal Barbot)   🟨 VISA 🟰 AE ⓪

4 r. Beethoven (16th) ⊠ 75016 – Ⓜ Passy – 𝒞 01 40 50 84 40
– Closed 27 April-13 May, 27 July-26 August, 1 week in November and at
Christmas, Saturday, Sunday, Monday and Bank Holidays   **N1**
Rest – (number of covers limited, pre-book) Menu 70 € (lunch), 120/210 € 🏵
♦ Creative ♦ Minimalist ♦ Elegant ♦
No menu or à la carte choices in this restaurant, where chef Pascal Barbot pro-
duces a different 'surprise menu' at each sitting. Sample the inventive cuisine of
a chef at the height of his art, who focuses on excellent ingredients and creative
flair. An unforgettable culinary experience.
➜ Foie gras mariné au verjus, millefeuille de champignons de Paris. Pigeon
cuit au sautoir, condiment griotte et amande, jus de cuisson. Guimauve safran, glace gingembre.

XXX

Pétrossian   🟨 ⇕ ⌂ VISA 🟰 AE ⓪

144 r. de l'Université (7th) – Ⓜ Invalides – 𝒞 01 44 11 32 32
– www.petrossian.fr
– Closed August, Sunday and Monday   **P1**
Rest – Menu 35/90 € – Carte 55/102 €
♦ Fish and seafood ♦ Formal ♦ Elegant ♦
The Petrossians have been serving Parisians caviar from the Caspian Sea since
1920. Enjoy fish and seafood in the elegant dining room above the boutique.

XX

සිසි **Jean-François Piège** – Rest. Thoumieux   🟨 VISA 🟰 AE

79 r. St-Dominique (1st floor) (7th) – Ⓜ La Tour Maubourg
– 𝒞 01 47 05 79 79 – www.thoumieux.com
– Closed August, Saturday and Sunday   **P1**
Rest – (number of covers limited, pre-book) Menu 99 € (lunch), 119/239 €
bi – Carte 120/150 € 🏵
♦ Modern ♦ Design ♦ Cosy ♦
Situated on the first floor of the Brasserie Thoumieux, this unusual restaurant is
run by the eponymous Jean-François (who made his reputation at the Crillon).
He greets guests as if they were visiting his home. Diners are invited to choose
an ingredient and a surprise dish is then cooked for them in the adjacent kit-
chen. A sublime experience.
➜ Sélection des plus beaux produits de saison.

XX

සි **Il Vino d'Enrico Bernardo**   🟨 ⌂ VISA 🟰 AE ⓪

13 bd La Tour-Maubourg (7th) – Ⓜ Invalides – 𝒞 01 44 11 72 00
– www.ilvinobyenricobernardo.com
– Closed Sunday and lunch   **P1**
Rest – Menu 98 € bi/150 € bi – Carte approx. 85 € 🏵
♦ Modern ♦ Design ♦ Cosy ♦
In his chic, design inspired restaurant, the 'World's Best Sommelier 2004' rever-
ses the trend of wine/food pairings by preparing cuisine in line with your choice
of wine.
➜ Homard breton rôti avec sa bisque, blettes confites et mousse aux épinards. Selle et carré d'agneau de lait rôtis, aubergine et fromage de chèvre
aux amandes. Crémeux au chocolat blanc, pêches et mangue, sorbet au
thé matcha.

XX

Les Ombres   ⩽ 🕎 � 🟨 🅿 VISA 🟰 AE ⓪

27 quai Branly (Quai Branly museum - 5th floor) (7th) – Ⓜ Alma Marceau
– 𝒞 01 47 53 68 00 – www.lesombres-restaurant.com   **O1**
Rest – Menu 38 € (lunch)/82 € – Carte 56/109 €
♦ Modern ♦ Design ♦ Trendy ♦
Perched on the roof of the Quai-Branly museum, this completely glass-fronted
restaurant – Jean Nouvel is behind both the interior and exterior design – stands
in the shadow of the nearby Eiffel Tower. The cuisine on offer is fine and subtle
with a contemporary flair.

XX ❀ **Le Violon d'Ingres** (Christian Constant) AC VISA ©© AE ①

135 r. St-Dominique (7th) – Ⓜ *École Militaire* – ✆ *01 45 55 15 05*
– *www.maisonconstant.com* O1
Rest – Menu 46 € (weekday lunch)
– Carte 61/87 €
♦ Modern ♦ Elegant ♦
The refined dining room, decorated in contemporary bistro-style, attracts keen gourmets. They are tempted by the high quality cuisine that showcases seasonal produce, while at the same time paying homage to tradition.
→ Salade façon César Ritz. Raviole de langoustine à l'estragon, concassé de tomate et bisque à l'armoricaine. Traditionnel millefeuille.

XX **Vin sur Vin** AC VISA ©©

20 r. de Monttessuy (7th) – Ⓜ *Pont de l'Alma*
– ✆ *01 47 05 14 20*
– *Closed 4 to 28 August, 22 December-8 January, Monday except dinner from September-March, Saturday lunch and Sunday* O1
Rest – *(number of covers limited, pre-book)* Menu 60 € (lunch)
– Carte 84/116 € ᰠ
♦ Classic ♦ Elegant ♦
This restaurant has friendly service, an elegant decor and the ambience of a private house. Its delicious, traditional cuisine is accompanied by an extensive (600-bin) wine list.

XX 🙊 **Chez les Anges** AC ⇄ VISA ©© AE

54 bd de la Tour-Maubourg (7th) – Ⓜ *La Tour Maubourg*
– ✆ *01 47 05 89 86* – *www.chezlesanges.com*
– *Closed Saturday and Sunday* P1
Rest – Menu 35/55 € – Carte 37/78 € ᰠ
♦ Traditional ♦ Design ♦
A contemporary decor provides the backdrop for the delicious, unfussy cuisine encompassing both tradition and modernity. Dishes include: pig's trotter pancakes, whiting fillet, calf's liver with braised red cabbage, and rum baba.

XX ❀ **Auguste** (Gaël Orieux) AC VISA ©© AE ①

54 r. Bourgogne (7th) – Ⓜ *Varenne* – ✆ *01 45 51 61 09*
– *www.restaurantauguste.fr*
– *Closed 1 to 22 August, Saturday and Sunday* Q2
Rest – Menu 35 € (lunch)/85 € – Carte 70/100 €
♦ Modern ♦ Design ♦ Elegant ♦
With its colourful and elegant designer decor, Auguste is a perfect match for the cuisine of Gaël Orieux. He is an impassioned chef who loves working with the best ingredients and who, in his quest for harmony and invention, creates a fine balance between the land and the sea. More modestly priced at lunchtime; you will need to push the boat out in the evening.
→ Foie gras de canard, enoki et chou pak-choï, consommé de crevettes au galanga. Lotte fleurée au thé vert, sabayon yuzu, mousseline de petits pois pistachée. Soufflé au chocolat pur Caraïbes, glace au miel.

XX **D'Chez Eux** 🍴 AC ⊏P VISA ©© AE

2 av. Lowendal (7th) – Ⓜ *École Militaire* – ✆ *01 47 05 52 55*
– *www.chezeux.com* P2
Rest – Menu 34 € (weekday lunch) – Carte 60/80 €
♦ South-West of France ♦ Rustic ♦ Friendly ♦
This restaurant has had a winning formula for over 40 years – and the place shows no sign of ageing! Sample the generous portions of dishes inspired by the southwest of France. These are made with quality ingredients and served by waiters in old-fashioned aprons in a provincial inn ambience.

XX **La Gauloise**   🍽 ⇄ VISA ⨀ AE

59 av. La Motte-Picquet (15th) – Ⓜ *La Motte Picquet Grenelle*
– ℰ 01 47 34 11 64   O3
Rest – Menu 29 € – Carte 35/75 €
♦ Traditional ♦ Elegant ♦ Retro ♦

This Belle Epoque brasserie boasts the delightful air of Parisian life from yesteryear. It has a menu that features dishes such as poached eggs and vegetable
pot-au-feu, pork crepinettes, turbot with a Béarnaise sauce, and onion soup. La
Gauloise's attractive terrace is also much appreciated by diners.

XX **L'Épopée**   AC VISA ⨀ AE

89 av. Émile-Zola (15th) – Ⓜ *Charles Michels – ℰ 01 45 77 71 37*
– www.lepopee.fr – Closed 9 to 17 August, 24 December-2 January,
Saturday lunch and Sunday dinner   N3
Rest – Menu 25 € (weekday lunch), 38/54 €
♦ Traditional ♦ Friendly ♦

L'Épopée's traditional approach has found favour with numerous regulars.
Dishes such as fricassée of Burgundy snails with blue cheese, country terrine
with morel mushrooms, and fresh tagliatelle with squid ink are on the menu,
accompanied by a good choice of estate wines.

X **Au Bon Accueil**   AC VISA ⨀ AE

14 r. Monttessuy (7th) – Ⓜ *Pont de l'Alma – ℰ 01 47 05 46 11*
– www.aubonaccueilparis.com
– Closed 3 weeks in August, Saturday and Sunday   O1
Rest – Menu 32 € – Carte 40/65 €
♦ Modern ♦ Bistro ♦ Cosy ♦

In the shadow of the Eiffel Tower, this chic and discreet restaurant serves appetising cuisine based around seasonal produce. Excellent value.

X **Les Fables de La Fontaine**   🍽 AC VISA ⨀ AE

131 r. St-Dominique (7th) – Ⓜ *École Militaire – ℰ 01 44 18 37 55*
– www.lesfablesdelafontaine.net
– Closed 23 to 28 December   O1
Rest – *(number of covers limited, pre-book)* Menu 35 € bi (weekday
lunch)/120 € – Carte 81/103 €
♦ Fish and seafood ♦ Bistro ♦ Intimate ♦

A pocket-sized bistro in which the chef gives a leading role to fish. Subtle gourmet cuisine is presented on a concise, inspired and well-structured menu,
accompanied by an impressive selection of wines by the glass.
➔ Croustillant de langoustines au basilic, émulsion d'agrumes et romaine
au parmesan. Rouget farci aux chipirons et mousseline de patate douce.
Parfait passion-praliné, minestrone de melon et nectarine.

X **Stéphane Martin**   AC ⇄ VISA ⨀ AE

67 r. des Entrepreneurs (15th) – Ⓜ *Charles Michels – ℰ 01 45 79 03 31*
– www.stephanemartin.com
– Closed 5 to 13 May, 4 to 26 August, 23 December-2 January, Sunday and Monday
Rest – Menu 22 € (weekday lunch)/35 € – Carte 41/63 €   N3
♦ Modern ♦ Friendly ♦

This Left Bank address is well known to gourmets. The cosy setting and tasteful
decor provide the backdrop for appetising traditional fare with a modern twist.
Enjoy the pleasure of dishes such as calf's liver meunière or knuckle of pork braised in spiced honey.

X **Le Clos des Gourmets**   ⇄ VISA ⨀

16 av. Rapp (7th) – Ⓜ *Alma Marceau – ℰ 01 45 51 75 61*
– www.closdesgourmets.com
– Closed 1 to 25 August, Sunday and Monday   O1
Rest – Menu 30 € (lunch), 32/37 € – Carte 35/60 € 🍯
♦ Modern ♦ Design ♦

Sleek and welcoming modern bistro where the chef loves good food and cares
enough to do it well. Asparagus crème brûlée, fennel slow cooked with mellow
spices: the cuisine is honest and full of delicious flavours.

Les Cocottes `VISA` `◉◉`

135 r. St-Dominique (7th) – **Ⓜ** *École Militaire – www.maisonconstant.com*
Rest – Menu 32 € – Carte 22/55 €   **O1**
♦ Modern ♦ Fashionable ♦
The concept in this friendly eatery is based around bistro cuisine with a modern touch cooked in cast-iron casserole pots (cocottes), including popular dishes such as country paté, roast veal etc. No advance booking.

Aida (Koji Aida) `AC` `⇔` `VISA` `◉◉` `AE`

1 r. Pierre Leroux (7th) – **Ⓜ** *Vaneau –* ℰ *01 43 06 14 18*
– www.aidaparis.com
– Closed 1 week in March, 3 weeks in August, Monday and lunch
Rest – *(number of covers limited, pre-book)* Menu 160 € 🏵   **Q3**
♦ Japanese ♦ Minimalist ♦
Be transported to the Land of the Rising Sun in this restaurant. It breathes authenticity and purity through its delicious Japanese cuisine full of finesse. The fish, presented alive and then prepared in front of you, couldn't be fresher. The art of simplicity and transparency at its best!
➜ Sashimi. Teppanyaki. Wagashi.

Le 122 `AC` `⇔` `VISA` `◉◉` `AE`

122 r. de Grenelle (7th) – **Ⓜ** *Solférino –* ℰ *01 45 56 07 42 – www.le122.fr*
– Closed 27 July-27 August, Saturday and Sunday   **Q2**
Rest – Menu 26 € (lunch), 39/59 € – Carte 33/68 €
♦ Modern ♦ Design ♦
A contemporary, designer inspired restaurant not far from government ministerial buildings. The owner heads to the Rungis market every day to source the best products, which the chef converts into inventive dishes very much in the bistronomy mould.

Kinnari `VISA` `◉◉`

8 r. Malar (7th) – **Ⓜ** *La Tour Maubourg –* ℰ *01 47 05 18 18*
– Closed Sunday   **P1**
Rest – Menu 22/39 € – Carte 30/45 €
♦ Thai ♦ Exotic ♦ Elegant ♦
Run by the brother of the owner of the Suan Thaï (4th arrondissement), Kinnari is inspired by the decor and recipes of his elder sibling. Dishes on the menu include: green papaya salad with prawns and duck breast with tamarind sauce.

L'Affriolé `AC` `VISA` `◉◉` `AE`

17 r. Malar (7th) – **Ⓜ** *Invalides –* ℰ *01 44 18 31 33*
– Closed 3 weeks in August, Sunday and Monday   **P1**
Rest – Menu 29 € (lunch)/35 €
♦ Modern ♦ Design ♦
With his daily specials board and monthly menu, the chef closely follows seasonal market availability. The contemporary designer decor adds a certain charm to the overall feel. A 'bento' menu is also available for those in a hurry.

Le Troquet `VISA` `◉◉`

21 r. François-Bonvin (15th) – **Ⓜ** *Cambronne –* ℰ *01 45 66 89 00*
– Closed 1 week in May, 3 weeks in August, 1 week in December, Sunday and Monday   **P3**
Rest – Menu 30 € (weekday lunch), 32/41 € – Carte 30/40 €
♦ Traditional ♦ Retro ♦ Bistro ♦
A typical Parisian 'troquet' (café-bar) in all its splendour! Although Christian Etchebest is no longer at the helm, a young promising chef is working with the same team. He has the same reliance on ultra-fresh ingredients and the same culinary focus on southwest France.

🍴 ☺

La Cantine du Troquet Dupleix ☂ VISA MC

53 bd de Grenelle (15th) – Ⓜ Dupleix – ✆ 01 45 75 98 00 **N2**
Rest – Carte 30/45 €
◆ Traditional ◆ Bistro ◆
Christian Etchebest's latest venture sticks to a tried and tested formula, and we certainly have no complaints. As with his restaurant in the 14th *arrondissement*, the menu strikes a balance between brasserie and bistro fare and lets its well-crafted recipes do the talking. Many of the dishes betray the owner's Basque heritage. A convivial place to eat.

🍴

Le Bistrot du 7ème VISA MC

56 bd de La Tour-Maubourg (7th) – Ⓜ La Tour Maubourg – ✆ 01 45 51 93 08 – www.bistrotdu7.com **P1**
Rest – Menu 17 € (weekday lunch)/25 € – Carte 29/39 €
◆ Traditional ◆ Rustic ◆
This authentic bistro has a traditional counter, old posters, paper napkins, and a typical brasserie-style menu. It features old favourites, such as rabbit terrine and duck confit.

🍴 ☺

Café Constant VISA MC

139 r. St-Dominique (7th) – Ⓜ École Militaire – www.maisonconstant.com
Rest – Menu 23 € (weekday lunch) – Carte 34/53 € **O1**
◆ Traditional ◆ Friendly ◆
This unpretentious and friendly brasserie run by Christian Constant occupies an old café. The gourmet bistro cuisine includes classics such as eggs mimosa, oyster tartare, roast lamb, rice pudding etc. No advance booking.

SAINT-GERMAIN DES PRES – QUARTIER LATIN – HOTEL DE VILLE

Plan V

🏨🏨🏨🏨

Lutetia 🏋 AC 📶 👥 VISA MC AE ⓓ

45 bd Raspail (6th) – Ⓜ Sèvres Babylone – ✆ 01 49 54 46 46 – www.lutetia.concorde-hotels.com **R2**
206 rm – 🚹550/750 € 🚹🚹550/750 €, ☕ 28 € – 25 suites
Rest *Paris* ✿ **Rest *Brasserie Lutetia*** – see restaurant listing
◆ Luxury ◆ Art Deco ◆
Built in 1910, this grand hotel on the left bank is a repository of French history and art. It brings together Art Deco-style and more modern elements (sculptures by César and Arman). The guestrooms are more or less recently done up. The Parisian smart set gathers in La Brasserie to enjoy the traditional atmosphere. Jazz evenings.

🏨🏨🏨🏨

Victoria Palace without rest ♿ AC 📶 👥 🚗 VISA MC AE ⓓ

6 r. Blaise-Desgoffe (6th) – Ⓜ St-Placide – ✆ 01 45 49 70 00 – www.victoriapalace.com **R3**
58 rm ☕ – 🚹300/365 € 🚹🚹300/365 € – 4 suites
◆ Traditional ◆ Stylish ◆
A hotel with a great tradition, featuring luxurious fabrics, Louis XVI furniture and marble bathrooms in the guestrooms. The well appointed junior suites are particularly recommended for a relaxing stay. The Victorian style lounge is equally restful.

🏨🏨🏨

Duc de St-Simon without rest ⛱ AC 📶 VISA MC AE ⓓ

14 r. St-Simon (7th) – Ⓜ Rue du Bac – ✆ 01 44 39 20 20 – www.hotelducdesaintsimon.com **R1**
29 rm – 🚹250/275 € 🚹🚹250/275 €, ☕ 15 € – 5 suites
◆ Luxury ◆ Personalised ◆
The small paved courtyard comes into view as you pass through the entrance, revealing the full beauty of this fine 18C townhouse. The fabrics, woodwork, old prints and antique furniture enhance the sense of an aristocratic property from bygone days. The charm here is on an equal par with the peace and quiet.

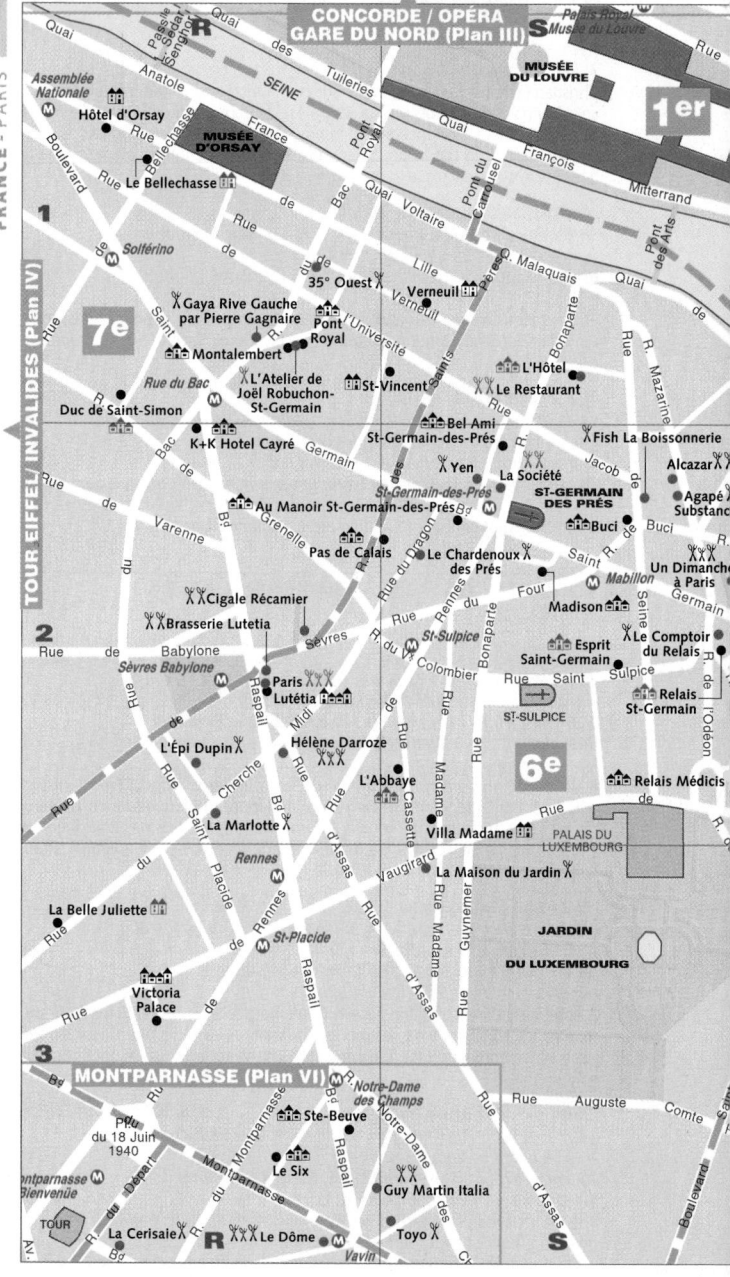

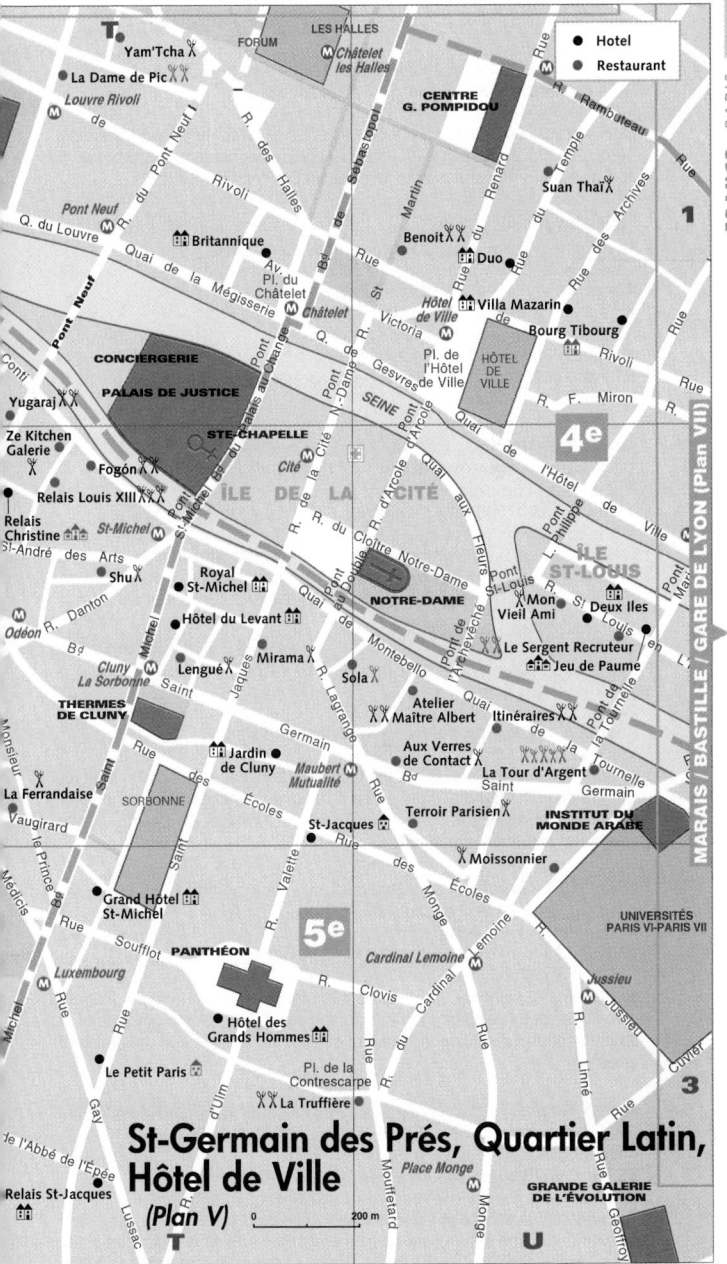

St-Germain des Prés, Quartier Latin, Hôtel de Ville

(Plan V)   0   200 m

Hotel
Restaurant

LES HALLES
FORUM
Yam'Tcha
T.
La Dame de Pic
Louvre Rivoli
Châtelet
les Halles
CENTRE
G. POMPIDOU
de
Rivoli
Q. du Louvre
Pont Neuf
R. du Pont Neuf
Rue des Halles
R. de Sébastopol
Martin
Renard
Rue du Temple
Rambuteau
Rue
Rue des Archives
Suan Thai
Benoit
Duo
Britannique
Av.
Pl. du
Châtelet
Rue de la Mégisserie
Châtelet
Hôtel
de Ville
Villa Mazarin
de
Victoria
Bourg Tibourg
Rue
Rivoli
Pl. de
l'Hôtel
de Ville
HÔTEL
DE
VILLE
R. F. Miron
CONCIERGERIE
PALAIS DE JUSTICE
Q. de la Mégisserie
Conti
Pont Neuf
Q. du Louvre
Yugaraj
Ze Kitchen
Galerie
Fogón
Relais Louis XIII
Relais
Christine
St-Michel
St-André des Arts
Shu
Royal
St-Michel
Hôtel du Levant
Cluny
La Sorbonne
Lengué
Mirama
Sola
Odéon
Bd
Danton
Michel
Rue
Saint
Jacques
STE-CHAPELLE
Cité
ÎLE DE LA CITÉ
R. du Cloître Notre-Dame
SEINE
Pont au Change
Pont N-Dame
Quai de la Corse
Quai aux Fleurs
Pont d'Arcole
NOTRE-DAME
Pont St-Louis
ÎLE
ST-LOUIS
Mon Vieil Ami
Deux Iles
St Louis en
Le Sergent Recruteur
Jeu de Paume
Montebello
Quai de l'Hôtel de Ville
Quai
L.-Philippe
Pont L.-Philippe
Pont Marie
Quai
de
l'Hôtel
de
Ville
THERMES
DE CLUNY
Rue
Saint
Germain
Jardin
de Cluny
Maubert
Mutualité
Atelier
Maître Albert
Itinéraires
Aux Verres
de Contact
La Tour d'Argent
Quai de la Tournelle
Pont de la Tournelle
INSTITUT DU
MONDE ARABE
SORBONNE
des
Écoles
St-Jacques
Terroir Parisien
Saint
Germain
Bd
Monsieur
Rue
Vaugirard
La Ferrandaise
le Prince
Médicis
Rue
Luxembourg
Grand Hôtel
St-Michel
Soufflot
PANTHÉON
Cardinal Lemoine
Clovis
R.
UNIVERSITÉS
PARIS VI-PARIS VII
Moissonnier
Écoles
des
Monge
Rue
Jussieu
Jussieu
Rue
Cuvier
3
Hôtel des
Grands Hommes
Le Petit Paris
Pl. de la
Contrescarpe
La Truffière
Rue
d'Ulm
Rue
Linné
Michel
Gay
Rue
de l'Abbé de l'Épée
Lussac
Relais St-Jacques
T
Mouffetard
Place Monge
Monge
GRANDE GALERIE
DE L'ÉVOLUTION
GRANDE GALERIE
DE L'ÉVOLUTION
Geoffroy
U

229

FRANCE - PARIS

L'Hôtel ⋙ 🅰🅲 🛜 𝘝𝘐𝘚𝘈 ⓸ 🅰🅴 ⓪

13 r. des Beaux-Arts (6th) – Ⓜ *St-Germain des Prés* – 𝒞 *01 44 41 99 00*
– www.l-hotel.com   **S1**
16 rm – ♦290/680 € ♦♦290/680 €, � 17 € – 4 suites
Rest Le Restaurant ❀ – see restaurant listing
◆ Luxury ◆ Historic ◆ Personalised ◆

It was at L'Hôtel that the great Oscar Wilde died in 1900. The atypical, aesthetic
decor, updated by Jacques Garcia, still manages to pay homage to artistic pomp
and splendour. There is a nod to Baroque, Empire and Oriental styles.

L'Abbaye without rest ⋙ 🅰🅲 🛜 𝘝𝘐𝘚𝘈 ⓸ 🅰🅴

10 r. Cassette (6th) – Ⓜ *St-Sulpice* – 𝒞 *01 45 44 38 11*
– www.hotel-abbaye.com   **S2**
40 rm ⊠ – ♦265/415 € ♦♦265/415 € – 4 suites
◆ Luxury ◆ Historic ◆ Personalised ◆

A hotel with a rare charm occupying a former 17C abbey. It features highly refined guestrooms, which are both bright and classically styled, as well as a peaceful and leafy courtyard where the only noise is from the bubbling fountain.
Thoughtful and attentive staff.

Relais Christine without rest ⋙ 🅵🅱 🅰🅲 🛜 🅰 🙢 𝘝𝘐𝘚𝘈 ⓸ 🅰🅴 ⓪

3 r. Christine (6th) – Ⓜ *St-Michel* – 𝒞 *01 40 51 60 80*
– www.relais-christine.com   **T2**
47 rm – ♦330/1000 € ♦♦330/1000 €, ⊠ 30 € – 4 suites
◆ Historic ◆ Personalised ◆

This historic property with its hushed lounges and attractively decorated
bedrooms has its own particular charm, including a breakfast room crowned
by 13C vaulting. The well-being area and loan of bicycles are added bonuses.

Relais St-Germain 🅰🅲 🛜 𝘝𝘐𝘚𝘈 ⓸ 🅰🅴 ⓪

9 carr. de l'Odéon (6th) – Ⓜ *Odéon* – 𝒞 *01 44 27 07 97*
– www.hotelrsg.com   **S2**
22 rm ⊠ – ♦220/440 € ♦♦285/440 €
Rest Le Comptoir du Relais – see restaurant listing
◆ Traditional ◆ Townhouse ◆ Personalised ◆

Life never seems to stand still at the Carrefour de l'Odéon – a good reason for
taking refuge in this refined hotel. The painted wood beams, shimmering fabrics and antique furniture bestow a unique character on the guestrooms, which
are perfect for literary inspiration!

Esprit St-Germain without rest 🅳 🅰🅲 🛜 𝘝𝘐𝘚𝘈 ⓸ 🅰🅴 ⓪

22 r. St-Sulpice (6th) – Ⓜ *Mabillon* – 𝒞 *01 53 10 55 55*
– www.espritsaintgermain.com   **S2**
23 rm – ♦340/610 € ♦♦340/610 €, ⊠ 28 € – 5 suites
◆ Townhouse ◆ Personalised ◆

The Orientalist paintings and leopard-skin carpet set the tone in the lounge-
cum-library of this elegant, comfortable and stylish hotel. Although simpler in
style, the guestrooms demonstrate real care for the comfort and well-being of
guests.

Pont Royal without rest 🅵🅱 🅳 🅰🅲 🛜 🅰 𝘝𝘐𝘚𝘈 ⓸ 🅰🅴 ⓪

7 r. Montalembert (7th) – Ⓜ *Rue du Bac* – 𝒞 *01 42 84 70 00*
– www.hotel-pont-royal.com   **R1**
75 rm – ♦420/560 € ♦♦420/560 €, ⊠ 25 € – 10 suites
◆ Historic ◆ Personalised ◆

This very Left Bank hotel still resonates with the voices of F Scott Fitzgerald and
his wife Zelda, who were regular guests here in the 1920s. Very much part of the
city's literary fabric, the Pont Royal is also resolutely contemporary and full of
charm!

FRANCE - PARIS

Bel Ami St-Germain des Prés without rest

7 r. St-Benoit (6th) – Ⓜ *St-Germain des Prés*
– ℰ 01 42 61 53 53
– www.hotel-bel-ami.com   **S2**
107 rm – †220/710 € ††220/710 €, ⊡ 25 € – 4 suites
♦ Townhouse ♦ Modern ♦

The name of this hotel has nothing to do with the famous novel by Maupassant, even if it is located in the literary district of St Germain. The hotel will suit guests looking for a chic, urban ambience. It has a trendy bar and simple, contemporary-style guestrooms, some of which have been renovated. Attractive well-being area.

Montalembert

3 r. Montalembert (7th) – Ⓜ *Rue du Bac – ℰ 01 45 49 68 68*
– www.montalembert.com   **R1**
50 rm – †280/660 € ††280/660 €, ⊡ 25 € – 5 suites
Rest – Carte 50/80 €
♦ Historic ♦ Personalised ♦ Design ♦

Located between St-Germain-des-Prés and the Orsay Museum, this particularly attractive building dates back to 1926. It has very pleasant guestrooms. Some are decorated in Louis-Philippe style, and the majority, in a chic and contemporary style bearing the hallmark of Christian Liaigre. A few even boast an attractive view of the city's rooftops.

K+K Hotel Cayré without rest

4 bd Raspail (7th) – Ⓜ *Rue du Bac – ℰ 01 45 44 38 88*
– www.kkhotels.com/cayre   **R1-2**
125 rm – †255/445 € ††295/480 €, ⊡ 29 €
♦ Business ♦ Modern ♦

The delightful Haussmann façade contrasts with the contemporary lounges and guestrooms, in which stylish elegance is very much to the fore. The basement is home to an attractive fitness centre featuring a sauna and massage room.

Madison without rest

143 bd St-Germain (6th) – Ⓜ *St-Germain des Prés – ℰ 01 40 51 60 00*
– www.hotel-madison.com   **S2**
48 rm ⊡ – †220/720 € ††350/720 € – 2 suites
♦ Townhouse ♦ Personalised ♦ Design ♦

Camus used to frequent this property, probably because of its perfect location at the heart of St-Germain-des-Prés. The guestrooms have all been renovated in a mix of contemporary styles with some boasting a view of the church.

Buci without rest

22 r. Buci (6th) – Ⓜ *Mabillon – ℰ 01 55 42 74 74 – www.buci-hotel.com*
19 rm – †160/340 € ††180/420 €, ⊡ 15 € – 5 suites   **S2**
♦ Traditional ♦ Personalised ♦

This intimate hotel is conveniently situated in a lively shopping street. It offers guestrooms of various styles including contemporary, romantic (with Pompadour-style drapes) and elegant boudoir. Ask for one of the renovated rooms if possible.

Relais Médicis without rest

23 r. Racine (6th) – Ⓜ *Odéon – ℰ 01 43 26 00 60 – www.relaismedicis.com*
17 rm – †142/172 € ††258/258 €   **S2**
♦ Traditional ♦ Personalised ♦ Cosy ♦

This delightful property is hidden behind a discreet façade just opposite the Théâtre de l'Odéon. Bright colours and antique furniture in the Provençal-style bedrooms ensure that guests feel right at home.

FRANCE - PARIS

Au Manoir St-Germain-des-Prés without rest   AC 📶   VISA 🌐 AE ①

153 bd St-Germain (6th) – Ⓜ *St-Germain des Prés*
– 🕾 *01 42 22 21 65*
– *www.hotelaumanoir.com*   **S2**
28 rm – 🛏210/380 € 🛏🛏210/380 €, ☲ 15 €
♦ Traditional ♦ Cosy ♦

Despite its name, this hotel opposite the Café de Flore is not quite a manor house but it is nonetheless a delightful, cosy place to stay. The guestrooms, some of which have a view of the church, are decorated in shimmering fabrics. Charming winter garden.

Pas de Calais without rest   AC 📶 VISA 🌐 AE ①

59 r. des Saints-Pères (6th) – Ⓜ *St-Germain des Prés* – 🕾 *01 45 48 78 74*
– *www.hotelpasdecalais.com*   **R2**
38 rm – 🛏160/340 € 🛏🛏170/340 €, ☲ 15 €
♦ Traditional ♦ Personalised ♦

Legend has it that Sartre and Beauvoir stayed here, perhaps enjoying the tranquil atmosphere of this quiet street. All the bedrooms are different, varying from very large to more compact, and traditional to those renovated in a more modern style. It is worth making your choice when you book.

Jeu de Paume without rest   ♿ AC 📶 ♨ VISA 🌐 AE ①

54 r. St-Louis-en-l'Ile (4th) – Ⓜ *Pont Marie* – 🕾 *01 43 26 14 18*
– *www.jeudepaumehotel.com*   **U2**
28 rm – 🛏185/255 € 🛏🛏285/360 €, ☲ 18 € – 2 suites
♦ Historic ♦ Business ♦ Personalised ♦

This 17C building on the Ile St-Louis, once a venue for real tennis, is now a charming boutique hotel. Entirely renovated in 2010, the rooms offer understated contemporary elegance with exposed beams and high ceilings.

Bourg Tibourg without rest   AC 📶 VISA 🌐 AE ①

19 r. Bourg Tibourg (4th) – Ⓜ *Hôtel de Ville* – 🕾 *01 42 78 47 39*
– *www.hotelbourgtibourg.com*   **U1**
30 rm – 🛏190 € 🛏🛏250/270 €, ☲ 16 €
♦ Luxury ♦ Townhouse ♦ Personalised ♦

Hotel entirely styled by Jacques Garcia. Each room has its own individual decor (neo-Gothic, Baroque, Eastern etc) and exudes luxury and refinement. A little gem in the heart of the Marais district.

Le Bellechasse without rest   AC 📶 VISA 🌐 AE ①

8 r. de Bellechasse (7th) – Ⓜ *Musée d'Orsay* – 🕾 *01 45 50 22 31*
– *www.lebellechasse.com*   **R1**
33 rm – 🛏179/430 € 🛏🛏179/430 €, ☲ 21 €
♦ Luxury ♦ Personalised ♦ Design ♦

A lovely hotel that has been entirely decorated by Christian Lacroix. The fashion house has created designer guestrooms with splashes of colour. They have old or contemporary details that often have a dreamlike quality. It makes for a 'journey within a journey' – fashionable and full of character!

La Belle Juliette without rest   ♿ AC 📶 VISA 🌐 AE

92 r. du Cherche-Midi (6th) – Ⓜ *Vaneau* – 🕾 *01 42 22 97 40*
– *www.labellejuliette.com*   **R3**
32 rm – 🛏220/650 € 🛏🛏220/650 €, ☲ 20 € – 2 suites
♦ Townhouse ♦ Elegant ♦

This hotel pays homage to the legendary beauty of the 18-19C celebrity Juliette Récamier. The setting is charming and combines the grace of the old with the bold colours of the new. A good spot for afternoon tea and the occasional Sunday piano concert.

FRANCE - PARIS

Villa Madame without rest   ⑤ 🆔 📶 🆅 ⓒ 🆎
44 r. Madame (6th) – Ⓜ *St-Sulpice* – ✆ *01 45 48 02 81*
– www.villa-madame.com   **S2**
28 rm – ♦235/344 € ♦♦235/344 €, ⌕ 18 €
♦ Townhouse ♦ Cosy ♦

Typical of the Left Bank in style, this small hotel is warm, elegant and full of character. The focus is on stylish details, restful colours and high-tech equipment. Enjoy browsing through an art book next to the fireplace.

Hôtel d'Orsay without rest   🆔 📶 🅂 🆅 ⓒ 🆎 ⓞ
93 r. de Lille (7th) – Ⓜ *Solférino* – ✆ *01 47 05 85 54*
– www.espritdefrance.com   **R1**
40 rm – ♦155/305 € ♦♦155/410 €, ⌕ 17 € – 1 suite
♦ Classic ♦

This hotel occupies two late-18C buildings. Find attractive and spacious rooms with period furniture. There is a welcoming lounge overlooking a small, leafy patio.

St-Vincent without rest   🆔 📶 🆅 ⓒ 🆎
5 r. Pré aux Clercs (7th) – Ⓜ *Rue du Bac* – ✆ *01 42 61 01 51*
– www.hotel-st-vincent.com   **S1**
22 rm – ♦180/200 € ♦♦290/310 €, ⌕ 15 €
♦ Historic ♦ Personalised ♦

This boutique hotel is in an attractive townhouse in the heart of a district of antique dealers and art galleries on the Left Bank. It is chic, tranquil and popular with a regular clientele. The decor in the welcoming and refined guestrooms is a modern evocation of the Napoleon III style.

Hôtel des Grands Hommes without rest   ≼ 🐾 🆔 📶 🅂
17 pl. du Panthéon (5th) – Ⓜ *Luxembourg*   📶 ⓒ 🆎 ⓞ
– ✆ 01 46 34 19 60 – www.hoteldesgrandshommes.com   **T3**
30 rm – ♦190/340 € ♦♦200/340 €, ⌕ 12 €
♦ Traditional ♦ Townhouse ♦ Historic ♦

This charming hotel enjoys a fine location near the Panthéon. The well-maintained guestrooms are furnished in Directoire-style and have plenty of character. Superb views from the balconies and terraces on the fifth and sixth floors.

Royal St-Michel without rest   🆔 📶 🆅 ⓒ 🆎 ⓞ
3 bd St-Michel (5th) – Ⓜ *St-Michel* – ✆ *01 44 07 06 06*
– www.hotelroyalsaintmichel.com   **T2**
39 rm – ♦180/290 € ♦♦190/320 €, ⌕ 16 €
♦ Business ♦ Townhouse ♦ Modern ♦

The full atmosphere of the Latin Quarter is right on the doorstep of this welcoming hotel just opposite the St-Michel fountain. Fortunately, the cosy and contemporary guestrooms are well-soundproofed, which is a detail not to be overlooked in this lively district.

Deux Îles without rest   🆔 📶 🆅 ⓒ
59 r. St-Louis-en-l'Île (4th) – Ⓜ *Pont Marie* – ✆ *01 43 26 13 35*
– www.hoteldesdeuxiles.com   **U2**
17 rm – ♦169/179 € ♦♦215 €, ⌕ 13 €
♦ Family ♦ Business ♦ Cosy ♦

This hotel has been fully renovated and offers small but pleasant rooms in soft colours (brown, ochre and bronze). Fine bathrooms with azulejo tiling.

Villa Mazarin without rest   🆔 📶 🆅 ⓒ 🆎 ⓞ
6 r. des Archives (4th) – Ⓜ *Hôtel de Ville* – ✆ *01 53 01 90 90*
– www.villamazarin.com   **U1**
29 rm – ♦220/350 € ♦♦220/350 €, ⌕ 12 €
♦ Family ♦ Townhouse ♦ Personalised ♦

This central hotel is a stone's throw from Notre Dame, Place des Vosges and Beaubourg. It offers a contemporary look at the Second Empire. There are a few split-level rooms.

Grand Hôtel St-Michel without rest

19 r. Cujas (5th) – Ⓜ *Luxembourg*
– ℰ 01 46 33 33 02 – www.grand-hotel-st-michel.com   **T3**
46 rm – 🛏215/350 € 🛏🛏215/350 €, ⌷ 20 € – 1 suite
♦ Business ♦ Modern ♦

Just a stone's throw from the lively Boulevard St-Michel, this hotel is a successful blend of designer-style and comfort. It has a minimalist decor, original details and restful colours. Relax in the fitness suite and hammam before enjoying a good night's sleep.

Relais St-Jacques without rest

3 r. Abbé-de-l'Épée (5th) – Ⓜ *Luxembourg – ℰ 01 53 73 26 00*
– www.relais-saint-jacques.com   **T3**
22 rm – 🛏350/375 € 🛏🛏350/375 €, ⌷ 17 €
♦ Family ♦ Traditional ♦ Cosy ♦

A very Parisian hotel in a relatively quiet street. Inspired by the castles of the Loire, the guestrooms come in varying styles (Directoire, Louis-Philippe etc). An intimate atmosphere, and a perfect base from which to explore this district.

Jardin de Cluny without rest

9 r. du Sommerard (5th) – Ⓜ *Maubert Mutualité – ℰ 01 43 54 22 66*
– www.hoteljardindecluny.com   **T2**
40 rm – 🛏130/210 € 🛏🛏130/300 €, ⌷ 15 €
♦ Business ♦ Townhouse ♦ Personalised ♦

Environmentally conscious travellers will enjoy staying at this Écolabel-certified hotel. The elegance and comfort in the guestrooms has not been sacrificed one bit. The vaulted room where breakfast is served has lots of charm.

Hôtel du Levant without rest

18 r. de la Harpe (5th) – Ⓜ *St-Michel – ℰ 01 46 34 11 00*
– www.hoteldulevant.com   **T2**
46 rm ⌷ **–** 🛏80/150 € 🛏🛏180/210 €
♦ Townhouse ♦ Business ♦ Personalised ♦

This reasonably priced hotel built in 1875 has guestrooms that are high in colour, with walls decorated in red, yellow and bright pink. A perfect location from which to explore the city.

Duo without rest

11 r. Temple (4th) – Ⓜ *Hôtel de Ville – ℰ 01 42 72 72 22*
– www.duoparis.com   **U1**
56 rm – 🛏140/225 € 🛏🛏235/420 €, ⌷ 15 € – 2 suites
♦ Townhouse ♦ Business ♦ Modern ♦

Well-preserved period features (listed staircase, 16C vaulted cellar) combined with elegant and trendy contemporary interior design: a winning Duo run by the same family since 1918.

Britannique without rest

20 av. Victoria (1st) – Ⓜ *Châtelet – ℰ 01 42 33 74 59*
– www.hotel-britannique.fr   **T1**
39 rm – 🛏185/207 € 🛏🛏207/330 €, ⌷ 14 €
♦ Traditional ♦ Family ♦ Cosy ♦

Established by an English family during the reign of Queen Victoria, this hotel has retained its British Imperial elegance. Richly furnished rooms with a refined and exotic feel. Charming lounge.

Verneuil without rest

8 r. de Verneuil (7th) – Ⓜ *Rue du Bac – ℰ 01 42 60 82 14*
– www.hotel-verneuil-saint-germain.com   **S1**
26 rm ⌷ **–** 🛏157 € 🛏🛏200/260 €
♦ Cosy ♦ Personalised ♦

This old building on the Left Bank is decorated in the style of a private house. Elegant rooms adorned with 18C prints. Serge Gainsbourg lived opposite.

FRANCE - PARIS

Le Petit Paris without rest   🕭 AC 🛜 VISA ⦿ AE

214 r. St-Jacques (5th) – Ⓜ *Luxembourg –* ✆ *01 53 10 29 29*
– www.hotelpetitparis.com   **T3**
20 rm – ♥250/370 € ♥♥250/370 €, ♒ 15 €
♦ Luxury ♦ Design ♦

With their elegant yet fun and colourful decor, the guestrooms in this hotel evoke the style of the Middle Ages, the 1920s, 1970s, or the Louis VX and Napoleon III periods.

St-Jacques without rest   AC 🛜 VISA ⦿ AE ⦿

35 r. des Écoles (5th) – Ⓜ *Maubert Mutualité –* ✆ *01 44 07 45 45*
– www.paris-hotel-stjacques.com   **T2**
36 rm – ♥110/168 € ♥♥151/292 €, ♒ 14 €
♦ Personalised ♦

This small, family-run hotel offers guests classic bedrooms with mouldings on the ceilings and romantic frescoes. The deluxe rooms have been attractively refurbished in a more opulent vein. The typically French-style will delight tourists passing through the city.

𝕏𝕏𝕏𝕏𝕏 La Tour d'Argent   ≤ AC ⇔ ☞ VISA ⦿ AE
❀

15 quai de la Tournelle (5th) – Ⓜ *Maubert Mutualité –* ✆ *01 43 54 23 31*
– www.latourdargent.com
– Closed August, Sunday and Monday   **U2**
Rest – Menu 70 € (lunch), 170/190 € – Carte 157/386 € ⅋
♦ Classic ♦ Luxury ♦ Elegant ♦

An unforgettable view of Notre-Dame cathedral and a quintessentially traditional restaurant serving classic dishes from the gastronomic hall of fame, including legendary Challans duck. Formal, elegant service, like in the old days. Superb wine list.
➜ Quenelles de brochet André Terrail. Caneton "Tour d'Argent". Crêpes Belle Époque.

𝕏𝕏𝕏 Paris – Hôtel Lutetia   🕭 AC ⇔ ☞ VISA ⦿ AE ⦿
❀

45 bd Raspail (6th) – Ⓜ *Sèvres Babylone –* ✆ *01 49 54 46 90*
– www.lutetia.concorde-hotels.com
– Closed school Holidays, August, Saturday, Sunday and Bank Holidays
Rest – Menu 50 € (lunch), 75/145 € – Carte dinner   **R2**
70/178 €
♦ Modern ♦ Cosy ♦ Elegant ♦

Faithful to the style of the Hotel Lutetia, which it occupies, the Art Deco-style dining room by Sonia Rykiel recreates the atmosphere of one of the lounges of the Normandie cruise liner. It is in this elegant setting that guests can savour masterful cuisine created using the finest seasonal ingredients.
➜ Cannelloni de foie gras de canard à la truffe noire du Périgord. Turbot de Bretagne cuit sur l'os, jeunes légumes à la dulce marine et à la laitue de mer. Le "tout-chocolat" d'un gourmand de cacao.

𝕏𝕏𝕏 Relais Louis XIII (Manuel Martinez)   AC ⇔ ☞ VISA ⦿ AE
❀❀

8 r. des Grands-Augustins (6th) – Ⓜ *Odéon –* ✆ *01 43 26 75 96*
– www.relaislouis13.com
– Closed August, Sunday, Monday and Bank Holidays   **T2**
Rest – Menu 50 € (lunch), 80/135 € – Carte approx. 115 € ⅋
♦ Classic ♦ Rustic ♦ Elegant ♦

In this 16C house the three Louis XIII-style dining rooms are teeming with character (stained-glass windows, exposed beams, half timbers etc). Fine classic cuisine, which is perhaps best experienced via the good-value lunchtime set menu.
➜ Ravioli de homard breton, foie gras et crème de cèpes. Caneton challandais cuisiné au grè de la saison. Millefeuille à la vanille de Tahiti.

Hélène Darroze

XXX
❀

4 r. d'Assas (6th) – Ⓜ Sèvres Babylone – ✆ 01 42 22 00 11
– www.helenedarroze.com   **R2**
Rest – (1st floor) (closed Sunday and Monday) Menu 52 € (lunch), 125/175 €
Rest Le Salon – (closed 3 weeks in August, Sunday and Monday)
Menu 28 € (lunch)/85 €
♦ Modern ♦ Cosy ♦

Hélène Darroze creates fine cuisine full of flavour, influenced by her native
Landes region. It is served in an elegant, hushed, contemporary-style dining
room. In the Salon on the ground floor the chef offers a selection of simple yet
chic dishes that are typical of southwest France.
➜ Seiche sautée au chorizo et tomates confites, riz carnaroli noir et crémeux.
Pigeonneau de Racan flambé au capucin, foie gras de canard grillé. Crème
mascarpone parfumée à la truffe blanche d'Alba, écume de lait d'amande.

Un Dimanche à Paris

XXX
❀

4 cours du Commerce-St-André (6th) – Ⓜ Odéon – ✆ 01 56 81 18 18
– www.un-dimanche-a-paris.com
– Closed 31 July-20 August, Sunday dinner and Monday   **T2**
Rest – Menu 35/105 € bi – Carte 53/76 €
♦ Modern ♦ Elegant ♦

Chocolate is king in this concept store! In the restaurant, the spicy hint of the
cocoa bean can even be detected in the meat and fish dishes. The delicious
desserts are a particular highlight. An elegant setting, which is equally perfect
for a mid- afternoon hot chocolate.

Le Restaurant – Hôtel L'Hôtel

XX
❀

13 r. des Beaux-Arts (6th) – Ⓜ St-Germain des Prés – ✆ 01 44 41 99 01
– www.l-hotel.com – Closed August, 23 to 28 December, Sunday and Monday
Rest – Menu 52 € (weekday lunch), 95/160 € bi – Carte 95/115 €   **S1**
♦ Modern ♦ Elegant ♦

In April 2011 a new chef took over the reins at Le Restaurant, part of L'Hôtel, with a
decor also created by Jacques Garcia. His cuisine revisits classic French gastronomy
with creative dishes based around evocative flavours and superb ingredients.
➜ Grenouilles, bouillon d'ail rose, fregola sarda cuisinée au vert. Ris de
veau, jus aux herbes, girolles et caviar d'aubergine fumé. Figue de Solliès,
glace à la brioche acidulée au cassis et pannacotta aux épices.

Le Sergent Recruteur

XX
❀

41 r. St-Louis (4th) – Ⓜ Pont Marie – ✆ 01 43 54 75 42
– www.lesergentrecruteur.fr
– Closed 1 to 16 August, 23 to 30 December, February Holidays, Sunday
and Monday   **U2**
Rest – Menu 65 € (lunch), 95/145 € ❀❀
♦ Creative ♦ Fashionable ♦ Elegant ♦

On Île St Louis, this very elegant and intimate restaurant is in a 13C building. The
food, by a chef who has an impressive CV to his name, turns out to be lively and
creative, as you embark on a set menu crafted with finesse. The place may have
only opened its doors in 2012 but it is already a sure bet.
➜ Cuisine du marché.

La Dame de Pic

XX
❀

20 r. du Louvre (1st) – Ⓜ Louvre Rivoli – ✆ 01 42 60 40 40
– www.ladamedepic.fr – Closed 30 July-26 August and Sunday
Rest – Menu 49 € (weekday lunch), 79/120 €   **T1**
♦ Creative ♦ Design ♦ Elegant ♦

Anne-Sophie Pic's Parisian restaurant was opened in 2012 and is a stone's throw
from the Louvre. The Valence-born chef's feeling for flavours is easily recognisable, as is the precision of her creations and her ability to combine unexpected
ingredients. Enjoy variations based on the leitmotiv of flavours and aromas.
➜ Berlingots fumés, chèvre frais fumé, champignons des bois et fève
tonka. Saint-pierre côtier, feuilles de cannelle, haricots cocos et café Bourbon pointu. Baba au rhum, fruit de la passion, gingembre et vanille.

La Société   🏠 AC ⌕ VISA ⦿ AE

4 pl. St-Germain-des-Prés (6th) – Ⓜ *St-Germain des Prés*
– ℰ *01 53 63 60 60 – www.restaurantlasociete.com*   **S2**
Rest – Carte 45/100 €
♦ Modern ♦ Design ♦ Luxury ♦

This stylish and glamorous address is part of the Costes empire. The terrace
opposite the church of St-Germain-des-Prés is a favourite meeting place for a
sophisticated clientele. They come here to enjoy a menu in keeping with the
setting, which features classic and Asian inspired dishes.

Cigale Récamier   🏠 AC VISA ⦿

4 r. Récamier (7th) – Ⓜ *Sèvres Babylone* – ℰ *01 45 48 86 58*
– *Closed Sunday*   **R2**
Rest – Carte 35/52 €
♦ Traditional ♦ Friendly ♦

A discreet and elegant address popular with politicians and publishers from this
exclusive district of Paris. In addition to classic bistro dishes, the kitchen is also
renowned for its delicious sweet and savoury soufflés, the flavours of which vary
with the seasons.

Benoit   AC ⟷ VISA ⦿ AE ①

20 r. St-Martin (4th) – Ⓜ *Châtelet-Les Halles* – ℰ *01 42 72 25 76*
– *www.alain-ducasse.com*
– *Closed August*   **U1**
Rest – Menu 38 € (lunch) – Carte 60/120 € 🍷
♦ Classic ♦ Bistro ♦ Retro ♦

Alain Ducasse runs this chic and lively bistro, one of the oldest in Paris. Classic
cuisine, respecting the soul of this fine, authentic establishment.
➜ Pâté en croûte, cœur de laitue à l'huile de noix et chapons aillés. Filet de sole
Nantua, épinards à peine crémés. Profiteroles Benoît, sauce chocolat chaud.

Yugaraj   AC VISA ⦿ AE ①

14 r. Dauphine (6th) – Ⓜ *Odéon* – ℰ *01 43 26 44 91*
– *Closed August and Monday*   **T1**
Rest – Menu 30/39 € – Carte 36/58 €
♦ Indian ♦ Exotic ♦

The wood panelling, silk drapes and antique furnishings lend a real exotic feel
to this temple of Indian gastronomy. Fans of cuisine from the sub-continent will
be in their element. Dishes such as butter chicken, grilled meats, and fish curry
with coconut milk feature on the menu.

La Truffière   AC ⟷ VISA ⦿ AE ①

4 r. Blainville (5th) – Ⓜ *Place Monge* – ℰ *01 46 33 29 82*
– *www.latruffiere.com*
– *Closed 23 to 30 December, Tuesday lunch in July-August, Sunday and Monday*
Rest – Menu 35 € (weekday lunch), 80/220 €   **T3**
– Carte 92/156 € 🍷
♦ Modern ♦ Intimate ♦

The standards are consistently high in this attractive 17C house. Enjoy recipes
full of finesse created with traditional produce and enhanced, in season, by
the exquisite flavours of black or white truffles. The wine list, featuring vintages
from around the world, is remarkable.
➜ Œuf mollet en croûte de pain et truffe noire. Parmentier de queue de
bœuf, pomme de terre truffée. Soufflé chaud à la truffe noire et glace yaourt.

Atelier Maître Albert   AC ⟷ VISA ⦿ AE ①

1 r. Maître Albert (5th) – Ⓜ *Maubert Mutualité* – ℰ *01 56 81 30 01*
– *www.ateliermaitrealbert.com*
– *Closed lunch Saturday and Sunday*   **U2**
Rest – Menu 30 € (lunch)/35 € – Carte 38/65 €
♦ Traditional ♦ Cosy ♦

An attractive medieval fireplace and roasting spits take pride of place in this
handsome interior designed by Jean-Michel Wilmotte. Guy Savoy is responsible
for the mouthwatering menu.

XX **Brasserie Lutetia** – Hôtel Lutetia   AC VISA ☺ AE ①
45 bd Raspail (6th) – Ⓜ *Sèvres Babylone* – ✆ *01 49 54 46 76*
– www.lutetia.concorde-hotels.com   **R2**
Rest – Menu 45 € (weekday lunch), 50/55 €
– Carte 60/81 €
♦ Traditional ♦ Brasserie ♦
The famous Hotel Lutetia also boasts a brasserie with its own inimitable atmosphere that has a chrome and mirrors decor. Enjoy delicious seafood platters and other classic brasserie dishes, such as sole meunière, bouillabaisse and rum baba.

XX **Alcazar**   �& AC ⇆ VISA ☺ AE
62 r. Mazarine (6th) – Ⓜ *Odéon* – ✆ *01 53 10 19 99*
– www.alcazar.fr   **S2**
Rest – Menu 37 € bi (weekday lunch)/42 € – Carte 45/60 €
♦ Modern ♦ Trendy ♦ Brasserie ♦
This restaurant owned by Sir Terence Conran also hosts 'electro chic' evenings, photo exhibitions and operatic events. The menu focuses on classic French cuisine, as well as specialities from outside France. Dishes such as fish and chips feature on the menu alongside quail stuffed with foie gras.

XX **Fogón**   AC ⌂☝ (dinner) VISA ☺
45 quai des Grands-Augustins (6th) – Ⓜ *St-Michel* – ✆ *01 43 54 31 33*
– www.fogon.fr
– Closed 29 July-20 August, 24 December-7 January, Monday and lunch except Saturday and Sunday   **T2**
Rest – Menu 50 € – Carte 45/77 €
♦ Spanish ♦ Design ♦
A taste of Spain on the banks of the Seine. Spanish cuisine is served in a trendy dining room with a chic, designer-style decor. Note that the set menus and paella rice dishes are only served for a minimum of two people.

XX **Itinéraires** (Sylvain Sendra)   �& AC ⇆ VISA ☺ AE
✿
5 r. de Pontoise (5th) – Ⓜ *Maubert Mutualité* – ✆ *01 46 33 60 11*
– www.restaurant-itineraires.com
– Closed 4 to 25 August, 20 to 29 December, Sunday and Monday
Rest – *(number of covers limited, pre-book)* Menu 35 €   **U2**
(weekday lunch), 59/79 € – Carte 40/60 € ✦
♦ Modern ♦ Fashionable ♦
This deservedly much talked about restaurant proposes fine modern cuisine in a contemporary setting.
➜ Tarte à l'oignon doux des Cévennes, foie gras, champignons de Paris et noix de muscade. Dos de cabillaud façon fish'n'chips, épinards et vieux parmesan. Soufflé au Grand Marnier, glace au chocolat.

X **L'Atelier de Joël Robuchon - St-Germain**   AC ⌂☝
✿✿
5 r. de Montalembert (7th) – Ⓜ *Rue du Bac*   VISA ☺ AE ①
– ✆ 01 42 22 56 56
– www.joel-robuchon.net
– Open from 11.30 am to 3.30 pm and 6.30pm to midnight. Reservations possible for certain times only: please enquire.   **R1**
Rest – Menu 165 € – Carte 62/132 € ✦
♦ Creative ♦ Design ♦ Minimalist ♦
Instead of normal tables, the original concept of the Rochon-designed decor features high stools facing the counter. Here diners can savour dishes served tapas-style. Superbly executed, in keeping with the art of simplicity!
➜ Langoustine en ravioli truffé à l'étuvée de chou vert. Agneau de lait en côtelettes à la fleur de thym. Fruit de la passion en soufflé chaud et sorbet exotique.

FRANCE - PARIS

Sola   AC VISA ᏏᏏ AE

12 r. de l' Hôtel-Colbert (5th) – Ⓜ *Maubert Mutualité –* ℰ *01 43 29 59 04*
– www.restaurant-sola.com
– Closed August, 30 December-7 January, Sunday and Monday   **T-U2**
Rest *–* Menu 48 € (lunch)/88 €
◆ Modern ◆ Exotic ◆ Elegant ◆
This restaurant is just a few yards from the banks of the Seine overlooking Notre Dame and yet you'd be forgiven for thinking you were already in Japan! The young Japanese chef is living proof that the cuisine of his home and adopted countries can combine to create harmonious and gracefully presented culinary creations. Ingredients sourced from France are transformed with traditional Far Eastern flavours.
➔ Truite mi-cuite, prune, radis, tomate sur une crème mascarpone. Bar, purée de carotte, girolles poêlées et vinaigrette de citron. Noisettes cara-mélisées, cookies sur crème chocolat et glace vanille.

Gaya Rive Gauche par Pierre Gagnaire   AC VISA ᏏᏏ AE

44 r. du Bac (7th) – Ⓜ *Rue du Bac –* ℰ *01 45 44 73 73*
– www.pierre-gagnaire.com
– Closed 12 to 19 August, 23 December-6 January and Sunday   **R1**
Rest *–* Menu 60 € (lunch) – Carte 60/100 €
◆ Fish and seafood ◆ Design ◆ Elegant ◆
This attractive and relaxed contemporary bistro has a grey-blue decor created by Christian Ghion. Savour dishes that are each more creative than the last. Fish and seafood to the fore, produced with finesse yet a laudable lack of pretention.
➔ Chair de tourteau, coquillages, salicornes, mayonnaise au raifort. Blanc de saint-pierre grillé, marinière de coques, couteaux à la nantaise. Gâteau chocolat au cru Cuba, crème glacée au cru Venezuela.

Ze Kitchen Galerie (William Ledeuil)   AC VISA ᏏᏏ AE

4 r. des Grands-Augustins (6th) – Ⓜ *St-Michel –* ℰ *01 44 32 00 32*
– www.zekitchengalerie.fr
– Closed 2 weeks in August, 1 week late December, Saturday lunch and Sunday
Rest *–* Menu 40 € bi (lunch), 70/82 € – Carte 75/82 €   **T2**
◆ Creative ◆ Design ◆
Attractive fusion cuisine with a hint of Asia, a minimalist, loft-style decor, con-temporary paintings on the walls and a view of the open kitchens. For over 10 years, Ze Kitchen has been one of the unmissable restaurants on the Left Bank.
➔ Bouillon thaï de canard, foie gras et condiment agrumes. Bœuf wagyu confit et grillé, condiment umeboshi-sésame. Glace chocolat blanc-wasabi et pistache-fraise.

Yam'Tcha (Adeline Grattard)   VISA ᏏᏏ

4 r. Sauval (1st) – Ⓜ *Louvre Rivoli –* ℰ *01 40 26 08 07 – www.yamtcha.com*
– Closed August, Christmas Holidays, Tuesday lunch, Sunday and Monday
Rest *–* (number of covers limited, pre-book) Menu 60 €   **T1**
(weekday lunch)/100 €
◆ Creative ◆ Cosy ◆
Enjoy remarkable cuisine produced by a young chef who trained in Hong Kong and at the Astrance. Simple, yet memorable dishes with both French and Asian influences, as well as an excellent selection of teas. Space for just twenty diners!
➔ Wonton de foie gras et de couteau servi dans un consommé. Turbot, trompettes-de-la-mort et émulsion de pétoncle. Crème de sésame noir, glace vanille et châtaigne.

Mon Vieil Ami   VISA ᏏᏏ AE ①

69 r. St-Louis-en-l'Île (4th) – Ⓜ *Pont Marie –* ℰ *01 40 46 01 35*
– www.mon-vieil-ami.com
– Closed 1 to 20 August, 1 to 20 January, Monday and Tuesday   **U2**
Rest *–* Menu 46 €
◆ Traditional ◆ Inn ◆ Elegant ◆
Old wooden beams and contemporary decor characterise this trendy, auberge-style restaurant. Delicious traditional recipes with a lovely modern touch and Alsace influences.

35° Ouest   `AC` `VISA` `CO` `AE` `O`

35 r. de Verneuil (7th) – **Ⓜ** *Rue du Bac* – *☏ 01 42 86 98 88*
– Closed 28 July-26 August, 27 December-2 January, Sunday and Monday
Rest – *(number of covers limited, pre-book)* Carte 60/100 €   **R1**
♦ Fish and seafood ♦ Minimalist ♦

The cuisine in this compact and discreet restaurant pays homage to the sea. The chef favours simplicity and the freshness and flavour of carefully selected ingredients. The result is cuisine prepared according to the rule book.
➔ Rémoulade de tourteau et Granny Smith. Sole poêlée meunière, pommes écrasées. Sorbet vanillé au muscat de Beaumes-de-Venise.

Moissonnier   `VISA` `CO`

28 r. des Fossés-St-Bernard (5th) – **Ⓜ** *Jussieu* – *☏ 01 43 29 87 65*
– Closed August, 25 December-2 January, Sunday and Monday   **U3**
Rest – Carte 30/60 €
♦ Lyonnaise ♦ Bistro ♦ Minimalist ♦

The decor in this bistro has resisted every passing trend with its gleaming zinc counter, walls showing the patina of age, and comfy banquettes. Calf sweetbread turnovers and oxtail terrine are just two examples of the specialities of the skilful chef.

Agapé Substance   `VISA` `CO` `AE`

66 r. Mazarine (6th) – **Ⓜ** *Odéon* – *☏ 01 43 29 33 83*
– www.agapesubstance.com
– Closed 15 July-21 August, Sunday and Monday   **S2**
Rest – *(number of covers limited, pre-book)* Menu 65 € (weekday lunch), 129/199 € bi
♦ Creative ♦ Design ♦ Simple ♦

In this annexe to the Agapé, opened in mid 2011, you can sense the very substance of the cuisine, as you follow the evolution of dishes as they are prepared in the kitchen. The menus are separated into different ingredients, for example: mushrooms, monkfish, peaches etc.

Le Chardenoux des Prés   `AC` `VISA` `CO` `AE`

27 r. du Dragon (6th) – **Ⓜ** *St-Germain des Prés* – *☏ 01 45 48 29 68*
– www.restaurantlechardenouxdespres.com   **S2**
Rest – Menu 27 € (weekday lunch) – Carte 47/69 €
♦ Traditional ♦ Retro ♦ Friendly ♦

Cyril Lignac has opened his second Le Chardenoux eatery in premises with a legendary culinary tradition. The blackboard highlights the concise daily menu, while bistro recipes (hearty casseroles and more contemporary dishes) cohabit the à la carte menu.

La Marlotte   `VISA` `CO` `AE`

55 r. du Cherche-Midi (6th) – **Ⓜ** *St-Placide* – *☏ 01 45 48 86 79*
– www.lamarlotte.com
– Closed 10 to 21 August   **R2**
Rest – Menu 27 € (lunch)/31 € – Carte 33/62 €
♦ Traditional ♦

This modern take on a provincial-style inn is not far from the Bon Marché department store and is a popular haunt for publishers and politicians. The copious and seasonal cuisine honours tradition with dishes such as herring and potatoes in oil, chicken liver terrine, and Grenoble-style skate.

L'Épi Dupin   `VISA` `CO`

11 r. Dupin (6th) – **Ⓜ** *Sèvres Babylone* – *☏ 01 42 22 64 56*
– www.epidupin.com
– Closed 1 to 24 August, Monday lunch, Saturday and Sunday   **R2**
Rest – *(number of covers limited, pre-book)* Menu 38/49 €
♦ Modern ♦ Friendly ♦

Stonework, half-timbers and exposed beams provide the welcoming setting for delicious cuisine that offers a new take on tradition. This pocket-sized restaurant has definitely won over the Bon Marché district!

La Maison du Jardin   AC VISA OO AE O

27 r. Vaugirard (6th) – ⓜ Rennes – ☏ 01 45 48 22 31
– Closed 1 to 22 August, Saturday lunch and Sunday   **S3**
Rest – (pre-book) Menu 32 €

♦ Traditional ♦ Bistro ♦

This bistro a stone's throw from the Luxembourg palace explores the flavours and simplicity of traditional cuisine. Try dishes such as homemade terrines, seasonal soups, lamb pastilla, cod with courgette polenta, and the chocolate dessert selection... all accompanied by sensibly priced wines.

Yen   AC VISA OO AE O

22 r. St-Benoît (6th) – ⓜ St-Germain-des-Prés – ☏ 01 45 44 11 18
– Closed 2 weeks in August and Sunday   **S2**
Rest – Menu 68 € (dinner)/85 € – Carte 40/80 €

♦ Japanese ♦ Minimalist ♦

The highly refined Japanese decor in this restaurant will appeal to fans of the minimalist look. The menu showcases the chef's speciality, soba – buckwheat noodles served hot or cold and prepared in front of you.

La Ferrandaise   ✧ VISA OO

8 r. de Vaugirard (6th) – ⓜ Odéon – ☏ 01 43 26 36 36
– www.laferrandaise.com
– Closed 3 weeks in August, Monday lunch, Saturday lunch and Sunday
Rest – Menu 34/55 € bi   **T2**

♦ Traditional ♦ Bistro ♦

This pretty restaurant close to the Luxembourg gardens pays homage to the cuisine of the Auvergne and the legendary Puy-de-Dôme. The owner has even developed a partnership with breeders of the traditional 'Ferrandaise' cattle from his homeland, while the Breton chef creates cuisine that is both honest and tasty. A winning combination.

Shu   VISA OO AE

8 r. Suger (6th) – ⓜ St-Michel – ☏ 01 46 34 25 88
– www.restaurant-shu.com
– Closed Easter Holidays, 2 weeks in August and Sunday   **T2**
Rest – (dinner only) (number of covers limited, pre-book) Menu 38/56 €

♦ Japanese ♦ Minimalist ♦

You will need to duck to get through the door that leads to this 17C cellar. To a backdrop of minimalist decor, discover authentic and impressively crafted Japanese cuisine here. The freshness of the ingredients is showcased to the full in dishes such as kushiage, sushi and sashimi.

Fish La Boissonnerie   AC VISA OO

69 r. de Seine (6th) – ⓜ Odéon – ☏ 01 43 54 34 69
– Closed 1 week in August and 20 December-2 January   **S2**
Rest – Menu 27 € (lunch)/35 € ⚇

♦ Traditional ♦ Bistro ♦

It is worth coming to this restaurant just to admire the mosaic façade! For the past 10 years this convivial restaurant has been paying homage to Bacchus, fish and seafood. The menu features dishes such as oyster vichyssoise, scallops with Paimpol beans, and sea bream with barigoule-style artichokes.

Le Comptoir du Relais – Hôtel Relais St-Germain   🛋 AC

5 carr. de l'Odéon (6th) – ⓜ Odéon   VISA OO AE O
– ☏ 01 44 27 07 50 – www.hotelrsg.com   **S2**
Rest – (bookings advisable at dinner) Menu 55 € (weekday dinner)
– Carte 23/86 €

♦ Traditional ♦ Bistro ♦

In this pocket-sized 1930s bistro, chef Yves Camdeborde delights customers with his copious traditional cuisine. Brasserie dishes are to the fore at lunchtime, with a more refined single menu available in the evening.

FRANCE - PARIS

Suan Thaï   *VISA* *◎◎* *AE*

35 r. Temple (4th) – **Ⓜ** *Rambuteau –* *ℰ 01 42 77 10 20 –* www.suanthai.fr
Rest – Menu 18 € (lunch)/29 € – Carte 32/55 €   **U1**
♦ Thai ♦ Exotic ♦

Now larger, more beautiful and more comfortable than before, the Suan Thaï moved 100m from its old address at the end of 2011. The Thai cuisine – delicate, authentic and reasonably priced – remains the same. Prior booking is now even more essential than ever!

Terroir Parisien   *&* *AC* *VISA* *◎◎* *AE*

20 r. St-Victor (5th) – **Ⓜ** *Maubert Mutualité –* *ℰ 01 44 31 54 54*
– Closed 2 weeks in August   **U2**
Rest – Carte 27/77 €
♦ Traditional ♦ Fashionable ♦

"My cooking is like my city, and my city is Paris." A Parisian chef if ever there was one, Yannick Alléno, head chef at Le Meurice, means to cultivate the specialities of Île-de-France, its produce and its forgotten recipes. Opening a bistro like this was the obvious step to take: *pâtés chauds* (Vietnamese puff pastries) and *matelote de Bougival* (fish stew).

Lengué   *⇧* *VISA* *◎◎*

31 r. Parcheminerie (5th) – **Ⓜ** *St-Michel –* *ℰ 01 46 33 75 10*
– Closed 3 weeks in August, Sunday lunch and Monday   **T2**
Rest – Menu 23 € (lunch) – Carte 40/60 €
♦ Japanese ♦ Intimate ♦

Named after a pink flower found in paddy fields. This charming Japanese restaurant is what they call an isakaya, specialising in food served in small portions – rather like tapas. And it is a tasty isakaya at that, as the dishes prove to be as delicate as they are delicious! Attentive service.

Aux Verres de Contact   *&* *VISA* *◎◎*

33 r. de Bièvre (corner of bd St-Germain) (5th) – **Ⓜ** *Maubert Mutualité*
– ℰ 01 46 34 58 02 – www.auxverresdecontact.com
– Closed Sunday   **U2**
Rest – Menu 31 €
♦ Modern ♦ Bistro ♦

The Jadis team, based in the 15th *arrondissement*, moved into these premises in 2011. A pleasant and colourful contemporary bistro where, despite the name, contact lenses aren't obligatory... but where you need to be adept at raising your glass! An appreciation of the finer things in life is also a must. Good value for money.

Mirama   *AC* *VISA* *◎◎*

17 r. St Jacques (5th) – **Ⓜ** *Cluny La Sorbonne –* *ℰ 01 43 54 71 77*
Rest – Carte 20/30 €   **T2**
♦ Chinese ♦ Simple ♦

A stone's throw from Boulevard St Michel, just behind the Eglise St Séverin church, Mirama is a mecca for those who love authentic Chinese food. Make sure you try the soups and the Peking duck, which are the house specialities.

MONTPARNASSE – DENFERT   *Plan VI*

Pullman Montparnasse   *≼ 🛜 ℔ & rm, AC 🛜 🎿*

19 r. du Cdt Mouchotte (14th)   *VISA* *◎◎* *AE* *◉*
– **Ⓜ** *Montparnasse Bienvenüe –* *ℰ 01 44 36 44 36*
– www.pullmanhotels.com   **V1**
918 rm – ♦165/517 € ♦♦165/517 €, ⬜ 25 € – 35 suites
Rest – Menu 41/44 € – Carte 46/60 €
♦ Business ♦ Functional ♦

In this hotel taken over by the Pullman chain in early 2011, it is worth asking for one of the newly renovated guestrooms, which are functional and soberly decorated. The Montparnasse's main selling points are its huge conference centre and its panoramic views of the capital.

Concorde Montparnasse   🏠 ⛤ 🅰 rm, 🛜 🎣 🚗

40 r. du Cdt Mouchotte (14th) – Ⓜ *Gaîté*   🆅🅸🆂🅰 ⓒⓞ 🅰🅴 ⓪
– ☎ 01 56 54 84 00
– www.concorde-montparnasse.com   **V1**
354 rm – ♦120/550 € ♦♦120/550 €, ⌂ 19 €
Rest – *(closed Saturday and Sunday)* Carte 35/45 €
♦ Business ♦ Modern ♦

Situated on Place de Catalogne, this hotel offers functional guestrooms that are ideal for business travellers. Guests can relax in the trendy bar or enjoy a meal in the 'salad bar' or on the outdoor patio.

Le Six *without rest*   🆚 ⛤ 🅰 🛜 🎣 🆅🅸🆂🅰 ⓒⓞ ⓪

14 r. Stanislas (6th) – Ⓜ *Notre-Dame des Champs – ☎ 01 42 22 00 75*
– www.hotel-le-six.com   **W1**
37 rm – ♦229/450 € ♦♦229/450 €, ⌂ 22 € – 4 suites
♦ Townhouse ♦ Design ♦

A contemporary hotel with a perfect location between the Luxembourg gardens, St-Germain-des-Prés and Montparnasse. The photos on the walls of the restrained yet well-appointed guestrooms pay homage to some of this district's legendary characters. Small but well-equipped spa.

Aiglon *without rest*   🅰 🛜 🚗 🆅🅸🆂🅰 ⓒⓞ 🅰🅴 ⓪

232 bd Raspail (14th) – Ⓜ *Raspail – ☎ 01 43 20 82 42*
– www.aiglon.com   **W1**
36 rm – ♦130/245 € ♦♦130/245 €, ⌂ 15 € – 10 suites
♦ Townhouse ♦ Personalised ♦

The Aiglon, where Giacometti and Buñuel once stayed, is gradually being modernised. There is a focus on bright colours and elegant details, such as mosaics in the bathrooms and photos on the walls. The renovated guestrooms are warm and more comfortable than before.

Ste-Beuve *without rest*   🅰 🛜 🆅🅸🆂🅰 🅰🅴

9 r. Ste-Beuve (6th) – Ⓜ *Notre-Dame des Champs – ☎ 01 45 48 20 07*
– www.hotelsaintebeuve.com   **W1**
22 rm – ♦169/327 € ♦♦169/327 €, ⌂ 16 €
♦ Townhouse ♦ Cosy ♦ Personalised ♦

Cosy and welcoming are the two adjectives that best describe this particularly tasteful hotel. In the guestrooms, antique furniture works well with the refined fabrics. A black and white decor predominates in the bathrooms. This is a very pleasant base from which to explore the city.

Lenox Montparnasse *without rest*   🅰 🛜 🚗 🆅🅸🆂🅰 ⓒⓞ 🅰🅴 ⓪

15 r. Delambre (14th) – Ⓜ *Vavin – ☎ 01 43 35 34 50*
– www.hotellenox.com   **W1**
52 rm – ♦130/400 € ♦♦130/400 €, ⌂ 17 €
♦ Business ♦ Classic ♦

A distinct ambience pervades this hotel in which the bar and lounges boast a tranquil charm and the stylish guestrooms are adorned with antique furniture, warm colours and delightful fabrics. If you prefer a little more space, opt for a junior suite.

Delambre *without rest*   🅰 🛜 🆅🅸🆂🅰 ⓒⓞ 🅰🅴

35 r. Delambre (14th) – Ⓜ *Edgar Quinet – ☎ 01 43 20 66 31*
– www.hoteldelambreparis.com   **W1**
30 rm – ♦90/160 € ♦♦90/160 €, ⌂ 11 €
♦ Business ♦ Functional ♦

The memory of André Breton and Paul Gauguin is still alive in this hotel situated near Montparnasse railway station. Relax in one of the simple, functional guestrooms before taking a stroll through this lively district.

FRANCE - PARIS

Mercure Raspail Montparnasse without rest   🕭 Ⓐ 🛜

207 bd Raspail (14th) – Ⓜ *Vavin* – ℰ *01 43 20 62 94*   🆅🆂🅰 ⓧⓧ 🅰🅴 🅞

– *www.mercure.com*   **W1**

63 rm – ♦145/230 € ♦♦145/230 €, ☲ 14 €

♦ Business ♦ Modern ♦

This hotel occupies a Haussmann-style building close to the Montparnasse district, famed for its brasseries and legendary nightlife. Small, functional bedrooms suitable for a weekend break.

Hôtel de la Paix without rest   Ⓐ 🛜 🆅🆂🅰 ⓧⓧ 🅰🅴

225 bd Raspail (14th) – Ⓜ *Raspail* – ℰ *01 43 20 35 82*

– *www.paris-montparnasse-hotel.com*   **W1**

39 rm – ♦99/255 € ♦♦99/255 €, ☲ 9 €

♦ Family ♦ Personalised ♦

Don't be fooled by the façade: this hotel renovated in 2010 has real charm. The owners have decorated the building with enthusiasm, using carefully chosen objects and old furniture. The guestrooms are bright, pretty and simple in style.

Apollon Montparnasse without rest   Ⓐ 🛜 🆅🆂🅰 ⓧⓧ 🅰🅴 🅞

91 r. Ouest (14th) – Ⓜ *Pernety* – ℰ *01 43 95 62 00*

– *www.apollon-montparnasse.com*   **V2**

33 rm – ♦118/130 € ♦♦130/152 €, ☲ 11 €

♦ Townhouse ♦ Functional ♦

A small family-run hotel with a decor dominated by stripes and floral curtains. Although the guestrooms are not overly spacious, they are gradually being renovated and are fine for a short stay. Friendly atmosphere and reasonable prices.

XXX   Le Dôme   Ⓐ ⇆ 🆅🆂🅰 ⓧⓧ 🅞

108 bd Montparnasse (14th) – Ⓜ *Vavin* – ℰ *01 43 35 25 81*   **W1**

Rest – Carte 85/110 €

♦ Fish and seafood ♦ Elegant ♦

One of the temples of literary and artistic bohemia from the Roaring Twenties with a legendary Art Deco setting. Le Dôme continues to serve the freshest fish and seafood in the best time-honoured fashion.

XXX   Cobéa (Philippe Bélissent)   Ⓐ 🆅🆂🅰 ⓧⓧ 🅰🅴

✤   *11 r. Raymond Losserand (14th)* – Ⓜ *Gaité* – ℰ *01 43 20 21 39*

– *www.cobea.fr*

– *Closed 28 April-6 May, August, 23 to 30 December, Sunday and Monday*

Rest – *(number of covers limited, pre-book)* Menu 44 €   **V2**

(lunch), 65/95 €

♦ Modern ♦ Elegant ♦

Monsieur Lapin changed its name to Cobéa in 2011. A simple, elegant decor of white and grey tones provides the backdrop for the subtle cuisine created by chef Philippe Bélissent, who has worked in many of the city's finest restaurants. Fine, honest cuisine that is full of flavour and focuses on excellent ingredients.
→ Courgettes et girolles, houmous et dattes. Pigeonneau fermier, céleri et truffe noire. Fraise-meringue.

XX   Guy Martin Italia   🕭 Ⓐ ⇆ 🆅🆂🅰 ⓧⓧ 🅰🅴

19 r. Bréa (6th) – Ⓜ *Vavin* – ℰ *01 43 27 08 80*

– *www.guymartinitalia.com*

– *Closed 3 weeks in August*   **W1**

Rest – Menu 50 € (weekday lunch), 75/100 € – Carte 40/55 €

♦ Italian ♦ Elegant ♦ Trendy ♦

The former Sensing has had a facelift! Still run by Guy Martin, this restaurant now pays tribute to Italian cucina. The chef, himself Italian, creates tasty dishes using good ingredients, for example the hearty burrata from Puglia served with thin slices of ham. Designer interior.

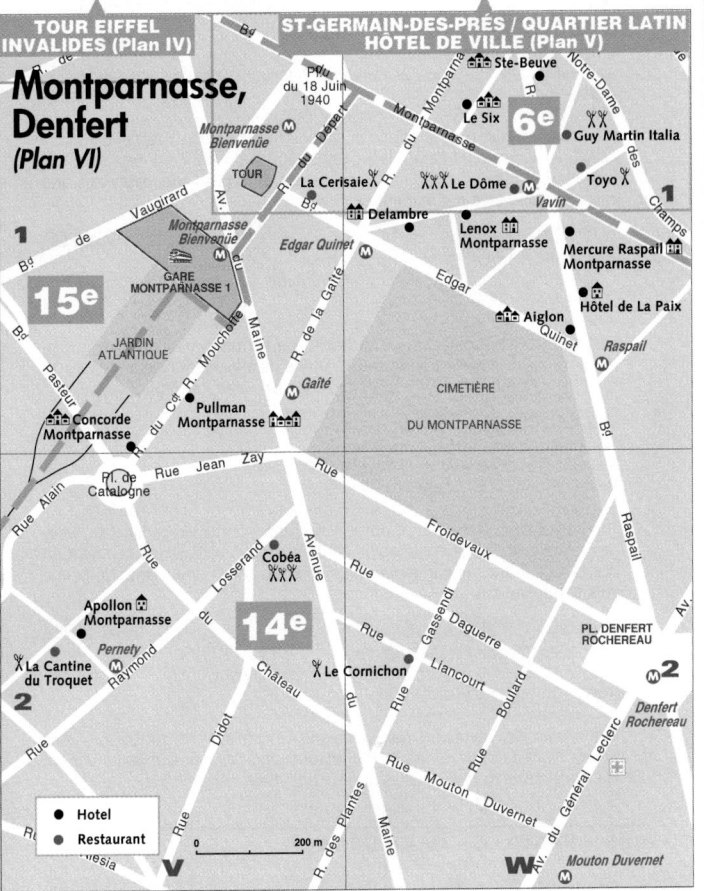

Montparnasse, Denfert
(Plan VI)

TOUR EIFFEL INVALIDES (Plan IV)

ST-GERMAIN-DES-PRÉS / QUARTIER LATIN HÔTEL DE VILLE (Plan V)

- Hotel
- Restaurant

0   200 m

✕ **Le Cornichon**   VISA ⊙⊙

🙂 *34 r. Gassendi (14th)*
- Ⓜ *Denfert-Rochereau*
- ✆ *01 43 20 40 19*
- *www.lecornichon.fr*
- *Closed August, 1 week Christmas Holidays, Saturday and Sunday*

Rest – Menu 32 € (lunch)/34 €   **W2**

♦ Modern ♦ Bistro ♦ Friendly ♦

This business is run by two real food lovers: the first is a computer engineer who has always wanted to get into the restaurant trade and the second is a well-trained young chef. They came together to create this bistro with a very modern feel. With its fine ingredients, appealing dishes, rich flavours etc, Le Cornichon is sure to win you over!

La Cerisaie
VISA ᴍᴏ

70 bd Edgard-Quinet (14th) – Ⓜ *Edgar Quinet –* ℰ *01 43 20 98 98*
– www.restaurantlacerisaie.com
– Closed 14 July-15 August, 25 December-1 January, Saturday and Sunday
Rest *– (pre-book)* Carte 34/42 €
V1

♦ South-West of France ♦ Bistro ♦

A fine ambassador for the cuisine of the southwest…in the heart of a traditionally Breton district of Paris! Classic dishes in this pocket-sized restaurant include seasonally inspired terrines, goose breast with spices and roast pears, and chocolate fondant tart. Charming service.

L'Ordonnance
VISA ᴍᴏ

51 r. Hallé (14th) – Ⓜ *Mouton Duvernet –* ℰ *01 43 27 55 85*
– Closed 1 to 15 August, Saturday except dinner in winter and Sunday
Rest *–* Menu 32 €
Plan I **B3**

♦ Traditional ♦ Bistro ♦

This new-wave bistro near Place Michel-Audiard is run by a friendly and welcoming owner. The honest and precise cuisine here includes favourites such as roast loin of lamb with thyme, poached eggs, pan-fried foie gras.

La Cantine du Troquet
🖂 VISA ᴍᴏ

101 r. de l'Ouest (14th) – Ⓜ *Pernety*
– Closed 2 weeks in August, Sunday and Monday
Rest *–* Menu 32 € – Carte 28/38 €
V2

♦ Traditional ♦ Friendly ♦ Bistro ♦

This typical Basque-style bistro oozes conviviality with its red banquettes, wooden tables and daily specials highlighted on a slate board. Diners can feast on dishes such as homemade terrine, pigs' ears and grilled razor clams. No phone and no reservations.

Toyo
AC 🖂 VISA ᴍᴏ ①

17 r. Jules Chaplain (6th) – Ⓜ *Vavin –* ℰ *01 43 54 28 03*
– Closed 3 weeks in August, Monday lunch and Sunday
Rest *–* Menu 35 € (lunch)/79 €
W1

♦ Creative ♦ Design ♦ Minimalist ♦

In a former life, Toyomitsu Nakayama was the private chef for the couturier Kenzo. Nowadays, he excels in the art of fusing flavours and textures from France and Asia to create dishes that are both fresh and delicate.

MARAIS – BASTILLE – GARE DE LYON
Plan VII

Pavillon de la Reine without rest
🐾 ᵴ ⊛ AC 🛜 ᴀ ⊜
28 pl. des Vosges (3rd) – Ⓜ *Bastille*
VISA ᴍᴏ ᴀᴇ ①
– ℰ *01 40 29 19 19 – www.pavillon-de-la-reine.com*
Y2
38 rm *–* †410/470 € ††410/470 €, � 34 € – 16 suites

♦ Luxury ♦ Historic ♦ Personalised ♦

This elegant and luxurious hotel showcases the discreet noble ambience of the Paris of yesteryear. Once through the vaulted arcades of Place des Vosges, the first feast for the eyes is the beautiful verdant courtyard. Inside, the guestrooms are both plush and elegant, with a small spa providing the icing on the cake.

Les Jardins du Marais
🛜 ᵴ rm, AC 🛜 ᴀ ⊜ VISA ᴍᴏ ᴀᴇ ①
74 r. Amelot (11th) – Ⓜ *St-Sébastien Froissart –* ℰ *01 40 21 22 23*
– www.lesjardinsdumarais.com
Y1
257 rm *–* †350/750 € ††350/750 €, ⊟ 20 € – 8 suites
Rest *– (closed Sunday dinner)* Menu 30/37 € – Carte 40/50 €

♦ Luxury ♦ Art Deco ♦

A little neighbourhood within another neighbourhood: the various buildings and rooms are dispersed along a pretty cobbled street. The entrance hall and bar have a designer aesthetic (red velvet, pendant chandeliers, furniture designed by Starck), and the rooms have Art Deco touches.

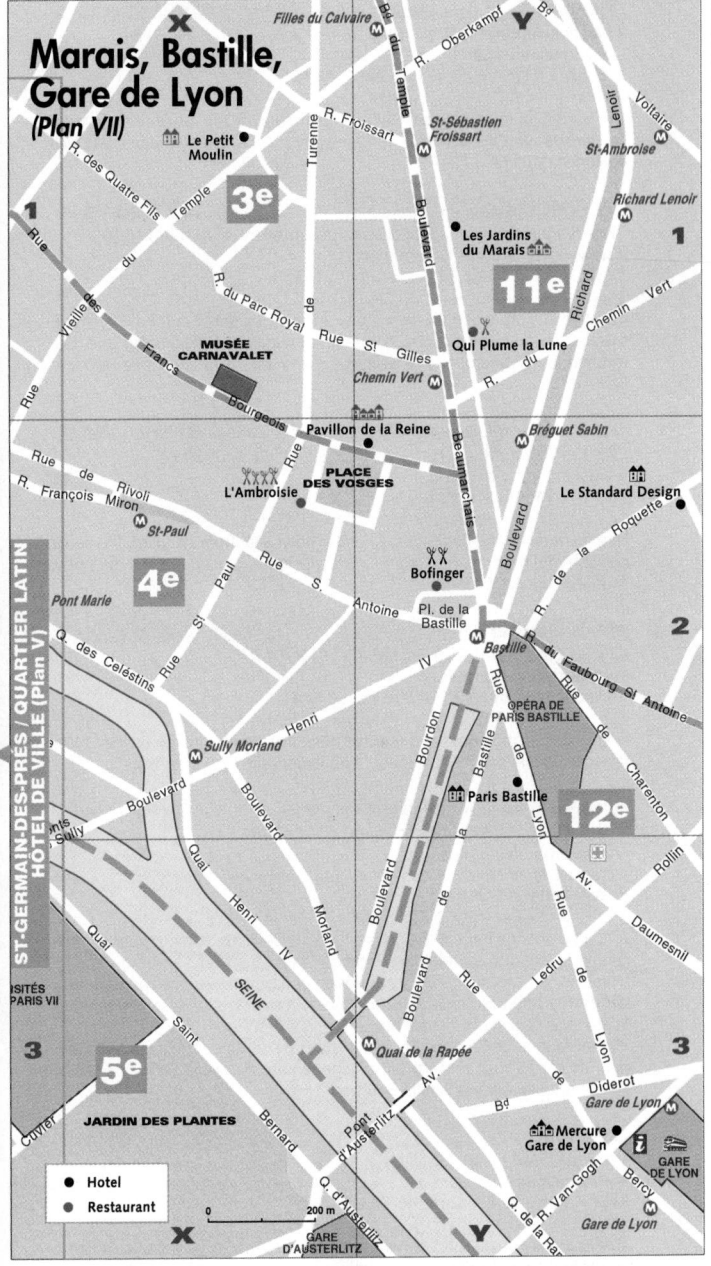

Marais, Bastille, Gare de Lyon
(Plan VII)

X

Filles du Calvaire

Bd. du Temple

R. Oberkampf

Y

Lenoir

Voltaire

St-Sébastien
Froissart

St-Ambroise

Le Petit
Moulin

R. Froissart

Turenne

R. des Quatre Fils

Temple

3e

Boulevard

Richard Lenoir

1

du

R. du Parc Royal

Rue

de

Les Jardins
du Marais

11e

Richard

Chemin Vert

Rue

St

Gilles

Qui Plume la Lune

MUSÉE
CARNAVALET

Vieille

des

Francs

Chemin Vert

R. Beaumarchais

Bréguet Sabin

Bourgeois

Rue

Pavillon de la Reine

Rue

de

Rivoli

Rue

R. François Miron

L'Ambroisie

PLACE
DES VOSGES

Le Standard Design

R. de la Roquette

St-Paul

4e

Paul

Rue

S.

Boulevard

Pont Marie

St

Antoine

Bofinger

R. de la Roquette

Q. des Célestins

Rue

Pl. de la
Bastille

Bastille

R. du Faubourg St Antoine

2

Henri

Bastille

Rue

de

Charenton

Sully Morland

IV

Rue

OPÉRA DE
PARIS BASTILLE

Bourdon

Bastille

Lyon

Rollin

Boulevard

Boulevard

Boulevard

Paris Bastille

12e

Av.

Daumesnil

louis

Sully

Quai

Henri

de

Morland

Rue

Ledru

de

Lyon

SEINE

IV

Quai

Saint

5e

Quai de la Rapée

Bd

Diderot

Gare de Lyon

JARDIN DES PLANTES

Bernard

Pont
d'Austerlitz

Mercure
Gare de Lyon

GARE
DE LYON

3

Cuvier

ITÉS
PARIS VII

3

● Hotel
● Restaurant

0   200 m

Q. d'Austerlitz

Q. de la R. Van-Gogh

Gare de Lyon

Bercy

Q. de la R.

X

GARE
D'AUSTERLITZ

Y

ST-GERMAIN-DES-PRÉS / QUARTIER LATIN
HÔTEL DE VILLE (Plan V)

Mercure Gare de Lyon without rest

2 pl. Louis-Armand (12th) – Ⓜ Gare de Lyon – ✆ 01 43 44 84 84 – www.mercure.com **Y3**

315 rm – †120/360 € ††120/360 €, ☕ 18 €

♦ Chain hotel ♦ Business ♦ Modern ♦

This hotel's contemporary architecture contrasts with the nearby bell tower of the gare de Lyon. Rooms of middling size which are resolutely modern and well equipped.

Le Petit Moulin without rest

29 r. du Poitou (3rd) – Ⓜ St-Sébastien Froissart – ✆ 01 42 74 10 10 – www.hoteldupetitmoulin.com **X1**

17 rm – †195/390 € ††195/390 €, ☕ 15 €

♦ Luxury ♦ Personalised ♦

Christian Lacroix is behind the unique and refined decor in this hotel in the Marais, which plays on the contrasts between the traditional and the modern. Every bedroom is a delight, with vibrant tones and free-standing bathtubs.

Le Standard Design without rest

29 r. des Taillandiers (11th) – Ⓜ Bastille – ✆ 01 48 05 30 97 – www.standard-design-hotel-paris.com **Y2**

36 rm – †100/300 € ††120/300 €, ☕ 15 €

♦ Traditional ♦ Cosy ♦ Design ♦

Despite its name, the designer style of this hotel is far from standard. The decor is stylish with bold motifs adorning the fabrics in the guestrooms and the lobby. Attic-style breakfast room.

Paris Bastille without rest

67 r. de Lyon (12th) – Ⓜ Bastille – ✆ 01 40 01 07 17 – www.hotelparisbastille.com **Y2**

37 rm – †195/301 € ††207/301 €, ☕ 14 €

♦ Business ♦ Townhouse ♦ Functional ♦

Fine fabrics, exotic woods and selected hues characterise the rooms and breakfast room in this comfortable modern hotel opposite Opera Bastille.

L'Ambroisie (Bernard et Mathieu Pacaud)

9 pl. des Vosges (4th) – Ⓜ St-Paul – ✆ 01 42 78 51 45 – www.ambroisie-paris.com – Closed 2 to 18 March, 27 July-27 August, Sunday and Monday

Rest – Carte 200/265 € **X2**

♦ Classic ♦ Luxury ♦ Elegant ♦

Ambrosia was the food of the gods on Mount Olympus. Without question, the cuisine of Bernard and Mathieu Pacaud – two generations working together – reaches similar heights with its explosion of flavours, scientific approach, and perfect execution. Incomparable classicism and an immortal feast for the senses in the regal setting of a private house on Place des Vosges.

→ Feuillantine de langoustine aux graines de sésame, sauce curry. Escalopine de bar à l'émincé d'artichaut, nage réduite au caviar. Tarte fine sablée au chocolat, glace à la vanille Bourbon.

Bofinger (dinner)

5 r. Bastille (4th) – Ⓜ Bastille – ✆ 01 42 72 87 82 – www.bofingerparis.com **Y2**

Rest – Menu 34 € – Carte 40/70 €

♦ Traditional ♦ Retro ♦ Brasserie ♦

This is a real Paris institution with a striking, Alsace-style decor, including a dome, inlaid wood, mirrors, and paintings by Hansi. Opened in 1864, this brasserie is as charming as ever.

Qui Plume la Lune   VISA ⬤⬤

50 r. Amelot (11th) – ⓜ *Chemin Vert* – ☏ *01 48 07 45 48*
– Closed August, 1 week late December, lunch Wednesday and Saturday,
Sunday, Monday and Bank Holidays   **Y1**
Rest – *(number of covers limited, pre-book)* Menu 41 € (lunch), 60/110 €
♦ Modern ♦ Cosy ♦

First, there is the place itself, which is very pretty, inviting and romantic and then there is the food, which is created by a passionate cook. It is fresh, full of vitality and made with carefully selected ingredients (organic produce, great vegetables etc). An enjoyable culinary moment.

MONTMARTRE – PIGALLE   *Plan VIII*

Terrass' Hôtel *without rest*   AC 🛜 🔧 VISA ⬤⬤ AE ⓪

12 r. J.-de-Maistre (18th) – ⓜ *Place de Clichy* – ☏ *01 46 06 72 85*
– www.terrass-hotel.com   **Z1**
93 rm – �atti185/455 € �attitti185/455 €, ⊑ 22 € – 6 suites
♦ Traditional ♦ Personalised ♦

This cosy hotel is located at the foot of Montmartre. It boasts an attractive lounge, piano bar and an open fire to warm you up after a long winter's walk around the city. Modern, colourful guestrooms of varying sizes.

Mercure Montmartre *without rest*   🔧 AC 🛜 🔧 VISA ⬤⬤ AE ⓪

3 r. Caulaincourt (18th) – ⓜ *Place de Clichy* – ☏ *01 44 69 70 70*
– www.mercure.com   **Z2**
305 rm – �attit145/350 € �attitt145/350 €, ⊑ 18 €
♦ Chain hotel ♦ Business ♦ Functional ♦

The major attraction of this chain hotel is its location close to Place Clichy, the Moulin Rouge and the Montmartre cemetery. The renovated bedrooms, furnished in a more contemporary style, are preferable.

Holiday Inn Paris Montmartre *without rest*   🔧 AC 🛜 🔧

23 r. Damrémont (18th) – ⓜ *Lamarck Caulaincourt*   VISA ⬤⬤ AE ⓪
– ☏ 01 44 92 33 40 – www.holiday-inn.com/paris-montmart
– www.holiday-inn.com/paris-montmart   **Z1**
54 rm – �attit129/279 € �attitt149/299 €, ⊑ 15 €
♦ Chain hotel ♦ Business ♦ Functional ♦

Although it is sometimes difficult to find somewhere to stay between Montmartre and Place Clichy, this hotel is a good option. The decor is modern and warm (brown tones), and the guestrooms are functional and well-maintained. A well-run hotel.

Relais Montmartre *without rest*   🌿 AC 🛜 VISA ⬤⬤ AE ⓪

6 r. Constance (18th) – ⓜ *Abbesses* – ☏ *01 70 64 25 25*
– www.relaismontmartre.fr   **Z2**
26 rm – �attit185/240 € �attitt185/240 €, ⊑ 15 €
♦ Traditional ♦ Cosy ♦

Not far from the shops on rue Lepic, this small hotel is a somewhat unexpected find in such a lively district. It is full of character and has all the charm of a bourgeois house. It offers charming guestrooms embellished with period furniture, not to mention the welcome peace and quiet.

Chamarré Montmartre   🍽 AC ↔ VISA ⬤⬤ AE

52 r. Lamarck (18th) – ⓜ *Lamarck Caulaincourt* – ☏ *01 42 55 05 42*
– www.chamarre-montmartre.com
– Closed Sunday dinner and Monday from 15 October-15 April   **AA1**
Rest – Menu 29 € (weekday lunch), 52/80 € – Carte 74/84 € 🍃
♦ Creative ♦ Fashionable ♦

This contemporary restaurant on Montmartre hill serves creative cuisine with a blend of culinary influences. Dishes include Seychelles-style sea bass, lobster in a calamansi sauce and rum baba, all of which can be enjoyed on the attractive terrace.

FRANCE - PARIS

✗ **L'Oriental** 🕸 AC ⇄ VISA ◯◯

47 av. Trudaine (9th) – ⓜ *Pigalle* – 𝒞 *01 42 64 39 80*
– www.loriental-restaurant.com
Rest – Menu 34 € – Carte 32/51 €   **AA2**
◆ Moroccan ◆ Exotic ◆
Choose from the pleasant outdoor terrace or the welcoming and comfortable
dining room with its oriental decor. Evocatively flavoured Moroccan cuisine, including signature couscous dishes.

✗ **La Table d'Eugène** VISA ◯◯

18 r. Eugène-Sue (18th) – ⓜ *Jules Joffrin* – 𝒞 *01 42 55 61 64*
– Closed 1 to 25 August, 24 December-3 January, Sunday and Monday
Rest – *(number of covers limited, pre-book)* Menu 38/78 €   **AA1**
◆ Modern ◆ Minimalist ◆
Foie gras ravioli with a truffle flavoured emulsion, bass fillet and courgette spaghetti, and absinthe baba all feature on the menu of this meticulous restaurant
near the town hall of the 18th arrondissement. The retro decor and excellent
value for money make this a popular haunt in the local neighbourhood and
beyond!

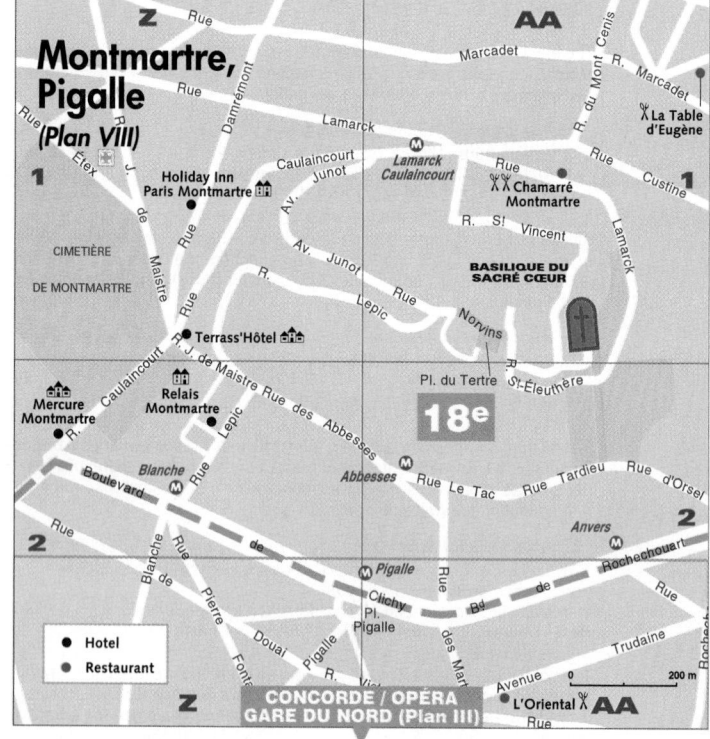

FRANCE - PARIS

St-James Paris

43 av. Bugeaud (16th) ⊠ 75116 – **Ⓜ** Porte Dauphine – ℰ 01 44 05 81 81
– www.saint-james-paris.com **A2**
18 rm – †340/500 € ††340/690 € – 30 suites – ††630/1550 €, ⊑ 35 €
Rest – *(closed Sunday and Bank Holidays) (dinner only)* Menu 95 €
– Carte 60/100 €

♦ Historic ♦ Luxury ♦ Personalised ♦

In 2011 this beautiful late-19C mansion was given a new look by Bambi Sloan.
Superb materials and luxurious fabrics endow it with a Napoleon III-style that
flirts with a typically British originality. The delightful library, majestic staircase
and harmonious volumes all add to the property's unique feel.

Pullman Paris Bercy

1 r. de Libourne (12th) – **Ⓜ** Cour St-Émilion – ℰ 01 44 67 34 00
– www.pullmanhotels.com **D3**
385 rm – †180/580 € ††180/580 €, ⊑ 25 € – 11 suites
Rest Café Ké – ℰ 01 44 67 34 71 *(closed 3 weeks in August and 1 week
late December)* Menu 35 € (weekdays) – Carte 58/73 €

♦ Chain hotel ♦ Business ♦ Functional ♦

A building that is readily recognisable on account of its imposing glazed façade.
The rooms, some of which have fine views over Paris, are contemporary in style.
Café Ké's ambience epitomises the pleasant 'village' atmosphere of the Bercy
district. Brunch on Sundays.

Square

3 r. Boulainvilliers (16th) ⊠ 75016 – **Ⓜ** Mirabeau – ℰ 01 44 14 91 90
– www.hotelsquare.com **A2**
18 rm – †300/700 € ††300/700 €, ⊑ 35 € – 4 suites
Rest Zébra Square – see restaurant listing

♦ Luxury ♦ Design ♦

This contemporary hotel is just opposite the Maison de la Radio. It has guestrooms that are spacious and quiet, thanks to the excellent soundproofing. The
high-tech facilities and modern art collection underline the Square's boutique
hotel image.

Kube

1-5 passage Ruelle (18th) – **Ⓜ** La Chapelle – ℰ 01 42 05 20 00
– www.kubehotel.com **C1**
41 rm – †189/900 € ††189/900 €, ⊑ 25 € **Rest** – Carte 50/100 €

♦ Luxury ♦ Design ♦ Minimalist ♦

Although not located in one of the city's most attractive districts, this resolutely
21C hotel with its designer look and high-tech gadgetry, will appeal to a more
contemporary clientele. Transparent glass, clean white lines and loft-style guestrooms provide the decor. It has a restaurant, as well as two bars, including the
Ice Kube (-10°C, warm clothing provided!).

Novotel Tour Eiffel

61 quai de Grenelle (15th) – **Ⓜ** Charles Michels – ℰ 01 40 58 20 00
– www.novotel-paris-convention.com **A2**
758 rm – †139/600 € ††139/600 €, ⊑ 18 € – 6 suites
Rest Benkay – see restaurant listing
Rest Novotel Café – ℰ 01 40 58 20 75 – Carte 36/60 €

♦ Chain hotel ♦ Business ♦ Modern ♦

This contemporary-style Novotel overlooking the Seine and surrounded by
1970s high-rise buildings boasts a high-tech conference centre. The main
bonus is that nearly all the guestrooms enjoy views of the river.

Océania without rest   🔥 🖥 ⚿ 🅰 🛜 🗓 🚗 🚗 **VISA ⓪ AE ⓪**

52 r. Oradour-sur-Glane (15th) – 🛇 *Porte de Versailles* – ☎ 01 56 09 09 09
– www.oceaniahotels.com   **A3**
232 rm – ♦145/350 € ♦♦145/350 €, ☲ 17 € – 18 suites
♦ Business ♦ Modern ♦
This elegant and contemporary hotel is a stone's throw from the exhibition centre. It offers pleasant bedrooms with parquet flooring and wenge wood furnishings. There is also a fully equipped fitness area (Jacuzzi, hammam, swimming pool) and an exotic garden where breakfast is served in fine weather.

Novotel Bercy   🏠 ⚿ rm, 🅰 🛜 🗓 **VISA ⓪ AE ⓪**

85 r. de Bercy (12th) – 🛇 *Bercy* – ☎ 01 43 42 30 00   **D3**
151 rm – ♦115/270 € ♦♦115/270 €, ☲ 15 €   **Rest** – Carte 22/50 €
♦ Chain hotel ♦ Business ♦ Functional ♦
These bright and contemporary rooms with balconies, near Bercy park, offer good value for money. During summer the restaurant terrace attracts those looking for peace and quiet. Traditional menu and a la plancha dishes.

Novotel Gare de Lyon   🔥 🖥 ⚿ 🅰 🛜 🗓 🚗 **VISA ⓪ AE ⓪**

2 r. Hector-Malot (12th) – 🛇 *Gare de Lyon* – ☎ 01 44 67 60 00
– www.accorhotels.com   **D2**
253 rm – ♦129/349 € ♦♦129/349 €, ☲ 17 € – 2 suites
Rest – Carte 21/51 €
♦ Chain hotel ♦ Business ♦ Functional ♦
Building of recent construction giving onto a peaceful square. Rooms in keeping with the latest chain standards, with terraces on the sixth floor. Pool, fitness facilities and good children's play area. Contemporary decor at the Novotel Café.

Mama Shelter   ⚿ 🅰 🛜 🗓 🚗 **VISA ⓪ AE**

109 r. de Bagnolet (20th) – 🛇 *Gambetta* – ☎ 01 43 48 48 48
– www.mamashelter.com   **D2**
171 rm – ♦79/129 € ♦♦109/169 €, ☲ 15 € – 1 suite
Rest *Mama Shelter* – see restaurant listing
♦ Design ♦
Philippe Starck is behind the refined, fantasy decor in this huge hotel, which is at the cutting edge of contemporary design. It is characterised by a young and slightly bohemian atmosphere in keeping with this district enjoying an urban revival.

Hôtel de Banville without rest   🅰 🛜 **VISA ⓪ AE ⓪**

166 bd Berthier (17th) – 🛇 *Porte de Champerret* – ☎ 01 42 67 70 16
– www.hotelbanville.fr   **B1**
38 rm – ♦159/450 € ♦♦159/450 €, ☲ 20 €
♦ Luxury ♦ Personalised ♦
This charming boutique hotel is decorated with great taste, with guestrooms embellished with shiny wood and opulent detail. Jazz evenings in the piano-bar every Tuesday.

Vice Versa without rest   ⚿ 🅰 🛜 **VISA ⓪ AE**

213 r. de la Croix-Nivert (15th) – 🛇 *Porte de Versailles* – ☎ 01 55 76 55 55
– www.viceversahotel.com   **A3**
37 rm – ♦149/315 € ♦♦149/315 €, ☲ 12 €
♦ Townhouse ♦ Personalised ♦ Design ♦
Greed, gluttony, pride, lust, wrath, sloth and envy: the guestrooms of this hotel decorated by Chantal Thomas illustrate the seven deadly sins! To get here, cross the hall with its heavenly feel. However, if you go down to the basement to visit the hammam, you will find yourself in hell... Diabolically inspired!

Hor without rest   🔥 📶 📶 🛜 VISA ⊙⊙ AE ⓪

160 r. La Fayette (10th) – Ⓜ *Gare du Nord* – 𝒞 01 40 05 18 05
– www.hotel-hor.com   **C1**
47 rm – 🛏289/399 € 🛏🛏289/399 €, ⌂ 15 €

♦ Business ♦ Modern ♦ Functional ♦

A brand new hotel (June 2012) between the Gare du Nord and Gare de l'Est train stations. The guestrooms are contemporary and functional; some even have a private terrace. In the morning, breakfast is served in a pretty room that opens onto a patio.

 Holiday Inn Express Canal de la Villette without rest

68 quai de Seine (19th) – Ⓜ *Crimée*   ≼ 🔥 📶 📶 🛜 VISA ⊙⊙
– 𝒞 01 44 65 01 01 – www.hiexpress.com/paris-canal   **D1**
144 rm ⌂ – 🛏110/334 € 🛏🛏110/334 €

♦ Business ♦ Modern ♦

Those who enjoy a stroll around the Bassin de la Villette know this building well: its twin (a warehouse dating from 1853) still stands on the opposite bank. The hotel, rebuilt in 2008, is striking for its unusual metal cladding and has a warm, friendly atmosphere. Some of the spacious guestrooms overlook the water.

 Windsor Home without rest   🛜 VISA ⊙⊙ AE

3 r. Vital (16th) ✉ 75016 – Ⓜ *La Muette* – 𝒞 01 45 04 49 49
– www.windsorhomeparis.fr   **A2**
8 rm – 🛏100/195 € 🛏🛏115/250 €, ⌂ 15 €

♦ Historic ♦ Family ♦ Personalised ♦

'A home from home for those of us who don't like hotels' is how some guests describe this hotel. It features antique furniture, mouldings, original colours, Baroque touches, a limited number of rooms and lots of charm.

 Le 20 Prieuré Hôtel without rest   🔥 📶 🛜 VISA ⊙⊙ AE

20 r. Grand Prieuré (11th) – Ⓜ *Oberkampf* – 𝒞 01 47 00 74 14
– www.hotel20prieure.com   **C2**
32 rm – 🛏99/195 € 🛏🛏109/195 €, ⌂ 13 €

♦ Design ♦

Renovated in 2007, this hotel subscribes to the urban contemporary look. It offers small yet agreeable rooms with shades of white, designer furniture, and huge photos of Paris.

 **Le Pré Catelan**   🚗 🔥 📶 ⇄ ⇄ 🅿 VISA ⊙⊙ AE ⓪

❁❁❁ *rte de Suresnes (16th)* ✉ 75016 – 𝒞 01 44 14 41 14 – www.precatelanparis.com
– Closed 3 to 18 March, 4 to 26 August, 27 October-4 November, Sunday and
Monday   **A2**
Rest – Menu 95 € (lunch), 195/250 € – Carte 212/282 € ⌂

♦ Creative ♦ Luxury ♦ Elegant ♦

Based on classic recipes that pay homage to the local produce, Frédéric Anton's inventive cuisine is perfectly accomplished. Each dish is a masterpiece, to be enjoyed to the full amid a magnificent decor of white and silver in the heart of the Bois de Boulogne.

➔ Langoustine en ravioli dans un bouillon à l'huile d'olive au parfum poivre et menthe. Turbot aux algues, pouces-pieds et crevettes grises façon dieppoise. Pomme soufflée croustillante, crème glacée caramel, cidre et sucre pétillant.

La Grande Cascade   🍴 ⇄ ⇄ 🅿 VISA ⊙⊙ AE ⓪

❁ *allée de Longchamp (16th)* ✉ 75016 – 𝒞 01 45 27 33 51
– www.grandecascade.com
Rest – Menu 75/185 € – Carte 140/190 € ⌂

♦ Modern ♦ Luxury ♦

A charming pavilion (1850) just a stone's throw from the large waterfall (Grande Cascade) in the Bois de Boulogne. To savour the refined cuisine here beneath the majestic rotunda or on the delightful terrace is a rare and elegant treat.

➔ Langoustines saisies au poivre sauvage, agnolettis de petits pois et pomme verte. Ris de veau saisi au beurre demi-sel, carottes fondantes et herbes à tortue en sauce. Fraîcheur exotique, émulsion de riz curry-banane.

FRANCE - PARIS

XXX **Relais d'Auteuil** (Patrick Pignol)   🅰🅲 ⌬ 🆅🅸🆂🅰 ⓬ 🅰🅴 ⓞ
£3   *31 bd Murat (16th)* ✉ 75016 – **Ⓜ** *Michel Ange Molitor* – ℰ 01 46 51 09 54
     – www.relaisdauteuil-pignol.com
     – Closed August, Christmas Holidays, Saturday lunch, Sunday and Monday
     Rest – Menu 100 € bi (lunch), 129/149 € – Carte 106/218 € ⅏   **A2**
     ♦ Modern ♦ Elegant ♦ Luxury ♦
     This restaurant's intimate setting highlights the numerous modern paintings
     and sculptures on display. The fine contemporary cuisine is inspired by top qua-
     lity produce, including game in season. Superb wine list, as well as an impres-
     sive choice of champagnes.
     ➜ Amandine de foie gras de canard du Gers et son lobe poêlé, petite
     salade d'herbes. Bar de ligne cuit au four, peau croustillante au poivre.
     Madeleines cuites minute au miel de bruyère, glace miel et noix.

XXX **Benkay** – Novotel Tour Eiffel   ⪜ 🅖 🅐🅒 ⌬ ⌬ 🆅🅸🆂🅰 ⓬ 🅰🅴 ⓞ
     61 quai de Grenelle (15th) – **Ⓜ** *Bir-Hakeim* – ℰ 01 40 58 21 26
     – www.restaurant-benkay.com
     – Closed August   **A2**
     Rest – Menu 39 € (lunch), 86/169 € – Carte 60/120 €
     ♦ Japanese ♦ Exotic ♦ Elegant ♦
     Overlooking the Seine, this restaurant owned by Japan Airlines serves a good
     selection of Japanese cuisine, including sushi, teppanyaki dishes (cooked on a
     grill at your table) and washoku (table service). An enjoyable culinary expe-
     rience.

XXX **Le Quinzième - Cyril Lignac**   🎐 🅰🅲 ⌬ 🆅🅸🆂🅰 ⓬ 🅰🅴
£3   *14 r. Cauchy (15th)* – **Ⓜ** *Javel* – ℰ 01 45 54 43 43
     – www.restaurantlequinzieme.com
     – Closed 2 weeks in August, Saturday and Sunday   **A2-3**
     Rest – Menu 49 € (lunch), 130/175 € bi – Carte 100/120 €
     ♦ Modern ♦
     Cyril Lignac's restaurant is certainly an attractive proposition. It features a chic,
     contemporary decor, a chef's table overlooking the kitchen and above all, ima-
     ginative and harmonious cuisine with a modern touch created with the finest
     ingredients.
     ➜ Grosses langoustines rôties, fine raviole au piment, crème de langous-
     tine au citron vert. Sole cuite doucement en viennoise d'herbes, crevettes
     grises, sauce au vin jaune. Madagascar.

XX   **Au Trou Gascon**   🅰🅲 🆅🅸🆂🅰 ⓬ 🅰🅴
£3   *40 r. Taine (12th)* – **Ⓜ** *Daumesnil* – ℰ 01 43 44 34 26
     – www.autrougascon.fr
     – Closed August, 22 December-1 January, Saturday and Sunday   **D3**
     Rest – Menu 40 € (lunch)/60 € – Carte 55/72 € ⅏
     ♦ South-West of France ♦ Elegant ♦ Fashionable ♦
     This place is well known to connoisuers of the cuisine of the South-West of
     France! More precisely, from the Adour River to the ocean, starting with the ine-
     vitable *cassoulet*, game, or cured ham served "off the bone". The menu also
     branches out to include more creative and contemporary dishes.
     ➜ Infusion de crevettes à la citronnelle et royale coraillée. Lièvre à la mode
     royale, enrichi de foie gras et parfumé à la truffe. Framboises façon vache-
     rin, sorbet de caillé de brebis, granité menthe fraîche.

XX   **Bon**   🎐 🅰🅲 ⌬ ⌬ 🆅🅸🆂🅰 ⓬ 🅰🅴
     25 r. de la Pompe (16th) ✉ 75116 – **Ⓜ** *La Muette* – ℰ 01 40 72 70 00
     – www.restaurantbon.fr   **A2**
     Rest – Menu 32 € bi (weekday lunch) – Carte 42/73 €
     ♦ Creative ♦ Design ♦ Trendy ♦
     This restaurant has three original dining halls designed by Philippe Starck. Each
     has a different ambience: the 'vinothèque', the fireplace room and the library.
     The short and appetising menu showcases fusion food with an array of Sou-
     theast Asian influences.

FRANCE - PARIS

Mansouria   AC VISA ©©

11 r. Faidherbe (11th) – Ⓜ Faidherbe Chaligny – ℰ 01 43 71 00 16
– www.mansouria.fr
– Closed Monday lunch and Sunday   **D2**
Rest – (pre-book) Menu 28/36 € – Carte 32/54 €

♦ Moroccan ♦ Exotic ♦

Tajines, couscous, and crème à la fleur d'oranger are among the aromatic dishes
prepared by the talented female chefs here under the baton of Fatema Hal, an
ethnologist, writer and leading figure in North African gastronomy.

Le Caroubier   AC VISA ©© AE

82 bd Lefèbvre (15th) – Ⓜ Porte de Vanves – ℰ 01 40 43 16 12
– www.restaurant-lecaroubier.com
– Closed 10 to 25 August   **B3**
Rest – Menu 18 € (weekday lunch), 28/55 € bi – Carte 31/45 €

♦ Moroccan ♦ Exotic ♦

Delicate couscous dishes, subtly flavoured and unfussy tajines, and pastillas
blessed with the sun from the Atlas mountains are on offer in this oasis of
calm close to the Porte de Versailles.

A et M Restaurant   🖼 ⌷ VISA ©© AE

136 bd Murat (16th) ✉ 75016 – Ⓜ Porte de St-Cloud – ℰ 01 45 27 39 60
– www.am-restaurant.com
– Closed August, Saturday lunch and Sunday   **A3**
Rest – Menu 34 € – Carte approx. 49 €

♦ Modern ♦ Elegant ♦ Friendly ♦

A true chef's bistro in a chic and welcoming setting. The menu includes dishes
such as calf's head with a ravigote sauce, and velouté of Paimpol beans with
haddock. The menu offers excellent value for money for a Parisian restaurant.

Zébra Square – Hôtel Square   ઙ AC VISA ©© AE ①

3 r. Boulainvilliers (16th) ✉ 75016 – Ⓜ Mirabeau – ℰ 01 44 14 91 91
– www.hotelsquare.com   **A2**
Rest – Carte 40/60 €

♦ Modern ♦ Design ♦

Boasting a decor of yellow walls brightened by contemporary photos and dark
leather banquettes, this restaurant proposes an international style cuisine with
salads, tartares, spring rolls and grilled meats all featuring on the menu.

L'Inattendu   AC VISA ©©

99 r. Blomet (15th) – Ⓜ Vaugirard – ℰ 01 55 76 93 12
– www.restaurant-inattendu.fr
– Closed 3 weeks in August, 2 to 10 January, Sunday and Monday
Rest – Menu 25 € (weekday lunch), 34/43 €   **B3**
– Carte 36/50 €

♦ Modern ♦ Elegant ♦

This small restaurant has a sophisticated, elegant decor. It is run by two experienced partners who opened a fishmonger's next door – a real guarantee of
fresh produce! Reliable, well-presented cuisine with the occasional unexpected
surprise.

Bigarrade   AC VISA ©© AE

106 r. Nollet (17th) – Ⓜ Brochant – ℰ 01 42 26 01 02
– Closed August, Christmas Holidays, Saturday lunch, Sunday and Monday
Rest – (number of covers limited, pre-book) Menu 35 €   **B1**
(lunch), 65/85 €

♦ Creative ♦ Fashionable ♦

A small, stylish restaurant decorated in white and green apple tones, watch the
team run the open kitchen. Impeccable presentation of dishes combining simplicity and invention. No à la carte or set menu choices – guests here trust the
chef's inspiration.
➔ Foie gras, homard rôti et jus pomme verte. Pigeon rôti, tamarin et
cèpes. Crème citron et gelée aux prunes.

FRANCE - PARIS

Mama Shelter – Hôtel Mama Shelter   🍴 🛴 AC VISA ☺☺ AE
109 r. de Bagnolet (20th) – Ⓜ *Gambetta* – ☏ *01 43 48 45 45*
– www.mamashelter.com   **D2**
Rest – Carte 33/58 €
♦ Modern ♦ Design ♦
The simple yet effective culinary options available in this very trendy restaurant bear the hallmark of Alain Senderens. The terrace and the huge 'table d'hôte' in the pizzeria (open non-stop) add to Mama Shelter's relaxed ambience.

Bon Kushikatsu   🛴 AC VISA ☺☺ AE
24 r. Jean-Pierre Timbaud (11th) – Ⓜ *Oberkampf* – ☏ *01 43 38 82 27*
– Closed Sunday and lunch   **C2**
Rest – *(number of covers limited, pre-book)* Menu 58 €
♦ Japanese ♦ Intimate ♦ Elegant ♦
This restaurant is an express trip to Osaka to discover the city's culinary speciality of kushikatsu (meat, vegetables or seafood skewers coated with breadcrumbs and deep-fried). Dish after dish reveals fine flavours, such as: beef sancho, peppered foie gras, and shiitake mushrooms. The courteous service transports you to Japan.

La Marée Passy   ⌐🍴 VISA ☺☺ AE
71 av. P. Doumer (16th) ✉ *75016* – Ⓜ *La Muette* – ☏ *01 45 04 12 81*
– www.lamareepassy.com   **A2**
Rest – Carte 42/56 €
♦ Fish and seafood ♦ Friendly ♦
With its wood panelling, red tones and maritime inspired backdrop, the decor is in perfect harmony with the cuisine, which focuses on fish and seafood. The daily specials board changes according to deliveries from the Atlantic coast.

La Régalade   AC VISA ☺☺
49 av. Jean-Moulin (14th) – Ⓜ *Porte d'Orléans* – ☏ *01 45 45 68 58*
– Closed 25 July-20 August, 1 to 10 January, Monday lunch, Saturday and Sunday   **B3**
Rest – *(pre-book)* Menu 34 € ❀
♦ Traditional ♦ Friendly ♦
A friendly and relaxed bistro serving well-presented and copious seasonal cuisine accompanied by an astutely compiled choice of wines. La Régalade is always full and it is easy to see why. Make sure you book ahead!

Jean-Pierre Frelet   AC VISA ☺☺
25 r. Montgallet (12th) – Ⓜ *Montgallet* – ☏ *01 43 43 76 65*
– Closed 20 to 27 May, 29 July-27 August, Saturday lunch and Sunday
Rest – Menu 30 € (dinner)/35 €   **D2**
♦ Traditional ♦ Friendly ♦ Bistro ♦
The minimalist decor and tightly packed tables create a friendly atmosphere here. Generous portions, with the emphasis firmly on seasonal produce.

Villaret   AC ⌐🍴 (dinner) VISA ☺☺ AE
13 r. Ternaux (11th) – Ⓜ *Parmentier* – ☏ *01 43 57 75 56*
– Closed 3 weeks in August, Saturday lunch and Sunday   **C2**
Rest – Menu 25 € (weekdays), 32/50 € – Carte 40/60 € ❀
♦ Traditional ♦ Friendly ♦ Bistro ♦
This convivial bistro serves appealing seasonal fare: baked eggs with foie gras, salted monkfish, and chocolate biscuits. Good choice of wines.

Auberge Pyrénées Cévennes   AC VISA ☺☺ AE
106 r. de la Folie-Méricourt (11th) – Ⓜ *République* – ☏ *01 43 57 33 78*
– Closed 30 July-20 August, Saturday lunch, Sunday and Bank Holidays
Rest – Menu 31 € – Carte 30/70 €   **C2**
♦ Regional/country ♦ Inn ♦
A fun atmosphere reigns in this restaurant popular with serious gourmets. The female owner's welcome is second to none, while the cuisine – a veritable gastronomic Tour de France – is both delicious and abundant.

FRANCE - PARIS

✗ **Afaria**   🏡 AC VISA ❶❸

15 r. Desnouettes (15th) – Ⓜ *Convention* – ✆ *01 48 42 95 90* – *www.afaria.fr*
– *Closed 6 to 29 August, February Holidays, Sunday and Monday*
Rest – Menu 26 € (weekday lunch)/45 € – Carte 36/54 €   **A-B3**
♦ Creative ♦ Rustic ♦
A welcoming bistro that honours the cuisine of the Basque country. Sample
superb tapas at the counter before feasting on creative gourmet dishes, which
do not shy away from incorporating flavours from around the world. Advance
booking recommended.

✗ **Beurre Noisette**   VISA ❶❸ AC
😊
68 r. Vasco-de-Gama (15th) – Ⓜ *Lourmel* – ✆ *01 48 56 82 49*
– *www.lebeurrenoisette.com* – *Closed 1 to 24 August, Sunday and Monday*
Rest – Menu 30 € (lunch), 35/50 €   **A3**
♦ Modern ♦ Friendly ♦
This warm and welcoming restaurant has been tastefully renovated and now features an enticing table d'hôte. The chef creates his blackboard of daily specials in
line with market availability and his inspiration. Impressive wine selection.

✗ **Le Bélisaire**   VISA ❶❸

2 r. Marmontel (15th) – Ⓜ *Vaugirard* – ✆ *01 48 28 62 24*
– *Closed 28 July-18 August, 24 December-1 January, Saturday lunch and Sunday*
Rest – Menu 24 € (lunch), 33/42 €   **B3**
♦ Traditional ♦ Retro ♦
The old-style bistro atmosphere makes this pleasant restaurant a popular
choice. The chef never misses the chance to revisit tradition through dishes
such as salmon stuffed with goat's cheese, braised ox cheek in red wine, and
peach sabayon, all generously prepared with the freshest ingredients.

✗ **Tintilou**   ⇦ VISA ❶❸
😊
37 bis r. de Montreuil (11th) – Ⓜ *Faidherbe-Chaligny* – ✆ *01 43 72 42 32*
– *www.tintilou.fr*
– *Closed 3 weeks in August, 1 week in February, Saturday lunch and Sunday*
Rest – Menu 25 € (lunch), 35/72 € bi – Carte 35/55 €   **D2**
♦ Modern ♦ Friendly ♦
Cherry red, anise green and saffron yellow all feature in the array of colours that
have transformed this former convenience store into a unique and contemporary restaurant. The ideal setting for refined cuisine with a global influence, with
an emphasis on the very finest ingredients.

✗ **Bistrot Paul Bert**   VISA ❶❸
😊
18 r. Paul-Bert (11th) – Ⓜ *Faidherbe Chaligny* – ✆ *01 43 72 24 01*
– *Closed August, Sunday and Monday*   **D2**
Rest – *(pre-book)* Menu 18 € (weekday lunch)/36 € – Carte 35/59 € ⅌
♦ Traditional ♦ Retro ♦ Bistro ♦
Home cooking is very much to the fore in this friendly bistro, with dishes such as beef
parmentier and steak on the menu. Make sure you save space for the rum baba!

✗ **L'Auberge Aveyronnaise**   🏡 AC VISA ❶❸ AE ⓪
😊
40 r. Gabriel-Lamé (12th) – Ⓜ *Cour St-Émilion* – ✆ *01 43 40 12 24*
– *Closed 1 to 15 August*   **D3**
Rest – Menu 26/32 € – Carte 35/72 €
♦ Regional/country ♦ Rustic ♦ Brasserie ♦
Checked tablecloths and rather rustic decoration help create this corner of the
Aveyron a stone's throw from Bercy Village, with specialities such as "tripoux"
(mutton tripe) and "aligot" (creamed potato with cheese).

✗ **Le Grand Pan**   VISA ❶❸ AE

20 r. Rosenwald (15th) – Ⓜ *Plaisance* – ✆ *01 42 50 02 50* – *www.legrandpan.fr*
– *Closed 1 week in May, 10 to 30 August, Christmas Holidays, Saturday and Sunday*
Rest – Menu 20 € (lunch) – Carte 30/50 €   **B3**
♦ Meats and grills ♦ Bistro ♦ Neighbourhood ♦
A neighbourhood bistro said to have been frequented by Georges Brassens, who
lived nearby. Delicious meat dishes, accompanied by salad or fries, embellish the
specials board, alongside lobster, scallops etc. All are of an undeniably high quality.

FRANCE - PARIS

※ **Pramil** VISA ⓪⓪

9 r. Vertbois (3rd) – Ⓜ Temple – ℰ 01 42 72 03 60
– www.pramilrestaurant.fr
– Closed 30 April-7 May, 19 August-2 September, 23 to 29 December, Sunday
lunch and Monday **C2**
Rest – Menu 33 € – Carte 38/48 €
♦ Modern ♦ Bistro ♦

The elegant yet restrained decor helps focus the senses on the attractive and honest seasonal cuisine conjured up by Alain Pramil. He is a self-taught chef passionate about food who, in another life, was a physics teacher!

※ **La Fourchette du Printemps** (Nicolas Mouton) VISA ⓪⓪
ⓢ
30 r. du Printemps (17th) – Ⓜ Wagram – ℰ 01 42 27 26 97
– Closed August, 24 December-1 January, Sunday and Monday **B1**
Rest – (number of covers limited, pre-book) Menu 49/75 €
– Carte lunch approx. 58 €
♦ Modern ♦ Bistro ♦

Enjoy springtime throughout the year in this contemporary bistro which stands out from the crowd, where the two young chefs, both trained in a number of top restaurants, accentuate the full flavour of their cuisine. Even simplicity is done with finesse here.
➔ Cuisine du marché.

※ **Les Cailloux** VISA ⓪⓪
ⓐ
58 r. des Cinq-Diamants (13th) – Ⓜ Corvisart – ℰ 01 45 80 15 08
– www.lescailloux.fr – Closed 1 week in August **C3**
Rest – Menu 18 € bi (lunch) – Carte 25/60 €
♦ Italian ♦ Bistro ♦

The Butte-aux-Cailles district is home to many restaurants, including this informal Italian bistro that serves delicious sun-blessed food at reasonable prices.

※ **L'Ourcine** VISA ⓪⓪
ⓐ
92 r. Broca (13th) (opening scheduled in springtime after renovation)
– Ⓜ Les Gobelins – ℰ 01 47 07 13 65
– Closed 3 weeks in August, Sunday and Monday **C3**
Rest – Menu 34 €
♦ Traditional ♦ Bistro ♦

L'Ourcine makes a virtue of quality ingredients and unpretentious cooking. A little bistro like they used to make them, offering inspired dishes that follow the seasons. Delicious daily set menu as well as specials on the blackboards.

※ **Jadis** VISA ⓪⓪ Ⓐ Ⓔ

208 r. de la Croix-Nivert (15th) – Ⓜ Convention – ℰ 01 45 57 73 20
– www.bistrot-jadis.com
– Closed 3 weeks in August, Saturday and Sunday **A3**
Rest – Menu 29 € (lunch), 36/65 € – Carte 45/65 €
♦ Modern ♦ Bistro ♦

Although its name translates as 'olden days', this bistro is very much contemporary in style. This image is heightened by its young, friendly and enthusiastic chef who proposes menu choices that change with the seasons. These include dishes such as: pike perch in sorrel broth and Basque pork with braised lettuce.

※ **Chez Marie-Louise** VISA ⓪⓪
ⓐ
11 r. Marie-et-Louise (10th) – Ⓜ Goncourt – ℰ 01 53 19 02 04
– www.chezmarielouise.com – Closed August, Saturday and Sunday
Rest – Menu 18 € (lunch) – Carte 28/38 € **C2**
♦ Traditional ♦ Bistro ♦

You will eat well in this small neo-bistro just a stone's throw from the St Martin canal. The simple, delicious dishes on the blackboard include salmon ceviche, shoulder of lamb with cumin, black pudding with herbs and spices, and a selection of tasty desserts.

FRANCE - PARIS

✗ **Schmidt - L'Os à Moelle** 🛜 VISA ⓒⓞ AE

3 r. Vasco-de-Gama (15th) – Ⓜ *Lourmel* – ℰ *01 45 57 27 27*
– Closed 2 weeks in August, Sunday and Monday **A3**
Rest – Menu 29 € (lunch), 38/43 € – Carte 45/57 €
♦ Traditional ♦ Friendly ♦ Bistro ♦

Pâté en croûte, sea bass with ceps and potatoes, honey and spice roasted quince... A young chef originally from Alsace proposes fresh and tasty market-inspired cuisine in this popular neighbourhood restaurant.

✗ **Impérial Choisy** AE VISA ⓒⓞ
☺

32 av. de Choisy (13th) – Ⓜ *Porte de Choisy* – ℰ *01 45 86 42 40*
Rest – Carte 18/32 € **C3**
♦ Chinese ♦ Minimalist ♦

A genuine Chinese restaurant frequented by many local Chinese who use it as their lunchtime canteen. Hardly surprising given the delicious Cantonese specials on offer!

✗ **Caffé dei Cioppi** 🛜 VISA ⓒⓞ
☺

159 r. du Faubourg-St-Antoine (11th) – Ⓜ *Ledru Rollin* – ℰ *01 43 46 10 14*
– Closed 3 weeks in August, Christmas Holidays, Saturday, Sunday and Monday
Rest – *(number of covers limited, pre-book)* Carte 26/41 € **C-D2**
♦ Italian ♦ Neighbourhood ♦

This tiny, spartan restaurant will take your breath away. She is from Milan, he is from Sicily and their cuisine has all the charm of their native country. Specialities include charcuterie, risotto and spaghetti with clams.

LA DÉFENSE *Plan I*

🏨 **Pullman La Défense** 🛜 ƙ ৬ rm, AE 🛜 🕍 🚗 VISA ⓒⓞ AE ⓞ

11 av. Arche (exit La Défense 6) ✉ *92081* – Ⓜ *La Défense*
– ℰ *01 47 17 50 00 – www.pullmanhotels.com*
381 rm – †185/580 € ††185/580 €, ☲ 25 € – 1 suite
Rest *Avant Seine* – ℰ *01 47 17 50 99 (closed Friday dinner, Saturday, Sunday and Bank Holidays)* Carte 60/88 €
♦ Luxury ♦ Business ♦ Modern ♦

Beautiful architecture, resembling a ship's hull, a combination of glass and ochre stonework. Spacious, elegant rooms, lounges and very well-equipped auditorium (with simultaneous translation booths). The Avant Seine offers you quality designer décor and spit-roast dishes.

🏨 **Renaissance La Défense** ƙ ৬ rm, AE 🛜 🕍 🚗 VISA ⓒⓞ AE

60 Jardin de Valmy (on the ring-road, exit La Défense 7) ✉ *92918*
– Ⓜ *La Défense* – ℰ *01 41 97 50 50 – www.renaissanceladefense.fr*
324 rm – †169/279 € ††184/294 €, ☲ 27 € – 3 suites
Rest – *(closed Saturday, Sunday and Bank Holidays) (dinner only)*
Menu 36 € – Carte 47/68 €
♦ Luxury ♦ Business ♦ Personalised ♦

Luxurious sophistication defines this contemporary hotel at the foot of the Grande Arche: quality materials, flawless comfort and inviting, perfectly equipped guestrooms. This brasserie serves traditional dishes and seasonal suggestions overlooking the Valmy gardens.

🏨 **Hilton La Défense** ƙ ৬ rm, AE 🛜 🕍 VISA ⓒⓞ AE ⓞ

2 pl. de la Défense ✉ *92053* – Ⓜ *La Défense* – ℰ *01 46 92 10 10*
– www.hilton.com
153 rm – †199/440 € ††199/440 €, ☲ 26 € – 9 suites
Rest *Côté Parvis* – *(closed lunch Saturday and Sunday)* Menu 55 € (lunch) – Carte 45/75 €
♦ Business ♦ Chain hotel ♦ Modern ♦

Hotel situated within the CNIT complex. Some of the rooms have been particularly designed with the business traveller in mind: work, rest, relaxation and Jacuzzi tubs in the bathrooms. At Côté Parvis, modern cuisine and a fine view of the Arch of La Défense.

Sofitel Paris La Défense
34 cours Michelet (on the ring-road, exit La Défense 4) ⊠ *92060 Puteaux*
– **Ⓜ** *Esplanade de la Défense* – ☎ *01 47 76 44 43*
– *www.sofitel-paris-ladefense.com*
151 rm – ♦205/575 € ♦♦205/575 €, ⊆ 27 €
Rest *L'Italian Lounge* – ☎ *01 47 76 72 40* – Menu 51 € (weekdays)
– Carte 55/85 €
♦ Luxury ♦ Chain hotel ♦ Design ♦
This business hotel not far from the CNIT and Grande Arche blends in perfectly with the high-rise buildings of the Défense district. Spacious, well-equipped guestrooms, as well as a restaurant (Mediterranean cuisine) and small fitness suite.

Novotel La Défense
2 bd Neuilly (exit La Défense 1) ⊠ *92081* – **Ⓜ** *Esplanade de la Défense*
– ☎ *01 41 45 23 23* – *www.novotel.com*   **A1**
280 rm – ♦139/390 € ♦♦139/490 €, ⊆ 17 €
Rest – Carte 25/40 €
♦ Business ♦ Chain hotel ♦ Modern ♦
This Novotel is situated on the edge of the La Défense district and overlooks the Seine. If travelling by car, don't miss the exit onto the circular boulevard. Around 30 rooms have been renovated in a resolutely contemporary style, as has the Novotel Café. Fitness centre on the 14th floor.

PARIS AIRPORT ORLY

Hilton Orly
(near Orly Sud airport) ⊠ *94544* – ☎ *01 45 12 45 12* – *www.hilton.fr*
340 rm – ♦99/400 € ♦♦99/400 €, ⊆ 20 €
Rest – Menu 30 € – Carte 42/110 €
♦ Chain hotel ♦ Business ♦
A popular choice for corporate clients, this 1960s hotel has a designer interior, discreet yet elegant bedrooms and state of the art business facilities. The Hilton's contemporary-style restaurant focuses on traditional cuisine.

Mercure Orly
allée Cdt Mouchotte (exit Orlytech) ⊠ *94547* – ☎ *01 49 75 15 50*
– *www.mercure.com*
192 rm – ♦110/230 € ♦♦110/230 €, ⊆ 16 €
Rest – *(closed lunch Saturday and Sunday)* Carte 32/42 €
♦ Chain hotel ♦ Functional ♦
This Mercure is a convenient option for stopover passengers. Friendly service, a pleasant verdant setting, and bedrooms which have been revamped in contemporary tones. Bar snacks and traditional dishes adapted to the timetables of travellers in transit.

PARIS AIRPORT ROISSY

À L'AÉROGARE N° 2

Sheraton Roissy
– ☎ *01 49 19 70 70* – *www.sheraton.com/parisairport*
252 rm – ♦189/499 € ♦♦189/499 €, ⊆ 32 €
Rest *Les Étoiles* – see restaurant listing
Rest *Les Saisons* – Carte 36/67 €
♦ Chain hotel ♦ Modern ♦
The only hotel at Roissy with a direct link to terminal 2, opposite the TGV station. The stopover is tempting in this futuristic building with its accent on comfort. Elegant guestrooms with views of the runway.

XXX **Les Étoiles** – Hôtel Sheraton

– ✆ 01 41 84 64 54 – www.sheraton.com/parisairport
– *Closed August, 20 December-5 January, Saturday, Sunday and Bank Holidays*
Rest – Menu 52 € (weekdays) – Carte 61/97 €

♦ Modern ♦ Elegant ♦

The fine dining restaurant at the Sheraton hotel, at the foot of terminal 2. Elegant setting, French cuisine: perfect for a business meal…and for those in a rush too, with the menu "served in 1 hour" (vegetarian option available).

À ROISSYPOLE

 Hilton Roissy

– ✆ 01 49 19 77 77 – www.hilton.com
385 rm – ♦160/600 € ♦♦160/600 €, ☲ 25 €
Rest *Les Aviateurs* – ✆ 01 49 19 77 95 – Menu 38 € (weekdays)
– Carte 40/65 €

♦ Business ♦ Modern ♦

Bold architecture, glass, light and space are the signatures of this huge hotel. Cutting-edge fixtures and fittings make it as pleasant for work as it is for leisure.

 Pullman Roissy

Zone centrale Ouest – ✆ 01 49 19 29 29 – www.pullmanhotels.com
339 rm – ♦135/570 € ♦♦135/570 €, ☲ 22 € – 5 suites
Rest *L'Escale* – Carte 40/60 €

♦ Business ♦ Classic ♦

The Pullman was the first hotel to be built at Roissy between the two terminals. It offers classic, comfortable rooms, in addition to an impressive range of services. These include seminar rooms, an indoor pool, a fitness area and fitness trail in the park.

À ROISSY-VILLE

 Marriott Roissy

allée du Verger – ✆ 01 34 38 53 53 – www.parismarriottcharlesdegaulle.fr
297 rm – ♦109/459 € ♦♦109/459 €, ☲ 22 € – 3 suites
Rest – Menu 35 € – Carte 35/60 €

♦ Business ♦ Classic ♦

Ideal for business travellers staying overnight in Paris who appreciate the good things in life. This establishment is both classic in style (colonnades, period furniture) and in comfort (fitness area, sauna, brasserie).

 Novotel Convention et Wellness

allée du Verger – ✆ 01 30 18 20 00
– www.novotel.com
295 rm – ♦99/450 € ♦♦99/450 €, ☲ 19 € – 7 suites
Rest – Carte 23/48 €

♦ Chain hotel ♦ Modern ♦

This modern hotel offers impressive services, ranging from a huge conference area with an integrated network to a kids' corner and a fully equipped business centre. In the contemporary setting of the spacious Novotel Café, guests can enjoy traditional brasserie fare and a menu focused on healthy eating.

Mercure Roissy

allée du Verger – ✆ 01 34 29 40 00
– www.mercure-paris-roissy-charles-de-gaulle.com
203 rm – ♦85/175 € ♦♦115/225 €, ☲ 18 € – 8 suites
Rest – Carte 27/50 €

♦ Business ♦ Classic ♦

This hotel reserves a particular welcome for the individual traveller (as opposed to seminars and groups). Spacious guestrooms in relaxing tones. The restaurant is worthy of note too, with its traditional cuisine and reasonable prices.

LYONS
LYON

Population: 479 803

Calzada/Fotolia.com

Lyons is a city that needs a second look, because the first one may be to its disadvantage: from the outlying autoroute, drivers get a vision of the petrochemical industry. But strip away that industrial façade and look what lies within: the gastronomic epicentre of France; a wonderfully characterful old town of medieval and Renaissance buildings with a World Heritage Site stamp of approval; and the peaceful flow of two mighty rivers. Lyons largely came of age in the 16C thanks to its silk industry; many of the city's finest buildings were erected by Italian merchants who flocked here at the time. What they left behind was the largest Renaissance quarter in France, with glorious architecture and an imposing cathedral.

Nowadays it's an energised city whose modern industries give it a 21C feel but that hasn't pervaded the three-hour lunch ethos of the older quarters. The rivers Saône and Rhône provide the liquid heart of the city. Modern Lyons in the shape of the new Villeurbanne and La Part Dieu districts are to the east of the Rhône. The medieval sector, the old town, is west of the Saône. Between the two rivers is a peninsula, the Presqu'ile, which is indeed almost an island. This area is renowned for its red-roofed 16C and 17C houses. Just north of here on a hill is the old silk-weavers' district, La Croix-Rousse.

LYONS IN...

→ **ONE DAY**
Old town including funicular up Fourvière hill, Musée des Beaux-Arts.

→ **TWO DAYS**
Musée des Tissus, La Croix-Rousse, evening river trip, Opera House.

→ **THREE DAYS**
Traboule hunting (map in hand), antique shops in rue Auguste Comte.

PRACTICAL INFORMATION

ARRIVAL-DEPARTURE

 Lyon Saint Exupéry Airport is 27km east of the city centre.
The Express Bus takes around 45min and runs every 20min.

GETTING AROUND

The transport system in the city includes the funicular, as well as the bus, tram and metro. The 'Liberty' ticket is valid for one day's travel on the network; you can also buy single tickets and a carnet of ten tickets. The Lyons City Card is available for 1, 2 or 3 days, and grants unlimited access to the transport network, plus many museums (including the Roman ruins in St-Romain-en-Gal), short river trips and guided city tours. The card is available from the tourist office and major public transport offices. Lyons boasts one of Europe's biggest 'swipe a bike' schemes: using a smart card, you can help yourself to a bicycle at one of two hundred places around town.

CALENDAR HIGHLIGHTS

March
International Fair.

May
Nuits Sonores (Electronic music).

June
Fête de la Musique, Fourvière Festival .

July
Bastille Day celebrations.

September
Lyons Dance Biennial.

October
Red Carpet Antiques Festival.

November
Baroque Music Festival.

December
Festival of Lights.

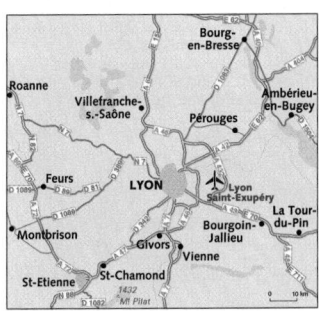

EATING OUT

Lyons is a great place for food. In the old town virtually every square metre is occupied by a restaurant but if you want a real encounter with the city, step inside a Lyonnais bouchon. These provide the true gastronomic heartbeat of the city - authentic little establishments where the cuisine revolves around the sort of thing the silk workers ate all those years ago: tripe, pigs' trotters, calf's head; fish lovers go for quenelles. For the most atmospheric example of the bouchon, try one in a tunnel-like recess inside a medieval building in the old town. Lyons also has plenty of restaurants serving dishes from every region in France and is a city that loves its wine: it's said that Lyons is kept afloat on three rivers: the Saône, the Rhône and the Beaujolais. Furthermore, the locals still enthusiastically embrace the true concept of lunch and so, unlike in many cities, you can enjoy a midday meal that continues for quite a few hours. With the reputation the city has for its restaurants, it's usually advisable to book ahead.

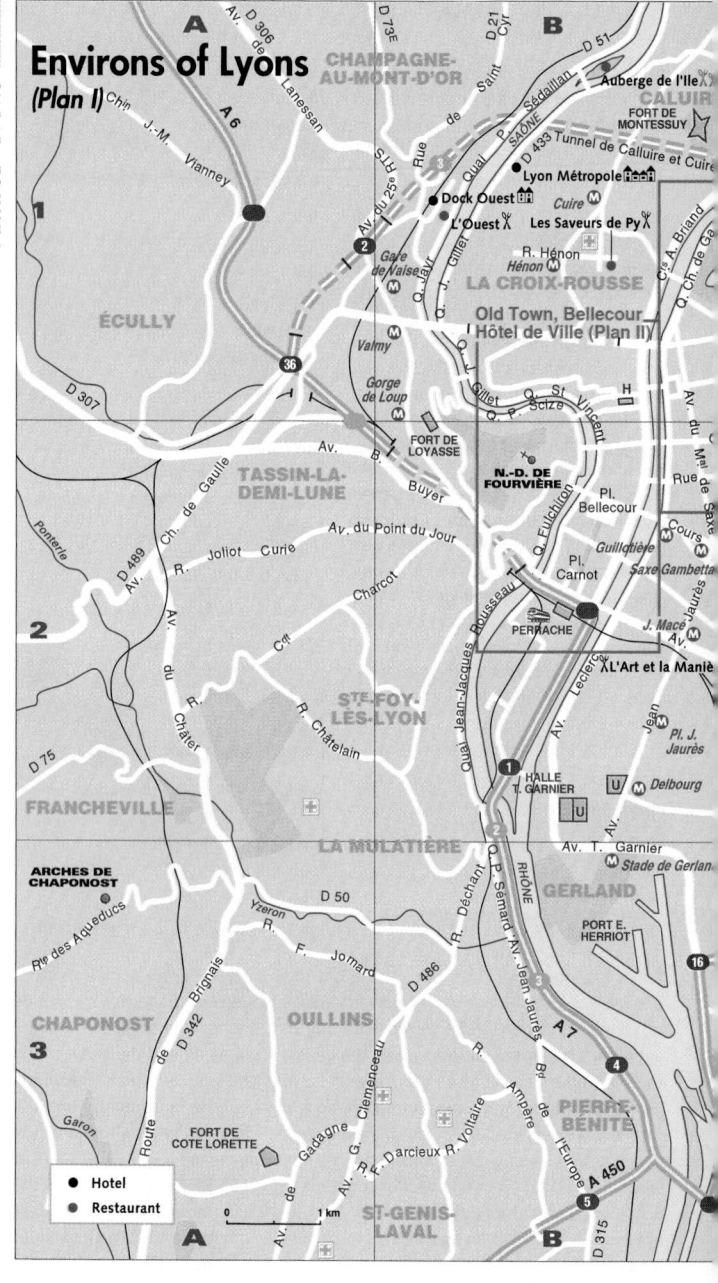

Environs of Lyons
(Plan I)

PARC DE LOISIRS DE MIRIBEL-JONAGE

ÎLE DE LA PAPE

D 48

D 483

RHÔNE

ET CUIRE

Rte de Strasbourg

N 346

A 42

Av. 8 Mai 1945

Bd L. Bonnevay

Canal de Jonage

VAULX-EN-VELIN

Av. M. Cachin

Av. Ch. de Gaulle

Av. S. Allende

Av. G. Péri

Marcelin

Av. Grandclément

D 317

PARC DE LA TÊTE D'OR

U

R. Salengro

D 383

Les Brotteaux, Cité Internationale, La Part-Dieu (Plan III)

République-Villeurbanne

Cours Émile Zola

Gratte-Ciel

Flachet

Cusset

L. Bonnevay

Av. de Bohlen

rs Vitton

VILLEURBANNE

R. du 4 Août 1789

Blum

R. de la Poudrette

Salengro

Av. F. Roosevelt D 112

Lafayette

ervient

LA PART-DIEU

Cours Tolstoï

R.

Léon

LA PART-DIEU

Garibaldi

R. J. Jaurès

Faure

Route

de

Bd L. Bonnevay

Genas

Av.

D 29

BRON

Av. F. Roosevelt

Bd Ch. de Gaulle

Gambetta

Av. Garibaldi

Sans-Souci

Montplaisir Lumière

A. Thomas

Cours

Grange-Blanche

Pinel

Av. P. Brossolette

Berthelot

CHÂTEAU LUMIÈRE

Av. Rockefeller

Avenue

Bd des États Unis

Bd Jean XXIII

Laënnec

U

Bd

FORT DE BRON

D 112

CHASSIEU

Route

Av. Mermoz

MONPLAISIR

Av. Paul Santy

Mermoz Pinel

A 43

Franklin

D 506

Roosevelt

D 306

de

Vienne

D 383

Bd L. Bonnevay

Joliot Curie

Parilly

Av. Ch. de Gaulle

Av. J. Guesde

PARC DE PARILLY

Bd de Parilly D 102

Rue du

Dauphiné

A 43

Av. J. Jaurès

VÉNISSIEUX

Av. de la République

R. G. Péri

Gare de Vénissieux

Bd A. Croizat

R. du Lyonnais

Chin du Charbonnier

D 318

ST-PRIEST

R. Gambetta

ST-FONS

Bd Av. M.

Thorez

Av. J. Cagne Av. M. Cachin

Yves D 307 Farge

R. A. Briand

LYON-ST EXUPÉRY

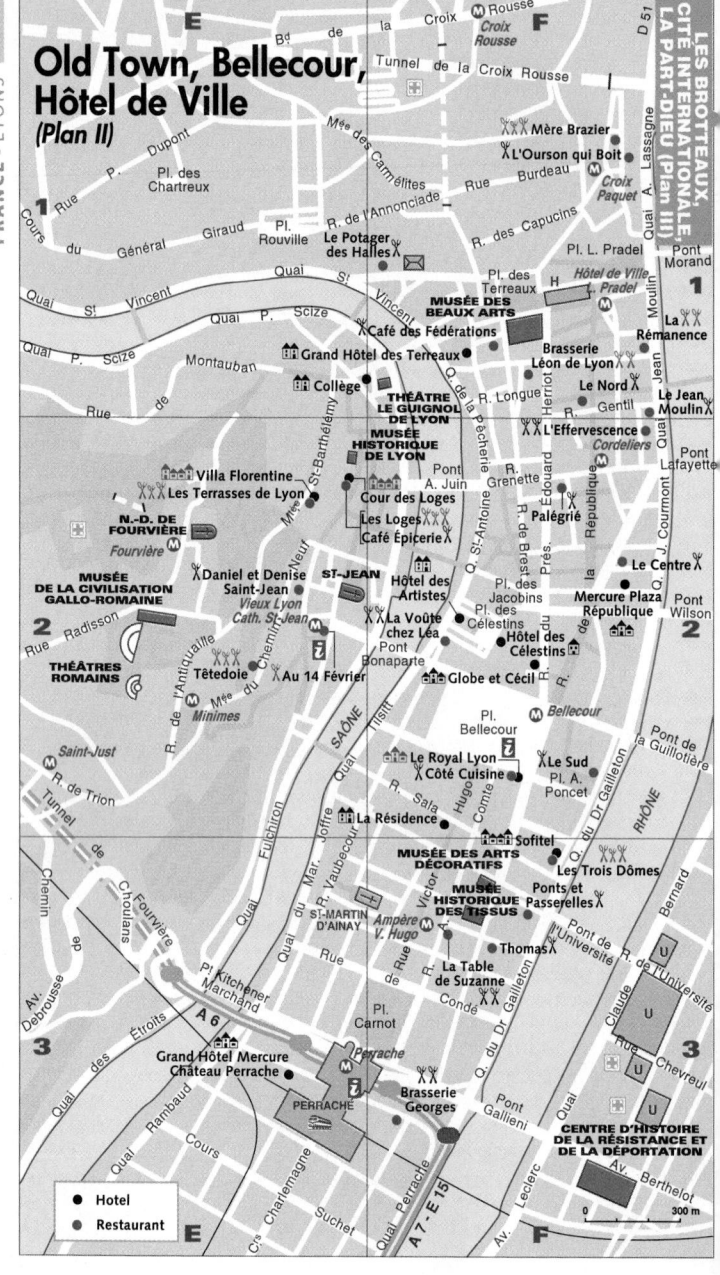

Old Town, Bellecour, Hôtel de Ville
(Plan II)

FRANCE - LYONS

Sofitel ⟨ 🛴 ⚲ & rm, 🄰 🛜 🦺 🕳 VISA ©© AE ①

20 quai Gailleton ✉ *69002* – Ⓜ *Bellecour* – 𝒞 *04 72 41 20 20*
– *www.sofitel.com*   **F3**
135 rm – †230/380 € ††230/380 €, � 26 € – 29 suites
Rest *Les Trois Dômes* ⊛ – see restaurant listing
Rest *Silk Brasserie* – 𝒞 *04 72 41 20 80* – Menu 26 € – Carte 31/54 €
♦ Business ♦ Luxury ♦ Modern ♦
A luxurious and elegant Sofitel in a contemporary building with futuristic facilities. Bill Clinton stayed in the presidential suite here. There are two options for dinner: the beautiful Trois Dômes restaurant or Le Silk restaurant (international menu, sleek setting).

Le Royal Lyon ⟨ 🄰 🛜 🕳 VISA ©© AE ①

20 pl. Bellecour ✉ *69002* – Ⓜ *Bellecour* – 𝒞 *04 78 37 57 31*
– *www.lyonhotel-leroyal.com*   **F2**
69 rm – †175/390 € ††175/390 €, ⊡ 25 € – 5 suites
Rest *Côté Cuisine* – see restaurant listing
♦ Luxury ♦ Traditional ♦ Elegant ♦
The Royal opened in 1912 and attracted visitors with its refined comfort. One hundred years later, it has lost none of its old-fashioned charm with its mouldings and toile de Jouy.

Globe et Cécil *without rest* 🄰 🛜 🦺 VISA ©© AE ①

21 r. Gasparin ✉ *69002* – Ⓜ *Bellecour* – 𝒞 *04 78 42 58 95*
– *www.globeetcecilhotel.com*   **F2**
60 rm ⊡ – †116/149 € ††148/186 €
♦ Traditional ♦ Classic ♦ Personalised ♦
This late 19C hotel right in the middle of the town centre has charming rooms (parquet flooring and fireplace in some).

Mercure Plaza République *without rest* & 🄰 🛜 🦺

5 r. Stella ✉ *69002* – Ⓜ *Cordeliers*   VISA ©© AE ①
– 𝒞 *04 78 37 50 50* – *www.mercure.com*   **F2**
78 rm – †119/219 € ††119/219 €, ⊡ 18 €
♦ Business ♦ Chain hotel ♦ Functional ♦
This pleasant chain hotel is well located and very popular with business travellers (meeting rooms).

Grand Hôtel des Terreaux *without rest* 🗔 🛜 VISA ©© AE ①

16 r. Lanterne ✉ *69001* – Ⓜ *Hôtel de Ville* – 𝒞 *04 78 27 04 10*
– *www.hotel-lyon.fr*   **F1**
53 rm – †77/107 € ††128/162 €, ⊡ 15 €
♦ Traditional ♦ Classic ♦
This 19C post house is conducive to relaxing in the centre of town. Find tastefully decorated rooms, a small indoor pool and attentive service.

Hôtel des Artistes *without rest* 🄰 🛜 VISA ©© AE ①

8 r. Gaspard-André ✉ *69002* – Ⓜ *Bellecour* – 𝒞 *04 78 42 04 88*
– *www.hoteldesartistes.fr*   **F2**
45 rm – †92/129 € ††125/149 €, ⊡ 12 €
♦ Business ♦ Modern ♦
It is impossible to miss the "curtain up" from this hotel next to the Célestins theatre. At bedtime, enjoy sweet dreams in one of the neat and fresh guestrooms.

La Résidence *without rest* & 🄰 🛜 VISA ©© AE ①

18 r. V. Hugo ✉ *69002* – Ⓜ *Bellecour* – 𝒞 *04 78 42 63 28*
– *www.hotel-la-residence.com*   **F2**
67 rm – †94 € ††94 €, ⊡ 8 €
♦ Business ♦ Traditional ♦ Functional ♦
Hotel run by the same family since the 1960s. The rooms are quite old-fashioned but comfortable and very clean.

Hôtel des Célestins without rest 🏨 🛜 VISA ⓒ

4 r. des Archers ✉ 69002 – Ⓜ Bellecour – ℰ 04 72 56 08 98
– www.hotelcelestins.com   F2
29 rm – †70/104 € ††84/114 €, � 10 €
♦ Traditional ♦ Functional ♦ Personalised ♦

A hotel in a residential building is rather unusual. Pleasant rooms including a
very attractive junior suite on the fifth floor (large Italian-style shower, flat screen
TV, etc).

Les Trois Dômes – Hôtel Sofitel ⩽ AC ⌀ VISA ⓒ AE ⓪

20 quai Gailleton (8th floor) ✉ 69002 – Ⓜ Bellecour – ℰ 04 72 41 20 97
– www.les-3-domes.com
– Closed 22 July-20 August, 3 to 11 March, Sunday and Monday
Rest – Menu 47 € (lunch), 79/125 € – Carte 113/136 € ⅋⅋   F3
♦ Modern ♦ Formal ♦

On the top floor of the hotel, you'll find flavourful and inventive cuisine, with well-
chosen food and wine pairings. The setting is elegant and minimalist, with a
theme recalling the craft of the Lyon silk weavers. Magical views over the city.
→ Quenelle de brochet aux écrevisses. Tourte de homard, sauce américaine au vin des Côtes du Rhône. Soufflé chaud guanaja intense, gourman-
dise jivara et crème glacée lactée.

Mère Brazier (Mathieu Viannay) AC ⌀ ⌀ VISA ⓒ AE

12 r. Royale ✉ 69001 – Ⓜ Hôtel de Ville – ℰ 04 78 23 17 20
– www.lamerebrazier.fr
– Closed 3 to 27 August, 1 week in February, Saturday and Sunday
Rest – Menu 50 € (lunch), 70/135 € – Carte 105/145 € ⅋⅋   F1
♦ Modern ♦ Elegant ♦ Formal ♦

The guardian of Lyon cuisine, Eugénie Brazier (1895-1977) is without doubt looking down on Mathieu Viannay – winner of the Meilleur Ouvrier de France
award – with pride. Emblematic restaurant where high-powered classics and
creativity continue to be served.
→ Artichaut et foie gras. Poularde de Bresse demi-deuil, petits légumes et
cerises au vinaigre. Paris-brest en ligne directe, glace aux noisettes caramélisées et pralin.

Brasserie Léon de Lyon 🍴 AC ⌀ VISA ⓒ AE

1 r. Pleney (corner of r. du Plâtre) ✉ 69001 – Ⓜ Hôtel de Ville
– ℰ 04 72 10 11 12 – www.leondelyon.com   F1
Rest – Menu 24 € (weekdays), 31/35 € – Carte 37/50 € ⅋⅋
♦ Traditional ♦ Brasserie ♦ Formal ♦

This Lyon institution founded in 1904 has kept its affluent setting and its convivial
atmosphere. Excellent ingredients combine to produce hearty gourmet dishes.

La Rémanence ⴟ AC ⌀ VISA ⓒ AE

31 r. du Bât-d'Argent ✉ 69001 – Ⓜ Hôtel de Ville – ℰ 04 72 00 08 08
– www.laremanence.fr
– Closed Sunday and Monday   F1
Rest – Menu 37/71 € – Carte 47/68 €
♦ Modern ♦ Elegant ♦ Fashionable ♦

Spinach cream and striped mullet, game pie with flaky pastry – modern day cuisine served with reverence under the vaults of this elegant 16C Jesuit refectory.

L'Effervescence (Christophe Hubert) VISA ⓒ AE

15 r. Claudia ✉ 69002 – Ⓜ Cordeliers – ℰ 04 78 37 23 89
– www.restaurant-effervescence.fr
– Closed 1 week in August, Saturday lunch and Sunday   F2
Rest – Menu 22 € (lunch), 29/41 €
♦ Modern ♦ Elegant ♦

Spontaneity and sparkle: L'Effervescence sums it up! Cooking is dynamic with
Christophe Hubert, a young but already experienced chef. His dishes are the result
of his inspiration, and the suggestions of his (quality) suppliers. He uses even the
simplest ingredients to good effect and cooks with accuracy and precision.
→ Menu du marché.

FRANCE - LYONS

XX **La Table de Suzanne**   🌿 AC VISA ⬤⬤ AE

37 r. Auguste-Comte ✉ *69002 –* Ⓜ *Ampère –* ✆ *04 78 37 49 83*
– www.latabledesuzanne.com
– Closed 28 July-20 August, Sunday and Monday   **F3**
Rest – Menu 22 € (lunch)/52 € – Carte 53/69 €
♦ Modern ♦ Elegant ♦
A refined restaurant in the antique district where "gastronomic" cuisine is brought
up to date. For example, the mushroom crémeux and the sea bass tartare.

XX **Brasserie Georges**   🌿 & ⇔ VISA ⬤⬤ AE

30 cours de Verdun ✉ *69002 –* Ⓜ *Perrache –* ✆ *04 72 56 54 54*
– www.brasseriegeorges.com   **F3**
Rest – Menu 20/26 € – Carte 25/50 €
♦ Traditional ♦ Brasserie ♦ Retro ♦
'Good beer and good cheer since 1836' in the jealously guarded Art Deco set-
ting of this brasserie that is a veritable institution.

XX **La Voûte - Chez Léa**   AC VISA ⬤⬤ AE

11 pl. A. Gourju ✉ *69002 –* Ⓜ *Bellecour –* ✆ *04 78 42 01 33*
– Closed Sunday and Bank Holidays   **F2**
Rest – Menu 19 € (weekday lunch), 30/41 € – Carte 35/44 €
♦ Traditional ♦ Friendly ♦ Traditional ♦
One of the oldest restaurants in Lyon. In a welcoming atmosphere, tradition car-
ries on with verve. Fine menu with tasty regional dishes and game in autumn.

X **Le Nord**   & AC ⇔ VISA ⬤⬤ AE

18 r. Neuve ✉ *69002 –* Ⓜ *Hôtel de Ville –* ✆ *04 72 10 69 69*
– www.nordsudbrasseries.com   **F1**
Rest – Menu 25 € (weekdays)/35 € – Carte 28/55 €
♦ Traditional ♦ Retro ♦ Brasserie ♦
Benches, mosaic floors, wood panelling, spherical lamps: a 1900 decor in this
brasserie – the first opened by the chef Paul Bocuse. The dishes are anchored
in tradition.

X **Le Sud**   🌿 AC VISA ⬤⬤ AE ⓿

11 pl. Antonin-Poncet ✉ *69002 –* Ⓜ *Bellecour –* ✆ *04 72 77 80 00*
– www.nordsudbrasseries.com   **F2**
Rest – Menu 25 € (weekdays), 33/49 € – Carte 30/55 €
♦ Traditional ♦ Brasserie ♦ Mediterranean ♦
This brasserie from the Paul Bocuse stable evokes the Mediterranean in its
colourful decor and sun-filled cuisine. The terrace in summer feels like the
south of France.

X **Thomas**   AC VISA ⬤⬤ AE

6 r. Laurencin ✉ *69002 –* Ⓜ *Bellecour –* ✆ *04 72 56 04 76*
– www.restaurant-thomas.com
– Closed 3 weeks in August, 24 December-2 January, Saturday and Sunday
Rest – Menu 19 € (lunch), 43/59 €   **F3**
Rest Comptoir Thomas – ✆ *04 72 41 92 99* – Carte 25/55 €
♦ Modern ♦ Bistro ♦ Friendly ♦
This cosy, modern bistro is under the auspices of a young chef who communi-
cates his passion for delicious, refined cuisine (monthly changing menu). Nea-
rby there are two annexes that are just as nice, including the trendy Comptoir
serving Spanish grill dishes.

X **Palégrié**   AC VISA ⬤⬤ AE

8 r. Palais-Grillet ✉ *69002 –* Ⓜ *Cordeliers –* ✆ *04 78 92 94 84 – www.palegrie.fr*
– Closed 5 to 25 August, Monday lunch, Saturday dinner and Sunday
Rest – *(number of covers limited, pre-book)* Menu 22 €   **F2**
(lunch), 28/38 €
♦ Modern ♦ Friendly ♦
Two thirtysomethings with flawless CVs – he as a chef, she as a sommelier
– created this restaurant full of freshness at the start of 2012, and clearly it becomes them. The wines enhance the dishes, which are spot on and show an
appreciation of the ingredients and a sense of finesse. Passion and conviviality...

X

Le Centre
                               🚫 📠 ⇄ 🆅🅸🆂🅰 ⊕ 🅰🅴 ①

14 r. Grolée ✉ *69002* – ⓜ *Cordeliers* – ℰ *04 72 04 44 44*
– *www.georgesblanc.com*   **F2**
Rest – Menu 22 € (weekday lunch)/26 € – Carte 38/75 €
♦ Modern ♦ Fashionable ♦ Friendly ♦

Georges Blanc, the renowned chef from Vonnas, is behind this contemporary brasserie launched in late 2012. On the menu, meat, and only the finest: charolais or Wagyu beef, lamb from the Aveyron, or Bresse poultry, with a large choice of sauces and garnishes to accompany. Carnivores take note!

X
☺

Ponts et Passerelles
                                    🍽 📠 🆅🅸🆂🅰 ⊕

5 pl. Dr.-Gailleton ✉ *69002* – ⓜ *Bellecour* – ℰ *04 78 38 70 70*
– *www.pontsetpasserelles.com*
– *Closed 11 August-2 September, 29 December-12 January, Sunday and Monday*   **F3**
Rest – *(number of covers limited, pre-book)* Menu 19 € (weekday lunch), 26/34 € – Carte 29/41 €
♦ Modern ♦ Friendly ♦ Bistro ♦

This friendly "neo-bistro" has a contemporary interior with some nice retro touches. The kitchen serves high quality seasonal food with the accent on local produce.

X

Côté Cuisine – Hôtel Le Royal Lyon
                               ⪡ 📠 🆅🅸🆂🅰 ⊕ 🅰🅴 ①

20 pl. Bellecour ✉ *69002* – ⓜ *Bellecour* – ℰ *04 78 37 57 31*
– *www.lyonhotel-leroyal.com*
– *Closed 14 July-20 August, Sunday and Monday*   **F2**
Rest – Menu 36 € – Carte approx. 40 €
♦ Modern ♦

Amid the refined, retro setting of Le Royal – one of Lyon's legendary hotels – the chef concocts well-crafted traditional cuisine. It is what you would expect from the Bocuse stable, with its unique take on French gastronomy!

X

Le Potager des Halles
                                📠 ⇄ 🆅🅸🆂🅰 ⊕ 🅰🅴

3 r. de la Martinière ✉ *69001* – ⓜ *Hôtel de Ville* – ℰ *04 72 00 24 84*
– *www.lepotagerdeshalles.com*
– *Closed 1 to 15 August, 1 week Christmas Holidays, Sunday and Monday*
Rest – Menu 18 € (weekday lunch), 35/52 € bi   **F1**
– Carte 35/50 €
♦ Traditional ♦ Bistro ♦ Friendly ♦

This bustling restaurant is between the Quais de la Saône and the Halles de la Martinière. It serves dishes like veal rump with heirloom carrots, and skate wing with samphire. Organic ingredients and fresh market produce take pride of place. Just next door is the tapas bar.

X
☺

Le Jean Moulin
                                             🆅🅸🆂🅰 ⊕

22 r. Gentil ✉ *69002* – ⓜ *Cordeliers* – ℰ *04 78 37 37 97*
– *Closed 2 weeks in August, Sunday and Monday*   **F1**
Rest – Menu 24 €
♦ Modern ♦ Friendly ♦ Elegant ♦

Find great value at this elegant, welcoming bistro, opened in late 2011 by a chef who trained at some of the top establishments (Bocuse, Viannay, Pic). The cooking is not so different from the man himself: lively, serious, tasteful, colourful and generous. Good enough to whet any appetite!

X
☺

L'Ourson qui Boit
                                        🆅🅸🆂🅰 ⊕ ①

23 r. Royale ✉ *69001* – ⓜ *Croix-Paquet* – ℰ *04 78 27 23 37*
– *Closed 4 weeks in July-August, 2 weeks in December, Wednesday and Sunday*
Rest – Menu 17 € (lunch)/25 €   **F1**
♦ Modern ♦ Friendly ♦ Bistro ♦

The Japanese chef at this contemporary bistro has worked in some of the finest restaurants. His cuisine blends the subtle flavours of yuzu and ginger with traditional French ingredients – all at reasonable prices. Not to be missed!

BOUCHONS *Regional wine tasting and local cuisine in a typical lyonnaise atmosphere*

Daniel et Denise

156 r. Créqui ✉ 69003 – Ⓜ Place Guichard – ✆ 04 78 60 66 53 – www.daniel-et-denise.fr – Closed 26 July-26 August, 22 December-2 January, Saturday, Sunday and Bank Holidays Plan III **G3**

Rest – Menu 27 € – Carte 37/48 €

♦ Lyonnaise ♦ Bistro ♦ Friendly ♦

A dyed-in-the-wool 'bouchon', smooth with the patina of age, serving tasty, generous cuisine with excellent ingredients. Unsurprisingly, typical dishes take pride of place.

Daniel et Denise Saint-Jean

32 r. Tramassac ✉ 69005 – Ⓜ Vieux Lyon – ✆ 04 78 42 24 62 – www.danieletdenise-stjean.com – Closed 2 weeks in August, Sunday and Monday **E2**

Rest – Menu 27/40 € – Carte 35/50 €

♦ Lyonnaise ♦ Friendly ♦

A stone's throw from Cathédrale St-Jean, La Machonnerie – emblematic bouchon of Lyon's Old Town – has been taken over by chef Joseph Viola (Meilleur Ouvrier de France). He is already known for his Daniel et Denise near Part-Dieu train station. The menu of this new place offers Lyonnaise cuisine that is no less delicious, hearty and tasty!

Café des Fédérations

8 r. Major Martin ✉ 69001 – Ⓜ Hôtel de Ville – ✆ 04 78 28 26 00 – www.lesfedeslyon.com – Closed 24 December-3 January and Sunday **F1**

Rest – *(pre-book)* Menu 19 € (lunch)/26 €

♦ Lyonnaise ♦ Bistro ♦ Friendly ♦

This is an indubitable academy of Lyonnaise cuisine. The decor has not changed for years, with its checked napkins and saucisson hanging from the ceiling, nor has its great ambience.

OLD TOWN *Plan II*

Villa Florentine

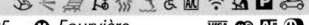

25 montée St-Barthélémy ✉ 69005 – Ⓜ Fourvière – ✆ 04 72 56 56 56 – www.villaflorentine.com **E2**

24 rm – †280/950 € ††280/950 €, ☕ 25 € – 4 suites

Rest *Les Terrasses de Lyon* ✿ – see restaurant listing

♦ Luxury ♦ Traditional ♦ Classic ♦

On the Fourvière hill, this 18C Renaissance inspired residence enjoys an incomparable view of the town. In the rooms, refinement and classic styling are the watchwords.

Cour des Loges

6 r. du Bœuf ✉ 69005 – Ⓜ Vieux Lyon – ✆ 04 72 77 44 44 – www.courdesloges.com **E2**

57 rm – †205/250 € ††265/390 €, ☕ 26 € – 4 suites

Rest *Les Loges* ✿ **Rest *Café-Épicerie*** – see restaurant listing

♦ Luxury ♦ Historic ♦ Personalised ♦

Vaults, galleries, passages... this magical place has all the character of the Renaissance in the middle of Vieux-Lyon with design and contemporary elegance as a bonus.

Collège without rest   ♿ AC 🛜 🏋 🛌 VISA ⓒⓞ AE

5 pl. St Paul ⊠ 69005 – Ⓜ Vieux Lyon – ℰ 04 72 10 05 05

– www.college-hotel.com   **E-F1**

39 rm – ♦125/155 € ♦♦125/155 €, ☑ 14 €

◆ Business ◆ Townhouse ◆ Contemporary ◆

Desks, a pommel horse, geography maps: everything here evokes the schools of yesteryear, and all in a designer style. Immaculately white rooms with balcony or terrace and pleasant bar serving 'gôneries' – Lyonnais tapas!

Les Terrasses de Lyon – Hôtel Villa Florentine   ≼ 🚗 🏠 ♿

25 montée St-Barthélémy ⊠ 69005   AC 🅿 VISA ⓒⓞ AE ⓞ

– Ⓜ Fourvière – ℰ 04 72 56 56 02 – www.villaflorentine.com

– Closed Sunday and Monday   **E2**

Rest – Menu 39 € (lunch), 49/98 € – Carte 74/120 €

◆ Modern ◆ Elegant ◆ Luxury ◆

Davy Tissot combines seasonal produce with refinement to produce heightened flavours – the delightful perfumes escape his kitchens! Splendid panorama from the terrace.

➔ Quenelle de langoustines, émulsion de têtes aux champignons sauvages. Risotto arborio cuit al dente aux copeaux de parmesan. Cocotte de fruits de saison rôtis au four, brioche feuilletée et sorbet maison.

Les Loges – Hôtel Cour des Loges   AC VISA ⓒⓞ AE ⓞ

6 r. du Bœuf ⊠ 69005 – Ⓜ Vieux Lyon – ℰ 04 72 77 44 44

– www.courdesloges.com

– Closed 27 July-29 August, Sunday and Monday   **E2**

Rest – (dinner only) Menu 75/95 € – Carte 75/108 €

◆ Modern ◆ Elegant ◆ Romantic ◆

Time seems to have stood still in this enchanting and romantic setting - a Florentine courtyard ringed by three floors of galleries and crowned by a contemporary glass ceiling. Savour the refined and inventive cuisine with flickering candlelight adding a final touch.

➔ Foie gras des Landes poché dans un consommé corsé, coing et oignon doux caramélisés. Pigeonneau et légumes de saison, essence de champignons. Cacao grand cru en chaud et froid, croustillant gianduja.

Têtedoie (Christian Têtedoie)   ≼ 🏠 ♿ AC ⇧ ⇨🍴 🅿 VISA ⓒⓞ AE

montée du Chemin-Neuf ⊠ 69005 – Ⓜ Minimes – ℰ 04 78 29 40 10

– www.tetedoie.com

– Closed Sunday   **E2**

Rest – Menu 36 € (weekday lunch), 58/108 € – Carte 78/106 € ⅍

Rest La Terrasse de l'Antiquaille – (open from mid-April to mid-October) Menu 40 €

◆ Modern ◆ Trendy ◆ Design ◆

On the Fourvière hill, this elegant and designer restaurant dominates Lyon. Christian Têtedoie explores French tradition with talent. The cellar is substantial and the cocktail bar is the place to be. Find a more relaxed atmosphere on the Terrasse, serving fine Mediterranean flavours and la plancha cuisine.

➔ Foie gras façon café gourmand. Homard et tête de veau. Croustillant gingembre, crémeux ananas, sauce et sorbet ananas-gingembre.

Au 14 Février   AC VISA ⓒⓞ AE

6 r. Mourguet ⊠ 69005 – Ⓜ Vieux Lyon – ℰ 04 78 92 91 39

– www.au14fevrier.com

– Closed 24 December-6 January, Sunday, Monday and lunch except Saturday

Rest – (number of covers limited, pre-book) (set menu only)   **E2**

Menu 75 €

◆ Creative ◆ Intimate ◆ Cosy ◆

This intimate restaurant is perfect for a Valentine's Day or romantic dinner! The young, Japanese-born chef focuses on fine French cuisine with a delicate modern touch.

➔ Velouté d'asperge blanche, tourteau, caviar osciètre et gelée de tomate. Turbot aux épices tandoori, mangue, gingembre et avocat. Mousse de champagne à la framboise façon kir royal.

Café-Épicerie – Hôtel Cour des Loges

6 r. du Bœuf ✉ 69005 – Ⓜ Vieux Lyon – ✆ 04 72 77 44 44
– www.courdesloges.com **E2**
Rest – Carte 39/61 €
◆ Modern ◆ Trendy ◆ Friendly ◆
In the marvellous setting of the Cour des Loges, this Café-Épicerie boasts a trendy bistro-style ambience. The locals come to enjoy unpretentious yet well-prepared dishes that change daily.

PERRACHE *Plan II*

Grand Hôtel Mercure Château Perrache

12 cours Verdun ✉ 69002 – Ⓜ Perrache
– ✆ 04 72 77 15 00 – www.mercure-lyon-centre-chateau-perrache.com
111 rm – †109/239 € ††109/239 €, ☕ 17 € – 2 suites **E3**
Rest *Les Belles Saisons* – *(closed 25 July-25 August, weekends and Bank Holidays)* Carte 30/40 €
◆ Chain hotel ◆ Historic ◆ Art Deco ◆
This hotel was built in 1900 and retains some of its character. Fine lobby with wood panelling, Art Nouveau frescos and mouldings, as well as authentic furniture in the most prestigious rooms. Majorelle elegance in the restaurant with a traditional French menu.

LES BROTTEAUX – CITÉ INTERNATIONALE – LA PART-DIEU *Plan III*

Hilton

70 quai Ch.-de-Gaulle ✉ 69006 – ✆ 04 78 17 50 50 – www.hilton.com
192 rm – †150/600 € ††150/600 €, ☕ 26 € – 5 suites **H1**
Rest *Blue Elephant* Rest *Brasserie* – see restaurant listing
◆ Chain hotel ◆ Business ◆ Modern ◆
Imposing hotel in glass and brick with a business centre. Very well-equipped rooms and suites overlooking the Tête-d'Or Park or the Rhône.

Radisson Blu

129 r. Servient (32th floor) ✉ 69003 – Ⓜ Part-Dieu – ✆ 04 78 63 55 00
– www.radissonblu.com/hotel-lyon **H3**
245 rm – †112/325 € ††112/325 €, ☕ 20 €
Rest *L'Arc-en-Ciel* – see restaurant listing
Rest *Bistrot de la Tour* – *(closed from late July-late August, Saturday and Sunday) (lunch only)* Menu 19 € – Carte 28/47 €
◆ Business ◆ Chain hotel ◆ Classic ◆
Business hotel where the reception is on the 32nd floor of the 'crayon' (pencil) skyscraper! In some of the rooms the view over the town is exceptional. Nearer the grounds, the Bistrot is very popular at lunchtime.

Hôtel de la Cité

22 quai Ch.-de-Gaulle ✉ 69006 – ✆ 04 78 17 86 86
– www.lyon.concorde-hotels.com **H1**
164 rm – †90/380 € ††90/380 €, ☕ 22 € – 5 suites
Rest – *(closed 27 July-18 August, Saturday and Sunday)* Carte 30/45 €
◆ Chain hotel ◆ Business ◆ Modern ◆
Recently constructed building designed by Renzo Piano. It has bright rooms overlooking the Tête-d'Or park or the Rhône. Traditional French cuisine and regional ingredients in the restaurant, as well as a pleasant terrace.

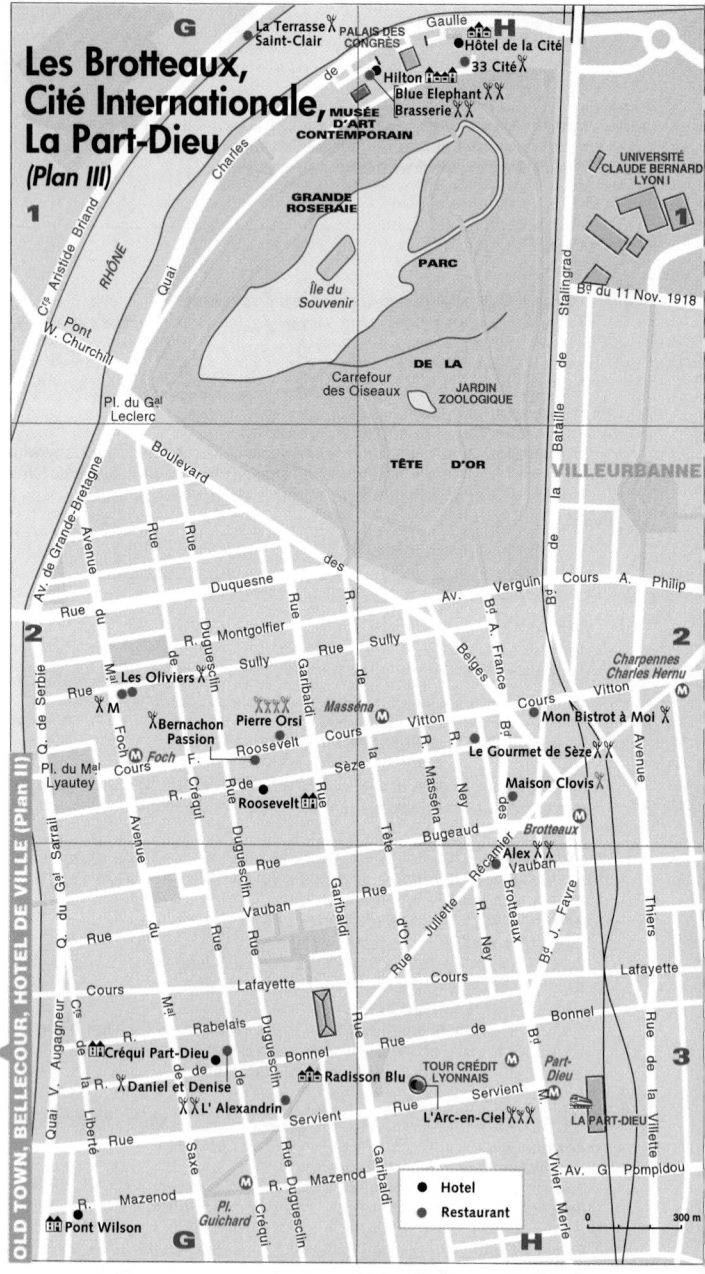

Les Brotteaux, Cité Internationale, La Part-Dieu
(Plan III)

G · **H**

La Terrasse Saint-Clair
PALAIS DES CONGRÈS
Gaulle
Hôtel de la Cité
33 Cité
Hilton
Blue Elephant
Brasserie
MUSÉE D'ART CONTEMPORAIN
Charles
de

GRANDE ROSERAIE

1

UNIVERSITÉ CLAUDE BERNARD LYON I

Île du Souvenir

PARC

Stalingrad
B⁰ du 11 Nov. 1918

RHÔNE
Q⁰ Aristide Briand
Quai
Charles
Pont W. Churchill

Carrefour des Oiseaux
JARDIN ZOOLOGIQUE

DE LA

Pl. du G⁰ Leclerc

Boulevard
Avenue
Rue
Rue
des
R.
TÊTE D'OR
de
la
Bataille
de
VILLEURBANNE

Av. de Grande-Bretagne
Duquesne
Av. Verguin
Cours A. Philip

2

Rue
du
Rue
Montgolfier
Rue
Sully
Bd A. France
Belges
Cours
Verguin
Charpennes Charles Hernu

Les Oliviers
M
R. Duguesclin
Sully
Garibaldi
Masséna
Rue
Vitton
Mon Bistrot à Moi

2

Bernachon Passion
Pierre Orsi
Roosevelt
Cours
Sèze
de
la
Masséna
Ney
Le Gourmet de Sèze

Pl. du M⁰ Lyautey
F.
de
Maison Clovis

Q⁰ de Serbie
Foch
Cours
Foch
R.
Crèqui
Rue
Duguesclin
Roosevelt
Rue
Tête
Bugeaud
Récamier
des
Brotteaux

Avenue
du
G⁰ Sarrail
Rue
Rue
Vauban
Garibaldi
Rue
d'Or
Juliette
R.
Ney
Bd J.-Favre
Alex
Vauban
Thiers

Cours
Rue
Lafayette
Rue
Rue
de
Cours
Bonnel
Lafayette

Rabelais
Duguesclin
Bonnel
Radisson Blu
TOUR CRÉDIT LYONNAIS
Part-Dieu
Rue de la Villette

Crèqui Part-Dieu
Daniel et Denise
L'Alexandrin
Servient
Rue
Servient
L'Arc-en-Ciel
LA PART-DIEU

Q⁰ V. Augagneur
C⁰ de la Liberté
R.
de
R.
Saxe
Rue
Mazenod
Pl. Guichard
Crèqui
R. Duguesclin
Mazenod
Garibaldi
Vivier Merle
Av. G. Pompidou

Pont Wilson

● Hotel
● Restaurant

0   300 m

G · **H**

FRANCE - LYONS

Créqui Part-Dieu   & rm, 🔳 🛜 🎛 💳 ⓒ AE ①

37 r. Bonnel ✉ *69003 –* Ⓜ *Place Guichard –* ℰ *04 78 60 20 47*
– www.bestwestern-lyonpartdieu.com   **G3**
46 rm – 🛉83/189 € 🛉🛉83/199 €, � 16 € – 3 suites
Rest *La Cantine du Palais* – ℰ *04 78 60 83 96 (closed August, Saturday and Sunday)* Menu 20 € (lunch), 21/24 € – Carte 28/50 €
♦ Business ♦ Functional ♦ Classic ♦

Opposite the judiciary centre and very near the Halles Paul-Bocuse. The rooms are comfortable and there is even a pretty flower-decked courtyard. In the Cantine, traditional French dishes and a decor on the theme of school.

Le Roosevelt *without rest*   & 🔳 🛜 🅿 🚗 💳 ⓒ AE ①

48 r. de Sèze ✉ *69006 –* Ⓜ *Foch –* ℰ *04 78 52 35 67*
– www.hotel-roosevelt.com
– Closed 10 to 18 August   **G2**
48 rm – 🛉94/206 € 🛉🛉94/206 €, ⊟ 15 €
♦ Traditional ♦ Family ♦ Modern ♦

Pleasant and comfortable hotel. On the courtyard side the rooms are more spacious and quiet. They overlook the famous Bernachon chocolate shop – only a few steps away for a delicious treat!

Pont Wilson *without rest*   🔳 🛜 🅿 💳 ⓒ AE ①

6 r. Mazenod ✉ *69003 –* Ⓜ *Guillotière –* ℰ *04 78 60 94 94*
– www.hotelwilson-lyon.com   **G3**
54 rm – 🛉79/305 € 🛉🛉89/315 €, ⊟ 15 €
♦ Business ♦ Chain hotel ♦ Functional ♦

This hotel is well located near the quayside and Wilson bridge and is suitable for business travellers. Quite spacious guestrooms.

Pierre Orsi   🛜 & 🔳 ⇩ ⇗ 💳 ⓒ AE

3 pl. Kléber ✉ *69006 –* Ⓜ *Masséna –* ℰ *04 78 89 57 68*
– www.pierreorsi.com
– Closed Sunday and Monday except Bank Holidays   **G2**
Rest – Menu 46 € (weekday lunch), 65/120 € – Carte 70/115 € ⅗
♦ Modern ♦ Formal ♦ Cosy ♦

An elegant old mansion with an air of quiet refinement in the lounges and a pretty flower-decked terrace. Pierre Orsi's cuisine is a symphony of classical offerings interpreted with finesse.
➜ Ravioles de foie gras de canard au jus de porto et truffe. Homard en carapace à la façon de Pierre Orsi. Crêpes Suzette au beurre d'orange.

L'Arc-en-Ciel – Hôtel Radisson Blu   ⩽ & 🔳 💳 ⓒ AE ①

129 r. Servient (32th floor) ✉ *69003 –* Ⓜ *Part-Dieu –* ℰ *04 78 63 55 00*
– Closed mid July-late August, 1 to 7 January, Saturday lunch and Sunday
Rest – Menu 49 € (weekdays), 57/97 € bi – Carte 68/104 € ⅗   **H3**
♦ Modern ♦ Elegant ♦ Romantic ♦

Located on the 32nd floor of the 'Pencil', the Arc-en-Ciel boasts 360° views of Lyon. Amid an elegant decor, the cuisine is highly influenced by the seasons and accompanied by an impressive choice of superb wines.

Le Gourmet de Sèze (Bernard Mariller)   🔳 💳 ⓒ AE

129 r. de Sèze ✉ *69006 –* Ⓜ *Masséna –* ℰ *04 78 24 23 42*
– www.le-gourmet-de-seze.com
– Closed 3 to 7 March, 26 July-22 August, Sunday, Monday and Bank Holidays
Rest – *(number of covers limited, pre-book)* Menu 36 €   **H2**
(weekday lunch), 50/115 €
♦ Modern ♦ Elegant ♦ Cosy ♦

Twenty years old in 2011 but the Gourmet remains untouched by age! Bernard Mariller's cuisine retains the ardour and freshness of youth and the finesse of classical cuisine.
➜ Croustillant de pied de cochon compoté à la moutarde en grains. Saint-Jacques d'Erquy grillées, velouté de lentilles vertes du Puy. Le grand dessert du gourmet.

XX **L'Alexandrin** · AC VISA ©© AE

83 r. Moncey ⊠ 69003 – ⓜ Place Guichard – 𝒞 04 72 61 15 69
– www.lalexandrin.fr
– Closed 4 to 27 August, Sunday and Monday **G3**
Rest – Menu 60/115 € ♨

♦ Modern ♦ Cosy ♦

This restaurant uses the fine produce of the region to create inventive, generous cuisine. Enjoy your meal either in the elegant dining room or on the pretty terrace.

XX **Alex** · ⤬ AC VISA ©© AE

44 bd des Brotteaux ⊠ 69006 – ⓜ Brotteaux – 𝒞 04 78 52 30 11
– Closed August, Sunday and Monday **H3**
Rest – Menu 25 € (weekday lunch), 30/67 € – Carte 47/62 €

♦ Modern ♦ Intimate ♦

Alex is the chef (and owner) of this chic and simple restaurant. He concocts well-crafted cuisine with beautifully fresh ingredients picked up at the market.

XX **Blue Elephant** – Hôtel Hilton · AC VISA ©© AE ⓞ

70 quai Ch.-de-Gaulle ⊠ 69006 – 𝒞 04 78 17 50 00 – www.hilton.com
– Closed August, Saturday lunch, Sunday and Monday **H1**
Rest – Menu 44 € (lunch) – Carte 34/58 €

♦ Thai ♦ Exotic ♦

The Blue Elephant prides itself on its excellent Thai cuisine prepared with ingredients imported directly from Bangkok. Lunchtime buffet, as well as suggestions that vary with market availability and the seasons.

XX **Brasserie** – Hôtel Hilton · AC VISA ©© AE ⓞ

70 quai Ch.-de-Gaulle ⊠ 69006 – 𝒞 04 78 17 51 00 – www.hilton.com
Rest – Carte 32/53 € **H1**

♦ Traditional ♦ Brasserie ♦ Friendly ♦

This brasserie is popular with regulars and business customers alike with its traditional menu, lunchtime buffet of starters and desserts, and 1900s-style decor. Very popular brunch on Sundays.

X **Maison Clovis** (Clovis Khoury) · AC VISA ©© AE ⓞ
❀
19 bd Brotteaux ⊠ 69006 – ⓜ Brotteaux – 𝒞 04 72 74 44 61
– www.maisonclovis.com
– Closed 5 to 13 May, 27 July-20 August, 1 to 8 January, Sunday and Monday
Rest – Menu 28 € (weekday lunch), 45/75 € **H2**
– Carte 70/100 €

♦ Modern ♦ Design ♦

This designer restaurant is elegant without being uptight. Clovis Khoury prepares delicious seasonal cuisine using fine ingredients. The menu is short, but the choice is nevertheless impossible.
➜ Oursin d'Islande, risotto aux supions et cuisses de grenouilles. Cailles des Vosges en chair et sans os farcie au chou braisé et foie gras. Millefeuille pure tradition.

X **33 Cité** · ⌂ ⤬ AC VISA ©© AE
☺
33 quai Charles-de-Gaulle ⊠ 69006 – 𝒞 04 37 45 45 45 – www.33cite.com
– Closed 5 to 25 August **H1**
Rest – Menu 23 € (weekdays)/27 € – Carte 35/51 € ♨

♦ Traditional ♦ Brasserie ♦ Fashionable ♦

Three talented chefs – Mathieu Viannay (Meilleur Ouvrier de France), Christophe Marguin and Frédéric Berthod (alumnus of the Bocuse) – joined forces to create this chic, tasty brasserie. It opens onto the Tête-d'Or Park. On the menu find the great brasserie specialities.

FRANCE - LYONS

La Terrasse St-Clair   🍴 🛋 VISA ⓪

2 Grande Rue St-Clair ✉ *69300 Caluire-et-Cuire –* ☏ *04 72 27 37 37*
– www.terrasse-saint-clair.com
– Closed 5 to 22 August, 23 December-7 January, Sunday and Monday
Rest – Menu 26 €   **G1**
  ◆ Traditional ◆ Bistro ◆ Friendly ◆
Restaurant with the air of an old-fashioned French café serving good, traditional cuisine. Terrace shaded by plane trees and, of course, a petanque ground!

Les Oliviers   ẬC VISA ⓪ AE

20 r. Sully ✉ *69006 –* Ⓜ *Foch –* ☏ *04 78 89 07 09 – www.lesoliviers-lyon.fr*
– Closed 1 to 8 May, August, Saturday, Sunday and Bank Holidays
Rest – Menu 24/36 € – Carte 34/44 €   **G2**
  ◆ Modern ◆ Fashionable ◆
A little corner of Provence tucked away in the 6th arrondissement. Appetising sun-drenched cuisine is served and the grilled fish counts among the stars of the show.

M   🍴 ẬC VISA ⓪ AE

47 av. Foch ✉ *69006 –* Ⓜ *Foch –* ☏ *04 78 89 55 19 – www.mrestaurant.fr*
– Closed 2 to 10 March, 3 to 25 August, Saturday and Sunday   **G2**
Rest – Menu 25/35 € – Carte approx. 43 €
  ◆ Modern ◆ Trendy ◆ Friendly ◆
The charming and fashionable M serves delicious gourmet cuisine full of flavour. The decor is slightly psychedelic.

Bernachon Passion   ẬC VISA ⓪ AE ⓪

42 cours Franklin-Roosevelt ✉ *69006 –* Ⓜ *Foch –* ☏ *04 78 52 23 65*
– www.bernachon.com
– Closed 20 July-21 August, Sunday, Monday and Bank Holidays
Rest *– (lunch only) (number of covers limited, pre-book)*   **G2**
Menu 27 € – Carte 34/49 €
  ◆ Traditional ◆ Family ◆
A restaurant run by the daughter and grandchildren of Paul Bocuse, owners of the famous chocolate shop. Traditional French recipes and lunchtime daily specials. Tea room.

Mon Bistrot à Moi   ẬC VISA ⓪

84 cours Vitton ✉ *69006 –* Ⓜ *Brotteaux –* ☏ *04 78 52 47 28*
– www.monbistrotamoi.fr
– Closed 1 to 23 August, 1 week in February, Saturday and Sunday
Rest *– (number of covers limited, pre-book)* Menu 23 €   **H2**
– Carte 29/47 €
  ◆ Traditional ◆ Bistro ◆ Friendly ◆
A pleasant contemporary bistro in the Brotteaux district. Find copper pans on the walls, hearty cuisine on the plate, wines on the blackboard and excellent value for money.

AROUND LYONS

Lyon Métropole   🍴 ẞ ⊕ ⊠ 🏊 ✕ ⑁ 占 rm, ẬC 🛜 🛁 🅿 🚗

85 quai J. Gillet ✉ *69004 –* ☏ *04 72 10 44 44*   VISA ⓪ AE ⓪
– www.lyonmetropole.com   **B1**
118 rm – ♥215/245 € ♥♥215/270 €, � 19 €
Rest *Le Lyon Plage –* ☏ *04 72 10 44 30 –* Menu 25 € – Carte 30/45 €
  ◆ Business ◆ Spa hotel ◆ Functional ◆
Hotel popular for its Olympic size swimming pool and sports facilities: superb spa, gym, tennis and squash courts, etc. Ask for one of the rooms renovated in 2009. In the restaurant, seafood and fish are to the fore.

Dock Ouest without rest   🔥 AC 📶 🚗 VISA ⓜ AE

39 r. des Docks ✉ *69009 –* 🚇 *Gare de Vaise –* 𝒞 *04 78 22 34 34*
– www.dockouest.com   **B1**
43 rm – †75/118 € ††97/140 €, ☲ 13 €
♦ Townhouse ♦ Business ♦ Contemporary ♦

Dock Ouest is located in an up-and-coming district of Lyon, just opposite Paul Bocuse's fast food outlet. The guestrooms are comfortable and decorated in a restrained style, with the added bonus of a kitchenette. Gourmet breakfast.

Auberge de l'Île (Jean-Christophe Ansanay-Alex)   ⇄
🕸 🕸

(on Barbe Island) ✉ *69009*   ⌷⤬ (dinner) P VISA ⓜ AE
– 𝒞 *04 78 83 99 49 – www.aubergedelile.com*
– Closed 11 to 25 August, 1 to 20 January, Sunday except Bank Holidays and Monday   **B1**
Rest – Menu 60 € (weekday lunch), 125/145 € – Carte 155/195 € 🕸
♦ Classic ♦ Cosy ♦ Luxury ♦

A country feel in the heart of the leafy île Barbe, an island in the Saône. The walls date from 1601 and there is a softly intimate atmosphere. The very refined cuisine has remarkable flavour associations and creative flights of fancy.
➜ Velouté des premières morilles comme un cappuccino. Selle d'agneau allaiton servie comme à Versailles. Soufflé chaud à la pêche blanche et sorbet pêche de vigne.

L'Ouest   🕸 AC VISA ⓜ AE
🕸

1 quai du Commerce (North via the banks of the Saône, D 51) ✉ *69009*
– 𝒞 *04 37 64 64 64 – www.nordsudbrasseries.com*   **B1**
Rest – Menu 25 € (weekdays)/33 € – Carte 30/55 €
♦ Traditional ♦ Friendly ♦

Designer brasserie (wood, concrete, metal, screens and open kitchen), pleasant Saône terrace and traditional dishes with occasional exotic influences. The famous chef Paul Bocuse goes en voyage…

Les Saveurs de Py   🕸 🔥 AC VISA ⓜ

8 r. Pailleron ✉ *69004 –* 🚇 *Hénon –* 𝒞 *04 78 28 80 86*
– www.saveursdepy.fr
– Closed August, Tuesday lunch, Sunday dinner and Monday   **B1**
Rest – Menu 16 € (lunch), 30/38 €
♦ Modern ♦ Friendly ♦ Bistro ♦

Right in the middle of the bustling district of La Croix-Rousse, this modern little bistro couldn't be more relaxed and friendly. On the menu find fresh ingredients and plenty of homemade produce, along with the occasional Japanese twist.

L'Art et la Manière   AC VISA ⓜ
🕸

102 Gde-Rue de la Guillotière ✉ *69007 –* 🚇 *Saxe-Gambetta*
– 𝒞 *04 37 27 05 83 – www.art-et-la-maniere.fr*
– Closed 3 weeks in August, Monday dinner, Saturday and Sunday
Rest – Menu 19 € (lunch), 26/37 € – Carte 34/45 €   **B-C2**
♦ Traditional ♦ Bistro ♦ Friendly ♦

A contemporary bistro that champions conviviality, seasonal cuisine and enticing, reasonably priced wines. It is also a great excuse for discovering the La Guillotière district. As it has a loyal local following, you are best advised to book ahead.

COLLONGES-AU-MONT-D'OR

Paul Bocuse   🔥 AC ⇄ ⌷⤬ P VISA ⓜ AE ⓞ
🕸 🕸 🕸

40 r. de la Plage, au pont de Collonges (12 km North via the banks of the Saône, D 433 and D 51) ✉ *69660 –* 𝒞 *04 72 42 90 90 – www.bocuse.fr*
Rest – Menu 147/235 € – Carte 130/215 € 🕸
♦ Classic ♦ Elegant ♦ Luxury ♦

A high temple of tradition and old-style service, which is oblivious to passing culinary trends. Paul Bocuse is still offering the same "presidential" truffle soup first served in 1975, and has had three Michelin stars since 1965!
➜ Soupe aux truffes noires V.G.E. Rouget en écailles de pomme de terre. Gâteau Président "Maurice Bernachon".

CHARBONNIÈRES-LES-BAINS

Le Pavillon de la Rotonde

3 av. Georges Bassinet – ℰ *04 78 87 79 79*
– www.pavillon-rotonde.com
16 rm – 335/565 € 365/565 €, ☕ 33 €
Rest *La Rotonde* ✿✿ – see restaurant listing
♦ Luxury ♦ Spa hotel ♦ Contemporary ♦

A stone's throw from the casino in wooded grounds, this luxurious hotel blends the contemporary with subtle Art Deco touches. Certain rooms boast hammam or terrace… A fine establishment on the outskirts of Lyon.

La Rotonde

au casino le Lyon Vert ✉ *69890 La Tour de Salvagny –* ℰ *04 78 87 79 79*
– www.pavillon-rotonde.com
– Closed August, 5 to 12 January, Sunday and Monday
Rest – *(dinner only)* Menu 127/157 € – Carte 110/200 € 🌿
♦ Modern ♦ Elegant ♦

On this impressive estate at the gates to the city, above the Lyon Vert casino – a legacy of the Art Deco period. An exquisite dining experience with excellent produce and fine flavours, orchestrated by chef Philippe Gauvreau.

➔ Œuf de poule fumé cuit mollet, truffe et girolles, sauce mousseuse. Canard de Challans cuit à la broche, en deux services. Cannellonis de chocolat amer à la glace de crème brûlée, sauce chocolat guanaja.

FRANCE - LYONS

STRASBOURG
STRASBOURG

Population: 272 975

DX/Fotolia.com

Would it be stretching things to call Strasbourg the ultimate European city? It can make an impressive claim. Although in France, it sits just across the Rhine from Germany; it's home to the Court of Human Rights and the Council of Europe; its stunning cathedral is the highest medieval building on the continent; and it's a major communications hub as it connects the Mediterranean with the Rhineland, Central Europe, the North Sea and the Baltic. Oh, and the Old Town is a UNESCO World Heritage Site. What's more, there's a real cosmopolitan buzz here. A large student population, courtesy of the city's ancient university, helps generate a year-round feeling of liveliness.

The name 'Strasbourg' translates as 'crossroads', and the city bounced back and forth between France and Germany for over three hundred years. Its unique geographical position also lends the city a great gastronomic tradition, with two cuisine cultures colliding head on and hungry visitors reaping the benefits. Meanwhile, street signs in both French and Alsatian add to a gently teasing schizophrenia, enhanced by distinct areas of medieval French and German architecture. The final brushwork of this striking picture is the handsome waterway that completely encircles the Old Town; the ideal setting for a lingering boat journey on a summer's afternoon.

STRASBOURG IN...

→ ONE DAY
Old Town, Notre-Dame Cathedral, Petite France.

→ TWO DAYS
Boat trip on the Ill, Museum of Modern and Contemporary Art, meal in a winstub.

→ THREE DAYS
Alsatian Museum (or Rohan Palace museum), European Parliament, Orangerie.

PRACTICAL INFORMATION

ARRIVAL-DEPARTURE

✈ Strasbourg Entzheim International Airport is 12km southwest of the city. The train to Central Station runs from Entzheim Station (a 5min walk from the terminal) and takes 15min.

GETTING AROUND

Strasbourg is covered by a bus and tram service. You can buy a single ticket or carnets (multipasses). There's also a Tour Pass which gives unlimited travel for 24hr. The city has impressive green credentials: buses run on natural gas, trams are slick and efficient, and there are 130,000 cyclists and 270 miles of cycle paths – hiring a bike is a great way of getting about here. If you're staying longer, invest in a Strasbourg Pass. This is a three-day pass which offers free travel, plus free admission or discounts to many city-wide monuments and visitor attractions.

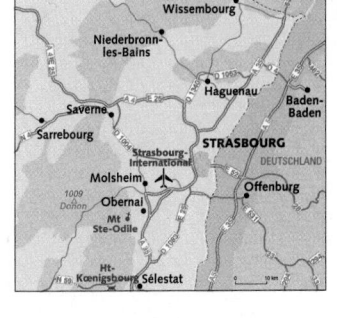

CALENDAR HIGHLIGHTS

May
Les Nuits de Musées.

June
Festival de Musique.

July
Les Nuits de Strasbourg, L'Ill aux Lumieres.

August
Route Romane Festival.

September
European Days of Heritage.

November
St-Art Contemporary Art Fair, Jazz d'Or.

December
Christmas Markets.

EATING OUT

Strasbourg is generally considered one of the best cities in France for great food. There's the attention to quality and detail that's the epitome of the French gourmet philosophy, allied to bold and hearty Alsatian fare with its roots firmly set across the Rhine. A favourite of the region is choucroute (or sauerkraut if you're leaning towards Germany), which is a rumbustious mixture of cabbage, potatoes, pork, sausage and ham; then there's baeckoffe, a tasty Alsace stew, which translates as 'ovenbake' and blends pieces of stewing lamb, beef and pork with liberal splashes of Riesling. Talking of which, the fragrant wines of the area have a distinct character of their own: they're white, spicy and floral. The local fruit liquor, eau de vie, has a definite Alsatian kick, too – it's sweetened entirely by fruit without a hint of sugar. A good place to try the local specialities is a typical Strasbourg winstub. Most of the city's smarter restaurants are around the cathedral, in the Petite France quarter, and along the canal and river banks.

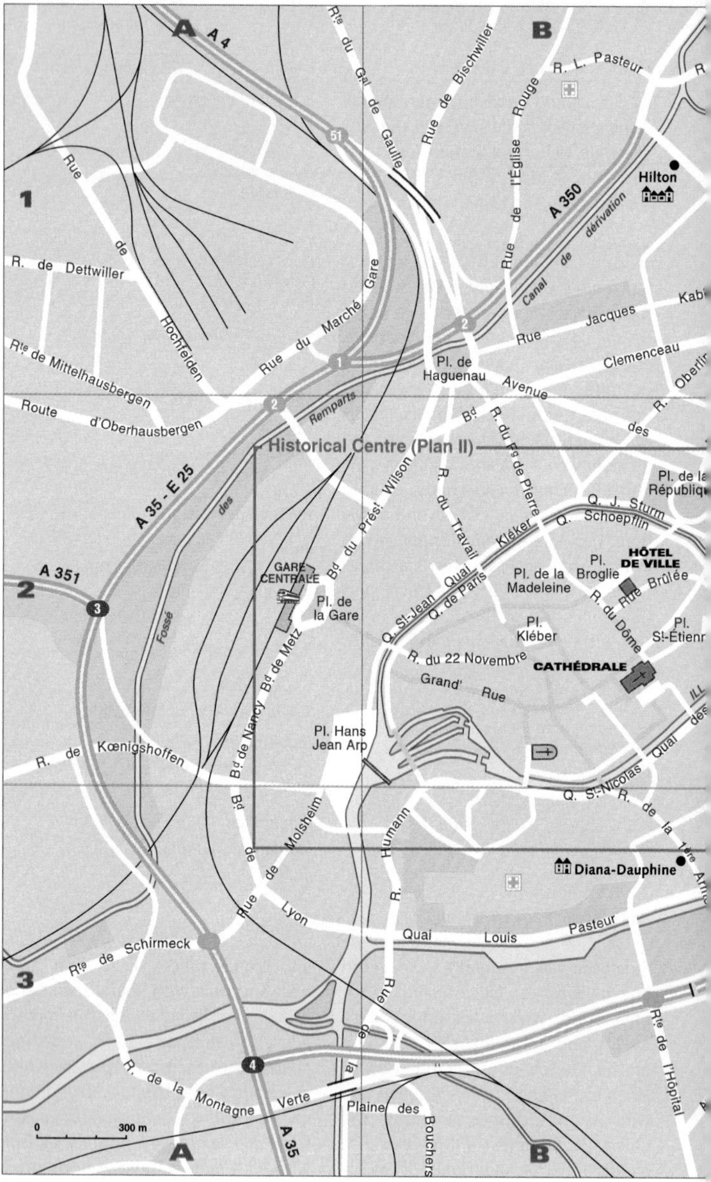
A
B
1
2
3
A 4
A 350
A 351
A 35 - E 25
A 35
Rte du Gal de Gaulle
Rue de Bischwiller
R. L. Pasteur
Rue de l'Église Rouge
Hilton
Canal de dérivation
Rue de Hochfelden
R. de Dettwiller
Rue du Marché Gare
Rue Jacques
Kab
Rte de Mittelhausbergen
Route d'Oberhausbergen
Remparts
Pl. de Haguenau
Avenue des Clemenceau
R. Oberlin
Bd
R. du Fg de Pierre
Historical Centre (Plan II)
Pl. de la République
Q. J. Sturm
Q. Schoepflin
Bd du Prést Wilson
R. du Travail
Quai Kléber
Fossé des
GARE CENTRALE
Pl. de la Gare
Q. St-Jean
Q. de Paris
Pl. de la Madeleine
Pl. Broglie
HÔTEL DE VILLE
Rue Brûlée
R. du Dôme
Pl. Kléber
Pl. St-Étienn
R. du 22 Novembre
CATHÉDRALE
Grand' Rue
ILL
Quai des
Bd de Nancy
Bd de Metz
Pl. Hans Jean Arp
R. de Kœnigshoffen
Q. St-Nicolas
R. de la 1ère Armée
Bd de Lyon
Rue de Molsheim
R. Humann
Diana-Dauphine
Quai Louis Pasteur
Rte de Schirmeck
Rue de la Plaine des Bouchers
Rte de l'Hôpital
R. de la Montagne Verte
0
300 m
STRASBOURG-INTERNATIONAL

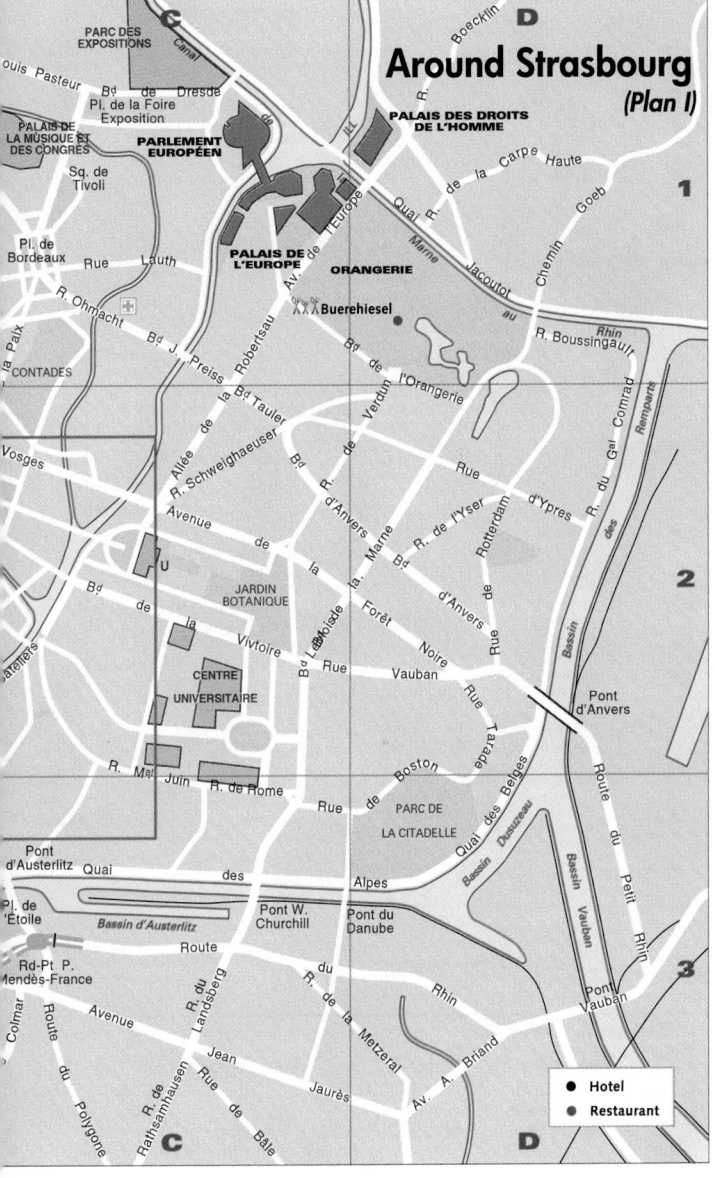

Around Strasbourg
(Plan I)

PARC DES
EXPOSITIONS

ouis Pasteur

Bd de Dresde
Pl. de la Foire
Exposition

PALAIS DE
LA MUSIQUE ET
DES CONGRÈS

PARLEMENT
EUROPÉEN

Sq. de
Tivoli

Pl. de
Bordeaux

Rue Lauth

R. Ohmacht

Bd J. Preiss

CONTADES

Bd Tauler

Allée de Robertsau

R. Schweighaeuser

Vosges

Avenue de

Bd de la

JARDIN
BOTANIQUE

Victoire

CENTRE
UNIVERSITAIRE

R. Mal Juin

R. de Rome

Pont
d'Austerlitz

Quai des Alpes

Pl. de
l'Etoile

Bassin d'Austerlitz

Pont W.
Churchill

Pont du
Danube

Route du

Rd-Pt P.
Mendès-France

Colmar

Route du Polygone

Avenue

R. du Landsberg

R. de Rathsamhausen

Rue de Bâle

Jean

Jaurès

R. de la Metzeral

Rhin

Av. A. Briand

PALAIS DES DROITS
DE L'HOMME

Canal

Boecklin

de la Carpe Haute

Goeb

Quai Marne

Jacoutot

Chemin au

PALAIS DE
L'EUROPE

ORANGERIE

Av. de l'Europe

XXX Buerehiesel

R. Boussingault

Rhin

Bd de l'Orangerie

Bd de Verdun

Rue

R. du Gal Conrad

Ramparts

des

Bassin

R. d'Anvers

Bd de la Marne

R. de l'Yser

d'Ypres

Rotterdam

d'Anvers

Rue de

Bd Leblois

Forêt

Noire

Rue Vauban

Rue Tarade

Pont
d'Anvers

Rue de Boston

PARC DE
LA CITADELLE

Quai des Belges

Bassin Dusuzeau

Bassin Vauban

Route du Petit Rhin

Pont
Vauban

● Hotel
● Restaurant

283

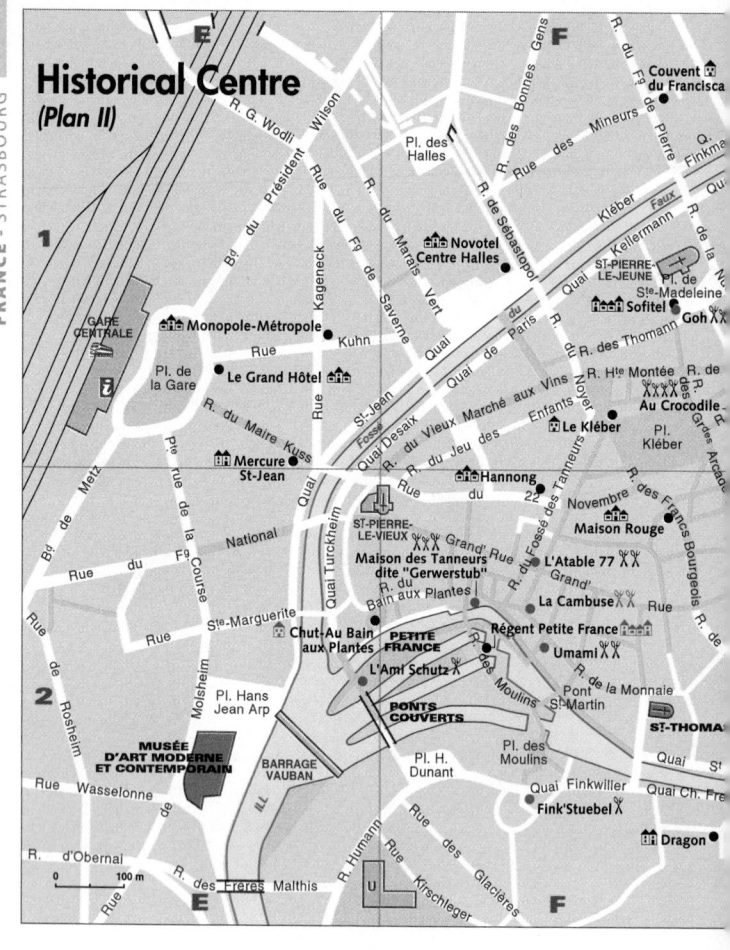

Historical Centre
(Plan II)

HISTORICAL CENTRE   *Plan II*

🏨 **Régent Petite France**   ⓢ ⓢ 🛎 ♨ ᵹ 🏧 📶 🛗 🚬

5 r. des Moulins – ℰ 03 88 76 43 43   *VISA* 💳 AE ①
– www.regent-petite-france.com   **F2**

72 rm – †165/520 € ††165/520 €, ☲ 23 € – 8 suites

Rest – *(closed Sunday, Monday and lunch except from June-September)*
Menu 38 € – Carte 52/66 €

♦ Grand Luxury ♦ Business ♦ Design ♦

A beautiful, large hotel occupying a former ice-making factory on the banks of
the river Ill in the historic Petite France district. Comfortable, modern, stylish and
unostentatious interior with pleasantly hushed rooms. A restaurant with a
modern menu, lounge bar and terrace over the river.

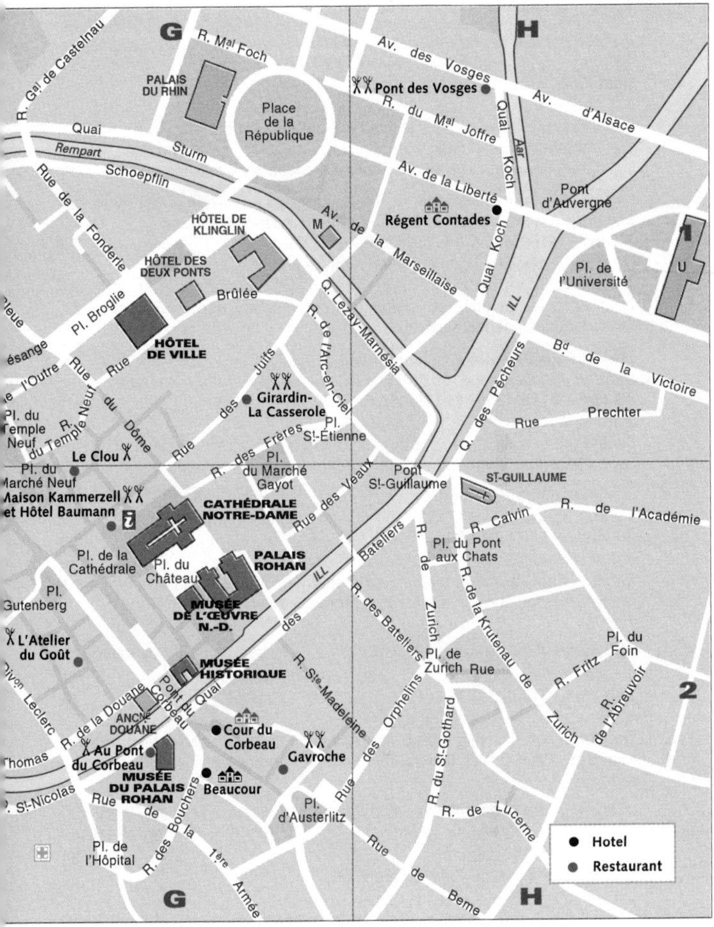

Map labels (reading the plan):

R. Gal de Castelnau
R. Mal Foch
Av. des Vosges
Av. d'Alsace
PALAIS DU RHIN
Place de la République
Quai Aar
Quai Koch
Quai
Rempart
Sturm
Schoepflin
R. de la Fonderie
Rue
R. du Mal Joffre
Av. de la Liberté
Pont d'Auvergne
✕✕ ● Pont des Vosges ●
Régent Contades
Pl. de l'Université
U
Av. de la Marseillaise
ILL
Q. Lezay-Marnésia
Bd. de la Victoire
Q. des Pêcheurs
HÔTEL DE KLINGLIN
HÔTEL DES DEUX PONTS
Pl. Broglie
Brûlée
HÔTEL DE VILLE
R. du Temple Neuf
R. des Juifs
R. de l'Arc-en-Ciel
Girardin-La Casserole
Pl. St.-Étienne
R. des Frères
Rue Prechter
Le Clou ✕
Pl. du Marché Neuf
Maison Kammerzell et Hôtel Baumann ✕✕
Pl. du Dôme
Pl. du Marché Gayot
CATHÉDRALE NOTRE-DAME
Rue des Veaux
Pont St-Guillaume
ST-GUILLAUME
R. Calvin
R. de l'Académie
Pl. de la Cathédrale
Pl. du Château
PALAIS ROHAN
R. des Bateliers
Pl. du Pont aux Chats
R. de la Krutenau
Pl. Gutenberg
MUSÉE DE L'ŒUVRE N.-D.
Rue de Zurich
Pl. de Zurich
Pl. du Foin
✕ L'Atelier du Goût
MUSÉE HISTORIQUE
R. Ste-Madeleine
Rue de Zurich
R. Fritz
de l'Abreuvoir
Quai Lederc
R. de la Douane
Cour du Corbeau ●
Gavroche ✕✕
R. des Orphelins
Pl. du
R. St-Gothard
R. de Lucerne
✕ Au Pont du Corbeau
MUSÉE DU PALAIS ROHAN
Beaucour
Pl. d'Austerlitz
Rue de Berne
St-Thomas
R. St-Nicolas
Rue des Bouchers
1re Armée
Pl. de l'Hôpital

● Hotel
● Restaurant

🏨 **Hilton**　🛜 ⎰ 🏊 ♿ rm, AC 📞 🧖 🅿 🚗 VISA ⑤ AE ①

av. Herrenschmidt
– 📞 03 88 37 10 10
– *www.strasbourg.hilton.fr*　　　　　　　*plan I* **B1**
245 rm – ♥299/369 € ♥♥299/369 €, ☕ 21 €
– 6 suites
Rest Carvi – 📞 03 88 37 41 42
– Carte 34/60 €
◆ Business ◆ Chain hotel ◆ Functional ◆
An impeccably designed glass and steel building opposite the Convention Centre, ideal for international business guests. Extremely comfortable guestrooms, meeting rooms, bar and restaurant.

285

Sofitel ⅃⁵ 🄰🄺 📶 🛍 🚘 📧 🅥🅘🅢🅐 ⓪ 🄰🄴

4 pl. St-Pierre-le-Jeune – ℰ *03 88 15 49 00* – *www.sofitel-strasbourg.com*
151 rm – †115/445 € ††115/445 €, ⌷ 24 € – 2 suites **F1**
Rest Goh – see restaurant listing
◆ Chain hotel ◆ Luxury ◆ Functional ◆
This modern establishment is located in a quiet neighbourhood to the north of the cathedral, and is 15min from the station. It offers space and flawless contemporary finishings. The pleasant rooms are ideal for a relaxing break.

Cour du Corbeau without rest ⅌ ♿ 🄰🄺 📶 📧 🅥🅘🅢🅐 ⓪ 🄰🄴

6 r. des Couples – ℰ *03 90 00 26 26* – *www.cour-corbeau.com*
57 rm – †165/520 € ††165/520 €, ⌷ 23 € – 8 suites **G2**
◆ Historic ◆ Design ◆ Personalised ◆
A stone's throw from the Pont du Corbeau and the cathedral, this attractive hotel occupies several 16C buildings. Contemporary decor and top of the range facilities. Friendly service.

Régent Contades without rest ⅏ ♿ 🄰🄺 📶 🛍 📧 🅥🅘🅢🅐 ⓪ 🄰🄴

8 av. de la Liberté – ℰ *03 88 15 05 05* – *www.regent-contades.com*
48 rm – †115/455 € ††115/455 €, ⌷ 20 € – 2 suites **H1**
◆ Luxury ◆ Historic ◆ Classic ◆
Behind the beautiful façade of this 19C townhouse is a refined, classical interior (wood panelling, paintings) with services to match.

Beaucour without rest 🄰🄺 📶 🛍 📧 🅥🅘🅢🅐 ⓪ 🄰🄴

5 r. des Bouchers – ℰ *03 88 76 72 00* – *www.hotel-beaucour.com*
49 rm – †77/112 € ††139/169 €, ⌷ 14 € **G2**
◆ Family ◆ Classic ◆ Personalised ◆
Two 18C Alsatian houses built around a charming flower-filled patio. Very comfortable Alsatian-style or classic rooms, some with wooden beams, spa bathtub etc.

Maison Rouge without rest ♿ 🄰🄺 📶 🛍 📧 🅥🅘🅢🅐 ⓪ 🄰🄴

4 r. des Francs-Bourgeois – ℰ *03 88 32 08 60* – *www.maison-rouge.com*
140 rm – †70/185 € ††70/185 €, ⌷ 15 € – 2 suites **F2**
◆ Luxury ◆ Business ◆ Stylish ◆
Traditional hotel offering top-quality comfort and service. Spacious, immaculate rooms (designer fabrics, top-quality furnishings), accessed via landings decorated with objets d'art.

Monopole-Métropole without rest ⅃⁵ ♿ 🄰🄺 📶 🛍 🚘

16 r. Kuhn – ℰ *03 88 14 39 14* 📧 🅥🅘🅢🅐 ⓪ 🄰🄴
– *www.bw-monopole.com* **E1**
81 rm ⌷ – †85/250 € ††92/250 €
◆ Family ◆ Rustic ◆ Design ◆
A smart 19C building located between the train station and the historic Petite France district. Charming features include Alsatian antiques and paintings by renowned local artists. Traditional or more contemporary rooms.

Hannong without rest 🄰🄺 📶 🛍 📧 🅥🅘🅢🅐 ⓪ 🄰🄴

15 r. du 22-Novembre – ℰ *03 88 32 16 22* – *www.hotel-hannong.com*
– Closed 1 to 6 January **F2**
72 rm – †69/119 € ††89/209 €, ⌷ 16 €
◆ Family ◆ Business ◆ Classic ◆
This hotel full of character is built on the site of the Hannong earthenware factory (18C). Objets d'art, contemporary facilities, quality materials and meticulous upkeep. Pleasant terrace area.

Le Grand Hôtel without rest 📶 🛍 📧 🅥🅘🅢🅐 ⓪ 🄰🄴

12 pl. de la Gare – ℰ *03 88 52 84 84* – *www.le-grand-hotel.com*
83 rm ⌷ – †79/355 € ††79/355 € **E1**
◆ Business ◆ Design ◆
This hotel opposite the TGV station is definitely on a modern track with its minimalist contemporary decor, understated yet plush furnishings, and meticulously maintained amenities. Five minutes from the city centre.

STRASBOURG - FRANCE

Novotel Centre Halles   ↳ & rm, 🅰 ⚹ 🔊 VISA 🚳 AE ①
4 quai Kléber – ℰ *03 88 21 50 50* – *www.novotel.com*   **F1**
96 rm – †87/300 € ††87/300 €, � 15 €
Rest – *(closed Sunday lunch)* Carte 22/40 €
♦ Chain hotel ♦ Modern ♦ Functional ♦
A hotel with bright, spacious rooms located in the Les Halles shopping centre. Gym on the top floor with a view of the cathedral.

Diana Dauphine *without rest*   🅰 ⚹ 🚗 VISA 🚳 AE
30 r. de la 1ère-Armée – ℰ *03 88 36 26 61*
– www.hotel-diana-dauphine.com
– Closed 23 December-2 January   *Plan I* **B3**
45 rm – †79/149 € ††79/149 €, ⊟ 11 €
♦ Business ♦ Design ♦ Personalised ♦
Located on the tram line leading to the old quarter, this hotel has a modern lobby-cum-lounge and understated contemporary rooms, most of which are spacious. Locked garage accessible 24 hours a day.

Mercure St-Jean *without rest*   🅰 ⚹ 🔊 VISA 🚳 AE ①
3 r. du Maire-Kuss – ℰ *03 88 32 80 80* – *www.mercure.com*   **E1**
63 rm – †79/199 € ††79/199 €, ⊟ 16 €
♦ Chain hotel ♦ Business ♦ Design ♦
Modern hotel with pleasant rooms offering contemporary comforts between the train station and old quarter. Try the "2030 room" for its imaginative and futuristic amenities.

Dragon *without rest*   ⚹ 🔊 VISA 🚳 AE ①
12 r. du Dragon – ℰ *03 88 35 79 80* – *www.dragon.fr*   **F2**
32 rm – †79/159 € ††89/159 €, ⊟ 12 €
♦ Family ♦ Modern ♦ Design ♦
Two 17C houses built around a flower-filled patio garden (where breakfast is served in summer) in a quiet area of the city. Comfortable, modern rooms, built into the eaves on the top floor.

Chut - Au Bain aux Plantes   🍴 & rm, ⚹ VISA 🚳 AE ①
4 r. Bain-aux-Plantes – ℰ *03 88 32 05 06* – *www.hote-strasbourg.fr*
8 rm – †95/200 € ††95/200 €, ⊟ 12 € – 1 suite   **E2**
Rest – *(closed 29 April-8 May, 12 to 21 August, 28 October-6 November, 23 to 27 December, Sunday and Monday)* Menu 22 € (weekday lunch)/ 38 € – Carte 36/54 €
♦ Inn ♦ Luxury ♦ Personalised ♦
Hotel with all the charm of a guesthouse, located in a picturesque street near the historic Petite France district. Contemporary and antique decorative objects and furniture in a tranquil, minimalist atmosphere. The spice-infused cuisine changes daily. Intimate dining room with a courtyard terrace.

Le Kléber *without rest*   ⚹ VISA 🚳 AE
29 pl. Kléber – ℰ *03 88 32 09 53* – *www.hotel-kleber.com*
37 rm – †65/90 € ††75/100 €, ⊟ 8.50 €   **F1**
♦ Family ♦ Personalised ♦ Cosy ♦
All the rooms here have a colourful, sweet and savoury theme (names include Meringue, Fraise and Cannelle). Unbeatable location on the famous Place Kléber.

Couvent du Franciscain *without rest*   & 🅰 ⚹ 🔊 🅿
18 r. du Fg-de-Pierre – ℰ *03 88 32 93 93*   VISA 🚳 AE
– www.hotel-franciscain.com   **F1**
43 rm – †50/80 € ††80/90 €, ⊟ 10 €
♦ Family ♦ Functional ♦ Retro ♦
This hotel on the site of an old convent at the end of a cul-de-sac offers simple, neat rooms at competitive rates. Breakfast is served in a winstub-style cellar with an amusing mural.

287

XXXX **Au Crocodile** (Philippe Bohrer)   ⏣ 📶 🅰 🄰🄴

🕸   *10 r. de l'Outre – ☎ 03 88 32 13 02 – www.au-crocodile.com*
– Closed 15 to 29 July, Sunday and Monday   **F1**
Rest – Menu 64 € (weekdays), 92/129 € – Carte 90/170 € ⏣

◆ Classic ◆ Romantic ◆ Formal ◆

Intimacy, elegance and harmony reign in this Strasbourg institution, which exudes a certain classicism. The same applies to the food: quality seasonal ingredients go into the delicious and well-executed concoctions.
→ Jambonnettes de cuisses de grenouille et chlorophylle d'ortie. Homard bleu rôti, cannelloni aux morilles et sauce à l'américaine. Streusel chocolat, crème glacée au Carambar et granité à la liqueur de cannelle.

XXX **1741**   🅰 ⏣ 📶 🅰

22 quai des Bateliers – ☎ 03 88 35 50 50 – www.1741.fr – Closed Sunday
Rest – Menu 57/97 € – Carte 25/50 €   **G2**

◆ Modern ◆ Elegant ◆ Cosy ◆

A fine Napoleonic Empire town house, opposite the Rohan château, with an elegant boudoir-style interior. Delicious cuisine, prepared with great attention to detail, and matched with an interesting selection of wines from Alsace.

XXX **Buerehiesel** (Eric Westermann)   ⏣ 🛋 🅰 🅿 📶 🅰 🄰🄴

🕸   *at the Orangerie park – ☎ 03 88 45 56 65 – www.buerehiesel.com*
– Closed 28 July-20 August, 31 December-15 January, 17 to 25 February,
Sunday and Monday   *Plan I* **D1**
Rest – Menu 35 € (weekday lunch), 68/90 € – Carte 65/95 € ⏣

◆ Modern ◆ Formal ◆ Friendly ◆

An exquisite restaurant housed in a beautiful half-timbered 17C farmhouse that was dismantled from its original location and rebuilt in the Parc de l'Orangerie (bucolic views from the conservatory dining room and terrace). Refined and reliable regional cuisine, accompanied by a wonderful choice of Alsace wines. Pleasant service.
→ Schniederspaetzle et cuisses de grenouilles poêlées au cerfeuil. Poulette pattes noires cuite entière comme un baeckeofe. Brioche caramélisée à la bière, glace à la bière et poire rôtie.

XXX **Maison des Tanneurs dite Gerwerstub**   📶 🅰 🄰🄴

42 r. Bain-aux-Plantes – ☎ 03 88 32 79 70
– www.maison-des-tanneurs.com
– Closed 28 July-12 August, 30 December-23 January, Sunday and Monday
Rest – Menu 20 € (weekday lunch), 26/45 € – Carte 34/52 €   **F2**

◆ Elegant ◆ Friendly ◆

This typical Alsace house with lots of character (1572) overlooking the river Ill in the historic Petite France district is an institution for sauerkraut and other famous regional specialities.

XXX **Goh** – Hôtel Sofitel   🛋 🅰 📶 🅰 🄰🄴

4 pl. St-Pierre-le-Jeune – ☎ 03 88 15 49 10 – www.sofitel-strasbourg.com
– Closed 3 weeks in August, 1 week in January, Saturday lunch, Sunday and
Bank Holidays   **F1**
Rest – Menu 34/89 € bi – Carte 47/71 €

◆ Modern ◆ Elegant ◆ Fashionable ◆

The elegant and contemporary decor is one of the main assets here, a setting that is perfectly suited to the cuisine that combines regional and modern influences.

XX **La Cambuse** (Elisabeth Lefebvre)   🅰 📶 ⏣

🕸   *1 r. des Dentelles – ☎ 03 88 22 10 22 – Closed 28 April-13 May, 28 July-19*
August, 22 December-6 January, Sunday and Monday   **F2**
Rest – *(number of covers limited, pre-book)* Carte 50/58 €

◆ Fish and seafood ◆ Cosy ◆ Intimate ◆

La Cambuse's intimate dining room is decorated in the style of a boat cabin. Simple yet refined fish and seafood are the specialities here, prepared in a fusion of French and Asian styles based around spices and a minimum of cooking time.
→ Tartare de crabe, écrevisse et dorade au wasabi. Bar coco à la feuille de banane. Tarte au chocolat amer et crème à la noix de coco.

XX **L'Atable 77**   🅰️ 🆅🅸🆂🅰 ⓔ 🅰🅴 ⓘ
77 Grand'Rue – ℰ 03 88 32 23 37
– www.latable77.com
*– Closed 29 April-8 May, 29 July-20 August, 1 to 10 January, Sunday, Monday
and Bank Holiday lunch*   **F2**
Rest – Menu 36/85 € bi 🍃
♦ Cosy ♦ Design ♦
An attractive, trendy restaurant with a resolutely contemporary feel throughout.
Sleek decor dotted with bright paintings, designer tableware and very appeti-
sing modern cuisine.

XX **Girardin - La Casserole** (Éric Girardin)   🅰️ 🆅🅸🆂🅰 ⓔ 🅰🅴
☸ *24 r. des Juifs – ℰ 03 88 36 49 68*
– www.restaurantlacasserole.fr
*– Closed 29 March-1 April, 5 to 13 May, 4 to 25 August, Tuesday lunch, Sunday
and Monday*   **G1**
Rest – *(number of covers limited, pre-book)* Menu 39 € (lunch), 75/95 €
– Carte approx. 85 € 🍃
♦ Creative ♦ Elegant ♦
A magical restaurant behind the cathedral where Éric Girardin creates refined,
harmonious dishes with striking skill. A hushed, contemporary setting and charming service.
➔ Émietté de tourteau et céleri, pomme fruit et nage de crustacés. Poitrine
de cochon confite, fromage blanc à la gentiane. Vanille de Madagascar en
"crousti'feuillage".

XX **Le Violon d'Ingres**   🛏️ 🆅🅸🆂🅰 ⓔ
1 r. Chevalier-Robert (at La Robertsau) – ℰ 03 88 31 39 50
– www.violondingres.com
– Closed Saturday lunch, Sunday dinner and Monday
Rest – Menu 32/65 € – Carte 54/66 €
♦ Elegant ♦ Classic ♦
This historic Alsace house in the Robertsau district near the European Parliament serves impeccably prepared modern cuisine in an elegant dining room
or on the shady terrace.

XX **Maison Kammerzell et Hôtel Baumann** with rm   🅰️ 🛜
16 pl. de la Cathédrale – ℰ 03 88 32 42 14   ♻️ 🆅🅸🆂🅰 ⓔ 🅰🅴 ⓘ
– www.maison-kammerzell.com   **G2**
9 rm – 🀫110/145 € 🀫🀫135/175 €, ☲ 10 €
Rest – Menu 28/46 € – Carte 29/50 €
♦ Traditional ♦ Inn ♦
A typical 16C Strasbourg house near the cathedral with an authentic medieval
feel, featuring stained-glass windows, paintings, wood carvings and Gothic vaulting. Local cuisine (sauerkraut is a speciality) and brasserie-style dishes. Plainly
decorated rooms.

XX **Gavroche** (Benoit Fuchs)   🅰️ 🆅🅸🆂🅰 ⓔ 🅰🅴 ⓘ
☸ *4 r. Klein – ℰ 03 88 36 82 89*
– www.restaurant-gavroche.com
– Closed 27 July-13 August, 23 December-3 January, Saturday and Sunday
Rest – Menu 42/62 € – Carte 65/80 €   **G2**
♦ Modern ♦ Elegant ♦
There's little fanfare in this restaurant offering a pleasant welcome and elegant,
contemporary decor. Beautifully presented modern and creative cuisine influenced by seasonal produce.
➔ Foie gras de canard poêlé aux amandes grillées. Selle et carré d'agneau
rôtis, charlotte à la coriandre et artichaut poivrade. Douceur café-caramel,
sorbet caramel.

XX
ξ3

Umami (René Fieger)   AC VISA ✱ AE

8 r. des Dentelles – ℰ 03 88 32 80 53 – www.restaurant-umami.com
– Closed 1 to 9 May, 4 to 19 September, 31 December-16 January, Sunday
dinner, Wednesday, Thursday and lunch except Saturday and Bank Holidays
Rest *– (number of covers limited, pre-book)* Menu 48/65 €   **F2**
♦ Creative ♦ Cosy ♦
Sweet, salty, sour, bitter and… "umami" (savoury), the fifth taste in Japanese cuisine and the hallmark of the cuisine here, which showcases flavours from around the world. Attractive modern decor.
→ Menu du marché.

XX

Pont des Vosges   🛜 VISA ✱ AE

15 quai Koch – ℰ 03 88 36 47 75 – www.lepont-des-vosges.fr
– Closed Sunday   **H1**
Rest *–* Carte 38/58 €
♦ Traditional ♦ Retro ♦ Friendly ♦
Located on the corner of an old building, this brasserie is renowned for its copious, traditional cuisine. Advertising posters and mirrors decorate the dining room.

X

L'Atelier du Goût   AC ⇔ VISA ✱

17 r. des Tonneliers – ℰ 03 88 21 01 01 – www.atelier-du-gout.fr
– Closed 1 week February Holidays, 2 weeks in August, Sunday and Bank
Holidays   **G2**
Rest *–* Menu 36 € *–* Carte 42/58 €
♦ Modern ♦ Trendy ♦ Design ♦
This pleasant restaurant in a picturesque area has a designer ambience. Blackboards featuring instructive pictures of cuts of beef and vegetables adorn the walls. Creative seasonal cuisine.

WINSTUBS *Regional specialities and wine tasting in a typical Alsatian atmosphere*

X

L'Ami Schutz   🛜 VISA ✱ AE ⓪

1 r. des Ponts-Couverts – ℰ 03 88 32 76 98 – www.ami-schutz.com
– Closed Christmas Holidays   **E2**
Rest *–* Menu 18 € (weekday lunch), 31/46 € *–* Carte 45/55 €
♦ Alsatian ♦ Rustic ♦ Friendly ♦
L'Ami Schutz enjoys a timeless setting on the river Ill in the historic Petite France district. Delightful shady terrace and two typical dining rooms (one rustic, the other more refined) with a menu to match.

X

Le Clou   AC VISA ✱ AE

3 r. du Chaudron – ℰ 03 88 32 11 67 – www.le-clou.com
– Closed Sunday   **G1-2**
Rest *– (pre-book)* Menu 19 € (weekday lunch) *–* Carte 28/55 €
♦ Alsatian ♦ Rustic ♦ Friendly ♦
Located a short distance from the cathedral, this authentic winstub (typical Alsace bistro) is packed with olde worlde objects and scenes from yesteryear (beautiful marquetry). Typical cuisine which pays homage to the region.

X

Fink'Stuebel with rm   🛜 VISA ✱

26 r. Finkwiller – ℰ 03 88 25 07 57 – www.finkstuebel.free.fr
– Closed 9 to 30 August, Sunday and Monday   **F2**
5 rm ⌂ *–* †79 € ††88 €   **Rest** *–* Carte 33/61 €
♦ Alsatian ♦ Family ♦ Inn ♦
Half-timbering, wooden floorboards, painted woodwork, regional furniture and floral tablecloths provide the decor in the Fink'Stuebel, the epitome of a traditional winstub. Local cuisine predominates here, of course, with foie gras to the fore. There are a few guestrooms above the winstub (just one per floor!), each decorated in an Alsatian style.

✗ **Au Pont du Corbeau** 　　　　　　　🛋 AC VISA ⊙⊙ AE

21 quai St-Nicolas – ✆ *03 88 35 60 68*
– Closed August, February Holidays, Sunday lunch and Saturday except in
December **G2**
Rest – Carte 25/40 € ❀

◆ Alsatian ◆ Rustic ◆ Inn ◆

Experience local gastronomic specialities and traditional decor (Renaissance
features, posters) in this restaurant next door to the Musée Alsacien, with its displays of popular art.

FRANCE - STRASBOURG

TOULOUSE
TOULOUSE

Population: 440 204

Rudiuk/Fotolia.com

The first thing you notice about Toulouse is its pink buildings, leaving you in little doubt as to why France's fourth biggest city has the enchanting epithet 'La Ville Rose'. The rouge shade of brickwork lends the place a distinctly sunny charm, enhanced by a lovely old town infused with 16C merchant houses and grand Romanesque churches. It's here that the Toulousains throng, particularly at dusk, when the town's bars and cafes are bathed in a sumptuous rosy glow.

This is a confident, easy-going city whose rich architectural heritage is matched by an intellectual verve: its 115,000 students make it second only to Paris as a French university centre. From the 10C to the 13C, the Counts of Toulouse ran a resplendent court populated by troubadours and poets whose works inspired the likes of Dante and Chaucer. Then in the 16C, it flourished again through the cultivation of woad, and newly enriched merchants built the most magnificent townhouses – *hôtels particuliers*. The visitor-friendly old town is bordered to the east by the Canal du Midi, and to the west by the gently curving River Garonne. This charming area is even more tightly hemmed in by a ring of 19C boulevards (d'Arcole, Strasbourg, Lazare Carnot, Verdier and Jules Guesde). A sharply defined 'cross' of streets cuts the centre into four quarters.

TOULOUSE IN...

→ **ONE DAY**
Place du Capitole, St-Sernin, Les Jacobins, Hôtel d'Assezat.

→ **TWO DAYS**
Musée des Augustins, Les Abattoirs (or Cité de l'Espace), Rue Croix-Baragnon, a stroll along the Canal du Midi.

→ **THREE DAYS**
Jardin des Plantes, Musée Paul-Dupuy.

PRACTICAL INFORMATION

ARRIVAL-DEPARTURE

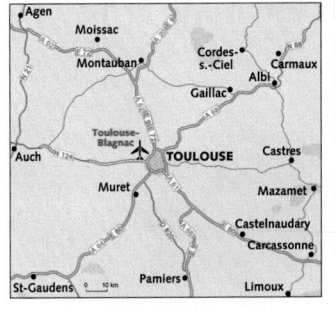

✈ Toulouse Blagnac Airport is located 7km west of the city centre. The Express bus takes 20min.
High speed trains to Paris go from Gare Matabiau.

GETTING AROUND

Toulouse has a bus and metro system to get you around. A one-trip red ticket allows you to travel anywhere on the network for an hour. There's a slightly more expensive round trip ticket, plus a day ticket and 10-12 trip tickets. The main railway station is situated in a picturesque setting by the Canal du Midi. It's a short five minute hop on the metro to the old town centre, but if you're not weighed down by luggage it's a pleasant twenty minute stroll over the canal on foot. On your walk into town, just before the central Place du Capitole, you'll find the main tourist office on the square Charles de Gaulle.

CALENDAR HIGHLIGHTS

February
International Violet Meeting.

March
International Fair.

June
The Garonne Festival,
Marathon des Mots.

July
Toulouse d'Éte Music Festival.

September
Piano Aux Jacobins Festival,
Printemps de Septembre,
Festival Occitania.

November
Antiques Fair.

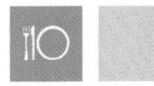

EATING OUT

The food of the Toulousain is not for the faint-hearted. Neck, brain, ears and liver find their way onto the menu – stuffed, slow-cooked or in eye-popping combinations. The mainstay of the southwest is cassoulet, a hearty stew with basic ingredients of pork, duck fat, beans and garlic. You need to be hungry to take it on, so you'll be pleased to know that evening dining in Toulouse doesn't really start till at least 8.30 in the evening, by which time your appetite should be whetted. Get there earlier and you'll be dining alone, as this is a city that lives the late life: it's only 60 miles from the Spanish border and its dining style is cheerily seen as 'la mode espagnole'. If you've been excited by an ingredient then stock up at the farmers' markets that are popular in the city: these are the places for sausages, cheeses, and bread the size of local rugby balls. There's a third element to the food scene here: wander down some of the narrower streets in the evening and you'll realise how close you are to North Africa, as exotic scents waft from darkened doorways.

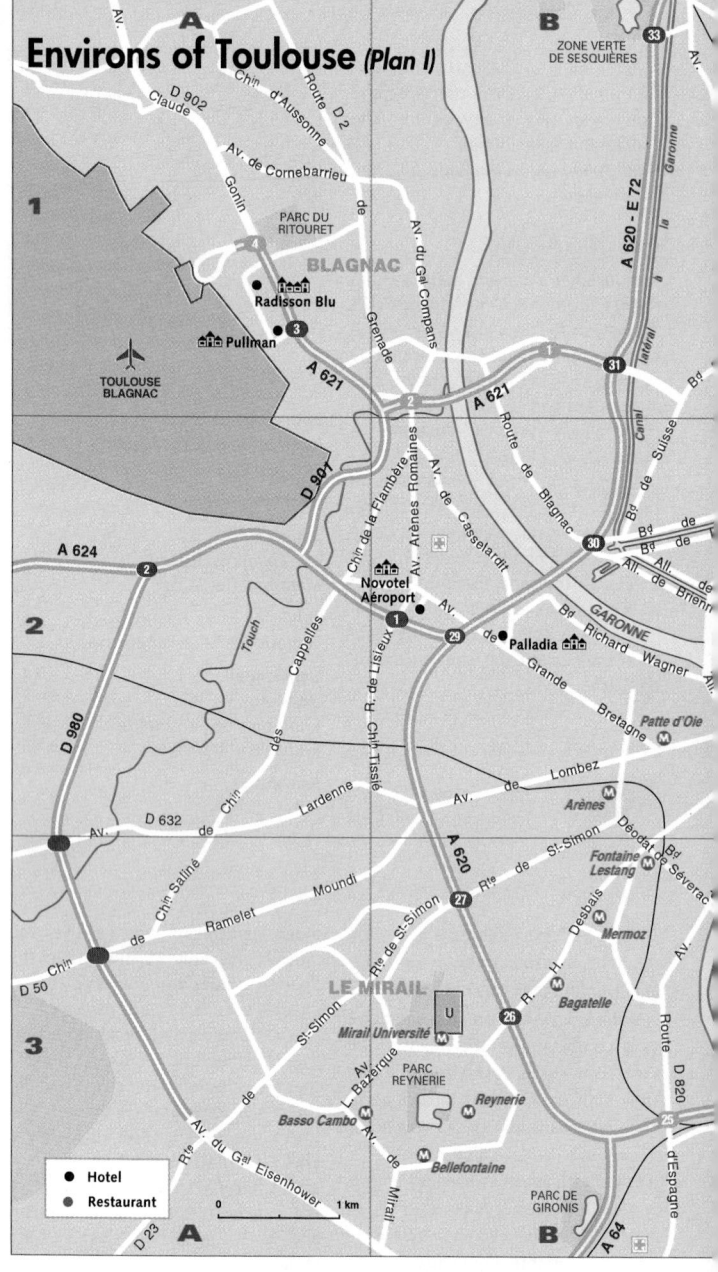

Environs of Toulouse *(Plan I)*

ZONE VERTE
DE SESQUIÈRES

FRANCE - TOULOUSE

Av. Claude
D 902
Chin d'Aussonne
Route D 2
Av. de Cornebarrieu
Gonin
PARC DU
RITOURET
BLAGNAC
Radisson Blu
Pullman
A 621
TOULOUSE
BLAGNAC
D 901
Av. du Gal Compans
Grenade
A 620 - E 72
Garonne
A 621
Canal latéral
Route de Blagnac
Bd de Suisse
A 624
Chin de la Flambère
Av. Arènes Romaines
Av. de Casselardit
Novotel
Aéroport
Touch
Cappelles
R. de Lisieux
Chin Tissié
D 980
Av. Palladia
GARONNE
Bd Richard Wagner
Grande Bretagne
Patte d'Oie
D 632
Chin de
Lardenne
Av. de Lombez
Arènes
Déodat de Séverac
Fontaine Lestang
Chin Saliné
Moundi
A 620
Rte de St-Simon
Desbals
Mermoz
D 50
Chin
Ramelet
LE MIRAIL
St-Simon
R. H.
Bagatelle
Mirail Université
PARC
REYNERIE
Reynerie
D 820
Av. L. Bazerque
Basso Cambo
Av. de Mirail
Bellefontaine
PARC DE
GIRONIS
Rte du Gal Eisenhower
D 23
d'Espagne
A 64

● Hotel
● Restaurant

0   1 km

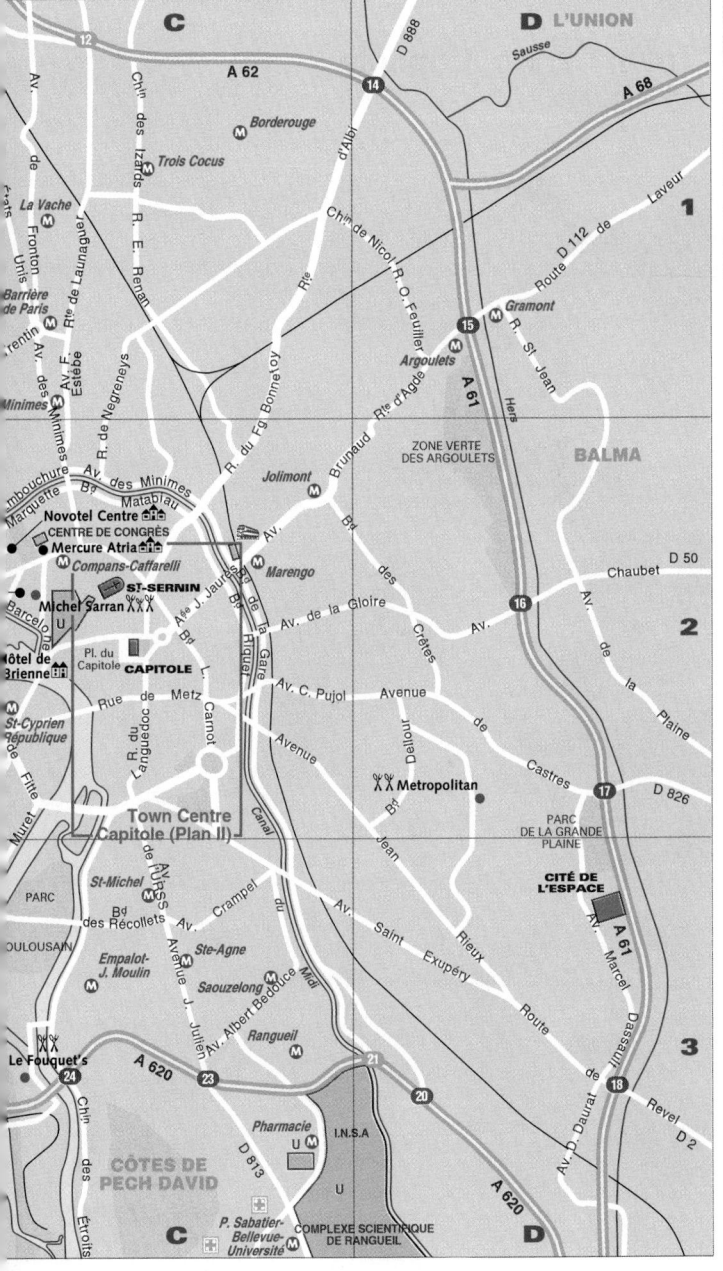

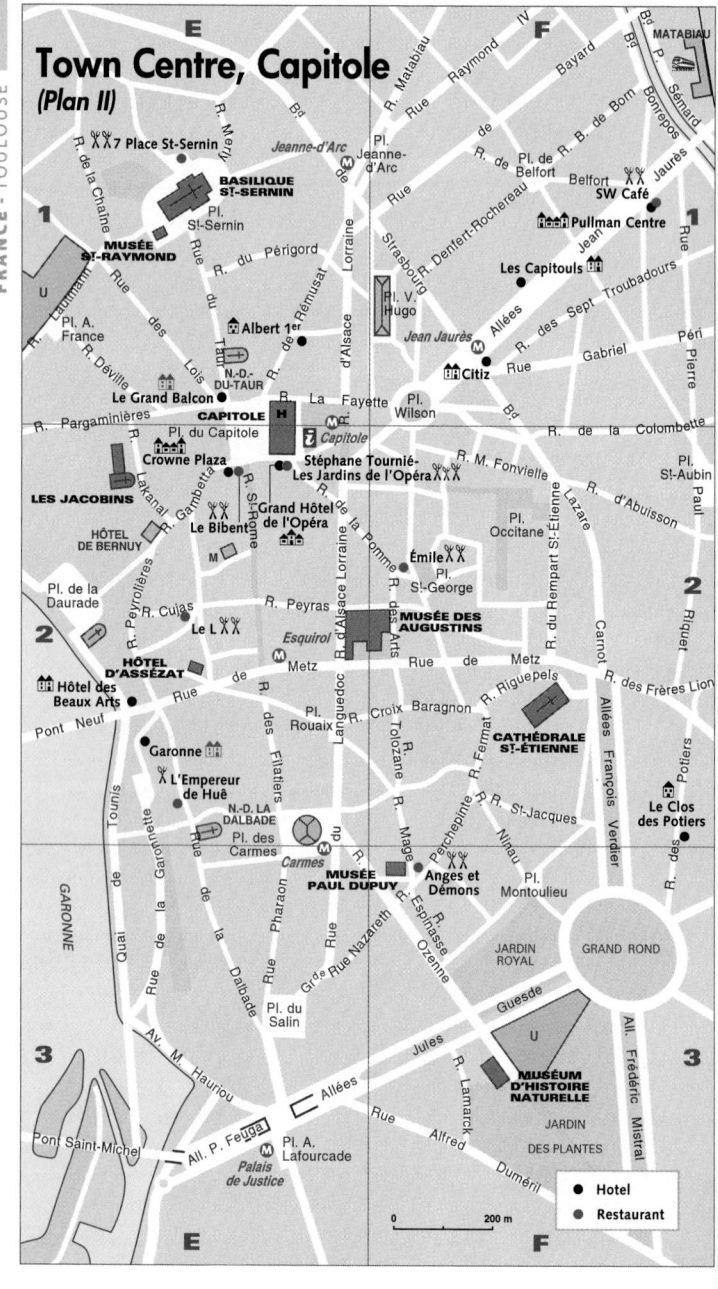

FRANCE - TOULOUSE

Pullman Centre 🖾 🖾 🛜 🗼 🚗 VISA ☎ AE

84 allées Jean-Jaurès – 𝒞 *05 61 10 23 10 – www.pullmanhotels.com*
– Closed 15 July-18 August **F1**
119 rm – †156/350 € ††156/350 €, � 25 € – 6 suites
Rest *S W Café* – 𝒞 *05 61 10 23 40 (closed lunch Saturday and Sunday)*
Menu 23 € – Carte 31/48 €
♦ Luxury ♦ Chain hotel ♦ Design ♦
Contemporary hotel slightly out of the city centre. Its refined style and high-tech equipment assure its popularity with an international clientele. Minimalist decor plus dishes showcasing regional produce and cosmopolitan flavours in the SW Café.

Crowne Plaza 🚗 🖾 🛁 🖾 rm, 🖾 🛜 🗼 VISA ☎ AE ①

7 pl. du Capitole – 𝒞 *05 61 61 19 19 – www.crowne-plaza-toulouse.com*
162 rm – †110/375 € ††110/375 €, ⊆ 24 € – 3 suites **E2**
Rest – *(closed August)* Menu 27/46 € – Carte 40/62 €
♦ Business ♦ Chain hotel ♦ Classic ♦
Perfectly situated on place du Capitole, this huge hotel is ideal for business travellers. It has a comprehensive business centre and rooms in a classic or contemporary style. The restaurant gives onto a lovely courtyard.

Grand Hôtel de l'Opéra *without rest* 🖾 🖾 🛜 🗼

1 pl. du Capitole – 𝒞 *05 61 21 82 66* VISA ☎ AE ①
– www.grand-hotel-opera.com **E2**
44 rm – †190/490 € ††220/490 €, ⊆ 19 € – 6 suites
♦ Luxury ♦ Cosy ♦ Stylish ♦
This 17C convent has style! Draperies, mahogany panelling, velvet... The decor is redolent of a stage set at the opera, which is entirely appropriate given that the latter is just a stone's throw away.

Mercure Atria 🚗 🖾 🖾 🛜 🗼 🚗 VISA ☎ AE ①

8 espl. Compans Caffarelli – 𝒞 *05 61 11 09 09*
– www.mercure-toulouse-compans-caffarelli.com *Plan I* **C2**
134 rm – †85/190 € ††85/190 €, ⊆ 17 € – 2 suites
Rest – *(closed 22 July-18 August)* Menu 20 € – Carte 24/44 €
♦ Chain hotel ♦ Modern ♦
This Mercure has direct access to the conference centre. After a busy day, guests will benefit from the tranquillity of the rooms, all of which give onto the courtyard or the garden.

Novotel Centre 🦮 🚗 🍽 🖾 rm, 🖾 🛜 🗼 🚗 VISA ☎ AE ①

5 pl. A. Jourdain – 𝒞 *05 61 21 74 74 – www.novotel.com* *Plan I* **C2**
135 rm – †78/195 € ††78/195 €, ⊆ 15 € – 2 suites **Rest** – Carte 20/45 €
♦ Chain hotel ♦ Functional ♦
In the city centre yet peacefully situated, this presentable Novotel is equally suitable for business travellers and families (special offers available to the latter).

Le Grand Balcon *without rest* 🖾 🖾 🛜 VISA ☎ AE ①

10 r. Romiguière – 𝒞 *05 34 25 44 09 – www.grandbalconhotel.com*
47 rm – †170/400 € ††170/400 €, ⊆ 18 € **E1**
♦ Luxury ♦ Design ♦
This renowned establishment hosted some of the great names during aviation's golden age. The decor – creatively designer in feel – pays homage to them. Room 32 is a carbon copy of the one used by Saint-Exupéry in the 1930s.

Garonne *without rest* 🖾 🖾 🛜 VISA ☎ AE

22 descente de la Halle-aux-Poissons – 𝒞 *05 34 31 94 80*
– www.hotelgaronne.com **E2**
14 rm – †95/260 € ††95/260 €, ⊆ 15 €
♦ Luxury ♦ Personalised ♦
A characterful 'boutique' hotel on an alley in old Toulouse. It is very contemporary in feel (wood, colour, oriental touches) and quite simply makes for an elegant and welcoming setting.

Citiz without rest   ⟨& AC ⟩ ⟨⟩ ⟨⟩ VISA ⟨◎⟩ AE ⟨①⟩

18 allées Jean-Jaurès – ℰ *05 61 11 18 18*
– *www.citizhotel.com*   **F1**
56 rm – †100/240 € ††115/255 €, � 18 €

♦ Business ♦ Modern ♦

Right in the city centre (near place Wilson), this brand new hotel has an urbane designer feel, plus a tea lounge for the peckish. Popular with business travellers and others.

Hôtel des Beaux Arts without rest   ⟨⇐ AC ⟩ ⟨⟩ VISA ⟨◎⟩ AE ⟨①⟩

1 pl. du Pont-Neuf – ℰ *05 34 45 42 42*
– *www.hoteldesbeauxarts.com*   **E2**
19 rm – †120/255 € ††120/255 €, ⊻ 14 €

♦ Business ♦ Modern ♦ Cosy ♦

Toile de Jouy giving a jewel box feel, or raffia backdrops lending exoticism... the decor here has been carefully chosen. Room 42 has its own terrace. The welcome does not disappoint either.

Les Capitouls without rest   ⟨& AC ⟩ ⟨⟩ VISA ⟨◎⟩ AE ⟨①⟩

29 allées Jean-Jaurès – ℰ *05 34 41 31 21*
– *www.bestwestern-capitouls.com*   **F1**
53 rm – †130/181 € ††130/181 €, ⊻ 15 € – 2 suites

♦ Chain hotel ♦ Classic ♦

An elegant building in the heart of Toulouse offering classic, practical and well-soundproofed accommodation.

Hôtel de Brienne without rest   ⟨& AC ⟩ ⟨⟩ ⟨⟩ P ⟨⟩ VISA ⟨◎⟩ AE ⟨①⟩

20 bd du Mar.-Leclerc – ℰ *05 61 23 60 60*
– *www.hoteldebrienne.com*   *Plan I* **C2**
77 rm – †90/140 € ††90/140 €, ⊻ 12 €

♦ Chain hotel ♦ Modern ♦ Functional ♦

Near the conference centre and the heart of Toulouse, this hotel is ideal for business travellers. The rooms are small but clean and practical (renovations began in 2010). Free parking.

Le Clos des Potiers without rest   ⟨⟩ P ⟨⟩ VISA ⟨◎⟩ AE

12 r. des Potiers – ℰ *05 61 47 15 15*
– *www.le-clos-des-potiers.com*   **F2**
10 rm – †105/150 € ††105/150 €, ⊻ 14 €

♦ Family ♦ Personalised ♦

Close to the city centre, this genteel residence stylishly exudes a distinct guest-house charm. It has tastefully classic accommodation and a very cosy atmosphere.

Albert 1er without rest   ⟨AC ⟩ ⟨⟩ ⟨⟩ VISA ⟨◎⟩ AE

8 r. Rivals – ℰ *05 61 21 17 91* – *www.hotel-albert1.com*
    E1
47 rm – †55/99 € ††69/120 €, ⊻ 10 €

♦ Family ♦ Functional ♦

This practical hotel is a stone's throw from place du Capitole. The functional rooms are well presented; opt for those at the rear, which are quieter.

Michel Sarran   ⟨⟩ AC ⟨⟩ ⟨⟩ VISA ⟨◎⟩ AE

21 bd A. Duportal – ℰ *05 61 12 32 32*
– *www.michel-sarran.com*
– *Closed August, Christmas Holidays, Wednesday lunch, Saturday and Sunday*
Rest – *(pre-book)* Menu 49 € bi (lunch), 98/165 € bi   *Plan I* **C2**
– Carte 100/145 €

♦ Creative ♦ Intimate ♦ Fashionable ♦

Michel Sarran has created a timeless ambience in this 19C manor house, adding elegant contemporary touches to a setting that is stylish without being fussy. This convivial atmosphere forms the backdrop for a fine culinary experience.
→ Fenouil en crème onctueuse à l'œuf, râpée de truffe et graines de maracuja. Foie gras aux pommes en cuisson basse température. Haricots tarbais en mousse légère au vieux rhum et lait de coco.

FRANCE - TOULOUSE

Stéphane Tournié Les Jardins de l'Opéra ⌘ ✧

1 pl. du Capitole – ☎ *05 61 23 07 76*   📶 ⬤⬤ 🅰🅴
– www.lesjardinsdelopera.com
– *Closed 1 to 7 January, Sunday, Monday and Bank Holiday lunch*
Rest – Menu 29 € (weekdays), 56/99 € – Carte 80/90 €   **E2**
♦ Modern ♦ Elegant ♦
Stéphane Tournié's restaurant offers consistent high quality. He focuses on the basics and does it extremely well. There is an emphasis on top quality ingredients (preferably organic), skill, expertise, finesse and good taste. The restaurant has an attractive inner courtyard crowned with a glass roof and is just a stone's throw from the Place du Capitole.
➔ Foie gras de canard poché dans un bouillon onctueux à la citronnelle et huître. Pigeon en deux cuissons fumé minute. Douceur litchi-rose, pomme verte et son sorbet.

Metropolitan 🍴 ♿ 🅰🅲 ✧ 🅿 📶 ⬤⬤ 🅰🅴

2 pl. Auguste-Albert – ☎ *05 61 34 63 11 – www.metropolitan-restaurant.fr*
– *Closed 3 to 18 August and Sunday*   *Plan I* **D2**
Rest – Menu 32 € (weekdays), 45/110 € – Carte 85/115 €
♦ Modern ♦ Design ♦
Passion and professionalism characterise this establishment's young chef and his team. In partial view of diners, they create contemporary cuisine using the finest produce. Sterling work, best enjoyed from the comfort of a Chesterfield.
➔ Fricassée de légumes oubliés en cocotte lutée. Truffe fraîche et poitrine de cochon confite. Barre glacée à la violette et chocolat ivoire.

Le Bibent 🍴 🅰🅲 ✧ 📶 ⬤⬤

5 pl. du Capitole – ☎ *05 34 30 18 37 – www.maisonconstant.com*
Rest – Carte 33/53 €   **E2**
♦ Traditional ♦ Elegant ♦ Brasserie ♦
A prime location in the heart of the pink city and a superb turn-of-the-20C interior characterise the historic interior of owner Christian Constant's bistro. The locals flock here to sample regional classics: authentic cassoulet, mimosa eggs, and so on.

Le Fouquet's 🍴 🅰🅲 ✧ 🅿 📶 ⬤⬤ 🅰🅴

18 chemin de la Loge – ☎ *05 61 33 37 77 – www.lucienbarriere.com*
Rest – Menu 32 € bi/36 € – Carte 38/75 €   **C3**
♦ Traditional ♦ Elegant ♦ Trendy ♦
Fouquet's most recent restaurant is situated on an island on the Garonne river. It serves contemporary cuisine amid a decor of gold leaf, discreet lighting and old photos.

Le L 🍴 🅰🅲 ✧ 📶 ⬤⬤

24 pl. de la Bourse – ☎ *05 61 21 69 05 – www.restaurantlel.com*
– *Closed 12 to 20 August, Sunday and Monday*   **E2**
Rest – Carte 34/68 €
♦ Creative ♦ Fashionable ♦
A contemporary designer restaurant in the heart of the old town. Find warm tones, dark wood and fine dining with a commensurate choice of wines. Creative cuisine served in a setting with atmosphere.

Anges et Démons 🅰🅲 ✧ 📶 ⬤⬤

1 r. Perchepinte – ☎ *05 61 52 66 69 – www.restaurant-angesetdemons.com*
– *Closed 1 to 15 July, 1 to 15 January, Sunday dinner, Monday and lunch except Sunday*   **F3**
Rest – Menu 48 € (weekdays), 55/75 € ⅜
♦ Classic ♦ Elegant ♦
Angels will be happiest on the ground floor, a happy blend of ancient and modern. Demons should head down to the cellar, with its magnificent 16C vaulting and vestiges of a bread oven. Classical cuisine.

XX **7 Place St-Sernin** 🛜 🔼 ⇄ 📧 🐠

7 pl. St-Sernin – 𝒞 *05 62 30 05 30*
– www.7placesaintsernin.com
– Closed 3 to 18 August, Monday lunch, Saturday lunch and Sunday
Rest – Menu 27/58 € – Carte 54/74 € **E1**
♦ Modern ♦ Friendly ♦
This typical Toulouse residence is bright and warm, with a terrace overlooking the basilica so dear to local singer Nougaro. The cuisine: tradition and regional with a modern twist.

XX **Émile** 🛜 🔼 📧 🐠 🔼 ①

13 pl. St-Georges – 𝒞 *05 61 21 05 56*
– www.restaurant-emile.com
– Closed Christmas Holidays, Monday except dinner from May-September and Sunday **F2**
Rest – Menu 22 € (lunch), 37/57 € – Carte 46/63 € ঌ
♦ Traditional ♦ Friendly ♦
An attractive wine list, good traditional cuisine that focuses on fresh produce and is 100% homemade, and – the icing on the cake – a pretty terrace overlooking a pleasant square. The star of the show is obviously the cassoulet!

X **L'Empereur de Huê** 🔼 📧 🐠

17 r. des Couteliers – 𝒞 *05 61 53 55 72*
– www.empereurdehue.com
– Closed Sunday and Monday **E2**
Rest – *(dinner only) (pre-book)* Menu 39 €
– Carte 47/60 €
♦ Vietnamese ♦ Minimalist ♦
This establishment counts salted lemongrass beef and caramelised pork among its classics. Against a resolutely Zen backdrop, the chef prepares fresh and colourful Vietnamese cuisine.

AROUND TOULOUSE
Plan I

BLAGNAC

🏨 **Radisson Blu**

2 r. Dieudonné-Costes – 𝒞 *05 61 16 18 30*
– www.lavieenrose-restaurant.com **A1**
200 rm – ♦110/320 € ♦♦145/370 €, ☑ 25 €
Rest – Menu 27 € (weekday lunch) – Carte 34/48 €
♦ Chain hotel ♦ Business ♦ Design ♦
Near the airport, this hotel is resolutely urban in character. The colourful rooms are designer and high-tech in feel. There is a superb patio planted with vines and oleander. In the restaurant, the menu is brief but truly original. Brunch on the first day of the month (with children's entertainment).

🏨 **Pullman** 🛜 🔼 📧 🛜 🔼 📧 🐠 🔼 ①

2 av. Didier Daurat (direction airport, exit 3) – 𝒞 *05 34 56 11 11*
– www.pullmanhotels.com **A1**
100 rm – ♦150/300 € ♦♦150/300 €, ☑ 22 €
Rest *Le Corridor* – *(closed 27 July-18 August, Friday dinner, Saturday, Sunday and Bank Holidays)* Menu 25 € – Carte 50/65 €
♦ Creative ♦ Contemporary ♦ Elegant ♦
This business hotel has cosy public areas, around 20 contemporary-style rooms (the rest are classic in feel) and up-to-the-minute equipment. Traditional menu and tapas-style service at the bar.

PURPAN

Palladia

271 av. de Grande Bretagne – *℘ 05 62 12 01 20* – *www.hotelpalladia.com*
89 rm – †91/280 € ††91/280 €, ⊑ 18 € – 1 suite   **B2**
Rest – *(closed Sunday and Bank Holidays)* Menu 25 € bi (weekday lunch), 33/66 € – Carte 43/69 €
♦ Business ♦ Modern ♦ Design ♦
Located between the airport and city centre, this hotel in concrete and glass primarily has business travellers in mind. The rooms are cosy, spacious and well soundproofed, and there is even a lecture theatre! Modern menu in the restaurant.

Novotel Aéroport

23 impasse Maubec – *℘ 05 61 15 00 00*
– www.novotel.com/0445   **B2**
123 rm – †85/192 € ††85/192 €, ⊑ 16 €
Rest – *(closed lunch Saturday and Sunday)* Carte 23/50 €
♦ Chain hotel ♦ Functional ♦
This Novotel is equally suitable for business travellers or families. It offers practical accommodation that was entirely renovated in 2010. There are also children's games and petanque.

COLOMIERS

L'Amphitryon (Yannick Delpech)

chemin de Gramont – *℘ 05 61 15 55 55* – *www.lamphitryon.com*
– Closed 2 weeks in August, 1 week Autumn school Holidays, 2 to 7 January and Saturday lunch
Rest – Menu 33 € (weekday lunch), 74/125 € – Carte 102/147 € ⅏
♦ Creative ♦ Fashionable ♦ Design ♦
Near the aeronautical site you will find this lovely chic place. It is bright, contemporary and surrounded by greenery. This is the preserve of Yannick Delpech, a high-flying young chef with talent beyond his years. His dishes are very fine and meticulous, and while remaining firmly rooted in the French classics and the Southwest, they also show plenty of creativity.
→ Caviar bio des Pyrénées, sardine taillée au couteau, crème de morue, raifort et vinaigre balsamique. Merlu de ligne à la poutargue, bouillon dashi aux légumes croquants. Bouchées gasconnes, glace pruneau et armagnac.

AUREVILLE

En Marge (Frank Renimel) with rm

1204 rte de la Croix-Falgarde (lieu-dit Birol) – *℘ 05 61 53 07 24*
– www.restaurantenmarge.com
6 rm – †170 € ††350 €, ⊑ 19 €
Rest – Menu 30 € (weekday lunch), 49/150 € ⅏
♦ Créative ♦
A new adventure for Frank Reminel who moved his "En Marge" from the city centre to this 19C farm, transformed into an elegant hôtel-restaurant…on the outskirts of Toulouse. At the helm, a talented and audacious chef who juggles flavours and textures with great dexterity.
→ Cappuccino de champignons et foie gras à la truffe noire. Homard, pigeon et crème de topinambour, sauce à fève de tonka. Sphère chocolat, sorbet au persil et lait de poule.

GERMANY
DEUTSCHLAND

→ **AREA:**
357 111 km² (137 735 sq mi).

→ **POPULATION:**
81 857 000 inhabitants.
Density = 229 per km².

→ **CAPITAL:**
Berlin.

→ **CURRENCY:**
Euro (€).

→ **GOVERNMENT:**
Parliamentary federal republic, comprising 16 states (Länder) since 1990. Member of European Union since 1957 (one of the 6 founding countries).

→ **LANGUAGE:**
German.

→ **PUBLIC HOLIDAYS:**
New Year's Day (1 Jan); Epiphany (6 Jan - certain regions only); Good Friday (late Mar/Apr); Easter Monday (late Mar/Apr); Labor Day (1 May); Ascension Day (May); Whit Monday (late May/June); Corpus Christi (late May/June – certain regions only); Assumption of the Virgin Mary (15 Aug); Day of German Unity (3 Oct); Reformation Day (31 Oct - new Federal States only); All Saints' Day (1 Nov); Day of Prayer & Repentance (21 Nov, certain regions only); Christmas Day (25 Dec); Boxing Day (26 Dec).

→ **LOCAL TIME:**
GMT+1 hour in winter and GMT +2 hours in summer.

→ **CLIMATE:**
Temperate continental, with cold winters and warm summers (Berlin: January 0°C; July 20°C).

→ **EMERGENCY:**
Police ℘ **110**; Medical Assistance and Fire Brigade ℘ **112**. (Dialling **112** within any EU country will redirect your call and contact the emergency services.)

→ **ELECTRICITY:**
230 volts AC, 50Hz; 2 round pin sockets.

→ **FORMALITIES**
Travellers from the European Union (EU), Switzerland, Iceland and the main countries of North and South America need a national identity card or passport (America: passport required) to visit Germany for less than three months (tourism or business purpose). For visitors from other countries a visa may be required, in addition to a passport, especially for those wishing to stay for longer than three months. We advise you to check with your embassy before travelling.

BERLIN
BERLIN

Population: 3 515 473

S. Guillot/MICHELIN

Berlin's parliament faces an intriguing dilemma when it comes to where to call its heart, as, although they are homogeneous in many other ways, the east and the west of the city still lay claim to separate centres after 40 years of partition. Following the tempestuous 1990s, Berlin sought to resolve its new identity, and it now stands proud as one of the most dynamic and forward thinking cities in the world. Alongside its idea of tomorrow, it's never lost sight of its bohemian past, and many parts of the city retain the arty sense of adventure that characterised downtown Berlin during the 1920s: turn any corner and you might find a modernist art gallery, a tiny cinema or a cutting-edge club.

The eastern side of the River Spree, around Nikolaiviertel, is the historic heart of the city, dating back to the 13C. Meanwhile, way over to the west of the centre lie Kurfürstendamm and Charlottenburg; smart districts which came to the fore after World War II as the heart of West Berlin. Between the two lie imposing areas which swarm with visitors: Tiergarten is the green lung of the city, and just to its east is the great boulevard of Unter den Linden. Continuing eastward, the self-explanatory Museum Island sits snugly and securely in the tributaries of the Spree. The most southerly of Berlin's sprawling districts is Kreuzberg, renowned for its bohemian, alternative character.

BERLIN IN...

→ **ONE DAY**
Unter den Linden, Museum Island, Nikolaiviertel, coffee at TV Tower.

→ **TWO DAYS**
Potsdamer Platz, Reichstag, Regierungsviertel including the Gemäldegalerie, concert at Philharmonie.

→ **THREE DAYS**
KaDeWe, Kurfürstendamm, Charlottenburg Palace.

PRACTICAL INFORMATION

ARRIVAL-DEPARTURE

 Berlin Tegel Airport lies 12km northwest.

 Berlin Schönefeld is 21km southeast.

U-Bahn and S-Bahn trains operate from both.

GETTING AROUND

The U- and S-Bahn trains are quick and efficient but the bus is another good alternative; routes 100 and 200 incorporate most of the top attractions. Trams operate mainly within East Berlin. There are various ticketing options - check with a tourist information office or simply invest in a Berlin-Potsdam Welcome Card, which provides unlimited travel on the S-Bahn, and discounts for selected theatres, museums, attractions and city tours; buy one from a public transport ticket desk, a tourist information office or one of many hotels. Cyclists are well looked after here; there are many cycling routes and most of the main roads have separate cycle lanes and special traffic lights at intersections.

CALENDAR HIGHLIGHTS

February
Berlin Film Festival (Berlinale).

May
Karneval der Kulturen.

May-September
Museumsinsel Festival.

August
Global City.

September
Musikfest Berlin, International Literary Festival.

October
Berlin Festival of Lights.

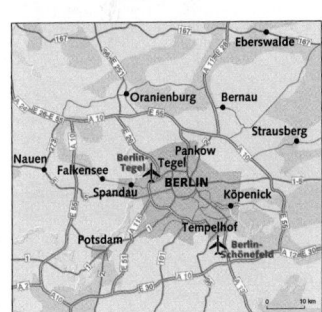

EATING OUT

Many of Berlin's best restaurants are found within the grand hotels and you only have to go to Savignyplatz near Ku'damm to realise how smart dining has taken off. Dinner is the most popular meal and you can invariably eat late, as lots of places stay open until 2 or 3am. Berlin also has a reputation for simple, hearty dishes, inspired by the long, hard winter and, when temperatures drop, the city's comfort food has an irresistible allure – there's pork knuckle, Schnitzel, Bratwurst in mustard, chunky dumplings... and the real Berlin favourite, Currywurst. Bread and potatoes are ubiquitous but since reunification, many dishes have also incorporated a more global influence, so produce from the local forests, rivers and lakes may well be given an Asian or Mediterranean twist (Berlin now claims a wider range of restaurants than any other German city). Service is included in the price of your meal but it's customary to round up the bill. Be sure to try the local 'Berliner Weisse mit Schuss' – a light beer with a dash of raspberry or woodruff.

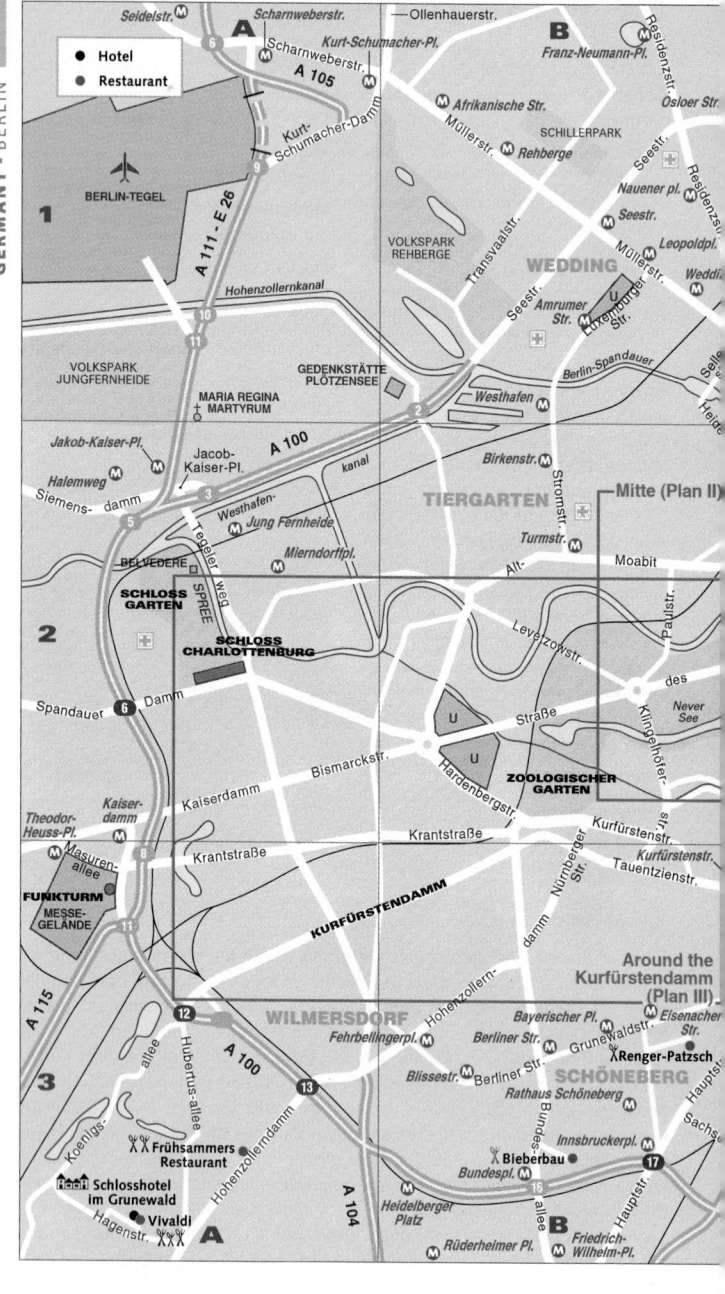

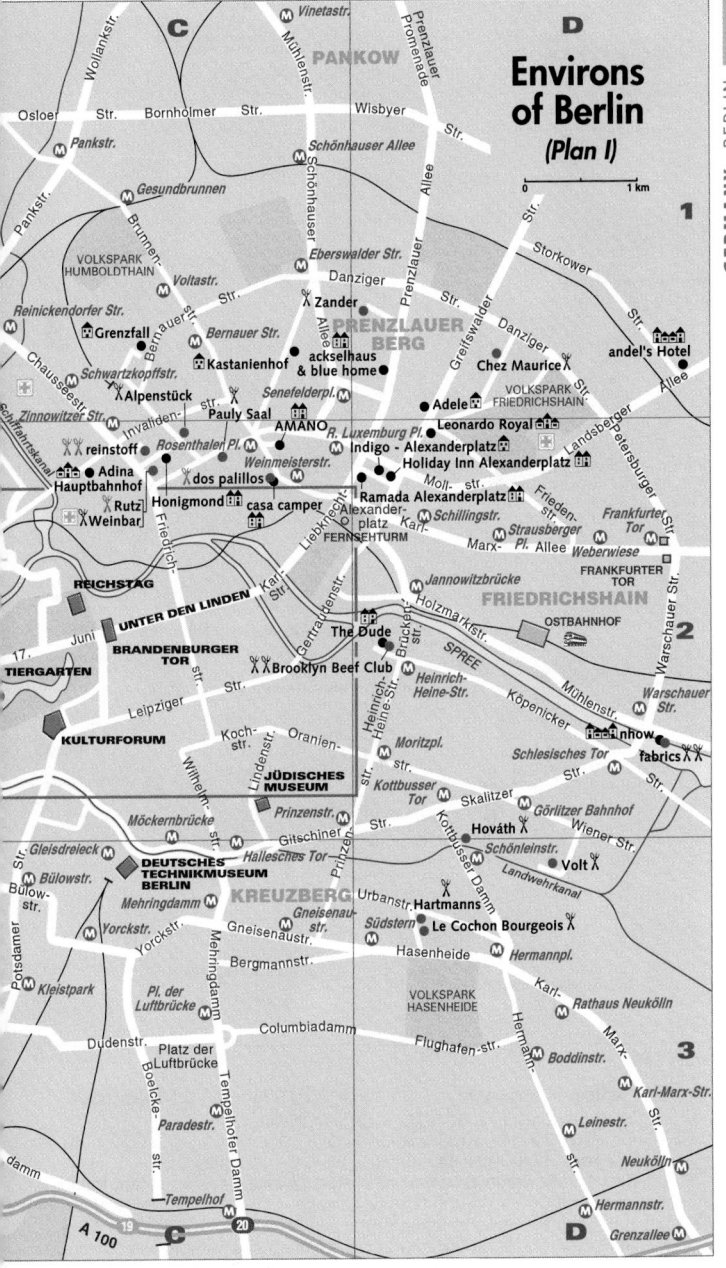

Environs of Berlin
(Plan I)

0   1 km

PANKOW

Vinetastr.
Mühlenstr.
Prenzlauer Promenade
Wisbyer
Str.
Bornholmer
Str.
Osloer
Str.
Pankstr.
Gesundbrunnen
Schönhauser Allee
Storkower
Str.
Reinickendorfer Str.
VOLKSPARK
HUMBOLDTHAIN
Voltastr.
Eberswalder Str.
Danziger
Str.
Danziger
Str.
Greifswalder Str.
Bernauer Str.
Grenzfall
Kastanienhof
Zander
PRENZLAUER
BERG
andel's Hotel
Chez Maurice
Schwartzkopffstr.
Zinnowitzer Str.
Alpenstück
Pauly Saal
ackselhaus
& blue home
Senefelderpl.
Adele
VOLKSPARK
FRIEDRICHSHAIN
Landsberger
Allee
AMANO
reinstoff
Rosenthaler Pl.
Weinmeisterstr.
Indigo - Alexanderplatz
R. Luxemburg Pl.
Leonardo Royal
Holiday Inn Alexanderplatz
Petersburger Str.
Adina
Hauptbahnhof
Rutz
Weinbar
dos palillos
Honigmond
casa camper
Ramada Alexanderplatz
Alexander-
platz
Moll-
str.
Schillingstr.
Frankfurter
Tor
Karl-
Strausberger
Pl.
Frankfurter
Tor
FERNSEHTURM
Marx-
Pl.
Weberwiese
REICHSTAG
UNTER DEN LINDEN
Jannowitzbrücke
Holzmarktstr.
FRANKFURTER
TOR
FRIEDRICHSHAIN
Juni
BRANDENBURGER
TOR
The Dude
Brückenstr.
OSTBAHNHOF
SPREE
Warschauer
Str.
17.
Brooklyn Beef Club
Heinrich-
Heine-Str.
Mühlenstr.
TIERGARTEN
Leipziger
Str.
Koch-
str.
Oranien-
Heinrich-Heine-Str.
Köpenicker
Str.
nhow
Warschauer
Str.
KULTURFORUM
Wilhelm-
str.
Moritzpl.
str.
Schlesisches Tor
fabrics
JÜDISCHES
MUSEUM
Prinzenstr.
Kottbusser
Tor
Skalitzer
Görlitzer Bahnhof
Wiener
Str.
Möckernbrücke
Gitschiner
Str.
Hováth
Landwehrkanal
Gleisdreieck
Hallesches Tor
Prinzenstr.
Kottbusser Damm
Schönleinstr.
Volt
DEUTSCHES
TECHNIKMUSEUM
BERLIN
Bülowstr.
Mehringdamm
KREUZBERG
Urbanstr.
Hartmanns
Yorckstr.
Yorckstr.
Gneisenau-
str.
Gneisenaustr.
Bergmannstr.
Südstern
Le Cochon Bourgeois
Hasenheide
Hermannpl.
Kleistpark
Pl. der
Luftbrücke
VOLKSPARK
HASENHEIDE
Rathaus Neukölln
Columbiadamm
Flughafen-str.
Karl-
Boddinstr.
Dudenstr.
Platz der
Luftbrücke
Tempelhofer Damm
Mehringdamm
Boelcke
Paradestr.
Leinestr.
Karl-Marx-Str.
Neukölln
damm
Tempelhof
Hermannstr.
A 100
19
20
Grenzallee

Potsdamer
Str.
Bülow-
str.

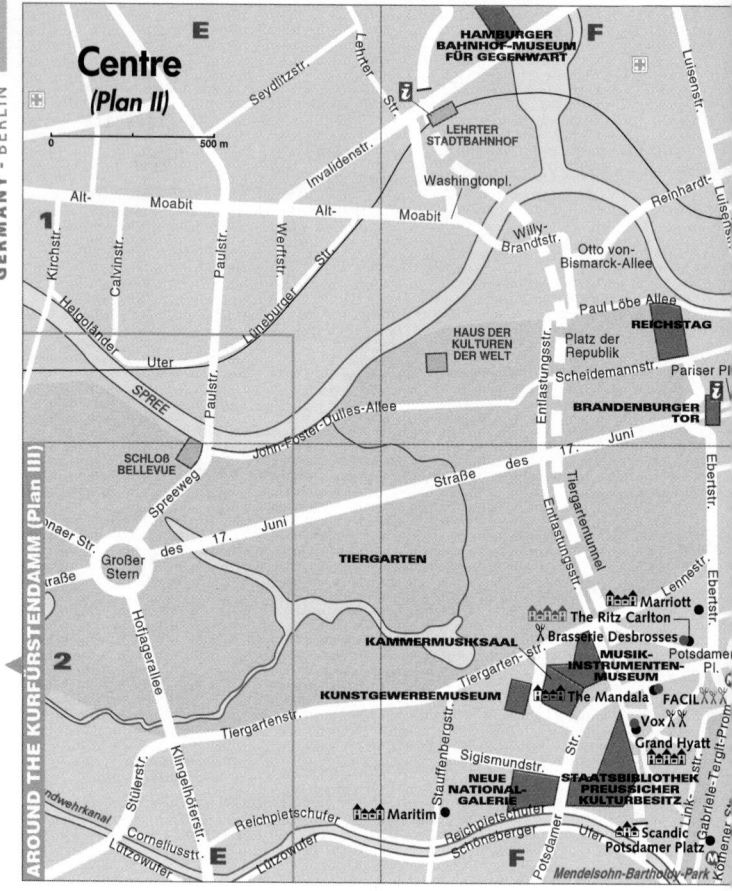

CENTRE Plan II

🏨 **Adlon Kempinski** 🛗 📶 🐕 📺 ⚥ 🅰️ 🛜 🏋️ 🚗 🏧 💳 🆎 ⓪

*Unter den Linden 77 ⌧ 10117 – Ⓜ Brandenburger Tor
– 𝒞 (030) 2 26 10 – www.hotel-adlon.de* **G1**
382 rm – †240/740 € ††240/740 €, ⌧ 39 € – 45 suites
Rest *Lorenz Adlon Esszimmer* ✿✿ **Rest** *Quarré* – see restaurant listing
♦ Grand Luxury ♦ Historic ♦ Classic ♦
Situated in the capital, this imposing grand hotel, which has hosted a list of
crowned heads far too long to cite here, is synonymous with glitz and glamour.
Magical, luxurious ambience, plus presidential suites with limousine and butler
service.

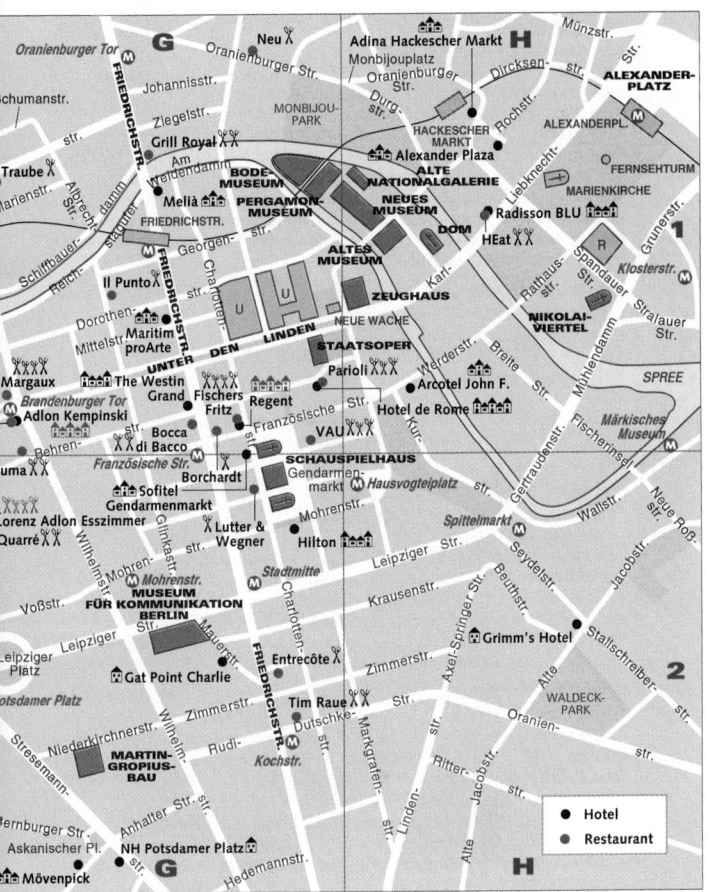

Hotel ●
Restaurant ●

The Ritz-Carlton

Potsdamer Platz 3 ✉ *10785*
– Ⓜ *Potsdamer Platz*
– ✆ *(030) 33 77 77*
– *www.ritzcarlton.de*
303 rm – ♥245/395 €, ♥♥245/395 €, ☲ 38 €
– **42 suites**
Rest *Brasserie Desbrosses* – see restaurant listing
♦ Grand Luxury ♦ Chain hotel ♦ Classic ♦
One of the most exclusive hotel addresses in Germany. The elegant lobby with its cantilevered marble staircase is home to a stylish lounge where guests gather for classic 'teatime' treats.

F2

309

Grand Hyatt ⛵ 🍽 🏋 ⊕ 🏊 📺 ♿ 🅰🅲 🛜 🐾 🚗 📼 💳 🅰🅴 ⓘ

Marlene-Dietrich-Platz 2 (Entrance on Eichhornstraße) ✉ 10785
– ⓜ *Potsdamer Platz* – 𝒞 *(030) 25 53 12 34* – www.berlin.grand.hyatt.com
342 rm – 🛏205/415 € 🛏🛏220/445 €, ⛄ 34 € – 16 suites **F2**
Rest Vox – see restaurant listing
Rest Tizian – 𝒞 *(030) 25 53 17 64* – Menu 39 € – Carte 46/56 €
Rest Mesa – 𝒞 *(030) 25 53 15 72* – Menu 15 € (lunch) – Carte 15/22 €
♦ Grand Luxury ♦ Chain hotel ♦ Design ♦
This trapezoidal-shaped hotel on the Potsdamer Platz boasts modern, minima-list guestrooms equipped with state-of-the-art technology. Apart from the Vox, the restaurants include Tizian (burgers and sandwiches) and Mesa (everything from curry sausage to beef olives).

Hotel de Rome 🏋 🏊 📺 ♿ 🅰🅲 🛜 🐾 🚗 📼 💳 🅰🅴 ⓘ

Behrenstr. 37 ✉ 10117 – ⓜ *Französische Str.* – 𝒞 *(030) 4 60 60 90*
– www.hotelderome.com **G1**
146 rm – 🛏415/495 € 🛏🛏415/495 €, ⛄ 30 € – 9 suites
Rest Parioli – see restaurant listing
♦ Grand Luxury ♦ Classic ♦
A luxury hotel on the Bebelplatz in the impressive framework of a building dating from 1889, formerly used by the Dresdner Bank. Today, the old strong-room is a pool.

Regent 🏋 🏊 📺 ♿ 🅰🅲 🛜 🐾 🚗 📼 💳 🅰🅴 ⓘ

Charlottenstr. 49 ✉ 10117 – ⓜ *Französische Str.* – 𝒞 *(030) 2 03 38*
– www.regenthotels.com/berlin **G1**
156 rm – 🛏295/495 € 🛏🛏295/495 €, ⛄ 35 € – 39 suites
Rest Fischers Fritz ✿✿ – see restaurant listing
♦ Grand Luxury ♦ Classic ♦
The guests here expect first class service and they are not disappointed. A plea-sant custom is the taking of tea – English-, Russian- or Saxony-style (the hotel's own blend) – on nothing but the finest Meissen porcelain in the elegant lounge.

The Westin Grand 🍽 🏋 ⊕ 🏊 📺 ♿ 🅰🅲 🛜 🐾 📼 💳 🅰🅴 ⓘ

Friedrichstr. 158 (Entrance on Behrenstraße) ✉ 10117
– ⓜ *Französische Str.* – 𝒞 *(030) 2 02 70* – www.westingrandberlin.com
400 rm – 🛏119/490 € 🛏🛏119/490 €, ⛄ 32 € – 16 suites **G1**
Rest Relish – 𝒞 *(030) 20 27 31 77* – Menu 20 € (lunch)/70 € – Carte 34/70 €
♦ Chain hotel ♦ Luxury ♦ Modern ♦
This classic grand hotel has an impressive lobby and modern rooms. Some of the suites are stylishly themed, as is the spa suite. A highlight is the 3,000m^2 garden in the middle of Berlin! The Relish restaurant serves contemporary, modern cuisine.

Radisson BLU 🏋 🏊 📺 ♿ 🅰🅲 🛜 🐾 🚗 📼 💳 🅰🅴 ⓘ

Karl-Liebknecht-Str. 3 ✉ 10178 – ⓜ *Alexanderplatz* – 𝒞 *(030) 23 82 80*
– www.radissonblu.de/hotel-berlin **H1**
427 rm – 🛏155/340 € 🛏🛏155/340 €, ⛄ 25 € – 1 suite
Rest HEat – see restaurant listing
♦ Business ♦ Chain hotel ♦ Modern ♦
What catches your eye when you look into the contemporary, atrium lobby of this hotel is the cylindrical aquarium 25m high. Some of the simply designed, modern, functional rooms have a view of the Spree or the AquaDom. The HEat restaurant serves international cuisine.

Hilton 🍽 🏋 ⊕ 🏊 📺 ♿ 🅰🅲 🛜 🐾 🚗 📼 💳 🅰🅴 ⓘ

Mohrenstr. 30 ✉ 10117 – ⓜ *Stadtmitte* – 𝒞 *(030) 20 23 00* – www.hilton.de/berlin
601 rm ⛄ – 🛏179/379 € 🛏🛏199/399 € – 16 suites **G2**
Rest Mark Brandenburg – 𝒞 *(030) 2 02 30 24 60* – Menu 45 € (lunch)
– Carte 26/53 €
♦ Chain hotel ♦ Luxury ♦ Functional ♦
This city hotel stands out for its impressive lobby, its wide range of wellness and fitness facilities, and its rooms, some of which look onto the Gendarmenmarkt. Mark Brandenburg offers regional dishes.

Marriott 🍴 🕭 🕅 🖼 🕭 🅰 🛜 🛁 🍴 🚾 🕾 🅰 🕦

Inge-Beisheim-Platz 1 ✉ *10785 –* Ⓜ *Potsdamer Platz –* ℰ *(030) 22 00 00*
– www.berlinmarriott.de **F2**
379 rm – ♦165/400 € ♦♦165/400 €, ☲ 32 € – 9 suites
Rest – Carte 29/72 €
◆ Chain hotel ◆ Luxury ◆ Contemporary ◆
The lobby of this typical American chain hotel is a 40m high atrium. The comfortable and luxurious rooms are ideally designed for the business guest. This bistro-style restaurant has an open kitchen and a large window façade.

Maritim 🍴 🕅 🖼 🕭 🅰 🕻 🍴 🚾 🕾 🅰 🕦

Stauffenbergstr. 26 ✉ *10785 –* Ⓜ *Mendelssohn-Bartholdy-Park*
– ℰ *(030) 2 06 50 – www.maritim.de* **F2**
505 rm – ♦97/257 € ♦♦112/272 €, ☲ 25 € – 58 suites
Rest *Grand Restaurant M* – ℰ *(030) 20 65 10 90 (closed Sunday)*
Menu 15 € (lunch)/50 € – Carte 29/60 €
◆ Conference hotel ◆ Elegant ◆ Contemporary ◆
This perfect business hotel boasts a tasteful, elegant lobby and extensive conference and event facilities. The highlight, however, is the 350m² Presidential Suite. The Grand Restaurant M is decorated in 1920s-style, while the Brasserie serves an 'Ambassador's Brunch' on Sundays (September to June).

The Mandala 🕭 🕮 🕅 🅰 🛜 🛁 🍴 🚾 🕾 🅰 🕦

Potsdamer Str. 3 ✉ *10785 –* Ⓜ *Potsdamer Platz –* ℰ *(030) 5 90 05 00*
– www.themandala.de **F2**
157 rm – ♦170/350 € ♦♦200/400 €, ☲ 28 € – 13 suites
Rest *FACIL* ❀ – see restaurant listing
◆ Business ◆ Design ◆
This hotel in the Potsdamer Platz (opposite the Sony Center) with its range of spacious and simple yet luxurious rooms and suites boasts an unusual spa. The trendy Bar Qiu serves business lunches.

andel's Hotel 🕭 🕅 🕭 🅰 🛜 🛁 🍴 🚾 🕾 🅰 🕦

Landsberger Allee 106 ✉ *10369 –* ℰ *(030) 4 53 05 30 – www.andelsberlin.com*
557 rm ☲ – ♦89/239 € ♦♦109/259 € – 23 suites *Plan I* **D1**
Rest *a.choice* – ℰ *(030) 45 30 53 26 21 (closed Sunday-Monday) (dinner only)* Menu 39/98 € – Carte 54/80 €
◆ Conference hotel ◆ Modern ◆
This remarkable building is an events and conference hotel. It has a modern design, very large lobby, and an excellent events area. Executive floors with free wi-fi. The restaurant decor is elegant with clean lines.

nhow 🕭 🕅 🕭 🅰 🛜 🛁 🅿 🍴 🚾 🕾 🅰

Stralauer Allee 3 ✉ *10245 –* Ⓜ *Warschauer Str. –* ℰ *(030) 2 90 29 90*
– www.nhow-hotels.com *Plan I* **D2**
304 rm – ♦125/330 € ♦♦125/340 €, ☲ 22 € – 1 suite
Rest *fabrics* – see restaurant listing
◆ Business ◆ Design ◆ Minimalist ◆
No other hotel in Berlin combines music and lifestyle in such an unconventional and cosmopolitan manner. Clean lines and functional architecture outside; upbeat design, curved forms and young, fresh colours inside. And with its recording studio looking out over the city, it really is one of a kind!

Arcotel John F. 🕅 🕭 🅰 🛜 🛁 🍴 🚾 🕾 🅰

Werderscher Markt 11 ✉ *10117 –* Ⓜ *Französische Str. –* ℰ *(030)*
4 05 04 60 – www.arcotelhotels.com/johnf **H1**
190 rm – ♦87/245 € ♦♦87/245 €, ☲ 20 € – 3 suites
Rest *Foreign Affairs* – ℰ *(030) 40 50 46 18 00* – Menu 19 € (lunch)/42 €
– Carte 29/60 €
◆ Business ◆ Modern ◆
This designer hotel located next to the German Foreign Office is dedicated to John F. Kennedy and offers attractive, modern rooms with rocking chairs, including themed 'Kennedy' and 'International Style' rooms. This restaurant serves international dishes.

GERMANY - BERLIN

Scandic Potsdamer Platz

Gabriele-Tergit-Promenade 19 ✉ *10963*
– Ⓜ *Mendelsohn-Bartholdy-Park* – ℰ *(030) 7 00 77 90*
– *www.scandichotels.de/berlin*   **F2**
563 rm – ♦89/240 € ♦♦89/240 €, ⌷ 20 € – 1 suite
Rest – Menu 33 € – Carte 32/50 €
♦ Business ♦ Minimalist ♦

The entrance is in Berlin-Mitte, but your room might be in Kreuzberg, as the
boundary between the two districts runs straight through the hotel! The style
is clean and minimalist, and the philosophy 'eco'. In the restaurant, the Nordic
tapas are a particular speciality.

Leonardo Royal

Otto-Braun-Str. 90 ✉ *10249* – Ⓜ *Alexanderplatz* – ℰ *(030) 7 55 43 00*
– *www.leonardo-hotels.com*   *Plan I* **D2**
343 rm – ♦80/199 € ♦♦80/199 €, ⌷ 19 € – 3 suites
Rest – *(closed Sunday)* Menu 29/49 € – Carte 30/49 €
♦ Business ♦ Modern ♦

This modern business hotel near Friedrichshain Park offers good transport links
and smart rooms including special "Ladies Rooms". It also has conference facilities
for up to 700 participants. This spacious restaurant serves international cuisine.

Maritim proArte

Friedrichstr. 151 (Access by Dorotheenstr. 55) ✉ *10117* – Ⓜ *Friedrichstr.*
– ℰ *(030) 2 03 35* – *www.maritim.de*   **G1**
403 rm – ♦101/221 € ♦♦116/236 €, ⌷ 23 € – 26 suites
Rest Atelier – ℰ *(030) 20 33 45 20 (closed Sunday-Monday) (dinner only)*
Menu 37/49 € – Carte 34/46 €
Rest Bistro media – ℰ *(030) 20 33 45 30* – Carte 19/30 €
♦ Chain hotel ♦ Business ♦ Modern ♦

This modern and functionally equipped hotel has good meeting facilities and
the pleasant Checkpoint Charlie bar. Throughout the hotel there are pictures
by Jungen Wilden. The Atelier is a modern, designer-style restaurant.,

Sofitel Gendarmenmarkt

Charlottenstr. 50 ✉ *10117* – Ⓜ *Französische Str.*
– ℰ *(030) 20 37 50* – *www.sofitel.com*   **G1-2**
92 rm – ♦145/295 € ♦♦170/330 €, ⌷ 28 €
Rest Aigner – Carte 38/49 €
♦ Chain hotel ♦ Business ♦ Modern ♦

This hotel is directly opposite the Gendarmenmarkt. It offers modern, designer-
style rooms and a small leisure area on the top floor. This restaurant has been decorated with the original fixtures and fittings from an old Viennese coffee house.

Meliá

Friedrichstr. 103 ✉ *10117* – Ⓜ *Friedrichstr.* – ℰ *(030) 20 60 79 00*
– *www.meliaberlin.com*   **G1**
364 rm – ♦79/187 € ♦♦89/197 €, ⌷ 22 € – 3 suites
Rest – Menu 31 € (lunch)/55 € – Carte 35/50 €
♦ Business ♦ Modern ♦

The modern rooms in the Spanish Sol-Meliá group's flagship Berlin hotel all feature the latest technology, with some enjoying views of the River Spree. Executive area on the seventh and eighth floors. International cuisine in the first-floor
Café Madrid restaurant, as well as an informal tapas bar.

Adina Hackescher Markt without rest

An der Spandauer Brücke 11 ✉ *10178*
– Ⓜ *Alexanderplatz* – ℰ *(030) 2 09 69 80* – *www.adina.eu*   **H1**
145 rm – ♦109/225 € ♦♦109/345 €, ⌷ 19 € – 55 suites
♦ Business ♦ Modern ♦

This hotel is resolutely fashionable. From the lobby and bar serving international
snacks, through to the guestrooms, each with its own cowhide cube stool. The
small fitness and sauna area has two indoor Jacuzzis crowned by a starlit ceiling.

GERMANY - BERLIN

Adina Hauptbahnhof 🔥 🕅 🖾 & 🕅 🛜 🔊 🚗 🚾 ⬧ 🅰🖲 ⑨

Platz vor dem Neuen Tor 6 (Access by Hannoversche Straße) ⊠ 10115
– ⓜ Zinnowitzer Str. – ℰ (030) 2 00 03 20 – www.adina.eu   *Plan I* **C2**
139 rm ⊑ – ✦95/209 € ✦✦105/229 € – 7 suites
Rest *Alto* – (dinner only) Carte 28/55 €
◆ Business ◆ Design ◆ Contemporary ◆
A non-smoking hotel opposite the Charité and not far from the main railway
station. Upmarket, contemporary and comfortable apartments with kitche-
nette. International and Australian cuisine and steaks in the Alto restaurant.

Mövenpick 🔥 🕅 & 🕅 🛜 🔊 🚗 🚾 ⬧ 🅰🖲 ⑨

Schönebergerstr. 3 ⊠ 10963 – ⓜ Potsdamer Platz – ℰ (030) 23 00 60
– www.moevenpick-hotels.com/berlin   **G2**
243 rm – ✦120/220 € ✦✦130/330 €, ⊑ 22 € – 1 suite
Rest – Menu 31 € – Carte 31/66 €
◆ Historic ◆ Design ◆
This former Siemens building combines external heritage architecture with a
modern interior. The lovely studio rooms on the top floor are particularly attractive; some have free-standing baths. This interior courtyard restaurant has a
glass roof that can be left open in summer.

Alexander Plaza 🔐 🕅 🕅 🛜 🔊 🚗 🚾 ⬧ 🅰🖲

Rosenstr. 1 ⊠ 10178 – ⓜ Alexanderplatz – ℰ (030) 24 00 10
– www.hotel-alexander-plaza.de   **H1**
94 rm ⊑ – ✦95/185 € ✦✦115/205 €   **Rest** – Carte 16/28 €
◆ Historic ◆ Design ◆ Modern ◆
This hotel occupies a restored 19C building between the Marienkirche and
Hackescher Markt. The bedrooms are pleasant and modern and the cuisine
international. The best tables in the restaurant are in the conservatory, occupying the glass-covered interior courtyard.

casa camper 🔥 🕅 & 🕅 🛜 🔊 🚾 ⬧ 🅰🖲 ⑨

Weinmeisterstr. 1 ⊠ 10178 – ⓜ Weinmeisterstr. – ℰ (030) 20 00 34 10
– www.casacamper.com   *Plan I* **C2**
51 rm ⊑ – ✦165/265 € ✦✦205/305 € – 3 suites
Rest *dos palillos* ⊛ – see restaurant listing
◆ Business ◆ Design ◆ Functional ◆
Fernando Amat and Jordi Tio are behind the design of this high quality interior.
The room are decorated in striking red and warm wood. Free snacks in "Ten-
tempié" on the seventh floor.

Ramada Alexanderplatz 🔐 🔥 🕃 & 🕅 🛜 🔊 🚗 🚾 ⬧ 🅰🖲

Karl-Liebknecht-Str. 32 ⊠ 10178 – ⓜ Alexanderplatz – ℰ (030)
30 10 41 10 – www.ramada.de   *Plan I* **D2**
337 rm – ✦79/259 € ✦✦79/259 €, ⊑ 15 € – 8 suites
Rest – Menu 32 € – Carte 26/52 €
◆ Chain hotel ◆ Contemporary ◆
With the Alexanderplatz on your doorstep and many other sights within walking distance, this is an ideal base from which to see Berlin. Don't miss the
manager broadcasting on the hotel's own radio station! Various restaurants ranging from the elegant to the rustic.

AMANO without rest & 🕅 🛜 🚗 🚾 ⬧ 🅰🖲 ⑨

Auguststr. 43 ⊠ 10119 – ⓜ Rosenthaler Platz – ℰ (030) 8 09 41 50
– www.hotel-amano.com   *Plan I* **C2**
163 rm – ✦60/380 € ✦✦60/380 €, ⊑ 15 € – 20 suites
◆ Business ◆ Modern ◆
Tailored perfectly for the business traveller, this smart, contemporary-style hotel
located close to the Hackesche Höfe boasts a panoramic roof terrace and bar.

The Dude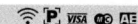

Köpenicker Str. 92 ✉ *10179 –* Ⓜ *Heinrich-Heine-Str.*
– ℰ (030) 4 11 98 81 00 – www.thedudeberlin.com *Plan I* **D2**
27 rm – 🛏129/180 € 🛏🛏169/220 €, ⚏ 18 €
Rest *Brooklyn Beef Club* – see restaurant listing
♦ Townhouse ♦ Elegant ♦
This is design in its purest form. The mix of historical detail (the building dates
back to 1822) and modern style is reminiscent of a mansion house. If you are in
search of a snack, the Deli serves sandwiches at lunchtime. Breakfast is also available.

Honigmond (with guest house)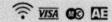

Tieckstr. 11 ✉ *10115 –* Ⓜ *Zinnowitzer Str. – ℰ (030) 2 84 45 50*
– www.honigmond.de *Plan I* **C2**
50 rm ⚏ – 🛏95/145 € 🛏🛏145/225 € – 3 suites
Rest – Carte 22/31 €
♦ Historic ♦ Classic ♦ Personalised ♦
Built in 1895 this house in a quiet side street has individually-styled rooms. The
Garden Hotel 350m away has a lovely inner courtyard garden. Pleasant coffee
shop-cum-restaurant in a classic setting.

Holiday Inn Alexanderplatz

Theanolte-Bähnisch Str. 2 ✉ *10178*
– Ⓜ *Schillingstr. – ℰ (030) 7 40 74 70*
– www.hiberlincenter.com *Plan I* **D2**
242 rm – 🛏89/299 € 🛏🛏94/304 €, ⚏ 17 € **Rest** – Carte 26/55 €
♦ Chain hotel ♦ Modern ♦
A good business hotel, this Holiday Inn combines a practical location close to
the Alexanderplatz with functional contemporary facilities. The restaurant serves Vietnamese cuisine.

ackselhaus & blue home without rest

Belforter Str. 21 ✉ *10405 –* Ⓜ *Senefelderplatz – ℰ (030) 44 33 76 33*
– www.ackselhaus.de *Plan I* **D1**
35 rm – 🛏100/250 € 🛏🛏140/330 €, ⚏ 15 € – 4 suites
♦ Townhouse ♦ Historic ♦ Personalised ♦
This establishment has a really special historical charm. It is Venetian in style
with blue tones. The green inner courtyards with their lounge feel are very
pretty.

Grimm's Hotel without rest

Alte Jakobstr. 100 ✉ *10179 –* Ⓜ *Spittelmarkt – ℰ (030) 28 44 41 00*
– www.grimms-hotel.de **H2**
36 rm – 🛏69/119 € 🛏🛏89/139 €, ⚏ 9 €
♦ Townhouse ♦ Modern ♦
What does the name Grimm mean to you? Probably not the smart modern lines
of the rooms but possibly the original wall motifs with their references to fairy-
tales, including The Golden Goose and Sleeping Beauty.

Indigo - Alexanderplatz

Bernhard-Weiß-Str. 5 ✉ *10178 –* Ⓜ *Schillingstr. – ℰ (030) 5 05 08 60*
– www.hotelindigoberlin.com *Plan I* **D2**
153 rm – 🛏89/120 € 🛏🛏99/120 €, ⚏ 19 €
Rest – (dinner only) Menu 15/25 €
♦ Chain hotel ♦ Modern ♦
Modern, urban and central... the ideal hotel for the young traveller. The restaurant serves only steaks as a main course, with diners invited to choose their own
starters and desserts.

GERMANY - BERLIN

⌂ **Adele** without rest   🛜 VISA ◉◉ AE

Greifswalder Str. 227 ✉ *10405* – **Ⓜ** *Alexanderplatz* – *ℰ (030) 44 32 43 10*
– www.adele-berlin.de   *Plan I* **D1**
16 rm ⌱ – ✝89/149 € ✝✝109/179 € – 2 suites
♦ **Townhouse** ♦ **Design** ♦
This small and very exclusive boutique hotel is furnished in Art Deco-style. It has
comfortable, pretty guestrooms and a very modern breakfast room.

⌂ **Kastanienhof** without rest   ℰ📶 ♨ P VISA ◉◉ AE

Kastanienallee 65 ✉ *10119* – **Ⓜ** *Senefelderpl.* – *ℰ (030) 44 30 50*
– www.kastanienhof.biz   *Plan I* **C1**
38 rm – ✝59/89 € ✝✝79/114 €, ⌱ 9 € – 2 suites
♦ **Townhouse** ♦ **Functional** ♦
This well-managed hotel offering functional rooms is run by a real Berliner who
has decorated it with a vast array of mementos of "his" city.

⌂ **NH Potsdamer Platz** without rest   ℰ 🅺 🛜 🚗 VISA ◉◉ AE ◍

Stresemannstr. 47 ✉ *10963* – **Ⓜ** *Potsdamer Platz* – *ℰ (030) 2 25 07 10*
– www.nh-hotels.com   **G2**
89 rm ⌱ – ✝89/139 € ✝✝99/149 €
♦ **Business** ♦ **Contemporary** ♦
This business hotel is close to Potsdamer Platz. It offers modern and freshly
designed rooms with parquet flooring and the latest technology. Good underground and local railway connections.

⌂ **Grenzfall**   🚞 🍽 ℰ rm, 📶 ♨ 🚗 VISA ◉◉ AE

Ackerstr. 136 ✉ *13355* – **Ⓜ** *Bernauer Str.* – *ℰ (030) 34 33 33 00*
– www.hotel-grenzfall.de   *Plan I* **C1**
37 rm – ✝63/109 € ✝✝83/119 €, ⌱ 11 €
Rest – *(dinner only)* Carte 16/26 €
♦ **Townhouse** ♦ **Functional** ♦
The Grenzfall's attractions include a friendly welcome, a 3 000m² garden and its
reasonable prices. The hotel, located in a quiet side street close to the site of the
former Berlin wall, provides employment opportunities for the disabled. The
contemporary feel also extends to the restaurant, which boasts a terrace overlooking the garden.

⌂ **Gat Point Charlie** without rest   ℰ 🅺 🛜 VISA ◉◉ AE

Mauerstr. 81 ✉ *10117* – **Ⓜ** *Kochstr.* – *ℰ (030) 20 67 17 47*
– www.gatrooms.com   **G2**
140 rm – ✝95/269 € ✝✝105/279 €, ⌱ 15 €
♦ **Townhouse** ♦ **Modern** ♦
Gat Point Charlie offers stylish minimalist decor, an ultra central location and
good prices. Fresh light green and white dominate throughout, matching the
informal atmosphere in the breakfast room and the small restaurant that serves
a range of tapas.

XXXX **Lorenz Adlon Esszimmer** – Hotel Adlon Kempinski   ℰ 🅺 ⇔
🕃🕃
Unter den Linden 77 ✉ *10117*   VISA ◉◉ AE ◍
*– **Ⓜ** Brandenburger Tor – ℰ (030) 22 61 19 60*
– www.hotel-adlon.de
– Closed 1-13 January, 8 July-4 August and Sunday-Monday   **G1**
Rest – *(dinner only)* Menu 110/160 € – Carte 98/129 € ⌀
♦ **Classic** ♦ **Luxury** ♦ **Elegant** ♦
You need to see it to believe it! The food delivers everything the name of Hend-
rik Otto promises and there are few chefs who manage to blend modern ele-
ments and classic cuisine with such skill. Will you be one of the lucky guests
with a view of the Brandenburg Gate?
→ Zander / Kalbsfuß-Lorbeerextrakt mit Sauerkraut, Blutwurst, Apfel und
Stockkartoffel. Caneton à la presse "Lorenz Adlon". Rhabarber / Joghurteis
mit Sauerklee, Blaumohn und Lakritz.

GERMANY - BERLIN

XXXX   **Margaux** (Michael Hoffmann)   ⅰ AC VISA ⚫ AE ⓪

ॐ   *Unter den Linden 78 (Entrance Wilhelmstraße)* ✉ *10117*
– ⓜ Brandenburger Tor – ℰ (030) 22 65 26 11 – www.margaux-berlin.de
– Closed 2 weeks July-August and Sunday-Monday   **G1**
Rest – *(dinner only)* Menu 95 € (Vegetarian)/195 € ❀
♦ Classic ♦ Minimalist ♦ Fashionable ♦
It is probably his respect for the natural world that gives Michael Hoffmann his special feel for fresh produce. Combined with his technical skills, his fine ingredients produce creative, considered dishes with an impressive range of tastes. The vegetarian options on both menus reveal his green fingers. The chef grows his own vegetables just outside the gates of Berlin.
➜ Makrele, Grapefruit & Rauchfleisch - Baiser, Sellerie. Gemüse - Textur & Bouillon. Aubergine, Süßkartoffel, Rauch - Pak Choi, Schnittlauch, roter Rübenfond.

XXXX   **Fischers Fritz** – Hotel Regent   ⅰ AC ⇄ VISA ⚫ AE ⓪

ॐ ॐ   *Charlottenstr. 49* ✉ *10117 – ⓜ Französische Str. – ℰ (030) 20 33 63 63*
– www.fischersfritzberlin.com   **G1**
Rest – *(booking advisable)* Menu 47 € (lunch)/180 € – Carte 97/155 € ❀
♦ Creative ♦ Elegant ♦
Holder of two Michelin stars since 2008, Christian Lohse's mastery of the technical aspects of his art is now firmly established. Working with great creativity he transforms classic dishes based on the highest quality produce into mouthwatering culinary masterpieces.
➜ Halber bretonischer Hummer vom Stahlgrill mit Kartoffel-Chorizosalat. Mittelstück vom Atlantik Steinbutt mit Beelitzer Spargel und Sauce Bérnaise. Gebackenes Demeter Onsenei mit Spitzmorcheln, jungen Erbsen und Bärlauchinfusion.

XXX   **FACIL** – Hotel The Mandala   🌳 ⅰ AC VISA ⚫ AE ⓪

ॐ   *Potsdamer Str. 3 (5th floor)* ✉ *10785 – ⓜ Potsdamer Platz*
– ℰ (030) 5 90 05 12 34 – www.facil.de – Closed 3 weeks January, 2 weeks end July-early August and Saturday-Sunday   **F2**
Rest – *(booking advisable)* Menu 39 € (lunch)/185 € – Carte 86/98 € ❀
♦ Creative ♦ Minimalist ♦
This restaurant has the feeling of an interior courtyard recreated on the 5th floor. When the glass frontage and roof are open in the summer, it is almost like being outside with fresh green foliage everywhere. Michael Kempf cooks creative dishes with Asian and Moroccan hints. Good value lunchtime menu.
➜ Bachforelle vom Ammersee, Kirschholz-Nussbutter, Erbsen und Buttermilch. Brust von der Taube mit Kohlrabi und Fichtensprossenasche. Karamell, Mandel und Ananas.

XXX   **Parioli** – Hotel de Rome   🌳 ⅰ AC ⇄ VISA ⚫ AE ⓪

ॐ   *Behrenstr. 37* ✉ *10117 – ⓜ Französische Str. – ℰ (030) 46 06 09 12 01*
– www.pariolirestaurant.de   **G1**
Rest – Menu 26 € (lunch)/86 € – Carte 57/73 €
♦ Mediterranean ♦ Elegant ♦
This elegant restaurant is decorated in dark wood and gold tones. It offers international cuisine with a Mediterranean influence. There is a terrace in the beautiful interior courtyard.

XXX   **VAU** (Kolja Kleeberg)   🌳 AC ⇄ VISA ⚫ AE ⓪

ॐ   *Jägerstr. 54* ✉ *10117 – ⓜ Französische Str. – ℰ (030) 2 02 97 30*
– www.vau-berlin.de – Closed Sunday   **G1**
Rest – Menu 65 € (lunch)/120 € – Carte 86/95 € ❀
♦ Creative ♦ Fashionable ♦
Kolja Kleeberg's cooking is at once light and fresh, fragrant and fully flavoured. But if for any reason this famous TV chef in not in the restaurant, rest assured he has a well-practiced team working with him. It is also worth noting that star architect Meinrad von Gerkan is responsible for the design.
➜ Thunfischbauch mit Aubergine, Raf-Tomate und Mandel. Heilbutt in der Schneckenkruste mit weißem Spargel, Rapsöl und Ponch Phoron. Croustillant und Parfait von Valrhôna Caraibe Schokolade.

XX **Grill Royal**   🍴 VISA ◎ AE

Friedrichstr. 105 b ⊠ 10117 – Ⓜ Oranienburger Tor – ℰ (030) 28 87 92 88
– www.grillroyal.com   **G1**
Rest – *(dinner only) (booking advisable)* Carte 36/127 € 🍴
♦ International ♦ Trendy ♦ Fashionable ♦

The place to eat on the River Spree, known for its grilled meats. Diners select the cuts themselves from a glass chiller cabinet! Great selection of Bordeaux and Italian wines.

XX **reinstoff** (Daniel Achilles)   🍴 & AC VISA ◎ AE
❀❀

Schlegelstr. 26c (Edison Höfe) ⊠ 10115 – Ⓜ Zinnowitzerstr.
– ℰ (030) 30 88 12 14 – www.reinstoff.eu
– Closed 2 weeks January, 2 weeks August and Sunday-Monday   *Plan I* **C2**
Rest – *(dinner only)* Menu 70/139 €
♦ Creative ♦ Fashionable ♦ Intimate ♦

Avoiding any feeling of sterility thanks to its 'room within a room' design and subdued lighting, the modern, minimalist style at reinstoff is the perfect match for the restaurant's post-industrial factory setting. Daniel Achilles offers two set menus dubbed 'Close to home' and 'Further afield', Ivo Ebert shares his knowledge of German and Spanish wines, while Sabine Demel provides the welcome front of house.
➜ Garnelen aus der Normandie, Buschbohne, Seemoos und Aioli. Wald und Wiese - Kronenstück vom Kalb, Salatspitzen, Knollenkerbel. Asiatisches Müsli und geeiste Zuckererbse.

XX **Tim Raue**   & AC VISA ◎ AE
❀❀

Rudi-Dutschke-Str. 26 ⊠ 10969 – Ⓜ Kochstr. – ℰ (030) 25 93 79 30
– www.tim-raue.com – Closed Sunday-Monday   **G2**
Rest – Menu 38 € (lunch)/148 € – Carte 106/142 €
♦ Asian ♦ Friendly ♦

Time Raue's cuisine is minimal and pared down, using a small number of high quality ingredients to perfect effect. Sweet and savoury, mild and sharp, soft and crispy, his dishes are a riot of different consistencies and fragrances, always combined with perfect balance. The lunchtime menu is also very popular.
➜ Zander / Perigord Trüffel / 20 Jahre alter Reiswein. Jasmin Taube / Erdnuss / Feige. Blauer Hummer / Karotte / Passionsfrucht.

XX **Quarré** – Hotel Adlon Kempinski   ⪡ 🍴 & AC VISA ◎ AE ⓞ

Unter den Linden 77 ⊠ 10117 – Ⓜ Brandenburger Tor
– ℰ (030) 22 61 15 55 – www.hotel-adlon.de   **G1**
Rest – Menu 26 € (lunch)/89 € – Carte 36/94 €
♦ Classic ♦ Brasserie ♦

A hotel like the Adlon naturally takes great pains to provide its guests with a suitably stylish setting for their stay. Here at Quarré, for example, they have succeeded in creating an elegant dining environment and cosmopolitan meeting place for a business lunch, dinner or Sunday brunch.

XX **Vox** – Hotel Grand Hyatt   🚗 🍴 & AC VISA ◎ AE ⓞ

Marlene-Dietrich-Platz 2 (Entrance on Eichhornstraße) ⊠ 10785
– Ⓜ Potsdamer Platz – ℰ (030) 25 53 17 72 – www.berlin.grand.hyatt.com
Rest – Carte 46/66 €   **F2**
♦ Modern ♦ Trendy ♦

The decor at Vox is bright and modern. The large show kitchen offers guests the chance to watch the team, including the sushi chefs, at work.

XX **Bocca di Bacco**   AC ⇄ VISA ◎ AE

Friedrichstr. 167 ⊠ 10117 – Ⓜ Französische Str. – ℰ (030) 20 67 28 28
– www.boccadibacco.de
– Closed Sunday lunch and Bank Holidays lunch   **G1**
Rest – Carte 36/61 €
♦ Italian ♦ Fashionable ♦

This restaurant with a modern design has a bar and lounge area where good Italian cuisine is served. Very friendly atmosphere. Beautiful function room on the first-floor.

XX **uma**   & 🆊 VISA ⓒ AE ⓪
Behrenstr. 72 ✉ 10117 – Ⓜ Brandenburger Tor – ℰ (030) 3 01 11 73 24
– www.hotel-adlon.de
– Closed Saturday lunch and Sunday   **G1**
Rest – (dinner only) – Carte 31/156 €
♦ Japanese ♦ Intimate ♦ Exotic ♦
In this restaurant and shochu bar located to the south of the Adlon Hotel. The
chef serves traditional Japanese food with a European spin.

XX **Il Punto**   🕌 & 🆊 ⇕ VISA ⓒ AE
Neustädtische Kirchstr. 6 ✉ 10117 – Ⓜ Friedrichstr. – ℰ (030) 20 60 55 40
– www.ilpunto.net
– Closed Saturday lunch and Sunday   **G1**
Rest – Menu 28 € (lunch)/70 € – Carte 38/63 €
♦ Italian ♦ Elegant ♦
Il Punto is a good place for fans of Italian cuisine. The 'paccheri alla Ciampi' owes
its existence to an official visit to the German capital by Italian President Dr A
Ciampi. The somewhat simpler 'Antica Lasagneria' is also open to diners.

XX **fabrics** – Hotel nhow   & 🆊 P VISA ⓒ AE
Stralauer Allee 3 ✉ 10245 – Ⓜ Warschauer Str. – ℰ (030) 2 90 29 90
– www.nhow-hotels.com
– Closed Saturday lunch and Sunday   **D2**
Rest – Carte 32/59 €
♦ Modern ♦ Minimalist ♦
Cool design throughout in white, pink and a trendy green, giving a light and
airy feel. The top quality produce in the kitchen is used to create house specials
including classics such as steak Chateaubriand. Small lunchtime menu.

XX **HEat** – Hotel Radisson BLU   🕌 & 🆊 VISA ⓒ AE ⓪
Karl-Liebknecht-Str. 3 ✉ 10178 – Ⓜ Alexanderplatz
– ℰ (030) 2 38 28 34 72 – www.radissonblu.de/hotel-berlin   **H1**
Rest – Menu 29 € (lunch)/39 € – Carte 18/50 €
♦ International ♦ Trendy ♦
With its finger well and truly on the pulse, the design at HEat is resolutely
modern with black leather furniture, rare woods and modern lighting. The ter-
race offers a view of Berlin Cathedral and the River Spree.

XX **Brooklyn Beef Club** – Hotel The Dude   VISA ⓒ AE
Köpenicker Str. 92 ✉ 10179 – Ⓜ Heinrich-Heine-Str. – ℰ (030) 20 21 58 20
– www.thedudeberlin.com
– Closed Sunday   Plan I **D2**
Rest – (dinner only) Carte 69/123 €
♦ International ♦ Individual ♦
The Brooklyn Beef Club provides the necessary New York-style to make sure
you really enjoy your American steak from the grill. It is worth taking a look at
the bar, where some 160 different whiskies are available by the glass.

X **Rutz**   🕌 🆊 VISA ⓒ AE
⁂ *Chausseestr. 8 (1st floor) ✉ 10115 – Ⓜ Oranienburger Tor*
– ℰ (030) 24 62 87 60 – www.weinbar-rutz.de
– Closed 2 weeks January and Sunday-Monday   Plan I **C2**
Rest – (dinner only) Menu 105/180 € ஐ
Rest Weinbar – see restaurant listing
♦ Modern ♦ Trendy ♦
'6 Inspirations - 12 Experiences' reads the subtitle of the 'inspiration' menu, each
course showcasing the creative gifts of Marco Müller. The expert advice provi-
ded by sommelier Billy Wagner – at work in both the restaurant and the wine
bar – is something akin to a wine tour.
➜ Macadamianuss - Königskrabbe & Vichygurke, Paprika, Sylter Royal &
Mangold, Beurre Blanc. Pfifferlinge - Runzelkarotte & Erbse, Tafelspitz &
Kohlrabi, Stroganoff. Manjari Schokolade - Sauerrahm & Ingwer Mole, Blut-
orange, Tarte & Grüner Tee, Papaya.

GERMANY - BERLIN

Hartmanns ☆ 🛜 VISA ⓸ AE

Fichtestr. 31 ✉ *10967 –* Ⓜ *Südstern –* ✆ *(030) 61 20 10 03*
– www.hartmanns-restaurant.de
– Closed 2 weeks end July-early August and Sunday Plan I **D3**
Rest *– (dinner only) (booking advisable)* Menu 58/90 € – Carte 66/76 €
♦ Modern ♦ Cosy ♦ Neighbourhood ♦

After spells in various restaurants in Germany and abroad, Stefan Hartmann has come home to Berlin. He has been cooking refined contemporary food for diners at the small tables in his cellar restaurant since 2007. The food is good, the service friendly, and the wine recommendations are excellent.
➜ Geräucherter Aal und wachsweicher Schweinebauch mit Gurke und Kresse. Glaciertes Kalbsbries mit marinierter Kalbshaxe, grüner Spargel und Champignons. Gebratenes Kalbsfilet mit weißem Spargel, Serrano-Gnocchi und Erbsen.

Brasserie Desbrosses – Hotel The Ritz-Carlton 🛜 ㋭ AC

Potsdamer Platz 3 ✉ *10785 –* Ⓜ *Potsdamer Platz* VISA ⓸ AE ⓿
– ✆ *(030) 3 37 77 63 41 – www.ritzcarlton.de* **F2**
Rest *–* Menu 45 € – Carte 26/62 €
♦ French ♦ Brasserie ♦

An eclectic group of diners meets here every day to savour the typically French bistro dishes on offer. The original 1875 interior comes from a brasserie in southern Burgundy.

Traube 🛜 VISA ⓸ AE

Reinhardtstr. 33 ✉ *10117 –* Ⓜ *Oranienburger Tor –* ✆ *(030) 27 87 93 93*
– www.traube-berlin.de
– Closed Saturday lunch and Sunday **G1**
Rest *–* Menu 19 € (lunch)/69 € – Carte 34/50 €
♦ International ♦ Friendly ♦

This very attractive, classically modern restaurant has a bistro area. It also serves international dishes on the terrace in the inner courtyard. There is also a small midday menu.

Pauly Saal 🛜 VISA ⓸ AE

Auguststr. 11 ✉ *10117 –* Ⓜ *Rosenthaler Pl. –* ✆ *(030) 33 00 60 70*
– www.paulysaal.com Plan I **C2**
Rest *–* Carte 51/69 €
♦ Modern ♦ Classic ♦

Enjoy fresh produce and well-prepared, unfussy cuisine at Pauly Saal. This former Jewish girls' school offers a reduced menu at lunchtimes and a more sophisticated and elaborate selection in the evenings. In the lovely high-ceiling dining room, your attention is bound to be drawn to the striking model of a rocket and the window to the kitchen.

dos palillos – Hotel casa camper 🛜 ㋭ AC VISA ⓸ AE ⓿

Weinmeisterstr. 1 (Entrance on Rosenthalerstr. 53) ✉ *10178*
– Ⓜ *Weinmeisterstr. –* ✆ *(030) 20 00 34 13 – www.dospalillos.com*
– Closed 1-14 January and Sunday-Tuesday lunch, Wednesday lunch
Rest *–* Menu 50/70 € – Carte 17/29 € Plan I **C2**
♦ Euro-asiatic ♦ Design ♦ Fashionable ♦

By its very shape, the long white bar invites guests to come and talk to the chefs, just as it was intended to do. Watch carefully as they prepare charcoal grilled or wok fried tapas-style Asian dishes. In short: good food, good value for money and plenty to talk about.

Borchardt 🛜 VISA ⓸ AE ⓿

Französische Str. 47 ✉ *10117 –* Ⓜ *Französische Str. –* ✆ *(030) 81 88 62 62*
– www.borchardt-restaurant.de **G1**
Rest *–* Carte 32/64 €
♦ International ♦ Brasserie ♦

A traditional townhouse in the Gendarmenmarkt is home to this trendy restaurant serving international cuisine with a charming interior courtyard terrace.

GERMANY - BERLIN

Chez Maurice ⬛ 🛜 *VISA* ⦿

Bötzowstr. 39 ✉ *10407* – ⓜ *Senefelder Platz* – ℰ *(030) 4 25 05 06*
– www.chez-maurice.de
– Closed Sunday lunch, Monday lunch Plan I **D1**
Rest – Carte 32/57 €

♦ French ♦ Brasserie ♦

The atmosphere here is relaxed and informal, just like a real French brasserie. The kitchen serves up simply prepared French classics (three-course lunch for €16) accompanied by good Bordeaux and Burgundy wines. If you fancy taking something home with you, you can also buy wine, cheese and saucisson on the premises.

Lutter & Wegner ⬛ 🛜 ⇔ *VISA* ⦿ **AE**

Charlottenstr. 56 ✉ *10117* – ⓜ *Französische Str.* – ℰ *(030) 20 29 54 15*
– www.l-w-berlin.de **G2**
Rest – Carte 34/63 € 🏛

♦ Austrian ♦ Wine bar ♦

This restaurant with its cosy wine bar-style rooms is a lively venue serving Austrian influenced cuisine. There is an additional seasonal menu on offer in the evenings. Extensive wine list featuring over 700 different wines across every price category.

Neu ⬛ 🛜 *VISA* ⦿

Oranienburgerstr. 32 (at Heckmannhöfen) ✉ *10117*
– ⓜ Oranienburger Tor – ℰ (030) 66 40 84 27 – www.restaurant-neu.de
– Closed 1-6 January and Sunday-Monday except Bank Holidays
Rest – *(October - May dinner only)* Menu 21 € (lunch)/73 € **G1**
– Carte 37/52 €

♦ International ♦ Trendy ♦

If you come here in summer, make sure you try the fresh seasonal dishes in the verdant interior courtyard. Dishes include entrecote served on cottage cheese and bread and the intriguingly named 'Knights who say Ni'. Reduced menu at lunchtimes.

Alpenstück ⬛ 🛜 ♿ *VISA* ⦿ **AE**
🏡

Gartenstr. 9 ✉ *10178* – ⓜ *Rosenthaler Platz* – ℰ *(030) 21 75 16 46*
– www.alpenstueck.de Plan I **C1**
Rest – *(dinner only) (booking advisable)* Menu 35 € – Carte 34/43 €

♦ Regional/country ♦ Fashionable ♦

This relaxed and friendly restaurant uses regional produce in dishes such as pan-fried fillet of trout with beetroot, yellow turnip and fondant potatoes. At lunchtimes the restaurant's own bakery over the road sells fine pastries and small snacks. In the delicatessen you can buy Maultaschen (Swabian pasta squares) and fond (caramelised meat dripping for making gravy) to take home.

Entrecôte ⬛ 🛜 ♿ *VISA* ⦿ **AE**

Schützenstr. 5 ✉ *10117* – ⓜ *Stadtmitte* – ℰ *(030) 20 16 54 96*
– www.entrecote.de
– Closed Christmas, Saturday lunch, Sunday lunch and Bank Holiday lunch
Rest – Menu 19 € – Carte 21/61 € **G2**

♦ French classic ♦ Brasserie ♦

This nice, pleasantly relaxed brasserie is a favourite address. A French flair characterises the food that is typically served.

Horváth ⬛ 🛜 ♿ *VISA* ⦿ **AE** ⓞ
🕸

Paul-Lincke-Ufer 44a ✉ *10999* – ⓜ *Schönleinstr.* – ℰ *(030) 61 28 99 92*
– www.restaurant-horvath.de
– Closed Monday Plan I **D2**
Rest – *(dinner only) (booking advisable)* Menu 56/114 € – Carte 52/65 €

♦ Creative ♦ Minimalist ♦

The highly motivated team at work here offer good, interesting cuisine that is creative but not overly fussy. The choice of 'Traditional', 'Vegetarian' and 'Innovation' menus hints at chef Sebastian Frank's Austrian roots. Good German wines.
➔ "Suppengrün" mit Liebstöckel, Kren und Schnittlauch. Brandenburger Rehkeule mit Germknödel, Heidelbeeren und Fichtennadel. Topfenknödel mit weißer Schokolade und Kürbiskernöl.

GERMANY - BERLIN

✗ **Volt** 🏠 ⚿ ♻ VISA ⦿⦿
Paul-Lincke-Ufer 20 ✉ *10999* – Ⓜ *Schönleinstr.* – ☏ *(030) 61 07 40 33*
– *www.restaurant-volt.de*
– *Closed 1 week end December-early January, 2 weeks June-July and Sunday*
Rest – *(dinner only)* Menu 38/56 € – Carte 42/58 €   *Plan I* **D3**
♦ Regional/country ♦ Fashionable ♦
Matthias Gleiß is back! With a new name and a new concept, this former elect-
ricity substation built in 1928 fits perfectly into the lively Kreuzberg food scene.
Harmonious industrial design and good cuisine with the accent on seasonal
vegetables.

✗ **Le Cochon Bourgeois** 🏠 VISA ⦿⦿ AE
Fichtestr. 24 ✉ *10967* – Ⓜ *Südstern* – ☏ *(030) 6 93 01 01*
– *www.lecochon.de*
– *Closed 1-15 January, 9-23 July and Sunday-Monday*   *Plan I* **D3**
Rest – *(dinner only)* Carte 38/60 €
♦ French classic ♦ Cosy ♦
French bistro-style cuisine is served in this fine historical setting with stucco-like
woodwork and parquet floors. The wine selection includes some little-known
gems.

✗ **Zander** 🏠 VISA ⦿⦿ AE
Kollwitzstr. 50 ✉ *10405* – Ⓜ *Senefelder Platz* – ☏ *(030) 44 05 76 79*
– *www.zander-restaurant.de*
– *Closed 3 weeks January and Monday*   *Plan I* **D1**
Rest – *(booking advisable)* Menu 38/49 € – Carte 34/50 €
♦ International ♦ Bistro ♦
This friendly restaurant located in a trendy residential area serves fresh, interna-
tional cuisine on two floors. Changing art exhibitions. Close to the underground.

✗ **Weinbar** – Restaurant Rutz 🏠 AK VISA ⦿⦿ AE
Chausseestr. 8 ✉ *10115* – Ⓜ *Oranienburger Tor* – ☏ *(030) 24 62 87 60*
– *www.weinbar-rutz.de*
– *Closed 2 weeks early January and Sunday-Monday*   *Plan I* **C2**
Rest – *(dinner only open from 4pm)* Menu 39/59 € – Carte 27/54 € ⌘
♦ Regional/country ♦ Wine bar ♦
This genuinely German restaurant has a regionally inspired menu. It offers tradi-
tional specialities such as, smoked Neuköllner Rauchknacker sausage and Man-
galitza ham hock, which provides a contrast to the more sophisticated Rutz.

AROUND THE KURFÜRSTENDAMM   *Plan III*

🏨 **Concorde** ⒑ 🏠 ⚿ AK 🛜 🍴 🌭 VISA ⦿⦿ AE ①
Augsburger Str. 41 ✉ *10789* – Ⓜ *Kurfürstendamm* – ☏ *(030) 8 00 99 90*
– *www.concorde-hotels.com/concordeberlin*   **K2**
311 rm ⌑ – ♦140/450 € ♦♦160/470 € – 22 suites
Rest *Brasserie Le Faubourg* – see restaurant listing
♦ Business ♦ Grand Luxury ♦ Modern ♦
This modern luxury hotel stands in the middle of the lively city centre. It has
spacious public areas and generously sized rooms. It also offers individual suites,
some of which have beautiful views. There is art throughout the hotel. The Brasserie Le Faubourg is elegant and modern.

🏨 **Palace** ⒑ ⓜ 🏠 ▯ ⚿ AK 🛜 🍴 🌭 VISA ⦿⦿ AE ①
Budapester Str. 45 ✉ *10787* – Ⓜ *Zoologischer Garten* – ☏ *(030) 2 50 20*
– *www.palace.de*   **K2**
278 rm – ♦135/325 € ♦♦155/515 €, ⌑ 26 € – 19 suites
Rest *First Floor* ⌘ – see restaurant listing
♦ Grand Luxury ♦ Classic ♦
This luxurious hotel is at the Europa Center. It offers a large lobby, attentive service and rooms in a classical or modern style, as well as elegant suites. It also
provides an 800m² Mediterranean spa area.

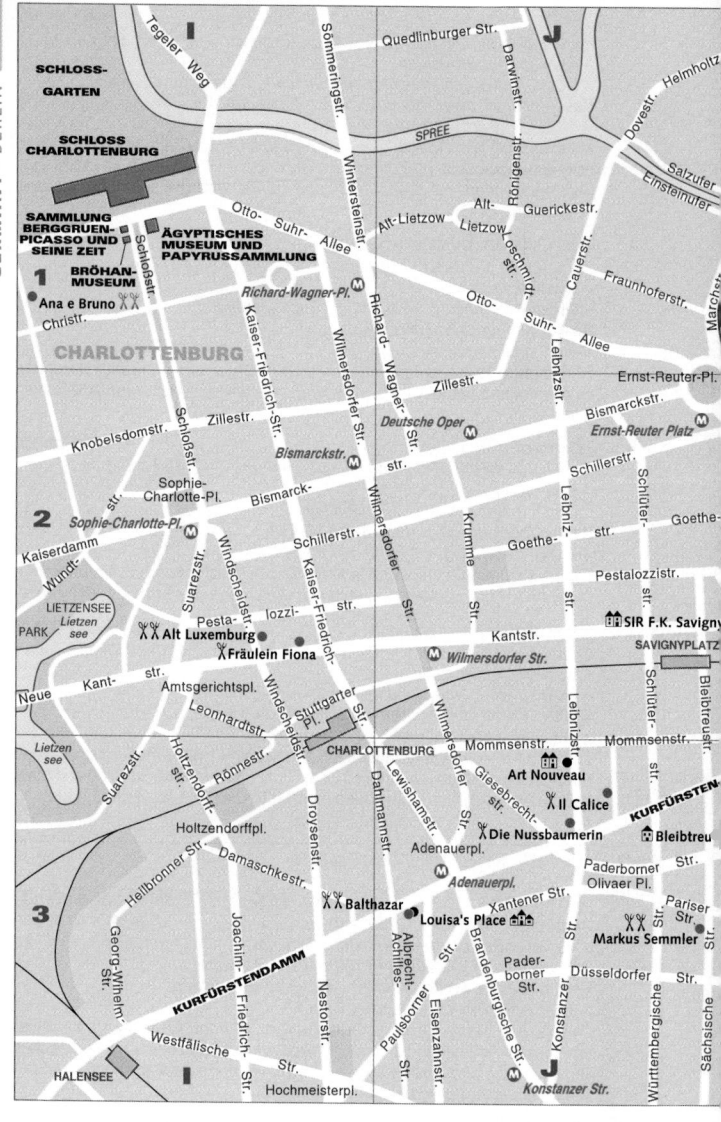

SCHLOSS-
GARTEN

SCHLOSS
CHARLOTTENBURG

SAMMLUNG
BERGGRUEN-
PICASSO UND
SEINE ZEIT

ÄGYPTISCHES
MUSEUM UND
PAPYRUSSAMMLUNG

BRÖHAN-
MUSEUM

Ana e Bruno

Christr.

CHARLOTTENBURG

Richard-Wagner-Pl.

Knobelsdomstr.

Zillestr.

Deutsche Oper

Bismarckstr.

Sophie-
Charlotte-Pl.

Sophie-Charlotte-Pl.

Kaiserdamm

LIETZENSEE
PARK

Lietzen
see

Alt Luxemburg

Fräulein Fiona

Neue   Kant-   str.

Lietzen
see

Amtsgerichtspl.

Leonhardtstr.

Holtzendorffpl.

Holtzendorfstr.

CHARLOTTENBURG

Damaschkestr.

Balthazar

KURFÜRSTENDAMM

Westfälische

HALENSEE

Hochmeisterpl.

Quedlinburger Str.

SPREE

Alt-
Lietzow

Guerickestr.

Fraunhoferstr.

Ernst-Reuter-Pl.

Bismarckstr.

Ernst-Reuter Platz

Schillerstr.

Goethe-

Pestalozzistr.

SIR F.K. Savigny

SAVIGNYPLATZ

Kantstr.

Wilmersdorfer Str.

Mommsenstr.

Art Nouveau

Il Calice

Die Nussbaumerin

Bleibtreu

KURFÜRSTEN

Adenauerpl.

Louisa's Place

Markus Semmler

Konstanzer Str.

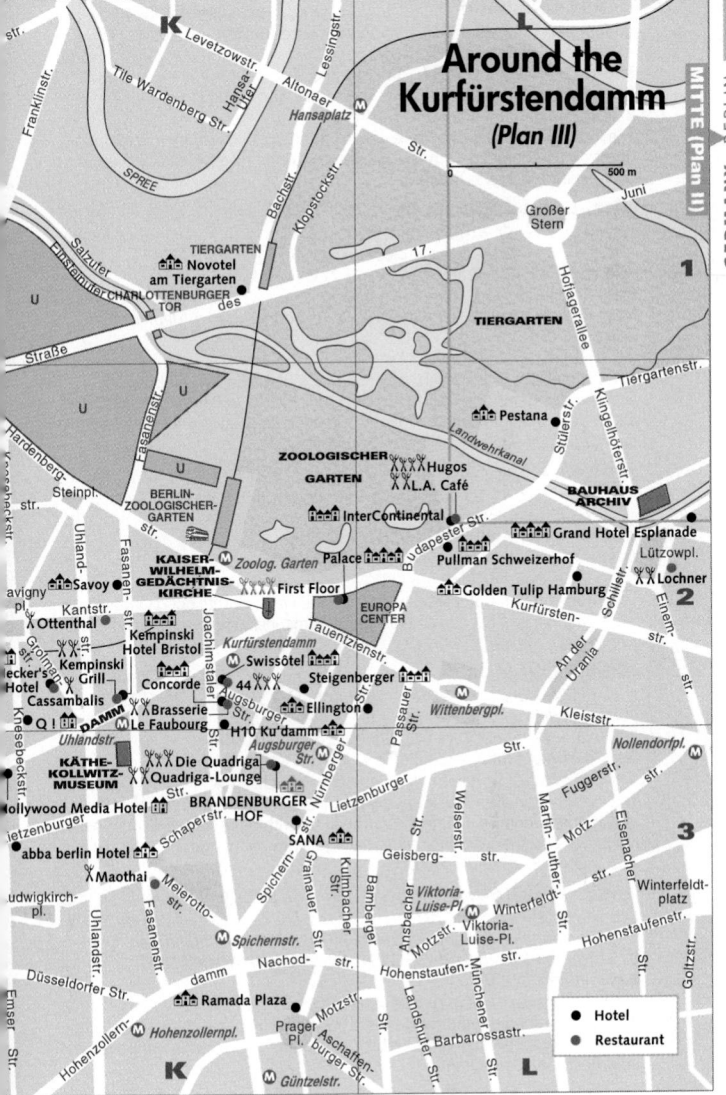

Around the Kurfürstendamm
(Plan III)

K Levetzowstr. Lessingstr. **L**

Franklinstr. Tile Wardenberg Str. Hansa Ufer Altonaer Str. Hansaplatz

SPREE Klopstockstr. Bachstr.

TIERGARTEN
🏨 **Novotel am Tiergarten**
CHARLOTTENBURGER TOR des

Straße 17.

Salzufer Einsteinufer

Hardenberg- str.

Fasanenstr.

TIERGARTEN

Großer Stern

Juni

0   500 m

1

🏨 **Pestana**

Landwehrkanal Tiergartenstr.

Klingelhöferstr.

Stülerstr.

BAUHAUS ARCHIV

ZOOLOGISCHER GARTEN 🍴 **Hugos**
🍴 **L.A. Café**

Steinpl. Uhlandstr.

BERLIN-ZOOLOGISCHER-GARTEN

🏨 **InterContinental**

🏨 **Grand Hotel Esplanade**
Lützowpl.
🍴 **Lochner**

KAISER-WILHELMS-GEDÄCHTNIS-KIRCHE

Zoolog. Garten **Palace** 🏨
Budapester Str.

Pullman Schweizerhof

An der Urania

Schillstr. Einemstr.

avigny pl.
🏨 **Savoy**
🍴 **First Floor**

EUROPA CENTER

🏨 **Golden Tulip Hamburg**

Kurfürsten-

2

🍴 **Ottenthal** Kantstr.

🏨 **Kempinski Hotel Bristol**

Joachimstaler str.

Kurfürstendamm

🏨 **Swissôtel**

Tauentzienstr.

🏨 **Steigenberger**

Kleiststr.

Wittenbergpl.

Nollendorfpl.

Fuggerstr.

Eisenacher str.

Martin-Luther-

ecker' Grill
🏨 **Kempinski**
Grolmanstr.
🍴 **Cassambalis**

🏨 **Concorde**
🍴 **44**

Augsburger Str.

🏨 **Ellington**

Passauer Str.

Str.

🏨 **Hotel**
Q 🏨
DAMM
🍴 **Brasserie Le Faubourg**

Uhlandstr.

🏨 **H10 Ku'damm**
Augsburger Str.

Nürnberger

Lietzenburger Str.

Weisestr.

Motzstr.

Knesebeckstr.

KÄTHE-KOLLWITZ-MUSEUM

🍴 **Die Quadriga**
🍴 **Quadriga-Lounge**

BRANDENBURGER HOF

Spichernstr. Grainauer Str.

Bamberger

Ansbacher str.

Welserstr.

Winterfeldt-

3

ollywood Media Hotel 🏨

ietzenburger

Schaperstr.

🏨 **SANA**

Geisberg-   str.

Viktoria-Luise-Pl.

Winterfeldt-str.

Winterfeldt-platz

Hohenstaufenstr.

🏨 **abba berlin Hotel**

🍴 **Maothai**

Meierotto-

Spichern-str.

Kulmbacher Str.

Münchener Str.

Motzstr.

Viktoria-Luise-Pl.

Hohenstaufenstr.

Golzstr.

udwigkirch-pl.

Uhlandstr.

Fasanenstr.

Spichernstr.

Nachod-   str.

Hohenzollern-

Landshuter Str.

Düsseldorfer Str.

🏨 **Ramada Plaza**
Prager Pl.

Motzstr.

Aschaffen-   burger Str.

Barbarossastr.

Emser Str.

Hohenzollerndamm

Hohenzollernpl.

Güntzelstr.

K **L**

● Hotel
● Restaurant

323

InterContinental 𝄢 ⊕ ⥀ ▣ & ⅄ 🛜 ⅍ 🚗 VISA ⊛ AE ⓞ

Budapester Str. 2 ✉ *10787* – ◍ *Zoologischer Garten* – ℰ *(030) 2 60 20*
– www.berlin.intercontinental.com **L2**
558 rm – ∲99/154 € ∲∲99/154 €, ⮺ 30 € – 13 suites
Rest *Hugos* ❀ **Rest** *L.A. Cafe* – see restaurant listing
♦ Chain hotel ♦ Luxury ♦ Classic ♦
The Intercontinental is smart and upmarket throughout. Elegant, contemporary
guestrooms equipped with the latest technology, tasteful Vitality Club, plus
conference and events facilities.

Grand Hotel Esplanade 🛜 𝄢 ⊕ ⥀ ▣ & ⅍ 🚗

Lützowufer 15 ✉ *10785* – ◍ *Wittenbergplatz* VISA ⊛ AE ⓞ
– ℰ (030) 25 47 80 – www.esplanade.de **L2**
394 rm – ∲99/399 € ∲∲99/399 €, ⮺ 22 € – 24 suites
Rest – Carte 30/55 €
Rest *Eckrestaurant* – *(closed 3 weeks July and Sunday) (dinner only)*
Carte 19/45 €
♦ Luxury ♦ Modern ♦
In this hotel on the Landwehr canal find a modern and lively lobby, very cosy
and friendly rooms and individual suites. Outside the building is the MS Espla-
nade yacht, home to events of all kinds. The Ellipse Lounge offers international
cuisine. Sample local specialities in the Eckrestaurant.

Swissôtel 𝄢 ⥀ ▣ ⅍ 🛜 ⅍ 🚗 VISA ⊛ AE ⓞ

Augsburger Str. 44 ✉ *10789* – ◍ *Kurfürstendamm* – ℰ *(030) 220100*
– www.swissotel.com/berlin **K2**
316 rm – ∲140/360 € ∲∲140/360 €, ⮺ 21 €
Rest *44* – see restaurant listing
♦ Business ♦ Modern ♦
This modern town hotel with its glass façade welcomes its guests with a spacious atrium hall. It has comfortable guestrooms, including business and executive rooms.

Steigenberger 🛜 ⥀ ▣ & ⅍ 🛜 ⅍ 🚗 VISA ⊛ AE ⓞ

Los-Angeles-Platz 1 ✉ *10789* – ◍ *Augsburger Str.* – ℰ *(030) 2 12 70*
– www.berlin.steigenberger.de **K2**
398 rm – ∲125/495 € ∲∲145/495 €, ⮺ 23 € – 10 suites
Rest *Berliner Stube* – ℰ *(030) 2 12 77 50* – Carte 29/63 €
♦ Conference hotel ♦ Business ♦ Modern ♦
This hotel has an attractive lobby area with bar and smokers' lounge and beautiful, modern rooms decorated in earthy tones with clean lines. Executive suites
are located on the sixth floor with access to a private lounge. This friendly Berliner Stube has a traditional touch.

Pullman Schweizerhof 🛜 𝄢 ⊕ ⥀ ▣ & ⅍ 🛜 🚗

Budapester Str. 25 ✉ *10787* VISA ⊛ AE ⓞ
– ◍ Zoologischer Garten – ℰ *(030) 26960 – www.pullmanhotels.com*
373 rm – ∲135/425 € ∲∲135/425 €, ⮺ 24 € – 10 suites **L2**
Rest – Carte 32/56 €
♦ Chain hotel ♦ Business ♦ Design ♦
A modern hotel designed for business travel and meetings. It features techni-
cally well-equipped and comfortable guestrooms, and a fashionable wellness
area. Bistro-style restaurant

Kempinski Hotel Bristol 🛜 𝄢 ⥀ ▣ 🛜 ⅍ 🚗

Kurfürstendamm 27 ✉ *10719* – ◍ *Uhlandstr.* VISA ⊛ AE ⓞ
– ℰ (030) 88 43 40 – www.kempinski-berlin.com **K2**
301 rm – ∲129/395 € ∲∲129/395 €, ⮺ 25 € – 22 suites
Rest *Kempinski Grill* – see restaurant listing
Rest *Reinhard's* – ℰ *(030) 88 43 52 61* – Carte 46/58 €
♦ Luxury ♦ Classic ♦
The impressive building on the renowned Ku'damm is an elegant luxury hotel,
which has already welcomed many a distinguished guest. The Kempinski Grill
has been a Berlin institution since 1952. Reinhard's has a pleasant brasserie style.

GERMANY - BERLIN

BRANDENBURGER HOF 🛜 🛁 🚗 VISA ☎ AE ⓪

Eislebener Str. 14 ⌧ *10789* – Ⓜ *Augsburger Str.* – 𝒞 *(030) 21 40 50*
– *www.brandenburger-hof.com*   **K3**
72 rm – ♦180/280 € ♦♦265/315 €, ⌁ 32 € – 8 suites
Rest *Quadriga-Lounge* **Rest** *Die Quadriga* – see restaurant listing
♦ Historic ♦ Design ♦ Elegant ♦
The Berlin City Palace retains all the classical elegance of the 19C in the simple,
clean lines of its rooms. It also boasts an exclusive Thaleia massage suite and a
lavish à-la-carte breakfast menu. There is a conservatory atmosphere in the light
and airy Quadriga Lounge.

abba Berlin Hotel 🛗 🛏 ♿ 🖥 🛜 🛁 🚗 VISA ☎ AE

Lietzenburger Str. 89 ⌧ *10719* – Ⓜ *Uhlandstr.* – 𝒞 *(030) 8 87 18 60*
– *www.abbaberlinhotel.com/de/*   **K3**
214 rm – ♦79/290 € ♦♦79/290 €, ⌁ 14 € – 4 suites
Rest *abba mia* – (dinner only) Menu 22 € – Carte 19/42 €
♦ Business ♦ Contemporary ♦ Functional ♦
This hotel is ideal for business travellers and conferences. There is a spacious
smart lobby, as well as modern, comfortable, pleasantly simple rooms, each
with a lovely crystal chandelier. The menu is Spanish and international.

Louisa's Place 🛗 🛏 🖥 ♿ 🛜 🛁 VISA ☎ AE ⓪

Kurfürstendamm 160 ⌧ *10709* – Ⓜ *Adenauerplatz* – 𝒞 *(030) 63 10 30*
– *www.louisas-place.de*   **J3**
47 suites – ♦135/595 € ♦♦135/595 €, ⌁ 20 €
Rest *Balthazar* – see restaurant listing
♦ Business ♦ Personalised ♦ Cosy ♦
This hotel has a friendly service and offers tasteful, spacious suites with kitchens.
There is also a stylish breakfast room and library.

H10 Ku'damm 🛗 🌐 ♿ 🖥 🛜 🛁 🚗 VISA ☎ AE

Joachimsthaler Str. 31 ⌧ *10178* – Ⓜ *Kurfürstendamm*
– 𝒞 *(030) 3 22 92 23 00* – *www.h10hotels.com*   **K2**
199 rm – ♦85/170 € ♦♦105/190 €, ⌁ 18 € – 7 suites
Rest – Menu 20 € (lunch)/56 € – Carte 21/40 €
♦ Business ♦ Modern ♦ Elegant ♦
A light, bright, modern hotel in which a restored school building (loft-style
rooms including some duplexes) has been cleverly combined with a new addi-
tion. The restaurant serves the house speciality: Berlin-style tapas.

Ramada Plaza 🍽 ♿ 🖥 🛜 🛁 🚗 VISA ☎ AE

Pragerstr. 12 ⌧ *10779* – Ⓜ *Güntzelstr.* – 𝒞 *(030) 2 36 25 00*
– *www.ramada-plaza-berlin.de*   **K3**
184 rm – ♦79/259 € ♦♦79/259 €, ⌁ 17 € – 67 suites
Rest – Menu 32 € – Carte 25/52 €
♦ Chain hotel ♦ Modern ♦
A business hotel providing elegant rooms and suites with American cherry
wood furnishings and the latest technical facilities. With executive suites on
the sixth floor. A classic style restaurant.

Ellington 🍽 🛗 ♿ 🖥 📞 🛁 🚗 VISA ☎ AE

Nürnberger Str. 50 ⌧ *10789* – Ⓜ *Wittenbergplatz* – 𝒞 *(030) 68 31 50*
– *www.ellington-hotel.com*   **L2**
285 rm – ♦118/208 € ♦♦128/228 €, ⌁ 20 € – 3 suites
Rest – Menu 15 € (lunch)/95 € – Carte 33/62 €
♦ Business ♦ Modern ♦ Minimalist ♦
Numerous photographs of the Duke Ellington, after whom the hotel is named,
adorn this simply furnished hotel. It has a beautiful lobby area and a lounge-
style interior courtyard. Many details preserve its historic charm. A restaurant
with a straightforward style.

SANA

Nürnberger Str. 33 ✉ 10777 – Ⓜ Augsburger Str. – ✆ (030) 20 05 15 10 – www.berlin.sanahotels.com **K3**

208 rm – †88/228 € ††88/228 €, ☕ 15 € – 1 suite

Rest – *(residents only)* Carte 30/46 €

♦ Business ♦ Modern ♦

Minimalist, urban design from top to toe, with a lounge in the interior courtyard. The top floor houses a small fitness suite with great views, while the hotel bar, the 'F8 – feight', has a terrace. In the restaurant the accent is on Portuguese cuisine.

Novotel am Tiergarten

Straße des 17. Juni 106 ✉ 10623 – Ⓜ Hansaplatz – ✆ (030) 60 03 50 – www.novotel-berlin.com **K1**

274 rm – †89/199 € ††89/199 €, ☕ 19 € – 11 suites

Rest – Carte 24/55 €

♦ Chain hotel ♦ Modern ♦

Located near the Tiergarten overland station, this business hotel provides modern rooms equipped with the latest technology and extensive fitness facilities as well as a lounge-style roof terrace.

Savoy

Fasanenstr. 9 ✉ 10623 – Ⓜ Zoologischer Garten – ✆ (030) 31 10 30 – www.hotel-savoy.com **K2**

125 rm ☕ – †92/121 € ††152/181 € – 7 suites

Rest *Weinrot* – *(closed Sunday)* Menu 35/50 €

♦ Business ♦ Modern ♦

The elegant lobby area of this traditional hotel has a personal feel and is dominated by red tones. The Casa del Habano has a good selection of cigars. Modern interior with a rugged, red wine colour scheme.

Golden Tulip Hamburg

Landgrafenstr. 4 ✉ 10787 – Ⓜ Wittenbergplatz – ✆ (030) 26 47 70 – www.goldentulipberlin.de **L2**

191 rm – †99/199 € ††119/239 €, ☕ 11 €

Rest – Menu 18/34 € – Carte 31/44 €

♦ Business ♦ Modern ♦

The Golden Tulip is contemporary and businesslike with comfortable rooms and a daytime bar, all decorated in warm earthy tones. The conference room is cleverly located on the 11th floor so that participants can enjoy peace, quiet and panoramic views over Berlin as they work.

Pestana

Stülerstr. 6 (corner Rauchstraße) ✉ 10787 – Ⓜ Nollendorfplatz – ✆ (030) 3 11 75 90 00 – www.pestana.com **L2**

142 rm – †99/179 € ††129/199 €, ☕ 14 €

Rest – Menu 21/60 € – Carte 24/56 €

♦ Business ♦ Contemporary ♦

The decor is simple and minimalistic throughout, from reception to the guestrooms, bar (which offers a wide selection of ports) and restaurant (tapas). The convenient location close to the Victory Column will suit all visitors to Berlin.

Hollywood Media Hotel

rm,

Kurfürstendamm 202 ✉ 10719 – Ⓜ Uhlandstr. – ✆ (030) 88 91 00 – www.filmhotel.de **K3**

182 rm ☕ – †95/129 € ††115/149 € – 7 suites **Rest** – Carte 22/53 €

♦ Business ♦ Modern ♦

The decor in this hotel follows a movie/Hollywood theme with film posters and photos of stars on the walls in the tasteful and contemporary bedrooms. In the same vein, it even has its own mini cinema. The Capone restaurant serves Italian fare.

GERMANY - BERLIN

Q!

🎐 🔥 rest, AC 🛜 🔏 VISA ⊛ AE ⓪

Knesebeckstr. 67 ⊠ 10623 – Ⓜ Uhlandstr. – ℰ (030) 8 10 06 60
– www.loock-hotels.com **K2**
77 rm – †105/205 € ††120/225 €, ☑ 15 €
Rest – (dinner for residents only) Carte 26/46 €
♦ Business ♦ Design ♦
Design reigns supreme. The modern, technically well laid out rooms are minimalist with their dark tones. Stylish restaurant with Euro-Asian fare.

Hecker's Hotel

🔥 AC 🛜 🔏 P 🚗 VISA ⊛ AE

Grolmanstr. 35 ⊠ 10623 – Ⓜ Uhlandstr. – ℰ (030) 8 89 00
– www.heckers-hotel.de **K2**
69 rm – †90/230 € ††100/330 €, ☑ 16 € – 1 suite
Rest *Cassambalis* – see restaurant listing
♦ Business ♦ Design ♦
This establishment offers contemporary living just a few steps from the Kurfürstendamm. The Bauhaus, Toskana and Colonial themed rooms are tastefully done out. There is a quiet sun terrace on the fourth-floor, and a modern breakfast room. The Cassambalis offers Mediterranean cuisine in a warm and charming atmosphere.

SIR F.K. Savigny without rest

AC 🛜 VISA ⊛ AE

Kantstr. 144 ⊠ 10623 – Ⓜ Uhlandstr. – ℰ (030) 3 23 01 56 00
– www.hotel-sirsavigny.de **J2**
44 rm – †119/189 € ††119/189 €, ☑ 18 €
♦ Townhouse ♦ Elegant ♦ Modern ♦
The smart black and white design is particularly striking and the many paintings are a little reminiscent of an English country house. Tapas and snacks available in the bar. The rear courtyard offers a small oasis of green.

Art Nouveau without rest

🛜 VISA ⊛ AE

Leibnizstr. 59 ⊠ 10629 – Ⓜ Adenauerplatz – ℰ (030) 3 27 74 40
– www.hotelartnouveau.de **J3**
18 rm ☑ – †96/156 € ††116/186 € – 3 suites
♦ Townhouse ♦ Personalised ♦ Cosy ♦
The lift of this very special and charming hotel on the fourth-floor dates back to 1906. Find individually decorated rooms, partly with antique furniture and wooden floorboards.

Bleibtreu

🎐 🎐 🔥 rm, 🛜 VISA ⊛ AE ⓪

Bleibtreustr. 31 ⊠ 10707 – Ⓜ Uhlandstr. – ℰ (030) 88 47 40
– www.bleibtreu.com **J3**
59 rm ☑ – †92/152 € ††121/181 €
Rest – (closed Sunday) Carte 33/45 €
♦ Business ♦ Design ♦
The welcoming guestrooms in this restored 19C patrician house are well furnished in a modern style and offer a free mini-bar and Wi-Fi access. The restaurant serves sandwiches, steaks and burgers. The terrace overlooks the street and the interior courtyard.

XXXX Hugos – Hotel InterContinental

≤ AC ⇆ VISA ⊛ AE ⓪

Budapester Str. 2 (14th floor) ⊠ 10787 – Ⓜ Zoologischer Garten
– ℰ (030) 26 02 12 63 – www.hugos-restaurant.de
– Closed 2 weeks early January, 1 week after Easter, 4 weeks August-September
and Sunday-Monday **L2**
Rest – (dinner only) Menu 95/220 € 🕭
♦ Modern ♦ Fashionable ♦ Elegant ♦
The phrase 'haute cuisine' takes on a whole new meaning here! Not only is Thomas Kammeier's cuisine highly rated, up on the 14th floor you will find your gaze drawn from your plate out over the rooftops of Berlin. Three menus on offer.
➜ Mangalitza Ferkel - krosser Bauch, Kokos-Chilischaum. Sesam Königslachs konfiert - Erbsennage, Minze. Valrhona-Schokoladen Soufflé - Ananas, Pfeffer, Tamarillo.

GERMANY - BERLIN

First Floor – Hotel Palace

XXXX
⍟

🏧 ↔ VISA ◉ AE ①

Budapester Str. 45 ✉ 10787 – Ⓜ *Zoologischer Garten*
– ℰ (030) 25 02 10 20 – www.firstfloor.palace.de
– Closed 1-15 January, 15 July-12 August and Sunday-Monday   K2
Rest – *(dinner only)* Menu 109/159 € – Carte 93/102 € ⍟
♦ French classic ♦ Elegant ♦

Michelin-starred since 1997, First Floor has been managed with great success by Berlin-born Matthias Diether for the past few years. The extensive wine list containing some 1 500 selections is particularly impressive. The suggestions from head sommelier Gunnar Tietz are a perfect match for the elegant, contemporary food.
➜ Lamm - Bärlauch - Orange. Taube - Gänseleber - kandierte Nüsse. Rinderfilet - Café de Paris - Frühlingsgemüse.

Die Quadriga – Hotel BRANDENBURGER HOF

XXX

🏧 ↔

Eislebener Str. 14 ✉ 10789 – Ⓜ *Augsburger Str.*   VISA ◉ AE ①
– ℰ (030) 21 40 56 51 – www.brandenburger-hof.com
– Closed 2-14 January, 20 July-24 August and Sunday-Monday   K3
Rest – *(dinner only)* Menu 85/135 € – Carte 66/96 € ⍟
♦ Creative ♦ Elegant ♦ Classic ♦

Following spells in a number of prestigious restaurants, Sebastian Voelz has now taken up the reins at Die Quadriga. His food is served by the well-versed front-of-house team directed by Annekatrin Simon. The elegant dining room is decorated in warm gold and olive.

44 – Hotel Swissôtel

XXX

🍴 ♿ 🏧 VISA ◉ AE ①

Augsburger Str. 44 ✉ 10789 – Ⓜ *Kurfürstendamm*
– ℰ (030) 2 20 10 22 88 – www.restaurant44.de
– Closed 1-13 January, 22 July-4 August and Sunday   K2
Rest – *(dinner only)* Menu 54/149 € – Carte 33/77 €
♦ Creative ♦ Fashionable ♦

This simple, modern and elegant restaurant serves imaginative food in the form of a tasting menu. Glass frontage and terrace overlooking the Kurfurstendamm.

Ana e Bruno

XX

🍴 🏧 VISA ◉

Sophie-Charlotten-Str. 101 ✉ 14059 – Ⓜ *Sophie-Charlotte-Pl.*
– ℰ (030) 3 25 71 10 – www.ana-e-bruno.de   I1
Rest – *(dinner only)* Menu 45/95 € – Carte 47/71 € ⍟
♦ Mediterranean ♦ Elegant ♦

Chef Bruno Pellegrini often appears front of house, exuding relaxed Italian charm. The Italian cuisine is ambitious and is accompanied by 500 wines from his homeland. You can look forward to a great espresso to round off your meal.

Kempinski Grill – Kempinski Hotel Bristol

XX

🍴 ♿ VISA ◉ AE ①

Kurfürstendamm 27 ✉ 10719 – Ⓜ *Uhlandstr. – ℰ (030) 88 43 47 67*
– www.kempinski-berlin.com
– Closed 4 weeks July-August   K2
Rest – Menu 65 € – Carte 43/76 €
♦ French classic ♦ Elegant ♦

A veritable institution on the Ku'Damm since 1952. Kempinski's classic period elegance remains (despite various refurbishments over the years), providing the restaurant with its unique charm.

L.A. Cafe – Hotel InterContinental

XX

🍴 ♿ 🏧 VISA ◉ AE ①

Budapester Str. 2 ✉ 10787 – Ⓜ *Zoologischer Garten – ℰ (030) 2 60 20*
– www.berlin.intercontinental.com   L2
Rest – Carte 26/82 €
♦ International ♦ Friendly ♦

A magnificent and brightly coloured glass dome bathes this spacious restaurant in a very special light. From early morning till late at night the L.A. Cafe makes the ideal place to dine with friends and family or colleagues and clients.

GERMANY - BERLIN

XX **Lochner** 🍴 VISA ◉◉ AE

Lützowplatz 5 ✉ *10785* – Ⓜ *Nollendorfplatz* – ✆ *(030) 23 00 52 20*
– *www.lochner-restaurant.com*
– *Closed 2 weeks end June-early July and Monday*   **L2**
Rest – *(dinner only)* Menu 48/85 € – Carte 45/62 €
♦ International ♦ Friendly ♦
This is a pleasant, family-run restaurant with many regular customers. Your host
cooks ambitiously, and friendly service is encouraged from the top down.

XX **Alt Luxemburg** AK ⇦ VISA ◉◉ AE ①

Windscheidstr. 31 ✉ *10627* – Ⓜ *Wilmersdorfer Str.* – ✆ *(030) 3 23 87 30*
– *www.altluxemburg.de* – *Closed Sunday*   **I2**
Rest – *(dinner only) (booking advisable)* Menu 53/75 € – Carte 53/67 €
♦ French classic ♦ Family ♦
Attractive, friendly colours contribute to the atmosphere of this restaurant. It
offers classic cuisine, and has been traditionally run by the Wannemacher family
since 1982.

XX **Quadriga-Lounge** – Hotel BRANDENBURGER HOF   🍴

Eislebener Str. 14 ✉ *10789* – Ⓜ *Augsburger Str.*
– ✆ *(030) 21 40 56 51* – *www.brandenburger-hof.com*   VISA ◉◉ AE ①   **K3**
Rest – Menu 45/68 € – Carte 39/66 €
♦ International ♦ Cosy ♦
With its wonderful winter garden atmosphere, the Quadriga-Lounge is one of
the jewels in the crown of this classy restaurant. Customers meet to eat and
drink while listening to live piano music. Jazz evening on Thursdays from 10pm.

XX **Balthazar** – Hotel Louisa's Place   🍴 & AK ⇦ VISA ◉◉ AE ①

Kurfürstendamm 160 ✉ *10709* – Ⓜ *Adenauerplatz* – ✆ *(030) 89 40 84 77*
– *www.balthazar-restaurant.de*   **J3**
Rest – *(dinner only)* Carte 40/80 €
♦ Classic ♦ Fashionable ♦ Trendy ♦
Holger Zurbrüggen's restaurant offers great food right on the Ku'damm. His
own particular brand of cooking, which he dubs 'Metropolitan Cuisine', is heavily influenced by South-East Asian and Mediterranean styles.

XX **Markus Semmler** 🍴 VISA ◉◉ AE

Sächsische Str. 7 ✉ *10707* – Ⓜ *Hohenzollernpl.* – ✆ *(030) 89 06 82 90*
– *www.kochkunst-ereignisse.de*
– *Closed 14-20 January, 3 weeks July and Saturday-Sunday*   **J3**
Rest – *(dinner only)* Menu 69/99 € – Carte 57/81 €
♦ Classic ♦ Trendy ♦
Markus Semmler cooks fresh classic cuisine including delicacies such as peppe-
red tuna with tomato and bread salad, and turbot with oxtail praline. The star-
ters and desserts are prepared in the open kitchen before your eyes.

XX **Brasserie Le Faubourg** – Hotel Concorde   🍴 & AK

Augsburger Str. 41 ✉ *10789* – Ⓜ *Kurfürstendamm*   VISA ◉◉ AE ①
– ✆ *(030) 80 09 99 77 00* – *www.concorde-hotels.com/concordeberlin*
Rest – Menu 15 € (lunch)/64 € – Carte 47/75 €   **K2**
♦ French classic ♦ Brasserie ♦
Inspired by modern Paris, the Brasserie exudes cool elegance with its teak
chairs, aubergine fabrics and striking artworks on the walls. Typical French bistro
cuisine and a great daily menu.

X **Bieberbau** 🍴 ⌷

Durlacher Str. 15 ✉ *10715* – Ⓜ *Bundesplatz* – ✆ *(030) 8 53 23 90*
– *www.bieberbau-berlin.de*
– *Closed mid June-mid July and Sunday-Monday*   *Plan I* **B3**
Rest – *(dinner only) (booking advisable)* Menu 35/60 €
♦ International ♦ Cosy ♦
This wonderful example of the stucco plasterer's art was created by Richard Bie-
ber in the 19C. The food prepared at the Molteni ranges is based on regional
products and fine herbs. So try not to fill up too much on the homemade
bread and flavoured butters!

GERMANY - BERLIN

Ottenthal
VISA ◯◯ **AE**

Kantstr. 153 ✉ *10623* – Ⓜ *Uhlandstr.* – ✆ *(030) 3 13 31 62*
– *www.ottenthal.com*
K2
Rest – *(dinner only) (booking advisable)* Menu 28/50 € – Carte 30/46 €
♦ Austrian ♦ Bistro ♦

Ottenthal's popularity speaks for itself. Its typically Austrian tavern fare is a great success. In his friendly bistro-style restaurant (named after his home town in Lower Austria) chef Arthur Schneller produces unfussy dishes including Wiener Tafelspitz (boiled rump of beef Viennese style) and apple strudel. Good wine selection.

Renger-Patzsch
🛏 *VISA* ◯◯

Wartburgstr. 54 ✉ *10823* – Ⓜ *Eisenacher Str.* – ✆ *(030) 7 84 20 59*
– *www.renger-patzsch.com*
Plan I **B3**
Rest – *(dinner only) (booking advisable)* Menu 29/46 € – Carte 25/43 €
♦ Traditional ♦ Inn ♦ Cosy ♦

This cosy restaurant is named after the pioneer of landscape photography – black and white pictures adorn the walls. Good traditional cooking and tarte flambée are on the menu.

Die Nussbaumerin
✄

Leibnizstr. 55 ✉ *10629* – Ⓜ *Adenauerpl.* – ✆ *(030) 50 17 80 33*
– *www.nussbaumerin.de*
– *Closed Sunday*
J3
Rest – *(dinner only) (booking advisable)* Carte 23/40 €
♦ Traditional ♦ Cosy ♦

This restaurant serves delicious home-cooked food of the sort you would like to eat more often. The owner herself serves up the freshly cooked Austrian classics including Wiener Schnitzel, boiled rump of beef and Marillenknödel apricot pastries. Unfortunately the good Austrian wines to accompany them are only available by the bottle.

Fräulein Fiona
✄

Fritschestr. 48 (corner Kantstr. 70) ✉ *10627* – Ⓜ *Wilmersdorfer Str.*
– ✆ *(030) 95 60 22 72*
– *Closed Sunday*
I2
Rest – *(dinner only)* Menu 36/55 € – Carte 31/52 €
♦ Regional/country ♦ Friendly ♦

Calf's tongue with wild garlic pesto and ox cheek with cream spätzle are perfect examples of the good contemporary German cuisine on offer in this small, friendly restaurant. In summer a couple of tables are set out on the street as a draw to passers-by.

Il Calice
🛏 *VISA* ◯◯ **AE**

Walter-Benjamin-Platz 4 ✉ *10629* – Ⓜ *Adenauerpl.* – ✆ *(030) 3 24 23 08*
– *www.ilcalice.de*
– *Closed Sunday*
J3
Rest – Carte 32/66 € ⅋
♦ International ♦ Friendly ♦ Brasserie ♦

By the Leibniz Kolonnaden, this friendly restaurant has a brasserie-like atmosphere. It features good Italian and international cuisine and more refined dining in the evening. The food is accompanied by very good Italian wines.

Cassambalis – Hecker's Hotel
AC **P** *VISA* ◯◯

Grolmanstr. 35 ✉ *10623* – Ⓜ *Uhlandstr.* – ✆ *(030) 8 85 47 47*
– *www.heckers-hotel.de*
K2
Rest – Menu 22 € (lunch)/65 € – Carte 29/50 €
♦ Mediterranean ♦ Friendly ♦

You can't get any closer to the action than this. Close to the Ku'Damm, this restaurant is reminiscent of a bright, friendly brasserie with lots of art on the walls, open wine shelves and bright colours. Mediterranean cuisine.

GERMANY - BERLIN

✗ **Maothai** 🏠 ✿ VISA ⚫ AE
Meierottostr. 1 ✉ 10719 – Ⓜ *Spichernstr. – ℰ (030) 8 83 28 23*
– www.maothai-am-fasanenplatz.de
Rest *– (dinner only)* Carte 19/49 €   **K3**

✦ Thai ✦ Exotic ✦

Enjoy the intimate, candle lit atmosphere in this restaurant near the Fasanen square. It serves authentic Thai cuisine, and there is a charming terrace dining area.

ENVIRONS OF BERLIN   *Plan I*

AT BERLIN-GRUNEWALD

🏨 **Schlosshotel im Grunewald** 🐾 🚗 🕭 🏠 ᛚ5 ♨ 🔲 🎬 🛜
Brahmsstr. 10 ✉ 14193 – ℰ (030) 89 58 40 ᛚ4 🅿 VISA ⚫ AE ①
– www.schlosshotelberlin.com   **A3**
53 rm – ❤239/399 € ❤❤239/399 €, ⌂ 26 € – 10 suites
Rest *Vivaldi* – see restaurant listing
Rest *Alter Wintergarten* – Menu 39/60 € – Carte 63/69 €

✦ Rural ✦ Luxury ✦ Design ✦

This 19C palace located in the upmarket Grunewald district offers a perfect combination of wonderful historical detail and refined, modern style. Remarkable library. Set in small grounds. A friendly welcome awaits in this lovely restaurant. A stylishly elegant restaurant with a pleasant terrace.

✗✗✗ **Vivaldi** – Schlosshotel im Grunewald 🕭 🏠 🎬 🅿 VISA ⚫ AE ①
Brahmsstr. 10 ✉ 14193 – ℰ (030) 89 58 47 34
– www.schlosshotelberlin.com
– Closed 2-22 January and Sunday-Monday   **A3**
Rest *– (dinner only)* Carte 63/70 €

✦ International ✦ Elegant ✦

This historical palace provides a sumptuous restaurant setting, even in the context of the magnificent Grunewald Forest. Guests never tire of the opulent interior (which is largely original) and elegant atmosphere.

✗✗ **Frühsammers Restaurant** 🏠 VISA ⚫ AE ①
Flinsberger Platz 8 ✉ 14193 – ℰ (030) 89 73 86 28
– www.fruehsammers-restaurant.de
– Closed 1-11 January, 1-10 April and Saturday lunch, Sunday-Monday
Rest *– (booking advisable)* Menu 34/110 € – Carte 38/88 €   **A3**
�
✦ International ✦ Friendly ✦

The Frühsammer family serve excellent international food along with the chef's wine recommendations in this elegant villa belonging to the Grunewalder Tennis Club. Good-value lunch menu.

AT AIRPORT SCHÖNEFELD South-East: 21 km

🏨 **Holiday Inn Airport** 🏠 ᛚ5 ♨ & 🎬 🛜 ᛚ4 🅿 🚗 VISA ⚫ AE ①
Hans-Grade-Allee 5 ✉ 12529 – ℰ (030) 63 40 10
– www.holidayinn-berlin.de
300 rm – ❤65/175 € ❤❤75/185 €, ⌂ 20 € – 4 suites
Rest *– Menu 18/54 € – Carte 25/52 €*

✦ Business ✦ Functional ✦ Modern ✦

The perfect hotel for business travellers arriving by plane who appreciate the Holiday Inn's contemporary and functional bedrooms and proximity to the airport. In addition to the restaurant, guests can also take advantage of the Hangar 16 bar and a smokers' lounge.

COLOGNE
KÖLN

Population: 1 010 269

F. Jürgen/Fotolia.com

Cologne is Germany's oldest city and its name was instigated by the Romans, who set up a 'colony' to fend off the Barbarians. It became a Free City, and later fell under the rule of Napoleon and then the Prussians; all of which has given the locals a cosmopolitan, laid-back and sociable outlook. Although it may never be described as Europe's prettiest city, it has an eye-catching old town (largely rebuilt after World War II) and some world-class museums. It also boasts one of the finest collections of medieval churches in Europe, and ploughs its own furrow by celebrating Carnival like it's Rio. Most famously, it has its Cathedral, a massive structure that took over half a millennium to build, stood tall during the War and remains the biggest tourist attraction in Germany to this day.

The River Rhine cuts a swathe right through the heart of Cologne, with four central bridges allowing plentiful passage from east to west. The main hub of the city is on the west bank, with the Altstadt (old town) practically on the river bank itself. Out to the west, the old medieval walls are now a ring road which neatly encircles the city centre and just northwest of the ring road is Mediapark, a brash modern development. To the east of the Rhine is the massive Trade Fair Centre, with its 80m-high tower, while to its north is Cologne's biggest and most popular park, Rheinpark.

COLOGNE IN...

→ **ONE DAY**
Altstadt, Dom, Romanesque churches.

→ **TWO DAYS**
Museum Ludwig, Wallraf-Richartz Museum (or Chocolate Museum), Stadtgarten (or Opera House).

→ **THREE DAYS**
Romano-Germanic Museum, Rheinpark.

PRACTICAL INFORMATION

ARRIVAL-DEPARTURE

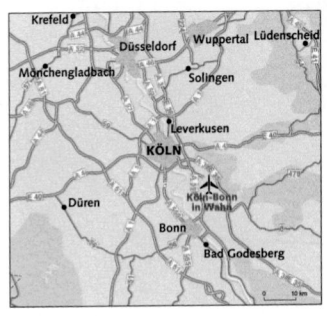

Cologne / Bonn Airport lies 17km southeast of the city centre. The S13 train takes about 15min.

GETTING AROUND

You can get around Cologne by bus, tram or metro. Validate your ticket by stamping it each time you board. Single and day tickets for Cologne not only take you from one side of the city to the other but are also valid for a journey to nearby Bonn. If you're in the city for a while, invest in a Köln Welcome Card, available from tourist information offices and many hotels. As well as providing free travel on the public transport network, it offers almost ninety deals and discounts at venues ranging from galleries and museums to shops, leisure facilities and eateries.

CALENDAR HIGHLIGHTS

February
Crazy Days (carnival).

March
lit.cologne (international literature festival).

July
Cologne Lights, Christopher Street Day (gay pride celebration), Summerjam.

August
Ringfest (two miles of rock stages along the Ringstrassen ring road).

October
Long Night of Cologne Museums.

November
Carnival begins.

EATING OUT

Cologne is known throughout Germany for its Kölsch. It's the name of the local people and it's the name of their brew, a light beer with the yeast risen to the top rather than sunk to the bottom of the glass. 20 local breweries produce their own versions and you can try them out in an old town brauhaus – atmospheric, dark wood-panelled places where buzzy waiters continuously refill your empty stangen (0.2 litre glass). After that, make the most of the city's ethnic diversity by selecting a restaurant from an impressive global range; pick of the bunch are the fine Italian, Japanese and Turkish establishments. If your preference is for something local, favoured dishes include Himmel un Äad (bloodsausage and mash), Sauerbraten vom Pferd (braised horse) or Töttchen (ragout of brains and calf's head, cooked with herbs). Bars, cafés and restaurants all stay open late, many until 11pm or midnight. Service charge is generally included but most people round up the bill. In summer, seek out an ice-cream parlour, sit under a parasol and tuck into a full-on sundae.

Environs of Cologne
(Plan I)

0   2 km

PESCH

LONGERICH

WEIDENPESCH

MAUENHEIM

OSSENDORF

BICKENDORF

Centre (Plan II)

VOGELSANG

EHRENFELD

MÜNGERSDORF

Aachener   Str.

WEIDEN

Maître im Landhaus Kuckuck

Landhaus Kuckuck

A 4-E 40

Brenner'scher Hof

STADTWALD

MUSEUM FÜR OSTASIATISCHE KUNST

JUNKERSDORF

Dürener

LINDENTHAL

SÜLZ

Dürener

Bonn-

KLETTENBERG

HÜRTH

Venloer

Militärringstr.

Neusser Landstr.

Industriestr.

Neusser

A 57-E 31

A 1-E 37

A 57

A 1-E 31

Militärringstr.

Venloer

Äußere   Kanalstr.

Ehrenfeld-gürtel

Innere   Kanalstr.

Melatengürtel   Str.

Universitätsstr.

Militärringstr.

Süzgürtel

Luxemburger

Klettenberg-gürtel

Zollstock-gürtel

Militärringstr.

A 4-E 40

Horbeller   Str.

Kölner   Str.

Frechener   Str.

Horbeller   Str.

Luxemburger   Str.

Parkgürtel

Kempene   Str.

Brühl

27

28

29

30

102

103

104

11

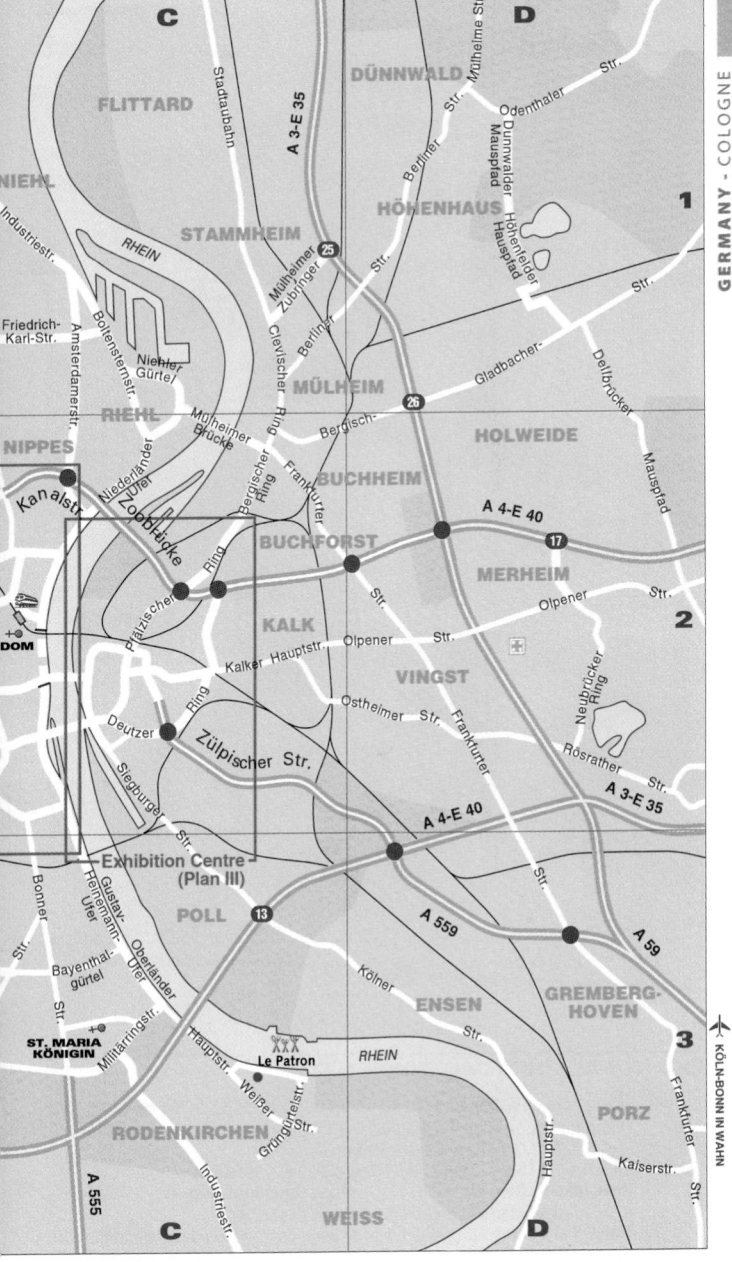

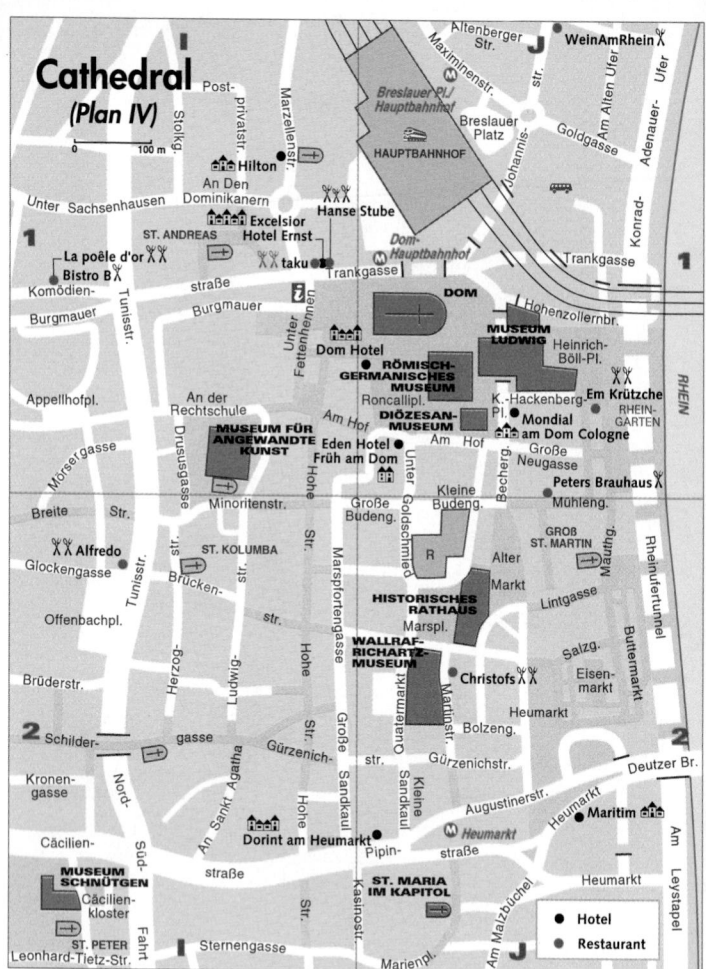

CATHEDRAL – HISTORIC TOWN HALL

Plan IV

Excelsior Hotel Ernst

🛁 � 📶 🛎 VISA 💳 AE ①

Domplatz/Trankgasse 1 ⊠ 50667 – Ⓜ *Dom-Hauptbahnhof*
– 𝒞 *(0221) 27 01 – www.excelsior-hotel-ernst.de*

I1

142 rm – 🕴180/400 € 🕴🕴200/470 €, � 29 € – 19 suites

Rest *taku* ❀ **Rest** *Hanse Stube* – see restaurant listing

♦ Grand Luxury ♦ Traditional ♦ Classic ♦

Traditional and modern elements have been combined with style and taste in this grand hotel by the cathedral. Exclusive reception area, elegant rooms. Particularly luxurious are the rooms in the Hanseflügel wing.

Dorint am Heumarkt

Pipinstr. 1 ⊠ 50667 – ⓜ Heumarkt – ☎ (0221) 2 80 60
– www.dorint.com/koeln-city   **J2**
262 rm ⊑ – ♦159/229 € ♦♦214/274 € – 9 suites
Rest – Menu 25/42 € – Carte 29/53 € ℬ

♦ Business ♦ Luxury ♦ Retro ♦

This hotel offers modern rooms ranging from standard up to the President Suite (many with a view of the cathedral). There are also good conference rooms and a concierge. There is also a large lobby with Harry's New York Bar, which features daily live music. International menu in the Maulbeers restaurant on the first floor.

Dom Hotel

Domkloster 2a ⊠ 50667 – ⓜ Dom-Hauptbahnhof – ☎ (0221) 2 02 40
– www.lemeridiendomhotelkoeln.com   **J1**
162 rm – ♦190/320 € ♦♦240/370 €, ⊑ 29 € – 13 suites
Rest – Carte 45/61 €

♦ Traditional ♦ Luxury ♦ Classic ♦

Established in 1857, this traditional grand hotel is in a prime position directly by the cathedral. It has nine room categories, all in a classic elegant style with modern technical facilities. Lively 'Ustinov' bar. Lovely window tables in the Le Merou restaurant with a terrace onto Roncalliplatz.

Hilton

Marzellenstr. 13 ⊠ 50668 – ⓜ Dom-Hauptbahnhof – ☎ (0221) 13 07 10
– www.hilton.de/koeln   **I1**
296 rm – ♦109/349 € ♦♦109/369 €, ⊑ 27 € – 2 suites
Rest – Carte 22/69 €

♦ Business ♦ Modern ♦

This business hotel is in the immediate vicinity of the cathedral. It offers contemporary design in the technically well-equipped rooms, in the 'Ice Bar' for smokers, and in the 'Fit & Well Health Club'. Unpretentious atmosphere and open kitchen in the Konrad restaurant.

Mondial Am Dom Cologne

Kurt-Hackenberg-Platz 1 ⊠ 50667
– ⓜ Dom-Hauptbahnhof – ☎ (0221) 2 06 30
– www.hotel-mondial-am-dom-cologne.com   **J1**
207 rm – ♦126/485 € ♦♦146/505 €, ⊑ 25 €
Rest – Carte 32/70 €

♦ Business ♦ Modern ♦

This hotel is in a prime central location by the cathedral. It offers modern functional rooms with all mod-cons, including large deluxe rooms. Habana cigar lounge. Restaurant with tapas bar, brasserie and fine dining. The Dom Pub is popular with opera goers.

Maritim

Heumarkt 20 ⊠ 50667 – ⓜ Heumarkt – ☎ (0221) 2 02 70
– www.maritim.de   **J2**
454 rm – ♦129/360 € ♦♦149/376 €, ⊑ 21 € – 12 suites
Rest *Bellevue* – ☎ (0221) 2 02 78 75 (closed Sunday dinner and Monday)
Menu 54 € (dinner)/89 € – Carte 59/81 €

♦ Chain hotel ♦ Functional ♦

This hotel is by the Deutz bridge at the edge of the old town. In the airy tall glass-roofed foyer there are various shops, and a good selection of cigars and whiskies in the Piano Bar. Functional rooms. The Bellevue restaurant has a roof terrace and view of the Rhine. Interesting selection of waters.

Eden Hotel Früh am Dom 🛅 🕭 rest, 🛜 🛠 VISA ⦿

Sporergasse 1 ✉ *50667* – ⓜ *Dom-Hauptbahnhof* – ℰ *(0221) 2 61 32 95*
– www.hotel-eden.de **J1**
74 rm ☐ – ♦100/125 € ♦♦125/150 €
Rest *Hof 18* – ℰ *(0221) 2 61 32 11* – Carte 28/52 €
♦ Townhouse ♦ Modern ♦
An established hotel close to the cathedral square. The rooms are up to date in terms of style and technology. Some also have a view of the cathedral – which can also be enjoyed while having breakfast. On the first floor the modern Hof 18 restaurant serves international cuisine.

XXX Hanse Stube – Excelsior Hotel Ernst 🛅 AC VISA ⦿ AE ⓘ

Domplatz/Trankgasse 1 ✉ *50667*
– ⓜ *Dom-Hauptbahnhof* – ℰ *(0221) 27 01*
– www.excelsior-hotel-ernst.com **I1**
Rest – Menu 29 € (lunch)/135 € – Carte 55/77 €
♦ Classic ♦ Elegant ♦
The Hanse Stube is one of the most elegant restaurants in the city and serves good classic cuisine. Many business people come for the fairly priced, daily changing business lunch.

XX taku – Excelsior Hotel Ernst AC VISA ⦿ AE ⓘ
❀

Domplatz (Trankgasse 1) ✉ *50667* – ⓜ *Dom-Hauptbahnhof*
– ℰ *(0221) 2 70 39 10* – *www.taku.de*
– Closed 4 weeks July-August and Monday **I1**
Rest – Menu 29 € (lunch)/98 € – Carte 54/95 €
♦ Asian ♦ Minimalist ♦ Fashionable ♦
The whole of Asia is represented on the menu of this bright, minimalist restaurant. A mixture of fine, authentic dishes are prepared by the kitchen team, who bring together knowledge and experience from many different regions. Friendly service.
➔ Pekingente. Bang Bang vom Schwarzfederhuhn. Filet vom Wagyu-Rind mit Szechuan Pfeffer, Wan-Tan und Schlangengurke.

XX Alfredo (Roberto Carturan) AC VISA ⦿ AE
❀

Tunisstr. 3 ✉ *50667* – ℰ *(0221) 2 57 73 80*
– www.ristorante-alfredo.com
– Closed 3 weeks July-August, Saturday-Sunday and Bank Holidays
Rest – *(booking advisable)* Menu 48/90 € – Carte 44/69 € **I2**
♦ Italian ♦ Friendly ♦
In the 1970s Alfredo Carturan showed that Italian cuisine was more than just pizzas. Today the restaurant's refined authentic dishes continue to grow in popularity under his son Roberto. Staff offer recommendations at the tables – the chef himself insists on this. On Friday evenings you will experience what it is to eat in a restaurant run by a trained singer!
➔ Catalana von Langustinen. Ravioli mit Kalbsbries gefüllt. Steinbutt in Guazetto.

XX La poêle d'or (Jean-Claude Bado) AC ⇄ VISA ⦿
❀

Komödienstr. 50 ✉ *50667* – ⓜ *Dom-Hauptbahnhof*
– ℰ *(0221) 13 98 67 77* – *www.lapoeledor.de*
– Closed 23 December-2 January, 2 weeks July-August, Sunday-Monday and Bank Holidays **I1**
Rest – Menu 52/95 € – Carte 58/73 € ※
Rest *Bistrot B*⌂ – see restaurant listing
♦ French classic ♦ Fashionable ♦
Jean-Claude Bado continues to combine classic cuisine and modern influences with great success and La poêle d'Or remains an essential address for food lovers. The same goes for the large selection of mainly French wines through which the expert service team will help you navigate.
➔ Langustine und Hummer mit Entengelée, Wildkräutern. Lammrücken mit Auberginen und schwarzer Knoblauchsauce. Quark-Zitrusfrüchte-Fantasie.

GERMANY - COLOGNE

Christofs 🍴🍴 🛱 ♿ *VISA* ⊚⊚

Martinstr. 32 ✉ 50667 – Ⓜ *Heumarkt –* ℰ *(0221) 27 72 95 30*
– www.christofsrestaurant.de
– Closed 1 week January   **J2**
Rest – Menu 55/79 € – Carte 42/68 €
♦ French classic ♦ Friendly ♦
This friendly restaurant is close to the cathedral and opposite the Wallraf Richartz Museum. Contemporary classic cuisine and at lunchtime a simpler bistro menu. Car parking close by.

Em Krützche 🍴🍴 🛱 ♿ *VISA* ⊚⊚ AE

Am Frankenturm 1 ✉ 50667 – Ⓜ *Dom-Hauptbahnhof*
– ℰ *(0221) 2 58 08 39 – www.em-kruetzche.de*
– Closed 23-25 December, 25 March-2 April and Monday   **J1**
Rest – Menu 34/58 € – Carte 36/51 €
♦ Regional/country ♦ Traditional ♦ Family ♦
Run for around 40 years by the Fehn family, this historic house has pretty rooms, ranging from rustic charm to elegant on two floors. Goose is the speciality in winter.

WeinAmRhein 🍴 *VISA* ⊚⊚ AE

Johannisstr. 64 ✉ 50668 – Ⓜ *Breslauer Pl./Hauptbahnhof*
– ℰ *(0221) 91 24 88 85 – www.weinamrhein.eu*
– Closed Saturday lunch, Sunday-Monday   **J1**
Rest – (Bank Holidays dinner only) Menu 43/54 € – Carte 33/62 € 🍴
♦ International ♦ Fashionable ♦
Rudolf Mützel prepares international but also German dishes with good products from local producers. The parental wine estate explains his love of wine – easily recognisable by the decoration in the restaurant and the wine selection of over 1000 bottles.

Bistrot B – Restaurant La poêle d'or 🍴 *VISA* ⊚⊚

Komödienstr. 50 ✉ 50667 – Ⓜ *Dom-Hauptbahnhof*
– ℰ *(0221) 13 98 67 77 – www.lapoeledor.de*
– Closed 23 December-2 January, 2 weeks July-August, Sunday-Monday and Bank Holidays   **I1**
Rest – Menu 28 € – Carte 30/35 €
♦ French classic ♦ Bistro ♦
An uncomplicated bistro in which chef and owner Jean-Claude Bado prepares flavoursome, French-inspired, classic cuisine. A number of attractively priced set menus are also available.

Peters Brauhaus 🍴 🛱 🚭

Mühlengasse 1 ✉ 50667 – Ⓜ *Dom-Hauptbahnhof –* ℰ *(0221) 2 57 39 50*
– www.peters-brauhaus.de
– closed during Christmas   **J1**
Rest – Carte 16/38 €
♦ Regional/country ♦ Cosy ♦
A rustic inn with a beautiful, decorated façade. Worth a look around: each room has a character of its own. Serves good, solid food with fresh Kölsch beer on draught.

CENTRE   *Plan II*

🏨🏨 Marriott 🛱 🏋 🐾 ♿ 🖿 📞 🛋 🚐 *VISA* ⊚⊚ AE ①

Johannisstr. 76 ✉ 50668 – Ⓜ *Breslauer Pl. / Hauptbahnhof*
– ℰ *(0221) 94 22 20 – www.koelnmarriott.de*   **F1-2**
365 rm – ♦135/505 € ♦♦135/560 €, ⊑ 25 € – 10 suites
Rest *Fou* – ℰ *(0221) 9 42 22 61 01 (closed Sunday dinner)* Carte 27/55 €
♦ Business ♦ Modern ♦
This comfortable and modern hotel has a touch of luxury. The Dom Suite is very pleasant with its large roof terrace and fantastic view. Various conference rooms. 'Plüsch-Bar' in the lobby. 'Fou' is the casual French brasserie-style restaurant.

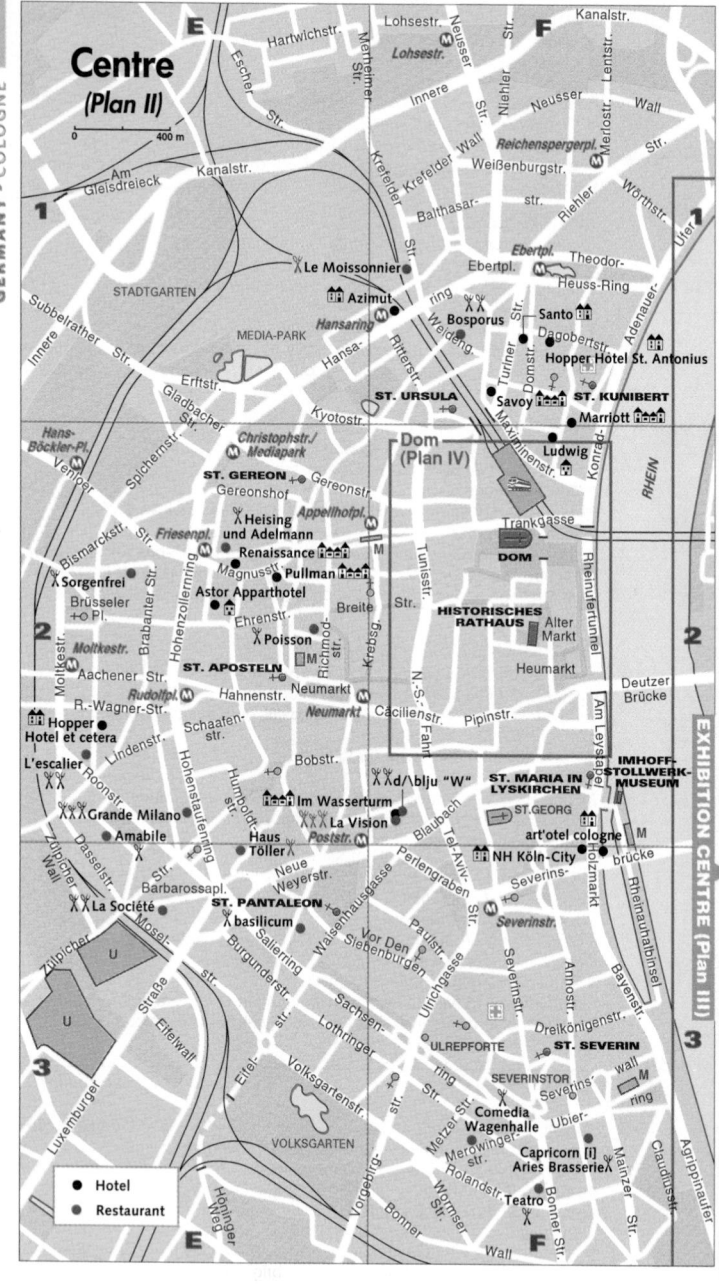

Centre
(Plan II)

0   400 m

GERMANY - COLOGNE

E   **F**

Hartwichstr.   Lohsestr.   Neusser   Str.   Kanalstr.

Escher   Memleiner   Str.

Lohsestr.

Innere   Niehler   Neusser   Str.   Wall

Am Gleisdreieck   Kanalstr.

Krefelder   Weißenburgstr.   Reichenspergerpl.   Wörthstr.

Subbelrather   Str.   Balthasar-   str.   Riehler

Innere   Str.   Ebertpl.   Theodor-Heuss-Ring   Adenauer

STADTGARTEN   𝕏 Le Moissonnier   Ebertpl.   ring

🏨 Azimut   Santo ●

MEDIA-PARK   Hansaring   Bosporus ●   Dagobertstr.

Weidengasse   Hopper Hôtel St. Antonius 🏨

Erftstr.   Hansa-   **ST. URSULA**   Savoy 🏨   **ST. KUNIBERT**

Gladbacher   Kyotostr.   Marriott 🏨

Hans-Böckler-Pl.   Christophstr./Mediapark   Ludwig ●

Spichernstr.   **ST. GEREON**   Gereonstr.   **Dom**   (Plan IV)

Bismarckstr.   Friesenpl.   Gereonshof   Appellhofpl.

𝕏 Heising und Adelmann   Trankgasse

𝕏 Sorgenfrei   Renaissance 🏨   **DOM**

Brüsseler Pl.   Magnusstr.   🏨 Pullman

Astor Apparthotel   **HISTORISCHES RATHAUS**

Aachener Str.   Ehrenstr.   𝕏 Poisson   Breite   Str.   Alter Markt

Moltkestr.   **ST. APOSTELN**   Richmod- str.   Heumarkt

R.-Wagner-Str.   Hahnenstr.   Neumarkt   Deutzer Brücke

Rudolfpl.   **Neumarkt**   Cäcilienstr.   Pipinstr.

🏨 Hopper Hotel et cetera ●   Schaafen- str.   Bobstr.

L'escalier 𝕏   **IMHOFF-STOLLWERK-MUSEUM**

𝕏𝕏 Grande Milano   Im Wasserturm 🏨   𝕏d/\blju "W"   **ST. MARIA IN LYSKIRCHEN**

● Amabile   Haus Töller 𝕏   𝕏𝕏 La Vision   **ST. GEORG**   art'otel cologne ●

Poststr.   Blaubach   🏨 NH Köln-City

Neue Weyerstr.   Perlengraben   Holzmarkt

𝕏𝕏 La Société   Barbarossapl.   **ST. PANTALEON**   𝕏 basilicum   Severins-   brücke

Sallierring   Burgunderstr.   Vor Den Siebenburgen   Severinstr.

Sachsen-   Ulrichgasse

U   Lothringer   Volksgartenstr.   **ULREPFORTE**   Dreikönigenstr.

U   Eifelwall   **ST. SEVERIN**

SEVERINSTOR

VOLKSGARTEN   Comedia Wagenhalle

Merowinger   Capricorn [i]

● Hotel   Aries Brasserie 𝕏

● Restaurant   Teatro 𝕏

Hönninger Weg   Bonner   Str.   Wall

E   **F**

Pullman

🛅 🐾 ৬ AC 🛜 🏊 🚗 VISA ⚫ AE ⓪

Helenenstr. 14 ⊠ 50667 – Ⓜ Friesenplatz – ℰ (0221) 27 50
– www.pullmanhotels.com
E2
275 rm – ♦146/436 € ♦♦146/456 €, ⛳ 24 € – 10 suites
Rest george M. – (closed 1 week end December, 5 weeks July-August
and Sunday-Monday) (dinner only) Menu 38/53 € – Carte 23/74 €
♦ Chain hotel ♦ Conference hotel ♦ Modern ♦
Sleek, modern business and conference hotel in the centre. Rooms with a hint
of luxury and lounge-style bar. Second largest ballroom in the city. In the evening the 'george M' restaurant on the 12th floor serves contemporary organic
cuisine, and a simpler menu at lunchtime.

Im Wasserturm

🐾 🛜 🏊 🚗 VISA ⚫ AE ⓪

Kaygasse 2 ⊠ 50676 – Ⓜ Poststr. – ℰ (0221) 2 00 80
– www.hotel-im-wasserturm.de
F2
88 rm – ♦154/353 € ♦♦184/383 €, ⛳ 28 € – 4 suites
Rest La Vision ❀❀ **Rest dΛblju "W"** – see restaurant listing
♦ Historic ♦ Business ♦ Design ♦
The imposing architecture of the over 130 year-old water tower is special here.
It offers tasteful and contemporary rooms, beauty treatments and massage in
the 'Atelier Beaut'. There is also a business centre. Clean-lined design in the
'dΛblju W' restaurant with a regional and international menu.

Renaissance

🚗 🐾 🖵 ৬ AC 🛜 🏊 🚗 VISA ⚫ AE ⓪

Magnusstr. 20 ⊠ 50672 – Ⓜ Friesenplatz – ℰ (0221) 2 03 40
– www.renaissancekoeln.de
E2
236 rm – ♦125/495 € ♦♦125/550 €, ⛳ 24 €
Rest Raffael – Carte 27/43 €
♦ Chain hotel ♦ Classic ♦
This hotel in the city centre has a refined foyer area with modern accessories, as
well as contemporary elegant rooms with very comfortable beds. Club floor
with its own lounge. The Raffael restaurant serves international dishes.

Savoy

🚗 🏧 🐾 AC 🛜 🚗 VISA ⚫ AE ⓪

Turiner Str. 9 ⊠ 50668 – Ⓜ Breslauer Pl. / Hauptbahnhof
– ℰ (0221) 1 62 30 – www.savoy.de
F1
94 rm – ♦147/425 € ♦♦194/500 €, ⛳ 18 € – 5 suites
Rest – Carte 38/67 €
♦ Business ♦ Personalised ♦
For guests looking for something special, Gisela and Daniela Ragge have crea-
ted very high quality and individual rooms with an eye to detail: New York,
Venice, Geisha... In the evening dine in the Mythos restaurant and at lunchtime
in the bar. Superb roof terrace.

art'otel cologne

🚗 🐾 ৬ rm, AC rm, 🛜 🏊 🚗 VISA ⚫ AE ⓪

Holzmarkt 4 ⊠ 50676 – Ⓜ Severinstr. – ℰ (0221) 80 10 30
– www.artotels.com
F3
218 rm ⛳ – ♦99/149 € ♦♦99/149 €   **Rest** – Carte 34/40 €
♦ Business ♦ Design ♦
Hotel and gallery in one: trendy designer interior, excellent technical facilities
with free wi-fi, as well as works by the Korean artist SEO throughout the building. The Chino Latino restaurant serves Asian cuisine and has a terrace with a
view of the Rhine port and Chocolate Museum.

Santo without rest

৬ AC 🛜 🚗 VISA ⚫ AE ⓪

Dagobertstr. 22 ⊠ 50668 – Ⓜ Ebertplatz – ℰ (0221) 9 13 97 70
– www.hotelsanto.de
F1
69 rm ⛳ – ♦89/114 € ♦♦98/124 €
♦ Business ♦ Modern ♦
Evident here is the interplay of minimalist design and Christian Türmer's 'Light
Emotion Concept'. The breakfast room is bright and clear with a sumptuous
buffet. Free wi-fi.

NH Köln-City 🛜 🕍 ⚙ AC rest, ☎ ⏷ 🚗 VISA ⬀ AE ①

Holzmarkt 47 ⊠ 50676 – ⓜ Severinstr. – ℰ (0221) 2 72 28 80
– www.nh-hotels.de   F3
204 rm – ♥79/349 €, ♥♥79/349 €, ☑ 19 €   **Rest** – Carte 19/48 €
♦ Chain hotel ♦ Modern ♦
This modern hotel is close to the Severin bridge and not far from the Stollwerck
chocolate museum. Some of the modern, functional rooms are superior in that
they face the peaceful interior courtyard. This modern restaurant has a small
conservatory.

Azimut without rest 🔊 🛜 ⚙ AC ☎ 🚗 VISA ⬀ AE

Hansaring 97 ⊠ 50670 – ⓜ Hansaring – ℰ (0221) 88 87 60
– www.azimuthotels.de   F1
190 rm – ♥90/435 € ♥♥90/435 €, ☑ 15 €
♦ Business ♦ Modern ♦
This modern business hotel in a historic brick building is equipped with good
technical facilities.

Hopper Hotel St. Antonius 🛜 🛜 🛜 🚗 VISA ⬀ AE ①

Dagobertstr. 32 ⊠ 50668 – ⓜ Ebertpl. – ℰ (0221) 1 66 00
– www.hopper.de   F1
54 rm ☑ – ♥110/135 € ♥♥160 € – 5 suites
Rest L. Fritz im Hopper – *(closed Saturday lunch, Sunday and Monday
dinner)* Carte 32/47 €
♦ Business ♦ Minimalist ♦ Modern ♦
A historic building fabric and a clear, modern style are combined in this former
Kolping guesthouse. Large and small suites are available. The Tiefrot theatre is
also housed here. Restaurant with a bistro atmosphere and a beautiful round
ceiling arch. It has a pleasant terrace in the interior courtyard.

Hopper Hotel et cetera 🛜 🔊 🛜 🚗 P 🚗 VISA ⬀ AE ①

Brüsseler Str. 26 ⊠ 50674 – ⓜ Moltkestr. – ℰ (0221) 92 44 00
– www.hopper.de
– Closed 21 December-6 January   E2
49 rm ☑ – ♥85/275 € ♥♥130/280 €
Rest – *(closed Sunday-Monday) (lunch only)* Menu 11 €
♦ Townhouse ♦ Personalised ♦
Former monastery located in the Belgian Quarter. All the rooms have design-
orientated furnishings, high quality eucalyptus parquet, marble bathrooms
and free wi-fi. The imposing altar painting catches the eye in the cosy restaurant. Inner courtyard terrace under the trees.

Astor Aparthotel without rest 🔊 🛜 P VISA ⬀ AE

Friesenwall 68 ⊠ 50672 – ⓜ Friesenplatz – ℰ (0221) 20 71 20
– www.hotelastor.de
– Closed 23 December-6 January   E2
50 rm ☑ – ♥95/195 € ♥♥115/235 €
♦ Townhouse ♦ Functional ♦
In this hotel the dedicated host offers comfortable modern or more functional
rooms. A good buffet selection awaits in the breakfast room.

Ludwig without rest 🛜 🚗 VISA ⬀ AE

Brandenburger Str. 24 ⊠ 50668 – ⓜ Breslauer Pl. / Hauptbahnhof
– ℰ (0221) 16 05 40 – www.hotelludwig.de   F2
55 rm ☑ – ♥95/105 € ♥♥119/135 € – 1 suite
♦ Townhouse ♦ Functional ♦
An informally-run hotel close to the old town with bright, cheerful and contem-
porary guestrooms. The position is ideal for rail travellers and city tourists.

XXX
❀ ❀ **La Vision** – Hotel Im Wasserturm   ⪡ 🛏 AC ✿ VISA ◐◉ AE ⓪

Kaygasse 2 (11th floor) ✉ *50676* – ⓜ *Poststr.* – 𝒫 *(0221) 2 00 80*
– *www.hotel-im-wasserturm.de*
– *Closed 2 weeks early January, 1 week after Easter, 4 weeks July-August and
Sunday-Monday*   **F2**
Rest – *(dinner only)* Menu 86/151 € – Carte 81/99 € ⅋

♦ Creative ♦ Elegant ♦

You might think the view of Cologne was the highlight at La Vision, but the
moment you finish your first course you will know that it is really Hans Hor-
berth's cooking. His two menus combine modern creativity and classic principles to achieve culinary harmony.

➔ Glasierte Weinbergschnecken aus Moers mit Birkenmelasse und Blattsa-
latcrème. Zanderfilet auf der Haut gebraten mit "gepufftem" Hahnenkamm,
Radieschen und Blaumohn. Weiße Schokolade - "Gefrorenes" von der
Ivoire-Schokolade mit Limettenkavier.

XXX **Grande Milano**   🛏 AC VISA ◐◉ AE ⓪

Hohenstaufenring 29 ✉ *50674* – ⓜ *Rudolfpl.* – 𝒫 *(0221) 24 21 21*
– *www.grandemilano.com*
– *Closed Saturday lunch and Sunday*   **E2**
Rest – Menu 59/81 € – Carte 41/75 €
Rest *Pinot di Pinot* – Menu 20 € – Carte 23/39 €

♦ Italian ♦ Elegant ♦ Friendly ♦

Owner and chef Alessandro Minotti prepares fine Italian dishes, which are particularly popular during the truffle season. Elegant ambience and good service.
For smokers the Pinot di Pinot is an informal alternative, also with a simpler
menu.

XX
❀ **La Société**   VISA ◐◉ AE

Kyffhäuser Str. 53 ✉ *50674* – 𝒫 *(0221) 23 24 64* – *www.lasociete.info*
– *Closed 2 weeks early August*   **E3**
Rest – *(dinner only) (booking advisable)* Menu 60/99 € – Carte 60/80 € ⅋

♦ Creative ♦ Individual ♦ Intimate ♦

With Dominic Jeske in the kitchen, this comfortable, intimate restaurant not far
from the Barbarossaplatz is guaranteed to provide fine fare. The food he serves
up in typical, friendly and uncomplicated style is both sophisticated and creative.

➔ Gänseleber. Suppenapotheke "La Société". Seeteufel im Ganzen für 2
Personen.

XX **Bosporus**   🛏 AC ✿ VISA ◐◉ AE ⓪

Weidengasse 36 ✉ *50668* – ⓜ *Hansaring* – 𝒫 *(0221) 12 52 65*
– *www.bosporus.de*
– *Closed Sunday lunch*   **F1**
Rest – Menu 29/42 € – Carte 26/39 €

♦ Turkish ♦ Classic ♦ Friendly ♦

The authentic Turkish dishes prepared from fresh produce, and the reasonable
prices are impressive at this restaurant. The service is led by the patron Ali Bala-
ban himself. In summer you can dine on the Mediterranean-style terrace.

XX **dΛblju "W"** – Hotel Im Wasserturm   🛏 AC VISA ◐◉ AE ⓪

Kaygasse 2 ✉ *50676* – ⓜ *Poststr.* – 𝒫 *(0221) 2 00 80*
– *www.hotel-im-wasserturm.de*
– *Closed Saturday*   **F2**
Rest – Menu 32/75 € – Carte 48/71 €

♦ International ♦ Fashionable ♦

The interior of this restaurant is light and modern, with the elegant light fittings
providing much of the atmosphere. The glass frontage offers a view of the terrace, which boasts an open-air kitchen in fine weather.

GERMANY - COLOGNE

GERMANY - COLOGNE

XX L'escalier

🏠 AC VISA ⓪ AE

Brüsseler Str. 11 ⊠ *50674 –* Ⓜ *Moltkestr. –* ✆ *(0221) 2 05 39 98*
– www.lescalier-restaurant.de
– Closed 2 weeks early January, 3 weeks end July-August and Sunday-Monday
Rest – Menu 64/97 € – Carte 51/82 €   E2
♦ Classic ♦ Fashionable ♦ Bistro ♦

As chef-owner of the famous L'escalier, Maximilian Lorenz puts to good use the experience he gleaned at various top gastronomic establishments; so expect contemporary, seasonal dishes made using good ingredients. The modern environment is a good spot for a business lunch.

X Le Moissonnier

AC VISA ⓪

❀❀ *Krefelder Str. 25* ⊠ *50670 –* Ⓜ *Hansaring –* ✆ *(0221) 72 94 79*
– www.lemoissonnier.de
– Closed 2 weeks Christmas-early January, 1 week Easter, 3 weeks July-August and Sunday-Monday except Bank Holidays   F1
Rest – *(booking advisable)* Menu 75/115 € – Carte 60/119 €
♦ Creative ♦ Bistro ♦ Friendly ♦

Liliane and Vincent Moissonnier, together with their compatriot Eric Menchon, prepare innovative and creative dishes without losing sight of their roots. They have made this place as appealing and charmingly French as any bistro in Paris. The wine list includes some rarities.
➔ Foie Gras Maison. Ris de veau. Pigeonneau rôti.

X Poisson

🏠 AC VISA ⓪

Wolfsstr. 6 ⊠ *50667 –* Ⓜ *Neumarkt –* ✆ *(0221) 27 73 68 83*
– www.poisson-restaurant.de
– Closed during Carnival, Sunday-Monday and Bank Holidays   E2
Rest – *(booking advisable)* Menu 55/85 € – Carte 50/81 €
♦ Fish and seafood ♦ Bistro ♦ Trendy ♦

Top quality products are deliciously prepared at this modern bistro with a fish orientated menu. The chef allows Asian, as well as Mediterranean and classic components to influence his food.

X Capricorn [i] Aries Brasserie

🏠 ✿ ⊘

☺ *Alteburgerstr. 31* ⊠ *50678 –* Ⓜ *Severinstr. –* ✆ *(0221) 3 97 57 10*
– www.capricorniaries.com
– Closed Saturday lunch and Sunday   F3
Rest – Menu 33/59 € – Carte 28/53 €
♦ French classic ♦ Bistro ♦ Cosy ♦

The brasserie-style restaurant in this corner building is everything it should be: friendly, uncomplicated and comfortable. The prices and quality are good too, whether you order the pikeperch in beurre blanc served on a bed of chard, the couscous with cucumber and tomatoes or a classic 'steak frites'.

X Sorgenfrei

AC VISA ⓪

☺ *Antwerpenerstr. 15* ⊠ *50672 –* Ⓜ *Moltkestr. –* ✆ *(0221) 3 55 73 27*
– www.sorgenfrei-koeln.com
– Closed during Carnival, during Christmas and Saturday lunch, Sunday
Rest – Menu 35/43 € (dinner) – Carte 34/55 € ❀   E2
♦ International ♦ Friendly ♦ Cosy ♦

A really appealing and lively address in the Belgian Quarter, next door to which is a wine dealer with a good European range. No-frills international dishes. The classic is Argentinean 'Black Ranch' entrecote steak. Simpler lunchtime menu.

X Amabile

🏠 VISA ⓪ AE

Görrestr. 2 ⊠ *50674 –* Ⓜ *Moltkestr. –* ✆ *(0221) 21 91 01*
– www.restaurant-amabile.de
– Closed during Carnival, 3 weeks September and Sunday-Monday
Rest – *(dinner only)* Menu 35/44 € – Carte 41/49 €   E2
♦ International ♦ Friendly ♦

You will find this lovingly decorated restaurant with a rustic touch between the Millowitsch Theatre and University. The best way to discover the seasonal cuisine is to order the surprise menu.

Heising und Adelmann   🍴 ⬆ 🚗 VISA ⓞⓞ AE

Friesenstr. 58 ✉ 50670 – Ⓜ Friesenplatz – ℰ (0221) 1 30 94 24
– www.heising-und-adelmann.de
– Closed Sunday-Monday and Bank Holidays   **E2**
Rest – *(dinner only)* Menu 36 € – Carte 33/48 €
♦ International ♦ Bistro ♦ Trendy ♦
Guests are served modern international cuisine in the relaxed atmosphere of this lively bistro restaurant with its delightful terrace. Pleasant lounge and large bar area.

Comedia Wagenhalle   🍴 VISA ⓞⓞ

Vondelstr. 4 ✉ 50677 – Ⓜ Severinstr. – ℰ (0221) 35 55 89 10
– www.comedia-wagenhalle.de   **F3**
Rest – Menu 30/50 € – Carte 27/57 €
♦ International ♦ Bistro ♦
This was formerly a fire station vehicle depot dating from 1904. Today it is a restaurant with a bistro feel where you can still sense the charm of the listed building that also incorporates the Comedia Theatre.

basilicum   🍴 VISA ⓞⓞ AE

Am Weidenbach 33 ✉ 50676 – Ⓜ Poststr. – ℰ (0221) 32 35 55
– www.basilicum.org
– Closed 7-12 February and Sunday   **E3**
Rest – *(dinner only) (booking advisable)* Menu 39/45 € – Carte 34/52 €
♦ International ♦ Friendly ♦
A very dedicatedly and personally-run small establishment with a bistro feel. Good seasonal and contemporary cuisine. The restaurant also has a lovely covered inner courtyard terrace.

Teatro   VISA ⓞⓞ

Zugweg 1 ✉ 50667 – Ⓜ Severinstr. – ℰ (0221) 80 15 80 20
– www.teatro-ristorante.de
– Closed 27 December-4 January, 2 weeks August and Tuesday, Saturday lunch,
Sunday lunch   **F3**
Rest – *(booking advisable)* Carte 24/53 €
♦ Italian ♦ Fashionable ♦ Family ♦
Italian dishes can be selected from a board at the Spatola family's vibrant restaurant. The decor features black and white photographs of film stars. Good value lunchtime menu.

Haus Töller   🍴 ⬆ 🍽

Weyerstr. 96 ✉ 50676 – Ⓜ Poststr. – ℰ (0221) 2 58 93 16 – www.haus-toeller.de
– Closed June-August, Sunday and Bank Holidays   **E3**
Rest – *(dinner only) (booking advisable)* Carte 19/28 €
♦ Regional/country ♦ Traditional ♦ Cosy ♦
The former 'Steynen Huys' dating from 1343 is really something for connoisseurs with its original wooden tables and floors, coffer ceiling and confession chair. Specialities include pork knuckles, Rhenish marinated roast (horsemeat) and on Friday evenings potato pancakes – all washed down with Päffgen Kölsch draught beer.

AT THE EXHIBITION CENTRE   *Plan III*

🏨 Hyatt Regency   ← 🛁 🕸 🗔 ᖚ 🄺 🛜 🚿 🅿 🚗 VISA ⓞⓞ AE ⓞ

Kennedy-Ufer 2a ✉ 50679 – Ⓜ Deutzer Freiheit – ℰ (0221) 8 28 12 34
– www.cologne.regency.hyatt.de   **G2**
306 rm – ♦190/450 € ♦♦220/500 €, ☲ 30 € – 17 suites
Rest *Glashaus* – ℰ (0221) 82 81 17 73 – Carte 49/83 €
♦ Chain hotel ♦ Luxury ♦ Classic ♦
Classic business hotel directly by the Rhine at the Hohenzollern bridge. The lobby is large and refined, the rooms sleek, modern, elegant and technically up to date. Even the standard rooms are 36m² in size. International cuisine in the bright Glashaus restaurant on the first floor.

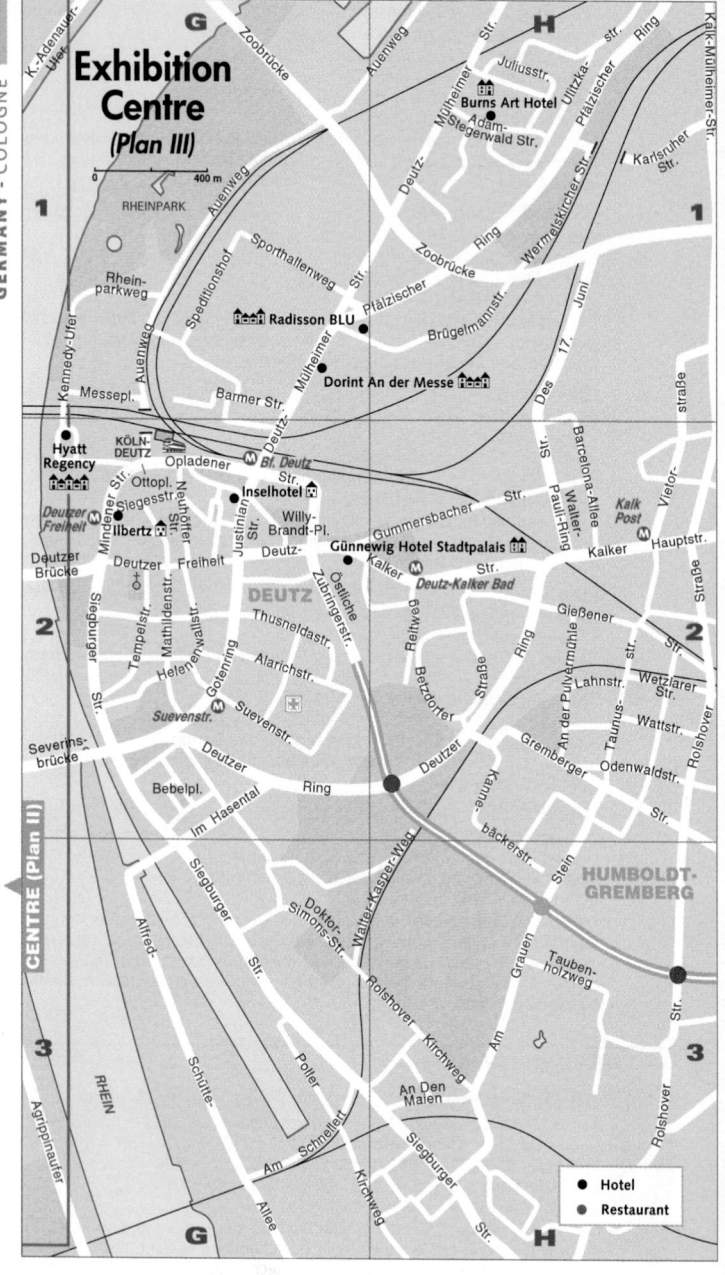

Exhibition Centre
(Plan III)

0 — 400 m

Burns Art Hotel
Radisson BLU
Dorint An der Messe
Hyatt Regency
Ilbertz
Inselhotel
Günnewig Hotel Stadtpalais

RHEINPARK

Rheinparkweg

KÖLN-DEUTZ

Bf. Deutz

Deutzer Freiheit

Deutzer Brücke

DEUTZ

Severins-brücke

Deutz-Kalker Bad

Kalk Post

HUMBOLDT-GREMBERG

RHEIN

CENTRE (Plan II)

● Hotel
● Restaurant

Dorint An der Messe

🖼 🛗 ⓔ 🏋 🗖 ⚅ 🖼 🛜 🕱 🚗

Deutz-Mülheimer-Str. 22 ✉ *50679 –* Ⓜ *Bf. Deutz* · 𝔙𝔦𝔰𝔞 ⬤◐ 𝔸𝔼 ⓞ
– 𝒞 (0221) 80 19 00 – www.dorint.com/koeln · **G1**
313 rm ⌫ – ♥139/219 € ♥♥159/239 € – 47 suites
Rest *Düx* – Carte 29/53 €

♦ Chain hotel ♦ Business ♦ Modern ♦

This elegant, modern hotel located opposite the Exhibition Centre has a 650m² spa and a bright and friendly breakfast room which also lays on a buffet lunch during trade fairs and exhibitions. For the ultimate in luxury try the exclusive Konrad Adenauer Suite. L'Adresse offers an upmarket menu. The Düx is a typical Cologne restaurant.

Radisson BLU

🛗 🏋 ⚅ 🖼 🛜 🕱 🚗 𝔙𝔦𝔰𝔞 ⬤◐

Messe Kreisel 3 ✉ *50679 –* Ⓜ *Bf. Deutz – 𝒞 (0221) 27 72 00*
– www.radissonblu.com/hotel-cologne · **G1**
393 rm – ♥125/500 € ♥♥150/500 €, ⌫ 25 € – 1 suite
Rest *– (closed Saturday lunch, Sunday lunch and Bank Holiday lunch)*
(June-August: dinner only) Carte 28/51 €

♦ Chain hotel ♦ Stylish ♦ Modern ♦

This ultra-modern business hotel next to the Exhibition Centre boasts an impressive glass lobby which houses the bar, and the luxury Capitolium Suite complete with cathedral view. Paparazzi serves Italian cuisine including pizzas fresh from its authentic pizza oven.

Günnewig Hotel Stadtpalais

🛗 🏋 rm, ⚅ 🛜 🕱 🚗

Deutz-Kalker-Str. 52 ✉ *50679 –* Ⓜ *Deutz-Kalker Bad* · 𝔙𝔦𝔰𝔞 ⬤◐ 𝔸𝔼
– 𝒞 (0221) 88 04 20 – www.guennewig.de · **G2**
115 rm ⌫ – ♥139/159 € ♥♥159/179 €
Rest *– (closed Sunday, July-August: Saturday-Sunday) (dinner only)* Menu 28/46 € – Carte 28/46 €

♦ Business ♦ Modern ♦

This attractive group of building directly opposite the LANXXES Arena combines historical and modern architecture. Technically well equipped rooms in purist style. Small range of dishes available in menu form.

Burns Art Hotel *without rest*

🛜 🅿 𝔙𝔦𝔰𝔞 ⬤◐ 𝔸𝔼 ⓞ

Adam-Stegerwald-Str. 9 ✉ *51063 –* Ⓜ *Bf. Deutz – 𝒞 (0221) 6 71 16 90*
– www.hotel-burns.de
– Closed 22-30 December · **H1**
95 rm ⌫ – ♥85/300 € ♥♥111/320 €

♦ Business ♦ Functional ♦

This hotel boasts a relatively calm location in a residential area. Guests can choose between contemporary "Fair & More" rooms and the pure lines of its designer "Burns Art" rooms.

Inselhotel *without rest*

🛜 𝔙𝔦𝔰𝔞 ⬤◐ ⓞ

Constantinstr. 96 ✉ *50679 –* Ⓜ *Bf. Deutz – 𝒞 (0221) 8 80 34 50*
– www.inselhotel-koeln.de · **G2**
42 rm ⌫ – ♥89/195 € ♥♥119/295 €

♦ Townhouse ♦ Functional ♦

This corner townhouse opposite Deutz railway station offers its guests friendly service and well-maintained, functional rooms. Close to the Exhibition Centre and Cologne Arena.

Ilbertz *without rest*

🛗 ⚅ 🛜 🕱 🚗 𝔙𝔦𝔰𝔞 ⬤◐ 𝔸𝔼 ⓞ

Mindener Str. 6 (Access by Siegesstr. 6) ✉ *50679 –* Ⓜ *Deutzer Freiheit*
– 𝒞 (0221) 8 29 59 20 – www.hotel-ilbertz.de
– Closed Christmas-6 January · **G2**
26 rm ⌫ – ♥97/159 € ♥♥116/199 €

♦ Family ♦ Functional ♦

This immaculate, family-run hotel with its characteristic yellow façade offers functional rooms equipped with the latest technology and a traditional breakfast room.

GERMANY - COLOGNE

Brenner'scher Hof without rest

Wilhelm-von-Capitaine-Str. 15 ⊠ *50858 – ℰ (0221) 9 48 60 00*
– www.brennerscher-hof.de **A2**
40 rm ⌁ – †95/250 € ††115/275 € – 2 suites
♦ Country house ♦ Historic ♦ Cosy ♦

This beautiful country house dating back to 1754 has been decorated in Mediterranean style. The guest accommodation is in a series of charming and comfortable individually designed rooms, suites and maisonettes.

Le Patron 🖾 ⇔ 🖾 ⦿ 🖾

Uferstr. 16 ⊠ *50996 – ℰ (0221) 3 48 06 55 – www.lepatron.de*
– Closed Sunday-Monday **C3**
Rest *– (dinner only)* Menu 69/95 € – Carte 54/76 €
♦ International ♦ Fashionable ♦

Great pains have been taken with the antique and modern furnishings in this upmarket restaurant, from the chandeliers to the table settings alike. To accompany the ambitious seasonal cuisine, try a bottle of Mouton Rothschild – they have all the vintages since 1934! Remember to book a window table with a view of the Rhine.

Maître im Landhaus Kuckuck (Erhard Schäfer) 🖾 ⅏ ⇔
🏵

Olympiaweg 2 (by Friedrich-Schmitt-Straße) 🅿 🖾 ⦿ 🖾 ⦿
⊠ *50933 – ℰ (0221) 48 53 60 – www.landhaus-kuckuck.de*
– Closed 4-13 February, 25 March-9 April, 22 July-20 August and Monday-Tuesday **A2**
Rest *– (dinner only) (booking essential)* Menu 99/119 € – Carte 73/81 €
Rest *Landhaus Kuckuck* – see restaurant listing
♦ French classic ♦ Elegant ♦ Classic ♦

Erhard Schäfer offers two menus at this restaurant, one 'classic', and the other 'seasonal'. There are only five tables, exactly the right number for this sophisticated – not to say exclusive – venue. It is located just a stone's throw from the home of FC Cologne.

➜ Trilogie vom Polarmeer Saibling mit mediterranen Aromen. Rehbockrücken mit Kruste von schwarzen Nüssen, Wirsing und Kartoffel-Kräutercrêpe. Schokoladensavarin mit spanischer Mispel, Mandel Panna Cotta, geeister Cappuccino.

Landhaus Kuckuck – Restaurant Maître im Landhaus Kuckuck

Olympiaweg 2 (by Friedrich-Schmitt- 🖾 ⅏ ⇔ 🅿 🖾 ⦿ 🖾 ⦿
Straße) ⊠ *50933 – ℰ (0221) 48 53 60 – www.landhaus-kuckuck.de*
– Closed 4-13 February and Monday-Tuesday **A2**
Rest – Menu 38 € – Carte 40/60 €
♦ Regional/country ♦ Elegant ♦ Luxury ♦

A real treasure on the outskirts of busy Cologne. This restaurant is the perfect place to relax and unwind with its magnificent countryside location and elegant English country house-style interior.

AT THE AIRPORT South-East: 17 km by A59 **D3**

Holiday Inn Airport 🖾 ⅏ 🖾 🕿 ⅏ 🅿 🖾 ⦿ 🖾 ⦿

Waldstr. 255 (at Köln/Bonn Airport) ⊠ *51147 – ℰ (02203) 56 10*
– www.koeln-bonn-airport-hi-hotel.de
177 rm – †139/169 € ††161/191 €, ⌁ 18 € **Rest** – Carte 30/45 €
♦ Chain hotel ♦ Functional ♦

Ideal for the business traveller, this hotel with its modern reception area and well-appointed contemporary rooms offers a free airport shuttle service. An elegant restaurant serving predominantly international cuisine with a great bar.

FRANKFURT

FRANKFURT AM MAIN

Population: 695 624

Tom Bayer/Fotolia.com

European travellers might feel there's no need to go all the way to New York when they've got Frankfurt. After all, it's earned itself the nickname 'Mainhattan', what with all those slinky, shiny skyscrapers reaching up from the banks of the River Main. This may be a city of big corporations, but you'll also find half-timbered medieval houses (admittedly rebuilt), and an array of museums along the south bank of the river. Located at the crossing point of Germany's north-south and east-west roads, Frankfurt is a city that takes its cultural scene very seriously. It's said that it spends more money on the arts per year than any other European city, and has also become something of a gourmet hotspot with a cuisine range that gets more eclectic by the month.

The centre of Frankfurt is Cathedral Hill, where the cathedral has stood for eight hundred years; it towers over Römerberg, the medieval square, rebuilt following the war. To the west, amongst the mighty skyscrapers of international banks and corporations, lie the main railway station and the Exhibition Centre, while south of the River Main is the famous 'museum embankment' and Frankfurt's oldest area, Sachsenhausen, full of bars, cafés and restaurants. Germany's great poet, novelist and dramatist, Johann Wolfgang von Goethe, was born and bred here; no doubt he wouldn't believe his eyes if he saw Frankfurt today.

FRANKFURT IN...

→ **ONE DAY**
Old Town, Römerberg, the view from Main Tower.

→ **TWO DAYS**
Goethe House, Museum Embankment, a restaurant in Sachsenhausen.

→ **THREE DAYS**
Boat trip on the Main, window shopping (Zeil), a concert at the Opera House.

PRACTICAL INFORMATION

ARRIVAL-DEPARTURE

✈ Frankfurt Airport is 9km southeast of the city centre. S-Bahn trains S8 and S9 leave every 15min for Frankfurt station and take just over 10min.

GETTING AROUND

Frankfurt runs an efficient bus, metro and tram system. You can buy a day ticket for one person or for a group (max. 5), which is valid until the last ride of the day. Tickets are available at vending machines and from bus drivers, but cannot be bought on trams, the U-Bahn or S-Bahn. A Frankfurt Card entitles you to free public transport, discounts at a variety of museums and attractions, and reductions of up to thirty per cent on selected boat trips. You can buy the Card at many travel agencies, at tourist information offices and in both terminals at the airport; it's valid for 24 or 48 hours.

EATING OUT

Not so long ago, Frankfurt's gastronomic fame came courtesy of its Apfelwein (a sweet or dry variant of cider), its Handkäs mit Musik (small yellow cheese with vinegar, oil and onions) and its Grüne Sauce (various herbs and sour cream served with boiled eggs). That's not the case now. Head along to the Fressgass (near Opernplatz) – which translates as 'Eatery Alley' or 'Glutton's Lane' – and you've got a pedestrian mile of eateries; choose from a whole range of food to take away or to graze over, all at good prices. Nearly thirty per cent of Frankfurt's citizens have come to the city from overseas,

CALENDAR HIGHLIGHTS

February
Carnival.

May
Forest Folk Festival.

June
Opernplatz Festival (music, cabaret and food), Rose and Light Festival (music and illuminations in the Palm Garden).

July
Sound of Frankfurt.

August
River Main Festival, Museum Quay Festival.

September
Autumn Dippe Fair (funfair and fireworks), IAA (Frankfurt motor show).

October
Book Fair.

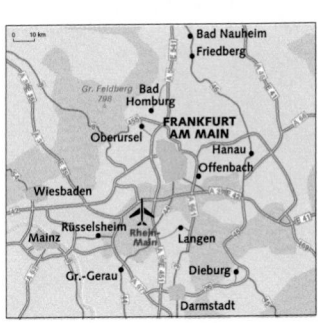

so a wealth of eating possibilities has been opened up. It's now easy to 'eat globally' all round the city and foreign communities have added a real touch of spice to the culinary landscape, with the likes of Turkish, Italian and Chinese establishments. Nevertheless, a visit to this city wouldn't be complete without a trip to the äppelwoilokale in Sachsenhausen, the casual but lively cafés where tradition is the key, and Apfelwein is served up in ceramic mugs.

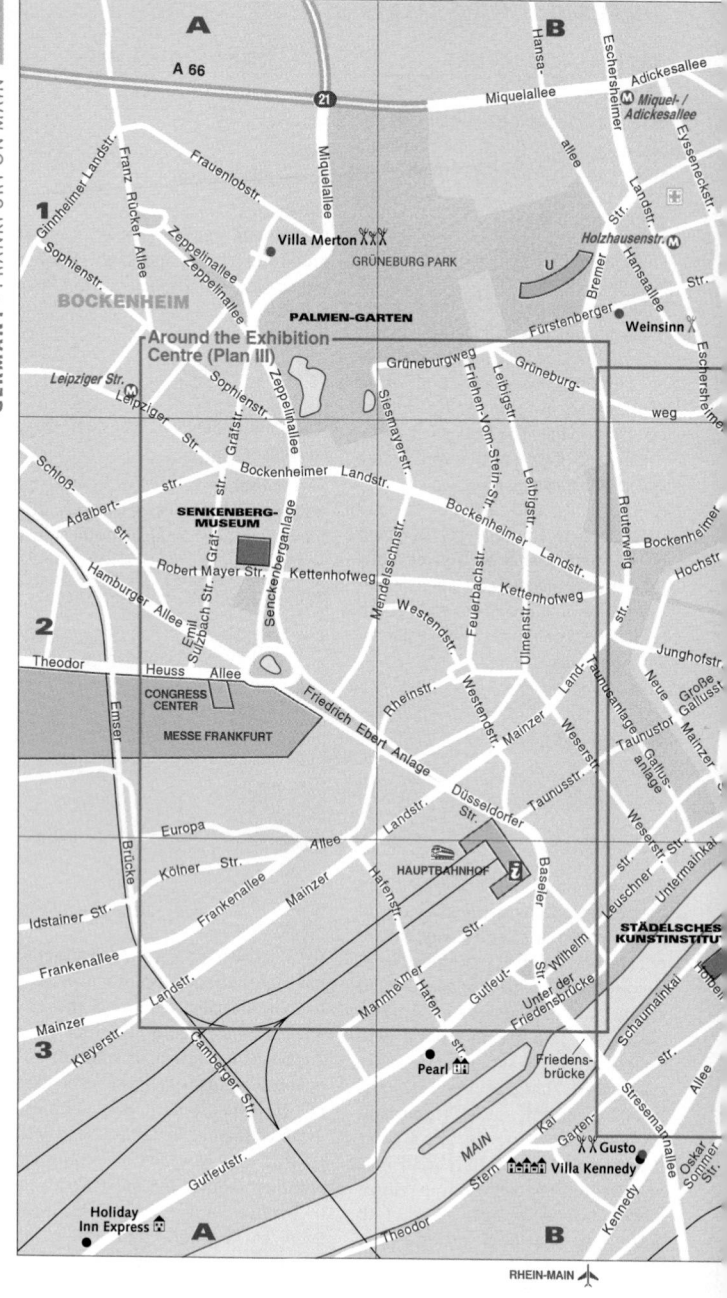

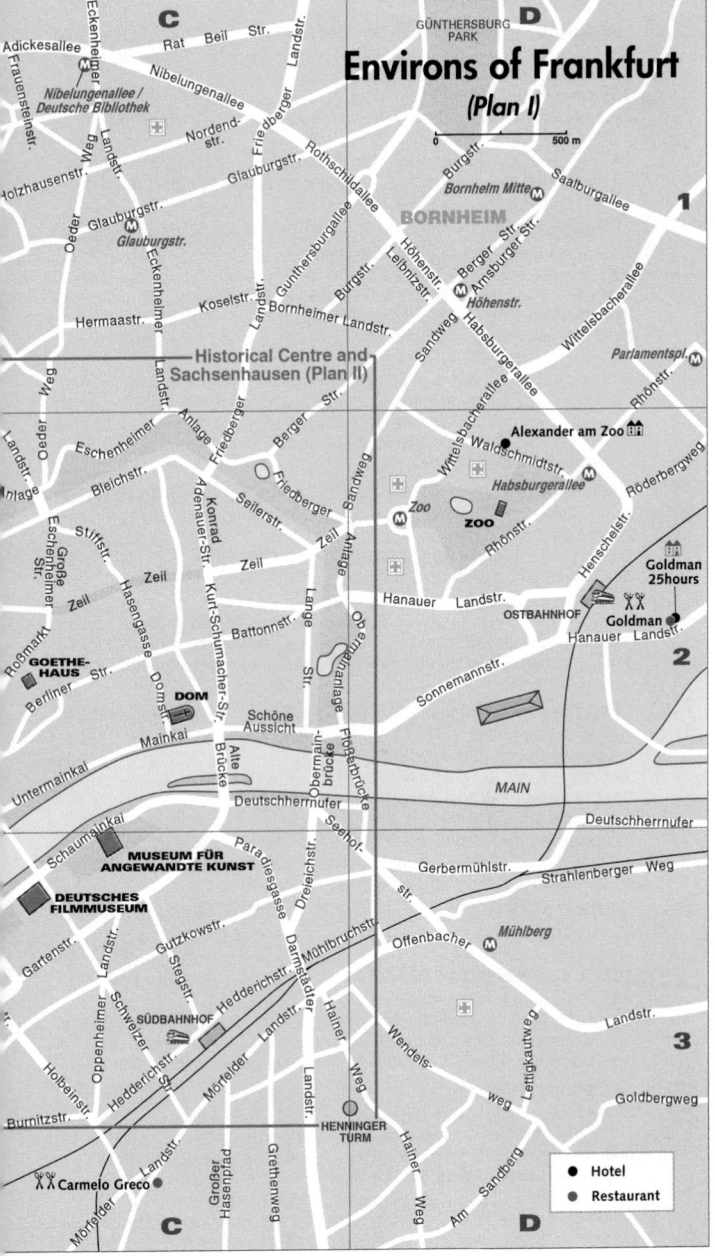

Environs of Frankfurt
(Plan I)

GÜNTHERSBURG PARK

BORNHEIM

Historical Centre and Sachsenhausen (Plan II)

Alexander am Zoo

ZOO

Goldman 25hours

OSTBAHNHOF

Goldman

GOETHE-HAUS

DOM

MAIN

MUSEUM FÜR ANGEWANDTE KUNST

DEUTSCHES FILMMUSEUM

SÜDBAHNHOF

Mühlberg

HENNINGER TURM

Carmelo Greco

● Hotel
● Restaurant

GERMANY - FRANKFURT ON MAIN

Steigenberger Frankfurter Hof
Am Kaiserplatz ⊠ *60311* – **Ⓜ** *Willy-Brandt-Platz*
– *𝒞 (069) 2 15 02 – www.steigenberger.com*   **E1**
303 rm – ♥195/706 € ♥♥195/706 €, � 32 € – 21 suites
Rest *Français* ❀ **Rest** *Oscar's* **Rest** *Iroha* – see restaurant listing
♦ Luxury ♦ Traditional ♦ Classic ♦
The origins of this luxury hotel date back to 1876. The impressive, historic façade sets the tone for the classic atmosphere inside where the lobby is decorated in feudal-style.

Jumeirah
Thurn-und-Taxis-Platz 2 (access via Groß Eschenheimer Str. 8) ⊠ *60313*
– **Ⓜ** *Hauptwache* – *𝒞 (069) 2 97 23 70 – www.jumeirah.com/frankfurt*
218 rm – ♥220/490 € ♥♥220/490 €, ⊑ 32 € – 57 suites   **E1**
Rest *Max on One* – see restaurant listing
Rest *Le Petit Palais* – *𝒞 (069) 2 97 23 74 24* – Menu 21 € – Carte 28/50 €
♦ Grand Luxury ♦ Modern ♦ Elegant ♦
At the Jumeirah the very best in comfort, technology and interior decor speak for themselves. No praise is too high for the 220m² Presidential Suite, which boasts its own massage and beauty facility, a Talise spa and direct access to the adjacent leisure centre. Breakfast and snacks are served in Le Petit Palais adjoining the MyZeil shopping mall.

Villa Kennedy
Kennedyallee 70 ⊠ *60596* – **Ⓜ** *Schweizer Platz* – *𝒞 (069) 71 71 20*
– *www.villakennedyhotel.de*   *Plan I* **B3**
163 rm – ♥220/685 € ♥♥220/685 €, ⊑ 32 € – 26 suites
Rest *Gusto* – see restaurant listing
♦ Grand Luxury ♦ Villa ♦ Classic ♦
The Villa Speyer, built in 1904, has been converted into an impressive luxury hotel with great architectural flair. The interior successfully combines the classic and the modern. The exquisite spa offers Éminence beauty treatments (the only one in Germany).

The Westin Grand
Konrad-Adenauer-Str. 7 ⊠ *60313* – **Ⓜ** *Konstablerwache* – *𝒞 (069) 2 98 10*
– *www.westingrandfrankfurt.com*   **F1**
371 rm – ♥149/775 € ♥♥149/810 €, ⊑ 31 € – 18 suites
Rest *san san* **Rest** *Sushimoto* – see restaurant listing
♦ Luxury ♦ Chain hotel ♦ Modern ♦
Enjoying a central location, this large international business hotel boasts comfortable, modern guestrooms and numerous conference areas. Executive club on the first floor. Swimming pool with great views of the city.

Hilton
Hochstr. 4 ⊠ *60313* – **Ⓜ** *Eschenheimer Tor* – *𝒞 (069) 13 38 00*
– *www.hilton.de/frankfurt*   **E1**
342 rm ⊑ – ♥239/279 € ♥♥239/279 € – 14 suites   **Rest** – Carte 25/70 €
♦ Business ♦ Chain hotel ♦ Contemporary ♦
A generous, impressive and airy atrium welcomes you into this hotel at the Bockenheimer centre. The 25m indoor pool, a former municipal swimming pool, is the largest hotel pool in Frankfurt. Restaurant with an international and American menu.

InterContinental
Wilhelm-Leuschner-Str. 43 ⊠ *60329* – **Ⓜ** *Willy-Brandt-Platz*
– *𝒞 (069) 2 60 50 – www.frankfurt.intercontinental.com*   **E2**
469 rm – ♥119/219 € ♥♥119/219 €, ⊑ 31 € – 62 suites
Rest *Signatures* – Menu 16/31 € (lunch) – Carte 36/76 €
♦ Business ♦ Conference hotel ♦ Functional ♦
This hotel, situated on the Main, offers classical-style guestrooms in its two buildings, the City Wing and River Wing. The best views are seen from the Club area on the 21st-floor. This restaurant has a modern conservatory. It serves international cuisine, mostly in buffet form.

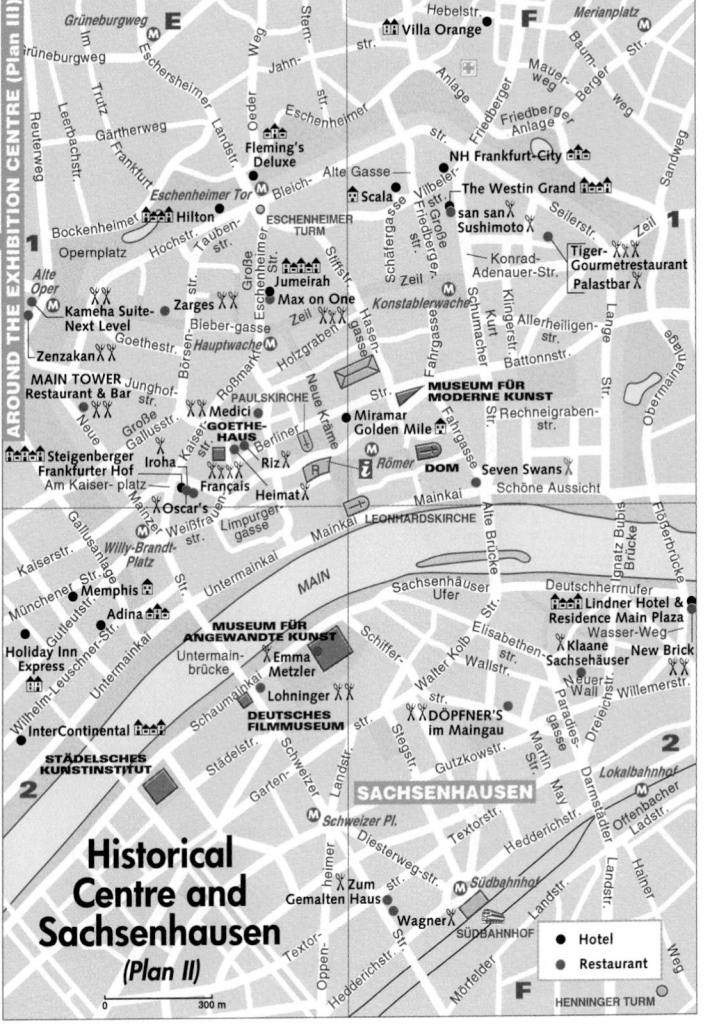

Historical Centre and Sachsenhausen (Plan II)

0 — 300 m

● Hotel
● Restaurant

Lindner Hotel & Residence Main Plaza ≤ ↱5 🏛 🛝 🖥

Walther-von-Cronberg Platz 1 ⒶⒸ 🛜 ⚕ 🚗 *VISA* 🆗 🇦🇪 ①
✉ 60594 – Ⓜ *Lokalbahnhof* – ℰ (069) 6 64 01 40 00 – www.lindner.de
118 rm – †199/599 € ††229/599 €, � 23 € – 7 suites **F2**
Rest New Brick – see restaurant listing

♦ Business ♦ Luxury ♦ Modern ♦

A striking redbrick tower on the banks of the Main. Generous, tasteful and elegant rooms, most with wonderful views over the city. Extensive beauty and spa suite. New Brick serves Californian cuisine from the show kitchen.

355

Fleming's Deluxe

Eschenheimer Tor 2 ⊠ 60318 – Ⓜ Eschenheimer Tor – ℰ (069) 4 27 23 20 – www.flemings-hotels.com **E1**

106 rm ⌓ – †128/178 € ††148/198 € – 6 suites

Rest – Carte 41/62 €

♦ Business ♦ Modern ♦

At the Eschenheimer centre find this listed, former office building from the 1950s with a still operating original Paternoster. It has modern furnishings with a bar and lounge on the seventh-floor. This roof top restaurant with its show kitchen offers a view of the Skyline.

NH Frankfurt-City

Vilbeler Str. 2 ⊠ 60313 – Ⓜ Konstablerwache – ℰ (069) 9 28 85 90 – www.nh-hotels.com **F1**

256 rm – †99/179 € ††99/179 €, ⌓ 24 € – 8 suites

Rest – Carte 28/45 €

♦ Chain hotel ♦ Contemporary ♦

Modern and function hotel also ideally suited to business travellers. Its plus points include the central location very close to the pedestrian zone. Restaurant with a large buffet on the first floor.

Adina

Wilhelm-Leuschner-Str. 6 ⊠ 60329 – Ⓜ Willy-Brandt-Platz – ℰ (069) 2 47 47 40 – www.adina.eu **E2**

134 rm – †169/349 € ††189/369 €, ⌓ 19 € – 75 suites

Rest – Carte 27/48 €

♦ Business ♦ Modern ♦

Apartment hotel close to the river Main and the city centre, with classic modern furnishings, clear cut lines and strong colours. All rooms have a kitchenette. Suites also have a washing machine and dryer. International dishes and tapas.

Alexander am Zoo *without rest*

Waldschmidtstr. 59 ⊠ 60316 – Ⓜ Habsburgerallee – ℰ (069) 94 96 00 – www.alexanderamzoo.de *Plan I* **D2**

66 rm ⌓ – †77/250 € ††97/250 € – 9 suites

♦ Business ♦ Contemporary ♦

Stay in timelessly styled, spacious rooms in this hotel near the zoo. From the conference floor there is direct access to the roof terrace with a view of the city.

Goldman 25hours

Hanauer Landstr. 127 ⊠ 60314 – ℰ (069) 40 58 68 90 – www.25hours-hotels.com *Plan I* **D2**

97 rm – †102/132 € ††102/132 €, ⌓ 15 €

Rest *Goldman* – see restaurant listing

♦ Business ♦ Design ♦ Personalised ♦

This hotel has all manner of endearing and stylish decor in the form of lamps, fabrics, paints etc. The very pleasant modern rooms could hardly be more individual.

Villa Orange *without rest*

Hebelstr. 1 ⊠ 60318 – Ⓜ Merianplatz – ℰ (069) 40 58 40 – www.villa-orange.de **F1**

38 rm ⌓ – †90/195 € ††115/275 €

♦ Family ♦ Modern ♦ Cosy ♦

This beautifully appointed villa-style townhouse is one of the Bio Hotels. Modern-style and warm tones from the foyer via the library to the rooms. Organic, quality breakfast.

GERMANY - FRANKFURT ON MAIN

Holiday Inn Express without rest 🔖 📶 ⚒ 🏊 VISA ⓒⓞ AE ①
Elbestr. 7 ⊠ *60329 –* Ⓜ *Willy-Brandt-Platz –* ℰ *(069) 87 00 38 83*
– www.hiexpress.com   **E2**
116 rm ⊑ *–* †79/399 € ††79/399 €
♦ Chain hotel ♦ Modern ♦
The great advantage of this modern hotel near the railway station is that the
rooms are more spacious than is usual for the chain. It offers all the features of
the latest generation Holiday Inn experience.

Miramar Golden Mile without rest 🔖 📶 VISA ⓒⓞ AE ①
Berliner Str. 31 ⊠ *60311 –* Ⓜ *Römer –* ℰ *(069) 9 20 39 70*
– www.miramar-frankfurt.de
– Closed 23-31 December   **E-F1**
39 rm ⊑ *–* †75/260 € ††85/280 €
♦ Townhouse ♦ Functional ♦
This well-kept and informally-run hotel is in a central location between Zeil and
Römer. The rooms are timeless and functional in style.

Memphis without rest 📶 🅿 VISA ⓒⓞ AE ①
Münchener Str. 15 ⊠ *60329 –* Ⓜ *Willy-Brandt-Platz –* ℰ *(069) 2 42 60 90*
– www.memphis-hotel.de   **E2**
42 rm *–* †75/90 € ††85/100 €, ⊑ 10 €
♦ Business ♦ Functional ♦
Only around 5min walk from the station. The rooms are not very large, but contemporary and functional in design. Those facing the inner courtyard are
quieter.

Scala without rest 📶 VISA ⓒⓞ AE
Schäfergasse 31 ⊠ *60313 –* Ⓜ *Konstablerwache –* ℰ *(069) 1 38 11 10*
– www.scala.bestwestern.de   **F1**
40 rm *–* †89/99 € ††109/139 €, ⊑ 14 €
♦ Business ♦ Townhouse ♦ Functional ♦
This hotel has a central location in the centre of the city. It offers functional,
though not overly large rooms. The reception and drinks service is staffed
24hrs a day.

Français – Hotel Steigenberger Frankfurter Hof 🍴 ♿ 🔖
Am Kaiserplatz ⊠ *60311 –* Ⓜ *Willy-Brandt-Platz* VISA ⓒⓞ AE ①
– ℰ *(069) 21 51 38 – www.frankfurter-hof.steigenberger.de*
*– Closed 2 weeks January, 5 weeks July-August, Saturday-Sunday and Bank
Holidays*   **E1**
Rest *– (booking advisable)* Menu 59 € (lunch)/135 € (dinner)
– Carte 66/120 € 🕸
♦ French classic ♦ Elegant ♦ Classic ♦
Someone here has both talent and technical skill, and that someone is Patrick
Bittner. He uses his expertise to transform high quality produce into creative
classic dishes. The Kaminzimmer and winter garden provide a touch of eleg-
ance, while the courtyard serves as a charming terrace.
➜ Elsässer Gänseleber / Kirsche / Caraque Schokolade / Brioche. Bretoni-
scher Steinbutt / Karotte / Liebstöckel / Sot-l'y-laisse. Apfelkuchen in Texturen / Hefeschaum / Vanille / Apfel.

Max on One – Hotel Jumeirah ♿ 🔖 VISA ⓒⓞ AE ①
Thurn-und-Taxis-Platz 2 (access via Groß Eschenheimer Str. 8, 1st. floor)
⊠ *60313 –* Ⓜ *Hauptwache –* ℰ *(069) 2 97 23 71 98*
– www.jumeirah.com/frankfurt   **E1**
Rest *– (booking advisable)* Menu 39 € (lunch)/98 € – Carte 44/68 €
♦ International ♦ Elegant ♦
Martin Steiner worked in a number of well-known restaurants including Jagd-
hof Glashütte and Johann Lafer's Stromburg before coming to Max on One.
Here he serves up Frankfurt classics and grilled dishes with a hint of his Austrian
homeland. The smart design comes courtesy of interior designer Takashi Sugi-
moto.

GERMANY - FRANKFURT ON MAIN

Tiger-Gourmetrestaurant   AC VISA ○○ AE ①
£3

Heiligkreuzgasse 20 ✉ *60313 –* **Ⓜ** *Konstablerwache*
– 𝒞 (069) 92 00 22 25 – www.tigerpalast.de
– Closed 23 December-14 January,10-13 February, 16 June-21 August and
Sunday-Monday   **F1**
Rest *– (dinner only) (booking essential)* Menu 90/125 € – Carte 72/112 € ❀
Rest *Palastbar* – see restaurant listing
◆ French classic ◆ Elegant ◆ Fashionable ◆
After many years at Brenners Park Restaurant, Andreas Krolik has returned to his
roots at the Tigerpalast and Varieté Theater. He prepares classically modern
cuisine.
→ Tatar vom Hedwigshofer Ochsen mit Steinpilzmousse, marinierter Gän-
seleber, Oxtailgelée und Anchovis-Gänselebereis. Angelkabeljau mit Cham-
pagnersauce, Zitronenspinat, Balsamicoschalotten und Kartoffelmousseline.
Kreation von Coppenauer Bio Grand Cru Schokolade mit Sanddorn, Karamell und Orangen-Sanddornsorbet.

Zenzakan   AC VISA ○○ AE ①

Taunusanlage 15 ✉ *60325 –* **Ⓜ** *Alte Oper – 𝒞 (069) 97 08 69 08*
– www.mook-group.de
– Christmas-New Year and Sunday   **E1**
Rest *– (dinner only)* Menu 90 € – Carte 44/110 €
◆ Asian ◆ Trendy ◆
A trendy chic and very international restaurant in striking black with a bar-
lounge. Contemporary Asian dishes are served, including modern sushi inter-
pretations.

Carmelo Greco   🏠 AC VISA ○○ AE
£3

Ziegelhüttenweg 1 ✉ *60598 –* **Ⓜ** *Südbahnhof – 𝒞 (069) 60 60 89 67*
– www.carmelo-greco.de
– Closed Saturday lunch, Sunday   *Plan I* **C3**
Rest *–* Menu 29 € (lunch)/82 € – Carte 57/71 €
◆ Mediterranean ◆ Fashionable ◆
Carmelo Greco has breathed new life into the slightly hidden away former
Bistro 77. You instantly feel at home in this tasteful, modern and elegant res-
taurant. Excellent Italian food and attentive service. Very good value lunch
menu.
→ Affettato vom Thunfisch in Sake mariniert, Essig-Gurkeneis. Atlantik
Hummer-Risotto, Sizilianische-Tomaten-Confettura. Steinbutt, Blutwurst,
Äpfel, Crostini.

MAIN TOWER Restaurant & Bar   ≤ AC VISA ○○ AE

Neue Mainzer Str. 52 (53rd floor, fee) ✉ *60311 –* **Ⓜ** *Alte Oper*
– 𝒞 (069) 36 50 47 77 – www.maintower-restaurant.de
– Closed Saturday lunch, Sunday-Monday   **E1**
Rest *– (booking essential)* Menu 30 € (lunch)/99 € (dinner)
– Carte 34/40 €
◆ International ◆ Fashionable ◆
187m above the ground, the Main Tower offers impressive views over Frankfurt,
and ambitious, international cuisine in a modern setting. Set menu only in the
evenings.

Lohninger   🏠 VISA ○○ AE

Schweizer Str. 1 ✉ *60594 –* **Ⓜ** *Schweizer Pl. – 𝒞 (069) 2 47 55 78 60*
– www.schmecken.net
– Closed 1-10 January, 24 March-1 April, 2 weeks early July and Bank Holidays
Rest *– (booking advisable)* Menu 88 € – Carte 39/73 €   **E2**
◆ Austrian ◆ Friendly ◆ Fashionable ◆
This modern restaurant can be found in the beautiful high-ceilinged rooms of a
classic townhouse. It offers Austrian cuisine with international influences.

XX **DÖPFNER'S im Maingau**   ఉ 🜨 ⇄ 𝚅𝙸𝚂𝙰 ⚫ 𝙰𝙴 ⓞ

Schifferstr. 38 ✉ *60594 –* ⓜ *Lokalbahnhof –* ☏ *(069) 61 07 52*
– www.maingau.de
– Closed Saturday lunch, Sunday dinner-Monday   **F2**
Rest – Menu 25/89 € – Carte 27/55 €
♦ International ♦ Friendly ♦
This family-run restaurant located close to the River Main offers a pleasant con-
temporary atmosphere and serves international and some classic cuisine. Good
value lunchtime menu.

XX **Kameha Suite - Next Level**   🜨 ⇄ 𝚅𝙸𝚂𝙰 ⚫ 𝙰𝙴 ⓞ

Taunusanlage 20 ✉ *60325 –* ⓜ *Alte Oper –* ☏ *(069) 4 80 03 70*
– www.kamehasuite.com
– Closed 2-7 January and Saturday lunch, Sunday   **E1**
Rest – Menu 49 € (dinner) – Carte 38/62 €
♦ International ♦ Trendy ♦ Fashionable ♦
The trendy restaurant in this imposing grand historical building is an ideal
place for a quick lunch or an evening meal, when contemporary and international cuisine features on the menu. Enjoy classic dishes such as Rossini beef
fillet, as well as more modern creations such as scallops on a carrot and ginger
purée.

XX **Medici**   🜓 🜨 𝚅𝙸𝚂𝙰 ⚫ 𝙰𝙴

Weißadlergasse 2 ✉ *60311 –* ⓜ *Hauptwache –* ☏ *(069) 21 99 07 94*
– www.restaurantmedici.de
– Closed Sunday and Bank Holidays   **E1**
Rest – Menu 40/62 € – Carte 42/61 €
♦ International ♦ Formal ♦
Two brothers are your hosts in this city centre restaurant. International dishes
with a Mediterranean influence are served in a modern atmosphere.

XX **Emma Metzler**   🜓 ⇄ 𝙿 𝚅𝙸𝚂𝙰 ⚫ 𝙰𝙴

Schaumainkai 17 ✉ *60594 –* ⓜ *Schweizer Platz –* ☏ *(069) 61 99 59 06*
– www.emma-metzler.com
– Closed Sunday dinner-Monday except during fairs   **E2**
Rest – Menu 58 € – Carte 46/55 €
♦ Modern ♦ Fashionable ♦
With its bright, modern interior the restaurant in the Frankfurt Museum of
Applied Art offers good seasonal cuisine with attentive service. Attractive ter-
race looking onto the park.

XX **New Brick** - Lindner Hotel & Residence Main Plaza   🜓 🜨

Walther-von-Cronberg Platz 1 ✉ *60594*   𝚅𝙸𝚂𝙰 ⚫ 𝙰𝙴 ⓞ
– ☏ *(069) 6 64 01 44 03*
– www.lindner.de   **F2**
Rest – Carte 37/69 €
♦ International ♦ Fashionable ♦
Sit back under the 'warm California sun' and enjoy... Not quite perhaps, but New
Brick does serve up a little slice of West Coast life along with its Californian cui-
sine in a pleasant atmosphere.

XX **Gusto** - Hotel Villa Kennedy   🜓 ఉ 🜨 𝚅𝙸𝚂𝙰 ⚫ 𝙰𝙴 ⓞ

Kennedyallee 70 ✉ *60596 –* ⓜ *Schweizer Platz –* ☏ *(069) 7 17 12 12 00*
– www.villakennedyhotel.de   **E2**
Rest – Menu 65/85 € – Carte 44/72 €
♦ International ♦ Fashionable ♦
Find tasteful design with a just hint of fashion and style within the venerable
walls of this villa. Enjoy the Italian cuisine and charming setting, particularly in
the impressive interior courtyard.

GERMANY - FRANKFURT ON MAIN

Zarges

🚇 AK ⟷ VISA ⊕⊕ AE

Kalbächer Gasse 10 ⊠ 60311 – Ⓜ Hauptwache – ℰ (069) 29 90 30
– www.zarges-frankfurt.com
– Closed Sunday and Bank Holidays except during fairs **E1**
Rest – Menu 35 € – Carte 39/66 €
• Classic • Cosy • Brasserie •
Located in Frankfurt's Fressgass, this townhouse has a pastry shop with all manner of dainty treats, and a cosy classic restaurant over three floors. To accompany the delicious French inspired dishes you can choose from around 500 wines.

Seven Swans

AK VISA ⊕⊕ AE

Mainkai 4 ⊠ 60311 – ℰ (069) 21 99 62 26 – www.sevenswans.de
– Closed Sunday-Tuesday **F1**
Rest – *(dinner only) (booking essential)* Menu 69/79 €
• Modern • Design •
Dining at the Seven Swans, built in 1838, is more like eating with your neighbours than in a restaurant. This is thanks to the charming staff and the intimate feel – with a surface area of 4 x 10m on each floor this is the narrowest building in the city. Young chef Kimberley Unser cooks ambitious cuisine ranging from Southeast Asian fare to international classics.

Heimat

🚇 VISA ⊕⊕ AE

Berliner Str. 70 ⊠ 60311 – Ⓜ Hauptwache – ℰ (069) 29 72 59 94
– www.restaurant-heimat.de
– Closed Christmas-New Year, during Easter and Whitsun **E1**
Rest – *(dinner only) (booking advisable)* Menu 39/85 € – Carte 39/56 € ⅏
• International • Trendy •
Situated centrally by the Goethe house in a former tram waiting room with kiosk is this lively and pleasantly relaxed restaurant. A good wine selection accompanies the delicious seasonal food.

Riz

🚇 ⊘

Berlinerstr. 72 (access via Groß Hirschgraben) ⊠ 60311 – ℰ (069) 28 24 39
– www.riz-frankfurt.de
– Closed Saturday lunch, Sunday **E1**
Rest – Menu 51/67 € – Carte 40/54 € ⅏
• International • Minimalist •
If you enjoy a glass of good wine with contemporary cuisine, you are sure to find what you are looking for here at Riz. Its comprehensive wine list offers 350 different selections, largely Spanish reds and German whites. Light and minimalist decor.

Goldman – Hotel Goldman 25hours

🚇 VISA ⊕⊕ AE

Hanauer Landstr. 127 ⊠ 60314 – ℰ (069) 40 58 68 98 06
– www.goldman-restaurant.com
– Closed Saturday lunch, Sunday and Bank Holidays *Plan I* **D2**
Rest – Menu 58 € – Carte 42/63 €
• Mediterranean • Design •
Comfortable dining in a smart, modern restaurant with an open kitchen and large glass frontage. Mediterranean dishes with a contemporary interpretation are served.

Palastbar – Tiger-Gourmetrestaurant

AK VISA ⊕⊕ AE ⓪

Heiligkreuzgasse 20 ⊠ 60313 – Ⓜ Konstablerwache – ℰ (069) 92 00 22 92
– www.tigerpalast.de
– Closed 23 December-14 January, 10-13 February, 16 June-21 August and Sunday-Monday **F1**
Rest – *(dinner only)* Menu 49/78 € – Carte 50/83 €
• International • Cosy •
With its comfortable bench seats upholstered in black leather, impressive brick arches and clever lighting, this restaurant is definitely the place to see and be seen.

✗ **Iroha** – Hotel Steigenberger Frankfurter Hof   ⅃ Ⓐ Ⓒ 🆅🅸🆂🅰 ⊛ Ⓐ🅴 Ⓞ
Bethmannstr. 35 ✉ *60311* – Ⓜ *Willy-Brandt-Platz* – ℰ *(069) 21 99 49 30*
– *www.iroha-frankfurt.de*
– *Closed Sunday and Bank Holidays*   **E1**
Rest – Menu 50/120 €
♦ Japanese ♦ Friendly ♦
There is a Japanese restaurant in the hotel cellar. In the Teppanyaki area food is prepared before your eyes on the traditional iron griddle. There is also a sushi bar.

✗ **Oscar's** – Hotel Steigenberger Frankfurter Hof   🍴 ⅃ Ⓐ
Am Kaiserplatz ✉ *60311* – Ⓜ *Willy-Brandt-Platz*   🆅🅸🆂🅰 ⊛ Ⓐ🅴 Ⓞ
– ℰ *(069) 2 15 02* – *www.frankfurter-hof.steigenberger.de*   **E1**
Rest – *(booking advisable)* Menu 30 € (lunch) – Carte 39/62 €
♦ Traditional ♦ Formal ♦
Informal, just as you would expect from a typical bistro, this is a popular meeting place for bankers and business people, so make sure you book ahead. The Wiener Schnitzel with cucumber salad and cranberries is particularly recommended.

✗ **san san** – Hotel The Westin Grand   ⅃ Ⓐ 🆅🅸🆂🅰 ⊛ Ⓐ🅴 Ⓞ
Konrad-Adenauer-Str. 7 ✉ *60313* – Ⓜ *Konstablerwache*
– ℰ *(069) 91 39 90 50* – *www.westingrandfrankfurt.com*
– *Closed Saturday lunch*   **F1**
Rest – Carte 28/50 €
♦ Chinese ♦ Exotic ♦
A restaurant offering typical Chinese fare in a Chinese setting with a choice of three dining options. The Bamboo Lounge, the Shanghai Suite or an intimate private dining room.

✗ **Sushimoto** – Hotel The Westin Grand   ⅃ Ⓐ 🆅🅸🆂🅰 ⊛ Ⓐ🅴 Ⓞ
Konrad-Adenauer-Str. 7 ✉ *60313* – Ⓜ *Konstablerwache*
– ℰ *(069) 1 31 00 57* – *www.westingrandfrankfurt.com*
– *Closed Monday, Sunday lunch*   **F1**
Rest – *(booking advisable)* Menu 40 € (Vegetarian) – Carte 34/103 €
♦ Japanese ♦ Minimalist ♦
The atmosphere is authentic and austere, just as you might expect from a Japanese restaurant. Explore the many facets of Japanese cuisine including sushi and teppanyaki.

✗ **Klaane Sachsehäuser**   🍴 🚫
Neuer Wall 11 (Sachsenhausen) ✉ *60594* – Ⓜ *Lokalbahnhof*
– ℰ *(069) 61 59 83* – *www.klaanesachsehaeuser.de*
– *Closed 24-31 December and Sunday*   **F2**
Rest – *(dinner only)* Carte 15/33 €
♦ Regional/country ♦ Rustic ♦
This popular pub-style restaurant reached through an interior courtyard has been serving traditional "Stöffche" brewed on the premises and good Frankfurt fare since 1876. And you'll always find someone to share your evening with!

✗ **Zum gemalten Haus**   🍴 🆅🅸🆂🅰 ⊛ Ⓐ🅴
Schweizer Str. 67 (Sachsenhausen) ✉ *60594* – Ⓜ *Schweizer Platz*
– ℰ *(069) 61 45 59* – *www.zumgemaltenhaus.de*
– *Closed Monday*   **F2**
Rest – Carte 11/20 €
♦ Regional/country ♦ Rustic ♦
Huddle up, talk shop and chat in the midst of these wall murals and mementoes from bygone days. The main thing is the "Bembel" is always full!

GERMANY - FRANKFURT ON MAIN

Wagner   🛋 ⅀ 🔠 VISA ⚫ AE

Schweizer Str. 71 (Sachsenhausen) ✉ *60594 –* ☏ *(069) 61 25 65*
– www.apfelwein-wagner.com   **F2**
Rest – Carte 13/25 €
♦ Regional/country ♦ Cosy ♦
Sit on old wooden benches at the heart of the apple wine area of Hochburg Sachsenhausen, and enjoy the golden liquid and a few tasty ribs ...!

WESTEND – EXHIBITION-CENTRE – STATION   *Plan III*

Hessischer Hof   🔠 ⅀ 🛁 P 🚗 VISA ⚫ AE ⓞ

Friedrich-Ebert-Anlage 40 ✉ *60325 –* Ⓜ *Hauptbahnhof –* ☏ *(069) 7 54 00*
– www.hessischer-hof.de   **G2**
119 rm – 🛏225/695 € 🛏🛏255/695 €, ⅀ 28 € – 7 suites
Rest *Sèvres* – see restaurant listing
♦ Luxury ♦ Classic ♦ Personalised ♦
Thanks to the excellent service, from the welcome drink, via the free minibar to the good quality breakfast, guests feel very well looked after here. New executive rooms in a classic-elegant style. The exhibition of fine Sèvre porcelain gives the restaurant an exclusive feel.

Marriott   ⪡ 🛁 🐾 🔠 ⅀ 🛁 🚗 VISA ⚫ AE ⓞ

Hamburger Allee 2 ✉ *60486 –* Ⓜ *Bockenheimer Warte –* ☏ *(069) 7 95 50*
– www.frankfurt-marriott.de   **G1**
588 rm – 🛏189/390 € 🛏🛏209/410 €, ⅀ 28 € – 11 suites
Rest – *(Closed Saturday-Sunday)* Carte 33/54 €
♦ Chain hotel ♦ Business ♦ Functional ♦
Opposite the exhibition centre, this hotel stands out for its well-equipped rooms in an elegant, classical style with views over the city. Increased privacy is offered on the executive floor. Restaurant with a pleasant brasserie ambience and French cuisine.

Radisson BLU   ⪡ 🛋 🐾 🔠 ▦ ⅀ 🔠 ⅀ 🛁 🚗 VISA ⚫ AE ⓞ

Franklinstr. 65 (by Theodor Heuss Allee A2) ✉ *60486 –* ☏ *(069) 7 70 15 50*
– www.radissonblu.com/hotel-frankfurt
428 rm – 🛏99/499 € 🛏🛏99/499 €, ⅀ 28 €
Rest *Gaia* – ☏ *(069) 77 01 55 22 00* – Carte 30/66 €
♦ Business ♦ Conference hotel ♦ Design ♦
Matteo Thun and Adam Tihany are behind the modern style of this unusual hotel. The rooms are named after their style of decoration. 'At home', 'Chic', 'Fashion' and 'Fresh'. The Gaia serves Mediterranean food.

Maritim   🐾 🔠 ▦ ⅀ 🔠 ⅀ 🛁 🚗 VISA ⚫ AE ⓞ

Theodor-Heuss-Allee 3 ✉ *60486 –* Ⓜ *Bockenheimer Warte*
– ☏ *(069) 7 57 80 – www.maritim.de*   **G2**
543 rm – 🛏139/490 € 🛏🛏169/520 €, ⅀ 28 € – 24 suites
Rest – *(dinner only)* Menu 36 € – Carte 38/57 €
♦ Chain hotel ♦ Conference hotel ♦ Functional ♦
This hotel, which is directly linked with the Exhibition and Congress Park, is an ideal conference venue with timeless rooms. The rooms on the upper floors have a particularly beautiful view. The Classico and SushiSho restaurants offer international cuisine.

Le Méridien Parkhotel   🛋 🐾 🔠 ⅀ 🛁 🚗 VISA ⚫ AE ⓞ

Wiesenhüttenplatz 28 ✉ *60329 –* Ⓜ *Hauptbahnhof –* ☏ *(069) 2 69 70*
– www.lemeridienparkhotelfrankfurt.com   **H2**
297 rm – 🛏145/519 € 🛏🛏145/539 €, ⅀ 27 € – 2 suites
Rest – Menu 38/48 € – Carte 39/58 €
♦ Luxury ♦ Chain hotel ♦ Design ♦
In the historic part of this hotel – a stately residence – you will find stylish rooms and a beautiful staircase. Modern, functional annexe. The Le Parc restaurant is in a bistro style. Garden bar at the front.

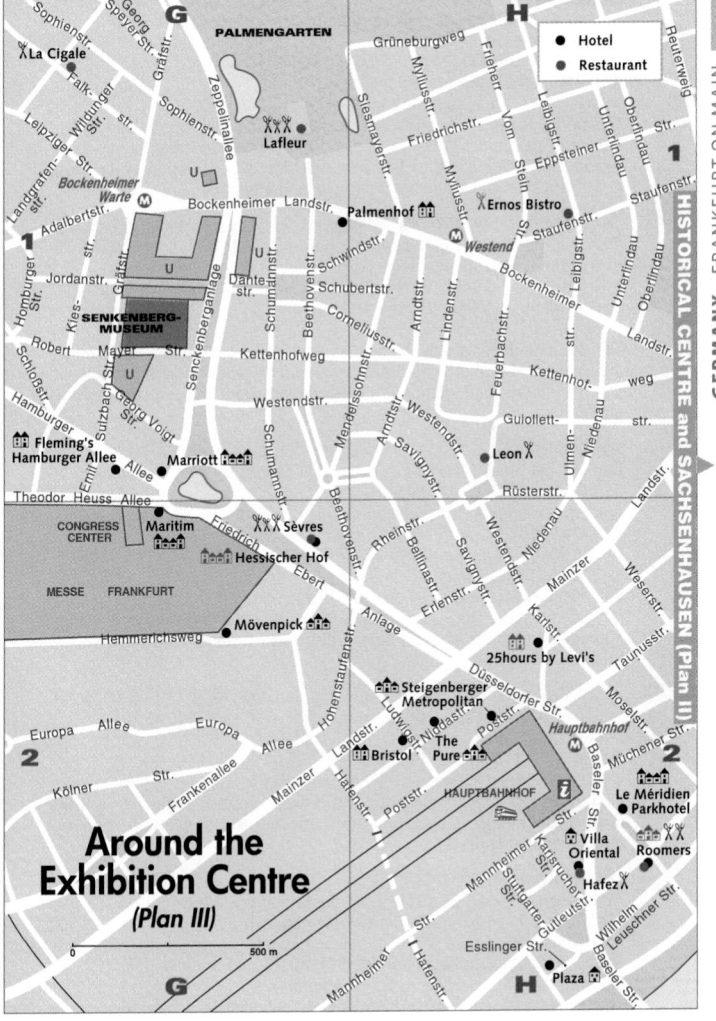

PALMENGARTEN

Hotel ●
Restaurant ●

La Cigale

Lafleur

Bockenheimer Warte

Bockenheimer Landstr.

Palmenhof

Ernos Bistro

Westend

SENKENBERG-MUSEUM

Kettenhofweg

Westendstr.

Guioflett-str.

Leon

Fleming's Hamburger Allee

Marriott

Rüsterstr.

Theodor Heuss Allee

CONGRESS CENTER

Maritim

Sèvres

Hessischer Hof

MESSE FRANKFURT

Mövenpick

Hemmerichsweg

25hours by Levi's

Steigenberger Metropolitan

Europa Allee

Europa

Bristol

The Pure

Hauptbahnhof

Kölner

Str.

HAUPTBAHNHOF

Le Méridien Parkhotel

Villa Oriental

Roomers

Around the Exhibition Centre
(Plan III)

Hafez

0   500 m

Esslinger Str.

Plaza

Roomers   🔥 🐾 🕹 🅰🅲 🛜 🐚 🚗 🆚🅸🆂🅰 ⓌⓈ 🅰🅴 ⓘ

Gutleutstr. 85 ⊠ 60329 – Ⓜ Hauptbahnhof – 𝒞 (069) 2 71 34 20
– www.roomers.eu   **H2**
117 rm – ♦150/500 € ♦♦190/700 €, ☷ 29 € – 1 suite
Rest *Roomers* – see restaurant listing
♦ Business ♦ Design ♦ Modern ♦
This trendy address impresses with its harmonious, high quality and tasteful interior in dark tones. Muted lights and music give the bar a lounge atmosphere. Guests are made to feel very welcome. Superb design in the sauna and fitness area. The restaurant is also chic and modern.

Steigenberger Metropolitan   🔥 🐾 🕹 🅰🅲 🛜 🐚

Poststr. 6 ⊠ 60329 – Ⓜ Hauptbahnhof – 𝒞 (069)   🆚🅸🆂🅰 ⓌⓈ 🅰🅴 ⓘ
5 06 07 00 – www.steigenberger.com   **H2**
131 rm ☷ – ♦119/699 € ♦♦139/699 € – 3 suites
Rest – Menu 39/69 € – Carte 34/65 €
♦ Business ♦ Contemporary ♦
This beautiful city palace by the main station dates from the 19C. It is fitted out in a modern style that is both functional and elegant. Art Deco components adorn the façade and interior. The Brasserie restaurant enjoys a contemporary atmosphere.

Mövenpick   🔥 🕹 🅰🅲 🛜 🐚 🚗 🆚🅸🆂🅰 ⓌⓈ 🅰🅴 ⓘ

Den Haager Str. 5 (near Tor Ost, Halle III) (access by Platz der Einheit)
⊠ 60327 – 𝒞 (069) 7 88 07 50
– www.moevenpick-hotels.com/frankfurt-city   **G2**
288 rm – ♦85/555 € ♦♦105/575 €, ☷ 23 €
Rest – Menu 55/70 € – Carte 22/62 €
♦ Chain hotel ♦ Contemporary ♦
This business hotel is directly on the exhibition ground and has a conspicuous red-green façade. The rooms feature clean, modern and functional design. There is a fitness area with roof terrace. Bistro-style restaurant with international menu.

The Pure *without rest*   🔥 🐾 🅰🅲 🛜 🚗 🆚🅸🆂🅰 ⓌⓈ 🅰🅴 ⓘ

Niddastr. 86 ⊠ 60329 – Ⓜ Hauptbahnhof – 𝒞 (069) 7 10 45 70
– www.the-pure.de   **H2**
50 rm ☷ – ♦150/160 € ♦♦170 €
♦ Townhouse ♦ Design ♦ Minimalist ♦
Find minimalist, modern elegance at this hotel, which is exclusively in white. Close to the railway station, the tasteful, modern and elegant rooms are not always generously sized.

Fleming's Hamburger Allee   🔥 🐾 🅰🅲 🛜 🚗 🆚🅸🆂🅰 ⓌⓈ 🅰🅴 ⓘ

Hamburger Allee 47 ⊠ 60486 – Ⓜ Bockenheimer Warte
– 𝒞 (069) 2 01 74 10 – www.flemings-hotels.com   **G1**
45 rm ☷ – ♦91/395 € ♦♦104/420 € – 2 suites
Rest – *(closed Christmas-2 January)* Menu 24/50 € – Carte 23/56 €
♦ Business ♦ Townhouse ♦ Modern ♦
The immediately proximity to the exhibition centre and its sleek modern rooms with open bathrooms distinguish this friendly business hotel. Trams stop right outside the door. Pleasant restaurant in a contemporary, bistro-style.

25hours by Levi's   🐚 🅰🅲 🛜 🐚 🅿 🆚🅸🆂🅰 ⓌⓈ 🅰🅴

Niddastr. 58 ⊠ 60329 – Ⓜ Hauptbahnhof – 𝒞 (069) 2 56 67 70
– www.25hours-hotels.com   **H2**
76 rm – ♦114/154 € ♦♦114/154 €, ☷ 15 €
Rest – *(Closed Sunday lunch)* Carte 19/52 €
♦ Townhouse ♦ Design ♦ Modern ♦
This designer hotel is by the main railway station. The floors have been individually decorated in the style of the jeans look of the 1930s to 1980s. There is a 'Gibson Music Room' in the basement. The cosy restaurant is colourful, trendy and lively.

GERMANY - FRANKFURT ON MAIN

Pearl without rest
🅰🅺 🛜 ♨ 🚗 🆅🅸🆂🅰 ⓪ 🅰🅴

Gutleutstr. 173 ✉ 60327 – ℰ (069) 27 13 66 90 – www.pearlhotel.de
55 rm ☕ – †89/399 € ††109/449 €   *Plan I* **B3**

♦ Business ♦ Design ♦

This business hotel is slightly outside the centre and not far from the station. Modern rooms in a striking minimalist style.

Bristol without rest
🛜 ♨ 🚗 🆅🅸🆂🅰 ⓪ 🅰🅴 ⓞ

Ludwigstr. 15 ✉ 60327 – Ⓜ Hauptbahnhof – ℰ (069) 24 23 90
– www.bristol-hotel.de   **H2**
145 rm ☕ – †85/300 € ††95/310 €

♦ Business ♦ Contemporary ♦

A conveniently located hotel with a modern interior in warm colours. The breakfast room has a pleasant terrace. There is also a cosy bar with snacks.

Palmenhof without rest
🛜 🅿 🆅🅸🆂🅰 ⓪ 🅰🅴

Bockenheimer Landstr. 89 ✉ 60325 – Ⓜ Westend – ℰ (069) 7 53 00 60
– www.palmenhof.com
– Closed Christmas-2 January   **G1**
45 rm – †125/155 € ††165/185 €, ☕ 16 €

♦ Townhouse ♦ Classic ♦

This privately run hotel in the banking quarter was built in 1890. Behind its Gründerzeit façade it houses pretty rooms furnished with antiques from various periods.

Plaza without rest
🛜 🅿 🚗 🆅🅸🆂🅰 ⓪ 🅰🅴

Esslinger Str. 8 ✉ 60329 – ℰ (069) 2 71 37 80
– www.plaza-frankfurt.bestwestern.de   **H2**
45 rm – †79/259 € ††99/299 €, ☕ 14 €

♦ Business ♦ Contemporary ♦

This well-kept hotel is in a relatively quiet location not far from the station. The rooms are large and furnished in a modern, functional style.

Holiday Inn Express without rest
♿ 🅰🅺 📞 ♨ 🅿 🚗

Gutleutstr. 296 ✉ 60327 – ℰ (069) 50 69 60
– www.hiexpress.com/exfrankfurtmes   🆅🅸🆂🅰 ⓪ 🅰🅴 ⓞ
175 rm ☕ – †79/145 € ††79/145 €   *Plan I* **A3**

♦ Chain hotel ♦ Functional ♦

The functional facilities and good connections to the A5 motorway make this an ideal business address. Bright, modern breakfast room in the lobby area.

Villa Oriental
🅰🅺 🛜 🆅🅸🆂🅰 ⓪ 🅰🅴

Baseler Str. 21 ✉ 60329 – Ⓜ Hauptbahnhof – ℰ (069) 27 10 89 50
– www.villa-oriental.com   **H2**
24 rm ☕ – †95/145 € ††115/165 €
Rest *Hafez* – see restaurant listing

♦ Townhouse ♦ Oriental ♦

This attractive townhouse hotel brings a touch of the Orient to Frankfurt. Its beautiful authentic interior includes round 15 000 highly decorative tiles from Morocco. Persian inspired ambience and cuisine in the Hafez restaurant.

Villa Merton
🍽 ✿ 🆅🅸🆂🅰 ⓪ 🅰🅴

❀❀

Am Leonhardsbrunn 12 (corner of Ditmarstraße) ✉ 60487
– ℰ (069) 70 30 33 – www.koflerkompanie.com
– Closed 21 December-14 January, Saturday-Sunday   *Plan I* **A1**
Rest – (booking advisable) Menu 85/129 €

♦ Innovative ♦ Classic ♦ Elegant ♦

This beautiful villa in the prestigious diplomatic quarter epitomises creative cuisine in a stylish and elegant setting. Matthias Schmidt leads the kitchen team. The small terrace also offers seating overlooking the garden.

→ Weißer Spargel mit Bucheckern, Gundermann, Blütenzucker und Leindotteröl. Flusskrebse mit Löwenzahnknospen, Radieschen und Meerrettich. Wacholder mit Schildampfer, Speierling und Vogelbeeren.

GERMANY - FRANKFURT ON MAIN

XXX   Lafleur   🍴 ♿ AC ⇔ P VISA ⬤ AE ⓘ
⭐

Palmengartenstr. 11 ✉ *60325 –* ✆ *(069) 90 02 91 00*
– www.restaurant-lafleur.de
– Closed 23 December-14 January, 2 weeks by Easter, 4 weeks July-August and
Saturday lunch, Sunday-Monday   **G1**
Rest – Menu 43 € (lunch)/135 € – Carte 89/122 € 🏵

♦ **French classic** ♦ **Elegant** ♦

Having left the Tigerpalast in favour of the company's sister restaurant at the
Palm Gardens, Alfred Friedrich – one of Frankfurt's greatest chefs – awaits you
in this brand new restaurant. His contemporary interpretations of classic dishes
are made using only the very best ingredients.
➜ Gänseleber gebraten / Rauchaal / Apfel / Holunder. Europäischer Hummer geröstet / Kalbsfuß / Steinpilz / Marone / Feige / Jabugo Schinken.
Rücken und Bauch vom Bunten Bentheimer Schwein / Aubergine / Blutwurst / Apfelkaramell.

XXX   Sèvres – Hotel Hessischer Hof   AC P VISA ⬤ AE ⓘ

Friedrich-Ebert-Anlage 40 ✉ *60325 –* Ⓜ *Hauptbahnhof –* ✆ *(069) 7 54 00*
– www.hessischer-hof.de   **G2**
Rest – Menu 39/99 € – Carte 48/86 €

♦ **French classic** ♦ **Elegant** ♦

A magnificent setting for a magnificent collection! An exhibition of precious
Sèvres porcelain has been artfully incorporated into the exquisite interior of
the eponymous restaurant. Good value with an 'all-inclusive' menu at lunchtimes.

XX   Roomers – Hotel Roomers   🍴 ♿ AC VISA ⬤ AE ⓘ

Gutleutstr. 85 ✉ *60329 –* Ⓜ *Hauptbahnhof –* ✆ *(069) 2 71 34 20*
– www.roomers.eu
– Closed Saturday-Sunday and Bank Holiday lunch   **H2**
Rest – Carte 44/88 €

♦ **International** ♦ **Trendy** ♦

This fashionable address in central 'Mainhattan' has a decor that is simply stunning. It features sand coloured upholstered sofas, indirect lighting and fine
materials combined with black accessories.

X   Ernos Bistro   🍴 VISA ⬤ AE
⭐

Liebigstr. 15 ✉ *60323 –* Ⓜ *Westend –* ✆ *(069) 72 19 97*
– www.ernosbistro.de
– Closed 2 weeks end December-early January, 1 week after Easter, 2 weeks
August, Saturday-Sunday and Bank Holidays   **H1**
Rest – *(booking advisable)* Menu 39 € (lunch)/125 € – Carte 65/111 € 🏵

♦ **French classic** ♦ **Bistro** ♦ **Cosy** ♦

Enjoy excellent French dishes in this authentic bistro with an appealing lively
atmosphere, not least because of the friendly service. Valéry Mathis is in charge
of the kitchen team.
➜ Schnecken mit Ricotta-Gnocchi, roten Zwiebeln und milder Knoblauch-
creme, Petersilienjus. Hausgemachte Gänsestopfleber mit Gewürztraminer-
Gelee und Brioche. Gratinierte Kalbskutteln à la mode de Caen mit Calvados flambiert.

X   Weinsinn   🍴 VISA ⬤ AE
⭐

Fürstenbergerstr. 179 ✉ *60322 –* Ⓜ *Holzhausenstr. –* ✆ *(069) 56 99 80 80*
– www.weinsinn-frankfurt.de
– Closed 25 March-7 April, 22 June-4 August, Sunday-Monday and Bank Holidays
Rest – *(dinner only)* Menu 46/62 € – Carte 47/57 € 🏵   *Plan I* **B1**

♦ **Modern** ♦ **Minimalist** ♦ **Retro** ♦

Notwithstanding a wine list boasting over 200 selections, Weinsinn is more than
just a treat for wine lovers. It also offers a feast for the eyes in its beautifully judged modern interior, as well as for the taste buds in the form of André Rickert's
contemporary, creative yet uncomplicated cuisine.
➜ Pulpo & Kaninchen mit Paprika, Artischocke, Pimenton. Weißer Heilbutt,
Blumenkohl, grüner Spargel, Curry. Kalbsfilet und Kalbsbäckchen mit Sellerie, Kirsche, PX-Essig.

La Cigale   🛒 VISA 🔒

Falkstr. 38 ✉ *60487 –* ☏ *(069) 70 41 11 – www.lacigale-restaurant.de*
– Closed 8-29 July and Sunday-Tuesday lunch, Friday lunch, Saturday lunch
Rest *– (bookings advisable at dinner)* Menu 35/56 €   **CV**
– Carte 31/56 €

♦ International ♦ Cosy ♦
La Cigale's many regulars are attracted here by the restaurant's friendly, welco-
ming atmosphere, as well as the fresh cuisine. This is prepared by chef Martin
Kofler, and his braised ox cheeks are a particular favourite.

Leon   🛒 VISA 🔒 AE

Feuerbachstr. 5 ✉ *60325 –* Ⓜ *Westend –* ☏ *(069) 15 34 48 50*
– www.leon-restaurant.de – Closed Saturday lunch, Sunday and Bank Holiday
Rest *–* Carte 36/54 €   **H1**

♦ International ♦ Neighbourhood ♦
This appealing basement restaurant with a small terrace is a pleasant two-man
business, serving international food.

Hafez *– Hotel Villa Oriental*   VISA 🔒 AE

Baseler Str. 21 ✉ *60329 –* Ⓜ *Hauptbahnhof –* ☏ *(069) 23 23 01*
– www.villa-oriental.com   **H2**
Rest *–* Menu 59 € *–* Carte 22/48 €

♦ International ♦ Exotic ♦
Brightly coloured lamps, embroidered cushions, cleverly selected colours and
Oriental accessories recreate the fairytale feeling of One Thousand and One
Nights. Step in and sample the Persian cuisine.

ENVIRONS OF FRANKFURT

AT THE RHEIN-MAIN AIRPORT by Kennedy Allee B3

Kempinski Hotel Gravenbruch

Graf zu Ysenburg und Büdingen-
Platz 1 ✉ *63263 –* ☏ *(069) 38 98 80 – www.kempinski.com/frankfurt*
241 rm *–* 🛏129/299 € 🛏🛏129/299 €, � 29 €
Rest *Forsthaus –* see restaurant listing
Rest *Torschänke –* ☏ *(069) 38 98 86 60 –* Carte 23/61 €

♦ Chain hotel ♦ Classic ♦
The hotel stands in pretty grounds with its own lake. The rooms are decorated in
classic country-house style or along clean modern lines. Beauty and massage parlour. The Torschänke restaurant, which has a beer garden, offers local specialities.

Hilton

Am Flughafen (The Squaire) ✉ *60549 –* ☏ *(0 69) 26 0120 00*
– www.hilton.de/frankfurtairport
249 rm *–* 🛏189/499 € 🛏🛏189/499 €, ⊻ 33 € *– 17 suites*
Rest *RISE –* Carte 40/80 €

♦ Chain hotel ♦ Design ♦
The Frankfurt Hilton offers the very best in urban chic. It is a 625m-long futuristic
glass and steel construction, designed as a recumbent skyscraper. The A3 could
hardly be closer and there is direct access to both the ICE station and the airport. There is also a ballroom that can accommodate 570 people!

Steigenberger Airport

Unterschweinstiege 16 ✉ *60549 –* ☏ *(069) 6 97 50*
– www.airporthotel-frankfurt.steigenberger.de
570 rm *–* 🛏109/189 € 🛏🛏109/189 €, ⊻ 28 € *– 20 suites*
Rest *Faces –* see restaurant listing
Rest *Unterschweinstiege –* ☏ *(069) 69 75 25 00 –* Carte 34/64 €

♦ Chain hotel ♦ Modern ♦
This hotel is characterised by its elegant hall, comfortable rooms (in particular
the modern Tower room) and the 'Open Sky' leisure area with fantastic views.
A cosy atmosphere in the Unterschweinstiege.

Sheraton Frankfurt Airport Hotel & Conference Center

Hugo-Eckener-Ring 15 ⚐ 🕸 ⚐ 🎦 🛜 🛱 **P** *VISA* **⬥** **AE** **①**
(Terminal 1) ✉ *60549 Frankfurt –* ℰ *(069) 6 97 70*
– www.sheratonfrankfurtairport.com
1008 rm – 🛉209/549 € 🛉🛉244/584 €, ☱ 32 € – 28 suites
Rest *Flavors* – ℰ *(069) 69 77 12 46* – Carte 47/98 €
Rest *Taverne* – ℰ *(069) 69 77 12 59 (closed Saturday - Sunday)*
Carte 28/52 €
♦ Business ♦ Chain hotel ♦ Modern ♦
Ideally situated for air travellers, the hotel – the largest in Germany – is located right opposite Terminal 1. If you need a little exercise before or after your flight, try the 24-hour fitness centre. There are two restaurants, the modern Flavors and the country-style Taverne.

Hilton Garden Inn

⚐ 🕸 ⚐ 🎦 🛜 🛱 🚗 *VISA* **⬥** **AE** **①**
Am Flughafen (The Squaire) ✉ *60549 Frankfurt –* ℰ *(069) 45 00 25 00*
– www.frankfurtairport.hgi.com
334 rm – 🛉119/329 € 🛉🛉119/329 €, ☱ 21 € – 2 suites
Rest – Carte 32/66 €
♦ Chain hotel ♦ Modern ♦
A little less comfortable than the Hilton proper next door, the Garden Inn is still unbeatable for its motorway, rail and airport connections – there is even a 'sky-walk' to take you straight to Terminal 1. It has ultramodern design and all the latest technology, including mattresses with adjustable firmness!

Forsthaus – Kempinski Hotel Gravenbruch

🚗 🌢 🛱 ✗ ⚐ 🎦 **P**
Graf zu Ysenburg und Büdingen-Platz 1 ✉ *63263*   *VISA* **⬥** **AE** **①**
– ℰ *(069) 38 98 80 – www.kempinski.com/frankfurt*
– Closed Monday-Tuesday
Rest – Menu 28/49 € – Carte 43/60 €
♦ International ♦ Elegant ♦
This restaurant is a treat for all the senses thanks to its classic cuisine and its sumptuous interior design. It also has views through the impressive glass windows into the wonderful greenery of the surrounding park.

Faces – Hotel Steigenberger Airport

🛱 ⚐ 🎦 **P** *VISA* **⬥** **AE** **①**
Unterschweinstiege 16 ✉ *60549 –* ℰ *(069) 69 75 24 00*
– www.airporthotel-frankfurt.steigenberger.de
– Closed 24 December-12 January, 25 March-6 April, 8 July-16 August, 15-27 Oktober, Saturday-Sunday and Bank Holidays
Rest – *(dinner only)* Menu 89 € – Carte 48/82 €
♦ International ♦ Design ♦
Behind the glass frontage lies a smart, modern restaurant with original lighting. It serves contemporary international cuisine focusing on high quality ingredients. Separate bar.

HAMBURG
HAMBURG

Population: 1 774 230

With a maritime role stretching back centuries, Germany's second largest city has a lively and liberal ambience. Hamburg is often described as 'The Gateway to the World', and there's certainly a visceral feel here, particularly around the big, buzzy and bustling port area. Locals enjoy a long-held reputation for their tolerance and outward looking stance, cosmopolitan to the core. Space to breathe is seen as very important in Hamburg: the city authorities have paid much attention to green spaces, and the city can proudly claim an enviable amount of parks, lakes and tree-lined canals.

There's no cathedral here (at least not a standing one, as war-destroyed St Nikolai remains a ruin), so the Town Hall acts as the central landmark. Just north of here are the Binnenalster (inner) and Aussenalster (outer) lakes. The old walls of the city, dating back over eight hundred years, are delineated by a distinct semicircle of boulevards that curve attractively in a wide arc south of the lakes. Further south from here is the port and harbour area, defined by Landungsbrücken to the west and Speicherstadt to the east. The district to the west of the centre is St Pauli, famed for its clubs and bars, particularly along the notorious Reeperbahn, which pierces the district from east to west. The contrastingly smart Altona suburb and delightful Blankenese village are west of St Pauli.

HAMBURG IN...

→ **ONE DAY**
Boat trip from Landungsbrücken, Speicherstadt, Kunsthalle, Fishmarket (Sunday morning).

→ **TWO DAYS**
Steamboat on the Alster, Hamburg History Museum, St Pauli by night.

→ **THREE DAYS**
Arts and Crafts Museum, canal trip, concert at Musikhalle.

PRACTICAL INFORMATION

ARRIVAL-DEPARTURE

✈ Hamburg Airport is 15km north of the city centre. Airport buses leave for Hamburg Hauptbahnhof every 15-20min and Altona Station every 30min; both take 20min.

GETTING AROUND

Hamburg Transport Authority controls all of the bus routes, the overground S-Bahn trains, the U-Bahn underground lines, and several river and ferry services. Tickets are available for single journeys, or for one-day or three-day duration; you can buy them from vending machines or bus drivers. The Hamburg Card is valid for the transport network, and offers discounts in museums, theatres and some restaurants, as well as for tours on land and water. Buy it from Tourist Information offices, vending machines, hotels or travel agents.

CALENDAR HIGHLIGHTS

March-April
Spring Market in St Pauli's Heiligengeistfeld.

April, August and November
Dom Festivals (huge funfairs).

May
Hafengeburtstag (harbour's birthday celebration), Long Night of Hamburg Museums.

September
Film Festival.

November
Art Mile Day.

EATING OUT

Being a city immersed in water, it's no surprise to find Hamburg is a good place for fish. Though its fishing industry isn't the powerhouse of old, the city still boasts a giant trawler's worth of seafood places to eat. Eel dishes are mainstays of the traditional restaurant's menu, as is the herring stew with vegetables called Labskaus. Also unsurprisingly, considering it's the country's gateway to the world, this is somewhere that offers a vast range of international dishes. Wherever you eat, the portions are likely to be generous. There's no problem with finding somewhere early: cafés are often open at seven, with the belief that it's never too early for coffee and cake. Bakeries also believe in an early start, and the calorie content here, too, can be pretty high. Bistros and restaurants, usually open by midday, are proud of their local ingredients, so keep your eyes open for Hamburgisch on the menu. Service charges are always included in the bill, so tipping is not compulsory, although most people will round it up and possibly add five to ten per cent.

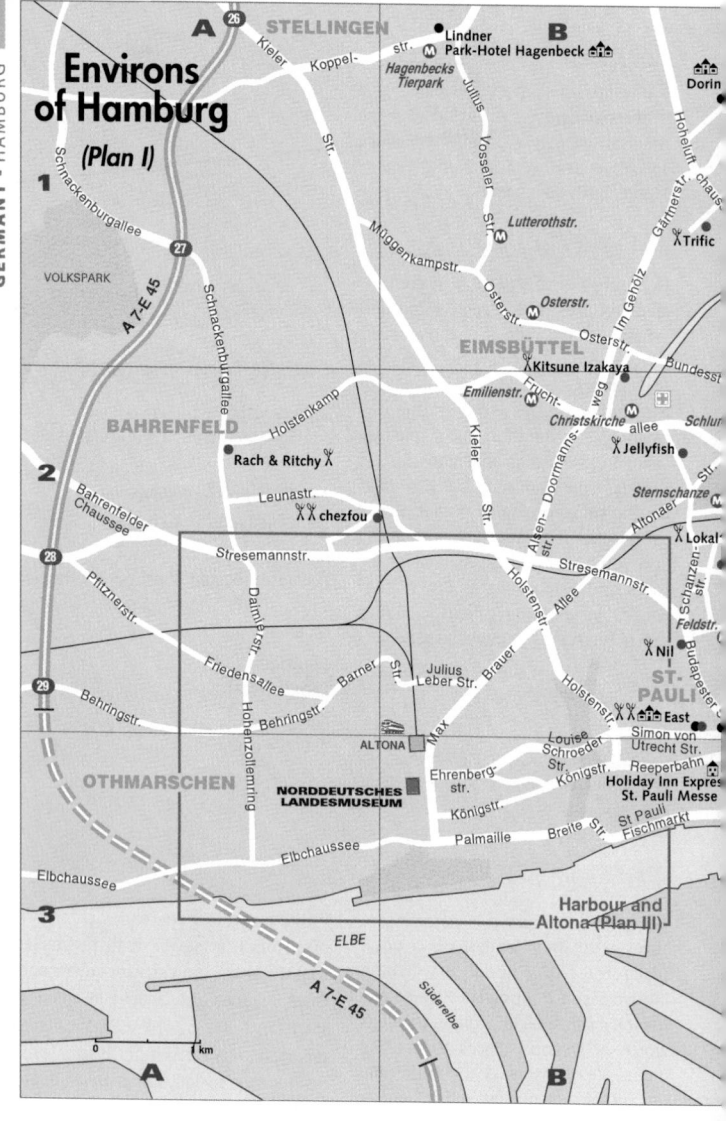

Environs of Hamburg
(Plan I)

A 26 STELLINGEN B

● Lindner
Park-Hotel Hagenbeck
Hagenbecks Tierpark

Dorin

VOLKSPARK

27

Schnackenburgallee

A 7-E 45

Schnackenburgallee

Kieler Str.

Koppel-str.

Julius Vosseler Str.

Müggenkampstr.

Osterstr.

Lutterothstr.

Osterstr.

Osterstr.

Im Gehölz

Trific

Hoheluft chaus.

Gärtner chaus.

EIMSBÜTTEL

Kitsune Izakaya

Bundesstr

1

BAHRENFELD

Holstenkamp

Emilienstr.

Fruchtallee

Doormanns weg

Christskirche allee

Jellyfish

Schlur

Rach & Ritchy

Leunastr.

chezfou

Kieler Str.

Sternschanze

Altonaer Str.

Lokal

2

Bahrenfelder Chaussee

Pfitznerstr.

28

Stresemannstr.

Daimlerstr.

Holstenstr.

Altonaer Str.

Stresemannstr.

Holstenstr. Allee

Schanzen-str.

Feldstr.

Nil

Budapester Str.

ST-PAULI

Friedensallee

Behringstr.

29

Behringstr.

Barner Str.

Max Brauer Allee

Julius Leber Str.

Holstenstr.

East

Simon von Utrecht Str.

OTHMARSCHEN

Hohenzollernring

ALTONA

NORDDEUTSCHES LANDESMUSEUM

Ehrenberg-str.

Louise Schroeder Str.

Königstr.

Reeperbahn

Holiday Inn Express St. Pauli Messe

Königstr.

Palmaille

Breite Str.

St Pauli Fischmarkt

Elbchaussee

Elbchaussee

Harbour and Altona (Plan III)

3

ELBE

A 7-E 45

Süderelbe

0   km   1

A   B

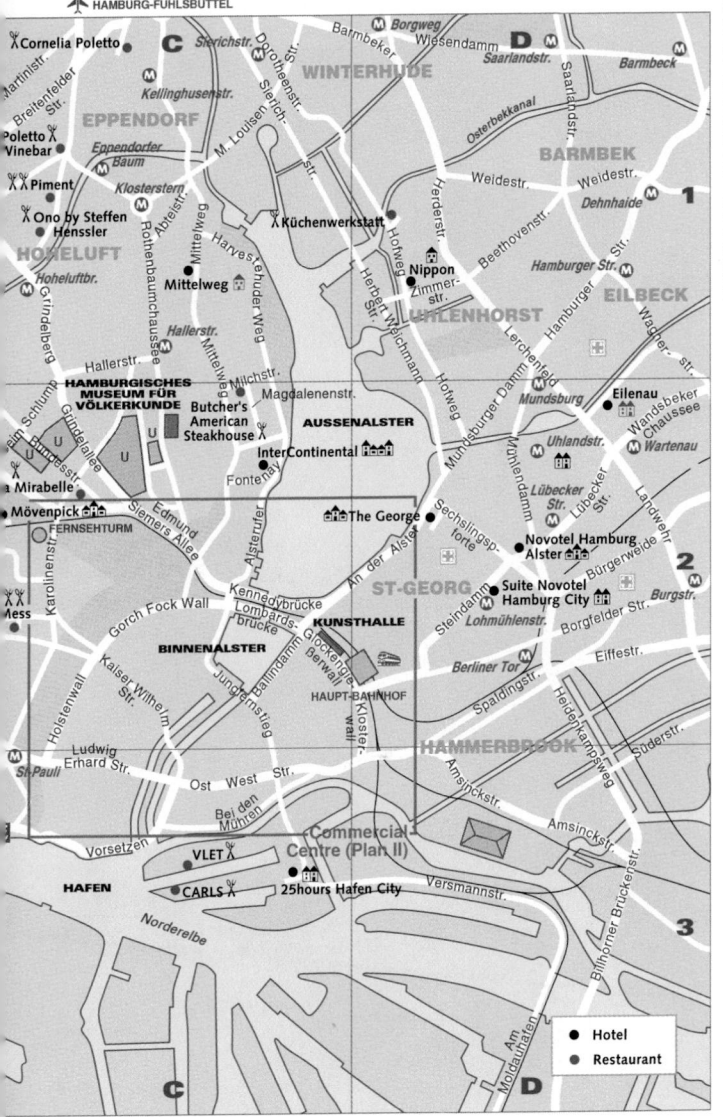

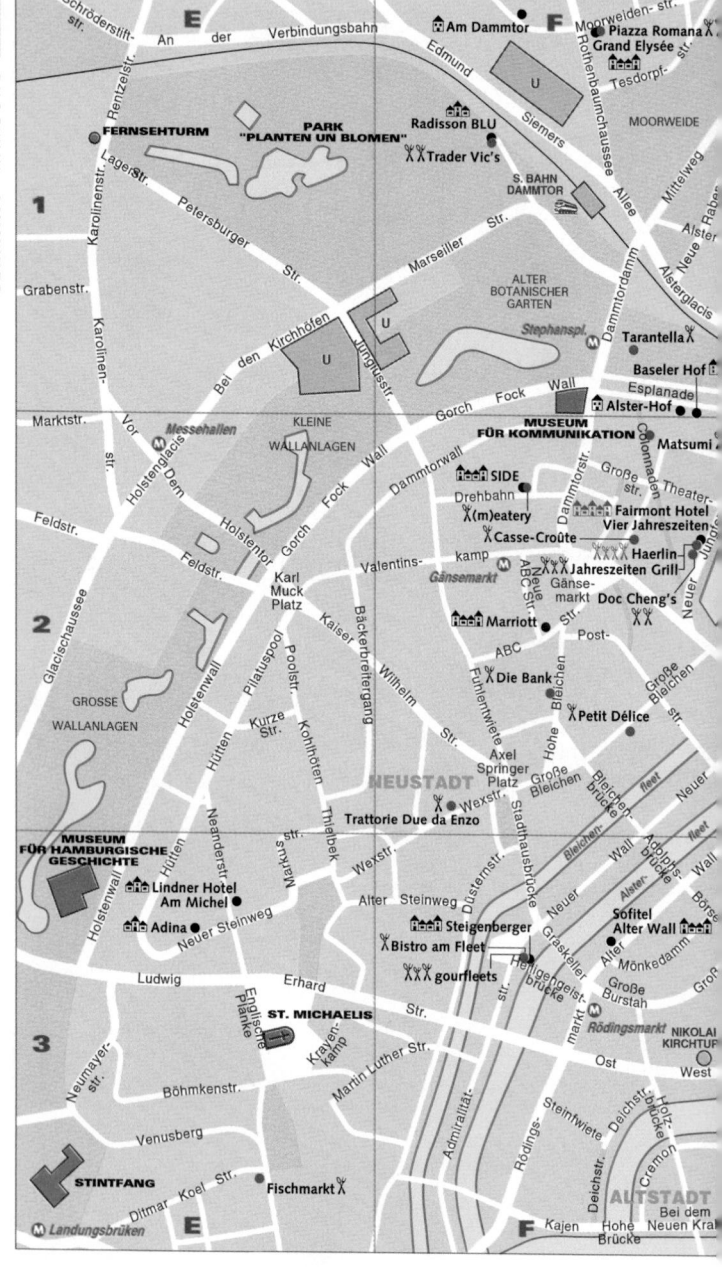

Schröderstift-str.
Rentzelstr.
An der Verbindungsbahn
Edmund
Moorweiden-str.
Piazza Romana
Grand Elysée
Rothenbaumchaussee
Tesdorpf-
MOORWEIDE
Mittelweg

Am Dammtor
U
Siemers

FERNSEHTURM
PARK "PLANTEN UN BLOMEN"
Radisson BLU
Trader Vic's
S. BAHN DAMMTOR
S. Bahn DAMMTOR

Karolinenstr.
Lager-Str.
Petersburger Str.
Str.
Marseiller Str.
ALTER BOTANISCHER GARTEN
Stephanspl.
Alster Neue Raben
Alsterglacis

Grabenstr.
Karolinen-str.

1

Tarantella
Baseler Hof
Esplanade
Alster-Hof

Marktstr.
Vor Holstenglacis
Messehallen
KLEINE WALLANLAGEN
Gorch Fock Wall
MUSEUM FÜR KOMMUNIKATION
Colonnaden Theater-
Matsumi

Feldstr.
Holstendamm
Dammtorwall
SIDE
Drehbahn
(m)eatery
Casse-Croûte
Große str.
Colonnaden
Fairmont Hotel
Vier Jahreszeiten
Haerlin
Jahreszeiten Grill
Doc Cheng's

Feldstr.
Holstenwall
Holstentor
Gorch
Fock
Wall
Karl Muck Platz
Valentins-kamp
Gänsemarkt
Neue ABC-Str.
Gänsemarkt
Post-

2
Glacischaussee
Pilatuspool
Kaiser-breitergang
Wilhelm
Str.
ABC
Fuhlentwiete
Bleichen
Marriott
Die Bank
Petit Délice
Große Bleichen str.

GROSSE WALLANLAGEN
Holstenwall
Hütten
Kurze Str.
Kohlhöfen
Axel Springer Platz
Hohe Bleichen
Große Bleichen
Bleicher Brücke
Reet
Neuer

NEUSTADT
Neanderstr.
Thielbek
Wexstr.
Trattorie Due da Enzo
Stadthausbrücke
Bleichen
Alster-Wall
Adolphs-Brücke
Börse

MUSEUM FÜR HAMBURGISCHE GESCHICHTE
Holstenwall
Hütten
Markus-str.
Neuer Steinweg
Alter Steinweg
Düsternstr.
Neuer Wall
Graskeller
Heiligengeist-brücke
Bleichen Wall
Alster
Sofitel
Alter Wall
Mönkedamm
Große Bur

Lindner Hotel Am Michel
Adina
Steigenberger
Bistro am Fleet
gourfleets
Große Burstah

Ludwig
Englische Planke
Erhard Str.
Heiligengeist-brücke
Rödingsmarkt
NIKOLAI KIRCHTUP
Ost West

3
Neumayer-str.
ST. MICHAELIS
Kraien-kamp
Martin Luther Str.
Steinwiete
Rödings-
Deichstr.
Holz-brücke
ALTSTADT

Böhmkenstr.
Venusberg

STINTFANG
Landungsbrücken
Ditmar Koel Str.
Fischmarkt
Admiralität-str.
Deichstr.
Kajen
Hohe Brücke
Bei dem Neuen Kra
Cremon

E
F
E
F

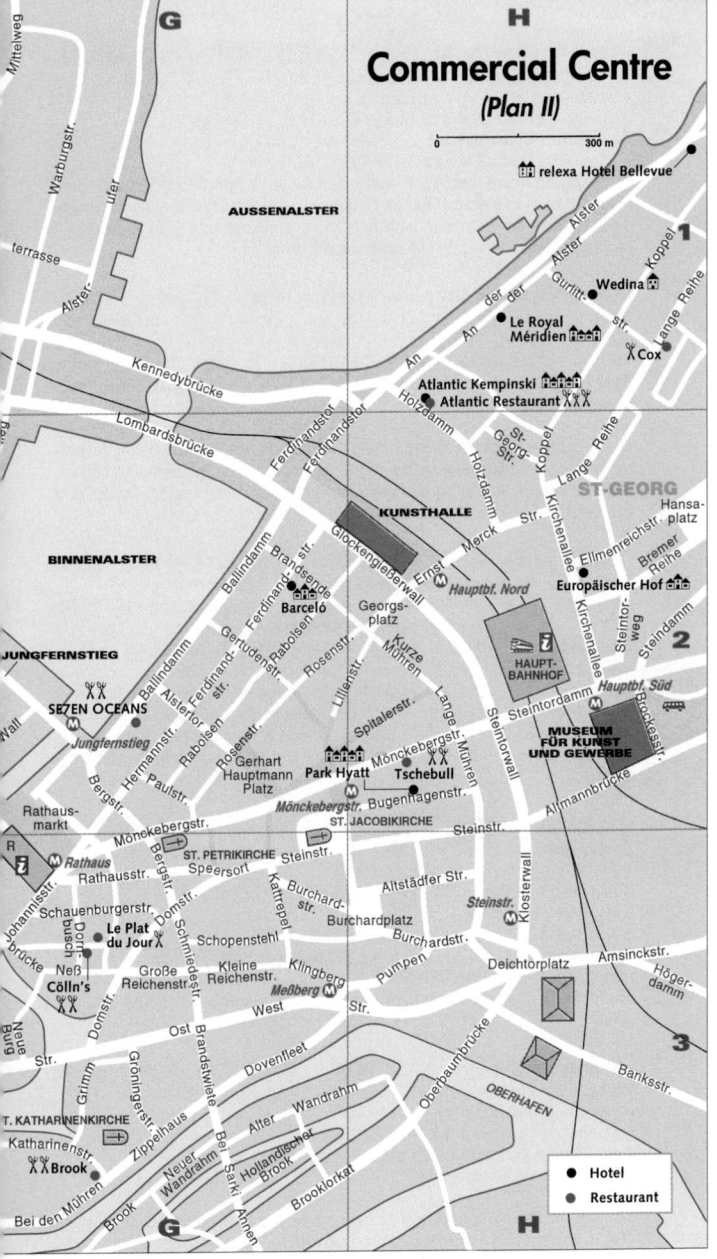

Commercial Centre
(Plan II)

0   300 m

🏨 relexa Hotel Bellevue

AUSSENALSTER

Wedina 🏨

Le Royal Méridien 🏨

✕ Cox

Atlantic Kempinski 🏨
Atlantic Restaurant ✕✕✕

ST-GEORG

Hansa-platz

KUNSTHALLE

Ellmenreichstr.

Bremer Reihe

Europäischer Hof 🏨

BINNENALSTER

Barceló

Georgs-platz

Hauptbf. Nord

HAUPT-BAHNHOF

JUNGFERNSTIEG

Hauptbf. Süd

SE7EN OCEANS

MUSEUM FÜR KUNST UND GEWERBE

Jungfernstieg

Gerhart Hauptmann Platz

Park Hyatt

Tschebull ✕✕

Rathaus-markt

ST. JACOBIKIRCHE

R

Rathaus

ST. PETRIKIRCHE

Le Plat du Jour ✕

Cölln's ✕✕

Steinstr.

Deichtörplatz

T. KATHARINENKIRCHE

Katharinenstr.

✕✕ Brook

OBERHAFEN

● Hotel
● Restaurant

375

Atlantic Kempinski ⟨ 🔥 ⟨ 🔲 ⬇ 🅰️ 🛜 🔁 🚗 🆚 🅐 🅐🅔 ⓘ

*An der Alster 72 ⊠ 20099 – ⓜ Hauptbf. Nord – ℰ (040) 2 88 80
– www.kempinski.com/hamburg* **H1**
245 rm – †199/589 € ††229/619 €, ⊊ 34 € – 30 suites
Rest *Atlantic Restaurant* – see restaurant listing
♦ Grand Luxury ♦ Traditional ♦ Modern ♦
Following extensive renovation work, the Atlantic Kempinski is now even more
magnificent than before. It has an elegant, classic lobby, timeless, sumptuously
decorated rooms (complete with fine ebony and state-of-the-art technology)
and stylish reception and conference facilities.

Fairmont Hotel Vier Jahreszeiten ⟨ 🔥 ⟨ 🅰️ 🛜 🚿 🚗

Neuer Jungfernstieg 9 ⊠ 20354 – ⓜ Jungfernstieg 🆚 🅐 🅐🅔 ⓘ
– ℰ (040) 3 49 40 – www.fairmont-hvj.de **F2**
156 rm – †260/360 € ††310/460 €, ⊊ 35 € – 20 suites
Rest *Haerlin* ❀❀ Rest *Jahreszeiten Grill* Rest *Doc Cheng's* – see res-
taurant listing
♦ Grand Luxury ♦ Traditional ♦ Classic ♦
The very epitome of the 'grand hotel'. The location, which could hardly be bet-
ter, is matched admirably by the high quality of its management and service.
Stylish furniture and antiques combine with fresh, contemporary fabrics and
the latest technology. The bar has genuine Rolls Royce seats.

Park Hyatt 🚿 🔥 🔊 🚿 🔲 ⬇ 🅰️ 🛜 🚿 🚗 🆚 🅐 🅐🅔 ⓘ

*Bugenhagenstr. 8 (im Levantehaus) ⊠ 20095 – ⓜ Mönckebergstr.
– ℰ (040) 33 32 12 34 – www.hamburg.park.hyatt.de* **H2**
283 rm – †180/280 € ††210/390 €, ⊊ 32 € – 21 suites
Rest *Apples* – ℰ (040) 33 32 17 11 – Menu 69 € – Carte 29/54 €
♦ Grand Luxury ♦ Chain hotel ♦ Modern ♦
This former Hanseatic League trading post welcomes guests on the first floor
where they can make themselves comfortable in the tasteful lounge. Combi-
ning high quality and modern elegance this is a luxury hotel without equal.
The Apples restaurant invites diners to watch the chef working in the show kitchen.

Le Royal Méridien 🔥 🔊 🚿 🔲 ⬇ 🅰️ 🛜 🚿 🚗 🆚 🅐 🅐🅔 ⓘ

*An der Alster 52 ⊠ 20099 – ⓜ Hauptbf. Nord – ℰ (040) 2 10 00
– www.leroyalmeridienhamburg.com* **H1**
284 rm – †159/419 € ††159/419 €, ⊊ 30 € – 12 suites
Rest – Carte 47/61 €
♦ Chain hotel ♦ Luxury ♦ Modern ♦
This modern hotel has an attractive, clear style extending from the brightly furnished rooms (with specially designed therapeutic beds) to the wellness area.
The restaurant on the ninth floor offers a fantastic view over the Außenalster
lake.

Grand Elysée 🚿 🔥 🔊 🚿 🔲 ⬇ 🅰️ 🛜 🚿 🚗 🆚 🅐 🅐🅔 ⓘ

*Rothenbaumchaussee 10 ⊠ 20148 – ⓜ Stephanspl. – ℰ (040) 41 41 20
– www.grand-elysee.com* **F1**
511 rm – †140/250 € ††160/270 €, ⊊ 20 € – 17 suites
Rest *Piazza Romana* – see restaurant listing
Rest *Brasserie Flum* – ℰ (040) 41 41 27 23 – Carte 24/49 €
♦ Luxury ♦ Classic ♦
The generous hotel lobby with its café greets you in boulevard style. It offers
classic, elegant rooms, quiet garden courtyard rooms, and south-facing rooms
on the Moorweiden park. Italian cuisine in the Piazza Romana, Brasserie and
oyster bar with seafood.

Sofitel Alter Wall

Alter Wall 40 ⊠ 20457 – **Ⓜ** Rödingsmarkt – ℰ (040) 36 95 00
– www.sofitel.com **F3**
241 rm – ♯150/345 € ♯♯175/345 €, ☲ 29 € – 10 suites
Rest – Carte 40/69 €

♦ Chain hotel ♦ Luxury ♦ Design ♦
The bright, modern style is both minimalist and luxurious. The Alsterfleet canal, which runs in front of the hotel, is best enjoyed from the terrace that has its own jetty. Lunch is served in the bistro and the sushi bar is open from 4pm.

Steigenberger

Heiligengeistbrücke 4 ⊠ 20459 – **Ⓜ** Rödingsmarkt – ℰ (040) 36 80 60
– www.hamburg.steigenberger.de **F3**
233 rm – ♯139/249 € ♯♯169/269 €, ☲ 28 € – 6 suites
Rest gourfleets ❀ **Rest Bistro am Fleet** – see restaurant listing

♦ Luxury ♦ Classic ♦
Right beside the Alster canal stands this well-run and elegant hotel in the shape of a ship. From the fitness area roof terrace there is a wonderful view over the city. International cuisine in the bistro.

SIDE

Drehbahn 49 ⊠ 20354 – **Ⓜ** Stephanspl. – ℰ (040) 30 99 90
– www.side-hamburg.de **F2**
178 rm – ♯170/325 € ♯♯170/325 €, ☲ 24 € – 10 suites
Rest (m)eatery – see restaurant listing

♦ Luxury ♦ Design ♦
Behind the natural stone and glass façade lays the impressive 30m high lobby, with a lighting design by Robert Wilson. The hotel has tasteful rooms designed in white and brown by Matteo Thun. The "(m)eatery" is a "high-end steakhouse" and bar.

Marriott

ABC-Str. 52 ⊠ 20354 – **Ⓜ** Gänsemarkt – ℰ (040) 3 50 50
– www.hamburgmarriott.com **F2**
278 rm – ♯179/239 € ♯♯189/239 €, ☲ 28 € – 3 suites
Rest – Carte 23/57 €

♦ Chain hotel ♦ Modern ♦ Contemporary ♦
This classic hotel is close to the Gänsemarkt. It has a sophisticated atmosphere in its lobby and guestrooms, and an attractive swimming, sauna and beauty area. Restaurant Speicher 52 has a friendly and modern presentation.

Radisson BLU

Marseiller Str. 2 ⊠ 20355 – **Ⓜ** Stephanspl. – ℰ (040) 3 50 20
– www.radissonblu.com/hotel-hamburg **F1**
556 rm – ♯119/399 € ♯♯119/399 €, ☲ 26 € – 9 suites
Rest Trader Vic's – see restaurant listing
Rest Filini – Carte 29/53 €

♦ Chain hotel ♦ Functional ♦
Business is made easy here with a conference centre adjoining the hotel and excellent railway connections. The 'Natural', 'Urban' and 'New York Mansion' themed rooms are interesting, and the view over the city unique. Filini serves international cuisine while Trader Vic's offers Polynesian fare.

Barceló

Ferdinandstr. 15 ⊠ 20095 – **Ⓜ** Hauptbf. Nord – ℰ (040) 2 26 36 20
– www.barcelohamburg.com **G2**
193 rm – ♯160/350 € ♯♯160/350 €, ☲ 22 € – 3 suites
Rest – Carte 20/36 €

♦ Chain hotel ♦ Modern ♦
This modern and thoroughly urban hotel enjoys a convenient location close to the River Alster and not far from the upmarket Jungfernstieg and Neuer Wall shopping streets. The lounge-style lobby takes you through to both the chic designer restaurant with its excellent tapas menus and the equally stylish, high-tech guestrooms.

The George   🛋 🐾 👤 rest, Ⓚ 🛜 🎿 🛋 VISA ⓪ AE

Barcastr. 3 ✉ *22087* – Ⓜ *Lohmühlenstr.* – ☎ *(040) 28 00 30 21 06*
– *www.thegeorge-hotel.de*   *Plan I* **D2**
125 rm – 📍145/175 € 📍📍165/195 €, ⌷ 16 € – 2 suites
Rest – *(closed Sunday)* Carte 24/74 €

◆ Townhouse ◆ Design ◆ Elegant ◆

Elegant, British-style meets young, modern design throughout this hotel. The library, bar and rooms are decorated in muted tones with feature pictures, fabrics and wallpapers. Highlights include the roof terrace with its view over Hamburg and the garden behind the hotel. The restaurant serves Mediterranean/Italian cuisine.

Mövenpick   ≤ 🛋 🛁 🐾 👤 Ⓚ 🕻 🎿 P 🛋 VISA ⓪ AE ⓪

Sternschanze 6 ✉ *20357* – Ⓜ *Sternschanze* – ☎ *(040) 3 34 41 10*
– *www.moevenpick-hotels.com/hamburg*   *Plan I* **C2**
226 rm – 📍129/169 € 📍📍149/189 €, ⌷ 23 € – 2 suites
Rest – Menu 33 € – Carte 24/51 €

◆ Chain hotel ◆ Historic ◆ Modern ◆

The guestrooms, in this former water tower from around 1900, have a modern style and technology. There is a very chic roof suite with a particularly impressive view over the city. International cuisine is served in this restaurant with a terrace facing the Schanzenpark.

Novotel Hamburg Alster   🐾 👤 Ⓚ 🛜 🎿 🛋 VISA ⓪ AE ⓪

Lübecker Str. 3 ✉ *22087* – Ⓜ *Lübecker Str.* – ☎ *(040) 39 19 00*
– *www.novotel.com*   *Plan I* **D2**
210 rm – 📍99/199 € 📍📍99/199 €, ⌷ 20 € – 2 suites
Rest – Carte 24/48 €

◆ Chain hotel ◆ Modern ◆

Business people in particular appreciate the functional, modern decor and good conference facilities, but at weekends they are joined by Hamburg citybreakers. From the nearby U-Bahn underground station it is just a short 2km hop into the city.

Europäischer Hof   🛁 ⓪ 🐾 🖻 Ⓚ rest, 🕻 🎿 🛋 VISA ⓪ AE ⓪

Kirchenallee 45 ✉ *20099* – Ⓜ *Hauptbahnhof Süd* – ☎ *(040) 24 82 48*
– *www.europaeischer-hof.de*   **H2**
275 rm ⌷ – 📍115/165 € 📍📍145/195 €
Rest *Paulaner's* – Carte 19/38 €

◆ Business ◆ Classic ◆

A large, dignified hall welcomes you to this hotel, which is located opposite the main station. Find the seven-storey 'Euro-therme' with a 150m waterslide over six floors. The atmosphere in Paulaner's is rustic and relaxed.

Lindner Hotel Am Michel   🛋 🛁 🐾 👤 rest, Ⓚ 🛜 🎿 🛋

Neanderstr. 20 ✉ *20459* – Ⓜ *St. Pauli*   VISA ⓪ AE ⓪
– ☎ *(040) 3 07 06 70* – *www.lindner.de*   **E3**
259 rm – 📍129/509 € 📍📍169/529 €, ⌷ 22 € – 8 suites
Rest – *(closed Sunday)* Menu 30 € – Carte 24/36 €

◆ Business ◆ Chain hotel ◆ Contemporary ◆

This brick building is in a relatively quiet and central location, close to the 'Michel'. It offers modern, well-appointed rooms in warm colours. There is a view over the city from the sauna area. The restaurant Sonnin serves international cuisine.

Adina   🛁 🐾 🖻 👤 Ⓚ 🛜 🎿 🛋 VISA ⓪ AE ⓪

Neuer Steinweg 26 ✉ *20549* – Ⓜ *St. Pauli* – ☎ *(040) 2 26 35 00*
– *www.adina.eu*   **E3**
128 rm – 📍139/259 € 📍📍139/259 €, ⌷ 19 € – 100 suites
Rest – *(dinner only)* Menu 27 € – Carte 23/54 €

◆ Business ◆ Contemporary ◆ Modern ◆

A quality business hotel. The apartment-style rooms are spacious and distinctive and have their own kitchenettes. The decor is bright and modern, and the technology is state-of-the-art. Close to Hamburg's landmark St Michaelis Church and the Reeperbahn.

Eilenau without rest   🛖 🛜 VISA ⦿ AE

Eilenau 36 ⊠ 22089 – Ⓜ Wartenau – ℰ (040) 2 36 01 30
– www.eilenau.de   *Plan I* **D2**
17 rm � – †126/160 € ††165/190 € – 5 suites

♦ Townhouse ♦ Personalised ♦ Elegant ♦

This establishment consists of two houses built in 1890, which have now been sumptuously restored. It has an atmosphere that would be difficult to find outside a historic townhouse. The antiques, stuccowork and old parquet flooring are beautifully set off by more modern elements. In summer, breakfast is served in the small, quiet garden.

25hours Hafen City   🛖 & 🅰 🛜 🚗 VISA ⦿ AE

Überseeallee 5 ⊠ 20457 – ℰ (040) 2 57 77 70 – www.25hours-hotels.com
170 rm – †105/205 € ††105/205 €, � 16 €   *Plan I* **C3**
Rest Heimat – ℰ (040) 2 57 77 78 40 – Carte 23/53 €

♦ Townhouse ♦ Cosy ♦

One thing is sure, for individuality and originality you can't beat this Hamburg hotel. Bright, new design meets warm wood and stories of the sea. Old records cover the walls in the lounge-style Vinyl Room and guests are given a sailor's kit bag for their personal belongings in the rooftop sauna. It's no surprise in a hotel full of seafaring references to find that all the rooms have a cabin feel.

relexa Hotel Bellevue   🛜 🅰 🅿 🚗 VISA ⦿ AE ⓪

An der Alster 14 (access via Koppel) ⊠ 20099 – Ⓜ Hauptbf. Nord
– ℰ (040) 28 44 40 – www.relexa-hotels.de   **H1**
83 rm ⊻ – †81/161 € ††112/202 € – 2 suites
Rest – Menu 23 € – Carte 25/37 €

♦ Villa ♦ Personalised ♦

This classic townhouse on the Alster, and two further buildings, accommodate cosy guestrooms and small, but modern, single rooms. There is also a pleasant cellar bar. During the day diners are served in the restaurant with a view of the Alster lake; and in the evening, in the cosy basement maritime restaurant.

Baseler Hof   🛖 🛜 🅰 VISA ⦿ AE ⓪

Esplanade 11 ⊠ 20354 – Ⓜ Stephansplatz – ℰ (040) 35 90 60
– www.baselerhof.de   **F1**
168 rm ⊻ – †89/135 € ††125/165 € – 5 suites
Rest Kleinhuis – ℰ (040) 35 33 99 – Menu 25/55 € – Carte 24/45 €

♦ Traditional ♦ Functional ♦

A great hotel located between the Outer Alster Lake and Botanical Gardens. A number of less grand rooms are available; those in the annexe are the quietest. Good wine selection in the Kleinhuis restaurant. The annual vintage car rally draws many aficionados.

Suite Novotel Hamburg City without rest   ≼ & 🅰 🛜 🚗

Lübeckertordamm 2 ⊠ 20099 – Ⓜ Lohmühlenstr.   VISA ⦿ AE ⓪
– ℰ (040) 27 14 00 – www.suitenovotel.com   *Plan I* **D2**
186 rm – †94/144 € ††94/144 €, ⊻ 12 €

♦ Business ♦ Functional ♦

The no-nonsense guestrooms in this hotel are quite spacious and functional. The internet and telephone can be used at no extra charge. Snacks are available to take away in the lobby.

Wedina without rest (with guesthouses)   🚲 🛜 🚗 VISA ⦿ AE ⓪

Gurlittstr. 23 ⊠ 20099 – Ⓜ Hauptbf. Nord – ℰ (040) 2 80 89 00
– www.hotelwedina.de
– Closed 22-27 December   **H1**
59 rm – †105/195 € ††125/225 €, ⊻ 18 € – 1 suite

♦ Family ♦ Cosy ♦

This establishment has Red, Blue, Green and Yellow Houses whose decors range from the sunny, fresh and Mediterranean through to the minimalist. Bedrooms have been designed on the theme of literary works. Try breakfast in the garden and explore the city on a bike rented from the hotel.

GERMANY - HAMBURG

Alster-Hof without rest 🛜 VISA ☻ AE ①

Esplanade 12 ⊠ 20354 – ⓜ *Stephansplatz*
– 𝒞 (040) 35 00 70
– www.alster-hof.de
– Closed 23 December-2 January   **F1**
111 rm �] – ✝85/105 € ✝✝125/165 € – 3 suites
♦ Traditional ♦ Functional ♦
This well cared for hotel is in the city centre, near to the Alster. It has functional guestrooms decorated in homely colours. These include sometimes rather small single rooms.

Am Dammtor without rest 🛜 🚗 VISA ☻ AE

Schlüterstr. 2 ⊠ 20146 – ⓜ *Stephanspl. – 𝒞 (040) 4 50 05 70*
– www.hotel-am-dammtor.de
– Closed 23-27 December   **F1**
40 rm – ✝89/149 € ✝✝99/189 €, ⊡ 12 €
♦ Townhouse ♦ Stylish ♦
Despite its fairly plain exterior, this townhouse built in 1897 hides a stylish and comfortable hotel with lots of atmosphere. Every room is different: one in bright red, another with a wooden floor, but all tastefully decorated and many with wonderful stucco ornamentation. Good central location.

XXXX **Haerlin** – Fairmont Hotel Vier Jahreszeiten ≼ ♿ AC VISA ☻ AE ①
🕸🕸

Neuer Jungfernstieg 9 ⊠ 20354 – ⓜ *Jungfernstieg*
– 𝒞 (040) 34 94 33 10
– www.fairmont-hvj.de
– Closed 2 weeks after Easter, 4 weeks June-July, 2 weeks October and Sunday-Monday   **F2**
Rest – *(dinner only)* Menu 98/144 € ⅋
♦ French classic ♦ Luxury ♦
Even though it is hard to tear your eyes away from the view of the Inner Alster Lake, there is nothing in this sumptuous restaurant to beat the sight – or the taste – of Christoph Rüffer's creative take on classic cuisine.
➜ Steinbuttschnitte mit warmem Gemüsesalat, gerösteter Hummer und Miso-Tamarinden-Hollandaise. Gänseleberkoralle mit Pink Grapefruit, Kaisergranat und Holunderblütenjoghurt. Mieral Wachtel mit gepfefferter Ananas, Ingwerjus und Süßkartoffel.

XXX **Jahreszeiten Grill** – Fairmont Hotel Vier Jahreszeiten 🍴 ♿ AC
Neuer Jungfernstieg 9 ⊠ 20354 – ⓜ *Jungfernstieg* VISA ☻ AE ①
– 𝒞 (040) 34 94 33 12
– www.fairmont-hvj.de   **F2**
Rest – Menu 69 € – Carte 34/103 €
♦ French classic ♦ Elegant ♦
The very epitome of elegance, this restaurant pays homage to the Art Deco style of the 1920s. Its original period pieces provide an upmarket backdrop for discerning diners.

XXX **Atlantic Restaurant** – Hotel Atlantic Kempinski ≼ 🍴
An der Alster 72 ⊠ 20099 – ⓜ *Hauptbf. Nord* VISA ☻ AE ①
– 𝒞 (040) 2 88 80
– www.kempinski.com/hamburg
– Closed Sunday   **H1**
Rest – Menu 29 € (lunch)/116 € – Carte 53/90 €
♦ Classic ♦ Elegant ♦
The elegant restaurant in this traditional Hamburg hotel doubles up as a meeting place for significant parts of Hamburg society. Thomas Wilken and his team serve classic cuisine of the very highest standard.

XXX
ꖥ **gourfleets** – Hotel Steigenberger   🛜 ᕫ 🅰🅺 𝗩𝗜𝗦𝗔 ⓿ 🅰🅴 ⓞ

Heiligengeistbrücke 4 ✉ *20459* – Ⓜ *Rödingsmarkt* – 𝒞 *(040) 36 80 60*
– *www.restaurant-fleets.de*
– *Closed 27 December-13 January, 15 July-11 August, Sunday-Monday and*
Bank Holidays   **F3**
Rest – Menu 49 € (lunch)/116 € – Carte 66/98 €
◆ Modern ◆ Elegant ◆ Fashionable ◆

In the Steigenberger's new little gourmet restaurant in the centre of the city, talented chef André Stolle produces his modern northern-style cuisine. It is characterised by its range of textures, temperatures and fine contrasts. The interior is modern and minimalist and there is an attractive terrace overlooking the canal. Smaller lunchtime menu.

➜ Arktischer Kaisergranat, Goldkiwi & Austern-Crème. Fläminger Reh - 60 Stunden geschmortes Bugblatt - gelierter Rhabarbersaft, Amaranth & Gelbsenf. Texturen vom Sanddorn - Eis & Jelly & Baiser.

XX
ꖥ **SE7EN OCEANS**   ⟨ ᕫ 🅰🅺 𝗩𝗜𝗦𝗔 ⓿ 🅰🅴

Ballindamm 40 (2nd floor) (Europa-Passage) ✉ *20095* – Ⓜ *Jungfernstieg*
– 𝒞 *(040) 32 50 79 44* – *www.se7en-oceans.de*
– *Closed 20 January-3 February, 11 August-1 September and Sunday-Tuesday*
Rest – Menu 37 € (lunch)/89 € – Carte 49/71 €   **G2**
◆ Modern ◆ Classic ◆

If you fancy a good meal after your shopping trip, this modern restaurant in the Europa-Passage shopping centre with its great view over the River Alster is the ideal solution. The refined, classic yet contemporary cuisine is thanks to chef Sebastian Andrée and his team.

➜ Kaviar Ei mit Tatar vom Stör und Crème Fraîche. Gebratene Bluttaube mit Petersilienwurzel und Pfifferlingen. Variation von Himbeeren und weißer Schokolade.

XX
🙂 **Tschebull**   ⟡ 𝗩𝗜𝗦𝗔 ⓿ 🅰🅴

Mönckebergstr. 7 (1st floor) (at Levantehaus) ✉ *20095*
– Ⓜ *Mönchebergstr.* – 𝒞 *(040) 32 96 47 96* – *www.tschebull.de*
– *Closed Sunday and Bank Holidays*   **H2**
Rest – Menu 26 € (lunch)/89 € (dinner) – Carte 30/59 €
◆ Austrian ◆ Cosy ◆

In the centre of this exclusive shopping arcade sits a little piece of Austria, courtesy of Carinthian chef Alexander Tschebull. As you would expect, the Austrian classics, such as Tafelspitz (Viennese-style boiled beef) and Fiaker (beef) goulash are excellent, as are the more modern dishes. These include skrei cod with potato and caper champ, radish and pearl onions.

XX
🙂 **Brook**   🛏 🅰🅴

Bei den Mühren 91 ✉ *20457* – Ⓜ *Meßberg* – 𝒞 *(040) 37 50 31 28*
– *www.restaurant-brook.de*
– *Closed Sunday*   **G3**
Rest – Carte 29/49 €
◆ International ◆ Fashionable ◆

The setting is modern and light, the cuisine fresh and seasonal. Classics such as rump steak and braised veal cheek and the very reasonably priced lunchtime menu are always popular. To cap it all, the view of the Speicherstadt warehouses provide a feast for the eyes – especially at night.

XX
Doc Cheng's – Fairmont Hotel Vier Jahreszeiten   ᕫ 🅰🅺

Neuer Jungfernstieg 9 ✉ *20354* – Ⓜ *Jungfernstieg*   𝗩𝗜𝗦𝗔 ⓿ 🅰🅴 ⓞ
– 𝒞 *(040) 3 49 43 33* – *www.fairmont-hvj.de*
– *Closed Sunday*   **F2**
Rest – *(dinner only)* Menu 53/79 € – Carte 34/61 €
◆ Asian ◆ Individual ◆

The Far East inspires both the design and cuisine of this restaurant. Euro-Asian cuisine is served here.

XX **Cölln's** 🖼️ ⇄ 𝗩𝗜𝗦𝗔 ⓿ 𝗔𝗘

Brodschrangen 1 ⊠ 20457 – Ⓜ Rathaus – ℰ (040) 36 41 53
– www.coellns-restaurant.de
– Closed Sunday and Bank Holidays **G3**
Rest – *(booking advisable)* Menu 40 € – Carte 38/64 €
♦ French classic ♦ Cosy ♦

Fish and oysters have been the order of the day here since 1760. Once they were sold over the shop counter, now they appear on the menu alongside other seafood specialities including lobster and caviar. The 13 charming small dining alcoves provide a historical atmosphere.

XX **Piazza Romana** – Hotel Grand Elysée 🔥 𝗔𝗖 𝗩𝗜𝗦𝗔 ⓿ 𝗔𝗘 ⓪

Rothenbaumchaussee 10 ⊠ 20148 – Ⓜ Stephanspl. – ℰ (040) 41 41 27 34
– www.grand-elysee.com **F1**
Rest – Carte 33/62 €
♦ Italian ♦ Classic ♦

If you fancy carpaccio di vitello, a plate of linguine or tiramisu, then the Italian cuisine on offer at this restaurant is for you.

XX **Trader Vic's** – Hotel Radisson BLU ⟨ 🔥 𝗔𝗖 𝗩𝗜𝗦𝗔 ⓿ 𝗔𝗘 ⓪

Marseiller Str. 2 ⊠ 20355 – Ⓜ Stephanspl. – ℰ (040) 3 50 20
– www.radissonblu.de/hotel-hamburg – Closed Sunday **F1**
Rest – *(dinner only)* Carte 31/62 €
♦ Polynesian ♦ Individual ♦

Take a culinary journey through the tastes and textures of Polynesian cuisine in this elegant and exotic setting – a breath of the South Seas in central Hamburg.

X **Tarantella** 🔥 🔥 ⇄ 𝗩𝗜𝗦𝗔 ⓿ 𝗔𝗘

Stephansplatz 10 (at Casino Esplanade) ⊠ 20354 – Ⓜ Stephanspl.
– ℰ (040) 65 06 77 90 – www.tarantella.cc **F1**
Rest – Carte 35/126 € 🍴
♦ International ♦ Fashionable ♦

Location, location, location... Close to the State Opera, the clean lines of this restaurant give the historical buildings of the casino a modern feel. Bistro area and leafy terrace. The house speciality is dry cured fish.

X **Die Bank** 🔥 𝗩𝗜𝗦𝗔 ⓿ 𝗔𝗘

Hohe Bleichen 17 ⊠ 20354 – Ⓜ Gänsemarkt – ℰ (040) 2 38 00 30
– www.diebank-brasserie.de
– Closed Sunday and Bank Holidays **F2**
Rest – Menu 53 € (dinner)/98 € – Carte 49/67 €
♦ International ♦ Brasserie ♦ Trendy ♦

This brasserie and bar are one of the city's hotspots. The banking hall on the first-floor of this former bank, built in 1897, is an impressive feature of this fashionable venue.

X **CARLS** 🔥 🔥 𝗔𝗖 ⇄ 𝗩𝗜𝗦𝗔 ⓿ 𝗔𝗘

Am Kaiserkai 69 ⊠ 20457 – Ⓜ Baumwall – ℰ (040) 3 00 32 24 00
– www.carls-brasserie.de *Plan I* **C3**
Rest – Menu 39 € (dinner) – Carte 28/73 €
♦ French classic ♦ Brasserie ♦

This elegant brasserie is at the New Elbe Philharmonic Hall. It serves up French cuisine with a North German slant alongside great views of the port. Savoury tarts and nibbles in the bistro; spices and other gourmet treats in the delicatessen.

X **La Mirabelle** 𝗩𝗜𝗦𝗔 ⓿ 𝗔𝗘

Bundesstr. 15 ⊠ 20146 – Ⓜ Hallerstr. – ℰ (040) 4 10 75 85
– www.la-mirabelle-hamburg.de
– Closed 1-6 January, 8-21 July, 7-13 October, Sunday and Bank Holidays
Rest – *(dinner only)* Menu 45/59 € – Carte 51/76 € *Plan I* **C2**
♦ French classic ♦ Cosy ♦

What else would a restaurateur with an evocative name like Pierre Moissonnier offer his guests if not impressions of his French home? When he is not at his stove, you will find him front of house.

✗ VLET

Sandtorkai 23 (1st Floor of the Markthalle) ✉ *20457* – Ⓜ *Baumwall*
– ℰ (040) 3 34 75 37 50 – www.vlet.de
– Closed Saturday lunch and Sunday   *Plan I* **C3**
Rest – Menu 53/67 € (dinner) – Carte 47/58 €
♦ Modern ♦ Trendy ♦
The deliberate warehouse feel, typical of Hamburg's Speicherstadt area, makes an ideal venue for fashionable cuisine. It is best to park in the Contipark and cross the Kibbelstegbrücke bridge to reach the restaurant.

✗ Fischmarkt

Ditmar-Koel-Str. 1 ✉ *20459* – Ⓜ *Landungsbrücken* – ℰ *(040) 36 38 09*
– www.restaurant-fischmarkt.de
– Closed Sunday   **E3**
Rest – *(booking advisable)* Menu 32/49 € – Carte 29/56 €
♦ Fish and seafood ♦ Bistro ♦
Here in the Schaarmarkt, close to the church of St Michaelis and the port, there is always a good selection of fish depending on what the season and the day's catch have to offer. This bistro is on two levels and has an open kitchen and enticing fish display.

✗ Le Plat du Jour

Dornbusch 4 ✉ *20095* – Ⓜ *Rathaus* – ℰ *(040) 32 14 14*
– www.leplatdujour.de   **G3**
Rest – *(booking advisable)* Carte 26/42 €
♦ French classic ♦ Bistro ♦
Lively, attractive and authentic – just what you would expect from a French bistro. Black and white photos adorn the walls and the many regulars chat away happily as they tuck into fresh, simple food such as stuffed chicken drumsticks at the tightly packed tables.

✗ Casse-Croûte

Büschstr. 2 ✉ *20354* – Ⓜ *Gänsemarkt* – ℰ *(040) 34 33 73*
– www.cassecroute.de
– Closed during Christmas, Sunday lunch and Bank Holidays lunch
Rest – *(booking advisable)* Menu 33 € – Carte 28/55 €   **F2**
♦ French classic ♦ Bistro ♦
Casse-Croûte combines French savoir vivre with a certain Hamburg touch to create a bustling yet pleasantly relaxed feel in a typical bistro setting. Try the 'Northern bouillabaisse', one of the classic dishes from Christian Möllers' repertoire or alternatively the Wiener Schnitzel or whole sole, which also feature on the menu.

✗ Petit Délice

Große Bleichen 21 ✉ *20354* – Ⓜ *Jungfernstieg* – ℰ *(040) 34 34 70*
– Closed Sunday and Bank Holidays   **F2**
Rest – *(booking advisable)* Menu 25 € (lunch)/98 € – Carte 34/91 €
Rest *Traiteur* – ℰ *(040) 33 44 19 80* – Carte 21/37 €
♦ French classic ♦ Friendly ♦
This small, bright restaurant is located in a passage in a shopping centre. It specialises in fresh, French dishes. Traiteur offers a bistro ambiance and good traditional and international food as well coffee and cakes.

✗ Cox

Lange Reihe 68 ✉ *20099* – Ⓜ *Hauptbf. Nord* – ℰ *(040) 24 94 22*
– www.restaurant-cox.de
– Closed Saturday lunch, Sunday lunch and Bank Holidays lunch
Rest – Carte 32/46 €   **H1**
♦ International ♦ Bistro ♦
The mood at Cox is more urban than chic and elegant, with a lively yet casual feel – a bistro in the best sense of the word. The cuisine is simple but good, featuring dishes such as delicious free-range meatballs and a less expensive menu at lunchtimes.

GERMANY - HAMBURG

Matsumi
🛜 **VISA** ⬤⬤ **AE**

Colonnaden 96 (1st floor) ✉ *20354* – ⓜ *Stephansplatz* – ☏ *(040) 34 31 25*
– www.matsumi.de
– Closed Christmas-early January, 2 weeks end July-early August, Sunday-Monday and Bank Holidays lunch   **F2**
Rest – Menu 45/62 € – Carte 21/77 €

✦ **Japanese** ✦ **Minimalist** ✦

Enjoy authentic Japanese cuisine just a stone's throw from the State Opera and the Alster. Food is served at tables, in the sushi bar or in the tatami room (groups only).

(m)eatery – Hotel SIDE
🅿 **AC** **VISA** ⬤⬤ **AE** ⓞ

Drehbahn 49 ✉ *20354* – ⓜ *Stephanspl.* – ☏ *(040) 30 99 90*
– www.meatery.de – Closed Saturday-Sunday and Bank Holidays
Rest – *(dinner only)* Carte 33/115 €   **F2**

✦ **International** ✦ **Trendy** ✦

The strong colours may shock some as the furniture and walls in this fashionable restaurant come in various shades of bright green. Steakhouse with glass-fronted meat maturing cabinet.

Bistro am Fleet – Hotel Steigenberger
🛜 🅿 **AC** **VISA** ⬤⬤ **AE** ⓞ

Heiligengeistbrücke 4 ✉ *20459* – ⓜ *Rödingsmarkt* – ☏ *(040) 36 80 60*
– www.hamburg.steigenberger.de   **F3**
Rest – Carte 27/62 €

✦ **International** ✦ **Bistro** ✦

The cool feel of this restaurant is due to the conservatory, which makes the transition from inside to outside almost seamless. A range of international dishes are on offer.

Trattoria Due da Enzo
🛜 **VISA** ⬤⬤

Großneumarkt 2 ✉ *20038* – ⓜ *Jungfernstieg* – ☏ *(040) 35 71 51 40*
– www.trattoria-enzo.de – Closed Sunday   **E3**
Rest – Carte 38/49 €

✦ **Italian** ✦ **Friendly** ✦

This friendly little trattoria offers charming uncomplicated service and good Italian food in the heart of Hamburg. In summer you can watch the comings and goings from the terrace. The main restaurant is located just 100m further down the street.

NORTH OF THE CENTRE
Plan I

Dorint
 🛜 Ⓕ 🐾 🅿 **AC** 🛜 🏊 🚗 **VISA** ⬤⬤ **AE**

Martinistr. 72 ✉ *20251* – ⓜ *Osterstr.* – ☏ *(040) 5 70 15 00*
– www.dorint.com/hamburg   **B1**
195 rm – ♦119/149 € ♦♦139/169 €, ⬚ 18 € – 14 suites
Rest *EPPO* – Menu 39/59 € – Carte 36/57 €

✦ **Business** ✦ **Functional** ✦

Whether they are travelling for business, pleasure or a conference, guests appreciate the Dorint. Its well-equipped rooms and clean, modern style gives it a light and airy feel throughout. For fitness enthusiasts, the hotel has its own gym, as well as attractive running routes nearby.

Lindner Park-Hotel Hagenbeck
 🛜 Ⓕ 🐾 🅿 **AC** 🛜 🏊 🚗

Hagenbeckstr. 150 ✉ *22527*
VISA ⬤⬤ **AE** ⓞ
– ⓜ Hagenbecks Tierpark – ☏ (040) 8 00 80 81 00
– www.lindner.de/de/parkhotel_hagenbeck_hamburg   **B1**
158 rm – ♦119/399 € ♦♦144/424 €, ⬚ 17 € – 2 suites
Rest – Carte 35/54 €

✦ **Business** ✦ **Holiday hotel** ✦ **Retro** ✦

Tasteful colonial-style is the main theme of this establishment. With selected authentic details, the themed floors reflect the exoticness of Africa and Asia. The colonial atmosphere of the hotel continues in the restaurant. Pretty terrace.

GERMANY - HAMBURG

Mittelweg without rest
Mittelweg 59 ⊠ 20149 – ⓜ Klosterstern – 𝒞 (040) 4 14 10 10
– www.hotel-mittelweg-hamburg.de **C1**
30 rm ⬝ – †100/125 € ††135/168 €
♦ Villa ♦ Cosy ♦
This 1890 villa is full of turn of the century charm, from the staircase, through to the stucco ceilings in the stylish breakfast room, and in the carefully selected combinations of colours, motifs and classic furniture in the bedrooms. Quiet, secluded garden.

Nippon without rest
Hofweg 75 ⊠ 22085 – 𝒞 (040) 2 27 11 40 – www.nipponhotel.de
– Closed Christmas-1 January **D1**
42 rm – †104/127 € ††122/158 €, ⬝ 15 €
♦ Townhouse ♦ Minimalist ♦
With a truly Far Eastern appearance, the rooms are furnished in a simple style with tatami floors, shoji walls and futons. The Wa-Yo restaurant with sushi bar offers classic Japanese cuisine and premium sake.

Piment (Wahabi Nouri)
Lehmweg 29 ⊠ 20251 – ⓜ Eppendorfer Baum – 𝒞 (040) 42 93 77 88
– www.restaurant-piment.de
– closed 4-15 March, end June-mid July and Sunday **C1**
Rest – (dinner only) (booking advisable) Menu 75/105 € – Carte 70/89 €
♦ Creative ♦ Friendly ♦
Those unfamiliar with Wahabi Nouri's cooking style might imagine something more exotic. Yet the influences of this chef's native Morocco play a subtle, measured role in his creations. They are sensitively combined with modern accents revealing his classic grounding. The food is accompanied with some excellent wine recommendations.
➔ Eismeerforelle in Kaffee-Aromen mit eingelegter Gurke und Kardamom-Panacotta. Gemüse Couscous mit Langustino und Arganöl-Nage. B´stilla von der Taube mit Schwarzen Oliven, Essig-Jus und Rhabarber.

Küchenwerkstatt (Gerald Zogbaum)
Hans-Henny-Jahnn-Weg 1 (entrance Hofweg) ⊠ 22085
– 𝒞 (040) 22 92 75 88 – www.kuechenwerkstatt-hamburg.de
– Closed 1-16 January, 1 week July, 1 week October and Sunday-Tuesday lunch, Saturday lunch **D1**
Rest – Menu 32 € (lunch)/125 €
♦ Creative ♦ Trendy ♦
It is possible to enjoy excellent food at reasonable prices – at least by Hamburg standards – as Gerald Zogbaum proves with his simple yet creative cuisine. Shorter version of the evening à la carte menu and daily specials at lunchtimes. The setting is a historic ferry house on the Osterbek Canal.
➔ Erdknollen: Zwiebel / Kartoffel / Trüffel. Kalb / Nelkenschwindling, Pom-Pom blanc & Champignon. Skrei / warme Misocreme / Sud von grünem Tee und Kombu.

Ono by Steffen Henssler
Lehmweg 17 ⊠ 20251 – ⓜ Hoheluftbr. – 𝒞 (040) 88 17 18 42
– www.onobysh.de
– Closed Christmas-7 January and Sunday **C1**
Rest – (booking advisable) Carte 23/46 €
♦ Asian ♦ Minimalist ♦
A lively and relaxed bistro serving East Asian food that is both good quality and affordable. Watch sushi being prepared in the show kitchen by genuine East Asian chefs. The reasonably priced lunch menu includes two courses and water. Make sure you try the pike-perch teriyaki.

Jellyfish
VISA *◎◎*

Weidenallee 12 ⊠ 20357 – Ⓜ Christkirche – ℰ (040) 4 10 54 14
– www.jellyfish-restaurant.de
– Closed 24 December-3 January and Monday
B2
Rest – Menu 79 € – Carte 51/119 €
♦ Fish and seafood ♦ Minimalist ♦

If you are looking for an alternative to Hamburg's long established fish restaurants, try Jellyfish. It has a cool, minimalist feel and simple yet ambitious cuisine. The delicious dishes chalked up on the blackboard are made using nothing but the highest quality ingredients.

Butcher's American Steakhouse
VISA *◎◎* *AE*

Milchstr. 19 ⊠ 20148 – ℰ (040) 44 60 82 – www.butchers-steakhouse.de
– Closed Saturday lunch, Sunday lunch and Bank Holidays lunch
Rest – Carte 55/100 €
C2
♦ International ♦ Trendy ♦

Here you can taste fine Nebraska beef that the chef presents to the table. A cosy restaurant with a decor dominated by dark wood and warm colours.

Cornelia Poletto
VISA *◎◎* *AE*

Eppendorfer Landstr. 80 ⊠ 20251 – Ⓜ Kellenhusenstr.
– ℰ (040) 4 80 21 59 – www.cornelia-poletto.de
– Closed 1 week January, Sunday and Bank Holidays
C1
Rest – (booking advisable) Carte 34/70 €
♦ Italian ♦ Friendly ♦ Cosy ♦

Cornelia Poletto (who Germans will know from the television if not from her previous restaurant) serves Italian specialities in the restaurant and sells them (spices, wine, pasta, cheese) in the shop. Booked out almost daily.

Poletto Winebar
🛏 🚭

Eppendorfer Weg 287 ⊠ 20251 – Ⓜ Eppendorfer Baum
– ℰ (040) 38 64 47 00 – www.poletto.de
C1
Rest – (bookings advisable at dinner) Menu 25 € (lunch)/43 €
– Carte 29/64 € ♨
♦ Italian ♦ Wine bar ♦

This lively wine bar is definitely one of the places to be in Eppendorf. The interior is simple but comfortable with a wine themed decor. The food is flavoursome and Italian in style, including classics such as vitello tonnato and tiramisu served alongside excellent cold meats straight from the Berkel meat slicer. Great wine selection in both the restaurant and the adjacent wine shop.

Trific
🛏 🚭

Eppendorfer Weg 170 ⊠ 20253 – Ⓜ Hoheluftbrücke – ℰ (040) 21 99 69 27
– www.trific.de – Closed Sunday-Monday
B1
Rest – (dinner only) (booking advisable) Menu 30 € – Carte 28/44 €
♦ Regional/country ♦ Fashionable ♦ Neighbourhood ♦

A light, bright and modern dining room with high ceilings run by 'food stylist' Oliver Trific in the kitchen and his charming wife Tanya in charge of front of house. Seasonal dishes ranging from fresh fish to breaded fried chicken feature on the menu.

HARBOUR – ALTONA
Plan III

Empire Riverside Hotel
⟨ 🏦 ᶜ 🖵 📞 🗳 🚗 *VISA* *◎◎* *AE*

Bernhard-Nocht-Str. 97 (via Davidstraße) ⊠ 20359 – Ⓜ Reeperbahn
– ℰ (040) 31 11 90 – www.empire-riverside.de
J1
327 rm – †129/349 € ††129/349 €, ☲ 20 €
Rest *Waterkant* – ℰ (040) 31 11 97 04 80 (dinner only) Carte 38/68 €
♦ Business ♦ Conference hotel ♦ Design ♦

Famous architect David Chipperfield designed this contemporary hotel close to the St Pauli pontoon bridges. Rooms have a view of either the river or the city as does "20", the panoramic bar on the 20th floor. This wharf-side restaurant offers international cuisine in a simple, contemporary setting.

East

Simon-von-Utrecht-Str. 31 ✉ 20359 – Ⓜ St. Pauli – ✆ (040) 30 99 30 – www.east-hamburg.de Plan I **B2**

128 rm – †160/200 € ††180/215 €, ☕ 20 € – 3 suites

Rest *East* – see restaurant listing

♦ Business ♦ Design ♦

The design in this former iron foundry is resolutely modern and trendy. It runs from the guestrooms through to the bar-lounge and the leisure and beauty area with its professionally staffed fitness club.

Boston

Missundestr. 2 ✉ 22769 – Ⓜ Feldstr. – ✆ (040) 5 89 66 67 00 – www.boston-hamburg.de **J1**

46 rm – †140/220 € ††160/240 €, ☕ 18 €

Rest – Menu 38 € – Carte 34/50 €

♦ Business ♦ Design ♦ Modern ♦

A modern business hotel with tasteful and straightforward fittings. Rooms are available in the categories Design and Business – the latter with a kitchenette. This trendy restaurant has an adjoining lounge and bar.

My Place without rest

Lippmannstr. 5 ✉ 22769 – Ⓜ Feldstr. – ✆ (040) 28 57 18 74 – www.myplace-hamburg.de **J1**

18 rm – †59/69 € ††80/94 €, ☕ 8 € – 5 suites

♦ Townhouse ♦ Personalised ♦ Contemporary ♦

Close to the trendy Schanze district the dedicated hostess runs a small hotel with individually styled, charming modern rooms named after districts of Hamburg.

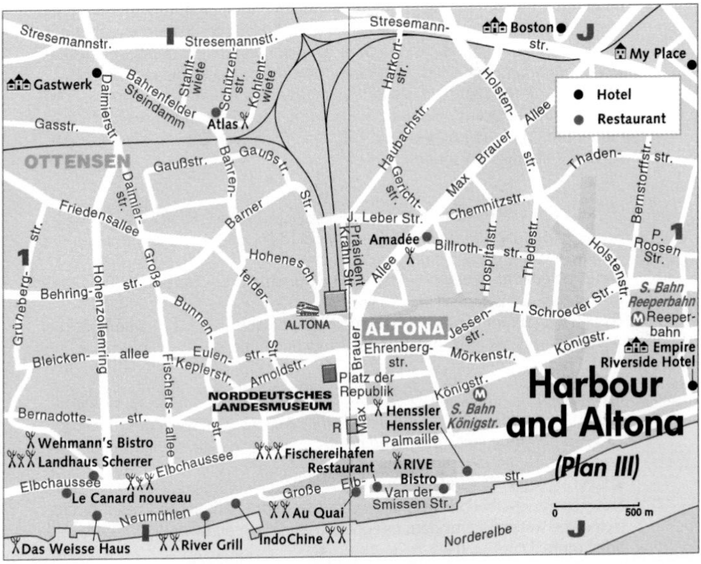
Harbour and Altona
(Plan III)
Hotel
Restaurant
Boston
My Place
Gastwerk
Atlas
Amadée
Empire Riverside Hotel
Henssler Henssler
Wehmann's Bistro
Landhaus Scherrer
Le Canard nouveau
Das Weisse Haus
River Grill
IndoChine
Au Quai
Fischereihafen Restaurant
RIVE Bistro
OTTENSEN
ALTONA
NORDDEUTSCHES LANDESMUSEUM
Platz der Republik
S. Bahn Reeperbahn
Reeperbahn
S. Bahn Königstr.
Stresemannstr.
Stresemann-str.
Bahrenfelder Steindamm
Gasstr.
Gaußstr.
Daimlerstr.
Friedensallee
Behring-str.
Bleicken-allee
Bernadotte-str.
Elbchaussee
Neumühlen
Große Elbstr.
Van der Smissen Str.
Palmaille
Norderelbe
Holsten-str.
Max Brauer Allee
Thaden-str.
Chemnitzstr.
Billroth-str.
Königstr.
Mörkenstr.
Ehrenberg-str.
Jessen-str.
Holstenstr.
L. Schroeder Str.
Bernstorffstr.
P. Roosen Str.
Hospitalstr.
Thedestr.
J. Leber Str.
Präsident Krahn Str.
Harkort-str.
Haubachstr.
Gerichtstr.
Hohenesch
Barner Str.
Bahren-felder-str.
Große Bergstr.
Hohenzollernring
Grüneberg-str.
Fischers-allee
Eulenstr.
Keplerstr.
Arnoldstr.
Stahlt-wiete
Schützen-str.
Kohlent-wiete
0 500 m
1
J

🏠

Holiday Inn Express St. Pauli Messe without rest   🕭 🔟

Simon-von-Utrecht-Str. 39a ✉ *20359*   🛜 🗚 🚗 ☒ ⓒ ☒ ⓞ
– Ⓜ *Reeperbahn* – ℰ *(040) 22 63 60 60* – *www.hiexpress.com*
120 rm ⌂ – †69/129 € ††69/129 €   *Plan I* **B2**
♦ Chain hotel ♦ Modern ♦
If you are looking for a modern, uncomplicated hotel in a good location, try this
Holiday Inn Express. It is just a 3min walk from the Reeperbahn and close to the
trade fair site and the city centre. The decor is clean and modern looking
throughout.

❌❌❌
❄

Landhaus Scherrer (Heinz O. Wehmann)   🔟 ↔ 🅿
Elbchaussee 130 ✉ *22763* – ℰ *(040) 8 83 07 00 30*   ☒ ⓒ ☒ ⓞ
– *www.landhausscherrer.de*
– *Closed Sunday*   **I1**
Rest – Menu 89/119 € – Carte 62/89 € ⅜
Rest *Wehmann's Bistro* – see restaurant listing
♦ French classic ♦ Elegant ♦
As their 30-year partnership undoubtedly shows, Emmi Scherrer and Heinz O
Wehmann have found the recipe for success. The wine list is a treasure trove
of great vintages, while the elegant restaurant is dominated by a large erotic
oil painting by Otto Bachmann.
➜ Flusskrebse und Kalbskopf mit Erbsenpüree, Zitronenmelisse, Curry
Aroma. Gedämpfter Angel Schellfisch auf Schmorgurken mit Estragon-
Senf-Vinaigrette. Rehnüsschen im Speckmantel mit Früchtebrot, glacierten
Kirschen und Pfifferlingen.

❌❌❌
❄

Le Canard nouveau (Ali Güngörmüs)   ≤ 🍴 ↔ 🅿 ☒ ⓒ ☒
Elbchaussee 139 ✉ *22763* – ℰ *(040) 88 12 95 31*
– *www.lecanard-hamburg.de*
– *Closed 1 week early January, 1 week mid March, 1 week early-mid October
and Sunday-Monday*   **I1**
Rest – Menu 44 € (lunch)/115 € – Carte 66/94 € ⅜
♦ Classic ♦ Fashionable ♦
Despite all the praise and recognition heaped upon him, this friendly chef
manages to keep his feet on the ground. His Turkish origins are revealed not
only by his name but also in the subtle oriental notes in his cuisine. The restaurant is bright and minimalist with views towards the River Elbe and the port.
➜ Thunfisch roh mariniert, gegrillt und gebacken mit Wasabi, Gurken, Pon-
zugelee und Avocado. Nordsee Steinbutt an der Gräte gebraten mit Zitro-
nenkartoffeln, Artischocken und Kalbsjus. Vierländer Ente in zwei Gängen
serviert - ab zwei Personen.

❌❌❌

Fischereihafen Restaurant   ≤ 🍴 ↔ 🅿 ☒ ⓒ ☒ ⓞ
Große Elbstr. 143 ✉ *22767* – ℰ *(040) 38 18 16*
– *www.fischereihafenrestaurant.de*   **J1**
Rest – *(booking advisable)* Menu 30 € (lunch)/55 € – Carte 31/80 €
♦ Fish and seafood ♦ Classic ♦
This fish restaurant overlooking the port is a veritable Hamburg institution. The
service is excellent as is the great value lunchtime menu.

❌❌

Au Quai   ≤ 🍴 ☒ ⓒ ☒
Große Elbstr. 145 b ✉ *22767* – ℰ *(040) 38 03 77 30* – *www.au-quai.com*
– *Closed Saturday lunch and Sunday*   **J1**
Rest – Carte 44/79 €
♦ Creative ♦ Trendy ♦
This popular establishment is situated close to the harbour and has a terrace
facing the water. The modern interior is complemented by designer items and
holographs.

GERMANY - HAMBURG

✕✕ IndoChine ← 🏠 ✿ P̄ 𝚅𝙸𝚂𝙰 ◑ AE

Neumühlen 11 ✉ 22763 – ✆ (040) 39 80 78 80 – www.indochine.de
– Closed Saturday lunch   I1
Rest – Menu 39/95 € – Carte 33/73 €

♦ Euro-asiatic ♦ Trendy ♦

This elegant modern restaurant with views over the Elbe serves wonderfully authentic Cambodian-, Laotian- and Vietnamese-inspired cuisine. The IceBar (pay on entry) is worth seeing and feeling!

✕✕ East – Hotel East 🏠 ♿ 𝚅𝙸𝚂𝙰 ◑ AE

Simon-von-Utrecht-Str. 31 ✉ 20359 – Ⓜ St. Pauli – ✆ (040) 30 99 30
– www.east-hamburg.de
– Closed Saturday lunch and Sunday lunch   Plan I **B2**
Rest – Carte 40/70 €

♦ Euro-asiatic ♦ Design ♦ Fashionable ♦

The atmosphere in this former factory building draws on many styles and influences. Far Eastern charm combines skilfully with Western industrial heritage. A restaurant not to be missed.

✕✕ Mess 🏠 𝚅𝙸𝚂𝙰 ◑ AE

Turnerstr. 9 ✉ 20038 – ✆ (040) 43 41 23 – www.mess.de
– Closed Saturday lunch and Sunday   Plan I **C2**
Rest – Menu 49/79 € – Carte 34/61 €

♦ International ♦ Friendly ♦

Located in the midst of the Karolinenviertel – once the centre of Hamburg's squatter community – chef Tobias Strauch's small restaurant is both warm and friendly despite its modern, minimalist design. For a taste of his ambitious, contemporary cuisine try the fillet of Husum beef with shallots in balsamic vinegar.

✕✕ River Grill ← 🏠 𝚅𝙸𝚂𝙰 ◑ AE

Neumühlen 17 ✉ 22763 – ✆ (040) 60 08 09 90 – www.river-grill.de
– Closed Saturday lunch and Sunday   I1
Rest – *(booking advisable)* Menu 22 € (lunch) – Carte 43/147 € 🏶

♦ International ♦ Minimalist ♦

The River Grill is a popular place to eat – hardly surprising given its good food and great views of the port. The glass and steel dominated interior is minimalist in style. The refined, contemporary cuisine is based on high quality ingredients and will delight fish fans – feast your eyes on the gleaming cooler cabinet.

✕ Henssler Henssler 🏠 AE
😊

Große Elbstr. 160 ✉ 22767 – Ⓜ Königstr. – ✆ (040) 38 69 90 00
– www.hensslerhenssler.de
– Closed Sunday   J1
Rest – *(booking advisable)* Carte 29/54 €

♦ Japanese ♦ Minimalist ♦

TV chef Steffen Henssler and his chef Tobias Frerks prepare an interesting selection of sushi and sashimi offerings at this Hamburg restaurant. These go alongside a number of other Japanese dishes and some contrasting non-fish alternatives, including entrecote of Australian beef.

✕ RIVE Bistro ← 🏠 AE
😊

Van-der-Smissen-Str. 1 (at Kreuzfahrt-Center) ✉ 22767 – Ⓜ Königstr.
– ✆ (040) 3 80 59 19 – www.rive.de   J1
Rest – *(booking advisable)* Menu 20 € (lunch)/37 € – Carte 29/52 €

♦ Fish and seafood ♦ Trendy ♦ Bistro ♦

Fish can't possibly taste better than here, right at the edge of the port. Specialities include the delicious 'Hamburger Pannfisch' (pan-fried pollack) with crispy roast potatoes and a Dijon mustard sauce), as well as oysters, sushi and sashimi served at the bar. NB: payment is by American Express and cash only.

Lokal1   AC VISA ⓶ ⓪
*Kampstr. 27 ✉ 20357 – **Ⓜ** Sternschanze – ℰ (040) 49 22 22 66*
– www.lokal1.com – Closed Sunday-Monday   *Plan I* **B2**
Rest – Menu 38/76 € (dinner) – Carte lunch 22/25 €
♦ Creative ♦ Minimalist ♦
After many years working in various well-known restaurants, Robert Wullkopf and Hagen Schäfer have now teamed up at the trendy Lokal1 in the Schanzenviertel. Their delicious modern food comes in the form of set menus (two to six courses) in the evenings – try the lamb from the wood-fired grill served with fennel and aubergine tart. There is a reduced selection at lunchtimes.

Nil   🏮 ⇔ ⊠
*Neuer Pferdemarkt 5 ✉ 20359 – **Ⓜ** Feldstr. – ℰ (040) 4 39 78 23*
– www.restaurant-nil.de – Closed Tuesday except in December
Rest – (dinner only) Menu 25/39 € – Carte 33/51 €   *Plan I* **B2**
♦ International ♦ Neighbourhood ♦ Friendly ♦
A little bit of a squeeze but comfortable nevertheless, this popular restaurant occupies three floors and is rightly renowned for its good, international cuisine. The 4-course menu is especially popular and offers good value for money. On warm days try the rear garden terrace. Adjoining cookery school.

Wehmann's Bistro – Restaurant Landhaus Scherrer   AC P
Elbchaussee 130 ✉ 22763 – ℰ (040) 8 83 07 00 50   VISA ⓶ AE ⓪
– www.wehmanns-bistro.de – Closed Sunday   **I1**
Rest – Menu 33 € – Carte 24/50 € 🌺
♦ Regional/country ♦ Bistro ♦
The decor in this lovely bistro gives the impression of classic comfort. Culinary delights are prepared by the owner, Heinz O Wehmann.

Amadée   🏮 VISA ⓶ AE
*Max-Brauer-Allee 80 ✉ 22765 – **Ⓜ** S. Bahn Königstr.*
– ℰ (040) 98 23 93 30 – www.restaurant-amadee.de
– Closed Monday   **J1**
Rest – (dinner only) Menu 33/45 € – Carte 28/54 €
♦ Austrian ♦ Classic ♦ Individual ♦
Restaurateur Karin Wege serves the good Austrian food prepared by her experienced kitchen team in the unusual setting of this former scene building workshop. The menu includes an excellent Wiener Schnitzel with potato and cucumber salad and pikeperch served on a bed of Styrian-style risotto.

Das Weisse Haus   VISA ⓶ AE ⓪
Neumühlen 50 ✉ 22763 – ℰ (040) 3 90 90 16 – www.das-weisse-haus.de
– Closed Sunday   **I1**
Rest – (booking advisable) Menu 30/75 € – Carte 32/58 €
♦ International ♦ Bistro ♦
In this little white building on the Elbpromenade Patrick Voelz treats his guests to delicious contemporary dishes served in a friendly, bistro-style atmosphere. A separate simpler menu is available at lunchtimes, with various set menus in the evenings.

ELBE-WESTERN DISTRICTS   *Plan III*

Louis C. Jacob   ⬅ 🦢 AC 🛜 �▲ 🚗 VISA ⓶ AE
Elbchaussee 401 (by Elbchaussee A3) ✉ 22609 – ℰ (040) 82 25 50
– www.hotel-jacob.de
85 rm – 🛏205/265 € 🛏🛏265/455 €, ⊡ 32 € – 10 suites
Rest *Jacobs Restaurant* ✿✿ **Rest** *Weinwirtschaft Kleines Jacob* ⓐ
– see restaurant listing
♦ Luxury ♦ Traditional ♦ Classic ♦
The successful management and services in this elegant hotel on the Elbe are exemplary. Equally pleasant is the classical furnishing of the rooms, some of which are as spacious as junior suites.

Gastwerk 🛏 🍴 🅰️ rm, 🛜 🛎️ 🅿️ 🚗 VISA 🅾️ 🅰️🅴 ①

Beim Alten Gaswerk 3 (corner Daimlerstraße) ✉️ 22761 – ☎️ *(040) 89 06 20*
– www.gastwerk.com **I1**
141 rm – 🛏120/200 € 🛏🛏120/200 €, � 18 € – 2 suites
Rest – *(closed Saturday lunch and Sunday lunch)* Menu 39 €
– Carte 22/49 €
♦ Business ♦ Design ♦
A successful combination of imposing industrial architecture and modern design. Pleasant rooms, lofts and suites – the suites have terraces. A modern restaurant serving international cuisine.

 Landhaus Flottbek 🚗 🛏 🛜 🛎️ 🅿️ 🚗 VISA 🅾️ 🅰️🅴

Baron-Voght-Str. 179 (by Stresemannstraße A2) ✉️ 22607 – ☎️ *(040)*
8 22 74 10 – www.landhaus-flottbek.de
25 rm – 🛏80/120 € 🛏🛏120/150 €, ⊑ 16 €
Rest – *(closed Saturday lunch and Sunday lunch)* Carte 29/54 €
♦ Family ♦ Cosy ♦
A group of 18C farmhouses set in a lovely garden with tasteful, individually furnished rooms. Two of the rooms have a terrace or winter garden. This comfortable restaurant serves seasonal cuisine and has a lovely terrace facing the garden.

 Strandhotel without rest  ≼ 🚗 🛜 🅿️ VISA 🅾️

Strandweg 13 (by Elbchaussee A3) ✉️ 22587 – ☎️ *(040) 86 13 44*
– www.strandhotel-blankenese.de
– Closed 28 December-16 January
14 rm – 🛏85/100 € 🛏🛏140/205 €, ⊑ 15 € – 2 suites
♦ Villa ♦ Classic ♦ Design ♦
Modern design paired with classic-historical flair. The white 19th century art-nouveau villa lies directly by the Elbe beach with views of the passing ships. This restaurant has a small menu and attractive terrace.

🍴🍴🍴🍴 **Jacobs Restaurant** – Hotel Louis C. Jacob ≼ 🛏 🅰️ VISA 🅾️
🏵️ 🏵️ *Elbchaussee 401 (by Elbchaussee A3)* ✉️ 22609 – ☎️ *(040) 82 25 54 07*
– www.hotel-jacob.de
– Closed Monday-Tuesday
Rest – *(booking advisable)* Menu 89 € (lunch)/164 € 🍷
♦ French classic ♦ Elegant ♦
Thomas Martin's 'Bewährt', 'Zeitgenössisch' and 'Natürlich' menus demand a stylish setting and that is exactly what they have here at Jacobs. Find high stucco ceilings, crystal chandeliers and fine tableware. The menus are also accompanied by an excellent wine list and knowledgeable staff to provide advice. The terrace with lime trees is a must in summer.
→ Roh marinierter Zander aus Nordpommern, Queller, Dill, Staudensellerie. Geschmorte Ochsenschulter, rote Zwiebel, Sellerie. Kräutergarten, Sauerrahm, Minze, Basilikum.

🍴🍴🍴🍴 **Süllberg - Seven Seas** (Karlheinz Hauser) with rm ≼ 🛏 ♿
🏵️ 🏵️ *Süllbergsterrasse 12 (by Elbchaussee A3)* rest, 🅰️ 🛜 🚗 VISA 🅾️ 🅰️🅴
✉️ 22587 – ☎️ *(040) 8 66 25 20 – www.suellberg-hamburg.de*
– Closed 1 January-6 February and Monday-Tuesday
10 rm – 🛏170/190 € 🛏🛏190/230 €, ⊑ 17 € – 1 suite
Rest – *(Wednesday-Saturday dinner only)* Menu 94/132 €
– Carte 86/102 € 🍷
Rest Deck 7 – see restaurant listing
♦ Modern ♦ Luxury ♦
Occupying the historic Süllberg Hotel, the Seven Seas restaurant offers a tasteful atmosphere and exemplary service – including a top sommelier in Christian Schäfer. This makes the perfect setting for the intense, refined cuisine of Karlheinz Hauser and his team. The overnight accommodation is no less exclusive.
→ Kaisergranat & Taschenkrebs - Waldmeister, Meeresalgen, Kaviar und Joghurt. Bretonischer Hummer - Eukalyptus, junge Mandeln und Chicorée. Gebratener Steinbutt & Eismeergarnele - Betetstrukturen, Radieschen, Lauch und Escabechesud.

XX **Deck 7** – Restaurant Süllberg - Seven Seas ← 🏠 AC ⇔ VISA ⑥ AE
Süllbergsterrasse 12 (by Elbchaussee A3) ✉ 22587 – 𝒞 *(040) 86 62 52 77*
– www.suellberg-hamburg.de
– Closed 1 January-6 February
Rest – Menu 30/45 € – Carte 38/78 €
♦ French classic ♦ Fashionable ♦
In defiance of many a passing trend, this restaurant with its smart, brown leather upholstered chairs and parquet flooring has opted for the versatility of a classic yet modern interior. In summer, eat outside with stunning views of the Elbe.

XX **Witthüs** 🏠 **P** VISA ⑥ AE
Elbchaussee 499a (access via Mühlenberg) (by Elbchaussee A3) ✉ 22587
– 𝒞 (040) 86 01 73 – www.witthues.com
– Closed Monday
Rest – *(dinner only)* Menu 33/36 € – Carte 34/46 €
♦ International ♦ Classic ♦
This historic farmhouse is idyllically located near the Elbe. Enjoy international cuisine and professional service in a classic, elegant setting with Nordic flair. Outdoor terrace.

XX **chezfou** 🏠 **P** VISA ⑥
Leverkusenstr. 54 ✉ 22761 – 𝒞 *(040) 88 30 22 03 – www.chezfou.de*
– Closed Sunday-Monday Plan I **A2**
Rest – Carte 46/60 €
♦ International ♦ Friendly ♦
The words chic, urban and industrial describe this restaurant and wine bar to perfection. The wines served to accompany the delicious fresh food are all organic, many from France, and there is even a wine shop.

X **Weinwirtschaft Kleines Jacob** – Hotel Louis C. Jacob 🏠
😊 *Elbchaussee 404 (by Elbchaussee A3)* ✉ 22609 VISA ⑥ AE
– 𝒞 (040) 82 25 55 10 – www.kleines-jacob.de
Rest – *(Monday to Saturday dinner only)* Menu 32 € – Carte 34/45 € ⅜
♦ Mediterranean ♦ Wine bar ♦ Cosy ♦
The atmosphere at Kleines Jacob is more casual and relaxed compared to its stylish gourmet counterpart. The Mediterranean and local fare is simpler here, though every bit as good. Try the Flammekueche, the cheese fondue or the veal involtini served on a bed of wild mushroom linguine.

X **Atlas** 🏠 **P** VISA ⑥
Schützenstr. 9a (entrance Phoenixhof) ✉ 22761 – 𝒞 *(040) 8 51 78 10*
– www.atlas.at
– Closed Saturday lunch and Sunday dinner I1
Rest – Menu 15 € (lunch)/49 € (dinner) – Carte 29/41 €
♦ International ♦ Bistro ♦
This former fish smokery is now a restaurant in the modern bistro style. Shorter menu available at lunchtimes. Pleasant ivy-covered terrace.

X **Rach & Ritchy** 🏠 **P** VISA ⑥ AE
Holstenkamp 71 ✉ 22525 – 𝒞 *(040) 89 72 61 70 – www.rach-ritchy.de*
– Closed Saturday lunch and Sunday Plan I **A2**
Rest – *(booking advisable)* Carte 32/60 €
♦ International ♦ Friendly ♦ Fashionable ♦
TV chef Christian Rach is now a household name. It is the second member of the duo, Richard 'Ritchy' Mayer, who does the cooking in his fashionable, modern grill restaurant. Specialities include succulent steaks from the glass-fronted maturing cabinet.

GERMANY - HAMBURG

Kitsune Izakaya

Eppendorfer Weg 62 ✉ *20259 –* ℰ *(040) 43 91 08 60*
– www.kitsune-izakaya.de
– Closed Monday-Tuesday   *Plan I* **B2**
Rest *– (dinner only) (booking advisable)* Menu 36/42 € – Carte 24/35 €
♦ Asian ♦ Minimalist ♦
Cooking in his own distinctive style, Leipzig-born Martin Schulz, a trained butcher and chef, combines traditional Japanese cuisine (following a valuable period in Osaka) with regional (and decidedly rustic) German elements. The set menus are probably the best way of trying a bit of everything.

AT THE AIRPORT

Radisson BLU Airport

Flughafenstr. 1 ✉ *22335 –* ℰ *(040) 3 00 30 00*
– www.radissonblu.com/hotel-hamburgairport
266 rm – ♥114/248 € ♥♥114/248 €, ☲ 20 € – 1 suite
Rest – Carte 20/44 €
♦ Business ♦ Modern ♦
Modern circular hotel complex with access to terminals 1 and 2. Purist design throughout, with rooms in "Ocean" and "Urban" style, including large business rooms. This bright, stylish restaurant has an integrated bar.

MUNICH
MÜNCHEN

Population: 1 378 176

Lichtblick/Fotolia.com

Situated in a stunning position not far north of the Alps, Munich is a cultural titan. Famously described as the 'village with a million inhabitants', its mix of German organisation and Italian lifestyle makes for a magical mix, with an enviable amount of Italian restaurants to seek out and enjoy. This capital of Southern Germany boasts over forty theatres and dozens of museums; temples of culture that blend charmingly with the Bavarian love of folklore and lederhosen. Perhaps in no other world location – certainly not in Western Europe – is there such an enjoyable abundance of folk festivals and groups dedicated to playing the local music. And there's an abundance of places to see them, too: Munich is awash with Bierhallen, Bierkeller, and Biergarten.

The heart of Munich is the Old Town, with its epicentre the Marienplatz in the south, and Residenz to the north: there are many fine historic buildings around here. Running to the east is the River Isar, flanked by fine urban thoroughfares and green areas for walks. Head north for the area dissected by the Ludwigstrasse and Leopoldstrasse – Schwabing – which is full of students as it's the University district. To the east is the English Garden, a denizen of peace. West of here, the Museums district, dominated by the Pinakothek, is characterised by bookshops, antique stores and galleries.

MUNICH IN...

➜ **ONE DAY**
The old town, Frauenkirche, English Garden, Wagner (if possible!) at the National Theatre.

➜ **TWO DAYS**
Schwabing, Pinakothek, Hofbräuhaus.

➜ **THREE DAYS**
Olympic Park, Schloss Nymphenburg, an evening in a traditional Bavarian inn.

PRACTICAL INFORMATION

ARRIVAL-DEPARTURE

✈ Airport Frank Josef Strauss is 28km northeast of the city. Munich S-Bahn Lines S1 or S8 take 45min to the centre.

GETTING AROUND

The underground network (U-Bahn) operates the same fare system as on Munich's buses and trams: it's divided into 4 ring-shaped price zones; zone 1 (the white zone) is the most important for visitors, as it covers the city centre. Prices rise in accordance with the amount of zones you intend to travel. If you plan to make several journeys, invest in a strip-card (Streifenkarte). You can also buy a 1 or 3-day Tageskarte: good value for tourists and available from tourist information offices, hotel receptions, travel agents and newsagents. The München Welcome Card is available for 1 or 3 days and gives free use of public transport as well as reduced entry to many museums, palaces and sights.

CALENDAR HIGHLIGHTS

March
Starkbierfest (Strong Beer Festival).

April
Biennale (contemporary music).

June
Münchner Opernfestspiele (opera and ballet), Jazz Summer.

July
Tollwood Festival (jazz and rock).

August
Theatron Music Summer.

September-October
Oktoberfest.

October
Long Night of Museums, Munich Media Marathon.

EATING OUT

Munich is a city in which you can eat well - especially if you're a meat-eater – and in large quantities. The local specialities are meat and potatoes, with large dollops of cabbage on the side; you won't have trouble finding roast pork and dumplings or meatloaf and don't forget the local white veal sausage, weisswurst. The meat is invariably succulent, and cabbage is often adorned with the likes of juniper berries. Potatoes, meanwhile, have a tendency to evolve into soft and buttery dumplings. And sausage? Take your pick from over 1,500 recognised species. Other specialities include Schweinshaxe (knuckle of pork) and Leberkäs (meat and offal pâté). Eating out in Munich, or anywhere in Bavaria, is an experience in itself, with the distinctive background din of laughter, singing and the clinking of mugs of Bavarian Weissbier. It's famous for the Brauereigaststätten or brewery inn; be prepared for much noise, and don't be afraid to fall into conversation with fellow diners and drinkers. The many Italian restaurants in the city provide an excellent alternative.

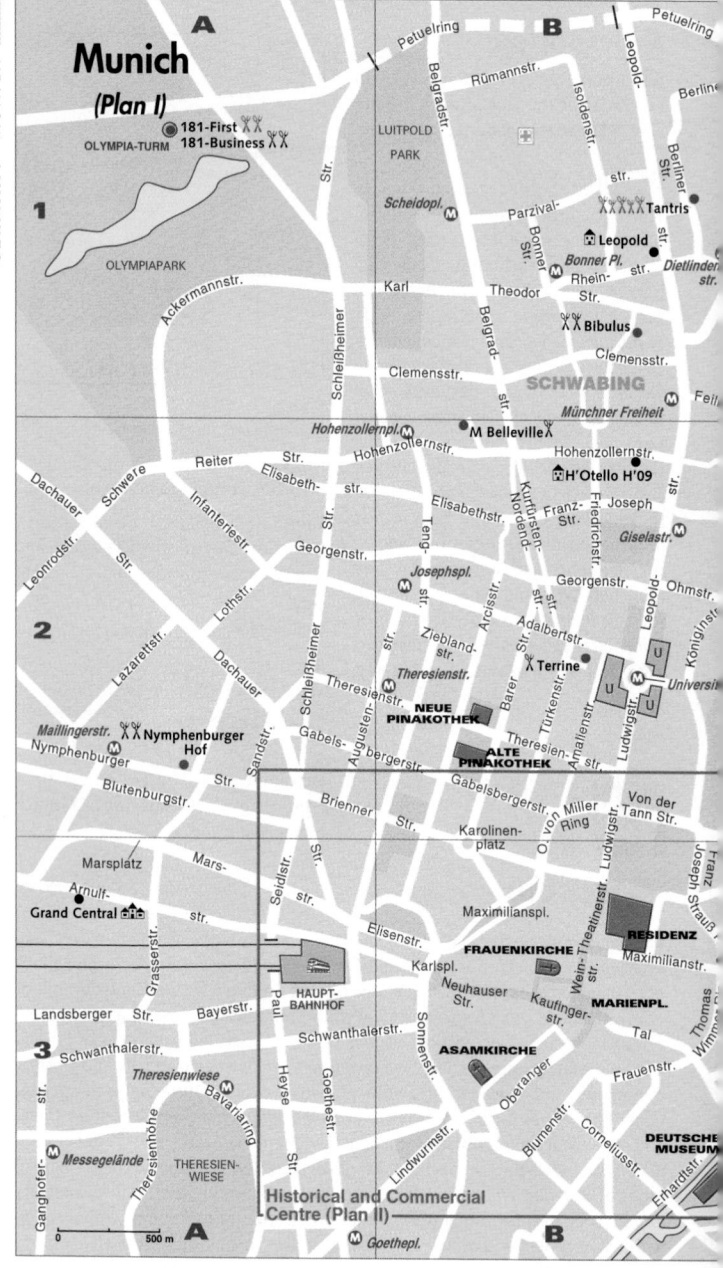

GERMANY - MUNICH

Munich
(Plan I)

● 181-First ✕✕
181-Business ✕✕

OLYMPIA-TURM

OLYMPIAPARK

Petuelring

LUITPOLD PARK

Scheidpl.

Belgradstr.

Rümannstr.

Isoldestr.

Leopold-

Berlin

Berliner Str.

str.

Parzival-

Bonner Str.

✕✕✕✕✕ Tantris

🏛 Leopold

Bonner Pl.

Rhein- Str.

Dietlinder str.

Karl

Theodor

Str.

✕✕ Bibulus

Clemensstr.

SCHWABING

Feile

Clemensstr.

Münchner Freiheit

Ackermannstr.

Schleißheimerstr.

Belgrad-str.

Hohenzollernpl. M

● M Belleville ✕

Hohenzollernstr.

Hohenzollernstr.

🏛 H'Otello H'09

Reiter

Str.

Elisabeth-

str.

Kurfürsten-Nordend-

Franz- Str.

Friedrichstr.

Joseph

Dachauer

Schwere

Infanteriestr.

Leonrodstr.

Str.

Lothstr.

Lazarettstr.

Dachauer

Str.

Elisabethstr.

Teng-

str.

Giselastr. M

Leopold-

Ohmstr.

Elisabeth- str.

Georgenstr.

Josephspl. M

str.

Arcisstr.

Georgenstr.

Adalbertstr.

Universi

Theresienstr.

Ziebland-str.

Theresienstr.

✕ Terrine

U

U

Königin

Universi

Maillingerstr. ✕✕ Nymphenburger Hof

Nymphenburger M

Str.

Theresienstr.

Schleißheimerstr.

Augusten-

Barer

NEUE PINAKOTHEK

Türkenstr.

Theresien-

Amalienstr.

str.

Ludwigstr.

M

U

U

U

Blutenburgstr.

Gabels-bergerstr.

ALTE PINAKOTHEK

Gabelsbergerstr.

von Miller

Von der Tann Str.

2

Brienner

Stf.

Sandstr.

Karolinen-platz

O

Ludwigstr.

Franz Joseph Strau

Marsplatz

Mars-

Arnulf-

Grand Central 🏛🏛

str.

Seidlstr.

str.

Brienner

Str.

Maximilianspl.

Wein-

Theatinerstr.

Maximilianstr.

RESIDENZ

Landsberger Str.

Bayerstr.

Paul

HAUPT-BAHNHOF

Elisenstr.

Karlspl.

FRAUENKIRCHE

Neuhauser Str.

MARIENPL.

Kaufinger-str.

Maximilianstr.

Thomas Wimmer

Schwanthalerstr.

Somenstr.

Tal

3

Schwanthalerstr.

str.

Theresienwiese

Bavariaring

Heyse

Goethestr.

ASAMKIRCHE

Oberanger

Frauenstr.

Cornellusstr.

Blumenstr.

DEUTSCHE MUSEUM

Ganghofer-str.

M Messegelände

Theresienhöhe

THERESIEN-WIESE

Str.

Lindwurmstr.

Erhardtstr.

Historical and Commercial Centre (Plan II)

0   500 m

A

M Goethepl.

B

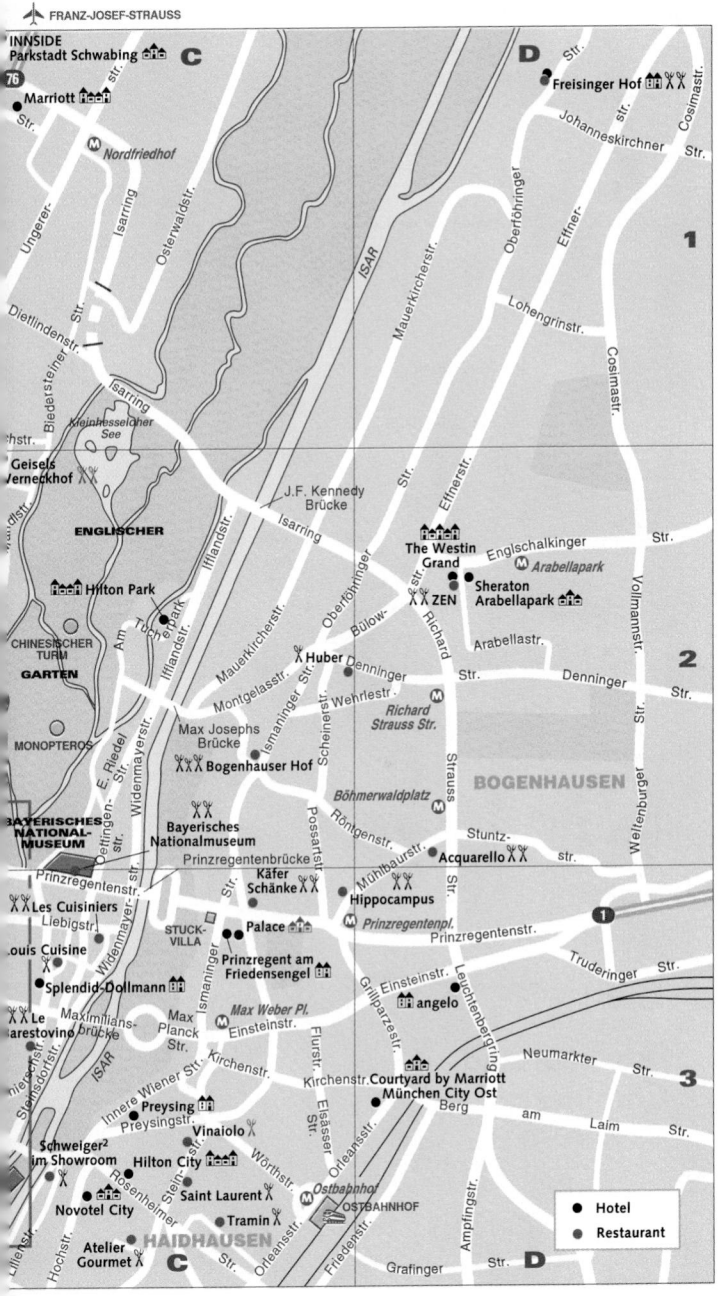

✈ FRANZ-JOSEF-STRAUSS

INNSIDE
Parkstadt Schwabing 🏨🏨 **C**
76
● Marriott 🏨🏨🏨

● Freisinger Hof 🏨🏨 ✕✕ **D**

Johanneskirchner str.

Cosimastr.

Ungerer Str.

Isarring

Osterwaldstr.

M Nordfriedhof

Dietlindenstr.

Oberföhringer

Efner-

Str.

ISAR

Mauerkircherstr.

Lohengrinstr.

Cosimastr.

Biedersteiner

Isarring

Kleinhesseloher
See

-hstr.

Geisels
Werneckhof ✕ 🏨

ENGLISCHER

J.F. Kennedy
Brücke

Isarring

Efnerstr.

Str.

🏨🏨🏨
**The Westin
Grand**

Englschalkinger Str.

M Arabellapark

🏨🏨🏨 Hilton Park

CHINESISCHER
TURM

GARTEN

Am Tucher Park

Ifflandstr.

Mauerkircherstr.

Oberföhringer str.

● ● **Sheraton
Arabellapark** 🏨🏨
✕✕ **ZEN**

Richard

Arabellastr.

Vollmannstr.

MONOPTEROS

E. Riedel
Str.

Widenmayerstr.

Ifflandstr.

Montgelasstr.

Ismaninger Str.

✕ **Huber** Denninger

Wehrlestr.

Str.

M
**Richard
Strauss Str.**

Denninger

Str.

2

BAYERISCHES
NATIONAL-
MUSEUM

Oettingen-
str.

Max Josephs
Brücke

Scheinerstr.

Strauss

✕✕✕ **Bogenhauser Hof**

Böhmerwaldplatz

BOGENHAUSEN

Wiesbadener Str.

Prinzregentenstr.

✕✕ **Les Cuisiniers**
Liebigstr.

ouis Cuisine

✕ Splendid-Dollmann 🏨

✕✕ Le
arestovino

Maximilians-
brücke

Widenmayer
str.

✕✕
**Bayerisches
Nationalmuseum**

Prinzregentenbrücke

Ismaninger

Str.

Possartstr.

Röntgenstr.

Möhlstr.

**Käfer
Schänke** ✕✕

● **Palace** 🏨🏨

STUCK-
VILLA

**Prinzregent am
Friedensengel** 🏨

Max
Planck
Str.

M Einsteinstr.

Stuntz-

str.

● **Acquarello** ✕ ✕

✕✕
Hippocampus

M Prinzregentenpl.

Prinzregentenstr.

1

Truderinger Str.

Einsteinstr.

🏨 **angelo**

Grillparzerstr.

Leuchtenbergring

ISAR

Sternstr.

-rich
str.

✕ Preysing 🏨
Preysingstr.

Innere Wiener Str.

Kirchenstr.

Elsässer
Str.

Kirchenstr. **Courtyard by Marriott
München City Ost** 🏨🏨

Berg

am

Laim

Neumarkter

Str.

3

Schweiger²
im Showroom

Hilton City 🏨🏨🏨

● Novotel City 🏨

✕ Saint Laurent ✕

● Tramin ✕

HAIDHAUSEN

Rosenheimer

Wörthstr.

Orleansstr.

Orleansplatz

M Ostbahnhof

🚉 **OSTBAHNHOF**

Ampfingstr.

Friedenstr.

Atelier
Gourmet ✕

C

Lilienstr.

Hochstr.

Grafinger

Str.

D

●	Hotel
●	Restaurant

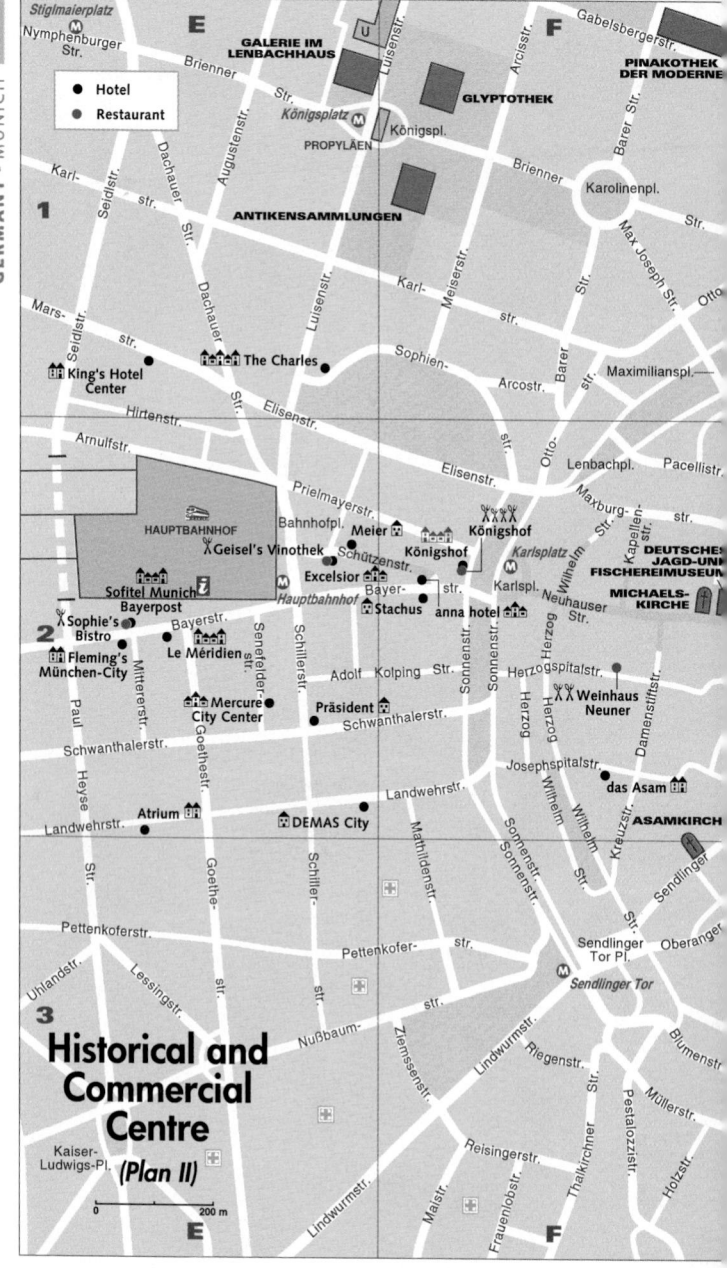

Stiglmaierplatz

Nymphenburger Str.

E

GALERIE IM LENBACHHAUS

Brienner Str.

● Hotel
● Restaurant

Königsplatz

PROPYLÄEN

Königspl.

GLYPTOTHEK

F

Gabelsbergerstr.

Luisenstr.

Arcisstr.

PINAKOTHEK DER MODERNE

Barer Str.

Brienner

Karolinenpl.

1

Karl-

Seidlstr.

Dachauer str.

Augustenstr.

Luisenstr.

ANTIKENSAMMLUNGEN

Karl-

Meiserstr.

str.

Max Joseph Str.

Otto

Mars-

Seidlstr.

str.

Dachauer

Sophien-

Karl-

str.

Barer

Arcostr.

Maximilianspl.

The Charles

King's Hotel Center

Hirtenstr.

Elisenstr.

Sophien-

Arnulfstr.

Elisenstr.

Lenbachpl.

Pacellistr.

Otto

Maxburg-str.

Kapellenstr.

DEUTSCHES JAGD-UND FISCHEREIMUSEUM

Prielmayerstr.

HAUPTBAHNHOF

Bahnhofpl.

Geisel's Vinothek

Schützenstr.

Meier

Königshof

Königshof

Karlsplatz

Karlspl.

Neuhauser Str.

Herzog

MICHAELS-KIRCHE

Sofitel Munich Bayerpost

Sophie's Bistro

Excelsior

Bayer-

str.

Stachus

anna hotel

2

Bayerstr.

Le Méridien

Senefelderstr.

Schillerstr.

Adolf Kolping Str.

Sonnenstr.

Sonnenstr.

Herzogspitalstr.

Herzog

Herzog

Weinhaus Neuner

Damenstiftstr.

Fleming's München-City

Mittererstr.

Paul Heyse

Mercure City Center

Goethestr.

Präsident

Schwanthalerstr.

Schwanthalerstr.

Josephspitalstr.

Wilhelm

Wilhelm

das Asam

Kreuzstr.

ASAMKIRCH

Schwanthalerstr.

Heyse

Atrium

Landwehrstr.

Goethe-

DEMAS City

Schillerstr.

Landwehrstr.

Mathildenstr.

Sonnenstr.

Sonnenstr.

Str.

Sendlinger

Str.

Uhlandstr.

Pettenkoferstr.

Lessingstr.

str.

Pettenkofer-

str.

Str.

Sendlinger Tor Pl.

Oberanger

Blumenstr.

3

Historical and Commercial Centre *(Plan II)*

Kaiser-Ludwigs-Pl.

Nußbaum-

Sendlinger Tor

Ziemssenstr.

Lindwurmstr.

Riegerstr.

Thalkirchner

Pestalozzistr.

Müllerstr.

0 ——— 200 m

Lindwurmstr.

Malstr.

Reisingerstr.

Frauenlobstr.

Thalkirchner Str.

Holzstr.

E

F

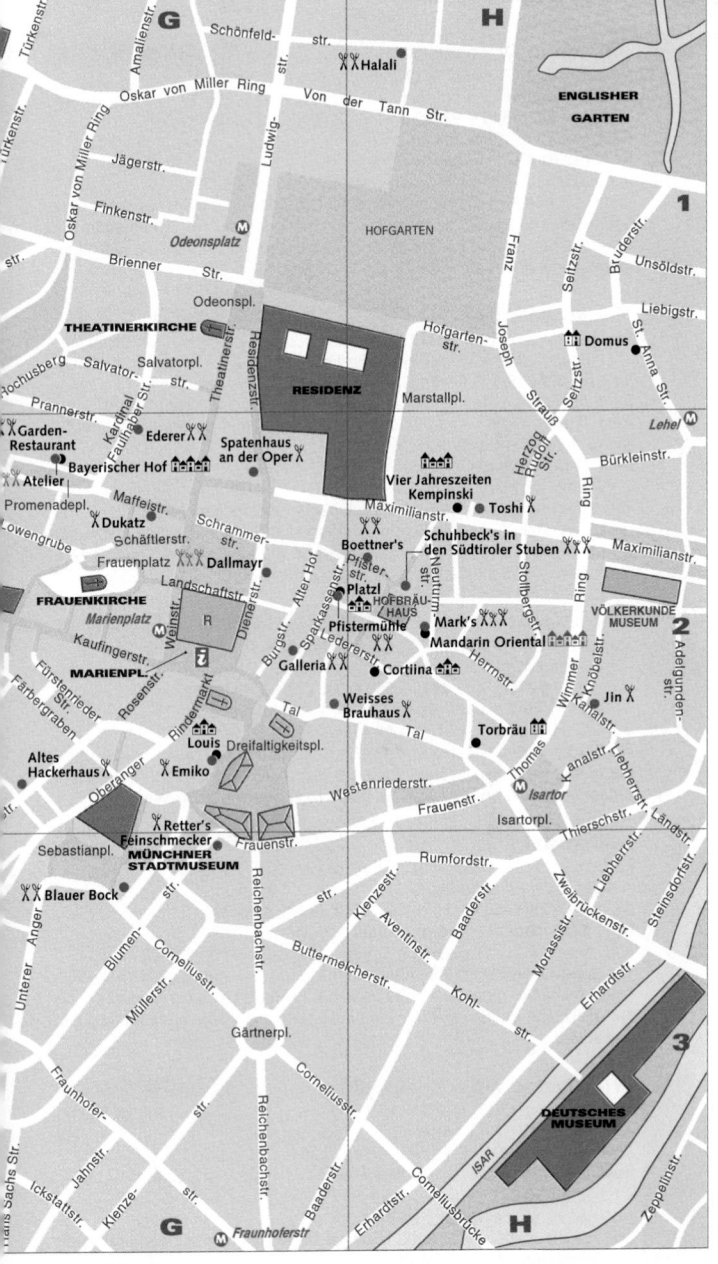

G
Schönfeld-   str.
Türkenstr.
Türkenstr.
Amalienstr.
Oskar von Miller Ring
H
Halali
Von der Tann Str.
ENGLISHER
GARTEN
Oskar von Miller Ring
Jägerstr.
Finkenstr.
Ludwig-
str.
1
Odeonsplatz
Brienner   Str.
Odeonspl.
HOFGARTEN
Franz
Joseph
Seitzstr.
Bruderstr.
Unsöldstr.
Liebigstr.
THEATINERKIRCHE
Salvatorpl.
Salvator-   str.
Theatinerstr.
Residenzstr.
Hofgarten-
str.
Domus
St. Anna Str.
Rochusberg
Prannerstr.
Kardinal
Faulhaber Str.
Ederer
RESIDENZ
Marstallpl.
Lehel
Herzog
Rudolf
Str.
Bürkleinstr.
str.
Garden-
Restaurant
Bayerischer Hof
Atelier
Spatenhaus
an der Oper
Vier Jahreszeiten
Kempinski
Toshi
Promenadepl.
Maffeistr.
Dukatz
Maximilianstr.
Maximilianstr.
Löwengrube
Schäftlerstr.
Schrammer-
str.
Boettner's
Schuhbeck's in
den Südtiroler Stuben
Ring
Stollbergstr.
Frauenplatz
Dallmayr
Landschaftstr.
Prister-
str.
Platzl
HOFBRÄU
HAUS
Mark's
VÖLKERKUNDE
MUSEUM
FRAUENKIRCHE
Marienplatz
R
Weinstr.
Dienerstr.
Sparkassenstr.
Alter Hof
Pfistermühle
Mandarin Oriental
Herrnstr.
Knöbelstr.
Adelgunden-
str.
Kaufingerstr.
Burgstr.
Ledererstr.
Galleria
Cortiina
MARIENPL.
Fürstenfelder
Str.
Rosenstr.
Rindermarkt
Tal
Weisses
Brauhaus
Tal
Kanalstr.
Liebherrstr.
Landstr.
Jin
Wimmer
Färbergraben
Louis
Dreifaltigkeitspl.
Torbräu
Thomas
Isartor
Altes
Hackerhaus
Oberanger
Emiko
Westenriederstr.
Frauenstr.
Isartorpl.
Thierschstr.
Zweibrückenstr.
Liebherrstr.
Steinsdorfstr.
Sebastianpl.
Retter's
Feinschmecker
MÜNCHNER
STADTMUSEUM
Frauenstr.
Rumfordstr.
Morassistr.
Erhardtstr.
Blauer Bock
Reichenbachstr.
str.
Klenzestr.
Baaderstr.
Unterer
Anger
Blumen-
str.
Corneliusstr.
Müllerstr.
Buttermelcherstr.
Kohl-
Erhardtstr.
3
DEUTSCHES
MUSEUM
Gärtnerpl.
Cornelius-
str.
ISAR
Fraunhofer-
str.
Reichenbachstr.
Baaderstr.
Corneliusbrücke
Zeppelinstr.
Hans Sachs Str.
Jahnstr.
Ickstattstr.
Klenze-   str.
G
Fraunhoferstr.
H
399

GERMANY - MUNICH

Mandarin Oriental   🖼 🕸 ⚲ 🅰🅲 rm, 🛜 🕸 🚗 VISA 🆗 AE 🄾

Neuturmstr. 1 ⊠ *80331 –* Ⓜ *Isartor – ✆ (089) 29 09 80*
– www.mandarinoriental.com   **H2**
73 rm – †425/545 € ††425/545 €, ⚄ 40 € – 11 suites
Rest *Mark's* ✿ – see restaurant listing
Rest *Bistro MO* – Carte 50/71 €
♦ Grand Luxury ♦ Historic ♦ Classic ♦
This classy hotel which occupies a beautiful period townhouse is one of the best
addresses in Germany. The exemplary service is perfectly complemented by the
luxurious but tasteful interior. With a heated pool on the roof. At lunchtime
international dishes are served in the Bistro MO.

Bayerischer Hof   🖼 🖼 🖼 🕸 🅲 🛜 rm, 🅰🅲 🛜 🕸 🚗

Promenadeplatz 2 ⊠ *80333 –* Ⓜ *Marienplatz*   VISA 🆗 AE 🄾
– ✆ (089) 2 12 00 – www.bayerischerhof.de   **G2**
340 rm – †285/525 € ††425/525 €, ⚄ 34 € – 17 suites
Rest *Atelier* ✿   **Rest** *Garden-Restaurant* – see restaurant listing
Rest *Trader Vic's* – ✆ (089) 2 12 09 95 (dinner only) (booking advisable)
Menu 50/83 € – Carte 33/77 €
Rest *Palais Keller* – ✆ (089) 2 12 09 90 – Carte 21/50 €
♦ Grand Luxury ♦ Traditional ♦ Classic ♦
This grand hotel set in a magnificent palace was first opened in 1841. The
rooms are exclusively designed in six different styles. The Blue Spa restaurant
with its small menu looks out over Munich to the Alps beyond. Other restau-
rants include Trader Vic's, which serves Polynesian food.

The Charles   🖼 🖼 🖼 🕸 🅲 rm, 🅰🅲 🛜 🕸 🚗 VISA 🆗 AE 🄾

Sophienstr. 28 ⊠ *80333 –* Ⓜ *Hauptbahnhof – ✆ (089) 5 44 55 50*
– www.roccofortecollection.com   **E1**
160 rm – †270/550 € ††270/550 €, ⚄ 30 € – 28 suites
Rest *DAVVERO* – Carte 48/69 €
♦ Grand Luxury ♦ Elegant ♦ Modern ♦
This luxury hotel is situated in the old botanic garden. Its fine decor has a simple, modern and elegant style. There is a high quality spa area, as well as every
service you could possibly wish for. Italian food is served at Davvero.

Königshof   🖼 🕸 🅰🅲 🛜 🕸 🚗 VISA 🆗 AE 🄾

Karlsplatz 25 ⊠ *80335 –* Ⓜ *Karlsplatz (Stachus) – ✆ (089) 55 13 60*
– www.geisel-privathotels.de   **F2**
87 rm – †280/460 € ††320/500 €, ⚄ 29 € – 8 suites
Rest *Königshof* ✿ – see restaurant listing
♦ Luxury ♦ Traditional ♦ Elegant ♦
The Geisel family have a long history in the hotel trade stretching back to 1900.
It has reached its pinnacle in this classic, luxury hotel in a choice location on the
Karlsplatz. The professional front of house team are always on hand to guide
and advise.

Vier Jahreszeiten Kempinski   🖼 🕸 🅲 🅰🅲 🛜 🕸 🚗

Maximilianstr. 17 ⊠ *80539 –* Ⓜ *Lehel*   VISA 🆗 AE 🄾
– ✆ (089) 2 12 50 – www.kempinski.com/munich   **H2**
300 rm – †230/960 € ††290/960 €, ⚄ 38 € – 30 suites
Rest *Vue Maximilian* – ✆ (089) 21 25 21 25 – Menu 40/80 €
– Carte 54/90 €
♦ Luxury ♦ Traditional ♦ Classic ♦
Ever since it opened in 1858 this hotel has been one of the classic grand hotels
in Munich, where historic charm combines with modern features. The lobby is a
lively meeting place for drinks, snacks or coffee and cakes.

GERMANY - MUNICH

Sofitel Munich Bayerpost 🛅 ⊛ 🏠 ⬚ ⭤ 🗚 🛜 🎿 🚗   VISA ⬤⬤ AE ⓞ

Bayerstr. 12 ✉ *80335 –* Ⓜ *Hauptbahnhof*
– ℰ *(089) 59 94 80*
– www.sofitel-munich.com   **E2**
396 rm – 🛉220/520 € 🛉🛉220/520 €, � 31 € – 8 suites
Rest *Sophie's Bistro* – see restaurant listing
Rest *Schwarz & Weiz* – *(closed 1-14 January, 29 June-2 September and Sunday-Monday) (dinner only)* Menu 99 € – Carte 52/76 €
◆ Chain hotel ◆ Luxury ◆ Design ◆
Modern architecture and contemporary design have been successfully combined in this imposing listed building. It is from Germany's period of rapid industrial expansion at the end of the 19C. The Schwarz & Weiz restaurant offers a mix of French and Bavarian cuisine. Alternatively, try Sophie's Bistro.

Hilton Park 🖾 🛅 ⊛ 🏠 ⬚ ⭤ 🗚 🛜 🎿 🚗 VISA ⬤⬤ AE ⓞ

Am Tucherpark 7 ✉ *80538 –* ℰ *(089) 3 84 50*
– www.hilton.de/muenchenpark   *Plan I* **C2**
484 rm – 🛉149/374 € 🛉🛉149/374 €, ⊻ 28 € – 9 suites
Rest *Tivoli & Club* – ℰ *(089) 38 45 27 69* – Carte 25/75 €
◆ Chain hotel ◆ Luxury ◆ Modern ◆
The Hilton Park's location (in the English Garden) and the comfortable accommodation, which includes business and executive rooms, are both excellent. The restaurant offers an international menu and there is beer garden on the River Eisbach.

Le Méridien 🖾 🛅 ⊛ 🏠 ⬚ ⭤ 🗚 📞 🎿 🚗 VISA ⬤⬤ AE ⓞ

Bayerstr. 41 ✉ *80335 –* Ⓜ *Hauptbahnhof –* ℰ *(089) 2 42 20*
– www.lemeridienmunich.com   **E2**
381 rm – 🛉169/559 € 🛉🛉169/559 €, ⊻ 28 € – 8 suites
Rest – Carte 46/59 €
◆ Chain hotel ◆ Luxury ◆ Design ◆
This hotel opposite the main railway station offers modern-style and simple elegance. The restaurant offers a view into the pretty, leafy interior courtyard, which is a small oasis from the bustling city outside. Room prices include entry to some of Munich's museums.

Grand Central 🖾 🛅 🏠 ⬚ ⭤ 🗚 🛜 🎿 🚗 VISA ⬤⬤ AE ⓞ

Arnulfstr. 35 ✉ *80636 –* Ⓜ *Maillingerstr. –* ℰ *(089) 5 16 57 40*
– www.eurostarsgrandcentral.com   *Plan I* **A3**
247 rm ⊻ – 🛉129/270 € 🛉🛉149/290 € – 8 suites
Rest – *(closed Saturday-Sunday) (dinner only)* Carte 41/72 €
◆ Business ◆ Modern ◆ Functional ◆
This business hotel is functional, ultra-modern and just an S-Bahn overground stop from the main railway station. The swimming pool on the roof is a highlight. International cuisine is served in 'Red' and in the lounge bar when the restaurant is closed.

Cortiina 🖾 🛅 🗚 🛜 🚗 VISA ⬤⬤ AE

Ledererstr. 8 ✉ *80331 –* Ⓜ *Isartor –* ℰ *(089) 2 42 24 90*
– www.cortiina.com   **H2**
75 rm – 🛉119/289 € 🛉🛉139/309 €, ⊻ 20 € – 4 suites
Rest – *(dinner only)* Menu 49 € – Carte 30/64 €
◆ Townhouse ◆ Business ◆ Elegant ◆
The interior of this hotel in its improbable but nonetheless central location comes as something of a surprise. It has beautiful materials including wood, slate and Jura marble, which are combined perfectly with natural colours. Some of the guestrooms are spacious and include their own kitchenette.

GERMANY - MUNICH

Louis ⓖ 🕍 🖾 🛜 ⅏ 🅥🅢🅐 ⓜⓓ 🅐🅔 ⓞ

Viktualienmarkt 6 ⊠ 80331 – ⓜ *Marienplatz –* ℰ *(089) 41 11 90 80*
– www.louis-hotel.com **G2**
72 rm – 🛏180/400 € 🛏🛏200/450 €, � 20 €
Rest *Emiko* – see restaurant listing
◆ Townhouse ◆ Elegant ◆
This hotel enjoys a splendid, very central location on the Viktualienmarkt. Time-lessly elegant rooms (including the 70m² 'Louis Room') with some boasting great views.

Excelsior 🛜 ⅏ 🚗 🅥🅢🅐 ⓜⓓ 🅐🅔 ⓞ

Schützenstr. 11 ⊠ 80335 – ⓜ *Hauptbahnhof –* ℰ *(089) 55 13 70*
– www.geisel-privathotels.de **E2**
118 rm – 🛏110/215 € 🛏🛏120/310 €, ⊝ 20 € – 3 suites
Rest *Geisel's Vinothek* – see restaurant listing
◆ Business ◆ Classic ◆
This hotel, with its individual and cosy rooms, is the sister enterprise of the Königshof, where you will also find the leisure area. There is a good breakfast buffet in a stylish atmosphere. This pleasant, rustic-style winery shop offers a wide range of wines.

Mercure City Center 🛁 🕭 rm, 🖾 🛜 ⅏ 🚗 🅥🅢🅐 ⓜⓓ 🅐🅔 ⓞ

Senefelder Str. 9 ⊠ 80336 – ⓜ *Hauptbahnhof –* ℰ *(089) 55 13 20*
– www.mercure.com **E2**
167 rm – 🛏109/199 € 🛏🛏109/219 €, ⊝ 19 € **Rest** – Carte 22/60 €
◆ Chain hotel ◆ Cosy ◆ Personalised ◆
Theatre is the theme that runs through this hotel, in which red tones dominate. It has extremely spacious guestrooms that are both comfortable and modern. The restaurant serves international cuisine and opens onto the lobby. Beer gar-den in the rear courtyard.

anna hotel 🛁 🖾 🛜 🚗 🅥🅢🅐 ⓜⓓ 🅐🅔 ⓞ

Schützenstr. 1 ⊠ 80335 – ⓜ *Karlsplatz (Stachus) –* ℰ *(089) 59 99 40*
– www.geisel-privathotels.de **F2**
75 rm ⊝ – 🛏200/365 € 🛏🛏220/385 € – 1 suite **Rest** – Carte 28/46 €
◆ Business ◆ Modern ◆
The clientele in this modern hotel right on the Karlsplatz – the 'Stachus' as it's known locally – is young or at least young at heart! For a panoramic view take a room on the top floor, and if you feel like some sushi, you need go no further than the hotel's bistro, which also boasts a popular bar.

Platzl 🛁 ⓖ 🕍 🕭 rm, 🖾 rm, 📞 ⅏ 🚗 🅥🅢🅐 ⓜⓓ 🅐🅔 ⓞ

Sparkassenstr. 10 ⊠ 80331 – ⓜ *Marienplatz –* ℰ *(089) 23 70 30*
– www.platzl.de **G2**
167 rm ⊝ – 🛏99/198 € 🛏🛏210/250 € – 1 suite
Rest *Pfistermühle* – see restaurant listing
Rest *Ayingers* – ℰ *(089) 23 70 36 66* – Carte 22/40 €
◆ Traditional ◆ Cosy ◆
This hotel is located in the centre of the old city. It has attractive, classically decorated rooms and a relaxation area in the style of Ludwig II's Moorish pavi-lion. Ayingers restaurant provides a more relaxed alternative to the formal Pfis-termühle.

Splendid-Dollmann without rest 🛜 🅥🅢🅐 ⓜⓓ 🅐🅔

Thierschstr. 49 ⊠ 80538 – ⓜ *Lehel –* ℰ *(089) 23 80 80*
– www.hotel-splendid-dollmann.de *Plan I* **C3**
36 rm – 🛏98/330 € 🛏🛏118/330 €, ⊝ 15 € – 1 suite
◆ Historic ◆ Personalised ◆
A haven of peace amid the hustle and bustle of the city, this hotel is set in a stylish old townhouse with a pretty terrace in the rear courtyard. In the eve-nings, light refreshments are served in the library. Two parking spaces and resi-dents' parking permits are available for guests with cars.

GERMANY - MUNICH

🏠 **das Asam** without rest   ♿ 🛜 🍽 🆚 ⓦ 🅰🅴
Josephspitalstr. 3 ⊠ 80331 – Ⓜ *Sendlinger Tor –* ℰ *(089) 2 30 97 00*
– www.hotel-asam.de
– Closed Christmas-early January   **F2**
25 rm – ♦151/170 € ♦♦183/202 €, � 19 € – 8 suites
◆ Business ◆ Classic ◆
Bright, cosy rooms with high quality baths can be found in this hotel in the city
centre - some face peacefully onto the interior court. There is a pleasant breakfast area with a small terrace.

🏠 **Torbräu**   🍽 🅰🅲 rm, 🛜 🔧 🅿 🍽 🆚 ⓦ 🅰🅴
Tal 41 ⊠ 80331 – Ⓜ *Isartor –* ℰ *(089) 24 23 40 – www.torbraeu.de*
90 rm ⊠ – ♦159/248 € ♦♦205/320 € – 3 suites   **H2**
Rest *Schapeau –* ℰ *(089) 22 80 75 23 – Carte 21/49 €*
◆ Traditional ◆ Classic ◆
The oldest hotel in Munich, Torbräu has been in business since 1490. Now a
smart, family-run property it is constantly being upgraded and modernised.
Attractive and bright breakfast room on the first floor. Bavarian and Mediterra-
nean food served in the Schapeau.

🏠 **Fleming's München-City**   🛗 🍽 ♿ 🅰🅲 🛜 🔧 🍽
Bayerstr. 47 ⊠ 80335 – Ⓜ *Hauptbahnhof*   🆚 ⓦ 🅰🅴 ⓞ
– ℰ (089) 4 44 46 60 – www.flemings-hotels.com   **E2**
112 rm ⊠ – ♦115/216 € ♦♦148/249 €   **Rest** – Carte 24/52 €
◆ Business ◆ Modern ◆
Centrally located near the main railway station, this hotel offers functional,
modern rooms. Bistro-style restaurant with bar and delicatessen.

🏠 **King's Hotel Center** without rest   ♿ 🅰🅲 🛜 🍽 🆚 ⓦ 🅰🅴 ⓞ
Marsstr. 15 ⊠ 80335 – Ⓜ *Hauptbahnhof –* ℰ *(089) 51 55 30*
– www.kingshotels.de
– Closed during Christmas   **E1**
90 rm – ♦99/270 € ♦♦140/400 €, ⊠ 14 €
◆ Business ◆ Cosy ◆
This hotel, close to the town centre, has comfortable rooms with four-poster
beds. The single rooms are rather small. The wood-panelled breakfast room
offers a good selection from the buffet.

🏠 **Atrium** without rest   🍽 🛜 🔧 🍽 🆚 ⓦ 🅰🅴 ⓞ
Landwehrstr. 59 ⊠ 80336 – Ⓜ *Theresienwiese –* ℰ *(089) 51 41 90*
– www.atrium-hotel.de   **E2**
162 rm ⊠ – ♦89/159 € ♦♦119/189 €
◆ Business ◆ Functional ◆
This hotel is located between the main station and Theresienwiese. It offers
practical rooms, a modern breakfast room with a generous buffet, and a beautifully planted interior courtyard with a lounge.

🏠 **Domus**   🍽 🛜 🍽 🆚 ⓦ 🅰🅴
St.-Anna-Str. 31 ⊠ 80538 – Ⓜ *Lehel –* ℰ *(089) 2 17 77 30*
– www.domus-hotel.de   **H1**
45 rm ⊠ – ♦85/210 € ♦♦120/280 €
Rest *Cupido –* ℰ *(089) 21 66 77 21 – Menu 13 € (lunch)/40 € (dinner)*
– Carte 30/46 €
◆ Business ◆ Functional ◆
This hotel is run with a personal touch and enjoys a relatively quiet location between Maximilianstraße and Prinzregentenstraße. The majority of rooms have a
balcony. In summer you can start the day on the pretty breakfast terrace. Clean,
straight-lined design and Italian cuisine in the Cupido restaurant.

GERMANY - MUNICH

🏠 DEMAS City without rest   🛜 🚗 VISA ⓬ AE

Landwehrstr. 19 ✉ *80336* – ⓜ *Hauptbahnhof* – ℰ *(089) 6 93 39 90*
– www.demas-city.de   **E2**
50 rm � – †59/359 € ††69/399 €
♦ Townhouse ♦ Modern ♦

DEMAS City boasts a great central position and impressive contemporary minimalist design. The rooms facing the courtyard are quieter. If you are looking for
a little more space, book one of the junior suites on the sixth floor.

🏠 Präsident without rest   🛜 ♨ VISA ⓬ AE ⓞ

Schwanthalerstr. 20 ✉ *80336* – ⓜ *Hauptbahnhof* – ℰ *(089) 5 49 00 60*
– www.hotel-praesident.de   **E2**
42 rm ☐ – †79/249 € ††93/289 €
♦ Business ♦ Functional ♦

This convenient hotel is diagonally opposite the Deutsche Theatre. It has practical, modern rooms and a breakfast buffet offering good food.

🏠 Stachus without rest   🛜 ♨ VISA ⓬ AE

Bayerstr. 7 ✉ *80335* – ⓜ *Hauptbahnhof* – ℰ *(089) 5 45 84 20*
– www.hotel-stachus.com – *Closed 20-28 December*   **F2**
73 rm – †79/109 € ††89/149 €, ☐ 10 €
♦ Business ♦ Functional ♦

This hotel guarantees an enjoyable stay, reasonable prices and a good location.
The Karlsplatz, or 'Stachus' as it is known locally, is right outside the door. The
rooms, though simple and in some cases quite small, are all modern. Ask for
the Superior rooms at the back.

🏠 Meier without rest   🛜 VISA ⓬ AE ⓞ

Schützenstr. 12 ✉ *80335* – ⓜ *Hauptbahnhof* – ℰ *(089) 5 49 03 40*
– www.hotel-meier.de   **E2**
50 rm ☐ – †80/250 € ††100/300 €
♦ Business ♦ Functional ♦

Ideal for anyone holidaying in the city, this smart and functional multi-storey
hotel is located on a shopping street between the main railway station and
the Karlsplatz or 'Stachus'. The breakfast buffet is both copious and varied.

🍴🍴🍴 Königshof – Hotel Königshof   ≤ AC VISA ⓬ AE ⓞ

Karlsplatz 25 (1st floor) ✉ *80335* – ⓜ *Karlsplatz (Stachus)*
– ℰ (089) 55 13 60 – www.geisel-privathotels.de
*– Closed 1 week early January, 1 week Easter, 1 week Whitsun, 4 weeks August-
early September and Sunday, January-September: Sunday-Monday*   **F2**
Rest – *(booking advisable)* Menu 42 € (lunch)/138 € – Carte 75/100 € ♨
♦ French classic ♦ Elegant ♦

The owners of the Königshof set great store by the art of fine dining. This is witnessed by the elegant style, beautifully laid tables and, most of all, by the excellent
dishes emanating from the kitchen staffed by Martin Fauster and his team. The
window tables are great for watching the bustling life on the Karlsplatz or 'Stachus'.
→ Gegrillte Lachsforelle mit Eiersalat und Sauerampfer. Brust und Keule von
der Bresse Taube mit Zwiebelkuchen und Petersilienwurzel. Rhabarber - Eis-
praline mit Karamellcrème, knuspriger Brioche und Waldmeister-Zitroneneis.

🍴🍴 Atelier – Hotel Bayerischer Hof   AC VISA ⓬ AE ⓞ

Promenadeplatz 2 ✉ *80333* – ⓜ *Marienplatz* – ℰ *(089) 2 12 07 43*
– www.bayerischerhof.de – Closed August and Sunday-Monday
Rest – *(dinner only)* Menu 80/135 € ♨   **G2**
♦ French creative ♦ Fashionable ♦

Every studio has its own art and it is the cuisine of Steffen Mezger that takes
centre stage here. The dishes are full of finesse and creativity. Such presentation
needs an appropriate setting and in this case it is a dining room decorated in
warm, calming and earthy tones staffed by a well-versed front of house team.
→ Zander mit weißer Zwiebel und Radieschen. Geschmortes Short-Rib
vom Wagyu mit Senfgurke und Rote Bete. Amedei Toscano White mit Rhabarber und Joghurt.

XXX **Dallmayr**   AC VISA OO AE

❀❀ *Dienerstr. 14 (1st floor)* ✉ *80331 –* ❶ *Marienplatz –* ☏ *(089) 2 13 51 00*
– www.dallmayr.de
– Closed 1 week 24 December-early January, 2 weeks Easter, 3 weeks early
August and Sunday-Monday   **G2**
Rest *– (dinner only) (booking advisable)* Menu 115/160 € ❀

◆ French classic ◆ Elegant ◆

While it is all hustle and bustle amid the heavily laden shelves of the delicatessen downstairs, on the first floor chef Diethard Urbansky reinvents classic dishes including calves' kidneys and pears Belle Hélène. For the perfect wine recommendation (there are a fine selection of Rieslings) who better than sommelier Andrej Grunert?

➔ Gefüllter Aal und Aalleber, Gewürzzwiebel und Radieschen. Zicklein - Marokkanisch gewürzt, Salzzitrone, Okra und Minzjoghurt. Rhabarber, Hüttenkäse und Arganöl.

XXX **Mark's** – Hotel Mandarin Oriental   AC VISA OO AE O

❀ *Neuturmstr. 1 (1st floor)* ✉ *80331 –* ❶ *Isartor –* ☏ *(089) 29 09 80*
– www.mandarinoriental.com
– Closed Monday   **H2**
Rest *– (dinner only)* Menu 65/119 € – Carte 60/103 €

◆ International ◆ Elegant ◆

Apparently just as influenced by Bangkok, Beijing and Shanghai as by his teachers in Germany, chef Simon Larese has developed his own contemporary culinary style with subtle Southeast Asian influences. The food served on the elegant gallery above the lobby is more than worthy of a restaurant of this standing.

➔ Wan Tan von der Entenleber mit Madeirasauce und weißem Trüffelschaum. Saibling mit Noilly Prat-Gelee, Brunnenkresse-Crème, sautierte Pfifferlinge, pochierte Gillardeau Austern und Yuzu-Schaum. Schokoladen-Zigarre mit geräuchertem Schokoladenmousse und Mojito-Granité.

XXX **Schuhbecks in den Südtiroler Stuben**   AC ⇄ VISA OO AE

❀ *Platzl 6* ✉ *80331 –* ❶ *Isartor –* ☏ *(089) 2 16 69 00 – www.schuhbeck.de*
– Closed 1 week early January and Sunday-Monday lunch   **H2**
Rest *– (booking advisable)* Menu 65 € *(lunch)/118 €* ❀

◆ International ◆ Rustic ◆ Elegant ◆

The atmosphere at the Platzl place is pleasant and lively and this feeling extends into Alfons Schuhbeck's elegant Alpine restaurant. Patrick Raaß offers two menus ('Schuhbeck's Classics' and 'World of Spices'). Next door, the restaurant's own shops sell ice cream, chocolate, spices and wine.

➔ Gebeizter Huchen mit Vanilleradi und Portulak. Filet und Tatar vom bayerischen Almochsen mit Seleriepürree und siebenerlei Pfeffer. Allerhand von der Himbeere mit Kardamom.

XX **Blauer Bock**   🏠 AE

Sebastiansplatz 9 ✉ *80331 –* ❶ *Marienplatz –* ☏ *(089) 45 22 23 33*
– www.restaurant-blauerbock.de
– Closed Sunday-Monday and Bank Holidays   **G3**
Rest *–* Menu 33 € *(lunch)/83 €* (dinner) – Carte 55/62 €

◆ International ◆ Minimalist ◆ Fashionable ◆

A chic modern restaurant with a bright, elegant interior located close to the Viktualienmarkt. The ambitious cuisine on offer combines French and international dishes.

XX **Ederer**   🏠 ⇄ VISA OO AE

Kardinal-Faulhaber-Str. 10 (1st floor) ✉ *80333 –* ❶ *Odeonsplatz*
– ☏ *(089) 24 23 13 10 – www.restaurant-ederer.de*
– Closed 1 week during Christmas, Sunday and Bank Holidays   **G2**
Rest *– (booking advisable)* Menu 30 € *(lunch)/55 €* (dinner) – Carte 44/65 € ❀

◆ International ◆ Fashionable ◆

This comfortable, chic and modern restaurant belongs to the 'Fünf Höfe' quarter of the city. Here, Karl Ederer offers international cuisine made from fresh products. There is a lovely interior courtyard.

GERMANY - MUNICH

XX **Halali**   *VISA* **⬤** **AE**

*Schönfeldstr. 22 ✉ 80539 – **Ⓜ** Odeonsplatz – ℰ (089) 28 59 09*
– www.restaurant-halali.de
– Closed Saturday lunch, Sunday and Bank Holidays   **H1**
Rest *– (booking advisable)* Menu 25 € (lunch)/62 € – Carte 36/67 €
♦ International ♦ Cosy ♦

The sophisticated restaurant in this 19C guesthouse has almost become an institution already. The dark wood panelling and lovely decoration has created a cosy atmosphere.

XX **Garden-Restaurant** – Hotel Bayerischer Hof   🛖 **AC**

*Promenadeplatz 2 ✉ 80333 – **Ⓜ** Marienplatz*   *VISA* **⬤** **AE** **①**
– ℰ (089) 2 12 09 93 – www.bayerischerhof.de   **G2**
Rest *– (booking advisable)* Menu 34 € (lunch)/65 € – Carte 46/90 €
♦ International ♦ Friendly ♦ Rurally ♦

Belgian designer Axel Vervoordt has given this restaurant a very particular look. The industrial-style conservatory design creates a setting reminiscent of an artist's studio.

XX **Boettner's**   🛖 **AC** *VISA* **⬤** **AE** **①**

*Pfisterstr. 9 ✉ 80331 – **Ⓜ** Marienplatz – ℰ (089) 22 12 10*
– www.boettners.de
– Closed Sunday and Bank Holidays   **H2**
Rest *– (booking advisable)* Menu 38 € (lunch)/89 € (dinner)
– Carte 39/95 €
♦ French classic ♦ Cosy ♦

Located close to the Platzl place, this family restaurant established in 1901 continues to serve classic cuisine. Diners appreciate the reasonably priced set menus (including wine), though you have to book in advance.

XX **Nymphenburger Hof**   🛖 *VISA* **⬤** **AE**

*Nymphenburger Str. 24 ✉ 80335 – **Ⓜ** Maillingerstr. – ℰ (089) 1 23 38 30*
– www.nymphenburgerhof.de
– Closed 24 December-8 January, Saturday lunch, Sunday and Bank Holidays
Rest *– (booking advisable)* Menu 25 € (lunch)/75 €   *Plan I* **A2**
– Carte 36/67 €
♦ International ♦ Friendly ♦

The Austrian inspired cuisine tastes just as good on the lovely terrace as it does in the friendly restaurant. Live piano music is also played on some evenings.

XX **Galleria**   **AC** *VISA* **⬤** **AE** **①**

*Sparkassenstr. 11 (corner Ledererstraße) ✉ 80331 – **Ⓜ** Marienplatz*
– ℰ (089) 29 79 95 – www.ristorante-galleria.de   **G2**
Rest *– (booking advisable)* Menu 25 € (lunch)/79 € (dinner)
– Carte 44/56 €
♦ Italian ♦ Cosy ♦

A cosy little restaurant in the city centre. It uses fresh, top quality produce in its ambitious Italian cuisine. The brightly coloured pictures on the walls change frequently.

XX **Bayerisches Nationalmuseum**   🛖 **P** *VISA* **⬤** **AE**

*Prinzregenstr. 3 (access via Lerchenfeldstraße) ✉ 80538 – **Ⓜ** Lehel*
– ℰ (089) 45 22 44 30 – www.bnmrestaurant.de
– Closed Sunday dinner-Monday   *Plan I* **C3**
Rest – Menu 59/75 € (dinner) – Carte 39/65 €
♦ Modern ♦ Minimalist ♦ Fashionable ♦

The pleasantly restrained design sets off the wonderful vaulted ceiling to perfection and despite all the modern elements it still manages to evoke the history of the building. The restaurant offers a concise menu at lunchtimes, handmade cakes throughout the day and ambitious contemporary-classic cuisine in the evenings.

✗✗ **Pfistermühle** – Hotel Platzl 🛜 VISA ⊕ AE ①
Pfisterstr. 4 ✉ 80331 – **Ⓜ** Marienplatz – ℰ (089) 23 70 38 65 – www.platzl.de
– Closed Sunday   **G2**
Rest – Menu 41/57 € – Carte 41/70 €
♦ Regional/country ♦ Rustic ♦
A separate entrance leads into this historic hostelry that started life as a ducal
mill in 1573. Stylish Bavarian bar crowned by a vaulted ceiling.

✗✗ **Weinhaus Neuner** ⇧ VISA ⊕ AE
Herzogspitalstr. 8 ✉ 80331 – **Ⓜ** Karlsplatz (Stachus) – ℰ (089) 2 60 39 54
– www.weinhaus-neuner.de
– Closed Sunday and Bank Holidays   **F2**
Rest – Carte 36/52 €
♦ International ♦ Traditional ♦
It is worth visiting this 1641 wine house to see the crossed vault 'Tirolian arches'.
There is also a beautiful wall painting, old panelling, and the preserved, original
carvings.

✗✗ **Les Cuisiniers** 🛜 VISA ⊕ AE
Reitmorstr. 21 ✉ 80538 – **Ⓜ** Lehel – ℰ (089) 23 70 98 90
– www.lescuisiniers.de
– Closed Saturday lunch, Sunday   Plan I **C3**
Rest – (booking advisable) Menu 23 € (lunch)/49 € (dinner)
– Carte 27/46 €
♦ French classic ♦ Bistro ♦
The atmosphere, service and food here are pleasantly uncomplicated – just as
you would imagine a French bistro should be. French and half-French respecti-
vely, the chef and owner serve authentic French food that is chalked up on a
blackboard menu.

✗✗ **Le Barestovino** 🛜 AC ⇧ VISA ⊕ AE
😊 Thierschstr. 35 ✉ 80538 – **Ⓜ** Lehel – ℰ (089) 23 70 83 55
– www.barestovino.de
– Closed Sunday-Monday   Plan I **C3**
Rest – (dinner only) Menu 46 € – Carte 29/50 €
♦ French classic ♦ Bistro ♦
'Patron' Joel Bousquet is French and not surprisingly the menu contains French,
as well as Mediterranean dishes. Alternatively you can sit in the Le Bouchon wine
bar at the front of the restaurant and order a light meal and wine by the glass.

✗ **Schweiger² im Showroom** 🛜 ✄
😾 Lilienstr. 6 ✉ 81669 – **Ⓜ** Isartor – ℰ (089) 44 42 90 82 – www.schweiger2.de
– Closed Christmas-early January, 2 weeks early August, Saturday, Sunday and
Bank Holidays   Plan I **C3**
Rest – (dinner only) (booking essential) Menu 95/135 €
♦ French classic ♦ Friendly ♦ Trendy ♦
Like his cooking and the atmosphere in this small restaurant, Andreas Schwei-
ger is young and unpretentious. He makes a personal appearance at every table
to announce his menus.
→ Konfierter Lachs auf Kohlrabi-Spaghetti mit Vanille-Kirschtomate und
Champagnerschaum. Geschmorte Schulter vom Ochsen auf Selleriepüree
mit Portweinschalotten. Lauwarmer Schwarzbrot-Schokoladengugl mit
Joghurt-Limoneneis und Rosenheimer Beeren.

✗ **Retter's Feinschmecker** 🛜 VISA ⊕
Frauenstr. 10 ✉ 80469 – **Ⓜ** Isartor – ℰ (089) 23 23 79 23 – www.retters.de
– Closed 1-14 January, 19 May-3 June, Sunday-Monday and Bank Holidays
Rest – Menu 27 € (lunch)/70 € (dinner) – Carte 36/57 € 🏵   **G3**
♦ Modern ♦ Cosy ♦
This restaurant is close to the Viktualienmarkt. Its clean, modern design meets
old Swiss pine panelling to create a welcoming, attractive interior. The weekly
seasonal menu is accompanied by over 300 different wines from chef Nicole
Retter's wine shop next door.

GERMANY - MUNICH

Jin
🕱 🛱 VISA ⓸ AE

Kanalstr. 14 ✉ *80538* – ⓶ *Isartor* – ℰ *(089) 21 94 99 70*
– *www.restaurant-jin.de*
– *Closed Monday*   **H2**
Rest – Menu 49/79 € – Carte 40/70 €
♦ Asian ♦ Exotic ♦ Elegant ♦
Hao Jin combines influences from various South-East Asian countries including China and Japan in his creative cuisine. Guests can choose from two menus, but the chef is always pleased to respond to individual wishes. The contents of the fish tank (including prawns and blue fin tuna) are particularly appetising.

Geisel's Vinothek – Hotel Excelsior
🕱 AC VISA ⓸ AE ⓸

Schützenstr. 11 ✉ *80335* – ⓶ *Hauptbahnhof* – ℰ *(089) 5 51 37 71 40*
– *www.geisel-privathotels.de*
– *Closed Sunday lunch and Bank Holidays lunch*   **H2**
Rest – Menu 40 € (dinner) – Carte 30/53 € ⌁
♦ Regional/country ♦ Rustic ♦
The Geisel family offer a great alternative to their Königshof restaurant with the focus on gourmet cuisine. Perfect for those who prefer a lighter regional or Mediterranean fare accompanied by a glass of good wine.

Toshi
AC VISA ⓸ AE ⓸

Wurzerstr. 18 ✉ *80539* – ⓶ *Lehel* – ℰ *(089) 25 54 69 42*
– *www.restaurant-toshi.de*
– *Closed 2 weeks August, Saturday lunch, Sunday and Bank Holidays lunch*
Rest – Menu 65/120 € – Carte 31/99 €   **H2**
♦ Japanese ♦ Minimalist ♦
It is just a short hop from the ritzy Maximilianstraße to this authentic Japanese restaurant. The menu – as characteristic as the minimalist design – offers fresh Far Eastern dishes. These include sushi, teppanyaki and 'pan-Pacific' cuisine.

Emiko – Hotel Louis
♿ AC VISA ⓸ AE ⓸

Viktualienmarkt 6 ✉ *80331* – ⓶ *Marienplatz* – ℰ *(089) 41 11 90 80*
– *www.louis-hotel.com*   **G2**
Rest – *(dinner only)* Menu 69 € – Carte 35/59 €
♦ Japanese ♦ Minimalist ♦
The simple, designer-style interior gives the restaurant a typical South-East Asian touch. The team in the kitchen prepares specialities from the Land of the Rising Sun.

Sophie's Bistro – Hotel Sofitel Munich Bayerpost
🕱 ♿ AC

Bayerstr. 12 ✉ *80335* – ⓶ *Hauptbahnhof*   VISA ⓸ AE ⓸
– ℰ *(089) 59 94 80* – *www.sofitel.com*   **H2**
Rest – Carte 42/61 €
♦ International ♦ Friendly ♦ Minimalist ♦
A very smart interior with furniture reminiscent of the 1970s. The high ceilings and floor-to-ceiling arched windows onto the street give the bistro a certain light and airy feel. Specialities from the lava grill.

Louis Cuisine
VISA ⓸

Tattenbachstr. 1 ✉ *80538* – ⓶ *Lehel* – ℰ *(089) 44 14 19 10*
– *www.restaurant-louis.de*
– *Closed 1 week early January, 1 week during Whitsun, 3 weeks end August-mid September and Saturday lunch, Sunday*   *Plan I* **C3**
Rest – Menu 20/63 €
♦ Classic ♦ Friendly ♦
Chef Stefan Schütz runs this pretty little restaurant in the old Lehel quarter of Munich together with his wife. Seating only 12, bookings for the good value lunch menu (three courses including water for €20) are highly sought after. In the evenings the classic cuisine comes in the form of set four- or five-course menus.

✗ **Altes Hackerhaus**   🏠 AC ✿ 🚾 ⚙ AE ①
Sendlinger Str. 14 ⊠ 80331 – Ⓜ Marienplatz – ℰ (089) 2 60 50 26
– www.hackerhaus.de   **G2**
Rest – Carte 20/49 €
◆ Regional/country ◆ Cosy ◆ Romantic ◆
A very cared-for and well-run rustic restaurant where Bavarian delicacies are served in warm and homely rooms. There is a beautiful covered interior courtyard.

✗ **Weisses Bräuhaus**   🏠 & ✿ 🚾 ⚙ AE ①
Tal 7 ⊠ 80331 – Ⓜ Isartor – ℰ (089) 2 90 13 80
– www.weisses-brauhaus.de   **G2**
Rest – Carte 17/42 €
◆ Regional/country ◆ Cosy ◆
This Bavarian hostelry is like something out of a picture book. People from Munich come here for the 'Kronfleisch' or skirt of beef – just one of the many specialities from the restaurant's own butchery. Squeezing together in the rustic dining areas is also traditional!

✗ **Spatenhaus an der Oper**   🏠 🚾 ⚙ AE
Residenzstr. 12 ⊠ 80333 – Ⓜ Marienplatz – ℰ (089) 2 90 70 60
– www.kuffler.de   **G2**
Rest – Carte 31/61 €
◆ Regional/country ◆ Traditional ◆
The attractive rooms in this townhouse, opposite the Bavarian State Opera, exude rural charm. On the ground floor the food is local; on the first-floor the menu is international.

ENVIRONS   *Plan I*

🏠🏠🏠🏠 **The Westin Grand**   ⇐ 🏠 ⅃♠ ⊕ 🛏 🖾 & AC 📞 🏊 🚗
Arabellastr. 6 ⊠ 81925 – Ⓜ Arabellapark   🚾 ⚙ AE ①
– ℰ (089) 9 26 40 – www.westingrandmunich.com   **D2**
627 rm – ♦149/449 € ♦♦149/449 €, 🖙 29 € – 28 suites
Rest ZEN – see restaurant listing
Rest Paulaner's – ℰ (089) 92 64 81 15 (closed Sunday lunch and Bank Holidays lunch) Carte 28/53 €
◆ Business ◆ Luxury ◆ Contemporary ◆
This luxury business hotel and conference venue boasts a wonderful 1500m² spa with adjoining fitness facilities. Great roof lounge for the executive rooms. ZEN offers Asian cuisine cooked in its open kitchen.

🏠🏠🏠 **Marriott**   ⅃♠ 🛏 🖾 & 🖾 ⧉ 🏊 🚗 🚾 ⚙ AE ①
Berliner Str. 93 ⊠ 80805 – Ⓜ Nordfriedhof – ℰ (089) 36 00 20
– www.marriott-muenchen.de   **C1**
348 rm – ♦109/349 € ♦♦109/349 €, 🖙 26 € – 1 suite
Rest – Carte 35/64 €
◆ Chain hotel ◆ Contemporary ◆
A comfortable business hotel in the contemporary style with pleasant, spacious lobby. Massage and beauty treatments available. Modern restaurant serving international cuisine and steaks. The Sportsbar offers a small selection of dishes.

🏠🏠🏠 **Hilton City**   🏠 ⅃♠ & 🖾 ⧉ 🏊 🚗 🚾 ⚙ AE ①
Rosenheimer Str. 15 ⊠ 81667 – Ⓜ Ostbahnhof – ℰ (089) 4 80 40
– www.hilton.de/munichcity   **C3**
480 rm – ♦149/374 € ♦♦149/374 €, 🖙 28 € – 20 suites
Rest – Carte 25/70 €
◆ Chain hotel ◆ Contemporary ◆
This business hotel with its contemporary, functional rooms is conveniently located for the conference centres and has a direct overland railway link to the airport. Regional and international cuisine is served in this rustic restaurant.

Palace 🛋 🛎 AC rm, 🛜 🏊 🚗 VISA ⑳ AE

Trogerstr. 21 ⊠ 81675 – Ⓜ Prinzregentenplatz – ℰ (089) 41 97 10
– www.muenchenpalace.de **C3**
74 rm – †170/330 € ††200/360 €, ⊑ 25 € – 4 suites
Rest – Carte 22/65 €
♦ Business ♦ Classic ♦ Elegant ♦
This tasteful, impeccably run hotel includes many musicians amongst its regulars. The natural tones and parquet floors combine to create a warm and friendly atmosphere. Pleasant garden and roof terrace. This restaurant serves classic international cuisine.

INNSIDE Parkstadt Schwabing 🛋 🛎 & rest, AC 🛜 🏊

Mies-van-der-Rohe-Str. 10 ⊠ 80807 🚗 VISA ⑳ AE ①
– Ⓜ Nordfriedhof – ℰ (089) 35 40 80 – www.innside.com **C1**
160 rm ⊑ – †149/459 € ††179/489 €
Rest – (closed Saturday lunch, Sunday lunch and Bank Holidays)
Carte 39/61 €
♦ Business ♦ Functional ♦
Designed by famous architect Helmut Jahn, this hotel enjoys a convenient location close to the striking HighLight Towers. The whole building is beautifully light, with clean modern lines. This bistro-style restaurant with its modern white interior serves international cuisine.

Courtyard by Marriott München City Ost 🛗 & AC 🛜

Orleansstr. 71 ⊠ 81667 – Ⓜ Ostbahnhof 🏊 🚗 VISA ⑳ AE ①
– ℰ (089) 5 58 91 90 – www.courtyardmunich-cityeast.com **D3**
225 rm – †169 € ††169 €, ⊑ 23 € – 1 suite
Rest max – Carte 21/57 €
♦ Chain hotel ♦ Modern ♦
The design concept in this comfortable hotel brings together straight lines, warm colours and all the latest technology. Long-term guests stay in the Residence Inn next door. The options on the international menu include burgers and steaks.

Novotel City 🛋 🛗 🛎 ▢ & AC 🛜 🏊 🚗 VISA ⑳ AE ①

Hochstr. 11 ⊠ 81669 – Ⓜ Ostbahnhof – ℰ (089) 66 10 70
– www.novotel.com **C3**
307 rm – †99/309 € ††122/332 €, ⊑ 19 € – 2 suites
Rest – Carte 28/51 €
♦ Business ♦ Modern ♦
This business hotel with its modern, well-equipped rooms is located close to the River Isar and the German Museum. The restaurant reflects the light and airy, contemporary design of the hotel.

Sheraton Arabellapark ≼ 🛋 🛎 ▢ & rm, AC 🛜 🏊 🚗

Arabellastr. 5 ⊠ 81925 – Ⓜ Arabellapark VISA ⑳ AE ①
– ℰ (089) 9 23 20 – www.sheratonarabellapark.com **D2**
446 rm – †129/369 € ††129/369 €, ⊑ 23 € – 41 suites
Rest – Carte 26/53 €
♦ Business ♦ Modern ♦
This hotel with its simple, modern rooms complete with balconies is situated close to the English Garden. Views over the city from the indoor pool on the 22nd floor. "Audrey's" and "66" offer international cuisine together with grilled meats and organic dishes.

Suite Novotel without rest 🛗 & AC 🛜 🚗 VISA ⑳ AE ①

Lyonel-Feininger-Str. 22 (by Isarring C1) ⊠ 80807 – ℰ (089) 35 81 90
– www.suitenovotel.com
149 rm – †104/149 € ††104/149 €, ⊑ 12 €
♦ Chain hotel ♦ Contemporary ♦
Contemporary hotel with modern design. The comfortable rooms are spacious and functional, with the state-of-the-art technology.

Prinzregent am Friedensengel without rest 🕸 📶 🛜 ♨

Ismaninger Str. 42 ✉ *81675* — 🚘 ᴠɪꜱᴀ ⑳ ᴀᴇ ⓪
– **Ⓜ** *Prinzregentenplatz* – ✆ *(089) 41 60 50*
– www.prinzregent.de **C3**
65 rm 🖵 – ♦95/450 € ♦♦125/500 € – 2 suites

♦ Business ♦ Cosy ♦

This lovely old hotel with its beautiful woodwork is full of Bavarian charm. The cosy, wood-panelled bar offers bar snacks.

Freisinger Hof 🕸 🛜 ♨ 🄿 🚘 ᴠɪꜱᴀ ⑳ ᴀᴇ

Oberföhringer Str. 191 ✉ *81925* – ✆ *(089) 95 23 02*
– www.freisinger-hof.de
– Closed 27 December-7 January **D1**
51 rm 🖵 – ♦118/178 € ♦♦148/205 €
Rest *Freisinger Hof*🍴 – see restaurant listing

♦ Country house ♦ Cosy ♦

The hotel annexe which has been added to this historical inn offers comfortable country-style rooms. The small lobby is bright and welcoming. Enjoy tasty regional food in this cosy inn dating from 1875. Boiled beef and other classic Austrian dishes served.

angelo 🕭 📶 🛜 ♨ 🄿 ᴠɪꜱᴀ ⑳ ᴀᴇ ⓪

Leuchtenbergring 20 ✉ *81677* – **Ⓜ** *Prinzregenpl.* – ✆ *(089) 1 89 08 60*
– www.angelo-munich.com **D3**
146 rm 🖵 – ♦74/409 € ♦♦99/434 € – 2 suites
Rest – Carte 22/43 €

♦ Business ♦ Contemporary ♦

This modern business hotel with direct access to the overland railway is located close to a large fitness and wellness studio for which it provides a daily menu. Bistro-style restaurant.

Preysing without rest 📶 🛜 ♨ 🚘 ᴠɪꜱᴀ ⑳ ᴀᴇ ⓪

Preysingstr. 1 / Stubenvollstr. 2 ✉ *81667*
– **Ⓜ** *Max Weber Pl.* – ✆ *(089) 45 84 50*
– www.hotel-preysing.de
– Closed Christmas-6 January **C3**
62 rm 🖵 – ♦128/250 € ♦♦179/290 € – 5 suites

♦ Townhouse ♦ Cosy ♦

This tip-top furnished hotel has up-to-date guestrooms with granite floors. It is very suited to business travellers.

H'Otello H'09 without rest 🕭 📶 🛜 ♨ 🚘 ᴠɪꜱᴀ ⑳ ᴀᴇ ⓪

Hohenzollernstr. 9 ✉ *80801* – **Ⓜ** *Hohenzollernpl.* – ✆ *(089) 3 09 07 70*
– www.hotello.de **B2**
71 rm 🖵 – ♦121/187 € ♦♦156/222 €

♦ Chain hotel ♦ Modern ♦

Set in the centre of Schwabing, H'Otello H'09 boasts modern, urban-style design and its own very practical underground car park. The hotel is just a 10min drive from the A8 and A96 motorways.

Leopold 🛏 🕸 🛜 ♨ 🄿 🚘 ᴠɪꜱᴀ ⑳ ᴀᴇ ⓪

Leopoldstr. 119 ✉ *80804* – **Ⓜ** *Dietlindenstr.* – ✆ *(089) 36 04 30*
– www.hotel-leopold.de – Closed 23-28 December **B1**
57 rm 🖵 – ♦89/168 € ♦♦115/215 €
Rest – Carte 18/38 €

♦ Family ♦ Contemporary ♦

This impeccably run, family hotel offers a range of well-appointed rooms furnished in different styles, some of which have lovely garden views. Rustic style restaurant, serving international cuisine.

Tantris 🛏️ 🅰️🅲 🅿️ 🆚🅰 ⓸⓸ 🅰️🅴 ⓸

Johann-Fichte-Str. 7 ✉️ *80805* – ⓶ *Dietlindenstr.* – ℰ *(089) 3 61 95 90*
– *www.tantris.de*
– *Closed 1-14 January, Sunday-Monday and Bank Holidays* **B1**
Rest – *(booking advisable)* Menu 75 € (lunch)/165 € – Carte 95/148 € 🍴
♦ French classic ♦ Retro ♦

Tantris has become as renowned for its legendary 1970s charm as it is for Hans Haas's classic cuisine. His guests' enthusiasm for his undisputed culinary skills remains as keen as it ever was.
➔ Langoustine mit mariniertem Chicorée und Yuzucrème. Pochierte Gänseleber mit pochiertem Ei und Périgord Trüffelsauce. Karamellsoufflé mit eingelegten Vanille-Äpfeln.

Bogenhauser Hof 🛏️ ↺ 🆚🅰 ⓸⓸ 🅰️🅴 ⓸

Ismaninger Str. 85 ✉️ *81675* – ⓶ *Böhmerwaldplatz* – ℰ *(089) 98 55 86*
– *www.bogenhauser-hof.de*
– *Closed Christmas-6 January, Sunday and Bank Holidays* **C2**
Rest – *(booking advisable)* Menu 45 € (lunch)/109 € – Carte 40/66 €
♦ Classic ♦ Traditional ♦ Cosy ♦

This modern elegant yet comfortable restaurant, housed in a building dating back to 1825 and serving classic cuisine prepared using the finest ingredients, has many regulars. Leafy garden complete with mature chestnut trees.

181 - First (Otto Koch) 🅰️🅲 🅿️ 🆚🅰 ⓸⓸ 🅰️🅴

Spiridon-Louis-Ring 7 (at Olympiaturm) ✉️ *80809* – ℰ *(089) 3 50 94 81 81*
– *www.restaurant181.com*
– *Closed 2 weeks January, 2 weeks during Easter, 2 weeks end August-early September and Saturday-Monday lunch, Bank Holidays* **A1**
Rest – *(booking essential)* Menu 69 € (lunch)/145 €
Rest 181 - Business – see restaurant listing
♦ Modern ♦ Elegant ♦

The tremendous view you get up here 181m above the ground is unforgettable. The panorama is ever-changing, as this small gourmet restaurant – it has only four tables – rotates the full 360° while you eat. No less remarkable is Otto Koch's creative menu, which is packed with surprises.
➔ Hummer Deluxe. Ente aus der Presse in der Luft tranchiert. Honeymoon.

Acquarello (Mario Gamba) 🛏️ 🅰️🅲 🆚🅰 ⓸⓸

Mühlbaurstr. 36 ✉️ *81677* – ⓶ *Böhmerwaldplatz* – ℰ *(089) 4 70 48 48*
– *www.acquarello.com*
– *Closed 1-3 January and Saturday lunch, Sunday lunch and Bank Holidays lunch* **D2**
Rest – Menu 39 € (lunch)/129 € – Carte 54/78 €
♦ Italian ♦ Friendly ♦ Mediterranean ♦

There is nothing Italian-born Mario Gamba likes more than paying a culinary tribute to his homeland. Bringing a little breath of the south into the setting as well, the decor is full of light Mediterranean touches. The attentive front of house team is all Italian.
➔ Hummer-Calamari-Ravioli mit grünem Spargel in Lardo di Colonnata auf Basilikumöl. Bretonische Rotbarbe in Zucchiniblüte mit Jakobsmuschelfarce, Tomatenragout, Safranschaum. Eukalyptusgelee mit Apfel-Koriandersorbet und Apfelspuma.

Käfer Schänke 🛏️ ↺ 🆚🅰 ⓸⓸ 🅰️🅴 ⓸

Prinzregentenstr. 73 (1st floor) ✉️ *81675* – ⓶ *Prinzregentenplatz*
– ℰ *(089) 4 16 82 47* – *www.feinkost-kaefer.de*
– *Closed Sunday and Bank Holidays* **C3**
Rest – *(booking essential)* Menu 37 € (lunch) – Carte 60/105 € 🍴
♦ International ♦ Cosy ♦ Individual ♦

In this popular restaurant with its 12 highly individual dining rooms the international menu is determined by the availability of the best quality produce. The delicatessen sells a range of fine foods.

XX
☺
Freisinger Hof – Hotel Freisinger Hof   🛖 P VISA ⓒⓞ AE

Oberföhringer Str. 189 ✉ *81925 –* ℰ *(089) 95 23 02 – www.freisinger-hof.de*
– Closed 27 December-7 January   **D1**
Rest – Carte 26/56 €
♦ Austrian ♦ Inn ♦

This is just what you imagine a traditional Bavarian restaurant to be like. Dating back to 1875, it stands just outside the city gates and serves typical Bavarian and Austrian cuisine. Dishes include Krosser saddle of suckling pig, and Vienna-style beef boiled in broth.

XX
Hippocampus   🛖 VISA ⓒⓞ AE ⓪

Mühlbaurstr. 5 ✉ *81677 –* Ⓜ *Prinzregentenplatz –* ℰ *(089) 47 58 55*
– www.hippocampus-restaurant.de
– Closed Monday and Saturday lunch   **C3**
Rest – Menu 50 € – Carte 42/56 €
♦ Italian ♦ Elegant ♦

Hippocampus offers friendly service, an informal atmosphere and ambitious Italian cuisine. Beautiful fixtures and fittings help create the elegant yet warm and welcoming interior.

XX
Geisels Werneckhof   AC VISA ⓒⓞ AE ⓪

Werneckstr. 11 ✉ *80802 –* Ⓜ *Münchner Freiheit –* ℰ *(089) 38 87 95 68*
– www.geisels-werneckhof.de
– Closed 3 weeks end July-August and Monday-Tuesday, Saturday lunch,
Sunday lunch   **C2**
Rest – *(booking advisable)* Menu 59/95 € – Carte 38/68 €
♦ Regional/country ♦ Cosy ♦

Geisels boasts a classic, comfortable decor, good food and a fine choice of wine, plus a friendly front-of-house team managed by Ireneo Tucci. In the kitchen, Michael Hüsken prepares fresh, flavoursome dishes that are available à la carte or from the good value two-course set lunch menu (including water and coffee).

XX
181 - Business – Restaurant 181 - First   AC P VISA ⓒⓞ AE

Spiridon-Louis-Ring 7 (at Olympiaturm, charge) ✉ *80809*
– ℰ *(089) 3 50 94 81 81 – www.restaurant181.com*
– Closed 2 weeks early January, 2 weeks during Easter, 2 weeks end August-
early September and Saturday-Monday lunch, Bank Holidays   **A1**
Rest – Menu 39 € (lunch)/68 € – Carte 36/67 €
♦ International ♦ Friendly ♦

Business is the second (and somewhat simpler) of the two revolving television tower restaurants. The journey up to it is quick but once you are there you probably won't be ready to leave the stunning views in a hurry!

XX
ZEN – Hotel The Westin Grand   ᵬ AC VISA ⓒⓞ AE ⓪

Arabellastr. 6 ✉ *81925 –* Ⓜ *Arabellapark –* ℰ *(089) 92 64 81 10*
– www.westingrandmunich.com
– Closed 3 weeks July-August and Sunday dinner   **D2**
Rest – Carte 29/50 €
♦ Asian ♦ Fashionable ♦

The warm brown wooden flooring throughout gives a certain harmony to this carefully designed interior. Characteristic flower arrangements add a South-East Asian feel. Open show kitchen.

XX
Bibulus   🛖 VISA ⓒⓞ AE

Siegfriedstr. 11 ✉ *80803 –* Ⓜ *Münchner Freiheit –* ℰ *(089) 39 64 47*
– www.bibulus-ristorante.de
– Closed Saturday lunch and Sunday   **B1**
Rest – Menu 43 € – Carte 36/52 €
♦ Italian ♦ Elegant ♦

It says something when a restaurant is popular with the locals, and the people of Schwabing clearly appreciate the uncomplicated and flavoursome Italian food. It is especially nice outside in the little square under the plane trees. Charming service.

GERMANY - MUNICH

X

Acetaia 🛱 _VISA_ **©©** **AE**
Nymphenburger Str. 215 (by A2) ✉ _80639_ – ℰ _(089) 13 92 90 77_
– _www.restaurant-acetaia.de_
– _Closed Saturday lunch_
Rest – Menu 29 € (lunch)/58 € – Carte 51/69 € 🕸
♦ Italian ♦ Cosy ♦

This friendly restaurant with its Art Nouveau decor offers Italian cuisine and the best espresso in the city. The olive oil and balsamic vinegar which gave the place its name are also very good. Attractive terrace.

X

Terrine 🛱 _VISA_ **©©** **AE** **①**
Amalienstr. 89 (at Amalien-Passage) ✉ _80799_ – Ⓜ _Universität_ – ℰ _(089) 28 17 80_ – _www.terrine.de_
– _Closed 2 weeks early January, 2 weeks June and Saturday lunch, Sunday-Monday lunch_   **B2**
Rest – Menu 39 € (lunch)/129 € – Carte 54/80 € 🕸
♦ Innovative ♦ Bistro ♦

Tucked away in an arcade under a large modern building, Terrine is a restaurant well worth finding. It combines a classic French bistro feel with a contemporary take on French cuisine. Chef Sebastian Heil and the entire front-of-house team demonstrate obvious dedication to their work. Excellent wine suggestions.

X
❀

Tramin _VISA_ **©©** **AE**
Lothringer Str. 7 ✉ _81667_ – Ⓜ _Ostbahnhof_ – ℰ _(089) 44 45 40 90_
– _www.tramin-restaurant.de_
– _Closed Sunday-Monday_   **C3**
Rest – _(dinner only)_ Menu 65/95 €
♦ Creative ♦ Fashionable ♦

This small restaurant with its friendly service and relaxed atmosphere can be very lively. Daniel Schimkowitsch's creative, modern cuisine is in the same vein.
➜ Huchen. Hühnerstall. Poltinger Maipock.

X

Huber 🛱 _VISA_ **©©** **AE**
Newtonstr. 13 ✉ _81679_ – Ⓜ _Richard Strauss Str._ – ℰ _(089) 98 51 52_
– _www.huber-restaurant.de_
– _Closed Saturday lunch, Sunday-Monday_   **C2**
Rest – Menu 25 € (lunch)/82 € (dinner) – Carte 40/53 €
♦ French classic ♦ Fashionable ♦

This appealing, modern restaurant offers friendly service and quality contemporary cuisine created by a young chef. The selection of Austrian wines is particularly good. The interior is by a Munich designer.

X

Saint Laurent 🛱 ⊠
Steinstr. 63 ✉ _81667_ – Ⓜ _Ostbahnhof_ – ℰ _(089) 47 08 40 00_
– _Closed 1-7 August and Monday_   **C3**
Rest – _(dinner only)_ Menu 25/58 € – Carte 35/62 €
♦ French ♦ Cosy ♦

A comfortable restaurant where the French-inspired atmosphere and French music provide the ideal backdrop to the chef's cooking style. There is a terrace some 50m from the restaurant.

X
☺

Atelier Gourmet 🛱 _VISA_ **©©** **AE**
Rablstr. 37 ✉ _81669_ – Ⓜ _Ostbahnhof_ – ℰ _(089) 48 72 20_
– _www.ateliergourmet.de_
– _Closed Sunday_   **C3**
Rest – _(dinner only) (booking advisable)_ Menu 35/63 € – Carte 45/51 €
♦ French classic ♦ Friendly ♦

The atmosphere in this modern restaurant is friendly and pleasantly casual. Find authentic French bistro cooking chalked up on a blackboard with dishes such as veal terrine in breadcrumbs. Good selection of wines.

Vinaiolo

🍴   VISA   ◍◑   AE

Steinstr. 42 ⊠ 81667 – Ⓜ Ostbahnhof – ℰ (089) 48 95 03 56
– www.vinaiolo.de
– Closed Saturday lunch   **C3**
Rest – Menu 21/64 € – Carte 44/54 €
♦ Italian ♦ Cosy ♦

Sample a taste of the 'dolce vita' in this restaurant. The service exudes southern charm, the food could not be better, even in Italy, and the lunchtime menu is very reasonably priced. The image of authentic Italy is completed by fixtures and fittings from an old grocer's shop in Trieste.

M Belleville

🍴   😀   ☆   VISA   ◍◑

Fallmerayerstr. 16 ⊠ 80796 – Ⓜ Hohenzollernpl. – ℰ (089) 30 74 76 11
– www.m-belleville.com
– Closed 4 weeks August-September and Sunday-Monday   **B2**
Rest – *(dinner only)* Menu 34 € – Carte 39/47 €
♦ French classic ♦ Bistro ♦ Brasserie ♦

So great is her love of Paris bistros that young chef Manina Panzer has brought their charm and simplicity to Munich. She prepares fresh, fragrant dishes. These include quail escabèche and Miéral guinea fowl, accompanied perhaps by a bottle from the carefully selected list of 'natural' wines.

AT THE EXHIBITION CENTRE

Prinzregent an der Messe

☆ 🄬 & rest, 🛜 🛋 ℙ 🚗   VISA ◍◑ AE ◐

Riemer Str. 350 (Industrialpark-West) ⊠ 81829
– ℰ (089) 94 53 90 – www.prinzregent.de
91 rm � – †85/450 € ††125/500 € – 4 suites   **Rest** – Carte 23/55 €
♦ Business ♦ Inn ♦ Cosy ♦

This lovely hotel, converted from a period inn, offers comfortable rooms in the Bavarian style and a great sauna. Located conveniently close to the exhibition centre. A cosy restaurant with a touch of elegance.

Innside München Neue Messe

☆ 🄬 & rest, 🄰🄲 rest, 🛜 🛋 🚗 VISA ◍◑ AE ◐

Humboldtstr. 12 (Gewerbegebiet-West)
⊠ 85609 – ℰ (089) 94 00 50 – www.innside.de
134 rm � – †99/459 € ††129/489 €   **Rest** – Carte 27/50 €
♦ Business ♦ Modern ♦

A modern design characterises this hotel, from the light hall area in atrium style, through to the cosy guestrooms. Unusual features include the freestanding glass showers. Bistro-style restaurant with international cuisine.

Novotel Messe

☆ & 🄰🄲 🛜 🛋 🚗 VISA ◍◑ AE ◐

Willy-Brandt-Platz 1 ⊠ 81829 – ℰ (089) 99 40 00
– www.novotel.com/5563
278 rm � – †69/499 € ††69/499 €   **Rest** – Carte 24/46 €
♦ Chain hotel ♦ Business ♦ Modern ♦

Located in the former airport grounds next to the convention centre, this hotel is modern and functional. Good transport connections with the motorway and underground. Bright, friendly restaurant with a glass frontage.

Schreiberhof

☆ 🄬 🛜 🛋 ℙ 🚗 VISA ◍◑ AE

Erdinger Str. 2 ⊠ 85609 – ℰ (089) 90 00 60 – www.schreiberhof.de
87 rm � – †97/115 € ††118/155 €
Rest – *(closed 3 weeks August and Sunday)* Carte 18/32 €
♦ Inn ♦ Conference hotel ♦ Functional ♦

Once a traditional inn, Schreiberhof has been developed into a modern city centre hotel with functional rooms. The light-flooded winter garden makes an unusual conference setting. This restaurant offers a number of dining rooms in different styles ranging from the stylish to the cosy and informal, and a beer garden set under mature trees.

Kempinski Airport München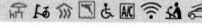

Terminalstraße Mitte 20 ✉ *85356 –* ℰ *(089) 9 78 20*
– www.kempinski-airport.de
389 rm – ♦170/450 € ♦♦170/450 €, ⌑ 32 € – 46 suites
Rest *charles lindbergh* – ℰ *(089) 97 82 45 00* – Carte 38/65 €
♦ Business ♦ Contemporary ♦
This business hotel has an imposing glass atrium complete with 18m-high palm trees. The rooms are contemporary but tasteful and the leisure facilities excellent. International cuisine features at the timeless Charles Lindbergh restaurant.

 Novotel

Nordallee 29 ✉ *85356 –* ℰ *(089) 9 70 51 30 – www.novotel.com/6711*
257 rm – ♦89/399 € ♦♦109/419 €, ⌑ 21 € **Rest** – Carte 26/55 €
♦ Chain hotel ♦ Contemporary ♦
Business hotel ideally located at the airport with a large modern lobby and straightforward functional rooms Restaurant offering international food.

STUTTGART
STUTTGART

Population: 601 650

Yuriy Davats/Fotolia.com

Baden-Württemberg, in Germany's south west, is one of the country's most popular tourist destinations and is defined by superb castles, delectable resorts and renowned wine-growing areas. The capital of the region, Stuttgart, sits easily within this framework. Its valley location, surrounded by steeply rising slopes, has allowed vineyards to approach the city centre from all around: the twisting branches of grapes are as much a part of the inner city picture as the sleek museums for Mercedes or Porsche.

There's an enviable amount of open space in Stuttgart and parks, forests and orchards cover more than half of its area. It seems appropriate that the city started life as a horse stud farm in the tenth century, growing to become Germany's most prosperous metropolis by way – incongruously or not – of its association with the world's sleekest cars. This is also a city of fine squares, majestic palaces, architecturally diverse buildings and cultural vigour. The city's museum of art is housed within a spectacular glass cube, while theatre, ballet and opera co-exist in the largest 'three function' building in Europe. Meanwhile, many visitors keep an eye open for Stuttgart's Beer Festival, which gives Munich's Oktoberfest a run for its money.

STUTTGART IN...

→ **ONE DAY**
Schlossplatz, Staatsgalerie, Mercedes-Benz Museum.

→ **TWO DAYS**
Kunstmuseum, Altes Schloss, amble through Schlossgarten, Porsche Museum, State Theatre Stuttgart.

→ **THREE DAYS**
Stroll in Rosenstein park, outing to Heidelberg or Baden-Baden.

PRACTICAL INFORMATION

ARRIVAL-DEPARTURE

✈ Stuttgart Airport is 13km South of the city centre.
S-Bahn commuter trains S2 and S3 run to the Central Station in 30min.

GETTING AROUND

There's an impressively integrated public transport system in Stuttgart, which covers nearby towns as well as the city itself. Once you've bought a ticket, you can switch between buses, trams, U-Bahn, mainline and S-Bahn trains. There are three types of ticket you might need: if you're here for a short time, buy a day ticket; if you're around for longer, invest in either a city explorer Stuttcard or a Stuttcard plus; these give free admission to most museums, reduced entry to theatres, and free travel on public transport for three days, including transport to the airport (the Stuttcard plus is more expensive, but offers more benefits).

CALENDAR HIGHLIGHTS

February
Stuttgart Bach Week.

March
Retroclassics (at the Messe Stuttgart), Long Art Night at the Museums.

April
Stuttgart Spring Beer Festival.

June
Christopher Street Day.

July
Jazz Open.

August
Summer Festival.

September
Stuttgarter Weindorf (wine festival).

October
Stuttgart Beer Festival.

EATING OUT

Württemberg's viniculture has a tradition of more than a thousand years and the most popular variety amongst the locals is the ruby red Trollinger. You might be surprised how it's served to you: in quarter litre glasses with handles. You won't be surprised that the 'Schwäbische Weinstuben' (local wine taverns) are rollicking good places to go. Beer is a flourishing trade too, with large Stuttgart breweries vying for your palate. That's not to say that food takes a back seat. There's a renowned 'local kitchen', with Gaisburger Marsch the pick of the dishes: it's a tasty stew made of Spätzle (the staple Stuttgart noodle), potatoes, beef pieces, vegetables, broth and roasted onions. Spätzles turn up everywhere, and are very popular 'mit Linsen' (lentils), especially when they're teamed up and served with warm sausages, or accompanying a Swabian roast, another hearty dish featuring slices of roast beef with lots of onions, served with Sauerkraut and Maultaschen (square dumplings with a savoury filling).

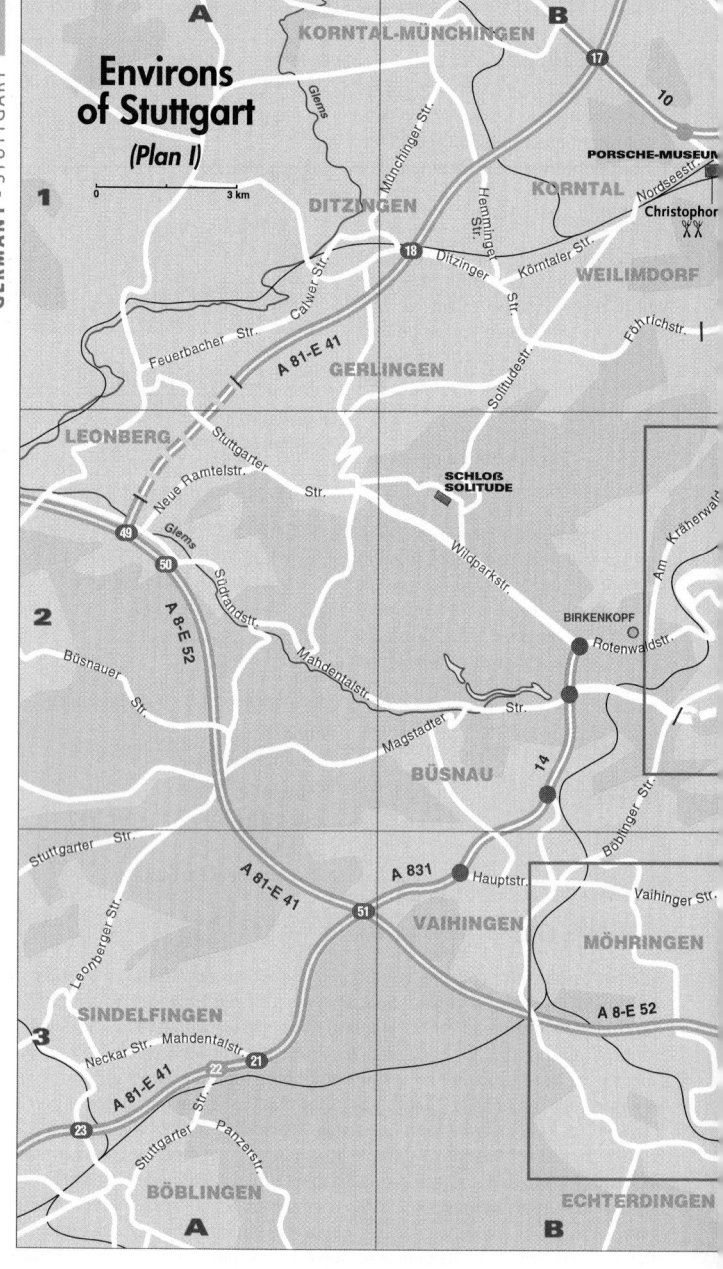

Environs of Stuttgart
(Plan I)

0   3 km

1

A

KORNTAL-MÜNCHINGEN

B

17

10

PORSCHE-MUSEUM

KORNTAL

Nordseestr.

Christophor

Glems

Münchinger Str.

DITZINGEN

18

Ditzinger

Hemminger Str.

Körntaler Str.

WEILIMDORF

Str.

Föhrichstr.

Feuerbacher Str.

Calwer Str.

GERLINGEN

A 81-E 41

Solitudestr.

LEONBERG

Stuttgarter Str.

SCHLOß
SOLITUDE

Am Krähenwald

Neue Ramtelstr.

49

Glems

Str.

Wildparkstr.

50

Südrandstr.

A 8-E 52

2

Büsnauer

Str.

Mahdentalstr.

BIRKENKOPF

Rotenwaldstr.

Str.

Magstadter

Str.

BÜSNAU

14

Böblinger Str.

Stuttgarter Str.

A 81-E 41

A 831

Hauptstr.

VAIHINGEN

Vaihinger Str.

Leonberger Str.

51

MÖHRINGEN

A 8-E 52

SINDELFINGEN

3

Neckar Str.

Mahdentalstr.

22

21

A 81-E 41

23

Stuttgarter Str.

Panzerstr.

BÖBLINGEN

ECHTERDINGEN

A

B

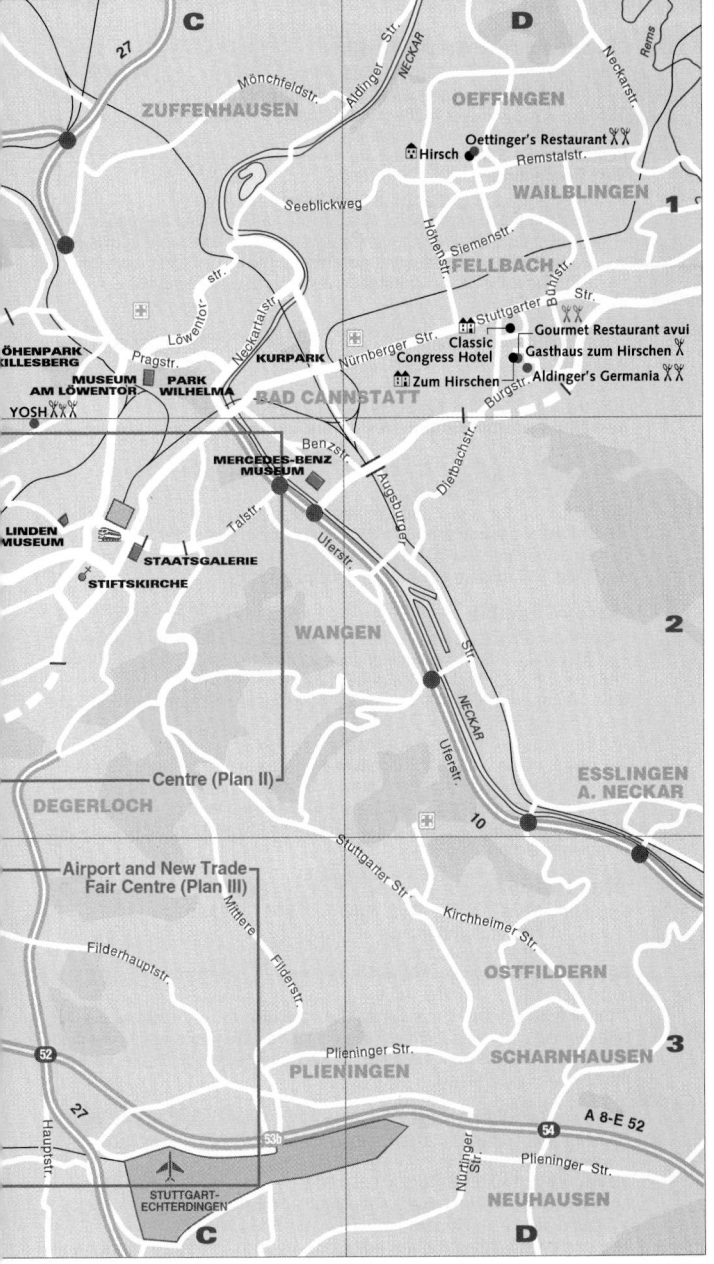

ZUFFENHAUSEN

OEFFINGEN

Mönchfeldstr.

Aldinger Str.

NECKAR

Neckarstr.

Rems

27

C

D

Oettinger's Restaurant ✕✕

Hirsch

Remstalstr.

WAILBLINGEN

Seeblickweg

Höhenstr.

Siemenstr.

FELLBACH

1

Löwentor str.

Neckartalstr.

Pragstr.

Stuttgarter Str.

Bühlstr.

Str.

Gourmet Restaurant avui ✕✕

ÖHENPARK
KILLESBERG

KURPARK

Nürnberger Str.

Classic
Congress Hotel

Gasthaus zum Hirschen ✕

MUSEUM
AM LÖWENTOR

PARK
WILHELMA

Zum Hirschen

Aldinger's Germania ✕✕

Burgstr.

YOSH ✕✕✕

BAD CANNSTATT

Benzstr.

Dietbachstr.

MERCEDES-BENZ
MUSEUM

Augsburger

LINDEN
MUSEUM

Talstr.

Uferstr.

STAATSGALERIE

Str.

WANGEN

2

STIFTSKIRCHE

NECKAR

Centre (Plan II)

Uferstr.

DEGERLOCH

ESSLINGEN
A. NECKAR

Airport and New Trade
Fair Centre (Plan III)

Stuttgarter Str.

10

Filderhauptstr.

Mittlere

Filderstr.

Kirchheimer Str.

OSTFILDERN

52

Plieninger Str.

SCHARNHAUSEN

3

27

PLIENINGEN

A 8-E 52

54

Hauptstr.

53b

Nürtinger Str.

Plieninger Str.

STUTTGART-
ECHTERDINGEN

NEUHAUSEN

C

D

GERMANY - STUTTGART

Steigenberger Graf Zeppelin 👐 🕸 🗏 🔥 🎿 🎷 📶 🚗
Arnulf-Klett-Platz 7 ⊠ *70173* – 🚇 *S. Bahn* 〔VISA〕〔🆖〕〔AE〕〔①〕
– 𝒞 (0711) 2 04 80 – www.stuttgart.steigenberger.de **N1**
155 rm – ♦189/259 € ♦♦189/259 €, ⊡ 26 € – 6 suites
Rest *OLIVO* ✿ – see restaurant listing
Rest *Zeppelin Stüble* – *(closed Sunday dinner-Monday)* Carte 20/47 €
Rest *Zeppelino'S* – Carte 29/63 €
♦ Chain hotel ♦ Elegant ♦ Modern ♦

The rooms in this business hotel opposite the railway station are modern and elegant. The technology in the junior suites is just a little more upmarket. If you fancy working out with a view of the city, there is a fitness room on the top floor. The rustic Zeppelin Stüble serves regional cuisine and you can enjoy a cigar in the Davidoff Lounge.

Am Schlossgarten 🎿 🔥 🎷 📶 🚗 VISA 🆖 AE ①
Schillerstr. 23 ⊠ *70173* – 🚇 *S. Bahn* – 𝒞 *(0711) 2 02 60*
– www.hotelschlossgarten.com **N1**
106 rm – ♦152/272 € ♦♦187/327 €, ⊡ 23 € – 4 suites
Rest *Schlossgarten Gourmetrestaurant Bernhard Diers* ✿ – see restaurant listing
Rest *Vinothek* – 𝒞 *(0711) 2 02 68 36* – Menu 25 € – Carte 26/49 €
♦ Townhouse ♦ Classic ♦

Opt for one of the newer, modern yet classic bedrooms that combine clean, simple lines and warm colours to good effect. Some have a view over the nearby Schlossgarten park. As well as the Schlossgarten Gourmetrestaurant Bernhard Diers, you can also enjoy the Vinothek or the Café.

Arcotel Camino 🔥 🕸 🔥 🔥 🕼 🎿 🅿 🚗 VISA 🆖 AE ①
Heilbronner Str. 21 (access via Im Kaisemer 1) ⊠ *70191* – 🚇 *S. Bahn*
– 𝒞 (0711) 25 85 80 – www.arcotelhotels.com/camino **M1**
168 rm – ♦139/299 € ♦♦139/299 €, ⊡ 20 € – 1 suite
Rest *Weissenhof* – 𝒞 *(0711) 2 58 58 42 00 (closed Saturday lunch, Sunday lunch)* Menu 30 € – Carte 23/50 €
♦ Business ♦ Design ♦ Contemporary ♦

The design of the hotel which operates in this beautifully restored 1890 sandstone building is inspired by the "Camino de Santiago" and the style of the Weißenhofsiedlung residential development. The rooms offer modern design and the latest technology. An elegant, contemporary restaurant decorated in shades of brown and ochre.

Kronen-Hotel without rest 🎾 🕸 🔥 🎷 🎿 🚗 VISA 🆖 AE ①
Kronenstr. 48 ⊠ *70174* – 🚇 *S. Bahn* – 𝒞 *(0711) 2 25 10*
– www.kronenhotel-stuttgart.de
– Closed Christmas-2 January **M1**
80 rm ⊡ – ♦110/135 € ♦♦156/180 €
♦ Business ♦ Functional ♦

Attentively run by the Berger family, this hotel near the city centre is popular with business travellers and weekend-breakers alike. Individually furnished rooms and the excellent breakfast (served on the terrace in the summer months) add to its charms.

Wörtz zur Weinsteige 🔥 🎷 🎿 🅿 🚗 VISA 🆖 AE
Hohenheimer Str. 30 ⊠ *70184* – 🚇 *Dobelstr.* – 𝒞 *(0711) 2 36 70 00*
– www.zur-weinsteige.de **N2**
30 rm – ♦95/120 € ♦♦110/130 €, ⊡ 10 €
Rest *Wörtz zur Weinsteige* – see restaurant listing
♦ Townhouse ♦ Rustic ♦ Contemporary ♦

Two dedicated brothers run this hotel. One of which breeds the koi carp you can admire in the large aquarium on the terrace. The rooms in the annexe, which also houses the stylish Louis XVI Suite, are more comfortable and elegant.

GERMANY - STUTTGART

Der Zauberlehrling 🏧 🛜 🚗🚫

Rosenstr. 38 ✉ *70182* – ⓜ *Olgaeck* – ℰ *(0711) 2 37 77 70*
– www.zauberlehrling.de   **N2**
17 rm – ♦135/250 € ♦♦180/290 €, ⭐ 19 € – 4 suites
Rest *Der Zauberlehrling* – see restaurant listing
♦ Townhouse ♦ Personalised ♦ Design ♦
This small hotel which occupies two townhouses is run by the Heldmann family.
The themed rooms are individually designed and furnished with particular
attention to detail. Some have roof terraces.

Unger without rest 🏧 📞 🧖 🚗 🆚🆒 🆎 ⓞ

Kronenstr. 17 ✉ *70173* – ⓜ *S. Bahn* – ℰ *(0711) 2 09 90*
– www.hotel-unger.de   **N1**
114 rm ⭐ – ♦106/148 € ♦♦146/189 €
♦ Townhouse ♦ Functional ♦
This hotel with its functional rooms is situated just off the pedestrian zone.
Some of the rooms on the top floor have balconies. The hotel's art exhibition
is particularly interesting.

City-Hotel without rest 🛜 📱 🆚 🆒 🆎 ⓞ

Uhlandstr. 18 ✉ *70182* – ⓜ *Olgaeck* – ℰ *(0711) 21 08 10*
– www.cityhotel-stuttgart.de   **N2**
31 rm ⭐ – ♦79/89 € ♦♦99/115 €
♦ Townhouse ♦ Functional ♦
This contemporary hotel close to the pedestrian zone offers individually designed rooms in the contemporary style and a light and airy breakfast room with
winter garden and terrace.

Abalon without rest 🛜 🚗 🆚 🆒 🆎

Zimmermannstr. 7 (access via Olgastr. 79) ✉ *70182* – ⓜ *Olgaeck*
– ℰ (0711) 2 17 10 – www.abalon.de   **N2**
42 rm ⭐ – ♦79/86 € ♦♦89/108 €
♦ Business ♦ Functional ♦
Located just north of the city centre, this hotel offers functional rooms (with fruit
juice and mineral water provided free of charge), a modern breakfast area and
leafy roof terrace.

Schlossgarten Gourmetrestaurant Bernhard Diers 🍴 🏧 ⇄ 🆚 🆒 🆎 ⓞ
🕸️

Schillerstr. 23 (1st floor) ✉ *70173*
– ⓜ S. Bahn – ℰ (0711) 2 02 68 30 – www.hotelschlossgarten.com
Rest – Menu 39 € (lunch)/142 € – Carte 88/131 €   **N1**
♦ Regional/country ♦ Elegant ♦
Just the presence of Bernhard Diers in the kitchen and his wife Susanne front of
house make a trip to Schlossgarten worthwhile. The carefully prepared, seaso-
nal cuisine adds to the attraction of this restaurant. It stands in a tasteful setting
near the entrance to the Schlosspark.
➜ Mosaik von Langoustino und Seeteufel. Poltinger Lamm in der Kräuter-
Senfkruste. Fürst Pückler in Schokoladensamt.

OLIVO – Hotel Steigenberger Graf Zeppelin ♿ 🏧 🆚 🆒 🆎 ⓞ
🕸️

Arnulf-Klett-Platz 7 ✉ *70173* – ⓜ *S. Bahn* – ℰ *(0711) 2 04 82 77*
– www.olivo-restaurant.de
– Closed July-early September, Sunday-Monday and Bank Holidays
Rest – Menu 60 € (lunch)/119 € – Carte 80/96 €   **N1**
♦ Creative ♦ Elegant ♦
Nico Burkhardt is the name of the talented young chef in charge in the kitchen
at OLIVO, which is on the first floor of this grand hotel. His meticulously prepared modern cuisine sits perfectly alongside the chic elegant setting and pleasantly casual professional service.
➜ Langostinos und Thunfisch mit Avocado / Gurke / Rosa Ingwer / Wasa-
bisorbet. Rücken vom Limousin Lamm mit Tomate / Powerade / gebacke-
ner Manchego / Olivenjus. Cannelloni von Crue de Cacao und Macadamia-
nuß.

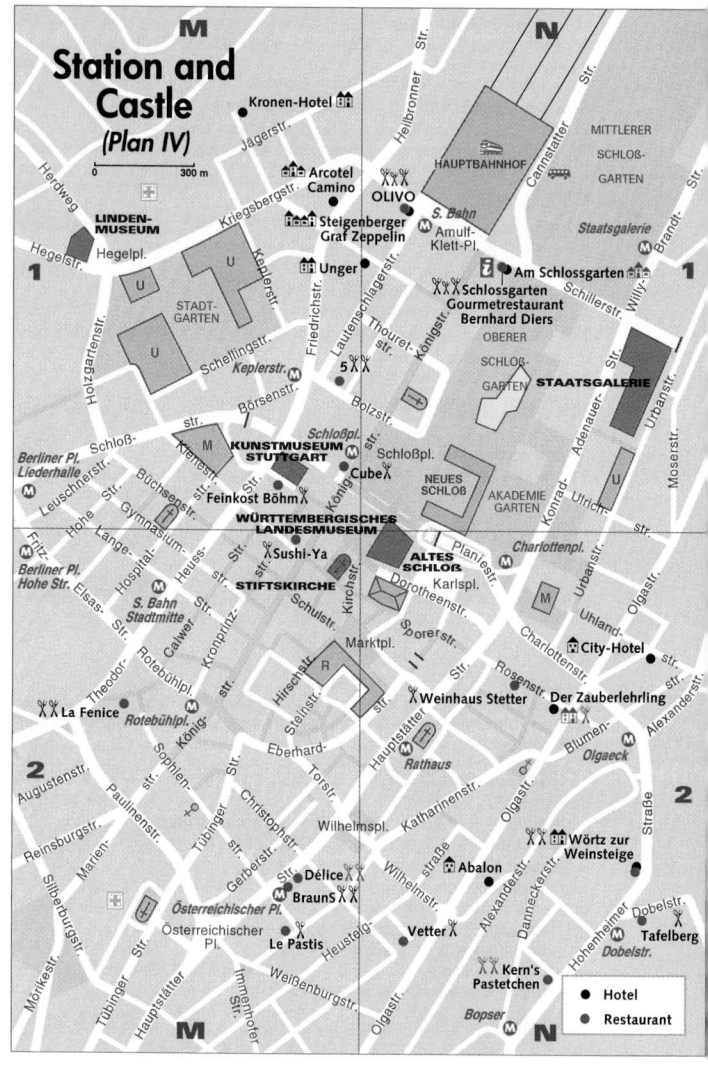

Station and Castle
(Plan IV)

0   300 m

Kronen-Hotel

Arcotel Camino
OLIVO
Steigenberger Graf Zeppelin
Unger

LINDEN-MUSEUM

HAUPTBAHNHOF

MITTLERER SCHLOß-GARTEN

S. Bahn
Amulf-Klett-Pl.

Staatsgalerie

Am Schlossgarten
Schlossgarten Gourmetrestaurant Bernhard Diers

STADT-GARTEN

OBERER
SCHLOß-GARTEN

STAATSGALERIE

5

SchloßPl.
KUNSTMUSEUM STUTTGART
Cube
Feinkost Böhm
SchloßPl.
NEUES SCHLOß
AKADEMIE GARTEN

Berliner Pl.
Liederhalle

WÜRTTEMBERGISCHES LANDESMUSEUM

Berliner Pl.
Hohe Str.

Sushi-Ya
STIFTSKIRCHE
ALTES SCHLOß

S. Bahn Stadtmitte

Charlottenpl.

City-Hotel

Marktpl.

La Fenice
Rotebühlpl.

Weinhaus Stetter
Der Zauberlehrling

Rathaus

Délice
Braun5
Österreichischer Pl.
Österreichischer Pl.
Le Pastis

Vetter

Abalon

Wörtz zur Weinsteige

Kern's Pastetchen

Tafelberg

Bopser

● Hotel
● Restaurant

Kern's Pastetchen

Hohenheimer Str. 64 ⊠ 70184 – ⓜ Bopser – ☎ (0711) 48 48 55
– www.kerns-pastetchen.de
– Closed 2 weeks end May, 2 weeks July-August and Sunday   **N2**
Rest *– (dinner only) (booking advisable)* Menu 48/68 € – Carte 44/62 €
♦ French classic ♦ Friendly ♦ Rustic ♦

Marieluise and Josef Kern are delightful hosts who always seem to manage to find the time for a quick chat with their guests. The characteristic appetisers and the wine selection give more than a passing nod to the chef's Austrian origins.

XX **La Fenice** 🏠 VISA ⬤⬤ AE

Rotebühlplatz 29 ✉ *70178 –* Ⓜ *Rotebühlpl. –* ☎ *(0711) 6 15 11 44*
– www.ristorante-la-fenice.de
– Closed Saturday lunch and Sunday except Bank Holidays **M2**
Rest – Menu 17 € (lunch)/55 € – Carte 36/56 €
♦ Italian ♦ Cosy ♦
This light, friendly restaurant with an elegant touch is where the Gorgoglione sisters offer Italian cuisine.

XX **Délice** AC VISA ⬤⬤ AE
🖧
Hauptstätter Str. 61 ✉ *70178 –* Ⓜ *Österreichischer Pl.*
– ☎ *(0711) 6 40 32 22 – www.restaurant-delice.de*
– Closed Christmas-6 January, 1 week Easter, 2 weeks Whitsun, 3 weeks August
and Saturday-Sunday **M2**
Rest – *(dinner only) (booking essential)* Menu 65/98 € – Carte 54/74 € 🍷
♦ Classic ♦ Friendly ♦
There are a number of reasons for eating at this small attractive restaurant. Not least of which are the personal service and wine suggestions from owner and sommelier Evangelos Pattas, and the highly recommended, produce centred cuisine created by chef Benjamin Schuster.
➔ Flusskrebse und Bries mit Rettich, Karotte, Erbsenschaum und Limonen-vinaigrette. Maibock mit Gänseleber und Blumenkohl-Chorizopüree, Balsa-mico-Nektarinen. Crème brûlée von Nougat mit marinierten Erdbeeren und Erdbeersorbet, Nougatschaum.

XX **5** AC VISA ⬤⬤ AE
🖧
Bolzstr. 8 (1st floor) ✉ *70173 –* Ⓜ *Keplerstr. –* ☎ *(0711) 65 55 70 11*
– www.5.fo
– Closed Sunday **M1**
Rest – *(dinner only)* Menu 59/99 €
♦ Modern ♦ Trendy ♦ Cosy ♦
Chic and informal, this restaurant offers a trendy bar downstairs and a lounge-style eatery upstairs. The committed culinary team works under the direction of Marc Müller to produce modern, creative cuisine. This is rich in contrast yet well balanced and perfectly suited to its urban setting.
➔ Schwäbischer Acker - Spargel/Estragon/Ziegenkäseschaum. Bretonisches Meer - Langoustine/Erbsen/Lardo. Wald - Maibock/Waldpilze/Sellerie/Birne.

XX **BraunS** AC VISA ⬤⬤ AE

Hauptstätter Str. 61 ✉ *70178 –* Ⓜ *Österreichischer Pl.*
– ☎ *(0711) 51 87 60 18 – www.restaurant-brauns.de*
– Closed Sunday and Bank Holidays **M2**
Rest – Carte 47/62 €
♦ International ♦ Elegant ♦
In March 2012 Michael Braun, no stranger to the world of gastronomy, opened his own restaurant in Stuttgart. Decorated in a striking red, BraunS sees classically based cuisine with a modern twist served by a friendly and dedicated front-of-house team.

XX **Wörtz zur Weinsteige** – Hotel Wörtz zur Weinsteige 🏠 ⅚
Hohenheimer Str. 30 ✉ *70184 –* Ⓜ *Dobelstr.* 🅿 VISA ⬤⬤ AE
– ☎ *(0711) 2 36 70 00 – www.zur-weinsteige.de*
– Closed 2 weeks early January, 2 weeks August, Sunday-Monday and Bank
Holidays except Christmas **N2**
Rest – Menu 35/85 € – Carte 41/68 € 🍷
♦ International ♦ Friendly ♦ Elegant ♦
Jörg Scherle is the chef in this welcoming restaurant, which he runs together with his brother. The cuisine is international in flavour, and the value for money lunchtime menu is always popular.

GERMANY - STUTTGART

✗ **Der Zauberlehrling** – Hotel Der Zauberlehrling   𝔸𝕂 ⊠
Rosenstr. 38 ⊠ 70182 – **Ⓜ** *Olgaeck – 𝒞 (0711) 2 37 77 70*
– www.zauberlehrling.de
– Closed Sunday   **N2**
Rest *– (dinner only) (booking advisable)* Menu 52/98 € – Carte 50/83 € 🍴
♦ Creative ♦ Trendy ♦ Fashionable ♦
Der Zauberlehrling is a lovely, bright little restaurant with a modern, minimalist
interior. It serves contemporary, creative cuisine with a regional influence. If you
are there on a Saturday night, try the set 'Candle Light Dinner' menu.

✗ **Feinkost Böhm**   ⛴ 𝒱𝒾𝒮𝒜 ⊕ 𝔸𝔼
Kronprinzstr. 6 ⊠ 70173 – **Ⓜ** *Schloßpl. – 𝒞 (0711) 2 27 56 28*
– www.feinkost-boehm.de
– Closed Sunday   **M1**
Rest *– (open to 8pm)* Menu 22 € – Carte 35/47 €
♦ International ♦ Fashionable ♦
As soon as you enter this minimalist, modern restaurant you are surrounded by
delicious things to eat, as it is located in a delicatessen. As a result, the chef has
all the ingredients he needs for his seasonal, classic cuisine right on the premises.

✗ **Le Pastis**   ⛴ 𝔸𝕂 ⇔ 𝒱𝒾𝒮𝒜 ⊕ 𝔸𝔼
Sophienstr. 3 ⊠ 70180 – **Ⓜ** *Österreichischer Pl. – 𝒞 (0711) 51 87 66 72*
– www.le-pastis.de
– Closed Sunday   **M2**
Rest *– (dinner only) (booking advisable)* Menu 32/46 € – Carte 36/59 €
♦ French ♦ Cosy ♦
A few steps down from the street you will find this cosy cellar restaurant. The
attractive setting of the old vaulted sandstone ceiling, combined with the
fresh French cuisine attracts a strong following.

✗ **Tafelberg**   ⇔ ⊠
Dobelstr. 2 ⊠ 70184 – **Ⓜ** *Dobelstr. – 𝒞 (0711) 51 89 02 68*
– www.tafelberg-stuttgart.de
– Closed 2 weeks end August and Sunday-Monday   **N2**
Rest *– (dinner only) (booking advisable)* Menu 40 € – Carte 24/37 €
♦ International ♦ Friendly ♦ Fashionable ♦
A friendly welcome from Nina Ruisinger awaits you in this contemporary style
restaurant where her husband prepares ambitious contemporary seasonal
dishes in the kitchen.

✗ **Cube**   ≼ ᵫ 𝔸𝕂 𝒱𝒾𝒮𝒜 ⊕ 𝔸𝔼
Kleiner Schlossplatz 1 (at Kunstmuseum, 4th floor) ⊠ 70173
– **Ⓜ** *Schloßpl. – 𝒞 (0711) 2 80 44 41 – www.cube-restaurant.de*
Rest *– Menu 30 € (lunch) – Carte 44/53 €*   **M1**
♦ Mediterranean ♦ Fashionable ♦
This cube-shaped, all-glass building designed by Heinz Witthöft with fantastic
views of the Schlosspark and city serves Mediterranean/Asian fusion cuisine.
There is also a good value lunchtime menu and snacks are served in the base-
ment bar.

✗ **Vetter**   ⛴ ⊠
☺ *Bopserstr. 18 ⊠ 70180 –* **Ⓜ** *Österreichischer Pl. – 𝒞 (0711) 24 19 16*
– Closed Sunday   **N2**
Rest *– (dinner only) (booking advisable)* Menu 29/57 € – Carte 29/57 €
♦ Regional/country ♦ Neighbourhood ♦
The menu in this warm and friendly city centre restaurant is as mixed as its
clientele. The food is good, whether you opt for something international or
one of the regional specialities. Try the Swabian-style beef with caramelised
onions and roast potatoes or spätzle.

STUTTGART
GERMANY -

✗ **Sushi - Ya**   ⚅ 🅰🅲 🆅🆂🅰 ⚉ 🅰🅴

Kronprinzenstr. 6 ✉ *70173 –* ⓜ *Schloßpl. –* ☏ *(0711) 2 27 56 29*
– www.feinkost-boehm.de
– Closed Sunday   M2
Rest – Menu 13 € (lunch)/30 € – Carte 12/39 €
♦ Japanese ♦ Trendy ♦
Make sure you get here early as once this trendy sushi bar has opened it fills up
in a matter of minutes! The authentic Japanese cuisine is much in demand and
they don't take reservations.

✗ **Weinhaus Stetter**   🈷 🚫

Rosenstr. 32 ✉ *70182 –* ⓜ *Rathaus –* ☏ *(0711) 24 01 63*
– www.weinhaus-stetter.de
*– Closed 2 weeks early January, 2 weeks end August-early September, Sunday
and Bank Holidays*   N2
Rest – *(Open from 3pm Monday-Friday)* Carte 16/33 € 🈸
♦ Regional/country ♦ Simple ♦
This rural style restaurant features regional cooking and a wine shop. The wine
selection includes around 600 offerings, with a good representation of Würt-
temberger and French wines.

CENTRE   *Plan II*

🏨 **Le Méridien**   🅰🅲 🎇 ⚉

Willy-Brandt-Str. 30 ✉ *70173 –* ⓜ *Neckartor –* ☏ *(0711) 2 22 10*
– www.lemeridienstuttgart.com   G1
292 rm – 🛏175/225 € 🛏🛏175/225 €, ☕ 25 € – 2 suites
Rest *Le Cassoulet* – see restaurant listing
♦ Luxury ♦ Business ♦ Classic ♦
This luxurious hotel is by the Schlossgarten. It has a spacious lobby and modern,
elegantly furnished rooms with good technical facilities. Pleasant spa area. Le
Cassoulet provides a range of international dishes.

🏨 **Maritim**   🈷 🏧 🖥 🅰🅲 🎇 ⚉

Seidenstr. 34 ✉ *70174 –* ⓜ *Rosenberg-/Seidenstr. –* ☏ *(0711) 94 20*
– www.maritim.de   F1
555 rm – 🛏99/219 € 🛏🛏119/239 €, ☕ 19 € – 12 suites
Rest – Carte 33/66 €
♦ Chain hotel ♦ Functional ♦
This spacious hotel connected to the Liederhalle cultural and congress centre is
ideal for conference visitors. Both suites and junior suites offer the height of
luxury with some rooms boasting "in-room saunas". As well as the Reuchlin restaurant, there is the rotisserie and buffet.

🏨 **Wald-Hotel**   🐕 🈷 ⚅ rest, 🅰🅲 🎇 🅿 🆅🆂🅰 ⚉ 🅰🅴 ⓞ

Guts-Muths-Weg 18 ✉ *70597 –* ⓜ *Waldau –* ☏ *(0711) 18 57 20*
– www.waldhotel-stuttgart.de   G3
96 rm – 🛏100/250 € 🛏🛏100/250 €, ☕ 18 €   **Rest** – Carte 29/60 €
♦ Traditional ♦ Modern ♦
Everything this hotel has to offer is right there for you to see, from the high quality furnishings to the latest modern technology. Its location too is perfect. It is
set on the edge of the woods but with good connections to Stuttgart, the trade
centre, the airport, and just around the corner from the Fernsehturm.

🏨 **Park Inn**   🈷 🅰🅲 🎇 ⚉ 🅰🅴 ⓞ

Hauptstätter Str. 147 ✉ *70178 –* ⓜ *Marienpl. –* ☏ *(0711) 32 09 40*
– www.parkinn.com/hotel-stuttgart   F2
181 rm – 🛏119/189 € 🛏🛏119/189 €, ☕ 16 €   **Rest** – Carte 25/49 €
♦ Business ♦ Functional ♦
Ideal for conference participants and business travellers – not least thanks to its
underground parking. The fitness suite and roof terrace offer wonderful views
over Stuttgart.

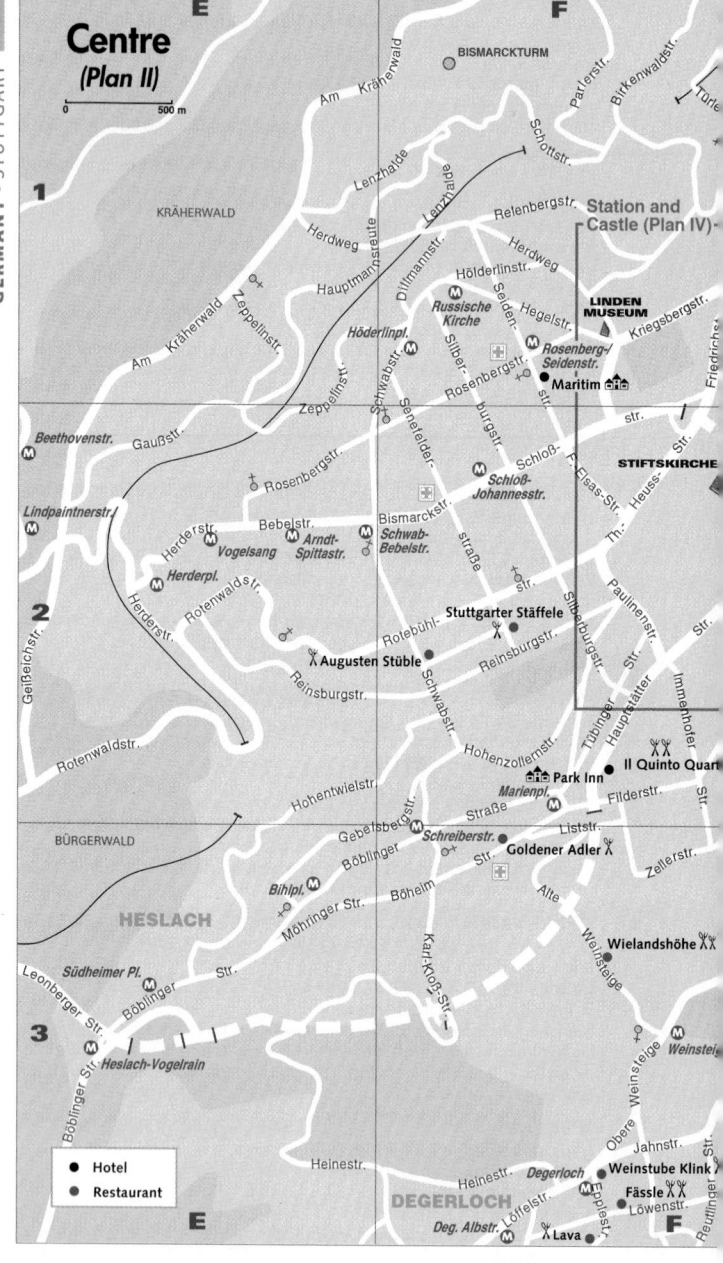

Centre
(Plan II)

0   500 m

E

F

BISMARCKTURM

Station and Castle (Plan IV)

KRÄHERWALD

1

Am Kräherwald

Lenzhalde

Herdweg

Relenbergstr.

Patlerstr.

Birkenwaldstr.

Türle

Zeppelinstr.

Hauptmannsreute

Dillmannstr.

Lenzhalde

Herdweg

Hölderlinstr.

Seiden-

Hegelstr.

LINDEN MUSEUM

Kriegsbergstr.

Am Kräherwald

Hölderlinpl.

Schwabstr.

Russische Kirche

Silber-

Rosenbergstr.

Friedrichs-

str.

Zeppelinstr.

Senefelder-

burgstr.

Rosenberg-/Seidenstr.

● **Maritim**

Beethovenstr.

Gaußstr.

Rosenbergstr.

Bebelstr.

Bismarckstr.

Schloß-

F.-Elsas-Str.

STIFTSKIRCHE

Schloß-Johannesstr.

Th.- Heuss-Str.

str.

Lindpaintnerstr.

Herderstr.

Vogelsang

Arndt-Spittastr.

Schwab-Bebelstr.

straße

Paulinenstr.

Silberburgstr.

2

Herderpl.

Rotenwaldstr.

Herderstr.

Rotebühl-

Stuttgarter Stäffele

str.

Tübinger

Hauptstätter

Immenhofer

Str.

Geißeichstr.

Reinsburgstr.

Str.

Reinsburgstr.

✗ **Augusten Stüble**

Schwabstr.

Hohenzollernstr.

Rotenwaldstr.

Hohentwielstr.

BÜRGERWALD

Hohentwielstr.

Gebelsbergstr.

Böblinger Str.

Straße

Marienpl.

Schreiberstr. ●

Park Inn

Filderstr.

● **Il Quinto Quart**

Liststr.

Zellerstr.

Bihlpl.

Möhringer Str.

Böblinger Str.

Böheim

Str.

Alte

Goldener Adler ✗

HESLACH

Karl-Kloß-Str.

Weinsteige

Wielandshöhe ✗✗

Südheimer Pl.

Leonberger Str.

Böblinger

Str.

3

Böblinger Str.

Heslach-Vogelrain

Obere Weinsteige

Weinstei

Heinestr.

Heinestr.

Degerloch

Jahnstr.

Weinstube Klink ✗

DEGERLOCH

Löffelstr.

Epplestr.

Fässle ✗✗

Löwenstr.

Peutlinger Str.

Deg. Albstr.

✗ **Lava**

● Hotel
● Restaurant

E

F

428

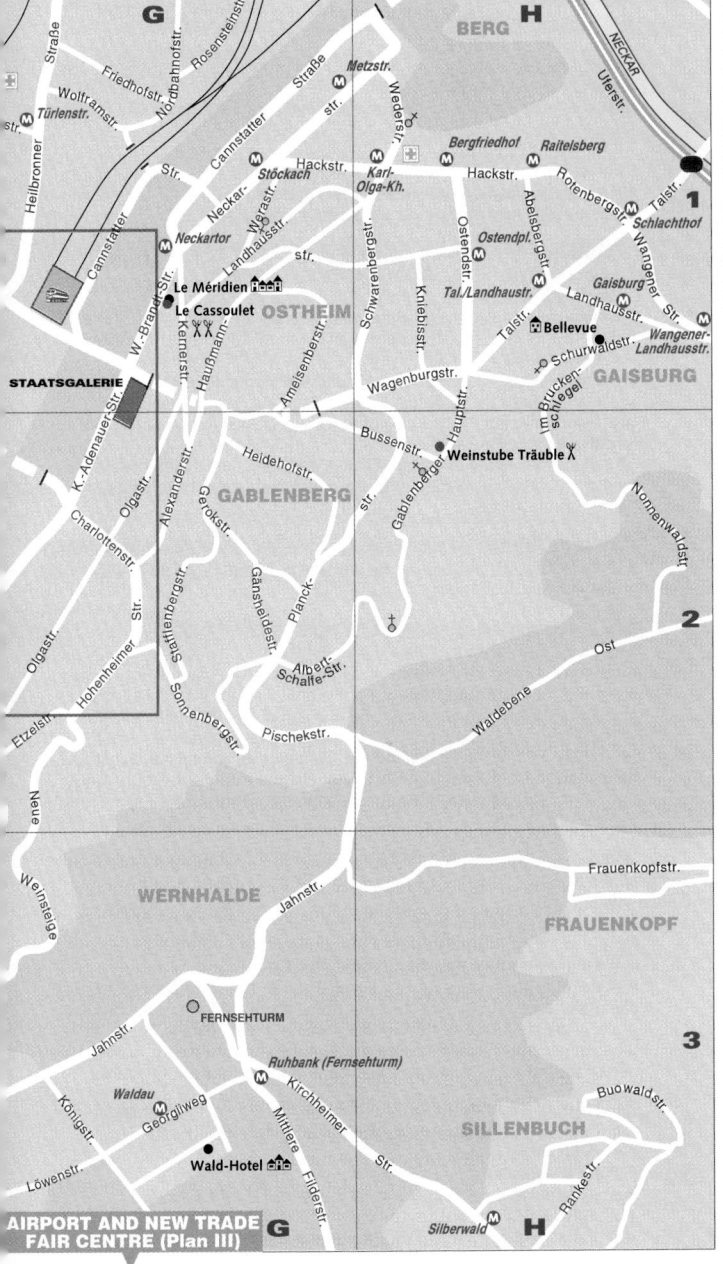

GERMANY - STUTTGART

Bellevue　　　　　　　📞 🅿 VISA ⓪ AE ⓪

Schurwaldstr. 45 ✉ *70186 –* ⓜ *Gaisburg –* ☎ *(0711) 48 07 60*
– www.bellevue-stuttgart.de
– Closed August　　　　　　　　　　　　　　　　**H1**
6 rm ☒ *–* ☦69/99 € ☦☦89/149 €
Rest *– (closed Monday lunch, Tuesday-Wednesday)* Menu 10/48 €
– Carte 23/61 €
♦ Family ♦ Functional ♦
Some of the rooms in this small hotel, which has been in family ownership since 1913, offer fine views. A daily newspaper is delivered to guests every morning. The hotel restaurant offers good, plain mainly regional food.

YOSH　　　　　　　　🛆 AC ⇄ VISA ⓪ AE

Feuerbacher Weg 101 ✉ *70192 –* ☎ *(0711) 6 99 69 60*
– www.yosh-stuttgart.de
– Closed mid August-early September and Monday-Tuesday　　*Plan I* **C2**
Rest *– (dinner only) (booking advisable)* Menu 98/139 € – Carte 62/99 € 🕸
♦ Classic ♦ Elegant ♦
If you fancy a good meal served in upmarket surroundings, then the upmarket YOSH could be the place for you. Start your meal with an aperitif in the garden, before enjoying the classic, seasonal cuisine created by chef Klaus Jäschke. Smokers' lounge also available.
➜ Langostinos ausgelöst, junge Erbsen, Karottenpüree. Kalbskotelett, Blumenkohl gebraten, La Ratte Kartoffeln, Sauce Bernaise. Schokobiskuit, marinierte Beeren, Minzeis.

Wielandshöhe (Vincent Klink)　　　⇐ 🏠 ⇄ VISA ⓪ AE ⓪

Alte Weinsteige 71 ✉ *70597 –* ⓜ *Weinsteige –* ☎ *(0711) 6 40 88 48*
– www.wielandshoehe.de
– closed Sunday-Monday　　　　　　　　　　　　　　**F3**
Rest *– (booking advisable)* Menu 78/110 € – Carte 54/102 € 🕸
♦ Classic ♦ Fashionable ♦
A classic chef cooks classic food. Vincent Klink (in the TV studio on Thursday afternoons, in the restaurant the rest of the time) belongs here just as much as his cooking style, which continues to focus on good, fresh ingredients. Although the food takes pride of place, the view is nevertheless impressive.
➜ Tranche vom Wildfang Steinbutt in Champagner, Florentiner Spinat und Kartoffeln. Elsässer Bauernhahn naturell gebraten mit Amalfi-Zitronensauce und Butter-Nudeln. Reis Trauttmannsdorff mit Zitrusfrüchte-Ragout und Vanilleglacé.

Fässle　　　　　　　　🏠 AC ⇄ VISA ⓪ AE ⓪

Löwenstr. 51 ✉ *70597 –* ⓜ *Degerloch –* ☎ *(0711) 76 01 00*
– www.faessle.de
– closed Sunday-Monday lunch　　　　　　　　　　　**F3**
Rest *– (booking advisable)* Menu 36 € (lunch)/55 € – Carte 27/47 €
♦ International ♦ Traditional ♦ Fashionable ♦
A glance at the menu tells you that Rudolf Schmölz intends to preserve the tradition that exudes from every pore of this wonderful old sandstone building, while at the same time gently introducing a note of modernity. For example, the roast joints and Topfenknödel (curd cheese dumplings) have now been joined on the menu by the more exotic tuna with southeast Asian vegetables.

Il Quinto Quarto　　　　　　　⇄ VISA ⓪ AE ⓪

Olgastr. 133b ✉ *70180 –* ⓜ *Marienpl. –* ☎ *(0711) 66 48 66 02*
– www.ilquintoquarto.de
– Closed 3 weeks August and Sunday dinner-Monday　　　　**F2**
Rest *– (booking advisable)* Menu 25 € (lunch) – Carte 33/62 €
♦ Italian ♦ Classic ♦ Elegant ♦
Attila Caprano learnt how to cook from his father and is now fulfilling a dream. In this tasteful restaurant he prepares lesser known Italian dishes based on meat from the restaurant's own butchery.

GERMANY - STUTTGART

XX **Le Cassoulet** – Hotel Le Méridien   🏠 ὲ. Ⓐ ᴍᴄ 🆅🆂🅰 ⓒⓞ ᴀᴇ ⓪

Willy-Brandt-Str. 30 ✉ *70173 –* Ⓜ *Neckartor –* 𝒸 *(0711) 2 22 10*
– www.lemeridienstuttgart.com   **G1**
Rest – Menu 65 € – Carte 34/72 €
♦ International ♦ Classic ♦
Bright, warm and earthy tones have been used to create an elegant interior for
this restaurant. Thanks to the international menu there really is something to
satisfy every taste.

X **Goldener Adler**   🏠 Ⓟ 🆅🆂🅰 ⓒⓞ ᴀᴇ

Böheimstr. 38 ✉ *70178 –* Ⓜ *Marienpl. –* 𝒸 *(0711) 6 33 88 02*
– www.goldener-adler-stuttgart.de   **F3**
Rest – *(dinner only) (booking advisable)* Carte 28/46 €
♦ Regional/country ♦ Fashionable ♦ Rustic ♦
Everything Rolf Hekeler and Christopher Oelkrug are doing here makes sense,
and tastes great. The cooking is down-to-earth and based on high quality
fresh produce. The many (regular) customers enjoy international dishes alongside tried and tested classics such as Wiener schnitzel with potato and cucumber salad.

X **Lava**   🆅🆂🅰 ⓒⓞ

Epplestr. 40 ✉ *70597 –* Ⓜ *Degerloch –* 𝒸 *(0711) 71 91 78 95*
– www.lava-stuttgart.de – Closed Sunday-Monday   **F3**
Rest – Menu 16 € (lunch)/66 € (dinner) – Carte 43/66 €
♦ International ♦ Fashionable ♦
This modern restaurant has direct access from its own underground car park. It
offers an extensive à la carte selection and a set 'Discovery' menu in the evenings. There is a simpler, value for money menu at lunchtimes.

X **Augusten Stüble**   🏠 ✍

Augustenstr. 104 ✉ *70197 –* Ⓜ *Schwab-Bebelstr. –* 𝒸 *(0711) 62 12 48*
– www.augustenstüble.de – Closed Sunday   **F2**
Rest – *(dinner only) (booking advisable)* Carte 36/43 €
♦ Regional/country ♦ Cosy ♦
This comfortable restaurant is located in a corner block on the edge of the town
centre. The seasonal menu features regional as well as classic dishes and a good
selection of wines. Daily specials are displayed on the board.

X **Weinstube Klink**   🏠 ✍

Epplestr. 1c (Degerloch) ✉ *70597 –* Ⓜ *Degerloch –* 𝒸 *(0711) 7 65 32 05*
– www.weinstube-klink.de – Closed Saturday lunch, Sunday and Bank Holidays
Rest – *(booking advisable)* Carte 18/42 €   **F3**
♦ Regional/country ♦ Rustic ♦
Regular guests appreciate this restaurant, which is somewhat hidden in an interior courtyard. It offers a small Swabian menu and a good wine selection. The
daily specials are displayed on a slate.

X **Stuttgarter Stäffele**   🏠 ⇔ Ⓟ 🆅🆂🅰 ⓒⓞ ᴀᴇ

Buschlestr. 2a ✉ *70178 –* Ⓜ *Schloß-Johannesstr. –* 𝒸 *(0711) 66 41 90*
– www.staeffele.de   **F2**
Rest – *(Saturday, Sunday and Bank Holidays: dinner only) (booking advisable)* Carte 23/39 €
♦ Regional/country ♦ Cosy ♦
This friendly Swabian restaurant and wine bar has several cosy dining rooms
lovingly decorated with various local artefacts. Parking service.

X **Weinstube Träuble**   🏠 ✍

Gablenberger Hauptstr. 66 (Entrance Bussenstraße) ✉ *70186 –* Ⓜ *Ostendpl.*
– 𝒸 *(0711) 46 54 28 – Closed 1 week early January, 2 weeks end August-
early September, Sunday and Bank Holidays*   **H2**
Rest – *(dinner only)* Carte 17/45 €
♦ Regional/country ♦ Wine bar ♦
The panelled dining room of this tiny 200-year-old house is extremely cosy.
Snacks and daily specials are available.

Mövenpick Hotel Airport & Messe   🛋 🧖 ⌂ 👌 🄰🄲 📶 🛗

Flughafenstr. 50 ✉ *70629 –* ✆ *(0711) 55 34 40*   🅿 💳 ⓥ 🄰🄴 ⓞ

– www.moevenpick-hotels.com/stuttgart-airport   **L2**

326 rm – 🛏120/450 € 🛏🛏145/475 €, ⌂ 22 € – 2 suites

Rest – Carte 24/56 €

◆ Conference hotel ◆ Business ◆ Design ◆

This ultra-modern business hotel at the airport offers great views from the upper storeys. Luxury corner junior suites. This clean-lined grey and white restaurant offers a view of the airport terminals.

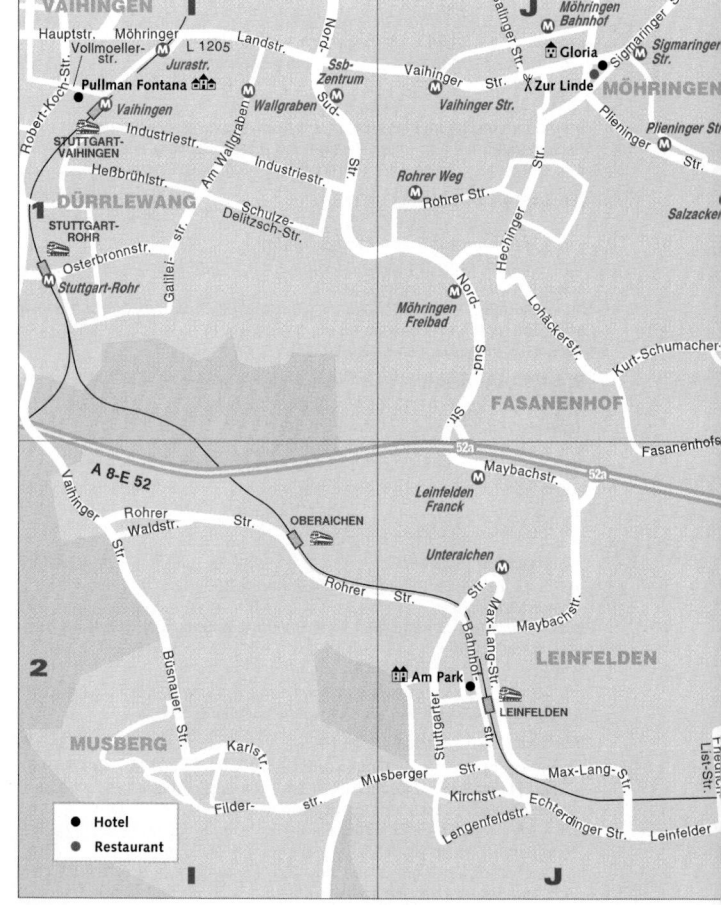

Hotel ●
Restaurant ●

Pullman Fontana 🚿 🅿 🐾 🖾 ♿ 🅰 🛜 🐾 🚗 💳 💳 💳 💳

Vollmoellerstr. 5 ⊠ 70563 – Ⓜ *Vaihingen*
– 𝒞 (07 11) 73 00
– www.pullmanhotels.com/5425
252 rm *–* **†**99/211 € **††**99/231 €, 🛋 22 €
– 2 suites
Rest – Carte 38/55 €

♦ **Chain hotel** ♦ **Business** ♦ **Classic** ♦

This convenient hotel offers comfortable rooms in the traditional style with fine views from the upper storeys. It also has offers bright and airy modern leisure facilities. An informal yet elegant restaurant with winter garden.

I1

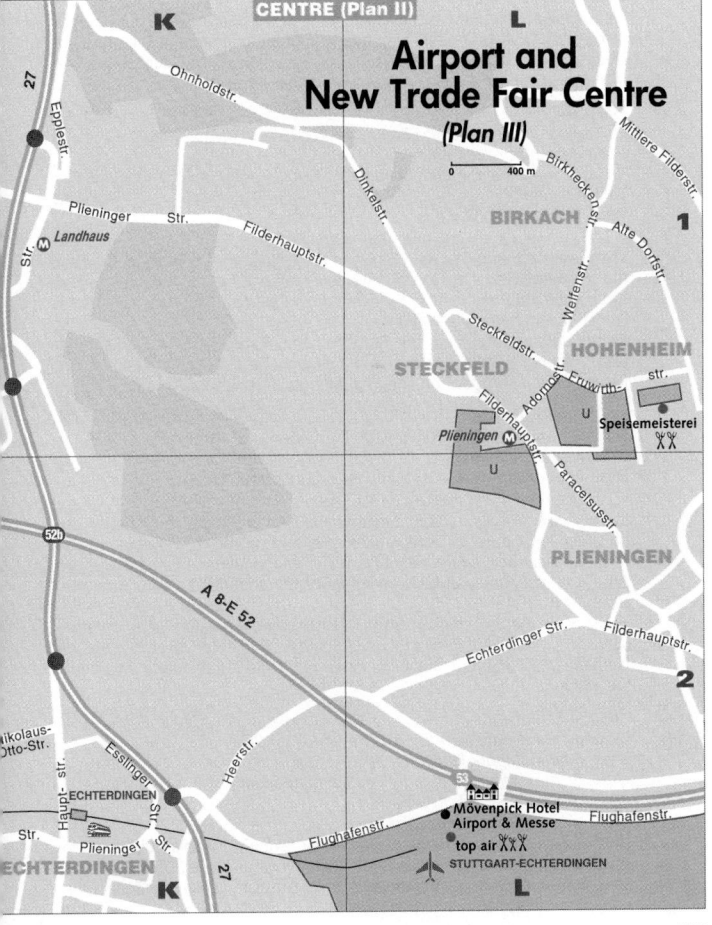

Airport and New Trade Fair Centre (Plan III)

Am Park 🐾 📶 🛁 P VISA ⦾ AE

Lessingstr. 4 (Leinfelden) ✉ *70771 – ℰ (0711) 90 31 00*
– www.hotelampark-leinfelden.de
– Closed 22 December-7 January   **J2**
42 rm ⌸ – **♦**85/120 € **♦♦**110/145 €
Rest Am Park🏵 – see restaurant listing
♦ Business ♦ Functional ♦
Run by the Schienle family, this hotel with its blue and white façade is situated
in a quiet location in a cul-de-sac near the park. Its rooms are meticulously maintained and well-equipped. Flavoursome regional food is served attentively in
the cosy dining rooms. A pretty beer garden also belongs to the restaurant.

Gloria 🎦 🏵 📶 🛁 P 🚗 VISA ⦾ AE

Sigmaringer Str. 59 ✉ *70567 – Ⓜ Sigmaringer Str. – ℰ (0711) 7 18 50*
– www.hotelgloria.de   **J1**
85 rm ⌸ – **♦**88/98 € **♦♦**100/115 €
Rest Möhringer Hexle – ℰ (0711) 7 18 51 17 (closed Sunday dinner and
Bank Holidays dinner) Carte 29/45 €
♦ Business ♦ Functional ♦
This excellent hotel with its convenient location has been run by Evelin Kraft for
more than 20 years. It offers high-quality contemporary rooms, the most spacious of which are located on the top floor. This informal restaurant serves Swa-
bian-Mediterranean cuisine and has a winter garden and terrace.

XXX top air 🔥 AK P VISA ⦾ AE ①
🅑

im Flughafen (Terminal 1, Level 4) ✉ *70629 – ℰ (0711) 9 48 21 37*
– www.restaurant-top-air.de
– Closed end December-early January, August, Saturday lunch, Sunday and
Bank Holidays   **L2**
Rest – Menu 74/118 €
♦ Creative ♦ Friendly ♦ Fashionable ♦
There are two things that draw diners to this restaurant: the excellent food and
the wonderful view – try to book a window table overlooking the runway. Well-
established after ten years in residence, chef Claudio Urru offers flavoursome
French-Mediterranean dishes.
→ Ungarische Entenleber mit Passionsfrucht, Popcorncrème, Pekkannüsse
und Chicorée. Weißer Heilbutt mit Spitzmorcheln, dreierlei Kartoffel und
Belper Knolle. Komposition von Thai Mango, Zitronengras und Basilikum.

XX Speisemeisterei (Frank Oehler) 🎦 🔥 ⇔ P VISA ⦾ AE ①
🅑

Schloss Hohenheim ✉ *70599 – Ⓜ Plieningen – ℰ (0711) 34 21 79 79*
– www.speisemeisterei.de   **L1**
Rest – (booking advisable) Menu 34 € (lunch)/108 €
♦ Modern ♦ Fashionable ♦ Classic ♦
Speisemeisterei boasts stucco, crystal chandeliers and old parquet flooring set
off skilfully by a decor of clean, modern lines and striking red velvet upholstery.
In the kitchen the creative duo of Frank Oehler and Markus Eberhardinger pro-
duce an equally impressive lunch menu. The art room offers a different type of
feast.
→ Loup de Mer in Schinkensud mit Artischocken, Spinatcrème und Parme-
sanravioli. Wildkräuter-Risotto mit Spargel und Bio-Onsenei von der
Domäne Weil. Steinbutt für 2 Personen mit Trüffel-Hollandaise und neuen
Kartoffeln.

XX Am Park – Hotel Am Park 🎦 ⇔ P VISA ⦾ AE
🅑

Lessingstr. 4 (Leinfelden) ✉ *70771 – ℰ (0711) 90 31 00*
– www.hotelampark-leinfelden.de
– Closed 22 December-7 January and Saturday-Sunday   **J2**
Rest – Menu 45 € – Carte 30/48 €
♦ Regional/country ♦ Friendly ♦
Diners know that they will always find their favourite Swabian dishes on the
menu here thanks to the efforts of chef Ulli Herkommer. The delicious beetroot
soup with smoked trout and horseradish is particularly recommended. In summer, dine alfresco on the garden terrace.

Zur Linde

Sigmaringer Str. 49 ✉ *70567 –* *Sigmaringer Str. –* ✆ *(0711) 7 19 95 90*
– www.joergmink.com – Closed Saturday lunch **J1**
Rest *– (booking advisable)* Carte 28/54 €

♦ **Regional/country** ♦ Inn ♦

The cosy dining rooms in this listed restaurant offer typical Swabian fare including home-made Maultaschen, a local speciality. Traditional vaulted basement room for functions.

ENVIRONS OF STUTTGART

Plan I

AT **FELLBACH**

Classic Congress Hotel *without rest*

Tainer Str. 9 ✉ *70734 –* ✆ *(0711) 5 85 90*
– www.bestwestern-fellbach.de
– Closed 21 December-5 January **D1**
149 rm ☐ *–* ♦114/154 € ♦♦144/184 €

♦ **Business** ♦ **Conference hotel** ♦ **Functional** ♦

This hotel's comfortable rooms, some with park views, are accessed via the bright, high-ceilinged atrium-style lobby. Conference rooms are available in the hotel itself and in the adjacent Schwabenlandhalle. In the evenings try the trendy Chilys bistro.

Zum Hirschen

Hirschstr. 1 ✉ *70734 –* ✆ *(0711) 9 57 93 70*
– www.zumhirschen-fellbach.de **D1**
9 rm ☐ *–* ♦88/98 € ♦♦118/138 €
Rest *Gourmet Restaurant avui* ✿ **Rest** *Gasthaus zum Hirschen*
– see restaurant listing

♦ Inn ♦ **Functional** ♦

Although the quality of the food and wine on offer at Zum Hirschen is hardly a secret, it is a little known fact that it is also possible to spend the night here after your meal. The chef and his wife provide a number of pretty, comfortable rooms with free telephone calls (landline) and Wi-Fi.

Hirsch

Fellbacher Str. 2 (Schmiden) ✉ *70736 –* ✆ *(0711) 9 51 30*
– www.hirsch-fellbach.de
– Closed 23 December-1 January **D1**
104 rm ☐ *–* ♦69/74 € ♦♦99/108 €
Rest *Oettinger's Restaurant* *– see restaurant listing*
Rest *Weinstube* *–* ✆ *(0711) 9 51 34 70 (closed 2 weeks Christmas-early January and Saturday-Sunday)* Carte 16/32 €

♦ **Family** ♦ **Modern** ♦

The Oetterings beautifully kept, traditional family hotel is in the centre of the village of Schmiden. If you are spending the night don't miss the charming, cosy wine bar in the adjoining listed farmhouse, which has its own beer garden. Serves good plain food.

Gourmet Restaurant avui *(Armin Karrer) – Hotel Zum Hirschen*

Hirschstr. 1 ✉ *70734 –* ✆ *(0711) 9 57 93 70*
– www.zumhirschen-fellbach.de
– Closed 2-5 January, 13-16 Februar, April-August and Sunday-Tuesday
Rest *– (dinner only) (booking essential)* Menu 98/138 € **D1**

♦ **Creative** ♦ **Elegant** ♦

It doesn't take long to realise that as well as an advocate of classic cuisine, Armin Karrer is also an innovator. The molecular starter gives the first hint of the tremendous effort that goes into his 'avant-garde' cuisine and the theme continues right up to the end of the meal.

➜ Kaninchen mit Auberginen und Blumenkohl-Aioli. US Prime Black Angus mit Buchweizen und Pack Choi. Warme Passionsfrucht und Kokos mit Gurken-Gazpacho.

GERMANY - STUTTGART

XX **Oettinger's Restaurant** – Hotel Hirsch   VISA ⓸ AE
Fellbacher Str. 2 (Schmiden) ⊠ *70736* – ℰ *(0711) 9 51 30*
– www.hirsch-fellbach.de
– Closed 2 weeks Christmas-early January, 6 weeks mid July-August and
Sunday-Monday   **D1**
Rest – *(Tuesday-Friday dinner only)* Menu 56/60 € – Carte 41/62 €
♦ International ♦ Elegant ♦
This is the upmarket dining option at the Hotel Hirsch. After spells cooking in a
number of good restaurants, 'Jeune Restaurateur' Michael Oettinger now offers
seasonal cuisine, including a set menu, here in his own premises.

XX **Aldinger's Germania**   🏠 ✿ 🚭
😊 *Schmerstr. 6* ⊠ *70734* – ℰ *(0711) 58 20 37* – *www.aldingers-germania.de*
– Closed 2 weeks February, 3 weeks August and Sunday-Monday
Rest – *(booking advisable)* Menu 39/49 € – Carte 24/58 €   **D1**
♦ Traditional ♦ Cosy ♦
Everything tastes good here, from the Maultaschen (Swabian ravioli) to the
roast meats and seasonal specials. With the Aldingers (now at the helm for the
third generation) you can be sure of a warm welcome. The vaulted cellar is ideal
for parties and events.

X **Gasthaus zum Hirschen** – Hotel Zum Hirschen   🏠 VISA ⓸
😊 *Hirschstr. 1* ⊠ *70734* – ℰ *(0711) 9 57 93 70*
– www.zumhirschen-fellbach.de
– Closed Monday   **D1**
Rest – *(booking advisable)* Menu 35/50 € – Carte 29/61 €
♦ Traditional ♦ Rurally ♦ Fashionable ♦
If you find the innovative gourmet cuisine of avui just a little over the top, here
Armin Karrer produces something more down to earth but no less flavoursome.
The menu includes handmade Maultaschen (a Swabian pasta speciality) and
pink roast rump of veal.

AT ZUFFENHAUSEN

XX **Christophorus**   🛆 🎿 ✿ VISA ⓸ AE ⓞ
Porscheplatz 5 (in the Porsche Museum) ⊠ *70435* – ℰ *(0711) 91 12 59 80*
– www.porsche.com
– Closed Sunday dinner-Monday   **B1**
Rest – Menu 38 € (lunch)/97 € – Carte 42/95 € ⌘
♦ Mediterranean ♦ Design ♦ Retro ♦
Located on the top floor of a futuristic building, this restaurant serves seasonal
cuisine focusing on prime cuts of US beef from the grill. There is also a bistro
and coffee bar, as well as a smokers' lounge on the ground floor.

GREECE
ELLÁDA

ATHENS

→ **AREA:**
131 944 km²
(50 944 sq mi).

→ **POPULATION:**
10 787 690 inhabitants.
Density = 82 per km².

→ **CAPITAL:** Athens.

→ **CURRENCY:** Euro (€).

→ **GOVERNMENT:**
Parliamentary republic
(since 1974). Member of European
Union since 1981.

→ **LANGUAGE:** Greek.

→ **PUBLIC HOLIDAYS:**
New Year's Day (1 Jan); Epiphany
(6 Jan); Orthodox Shrove Monday
(late Feb-Mar); Independence Day
(25 Mar); Orthodox Good Friday
(late Mar/Apr); Orthodox Easter
Monday (late Mar/Apr); Labor Day
(1 May); Pentecost Sunday (late
May/June); Orthodox Whit Monday
(late May/June); Assumption of
the Virgin Mary (15 Aug); Ochi Day
(28 Oct); Christmas Day (25 Dec);
Boxing Day (26 Dec).

→ **LOCAL TIME:**
GMT+2 hours in winter and GMT
+3 hours in summer.

→ **CLIMATE:**
Temperate Mediterranean, with
mild winters and hot, sunny
summers (Athens: January 10°C;
July 27°C).

→ **EMERGENCY:**
Police ℓ **100**; Medical Assistance
ℓ **166**; Fire Brigade ℓ **199**;
Tourist Police ℓ **171**.
(Dialing **112** within any EU country
will redirect your call and contact
the emergency services.)

→ **ELECTRICITY:**
230 volts AC, 50Hz; 2 round pin
sockets.

→ **FORMALITIES:**
Travellers from the European Union
(EU), Switzerland, Iceland and
the main countries of North and
South America need a national
identity card or passport (America:
passport required) to visit Greece
for less than three months (tourism
or business purpose). For visitors
from other countries a visa may be
required, in addition to a passport,
especially for those wishing to
stay for longer than three months.
We advise you to check with your
embassy before travelling.

ATHENS
ATHÍNA
Population: 750 982

Stefanos Kyriazis/Fotolia.com

Inventing democracy, the theatre and the Olympic Games… and planting the seeds of philosophy and Western Civilisation – Athens was central to all of these, a city that became a byword for glory and learning, a place whose golden reputation could inspire such awe that centuries later just the mention of its name was enough to turn people misty-eyed. It's a magical place, built upon eight hills and plains, with a history stretching back at least 3,000 years. Its short but highly productive golden age resulted in the architectural glory of The Acropolis, while the likes of Plato, Aristotle and Socrates were in the business of changing the mindset of society.

The Acropolis still dominates Athens and can be seen peeking through alleyways and turnings all over the city. Beneath it lies a teeming metropolis, part urban melting pot, part über-buzzy neighbourhood. Plaka, below the Acropolis, is the old quarter, and the most visited, a mixture of great charm and cheap gift shops. North and west, Monastiraki and Psiri have become trendy zones; to the east, Syntagma and Kolonaki are notably modern and smart, home to the Greek parliament and the famous. The most northerly districts of central Athens are Omonia and Exarcheia, distinguished by their rugged appearance and steeped in history; much of the life in these parts is centred round the polytechnic and the central marketplace.

ATHENS IN...

→ **ONE DAY**
Acropolis (Parthenon), Agora and Temple of Hephaestus, Plaka.

→ **TWO DAYS**
Kolonaki, National Archaeological Museum, Filopappou Hill.

→ **THREE DAYS**
Monastiraki flea-market (Sunday), Benaki Museum, Technopolis, National Gardens, Lykkavittos Hill.

PRACTICAL INFORMATION

ARRIVAL-DEPARTURE

 Athens International Airport is 33km east of the city. Metro Line 3 takes you to Monastiraki.

Piraeus Port is the third largest port in the Mediterranean and is 10km southwest of Athens. Metro Line 1 takes you to Monastiraki.

GETTING AROUND

The most sensible way of getting around town is by the metro; buses and trolley-buses run an excellent service but are hampered by traffic. Carnets of 10 tickets are available from newsstands, OASA booths and kiosks, and at metro or subway stations.

Be sure to have some Euros in your wallet when you arrive, as tickets for all forms of public transport can only be paid for in cash; cards are not accepted by either ticket agents or ticket machines.

CALENDAR HIGHLIGHTS

March/April
Candlelit procession up Lykavittos Hill to the chapel of Agios Georgos.

May-September
Greek folk dances at Dora Stratou Theatre.

June
European Jazz Festival, Rockwave Festival (rock music).

June-September
International Petra Festival (music and theatre), Hellenic Festival.

August
Nights Under The Full Moon (moonlit classical performances at monuments and archaeological sites).

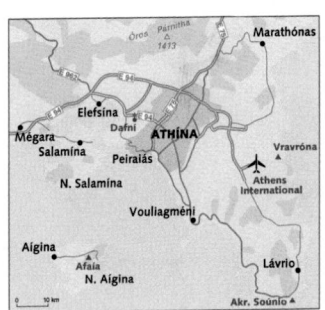

EATING OUT

In recent times, a smart wave of restaurants has hit the city and, with many chefs training abroad before returning home, this is a good time to eat out in the shadow of The Acropolis. If you want the full experience, dine with the locals rather than the tourists and make your reservation for late evening, as Greeks rarely go out for dinner before 10pm. The trend towards a more eclectic restaurant scene now means that you can find everything from classical French and Italian cuisine to Asian and Moroccan dishes, and even sushi. Modern tavernas offer good attention to detail, but this doesn't mean they're replacing the wonderfully traditional favourites. These older tavernas, along with mezedopoleia, are the backbone of Greek dining, and most visitors wouldn't think their trip was complete without eating in one; often the waiter will just tell you what's cooking that day - and you're usually very welcome to go into the kitchen and make your selection. Greece is a country where it is customary to tip good service; ten per cent is the normal rate.

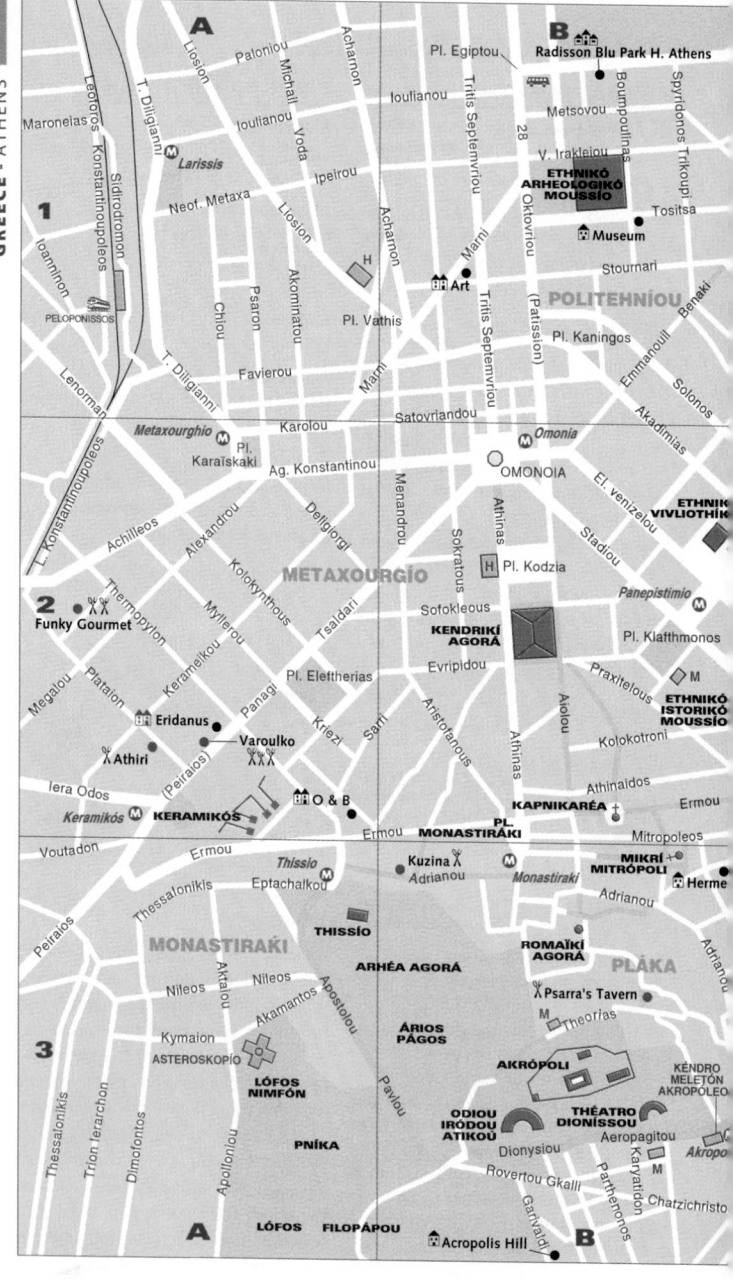

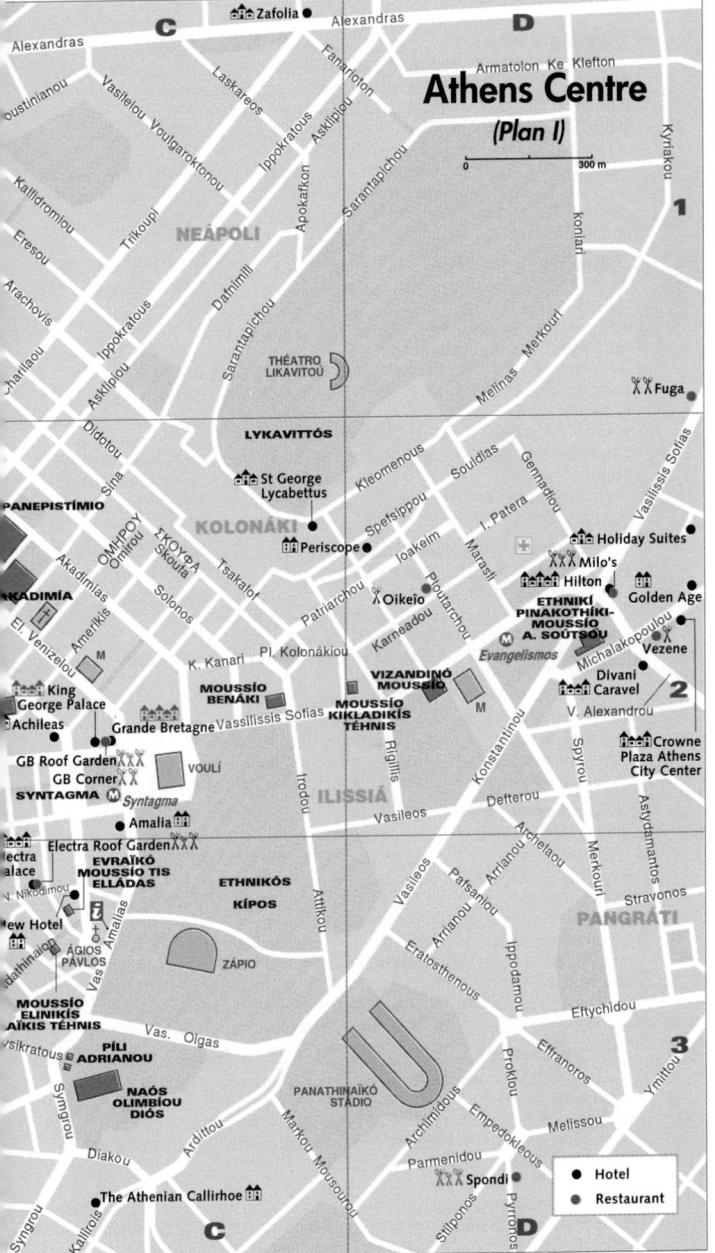

Athens Centre
(Plan I)

0   300 m

Alexandras
Zafolia
Alexandras
Armatolon Ke Klefton
Kyriakou

Ioustinianou
Vasileiou Voulgaroktonou
Laskareos
Fanarioton
Apokafkon
Asklipiou
Sarantapichou
Ionari

Kallidromiou
Trikoupi
Ippokratous
NEÁPOLI
Melinas · Merkouri

Eresou
Dafnimili

Arachovis
Charilaou
Asklipiou
Sarantapichou
THÉATRO
LIKAVITOÚ
Fuga

LYKAVITTÓS

Didotou
Sina
Kleomenous
Soulidias
Gennadiou
Vasillis Sofias

PANEPISTÍMIO
St George
Lycabettus
Spefsippou
I. Patera
Holiday Suites

OMHPOY
Onirou
TKOYΦA
Skoufa
KOLONÁKI
Periscope
Ioakeim
Marasli
Milo's
Hilton

Akadimias
Tsakalof
Patriarchou
Ploutarchou
ETHNIKÍ
PINAKOTHÍKI-
MOUSSÍO
A. SOÚTSOU
Golden Age

AKADIMÍA
El. Venizelou
Amerikis
Solonos
Oikeío
Karneadou
Evangelismos
Michalakopoulou
Vezene

King
George Palace
Achileas
K. Kanari
Pl. Kolonákiou
MOUSSÍO
BENÁKI
VIZANDINÓ
MOUSSÍO
MOUSSÍO
KIKLADIKÍS
TÉHNIS
Divani
Caravel

Grande Bretagne
Vassilissis Sofias
Figilitis
V. Alexandrou

GB Roof Garden
GB Corner
SYNTAGMA
Syntagma
VOULÍ
ILISSIÁ
Konstantinou
Defterou
Crowne
Plaza Athens
City Center

Amalia
Irodou
Vasileos
Astydamantos

Electra Roof Garden
V. Nikodimou
Electra
Palace
EVRAÏKÓ
MOUSSÍO TIS
ELLÁDAS
ETHNIKÓS
KÍPOS
Vasileos
Pafsaniou
Arrianou
Archelaou
Merkouri
Stravonos
PANGRÁTI

New Hotel
Vas. Amalias
Adrianou
ÁGIOS
PÁVLOS
Attikou
Arrianou
Ippodamou
Eratosthenous
Eftychidou

MOUSSÍO
ELINIKÍS
LAÏKÍS TÉHNIS
Ysikratous
PÍLI
ADRIANOU
Vas. Olgas
ZÁPIO
Archimidous
Empedokleous
Effranoros
Proklou
Melissou

NAÓS
OLIMBÍOU
DIÓS
PANATHINAÏKÓ
STÁDIO
Markou · Mousouri
Parmenidou
Ymitou

Diakou
Ardittou
Sitiponos
Pyrrhonos
Spondi

Symgrou
Kallirois
The Athenian Callirhoe
Syngrou
Stilponos

● Hotel
● Restaurant

441

Grande Bretagne

1 Vas Georgiou A, Constitution Sq ⊠ *105 64*
– **Ⓜ** *Syntagma* – *𝒞 (210) 3330 000* – *www.grandebretagne.gr*
272 rm – **♦**248/463 € **♦♦**269/485 €, ☐ 25 € – 48 suites   **C2**
Rest *GB Roof Garden* **Rest** *GB Corner* – see restaurant listing
♦ **Grand Luxury** ♦ **Palace** ♦ **Stylish** ♦

Impressive 19C city centre hotel, affording fantastic views of the surrounding area. Grand interior displays elegant handmade furnishings. Luxurious, individually styled bedrooms boast extremely spacious bathrooms. Excellent spa and wellness facilities; professional service.

Hilton

46 Vas Sofias Ave ⊠ *115 28* – **Ⓜ** *Evangelismos* – *𝒞 (210) 7281 000*
– *www.hiltonathens.gr*   **D2**
472 rm – **♦**179/299 € **♦♦**179/299 €, ☐ 35 € – 34 suites
Rest *Milo's* – see restaurant listing
Rest *Byzantine* – *𝒞 (210) 7281 400* – Menu 38 € – Carte 42/69 €
Rest *Galaxy Roof* – *𝒞 (210) 7281 403 (May-October) (dinner only)*
Carte 49/100 €
♦ **Chain hotel** ♦ **Grand Luxury** ♦ **Modern** ♦

Corporate hotel near Kolonaki Square, with smart guest areas, well-equipped fitness centre and two business floors. Modern, uniform bedrooms boast balconies and sea or mountain views. Local and international dishes served in informal Byzantine; similar theme in rooftop Galaxy; seafood in Milo's.

Athenaeum Inter-Continental

89-93 Syngrou Ave (Southwest : 2.5 km)
⊠ *117 45* – *𝒞 (210) 9206 000* – *www.athens.intercontinental.com*
483 rm – **♦**200/280 € **♦♦**200/280 €, ☐ 33 € – 60 suites
Rest *Première* – see restaurant listing
Rest *Cafezoe* – *𝒞 (210) 9206 655 (lunch only and dinner Sunday-Monday)* Menu 40 € – Carte 42/64 €
♦ **Grand Luxury** ♦ **Business** ♦ **Modern** ♦

Corporate hotel near the business district. Elegant lobby with newspaper, jewellery and gift shops; impressive meeting spaces and business centre. Spacious bedrooms boast the latest facilities – the Club floors offer dedicated services. Fine dining in modern Première. Buffet lunches in informal Cafezoe.

King George Palace

3 Vas Georgiou A, Syntagma Sq ⊠ *105 64*
– **Ⓜ** *Syntagma* – *𝒞 (210) 3222 210* – *www.kinggeorgepalace.com*
89 rm ☐ – **♦**230/260 € **♦♦**260/290 € – 13 suites   **C2**
Rest *Tudor Hall* – *(closed Sunday)* Menu 29 € (lunch) – Carte 39/73 €
♦ **Palace** ♦ **Grand Luxury** ♦ **Classic** ♦

Luxurious converted mansion set in Syntagma Square. Cosy, classically furnished bedrooms come with smart marble bathrooms; the rooftop suite boasts a private pool and panoramic views. Stylish, informal lounge-bar serves light bites, while the 7th floor Tudor Hall offers a greater sense of occasion, featuring a smart terrace and modern Mediterranean menu.

Divani Caravel

2 Vas Alexandrou Ave ⊠ *161 21* – **Ⓜ** *Evelangismos* – *𝒞 (210) 7207 000*
– *www.divanis.com*   **D2**
427 rm – **♦**390/500 € **♦♦**410/530 €, ☐ 29 € – 44 suites
Rest *Brown's* – *(closed August and Sunday) (dinner only)* Carte 48/65 €
Rest *Café Constantinople* – Menu 23 € – Carte 37/54 €
♦ **Business** ♦ **Luxury** ♦ **Classic** ♦

Set close to Kolonaki, boasting a lovely marble lobby with an impressive chandelier and a rooftop pool offering breathtaking views of The Acropolis and Lykavittos Hill. Bedrooms combine classical charm with mod cons; the higher grades come in a colonial style. Chic Brown's serves modern Mediterranean cuisine; Café Constantinople offers casual, all-day dining.

Crowne Plaza Athens City Center

50 Michalakopoulou Ave ⊠ 115 28
– Ⓜ Megaro Moussikis – ℰ (210) 7278 000 – www.cpathens.com
188 rm ⊡ – ♦110/220 € ♦♦129/259 € – 5 suites   **D2**
Rest *Ambrosia* – Menu 31/34 € – Carte 23/47 €
♦ Chain hotel ♦ Business ♦ Modern ♦

Centrally located business hotel with smart, modern interior and a range of well-equipped conference rooms. Contemporary bedrooms; stylish 'executive' level display seating areas, large desks and a good level of facilities. Appealing menu in smart Ambrosia, which moves to the poolside roof garden in summer.

Electra Palace

18-20 Nikodimou St ⊠ 105 57 – Ⓜ Syntagma
– ℰ (210) 3370 000 – www.electrahotels.gr   **C3**
144 rm ⊡ – ♦105/175 € ♦♦115/195 € – 11 suites
Rest *Electra Roof Garden* – see restaurant listing
Rest – Menu 35 € – Carte 46/66 €
♦ Luxury ♦ Classic ♦

Attractive hotel on a peaceful city street – its classical façade concealing a much more contemporary interior. Fantastic panoramas from the rooftop pool. Smart, well-kept bedrooms; some with balconies and Acropolis views. Motivo restaurant opens onto a terrace and serves classical Greek and international fare. Roof Garden offers a modern menu and beautiful vistas.

Ledra Marriott

115 Syngrou Ave (Southwest : 3 km) ⊠ 117 45 – ℰ (210) 9300 000
– www.athensmarriott.com
308 rm – ♦182/268 € ♦♦182/268 €, ⊡ 28 € – 6 suites
Rest *Kona Kai* – (closed July-August, Sunday and Monday) (dinner only)
Menu 45 € – Carte 41/93 €
Rest *Zephyros* – Menu 25 € – Carte 31/58 €
♦ Chain hotel ♦ Business ♦ Contemporary ♦

On the road from the city to the sea, with panoramic views from the rooftop terrace. Traditional guest areas and classically styled bedrooms; superior furnishings in executive rooms. Authentic Polynesian dishes, sushi and teppan-yaki in atmospheric Kona Kai. Local and global fare in contemporary Zephyros.

St George Lycabettus

2 Kleomenous St ⊠ 106 75 – Ⓜ Evangelismos
– ℰ (210) 7416000 – www.sgl.gr   **C2**
148 rm – ♦130/160 € ♦♦150/170 €, ⊡ 22 € – 6 suites
Rest *Le Grand Balcon* – Carte 51/70 €
Rest *Frame Garden* – (May-October) Menu 25 € – Carte 35/56 €
♦ Business ♦ Personalised ♦ Modern ♦

Elegant hotel in an exclusive district. Smart gold and black interior with Greek artefacts and modern art. Bedrooms mix the classic and contemporary, displaying different colour schemes on every floor; some have balconies and views. Fine dining in Le Grand Balcon; more casual feel to stylish Frame Garden.

Radisson Blu Park H. Athens

10 Alexandras Ave ⊠ 106 82 – Ⓜ Victoria
– ℰ (210) 8894 500 – www.radissonblu.com/hotel-athens   **B1**
152 rm – ♦95/120 € ♦♦105/200 €
Rest *St' Astra East* – (closed mid June-September, Sunday and Monday)
(dinner only) Carte 31/52 €
Rest *Gallo Nero* – (closed mid June-September) Carte 20/56 €
♦ Business ♦ Contemporary ♦ Personalised ♦

In the family since 1976: its décor inspired by the park opposite, with tree trunk pillars and colour-changing leaves. Contemporary bedrooms come in browns and greens; most have park views. Meeting and leisure facilities are well-equipped. Asian restaurant overlooks The Acropolis and serves BBQ/pasta dishes on the roof in summer. Casual Gallo Nero offers Tuscan fare.

Holiday Suites without rest

🔲 📶 💳 ⦾ 🅰🅴 ⓞ

4 Arnis St (by Mihalakopoulou) ✉ 115 28 – Ⓜ *Megaro Moussikis*
– ☎ (210) 7278 690 – www.holiday-suites.com
34 rm – �95/180 € ♦♦95/180 €, 🍽 16 €

D2

♦ Business ♦ Modern ♦ Functional ♦

Converted apartments in quiet residential street. All rooms are spacious, contemporary suites with work and kitchen areas, comfy seating, and pink and white marble bathrooms. Meeting and leisure facilities are shared with the Crowne Plaza.

Zafolia

⬅ 🛁 🏠 🏊 ⅍ 🔲 ⅍ 📶 🧖 🚗 💳 ⦾ 🅰🅴 ⓞ

87-89 Alexandras Ave ✉ 114 74 – Ⓜ *Ambelokipi* – ☎ (210) 6449 002
– www.zafoliahotel.gr

C1

185 rm 🍽 – ♦115/158 € ♦♦122/165 € – 7 suites
Rest – *(residents only)* Menu 25 € – Carte 25/45 €

♦ Business ♦ Functional ♦

Privately owned business hotel to the north of the city, run by an organised team. Contemporary lounge; excellent views from the rooftop pool and bar. Well-equipped, modern bedrooms – those on the 6th and 7th floors boast balconies. Mezzanine dining room serves buffet of Greek and Mediterranean dishes.

Eridanus

🏨 🛁 🏠 🔲 ⅍ 📶 🧖 🚗 💳 ⦾ 🅰🅴

78 Pireaus Ave, Keramicos ✉ 104 35 – Ⓜ *Thissio* – ☎ (210) 5205 360
– www.eridanus.gr

A2

36 rm 🍽 – ♦75/115 € ♦♦85/130 € – 3 suites
Rest – Menu 35/55 € – Carte 24/45 €

♦ Townhouse ♦ Business ♦ Contemporary ♦

Contemporary design hotel named after a river from Greek mythology; located on a busy main street. Charming guest areas feature original ceiling frescoes. Elegant bedrooms come in refined, modern-classical designs and offer plenty of extras; all have hydro-massage showers, some boast Acropolis views. Mediterranean restaurant moves to the top floor terrace in summer.

New Hotel

⅍ 🔲 ⅍ 📶 🧖 💳 ⦾ 🅰🅴 ⓞ

16 Filellinon ✉ 105 57 – Ⓜ *Syntagma* – ☎ (210) 327 3000
– www.yeshotels.gr

C3

79 rm 🍽 – ♦160/185 € ♦♦175/295 €
Rest *New Taste* – ☎ (210) 327 3170 – Carte 36/72 €

♦ Business ♦ Design ♦ Minimalist ♦

Modern hotel designed by the Campana brothers, set close to Syntagma Square. Quirky lobby walls feature wood reclaimed from old bedsteads. Minimalist bedrooms boast balconies overlooking the city and furnishings made from recycled materials. All-day dining at white marble tables from an international menu.

Athenian Callirhoe

🛁 🏠 🔲 ⅍ 📶 🧖 💳 ⦾ 🅰🅴 ⓞ

32 Kallirois Ave and Petmeza ✉ 117 43 – Ⓜ *Syngrou-Fix*
– ☎ (210) 9215 353 – www.tac.gr

C3

84 rm 🍽 – ♦79/209 € ♦♦80/250 €
Rest *Callirhoe VIP* – Menu 25 € – Carte 40/61 €
Rest *Café Degli Artisti* – Menu 25 € – Carte 40/61 €

♦ Business ♦ Modern ♦

Contemporary hotel near the city centre, its elegant lobby filled with smart design furniture. Comfortable wood-furnished bedrooms, with spacious executives and suites – some have jacuzzis and balconies. Roof garden bar and restaurant serves modern Mediterranean cuisine; Café Degli Artisti boasts a water feature, live piano music and an Italian menu.

O & B
🖩 ↳ 🛜 📈 ⦾ 𝔸𝔼

7 Leokoriou St ✉ 105 54 – Ⓜ Thissio – ℰ (210) 331 2940
– www.oandbhotel.com
A2
21 rm ⌨ – ♦150/190 € ♦♦150/190 € – 1 suite   **Rest** – Carte 19/34 €
♦ Townhouse ♦ Design ♦ Minimalist ♦
Stylish boutique hotel in downtown Athens, with an 'O'chre & 'B'rown colour
scheme. Spacious bedrooms boast quality furnishings, good attention to detail
and smart marble bathrooms. All-day restaurant offers Greek and Mediterranean cuisine in a minimalist setting. Lively lounge-bar for music and cocktails.

Amalia
🖩 ↳ 🛜 🕍 📈 ⦾ 𝔸𝔼 ⓞ

10 Amalias Ave ✉ 105 57 – Ⓜ Syntagma – ℰ (210) 3237 300
– www.amaliahotels.gr
C2
97 rm ⌨ – ♦90/140 € ♦♦100/180 € – 1 suite   **Rest** – Carte 31/46 €
♦ Business ♦ Modern ♦ Functional ♦
Well-kept, minimalist hotel close to the plazas and Parliament buildings. Light,
modern lobby and lounge-bar; well-equipped, contemporary bedrooms exude
a relaxing ambience – those to the front have balconies overlooking the National Gardens. Large, modern restaurant serves both Mediterranean and local
fare.

Art
🛋 🖩 ↳ 🛜 🕍 📈 ⦾ 𝔸𝔼 ⓞ

27 Marni St ✉ 104 32 – Ⓜ Omonia – ℰ (210) 5240 501
– www.arthotelathens.gr
B1
30 rm ⌨ – ♦59/69 € ♦♦69/111 €
Rest – (dinner only residents only) Menu 35/50 €
♦ Family ♦ Personalised ♦
Family-run hotel on a busy central street, hiding behind a residential 1820s
façade. Intimate lobby with marble floor, piano, Greek paintings and sculptures.
Individually designed, simply furnished bedrooms with parquet floors, in classi-
cal or minimalist styles. Set menus offer Greek and Mediterranean cuisine.

Periscope
🖩 ↳ 🛜 🕍 📈 ⦾ 𝔸𝔼 ⓞ

22 Charitos St ✉ 106 75 – Ⓜ Evangelismos – ℰ (210) 7297 200
– www.yeshotels.gr
D2
21 rm ⌨ – ♦130/140 € ♦♦145/385 €
Rest P Box – ℰ (210) 7298 556 – Carte 30/47 €
♦ Business ♦ Modern ♦ Minimalist ♦
Modern, minimalist hotel on a quiet residential street in an elegant district. Individually designed bedrooms come with balconies: executives display enlarged
aerial photos of Athens on the ceiling. Stylish bar with Mini Cooper seating. Simple restaurant uses good ingredients in generously portioned dishes.

Golden Age
🖩 ↳ 🛜 🕍 📈 ⦾ 𝔸𝔼 ⓞ

57 Michalakopoulou Ave ✉ 115 28 – Ⓜ Megaro Moussikis
– ℰ (210) 7240 861 – www.hotelgoldenage.com
D2
122 rm ⌨ – ♦65/108 € ♦♦73/130 €   **Rest** – Carte 31/50 €
♦ Business ♦ Functional ♦
Modern city centre hotel with contemporary steel façade and minimalist interior; best suited to business clientele. Internet corner, cosy lounge and good-
sized, functional bedrooms with up-to-date facilities and compact bathrooms;
some have balconies. Small restaurant serves Greek and Mediterranean cuisine.

Acropolis Hill without rest
🏊 ⅄ ↳ 🛜 🕍 📈 ⦾ 𝔸𝔼 ⓞ

7 Mousson St ✉ 117 42 – Ⓜ Singrou-Fix – ℰ (210) 9235 151
– www.acropolishill.gr
B3
37 rm ⌨ – ♦55/80 € ♦♦65/105 €
♦ Traditional ♦ Business ♦ Contemporary ♦
Sister to Achilleas, a boutique hotel set close to the Philopappos Monument.
Contemporary lounge-bar and breakfast room. Simple, practical bedrooms
with large showers – front rooms have balconies and Acropolis views. Pleasant
outdoor pool.

Hermes without rest
19 Apollonos St ⊠ 105 57 – Ⓜ Syntagma – ℰ (210) 3235 514
– www.hermeshotel.gr   **B3**
45 rm ⊑ – ♦90/109 € ♦♦95/150 €
♦ Family ♦ Functional ♦
Compact, modern hotel located between Monastiraki and Syntagma Square. Well-kept, contemporary interior with light lobby, comfortable lounge and discreet first floor breakfast room. Functional, wood-furnished bedrooms; some have balconies.

Achilleas without rest
21 Lekka St ⊠ 105 62 – Ⓜ Syntagma – ℰ (210) 3233197
– www.achilleashotel.gr   **C2**
34 rm ⊑ – ♦50/70 € ♦♦60/90 €
♦ Family ♦ Functional ♦
Friendly hotel in small street that's well-known for its silversmiths, close to Constitution Square. Spacious, comfy bedrooms in uniform styles with well-kept, up-to-date bathrooms; ideal for families. Self-service breakfast on mezzanine.

Museum without rest
16 Bouboulinas St ⊠ 106 82 – Ⓜ Victoria – ℰ (210) 3805 611
– www.hotelsofathens.com   **B1**
93 rm ⊑ – ♦50/65 € ♦♦60/120 €
♦ Family ♦ Traditional ♦ Functional ♦
Small but reasonably priced hotel, made up of two buildings overlooking the National Archaeological Museum. Simple, functional style throughout: half the bedrooms are larger and in a contemporary vein; the rest are more classically styled.

Spondi
5 Pyronos, off Varnava Sq, Pangrati ⊠ 116 36 – ℰ (210) 7564 021
– www.spondi.gr
– Closed Easter and 1 week mid-August   **D3**
Rest – *(dinner only)* Menu 69/128 € – Carte 87/115 € 錄
♦ French ♦ Romantic ♦ Elegant ♦
Well-known restaurant with 2 courtyards and 2 dining rooms: one is intimate; the other, elegantly designed from reclaimed bricks in the style of a vaulted cellar, complete with a wine cave. Top quality produce is used to create imaginative, deftly executed and stunningly presented modern French dishes.
➔ Crab with mint, cauliflower and apple. Cod with coco beans, shiitake and tamarind. Puff pastry with vanilla, caramel and fleur de sel.

GB Roof Garden – at Grande Bretagne Hotel
1 Vas Georgiou A, Constitution Sq ⊠ 105 64
– Ⓜ Syntagma – ℰ (210) 3330 766 – www.gbroofgarden.gr
Rest – *(booking essential)* Carte 46/81 € 錄   **C2**
♦ Mediterranean ♦ Friendly ♦ Elegant ♦
Smart, comfortable and smoothly run restaurant on the rooftop of the elegant Grand Bretagne hotel, boasting a lovely terrace and spectacular views over Syntagma Square and out towards The Acropolis. Sunny, modern Mediterranean cooking is accompanied by an extensive wine list.

Première – at Athenaeum Inter-Continental Hotel
89-93 Syngrou Ave (9th floor) (Southwest : 2.5 km)
⊠ 117 45 – ℰ (210) 9206 981 – www.athens.intercontinental.com
– Closed Sunday-Monday
Rest – *(dinner only)* Menu 65 € – Carte 62/84 € 錄
♦ Mediterranean ♦ Elegant ♦ Minimalist ♦
Elegant, modern restaurant with cocktail bar and terrace, set on the 9th floor and offering panoramic views which take in The Acropolis. Interesting Mediterranean dishes are carefully crafted from quality produce and have a delicate touch.

Varoulko (Lefteris Lazarou)

80 Pireaus Ave, Keramikos ✉ 104 35 – ⓂThissio – ℰ (210) 5228 400
– www.varoulko.gr – Closed Easter, 25 and 31 December and Sunday
Rest *– (dinner only) (booking essential)* Menu 50 € – Carte 44/56 €   A2
◆ **Fish and seafood** ◆ **Fashionable** ◆ **Elegant** ◆
Set on a busy avenue; a sleek, minimalist, split-level restaurant with a part-glass roof and areas of glass flooring. Well-balanced, appealingly presented seafood dishes showcase quality produce. Knowledgeable team personalise the modern 'Degustation' menu for each guest. Remarkable views from the roof terrace.
➜ Marinated salmon with fennel sorbet. Market fish with aioli and rocket. Olive oil chocolate mousse and vanilla ice cream.

Milo's – at Hilton Hotel

46 Vas Sofias Ave ✉ 115 28 – ⓂEvangelismos – ℰ (210) 7244 400
– www.milos.ca – Closed Christmas, New Year, 3-6 May and Sunday dinner
Rest – Menu 25 € – Carte 56/91 €   D2
◆ **Fish and seafood** ◆ **Fashionable** ◆
Superb seafood restaurant set in the Hilton, with sister establishments in New York, Las Vegas and Montreal. Modern room with central bar, open kitchen and fresh produce on display. Tasty, top quality fish and shellfish from the day boats.

Electra Roof Garden – at Electra Palace Hotel

18-20 Nikodimou St ✉ 105 57 – ⓂSyntagma
– ℰ (210) 3370 000 – www.electrahotels.gr   C3
Rest *– (dinner only)* Menu 35 € – Carte 46/66 €
◆ **Mediterranean** ◆ **Romantic** ◆ **Elegant** ◆
Stunningly located 5th floor restaurant offering unrivalled views of The Acropolis and Athens. Innovative menu features traditional Greek flavours in modern interpretations. Attentive service, with many dishes delivered by the chef himself.

Funky Gourmet (Georgianna Chiliadaki and Nikos Roussos)

13 Paramythias St and Salaminos, Keramikos
✉ 104 35 – ⓂKeramikós – ℰ (210) 5242 727 – www.funkygourmet.com
– Closed August, Sunday and Monday   A2
Rest *– (dinner only) (booking essential)* Menu 68/118 €
◆ **Innovative** ◆ **Minimalist** ◆ **Intimate** ◆
Charming neoclassical house off the main tourist track, with marble-floored reception, art deco lounge, and minimalist first floor dining room in white, black and grey. Well-crafted, creative dishes presented in unusual but well-thought-through combinations. Degustation menu offers interesting wine pairings.
➜ Greek salad. Scallop in the sea. Very berry dessert.

GB Corner – at Grande Bretagne Hotel

1 Vas Georgiou A, Constitution Sq ✉ 105 64 – ⓂSyntagma
– ℰ (210) 3330 750 – www.gbcorner.gr   C2
Rest – Carte 32/74 €
◆ **Greek** ◆ **Friendly** ◆
Luxurious brasserie on the ground and mezzanine levels of an impressive hotel, where affluent local businessmen like to lunch. Exclusively Greek menu presents top quality products in an unfussy manner; cooking is respectful of natural flavours. Efficient, welcoming team.

Hytra

6th Floor, Onassis Cultural Centre, 107-109 Syngrou Ave (Southwest :
2.5 km) ✉ 11745 – ℰ (210) 7071 118 – www.hytra.gr – Closed Monday
Rest *– (dinner only)* Menu 62 € – Carte 56/68 €
◆ **Modern** ◆ **Design** ◆ **Fashionable** ◆
Slick, modern bar and stylish, sultry restaurant on the 6th floor of the arts centre – the best tables look across Singrou towards The Acropolis. Choose from the degustation menu or the concise à la carte; well-executed dishes employ modern techniques and are executed with finesse. Service is smooth.
➜ Beetroot and goat's cheese with sour honey and fig vinaigrette. Black pork with celeriac purée and orange. Tiramisu, coffee caviar and bitter almond ice cream.

Fuga

⛶ AC VISA ⬤⬤ AE ⬤

Vas Sofias & Kokkali 1 (at the Megaro Moussikis) ✉ 115 21
– Ⓜ *Megaro Moussikis* – ✆ (210) 7242 979 – www.fugarestaurant.com
Rest – *(dinner only)* Carte 51/68 €   D1
♦ Italian ♦ Minimalist ♦ Elegant ♦

Set in the garden of the Concert Hall; its name means harmony. Simple yet elegant room displays projections of classical composers; large windows open onto a terrace. Experienced chef prepares modern Italian dishes with care and precision.

Luna Rossa

VISA ⬤⬤ AE

213 Sokratous, Kallithea (Southwest : 4 km) ✉ 176 74 – ✆ (210) 9423 777
– www.lunarossa.gr
– *Closed Easter, July, August, 31 December and Sunday*
Rest – *(dinner only) (booking essential)* Menu 40 € – Carte 29/70 € ⅜
♦ Italian ♦ Family ♦ Elegant ♦

Discreet, intimate, family-run restaurant, unusually set in a residential property. Elegant handmade furnishings and personal service. Three romantic, classical rooms – two containing just 1 table each. Authentic cooking from Italian chef.

Athiri

⛶ AC VISA ⬤⬤

15 Plateon ✉ 104 35 – Ⓜ *Keramikós* – ✆ (210) 3462 983
– www.athirirestaurant.gr
– *Closed 10 days August, 1 week Easter, 1-5 January and Monday*
Rest – *(dinner only and Sunday lunch)* Carte 18/31 €   A2
♦ Greek ♦ Neighbourhood ♦

Discreet address to the west of the city. Dine in the minimalist inner or outdoors amongst the greenery. Seasonal ingredients are simply prepared in order to reveal their natural flavours. Dishes are generous and display creative touches.

Kuzina

⛶ AC VISA ⬤⬤ ⬤

9 Adrianou St ✉ 105 55 – Ⓜ *Thissio* – ✆ (210) 3240 133 – www.kuzina.gr
– *Closed Easter, 25 December and 1 January*   B3
Rest – Menu 20 € – Carte 25/50 €
♦ Mediterranean ♦ Friendly ♦ Bistro ♦

Large, lively, split-level restaurant with an open kitchen, shelves filled with alcohol and preserves, and panoramic views from the terrace. Contemporary Greek cooking displays some Asian influences and makes good use of local produce.

Vezene

⛶ AC VISA ⬤⬤

Vrasida 11 ✉ 115 28 – ✆ (210) 723 2002 – www.vezene.gr
– *Closed Easter, 24-25 and 31 December, 1 January and Sunday*
Rest – *(dinner only)* Carte 25/99 €   D2
♦ Meats and grills ♦ Friendly ♦ Minimalist ♦

Easy-going eatery specialising in unfussy steak and seafood dishes. Dark wood interior leads to a glass veranda and terrace. The friendly team guide guests as the menu evolves. Try the mini Wagyu burger and the sliced-to-order salumi.

Oikeîo

⛶ AC VISA ⬤⬤ ⬤

15 Ploutarhou St ✉ 106 75 – Ⓜ *Evangelismos* – ✆ (210) 7259 216
– *Closed 25 December, 1 January, Easter and Sunday*   D2
Rest – Carte 15/25 €
♦ Greek ♦ Rustic ♦ Traditional ♦

Small neighbourhood restaurant with loft room and outside tables, set in a smart quarter of Athens. Warm, cosy dining room with simply laid tables, exposed red-brick walls, and country objects hanging from the ceiling. Simple Greek cooking.

Psarra's Tavern

⛶ VISA ⬤⬤ AE ⬤

16 Erechtheos and Erotokritou St, Plaka ✉ 105 56 – Ⓜ *Monastiraki*
– ✆ (210) 3218 733 – www.psaras-taverna.gr   B3
Rest – Menu 15/20 € – Carte 13/28 €
♦ Greek ♦ Rustic ♦

Rustic Greek taverna dating back to 1898, set in a small side street of a characterful district close to The Acropolis. Various wood-furnished, stone-walled dining rooms and terraces are spread over 3 different houses. Simple local cuisine.

GREECE - ATHENS

Pentelikon

66 Diligianni St, Kefalari (off Harilaou Trikoupi, follow signs to Politia) ⊠ 145 62 – Ⓜ Kifissia – ℰ (210) 6230 650 – www.pentelikon.gr

89 rm ⊊ – ♦165/350 € ♦♦370 € – 12 suites

Rest *La Locanda Italiana* – Menu 30/35 € – Carte 33/49 €

♦ Palace ♦ Luxury ♦ Classic ♦

Elegant 1920s hotel with pleasant gardens, in an affluent residential area close to the shopping streets. Classically styled throughout, boasting marble, hand-made furniture, heavy drapes, antiques and oil paintings. The most luxurious bedrooms are in the annexes. Creative Italian cuisine in La Locanda Italiana.

Kefalari Suites without rest

1 Pentelis and Kolokotroni St, Kefalari ⊠ 145 62 – Ⓜ Kifissia – ℰ (210) 6233 333 – www.yeshotels.gr

12 rm ⊊ – ♦140/155 € ♦♦155/195 € – 1 suite

♦ Townhouse ♦ Villa ♦ Elegant ♦

Early 20C villa in a smart residential area, just a stone's throw from the main square. Small but stylish lobby and breakfast room. Individually designed, ele-gantly furnished bedrooms boast kitchens and marble bathrooms; two take on a nautical style. Roof terrace comes complete with jacuzzi and sun loungers.

Semiramis

48 Charilaou Trikoupi St, Kefalari ⊠ 145 62 – Ⓜ Kifissia – ℰ (210) 6284 400 – www.yeshotels.gr

50 rm ⊊ – ♦160/170 € ♦♦175/185 € – 1 suite   **Rest** – Carte 28/59 €

♦ Business ♦ Design ♦ Minimalist ♦

Contemporary design hotel on the main plaza of a leafy suburb. Flamboyant colour schemes feature inside and out, and are complemented by vibrant modern furnishings. Bedrooms boast hi-tech facilities, balconies and LED 'do not disturb' signs. Mediterranean restaurant overlooks the pool and decked terrace.

Twenty One

21 Kolokotroni and Mykonou St, Kefalari ⊠ 145 62 – Ⓜ Kifissia – ℰ (210) 6233 521 – www.yeshotels.gr

16 rm ⊊ – ♦135/140 € ♦♦150/155 € – 5 suites

Rest – (dinner only and lunch Saturday and Sunday) Carte 34/65 €

♦ Business ♦ Minimalist ♦ Modern ♦

Modern, slate-grey city hotel – formerly a water mill – in a pleasant residential area by the main square. Choice of 16 minimalist bedrooms with parquet floors and feature walls or 5 spacious, stylish loft suites. Modern Greek and Mediterra-nean cuisine served in contemporary restaurant and on the terrace.

P Box

11 Levidou St ⊠ 145 62 – Ⓜ Kifissia – ℰ (210) 8088 818 – www.p-box.gr – Closed 25 December, 1 January and Easter

Rest – (bookings not accepted) Carte 28/54 €

♦ International ♦ Fashionable ♦ Friendly ♦

Set on the main shopping street of a wealthy suburb and frequented by the 'desig-ner' set. Easy-going atmosphere and popular terrace. Unfussy, modern cooking with Asian overtones; dishes range from pastas to grilled meats. Efficient service.

Pandeli

3 Pendelis St, Kefalari ⊠ 145 62 – Ⓜ Kifissia – ℰ (210) 8080 787 – www.pandeli.gr – Closed 1 week Easter, 3 weeks August, 25 December, 1 January and Sunday dinner

Rest – (dinner only and Sunday lunch) Menu 25 € – Carte 22/40 €

♦ Turkish ♦ Traditional ♦

Welcoming Turkish restaurant following in the footsteps of the Istanbul original. Large room with red-tiled floor and turquoise-tiled walls opens out onto the street. Generous, authentic Turkish dishes display the occasional Greek touch.

AT HALANDRI   Northeast : 11 km by Vas. Sofias

XXX   **Botrini's**   📶 AC 🚭 AE ①

24b Vasileos Georgiou ✉ *10435 –* Ⓜ *Halandri –* ℰ *(210) 6857323*
– www.botrinis.com
– Closed 5-20 August, Monday in low season and Sunday dinner in winter
Rest *– (dinner only and Sunday lunch in winter)* Menu 40/65 €
– Carte 58/69 €
♦ Mediterranean ♦ Design ♦ Friendly ♦
Converted school in a quiet suburb – passionately run, with an ultra-modern
interior, a sleek glass-fronted kitchen and lush terraces. Appealing modern
menus include a good value set option. Oils and salamis are produced by the
family.

AT MAROUSSI   Northeast : 12.5 km by Vas. Sofias

XX   **Aneton**   AC VISA 🚭 AE ①

19 Stratigou Lekka ✉ *151 22 –* Ⓜ *Maroussi –* ℰ *(210) 8066 700*
– www.aneton.gr
– Closed August, 25 December, 1 January and Easter
Rest *– (dinner only) (booking essential)* Carte 21/33 €
♦ Greek ♦ Friendly ♦
Well-regarded, vintage-style restaurant in a smart suburb. Retro interior with
subtle lighting and 1950s/60s inspired furniture. Concise menus rely on fresh
market produce; classical dishes are interpreted in an imaginative, modern
manner.

AT ATHENS INTERNATIONAL AIRPORT   East : 35 km by Vas. Sofias

🏨   **Sofitel Athens Airport**   ƒ₆ 🎐 🕥 🖭 ᕗ AC ⇄ 🛜 🏋 🚗

✉ *190 19 –* Ⓜ *Airport –* ℰ *(210) 3544 000*   VISA 🚭 AE ①
– www.sofitel-athens-airport.com
332 rm – ♥95/345 € ♥♥95/345 €, ⌻ 25 € – 13 suites
Rest *Karavi* *– (dinner only)* Carte 59/93 €
Rest *Mesoghaia* – Carte 45/55 €
♦ Chain hotel ♦ Business ♦ Contemporary ♦
Modern business hotel set 30m from the airport terminal. Spacious bedrooms
are well-equipped and well-soundproofed; executive floors have private
check-in and a lounge with all-day snacks. Small wellness centre. Choice of cuisine: modern French in 9th floor Karavi or Greek and Mediterranean in 24hr
Mesoghaia.

AT VOULIAGMENI   South : 18 km by Singrou

🏨   **Westin Athens**   ≤ 🛥 🐬 ƒ₆ 🎐 🕥 ☒ 🖭 🌿 ᕗ AC ⇄ 🐾 🏋 🅿

40 Apollonos St (Vouliagmeni) ✉ *166 71*   VISA 🚭 AE ①
– ℰ *(210) 8902 000*
– www.westin.com/athens
155 rm ⌻ – ♥105/395 € ♥♥135/425 € – 7 suites
Rest *Galazia Hytra* ❀ – see restaurant listing
Rest *Kymata* *–* ℰ *(210) 8901 548 (May-September) (lunch only)*
Carte 40/58 €
♦ Luxury ♦ Palace ♦ Modern ♦
Professionally run hotel set within a 75 acre complex on a private peninsula.
Extensive facilities include private beaches, a spa and a wide range of water
sports. Spacious bedrooms boast sea views and either a balcony or terrace.
Mediterranean dishes served by the pool in casual Kymata. Inventive southern
European dishes in Galazia Hytra.

Arion Resort & Spa

40 Apollonos St (Vouliagmeni) ⊠ *166 71*
– ℰ *(210) 8902 000 – www.luxurycollection.com/arion*
165 rm ⬚ – ♦115/405 € ♦♦145/435 € – 16 suites
Rest *Il Tramonto* – ℰ *(210) 8901 794 (dinner only)* Carte 31/68 €
Rest *Taverna 37* – ℰ *(210) 8901 737 (lunch only mid May-late September)* Carte 31/68 €

♦ Luxury ♦ Spa hotel ♦ Elegant ♦

Set in the same complex as the Westin and sharing many of the excellent facilities. Choose between large, stylish bedrooms with balconies and sea/marina views or contemporary bungalows with marble bathrooms – some with private pools. Traditional lunches in Taverna 37; modern Greek dinners in elegant Il Tramonto.

Divani Apollon Palace & Spa

10 Ag Nikolaou and Iliou St
(Kavouri) off Athinas ⊠ *16671* – ℰ *(210) 8911 100 – www.divanis.com*
273 rm ⬚ – ♦420/560 € ♦♦420/560 € – 7 suites
Rest *Mythos* – Carte 56/70 €
Rest *Anemos* – Carte 41/57 €

♦ Palace ♦ Luxury ♦ Classic ♦

Fashionable resort hotel with a walkway to its own private beach. Luxurious bedrooms boast balconies and gulf views. Impressive spa and thalassotherapy centre, and two indoor and two outdoor pools. All-day snacks in the coffee lounge; fresh seafood in beachside Mythos; international dishes in modern Anemos.

Apollon Suites *without rest*

11 Nikolaou St ⊠ *166 71* – ℰ *(210) 8911 100 – www.divanis.com*
– *Restricted opening in winter*
56 rm – ♦420/560 € ♦♦420/950 €

♦ Luxury ♦ Contemporary ♦

Peaceful annexe of the Divani Apollon, with a more intimate atmosphere. Large, well-equipped bedrooms boast contemporary décor, hand-chosen fabrics and furnished terraces; some have sea views. Facilities are shared with its bigger sister.

Margi

11 Litous St ⊠ *166 71* – ℰ *(210) 8929 000 – www.themargi.gr*
81 rm ⬚ – ♦134/209 € ♦♦144/231 € – 8 suites
Rest – Menu 28 € – Carte 35/60 €

♦ Traditional ♦ Personalised ♦ Mediterranean ♦

Stylish hotel on the peninsula, close to the beach. Elegant lobby has a Mediterranean feel. Antique-furnished, modern colonial style bedrooms boast smart marble bathrooms and balconies with sea/forest views. Greek cooking displays Mediterranean influences; meals can be taken on the poolside terrace in summer.

Matsuhisa

40 Apollonos St (Vouliagmeni) ⊠ *16671* – ℰ *(210) 8960 510*
– *www.matsuhisaathens.com*
– *Closed Easter*
Rest – *(dinner only and lunch Saturday-Sunday) (booking essential)*
Menu 50/75 € – Carte 25/89 €

♦ Japanese ♦ Fashionable ♦ Trendy ♦

Sophisticated restaurant with a bustling atmosphere, polished service, a small upstairs cocktail bar and a stunning terrace boasting sea and island views. Contemporary Japanese cooking in the typical Nobu style: original, well-thought-through dishes come from the sushi counter, wood-fired oven or robata grill.

XXX ✿
Galazia Hytra – at Westin Athens H.   🛖 ㅊ AC VISA ∞ AE ①
40 Apollonos St (Vouliagmeni) ✉ *16671 –* ✆ *(210) 8902 137*
– www.hytra.gr
Rest *– (closed 15 September-25 May) (dinner only)* Carte 60/69 €
♦ Mediterranean ♦ Elegant ♦ Minimalist ♦
Slick, understated dining room leading to a lovely terrace with wonderful sea views. Innovative, modern Mediterranean dishes are carefully prepared and smartly presented, featuring top quality products in well-considered combinations.
→ Moussaka. Red mullet with cauliflower and cucumber sauce. The 'Anthotyro' tiramisu with coffee and bitter almond.

AT KALAMAKI   Southwest : 14 km by Singrou

XXX
Akrotiri   ← 🛖 AC ㅁ️ P VISA ∞ AE ①
Vas. Georgiou B5, Agios Kosmas, Helliniko ✉ *167 77 –* ✆ *(210) 9859 147*
– www.akrotirilounge.gr
– 7 April-October
Rest *– (dinner only)* Carte 43/74 €
♦ Mediterranean ♦ Fashionable ♦ Musical ♦
Fashionable, open-air, seafront restaurant boasting stylish furnishings, modern lighting and contemporary designs. Appealing Greek and Mediterranean dishes. Club area boasts a pool, bridge and disco ball; the whole place gets busy at midnight.

AT PIRAEUS   Southwest: 8 km by Singrou

🏨
Piraeus Theoxenia   ♨ AC ⇔ 🛜 🖄 🚗 VISA ∞ AE ①
23 Karaoli and Dimitriou St ✉ *185 31 –* Ⓜ *Pireaus –* ✆ *(210) 4112 550*
– www.theoxeniapalace.com
75 rm 🖃 – 🛏99/107 € 🛏🛏99/107 € – 1 suite
Rest *Incognito* – Menu 25 € – Carte 29/36 €
♦ Business ♦ Contemporary ♦ Functional ♦
Corporate hotel in the heart of town, close to the harbour and bustling local markets. Well-equipped gym and business centre. Spacious bedrooms combine traditional and modern styles; some have work desks and comfy seating areas. Classical restaurant offers an international menu with Mediterranean influences.

X
Papaioannou   🛖 AC VISA ∞ ①
Akti Koumoumdourou 42.1, Microlimano (West 1.5 km by coastal road)
✉ *185 33 –* ✆ *(210) 4225 059*
– Closed Easter, dinner 25 and 31 December and Sunday dinner
Rest – Carte 36/41 €
♦ Fish and seafood ♦ Traditional ♦
Traditional seafood restaurant. Diners select the type, weight and cooking style of their fish; while shrimp, mussels and crayfish come 'saganaki' style – in tomato sauce with feta cheese. Menus evolve as more fresh fish arrives.

HUNGARY
MAGYARORSZÁG

● BUDAPEST

→ **AREA:**
93 032 km² (35 920 sq mi).

→ **POPULATION:**
9 971 000 inhabitants.
Density = 107 per km².

→ **CAPITAL:**
Budapest.

→ **CURRENCY:**
Hungarian Forint (Ft or HUF).

→ **GOVERNMENT:**
Parliamentary republic (since 1989). Member of European Union since 2004.

→ **LANGUAGE:**
Hungarian; many Hungarians also speak English and German.

→ **PUBLIC HOLIDAYS:**
New Years' Day (1 Jan); 1848 Revolution Day (15 Mar); Easter Monday (late Mar/Apr); Labor Day (1 May); Whit Monday (late May/June); St Stephen's Day (20 Aug); 1956 Uprising Remembrance Day (23 Oct); All Saints' Day (1 Nov); Christmas Eve (24 Dec); Christmas Day (25 Dec); Boxing Day (26 Dec).

→ **LOCAL TIME:**
GMT+1 hour in winter and GMT+2 hours in summer.

→ **CLIMATE:**
Temperate continental with cold winters and warm summers (Budapest: January -1°C; July 22°C).

→ **EMERGENCY:**
Police ☏ **107**; Medical Assistance ☏ **104**; Fire Brigade ☏ **105**; Roadside breakdown service ☏ **188**.
(Dialling **112** within any EU country will redirect your call and contact the emergency services.)

→ **ELECTRICITY:**
230 volts AC, 50Hz; 2 round pin sockets.

→ **FORMALITIES:**
Travellers from the European Union (EU), Switzerland, Iceland and the main countries of North and South America need a national identity card or passport (America: passport required) to visit Hungary for less than three months (tourism or business purpose).
For visitors from other countries a visa may be required, in addition to a passport, especially for those wishing to stay for longer than three months. We advise you to check with your embassy before travelling.

BUDAPEST
BUDAPEST

Population: 1 740 041

Jonathan/Fotolia.com

No one knows quite where the Hungarian language came from: it's not quite Slavic, not quite Turkic, and its closest relatives appear to be in Finland and Siberia. In much the same way, Hungary's capital is a bit of an enigma. A lot of what you see is not as old as it appears. Classical and Gothic buildings are mostly neoclassical and neo-Gothic, and the fabled baroque of the city is of a more recent vintage than in other European capitals. That's because Budapest's frequent invaders and conquerors, from all compass points of the map, left little but rubble behind them when they left; the grand look of today took shape for the most part no earlier than the mid-19C.

It's still a beautiful place to look at, with hilly Buda keeping watch – via eight great bridges – over sprawling Pest on the other side of the lilting, bending Danube. These were formerly two separate towns, united in 1873 to form a capital city. It enjoyed its heyday around that time, a magnificent city that was the hub of the Austro-Hungarian Empire. Defeats in two world wars and fifty years behind the Iron Curtain put paid to the glory, but battered Budapest is used to rising from the ashes and now it's Europe's most earthily beautiful capital, particularly when winter mists rise from the river to shroud it in a thick white cloak. In summer the days can swelter, and the spas are definitely worth a visit.

BUDAPEST IN...

→ **ONE DAY**
Royal Palace, the Parliament Building, a trip on the Danube.

→ **TWO DAYS**
Gellert Baths, a stroll down Váci utca, a concert at the State Opera House.

→ **THREE DAYS**
Museum of Applied Arts, Margaret Island, coffee and cake at Gerbeaud.

PRACTICAL INFORMATION

ARRIVAL-DEPARTURE

✈ Liszt Ferenc National Airport is 24km southeast of the city. A taxi will take about 45min. Shuttle Minibuses do the rounds of the hotels. A train will take you from Terminal 1 to the Western Railway Station.

GETTING AROUND

Budapest has an extensive public transport system, with a three-line metro, buses, trolley buses and trams. Tickets must be bought in advance and validated in the ticket stampers at the start of the journey. Buy your tickets at metro stations, ticket machines, newsagents or tobacconists.

The Budapest Card includes unlimited travel on public transport; free or reduced price admission to many museums and sights, cultural and folklore programmes; and discounts in some shops, restaurants and thermal baths. Valid for two or three days, it can be bought at the airport, main metro stations, tourist offices and some hotels.

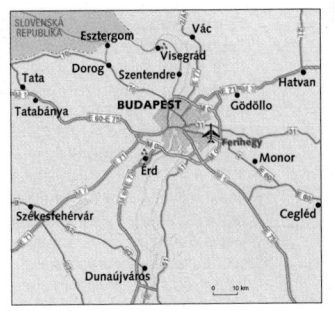

CALENDAR HIGHLIGHTS

March
Spring Festival (classical, opera and folk music).

June-August
Summer Festival (open-air theatre).

August
Sziget Festival (rock music).

October
Autumn Festival (cutting edge theatre, dance, music and film).

November-December
Christmas Fair at Vörösmarty tér.

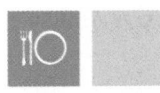

EATING OUT

The city is most famous for its coffee houses so, before you start investigating restaurants, find time to tuck into a cream cake with a double espresso in, say, the Ruszwurm on Castle Hill, the city's oldest, and possibly cosiest, café. In tourist areas, it's not difficult to locate goulash on your menu, and you never have to travel far to find beans, dumplings and cabbage in profusion. Having said that, Budapest's culinary scene has moved on apace since the fall of communism, and Hungarian chefs have become much more inventive with their use of local, seasonal produce. Pest is where you'll find most choice but even in Buda there are plenty of worthy restaurants. Lots of locals like to eat sausage on the run and if you fancy the idea, buy a pocket knife. Sunday brunch is popular in Budapest, especially at the best hotels. Your restaurant bill might well include a service charge; don't feel obliged to pay it, as tipping is entirely at your own discretion – though you may find the persistence of the little folk groups that pop up in many restaurants hard to resist.

Four Seasons Gresham Palace

Szechenyi István tér 5-6 ⊠ *1051*
– **Ⓜ** *Vörösmarty tér* – *ℰ (01) 268 6000*
– *www.fourseasons.com/budapest*   **E2**
169 rm ☐ – †77350/182900 HUF ††77350/182900 HUF – 10 suites
Rest *Gresham* – *ℰ (01) 268 5110* – Menu 4640/112500 HUF
– Carte 7900/15300 HUF
♦ Grand Luxury ♦ Palace ♦ Art Deco ♦
Beautifully renovated art nouveau building constructed for the Gresham Insurance Company in 1906; located opposite the Chain Bridge, with superb river views. Stunning lobby with a mosaic floor and cupola roof; impressive rooftop spa. Luxurious bedrooms and high quality service. Menus reflect the chef's Italian roots; Hungarian and international dishes also feature.

Corinthia Budapest

Erzsébet krt 43-49 ⊠ *1073* – **Ⓜ** *Oktogon*
– *ℰ (01) 479 4000* – *www.corinthia.com/budapest*   **F1**
390 rm – †39040/129320 HUF ††39040/129320 HUF, ☐ 8000 HUF
– 24 suites
Rest *Brasserie* – *ℰ (01) 479 4850* – Menu 6900 HUF
– Carte 7600/13500 HUF
Rest *Rickshaw* – *ℰ (01) 479 4855 (dinner only)* Menu 3900 HUF
– Carte 6100/12800 HUF
♦ Grand Luxury ♦ Classic ♦ Elegant ♦
Originally built in the late 19C, a beautifully restored and comprehensively equipped hotel with a splendid façade, a spectacular atrium, a marble staircase and large bedrooms, along with a stunning swimming pool and spa facilities, and even a patisserie. International menu in spacious Brasserie; Asian décor and regularly changing Cantonese dishes in intimate Rickshaw.

Kempinski H. Corvinus

Erzsébet tér 7-8 ⊠ *1051* – **Ⓜ** *Deák Ferenc tér*
– *ℰ (01) 429 3777* – *www.kempinski.com/budapest*   **E2**
337 rm – †32200/100800 HUF ††32200/100800 HUF, ☐ 7840 HUF
– 18 suites
Rest *Nobu Budapest* – see restaurant listing
Rest *Ristorante Giardino* – Menu 7600/8400 HUF
– Carte 7600/28750 HUF
♦ Business ♦ Luxury ♦ Modern ♦
Modern, well-equipped and stylishly built hotel overlooking a central square; named after the charismatic, late 15C Hungarian king, Matthias Corvinus. Spacious bedrooms feature Empire-style furniture and boast a good range of luxury facilities. International menu offered in Ristorante Giardino.

Le Meridien

Erzsébet tér 9-10 ⊠ *1051* – **Ⓜ** *Deák Ferenc tér* – *ℰ (01) 429 5500*
– *www.lemeridien.com/budapest*   **E2**
203 rm – †67300/149000 HUF ††67300/149000 HUF, ☐ 7045 HUF
– 15 suites
Rest *Le Bourbon* – Menu 3600/8900 HUF
– Carte 8200/15800 HUF
♦ Business ♦ Luxury ♦ Classic ♦
An imposing façade hides a classical Hungarian interior with cornicing and rug-covered wooden floors. Very spacious bedrooms boast high ceilings, traditional furniture and chandeliers. Atrium-styled Le Bourbon, with an art deco glass dome, serves a French-influenced menu.

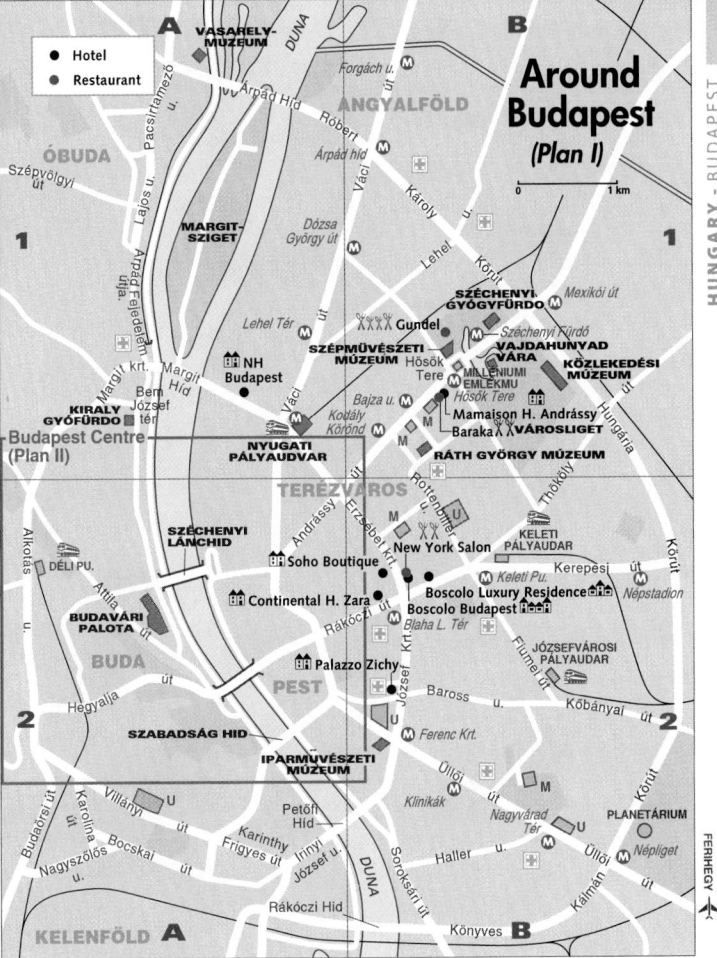

Around Budapest (Plan I)

Legend:
● Hotel
● Restaurant

ÓBUDA
Szépvölgyi út
VASARELY-MÚZEUM
DUNA
Forgách u.
ANGYALFÖLD
Róbert
Árpád híd
Károly
Váci
Lehel
Körút
Mexikói út
SZÉCHENYI GYÓGYFÜRDO
Széchenyi Fürdő
VAJDAHUNYAD VÁRA
KÖZLEKEDÉSI MÚZEUM
Hungária
MARGIT-SZIGET
Dózsa György út
Lehel Tér
Gundel
SZÉPMŰVÉSZETI MÚZEUM
Hősök Tere
MILLENIUMI EMLÉKMŰ
Hősök Tere
Bajza u.
Mamaison H. Andrássy
Baraka
VÁROSLIGET
KIRÁLY GYÓFÜRDŐ
NH Budapest
Kodály Körönd
RÁTH GYÖRGY MÚZEUM
Budapest Centre (Plan II)
NYUGATI PÁLYAUDVAR
TERÉZVÁROS
Rottenbiller
Thököly
DÉLI PU.
SZÉCHENYI LÁNCHID
Andrássy
Erzsébet krt.
New York Salon
KELETI PÁLYAUDAR
Keleti Pu.
Kerepesi út
Népstadion
Soho Boutique
Continental H. Zara
Boscolo Luxury Residence
Boscolo Budapest
Rákóczi
Blaha L. Tér
Körút
BUDAVÁRI PALOTA
BUDA
Hegyalja út
Palazzo Zichy
PEST
JÓZSEF
Baross
JÓZSEFVÁROSI PÁLYAUDAR
Kőbányai út
SZABADSÁG HID
IPARMŰVÉSZETI MÚZEUM
Ferenc Krt.
Üllői
Klinikák
Nagyvárad Tér
PLANETÁRIUM
Népliget
Petőfi Hid
Karinthy Frigyes út
Irinyi József u.
Sorоksári út
Haller
Üllői út
Kálmán
Rákóczi Hid
KELENFÖLD
Könyves
DUNA

0 --- 1 km

🏨🏨🏨 **Sofitel Budapest Chain Bridge**   ⟨ 🍴 👗 🐾 🖼 ⚙ 🆎 🔌

Széchenyi István tér 2 ✉ *1051*   rm, 📶 🏋 🚗 **VISA** **◎** **AE** **①**
– **Ⓜ** *Vörösmarty tér* – ✆ *(01) 235 1234* – www.sofitel.com   **E2**
323 rm – 🛏40600/99000 HUF 🛏🛏40600/99000 HUF, ☕ 7560 HUF
– 34 suites
Rest *Paris Budapest* – Menu 2900/7950 HUF – Carte 6100/14650 HUF
◆ Business ◆ Modern ◆ Stylish ◆
Modern hotel with a vast atrium, a stylish lobby-cum-lounge and a pretty terrace. Compact bedrooms boast the latest mod cons; those on the northwest corners have Buda views. Fashionable Paris Budapest blends French and Hungarian cuisine; unusual open kitchen and stunning castle and Danube views.

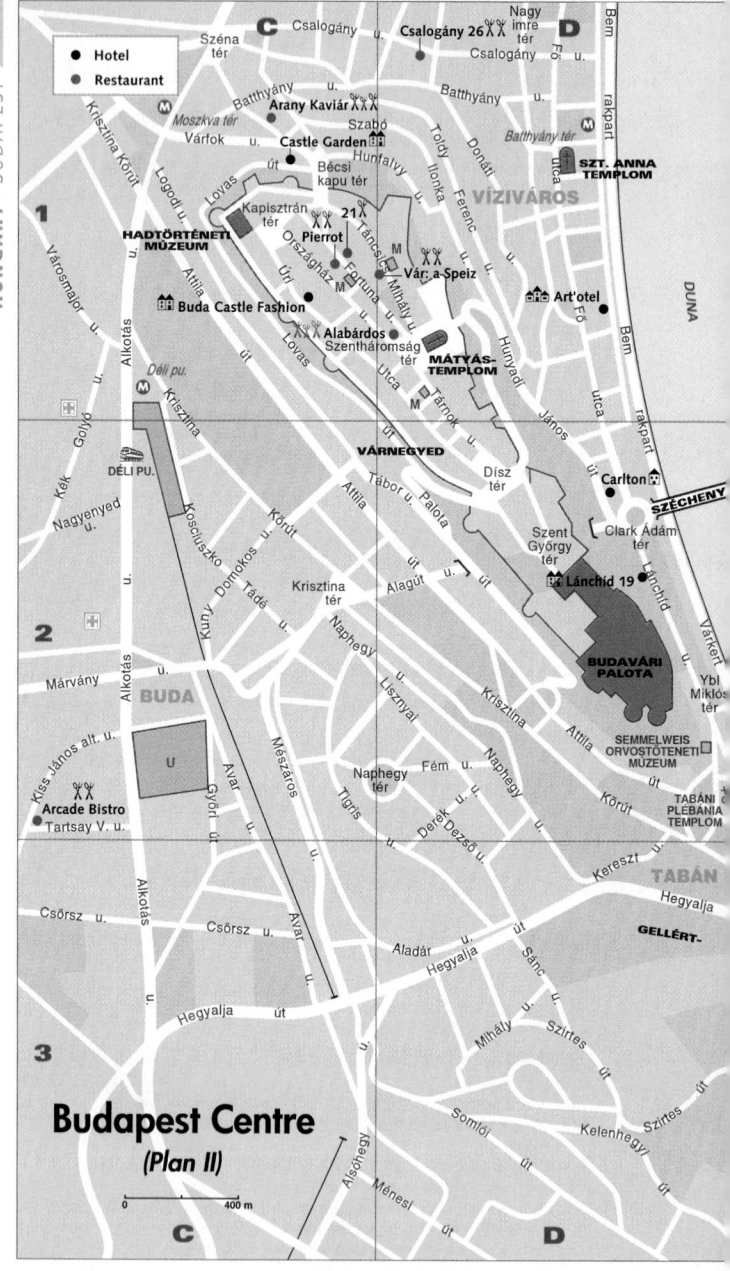

Hotel
Restaurant

Csalogány u.

Csalogány 26

Nagy imre tér

Csalogány u.

Széna tér

Batthyány u.

Moszkva tér

Arany Kaviár

Szabó Ilonka u.

Batthyány tér

Várfok u.

Bécsi kapu tér

Hunfalvy u.

SZT. ANNA TEMPLOM

Krisztina Körút

Logodi u.

Lovas út

Kapisztrán tér

21

Pierrot

Táncsics Mihály u.

VÍZIVÁROS

HADTÖRTÉNETI MÚZEUM

Országház

Fortuna

Vár: a Speiz

Art'otel

Attila

Buda Castle Fashion

Alabárdos

Szentháromság tér

MÁTYÁS-TEMPLOM

Déli pu.

DÉLI PU.

Krisztina

Lovas

Tárnok u.

VÁRNEGYED

Dísz tér

Carlton

SZÉCHENYI

Kék Golyó

Nagyenyed u.

Kosciuszko Tádé u.

Kuny Domokos u.

Krisztina Körút

Attila

Tábor u.

Palota út

Szent György tér

Clark Ádám tér

Lánchíd 19

Lánchíd

Krisztina tér

Alagút u.

BUDAVÁRI PALOTA

Márvány u.

BUDA

U

Mészáros

Naphegy u.

Lisznyai

Ybl Miklós tér

Kiss János alt. u.

Arcade Bistro

Tartsay V. u.

Avar

Győri út

Naphegy tér

Fém u.

Tigris

Derék Dezső u.

Naphegy

Krisztina

Attila

SEMMELWEIS ORVOSTÖRTÉNETI MÚZEUM

Körút

TABÁNI PLÉBÁNIA TEMPLOM

Csörsz u.

Alkotás u.

Csörsz u.

Avar út

Aladár

Hegyalja

Sánc u.

Mihály

Szirtes

TABÁN

Keresztúr út

Hegyalja

GELLÉRT-

Hegyalja út

Somlói út

Kelenhegyi

Szirtes

Alsóhegy

Ménesi út

Budapest Centre
(Plan II)

0   400 m

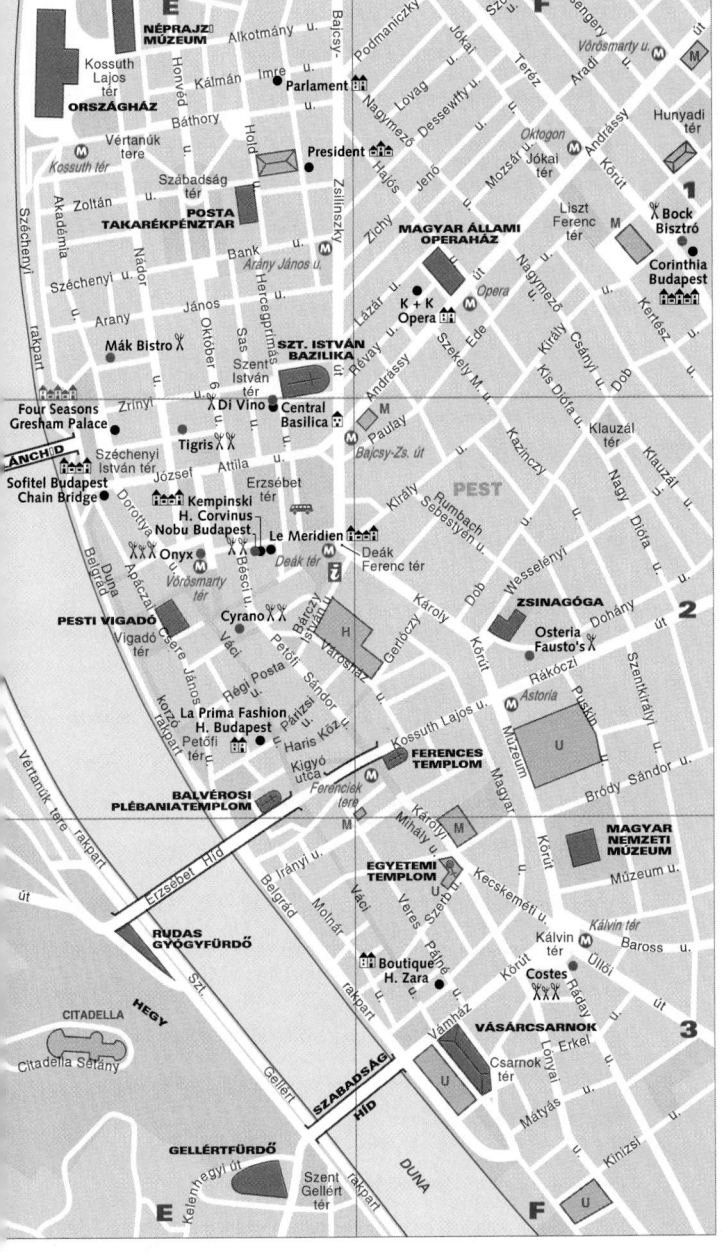

NÉPRAJZI MÚZEUM

Kossuth Lajos tér

ORSZÁGHÁZ

Kossuth tér

Alkotmány u.

● Parlament

Vértanúk tere

Szabadság tér

● President

POSTA TAKARÉKPÉNZTAR

Hunyadi tér

Oktogon

Jókai tér

Liszt Ferenc tér

Bock Bisztró

Corinthia Budapest

MAGYAR ÁLLAMI OPERAHÁZ

Opera

K + K Opera

Szent István tér

SZT. ISTVÁN BAZILIKA

Four Seasons Gresham Palace

Széchenyi István tér

LÁNCHÍD

Sofitel Budapest Chain Bridge

● Mák Bistro X

● Dí Vino

Tigris X X

Central Basilica

PEST

Paulay

Bajcsy-Zs. út

József

Attila

Erzsébet tér

● Kempinski H. Corvinus
Nobu Budapest

● Le Meridien

Deák Ferenc tér

X X X Onyx ●

Vörösmarty tér

ZSINAGÓGA

Osteria Fausto's X

PESTI VIGADÓ

Vigadó tér

● Cyrano X X

H

Astoria

2

Kossuth Lajos u.

La Prima Fashion H. Budapest

Haris Köz.

Petőfi

FERENCES TEMPLOM

Kígyó utca

BALVÉROSI PLÉBANIATEMPLOM

Ferenciek tere

MAGYAR NEMZETI MÚZEUM

Múzeum u.

EGYETEMI TEMPLOM

RUDAS GYÓGYFÜRDŐ

● Boutique H. Zara

Kálvin tér

Baross u.

Costes

X X X Ráday

Üllői út

CITADELLA

Citadella Sétány

HEGY

Erzsébet Hid

VÁSÁRCSARNOK

Vámház

Csarnok tér

Erkel

3

GELLÉRTFÜRDŐ

Kelenhegyi út

Szent Gellért tér

SZABADSÁG HÍD

DUNA

Kinizsi

U

E

F

Boscolo Budapest ᛋᚼ ⚙ 🕸 ⬚ ⅗ AC 🛜 ⅛ ⛱ VISA ⓞ AE ①

Erzsébet krt. 9-11 ✉ *1073* – Ⓜ *Blaha Lujza tér* – ☏ *(01) 886 6111*
– *www.boscolohotels.com* Plan I **B2**
179 rm – ♦113881/142320 HUF ♦♦119547/148011 HUF, ⌚ 5812 HUF
– 6 suites
Rest *New York Salon* – see restaurant listing
♦ Grand Luxury ♦ Stylish ♦ Design ♦

Former insurance company building constructed in 1891, set around an impressive atrium with an Italian Renaissance style. A feeling of luxury pervades, with vast bedrooms featuring silk wallpaper, chandeliers and marble bathrooms.

President ᛋᚼ 🕸 ⬚ ⅗ rm, AC ⅛ 🕻 ⅛ VISA ⓞ AE

Hold utca 3-5 ✉ *1054* – Ⓜ *Arány Janos utca* – ☏ *(01) 373 8200*
– *www.hotelpresident.hu* **E1**
106 rm ⌚ – ♦22955/28767 HUF ♦♦25861/34578 HUF – 4 suites
Rest – Menu 5811 HUF – Carte 8717/17434 HUF
♦ Business ♦ Design ♦ Modern ♦

Stylish hotel with a luxurious presidential suite, a delightful spa and pool, and a rooftop helipad which doubles as a restaurant. Garden City bedrooms have mirrored ceilings and murals of the city skyline; Avenue bedrooms boast balconies. Informal, Mediterranean-themed restaurant; international menu.

Boscolo Luxury Residence without rest ᛋᚼ ⚙ 🕸 ⬚ ⅗ AC
Osvat utca 2-8 ✉ *1073* ⅛ 🛜 ⛱ VISA ⓞ AE ①
– Ⓜ *Blaha Lujza tér* – ☏ *(01) 4244700*
– *www.budapest.boscolohotels.com/hotel/residence* Plan I **B2**
138 suites – ♦38214/55611 HUF ♦♦52474/90404 HUF, ⌚ 3422 HUF
♦ Business ♦ Modern ♦ Stylish ♦

Huge new-build hotel with an open-plan atrium. Spacious, very comfortable, state-of-the-art suites have a kitchen, a lounge and 1-3 bedrooms; rates are by the night, week or month. Adjacent is Boscolo Budapest, whose facilities can be used.

La Prima Fashion H. Budapest without rest ᛋᚼ ⅗ AC 🛜
Pesti Barnabás utca 6 ✉ *1052* – Ⓜ *Ferenciek ter* VISA ⓞ AE
– ☏ *(01) 799 0088* – *www.laprimahotelbudapest.hu* **E2**
80 rm ⌚ – ♦19435/72950 HUF ♦♦22251/72950 HUF
♦ Townhouse ♦ Modern ♦ Cosy ♦

Simple, modern hotel, centrally located near Elizabeth Bridge. Beige and duck egg blue bedrooms with feature walls and compact, functional bathrooms; all are the same price, irrespective of size or location. Small basement breakfast room.

Mamaison H. Andrássy AC ⅛ 🛜 ⅛ P VISA ⓞ AE
Andrássy utca 111 ✉ *1063* – Ⓜ *Bajza utca* – ☏ *(01) 462 2100*
– *www.mamaison.com* Plan I **B1**
63 rm – ♦25000/53200 HUF ♦♦25000/53200 HUF, ⌚ 4800 HUF – 5 suites
Rest *Baraka* – see restaurant listing
♦ Business ♦ Stylish ♦ Functional ♦

Classical Bauhaus building in a superb location on the elegant main street. Lobby-cum-lounge with feature pillars of stainless filigree. Spacious, modern bedrooms have good facilities; some feature balconies and baths.

Palazzo Zichy without rest ᛋᚼ 🕸 ⅗ AC ⅛ 🛜 ⅛ VISA ⓞ AE
Lorinc pap tér 2 ✉ *1088* – Ⓜ *Ferenc körűt* – ☏ *(01) 235 4000*
– *www.hotel-palazzo-zichy.hu* Plan I **B2**
80 rm ⌚ – ♦22469/65132 HUF ♦♦25314/67987 HUF
♦ Business ♦ Design ♦ Modern ♦

Rococo building with impressive 1899 façade: formerly the home of writer Count Zichy. Stylish atrium lobby with striking modern design. Bedrooms are generously sized, well-equipped and minimalistic in style; good bathrooms.

Parlament without rest   🈁 ⅙ 🆔 ↳ 🛜 🔩 VISA ⚫ AE

Kálmán Imre utca 19 ✉ *1054 –* Ⓜ *Arany János utca –* ✆ *(01) 374 6000*
– www.parlament-hotel.hu   **E1**
65 rm ⬚ – ♦19620/56615 HUF ♦♦19620/70890 HUF
♦ Business ♦ Design ♦ Modern ♦
Well-run hotel; its stylish, modern interior a contrast to its classical 19C exterior.
Splendid open-plan atrium with an unusual display featuring famous Hungarians. Compact bedrooms have a clean, crisp design.

 Continental H. Zara   🔥 🈁 ⍓ 🗔 ⅙ rm, 🆔 ↳ 🛜 🔩 🚗

Dohány utca 42-44 ✉ *1074 –* Ⓜ *Blaha Lujza tér*   VISA ⚫ AE Ⓞ
– ✆ *(01) 8151000 – www.continentalhotelbudapest.com*   *Plan I* **B2**
272 rm – ♦25381/68159 HUF ♦♦25381/94966 HUF, ⬚ 4277 HUF
Rest – Menu 1490 HUF (lunch) – Carte 4600/9850 HUF
♦ Business ♦ Modern ♦ Functional ♦
Modern hotel which blends contemporary and art nouveau styling; built to
reflect its former use as a public baths. Impressive copper entrance and 7th
floor roof garden with loungers. Both indoor and outdoor pools. Restaurant
offers Hungarian and international dishes.

 NH Budapest   🔥 🈁 ⅙ 🆔 ↳ rm, 🛜 🔩 🚗 VISA ⚫ AE

Vigszinház utca 3 ✉ *1137 –* Ⓜ *Nyugati pályaudvar –* ✆ *(01) 814 0000*
– www.nh-hotels.com   *Plan I* **A1**
160 rm – ♦23000/42200 HUF ♦♦23000/42200 HUF, ⬚ 4800 HUF
Rest – *(closed Saturday and Sunday)* Menu 3650/6000 HUF – Carte 3650/
13350 HUF
♦ Business ♦ Chain hotel ♦ Modern ♦
Modern, purpose-built hotel located in the city suburbs. Bright, comfortable,
well-equipped bedrooms; some with balconies. Impressive atrium complete
with café-bar. Informal restaurant offers a mix of Hungarian and more international dishes.

 K + K Opera without rest   🔥 🈁 ⅙ 🆔 ↳ 🛜 🔩 🚗 VISA ⚫ AE

Révay utca 24 ✉ *1065 –* Ⓜ *Opera –* ✆ *(01) 269 0222*
– www.kkhotels.com   **F1**
198 rm ⬚ – ♦22498/39372 HUF ♦♦25310/42197 HUF – 2 suites
♦ Business ♦ Modern ♦ Functional ♦
Friendly hotel, handily situated next door to the Opera House and near the
smart shops of Andrassy utca. Uniform bedrooms are comfortable and up-to-
date. Cool bar-lounge and comprehensive breakfast buffets.

 Soho Boutique without rest   🆔 ↳ 🛜 VISA ⚫ AE

Dohány utca 64 ✉ *1074 –* Ⓜ *Blaha Lujza tér –* ✆ *(01) 872 8292*
– www.sohohotel.hu   *Plan I* **B2**
74 rm ⬚ – ♦39115/53186 HUF ♦♦41931/56000 HUF
♦ Business ♦ Stylish ♦ Design ♦
Well-located for tourists, with a vibrantly coloured lobby and funky bar; Polans-
ki's 'Dance of the Vampires' theme runs throughout. Modern bedrooms boast
stylish furniture – their size means they're more suited to sleeping than relaxing.

Boutique H. Zara   ⅙ rm, 🆔 ↳ 🛜 🚗 VISA ⚫

Só utca 6 ✉ *1056 –* Ⓜ *Kálvin tér –* ✆ *(01) 577 0700*
– www.zeinahotels.com   **F3**
74 rm ⬚ – ♦22500/84000 HUF ♦♦25300/84000 HUF
Rest *Araz Bistro* – Menu 1490/3990 HUF – Carte 3770/8990 HUF
♦ Business ♦ Modern ♦
Purpose-built hotel hidden away in a bohemian area adjacent to the river and
the main shopping street. Mirrored glass façade and compact, stylish, up-to-
date bedrooms with modern fabrics and good levels of comfort. All-encompassing menu served in Araz Bistro.

HUNGARY - BUDAPEST

⌂ **Central Basilica** without rest   & 🏧 ⇄ 🛜 🏋 💳 ⓪ 🅰

Hercegprímás utca 8 ✉ *1051 –* Ⓜ *Bajcsy-Zs. út –* ✆ *(01) 328 5010*
– www.hotelcentral-basilica.hu   **E2**
43 rm ⌑ – ♦16815/25365 HUF ♦♦19665/28215 HUF – 3 suites
  ♦ Conference hotel ♦ Functional ♦ Minimalist ♦

Good value hotel, superbly located close to the Basilica and perfect for the short-stay tourist: its exterior may look a tad dated, but inside it's a stylish blend of old and new. Simple modern bedrooms; some are slightly on the small side.

XXXX **Gundel**   🏧 🏧 ⇄ 💳 ⓪ 🅰 ⓪

Gundel Károly utca 4 ✉ *1146 –* Ⓜ *Hősök tere –* ✆ *(01) 889 8100*
– www.gundel.hu
– Closed 24-25 December   Plan I **B1**
Rest – *(booking essential)* Menu 3800 HUF (lunch)
– Carte 8150/16750 HUF
  ♦ Traditional ♦ Romantic ♦ Luxury ♦

Overlooking the city park, this impressive floodlit villa is home to a veritable culinary institution. Spacious columned salon with mahogany panelling, ornate ceiling and paintings by Hungarian masters. Huge choice of traditional cuisine; the famous Gundel pancakes are a favourite. Live gypsy band at dinner.

XXX **Costes**   🏧 💳 ⓪
£3

Ráday utca 4 ✉ *1092 –* Ⓜ *Kálvin tér –* ✆ *(01) 219 0696 – www.costes.hu*
– Closed Christmas, Monday and Tuesday   **F3**
Rest – *(dinner only) (booking essential)* Menu 19056/27589 HUF
– Carte 13368/22469 HUF
  ♦ Modern ♦ Design ♦ Elegant ♦

Sophisticated restaurant offering immaculately dressed tables, quality glassware and assured, formal service from an experienced team. The talented chef displays a deft touch, producing accomplished, confident cooking, with modern techniques and clear flavours. Most diners choose the set 5 or 8 course menus.
→ Lobster with green apple and celeriac remoulade. Assiette of pork with swiss chard. Poire Belle Hélène.

XXX **Onyx**   🏧 ⇄ 💳 ⓪ 🅰
£3

Vörösmarty tér 7-8 ✉ *1051 –* Ⓜ *Vörösmarty tér –* ✆ *30 508 0622*
– www.onyxrestaurant.hu
– Closed 3 weeks August, 2 weeks January, Saturday lunch, Sunday and
Monday   **E2**
Rest – *(booking essential)* Menu 4590/25900 HUF – Carte dinner 13300/24900 HUF
  ♦ Modern ♦ Design ♦ Elegant ♦

Stylish, intimate restaurant featuring a black tiled floor and a silver ceiling, with chandeliers, orchids and onyx adornments. Precise, highly skilled cooking and formal service. Classical Hungarian flavours to the fore but with interesting modern twists and some unusual combinations.
→ Caviar with cauliflower and black soup. Veal tenderloin with tuna tataki. 21C Somló sponge cake.

XX **New York Salon** – at Boscolo Budapest Hotel   🏧 💳 ⓪ 🅰 ⓪

Erzsébet krt. 9-11 ✉ *1073 –* ✆ *(01) 886 6167 – www.boscolohotels.com*
– Closed Sunday and Monday   Plan I **B2**
Rest – *(dinner only)* Menu 12098 HUF – Carte 9108/13094 HUF
  ♦ International ♦ Intimate ♦ Luxury ♦

Stunning baroque salon in a luxurious hotel; admire the architecture and ornate gilding as you dine. There's something for everyone here: choose from the light, café-style menu or more formal list of international and Hungarian classics.

XX **Baraka** – at Mamaison H. Andrássy 🍴 AC P VISA OO AE

Andrássy utca 111 ⊠ 1062 – Ⓜ Bajza utca – 𝒞 (01) 483 1355
– www.barakarestaurant.hu   Plan I **B1**
Rest – Carte 9000/12900 HUF
♦ Modern ♦ Intimate ♦ Design ♦
Seductive, stylish restaurant with slick, professional service. Cooking uses interesting combinations of high quality ingredients; dishes are modern, or classical
with an innovative twist. Excellent value lunch menu. Delightful terrace.

XX **Tigris** AC ⇔ VISA OO AE ①

Mérleg utca 10 ⊠ 1051 – Ⓜ Bajcsy-Zs. út – 𝒞 (01) 317 3715
– www.tigrisrestaurant.hu
– Closed 1 week August, 24 December and Sunday   **E2**
Rest – Carte 5560/10007 HUF 🍷
♦ Hungarian ♦ Brasserie ♦ Neighbourhood ♦
Busy bistro, well-run by passionate owner, serving carefully prepared, classic
Hungarian dishes with an appealing, earthy quality. Informal, efficient service
and relaxed atmosphere. Excellent choice of wine from country's top producers.

XX **Cyrano** 🍴 AC ⇔ VISA OO AE

Kristóf tér 7-8 ⊠ 1052 – Ⓜ Vörösmarty tér – 𝒞 (01) 266 4747
– www.cyrano.hu
– Closed 24 December   **E2**
Rest – Menu 4505 HUF (lunch) – Carte 2885/12109 HUF
♦ International ♦ Trendy ♦ Fashionable ♦
Fashionable, modern restaurant named after the duellist and poet, with ornate
plaster ceiling and dimly lit, intimate interior. Selection of Hungarian and inter-
national dishes. Choose a table on the mezzanine floor.

XX **Nobu Budapest** – at Kempinski H. Corvinus AC ⇔ VISA OO AE ①

Erzsébet tér 7-8 ⊠ 1051 – Ⓜ Deák Ferenc tér – 𝒞 (01) 429 4242
– www.noburestaurants.com
– Closed 25 December   **E2**
Rest – Menu 7500/25000 HUF – Carte 7600/22300 HUF
♦ Japanese ♦ Minimalist ♦ Fashionable ♦
Located on the ground floor of a stylish hotel, with well-spaced wooden tables,
Japanese lanterns and an open kitchen. Numerous menus offer an almost
bewildering array of dishes; some have matching sake or wine flights.

X **Mák Bistro** VISA OO AE ①

Vigyázó Ferenc utca 4 ⊠ 1051 – Ⓜ Vörösmarty tér – 𝒞 307 239383
– www.makbistro.hu
– Closed first 2 weeks August, 24 December-2 January, Sunday and Monday
Rest – Menu 3500/9000 HUF – Carte 6200/11300 HUF   **E1**
♦ Mediterranean ♦ Rustic ♦ Intimate ♦
Simple, rustic restaurant with whitewashed brickwork and semi-vaulted ceilings: its name means 'poppy seed' in Hungarian. Strong Spanish and Italian
influences on the menu; flavours are pure and the cooking, both skilful and
playful.

X **Bock Bisztró** AC VISA OO
🐷

Erzsébet krt. 43-49 ⊠ 1073 – Ⓜ Oktogon – 𝒞 (01) 321 0340
– www.bockbisztro.hu
– Closed Sunday and bank holidays   **F1**
Rest – (booking essential) Carte 5550/11900 HUF 🍷
♦ Hungarian ♦ Bistro ♦ Rustic ♦
A family-orientated restaurant with many regular diners and a rustic, bistro feel.
Honest, tasty cooking; go for the simple, seasonal Hungarian dishes or let the
friendly, knowledgeable staff guide your choices. The homemade bread is a
winner; as is the ham they cure themselves from Mangalitza pigs.

HUNGARY - BUDAPEST

🍴 **Osteria Fausto's**   ᴀᴄ 🌿 𝘝𝘐𝘚𝘈 ⓄⓄ 𝔸𝔼

Dohány utca 5 ⊠ 1072 – Ⓜ Astoria – 𝒞 (01) 269 6806 – www.osteria.hu
– Closed 24-26 December and Sunday   **F2**
Rest – Menu 3000/9000 HUF – Carte 5372/10054 HUF
♦ Italian ♦ Bistro ♦ Neighbourhood ♦

Informal, personally run restaurant and wine bar serving simple, rustic Italian classics; go for the daily homemade pasta listed on the blackboard specials. Quality Hungarian and Italian wines. Expect a friendly welcome.

🍴 **Di Vino**   🛋 ᴀᴄ 𝘝𝘐𝘚𝘈 ⓄⓄ 𝔸𝔼 Ⓞ

Szent István tér 3 ⊠ 1051 – Ⓜ Bajcsy-Zs. út – 𝒞 (70) 935 3980
– www.divinowinebar.hu
– Closed 25-26 December   **E2**
Rest – Carte 3333/6111 HUF ⁂
♦ Hungarian ♦ Wine bar ♦ Trendy ♦

Buzzing wine bar located right in front of the Basilica. There is a small selection of light and tasty dishes, but the big draw here is the superb selection of Hungarian wines, including many by the glass. Knowledgeable, helpful staff.

BUDA   *Plan II*

🏨 **Art'otel** without rest ≤ ℔ 🍽 ⅙ ᴀᴄ 🌿 🤏 🏋 🏊 𝘝𝘐𝘚𝘈 ⓄⓄ 𝔸𝔼

Bem rkp. 16-19 ⊠ 1011 – Ⓜ Batthyány tér – 𝒞 (01) 487 9487
– www.artotels.com   **D1**
156 rm – †27804/41849 HUF ††27804/41849 HUF, � 3932 HUF – 9 suites
♦ Business ♦ Design ♦ Contemporary ♦

Modern, purpose-built hotel on the banks of the Danube: ideal for businesspeople. Stylish interior in cool shades, with 700+ pieces of art by Donald Sultan. Rooms in converted baroque houses are more spacious; those overlooking the courtyard are quieter. Room service only.

🏨 **Lánchíd 19** ≤ 🛋 ⅙ ᴀᴄ 🌿 🤏 🏋 𝘝𝘐𝘚𝘈 ⓄⓄ 𝔸𝔼

Lánchíd utca 19 ⊠ 1013 – 𝒞 (01) 419 1900 – www.lanchid19hotel.hu
48 rm – †22050/60000 HUF ††82500/138000 HUF,   **D2**
⊒ 3700 HUF
Rest L19 – Menu 1499 HUF (lunch) – Carte 4500/8200 HUF
♦ Business ♦ Design ♦ Retro ♦

Stylish hotel overlooking Danube and castle; pay more for a front bedroom to ensure an impressive view. Bedrooms boast designer chairs, feature walls and modern facilities and the glass-floored lounge looks down onto ruins of a 14C water tower. Mezzanine restaurant with good river views; international menu.

🏨 **Buda Castle Fashion** without rest   ᴀᴄ 🌿 🤏 𝘝𝘐𝘚𝘈 ⓄⓄ 𝔸𝔼

Úri utca 39 ⊠ 1014 – Ⓜ Moszkva tér – 𝒞 (01) 224 7900
– www.budacastlehotel.eu   **C1**
20 rm ⊒ – †18200/35264 HUF ††22466/53747 HUF – 5 suites
♦ Townhouse ♦ Stylish ♦ Personalised ♦

15C merchant's house and former HQ for the Hungarian Hunting Association, set on a quiet street in the heart of Old Buda. Spacious, comfortable bedrooms boast pleasant, modern décor. Delightfully peaceful central courtyard terrace.

🏨 **Castle Garden**   🛋 🍽 ⅙ ᴀᴄ 🌿 🤏 🏊 𝘝𝘐𝘚𝘈 ⓄⓄ 𝔸𝔼

Lovas útca 41 ⊠ 1012 – Ⓜ Moszkva tér – 𝒞 (01) 224 7420
– www.hotelcastlegarden.hu   **C1**
39 rm ⊒ – †14060/22495 HUF ††16872/28120 HUF
Rest Riso – Menu 2250/3937 HUF – Carte 4500/9842 HUF
♦ Business ♦ Modern ♦ Functional ♦

Contemporary hotel just outside the castle walls. Comfortable bedrooms, in natural hues, boast a good level of facilities; superior rooms have enclosed terraces and views. Colourful tiled Riso serves a few Hungarian classics but the menu is mainly Italian, with an emphasis on pizza. Pleasant terrace.

🏠 **Carlton** without rest   🔼 ⇖ 🛜 🚗 VISA ⓞ AE ⓞ
Apor Péter utca 3 ⊠ 1011 – ℰ (01) 224 0999 – www.carltonhotel.hu
95 rm ⬒ – †15000/30000 HUF ††18000/42000 HUF   **D2**
◆ Traditional ◆ Classic ◆
Friendly hotel in quiet location between the Danube and the castle. Neat, well-equipped, traditionally styled bedrooms; half with baths, half with showers. Extensive buffet breakfast overlooking the garden.

XXX **Alabárdos**   🏡 🔼 ⇖ ⇔ VISA ⓞ AE
Országház utca 2 ⊠ 1014 – Ⓜ Moszkva tér – ℰ (01) 356 0851
– www.alabardos.hu
– Closed 25-26 December and Sunday   **D1**
Rest *– (dinner only and Saturday lunch) (booking essential)*
Menu 11000 HUF – Carte 6700/12100 HUF ⅏
◆ Hungarian ◆ Formal ◆ Elegant ◆
Long-standing, professionally run restaurant, named after the guards of the castle and set in a series of 15C buildings opposite it. It's formal yet atmospheric, with vaulted ceilings, detailed service and a delightful terrace. Cooking is rich and flavourful; classic Hungarian dishes have a modern edge.

XXX **Arany Kaviár**   🏡 🔼 VISA ⓞ AE
Ostrom utca 19 ⊠ 1015 – Ⓜ Moszkva tér – ℰ (01) 201 6737
– www.aranykaviar.hu
– Closed 24-25 December   **C1**
Rest – Menu 4900/30000 HUF – Carte 7090/19900 HUF
◆ Russian ◆ Intimate ◆ Elegant ◆
Lavishly furnished restaurant serving menu of Russian and Hungarian dishes. Caviar is a speciality – they even offer their own range. Rich, well-executed, accomplished cooking uses fine ingredients. Candlelit and intimate in the evening.

XX **Csalogány 26**   🏡 VISA ⓞ AE
😊 *Csalogány utca 26 ⊠ 1015 – Ⓜ Batthyány tér – ℰ (01) 201 7892*
– www.csalogany26.hu
– Closed 2 weeks summer, 1 week winter, Sunday, Monday and bank holidays
Rest *– (booking advisable)* Menu 2500/12000 HUF – Carte   **D1**
6100/10800 HUF
◆ Modern ◆ Bistro ◆ Friendly ◆
Simple neighbourhood restaurant with a homely, bistro style. A passionate father and son team offer two daily changing menus; go for either 4 or 8 courses, or choose your dishes from the à la carte. The cooking is full of flavour and presented in a modern style; service is knowledgeable and helpful.

XX **Pierrot**   🏡 🔼 ⇖ VISA ⓞ AE
Fortuna utca 14 ⊠ 1014 – Ⓜ Moszkva tér – ℰ (01) 375 6971
– www.pierrot.hu   **C1**
Rest – Carte 5860/12420 HUF
◆ Hungarian ◆ Elegant ◆ Intimate ◆
Elegant, vaulted, two-roomed restaurant in historic property within the castle walls. European and Hungarian classics prepared with a contemporary touch; efficient service. Pierrot theme and live piano.

XX **Arcade Bistro**   🏡 🔼 VISA ⓞ AE
😊 *Kiss Janos Alt utca 38 ⊠ 1126 – Ⓜ Déli pu. – ℰ (01) 225 1969*
– www.arcadebistro.hu
– Closed 24-26 December, 1 January, Easter and bank holidays   **C2**
Rest – Carte 7314/9232 HUF
◆ Hungarian ◆ Bistro ◆ Neighbourhood ◆
Friendly, well-run neighbourhood restaurant with warm Mediterranean décor and pretty, spacious terrace; hidden away beneath apartment blocks in a residential area. International dishes and Hungarian classics delivered in a delicate, modern manner; sizeable list of daily specials.

Vár: a Speiz ⟨♨⟩ ⟨VISA⟩ ⟨◑◑⟩ ⟨AE⟩

Hess András tér 6 ✉ *1014 –* Ⓜ *Moszkva tér – ☎ (01) 488 7416*
– www.speiz.hu
– Closed 24-26 December　　　　　　　　　　　　　　　　**D1**
Rest – Carte 5800/15000 HUF
♦ Hungarian ♦ Fashionable ♦ Romantic ♦

Located close to the castle in the heart of beautiful Buda; its name meaning 'castle pantry' in German. Large, seasonally changing menu; cooking is rustic, wholesome and full of flavour. A relaxing ambience and professional service.

21 ⟨♨⟩ ⟨AC⟩ ⟨≠⟩ ⟨VISA⟩ ⟨◑◑⟩ ⟨AE⟩

Fortuna utca 21 ✉ *1014 –* Ⓜ *Moszkva tér – ☎ (01) 202 2113*
– www.21restaurant.hu　　　　　　　　　　　　　　　　**C1**
Rest – Menu 7900 HUF – Carte 5740/9290 HUF
♦ Hungarian ♦ Fashionable ♦ Bistro ♦

Situated within the castle walls; a contemporary take on a traditional bistro, with wood floors, rustic touches and a relaxed style. Classic Hungarian dishes, subtly reinvented with an appealing contemporary touch; blackboard specials. Efficient, friendly service.

Republic of IRELAND
ÉIRE

→ **AREA:**
70 284 km² (27 137 sq mi).

→ **POPULATION:**
4 588 252 inhabitants.
Density = 65 per km².

→ **CAPITAL:** Dublin.

→ **CURRENCY:** Euro (€).

→ **GOVERNMENT:**
Parliamentary republic
(since 1921). Member of
European Union since 1973.

→ **LANGUAGES:**
Irish and English.

→ **PUBLIC HOLIDAYS:**
New Year's Day (1 Jan);
St Patrick's Day (17 Mar); Easter
Monday (late Mar/Apr); May Bank
Holiday (first Mon in May); June
Bank Holiday (first Mon in June);
August Bank Holiday (first Mon
in Aug); October Bank Holiday (last
Mon in Oct); Christmas Day
(25 Dec); St Stephen's Day (26 Dec).

→ **LOCAL TIME:**
GMT in winter and GMT+1 hour in
summer.

→ **CLIMATE:**
Temperate maritime with cool
winters and mild summers (Dublin:
January 5°C; July 15°C), fairly high
rainfall.

→ **EMERGENCY:**
Police, Medical Assistance, Fire
Brigade ✆ **999** – also used for
Mountain, Cave, Coastguard and
Sea Rescue.
(Dialling **112** within any EU country
will redirect your call and contact
the emergency services.)

DUBLIN ●

→ **ELECTRICITY:**
230 volts AC, 50 H; 3 flat pin
sockets.

→ **FORMALITIES:**
Travellers from the European Union
(EU), Switzerland, Iceland and the
main countries of North and South
America need a national identity
card or passport (except for British
nationals travelling from the UK;
America: passport required) to visit
Ireland for less than three months
(tourism or business purpose).
For visitors from other countries a
visa may be required, in addition
to a passport, especially for those
wishing to stay for longer than
three months. We advise you to
check with your embassy before
travelling.

DUBLIN
BAILE ÁTHA CLIATH

Population: 527 612

Marek Slusarczyk/Fotolia.com

For somewhere touted as the finest Georgian city in the British Isles, Dublin enjoys a very young image. When the 'Celtic Tiger' roared to prominence in the 1990s, Ireland's old capital took on a youthful expression, and for the first time revelled in the epithets 'chic' and 'trendy'. Nowadays it's not just the bastion of Guinness drinkers and those here for the 'craic', but a twenty-first century city with smart restaurants, grand new hotels, modern architecture and impressive galleries. Its handsome squares and façades took shape 250 years ago, designed by the finest architects of the time. Since then, it's gone through uprising, civil war and independence from Britain, and now holds a strong fascination for foreign visitors.

The city can be pretty well divided into three. Southeast of the river is the classiest, defined by the glorious Trinity College, St Stephen's Green, and Grafton Street's smart shops. Just west of here is the second area, dominated by Dublin Castle and Christ Church Cathedral – ancient buildings abound, but it doesn't quite match the sleek aura of the city's Georgian quarter. Across the Liffey, the northern section was the last part to be developed and, although it lacks the glamour of its southern neighbours, it does boast the city's grandest avenue, O'Connell Street, and its most celebrated theatres.

DUBLIN IN...

→ **ONE DAY**
  Trinity College, Grafton Street, St Stephen's Green, Merrion Square, Temple Bar.

→ **TWO DAYS**
  Christ Church Cathedral, Dublin Castle, Chester Beatty Library, the quayside.

→ **THREE DAYS**
  O'Connell Street, Parnell Square, Dublin Writers' Museum, DART train to the coast.

PRACTICAL INFORMATION

ARRIVAL-DEPARTURE

✈ Dublin Airport is 7 miles north. There are a number of coaches and buses, including Airlink and Aircoach, which take approximately 30mins.

GETTING AROUND

The bus network covers the whole city from the Central Bus Station in Store Street and is cheap and efficient, while the exciting LUAS (meaning 'speed') light rail network will get you to places a little quicker; ticket prices for both relate to the number of stages travelled. If you want to visit the coast, then jump on a DART (Dublin Area Rapid Transport) train. They operate at regular intervals, are amazingly efficient, and leave central Dublin from Connolly, Tara Street and Pearse stations. If you'd rather spend your time in the city, the Dublin Pass provides access to over thirty attractions, and ranges from one to six days.

EATING OUT

It's still possible to indulge in Irish stew but nowadays you can also dine on everything from tacos and Thai to Malaysian and Middle Eastern cuisine, particularly in the Temple Bar area. The city makes the most of its bay proximity, so seafood features highly, with smoked salmon and oysters the favourites; the latter washed down with a pint of Guinness. Meat is particularly tasty in Ireland, due to the healthy livestock and a wet climate, and Irish beef is world famous for its fulsome flavour. However, there's never been a better time to be a vegetarian

CALENDAR HIGHLIGHTS

March
St Patrick's Day, Celtic Flame, Temple Bar Fleadh (traditional music)

April
Colours Boat Race, Feis Ceoil (classical music).

June
Bloomsday.

July-August
Diversions (free concerts and open-air theatre).

August
Horse Show.

September
Fringe Theatre Festival.

October
Dublin Theatre Festival.

November
Opera Ireland.

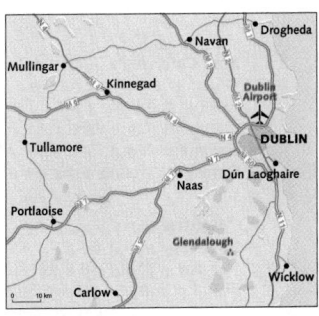

in Dublin, as every type of veg from spinach to seaweed now features, and chefs insist on the best seasonal produce, cooked for just the right amount of time to savour all the taste and goodness. Dinner here is usually served until about 10pm, though many global and city centre restaurants stay open later. If you make your main meal at lunchtime, you'll pay considerably less than in the evening: the menus are often similar, but the bill in the middle of the day will probably be about half the price.

Shelbourne

27 St Stephen's Grn. ✉ *D2 – ✆ (01) 6634500 – www.theshelbourne.ie* **E3**
250 rm – 🚹199/525 € 🚹🚹199/525 €, ☕ 29 € – 12 suites
Rest *Saddle Room* – see restaurant listing
♦ Luxury ♦ Classic ♦
Landmark Georgian hotel with elegant guest areas, contemporary furnishings and state-of-the-art facilities. Bedrooms in original house are most characterful. High level of services and extras.

Merrion

Upper Merrion St ✉ *D2 – ✆ (01) 6030600 – www.merrionhotel.com*
133 rm – 🚹485 € 🚹🚹505 €, ☕ 29 € – 9 suites **F3**
Rest *Cellar* – *✆ (01) 6030630 (closed Saturday lunch)* Menu 30 € – Carte 37/57 €
Rest *Cellar Bar* – *(closed Sunday)* Carte 22/42 €
♦ Luxury ♦ Classic ♦
Elegant hotel boasting opulent lounges, a stylish, intimate cocktail bar and a characterful barrel-ceilinged bar in the 18C wine vaults. Spacious bedrooms – some with original features, some more corporate in style – boast smart marble bathrooms and good facilities. Restaurant offers an accessible menu.

The Westbury

Grafton St ✉ *D2 – ✆ (01) 679 1122 – www.doylecollection.com*
185 rm – 🚹199/519 € 🚹🚹199/519 €, ☕ 25 € – 20 suites **E2**
Rest *Wilde* – *(closed Sunday and Monday) (dinner only)* Menu 45 € – Carte 36/72 €
Rest *Café Novo* – *(closed 25 December)* Menu 12/19 € – Carte 25/42 €
♦ Business ♦ Luxury ♦ Contemporary ♦
Well-run hotel with a stylish bar, a comfy lounge (popular for afternoon tea) and state-of-the-art conference facilities; modern artwork features throughout. Well-equipped, elegant bedrooms come in browns and creams. Excellent service. Formal Wilde offers a modern Irish menu; Café Novo serves old favourites.

Westin

Westmoreland St ✉ *D2 – ✆ (01) 6451000 – www.thewestindublin.com*
153 rm – 🚹180/250 € 🚹🚹180/250 €, ☕ 20 € – 10 suites **E2**
Rest *Exchange* – *(closed Sunday dinner and Monday) (dinner only and lunch Saturday-Sunday)* Menu 19 € – Carte 24/55 €
Rest *Mint* – Carte 24/37 €
♦ Luxury ♦ Classic ♦
Built in 1860 as a bank; now a smart hotel set over 6 period buildings, with comfy lounges, impressive conference rooms and good facilities. Bedroom styles range from classic, with mahogany furniture, to contemporary, with leather furnishings and media hubs. Modern European cooking in semi-formal Exchange. Accessible menu in The Mint, which was once the bank's vaults.

Dylan

Eastmoreland Pl ✉ *D4 – ✆ (01) 6603000 – www.dylan.ie – Closed 24-26 December* *Plan III* **H1**
44 rm – 🚹395 € 🚹🚹395 €, ☕ 25 €
Rest – Menu 22 € (weekdays)/40 € – Carte 32/54 €
♦ Townhouse ♦ Stylish ♦
Modern boutique hotel with vibrant use of colour. Supremely comfortable, individually decorated bedrooms boast an opulent feel and a host of unexpected extras. French-influenced menus served in warm, stylish dining room.

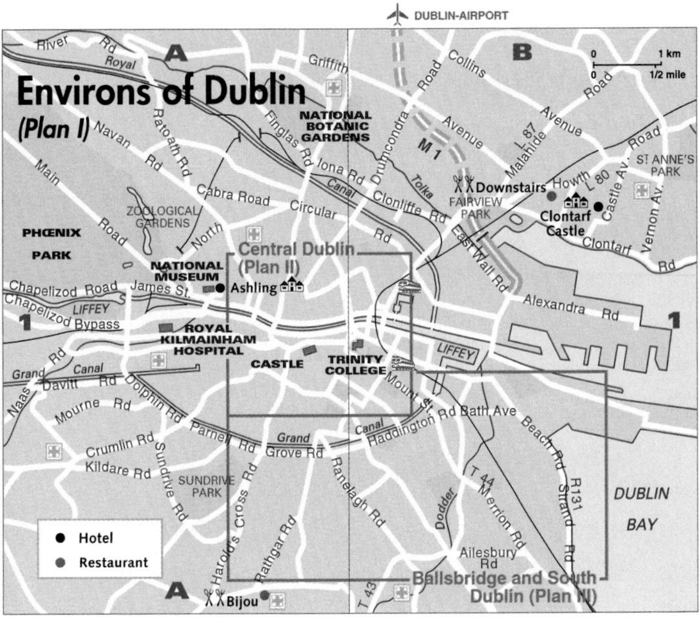

Environs of Dublin
(Plan I)

DUBLIN-AIRPORT

River Rd · Royal

Navan Rd · Ratoath Rd · Main Rd · Finglas Rd · Griffith Av

NATIONAL BOTANIC GARDENS

Iona Rd · Drumcondra Rd · Clonliffe Rd · Tolka

Cabra Road · North Circular Rd

PHŒNIX PARK

ZOOLOGICAL GARDENS

Phoenix Road

Collins Av · Malahide Rd · Howth Rd · Castle Av · Vernon Av

M 1

Downstairs

FAIRVIEW PARK

Clontarf Castle · Clontarf Rd

ST ANNE'S PARK

Chapelizod Road · Chapelizod Bypass

LIFFEY · James St

NATIONAL MUSEUM · **Ashling**

Central Dublin (Plan II)

ROYAL KILMAINHAM HOSPITAL

CASTLE · **TRINITY COLLEGE**

LIFFEY

Alexandra Rd

Grand Canal · Naas Rd · Davitt Rd · Dolphin Rd · Mourne Rd · Parnell Rd · Crumlin Rd · Kildare Rd · Sundrive Rd · Harold's Cross Rd · Rathgar Rd · Ranelagh Rd · Grand Grove Rd · Mount · Haddington Rd · Bath Av · Beach · Canal · Merrion Strand · Dodder

SUNDRIVE PARK

DUBLIN BAY

Ailesbury Rd

T 44 · T 43 · R131

● Hotel
● Restaurant

Bijou

Ballsbridge and South Dublin (Plan II)

0 1 km / 1/2 mile

Brooks
♨ ⅏ ⚒ ⶌ 🛜 ⌖ VISA ⚙ AE

Drury St ⊠ D2 – ℰ (01) 6704000 – www.brookshotel.ie   **E2**
97 rm 🖙 – ∲135/385 € ∲∲150/450 € – 1 suite
Rest *Francesca's* – see restaurant listing
♦ Business ♦ Stylish ♦

Smart, boutique-style townhouse hidden down a backstreet. Traditional basement lounge and stylish bedrooms with modern artwork; executives boast fresh flowers and other homely touches. Experienced owner keeps a keen eye over proceedings.

Clarence
⟨ ♨ ⚒ 🛜 ⌖ 🚗 VISA ⚙ AE ①

6-8 Wellington Quay ⊠ D2 – ℰ (01) 4070800 – www.theclarence.ie
44 rm – ∲139/209 € ∲∲179/259 €, 🖙 10 € – 5 suites   **D2**
Rest *Tea Room* – see restaurant listing
♦ Luxury ♦ Design ♦

Attractive riverside hotel, formerly a warehouse. Stylish and well-run, with art deco reception, comfy lounge and famous domed bar. Plainly decorated, understated bedrooms; good facilities.

Fitzwilliam
⟨ ♨ ⚒ 🛜 ⌖ 🚗 VISA ⚙ AE ①

St Stephen's Grn ⊠ D2 – ℰ (01) 478 70 00 – www.fitzwilliamhotel.com
136 rm – ∲189/480 € ∲∲209/500 €, 🖙 22.50 € – 3 suites   **E3**
Rest *Thornton's* ✿ – see restaurant listing
Rest *Citron* – Menu 20/30 € – Carte 36/50 €
♦ Business ♦ Modern ♦

Stylish, U-shaped hotel set around a huge roof garden – the largest in Europe. Contemporary bedrooms display striking bold colours and good facilities; half overlook the garden and half, the green. Modern first floor brasserie offers an international menu.

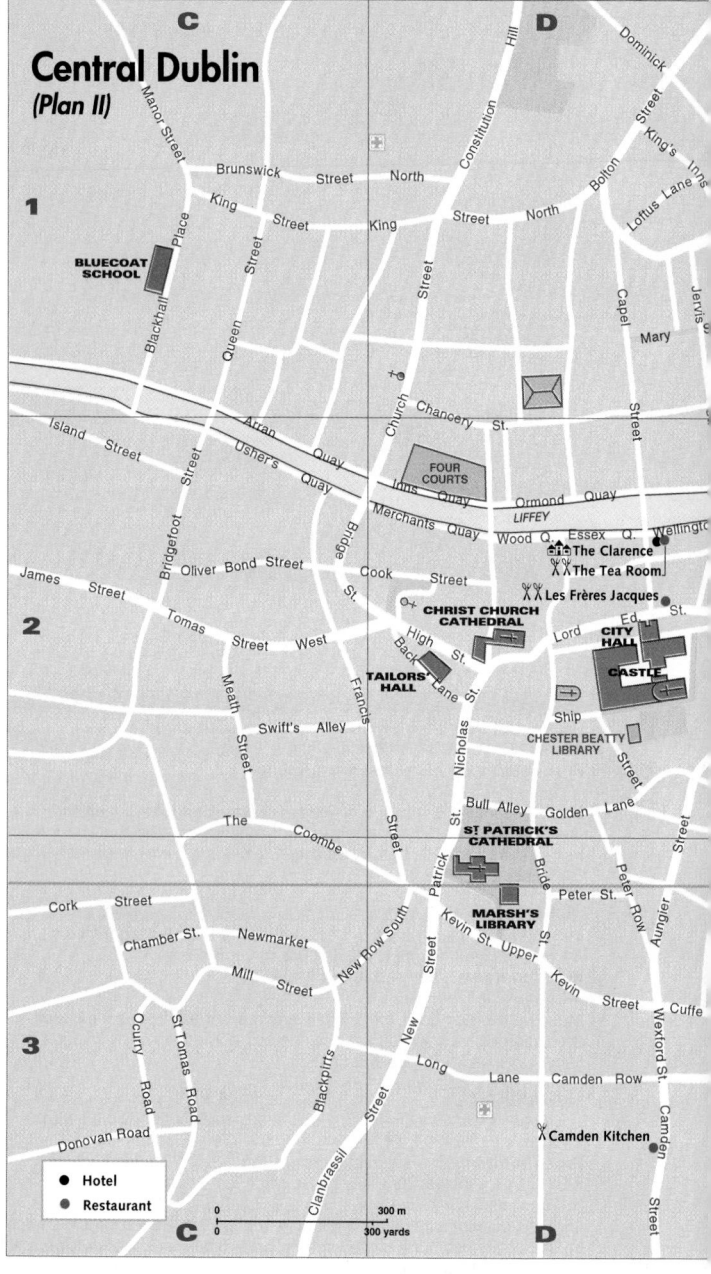

Central Dublin
(Plan II)

BLUECOAT
SCHOOL

Manor Street

Brunswick   Street   North

King   Street

King   Street   North

Constitution   Hill

Dominick   Street

King's   Inns

Loftus   Lane

Bolton   Street

Blackhall   Place

Queen   Street

Capel   Street

Mary

Jervis

Chancery   St.

Church   Street

Island   Street

Arran   Quay

Usher's   Quay

FOUR
COURTS

Inns   Quay

Merchants   Quay

Ormond   Quay

LIFFEY

Wood   Q.   Essex   Q.   Wellington

The Clarence
The Tea Room
Les Frères Jacques

Bridgefoot   Street

Oliver   Bond   Street

Cook   Street

James   Street

Tomas   Street   West

Meath   Street

Bridge   St.

High   St.

Back   Lane   St.

Lord   Ed   St.

CHRIST CHURCH
CATHEDRAL

CITY
HALL

CASTLE

TAILORS'
HALL

Francis   Street

Swift's   Alley

Ship   Street

Nicholas   Street

CHESTER BEATTY
LIBRARY

The   Coombe

Bull   Alley   Golden   Lane

St PATRICK'S
CATHEDRAL

Patrick   Street

Bride   St.

Peter   St.

Peter   Row

Aungier   Street

Cork   Street

Chamber St.

Newmarket

Mill   Street

MARSH'S
LIBRARY

Kevin   St.   Upper

Kevin   Street

Cuffe

New Row South

New Row   Street

Wexford St.

Ocurry   Road

St Tomas   Road

Blackpirts

Long   Lane   Camden Row

Donovan Road

Clanbrassil   Street

Camden Kitchen

Camden

Camden   Street

| ● | Hotel |
| ● | Restaurant |

0   300 m
0   300 yards

C   D

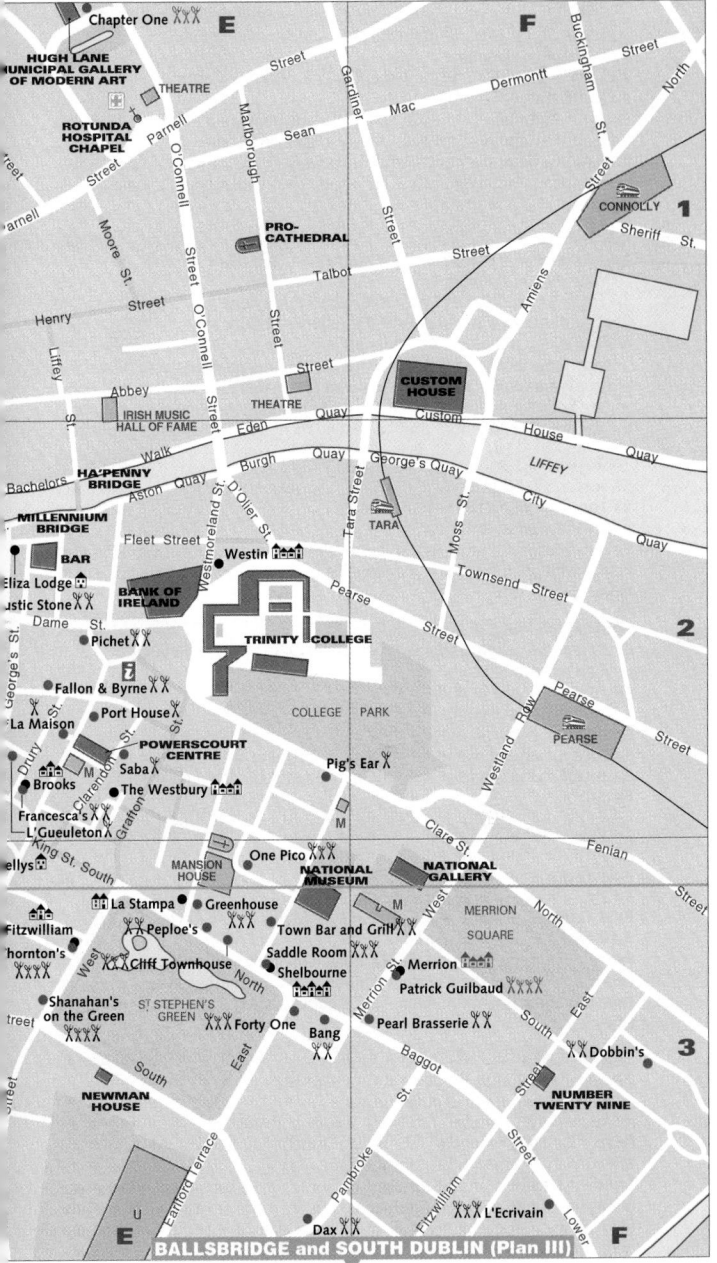

BALLSBRIDGE and SOUTH DUBLIN (Plan III)

Ashling   ⅙ rm, 🛜 ⅍ 🅿 VISA 🝙 AE

Parkgate St. ✉ *D8 –* ✆ *(01) 677 2324 – www.ashlinghotel.ie*
– Closed 24-26 December   **A1**
225 rm – ♦99/250 € ♦♦99/340 €, ⚏ 15 €   **Rest** – Carte 28/51 €
♦ Business ♦ Functional ♦

Smartly refurbished hotel with sleek, modern frontage and cheery team; set close to the tram and rail links. Mix of classic and contemporary bedrooms; front rooms boast river and Guinness Brewery views. Large bar-lounge serves all-day menu. Restaurant offers carvery lunches and accessible evening à la carte.

La Stampa   🝙 AC rm, 🛜 VISA 🝙

35-36 Dawson St ✉ *D2 –* ✆ *(01) 6774444 – www.lastampa.ie*
– Closed 25-26 December   **E3**
36 rm – ♦120/270 € ♦♦120/270 €, ⚏ 15 € – 1 suite
Rest – Menu 23 € (weekdays)/60 € – Carte 31/51 €
♦ Townhouse ♦ Personalised ♦

Georgian townhouse with Art Nouveau exterior and quirky, eclectic décor. Stylish guest areas and characterful spa with Far Eastern feel. Spacious bedrooms feature bespoke Asian or opulent French furnishings; the suite has a Moroccan theme. Grand dining room with interesting menu of original modern cooking.

Number 31 without rest   🚲 🛜 VISA 🝙 AE

31 Leeson Cl. ✉ *D2 –* ✆ *(01) 6765011 – www.number31.ie*   *Plan III* **H1**
21 rm ⚏ – ♦120/180 € ♦♦160/280 €
♦ Townhouse ♦ Retro ♦

Unique house with retro styling, personally run by hospitable couple. Sunken lounge with open fire; quirky, comfortable bedrooms. Communal breakfast includes The Full Irish.

Kellys without rest   🛜 ⊄

First Floor, 36 South Great George's St ✉ *D2 –* ✆ *(01) 648 0010*
– www.kellysdublin.com   **E2**
16 rm – ♦70/130 € ♦♦200/240 €
♦ Townhouse ♦ Minimalist ♦

Shabby-chic hotel set among trendy boutiques and bars, in a bustling area. Stripped paint and white emulsioned walls hung with funky artwork; airy, open-plan lounge and bar; spacious, minimalist bedrooms. Breakfast in the restaurant below.

Eliza Lodge   ≤ AC 🛜 VISA 🝙 AE ⓞ

23-24 Wellington Quay ✉ *D2 –* ✆ *(01) 6718044*
– www.elizalodge.com   **E2**
18 rm – ♦49/150 € ♦♦59/200 €, ⚏ 9 €
Rest *Italian Corner* – ✆ *(01) 6719114* – Menu 11 € – Carte 22/47 €
♦ Family ♦ Functional ♦

Friendly, family-owned hotel ideally situated for lively Temple Bar area. Uniform bedrooms; those at the top have the best outlook over the city and river; two have balconies. Bright restaurant serves popular Italian menus overlooking the Liffey.

Patrick Guilbaud (Guillaume Lebrun)   AC ⇔ VISA 🝙 AE ⓞ
🛇🛇 (XXXX)

21 Upper Merrion St ✉ *D2 –* ✆ *(01) 6764192*
– www.restaurantpatrickguilbaud.ie
– Closed 25-26 December, 17 March, Sunday and Monday   **F3**
Rest – *(booking essential)* Menu 50 € (lunch)/130 € ⅏
♦ French classic ♦ Design ♦ Elegant ♦

Stylish restaurant in an elegant Georgian house, where contemporary art stands out against white walls. Regulars and visitors are made equally welcome by the efficient, knowledgeable team. Cooking has a classical French base but a refined, modern style; the balance of textures and flavours is superb.
➜ Lobster ravioli with split curry dressing. Roast veal sweetbread with cabernet sauvignon vinegar and star anise. 'Coeur de Guanaja'.

XXXX **Thornton's** (Kevin Thornton) – Fitzwilliam Hotel   [AC] [VISA] [◉◉] [AE] [①]

£3 *128 St Stephen's Grn. ⊠ D2 – ℰ (01) 4787008*
– www.thorntonsrestaurant.com
– Closed 25 December-3 January, Sunday, Monday and lunch Tuesday-
Wednesday   **E3**
Rest – Menu 45/76 € ஃ
♦ Modern ♦ Formal ♦
Elegant hotel restaurant where smart glass panels divide the room; eye-catching food photos adorn the walls. Choice of classical à la carte, or modern tasting menu displaying innovative texture and flavour combinations. Knowledgeable service.
➜ Dublin Bay prawns with truffle sabayon and prawn bisque. Milk-fed lamb with glazed turnips, wild garlic and bog oak sauce. Tarte Tatin, pressed apple terrine and pain d'épice ice cream.

XXXX **Shanahan's on the Green**   [AC] [VISA] [◉◉] [AE] [①]

119 St Stephen's Grn ⊠ D2 – ℰ (01) 4070939 – www.shanahans.ie
– Closed 25-27 December, Good Friday and Sunday   **E3**
Rest – *(dinner only and lunch Friday-Saturday) (booking essential)*
Menu 45 € (early dinner) – Carte 59/82 €
♦ Meats and grills ♦ Formal ♦
Sumptuous Georgian townhouse; upper floor window tables survey the Green. Supreme comfort enhances your enjoyment of strong seafood dishes and choice cuts of Irish beef.

XXX **Chapter One** (Ross Lewis)   [AC] [⇔] [☜] [VISA] [◉◉] [AE]

£3 *The Dublin Writers Museum, 18-19 Parnell Sq ⊠ D1 – ℰ (01) 8732266*
– www.chapteronerestaurant.com
– Closed 2 weeks August, 2 weeks Christmas, Sunday, Monday and bank
holidays   **E1**
Rest – *(booking essential)* Menu 37/85 €
♦ Modern ♦ Formal ♦ Design ♦
Stylish basement restaurant under the Writers Museum, with a modern lounge and two smart dining rooms hung with specially commissioned art. Various set and tasting menus offer flavoursome, classically based dishes prepared using modern techniques; the kitchen table offers its own menu. Pleasant, formal service.
➜ Scallops with a light potato mousseline and smoked bacon. Pork with parsley creamed barley, carrots and pickled thistle. Spiced rhubarb with a maple syrup baked custard and gingerbread crumb.

XXX **L'Ecrivain** (Derry Clarke)   [☝] [AC] [⇔] [VISA] [◉◉] [AE]

£3 *109a Lower Baggot St ⊠ D2 – ℰ (01) 6611919 – www.lecrivain.com*
– Closed Sunday and bank holidays   **F3**
Rest – *(dinner only and lunch Thursday-Friday) (booking essential)* Menu
25/90 €
♦ Modern ♦ Formal ♦
Three-floored, former warehouse with piano bar, whiskey-themed private dining room, mezzanine and attractive terrace. Refined cooking arrives with modern touches and contemporary presentation. Service is formal but comes with personality.
➜ Rabbit terrine and loin with sweetcorn beignet and foie gras emulsion. Skate with pine nut, orange and raisin butter and artichoke gnocchi. Chocolate and blood orange mousse, parfait and marmalade.

XXX **Forty One**   [⇔] [VISA] [◉◉] [AE]

41 St. Stephen's Grn. ⊠ D2 – ℰ (01) 6620000 – www.fortyone.ie
– Closed Good Friday, 25-30 December, Sunday and Monday   **E3**
Rest – *(booking advisable)* Menu 30/75 € – Carte 57/70 €
♦ Modern ♦ Elegant ♦ Intimate ♦
Intimate, richly furnished restaurant on the first floor of an attractive, creeper-clad townhouse, in a corner of St Stephen's Green. Accomplished, classical cooking features luxurious Irish ingredients and personal, modern touches.

IRELAND - DUBLIN

XXX **Cliff Townhouse** with rm ☒ rest, 🛜 ▩ ◑ 🅰 ⓪

22 St Stephen's Grn ⊠ *D2* – ℰ *(01) 6383939*
– *www.theclifftownhouse.com*
– *Closed 25-27 December and 1 January*   **E3**
9 rm ☷ – †99/145 € ††99/195 €
Rest – *(booking advisable)* Menu 25 € (weekdays) – Carte 26/88 €
♦ Modern ♦ Brasserie ♦

Impressive Georgian townhouse overlooking the green. Large dining room with marble-topped bar and blue leather seating. Good value fixed price menus offer straightforward, classical combinations. Bedrooms display contemporary colour schemes and good comforts.

XXX **Saddle Room** – Shelbourne Hotel 🅰 ⇄ ▩ ◑ 🅰 ⓪

27 St Stephen's Grn. ⊠ *D2* – ℰ *(01) 6634500* – *www.theshelbourne.ie*
Rest – Menu 24 € (dinner) – Carte 38/77 €   **E3**
♦ Meats and grills ♦ Formal ♦

Smart restaurant with well-spaced, linen-laid tables: some are set by the window; some are in booths; and some, in glass-walled private rooms. Open kitchen specialises in seafood and steaks.

XXX **Greenhouse** 🅰 ▩ ◑ 🅰

Dawson St ⊠ *D2* – ℰ *(01) 676 7015* – *www.thegreenhouserestaurant.ie*
– *Closed 2 weeks Christmas, Sunday and Monday*   **E3**
Rest – Menu 30/56 €
♦ Modern ♦ Elegant ♦ Fashionable ♦

Stylish restaurant with bold turquoise chairs and smooth service. 'Set', 'Surprise' and 'Tasting' menus come with suggested wine flights. Attractive, flavoursome dishes feature original combinations and many have Scandinavian touches.

XXX **One Pico** 🅰 ⇄ ▩ ◑ 🅰

5-6 Molesworth Pl ⊠ *D2* – ℰ *(01) 6760300* – *www.onepico.com*
– *Closed bank holidays*   **E3**
Rest – Menu 25/45 € – Carte 51/66 €
♦ Modern ♦ Fashionable ♦

Stylish, modern restaurant with a muted colour scheme, mirrors and comfy banquettes. An array of menus showcase a range of cooking styles, from traditional combinations to more modern dishes with an Asian twist.

XX **Pichet** 🅰 ▩ ◑ 🅰
😊
14-15 Trinity St ⊠ *D2* – ℰ *(01) 6771060* – *www.pichetrestaurant.ie*
– *Closed 25-26 December and 1-7 January*   **E2**
Rest – *(booking advisable)* Menu 25/45 € – Carte 34/52 €
♦ Modern ♦ Fashionable ♦ Bistro ♦

Popular brasserie with an open-plan kitchen and a buzzy atmosphere, run by a friendly team. Neat, flavoursome, modern European cooking from good value, daily changing menus. Wines available by the glass or in a 500ml 'pichet'. Front café-cum-bar offers light snacks and they open for breakfast too.

XX **Pearl Brasserie** 🅰 ▩ ◑ 🅰

20 Merrion St Upper ⊠ *D2* – ℰ *(01) 6613572* – *www.pearl-brasserie.com*
– *Closed 25 December and Sunday*   **F3**
Rest – Menu 22 € (weekdays) – Carte 34/59 €
♦ French classic ♦ Brasserie ♦

Basement restaurant with small bar-lounge and two surprisingly airy dining rooms; choose one of the stylish booths set in the old coal bunkers. Modern menus of elaborate, stylishly presented dishes and a simpler market menu. Formal service.

XX **Brasserie Le Pont** 🛜 🅰 ▩ ◑ 🅰 ⓪

25 Fitzwilliam Pl ⊠ *D2* – ℰ *(01) 669 4600* – *www.brasserielepont.ie*
– *Closed Saturday lunch and Monday dinner and Sunday*   *Plan III* **H1**
Rest – *(bookings advisable at dinner)* Menu 25/40 € – Carte 29/55 €
♦ French ♦ Brasserie ♦ Intimate ♦

Cosy, L-shaped restaurant in the basement of a Georgian townhouse. Cooking has a classical base but is presented in a light modern manner; sit at the counter to try snacks from the grazing menu. Resident jazz band plays Thursday and Friday.

XX **Dax** `VISA` `OO` `AE`

23 Pembroke St Upper ⊠ *D2 – ℰ (01) 6761494 – www.dax.ie*
– Closed 2 weeks August, 1 week Easter, 10 days Christmas, Saturday lunch,
Sunday and Monday **E3**
Rest *– (booking essential)* Menu 26 € (weekdays)/30 € – Carte 37/60 €
♦ French ♦ Rustic ♦
Simply furnished restaurant hidden in the basement of a Georgian terraced
house not far from Fitzwilliam Square. Rustic inner with smart linen-laid tables
and wine cellar. French-inspired menus include a six course 'surprise' selection.

XX **Dobbin's** `AC` ⇔ `VISA` `OO` `AE` `OD`

15 Stephen's Ln, (off Stephen's Pl) off Lower Mount St ⊠ *D2*
– ℰ (01) 6619536 – www.dobbins.ie
– Closed 24 December-2 January, Saturday lunch, Sunday dinner, Mondays
except December and bank holidays **F3**
Rest *– (booking essential)* Menu 25/26 € – Carte 36/52 €
♦ Traditional ♦ Neighbourhood ♦
Smart, well-established restaurant in residential area. Small bar with booths
leads to spacious, neatly laid dining room with warm, modern décor. Large
menu displays international influences.

XX **Tea Room** – Clarence Hotel `VISA` `OO` `AE` `OD`

6-8 Wellington Quay ⊠ *D2 – ℰ (01) 4070813 – www.theclarence.ie*
Rest *– (booking essential)* Menu 15/27 € – Carte 20/34 € **D2**
♦ Modern ♦ Brasserie ♦
Spacious hotel restaurant, where small mezzanine level overlooks larger main
room with central banquette island. Ambitious cooking displays Gallic influen-
ces. Polite, formal service.

XX **Les Frères Jacques** `AC` `VISA` `OO` `AE`

74 Dame St ⊠ *D2 – ℰ (01) 679 4555 – www.lesfreresjacques.com*
– Closed 24-30 December, Saturday lunch, Sunday and bank holidays
Rest *–* Menu 18 € (weekdays)/35 € – Carte 44/66 € **D2**
♦ French classic ♦ Bistro ♦
Long-standing restaurant on narrow cobbled alley, with typical French styling
and team. Classical Gallic cooking with seafood a speciality: daily fresh fish and
lobster tank on display.

XX **Peploe's** `AC` `VISA` `OO` `AE`

16 St Stephen's Grn. ⊠ *D2 – ℰ (01) 6763144 – www.peploes.com*
– Closed 25-26 December, Good Friday and lunch bank holidays **E3**
Rest *– (booking essential)* Menu 25 € (weekday lunch) – Carte 34/56 €
♦ Mediterranean ♦ Fashionable ♦ Brasserie ♦
Well-run, atmospheric brasserie named after Scottish artist and set in former
bank vault. Small bar; main room with smart mural and linen-laid tables. Exten-
sive menu with influences from the Med.

XX **Town Bar and Grill** `AC` `♥♥` `VISA` `OO` `AE`

21 Kildare St ⊠ *D2 – ℰ (01) 662 4800 – www.townbarandgrill.com*
– Closed Good Friday, 25-27 December and bank holidays **E3**
Rest *– (booking advisable)* Menu 30/45 € – Carte 34/59 €
♦ Modern ♦ Rustic ♦
Located in the old cellars of a famous city wine merchant, with a small bar and
high stools at entrance, more intimate tables to the rear and a pianist at wee-
kends. Menus display a mix of modern and classic dishes and have Irish overtones.

XX **Fallon & Byrne** `VISA` `OO` `AE`

First Floor, 11-17 Exchequer St ⊠ *D2 – ℰ (01) 4721000*
– www.fallonandbyrne.com
– Closed Good Friday, 25-26 December and Sunday dinner **E2**
Rest *–* Menu 24/39 € – Carte 30/49 €
♦ French classic ♦ Friendly ♦
Food emporium boasting vast basement wine cellar, ground floor full of fresh
quality produce, and first floor French-style bistro with banquettes, mirrors and
tasty bistro food.

Bang

🛱 AC ⇪ VISA ◎ AE ①

11 Merrion Row ✉ *D2 –* 𝒞 *(01) 4004229 – www.bangrestaurant.com*
– Closed 25 December, 1 January, Monday lunch and Sunday   **E3**
Rest *– (booking essential)* Menu 26/35 € – Carte 33/55 €

♦ Modern ♦ Fashionable ♦

Stylish three floor restaurant displaying impressive modern artwork by leading Irish and international artists. Good value lunch and early evening menus; more luxurious, modern dishes on the à la carte.

Francesca's – Brooks Hotel

ఈ AC ☜ VISA ◎ AE

Drury St ✉ *D2 –* 𝒞 *(01) 6704000 – www.brookshotel.ie*   **E2**
Rest *– (dinner only)* Menu 28 € – Carte 31/48 €

♦ Modern ♦ Fashionable ♦

Fine dining room with an open-plan kitchen, set in a smart, boutique-style townhouse. Interesting menu offers plenty of choice and relies on local produce; good value pre-theatre selection.

Locks Brasserie

⇪ VISA ◎ AE

1 Windsor Terr. ✉ *D8 –* 𝒞 *(01) 4200555 – www.locksbrasserie.com*
– Closed 25-28 December and bank holiday Mondays   *Plan III* **G1**
Rest *– (dinner only and lunch Thursday-Sunday)* Menu 29 €
– Carte 30/51 €

♦ Modern ♦ Fashionable ♦ Neighbourhood ♦

Relaxed, neighbourhood restaurant on a quiet corner site. The pastel-hued room is full of natural light, with comfy banquette seating and a cocktail bar. Appealing menu of modern European dishes; cooking is technically confident, with some innovative combinations. Professional, engaging service.
➜ Veal sweetbreads with ox tongue and pickled shallots. Scallops with suckling pig, celeriac purée and asparagus. Tonka bean and blood orange panna cotta.

Pig's Ear

⇪ VISA ◎ AE

4 Nassau St ✉ *D2 –* 𝒞 *(01) 6703865 – www.thepigsear.ie*
– Closed first week January, Sunday and bank holidays   **E2**
Rest *– (booking essential)* Menu 16 € (weekdays)/25 € – Carte 29/47 €

♦ Modern ♦ Bistro ♦ Friendly ♦

Well-established restaurant in a Georgian townhouse. Bustling dining rooms with porcine-themed memorabilia and hearty bistro dishes on the first two floors; a Scandinavian-style private room with a chef's table and more ambitious 12 course tasting menu on the third. Window tables overlook Trinity College.

La Maison

🛱 AC VISA ◎

15 Castlemarket ✉ *D2 –* 𝒞 *(01) 672 7258 – www.lamaisonrestaurant.ie*
– Closed 24 December-5 January   **E2**
Rest *–* Menu 24 € (lunch and early dinner) *–* Carte 25/42 €

♦ French classic ♦ Bistro ♦

Appealing French bistro with light blue façade, tables on the pavement and original posters decorating the walls inside. Breton-born chef offers carefully prepared, seasonal Gallic classics at a good price, which are brought to the table by a personable team.

Rustic Stone

🛱 AC ⊄

17 Great George's St ✉ *D2 –* 𝒞 *(01) 707 9596 – www.rusticstone.ie*
– Closed Good Friday, 1 January and 24-26 December   **E2**
Rest *–* Menu 15 € (weekdays)/50 € – Carte 21/61 €

♦ Modern ♦ Fashionable ♦

Split-level restaurant offering something a little bit different. Good quality ingredients are cooked simply to retain their natural flavours and menus point out the healthier options; some meats and fish arrive on a sizzling hot stone.

IRELAND - DUBLIN

X **L'Gueuleton**   🏠 VISA ⓒ⃝

1 Fade St ☒ D2 – ℰ (01) 6753708 – www.lgueuleton.com
– Closed 25-27 December, 1 January and Good Friday   **E2**
Rest – *(bookings not accepted)* Menu 25/35 € – Carte 30/47 €
♦ French classic ♦ Bistro ♦

Rustic restaurant with beamed ceilings, Gallic furnishings and rear terrace. Interesting French menus use local, seasonal produce. Flavoursome country cooking; friendly, efficient service.

X **Camden Kitchen**   🔄 VISA ⓒ⃝

3a Camden Mkt, Grantham St ☒ D8 – ℰ (01) 4760125
– www.camdenkitchen.ie
– Closed 24-26 December, Sunday dinner and Monday   **D3**
Rest – Menu 24 € (early dinner) – Carte 30/46 €
♦ Modern ♦ Rustic ♦

Appealing bistro with canopied façade and rustic inner, set over two floors. Open kitchen serving gutsy menu of robust, modern dishes. Relaxed, friendly service from a young team.

X **Saba**   Ⓐ⃝ VISA ⓒ⃝ AE

26-28 Clarendon St ☒ D2 – ℰ (01) 679 2000 – www.sabadublin.com
– Closed Good Friday and 25-26 December   **E2**
Rest – Menu 24 € (weekdays)/30 € – Carte 25/43 €
♦ Thai ♦ Fashionable ♦

Very trendy, buzzy Thai restaurant and cocktail bar. Simple yet stylish rooms with refectory tables in the centre and banquette seating around the walls. Fresh, clean, visual cooking from an all-Thai team who like to keep things authentic.

X **Port House**   VISA ⓒ⃝

64a South William St ☒ D2 – ℰ (01) 677 0298 – www.porthouse.ie
– Closed 25-26 December   **E2**
Rest – *(bookings not accepted)* Carte 12/38 €
♦ Spanish ♦ Rustic ♦

Characterful Spanish tapas bar serving a vast array of authentic, flavoursome dishes. Rustic, candlelit interior with exposed brick, semi-vaulted ceiling and tightly packed tables; small bar upstairs. Imported meats, cheeses and olives.

BALLSBRIDGE   *Plan III*

🏨🏨🏨🏨 **Four Seasons**   🚗 Ⅰゟ ⊕ 🎱 🔲 👌 Ⓐ⃝ 🛜 🏊 🅿 🔁 VISA ⓒ⃝ AE ⓞ

Simmonscourt Rd. ☒ D4 – ℰ (01) 665 4000
– www.fourseasons.com/dublin   **J2**
156 rm – †200/280 € ††220/300 €, � 29 € – 40 suites
Rest *Seasons* – Menu 23 € (weekdays)/57 € – Carte 34/84 €
♦ Grand Luxury ♦ Classic ♦

Set in grounds of the RDS arena. Elegant guest areas, state-of-the-art meeting rooms and impressive ballrooms boast ornate décor, antiques and Irish art. Spacious bedrooms; plenty of extras. Fine dining with fountain/garden views in Seasons.

🏨🏨🏨 **Herbert Park**   Ⅰゟ 👌 Ⓐ⃝ 🛜 🏊 🅿 VISA ⓒ⃝ AE ⓞ

☒ D4 – ℰ (01) 667 2200 – www.herbertparkhotel.ie   **J2**
151 rm – †109/250 € ††109/295 €, ⊟ 20 € – 2 suites
Rest *The Pavilion* – Menu 29/35 €
♦ Business ♦ Modern ♦

Contemporary hotel overlooking suburban park, with smart marble-floored reception, stylish seating areas and chic bar. Modern bedrooms display quality furnishings and marble bathrooms. Sizeable, formal restaurant offers interesting menu.

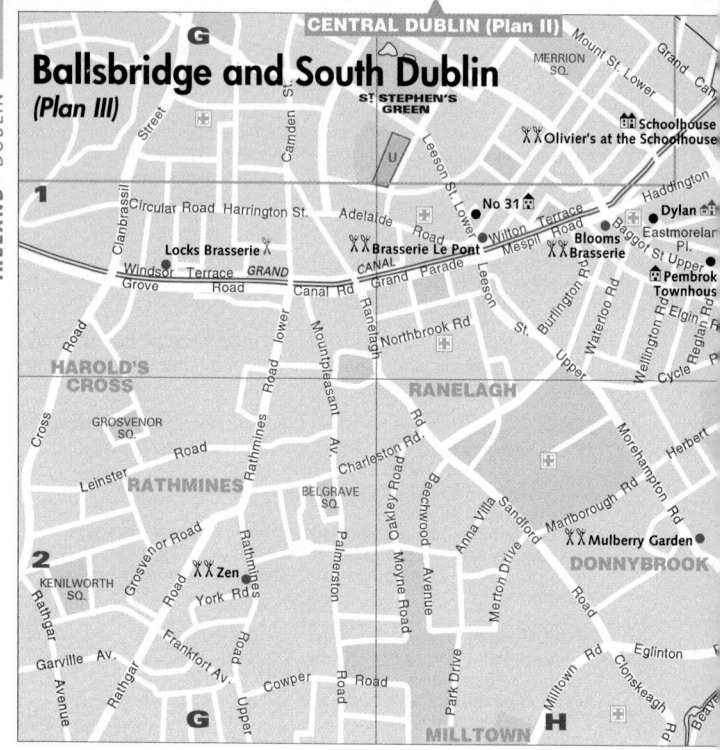

Ballsbridge and South Dublin
(Plan III)

🏨 Schoolhouse 🚗 🛏 AC 🛜 P VISA ⚫ AE ①

2-8 Northumberland Rd ⊠ D4 – ℰ (01) 667 5014
– www.schoolhousehotel.com
– Closed 24-26 December

31 rm ⊊ – †99/269 € ††109/279 €
Rest – Menu 23 € (dinner) – Carte 18/42 €

♦ Business ♦ Historic ♦

H1

Dating back to 1861 and formerly the St Stephens Parochial School. Spacious, well-kept bedrooms – most in the extension – boast William Morris designed fabrics and locally built Mackintosh-style furniture; some have half-tester beds. Busy bar with vaulted ceiling; formal restaurant serves classic dishes.

🏠 Ariel House without rest 🛜 P VISA ⚫ AE

50-54 Lansdowne Rd ⊠ D4
– ℰ (01) 668 5512
– www.ariel-house.net
– Closed 22 December-3 January

37 rm ⊊ – †59/290 € ††59/290 €

♦ Townhouse ♦ Classic ♦

J1

Personally run Victorian townhouse with comfy, traditionally styled guest areas and antique furnishings. Warmly decorated bedrooms have modern facilities and smart bathrooms; some four-posters.

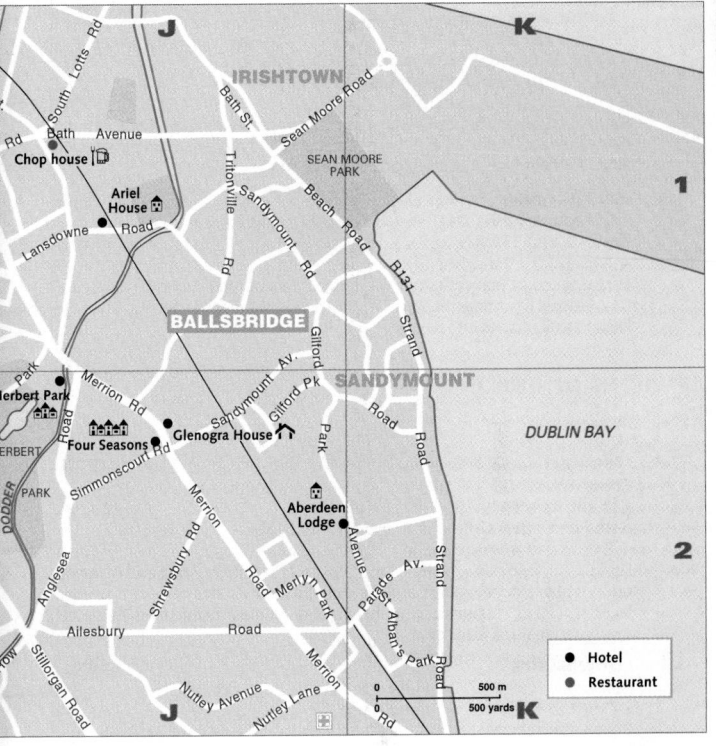

🏠 **Aberdeen Lodge** without rest   🚗 🛜 P VISA ⦿ AE ⓪
53-55 Park Ave. ⊠ *D4* – ℰ *(01) 283 8155 – www.halpinsprivatehotels.com*
16 rm ⌷ – ✚90/159 € ✚✚139/299 €   **J2**
♦ Townhouse ♦ Classic ♦
Two Edwardian townhouses in a smart suburban setting, knocked through into
one impressive hotel. Comfy lounge, warm homely atmosphere and well-equipped bedrooms – some with garden views.

🏠 **Pembroke Townhouse** without rest   🛜 P VISA ⦿ AE
90 Pembroke Rd ⊠ *D4* – ℰ *(01) 66 00 277 – www.pembroketownhouse.ie*
– Closed 2 weeks Christmas-New Year   **H1**
48 rm – ✚79/159 € ✚✚79/199 €, ⌷ 10 €
♦ Townhouse ♦ Classic ♦
Formerly three Georgian houses, now a friendly hotel with traditional styling,
comfy lounge and sunny breakfast room. Bedrooms vary in shape and size;
duplex rooms are the cosiest.

🏠 **Glenogra House** without rest   🛜 P VISA ⦿ AE ⓪
64 Merrion Rd ⊠ *D4* – ℰ *(01) 668 3661 – www.glenogra.com*
13 rm ⌷ – ✚59/99 € ✚✚79/179 €   **J2**
♦ Family ♦ Cosy ♦
Personally run red-brick Victorian house with informal reception, comfy lounge
and homely furnishings. Simply decorated bedrooms vary in shape and size; all
boast modern facilities.

481

XX **Bloom Brasserie** 🖹 AC VISA ⦿⦿

11 Upper Baggot St ✉ *D4 –* ✆ *(01) 668 7170 – www.bloombrasserie.ie*
– Closed 25 December, Sunday and bank holidays **H1**
Rest – Menu 25 € (dinner) – Carte 27/54 €
♦ Modern ♦ Brasserie ♦

Sizeable basement brasserie with cool, contemporary styling, vibrant art and
garden terrace. Menus offer a mix of traditional and more modern dishes; with
an additional small plate selection in the evening.

🍴 **Chop House** 🖹 VISA ⦿⦿ AE ⦿

2 Shelbourne Rd ✉ *D4 –* ✆ *(01) 6602390 – www.thechophouse.ie*
Rest – Menu 15/35 € **J1**
♦ Modern ♦ Pub ♦

Imposing square pub with small side terrace, dark bar and bright, airy conservatory. Relaxed lunchtime menu; more ambitious dishes in the evening, when the
kitchen really comes into its own.

ENVIRONS OF DUBLIN

AT CLONTARF

🏨 **Clontarf Castle** 🖫 ⅙ AC 🛜 🖎 P VISA ⦿⦿ AE ⦿

Castle Ave. ✉ *D3 –* ✆ *(01) 833 2321 – www.clontarfcastle.ie*
111 rm ⌑ – †109/189 € ††119/199 € *Plan I* **B1**
Rest *Fahrenheit Grill* – (dinner only) Menu 20 € – Carte 29/50 €
♦ Business ♦ Historic ♦

Set in an historic castle, partly dating back to 1172. Striking medieval style entrance lobby. Modern rooms and characterful luxury suites with cutting edge
facilities. Grand restaurant reminiscent of a knights' banqueting hall; local
meats and seafood feature.

XX **Downstairs** AC VISA

Hollybrook Park ✉ *D3 –* ✆ *(01) 833 8883 – www.downstairs.ie*
– Closed 25 December and Good Friday *Plan I* **B1**
Rest – (dinner only and Sunday lunch) Menu 27 € – Carte 31/41 €
♦ Modern ♦ Brasserie ♦ Neighbourhood ♦

Smart, modern, basement restaurant underneath a pub, in a lovely neighbourhood close to the sea. Classical menus offer plenty of choice and change with
the seasons. Refined, honest, balanced cooking shows respect for natural flavours.

AT DONNYBROOK

XX **Mulberry Garden** ⦿⦿ AE

Mulberry Ln (off Donnybrook Rd) ✉ *D4 –* ✆ *(01) 269 3300*
– www.mulberrygarden.ie – Closed Sunday-Wednesday *Plan III* **H2**
Rest – (dinner only and Sunday lunch in summer) (booking essential)
Menu 40 €
♦ Modern ♦ Friendly ♦ Neighbourhood ♦

Smart restaurant behind a parade of shops in the city suburbs, with a large L-
shaped dining room set around a terrace. Choice of two dishes per course on
the weekly changing menu; ambitious cooking features fresh, local produce.

AT DUBLIN AIRPORT

🏨 **Carlton H. Dublin Airport** ⩽ 🖫 ⅙ AC 🛜 🖎 P VISA ⦿⦿ AE

Old Airport Rd., Cloughran (on R 132 Santry rd) – ✆ *(01) 866 7500*
– www.carlton.ie/dublinairport – Closed 24-26 December
100 rm – †59/150 € ††69/190 €, ⌑ 14 € – 1 suite
Rest *Kittyhawks* – Menu 20/25 € – Carte 22/42 €
♦ Business ♦ Modern ♦

Modern commercial hotel with spacious marbled reception and comfy guest areas.
Uniform bedrooms display good facilities and smart bathrooms. Some rooms overlook airfield; some have balconies. Informal all-day brasserie offers popular menu.

Bewleys   ⓖ 📠 🛜 🅿 🚗 VISA ⦿ AE ①
Baskin Ln. (East : 1.5 km on N 32) – ℰ *(01) 871 1000*
– www.bewleyshotels.com
466 rm – †89/199 € ††89/199 €, ⌣ 10 €
Rest *The Brasserie* – Menu 26 € (dinner) – Carte 25/55 €
♦ **Business** ♦ **Functional** ♦
Immense eight floor hotel, ten minutes from the airport, with selection of small
meeting rooms. Immaculately kept bedrooms; good value for money. Wide-ranging menu served in The Brasserie.

AT RATHGAR

℣   Bijou   🛖 📠 VISA ⦿ AE ①
46 Highfield Rd ✉ *D6* – ℰ *(01) 496 1518* – *www.bijourathgar.ie*
– Closed 25-26 December   *Plan I* **A1**
Rest – Carte 31/46 €
♦ **British modern** ♦ **Brasserie** ♦ **Classic** ♦
Friendly, split-level restaurant with a heated terrace and a clubby feel; the expe-
rienced owners also run the nearby deli. Local ingredients feature in accomplis-
hed, full-flavoured, classically based dishes with modern touches.

AT RATHMINES

℣℣   Zen   📠 VISA ⦿ AE ①
89 Upper Rathmines Rd ✉ *D6* – ℰ *(01) 4979428* – *www.zenrestaurant.ie*
– Closed 25-27 December   *Plan III* **G2**
Rest – *(dinner only and Friday lunch)* Menu 15/24 € – Carte 23/32 €
♦ **Chinese** ♦ **Exotic** ♦
Renowned family run Chinese restaurant in the unusual setting of an old church
hall. Imaginative, authentic oriental cuisine with particular emphasis on spicy
Sichuan dishes.

ITALY
ITALIA

→ **AREA:**
301 262 km² (116 317 sq mi).

→ **POPULATION:**
60 849 247 inhabitants.
Density = 202 per km².

→ **CAPITAL:**
Rome.

→ **CURRENCY:**
Euro (€).

→ **GOVERNMENT:**
Parliamentary republic with two chambers (since 1946). Member of European Union since 1957 (one of the 6 founding countries).

→ **LANGUAGE:**
Italian.

→ **PUBLIC HOLIDAYS:**
New Year's Day (1 Jan); Epiphany (6 Jan); Easter Monday (late Mar/Apr); Liberation Day (25 Apr); Labor Day (1 May); Republic Day (2 June); Assumption of the Virgin Mary (15 Aug); All Saints' Day (1 Nov); Immaculate Conception (8 Dec); Christmas Day (25 Dec); St Stephen's Day (26 Dec).

→ **LOCAL TIME:**
GMT+1 hour in winter and GMT +2 hours in summer.

→ **CLIMATE:**
Temperate Mediterranean with mild winters and hot, sunny summers (Rome: January 8°C; July 25°C).

→ **EMERGENCY:**
Police ✆ **112**; Medical Assistance ✆ **118**; Fire Brigade ✆ **115**.
(Dialling **112** within any EU country will redirect your call and contact the emergency services.)

→ **ELECTRICITY:**
230 volts AC, 50Hz; 2 round pin sockets.

→ **FORMALITIES:**
Travellers from the European Union (EU), Switzerland, Iceland and the main countries of North and South America need a national identity card or passport (America: passport required) to visit Italy for less than three months (tourism or business purpose). For visitors from other countries a visa may be required, in addition to a passport, especially for those wishing to stay for longer than three months. We advise you to check with your embassy before travelling.

ROME
ROMA

Population: 2 761 477

Marie-Louise Detoux/Fotolia.com

Rome wasn't built in a day, and, when visiting, it's pretty hard to do it justice in less than three. The Italian capital is richly layered in Imperial, Renaissance, baroque and modern architecture, and its broad piazzas, hooting traffic and cobbled thoroughfares all lend their part to the heady fare: a theatrical stage cradled within seven famous hills. Being Eternal, Rome never ceases to feel like a lively, living city, while at the same time a scintillating monument to Renaissance power and an epic centre of antiquity. Nowhere else offers such a wealth of classical remains; set alongside palaces and churches, and bathed in the soft, golden light for which it is famous. When Augustus became the first Emperor of Rome, he could hardly have imagined the impact his city's language, laws and calendar would have upon the world.

The River Tiber snakes its way north to south through the heart of Rome. On its west bank lies the characterful and 'independent' neighbourhood of Trastevere, while north of here is Vatican City. Over the river the Piazza di Spagna area to the north has Rome's smartest shopping streets, while the southern boundary is marked by the Aventine and Celian hills, the latter overlooking the Colosseum. Esquiline's teeming quarter is just to the east of the city's heart; that honour goes to The Capitol, which gave its name to the concept of a 'capital' city.

ROME IN...

→ **ONE DAY**
Capitol, Forum, Colosseum, Pantheon, Trevi Fountain, Spanish Steps.

→ **TWO DAYS**
Via Condotti, Piazza Navona and surrounding churches, Capitoline museums.

→ **THREE DAYS**
A day on the west bank of the Tiber at Trastevere, Vatican City.

PRACTICAL INFORMATION

ARRIVAL-DEPARTURE

✈ Leonardo da Vinci Airport at Fiumicino is 32km southwest of Rome. The Fiumicino Leonardo Express train to Stazione Termini runs every 30min and takes 35min. Every 30min the Cotral bus travels to Cornelia Station (Metro Line A).

GETTING AROUND

Rome is served by a metro, bus and tram system. Tickets are available from metro stations, bus terminals, ticket machines, tobacconists, newsagents, cafés and tourist information centres. Choose your ticket type: a single ticket, which must be time stamped on board, or travelcards for one, three or seven days. Rome is best seen on foot, so make sure you have a good pair of walking shoes. Avoid the likes of sleeveless tops, shorts and miniskirts if you want to visit religious sites.

CALENDAR HIGHLIGHTS

February
Carnival.

March
Spring Festival, Independent Film Festival, Cultural Heritage Week.

April
Rome's Birthday, Parklife Festival.

June-August
Cinema Isle.

June-September
The Roman Summer.

July
Festa de Noantri, Tevere Expo.

July-August
Secret Passages.

July-September
New Operafestival.

September
White Night.

October
Rome Film Festival.

November
Romaeuropa Festival.

EATING OUT

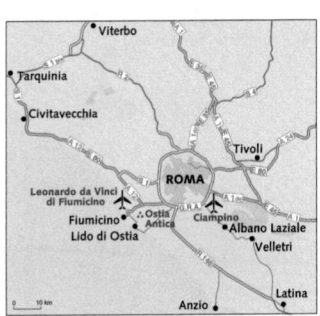

Despite being Italy's capital, Rome largely favours a local, traditional cuisine, typically found in an unpretentious trattorie or osterie. Although not far from the sea, the city doesn't go in much for fish, and food is often connected to the rural, pastoral life with products coming from the surrounding Lazio hills, which also produce good wines. Pasta, of course, is not to be missed, and lamb is favoured among meats for the main course. So too, the 'quinto quarto': a long-established way of indicating those parts of the beef (tail, tripe, liver, spleen, lungs, heart, kidney) left over after the best bits had gone to the richest families. For international cuisine combined with a more refined setting, head for the elegant hotels: very few other areas of Italy have such an increasing number of good quality restaurants within a hotel setting. Locals like to dine later in Rome than say, Milan, with 1pm, or 8pm the very earliest you'd dream of appearing for lunch or dinner. In the tourist hot-spots, owners are, of course, only too pleased to open that bit earlier.

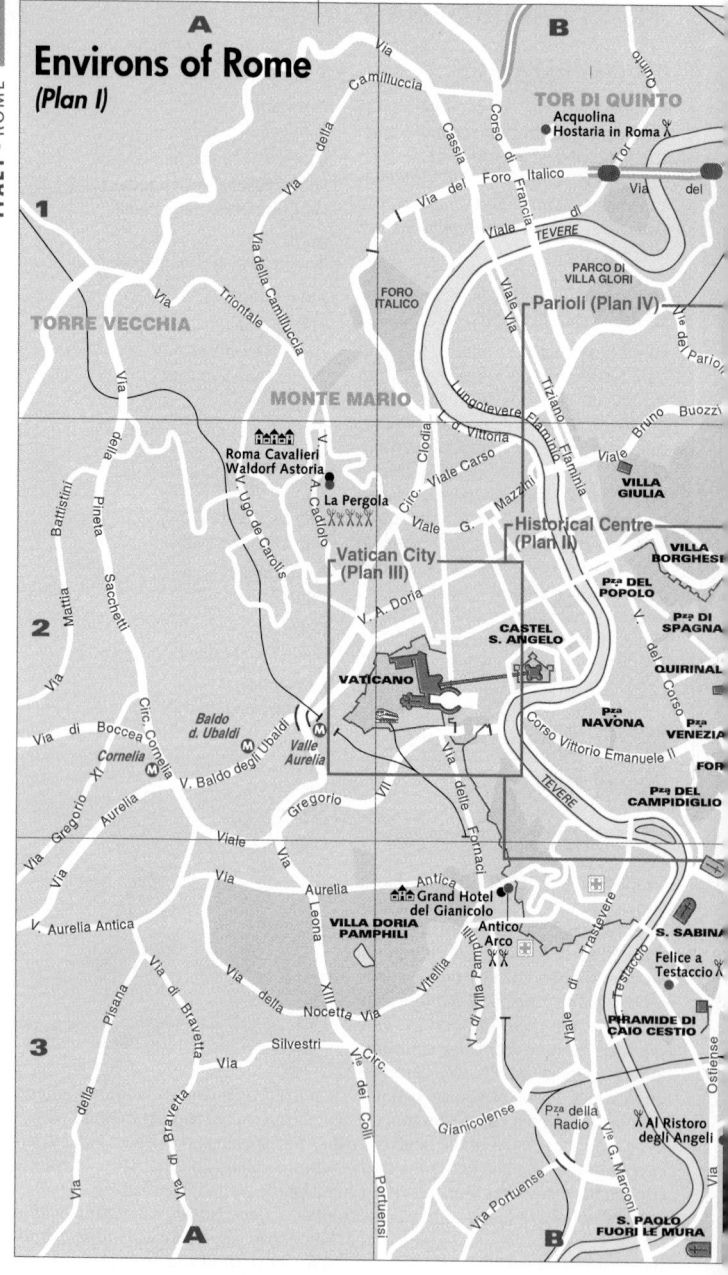

Environs of Rome
(Plan I)

TOR DI QUINTO
Acquolina
Hostaria in Roma

FORO ITALICO

PARCO DI VILLA GLORI

Parioli (Plan IV)

TORRE VECCHIA

MONTE MARIO

Roma Cavalieri Waldorf Astoria
La Pergola

VILLA GIULIA

Historical Centre (Plan II)

VILLA BORGHESE

Vatican City (Plan III)

CASTEL S. ANGELO

P.za DEL POPOLO

P.za DI SPAGNA

VATICANO

QUIRINAL

Baldo d. Ubaldi
Valle Aurelia

P.za NAVONA

Corso Vittorio Emanuele II

P.za VENEZIA

Cornelia

FOR

P.za DEL CAMPIDIGLIO

Grand Hotel del Gianicolo
Antico Arco

VILLA DORIA PAMPHILI

S. SABINA

Felice a Testaccio

PIRAMIDE DI CAIO CESTIO

P.za della Radio

Al Ristoro degli Angeli

S. PAOLO FUORI LE MURA

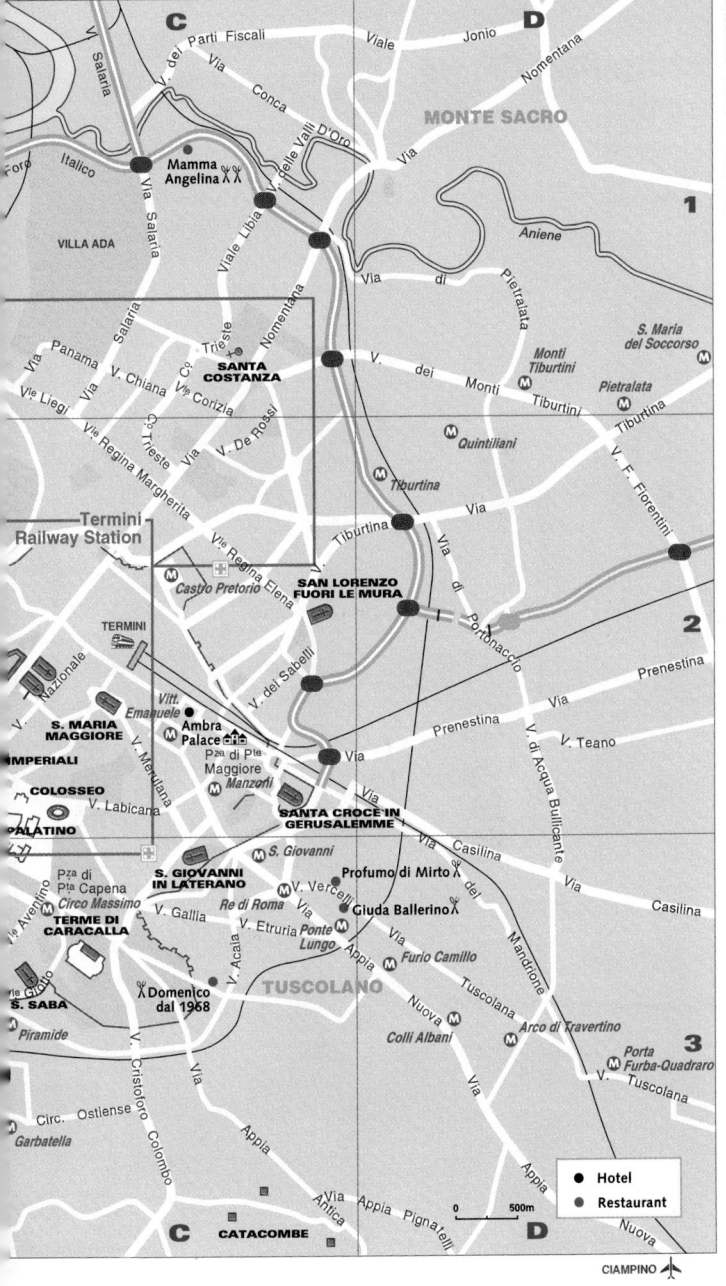

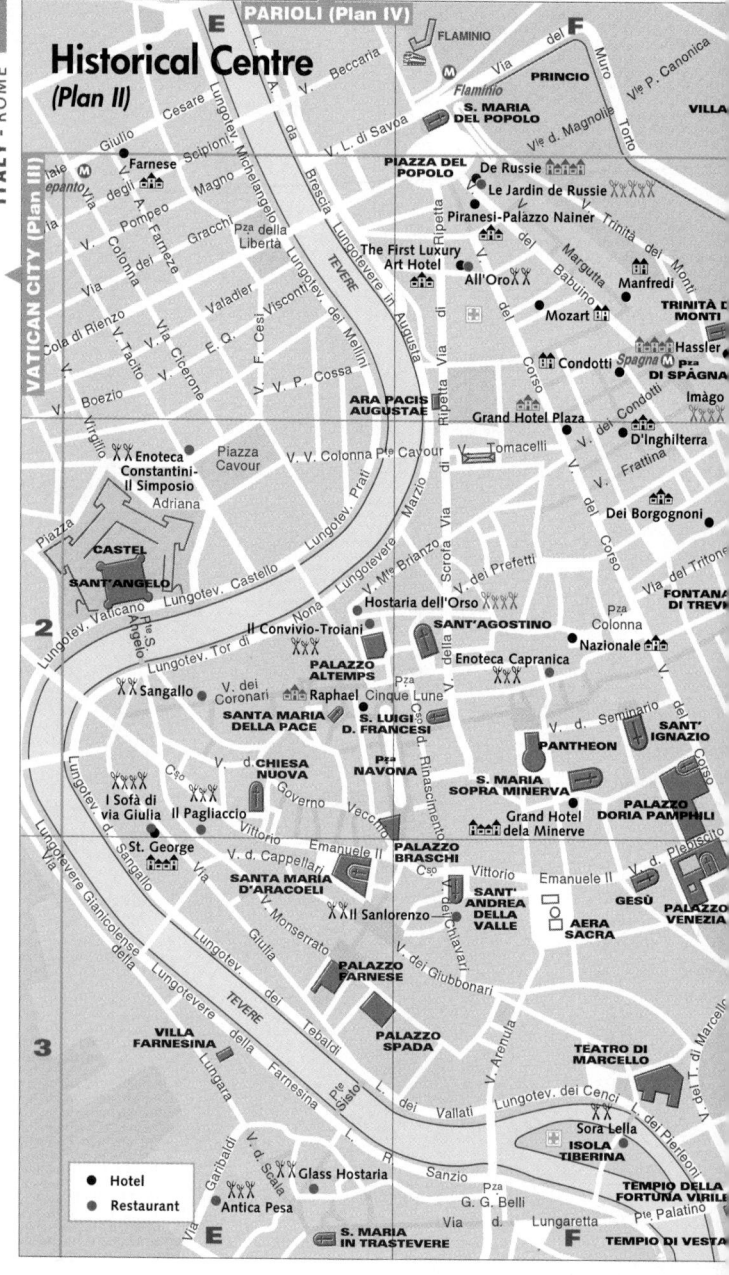

Historical Centre
(Plan II)

PARIOLI (Plan IV)

FLAMINIO

PRINCIO

VILLA

S. MARIA DEL POPOLO

PIAZZA DEL POPOLO

De Russie

Le Jardin de Russie

Piranesi-Palazzo Nainer

The First Luxury Art Hotel

All'Oro

Manfredi

TRINITÀ DI MONTI

Mozart

Hassler

Condotti

Spagna Pza DI SPAGNA

ARA PACIS AUGUSTAE

Imàgo

Grand Hotel Plaza

D'Inghilterra

Piazza Cavour

Enoteca Constantini-Il Simposio

Adriana

Dei Borgognoni

CASTEL SANT'ANGELO

FONTANA DI TREVI

Hostaria dell'Orso

SANT'AGOSTINO

Pza Colonna

Nazionale

Il Convivio-Troiani

Enoteca Capranica

Sangallo

PALAZZO ALTEMPS

Raphael   Cinque Lune

SANTA MARIA DELLA PACE

S. LUIGI D. FRANCESI

SANT' IGNAZIO

PANTHEON

CHIESA NUOVA

Pza NAVONA

S. MARIA SOPRA MINERVA

PALAZZO DORIA PAMPHILI

I Sofà di via Giulia

Il Pagliaccio

Grand Hotel dela Minerve

St. George

PALAZZO BRASCHI

SANTA MARIA D'ARACOELI

Il Sanlorenzo

SANT' ANDREA DELLA VALLE

AERA SACRA

GESÙ

PALAZZO VENEZIA

PALAZZO FARNESE

VILLA FARNESINA

PALAZZO SPADA

TEATRO DI MARCELLO

Sora Lella

ISOLA TIBERINA

TEMPIO DELLA FORTUNA VIRILE

Glass Hostaria

Antica Pesa

S. MARIA IN TRASTEVERE

TEMPIO DI VESTA

● Hotel

● Restaurant

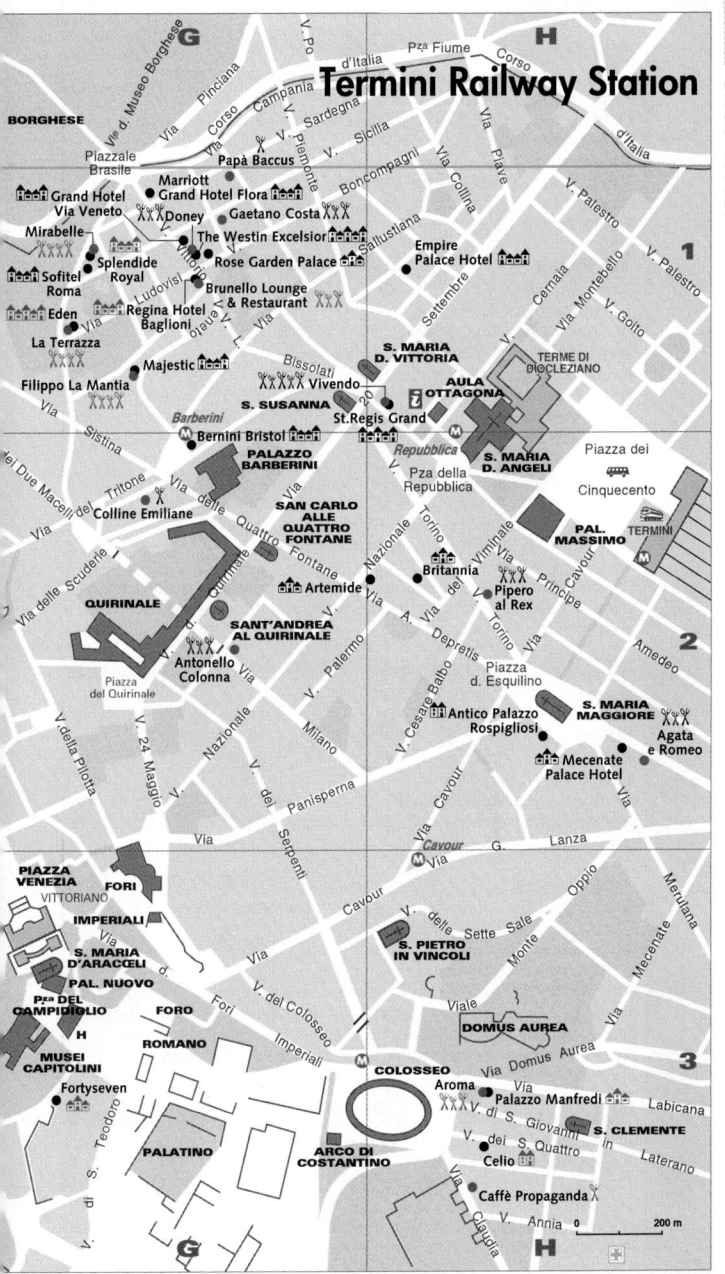

Termini Railway Station

G **H**

Pza Fiume
d'Italia
Corso
d'Italia

BORGHESE

V. Po
Piaciana
Campania
Corso
V. Piemonte
V. Sardegna
V. Sicilia
V. Piave
V. Palestro

Piazzale
Brasile

Papà Baccus

Grand Hotel
Via Veneto
Marriott
Grand Hotel Flora
Doney
Gaetano Costa
The Westin Excelsior
Rose Garden Palace
Empire
Palace Hotel
Boncompagni
V. Collina
V. Palestro

Mirabelle
Splendide
Royal
Sofitel
Roma
Brunello Lounge
& Restaurant
Sallustiana
V. Cernaia
V. Montebello
V. Goito

Eden
Regina Hotel
Baglioni
Settembre

La Terrazza

Majestic
Bissolati
S. MARIA
D. VITTORIA
TERME DI
DIOCLEZIANO

Filippo La Mantia
Vivendo
AULA
OTTAGONA

S. SUSANNA
St.Regis Grand

Barberini
Bernini Bristol
Repubblica
S. MARIA
D. ANGELI
Piazza dei

PALAZZO
BARBERINI
Pza della
Repubblica
Cinquecento

Colline Emiliane
SAN CARLO
ALLE
QUATTRO
FONTANE
PAL.
MASSIMO
TERMINI

QUIRINALE
Artemide
Nazionale
Torino
Viminale
Principe
Cavour

Britannia
Pipero
al Rex
Amedeo

SANT'ANDREA
AL QUIRINALE
V. Palermo
A. Via
Depretis

Antonello
Colonna
Piazza
d. Esquilino

Piazza
del Quirinale
Nazionale
Milano
V. Cesare Balbo
S. MARIA
MAGGIORE
Agata
e Romeo

Via
Antico Palazzo
Rospigliosi
Mecenate
Palace Hotel

Panisperna
Via Cavour

PIAZZA
VENEZIA
FORI
Cavour
G. Lanza
Oppio
Merulana

VITTORIANO
IMPERIALI
Cavour

S. MARIA
D'ARACŒLI
PAL. NUOVO
V. delle
Sette Sale
Monte
Mecenate

Pza DEL
CAMPIDOGLIO
S. PIETRO
IN VINCOLI

MUSEI
CAPITOLINI
FORO
ROMANO
DOMUS AUREA

Fortyseven
COLOSSEO
Via Domus Aurea

Aroma
Palazzo Manfredi
Labicana
S. CLEMENTE

PALATINO
ARCO DI
COSTANTINO
Celio
Laterano

Caffè Propaganda
V. Annia

200 m
0

G **H**

491

Hassler

piazza Trinità dei Monti 6 ✉ *00187* – Ⓜ *Spagna* – ☏ *06 699340*
– www.hotelhasslerroma.com F1
96 rm – 🛉440/500 € 🛉🛉560/900 €, ☑ 38 € – 14 suites
Rest *Imàgo* ✿ – see restaurant listing
♦ Grand Luxury ♦ Stylish ♦
With its superb location at the top of the Spanish Steps, this hotel combines
elegance, luxury and tradition. Unusual interpretation of the classical style on
the fifth floor.

De Russie

via del Babuino 9 ✉ *00187* – Ⓜ *Flaminio* – ☏ *06 328881*
– www.roccofortehotels.com F1
122 rm – 🛉358/750 € 🛉🛉475/1050 €, ☑ 35 € – 25 suites
Rest *Le Jardin de Russie* – see restaurant listing
♦ Grand Luxury ♦ Modern ♦
Designed by Valadier during the early 19C, this hotel is furnished in a simple
and harmonious style. It features elegant guestrooms and an attractive 'secret
garden' scented with roses and jasmine. One of the best hotels in Rome.

St. George

via Giulia 62 ✉ *00186* – ☏ *06 686611* – *www.stgeorgehotel.it*
64 rm – 🛉230/420 € 🛉🛉270/460 € E2
Rest *I Sofà di Via Giulia* – see restaurant listing
♦ Luxury ♦ Modern ♦
This boutique, designer-style hotel is in one of the most beautiful streets in
Rome. It offers an elegant ambience and luxurious furnishings in its public
areas and spacious guestrooms.

Grand Hotel de la Minerve

piazza della Minerva 69 ✉ *00186* – ☏ *06 695201*
– www.grandhoteldelaminerve.com F2
123 rm – 🛉235/595 € 🛉🛉285/645 €, ☑ 35 € – 12 suites
Rest – Carte 58/154 €
♦ Luxury ♦ Stylish ♦
An historic building surrounded by ancient monuments. Elegant atmosphere
and an imaginative menu of traditional cuisine. Attractive views from the terrace.

Raphaël

largo Febo 2 ✉ *00186* – ☏ *06 682831* – *www.raphaelhotel.com*
49 rm ☑ – 🛉200/600 € 🛉🛉250/800 € – 1 suite E2
Rest – Carte 46/102 €
♦ Luxury ♦ Personalised ♦
With its collection of porcelain, antiquarian artefacts and sculptures by famous
artists, the entrance to this hotel resembles a museum. The recently renovated
guestrooms are modern in style. The menu in this attractive restaurant with a
panoramic terrace focuses mainly on Italian cuisine, along with some French
dishes.

Grand Hotel Plaza

via del Corso 126 ✉ *00186* – Ⓜ *Spagna* – ☏ *06 67495*
– www.grandhotelplaza.com F2
200 rm ☑ – 🛉220/260 € 🛉🛉240/650 € – 20 suites **Rest** – Carte 50/70 €
♦ Luxury ♦ Stylish ♦
This hotel boasts huge, stunning, late-19C lounges decorated in Art Nouveau-
style with coffered ceilings and a profusion of marble, frescoes and glass. The
guestrooms are also furnished in period style, as is the atmospheric dining
room. Panoramic terrace with a Champagne bar.

ITALY - ROME

Piranesi-Palazzo Nainer *without rest* 🖼 🕸 AC 🛜
via del Babuino 196 ✉ *00187* – **Ⓜ** *Flaminio* VISA ⓒⓞ AE ⓪
– ℰ *06 328041* – *www.hotelpiranesi.com* F1
32 rm ⌷ – ♦158/168 € ♦♦198/398 € – 8 suites
♦ Traditional ♦ Classic ♦
The lobby, guestrooms and corridors of this hotel are decorated with marble, elegant furnishings and an unusual exhibition of old fabrics. The hotel also boasts a roof garden and sun terrace.

The First Luxury Art Hotel ⅙ AC 🛜 VISA ⓒⓞ AE ⓪
via del Vantaggio 14 ✉ *00186* – **Ⓜ** *Flaminio* – ℰ *06 45617070*
– *www.thefirsthotel.com* F1
18 rm – ♦341/671 € ♦♦385/715 €, ⌷ 30 € – 11 suites
Rest *All'Oro* 🌼 – see restaurant listing
♦ Luxury ♦ Stylish ♦
This elegant 19C palazzo features refined guestrooms and panoramic terraces overlooking the rooftops of the city centre. The interior decor is light and modern with contemporary artwork on display.

Dei Borgognoni *without rest* AC 🛜 ⅙ 🛋 VISA ⓒⓞ AE ⓪
via del Bufalo 126 ✉ *00187* – **Ⓜ** *Spagna* – ℰ *06 69941505*
– *www.hotelborgognoni.it* F2
51 rm ⌷ – ♦215/255 € ♦♦220/330 €
♦ Traditional ♦ Classic ♦
Occupying a 19C palazzo, this elegant hotel's spacious, modern public rooms and comfortable guestrooms combine both traditional and modern features.

Nazionale AC 🛜 ⅙ VISA ⓒⓞ AE ⓪
piazza Montecitorio 131 ✉ *00186* – ℰ *06 695001*
– *www.hotelnazionale.it* F2
100 rm ⌷ – ♦220/290 € ♦♦380/560 € – 1 suite
Rest *31 al Vicario* – *(closed August, Sunday and Monday lunch)*
♦ Traditional ♦ Classic ♦
This hotel is housed in an 18C building on Piazza di Montecitorio. It offers elegant public areas and guestrooms furnished with individual touches. Guests will enjoy traditional Italian cuisine in this elegant, comfortable restaurant.

Grand Hotel del Gianicolo 🚗 ⅃ AC 🛜 ⅙ 🛋
viale Mura Gianicolensi 107 ✉ *00152*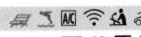
– **Ⓜ** *Cipro Musei Vaticani* – ℰ *06 58333405*
– *www.grandhotelgianicolo.it* *Plan I* **B3**
48 rm ⌷ – ♦103/380 € ♦♦113/410 €
Rest *Corte degli Archi* – Carte 45/61 €
♦ Traditional ♦ Classic ♦
A stylish hotel on the Gianicolo offering comfortable guestrooms and elegant public areas. You also have the illusion of being a guest in a smart country house, thanks to the beautiful outdoor pool – an unusual sight in Rome. Contemporary cuisine is served in the Corte degli Archi.

D'Inghilterra ⅙ rm, AC rm, 🛜 VISA ⓒⓞ AE ⓪
via Bocca di Leone 14 ✉ *00187* – ℰ *06 699811* – *www.royaldemeure.com*
88 rm ⌷ – ♦460/750 € ♦♦490/750 € – 7 suites F2
Rest *Caffè Romano* – Carte 44/67 €
♦ Luxury ♦ Classic ♦
A haven for tourists from around the world since as early as the 17C, this hotel has the charming ambience of an elegant private house with delightful, individual-style guestrooms. Find elegant lounges, an atmospheric bar, and a restaurant serving simple, classic cuisine at lunchtime and more elaborate, ambitious fare in the evening.

ITALY - ROME

Manfredi without rest 〔AC〕〔WiFi〕〔VISA〕〔MC〕〔AE〕〔DC〕
via Margutta 61 ⊠ *00187 –* Ⓜ *Spagna –* ℰ *06 3207676*
– www.hotelmanfredi.it **F1**
28 rm ⌷ – †75/199 € ††99/299 € – 1 suite
♦ Traditional ♦ Classic ♦

Housed on the third floor of a palazzo on the famous Via Margutta. Elegant, individually furnished guestrooms, all of which boast the latest in modern facilities. Excellent international breakfast of natural products, including yoghurt and homemade pastries.

Mozart without rest 〔AC〕〔WiFi〕〔VISA〕〔MC〕〔AE〕〔DC〕
via dei Greci 23/b ⊠ *00187 –* Ⓜ *Spagna –* ℰ *06 36001915*
– www.hotelmozart.com **F1**
56 rm ⌷ – †64/359 € ††84/514 €
♦ Traditional ♦ Classic ♦

Housed in a 19C palazzo, this hotel boasts elegant public areas and stylish guestrooms. Those in the annexe are more modern and spacious.

Condotti without rest 〔AC〕〔WiFi〕〔VISA〕〔MC〕〔AE〕〔DC〕
via Mario dè Fiori 37 ⊠ *00187 –* Ⓜ *Spagna –* ℰ *06 6794661*
– www.hotelcondotti.com **F1**
16 rm ⌷ – †79/299 € ††99/489 €
♦ Traditional ♦ Classic ♦

The lobby of this hotel is decorated in marble and adorned with elegant chandeliers. Find small, comfortable guestrooms, some of which are in a separate building nearby.

Le Jardin de Russie – Hotel De Russie 〔🚗〕〔🏡〕〔&〕〔AC〕〔VISA〕〔MC〕〔AE〕〔DC〕
via del Babuino 9 ⊠ *00187 –* Ⓜ *Piazzale Flaminio*
– ℰ 06 32888870 – www.roccofortehotels.com **F1**
Rest – Carte 70/133 €
♦ Modern ♦ Elegant ♦

Despite its French name, this restaurant serves creative reinterpretations of distinctly Italian cuisine. This is prepared by Fulvio Pierangelini, one of Italy's great chefs. Extremely elegant atmosphere.

Imàgo – Hotel Hassler 〔AC〕〔VISA〕〔MC〕〔AE〕〔DC〕
🕸
piazza Trinità dei Monti 6 ⊠ *00187 –* Ⓜ *Spagna –* ℰ *06 69934726*
– www.imagorestaurant.com **F1**
Rest – *(dinner only)* Menu 100/140 € – Carte 85/152 €
♦ Creative ♦ Elegant ♦

This restaurant continues to be a perennial favourite, thanks to its large windows and unforgettable views of Rome. Modern cuisine made with high quality ingredients.
➜ Fusilloni alla carbonara con ragù di quaglia. Merluzzo carbonaro glassato al sake, schiacciatina di fagioli cannellini. Sfogliatelle calde di pasta di riso con salsa di ciliegie e gelato al tè verde.

Hostaria dell'Orso 〔🏡〕〔AC〕〔⇄〕〔VISA〕〔MC〕〔AE〕〔DC〕
via dei Soldati 25/c ⊠ *00186 –* ℰ *06 68301192 – www.hdo.it*
– Closed August and Sunday **E-F2**
Rest – *(booking advisable)* Menu 45/95 € – Carte 50/68 € 🐌
♦ Modern ♦ Elegant ♦

Housed in an historic building, this restaurant has intimate, romantic dining rooms decorated in a simple, elegant style. The elegant cuisine is based around the highest quality ingredients.

I Sofà di Via Giulia – Hotel St. George 〔&〕〔AC〕〔VISA〕〔MC〕〔AE〕〔DC〕
via Giulia 62 ⊠ *00186 –* ℰ *06 686611 – www.isofadiviagiulia.com*
– Closed Sunday, Monday and for dinner during the Summer **E2**
Rest – Menu 30 € – Carte 65/88 €
♦ Modern ♦ Elegant ♦

Typical Italian dishes and regional specialities featuring meat, fish and vegetables are served in this restaurant. Excellent wine list.

ITALY - ROME

XXX ✿

Il Convivio-Troiani (Angelo Troiani)   🔲 ⬄ 💳 💳 💳 🅾

vicolo dei Soldati 31 ✉ *00186* – ☎ *06 6869432*
– *www.ilconviviotroiani.com* – *Closed 1 week in August and Sunday*
Rest – *(dinner only)* Carte 70/132 € ▒   **E2**
♦ Creative ♦ Classic ♦

This elegant restaurant is in the heart of the historic centre. Amid a decor of fres-coes, paintings and modern minimalism, enjoy quintessential Italian cuisine. Choose from risottos and pasta, as well as a selection of specialities from the Lazio region.
➜ Vermicelli bucati alla amatriciana. Poker di piccione. Semifreddo di zabaione con frutta secca caramellata e aceto balsamico tradizionale di Modena.

XXX ✿✿

Il Pagliaccio (Anthony Genovese)   🔲 💳 💳 💳 🅾

via dei Banchi Vecchi 129 ✉ *00186* – ☎ *06 68809595*
– *www.ristoranteilpagliaccio.it*
– *Closed 8-31 August, 9-17 January, Sunday, Monday, Tuesday lunch*
Rest – *(bookings advisable at dinner)* Menu 75 € (lunch)/   **E2**
160 € – Carte 95/150 € ▒
♦ Creative ♦ Friendly ♦

This restaurant is a breath of modernity in the heart of Renaissance Rome. It is constantly on the lookout for new products, creating innovative dishes from tra-ditional favourites.
➜ Ziti con stoccafisso e salsa di 'nduja. Piccione laccato, latte e soffice alle nocciole. Albicocche al timo, crema di riso alla vaniglia, sorbetto di albicocche.

XXX

Enoteca Capranica   🔲 ⬄ 💳 💳 💳 🅾

piazza Capranica 99/100 ✉ *00186* – ☎ *06 69940992*
– *www.enotecacapranica.it* – *Closed Saturday lunch, Sunday*
Rest – Menu 65/75 € – Carte 54/104 € ▒   **F2**
♦ Mediterranean ♦ Formal ♦

This 15C palazzo near Montecitorio has been transformed into an elegant res-taurant serving Mediterranean cuisine. Colourful vaulted ceiling plus an impres-sive wine list.

XXX

Antica Pesa   🏠 🔲 💳 💳 💳 🅾

via Garibaldi 18 ✉ *00153* – ☎ *06 5809236* – *www.anticapesa.it*
– *Closed Sunday*   **E3**
Rest – *(dinner only)* Carte 107/143 € ▒
♦ Roman ♦ Formal ♦

Typical Roman dishes made from carefully selected ingredients grace the menu of this restaurant, which is housed in a grain storehouse that once belonged to the neighbouring Papal State. Large paintings by contemporary artists hang on the walls and there is a small lounge with a fireplace near the entrance.

XXX

Il Sanlorenzo   🔲 ⬄ 💳 💳 💳

via dei Chiavari 4/5 ✉ *00186* – ☎ *06 6865097* – *www.ilsanlorenzo.it*
– *Closed 12-26 August, for lunch on Saturday, Sunday, Monday, also for dinner on Sunday in June, July and August*   **F3**
Rest – Carte 64/127 € ▒
♦ Modern ♦ Fashionable ♦

Built over the foundations of the Teatro Pompeo, this palazzo now houses an atmospheric restaurant, which combines a sense of history with contemporary style. Modern cuisine and fish specialities.

XX ✿

All'Oro (Riccardo Di Giacinto) - The First Luxury Art Hotel   🔲

via del Vantaggio 14 ✉ *00186* – Ⓜ *Flaminio*   💳 💳 💳
– ☎ *06 97996907* – *www.ristoranteallloro.it* – *Closed Sunday dinner*
Rest – Menu 68 € – Carte 64/91 €   **F1**
♦ Creative ♦ Design ♦

This restaurant has a simple, modern décor. The inventive, personalised cuisine highlights authentic Roman traditions and flavours.
➜ Cappelletti in brodo "asciutto", parmigiano e zafferano. Quaglia: petto farcito al ciauscolo e coscia laccata con miele e 'nduja. Tiramisù all'Oro.

XX **Sangallo** 🛋 AC ⇔ VISA ⚫⚫ AE ⓘ
via dei Coronari 180 ✉ *00186* – ☎ *06 68134055*
– www.ristorantesangallo.com **E2**
Rest – Menu 40 € (lunch)/70 € (dinner) – Carte 59/86 €
♦ Mediterranean ♦ Formal ♦
This 16C palazzo, near San Salvatore church in Lauro, has an interesting contrast of
old and new. It houses an elegant restaurant serving modern, innovative cuisine.

XX **Glass Hostaria** (Cristina Bowerman) AC VISA ⚫⚫ AE ⓘ
❀ *vicolo del Cinque 58* ✉ *00153* – ☎ *06 58335903* – *www.glasshostaria.it*
– Closed 8-30 July, 24-26 December, 14-29 January and Monday
Rest – (dinner only) Menu 65/90 € – Carte 59/95 € 🍷 **E3**
♦ Modern ♦ Design ♦
Situated in the heart of Trastevere, this restaurant boasts an ultra-modern
design with an interesting play of light and a slightly unsettling atmosphere.
The excellent cuisine also features highly modern touches.
➔ Raviolini ripieni di parmigiano 60 mesi con funghi e burro d'Isigny.
Astice con mango, cipolle rosse e yogurt alla menta. Torcione di caprino
con pistacchi di Bronte, amarena e rosmarino.

XX **Sora Lella** AC VISA ⚫⚫ AE
via di Ponte Quattro Capi 16 (Tiber Island) ✉ *00186* – ☎ *06 6861601*
– www.soralella.com
– Closed Christmas Holidays **F3**
Rest – Menu 48/80 € – Carte 34/68 €
♦ Roman ♦ Family ♦
Son and grandchildren of the famous late "Sora Lella", perpetuate in a dignified
way the tradition both in the warmth of the welcome and in the typical Roman
elements of the cooking.

XX **Antico Arco** AC ⇔ VISA ⚫⚫ AE ⓘ
piazzale Aurelio 7 ✉ *00152* – ☎ *06 5815274* – *www.anticoarco.it*
Rest – Carte 49/77 € 🍷 *Plan I* **B3**
♦ Creative ♦ Fashionable ♦
The chef at this modern, bright and fashionable restaurant selects the best
Italian ingredients to create innovative dishes based on traditional specialities.

X **Felice a Testaccio** AC VISA ⚫⚫ AE ⓘ
🚇 *via Mastrogiorgio 29* ✉ *00153* – ☎ *06 5746800*
– www.feliceatestaccio.com
– Closed August *Plan I* **B3**
Rest – (booking advisable) Carte 28/53 €
♦ Roman ♦ Family ♦
One of the standard-bearers of cuisine from Lazio, this simple trattoria with a
family atmosphere is now so popular that it is advisable to book your table in
advance. Make sure you try the legendary pasta all'amatriciana (bacon and
tomato sauce).

TERMINI RAILWAY STATION *Plan II*

🏨 **Eden** ≤ ⅙ AC 🛜 🏋 VISA ⚫⚫ AE ⓘ
via Ludovisi 49 ✉ *00187* – Ⓜ *Barberini* – ☎ *06 478121*
– www.edenroma.com **G1**
108 rm – ♦245/438 € ♦♦324/618 €, ⊔ 49 € – 13 suites
Rest *La Terrazza* ❀ – see restaurant listing
♦ Luxury ♦ Stylish ♦
This large, top-end hotel has a formal atmosphere but the service is warm and
friendly. Some of the rooms on the upper floors have what is perhaps the best
view of Rome.

ITALY - ROME

The St. Regis Rome 🔥 🕸 ⅙ 🗛 🛜 ⅔ 𝚅𝙸𝚂𝙰 ⊙⊙ 𝙰𝙴 ⊙

via Vittorio Emanuele Orlando 3 ✉ *00185* – ⓜ *Repubblica* – ℰ *06 47091*
– www.stregisrome.com
H1
161 rm – ♦310/930 € ♦♦330/1020 €, � 43 € – 23 suites
Rest *Vivendo* – see restaurant listing
♦ Grand Luxury ♦ Classic ♦
Frescoes, fine fabrics and Empire-style antique pieces adorn the luxurious guest-rooms and lavish lounges of this hotel, which has retained the splendid atmosphere of its early years (1894). The only concession to the modern age is the attractive and well-equipped spa.

The Westin Excelsior 🔥 ⊕ 🕸 🖾 🗛 🛜 ⅔ 𝚅𝙸𝚂𝙰 ⊙⊙ 𝙰𝙴 ⊙

via Vittorio Veneto 125 ✉ *00187* – ⓜ *Barberini* – ℰ *0647081*
– www.westinrome.com
G1
281 rm – ♦270/600 € ♦♦360/1200 €, ☐ 29 € – 35 suites
Rest *Doney* – see restaurant listing
♦ Luxury ♦ Classic ♦
Spoil yourself with a stay in the royal suite (the largest in Europe) or choose one of the luxurious guestrooms, where elegant and comfortable furnishings are complemented by the very latest technology. The "dolce vita" at its best!

Grand Hotel Via Veneto 🕼 🔥 ⊕ 🕸 ⅙ 🗛 🛜 ⅔

via Vittorio Veneto 155 ✉ *00187* – ⓜ *Barberini*   𝚅𝙸𝚂𝙰 ⊙⊙ 𝙰𝙴 ⊙
– ℰ 06 487881
G1
106 rm – ♦380/700 € ♦♦380/700 €, ☐ 33 € – 10 suites
Rest *Magnolia* – Carte 75/145 €
Rest *Time* – Carte 40/60 €
♦ Luxury ♦ Classic ♦
Situated on one of Rome's most famous streets, this hotel offers luxury in the true sense of the word, with superb, retro-style guestrooms and a collection of more than 500 original paintings on display. A love of Italian flavours and traditions is clearly evident in the cuisine served in this restaurant, which serves Italian and international cuisine, as well as a good choice of cocktails.

Regina Hotel Baglioni 🔥 ⅙ 🗛 🛜 ⅔ 𝚅𝙸𝚂𝙰 ⊙⊙ 𝙰𝙴 ⊙

via Vittorio Veneto 72 ✉ *00187* – ⓜ *Barberini* – ℰ *06 421111*
– www.baglionihotels.com
G1
125 rm ☐ – ♦250/676 € ♦♦350/850 € – 9 suites
Rest *Brunello Lounge & Restaurant* – see restaurant listing
♦ Luxury ♦ Stylish ♦
A historic hotel in an Art Nouveau-style building, with an elegant interior decor of stuccowork, period furniture and an imposing bronze and marble staircase. The only concessions to the modern day are the levels of comfort and facilities, as well as the superb guestrooms, some of which are decorated in a contemporary designer style.

Majestic 🔥 ⅙ 🗛 🛜 ⅔ 𝚅𝙸𝚂𝙰 ⊙⊙ 𝙰𝙴 ⊙

via Vittorio Veneto 50 ✉ *00187* – ⓜ *Barberini* – ℰ *06 421441*
– www.hotelmajestic.com
G1
93 rm – ♦210/540 € ♦♦250/640 €, ☐ 30 € – 4 suites
Rest *Filippo La Mantia* – see restaurant listing
♦ Traditional ♦ Classic ♦
Film-buffs may recognise the backdrop to the famous Italian movie 'La Dolce Vita' at this hotel, which was opened in the late 19C. The Majestic remains one of the bastions of luxury accommodation on the Via Veneto, with its antique furniture, tapestries and frescoes, nowadays accompanied by modern comforts and facilities.

Sofitel Rome Villa Borghese 🛏 ⓘ ℗ 🅰️ 🤶 VISA ⑩ AE ①

via Lombardia 47 ✉ *00187* – Ⓜ *Barberini* – 𝒞 *06 478021* – *www.sofitel.com*
100 rm – †200/290 € ††230/390 €, ⊆ 30 € – 4 suites   **G1**
Rest *La Terrasse* – Carte 67/108 €
♦ Luxury ♦ Classic ♦

The neo-Classical style dominates in this hotel just a stone's throw from the cosmopolitan Via Veneto. Superb guestrooms and elegant public areas. Situated on the top floor, the panoramic restaurant with its Lounge Bar boasts romantic views of the Villa Medici.

Splendide Royal ⓘ ℗ 🅰️ 🤶 VISA ⑩ AE ①

via di porta Pinciana 14 ✉ *00187* – Ⓜ *Barberini* – 𝒞 *06 421689*
– *www.splendideroyal.com*   **G1**
68 rm – †360/630 € ††400/850 €, ⊆ 35 € – 9 suites
Rest *Mirabelle* – see restaurant listing
♦ Luxury ♦ Classic ♦

Gilded stucco, damask fabrics and sumptuous antique furnishings contribute to the Roman Baroque style of this hotel, which is in sharp contrast to the contemporary trend for minimalist design. Shades of periwinkle blue, golden yellow and cardinal red dominate in the guestrooms, creating an ambience of traditional luxury.

Bernini Bristol 🛏 ⓘ 🦮 rm, ℗ 🤶 🤶 VISA ⑩ AE ①

piazza Barberini 23 ✉ *00187* – Ⓜ *Barberini* – 𝒞 *06 488931*
– *www.berninibristol.com*   **G2**
127 rm ⊆ – †230/400 € ††330/660 € – 10 suites
Rest *L'Olimpo* – 𝒞 *06 488933288* – Carte 56/102 €
♦ Traditional ♦ Classic ♦

A key feature of the famous square on which it stands, this elegant hotel offers traditionally furnished and contemporary-style guestrooms. Ask for a room with a view on one of the upper floors. Roof-garden restaurant, with outdoor dining in the summer and a superb view of the Eternal City.

Marriott Grand Hotel Flora ⓘ 🦮 rest, ℗ 🤶 🤶

via Vittorio Veneto 191 ✉ *00187* – Ⓜ *Spagna*   VISA ⑩ AE ①
– 𝒞 *06 489929* – *www.grandhotelflora.net*   **G1**
156 rm – †319/389 € ††319/389 €, ⊆ 30 € – 3 suites
Rest *The Cabiria* – 𝒞 *06 48992548* – Carte 42/77 €
♦ Traditional ♦ Modern ♦

One of the symbolic buildings of the Italian capital, the Marriott Grand Hotel Flora is situated at the end of Via Vittorio Veneto. It boasts an elegant neo-Classical ambience with the occasional contemporary feature. Rather than the usual hotel fare, the restaurant serves traditional Italian cuisine with the influence of the Campania region.

Empire Palace Hotel 🛏 ⓘ 🦮 ℗ 📞 🤶 VISA ⑩ AE ①

via Aureliana 39 ✉ *00187* – 𝒞 *06 421281*
– *www.empirepalacehotel.com*   **H1**
110 rm ⊆ – †360 € ††512 € – 5 suites
Rest *Aureliano* – *(closed Sunday)* Carte 40/70 €
♦ Traditional ♦ Personalised ♦

Sophisticated combination of elements in the 19C building and its contemporary design, with a collection of modern art in the public areas; simple, classic bedrooms. This restaurant features cherry wood decor, tables set close together and red and blue chandeliers. Mediterranean specialities take pride of place on the menu.

Rose Garden Palace ⓘ 🦮 ℗ 🤶 🤶 VISA ⑩ AE ①

via Boncompagni 19 ✉ *00187* – Ⓜ *Barberini* – 𝒞 *06 421741*
– *www.rosegardenpalace.com*   **G1**
65 rm – †180/260 € ††240/370 €, ⊆ 15 €
Rest – *(closed lunch Sunday)* Carte 51/80 €
♦ Traditional ♦ Modern ♦

A modern, minimalist design is the inspiration behind the furnishing of this hotel housed in an early-20C palazzo. The building has nonetheless retained some of its original architectural features, such as its high ceilings and marble decor.

ITALY - ROME

 Mecenate Palace Hotel 🛗 ⚙ Ⓜ 🛜 📶 VISA ⓪ AE ①

via Carlo Alberto 3 ✉ *00185 –* Ⓜ *Vittorio Emanuele –* 𝒞 *06 44702024*
– www.mecenatepalace.com H2
71 rm ⊆ – ♦100/315 € ♦♦180/410 € – 3 suites
Rest – *(dinner only)* Carte 33/47 €
♦ Traditional ♦ Stylish ♦
The warm and elegant period-style interiors are in perfect keeping with the spirit of the 19C building, which houses this hotel. Fine views of Santa Maria Maggiore from the terrace and some of the guestrooms. The restaurant on the top
floor serves typical Italian cuisine.

 Artemide 🕭 ⋒ ⚙ Ⓜ 🛜 VISA ⓪ AE ①

via Nazionale 22 ✉ *00184 –* Ⓜ *Repubblica –* 𝒞 *06 489911*
– www.hotelartemide.it G-H2
85 rm ⊆ – ♦119/419 € ♦♦139/449 €
Rest – *(residents only)* Carte 37/90 €
♦ Business ♦ Classic ♦
Housed in a delightful 19C Art Nouveau building, the Artemide offers all the
usual comforts of a modern hotel, as well as excellent conference facilities.

 Ambra Palace without rest ⚙ Ⓜ 🛜 📶 VISA ⓪ AE ①

via Principe Amedeo 257 ✉ *00185 –* Ⓜ *Vittorio Emanuele –* 𝒞 *06 492330*
– www.ambrapalacehotel.com Plan I **C2**
78 rm ⊆ – ♦79/190 € ♦♦89/330 €
♦ Traditional ♦ Classic ♦
Occupying a mid-19C palazzo in a lively, multi-ethnic district behind the station,
this hotel has been furnished and equipped to meet the requirements of a
mainly business clientele.

 Palazzo Manfredi ⩽ ⚙ Ⓜ 🛜 VISA ⓪ AE ①

via Labicana 125 ✉ *00184 –* Ⓜ *Colosseo –* 𝒞 *06 77591380*
– www.palazzomanfredi.com H3
15 rm – ♦300/710 € ♦♦300/710 €, ⊆ 30 € – 1 suite
Rest *Aroma* – see restaurant listing
♦ Luxury ♦ Classic ♦
The elegant rooms and superb suites of this hotel overlook the Colosseum and
the Domus Aurea. Without a doubt the hotel's most striking feature is its
delightful roof-garden terrace, which is perfect for a relaxing breakfast or
romantic dinner.

 Fortyseven 🛗 🕭 ⚙ Ⓜ 🛜 📶 VISA ⓪ AE ①

via Luigi Petroselli 47 ✉ *00186 –* 𝒞 *06 6787816*
– www.fortysevenhotel.com G3
59 rm ⊆ – ♦190/240 € ♦♦200/250 € – 2 suites
Rest *Circus* – Carte 49/76 €
♦ Luxury ♦ Art Deco ♦
The name of this hotel housed in an austere 1930s palazzo refers to the number
of the street which leads down to the Teatro di Marcello. Each of the five floors
here is dedicated to a 20C Italian artist (Greco, Quagliata, Mastroianni, Modig-
liani and Guccione) and the hotel is adorned with a collection of paintings,
sculptures and lithographs.

 Britannia without rest Ⓜ 🛜 VISA ⓪ AE ①

via Napoli 64 ✉ *00184 –* Ⓜ *Repubblica –* 𝒞 *06 4883153*
– www.hotelbritannia.it H2
33 rm ⊆ – ♦150/330 € ♦♦160/380 €
♦ Traditional ♦ Classic ♦
Attentive service and stylish personalised decor are some of the features of this
small hotel, which offers comfortable guestrooms, most of which are brightened by a small aquarium.

Celio without rest   ⟨icons⟩ AC 📶 ⚲ VISA ⊙

via dei Santi Quattro 35/c ✉ *00184* – **Ⓜ** *Colosseo* – ✆ *06 70495333*
– www.hotelcelio.com   **H3**
19 rm ⊑ – 🛏110/180 € 🛏🛏130/250 € – 1 suite
♦ Traditional ♦ Classic ♦
Delightful artistic touches create an elegant atmosphere in this hotel situated
opposite the Colosseum. Stylish guestrooms with individual touches, as well as
a hammam and relaxation zone.

Antico Palazzo Rospigliosi without rest   ⟨icons⟩ AC 📶 ⚲ 🅿

via Liberiana 21 ✉ *00185* – **Ⓜ** *Cavour*   VISA ⊙ AE ⓪
– ✆ 06 48930495 – www.hotelrospigliosi.com   **G2**
39 rm ⊑ – 🛏115/195 € 🛏🛏140/290 €
♦ Historic ♦ Classic ♦
This 16C mansion has retained much of its period elegance in its large lounges,
as well as in the fine detail of its beautiful bedrooms. The cloister-garden, with
its bubbling fountain and splendid 17C chapel, is particularly delightful.

Vivendo – Hotel The St. Regis Rome   ⟨icons⟩ AC ⇄ VISA ⊙ AE ⓪

via Vittorio Emanuele Orlando 3 ✉ *00185* – **Ⓜ** *Repubblica*
– ✆ 06 47092736 – www.stregisrome.com/en/vivendo
– Closed Sunday and Monday   **H1**
Rest – *(dinner only)* Carte 70/92 € ⅜
♦ Mediterranean ♦ Luxury ♦
Although the hotel is traditional in style, the restaurant boasts a completely dif-
ferent feel with its bright, eclectic decor. The cuisine follows the same pattern,
focusing on Mediterranean dishes reinterpreted with a contemporary flavour.

Mirabelle – Hotel Splendide Royal   ⟨icons⟩ ☕ ⟨icons⟩ AC ⇄ VISA ⊙ AE ⓪

via di porta Pinciana 14 ✉ *00187* – **Ⓜ** *Barberini* – ✆ *0642168838*
– www.mirabelle.it   **G1**
Rest – Carte 113/174 €
♦ Modern ♦ Elegant ♦
With one of the most spectacular roof gardens in Rome and views of the Vatican Gardens, this restaurant serves an interesting blend of regional and international cuisine.

La Terrazza – Hotel Eden   ⟨icons⟩ AC ⇄ VISA ⊙ AE ⓪

via Ludovisi 49 ✉ *00187* – **Ⓜ** *Barberini* – ✆ *06 47812752*
– www.edenroma.it   **G1**
Rest – Carte 100/180 € ⅜
♦ Modern ♦ Elegant ♦ Romantic ♦
La Terrazza boasts a stunning view of the historic centre. It also has the added
attraction of delicious and varied cuisine created by the restaurant's young chef.
The extraordinary array of specialities includes international dishes and produce
from France to the Mediterranean. Nothing is missing, including caviar.
→ Capesante marinate con vinaigrette di mango e frutto della passione,
sorbetto di sedano e caviale. Rombo chiodato in crosta di sale nero, fagot-
tino di acetosella e salsa di Franciacorta. Lingotto di tiramisù al caffè con
gelato al caffè.

Filippo La Mantia – Hotel Majestic   ⟨icons⟩ ⟨icons⟩ AC ⇄ VISA ⊙ AE ⓪

via Vittorio Veneto 50 ✉ *00187* – **Ⓜ** *Barberini* – ✆ *06 42144715*
– www.filippolamantia.com
– Closed 5-30 August, 1°-10 January, lunch Saturday and Sunday
Rest – Menu 40 € (lunch)/120 € – Carte 60/90 €   **G1**
♦ Sicilian ♦ Luxury ♦
A Sicilian landmark in the heart of Rome situated on the top floor of one of the
famous hotels on the Via Veneto, this restaurant revolves around the origins
and personality of its chef, Filippo La Mantia. The typical Sicilian specialities are
occasionally given a fresh reinterpretation but are mostly served in the traditional way (with the exception of garlic and onion which are banned by the chef).

ITALY - ROME

Open Colonna   🔲 VISA ⦾ AE ⑩

scalinata di via Milano 9/a ✉ *00184 –* Ⓜ *Termini –* 𝒞 *06 47822641*
– www.antonellocolonna.it
– Closed August, Sunday and Monday   **G2**
Rest *– (dinner only) (booking advisable)* Carte 91/129 €
♦ Creative ♦ Design ♦ Luxury ♦
This open-plan, glass-walled restaurant is within the imposing Palazzo delle Esposizioni. It serves inventive cuisine inspired by traditional dishes, which will please the most discerning guests.
➔ Cannolo di baccalà, panna acida e limone candito. Negativo di carbonara. Diplomatico crema e cioccolato, caramello al sale.

Agata e Romeo *(Agata Parisella)*   🔲 VISA ⦾ AE ⑩

via Carlo Alberto 45 ✉ *00185 –* Ⓜ *Vittorio Emanuele –* 𝒞 *06 4466115*
– www.agataeromeo.it
– Closed 5-25 August, lunch Saturday, Sunday, lunch Monday   **H2**
Rest *–* Menu 35 € (weekday lunch)/150 € – Carte 80/110 € 🍴
♦ Classic ♦ Formal ♦
Situated in a district that is becoming more and more multicultural, this restaurant continues to showcase Roman and Italian produce and cuisine. One of the capital's culinary institutions!
➔ Paccheri all'amatriciana. Baccalà cucinato in 5 modi diversi. Il millefoglie di Agata.

Aroma *– Hotel Palazzo Manfredi*   ⟨ 🏠 🔲 VISA ⦾ AE ⑩

via Labicana 125 ✉ *00184 –* Ⓜ *Colosseo –* 𝒞 *06 77591380*
– www.aromarestaurant.it   **H3**
Rest *– (bookings advisable at dinner)* Carte 98/138 €
♦ Mediterranean ♦ Design ♦
The name of this restaurant pays tribute both to the city of Rome and to the aromas of Mediterranean cuisine. Situated on the top floor of the Palazzo Manfredi hotel, the restaurant boasts breathtaking views of Ancient Rome, from the Colosseum to the dome of St Peter's.

Brunello Lounge & Restaurant *– Regina Hotel Baglioni*   ♿

via Vittorio Veneto 72 ✉ *00187*   🔲 ⇔ VISA ⦾ AE ⑩
– Ⓜ *Barberini –* 𝒞 *06 48902867 – www.brunellorestaurant.com*
– Closed Sunday   **G1**
Rest *–* Carte 66/119 €
♦ Modern ♦ Design ♦
This warm, elegant restaurant has a faintly Oriental feel. It provides the perfect setting to enjoy superb Mediterranean cuisine, as well as international dishes that will appeal to foreign visitors to the capital.

Doney *– Hotel The Westin Excelsior*   🔲 VISA ⦾ AE ⑩

via Vittorio Veneto 125 ✉ *00187 –* Ⓜ *Barberini –* 𝒞 *06 47082783*
Rest *–* Carte 48/78 €   **G1**
♦ Italian ♦ Classic ♦
This restaurant is a fusion of the classic and the contemporary, where every detail component has been studied in attentive detail. The same is true of the H Club›Doney lounge bar, which also offers a concise, attractively priced organic menu.

Gaetano Costa   🔲 ⇔ VISA ⦾ AE ⑩

via Sicilia 45 ✉ *00186 –* 𝒞 *06 42016822*
– www.gaetanocostarestaurant.com   **G1**
Rest *–* Menu 39/100 € – Carte 55/88 €
♦ Modern ♦ Design ♦
A new, modern restaurant, both in terms of its decor and menu, which includes fish and meat dishes. Fixed menus are available at lunchtime, in addition to the gourmet à la carte menu. The elegant dining room becomes a popular tea room in the afternoon.

XXX

Pipero al Rex   🅰🅲 🆅🅸🆂🅰 ⊚⊙ 🅰🅴 ⓪

via Torino 149 ✉ 00184 – 𝒞 06 4815702 – www.alessandropipero.com
– Closed dinner Sunday and Monday   **H2**
Rest *– (number of covers limited, pre-book)* Menu 50/80 € – Carte 65/85 €
♦ Modern ♦ Intimate ♦ Romantic ♦

You walk through the lobby of the Hotel Rex to get to this elegant and intimate restaurant with its muted lighting. The superb cuisine is prepared by a young yet experienced chef, and the wine list features a selection of excellent wines.
➜ Crudo d'oca, mela e senape. Spaghetti mantecati di mare. Coniglio tonnato.

XX

Giuda Ballerino (Andrea Fusco)   🏠 🅰🅲 🆅🅸🆂🅰 ⊚⊙ 🅰🅴 ⓪

largo Appio Claudio 346 ✉ 00174 – Ⓜ Giulio Agricola – 𝒞 06 71584807
– www.giudaballerino.com – Closed 1-10 January and Wednesday
Rest *– (dinner only except Sunday) (booking advisable)*   *Plan I* **C3**
Menu 70/95 € – Carte 65/102 € 🍴
Rest L'Osteria – Menu 40 € – Carte 24/48 €
♦ Creative ♦ Friendly ♦

This restaurant has an unusual dual function – on one side the Osteria has a rustic feel and serves regional fare, while on the other a small, modern dining room focuses on creative, gourmet cuisine. The walls of the latter are covered with cartoons, especially of Dylan Dog, a huge favourite of the owners.
➜ Risotto cacio e pepe con culatello di Zibello e tartufo. Pollo al latte e tabacco con gamberi d'Anzio crudi e arachidi. Cioccolando.

X

Caffè Propaganda   🅰🅲 🆅🅸🆂🅰 ⊚⊙ 🅰🅴 ⓪

via Claudia 15 ✉ 00186 – Ⓜ Colosseo – 𝒞 06 94534255
– www.caffepropaganda.it – Closed lunch Monday   **H3**
Rest – Carte 34/66 €
♦ Lazio ♦ Bistro ♦

This restaurant evokes a Parisian bistro of the early 20C with its zinc bar and tiles, although its cuisine is resolutely Roman. Cured meats, salads and a few daily specials are served at lunchtime.

X

Domenico dal 1968   🏠 🅰🅲 🆅🅸🆂🅰 ⊚⊙ 🅰🅴

via Satrico 23/25 ✉ 00183 – 𝒞 06 70494602 – www.domenicodal1968.it
– Closed 20 days August, Sunday and Monday lunch May-September, Sunday
dinner and Monday rest of year   *Plan I* **C3**
Rest – Carte 28/74 €
♦ Roman ♦ Family ♦

It is worth heading off the tourist track to experience this authentic Roman trattoria. The fritto (fried seafood and vegetables) and linguine with mullet roe and clams are the house specialities.

X

Profumo di Mirto   🅰🅲 🆅🅸🆂🅰 ⊚⊙ 🅰🅴

viale Amelia 8/a ✉ 00181 – 𝒞 06 786206 – www.profumodimirto.it
– Closed August and Monday   *Plan I* **C3**
Rest – Menu 25 € (lunch)/65 € – Carte 22/77 €
♦ Fish and seafood ♦ Cosy ♦

The name of this restaurant pays tribute to Sardinia, the owner's native region. Fish from the Mediterranean takes pride of place on the menu. It is prepared in delicious, home-style dishes such as the excellent octopus ravioli served with a crayfish sauce.

X

Papà Baccus   🏠 🅰🅲 ♿ 🆅🅸🆂🅰 ⊚⊙ 🅰🅴 ⓪

via Toscana 32/36 ✉ 00187 – Ⓜ Barberini – 𝒞 06 42742808
– www.papabaccus.com
– Closed Saturday lunch, Sunday and Bank Holidays   **G1**
Rest – Carte 52/82 €
♦ Italian ♦ Formal ♦

Although the decor of this restaurant in the Via Veneto district is traditional, the management is young and enthusiastic. The menu features delicious seafood dishes, as well as specialities from Tuscany (including Chianina beef and Cinta Senese pork), Lazio and other regions of Italy.

✗ **Colline Emiliane**   AK ↔ VISA ◉

via degli Avignonesi 22 ⊠ 00187 – Ⓜ *Barberini – ☏ 06 4817538*
– Closed August, Sunday dinner, Monday   **G2**
Rest – *(booking advisable)* Carte 26/62 €

♦ Emilian ♦ Family ♦

Just a stone's throw from Piazza Barberini, this simple, friendly, family-run restaurant has just a few tables arranged close together. It serves typical dishes
from the Emilia region, including fresh pasta stretched by hand in the traditional
way.

✗ **Al Ristoro degli Angeli**   🏠 AK VISA ◉ AE
☺

via Luigi Orlando 2 ⊠ 00154 – ☏ 06 51436020 – www.ristorodegliangeli.it
– Closed 1 August-15 September, 1-10 January, Sunday and Monday
Rest – *(dinner only)* Carte 36/48 €   *Plan I* **B3**

♦ Roman ♦ Bistro ♦

Housed in premises occupied immediately after the war by the Ente Comunale
di Consumo and then later by a grocery store, this unusual restaurant has a
bistro-style ambience. The cuisine is mainly Roman. There is the occasional
gourmet speciality such as grilled beef steak served in a red wine sauce or
with Himalayan crystal salt.

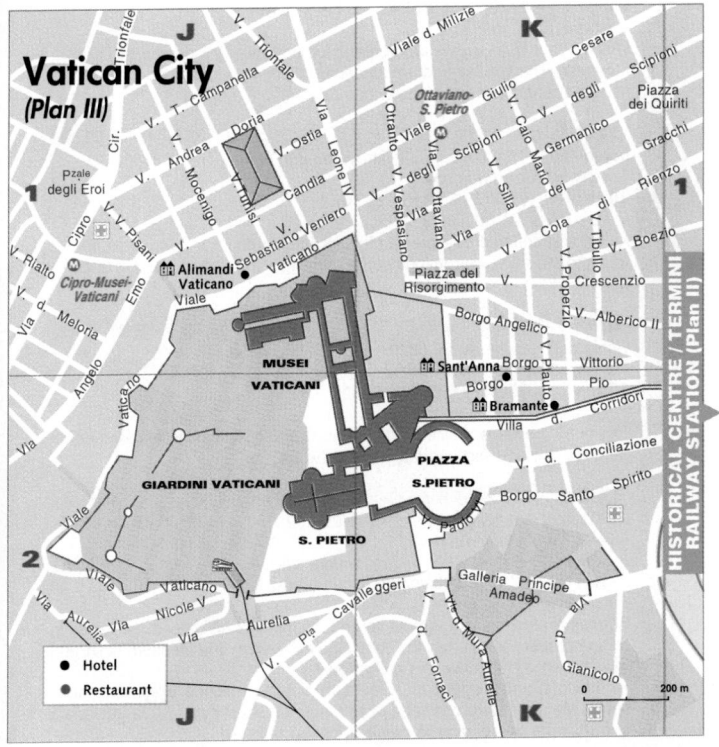

Rome Cavalieri Waldorf Astoria   ≤ 👤 🏠 🖼 👥 🏠 🏊 🔳

via Cadlolo 101 ✉ *00136*   ※ 🔥 🖼 🛜 🏄 **P** 🚗 🆚 💳 🅰🅴 ⓘ
– 𝒞 *06 35091* – *www.romecavalieri.com*   *Plan I* **A2**
366 rm 🖵 – 🕴380/990 € 🕴🕴410/1020 € – 4 suites
Rest *La Pergola* ✿✿✿ – see restaurant listing
Rest *L'Uliveto* – Carte 65/130 €
♦ Luxury ♦ Classic ♦

This imposing building overlooks the entire city of Rome. The hotel has excellent facilities, including extensive gardens, an outdoor swimming pool, plus a fine art collection. Restaurant with an informal atmosphere by the edge of the swimming pool for dining with live music.

Farnese without rest   🖼 🛜 **P** 🆚 💳 🅰🅴 ⓘ

via Alessandro Farnese 30 ✉ *00192* – 🚇 *Lepanto* – 𝒞 *06 3212553*
– *www.hotelfarnese.com*   *Plan II* **E1**
23 rm 🖵 – 🕴90/220 € 🕴🕴120/350 €
♦ Traditional ♦ Classic ♦

Decorated in period style, this hotel has elegant rooms and an attractive lobby housing a 17C polychrome marble frontal. Fine views of St Peter's from the terrace.

Alimandi Vaticano without rest   🖼 🛜 🚗 🆚 💳 🅰🅴 ⓘ

viale Vaticano 99 ✉ *00165* – 🚇 *Ottaviano-San Pietro* – 𝒞 *06 39745562*
– *www.alimandi.it*   **J1**
24 rm 🖵 – 🕴120/200 € 🕴🕴140/220 € – 3 suites
♦ Family ♦ Classic ♦

This pleasant hotel enjoys an excellent location directly opposite the Vatican Museums. The marble and wood decor in the well-appointed guestrooms adds to their elegant atmosphere.

Sant'Anna without rest   🖼 🛜 🆚 💳 🅰🅴 ⓘ

borgo Pio 133 ✉ *00193* – 🚇 *Ottaviano-San Pietro* – 𝒞 *06 68801602*
– *www.hotelsantanna.com*   **K1-2**
20 rm 🖵 – 🕴90/180 € 🕴🕴130/230 €
♦ Traditional ♦ Classic ♦

An original coffered ceiling and pleasant interior courtyard add a decorative touch to this small, welcoming hotel occupying a 16C building a short distance from St Peter's.

Bramante without rest   🖼 🛜 🆚 💳 🅰🅴 ⓘ

vicolo delle Palline 24 ✉ *00193* – 🚇 *Ottaviano-San Pietro*
– 𝒞 *06 68806426* – *www.hotelbramante.com*   **K2**
16 rm 🖵 – 🕴50/170 € 🕴🕴80/250 €
♦ Traditional ♦ Classic ♦

This historic hotel is situated in the heart of the typical, pedestrianised Borgo district. The oldest sections date back to the 15C.

La Pergola – Hotel Rome Cavalieri Waldorf Astoria   ≤ 🏠 🔥 🖼
✿✿✿ *via Cadlolo 101* ✉ *00136* – 𝒞 *06 35092152*   ⇔ **P** 🆚 💳 🅰🅴 ⓘ
– *www.romecavalieri.com*
– *Closed 5-20 August, 1-23 January, Sunday and Monday*   *Plan I* **A2**
Rest – *(dinner only) (booking essential)* Menu 175 € – Carte 125/183 € 🕸
♦ Creative ♦ Luxury ♦

German chef Heinz Beck is more Italian than many of his colleagues! Served in the panoramic roof garden, the cuisine here is Roman and Mediterranean, and the service both attentive and professional.

➜ Infuso di erbe e fava di Tonka con tartare di tonno e sorbetto al tè verde. Merluzzo nero con salsa di sedano e crosta al curry. Sfera ghiacciata ai frutti rossi su crema al tè con lamponi cristallizzati.

ⵝⵝ **Enoteca Costantini-Il Simposio** `AC` `VISA` `ⓒⓞ` `AE`

piazza Cavour 16 ✉ 00193 – **Ⓜ** *Lepanto –* ✆ *06 32111131*
– www.pierocostantini.it
– Closed August, Saturday lunch and Sunday *Plan II* **E2**
Rest – Menu 40/70 € – Carte 49/98 € ⅜
♦ Creative ♦ Formal ♦

An evocative wrought-iron vine marks the entrance to this restaurant-cum-wine bar, which serves specialities such as foie gras, as well as a selection of different cheeses, accompanied by a glass of wine.

ITALY - ROME

PARIOLI   *Plan IV*

🏨 **Grand Hotel Parco dei Principi**   `←` `🛏` `🛗` `👶` `🐾` `🏊` `🗄` `♿`
via Gerolamo Frescobaldi 5 ✉ 00198   `AC` `📶` `🛁` `🚗` `VISA` `ⓒⓞ` `AE` `Ⓘ`
– ✆ 06 854421 – www.parcodeiprincipi.com **M2**
165 rm – 🛇205/415 € 🛇🛇245/540 €, ⚏ 23 € – 14 suites
Rest *Pauline Borghese* – see restaurant listing
♦ Grand Luxury ♦ Classic ♦

This hotel is situated in a quiet, residential district not far from the Villa Borghese gardens. The dome of St Peter's is visible from the top floor rooms. Wood panelling, carpets and reproductions of famous paintings contribute to the luxurious ambience, while the 2 000m² spa offers all the latest treatments and technology.

🏨 **Aldrovandi Villa Borghese**   `🚗` `🛗` `🏊` `♿` `AC` `📶` `🛁` `P`
via Ulisse Aldrovandi 15 ✉ 00197 – ✆ 06 3223993   `VISA` `ⓒⓞ` `AE` `Ⓘ`
– www.aldrovandi.com **M2**
108 rm ⚏ – 🛇200/600 € 🛇🛇200/800 € – 16 suites
Rest *Oliver Glowig* ❀❀ – see restaurant listing
♦ Luxury ♦ Classic ♦

Off the beaten track, yet exclusive, this hotel situated in a smart district a stone's throw from the Villa Borghese boasts classic rooms, the best of which have been recently renovated.

🏨 **Lord Byron**   `❦` `AC` `📶` `VISA` `ⓒⓞ` `AE` `Ⓘ`
via G. De Notaris 5 ✉ 00197 – **Ⓜ** *Flaminio –* ✆ *06 3220404*
– www.lordbyronhotel.com **L-M1**
26 rm ⚏ – 🛇200/413 € 🛇🛇210/542 € – 6 suites
Rest *Sapori del Lord Byron* – see restaurant listing
♦ Luxury ♦ Art Deco ♦

Situated just a few metres from the greenery of the Villa Borghese gardens, this elegant aristocratic hotel is adorned with Art Deco features. The guestrooms and public areas have been carefully decorated with fabrics and furniture that bring out the original character of the building.

🏨 **The Duke Hotel**   `♿` rm, `AC` `📶` `🛁` `🚗` `VISA` `ⓒⓞ` `AE` `Ⓘ`
via Archimede 69 ✉ 00197 – ✆ 06 367221
– www.thedukehotel.com **L1**
78 rm ⚏ – 🛇110/340 € 🛇🛇160/420 € – 7 suites
Rest – Carte 51/78 €
♦ Traditional ♦ Classic ♦

Situated in a quiet residential area, this hotel has the discreet, muted atmosphere of an elegant English club. Decorated in typical period style, but with all the latest modern comforts. Afternoon tea is served in front of the fireplace. Italian and international dishes are reinterpreted with a creative flair at this restaurant.

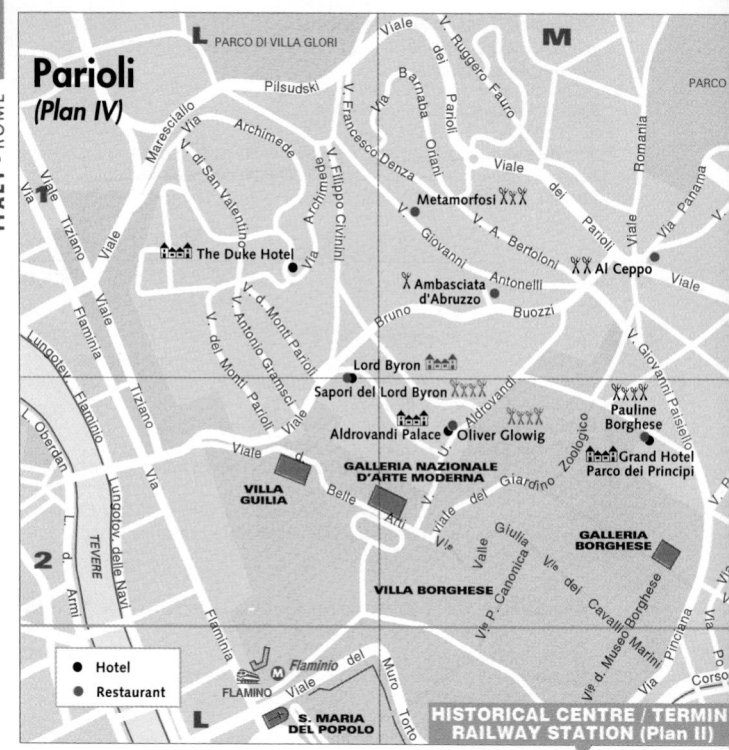

Parioli
(Plan IV)

🏨 **Villa Morgagni** without rest   🕌 🔥 🅰️ 🛜 🅿️ 🚗 📶 ⓿ 🅰️🄴 ⓪

via G.B. Morgagni 25 ✉️ *00161 –* Ⓜ️ *Policlinico – ℰ 06 44202190*
– www.villamorgagni.it   **O2**

34 rm ⬚ – 🛏75/150 € 🛏🛏90/250 €

♦ Luxury ♦ Classic ♦

Private and quiet in an elegant Art Nouveau setting with comfortable rooms. In summer or winter, the first meal of the day is prepared in the panoramic roof garden.

XXXX **Oliver Glowig** – Hotel Aldrovandi Villa Borghese   🏡 🅰️ 🅿️

💠💠 *via Ulisse Aldrovandi 15* ✉️ *00197*   📶 ⓿ 🅰️🄴 ⓪
– ℰ 06 3216126
– www.oliverglowig.com
– Closed 7 January-28 February and Sunday, also Monday from October-May

Rest – Menu 110/130 € – Carte 96/146 €   **M2**

♦ Creative ♦ Elegant ♦

Originally from Germany, the chef at this restaurant is one of the best interpreters of Italian cuisine. He demonstrates a real passion for fish and seafood, as well as a typical Roman love for offal dishes. Charming outdoor dining area surrounded by century-old trees.

➜ Eliche cacio e pepe con ricci di mare. Quaglia e fegato grasso d'oca in croccante frutta secca con sedano. Macaron al wasabi con crema di patata dolce e soia.

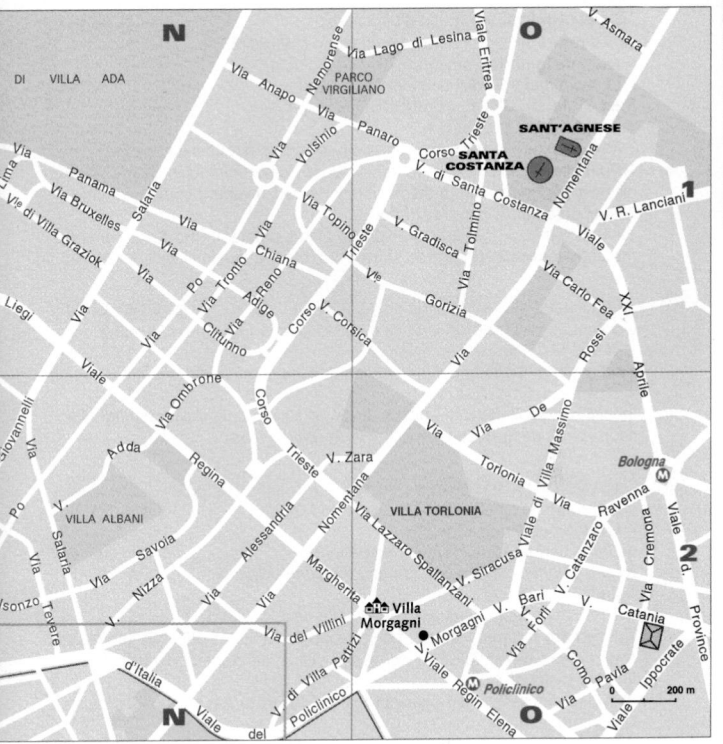

XXXX **Sapori del Lord Byron** – Hotel Lord Byron   🅰🅺 ✚
via G. De Notaris 5 ✉ *00197*   🆅🅸🆂🅰 ⦿ 🅰🅴 ⓪
– Ⓜ *Flaminio*
– ℰ *06 3220404*
– *www.lordbyronhotel.com*
– *Closed lunch Monday and Sunday*   **L-M1**
Rest – Menu 50 € – Carte 46/69 €
 ♦ Modern ♦ Luxury ♦
Be prepared to be stunned by the opulence of this luxury restaurant, which is
adorned with mirrors, paintings and white marble. The skills of the chef com-
bine with a respect for tradition to bring out the very best of Italian cuisine.
The menu includes original dishes such as carpaccio of beetroot with crayfish
and wasabi.

XXXX **Pauline Borghese** – Grand Hotel Parco dei Principi   🚗 🏠 ♿
via Gerolamo Frescobaldi 5 ✉ *00198*   🅰🅺 ✚ 🆅🅸🆂🅰 ⦿ 🅰🅴 ⓪
– ℰ *06 85442804*
– *www.parcodeiprincipi.com*   **M2**
Rest – Carte 55/62 €
 ♦ International ♦ Classic ♦
Well-prepared, eclectic dishes influenced by Mediterranean, classic French and
international cuisine are served in a delightful dining room overlooking an
Italian-style garden. Typical hotel-restaurant ambience.

ITALY - ROME

✕✕✕ Metamorfosi (Roy Caceres)   🔲 ⇕ 💳 ⓒ AE ①
❀

via Giovanni Antonelli 30/32 ✉ *00197 –* ☎ *06 8076839*
– www.metamorfosiroma.it
– Closed August, Sunday and lunch Saturday   M1
Rest – Menu 70/90 € – Carte 59/95 €

♦ Creative ♦ Design ♦

With a clean design and comfortable feel, this modern restaurant opened in late 2010 is already one of the most renowned in Rome. Colombian chef Roy adds his own personal touch to the expertly prepared, inventive cuisine, creating a host of occasionally complex dishes.

→ Mont Blanc di foie gras. Manzo alla pietra, patate al "pro-fumo" di noce moscata, tartufo e salsa verde. Cioccolato, banane caramellate e Armagnac.

✕✕ Al Ceppo   🔲 💳 ⓒ AE ①

via Panama 2 ✉ *00198 –* ☎ *06 8551379 – www.ristorantealceppo.it*
– Closed 12-25 August   M1
Rest – Carte 45/83 € ⅍

♦ Italian ♦ Rustic ♦

Innovative Mediterranean cuisine served in an elegantly rustic setting. Main courses include meat and fish grilled in the dining room.

✕✕ Acquolina Hostaria in Roma (Giulio Terrinoni)   🏠 🔲 ⇕
❀

via Antonio Serra 60 ✉ *00191 –* ☎ *06 3337192*   💳 ⓒ AE ①
– www.acquolinahostaria.it
– Closed Christmas Holidays, 10 days August   Plan I **B1**
Rest – *(dinner only except Sunday) (booking advisable)* Menu 58/100 €
– Carte 59/115 € ⅍

♦ Fish and seafood ♦ Cosy ♦

This recently restored restaurant on the outskirts of Rome offers an impressive choice of raw fish antipasti, as well as more elaborate dishes. Unequalled for its fish and seafood!

→ Spaghettone alla carbonara di mare. Gran fritto Acquolina. Ricotta, visciole, limone, miele.

✕✕ Mamma Angelina   🏠 🔲 💳 ⓒ AE
☺

viale Arrigo Boito 65 ✉ *00199 –* ☎ *06 8608928*
– Closed August and Wednesday   Plan I **C1**
Rest – Menu 25 € – Carte 23/38 € ⅍

♦ Fish and seafood ♦ Formal ♦

After the antipasto buffet, the cuisine in this restaurant follows two distinct styles – fish and seafood, or Roman specialities. The paccheri pasta with seafood and fresh tomatoes sits in both camps!

✕ Ambasciata d'Abruzzo   🏠 🔲 💳 ⓒ AE ①
☺

via Pietro Tacchini 26 ✉ *00197 –* Ⓜ *Euclide –* ☎ *06 8078256*
– www.ambasciatadiabruzzo.com
– Closed 5-26 August   M1
Rest – *(pre-book)* Carte 29/63 €

♦ Abruzzian ♦ Rustic ♦

This family-run trattoria in the heart of a residential district seems to appear from nowhere. The menu focuses on cuisine from the Abruzzo region, as well as fish dishes and specialities from Lazio, such as the famous maccheroni alla chitarra cacio e pepe (pasta with cheese and pepper).

FLORENCE
FIRENZE

Population: 371 282

Giovanni Simeone/Sime/Photononstop

Florence has always stood for beauty, and represents Italy's greatest contribution to the world of arts: the Renaissance. It is said that Cupid lives in Florence and it's hard to imagine a city more romantic than this; lovers visit from around the world, while those not yet in love are thought to find their match here. Florence is surrounded by a ring of hills, and winding streets flanked with cypress and olive trees lead you to the heart of Dante's beloved hometown. The city centre and many of its monuments lie on the northern side of the Arno, a river closely connected with Florence's history and celebrated by poets throughout the years. The river is crossed by many delightful bridges, Ponte Vecchio being the most famous, but, despite its charm, the Arno has in the past wreaked havoc in the form of regular flooding, which has caused huge amounts of damage.

In each area of Florence, civic and religious powers occupy their own distinct site. Piazza della Signoria is home to the town hall, while the Duomo sits in the piazza of the same name at the end of Via Calzaiuoli, the city's most famous shopping street. Cross one of the bridges to the south side of the city for a more relaxed, village-like atmosphere; here you will find the Palazzo Pitti and the Giardino di Boboli. Walking eastwards will bring you to the Piazzale Michelangelo, which boasts probably the best views in Florence.

FLORENCE IN...

→ ONE DAY
Piazza della Signoria, Via Calzaiuoli, the Duomo, Santa Croce, Ponte Vecchio.

→ TWO DAYS
The Uffizi, Santa Maria Novella, San Lorenzo.

→ THREE DAYS
Palazzo Pitti/Galleria Palatina, Giardino di Boboli, Santa Maria del Carmine, Piazzale Michelangelo.

PRACTICAL INFORMATION

ARRIVAL-DEPARTURE

✈ Amerigo Vespucci, Florence's airport, lies 5km outside of the city. A bus will take you to the Santa Maria Novella Railway Station.

GETTING AROUND

If you are staying in the city centre, the best and most interesting way to see Florence is by foot, as most of the sights are within easy walking distance. Alternatively, one of the municipal orange buses will take you everywhere you need. There are two main tourist offices in Florence; one is in Piazza Stazione (Santa Maria Novella), 4/a; the other is in Via Cavour 1r.

CALENDAR HIGHLIGHTS

January
Pitti Immagine Fashion Fair.

February
Carnival.

April
Easter Sunday Celebration in the Piazza del Duomo, Arts and Crafts exhibition.

May
Trofeo Marzocco (flag-waving competition).

June
Festa di San Giovanni (Feast of St John the Baptist – fireworks and a football match).

August
Festa di San Lorenzo (Feast of St Lawrence).

September
Festa della Rificolona (paper lantern festival).

November
Florence Marathon.

EATING OUT

Tuscan food is one of the most famous and highly regarded of Italy's regional cuisines, and it will come as no surprise to learn that some of the best examples are to be found here in Florence. Soups are particularly renowned; don't miss pappa col pomodoro – made with bread and tomatoes – or ribollita – made from cannellini, a local variety of beans, black cabbage, bread and other vegetables. Pasta can certainly not be ignored; pappardelle con la lepre (with hare) and pici (a sort of spaghetti) are two of the most popular.

Meat is a favourite for second courses: the fiorentina, a grilled T-bone steak which takes its name from the city, has now become a favourite nationwide. Restaurants in tourist areas can be very pricey – for a quick, inexpensive meal you're better off opting for a pizza. Wines are equally important in Florence as the cooking: a Chianti, a Morellino di Scansano or a Nobile di Montepulciano will give you good value for money but, if price is not an issue, opt for the Super Tuscans – Ornellaia, Sassicaia, Solaia or Tignanello.

ITALY - FLORENCE

The Westin Excelsior   Ló ఉ 🕅 🛜 🔊 VISA ෮ AE ①
piazza Ognissanti 3 ⊠ *50123* – ℰ *055 27151* – *www.westinflorence.com*
155 rm – †400/800 € ††400/800 €, ⊆ 39 € – 16 suites   **C2**
Rest *SE.STO* – see restaurant listing
♦ Grand Luxury ♦ Palace ♦ Historic ♦

Sumptuous interiors of an old nobleman's dwelling on the Arno, where history
and tradition combine with more modern accessories for an exclusive aristocratic stay. The dining hall of this restaurant is princely. Among its features are the
boxed ceilings and decor in Carrara marble.

Four Seasons Hotel Firenze   🕅 Ló ⊛ 🕅 ఉ 🕅 🛜 🔊
borgo Pinti 99 – ℰ *055 2626470*   VISA ෮ AE ①
98 rm – †595/895 € ††595/895 €, ⊆ 38 € – 18 suites   **F2**
Rest *Il Palagio* ❀ – see restaurant listing
Rest *Trattoria al Fresco* – (open 1° May-30 September) Carte 50/80 €
♦ Chain hotel ♦ Grand Luxury ♦ Historic ♦

Situated in attractive botanical gardens, this hotel comprises of two buildings,
the 'Palazzo della Gherardesca' and the 'Conventino'. Both are extremely elegant with frescoes, low reliefs and silk-papered walls forming part of the decor.
The Palagio restaurant serves gourmet cuisine, while lighter meals are available
in the Al Fresco. A truly exclusive place to stay.

The St. Regis Florence   Ló 🕅 ఉ rm, 🕅 🛜 🔊 VISA ෮ AE
piazza Ognissanti 1 ⊠ *50123* – ℰ *055 27161* – *www.stregisflorence.com*
89 rm – †750/1180 € ††990/1250 €, ⊆ 39 € – 11 suites   **C2**
Rest – Carte 63/88 €
♦ Grand Luxury ♦ Historic ♦ Personalised ♦

This hotel is even more luxurious and exclusive after its recent renovation. It
offers spacious guestrooms, where modern accessories provide a contrast with
the classic decor of frescoes, Murano glass chandeliers and antique furniture.

Savoy   🕅 Ló ఉ 🕅 🛜 🔊 VISA ෮ AE ①
piazza della Repubblica 7 ⊠ *50123* – ℰ *055 27351* – *www.hotelsavoy.it*
102 rm – †315/470 € ††382/570 €, ⊆ 30 € – 14 suites   **D2**
Rest *L'Incontro* – ℰ *055 2735891* – Carte 49/88 €
♦ Luxury ♦ Palace ♦ Historic ♦

This elegant, historic hotel is situated near the Duomo, the city's museums and
luxury fashion boutiques. It offers spacious, comfortable guestrooms with
mosaic adorned bathrooms.

Montebello Splendid   🚗 🕅 ఉ 🕅 🛜 🔊 VISA ෮ AE ①
via Garibaldi 14 ⊠ *50123* – ℰ *055 27471* – *www.montebellosplendid.com*
58 rm ⊆ – †180/380 € ††235/650 € – 3 suites   **C2**
Rest – Carte 45/79 €
♦ Traditional ♦ Functional ♦ Modern ♦

This stylishly modern hotel is the much frequented haunt of tourists and business people; common areas are spacious and attractively furnished and give
onto a delightful internal garden.

Relais Santa Croce   🕅 🛜 VISA ෮ AE ①
via Ghibellina 87 ⊠ *50122* – ℰ *055 2342230* – *www.relaisantacroce.com*
21 rm ⊆ – †300/350 € ††400/700 € – 3 suites   **E3**
Rest – Carte 49/95 €
♦ Palace ♦ Personalised ♦

This hotel forms part of an 18th century mansion that also houses the famous
Pinchiorri Wine library; it is characterised by a fascinating atmosphere, frescoed
halls and elegantly furnished rooms. The passion for old recipes and Tuscan
herbs and flavours are evident in this restaurant.

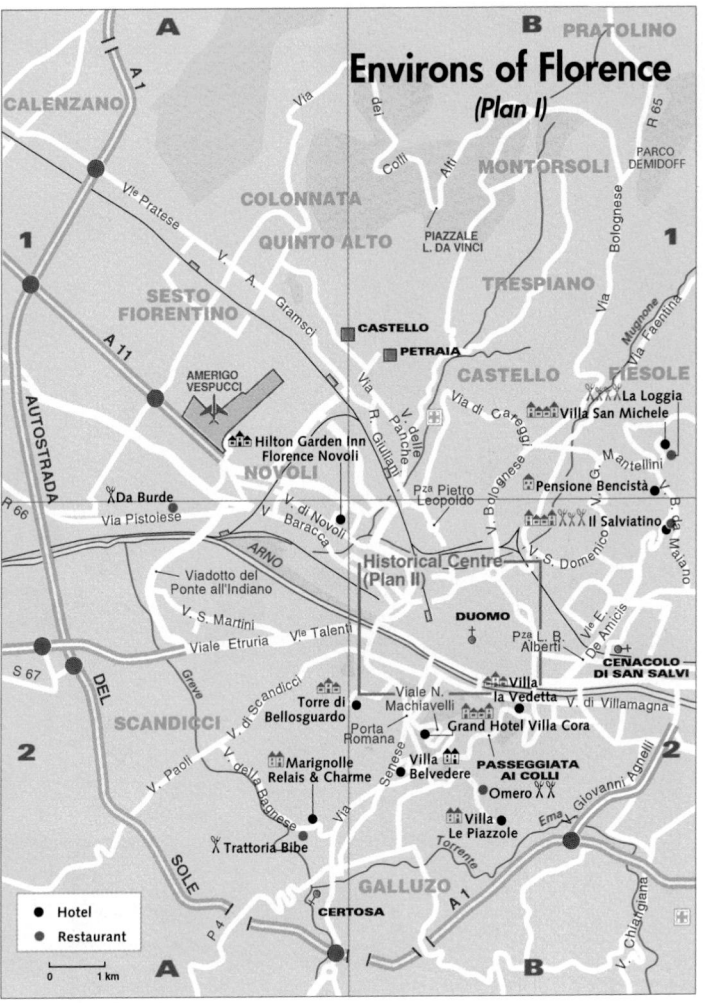

Environs of Florence
(Plan I)

A **B** PRATOLINO

CALENZANO

Via dei Colli

MONTORSOLI

PARCO DEMIDOFF

R 65

1

COLONNATA

PIAZZALE L. DA VINCI

QUINTO ALTO

TRESPIANO

1

Vle Pratese

V. A. Gramsci

SESTO FIORENTINO

A 11

AUTOSTRADA

AMERIGO VESPUCCI

CASTELLO

PETRAIA

CASTELLO

FIESOLE

La Loggia

Villa San Michele

R 66

Hilton Garden Inn Florence Novoli

NOVOLI

V. delle Panche

V. di Careggi

M. antellini

Pensione Bencistà

Da Burde

Via Pistolese

V. di Novoli

V. Baracca

Pza Pietro Leopoldo

V. Bolognese

Il Salvatino

B. di Maiano

ARNO

Viadotto del Ponte all'Indiano

Historical Centre (Plan II)

V. S. Domenico

V. E. De Amicis

S 67

V. S. Martini

Viale Etruria

Vle Talenti

DUOMO

Pza L. B. Alberti

CENACOLO DI SAN SALVI

DEL

Greve

V. di Scandicci

Torre di Bellosguardo

Viale N. Machiavelli

Villa la Vedetta

V. di Villamagna

2

SCANDICCI

Porta Romana

Grand Hotel Villa Cora

2

V. Paoli

V. della Bagnese

Marignolle Relais & Charme

V. Senese

Villa Belvedere

PASSEGGIATA AI COLLI

Omero

SOLE

P. 4

Trattoria Bibe

Villa Le Piazzole

V. Ema Giovanni Agnelli

Torrente

GALLUZO

A 1

V. Chiargiana

CERTOSA

A **B**

● Hotel
● Restaurant

0 ————— 1 km

🏨 **Regency** 🚗 AC 🛜 🍴 VISA ⑤ AE ①

piazza Massimo D'Azeglio 3 ✉ *50121*
– ✆ *055 245247*
– *www.regency-hotel.com* **F2**
31 rm ⬝ – 🛏200/413 € – 🛏🛏210/542 € – 3 suites
Rest *Relais le Jardin* – see restaurant listing

◆ Luxury ◆ Personalised ◆

This elegant hotel was built to offer accommodation to local political figures. It boasts a tranquil, comfortable atmosphere and has retained much of its traditional charm.

513

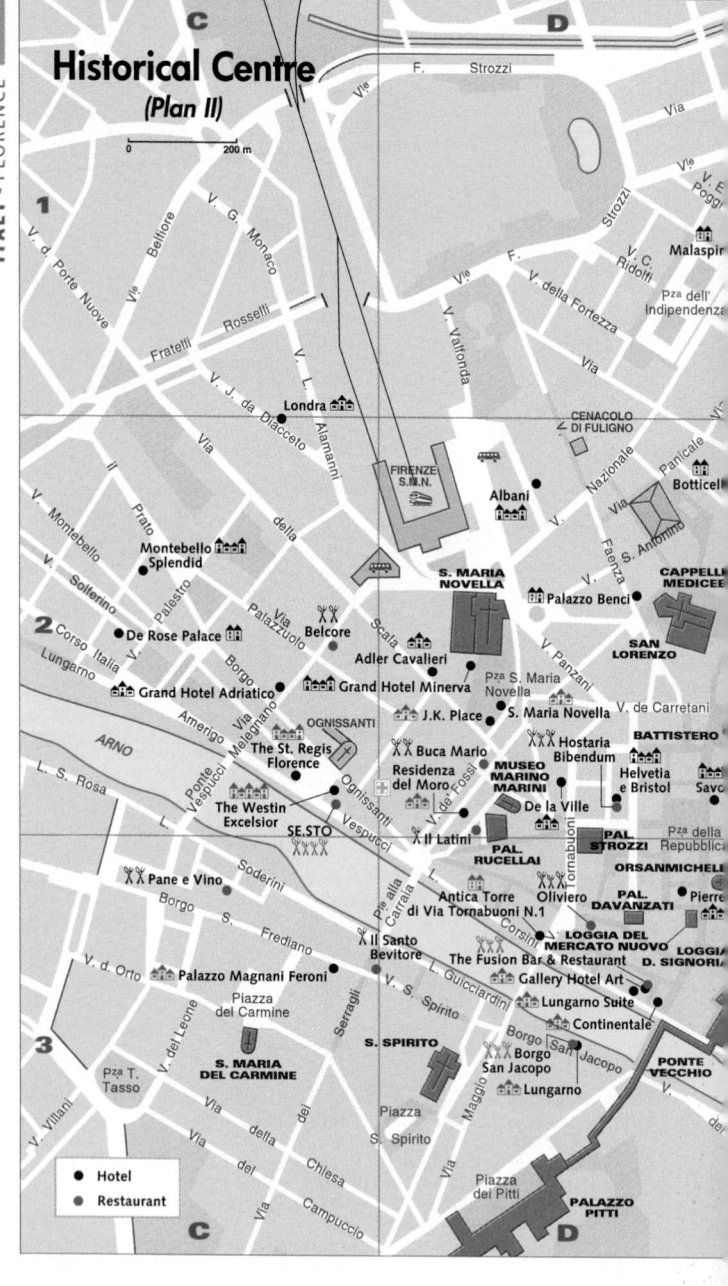

Historical Centre
(Plan II)

0 ——— 200 m

C
D

F. Strozzi

V^{le}

Via

V^{le} E. Poggi

V. C. Ridolfi

Malaspir

Pza dell' Indipendenza

V. d. Porte Nuove

Belfiore

V. G. Monaco

Rosselli

Fratelli

V. L.

V. J. da Diacceto

della

Londra 🏨

FIRENZE S.M.N.

CENACOLO DI FULIGNO

Nazionale

Panicale

Botticell

Albani 🏨

Via

S. Antonino

Faenza

CAPPELLE MEDICEE

Il Prato

V. Montebello

V. Solferino

Montebello Splendid 🏨

De Rose Palace 🏨

Palestro

Corso Italia

Lungarno

Via Palazzuolo

Borgo

Belcore ✗✗

Adler Cavalieri

S. MARIA NOVELLA

🏨 Palazzo Benci

V. Panzani

SAN LORENZO

Pza S. Maria Novella

Grand Hotel Minerva 🏨

V. de Carretani

Grand Hotel Adriatico 🏨

ARNO

L. S. Rosa

Amerigo

Via Melarancio

Ponte Vespucci

Borgo

OGNISSANTI

The St. Regis Florence 🏨

The Westin Excelsior 🏨

Ognissanti

SE.STO ✗✗✗

Vespucci

L.

🏨 J.K. Place   S. Maria Novella 🏨

BATTISTERO

✗✗ Buca Mario

Residenza del Moro

MUSEO MARINO MARINI

V. de Fossi

✗✗✗ Hostaria Bibendum

Helvetia e Bristol 🏨

Savo

De la Ville 🏨

✗ Il Latini

Pza della Repubblica

PAL. STROZZI

ORSANMICHELE

✗✗ Pane e Vino

Soderini

Borgo   S. Frediano

V. d. Orto

Palazzo Magnani Feroni 🏨

Pza T. Tasso

V. del Leone

V. Villani

S. MARIA DEL CARMINE

Piazza del Carmine

✗ Il Santo Bevitore

P^{te} alla Caraia

Antica Torre di Via Tornabuoni N.1 🏨

Oliviero ✗✗✗

The Fusion Bar & Restaurant

Corso

Tornabuoni

PAL. RUCELLAI

PAL. DAVANZATI

LOGGIA DEL MERCATO NUOVO

Gallery Hotel Art 🏨

Pierre

LOGGIA D. SIGNORIA

V. Guicciardini

Lungarno Suite 🏨

Continentale 🏨

Borgo San Jacopo

V. S. Spirito

S. SPIRITO

Serragli

Maggio

✗✗✗ Borgo San Jacopo

Lungarno 🏨

PONTE VECCHIO

Via   del

V. del Leone

Via   della   Chiesa

Via   del   Campuccio

Piazza S. Spirito

Piazza dei Pitti

PALAZZO PITTI

● Hotel
● Restaurant

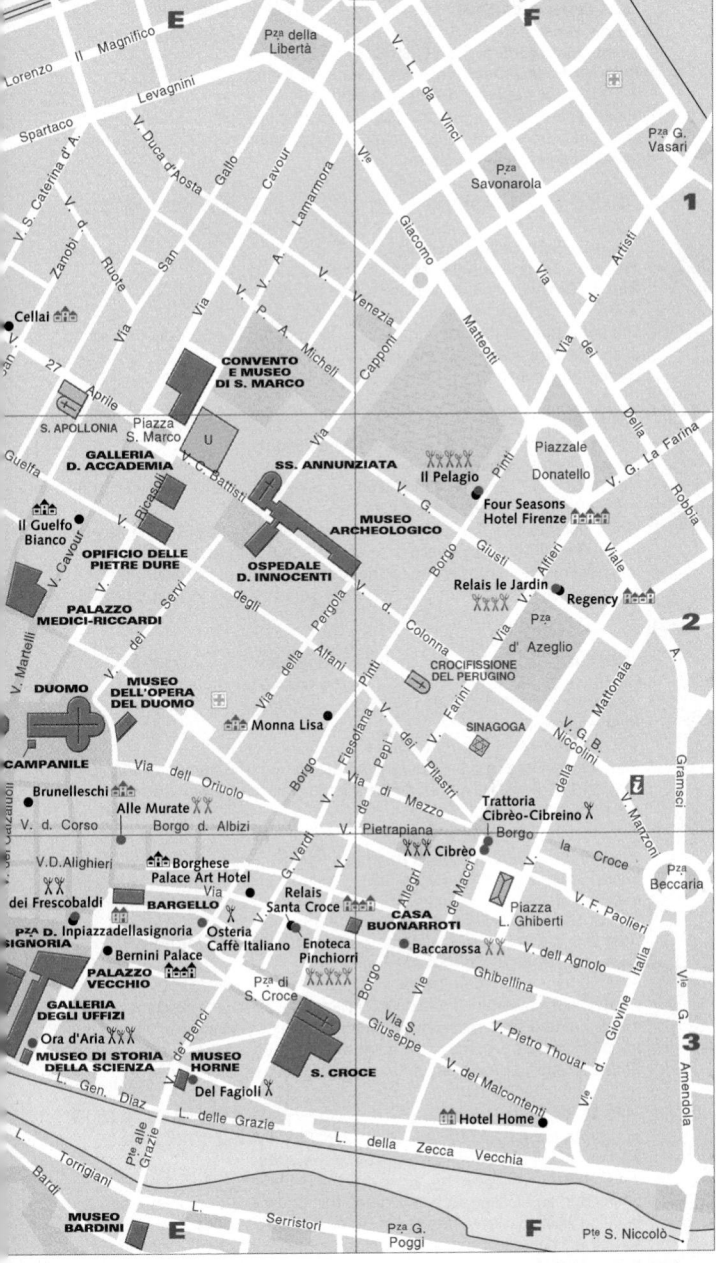

ITALY - FLORENCE

Helvetia e Bristol ⬚ 🛜 VISA ⊙⊙ AE ⓪
via dei Pescioni 2 ⬚ *50123 –* 𝒞 *055 26651 – www.royaldemeure.com*
67 rm ⬚ – †385/506 € ††539/825 € – 15 suites   **D2**
Rest *Hostaria Bibendum* – see restaurant listing
♦ Palace ♦ Luxury ♦ Personalised ♦
Situated near the Duomo and Palazzo Strozzi, this elegant 19C hotel evokes the
charm of bygone days. It has personalised guestrooms decorated with period
paintings and antique furniture.

Grand Hotel Minerva ⬚ ⅃ ⅍ ⬚ 🛜 ⅍ VISA ⊙⊙ AE ⓪
piazza Santa Maria Novella 16 ⬚ *50123 –* 𝒞 *055 27230*
– www.grandhotelminerva.com   **D2**
102 rm ⬚ – †120/300 € ††180/500 € – 5 suites
Rest *I Chiostri* – *(closed Sunday)* Carte 47/99 €
♦ Palace ♦ Modern ♦
This hotel is one of the oldest in the city. Elegantly furnished guestrooms, works
of art, a terrace with a swimming pool and fine views all contribute to the welcoming atmosphere.

Bernini Palace ⬚ 🛜 ⅍ VISA ⊙⊙ AE ⓪
piazza San Firenze 29 ⬚ *50122 –* 𝒞 *055 288621*
– www.duetorrihotels.com   **E3**
74 rm ⬚ – †130/250 € ††150/350 € – 5 suites   **Rest** – Carte 36/108 €
♦ Historic ♦ Personalised ♦
When Florence was the capital of Italy, members of parliament and senators
would meet in the Sala Parlamento of this hotel. With its spacious corridors,
magnificent guestrooms (those on the Tuscan Floor are particularly impressive),
and an excellent restaurant, this hotel now attracts visitors looking for the highest quality.

Albani 🛖 ⅃ 🐾 ⬚ ⬚ 🛜 ⅍ VISA ⊙⊙ AE ⓪
via Fiume 12 ⬚ *50123 –* 𝒞 *055 26030 – www.albanihotels.com*
96 rm ⬚ – †100/400 € ††120/450 € – 2 suites   **D2**
Rest – Carte 29/62 €
♦ Traditional ♦ Functional ♦
Near the station, in a prestigious palace dating from the start of the 20th Century, strict neo-classical refined features in the Imperial style ambience of an extremely fascinating hotel.

Brunelleschi ⇐ ⅃ ⅍ rm, ⬚ 🛜 ⅍ VISA ⊙⊙ AE ⓪
piazza Santa Elisabetta 3 ⬚ *50122 –* 𝒞 *055 27370*
– www.hotelbrunelleschi.it   **E2**
82 rm ⬚ – †234/674 € ††262/699 € – 13 suites
Rest *Santa Elisabetta* – *(closed Sunday) (dinner only)* Carte 54/97 €
Rest *Osteria della Pagliazza* – Carte 54/71 €
♦ Historic ♦ Functional ♦
Housed in the Byzantine Torre della Pagliazza, this hotel with welcoming guestrooms boasts a small museum with Roman remains. A dining room partly enclosed by old walls is home to the gourmet Santa Elisabetta restaurant, while the
hotel also offers bistro dining in the elegant Osteria della Pagliazza.

De la Ville *without rest* ⬚ 📞 ⅍ VISA ⊙⊙ AE ⓪
piazza Antinori 1 ⬚ *50123 –* 𝒞 *055 2381805 – www.hoteldelaville.it*
54 rm ⬚ – †100/280 € ††120/420 € – 14 suites   **D2**
♦ Historic ♦ Classic ♦
Situated in an elegant shopping street, this luxury hotel occupies a historical
building which has been restored in classic modern style. Spacious guestrooms,
as well as a new collection of suites and junior suites which will delight the most
demanding of guests. Superb 180m^2 penthouse with a large terrace and 360°
views of the city.

ITALY - FLORENCE

Lungarno ⟨ 🄰🄲 📶 🏋 VISA ⓒⓞ 🄰🄴 ⓞ
borgo San Jacopo 14 ✉ *50125* – ℰ *055 281661*
– www.lungarnocollection.com   **D3**
70 rm – ♦160/350 € ♦♦240/750 €, ☷ 25 € – 3 suites
Rest *Borgo San Jacopo* – see restaurant listing
♦ Luxury ♦ Personalised ♦ Classic ♦
The name of this hotel situated between Ponte Vecchio and Santa Trinità refers to its excellent location overlooking the River Arno. Every corner of the hotel is stylish and elegant. It has numerous terraces and balconies and many of the guestrooms offer views of the river.

J.K. Place Firenze without rest ⟨ 🄰🄲 📶 VISA ⓒⓞ 🄰🄴
piazza Santa Maria Novella 7 ✉ *50123* – ℰ *055 2645181*
– www.jkplace.com   **D2**
17 rm ☷ – ♦380 € ♦♦380 € – 3 suites
♦ Grand Luxury ♦ Historic ♦
This stylish hotel overlooks the historical Piazza Santa Maria Novella. Recently restored by the architect Michele Bönan, the building now offers a surprising mix of luxury and individual details which combine to create an elegant, yet welcoming atmosphere.

Continentale without rest 🕭 🕭 🄰🄲 📶 VISA ⓒⓞ 🄰🄴 ⓞ
vicolo dell'Oro 6 r ✉ *50123* – ℰ *055 27262* – *www.lungarnocollection.com*
43 rm – ♦180/700 € ♦♦180/700 €, ☷ 25 € – 1 suite   **D3**
♦ Traditional ♦ Modern ♦
This hotel has been built up around a medieval tower. There is a fine view of the Ponte Vecchio from the flower-filled terrace and from some of the attractively furnished rooms.

Santa Maria Novella without rest ⟨ 🛏 🕭 🕭 🄰🄲 📶
piazza Santa Maria Novella 1 ✉ *50123*   VISA ⓒⓞ 🄰🄴 ⓞ
– ℰ 055 271840 – www.hotelsantamarianovella.it   **D2**
69 rm ☷ – ♦150/290 € ♦♦178/450 € – 2 suites
♦ Traditional ♦ Modern ♦
Overlooking Piazza Santa Maria Novella, this welcoming hotel offers small lounge areas and elegant guestrooms, all of which have different decor and furnishings. Enjoy superb views of this magical city from the hotel's delightful panoramic terrace.

Gallery Hotel Art 🕭 🄰🄲 📶 VISA ⓒⓞ 🄰🄴 ⓞ
vicolo dell'Oro 5 ✉ *50123* – ℰ *055 27263* – *www.lungarnocollection.com*
69 rm – ♦180/600 € ♦♦180/600 €, ☷ 25 € – 5 suites   **D3**
Rest *The Fusion Bar & Restaurant* – see restaurant listing
♦ Business ♦ Modern ♦
Contemporary design by a well known architect and cosmopolitan art exhibited as if in a museum, are the ingredients of the uniqueness and fascination of this really "modern" hotel. Decorated in the same contemporary style as the hotel, the restaurant serves "fusion cuisine". Fixed-price buffet at lunchtime with brunch served at the weekend.

Monna Lisa without rest 🕭 🕬 🛏 🄰🄲 📶 🏋 VISA ⓒⓞ 🄰🄴 ⓞ
via Borgo Pinti 27 ✉ *50121* – ℰ *055 2479751* – *www.monnalisa.it*
45 rm ☷ – ♦89/209 € ♦♦139/279 € – 4 suites   **E2**
♦ Luxury ♦ Historic ♦
Situated in the historic centre, this hotel occupies an original medieval palazzo with an imposing staircase, brick flooring and coffered ceilings. Rooms and communal areas have Renaissance-style furnishings. The newer rooms, which are just as elegant as the rest of the hotel, can be found in the two annexes in the splendid garden.

ITALY - FLORENCE

Londra

🛗 🕬 ᵹ 🄰🄲 📶 🛎 🄿 🚗 🆅🅸🆂🅰 🆆 🄰🄴 🄾

via Jacopo da Diacceto 18-20 ✉ 50123 – ✆ 055 27390
– www.concertohotels.com   C1-2

166 rm ☲ – 📍170/280 € 📍📍210/395 €   **Rest** – Carte 33/60 €

♦ Palace ♦ Modern ♦

Near the station - a recently constructed building which is both practical and comfortable, endowed with vast public areas, business centre and conference facilities; rooms with modern furnishings. Contemporary style dining room adjoining a patio with a more romantic atmosphere.

Borghese Palace Art Hotel without rest

🛗 🕬 ᵹ 🄰🄲 📞 🛎

via Ghibellina 174/r ✉ 50122 – ✆ 055 284363   🆅🅸🆂🅰 🆆 🄰🄴 🄾
– www.borghesepalace.com   E3

25 rm ☲ – 📍100/200 € 📍📍120/240 €

♦ Historic ♦ Functional ♦

Housed in the 19C mansion that was once the residence of Carolina Bonaparte, this attractive hotel blends classical elegance and modern furnishings, with contemporary art exhibitions often held in the public areas. The relaxation area is pretty and full of character.

Adler Cavalieri without rest

🛗 🕬 ᵹ 🄰🄲 📶 🛎 🆅🅸🆂🅰 🆆 🄰🄴

via della Scala 40 ✉ 50123 – ✆ 055 277810
– www.hoteladlercavalieri.com   D2

60 rm ☲ – 📍115/295 € 📍📍145/370 €

♦ Traditional ♦ Functional ♦

This pleasant hotel is located in the immediate vicinity of the station. The soundproofing is excellent and wood has been used to very good effect. The management is youthful and competent.

Grand Hotel Adriatico

🚗 ᵹ rm, 🄰🄲 📞 🛎 🄿 🆅🅸🆂🅰 🆆 🄰🄴

via Maso Finiguerra 9 ✉ 50123 – ✆ 055 27931 – www.hoteladriatico.it

126 rm ☲ – 📍80/230 € 📍📍100/350 € – 3 suites   C2

Rest *Opera* – *(closed Sunday)* Carte 25/65 €

♦ Traditional ♦ Functional ♦

Conveniently situated in the city centre, this hotel has a large lobby and modern guestrooms decorated in simple, yet elegant style. Tuscan and Italian cuisine is served in the quiet, recently renovated dining room, as well as in the attractive garden.

Lungarno Suites without rest

≤ ᵹ 🄰🄲 📶 🆅🅸🆂🅰 🆆 🄰🄴 🄾

lungarno Acciaiuoli 4 ✉ 50123 – ✆ 055 27268000
– www.lungarnocollection.com   D3

32 suites – 📍255/740 € 📍📍255/740 €, ☲ 25 €

♦ Luxury ♦ Functional ♦

As the name suggests, the rooms in this hotel are actually apartment suites with their own kitchen area. An ideal place for families and long-stay guests, as well as for visitors looking for spacious accommodation with hotel standard service.

Il Guelfo Bianco

ᵹ rm, 🄰🄲 rm, 📶 🆅🅸🆂🅰 🆆 🄰🄴 🄾

via Cavour 29 ✉ 50129 – ✆ 055 288330 – www.ilguelfobianco.it

40 rm ☲ – 📍90/155 € 📍📍99/250 €   E2

Rest *Il Desco* – *(lunch only)* Carte 23/42 €

♦ Traditional ♦ Personalised ♦

Situated in the heart of Medici Florence, this hotel offers contemporary-style public areas and spacious guestrooms, some of which have frescoes on the ceilings. Small bistro selling hot food from 12-3pm.

Palazzo Magnani Feroni without rest

🛗 🄰🄲 📶 🚗

borgo San Frediano 5 ✉ 50124 – ✆ 055 2399544   🆅🅸🆂🅰 🆆 🄰🄴
– www.palazzomagnaniferoni.it   C3

12 suites ☲ – 📍200/800 € 📍📍200/800 €

♦ Luxury ♦ Historic ♦

Located in the Oltrarno, inside a 16C building, centring on a small internal courtyard. Offering terraces with an all-round panoramic view of the city.

Cellai without rest   AC 🛜 ⚐ VISA ⦿ AE ⓪

via 27 Aprile 14 ✉ *50129 –* ☎ *055 489291 – www.hotelcellai.it*
68 rm ⌷ **– ♦110/169 € ♦♦110/249 €**   **E1**
♦ Traditional ♦ Classic ♦
This luxurious hotel in Florence offers a welcoming atmosphere, period furnishings and antique prints of plants and animals. The top floor is home to an attractive terrace decked with jasmine, which acts as an open-air lounge in which to relax and enjoy views of the city.

Residenza del Moro without rest   🚗 AC 🛜 VISA ⦿ AE ⓪

via del Moro 15 ✉ *50123 –* ☎ *055 290884 – www.residenzadelmoro.com*
6 rm ⌷ **– ♦250/350 € ♦♦305/810 € – 5 suites**   **D2**
♦ Luxury ♦ Personalised ♦
This palazzo built in the 16C for the marquises of Niccolini-Bourbon has been carefully restored to its former glory. Original frescoes and stunning contemporary works of art combine to create a luxurious hotel right in the centre of Florence.

Pierre without rest   ♿ AC 🛜 VISA ⦿ AE ⓪

via Dè Lamberti 5 ✉ *50123 –* ☎ *055 216218 – www.remarhotels.com*
49 rm ⌷ **– ♦180/370 € ♦♦180/370 € – 1 suite**   **D3**
♦ Traditional ♦ Classic ♦
Ancient façade and interiors, recently restored, in this comfortable hotel right in the historical centre; rooms have been recently refurbished but in a Florentine or Venetian style.

Antica Torre di via Tornabuoni N. 1 – Residenza d'epoca without

via Tornabuoni 1 ✉ *50123*   AC 🛜 VISA ⦿ AE ⓪
– ☎ *055 2658161 – www.tornabuoni1.com*   **D3**
17 rm ⌷ **– ♦260/600 € ♦♦260/600 € – 5 suites**
♦ Luxury ♦ Historic ♦
The hotel premises include the upper floors of the building. The rooms are spacious and bright and an outstanding feature is the breathtaking view from the two terraces of the entire town.

Home without rest   🛗 ♿ AC 🛜 ⚐ VISA ⦿ AE ⓪

piazza Piave 3 ✉ *50122 –* ☎ *055 243668 – www.hhflorence.it*
38 rm ⌷ **– ♦99/200 € ♦♦119/250 €**   **F3**
♦ Townhouse ♦ Design ♦
This charming small palazzo with a predominantly white decor has a young, fashionable feel while at the same time – as the name suggests – manages to retain a homely atmosphere. Breakfast is served on three shared tables.

De Rose Palace without rest   AC 🛜 VISA ⦿ AE

via Solferino 5 ✉ *50123 –* ☎ *055 2396818 – www.florencehotelderose.com*
18 rm ⌷ **– ♦90/200 € ♦♦120/260 €**   **C2**
♦ Traditional ♦ Classic ♦
In a renovated 19th Century building a hotel with a simple, elegant interior, with period style furnishings and beautiful Venetian lamps; pleasant family atmosphere.

Botticelli without rest   ♿ AC 🛜 VISA ⦿ AE ⓪

via Taddea 8 ✉ *50123 –* ☎ *055 290905 – www.hotelbotticelli.it*
34 rm ⌷ **– ♦70/150 € ♦♦120/240 € – 1 suite**   **D2**
♦ Traditional ♦ Classic ♦
Near to the S.Lorenzo market, in a 16th Century building, is a charming hotel with frescoes in the public areas and a small covered balcony; bedrooms recently refurbished.

Inpiazzadellasignoria – Residenza d'epoca without rest 🔳

via de' Magazzini 2 ⊠ *50122* – *☎ 055 2399546* 📶 💳 💳 📧 📧
– *www.inpiazzadellasignoria.com* **E3**
10 rm ☲ – **†**200/250 € **††**250/320 € – 2 suites
♦ Luxury ♦ Historic ♦

As the name implies, this establishment faces the Piazza della Signoria, the political centre of old Florence. It is welcoming and pleasantly elegant.

Malaspina without rest 🔳 🔳 📶 💳 💳 📧

piazza dell'Indipendenza 24 ⊠ *50129* – *☎ 055 489869*
– *www.malaspinahotel.it* **D1**
31 rm ☲ – **†**54/168 € **††**72/250 €
♦ Traditional ♦ Classic ♦

In the 13C the Malaspina family received Dante as their guest at the Castello di Fosdinovo. This tradition of hospitality is upheld by the descendants of the Malaspina, who run this 20C hotel decorated in period style. Spacious, well-equipped guestrooms.

Palazzo Benci without rest 🔳 🔳 📶 🔳 💳 💳 📧

piazza Madonna degli Aldobrandini 3 ⊠ *50123* – *☎ 055 213848*
– *www.palazzobenci.com*
– *Closed 1-26 August and 24-26 December* **D2**
35 rm ☲ – **†**60/140 € **††**90/195 €
♦ Traditional ♦ Classic ♦

This restored historic 16C palazzo, once the residence of the Benci family, now houses an elegant hotel with coffered ceilings and original bas-reliefs adorning the communal areas. The guestrooms are comfortable and furnished with modern elegance. Delightful inner courtyard.

Enoteca Pinchiorri (Annie Féolde) 🔳 🔳 ⟷ 💳 💳 📧

via Ghibellina 87 ⊠ *50122* – *☎ 055 242777* – *www.enotecapinchiorri.com*
– *Closed August, 18-27 December, Sunday, Monday* **E3**
Rest – *(dinner only) (booking advisable)* Carte 165/285 € ❀
♦ Modern ♦ Luxury ♦

One of Florence's temples of gourmet dining, this elegant restaurant boasts a legendary wine list that will delight wine enthusiasts. The chef uses Tuscan specialities as the inspiration for his highly skilful, imaginative and innovative cuisine.
➔ Uovo in camicia, burro alle acciughe e bietole all'aglio. Maialino di razza mora romagnola con pomodoro, zucchine, melanzane e cipolla fondente. Arancia di Sicilia in gelatina di litchi, morbido alle fave di Tonka e cremoso di cioccolato.

Il Palagio – Four Seasons Hotel Firenze 🔳 🔳 🔳 🔳 🔳

borgo Pinti 99 ⊠ *50121* – *☎ 055 2626450* 💳 💳 📧 📧
– *www.fourseasons.com/florence*
– *Closed January, February and Sunday* **F2**
Rest – *(dinner only)* Menu 75 € – Carte 151/203 € ❀
♦ Luxury ♦ Elegant ♦ Creative ♦

Admire the high, vaulted ceilings and majestic chandeliers of this restaurant housed in the old Palazzo della Gherardesca. Attentive service, as well as deliciously eclectic cuisine created by a talented chef.
➔ Insalata di lesso rifatto con tartufo nero. Cavatelli cacio e pepe con gamberi rossi marinati e calamaretti spillo. Soufflé al Cassis con gelato al fior di latte.

SE.STO – Hotel The Westin Excelsior 🔳 🔳 ⟷ 💳 💳 📧 📧

piazza Ognissanti 3 ⊠ *50123* – *☎ 055 27151* – *www.westinflorence.com*
Rest – *(booking advisable)* Menu 28 € (weekday lunch)/120 € **C2**
– Carte 48/90 €
♦ Modern ♦ Formal ♦

This restaurant boasts the highest terrace in Florence, offering stunning views of the Duomo, Giotto's bell tower, the Palazzo della Signoria and Ponte Vecchio. The Mediterranean cuisine, which is reinterpreted with a contemporary twist, provides a real treat for the taste buds.

ITALY - FLORENCE

XXXX **Relais le Jardin** – Hotel Regency
piazza Massimo D'Azeglio 3 ✉ *50121* – ☎ *055 245247*
– www.regency-hotel.com   **F2**
Rest – Carte 50/79 €
♦ Italian ♦ Luxury ♦
Whether you choose to dine in the elegantly furnished Sala Zodiaco or in the
Veranda overlooking the private garden, you are sure to enjoy the cuisine at
this restaurant. It combines excellent Tuscan traditions with a light contemporary touch.

XXX **Ora D'Aria** (Marco Stabile)
✿ *via de' Georgofili 11/13 r* ✉ *50122* – ☎ *055 2001699*
– www.oradariaristorante.com
– Closed 11-26 August, 28 January-12 February, Monday lunch and Sunday
Rest – *(booking advisable)* Menu 23/75 € – Carte 54/90 €   **F3**
♦ Creative ♦ Formal ♦
The young Tuscan chef at this restaurant boasts experience acquired in some of
the region's best addresses. He makes full use of Tuscany's superb produce,
delighting fans of strong flavours with his excellent game specialities. The
menu also makes room for a selection of fish dishes.
→ Zuppa di asparagi con burrata e caviale di tartufo nero. Maialino morbido croccante con salsa d'aglio e lavanda. Tiramisù "espresso".

XXX **The Fusion Bar & Restaurant** – Gallery Hotel Art
vicolo dell'Oro 5 ✉ *50123* – ☎ *055 27266987*
– www.lungarnocollection.com   **D3**
Rest – Menu 14 € (lunch) – Carte 36/62 €
♦ Modern ♦ Design ♦
Stylish and innovative are the best adjectives to describe both the cuisine in this
restaurant and its sophisticated atmosphere. The fusion menu is highly varied. It
successfully combines different ingredients such as sushi, soups made from seaweed, yuzu, curry, foie gras, and a wide variety of fish and meat.

XXX **Borgo San Jacopo** – Hotel Lungarno
borgo San Jacopo 14 ✉ *50125* – ☎ *055 281661*
– www.lungarnocollection.com   **D3**
Rest – Carte 67/101 € ❦
♦ Modern ♦ Fashionable ♦
The flavours of the region have been given a lighter touch in this restaurant,
which also offers an excellent wine list of over 600 labels. In summer, treat yourself to dinner on the delightful small terrace overlooking the Arno, where the
candlelight is reflected on the surface of the water.

XXX **Hostaria Bibendum** – Hotel Helvetia e Bristol
via dei Pescioni 8/r ✉ *50123* – ☎ *0552665620* – *www.royaldemeure.com*
Rest – Carte 49/73 €   **D2**
♦ Modern ♦ Trendy ♦
The terrace at this restaurant directly overlooks Piazza Strozzi. The dining room
is a real melting pot of styles with a mix of warm colours, exotic decor and Art
Nouveau details. There is no mistaking the style of the cuisine however, which is
resolutely Tuscan in flavour with the occasional imaginative twist.

XXX **Oliviero**
via delle Terme 51 r ✉ *50123* – ☎ *055 287643* – *www.ristorante-oliviero.it*
– Closed 3 weeks in August, Sunday   **D3**
Rest – *(dinner only)* Menu 55/65 € – Carte 45/73 €
♦ Tuscan ♦ Modern ♦ Formal ♦
Situated in the heart of the old town, this renowned local restaurant is now
under new management. Two distinct types of cuisine are on offer here – one
traditional, the other a little more imaginative in style.

ITALY - FLORENCE

XXX **Cibrèo**   &. AC ⇔ VISA ⓪ AE ⓪

via A. Del Verrocchio 8/r ✉ *50122 –* ✆ *055 2341100*
– www.edizioniteatrodelsalecibreofirenze.it
– Closed 1 week in July, August, 2 weeks in February and Monday
Rest *– Carte 60/80 €* 🕸   **F3**
♦ Tuscan ♦ Formal ♦
This restaurant has an informal, fashionable atmosphere, with young, confident staff and fine, inventive cuisine inspired by traditional dishes.

XX **Alle Murate**   AC VISA ⓪ AE ⓪

via del Proconsolo 16 r ✉ *50122 –* ✆ *055 240618*
– www.allemurate.it
– Closed lunch Sunday and Monday   **E2-3**
Rest *– (bar lunch Monday-Saturday) Menu 16 € (lunch)/90 €*
– Carte 61/98 €
♦ Regional ♦ Intimate ♦
This restaurant is open to visitors during the day and in the evening (upon request); an audio-guide provides information on the frescoes and archaeological ruins visible here. The menu is also influenced by the past, with its emphasis on traditional, regional cuisine. A unique experience!

XX **Baccarossa**   AC VISA ⓪ AE

via Ghibellina 46/r ✉ *50122 –* ✆ *055240620 – www.baccarossa.it*
– Closed Monday   **F3**
Rest *– (dinner only) (booking advisable) Menu 35 € (weekdays)/85 €*
– Carte 43/93 €
♦ Mediterranean ♦ Family ♦
This elegant, bistro-style, wine bar is decorated in bright colours and furnished with wooden tables. It serves delicious Mediterranean cuisine including fish specialities, homemade pasta and some meat dishes. All the wines available can be be ordered by the glass.

XX **Belcore**   AC VISA ⓪ ⓪

via dell'Albero 30r ✉ *50123 –* ✆ *055 211198 – www.ristorantebelcore.it*
– Closed 16-25 August   **C2**
Rest *– (Monday to Friday dinner only) Menu 35/55 € – Carte 34/52 €*
♦ Classic ♦ Neighbourhood ♦
An excellent selection of wines complement the different types of cuisine served in this restaurant. Taste the fish specialities, traditional favourites from Italy and Tuscany, and more modern dishes.

XX **Buca Mario**   AC VISA ⓪ AE ⓪

piazza Degli Ottaviani 16 r ✉ *50123 –* ✆ *055 214179 – www.bucamario.it*
– Closed 10-21 December   **D2**
Rest *– (Monday to Friday dinner only) Carte 38/91 €*
♦ Tuscan ♦ Family ♦
This typical Florentine restaurant opened in 1886. Housed in the cellars of the Palazzo Niccolini in the heart of Florence, it is popular for its excellent, traditional Tuscan cuisine.

XX **Pane e Vino**   AC VISA ⓪ ⓪

piazza di Cestello 3 r ✉ *50124 –* ✆ *055 2476956*
– www.ristorantepaneevino.it
– Closed 10 days August and Sunday   **C3**
Rest *– (dinner only) Menu 30/45 € – Carte 31/53 €*
♦ Tuscan ♦ Formal ♦
Friendly, well maintained and furnished with an unusual wooden mezzanine, this pleasant restaurant offers traditional regional cuisine with a creative twist.

ITALY - FLORENCE

XX **dei Frescobaldi** AC VISA ⬤⬤

via dè Magazzini 2/4 r ✉ *50122 –* ✆ *055 284724*
– www.deifrescobaldi.it
– Closed 8 August-2 September, Sunday and Monday lunch   E3
Rest – Carte 40/69 € ✦
✦ Tuscan ✦ Friendly ✦
Owned by a wine producer, this restaurant boasts two welcoming rooms ador-
ned with stone and frescoes. The menu here focuses on regional cuisine, as well
as dishes from elsewhere. Simpler fare is served in the adjacent wine bar.

X **Il Santo Bevitore** ⬦ VISA ⬤⬤

via Santo Spirito 64/66 r ✉ *50125 –* ✆ *055 211264*
– www.ilsantobevitore.com
– Closed 10-20 August and Sunday at midday   C3
Rest – Carte 24/55 €
✦ Tuscan ✦ Fashionable ✦ Wine bar ✦
A young, welcoming restaurant with a good location in the Sanfrediano district.
The home-style cooking includes dishes such as fresh pasta, 'nduja di Spilinga
(smoked pork sausage) and mature pecorino cheese, as well as more inventive
fare. Good value for money.

X **Osteria Caffè Italiano** AC ⬦ VISA ⬤⬤

via Isola delle Stinche 11 ✉ *50122 –* ✆ *055 289368*
– www.caffeitaliano.it
– Closed Monday   E3
Rest – Menu 50 € – Carte 34/60 €
✦ Tuscan ✦ Friendly ✦
These fine premises are part of a historic building. Wood furnishings predomi-
nate in the three small dining halls where the cuisine is largely based on Tuscan
recipes. There is a fine wine list.

X **Trattoria Cibrèo-Cibreino** AC

via dei Macci 122/r ✉ *50122 –* ✆ *0552341100*
– www.edizioniteatrodelsalecibreofirenze.it
– Closed 29 July-31 August, 2 weeks February and Monday   F3
Rest – Carte 28/35 €
✦ Modern ✦ Friendly ✦
This trattoria is named after the famous cibreo, a typical stew from Florence,
which Catherine of Medici was said to enjoy so much that she even attempted,
unsuccessfully, to export it to France. Although it is often crowded, there is no
point calling ahead as the restaurant doesn't take reservations.

X **Il Latini** AC VISA ⬤⬤ ⓘ

via dei Palchetti 6 r ✉ *50123 –* ✆ *055 210916 – www.illatini.com*
– Closed 20 December-2 January and Monday   D2
Rest – Carte 25/80 €
✦ Tuscan ✦ Family ✦
Locals and tourists alike join the queue to eat at this trattoria. It is popular both
for its cuisine (excellent wild boar stew) and its informal, lively atmosphere.
Always busy, even at lunchtime.

X **Del Fagioli** AC

corso Tintori 47 r ✉ *50122 –* ✆ *055 244285 – www.localistorici.it*
– Closed August, Saturday and Sunday   E3
Rest – Carte 22/38 €
✦ Family ✦ Tuscan ✦
A typical, family-run Tuscan trattoria in the centre of Florence, which is popular
with tourists and locals alike. Enjoy delicious local specialities such as the legen-
dary ribollita (Tuscan bean soup) while you soak up the authentic ambience.

ITALY - FLORENCE

Grand Hotel Villa Cora

viale Machiavelli 18 ✉ _50125_
– ☎ _055 228790_ – _www.villacora.it_ **B2**
40 rm – †300/450 € ††350/650 €, ⊡ 25 € – 6 suites
Rest _Il Pasha_ – Carte 60/113 €
♦ Historic ♦ Grand Luxury ♦ Stylish ♦
This elegant late-19C villa surrounded by century-old gardens offers a profusion of frescoed lounges and marble and stucco decor. Modern well-equipped spa, outdoor swimming pool and refined cuisine in the restaurant, where you can dine on the veranda in summer.

Torre di Bellosguardo _without rest_

via Roti Michelozzi 2 ✉ _50124_ – ☎ _055 2298145_
– _www.torrebellosguardo.com_ **A2**
16 rm – †160/290 € ††290 €, ⊡ 20 € – 7 suites
♦ Historic ♦ Personalised ♦
There's a hint of the past in the lounge areas and guestrooms of this simple yet elegant hotel, which has breathtaking views of Florence. It has a magical, fairy tale atmosphere. There is a park with a botanical garden, an aviary and a swimming pool.

Villa La Vedetta

viale Michelangiolo 78 ✉ _50125_ – ☎ _055 681631_
– _www.villalavedettahotel.com_ **B2**
11 rm ⊡ – †150/1100 € ††150/1100 € – 7 suites
Rest _Onice Lounge e Restaurant_ – _(booking advisable)_ Carte 47/72 € 綴
♦ Grand Luxury ♦ Personalised ♦ Design ♦
This deluxe hotel is noteworthy for its well-kept rooms, each of which is different. Outside there is a fine Italian-style garden with stepped terraces.

Villa Le Piazzole

via Suor Maria Celeste 28 – ☎ _055 223520_ – _www.lepiazzole.com_
– _Closed 20 December-14 January_ **B2**
7 rm ⊡ – 7 suites **Rest** – _(booking essential) (residents only)_
♦ Traditional ♦ Personalised ♦
Enjoying a panoramic location overlooking the Ema valley with its old churches and farms, this extensive olive oil and wine estate offers individually decorated rooms with elegant period furnishings. The hotel is surrounded by a delightful Italian-style garden.

Marignolle Relais & Charme _without rest_

via di San Quirichino 16, località Marignolle
– ☎ _055 2286910_ – _www.marignolle.com_ **A2**
8 rm ⊡ – †115/225 € ††130/275 € – 1 suite
♦ Family ♦ Personalised ♦
The pleasant rooms in this rustic dwelling in a holding in the hills are all different from one another and are characterized by refined blends of lively materials; panoramic swimming pool in the greenery.

Villa Belvedere _without rest_

via Benedetto Castelli 3 ✉ _50124_ – ☎ _055 222501_
– _www.villabelvederefirenze.it_
– _Open 1° March-20 November_ **B2**
26 rm ⊡ – †80/100 € ††100/180 €
♦ Historic ♦ Personalised ♦
Villa dating from the 1950s, with a swimming pool in the gardens and a splendid view over the town and the hills, for a quiet stay in a luxury but family orientated environment.

XX **Omero** ⟨ ⌂ VISA ◐ AE ⓪

via Pian de' Giullari 49 – ℰ 055 220053 – www.ristoranteomero.it
Rest – Menu 35/55 € – Carte 48/70 € ⅜   **B2**
♦ Tuscan ♦ Friendly ♦

Passing under the hams hung in a pork butcher's shop you enter a country trattoria with a view over the hills and service in summer on the terrace; typical cuisine.

X **Trattoria Bibe** with rm   ⌂ P VISA ◐ AE
⊕
via delle Bagnese 15 – ℰ 055 2049085 – www.trattoriabibe.com
– Closed 1 week in November, 2 weeks in February and Wednesday
3 rm ⌴ – ♦50/70 € ♦♦70/120 €   **A2**
Rest – *(dinner only except Saturday and Bank Holidays)* Carte 27/52 €
♦ Tuscan ♦ Family ♦

Immortalised by the Italian writer Montale in his poetry, this trattoria has been run by the same family for almost two centuries. The menu features traditional Tuscan dishes, such as pici pasta with cheese and pepper served with fried leeks. There is alfresco dining in summer, as well as apartments with kitchens available for guests wishing to extend their stay.

AT BAGNO A RIPOLI

🏨 **Villa La Massa** ⟡ ⟨ ⇌ ⅙ ⌶ ⅙ 🄚 ⌂ ⅍ P VISA ◐ AE ⓪

via della Massa 24 – ℰ 055 62611 – www.villalamassa.it
– Open 20 March-3 November
23 rm ⌴ – ♦450 € ♦♦550 € – 14 suites
Rest *Il Verrocchio* – see restaurant listing
♦ Palace ♦ Luxury ♦ Historic ♦

Surrounded by tranquil green hills, this 17C Medici villa offers superb views of the Arno. Period-style decor, as well as a shuttle service to central Florence.

🏨 **Villa Olmi Resort** ⇌ ⅙ ⌶ ⅙ 🄚 ⅍ ⅍ P VISA ◐ AE

via degli Olmi 4/8 – ℰ 055 637710 – www.villaolmiresort.com
59 rm ⌴ – ♦119/310 € ♦♦134/450 € – 3 suites   **Rest** – Carte 54/70 €
♦ Luxury ♦ Historic ♦ Elegant ♦

An 18C villa with a recent addition, connected via an underground passage. Offers elegant and personalised rooms, furnished with antique pieces. In the dining room find antique chandeliers on the ceiling, a natural finish on the walls and fanciful Italian cuisine.

XXX **Il Verrocchio** – Hotel Villa La Massa   ⇌ ⌂ ⅙ 🄚 ⇔ P
VISA ◐ AE ⓪
via della Massa 24 – ℰ 055 62611
– www.villalamassa.it
– Open 20 March-3 November
Rest – Carte 63/123 €
♦ Modern ♦ Elegant ♦ Luxury ♦

This restaurant is named after the Florentine artist in whose studio the great Leonardo da Vinci trained. It boasts an elegant dining room with a vaulted ceiling, as well as a delightful terrace overlooking the Arno for alfresco dining. Regional specialities and traditional Italian favourites are on the menu.

AT FIESOLE   *Plan I*

🏨 **Villa San Michele** ⟡ ⟨ ⇌ ⅙ ⌶ ⅍ ⅍ P VISA ◐ AE ⓪

via Doccia 4 – ℰ 055 5678200 – www.villasanmichele.com
– Open 21 March-12 November   **B1**
46 rm ⌴ – ♦605 € ♦♦946/1177 € – 24 suites
Rest *La Loggia* – see restaurant listing
♦ Grand Luxury ♦ Historic ♦ Elegant ♦

A free shuttle bus takes guests from this hotel to the heart of Florence (10min). Or you may prefer simply to relax in the tranquil grounds of this elegant 15C building and enjoy the superb views of the city below.

Il Salviatino

🎀 🗑 ⚞ 🌿 🏛 🍴 🈁 🌐 📡 **P** **VISA** 🅾 **AE** ⓪

via del Salviatino 21 – 𝒞 055 9041111 – www.salviatino.com

45 rm ⌑ – **†**330/1080 € **††**330/1080 € – 4 suites   **B2**

Rest *Il Salviatino* – see restaurant listing

◆ **Grand Luxury** ◆ **Historic** ◆ **Stylish** ◆

Luxury is evident not only in the rooms of this 16C villa – which is surrounded by gardens and boasts fine views of the city – but also in its "service ambassadors", who are on hand to deal with guests' requests 24 hours a day. A truly idyllic place to stay!

Pensione Bencistà

🎀 🗑 ⚞ 🌿 🏛 🍴 🌐 **P** **VISA** 🅾

via Benedetto da Maiano 4 – 𝒞 055 59163 – www.bencista.com
– Open 15 March-15 November   **B1**

41 rm ⌑ – **†**82/132 € **††**147/204 € – 2 suites   **Rest** – Carte 19/39 €

◆ **Family** ◆ **Historic** ◆

Surrounded by extensive grounds and olive trees, this 14C villa boasts elegant public rooms decorated with period furnishings, where afternoon tea is served daily. Attractive guestrooms. The hotel's simple, spotless dining room is the setting for typical Tuscan cuisine at breakfast, lunch and dinner.

XXXX   La Loggia – Hotel Villa San Michele

🚗 🏮 🏛 ⇕ **P** **VISA** 🅾 **AE** ⓪

via Doccia 4 – 𝒞 055 5678200 – www.villasanmichele.com
– Open 21 March-12 November   **B1**

Rest – Carte 82/162 €

◆ **Modern** ◆ **Luxury** ◆

In summer, meals are served under the loggia with views of Florence, whereas in winter guests dine either in the cloisters or the cenacle. Tuscan produce takes pride of place on the menu with homemade pasta, meat and mushrooms (in season) to delight the palate.

XXX   Il Salviatino – Hotel Salviatino

⚞ 🌿 🏮 🏛 **P** **VISA** 🅾 **AE** ⓪

via del Salviatino 21 – 𝒞 055 9041111 – www.salviatino.com

Rest – Carte 61/110 €   **B2**

◆ **Creative** ◆ **Elegant** ◆

This restaurant has classic furnishings in shades of white, as well as a beautiful outdoor terrace overlooking the lovely gardens. The menu focuses on elaborate dishes made from the best ingredients, which are presented in a simple yet elegant way.

X   Tullio a Montebeni

🏮 **VISA** 🅾 **AE**

via Ontignano 48 – 𝒞 055 697354 – www.ristorantetullio.it
– Closed August, Monday and Tuesday lunch

Rest – Carte 24/59 €

◆ **Tuscan** ◆ **Family** ◆

This restaurant started as a simple grocery shop and in 1958 it began serving simple meals to locals and hunters in the region. Today the restaurant is enthusiastically run by Tullio's children, who continue to offer regional cuisine accompanied by their own home produced wine.

AT SAN CASCIANO IN VAL DI PESA

Villa il Poggiale

⚞ 🚗 🏮 🌿 🍴 🏛 🌐 🈁 **P** **VISA** 🅾 **AE**

via Empolese 69 (North-West: 1 km) – 𝒞 055 828311
– www.villailpoggiale.it
– Closed 9 January-9 February

24 rm ⌑ – **†**80/200 € **††**90/290 € – 3 suites

Rest – *(open 1° Avril-31 October)* Carte 22/60 €

◆ **Historic** ◆ **Stylish** ◆

This delightful villa is reminiscent of the Tuscany of E.M. Forster and Merchant Ivory, with its hundred-year-old cypress trees, Italian-style garden and Renaissance loggia. Superb guestrooms, as well as massages and beauty treatments available by prior appointment.

XXX **La Tenda Rossa** (Salcuni e Santandrea)
£3 *piazza del Monumento 9/14 – 𝒞 055 826132 – www.latendarossa.it*
– Closed 19 August-5 September, Sunday and Monday lunch
Rest – Menu 45 € (lunch)/110 € – Carte 62/111 € ❀
♦ Creative ♦ Elegant ♦
Italian restaurants are traditionally family-run, and three families run this one! Its
quality of service and the food is three times as good.
→ Perline di patate di montagna con carciofo e ragù di finocchiona. Cubo
di baccalà in velo di lardo di Colonnata con cremoso di fagioli all'uccelletto.
Meringa ghiacciata al lime e crema soffice di muesli.

AT THE AIRPORT   *Plan I*

🏠 **Hilton Garden Inn Florence Novoli**   ⅃ & 🖩 🛜 🚗
via Sandro Pertini 2/9, Novoli ⊠ 50127   VISA ⓪ AE ⓪
– 𝒞 055 42401 – www.florencenovoli.hgi.com   **A1**
119 rm – ♥105/210 € ♥♥117/210 €, ⊡ 12 € – 2 suites
Rest *City* – Carte 37/63 €
♦ Chain hotel ♦ Business ♦ Modern ♦
This modern hotel near the motorway offers bright and airy public areas, as well
as comfortable guestrooms furnished in tasteful modern style and equipped
with all the latest facilities.

X **Da Burde**   🖩 VISA ⓪ AE
🍴 *via Pistoiese 154 ⊠ 50122 – 𝒞 055 317206 – www.burde.it*
– Closed 10-17 August   **A2**
Rest – *(lunch only except Friday)* Carte 23/39 €
♦ Regional ♦ Family ♦
Opened in the early 20C as a grocery store and trattoria, this historic restaurant
lies well off the usual tourist trail. The two brothers who currently run the restaurant have retained its original style. It has cured meats for sale, a bar selling
tobacco and, to the rear, a small family-style dining room. Here, authentic Florentine dishes are served, such as the legendary bistecca alla fiorentina.

MILAN
MILANO

Population: 1 324 110

Bruno Bernier/Fotolia.com

If it's the romantic charm of places like Venice, Florence or Rome you're looking for, then best avoid Milan. If you're hankering for a permanent panorama of Renaissance chapels, palazzi, shimmering canals and bastions of fine art, then you're in the wrong place. What Milan does is relentless fashion, churned out with oodles of attitude and style. Italy's second largest city is constantly reinventing itself, and when Milan does a makeover, it invariably does it with flair and panache. That's not to say that Italy's capital of fast money and fast fashion doesn't have an eye for its past. The centrepiece of the whole city is the magnificent gleaming white Duomo, which took five hundred years to complete, while up la via a little way, La Scala is quite simply the world's most famous opera house. But this is a city known primarily for its sleek and modern towers, many housing the very latest threads from the very latest fashion gurus.

Just north of Milan's centre lies Brera, with its much prized old-world charm, and Quadrilatero d'Oro, with no little new-world glitz; the popular Giardini Pubblici are a little further north east from here. South of the centre is the Navigli quarter, home to rejuvenated Middle Age canals, while to the west are the green lungs of the Parco Sempione. The artily trendy neighbourhood of Lambrate is way up to the north east of Milan.

MILAN IN...

→ **ONE DAY**
Duomo, The Last Supper (remember to book first), Brera, Navigli.

→ **TWO DAYS**
Pinacoteca Brera, Castello Sforzesco, Parco Sempione, a night at La Scala.

→ **THREE DAYS**
Giardini Pubblici and its museums, trendy Lambrate district.

PRACTICAL INFORMATION

ARRIVAL-DEPARTURE

 Malpensa Airport is 48km north-west of the city and Linate Airport, 7km east. A train connects Malpensa with Stazione Cadorna every 30min, which takes 40min. From Linate take the Airport Bus No. 73 to Piazza San Babila metro station (every 10min, it takes 25min).

GETTING AROUND

The best way to get about Milan is by bus, tram or metro. Tickets are valid for one metro ride, or seventy five minutes of travel on buses or trams. You can also purchase books of ten tickets, or unlimited one-day or two-day passes. Buy them at metro stations, kiosks, bars or tobacconists. The metro provides a fast and efficient service, with frequent trains running on three different lines. Walking is a good alternative: most of Milan's attractions are based in the small and compact centre.

CALENDAR HIGHLIGHTS

March
MiArt (international modern art fair).

April
Naviglio Grande Flower Market.

June
Gods of Metal Festival, Festival Latino Americano, Festa del Naviglio, Notte Bianca.

September
September Music, Panoramica (film festival).

October
Wellness World Exhibition, Celtic New Year celebrations.

December
Opera season at La Scala gets underway.

EATING OUT

For a taste of Italy's regional cuisines, Milan is a great place to be. The city is often the goal of those leaving their home regions in the south or centre of the country; many open trattoria or restaurants, with the result that Milan offers a wide range of provincial menus. Excellent fish restaurants, inspired by recipes from the south, are a big draw despite the fact that the city is a long way from the sea. Going beyond the local borders, the emphasis on really good food continues and the quality of internationally diverse places to eat is better in Milan than just about anywhere else in Italy, including Rome. You'd expect avant-garde eating destinations to be the thing in this city of fashion and style, and you'd be right: there are some top-notch cutting-edge restaurants, thanks to Milan's famous tendency to reshape and experiment as it goes. For those who want to try out the local gastronomic traditions, risotto allo zafferano is not to be missed, nor is the cotoletta alla Milanese (veal cutlet) or the casoeula (a winter special made with pork and cabbage).

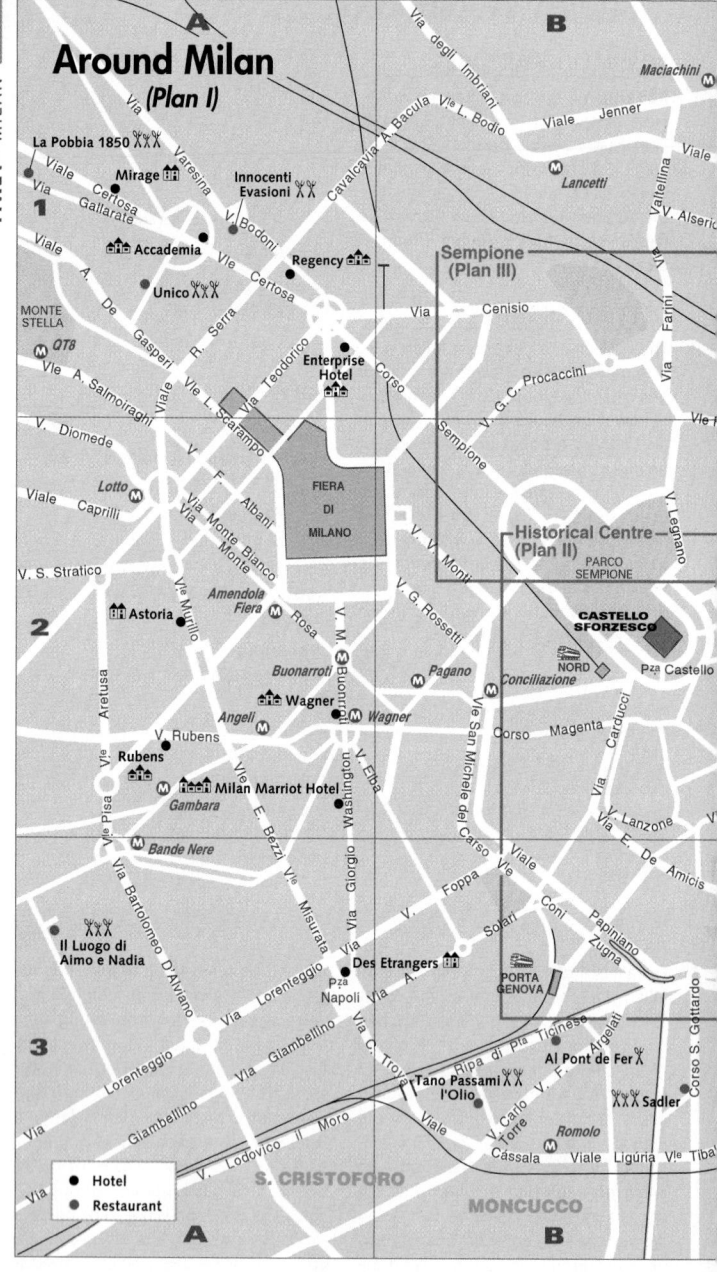

Around Milan
(Plan I)

ITALY - MILAN

La Pobbia 1850

Mirage

Innocenti Evasioni

Via Varesina

Via Certosa

Viale Certosa

Via degli Imbriani

Via L. Bodio

Viale Jenner

Maciachini

Lancetti

Cavalcavia A. Bacula

Via Gallarate

Accademia

Unico

Regency

Via Bodoni

Via Serra

Enterprise Hotel

Via Teodorico

Via L. Scarampo

Corso Sempione

Sempione
(Plan III)

Via Cenisio

Vle G. C. Procaccini

Viale F

MONTE STELLA

QT8

Vle A. Salmoiraghi

V. Diomede

V. A. De Gasperi

V. F. Albani

V. S. Stratico

Lotto

Viale Caprilli

Via Monte Bianco

Via Monte

FIERA DI MILANO

V. V. Monti

V. G. Rossetti

Historical Centre
(Plan II)

PARCO SEMPIONE

Viale Legnano

Astoria

Via Murillo

Amendola Fiera

Rosa

V. M. Buonarroti

Pagano

CASTELLO SFORZESCO

NORD

Pza Castello

Aretusa

Buonarroti

Wagner

V. Elba

Conciliazione

Corso Magenta

Carducci

Angeli

V. Rubens

Wagner

Washington

Corso San Michele del Carso

Via Lanzone

Via E. De Amicis

Rubens

Via Pisa

Milan Marriot Hotel

Gambara

Via E. Bezzi

Via Giorgio

Viale

Via Foppa

Bande Nere

Via Bartolomeo D'Alviano

Via Misurata

V. Solari

Coni

Papiniano

Zugna

Il Luogo di Aimo e Nadia

Lorenteggio

Des Etrangers

Pza Napoli

Via A.

PORTA GENOVA

Via Giambellino

Via C. Troya

Ripa di Pta Ticinese

Al Pont de Fer

Corso S. Gottardo

Lorenteggio

Via Giambellino

Tano Passami l'Olio

V. Carlo Torre

Sadler

Via

V. Lodovico Il Moro

Viale

Romolo

Cassala

Viale Liguria

Vle Tiba

S. CRISTOFORO

MONCUCCO

● Hotel
● Restaurant

A   B

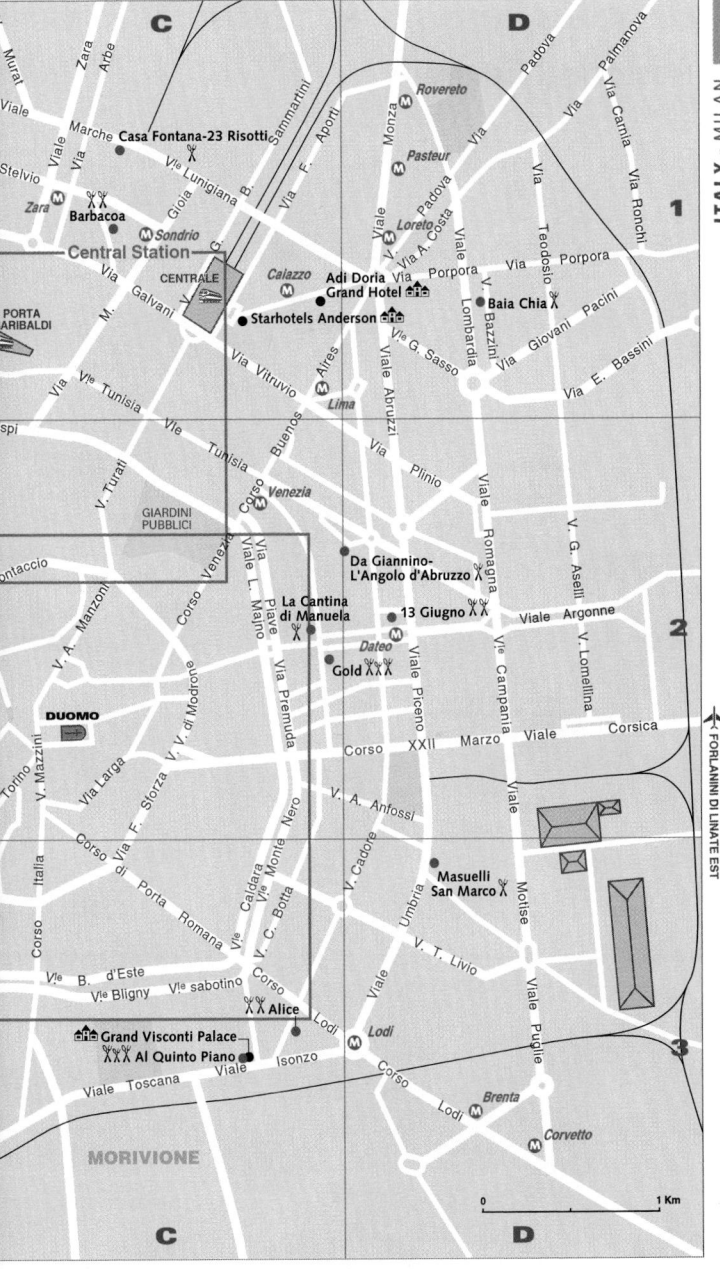

FORLANINI DI LINATE EST

531

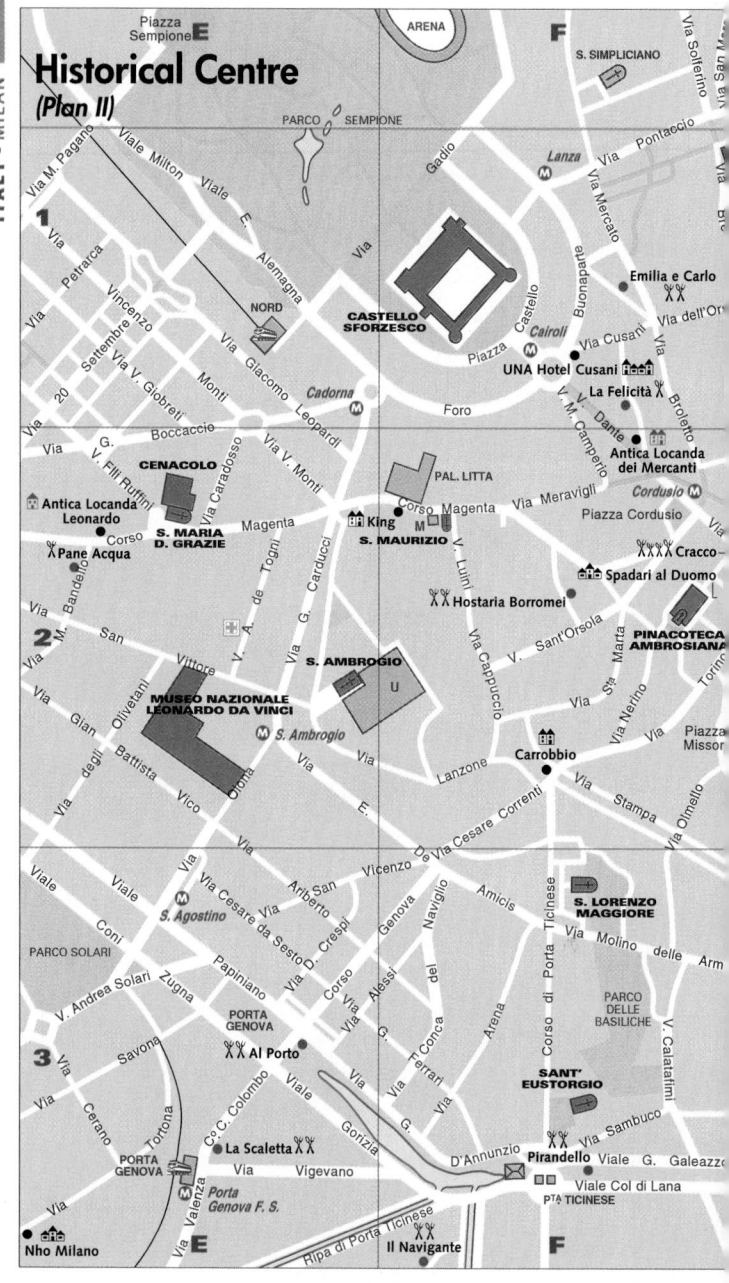

Historical Centre
(Plan II)

ARENA

S. SIMPLICIANO

Piazza Sempione

PARCO SEMPIONE

PARCO SEMPIONE

Lanza

Via Pontaccio

Gadio

Via Mercato

Via M. Pagano

Viale Milton

Viale E.

Via Alemagna

Via Petrarca

Via Vincenzo

Via V. Giobetti

Via Monti

Via Giacomo

Via Giacomo

NORD

Buonaparte

Emilia e Carlo

Castello

CASTELLO SFORZESCO

Cairoli

Via Cusani

Via dell'Or

UNA Hotel Cusani

Piazza

V. M. Dante

La Felicità

20 Settembre

Boccaccio

Leopardi

Cadorna

Foro

V. M. Camperio

Brletto

CENACOLO

Via Caradosso

V. V. Monti

Antica Locanda dei Mercanti

Antica Locanda Leonardo

S. MARIA D. GRAZIE

Corso

Magenta

PAL. LITTA

Corso Magenta

Via Meravigli

Corsusio

Piazza Cordusio

Pane Acqua

Magenta

Via G. Carducci

King

M

S. MAURIZIO

V. Luini

Cracco

Via de Togni

V. A. de Togni

S. MAURIZIO

Hostaria Borromei

Spadari al Duomo

L

Via Bandello

San

Vittore

V. A. de Togni

Via G. Carducci

S. AMBROGIO

Via Sant'Orsola

Via Sta Marta

PINACOTECA AMBROSIANA

Via M.

Via Gian

Olivetani

MUSEO NAZIONALE LEONARDO DA VINCI

U

Via Cappuccio

Via Nerino

Torino

Piazza Misso

degli

Battista

Vico

Olona

M S. Ambrogio

Via

Via

Lanzone

Carrobbio

Via Stampa

Via Olmetto

Viale

Viale

Via San

Ariberto

Vicenzo

De

Via Cesare Correnti

Via Cesare da Sesto

Crespi

Genova

Navigle

Amicis

Porta Ticinese

S. LORENZO MAGGIORE

Coni

S. Agostino

Via Molino

delle

Arm

PARCO SOLARI

Papiniano

Corso

Via Alessi

del

Corso di Porta

PARCO DELLE BASILICHE

V. Andrea Solari

Zugna

PORTA GENOVA

Via F. Conca

Atena

V. Calatafimi

Via

Al Porto

Via G. Ferrari

SANT' EUSTORGIO

Savona

Cerano

C.C. Colombo

Viale

Gorizia

Via Sambuco

Via

Tortona

La Scaletta

Via

Via Vigevano

D'Annunzio

Pirandello

Viale G. Galeazzo

PORTA GENOVA

Porta Genova F. S.

PTA TICINESE

Viale Col di Lana

Nho Milano

Ripa di Porta Ticinese

Il Navigante

E

F

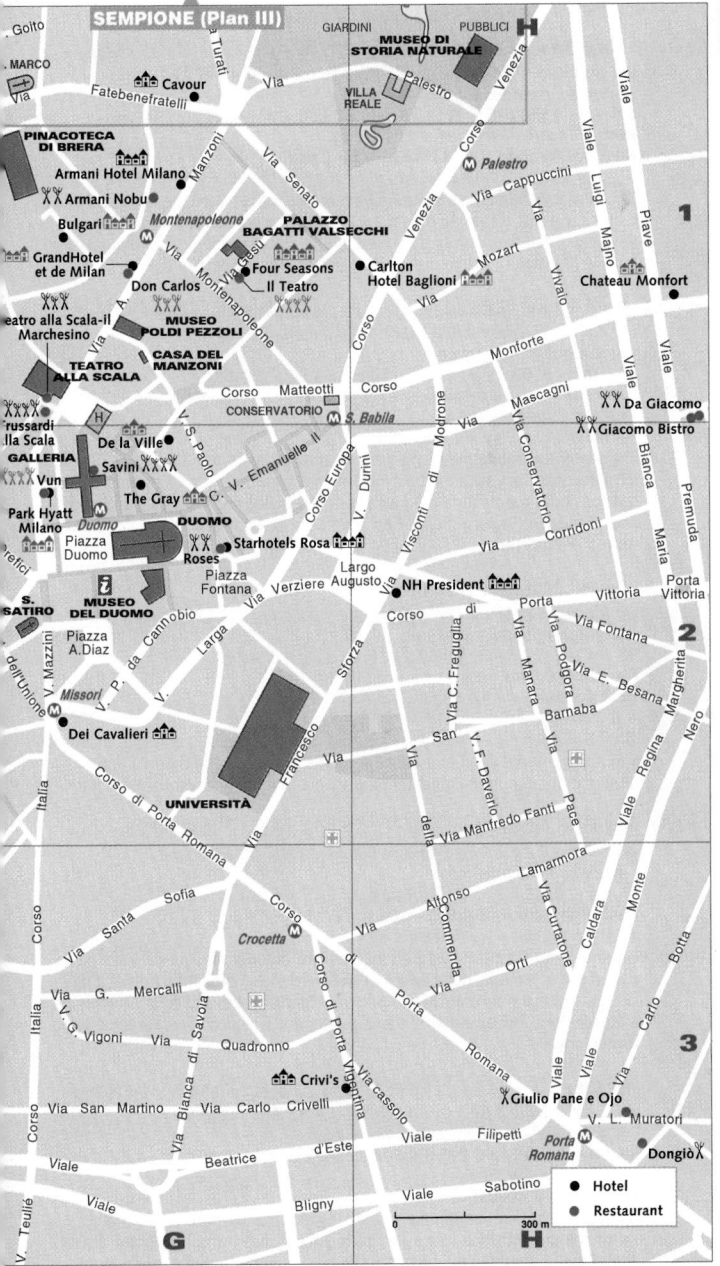

SEMPIONE (Plan III)

GIARDINI PUBBLICI
MUSEO DI STORIA NATURALE

Goito
MARCO
Via
Cavour
Fatebenefratelli
Via Turati

VILLA REALE
Palestro
Venezia

Viale
Viale Luigi
Viale Plave

PINACOTECA DI BRERA
Armani Hotel Milano
Armani Nobu
Bulgari
Montenapoleone
GrandHotel et de Milan
Don Carlos
Il Teatro
Four Seasons

Via Manzoni
Via Senato
Via Gesù

PALAZZO BAGATTI VALSECCHI
Carlton Hotel Baglioni
Chateau Monfort

Palestro
Via Cappuccini
Mozart
Vivaio
Via

eatro alla Scala-il Marchesino
MUSEO POLDI PEZZOLI
CASA DEL MANZONI
TEATRO ALLA SCALA

Monforte
Mascagni

Da Giacomo
Giacomo Bistro

Corso Matteotti
Corso
CONSERVATORIO
S. Babila

Via Modrone
Via Conservatorio

Via Bianca
Premuda

russardi lla Scala
GALLERIA
Vun
Park Hyatt Milano
retici
De la Ville
Savini
The Gray
DUOMO
Duomo
Piazza Duomo
Roses
Starhotels Rosa

V. S. Paolo
Corso V. Emanuele II
Corso Europa
V. Durini

NH President

Via Corridoni
Via

Via Maria
Porta Vittoria

S. SATIRO
MUSEO DEL DUOMO
Piazza Fontana
Piazza A.Diaz
V. P. da Cannobio

Largo Augusto
Corso Verziere

Corso
di
Porta Vittoria

delfunione
V. Mazzini
Missori
Dei Cavalieri
Larga

Via Sforza
Via C. Freguglia
San Francesco
V. F. Daverio
Via della

Via Manara
Via Podgora
Via Fontana
Barnaba
Via E. Besana

Viale Regina Margherita
Nero

UNIVERSITÀ
Corso di Porta Romana

Via Manfredo Fanti
Pace

Lamarmora
Via Curtatone
Alfonso d'Commenda
Orti
Caldara
Monte

Corso
Via Santa Sofia
Crocetta
Corso di Porta Vigentina
Via di Porta Romana

Italia
Via G. Mercalli
V.V.G. Vigoni
Via
Quadronno
Via Bianca di Savoia

Carlo Botta

Crivi's
Via San Martino
Via Carlo Crivelli
d'Este

Giulio Pane e Ojo
V. L. Muratori
Porta Romana
Dongiò

Italia
Corso
Viale
Beatrice
Viale
Bligny
Filipetti
Sabotino

V. Teulié
Viale

G
H
1
2
3

0   300 m

● Hotel
● Restaurant

531

Four Seasons   🚗 ⅃⚹ ⅙ rm, 📶 🛜 🏋 🚘 VISA ⚙ AE ①

*via Gesù 6/8 ⊠ 20121 – Ⓜ Montenapoleone – ℰ 02 77088
– www.fourseasons.com/milan*   **G1**
67 rm – †530/610 € ††530/610 €, ⊑ 32 € – 51 suites
Rest *Il Teatro* – see restaurant listing
Rest *La Veranda* – ℰ 02 7788 1478 – Carte 67/115 €
♦ Grand Luxury ♦ Stylish ♦
This evocative hotel has achieved a perfect balance between the original architectural features of the 15C monastery in which it is housed and its elegant contemporary design. Don't be surprised by the highly modern technology available in the superb guestrooms that occupy the former monks' cells.

Park Hyatt Milano   ⅃⚹ ⚙ ⅙ 📶 🛜 🏋 VISA ⚙ AE ①

*via Tommaso Grossi 1 ⊠ 20121 – Ⓜ Duomo – ℰ 02 88211234
– www.milano.park.hyatt.it*   **G2**
106 rm – †500/750 € ††500/750 €, ⊑ 35 € – 16 suites
Rest *Vun* ❀ – see restaurant listing
Rest *La Cupola* – Carte 61/95 €
♦ Grand Luxury ♦ Modern ♦
The contemporary design of this hotel occupying a palazzo dating from 1870 is in perfect harmony with the building's architecture. Excellent modern facilities, spacious guestrooms decorated with Venetian stucco and Murano glass lamps, and an elegant Imperial Suite. Find traditional or buffet cuisine at La Cupola from 11am to 11pm.

Grand Hotel et de Milan   ⅃⚹ ⅙ rm, 📶 🛜 🏋 VISA ⚙ AE ①

*via Manzoni 29 ⊠ 20121 – Ⓜ Montenapoleone – ℰ 02 723141
– www.grandhoteletdemilan.it*   **G1**
95 rm – †391/644 € ††457/710 €, ⊑ 35 € – 6 suites
Rest *Don Carlos* – see restaurant listing
Rest *Caruso* – (lunch only) Carte 47/86 €
♦ Luxury ♦ Traditional ♦ Stylish ♦
This hotel opened over 150 years ago. Big names in the field of music, theatre and politics have stayed in its elegant rooms that are full of charm. Bright restaurant dedicated to the great tenor, who recorded his first record in this hotel.

Carlton Hotel Baglioni   🍴 ⅃⚹ 📶 🛜 🏋 🚘 VISA ⚙ AE ①

*via Senato 5 ⊠ 20121 – Ⓜ San Babila – ℰ 02 77077
– www.baglionihotels.com*   **H1**
83 rm – †340/630 € ††390/680 €, ⊑ 26 € – 9 suites
Rest *Il Baretto al Baglioni* – Carte 70/141 €
♦ Grand Luxury ♦ Classic ♦
Celebrities and well-known personalities are among the guests who have stayed in this splendid hotel, which describes itself as 'home from home'. It provides luxury in a warm, family atmosphere. Antique pieces and original works of art grace the public areas, while the guestrooms offer stucco decor and modern technology.

Bulgari   🚗 🍴 ⅃⚹ ⚙ 🖥 ⅙ 📶 🛜 🏋 🚘 VISA ⚙ AE ①

*via privata Fratelli Gabba 7/b ⊠ 20121 – Ⓜ Montenapoleone
– ℰ 02 805805 1 – www.bulgarihotels.com*   **G1**
58 rm – †530/850 € ††530/850 €, ⊑ 24 € – 11 suites
Rest – Carte 59/120 €
♦ Luxury ♦ Stylish ♦
Owned by the famous jewellery company, this luxury hotel is decorated in warm colours with fine materials gracing the guestrooms. The hotel boasts one of the best spas in the city with a hammam whose green glass decor evokes an emerald. Exclusive terrace overlooking an unexpected garden.

Armani Hotel Milano ← ⅃ᵬ ⅏ ⌂ ⌘ 🛁 VISA ⚫ AE ⓞ

via Manzoni 31 ⊠ *20123* – Ⓜ *Montenapoleone* – ℰ *02 8883 8888*
– *www.armanihotels.com* **G1**
64 rm – ♦605/1320 € ♦♦605/1320 € – 31 suites
Rest – *(booking advisable)* Carte 70/115 €
♦ Luxury ♦ Design ♦
This innovative hotel is housed in an austere building dating from 1937, typical
of the Armani style. It is run by a 'lifestyle manager' who offers a warm welcome
to guests. Luxurious 1 000m² spa and very spacious guestrooms.

 Starhotels Rosa Grand ⅃ᵬ ⅊ ⅏ ⌂ ⌘ ⅊ VISA ⚫ AE ⓞ

piazza Fontana 3 ⊠ *20122* – Ⓜ *Duomo* – ℰ *02 88311*
– *www.starhotels.com* **G2**
320 rm – ♦165/900 € ♦♦300/1300 €, ⌓ 25 € – 7 suites
Rest *Roses* – see restaurant listing
♦ Chain hotel ♦ Classic ♦
Situated in the heart of Milan, this hotel has recently undergone a major refurbishment. The interior is arranged around a courtyard, with simple, square shapes creating a naturally elegant look. The guestrooms here are comfortable and
stylish, although only a few offer views of the Duomo.

 NH President ⅊ rm, ⅏ ⌂ ⌘ VISA ⚫ AE ⓞ

largo Augusto 10 ⊠ *20122* – Ⓜ *San Babila* – ℰ *02 77461*
– *www.nh-hotels.it* **H2**
262 rm ⌓ – ♦390/630 € ♦♦400/780 € – 12 suites
Rest *Il Verziere* – Carte 45/81 €
♦ Chain hotel ♦ Modern ♦
An international standard hotel for business travellers or tourists. It has attractive, spacious lounge areas as well as facilities for fashion shows, business lunches and conferences. The restaurant serves specialities from Lombardy, as well
as Mediterranean-style dishes.

 UNA Hotel Cusani ⅊ rm, ⅏ ⌂ ⌘ VISA ⚫ AE ⓞ

via Cusani 13 ⊠ *20121* – Ⓜ *Cairoli* – ℰ *02 85601* – *www.unahotels.it*
92 rm ⌓ – ♦189/900 € ♦♦199/1100 € – 6 suites **F1**
Rest – *(closed lunch Saturday and Sunday)* Carte 36/74 €
♦ Business ♦ Classic ♦
Located in the heart of the historic town centre, this hotel is in an ideal location
for business and sightseeing. It has simple and modern, very large attractive
rooms. Choose from classic Italian or international dishes at this cosy restaurant.

 De la Ville ⅃ᵬ ⅏ ⅂ ⅊ rm, ⅏ ⌂ ⌘ VISA ⚫ AE ⓞ

via Hoepli 6 ⊠ *20121* – Ⓜ *Duomo* – ℰ *02 8791311*
– *www.sinahotels.com* **G2**
109 rm ⌓ – ♦200/450 € ♦♦300/490 € – 1 suite
Rest *L'Opera* – ℰ *02 8051231* – Carte 48/73 €
♦ Luxury ♦ Classic ♦
Despite its location in the bustling centre of Milan, there's nothing Milanese
about this hotel, which has a French name and a distinctly British decor. It features wood panelling, fireplaces and attractive prints depicting horses and fox
hunting. The same stylish elegance is evident in the guestrooms.

 Château Monfort ⅏ ⅂ ⅊ rm, ⅏ rm, ⌂ ⌘ VISA ⚫ AE

corso Concordia 1 ⊠ *20129* – ℰ *02 776761* – *www.chateaumonfort.com*
77 rm – ♦195/705 € ♦♦195/705 €, ⌓ 25 € **H1**
Rest *Rubacuori* – *(booking advisable)* Carte 47/79 €
♦ Historic ♦ Classic ♦
Discreet elegance characterises this splendid Art Nouveau-style palazzo that
bears the hallmark of the architect Paolo Mezzanotte. The guestrooms are chic
and glamorous (those inspired by the opera are truly magical), and there is a
small spa in which to rest and relax. Mediterranean cuisine is to the fore in the
hotel restaurant.

The Gray   🚫 AC 🛜 VISA ⑳ AE ⓪

via San Raffaele 6 ✉ 20121 – ⓜ *Duomo –* ✆ *02 7208951*
– www.sinahotels.com
– Closed August   **G2**
21 rm – ♛350/600 € ♛♛450/750 €, � 33 € – 5 suites
Rest – Carte 68/96 €
♦ Luxury ♦ Design ♦
All different in style, the rooms in this hotel feature a host of interesting details, as well as up-to-date technology such as Wi-Fi internet connection and LCD televisions. 'Gray' in name only (perhaps an ironic reference to Milan's occasional dull weather?), this hotel is one of the most stylish and elegant in the city.

Grand Visconti Palace   🚗 🖙 ⊛ ⍦ 🔲 🚫 AC 🛜 🐴 🚍

viale Isonzo 14 ✉ 20135 – ⓜ *Lodi TIBB*   VISA ⑳ AE ⓪
– ✆ *02 540341 – www.grandviscontipalace.com*   *Plan I* **C3**
166 rm ⊵ **–** ♛149/650 € ♛♛169/1100 € – 6 suites
Rest Al Quinto Piano – see restaurant listing
♦ Palace ♦ Classic ♦
This elegant, grand hotel occupies a large former industrial mill. It boasts a welcoming wellbeing centre, conference rooms and a charming garden.

Nhow Milano   🖙 🚫 rm, AC 🛜 🐴 P VISA ⑳ AE ⓪

via Tortona 35 ✉ 20144 – ✆ *02 4898861 – www.nhow-hotels.com*
246 rm ⊵ **–** ♛104/594 € ♛♛113/603 € – 1 suite   **E3**
Rest – Carte 40/55 €
♦ Chain hotel ♦ Modern ♦
This designer-style hotel located in a former industrial district has plenty of charm, and acts as a permanent showcase for artistic and stylistic excellence. Eclectic guestrooms offering impeccable standards of comfort.

Spadari al Duomo *without rest*   AC 🛜 VISA ⑳ AE ⓪

via Spadari 11 ✉ 20123 – ⓜ *Duomo –* ✆ *02 72002371*
– www.spadarihotel.com
– Closed 23-27 December   **F2**
39 rm ⊵ **–** ♛140/200 € ♛♛180/380 € – 1 suite
♦ Business ♦ Design ♦
This modern hotel has the twin advantage of a central location, as well as a fine display of contemporary art collected by its art enthusiast owners. Note the Giò Pomodoro fireplace in the lobby and the careful play of light throughout the hotel.

Cavour   AC 🛜 🐴 VISA ⑳ AE ⓪

via Fatebenefratelli 21 ✉ 20121 – ⓜ *Turati –* ✆ *02 620001*
– www.hotelcavour.it
– Closed August   **G1**
121 rm ⊵ **–** ♛110/260 € ♛♛120/300 € – 6 suites
Rest Conte Camillo – ✆ *02 6570516 (closed Saturday and Sunday)*
Carte 44/70 €
♦ Business ♦ Functional ♦
High quality flooring and fine wood panelling contribute to the simple yet elegant atmosphere in this hotel. It is situated not far from the city's main sights. Traditional cuisine with a modern edge is to the fore in the Conte Camillo restaurant.

Dei Cavalieri   🚫 rm, AC rm, 🛜 🐴 VISA ⑳ AE ⓪

piazza Missori 1 ✉ 20123 – ⓜ *Missori –* ✆ *02 88571*
– www.hoteldeicavalieri.com   **G2**
165 rm ⊵ **–** ♛129/720 € ♛♛129/720 € – 2 suites
Rest – *(closed Sunday) (dinner only)* Carte 33/62 €
♦ Traditional ♦ Functional ♦
You are sure to find a relaxing atmosphere in this hotel that has stylish, comfortably furnished rooms with contemporary décor and facilities for conferences, business lunches and banquets.

ITALY - MILAN

Crivi's without rest

corso Porta Vigentina 46 ✉ *20122 –* **Ⓜ** *Crocetta –* ☏ *02 582891*
– www.crivis.com
– Closed August and Christmas Holidays   **G3**
86 rm ☑ *–* **†**120/250 € **††**140/350 €
♦ **Business** ♦ **Modern** ♦

In a convenient location near the metro, this comfortable hotel has pleasant public areas and traditionally furnished, reasonably comfortable and spacious guestrooms.

Carrobbio without rest
&. 🔲 🛜 📠 ⊙⊙ 🆎 ⓪

via Medici 3 ✉ *20123 –* **Ⓜ** *Duomo –* ☏ *02 89010740*
– www.hotelcarrobbiomilano.com
– Closed August and Christmas Holidays   **F2**
56 rm ☑ *–* **†**117/198 € **††**147/356 €
♦ **Business** ♦ **Classic** ♦

This recently renovated hotel is in a quiet area and near the historic town centre. It has a small and relaxing winter garden.

King without rest
🔲 🛜 📠 ⊙⊙ 🆎 ⓪

corso Magenta 19 ✉ *20123 –* **Ⓜ** *Cadorna F.N.M. –* ☏ *02 874432*
– www.mokinba.it   **F2**
48 rm ☑ *–* **†**129/385 € **††**275/498 €
♦ **Business** ♦ **Classic** ♦

This six-floor building not far from the Duomo has been recently refurbished. It boasts some magnificent touches in the public areas and compact but comfortable guestrooms.

Antica Locanda dei Mercanti without rest
🔲 🛜 📠 ⊙⊙ 🆎

via San Tomaso 6 ✉ *20121 –* **Ⓜ** *Cordusio –* ☏ *02 8054080*
– www.locanda.it   **F2**
12 rm *–* **†**205/315 € **††**205/315 €, ☑ 10 € *– 7 suites*
♦ **Townhouse** ♦ **Family** ♦ **Personalised** ♦

A small, cosy hotel, simple and elegant in style, and furnished with antique furniture. Many of the light and spacious guestrooms have a small terrace.

XXXX
❀

Vun – Hotel Park Hyatt Milano

via Silvio Pellico 3 ✉ *20121 –* **Ⓜ** *Duomo –* ☏ *02 88211234*
– www.ristorante-vun.it
– Closed 3 weeks August, 1 week January, lunch Saturday and Sunday
Rest *–* Menu 52 € (weekday lunch)/100 € *–* Carte 71/116 €   **G2**
✿✿
♦ **Modern** ♦ **Classic** ♦

The young Neapolitan chef creates dishes influenced by the flavours and produce of Naples, as well as providing guests with an extraordinary introduction to some of Italy's best ingredients. A sumptuous, austere and minimalist restaurant.

➔ Pappa al pomodoro "solida e liquida", ricotta di bufala e acciughe. Coppa di maiale nero, cipollotto, melanzane affumicate e prugne. Gianduia e i lamponi.

XXXX
❀❀

Cracco
🔲 📠 ⊙⊙ 🆎

via Victor Hugo 4 ✉ *20123 –* **Ⓜ** *Duomo –* ☏ *02 876774*
– www.ristorantecracco.it
– Closed 3 weeks in August, 24 December-11 January, Saturday lunch, Sunday, Monday lunch   **F2**
Rest *–* Menu 140/165 € *–* Carte 93/185 € ✿✿
♦ **Creative** ♦ **Elegant** ♦

Decorated in a simple, modern style, this restaurant serves excellent contemporary cuisine with a focus on innovative and inventive dishes.

➔ Risotto allo zafferano con midollo alla piastra. Vitello impanato alla milanese. Nuvola di mascarpone.

XXXX **Il Teatro** – Hotel Four Seasons   🏧 ⇄ 💳 📧 🅰🅴 ⓘ
via Gesù 6/8 ✉ *20121* – **Ⓜ** *Montenapoleone* – ☏ *02 77081435*
– *www.fourseasons.com/milan/dining*
– *Closed 17 July-5 September and Sunday*   **G1**
Rest – *(dinner only) (booking advisable)* Menu 85 €
– Carte 80/96 €
♦ Modern ♦ Formal ♦ Luxury ♦
The restaurant, contained in the splendid premises of the Four Seasons hotel, is characterised by exclusiveness and class. The cuisine highlights interpretive creativity.

XXXX **Savini**   ♿ 🏧 ⇄ 🅿 💳 📧 🅰🅴 ⓘ
galleria Vittorio Emanuele II ✉ *20121* – **Ⓜ** *Duomo*
– ☏ *02 72003433*
– *www.savinimilano.it*
– *Closed 20 days in August, 10 days in January, Saturday lunch and Sunday*
Rest – Carte 78/132 € ❀   **G2**
Rest *Bistrot* – Carte 65/125 € ❀
♦ Italian ♦ Classic ♦ Luxury ♦
This restaurant is the perfect embodiment of fine dining with its exclusive, elegant ambience and reinterpretations of classic Milanese cuisine. The Bistrot offers a delightful outdoor dining area, facing out onto the Galleria with views of the historic glass roof of the Ottagono.

XXXX **Trussardi alla Scala**   ♿ 🏧 💳 📧 🅰🅴 ⓘ
❀
piazza della Scala 5 (palazzo Trussardi) ✉ *20121*
– **Ⓜ** *Duomo* – ☏ *02 80688201*
– *www.trussardiallascala.com*
– *Closed 3 weeks in August, 3 weeks in January, Saturday lunch, Sunday, and the first Monday each month*   **G1**
Rest – Menu 55 € *(weekday lunch)* – Carte 130/150 €
♦ Modern ♦ Trendy ♦
There has been a change in the style of cuisine served at this modern restaurant, which overlooks one of the most famous squares in Milan. A careful selection of produce and imaginative creativity are the hallmarks of the young, talented chef, Luigi Taglienti.
➔ Orata, oro, ginger e zafferano. Riso alla milanese con lacrima di midollo alla brace. Petto di piccione alla coque, okra, kakavia e frittura di calamari

XXX **Don Carlos** – Grand Hotel et de Milan   🏧 💳 📧 🅰🅴 ⓘ
via Manzoni 29 ✉ *20121* – **Ⓜ** *Montenapoleone* – ☏ *02 72314640*
– *www.ristorantedoncarlos.it*
– *Closed August*   **G1**
Rest – *(dinner only)* Menu 90 € – Carte 65/113 €
♦ Historical ♦ Modern ♦
Named after one of Verdi's operas, this charming restaurant has a quiet atmosphere and elegant decor, including wood panelling, red appliqué and old photos. The menu focuses on traditional cuisine from Lombardy and Piedmont with a creative touch.

XXX **Al Quinto Piano** – Hotel Grand Visconti Palace   🏧
via Mantova 12 ✉ *20135* – **Ⓜ** *Lodi*   💳 📧 🅰🅴 ⓘ
– ☏ *02 54069515* – *www.grandviscontipalace.com*
– *Closed 5-26 August*   *Plan I* **C3**
Rest – *(booking advisable)* Carte 49/80 €
♦ Modern ♦ Formal ♦
Decorated in soft pastel shades with a dash of red here and there to brighten the ambience, this elegant restaurant delights diners with its fine cuisine, which is imaginatively and carefully prepared.

ITALY - MILAN

XXX
$\mathbb{ABC}$ $\mathbb{ABC}$ **Sadler**   AC ⇔ 🆅🆂🅰 ⚛ AE

via Ascanio Sforza 77 ☒ *20141* – Ⓜ *Romolo* – ℰ *02 58104451*
– *www.sadler.it*
– *Closed 4-22 August, 1-8 January and Sunday*   *Plan I* **B3**
Rest – *(dinner only)* Menu 75/140 € – Carte 82/154 € ⒢
♦ Creative ♦ Formal ♦
Harmony is the hallmark of this restaurant, with its clean lines, carefully chosen
fabrics, large windows and effective lighting. Balance is also evident in the cui-
sine, which is a fine blend of the traditional and the innovative.
➔ Tortelli farciti di guancia di vitello stufata, topinambur e tartufo nero.
Padellata di crostacei con crema di broccoletti e patate croccanti. Ciocco-
lato d'alta qualità in varie forme, sapori e temperature.

XXX   **Teatro alla Scala - il Marchesino**   ♿ AC ⇔ 🆅🆂🅰 ⚛ AE ⓞ

piazza della Scala ☒ *20121* – Ⓜ *Duomo* – ℰ *02 72 09 43 38*
– *www.ilmarchesino.it*
– *Closed 11-31 August, 31 December-6 January and Sunday*   **G1**
Rest – *(booking advisable)* Carte 72/126 € ⒢
♦ Modern ♦ Elegant ♦
Housed in the La Scala opera house, this attractive restaurant also doubles as a
cafeteria and tea room. Elegant and informal at the same time, it serves fine tra-
ditional cuisine.

XX   **Armani/Nobu**   AC ⇔ 🆅🆂🅰 ⚛ AE ⓞ

via Pisoni 1 ☒ *20121* – Ⓜ *Montenapoleone* – ℰ *02 62312645*
– *Closed 12-26 August and Sunday lunch*   **G1**
Rest – Menu 30 € (lunch)/140 € – Carte 44/87 €
♦ Japanese ♦ Trendy ♦
This unique restaurant is the result of collaboration between the designer
Armani and one of the best Japanese chefs in the world, Nobuyuki. Minimalist,
Japanese-style decor and fusion cuisine with south American influences.

XX   **Emilia e Carlo**   AC 🆅🆂🅰 ⚛ AE ⓞ

via Sacchi 8 ☒ *20121* – Ⓜ *Cairoli* – ℰ *02 875948* – *www.emiliaecarlo.it*
– *Closed August, Saturday lunch, Sunday*   **F1**
Rest – Carte 53/74 € ⒢
♦ Modern ♦ Formal ♦
Housed in an early 19C palazzo, this trattoria has a rustic feel with arches and
wooden beams. Creative contemporary cuisine, and a fine choice of wines.

XX   **Roses** – Starhotels Rosa Grand   AC 🆅🆂🅰 ⚛ AE ⓞ

piazza Fontana 3 ☒ *20122* – Ⓜ *Duomo* – ℰ *02 88311*
– *www.starhotels.com*   **G2**
Rest – Menu 30 € (lunch) – Carte 46/80 €
♦ Italian ♦ Friendly ♦
Impeccable service, imaginative cuisine and excellent ingredients all contribute
to the success of this restaurant, which also boasts a delightful atmosphere.
With its flowing spaces and chic decor, this is an ideal venue for a romantic din-
ner or business lunch.

XX   **Al Porto**   AC 🆅🆂🅰 ⚛ AE ⓞ

piazzale Generale Cantore ☒ *20123* – Ⓜ *Porta Genova FS*
– ℰ *02 89407425* – *www.alportomilano.it*
– *Closed August, 24 December-3 January, Sunday, Monday lunch*
Rest – Carte 48/88 €   **E3**
♦ Fish and seafood ♦ Formal ♦
There is a definite maritime flavour to this restaurant, which occupies the old
19C Porta Genova toll house. Always busy, Al Porto specialises exclusively in
fresh fish dishes, including raw fish.

XX **Il Navigante**　　　　　　　　　　 AC P VISA ◎◎ AE

via Magolfa 14 ⊠ 20143 – 𝒞 02 89406320 – www.navigante.it
– Closed 6-26 August, Saturday lunch and Sunday　　　　　　　**F3**
Rest – Carte 43/96 €
♦ Fish and seafood ♦ Intimate ♦

On a road at the back of the waterway, live music every evening in an establishment, managed by an ex-ship's cook, with an unusual aquarium on the floor; seafood cuisine.

XX **Pirandello**　　　　　　　　　　　 AC VISA ◎◎ AE

viale Gian Galeazzo 6 ⊠ 20136 – 𝒞 02 89402901
– Closed 7-30 August, Saturday lunch, Sunday　　　　　　　**F3**
Rest – Carte 44/60 €
♦ Sicilian ♦ Formal ♦

This restaurant has a decidedly Sicilian atmosphere, management and cuisine. Sample the tasty fish dishes and traditional Sicilian cuisine in both dining rooms.

XX **La Scaletta**　　　　　　　　　　 🍽 AC VISA ◎◎ AE

piazzale Stazione Genova 3 ⊠ 20144 – 𝒞 02 43986316
– www.lascalettamilano.it
– Closed 12-19 August, 25 December-1 January, Saturday lunch and Sunday
Rest – Menu 15 € (weekday lunch)/45 € – Carte 36/61 €　　　**E3**
♦ Modern ♦ Traditional ♦

This elegant restaurant is run by three young brothers who have created a lively, friendly atmosphere. Original silk-screen paintings depicting images of the city adorn the dining room. The menu features cuisine from Lombardy and the Mediterranean, including a few traditional dishes with a particularly successful contemporary twist.

XX **Hostaria Borromei**　　　　　　　 🍽 ⇔ VISA ◎◎ AE

via Borromei 4 ⊠ 20123 – Ⓜ Cordusio – 𝒞 02 86453760
– Closed 9-18 August, 24 December-7 January and lunch Saturday and Sunday
Rest – Menu 10/20 € (weekday lunch) – Carte 30/63 €　　　**F2**
♦ Italian ♦ Family ♦

Housed in an 18C palazzo in the heart of the historic centre, this small restaurant serves traditional, regional cuisine, with the accent on dishes from Mantua. Outdoor dining in the courtyard in summer.

XX **Da Giacomo**　　　　　　　　　　 AC VISA ◎◎

via B. Cellini ang. via Sottocorno 6 ⊠ 20129 – 𝒞 02 76023313
– www.giacomomilano.com
– Closed 2 weeks in August and Christmas Holidays　　　　**H1**
Rest – Carte 58/83 €
♦ Fish and seafood ♦ Traditional ♦

This old Milanese trattoria dates from the early 20C. Seafood enthusiasts will be delighted by the numerous fish specialities on offer. The menu also includes a few meat dishes, as well as Alba truffles, Caesars' mushrooms and cep mushrooms in season.

XX **Giacomo Bistrot**　　　　　　　　 AC VISA ◎◎

via Sottocorno 6 ⊠ 20129 – 𝒞 02 76022653 – www.giacomomilano.com
– Closed 2 weeks August, 24 December-2 January　　　　　　**H1**
Rest – Carte 48/66 €
♦ Classic ♦ Trendy ♦

This restaurant, which stays open until late at night, boasts tables set close together in French-bistro style, while its shelves of leather-bound volumes evoke the distinctly British ambience of a traditional bookshop. The menu features meat dishes, game, oysters and truffles (in season).

XX
£3
Alice   AC VISA ⦿ AE ⊙

*via Adige 9 ⊠ 20135 – **Ⓜ** Porta Romana – 𝒞 02 5462930*
– www.aliceristorante.it – Closed 2 weeks August, Sunday, Monday lunch
Rest – *(bookings advisable at dinner)*   *Plan I* **C3**
Menu 25 € (weekday lunch)/85 € – Carte 57/94 €
♦ Fish and seafood ♦ Friendly ♦
Both the chef and the sommelier are female in this restaurant, which specialises
in fish and seafood (the name Alice is the Italian for anchovy) prepared in a
range of imaginative dishes. Meat lovers will be pleased to learn that Fassone
beef and other meat dishes are also available on the menu.
➜ Spaghettini in brodo affumicato con vongole, calamari e scorza di
limone. Bocconcini di razza con foie gras e crema di finocchi. Universo:
mousse al cioccolato con cuore di liquirizia su salsa inglese allo zafferano.

X
Pane Acqua   ♿ AC VISA ⦿

*via Bandello 14 ⊠ 20123 – **Ⓜ** Conciliazione – 𝒞 02 48198622*
– www.paneacqua.com
– Closed 3 weeks August, 24 December-6 January, Sunday and Monday lunch
Rest – Menu 55 € – Carte 59/75 €   **E2**
♦ Modern ♦ Fashionable ♦
If you're looking for an unusual address, look no further! Thanks to an agree-
ment with a modern art gallery, the furnishings and decor in this small bistro-
style restaurant change on a regular basis. Not so the cuisine, however, which is
always full of flavour and imaginative flair.

X
La Felicità   ♿ AC VISA ⦿ AE ⊙

*via Rovello 3 ⊠ 20121 – **Ⓜ** Cordusio – 𝒞 02 865235*   **F1**
Rest – Menu 17/22 € – Carte 15/51 €
♦ Chinese ♦ Family ♦
This simple, well-run Chinese restaurant also serves Vietnamese, Thai and
Korean cuisine. Elegant furnishings which are broadly Oriental in style.

X
Masuelli San Marco   AC VISA AE

*viale Umbria 80 ⊠ 20135 – **Ⓜ** Lodi TIBB – 𝒞 02 55184138*
– www.masuellitrattoria.it
– Closed 3 weeks in August, 25 December-6 January, Sunday, Monday midday
Rest – Carte 36/65 €   **D3**
♦ Lombardian ♦ Friendly ♦
A rustic atmosphere with a luxurious feel in a typical trattoria, with the same
management since 1921; cuisine strongly linked to traditional Lombardy and
Piedmont recipes.

X
£3
Al Pont de Ferr   AC VISA ⦿

*Ripa di Porta Ticinese 55 ⊠ 20143 – **Ⓜ** Porta Genova FS*
– 𝒞 02 89406277 – www.pontdeferr.it
– Closed 10-18 August, 1-10 January   *Plan I* **B3**
Rest – Menu 70 € – Carte 55/73 €
♦ Creative ♦ Rustic ♦
Situated on the Naviglio Grande promenade in front of the old iron bridge, this sim-
ple, rustic-style restaurant serves elegant, yet reasonably priced gourmet cuisine.
Simpler menu available at lunchtime (the à la carte menu can also be requested).
➜ Cipolla rossa di Tropea caramellata al formaggio di capra. Gnocchi di
patate alla brace con zucchine grigliate e gamberoni. Maiale iberico con
crema di burrata e ricci di mare.

X
⊛
Giulio Pane e Ojo   AC ⇔ VISA ⦿ AE ⊙

*via Muratori 10 ⊠ 20135 – **Ⓜ** Porta Romana – 𝒞 02 5456189*
– www.giuliopaneojo.com
– Closed Sunday except December   **H3**
Rest – *(booking advisable)* Menu 10 € (weekday lunch) – Carte 27/41 €
♦ Roman ♦ Friendly ♦
The cuisine here is typical of Rome with its generous portions and full-bodied
flavours. Specialities include spaghetti all'amatriciana, spring lamb with pota-
toes and the ever-popular oxtail stew.

ITALY - MILAN

Dongiò ✂ 🚇 AC VISA 🚫 AE ①

via Corio 3 ✉ *20135 –* 🚇 *Porta Romana – ℰ 02 5511372*
– Closed 3 weeks August, Saturday lunch, Sunday **H3**
Rest *– (booking advisable) Carte 27/37 €*
♦ Calabrian ♦ Family ♦

This family-run restaurant introduces a flavour of traditional Calabria to Milan with a simple, lively atmosphere that is quite rare nowadays. Home cooking based on fresh pasta, 'nduja (spicy sausage) and the ubiquitous peperoncino (chilli pepper).

CENTRAL STATION *Plan III*

Principe di Savoia 🛗 🚇 🏖 🔲 AC 🛜 🔥 VISA 🚫 AE ①

piazza della Repubblica 17 ✉ *20124 –* 🚇 *Repubblica – ℰ 02 62301*
– www.hotelprincipedisavoia.com **M2**
400 rm – ♥219/900 € ♥♥246/928 €, ⚓ 41 € – 54 suites
Rest Acanto – see restaurant listing
♦ Grand Luxury ♦ Palace ♦ Stylish ♦

Overlooking Piazza della Repubblica, this majestic white building dating from the 19C is an imposing sight. With a truly international atmosphere, this luxury hotel boasts superb guestrooms, a well-equipped fitness area and a wellbeing centre. Perfect for a relaxing stay.

The Westin Palace 🛗 ♿ AC 🛜 🔥 🚗 VISA 🚫 AE ①

piazza della Repubblica 20 ✉ *20124 –* 🚇 *Repubblica – ℰ 02 63361*
– www.westinpalacemilan.it **M2**
228 rm – ♥100/999 € ♥♥110/1100 €, ⚓ 40 € – 5 suites
Rest Casanova – see restaurant listing
♦ Grand Luxury ♦ Stylish ♦

The Milanese apotheosis of the Imperial style – a luxury hotel with sober, austere decor. Some of the rooms have views of the Duomo, while all guests can enjoy the roof terrace in summer. Recently refurbished and just as elegant as ever, the restaurant now also offers a private dining area. Mediterranean dishes dominate the menu.

Atahotel Executive ♿ rm, AC rm, 🛜 🔥 VISA 🚫 AE ①

viale Luigi Sturzo 45 ✉ *20154 –* 🚇 *Porta Garibaldi FS – ℰ 02 62941*
– www.atahotels.it **L1**
414 rm ⚓ – ♥100/650 € ♥♥150/850 € – 6 suites
Rest *– (closed Saturday, Sunday lunch) Carte 37/49 €*
♦ Chain hotel ♦ Business ♦ Classic ♦

This modern hotel is situated opposite the Garibaldi railway station. Its well-equipped conference centre is ideal for business clients and meetings. Attractive and comfortable guestrooms.

Four Points Sheraton Milan Center 🛗 ♿ AC 🛜 🔥

via Cardano 1 ✉ *20124 –* 🚇 *Gioia – ℰ 02 667461* VISA 🚫 AE ①
– www.fourpoints.com/milan **M1**
254 rm ⚓ – ♥150/550 € ♥♥200/700 € – 11 suites
Rest Nectare – Carte 36/72 €
♦ Business ♦ Palace ♦ Classic ♦

Housed in a modern building in the centre of Milan, this hotel offers relaxing public areas furnished in a simple, elegant style, as well as pleasant and comfortable guestrooms. A bright dining room with tasteful decor.

UNA Hotel Tocq 🍴 AC 🛜 🔥 VISA 🚫 AE ①

via A. de Tocqueville 7/D ✉ *20154 –* 🚇 *Porta Garibaldi FS – ℰ 02 62071*
– www.unahotels.it **L1**
121 rm ⚓ – ♥124/613 € ♥♥124/633 € – 1 suite
Rest *– (closed Saturday and Sunday lunch) Carte 32/60 €*
♦ Business ♦ Chain hotel ♦ Design ♦

Not far from the huge building site that is changing the face of Milan, this modern, minimalist-style hotel is ideal for business travellers. Enjoy an aperitif in the fashionable lounge bar, or for a late night out head to the nearby Hollywood nightclub.

Holiday Inn Milan Garibaldi Station 🖪 ⴺ rm, 🔠 🛜 ⴽ

via Ugo Bassi 1 angolo via Farini ✉ *20159* 🚗 VISA ⓪ AE ⑩
– Ⓜ *Porta Garibaldi FS* – ☏ *02 6076801* – *www.himilangaribaldi.com*
129 rm ☲ – ♦120/250 € ♦♦134/264 € **K1**
Rest – Menu 23/50 € – Carte 35/68 €
♦ Chain hotel ♦ Business ♦ Modern ♦
This light, welcoming hotel decorated in a minimalist style continues to be a
good choice for accommodation in Milan. The pleasant breakfast room has a
glass cupola. Modern decor and traditional cuisine.

Starhotels Anderson 🖪 ⴺ rm, 🔠 🛜 ⴽ VISA ⓪ AE

piazza Luigi di Savoia 20 ✉ *20124* – Ⓜ *Centrale FS* – ☏ *02 6690141*
– *www.starhotels.com* *Plan I* **C1**
106 rm ☲ – ♦99/800 € ♦♦99/800 € **Rest** – Carte 37/67 €
♦ Chain hotel ♦ Classic ♦
This hotel has a warm, designer-style atmosphere, with fashionable and intimate public rooms and welcoming guestrooms offering all the usual comforts
of a hotel of this standard. The elegant lounge is home to a small restaurant
(open only in the evenings) which serves contemporary-style cuisine.

NH Machiavelli ⴺ 🔠 🛜 ⴽ VISA ⓪ AE ⑩

via Lazzaretto 5 ✉ *20124* – Ⓜ *Repubblica* – ☏ *02 631141*
– *www.nh-hotels.com* **M2**
103 rm ☲ – ♦100/490 € ♦♦110/500 € – 3 suites
Rest – *(closed Saturday and Sunday)* Carte 75/118 €
♦ Chain hotel ♦ Classic ♦
A modern hotel with simple, airy guestrooms. There is an open-plan layout that
encompasses a number of sitting areas in one large space. Excellent breakfast.

ADI Doria Grand Hotel ⴺ 🔠 🛜 ⴽ VISA ⓪ AE ⑩

viale Andrea Doria 22 ✉ *20124* – Ⓜ *Caiazzo* – ☏ *02 67411411*
– *www.adihotels.com* *Plan I* **C1**
122 rm ☲ – ♦101/489 € ♦♦101/560 € – 2 suites
Rest – *(closed August, 24 December-6 January and Sunday)* Carte 39/55 €
♦ Chain hotel ♦ Classic ♦
This classical building has an elegant lobby furnished in early 20C-style and
large, comfortable guestrooms. Cultural and musical events are occasionally
held in the spacious public areas. This elegant restaurant serves fine regional
and international cuisine.

Auriga *without rest* 🔠 🛜 ⴽ VISA ⓪ AE ⑩

via Giovanni Battista Pirelli 7 ✉ *20124* – Ⓜ *Centrale FS* – ☏ *02 66985851*
– *www.auriga-milano.com*
– *Closed 2-25 August and 1-6 January* **M1**
52 rm ☲ – ♦90/270 € ♦♦120/360 €
♦ Business ♦ Modern ♦
The mix of styles, unusual façade and bright colours of this hotel combine to
create a striking exterior. Comfortable facilities and efficient service for tourists
and business travellers alike.

XXXX Acanto – *Hotel Principe di Savoia* 🔠 ⟷ VISA ⓪ AE ⑩

piazza della Repubblica 17 ✉ *20124* – Ⓜ *Repubblica* – ☏ *02 62302026*
– *www.hotelprincipedisavoia.it* **M2**
Rest – Menu 42 € *(weekday lunch)*/100 € – Carte 79/132 €
♦ Italian ♦ Elegant ♦
Enjoy classic-contemporary cuisine in this modern restaurant with large windows overlooking an unexpected garden. The mouthwatering dishes on offer
include pasta with prawns and lemon, tempura of squid, prawns and mullet
with courgettes and a sweet and sour sauce, and apple strudel with Malaga
wine-flavoured ice cream.

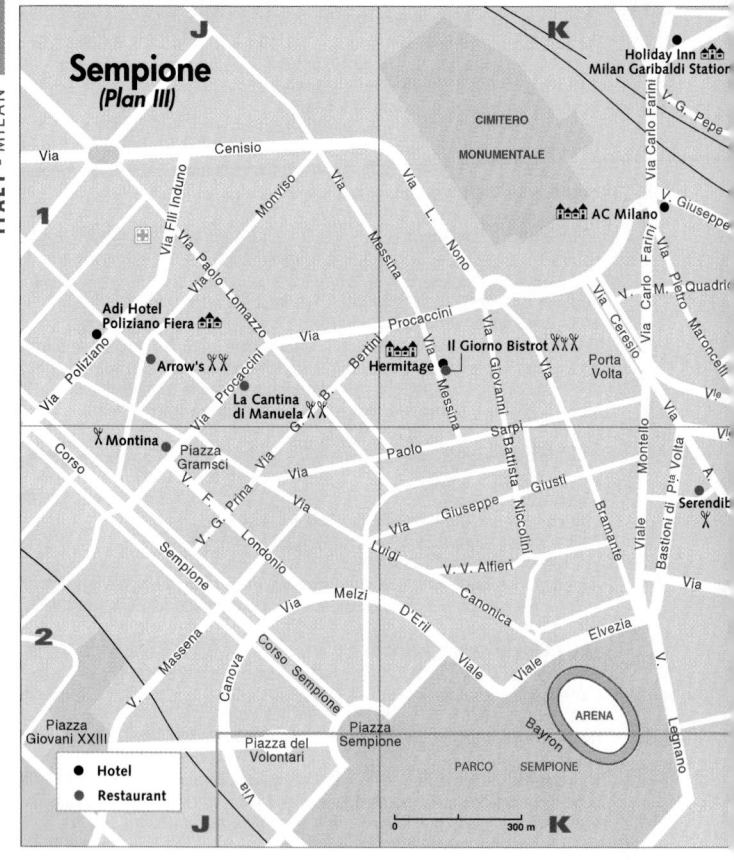

XXXX **Casanova** – Hotel The Westin Palace   🚫 🅐🅒 ⇆ 🆅🅸🆂🅰 ⊕ 🅰🅴 ⓪

piazza della Repubblica 20 ⊠ *20124* – Ⓜ *Repubblica* – ℰ *02 63361*
– *www.westin.com/palacemilan*   **M2**

Rest – Carte 59/109 € 🕸

♦ Italian ♦ Elegant ♦

The cuisine at the Casanova is predominantly Mediterranean in style, with particular attention paid to specialities from Lombardy, Piedmont and Liguria. Elegant restaurant with a new private dining area.

XXX **Gold**   🅐🅒 ⇆ 🆅🅸🆂🅰 ⊕ 🅰🅴 ⓪

piazza Risorgimento,angolo via Poerio ⊠ *20129* – Ⓜ *Porta Venezia*
– ℰ *02 7577771* – *www.dolcegabbanagold.it*
– *Closed August and Sunday*   **C2**

Rest – Menu 70/132 € – Carte 42/88 € 🕸

♦ Italian ♦ Fashionable ♦

Still considered one of the trendiest restaurants in Milan, Gold has a distinctive character that lives up to its name. Glitzy, luxurious surroundings, where, if you're lucky, you may even catch a glimpse of famous diners such as Louise Veronica Ciccone, otherwise known as Madonna.

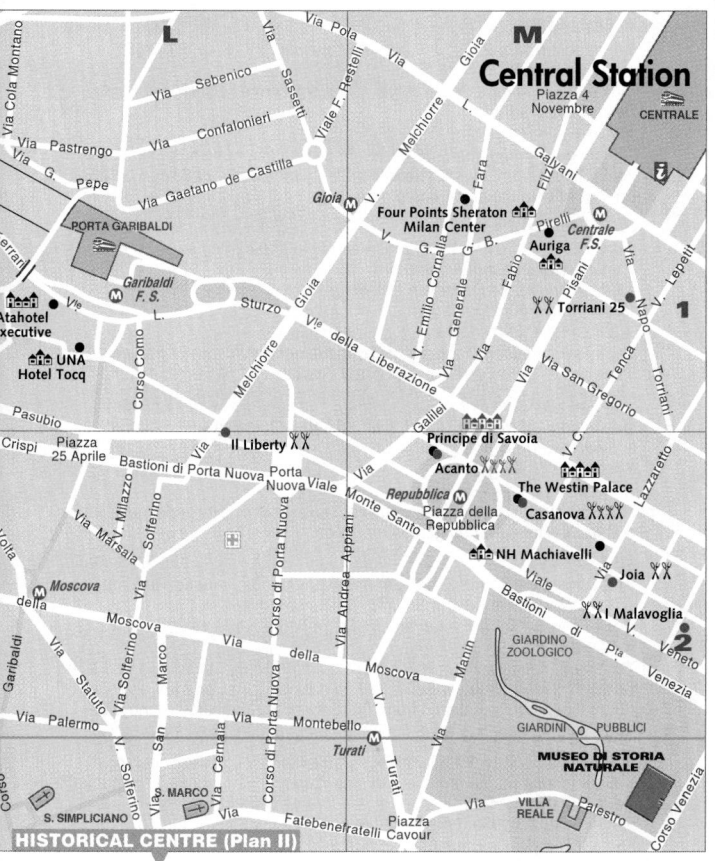

Central Station

Piazza 4 Novembre

CENTRALE

HISTORICAL CENTRE (Plan II)

✗✗ **Joia** (Pietro Leemann) AC ☐ VISA ④ AE ①

✿ *via Panfilo Castaldi 18*
  ⊠ *20124 –* **Ⓜ** *Repubblica*
  – ✆ *02 29522124 – www.joia.it*
  – *Closed 7-30 August, 25 December-8 January, Saturday lunch, Sunday*
  Rest – Menu 65/100 € – Carte 67/93 € ⌀   **M2**
  ♦ Vegetarian ♦ Formal ♦

This restaurant focuses on beautifully presented vegetarian cuisine with a hint of Eastern flavour. Less ambitious, reasonably priced dishes are served in the evening in the bistro-style dining room facing the open-view kitchen. Simple, plain decor.

➔ Gnocchi di patate senza farina, farciti di casera (formaggio) con fonduta di piselli. Muffin di grano saraceno, verdure e casera, patate, ricotta e camomilla. Torta senza zucchero con fragole, datteri e sorbetto di rabarbaro.

XX **Torriani 25**   AC ⇄ VISA ◯◯ AE ◯

via Napo Torriani 25 ☒ 20124 – ◍ Centrale FS – ☎ 02 67078183
– www.torriani25.it
– Closed 6-28 August, 24 December-1 January, Saturday lunch and Sunday
Rest – Carte 38/86 €   M1
♦ Italian ♦ Friendly ♦
This modern restaurant is decorated in warm colours, with plenty of natural
light. Choose from a wide selection of fish - the house speciality - on display
on the buffet in the dining room.

XX **I Malavoglia**   AC VISA ◯◯ AE ◯

via Lecco 4 ☒ 20124 – ◍ Porta Venezia – ☎ 02 29531387
– www.ristoranteimalavoglia.com
– Closed August, 24 December-7 January, Sunday, Monday lunch
Rest – Carte 40/83 €   M2
♦ Sicilian ♦ Formal ♦
This classic restaurant has been run by the same team for over thirty years. They
serve typical Sicilian dishes in Lombardy's capital.

XX **13 Giugno**   AC ⇄ VISA ◯◯ AE ◯

via Goldoni 44 ang.via Uberti 5 ☒ 20129 – ◍ Dateo – ☎ 02 719654
– www.ristorante13giugno.it   Plan I **D2**
Rest – Carte 50/84 €
♦ Sicilian ♦ Classic ♦
This restaurant has a subdued elegance, serves seafood and Sicilian specialities,
and has a veranda-winter garden extension.

XX **Il Liberty**   AC VISA ◯◯ AE

viale Monte Grappa 6 ☒ 20124 – ☎ 02 29011439 – www.il-liberty.it
– Closed 2 weeks in August, Saturday lunch, Sunday   **L2**
Rest – Menu 60/70 € – Carte 47/68 €
♦ Modern ♦ Friendly ♦
This small, friendly restaurant is housed in an Art Nouveau-style palazzo. It has
two dining rooms and a mezzanine. The cuisine focuses on meat and seafood
dishes. The former is sourced from the surrounding Lombardy countryside.

XX **Barbacoa**   ⌂ & AC ⇄ VISA AE

via delle Abbadesse 30 ☒ 20123 – ☎ 02 6883883 – www.barbacoa.it
– Closed for lunch Saturday, Sunday and August   Plan I **C1**
Rest – Menu 43/48 €
♦ International ♦ Minimalist ♦
The first European restaurant of a Brazilian chain, Barbacoa is a true celebration
of meat. Beef takes pride of place, although chicken, pork and lamb also feature
on the menu. The traditional caipirinha, a cocktail based on cane sugar and
lime, continues the Brazilian theme, while mixed salads and exotic fruit desserts
complete the picture.

X **Casa Fontana-23 Risotti**   AC VISA ◯◯

piazza Carbonari 5 ☒ 20125 – ◍ Sondrio – ☎ 02 6704710
– www.23risotti.it
– Closed 1-4 April, 1-26 August, 24 December-9 January, Saturday lunch,
Monday   Plan I **C1**
Rest – Menu 30 € – Carte 40/60 €
♦ Lombardian ♦ Family ♦
Despite the obligatory 25min wait for your food, this restaurant is well worth a
visit for its excellent risottos. Attractive pictures of rice fields on the walls.

X **Serendib**   AC VISA ◯◯
⊛
via Pontida 2 ☒ 20121 – ◍ Moscova – ☎ 02 6592139 – www.serendib.it
– Closed 10 -20 August   **K2**
Rest – *(dinner only)* Menu 25 € – Carte 27/48 €
♦ Indian ♦ Friendly ♦
Serendib, the old name for Sri Lanka, means "to make happy" – an ambitious
promise, but one which this restaurant manages to keep! True to its origins,
the tempting menu focuses on Indian and Sri Lankan cuisine.

ITALY - MILAN

La Cantina di Manuela   🔥 AC VISA ⬤⬤ AE

via Carlo Poerio 3 ✉ *20129*
– ⓜ Porta Venezia – ℰ 02 76318892
– www.lacantinadimanuela.it
– Closed 2 week August, 25 December-1 January, Sunday lunch   *Plan I* **C2**
Rest *– Carte 34/48 €* 🍷
♦ Italian ♦ Wine bar ♦

The dining room in this young, dynamic restaurant is surrounded by bottles of wine. Elaborate dishes feature on the menu, with antipasti available in the evening. At lunchtime these are replaced by various salads aimed at a business clientele in a hurry. Milanese-style cutlets are the house speciality.

Da Giannino-L'Angolo d'Abruzzo   AC VISA ⬤⬤

via Pilo 20 ✉ *20129 – ⓜ Porta Venezia – ℰ 02 29406526*   *Plan I* **D2**
Rest *– Carte 26/34 €*
♦ Abruzzian ♦ Family ♦

A warm welcome combined with a simple but lively atmosphere and typical dishes from the Abruzzo region make this a popular place to eat. Generous portions and excellent roast dishes.

Baia Chia   AC ⇄ VISA ⬤⬤

via Bazzini 37 ✉ *20131 – ⓜ Piola – ℰ 02 2361131*
– www.ristorantesardobaiachia.it
– Closed Easter Holidays, 6-25 August, Christmas Holidays, Sunday, Monday lunch   *Plan I* **D1**
Rest *– Carte 29/41 €*
♦ Sardinian ♦ Rustic ♦

This pleasant restaurant with a family atmosphere is divided into two small dining rooms, plus a veranda which can also be used in winter. Excellent fish dishes and Sardinian specialities on the menu. Many of the wines also come from Sardinia.

FIERA-SEMPIONE AT NAVIGLI (viale Certosa, San Siro, via Novara, corso Sampione, piazza Carlo Magno, via Monte Rosa, via Washington, viale Fulvio Testi, Niguarda, viale Fermi)   *Plan I*

Hermitage   🅰 AC 🛜 🛁 🍽 VISA ⬤⬤ AE ⓪

via Messina 10 ✉ *20154 – ⓜ Porta Garibaldi FS – ℰ 02 318170*
– www.monrifhotels.it
– Closed August   **K1**
122 rm ⌑ – †100/320 € ††120/340 € – 9 suites
Rest *Il Giorno Bistrot* – see restaurant listing
♦ Business ♦ Classic ♦

Style and comfort are the trademarks of this hotel, which combines the atmosphere of elegant period-style interiors with modern facilities. Situated in a quarter bustling with activity and shops.

Milan Marriott Hotel   🅵 AC 🕻 🛁 VISA ⬤⬤ AE ⓪

via Washington 66 ✉ *20146 – ⓜ Wagner – ℰ 02 48521*
– www.milanmarriotthotel.com   **A2**
321 rm – †99/545 € ††99/545 €, ⌑ 20 €
Rest *La Brasserie de Milan* – ℰ 02 48522834 – Carte 39/86 €
♦ Business ♦ Classic ♦

Not far from the bustling Corso Vercelli, this hotel combines a modern exterior with a more traditional interior decor. Functional guestrooms. Enjoy regional dishes and Mediterranean cuisine in the La Brasserie de Milan restaurant.

ITALY - MILAN

AC Milano   ♪₅ ♿ 🅰🅲 🛜 ⚙ 🚗 🆅🅸🆂🅰 ⓑ 🅰🅴 ⓞ

via Tazzoli 2 ✉ *20154 –* ✆ *02 20424211 – www.ac-hotels.com*
156 rm ⊆ – ♦120/500 € ♦♦130/510 € – 2 suites   *Plan III* **K1**
Rest – *(residents only)* Carte 44/57 €
♦ Business ♦ Design ♦
A stone's throw from Corso Como and Milan's nightlife, this modern, designer-style hotel is popular with an upmarket business clientele. Spacious, well-appointed bedrooms in keeping with the high standards of this hotel chain.

Wagner *without rest*   🅰🅲 🛜 🆅🅸🆂🅰 ⓑ 🅰🅴 ⓞ

via Buonarroti 13 ✉ *20149 –* Ⓜ *Buonarroti –* ✆ *02 463151*
– www.roma-wagner.com
– Closed 12-19 August   **A2**
48 rm ⊆ – ♦105/698 € ♦♦149/698 € – 1 suite
♦ Business ♦ Personalised ♦
This hotel, next to the eponymous metro station, has attractive rooms with marble and modern furnishings.

Enterprise Hotel   🏠 ♪₅ 🐾 ♿ 🅰🅲 🛜 ⚙ 🚗 🆅🅸🆂🅰 ⓑ 🅰🅴 ⓞ

corso Sempione 91 ✉ *20149 –* ✆ *02318181 – www.enterprisehotel.com*
126 rm ⊆ – ♦133/820 € ♦♦143/820 € – 2 suites   **A1**
Rest *Sophia's* – Carte 42/70 €
♦ Business ♦ Design ♦
Attention to detail and design is evident in every aspect of this elegant modern hotel, from the marble and granite exterior to its bespoke furnishings and pleasing geometrical lines. A pleasant and original restaurant for lunch and dinner. Outdoor dining in summer.

Regency *without rest*   ♪₅ 🅰🅲 🛜 ⚙ 🆅🅸🆂🅰 ⓑ 🅰🅴 ⓞ

via Arimondi 12 ✉ *20155 –* ✆ *02 39216021 – www.regency-milano.com*
– Closed 2-25 August and 21 December-6 January   **A1**
71 rm ⊆ – ♦80/290 € ♦♦100/390 €
♦ Business ♦ Classic ♦
This charming and unusual mansion dating from the late-19C is built in the style of a small castle. Delightful courtyard and stylish interior furnishings.

Rubens   ♪₅ 🅰🅲 🛜 ⚙ 🅿 🆅🅸🆂🅰 ⓑ 🅰🅴 ⓞ

via Rubens 21 ✉ *20148 –* Ⓜ *Gambara –* ✆ *02 40302*
– www.hotelrubensmilano.com
– Closed 5-19 August   **A2**
87 rm ⊆ – ♦89/320 € ♦♦99/450 €
Rest – *(residents only)* Carte 36/60 €
♦ Business ♦ Personalised ♦
The spacious, comfortable guestrooms in this elegant hotel are adorned with frescoes by contemporary artists and furnished in stylish beige, golden and pastel-coloured tones. To get the day off to a good start, enjoy a copious breakfast in the evocatively named Sala delle Nuvole (Room in the Clouds) on the top floor.

Accademia   ♪₅ 🅰🅲 🛜 ⚙ 🚗 🆅🅸🆂🅰 ⓑ 🅰🅴 ⓞ

viale Certosa 68 ✉ *20155 –* ✆ *02 39211122 – www.antareshotels.com*
– Closed 9-23 August   **A1**
65 rm ⊆ – ♦89/320 € ♦♦99/400 € – 1 suite
Rest – *(residents only)*
♦ Business ♦ Classic ♦
Following major renovation work, this hotel features new guestrooms in warm tones with designer-style furnishings and excellent levels of comfort thanks to the careful use of the space available. Note the typical mosaic which frames the lift doors.

ITALY - MILAN

ADI Hotel Poliziano Fiera   &rm, 🛗 📶 🖫 🌐 🖭 ⓘ
via Poliziano 11 ✉ *20154 –* ☎ *02 3191911 – www.adihotels.com*
– Closed August and 28 December-8 January   *Plan III* **J1**
98 rm ☕ **–** ●73/336 € ●●80/397 € – 2 suites
Rest *– (closed Sunday) (residents only)* Carte 25/42 €
♦ Business ♦ Classic ♦
This modern hotel offers friendly, attentive service and spacious guestrooms
furnished in light green and sand-coloured tones, as well as attractive public
rooms.

Astoria *without rest*   🛗 📶 🖫 🖾 🌐 🖭
viale Murillo 9 ✉ *20149 –* Ⓜ *Lotto –* ☎ *02 40090095*
– www.astoriahotelmilano.com   **A2**
68 rm ☕ – ●75/300 € ●●95/400 €
♦ Chain hotel ♦ Modern ♦
This hotel that caters mostly to business travellers is located along a ring road.
The rooms are modern and soundproof.

Mirage   ᷃Ł &rm, 🛗 📶 🖫 ᷃ 🖾 🌐 🖭 ⓘ
viale Certosa 104/106 ✉ *20156 –* ☎ *02 39210471*
– www.hotelmirage-milano.com
– Closed 26 July-18 August and 24-31December   **A1**
86 rm ☕ – ●●114/344 €
Rest *– (closed Friday, Saturday) (dinner only)* Carte 21/36 €
♦ Business ♦ Classic ♦
Thanks to its strategic location near major motorways and not far from the Rho-
Pero exhibition complex, this hotel is ideal for business travellers. The guestrooms, some of which have parquet floors, have been renovated in traditional
style.

Des Etrangers *without rest*   & 🛗 📶 🖫 ᷃ 🖾 🌐 🖭 ⓘ
via Sirte 9 ✉ *20146 –* ☎ *02 48955325 – www.hoteldesetrangers.it*
– Closed 9-25 August   **A3**
94 rm ☕ – ●50/200 € ●●70/380 €
♦ Business ♦ Classic ♦
This well-maintained hotel in a quiet street offers its guests functional and comfortable public areas and guestrooms, as well as convenient underground parking.

Antica Locanda Leonardo *without rest*   🚗 🛗 📶
corso Magenta 78 ✉ *20123 –* Ⓜ *Conciliazione*   🖾 🌐 🖭 ⓘ
– ☎ *02 48014197 – www.anticalocandaleonardo.com*
– Closed 5-25 August, 31 December-6 January   *Plan II* **E2**
16 rm ☕ – ●95/120 € ●●170/265 €
♦ Townhouse ♦ Personalised ♦
The luxury atmosphere combines with the family-style welcome in a hotel
which overlooks a small inner courtyard, in an ideal location near the place
where Leonardo da Vinci's painting of the "Last Supper" is housed.

Il Luogo di Aimo e Nadia *(Aimo Moroni)*   🛗 ✿
ꔸꔸ ꔸꔸ   *via Montecuccoli 6* ✉ *20147 –* Ⓜ *Primaticcio*   🖾 🌐 🖭 ⓘ
– ☎ *02 416886 – www.aimoenadia.com*
– Closed 3 weeks August, 1-8 January, Saturday lunch, Sunday   **A3**
Rest – Menu 39 € *(weekday lunch)*/120 € – Carte 78/160 € ⅋
♦ Creative ♦ Formal ♦
Tuscan cuisine was brought to Milan, and later to other regions. Faithful to this,
the selection of Italian products that the restaurant offers today is difficult to
equal.
→ Vermicelli con bottarga di tonno, seppioline arricciate, fave fresche,
limoni e mandorle. Anatra al leggero fumo di zucchero di canna e ridu-
zione di ciliegie di Vignola. Dolci ortaggi: tuberi e tartufi.

ITALY - MILAN

XXX **La Pobbia 1850**

via Gallarate 92 ⊠ 20151 – ☎ 02 38006641
– www.lapobbia.com
– Closed 5-26 August, 1-10 January, Sunday   **A1**
Rest – Menu 25 € – Carte 43/73 €
♦ Lombardian ♦ Formal ♦

The name of this restaurant refers to the poplar trees that once lined the road
through what was still open countryside in the late 19C. The old inn, now converted into an elegant restaurant with an internal garden, continues to offer traditional specialities from Lombardy, as well as a selection of fish dishes.

XXX **Unico** (Fabio Baldassarre)

via Achille Papa 30, palazzo World Join Center ⊠ 20149 – Ⓜ Lotto
– ☎ 02 39261025 – www.unicorestaurant.it
– Closed 2 weeks August and Saturday lunch   **A1**
Rest – Menu 60/120 € – Carte 64/93 €
♦ Creative ♦ Trendy ♦

Situated in the Portello district, this restaurant on the 20th floor of the World
Join Center boasts breathtaking views. The delightful culinary combinations on
the menu are just as impressive as the setting.
➔ Spaghetti "cacio e pepe" con porri e ricci di mare. Filetto di fassona al
pepe verde, patate al burro e agretti. Sorbetto al sedano su infusione di
mango, arance e zenzero.

XX **Il Giorno Bistrot** – Hotel Hermitage

via Messina 10 ⊠ 20154 – Ⓜ Porta Garibaldi FS – ☎ 02 318170
– Closed August, Saturday and Sunday lunch   Plan III **K1**
Rest – Menu 25 € (weekday lunch)/60 € – Carte 35/61 €
♦ Classic ♦ Formal ♦

Like the hotel of which it is a part, this restaurant is characterised by elegant
decor and attentive service. The cuisine is renowned for its seafood specialities
and, on Mondays, for its dishes of boiled meat.

XX **Innocenti Evasioni** (Arrigoni e Picco)

via privata della Bindellina ⊠ 20155
– ☎ 02 33001882 – www.innocentievasioni.com
– Closed August, 1-10 January and Sunday   **A1**
Rest – (dinner only) (booking advisable) Menu 28/68 € – Carte 47/71 € ♨
♦ Creative ♦ Formal ♦ Intimate ♦

This pleasant establishment, with large windows facing the garden, offers classic cuisine reinterpreted with imagination. Enjoyable outdoor summer dining.
➔ Tagliolini al nero di seppia con filetti di rombo, barba dei frati e pomodorini. Ombrina dorata, cous-cous con pomodori essicati, olive, uvetta e
salsa allo zafferano. Cheese-cake alla vaniglia con sorbetto di ciliegia al
Porto.

XX **Tano Passami l'Olio** (Gaetano Simonato)

via Villoresi, 16 ⊠ 20143 – ☎ 02 8394139
– www.tanopassamilolio.it
– Closed August, 24 December-6 January and Sunday   **B3**
Rest – (dinner only) (booking advisable) Menu 68/110 € – Carte 81/115 €
♦ Creative ♦ Intimate ♦

The key features here are the soft lighting, romantic atmosphere and creative
fish and meat dishes, flavoured with a choice of extra-virgin olive oils on display
in the dining room. Smoking lounge with a sofa.
➔ Uova di quaglia caramellate su mousse di tonno, bottarga di tonno e
tonno crudo marinato. Carrè d'agnello in crosta di mandorle col suo
fondo alla liquirizia. Mousse di nocciola con crema solida di cioccolato in
salsa di pistacchi.

XX **Arrow's**   🛋 ᓬ 🅰🅲 ꜰꜱꜰ ⓿ 🅰🅴 ⓿

via A.Mantegna 17/19 ✉ *20154 – 🕻 02 341533 – www.ristorantearrows.it*
– Closed 3 weeks August, Sunday, Monday lunch   *Plan III* **J1**
Rest – Carte 34/76 €
◆ Fish and seafood ◆ Family ◆
Packed, even at midday, the atmosphere becomes cosier in the evening but the seafood cuisine, prepared according to tradition, remains the same.

XX **La Cantina di Manuela**   ᓬ 🅰🅲 ꜰꜱꜰ ⓿

😊 *via Procaccini 41* ✉ *20154 – 🕻 02 3452034 – www.lacantinadimanuela.it*
– Closed Sunday lunch   *Plan III* **J1**
Rest – Carte 32/52 € ☆
◆ Italian ◆ Friendly ◆
This restaurant-cum-wine bar is not far from FieraMilanoCity. Lasagne with aubergines, gilthead fish, smoked scamorza cheese, cherry tomatoes and rocket pesto all feature on the menu, as well as other traditional dishes reinterpreted with a light touch.

X **Trattoria Montina**   🛋 🅰🅲 ꜰꜱꜰ ⓿ 🅰🅴 ⓿

via Procaccini 54 ✉ *20154 –* Ⓜ *Porta Garibaldi FS – 🕻 02 3490498*
– www.trattoriamontina.it
– Closed 8-30 August, 25 December-5 January, Sunday, Monday lunch
Rest – Carte 31/57 €   *Plan III* **J2**
◆ Lombardian ◆ Intimate ◆
Nice bistro atmosphere, tables close together, defused lighting in the evening in an establishment managed by twin brothers; seasonal national and Milanese dishes.

TURIN
TORINO

Population: 907 563

Piazza Castello, the square from which some of Turin's most celebrated avenues start, may well be considered the heart of the city; while the city's landmark building has to be the Mole Antonelliana – originally designed as a Jewish synagogue. Named after an ancient Roman settlement, the Quadrilatero Romano is the most fashionable quarter of Turin and boasts some of its most elegant shops; its narrow medieval streets are a fascinating interlude to the city's orthogonal plan. Less fashionable but equally interesting is Borgo Dora, the quarter north of the Piazza della Repubblica – a popular area that has been given a facelift but still retains its old, bohemian atmosphere – and don't miss the Cortile del Maglio, inside the arsenal in Piazza Borgo Dora, with its markets and art.

At the other end of the scale, la Collina provides some of the city's smartest addresses, while crossing the River Po – the longest in Italy – at Piazza Vittorio Veneto will lead you to Turin's luxurious period houses. Those interested in residential architecture can also find some of the city's most beautiful houses – dating back to the 19C – in the Via Galileo Ferrari area of the Crocetta quarter. For a more vibrant atmosphere, head for the embankment between Piazza Vittorio Veneto and Corso Vittorio Emanuele and you will find the 'murazzi', where you will get the best of Turin's nightlife with its bars and clubs.

TURIN IN...

→ **ONE DAY**
Piazza Castello, Via Roma, Piazza San Carlo, Mole Antonelliana, Piazza Vittorio Veneto, Duomo, Sacra Sindone.

→ **TWO DAYS**
Egyptian Museum, Sabaudia Gallery, Palazzo Carignano & Madama.

→ **THREE DAYS**
Valentino Park, Reggia di Venaria, Museum of Cinema.

PRACTICAL INFORMATION

ARRIVAL-DEPARTURE

 Better known as Caselle – after the nearby town – Turin's airport, Sandro Pertini, is 16km north of the city.

Trains run every 30min and bring you into Torino Dora Railway Station in 19min. A shuttle bus takes 50min to the centre. A taxi will take about 40min.

GETTING AROUND

Turin has a very efficient public transport network, with buses and trams crossing the city from 5am until midnight. Tickets for buses, trams and the underground can be bought at tobacconists, newsagents and other places exhibiting a special GTT sign, and must be stamped on board. Options range from 90min travel to unlimited daily use, as well as blocks of 5 or 25 tickets.

CALENDAR HIGHLIGHTS

February
CioccolaTò Chocolate Festival.

May
Fiera Internazionale del Libro (International Book Fair).

June
Feast of Patron Saint John the Baptist.

September
Mito (over 200 music events).

October
Salone del Gusto (biennial food fair, organised by the Slow Food Movement).

November
Torino Film Festival.

EATING OUT

Turin can rightly boast of being one of Italy's gastronomic centres. Not to be missed are the fresh egg pastas, and the local braised beef, lamb and pigeons. White truffles deserve a mention, although they've become so rare that prices are often incredibly high; they are usually served with pasta or fonduta (melted cheese, milk and egg yolks). With some of the best Italian chocolate produced in Turin, desserts are a real treat. You might find bonèt (chocolate pudding with almond biscuits), torta di nocciole (hazelnut cake) or panna cotta (cooked cream). Alongside Tuscany, Piedmont's red wines are indisputably the best in Italy; try a local Barbera, a reliable Nebbiolo or a world famous Barbaresco or Barolo. Cafés have a long tradition in Turin; try a bicerin (a drink made from coffee, cream and chocolate) with a gianduiotto (a chocolate made with 'tonda gentile', a famous variety of hazelnut). Look out for the world's biggest food market, 'Eataly': 2,500m² of delicacies brought to you by local producers, who pride themselves on their excellent, often rare, ingredients.

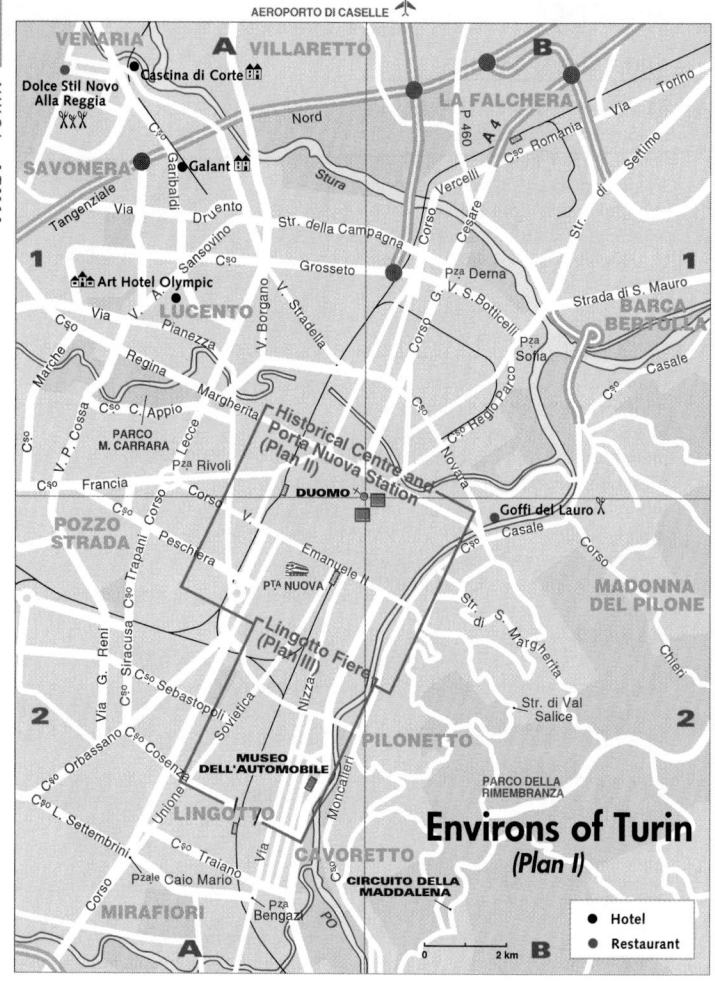

AEROPORTO DI CASELLE ✈

VENARIA   A   VILLARETTO   B

Dolce Stil Novo
Alla Reggia
XXX   ■Cascina di Corte 🏠

Nord   LA FALCHERA

SAVONERA   ■Garibaldi   ■Galant 🏠

Tangenziale   Via   Druento   Stura

Str. della Campagna

Sansovino   Grosseto

1   ♨ Art Hotel Olympic   Pza Derna   **1**

LUCENTO   Pza Sofia   BARCA BERTOLLA

Pianezza   Strada di S. Mauro

Regina   Margherita

PARCO M. CARRARA   Pza Rivoli

Francia   Corso   Historical Centre and Porta Nuova Station (Plan II)

POZZO STRADA   DUOMO   ■Goffi del Lauro

Peschera   Emanuele II   Casale   MADONNA DEL PILONE

PTA NUOVA

Lingotto Fiere (Plan III)

2   Nizza   PILONETTO   **2**

MUSEO DELL'AUTOMOBILE   PARCO DELLA RIMEMBRANZA

LINGOTTO   CAVORETTO

MIRAFIORI   Pza Bengazi   CIRCUITO DELLA MADDALENA

Environs of Turin
(Plan I)

0   2 km

● Hotel
● Restaurant

HISTORICAL CENTRE   *Plan II*

🏨   **Golden Palace**   ⅃ 🕤 🐾 🗔 & 🗛 🤶 🛗 VISA ⬥⬤ AE ⑩

via dell'Arcivescovado 18 ✉ *10121* – Ⓜ *Re Umberto* – ✆ *011 5512111*
– www.goldenpalace.it   **D2**

166 rm ⌑ – ♦199€ ♦♦219€ – 14 suites

Rest *Winner* – see restaurant listing

♦ Grand Luxury ♦ Design ♦

When Palazzo Toro (the present location of this hotel) was built after the Second
World War, the building was cited for its design and structure in some of the
best books on architecture. Half a century later, its Art Deco influence and minimalist style continues to delight guests. A hotel fit for a king!

ITALY - TURIN

Grand Hotel Sitea

via Carlo Alberto 35 ✉ *10123* – ⓜ *Porta Nuova* – ✆ *011 5170171*
– *www.grandhotelsitea.it*   **E2**
120 rm ⌂ – †139/270 € ††178/370 € – 1 suite
Rest *Carignano* – see restaurant listing
♦ Palace ♦ Traditional ♦ Classic ♦
Founded in 1925, this hotel keeps the traditions of elegant hospitality alive. It has a stylish, classic and period decor that contributes to its delightful atmosphere.

Principi di Piemonte

via Gobetti 15 ✉ *10123* – ⓜ *Porta Nuova* – ✆ *011 55151*
– *www.atahotels.it*   **E2**
99 rm ⌂ – †200/750 € ††200/750 € – 18 suites
Rest *Casa Savoia* – see restaurant listing
♦ Luxury ♦ Business ♦ Modern ♦
This historic 1930s building is situated just a stone's throw from the centre. It offers spacious guestrooms decorated in marble, an elegant atmosphere and resolutely modern comfort.

Victoria *without rest*

via Nino Costa 4 ✉ *10123* – ⓜ *Porta Nuova* – ✆ *011 5611909*
– *www.hotelvictoria-torino.com*   **E2**
106 rm ⌂ – †175/220 € ††290/330 € – 4 suites
♦ Traditional ♦ Personalised ♦
Antique furniture, symphonies of colours, four poster beds, an exacting attention to details in the personalised environment of an elegant residence with few rivals for fascination and atmosphere.

NH Ambasciatori

corso Vittorio Emanuele II 104 ✉ *10121* – ⓜ *Vinzaglio* – ✆ *011 57521*
– *www.nh-hotels.it*   **C2**
199 rm – †163/260 € ††183/290 €, ⌂ 20 € – 4 suites
Rest *Il Diplomatico* – see restaurant listing
♦ Chain hotel ♦ Business ♦ Classic ♦
A modern hotel in a square building, ideal for conferences, fashion shows or receptions. Comfortable, elegant guestrooms with a 1980s decor.

Art Hotel Boston

via Massena 70 ✉ *10128* – ✆ *011 500359* – *www.arthotelboston.it*
86 rm ⌂ – †80/250 € ††100/300 € – 1 suite   **D3**
Rest – *(residents only)* Carte 33/60 €
♦ Business ♦ Design ♦
The renovation of this hotel has fully satisfied not only the requirements of comfort but also those of good taste. There is an art collection in the hall and oriental-style ornaments in the newly furnished rooms.

Genova *without rest*

via Sacchi 14/b ✉ *10128* – ⓜ *Porta Nuova* – ✆ *011 5629400*
– *www.albergogenova.it*   **E2**
78 rm ⌂ – †70/180 € ††90/260 € – 1 suite
♦ Traditional ♦ Personalised ♦
At Porta Nuova, luxury atmosphere in an 19th century building where restorations have skilfully combined a classical interior with all the modern requirements of comfort.

Genio *without rest*

corso Vittorio Emanuele II 47 ✉ *10125* – ⓜ *Porta Nuova*
– ✆ *011 6505771* – *www.hotelgenio.it*   **E2**
116 rm ⌂ – †75/150 € ††95/280 €
♦ Traditional ♦ Classic ♦
Housed in a late-19C palazzo which was extended for the Olympics, this hotel features well-maintained guestrooms decorated with individual touches. Artistic flooring in the corridors and rooms adds a touch of elegance to the building.

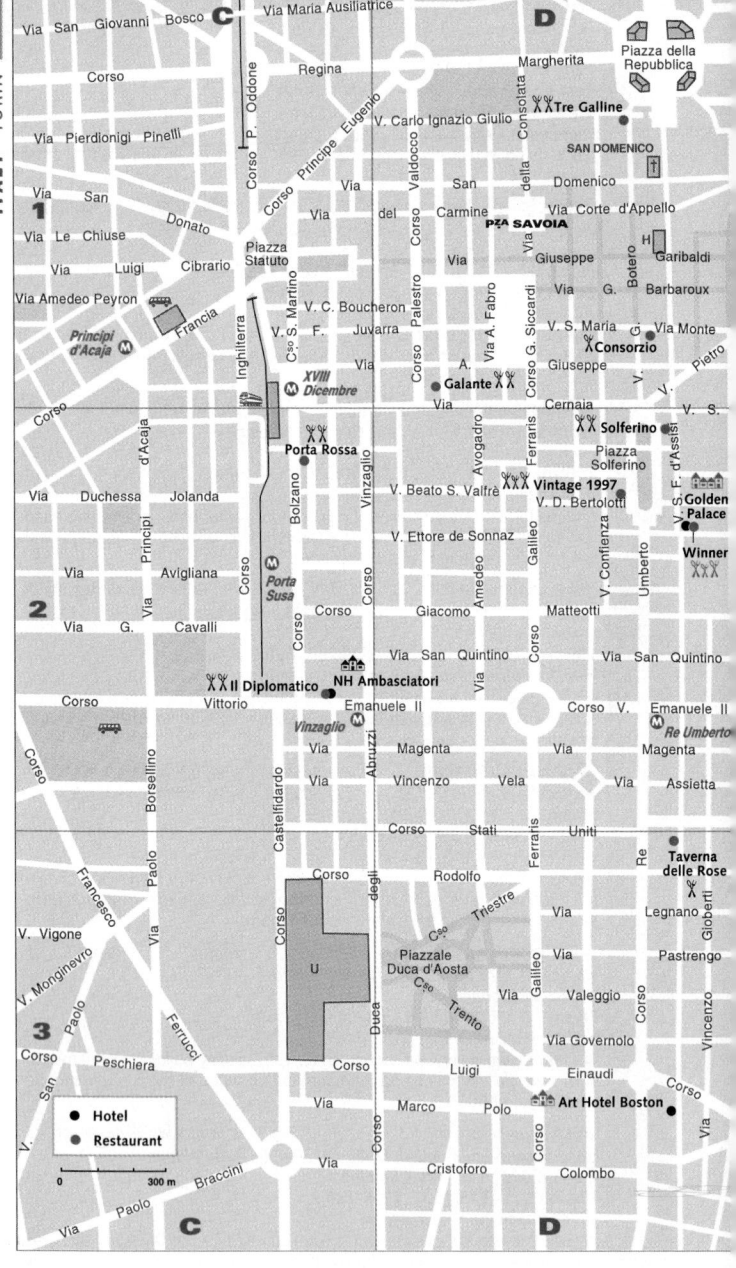

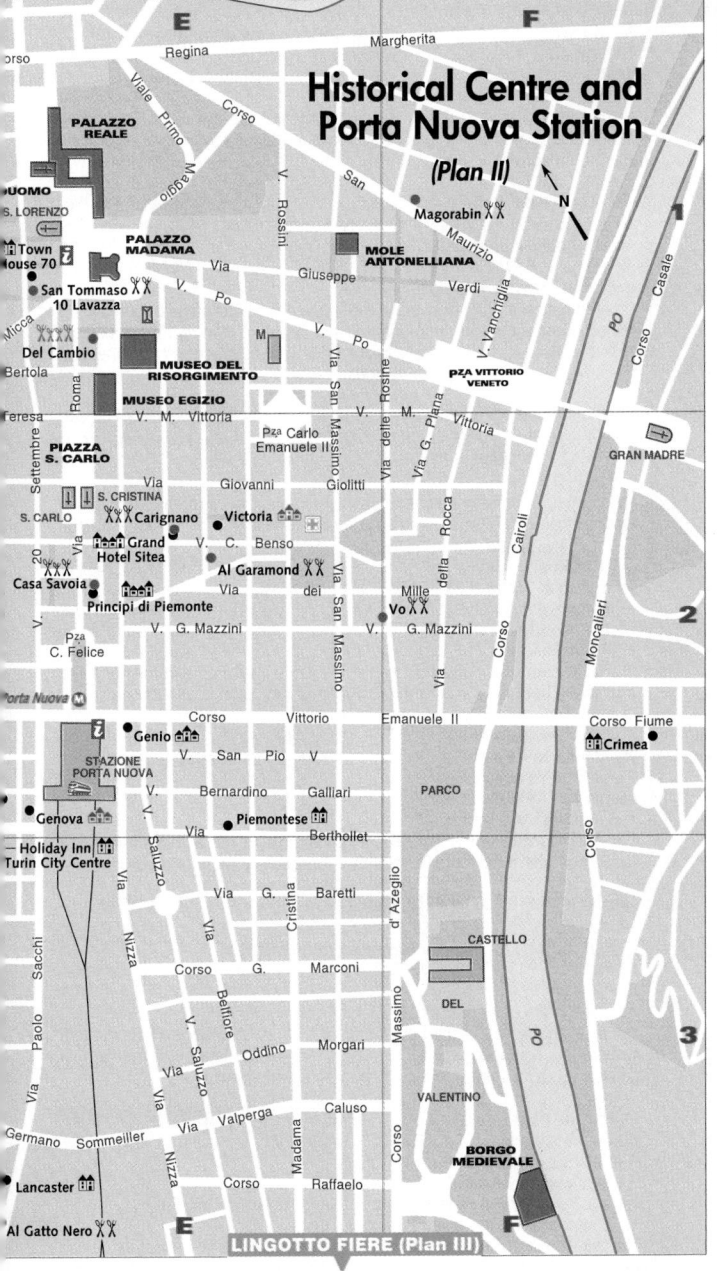

Historical Centre and Porta Nuova Station
(Plan II)

N

PALAZZO REALE

DUOMO

S. LORENZO

Town House 70

PALAZZO MADAMA

San Tommaso
10 Lavazza

Del Cambio

Bertola

Teresa

Roma

Settembre

Micca

MUSEO DEL RISORGIMENTO

MUSEO EGIZIO

V. M. Vittoria

PIAZZA S. CARLO

Via
S. CRISTINA
Carignano

S. CARLO

Casa Savoia

Grand Hotel Sitea

Principi di Piemonte

Pza C. Felice

Porta Nuova

Genio

STAZIONE PORTA NUOVA

Genova

Holiday Inn Turin City Centre

Sacchi

Paolo

Via

Germano Sommeiller

Lancaster

Al Gatto Nero

Regina

Viale Primo Maggio

Corso

V. Rossini

San

Margherita

Magorabin

Maurizio

MOLE ANTONELLIANA

Via

Giuseppe

V. Po

Verdi

V. Vanchiglia

PZA VITTORIO VENETO

V. San Massimo

V. delle Rosine

Vittoria

Via G. Plana

V. M.

Pza Carlo Emanuele II

Giovanni

Giolitti

Victoria

V. C. Benso

Al Garamond

Via dei

Rocca

della

Mille

Vo

V. G. Mazzini

V. G. Mazzini

Corso

Cairoli

GRAN MADRE

Moncalieri

PO

Corso

Casale

Corso

Corso Vittorio Emanuele II

V. San Pio V

V. Bernardino Galliari

Piemontese

Berthollet

PARCO

Corso Fiume

Crimea

Corso

Via

Nizza

Via

Saluzzo

Via G.

Via Cristina

Baretti

Corso G. Marconi

V. Belfiore

Oddino

Via Saluzzo

Via Valperga

Nizza

Caluso

Via Madama

Corso Raffaello

d' Azeglio

Corso Massimo

Morgari

CASTELLO DEL

VALENTINO

BORGO MEDIEVALE

PO

LINGOTTO FIERE (Plan III)

Art Hotel Olympic 🏠 🅰️ 🛜 🚗 VISA 🅾️ AE ①

via Verolengo 19 ✉ 10149 – ✆ 011 39997 – www.arthotelolympic.it
147 rm 🛏 – 🛏80/150 € 🛏🛏100/300 €   *Plan I* **A1**
Rest – Carte 27/56 €
♦ Business ♦ Minimalist ♦

As the name suggests, the hotel brings together art and sport. Established during the recent winter games, it boasts designer rooms and communal areas adorned with artwork.

Piemontese *without rest* 🅰️ 🛜 VISA 🅾️ AE ①

via Berthollet 21 ✉ 10125 – Ⓜ Porta Nuova – ✆ 011 6698101
– www.hotelpiemontese.it
37 rm 🛏 – 🛏59/150 € 🛏🛏79/180 €   **E2**
♦ Traditional ♦ Personalised ♦

Situated between Porta Nuova and the Po river, this hotel offers colourfully furnished guestrooms with individual touches; the attic-style rooms are particularly attractive with their exposed beams and hydro-massage baths. In fine weather, breakfast is served on the veranda.

Town House 70 *without rest* 🅰️ 🛜 🚿 VISA 🅾️ AE ①

via XX Settembre 70 ✉ 10122 – ✆ 011 19700003 – www.townhouse.it
48 rm 🛏 – 🛏79/395 € 🛏🛏89/452 € – 1 suite   **E1**
♦ Business ♦ Minimalist ♦

This centrally located hotel offers attractive, spacious guestrooms decorated in modern style. Breakfast is served on one large table in the small breakfast room.

Lancaster *without rest* 🅰️ 🛜 🚿 VISA 🅾️ AE ①

corso Filippo Turati 8 ✉ 10128 – ✆ 011 5681982 – www.lancaster.it
– Closed 5-20 August   **E3**
83 rm 🛏 – 🛏72/95 € 🛏🛏95/137 €
♦ Traditional ♦ Personalised ♦

In a fairly central residential district, a luxury hotel with modern comforts and with stylish furnishing in both the public areas and upper floor bedrooms.

Crimea *without rest* 🅰️ 🛜 🚿 VISA 🅾️ AE ①

via Mentana 3 ✉ 10133 – ✆ 011 6604700 – www.hotelcrimea.it
– Closed 12-19 August   **F2**
48 rm 🛏 – 🛏75/140 € 🛏🛏89/210 €
♦ Business ♦ Classic ♦

Pleasantly discreet and simply elegant interiors in a hotel in a quiet position in a residential area in the foothills; recently refurbished comfortable bedrooms.

Holiday Inn Turin City Centre 🚿 rm, 🅰️ 🛜 🚿 🚗

via Assietta 3 ✉ 10128 – Ⓜ Porta Nuova   VISA 🅾️ AE ①
– ✆ 011 5167111 – www.holidayinn.com/turin-cityctr   **E2**
57 rm 🛏 – 🛏175/200 € 🛏🛏200/230 €
Rest – *(dinner only)* Carte 26/62 €
♦ Chain hotel ♦ Traditional ♦ Modern ♦

Not far from the station, this hotel occupies a 19C palazzo which offers modern guestrooms equipped with all the latest technology. The hotel has its own garage. This restaurant is modern in both tone and layout.

XXX Del Cambio 🏠 🅰️ ⇔ VISA 🅾️ AE

piazza Carignano 2 ✉ 10123 – ✆ 011 546690
– www.ristorantedelcambio.it
– Closed February-April   **E1**
Rest – *(booking advisable)* Menu 55/80 € – Carte 73/106 € 🍴
♦ Regional ♦ Luxury ♦ Retro ♦

The regal history of Turin and the spirit of Cavour is still ever present in the rich interiors with 19th Century decorations of this historic building; great traditional cuisine also.

XXX ⊗

Vintage 1997 (Pierluigi Consonni)   🔟 💳 🆗 🆎 ⓪
piazza Solferino 16/h ✉ *10121 –* Ⓜ *Re Umberto –* ☎ *011 535948*
– www.vintage1997.com
– Closed 3 weeks August, 1-6 January, Saturday lunch, Sunday   **D2**
Rest – Menu 40/75 € – Carte 50/116 € 🏵

♦ Italian ♦ Formal ♦

Scarlet fabrics, lampshades and elegant wood panelling all add to the muted ambience of this elegant restaurant. It serves imaginative cuisine inspired by traditional favourites using carefully selected ingredients. Champagne imported from France.
→ Linguine con nero di seppia, carciofi, peperoncino e seppie. Trittico di baccalà alle olive, ai porri e alle patate. Pistakkiando: pistacchi in cinque diverse declinazioni.

XXX

Casa Savoia – Hotel Principi di Piemonte   🆗 💳 💳 🆎 ⓪
via Gobetti 15 ✉ *10123 –* Ⓜ *Porta Nuova –* ☎ *011 55151*
– www.atahotels.it   **CY**
Rest – Carte 40/79 €

♦ Mediterranean ♦ Luxury ♦

The splendid decor of the hotel is echoed in the restaurant. No detail is left to chance, ensuring that your gastronomic experience is a memorable one. Mediterranean cuisine.

XXX

Winner – Hotel Golden Palace   🛜 ♿ 🆗 💳 💳 🆎 ⓪
via dell'Arcivescovado 18 ✉ *10121 –* Ⓜ *Re Umberto –* ☎ *011 5512111*
– www.goldenpalace.it
– Closed 22 July-20 August   **D2**
Rest – Carte 49/72 €

♦ Modern ♦ Minimalist ♦ Luxury ♦

This restaurant specialises in sophisticated yet unpretentious cuisine. The menu features light dishes that focus on the use of local ingredients blended with the scents and fragrances of exotic spices. This results in delicious and unusual dishes that are full of flavour.

XXX

Carignano – Grand Hotel Sitea   🆗 ↔ 💳 💳 🆎 ⓪
via Carlo Alberto 35 ✉ *10123 –* Ⓜ *Porta Nuova –* ☎ *011 5170171*
– www.grandhotelsitea.it
– Closed August, 1-7 January, Saturday lunch and Sunday   **CY**
Rest – Menu 50/120 € – Carte 40/80 €

♦ Mediterranean ♦ Luxury ♦

Natural light filters through the large windows of this restaurant that overlooks the greenery outside. Mediterranean cuisine and Piedmontese specialities take pride of place on the menu. These are supplemented by tasting menus (Principe Amedeo, Re Umberto, Vittorio Emanuele) for guests who like to be 'guided' in their choice of dishes.

XX ⊗

Vo (Stefano Borra)   🆗 💳 💳
via Provana 3/d ✉ *10123 –* ☎ *011 8390288*
– www.ristorantevo.it
– Closed 3 weeks August, Saturday lunch and Sunday   **E2**
Rest – *(booking advisable)* Carte 41/74 €

♦ Creative ♦ Minimalist ♦

His culinary expertise may have been acquired in France, but the gastronomic passion of the young chef at this modern, minimalist restaurant is completely Piedmontese. Fresh stuffed pastas and the famous Fassone beef are the main specialities on the menu, which also includes fish dishes.
→ Insalata di mare con fagioli borlotti e vinaigrette allo zenzero. Degustazione d'agnello: costolette dorate al pain brioche, cosciotto in pasta croccante, sella confit. Tortino al gianduja.

Magorabin (Marcello Trentini) 🕭 ⒶⒸ 🆅🆂🅰 ⓒⓔ ⒶⒺ

corso San Maurizio 61/b ✉ 10124 – ℰ 011 8126808 – www.magorabin.com
– Closed Sunday and Monday lunch **F1**
Rest – (booking advisable) Menu 40/80 € – Carte 51/69 € 🕸

♦ Modern ♦ Formal ♦

Forget the noisy, traffic-filled avenue and soak up the atmosphere of this enchanting restaurant. It serves imaginative, creative cuisine with the occasional hint of the Piedmont. A real contrast to conservative, traditional Turin.

➜ Lingua, gamberi e mandarino. Rombo al sale e scaloppa di fegato grasso. Langhe: zabajone, nocciola e torroncino.

Al Garamond ⒶⒸ ⇔ 🆅🆂🅰 ⓒⓔ

via Pomba 14 ✉ 10123 – Ⓜ Porta Nuova – ℰ 011 8122781
– www.algaramond.it – Closed August, Saturday lunch, Sunday
Rest – Carte 43/85 € 🕸 **E2**

♦ Modern ♦ Formal ♦ Intimate ♦

Bearing the name of a lieutenant in Napoleon's Dragoons, this restaurant offers creative modern cuisine and is run by young, skilled and enthusiastic management.

San Tommaso 10 Lavazza ⒶⒸ 🆅🆂🅰 ⓒⓔ ⒶⒺ ⓪

via San Tommaso 10 ✉ 10122 – ℰ 011 534201 – www.lavazza.it
– Closed August and Sunday **E1**
Rest – Menu 45/60 €

♦ Classic ♦ Mediterranean ♦ Trendy ♦

Right behind the bar, beauty is the element that characterises every creation. The pleasure of looking out at the view and tempting the palate with Italian cuisine that reinterprets fantasy into delicate and intriguing recipes.

Al Gatto Nero ⒶⒸ 🆅🆂🅰 ⓒⓔ ⒶⒺ

corso Filippo Turati 14 ✉ 10128 – ℰ 011 590414 – www.gattonero.it
– Closed Sunday **E3**
Rest – (pre-book) Carte 42/77 € 🕸

♦ Classic ♦ Retro ♦

This restaurant has built up a reputation for fine dining, with a focus on Piedmontese and Tuscan dishes, as well as Mediterranean cuisine. Excellent wine list offering a selection of around 1 000 different wines.

Galante ⒶⒸ 🆅🆂🅰 ⓒⓔ ⒶⒺ ⓪

corso Palestro 15 ✉ 10122 – Ⓜ XVIII Dicembre – ℰ 011532163
– www.ristorantegalante.it
– Closed 9 August-2 September, 26 December-5 January, Saturday lunch, Sunday
Rest – Menu 42 € – Carte 34/63 € **E1**

♦ Fish and seafood ♦ Formal ♦

Soft shades and padded seating in the small, well-cared for elegant hotel with neo classical setting; on the menu with its wide selection there are both meat and fish dishes.

Porta Rossa ⒶⒸ 🆅🆂🅰 ⓒⓔ ⒶⒺ

via Passalacqua 3/b ✉ 10122 – Ⓜ XVIII Dicembre – ℰ 011 530816
– www.laportarossa.it
– Closed 26 December-6 January, Saturday lunch, Sunday
Rest – Menu 25 € (weekday lunch)/70 € – Carte 40/79 € 🕸 **C2**

♦ Fish and seafood ♦ Intimate ♦

Near to piazza Statuto, with tables placed close to one another and a lively atmosphere in a modern and well-maintained establishment; choose from the carte or from the cleverly formulated tasting menu, fish is always very fresh.

Tre Galline ⒶⒸ ⇔ 🆅🆂🅰 ⓒⓔ ⒶⒺ ⓪

via Bellezia 37 ✉ 10122 – ℰ 011 4366553 – www.3galline.it
– Closed 3 weeks August, 1 week January, Sunday, Monday lunch
Rest – Carte 36/70 € 🕸 **D1**

♦ Regional ♦ Family ♦

Well cared-for rustic environment in the dining rooms, with wooden ceiling beams characterising this historic city restaurant, where you can sample typical and tasty Piedmonts cuisine.

XX **Solferino**   🛆 AC VISA ⊕ AE

piazza Solferino 3 ⊠ *10121 – ℰ 011 535851 – www.ristorantesolferino.com*
Rest – Menu 40/52 € – Carte 31/61 €   **D2**
♦ Regional ♦ Family ♦ Formal ♦

In a beautiful Turin square, competently managed for almost 30 years you will find
a classic restaurant, renowned and popular - even at lunchtime; traditional cuisine.

XX **Il Diplomatico** – Hotel NH Ambasciatori   AC VISA ⊕ AE ⓪

corso Vittorio Emanuele II 104 ⊠ *10121 –* Ⓜ *Vinzaglio – ℰ 011 57521*
– www.nh-hotels.com   **C2**
Rest – Carte 29/56 €
♦ Classic ♦ Traditional ♦

Known as the 'city of the car', Turin also has much to offer in terms of its cuisine.
This elegant restaurant with large windows offers a selection of regional specialities, as well as international cuisine for non-Italian guests.

X **Consorzio**   AC VISA ⊕

ⓐ *via Monte di Pietà 23* ⊠ *10122 – ℰ 011 2767661 – www.ristoranteconsorzio.it*
– Closed 3 weeks August, Saturday lunch, Sunday   **D1**
Rest – *(booking advisable)* Carte 27/49 € 🍸
♦ Piedmontese ♦ Neighbourhood ♦

Two young associates run this simple, informal restaurant that serves delicious
Piedmontese specialities and traditional regional cuisine. This includes a selection of local wines and cheeses. If you want to try something really special, ask
for the Fassone beef casserole cooked in Ruché wine.

X **Taverna delle Rose**   AC VISA ⊕ AE ⓪

via Massena 24 ⊠ *10128 –* Ⓜ *Re Umberto – ℰ 011 538345*
– Closed August, Saturday lunch, Sunday   **D3**
Rest – Carte 26/62 €
♦ Regional ♦ Friendly ♦

Typical regional cuisine served in a charming, informal atmosphere. The dining
room is particularly romantic in the evening, with its exposed brickwork and
soft lighting.

X **Goffi del Lauro**   🛆 AC VISA ⊕

ⓐ *corso Casale 117* ⊠ *10132 – ℰ 011 8190619 – www.ristorantegoffi.it*
– Closed 15 September-5 October and Tuesday   *Plan I* **B2**
Rest – Carte 27/39 €
♦ Piedmontese ♦ Friendly ♦ Family ♦

Run by the same family since 1893, this authentic trattoria keeps the gastronomic traditions of the Piedmont alive. It features an antipasto buffet, pastas, and
braised and boiled meats.

LINGOTTO FIERE   *Plan III*

🏨 **NH Lingotto Tech**   🛆 AC 🛜 �️ 🅿 🏊 VISA ⊕ AE ⓪

via Nizza 230 ⊠ *10126 –* Ⓜ *Lingotto – ℰ 011 6642000 – www.nh-hotels.it*
– Closed August   **H2**
139 rm � – ♦99/310 € ♦♦99/310 € – 1 suite   **Rest** –
♦ Palace ♦ Design ♦

A panoramic lift takes guests from the small lobby to the top floor leading to
the balcony that gives access to the rooms. The effect of this innovative layout
is surprising. This restaurant combines elegance with a pleasantly informal
atmosphere; the decor is in cherry wood.

🏨 **NH Lingotto**   🚆 🛗 ⊕ 🛆 AC 🛜 🚌 🅿 VISA ⊕ AE ⓪

via Nizza 262 ⊠ *10126 –* Ⓜ *Lingotto – ℰ 011 6642000 – www.nh-hotels.it*
226 rm ⊒ – ♦99/270 € ♦♦99/310 € – 14 suites   **H2**
Rest *Torpedo* – see restaurant listing
♦ Palace ♦

This modern hotel in the Palazzo del Lingotto provides a good example of the
successful restoration of an industrial building. Guestrooms designed by Renzo
Piano, as well as a tropical garden.

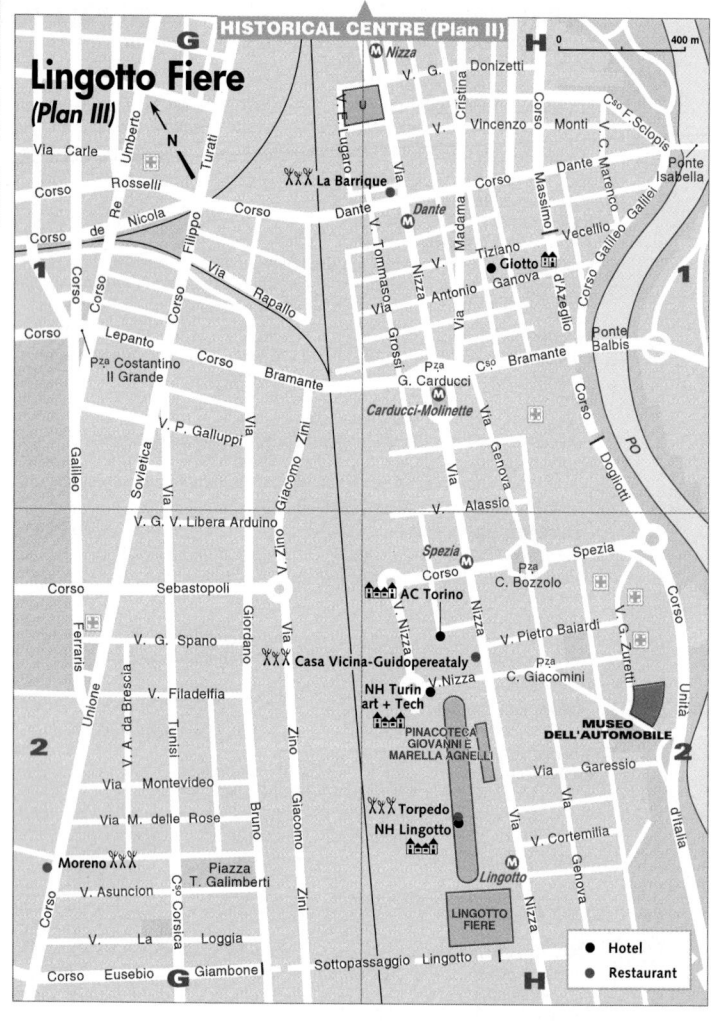

Lingotto Fiere
(Plan III)

HISTORICAL CENTRE (Plan II)

🏨🏨🏨 **AC Torino**   ♿ 🏧 📶 🍴 🅿 🚗 🚭 VISA ⑩ AE ⓪

via Bisalta 11 ✉ 10126 – Ⓜ *Lingotto*
– 𝒞 011 6395091
– www.ac-hotels.com   **H2**
83 rm ☑ – †100/300 € ††110/310 € – 6 suites
Rest – *(residents only)* Carte 39/63 €
♦ Chain hotel ♦ Luxury ♦ Minimalist ♦
Once a pasta factory, this early 20th century building in the Lingotto area is
now an up-to-date hotel that offers ideal comfort and completely modern
facilities.

ITALY - TURIN

Giotto without rest   〈AC〉 〈wifi〉 〈X〉 〈VISA〉 〈MC〉 〈AE〉 〈DC〉

via Giotto 27 ⊠ *10126 –* Ⓜ *Dante – ℰ 011 6637172*
– www.hotelgiottotorino.com   **H1**
50 rm ⊡ – †69/141 € ††79/175 €
♦ Traditional ♦ Modern ♦
Situated on the outskirts, not far from Lingotto and Valentino, a modern hotel
with refurbished interior; bedrooms with all comforts including bath or hydro-
massage baths or shower.

𝕏𝕏𝕏 Casa Vicina-Guidopereataly (Claudio Vicina Mazzaretto)   〈&〉
𝔈𝔈
via Nizza 224 ⊠ *10126 –* Ⓜ *Lingotto*   〈AC〉 〈VISA〉 〈MC〉 〈AE〉
– ℰ 011 19506840 – www.casavicina.it
– Closed 10 August-8 September, Christmas Holidays, Sunday dinner, Monday
Rest – Menu 38 € (lunch)/90 € – Carte 53/113 € 𝔅𝔅   **H2**
♦ Regional ♦ Formal ♦
This restaurant in Eattaly, the first Italian supermarket to sell specialist food pro-
ducts, is minimalist in style and serves a wide range of creative cuisine.
➜ Agnolotti pizzicati a mano al sugo d'arrosto. Faraona novella composta
in salmì. Torrone piemontese semifreddo.

𝕏𝕏𝕏 La Barrique (Stefano Gallo)   〈AC〉 〈⇔〉 〈VISA〉 〈MC〉
𝔈𝔈
corso Dante 53 ⊠ *10126 –* Ⓜ *Dante – ℰ 011 657900*
– www.labarriqueristorante.it
– Closed 2 weeks August, Sunday, Monday lunch   **H1**
Rest – Menu 35 € (weekday lunch)/85 € – Carte 51/98 € 𝔅𝔅
♦ Modern ♦ Formal ♦
Friendly, family management in this restaurant that blends classical regional
dishes, fresh pastas, fish, meat and the inevitable triumph of chocolate, for
more creative fare.
➜ Ravioli di patate affumicate con caviale di salmone e limone. Agnello da
latte ai peperoni canditi e melanzane. Gran dessert al cioccolato.

𝕏𝕏𝕏 Moreno   〈AC〉 〈⇔〉 〈VISA〉 〈MC〉 〈DC〉

corso Unione Sovietica 244 ⊠ *10134 – ℰ 011 3179191*
– www.marachellagruppo.it
– Closed August and Monday lunch   **G2**
Rest – Carte 42/102 €
♦ Classic ♦ Formal ♦
From the suburban road an unexpected lane leads into the greenery to an ele-
gant and well-maintained establishment; pleasantly situated tables near to the
glass doors looking out over the garden; traditional cuisine.

𝕏𝕏𝕏 Torpedo – Hotel NH Lingotto   〈⌂〉 〈&〉 〈AC〉 〈P〉 〈VISA〉 〈MC〉 〈AE〉 〈DC〉

via Nizza 262 ⊠ *10126 –* Ⓜ *Lingotto – ℰ 011 6642714*
– www.nh-hotels.it   **H2**
Rest – Menu 28/50 € – Carte 38/64 €
♦ Traditional ♦ Classic ♦
Housed in what was once a car factory belonging to Fiat (the emblem of Turin
in the 20C), this elegant restaurant serves high quality cuisine. Don't miss the
Vialone Piedmontese-style rice with leeks, pancetta ham, potatoes and Toma
cheese.

AT CASELLE TORINESE

Jet Hotel   〈AC〉 〈wifi〉 〈X〉 〈P〉 〈VISA〉 〈MC〉 〈AE〉 〈DC〉

via Della Zecca 9 – ℰ 0119913733 – www.jet-hotel.com
80 rm ⊡ – †68/120 € ††70/180 €
Rest *Antica Zecca* – see restaurant listing
♦ Business ♦ Traditional ♦ Classic ♦
Situated near the airport, this pleasant hotel is housed in an attractive 16C buil-
ding. It has an elegant atmosphere, good service and well-equipped guestrooms.

XX **Antica Zecca** – Jet Hotel · AC ⇄ P VISA ⊚ AE ⓪

via Della Zecca 9 – ☏ 011 9913733 – www.jet-hotel.com
Rest – Carte 31/59 €
♦ Modern ♦ Classic ♦

Don't be fooled by the appearance of this restaurant, which at first glance appears to cater solely for a business clientele. The ambience is welcoming, while the menu features delicious regional cuisine with a contemporary flavour. Meat grill in the dining room.

AT RIVOLI

XXXX **Combal.zero** (Davide Scabin) ≤ AC VISA ⊚ AE ⓪
❀❀
piazza Mafalda di Savoia – ☏ 011 9565225 – www.combal.org
– Closed August, 25 December-6 January, Sunday and Monday
Rest – *(dinner only)* Menu 115/200 € – Carte 125/165 € 🍴
♦ Modern ♦ Elegant ♦

The modern design of this restaurant echoes that of the nearby contemporary art museum. The cuisine is eclectic in style, featuring traditional dishes from the Piedmont, alongside more original fare.
➜ Ostriche con carpaccio di animelle e crema parmentier. Ravioli di burrata e basilico con pomodorini glassati. Filetto di cervo brasato al Barolo con frappé di peperoni di Carmagnola.

AT VENARIA REALE *Plan I*

🏠 **Galant** without rest · AC 🛜 P VISA ⊚ AE ⓪
corso Garibaldi 155 – ☏ 011 4551021 – www.hotelgalant.it
– Closed 15 days in August and Christmas Holidays A1
39 rm ⊇ – ♦60/150 € ♦♦88/183 €
♦ Family ♦ Classic ♦

A modern-style structure, ideal for business clientele. Pleasant and functional common areas, comfortable bedrooms with large writing desks. There is also a meeting room.

🏠 **Cascina di Corte** · 🛜 AC 🛜 VISA ⊚ AE
via Amedeo di Castellamonte 2 – ☏ 011 4593278 – www.cascinadicorte.it
10 rm ⊇ – ♦110/160 € ♦♦130/190 € – 2 suites A1
Rest – *(closed August)* Menu 25/38 € – Carte 29/49 €
♦ Historic ♦ Rustic ♦

Not far from the famous palace, this 19C farmhouse with adjoining ice-cream parlour has a simple architectural style that is typical of the region. A rustic interior with exposed brickwork in the bedrooms goes hand-in-hand with modern, comfortable furnishings and facilities.

XXX **Dolce Stil Novo alla Reggia** (Alfredo Russo) · 🛜 🛜 AC ⇄
❀
piazza della Repubblica 4 – ☏ 011 4992343 VISA ⊚ AE ⓪
– www.dolcestilnovo.com
– Closed 2 weeks August, 2 weeks January, Sunday dinner, Monday, Tuesday lunch
Rest – *(number of covers limited, pre-book)* A1
Menu 38 € (weekday lunch)/90 € – Carte 77/127 €
♦ Innovative ♦ Elegant ♦

Located inside the Torrione del Garove, this restaurant boasts a pretty terrace overlooking the Reggia di Venaria garden. There are two ample dining rooms with spacious tables, which are contrasted by minimalist furnishings. Sample the welcoming local cuisine with several seafood specialities.
➜ Ravioli di "barbabuc" (scorzabianca) con ricotta di montagna. Stracotto di fassone piemontese in cottura lunga con pomodoro fresco. Semifreddo di agrumi con biscotto all'acqua, profumato al finocchietto.

LUXEMBOURG
LËTZEBUERG

→ **AREA:**
2 586 km² (998 sq mi).

→ **POPULATION:**
516 000 inhabitants (nearly 62% nationals, 38% resident foreigners). Density = 200 per km².

→ **CAPITAL:** Luxembourg.

→ **CURRENCY:** Euro (€).

→ **GOVERNMENT:**
Constitutional parliamentary monarchy (since 1868). Member of European Union since 1957 (one of the 6 founding countries).

→ **LANGUAGES:**
The official language is Lëtzebuergesch, a variant of German, similar to the Frankish dialect of the Moselle valley; High German is used for general purposes and is the first language for teaching; French is the literary and administrative language.

→ **PUBLIC HOLIDAYS:**
New Year's Day (1 Jan); Easter Monday (late Mar/Apr); Labor Day (1 May); Ascension Day (May); Whit Monday (late May/June); National Day (23 June); Assumption of the Virgin Mary (15 Aug); All Saints' Day (1 Nov); Christmas Day (25 Dec); St Stephen's Day (26 Dec).

→ **LOCAL TIME:**
GMT+1 hour in winter and GMT +2 hours in summer.

LUXEMBOURG

→ **CLIMATE:**
Temperate continental with cold winters and mild summers (Luxembourg: January 1°C; July 17°C).

→ **EMERGENCY:**
Police ☎ **113**; Medical Assistance ☎ **112**; Fire Brigade ☎ **118**. (Dialling **112** within any EU country will redirect your call and contact the emergency services.)

→ **ELECTRICITY:**
230 volts AC, 50Hz; 2 round pin sockets.

→ **FORMALITIES:**
Travellers from the European Union (EU), Switzerland, Iceland and the main countries of North and South America need a national identity card or passport (America: passport required) to visit the Grand Duchy of Luxembourg for less than three months (tourism or business purpose). For visitors from other countries a visa may be required, in addition to a passport, especially for those wishing to stay for longer than three months. We advise you to check with your embassy before travelling.

565

LUXEMBOURG
LËTZEBUERG

Population: 100 000

Raymond Thill/Fotolia.com

Luxembourg may be small but it's perfectly formed. Standing high above two rivers on a sandstone bluff, its commanding position over sheer gorges may be a boon to modern visitors, but down the centuries that very setting has rendered it the subject of conquest on many occasions. Its eye-catching geography makes it a city of distinctive districts, linked by spectacular bridges spanning lush green valleys.

The absolute heart of the city is the old town, its most prominent landmarks the cathedral spires and the city squares with their elegant pastel façades – an ideal backdrop to the 'café culture' and a worthy recipient of UNESCO World Heritage Status. Winding its way deep below to the south west is the river Pétrusse, which has its confluence with the river Alzette in the south east. Follow the Chemin de la Corniche, past the old city walls and along the Alzette's narrow valley to discover the ruins of The Bock, the city's first castle, and the Casemates, a labyrinth of rocky 17C and 18C underground defences. Directly to the south of the old town is the railway station quarter, while down at river level to the east is the altogether more attractive Grund district, whose northerly neighbours are Clausen and Pfaffenthal. Up in the north east, connected by the grand sounding Pont Grand-Duchesse Charlotte, is Kirchberg Plateau, a modern hub of activity for the EU.

LUXEMBOURG CITY IN...

➜ **ONE DAY**
Place d'Armes, Ducal Grand Palace, National Museum of History and Art, Chemin de la Corniche.

➜ **TWO DAYS**
Luxembourg City History Museum, Bock Casemates, the Grund.

➜ **THREE DAYS**
Kirchberg Plateau, Museum of Modern Art, concert at Luxembourg Philharmonic Hall.

PRACTICAL INFORMATION

ARRIVAL-DEPARTURE

✈ Luxembourg Findel Airport is 6km northeast of the city centre. City bus Number 16 runs every 20min and takes 25min.

GETTING AROUND

Buses run from 5am to 10pm and there's an additional late night service on Fridays and Saturdays (there's no metro). The most convenient bus stations are at the exit of the Gare Centrale and on Place Hamilius in the old town. The fare system (valid for trains too) is simple enough: for trips of 10km or less you buy a 'short' ticket; for an unlimited day ticket (valid until 8am the next day) you buy a Billet Reseau. Available from Easter-October, the Luxembourg Card offers unlimited travel and free admission to many attractions countrywide. In winter, the Stater Museeskaart offers three days of free admission to important sights in the city.

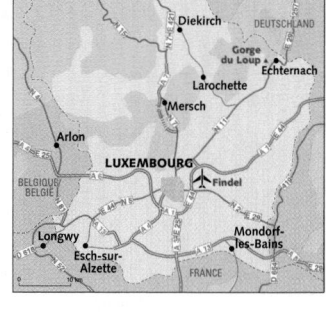

CALENDAR HIGHLIGHTS

March-June
Printemps Festival.

May
Luxembourg Marathon.

June
National Day Eve - Fireworks over the Pétrusse Valley and partying on Place d'Armes and Place Guillaume II.

August-September
Schueberfouer (One of Europe's biggest funfairs).

November-January
Winter Lights Festival.

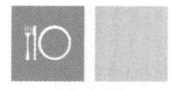

EATING OUT

The taste buds of Luxembourg have been very much influenced by French classical cuisine, particularly around and about the old town, an area that becomes a smart open-air terrace in summer. Look out for the local speciality Judd mat Gaardebounen, smoked neck of pork with broad beans. The centre of town is an eclectic place to eat as it runs the gauntlet from fast-style pizzeria to expense account restaurants favoured by businessmen. A good bet for atmosphere is the Grund, which offers a wide variety of restaurants and price ranges, and is

certainly the area that boasts the most popular cafés and pubs. A few trendy places have sprouted over recent times near the Casemates, and these too are proving to be pretty hot with the younger crowd. A service charge is included in your bill but if you want to tip, ten per cent is reasonable. The Grand Duchy produces its own white and sparkling wines on the borders of the Moselle. Over the last decade it has produced some interesting varieties but you'll rarely find these abroad, as they're eagerly snapped up by the locals.

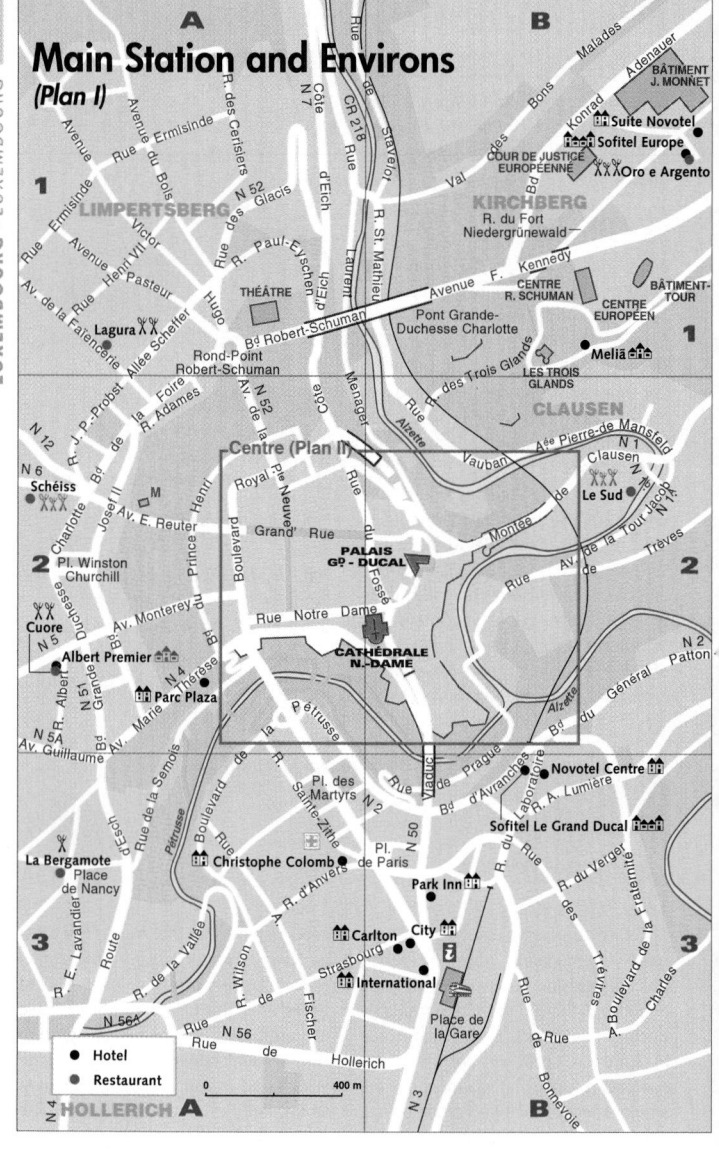

Main Station and Environs
(Plan I)

A

B

Rue des Malades

Adenauer

BÂTIMENT
J. MONNET

Konrad

Suite Novotel

Sofitel Europe

COUR DE JUSTICE
EUROPÉENNE

Oro e Argento

Val des Bons

KIRCHBERG

R. du Fort
Niedergrünewald

Avenue F. Kennedy

CENTRE
R. Schuman

BÂTIMENT-
TOUR

CENTRE
EUROPÉEN

THÉÂTRE

Pont Grande-
Duchesse Charlotte

LES TROIS
GLANDS

Lagura

Rond-Point
Robert-Schuman

LIMPERTSBERG

1

1

Aée Pierre-de-Mansfeld

Centre (Plan II)

CLAUSEN

Le Sud

Schéiss

Pl. Winston
Churchill

Royal Pie Neuve

Grand' Rue

PALAIS
Gd - DUCAL

Rue Notre Dame

CATHÉDRALE
N.-DAME

2

Cuore

Albert Premier

Parc Plaza

2

La Bergamote
Place
de Nancy

Christophe Colomb

Pl. des
Martyrs

Pl.
de Paris

Novotel Centre

Sofitel Le Grand Ducal

Park Inn

Carlton

City

International

3

3

	Hotel
●	Hotel
●	Restaurant

0   400 m

HOLLERICH A

B

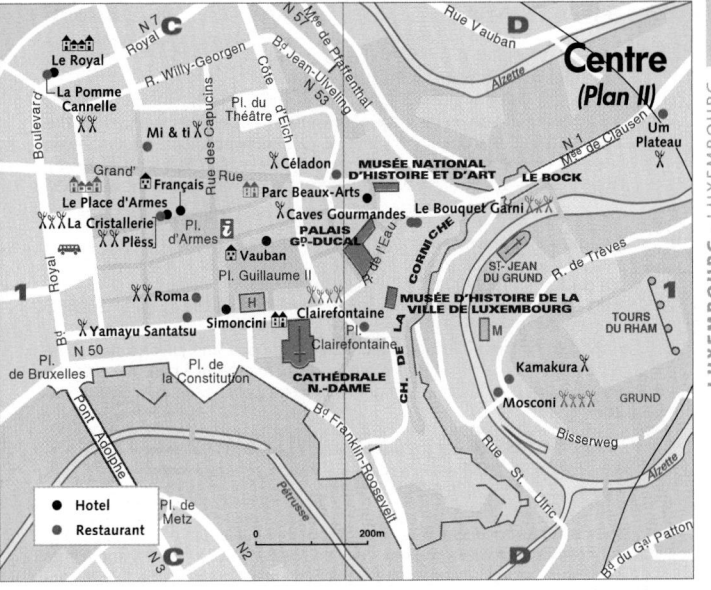

CENTRE
Plan II

Le Royal
🛗 ⊕ 🕭 📺 🅰🅲 📶 🔁 🚗 VISA 🆖 AE ⓪

12 bd Royal ⊠ *2449* – 𝒞 *241 61 61* – www.leroyalluxembourg.com
190 rm – 🛏390/530 € 🛏🛏390/530 €, � 29 € – 20 suites **C1**
Rest *La Pomme Cannelle* – see restaurant listing
♦ Palace ♦ Grand Luxury ♦ Personalised ♦

Nothing in this hotel is left to chance, to such an extent that a king would feel perfectly at home! Guests are waited on hand and foot by an army of staff that are available day and night. It is ideally located in the city's 'Wall Street' neighbourhood.

Le Place d'Armes
🛗 🅰🅲 📶 🔁 🚗 VISA 🆖 AE

18 pl. d'Armes ⊠ *1136* – 𝒞 *27 47 37* – www.hotel-leplacedarmes.com
18 rm – 🛏295/425 € 🛏🛏295/425 €, ⊡ 22 € – 10 suites **C1**
Rest *La Cristallerie* Rest *Plëss* – see restaurant listing
♦ Historic ♦ Grand Luxury ♦ Personalised ♦

Although on the liveliest square in the town centre, this establishment is a real haven of peace. This former townhouse has been given a complete makeover. It exudes charm and an old Luxembourg atmosphere without feeling stuffy. A must.

Sofitel Le Grand Ducal
⩽ 🛗 🅰🅲 📶 🔁 VISA 🆖 AE ⓪

40 bd d'Avranches ⊠ *1160* – 𝒞 *24 87 71* – www.sofitel.com
126 rm – 🛏120/550 € 🛏🛏120/550 €, ⊡ 27 € – 2 suites *Plan I* **B3**
Rest *Top Floor* – 𝒞 *24 87 73 10 (closed Monday in August, Saturday lunch and Sunday)* Menu 45/80 € – Carte 45/80 €
♦ Chain hotel ♦ Business ♦ Modern ♦

This Sofitel has everything you would expect from a top class, international hotel. The plush, understated ambience is set off by an interior that combines designer details with luxurious comfort. It also has a view over the town and the lush gardens of the Pétrusse Valley (from the bathtub of some rooms).

LUXEMBOURG - LUXEMBOURG

Albert Premier

2a r. Albert Ier ⊠ 1117 Belair – 𝒞 442 44 21 – www.albertpremier.lu
40 rm – †110/540 € ††120/1080 €, ⊊ 22 €   *Plan I* **A2**
Rest *Cuore* – see restaurant listing
♦ Luxury ♦ Modern ♦

This noble residence on the edge of town has a very high-tech extension. This creates a blend of styles in this very chic establishment. Choose a classic room, like a bijou apartment, or one of the equally impeccable ultra-modern rooms. Add the wellness area and you are on the way to relaxing both mind and body.

Parc Belair

*111 av. du X Septembre ⊠ 2551 Belair – 𝒞 44 23 23
– www.goeres-group.com*
57 rm ⊊ – †139/400 € ††139/425 € – 1 suite
Rest – *(closed lunch Saturday, Sunday and Bank Holidays)* Carte 38/58 €
♦ Luxury ♦ Personalised ♦

A modern building offering comfortable guestrooms and junior suites, some with a themed decor. Quieter rooms with more attractive park views to the rear. Pleasant lounge bar. This bistro has a menu that focuses on traditional cuisine.

Parc Beaux-Arts without rest

1 r. Sigefroi ⊠ 2536 – 𝒞 26 86 76 – www.goeres-group.com
10 rm ⊊ – †159/475 € ††159/500 €   **D1**
♦ Luxury ♦ Stylish ♦

This delightful hotel stands right next door to the Museum of Art and History and the Grand Ducal Palace, with whom it shares a taste for beauty and refinement. Each individually appointed spacious room has its own distinctive character. For lovers of sophisticated art de vivre!

Novotel Centre

*35 r. Laboratoire ⊠ 1911 – 𝒞 24 87 81
– www.novotel.com/fr/hotel-5556-novotel-luxembourg-centre/ind*
150 rm – †99/270 € ††99/270 €, ⊊ 20 €   *Plan I* **B3**
Rest – *(closed lunch Saturday and Sunday)* *(open until 11pm)* Menu 22 € bi (lunch) – Carte 30/56 €
♦ Chain hotel ♦ Business ♦ Functional ♦

This contemporary, highly practical hotel is just a 2min walk from the station and only a few steps from the historic centre.

Parc Plaza

5 av. Marie-Thérèse ⊠ 2132 – 𝒞 456 14 11 – www.goeres-group.com
89 rm ⊊ – †109/255 € ††129/275 €   *Plan I* **A2**
Rest – *(closed lunch Saturday, Sunday and Bank Holidays)* Menu 13 € (lunch)/21 € – Carte approx. 40 €
♦ Business ♦ Classic ♦

A hotel outside the bustling city centre can in fact be a bonus, as this establishment demonstrates by its tranquillity and fine view of the city. Although the concrete structure can hardly be deemed charming, the rooms are spacious.

Parc Belle-Vue 🏠

58 rm ⊊ – †85/195 € ††85/215 €
♦ Business ♦ Functional ♦

This annexe of the Parc Plaza offers a less ostentatious level of comfort, but the prices are also less extravagant.

Simoncini without rest

6 r. Notre-Dame ⊠ 2240 – 𝒞 22 28 44 – www.hotelsimoncini.lu
35 rm ⊊ – †115/160 € ††135/180 €   **C1**
♦ Business ♦ Minimalist ♦

This fashionable establishment, which is half hotel, half art gallery, is something of a wild card in Luxembourg's traditional hotel landscape. Well located right in the centre, it is ideal for a city trip and has a public car park nearby.

LUXEMBOURG - LUXEMBOURG

Français   🏠 🛜 ⚗ VISA ⓒ AE ⓞ

14 pl. d'Armes ⊠ 1136 – 𝒞 47 45 34 – www.hotelfrancais.lu
24 rm � – †90/120 € – ††90/140 €   **C1**
Rest – *(closed dinner 24 and 31 December) (open until 11pm)* Menu
28/34 € – Carte 34/65 €
◆ Family ◆ Functional ◆

Located on one of the city's most beautiful squares, the Français has been run
by the same family since 1970. The owner organises regular art exhibitions on
the premises. The café and restaurant (French cuisine and terrace) are similarly
representative of the arty ambience.

Vauban *without rest*   🛜 VISA ⓒ AE ⓞ

10 pl. Guillaume II ⊠ 1648 – 𝒞 22 04 93 – www.hotelvauban.lu
16 rm ⊠ – †60/120 € ††100/140 €   **C1**
◆ Inn ◆ Functional ◆

Put on your walking shoes: this traditional hotel could not be better located to
explore the historic centre. After exploring every avenue and back alley of
Luxembourg, take a seat on the hotel's terrace overlooking a lively square and
quench your thirst.

Clairefontaine (Arnaud Magnier)   🛜 🅰🅲 ⇄ 🅿 VISA ⓒ AE ⓞ

9 pl. de Clairefontaine ⊠ 1341 – 𝒞 46 22 11
– www.restaurantclairefontaine.lu
– closed Easter week, last 2 weeks August-first week September, Christmas
week-first week January, Bank Holidays, Saturday and Sunday   **D1**
Rest – Menu 53/125 € bi – Carte 70/103 € ⅏
◆ Creative ◆ Elegant ◆

This attractive restaurant with a terrace stands on an elegant square. It has a traditional decor with old wooden panelling and contemporary furnishings. Creative, modern cuisine and astute wine pairings.
➔ Fricassée de jambonnettes de grenouilles au persil plat, poêlée de girolles et gnocchis, écume à l'ail doux Poularde farcie au foie gras contisée à la
truffe et cuite en vessie, purée crémeuse à la truffe et sauce Albufera Diffé-
rentes sortes de pêches et espuma à la verveine

Mosconi (Ilario Mosconi)   🛜 ⇄ 🍽 VISA ⓒ AE ⓞ

13 r. Münster ⊠ 2160 – 𝒞 54 69 94 – www.mosconi.lu
– closed 1 week at Easter, last 3 weeks August, 24 December-early January,
Bank Holidays, Saturday lunch, Sunday and Monday   **D1**
Rest – Menu 44/130 € – Carte 97/127 € ⅏
◆ Italian ◆ Cosy ◆

Illario and Simonetta Mosconi are an enthusiastic couple that proudly pay
homage to the gastronomic traditions of Italy. Their Italian cuisine is as full of
flair as it is steeped in flavours. The secret of their success no doubt lies in the
infinite care and attention they devote to choosing their suppliers.
➔ Pâté de foies de volaille à la crème de truffe blanche, polenta rôtie et
câpres caramélisées. Maialino di latte : porcelet. Caramel à la sicilienne,
sauce à l'orange et aux pistaches.

Le Bouquet Garni (Thierry Duhr)   🛜 ⇄ 🍽 (dinner) VISA ⓒ AE

32 r. Eau ⊠ 1449 – 𝒞 26 20 06 20 – www.lebouquetgarni.lu
– closed Saturday lunch, Sunday and Bank Holidays   **D1**
Rest – Menu 60 € (lunch), 65/85 €
◆ Classic ◆ Rustic ◆ Cosy ◆

As the establishment's name suggests, the dishes are steeped in the aroma of
French cuisine. Chef Thierry Duhr demonstrates his masterful talent by the quality, sophistication and generosity of his recipes. The dining room, both elegant
and rustic, provides the perfect backdrop to the menu.
➔ Espadon à la plancha, fin ragoût de févettes et petits pois à la tomate
confite. Côte de veau en cocotte dans son jus de cuisson, asperges et
morilles au vin jaune. Poire Belle-Hélène "revisitée".

LUXEMBOURG - LUXEMBOURG

Schéiss 🏠 ✿ 🅿 VISA ⊕ AE

142 r. Val Sainte Croix ✉ *1370 Belair –* ℰ *24 61 82 – www.scheiss.lu*
Rest – Menu 24 € (lunch) – Carte 43/64 €   Plan I **A2**
♦ Modern ♦ Design ♦

Despite the elegant minimalist interior, you need have no fear of the usual hefty bill associated with such decors. Enjoy the delicious, contemporary cuisine that is steeped in simplicity.

La Cristallerie – Hôtel Le Place d'Armes 🔤 ⌀ VISA ⊕ AE

18 pl. d'Armes (1ᵗʰ floor) ✉ *1136 –* ℰ *27 47 37*
– www.hotel-leplacedarmes.com
– closed Saturday lunch, Sunday and Monday   **C1**
Rest – Menu 45/85 € – Carte 64/81 €
♦ Classic ♦ Elegant ♦

An elegant dining room surrounded by a superb Art Nouveau glass wall. Contemporary cuisine drawing from classical sources. The chef has a predilection for fine ingredients, in keeping with the setting.

Roma 🏠 ✿ VISA ⊕ AE ①

5 r. Louvigny ✉ *1946 –* ℰ *22 36 92 – www.roma.lu*
– closed Sunday dinner and Monday   **C1**
Rest – Carte 51/64 €
♦ Italian ♦ Friendly ♦

The Roma, Luxembourg's first Italian restaurant, specialises in homemade pasta, ultra fresh ingredients, and more unusually, theme festivals. All of which have enabled it to become a firm favourite with the locals. There is a popular range of daily specials.

Plëss – Hôtel Le Place d'Armes 🔤 VISA ⊕ AE

18 pl. d'Armes ✉ *1136 –* ℰ *27 47 37 – www.hotel-leplacedarmes.com*
Rest – Menu 34 € – Carte 43/63 €   **C1**
♦ Classic ♦ Brasserie ♦ Elegant ♦

Plëss means 'square' in Luxembourgish – an obvious reference to the Place d'Armes. This is where this lovely contemporary brasserie is located, in the heart of town. Glamorous, urban atmosphere.

La Pomme Cannelle – Hôtel Le Royal ⚬ 🔤 ✿ ⌀

12 bd Royal ✉ *2449 –* ℰ *241 61 67 36*   VISA ⊕ AE ①
– www.leroyalluxembourg.com
– closed 27 July-25 August, 1-6 January, Saturday, Sunday and Bank Holidays
Rest – Menu 56 € (lunch)/79 € – Carte 71/93 € ⅜   **C1**
♦ Classic ♦ Formal ♦ Exotic ♦

La Pomme Cannelle represents a culinary marriage between French traditions and oriental flavours. The Indian Empire interior echoes that of the hotel to which it belongs.

Cuore – Hôtel Albert Premier 🏠 🔤 ✿ VISA ⊕ AE ①

2a r. Albert Ier ✉ *1117 Belair –* ℰ *442 44 26 00 – www.albertpremier.lu*
– closed Saturday lunch and Sunday   Plan I **A2**
Rest – Menu 16 € (lunch) – Carte 36/60 €
♦ Italian ♦ Design ♦ Trendy ♦

The sophisticated charm of the Albert Premier Hotel is echoed by its restaurant, the Cuore ('choir' in Italian), which specialises in up-to-the-minute Italian cuisine. Ask the sommelier about his treasure trove.

Mi & Ti 🏠 🔤 VISA ⊕

☺

8 av. de la Porte-Neuve ✉ *2227 –* ℰ *26 26 22 50*
– closed 1 week at Easter, last 3 weeks August, 1 week late December, Monday dinner, Tuesday dinner and Sunday   **C1**
Rest – Menu 18 € (lunch)/35 € – Carte 45/53 €
♦ Italian ♦ Fashionable ♦

A trendily decorated Italian restaurant occupying the first floor of a modern building. Authentic produce imported directly from Italy. Simplified menu at the downstairs Bottega. Busy street terrace.

La Bergamote
🗡 ☺ VISA ⓒⓒ AE

2 pl. de Nancy ✉ *2212 –* ☎ *26 44 03 79 – www.labergamote.lu*
– closed first 2 weeks August, Monday dinner, Saturday and Sunday
Rest – Menu 27 € (lunch)/30 € – Carte 46/61 €   *Plan I* **A3**
♦ Modern ♦ Trendy ♦

Have you tasted bergamot before? All the subtlety and freshness of this little citrus fruit can be found in Guillaume Lempens' cooking. He concocts sun-drenched dishes: vitello tonnato, roast sea bream or polenta with prawns, also with French and modern touches.

Céladon
🗡 ⟷ VISA ⓒⓒ AE ⓞ

1 r. Nord ✉ *2229 –* ☎ *47 49 34 – www.thai.lu*
– closed Saturday lunch and Sunday   **C1**
Rest – Menu 23 € (lunch), 45/55 € – Carte approx. 44 €
♦ Thai ♦ Exotic ♦ Trendy ♦

Lovers of Thai cuisine won't be disappointed by the fresh produce and authentic Asian flavours of the Céladon. Vegetarians will no doubt be in seventh heaven with the range that is on offer.

Kamakura
🗡 ☺ ⟷ VISA ⓒⓒ AE ⓞ

4 r. Münster ✉ *2160 –* ☎ *47 06 04 – www.kamakura.lu*
– closed 2 weeks at Easter, last 3 weeks August, 23 December-2 January, Bank Holidays, Saturday lunch and Sunday   **D1**
Rest – Menu 12 € (lunch), 31/68 € – Carte 38/78 €
♦ Japanese ♦ Minimalist ♦

The minimalist design of this Japanese restaurant has made no concessions to the West. It is named after the former capital of the Land of the Rising Sun and embodies the essence of Japanese cooking: understated, low-key presentation and virtuoso preparation. Kamakura celebrates its 25th anniversary in 2013.

Caves Gourmandes
🗡 ☺ 🌳 ⟷ VISA ⓒⓒ AE

32 r. Eau ✉ *1449 –* ☎ *46 11 24 – www.caves-gourmandes.lu*
– closed Saturday and Sunday except 21 June-15 September   **D1**
Rest – Menu 22 € (lunch)/35 € – Carte approx. 50 €
♦ Traditional ♦ Neighbourhood ♦ Rustic ♦

Tucked away in a neighbourhood that is sometimes likened to the capital's belly, these epicurean cellars serve delicious regional fare, in which casserole dishes take pride of place. The lunch menu is excellent value.

Yamayu Santatsu
🗡 ⟷ VISA ⓒⓒ AE ⓞ

26 r. Notre-Dame ✉ *2240 –* ☎ *46 12 49*
– closed mid July-mid August, late December-early January, Sunday and Monday   **C1**
Rest – Menu 15 € (lunch)/32 € – Carte 31/50 €
♦ Japanese ♦ Neighbourhood ♦

Yamayu Santatsu's sushi is fully equal to those of Tokyo, explaining the establishment's popularity by gourmets who know how to appreciate the subtlety of Japanese cuisine. It has an understated decor and private rooms for business meetings.

MAIN STATION   *Plan I*

International
🏠 🌳 VISA ⓒⓒ AE ⓞ

20 pl. de la Gare ✉ *1616 –* ☎ *48 59 11 – www.hotelinter.lu*   **B3**
69 rm ⌷ – †80/300 € ††80/300 € – 1 suite
Rest – *(closed 21 December-6 January, Saturday and Sunday)* Menu 25/38 € – Carte 24/63 €
♦ Family ♦ Classic ♦

The Klein family has been running this establishment for four generations and it is an understatement to say that the hotel is well looked after. It is a must if you are looking for a reliable address in the vicinity of the station.

Park Inn without rest   🔗 🕸 🛜 🖳 🅿 🆅🆂🅰 ⑩ 🅰🅴

45 av. de la Gare ✉ *1611* – ℰ *268 91 81*
– www.parkinn.com/hotel-luxembourg   **B3**
99 rm – 🛏67/215 € 🛏🛏67/215 €, ⌷ 19 €
♦ Chain hotel ♦ Business ♦ Modern ♦

Anyone in search of the modernity and comfort of a hotel chain will appreciate the recently created Park Inn.

City without rest   🔗 🕸 🛜 🖳 🍽 🆅🆂🅰 ⑩ 🅰🅴 ⑩

1 r. Strasbourg ✉ *2561* – ℰ *29 11 22* – *www.cityhotel.lu*   **B3**
35 rm ⌷ – 🛏91/141 € 🛏🛏122/187 €
♦ Business ♦ Family ♦ Functional ♦

This well-located hotel is at the crossroads of two main streets near the railway station. Start the day with the excellent buffet breakfast.

Carlton without rest   🛜 🍽 🆅🆂🅰 ⑩ 🅰🅴

9 r. Strasbourg ✉ *2561* – ℰ *29 96 60* – *www.carlton.lu*
– closed 24-27 December   **B3**
48 rm ⌷ – 🛏95/130 € 🛏🛏115/150 €
♦ Business ♦ Family ♦ Functional ♦

The Carlton continues to embody a certain image of the Grand Duchy. Behind its fine Art Deco façade the visitor can admire a spacious interior that is steeped in 'turn of the last century' nostalgia. Well located near the station and in a quiet neighbourhood.

Christophe Colomb without rest   🛜 🖳 🍽 🆅🆂🅰 ⑩ 🅰🅴 ⑩

10 r. Anvers ✉ *1130* – ℰ *408 41 41* – *www.christophe-colomb.lu*
24 rm ⌷ – 🛏75/170 € 🛏🛏85/185 €   **A3**
♦ Family ♦ Functional ♦

This hotel has built up a regular clientele over the years. They appreciate both the spacious guestrooms and the location, which is just 500m from the station.

ENVIRONS OF LUXEMBOURG   *Plan I*

Sofitel Europe   🦢 🔗 🕭 rm, 🗚 🛜 🖳 🅿 🍽 🆅🆂🅰 ⑩ 🅰🅴 ⑩

4 r. Fort Niedergrünewald (European Centre) ✉ *2015 Kirchberg*
– ℰ 43 77 61 – www.sofitel.com   **B1**
105 rm – 🛏100/450 € 🛏🛏100/450 €, ⌷ 25 € – 4 suites
Rest *Oro e Argento* – see restaurant listing
Rest *Le Stübli* – ℰ *43 77 68 83 (closed school holidays)* Menu 33 €
– Carte 39/48 €
♦ Chain hotel ♦ Business ♦ Stylish ♦

A bold, oval shaped hotel at the heart of the European Institutions district. Central atrium and spacious, extremely comfortable guestrooms. The attentive, friendly service you would expect from this upmarket chain. A typical restaurant serving regional cuisine. A warm atmosphere enhanced by the staff in traditional costume.

Meliã   🦢 ≤ 🔗 🕸 🕭 🗚 🛜 🖳 🆅🆂🅰 ⑩ 🅰🅴 ⑩

1 Park Dräi Eechelen ✉ *1499 Kirchberg* – ℰ *27 33 31*
– www.melia.com   **B1**
161 rm ⌷ – 🛏145/350 € 🛏🛏165/370 € – 1 suite
Rest *Aqua* – *(closed Saturday and Sunday) (open until 11pm)* Menu 18 €
(lunch), 24/35 € – Carte 34/60 €
♦ Business ♦ Design ♦

The first hotel in this Spanish chain in Benelux, located next to the conference centre. Rooms are stylish, comfortable and functional. Lovely view of the city.

🏨 **Suite Novotel** without rest 🖪 🌿 🛜 🏋 🍴 🚗 VISA ⓞⓞ AE ⓞ

13 av. J.F. Kennedy ✉ 1855 Kirchberg – ℰ 2 70 40
– www.suitenovotel.com **B1**
110 rm – †129/285 € ††139/295 €, ☕ 14 €
♦ Business ♦ Design ♦

Seasoned travellers will no doubt appreciate the fixtures and fittings of this trendy hotel, which is 5min from the centre. Music and film are on demand to satisfy the mind, and there are microwave and ready-to-eat dishes for the body.

XXX **Le Sud** ≤ 🌿 🗽 P VISA ⓞⓞ AE

8 Rives de Clausen (at the former brasserie Mousel, parking Clausen)
✉ 6521 Clausen – ℰ 26 47 87 50
– www.le-sud.lu
– closed 5-25 August, Sunday and Monday **B2**
Rest – (dinner only) (set menu only) Menu 75 €
♦ Provençal ♦ Elegant ♦

With dishes like cappuccino of scallops, barigoule d'artichauts du Var and croustillant of cod served with bouillabaisse jus, you may well think you are in the South of France!

XXX **Oro e Argento** – Hôtel Sofitel Europe 🌿 P VISA ⓞⓞ AE ⓞ

6 r. Fort Niedergrünewald (European Centre) ✉ 2015 Kirchberg
– ℰ 43 77 68 70 – www.sofitel.com
– closed weekends in July-August, Bank Holidyas and Saturday **B1**
Rest – Carte 45/75 €
♦ Italian ♦ Elegant ♦

An attractive Italian restaurant in a luxury hotel. Contemporary cuisine served to a backdrop of plush interior decor with a Venetian touch. Intimate atmosphere and stylish service.

XX **The Last Supper** 🌿 P VISA ⓞⓞ AE

33 av. J.F. Kennedy (Ellipse Kirchberg 2) ✉ 1855 Kirchberg – ℰ 27 04 54
– www.thelastsupper.lu
– closed Saturday lunch, Sunday and Bank Holidays
Rest – Menu 13 € (lunch) – Carte 39/61 €
♦ Modern ♦ Trendy ♦ Brasserie ♦

Despite its biblical name, the Last Supper is not frequented by pious disciples but by a group of pleasure-seeking fashionistas. The interior represents a stunning marriage between contemporary and boudoir styles. Modern cuisine with classical roots.

XX **Lagura** 🌿 ⇄ VISA ⓞⓞ AE ⓞ

18 av. de la Faïencerie ✉ 1510 Limpertsberg – ℰ 26 27 67
– www.lagura.lu
– closed 25 and 26 December, Saturday lunch and Sunday **A1**
Rest – Menu 24 € (lunch), 38/45 € – Carte 45/72 €
♦ Italian ♦ Fashionable ♦

The Lagura is not your run-of-the-mill Italian restaurant. The pasta may well be homemade but the recipes are far from traditional (for example, grapefruit jelly or basil flavoured ice cream). Whatever the dish, everything is delicate and flavoursome and further enhanced by the sophisticated dining room.

X **Um Plateau** 🌿 🌿 ⇄ 🍴 VISA ⓞⓞ AE

6 Plateau Altmunster ✉ 1123 Clausen – ℰ 26 47 84 26
– www.umplateau.lu
– closed Saturday lunch and Sunday Plan II **D1**
Rest – Menu 25 € (lunch) – Carte 38/55 €
♦ Modern ♦ Trendy ♦

An elegant neo-bistro with designer chairs, pop lighting, warm colours and, for a retro touch, stained-glass windows. Contemporary cuisine: black rice risotto, salmon tartare with fennel…

NETHERLANDS
NEDERLAND

→ **AREA:**
41 543 km² (16 163 sq mi).

→ **POPULATION:**
16 751 323 inhabitants.
Density = 403 per km².

→ **CAPITAL:**
Amsterdam; The Hague
is the seat of government
and Parliament.

→ **CURRENCY:**
Euro (€).

→ **GOVERNMENT:**
Constitutional parliamentary
monarchy (since 1815). Member
of European Union since 1957
(one of the 6 founding countries).

→ **LANGUAGE:**
Dutch; many Dutch people also
speak English.

→ **PUBLIC HOLIDAYS:**
New Year's Day (1 Jan); Good Friday
(late Mar/Apr); Easter Monday
(late Mar/Apr); Queen's Day (30 Apr);
Liberation Day (5 May); Ascension
Day (May); Pentecost (late May/
June); Christmas Day (25 Dec);
St Stephen's Day (26 Dec).

→ **LOCAL TIME:**
GMT+1 hour in winter and GMT
+2 hours in summer.

→ **CLIMATE:**
Temperate maritime with cool
winters and mild summers
(Amsterdam: January 2°C; July
17°C), rainfall evenly distributed
throughout the year.

AMSTERDAM

● The Hague
● Rotterdam

→ **EMERGENCY:**
Police, Medical Assistance and Fire
Brigade ☏ **112**.

→ **ELECTRICITY:**
230 volts AC, 50Hz; 2 round pin
sockets.

→ **FORMALITIES:**
Travellers from the European Union
(EU), Switzerland, Iceland and the
main countries of North and South
America need a national identity
card or passport (America: passport
required) to visit the Netherlands
for less than three months (tourism
or business purpose). For visitors
from other countries a visa may be
required, in addition to a passport,
especially for those wishing to
stay for longer than three months.
We advise you to check with your
embassy before travelling.

AMSTERDAM
AMSTERDAM

Population: 792 490

Packshot/Fotolia.com

Once visited, never forgotten; that's Amsterdam's great claim to fame. Its endearing horseshoe shape – defined by 17C canals cut to drain land for a growing population – allied to finely detailed gabled houses, has produced a compact city centre of aesthetically splendid symmetry and matchless consistency. Exploring the city on foot or by bike is the real joy here and visitors rarely need to jump on a tram or bus.

'The world's biggest small city' displays a host of distinctive characteristics, ranging from the world-famous red light district to the cosy and convivial brown cafés, from the wonderful art galleries and museums to the quirky shops, and the medieval churches to the tree-lined waterways with their pretty bridges. There's the feel of a northern Venice, but without the hallowed and revered atmosphere. It exists on a human scale, small enough to walk from one end to the other. Those who might moan that it's just too small should stroll along to the former derelict docklands on the east side and contemplate the shiny new apartments giving the waterfront a sleek, 21C feel. Most people who come here, though, are just happy to cosy up to old Amsterdam's sleepy, relaxed vibe. No European city does snug bars better: this is the place to go for cats kipping on beat-up chairs and candles flickering on wax-encrusted tables…

AMSTERDAM IN...

→ **ONE DAY**
A trip on a canal boat, Rijksmuseum, Anne Frank Museum, Van Gogh Museum.

→ **TWO DAYS**
Begijnhof, shopping in the '9 Straatjes', Vondelpark, evening in a brown café.

→ **THREE DAYS**
The Jordaan, Plantage and Entrepotdok, red light district.

PRACTICAL INFORMATION

ARRIVAL-DEPARTURE

 Schipol International Airport is 18km southwest of the city. Trains run regularly to Amsterdam Central Station, and take 20min.

GETTING AROUND

With its narrow streets and canals, this is a city geared to walking. It's also one of the most bike-friendly capitals in the world, so rent one if you want to experience life as a local. Trams and buses run mostly from the central station; the metro has four short lines, mostly used by commuters. The Amsterdam Card entitles the holder to free public transport, admission to major museums, a canal cruise and discounts in some restaurants. Valid for 24hr, 48hr, or 72hr, it is available from the Tourist Information Office opposite the central station.

CALENDAR HIGHLIGHTS

May
Kunst RAI (modern art exhibition).

June
Holland Festival (theatre, concerts and ballets), Roots Festival (music and dance), Open Garden Days.

July-August
Concertgebouw (classical music).

August
Uitmarkt (theatrical/musical shows), Gay Pride's Canal Parade, Grachtenfestival (classical concerts).

September
Jordaan Festival (musical shows and fairs).

November
Museumnacht (many museums stay open during the night).

EATING OUT

Amsterdam is a vibrant and multicultural city and, as such, has a wide proliferation of restaurants offering a varied choice of cuisines, where you can eat well without paying too much. Head for an eetcafe and you'll get a satisfying three course meal at a reasonable price. The Dutch consider the evening to be the time to eat your main meal, so some restaurants shut at lunchtime. Aside from the eetcafe, you can top up your middle-of-day fuel levels with simple, home-cooked meals and local beers at a bruin (brown) café, or for something lighter, a café specialising in coffee and cake. If you wish to try local specialities, number one on the hit list could be rijsttafel or 'rice table', as the Dutch have imported much from their former colonies of Indonesia. Fresh raw herring from local waters is another nutritious local favourite, as are apple pies and pancakes of the sweet persuasion; often enjoyed with a hot chocolate. Restaurants are never too big but are certainly atmospheric and busy, so it's worth making reservations.

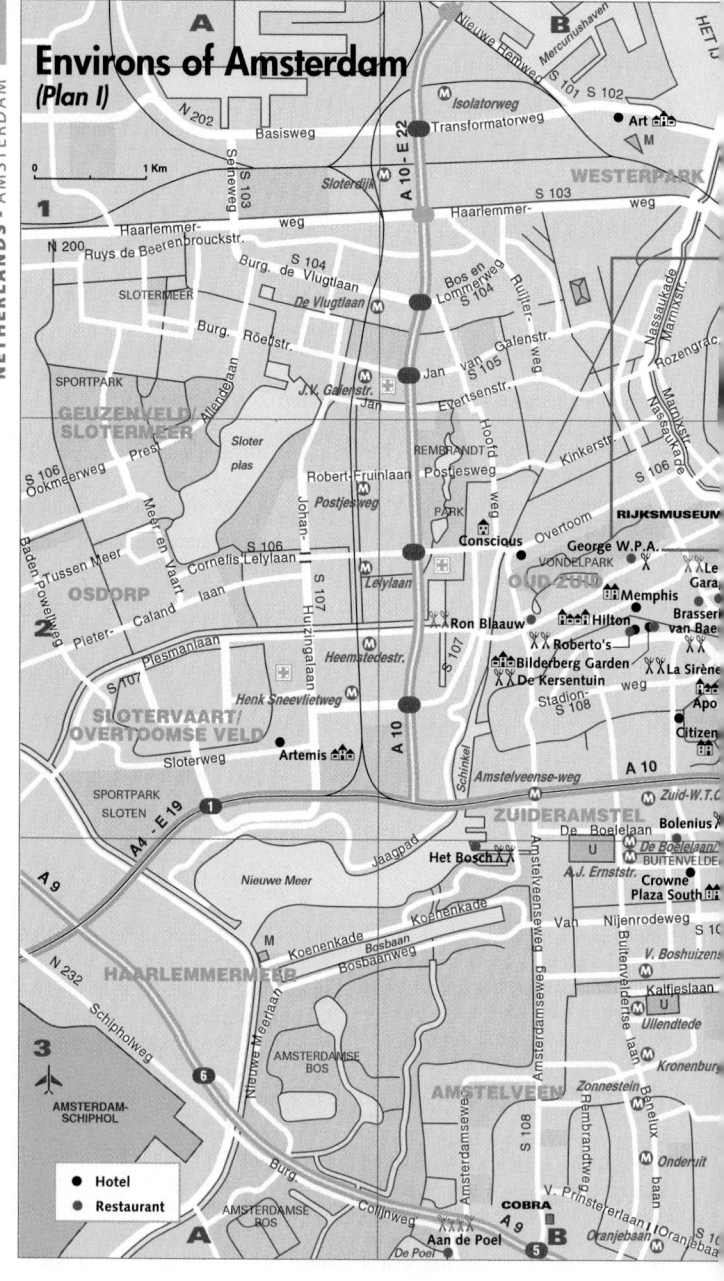

Environs of Amsterdam
(Plan I)

0   1 Km

● Hotel
● Restaurant

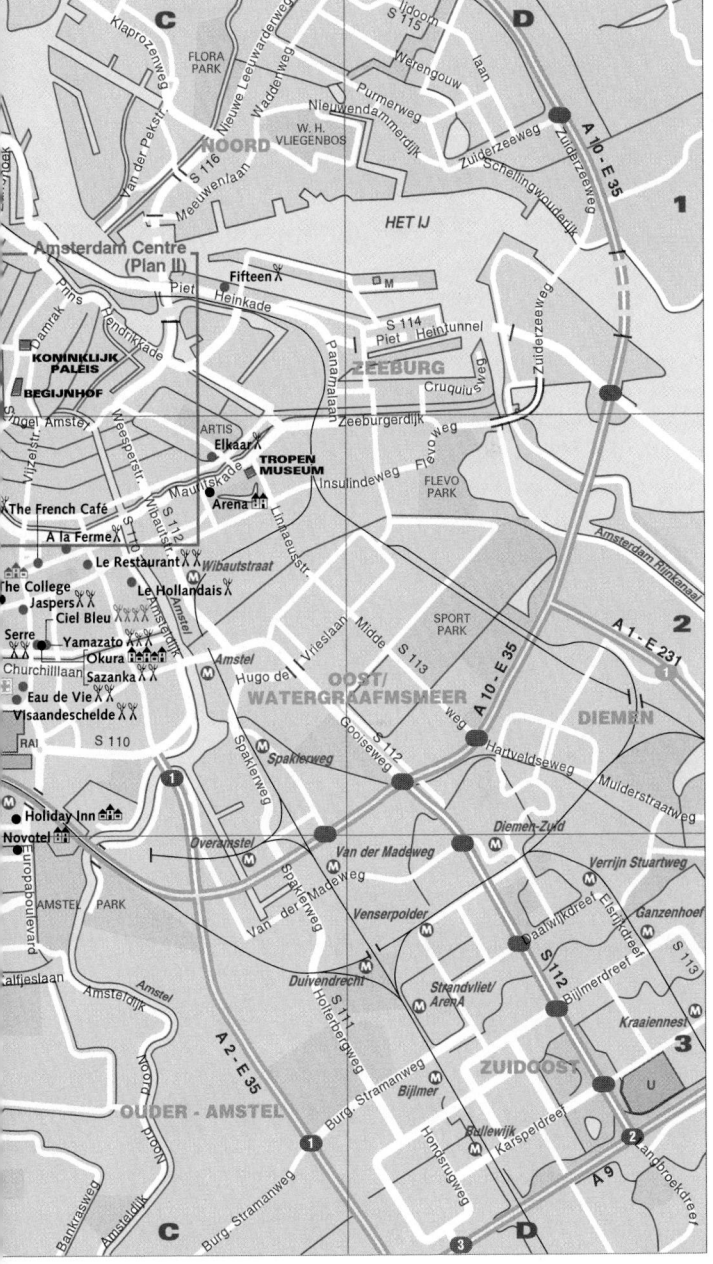

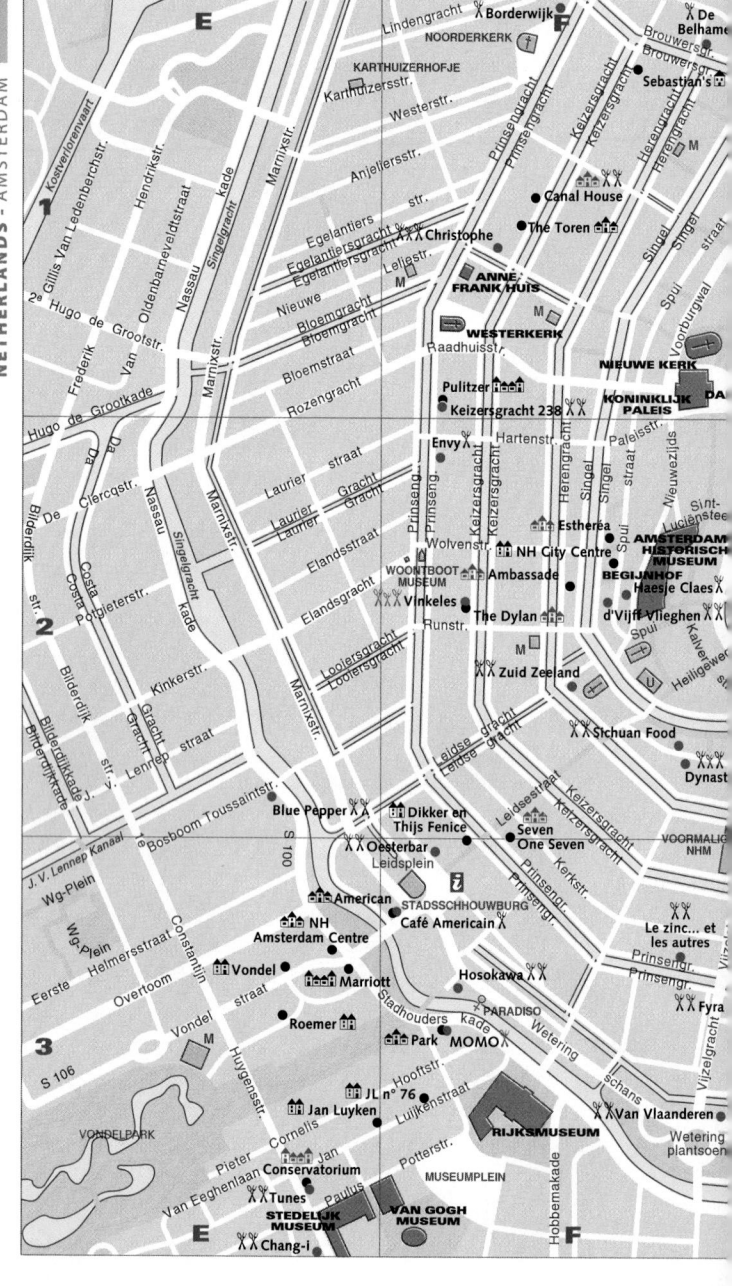

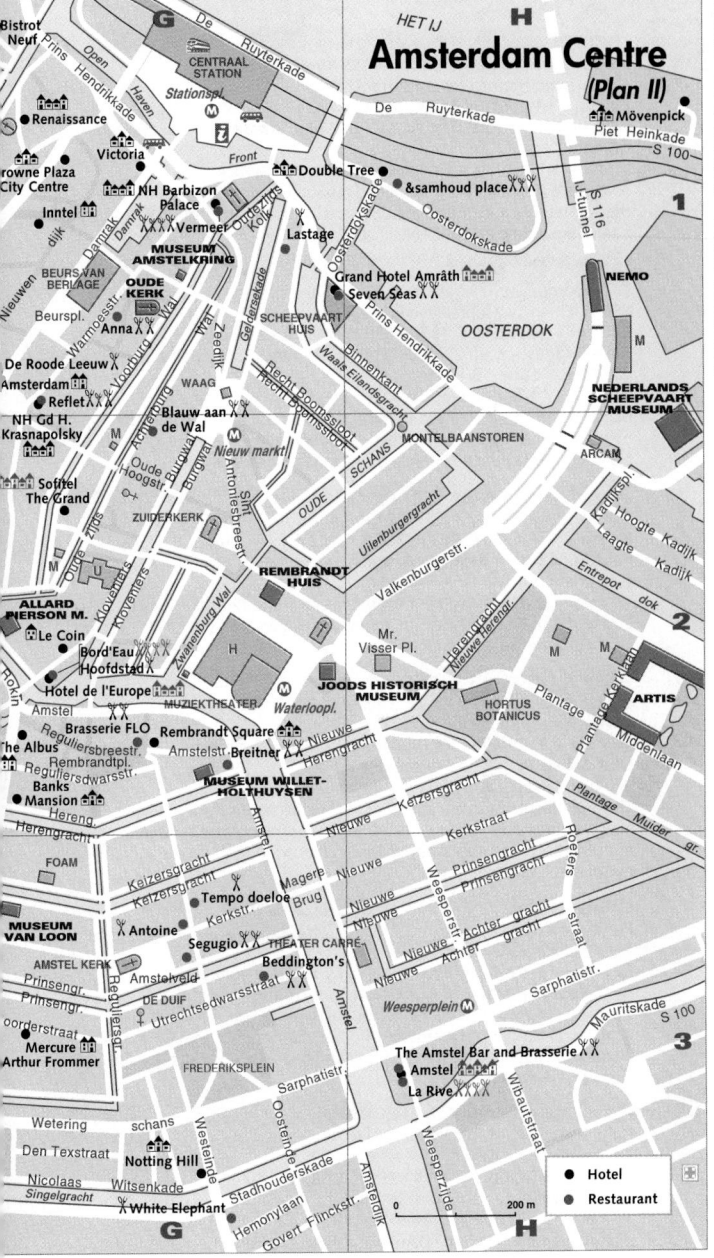

Amsterdam Centre
(Plan II)

HET IJ

De Ruyterkade

Piet Heinkade

S 100

Mövenpick

CENTRAAL STATION
Stationspl.

Front

Double Tree

&samhoud place

Oosterdokskade

Renaissance

Victoria

Crowne Plaza City Centre

NH Barbizon Palace

Inntel

Vermeer

Lastage

Oosterdokstraat

S 116

IJ-tunnel

NEMO

M

Danrak

dijk

Oudezijds Kolk

Grand Hotel Amrâth

Seven Seas

Prins Hendrikkade

OOSTERDOK

MUSEUM AMSTELKRING

BEURS VAN BERLAGE

OUDE KERK

Beurspl.

Anna

SCHEEPVAART HUIS

Binnenkant

NEDERLANDS SCHEEPVAART MUSEUM

ARCAM

Nieuwen

Warmoesstr.

Voorburg

Zeedijk

Gel. Oosterdok

Waals Eilandsgracht

De Roode Leeuw

Amsterdam

Reflet

WAAG

Recht Boomssloot

Krom Boomssloot

MONTELBAANSTOREN

M

NH Gd H. Krasnapolsky

Blauw aan de Wal

Nieuwmarkt!

Sint Antoniebreestr.

SCHANS

OUDE

Kloveniersburgwal

Oude Hoogstr.

ZUIDERKERK

Uilenburgergracht

Sofitel The Grand

Oude Zijds

Kadijksplein

Hoogte Kadijk

Laagte Kadijk

Entrepot dok

ALLARD PIERSON M.

Le Coin

Bord'Eau

Hoofdstad

Kouwen...

Zwanenburg Wal

REMBRANDT HUIS

Rokin

Amstel

Hotel de l'Europe

Mr. Visser Pl.

Valkenburgerstr.

M

ARTIS

Brasserie FLO

The Albus

Reguliersbreestr.

Rembrandtpl.

Reguliersdwarsstr.

Banks

Mansion

Hereng.

Herengracht

MUZIEKTHEATER

Waterlooplein

JOODS HISTORISCH MUSEUM

HORTUS BOTANICUS

Plantage

Middenlaan

Rembrandt Square

Breitner

Amstelstr.

Nieuwe Herengracht

Herengracht

Nieuwe Keizersgracht

MUSEUM WILLET-HOLTHUYSEN

Kerkstraat

Plantage Kerklaan

Plantage Muidergr.

FOAM

Keizersgracht

Magere Brug

Nieuwe

Prinsengracht

Roeters...

Tempo doeloe

Keizersgr.

Kerkstr.

Nieuwe

Weesperstr.

Achter gracht

Sarphatistr.

MUSEUM VAN LOON

Antoine

Segugio

THEATER CARRÉ

Nieuwe

Achter gracht

AMSTEL KERK

Prinsengr.

Prinsengr.

oorderstraat

Amstelveld

Beddington's

Utrechtsedwarsstraat

Amstel

Weesperplein

S 100

Mauritskade

Mercure Arthur Frommer

DE DUIF

FREDERIKSPLEIN

Sarphatistr.

The Amstel Bar and Brasserie

Amstel

La Rive

Wibautstraat

Wetering schans

Den Texstraat

Notting Hill

Westeinde

Oosteinde

Stadhouderskade

Amsteldijk

Weesperzijde

Nicolaas

Singelgracht

Witsenkade

White Elephant

Hemonylaan

Govert Flinckstr.

| ● | Hotel |
| ● | Restaurant |

0   200 m

NETHERLANDS - AMSTERDAM

Amstel   ← ↳ 🕏 ▣ 🎵 🎐 🛋 🅿 ☁ 🚾 ⑩ 🄰🄴 ⑩

Prof. Tulpplein 1 ⊠ 1018 GX – ℰ (0 20) 622 60 60
– www.amsterdam.intercontinental.com   **H3**
63 rm – ♦395/650 € ♦♦395/650 €, ☲ 33 € – 16 suites
Rest *La Rive* ✿ **Rest** *The Amstel Bar and Brasserie* – see restaurant
listing
♦ Grand Luxury ♦ Palace ♦ Personalised ♦
A veritable haven of luxury and good taste in this grand hotel on the banks of
the Amstel. The vast rooms are decorated with attention to detail and stylish
furnishings. Complete, efficient service.

Sofitel The Grand   🕭 🚗 🕏 ↳ 🕏 ▣ 🎵 🎐 🛋 🍽 ☁

O.Z. Voorburgwal 197 ⊠ 1012 EX – ℰ (0 20)   🚾 ⑩ 🄰🄴 ⑩
555 31 11 – www.sofitel-legend-thegrand.com   **G2**
148 rm – ♦265/550 € ♦♦265/550 €, ☲ 35 € – 29 suites
Rest *Bridges* – ℰ (0 20) 555 35 60 (open until 11pm) Menu 35 € (lunch),
49/105 € – Carte 58/170 €
♦ Luxury ♦ Palace ♦ Historic ♦
Maria de Medici once stayed in this superb historic building, formerly Amsterdam's town hall. Stylish, refurbished guestrooms, lounges and a beautiful courtyard. Chic restaurant with fish and seafood in their purest form.

Hotel de l'Europe   ← ↳ 🕭 🕏 ▣ 🕭 🎵 🎐 🛋 🅿 🚾 ⑩ 🄰🄴 ⑩

Nieuwe Doelenstraat 2 ⊠ 1012 CP – ℰ (0 20) 531 17 77 – www.leurope.nl
88 rm – ♦309/750 € ♦♦309/750 €, ☲ 32 € – 23 suites   **G2**
Rest *Bord'Eau* ✿ **Rest** *Hoofdstad* ⌂ – see restaurant listing
♦ Luxury ♦ Palace ♦ Personalised ♦
This luxury hotel, which dates back to the end of the 19C, offers a chic combination of charm and tradition. The rooms are elegant and the junior suites were
inspired by Mondrian, the Dutch painter. Views of the canals.

Grand Hotel Amrâth   ↳ 🎵 ▣ 🕭 🎐 🎐 🛋 🅿 🚾 ⑩ 🄰🄴 ⑩

Prins Hendrikkade 108 ⊠ 1011 AK – ℰ (0 20) 552 00 00
– www.amrathamsterdam.com   **G1**
165 rm – ♦190/400 € ♦♦190/450 €, ☲ 25 € – 7 suites
Rest *Seven Seas* – see restaurant listing
♦ Chain hotel ♦ Business ♦ Art Deco ♦
The monumental staircase of this impressive, luxury Art Nouveau hotel is a true
"stairway to heaven" and guests will want for nothing here. It offers a convenient central location, pleasantly spacious and comfortable rooms and excellent,
personalised service.

Pulitzer   🚗 ↳ 🕭 🎐 🎐 🛋 ☁ 🚾 ⑩ 🄰🄴 ⑩

Prinsengracht 323 ⊠ 1016 GZ – ℰ (0 20) 523 52 35
– www.luxurycollection.com/pulitzer   **F1**
227 rm – ♦249/489 € ♦♦274/514 €, ☲ 29 € – 3 suites
Rest *Keizersgracht 238* – see restaurant listing
♦ Chain hotel ♦ Luxury ♦ Historic ♦
A group of 25 admirably-restored houses, dating from the 17 and 18C, set
around a well-tended garden. Public areas filled with works of art; refined, indi-
vidualized bedrooms.

NH Grand Hotel Krasnapolsky   ↳ 🎵 🕭 🎐 🎐 🛋 ☁

Dam 9 ⊠ 1012 JS – ℰ (0 20) 554 91 11   🚾 ⑩ 🄰🄴 ⑩
– www.nh-hotels.com   **G1**
468 rm – ♦149/399 € ♦♦149/399 €, ☲ 30 € – 1 suite
Rest *Reflet* – see restaurant listing
♦ Luxury ♦ Traditional ♦ Classic ♦
Historic grand hotel on the Dam with various categories of rooms, apartments
for rent by the week and buffet breakfast served under a magnificent glass roof
dating from 1879.

NETHERLANDS - AMSTERDAM

Renaissance ᴸᵃ 🏠 🕭 🄰🄲 🤶 🔊 🖙 🚗 𝚅𝚂𝙰 🅾🅾 🄰🄴 ⓞ

Kattengat 1 ⊠ 1012 SZ – ℰ (0 20) 621 22 23
– www.renaissanceamsterdamhotel.com   **G1**
402 rm – ♦150/425 € ♦♦150/425 €, ⊡ 27 € – 6 suites
Rest *– (closed Sunday) (dinner only)* Menu 28/35 € – Carte 28/49 €
♦ Chain hotel ♦ Business ♦ Modern ♦
Rooms, suites and junior suites with modern comfort and numerous services on
offer. Excellent conference facilities underneath the dome of an old Lutheran
church dating from 1671. Restaurant with an international menu; simplified
dining in the "brown café".

NH Barbizon Palace ᴸᵃ 🏠 🕭 🄰🄲 🤶 🔊 🖙 🚗 𝚅𝚂𝙰 🅾🅾 🄰🄴 ⓞ

Prins Hendrikkade 59 ⊠ 1012 AD – ℰ (0 20) 556 45 64
– www.nh-hotels.com   **G1**
271 rm – ♦150/300 € ♦♦150/300 €, ⊡ 26 € – 3 suites
Rest *Vermeer* ❀ – see restaurant listing
Rest – Menu 40 € (lunch), 43/65 € – Carte 28/45 €
♦ Chain hotel ♦ Business ♦ Modern ♦
Luxury accommodation right opposite the station. It offers a hint of 17C charm
combined with modern and fashionable comfort. Step onto the hotel's private
jetty to explore the famous Amsterdam canals. The menu at Hudson's restaurant is international.

Marriott ᴸᵃ 🏠 🕭 rm, 🄰🄲 🤶 🔊 🖙 🚗 𝚅𝚂𝙰 🅾🅾 🄰🄴 ⓞ

Stadhouderskade 12 ⊠ 1054 ES – ℰ (0 20) 607 55 55
– www.amsterdammarriott.com   **E3**
395 rm – ♦150/425 € ♦♦150/425 €, ⊡ 27 € – 5 suites
Rest *– (dinner only)* Carte 34/61 €
♦ Chain hotel ♦ Business ♦ Cosy ♦
A high-class, American-style hotel on a major thoroughfare. The rooms are vast
and well-equipped. A good seminar infrastructure and business centre. Modern
steak house specialising in grilled Black Angus Beef.

Conservatorium 🤶 ᴸᵃ 🌐 🏠 🔲 🕭 rest, 🄰🄲 🤶 🔊 𝚅𝚂𝙰 🅾🅾 🄰🄴

Van Baerlestraat 27 ⊠ 1071 AN – ℰ (0 20) 570 00 00
– www.conservatoriumhotel.com   **E3**
129 rm – ♦305/515 € ♦♦305/515 €, ⊡ 28 €
Rest *Tunes* – see restaurant listing
Rest – Menu 38 € bi/85 € bi – Carte 36/75 €
♦ Grand Luxury ♦ Historic ♦
The Conservatorium is one of Amsterdam's finest hotels. Neither expense nor
effort was spared in the renovation of this neo-Classical jewel that dates back
to the end of the 19C. Excellent service, with staff at hand to meet your every
need. Pure, unadulterated luxury.

Crowne Plaza City Centre ᴸᵃ 🏠 🕭 🄰🄲 🔊 🔊 🖙 🚗

N.Z. Voorburgwal 5 ⊠ 1012 RC   𝚅𝚂𝙰 🅾🅾 🄰🄴 ⓞ
– ℰ (0 20) 620 05 00 – www.amsterdam-citycentre.crowneplaza.com
268 rm – ♦129/380 € ♦♦139/380 €, ⊡ 25 € – 2 suites   **G1**
Rest *– (open until 11pm)* Carte 32/46 €
♦ Chain hotel ♦ Business ♦ Modern ♦
This fully renovated member of a hotel chain has modern, functional rooms. It
also offers a sauna, gym, meeting rooms and valet parking. Attractive roof garden. Contemporary-style cuisine and Dutch specialities are served in the restaurant.

Ambassade without rest ⩽ 🄰🄲 🔊 𝚅𝚂𝙰 🅾🅾 🄰🄴 ⓞ

Herengracht 341 ⊠ 1016 AZ – ℰ (0 20) 555 02 22
– www.ambassade-hotel.nl   **F2**
53 rm – ♦185/225 € ♦♦185/350 €, ⊡ 18 € – 3 suites
♦ Luxury ♦ Family ♦ Stylish ♦
The Cobra collection and the books in the library signed by authors who have
stayed here all testify to the artistic style of this hotel. It is just perfect for art
loving Amsterdam!

NETHERLANDS - AMSTERDAM

The Dylan
Keizersgracht 384 ☒ *1016 GB –* ℰ *(0 20) 530 20 10*
– www.dylanamsterdam.com   **F2**
32 rm – ♥295/350 € ♥♥325/1250 €, ☲ 28 € – 8 suites
Rest *Vinkeles* ✿ – see restaurant listing
♦ Grand Luxury ♦ Design ♦
Discover the intimate harmony of this 17C boutique hotel with its surprising design decor. Gorgeous rooms and personal service make this a very special place to stay.

American
Leidsekade 97 ☒ *1017 PN –* ℰ *(0 20) 556 30 00*
– www.amsterdamamerican.com   **F3**
174 rm – ♥120/385 € ♥♥120/385 €, ☲ 20 € – 1 suite
Rest *Café Americain* – see restaurant listing
♦ Palace ♦ Business ♦ Art Deco ♦
This historic building, which is situated on a lively square, is not easily missed: its impressive frontage has a real majestic air.

Banks Mansion without rest
Herengracht 519 ☒ *1017 BV –* ℰ *(0 20) 420 00 55*
– www.banksmansion.nl   **G2**
50 rm ☲ – ♥199/259 € ♥♥199/299 € – 1 suite
♦ Chain hotel ♦ Business ♦ Modern ♦
The handsome Berlage architecture of this hotel hints at the elegant accommodation on offer here. As an added attraction, the minibar and the whisky are included in the price of the room.

Seven One Seven without rest
Prinsengracht 717 ☒ *1017 JW –* ℰ *(0 20) 427 07 17 – www.717hotel.nl*
9 rm ☲ – ♥300/500 € ♥♥300/650 €   **F2-3**
♦ Grand Luxury ♦ Traditional ♦ Classic ♦
Attractive 18C house converted into an intimate and select place to stay. The guestrooms are veritable gems. Romantic lounges; leafy courtyard where breakfast is served in summer.

Victoria
Damrak 1 ☒ *1012 LG –* ℰ *(0 20) 623 42 55 – www.parkplaza.com*
296 rm – ♥105/360 € ♥♥105/360 €, ☲ 24 € – 10 suites   **G1**
Rest – Menu 33 € – Carte approx. 47 €
♦ Chain hotel ♦ Traditional ♦ Classic ♦
Near the station, a neoclassical 19C luxury hotel and extension dating from the 1980s. Domed lobby with modern stained glass. Refurbished rooms. Tavern-restaurant with traditional menu.

Mövenpick
Piet Heinkade 11 ☒ *1019 BR –* ℰ *(0 20) 519 12 00*
– www.moevenpick-amsterdam.com   **H1**
408 rm – ♥149/280 € ♥♥149/280 €, ☲ 23 € – 1 suite
Rest – *(open until 11pm)* Menu 25/95 € – Carte 28/77 €
♦ Chain hotel ♦ Business ♦ Modern ♦
Modern chain hotel inaugurated in 2006 in a modern district. The rooms have panoramic views. Concert hall, jazz club and congress centre next door. Restaurant serving Asian cuisine: Chinese, Thai and Indonesian.

Canal House
Keizersgracht 148 ☒ *1015 CX –* ℰ *(0 20) 622 51 82 – www.canalhouse.nl*
23 rm ☲ – ♥175/525 € ♥♥550/700 € – 1 suite   **F1**
Rest *Canal House* – see restaurant listing
♦ Luxury ♦ Personalised ♦ Modern ♦
Canal House is synonymous with luxurious accommodation beside the Amsterdam canals. There is a choice between various room categories (ranging from good, to better and best!), offering the ultimate in indulgence – it all depends on how much pampering you want! The rooms are designed so that their modern character complements the historic setting of the hotel beautifully.

AMSTERDAM - NETHERLANDS

Estheréa without rest   🔲 🛜 ⅍ 🚗 VISA ⚫ AE ①

Singel 305 ⊠ 1012 WJ – ℰ (0 20) 624 51 46 – www.estherea.nl
91 rm – †99/280 € ††125/360 €, ⌑ 18 €   **F2**
♦ Family ♦ Traditional ♦ Personalised ♦
The Estherea is a beautiful, elegant hotel full of charm. The restaurant's warm, classic interior clad in red velvet will tempt diners, and its excellent breakfast will win them over completely.

The Toren without rest   🚙 🔲 🛜 VISA ⚫ AE ①

Keizersgracht 164 ⊠ 1015 CZ – ℰ (0 20) 622 63 52 – www.thetoren.nl
35 rm – †90/200 € ††150/450 €, ⌑ 14 € – 3 suites   **F1**
♦ Traditional ♦ Cosy ♦ Retro ♦
A charming hotel composed of several old houses, near the Anne Frank House. Neo-baroque bedrooms, elegant breakfast room with an attractive bar.

Rembrandt Square   🔲 📞 ⅍ VISA ⚫ AE ①

Amstelstraat 17 ⊠ 1017 DA – ℰ (0 20) 890 47 47
– www.hamshire-hotels.com   **G2**
166 rm – †90/450 € ††90/450 €, ⌑ 18 €
Rest *Brasserie FLO* – see restaurant listing
♦ Chain hotel ♦ Modern ♦
Set on a lively square, the vintage façade hides a modernised interior. Contemporary, well-equipped guestrooms. Seminar facilities and bicycles available.

Eden 🏨   🔲 📞 VISA ⚫ AE ①

Amstel 144 ⊠ 1017 AE – ℰ (0 20) 530 78 70 – www.hampshire-hotels.com
218 rm – †90/450 € ††90/450 €, ⌑ 18 €
♦ Chain hotel ♦ Functional ♦
The guestrooms in the adjoining outbuilding are pleasantly comfortable.

Notting Hill   🛋 ⅗ rm, 🔲 rm, 🛜 VISA ⚫ AE ①

Westeinde 26 ⊠ 1017 ZP – ℰ (0 20) 523 10 30 – www.hotelnottinghill.nl
67 rm – †135/215 € ††145/225 €, ⌑ 24 €   **G3**
Rest – Carte 40/60 €
♦ Luxury ♦ Stylish ♦
A pleasant stay awaits in this boutique hotel. It offers a full range of modern comforts in a quiet neighbourhood on the Kleine Singel. Handsomely appointed bedrooms, which not only look attractive but also have been created using high quality materials.

Double Tree   ≤ 🛋 ⅙ ⅗ rm, 🛜 ⅍ VISA ⚫ AE ①

Oosterdoksstraat 4 ⊠ 1011 DK – ℰ (0 20) 530 08 00
– www.amsterdam.doubletree.com   **H1**
553 rm – †159/425 € ††159/425 €, ⌑ 25 €
Rest – *(open until 11pm)* Menu 30 € – Carte 37/54 €
♦ Chain hotel ♦ Business ♦ Functional ♦
This hotel with its huge windows boasts dazzling views to tempt the curious traveller, as well as a great location close to the river IJ and the station. The bedrooms of this rather futuristic hotel are light and airy. Impressive Sky bar.

NH Amsterdam Centre   🛋 🕌 ⅗ 🔲 🛜 ⅍ ▱ VISA ⚫ AE

Stadhouderskade 7 ⊠ 1054 ES – ℰ (0 20) 685 13 51 – www.nh-hotels.com
232 rm – †119/400 € ††119/400 €, ⌑ 20 € – 2 suites   **E3**
Rest – *(closed Sunday and Monday) (dinner only)* Menu 40 € – Carte approx. 55 €
♦ Chain hotel ♦ Business ♦ Modern ♦
Renovated chain hotel built to host athletes attending the Amsterdam Olympic Games in 1928. Designer public areas. Large modern bedrooms. Italian menu, contemporary décor and view of the Leidseplein at Sogno.

NETHERLANDS - AMSTERDAM

Park 🛏 ♿ Ⓜ 🛜 🏊 🚗 ᴠ𝙸𝚂𝙰 ⓞⓞ Ⓐ𝙴 ⓘ

Stadhouderskade 25 ⊠ 1071 ZD – ℰ (0 20) 671 12 22 – www.parkhotel.nl
189 rm – ♦99/375 € ♦♦99/375 €, ☲ 24 € **F3**
Rest MOMO – see restaurant listing
♦ Luxury ♦ Modern ♦
Fully renovated hi-tech hotel set between Vondelpark and the busy centre. Five types of spacious and pleasant trendy rooms. Meeting and fitness facilities. Stylish service.

Amsterdam Ⓜ 🛜 ᴠ𝙸𝚂𝙰 ⓞⓞ Ⓐ𝙴 ⓘ

Damrak 93 ⊠ 1012 LP – ℰ (0 20) 555 06 66 – www.hotelamsterdam.nl
79 rm – ♦89/390 € ♦♦99/400 €, ☲ 15 € **G1**
Rest De Roode Leeuw – see restaurant listing
♦ Traditional ♦ Classic ♦
This traditional Amsterdam hotel is located on a central section of the busy Damrak. Very comfortable rooms. Public car parks nearby.

Dikker en Thijs Ⓜ rm, 🛜 ᴠ𝙸𝚂𝙰 ⓞⓞ Ⓐ𝙴

Prinsengracht 444 ⊠ 1017 KE – ℰ (0 20) 620 12 12 – www.dtfh.nl
42 rm – ♦125/245 € ♦♦150/345 €, ☲ 18 € **F2-3**
Rest – *(closed Sunday) (dinner only)* Menu 33/44 € – Carte 40/49 €
♦ Business ♦ Traditional ♦ Classic ♦
Facing the canal, this complex features a 17C house and a huge 1921 building, where a pupil of famous French chef Escoffier once owned a food shop. Large guestrooms, studio and penthouse.

Inntel without rest Ⓜ 🛜 ᴠ𝙸𝚂𝙰 ⓞⓞ Ⓐ𝙴 ⓘ

Nieuwezijdskolk 19 ⊠ 1012 PV – ℰ (0 20) 530 18 18 – www.inntelhotels.nl
239 rm – ♦95/370 € ♦♦95/370 €, ☲ 15 € **G1**
♦ Chain hotel ♦ Modern ♦
A modern glass-fronted establishment in the heart of the busy Nieuwe Zijde, the shopping area next to the station. Well sound-proofed rooms. Breakfast area entirely surrounded by glass.

The Albus 🛜 ᴠ𝙸𝚂𝙰 ⓞⓞ Ⓐ𝙴 ⓘ

Vijzelstraat 49 ⊠ 1017 HE – ℰ (0 20) 530 62 00 – www.albushotel.com
74 rm – ♦99/269 € ♦♦99/269 €, **G2**
Rest – Menu 23 € (lunch), 30/49 € bi – Carte 27/46 €
♦ Business ♦ Design ♦
This smart design hotel is in an interesting location. The restaurant offers an up-to-date menu.

NH City Centre without rest ♿ 🛜 🚗 ᴠ𝙸𝚂𝙰 ⓞⓞ Ⓐ𝙴 ⓘ

Spuistraat 288 ⊠ 1012 VX – ℰ (0 20) 420 45 45 – www.nh-hotels.com
209 rm – ♦119/179 € ♦♦119/179 €, ☲ 20 € **F2**
♦ Chain hotel ♦ Business ♦ Functional ♦
Slotted between the Singel canal and the Béguine convent, this hotel has neutral, contemporary-style bedrooms typical of the NH chain. Spacious and comfortable lounge.

Mercure Arthur Frommer without rest Ⓜ 🛜 🅿

Noorderstraat 46 ⊠ 1017 TV – ℰ (0 20) 622 03 28 ᴠ𝙸𝚂𝙰 ⓞⓞ Ⓐ𝙴 ⓘ
– www.accorhotels.com **G3**
93 rm – ♦79/269 € ♦♦79/269 €, ☲ 19 €
♦ Chain hotel ♦ Modern ♦
Belonging to a national chain, this hotel was once part of a group of weavers' cottages and is now situated in a residential area, close to the Rijks Museum. The modern rooms, some of which boast designer-style furniture, have all been fully renovated.

NETHERLANDS - AMSTERDAM

 Roemer without rest

Roemer Visscherstraat 10 ⊠ *1054 EX* – ✆ *(0 20) 589 08 00*
– www.vondelhotels.com   **E3**
23 rm – ♦150/520 € ♦♦170/550 €, � 20 €
♦ Business ♦ Design ♦

An attractive hotel with an elegant, designer-style interior, in an early 20C town-house situated close to the Vondel Park. Modern interior, immaculate rooms and breakfast served in the garden in summer.

 Vondel

Vondelstraat 26 ⊠ *1054 GD* – ✆ *(0 20) 612 01 20*
– www.vondelhotels.com   **E3**
86 rm – ♦90/405 € ♦♦105/420 €, ⊽ 20 €
Rest – Menu 30/44 € – Carte 37/44 €
♦ Business ♦ Luxury ♦ Modern ♦

This boutique hotel was created out of seven 1900s houses. Communal areas, bedrooms and conference room in a decidedly contemporary style. Breakfasts on the stylish patio when the weather is good. Hip, stylish bistro serving local and international cuisine.

 Jan Luyken without rest

Jan Luykenstraat 58 ⊠ *1071 CS* – ✆ *(0 20) 573 07 30*
– www.janluyken.nl   **E3**
62 rm – ♦109/219 € ♦♦129/289 €, ⊽ 20 €
♦ Chain hotel ♦ Traditional ♦ Cosy ♦

Three 1900s houses make up this hotel with contemporary interior décor. Modern bedrooms, designer bar with a few period touches and small courtyard terrace.

 JL n° 76 without rest

Jan Luijkenstraat 76 ⊠ *1071 CT*
– ✆ (0 20) 348 55 55
– www.vondelhotels.com   **F3**
39 rm – ♦110/350 € ♦♦110/350 €, ⊽ 20 €
♦ Luxury ♦ Cosy ♦

Two 18C townhouses have been converted into one at Jan Luijkenstraat 76, hence the name. Comfortable accommodation, which might not be the ulti-mate in luxury but is definitely stylish and elegant. This hotel is situated in the fashion and museum district, so there is plenty to do in the neighbour-hood.

 Le Coin without rest

Nieuwe Doelenstraat 5 ⊠ *1012 CP* – ✆ *(0 20) 524 68 00*
– www.lecoin.nl   **G2**
42 rm – ♦120/125 € ♦♦120/185 €, ⊽ 12 €
♦ Traditional ♦ Functional ♦

Seven houses next to the University of Amsterdam make up this hotel. Rooms of various shapes and sizes, but all decorated in a contemporary style and equipped with a kitchenette.

 Sebastian's without rest

Keizersgracht 15 ⊠ *1055 CC* – ✆ *(0 20) 423 23 42*
– www.hotelsebastians.nl   **F1**
26 rm – ♦70/140 € ♦♦90/240 €, ⊽ 10 €
♦ Traditional ♦ Modern ♦

A boutique hotel with an adventurous, yet warm colour scheme. Its convenient location on the Keizersgracht canal, close to the Jordaan area, will suit business travellers and night-owls alike. Trendy bar.

XXXX **La Rive** – Hotel Amstel   ⬉ 🏠 🄰🄺 ⇵ 🖼 **P** **VISA** 🆎 **①**
⌘
Prof. Tulpplein 1 ✉ *1018 GX* – 𝒞 *(0 20) 520 32 64* – *www.restaurantlarive.com*
– *closed 30 April, 9 May, 22 July-13 August, 1-15 January, Saturday lunch,*
Sunday and Monday   **H3**
Rest – Menu 49 € (lunch), 90/112 € – Carte 112/184 € 🏵
♦ Creative ♦ Formal ♦
Intimate ambience, sophisticated decor, wonderful wines and sublime comfort
characterise this gastronomic restaurant at the Amstel Hotel. The cuisine is inno-
vative with the flavours of Asia as an underlying motif. The front looks out over
the water.
➜ Zalm met avocado, limoen en komkommer. Wagyu-entrecote met kai-
lan, pompoen en laurier. Aardbei met Tasmaanse peper en crème fraîche.

XXXX **Bord'Eau** – Hotel de l'Europe   ⬉ 🏠 🄰🄺 ⇵ 🖼 **P** **VISA** 🆎 **①**
⌘
Nieuwe Doelenstraat 2 ✉ *1012 CP* – 𝒞 *(0 20) 531 17 77* – *www.bordeau.nl*
– *closed Saturday lunch, Sunday and Monday*   **G2**
Rest – Menu 38 € (lunch), 73/93 € – Carte 65/117 €
♦ Innovative ♦ Formal ♦
Delicious and sophisticated, or deliciously sophisticated is the best way of sum-
ming up the hallmarks of this restaurant. The chef makes every effort to please
his demanding clientele by serving well-sourced produce in dishes that reflect
the spirit of the times completely.
➜ Krokante zwezerik met eigen jus, taggiasche olijf en knolselderij risotto-
stijl. Blauwe kreeft met lauwwarme salade, bouillon van koraal en pompel-
moes. Roomijs van pure chocolade verrijkt met roquefortkaas.

XXXX **Vermeer** – Hotel NH Barbizon Palace   ♿ 🄰🄺 ⇵ 🖼 **P**
⌘
Prins Hendrikkade 59 ✉ *1012 AD*   **VISA** 🆎 **①**
– 𝒞 *(0 20) 556 48 85* – *www.restaurantvermeer.nl*
– *closed 28 July-25 August, 22 December-6 January, Sunday and Bank Holidays*
Rest – *(dinner only)* Menu 80/110 € – Carte approx. 80 € 🏵   **G1**
♦ Modern ♦ Elegant ♦ Formal ♦
Classy restaurant of a luxury hotel where the chef creates inventive dishes with
a bold personal touch. Fine à la carte menu with a wine list and expert sommelier to match.
➜ Zee-egel en sepia met aardappelpuree, rauwe venkelslaatje en zoe-
thout, yoghurtdressing met dille. Palet van groenten, individueel bereid:
rauw, gegaard en gemarineerd. Bladerdeeggebakje van peer in zoutkorst
gebraden met anijs en kruidnagel, sorbet van trappistenbier.

XXX   **Vinkeles** – Hotel The Dylan   🖼 🖼 **VISA** 🆎 **①**
⌘
Keizersgracht 384 ✉ *1016 GB* – 𝒞 *(0 20) 530 20 10* – *www.vinkeles.com*
– *closed 26 December-13 January, Sunday and Bank Holidays*   **F2**
Rest – *(dinner only)* Menu 70/125 € – Carte 74/168 €
♦ Modern ♦ Elegant ♦
Smart restaurant set in a characterful hotel. Creative, tasty cuisine, served sty-
lishly in the former bakery (view of the old ovens) or facing the courtyard.
➜ Oosterscheldekreeft met witte asperges, doperwten, lamsoren, morieljes en
daslookolie. Vijf stukken van het kalf: lende, lever, nier, zwezerik en tong.
Bleekselderie in diverse structuren, zuring, stroop, peer en piment d'Espelette.

XXX   **&samhoud places** (Moshik Roth)   🄰🄺 ⇵ **VISA** 🆎 🆎
⌘⌘
Oosterdokskade 5 (1st floor) ✉ *1011 AD* – 𝒞 *(0 20) 260 20 94*
– *www.samhoudplaces* – *closed last week July-first week August,*
first 2 weeks January, Saturday lunch, Sunday and Monday   **H1**
Rest – Menu 65 € (lunch), 115/155 € – Carte 110/215 €
♦ Innovative ♦ Fashionable ♦
Moshik Roth has left Overveen and moved into an animated new neighbourhood in the centre of the city. Start with an aperitif in the chic ground floor
bar, then head upstairs to the trendy restaurant, where you can watch the
chefs preparing highly inventive dishes in the open kitchen.
➜ Gebakken eendenlever met paddestoelen, paletje van groenten en
mousaka. Entrecote van Wagyurund, jus met zwarte knoflook, Pont-Neuf
aardappel en Choronsaus. Appel met karamel, calvados, steranijs en kaneel.

XXX **Christophe**   🔲 AC ⇄ VISA ⚌ AE

Leliegracht 46 ⊠ 1015 DH – 𝒞 (0 20) 625 08 07
– www.restaurantchristophe.nl
– closed 30 April, 1 January, Sunday and Monday   **F1**
Rest – *(dinner only)* Menu 36/66 € – Carte 54/83 €
♦ Classic ♦ Elegant ♦ Cosy ♦
This low-key, refined restaurant in a traditional building on the banks of the canal Lys serves good classic to modern cuisine.

XXX **Dynasty**   🏠 AC ⇄ VISA ⚌ AE ➊

Reguliersdwarsstraat 30 ⊠ 1017 BM – 𝒞 (0 20) 626 84 00 – www.fer.nl
– closed 27 December-3 February and Tuesday   **F2**
Rest – *(dinner only until 11pm)* Menu 43/66 €
♦ Asian ♦ Exotic ♦
A pleasant, longstanding restaurant featuring cuisine from around Asia. The trendy exotic décor is warm and colourful. Lovely terrace in the back and attentive service.

XXX **Reflet** – Hotel NH Grand Hotel Krasnapolsky   ⚹ AC ⌁

Dam 9 ⊠ 1012 JS – 𝒞 (0 20) 554 60 26 – www.reflet.nl   VISA ⚌ AE ➊
– closed Sunday and Monday   **G1**
Rest – *(dinner only)* Menu 45/80 € – Carte 50/61 €
♦ Italian ♦ Retro ♦
This Baroque-style restaurant dates back to 1883. Today it offers dishes from a more classic menu served in a stylish decor and a luxurious ambience right in the heart of the city.

XX **d'Vijff Vlieghen**   AC ⇄ VISA ⚌ AE ➊

Spuistraat 294 (via Vlieghendesteeg 1) ⊠ 1012 VX – 𝒞 (0 20) 530 40 60
– www.vijffvlieghen.nl
– closed 30 April, 29 July-12 August and 24 and 31 December-1 January
Rest – *(dinner only)* Menu 36/108 € bi – Carte 54/61 €   **F2**
♦ Traditional ♦ Rustic ♦
The innovative dishes on offer at these charming 17C premises are all prepared with typical Dutch products. A set menu is served in various attractive, country-style dining rooms where original Rembrandt sketches decorate the walls.

XX **Breitner**   ⪜ VISA ⚌ AE

Amstel 212 ⊠ 1017 AH – 𝒞 (0 20) 627 78 79 – www.restaurant-breitner.nl
– closed 22 July-5 August, 25 December-2 January and Sunday   **G2**
Rest – *(dinner only)* Menu 40/58 € – Carte 51/70 €
♦ Classic ♦ Formal ♦
Creative and elaborate meals served in a classical modern setting. There are views over the Amstel with sightseeing boats and monuments (drawbridges, Amstelhof) in the background.

XX **Beddington's**   🏠 VISA ⚌ AE

Utrechtsedwarsstraat 141 ⊠ 1017 WE – 𝒞 (0 20) 620 73 93
– www.beddington.nl
– closed 28 April-6 May, 28 July-19 August, 22 December-1 January, Sunday and Monday   **G3**
Rest – *(dinner only)* Menu 48/55 €
♦ Modern ♦ Fashionable ♦
A British chef runs the open kitchen of this modern restaurant serving contemporary cuisine in her adopted home of Amsterdam. Black and white décor.

XX **Blauw aan de Wal**   🏠 AC ⇄ VISA ⚌ AE

O.Z. Achterburgwal 99 ⊠ 1012 DD – 𝒞 (0 20) 330 22 57
– closed Sunday and Monday   **G2**
Rest – *(dinner only until 11.30pm) (booking advisable) (set menu only)*
Menu 55 € 🌿
♦ Classic ♦ Cosy ♦
A popular restaurant at the end of a cul-de-sac in the lively red light district. Discreet décor, simple and tasty modern cuisine, good wine selection and a shady terrace.

Le zinc... et les autres ⬡ VISA ⓸ AE ⓞ

*Prinsengracht 999 ✉ 1017 KM – ℰ (0 20) 622 90 44 – www.lezinc.nl
– closed 30 April, 31 December-7 January and Sunday* **F3**
Rest – *(dinner only until 11pm)* Menu 38 € – Carte 45/58 €
♦ Modern ♦ Rustic ♦
This stylish 17C warehouse is on the Prinsengracht canal. The interior has been modernised but the rustic bar and beams have been left just as they were. Diners looking for a quieter meal should choose the lower room. Well-chosen menu and an interesting assortment of wines available by the glass.

Anna AC VISA ⓸ AE

*Warmoesstraat 111 ✉ 1012 JA – ℰ (0 20) 428 11 11
– www.restaurantanna.nl
– closed Saturday lunch and Sunday* **G1**
Rest – *(open until 11pm)* Menu 30 € (lunch)/48 € – Carte 49/57 €
♦ Modern ♦ Fashionable ♦
There is no lack of vitality at Anna given its location in the middle of the vibrant red-light district. This cosmopolitan restaurant has a relaxed and informal atmosphere – a choice setting for balanced, modern cooking.

Fyra VISA ⓸ ⓞ

*Noorderstraat 19 ✉ 1017 TR – ℰ (0 20) 428 36 32
– www.restaurantfyra.nl
– closed 2 weeks in August, 22 December-2 January and Tuesday*
Rest – *(dinner only)* Menu 38/55 € – Carte 41/57 € **F3**
♦ Modern ♦ Friendly ♦ Cosy ♦
Fyra means four and refers to the two couples that run this establishment. The interior is cosy and pleasant in a living room style. Current dishes with a mediteranean streak decorate the plates.

Zuid Zeeland 🍴 VISA ⓸ AE

*Herengracht 413 ✉ 1017 BP – ℰ (0 20) 624 31 54 – www.zuidzeeland.nl
– closed lunch Saturday and Sunday* **F2**
Rest – *(open until 11pm)* Menu 36/85 € – Carte 52/69 €
♦ Modern ♦ Friendly ♦
This old establishment overlooks an attractive section of the Herengracht canal on one side and a patio on the other. Good, reasonably priced menu (simpler at lunchtimes). Pavement terrace on the canal.

Hosokawa AC ⬡ VISA ⓸ AE

*Max Euweplein 22 ✉ 1017 MB – ℰ (0 20) 638 80 86 – www.hosokawa.nl
– closed Tuesday* **F3**
Rest – Menu 60 € – Carte 32/90 €
♦ Japanese ♦ Minimalist ♦
A sober, modern Japanese restaurant with cooking tables, worth a detour to watch the entertaining show of food rotating past your eyes! At lunchtimes, only sushi is available.

Segugio AC ⬡ VISA ⓸ AE ⓞ

*Utrechtsestraat 96 ✉ 1017 VS – ℰ (0 20) 330 15 03 – www.segugio.nl
– closed 30 April, 24, 25 and 31 December-1 January and Sunday*
Rest – *(dinner only)* Menu 42/55 € – Carte 52/63 € **G3**
♦ Italian ♦ Design ♦
This establishment with three modern dining rooms on several levels features sunny Italian cuisine made right before your eyes. Good selection of regional wines.

Oesterbar AC ⬡ VISA ⓸ AE ⓞ

*Leidseplein 10 ✉ 1017 PT – ℰ (0 20) 623 29 88 – www.oesterbar.nl
– closed 30 April* **F3**
Rest – *(open until 11pm)* Menu 33 € (lunch)/35 € – Carte 46/96 €
♦ Fish and seafood ♦ Retro ♦
A seafood restaurant with a new twist, featuring classic (Oude school) and evolving (Nieuwe school) cuisine served on three levels. Aquariums and lobster tanks.

XX **Brasserie FLO** – Hotel Rembrandt Square   VISA ❿ AE ⓘ

Amstelstraat 9 ✉ *1017 DA* – ✆ *(0 20) 890 47 57*
– www.floamsterdam.com
– closed lunch Saturday and Sunday   **G2**
Rest – *(dinner only 17 July-26 August) (open until 11.30pm)* Menu 33 €
– Carte 36/70 €
♦ Fish and seafood ♦ Brasserie ♦
Brasserie/oyster bar with a chic Parisian look featuring red velvet banquettes, sparkling brass, retro lighting and white apron service. Typical brasserie fare and good set menus.

XX **Sichuan Food**   AC ⇕ VISA ❿ AE

Reguliersdwarsstraat 35 ✉ *1017 BK* – ✆ *(0 20) 626 93 27*
– www.sichuanfood.nl
– closed 31 December   **F2**
Rest – *(dinner only)* Menu 31/43 € – Carte 34/42 €
♦ Chinese ♦ Family ♦
Small oriental restaurant with good local reputation situated in a lively area. Beijing Duck prepared and served in the dining room.

XX **Van Vlaanderen**   ⇱ AC ⇕ VISA ❿ AE
☺
Weteringschans 175 ✉ *1017 XD* – ✆ *(0 20) 622 82 92*
– www.restaurant-vanvlaanderen.nl
– closed Saturday lunch, Sunday and Monday   **F3**
Rest – Menu 30 € (lunch)/36 € – Carte 49/59 €
♦ Modern ♦ Fashionable ♦
Van Vlaanderen has long been recognised as the place to go for the good things in life. It has a pleasant location in the centre of Amsterdam with its own jetty on the patio. The restaurant's success lies in attentive service and a young, spirited team whose enthusiasm is evident in the modern, original versions of the classic dishes served here.

XX **Canal House** – Hotel Canal House   ⇲ AC VISA ❿ AE

Keizersgracht 148 ✉ *1015 CX* – ✆ *(0 20) 622 51 82* – *www.canalhouse.nl*
Rest – Carte 35/50 €   **F1**
♦ Modern ♦ Elegant ♦
The Great Room richly deserves its name: a suitably sophisticated ambience in a dark hued setting. The menu lists finger food, beautifully presented snacks and a more extensive choice from the à la carte selection.

XX **The Amstel Bar and Brasserie** – Hotel Amstel   ≤ AC ⇲

Prof. Tulpplein 1 ✉ *1018 GX*   P VISA ❿ AE ⓘ
– ✆ (0 20) 520 32 69 – www.amsterdam.intercontinental.com
Rest – *(open until 11pm)* Menu 49 € – Carte 50/103 €   **H3**
♦ Classic ♦ Elegant ♦
This brasserie is, in its own words, the epitome of unpretentious, nautical elegance. It is inspired by its location close to the rhythm of passing boats. Classy interior and 'casual' brasserie kitchen.

XX **Blue Pepper**   AC VISA ❿ AE

Nassaukade 366h ✉ *1054 AB* – ✆ *(0 20) 489 70 39*
– www.restaurantbluepepper.com   **E2**
Rest – *(dinner only)* Menu 40/70 € – Carte 50/56 €
♦ Indonesian ♦ Fashionable ♦
An intimate modern setting and up-to-date Indonesian cuisine are featured at this establishment popular with romantic diners. Three menus. Attentive service.

XX **Keizersgracht 238** – Hotel Pulitzer   ⇲ & AC ⇲ VISA ❿ AE ⓘ

Keizersgracht 238 ✉ *1016 DZ* – ✆ *(0 20) 523 52 82*
– www.restaurantkeizersgracht238.nl   **F1**
Rest – Carte 38/69 €
♦ Meats and grills ♦ Friendly ♦
From beef to tuna, everything finds its way onto the lava stone at this grill restaurant. The dining area has a huge Frans Hals painting for a humorous touch.

XX **Seven Seas** – Hotel Grand Hotel Amrâth   AC P VISA ⬤⬤ AE ⓞ

Prins Hendrikkade 108 ✉ *1011 AK –* ☏ *(0 20) 552 00 00*
– *www.amrathamsterdam.com*   **G1**
Rest – Menu 36/64 € – Carte 34/63 €
♦ Modern ♦ Retro ♦

A hint of retro in the decor and an international flair in the cuisine – this is, after all, the Seven Seas. Choose freely from a menu with a fixed price for each course.

XX **Tunes** – Hotel Conservatorium   ⅋ AC VISA ⬤⬤ AE

Van Baerlestraat 27 ✉ *1071 AN –* ☏ *(0 20) 570 00 00*
– *closed Sunday*   **E3**
Rest – *(dinner only until 11pm)* Menu 68/105 €
♦ Modern ♦ Elegant ♦

Tunes got off to a flying start even at its opening and it is easy to see why. It is the place to be – with a modern heart, a trendy soul and especially, contemporary high quality cuisine. Lobster cappuccino, tomato specialities and many other delicious dishes are featured.

X **Bordewijk**   ⅋ AC VISA ⬤⬤ AE ⓞ

Noordermarkt 7 ✉ *1015 MV –* ☏ *(0 20) 624 38 99*
– *www.restaurantbordewijk.nl*
– *closed mid July-mid August, 24 December-early January, Sunday and Monday*
Rest – *(dinner only)* Menu 39/59 € – Carte 48/66 €   **F1**
♦ Classic ♦ Minimalist ♦

Popular restaurant due to its modern menu with inventive touches and minimalist décor: bare floorboards, Formica tables and designer chairs. Noisy atmosphere when busy.

X **Antoine**   AC ⬌ VISA ⬤⬤ AE

Kerkstraat 377 ✉ *1017 HW –* ☏ *(0 20) 422 27 66*
– *www.restaurantantoine.nl*
– *closed Sunday and Monday*   **G3**
Rest – *(dinner only)* Menu 35/55 € – Carte 49/59 €
♦ Modern ♦ Fashionable ♦

Up-to-date cuisine served in two modern rooms, one a mezzanine, the other with a view outside. Neat tables, banquettes and comfortable seats.

X **Lastage** (Rogier Van Dam)   AC VISA ⬤⬤
✿ *Geldersekade 29* ✉ *1011 EJ –* ☏ *(0 20) 737 08 11*
– *www.restaurantlastage.nl*
– *closed 22 July-13 August, 26 December-3 January, Monday and Tuesday*
Rest – *(dinner only) (booking essential)* Menu 38/62 €   **G1**
♦ Modern ♦ Cosy ♦

At Lastage you'll find a concise selection of tempting dishes full of character and depth, like vichyssoise of potato with mackerel tartare or veal cheek confit with lobster. The relatively small bill at the end will make the experience even more enjoyable.

→ Tartaar van makreel met een terrine van kreeft, rode biet, waterkers en appel. Wilde zeebaars en cannelloni van garnalen met een crème en slaatje van selderie. Tarte tatin en karamelroomijs, witte chocoladecake met vanillecreme.

X **Envy**   AC VISA ⬤⬤ AE
☻ *Prinsengracht 381* ✉ *1016 HL –* ☏ *(0 20) 344 64 07 – www.envy.nl*
– *open until 11pm*   **F2**
Rest – *(dinner only except weekend)* Menu 28 € (lunch), 36/60 € – Carte approx. 45 €
♦ Creative ♦ Design ♦

A new-style brasserie with dining on either side of a long refectory table under low, spherical lights or standing at one of the smaller tables. All the food is on display in glass showcases.

De Belhamel   ⪦ 🛆 AC ⇦ VISA ⬤⬤ AE

Brouwersgracht 60 ✉ *1013 GX* – ☎ *(0 20) 622 10 95* – *www.belhamel.nl*
Rest – Menu 36 € – Carte 46/56 €   **F1**

♦ Classic ♦ Bistro ♦

This local brasserie is at the confluence of delightful canals. Small traditional choice plus a blackboard menu (simpler at lunchtimes). Belle Epoque-style dining room with a mezzanine. Terrace near the bridge.

Tempo doeloe   AC VISA ⬤⬤ AE ①

Utrechtsestraat 75 ✉ *1017 VJ* – ☎ *(0 20) 625 67 18*
– *www.tempodoeloerestaurant.nl*
– *closed 30 April, 25, 26 and 31 December-1 January and Sunday*
Rest – *(dinner only until 11pm)* Menu 35/68 €   **G3**
– Carte 36/69 €

♦ Indonesian ♦ Friendly ♦

Regular diners at Tempo Doeloe or 'Times Gone By' find it difficult to hide their enthusiasm when they visit this restaurant. They know that an Indonesian feast like no other in Amsterdam awaits them. The food here is authentically Indonesian, with no concessions to Western taste. Selamat Makan!

Hoofdstad – Hotel de l'Europe   🛆 AC VISA ⬤⬤ AE ①

Nieuwe Doelenstraat 2 ✉ *1012 CP* – ☎ *(0 20) 531 17 77* – *www.leurope.nl*
Rest – Menu 35 € – Carte approx. 42 €   **G2**

♦ Modern ♦ Brasserie ♦

Watch Amsterdam come to life from the terrace of this luxury brasserie, located close to the city's canal bridges and boats. Inside, enjoy mouthwatering dishes, never contrived and always full of flavour. Spotted ray fin, rigatoni and beef tartare are just a few of the appetising dishes served here.

Fifteen   🛆 ᠖ AC VISA ⬤⬤ AE

Jollemanhof 9 ✉ *1019 GW* – ☎ *(0 20) 509 50 15* – *www.fifteen.nl*
– *closed 30 April, 1 January and Sunday lunch*   Plan I **C1**
Rest – *(dinner only mid July-mid August)* Carte 33/43 €

♦ Modern ♦ Brasserie ♦

Jamie Oliver is behind the concept of this popular restaurant with a mission to give disadvantaged youngsters opportunities. Parking at the Piet Hein parking.

Bistrot Neuf   AC VISA ⬤⬤ AE

Haarlemmerstraat 9 ✉ *1013 EH* – ☎ *(0 20) 400 32 10*
– *www.bistrotneuf.nl*   **G1**
Rest – *(open until 11pm)* Menu 19 € (lunch), 30/48 € – Carte 34/62 €

♦ Traditional ♦ Bistro ♦ Fashionable ♦

With its clean, modern design, this relaxed bistro is ideally located in a lively area of Amsterdam. Enjoy original Amsterdam flair expressed in traditional French dishes, impeccably cooked to bring out the true flavours of the ingredients. Efficient service.

Café Americain – Hotel American   ᠖ VISA ⬤⬤ AE ①

Leidsekade 97 ✉ *1017 PN* – ☎ *(0 20) 556 30 10* – *www.cafeamericain.com*
Rest – Menu 28 € (lunch)/35 € – Carte 42/77 €   **F3**

♦ Classic ♦ Retro ♦ Brasserie ♦

Café Americain is a stylish Art Deco restaurant featuring a magnificent ceiling, with fine brasserie cuisine which attracts a mixed crowd. Jazz brunch on Sundays.

De Roode Leeuw – Hotel Amsterdam   AC VISA ⬤⬤ AE ①

Damrak 93 ✉ *1012 LP* – ☎ *(0 20) 555 06 66*
– *www.restaurantderoodeleeuw.nl*
– *closed dinner 31 December*   **G1**
Rest – Menu 33/55 € – Carte 36/52 €

♦ Traditional ♦ Brasserie ♦

Herring salad and pork medallions with wholegrain mustard: this is the place for traditional Dutch fare. There is a warm ambience thanks to its interior of red and brown.

✗ **MOMO** – Hotel Park   🏢 🕙 💳 😔 🄰🄴 ①
Hobbemastraat 1 ✉ *1071 XZ – ℰ (0 20) 671 74 74*
– www.momo-amsterdam.com   **F3**
Rest – Menu 54/65 € – Carte 40/107 €
♦ Asian ♦ Trendy ♦
Momo is still one of the city's hot spots, with fusion cuisine in a fashionable setting. Bento (Japanese lunch box) at lunchtime and a menu designed for sharing in the evening.

✗ **Haesje Claes**   🏠 🏢 ⇧ 💳 😔 🄰🄴 ①
Spuistraat 275 ✉ *1012 VR – ℰ (0 20) 624 99 98 – www.haesjeclaes.nl*
– closed 30 April and 25, 26 and 31 December   **F2**
Rest – Menu 24/30 € – Carte 28/49 €
♦ Traditional ♦ Rustic ♦
A popular restaurant reflecting the city's atmosphere. Simple and copious Dutch cuisine served in a cheerful setting. Historical museum nearby.

SOUTH and WEST QUARTERS   *Plan I*

🏨🏨🏨 **Okura**   🛎 ← 🕙 🏢 🕙 🖥 💳 🏢 🛜 🚣 🅿 🛋 💳 😔 🄰🄴 ①
Ferdinand Bolstraat 333 ✉ *1072 LH – ℰ (0 20) 678 71 11 – www.okura.nl*
293 rm – †185/470 € ††185/470 €, ⌕ 33 € – 8 suites   **C2**
Rest *Ciel Bleu* ❀❀ **Rest** *Yamazato* ❀ **Rest** *Serre* ❀ **Rest** *Sazanka* – see restaurant listing
♦ Grand Luxury ♦ Business ♦ Modern ♦
A luxurious Japanese-style hotel set in a modern tower building. Various types of rooms and suites, superb wellness centre, extensive conference facilities and a full range of services.

🏨🏨🏨 **Hilton**   ← 🚗 🕙 🏢 🕙 🏢 🛜 🚣 🅿 💳 😔 🄰🄴 ①
Apollolaan 138 ✉ *1077 BG – ℰ (0 20) 710 60 00*
– www.amsterdam.hilton.com   **B2**
271 rm – †209/499 € ††209/499 €, ⌕ 28 € – 4 suites
Rest *Roberto's* ❀ – see restaurant listing
♦ Chain hotel ♦ Business ♦ Modern ♦
A modern apartment-style building with a waterside garden and several terraces. Contemporary rooms and suites with panoramic views, one of which was the scene of 'John and Yoko's bed-in' in 1969.

🏨🏨🏨 **Apollo**   ← 🕙 🏢 🛜 🚣 🅿 💳 😔 🄰🄴 ①
Apollolaan 2 ✉ *1077 BA – ℰ (0 20) 673 59 22 – www.wyndham.nl*
223 rm – †65/350 € ††75/400 €, ⌕ 23 €   **B2**
Rest *La Sirène* ❀ – see restaurant listing
♦ Chain hotel ♦ Business ♦ Stylish ♦
An international chain hotel located at the intersection of five canals. Guestrooms designed with the business traveller in mind. Waterside bar, terrace and landing stage.

🏨🏨🏨 **Bilderberg Garden**   🏢 🛜 🚣 🅿 💳 😔 🄰🄴 ①
Dijsselhofplantsoen 7 ✉ *1077 BJ – ℰ (0 20) 570 56 00*
– www.bilderberg.nl/hotels/garden-hotel   **B2**
122 rm – †139/339 € ††139/339 €, ⌕ 23 € – 2 suites
Rest *De Kersentuin* – see restaurant listing
♦ Business ♦ Luxury ♦ Stylish ♦
Chain hotel catering mainly to corporate customers in the business district. Inviting interior, spacious and comfortable guestrooms, meeting facilities and valet parking.

Art 🏠 ⌇ 🆊 📶 🛄 📠 🆅🆂🅰 ⓒ 🆎 ⓞ

Spaarndammerdijk 302 (Westerpark) ✉ *1013 ZX* – ℰ *(0 20) 410 96 70*
– www.westcordhotels.nl   **B1**
187 rm – ♦89/299 € ♦♦89/299 €, ☲ 18 € – 3 suites
Rest – Menu 35/60 € – Carte 29/60 €
♦ **Chain hotel** ♦ **Business** ♦ **Stylish** ♦
Near a slip road off the ring, a modern hotel with very contemporary guestrooms, available in two sizes. Exhibition of paintings in the public areas. A la
carte meals served in a trendy atmosphere; simpler set menu in the "eetcafé".

 The College 🚋 🏠 ♿ rest, 🆊 📶 🛄 ⌂ 📠 🆅🆂🅰 ⓒ 🆎 ⓞ

Roelof Hartstraat 1 (Hotel school training facility) ✉ *1071 VE*
– ℰ *(0 20) 571 15 11 – www.thecollegehotel.com*   **C2**
40 rm – ♦215/560 € ♦♦235/560 €, ☲ 25 €
Rest – Menu 35/60 € – Carte 54/63 €
♦ **Grand Luxury** ♦ **Design** ♦
This hotel is located in a former 19C "college", redecorated with refinement.
Chic and fashionable lounge bar and rooms in the same style. The modern res-
taurant installed in a former gym serves modern cuisine.

 Holiday Inn 🛁 ♿ rm, 🆊 📶 🛄 🅿 🆅🆂🅰 ⓒ 🆎 ⓞ

De Boelelaan 2 ✉ *1083 HJ* – ℰ *(0 20) 646 23 00*
– www.holidayinn.com/amsterdam   **C2**
264 rm – ♦150/350 € ♦♦195/550 €, ☲ 22 €
Rest – *(open until 11pm)* Menu 25 € (lunch), 30/49 € bi – Carte 38/52 €
♦ **Chain hotel** ♦ **Business** ♦ **Functional** ♦
Chain hotel close to the RAI. Enjoy the discreet luxury and spaciousness of the
communal areas and the comfortable guestrooms. Lounge-bar and restaurant
in a modern setting evocative of New England. International and American cuisine.

 Novotel 🏠 🍴 ♿ rm, 🆊 📶 🛄 🅿 🆅🆂🅰 ⓒ 🆎 ⓞ

Europaboulevard 10 ✉ *1083 AD* – ℰ *(0 20) 541 11 23*
– www.novotelamsterdamcity.com   **C3**
610 rm – ♦119/249 € ♦♦119/249 €, ☲ 23 €
Rest – *(open until 11pm)* Menu 22 € (lunch), 28/34 € – Carte 28/51 €
♦ **Chain hotel** ♦ **Business** ♦ **Functional** ♦
An imposing hotel complex with one of the largest accommodation capacities
in Benelux. The interior has been fully refurbished and the rooms are modern
and functional. A lounge restaurant serves international and pan-Asian dishes.

 Citizen M without rest 🆊 📶 🆅🆂🅰 ⓒ 🆎 ⓞ

Prinses Irenestraat 30 ✉ *1077 WX* – ℰ *(0 20) 811 70 90*
– www.citizenm.com   **B2**
215 rm – ♦79/169 € ♦♦79/169 €
♦ **Chain hotel** ♦ **Functional** ♦ **Design** ♦
The M in Citizen M stands for mobile: this slightly eccentric hotel focuses on
independent travellers open to new concepts. The guestrooms have been
kept bright and functional and the public areas very attractive. CanteenM offers
'grab and go' food for those in need of a light snack.

 Memphis ♿ rm, 🆊 rm, 📶 🆊 🆅🆂🅰 ⓒ 🆎 ⓞ

De Lairessestraat 87 ✉ *1071 NX* – ℰ *(0 20) 673 31 41*
– www.memphishotel.nl   **B2**
78 rm – ♦79/199 € ♦♦99/219 €, ☲ 13 €
Rest – *(closed Sunday) (dinner only)* Menu 25 € – Carte 33/48 €
♦ **Chain hotel** ♦ **Business** ♦ **Modern** ♦
The tram line to the city centre runs in front of this ivy-covered hotel. Modern
and intimate lounge bar with hushed atmosphere. Fresh bedrooms and pleasant breakfast area.

NETHERLANDS - AMSTERDAM

NETHERLANDS - AMSTERDAM

Arena
🚃 🏠 Ⓜ 🛜 ⚐ P VISA ⓒⓞ AE ⓞ

's-Gravesandestraat 51 ☒ 1092 AA – ℰ (0 20) 850 24 00
– www.hotelarena.nl   **C2**
116 rm – ♦89/229 € ♦♦89/229 €, ☲ 19 €
Rest – (closed Sunday and Monday) (bar lunch) Menu 23 € (lunch)
– Carte approx. 35 €
♦ Business ♦ Design ♦ Minimalist ♦

Formerly an orphanage (1890), now an ultra-trendy hotel. 3 fantastic old stairca-ses, designer bar and guestrooms of various styles and levels of comfort. Week-end nightclub (separate access). Designer setting and modern cuisine in the restaurant.

Crowne Plaza South
🏠 ⅃⅚ ⅍ Ⓜ 🛜 ⚐ 🚗 VISA ⓒⓞ AE

George Gershwinlaan 101 ☒ 1082 MT – ℰ (0 20) 504 36 66
– www.crowneplaza.com/amstsouth   **B3**
207 rm – ♦99/340 € ♦♦119/360 €, ☲ 23 € – 5 suites
Rest – Menu 50 € – Carte 34/53 €
♦ Chain hotel ♦ Business ♦ Functional ♦

This hotel in a rapidly expanding part of Amsterdam is ideal for business travel-lers. It has a fresh feel and a bright, minimalist decor. The airport and RAI con-gress centre are only minutes away by public transport.

Conscious without rest
⅍ 🛜 🚗 VISA ⓒⓞ AE ⓞ

Overtoom 519 ☒ 1054 LH – ℰ (0 20) 820 33 33
– www.conscioushotels.com   **B2**
81 rm – ♦45/295 € ♦♦50/300 €, ☲ 14 €
♦ Chain hotel ♦ Functional ♦

Green and sustainable, that's the innovative philosophy behind this hotel. "So that you can be kind to the planet even when you're away from home" and still want for nothing during your stay. Conscious proves that ecology and com-fort can go hand in hand.

Ciel Bleu – Hotel Okura, 23th floor
← Ⓜ ⇔ ⊶ P VISA ⓒⓞ AE ⓞ

🕸🕸🕸 ⬡⬡
Ferdinand Bolstraat 333 ☒ 1072 LH – ℰ (0 20) 678 74 50 – www.cielbleu.nl
– closed 28 July-18 August, 1-6 January and Sunday   **C2**
Rest – (dinner only) Menu 95/165 € – Carte 129/193 € 🥂
♦ Creative ♦ Formal ♦

A chic restaurant at the top of the Okura Hotel with a superb contemporary décor and a fascinating urban panorama. Experience stylish service, delicious creative cuisine with exotic touches, a fine wine list and sunset views from the lounge.
→ Koningskrab en kaviaar. Heilbot 2006. Exotisch fruit 2010.

Yamazato – Hotel Okura
Ⓜ ⇔ ⊶ P VISA ⓒⓞ AE ⓞ

🕸🕸 ⬡
Ferdinand Bolstraat 333 ☒ 1072 LH – ℰ (0 20) 678 74 50
– www.yamazato.nl
– closed 8-22 July   **C2**
Rest – Menu 40 € (lunch), 75/115 € – Carte 27/128 €
♦ Japanese ♦ Minimalist ♦

Excellent Japanese restaurant featuring authentic Kaiseki cuisine in a Sukiya décor. Sushi bar. Meticulous and friendly service. Simplified lunch menu (lunchbox).
→ Tempura van kreeft Wagyu-ribeye Sumibi Yaki, op houtskool gegrild. Soepje van zoete rode bonen met rijstcake, warm opgediend.

Eau de Vie
🏠 Ⓜ VISA ⓒⓞ AE ⓞ

🕸🕸
Maasstraat 20 ☒ 1078 HK – ℰ (0 20) 662 95 88
– www.restaurant-eaudevie.nl
– closed 31 December-1 January   **C2**
Rest – Menu 30 € (lunch), 38/55 € – Carte 44/81 €
♦ Modern ♦ Friendly ♦

The elixir of life in this restaurant is its love of modern cuisine. Taken over by a new, enthusiastic team in March 2012, the restaurant now serves French cuisine with a distinctly contemporary flavour.

XX
❀❀ **Ron Blaauw**   🏠 🅐🅒 ⟷ ⟶ 📶 🆚 ⓒⓒ 🅰🅔

Sophialaan 55 ✉ 1075 BP – ℰ (0 20) 496 19 43 – www.ronblaauw.nl
– closed Saturday lunch, Sunday and Monday   **B2**
Rest – Menu 48 € (lunch), 75/110 € – Carte approx. 81 €
♦ Innovative ♦ Design ♦ Fashionable ♦
Phenomenal is the best way of describing this restaurant's value for money.
Nowhere else in Benelux will you find as much sophistication, elegance and
top quality for the price you pay at Ron Blaauw's. The inventive, surprising coo-
king comes exquisitely to life in a playful setting that exudes luxury.
➜ Geroosterde bloemkool met Messekleverskaas, geroosterde ui en truffel.
Gebraden longhaas met zoetzuur van groenten en piccalilly. "Baileys" 2012.

XX
❀ **Le Restaurant** (Jan de Wit)   🅐🅒 🆚 ⓒⓒ

2ᵉ Jan Steenstraat 3 ✉ 1073 VK – ℰ (0 20) 379 22 07
– www.lerestaurant.nl
– closed 28 April-7 May, 3 weeks in August, late December-early January,
Sunday and Monday   **C2**
Rest – *(dinner only) (number of covers limited, pre-book) (set menu only)*
Menu 70 € 🍷
♦ Creative ♦ Elegant ♦
A deliciously small grand restaurant! Appetising market-fresh set menu, poised
between tradition and modernity. Made with sumptuous produce, the dishes
are served in an intimate and distinguished setting. Bookings essential.
➜ Kabeljauw en bloemkool met een sausje van langoustines. Gebraden
eend met amandelen, abrikozen, cantharellen en een jus met rasel-hanout-
kruiden. Trio van fruit, groenten en chocolade.

XX
Visaandeschelde   🏠 🅐🅒 ⟶ (dinner) 🆚 ⓒⓒ 🅰🅔 ⓪

Scheldeplein 4 ✉ 1078 GR – ℰ (0 20) 675 15 83 – www.visaandeschelde.nl
– closed 30 April, 24, 25, 26 and 31 December-1 January, Saturday lunch and
Sunday lunch   **C2**
Rest – *(open until 11pm)* Menu 35 € (lunch), 40/60 € – Carte 66/105 €
♦ Fish and seafood ♦ Fashionable ♦ Trendy ♦
Opposite the RAI congress centre, this restaurant is popular with Amsterdam-
mers for its dishes full of the flavours of the sea, contemporary brasserie décor
and lively atmosphere.

XX
😊 **Roberto's** – Hotel Hilton   🏠 🅐🅒 🅿 🆚 ⓒⓒ 🅰🅔 ⓪

Apollolaan 138 ✉ 1077 BG – ℰ (0 20) 710 60 25
– www.robertosrestaurant.nl   **B2**
Rest – Menu 35/95 € – Carte 43/138 €
♦ Italian ♦ Formal ♦
Located in the Hilton, Roberto's is one of the best Italian restaurants in the city.
No fancy decor, just an understated modern dining room with smart service,
top class and authentic Italian cuisine, and a menu that upholds the Bib philo-
sophy.

XX
😊 **Serre** – Hotel Okura   🅐🅒 ⟶ 🅿 🆚 ⓒⓒ 🅰🅔 ⓪

Ferdinand Bolstraat 333 ✉ 1072 LH – ℰ (0 20) 678 74 50 – www.okura.nl
Rest – Menu 35/59 € – Carte 54/85 €   **C2**
♦ Classic ♦ Brasserie ♦
Luxurious, French brasserie ambience, select menus, sensible prices and a
young enthusiastic team in the kitchen. A favourite hotel restaurant for locals.

XX
Sazanka – Hotel Okura   🅐🅒 ⟶ 🅿 🆚 ⓒⓒ 🅰🅔 ⓪

Ferdinand Bolstraat 333 ✉ 1072 LH – ℰ (0 20) 678 74 50 – www.okura.nl
Rest – *(dinner only)* Menu 85/115 € – Carte 38/108 €   **C2**
♦ Japanese ♦ Exotic ♦
If you are looking for more than just a simple dining experience and enjoy a
good show, come and watch the juggling skills that accompany dinner around
Sazanka's teppanyaki.

NETHERLANDS - AMSTERDAM

XX Bolenius
🎐 ⇔ VISA ◎◎ AE

George Gershwinlaan 30 ✉ *1082 MT –* ☎ *(0 20) 404 44 11*
– www.bolenius-restaurant.nl
– closed 1 April, 30 April, 20 May, 3-19 August and Sunday   **B2-3**
Rest – Menu 35 € (lunch), 59/99 € – Carte 55/69 €
♦ Creative ♦ Minimalist ♦ Design ♦

This restaurant has an 'open space' minimalistic design reminiscent of Scandi-navia. Bolenius has a vision of being open and transparent and completely in touch with contemporary gastronomy. Delightful, creative presentations that are a joy to behold.

XX Le Garage
🔠 ⇔ ⊃⁴ VISA ◎◎ AE

Ruysdaelstraat 54 ✉ *1071 XE –* ☎ *(0 20) 679 71 76*
– www.restaurantlegarage.nl
– closed lunch Saturday and Sunday   **B2**
Rest – *(open until 11pm)* Menu 27 € (lunch)/36 € – Carte 55/84 €
♦ Modern ♦ Trendy ♦

Excellent up-to-date establishment with an original décor. The entertainment and business clientele come to see and be seen as well as to enjoy the great food.

XX Brasserie van Baerle
🎐 ⇔ VISA ◎◎ AE

Van Baerlestraat 158 ✉ *1071 BG –* ☎ *(0 20) 679 15 32*
– www.brasserievanbaerle.nl
– closed 30 April, 25, 26 and 31 December-1 January, Monday lunch and Saturday lunch   **B2**
Rest – *(open until 11pm)* Menu 25 € (lunch), 36/45 € – Carte 48/63 €
♦ Classic ♦ Retro ♦

This retro brasserie attracts regular customers, mainly from the local area because of its attractive menu, tasty steak tartare and well-matched wines. Courtyard terrace.

XX Chang-i
🔠 ⇔ VISA ◎◎ AE

Jan Willem Brouwersstraat 7 (adjacent to the artists' entrance to the Concertgebouw) ✉ *1071 LH –* ☎ *(0 20) 470 17 00 – www.chang-i.nl*
– closed 29 July-11 August and Bank Holidays   *Plan II* **E3**
Rest – *(dinner only) (booking advisable)* Menu 37/52 € – Carte 32/90 €
♦ Asian ♦ Trendy ♦

The 'i' in the name highlights the innovative nature of this chef's Asian cuisine. Trendy and intimate lounge atmosphere. Near a theatre.

XX Het Bosch
≤ 🎐 P VISA ◎◎ AE

Jollenpad 10 ✉ *1081 KC –* ☎ *(0 20) 644 58 00 – www.hetbosch.com*
– closed 26 December-6 January, Saturday lunch October-March and Sunday
Rest – Menu 40 € (lunch), 45/60 € – Carte 41/56 €   **B3**
♦ Traditional ♦ Formal ♦

The restaurant and patio of this cube-shaped, up-to-the-minute restaurant offer views of the marina at Nieuwe Meer. Classic dishes with an adventurous twist feature on the menu. In summer, Het Bosch Waterfront serves cocktails and bar-becued choices on – as its name suggests – the waterfront.

XX La Sirène – Hotel Apollo
≤ 🎐 🔠 ⇔ P VISA ◎◎ AE ◍

Apollolaan 2 ✉ *1077 BA –* ☎ *(0 20) 570 57 24 – www.lasirene.nl*
– closed 5-25 August, 27 December-6 January, Saturday lunch and Sunday
Rest – Menu 25 € (lunch), 35/75 € bi – Carte 42/57 €   **B2**
♦ Fish and seafood ♦ Formal ♦

It is not easy finding somewhere for a delicious lunch at a reasonable price in Amsterdam. The chic La Sirène restaurant at Wyndham Apollo Hotel is the ans-wer, offering fresh, contemporary cuisine at attractive prices. It offers either à la carte or 3 or 4-course menus. The terrace offers views of Amsterdam's typical wooden yachts.

XX Jaspers ⇔ VISA ◑◐ AE

Ceintuurbaan 196 ⊠ *1072 GC –* ☎ *(0 20) 471 52 33*
– www.restaurantjaspers.nl   **C2**
Rest *– (dinner only until midnight) (set menu only)* Menu 46/76 €
♦ Modern ♦ Fashionable ♦

Although there is no choice on offer in this restaurant (only a set menu), this is
more than compensated for by the fresh ingredients used. Jaspers' cooking style
demonstrates French roots with a modern twist. Dishes such as poached egg with
asparagus, Comté cheese and hazelnut-truffle tapenade feature on the menu.

XX De Kersentuin – Hotel Bilderberg Garden AC ⊷ P

Dijsselhofplantsoen 7 ⊠ *1077 BJ*   VISA ◑◐ AE ◐
– ☎ *(0 20) 570 56 00 – www.dekersentuin.nl*
– closed Saturday lunch and Sunday   **B2**
Rest *–* Menu 28 € (lunch), 33/43 € – Carte 45/69 €
♦ Modern ♦ Brasserie ♦

The poetic name of De Kersentuin conceals a chic brasserie. The cuisine is now
contemporary, presenting fresh combinations based on original techniques.

X Le Hollandais ⏰ AC ⇔ VISA ◑◐ AE
☺

Amsteldijk 41 ⊠ *1074 HV –* ☎ *(0 20) 679 12 48 – www.lehollandais.nl*
– closed 3 weeks August, Sunday and Monday   **C2**
Rest *– (dinner only)* Menu 36/59 € – Carte 49/59 €
♦ Classic ♦ Trendy ♦

The 1970s furniture and lighting, wooden floors and panelling create a charming setting. The menu features traditional simmered dishes, offal, blood sausage and homemade cold meats.

X A la Ferme ⏰ ⇔ VISA ◑◐ AE

Govert Flinckstraat 251 ⊠ *1073 BX –* ☎ *(0 20) 679 82 40*
– www.alaferme.nl
– closed Sunday and Monday   **C2**
Rest *– (dinner only)* Menu 33 € – Carte 43/54 €
♦ Classic ♦ Friendly ♦

Monthly menus feature in the contemporary dining room, in one of the smaller,
more intimate rooms in the back, or under the grape arbour in summer.

X The French Café ⏰ AC VISA ◑◐ AE

Gerard Doustraat 98 ⊠ *1072 VX –* ☎ *(0 20) 470 03 01*
– www.thefrenchcafe.nl
– closed Bank Holidays except Christmas, Sunday and Monday   **C2**
Rest *– (dinner only)* Menu 37/63 € – Carte 40/68 €
♦ Classic ♦ Friendly ♦

With its neo-retro wallpaper, this modern bistro near the vibrant Pijp area of
Amsterdam exudes the ambience of France. Delicious cuisine at reasonable prices. Pleasant summer terrace.

X White Elephant ⏰ VISA ◑◐

Van Woustraat 3 ⊠ *1074 AA –* ☎ *(0 20) 679 55 56*
– www.whiteelephant.nl
– closed 31 December and 1 January   *Plan II* **G3**
Rest *–* Menu 35 € – Carte 34/50 €
♦ Thai ♦ Exotic ♦

Thai restaurant with matching décor: panelling, orchids, bar in a traditional "hut",
exotic terrace and friendly waiters in traditional costume. Authentic cuisine.

X Elkaar ⏰ AC VISA ◑◐ AE ◐
☺

Alexanderplein 6 ⊠ *1018 CG –* ☎ *(0 20) 330 75 59 – www.etenbijelkaar.nl*
– closed 30 April, 25 and 31 December-1 January and Saturday lunch
Rest *–* Menu 30 € (lunch), 36/55 € – Carte 44/56 €   **C2**
♦ Classic ♦ Cosy ♦

Refined lunches and menus are offered at this restaurant in a large townhouse.
Enthusiastic young team, bistro comforts, modern paintings and a teak terrace
facing the Tropenmuseum.

NETHERLANDS - AMSTERDAM

George W.P.A. 🏠 AC VISA ⊛ AE

Willemsparkweg 70 ⊠ *1071 HK –* ℰ *(0 20) 470 25 30*
– www.georgewpa.nl   **B2**
Rest – *(open until 11pm)* Carte 29/51 €
♦ Classic ♦ Bistro ♦
This restaurant is made up of three little buildings and a sunny outdoor seating area on a small square. A bistro-style interior with small tables, some art-nouveau details and an open kitchen give it an American atmosphere.

AT SCHIPHOL AIRPORT   *Plan I*

Sheraton Airport 🛗 🐕 🏠 🛁 rm, AC 🛜 🖴 🚗 VISA ⊛ AE ⓞ

Schiphol bd 101 ⊠ *1118 BG Schiphol –* ℰ *(0 20) 316 43 00*
– www.sheraton.com/amsterdamair
405 rm – ♥189/449 € ♥♥214/474 €, � 29 € – 1 suite
Rest – *(closed lunch Saturday and Sunday) (open until 11pm)*
Carte 54/75 €
♦ Chain hotel ♦ Business ♦ Modern ♦
Modern hotel complex near the airport, designed for a globe-trotting business clientèle. Guestrooms offer every comfort. Fine atrium. Full service. Modern restaurant with a bluish dome reminiscent of the Paris Zénith concert hall. International menu.

Radisson Blu Airport 🐕 🏠 🛗 🏠 🛁 rm, AC 🛜 🖴 🅿 🚗 VISA ⊛ AE ⓞ

Boeing Avenue 2 (Rijk) (South: 4 km via N201)
⊠ *1119 PB Schiphol –* ℰ *(0 20) 655 31 31*
– www.radissonblu.com/hotel-amsterdamairport
279 rm – ♥95/399 € ♥♥95/399 €, � 25 € – 2 suites
Rest – *(open until 11pm)* Carte 31/52 €
♦ Chain hotel ♦ Business ♦ Modern ♦
This hotel is ideal for business trips. It is spacious, close to the airport and motorway, with a cosy bar, meeting rooms and modern guestrooms lacking nothing in comfort. The restaurant menu offers international cuisine, dominated by Mediterranean dishes.

Crowne Plaza Amsterdam-Schiphol 🛗 🖥 🛁 rm, AC 🛜 🖴 🅿 VISA ⊛ AE ⓞ

Planeetbaan 2 ⊠ *2132 HZ Hoofddorp*
– ℰ *(0 23) 565 00 00*
– www.crowneplaza.com/ams-schiphol
238 rm – ♥119/250 € ♥♥139/350 €, � 22 € – 4 suites
Rest – Menu 33 € – Carte approx. 55 €
♦ Chain hotel ♦ Business ♦ Functional ♦
Establishment in a modern building, popular with business and conference clientele. Huge lobby, superb swimming pool, health club, large guestrooms and suites with lounges. "Sleep advantage" programme. Restaurant offering an international menu in several rooms.

Courtyard by Marriott - Amsterdam Airport 🛗 🛁

Bosweg 15 ⊠ *2131 LX Hoofddorp* 🏠 🛁 🛜 🖴 🅿 VISA ⊛ AE ⓞ
– ℰ *(0 23) 556 90 00 – www.claus.nl*
140 rm – ♥99/259 € ♥♥99/259 €, � 22 € – 8 suites
Rest – Menu 16/52 € – Carte 24/49 €
♦ Chain hotel ♦ Business ♦ Modern ♦
A modern-style business hotel next to a wooded area and lake, ideal for running. Spacious and contemporary guestrooms with king-size beds. Designer fireside lounge. Brasserie serving intercontinental cuisine.

Artemis 🏠 ⅄ ⅙ 🅰 🛜 ♨ 🛢 🚗 VISA 💳 AE
John M. Keynesplein 2 (exit ① Sloten) ✉ *1066 EP* – 🕿 *(0 20) 714 10 00*
– www.artemisamsterdam.com **A2**
247 rm – ♥85/325 € ♥♥85/325 €, ⊊ 20 € – 9 suites
Rest – Menu 32 € (lunch) – Carte 32/48 €
♦ Luxury ♦ Design ♦
This modern building of original design in the business district features Dutch designer-style décor. There is an art gallery to explore the subject in more detail. A large restaurant with ultra-modern décor and a big waterside terrace. Contemporary menu.

De Herbergh 🏠 🛜 🅿 VISA 💳 AE
Sloterweg 259 ✉ *1171 CP Badhoevedorp* – 🕿 *(0 20) 659 26 00*
– www.herbergh.nl
24 rm – ♥80/140 € ♥♥85/145 €, ⊊ 15 €
Rest *Brasserie la Bouche* – see restaurant listing
Rest – Menu 29 € (lunch)/28 € – Carte 37/50 €
♦ Family ♦ Functional ♦
If you are visiting Amsterdam by car, you will appreciate the easy, free parking at this restaurant. It is perfect for visitors to the Keukenhof, and the shuttle service to Schiphol makes it ideal for holidaymakers who have to catch an early flight. Italian cuisine in Trattoria La Bocca.

Aan de Poel (Stefan van Sprang) ≤ 🏠 🅰 ⇌ ⌂↟ VISA 💳 AE ①
🕸🕸
Handweg 1 ✉ *1185 TS Amstelveen* – 🕿 *(0 20) 345 17 63*
– www.aandepoel.nl
– closed 30 April-1 May, 14-29 July, 27 December-3 January, Saturday lunch, Sunday and Monday **B3**
Rest – Menu 42 € (lunch), 62/89 € – Carte 65/85 € ℬ
♦ Creative ♦ Design ♦
A delightful lakeside location with a chic and sophisticated interior design and a lovely terrace on the water. Delicious modern cuisine, a clever sommelier and pleasant service.
➜ Langouste van de plancha en een witteportsaus. Gebakken entrecote met brioche, paddenstoelen en rodewijnjus. Krokante kokos, karamel met mangosorbet en meringue.

Marktzicht 🏠 ⇌ VISA 💳 AE ①
Marktplein 31 ✉ *2132 DA Hoofddorp* – 🕿 *(0 23) 561 24 11*
– www.restaurant-marktzicht.nl
– closed 25 and 26 December, 1 January and Sunday
Rest – Menu 35 € – Carte 40/65 €
♦ Traditional ♦ Rustic ♦
A wind of change is blowing through this old 19C inn on the Markt, built when the polder was erected. Up-to-date menu and welcoming terrace.

Brasserie la Bouche – Hotel De Herbergh 🏠 🅰 ⇌ 🅿
Sloterweg 259 ✉ *1171 CP Badhoevedorp* VISA 💳 AE
– 🕿 (0 20) 659 26 00 – www.herbergh.nl
Rest – Menu 29 € (lunch)/28 € – Carte 37/50 €
♦ Modern ♦ Cosy ♦
French cooking combines with global flavours and exotic ingredients on the menu at Brasserie la Bouche. Ask for the vegetable tempura salad to start; follow it with lamb souvlaki; and for dessert, try a classic tarte Tatin.

NETHERLANDS - AMSTERDAM

THE HAGUE
DEN HAAG –'S GRAVENHAGE

Population: 500 000

Iconotec/PHOTONONSTOP

The Hague appears to be a city of anomalies. Although the seat of Dutch government, it's not the capital of the Netherlands (which is Amsterdam); although a city of Europe-wide importance, it's just as famous for its modern seaside resort of Scheveningen; and although populated for hundreds of years by the well-to-do, its canal-side houses share little of Amsterdam's flamboyance. The Hague earned its nickname 'the biggest village in Europe' because of its relatively small population sprawled about a large area: that 'village' is marked by an aristocratic charm, which is why it's rightly obtained another title – Holland's most elegant town.

The Hague is also doffing its neatly tailored cap to the 21C: parts of the centre now shoot skywards courtesy of shiny government high-rises, while a rash of reasonably priced, buzzy restaurants and bars has brightened the streets. An outward-thinking city council has helped loosen the staid image with a lively programme of concerts and events, and there's an enticing range of museums clustered in the centre. A village, however large, wouldn't be a village without its sections of green and pleasant land, and The Hague doesn't disappoint, with a kaleidoscope of leafy lanes and large parks. The air of gentle manners is all-pervasive, and bureaucrats and bankers know that in a few minutes they can be sitting in a deckchair on a sandy beach.

THE HAGUE IN...

→ **ONE DAY**
Binnenhof, Mauritshuis, Panorama Mesdag.

→ **TWO DAYS**
Gemeentemuseum, 'The Fred', a stroll around Noordeinde, a show at Lucent Dans Theater.

→ **THREE DAYS**
A day out by the sea at Scheveningen, Madurodam.

PRACTICAL INFORMATION

ARRIVAL-DEPARTURE

✈ Rotterdam Airport is 16km southeast of The Hague. A shuttle service to Central Station takes 45min. The train takes 30min.

GETTING AROUND

Single tickets can be purchased from the bus driver but saver tickets must be bought in advance from the tourist information office, post offices, tobacconists, newsagents and hotels. You can buy good value stripcards in two varieties – as a 15-stripcard or a 45-stripcard – and these are valid throughout the country on buses, trams and metro. A one-day pass is also available; with the price dependent on the amount of zones to be covered. The only rail travel within the city is the line linking the two stations, Den Haag Centraal Station and Den Haag Hollands Spoor, which is a kilometre to the south of the centre.

EATING OUT

Locals like to think that their 'biggest village in Europe' is the result of a lot made from a little; they call it the Hague Bluff. But what's that got to do with food? Well, the Hague Bluff is also a local pudding, a gooseberry fool made with eggs and sugar, representing the idea that something grand can be made from humble ingredients. There's no bluff, though, about the city's restaurant scene. It's first rate in every respect, and although some establishments are targeted full-on at the embassy army, many more are very affordable. With the cuisine

CALENDAR HIGHLIGHTS

April
Queen's Night Festival.

April-June
International Sand Sculpture Festival.

May
North Sea Regatta.

June
Music In My Head.

July
De Parade (fairground rides, music, theatre, film, dance and opera).

August
International Fireworks Festival.

September
Todaysart Festival.

November
Crossing Border Festival (literature, music and visual arts).

of more than 20 nationalities on offer, the choice is broad and pleasingly sophisticated, and the number of exotic restaurants reflects the many cultures found here. Asian influences are everywhere, but in particular, the Indonesian connection is clear. There's a host of top-notch restaurants in the area just beyond Lange Voorhout, around Denneweg and Frederikstraat. If you can't find what you want there, then head to Molenstraat, near the Noordeinde Palace, for another exciting cluster.

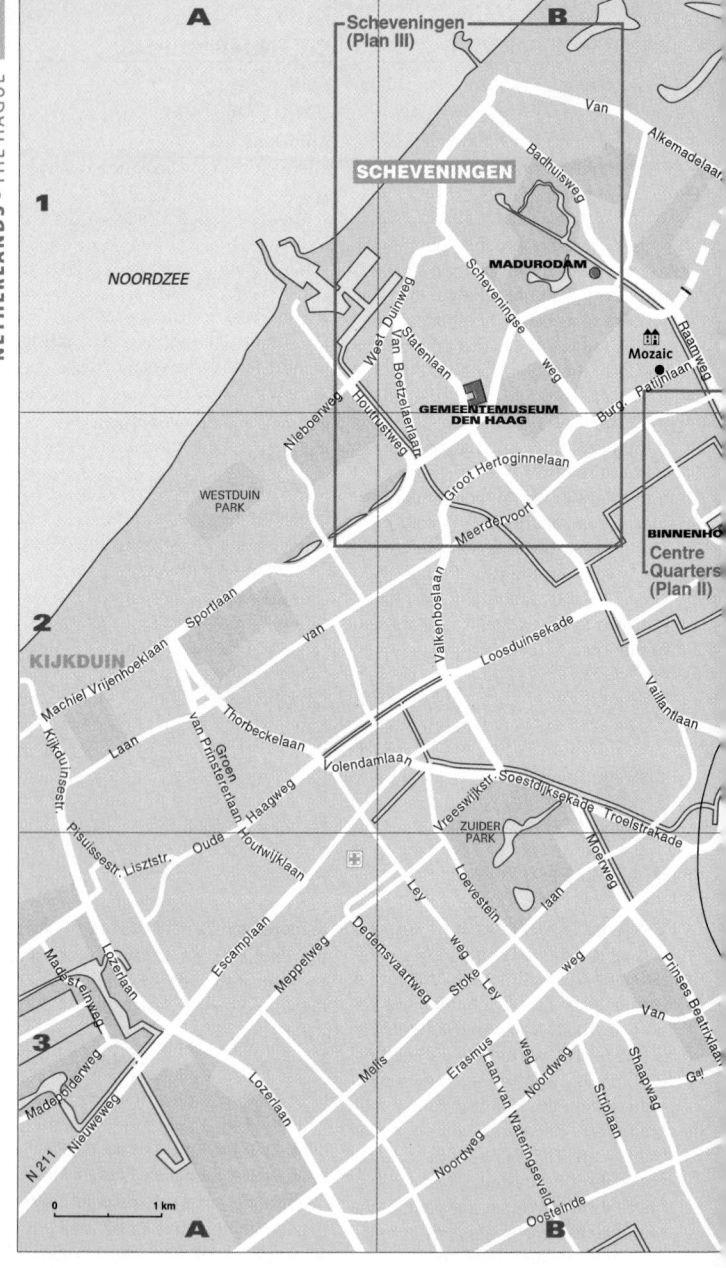

A

B

Scheveningen
(Plan III)

1

SCHEVENINGEN

Van

Badhuisweg

Alkemadelaan

NOORDZEE

MADURODAM

Scheveningse weg

Mozaic

Baamweg

Batijnlaan

Statenlaan

Van Boetzelaerlaan

West Duinweg

Nieboerweg

Houtrustweg

**GEMEENTEMUSEUM
DEN HAAG**

Groot Hertoginnelaan

Burg.

WESTDUIN
PARK

Meerdervoort

BINNENHO
Centre
Quarters
(Plan II)

2

KIJKDUIN

Machiel Vrijenhoeklaan

Sportlaan

van

Valkenboslaan

Loosduinsekade

Vaillantlaan

Laan

Thorbeckelaan

Groen van Prinstererlaan

Haagweg

Volendamlaan

Kijkduinsestr.

Vreeswijkstr.

Soestdijksekade

Troelstrakade

Moerweg

Pisuissestr. Lisztstr.

Oude Houtwijklaan

**ZUIDER
PARK**

Loevestein

laan

Prinses Beatrixlaan

Lozerlaan

Escamplaan

Meppelweg

Dedemsvaartweg

Ley

weg

Stoke Ley

Ley

weg

Van

Shaapwag

Ge

3

Madesteinweg

Lozerlaan

Melis

Erasmus

weg

Laan van Wateringseveld

Noordweg

Striplaan

Maderoiderweg Nieuweweg

Lozerlaan

N 211

Noordweg

Oosteinde

0   1 km

A

B

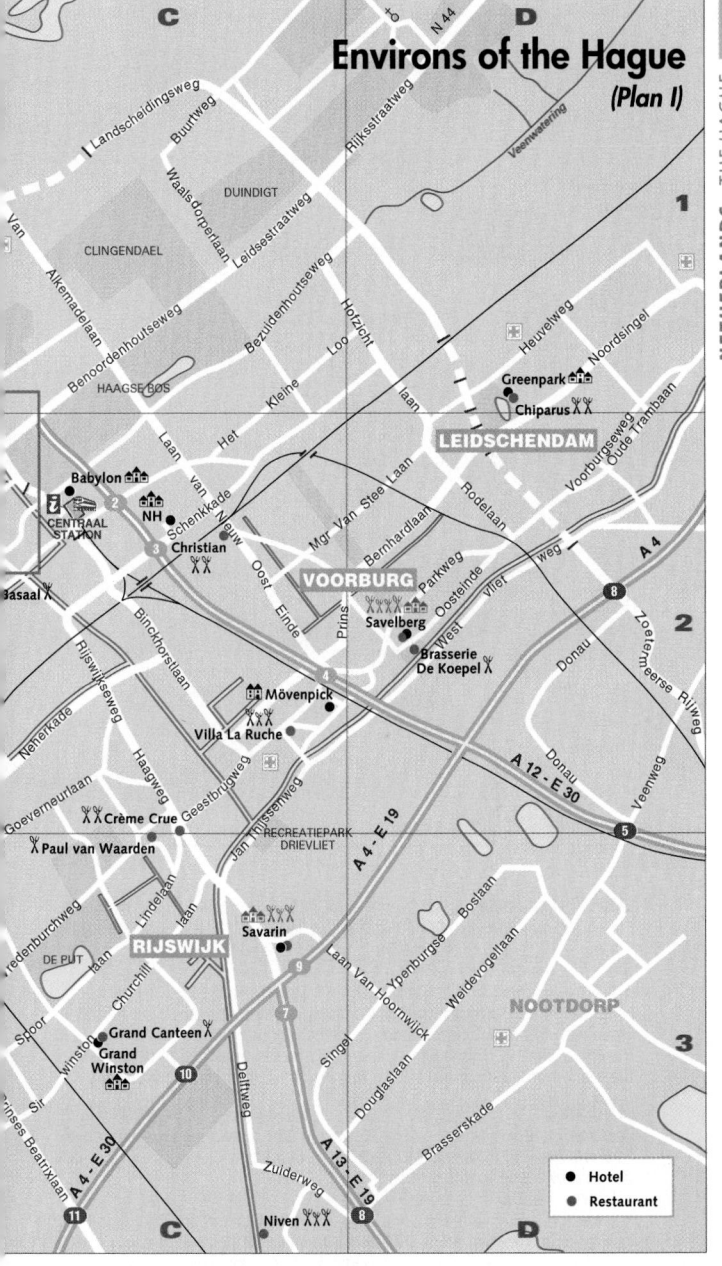

Environs of the Hague
(Plan I)

Landscheidingsweg

Buurtweg

Waalsdorperlaan

DUINDIGT

Leidsestraatweg

Rijksstraatweg

N 44

Veenwatering

CLINGENDAEL

Van Alkemadelaan

Benoordenhoutseweg

Bezuidenhoutseweg

Horizicht

Heuvelweg

Noordsingel

HAAGSE BOS

Laan

Het

Kleine

Loo

Greenpark

Chiparus ××

LEIDSCHENDAM

Babylon

NH

Schenkkade

Laan van Nieuw Oost-Einde

Mgr. Van Steel Laan

Bernhardlaan

Rodelaan

Voorburgseweg

Oude Trambaan

A 4

CENTRAAL STATION

Christian ××

VOORBURG

Parkweg

Oosteinde

West

Vliet

Weg

8

Basaal ×

Savelberg ××××

Brasserie De Koepel ×

Donau

A 2

Rijswijkseweg

Binckhorstlaan

Mövenpick

4

Neherkade

Haagweg

Villa La Ruche

Geestbrugweg

A 12 - E 30

Donau

Veenweg

Goeverneurlaan

×× Crème Crue

Jan Thijssenweg

RECREATIEPARK DRIEVLIET

A 4 - E 19

5

× Paul van Waarden

Lindelaan

laan

Churchill

Savarin

RIJSWIJK

9

Laan Van Ypenburgse

Boslaan

Weidevogellaan

NOOTDORP

3

Vredenburchweg

DE PUT

Spoor

Winston

Sir

Grand Canteen ×

Grand Winston

10

Delftweg

7

Singel

Laan Van Hoornwijck

Douglaslaan

Brasserskade

Prinses Beatrixlaan

A 4 - E 30

11

Zuiderweg

A 13 - E 19

Niven ×××

8

	Hotel
	Restaurant

607

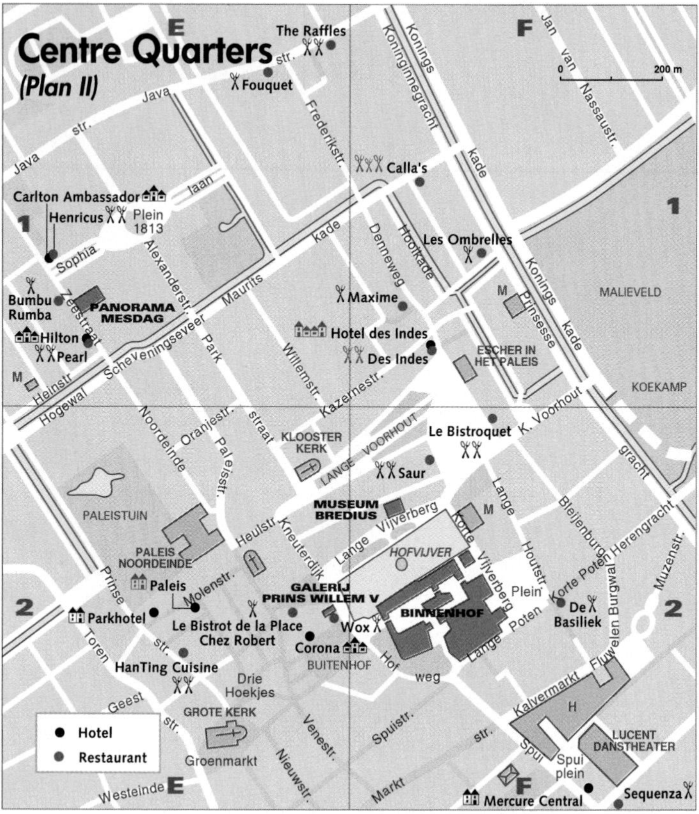
Centre Quarters
(Plan II)
E
F
1
2
0
200 m
The Raffles
Fouquet
Calla's
Les Ombrelles
Maxime
Hotel des Indes
Des Indes
Le Bistroquet
Saur
Carlton Ambassador
Henricus
Plein 1813
Bumbu
Rumba
Hilton
Pearl
PANORAMA MESDAG
ESCHER IN HET PALEIS
MALIEVELD
KOEKAMP
KLOOSTER KERK
MUSEUM BREDIUS
HOFVIJVER
PALEISTUIN
PALEIS NOORDEINDE
Paleis
Parkhotel
Le Bistrot de la Place Chez Robert
GALERIJ PRINS WILLEM V
Wox
Corona
BINNENHOF
BUITENHOF
HanTing Cuisine
Drie Hoekjes
GROTE KERK
Groenmarkt
De Basiliek
LUCENT DANSTHEATER
Spui plein
Mercure Central
Sequenza
Hotel
Restaurant
Java
str.
Sophia
laan
Alexanderstr.
Zeestraat
Mauritskade
Scheveningseveer
Park
Heinstr.
Hogewal
Noordeinde
Oranjestr.
Paleisstr.
straat
Willemstr.
Kazernestr.
Lange Voorhout
K. Voorhout
Denneweg
Hooikade
Frederikstr.
Koningsgracht
Koninginnegracht
Koningskade
Jan van Nassaustr.
Prinsessegracht
Heulstr.
Kneuterdijk
Lange Vijverberg
Korte Vijverberg
Lange Houtstr.
Plein
Korte Poten
Lange Poten
Herengracht
Bleijenburg
Muzenstr.
Fluwelen Burgwal
Kalvermarkt
Spui
Spuistr.
Hofweg
Molenstr.
Prinsestr.
Torenstr.
Geeststr.
Westeinde
Venestr.
Nieuwstr.
Markt
H
M

CENTRE

Plan II

Hotel des Indes

Lange Voorhout 54 ✉ 2514 EG – ✆ (0 70) 361 23 45 – www.hoteldesindes.nl
90 rm – 🚹185/455 € 🚹🚹195/455 €, ☕ 33 € – 2 suites **F1**
Rest *Des Indes* – see restaurant listing
♦ Grand Luxury ♦ Traditional ♦ Classic ♦

Hotel des Indes describes itself as the hotel in The Hague and it is difficult to argue with this description. Already renowned for its beauty when it opened at the end of the 19C, this fairytale palace has become simply more stunning over the years. It boasts an opulent decor that is characteristic of its colonial past.

Hilton

Zeestraat 35 ✉ 2518 AA – ✆ (0 70) 710 70 00 – www.thehague.hilton.com
195 rm ☕ – 🚹119/279 € 🚹🚹119/279 € – 6 suites **E1**
Rest *Pearl* – see restaurant listing
♦ Luxury ♦ Business ♦ Design ♦

The hotel is conveniently situated close to the city centre and the diplomatic quarter and offers excellent conference facilities. Its decor is modern with a hint of 1960s' style and the service is just what you would expect from a member of this group of hotels.

Babylon

Bezuidenhoutseweg 53 ⊠ *2594 AC* – ⚲ *(0 70) 381 49 01*
– www.hampshire-hotels.com/babylon   *Plan I* **C2**
143 rm – †95/185 €, ††95/185 €, � 18 € – 1 suite
Rest – Carte 38/49 €
♦ Chain hotel ♦ Business ♦ Design ♦
Hotel Babylon provides the typical modern hotel comfort so prized by business travellers. Its trendy lounge bar and location close to the station are added attractions.

Bel Air

Johan de Wittlaan 30 ⊠ *2517 JR* – ⚲ *(0 70) 352 53 54*
– www.belairhotel.nl
– closed 25, 26 and 31 December-1 January   *Plan III* **H3**
319 rm – †105/235 € ††105/235 €, ⊻ 21 € – 8 suites
Rest – Menu 13 € (lunch), 30/35 € – Carte 38/52 €
♦ Chain hotel ♦ Classic ♦
The Bel Air hotel boasts a range of facilities ranging from organising conferences to accommodating visitors to the neighbouring World Forum. Characterised by a fresh feel throughout, the hotel also offers a bar with a jazz-style ambience.

Crowne Plaza Promenade

van Stolkweg 1 ⊠ *2585 JL* – ⚲ *(0 70) 352 51 61*
– www.crowneplazadenhaag.nl   *Plan III* **H2**
173 rm – †99/345 € ††99/345 €, ⊻ 23 € – 1 suite
Rest – Menu 20 € (lunch) – Carte approx. 55 €
♦ Chain hotel ♦ Functional ♦
Whether you are here to visit the International Court of Justice and the diplomatic quarter, the beach at Scheveningen or the miniature village at Madurodam, this hotel is conveniently situated for business and pleasure alike. Don't be deceived by the flashy lobby – the interior decor is more classic in style.

NH

Prinses Margrietplantsoen 100 ⊠ *2595 BR* – ⚲ *(0 70) 381 23 45*
– www.nh-hotels.com   *Plan I* **C2**
205 rm – †150/225 € ††150/225 €, ⊻ 19 €
Rest – Menu 18 € (lunch), 35/55 € – Carte approx. 66 €
♦ Chain hotel ♦ Business ♦ Modern ♦
This hotel in the centre of The Hague's 'Manhattan' district offers all comforts expected of this Spanish chain. The Hague is just a stone's throw away.

Carlton Ambassador

Sophialaan 2 ⊠ *2514 JP* – ⚲ *(0 70) 363 03 63*
– www.carlton.nl/ambassador   **E1**
77 rm – †95/250 € ††95/250 €, ⊻ 24 € – 1 suite
Rest *Henricus* – see restaurant listing
♦ Palace ♦ Classic ♦
Dozens of ancient chestnut trees surround this small luxury hotel in the Mesdag diplomatic district. Charming lobby, Dutch- and English-style bedrooms.

Corona

Buitenhof 42 ⊠ *2513 AH* – ⚲ *(0 70) 363 79 30* – *www.corona.nl*
35 rm – †112 € ††127/137 €, ⊻ 14 € – 1 suite   **E2**
Rest – Menu 26 € (lunch), 29/79 € bi – Carte approx. 55 €
♦ Traditional ♦ Luxury ♦ Modern ♦
This cosmopolitan hotel is situated in the heart of The Hague across the road from the Dutch Parliament and has a history dating back more than 300 years. It is the ideal place to drop in for a cup of coffee or a bite to eat at any time of the day.

NETHERLANDS - THE HAGUE

Parkhotel *without rest*

Molenstraat 53 ⊠ *2513 BJ* – ℰ *(0 70) 362 43 71*
– *www.parkhoteldenhaag.nl*   **E2**
120 rm – †79/100 € ††89/279 €, ⊆ 20 €
♦ Traditional ♦ Functional ♦

This hotel offers pleasant accommodation and has been a feature of the hospitality scene in The Hague for over a century. The Berlage-style staircase bears witness to its rich history. The hotel oozes historic charm whilst providing all the comforts you would expect of a modern hotel.

Paleis *without rest*

Molenstraat 26 ⊠ *2513 BL* – ℰ *(0 70) 362 46 21* – *www.paleishotel.nl*
20 rm – †155/245 € ††175/295 €, ⊆ 17 €   **E2**
♦ Luxury ♦ Classic ♦

A canopy at the head of the bed and a sumptuous ottoman at the foot are just two of the luxurious details in the guestrooms at the Paleis. This luxury hotel offers its guests a royal welcome in genuine Louis XVI-style, including a king-size bed.

Mercure Central

Spui 180 ⊠ *2511 BW* – ℰ *(0 70) 363 67 00* – *www.mercure.com*
156 rm – †99/214 € ††99/214 €, ⊆ 20 € – 3 suites   **F2**
Rest – Menu 20 € (lunch), 28/33 € – Carte approx. 36 €
♦ Chain hotel ♦ Business ♦ Design ♦

The aptly named Mercure Central is situated in the heart of The Hague, close to the Music and Dance Theatre. It features the usual functional comfort offered by this hotel chain.

Mozaic *without rest*

Laan Copes van Cattenburgh 40 ⊠ *2585 GB* – ℰ *(0 70) 352 23 35*
– *www.mozaic.nl*
– *closed 25 and 26 December*   *Plan I* **B1**
25 rm – †79/125 € ††129/159 €, ⊆ 13 €
♦ Family ♦ Design ♦

The team at Mozaic offer their guests that little bit extra. Find a warm personal welcome, a townhouse with a hint of history and a touch of modern design in the bedrooms. An inspired alternative to the usual chain hotels.

Calla's (Marcel van der Kleijn)

Laan van Roos en Doorn 51a ⊠ *2514 BC* – ℰ *(0 70) 345 58 66*
– *www.restaurantcallas.nl*
– *closed 21 July-19 August, 22 December-2 January, Saturday lunch, Sunday and Monday*   **F1**
Rest – Menu 48/105 € – Carte 83/113 € ❀
♦ Classic ♦ Elegant ♦

'Calla' refers to a Mexican lily, which derives its name from the Greek word for beauty. To continue with the international theme, the cuisine is French and the wine list a combination of the Old World and the New. The delicious, simple yet refined cuisine served here provides a truly memorable dining experience.
→ Taartje met coquilles, parmezaanse kaas en seizoenstruffel. Gepocheerde zeetong met langoustines, aardappelmousseline en een sausje van schaaldieren. Moelleux van bittere chocolade met kersen en specerijenroomijs.

Le Bistroquet

Lange Voorhout 98 ⊠ *2514 EJ* – ℰ *(0 70) 360 11 70* – *www.bistroquet.nl*
– *closed 24-31 December, Saturday lunch and Sunday*   **F2**
Rest – Menu 35 € (lunch)/45 € – Carte 59/77 €
♦ Modern ♦ Cosy ♦ Elegant ♦

A glass of Bolli, served with scallops followed by crispy sweetbreads? The up-to-the-minute menu betrays the fact that this luxurious bistro is situated in the heart of diplomatic The Hague where the clientele is both discerning and demanding. In the summer, dine alfresco under the lime trees.

NETHERLANDS - THE HAGUE

XX
 සු **HanTing Cuisine** (Xiaohan Ji)   AC ⇆ VISA ◎ AE

Prinsestraat 33 ⊠ *2513 CA –* ℰ *(0 70) 362 08 28 – www.hantingcuisine.nl*
– closed Monday   **E2**
Rest *– (dinner only)* Menu 34 € *–* Carte 36/65 €
♦ Innovative ♦ Intimate ♦ Exotic ♦

HanTing Cuisine is certainly the place to discover fusion cooking at its best. Han, the chef, brings all his expertise to bear in balancing the flavours of China with those of the West. He creates cuisine that is delicate and pleasingly harmonious. Not surprisingly, it is also very popular.

➙ Rauwe zalm met appel, rode biet met creme fraîche, zeewier en grijze garnalen. Eendenborst in een lotusblad met shii-takechampignons, eendenbout en eendenlever. Parfait van mango met een kokosmousse en straciatella van chocoladeganache en chocoladesaus.

XX
Saur   ⛱ AC ⇆ VISA ◎ AE

Lange Voorhout 51 ⊠ *2514 EC –* ℰ *(0 70) 361 70 70 – www.saur.nl*
– closed Sunday   **F2**
Rest *–* Menu 35 € (lunch), 39/99 € *–* Carte 48/85 € ⅏
♦ Traditional ♦ Brasserie ♦

Few businesses can boast as long a history as Saur. After undergoing extensive renovation, this restaurant has reopened its doors on the grand Lange Voorhout. The menu features French cuisine, occasionally with a Japanese flavour, and a focus on fish dishes.

XX
☺ **Rousseau**   ⛱ ⇆ VISA ◎ AE

Van Boetzelaerlaan 134 ⊠ *2581 AX –* ℰ *(0 70) 355 47 43*
– www.restaurantrousseau.com
– closed 28 April-6 May, 4-26 August, 23 December-7 January, 16-25 February,
Sunday and Monday   *Plan III* **G3**
Rest *– (dinner only)* Menu 35/68 € *–* Carte approx. 62 €
♦ Traditional ♦ Friendly ♦

As a Frenchman born and bred, owner-chef Jean Marc Rousseau creates delicious, classic French cuisine like no other. A fact demonstrated by his popularity with French diplomats who often come here for a taste of home. The frescoes add a light-hearted touch to the decor in the dining room.

XX
Christian   ⛱ ⇆ VISA ◎ AE

Laan van Nieuw Oost Indië 1f ⊠ *2593 BH –* ℰ *(0 70) 383 88 56*
– www.restaurantchristian.nl
– closed 19 July-8 August, 28 December-6 January, Saturday lunch and Sunday
Rest *–* Menu 33/100 € bi *–* Carte 55/67 €   *Plan I* **C2**
♦ Modern ♦ Friendly ♦

Christian has a real style of his own, which culminates in a festival of home-grown vegetables complemented with a daily supply of fresh fish and meat. The passionate enthusiasm he shows for simple cuisine with an ecological heart is truly praiseworthy.

XX
The Raffles   AC VISA ◎ AE ◑

Javastraat 63 ⊠ *2585 AG –* ℰ *(0 70) 345 85 87*
– www.restauraffles.com
– closed 1 week in February, last 2 weeks July-early August, Sunday and
Monday   **E1**
Rest *– (dinner only)* Menu 39/53 € *–* Carte 37/63 €
♦ Indonesian ♦ Friendly ♦ Exotic ♦

Chef Vichai Boonyuen, whose name is as authentic as his dishes, takes diners on a journey to the Indonesian archipelago in a decor that evokes the Dutch East Indies. A perfect setting for the satay babi, udang opor and other delicious Indonesian specialities that feature on the menu here.

XX **Des Indes** – Hotel des Indes   ⚑ ✢ ⛩ 🅿 VISA ◑◐ AE ⓪

Lange Voorhout 54 ⊠ *2514 EG –* ✆ *(0 70) 361 23 45*
– www.hoteldesindes.nl   **F1**
Rest *– (open until 11pm)* Carte 55/88 €
♦ Modern ♦ Formal ♦ Elegant ♦

The Des Indes hotel is considered the 'grande dame' of hotels in The Hague,
and it is fair to say that its restaurant can claim similar status among the city's
eateries. The cosmopolitan clientele is completely at home in the opulent decor
where contemporary cuisine is served with the subtle flavours of the spice
route.

XX **Pearl** – Hotel Hilton   😐 ⚑ AC ✢ VISA ◑◐ AE ⓪

Zeestraat 35 ⊠ *2518 AA –* ✆ *(0 70) 710 70 00*
– www.thehague.hilton.com   **E1**
Rest *–* Menu 33 € (lunch)/42 € – Carte 45/77 €
♦ Modern ♦ Trendy ♦ Brasserie ♦

Pearl's interior design is inspired by Vermeer's Girl with a Pearl Earring. In the
kitchen, French and contemporary cooking serve as the model for the dishes,
prepared under the close supervision of an experienced executive chef.

XX **Henricus** – Hotel Carlton Ambassador   AC ✢ 🅿 VISA ◑◐ AE ⓪

Sophialaan 2 ⊠ *2514 JP –* ✆ *(0 70) 363 03 63*
– www.carlton.nl/ambassador   **E1**
Rest *– (open until 11.30pm)* Menu 35 € – Carte 49/60 €
♦ Classic ♦ Cosy ♦

The menu at the Henricus takes the form of a 'mood book'. Whatever you are in
the mood for – whether it is 'light & easy' or 'delightful' – you will be given suggestions to suit from a range of light meals and international dishes.

X **Maxime**   AC VISA ◑◐ AE
🙂

Denneweg 10b ⊠ *2514 CG –* ✆ *(0 70) 360 92 24*
– www.restaurantmaxime.nl
– closed 25, 26 and 31 December-1 January   **F1**
Rest *–* Menu 35 €
♦ Modern ♦ Bistro ♦

Exchange The Hague for Paris: this chic bistro with a distinctive French flavour is
a popular place to eat in The Hague. There are two sittings at weekends, the first
from 6pm to 8pm and the second from 8pm to 10pm. The cuisine is authentic,
fresh and contemporary with no unnecessary frills. Shorter menu served at
lunchtimes.

X **Wox**   AC ✢ VISA ◑◐ AE

Buitenhof 36 ⊠ *2513 AH –* ✆ *(0 70) 365 37 54 – www.wox.nl*
– closed Bank Holidays, Sunday and Monday   **E2**
Rest *– (dinner only)* Carte 45/67 € 🍸
♦ Modern ♦ Trendy ♦

The name gives you an inkling of the ambience here and the interior confirms it:
this flashy brasserie is an ultra trendy venue. Fashionable Franco-Asian dishes
feature on the menu, as well as phenomenal wines with a good selection available by the glass.

X **De Basiliek**   😐 ✢ VISA ◑◐ AE

Korte Houtstraat 4a ⊠ *2511 CD –* ✆ *(0 70) 360 61 44 – www.debasiliek.nl*
– closed Saturday lunch and Sunday   **F2**
Rest *–* Menu 30/55 € – Carte 36/50 €
♦ Modern ♦ Brasserie ♦

This is the perfect place to kick off a Saturday night with friends. Friendly bustling ambience, smart contemporary cuisine and an attractive formula allowing
you to choose from the entire menu: the tone is set for a great night out.

Bumbu Rumba   _VISA_ **☾**

Zeestraat 58 ⊠ *2518 AB –* ℰ *(0 70) 360 06 50*
– www.bumburumba.com
– closed Monday and Tuesday   **E1**
Rest – *(dinner only)* Menu 35/45 € – Carte 35/45 €
♦ Indonesian ♦ Exotic ♦

Bumbu Rumba is Bali at its best. It serves a surprising fusion of traditional and innovative cuisine, surrounded by Buddha statues and bamboo.

Basaal   🛏 _VISA_ **☾**

Dunne Bierkade 3 ⊠ *2512 BC –* ℰ *(0 70) 427 68 88 – www.basaal.net*
– closed first week January, Monday and Tuesday   *Plan I* **C2**
Rest – *(dinner only until 11pm)* Menu 35/50 € – Carte 40/48 €
♦ Modern ♦ Bistro ♦

Basaal focuses on European cuisine, with a menu featuring delicious dishes such as roast duck breast with smoked sausage, smoked beetroot salad and North Sea fish soup. The pavement terrace facing the canal is open in the summer. The engaging couple that own this elegant restaurant had it licensed as an official wedding venue for their own wedding – it is now open to others as well.

Les Ombrelles   🛏 ⇄ ⊶ (dinner) **P** _VISA_ **☾** **AE** **①**

Hooistraat 4a ⊠ *2514 BM –* ℰ *(0 70) 365 87 89*
– www.lesombrelles.nl
– closed 25 December-3 January, Saturday lunch and Sunday lunch
Rest – Menu 33/50 € – Carte 43/70 €   **F1**
♦ Fish and seafood ♦ Bistro ♦

You don't need to be an expert in Molière's language to know the meaning of Ombrelles – just glance at the ceiling full of umbrellas to find the clue. The chef focuses on fish and shellfish dishes, adding his own original touches to traditional French recipes.

Le Bistrot de la Place Chez Norbert   🛏 _VISA_ **☾**

Plaats 27 ⊠ *2513 AD –* ℰ *(0 70) 364 33 27 – www.bistrotdelaplace.nl*
– closed Saturday lunch and Sunday   **E2**
Rest – Menu 35/50 € – Carte 39/56 €
♦ Traditional ♦ Bistro ♦

The record sleeves on the walls, the French music in the background and the flavours of archetypal French cuisine: the spirit of France has penetrated every fibre of this exceptional bistro. On Saturdays, the owner performs French songs.

Sequenza   🛏 _VISA_ **☾** **AE**

Spui 224 ⊠ *2511 BX –* ℰ *(0 70) 345 28 53*
– closed Sunday and Monday   **F2**
Rest – *(dinner only until 11pm) (set menu only)* Menu 43 €
♦ Classic ♦ Friendly ♦

The cosy atmosphere of Sequenza has won the hearts of its many regular customers. They return time and time again for the French inspired cuisine made from fresh, market-sourced produce. The restricted menu may offer only a small selection of dishes, but the food is full of flavour.

Fouquet   🛏 ⇄ _VISA_ **☾** **①**

Javastraat 31a ⊠ *2585 AC –* ℰ *(0 70) 360 62 73 – www.fouquet.nl*
– closed Sunday   **E1**
Rest – *(dinner only)* Menu 28/75 € bi – Carte 43/64 €
♦ Traditional ♦ Trendy ♦ Friendly ♦

The enthusiastic new owner-chef of this well-known restaurant continues along the French course to which it owes its success. This is the place for 'cuisine du marché', prepared with respect for traditions. Pavement terrace in summer.

NETHERLANDS - THE HAGUE

Steigenberger Kurhaus

Gevers Deynootplein 30 ⊠ *2586 CK* VISA ⊙⊙ AE ①
– ℰ (0 70) 416 26 36 – www.kurhaus.nl **G1**
245 rm – ✚145/400 € ✚✚145/400 €, ⊑ 25 € – 8 suites
Rest *Kurzaal* – see restaurant listing
♦ Palace ♦ Luxury ♦ Historic ♦

This 'kurhaus' or spa hotel is a real Scheveningen institution. Its reputation is fully justified by its elegant atmosphere, wonderful spa and exquisite seaside location.

Carlton Beach

Gevers Deynootweg 201 ⊠ *2586 HZ – ℰ (0 70) 354 14 14*
– www.carlton.nl/beach **H1**
183 rm – ✚125/275 € ✚✚150/300 €, ⊑ 18 €
Rest – *(open until 11pm)* Carte approx. 38 €
♦ Business ♦ Classic ♦

Despite its typical 1980s exterior, the Carlton Beach boasts smart modern rooms with views of the dunes, the beach or the promenade. In summer, the hotel beach club makes full use of the hotel's superb location.

Europa

Zwolsestraat 2 ⊠ *2587 VJ – ℰ (0 70) 416 95 95 – www.bilderberg.nl*
174 rm – ✚109/189 € ✚✚109/189 €, ⊑ 20 € **H1**
Rest – Menu 28 € (lunch), 40/99 € – Carte 35/83 €
♦ Chain hotel ♦ Functional ♦

A comfortable modern hotel, 300m from the jetty, overlooking a busy boulevard. Some of the rooms have views of the dunes and the sea. Colourful contemporary brasserie with an international à la carte menu and city terrace.

Badhotel

Gevers Deynootweg 15 ⊠ *2586 BB – ℰ (0 70) 351 22 21*
– www.badhotelscheveningen.nl **G1**
90 rm – ✚113/168 € ✚✚128/168 €, ⊑ 16 €
Rest – *(dinner only)* Menu 33 € – Carte 34/41 €
♦ Traditional ♦ Classic ♦

Whether you are travelling for business or pleasure, Badhotel is an excellent choice for visitors looking for a well-maintained, reputable hotel.

Ibis without rest

Gevers Deynootweg 63 ⊠ *2586 BJ – ℰ (0 70) 354 33 00*
– www.ibishotel.com **G1**
88 rm – ✚79/155 € ✚✚79/155 €, ⊑ 16 €
♦ Chain hotel ♦ Functional ♦

Centrally located and close to all the resort's main amenities, this chain hotel stands on a main street parallel to the dyke (Strandweg). Two sizes of rooms.

Seinpost

Zeekant 60 ⊠ *2586 AD – ℰ (0 70) 355 52 50 – www.seinpost.nl*
– closed Saturday lunch, Sunday and Bank Holidays **G1**
Rest – Menu 35 € (lunch), 49/69 € – Carte 68/95 € ⌂
♦ Fish and seafood ♦ Design ♦

The market-sourced menus at Seinpost prove that restaurants with stars are not just for the happy few. Refined cuisine inspired by the sea is served in a delightful location overlooking the water. For visitors not in the mood for fine dining but still wanting good quality food, Brasserie L'Entrée offers simpler cuisine.
➜ Lauwwarme zalm "en torchon", nage van scheermessen, alikruiken, ijzerkruid en raapstelen. Zeebaars in zoutkorst gegaard met tomaat en ansjovis, olijvenvinaigrette met saffraan. Diverse bereidingen van chocolade met lavendel en sinaasappelbloesem.

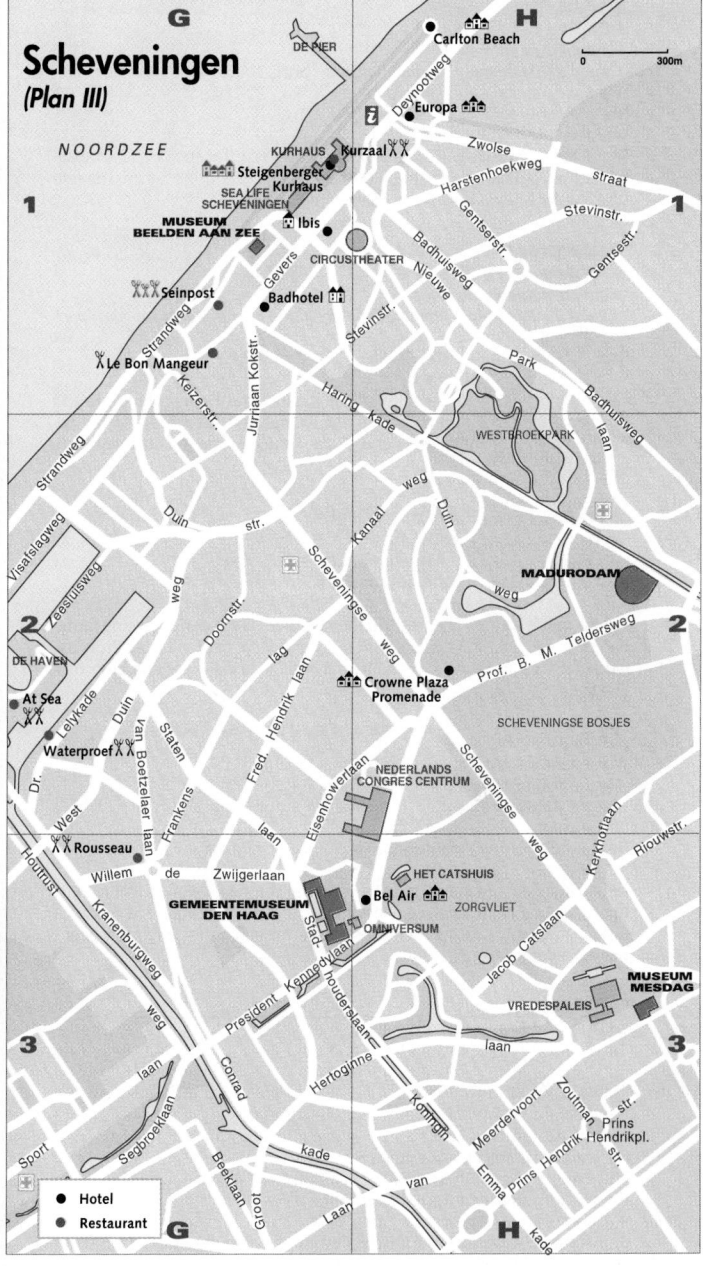

Scheveningen
(Plan III)

NOORDZEE

DE PIER

Carlton Beach

Europa

KURHAUS **Kurzaal**
Steigenberger Kurhaus
SEA LIFE SCHEVENINGEN
MUSEUM BEELDEN AAN ZEE
Ibis
CIRCUSTHEATER

Zwolse straat

Deynootweg

Harstenhoekweg

Stevinstr.

Gentsestr.
Gentsestr.

Seinpost

Badhotel

Badhuisweg

Nieuwe Stevinstr.

Haring kade

Le Bon Mangeur

Strandweg
Keizerstr.
Jurriaan Kokstr.
Gevers

Park

Badhuisweg laan

WESTBROEKPARK

weg

Strandweg

Visafslagweg
Zeesluisweg

Duin str.

Duin weg

Kanaal weg

Scheveningse weg

Duin weg

MADURODAM

DE HAVEN

At Sea

Waterproef

Lelykade
Duin
van Boetzelaer laan
Doornstr.
Staten
Frankens
Slag
Fred. Hendrik laan

Scheveningse weg

Prof. B. M. Teldersweg

Crowne Plaza Promenade

SCHEVENINGSE BOSJES

Rousseau

West
Houtrust
Kranenburgweg
Willem de Zwijgerlaan

laan

Eisenhowerlaan

NEDERLANDS CONGRES CENTRUM

Scheveningse weg

Kerkhoflaan
Riouwstr.

GEMEENTEMUSEUM DEN HAAG

Stadh
President Kennedylaan
houderslaan

HET CATSHUIS

Bel Air
OMNIVERSUM

ZORGVLIET

Jacob Catslaan

VREDESPALEIS

MUSEUM MESDAG

Sport laan
Segbroeklaan
Conrad kade
Beeklaan
Groot
Hertoginne laan

Koningin

laan

van

Emma kade
Meerdervoort
Zoutman str.
Prins Hendrik Prins Hendrikpl.

●	Hotel
●	Restaurant

0 300m

NETHERLANDS - THE HAGUE

XX **At Sea** _VISA_ ⓪ AE

Hellingweg 138 ⊠ *2583 DX –* ℰ *(0 70) 331 74 45*
– www.restaurantatsea.nl
– closed 27 December-1 January, Saturday lunch, Sunday lunch, Monday and
Tuesday **G2**
Rest – Menu 40/55 € – Carte 60/66 € ⅍
♦ Modern ♦ Trendy ♦

The At Sea team skilfully creates innovative dishes such as tuna sashimi, zabaglione of eel or Bounty with ravioli of mango and coconut ice cream. The loft-style interior boasts views of the boats in the dry-dock.

XX **Waterproef** ⌂ AC ⇔ _VISA_ ⓪ AE

Dr. Lelykade 25 ⊠ *2583 CL –* ℰ *(0 70) 358 87 70*
– www.restaurantwaterproef.nl
– closed 27 December-2 January, Saturday lunch, Sunday lunch, Monday lunch
and Wednesday **G2**
Rest – Menu 30 € (lunch), 40/65 € – Carte 47/63 €
♦ Modern ♦ Family ♦ Friendly ♦

This restaurant is a real quayside stunner. It is an attractive mix of modern and traditional and can accommodate up to a 100 guests. The cuisine is contemporary (the menus are attractively priced), the service relaxed and the ambience guaranteed.

XX **Kurzaal** – Hotel Steigenberger Kurhaus ⇐ & AC ⌂♥ P

Gevers Deynootplein 30 ⊠ *2586 CK* _VISA_ ⓪ AE ⓪
– ℰ *(0 70) 416 27 13 – www.kurhaus.nl* **G1**
Rest – Menu 35 € – Carte approx. 60 €
♦ Modern ♦ Brasserie ♦

A drink in the bar or a light meal in the restaurant is the perfect excuse for sitting back and enjoying the impressive, historic decor of the Kurzaal. Breakfast, lunch, high tea or dinner from the international menu in the evening. Brunch on Sundays.

X **Le Bon Mangeur** _VISA_ ⓪

Wassenaarsestraat 119 ⊠ *2586 AM –* ℰ *(0 70) 355 92 13*
– www.lebonmangeur.nl
– closed 22 July-14 August, 31 December-16 January, Monday
and Tuesday **G1**
Rest – *(dinner only)* Menu 35/60 € bi – Carte 50/60 €
♦ Classic ♦ Friendly ♦

Le Bon Mangeur restaurant is run by Theo and Patricia Pronk who aim to introduce their guests to French cuisine with an international flavour. This congenial restaurant opens its doors wide to everyone, making it the perfect place for a friendly, informal dinner.

ENVIRONS OF THE HAGUE *Plan I*

🏛 **Grand Winston** ƒ& & AC 🛜 ⅍ P _VISA_ ⓪ AE ⓪

Generaal Eisenhowerplein 1 ⊠ *2288 AE Rijswijk*
– ℰ *(0 70) 414 15 00*
– www.worldhotelgrandwinston.com **C3**
252 rm – ♦133/232 € ♦♦143/242 €, ⧠ 20 € – 7 suites
Rest *Grand Canteen* – see restaurant listing
♦ Business ♦ Modern ♦ Functional ♦

Sir Winston Churchill keeps a watchful eye on the reception area of this designer hotel next to the station. The rooms are housed in two towers and, like the public areas, are very well maintained.

NETHERLANDS - THE HAGUE

Savarin 🕯️ 🌐 ⓦ 🖼️ 🐧 🗺️ 🛜 🖧 🅿 VISA ⓒⓞ AE ①

Laan van Hoornwijck 29 ⊠ *2289 DG Rijswijk* – ℰ *(0 70) 307 20 50*
– www.savarin.nl   **C3**
35 rm – ♦175/225 € ♦♦175/225 €, � 20 €
Rest *Savarin* – see restaurant listing
♦ Business ♦ Luxury ♦ Design ♦

Despite its location between motorways and large office buildings, this oasis of calm offers a wonderful combination of relaxation, personal service and wellness facilities. The special beds and bright interiors of the rooms add to the appeal.

Greenpark ← 🕯️ 🌐 🖼️ 🛜 🖧 VISA ⓒⓞ AE ①

Weigelia 22 ⊠ *2262 AB Leidschendam* – ℰ *(0 70) 320 92 80*
– www.greenpark.nl   **D1**
92 rm – ♦70/214 € ♦♦70/224 €, ⊻ 20 € – 4 suites
Rest *Chiparus* – see restaurant listing
♦ Chain hotel ♦ Business ♦ Classic ♦

This lakeside hotel stands on stilts and is close to a large shopping mall. The reception area in the atrium welcomes guests with a lighting feature consisting of no fewer than 2 048 LED light bulbs. The best rooms have balconies with views over the water.

Savelberg 🐧 ← 🅿 🅿 VISA ⓒⓞ AE ①

Oosteinde 14 ⊠ *2271 EH Voorburg* – ℰ *(0 70) 387 20 81*
– www.restauranthotelsavelberg.nl
– closed late December   **D2**
14 rm – ♦150/190 € ♦♦150/190 €, ⊻ 19 €
Rest *Savelberg* ✿ – see restaurant listing
♦ Luxury ♦ Classic ♦

If you are looking for timeless, top class elegance, then the Savelberg is the perfect place for you. Inhabited by a noble family in the 18C, this fine building has been converted into a delightful hotel. What could be more enjoyable than to spend an afternoon reading in the sun-drenched garden among the hydrangeas?

Mövenpick 🚿 🛜 🖼️ 🛜 🖧 🍽️ VISA ⓒⓞ AE ①

Stationsplein 8 ⊠ *2275 AZ Voorburg* – ℰ *(0 70) 337 37 37*
– www.moevenpick-hotels.com/denhaag-voorburg   **C2**
125 rm – ♦99/160 € ♦♦99/160 €, ⊻ 18 €
Rest – Carte 28/46 €
♦ Chain hotel ♦ Functional ♦

This chain hotel is housed in a modern building whose semicircular façade faces the station. Functional rooms (those to the rear are preferable), plus easy access for wheelchair users. Designer-style bar. Modern brasserie with Italian-Asian cuisine (pasta and wok dishes). Terrace in front of the hotel.

Savelberg – Hotel Savelberg ← 🅿 🚿 🐧 ⇄ 🅿 VISA ⓒⓞ AE ①
✿✿

Oosteinde 14 ⊠ *2271 EH Voorburg* – ℰ *(0 70) 387 20 81*
– www.restauranthotelsavelberg.nl
– closed late December, Saturday lunch, Sunday and Monday   **D2**
Rest – Menu 58 € (lunch), 83/125 € – Carte 80/120 € 🍷
♦ Modern ♦ Formal ♦ Elegant ♦

The sumptuous decor of this elegant restaurant provides the ideal setting for a stylish meal out. The chef skilfully transforms high quality ingredients into simple yet exceptional dishes, while the sommelier is on hand to offer sound advice.

→ Slaatje van kreeft met artisjokharten, groene boontjes en truffel. Op het karkas gegaarde duif met taartje van de orgaantjes en eigen braadjus. Soufflé van kwark en pruimedanten, vanilleroomijs en pruimencompote.

617

XXX

Savarin – Hotel Savarin

Laan van Hoornwijck 29 ✉ 2289 DG Rijswijk – ✆ (0 70) 307 20 50
– www.savarin.nl
– closed Saturday lunch and Sunday **C3**

Rest – Menu 35/90 € – Carte 45/70 €

♦ Modern ♦ Formal ♦

Serving French cuisine with an international twist, this restaurant occupies a modernised farmhouse that has retained its traditional charm. Original flavours add a fresh touch to the occasionally playfully prepared dishes.

XXX ✿

Niven (Niven Kunz)

Delftweg 58a ✉ 2289 AL Rijswijk – ✆ (0 70) 307 79 70
– www.restaurantniven.nl
– closed first week August, Tuesday lunch, Sunday and Monday **C3**

Rest – Menu 55/100 € – Carte 58/80 €

♦ Modern ♦ Elegant ♦

This restaurant features creative delicacies from a young chef. They are served in a bright, modern setting (white beams, modern paintings, padded seating and designer lighting) or on the patio overlooking the golf course. Elegant ambience.

➜ Rode bietjes met sorbet van rodewijnazijn en framboos. Asperges en Opperdoezer Ronde-aardappel met een kwartelei en hollandaisesaus. Diverse structuren van chocolade.

XXX

Villa la Ruche

Prinses Mariannelaan 71 ✉ 2275 BB Voorburg – ✆ (0 70) 386 01 10
– www.villalaruche.nl
– closed 26 and 31 December-1 January, Saturday lunch, Sunday and Monday

Rest – Menu 35 € (lunch), 43/85 € – Carte 61/78 € **C2**

♦ Modern ♦ Formal ♦ Elegant ♦

Villa la Ruche is a villa from the 19C with a modernised interior. It treats its guests to up-to-the-minute cuisine, served either in the atmospheric restaurant with a conservatory or on the patio under the shade of the plane trees.

XX

Chiparus – Hotel Greenpark

Weigelia 22 ✉ 2262 AB Leidschendam – ✆ (0 70) 320 92 80
– www.greenpark.nl **D1**

Rest – Menu 20 € (lunch), 33/50 € – Carte 44/56 €

♦ Modern ♦ Elegant ♦

This restaurant, treated to a smart, modern makeover, also boasts a lakeside terrace. Seasonal and à la carte menu. A glass of wine is suggested with each dish.

XX

Crème Crue

Haagweg 114 ✉ 2282 AG Rijswijk – ✆ (0 70) 365 10 80
– www.cremecrue.nl
– closed 27 December-3 January, Monday and Tuesday **C2**

Rest – *(dinner only except Thursday and Friday)* Menu 38 € (lunch), 47/125 € bi – Carte approx. 65 €

♦ Modern ♦ Trendy ♦

Wood is used to full effect in this restaurant, where an ingenious wooden wall dominates the interior and creates a wonderfully warm atmosphere. The contrasting sweet-sour flavours and the interplay of textures give the modern cuisine a truly contemporary appeal.

X

Paul van Waarden

Tollensstraat 10 ✉ 2282 BM Rijswijk – ✆ (0 70) 414 08 12
– www.paulvanwaarden.nl
– closed 2 weeks in May, late December-early January, Saturday lunch, Sunday and Monday **C3**

Rest – Menu 40/55 € – Carte 63/77 €

♦ Classic ♦ Brasserie ♦

A renovated house near the church tower offering tasty seasonal dishes at reasonable prices, served in three simple and airy dining rooms (bare tables, gastronomic photographs, cast iron basins) or on the patio in summer.

X **Brasserie De Koepel**   🔌 ☂ ✿ 𝘝𝘐𝘚𝘈 ⓸ 𝗔𝗘

Oosteinde 1 ✉ 2271 EA Voorburg – ☎ (0 70) 369 35 72
– www.brasseriedekoepel.nl
– closed 27-31 December   **D2**
Rest – *(dinner only except Sunday)* Menu 30 € – Carte 41/51 €
♦ Modern ♦ Brasserie ♦
Former orangery in Vreugd en Rust park featuring a rotunda with columns, high
bay windows, a cupola adorned with whimsical frescoes, red velvet padding,
candlelight dinners, and a summer terrace.

X **Grand Canteen** – Hotel Grand Winston   𝗔𝗖 𝗣 𝘝𝘐𝘚𝘈 ⓸ 𝗔𝗘 ⓪

Generaal Eisenhowerplein 1 ✉ 2288 AE Rijswijk – ☎ (0 70) 414 15 00
– www.worldhotelgrandwinston.com   **C3**
Rest – Menu 22 € (lunch)/29 € – Carte 25/51 €
♦ International ♦ Brasserie ♦ Trendy ♦
The Grand Canteen's menu adopts a trendy, modern approach to food, with
snacks and international classics served in a relaxed setting.

NETHERLANDS - THE HAGUE

ROTTERDAM
ROTTERDAM

Population: 617 347

Jérôme Dancette/Fotolia.com

Rotterdam trades on its earthy appeal, on a rough and ready grittiness that ties in with its status as the largest seaport in the world; it handles 350 million tonnes of goods a year, with over half of all the freight that is heading into Europe passing through it. Flattened during the Second World War, Rotterdam was rebuilt on a grand scale, jettisoning the idea of streets full of terraced houses in favour of a modern cityscape of concrete and glass, and there are few places in the world that have such an eclectic range of buildings to keep you entertained (or bewildered): try the Euromast Space Tower, the Groothandelsgebouw (which translates as 'large business building'), the 'Cube Houses' or the fabulous sounding Boompjestorens for size. The city is located on the Nieuwe Maas but is centred around a maze of other rivers – most importantly the Rhine and the Maas – and is only a few dozen kilometres inland from the North Sea. It spills over both banks, and is linked by tunnels, bridges and the metro; the most stunning connection across the water is the modern Erasmusbridge, whose graceful, angular lines of silver tubing have earned it the nickname 'The Swan', and whose sleek design has come to embody the Rotterdam of the new millennium. It's mirrored on the southern banks by the development of the previously rundown Kop Van Zuid area into a zone of new build and sleek promise.

ROTTERDAM IN...

➜ ONE DAY
Blaak area including Kijk-Kubus and Boompjestorens, Oude Haven, Museum Boijmans Van Beuningen.

➜ TWO DAYS
More Museumpark, Delfshaven, take in the view from Euromast, cruise along the Nieuwe Maas.

➜ THREE DAYS
Kop Van Zuid, a show at the Luxor Theatre.

PRACTICAL INFORMATION

ARRIVAL-DEPARTURE

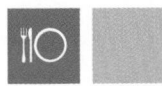 The Airport is 8km northwest of the city. Shuttle buses No.33 and 43 run every 10min and take 20min to Centraal Railway Station.

GETTING AROUND

There are a variety of stripcards to ease your way around on metro, bus, tram and train: from two-strip right up to forty-five strip tickets. That could entail a lot of fiddling about and franking. A better bet could be to invest in a one-day, two-day, or three-day card, which gives you unlimited travel on any form of transport. A Rotterdam Card provides unlimited use of the transport network as well as free admission to most attractions and is available for either 24 or 72 hours. You can hire bicycles from the Centraal Station cycle shop. These work out at good value, and can be hired for either a day or a week.

CALENDAR HIGHLIGHTS

January
International Film Festival.

March
Museum Night.

May
Dunya Festival (music, storytelling and performance).

June
Poetry International Festival.

July
North Sea Jazz Festival,
Summer Carnival (street parade).

August
Dance Parade.

September
Chocolad's Amour, KunsthalCOOKING, World Port Festival (ship tours, demos and cruises).

EATING OUT

Rotterdam is a hot place for dining, in the literal and metaphorical sense. There are lots of places to tuck into the flavours of Holland's colonial past, in particular the spicy delicacies of Indonesia and Surinam. The long east/west stretch of Oude and Nieuwe Binnenweg is not only handy for many of the sights, it's also chock-full of good cafés, café-bars and restaurants, and the canal district of Oudehaven has introduced to the city a good selection of places to eat while taking in the relaxed vibe. Along the waterfront, various warehouses have been transformed into mega-restaurants, particularly around the Noordereiland isle in the middle of the river, while in Kop Van Zuid, the Wilhelminapier Quay offers quality restaurants and tasty views too. Many establishments are closed at lunchtime, except business restaurants and those that set a high gastronomic standard and like to show it off in the middle of the day as well as in the evening. The bill includes a service charge, so tipping is optional: round up the total if you're pleased with the service.

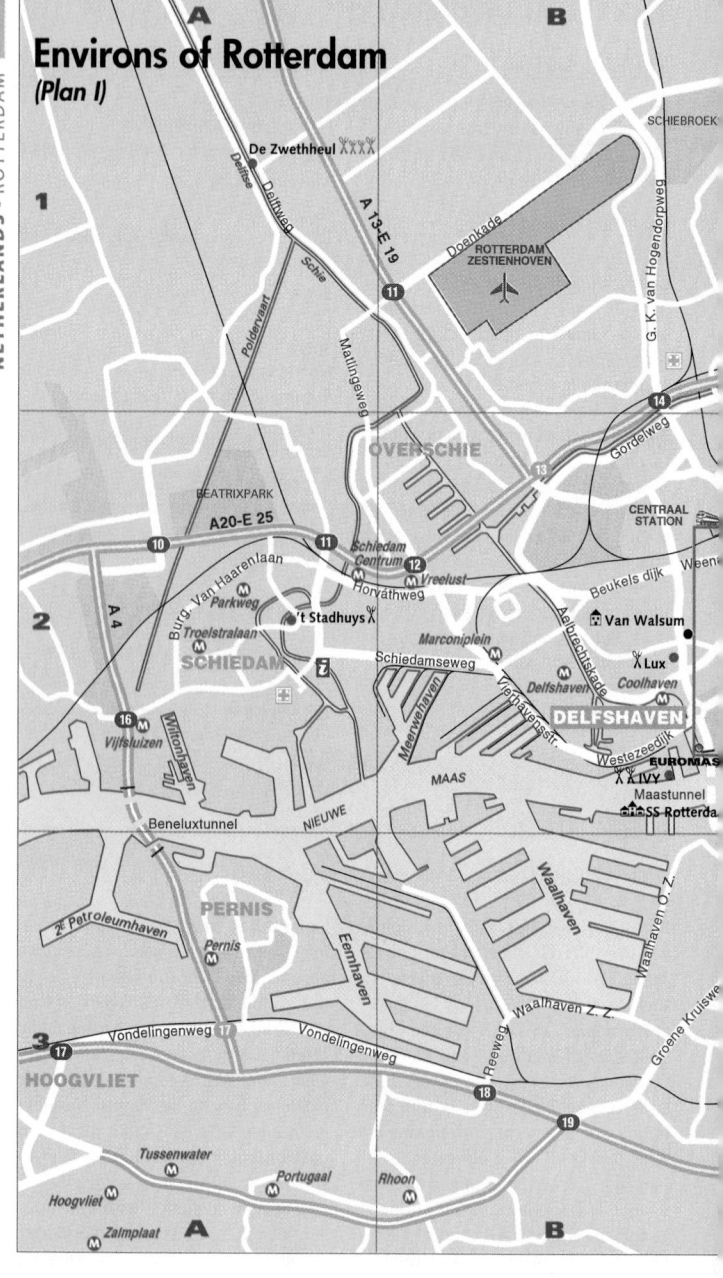

Environs of Rotterdam
(Plan I)

SCHIEBROEK

De Zwethheul ✗✗✗✗

Delftse

Delftweg

Schie

A 13-E 19

Doenkade

ROTTERDAM
ZESTIENHOVEN

G. K. van Hogendorpweg

11

1

Poldervaart

Matlingeweg

14

BEATRIXPARK

A20-E 25

OVERSCHIE

13

Gordelweg

CENTRAAL
STATION

10

11

Schiedam
Centrum

12

Vreelust

Horváthweg

Beukels dijk

Ween

Burg. Van Haarenlaan

Parkweg

Van Walsum

A 4

Troelstralaan

't Stadhuys ✗

Marconiplein

Schiedamseweg

Lux

Coolhaven

SCHIEDAM

Delfshaven

DELFSHAVEN

16

Vlaardingerdijk

Vijfsluizen

Wiltonhaven

Meeuwenhaven

Vlaardingerstr.

Westzeedijk

EUROMAS

✗ Ivy

MAAS

Maastunnel

Beneluxtunnel

NIEUWE

SS Rotterda

2

PERNIS

Waalhaven

Waalhaven O. Z.

Petroleumhaven

Pernis

Eemhaven

Groene Kruiswe

3

17

Vondelingenweg

17

Vondelingenweg

Waalhaven Z. Z.

Reeweg

18

HOOGVLIET

19

Tussenwater

Portugaal

Rhoon

Hoogvliet

Zalmplaat

A

B

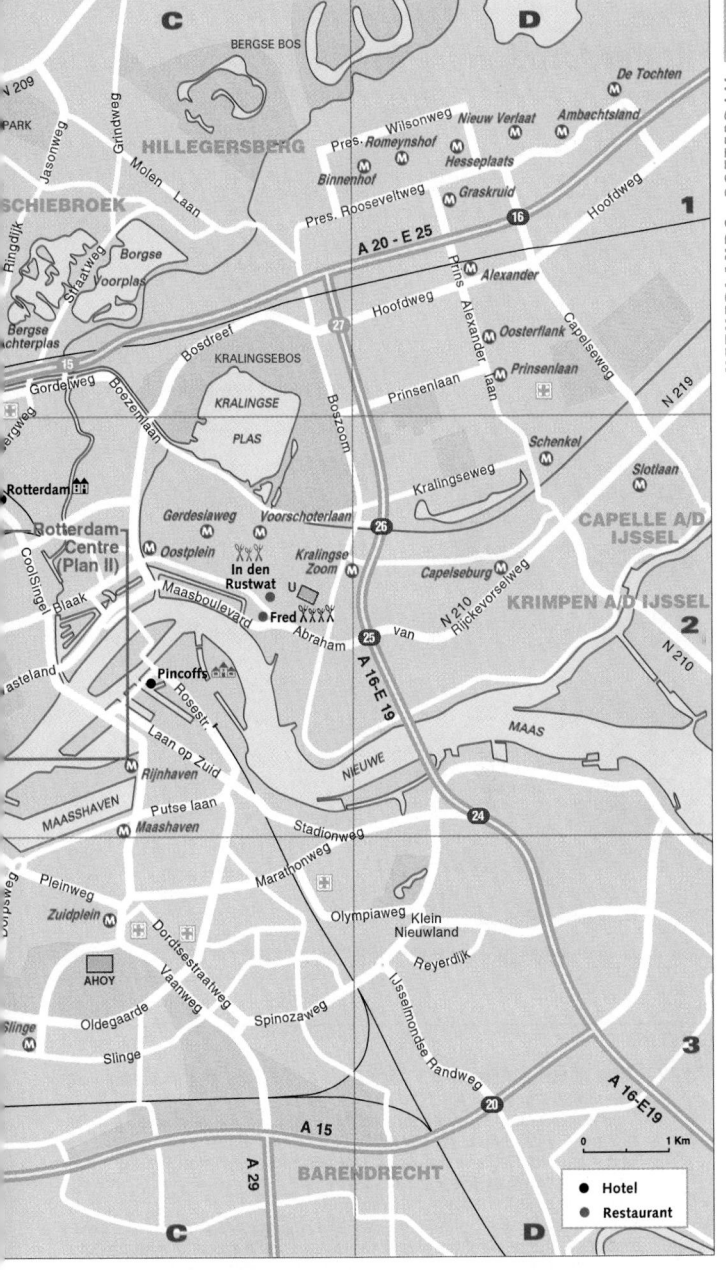

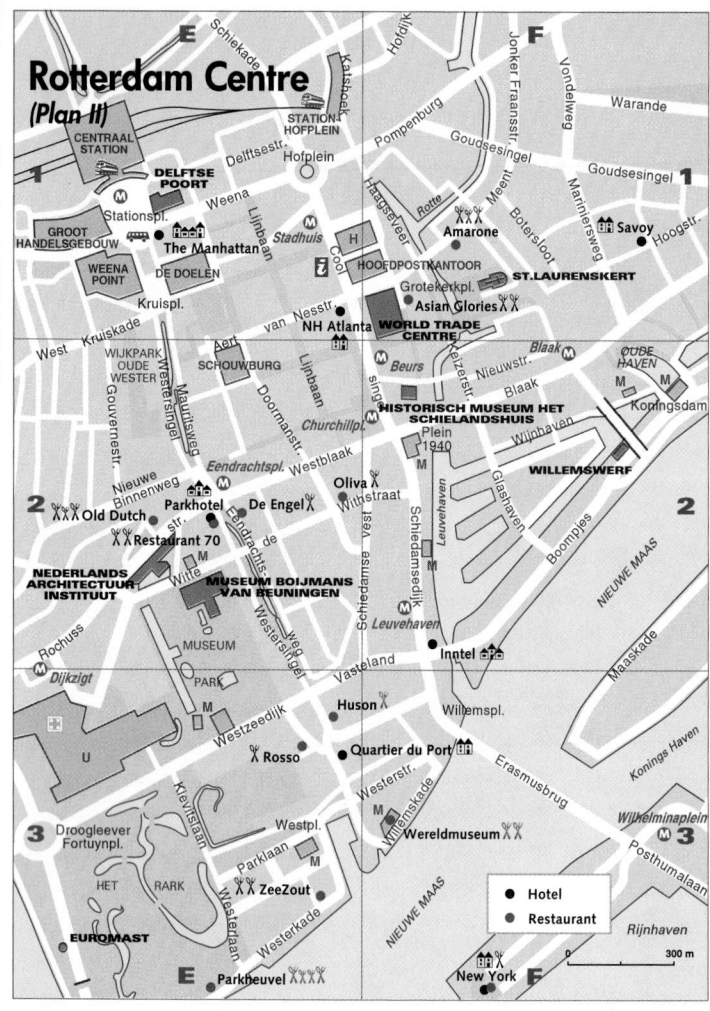

NETHERLANDS - ROTTERDAM

Rotterdam Centre
(Plan II)

CENTRE   *Plan II*

The Manhattan   ⬅ 🛁 🕭 🅰🅲 🛜 🏖 ⛑ 📶 *VISA* 🏧 AE ①

Weena 686 ☒ 3012 CN – ℰ (0 10) 430 20 00
– www.manhattanhotelrotterdam.com   **E1**
230 rm – 🛏199/369 € 🛏🛏199/369 €, ⌑ 29 € – 3 suites
Rest – *(closed 23 December-4 January, Saturday lunch and Sunday lunch)*
Menu 28 € (lunch)/35 € – Carte 33/63 €

♦ Business ♦ Luxury ♦ Modern ♦

A colossal skyscraper opposite the station. Large guestrooms with all modern
comforts, a business centre, plus all the facilities you'd expect of a luxury hotel.
The top floors offer wonderful views over the city. Seasonal cuisine with a focus
on fish, served in a restaurant with panoramic windows and a modern decor.

Parkhotel   ≤ ⅃₅ ⚄ 瓜 ⹂ ⾑ 𝗣 ⅶ⅛ ⬤⬤ 𝗔𝗘 ⓪
Westersingel 70 ⊠ *3015 LB* – ℰ *(0 10) 436 36 11*
– www.parkhotelrotterdam.nl   **E2**
187 rm – ♥79/210 € ♥♥79/210 €, �ⶲ 25 € – 2 suites
Rest *Restaurant 70* – see restaurant listing
♦ Business ♦ Classic ♦
With part of the hotel dating back to 1922, Parkhotel presents a slice of hotel history in the centre of modern Rotterdam. The two tower blocks dating back to the 1980s offer panoramic views of the 'Architectural Capital of the Netherlands'.

Inntel   ≤ ⅃₅ ⚄ ⾑ ⅙ rest, 瓜 ⹂ ⾑ 𝗣 ⅶ⅛ ⬤⬤ 𝗔𝗘 ⓪
Leuvehaven 80 ⊠ *3011 EA* – ℰ *(0 10) 413 41 39*
– www.inntelhotelsrotterdamcentre.nl   **F2**
263 rm – ♥100/255 € ♥♥100/255 €, �ⶲ 24 €
Rest – *(closed Sunday dinner)* Menu 28 € (lunch), 40/47 € – Carte approx. 38 €
♦ Chain hotel ♦ Business ♦ Modern ♦
The only hotel in the city with its own swimming pool, the Inntel also boasts superb views of the Erasmus Bridge and the museum harbour, making this a delightful place to stay. Enjoy a drink in the aptly named 'Water' bar-brasserie.

Pincoffs without rest   瓜 ⾑ ⅙ 𝗣 ⅶ⅛ ⬤⬤ 𝗔𝗘
Stieltjesstraat 34 (on the left bank area called "Kop van Zuid") ⊠ *3071 JX*
– ℰ (0 10) 297 45 00 – www.hotelpincoffs.nl
– closed 24-27 December   *Plan I* **C2**
16 rm – ♥125/145 € ♥♥125/204 €, �ⶲ 18 € – 1 suite
♦ Historic ♦ Modern ♦
This trendy renovated customs office is the place to be for visitors wanting to explore the city and indulge in a little pampering. Bulgari accessories in the bathroom, your favourite music on the iPod docking station and impeccable, friendly service all add to the appeal.

SS Rotterdam   ⅙ ⾑ ⅙ ⅶ⅛ ⬤⬤ 𝗔𝗘
3e Katendrechtsehoofd 25 ⊠ *3072 AM* – ℰ *(0 10) 297 30 90*
– www.ssrotterdam.nl   *Plan I* **B2**
254 rm – ♥90/200 € ♥♥90/250 €, �ⶲ 19 €
Rest – Menu 25 € (lunch)/45 € – Carte 62/70 €
♦ Historic ♦ Personalised ♦
This former cruise ship makes a great base from which to explore the port of Rotterdam. Guests can relive the history of this ocean-going steamer in the themed rooms. All aboard!

NH Atlanta   ⅃₅ ⅙ 瓜 ⾑ ⅙ ⌬ ⅶ⅛ ⬤⬤ 𝗔𝗘 ⓪
Aert van Nesstraat 4 ⊠ *3012 CA* – ℰ *(0 10) 206 78 00*
– www.nh-hotels.com   **E1**
215 rm – ♥69/200 € ♥♥69/200 €, �ⶲ 19 €
Rest – *(closed lunch Saturday and Sunday)* Menu 16 € (lunch)
– Carte 31/44 €
♦ Chain hotel ♦ Business ♦ Functional ♦
A hotel offering all the comforts you would expect from this hotel chain, with just a hint of Art Deco style in the public areas. Dine either in the brasserie or the Chinese restaurant.

Savoy without rest   ⅃₅ 瓜 ⾑ ⅙ ⅶ⅛ ⬤⬤ 𝗔𝗘
Hoogstraat 81 ⊠ *3011 PJ* – ℰ *(0 10) 413 92 80*
– www.hampshire-hotels.com/rotterdam   **F1**
94 rm ⊽ – ♥99 € ♥♥113 €
♦ Business ♦ Modern ♦
This functional, modern hotel is ideally located for a visit to Rotterdam's famous cube houses, making this the perfect choice for visitors to the city.

New York

Koninginnenhoofd 1 (Wilhelminapier) ✉ *3072 AD*
– ℰ (0 10) 439 05 00
– www.hotelnewyork.nl   **F3**
72 rm – †99/270 € ††99/270 €, ⊊ 18 €
Rest *New York* – see restaurant listing
♦ Traditional ♦ Retro ♦

Stay at the New York hotel and experience the excitement of the fortune-seekers who came to buy their tickets here for the ocean crossing to New York. From the bar and restaurant to the elegant guestrooms, this lively hotel is full of character.

Rotterdam

Schiekade 658 ✉ *3032 AK* – *ℰ (0 10) 466 33 44*
– www.hotel-rotterdam-city.nl   *Plan I* **C2**
115 rm ⊊ – †45/145 € ††65/195 €
Rest – *(closed Saturday and Sunday) (dinner only)*
Carte 28/49 €
♦ Chain hotel ♦ Traditional ♦ Functional ♦

On a busy main street, the hotel is made up of three old houses and a modern wing at the rear, where rooms are just as comfortable, but quieter. Restaurant offering an international menu in a contemporary setting.

Quartier du Port

Van Vollenhovenstraat 48 ✉ *3016 BJ* – *ℰ (0 10) 240 04 25*
– www.quartierduport.nl   **E3**
20 rm – †90/140 € ††90/140 €, ⊊ 17 €
Rest – *(closed last week July-first week August)* Menu 25 €
– Carte 28/45 €
♦ Inn ♦ Retro ♦ Functional ♦

This boutique hotel has a warm, welcoming atmosphere. It has a feeling of space and openness in the guestrooms, and just a hint of nostalgia in the reception area. The better rooms are situated to the rear of the hotel.

Van Walsum

Mathenesserlaan 199 ✉ *3014 HC* – *ℰ (0 10) 436 32 75*
– www.hotelvanwalsum.nl
– closed 23 December-1 January   *Plan I* **B2**
28 rm – †75/140 € ††80/160 €, ⊊ 14 €
Rest – *(residents only)*
♦ Family ♦ Classic ♦

The Van Dam family, who have been running this hotel for three generations, don't believe in standing still. Renovations take place here on a regular basis, so it is worth asking for a refurbished room when you book.

Parkheuvel (Erik van Loo)

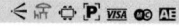

Heuvellaan 21 ✉ *3016 GL* – *ℰ (0 10) 436 07 66*
– www.parkheuvel.nl
– closed 29 July-18 August, 27 December-6 January, 11-14 February, Bank Holidays, Saturday lunch and Sunday   **E3**
Rest – Menu 53/135 € – Carte 79/133 € ℬ
♦ Creative ♦ Formal ♦

A semicircular modern pavillion located on the Maas by a park with bay windows and a terrace overlooking the harbour. Lovely remodelled art deco interior, extensive menu and wine list, as well as impeccable service.
→ Krokante open sandwich van noordzeekrab met een frisse brandade en grijze garnaaltjes. Wilde zeebaars, gegrild, op een bloemige aardappelsalade en zomergroenten en "Thousand Island"-dressing. Aardbeien met een granité van droge gin en verse dragon, cocktail Romanoff.

NETHERLANDS - ROTTERDAM

XXXX **Fred** (Fred Mustert) [AC] ⊐¶ (dinner) [VISA] [CO] [AE]

⅜ *Honingerdijk 263 ⊠ 3063 AM Kralingen – ℰ (0 10) 212 01 10*
– www.restaurantfred.nl
– closed 5-25 August, 25 December-1 January, Saturday lunch and Sunday
Rest – Menu 45 € (lunch), 79/92 € – Carte 74/94 €   **C2**
♦ Modern ♦ Design ♦

Providing a feast for the eyes as well as the palate, this restaurant boasts a spectacular dining room decorated in a dazzling neo-Baroque style. The menu is
contemporary with a French flavour, featuring skilfully prepared dishes made
from the best ingredients.
→ In briochebrood gebakken groene asperges met een jus van morieljes,
Parmezaanse kaas en sel de Guérande. Geroosterde zeebaars met zachtge-
gaarde kreeft, paksoi en een dressing van oude sherry en sjalotten. "Delice"
van karamel, witte chocolade, wasabi en eucalyptusroomijs.

XXX **Old Dutch** ⌂ ⇔ ⊐¶ [P] [VISA] [CO] [AE]

Rochussenstraat 20 ⊠ 3015 EK – ℰ (0 10) 436 03 44 – www.olddutch.net
– closed Bank Holidays, Saturday and Sunday   **E2**
Rest – Menu 38 € (lunch), 43/63 € – Carte 49/83 €
♦ Modern ♦ Formal ♦

The aptly named Old Dutch restaurant is the perfect place to enjoy a traditional
Dutch atmosphere. In contrast, the menu is resolutely modern with dishes such
as giant prawn tempura and grilled lobster with lime sauce. Good-sized outdoor
terrace.

XXX **Amarone** (Gert Blom) [AC] [VISA] [CO] [AE]

⅜ *Meent 72a ⊠ 3011 JN – ℰ (0 10) 414 84 87 – www.restaurantamarone.nl*
– closed 22 July-10 August, 30 December-2 January, Bank Holidays, Saturday
lunch and Sunday   **F1**
Rest – Menu 35 € (lunch), 58/75 € – Carte 59/84 € ⅜
♦ Modern ♦ Formal ♦

This fashionable city restaurant emanates the same elegance and superior quality as the fine wine from which it takes its name. Inventive cuisine made from
the best ingredients.
→ Geroosterde langoustines met zalfje van bospeen, krokante aardappel,
tuinkers en een nage van sake. In de oven gegaarde tarbot met citroenbo-
ter, cantharellen, paksoi en limoen. Warme amandelmadeleine met bereidingen van mango en chocolade, stacciatellaroomijs.

XXX **In den Rustwat** ⌂ [AC] ⇔ [VISA] [CO] [AE]

⊚ *Honingerdijk 96 ⊠ 3062 NX Kralingen – ℰ (0 10) 413 41 10 – www.idrw.nl*
– closed 5-23 August, 25 December-9 January, Saturday lunch, Sunday and
Monday   *Plan I* **C2**
Rest – Menu 33 € (lunch), 35/58 € – Carte 52/64 €
♦ Modern ♦ Formal ♦

In den Rustwat adds an exotic touch to metropolitan Rotterdam with its thatched roof, history dating back to the 16C and an idyllic setting close to an arbo-
retum. The food here is anything but traditional, offering contemporary-style
dishes with an abundance of ingredients and cooking methods.

XX **IVY** (Francois Geurds) [AC] [P] [VISA] [CO]

⅜ *Lloydstraat 204 ⊠ 3024 EA – ℰ (0 10) 425 05 20 – www.restaurantivy.nl*
– closed first 3 weeks July, late December-early January, Sunday and Monday
Rest – Menu 35 € (lunch), 78/146 € – Carte 77/142 €   *Plan I* **B2**
♦ Innovative ♦ Fashionable ♦

This exclusive and spectacular restaurant could hardly be more impressive. Chef
François Geurds' style of cooking is not only clever and highly innovative, but
also demonstrates a convincing combination of flavours. Therefore, it comes
as no surprise to learn that this culinary genius learnt his craft at The Fat Duck.
Contemporary decor in the dining room.
→ Oester, foie en rabarber. Duif, foie en kersensorbet. Macadamia, foie,
vanille en olijfolie.

XX **Zeezout** 🛣 AC VISA ⓐ AE

Westerkade 11b ⊠ *3016 CL – ℰ (0 10) 436 50 49*
– www.restaurantzeezout.nl
– closed Sunday lunch and Monday   **E3**
Rest – Menu 30 € (lunch), 45/68 € – Carte 50/62 €
♦ Fish and seafood ♦ Formal ♦

Situated in the marine quarter of one of the world's most important ports, it's no surprise that this restaurant focuses on fish, fish… and more fish. Stylish decor, plus a riverside terrace overlooking the harbour.

XX **Wereldmuseum** ⴲ AC VISA ⓐ AE

Willemskade 25 ⊠ *3016 DM – ℰ (0 10) 270 71 85*
– www.wereldmuseum.nl
– closed 30 April, 29 July-19 August, 24 December-2 January, Saturday lunch and Monday   **F3**
Rest – Menu 30 € (lunch), 43/80 € – Carte 50/71 €
♦ Modern ♦ Elegant ♦

This restaurant is set in a stylish dining room and reflects the feel of the city. The chef presents an ambitious and interesting style of cooking inspired by modern, Mediterranean cuisine. Impeccable service. Reservations are advised.

XX **Asian Glories** AC ⬄ VISA ⓐ AE ⓞ

Leeuwenstraat 15 ⊠ *3011 AL – ℰ (0 10) 411 71 07*
– closed Wednesday   **F1**
Rest – Menu 32/49 € – Carte 30/59 €
♦ Chinese ♦ Family ♦ Friendly ♦

It is hard not to be a fan of chef Fan's authentic, high quality Chinese cuisine, which focuses on the culinary traditions of Canton and Szechuan. Specialities on the menu include the delicious dim sum, a type of Oriental dumpling that is served either boiled or fried. Parking is available opposite the restaurant.

XX **Restaurant 70** – Hotel Parkhotel ⬰ ⴲ AC ⬄ P VISA ⓐ AE ⓞ

Westersingel 70 ⊠ *3015 LB – ℰ (0 10) 436 36 11*
– www.parkhotelrotterdam.nl
– closed 1-15 August and Sunday dinner   **E2**
Rest – Menu 29 € (lunch)/35 € – Carte 40/59 €
♦ International ♦ Formal ♦

Restaurant 70 is a cosy, informal hotel-restaurant offering French-Mediterranean cooking. In the summer, the courtyard garden is a delightful place to sit.

X **Huson** 🛣 AC VISA ⓐ AE

Scheepstimmermanslaan 14 ⊠ *3011 BS – ℰ (0 10) 413 03 71*
– www.huson.info
– closed last week July-first 2 weeks August, 28 December-12 January, Saturday lunch and Sunday   **E3**
Rest – Menu 32 € (lunch)/35 € – Carte approx. 40 €
♦ Modern ♦ Brasserie ♦

This trendy restaurant has a lively, lounge-bar ambience and the same friendly buzz as the nearby harbour. The menu features the sort of ultra-modern, brasserie-style dishes you would expect from such a contemporary venue.

X **De Engel** AC ⬄ VISA ⓐ AE

Eendrachtsweg 19 ⊠ *3012 LB – ℰ (0 10) 413 82 56*
– www.restaurant-deengel.nl
– closed 30 April, 1 January, Saturday lunch and Sunday   **E2**
Rest – Menu 29 € (lunch), 46/73 €
♦ Modern ♦ Friendly ♦

The relaxed ambience and hint of old-fashioned grandeur in this welcoming townhouse make it the perfect place for an enjoyable meal. Seasonal cuisine with a French flavour and numerous options on the menu.

NETHERLANDS - ROTTERDAM

✗ **Lux**   ☞ VISA ⓪

's-Gravendijkwal 133 ⊠ 3021 EK – ℰ (0 10) 476 22 06
– www.restaurantlux.nl
– closed 25, 26 and 31 December-1 January   *Plan I* **B2**
Rest – *(dinner only)* Carte 26/39 €
♦ Italian ♦ Brasserie ♦

This trendy version of a traditional Italian restaurant has retained the lively, friendly ambience and good, local food of a typical trattoria, while creating a contemporary and up-to-date ambience.

✗ **Oliva**   ☞ AC ⇔ VISA ⓪

Witte de Withstraat 15a ⊠ 3012 BK – ℰ (0 10) 412 14 13
– www.restaurantoliva.nl
– closed 25 December-1 January   **E2**
Rest – *(dinner only)* Menu 34/44 € – Carte 27/47 €
♦ Italian ♦ Bistro ♦

Lively Italian restaurant with a loft-inspired ambience. Open kitchen, simple menu and daily specials chalked on a board.

✗ **Rosso**   AC ⇔ VISA ⓪ AE

Van Vollenhovenstraat 15 (access via Westerlijk Handelsterrein)
⊠ 3016 BE – ℰ (0 10) 225 07 05 – www.rossorotterdam.nl
– closed first 2 weeks August, Sunday and Monday   **E3**
Rest – *(dinner only until 11pm)* Menu 50/75 € – Carte 44/65 €
♦ Modern ♦ Fashionable ♦

Enjoy the intimate atmosphere in the wine bar at this restaurant, or treat yourself to fine cuisine in the contemporary-style dining room. And if you are looking for a night out, then Club Rosso is the perfect venue.

✗ **New York** – Hotel New York   ≤ 🕭 ⇔ VISA ⓪ AE

Koninginnenhoofd 1 (Wilhelminapier) ⊠ 3072 AD – ℰ (0 10) 439 05 25
– www.hotelnewyork.nl   **F3**
Rest – *(open until 11pm)* Carte 24/65 €
♦ Traditional ♦ Friendly ♦

A historic grand café with a post-industrial look. Modern menu with brasserie dishes that change twice a year, in summer and winter.

ENVIRONS OF ROTTERDAM   *Plan I*

✗✗✗✗ **De Zwethheul** (Mario Ridder)   ≤ 🕭 AC ⇔ P VISA ⓪ AE ⓪
⌘⌘   Rotterdamseweg 480 (beside the canal in Zweth) ⊠ 2636 KB Schipluiden
– ℰ (0 10) 470 41 66 – www.zwethheul.nl
– closed 2 weeks construction industry holidays, 26 December-3 January,
Saturday lunch and Monday   **A1**
Rest – Menu 53 € (lunch), 85/145 € – Carte 80/172 € ⌂
♦ Innovative ♦ Design ♦

This remodelled former inn (1685) serves dazzling contemporary cuisine and select wines. Breathtaking views of the boats from the dining room and the shaded waterside terrace.
➜ Brioche van ganzenlever met truffel en perigordjus. Likkepot van noordzeekrab met kaviaar en knolselderie. Reerug met amandel en sinaasappel, jus met peperkoek.

✗ **'t Stadhuys**   🕭 ⇔ VISA ⓪ AE ⓪

Grote Markt 1a ⊠ 3111 NG Schiedam – ℰ (0 10) 426 55 33
– www.restauranthetstadhuys.nl   **A2**
Rest – Menu 33/60 € – Carte 40/55 €
♦ Modern ♦ Brasserie ♦

A pretty baroque building, once Schiedam's town hall. Tavern-style meals at noon and gastronomic dishes for dinner. Terrace on the square. Popular "proeverij" menu (six small à la carte dishes).

→ **AREA:**
323 878 km² (125 049 sq mi).

→ **POPULATION:**
5 033 675 inhabitants. Density = 16 per km².

→ **CAPITAL:**
Oslo.

→ **CURRENCY:**
Norwegian Krone (kr or NOK) divided into 100 øre.

→ **GOVERNMENT:**
Constitutional parliamentary monarchy with single-chamber Parliament (since 1945).

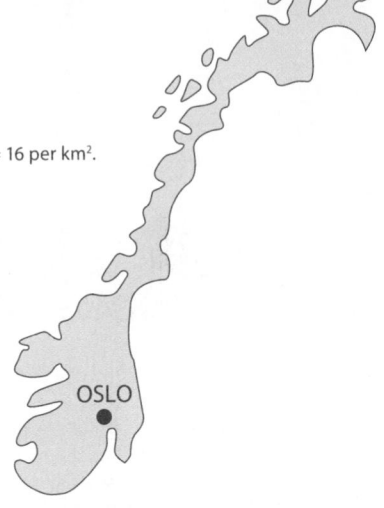

→ **LANGUAGES:**
Norwegian has two written variants: Bokmål - influenced by Danish and spoken by 80% of the population - and Nynorsk (New Norwegian). Sami is the language of the Sami people in the far north. English is widely spoken.

→ **PUBLIC HOLIDAYS:**
New Year's Day (1 Jan); Maundy Thursday and Good Friday (late Mar/Apr); Easter Monday (late Mar/Apr); Labor Day (1 May); Constitution Day (17 May); Ascension Day (May); Whit Monday (late May/June); Christmas Day (25 Dec); St Stephen's Day (26 Dec).

→ **LOCAL TIME:**
GMT+1 hour in winter and GMT +2 hours in summer.

→ **CLIMATE:**
Temperate northern maritime with cold winters and mild summers (Oslo: January -4°C; July 16°C). Colder interior, fairly high precipitation in the coastal regions.

→ **EMERGENCY:**
Police ☏ **112**; Medical Assistance ☏ **113**; Fire Brigade ☏ **110**. (Dialling **112** within any EU country will redirect your call and contact the emergency services.)

→ **ELECTRICITY:**
230 volts AC, 50Hz; 2 round pin sockets.

→ **FORMALITIES:**
Travellers from the European Union (EU), Switzerland, Iceland and the main countries of North and South America need a national identity card or passport (America: passport required) to visit Norway for less than three months (tourism or business purpose). For visitors from other countries a visa may be required, in addition to a passport, especially for those wishing to stay for longer than three months. We advise you to check with your embassy before travelling.

OSLO
OSLO

Population: 613 285

Oslo has a lot going for it – and one slight downside: it's one of the world's most expensive cities. It also ranks high when it comes to its standard of living, however, and its position at the head of Oslofjord, surrounded by steep forested hills, is hard to match for drama and beauty. It's a charmingly compact place to stroll round, particularly in the summer, when the daylight hours practically abolish the night and, although it may lack the urban cool of some other Scandinavian cities, it boasts its fair share of trendy clubs and a raft of Michelin starred restaurants. There's a real raft, too: Thor Hyerdahl's famous Kon-Tiki – one of the star turns in a city that loves its museums.

Oslo's uncluttered feel is enhanced by parks and wide streets and, in the winter, there are times when you feel you have the whole place to yourself. Drift into the city by boat and land at the smart harbour of Aker Brygge; to the west lies the charming Bygdøy peninsula, home to museums permeated with the smell of the sea. Northwest is Frogner, with its famous sculpture park, the place where locals hang out on long summer days. The centre of town, the commercial hub, is Karl Johans Gate, bounded at one end by the Royal Palace and at the other by the Cathedral, while further east lie two trendy multi-cultural areas, Grunerlokka and Grønland, the former also home to the Edvard Munch Museum.

OSLO IN...

→ **ONE DAY**
Aker Brygge, Karl Johans Gate, Oslo Opera House.

→ **TWO DAYS**
Akershus, Astrup Fearnley Museum, ferry trip to Bygdøy.

→ **THREE DAYS**
Vigeland Park, Holmenkollen Ski Jump, Grunerlokka, Munch Museum.

PRACTICAL INFORMATION

ARRIVAL-DEPARTURE

 Oslo International Airport, Gardermoen, is 47km north of the city. The train station is located beneath the terminal and the Flytoget train takes 19min to Oslo's central station. The Express Bus to Galleri bus terminal leaves every 20min and takes 45min.

GETTING AROUND

The integrated transport system comprises bus, tram or metro and you can obtain single or day tickets. You can get an electronic 'Tourist Card' for a small deposit from a tourist information centre and hire one of the many free Citybike scheme bicycles parked at different points around the city. You pay a toll if you arrive by car. The Oslo Pass, which covers the transport system and entry to all museums, is valid for one to three days and is available from the Information Centre next to Oslo Central Station.

CALENDAR HIGHLIGHTS

February–March
Winter Night Festival (classical music), Oslo International Church Music Festival.

May
St Hallvard's Day (concerts and theatre productions).

June
Norwegian Wood Rock Festival.

August
International Jazz Festival;

November
Oslo World Music Festival.

December
Nobel Peace Prize awarded (parades and festivities).

EATING OUT

Oslo has a very vibrant dining scene, albeit one that is somewhat expensive, particularly if you drink wine. The cooking can be quite classical and refined but there are plenty of restaurants offering more innovative menus too. What is in no doubt is the quality of the produce used, whether that's the ever-popular game or the superlative shellfish, which comes from very cold water, giving it a clean, fresh flavour. Classic Norwegian dishes often include fruit, such as lingonberries with venison. Lunch is not a major affair; most prefer just a snack or sandwich at midday while making dinner the main event of the day. You'll find most diners are seated by 7pm and are offered a 6, 7 or 8 course menu which they can reduce at their will, with a paired wine menu alongside. It doesn't have to be expensive, though. Look out for konditoris (bakeries) where you can pick up sandwiches and pastries, and kafeterias which serve substantial meals at reasonable prices. Service is a strength; staff are generally very polite, speak English and are fully versed in the menu.

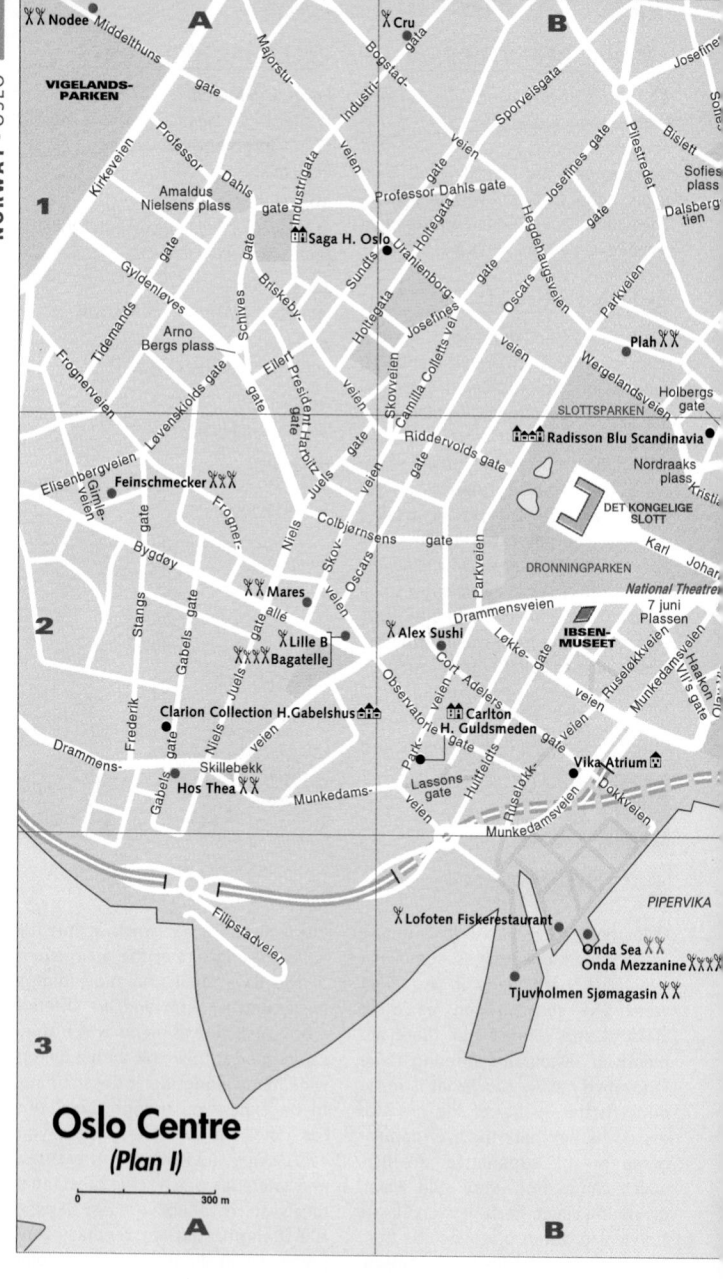

X X Nodee Middelthuns

X Cru gata

B

Josefine

VIGELANDS-
PARKEN

Majorstu-

Bogstad-

veien

Sporveisgata

Bislett

Kirkeveien

Professor Dahls

gate

Industrigata

Industri-

veien

Josefines gate

Pilestredet

Sofies
plass

Dalsberg
tien

1

Amaldus
Nielsens plass

gate

Professor Dahls gate

Uranienborg

Holtegata

Oscars

gate

Parkveien

Gyldenløves

gate

Schives

Briskeby-

Sundts

Josefines veien

gate

Saga H. Oslo

Arno
Bergs plass

Ellert

President Harbitz

gate

Skovveien

Holtegata

Camilla Colletts veien

Oscars

veien

Plah X X

Frognerveien

Tidemands

gate

Løvenskiolds

gate

Niels

gate

Riddervolds gate

Weigelandsveien

Holbergs
gate

SLOTTSPARKEN

Radisson Blu Scandinavia

Elisenbergveien

Gimle-

Feinschmecker X X X

Colbjørnsens

gate

Nordraaks
plass

Kristia

veien

Frogner-

Skov-

gate

DET KONGELIGE
SLOTT

Bygdøy

Stangs

gate

Gabels gate

Mares X X

Niels Juels gate

Oscars
veien

Lille B

X X X X Bagatelle

Alex Sushi X

Drammensveien

Løkke-

gate

Parkveien

DRONNINGPARKEN

Karl

Johan

National Theatre

7 juni
Plassen

IBSEN-
MUSEET

Ruseløkkveien

Haakon
VII's gate

Munkedamsveien

Frederik

gate

Niels
Juels

veien

Clarion Collection H.Gabelshus

Carlton

H. Guldsmeden

Cort Adelers

gate

Observatorie

Ruseløkk-

veien

Vika Atrium

Drammens-

Gabels

gate

Skillebekk

Hos Thea X X

Munkedams-

Lassons
gate

Park-

Hltfeldts

gate

Ruseløkk-

Munkedamsveien

Dokkveien

PIPERVIKA

Filipstadveien

X Lofoten Fiskerestaurant

Onda Sea X X
Onda Mezzanine X X X X

Tjuvholmen Sjømagasin X X

3

Oslo Centre
(Plan I)

0   300 m

A   B

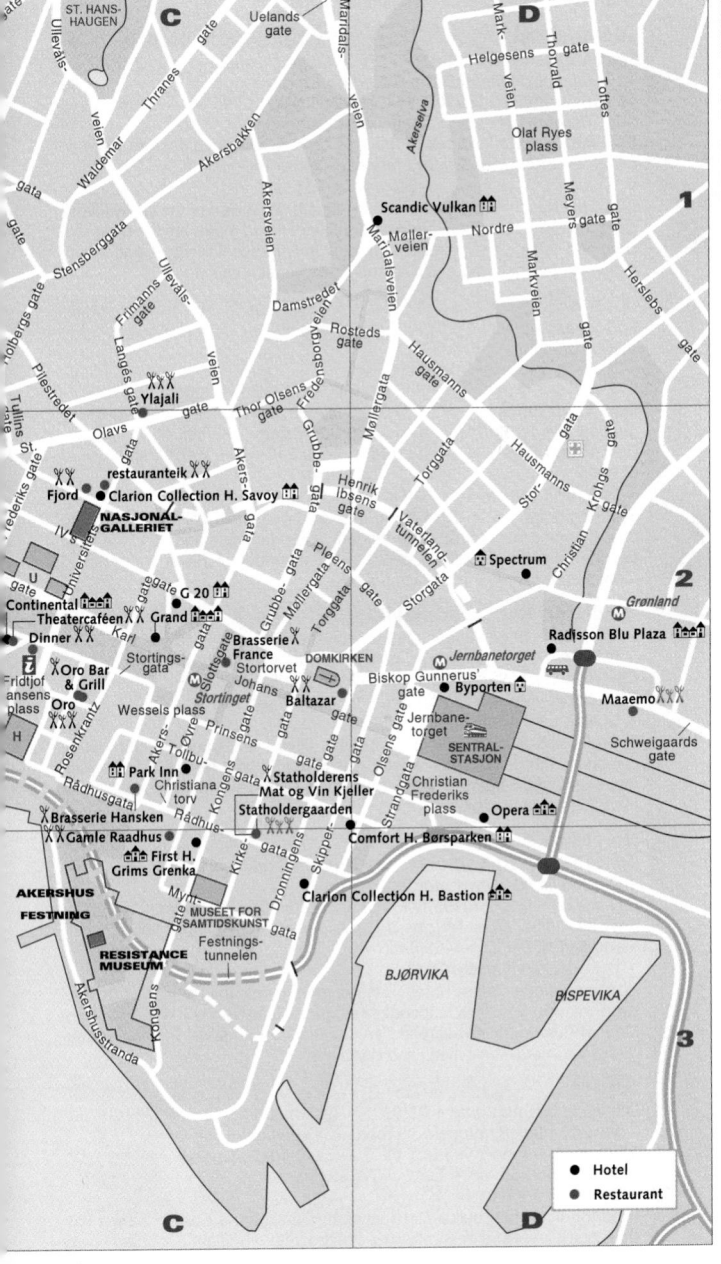

ST. HANS-HAUGEN

Scandic Vulkan

Olaf Ryes plass

Ylajali

restauranteik

Fjord
Clarion Collection H. Savoy

NASJONAL-GALLERIET

Spectrum

Continental
Theatercaféen
Dinner
G 20
Grand
Brasserie France
Oro Bar & Grill
Oro
Stortinget
Stortorvet
Johans
DOMKIRKEN
Baltazar
Radisson Blu Plaza
Grønland
Jernbanetorget
Biskop Gunnerus' gate
Byporten
Maaemo
Park Inn
Christiana torv
Statholderens Mat og Vin Kjeller
SENTRAL-STASJON
Schweigaards gate
Brasserie Hansken
Gamle Raadhus
Statholdergaarden
Christian Frederiks plass
Opera
First H. Grims Grenka
Comfort H. Børsparken
MUSEET FOR SAMTIDSKUNST
Clarion Collection H. Bastion
AKERSHUS FESTNING
RESISTANCE MUSEUM
BJØRVIKA
BISPEVIKA

● Hotel
● Restaurant

635

NORWAY - OSLO

Continental 🔥 🕭 🅰️ ↯ 🛜 🦺 🛌 💳 🟠 🔴

Stortingsgaten 24-26 ⊠ 0117 – Ⓜ National Theatret – ℰ 22 82 40 00
– www.hotelcontinental.no – Closed Christmas **C2**
152 rm – ♦1465/2735 NOK ♦♦1640/3300 NOK, ⊊ 195 NOK – 3 suites
Rest *Theatercaféen* – see restaurant listing
Rest *Restauranteik Annen Etage* – ℰ 22 54 79 70 (closed 4 weeks summer, Easter, Christmas, Sunday and Monday) (dinner only) Menu 395 NOK ⸙
♦ Grand Luxury ♦ Traditional ♦ Classic ♦
Set by the National Theatre and run by the 4th generation of the family. Classical lounge-bar and bright, modern bedrooms; Deluxe rooms are the most spacious and come with bathrobes and sofas. Very personal service. Large restaurant with opulent baroque styling and inventive set menu.

Grand 🔥 🕭 🕭 🖾 🚭 rm, 🅰️ ↯ rm, 🛜 🦺 🛌 💳 🟠 🔴

Karl Johans Gate 31 ⊠ 0159 – Ⓜ Stortinget – ℰ 23 21 20 00
– www.grand.no
– Closed 25 December and 1 January **C2**
292 rm ⊊ – ♦1450/2675 NOK ♦♦1895/2925 NOK – 9 suites
Rest *Julius Fritzner* – ℰ 23 21 25 70 (closed July, Easter, Christmas and Sunday) (dinner only) Menu 615/990 NOK – Carte 585/895 NOK
Rest *Grand Café* – ℰ 23 21 20 18 – Menu 310/470 NOK – Carte 395/650 NOK
♦ Grand Luxury ♦ Traditional ♦ Classic ♦
Imposing hotel built in 1874; the guest areas and grand ballrooms reflecting this. Charming bedrooms: some modern, some feminine and others in belle époque style. Smart wellness centre. Contemporary cuisine in stylish dining room. Brasserie dishes in characterful café.

Radisson Blu Scandinavia ⋸ 🔥 🕭 🖾 🚭 🅰️ ↯ rm, 🛜 🦺

Holbergsgate 30 ⊠ 0166 – Ⓜ National Theatret 🛌 💳 🟠 🔴
– ℰ 23 29 30 00 – www.radissonblu.com/scandinaviahotel-oslo
496 rm ⊊ – ♦895/2695 NOK ♦♦895/2995 NOK – 1 suite **B2**
Rest *Enzo* – Menu 385/450 NOK – Carte 540/705 NOK
♦ Luxury ♦ Modern ♦
One of Oslo's tallest buildings. Vast lobby filled with boutiques, and lounge complete with pianist. Pale wood-furnished bedrooms have a Scandinavian feel. 21st floor bar boasts magnificent fjord and city views. Minimalist restaurant offers Mediterranean menu.

Radisson Blu Plaza ⋸ 🔥 🕭 🖾 🚭 🅰️ ↯ 🛜 🦺 🛌

Sonja Henies Plass 3 ⊠ 0134 – Ⓜ Jernbanetorget 💳 🟠 🔴
– ℰ 22 05 80 00 – www.radissonblu.com **D2**
657 rm ⊊ – ♦1295/2995 NOK ♦♦1295/2995 NOK – 19 suites
Rest *34* – ℰ 22 05 80 34 (closed Easter and Sunday) (dinner only) Menu 545 NOK – Carte 465/945 NOK
♦ Business ♦ Modern ♦
Northern Europe's tallest hotel, boasting more rooms than any other in Oslo. Large marble lobby with lounge and bar; extensive conference facilities. Modern 'Business' level bedrooms are the most comfortable. Top floor restaurant offers international menu and city views.

Opera ⋸ 🔥 🕭 🚭 🅰️ ↯ rm, 🛜 🦺 💳 🟠 🔴

Dronning Eufemias gate 4 ⊠ 0191 – Ⓜ Jernbanetorget – ℰ 24 10 30 00
– www.thonhotels.no/opera – Closed 22 December-3 January
478 rm ⊊ – ♦995/1995 NOK ♦♦1250/2250 NOK – 2 suites **D2**
Rest – Menu 385 NOK – Carte 440/525 NOK
♦ Business ♦ Modern ♦
Imposing, light-stone building in front of the Opera House, close to the sea. Spacious guest areas and classically styled bedrooms with bright décor and cherry wood furnishings. Classical restaurant boasts huge windows and panoramic views; international menu and buffet-style lunches.

NORWAY - OSLO

First H. Grims Grenka [K̲] 🛜 [VISA] 🅾🅾 AE ⓪

Kongensgate 5 ✉ *0152 –* Ⓜ *Stortinget –* ☏ *23 10 72 00*
– www.firsthotels.no/grimsgrenka **C3**
55 rm ⌶ *–* ♦*1495/2595 NOK* ♦♦*1695/2795 NOK –* **10 suites**
Rest *Madu – (closed Sunday and Monday) (dinner only)* Menu 475/735 NOK
♦ Business ♦ Stylish ♦

Smart design hotel set between the main shopping street and the castle. Boutique interior with a trendy bar and superb summer terrace. Well-equipped 'Summer' and 'Winter' bedrooms afford atrium and outside views respectively; all come with glass shower rooms. Innovative cuisine uses fine Nordic ingredients.

Clarion Collection H. Bastion *without rest* ♭♪ 🗌 [K̲] ↳ 🛜

Skippergaten 5 ✉ *0152 –* Ⓜ *Jernbanetorget* 🕭 [VISA] 🅾🅾 AE ⓪
– ☏ *22 47 77 00 – www.hotelbastion.no*
– Closed Easter and Christmas **C3**
94 rm ⌶ *–* ♦*780/1990 NOK* ♦♦*980/2190 NOK –* **5 suites**
♦ Business ♦ Modern ♦

On the edge of the city, close to the port. Charming English lobby, cosy lounge and friendly staff. Bedrooms vary in size and are furnished in either a classic or a modern style; the latter decorated in silver and purple hues.

Clarion Collection H. Gabelshus *without rest* ⚘ 🌐 🗌

Gabelsgate 16 ✉ *0272 –* ☏ *23 27 65 00* ↳ 🛜 🕭 🅿 [VISA] 🅾🅾 AE ⓪
– www.choicehotels.no/no094
– Closed 22 December-2 January and 23 March-2 April **A2**
113 rm ⌶ *–* ♦*790/1990 NOK* ♦♦*1090/2240 NOK –* **1 suite**
♦ Traditional ♦ Classic ♦

Beautiful red-brick, ivy-covered house in smart, residential neighbourhood. Peaceful atmosphere with classical, wood-furnished lounge and library. Charming bedrooms offer pleasing contrast between the old and new; some overlook the garden.

G 20 *without rest* ♿ ↳ 🛜 [VISA] 🅾🅾 AE ⓪

Grensen 20 ✉ *0180 –* Ⓜ *Stortinget –* ☏ *22 01 64 00*
– www.rica-hotels.com
– Closed 19 December-1 January **C2**
96 rm ⌶ *–* ♦*765/1865 NOK* ♦♦*965/2115 NOK*
♦ Business ♦ Chain hotel ♦ Modern ♦

Hip, new-build hotel with a smart glass façade, set in the heart of the city among shops and restaurants. Compact, modern interior. Pale wood furnished bedrooms feature flat screens, desks and iPod docks; those to the rear are quieter.

Saga H. Oslo *without rest* ↳ 🛜 🅿 [VISA] 🅾🅾 AE

Eilert Sundstgate 39 ✉ *0259 –* ☏ *22 55 44 90 – www.sagahoteloslo.no*
– Closed 23 December-2 January and Easter **B1**
47 rm ⌶ *–* ♦*795/1550 NOK* ♦♦*995/1750 NOK*
♦ Townhouse ♦ Historic ♦ Stylish ♦

Late Victorian townhouse with a smart, contemporary interior; set in a quiet suburb of the city. Bedrooms vary in size but most are very spacious; they have bold feature walls and modern facilities, including compact, shower-only ensuites.

Carlton H. Guldsmeden *without rest* 🗌 ↳ 🛜 [VISA] 🅾🅾 AE

Parkveien 78 ✉ *0254 –* Ⓜ *National Theatret –* ☏ *23 27 40 00*
– www.hotelguldsmeden.com
– Closed 2 weeks Christmas **B2**
53 rm ⌶ *–* ♦*695/1695 NOK* ♦♦*895/1895 NOK*
♦ Townhouse ♦ Business ♦ Rustic ♦

A relaxing, design-led hotel close to the Royal Palace. Bohemian-style bedrooms boast iMacs, and wood furniture made from sustainable sources. Unique breakfasts offer organic, fair trade, largely local produce. Friendly, approachable staff.

Scandic Vulkan ≤ 🛏 ᏝᏖ ᏖᏖ rm, 🖥 ↳ 🛜 ᏕᏖ 𝘝𝘐𝘚𝘈 ⓒ AE ⓞ

Maridalsveien 13 ⊠ 0178 – ℰ 21 05 71 00
– www.scandichotels.com/vulkan   **D1**
149 rm ⌑ – †690/1990 NOK ††890/2190 NOK
Rest V – Menu 175/349 NOK – Carte 265/525 NOK
♦ Business ♦ Chain hotel ♦ Design ♦
New-build hotel on the site of a former silver mine, in an up-and-coming part of the city. Modern bedrooms have shower-only bathrooms; ask for an external-facing room as they have full length windows. Light, airy restaurant with trendy bar and deli. Accessible menus and daily Norwegian specials.

Clarion Collection H. Savoy ↳ 🛜 𝘝𝘐𝘚𝘈 ⓒ AE ⓞ

Universitetsgata 11 ⊠ 0164 – ⓜ National Theatret – ℰ 23 35 42 00
– www.nordichotels.no   **C2**
93 rm ⌑ – †670/2080 NOK ††870/2780 NOK
Rest restauranteik⊛ – see restaurant listing
♦ Business ♦ Classic ♦
Next to the National Gallery, in a building dating back to 1850. Small, modern lobby and elegant attic room. Variously sized bedrooms: some are decorated in a classic style; others are more contemporary, with 'action photos' as focal points.

Comfort H. Børsparken without rest ᏝᏖ ᏖᏖ ↳ 🛜 ᏕᏖ

Tollbugata 4 ⊠ 0152 – ⓜ Jernbanetorget   𝘝𝘐𝘚𝘈 ⓒ AE ⓞ
– ℰ 22 47 17 17 – www.nordicchoicehotels.no   **C/D2**
248 rm ⌑ – †680/1780 NOK ††880/1980 NOK
♦ Business ♦ Chain hotel ♦ Functional ♦
Centrally-located, with pleasant gardens in front. Modern guest areas. Uniformly decorated bedrooms with contemporary furnishings and designer lighting – front rooms have Opera House views.

Park Inn without rest ᏖᏖ 🖥 ↳ 🛜 ᏕᏖ 𝘝𝘐𝘚𝘈 ⓒ AE ⓞ

Øvre Slottsgate 2c ⊠ 0157 – ⓜ Stortinget – ℰ 22 40 01 00
– www.parkinn.com/hotel-oslo   **C2**
118 rm ⌑ – †995/1395 NOK ††1095/1595 NOK
♦ Business ♦ Chain hotel ♦ Functional ♦
Converted apartment block near Karl Johans Gate. Modern lobby with red leather armchairs. Good-sized, functional bedrooms with pale wood furniture and modern lighting; top floor rooms have balconies.

Byporten without rest ᏖᏖ ↳ 🛜 🚭 𝘝𝘐𝘚𝘈 ⓒ AE ⓞ

Jernbanetorget 6 ⊠ 0154 – ⓜ Jernbanetorget – ℰ 23 15 55 00
– www.scandichotels.com/byporten   **D2**
235 rm ⌑ – †690/2190 NOK ††890/2390 NOK – 5 suites
♦ Business ♦ Modern ♦
Set inside a shopping arcade, with bus and train stops nearby. Small boutique and seating area in lobby. Smart Scandinavian-style bedrooms with modern furnishings and excellent soundproofing.

Vika Atrium without rest ᏝᏖ 🐕 ↳ 🛜 ᏕᏖ 𝘝𝘐𝘚𝘈 ⓒ AE ⓞ

Munkedamsveien 45 ⊠ 0250 – ⓜ National Theatret – ℰ 22 83 33 00
– www.thonhotels.no/vikaatrium   **B2**
79 rm ⌑ – †895/1925 NOK ††1095/2125 NOK
♦ Business ♦ Functional ♦
Located in a large office block by the harbour, in a redeveloped area. Bright lobby and glass-walled breakfast room. Bedrooms are set over 7 floors and have smart, modern styling and marble bathrooms.

Spectrum without rest ᏖᏖ ↳ 🛜 𝘝𝘐𝘚𝘈 ⓒ AE ⓞ

Brugata 7 ⊠ 0186 – ⓜ Grønland – ℰ 23 36 27 00
– www.thonhotels.no/spectrum – Closed Christmas   **D2**
151 rm ⌑ – †695/1225 NOK ††845/1425 NOK
♦ Business ♦ Functional ♦
Budget hotel in a pedestrianised shopping street, close to the station. Unassuming exterior conceals a modern lobby and spacious breakfast room. Light-hued bedrooms offer basic comforts.

XxXxX
✿
Bagatelle
🔲 ⇇ ⇵ 🅅🅸🅂🅰 ⓒⓞ 🅰🅴 ⓞ

Bygdøy Allé 3 ✉ *0257* – Ⓜ *National Theatret* – 𝒞 *22 44 40 40*
– www.bagatelle.no
– Closed 23 December-10 January, Easter, Monday and Sunday **A2**
Rest *– (dinner only) (booking essential)* Menu 1350 NOK ✿
♦ Modern ♦ Design ♦ Formal ♦
This legendary restaurant offers a charmingly discreet entrance, an impressive wine cellar and an elegant, art-filled dining room, with formal service and a tranquil atmosphere. Contemporary cooking uses top quality produce and the intricate, creative, well-crafted dishes allow the flavours to shine through.
➜ Foie gras terrine. Lamb roulade and sweetbreads. Chocolate Nemesis.

XxXxX
✿
Onda Mezzanine
🔲 ⇇ ⇵ 🅅🅸🅂🅰 ⓒⓞ 🅰🅴 ⓞ

Stranden 30 ✉ *0250* – 𝒞 *47 66 07 00* – *www.onda.no*
– Closed 21 December-6 January, Easter and Sunday **B3**
Rest *– (booking essential)* Menu 1595 NOK (dinner) – Carte 755/2085 NOK
♦ French ♦ Intimate ♦ Elegant ♦
Stylish, comfortable, fine dining restaurant on upper level gallery of the 3-restaurant Onda complex, with open kitchen, serene ambience and structured service. Classic, French-based cooking utilises the finest produce; prices reflect this.

XxXx
✿✿
Maaemo (Esben Bang)
🔲 ⇇ ⇵ 🅅🅸🅂🅰 ⓒⓞ 🅰🅴

Schweigaardsgate 15B (entrance via staircase) ✉ *0191* – Ⓜ *Grønland*
– 𝒞 91 99 48 05 – *www.maaemo.no*
– Closed Easter, Christmas, Sunday, Monday and public holidays
Rest *– (dinner only) (booking essential) (set menu only)* **D2**
Menu 1600 NOK
♦ Innovative ♦ Design ♦ Fashionable ♦
Sleek, modern, professionally run restaurant; 3 walls of glass ensure a bright feel and a mezzanine-level kitchen allows diners to view chefs at work. Nine course, no-choice menu: intricate, original, visually stimulating dishes offer wonderful taste and texture combinations. Attentive, knowledgeable service.
➜ Langoustine from Frøya with last year's pine. Spring chicken with elderflower and grilled wheat grass. Butter from Røros.

XxXx
✿
Statholdergaarden (Bent Stiansen)
⇵ 🅅🅸🅂🅰 ⓒⓞ 🅰🅴 ⓞ

Rådhusgate 11, (entrance on Kirkegate) ✉ *0151* – Ⓜ *Stortinget*
– 𝒞 22 41 88 00 – *www.statholdergaarden.no*
– Closed 24 March-2 April, 1,9,17 and 20 May, 14 July-6 August, 23 December-2 January and Sunday **C2**
Rest *– (dinner only) (booking essential)* Menu 995 NOK – Carte 935/1095 NOK ✿
Rest Statholderens Mat og Vin Kjeller – see restaurant listing
♦ Modern ♦ Formal ♦ Elegant ♦
Attractive 17C house in the heart of the city, boasting an elegant interior with a wonderfully ornate stucco ceiling and chandeliers. Expertly rendered, classically based cooking with modern touches; highly seasonal menu lists every ingredient used. Service strikes a good balance between friendly and formal.
➜ Langoustine with mushroom samosa and bell pepper cream. Reindeer fillet with hazelnut crunch chanterelles. Coast berry soufflé, pickled apricots and cardamom strudel.

XxX
Feinschmecker
🔲 ⇵ 🅅🅸🅂🅰 ⓒⓞ 🅰🅴 ⓞ

Balchensgate 5 ✉ *0265* – 𝒞 *22 12 93 80* – *www.feinschmecker.no*
– Closed 8 July-3 August, Christmas, Easter, and Sunday **A2**
Rest *– (dinner only)* Carte 785/885 NOK ✿
♦ Traditional ♦ Classic ♦ Neighbourhood ♦
Long-standing restaurant with charming chef-owner and a loyal local following; it has the feel of a Scandinavian country cabin, with wood, warm fabrics and a welcoming atmosphere. Well-presented, classically based cooking; friendly service.

XXX Oro
☒☒ ⇔ ☒☒ ☒☒ ☒☒ ☒

Tordenskioldsgate 6A ⊠ 0160 – ⓜ *Stortinget – ℰ 23 01 02 40*
– www.ororestaurant.no
– Closed 22 December-4 January, 7-31 July and Sunday   **C2**
Rest *– (booking essential)* Menu 795 NOK ⅋
♦ International ♦ Design ♦ Elegant ♦
Warm, elegant restaurant not far from the City Hall; its cosy, modern interior
decorated in pale tones. Classically based, seasonal set menus cooked in open
rear kitchen. Lively atmosphere and attentive, formal service.

XXX Ylajali
☒☒ ☒☒ ☒☒ ☒☒ ☒

St Olavs plass 2 ⊠ 0165 – ⓜ *National Theatret – ℰ 22 20 64 86*
– www.ylajali.no
– Closed 4 weeks summer, Easter, Christmas and Sunday   **C2**
Rest *– (dinner only) (booking essential)* Menu 1100 NOK
♦ Innovative ♦ Intimate ♦
In a former apartment building, with high ceilings and a mosaic floor; its name a
reference to a character from the novel 'Hunger'. Set menus of 6 or 9 courses;
visually impressive dishes offer innovative combinations. Attentive service.

XX Onda Sea
⪉ ☒ ☒☒ ↯ ☒☒ ☒☒ ☒

Stranden 30 ⊠ 0250 – ℰ 45 50 20 00 – www.onda.no
– Closed 23-26 December   **B3**
Rest – Menu 595 NOK (dinner) – Carte 435/655 NOK
Rest Onda Asia *– (closed Sunday)* Menu 445 NOK – Carte 485/570 NOK
♦ Fish and seafood ♦ Fashionable ♦ Design ♦
An eye-catching, sea shell shaped building: home to three restaurants under
one roof. Stylish, tactile Onda Sea is the largest, with wonderful views over the
marina and fjord through tinted windows and from the decked terrace. Beauti-
fully fresh seafood is simply cooked; service is polite and friendly. Onda Asia
offers oriental food cooked in an open kitchen.

XX Gamle Raadhus
☒☒ ☒☒ ☒☒ ☒

Nedre Slottsgate 1 ⊠ 0157 – ⓜ *Stortinget – ℰ 22 42 01 07*
– www.gamleraadhus.no
– Closed Easter, 3 weeks July, 22 December-3 January and Sunday
Rest – Menu 445 NOK (dinner) – Carte 435/680 NOK   **C3**
♦ Traditional ♦ Rustic ♦
Brightly painted house dating from 1641. Charming, antique-filled interior with
a library, an open-fired lounge and a lovely terrace. Lunch served in the bar;
classical dinners, in the traditional dining room.

XX Fjord
☒☒ ☒☒ ☒☒ ☒☒ ☒

Kristian Augusts Gt. 11 ⊠ 0164 – ⓜ *National Theatret – ℰ 22 98 21 50*
– www.restaurantfjord.no
– Closed 4 weeks summer, Easter and Christmas   **C2**
Rest *– (dinner only) (set menu only)* Menu 445 NOK
♦ Fish and seafood ♦ Design ♦ Fashionable ♦
Contemporary restaurant opposite the National Gallery. Dimly lit interior with
open kitchen, blue glass walls and buffalo horns on the ceiling. Weekly set
menu of flavoursome seafood dishes.

XX Dinner
☒☒ ⇔ ☒☒ ☒☒ ☒☒ ☒

Stortingsgata 22 ⊠ 0161 – ⓜ *National Theatret – ℰ 23 10 04 66*
– www.dinner.no
– Closed Christmas and Easter   **C2**
Rest – Menu 348/699 NOK – Carte 388/427 NOK
♦ Chinese ♦ Design ♦
Set on the central square, close to the National Theatre. Black façade masks a
modern, split-level interior. Cooking focuses on the Sichuan and Cantonese
regions, with dim sum offered at lunch.

NORWAY - OSLO

XX **Nodee** ⌂ AC ⇔ VISA ⊙ AE ⓪

Middelthunsgt 25 ✉ *0368 –* ⓜ *Majorstuen – ☏ 22 93 34 50*
– www.nodee.no
– Closed Christmas and Easter   **A1**
Rest – Menu 168/750 NOK – Carte 489/868 NOK
◆ Asian ◆ Fashionable ◆
Smart, modern restaurant with lounge, sushi bar and large pavement terrace, set opposite Vigeland Sculpture Park. Extensive menu of Chinese, Japanese and Thai dishes. Knowledgeable service.

XX **Tjuvholmen Sjømagasin** ⌂ ⇔ VISA ⊙ AE ⓪

Tjuvholmen Allé 14 ✉ *0252 – ☏ 23 89 77 77 – www.sjomagasinet.no*
– Closed Easter, 21 December-6 January and Sunday   **B3**
Rest – Menu 325/475 NOK – Carte 375/735 NOK
◆ Fish and seafood ◆ Design ◆
Vast, split-level restaurant with a lounge, an open kitchen, a lobster tank at the entrance and even a fish shop; its name means 'island of the thieves' and 'sea store'. 5 course seafood menu; some fjord views.

XX **restauranteik** – at Clarion Collection H. Savoy AC ⇔
⊛
Universitetsgata 11 ✉ *0164 –* ⓜ *National Theatret*   VISA ⊙ AE ⓪
– ☏ 22 36 07 10 – www.restauranteik.no
– Closed 4 weeks summer, Easter, Christmas, Sunday and Monday
Rest – *(dinner only) (set menu only)* Menu 375 NOK   **C2**
◆ Modern ◆ Fashionable ◆
Modern, minimalist dining room with an open kitchen, a glass-walled wine cellar and a friendly atmosphere. The larger tables are towards the front, with more intimate banquette seating to the rear. The set menu of inventive, international cuisine changes every Tuesday.

XX **Mares** AC VISA ⊙ AE ⓪

Skovveien 1 ✉ *0257 – ☏ 22 54 89 80 – www.mares.no*
– Closed 28 March-3 April, 7 July-6 August, 22 December-2 January and Sunday
Rest – *(bookings advisable at dinner)* Menu 295/475 NOK   **A2**
– Carte 473/645 NOK
◆ French ◆ Neighbourhood ◆ Brasserie ◆
Welcoming neighbourhood restaurant with deli and fish shop; bright, modern and open-plan with white furniture and a slightly industrial feel. French-based menus with Spanish and Italian influences; tasty dishes rely on classic combinations.

XX **Theatercaféen** – at Continental Hotel ⇔ VISA ⊙ AE ⓪

Stortingsgaten 24-26 ✉ *0117 –* ⓜ *National Theatret – ☏ 22 82 40 50*
– www.theatercafeen.no
– Closed July, Christmas and Easter   **C2**
Rest – Menu 340/645 NOK – Carte 525/764 NOK
◆ Traditional ◆ Brasserie ◆
Prestigious Oslo institution. Charming Viennese 'grand café' interior with pillars, black banquettes and art nouveau lighting. Elaborate lunchtime sandwiches make way for ambitious dinner menu.

XX **Baltazar** ⌂ AC VISA ⊙ AE ⓪

Dronningensgate 27 ✉ *0154 –* ⓜ *Jernbanetorget – ☏ 23 35 70 60*
– www.baltazar.no
– Closed July, Christmas, Easter and Sunday   **C2**
Rest – *(dinner only)* Menu 795 NOK – Carte 625/1070 NOK ⌘
Rest *Enoteca* – Carte 323/915 NOK
◆ Italian ◆ Friendly ◆
First-floor restaurant under the arches of a 19C brick market beside the cathedral. Smart interior with designer chairs and open kitchen. Two set menus of innovative, Italian dishes. Informal, ground floor eatery boasts a terrace and glass-covered wine cellar.

XX **Hos Thea**   `VISA` `CO` `AE` `O`

Gabelsgate 11 ✉ *0272 –* 𝒞 *22 44 68 74 – www.hosthea.no*
– Closed July, Easter and Christmas   **A2**
Rest *– (dinner only)* Menu 485/685 NOK – Carte 450/635 NOK
♦ Italian ♦ Family ♦
Small neighbourhood restaurant with black façade, set in a charming residential area. Beige colour scheme and views into the kitchen. Concise menu of Mediterranean dishes; good homemade bread.

XX **Plah**   `HiFi` `AC` `⇔` `VISA` `CO` `AE` `O`

Hegdehaugsveien 22 ✉ *0167 –* 𝒞 *22 56 43 00 – www.plah.no*
– Closed Christmas, Easter and Sunday   **B1**
Rest *– (dinner only)* Carte 445/565 NOK
♦ Thai ♦ Neighbourhood ♦ Friendly ♦
Welcoming neighbourhood restaurant offering tasty Westernised dishes – its name means 'fish' in Thai. Go for one of the good value tasting menus with wines available to match. Attractive summer terrace and knowledgeable, friendly service.

X **Lille B**   `AC` `½` `VISA` `CO` `AE` `O`
🙂
Bygdøy Allé 3 ✉ *0257 –* ⓜ *National Theatret –* 𝒞 *22 44 40 40*
– www.bagatelle/lilleb.no
– Closed Easter, 23 December-10 January and Sunday   **A2**
Rest *– (booking advisable)* Menu 190/220 NOK – Carte 275/625 NOK
♦ French ♦ Design ♦ Cosy ♦
Smart, compact brasserie with well-stocked bar, leather banquettes and striking modern artwork. Reasonably priced menus offer hearty, filling, flavoursome cooking, which mixes French brasserie dishes with Norwegian favourites. Interesting choice of wines by the glass or flaske. Service is bright and breezy.

X **Statholderens Mat og Vin Kjeller** – at Statholdergaarden

Rådhusgate 11 (entrance from Kirkengaten)   `VISA` `CO` `AE` `O`
✉ *0151 –* ⓜ *Stortinget –* 𝒞 *22 41 88 00 – www.statholdergaarden.no*
– Closed 24 March-2 April, 1,9,17 and 20 May, 7 July-7 August, 23 December-2 January, Sunday and Monday   **C2**
Rest *– (dinner only)* Menu 625 NOK – Carte 569/640 NOK
♦ Norwegian ♦ Rustic ♦ Simple ♦
Three-roomed vaulted cellar set below, and run by the owner of, Statholdergaarden. Relaxed inner with large entrance wall filled with wine bottles. 10 course 'themed' set menu or à la carte.

X **Cru**   `VISA` `CO` `AE` `O`

Ingelbrecht, Knudssønsgt 1 ✉ *0365 –* 𝒞 *23 98 98 98 – www.cru.no*
– Closed 3 weeks July and Christmas   **B1**
Rest *– (dinner only)* Menu 395/745 NOK – Carte 427/527 NOK 🍷
♦ Traditional ♦ Wine bar ♦ Trendy ♦
Trendy, informal wine bar offering over 800 bins. Downstairs boasts an open fire and is great for a traditional dish or an aperitif. Upstairs displays light wood furniture and a daily menu of gutsy local dishes with the odd delicate touch.

X **Oro Bar & Grill**   `VISA` `CO` `AE` `O`
🙂
Tordenskioldsgate 6A ✉ *0160 –* ⓜ *Stortinget –* 𝒞 *23 01 02 40*
– www.ororestaurant.no
– Closed 7-31 July, 22 December-4 January and Sunday   **C2**
Rest *–* Menu 299 NOK (lunch) – Carte 313/593 NOK
♦ Modern ♦ Trendy ♦ Fashionable ♦
Easy-going counterpart to adjoining Oro restaurant, featuring a central bar and polished wood tables. Lunch offers a set selection of earthy dishes. Grills feature in the evening, alongside daily specials – try the house dishes of gravadlax and Iberico pork.

Brasserie Hansken ⇌ VISA ◎ AE ⑪

Akersgate 1 ⊠ *0158 –* Ⓜ *Stortinget –* ✆ *22 42 60 88*
– www.brasseriehansken.no
– Closed 23 March-3 April, 15 July-5 August, 22 December-3 January
and Sunday   C2
Rest – Menu 225/495 NOK – Carte 415/655 NOK
◆ Modern ◆ Elegant ◆
Traditional, wood-furnished brasserie with large terrace, not far from City Hall.
Counter with bar stools to one side; tables set at black banquettes on the
other. Contemporary brasserie menu.

Brasserie France 斋 AC VISA ◎ AE ⑪

Øvre Slottsgate 16 ⊠ *0157 –* Ⓜ *Stortinget –* ✆ *23 10 01 65*
– www.brasseriefrance.no
– Closed 23 December-2 January and Sunday   C2
Rest – *(dinner only and light lunch Saturday)* Menu 350 NOK
– Carte 395/600 NOK
◆ French ◆ Brasserie ◆
Lively French brasserie in pedestrianised shopping street. Main restaurant and
terrace on ground floor; private rooms above. Brasserie classics and an 'eat-as-
much-as-you-like' pastry trolley.

Alex Sushi ⇌ VISA ◎ AE ⑪

Cort Adelers Gate 2 ⊠ *0254 –* Ⓜ *National Theatret –* ✆ *22 43 99 99*
– www.alexsushi.no
– Closed Easter and Christmas   B2
Rest – *(dinner only)* Menu 355/1240 NOK
– Carte 395/705 NOK
◆ Japanese ◆ Design ◆ Minimalist ◆
Glass-fronted, two-floored Japanese restaurant in a busy location; its bright inte-
rior made of wood, steel and glass. Eat at the unique, boat-shaped sushi bar; go
for the set 'white', 'red' or 'black' menus, which offer the best value.

Lofoten Fiskerestaurant ⇐ 斋 VISA ◎ AE ⑪

Stranden 75 ⊠ *0250 –* ✆ *22 83 08 08*
– www.lofotenfiskerestaurant.no
– Closed 22 December-2 January   B3
Rest – Menu 625 NOK (dinner) – Carte 560/675 NOK
◆ Fish and seafood ◆ Brasserie ◆ Fashionable ◆
Modern, fjord-side restaurant in bright, maritime colours, offering lovely views
from its large windows and terrace. Traditional seafood menu. Semi-open kit-
chen and lobster tank on display.

ENVIRONS OF OSLO

AT GREFSEN **North : 10 km by Ring 3**

Grefsenkollen ⇐ 斋 ⇌ VISA ◎ AE

Grefsenkollveien 100 ⊠ *0490 –* ✆ *22 79 70 60*
– www.grefsenkollen.no
– Closed July, 23 December-2 January, Sunday dinner and Monday
Rest – *(booking essential at dinner)* Menu 550 NOK (dinner)
– Carte lunch approx. 440 NOK
◆ Modern ◆ Friendly ◆
Large wooden chalet with spacious terrace and lovely views over the city and
fjord. Characterful, open-fired restaurant with dark wood furnishings, modern
counter and open kitchen; smaller room at the end open for lunch. Evening
set menu comes with wine pairings.

AT OSLO AIRPORT Northeast : 45 km by E 6 at Gardermoen

Clarion Oslo Airport 🕭 🕅 ఈ ఈ rm, 🛜 🔊 **P** 🌇 ⓪ 🄰🄴 ⓪

Hans Gaarderveg 15 (West : 6 km) ✉ *2060* – ℰ *63 94 94 94*
– www.clarionosloairport.no
430 rm 🖵 – 👤680/1990 NOK 👫880/2190 NOK – 2 suites
Rest – Carte 409/465 NOK
♦ Business ♦ Functional ♦

Typical, two-storey Norwegian house, accessed from the airport by a shuttle bus. Modern Scandinavian bedrooms in pale hues. One of the largest conference capacities in the country. Bar and open-fired lounges with live bands. Buffet meals in traditional restaurant.

AT HOLMENKOLLEN Northwest : 10 km by Bogstadveien, Sørkedalsveien and Holmenkollveien

Holmenkollen Park 🕭 ≤ 🕭 🕭 🕅 🖵 ఈ 🔟 ఈ rm, 🛜 🔊 **P**

Kongeveien 26 ✉ *0787* – ⓜ *Holmenkollen* 🚗 🌇 ⓪ 🄰🄴 ⓪
– ℰ 22 92 20 00 – www.holmenkollenparkhotel.no
– Closed Christmas and New Year
325 rm 🖵 – 👤835/2575 NOK 👫1385/2825 NOK – 11 suites
Rest *De Fem Stuer* – ℰ *22 92 27 34* – Menu 425/585 NOK
♦ Traditional ♦ Personalised ♦

Impressive 1894 red wood building once used as a sanitorium for TB patients. Mix of classic and modern bedrooms with good comfort levels; some with city or fjord views. Extensive conference and wellness facilities. Buffet lunch is followed by a choice of two set evening menus.

POLAND
POLSKA

WARSAW ●

● Cracow

→ **Area:**
312 677 km²
(120 725 sq mi).

→ **Population:**
38 538 447 inhabitants.
Density = 123 per km².

→ **Capital:**
Warsaw.

→ **Currency:**
Polish Złoty (zl or PLN).

→ **Government:**
Parliamentary republic (since 1990).
Member of European Union since
2004.

→ **Language:**
Polish.

→ **Public holidays:**
New Year's Day (1 Jan); Easter
Monday (late Mar/Apr); Labor Day
(1 May); Constitution Day (3 May);
Pentecost Monday (late May/June);
Corpus Christi (late May/June);
Assumption of the Virgin Mary (15
Aug); All Saints' Day
(1 Nov); Independence Day (11 Nov);
Christmas Day (25 Dec); Boxing Day
(26 Dec).

→ **Local Time:**
GMT+1 hour in winter and GMT
+2 hours in summer.

→ **Climate:**
Temperate continental with
cold winters and warm summers
(Warsaw: January -2°C; July 20°C).

→ **Emergency:**
Police ✆ **997;**
Medical Assistance ✆ **999;**
Fire Brigade ✆ **998.**
(Dialling **112** within any
EU country will redirect your
call and contact the emergency
services.)

→ **Electricity:**
230 volts AC, 50Hz; 2 round pin
sockets.

→ **Formalities:**
Travellers from the European Union
(EU), Switzerland, Iceland and
the main countries of North and
South America need a national
identity card or passport (America:
passport required) to visit Poland
for less than three months (tourism
or business purpose). For visitors
from other countries a visa may be
required, in addition to a passport,
especially for those wishing to
stay for longer than three months.
We advise you to check with your
embassy before travelling.

645

WARSAW
WARSZAWA

Population: 1 714 400

Céline Lecardonnel/Fotolia.com

When UNESCO added Warsaw to its World Heritage list, it was a fitting seal of approval for its inspired rebuild, after eighty per cent of the city was destroyed during World War II. Using plans of the old city, architects painstakingly rebuilt the shattered capital throughout the 1950s, until it became an admirable mirror image of its former self. Now grey communist era apartment blocks sit beside pretty, pastel-coloured aristocratic buildings, their architecture ranging from Gothic to baroque, rococo to secession.

Nestling against the River Vistula, the Old Town was established at the end of the 13C, around what is now the Royal Castle, and a century later the New Town, to the north, began to take shape. To the south of the Old Town runs 'The Royal Route', so named because, from the late middle ages, wealthy citizens built summer residences with lush gardens along these rural thoroughfares. Continue southwards and you're in Lazienki Park with its palaces and pavilions, while to the west lie the more commercial areas of Marshal Street and Solidarity Avenue, once the commercial heart of the city. The northwest of Warsaw was traditionally the Jewish district, until it was destroyed during the war; today it has been redeveloped with housing estates and the sobering Monument to the Ghetto Heroes.

WARSAW IN...

→ **ONE DAY**
Royal Castle, Warsaw History Museum, National Museum, Lazienki Park.

→ **TWO DAYS**
Monument to the Ghetto Heroes, Saxon Gardens, concert at Grand Theatre or Philharmonic Hall.

→ **THREE DAYS**
The Royal Route, Marshal Street, Solidarity Avenue, Wilanow.

ARRIVAL-DEPARTURE

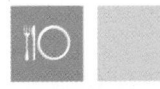 Warsaw Frederic Chopin Airport is 10km southwest. Bus 175 or 188 takes 20min. Trains run every 10-12min and take 25min. If travelling by taxi, ensure you take one from the rank outside arrivals.

Warsaw Modlin Airport is 40km northwest. Modlinbus operate a regular service to the Central Station that takes 60min.

GETTING AROUND

If you are visiting the central attractions, go on foot; otherwise, take the metro, bus or tram. The RUCH kiosks are often closed in the evenings and at weekends, so it's best to buy tickets in a pack of ten. A flat rate fare for all single journeys applies, and one-day, seven-day and family tickets are also available. The Warsaw Tourist Card is available from tourist information offices; it entitles you to free travel on public transport, free admission to 21 museums, and discounts in some shops, restaurants and leisure centres. (All museums offer free entry on a Sunday.)

CALENDAR HIGHLIGHTS

April
Beethoven Easter Festival.

June
Chopin concerts in Lazienki Park.

June/July
Mozart Festival.

July-August
Summer Jazz Days.

October
International Film Festival (WIFF), Baroque Opera Festival, Jazz Festival.

November
Piano Festival.

EATING OUT

The centuries-old traditional cuisine of Warsaw was influenced by neighbouring Russia, Ukraine and Germany, while Jewish dishes were also added to the mix. Over the years there has been a growing sophistication to the cooking and a lighter, more contemporary style has become evident, with time-honoured classics - such as the ubiquitous pierogi (dumplings with various fillings) and the assorted pork dishes - having been updated with flair. These are accompanied, of course, by chilled Polish vodka, which covers a bewildering range of styles. Warsaw also has a more global side, with everything from stalls selling falafel to restaurants serving Vietnamese, and a large Italian business community has ensured there are a good number of Italian restaurants too. Asian food is also well represented, with Japanese restaurants being particularly plentiful. Stylised settings are popular, such as a burghers' houses or vaulted cellars; wherever you eat, check that VAT has been included within the prices (it's not always) and add a ten per cent tip.

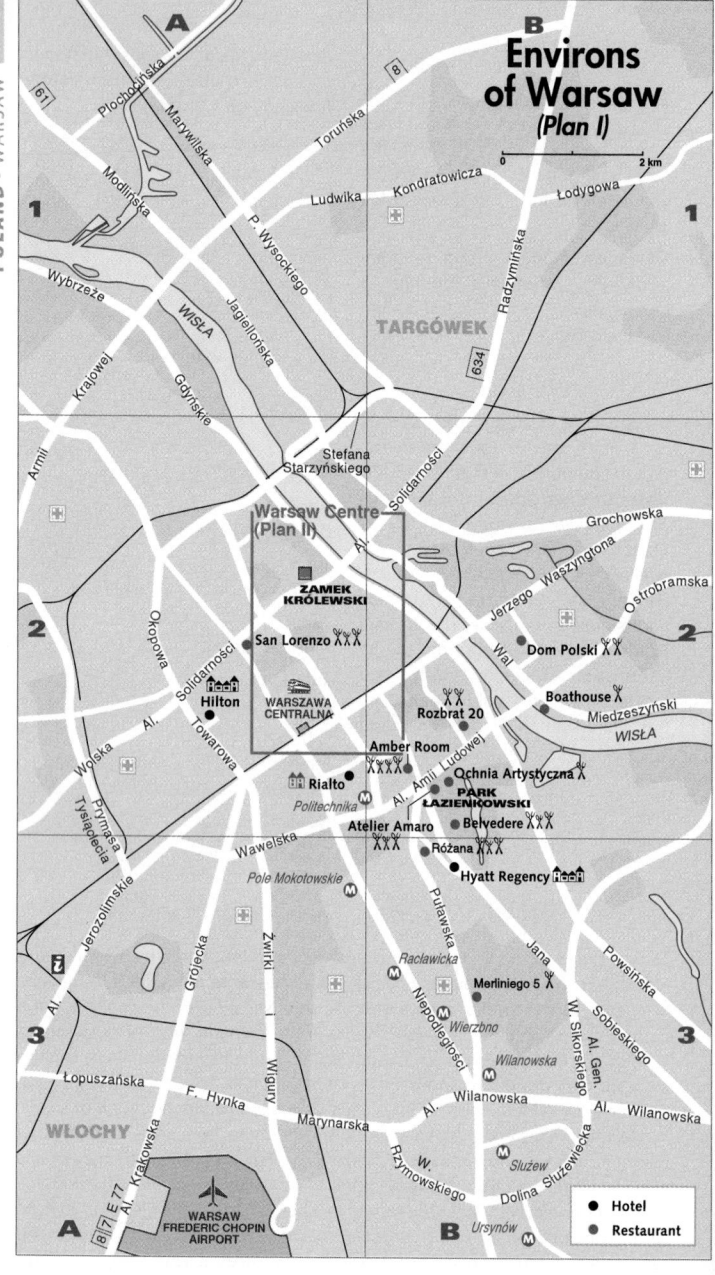

Environs
of Warsaw
(Plan I)

0   2 km

A

B

1

TARGÓWEK

Płochocińska

Toruńska

Ludwika

Kondratowicza

Łodygowa

Modlińska

Marywilska

P. Wysockiego

Wybrzeże

WISŁA

Jagiellońska

Radzymińska

634

Armii

Krajowej

Gdyńskie

Stefana
Starzyńskiego

Solidarności

Grochowska

Warsaw Centre
(Plan II)

Jerzego Waszyngtona

Ostrobramska

2

**ZAMEK
KRÓLEWSKI**

San Lorenzo

Okopowa

Solidarności

Hilton

**WARSZAWA
CENTRALNA**

Towarowa

Wał

Dom Polski

Boathouse

Międzeszyński

WISŁA

Rozbrat 20

Amber Room

Ochnia Artystyczna

Al. Armii Ludowej

**PARK
ŁAZIENKOWSKI**

Wolska

Prymasa
Tysiąclecia

Rialto

Politechnika

Atelier Amaro

Belvedere

Różana

Wawelska

Pole Mokotowskie

Hyatt Regency

Jerozolimskie

Grójecka

Żwirki

Puławska

Racławicka

Merliniego 5

Jana

W. Sikorskiego

Al. Gen.

Sobieskiego

Powsińska

3

Niepodległości

Wierzbno

Wilanowska

Łopuszańska

F. Hynka

Wigury

Marynarska

Al. Wilanowska

Al. Wilanowska

WŁOCHY

E 77

Al. Krakowska

Rzymowskiego

W.

Dolina Służewiecka

Służew

Ursynów

**WARSAW
FREDERIC CHOPIN
AIRPORT**

A

B

● Hotel
● Restaurant

POLAND - WARSAW

Intercontinental
ul. Emilii Plater 49 ✉ *00 125 –* Ⓜ *Centrum*
– ℰ (022) 328 8888 – www.warsaw.intercontinental.com **C2**
328 rm – †262/831 PLN **††**262/831 PLN, ⌷ 91 PLN – 76 suites
Rest *Platter by Karol Okrasa* – see restaurant listing
Rest *Downtown* – ℰ *(022) 328 8740 (closed Sunday dinner)*
Menu 109 PLN (buffet) – Carte 75/280 PLN
♦ Grand Luxury ♦ Business ♦ Modern ♦
Striking high-rise hotel in central location. Smart guest areas include a modern lobby, lounge and clubby bar. Impressive health and leisure club on 43rd and 44th floors boasts fantastic views. Comfy, contemporary bedrooms. Informal brasserie with accessible menu.

Hyatt Regency
ul. Belwederska 23 ✉ *00 761 – ℰ (022) 558 12 34*
– www.warsaw.regency.hyatt.com *Plan I* **B3**
231 rm ⌷ *–* †340/1600 PLN **††**400/1660 PLN – 19 suites
Rest *Venti Tre* – ℰ *(022) 558 10 94* – Carte 112/166 PLN
♦ Luxury ♦ Business ♦ Modern ♦
Contemporary hotel with impressive open-plan lobby and glass-roofed lounge-bar. Spacious bedrooms boast top quality furniture, smart bathrooms and excellent facilities. Large, split-level restaurant offers extensive Mediterranean menu and wood-fired specialities.

Hilton
ul. Grzybowska 63 ✉ *00 844 – ℰ (022) 356 55 55 – www.hilton.com*
303 rm – †250/1100 PLN **††**250/1100 PLN, ⌷ 88 PLN *Plan I* **A2**
– 11 suites
Rest *Meza* – Carte 115/250 PLN
♦ Business ♦ Modern ♦
Large, modern hotel in the financial district. Bright atrium houses shops and lounge-bar; extensive business and leisure facilities include a casino. Well-equipped, contemporary bedrooms and smart club lounge. Informal restaurant serves Mediterranean cuisine.

Sheraton
ul. Boleslawa Prusa 2 ✉ *00 493 – ℰ (022) 450 6100 – www.sheraton.pl*
336 rm – †324/1350 PLN **††**324/1350 PLN, ⌷ 99 PLN **D2**
– 14 suites
Rest *Oriental* – ℰ *(022) 450 67 05 (closed August and Sunday dinner)*
(dinner only and Sunday lunch) Menu 120 PLN – Carte 118/408 PLN
Rest *Olive* – ℰ *(022) 450 67 06 (lunch only)* Carte 140/220 PLN
♦ Luxury ♦ Business ♦ Classic ♦
Spacious corporate hotel on the historic Three Cross Square, with large, open-plan lobby and leather-furnished lounge-bar. Good conference and leisure facilities. Modern, well-equipped bedrooms. Asian dishes in Oriental. Mediterranean menu and buffet lunches in Olive.

Le Meridien Bristol
ul. Krakowskie Przedmiescie 42-44 ✉ *00 325 – ℰ (022) 551 10 00*
– www.lemeridien.pl **D1**
175 rm – †450/1350 PLN **††**530/1350 PLN, ⌷ 110 PLN – 31 suites
Rest *Marconi* – ℰ *(022) 551 11 832* – Carte 90/210 PLN
♦ Grand Luxury ♦ Classic ♦
Early 20C hotel next to the Presidential Palace, boasting an elegant, marble-floored reception and impressive columned bar. Good-sized, luxurious bedrooms with a high level of facilities and marble bathrooms. Smart restaurant offers a Mediterranean-based menu.

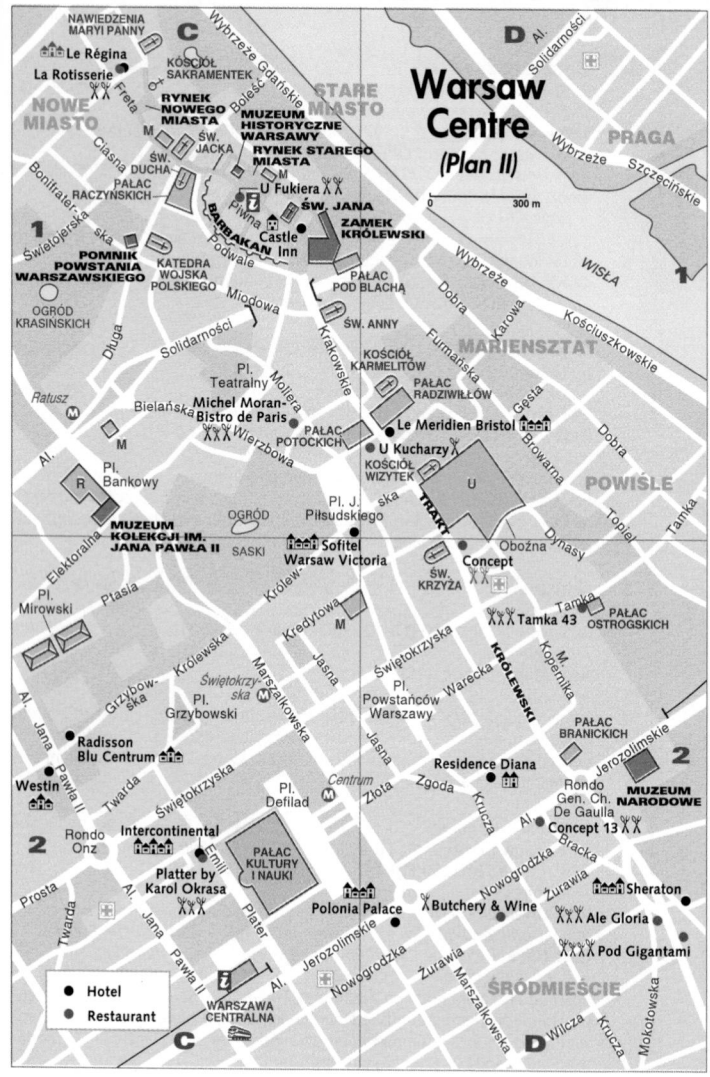

Warsaw Centre
(Plan II)

0   300 m

NAWIEDZENIA
MARYI PANNY
Le Régina
La Rotisserie
KOŚCIÓŁ
SAKRAMENTEK
STARE
MIASTO
NOWE
MIASTO
Wybrzeże Gdańskie
Boles.
Freta
RYNEK
NOWEGO
MIASTA
MUZEUM
HISTORYCZNE
WARSZAWY
PRAGA
ŚW.
JACKA
ŚW.
DUCHA
Wybrzeże
Szczecińskie
RYNEK STAREGO
MIASTA
Ciasna
KOŚCIÓŁ
RACZYŃSKICH
PAŁAC
RACZYŃSKICH
U Fukiera
ŚW. JANA
Boniftaterska
Długa
Świętojerska
BARBAKAN
Piwna
Castle
Inn
ZAMEK
KRÓLEWSKI
WISŁA
POMNIK
POWSTANIA
WARSZAWSKIEGO
KATEDRA
WOJSKA
POLSKIEGO
Podwale
PAŁAC
POD BLACHĄ
OGRÓD
KRASIŃSKICH
Miodowa
ŚW. ANNY
Dobra
Furmańska
Karowa
Kościuszkowskie
Długa
Solidarności
KOŚCIÓŁ
KARMELITÓW
MARIENSZTAT
Pl.
Teatralny
Moliera
PAŁAC
RADZIWIŁŁÓW
Gęsta
Ratusz
Bielańska
Michel Moran-
Bistro de Paris
Wierzbowa
PAŁAC
POTOCKICH
Krakowskie
Le Meridien Bristol
Dobra
Browarna
POWIŚLE
Wierzbowa
U Kucharzy
KOŚCIÓŁ
WIZYTEK
Tamka
Pl.
Bankowy
OGRÓD
Pl. J.
Piłsudskiego
ska
TRAKT
U
Topiel
Dynasy
MUZEUM
KOLEKCJI IM.
JANA PAWŁA II
SASKI
Sofitel
Warsaw Victoria
ŚW.
KRZYŻA
Oboźna
Concept
Elektoralna
Pl.
Mirowski
Ptasia
Królew.
Kredytowa
Tamka 43
PAŁAC
OSTROGSKICH
Kopernika
KRÓLEWSKI
Grzybow-
ska
Królewska
Świętokrzy-
ska
Marszałkowska
Jasna
Świętokrzyska
Pl.
Powstańców
Warszawy
Warecka
PAŁAC
BRANICKICH
Jerozolimskie
Pl.
Grzybowski
Jasna
Radisson
Blu Centrum
Centrum
Residence Diana
Rondo
Gen. Ch.
De Gaulla
MUZEUM
NARODOWE
Westin
Twarda
Świętokrzyska
Zgoda
Złota
Krucza
Concept 13
Bracka
Al. Jana Pawła II
2
Rondo
Onz
Intercontinental
PAŁAC
KULTURY
I NAUKI
Emilii
Pl.
Defilad
Al.
Nowogrodzka
Żurawia
Sheraton
Prosta
Twarda
Platter by
Karol Okrasa
Plater
Polonia Palace
Butchery & Wine
Ale Gloria
Pod Gigantami
Jerozolimskie
Nowogrodzka
Żurawia
Marszałkowska
ŚRÓDMIEŚCIE
Mokotowska
WARSZAWA
CENTRALNA
Wilcza
Krucza

● Hotel
● Restaurant

650

POLAND - WARSAW

Polonia Palace

al. Jerozolimskie 45 ✉ *00 692* – **Ⓜ** *Centrum* – 𝒞 *(022) 318 2800*
– *www.poloniapalace.com*
203 rm – 🛏260/915 PLN 🛏🛏260/915 PLN, 🍴 80 PLN – 3 suites
Rest Strauss – 𝒞 *(022) 318 2834 (closed lunch Saturday and Sunday)*
Carte 107/198 PLN

D2

♦ Business ♦ Classic ♦

Striking hotel dating from 1913, set on a busy central street. Elegant interior with lovely glass-roofed lobby, comfy lounge-bar and beautifully ornate, gilded ballroom. Modern, well-equipped bedrooms in browns and creams. International menu in formal restaurant.

Sofitel Warsaw Victoria

ul. Krølewska 11 ✉ *00 065* – **Ⓜ** *Świętokrzyska*
– 𝒞 *(022) 657 80 11* – *www.sofitel.com*
291 rm – 🛏325/995 PLN 🛏🛏325/995 PLN, 🍴 95 PLN – 52 suites
Rest Canaletto – 𝒞 *(022) 657 8382 (closed Sunday) (dinner only)* Carte 127/175 PLN

C1/2

♦ Business ♦ Classic ♦

Set next to Pilsudski Square, overlooking the Saxon Gardens. Spacious, contemporary guest areas feature lots of marble; bedrooms are comfy and well-equipped. Large conference centre and very pleasant leisure suite. Bright restaurant offers Italian-based menus.

Le Régina

ul. Koscielna 12 ✉ *00 218* – 𝒞 *(022) 531 60 00*
– *www.mamaison.com/leregina*
59 rm – 🛏1045/1425 PLN 🛏🛏1045/1425 PLN, 🍴 86 PLN – 2 suites
Rest La Rotisserie – see restaurant listing

C1

♦ Luxury ♦ Design ♦

Stylish boutique hotel housed in a neo-18C building, close to the Old Town. Comfortable, contemporary guest areas in natural hues. Understated bedrooms with smart bathrooms; 'Superior' boast balconies and hand-painted frescoes on the bed heads. Friendly service.

Radisson Blu Centrum

ul. Grzybowska 24 ✉ *00 132* – **Ⓜ** *Świętokrzyska*
– 𝒞 *(022) 321 88 88* – *www.radissonblu.com/hotel-warsaw*
292 rm – 🛏246/2460 PLN 🛏🛏246/2460 PLN, 🍴 80 PLN – 19 suites
Rest Brasserie at Ferdy's – 𝒞 *(022) 321 88 22* – Menu 38/128 PLN
– Carte 85/219 PLN

C2

♦ Business ♦ Modern ♦

Glass-fronted hotel in the business district, boasting state-of-the-art conference facilities. Leather-furnished bar and well-equipped leisure centre. Smart Maritime, Scandinavian or Italian themed bedrooms. All-day brasserie offers Polish and Mediterranean fare.

Westin

al. Jana Pawla II 21 ✉ *00 854* – **Ⓜ** *Świętokrzyska* – 𝒞 *(022) 450 80 00*
– *www.westin.pl*
348 rm – 🛏300/1250 PLN 🛏🛏300/1250 PLN, 🍴 99 PLN – 13 suites
Rest Fusion – 𝒞 *(022) 450 86 31* – Menu 99/165 PLN – Carte 110/227 PLN

C2

♦ Luxury ♦ Business ♦ Modern ♦

Eye-catching modern building on a busy street, boasting an impressive glass atrium and glass lifts. Bright, open-plan lobby and lounge-bar; large conference capacity. Smart, contemporary bedrooms come with good facilities. East meets West in the restaurant.

POLAND - WARSAW

Rialto
ul. Wilcza 73 ⊠ *00 670* – Ⓜ *Politechnika* – ℰ *(022) 584 87 00*
– www.rialto.pl
Plan I **A2**
33 rm – †251/1005 PLN †† 251/1089 PLN, ⊆ 75 PLN – 11 suites
Rest – Menu 92 PLN – Carte 92/147 PLN
♦ Business ♦ Art Deco ♦
Attractive converted townhouse dating back to 1906. Elegant, sympathetically refurbished interior boasts original art deco and art nouveau features. Well-sized, classical bedrooms offer good facilities and boast beautiful marble-floored bathrooms. Intimate cigar room and smart bar. Brasserie serves modern Polish menu.

Residence Diana without rest
ul Chmielna 13a ⊠ *00 021* – Ⓜ *Centrum* – ℰ *(022) 505 9100*
– www.mamaison.com
D2
12 rm – †286/362 PLN †† 286/362 PLN – **34 suites** – †† 362/1555 PLN, ⊆ 54 PLN
♦ Townhouse ♦ Cosy ♦
Set in a quiet courtyard off a busy central shopping street, with a spacious reception and lounge, and a smart, black wood furnished bar. Large, modern bedrooms have small kitchen areas and good facilities.

Castle Inn without rest
Plac Zamkowy, ul Swietojanska 2 ⊠ *00 288* – ℰ *(022) 4250100*
– www.castleinn.pl
C1
22 rm – †177/355 PLN †† 199/438 PLN, ⊆ 35 PLN
♦ Family ♦ Historic ♦
Small 16C property on a cobbled street in the heart of the Old Town – a stone's throw from the castle. Very unique bedrooms: designed by local artists, they range from bohemian to contemporary.

Amber Room
al Ujazdowskie 13 ⊠ *00 567* – ℰ *(022) 523 6664* – *www.amber-room.pl*
– Closed 24-26 December, 1 January, Easter and 11 November
Plan I **B2**
Rest – Menu 79 PLN (lunch) – Carte 123/356 PLN
♦ Modern ♦ Formal ♦
Set in an attractive villa; home to the exclusive 'Round Table of Warsaw' club. Stylish dining room and pleasant summer terrace. Attentive, well-paced service. Modern cooking relies on quality ingredients and displays original touches.

Pod Gigantami
al. Ujazdowskie 24 ⊠ *00 478* – ℰ *(022) 629 23 12* – *www.podgigantami.pl*
– Closed Christmas and Easter
D2
Rest – Menu 40 PLN (lunch) – Carte 118/156 PLN
♦ Modern ♦ Formal ♦
Elegant restaurant in a grand property close to the embassies. Three beautifully styled dining rooms with large, well-spaced tables. Extensive classical menu of Polish and Mediterranean dishes.

Atelier Amaro (Wojciech Amaro)
ऄ
ul. Agrykola 1 ⊠ *00 460* – ℰ *(022) 6285747* – *www.atelieramaro.pl*
– Closed 23 December-3 January, 29 March-3 April, 28 July-11 August, Sunday and lunch Saturday and Monday
Plan I **B2**
Rest – (booking essential) Menu 120/280 PLN
♦ Innovative ♦ Design ♦ Individual ♦
Discreet restaurant with a chic black and white interior, housed in a stylish glass cube overlooking the park. 3, 5 or 8 course 'Moments' menus give little away; cooking is modern and highly original, using carefully sourced and 'forgotten' ingredients in unusual combinations. Meticulous, unobtrusive service.
→ Tomato, cress and pine kernels. Lamb, cumin and chanterelles. Wild strawberry, boletus and chocolate.

POLAND - WARSAW

XXX　Belvedere　🏮 📶 ⇪ ⇄ 🅿 🆚 ⓒ🅰 🅰🅴 ⓞ

Lazienki Park, ul. Agrykoli 1 (entry from ul Parkowa) ✉ 00 460 – ☏ (022)
55 86 700 – www.belvedere.com.pl
– Closed until 1 May for renovations *Plan I* **B2**
Rest – *(booking essential)* Menu 65 PLN (lunch) – Carte 117/224 PLN
♦ Modern ♦ Formal ♦

Impressive Victorian orangery in Lazienki Park. Spacious, split-level dining room
with large arched windows and tables hidden among the foliage. Light, refined
Polish and international dishes.

XXX　Michel Moran - Bistro de Paris　📶 ⇄ 🆚 ⓒ🅰 🅰🅴 ⓞ

pl. Pilsudskiego 9 ✉ 00 078 – Ⓜ *Ratusz* – ☏ *(022) 826 01 07*
– www.restaurantbistrodeparis.com
– Closed Sunday and bank holidays **C1**
Rest – Menu 86/150 PLN – Carte 128/237 PLN
♦ French ♦ Elegant ♦

Smart, marble-floored restaurant in a striking columned building on the edge of
the Old Town. Large menu of Polish and French dishes; the 'Classics' are a hit,
with produce imported from France.

XXX　Platter by Karol Okrasa　– at Intercontinental Hotel　📶 ⇪

ul. Emilii Plater 49 ✉ 00 125 – Ⓜ *Centrum*　🆚 ⓒ🅰 🅰🅴 ⓞ
– ☏ (022) 328 8730 – www.platter.pl
– Closed lunch Saturday, Sunday and bank holidays **C2**
Rest – Menu 105 PLN (lunch) – Carte 150/322 PLN
♦ Modern ♦ Formal ♦

Modern hotel restaurant with smart red and black décor and an open kitchen.
Well-balanced menus change with the seasons and are classically based. Dishes
are sophisticated, refined and flavoursome.

XXX　San Lorenzo　🏮 📶 ⇪ 🆚 ⓒ🅰 🅰🅴

al. Jana Pawla II 36, (1st Floor) ✉ 00 141 – ☏ (022) 652 16 16
– www.sanlorenzo.pl
– Closed 25 December, Easter and 1-3 May *Plan I* **A2**
Rest – Carte 60/250 PLN
♦ Italian ♦ Formal ♦

Imposing classical building with ground floor bistro and wide marble staircase
up to the elegant restaurant. Extensive menus of flavoursome Italian dishes,
with Tuscan influences to the fore.

XXX　Rózana　🏮 📶 ⇪ ⇄ 🆚 ⓒ🅰 ⓞ

ul. Chocimska 7 ✉ 00 791 – ☏ (022) 848 12 25
– www.restauracjarozana.com.pl
– Closed 24 and 31 December *Plan I* **B3**
Rest – *(booking essential)* Menu 42/59 PLN – Carte 77/151 PLN
♦ Traditional ♦ Friendly ♦

Attractive villa with a lovely enclosed terrace and early 20C Polish décor. Deceptively large interior with various rooms set over two floors. Extensive menus of
hearty Polish dishes and homemade desserts.

XXX　AleGloria　📶 ⇄ 🆚 ⓒ🅰 🅰🅴 ⓞ

pl. Trzech Krzyzy 3 ✉ 00 535 – ☏ (022) 584 70 80 – www.alegloria.pl
– Closed 25 December **D2**
Rest – Carte 104/246 PLN
♦ Polish ♦ Design ♦

Boutique shopping arcade with steep steps down to this spacious restaurant;
formerly cellars and stables. Various charming, elegant dining rooms. Extensive
menu of hearty Polish classics.

XXX **Tamka 43**　　　　　　　　　　　AC ↳ VISA ◉ AE ⓪

ul. Tamka 43 (1st Floor) ✉ *00 355* – Ⓜ *Świętokrzyska* – ✆ *(022) 4416234*
– www.tamka43.pl
– Closed Christmas-New Year and Easter　　　　　　　　**D2**
Rest – Menu 49/150 PLN – Carte 85/203 PLN
♦ Modern ♦ Design ♦

Minimalist, industrial styling, with bare brick, concrete and steel girders; floor to ceiling windows at one end overlook the Chopin Museum. Passionate chef brings molecular dining to the city: adventurous cooking uses local ingredients.

XX **Concept**　　　　　　　　　　　AC ↳ ⟲ VISA ◉ AE ⓪

ul Krakowskie Przedmiescie 16-18 ✉ *00 325* – ✆ *(022) 492 7409*
– www.likusrestauracja.pl
– Closed Christmas, Easter, Sunday and bank holidays　　　　　**D1**
Rest – Carte 153/193 PLN
♦ Modern ♦ Design ♦

Characterful restaurant in a columned, glass-roofed room; part of a small complex within the old Central Baths, consisting of a wine shop, a cigar room and a fashion boutique set around a sunken pool. Good-sized menu of refined, modern Mediterranean dishes.

XX **Dom Polski**　　　　　　　　　　🍴 AC ↳ ⟲ VISA ◉ AE ⓪

ul. Francuska 11 ✉ *03 906* – ✆ *(022) 616 24 32*
– www.restauracjadompolski.pl
– Closed 24 December　　　　　　　　　　*Plan I* **B2**
Rest – Menu 70 PLN (lunch) – Carte 75/194 PLN
♦ Traditional ♦ Friendly ♦

Mediterranean-style villa with a lovely terrace to the rear, located in a smart residential area. Various small rooms are set over two floors. Extensive, Polish-based menus offer weekly specials and a refined touch.

XX **Concept 13**　　　　　　　　　🍴 ⅊ AC ↳ ⟲ VISA ◉ AE ⓪

Vitkac (5th Floor), ul. Bracka 9 ✉ *00 501* – Ⓜ *Centrum*
– ✆ (022) 3107373 – www.likusrestauracja.pl
– Closed Christmas, Easter and bank holidays　　　　　　**D2**
Rest – Menu 50 PLN (lunch) – Carte 143/203 PLN
♦ Modern ♦ Design ♦ Fashionable ♦

Spacious restaurant above a luxurious home and fashion store, with stylish black furnishings, a glass-walled kitchen and a smart terrace. Appealing, attractively presented dishes feature some unusual combinations. Wine bar and deli below.

XX **La Rotisserie** – at Le Régina Hotel　　🍴 ⅊ AC ↳ VISA ◉ AE ⓪

ul. Koscielna 12 ✉ *00 218* – ✆ *(022) 531 60 00*
– www.mamaison.com/leregina
– Closed dinner 24 December　　　　　　　　**C1**
Rest – *(booking essential)* Menu 80/224 PLN – Carte 158/232 PLN
♦ Modern ♦ Mediterranean ♦

Small but stylish hotel restaurant in neutral hues, with an arched ceiling, an enclosed courtyard terrace and Mediterranean villa styling. Refined, flavoursome modern dishes have Polish origins.

XX **Rozbrat 20**　　　　　　　　　　　🍴 VISA ◉ AE

ul. Rozbrat 20 ✉ *00 447* – ✆ *(022) 628 0295 – www.rozbrat20.pl*
– Closed Easter, 24-25 December and 1 January　　　*Plan I* **B2**
Rest – Menu 35/85 PLN – Carte 110/158 PLN
♦ International ♦ Brasserie ♦ Neighbourhood ♦

Relaxed, cosy, corner restaurant – popular with the locals – boasting a modern brasserie feel, monochrome décor and floor to ceiling doors opening onto a pavement terrace. Carefully prepared international dishes; efficient service.

POLAND - WARSAW

XX U Fukiera

🛱 AC ↳ ⇄ VISA ◑ AE ①

Rynek Starego Miasta 27 ✉ *00 272 –* ☎ *(022) 831 10 13 – www.ufukiera.pl*
– Closed 24-25 and 31 December   **C1**
Rest – Carte 90/231 PLN
♦ Polish ♦ Rustic ♦
Traditional house with an enclosed courtyard, located on a historic cobbled
square. Spacious interior is made up of several intimate, homely rooms, inclu-
ding a 17C vaulted cellar. Hearty, classical cooking.

X Butchery and Wine

↳ VISA ◑ AE ①

ul. Zurawia 22 ✉ *00 515 –* Ⓜ *Centrum –* ☎ *(022) 5023118*
– www.butcheryandwine.pl
– Closed Christmas, Sunday and public holidays   **D2**
Rest – *(booking essential)* Carte 54/195 PLN ⅋
♦ Meats and grills ♦ Friendly ♦ Trendy ♦
Modern, keenly run bistro in a narrow room with an open kitchen: their mantra
is 'love what you eat' and their customers certainly do. As the name suggests,
the emphasis is on meat – particularly beef – which is served on wooden
boards. The wine is on display in glass cabinets and staff wear butcher's aprons.

X Boathouse

🚘 🛱 ↳ ⇄ P VISA ◑ AE ①

Wal Miedzeszynski 389a ✉ *03 975 –* ☎ *(022) 616 32 23*
– www.boathouse.pl   Plan I **B2**
Rest – Carte 113/131 PLN ⅋
♦ Mediterranean ♦ Rustic ♦
Wooden boathouse with a rustic, two-floored interior complete with a wine bar,
and lawns leading down to the river. Appealing Mediterranean menus; seasonal
themes often feature, such as dedicated shrimp menus.

X Qchnia Artystyczna

🛱 ↳ VISA ◑ AE ①

ul. Jazdow 2 ✉ *00 467 –* ☎ *(022) 625 76 27 – www.qchnia.pl*
– Closed Christmas, Easter and bank holidays   Plan I **B2**
Rest – Carte 90/142 PLN
♦ Modern ♦ Fashionable ♦
Busy, two-roomed restaurant with simple furnishings, in a contemporary art gal-
lery by the Royal Park. Short menus mix classical Polish and international influ-
ences; dishes are full of flavour.

X Merliniego 5

🛱 ↳ VISA ◑ AE ①

ul. Merliniego 5 ✉ *02 511 –* ☎ *(022) 6460849 – www.merliniego5.pl*
– Closed 25 December   **B3**
Rest – *(booking essential at dinner)* Menu 25 PLN (lunch)
– Carte 90/163 PLN
♦ Traditional ♦ Bistro ♦ Neighbourhood ♦
Cosy, passionately run neighbourhood bistro, with low lighting and neat tables
set over two levels. The large menu offers carefully prepared French and Italian
classics, along with the occasional Polish dish. Ingredients are well-sourced.

X U Kucharzy

AC ↳ ⇄ VISA ◑ AE

ul. Ossolinskich 7 ✉ *00 071 –* ☎ *(022) 826 79 36 – www.gessler.pl*
– Closed 24-26 and 31 December   **D1**
Rest – *(booking essential)* Menu 20 PLN (lunch) – Carte 54/123 PLN
♦ Traditional ♦ Neighbourhood ♦
Large, lively restaurant in the old kitchens of a 19C former hotel. Tables overlook
the chefs hard at work. Small, well-priced menus feature produce from the
enthusiastic owner's nearby farm.

CRACOW
KRAKÓW
Population: 757 430

B. Brillion/MICHELIN

Cracow was deservedly included in the very first UNESCO World Heritage List. Unlike much of Poland, this beautiful old city – the country's capital from the 11C to the 17C – was spared Second World War destruction because the German Governor had his HQ here. So Cracow is still able to boast a hugely imposing market square – the biggest medieval square Europe – and a hill that's crowned not just with a castle, but a cathedral too. Not far away there's even a glorious chapel made of salt, one hundred metres under the ground.

Cracow is a city famous for its links with Judaism and its Royal Route, but also for its cultural inheritance. During the Renaissance, it became a centre of new ideas that drew the most outstanding writers, thinkers and musicians of the day. It has thousands of architectural monuments and millions of artefacts displayed in its museums and churches; but it's a modern city too, with an eye on the 21C. The heart and soul of Cracow is its old quarter, which received its charter in 1257. It's dominated by the Market Square and almost completely encircled by the Planty gardens. A short way to the south, briefly interrupted by the curving streets of the Okol neighbourhood, is Wawel Hill, and further south from here is the characterful Jewish quarter of Kazimierz. The smart residential areas of Piasek and Nowy Swiat are to the west.

CRACOW IN...

→ **ONE DAY**
St Mary's Church, Cloth Hall, Wawel, main building of National Museum.

→ **TWO DAYS**
Kazimierz, Czartoryski Museum, stroll round Planty.

→ **THREE DAYS**
Auschwitz-Birkenau, Wieliczka salt mine.

PRACTICAL INFORMATION

ARRIVAL-DEPARTURE

✈ John Paul II International Airport is 13km west of the city centre. Bus 292 goes to the central bus station. There's a free shuttle to the train station; trains to the centre take 15min. A taxi takes 20min.

GETTING AROUND

The historic city centre is a largely pedestrian precinct, so getting about on foot here is a traffic-free pleasure; the streets in the old quarter are laid out in a grid pattern, which makes orientation even easier. The public transport system is made up of an extensive network of buses and trams – you can use your tickets on both, and there several types available, from 15-minute timed tickets to 7-day passes. Be sure to stamp your ticket upon boarding. The Cracow Tourist Card includes unlimited free travel, as well as free entry to many museums, offers on excursions, and discounts in shops and restaurants; it's valid for 48 or 72 hours.

CALENDAR HIGHLIGHTS

June
The Lajkonik Parade, Wianki (flowers floated down the river, music and fireworks).

June/July
Cracow Jewish Culture Festival.

August
Music in Old Cracow.

September
Sacrum Profanum (concerts in post-industrial spaces).

EATING OUT

Even during the communist era, Cracow had a reputation as a good place to eat. In the 1990s, hundreds of new restaurants opened their doors, often in pretty locations with medieval or Renaissance interiors or in intimate cellars. Many Poles go misty-eyed at the thought of Bigos on a cold winter's day; it's a game, sausage and cabbage stew that comes with sauerkraut, onion, potatoes, herbs and spices, and is reputed to get better with reheating on successive days. Pierogi is another local favourite: crescent-shaped dumplings which come in either savoury or sweet style. Barszcz is a lemon and garlic flavoured beetroot soup that's invariably good value, while in Kazimierz, specialities include Jewish dumplings - filled with onion, cheese and potatoes - and Berdytchov soup, which imaginatively mixes honey and cinnamon with beef. There are plenty of restaurants specialising in French, Greek, Vietnamese, Middle Eastern, Indian, Italian and Mexican food too. Most restaurants don't close until around midnight and there's no pressure to rush your drinks and leave.

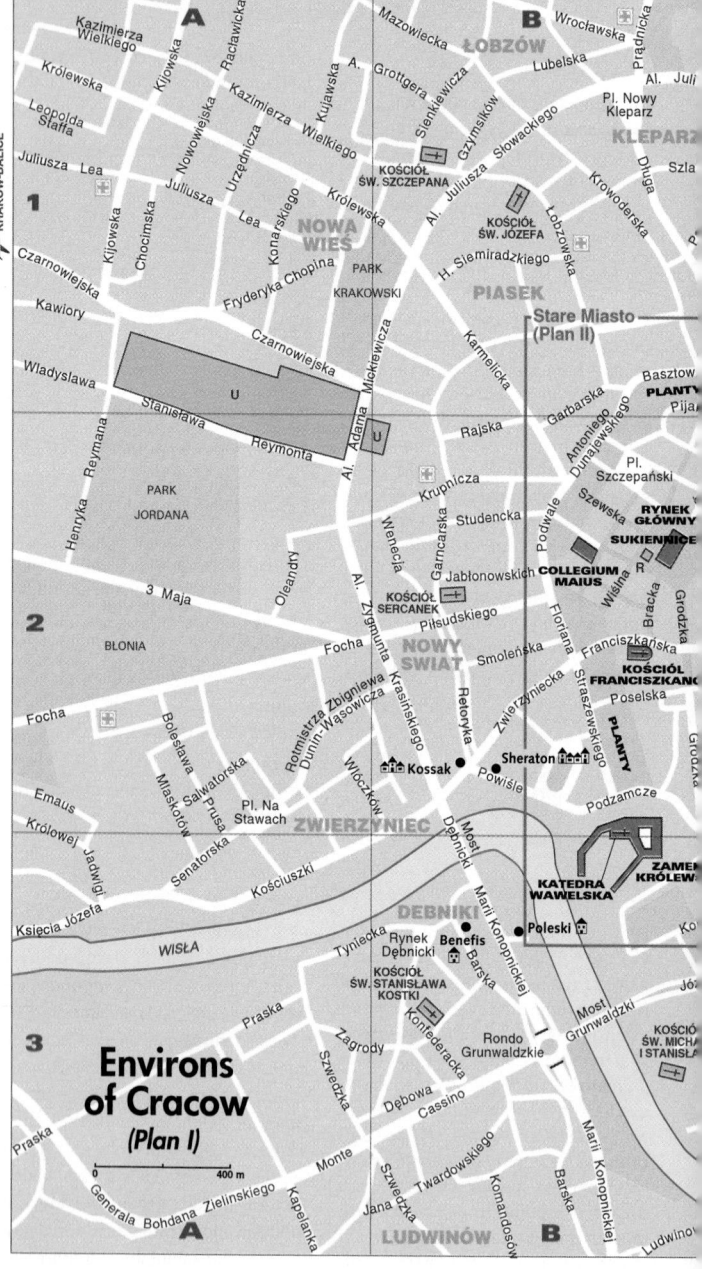

Environs of Cracow
(Plan I)

0 ———— 400 m

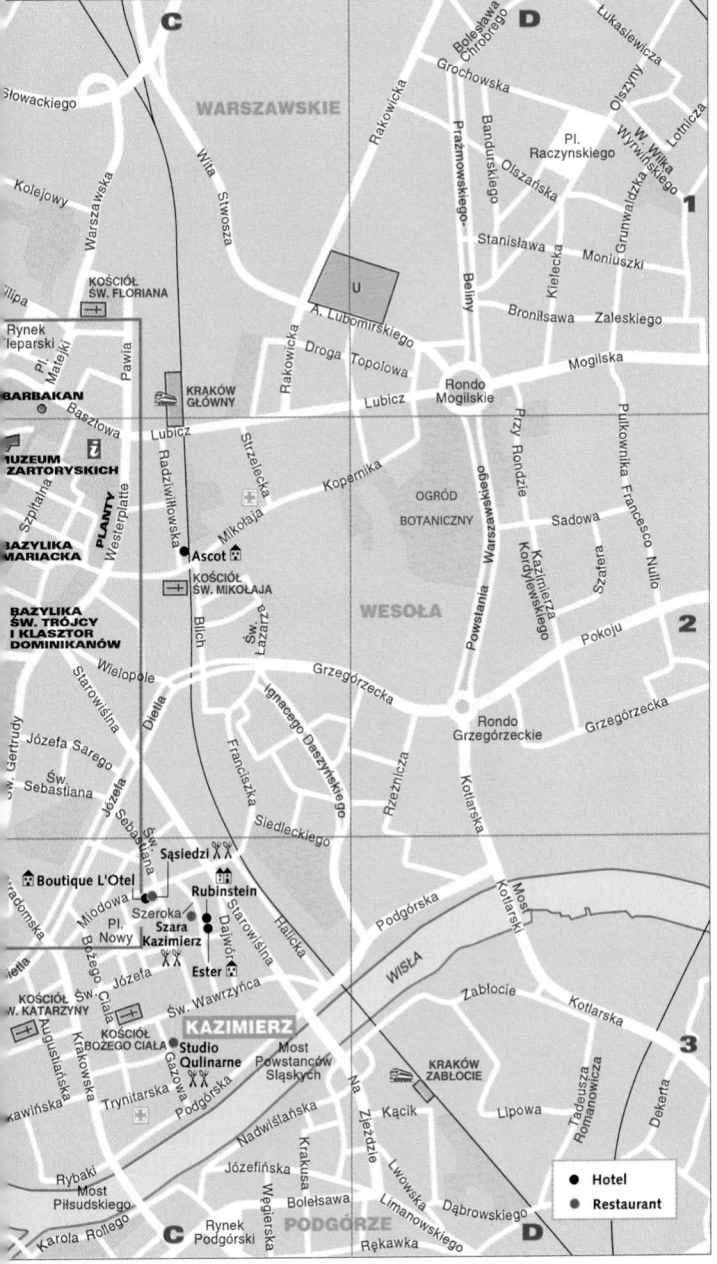

C
D

Słowackiego

Łukasiewicza

Bolesława Chrobrego

Grochowska

Rakowicka

WARSZAWSKIE

Olszańska

Bandurskiego

Przmowskiego

Pl. Raczyńskiego

Olszyny

W. Wilka Wyrwińskiego

Lotnicza

1

Kolejowy

Wila Stwosza

Warszawska

Stanisława

Kielecka

Moniuszki

Grunwaldzka

Filipa

KOŚCIÓŁ ŚW. FLORIANA

A. Lubomirskiego

Balmy

Bronisława

Zaleskiego

Rynek Kleparski

Pawia

Pl. Matejki

KRAKÓW GŁÓWNY

Rakowicka

Droga Topolowa

Rondo Mogilskie

Mogilska

BARBAKAN

Basztowa

Lubicz

Lubicz

Przy Rondo

Pułkownika Francesco Nullo

MUZEUM CZARTORYSKICH

Westerplatte

Strzelecka

Kopernika

OGRÓD BOTANICZNY

Warszawskiego

Sadowa

Szpitalna

PLANTY

Radziwiłłowska

Mikołaja

Kazimierza Kordylewskiego

Szafera

BAZYLIKA MARIACKA

Ascot

KOŚCIÓŁ ŚW. MIKOŁAJA

WESOŁA

Powstania

Pokoju

2

BAZYLIKA ŚW. TRÓJCY I KLASZTOR DOMINIKANÓW

Blich

Św. Łazarza

Wielopole

Starowiślna

Dietla

Ignacego Daszyńskiego

Grzegórzecka

Rondo Grzegórzeckie

Grzegórzecka

Św. Gertrudy

Józefa Sarego

Franciszka

Rzeźnicza

Kotlarska

Św. Sebastiana

Józefa Sebastiana

Siedleckiego

Sąsiedzi

Boutique L'Otel

Rubinstein

Most Kotlarski

Miodowa

Szeroka

Szara Kazimierz

Dajwór

Halicka

Podgórska

Wradomska

Pl. Nowy

Ester

Starowiślna

WISŁA

Kotlarska

Józefa

Św. Wawrzyńca

Zabłocie

KOŚCIÓŁ ŚW. KATARZYNY

KOŚCIÓŁ BOŻEGO CIAŁA

Studio Qulinarne

KAZIMIERZ

Most Powstańców Śląskich

KRAKÓW ZABŁOCIE

Kotlarska

3

Augustiańska

Krakowska

Gazowa

Podgórska

KRAKÓW ZABŁOCIE

Tadeusza Romanowicza

Dekerta

Kawińska

Trynitarska

Nadwiślańska

Na Zjeździe

Kącik

Lipowa

Lwowska

Rybaki

Most Piłsudskiego

Józefińska

Krakusa

Bolesława

Dąbrowskiego

Karola Rollego

Rynek Podgórski

Węgierska

PODGÓRZE

Limanowskiego

Rękawka

● Hotel

● Restaurant

C
D

659

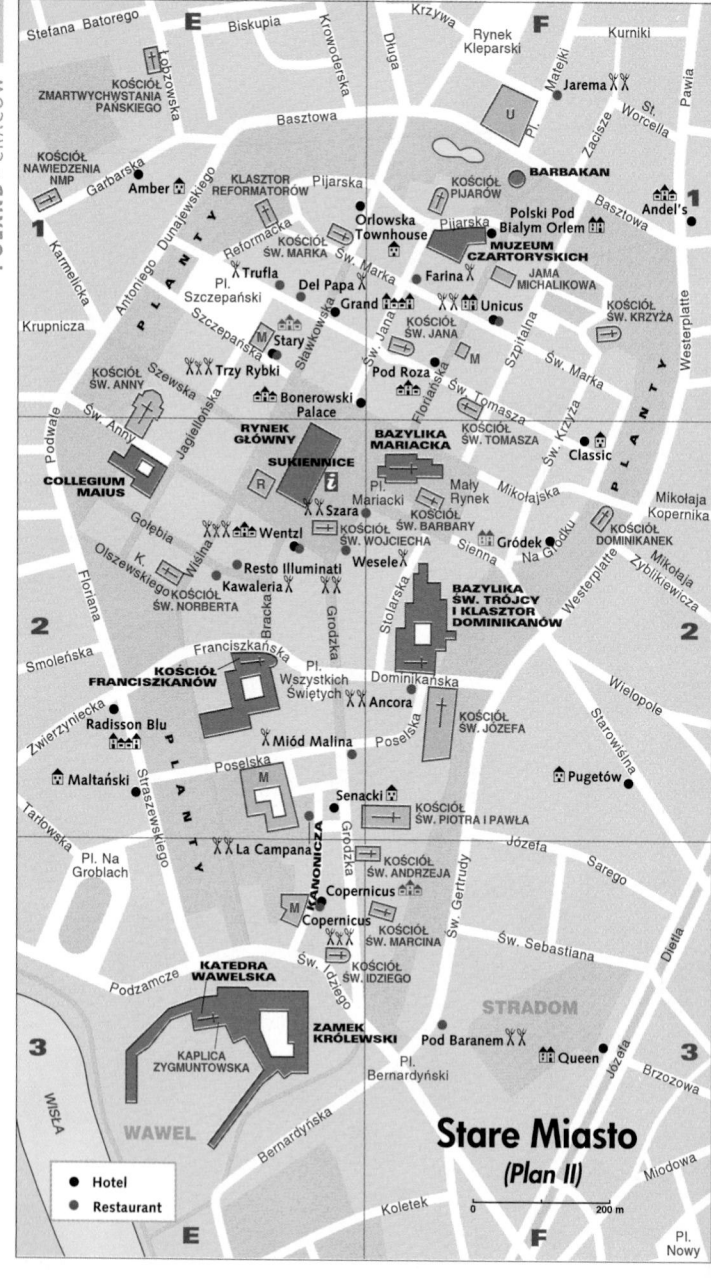

Stare Miasto
(Plan II)

- ● Hotel
- ● Restaurant

0   200 m

POLAND - CRACOW

Sheraton ⫷ ⌂ ⛷ 🐾 🔲 ⅗ 🔲 ↯ 🛜 ⅍ 🅿 🍽 𝖵𝖨𝖲𝖠 ⓒⓓ 🄰🄴 ⓞ

ul. Powisle 7 ⊠ 31 101 – ☎ (12) 662 10 00
– www.sheraton.pl/krakow *Plan I* **B2**
229 rm 🖘 – ♥535/1183 PLN ♥♥600/1248 PLN – 3 suites
Rest Olive – ☎ (12) 662 16 60 – Menu 80/130 PLN – Carte 118/183 PLN
Rest Someplace Else – Menu 50/90 PLN – Carte 87/183 PLN
♦ Luxury ♦ Business ♦ Modern ♦
Well-located, international hotel with impressive glass-roofed atrium at its centre. Luxuriously appointed, well-equipped bedrooms; 'Club' and 'Deluxe' boast
river and castle views. Compact basement fitness facilities and extensive event
space. Olive offers accessible global menu with Polish specialities. Sports bar
serves a broad range of humorously-named dishes.

Radisson Blu 🐾 🔲 ⅗ 🔲 ↯ 🛜 ⅍ 🍽 𝖵𝖨𝖲𝖠 ⓒⓓ 🄰🄴 ⓞ

ul. Straszewskiego 17 ⊠ 31 101 – ☎ (12) 618 88 88
– www.radissonblu.com/hotel-krakow **E2**
177 rm 🖘 – ♥460/1000 PLN ♥♥460/1000 PLN – 19 suites
Rest – Carte 62/234 PLN
♦ Business ♦ Modern ♦
Purpose-built business hotel next to the Planty, not far from the castle and main
square. Spacious, well-appointed bedrooms: 'City' in warm red hues, 'Harmony'
in cool blues. Extensive conference facilities and basement fitness centre. Informal, international dining; themed buffets (e.g. Thai) at weekends.

Grand 🐾 🔲 ⅗ rm, 🔲 ↯ 🛜 𝖵𝖨𝖲𝖠 ⓒⓓ 🄰🄴 ⓞ

ul. Slawkowska 5/7 ⊠ 31 014 – ☎ (12) 424 08 00 – www.grand.pl
55 rm 🖘 – ♥390/975 PLN ♥♥429/1014 PLN – 9 suites **E1**
Rest Mirror Hall – Menu 69/130 PLN – Carte 106/150 PLN
Rest Vienna Cafe – Menu 69/130 PLN – Carte 106/150 PLN
♦ Traditional ♦ Historic ♦ Classic ♦
Once Duke Czartoryski's palace, now the city's oldest hotel. Classic façade masks
a columned lobby with polished parquet floor and grand staircase, and rooms
filled with gold leaf and stained glass. Bedrooms are spacious and suites, vast,
opulent and impressively furnished. Former ballroom serves fittingly formal
menu. Traditional Viennese café offers Polish cuisine.

Copernicus 🐾 🔲 ↯ 🛜 𝖵𝖨𝖲𝖠 ⓒⓓ 🄰🄴

ul. Kanonicza 16 ⊠ 30 002 – ☎ (12) 424 34 00 – www.hotel.com.pl
23 rm – ♥560/800 PLN ♥♥630/900 PLN, 🖘 70 PLN – 6 suites **E3**
Rest Copernicus – see restaurant listing
♦ Historic ♦ Luxury ♦ Stylish ♦
Charming townhouse in the castle's shadow, on one of the city's oldest streets.
Central atrium with comfy lounge and small patio for breakfast/light lunch; inti-
mate pool and fitness suite in medieval cellars. Luxurious, beamed bedrooms
boast handmade furniture and excellent comforts. Lovely rooftop terrace.

Stary 🐾 🔲 ⅗ 🔲 ↯ 🛜 ⅍ 𝖵𝖨𝖲𝖠 ⓒⓓ 🄰🄴

ul. Szczepanska 5 ⊠ 31 011 – ☎ (12) 384 08 08
– www.hotel.com.pl **E1**
46 rm 🖘 – ♥650/870 PLN ♥♥720/1040 PLN – 7 suites
Rest Trzy Rybki – see restaurant listing
♦ Luxury ♦ Design ♦ Modern ♦
Behind a traditional townhouse façade, dramatic modern glass and steel struc-
tures blend cleverly with 15C features. Contemporary atrium, bar and rooftop
terrace sit alongside original brick and stonework. Stylish bedrooms boast
handmade furniture, impressive marble bathrooms and state-of-the-art lighting.

Wentzl ⟨ AC ⇔ 🛜 VISA ⚬⚬ AE ①

Rynek Główny 19 ✉ *31 008* – ℰ *(12) 430 26 64* – *www.wentzl.pl*
18 rm ⌣ – 📞510/760 PLN 📞📞580/830 PLN   **E2**
Rest *Wentzl* – see restaurant listing
♦ Luxury ♦ Historic ♦ Elegant ♦
Superbly set 15C tenement house, affording excellent views over the market
square to St Mary's Basilica. Individually furnished bedrooms feature four-posters, antiques and interesting art: some have balconies; top floor are the most
modern.

 Bonerowski Palace 🏠 AC ⇔ 🛜 🏊 VISA ⚬⚬ AE ①

ul. Sw. Jana 1 ✉ *31 013* – ℰ *(12) 374 13 00*
– *www.palacbonerowski.pl*   **E1**
8 rm ⌣ – 📞624/1039 PLN 📞📞748/1371 PLN – 6 suites
Rest *Milano* – Carte 108/191 PLN
♦ Palace ♦ Historic ♦ Personalised ♦
Former palace, superbly located on the main square, featuring medieval por-
tals, ornate ceilings, restored polychrome décor, an impressive staircase and
the largest Swarovski chandelier in Europe. Large, antique-furnished
bedrooms and marble bathrooms; chic suites. Country-style Milano offers
Italian menu.

 Kossak ⟨ 🍴 ⅃⅃ 🏠 ⅗ AC ⇔ 🛜 🏊 VISA ⚬⚬ AE ①

Plac Kossaka 1 ✉ *31 106* – ℰ *(12) 379 59 00*
– *www.hotelkossak.pl*   *Plan I* **B2**
55 rm ⌣ – 📞710/810 PLN 📞📞760/860 PLN – 5 suites
Rest *Percheron* – ℰ *(12) 379 58 50* – Carte 57/132 PLN
Rest *Cafe Oranzeria* – ℰ *(12) 379 59 50* – Carte 68/138 PLN
♦ Business ♦ Modern ♦
Contemporary business hotel named after the famous Polish painter and offering views over the river towards the castle. Each of its well-equipped, modern
bedrooms features a piece of Kossak's art; opt for one of the comfortable corner
suites. Ground floor restaurant offers Polish specialities. 7th floor café with terrace serves modern international menu.

 Pod Róza ⅃⅃ 🏠 AC ⇔ rest, 🛜 🏊 VISA ⚬⚬ AE

ul. Florianska 14 ✉ *31 021* – ℰ *(12) 424 33 00* – *www.hotel.com.pl*
53 rm ⌣ – 📞390/650 PLN 📞📞440/720 PLN – 4 suites   **F1**
Rest *Pod Róza* – ℰ *(12) 424 33 81* – Carte 125/175 PLN ❀
Rest *Amarone* – ℰ *(12) 424 33 81* – Menu 50 PLN (weekday lunch)
– Carte 99/125 PLN
♦ Historic ♦ Classic ♦
A discreet entrance leads to a surprisingly large glass-covered courtyard, complete with a formal modern restaurant and a laid-back Italian trattoria. Classically
appointed bedrooms feature silhouette artwork and modern bathrooms, and
many have jacuzzi baths. 4th floor rooms are cosiest and boast city skyline
panoramas; the top floor fitness suite shares the view.

 Andel's 🍴 ⅃⅃ 🏠 ⅗ AC ⇔ rm, 🛜 🏊 🚗 VISA ⚬⚬ AE ①

ul. Pawia 3 ✉ *31 154* – ℰ *(12) 660 01 00*
– *www.andelscracow.com*   **F1**
153 rm ⌣ – 📞300/920 PLN 📞📞380/1000 PLN – 6 suites
Rest *Delight* – Menu 48/60 PLN – Carte 79/137 PLN
♦ Business ♦ Modern ♦
Striking modern building opposite the station, its spacious interior decorated in
bold colours. Stylish bedrooms are well-equipped for business travellers, with
wi-fi, DVD players and foreign TV channels. Live music in chic bar. Bright restaurant with curvaceous designs, global menu and tables on the square.

POLAND - CRACOW

Gródek 　　　🛖 & 🅰🅲 ↳ 🛜 VISA ⦿ 🅰🅴 ①
ul. Na Gródku 4 ✉ *31 028 –* ℰ *(12) 431 90 30 – www.donimirski.com*
21 rm ⌑ – 🛈570/650 PLN 🛈🛈650/960 PLN – 2 suites　　**F2**
Rest *Restaurant Gródek* – ℰ *(12) 431 20 41 (dinner only)* Carte 87/
123 PLN

◆ Historic ◆ Townhouse ◆ Elegant ◆

Charming townhouse hidden in a quiet side street close to the square; seek out the pleasant country house bar in the library or relax on the roof terrace. Stylish bedrooms have their own individual characters and strong comforts. Formal restaurant exhibits 12-14C artefacts found during its excavation and offers classic Polish and Hungarian dishes with modern touches.

Unicus 　　　🛖 🅰🅲 ↳ 🛜 🛁 VISA ⦿ 🅰🅴 ①
Sw. Marka 20 ✉ *31 020 –* ℰ *(12) 433 71 11 – www.hotelunicus.pl*
35 rm ⌑ – 🛈500/600 PLN 🛈🛈600/1200 PLN　　**F1**
Rest *Unicus* – see restaurant listing

◆ Business ◆ Townhouse ◆ Modern ◆

Stylish, modern boutique hotel converted from old tenement houses. Spacious, well-appointed bedrooms range in colour from green to gold and boast state-of-the-art shower rooms; 'Double Deluxe', overlooking Florianska Street, are the best.

Queen 　　　& 🅰🅲 ↳ 🛜 🛁 VISA ⦿ 🅰🅴 ①
ul. Józefa Dietla 60 ✉ *31 039 –* ℰ *(12) 433 33 33 – www.queenhotel.pl*
30 rm ⌑ – 🛈280/840 PLN 🛈🛈340/880 PLN – 1 suite　　**F3**
Rest *Amarylis* – Carte 55/121 PLN

◆ Business ◆ Design ◆ Stylish ◆

Smart boutique hotel with minimalist lobby and chic styling. Bedrooms come in brown and silver, boasting the latest mod cons and smart shower rooms. 'Sky' rooms afford views over the castle; 3rd floor rooms have balconies. Global menu: dine in either the traditional brick or modern black & white cellar.

Polski Pod Bialym Orlem without rest 　　🛁 ↳ 🛜 🛁
ul. Pijarska 17 ✉ *31 015 –* ℰ *(12) 422 11 44*　　VISA ⦿ 🅰🅴 ①
– www.podorlem.com.pl　　**F1**
54 rm ⌑ – 🛈310/350 PLN 🛈🛈389/575 PLN – 3 suites

◆ Historic ◆ Classic ◆

Traditional hotel with colourful flower boxes, overlooking the city walls. Beams date from the 17C; the cosy brick bar, from the 16C. Warm breakfast room and well-equipped conference rooms are in keeping. Bedrooms exhibit a mix of styles.

Orlowska Townhouse without rest 　　　↳ 🛜 VISA ⦿
ul. Slawkowska 26 ✉ *31 014 –* ℰ *(12) 429 54 45*
– www.orlowskatownhouse.com　　**E/F1**
6 rm – 🛈330/413 PLN 🛈🛈330/578 PLN, ⌑ 30 PLN

◆ Historic ◆ Townhouse ◆ Elegant ◆

17C townhouse on a peaceful central street, with an intimate French piano bar. Spacious apartment-style bedrooms boast small kitchenettes and modern bathrooms, and are furnished according to themes; from 'Art Deco' to 'Poets' and 'Boudoir'.

Pugetów without rest 　　　🅰🅲 ↳ 🛜 🅿 VISA ⦿ 🅰🅴 ①
ul. Starowislna 15a ✉ *31 038 –* ℰ *(12) 432 49 50 – www.donimirski.com*
4 rm ⌑ – 🛈350/390 PLN 🛈🛈630/680 PLN – 2 suites　　**F2**

◆ Historic ◆ Classic ◆

19C former coach house set back from the main street, in the shadow of Pugetów Palace. Calm, intimate interior feels like a private residence. Classic, antique-filled bedrooms. Small lounge and breakfast tables in cool, characterful cellar.

Senacki without rest
⟜ 🏨 📶 ⓗⓐ 🅿️ VISA ⓪ AE ⓪

ul. Grodzka 51 ✉ *31 001 –* ℘ *(12) 422 76 86 – www.hotelsenacki.pl*
18 rm ⌴ – †420/510 PLN ††530/650 PLN – 2 suites   **E2**
♦ Townhouse ♦ Classic ♦

Peaceful hotel with ornate stone façade, set opposite a 17C church on the Royal Way. Classical bedrooms – upper floors boast rooftop views and air con; opt for a suite as they have baths. Buffet breakfast in hugely atmospheric 13C cellar.

Maltanski without rest
ⓗⓐ 🏨 🅿️ VISA ⓪ AE ⓪

ul. Straszewskiego 14 ✉ *31 101 –* ℘ *(12) 431 00 10 – www.donimirski.com*
16 rm ⌴ – †510/590 PLN ††590/650 PLN   **E2**
♦ Traditional ♦ Personalised ♦

Lovely little hotel named after the previous owners, the Knights of Malta; next to the Planty, with the castle and square just a stroll away – a great base for exploring. Charming bedrooms have traditional furniture, wood floors and baths.

Amber without rest
🛎 ⟜ 📺 ⓗⓐ 🏨 VISA ⓪ AE ⓪

ul. Garbarska 10 ✉ *31 131 –* ℘ *(12) 421 06 06 – www.hotel-amber.pl*
38 rm ⌴ – †229/349 PLN ††329/879 PLN   **E1**
♦ Townhouse ♦ Modern ♦ Functional ♦

Traditional townhouse in a residential street, run by a pleasant team. Surprisingly contemporary interior, including a modern breakfast room, cellar lounge and sauna. Well-equipped bedrooms come complete with complimentary cherry vodka.

Poleski
⟜ 🏨 📺 ⓗⓐ rm, 🏨 🧖 VISA ⓪ AE ⓪

ul. Sandomierska 6 ✉ *30 301 –* ℘ *(12) 260 54 05 – www.hotelpoleski.pl*
16 rm ⌴ – †225/305 PLN ††275/385 PLN – 4 suites   *Plan I* **B3**
Rest – Carte 49/99 PLN
♦ Modern ♦ Functional ♦

Simple, affordable hotel in an enviable position on the banks of the river. Spacious bedrooms have a slight Scandinavian feel and many share the view. Fantastic outlook towards the castle from the fourth floor bar and terrace. Smart, first floor restaurant offers a mix of international and Polish dishes.

Benefis without rest
⟜ ⓗⓐ 🏨 🅿️ VISA ⓪ AE ⓪

ul. Barska 2 ✉ *30 307 –* ℘ *(12) 252 07 10 – www.hotelbenefis.pl*
12 rm ⌴ – †230/340 PLN ††270/390 PLN – 8 suites   *Plan I* **B3**
♦ Modern ♦ Functional ♦

Small, purpose-built hotel just over the Wisla River, a short walk from town. Surprisingly spacious, modern bedrooms, most with balconies; 4th floor rooms come with air con and distant castle views. Small bar in smartly furnished basement.

Ascot without rest
⟜ 📺 ⓗⓐ 🏨 VISA ⓪ AE

ul. Radziwillowska 3 ✉ *31 026 –* ℘ *(12) 384 06 06 – www.hotelascot.pl*
49 rm ⌴ – †309/392 PLN ††371/495 PLN   *Plan I* **C2**
♦ Business ♦ Functional ♦

Modern hotel located in a residential area, 5 minutes' walk from town. Bold, contemporary art lines the lobby walls and there's a small corner bar. Uniform, up-to-date bedrooms; those to the front are quieter. Family rooms come with baths.

Classic without rest
📺 ⓗⓐ 🏨 VISA ⓪ AE ⓪

ul. Sw. Tomasza 32 ✉ *31 014 –* ℘ *(12) 424 03 03 – www.hotel-classic.pl*
30 rm ⌴ – †250/390 PLN ††290/590 PLN   **F2**
♦ Business ♦ Functional ♦

Well-run by a friendly team, a simple, purpose-built hotel on a fairly peaceful, central street. Rear bedrooms overlook a central garden; suites come with baths and mini bars. Hot and cold buffet breakfasts in the light, airy basement.

POLAND - CRACOW

XXX **Trzy Rybki** – at Stary Hotel   `AC` `¼` `VISA` `OO` `AE`
ul. Szczepanska 5 ✉ *31 011* – ☎ *(12) 384 08 01* – *www.hotel.com.pl*
Rest – Carte 143/203 PLN ❀   **E1**
♦ Fish and seafood ♦ Elegant ♦ Design ♦
Airy, two-roomed restaurant in a uniquely designed hotel. Impressive vaulted
stone ceiling and dramatic flower arrangements dominate. Cooking is modern,
original and uncluttered; fish features highly. Superb collection of Italian wines.

XXX **Copernicus** – at Copernicus Hotel   `AC` `¼` `VISA` `OO` `AE`
ul. Kanonicza 16 ✉ *30 002* – ☎ *(12) 424 34 21* – *www.hotel.com.pl*
Rest – *(dinner only) (booking essential)* Menu 99/229 PLN   **E3**
– Carte 167/217 PLN ❀
♦ Polish ♦ Intimate ♦
Intimate, split-level restaurant of less than 10 tables, tucked away in the atrium
of a charming hotel. Lovely hand-painted wooden ceiling from the Renaissance.
Formal menu of Polish and European dishes prepared with a light, modern
touch.

XXX **Wentzl** – at Wentzl Hotel   `舟` `AC` `¼` `VISA` `OO` `AE` `①`
Rynek Główny 19 ✉ *31 008* – ☎ *(12) 429 5299* – *www.wentzl.pl*
Rest – Menu 90/140 PLN – Carte 78/190 PLN   **E2**
♦ International ♦ Elegant ♦ Formal ♦
Grand first floor restaurant boasting polished parquet floors, a stunning 15C ceil-
ing, superb market square views and a lovely terrace. Classical French menu
also features a few Polish dishes. Tables are crisply laid and service is formal.

XX **Ancora**   `AC` `¼` `VISA` `OO` `AE` `①`
ul. Dominikánska 3 ✉ *31 043* – ☎ *(12) 357 33 55*
– *www.ancora-restaurant.com*
– *Closed Good Friday, 1 November and 25 December*   **F2**
Rest – Carte 96/153 PLN ❀
♦ Polish ♦ Fashionable ♦ Design ♦
Spacious, contemporary restaurant in subtle hues, with two chef's tables and an
appealing cellar for a more intimate experience. Classical Polish combinations
interpreted in an original, modern style; 5 and 7 course chef's menus available.

XX **Unicus** – at Unicus Hotel   `AC` `¼` `VISA` `OO` `AE` `①`
Sw. Marka 20 ✉ *31 020* – ☎ *(12) 433 71 11* – *www.hotelunicus.pl*
Rest – Menu 65/85 PLN – Carte 78/126 PLN   **F1**
♦ Modern ♦ Design ♦ Individual ♦
Smart restaurant and small bar, set in the cellars of a boutique hotel. Contempo-
rary styling and clever lighting create a bright, open feel. Concise menu changes
with the seasons, offering a mix of modern Polish and international dishes.

XX **Resto Illuminati**   `AC` `¼` `VISA` `OO` `AE` `①`
ul. Golebia 2 ✉ *31 007* – ☎ *(12) 430 73 73* – *www.restoilluminati.pl*
– *Closed dinner 24 December*   **E2**
Rest – Carte 93/127 PLN
♦ International ♦ Musical ♦ Trendy ♦
Cosy restaurant run by a husband and wife team, featuring live piano every eve-
ning and offering an extensive range of cocktails in the bar. Cooking is interna-
tional with Italian overtones; daily specials are chalked on the board.

XX **Szara**   `舟` `¼` `VISA` `OO` `AE` `①`
Rynek Główny 6 ✉ *31 042* – ☎ *(12) 421 66 69* – *www.szara.pl*
– *Closed 24 December*   **E/F2**
Rest – Carte 98/148 PLN
♦ International ♦ Brasserie ♦ Classic ♦
Well-regarded, family-run restaurant in the 10 acre Grand Square. Lovely ter-
race, hand-painted Gothic ceiling and pleasant brasserie atmosphere. Unusual
mix of classic Swedish and Polish dishes; cooking is authentic, hearty and
good value.

XX **Pod Baranem**   🏧 ↳ 🆅🆂🅰 ⓪ 🄰🄴

ul. Sw. Gertrudy 21 ✉ *31 049 –* ℰ *(12) 429 40 22*
– www.podbaranem.com
– Closed 25-26 December   **F3**
Rest – Menu 70/80 PLN – Carte 46/114 PLN
◆ Polish ◆ Neighbourhood ◆ Family ◆

Traditional, family-run restaurant with rug-covered stone floors, local art on the
walls and old beams hung with herbs. Large menu offers classic Polish cuisine;
sharing dishes must be ordered in advance. Passionate, brightly dressed team.

XX **Jarema**   🏠 🏧 ↳ 🆅🆂🅰 ⓪ 🄰🄴

Pl. Matejki 5 ✉ *30 157 –* ℰ *(12) 429 36 69 – www.jarema.pl*
Rest – Menu 35/60 PLN – Carte 48/152 PLN   **F1**
◆ Polish ◆ Musical ◆ Rustic ◆

Three-roomed restaurant with a homely feel. Hunting trophies fill the walls and
live violin and piano music features every night. Family recipes are handed
down through the generations and focus on dishes from the east of the
country.

X **Trufla**   🏠 ↳ 🆅🆂🅰 ⓪

ul. Sw. Tomasza 2 ✉ *31 014 –* ℰ *(12) 422 16 41 – www.truflakrakow.pl*
– Closed 1 November and 24-26 December   **E1**
Rest – Menu 20/30 PLN – Carte 30/85 PLN
◆ Italian ◆ Bistro ◆ Individual ◆

Hidden behind a small façade, this simple little Italian restaurant boasts a charming walled garden and a conservatory. Cooking is inspired by Tuscany and
dishes are authentic and classically based; save room for the tasty homemade
cake.

X **La Campana**   🏠 ↳ 🆅🆂🅰 ⓪ 🄰🄴

ul. Kanonicza 7 ✉ *31 002 –* ℰ *(12) 430 22 32 – www.lacampana.pl*
– Closed Easter and 24-25 December   **E1**
Rest – Menu 50/90 PLN – Carte 67/96 PLN
◆ Italian ◆ Cosy ◆ Rustic ◆

Discretely set under an arch with a charming, country style interior, pine dres-
sers and olive branch frieze. Beautiful walled garden with tables dotted between the bushes. Wide range of flavoursome Italian dishes; try the prosciutto
plate.

X **Farina**   🏧 🆅🆂🅰 ⓪ 🄰🄴 ⓪

ul. Sw. Marka 16 ✉ *31 017 –* ℰ *(12) 422 16 80 – www.farina.com.pl*
– Closed 24-25 December   **F1**
Rest – Menu 55/150 PLN – Carte 61/241 PLN
◆ Fish and seafood ◆ Cosy ◆ Friendly ◆

Pretty little restaurant set over three rooms; all cosy and candlelit but each with
its own character. Seafood is a speciality, with fish arriving from France twice a
week. Mussels come 12 ways and fish is cooked whole over salt and herbs.

X **Wesele**   🏠 🏧 ↳ ⇄ 🆅🆂🅰 ⓪ 🄰🄴

Rynek Główny 10 ✉ *31 042 –* ℰ *(12) 422 74 60*
– www.weselerestauracja.pl
– Closed Easter and 24-25 December   **E2**
Rest – Menu 40/60 PLN – Carte 53/122 PLN
◆ Polish ◆ Rustic ◆

Friendly, country-style restaurant on the central square, complete with beams,
wooden panelling and a decked terrace. Menu offers a good range of generously portioned, authentically prepared Polish classics, including herring and
perogi.

POLAND - CRACOW

✕ Miód Malina 🛜 AC ↳ VISA ⦿ AE

ul. Grodzka 40 ✉ *31 044* – ✆ *(12) 430 04 11* – *www.miodmalina.pl*
– *Closed Easter and 24-25 December* **E2**
Rest – *(booking essential at dinner)* Menu 50/70 PLN – Carte 58/108 PLN
◆ Polish ◆ Rustic ◆

Rustic restaurant with a tiled floor, vaulted ceiling, chunky wood furnishings and a courtyard terrace. Cooking is Polish with Italian touches and sticks to tried-and-tested classics. Some dishes are finished on the wood-burning stove.

✕ Kawaleria 🛜 AC ↳ VISA ⦿ AE ⦿

ul. Golebia 4 ✉ *31 007* – ✆ *(12) 430 24 32* – *www.kawaleria.com.pl*
– *Closed 24-26 December* **E2**
Rest – Menu 31/46 PLN – Carte 48/95 PLN
◆ Polish ◆ Cosy ◆ Traditional ◆

Its name means 'cavalry' – a tribute to the owner's great-grandfather, who was a commanding officer – and swords, hats and photos line the walls. Dine on traditional Polish dishes in one of the cosy front rooms or on the charming terrace.

✕ Del Papa 🛜 AC ↳ VISA ⦿ AE ⦿

ul. Sw. Tomasza 6 ✉ *31 014* – ✆ *(12) 421 83 43* – *www.delpapa.pl*
– *Closed 24-25 December* **E1**
Rest – Carte 50/106 PLN
◆ Italian ◆ Bistro ◆

Simple Italian trattoria; dine in the front, bistro-style room, the characterful Italian 'street' or on the partially covered rear terrace. Menus follow the seasons, offering a good range of honest Italian classics and a fat free selection.

---

at KAZIMIERZ *Plan I*

🏠🏠 Rubinstein Residence 🛜 🕸 AC ↳ rm, 🛜 🛇 VISA ⦿ AE ⦿

ul. Szeroka 12 ✉ *31 053* – ✆ *(12) 384 00 00* – *www.rubinstein.pl*
22 rm ⌑ – 🛇250/700 PLN 🛇🛇300/800 PLN – 4 suites **C3**
Rest – Carte 87/150 PLN
◆ Historic ◆ Townhouse ◆ Stylish ◆

Named after Helena Rubinstein – who lived nearby – and located in a pleasant square, this pair of restored townhouses is joined by a bright, glass-roofed restaurant. Characterful bedrooms are well-equipped, with luxurious bathrooms featuring alabaster and marble. The roof terrace affords panoramic city views.

🏠 Ester 🛜 🕸 & rm, AC ↳ rm, 🛜 🛇 VISA ⦿ AE ⦿

ul. Szeroka 20 ✉ *31 053* – ✆ *(12) 429 11 88* – *www.hotel-ester.krakow.pl*
32 rm – 🛇250/600 PLN 🛇🛇280/1400 PLN, ⌑ 35 PLN **C3**
Rest – Menu 35/50 PLN – Carte 62/119 PLN
◆ Townhouse ◆ Homely ◆

Cosy little hotel overlooking a pleasant square in the Jewish quarter, with a traditionally furnished interior and bird cages dotted about the place. Comfortable bedrooms are colour themed and boast both baths and showers. Simple café has a terrace and serves a mix of traditional Polish and Jewish dishes.

🏠 Boutique L'Otel *without rest* ↳ 🛜 VISA ⦿

ul. Miodowa 25 ✉ *31 055* – ✆ *(12) 633 34 44*
– *www.apartmenty.oberza.pl*
– *Closed 24-28 December* **C3**
15 rm – 🛇165/180 PLN 🛇🛇195 PLN, ⌑ 20 PLN – 1 suite
◆ Townhouse ◆ Design ◆ Stylish ◆

Discreet, former tenement house in the heart of Kazimierz. An impressive staircase leads to stylish, individually themed bedrooms ranging from 'Art Deco' to 'Crystal' and boasting smart, modern bathrooms. Breakfast is served in next door Sasiedzi restaurant.

POLAND - CRACOW

XX **Studio Qulinarne**   🛗 🗚 ⅋ 𝘝𝘐𝘚𝘈 ⓒⓞ 🆎 ⓪

ul. Gazowa 4 ✉ *31 060 – ℰ (12) 430 69 14 – www.studioqulinarne.pl*
– Closed 25 December and Good Friday   **C3**
Rest – Carte 62/138 PLN
   ♦ International ♦ Individual ♦ Neighbourhood ♦

Passionately run, restyled bus garage with folding glass doors, a cocktail bar and an intimate garden. Airy inner features exposed timbers, unusual lighting and black linen. Monthly menu offers well-presented, modern international dishes.

XX **Sasiedzi**   🛗 ⅋ 𝘝𝘐𝘚𝘈 ⓒⓞ

ul. Miodowa 25 ✉ *31 055 – ℰ (12) 654 83 53 – www.oberza.pl*
– Closed 24-28 December   **C3**
Rest – Menu 17 PLN (lunch) – Carte 47/121 PLN
   ♦ Polish ♦ Intimate ♦ Rurally ♦

Owned by an experienced family, with a relaxed, welcoming atmosphere – its name, 'Neighbour', sums it up well. Dine on the small terrace or in one of several charming cellar rooms. Honest, good value cooking uses traditional Polish recipes.

XX **Szara Kazimierz**   🛗 ⅋ 𝘝𝘐𝘚𝘈 ⓒⓞ

ul. Szeroka 39 ✉ *31 053 – ℰ (12) 429 12 19 – www.szarakazimierz.pl*
– Closed 24-25 December   **C3**
Rest – Menu 33/62 PLN – Carte 66/120 PLN
   ♦ Polish ♦ Brasserie ♦

French brasserie in a pleasant spot on the square; a sister to Szara in the Old Town. Sit on the pavement, the rear terrace or inside among photos of Gaultier models. Reflecting the owners' heritage, menus mix Polish and Swedish classics.

→ **AREA:**
92 391 km² (35 521 sq mi).

→ **POPULATION:**
10 561 614. Density = 114 per km².

→ **CAPITAL:**
Lisbon.

→ **CURRENCY:**
Euro (€).

→ **GOVERNMENT:**
Parliamentary republic (since 1976).
Member of European Union since 1986.

→ **LANGUAGE:**
Portuguese.

→ **PUBLIC HOLIDAYS:**
New Year's Day (1 Jan); Good Friday (late Mar/Apr); Liberation Day (25 Apr); Labor Day (1 May); Corpus Christi (May/June – currently suspended); Portugal Day (10 June); Assumption of the Virgin Mary (15 Aug); Republic Day (5 Oct – currently suspended); All Saints' Day (1 Nov – currently suspended); Restoration of Independence Day (1 Dec – currently suspended); Immaculate Conception (8 Dec); Christmas Day (25 Dec).

→ **LOCAL TIME:**
GMT in winter and GMT+1 hour in summer.

→ **CLIMATE:**
Temperate Mediterranean with warm winters and hot summers (Lisbon: January 15°C; July 26°C).

LISBON

→ **EMERGENCY:**
Police, Medical Assistance and Fire Brigade ☎ **112**.

→ **ELECTRICITY:**
230 volts AC, 50Hz; 2 round pin sockets.

→ **FORMALITIES:**
Travellers from the European Union (EU), Switzerland, Iceland and the main countries of North and South America need a national identity card or passport (America: passport required) to visit Portugal for less than three months (tourism or business purpose). For visitors from other countries a visa may be required, in addition to a passport, especially for those wishing to stay for longer than three months. We advise you to check with your embassy before travelling.

LISBON
LISBOA

Population: 547 631

Alain Rapoport/Fotolia.com

Sitting on the north bank of the River Tagus, beneath huge open skies and surrounded by seven hills, Lisbon boasts an atmosphere that few cities can match. An enchanting walk around the streets has an old-time ambience all of its own, matched only by a jaunt on the trams and funiculars that run up and down the steep hills. At first sight Lisbon is all flaky palaces, meandering alleyways and castellated horizon quarried from medieval stone; but there's a 21C element, too. Slinky new developments line the riverside, linking the old and new in a glorious jumble which spills down the slopes to the water's edge. The views of the water from various vantage points all over Lisbon and the vistas of the 'Straw Sea' – so named because of the golden reflections of the sun – reach out to visitors, along with the sounds of fado, the city's alluring folk music, which conjures up a melancholic yearning.

The compact heart of the city is the Baixa, a flat, 18C grid of streets flanked by the hills. To the west is the elegant commercial district of Chiado and the funky hilltop Bairro Alto, while immediately to the east is Alfama, a tightly packed former Moorish quarter with kasbah-like qualities. North of here is the working-class neighbourhood of Graça and way out west lies the spacious riverside suburb of Belém, while up the river to the east can be found the ultra-modern Parque das Nações.

LISBON IN...

→ **ONE DAY**
Alfama, Castelo São Jorge, Bairro Alto.

→ **TWO DAYS**
Baixa, Calouste Gulbenkian Museum, Parque das Nações.

→ **THREE DAYS**
Museu Nacional de Arte Antiga, Belém.

PRACTICAL INFORMATION

ARRIVAL-DEPARTURE

✈ Lisbon Portela Airport is 7km north of the town centre. The Metro Red Line takes about 20min. The Aerobus runs every 20-30min.

GETTING AROUND

Lisbon is easy to get around. Four metro lines cover much of the central part of the city and there are six main bus routes and three funiculars. Buses and trams operate every 11-15 minutes; tram routes 15 and 28 serve the main sights. Tickets can be bought as a single fare but it might be worthwhile investing in a 7 Colinas or Viva Viagem Card, which can be loaded with various tickets (which give discounts on standard single fares) or with pre-pay credit for 'zapping'. The 24, 48 or 72 hr Lisboa Card is valid for unlimited travel on public transport and for free or reduced admission to most museums and cultural sites.

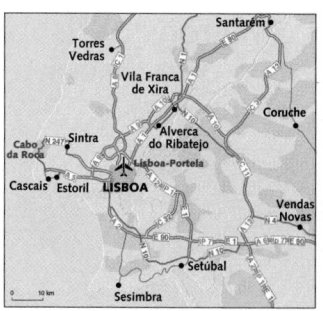

CALENDAR HIGHLIGHTS

February
Carnaval.

March
Spring Festival.

April
CCB Music Festival.

June
Festas dos Santos Populares (Feast Days of the Popular Saints), National Day, Lisbon Book Fair, Alkantara Festival (17-day jamboree).

July
Super Bock Super Rock Festival, Almada International Theatre Festival.

November
Arte Lisboa.

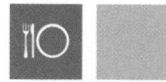

EATING OUT

Lisboetas love their local agricultural produce and the cuisine of the region can be characterised by its honesty and simplicity. The city has an age-old maritime tradition and there are a number of fishing ports nearby, so ocean-fresh fish and seafood features in a range of dishes. One thing the locals love in particular is bacalhau (cod), and it's said that in Lisbon, there's a different way to prepare it for every day of the year: it may come oven-baked, slow-cooked or cooked in milk, and it can be served wrapped in cabbage, with tocino belly pork or in a myriad of other ways. While eating in either a humble tasca, a casa de pasto or a restaurante, other specialities to keep an eye out for are clams cooked with garlic and coriander, traditional beef, chicken and sausage stew with vegetables and rice, bean casserole with tocino belly pork, and lamprey eel with rice. Enjoy them with a vinho verde, the wine of the region. A service charge will be included on your bill but it's customary to leave a tip of about ten per cent.

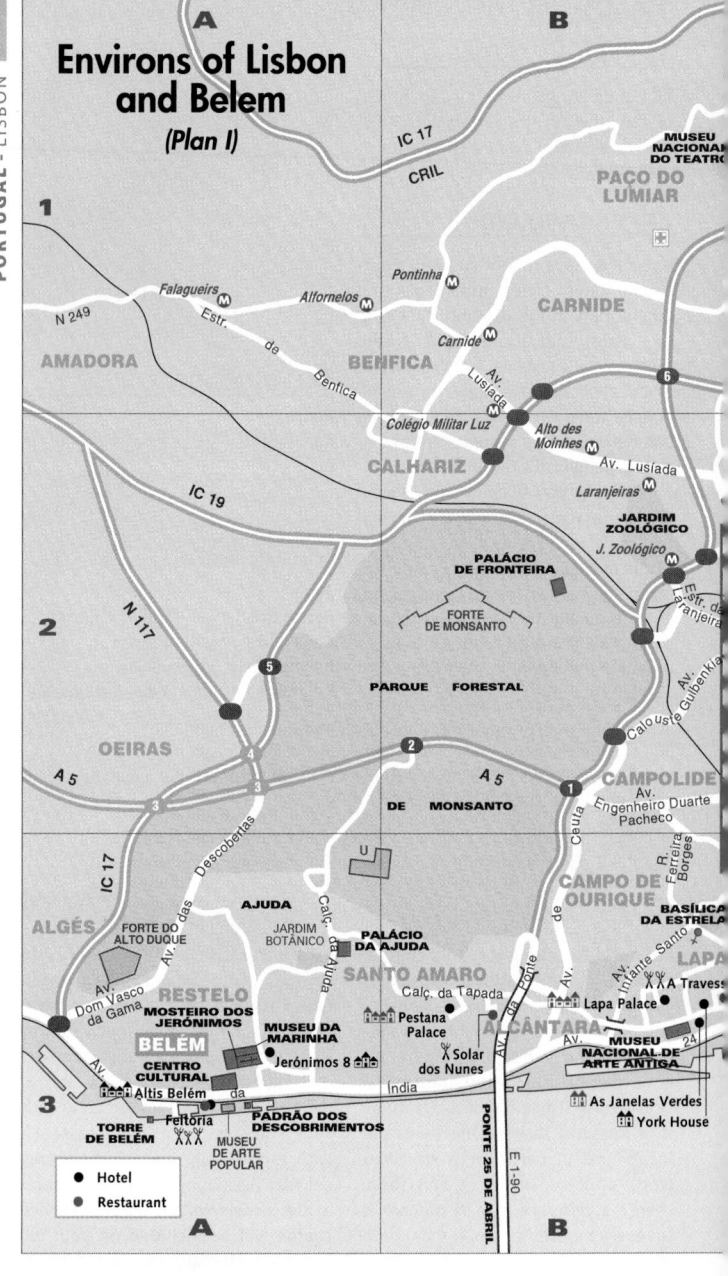

Environs of Lisbon and Belém
(Plan I)

A **B**

MUSEU NACIONAL DO TEATRO

PAÇO DO LUMIAR

IC 17
CRIL

1

N 249

Falagueirs *Alfornelos*

Pontinha

Estr. de Benfica

AMADORA

BENFICA

Carnide

CARNIDE

Av. Lusíada

Colégio Militar Luz

Alto des Moinhes

6

CALHARIZ

Av. Lusíada

IC 19

Laranjeiras

JARDIM ZOOLÓGICO

N 117

PALÁCIO DE FRONTEIRA

J. Zoológico

2

FORTE DE MONSANTO

PARQUE FORESTAL

5

OEIRAS

4

2

Calouste Gulbenkian

A 5

3

3

A 5

DE MONSANTO

1

CAMPOLIDE

Av. Engenheiro Duarte Pacheco

IC 17

Av. das Descobertas

CAMPO DE OURIQUE

BASÍLICA DA ESTRELA

ALGÉS

FORTE DO ALTO DUQUE

AJUDA

JARDIM BOTÂNICO

Calç. da Ajuda

PALÁCIO DA AJUDA

SANTO AMARO

LAPA

Av. Dom Vasco da Gama

RESTELO

Calç. da Tapada

A Travess

MOSTEIRO DOS JERÓNIMOS

MUSEU DA MARINHA

Pestana Palace

Lapa Palace

MUSEU NACIONAL DE ARTE ANTIGA

BELÉM

CENTRO CULTURAL

Jerónimos 8

Solar dos Nunes

ALCÂNTARA

Altis Belém

da

Índia

As Janelas Verdes

3

TORRE DE BELÉM

Feitoria

PADRÃO DOS DESCOBRIMENTOS

MUSEU DE ARTE POPULAR

York House

PONTE 25 DE ABRIL

E 1-90

● Hotel
● Restaurant

A **B**

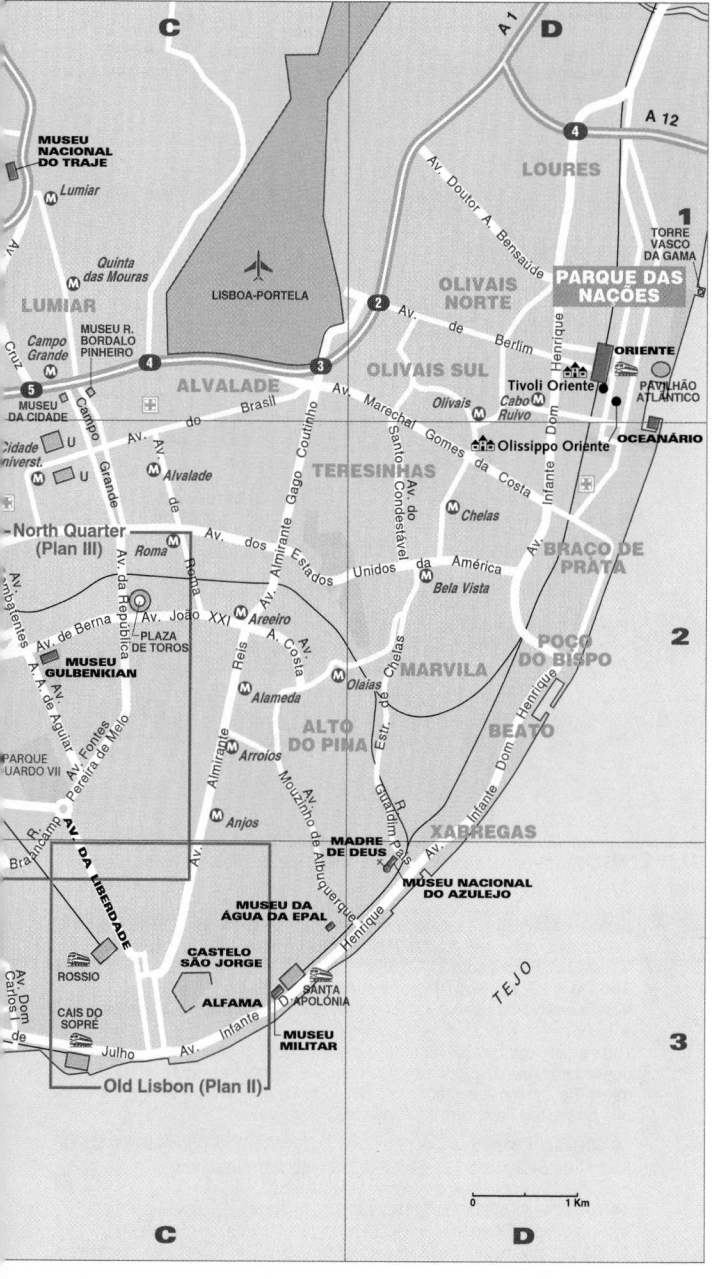

MUSEU NACIONAL DO TRAJE

Lumiar

Quinta das Mouras

LISBOA-PORTELA

LOURES

TORRE VASCO DA GAMA

PARQUE DAS NAÇÕES

LUMIAR

Campo Grande

MUSEU R. BORDALO PINHEIRO

Av. de Berlim

ORIENTE

MUSEU DA CIDADE

ALVALADE

OLIVAIS NORTE

Tivoli Oriente

PAVILHÃO ATLÂNTICO

Cidade Universit.

Brasil

OLIVAIS SUL

Olivais

Cabo Ruivo

OCEANÁRIO

Av. Marechal Gomes da Costa

Olissippo Oriente

Alvalade

North Quarter (Plan III)

TERESINHAS

Chelas

BRAÇO DE PRATA

Roma

Av. dos Estados Unidos da América

Bela Vista

POÇO DO BISPO

MUSEU GULBENKIAN

Av. João XXI

PLAZA DE TOROS

Areeiro

A. Costa

Olaias

MARVILA

BEATO

PARQUE EDUARDO VII

Alameda

ALTO DO PINA

Arroios

Anjos

MADRE DE DEUS

XABREGAS

AV. DA LIBERDADE

MUSEU NACIONAL DO AZULEJO

MUSEU DA ÁGUA DA EPAL

ROSSIO

CASTELO SÃO JORGE

SANTA APOLÓNIA

TEJO

CAIS DO SODRÉ

ALFAMA

Av. Infante

MUSEU MILITAR

Julho

Old Lisbon (Plan II)

0   1 Km

OLD LISBON (Alfama, Castelo de São Jorge, Rossio, Baixa, Chiado, Bairro Alto) *Plan II*

🏨🏨🏨 Tivoli Lisboa ≤ 🍴 💆 ⌂ & 🅰 🛜 🕍 🛏 VISA ⨌ AE ①

*Av. da Liberdade 185 ⊠ 1269-050 – ⓜ Avenida – 𝒞 213 19 89 00
– www.tivolihotels.com* **E1**
306 rm ⌿ – †135/670 € – 15 suites
Rest *Brasserie Flo Lisboa* – Carte approx. 42 € **Rest** *Terraço* – Carte approx. 45 €
◆ Business ◆ Classic ◆
This elegant, comfortable hotel has a delightful lounge area. The well-appointed guestrooms are cosy and stylish. Attractive swimming pool surrounded by trees. The Terraço restaurant has a dining room enclosed by large glass windows on the top floor, with stunning views of the city.

🏨🏨🏨 Avenida Palace without rest 💆 🅰 🛜 🕍 VISA ⨌ AE ①

*Rua 1° de Dezembro 123 ⊠ 1200-359 – ⓜ Restauradores
– 𝒞 213 21 81 00 – www.hotelavenidapalace.pt* **E1**
64 rm ⌿ – †150/350 € ††180/400 € – 18 suites
◆ Historic ◆ Elegant ◆
An elegant, prestigious building dating from 1892. This hotel has a magnificent lounge area, delightful English-style bar and well-maintained, classical-style guestrooms.

PORTUGAL - LISBON

Sofitel Lisbon Liberdade

Av. da Liberdade 127 ✉ *1269-038 –* Ⓜ *Avenida –* ℰ *213 22 83 00*
– www.sofitel.com **E1**
165 rm – ♦♦150/460 €, ♀ 22 € – 6 suites
Rest *Ad Lib* – see restaurant listing
♦ Chain hotel ♦ Modern ♦
This hotel is decorated in contemporary-style with numerous designer details. It has fully equipped guestrooms furnished with top-quality materials.

Bairro Alto H

Praça Luis de Camões 2 ✉ *1200-243 –* Ⓜ *Baixa-Chiado –* ℰ *213 40 82 88*
– www.bairroaltohotel.com **E2**
51 rm ♀ – ♦160/340 € ♦♦185/395 € – 4 suites
Rest – Menu 21/55 € – Carte 32/46 €
♦ Historic ♦ Modern ♦
An attractively restored building in the city's historic quarter. Contemporary decor with minimalist touches, and a roof terrace with views. A simple restaurant with large windows overlooking the square.

Heritage Av Liberdade without rest

Av. da Liberdade 28 ✉ *1250-145 –* Ⓜ *Avenida –* ℰ *213 40 40 40*
– www.heritage.pt **E1**
42 rm – ♦150/295 € ♦♦163/325 €, ♀ 14 €
♦ Business ♦ Contemporary ♦
The Heritage has a classic façade and a multipurpose public area, which also serves as the breakfast room. Well-appointed guestrooms that are contemporary in style.

Internacional Design H. without rest

Rua da Betesga 3 ✉ *1100-090 –* Ⓜ *Rossio –* ℰ *213 24 09 90*
– www.idesignhotel.com **E2**
55 rm ♀ – ♦♦100/500 €
♦ Business ♦ Design ♦
In keeping with the hotel name, the decor here is very much designer focused. The guestrooms are on four floors, each with its own style: urban, tribal, zen and pop.

Do Chiado without rest

Rua Nova do Almada 114 ✉ *1200-290 –* Ⓜ *Baixa-Chiado*
– ℰ *213 25 61 00 – www.hoteldochiado.pt* **E2**
38 rm ♀ – ♦♦195/300 € – 1 suite
♦ Business ♦ Oriental ♦
A hotel with well-appointed guestrooms in the heart of the Chiado district. Those on the seventh floor have private balconies with splendid views of the city.

Britania without rest

Rua Rodrigues Sampaio 17 ✉ *1150-278 –* Ⓜ *Avenida –* ℰ *213 15 50 16*
– www.heritage.pt **E1**
33 rm – ♦130/230 € ♦♦143/255 €, ♀ 14 €
♦ Business ♦ Art Deco ♦
The only public area in this hotel is the bar with its lovely wood floor and paintings of Portugal's former colonies. Spacious guestrooms with an Art Deco feel.

NH Liberdade

Av. da Liberdade 180-B ✉ *1250-146 –* Ⓜ *Avenida –* ℰ *213 51 40 60*
– www.nh-hotels.com **E1**
83 rm ♀ – ♦272/300 € ♦♦303/330 €
Rest – *(dinner only weekend)* Carte approx. 40 €
♦ Chain hotel ♦ Modern ♦
A good choice in Lisbon's business district. Highlights include the comfortable guestrooms designed in a contemporary style and the rooftop terrace boasting magnificent views of the old city. The multi-function restaurant offers Portuguese à la carte options alongside a selection of pasta dishes.

Tivoli Jardim 🔏 & 🖾 🛜 🛂 🅿 🚗 🚾 ⓪ 🔠 ⓪

Rua Julio Cesar Machado 7 ✉ *1250-135 –* Ⓜ *Avenida –* 𝒞 *213 59 10 00*
– www.tivolihotels.com   **E1**
119 rm 🛏 – 🛌130/270 € 🛏🛏140/290 €   **Rest** – Menu 34/51 €
◆ Business ◆ Functional ◆

The Tivoli Jardim's modern, functional and state-of-the-art facilities cater perfectly to its business guests. Contemporary accommodation with superior rooms that are more spacious and feature a terrace. The restaurant, which is also the venue for breakfast, offers an updated traditional menu.

Olissippo Castelo without rest ⩽ & 🖾 🛜 🚾 ⓪ 🔠 ⓪

Rua Costa do Castelo 120 ✉ *1100-179 –* Ⓜ *Rossio –* 𝒞 *218 82 01 90*
– www.olissippohotels.com   **F2**
24 rm 🛏 – 🛌200/220 € 🛏🛏220/240 €
◆ Holiday hotel ◆ Classic ◆

Located on a hill next to the San Jorge castle, part of this hotel is built up against the castle ramparts. Very comfortable guestrooms, a dozen of which have their own garden terrace and magnificent views.

Solar do Castelo without rest ⌘ 🖾 🛜 🚾 ⓪ 🔠 ⓪

Rua das Cozinhas 2 ✉ *1100-181 –* 𝒞 *218 80 60 50 – www.heritage.pt*
20 rm – 🛌162/310 € 🛏🛏176/340 €, 🛏 14 €   **F2**
◆ Palace ◆ Contemporary ◆

This hotel partially occupies a small 18C palace. It boasts a pretty paved patio with peacocks and a tiny ceramics museum. The classic yet contemporary guestrooms have seven personalised rooms in the palace itself and these offer greater comfort.

Solar dos Mouros without rest ⌘ ⩽ 🖾 🚾 ⓪ 🔠 ⓪

Rua do Milagre de Santo António 6 ✉ *1100-351 –* 𝒞 *218 85 49 40*
– www.solardosmouros.com   **F2**
13 rm – 🛌109/215 € 🛏🛏145/248 €, 🛏 13.90 €
◆ Business ◆ Holiday hotel ◆ Contemporary ◆

A traditional-style hotel with an original decor, a somewhat irregular layout and a modern interior. Colourful guestrooms, some enjoying excellent views.

Albergaria Senhora do Monte without rest ⩽ 🖾 🛜

Calçada do Monte 39 ✉ *1170-250*   🚾 ⓪ 🔠 ⓪
– Ⓜ *Martim Moniz –* 𝒞 *218 86 60 02*
– www.albergariasenhoradomonte.com   **F1**
28 rm 🛏 – 🛌59/99 € 🛏🛏60/150 €
◆ Townhouse ◆ Classic ◆

This quiet hotel is in the Graça residential district. It has cosy, functional guestrooms that are classic in feel. There is a terrace-bar with splendid views of Lisbon.

Tavares 🖾 🚾 ⓪ 🔠

Rua da Misericórdia 37 ✉ *1200-270 –* Ⓜ *Baixa-Chiado –* 𝒞 *213 42 11 12*
– www.restaurantetavares.net
– Closed Sunday and Monday   **E2**
Rest – Menu 40/89 € – Carte 81/113 € 🏶
◆ Traditional ◆ Classic ◆

Founded in 1784, this emblematic address is renowned for its history and elegance. It has an attractive entrance hall and majestic dining room with large mirrors, superb gilded work and chandeliers. Creative dishes with a solid base in traditional cuisine.

Gambrinus 🖾 🚾 ⓪ 🔠 ⓪

Rua das Portas de Santo Antão 25 ✉ *1150-264 –* Ⓜ *Restauradores*
– 𝒞 *213 42 14 66 – www.gambrinuslisboa.com*   **E1**
Rest – Carte 54/85 €
◆ Traditional ◆ Classic ◆

This renowned Lisbon restaurant has an attractive bar and a dining room with a fireplace. Traditional Portuguese specialities, international cuisine and seafood.

PORTUGAL - LISBON

XXX **Tágide**   ⇐ 🅰️ ⇔ 💳 😊 🅰️🅴 ⓞ

Largo da Academia Nacional de Belas Artes 18-20 ⊠ *1200-005*
– Ⓜ *Baixa-Chiado –* ℰ *213 40 40 10 – www.restaurantetagide.com*
– Closed August, Sunday and Monday   **E2**
Rest – Menu 23/42 € – Carte 33/47 €
♦ Modern ♦ Classic ♦

Tágide occupies an aristocratic building. Its main dining room exudes a certain charm with its delightful Portuguese tiling. Traditional cuisine with a modern touch.

XXX **Casa do Leão**   ⇐ 🍴 🅰️ 💳 😊 🅰️🅴 ⓞ

Castelo de São Jorge ⊠ *1100-129 –* ℰ *218 87 59 62 – www.pousadas.pt*
Rest – Carte 35/54 €   **F2**
♦ Traditional ♦ Classic ♦

A unique location inside the defensive walls of the Castle of São Jorge. Typical Portuguese style dining room with a fireplace and vaulted roof, as well as a terrace with spectacular views.

XXX **Belcanto** (José Avillez)   🅰️ 💳 😊 🅰️🅴

⛉ *Largo de São Carlos 10* ⊠ *1200 - 410 –* Ⓜ *Baixa-Chiado –* ℰ *213 42 06 07*
– www.belcanto.pt
– Closed August, Sunday and Monday   **E2**
Rest – Menu 60/80 € – Carte 55/70 € ⅋
♦ Creative ♦ Classic ♦

Belcanto is situated behind a discreet façade in the Bairro Alto district. It has two attractively decorated dining rooms. Both are furnished in a classic, contemporary style and both boast views of the kitchen. Traditional dishes form the basis of the menu, alongside more creative cuisine with an innovative touch.
➜ Rebentação, bivalves, gamba da costa, agua do mar e areia de algas. Mergulho no mar, robalo com algas e bivalves. Tangerina.

XX **Solar dos Presuntos**   🅰️ 💳 😊 🅰️🅴 ⓞ

Rua das Portas de Santo Antão 150 ⊠ *1150-269 –* Ⓜ *Avenida*
– ℰ *213 42 42 53 – www.solardospresuntos.com*
– Closed August, Christmas, Sunday and Bank Holidays   **E1**
Rest – Menu 43 € – Carte 42/65 € ⅋
♦ Traditional ♦ Inn ♦

Run by its owners, this pleasant restaurant has an attractive counter of fresh produce on display. Large selection of traditional dishes and seafood specialities, as well as an excellent wine list.

XX **Ad Lib** – Hotel Sofitel Lisbon Liberdade   🅰️ 💳 😊 🅰️🅴 ⓞ

Av. da Liberdade 127 ⊠ *1269-038 –* Ⓜ *Avenida –* ℰ *213 22 83 50*
– www.restauranteadlib.pt
– Closed Saturday dinner and Sunday dinner   **E1**
Rest – Menu 25 € – Carte 39/55 €
♦ Modern ♦ Trendy ♦

Contemporary dining with a colonial touch. Two types of menu are offered here. The menu at lunchtime combines traditional cuisine with French brasserie-style dining. The menu in the evening is a more elaborate affair.

X **100 Maneiras**   🅰️ 💳 😊 🅰️🅴

Rua do Teixeira 35 ⊠ *1200-459 –* ℰ *210 99 04 75*
– www.restaurante100maneiras.com
– Closed Sunday   **E1**
Rest – *(dinner only)* Menu 40 €
♦ Creative ♦ Rustic ♦

A small restaurant in a narrow street in the Barrio Alto district. The young chef offers a creative tasting menu, which is fresh, light and imaginatively presented.

Four Seasons H. Ritz Lisbon ⟨ 🛬 ɫ⚂ 🖼 ℅ rm, 🛗 🛜 🛁 🅿 🚗 VISA ⓪ AE ⓪

Rua Rodrigo da Fonseca 88 ✉ 1099-039
– Ⓜ Marquês de Pombal – ℰ 213 81 14 00
– www.fourseasons.com   G3
241 rm – 🛏🛏455/560 €, 🍽 37 € – 41 suites
Rest *Varanda* – Carte 73/98 €

◆ Grand Luxury ◆ Classic ◆

Everything at the Four Seasons has been designed to ensure a perfect stay for its guests. The building's modern exterior is in contrast to the classic, elegant feel of the interior. The delightful restaurant offers an extensive lunchtime buffet and contemporary influenced à la carte dining in the evening.

Tiara Park Atlantic Lisboa ⟨ ɫ⚂ ℅ rm, 🛗 🛜 🛁 🚗 VISA ⓪ AE ⓪

Rua Castilho 149 ✉ 1099-034
– Ⓜ Marquês de Pombal – ℰ 213 81 87 00 – www.tiara-hotels.com
314 rm – 🛏🛏120/450 €, 🍽 23 € – 17 suites   G3
Rest *L'Appart* – Carte 38/50 €

◆ Business ◆ Contemporary ◆

Excellent facilities and professional staff in this well-maintained hotel with modern guestrooms and suites. Marble bathrooms and quality furniture. An attractively decorated restaurant with four different dining areas. Options include a buffet, à la carte menu and daily specials.

Eurostars Das Letras 🛬 ɫ⚂ ℅ rm, 🛗 rm, 🛜 🛁 🚗 VISA ⓪ AE ⓪

Rua Castilho 6-12 ✉ 1250-069 – ℰ 213 57 30 94
– www.eurostarshotels.com   G3
107 rm 🍽 – 🛏130/799 € 🛏🛏140/799 € – 6 suites
Rest – Menu 28/40 € – Carte 25/41 €

◆ Business ◆ Contemporary ◆

The modern look and designer detail in the hotel's public areas compete with the crisp aesthetics of its classic guestrooms, which are comfortable and contemporary in style. The multi-function restaurant offers a choice of traditional cuisine.

CS Vintage Lisboa ɫ⚂ ℅ rm, 🛗 🛜 🛁 🚗 VISA ⓪ AE ⓪

Rua Rodrigo da Fonseca 2 ✉ 1250-191 – Ⓜ Rato – ℰ 210 40 54 00
– www.cshotelandresorts.com   G3
53 rm 🍽 – 🛏197/256 € 🛏🛏220/265 € – 3 suites
Rest – Menu 18 € – Carte 24/35 €

◆ Business ◆ Contemporary ◆

Strong attention to detail has resulted in a look that is both personalised and welcoming. The guestrooms are classic yet contemporary in style with top quality fixtures and furnishings. The multi-function restaurant is the setting for breakfast, lunch and dinner. Small spa.

Aviz ℅ rm, 🛗 📞 🛁 🚗 VISA ⓪ AE ⓪

Rua Duque de Palmela 32 ✉ 1250-098
– Ⓜ Marquês de Pombal – ℰ 210 40 20 00
– www.hotelaviz.com   G3
70 rm 🍽 – 🛏90/120 € 🛏🛏100/220 € – 14 suites
Rest *Aviz* – Menu 18 € – Carte 31/55 €

◆ Traditional ◆ Classic ◆

This classically designed hotel features an elegant lobby and meticulously furnished and equipped guestrooms. Each one is dedicated to a character from history who has stayed here.

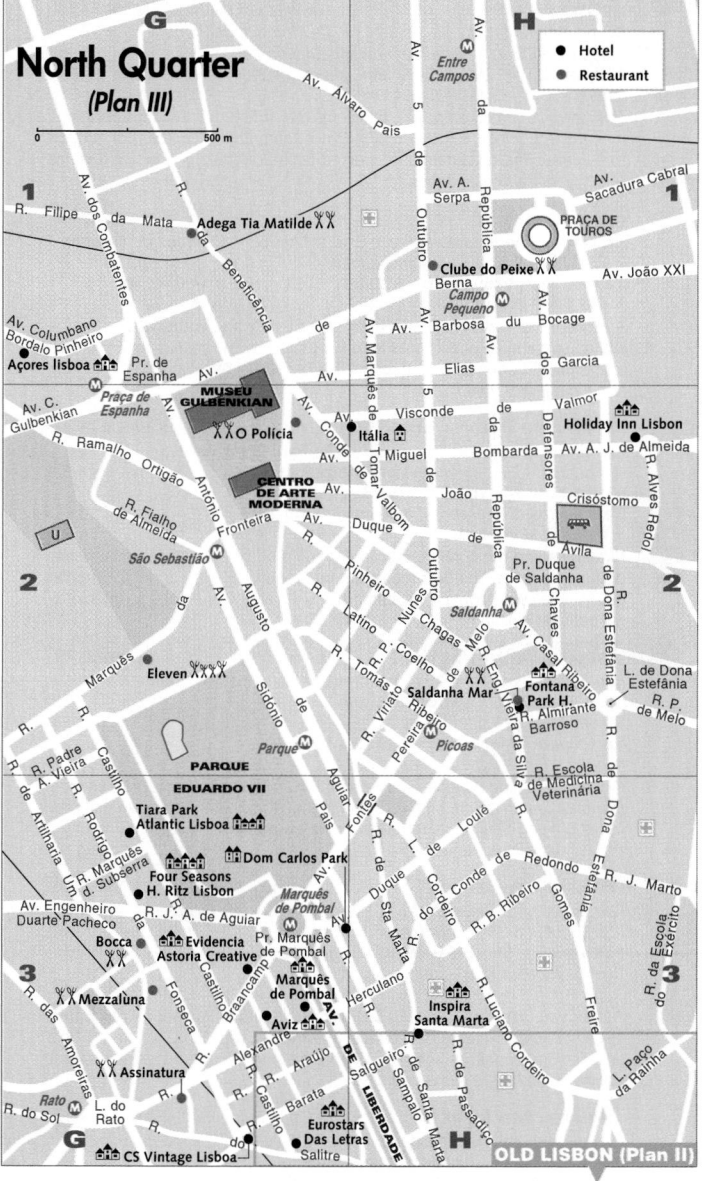

North Quarter
(Plan III)

0   500 m

Hotel ●   **Restaurant** ●

G   **H**

1

Av. Álvaro Pais

Av. Entre Campos

Av. Sacadura Cabral

R. Filipe   da   Mata

Av. dos Combatentes

Adega Tia Matilde ✗✗

Av. A. Serpa

Av. 5 de Outubro

Av. da República

PRAÇA DE TOUROS

Clube do Peixe ● ✗✗

Av. João XXI

Berna   Campo Pequeno

R. da Beneficência

Av. C. Gulbenkian

Av. Columbano Bordalo Pinheiro

Açores lisboa 🏨

Pr. de Espanha

Praça de Espanha

MUSEU GULBENKIAN

✗✗ **O Polícia**

Av. Marquês de

Av. Conde de Valbom

Av. Barbosa du Bocage

Elias

Av. Miguel Bombarda

dos Garcia

Itália 🏨

Visconde de

Valmor

Holiday Inn Lisbon 🏨

Av. A. J. de Almeida

Defensores de

R. Ramalho Ortigão

R. Fialho de Almeida

CENTRO DE ARTE MODERNA

Av. António

Av. Fonteira

Av. Duque de

Miguel

João

de

República

Crisóstomo

Pr. Duque de Saldanha

Av. Casal Ribeiro

Avila

U

São Sebastião Ⓜ

2

dp

Av. Augusto

R. Pinheiro

R. Latino

R. Tomás

R. P. Coelho

R. Viriato

Nunes

Chagas

Meio

R. Eng.

Vieira da Silva

Av. Chaves

Ⓜ Saldanha

Saldanha Mar

Fontana Park H. 🏨

L. de Dona Estefânia

R. P. de Melo

Marquês ●

Eleven ✗✗✗✗

Sidónio

Ⓜ Parque

Ribeiro

Pereira

Ⓜ Picoas

R. Almirante Barroso

R. de Dona Estefânia

R. P. de Melo

PARQUE

EDUARDO VII

R. Escola de Medicina Veterinária

R. Padre A. Vieira

R. Castilho

R. Rodrigo d. Subserra

Tiara Park Atlantic Lisboa 🏨

H. Ritz Lisbon 🏨

Four Seasons

🏨 **Dom Carlos Park**

Av. Fontes

R. de Loulé

R. Duque de Palmela

Av. Aguiar

R. Castilho

Av. Engenheiro Duarte Pacheco

R. J. A. de Aguiar

Marquês de Pombal

Bocca ● ✗✗

Evidencia Astoria Creative 🏨

Pr. Marquês de Pombal

Marquês de Pombal Ⓜ

R. Castilho

R. Braancamp

R. Fonseca

Marquês de Pombal 🏨

Av. da

R. S. de Sta Marta

R. Conde de Redondo

R. B. Ribeiro Gomes

R. Luciano Cordeiro

R. J. Marto

R. da Escola do Exército

3

✗✗ **Mezzalùna**

R. das Amoreiras

✗✗ **Assinatura**

Aviz 🏨

R. Alexandre Araújo

R. Barata

R. Herculano

Inspira Santa Marta 🏨

R. de Passadiço

R. de Santa Marta

L. Paço da Rainha

Rato ● L. do Rato

R. do Sol

🏨 **CS Vintage Lisboa**

Salgueiro Sampaio

do

Salitre

Eurostars Das Letras 🏨

LIBERDADE

OLD LISBON (Plan II)

G   **H**

Marquês de Pombal

Av. da Liberdade 243 ✉ *1250-143 –* Ⓜ *Marquês de Pombal*
– ☎ 213 19 79 00 – www.hotel-marquesdepombal.pt   **G3**
120 rm ⊷ – ♦138/172 € ♦♦150/184 € – 3 suites   **Rest** – Carte 26/46 €
♦ Business ♦ Contemporary ♦

This hotel has a contemporary, functional feel. It features elegant furnishings,
modern technology, a modular conference room and good levels of comfort
throughout. The restaurant is connected to the cafeteria and serves a varied
selection of traditional dishes.

Açores Lisboa

Av. Columbano Bordalo Pinheiro 3 ✉ *1070-060 –* Ⓜ *Praça de Espanha*
– ☎ 217 22 29 20 – www.bensaude.pt   **G1**
123 rm ⊷ – ♦69/199 € – 5 suites   **Rest** – Menu 14 € – Carte 18/32 €
♦ Chain hotel ♦ Business ♦ Contemporary ♦

A modern and functional chain hotel with friendly and enthusiastic staff. The
limited space in its public areas is compensated by the well-appointed guestrooms and fully equipped bathrooms. The restaurant offers a buffet at midday,
and a traditional menu at night.

Evidencia Astoria Creative

Rua Braamcamp 10 ✉ *1250-050 –* Ⓜ *Marquês de Pombal*
– ☎ 213 86 13 17 – www.evidenciaastoria.com   **G3**
91 rm ⊷ – ♦85/105 € ♦♦115/135 €
Rest – *(closed weekend) (lunch only)* Menu 12 €
♦ Business ♦ Minimalist ♦

Hidden behind the hotel's classic façade is a modern interior decked out with
designer features. The best rooms are those with a lounge and glass-fronted
gallery. The contemporary restaurant serves breakfast, as well as an international buffet at lunchtime.

Inspira Santa Marta

Rua Santa Marta 48 ✉ *1150-297 –* Ⓜ *Marqúes de Pombal*
– ☎ 210 44 09 00 – www.inspirahotels.com   **H3**
89 rm ⊷ – ♦♦125/180 €
Rest Open – Menu 15 € – Carte 20/36 €
♦ Business ♦ Modern ♦

A hotel combining designer features, comfort and a spa. Its aim is to be environmentally sustainable and it has rooms arranged according to the oriental principles of Feng Shui. In its restaurant, dine on modern, healthy cuisine based
around organic produce.

Fontana Park H.

Rua Engenheiro Vieira da Silva 2 ✉ *1050-105 –* Ⓜ *Picoas*
– ☎ 210 41 06 00 – www.fontanaparkhotel.com   **H2**
139 rm ⊷ – ♦90/215 € ♦♦105/235 €
Rest Saldanha Mar – see restaurant listing
♦ Business ♦ Modern ♦

A hotel with a minimalist decor, designer details and an interior garden faithful
to Zen philosophy. It has comfortable guestrooms, with those on the top floor
enjoying the benefit of a terrace. Choose between Portuguese and Japanese
cuisine in the hotel's two restaurants.

Holiday Inn Lisbon

Av. António José de Almeida 28-A ✉ *1000-044 –* Ⓜ *Saldanha*
– ☎ 210 04 40 00 – www.holiday-inn.com   **H2**
161 rm – ♦70/250 € ♦♦80/260 €, ⊷ 14.50 € – 9 suites
Rest – Carte 30/37 €
♦ Business ♦ Contemporary ♦

Contemporary-style hotel geared to business travellers. Pleasant lounge and
public areas, in addition to well-appointed guestrooms with classic modern furnishings. The hotel's restaurant serves a varied choice of traditional dishes.

PORTUGAL - LISBON

Dom Carlos Park without rest 🔠 🛜 🔊 ⅷ 🆚 🌀 🆎 🆔

Av. Duque de Loulé 121 ⌷ *1050-089 –* ❶ *Marquês de Pombal*
– 𝒞 213 51 25 90 – www.domcarloshoteis.com G-H3
76 rm ⬚ – †64/147 € ††70/196 €

◆ Business ◆ Classic ◆

A classic, elegant address with a privileged location and tranquil ambience. Comfortable bedrooms designed along traditional lines; the majority adorned with functional furnishings.

Itália without rest 🔠 ⅷ 🆚 🌀 🆎 🆔

Av. Visconde de Valmor 67 ⌷ *1050-239 –* ❶ *Saldanha – 𝒞 217 97 77 36*
– www.hotelitalia.pt G-H2
44 rm ⬚ – †36/99 € ††45/99 €

◆ Family ◆ Business ◆ Functional ◆

The attractive patio with its tables, lawn and orange trees comes as a pleasant surprise in the centre of the city. The guestrooms are modern, simple and functional.

Eleven ≤ 🔠 ⇧ 🅿 ⅷ 🌀 🆎 🆔

Rua Marquês de Fronteira ⌷ *1070 –* ❶ *São Sebastião – 𝒞 213 86 22 11*
– www.restauranteleven.com
– closed Sunday G2
Rest – Menu 38/89 € – Carte 60/100 € ⅍

◆ Creative ◆ Trendy ◆

This restaurant is housed in a building where the design element predominates. In the modern and bright dining room, boasting magnificent views of both the park and the city, the emphasis is very much on creative cuisine.

Assinatura 🔠 ⇧ ⅷ 🌀 🆎 🆔

Rua Vale do Pereiro 19 ⌷ *1250-270 –* ❶ *Rato – 𝒞 213 86 76 96*
– www.assinatura.com.pt
– Closed Saturday lunch, Sunday and Monday lunch G3
Rest – Menu 25/44 € – Carte 41/60 €

◆ Modern ◆ Minimalist ◆

A restaurant with a minimalist atmosphere, a colour scheme focusing on red and white tones, and a private room called 'The Chef's Table'. Updated traditional cuisine.

Saldanha Mar – Hotel Fontana Park H. ⅷ 🌀 🆎 🆔

Rua Engenheiro Vieira da Silva 2 ⌷ *1050-105 –* ❶ *Picoas*
– 𝒞 210 41 06 00 – www.fontanaparkhotel.com H2
Rest – Menu 30 € – Carte 27/67 €

◆ Traditional ◆ Minimalist ◆

The Saldanha Mar is minimalist in style and dominated by varying tones of white, with a kitchen visible to diners. Two types of menu: one for lunch, based around fresh fish and daily suggestions; the other, more elaborate in composition, for the evening.

Bocca 🔠 ⅷ 🌀 🆎 🆔

Rua Rodrigo da Fonseca 87 D ⌷ *1250-190 –* ❶ *Marquês de Pombal*
– 𝒞 213 80 83 83 – www.bocca.pt
– Closed Sunday and Monday G3
Rest – *(dinner only)* Menu 38/65 € – Carte 34/68 €

◆ Creative ◆ Fashionable ◆

The Bocca has two contemporary dining rooms with the first having views of the kitchen. There is also a gastro-bar area in the basement for tapas and raciones. Creative cuisine.

Clube do Peixe 🔠 ⅷ 🌀 🆎

Av. 5 de Outubro 180 ⌷ *1050-063 –* ❶ *Campo Pequeno – 𝒞 217 97 34 34*
– www.clube-do-peixe.com – closed Sunday H1
Rest – Menu 28 € – Carte 35/45 €

◆ Fish and seafood ◆ Classic ◆

A popular local restaurant with an attractive display of fish and seafood at the entrance. The dining room is classic-contemporary in style with the occasional maritime detail in the decor.

XX **Adega Tia Matilde**   AC ⇔ 🚗 VISA ◎ AE ①
Rua da Beneficéncia 77 ✉ 1600-017 – ⓜ Praça de Espanha
– ☏ 217 97 21 72 – www.adegatiamatilde.com
– Closed Saturday dinner and Sunday   G1
Rest – Menu 29/35 € – Carte 20/42 €
♦ Traditional ♦ Classic ♦

Family-run restaurant with a good local reputation. Spacious dining rooms and traditional cuisine. The large underground car park makes up for the location.

XX **O Polícia**   AC VISA ◎ AE ①
Rua Marquês Sá da Bandeira 112 ✉ 1050-150 – ⓜ São Sebastião
– ☏ 217 96 35 05 – www.restauranteopolicia.com
– Closed Saturday dinner, Sunday and Bank Holidays   G2
Rest – Menu 25/33 € – Carte 22/45 €
♦ Traditional ♦ Simple ♦

The quality of the fish here is well known throughout the city. Although functional in appearance, the food display counters are hugely enticing. Advance booking recommended.

XX **Mezzaluna**   ⅇ AC VISA ◎ AE ①
Rua Artilharia Um 16 ✉ 1250-039 – ⓜ Rato – ☏ 213 87 99 44
– www.mezzalunalisboa.com
– Closed Christmas, Saturday lunch and Sunday   G3
Rest – Menu 35/45 € – Carte 25/41 €
♦ Italian ♦ Classic ♦

The owner-chef runs this restaurant with a casual yet chic feel. The focus here is
on traditional Italian cuisine with a few Italian-Portuguese variations.

PARQUE DAS NAÇÕES   *Plan I*

🏠 **Tivoli Oriente**   ⅙ 🖳 ⅇ rm, AC 🛜 🖴 🚗 VISA ◎ AE
Av. D. João II (Parque das Nações) ✉ 1990-083 – ⓜ Oriente
– ☏ 218 91 51 00 – www.tivolihotels.com   D1
277 rm – ♛♛80/120 €, � 10 € – 2 suites   **Rest** – Carte approx. 32 €
♦ Chain hotel ♦ Classic ♦

Housed in an attractively designed tower in the Expo district, the Tivoli Oriente has
a modern lobby and comfortable guestrooms. The renovated rooms are more
contemporary in feel, and the remainder are more classic and functional in appearance. The simple restaurant next to reception specialises in grilled meats.

🏠 **Olissippo Oriente**   ⅇ rm, AC 🛜 🖴 🚗 VISA ◎ AE ①
Rua D. João II (Parque das Nações) ✉ 1990-083 – ⓜ Oriente
– ☏ 218 92 91 00 – www.olissippohotels.com   D1
182 rm ⊆ – ♛102/120 € ♛♛115/140 €   **Rest** – Carte 21/39 €
♦ Chain hotel ♦ Modern ♦

Situated on the Expo site, this hotel boasts modern facilities. It includes extensive public areas and lounges, meeting rooms and comfortable guestrooms. A
refined dining room where guests can enjoy a full buffet or a menu featuring
traditional cuisine.

WEST   *Plan I*

🏠 **Pestana Palace**   🌿 🚲 ⅙ 🏊 🖳 ⅇ rm, AC 🛜 🖴 🚗 VISA ◎ AE
Rua Jau 54 ✉ 1300-314 – ☏ 213 61 56 00 – www.pestana.com
177 rm ⊆ – ♛180/260 € – 17 suites   B3
Rest *Valle Flor* – Menu 25/80 € – Carte 37/82 €
♦ Grand Luxury ♦ Palace ♦ Elegant ♦

A beautiful 19C palace decorated in line with the period with sumptuous lounges, guestrooms featuring an array of decorative detail, and grounds that have
the feel of a botanical garden. In the restaurant, choose from several set menus
at lunchtime and traditional à la carte choices with a modern flair in the evening. A small private room is also available in the old kitchen.

PORTUGAL - LISBON

Lapa Palace ⌚ ≤ 🚗 🏠 ⅃ ☒ 🍴 & rm, 🔲 🛜 🐕 🅿 🚘

Rua do Pau de Bandeira 4 ✉ *1249-021 –* ⓜ *Rato* 🆅🆂🅰 ⓒⓞ 🄰🄴 ⓞ
– 𝒞 213 94 94 94 – www.olissippohotels.com **B3**
102 rm ⌤ – ♥♥370/430 € – 7 suites **Rest** – Carte 48/68 €
♦ Grand Luxury ♦ Classic ♦
This 19C palace combines lavish style and classic splendour on a hill overlooking the Tagus. It has delightful gardens full of intimate corners and even a waterfall between the trees. In the bright and elegant restaurant, embellished with chandeliers, the menu offers a successful modern take on traditional Portuguese cuisine.

As Janelas Verdes without rest & 🔲 🛜 🆅🆂🅰 ⓒⓞ 🄰🄴 ⓞ

Rua das Janelas Verdes 47 ✉ *1200-690 – 𝒞 213 96 81 43*
– www.heritage.pt **B3**
29 rm – ♥143/280 € ♥♥157/298 €, ⌤ 14 €
♦ Villa ♦ Classic ♦
Partially housed in an 18C mansion, this welcoming hotel has a delightful lounge-library and beautiful views. A romantic feel and classic style.

York House 🏠 🔲 🛜 🕍 🆅🆂🅰 ⓒⓞ 🄰🄴 ⓞ

Rua das Janelas Verdes 32 ✉ *1200-691 –* ⓜ *Cais do Sodré*
– 𝒞 213 96 24 35 – www.yorkhouselisboa.com **B3**
32 rm – ♥80/220 € ♥♥90/250 €, ⌤ 12 €
Rest – *(closed January, Monday and Tuesday)* Carte 25/46 €
♦ Historic ♦ Contemporary ♦
Housed in a 17C convent, this hotel has a comfortable, contemporary interior. Its modern decor is furnished with period pieces. Classic-style restaurant adorned with an attractive frieze of old azulejo tiles.

✗✗ A Travessa 🏠 🆅🆂🅰 ⓒⓞ 🄰🄴

Travessa do Convento das Bernardas 12 ✉ *1200-638 – 𝒞 213 90 20 34*
– www.atravessa.com
– Closed Sunday **B3**
Rest – Carte 45/52 €
♦ International ♦ Cosy ♦
This restaurant occupies a 17C monastery. The dining room has a lovely vaulted ceiling, rustic-style flooring and an attractive terrace in the cloister.

✗ Solar dos Nunes 🔲 ⌂📶 🆅🆂🅰 ⓒⓞ 🄰🄴 ⓞ

Rua dos Lusíadas 68-72 ✉ *1300-372 – 𝒞 213 64 73 59*
– www.solardosnunes.pt
– Closed 7-31 August and Sunday **B3**
Rest – Menu 25/65 € – Carte approx. 30 €
♦ Traditional ♦ Neighbourhood ♦
This restaurant has a friendly atmosphere, traditional-style dining rooms and a lovely paved floor. Wide choice of traditional Portuguese dishes and a good wine list.

BELÉM *Plan I*

Altis Belém ≤ 🍴 🏀 & rm, 🔲 🛜 🕍 🅿 🚘 🆅🆂🅰 ⓒⓞ 🄰🄴 ⓞ

Doca do Bom Sucesso ✉ *1400-038 – 𝒞 210 40 02 00*
– www.altisbelemhotel.com **A3**
45 rm ⌤ – ♥150/300 € ♥♥190/450 € – 5 suites
Rest *Feitoria* ✿ – see restaurant listing
Rest – Carte 36/51 €
♦ Luxury ♦ Business ♦ Modern ♦
A combination of luxury and modernity with facilities that include a fully equipped spa and a chill-out zone on the roof terrace. It has particularly spacious guestrooms with personalised decor and river views. Enjoy a range of contemporary dishes in the roomy and elegant restaurant.

Jerónimos 8 without rest   🔓 📶 🛜 🗚 VISA ⓒ AE ①

Rua dos Jerónimos 8 ⊠ *1400-211 – ℰ 213 60 09 00*
– www.almeidahotels.com   **A3**
65 rm ⊆ – †100/240 € ††110/250 €

♦ Business ♦ Modern ♦

This comfortable hotel is located next to the Monasterio de Los Jerónimos. It occupies an old building that has been completely renovated with a minimalist feel.

Feitoria – Hotel Altis Belém   🛜 📶 🅿 VISA ⓒ AE ①

Doca do Bom Sucesso ⊠ *1400-038 – ℰ 210 40 02 07*
– www.altisbelemhotel.com
– Closed 7-23 August, Sanday and Monday   **A3**
Rest – Menu 45/70 € – Carte 68/82 € 🕸

♦ Modern ♦ Inn ♦

The Feitoria features a modern dining room on two floors, an attractive ent-rance hall, a bar for a pre-dinner drink and a terrace. Creative cuisine centred around quality ingredients, meticulous presentation, and a panoply of flavours.
➜ Lagostins com espargos brancos e verdes, pequenos torresmos de leitão. Alfaquique corado com grelos e ovas, açorda lisboeta de alho e coentros, sal e cêra de limão. Parfait de baunilha e alfazema recheado com coulis de alperce, gelado "pèche de vigne"

SPAIN
ESPAÑA

→ **AREA:**
504 645 km² (194 595 sq mi).

→ **POPULATION:**
47 190 493 inhabitants.
Density = 94 per km².

→ **CAPITAL:** Madrid.

→ **CURRENCY:**
Euro (€).

→ **GOVERNMENT:**
Constitutional parliamentary monarchy (since 1978). Member of European Union since 1986.

→ **LANGUAGES:**
Spanish (Castilian) but also Catalan in Catalonia, Gallego in Galicia, Euskera in the Basque Country, Valencian in the Valencian Region and Mallorquin in the Balearic Isles.

→ **PUBLIC HOLIDAYS:**
New Year's Day (1 Jan); Epiphany (6 Jan); Maundy Thursday (late Mar/Apr); Good Friday (late Mar/Apr); Labor Day (1 May); Assumption of the Virgin Mary (15 Aug); National Day (12 Oct); All Saints' Day (1 Nov); Constitution Day (6 Dec); Immaculate Conception (8 Dec); Christmas Day (25 Dec). Autonomous communities may replace some dates.

→ **LOCAL TIME:**
GMT+1 hour in winter and GMT +2 hours in summer.

→ **CLIMATE:**
Temperate Mediterranean with mild winters (colder in interior) and sunny, hot summers (Madrid: January 6°C; July 25°C).

→ **EMERGENCY:**
Police ☎ **091**; Medical Assistance and Fire Brigade ☎ **112.** (Dialling **112** within any EU country will redirect your call and contact the emergency services.)

→ **ELECTRICITY:**
230 volts AC, 50Hz; 2 round pin sockets.

→ **FORMALITIES:**
Travellers from the European Union (EU), Switzerland, Iceland and the main countries of North and South America need a national identity card or passport (America: passport required) to visit Spain for less than three months (tourism or business purpose). For visitors from other countries a visa may be required, in addition to a passport, especially for those wishing to stay for longer than three months. We advise you to check with your embassy before travelling.

MADRID

MADRID

Population: 3 265 038

Aidas Zubkonis/Fotolia.com

The renaissance of Madrid has seen it develop as a big player on the world cultural stage, attracting more international music, theatre and dance than it would have dreamed of a few decades ago. The nightlife in Spain's proud capital is second to none and the superb museums of art which make up the city's 'golden triangle' have all undergone thrilling reinvention in recent years. This is a city that might think it has some catching up to do: it was only made the capital in 1561 on the whim of ruler, Felipe II. But its position was crucial: slap bang in the middle of the Iberian Peninsula. Ruled by Habsburgs and Bourbons, it soon made a mark in Europe, and the contemporary big wigs of Madrid are now having the same effect – this time with a 21C twist.

The central heart of Madrid is compact, defined by the teeming Habsburg hubs of Puerta del Sol and Plaza Mayor, and the mighty Palacio Real – the biggest official royal residence in the world, with a bewildering three thousand rooms. East of here are the grand squares, fountains and fine museums of the Bourbon District, with its easterly boundary, the Retiro park. West of the historical centre are the capacious green acres of Casa de Campo, while the affluent, regimented grid streets of Salamanca are to the east. Modern Madrid is just to the north, embodied in the grand north-south boulevard Paseo de la Castellana.

MADRID IN...

→ **ONE DAY**
Puerta del Sol, Plaza Mayor, Palacio Real, Prado.

→ **TWO DAYS**
Museo Thyssen-Bornemisza, Retiro, Gran Vía, tapas at a traditional taberna.

→ **THREE DAYS**
Chueca, Malasaña, Centro de Arte Reina Sofía.

PRACTICAL INFORMATION

ARRIVAL-DEPARTURE

 Madrid Barajas Airport is 13km east of the city. Metro Line 8 runs every 4-7min and takes 50min. Commuter rail service C-1 connects T4 with Chamartin and Atocha Railway Stations (frequency 30min); Chamartin for services to the north of Spain and France; Atocha for those to the south.

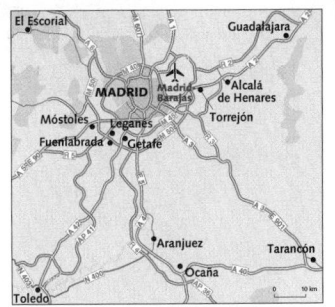

GETTING AROUND

You can buy single journey tickets, but better value for longer visits is a ten-trip Metrobus ticket, valid on both bus and metro networks, and available from underground stations, bus ticket offices, newsstands and tobacconists. The Tourist Travel Pass is valid from one to seven days for unlimited travel on all public transport in either Zone A or Zone T. A Madrid Card, valid for one, two, three or five day periods, entitles you to travel on all forms of public transport, and grants admission to more than fifty museums. It is also valid for discounts in some nightclubs, shops and restaurants.

CALENDAR HIGHLIGHTS

January
Twelfth Night Procession.

February
ARCO (contemporary art fair), Carnaval.

April
Día de Cervantes (book fair).

May
Dos de Mayo, Fiesta de San Isidro, Madrid Book Fair.

July–August
Los Veranos de la Villa.

September
Festival de Otoño.

EATING OUT

Madrileños know how to pace themselves. Breakfast is around 8am, lunch 2pm or 3pm; the afternoon begins at 5pm and dinner won't be until 10pm or 11pm. Madrid is the European capital which has best managed to absorb the regional cuisine of the country, largely due to massive internal migration to the city, and it claims to have highest number of bars and restaurants per capita than anywhere else in the world. If you want to tuck into local specialities, you'll find them everywhere around the city. Callos a la Madrileña is Madrid-style tripe, dating back to 1559, while sopas de ajo (garlic soup) is a favourite on cold winter days. Another popular soup (also a main course) is cocido Madrileño, hearty and aromatic and comprised of chickpeas, meat, tocino belly pork, potatoes and vegetables, slowly cooked in a rich broth. To experience the real Madrid dining ambience, get to a traditional taberna in the heart of the old neighbourhood: these are distinguished by a large clock, a carved wooden bar with a zinc counter, wine flasks, marble-topped tables and ceramic tiles.

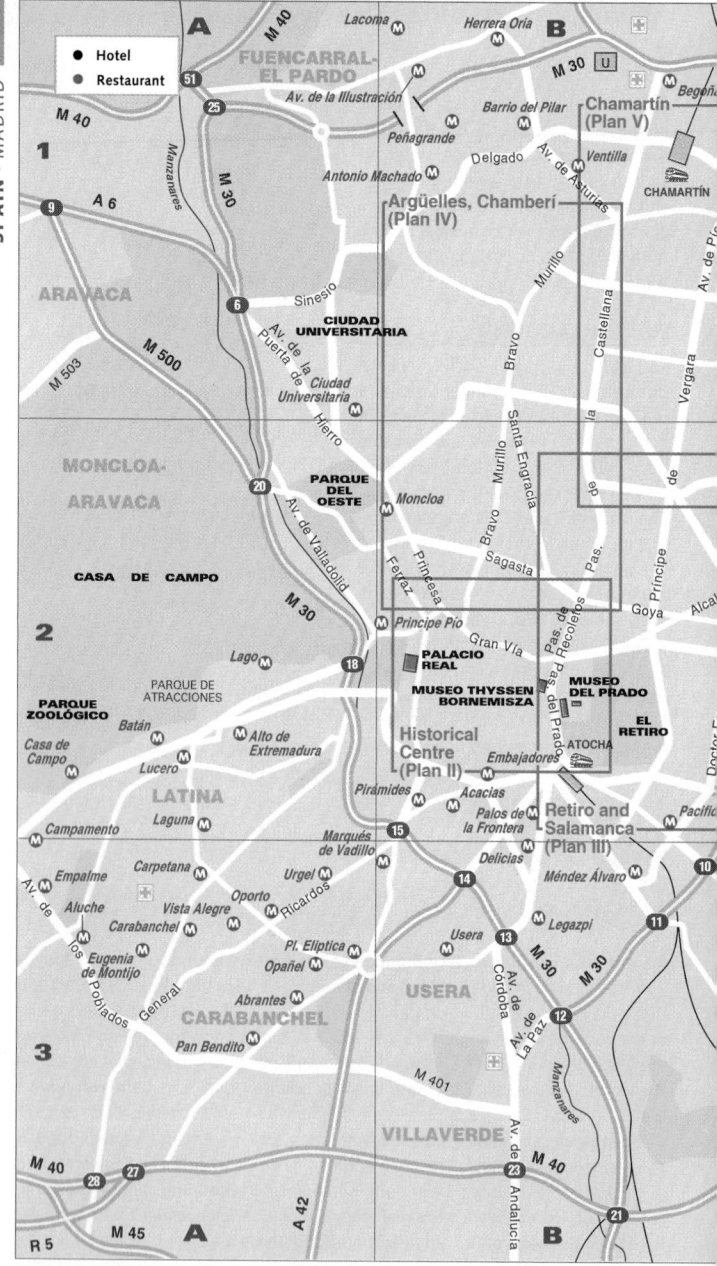

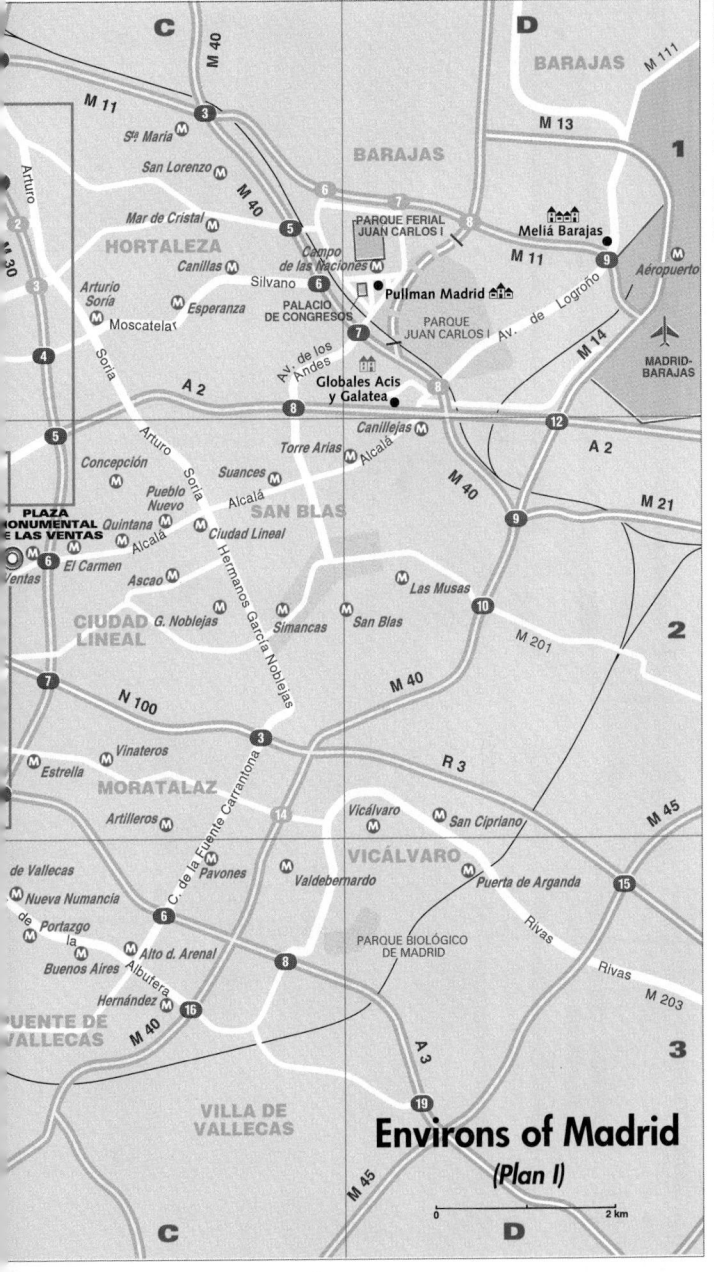

Environs of Madrid
(Plan I)

0   2 km

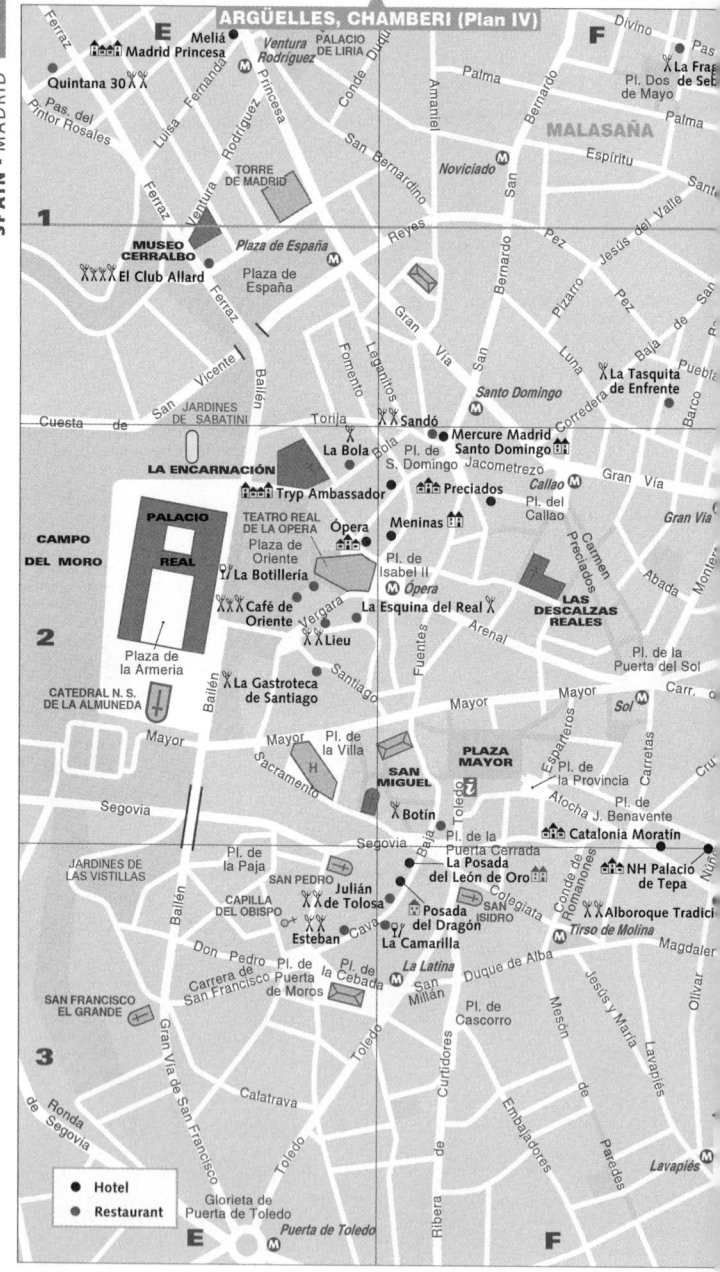

ARGÜELLES, CHAMBERI (Plan IV)

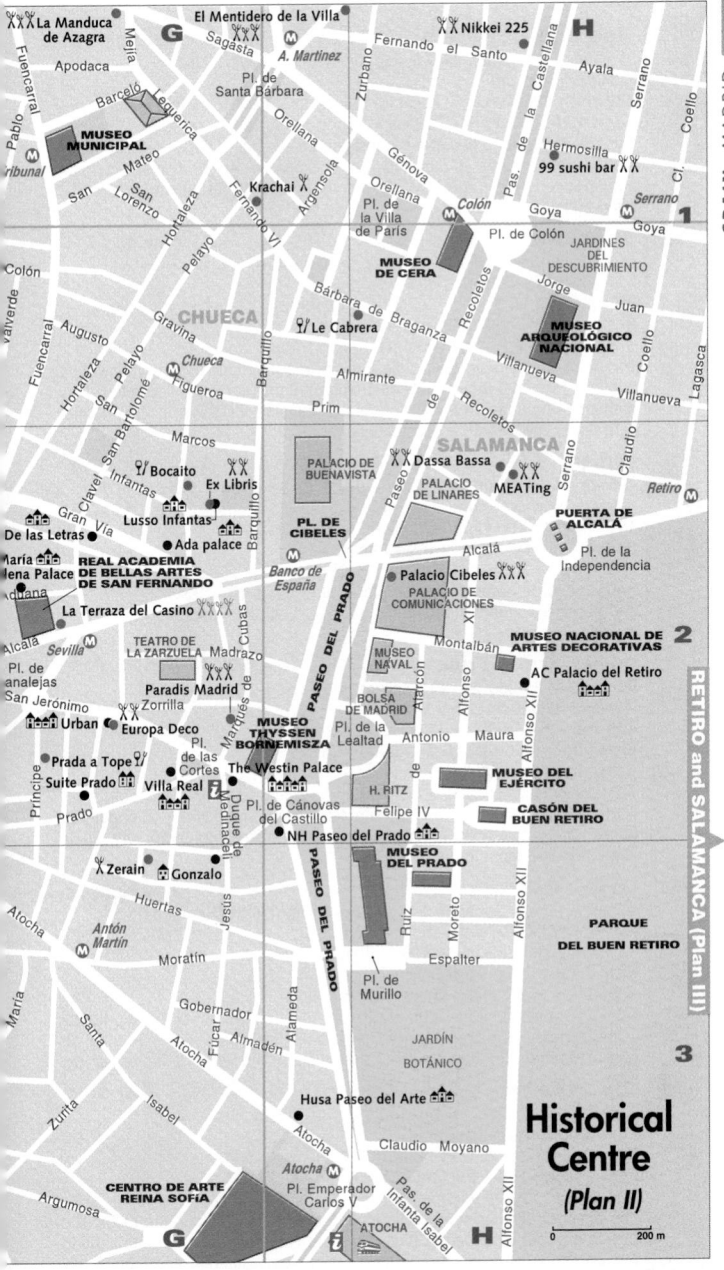

Historical
Centre
(Plan II)

0   200 m

The Westin Palace   🛗 ᕹ rm, 🅐🅒 🛜 🛅 🚗 🆅🅸🆂🅰 ⓪ 🅰🅴 ⓪
pl. de las Cortes 7 ⊠ 28014 – ⓜ Sevilla – ℰ 913 60 80 00
– www.westin.com   G2
420 rm – ♥♥550/630 €, ☲ 34 € – 47 suites   **Rest** – Carte 31/55 €
♦ Grand Luxury ♦ Classic ♦ Elegant ♦
This elegant, historic building is considered a symbol of the Belle Époque. Its
unusual lounge area is crowned by an expansive Art Nouveau-style glass
atrium. Superb guestrooms furnished in classic-style. Its restaurant, La Rotonda,
offers an international menu.

Villa Real   🅐🅒 🛜 🛅 🚗 🆅🅸🆂🅰 ⓪ 🅰🅴 ⓪
pl. de las Cortes 10 ⊠ 28014 – ⓜ Sevilla – ℰ 914 20 37 67
– www.derbyhotels.com   G2
96 rm – ♥410 € ♥♥460 €, ☲ 21 € – 19 suites
Rest – Menu 32/38 € – Carte 40/60 € 🕸
♦ Business ♦ Personalised ♦
This hotel displays a valuable collection of Greek and Roman art in many of its
public areas. The comfortable guestrooms are attractively decorated with
mahogany furniture. This informal restaurant with an abundance of natural
light serves cuisine with an international flavour.

Urban   🛗 ⛲ ᕹ 🅐🅒 🛜 🛅 🚗 🆅🅸🆂🅰 ⓪ 🅰🅴 ⓪
Carrera de San Jerónimo 34 ⊠ 28014 – ⓜ Sevilla – ℰ 917 87 77 70
– www.derbyhotels.com   G2
102 rm – ♥480 € ♥♥535 €, ☲ 21 € – 21 suites
Rest *Europa Decó* – see restaurant listing
♦ Business ♦ Design ♦
An avant-garde hotel with high quality furnishings, attractive lighting effects
and numerous works of art on display. Well-equipped guestrooms with real
attention to detail.

Meliá Madrid Princesa   🛗 ᕹ 🅐🅒 🛜 🛅 🆅🅸🆂🅰 ⓪ 🅰🅴 ⓪
Princesa 27 ⊠ 28008 – ⓜ Ventura Rodríguez – ℰ 915 41 82 00
– www.meliamadridprincesa.com   E1
269 rm – ♥♥135/305 €, ☲ 25 € – 5 suites
Rest *Uno* – Menu 20/60 € – Carte 40/65 €
♦ Business ♦ Contemporary ♦
This emblematic hotel has been pleasantly modernised. Attractive public areas
combining contemporary and antique furnishings, along with well-appointed
guestrooms with a modern feel. The restaurant offers a contemporary menu,
in addition to a tapas lounge.

Tryp Ambassador   🅐🅒 🛜 🛅 🆅🅸🆂🅰 ⓪ 🅰🅴 ⓪
cuesta de Santo Domingo 5-7 ⊠ 28013 – ⓜ Santo Domingo
– ℰ 915 41 67 00 – www.solmelia.com   E-F2
183 rm – ♥♥80/220 €, ☲ 19 € – 3 suites
Rest – Menu 32 € – Carte 32/47 €
♦ Business ♦ Chain hotel ♦ Classic ♦
The Tryp Ambassador has a stately atmosphere with an attractive patio typical
of this exclusive district of the city. Comfortable guestrooms with elegant, high
quality furniture. Restaurant with a glass ceiling, in the style of a winter garden.

De las Letras   ᕹ rm, 🅐🅒 🛜 🛅 🆅🅸🆂🅰 ⓪ 🅰🅴
Gran Vía 11 ⊠ 28013 – ⓜ Gran Vía – ℰ 915 23 79 80
– www.hoteldelasletras.com   G2
109 rm – ♥110/425 € ♥♥115/430 €, ☲ 17 € – 1 suite
Rest – Menu 18/55 € – Carte 58/81 €
♦ Business ♦ Design ♦
The restored exterior contrasts with a contemporary, colourful interior. The
guestrooms are described as having a 'New York' style with intimate lighting
and poems on the walls. The cuisine in this modern restaurant, which practically
forms one room with the lounge-bar, is mainly focused around two menus.

NH Palacio de Tepa
🍴 ⅃ᵳ ⅂ rm, 🄰🄲 🛜 ⅍ ᗑ 🆅🅸🆂🅰 ₵₵ 🄰🄴 ⓪

San Sebastian 2 ✉ 28012 – Ⓜ *Sol* – ℰ 913 89 64 90
– *www.nh-hotels.com*   **F2-3**
85 rm – ♦139/410 € ♦♦149/420 €, ⌑ 29 €
Rest *Estado Puro* – Menu 15/49 € – Carte 20/30 €
♦ Historic ♦ Minimalist ♦

A hotel occupying an aristocratic 18C building with a superb location in the
heart of the city's Las Letras district. Although it has retained its original structure, the interior nowadays features very contemporary public areas and minimalist guestrooms, some of which are attic in style. The decor in the gastro-bar
comes as something of a surprise!

María Elena Palace
⅂ rm, 🄰🄲 🛜 ⅍ 🆅🅸🆂🅰 ₵₵ 🄰🄴

Aduana 19 ✉ 28013 – Ⓜ *Sol* – ℰ 913 60 49 30 – *www.chh.es*
87 rm – ♦120/150 € ♦♦150/250 €, ⌑ 18 €   **G2**
Rest – Menu 19/23 € – Carte approx. 30 €
♦ Traditional ♦ Business ♦ Classic ♦

This hotel has an open lobby and a magnificent patio crowned by a glass dome.
Classical-style bedrooms with quality furnishings, carpets and marble baths. The
cuisine in this hotel's traditional yet welcoming restaurant is based on contemporary à la carte choices and a daily set menu.

NH Paseo del Prado
🍴 ⅃ᵳ ⅂ rm, 🄰🄲 🛜 ⅍ 🆅🅸🆂🅰 ₵₵ 🄰🄴 ⓪

pl. Cánovas del Castillo 4 ✉ 28014 – Ⓜ *Banco de España*
– ℰ 913 30 24 00 – *www.nh-hotels.com*   **G2**
114 rm – ♦140/320 € ♦♦200/500 €, ⌑ 27 €
Rest *Estado Puro* – Menu 15/49 € – Carte 20/30 €
♦ Chain hotel ♦ Business ♦ Classic ♦

This chain hotel enjoys an excellent location and as such is perfect for business
and leisure travellers. Although a little on the small side, the guestrooms are of a
high quality with modern furnishings. This lively restaurant offers a varied
choice of raciones, classic tapas and main dishes.

Ópera
⅂ rm, 🄰🄲 rm, 🛜 ⅍ 🆅🅸🆂🅰 ₵₵ 🄰🄴 ⓪

cuesta de Santo Domingo 2 ✉ 28013 – Ⓜ *Ópera* – ℰ 915 41 28 00
– *www.hotelopera.com*   **E2**
79 rm – ♦75/130 € ♦♦85/170 €, ⌑ 15 €
Rest *El Café de La Ópera* – Menu 54 € – Carte 37/54 €
♦ Business ♦ Modern ♦

This hotel has a traditional bar with a lively ambience, one multi-purpose breakfast room and one room for meetings. Modern bedrooms with contemporary
furnishings. One of the specific attractions of this restaurant is its live evening
performances of opera and zarzuela.

Lusso Infantas
⅂ 🄰🄲 🛜 ⅍ 🆅🅸🆂🅰 ₵₵ 🄰🄴 ⓪

Infantas 29 ✉ 28004 – Ⓜ *Chueca* – ℰ 915 21 28 28
– *www.hotelinfantas.com*   **G2**
40 rm – ♦♦76/234 €, ⌑ 13 €
Rest *Ex Libris* – see restaurant listing
♦ Business ♦ Modern ♦

The Infantas occupies an old building that has been completely renovated in a
contemporary-style. Well-appointed guestrooms and bathrooms.

Husa Paseo del Arte
⅃ᵳ ⅂ rm, 🄰🄲 🛜 ⅍ ᗑ ₵₵ 🄰🄴 ⓪

Atocha 123 ✉ 28012 – Ⓜ *Atocha* – ℰ 912 98 48 00
– *www.hotelhusapaseodelarte.com*   **G3**
254 rm – ♦♦95/300 €, ⌑ 20 € – 6 suites
Rest – *(Closed August and weekend)* Menu 22/60 €
♦ Business ♦ Functional ♦

As the name suggests, this hotel is extremely well placed for visiting Madrid's
most famous museums. Bright and airy public areas and functional, high quality
bedrooms. The restaurant occupies the interior patio with its glass ceiling and
small garden.

Preciados   rm, 🏧 📶 🔈 🚗 VISA 🟠 AE ①

Preciados 37 ✉ 28013 – ⓜ Callao – ☏ 914 54 44 00
– www.preciadoshotel.com   **F2**
69 rm – ♦85/150 € ♦♦90/160 €, ⌧ 15 € – 5 suites
Rest – Menu 16 € – Carte 26/43 €
♦ Business ♦ Modern ♦
The plain classic architectural style of this building, dating back to the 19C, contrasts with the modern, fully equipped interior. Smallish, cosy lounge area. This versatile restaurant offers a choice between traditional à la carte dining and two set menus.

Catalonia Moratín without rest   🏧 🔈 VISA 🟠 AE ①

Atocha 23 ✉ 28012 – ⓜ Sol – ☏ 913 69 71 71
– www.hoteles-catalonia.com   **F2-3**
63 rm ⌧ – ♦♦70/515 €
♦ Business ♦ Chain hotel ♦ Functional ♦
Housed in an 18C building, this hotel has retained some of its original decor, such as the staircase, and combined them with more modern features. Contemporary-style bedrooms, plus a lounge area occupying the carriage courtyard.

Ada Palace   🔈 rm, 🏧 📶 VISA 🟠 AE

Marqués de Valdeiglesias 1 ✉ 28004 – ⓜ Banco de España
– ☏ 917 01 19 19 – www.chh.es   **G2**
78 rm – ♦80/320 € ♦♦90/360 €, ⌧ 15 €
Rest – Menu 24 € – Carte 40/60 €
♦ Historic ♦ Classic ♦
The Ada Palace occupies an historic building, which brings with it advantages and a few disadvantages, such as the small size of the reception area. Classic bedrooms offering acceptable levels of comfort. The restaurant is situated on the sixth floor, next to the cafeteria and the popular small terraces.

Mercure Madrid Santo Domingo   🍽 🏧 📶 🔈 🚗

San Bernardo 1 ✉ 28013 – ⓜ Santo Domingo   VISA 🟠 AE
– ☏ 915 47 98 00 – www.hotelsantodomingo.es   **F1-2**
200 rm – ♦90/170 € ♦♦110/220 €, ⌧ 14 €
Rest Sandó – see restaurant listing
♦ Business ♦ Contemporary ♦
This chain hotel houses the world's largest vertical garden with over 200 species of plants and even a waterfall. It offers a spacious café, a striking cocktail bar occupying caves from the 16C, as well as a variety of meeting rooms. Contemporary guestrooms, which despite being on the small side, show a personal touch.

Suite Prado without rest   🏧 📶 VISA 🟠 AE ①

Manuel Fernández y González 10 ✉ 28014 – ⓜ Antón Martín
– ☏ 914 20 23 18 – www.suiteprado.com   **G2**
9 rm – ♦76/136 € ♦♦91/216 €, ⌧ 10 € – 9 suites
♦ Family ♦ Contemporary ♦
This hotel has a classic contemporary façade and a delightful old staircase. Family atmosphere and apartment-style bedrooms, each with their own lounge and kitchen.

Meninas without rest   🔈 🏧 📶 VISA 🟠 AE ①

Campomanes 7 ✉ 28013 – ⓜ Ópera – ☏ 915 41 28 05
– www.hotelmeninas.com   **F2**
37 rm – ♦79/130 € ♦♦89/170 €, ⌧ 15 €
♦ Family ♦ Cosy ♦
This hotel occupying a residential building is renowned for its friendly and personalised service. It has a welcoming public area with a library, in addition to modern guestrooms.

La Posada del Léon de Oro   rm, 🛜 VISA ④ AE

Cava Baja 12 ⊠ *28005* – Ⓜ *La Latina* – 𝒞 *911 19 14 94*
– www.posadadelleondeoro.com   **F3**
17 rm – ♥♥99/243 €, � 12 €   **Rest** – Carte 25/40 € ℬ

◆ Historic ◆ Personalised ◆

This hotel is teeming with charm. Find it both in its individually furnished guest-rooms with their abundance of design features, and the 19C courtyard, nowadays crowned by a glass roof. The restaurant, which offers a traditional à la carte menu, has a glass floor, enabling guests to admire the remains of a 12C wall below.

Gonzalo without rest   AK 🛜 VISA ④

Cervantes 34 (3th floor) ⊠ *28014* – Ⓜ *Antón Martín* – 𝒞 *914 29 27 14*
– www.hostalgonzalo.com   **G3**
15 rm – ♥45/50 € ♥♥55/60 €

◆ Family ◆ Functional ◆

This typical, family-run guesthouse occupies a residential building in the Las Letras district. Spacious guestrooms with simple, functional furnishings.

Posada del Dragón   AK rm, 🛜 VISA ④ AE

Cava Baja 14 ⊠ *28005* – Ⓜ *La Latina* – 𝒞 *911 19 14 24*
– www.posadadeldragon.com   **F3**
27 rm – ♥79/223 € ♥♥89/243 €, ⊕ 12 €
Rest – Menu 11 € – Carte 30/50 €

◆ Historic ◆ Personalised ◆

Although it occupies the site of one of the oldest inns in the city, this hotel is a cutting-edge property. It has only retained the framework and 19C courtyard from the original building. The restaurant, which embraces the 'show cooking' concept, occupies what was once the La Antoñita soap factory, from which it takes its name.

XXXX ℬℬ ### La Terraza del Casino *(Paco Roncero)*   🛜 AK ⇔ VISA ④ AE ①

Alcalá 15 (3th floor) ⊠ *28014* – Ⓜ *Sevilla* – 𝒞 *915 32 12 75*
– www.casinodemadrid.es
– Closed August, Saturday lunch, Sunday and Bank Holidays   **G2**
Rest – Menu 65/135 € – Carte 69/90 € ℬ

◆ Creative ◆ Elegant ◆

A palatial 19C setting for this restaurant that nowadays has a more contemporary look. The chef adopts a restrained approach to creative cuisine with an end result that reaches perfection. One of the best terraces in the capital.

➜ Tartar de ostras con huevas de salmón, crema de tuétano y aire de yema. Rape con puré de apio, nabo y consomé de garbanzos. Sabores y aromas de Madrid.

XXXX ℬℬ ### El Club Allard *(Diego Guerrero)*   AK ⇔ ⊡♥ VISA ④ AE ①

Ferraz 2 ⊠ *28008* – Ⓜ *Plaza España* – 𝒞 *915 59 09 39* – *www.elcluballard.com*
– Closed August, Saturday lunch, Sunday, Monday dinner and Bank Holidays
Rest – *(set menu only)* Menu 74/99 € ℬ   **E1**

◆ Creative ◆ Classic ◆

A restaurant housed in a listed Modernist building, hence the lack of signage outside. The classically elegant interior provides the backdrop for creative, delicately presented cuisine featuring skilful fusions of ingredients and impressive technical ability.

➜ Cococha de salmón ahumada con caldo corto de azafrán, erizo de mar y aire de coco. Taco de liebre. Huevo poché.

XXX ### Palacio Cibeles   🛜 AK VISA ④ AE ①

pl. de Cibeles 1 (6th floor) ⊠ *28014* – Ⓜ *Banco de España*
– 𝒞 915 23 14 54 – *www.grupoadolfo.com*   **H2**
Rest – Menu 48 € – Carte 59/75 €

◆ Traditional ◆ Formal ◆

The Palacio Cibeles enjoys a marvellous location on the sixth floor of the city's emblematic city hall (Ayuntamiento). In addition to the modern-style dining room, the restaurant has two attractive terraces where guests can dine or simply enjoy a drink. The cooking is of a traditional flavour.

SPAIN - MADRID

XXX Paradis Madrid
AC ⇔ VISA ◯◯ AE ①

Marqués de Cubas 14 ⊠ *28014 –* Ⓜ *Banco de España –* 𝒞 *914 29 73 03*
– www.restauranteparadismadrid.es
– Closed Saturday lunch, Sunday and Bank Holidays   **G2**
Rest – Carte 40/50 €
♦ Mediterranean ♦ Classic ♦
A modern restaurant next to the conference centre, with access via a delicatessen shop. Spacious dining room plus a tapas area.

XXX Café de Oriente
🍴 AC ⇔ VISA ◯◯ ①

pl. de Oriente 2 ⊠ *28013 –* Ⓜ *Ópera –* 𝒞 *915 41 39 74*
– www.grupolezama.es   **E2**
Rest – Menu 49/82 € – Carte 41/65 € 🍷
♦ Traditional ♦ Classic ♦
This famous address opposite the royal palace offers its guests several different atmospheres including a luxurious cafeteria, an attractive wine bar-cum-dining room, and a number of elegant private rooms. The traditional à la carte menu shows the influence of the Basque country.

XXX La Manduca de Azagra
AC ⇔ VISA ◯◯ AE ①

Sagasta 14 ⊠ *28004 –* Ⓜ *Alonso Martínez –* 𝒞 *915 91 01 12*
– www.lamanducadeazagra.com
– Closed August, Sunday and Bank Holidays   **G1**
Rest – Carte approx. 45 €
♦ Traditional ♦ Minimalist ♦
This spacious, well-located restaurant is decorated in minimalist style with particular attention paid to the design and lighting. The menu focuses on high quality produce.

XX Julián de Tolosa
AC VISA ◯◯ AE ①

Cava Baja 18 ⊠ *28005 –* Ⓜ *La Latina –* 𝒞 *913 65 82 10*
– www.casajuliandetolosa.com – Closed Sunday dinner   **F3**
Rest – Menu 65 € – Carte 47/58 €
♦ Meats and grills ♦ Rustic ♦
This famous carvery restaurant serves some of the best T-bone steaks in the city. The neo-rustic-style decor provides a backdrop for a concise menu based around high-quality ingredients.

XX Europa Decó – Hotel Urban
AC VISA ◯◯ AE ①

Carrera de San Jerónimo 34 ⊠ *28014 –* Ⓜ *Sevilla –* 𝒞 *917 87 77 80*
– www.derbyhotels.com – Closed August, Saturday lunch and Sunday
Rest – Menu 35 € – Carte 40/65 € 🍷   **G2**
♦ Creative ♦ Fashionable ♦
Increasingly popular for its innovative design and excellent service. Mediterranean and ethnic cuisine prepared using fresh and exotic produce.

XX Lieu
AC VISA ◯◯ AE

Amnistía 10 ⊠ *28013 –* 𝒞 *915 41 74 81 – www.lieu.es*
– Closed Christmas, 15 August-7 September, Sunday dinner and Monday
Rest – Menu 50/60 € – Carte 42/51 €   **E2**
♦ Modern ♦ Elegant ♦
Located close to the city's Teatro Real, this restaurant surprises passers-by as the kitchen is visible from the street. There is a bar at the entrance and a stylishly decorated dining room. The contemporary menu highlights delicate presentation and culinary skill in every dish.

XX Sandó – Hotel Mercure Madrid Santo Domingo
AC VISA ◯◯ AE

Isabel la Católica 2 ⊠ *28013 –* Ⓜ *Santo Domingo –* 𝒞 *915 47 99 11*
– www.restaurantesando.es – Closed August, Sunday dinner and Monday
Rest – Menu 49 € – Carte 40/51 €   **F1-2**
♦ Modern ♦ Classic ♦
An attractive, classically furnished interior enhanced by interesting contemporary and designer detail. With Juan Mari Arzak's influence in the kitchen, guests can enjoy an adaptation of the renowned cuisine of this famous chef.

XX **Ex Libris** – Hotel Lusso Infantas   AC VISA ⊙⊙ AE ①

Infantas 29 ✉ *28004* – ⓜ *Chueca* – ℰ *915 21 28 28*
– www.restauranteexlibris.com   **G2**
Rest – Menu 13 € – Carte 35/50 €
♦ Modern ♦ Neighbourhood ♦
An original and contemporary decor showing great attention to detail provides the backdrop for traditional cuisine with a modern touch. There are also a variety of set menus.

XX **Quintana 30**   AC ⇔ ⊂⌐ VISA ⊙⊙ AE ①
⊛

Quintana 30 ✉ *28008* – ⓜ *Argüelles* – ℰ *915 42 65 20*
– www.quintana30.es
– *Closed Holy Week, 15-31 August and Sunday dinner*   **E1**
Rest – Carte 30/35 €
♦ Traditional ♦ Fashionable ♦
This modern and contemporary restaurant has a dining area on two floors with two different atmospheres, as well as a small private room. Extensive menu of traditional dishes from the Basque country and Navarra.

XX **Alboroque Tradición**   AC VISA ⊙⊙ AE ①
⊛

Atocha 34 ✉ *28012* – ⓜ *Antón Martín* – ℰ *913 89 65 70*
– www.alboroquetradicion.es
– *Closed August, Sunday and Monday dinner*   **F3**
Rest – Menu 27/35 € – Carte 33/39 €
♦ Traditional ♦ Formal ♦
Accessed via a courtyard once used by horse-drawn carriages, this restaurant occupies a former art gallery. It has several interconnecting dining rooms with Modernist paintings hanging from the walls. Well-presented and tasty, traditional cuisine with a contemporary touch is served.

XX **Esteban**   AC ⇔ VISA ⊙⊙

Cava Baja 36 ✉ *28005* – ⓜ *La Latina* – ℰ *913 65 90 91*
– www.rte-esteban.com
– *Closed 20 July-10 August, Sunday dinner, Monday dinner and Tuesday dinner*
Rest – Carte 40/50 €   **E3**
♦ Traditional ♦ Rustic ♦
A welcoming hotel decorated in typical Castilian style with photos of famous characters on the walls. The restaurant serves traditional cuisine.

X **La Esquina del Real**   AC VISA ⊙⊙ AE ①

Amnistía 4 ✉ *28013* – ⓜ *Ópera* – ℰ *915 59 43 09*
– www.laesquinadelreal.es
– *Closed 15 August-15 September, Saturday lunch, Sunday and Bank Holidays*
Rest – Menu 40 € – Carte 38/55 €   **E-F2**
♦ French ♦ Cosy ♦
A charming and intimate restaurant decorated in a rustic style with stone and brick walls. Good service and an attractive menu with an emphasis on French cuisine.

X **Zerain**   AC ⇔ VISA ⊙⊙ AE ①

Quevedo 3 ✉ *28014* – ⓜ *Antón Martín* – ℰ *914 29 79 09*
– www.restaurante-vasco-zerain-sidreria.es
– *Closed Sunday dinner*   **G3**
Rest – Menu 29/57 € – Carte approx. 40 €
♦ Basque ♦ Rustic ♦
Typical Basque cider bar decorated with large barrels. Friendly atmosphere and cheerful decor with photographs of typical towns and villages. Affordable menu with an emphasis on roasted meats.

X **Krachai** AC VISA ◎◎ AE

Fernando VI-11 ✉ *28004 –* Ⓜ *Alonso Martínez – ℰ 918 33 65 56*
– www.krachai.es
– Closed August and Sunday dinner   **G1**
Rest – Menu 13/30 € – Carte 25/40 €
♦ Thai ♦ Exotic ♦

The Krachai is split between two dining rooms, each with attractive lighting and a contemporary feel. The Thai cuisine on offer is listed on the menu according to the way it is prepared.

X **La Gastroteca de Santiago** AC VISA ◎◎ AE ①

pl. Santiago 1 ✉ *28013 –* Ⓜ *Ópera – ℰ 915 48 07 07*
– www.lagastrotecadesantiago.es
– Closed Holy Week, 15-31 August, Sunday dinner and Monday   **E2**
Rest – Menu 20 € – Carte 48/66 €
♦ Modern ♦ Cosy ♦

A small, cosy restaurant with two large French windows and a modern decor. Friendly staff, contemporary cuisine and a kitchen that is partially visible to diners.

X **La Fragua de Sebín** 🔆 AC VISA ◎◎ AE
☺

Divino Pastor 21 ✉ *28004 –* Ⓜ *San Bernardo – ℰ 914 45 95 97*
– www.fraguadesebin.com
– Closed Sunday dinner and Monday in October-Mars   **F1**
Rest – Menu 30/47 € – Carte 26/39 €
♦ Traditional ♦ Formal ♦

Run by two brothers who pride themselves on the quality of their ingredients. There is a small tapas area and three interconnecting dining rooms, each laid out in contemporary-style. A successful modern take on traditional cuisine.

X **La Tasquita de Enfrente** AC VISA ◎◎ AE ①

Ballesta 6 ✉ *28004 –* Ⓜ *Gran Vía – ℰ 915 32 54 49*
– www.latasquitadeenfrente.com
– Closed August, Sunday and Monday   **F1**
Rest – *(booking essential)* Menu 65 € – Carte 50/80 €
♦ Traditional ♦ Family ♦

This small family-run restaurant continues to attract a loyal clientele. Enjoy the good, seasonal cuisine produced with simplicity, great care and intelligence.

X **La Bola** AC ⇗

Bola 5 ✉ *28013 –* Ⓜ *Santo Domingo – ℰ 915 47 69 30 – www.labola.es*
– Closed Sunday dinner   **E2**
Rest – Menu 27/40 € – Carte 30/48 €
♦ Traditional ♦ Neighbourhood ♦

This family-run restaurant maintains the typical culinary traditions of old Madrid. The interior is traditional in character with old photos on the walls. If stews are your thing, make sure you order the cocido madrileño!

X **Botín** AC ⇔ VISA ◎◎ AE ①

Cuchilleros 17 ✉ *28005 –* Ⓜ *Sol – ℰ 913 66 42 17 – www.botin.es*
Rest – Menu 44 €   **F2**
♦ Traditional ♦ Rustic ♦

Founded in 1725, Botín has made it to the Guinness Book of Records as the oldest restaurant in the world. Its decor evokes the essence of old Madrid.

ℙ/ **Le Cabrera** AC VISA ◎◎ AE ①

Bárbara de Braganza 2 ✉ *28004 –* Ⓜ *Colón – ℰ 915 77 59 55*
– www.lecabrera.com
– Closed Sunday   **H1**
Ración approx. 9 €
♦ Modern ♦ Design ♦ Fashionable ♦

This original restaurant with its trendy decor is divided into two sections. One has access to the chef who prepares dishes behind a counter, and the other, in the basement, is designed primarily for drinks.

SPAIN - MADRID

Y/ **La Botillería del Café de Oriente** ⌂ AC ⇔ VISA ☺ AE ①
pl. de Oriente 4 ⊠ 28013 – Ⓜ Ópera – ☏ 915 48 46 20
– www.grupolezama.es   E2
Tapa 4 € **Ración** approx. 12 €
♦ Traditional ♦ Tapas bar ♦
Situated in a lively area of bars and restaurants. This Viennese-style café serves a
wide variety of snacks and canapés, as well as excellent wines by the glass.

Y/ **La Camarilla** AC VISA ☺ AE ①
Cava Baja 21 ⊠ 28005 – Ⓜ Latina – ☏ 913 54 02 07
– www.lacamarillarestaurante.com
– Closed 21 days July and Wednesday lunch   F3
Tapa 5 €
♦ Traditional ♦ Fashionable ♦
A great place for tapas. It has a large bar – where you can sit and choose what
you want to eat – that leads to a modern, informal dining room.

Y/ **Bocaito** AC ⇔ VISA ☺ AE ①
Libertad 6 ⊠ 28004 – Ⓜ Chueca – ☏ 915 32 12 19 – www.bocaito.com
– closed August, Saturday lunch and Sunday   G2
Tapa 6 € **Ración** approx. 10 €
♦ Traditional ♦ Rustic ♦
This restaurant is split between two premises which are connected to each
other. Four dining rooms in total, each furnished in rustic Castilian style with a
few bullfighting mementoes as part of the decor. Traditional cuisine.

Y/ **Prada a Tope** AC VISA ☺ ①
Príncipe 11 ⊠ 28012 – Ⓜ Sevilla – ☏ 914 29 59 21 – www.pradaatope.es
Tapa 5 € **Ración** approx. 10 €   G2
♦ Traditional ♦ Neighbourhood ♦
This restaurant follows the typical decor found throughout this chain. A bar, rus-
tic-style tables and a plethora of wood in the dining room, which is adorned
with old photos and typical products from the El Bierzo region.

Y/ **Taberna de San Bernardo** AC VISA ☺ AE
San Bernardo 85 ⊠ 28015 – Ⓜ San Bernardo – ☏ 914 45 41 70
– Closed Monday   *Plan IV* **K3**
Tapa 2 € **Ración** approx. 7 €
♦ Traditional ♦ Neighbourhood ♦
A tavern-style bar with an authentic atmosphere. Large bar, a main dining room
and two private rooms, the one in the basement surrounded by exposed brick
walls. Popular dishes include papas con huevo (potatoes and eggs) and fritura
de verduras (fried vegetables).

Y/ **Kulto al Plato** ⌂ AC VISA ☺ AE
Serrano Jover 1 ⊠ 28015 – Ⓜ Argüelles – ☏ 663 18 80 27
– www.kultoalplato.com – Closed Sunday   *Plan IV* **K3**
Tapa 3 € **Ración** approx. 12 €
♦ Modern ♦ Fashionable ♦
A bar with a modern atmosphere split between several floors. Two dining areas,
one for its tapas based tasting menus, the other, with higher tables, for indivi-
dual tapas.

RETIRO – SALAMANCA   *Plan III*

🏨 **Ritz** ⌂ Ⅰ₆ ♿ rm, AC 🛜 ♨ VISA ☺ AE ①
pl. de la Lealtad 5 ⊠ 28014 – Ⓜ Banco de España – ☏ 917 01 67 67
– www.ritzmadrid.com   I2
137 rm – ♙♙255/590 €, � 34 € – 30 suites
Rest *Goya* – Menu 61/100 € – Carte 63/110 € ⌘
♦ Grand Luxury ♦ Elegant ♦
This elegant, internationally renowned hotel occupies an early 20C mansion.
Stunning lounge areas, with lavish decor in the guestrooms. The Ritz's restaurant boasts an elegant dining room and pleasant summer terrace.

Retiro and Salamanca
(Plan III)

ARGÜELLES, CHAMBERÍ (Plan IV)

HISTORICAL CENTRE (Plan II)

CHAMARTÍN (Plan V)

José Abascal

Gregorio Marañón

López de Hoyos

Vergara

Cartagena

Cartagena

América

Avenida de América

José

Maria

de

Molina

Pas. del General Martínez Campos

MUSEO L. GALDIANO

Cinco Jotas

Tasca
La Farmacia

Diego de León

Diego de León del Río

Ferrer del Río

Azcona

1

Rubén Darío

Maldonado 14

Juan Bravo

Juan Bravo 25

Cañadio

Pedro Larumbe

N. de Balboa

Juan Bravo

Diego de León

Toreros

La Torcaz

José Ortega

y

Lista

El Barril de Alcántara

Villa Magna

Oter Epicure

Sanxenxo

Gasset

Pl. de Manuel Becerra

Astrid & Gastón

Ayala

SALAMANCA

Ramón Freixa Madrid

Taberna de la Daniela

Manuel Becerra

Único Madrid

Gran Meliá Fénix

Colón

Serrano Goya

Ayala

Adler

Velázquez

Bauzá

Príncipe

Alcalá

Goya

El Barril de Goya

Goya

MUSEO DE CERA

MUSEO ARQUEOLÓGICO NACIONAL

Cinco Jotas

La Paloma

Castelló 9

O'Donnell

2

Jardín de Recoletos

Sula

El Chiscó de Castelló

2

Pelotari

Wellington

Goizeko Wellington

P. de Vergara

Hospes Madrid

Shikku

Retiro

Alcalá

Kabuki Wellington

O'Donnell

O'Donnell

Banco de España

PUERTA DE ALCALÁ

Pl. de la Independencia

La Castela

La Hoja

Ritz

Pl. de la Lealtad
A. Maura

Alfonso XII

MUSEO DEL EJÉRCITO

Ibiza

O'Grelo

Ibiza

Doctor

Sáinz de Baranda

Felipe IV

CASÓN DEL BUEN RETIRO

Alcalde

PAS. DEL PRADO

MUSEO DEL PRADO

PARQUE

Sáinz de Baranda

MUSEO DEL PRADO

DEL BUEN RETIRO

Menéndez

JARDÍN BOTÁNICO

Alfonso XII

PALACIO DE CRISTAL

PARQUE DE ROMA

Atocha

RETIRO

Pelayo

Nazaret

Astros

Pas. de la Infanta Isabel

Esguerdo

Pez Volador

Espalduí

Atocha Renfe

Pl. de Mariano de Cavia

Conde de Casal

Plaza del Conde de Casal

ATOCHA

Pas. de la Reina Cristina

Av. del Mediterráneo

M 30

Menéndez Álvaro

Av. de la Ciudad de Barcelona

Menéndez Pelayo

Claridge

A 3

Comercio

Dr.

● Hotel
● Restaurant

0   400 m

Villa Magna 🍴 ⅃ᵟ ₲ rm, 🕮 🕻 ⅏ 🚗 🚘 🆚 💳 🔤 ①

paseo de la Castellana 22 ✉ *28046* – ⓜ *Rubén Darío* – ℰ *915 87 12 34*
– www.hotelvillamagna.es **I1**
164 rm – †290/550 € †290/610 €, ⌑ 37 € – 17 suites
Rest *Villa Magna* – *(Closed August)* Carte 44/64 €
Rest *Tsé Yang* – Carte 53/70 €

♦ Grand Luxury ♦ Classic ♦

After a major renovation, this has a much brighter social area and contemporary-style bedrooms. Top floor suites boast stunning terraces. Enjoy delicious, innovative cuisine at the Villa Magna restaurant.

Hospes Madrid ⅃ᵟ ⊛ ₲ 🕮 🛜 🚗 🆚 💳 🔤 ①

pl. de la Independencia 3 ✉ *28001* – ⓜ *Retiro* – ℰ *914 32 29 11*
– www.hospes.com **I2**
40 rm – ††165/396 €, ⌑ 25 € – 1 suite   **Rest** – Menu 17/86 €

♦ Luxury ♦ Contemporary ♦

This establishment is set in a building dating from 1883, with the lobby occupying what was once the carriage entrance. Many of the modern bedrooms overlook the Puerta de Alcalá. There are two meeting rooms and a spa. This restaurant has a modern layout and serves a menu of contemporary cuisine.

Gran Meliá Fénix ⅃ᵟ ₲ rm, 🕮 🛜 🚗 🆚 💳 🔤 ①

Hermosilla 2 ✉ *28001* – ⓜ *Serrano* – ℰ *914 31 67 00*
– www.granmeliafenix.com **I2**
212 rm – †180/450 € ††200/500 €, ⌑ 28 € – 12 suites
Rest – Menu 30 € – Carte 37/70 €

♦ Luxury ♦ Elegant ♦

This smart, distinctive hotel has bedrooms in an elegant, classical style equipped to a very high standard. Spacious public areas, including an impressive lounge crowned by a domed ceiling. This restaurant has a relaxed atmosphere and serves cuisine with Mediterranean overtones.

Wellington ⅃ᵟ ⅃ 🕮 🛜 🚗 🆚 💳 🔤 ①

Velázquez 8 ✉ *28001* – ⓜ *Retiro* – ℰ *915 75 44 00*
– www.hotel-wellington.com **I2**
255 rm – ††140/325 €, ⌑ 22 € – 19 suites
Rest *Kabuki Wellington* ❀ **Rest** *Goizeko Wellington* – see restaurant listing

♦ Luxury ♦ Classic ♦

This smart area next to the Retiro is famous as the place where many bullfighters stay during the Feria de San Isidro. The interior is classically elegant with bedrooms offering a high level of comfort. A gym is available for guests.

Adler 🕮 🛜 🚗 🆚 💳 🔤 ①

Velázquez 33 ✉ *28001* – ⓜ *Velázquez* – ℰ *914 26 32 20*
– www.hoteladler.es **I2**
44 rm – †200/400 € ††250/495 €, ⌑ 27 €
Rest – Menu 55 € – Carte 58/69 €

♦ Luxury ♦ Elegant ♦

This exclusive, select hotel has an elegant interior decorated with high quality furnishings. Comfortable guestrooms equipped to the highest standard. Restaurant with a charming atmosphere and impressive attention to detail in its decor.

AC Palacio del Retiro ⅃ᵟ ₲ rm, 🕮 🛜 🚗 🆚 💳 🔤 ①

Alfonso XII-14 ✉ *28014* – ⓜ *Retiro* – ℰ *915 23 74 60*
– www.ac-hotels.com Plan II **H2**
50 rm – †195/305 € ††210/320 €, ⌑ 29 €
Rest – Menu 36 € – Carte 38/49 €

♦ Palace ♦ Classic ♦

Early-20C mansion with a reception area situated in what was once a passageway for horse-drawn carriages. Elegant public area and superb guestrooms. The restaurant, which is clearly focused towards the hotel's guests, serves a mix of traditional and contemporary dishes.

SPAIN - MADRID

Único Madrid

Claudio Coello 67 ✉ *28001* – **Ⓜ** *Serrano* – ☏ *917 81 01 73*
– www.unicohotelmadrid.com

I2

44 rm – ♛♛185/255 €, ⌷ 26 € – 1 suite
Rest *Ramón Freixa Madrid* ❀ ❀ – see restaurant listing
♦ Business ♦ Contemporary ♦

Behind this establishment's attractive, classical façade is a designer reception hall and an elegant social area. The comfortable bedrooms all have classical, avant-garde elements.

Claridge

pl. Conde de Casal 6 ✉ *28005* – **Ⓜ** *Conde de Casal* – ☏ *915 51 94 00*
– www.hotelclaridge.com

J3

112 rm ⌷ – ♛75/160 € ♛♛90/180 € – 2 suites
Rest – Menu 13 € – Carte 30/40 €
♦ Business ♦ Classic ♦

Following a complete renovation, the Claridge now offers a modern setting with a decorative homage to classic British and American images. It has elegant and spacious guestrooms geared towards a business clientele. The restaurant, which includes a private dining room, offers a menu catering to international tastes.

Vincci Soma

Goya 79 ✉ *28001* – **Ⓜ** *Goya* – ☏ *914 35 75 45* – *www.vinccihoteles.com*
176 rm – ♛57/465 € ♛♛78/486 €, ⌷ 18 €

J2

Rest – *(Closed August)* Menu 25 € – Carte 32/54 €
♦ Business ♦ Modern ♦

This centrally located hotel has modern facilities. It offers fully equipped guest-rooms, some of which have their own terrace. There is also an attractive lounge-library with a fireplace. This bright, modern restaurant is decorated in varying shades of white. It serves innovative, creative cuisine.

Jardín de Recoletos

Gil de Santivañes 4 ✉ *28001* – **Ⓜ** *Serrano* – ☏ *917 81 16 40*
– www.vphoteles.com

I2

43 rm – ♛♛89/479 €, ⌷ 19 €
Rest – Menu 25 € – Carte 35/45 €
♦ Traditional ♦ Classic ♦

Attractive façade with balustraded balconies. The hotel has an elegant recep-tion hall with a glass ceiling, large studio-style guestrooms and an attractive patio-terrace. This small, classic-style dining room has a menu based around tra-ditional cuisine.

Ramón Freixa Madrid – Hotel Único Madrid

❀ ❀

Claudio Coello 67 ✉ *28001* – **Ⓜ** *Serrano*
– ☏ 917 81 82 62 – www.ramonfreixamadrid.com
– Closed Holy Week, August, Sunday and Monday

I2

Rest – Menu 75/125 € – Carte 75/100 € ❀
♦ Creative ♦ Design ♦

Fronted by a pleasant terrace, this restaurant has a thoroughly modern look and a limited number of tables. In the kitchen, the focus is on impressively consistent cuisine, which is superbly presented and prepared using high quality ingredients.
➜ Parmentier crujiente con queso al vino. Rape, limón en salmuera con zanahoria sinfín y naranjas. El chocolate 2013.

Pedro Larumbe

paseo de la Castellana 38 ✉ *28006* – **Ⓜ** *Rubén Darío* – ☏ *915 75 11 12*
– www.larumbe.com
– Closed 15 days August, Sunday and Bank Holidays

I1

Rest – Menu 55 € – Carte 43/70 €
♦ Modern ♦ Classic ♦

Following a change in location, this restaurant has improved in every aspect. It has a waiting area for a pre-meal drink, as well as a large, classically decorated and contemporary dining room with high quality furniture and excellent at-table service. Modern cuisine with its roots in traditional cooking.

XXX **Sanxenxo**

José Ortega y Gasset 40 ✉ *28006 –* Ⓜ *Núñez de Balboa –* ✆ *915 77 82 72*
– www.sanxenxo.com.es
– Closed Holy Week, 15 days August and Sunday dinner **J1**
Rest – Carte 45/60 €
♦ Fish and seafood ♦ Classic ♦
This restaurant serves traditional Galician cuisine based on quality fish and sea-food. Covering two floors, the superb dining rooms are decorated with a profu-sion of granite and wood.

XXX **Castelló 9**

Castelló 9 ✉ *28001 –* Ⓜ *Príncipe de Vergara –* ✆ *914 35 00 67*
– www.castello9.es
– Closed Holy Week, August, Sunday and Bank Holidays **I2**
Rest – Carte approx. 46 €
♦ International ♦ Classic ♦
Classically elegant decor in a location just a stone's throw from the Retiro. Enjoy a menu of classic international dishes and a good tasting menu, with a variety of dishes and half portions available.

XXX **Kabuki Wellington** (Ricardo Sanz) – Hotel Wellington
❄️
Velázquez 6 ✉ *28001 –* Ⓜ *Retiro –* ✆ *915 77 78 77*
– www.restaurantekabuki.com
– Closed Holy Week, 1-21 August, Saturday lunch, Sunday and Bank Holidays
Rest – Menu 91 € – Carte 59/80 € ⓑ **I2**
♦ Japanese ♦ Design ♦
This restaurant enjoys great success in the capital. There is a large, contempo-rary-style dining room on two floors that features designer detail and a sushi bar. Japanese cuisine skilfully prepared with top quality ingredients, and always superbly presented.
→ Usuzukuri de "pa amb tomaca". Atún picante con huevo frito. Chocolate con churros.

XXX **Goizeko Wellington** – Hotel Wellington

Villanueva 34 ✉ *28001 –* Ⓜ *Retiro –* ✆ *915 77 01 38*
– www.goizekogaztelupe.com
– Closed Saturday lunch July-August and Sunday **I2**
Rest – Menu 50 € – Carte 50/80 € ⓑ
♦ International ♦ Classic ♦
The contemporary-classic dining room and the two private rooms have been exquisitely designed. The cuisine on offer is a fusion of traditional, international and creative cooking, and is enriched with a few Japanese dishes.

XXX **Astrid & Gastón**

paseo de la Castellana 13 ✉ *28046 –* Ⓜ *Serrano –* ✆ *917 02 62 62*
– www.astridygastonmadrid.com **I1-2**
Rest – Menu 48/72 € – Carte approx. 56 €
♦ International ♦ Friendly ♦
Extending over two floors, this restaurant has spacious dining areas decorated in a contemporary-style. Bar for pre-dinner cocktails, and a menu specialising in Peruvian cuisine.

XX **La Paloma**

Jorge Juan 39 ✉ *28001 –* Ⓜ *Príncipe de Vergara –* ✆ *915 76 86 92*
– www.rtelapaloma.com
– Closed Holy Week, August, Sunday and Bank Holidays **I2**
Rest – Menu 45/60 € – Carte 46/61 €
♦ Traditional ♦ Classic ♦
A professionally run restaurant catering to a sophisticated clientele. Dining room on two levels, where the focus is on international and traditional cuisine. Excellent service.

XX **O'Grelo**   AC ⇄ VISA ⊕ AE ⓪

Menorca 39 ⊠ 28009 – Ⓜ *Ibiza – 𝒞 914 09 72 04*
– www.restauranteogrelo.com
– Closed Sunday dinner   **J2**
Rest – Carte 40/72 €
♦ Galician ♦ Rustic ♦
Enjoy excellent traditional Galician cuisine in this restaurant decorated in a neo-rustic style. Wide selection of fish and seafood and a tapas bar at the entrance.

XX **Maldonado 14**   AC VISA ⊕ AE

Maldonado 14 ⊠ 28006 – Ⓜ *Núñez de Balboa – 𝒞 914 35 50 45*
– www.maldonado14.com
– Closed 10-28 August, Sunday and Bank Holidays dinner   **I1**
Rest – Menu 35/52 € – Carte 45/60 €
♦ Traditional ♦ Classic ♦
A single dining room on two levels, both featuring a classic decor, quality furnishings and wood floors. The à la carte menu has a traditional feel and includes delicious homely desserts, such as the outstanding apple tart.

XX **La Torcaz**   AC ⇄ VISA ⊕ AE ⓪

Lagasca 81 ⊠ 28006 – Ⓜ *Núñez de Balboa – 𝒞 915 75 41 30*
– www.latorcaz.com
– Closed 4-25 August and Sunday   **I1**
Rest – Menu 41/50 € – Carte 35/52 €
♦ Classic ♦ Classic ♦
Friendly restaurant with an attractive wine display. The dining room, decorated in classical-contemporary style, is divided into three different ambiences. Excellent service and an extensive wine list.

XX **Dassa Bassa**   AC VISA ⊕ AE ⓪

Villalar 7 ⊠ 28001 – Ⓜ *Retiro – 𝒞 915 76 73 97 – www.dassabassa.com*
– Closed Holy Week, August, Sunday and Monday   *Plan II* **H2**
Rest – Menu 25/80 € – Carte 50/65 €
♦ Modern ♦ Design ♦
This restaurant occupies what was once a coal merchant's property. It has an attractive tapas bar at the entrance and four modern dining rooms decorated with designer detail. Contemporary cuisine with a focus on distinct flavours.

XX **99 sushi bar**   AC ⇄ VISA ⊕ AE ⓪

Hermosilla 4 ⊠ 28001 – Ⓜ *Serrano – 𝒞 914 31 27 15*
– www.99sushibar.com
– Closed 1-23 August, Saturday lunch, Sunday and Bank Holidays
Rest – Menu 75 € – Carte 55/65 €   *Plan II* **H1**
♦ Japanese ♦ Exotic ♦
A good address in which to discover the flavours and textures of Japanese cuisine. There is a small bar where sushi is prepared in front of diners, an attractive glass-fronted wine cellar, and a modern dining room featuring typical Japanese decor and furnishings.

XX **Oter Epicure**   AC ⇄ VISA ⊕ AE ⓪

Claudio Coello 71 ⊠ 28001 – Ⓜ *Serrano – 𝒞 914 31 67 70*
– www.oterepicure.com
– Closed Sunday dinner   **I1**
Rest – Carte 40/50 €
♦ Traditional ♦ Bistro ♦ Rustic ♦
This restaurant has a bar at the entrance, and a long bistro-style dining room with a rustic ambience and tables set somewhat close together. Tempting chef's suggestions enhances the extensive à la carte options.

XX **Shikku**   AC VISA ⊙⊙ AE

Lagasca 5 ⊠ 28001 – Ⓜ *Retiro –* ℰ *914 31 93 08 – www.shikku.es*
– Closed Friday lunch and Saturday lunch in August, Sunday ant Bank Holidays
Rest – Carte 45/65 €   **I2**
♦ Japanese ♦ Minimalist ♦

This restaurant has a bar at its entrance plus a dining room with a modern decor and carpeted floors. Japanese cuisine prepared with high quality ingredients.

XX **El Chiscón de Castelló**   AC VISA ⊙⊙ ⊙

Castelló 3 ⊠ 28001 – Ⓜ *Príncipe de Vergara –* ℰ *915 75 56 62*
– www.elchiscon.com
– Closed August, Sunday and Monday dinner   **I2**
Rest – Menu 25/30 € – Carte 30/42 €
♦ Traditional ♦ Classic ♦

Behind the typical façade is a warmly decorated interior similar in style to a private home, especially in the first floor dining rooms. Reasonably priced traditional cuisine.

XX **La Hoja**   AC VISA ⊙⊙ AE

Doctor Castelo 48 ⊠ 28009 – Ⓜ *O'Donnell –* ℰ *914 09 25 22*
– www.lahoja.es
– Closed Sunday dinner   **J2**
Rest – Menu 40/50 € – Carte 42/53 €
♦ Asturienne ♦ Neighbourhood ♦

This restaurant has two classic-style dining rooms. Enjoy generous portions of traditional Asturian cooking, including bean dishes and chicken raised on the owner's farm. Delicatessen shop.

XX **Cañadío**   🍴 AC ⇔ VISA ⊙⊙ AE ⊙

Conde Peñalver 86 ⊠ 28005 – Ⓜ *Diego de León –* ℰ *912 81 91 92*
– www.restaurantecanadio.com
– Closed Sunday dinner   **J1**
Rest – Carte 40/55 €
♦ Traditional ♦ Formal ♦

The name will ring a bell with those familiar with Santander, given the location of this, the original Cañadío restaurant, on one of the city's most famous squares. Café-bar for tapas, two contemporary dining rooms, and well-prepared traditional cuisine.

XX **MEATing**   AC VISA ⊙⊙

Villalar 4 ⊠ 28005 – Ⓜ *Retiro –* ℰ *914 31 69 97*
– www.restaurantemeating.com
– Closed Holy Week, 21 days August, Sunday and Monday dinner
Rest – Carte 35/55 €   *Plan II* **H2**
♦ Meats and grills ♦ Formal ♦

A restaurant with a contemporary look that takes high quality ingredients as the basic philosophy for its cuisine. Enjoy traditional cooking that specialises in Galician beef dishes and delicious vegetables from the Basque Country and Navarra.

X **Pelotari**   AC ⇔ VISA ⊙⊙ AE ⊙

Recoletos 3 ⊠ 28001 – Ⓜ *Colón –* ℰ *915 78 24 97*
– www.pelotari-asador.com
– Closed Sunday   **I2**
Rest – Menu 45/67 € – Carte 40/60 €
♦ Basque ♦ Rustic ♦

This typical Basque eatery specialising in roasted meats is run by its owners, with one in the kitchen and the other front of house. Four regional style dining rooms, two of which can be used as private rooms.

La Castela
%   AC VISA ©©

Doctor Castelo 22 ✉ *28009 –* Ⓜ *Ibiza –* ℰ *915 74 00 15*
– www.lacastela.com
– closed Holy Week, 15 days August and Sunday   **J2**
Rest – Menu 40 € – Carte 26/41 €
♦ Traditional ♦ Neighbourhood ♦
A traditional Madrid style tavern with a tapas bar at the entrance. The menu in the traditional dining room is centred on international cuisine.

Sula
%   🌿 AC ⇔ VISA ©© AE ①

Jorge Juan 33 ✉ *28001 –* Ⓜ *Velázquez –* ℰ *917 81 61 97 – www.sula.es*
– Closed August and Sunday   **I2**
Rest – Menu 35 € – Carte approx. 45 €
♦ Modern ♦ Design ♦
Designed with the gastro-bar concept in mind, Sula offers a modern setting embellished with designer details. Two high quality products feature prominently on the menu here: Iberian hams and vegetables from Navarra.

Juan Bravo 25
%/   🌿 AC VISA ©© AE ①

Juan Bravo 25 ✉ *28006 –* Ⓜ *Núñez de Balboa –* ℰ *914 11 60 25*
– www.juanbravo25.com
– Closed 15 days August and Sunday   **J1**
Tapa 3.80 € **Ración** approx. 17 €
♦ Traditional ♦ Classic ♦
This restaurant has a pleasant terrace in the middle of the street. The bar heaves with Basque-style tapas and pinchos, and there is a classic dining room with decoration that pays homage to Art Nouveau. Extensive traditional menu.

Cinco Jotas
%/   🌿 AC VISA ©© AE ①

Puigcerdá ✉ *28001 –* Ⓜ *Serrano –* ℰ *915 75 41 25*
– www.mesoncincojotas.com   **I2**
Tapa 3 € **Ración** approx. 15 €
♦ Traditional ♦ Tapas bar ♦
This mesón is renowned for its excellent hams and tapas. The restaurant has a splendid terrace, and three cosy dining rooms spread across three floors.

Tasca La Farmacia
%/   AC VISA ©© AE ①

Diego de León 9 ✉ *28006 –* Ⓜ *Diego de León –* ℰ *915 64 86 52*
– www.asadordearanda.com
– Closed 28 July-18 August and Sunday   **I1**
Tapa 4 € **Ración** approx. 12 €
♦ Traditional ♦ Exotic ♦
Traditional style tasca, with a beautifully tiled bar adorned with elegant motifs. House specialities include cod and 'zancarrón' (meat on the bone) tapas and snacks.

Cinco Jotas
%/   AC VISA ©© AE ①

Serrano 118 ✉ *28006 –* Ⓜ *Núñez de Balboa –* ℰ *915 63 27 10*
– www.mesoncincojotas.com   **I1**
Tapa 3 € **Ración** approx. 15 €
♦ Traditional ♦ Tapas bar ♦
Contemporary-style mesón serving a varied array of tapas, snacks and sandwiches with an emphasis on Spanish hams and pork. Attractive dining room.

El Barril de Goya
%/   AC VISA ©© AE ①

Goya 86 ✉ *28009 –* Ⓜ *Goya –* ℰ *915 78 39 98 – www.elbarrildegoya.com*
– Closed Sunday dinner   **J2**
Tapa 12 € **Ración** approx. 18 €
♦ Fish and seafood ♦ Tapas bar ♦
Good seafood restaurant with an air-conditioned bar displaying an impressive range of high quality products. Dining room with a more substantial menu to the rear of the building.

Taberna de la Daniela 🛅 VISA ⊙⊙ AE ①
General Pardiñas 21 ⊠ *28001 –* ⓜ *Goya –* ✆ *915 75 23 29*
– www.tabernaladaniela.com   J2
Ración approx. 12 €
◆ Traditional ◆ Tapas bar ◆
A typical taberna in the Salamanca district, with a tiled façade and various dining rooms in which to enjoy a range of tapas. The restaurant is particularly famous for its cocido madrileño (a meat, potato and chickpea stew) that is traditionally eaten in three stages.

El Barril de Alcántara 🛅 VISA ⊙⊙ AE ①
Don Ramón de la Cruz 91 ⊠ *28006 –* ⓜ *Manuel Becerra*
– ✆ *914 01 33 05 – www.elbarrilalcantara.com*   J1
Tapa 7 € **Ración** approx. 15 €
◆ Fish and seafood ◆ Tapas bar ◆
Renowned seafood restaurant with an excellent reputation for its cuisine and service. Enjoy seafood specialities and snacks either in the pub or in one of the two dining rooms.

ARGÜELLES   *Plan IV*

El Barril de Argüelles 🛅 VISA ⊙⊙ AE ①
Andrés Mellado 69 ⊠ *28015 –* ⓜ *Islas Filipinas –* ✆ *915 44 36 15*
– www.grupo-oter.com   K2
Rest – Carte 40/55 €
◆ Fish and seafood ◆ Mediterranean ◆
The long tapas bar, featuring enticing displays of seafood, leads to a stylish and modern dining room with a maritime inspired design. Shellfish and octopus are the house specialities.

El Barril de Argüelles 🛅 VISA ⊙⊙ AE ①
Andrés Mellado 69 ⊠ *28015 –* ⓜ *Islas Filipinas –* ✆ *915 44 36 15*
– www.grupo-oter.com   K2
Ración approx. 15 €
◆ Fish and seafood ◆ Mediterranean ◆
This impressive seafood restaurant has an elegant layout and extremely popular bar. Superb fish and seafood, including octopus and delicious Andalucian-style fresh fish, is served.

CHAMBERÍ   *Plan IV*

AC Santo Mauro 🛅 VISA ⊙⊙ AE ①
Zurbano 36 ⊠ *28010 –* ⓜ *Alonso Martínez –* ✆ *913 19 69 00*
– www.ac-hotels.com   L3
43 rm – ✝235/325 € ✝✝260/350 €, � 30 € – 8 suites
Rest – *(Closed August, Sunday and Monday)* Carte 41/64 €
◆ Palace ◆ Grand Luxury ◆ Contemporary ◆
This delightful, French-style mansion is located in the city's aristocratic and embassy district. Find luxurious features, and an elegant setting surrounded by an attractive garden. This highly distinguished restaurant occupies a stunning library-lounge.

InterContinental Madrid 🛅 VISA ⊙⊙ AE ①
paseo de la Castellana 49 ⊠ *28046*
– ⓜ *Gregorio Marañón –* ✆ *917 00 73 00*
– www.madrid.intercontinental.com   L3
279 rm – ✝✝155/550 €, ⊆ 32 € – 33 suites
Rest – Menu 27/60 € – Carte 59/75 €
◆ Chain hotel ◆ Classic ◆
This hotel has an elegant marble adorned lobby crowned with a cupola. Attractive inner terrace-patio and extremely comfortable guestrooms. The restaurant, located next to the bar, serves fine international cuisine.

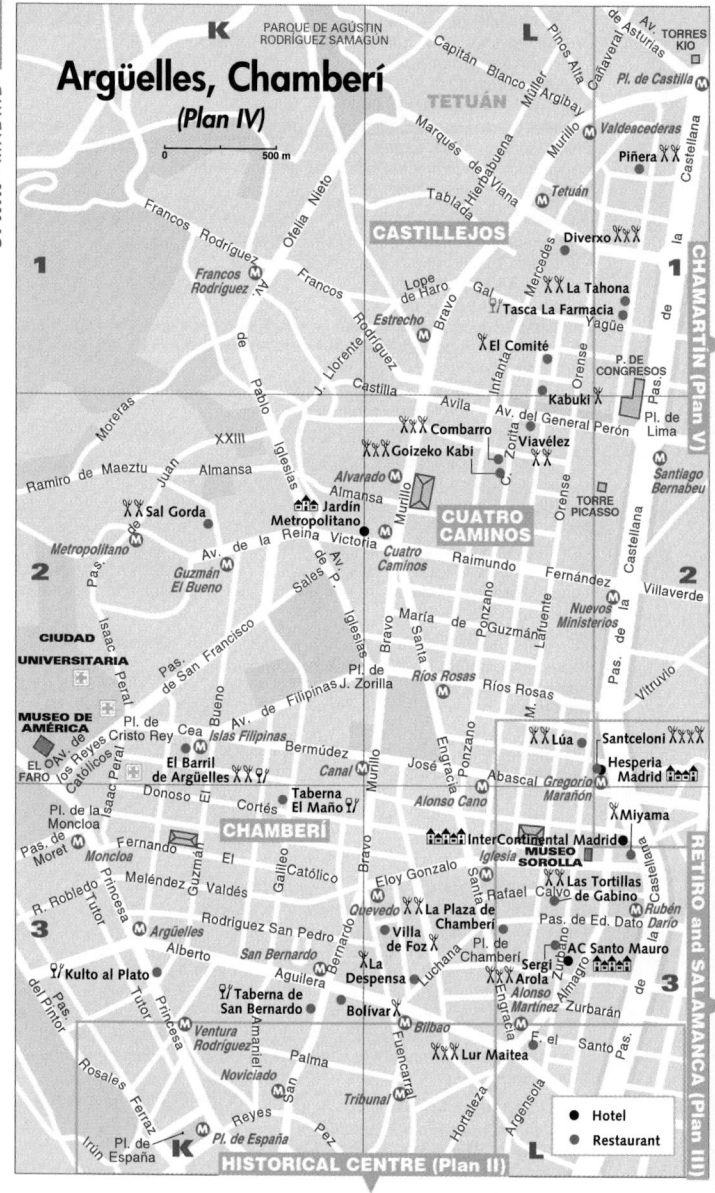

Argüelles, Chamberí
(Plan IV)

0   500 m

PARQUE DE AGUSTÍN
RODRÍGUEZ SAMAGUN

TETUÁN

CASTILLEJOS

CUATRO
CAMINOS

CIUDAD
UNIVERSITARIA

MUSEO DE
AMÉRICA

EL FARO

CHAMBERÍ

TORRES
KIO

Pl. de Castilla

Valdeacederas

Piñera

Diverxo

La Tahona
Tasca La Farmacia

El Comité

Kabuki

Combarro

Goizeko Kabi

Viavélez

P. DE
CONGRESOS

Pl. de
Lima

Santiago
Bernabeu

TORRE
PICASSO

Sal Gorda

Jardín
Metropolitano

Nuevos
Ministerios

Lúa   Santceloni

Hesperia
Madrid

Miyama

El Barril
de Argüelles

Taberna
El Maño

InterContinental Madrid

MUSEO
SOROLLA

Las Tortillas
de Gabino

Kulto al Plato

La Plaza de
Chamberí

Villa
de Foz

La
Despensa

Taberna de
San Bernardo

Bolívar

Sergi
Arola

AC Santo Mauro

Ventura
Rodríguez

Lur Maitea

Pl. de España

HISTORICAL CENTRE (Plan II)

CHAMARTÍN (Plan VI)

RETIRO and SALAMANCA (Plan III)

● Hotel
● Restaurant

Hesperia Madrid 𝄪𝄪 rm, Ⓐ 🛜 🏋 VISA ⓪ AE ⓪

paseo de la Castellana 57 ✉ *28046* – Ⓜ *Gregorio Marañón*
– ✆ *912 10 88 00* – *www.hesperia-madrid.com* L2
139 rm – 👫185/285 €, 🛏 30 € – 32 suites
Rest *Santceloni* ✿✿ – see restaurant listing
Rest – *(Closed August, Saturday lunch, Sunday and Bank Holidays) (lunch only)* Menu 32/60 € – Carte 47/70 €
♦ Chain hotel ♦ Classic ♦

Conveniently located in a central business district, this hotel has a small lobby and a number of different lounge areas. Elegant guestrooms that are in traditional in style. The restaurant in the internal patio also serves as the hotel's breakfast room.

Santceloni – Hotel Hesperia Madrid Ⓐ ⇔ VISA ⓪ AE ⓪

paseo de la Castellana 57 ✉ *28046* – Ⓜ *Gregorio Marañón*
– ✆ *912 10 88 40* – *www.restaurantesantceloni.com* L2
Rest – *(Closed Holy Week, August, Saturday lunch, Sunday and Bank Holidays)* Menu 150/180 € – Carte 110/146 € ⅜
♦ Creative ♦ Classic ♦

A great gastronomic experience. This elegant restaurant boasts a superbly arranged classic-contemporary dining room split between two floors. The culinary focus is on updated traditional cuisine that is well presented and comes with a creative touch.
→ Ravioli de ricota ahumada con caviar imperial. Carré de cochinillo asado al momento con aroma de tomillo. Crema de café con la mousse de chocolate cocida.

Sergi Arola Ⓐ VISA ⓪ AE ⓪

Zurbano 31 ✉ *28010* – Ⓜ *Rubén Darío* – ✆ *913 10 21 69*
– *www.sergiarola.es*
– *Closed 8-12 January, Holy Week, 15 days August, Sunday and Monday*
Rest – Menu 105/135 € – Carte 83/100 € ⅜ L3
♦ Creative ♦ Design ♦

The impressive set-up includes a cocktail bar, a modern dining room and an impressive private room next to the kitchen. The innovative cuisine stands out for its technical skill, the delicacy of its dishes and its perfect culinary combinations.
→ Crema Ligera de tupinambo, mascarpone con finas hierbas y mousse de ave trufada. Lomo de ternera ahumado al romero, ragout de morillas, puré granny smith y mostaza antigua. El chocolate "Da la vida".

Lur Maitea Ⓐ ⇔ VISA ⓪ AE ⓪

Fernando el Santo 4 ✉ *28010* – Ⓜ *Alonso Martínez* – ✆ *913 08 03 50*
– *www.lurmaitearestaurante.com*
– *Closed August and Sunday* L3
Rest – Menu 40 € – Carte 42/67 €
♦ Basque ♦ Formal ♦

Lur Maitea has become one of the city's best-known restaurants. It serves contemporary Basque cuisine in an elegant dining room with blue-inspired decor and wood flooring.

El Mentidero de la Villa 🛜 Ⓐ ⇔ ⊡ VISA ⓪ AE ⓪

Almagro 20 ✉ *28010* – Ⓜ *Alonso Martínez* – ✆ *913 08 12 85*
– *www.mentiderodelavilla.es* *Plan II* **G-H1**
Rest – Menu 50 € – Carte approx. 55 €
♦ Traditional ♦ Elegant ♦

Hidden behind the attractive classical façade is this elegant and contemporary restaurant with a pleasant main dining room and several private sections. It serves updated traditional cuisine where the best possible ingredients act as the guiding principle.

XX **Nikkei 225**   AC ⌂ VISA ⑩ AE

paseo de la Castellana 15 (entrance door Fernando El Santo St)
⊠ 28046 – Ⓜ *Colón* – ℰ 913 19 03 90
– *www.nikkei225.es*
– *Closed Sunday and Bank Holidays*   *Plan II* **H1**
Rest – Menu 45/75 € – Carte 50/75 €
♦ Japanese ♦ Design ♦
This particularly interesting dining option is set in an elegant, designer inspired setting. Explore the flavours of Japanese cuisine with a Peruvian influence, developed by Japanese descendants who emigrated to South America.

XX **Lúa**   AC VISA ⑩ AE ①

Eduardo Dato 5 ⊠ 28003 – Ⓜ *Rubén Darío* – ℰ 913 95 28 53
– *www.restaurantelua.com*   **L2**
Rest – Menu 35/78 € – Carte 38/47 €
♦ Modern ♦ Fashionable ♦
This small, trendy restaurant has a lively atmosphere with the dining room separated into three sections. Creative, contemporary cuisine, including a tasting menu.

XX **La Plaza de Chamberí**   AC VISA ⑩ AE ①

pl. de Chamberí 10 ⊠ 28010 – Ⓜ *Iglesia* – ℰ 914 46 06 97
– *www.restaurantelaplazadechamberi.com*
– *Closed Sunday dinner*   **L3**
Rest – Menu 30/50 € – Carte 36/41 €
♦ Traditional ♦ Classic ♦
A well-established and popular restaurant with an old-style dining room extending over two floors. The culinary focus here is on traditional cuisine.

XX **Las Tortillas de Gabino**   AC VISA ⑩ AE ①
⊛

Rafael Calvo 20 ⊠ 28010 – Ⓜ *Rubén Darío* – ℰ 913 19 75 05
– *www.lastortillasdegabino.com*
– *Closed Sunday*   **L3**
Rest – Carte 25/34 €
♦ Traditional ♦ Formal ♦
Two brothers run this restaurant. It has an entrance hall, two contemporary rooms with wooden panels, and a private room. Traditional menu with a selection of tortillas.

X **Bolívar**   AC VISA ⑩ AE ①
⊛

Manuela Malasaña 28 ⊠ 28004 – Ⓜ *San Bernardo* – ℰ 914 45 12 74
– *www.restaurantebolivar.com*
– *Closed August and Sunday*   **K3**
Rest – Menu 38 € – Carte 30/45 €
♦ Traditional ♦ Trendy ♦
This family-run restaurant in the traditional Malasaña district has excellent service and a reasonably priced, varied menu. Welcoming dining room with a modern feel.

X **Miyama**   AC VISA ⑩ AE

paseo de la Castellana 45 ⊠ 28013
– Ⓜ *Gregorio Marañón* – ℰ 913 91 00 26
– *www.restaurantemiyama.com*
– *Closed 7-31 August, Sunday and Bank Holidays*   **L3**
Rest – Carte approx. 50 €
♦ Japanese ♦ Minimalist ♦
A Japanese restaurant that is hugely popular in the city, including with Japanese visitors. An extensive sushi bar and simply laid tables share space in the single dining area. High quality, traditional Japanese cuisine.

X **Villa de Foz**　　　　　　　　　　　AC ⇄ 🛇 VISA ⓪⑤ AE ⓪

Gonzálo de Córdoba 10 ⊠ *28010 –* ⓜ *Bilbao –* ☏ *914 46 89 93*
– www.villadefoz.com
– closed August　　　　　　　　　　　　　　　　　　**L3**
Rest – Menu 33/55 € – Carte 35/41 €
♦ Galician ♦ Classic ♦
The Villa de Foz has two pleasant dining rooms, both decorated in a style that reflects traditional and contemporary influences. Its à la carte menu of traditional Galician cuisine is enhanced by a fine choice of raciones and home-made desserts.

Ⴒ **Taberna El Maño**　　　　　　　　　　　🛏 VISA ⓪⑤

Vallehermoso 59 ⊠ *28015 –* ⓜ *Canal –* ☏ *914 48 40 35*
– closed Sunday dinner　　　　　　　　　　　　　　　**K3**
Tapa 3 € **Ración** approx. 10 €
♦ Traditional ♦ Tapas bar ♦
Old, traditional restaurant decorated with a bullfighting theme. Tapas and snacks of a high quality.

CASTILLEJOS – CUATRO CAMINOS　　　　　　　　　*Plan IV*

🏨 **Jardín Metropolitano**　　　&. rm, AC 🛜 ⚒ 🛇 VISA ⓪⑤ AE ⓪

av. Reina Victoria 12 ⊠ *28003 –* ⓜ *Cuatro Caminos –* ☏ *911 83 18 10*
– www.metropolitano-hotel.com　　　　　　　　　　　**K-L2**
101 rm – ♥♥69/245 €, ☲ 13 € – 7 suites
Rest – *(Closed August) (lunch only)* Menu 18 € – Carte approx. 30 €
♦ Business ♦ Classic ♦
Attractively laid out around a patio, this hotel offers guests well-appointed, classically styled bedrooms, with the suites on the top floor the pick of the bunch. The restaurant, serving typical cuisine, comprises of a traditional dining area and an attractive room with the feel of a winter garden.

XXX **Combarro**　　　　　　　　　　　AC ⇄ VISA ⓪⑤ AE ⓪

Reina Mercedes 12 ⊠ *28020 –* ⓜ *Nuevos Ministerios –* ☏ *915 54 77 84*
– www.combarro.com
– Closed Holy Week, 15 days August and Sunday dinner　　　　**L2**
Rest – Carte 45/60 €
♦ Fish and seafood ♦ Classic ♦
Galician cuisine with an emphasis on fresh quality produce, including live fish tanks. Public bar, dining on the first floor and a number of rooms in the basement. Classic and elegant in style.

XXX **Diverxo** (David Muñoz)　　　　　　　AC VISA ⓪⑤ AE
🏵🏵

Pensamiento 28 ⊠ *28020 –* ⓜ *Cuzco –* ☏ *915 70 07 66*
– www.diverxo.com
– Closed Holy Week, 21 days August, Sunday and Monday　　　**L1**
Rest – *(booking essential) (set menu only)* Menu 75/145 €
♦ Creative ♦ Trendy ♦
Modern and welcoming, the Diverxo is accessed via a cocktail bar. In the bright, contemporary-style dining room, choose between various tasting menus. These reflect the highly original and creative cuisine with a marked Asian slant.
➜ Patatas cenarias guisadas con erizos, miso y morcilla. Lenguado a la romana en wok sin harina. Chocolate, lapsang souchang, yuzu, wasabi y pimienta sansho.

XXX **Goizeko Kabi**　　　　　　　　　AC VISA ⓪⑤ AE ⓪

Comandante Zorita 37 ⊠ *28020 –* ⓜ *Alvarado –* ☏ *915 33 01 85*
– www.goizekogaztelupe.com
– Closed Sunday dinner　　　　　　　　　　　　　　**L2**
Rest – Menu 35 € – Carte 44/51 €
♦ Basque ♦ Classic ♦
Prestigious address serving modern Basque cuisine. Although the tables are somewhat close together, the overall feel is one of refined elegance.

XX **Piñera**   AC ⇄ VISA ⊛ AE ⓪
Rosario Pino 12 ⊠ 28012 – **Ⓜ** *Valdeacederas – ℰ 914 25 14 25*
– www.restaurantepinera.com – Closed 15 days August   **L1**
Rest – Carte 45/65 € ⊛
♦ Classic ♦ Formal ♦
The Piñera has an attractive entrance hall with a bar, in addition to two contemporary-style dining rooms and two private rooms. Traditional and international cuisine with a modern touch.

XX **Viavélez**   AC VISA ⊛ AE ⓪
av. General Perón 10 ⊠ 28020 – **Ⓜ** *Santiago Bernabeu*
– www.restauranteviavelez.com – Closed August and Sunday
Rest – Menu 28/60 € – Carte 37/54 €   **L2**
♦ Creative ♦ Fashionable ♦
This tavern-restaurant features a select tapas bar at the entrance and a modern and intimate dining room in the basement. Its creative cuisine is based on traditional Asturian recipes.

XX **La Tahona**   AC ⇄ VISA ⊛ AE ⓪
Capitán Haya 21 (on the side) ⊠ 28020 – **Ⓜ** *Cuzco – ℰ 915 55 04 41*
– www.asadordearanda.com – closed August and Sunday dinner
Rest – Menu 35/55 € – Carte 33/49 €   **L1**
♦ Meats and grills ♦ Rustic ♦
Bar in the entrance with a wood oven and wood panelling, followed by various dining rooms decorated in medieval Castilian style. Enjoy traditional roast dishes accompanied by the restaurant's own house red.

XX **Sal Gorda**   AC VISA ⊛ AE ⓪
Beatriz de Bobadilla 9 ⊠ 28040 – **Ⓜ** *Guzmán El Bueno – ℰ 915 43 95 06*
– www.restaurantesalgorda.es – Closed Holy Week, August and Sunday
Rest – Menu 35/45 € – Carte 30/45 €   **K2**
♦ International ♦ Classic ♦
Renowned professionals run this small restaurant. Find carefully prepared, classical cuisine based on traditional recipes, as well as some international dishes.

X **El Comité**   AC VISA ⊛ AE
pl. de San Amaro 8 ⊠ 28020 – **Ⓜ** *Nuevos Ministerios – ℰ 915 71 87 11*
– Closed Saturday lunch and Sunday   **L1**
Rest – Menu 35/50 € – Carte 37/55 €
♦ French ♦ Bistro ♦
Cosy bistro-restaurant with café style furniture and a huge collection of old photographs. The menu here focuses on French cuisine.

X **Kabuki**   ⌂ AC VISA ⊛ AE ⓪
£³
av. Presidente Carmona 2 ⊠ 28020 – **Ⓜ** *Santiago Bernabeu*
– ℰ 914 17 64 15
– Closed Holy Week, 12-31 August, Saturday lunch, Sunday and Bank Holidays
Rest – Carte 48/65 €   **L1-2**
♦ Japanese ♦ Minimalist ♦
An intimate Japanese restaurant with a minimalist feel. Modern terrace, as well as a kitchen-bar serving a range of dishes including a wide choice of nigiri sushi. It is best to book ahead as it is often full.
➜ Navajas con vinagreta de yuzu. Selección de nigiris. Cremoso de yuzu con fresas y pipas de calabaza.

Y/ **Tasca La Farmacia**   AC VISA ⊛ AE ⓪
Capitán Haya 19 ⊠ 28020 – **Ⓜ** *Cuzco – ℰ 915 55 81 46*
– www.asadordearanda.com
– Closed 11 August-3 September and Sunday   **L1**
Tapa 4 € **Ración** approx. 12 €
♦ Traditional ♦ Exotic ♦
Delightful restaurant decorated with azulejo tiles, stone arches, exposed brickwork, wrought iron lattice windows and an impressive glass ceiling. La Farmacia is famous for its cod dishes.

Puerta América 🖪 🖵 🕭 rm, 🖾 🎅 🖄 🖜 🚾 🐠 🆎 ⓪

av. de América 41 ✉ *28002* – 🅜 *Cartagena* – 𝄞 *917 44 54 00*
– *www.hotelpuertamerica.com* **N3**
315 rm – 🛉🛉120/200 €, 🖙 25 € – 12 suites
Rest *Lágrimas Negras* – *(Closed 25 July-22 August and Sunday)* Menu
35/75 € – Carte 50/66 € 🕸

♦ Business ♦ Design ♦

Colourfully decorated and with numerous designer features, each of the floors
of this hotel reflects the creativity of a renowned artist. The guestrooms are very
original in style. This modern restaurant has a certain New York feel, with its bar
area and high ceilings.

 NH Eurobuilding 🖪 🌐 🕭 rm, 🖾 🎅 🖄 🖜 🚾 🐠 🆎 ⓪

Padre Damián 23 ✉ *28036* – 🅜 *Cuzco* – 𝄞 *913 53 73 00*
– *www.nh-hotels.com* **M2**
426 rm – 🛉🛉75/306 €, 🖙 23 € – 4 suites
Rest – Menu 22/52 € – Carte 34/49 €

♦ Business ♦ Chain hotel ♦ Classic ♦

The decor here upholds the philosophy of this hotel chain, with comfortable,
well-appointed and spacious guestrooms. Additional facilities include several
meeting rooms and a modern spa. The cuisine in this restaurant remains faithful
to traditional recipes.

 Don Pío without rest 🖪 🖾 🎅 🖄 🄿 🚾 🐠 🆎 ⓪

av. Pío XII-25 ✉ *28016* – 🅜 *Pio XII* – 𝄞 *913 53 07 80*
– *www.hoteldonpio.com* **N2**
41 rm 🖙 – 🛉78/128 € 🛉🛉99/150 €

♦ Family ♦ Classic ♦

Attractive patio-lobby crowned by a modern skylight and overlooked by all the
guestrooms. These are spacious and include features such as hydromassage
bathtubs.

Castilla Plaza 🖪 🕭 rm, 🖾 🎅 🖄 🖜 🚾 🐠 🆎 ⓪

paseo de la Castellana 220 ✉ *28046* – 🅜 *Plaza Castilla* – 𝄞 *915 67 43 00*
– *www.abbacastillaplaza.com* **M1**
228 rm – 🛉🛉65/150 €, 🖙 17 €   **Rest** – Menu 25 € – Carte 40/60 €

♦ Business ♦ Classic ♦

Beautiful glass fronted building, which along with the Kio Towers, is part of the
Puerta de Europa complex. Comfortable, contemporary-style with a wealth of
decorative detail. This restaurant serves cuisine with a Mediterranean flavour,
including interesting daily specials.

XXXXX **Zalacaín** 🖾 ⟷ 🚾 🐠 🆎 ⓪
🕸

Álvarez de Baena 4 ✉ *28006* – 🅜 *Gregorio Marañón* – 𝄞 *915 61 48 40*
– *www.restaurantezalacain.com*
– *Closed Holy Week, August, Saturday lunch, Sunday and Bank Holidays*
Rest – Menu 90/99 € – Carte 58/100 € 🕸 **M3**

♦ Classic ♦ Elegant ♦

One of the most prestigious and elegant restaurants in Spain. It has an attractive
entrance, private bar and refined dining rooms with a classic air. Ever faithful to
its demanding principles, Zalacaín is superbly run and remains a standard bea-
rer for traditional dining.

➔ Pequeño búcaro "Don Pío". Bacalao Tellagorri. Crepes Zalacain.

XXXX **El Bodegón** 🖾 ⟷ 🚾 🐠 🆎

Pinar 15 ✉ *28006* – 🅜 *Gregorio Marañón* – 𝄞 *915 62 88 44*
– *www.el-bodegon.es*
– *Closed August, Saturday lunch and Sunday* **M3**
Rest – Menu 60 € – Carte 60/78 €

♦ Traditional ♦ Classic ♦

Elegant restaurant in classical style with a private bar and dining rooms on
various levels. The menu here focuses on traditional cuisine.

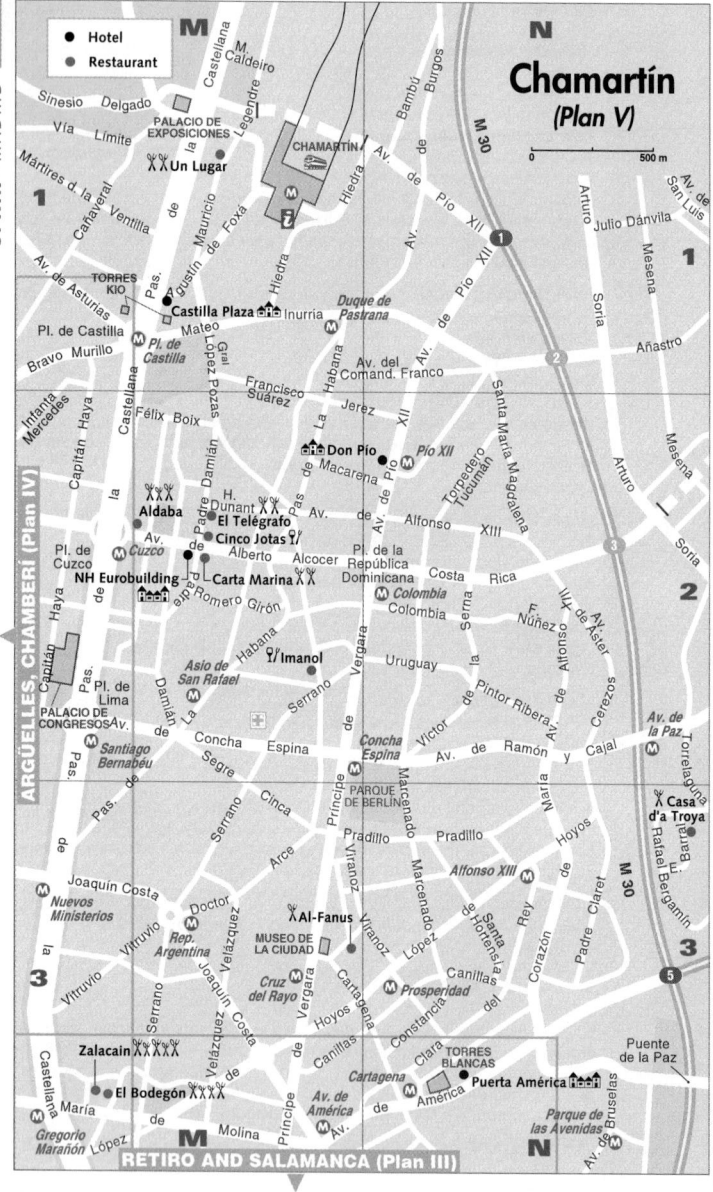

XXX **Aldaba** 🔲 ⛤ 🔄 VISA ⓸ AE ⓪
av. Alberto Alcocer 5 ⊠ 28036 – **Ⓜ** *Cuzco –* ℰ *913 59 73 86*
– www.aldaba-restaurante.com
– Closed Holy Week, August, Saturday lunch, Sunday and Bank Holidays
Rest – Carte 52/75 € 🏵   M2
♦ Traditional ♦ Classic ♦
This restaurant has a bar at the entrance, followed by an attractive dining room
in classic-modern style and several small rooms for private dining. Excellent
wine list.

XX **Un Lugar** 🏠 🔲 VISA ⓸ AE ⓪
Mauricio Legendre 33 ⊠ 28046 – **Ⓜ** *Chamartín –* ℰ *913 14 77 27*
– www.unlugarmadrid.com
– Closed 15 days August and Sunday   M1
Rest – Menu 15/50 € – Carte 40/55 €
♦ Traditional ♦ Design ♦
This restaurant occupies a detached cube-like building with a carefully pack-
aged design and contemporary look. It offers a traditional à la carte, including
dishes from Rioja, in addition to several set menus. Make sure you try the grilled
wild turbot and T-bone steak.

XX **El Telégrafo** 🏠 🔲 ⛤ VISA ⓸ AE ⓪
Padre Damián 44 ⊠ 28036 – **Ⓜ** *Cuzco –* ℰ *913 59 70 83*
– www.eltelegrafomarisqueria.com   M2
Rest – Carte approx. 50 €
♦ Fish and seafood ♦ Mediterranean ♦
This seafood restaurant imitates the decor of the inside of a boat with dining
rooms separated into different areas and levels. Attractive bar at the entrance
with a seafood counter.

XX **Carta Marina** 🏠 🔲 ⛤ VISA ⓸ AE ⓪
Padre Damián 40 ⊠ 28036 – **Ⓜ** *Cuzco –* ℰ *914 58 68 26*
– www.restaurantecartamarina.com
– Closed Holy Week, August and Sunday dinner   M2
Rest – Menu 45 € – Carte 35/70 €
♦ Galician ♦ Classic ♦
This restaurant has an attractive wood decor, private bar, and cosy dining rooms
with a summer and winter terrace. Traditional Galician menu.

X **Al-Fanus** 🔲 VISA ⓸ AE ⓪
Pechuán 6 ⊠ 28002 – **Ⓜ** *Cruz del Rayo –* ℰ *915 62 77 18*
– www.alfanus.es
– Closed Sunday dinner   M3
Rest – Menu 21/33 € – Carte 34/48 €
♦ International ♦ Classic ♦
Authentic Syrian cuisine is on offer in this restaurant with a bar at the entrance
and a Moorish-style dining room. The intimate lighting is provided by hand-
made metal wall lamps.

X **Casa d'a Troya** 🔲 VISA ⓸ AE ⓪
Emiliano Barral 14 ⊠ 28043 – **Ⓜ** *Avenida de la Paz –* ℰ *914 16 44 55*
– www.casadatroya.es
*– Closed 24 December 2-January, Holy Week, 25 July-August, Sunday and Bank
Holidays*   N3
Rest – *(lunch only except Friday and Saturday)* Menu 30/68 €
– Carte 41/48 €
♦ Galician ♦ Family ♦
A family-run restaurant with a bar at the entrance and two comfortable dining
rooms. Tasty, well-prepared Galician cooking, always made with the best quality
ingredients.

SPAIN - MADRID

⊻/ **Imanol**   AC VISA ⊛ AE

Víctor Andrés Belaúnde 3 ✉ *28016 –* **Ⓜ** *Colombia –* ℰ *914 57 77 57*
– *www.asadorimanol.com*
– *Closed Sunday dinner*   **M2**
Tapa 2.30 € **Ración** approx. 8 €
♦ **Basque** ♦ **Tapas bar** ♦

Extensive bar displaying Basque inspired tapas, as well as a small dining room
where you can choose from a menu focusing on the Basque Country and
Navarra. It always seems to be full... and for good reason.

⊻/ **Cinco Jotas**   🛜 AC VISA ⊛ AE ⓪

Padre Damián 42 ✉ *28036 –* **Ⓜ** *Cuzco –* ℰ *913 50 31 73*
– *www.mesoncincojotas.com*   **M2**
Tapa 3 € **Ración** approx. 15 €
♦ **Traditional** ♦ **Tapas bar** ♦

This chain restaurant specialises in top quality Iberian ham and chorizos. Varied
tapas and à la carte menus served in two pleasant dining rooms.

PARQUE FERIAL   *Plan I*

🏛 **Pullman Madrid**   ⯑ ⅍ rm, AC 🛜 ⯑ ⯑ VISA ⊛ AE ⓪

av. Capital de España 10 ✉ *28042 –* ℰ *917 21 00 70*
– *www.pullmanhotels.com*   **D1**
174 rm ⯑ – ⯑105/170 € – 5 suites
Rest *Mare Nostrum* – *(Closed August, Saturday and Sunday)* Menu
15/35 € – Carte approx. 35 €
♦ **Business** ♦ **Modern** ♦

This hotel is next to IFEMA and aimed predominantly at a business clientele. It
offers a wide range of meeting rooms and comfortable bedrooms with a contemporary, classic decor. Free airport transfers. The Mare Nostrum, serving
updated versions of traditional dishes, stands out among its various restaurants.

🏨 **Globales Acis y Galatea** without rest   ⯑ AC 🛜 P VISA ⊛ ⓪

Galatea 6 ✉ *28042 –* **Ⓜ** *Canillejas –* ℰ *917 43 49 01*
– *www.hotelesglobales.com*   **D1**
25 rm ⯑ – ⯑62/98 € ⯑66/102 €
♦ **Family** ♦ **Modern** ♦

The combination of friendly, family management and a decor in contrasting
colours gives this hotel a certain charm. Bedrooms designed along contemporary-classic lines – it is worth requesting one of the three with their own private
balcony.

AT BARAJAS AIRPORT   *Plan I*

🏨 **Meliá Barajas**   ⯑ ⅍ ⯑ ⅍ rm, AC 🛜 ⯑ P VISA ⊛ AE ⓪

av. de Logroño 305 (A 2, then towards Barajas Town: 15 km) ✉ *28042*
– **Ⓜ** *Barajas –* ℰ *917 47 77 00 – www.melia-barajas.com*   **D1**
221 rm – ⯑99/275 €, ⯑ 19 € – 8 suites
Rest – Menu 26 € – Carte 28/48 €
♦ **Business** ♦ **Classic** ♦

Comfortable, classically furnished facilities, including fully equipped guestrooms
and a wide choice of meeting rooms arranged around the garden and pool
area. International dining with the occasional Asian influence is to the fore in
the restaurant.

BARCELONA
BARCELONA

Population: 1 615 448

B. Brillion/MICHELIN

It can't be overestimated how important Catalonia is to the locals of Barcelona: pride in their region of Spain runs deep in the blood. Barcelona loves to mix the traditional with the avant-garde, and this exuberant opening of arms has seen it grow into a pulsating city for visitors. Its rash of theatres, museums and concert halls is unmatched by most other European cities, and many artists and architects, including Picasso, Miró, Dalí, Gaudí and Subirachs, have chosen to live here.

The 19C was a golden period in the city's artistic development, with the growth of the great Catalan Modernism movement, but it was knocked back on its heels after the Spanish Civil War and the rise to power of the dictator Franco, who destroyed hopes for an independent Catalonia. After his death, democracy came to Spain and since then, Barcelona has relished its position as the capital of a restored autonomous region. Go up on the Montjuïc to get a great overview of the city below. Barcelona's atmospheric old town is near the harbour and reaches into the teeming streets of the Gothic Quarter, while the newer area is north of this; its elegant avenues in grid formation making up Eixample. The coastal quarter of Barça has been transformed with the development of trendy Barceloneta. For many, though, the epicentre of this bubbling city is Las Ramblas, scything through the centre of town.

BARCELONA IN...

→ **ONE DAY**
Catedral de Santa Eulalia, Las Ramblas, La Pedrera, Museu Picasso, Sagrada Familia.

→ **TWO DAYS**
Montjuïc, Parc Güell, Nou Camp Stadium, Barceloneta Waterfront, Tibidabo.

→ **THREE DAYS**
Barri Gotic and Palau de la Musica Catalana, Via Laietana, Sitges.

PRACTICAL INFORMATION

ARRIVAL-DEPARTURE

✈ Barcelona Airport is located 13km southwest of the city. The Renfe train (Line 2, suburban train) runs every 30min. The Aerobus runs every 5min.

GETTING AROUND

The Barcelona Card offers two to five days of unlimited travel on the metro and buses, discounts on airport buses and cable cars, reduced entry to museums and attractions and discounts in some restaurants, bars and shops; it is sold at the airport, tourist offices and various other venues. The Articket gives free entry to seven museums and galleries over six months and is available from tourist offices. Look out for two tourist buses – the Barcelona City Tour and the Bus Turistic.

CALENDAR HIGHLIGHTS

May
Ciutat Flamenco, Barcelona Guitar Festival.

June
Bicycle Week, Saint John's Day (concerts, dances and bonfires).

September
Fiesta de la Merce (Feast of Our Lady of Mercy), Barcelona Book Market.

October
International Jazz Festival.

October–July
Classical performances at Gran Teatre del Liceu.

EATING OUT

Barcelona has long had a good gastronomic tradition, and geographically it's been more influenced by France and Italy than other Spanish regions. But these days the sensual enjoyment of food has become something of a mainstream religion here. The city has hundreds of tapas bars; a type of cuisine which is very refreshing knocked back with a draught beer. The city's location brings together produce from the land and the sea, with a firm emphasis on seasonality and quality produce. This explains why there are myriad markets in the city, all in great locations. Specialities to look out for include Pantumaca: slices of toasted bread with tomato and olive oil; Escalibada, which is made with roasted vegetables; Esqueixada, a typically Catalan salad, and Crema Catalana, a light custard. One little known facet of Barcelona life is its exquisite chocolate and sweet shops. Two stand out: Fargas, in the Barri Gothic, is the city's most famous chocolate shop, while Cacao Sampaka is the most elegant chocolate store you could ever wish to find.

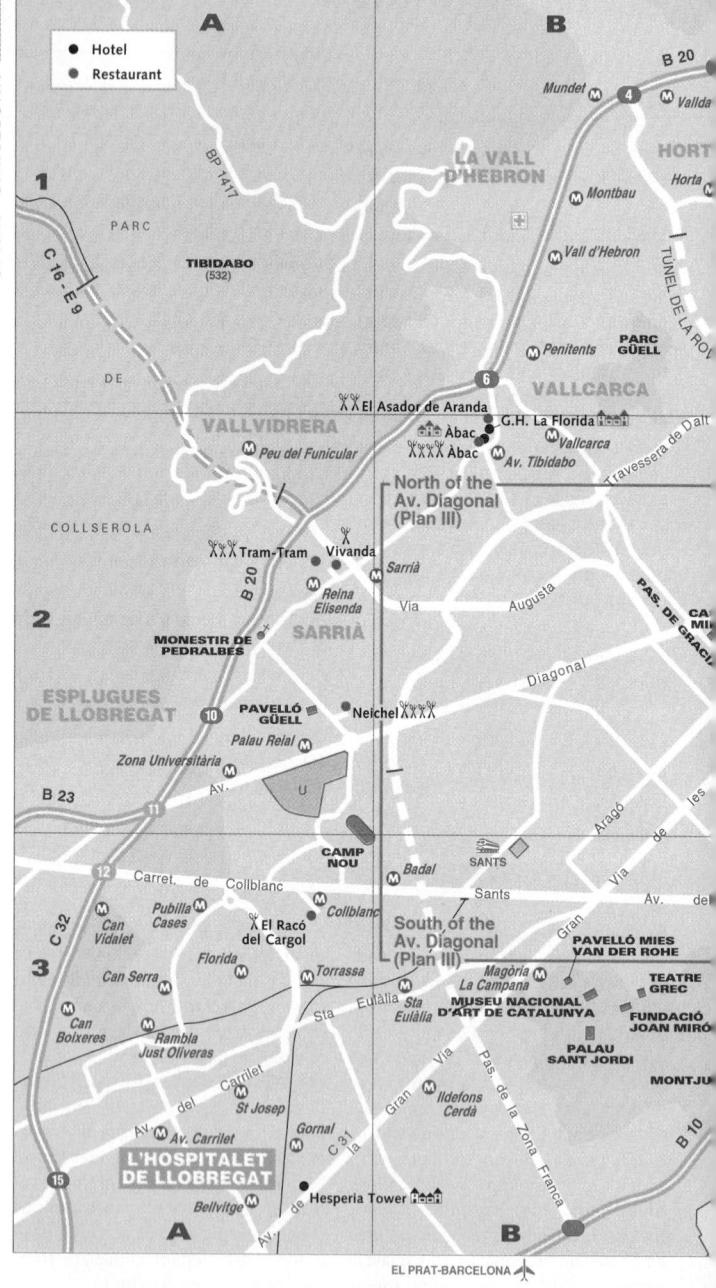

EL PRAT-BARCELONA ✈

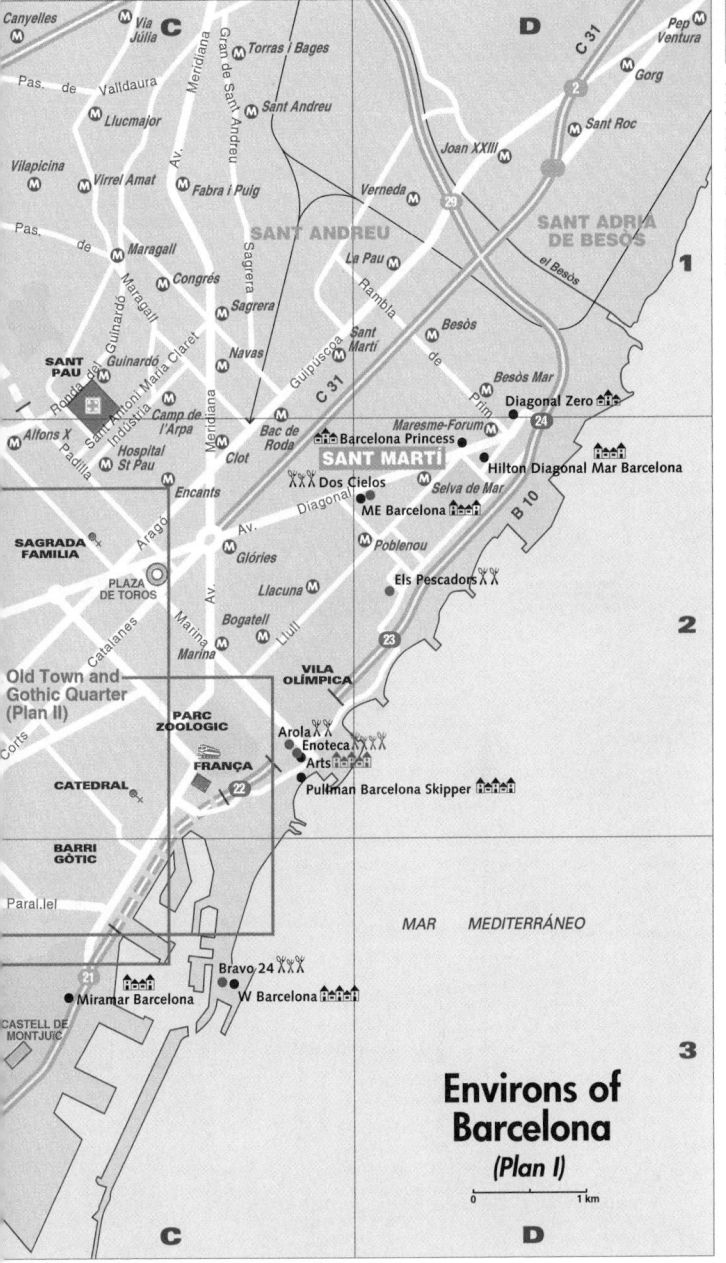

Environs of
Barcelona
(Plan I)

MAR   MEDITERRÁNEO

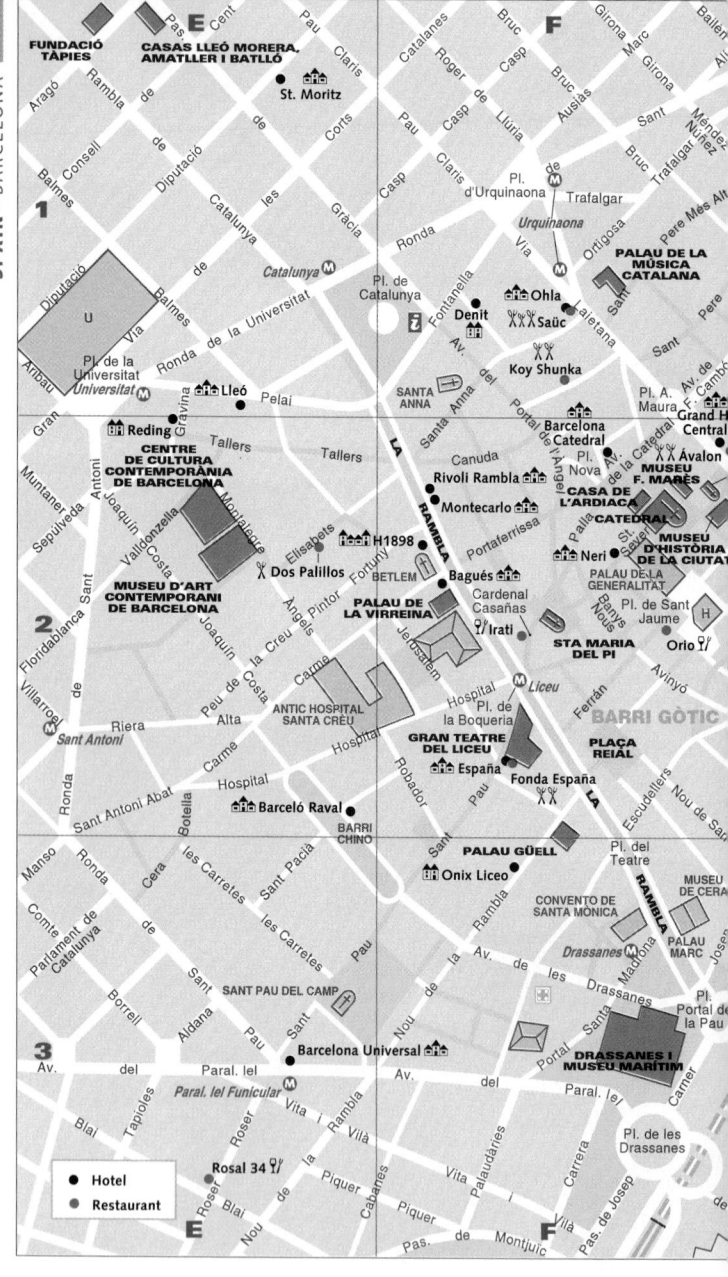

FUNDACIÓ
TÀPIES

CASAS LLEÓ MORERA,
AMATLLER I BATLLÓ

St. Moritz

Pl.
d'Urquinaona — Trafalgar

Urquinaona

PALAU DE LA
MÚSICA
CATALANA

Catalunya Ⓜ

Pl. de
Catalunya

Ohla

Denit   Saüc

Koy Shunka

U

Pl. de la
Universitat

Universitat Ⓜ

Lleó

SANTA
ANNA

Pl. A.
Maura

Grand H

Reding

Barcelona
Catedral

Central

CENTRE
DE CULTURA
CONTEMPORÀNIA
DE BARCELONA

Tallers

Pl.
Nova

MUSEU
F. MARÉS

Àvalon

Rivoli Rambla

Montecarlo

CASA DE
L'ARDIACA

CATEDRAL

H1898

Dos Palillos

BETLEM

Bagués

Neri

MUSEU
D'HISTÒRIA
DE LA CIUTAT

MUSEU D'ART
CONTEMPORANI
DE BARCELONA

PALAU DE
LA VIRREINA

Cardenal
Casañas

Irati

PALAU DE LA
GENERALITAT

Pl. de Sant
Jaume

STA MARIA
DEL PI

Orio

ANTIC HOSPITAL
SANTA CREU

Pl. de
la Boqueria

Liceu Ⓜ

BARRI GÒTIC

GRAN TEATRE
DEL LICEU

España

Fonda España

PLAÇA
REIAL

Barceló Raval

BARRI
CHINO

PALAU GÜELL

Pl. del
Teatre

Onix Liceo

MUSEU
DE CERA

CONVENTO DE
SANTA MÓNICA

PALAU
MARC

SANT PAU DEL CAMP

Drassanes Ⓜ

Pl.
Portal de
la Pau

Barcelona Universal

DRASSANES I
MUSEU MARÍTIM

Paral. lel Funicular Ⓜ

Pl. de les
Drassanes

Rosal 34

● Hotel
● Restaurant

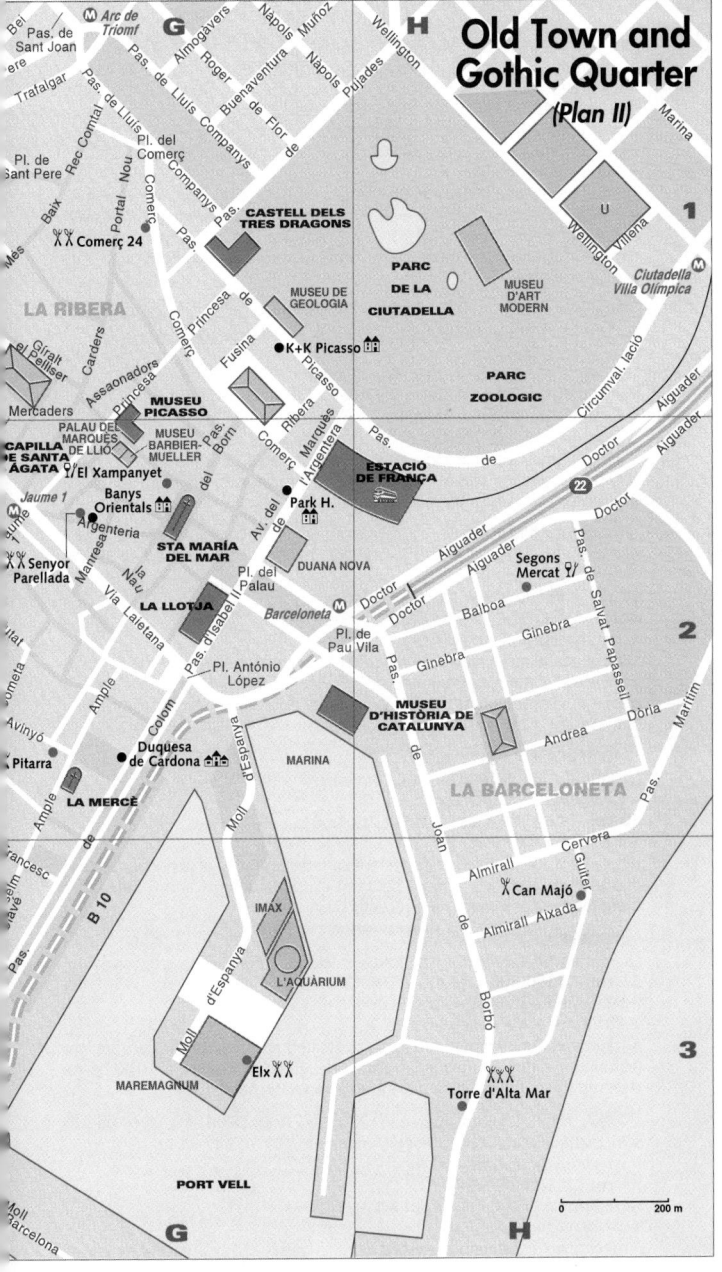

Old Town and Gothic Quarter
(Plan II)

LA RIBERA

CASTELL DELS TRES DRAGONS

MUSEU DE GEOLOGIA

K+K Picasso

PARC DE LA CIUTADELLA

PARC ZOOLOGIC

MUSEU D'ART MODERN

Ciutadella Villa Olímpica

Comerç 24

Girat el Pellisser

Mercaders

MUSEU PICASSO

PALAU DEL MARQUÈS DE LLIÓ

CAPILLA DE SANTA ÀGATA

El Xampanyet

MUSEU BARBIER-MUELLER

Banys Orientals

Senyor Parellada

STA MARÍA DEL MAR

Park H.

ESTACIÓ DE FRANÇA

Segons Mercat

LA LLOTJA

Pl. del Palau

DUANA NOVA

Barceloneta

Pl. de Pau Vila

Pl. António López

Pitarra

Duquesa de Cardona

MUSEU D'HISTÒRIA DE CATALUNYA

LA MERCÈ

MARINA

LA BARCELONETA

Can Majó

IMAX

L'AQUÀRIUM

MAREMAGNUM

Elx

Torre d'Alta Mar

PORT VELL

0   200 m

SPAIN - BARCELONA

W Barcelona ⟨icons⟩

pl. de la Rosa dels Vents 1 (Moll De Llevant) ⊠ *08039* – ℰ *932 95 28 00*
– www.w-barcelona.com Plan I **C3**
473 rm – †‡250/650 €, ⊡ 30 € – 67 suites
Rest *Bravo 24* – see restaurant listing
Rest – Menu 85 € – Carte 52/162 €
♦ Luxury ♦ Design ♦
This hotel designed by Ricardo Bofill is located in the city's port area. It comprises of two glass buildings: one a cube, the other a huge sail rising impressively above the Mediterranean. Extensive spa facilities. This contemporary looking gastronomic restaurant offers guests an à la carte menu based around high quality products.

H1898 ⟨icons⟩

La Rambla 109 ⊠ *08002* – ⓜ *Catalunya* – ℰ *935 52 95 52*
– www.hotel1898.com **F2**
166 rm – †‡195/486 €, ⊡ 23 € – 3 suites
Rest – Menu 27/54 € – Carte 36/78 €
♦ Chain hotel ♦ Classic ♦
The decor in this hotel occupying the former Tabacos de Filipinas headquarters is a mix of the traditional and contemporary. Spa area, guestrooms offering the very best amenities, plus a rooftop solarium with views of the city. This resolutely contemporary restaurant offers an à la carte menu of international dishes.

Miramar Barcelona ⟨icons⟩

pl. Carlos Ibáñez 3 ⊠ *08038* – ℰ *932 81 16 00* ⟨icons⟩
– www.hotelmiramarbarcelona.com Plan I **C3**
67 rm – †‡150/370 €, ⊡ 27 € – 8 suites
Rest – Menu 32 € – Carte approx. 35 €
♦ Business ♦ Contemporary ♦
In an outstanding location with magnificent views of the port and the city from its peaceful vantage point on the side of Montjuïc hill. Modern public areas, a good spa and bedrooms that combine designer detail and high quality. Panoramic restaurant, as well as a conservatory-style area for large functions.

Montecarlo *without rest* ⟨icons⟩

La Rambla 124 ⊠ *08002* – ⓜ *Catalunya* – ℰ *934 12 04 04*
– www.montecarlobcn.com **F2**
50 rm – †61/160 € †‡150/332 €, ⊡ 13 €
♦ Palace ♦ Classic ♦
Housed in a 19C mansion, this hotel is a harmonious blend of period furnishings and modern comforts. Choose between classic bedrooms and those with a more modern look which have recently been renovated.

Bagués ⟨icons⟩

La Rambla 105 ⊠ *08002* – ⓜ *Liceu* – ℰ *933 43 50 00* – www.derbyhotels.com
31 rm – †150/500 € †‡200/750 €, ⊡ 21 € **F2**
Rest – Menu 25/50 € – Carte 42/54 €
♦ Business ♦ Personalised ♦
An authentic hotel-museum that has recreated an Art Nouveau-style interior featuring a variety of unique jewellery inspired decorative pieces. The bistrostyle restaurant offers a high quality, contemporary menu.

Ohla ⟨icons⟩

Vía Laietana 49 ⊠ *08003* – ⓜ *Urquinaona* – ℰ *933 41 50 50*
– www.ohlahotel.com **F1**
74 rm ⊡ – †‡215/397 €
Rest *Saüc* ⟨icon⟩ – see restaurant listing
♦ Business ♦ Design ♦
A modern hotel featuring interesting designer details and an attractive façade. All the guestrooms are contemporary in feel and half of them are fitted with glass doors giving onto open-plan showers. Bar and swimming pool on the roof terrace.

SPAIN - BARCELONA

 Neri `AC` `📶` `VISA` `◍◍` `AE` `◍`

Sant Sever 5 ✉ *08002 –* Ⓜ *Liceu –* ✆ *933 04 06 55 – www.hotelneri.com*
21 rm – ⍦⍦240/800 €, 🍽 23 € – 1 suite   **F2**
Rest – Menu 23/60 € – Carte 44/66 €
◆ Palace ◆ Design ◆
The modern interior of this hotel occupying an 18C mansion comes as something of a surprise. Library-lounge, designer-inspired guestrooms and a rooftop terrace. In the dining room, embellished with two 12C stone arches, diners can choose from a selection of contemporary Mediterranean cuisine.

 España `&` `AC` `📶` `⛲` `VISA` `◍◍` `AE` `◍`

Sant Pau 9 ✉ *08001 –* Ⓜ *Liceu –* ✆ *935 50 00 00*
– www.hotelesespanya.com   **F2**
82 rm – ⍦⍦135/315 €, 🍽 14 €
Rest *Fonda España* – see restaurant listing
◆ Holiday hotel ◆ Historic ◆
Located right in the heart of the old quarter and easy to find since it occupies a 19C building next to the Liceu. Pleasant lounge area with some historical details, plus comfortable, albeit rather small guestrooms with a contemporary design.

 Grand H. Central `🛏` `🏊` `&` `AC` `📶` `⛲` `VISA` `◍◍` `AE`

Via Laietana 30 ✉ *08003 –* Ⓜ *Jaume I –* ✆ *932 95 79 00*
– www.grandhotelcentral.com   **F2**
147 rm – ⍦⍦185/300 €, 🍽 22 € – 6 suites
Rest *Ávalon*⍟ – see restaurant listing
◆ Business ◆ Design ◆
This contemporary hotel emphasises modern design and functionality. Guestrooms feature great attention to detail. Terrace with a swimming pool and panoramic views.

 St. Moritz `🛏` `&` rm, `AC` `📶` `⛲` `🍽` `VISA` `◍◍` `AE` `◍`

Diputació 264 ✉ *08007 –* Ⓜ *Passeig de Gràcia –* ✆ *934 12 15 00*
– www.hcchotels.es   **E1**
91 rm – ⍦141/255 € ⍦⍦141/313 €, 🍽 22 €
Rest – *(Closed August and Weekend) (set menu only)* Menu 31/47 €
◆ Traditional ◆ Classic ◆
This city centre hotel occupies a listed building that dates back to 1883 and breathes classicism from every pore. Pleasant lobby area with a monumental staircase, and attractively refurbished guestrooms, all with functional, contemporary furnishings. The restaurant offers a traditional menu.

 Duquesa de Cardona `&` rm, `AC` `📶` `⛲` `VISA` `◍◍` `AE` `◍`

passeig de Colom 12 ✉ *08002 –* Ⓜ *Drassanes –* ✆ *932 68 90 90*
– www.hduquesadecardona.com   **G2**
40 rm – ⍦140/245 € ⍦⍦160/265 €, 🍽 17 €   **Rest** – Carte 29/46 €
◆ Historic ◆ Cosy ◆
This hotel occupies a charming 19C mansion that has retained many of its original features. Excellent guestrooms and an attractive terrace-solarium on the roof. A restaurant that is impressively classical in style with large arches and vaults.

 Rivoli Ramblas `🛏` `&` rm, `AC` `📶` `⛲` `VISA` `◍◍` `AE` `◍`

La Rambla 128 ✉ *08002 –* Ⓜ *Catalunya –* ✆ *934 81 76 76*
– www.rivolihotels.com   **F2**
120 rm – ⍦150/305 € ⍦⍦150/340 €, 🍽 16 € – 5 suites
Rest – Menu 14/35 € – Carte 17/41 €
◆ Business ◆ Classic ◆
This historical building has an attractive façade and a classic-contemporary décor with Art Deco features. Comfortable guestrooms and a pleasant interior terrace. In this restaurant guests can enjoy classic à la carte dishes with an international slant, alongside two set menus.

Barcelona Catedral 🛏 🖪 🗗 🕭 rm, 🗚 📶 🕍 📨 🥢 🖭 🕦

Dels Capellans 4 ✉ *08002* – **Ⓜ** *Catalunya* – 𝒞 *933 04 22 55*
– *www.barcelonacatedral.com*   F2
80 rm – ♥♥113/323 €, 🖵 18 €
Rest – *(Closed August, Saturday, Sunday and Bank Holidays)* Menu 19 €
– Carte 26/41 €

♦ **Business** ♦ **Modern** ♦

Behind the modern façade is a contemporary hotel that stands out for its high class decor and guestrooms equipped with all mod cons. Impressive terrace on the interior patio. The restaurant, located next to the bar, combines traditional à la carte choices with a good set menu. Guided tours of the Gothic quarter available.

Barcelona Universal 🖪 🗗 🕭 rm, 🗚 📶 🕍 📨 🥢 🖭 🕦

av. del Paral.lel 80 ✉ *08001* – **Ⓜ** *Paral.lel* – 𝒞 *935 67 74 47*
– *www.hotelbarcelonauniversal.com*   E3
165 rm – ♥♥110/800 €, 🖵 15 € – 2 suites
Rest – *(dinner only)* Menu 23 €

♦ **Chain hotel** ♦ **Contemporary** ♦

This modern hotel offers spacious, well-appointed guestrooms and a lounge area with bar. Panoramic swimming pool with a solarium on the top floor. A simply furnished restaurant serving a buffet of grilled meats.

Lleó without rest 🗗 🕭 🗚 📶 🕍 📨 🥢 🖭

Pelai 22 ✉ *08001* – **Ⓜ** *Universitat* – 𝒞 *933 18 13 12* – *www.hotel-lleo.com*
92 rm – ♥135/160 € ♥♥165/195 €, 🖵 14 €   E1

♦ **Holiday hotel** ♦ **Functional** ♦

A well-run hotel with an elegant façade and functional appearance. Comfortable guestrooms, spacious lounge area and a small rooftop pool.

Barceló Raval without rest 🖪 🕭 🗚 📶 🕍 🖾 📨 🥢 🖭 🕦

rambla del Raval 17-21 ✉ *08001* – **Ⓜ** *Liceu* – 𝒞 *933 20 14 90*
– *www.barceloraval.com*   E2
182 rm – ♥♥120/370 €, 🖵 18 € – 4 suites

♦ **Business** ♦ **Retro** ♦

This surprising building has an elliptical floor plan, avant-garde interior, a layout that favours wide-open spaces, and design features wherever you look!

K+K Picasso without rest 🗗 🕭 🗚 📶 🕍 🖾 📨 🥢 🖭 🕦

passeig de Picasso 26 ✉ *08003* – **Ⓜ** *Barceloneta* – 𝒞 *935 47 86 00*
– *www.kkhotels.es*   G1
92 rm 🖵 – ♥160/390 € ♥♥160/410 €

♦ **Business** ♦ **Functional** ♦

This hotel with a classical façade is located opposite the Parc de la Ciutadella. It offers a highly colourful reception area, a tapas bar and several meeting rooms. The guestrooms have a functional, contemporary feel. The rooftop solarium enjoys good views of the city.

Onix Liceo without rest 🕭 🗚 📶 🕍 🖾 📨 🥢 🖭 🕦

Nou de la Rambla 36 ✉ *08001* – **Ⓜ** *Liceu* – 𝒞 *934 81 64 41*
– *www.hotelonixliceo.com*   F3
45 rm – ♥♥90/165 €, 🖵 9 €

♦ **Business** ♦ **Contemporary** ♦

This establishment occupies a 19C renovated building, whose façade, light well and original marble staircase have been preserved. It has a modern social area and bedrooms in a functional style.

Park H. without rest 🕭 🗚 📶 🕍 📨 🥢 🖭 🕦

av. Marqués de l'Argentera 11 ✉ *08003* – **Ⓜ** *Barceloneta*
– 𝒞 *933 19 60 00* – *www.parkhotelbarcelona.com*   G2
91 rm – ♥79/114 € ♥♥93/151 €, 🖵 14 €

♦ **Business** ♦ **Functional** ♦

A hotel occupying a listed building dating back to 1953. Delightful spiral staircase, lounge, and a majority of rooms which have been upgraded, some with a balcony.

Reding
                                          ♿ rm, AC 🛜 VISA ◑◐ AE ⓪

Gravina 5-7 ✉ *08001* – Ⓜ *Universitat* – ℰ *934 12 10 97*
– www.hotelreding.com   **E1-2**
44 rm – †87/351 € ††98/378 €, ⌂ 16 €
Rest – *(Closed August, Saturday dinner, Sunday and Bank Holidays)*
Menu 16/65 € – Carte 15/35 €
♦ Business ♦ Functional ♦
A hotel with a traditional façade located close to Plaça de Catalunya. Modern reception, a lounge area and attractively renovated guestrooms with functional furnishings. The simply designed dining room offers a menu featuring traditional and Catalan dishes.

Banys Orientals
                              ♿ AC 🛜 VISA ◑◐ AE ⓪

L'Argenteria 37 ✉ *08003* – Ⓜ *Jaume I* – ℰ *932 68 84 60*
– www.hotelbanysorientals.com   **G2**
43 rm – †88 € ††105 €, ⌂ 10 €
Rest Senyor Parellada 😊 – see restaurant listing
♦ Business ♦ Design ♦
This hotel has comfortable, minimalist-style rooms. They feature plenty of design features, wooden floors and canopies above the beds. No lounge.

Denit *without rest*
                                ♿ AC 🛜 VISA ◑◐ AE ⓪

Estruc 24 ✉ *08002* – Ⓜ *Urquinaona* – ℰ *935 45 40 00*
– www.denit.com   **F1**
36 rm ⌂ – †89/189 € ††99/229 €
♦ Business ♦ Functional ♦
Although fronting one of the city's less-known streets, the Denit enjoys a central location next to Plaça de Catalunya. The rooms, spread across five floors, are all modern, neat and functional.

Torre d'Alta Mar
                                    ⬅ AC VISA ◑◐ AE ⓪

passeig Joan de Borbó 88 ✉ *08039* – Ⓜ *Barceloneta* – ℰ *932 21 00 07*
– www.torredealtamar.com
– Closed 23-27 December, Sunday and Monday lunch   **H3**
Rest – Menu 48 € – Carte 50/85 €
♦ Modern ♦ Formal ♦
A striking location at the top of a 75m metal tower. Modern circular dining room with large glass windows and spectacular views.

Bravo 24 – Hotel W Barcelona
                                ⛱ ♿ AC VISA ◑◐ AE ⓪

pl. de la Rosa dels Vents 1 (Moll De Llevant) ✉ *08039* – ℰ *932 95 26 36*
– www.carlesabellan.com   *Plan I* **C3**
Rest – Menu 85 € – Carte 44/75 € 🍴
♦ Modern ♦ Design ♦
Bravo 24, located on the mezzanine of the W hotel in Barcelona, has a thoroughly modern look featuring lots of wood, as well as an attractive summer terrace. Traditionally based cuisine enhanced with contemporary touches. The larger dishes of tapas (raciones) are particularly plentiful!

Saüc *(Xavier Franco)* – Hotel Ohla
                                    AC VISA ◑◐ AE ⓪

Vía Laietana 49 ✉ *08003* – Ⓜ *Urquinaona* – ℰ *933 21 01 89*
– www.saucrestaurant.com
– Closed Sunday and Monday   **F1**
Rest – Menu 37/118 € – Carte 60/85 €
♦ Modern ♦ Fashionable ♦
A restaurant with a good reputation in the city. Ther is a modern gastro-bar and a contemporary, almost minimalist dining room upstairs. The chef offers innovative cuisine, in addition to several tasting menus, which combine traditional and up-to-date dishes.
➜ Gambas a la sal con alcachofas, papada ibérica y jugo del asado. Pichón de Bresse en "capraudine" con wok de endivias trufado. Pastel de queso de oveja con peras de Puigcerdà asadas.

SPAIN - BARCELONA

Comerç 24 (Carles Abellán)

A/C VISA ◑ AE ⓪

Comerç 24 ✉ 08003 – Ⓜ Arc de Triomf – ℰ 933 19 21 02
– www.carlesabellan.com
– Closed Christmas, Sunday and Monday   G1
Rest – Menu 84/106 € – Carte 56/83 € ▒

♦ Creative ♦ Design ♦

This restaurant has a contemporary decor, including a kitchen visible to diners.
It offers two tasting menus and a creative à la carte menu of delicious tapas,
tostas and raciones. All of which are well prepared using the very best ingredients.
→ Semillas de berenjena. Raya de Barcelona amazónica. "Mel i mató" con
trufa.

Senyor Parellada – Hotel Banys Orientals

A/C VISA ◑ AE ⓪

L'Argenteria 37 ✉ 08003 – Ⓜ Jaume I – ℰ 933 10 50 94
– www.senyorparellada.com   G2
Rest – Carte 20/35 €

♦ Regional ♦ Cosy ♦

This attractive restaurant has a classic-colonial style and various dining rooms in
which time seems to have stood still. The small patio with a glass roof is a particularly impressive feature. Moderately priced, traditional Catalan cuisine.

Elx

≤ 🏠 A/C VISA ◑ AE ⓪

Moll d'Espanya 5-Maremagnum, Local 9 ✉ 08039 – Ⓜ Drassanes
– ℰ 932 25 81 17 – www.elxrestaurant.com   G3
Rest – Carte 30/44 €

♦ Traditional ♦ Formal ♦

A restaurant graced with views of the fishing port. Modern dining room and an
attractive terrace, where the focus is on fish and a good selection of savoury rice
dishes.

Koy Shunka (Hideki Matsuhisa)

A/C VISA ◑ AE

Copons 7 ✉ 08002 – Ⓜ Urquinaona – ℰ 934 12 79 39
– www.koyshunka.com
– Closed 7 days Christmas, Holy Week, 21 days August, Sunday dinner and
Monday   F1
Rest – Menu 72/108 € – Carte 48/109 €

♦ Japanese ♦ Minimalist ♦

The perfect place to watch delicious nigiri and other types of sushi being prepared in front of you, as one of the dining rooms has an open-view kitchen in the
middle of it. Japanese gastronomy created with ingredients from the Mediterranean.
→ Fideos japoneses somen con "espardenyes". Atún toro con erizo de mar
y trufa. Canelones de ternera wagyu rellenos de calçots.

Ávalon – Hotel Grand H. Central

A/C ✪ VISA ◑ AE

Pare Galifa 3 ✉ 08003 – Ⓜ Jaume I – ℰ 932 95 79 05
– www.avalonrestaurant.es   F2
Rest – (dinner only in August) Menu 19 € – Carte approx. 35 €

♦ Modern ♦ Fashionable ♦

This restaurant has its own distinctive personality, where young and friendly
staff serve a creative set price menu. Modern facilities with many design elements.

Fonda España – Hotel España

A/C VISA ◑ AE ⓪

Sant Pau 9 ✉ 08001 – Ⓜ Liceu – ℰ 935 50 00 00
– www.hotelespanya.com   F2
Rest – (Closed 21 days August and Sunday dinner) Menu 25 €
– Carte 29/59 €

♦ Traditional ♦ Retro ♦

The main selling points of this restaurant are its location in a listed building and
the fact that the Modernist dining room, decorated with stunning mosaics, was
designed by Domènech i Montaner. Its updated take on traditional cuisine is
overseen by renowned chef Martín Berasategui.

Pitarra

⌧ ⇧ VISA ⦿⦿ AE ⓞ

Avinyó 56 ⊠ *08002 –* Ⓜ *Liceu – ℰ 933 01 16 47*
– www.restaurantpitarra.cat
– Closed 2-18 August, Sunday and Bank Holidays dinner G2
Rest – Menu 20/100 € – Carte 21/47 €

♦ Traditional ♦ Cosy ♦

It was in these premises that Frederic Soler, a leading figure from the world of Catalan theatre, once had his watchmaker's shop. Dining rooms with an old-fashioned feel, including two rooms for private parties. Traditional cuisine.

Can Majó

⌂ ⌧ VISA ⦿⦿ AE ⓞ

Almirall Aixada 23 ⊠ *08003 –* Ⓜ *Barceloneta – ℰ 932 21 54 55*
– www.canmajo.es
– Closed Sunday dinner and Monday H3
Rest – Carte 28/50 €

♦ Fish and seafood ♦ Mediterranean ♦

Renowned, family-run restaurant serving an excellent menu focusing on seafood and rice dishes, hence the impressive seafood counter. Terrace.

Dos Palillos (Albert Raurich)

⌧ VISA ⦿⦿ ⓞ

❀

Elisabets 9 ⊠ *08001 –* Ⓜ *Catalunya – ℰ 933 04 05 13*
– www.dospalillos.com
– Closed 24 December-2 January, 6-27 August, Tuesday lunch, Wednesday lunch, Sunday and Monday E2
Rest – Menu 55/70 €

♦ Creative ♦ Fashionable ♦

At this restaurant the cooks work in front of your very eyes! The result will surprise guests, both in terms of the culinary philosophy and the cuisine itself, which is based on a fusion of Oriental cooking and Spanish ingredients. À la carte tapas choices and two tasting menus.

→ Gamba fría y caliente. Salmonete con ensalada de escabeches. Makis de atún rojo.

Irati

⌧ VISA ⦿⦿ AE ⓞ

Cardenal Casanyes 17 ⊠ *08002 –* Ⓜ *Liceu – ℰ 902 52 05 22*
– www.iratitavernabasca.com F2
Tapa 3 € **Ración** approx. 15 €

♦ Basque ♦ Tapas bar ♦

A typical Basque tavern close to the Gran Teatre del Liceu. Traditional carvery-style dining room where the menu focuses on innovative Basque cuisine. Good selection of tapas at the bar.

El Xampanyet

VISA ⦿⦿

Montcada 22 ⊠ *08003 –* Ⓜ *Jaume I – ℰ 933 19 70 03*
– Closed January, August, Saturday dinner, Sunday and Monday lunch Holy Week-July, Sunday dinner and Monday for rest of the year G2
Tapa 5 €

♦ Traditional ♦ Tapas bar ♦

This old tavern with a long-standing family tradition is decorated with typical azulejo tiles. Varied selection of tapas with an emphasis on cured meats and high-quality canned products.

Rosal 34

⌧ VISA ⦿⦿ ⓞ

Roser 34 ⊠ *08004 –* Ⓜ *Paral.lel – ℰ 933 24 90 46 – www.rosal34.com*
– Closed Sunday dinner and Monday E3
Tapa 5 € **Ración** approx. 12 €

♦ Creative ♦ Rustic ♦

Rosal 34 is located in an old family wine cellar, where the rustic stonework blends in with the contemporary decor. Seasonal dishes plus interesting tapas with a creative touch.

SPAIN - BARCELONA

Segons Mercat 🛋 𝔸ℂ 𝒱𝐼𝒮𝒜 ⊙⊙

Balboa 16 ✉ *08003 –* Ⓜ *Barceloneta –* ✆ *933 10 78 80*
– www.segonsmercat.com **H2**
Tapa 5.50 € **Ración** approx. 14 €
♦ Traditional ♦ Tapas bar ♦
This restaurant has a bar with an impressive display of fresh produce, in particular fish and seafood. A separate room is available for tapas, snacks and daily specials.

Orio 𝔸ℂ 𝒱𝐼𝒮𝒜 ⊙⊙ 𝔸𝔼 ⓪

Ferran 38 ✉ *08002 –* Ⓜ *Jaume I –* ✆ *933 179 407*
– www.oriogastronomiavasca.com **F2**
Tapa 2 € **Ración** approx. 12 €
♦ Basque ♦ Tapas bar ♦
Well-located in a pedestrian street, the Orio has an appealing bar laden with tapas, an oyster section and a dining room with high tables in the basement.

SOUTH of AV. DIAGONAL — *Plan III*

El Palace ƒ₆ ⊕ ⅙ 𝔸ℂ ℭℓ 𝔰𝔸 ⌂ 𝒱𝐼𝒮𝒜 ⊙⊙ 𝔸𝔼 ⓪

Gran Via de les Corts Catalanes 668 ✉ *08010 –* Ⓜ *Urquinaona*
– ✆ *935 10 11 30 – www.hotelpalacebarcelona.com* **L2**
119 rm – †‡215/560 €, ⌷ 28 € – 6 suites
Rest *Caelis* ✿ – see restaurant listing
♦ Grand Luxury ♦ Classic ♦
This emblematic hotel, occupying an old building that has recently been restored, is steeped in tradition. Refined public areas, and hugely comfortable guestrooms embellished with elegant wallpaper.

Mandarin Oriental Barcelona ƒ₆ ⊡ ⅙ rm, 𝔸ℂ 🛜 𝔰𝔸

passeig de Gràcia 38-40 ✉ *08007* 𝒱𝐼𝒮𝒜 ⊙⊙ 𝔸𝔼
– Ⓜ *Passeig de Gràcia –* ✆ *931 51 88 88*
– www.mandarinoriental.com/barcelona **K2**
98 rm – †‡355/505 €, ⌷ 39 € – 10 suites
Rest *Moments* ✿✿ – see restaurant listing
Rest – Menu 29/42 € – Carte 39/77 €
♦ Luxury ♦ Design ♦
This top class hotel occupies a former bank building that has undergone a complete transformation. It has a designer interior, fully equipped spa, and guestrooms offering high levels of comfort. In the restaurant, dine on fusion cuisine, including dishes from Asia and the Mediterranean

Majestic ƒ₆ ⊕ ⅃ ⅙ rm, 𝔸ℂ 🛜 𝔰𝔸 ⌂ 𝒱𝐼𝒮𝒜 ⊙⊙ 𝔸𝔼 ⓪

passeig de Gràcia 68 ✉ *08007 –* Ⓜ *Passeig de Gràcia –* ✆ *934 88 17 17*
– www.hotelmajestic.es **K2**
271 rm – †‡199/499 €, ⌷ 25 € – 32 suites
Rest – Menu 18/55 € – Carte 31/45 €
♦ Traditional ♦ Classic ♦
A renovated classic hotel on the Paseo de Gràcia. Superbly appointed guestrooms, although some are not particularly spacious. Impeccable service. Functional dining room offering both a set menu and buffet service.

Fira Palace ƒ₆ ⊡ ⅙ rm, 𝔸ℂ 🛜 𝔰𝔸 ⌂ 𝒱𝐼𝒮𝒜 ⊙⊙ 𝔸𝔼 ⓪

av. Rius i Taulet 1 ✉ *08004 –* Ⓜ *Espanya –* ✆ *934 26 22 23*
– www.fira-palace.com **J-K3**
258 rm – †182/405 € †‡199/430 €, ⌷ 13 € – 18 suites
Rest *El Mall* – Menu 28 € – Carte 33/60 €
♦ Conference hotel ♦ Classic ♦
Located right next to the city's exhibition centre, this contemporary-classic hotel stands out for its superbly maintained facilities and the quality of the materials used. Numerous meeting rooms and reasonably spacious guestrooms. The restaurant, decorated in rustic-style, offers an international menu.

SPAIN - BARCELONA

Alma Barcelona

Mallorca 271 ✉ *08008* – Ⓜ *Passeig de Gràcia* – ✆ *932 16 44 90*
– www.almahotels.com   K2
72 rm – ♦♦205/295 €, ☐ 25 € – 2 suites   **Rest** – Carte 33/60 €
♦ Business ♦ Design ♦
A highly contemporary hotel in which the pure lines of the design manage to
combine style and maximum comfort. This is the case both in the multi-purpose
lobby and the hotel's guestrooms. In the restaurant, enjoy traditionally based
cuisine with a contemporary touch.

Condes de Barcelona – (Monument i Center)

passeig de Gràcia 73-75 ✉ *08008*
– Ⓜ *Passeig de Gràcia* – ✆ *934 45 00 00 – www.condesdebarcelona.com*
232 rm – ♦♦135/315 €, ☐ 21 € – 3 suites   K2
Rest *Lasarte* ✿✿ **Rest** *Loidi* – see restaurant listing
♦ Historic ♦ Classic ♦
An emblematic hotel occupying two historic buildings, the Casa Batlló and Casa
Daurella. At night, the attractive rooftop sun terrace is transformed into a trendy
bar.

Claris

Pau Claris 150 ✉ *08009* – Ⓜ *Passeig de Gràcia* – ✆ *934 87 62 62*
– www.derbyhotels.com   K2
124 rm – ♦159/445 € ♦♦159/500 €, ☐ 23 € – 40 suites
Rest – Menu 25 € – Carte 51/79 €
♦ Traditional ♦ Modern ♦
This elegant, stately hotel occupies the former Vedruna palace. It offers a perfect
fusion of tradition, cutting-edge design and technology. Impressive archaeological collection. The attractively presented restaurant is decorated in a style that
recalls the work of Andy Warhol.

Barcelona Center

Balmes 103 ✉ *08008* – Ⓜ *Diagonal* – ✆ *932 73 00 00*
– www.hotelescenter.com   K2
129 rm – ♦♦80/925 €, ☐ 17 € – 3 suites
Rest – Menu 17 € – Carte 25/37 €
♦ Chain hotel ♦ Classic ♦
Sheltered behind a striking, well-maintained façade, this hotel boasts superbly
equipped modern guestrooms, impressive public areas and a huge solarium on
the roof terrace.

Omm

Rosselló 265 ✉ *08008* – Ⓜ *Diagonal* – ✆ *934 45 40 00*
– www.hotelomm.es   K1
87 rm – ♦♦215/450 €, ☐ 25 € – 4 suites
Rest *Moo* ✿ – see restaurant listing
♦ Business ♦ Design ♦
Hidden behind the original façade is a highly contemporary hotel with spacious
public areas divided into three sections. Extremely well-appointed guestrooms,
and an attractive spa.

Cram

Aribau 54 ✉ *08011* – Ⓜ *Universitat* – ✆ *932 16 77 00*
– www.hotelcram.com   K2
67 rm – ♦♦99/224 €, ☐ 21 €
Rest *Gaig* ✿ – see restaurant listing
♦ Business ♦ Design ♦
Although the guestrooms are on the small side, this is counter balanced by cutting-edge technology and the superb contemporary interior – the work of
several famous designers.

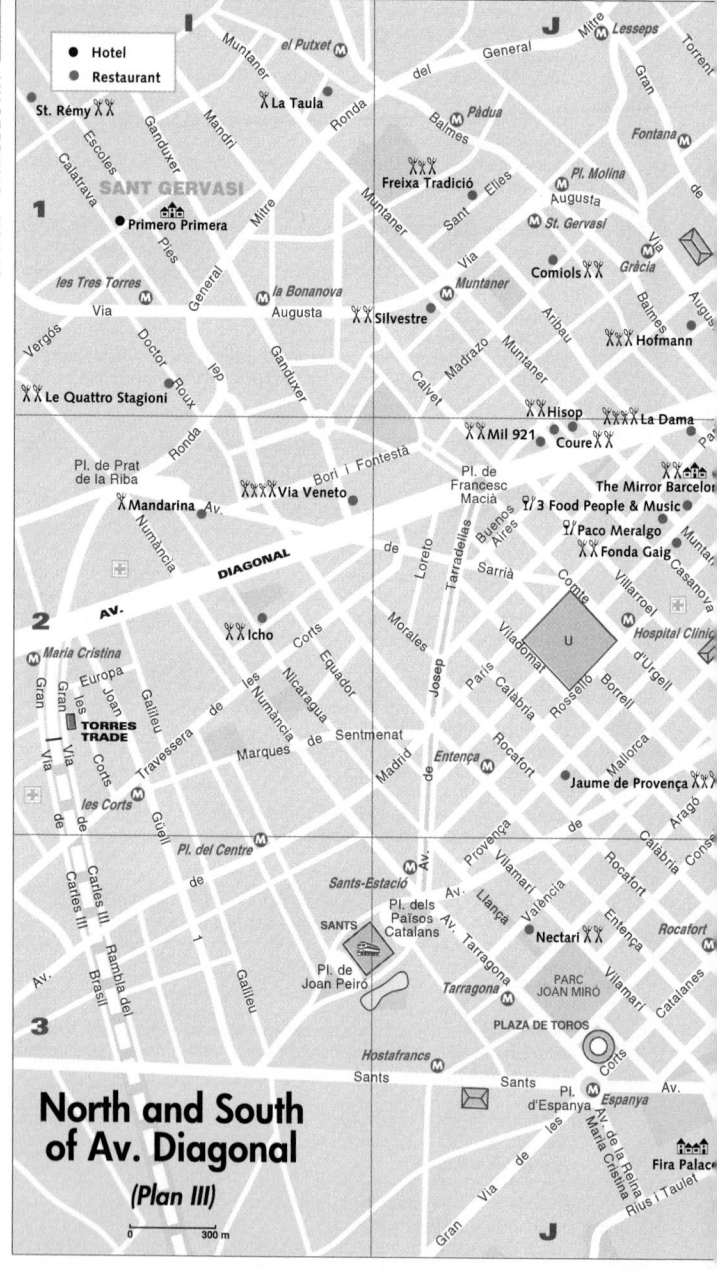

Hotel
Restaurant

St. Rémy
La Taula
SANT GERVASI
Primero Primera
les Tres Torres
la Bonanova
Silvestre
Le Quattro Stagioni
Mandarina
Via Veneto
Pl. de Prat de la Riba
DIAGONAL
AV.
Maria Cristina
Europa
TORRES TRADE
Icho
les Corts
Pl. del Centre
Sants-Estació
SANTS
Pl. dels Països Catalans
Pl. de Joan Peiró
Hostafrancs
Sants

el Putxet
Lesseps
General
Pàdua
Freixa Tradició
Pl. Molina
Augusta
St. Gervasi
Comiols
Gràcia
Fontana
Hofmann
Muntaner
Hisop
La Dama
Mil 921
Coure
Pl. de Francesc Macià
The Mirror Barcelon
3 Food People & Music
Paco Meralgo
Fonda Gaig
Hospital Clinic
Jaume de Provença
Nectari
PARC JOAN MIRÓ
PLAZA DE TOROS
Pl. d'Espanya
Espanya
Fira Palace

North and South
of Av. Diagonal
(Plan III)

0   300 m

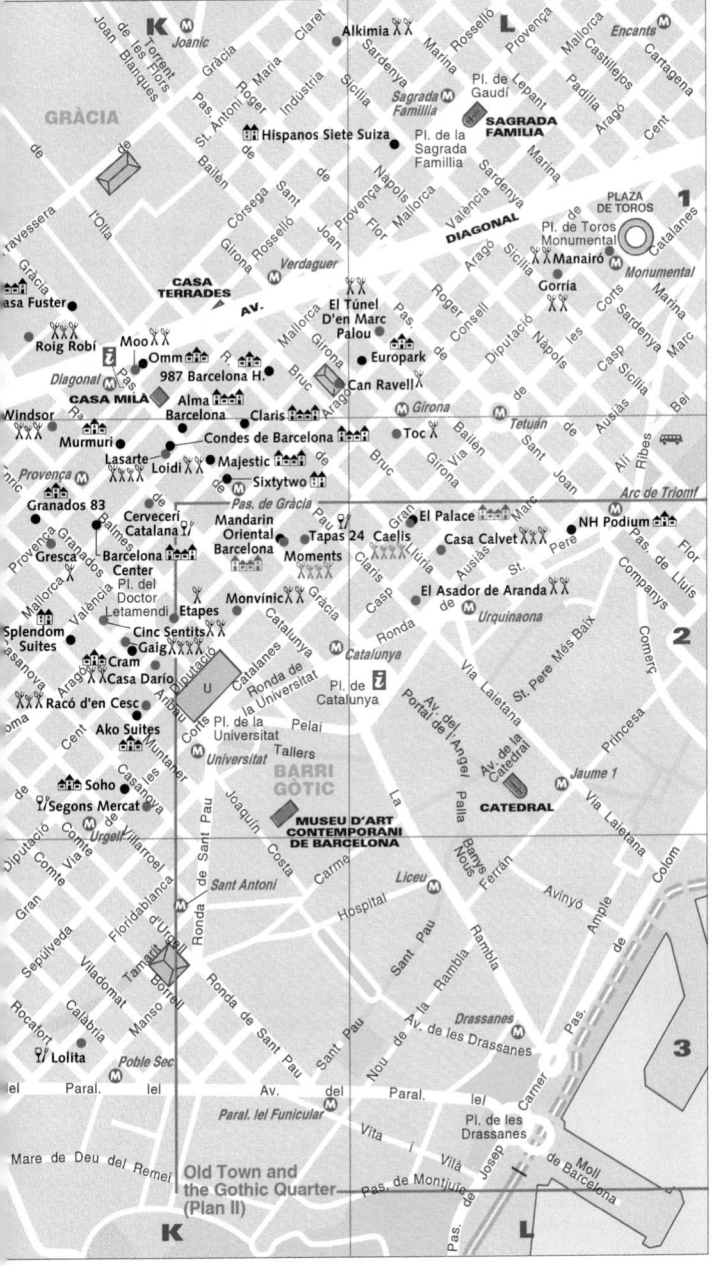

GRÀCIA

Joanic

Alkimia

Pl. de Lepant

Sagrada Família

Hispanos Siete Suiza

Pl. de la Sagrada Família

SAGRADA FAMILIA

PLAZA DE TOROS

DIAGONAL

Pl. de Toros Monumental

Manairó

Gorria

CASA TERRADES

Casa Fuster

AV.

El Túnel D'en Marc Palou

Europark

Roig Robí

Moo

Can Ravell

Omm

987 Barcelona H.

CASA MILA

Alma Barcelona

Claris

Girona

Windsor

Condes de Barcelona

Toc

Tetuán

Murmuri

Lasarte

Majestic

Arc de Triomf

Loidi

Sixtytwo

Pas. de Gràcia

Granados 83

Cerveceri Catalana

Mandarin Oriental Barcelona

El Palace

NH Podium

Gresca

Barcelona Center

Tapas 24

Caelis

Casa Calvet

Moments

Pl. del Doctor Letamendi

Monvínic

El Asador de Aranda

Splendom Suites

Etapes

Cinc Sentits

Urquinaona

Gaig

Catalunya

Cram

Casa Darío

Pl. de Catalunya

Ako Suites

Racó d'en Cesc

U

Pl. de la Universitat

Soho

Pelai

Universitat

Segons Mercat

Tallers

BARRI GÒTIC

MUSEU D'ART CONTEMPORANI DE BARCELONA

CATEDRAL

Sant Antoni

Liceu

Lolita

Hospital

Poble Sec

La Rambla

Ferrán

Avinyó

Colom

Paral.

Av. de les Drassanes

Drassanes

Pl. de les Drassanes

Moll de Barcelona

Mare de Deu del Remei

Old Town and the Gothic Quarter (Plan II)

Granados 83 🛗 ⚹ rm, 🅰 🤶 🏊 🍴 VISA ◍ AE ①

Enric Granados 83 ⊠ *08008 –* Ⓜ *Provença –* ☏ *934 92 96 70*
– www.derbyhotels.com   K2
77 rm – ✦110/260 € ✦✦130/300 €, ⊑ 18 €
Rest – *(Closed August and Sunday)* Menu 21/55 € – Carte 37/44 €
♦ Business ♦ Design ♦
This cutting-edge hotel is characterised by a predominance of glass, steel and
brick. The superbly appointed bedrooms are decorated with Asian antiques.
This restaurant has a terrace and a simple fusion-style menu.

Murmuri ⚹ 🅰 🤶 VISA ◍ AE ①

Rambla de Catalunya 104 ⊠ *08008 –* Ⓜ *Diagonal –* ☏ *935 50 06 00*
– www.murmuri.com   K2
53 rm – ✦149/449 € ✦✦179/509 €, ⊑ 16 € – 5 suites
Rest – Menu 19/56 € – Carte 30/45 €
♦ Business ♦ Modern ♦
Building with a classical façade in the middle of Las Ramblas. The lobby is in a
contemporary style, just like its simply decorated bedrooms. It features an
attractive solarium-terrace. Taste carefully prepared Asian fusion cuisine in this
restaurant.

Ako Suites *without rest* ⚹ 🅰 🤶 🏊 VISA ◍ AE ①

Diputació 195 ⊠ *08011 –* Ⓜ *Hospital Clínic –* ☏ *934 53 34 19*
– www.akosuite.com   K2
28 suites – ✦✦150/450 €, ⊑ 12 €
♦ Family ♦ Modern ♦
Located in the city's L'Eixample district, this hotel is a good option for families
and couples. High quality apartments, all modern in style and with fully equipped kitchens. Half of the bathrooms are equipped with relaxing rain-type showers.

987 Barcelona H. *without rest* ⚹ 🅰 🤶 🏊 VISA ◍ AE ①

Mallorca 288 ⊠ *08037 –* Ⓜ *Diagonal –* ☏ *934 76 33 96*
– www.987barcelonahotel.com   K1
88 rm – ✦99/346 € ✦✦99/368 €, ⊑ 16 €
♦ Business ♦ Design ♦
Designer decor is to the fore here, with coloured lights in the public areas, a
pleasant internal patio and modern and functional guestrooms.

Europark *without rest* 🅸 🏊 ⚹ 🅰 🤶 🏊 VISA ◍ AE ①

Aragó 325 ⊠ *08009 –* Ⓜ *Girona –* ☏ *934 57 92 05*
– www.hoteleuropark.com   L1
103 rm – ✦✦90/210 €, ⊑ 12 € – 2 suites
♦ Business ♦ Contemporary ♦
This contemporary hotel is in the very heart of town. Its small, social area is offset by well-equipped bedrooms. On the top floor are two suites with terraces
and good views.

NH Podium 🅸 🏊 ⚹ rm, 🅰 rm, 🤶 🏊 🍴 VISA ◍ AE ①

Bailén 4 ⊠ *08010 –* Ⓜ *Arc de Triomf –* ☏ *932 65 02 02*
– www.nh-hotels.com   L2
140 rm – ✦90/290 € ✦✦100/340 €, ⊑ 19 € – 5 suites
Rest – *(lunch only) (set menu only)* Menu 26/60 €
♦ Business ♦ Functional ♦
Located in the Modernist Ensanche district, the Podium has a classical façade
with a contemporary interior and cosy guestrooms. Swimming pool and a fitness room with sauna on the top floor. A restaurant with a contemporary layout
featuring quality furnishings, with an à la carte menu of international dishes.

The Mirror Barcelona   ⮝ ⟐ ⎙ 🛜 𝚅𝙸𝚂𝙰 ⚭ 𝔸𝔼 ⓘ

Còrsega 255 ✉ *08036 –* Ⓜ *Provença –* ℰ *932 02 86 86*
– www.themirrorbarcelona.com   J2
63 rm – ♥♥99/224 €, ⚏ 23 €
Rest *The Mirror Barcelona* – see restaurant listing
♦ Business ♦ Design ♦
The most striking aspect of this hotel is its design, which will appeal to guests
keen on this type of minimalist decor. Everything is dominated by mirrors, the
colour white and the use of simple, clean lines.

Soho without rest   ⟐ ⎙ 🛜 ⌂ 𝚅𝙸𝚂𝙰 ⚭ 𝔸𝔼 ⓘ

Gran Via de les Corts Catalanes 543-545 ✉ *08011 –* Ⓜ *Urgell*
– ℰ *935 52 96 10 – www.hotelsohobarcelona.com*   K2
51 rm – ♥♥108/335 €, ⚏ 14 €
♦ Business ♦ Design ♦
The Soho Hotel combines an avant-garde look with design details, decorative
lighting effects and an interesting use of space. A happy marriage of comfort
and technology.

Sixtytwo without rest   ⟐ ⎙ 🛜 𝚅𝙸𝚂𝙰 ⚭ 𝔸𝔼 ⓘ

Passeig de Gràcia 62 ✉ *08007 –* Ⓜ *Passeig de Gràcia –* ℰ *932 72 41 80*
– www.sixtytwohotel.com   K2
45 rm – ♥♥125/330 €, ⚏ 18.50 €
♦ Holiday hotel ♦ Modern ♦
This small hotel, with its attractive façade and modern interior, is situated along
the Paseo de Gràcia. Well-equipped guestrooms, albeit a little on the small side.

Splendom Suites without rest   ⟐ 🛜 𝚅𝙸𝚂𝙰 ⚭ 𝔸𝔼

Valencia 194 ✉ *08011 –* Ⓜ *Universitat –* ℰ *934 52 10 30*
– www.splendomsuites.com   K2
11 suites – ♥♥110/400 €
♦ Business ♦ Contemporary ♦
Occupying a listed building with a classic Modernist façade in the heart of the
Eixample district. Its apartments are spread across six floors, the majority of
which have well-equipped kitchens, sitting rooms with sofa beds and comfortable bedrooms.

Caelis (Romain Fornell) – Hotel El Palace   ⟐ ⟷ 𝚅𝙸𝚂𝙰 ⚭ 𝔸𝔼 ⓘ

Gran Via de les Corts Catalanes 668 ✉ *08010 –* Ⓜ *Urquinaona*
– ℰ *935 10 11 30 – www.caelis.com*
– Closed Holy Week, 15 days August, Sunday, Monday and Tuesday lunch
Rest – Menu 85/120 € – Carte 70/102 € ❀   L2
♦ Creative ♦ Elegant ♦
This restaurant is a pleasant surprise both in terms of its elegant 19C ambience
and spacious surroundings. Separate access to the hotel, a classically contem-
porary dining room, and a private section. Enjoy top-notch, meticulously pre-
sented creative cuisine.
➙ El caviar, vichyssoise en plato de hielo, apio y buey de mar, salmón
marinado. Los macarrones rellenos como un "mar y montaña", bogavante
y foie gras. Sorbete de tequila, yuzu y petazeta.

La Dama   ⟐ ⟷ 𝚅𝙸𝚂𝙰 ⚭ 𝔸𝔼 ⓘ

av. Diagonal 423 ✉ *08036 –* Ⓜ *Diagonal –* ℰ *932 02 06 86*
– www.restaurantladama.com   J2
Rest – Menu 69/99 € – Carte 40/91 € ❀
♦ International ♦ Classic ♦
La Dama has a classically elegant atmosphere with splendid Modernist detail
both on the façade and within its walls. Excellent service.

SPAIN - BARCELONA

SPAIN - BARCELONA

XXXX ✿✿ **Moments** – Hotel Mandarin Oriental Barcelona   🅰🅲 🆅🅸🆂🅰 ⓒⓞ 🅰🅴
passeig de Gràcia 38-40 ✉ *08007 –* Ⓜ *Passeig de Gràcia*
– ℰ 931 51 87 81 – www.mandarinoriental.com
– Closed August, Sunday and Monday   **K2**
Rest – Menu 43/125 € – Carte 88/112 € 🎇
♦ Creative ♦ Design ♦
Access to this restaurant, which stands out for its originality and open-view kit-
chen, is via the hotel reception. The chef prepares skilful and creative cuisine
that respects flavours, embraces textures and pays great attention to delicate
presentation.
➔ Arroz caldoso de gambas. Albóndiga "coulant". Pijama.

XXXX ✿ **Gaig** (Carles Gaig) – Hotel Cram   🅰🅲 ⇔ 🆅🅸🆂🅰 ⓒⓞ 🅰🅴 ⓞ
Aragó 214 ✉ *08011 –* Ⓜ *Universitat – ℰ 934 29 10 17*
– www.restaurantgaig.com
*– Closed Holy Week, 3 weeks August, Saturday lunch, Sunday, Monday lunch
and Bank Holidays*   **K2**
Rest – Menu 94/119 € – Carte 65/96 € 🎇
♦ Modern ♦ Design ♦
A restaurant with a contemporary look and superb decor. Guests can savour
cuisine of the highest level combining the cutting-edge and the traditional,
and encompassing fine presentation and carefully selected ingredients.
➔ Escabeche fino de marisco y verduras. Pichón en dos servicios. Homenaje a Gaudí.

XXXX ✿✿ **Lasarte** – Hotel Condes de Barcelona   🅰🅲 🆅🅸🆂🅰 ⓒⓞ 🅰🅴 ⓞ
Mallorca 259 ✉ *08008 –* Ⓜ *Passeig de Gràcia – ℰ 934 45 32 42*
– www.restaurantlasarte.com
– Closed Holy Week, August, Sunday, Monday and Bank Holidays
Rest – Menu 75/120 € – Carte 77/111 € 🎇   **K2**
♦ Creative ♦ Trendy ♦
Lasarte bears the personal stamp of Martín Berasategui and his team. It features
an attractive entrance hall and two delightfully laid-out dining rooms, both
designed in a reasonably contemporary style. The menu is highly creative, featuring inventive dishes and traditional Basque specialities.
➔ Ostra ahumada a la parrilla, espinacas guisadas al sésamo y tubérculos
crujientes. Pichón asado sobre estofado de trigo, toques de patata trufada
y salsa especiada. Pastel de cacao y su polvo helado, trufa de frambuesa y
helado de cerveza negra.

XXX **Casa Calvet**   🅰🅲 ⇔ 🆅🅸🆂🅰 ⓒⓞ 🅰🅴 ⓞ
Casp 48 ✉ *08010 –* Ⓜ *Urquinaona – ℰ 934 12 40 12 – www.casacalvet.es*
– Closed Sunday and Bank Holidays   **L2**
Rest – Menu 40/70 € – Carte 49/61 €
♦ Mediterranean ♦ Classic ♦
Housed in an attractive Modernist building designed by Gaudí. Well-presented
traditional cuisine with a contemporary flavour, centred around the very best
ingredients.

XXX **Windsor**   🅰🅲 ⇔ 🆅🅸🆂🅰 ⓒⓞ 🅰🅴 ⓞ
Còrsega 286 ✉ *08008 –* Ⓜ *Diagonal – ℰ 932 37 75 88*
– www.restaurantwindsor.com
*– Closed 1-7 January, Holy Week, August, Saturday lunch, Sunday and Bank
Holidays*   **K2**
Rest – Menu 29/60 € – Carte 41/60 € 🎇
♦ Modern ♦ Classic ♦
Elegant, classical style restaurant with several private rooms and a main dining
room that overlooks a garden. Good selection of contemporary Catalan dishes,
as well as an excellent wine list.

XXX **Jaume de Provença** $\boxed{AC}$ ⇔ $\boxed{VISA}$ ⓸ $\boxed{AE}$ ⓞ

Provença 88 ✉ 08029 – Ⓜ Entença – ☏ 934 30 00 29
– www.jaumeprovenza.com
– Closed August, Sunday dinner and Monday   **J2**
Rest – Menu 22/50 € – Carte 35/60 €
♦ International ♦ Classic ♦
Run by its owner, this classical style restaurant has a bar, various wine cellars and a pleasant dining room with wood panelled walls.

XXX **Racó d'en Cesc** $\boxed{AC}$ ⇔ $\boxed{VISA}$ ⓸ $\boxed{AE}$ ⓞ

Diputació 201 ✉ 08011 – Ⓜ Universitat – ☏ 934 51 60 02
– www.elracodencesc.com
– Closed Holy Week, August, Sunday and Bank Holidays   **K2**
Rest – Menu 35/62 € – Carte 30/40 € 🍃
♦ Modern ♦ Classic ♦
This restaurant has an entrance hall, a resolutely traditional main dining room and various private rooms. Creative menu based on daily recommendations, accompanied by a comprehensive choice of wines.

XX **The Mirror Barcelona** – Hotel The Mirror Barcelona $\boxed{AC}$

Còrsega 255 ✉ 08036 – ☏ 932 02 86 86 $\boxed{VISA}$ ⓸ $\boxed{AE}$ ⓞ
Rest – (Closed August, Sunday and Monday) Menu   **J2**
45/115 € – Carte 39/85 €
♦ Modern ♦ Fashionable ♦
In keeping with the hotel that it occupies, the decor of this restaurant is resolutely modern and defined by white tones and the presence of numerous mirrors. Cuisine with a maritime flavour, updated with contemporary techniques.

XX **Fonda Gaig** $\boxed{AC}$ ⇔ $\boxed{VISA}$ ⓸ $\boxed{AE}$ ⓞ

Còrsega 200 ✉ 08036 – Ⓜ Hospital Clinic – ☏ 934 53 20 20
– www.fondagaig.com
– Closed Bank Holiday dinner   **J2**
Rest – Menu 25 € – Carte 32/76 €
♦ Regional ♦ Fashionable ♦
The name refers to the former family-run inn, now closed. It features a glass façade, lots of natural light in the two-floor dining room, and three private dining rooms. Catalan cuisine.

XX **Cinc Sentits** (Jordi Artal) $\boxed{AC}$ $\boxed{VISA}$ ⓸
❀

Aribau 58 ✉ 08011 – Ⓜ Universitat – ☏ 933 23 94 90
– www.cincsentits.com
– Closed 15 days August, Sunday, Monday and Bank Holidays   **K2**
Rest – (set menu only) Menu 59/109 €
♦ Creative ♦ Minimalist ♦
The Cinc Sentits combines a meticulous layout and a highly original look that is dominated by darker tones. Its cuisine is centred on three menus: Sensaciones, Esencia and Degustación. Inventive culinary creations based around carefully selected Catalan products.
→ Sardinas marinadas, leche de almendras, cerezas y sorbete de piñón de cereza. Zarzuela de pescado de lonja, esferificación de almeja, gamba y calamar encebollado. Cremoso de chocolate ecológico, violetas, cítricos y fresas del Maresme.

XX **El Asador de Aranda** $\boxed{AC}$ ⇔ $\boxed{VISA}$ ⓸ $\boxed{AE}$ ⓞ

Londres 94 ✉ 08036 – Ⓜ Hospital Clínic – ☏ 934 14 67 90
– www.asadordearanda.com
– Closed Sunday dinner   **L2**
Rest – Menu 34/51 € – Carte 28/42 €
♦ Meats and grills ♦ Rustic ♦
This spacious restaurant is decorated in Castilian style with a wood oven in full view of the dining room. Traditional cuisine with a particular focus on roast dishes.

XX **El Túnel d'en Marc Palou** [AC] [VISA] [OO] [AE] [O]

Bailén 91 ✉ 08009 – **M** *Girona – ℰ 932 65 86 58*
– www.eltuneldenmarc.com
– Closed August, Sunday and Monday dinner   **L1**
Rest – Menu 24/40 € – Carte 33/41 €
♦ Traditional ♦ Fashionable ♦
Located in a busy street, this restaurant has two contemporary-style dining rooms on two floors and a wine cellar which doubles as a private room. Traditional cuisine with a creative touch.

XX **Moo** – Hotel Omm [AC] [VISA] [OO] [AE] [O]
❀
Rosselló 265 ✉ 08008 – **M** *Diagonal – ℰ 934 45 40 00*
– www.hotelomm.es
– Closed 7 days January, 3 weeks August and Sunday   **K1**
Rest – Menu 45/100 € – Carte 43/53 € ℬ
♦ Creative ♦ Design ♦
A cosmopolitan ambience pervades the café and bright dining room. Contemporary decor defined by skylights and designer details. Signature cuisine, a good combination of flavours and a very original wine list.
→ Fideua sin fideos. Pichón con guisado de cereales. Chocolates del mundo.

XX **Gorría** [AC] [⇔] [VISA] [OO] [AE] [O]

Diputació 421 ✉ 08013 – **M** *Monumental – ℰ 932 45 11 64*
– www.restaurantegorria.com
– Closed Holy Week, August, Sunday, Monday dinner and Bank Holidays dinner
Rest – Carte 27/55 €   **L1**
♦ Basque ♦ Rustic ♦
A well-established Basque restaurant with rustic style decor. The excellent menu is complemented by an extensive wine list. Attentive service.

XX **Icho** [⇱] [AC] [⇔] [VISA] [OO] [AE]

Deu i Mata 69-95 ✉ 08029 – **M** *Les Corts – ℰ 934 44 33 70*
– www.ichobcnjapones.com
– Closed Sunday   **I2**
Rest – Menu 33/60 € – Carte 37/62 €
♦ Japanese ♦ Fashionable ♦
The restaurant is named after a traditional Japanese tree. Its style is contemporary, service and cuisine are to a high standard, and the cuisine respects both technique and the product.

XX **Nectari** (Jordi Esteve) [AC] [⇔] [VISA] [OO] [AE] [O]
❀
València 28 ✉ 08015 – **M** *Tarragona – ℰ 932 26 87 18 – www.nectari.es*
– Closed 15 days August and Sunday   **J3**
Rest – Menu 25/76 € – Carte 27/56 €
♦ Modern ♦ Fashionable ♦
Hidden behind the discreet façade of this family-run restaurant is an interior with two contemporary dining rooms and a private section. The owner-chef offers a Mediterranean inspired menu with innovative touches.
→ Huevo ahumado nacido en tierra de trufas con miga de pan y boletus. Carré de cordero con costra de boletus, alcachofas, mangostán y mini verduritas. Tatin de manzana con helado de vainilla y nata.

XX **Casa Darío** [AC] [⇔] [VISA] [OO] [AE] [O]

Consell de Cent 256 ✉ 08011 – **M** *Universitat – ℰ 934 53 31 35*
– www.casadario.com
– Closed 3 weeks August and Sunday dinner   **K2**
Rest – Menu 37/72 € – Carte 45/75 €
♦ Galician ♦ Classic ♦
A well-established restaurant with a good reputation for the quality of its ingredients. The restaurant has a private bar, three dining rooms and three private rooms. Galician dishes and seafood are the house specialities.

XX **Monvínic** [AC] [✣] [VISA] [OO] [AE]

Diputació 249 ✉ *08007 –* Ⓜ *Catalunya –* ℰ *932 72 61 87*
– www.monvinic.com
– Closed August, Saturday, Sunday and Bank Holidays **K2**
Rest – Carte 41/80 € ⅌
♦ Modern ♦ Design ♦
A highly original, cutting-edge restaurant with the world of wine as its leitmotiv!
Designer inspired tapas bar, a single dining room with two large tables, and an
area reserved for tastings. Updated traditional cuisine and an impressive wine
cellar.

XX **Loidi** – Hotel Condes de Barcelona [AC] [VISA] [OO] [AE] [O]

Mallorca 248 ✉ *08008 –* Ⓜ *Passeig de Gràcia –* ℰ *934 92 92 92*
– www.loidi.com **K2**
Rest – *(Closed 3 weeks August and Sunday dinner) (set menu only)* Menu
27/62 €
♦ Modern ♦ Trendy ♦
The concept behind this restaurant favours cuisine that is economical, light and
quick. Various set menus are offered, although the menu named after Martín
Berasategui is dedicated to the culinary origins of this extraordinary chef.

XX **Manairó** (Jordi Herrera) [AC] [VISA] [OO] [AE] [O]
✿

Diputació 424 ✉ *08013 –* Ⓜ *Monumental –* ℰ *932 31 00 57*
– www.manairo.com
– Closed 1-7 January, Sunday and Bank Holidays **L1**
Rest – Menu 58/78 € – Carte 46/74 €
♦ Creative ♦ Fashionable ♦
Although somewhat on the small side, the Manairó is a renowned address in
this part of the city. In its elongated contemporary dining room, works by a
variety of artists grace its walls. The emphasis is on creative, traditionally based
cuisine featuring surprisingly innovative touches.
→ Huevo, patata chip y chorizo de mar y montaña. Filete de buey al clavo
ardiente. Torrija de uvas secas y helado de queso.

X **Toc** [AC] [VISA] [OO] [AE]
☺

Girona 59 ✉ *08009 –* Ⓜ *Girona –* ℰ *934 88 11 48 – www.tocbcn.com*
– Closed August, Saturday and Sunday **L2**
Rest – Menu 25 € – Carte approx. 35 €
♦ Modern ♦ Fashionable ♦
This restaurant is split between two floors, each with a contemporary, minima-
list look; although the upper of the two is recommended for its enhanced pre-
sentation and designer detail. Enjoy cooking with its roots in Catalan cuisine
that has been brought bang up-to-date.

X **Gresca** [AC] [VISA] [OO]

Provença 230 ✉ *08036 –* Ⓜ *Diagonal –* ℰ *934 51 61 93 – www.gresca.net*
– Closed 7 days Christmas, Holy Week, 15 days August, Saturday lunch and
Sunday **K2**
Rest – Menu 19/50 € – Carte 32/45 €
♦ Modern ♦ Fashionable ♦
The discreet façade leads to a spacious, minimalist-style dining room, decorated
in contrasting shades of black and white. Contemporary cuisine from the cons-
cientious chef.

X **Etapes** [⌂] [AC] [VISA] [OO] [AE] [O]
☺

Enrique Granados 10 ✉ *08007 –* ℰ *933 23 69 14*
– www.etapesrestaurant.com
– Closed Sunday **K2**
Rest – Menu 16/45 € – Carte approx. 35 €
♦ Modern ♦ Elegant ♦
An address that is well worth bearing in mind! This small restaurant has a
modern yet informal look featuring an elongated dining room with a decor
that combines wood, iron and glass. Enjoy contemporary cuisine with an
emphasis on meticulous presentation and carefully selected ingredients.

SPAIN - BARCELONA

SPAIN - BARCELONA

X **Can Ravell**   AC VISA ⊕⊗ AE ⊙

Aragó 313 ⊠ *08009* – Ⓜ *Girona* – 𝒞 *934 57 51 14* – *www.ravell.com*
– *Closed Sunday dinner and Monday*   **K1**
Rest – *(lunch only)* Menu 30 € – Carte 30/42 € ⅏
♦ Traditional ♦ Family ♦
This unusual restaurant has a charcuterie at the entrance and a small kitchen
which guests have to walk through to get to the dining room and private
rooms. Traditional cuisine.

Ⴤ/ **3 Food People & Music**   ⌂ AC VISA ⊕⊗ AE

Còrcega 231-233 ⊠ *08002* – 𝒞 *671 09 55 99* – *www.3fpm.com*
– *Closed Saturday lunch, Sunday, Monday lunch and Bank Holidays*
Tapa 6 € **Ración** approx. 9 €   **J2**
♦ Modern ♦ Friendly ♦
Split between two floors, this gastro-bar boasts a young and relaxed atmo-
sphere. The street level bar is dedicated to contemporary raciones and cocktails,
while the main dining room, with its open kitchen and low tables, is upstairs.

Ⴤ/ **Cervecería Catalana**   ⌂ AC VISA ⊕⊗ AE ⊙

Mallorca 236 ⊠ *08008* – Ⓜ *Diagonal* – 𝒞 *932 16 03 68*   **K2**
Tapa 4 € **Ración** approx. 12 €
♦ Traditional ♦ Tapas bar ♦
This popular local pub, decorated with racks full of bottles, serves a comprehen-
sive choice of top quality tapas.

Ⴤ/ **Paco Meralgo**   AC ⇆ VISA ⊕⊗ AE

Muntaner 171 ⊠ *08036* – Ⓜ *Hospital Clínic* – 𝒞 *934 30 90 27*
– *www.pacomeralgo.com*   **J2**
Tapa 4 € **Ración** approx. 15 €
♦ Traditional ♦ Fashionable ♦
The Paco Meralgo has two bars and two separate entrances. Its most impressive
features are its seafood display cabinets with a varied, fresh and top quality
choice of options. A private room is also available.

Ⴤ/ **Segons Mercat**   VISA ⊕⊗

Gran Via de les Corts Catalanes 552 ⊠ *08010* – 𝒞 *934 51 16 98*
– *www.segonsmercat.com*   **K2**
Tapa 5 € **Ración** approx. 9 €
♦ Traditional ♦ Tapas bar ♦
This rustic-cum-contemporary restaurant has a bar and an elongated dining
room. The walls of the latter are adorned with black and white photos, printed
panels and menu boards. Traditional cuisine with its roots in the sea.

Ⴤ/ **Tapas 24**   AC VISA ⊕⊗

Diputació 269 ⊠ *08007* – 𝒞 *934 88 09 77* – *www.projectes24.com*
– *Closed Sunday*   **K2**
Tapa 8 € **Ración** approx. 14 €
♦ Traditional ♦ Fashionable ♦
This bar is located in a half-basement. It creates a contemporary atmosphere
with two bars and walls decorated with mosaics. Choose from its delicious
menu of tapas and side dishes.

Ⴤ/ **Lolita**   AC VISA ⊕⊗ AE

Tamarit 104 ⊠ *08015* – Ⓜ *Poble Sec* – 𝒞 *934 24 52 31*
– *www.lolitataperia.com*
– *Closed 10 days Christmas, Holy Week, August, Sunday and Monday*
*(dinner only except Friday and Saturday)***Tapa** 7 €   **K3**
♦ Traditional ♦ Inn ♦
Situated close to the city's exhibition site, this restaurant stands out for its personalised decor. Traditional tapas created using top quality ingredients.

Arts   🐎 ⇜ ⌚ 🛏 🔒 👓 🅰️🅲 📶 🧖 🅿️ 💳 🆎 ⓪

*Marina 19 ⊠ 08005 – Ⓜ Ciutadella-Vila Olímpica – ℰ 932 21 10 00
– www.hotelartsbarcelona.com*   **C2**
397 rm – ♦♦325/460 €, 🖵 32 € – 114 suites
Rest *Enoteca* ✿✿ **Rest** *Arola* – see restaurant listing
♦ **Luxury** ♦ **Contemporary** ♦

Splendid hotel occupying a glass tower overlooking the Olympic port. It has magnificent views of the city and rooms that combine luxury and ultramodern design. Arola is renowned for its top quality cuisine.

Hilton Diagonal Mar Barcelona   ⇜ ⌚ 🛏 🔒 👓 rm, 🅰️🅲 📶

passeig del Taulat 262-264 ⊠ 08019   🧖 🛎️ 💳 🆎 ⓪
– Ⓜ El Maresme Fòrum – ℰ 935 07 07 07
– www.hiltondiagonalmarbarcelonahotel.es   **D2**
425 rm – ♦150/431 € ♦♦170/452 €, 🖵 24 € – 8 suites   **Rest** – Carte 40/50 €
♦ **Conference hotel** ♦ **Contemporary** ♦

Located near the Fórum, the Hilton is a popular conference venue. The guestrooms have a clean, contemporary design, with high-quality modern furnishings ensuring a comfortable stay. The functional restaurant doubles as the breakfast buffet room and a dining room offering an international à la carte menu.

Pullman Barcelona Skipper without rest   👓 🛏 🔒 🅰️🅲 📶

av. del Litoral 10 ⊠ 08005   🧖 🛎️ 💳 🆎 ⓪
– Ⓜ Ciutadella-Vila Olímpica – ℰ 932 21 65 65
– www.pullman-barcelona-skipper.com   **C2**
235 rm 🖵 – ♦150/325 € ♦♦165/350 € – 6 suites
♦ **Business** ♦ **Modern** ♦

This hotel combines designer detail and technology with a warm and welcoming setting. A varied lounge area, guestrooms offering modern creature comforts, a spa, plus an attractive rooftop terrace with a swimming pool. A bright, contemporary-style restaurant with views of the terrace. International cuisine.

ME Barcelona   ⇜ ⌚ 👓 🛏 🔒 rm, 🅰️🅲 📶 🧖 🛎️ 💳 🆎 ⓪

Pere IV-272 ⊠ 08005 – Ⓜ Poblenou – ℰ 933 67 20 50 – www.melia.com
258 rm 🖵 – ♦425 € ♦♦445 € – 9 suites   **D2**
Rest *Dos Cielos* ✿ – see restaurant listing
Rest *Dos* – Menu 30/42 € – Carte approx. 42 €
♦ **Business** ♦ **Design** ♦

The hotel is set in a 30-floor glazed building. It has a modern lobby with designer details, a lounge-bar, and contemporary bedrooms all with views. The cuisine in the hotel's contemporary restaurant is firmly geared towards international tastebuds.

Diagonal Zero   👓 📵 🛏 🔒 rm, 🅰️🅲 📶 🧖 🛎️ 💳 🆎 ⓪

pl. de Llevant ⊠ 08019 – Ⓜ El Maresme Fòrum – ℰ 935 07 80 00
– www.hoteldiagonalzero.com   **D1-2**
260 rm – ♦♦90/378 €, 🖵 18 € – 2 suites
Rest – *(Closed Sunday)* Menu 24/42 € – Carte 37/48 €
♦ **Business** ♦ **Modern** ♦

This hotel is well located next to the Barcelona Conference Centre. It offers guests bright and modern rooms equipped with the latest technology. Large gym and spa. The set menu and concise à la carte choices in this restaurant are based around Mediterranean cuisine.

Barcelona Princess   ⇜ 👓 🛏 🔒 rm, 🅰️🅲 📞 🧖 🛎️ 💳 🆎 ⓪

av. Diagonal 1 ⊠ 08019 – Ⓜ El Maresme Fòrum – ℰ 933 56 10 00
– www.hotelbarcelonaprincess.com   **D2**
316 rm – ♦98/318 € ♦♦110/330 €, 🖵 19 € – 48 suites
Rest – *(October-March)* Menu 20 € – Carte 25/32 €
♦ **Business** ♦ **Contemporary** ♦

The Princess occupies two modern tower blocks in the Fórum district of the city. Colourful lobby and contemporary-style guestrooms with good views and glass-enclosed bathrooms. Traditional à la carte choices are on offer in the bright and functional restaurant.

SPAIN - BARCELONA

XXXX **Enoteca** – Hotel Arts   🍴 AC VISA ⊕ AE ⊕
❀❀ *Marina 19 ⊠ 08005 –* Ⓜ *Ciutadella-Vila Olímpica –* ☎ *934 83 81 08*
– www.hotelartsbarcelona.com
– Closed 13-28 August and Sunday   **C2**
Rest *– (dinner only except Monday and Tuesday)* Menu 110 €
– Carte 67/99 € ❀
◆ Modern ◆ Classic ◆
The Enoteca's luminous dining room has a white-dominated colour scheme and attractive, decorative wine racks. This is the backdrop for perfectly prepared contemporary cuisine with its roots in traditional cooking. Top quality ingredients and excellent attention to detail.
➔ Colmenillas guisadas, panceta ibérica y "espardenyes". Gallo San Pedro, "un paseo por la Boquería". Selva negra.

XXX **Dos Cielos** (Sergio y Javier Torres) – Hotel ME Barcelona   ← 🍴
❀ *Pere IV-272 ⊠ 08005 –* Ⓜ *Poblenou*   ⇔ VISA ⊕ AE ⊕
– ☎ *933 67 20 50 – www.me-barcelona.com*   **D2**
Rest *– (Closed 15 days January, 15 days August, Sunday and Monday)*
Menu 95/125 € *– Carte 82/115 €* ❀
◆ Modern ◆ Trendy ◆
This restaurant is on the 24th floor of the ME Barcelona hotel. Unique features include the kitchen built into the dining room, a steel counter that doubles as a table for guests, as well as a terrace. Savour innovative cuisine that continues to embrace new flavours, while enjoying the superb views!
➔ Buey de mar hembra, pan de algas negras y flores. Bogavante azul, cítricos y aceite de dendé. La joya.

XX **Els Pescadors**   🍴 AC VISA ⊕
pl. Prim 1 ⊠ 08005 – Ⓜ *Poblenou –* ☎ *932 25 20 18*
– www.elspescadors.com
– Closed 22 December - 4 January   **D2**
Rest *– Carte 41/56 €*
◆ Fish and seafood ◆ Fashionable ◆
This restaurant has three dining rooms, one in early-20C café style and two with a more modern decor. A generous menu based on fish and seafood with rice dishes and cod to the fore.

XX **Arola** – Hotel Arts   ← 🍴 ☒ AC ⇔ VISA ⊕ AE ⊕
Marina 19 ⊠ 08005 – ☎ *934 83 80 90*
– www.hotelartsbarcelona.com   **C2**
Rest *– (Closed 2-29 January, Monday and Tuesday)* Menu 52/75 €
– Carte 45/75 € ❀
◆ Creative ◆ Friendly ◆
This restaurant is modern, urban and with a thoroughly young feel. It features a glass-fronted dining room, a terrace that doubles as a chill-out area, as well as a single large table for private dining in the kitchen. Creative à la carte options and two more popular set menus.

NORTH of AV. DIAGONAL   *Plan III*

🏨 **Casa Fuster**   ♨ 🕭 rm, AC 🕭 ♨ VISA ⊕ AE ⊕
passeig de Gràcia 132 ⊠ 08008
– Ⓜ *Diagonal –* ☎ *932 55 30 00*
– www.hotelcasafuster.com   **K1**
96 rm – ♦♦160/1200 €, ☒ 25 € – 20 suites
Rest *Galaxó* – Carte 45/77 €
◆ Luxury ◆ Historic ◆ Contemporary ◆
This magnificent hotel occupies a beautiful Modernist building. Attractive lounge-café, top-quality guestrooms and a panoramic bar on the roof terrace. The culinary focus in this elegant restaurant is on traditional Catalan cuisine with a contemporary twist.

G.H. La Florida 🐾 ⪡ 🚗 ⪢ 🛗 ⊗ 🛎 🗂 ₺ rm. 🖾 🛜 🏊 🅿️

carret. Vallvidrera al Tibidabo 83-93 ✉ *08035*   🚗 VISA ◉◎ AE ①
– ℰ 932 59 30 00 – www.hotellaflorida.com   Plan I **B2**
53 rm – ♦♦155/400 €, � 28 € – 17 suites
Rest L'Orangerie – Menu 80 € – Carte approx. 60 € ⍥
♦ Traditional ♦ Design ♦

Luxurious facilities on top of Mount Tibidabo. Guest rooms arranged by renowned interior designers, combining elegance, comfort and avant-garde taste. The restaurant has an outstanding set-up and a gorgeous view of the city.

Àbac ⊛ 🖾 🛜 🚗 VISA ◉◎ AE ①

av. del Tibidabo 1 ✉ *08022* – Ⓜ *Av. Tibidabo* – ℰ *933 19 66 00*
– www.abacbarcelona.com   Plan I **B2**
15 rm – ♦♦225/540 €, � 30 €   **Rest Àbac** ⍟⍟ – see restaurant listing
♦ Luxury ♦ Modern ♦

Spectacular guestrooms with a contemporary look, featuring top-quality furnishings, the latest technology and even colour therapy in the bathrooms. Modern spa.

Primero Primera without rest 🛗 ₺ 🖾 🛜 🏊 🚗 VISA ◉◎ AE ①

Doctor Carulla 25-29 ✉ *08017* – Ⓜ *Tres Torres* – ℰ *934 17 56 00*
– www.primeroprimera.com   **I1**
25 rm ⊑ – ♦♦160/300 € – 5 suites
♦ Historic ♦ Elegant ♦

Originally a series of apartments that have been restored and adapted, the Primero Primera is accessed via a passageway that calls to mind carriage entrances from the past. It offers bedrooms with a contemporary look and some have a pleasant terrace.

Hispanos Siete Suiza ₺ rm. 🖾 🛜 🚗 VISA ◉◎ AE ①

Sicilia 255 ✉ *08025* – Ⓜ *Sagrada Familia* – ℰ *932 08 20 51*
– www.hispanos7suiza.com   **L1**
20 suites – ♦♦105/220 €, ⊑ 5 €
Rest La Cúpula – ℰ *932 08 20 61 (Closed Sunday dinner)* Menu 12/59 €
– Carte 37/49 €
♦ Traditional ♦ Classic ♦

This comfortable, traditional property has apartments with two bedrooms, two bathrooms, a lounge and fully equipped kitchen. Most of the apartments have a terrace. The restaurant has two dining rooms, both exquisitely decorated in classical style with high-quality furniture.

XXXX Via Veneto 🖾 ⇆ VISA ◉◎ AE ①
⍟

Ganduxer 10 ✉ *08021* – Ⓜ *Hospital Clínic* – ℰ *932 00 72 44*
– www.viavenetorestaurant.com
– Closed 1-20 August, Saturday lunch and Sunday   **I2**
Rest – Menu 80/118 € – Carte 61/109 € ⍥
♦ Classic ♦ Retro ♦

This emblematic house has re-created a delightful Belle Epoque-style setting. It has a dining room laid out on several floors where the table service is impeccable. Traditional cuisine with a modern twist, prepared using the very finest products.
➜ "Espardenyes" salteadas con "rossejat" de fideos. Pato asado en su propio jugo "a la presse". Buñuelos de chocolate y avellana con velo de cacao y helado thai.

XXXX Àbac – Hotel Àbac 🖾 ⇆ VISA ◉◎ AE ①
⍟⍟

av. del Tibidabo 1 ✉ *08022* – Ⓜ *Av. Tibidabo* – ℰ *933 19 66 00*
– www.abacbarcelona.com   Plan I **B2**
Rest – *(Closed Sunday and Monday)* Menu 125/145 € – Carte 93/124 € ⍥
♦ Creative ♦ Trendy ♦

A memorable gastronomic experience awaits at Àbac, which occupies a contemporary building in the upper section of the city. It has a terrace, designer bar and an elegant, classically styled dining room. Creative cuisine featuring unique textures and flavours with top-notch presentation.
➜ Tomates rama desecados con agua de pimientos, sardina ahumada, piel de pan y albahaca. Liebre a la Royal, farsa guisada, lomo asado, foie-gras, piña y piñones. Sobre crujientes galletas, nieve de yogur, néctar de flores y violetas.

XXXX ✧

Neichel (Jean Louis Neichel)   `AK` ⇄ `VISA` `OO` `AE` `O`

Beltran i Rózpide 1 ✉ *08034 –* Ⓜ *Maria Cristina –* ☎ *932 03 84 08*
– www.neichel.es
– Closed 7 days January, Holy Week, 1-24 August, Sunday, Monday and Bank
Holidays   Plan I **A2**
Rest – Menu 43/90 € – Carte 57/78 € ♫
♦ International ♦ Classic ♦

An elegant restaurant with a classic ambience. In the kitchen, the father and son team perpetuates their commitment to international dishes, yet with an ever-increasing reliance on locally sourced ingredients. Enticing cheese trolley and a tempting choice of traditional homemade desserts.

➡ Huevo poché sobre parmentier cremoso de trufa fresca de Graus. "Trinxat" de mar con papada a la plancha, gambas, vieiras y "esparden-yes". Torrija de brioche con cremoso de cacao, pera y crema de Ratafia de Olot.

XXX ✧

Hofmann (Mey Hofmann)   `AK` ⇄ `VISA` `OO` `AE` `O`

La Granada del Penedès 14-16 ✉ *08006*
– Ⓜ *Diagonal –* ☎ *932 18 71 65*
– www.hofmann-bcn.com
– Closed Christmas, Holy Week, August, Saturday, Sunday and Bank Holidays
Rest – Menu 47/85 € – Carte 59/87 €   **J1**
♦ Creative ♦ Elegant ♦

The Hofmann reflects a contemporary gastronomic philosophy with its semi-private small rooms and an attractive main dining room with views of the kitchen via a large window. Creative cuisine that attracts a sizeable business clientele.

➡ Canelón de ternera, crema trufada y teja de parmesano. Pies de cerdo deshuesados, rellenos de foie y trufa, en crepina glaseada con salsa de Oporto. Crujientes templados de vainilla con uvas pasas.

XXX ☺

Freixa Tradició   `AK` `VISA` `OO` `AE` `O`

Sant Elíes 22 ✉ *08006 –* Ⓜ *Plaça Molina –* ☎ *932 09 75 59*
– www.freixatradicio.com
– Closed Holy Week, 21 days August, Sunday and Monday   **J1**
Rest – Menu 35 € – Carte 29/35 €
♦ Regional ♦ Fashionable ♦

Run by the couple that owns the restaurant, the Freixa Tradició has, over the years, established itself as one of the city's culinary institutions. In its minimalist interior enjoy the high quality and well-prepared traditional Catalan cuisine.

XXX

Roig Robí   🛋 `AK` ⇄ `VISA` `OO` `AE` `O`

Sèneca 20 ✉ *08006 –* Ⓜ *Diagonal –* ☎ *932 18 92 22 – www.roigrobi.com*
– Closed 7 days January, 21 days August, Saturday lunch and Sunday
Rest – Menu 36/64 € – Carte 32/70 € ♫   **K1**
♦ Regional ♦ Classic ♦

A classic restaurant in a particularly pleasant setting, with a conservatory-style dining room arranged around a patio-garden. Traditional Catalan cuisine of a consistently high quality.

XXX

Tram-Tram   🛋 `AK` ⇄ `VISA` `OO` `AE` `O`

Major de Sarrià 121 ✉ *08017 –* ☎ *932 04 85 18 – www.tram-tram.com*
– Closed Christmas, Holy Week, 15 days August, Sunday, Monday and Bank
Holidays   Plan I **A2**
Rest – Menu 22/65 € – Carte 40/60 €
♦ Modern ♦ Family ♦

Located in the upper part of the city, Tram-Tram's dining room is classic in style and divided into two sections with two private rooms and a terrace-patio with a glass-fronted gallery. Creative cuisine.

SPAIN - BARCELONA

XX **El Asador de Aranda** 🛋 AC ⇔ P VISA ⓪ AE ①

av. del Tibidabo 31 ✉ *08022 –* 𝒞 *934 17 01 15*
– www.asadordearanda.com
– Closed Sunday dinner   *Plan I* **B1-2**
Rest – Menu 34/51 € – Carte 28/42 €
♦ Meats and grills ♦ Rustic ♦
This restaurant occupies the incomparable Casa Roviralta, a Modernist building also known as El Frare Blanc. The culinary focus here is on typical Castilian cuisine, with a house speciality of roast lamb cooked in a clay oven.

XX **Alkimia** (Jordi Vilá)   AC VISA ⓪ ①
ঞ
Indústria 79 ✉ *08025 –* Ⓜ *Sagrada Familia –* 𝒞 *932 07 61 15*
– www.alkimia.cat
– Closed Holy Week, 21 days August, Saturday, Sunday and Bank Holidays
Rest – Menu 38/84 €   **K1**
♦ Creative ♦ Minimalist ♦
Family run, the Alkimia has a single dining room with a minimalist look. The cooking is based around two tasting menus: one more innovative, the other more traditional. Guests can choose single dishes from these if they prefer dining à la carte.
→ Ostra escabechada, careta y espinacas. Mediana de vaca vieja. Ciruelas con mató y lichies.

XX **Coure**   AC VISA ⓪ AE

passatge de Marimon 20 ✉ *08021 –* Ⓜ *Hospital Clínic –* 𝒞 *932 00 75 32*
– www.restauantcoure.es
– Closed Holy Week, 21 days August, Sunday and Monday   **J2**
Rest – Menu 35/50 € – Carte 27/49 €
♦ Modern ♦ Fashionable ♦
A modern restaurant with bright colours and a minimalist inspired decoration. Interesting and innovative cuisine from the owner-chef.

XX **Hisop** (Oriol Ivern)   AC VISA ⓪ AE ①
ঞ
passatge de Marimon 9 ✉ *08021 –* Ⓜ *Hospital Clínic –* 𝒞 *932 41 32 33*
– www.hisop.com
– Closed 1-7 January, 21 days August, Saturday lunch, Sunday and Bank Holidays   **J2**
Rest – Menu 27/50 € – Carte 49/57 €
♦ Creative ♦ Minimalist ♦
A contemporary restaurant which, given its size, has an understandably intimate atmosphere. The dining room features an abundance of wood. Enjoy creative cuisine based around traditional recipes, all of which are produced using local or seasonal ingredients.
→ Gambas de Palamós con habitas a la catalana. Pollo asado con "espardenyes". Rebozuelos con maracuyá y chocolate.

XX **St. Rémy**   AC ⇔ VISA ⓪ AE ①

Iradier 12 ✉ *08017 –* 𝒞 *934 18 75 04 – www.stremyrestaurant.com*
– Closed Sunday dinner   **I1**
Rest – Menu 30 € – Carte 26/45 €
♦ Regional ♦ Trendy ♦
The St Rémy occupies a small mansion with spacious dining rooms, modern furniture and elegant lighting. Catalan inspired cuisine.

XX **Comiols**   AC ⇔ VISA ⓪ AE ①

Madrazo 68-70 ✉ *08006 –* 𝒞 *932 09 07 91 – www.comiols.es*
– Closed 5-29 August, Saturday lunch and Sunday   **J1**
Rest – Menu 40/50 € – Carte 34/57 €
♦ Modern ♦ Trendy ♦
Although at first glance it may come across as modern and somewhat informal, this restaurant is run with great professionalism. It features traditional dishes with a modern flair and a focus on light and healthy cuisine.

XX **Le Quattro Stagioni**　　　🏠 AC 🔄 VISA 🐼 AE ⓞ

Dr. Roux 37 ✉ *08017* – ⓜ *Tres Torres* – ☏ *932 05 22 79*
– www.4stagioni.com
– Closed Holy Week, Sunday and Monday lunch (July-August), Sunday dinner and Monday rest of year　　　I1
Rest – Carte 29/42 €
♦ Italian ♦ Fashionable ♦
Dining rooms on two floors with a glass-fronted terrace and outdoor patio. Mediterranean ambience, Italian cuisine and a wide selection of Italian wines.

XX **Silvestre**　　　AC 🔄 VISA 🐼 AE ⓞ
😊

Santaló 101 ✉ *08021* – ⓜ *Muntaner* – ☏ *932 41 40 31*
– www.restaurantesilvestre.com
– Closed Holy Week, 21 days August, Saturday July -August, Saturday lunch, Sunday and Bank Holidays rest of year　　　J1
Rest – Menu 21/42 € – Carte 30/35 €
♦ Traditional ♦ Classic ♦
The couple who own the Silvestre have created a classic setting with several separate areas that endow the property with a certain intimacy. Traditional, market-influenced cuisine is served. The pigs' trotters filled with mushrooms and the port flavoured Catalan sausage (butifarra) are definitely worth trying here.

XX **Mil921**　　　🏠 AC VISA 🐼

Casanova 211 ✉ *08021* – ⓜ *Hospital Clinic* – ☏ *934 14 34 94*
– www.mil921.com
– Closed Sunday and Monday dinner　　　J2
Rest – Menu 15/65 € – Carte 34/48 €
♦ Modern ♦ Fashionable ♦
A cosy and intimate restaurant that is well run by its owner-chef. It has two dining rooms that are both modern in feel. Enjoy contemporary cuisine prepared using locally sourced and market-fresh ingredients… and always presented in a highly creative way.

X **Vivanda**　　　🏠 AC 🔄 VISA 🐼
😊

Major de Sarrià 134 ✉ *08017* – ⓜ *Sarrià* – ☏ *932 03 19 18 – www.vivanda.cat*
– Closed Sunday dinner and Monday　　　*Plan I* **A2**
Rest – Menu 15 € – Carte 24/35 €
♦ Traditional ♦ Trendy ♦
The Vivanda boasts a modern-style main dining room, as well as a tree-shaded patio-terrace that is hugely popular with locals. The chef focuses on traditional Catalan cuisine, using contemporary techniques to rekindle the flavours of yesteryear.

X **La Taula**　　　AC VISA 🐼 AE ⓞ
😊

Sant Màrius 8-12 ✉ *08022* – ⓜ *El Putxet* – ☏ *934 17 28 48*
– www.lataula.com
– Closed Holy Week, August, Saturday lunch, Sunday and Bank Holidays
Rest – Menu 15/37 € – Carte approx. 35 €　　　I1
♦ International ♦ Classic ♦
Small, welcoming and full of interesting detail, La Taula boasts a busy and lively atmosphere. The cuisine has an international slant, centred around three highly distinct menus and a series of chef's recommendations.

X **Mandarina**　　　AC 🔄 VISA 🐼 AE
😊

Caravel.la "La Niña" ✉ *08017* – ☏ *932 05 60 04*
– www.mandarinarestaurant.com
– Closed 5-31 August, Saturday and Sunday　　　I2
Rest – *(lunch only)* Menu 15/35 € – Carte approx. 35 €
♦ Modern ♦ Trendy ♦
The Mandarina has a fresh, young feel, giving diners the sensation of eating both modestly and healthily. Split between two floors, the restaurant also boasts a semi-visible kitchen, as well as a delicatessen-style boutique. Enjoy creative and contemporary dishes based around meticulously prepared ingredients.

SPAIN - BARCELONA

AT SANTA COLOMA de GRAMENET

Lluerna (Víctor Quintillà) 🔲 ⇔ VISA ⑧ 🖭

Rafael Casanovas 31 ⊠ 08921 Santa Coloma de Gramenet
– Ⓜ Santa Coloma – ℰ 933 91 08 20 – www.lluernarestaurant.com
– Closed Holy Week, 12-26 August, Sunday and Monday
Rest – Menu 30 €, 48/48 € – Carte 34/59 €
♦ Modern ♦ Minimalist ♦
Well run by the couple that owns the restaurant, the Lluerna has a small, minimalist-style dining room. The focus is on a contemporary interpretation of traditional recipes, alongside two tasting menus. Enjoy the perfectly prepared and attractively presented cuisine that shows good attention to detail.
➜ Mollejas de ternera crujientes con sepietas. Pescado de playa con "calçots" y romesco. La torrija, café y cacao.

AT L'HOSPITALET de LLOBREGAT   *Plan I*

Hesperia Tower ⇐ ᴌᴓ 🔲 ᵭ rm, 🔲 🛜 🔐 🖘 VISA ⑧ 🖭 ①

Gran Via 144 ⊠ 08907 L'Hospitalet de Llobregat – Ⓜ Hospital de Bellvitge
– ℰ 934 13 50 00 – www.hesperia-tower.com   A3
280 rm – ♛♛100/400 €, ☲ 24 € – 41 suites
Rest Bouquet – (dinner only) Carte 77/92 €
♦ Chain hotel ♦ Business ♦ Modern ♦
This hotel occupying a tower block designed by the famous architect Richard Rogers boasts spacious public areas, a convention centre and contemporary guestrooms. The emphasis in this first-floor restaurant is on traditional cuisine prepared using seasonal products.

El Racó del Cargol 🔲 VISA ⑧

Dr. Martí Julià 54 ⊠ 08903 L'Hospitalet de Llobregat – Ⓜ Collblanc
– ℰ 934 49 77 18 – www.rocxi.es
– Closed Christmas, 15 days August and Sunday   A3
Rest – Menu 15/42 € – Carte 22/35 €
♦ Regional ♦ Classic ♦
This restaurant has a bar area, a classically furnished main dining room, as well as two additional rooms upstairs. It serves extensive, traditional à la carte options, including typical Catalan dishes, enticing daily specials and different set menus.

AT EL PRAT AIRPORT

Tryp Barcelona Aeropuerto without rest ᴌᴓ ᵭ 🔲 🕻 🔐

🖘 VISA ⑧ 🖭 ①
pl. del Pla de L'Estany 1-2 ⊠ 08820 El Prat de
Llobregat – ℰ 933 78 10 00 – www.trypbarcelonaaeropuerto.melia.com
196 rm – ♛80/270 € ♛♛105/310 €, ☲ 15 € – 9 suites
♦ Business ♦ Contemporary ♦
A modern, functional hotel located in a business park near the airport. The large lobby, open to the ceiling several floors above, is enclosed by functional and well-appointed guestrooms.

VALENCIA
VALÈNCIA

Population: 800 469

Gregory Gerault/hemis.fr

Spain's third largest city offers undeniable character and charm, with unspoilt beaches, numerous museums, amazing nightlife and rip roaring fiestas. The city sits in an enviable position on the Mediterranean coast, with its port and its long golden beach to the east. A mile or so inland is the heart of the city, its beautiful old town; a labyrinth of ancient cobbled streets which pay testament to its rich history, with medieval churches, Renaissance halls of trade and baroque mansions layered on top of an earlier Roman city.

Valencia is the home of paella, and a thriving café scene gives you ample opportunity to tuck into it. The sun shines most of the time here, but if you want shelter there are plenty of museums on hand to offer a cool escape. Culturally, the city has been propelled into the major league in the last few decades. What's taken it there is the exciting City of Arts and Sciences complex, a 21C addition to the city's skyline built within the confines of the Turia River Park; the fabulous nine-mile green space created when the river was diverted after flooding in 1957. This futuristic 'city' draws over four million visitors each year, is made up of four stunning buildings and is home to a science museum, an opera house, an aquarium and an Imax cinema with a planetarium and laserium.

VALENCIA IN...

➜ **ONE DAY**
Plaza de la Virgen, La Lonja, Central Market, a trip to the beach.

➜ **TWO DAYS**
IVAM (Valencian Institute of Modern Art), City of Arts and Sciences, Carmen district nightlife.

➜ **THREE DAYS**
A stroll along the Turia River Park.

PRACTICAL INFORMATION

ARRIVAL-DEPARTURE

 Valencia Manises Airport is 8km west of the city. Metro trains (lines 3 and 5) take about 25min. The Airport bus, which runs every 20min, takes around 15min.

GETTING AROUND

Valencia has an integrated transport system with metro, buses and trams. Single tickets for the metro, which has five lines, are cheap and can be purchased from station machines or ticket offices. You can buy a one day pass for the metro, trams and buses or, alternatively, a more cost-effective 10-trip pass. Another useful investment is the Valencia Tourist Card, available from tourist offices, hotels, tobacconists and kiosks. It offers free travel on all forms of public transport, as well as discounts in museums, shops, restaurants and on various leisure activities; the cards last for one, two, or three days.

CALENDAR HIGHLIGHTS

January
Epiphany, St Vincent's Day.

March
Las Fallas (the arrival of spring).

April
Semana Santa Marinera (Holy Week).

May
The Crosses of May, Feast of Our Lady of the Forsaken.

June
Corpus Christi.

July
Feria de Julio (July Fair).

August
La Tomatina (battle of the tomatoes).

EATING OUT

Valencia is the city of paella. It was invented here, and this is the place to try it in infinite varieties. For a gargantuan helping, head off to the Las Arenas beach promenade, which is lined with a whole legion of seafood restaurants. On a hot day, the traditional liquid accompaniment is agua de Valencia, a potentially lethal combination of orange juice, Cava and vodka. Most restaurants remain very Spanish in character, and if you're not eating paella, then you'll probably be enjoying tapas, with an emphasis on the excellent local cured hams and cheeses. A little different is the

local delicacy of all i pebre, a mouth-watering meal of stewed eels from the local wetlands, served in a garlic and red pepper sauce. The drink to cool down with is horchata: it's tigernut milk – a mixture of nuts, cinnamon, sugar and water – and is best enjoyed with a doughy cake. Meal times can throw the unwary visitor: lunch is often not served until two in the afternoon, and dinner, in general, is never eaten before nine at night.

A   GODELLA   B   Palmaret

5   Burjassot-Godella   BORBÒTO

Llíria   Montcada

TVV   V. Andrés E.   BURJASSOT

Fira   Campus   Burjassot

Ctra del Pla del Pou   U   St. Joan

CV 31   La Granja

Benimàmet   Juan   XXIII   de   los

Les Carolines   Cantereria   Empalme

PATERNA   CV 31   PALACIO DE   Palau de Congressos   Av.   de   Juan XXIII

Campament   CONGRESOS   Florista

CV 31   Av.   Palacio de Congresos   Trànsits

Sorolla Palace   Novotel Valencia

Camp   Garbi   Benicalap   Av. Dr. Peset Aleixandre

Meliá València   Beniferri   Marxalenes

del   Túria   Safor   Avilés   Reus   Sagun

Maestro   Cortes   Reus

Kaymus   Campanar   Sagunto

Valencianes   Av.   Buriassot

Valencia Centre

CAMPANAR   (Plan II)

MISLATA   Av. M.   Rodrigo

Mislata-Almassil   de Falla   Pechina   CATEDRAL

San   Antonio   Paseo   ESTACIÓN

Nuevo   Ronda   Mislata   DEL NORTE

Ronda   Nou d'Octubre   Gran Vía de Fernando el Católico

338   Av.   del   Cid   Gran Vía de Ramón y Cajal

XIRIVELLA   del   Av. del Cid   Jesús

Cruce   Av.   Tres   Forques   Av.   Giorgeta

Río   Marginal   Picaña   Archiduque Carlos   Av.   de   Pe

Turia   Cruces   Hospital   Patraix   San   Vicente   Av.

de   Nuevo   Sant Isidre   Av. de G. Aguilar   Martí

Camino   V 30   Av. del Pianista M. Carrasco

CV 36   Barranc   València-Sud   V 30   Ronda

Picanya   PICANYA   Paiporta   Ronda

Picanya   V 400   Av. del País Valenciano   Av. del

PAIPORTA   Xiva   BENETÚSSER   SEDAVÍ   V 31

| ● Hotel |
| ● Restaurant |

A   B

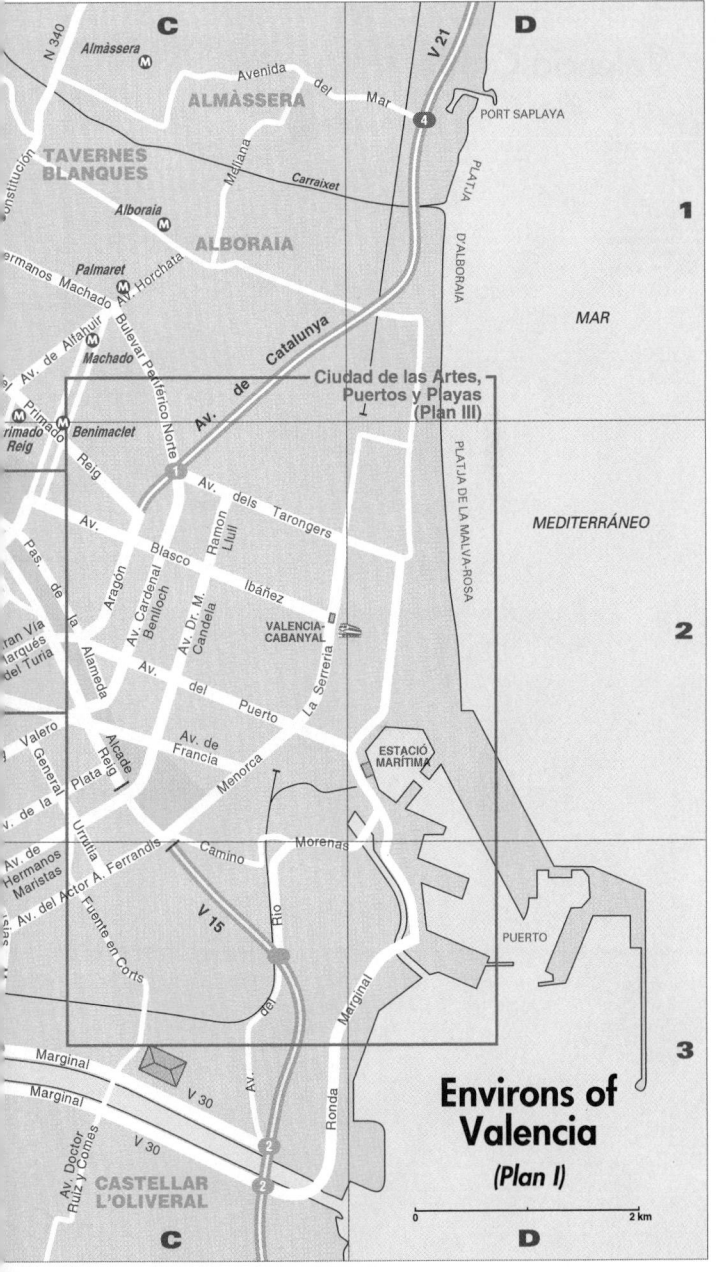

Environs of Valencia
(Plan I)

0   2 km

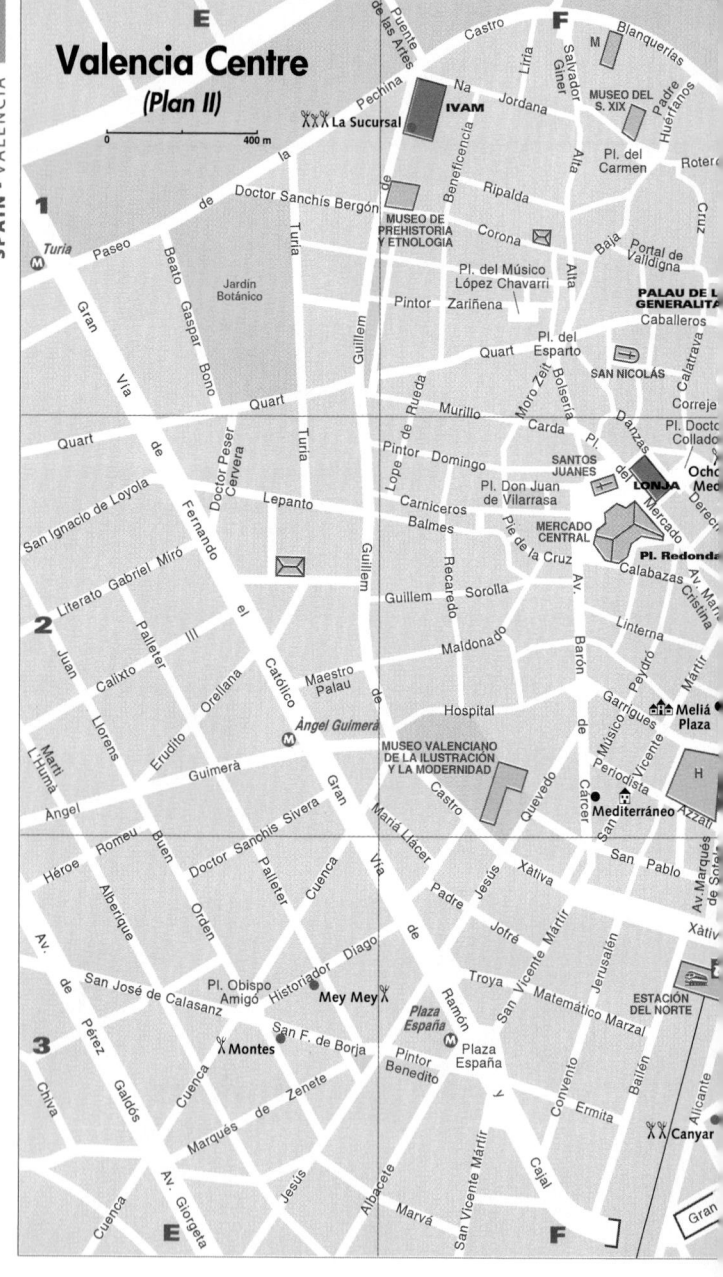

Valencia Centre
(Plan II)

0   400 m

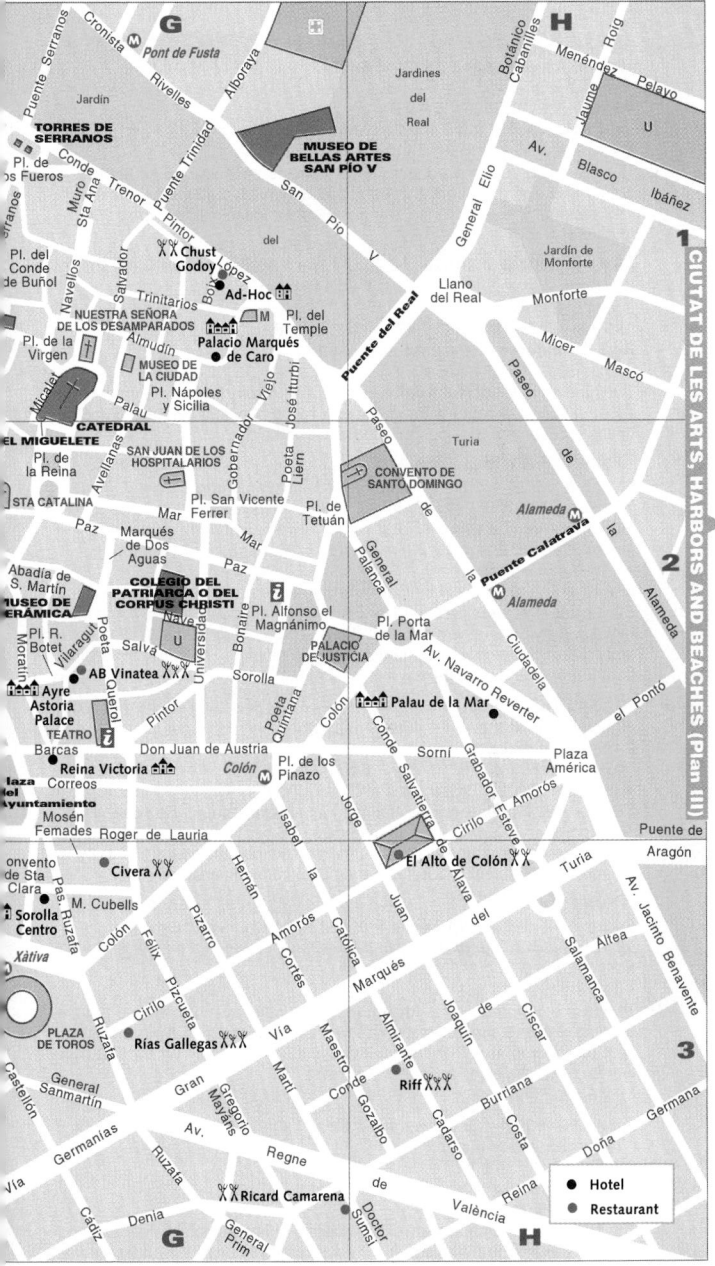

G   Pont de Fusta

Jardines
del
Real

Cronista
Puente Serranos
Rivelles
Alboraya

Jardin

TORRES DE
SERRANOS
Pl. de
os Fueros
Conde
Trenor
Muro
Sta Ana
Puente Trinidad
Pintor
San Pío V

MUSEO DE
BELLAS ARTES
SAN PÍO V

Botánico
Cabanilles
Menéndez
Roig
Pelayo

Jaume
U

Av.
Blasco

Ibáñez

General Elío

Jardín de
Monforte

Monforte

Micer

Mascó

Paseo

Navellos
Salvador
Pl. del
Conde
de Buñol
Trinitarios
López
X X Chust
Godoy
Ad-Hoc
M
Pl. del
Temple
Palacio Marqués
de Caro

NUESTRA SEÑORA
DE LOS DESAMPARADOS
Pl. de la
Virgen
Almudín
MUSEO DE
LA CIUDAD
Pl. Nápoles
y Sicilia
Palau
Gobernador Viejo
José Iturbi
Puente del Real

CATEDRAL
EL MIGUELETE
Micalet

Puente del Real

Llano
del Real

STA CATALINA
Pl. de
la Reina
SAN JUAN DE LOS
HOSPITALARIOS
Avellanas
Paz
Mar
Pl. San Vicente
Ferrer
Pl. de
Tetuán

CONVENTO DE
SANTO DOMINGO

Turia

Paseo
de
la
Alameda M

Puente Calatrava
Alameda M

Abadía de
S. Martín
MUSEO DE
CERÁMICA
Pl. R.
Botet
Moratín
Vilaragut
Poeta
Querol
Salva
Nave
U
Pl. Alfonso el
Magnánimo
Bonaire
COLEGIO DEL
PATRIARCA O DEL
CORPUS CHRISTI
Marqués
de Dos
Aguas
Paz
Mar
General
Palanca
Pl. Porta
de la Mar
PALACIO
DE JUSTICIA
Av. Navarro Reverter
Ciudadela
el Pontó

Ayre
Astoria
Palace
AB Vinatea X X X
Universidad
Sorolla
Colón
Palau de la Mar

TEATRO
Barcas
Reina Victoria
Don Juan de Austria
Colón M
Pl. de los
Pinazo
Poeta
Quintana
Conde
Salvatierra
de Álava
Sorní
Amorós
Grabador Esteve
Cirilo
Plaza
América

laza
del
Ayuntamiento
Mosén
Femades
Roger de Lauria
Isabel
la
Jorge
Puente de
Aragón

onvento
de Sta
Clara
M. Cubells
Pas. Ruzafa
Civera X X
Hernán
Católica
Juan
El Alto de Colón X X
Turia
Altea

Sorolla
Centro
Xàtiva
Colón
Félix
Pizarro
Amorós
Cortés
Marqués
de
Almirante
Joaquín
Ciscar
Costa
Av. Jacinto Benavente
Salamanca
Germana
Doña

PLAZA
DE TOROS
Castelón
General
Sanmartín
Cirilo
Ruzafa
Pizcueta
Rías Gallegas X X X
Maestro
Martí
Conde
Gozalbo
Riff X X X
Burriana
Cadarso
Reina
Valéncia

Germanias
Av.
Gran
Gregorio
Mayans
Regne
Ricard Camarena X X
de
Doctor
Sums

Via
Cádiz
Denia
Ruzafa
General
Prim
G
H

● Hotel
● Restaurant

Palau de la Mar   ⚫ 𝆏 ⬚ & rm, 🆔 📶 🏊 🅿 🆅🅸🆂🅰 ⚫ 🅰🅴 ①

Navarro Reverter 14 ✉ *46004* – ⓜ *Colón* – ℰ *963 16 28 84*
– www.fuenso.com   **H2**
65 rm – 🛏🛏110/300 €, ☲ 19 € – 1 suite
Rest *Senzone* – *(Closed Sunday)* Menu 25/60 € – Carte 25/46 €
♦ Palace ♦ Business ♦ Modern ♦

The 'Sea Palace' partially occupies two 19C mansions. These house the hotel's public areas and most of its fully equipped, minimalist-style rooms. Spa centre. This restaurant specialises in creative Mediterranean cuisine, including an impressive choice of rice dishes.

Ayre Astoria Palace   𝆏 & 🆔 📶 🏊 🆅🅸🆂🅰 ⚫ 🅰🅴 ①

pl. Rodrigo Botet 5 ✉ *46002* – ⓜ *Colón* – ℰ *963 98 10 00*
– www.ayrehoteles.com   **G2**
196 rm – 🛏75/450 € 🛏🛏90/475 €, ☲ 15 € – 8 suites
Rest *AB Vinatea* – see restaurant listing
♦ Business ♦ Classic ♦

Two types of guestroom are on offer at the Ayre Astoria Palace: one more traditional in style, the other with a decidedly modern look. Bright and attractive dining room on the top floor enjoying views of the city.

Palacio Marqués de Caro   & rm, 🆔 📶 🆅🅸🆂🅰 ⚫ 🅰🅴 ①

Almirante 14 ✉ *46003* – ℰ *963 05 90 00* – *www.carohotel.com*
25 rm – 🛏130/250 € 🛏🛏140/280 €, ☲ 20 € – 1 suite   **G1**
Rest *Alma del Temple* – *(Closed Sunday dinner, Monday dinner and Tuesday dinner)* Menu 19/30 € – Carte 25/40 €
♦ Palace ♦ Modern ♦

A small 19C palace full of fascinating historical interest. Important archaeological remains have been preserved in almost every guestroom, where contemporary urban style sits in harmony with Roman and Moorish artefacts. The restaurant combines perfectly these vestiges of the past with a more modern setting. Contemporary à la carte menu.

Meliá Plaza   🛋 𝆏 & rm, 🆔 📶 🏊 🅿 🆅🅸🆂🅰 ⚫ 🅰🅴 ①

pl. del Ayuntamiento 4 ✉ *46002* – ⓜ *Xàtiva* – ℰ *963 52 06 12*
– www.solmelia.com   **F2**
101 rm – 🛏🛏85/300 €, ☲ 18 €   **Rest** – Menu 23 € – Carte 28/45 €
♦ Chain hotel ♦ Business ♦ Classic ♦

This centrally located hotel has limited lounge space but its classically styled guestrooms make up for this and offer excellent facilities for the price. There is also a fully equipped fitness centre on the top floor boasting views of the city. In the modern restaurant choose from a set menu or traditional à la carte.

Reina Victoria   & rm, 🆔 📶 🏊 🆅🅸🆂🅰 ⚫ 🅰🅴 ①

Barcas 4 ✉ *46002* – ⓜ *Xàtiva* – *www.husa.es*
96 rm – 🛏67/333 € 🛏🛏70/350 €, ☲ 13 €   **G2**
Rest – *(Closed August)* Menu 20/48 €
♦ Business ♦ Classic ♦

The 'Queen Victoria', fronted by a fine façade in keeping with such a historic building, enjoys a superb location a few steps from the city's main museums. Spacious bedrooms with a classic design and a dining room on the first floor where guests can enjoy an impressive buffet.

Ad-Hoc   🆔 📶 🆅🅸🆂🅰 ⚫ 🅰🅴 ①

Boix 4 ✉ *46003* – ⓜ *Alameda* – ℰ *963 91 91 40*
– www.adhochoteles.com   **G1**
28 rm – 🛏71/114 € 🛏🛏83/135 €, ☲ 13 €
Rest – *(Closed Sunday) (dinner only)* Menu 11/16 €
♦ Cosy ♦ Rustic ♦

This hotel occupies an attractive 19C building. It has a small lounge area and rooms decorated in neo-rustic style with exposed brickwork, wooden beams and clay tiles. The restaurant has a pleasant and relaxing atmosphere, making it the perfect place for an after dinner cocktail.

Sorolla Centro without rest   🅰️ 🛜 ⚐ 💳 ⑨ ⑩

Convento Santa Clara 5 ⊠ *46002 –* Ⓜ *Xàtiva –* 𝒞 *963 52 33 92*
– www.hotelsorollacentro.com   **G3**
58 rm – ♦65/162 € ♦♦76/249 €, ⌷ 11 €

♦ **Business** ♦ **Functional** ♦

As the name would suggest, this hotel enjoys a central location a stone's throw from the best shopping areas in the city. Guest facilities include a bright breakfast room and functional, yet well-appointed bedrooms.

Mediterráneo without rest   🅰️ 🛜 💳 ⑨ ⑩

Barón de Cárcer 45 ⊠ *46001 –* Ⓜ *Xàtiva –* 𝒞 *963 51 01 42*
– www.hotel-mediterraneo.es   **F2**
34 rm – ♦50/145 € ♦♦50/200 €, ⌷ 8 €

♦ **Business** ♦ **Functional** ♦

This centrally located hotel has a breakfast room on the first floor and classic bedrooms. Each of these has a fitted carpet and the full range of facilities you would expect of a hotel of this standard.

XXX

🕸️

La Sucursal   🅰️ 💳 ⑨ ⑩

Guillém de Castro 118 ⊠ *46003 –* Ⓜ *Túria –* 𝒞 *963 74 66 65*
– www.restaurantelasucursal.com
– Closed 12-26 August, Saturday lunch and Sunday   **F1**
Rest – Menu 48/70 € – Carte 43/65 € ❦

♦ **Creative** ♦ **Fashionable** ♦

This restaurant is located inside the Instituto Valenciano de Arte Moderno. It has a café on the ground floor and a minimalist inspired dining room upstairs. The chef combines traditional and cutting-edge dishes to perfection.

→ Micro verduras de nuestra huerta en ligero escabeche, yogur de trufa y sardina. Pescado de lonja, edamame, cuscús vegetal y cebolla confitada. Nuestro homenaje al vino, sorbete de melocotón de viña con sarmientos y taninos dulces.

XXX

Rías Gallegas   🅰️ ⇆ 🅿️ 💳 ⑨ ⑩

Cirilo Amorós 4 ⊠ *46004 –* Ⓜ *Xàtiva –* 𝒞 *963 52 51 11*
– www.riasgallegas.es
– Closed Sunday and Monday dinner   **G3**
Rest – Menu 35 € – Carte 48/60 €

♦ **Traditional** ♦ **Fashionable** ♦

A family-run restaurant with an impeccable appearance. The cuisine is focused on tradition, hence the typical Galician dishes with a contemporary touch.

XXX

🕸️

Riff (Bernd Knöller)   🅰️ 💳 ⑨ ⑩

Conde de Altea 18 ⊠ *46005 –* Ⓜ *Colón –* 𝒞 *963 33 53 53*
– www.restaurante-riff.com
– Closed Holy Week, August, Sunday and Monday   **H3**
Rest – Menu 30/85 € – Carte 54/79 € ❦

♦ **Creative** ♦ **Trendy** ♦

A restaurant with a meticulous, minimalist feel now complemented by the deli next door. Riff's owner-chef concocts innovative cuisine based around seasonal products that are always of the highest quality.

→ Arroz meloso de champiñones y foie. Pagre con semillas y ragú de clochinas. Mousse de chocolate caliente con aceite de oliva, sal y helado de achicoria.

XXX

AB Vinatea – Hotel Ayre Astoria Palace   🅰️ ⇆ 💳 ⑨ ⑩

Vilaragut 4 ⊠ *46002 –* Ⓜ *Colón –* 𝒞 *963 98 10 00*
– www.ayrehoteles.com
– Closed Sunday, Monday and Tuesday dinner   **G2**
Rest – Menu 20 € – Carte 35/45 €

♦ **Traditional** ♦ **Trendy** ♦

This restaurant has its own separate entrance. The modern dining room serves traditional and local cuisine with a modern touch, plus an excellent choice of rice dishes.

SPAIN - VALENCIA

XX + **Ricard Camarena**   [AC] [VISA] [⦿⦿] [AE]

Doctor Sumsi 4 ✉ *46005* – ☏ *963 35 54 18* – *www.ricardcamarena.com*
– Closed Sunday and Monday   **G3**
Rest – Menu 85 € – Carte 65/75 €
♦ Modern ♦ Design ♦
A restaurant boasting a thoroughly modern and meticulous look. There is a unique private section and highly original table that dominates the room from its position opposite the open-view kitchen. The concise choice of daily à la carte dishes and the tasting menu demonstrate excellent culinary skill.
➔ Tomate-anchoa-pesto. Atún de almadraba-nabo aliñado. Lomo de vaca-tendones-manteca negra.

XX **El Alto de Colón**   [AC] [VISA] [⦿⦿] [AE] [①]

Jorge Juan 19 ✉ *46004* – Ⓜ *Colón* – ☏ *963 53 09 00*
– www.grupoelalto.com
– Closed Holy Week, August, Saturday lunch and Sunday   **H3**
Rest – Menu 35/69 € – Carte approx. 55 €
♦ Mediterranean ♦ Trendy ♦
This remarkable restaurant located in one of the towers of the Colón market is resolutely modern in style. Attractive tiled ceilings and contemporary Mediterranean cuisine.

XX **Civera**   [⛶] [AC] [⟺] [VISA] [⦿⦿] [AE] [①]

Mosén Femades 10 ✉ *46002* – Ⓜ *Colón* – ☏ *963 52 97 64*
– www.marisqueriascivera.com
– Closed 1-7 August   **G3**
Rest – Carte 45/80 €
♦ Fish and seafood ♦ Mediterranean ♦
The Civera specialises in fish, seafood and savoury rice dishes. It has a bar with several tables, enticing display cabinets and a dining room with a maritime ambience. Interesting glass-fronted wine cellar.

XX **Canyar**   [AC] [⟺] [VISA] [⦿⦿] [AE] [①]

Segorbe 5 ✉ *46004* – Ⓜ *Bailén* – ☏ *963 41 80 82*
– www.canyarrestaurante.com
– Closed August and Sunday   **F3**
Rest – Menu 55/73 € – Carte approx. 42 € ⍁
♦ Traditional ♦ Classic ♦
The Canyar is somewhat unusual in that it combines old-style decor with modernist detail. It features an astutely selected wine list and high quality fish that arrives daily from Denia.

XX **Chust Godoy**   [AC] [⟺] [VISA] [⦿⦿] [AE]

Boix 6 ✉ *46003* – Ⓜ *Alameda* – ☏ *963 91 38 15* – *www.chustgodoy.com*
– Closed Holy Week, August and Sunday   **G1**
Rest – Carte 30/45 €
♦ Traditional ♦ Cosy ♦
The owner-chef and his wife run this well-respected restaurant. It has a neo-rustic dining room and an attractive private room upstairs. Market-based menu including a good selection of savoury rice dishes.

X ☺ **Montes**   [AC] [VISA] [⦿⦿] [AE] [①]

pl. Obispo Amigó 5 ✉ *46007* – Ⓜ *Pl. España* – ☏ *963 85 50 25*
– Closed Holy Week, August, Sunday dinner, Monday and Tuesday dinner
Rest – Menu 13/25 € – Carte 24/35 €   **E3**
♦ Traditional ♦ Classic ♦
This restaurant serves traditional cuisine at reasonable prices. It has a small entrance hall, a long dining room, and at the back of the building, the main restaurant is decorated in classical style with regionally inspired decor.

SPAIN - VALENCIA

✂ **Mey Mey**   🅰🅲 ᵛⁱˢᵃ ⓒⓞ 🅰🅴 ⓞ

Historiador Diago 19 ⊠ *46007* – Ⓜ *Pl. Espanya* – ☎ *963 84 07 47*
– *www.mey-mey.com*
– *Closed Sunday dinner*   **E3**
Rest – Menu 15 € – Carte 20/35 €
♦ Chinese ♦ Exotic ♦
Decorated in typical Chinese style, this well-run restaurant has an attractive circular fountain with colourful fish. Cantonese cuisine with an emphasis on steamed dishes.

✂ **Ocho y Medio**   🍴 🅰🅲 ⇕ ᵛⁱˢᵃ ⓒⓞ 🅰🅴

pl. Lope de Vega 5 ⊠ *46001* – ☎ *963 92 20 22* – *www.elochoymedio.com*
Rest – Carte 35/42 €   **F2**
♦ Traditional ♦ Cosy ♦
The major selling point of this restaurant is its location fronting a charming small square. Pleasant terrace and two dining rooms, where guests can choose from a traditional menu featuring a selection of sweet and savoury rice dishes.

CIUDAD DE LAS ARTES – HARBOURS – BEACHES   *Plan III*

 The Westin València 🍴 ℔ 🌐 🖥 ㋐ rm, 🅰🅲 🔱 🚗
Amadeo de Saboya 16 ⊠ *46010* – Ⓜ *Alameda* ᵛⁱˢᵃ ⓒⓞ 🅰🅴 ⓞ
– ☎ *963 62 59 00* – *www.westinvalencia.com* **J1**
130 rm – ♥♥150/585 €, ⊑ 23 € – 5 suites
Rest *The Gourmet* – Menu 20/50 € – Carte approx. 45 €
♦ Luxury ♦ Classic ♦
The Westin is housed in one of the city's historic buildings. Large patio, magnificent spa and spacious, superbly appointed guestrooms decorated in a classic, elegant style. The gastronomic restaurant has an exclusive feel with three private rooms, an open kitchen and a traditional menu.

 Las Arenas ≤ 🛏 🍴 ℔ 🎿 🖥 🅰🅲 🛜 🔱 🚗 ᵛⁱˢᵃ ⓒⓞ 🅰🅴 ⓞ
Eugenia Viñes 22 ⊠ *46011* – Ⓜ *Neptú* – ☎ *963 12 06 00*
– *www.h-santos.es* **K2**
243 rm – ♥♥145/555 €, ⊑ 23 € – 10 suites
Rest *Brasserie Sorolla* – Carte 42/60 €
♦ Luxury ♦ Business ♦ Classic ♦
This luxury hotel, located right on the beach, is divided between three buildings and features welcoming public areas, superb meeting rooms, and well-appointed guestrooms. In the elegant Brasserie Sorolla the focus is very much on creative cuisine.

 Neptuno ≤ ℔ ㋐ 🅰🅲 🛜 🚗 ᵛⁱˢᵃ ⓒⓞ 🅰🅴 ⓞ
paseo de Neptuno 2 ⊠ *46011* – Ⓜ *Neptú* – ☎ *963 56 77 77*
– *www.hotelneptunovalencia.com* **K2**
50 rm ⊑ – ♥115/135 € ♥♥135/150 €
Rest *Tridente* – see restaurant listing
♦ Holiday hotel ♦ Business ♦ Modern ♦
This contemporary-style hotel on the beach offers extremely bright bedrooms with a minimalist theme. They are all decorated with teak furniture and fitted with hydromassage bathtubs. The interesting and traditional restaurant menu includes several rice dishes.

Abba Acteón ℔ ㋐ rm, 🅰🅲 🛜 🔱 🚗 ᵛⁱˢᵃ ⓒⓞ 🅰🅴 ⓞ
Escultor Vicente Beltrán Grimal 2 ⊠ *46023* – Ⓜ *Ayora* – ☎ *963 31 07 07*
– *www.abbahoteles.com* **J2**
182 rm – ♥55/309 € ♥♥55/329 €, ⊑ 15 € – 5 suites
Rest *Amalur* – (Closed Sunday) Menu 15/21 € – Carte 27/44 €
♦ Chain hotel ♦ Contemporary ♦
A chain hotel with a good choice of meeting rooms and spacious, external-facing bedrooms that are both bright and functional. The simply furnished restaurant offers an à la carte menu featuring an impressive choice of traditional dishes.

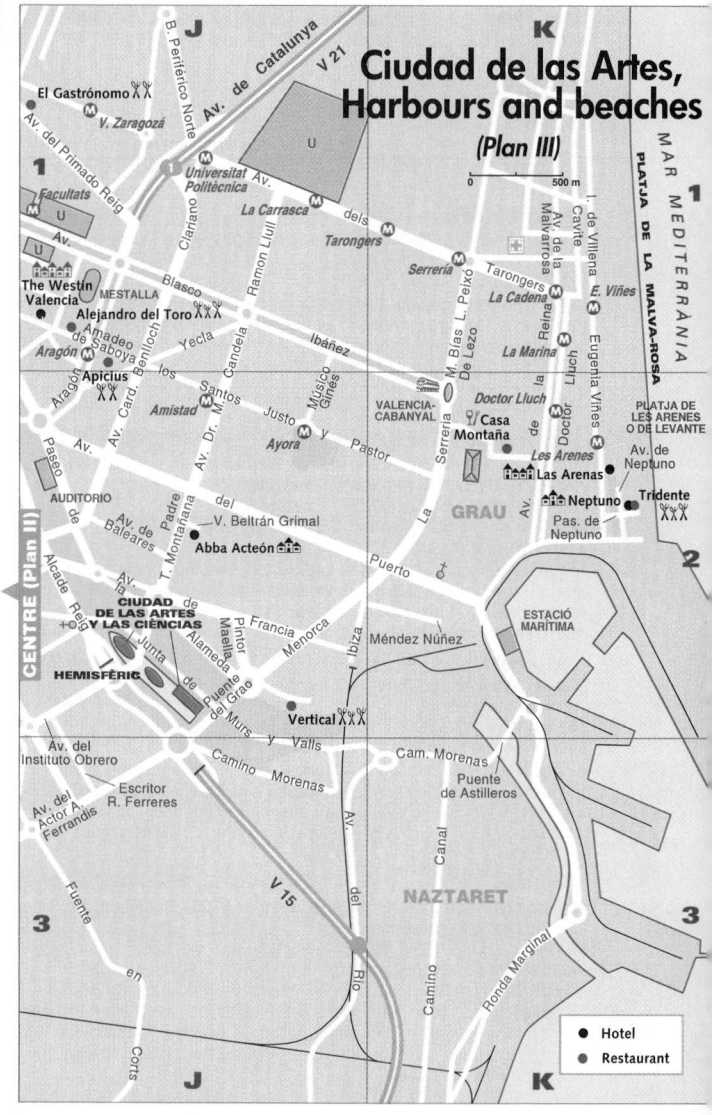

Ciudad de las Artes, Harbours and beaches
(Plan III)

El Gastrónomo
V. Zaragozá
Facultats
Universitat Politècnica
La Carrasca
The Westin Valencia
MESTALLA
Alejandro del Toro
Amadeo de Savoya
Apicius
Aragón
Amistad
Ayora
AUDITORIO
V. Beltrán Grimal
Abba Acteón
CIUDAD DE LAS ARTES Y LAS CIÈNCIES
HEMISFÈRIC
Vertical

Serrería
La Cadena
La Marina
VALENCIA-CABANYAL
Doctor Lluch
Casa Montaña
Les Arenes
Las Arenas
Neptuno
Tridente
GRAU
ESTACIÓ MARÍTIMA
Méndez Núñez
Puente de Astilleros
NAZTARET

MAR MEDITERRÀNIA
PLATJA DE LA MALVA-ROSA
E. Viñes
PLATJA DE LES ARENES O DE LEVANTE
Av. de Neptuno
Pas. de Neptuno

0   500 m

● Hotel
● Restaurant

XXX **Alejandro del Toro** 〔AK〕〔✿〕〔VISA〕〔AE〕

Amadeo de Saboya 15 ✉ *46010 –* Ⓜ *Aragón –* ☏ *963 93 40 46*
– www.restaurantealejandrodeltoro.com
– Closed 1-15 September, Sunday and Monday **J1**
Rest – Menu 35/82 € – Carte 45/75 €
♦ Creative ♦ Trendy ♦
The owner-chef here serves creative cuisine in a spacious dining room with a minimalist aesthetic. Glazed wine cellar that leaves the kitchen visible to diners.

XXX **Vertical** (Jorge de Andrés) 〔≼〕〔AK〕〔VISA〕〔◎◎〕〔AE〕〔⓪〕
🏵️
Luis García Berlanga 19 ✉ *46013 –* ☏ *963 30 38 00*
– www.restaurantevertical.com
– Closed Sunday lunch **J2**
Rest – *(set menu only)* Menu 35/63 €
♦ Creative ♦ Trendy ♦
In addition to its interesting creative cuisine, which is reflected in its gastronomic menus, Vertical stands out for its attractive decor and excellent views from its location on the top floor of the Confortel Aqua 4 hotel. Contemporary look in the dining room, as well as an unusual chill-out terrace.
➜ Ensalada de moluscos y micro vegetales con licuado de ensalada valenciana. Buey a la royal. Naranja, almendra y azafrán.

XXX **Tridente** – Hotel Neptuno 〔≼〕〔AK〕〔VISA〕〔◎◎〕〔AE〕〔⓪〕

paseo de Neptuno 2 ✉ *46011 –* Ⓜ *Neptú –* ☏ *963 56 77 77*
– www.hotelneptunovalencia.com
– Closed 7-31 January and Sunday dinner **K2**
Rest – Menu 29/49 € – Carte 67/74 €
♦ Traditional ♦ Fashionable ♦
A major selling point for this hotel is its beachfront location. There is a partitionable dining room with an avant-garde design. Enjoy interesting and innovative à la carte choices alongside several tasting menus and savoury rice dishes.

XX **El Gastrónomo** 〔AK〕〔VISA〕〔◎◎〕〔AE〕

av. Primado Reig 149 ✉ *46020 –* Ⓜ *Benimaclet –* ☏ *963 69 70 36*
– www.elgastronomorestaurante.com
– Closed August, Sunday and Monday dinner **J1**
Rest – Menu 25/40 € – Carte 34/42 €
♦ International ♦ Classic ♦
An old-fashioned, highly professional restaurant with traditional decor. Good choice of dishes, including the house speciality, steak tartare.

XX **Apicius** 〔AK〕〔VISA〕〔◎◎〕〔AE〕

Eolo 7 ✉ *46021 –* Ⓜ *Aragón –* ☏ *963 93 63 01*
– www.restaurante-apicius.com
– Closed Holy Week, August, Saturday lunch and Sunday **J1-2**
Rest – Menu 25/46 € – Carte 36/50 € ❀
♦ Traditional ♦ Fashionable ♦
The single dining room is both spacious and contemporary in feel with an emphasis on modern, seasonal cuisine. The extensive wine cellar has a particularly fine selection of German whites.

Y/ **Casa Montaña** 〔AK〕〔VISA〕〔◎◎〕〔AE〕

José Benlliure 69 ✉ *46011 –* Ⓜ *Cabañal –* ☏ *963 67 23 14*
– www.emilianobodega.com
– Closed Sunday dinner **K2**
Tapa 4 € **Ración** approx. 12 €
♦ Traditional ♦ Wine bar ♦
An old tavern-style eatery decorated in typical style, including large wine barrels. Various private rooms, an impressive tapas menu and a wine list featuring several prestigious labels.

SPAIN - VALENCIA

Meliá València ≤ ⅃ 📶 🛜 🛁 🚗 🚗 🅥🅢🅐 ⓪ 🅐🅔

av. Cortes Valencianas 52 ⊠ *46015* – ℰ *963 03 00 00* – *www.melia.com*
265 rm – ♂♀75/200 €, ⌷ 17 € – 38 suites **B1**
Rest – Menu 25 € – Carte approx. 50 €
♦ Chain hotel ♦ Modern ♦

This impressive modern building stands alongside the city's Palacio de Congresos. It has a large lobby and attractive panoramic lifts. Superbly appointed guestrooms, with those on the upper floors enjoying magnificent views. Choose from a contemporary à la carte menu in the informal, multi-purpose restaurant.

Sorolla Palace 🝳 🝴 🝵 ⅃ rm, 📶 🛜 🛁 🚗 🅥🅢🅐 ⓪ 🅐🅔

av. Cortes Valencianas 58 ⊠ *46015* – ⓜ *Beniferri* – ℰ *961 86 87 00*
– *www.hotelsorollapalace.com* **B1**
272 rm – ♂♀65/324 €, ⌷ 15 € – 22 suites
Rest – Menu 18/36 € – Carte 23/49 €
♦ Business ♦ Functional ♦

Popular with business travellers thanks to its modern facilities and proximity to the city's conference centre. Guestrooms with a contemporary, functional feel. The restaurant is decorated in a similar style occupying a partitionable dining room complemented by three private dining areas.

Novotel València Palacio de Congresos 🝳 🝴 ⅃

Valle de Ayora 1 ⊠ *46015* rm, 📶 🛜 🛁 🚗 🅥🅢🅐 ⓪ ⓞ
– ⓜ *Beniferri* – ℰ *963 99 74 00* – *www.novotel.com* **B1**
151 rm – ♂♀62/210 €, ⌷ 15 €
Rest – *(Closed Saturday and Sunday lunch except Summer)* Menu 13/16 €
– Carte approx. 30 €
♦ Chain hotel ♦ Business ♦ Functional ♦

This hotel has a decent sized lobby, a variety of lounge areas and pleasantly equipped guestrooms, all with desks and fully equipped bathrooms. The kitchen in this contemporary-style restaurant is in full view of the dining room.

Kaymus ⟳ 🅥🅢🅐 ⓪ 🅐🅔 ⓞ

av. Maestro Rodrigo 44 ⊠ *46015* – ⓜ *Beniferri* – ℰ *963 48 66 66*
– *www.kaymus.es*
– *Closed Monday dinner* **B2**
Rest – Menu 25/59 € – Carte 32/54 € ⅊
♦ Traditional ♦ Fashionable ♦

A modern restaurant known for its high quality cuisine, which is prepared simply yet with great finesse. The wine cellar benefits from similar attention to detail.

SWEDEN
SVERIGE

→ **AREA:**
449 964 km² (173 731 sq mi).

→ **POPULATION:**
9 532 634 inhabitants.
Density = 21 per km².

→ **CAPITAL:**
Stockholm.

→ **CURRENCY:**
Swedish Krona (Skr or SEK).

→ **GOVERNMENT:**
Constitutional parliamentary
monarchy (since 1950).
Member of
European Union since 1995.

→ **LANGUAGE:**
Swedish; many Swedes also speak
good English.

→ **PUBLIC HOLIDAYS:**
New Year's Day (1 Jan); Epiphany
(6 Jan); Good Friday (late Mar/
Apr); Easter Monday (late Mar/Apr);
Labor Day (1 May); Ascension Day
(May); Whit Sunday (late May/June);
National Day (6 June); Midsummer's
Day (Sat between 20-26 June);
All Saints' Day (1 Nov); Christmas
Day (25 Dec); St Stephen's Day
(26 Dec).

→ **LOCAL TIME:**
GMT+1 hour in winter and GMT
+2 hours in summer.

→ **CLIMATE:**
Temperate continental with
cold winters and mild summers
(Stockholm: January -3°C; July 16°C).

→ **EMERGENCY:**
Police, Medical Assistance and Fire
Brigade ☎ **112** – also on-call doctors
and roadside breakdown service.

STOCKHOLM

Gothenburg

→ **ELECTRICITY:**
230 volts AC, 50Hz; 2 round pin
sockets.

→ **FORMALITIES:**
Travellers from the European Union
(EU), Switzerland, Iceland and the
main countries of North and South
America need a national identity
card or passport (America: passport
required) to visit Sweden for less
than three months (tourism or
business purpose). For visitors
from other countries a visa may be
required, in addition to a passport,
especially for those wishing to
stay for longer than three months.
We advise you to check with your
embassy before travelling.

STOCKHOLM
STOCKHOLM

Population: 851 155

imagepassion/Fotolia.com

Stockholm is the place to go for clean air, big skies and handsome architecture. And water. One of the great beauties of the city is the amount of water that runs through and around it; it's built on 14 islands, and looks out on 24,000 of them. An astounding two-thirds of the area within the city limits is made up of water, parks and woodland, and there are dozens of little bridges to cross to get from one part of town to another. It's little wonder Swedes appear so calm and relaxed.

It's in Stockholm that the salty waters of the Baltic meet head-on the fresh waters of Lake Mälaren, reflecting the broad boulevards and elegant buildings that shimmer along their edge. Domes, spires and turrets dot a skyline that in the summertime never truly darkens. The heart of the city is the Old Town, Gamla Stan, full of alleyways and lanes little changed from their medieval origins. Just to the north is the modern centre, Norrmalm: a buzzing quarter of shopping malls, restaurants and bars. East of Gamla Stan you reach the small island of Skeppsholmen, which boasts fine views of the waterfront; directly north from here is Östermalm, an area full of grand residences, while southeast you'll find the lovely park island of Djurgården. South and west of Gamla Stan are the two areas where Stockholmers particularly like to hang out, the trendy (and hilly) Södermalm, and Kungsholmen.

STOCKHOLM IN...

→ **ONE DAY**
Gamla Stan, City Hall, Vasa or Skansen museums, an evening in Södermalm.

→ **TWO DAYS**
Coffee in Kungsholmen, museums in Skeppsholmen, a stroll around Djurgården.

→ **THREE DAYS**
Shopping in Norrmalm, boat trip round the archipelago.

ARRIVAL-DEPARTURE

 Stockholm Arlanda Airport is 40km north of the city. The Arlanda Express train takes 20min to Centralstation and departs every 15min. The airport bus (Flygbuss) to Cityterminalen takes 40min.

 Bromma Stockholm Airport is 7km northwest of the city.

GETTING AROUND

Invest in a Stockholm Card, available from tourist offices. It is valid for 1, 2 or 3 days and offers free travel on public transport, including sightseeing boats, and free entry to over 70 attractions (museums, galleries and castles). The efficient metro system offers a more direct route than the buses. The No. 7 tram, which runs throughout the summer, takes in quite a few of the main attractions. You can buy single tickets for the bus, tram and metro, but if you're planning to do lots of travelling about the city, you can also get passes which cover one or three days.

CALENDAR HIGHLIGHTS

January
The Viking Run (ski race).

April
Walpurgis Night.

May
Stockholm Marathon.

June
Midsummer's Eve celebrations.

July
Jazz Festival, Tall Ships' Races.

August
Festival of Culture.

November
Boat Show.

December
Nobel Prize Day.

SWEDEN – STOCKHOLM

EATING OUT

Everyone thinks that eating out in Stockholm is invariably expensive, but with a little forward planning it doesn't have to be. In the middle of the day, most restaurants and cafés offer very good value set menus. Keep in mind that, unlike in Southern Europe, the Swedes like to eat quite early, so lunch can often begin at around 11am and dinner may start from 6pm. Picking wild food is a birthright of Swedes, and there's no law to stop you going into forest or field to pick blueberries, cloudberries, cranberries, strawberries, mushrooms and the like. This love of outdoor, natural fare means that Stockholmers have a special bond with menus which relate to the seasons: keep your eyes open for restaurants that feature husmanskost (traditional Swedish dishes). While you are here make sure you try somewhere with a good smörgåsbord: if you're lucky, this should include soup, herring, warm potatoes and gravlax, followed by salads, cold meats, meatballs, beef and chicken – perfect with a glass of beer.

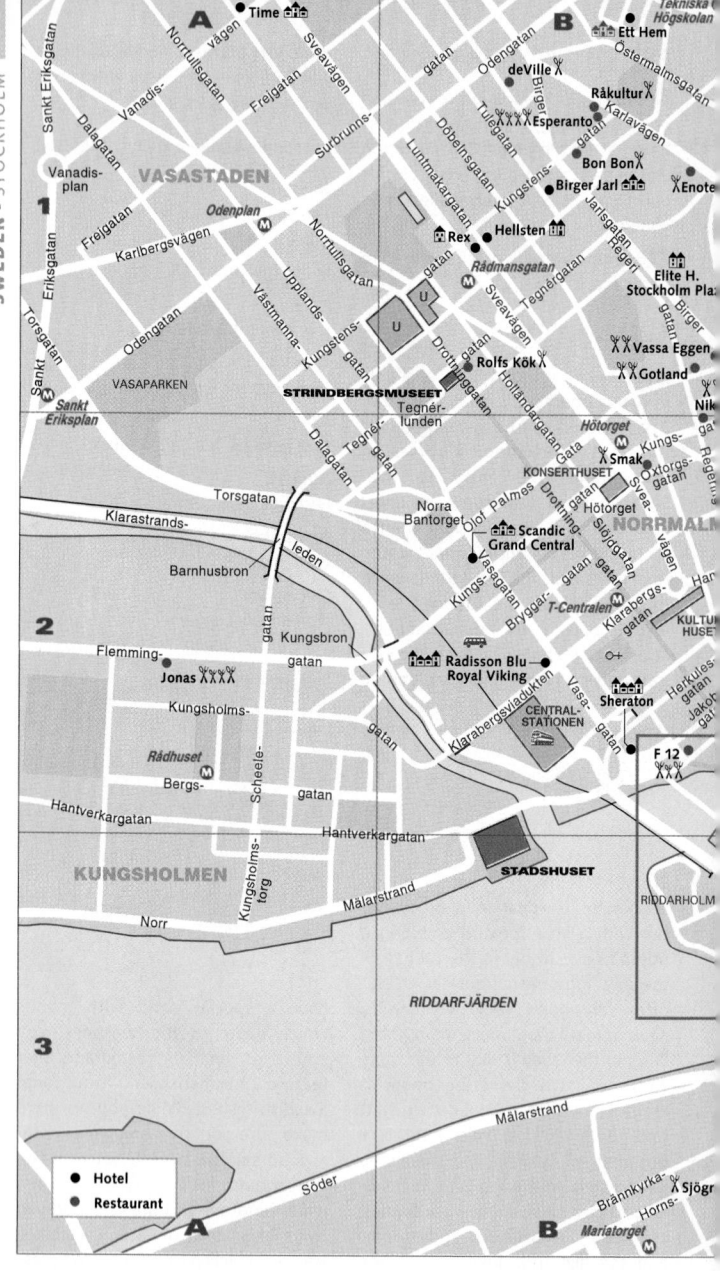

A

Time 🏠🏠

B

Tekniska Högskolan

🏠🏠 Ett Hem

Odengatan

deVille ✕

Råkultur ✕

Esperanto ✕✕✕✕

Bon Bon ✕

Birger Jarl 🏠🏠

✕ Enote

Rex 🏛

Hellsten 🏛

Elite H. Stockholm Plaz

1

VASASTADEN

Odenplan Ⓜ

Rådmansgatan Ⓜ

Vassa Eggen ✕✕

✕✕ Gotland

Rolfs Kök ✕

Nik

STRINDBERGSMUSEET

Tegnér-lunden

Hötorget Ⓜ

Smak ✕

KONSERTHUSET

Torsgatan

Klarastrands-

Norra Bantorget

Scandic 🏠🏠 Grand Central

Hötorget

NORRMALM

leden

Barnhusbron

T-Centralen Ⓜ

KULTUR HUSET

2

Flemming-

Jonas ✕✕✕✕

Radisson Blu 🏠🏠 Royal Viking

Sheraton 🏠🏠

Kungsbron

Kungsholms-

Rådhuset Ⓜ

Bergs-

CENTRAL-STATIONEN

F 12 ✕✕✕

Hantverkargatan

Hantverkargatan

KUNGSHOLMEN

STADSHUSET

Norr

Mälarstrand

RIDDARHOLM

RIDDARFJÄRDEN

3

Mälarstrand

● Hotel
● Restaurant

Söder

✕ Sjögr

A

Brännkyrka-

B

Mariatorget Ⓜ

764

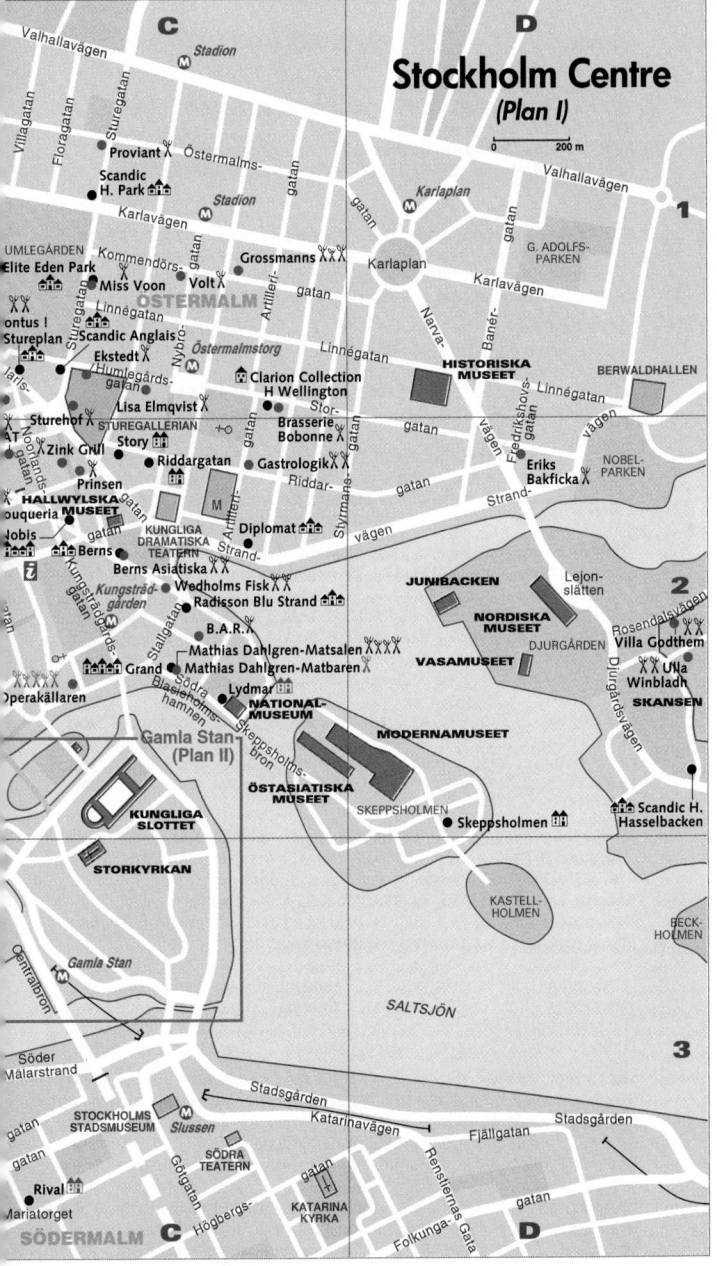

Stockholm Centre
(Plan I)

0   200 m

Valhallavägen

Stadion

Valhallavägen

Karlaplan

Karlaplan

G. ADOLFS-
PARKEN

Karlavägen

BERWALDHALLEN

Proviant
Scandic
H. Park

UMLEGÅRDEN
Elite Eden Park
Miss Voon
Volt
Grossmanns

ÖSTERMALM

Kommendörs-
gatan

Linnégatan

Sturegatan

Linnégatan

Scandic Anglais
Ekstedt

Östermalmstorg

Clarion Collection
H Wellington

HISTORISKA
MUSEET

Linnégatan

Fredrikshovs-
gatan

Lisa Elmqvist

Sturehof
Zink Grill
Story

Stor-
Brasserie
Bobonne

Eriks
Bakficka

NOBEL-
PARKEN

Prinsen
Riddargatan
Gastrologik

Riddar-

HALLWYLSKA
MUSEET

Diplomat

KUNGLIGA
DRAMATISKA
TEATERN

Berns
Berns Asiatiska
Kungsträd-
gården
Wedholms Fisk
Radisson Blu Strand

JUNIBACKEN

NORDISKA
MUSEET

Lejons-
slätten

Villa Godthem

Ulla
Winbladh

SKANSEN

B.A.R.
Mathias Dahlgren-Matsalen
Grand
Mathias Dahlgren-Matbaren
Lydmar

VASAMUSEET

DJURGÅRDEN

Operakällaren

NATIONAL-
MUSEUM

MODERNAMUSEET

Gamla Stan-
(Plan II)

ÖSTASIATISKA
MUSEET

SKEPPSHOLMEN

Skeppsholmen

Scandic H.
Hasselbacken

KUNGLIGA
SLOTTET

STORKYRKAN

KASTELL-
HOLMEN

BECK-
HOLMEN

Gamla Stan

SALTSJÖN

Söder
Mälarstrand

Stadsgården

STOCKHOLMS
STADSMUSEUM
Slussen

Katarinavägen

Fjällgatan

Stadsgården

SÖDRA
TEATERN

Rival

KATARINA
KYRKA

Mariatorget

SÖDERMALM

765

SWEDEN - STOCKHOLM

🏚🏚🏚 Grand ⟨ 🛦 ⏻ 🏊 ☒ & ↳ 🎧 ⚿ 🚗 🆚🆂🅰 ⬢ 🅰🅴 ⬤

Södra Blasieholmshamnen 8 ☒ *S-103 27* – 🅜 *Kungsträdgården* – ℰ *(08) 679 35 00* – *www.grandhotel.se* **C2**

269 rm – 🛏1800/3800 SEK 🛏🛏2800/5200 SEK, ☲ 292 SEK – 31 suites

Rest Mathias Dahlgren-Matsalen 🌼🌼

Rest Mathias Dahlgren-Matbaren 🌼 – see restaurant listing

Rest Verandan – ℰ *(08) 679 35 86* – Menu 615 SEK (dinner) – Carte 415/895 SEK

♦ Grand Luxury ♦ Classic ♦

Majestic waterfront hotel made up of 3 buildings, the oldest dating back to 1874. Impressive conference rooms and splendid spa. Bedrooms range in style and some boast sea views. Stylish all-day bar displays wooden carvings. Classical Verandan restaurant has a pleasant harbour outlook; its buffets are renowned.

🏚🏚🏚 Sheraton ⟨ 🎇 🛦 🏊 & 🎞 ↳ 🎧 🚿 🚗 🆚🆂🅰 ⬢ 🅰🅴 ⬤

Tegelbacken 6 ☒ *S-101 23* – 🅜 *T-Centralen* – ℰ *(08) 412 34 00* – *www.sheratonstockholm.com* **B2**

458 rm – 🛏1295/4995 SEK 🛏🛏1295/4995 SEK, ☲ 259 SEK – 7 suites

Rest 360° – ℰ *(08) 412 34 72* – Menu 259 SEK (lunch) – Carte 415/630 SEK

♦ Business ♦ Modern ♦

Well-run hotel: the first Sheraton to open in Europe. Spacious, well-equipped, modern bedrooms – ask for one with Gamla Stan views or opt for the 7th floor with its dedicated business lounge. Lively restaurant with central open kitchen offers international buffet lunches and traditional Swedish dinners.

🏚🏚🏚 Nobis 🎇 🛦 🏊 & rm, 🎧 🚿 🚗 🆚🆂🅰 ⬢ 🅰🅴 ⬤

Norrmalmstorg 2-4 ☒ *S-111 86* – 🅜 *Östermalmstorg* – ℰ *(08) 614 10 00* – *www.nobishotel.com* **C2**

200 rm – 🛏1490/2690 SEK 🛏🛏2090/3290 SEK, ☲ 175 SEK – 1 suite

Rest Caina – ℰ *(08) 614 10 30 (closed Sunday) (dinner only)* Carte 320/705 SEK

Rest Bistro – ℰ *(08) 614 10 30* – Carte 265/405 SEK

♦ Historic ♦ Design ♦

Formerly two 19C Royal Palaces, then later the bank where the famous 'Stockholm Syndrome' robbery took place. Spacious bedrooms offer clean lines, neutral hues, African wood furniture and Italian marble bathrooms. Small gym and sauna. Rustic Italian menu in basement Caina; informal, all-day Bistro has a pavement terrace.

🏚🏚🏚 Radisson Blu Royal Viking 🛦 🏊 ☒ & 🎞 ↳ 🎧 🚿 🚗

Vasagatan 1 ☒ *S-101 24* – 🅜 *T-Centralen* 🆚🆂🅰 ⬢ 🅰🅴 ⬤ – ℰ *(08) 506 540 00* – *www.royalvikinghotel.com* **B2**

456 rm ☲ – 🛏995/3195 SEK 🛏🛏1095/3295 SEK – 3 suites

Rest Stockholm Fisk – ℰ *(08) 580 01730 (closed Saturday and Sunday lunch)* Menu 455 SEK (dinner) – Carte 278/755 SEK

♦ Business ♦ Modern ♦

Large, central hotel boasting good leisure and meeting facilities. Bedroom styles vary greatly – from classical to newly refurbished with dark wood furnishings and bright, modern fabrics; one suite even has a jacuzzi and a sauna. Contemporary restaurant focuses on seafood; sky bar affords city views.

🏚🏚🏚 Ett Hem 🚗 🛦 🎞 🎧 🆚🆂🅰 ⬢ 🅰🅴 ⬤

Sköldungagatan 2 ☒ *S 114 27* – 🅜 *Tekniska Högskolan* – ℰ *(8) 20 05 90* – *www.etthem.se* **B1**

10 rm ☲ – 🛏3800/4900 SEK 🛏🛏6500 SEK – 2 suites

Rest – *(residents only)* Menu 425/895 SEK – Carte 725/1295 SEK

♦ Luxury ♦ Design ♦ Classic ♦

Charming Arts and Crafts townhouse in a peaceful residential area; built as a private residence in 1910. Cosy lounge with a piano and stove. Bedrooms are spread over 3 floors and come with iPads, wi-fi and marble bathrooms; some have open fires. Meals are served in the kitchen, in the library or on the heated veranda overlooking the sunken garden.

Elite Eden Park   🗲 🍸 ₺ 🅰️ 🛜 👙 🚗 VISA ⓞⓞ AE ⓪

Sturegatan 22 ⊠ *S114 36 –* Ⓜ *Östermalmstorg –* ✆ *(08) 5556 2700*
– www.elite.se   **C2**
126 rm ⌕ – 🛏1480/3990 SEK 🛏🛏1380/4190 SEK – 1 suite
Rest *Miss Voon* – see restaurant listing
♦ Business ♦ Contemporary ♦ Stylish ♦

Smart hotel in a converted office block, designed with the business traveller in
mind. Stylish bedrooms boast comfy beds and large showers – some rooms
overlook the park and some have small balconies. Choose from an Asian-inspired menu in the restaurant or traditional pub-style dishes in their "British pub".

 Scandic Grand Central   🗲 🍸 ₺ rm, 🅰️ rm, 🛜 👙

Kungsgatan 70 ⊠ *S-111 20 –* Ⓜ *T-Centralen*   VISA ⓞⓞ AE ⓪
– ✆ (08) 5125 2000 – www.scandichotels.com/grandcentral   **B2**
387 rm ⌕ – 🛏990/3890 SEK 🛏🛏1540/3990 SEK – 4 suites
Rest *Teaterbrasseriet* – *(closed Saturday and Sunday lunch)* Carte 390/
605 SEK
♦ Chain hotel ♦ Business ♦ Contemporary ♦

Contemporary hotel on the site of the first university in Stockholm (1885), next
to the theatres; its décor tying in with the arts theme of the area. Modern
bedrooms range from cabin bunks to well-equipped suites. The coffee shop
offers snacks, the restaurant serves Swedish classics and the bar has live music.

 Courtyard by Marriott   🗲 ₺ rm, 🅰️ rm, 🛜 👙 🚗

Rålambshovsladen 50 (West : 4 km by Norr   VISA ⓞⓞ AE ⓪
Malastrand A 3) ⊠ *S-112 19 – ✆ (08) 441 3100*
– www.stockholmcourtyard.com
278 rm ⌕ – 🛏1190/3590 SEK 🛏🛏1290/5190 SEK
Rest – Menu 215/444 SEK – Carte 272/544 SEK
♦ Chain hotel ♦ Modern ♦ Functional ♦

Extremely spacious, new-build hotel set just outside the city centre, opposite a
park and lake. Choice of 12 well-equipped meeting rooms. Generously proportioned modern bedrooms boast huge beds and the latest mod cons. The open-
plan dining room is popular with the locals, offering menus with Swedish roots.

 Radisson Blu Strand   🗲 🍸 ₺ 🅰️ 👙 🛜 👙 VISA ⓞⓞ AE ⓪

Nybrokajen 9 ⊠ *S-103 27 –* Ⓜ *Kungsträdgården – ✆ (08) 506 640 00*
– www.radissonblu.se/strandhotell-stockholm   **C2**
152 rm – 🛏1300/2900 SEK 🛏🛏1500/3400 SEK, ⌕ 170 SEK
Rest *Strand* – Carte 265/515 SEK
♦ Chain hotel ♦ Contemporary ♦

Well-run hotel in a lively harbourside setting, part-dating from the 1912 Olympics. Choose from modern, masculine or fresh New England style bedrooms:
many have water views and balconies; the impressive Tower Suite boasts a private roof terrace. The courtyard restaurant mixes Swedish and international cuisine.

 Diplomat   🗲 🍸 🍸 👙 🛜 👙 VISA ⓞⓞ AE ⓪

Strandvägen 7c ⊠ *S-104 40 –* Ⓜ *Kungsträdgården – ✆ (08) 459 68 00*
– www.diplomathotel.com
– Closed 23-26 December   **C2**
126 rm – 🛏2750/2900 SEK 🛏🛏3150/3700 SEK, ⌕ 195 SEK – 4 suites
Rest *T Bar* – ✆ *(08) 459 68 02* – Carte 385/690 SEK
♦ Traditional ♦ Classic ♦

Attractive 1911 art nouveau building blending early 20C charm with contemporary furnishings and facilities. Cosy library-lounge and lovely preserved cage lift.
Elegant bedrooms in pastel hues: all boast marble bathrooms and some have
harbour views. Scandinavian-inspired brasserie dishes in all-day T Bar.

Berns ⇔ 🤶 🕸 VISA ⓪ AE ⓪

Näckströmsgatan 8, Berzelii Park ⊠ *S-111 47* – Ⓜ *Kungsträdgården*
– ℰ *(08) 566 322 00* – *www.berns.se*　　　　　　　　　　　　**C2**
79 rm – ♦1290/2490 SEK ♦♦1690/2890 SEK, ⊑ 220 SEK – 3 suites
Rest *Berns Asiatiska* – see restaurant listing
♦ Business ♦ Historic ♦ Stylish ♦

Originally a theatre built in 1863 by the Royal Family tailor, this building was the venue for the first cancan dance performance in Sweden. Its interior is now modern and minimalist; the newer bedrooms are the largest and most comfortable.

 ## Scandic H. Park 🕸 🛗 🕸 ♿ AC ⇔ 🤶 🕸 🛌 VISA ⓪ AE ⓪

Karlavägen 43 ⊠ *S-102 46* – Ⓜ *Stadion* – ℰ *(08) 517 348 00*
– *www.scandichotels.com/park*　　　　　　　　　　　　**C1**
199 rm ⊑ – ♦1090/3350 SEK ♦♦1190/3450 SEK – 2 suites
Rest *Park Village* – Menu 139 SEK (lunch) – Carte 245/455 SEK
♦ Business ♦ Chain hotel ♦ Functional ♦

Up-to-date hotel in a chic neighbourhood, facing Humlegården Park. Dark furniture contrasts with light walls in large, functional bedrooms; contemporary suites afford lovely park or avenue views. Park Village offers a French-orientated menu and boasts oversized windows and a pleasant summer terrace.

 ## Scandic Anglais 🛗 🕸 ♿ AC ⇔ 🤶 🛌 🕸 VISA ⓪ AE ⓪

Humlegårdsgatan 23 ⊠ *S-102 44* – Ⓜ *Östermalmstorg* – ℰ *(08)*
517 340 00 – *www.anglais.se*　　　　　　　　　　　　**C1**
218 rm ⊑ – ♦1290/3000 SEK ♦♦1550/3200 SEK – 12 suites
Rest – *(closed Christmas and Sunday)* Menu 135/285 SEK – Carte 305/625 SEK
♦ Chain hotel ♦ Business ♦ Modern ♦

Modern hotel right in the heart of town, with a stylish, open-plan lobby, well-equipped conference rooms and a choice of bars. Bedrooms range from tiny, windowless cellar rooms to spacious suites with balconies and park views. Open-plan restaurant offers buffet lunches and classic Swedish staples at dinner.

 ## Stureplan ⇔ 🤶 🛌 VISA ⓪ AE ⓪

Birger Jarlsgatan 24-26 ⊠ *S-114 34* – Ⓜ *Östermalmstorg* – ℰ *(08)*
440 66 00 – *www.hotelstureplan.se*　　　　　　　　　　　　**C1**
101 rm ⊑ – ♦1195/3100 SEK ♦♦1395/4195 SEK
Rest *Ostra Matsal* – ℰ *(08) 6788009 (closed Sunday lunch)* Carte 325/720 SEK
♦ Traditional ♦ Classic ♦

Ornate 19C building with a Gustavian-style interior and up-to-date amenities. Charming, individually styled bedrooms: choose from compact 'Cabin' (in the basement); functional, modern 'Loft'; or more spacious 'Classic'. Laid-back restaurant offers traditional seafood dishes in unfussy flavour combinations.

 ## Birger Jarl 🛗 ♿ ⇔ 🤶 🛌 🕸 VISA ⓪ AE ⓪

Tulegatan 8 ⊠ *S - 104 32* – Ⓜ *Rådmansgatan* – ℰ *(08) 674 18 00*
– *www.birgerjarl.se*　　　　　　　　　　　　**B1**
263 rm ⊑ – ♦1090/2790 SEK ♦♦1190/2990 SEK – 8 suites
Rest – *(closed lunch Saturday and Sunday)* Carte 288/508 SEK
♦ Business ♦ Design ♦ Modern ♦

1970s building set in a residential area and named after the city's founder. An unassuming façade belies its chic interior: the lobby features modern Swedish art and 17 of the chic bedrooms are styled by famous native designers. Regional dishes and express business lunches offered in the bright restaurant.

Time without rest 🕭 ᕒ ⇞ 🛜 🚿 🚗 📟 🔟 📟 🆔

Vanadisvägen 12 ⊠ S-113 46 – ⓜ Odenplan – ℰ (08) 54 54 73 00
– www.timehotel.se   **A1**
144 rm ⌷ – **†**750/2850 SEK **††**950/3550 SEK
♦ Business ♦ Modern ♦

Spacious, purpose-built business hotel in a pleasant residential area on the edge of town. High-ceilinged lobby and modern buffet breakfast room. Large, functional bedrooms and studios; some with comfy chairs or balconies. Friendly team.

 Lydmar ⇐ 🕭 ᕒ 🖾 ⇞ 🛜 📟 📟 🆔

Södra Blasieholmshamnen 2 ⊠ S-103 24 – ⓜ Kungsträdgården – ℰ (08)
22 31 60 – www.lydmar.com   **C2**
40 rm ⌷ – **†**3200 SEK **††**3200 SEK – 6 suites   **Rest** – Carte 318/605 SEK
♦ Townhouse ♦ Stylish ♦ Design ♦

Charming townhouse, superbly located opposite the Palace; once a store for the adjacent museum's archives. The gallery entrance sets the scene with eclectic art and unusual décor. Spacious bedrooms boast funky furnishings and stylish bathrooms. Casual lounge and smart roof terrace with a cocktail bar. Attractive restaurant offers modern European brasserie menu.

 Story ᕒ 🛜 📟 📟 🆔

Riddargatan 6 ⊠ S-114 35 – ⓜ Östermalmstorg – ℰ (08) 545 039 40
– www.storyhotels.com   **C2**
83 rm ⌷ – **†**1190/1990 SEK **††**2380/7990 SEK
Rest Story Kitchen – (closed Sunday) Carte 354/648 SEK
♦ Townhouse ♦ Personalised ♦ Design ♦

Collection of converted townhouses with a stylish, bohemian feel. Modern bedrooms display interesting designer touches, including headboards made from the old house doors. Delightful bathrooms boast monsoon showers. Casual restaurant offers an eclectic global menu; live music is a feature in the funky bar.

 Riddargatan without rest ⇞ 🛜 🚿 📟 📟 🆔

Riddargatan 14 ⊠ S-114 35 – ⓜ Östermalmstorg – ℰ (08) 555 730 00
– www.profilhotels.se   **C2**
74 rm ⌷ – **†**995/2130 SEK **††**1250/2530 SEK – 4 suites
♦ Business ♦ Modern ♦ Stylish ♦

Smart hotel close to the shops, restaurants and theatres. Bedrooms in the newer wing have bright, bold designs and modern wet rooms; all have exercise DVDs, weights and maps for joggers. Contemporary breakfast room doubles as a lively bar.

 Elite H. Stockholm Plaza 🕭 ᕒ ⇞ 🛜 🚿 📟 📟 🆔

Birger Jarlsgatan 29 ⊠ S-103 95 – ⓜ Östermalmstorg – ℰ (08)
566 220 00 – www.elite.se
– Closed 23-26 December   **B1**
131 rm ⌷ – **†**1290/3190 SEK **††**1690/3790 SEK – 12 suites
Rest Vassa Eggen – see restaurant listing
♦ Business ♦ Chain hotel ♦ Functional ♦

Attractive building dating from 1884; located right in the centre of the city with the shops nearby. Bright lobby and basement conference facilities. Modern, functional bedrooms come in neutral hues – opt for one of the contemporary suites.

 Hellsten without rest 🛏 🕭 ᕒ ⇞ 🛜 🚿 📟 📟 🆔

Luntmakargatan 68 ⊠ S-113 51 – ⓜ Rådmansgatan – ℰ (08) 661 86 00
– www.hellsten.se   **B1**
78 rm ⌷ – **†**990/1590 SEK **††**1290/3090 SEK
♦ Townhouse ♦ Personalised ♦ Cosy ♦

Quirky hotel filled with interesting pieces from the owner's globetrotting adventures. Choose from large, high-ceilinged bedrooms or smaller, more uniquely styled rooms. Snacks are served in the bar, which features live jazz on Thursdays.

SWEDEN - STOCKHOLM

Clarion Collection H. Wellington without rest 🛜 🚗 VISA ⚫ AE ⓿ 🏡 ♿ ↩

Storgatan 6 ✉ *S-114 51*
– ⓜ *Östermalmstorg* – ✆ *(08) 667 09 10* – *www.wellington.se*
– *Closed 21 December-3 January*   **C1**
58 rm ⌖ – †820/2580 SEK ††1120/3120 SEK – 2 suites
♦ Business ♦ Functional ♦

Well-run, centrally located former office block, ideally set for shopping and tourism. Contemporary lounge and pleasant breakfast room. Compact but well-equipped bedrooms come in pastel hues; many have balconies and city or courtyard views.

Rex without rest ↩ 🛜 VISA ⚫ AE ⓿

Luntmakargatan 73 ✉ *S-113 51* – ⓜ *Rådmannsgatan* – ✆ *(08) 16 00 40*
– *www.rexhotel.se*   **B1**
55 rm ⌖ – †890/1490 SEK ††990/2190 SEK
♦ Townhouse ♦ Classic ♦ Personalised ♦

Simple, suburban hotel dating from 1866, exhibiting an eclectic style. Compact bedrooms: those in the annexe are modern and functional; those in the main building, more characterful. Have breakfast on the veranda overlooking the courtyard.

🅇🅇🅇🅇🅇 Operakällaren ↩ ♻ VISA ⚫ AE ⓿

Operahuset, Karl XII's Torg ✉ *S 111 86* – ⓜ *Kungsträdgården* – ✆ *(08)*
676 58 01 – *www.operakallaren.se*
– *Closed July, 23 December-15 January, Sunday and Monday*   **C2**
Rest – *(dinner only)* Carte 606/1559 SEK ✿
♦ Classic ♦ Formal ♦ Luxury ♦

Set in the historic Opera House, this is one of the most opulent restaurants in town. Stunning high-ceilinged room displays 19C wood carvings, original fresco paintings and elegant chandeliers. Seasonal cooking uses complex preparations in ambitious combinations. Modern lounge boasts Royal Palace views.

🅇🅇🅇 Mathias Dahlgren-Matsalen – at Grand Hotel 🅐🅒 ↩
✿✿

Södra Blasieholmshamnen 6 ✉ *S-103 27*   VISA ⚫ AE ⓿
– ⓜ *Kungsträdgården* – ✆ *(08) 679 35 84* – *www.mdghs.com*
– *Closed 12 July-5 August, 23 December-7 January, Sunday and Monday*
Rest – *(dinner only) (booking essential) (set menu only)*   **C2**
Menu 1500/1650 SEK ✿
♦ Innovative ♦ Elegant ♦ Luxury ♦

Ultra-stylish waterfront restaurant in the city's top hotel, which mixes elegant architectural features and contemporary furnishings. Two 8 course menus are presented on an iPad; cooking is light and focuses on textures and natural flavours. Slick, unobtrusive service. Beautiful wine cellar and chef's table.
→ Scandinavian sashimi. Sweetbreads with asparagus and morels. Rhubarb with new potatoes.

🅇🅇🅇 Esperanto (Sayan Isaksson) 🅐🅒 ↩ VISA ⚫ AE ⓿
✿

Kungstensgatan 2, (1st floor) ✉ *S-114 25* – ⓜ *Tekniska Högskolan*
– ✆ *(08) 696 23 23* – *www.esperantorestaurant.se*
– *Closed Christmas and Sunday-Tuesday*   **B1**
Rest – *(dinner only)* Menu 1275 SEK – Carte 585/785 SEK
♦ Innovative ♦ Formal ♦ Luxury ♦

Understated, candlelit restaurant on the first floor of a converted theatre, boasting an impressive curved ceiling and a pleasant lounge-bar. Creative, original cooking is light and flavours are well-defined. Choice of two set menus: one Swedish, the other Oriental. Service is professional and engaging.
→ Roasted langoustine with foie gras and pickled daikon. Sweetbreads glazed in white miso with truffles and Jerusalem artichoke. Braised fennel root with marzipan and blueberries.

XXXX **Jonas** ⓐⓚ ⓥⓘⓢⓐ ⓞⓞ ⓐⓔ

Flemminggatan 39 ✉ *112 32* – ⓜ *Rådhuset* – ℰ *(08) 650 2220*
– www.restaurangjonas.se
– Closed Easter, July, Christmas, Sunday and Monday **A2**
Rest *– (dinner only) (booking essential) (set menu only)* Menu 590/
1175 SEK
Rest *Food and Wine* *– (dinner only)* Carte 335/680 SEK

◆ Innovative ◆ Elegant ◆ Design ◆

Turn left for a cool, formal restaurant serving 6 or 9 uniquely presented dishes featuring modern texture and flavour combinations. Turn right for a relaxed, dark wood furnished room offering fresh, modern dishes cooked on the Josper grill.

XXX **F12** (Danyel Couet) Ⓨ ⓥⓘⓢⓐ ⓞⓞ ⓐⓔ ⓞ
ⓒ *Rödbotorget 2* ✉ *S-111 52* – ⓜ *T-Centralen* – ℰ *(08) 24 80 52*
– www.f12.se
– Closed 24 December, Saturday lunch and Sunday **B2**
Rest *– (booking essential)* Menu 390/1250 SEK – Carte 760/845 SEK

◆ Innovative ◆ Fashionable ◆ Design ◆

Stylish restaurant in the Academy of Arts, with warm green hues and spacious bar. Choice of tasting menu or monthly themed à la carte – both feature a well-balanced mix of traditional and innovative dishes crafted from quality ingredients. Set 'Chef's Choice' and a concise version of the à la carte at lunch.
➜ Sweetbreads with broad beans, caramel and sherry vinegar. Wagyu beef with chanterelles. Blackcurrant and meringue chocolate crisp.

XXX **Grossmanns** Ⓨ ⓒ ⓥⓘⓢⓐ ⓞⓞ ⓐⓔ ⓞ
Kommendörsgatan 23 ✉ *S-114 48* – ⓜ *Stadion* – ℰ *(08) 545 674 30*
– www.grossmanns.se
– Closed 22 December-9 January, Easter, Sunday, Monday and bank holidays
Rest *– (dinner only)* Carte 480/740 SEK ⓑ **C1**

◆ Swedish ◆ Elegant ◆

Candlelit restaurant and wine bar run by a passionate, knowledgeable team. Classically based, French-inspired dishes display modern touches and arrive artfully presented; set menus come with wine pairings. Lighter bites served in the bar.

XX **Gastrologik** (Jacob Holmström and Anton Bjuhr) ⓥⓘⓢⓐ ⓞⓞ ⓐⓔ ⓞ
ⓒ *Artillerigatan 14* ✉ *S 114 51* – ⓜ *Östermalmstorg* – ℰ *(08) 662 3060*
– www.gastrologik.se
– Closed 3 weeks in summer, Christmas, Sunday and Monday **C2**
Rest *– (dinner only) (booking advisable) (set menu only)* Menu 795/
1095 SEK ⓑ

◆ Innovative ◆ Design ◆ Individual ◆

Intimate restaurant owned by two skilled chefs. The evening's produce is displayed on a table, explained by the chefs, and offered in 3 or 6 courses. The emphasis is on top quality Swedish ingredients with minimal accompaniments. The adjoining artisan bakery offers fresh bread and groceries, as well as lunch.
➜ Oyster with fermented cucumber. Medallions of veal with goat's cheese and burnt butter. Crème de panais, salted caramel ice cream.

XX **Wedholms Fisk** ⓡ ⓐⓚ Ⓨ ⓒ ⓥⓘⓢⓐ ⓞⓞ ⓐⓔ ⓞ
Nybrokajen 17 ✉ *S-111 48* – ⓜ *Kungsträdgården* – ℰ *(08) 611 78 74*
– www.wedholmsfisk.se
– Closed Easter, 22 December-2 January, 6 January, Saturday lunch, Sunday and bank holidays **C2**
Rest *– (booking essential)* Menu 995/1350 SEK (dinner) – Carte 495/
1080 SEK

◆ Fish and seafood ◆ Formal ◆

Set on Stockholm's 'little Wall Street', an impressive 19C harbourside building with an elegant interior and friendly service. Unfussy seafood menu lists the likes of turbot, halibut, prawns and scallops, prepared in several different ways.

XX **Berns Asiatiska** – at Berns Hotel   ⇖ ⇔ 🅥🅘🅢🅐 ⓄⒶⒺ ⓄⒾ

Näckströmsgatan 8, Berzelii Park ✉ *S-111 47 –* Ⓜ *Kungsträdgården*
– 𝒞 (08) 566 322 22 – www.berns.se   **C2**
Rest – Carte 235/705 SEK
♦ Asian ♦ Fashionable ♦ Elegant ♦

Stunningly restored rococo ballroom from 1863, boasting a pleasant terrace overlooking Berzelii Park. Extensive Asian fusion menu and a wide-ranging sushi selection at dinner; bento boxes are offered at lunch and a traditional buffet on Sundays. Cooking follows the kaiseki concept of sharing and well-being.

XX **Gotland**   🅥🅘🅢🅐 ⓄⒶⒺ ⓄⒾ

Brunnsgatan 6 ✉ *S-111 38 –* Ⓜ *Östermalmstorg – 𝒞 (08) 20 22 36*
– www.restauranggotland.se
– Closed mid June-mid August, 21 December-6 January, Sunday and Monday
Rest – *(dinner only) (booking essential)* Menu 725 SEK   **B1**
– Carte 510/735 SEK
♦ Swedish ♦ Rustic ♦ Cosy ♦

Intimate restaurant sourcing all of its produce and many furnishings from a small island to the east. Concise menu changes every 6 weeks and offers appealing, flavoursome dishes with a classical base; tasting menu provides the best value.

XX **AG**   🅐🅒 🅥🅘🅢🅐 ⓄⒶⒺ ⓄⒾ

Kronobergsgatan 37 (2nd Floor), Kungsholmen (via Flemminggatan A2)
✉ *112 33 –* Ⓜ *Fridshemsplan – 𝒞 (08) 410 681 00*
– www.restaurangag.se
– Closed July and Sunday
Rest – *(dinner only)* Carte 305/800 SEK 🍴
♦ Meats and grills ♦ Rustic ♦ Fashionable ♦

Industrial, New York style eatery on the 2nd floor of an old silver factory. Swedish, American and Scottish beef is displayed in huge cabinets: choose your accompaniments; maybe opt for a cut for two. Great wine list and smooth service.

XX **Pontus!**   🅐🅒 ⇖ ⇔ 🅥🅘🅢🅐 ⓄⒶⒺ ⓄⒾ

Brunnsgatan 1 ✉ *S-111 38 –* Ⓜ *Östermalmstorg – 𝒞 (08) 545 27300*
– www.pontusfrithiof.com
– Closed Easter, Christmas, midsummer and Sunday
Rest – *(booking essential)* Carte 285/1150 SEK   **C1**
♦ Modern ♦ Fashionable ♦ Brasserie ♦

Lively '3-in-1' eatery that's a hit with the locals. Sample Swedish dishes in the library dining room, or sushi and sashimi at the counter while watching the chefs at work. The bustling bar offers modern Asian cuisine and Friday night tapas.

XX **Niklas**   ⇖ 🅥🅘🅢🅐 ⓄⒶⒺ ⓄⒾ

Regeringsgatan 66 ✉ *S-111 39 –* Ⓜ *Hötorget – 𝒞 (08) 20 60 10*
– www.niklas.se
– Closed Christmas, Easter, Saturday lunch and Sunday
Rest – Carte 345/535 SEK   **B2**
♦ Modern ♦ Fashionable ♦ Friendly ♦

Modern, industrial-style bistro with grey banquettes, sage green chairs and large blackboards on the walls. The owner regularly travels to different regions of the world and uses this inspiration to guide the menus for the next 6 months.

XX **Vassa Eggen** – at Elite H. Stockholm Plaza   🅐🅒 ⇖ 🅥🅘🅢🅐 ⓄⒶⒺ ⓄⒾ

Birger Jarlsgatan 29 ✉ *S-103 95 –* Ⓜ *Östermalmstorg – 𝒞 (08) 21 61 69*
– www.vassaeggen.com
– Closed 23-26 December, Saturday lunch and Sunday   **B1**
Rest – Menu 485/595 SEK – Carte 440/805 SEK
♦ Meats and grills ♦ Fashionable ♦ Rustic ♦

Large, contemporary restaurant and bar in an attractive hotel, with an open kitchen, regularly changing art and a laid-back atmosphere. The appealing steakhouse menu features a mix of meat and seafood dishes; try the tasty Wagyu steaks.

Mathias Dahlgren-Matbaren – at Grand Hotel

Södra Blasieholmshamnen 6 ✉ *S-103 27*   VISA ◯◯ AE ◯
– ◍ *Kungsträdgården* – ℰ *(08) 679 35 84 – www.mdghs.com*
– *Closed 12 July-5 August, 23 December-7 January, Saturday lunch and Sunday*
Rest – Carte 380/755 SEK   **C2**
♦ Modern ♦ Fashionable ♦ Design ♦

Vibrant restaurant featuring stylish design furniture, where you can have anything from one course to a full meal. The concise, modern menu changes up to twice a day, featuring carefully crafted, perfectly balanced recipes with a simple yet playful style. Each dish is prepared and delivered within 7 minutes.
➜ Beetroot, Jerusalem artichoke, truffle and hazelnuts. Seared wild duck with forest mushrooms. Apple crumble with vanilla ice cream.

Ekstedt

                                                                    VISA ◯◯ AE ◯
Humlegårdsgatan 17 ✉ *11 446* – ◍ *Östermalmstorg* – ℰ *(08) 611 1210*
– *www.ekstedt.nu – Closed July, Christmas, Sunday and Monday*
Rest – *(dinner only) (booking advisable)* Menu 650/850 SEK 🍸   **C1**
♦ Meats and grills ♦ Individual ♦ Neighbourhood ♦

Relaxed brasserie where dishes are cooked in a wood-burning oven, over a fire-pit or are smoked through a chimney; the woods range from apple to rowanberry. Choose from the day's set choice or 6 'salt' and 3 'sweet' dishes; all are given their finishing touches at the slate bar. Friendly, professional service.
➜ Chimney-smoked lobster. Spring lamb from the fire pit. Baked rhubarb with vanilla doughnut.

Brasserie Bobonne

                                                               ↳ VISA ◯◯ AE
Storgatan 12 ✉ *S-114 44* – ◍ *Östermalmstorg* – ℰ *(08) 660 03 18*
– *www.bobonne.se – Closed Sunday and bank holidays*   **C1**
Rest – *(booking essential)* Menu 245/495 SEK – Carte 210/595 SEK
♦ French ♦ Cosy ♦ Bistro ♦

Sweet little two-roomed restaurant with comfy chairs, period floor tiles and a homely feel. Open-plan kitchen fills the room with pleasant aromas. Blackboard lists tasty, well-balanced dishes crafted from fresh ingredients. Menus are French-inspired, with modern touches and the odd Swedish recipe featuring.

Proviant

                                                           ↳ VISA ◯◯ AE
Sturegatan 19 ✉ *S-114 36* – ◍ *Stadion* – ℰ *(08) 22 60 50*
– *www.proviant.se*
– *Closed Easter, July, Christmas-New Year, lunch Saturday and Sunday*
Rest – Menu 575 SEK *(dinner)* – Carte 365/645 SEK   **C1**
♦ Swedish ♦ Bistro ♦ Intimate ♦

Lively restaurant boasting smart, contemporary décor, a small counter and an adjoining foodstore; located in a chic residential area by Sture Park. Swedish ingredients feature highly – choose from the rustic, classically based dishes on the blackboard, the French-inspired à la carte or the house specialities.

Sturehof

                                              ⌂ ↳ ✿ VISA ◯◯ AE ◯
Stureplan 2-4 ✉ *S-114 46* – ◍ *Östermalmstorg* – ℰ *(08) 440 57 30*
– *www.sturehof.com*   **C1**
Rest – Carte 276/1044 SEK 🍸
♦ Fish and seafood ♦ Brasserie ♦

A city institution dating back to 1896. The modern interior has a bold, buzzy feel and consists of several rooms; a large glass screen separates the bar and the restaurant. Fresh, unfussy seafood dishes and a superb wine list. Open late.

Miss Voon – at Elite Eden Park Hotel

                                                    AC VISA ◯◯ AE ◯
Sturegatan 22 ✉ *S 114 36* – ◍ *Östermalmstorg* – ℰ *(08) 5052 4470*
– *www.missvoon.se – Closed mid July-mid August*   **C2**
Rest – Carte 415/665 SEK
♦ Asian ♦ Trendy ♦ Design ♦

Smart, Asian-inspired restaurant and large bar, set within a stylish hotel. Simple but tasty selection of bento boxes offered at lunch; the evening à la carte is influenced by Japan, Vietnam and Thailand, with dishes designed for sharing.

✗ ### Eriks Bakficka
🛜 ½↗ 🅅🅸🅂🅰 ⑩ 🅰🅴 ⑩

Fredrikshovsgatan 4 ✉ *S-115 23 –* ℰ *(08) 660 15 99 – www.eriks.se*
– Closed Easter, early July-mid August, Christmas, New Year, Saturday
lunch and Sunday **D2**
Rest – Menu 495 SEK (dinner) – Carte 340/675 SEK
◆ Swedish ◆ Bistro ◆

Set in a residential area close to Djurgårdsbron Bridge; a favourite with the
locals. Bistro-style interior with wood-panelling and marble-topped tables. Simple, unpretentious cooking features old Swedish classics and a 'dish of the day'.

✗ ### Volt
🅅🅸🅂🅰 ⑩ 🅰🅴 ⑩

Kommendörsgatan 16 ✉ *S 114 48 –* ⑩ *Stadion –* ℰ *(08) 662 34 00*
– www.restaurangvolt.se
– Closed 4 weeks summer, Christmas, Sunday and Monday **C1**
Rest – *(dinner only) (booking essential)* Menu 550 SEK
◆ Innovative ◆ Intimate ◆ Neighbourhood ◆

Small restaurant run by a young but experienced team – named after the
phrase 'High Voltage'. Dishes are rustic and boldly flavoured; ingredients are
arranged on the plate in layers, so that each forkful contains a little of everything.

✗ ### deVille
🅅🅸🅂🅰 ⑩ 🅰🅴 ⑩

Roslagsgatan 6 ✉ *S-113 55 –* ⑩ *Tekniska Högskolan –* ℰ *(08) 10 01 53*
– www.restaurangdeville.se
– Closed midsummer, July and Christmas **B1**
Rest – *(dinner only)* Carte 370/615 SEK
◆ French ◆ Bistro ◆

Double-fronted neighbourhood restaurant with colourful rugs on the floor and
a bohemian feel; set in a residential area just north of the city. Flavoursome
dishes have a classical base and display French influences. Open for dinner only.

✗ ### Prinsen
🛜 ½↗ ⇄ 🅅🅸🅂🅰 ⑩ 🅰🅴 ⑩

Mäster Samuelsgatan 4 ✉ *S-111 44 –* ⑩ *Östermalmstorg –* ℰ *(08)*
611 13 31 – www.restaurangprinsen.se
– Closed midsummer, 24-25 December and 1 January
Rest – *(booking essential)* Carte 437/763 SEK **C2**
◆ Traditional ◆ Brasserie ◆ Retro ◆

Characterful eatery with a bustling bistro style and a large basement bar serving
seafood and snacks. Since opening in 1897, it's been frequented by literary and
artistic figures. Menus mix French, Swedish and Mediterranean influences.

✗ ### B.A.R.
🅰🅲 ½↗ 🅅🅸🅂🅰 ⑩ 🅰🅴 ⑩

Blasieholmsgatan 4A ✉ *S-111 48 –* ⑩ *Kungsträdgården –* ℰ *(08)*
611 53 35 – www.restaurangbar.se
– Closed 10 days Christmas-New Year, lunch mid-July to mid-August and lunch
Saturday and Sunday **C2**
Rest – Carte 320/595 SEK
◆ Fish and seafood ◆ Brasserie ◆ Trendy ◆

Spacious, canteen-style restaurant with an industrial feel. Wide-ranging menu
changes with each season and offers some interesting side dishes. For the
daily specials, head to the counter and select your meat or fish from the ice display.

✗
☺ ### EAT
🛜 ₲ 🅅🅸🅂🅰 ⑩ 🅰🅴 ⑩

Jakobsbergsgatan 15 ✉ *111 44 –* ⑩ *Hötorget –* ℰ *(08) 50920300*
– www.eatrestaurant.se
– Closed Christmas and New Year **C2**
Rest – *(bookings advisable at dinner)* Menu 475/545 SEK – Carte 285/
635 SEK
◆ Asian ◆ Brasserie ◆ Fashionable ◆

Slick, modern, Oriental-style bistro with a central cocktail bar; set in an upmarket
shopping mall and offering a fusion of British, French and Asian cuisine – hence
the name 'European Asian Taste'. Dishes are flavoursome and well-executed;
choose from the à la carte or a range of themed set menus for 2+.

X **Boqueria** ⌂ 🕭 VISA ⊚ AE ⓘ

Jakobsbergsgatan 17 ⊠ *S-111 44 –* ⓜ *Hötorget –* ✆ *(08) 307400*
– www.boqueria.se
– Closed 30-31 March, midsummer and 24-25 December **C2**
Rest – Carte 435/860 SEK
◆ Spanish ◆ Tapas bar ◆ Fashionable ◆
Vibrant, bustling tapas bar with high-level, counter-style seating. Appealing menu offers a wide range of authentic Spanish dishes and daily tapas specials. Sangria and pintxos can be enjoyed in the reservation-free, shopping mall area.

X **Enoteca** ⌂ 🕭 VISA ⊚ AE

Karlavägen 28 ⊠ *114 31 –* ⓜ *Tekniska Högskolan –* ✆ *(08) 611 02 99*
– www.enoteca.se
– Closed 22-26 December, first week January, Easter, midsummer and Sunday
Rest – Menu 105/155 SEK – Carte 275/600 SEK ⏣ **B1**
◆ Italian ◆ Wine bar ◆ Friendly ◆
Smart restaurant set in a chic neighbourhood. Authentic Italian cooking; the nightly specials are chalked on blackboards. An 'enoteca' is a regional Italian wine shop – unsurprisingly, the appealing wine list is passionately compiled.

X **Råkultur** ⇔ ⟳ VISA ⊚ AE

Kungstensgatan 2 ⊠ *S-114 25 –* ⓜ *Tekniska Högskolan –* ✆ *(08)*
696 23 25 – www.rakultur.se
– Closed 24 December and Sunday **B1**
Rest – Menu 350/520 SEK (dinner) – Carte 157/536 SEK
◆ Japanese ◆ Trendy ◆
In the same building and run by the same team as Esperanto. The name means 'Raw Culture' and the menu reflects this, focusing on sushi, sashimi and maki, plus some more contemporary Japanese and Swedish recipes. Friendly, informal service.

X **Rolfs Kök** ⇔ VISA ⊚ AE ⓘ
☺
Tegnérgatan 41 ⊠ *S-111 61 –* ⓜ *Rådmansgatan –* ✆ *(08) 10 16 96*
– www.rolfskok.se
– Closed July, 25 and 31 December and lunch Saturday-Sunday **B1**
Rest – *(booking essential)* Carte 385/735 SEK ⏣
◆ Modern ◆ Bistro ◆ Rustic ◆
Buzzy restaurant in a lively commercial district, run by a passionate chef-owner and attracting a loyal local following. Contemporary interior designed by famous Swedish artists. Open kitchen involves guests in the preparation; dishes include homely Swedish classics and blackboard specials. Superb wine list.

X **Smak** ⇔ VISA ⊚ AE ⓘ

Oxtorgsgatan 14 ⊠ *S-111 57 –* ⓜ *Hötorget –* ✆ *(08) 22 09 52*
– www.restaurangentm.com
– Closed July, 24-30 December, Saturday lunch and Sunday **B2**
Rest – *(booking essential)* Menu 130/400 SEK
◆ Innovative ◆ Trendy ◆
Large, contemporary restaurant from the same owners as F12. Express-style light lunches. Interesting dinners consist of innovative tasting plates with Asian influences; choose 3, 5 or 7 dishes by 'flavour', along with a flavour of drink.

X **Bon Bon** VISA ⊚ AE

Kungstensgatan 9 ⊠ *S-114 25 –* ⓜ *Rådmansgatan –* ✆ *(08) 20 17 10*
– www.restaurangbonbon.se
– Closed July, Christmas-New Year and Sunday **B1**
Rest – *(dinner only) (booking advisable)* Carte 165/265 SEK
◆ Modern ◆ Simple ◆ Neighbourhood ◆
Lively, split-level restaurant with a large open kitchen and bar; simply furnished in a modern Scandic style. There's no menu; instead a repertoire of tapas-sized dishes are brought round for you to accept or decline. Go in a group.

※ **Zink Grill** 🛜 ↳ 𝕍𝕀𝕊𝔸 ⊕ 🄰🄴 ⓪

Biblioteksgatan 5 ⊠ *S-111 46* – Ⓜ *Östermalmstorg* – ℰ *(08) 611 42 22*
– www.zinkgrill.se
– Closed 24-25 and 31 December, 1 January and midsummer eve
Rest – Carte 367/588 SEK
C2
♦ French ♦ Bistro ♦

Lively bistro with a French, zinc-topped bar, Spanish tiles and vintage furnishings. Open from early till late, it offers an eclectic French and Italian menu. Charcuterie hangs from the ceiling; fish and meat are cooked on a charcoal grill.

※ **Lisa Elmqvist** ↳ 𝕍𝕀𝕊𝔸 ⊕ 🄰🄴 ⓪

Östermalms Saluhall ⊠ *S-114 39* – Ⓜ *Östermalmstorg* – ℰ *(08)*
553 40410 – *www.lisaelmqvist.se*
– Closed Easter, 24-26 December, Sunday and bank holidays
Rest – *(lunch only)* Carte 263/634 SEK
C1
♦ Fish and seafood ♦ Minimalist ♦

Family-run for over 80 years, a lively, informal operation in an impressive 19C red-brick market hall, complete with a fish counter and deli. Dishes are based on the day's catch and feature quality seafood in unfussy, classical combinations.

AT GAMLA STAN (OLD STOCKHOLM) *Plan II*

🏛 **First H. Reisen** ⇐ 🕅 🕭 rm, 🄰🄲 rest, ↳ 🛜 🕍 𝕍𝕀𝕊𝔸 ⊕ 🄰🄴 ⓪

Skeppsbron 12 ⊠ *S-111 30* – Ⓜ *Gamla Stan* – ℰ *(08) 22 32 60*
– www.firsthotels.com/reisen
F1
138 rm ☲ – 🛉1345/2695 SEK 🛉🛉1525/3250 SEK – 6 suites
Rest *Reisen Bar and Dining Room* – *(dinner only)* Carte 325/585 SEK
♦ Business ♦ Classic ♦

19C waterfront hotel with contemporary black and white décor, a library lounge and a rustic bar. Comfy, functional bedrooms with panelling and dark wood furnishings; some have quayside views. Small leisure facility in 17C vaulted cellar. Bright, modern restaurant; menus mix Swedish and international flavours.

🏨 **Rica H. Gamla Stan** without rest ↳ 🛜 🕍 𝕍𝕀𝕊𝔸 ⊕ 🄰🄴 ⓪

Lilla Nygatan 25 ⊠ *S-111 28* – Ⓜ *Gamla Stan* – ℰ *(08) 723 72 50*
– www.rica.se
F1
50 rm ☲ – 🛉995/2995 SEK 🛉🛉1195/3095 SEK – 1 suite
♦ Historic ♦ Classic ♦ Cosy ♦

Characterful 17C house in a pleasant Old Town setting. Cosy bedrooms are classically styled, well-maintained and equipped with good modern facilities; bathrooms are compact but smart. Top-floor terrace offers superb rooftop and city views.

🏠 **Lady Hamilton** without rest 🕅 ↳ 🛜 🕍 𝕍𝕀𝕊𝔸 ⊕ 🄰🄴 ⓪

Storkyrkobrinken 5 ⊠ *S-111 28* – Ⓜ *Gamla Stan* – ℰ *(08) 506 401 00*
– www.ladyhamiltonhotel.se
E/F1
34 rm ☲ – 🛉1290/3690 SEK 🛉🛉1790/3990 SEK
♦ Historic ♦ Cosy ♦

15C building near the Royal Palace, packed with nautical curios. Charming, classical breakfast room; compact bedrooms with functional furniture and modern bathrooms. The sauna is in the vaulted cellar; the plunge pool is in an old well.

XXX **Brasserie Le Rouge** ↳ 𝕍𝕀𝕊𝔸 ⊕ 🄰🄴 ⓪

Brunnsgränd 2-4 ⊠ *111 30* – Ⓜ *Gamla Stan* – ℰ *(08) 505 244 30*
– www.lerouge.se
– Closed 25 December, Saturday lunch and Sunday dinner
F1
Rest – Menu 145/530 SEK – Carte 345/710 SEK
Rest *Le Bar Rouge* – see restaurant listing
♦ French ♦ Musical ♦ Exotic ♦

In the cellars of a grand old house, a richly decorated restaurant with an extravagant burlesque theme and an exuberant atmosphere. Carefully prepared, classic French dishes have the odd Italian touch and are served by a professional team.

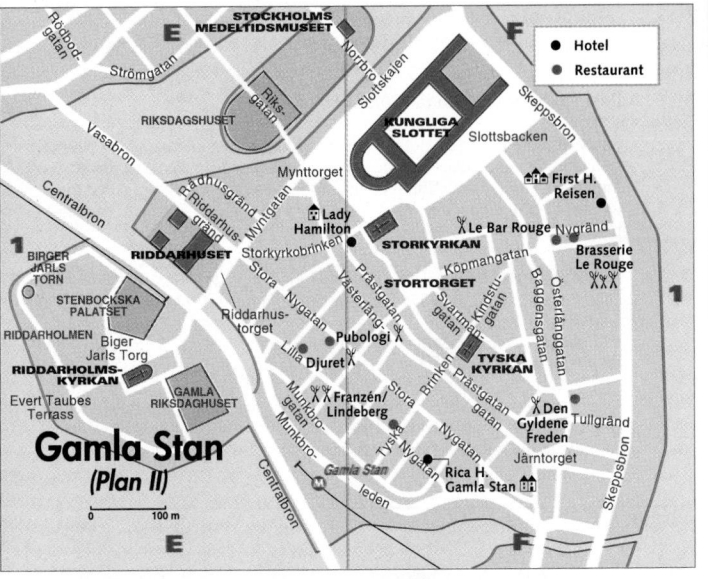

Gamla Stan
(Plan II)

0   100 m

XX   **Frantzén/Lindeberg** (Björn Frantzén/Daniel Lindeberg)   ⊬

❋ ❋   *Lilla Nygatan 21* ⊠ *S-111 28 –* Ⓜ *Gamla Stan*   ⇔ 𝘝𝘐𝘚𝘈 ⓪③ 𝘈𝘌 ⓪
– ℞ *(08) 20 85 80 – www.frantzen-lindeberg.com*
– *Closed mid July-mid August, 2 weeks Christmas-New Year, Sunday and Monday*
Rest – *(dinner only and Saturday lunch) (booking essential)*   **F1**
(set menu only) Menu 2100 SEK ♭
◆ Innovative ◆ Romantic ◆ Fashionable ◆

Intimate restaurant serving just 17 guests an evening, with the experienced chefs on show in the open kitchen. Dishes change daily and are formed around the finest seasonal produce, used at its peak. Refined, creative cooking employs some well-mastered, inventive techniques; flavour combinations are sublime.
➔ Langoustine with melting pig's fat, fennel, celery and caviar. Sweetbreads with flavours of hay and bay leaves. Bark flour pancake with birch ice cream and moss mousse.

XX   **Djuret**   ⊬ 𝘝𝘐𝘚𝘈 ⓪③ 𝘈𝘌 ⓪

Lilla Nygatan 3 ⊠ *S-111 28 –* Ⓜ *Gamla Stan –* ℞ *(08) 506 400 84 – www.djuret.se*
– *Closed two months in summer, Christmas, New Year and Sunday*
Rest – *(dinner only) (booking essential)* Menu 795 SEK – Carte 420/695 SEK ♭
◆ Meats and grills ◆ Rustic ◆ Neighbourhood ◆

Set within a hotel and centred around all things meat. Sit at the bar counter, in the 'Meat' room or in the trophy-filled 'Hunting' room. A concise but appealing menu features a different beast every two weeks. Excellent wine list.

X   **Den Gyldene Freden**   ⊬ ⇔ 𝘝𝘐𝘚𝘈 ⓪③ 𝘈𝘌 ⓪

☺   *Österlånggatan 51* ⊠ *S-103 17 –* Ⓜ *Gamla Stan –* ℞ *(08) 24 97 60*
– *www.gyldenefreden.se – Closed Sunday*   **F1**
Rest – *(booking essential)* Menu 395/450 SEK *(dinner)* – Carte 290/740 SEK
◆ Traditional ◆ Rustic ◆ Inn ◆

Dating back to 1722 and reputedly the city's oldest restaurant; the Swedish Academy – who award the Nobel Prize for literature – meet here weekly. Two rustic, café style, candle-filled dining rooms. Good choice of refined Swedish dishes with modern influences, accompanied by a thoughtfully compiled wine list.

Pubologi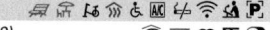

Stora Nygatan 20 ✉ *S-111 27 –* ⓜ *Gamla Stan –* ✆ *(08) 506 400 86*
– www.pubologi.se
– Closed Christmas, New Year, Easter, July and Sunday   **E1**
Rest *– (dinner only)* Carte 470/535 SEK
♦ Innovative ♦ Individual ♦ Rustic ♦

Buzzy restaurant-cum-gastropub with one long, communal table and several smaller ones; each place setting has an illuminated drawer containing the menu and cutlery. Tasty dishes are half usual size and range from cured meat platters to crab croquettes. Wine is displayed on shelves and there are 8 cask beers.

Le Bar Rouge

Österlänggatan 17 ✉ *S-111 31 –* ⓜ *Gamla Stan –* ✆ *(08) 505 244 60*
– www.lerouge.se
– Closed 25 December, Saturday lunch and Sunday   **F1**
Rest – Menu 145/250 SEK – Carte 265/500 SEK
♦ Swedish ♦ Cosy ♦

More casual counterpart to Le Rouge, boasting velvet fabrics, baroque furniture and a charming summer terrace. Have a cocktail before following the sweeping staircase to the restaurant for a classical Swedish dish with a French twist.

AT DJURGÅRDEN   *Plan I*

Scandic H. Hasselbacken

Hazeliusbacken 20 ✉ *S-100 55 –* ✆ *(08)*
517 343 00 – www.scandichotels.com/hasselbacken   **D2**
112 rm ☳ **–** ♠1190/3150 SEK ♠♠1290/3250 SEK – 1 suite
Rest *Restaurang Hasselbacken* *–* ✆ *(08) 517 343 07 (closed Sunday dinner) (dinner only and buffet lunch)* Menu 145/430 SEK – Carte dinner 583/605 SEK
♦ Business ♦ Functional ♦

Located just outside the city centre in Djurgården Park, close to the Vasa Museum; a popular hotel for hosting conferences and events. Simply furnished, functional bedrooms have desks, partial park views and compact bathrooms. The grand restaurant boasts an ornate mirrored ceiling and a pleasant summer terrace.

Ulla Winbladh

Rosendalsvägen 8 ✉ *S-115 21 –* ✆ *(08) 534 897 01*
– www.ullawinbladh.se
– Closed 24-25 December   **D2**
Rest *– (booking essential)* Carte 242/655 SEK
♦ Swedish ♦ Classic ♦ Cosy ♦

Set in a charming park location and originally built as a steam bakery for the 1897 Stockholm World Fair. Choose between several knick-knack filled rooms and a large summer terrace. Traditional Swedish menu features plenty of herring and fish roe in sweet and sour combinations. Buffet-style dining in winter.

Villa Godthem

Rosendalsvägen 9 ✉ *S-115 21 –* ✆ *(08) 505 244 15*
– www.villagodthem.se   **D2**
Rest – Carte 425/710 SEK
♦ Swedish ♦ Cosy ♦

Homely Swiss-style chalet with ornate woodwork, a terrace and a cocktail bar; built in 1874 for opera singer Carl Johan Uddman. Menus features French and Swedish classics, as well as reviving traditional cedar wood 'Planks' of meat and fish.

Skeppsholmen

Grona Gången 1 ⊠ S-111 86 – ℰ (08) 407 23 00
– www.hotelskeppsholmen.se   D2
78 rm ⊑ – **†**1595/2195 SEK **††**1795/2695 SEK – 3 suites
Rest – Carte 335/635 SEK
◆ Historic ◆ Design ◆
Passionately run, 17C hotel, set by a beautiful park on a small, peaceful island;
built by the king in 1699 for his soldiers. Modern Scandinavian art, décor and
furnishings feature throughout; white bedrooms display minimalist influences
and sea or park views. Dining room offers traditional Swedish cuisine.

Clarion H. Stockholm

Ringvägen 98 (South: 3 Km by C3) ⊠ S-104 60
– Ⓜ Skanstull – ℰ (08) 462 1000 – www.clarionstockholm.com
522 rm ⊑ – **†**780/2380 SEK **††**980/2580 SEK – 10 suites
Rest Minami – (closed mid June-mid August, Christmas, Saturday lunch
and Sunday) Carte 265/465 SEK
◆ Business ◆ Modern ◆
Purpose-built hotel with well-equipped conference facilities and a modern, functional style. Spacious lobby and breakfast room; smart spa. Bright bedrooms vary
from singles to sizeable suites. Restaurant offers a wide-ranging, Asian-inspired
menu; eat here, in the lobby or in your room. Live music at weekends.

Rival

Mariatorget 3 ⊠ S-118 91 – Ⓜ Mariatorget – ℰ (08) 545 789 00 – www.rival.se
97 rm – **†**1395/3295 SEK **††**1595/3495 SEK, ⊑ 175 SEK – 2 suites   C3
Rest The Bistro – ℰ (08) 545 789 15 (dinner only and Sunday lunch)
Carte 333/570 SEK
◆ Business ◆ Stylish ◆
Warm, stylish hotel opposite a beautiful square and gardens in a charming
neighbourhood; owned by ABBA's Benny Andersson. Colourful, movie-themed
bedrooms with a pillow menu, DVD player and teddy bear; some have balconies. 700-seater art deco theatre hosts events and shows. Restaurant serves a
wide-ranging global menu; café and artisan bakery offer tempting snacks.

Sjögräs

Timmermansgatan 24 ⊠ S-118 55 – Ⓜ Mariatorget – ℰ (08) 84 12 00
– www.sjogras.com
– Closed 15 July-4 August, 23 December-4 January and Sunday   B3
Rest – (dinner only) (booking essential) Carte 475/670 SEK ❀
◆ French ◆ Bistro ◆ Friendly ◆
Lively restaurant in a pleasant residential area by Mariatorget Park. An open kitchen
dominates the room, which blends Gallic and Scandic styling. Concise, French-influ-
enced menu features some complex combinations. Over 300 choices of rum.

Radisson Blu Sky City

at Terminals 4-5, 2nd floor above street level (Stockholm-Arlanda, Sky City)
⊠ S-190 45 – ℰ (08) 50 67 4000 – www.stockholmfisk.se
229 rm – **†**1350/2350 SEK **††**1600/2600 SEK, ⊑ 145 SEK – 1 suite
Rest Stockholm Fisk – ℰ (08) 506 740 25 – Menu 200/250 SEK
– Carte approx. 405 SEK
◆ Business ◆ Modern ◆ Functional ◆
Comfortable, corporate hotel built into the airport between terminals 4 and 5,
and offering good facilities. Fully soundproofed bedrooms come in three diffe-
rent styles – Ocean, Urban and Chilli; some look out over the runway. Open-plan
bistro looks down onto the shopping plaza and serves a seafood-based menu.

SWEDEN - STOCKHOLM

AT **NORRTULL** North : 2 km by Sveavägen (at beginning of E4)

 Stallmästaregården 🚗 🛏 ⅄ 🛜 🕍 **P** 💳 🟢 🅰🄴 🅞

☒ SE-113 47 – ⓜ Karlberg – 𝒞 (08) 610 13 00 – www.stallmastaregarden.se
– Closed 25 December and 1 January
46 rm ⚏ – †1195/1495 SEK ††1695/2595 SEK – 3 suites
Rest – Menu 295/615 SEK – Carte 515/690 SEK
♦ Inn ♦ Cosy ♦

Brightly painted 17C inn, consisting of several buildings set around a courtyard
and boasting Royal Park, Palace and water views. Swedish décor in guest areas;
good modern comforts in cosy, oriental-themed bedrooms. Large restaurant
offers modern Swedish cuisine influenced by classic Tore Wretman recipes.

AT **LADUGÅRDSGÄRDET** East : 3 km by Strandvägen

 Villa Källhagen 🍴 ⬅ 🚗 🛏 🐾 ⅄ 🛜 🕍 **P** 💳 🟢 🅰🄴 🅞

Djurgårdsbrunnsvägen 10 ☒ S-115 27 – 𝒞 (08) 665 03 00
– www.kallhagen.se
33 rm ⚏ – †1195/2595 SEK ††1395/2795 SEK – 3 suites
Rest – (closed Sunday dinner and lunch in July) Carte 365/665 SEK
♦ Inn ♦ Business ♦ Modern ♦

Well-run hotel in an idyllic waterside location, surrounded by a park and walking
trail. Comfortable guest areas; quiet bedrooms in four contemporary colour schemes inspired by the seasons. Great views from the restaurant and terrace.
Modern Swedish menu has a Mediterranean edge and comes with wine pairings.

AT **FJÄDERHOLMARNA ISLAND** East: 25 minutes by boat from Sodermalm,
or 5 minutes from Nacka Strand

❌❌ **Fjäderholmarnas Krog** ⬅ 🛏 ⅄ 💳 🟢 🅰🄴 🅞

Stora Fjäderholmen ☒ S-111 15 – 𝒞 (08) 718 33 55
– www.fjaderholmarnaskrog.se
– Closed 9 September-26 November and 21 December
Rest – (booking essential) Menu 385/490 SEK – Carte 335/705 SEK
♦ Fish and seafood ♦ Friendly ♦ Rustic ♦

Large restaurant with a cosy bar and spacious terrace, on a lovely island in a
delightful harbourside location. Classical Swedish menu focuses on seafood and
plank steaks; in December it is replaced by a traditional Christmas buffet table.

AT **ENSKEDEDALEN** Southeast : 9 kms by Nynasvagen

❌ **Enskede Krog** 🛏 💳 🟢

Gamla Tyresövägen 326 ☒ S-121 33 – ⓜ Sandsborg – 𝒞 (08) 394 300
– www.enskedekrog.se – Closed Easter, 15 July-6 August, 22 December-3
January, Saturday lunch and Monday dinner
Rest – (booking advisable) Menu 84/236 SEK (lunch)
– Carte dinner 227/463 SEK
♦ Swedish ♦ Neighbourhood ♦ Cosy ♦

Popular neighbourhood restaurant with a small terrace, set on a quiet residential street. Buffet-style lunches feature four hot choices and a fresh salad selection. Classical Swedish dinners rely on seasonal, locally foraged ingredients.

AT **NACKA STRAND** Southeast : 10 km by Stadsgården or 20 mins by boat
from Nybrokajen

🏨 **Hotel J** 🍴 ⬅ 🚗 ♿ 🎛 ⅄ 🛜 🕍 **P** 💳 🟢 🅰🄴 🅞

Ellensviksvägen 1 ☒ S-131 52 – 𝒞 (08) 601 30 00 – www.hotelj.com
154 rm ⚏ – †1245/2595 SEK ††1545/2895 SEK – 4 suites
Rest Restaurant J – see restaurant listing
♦ Historic ♦ Design ♦

20C red-brick hotel with modern extensions and numerous event rooms, set in a
quiet park overlooking the sea. Charming guest areas display characterful maritime knick-knacks. Bedrooms and duplex suites boast quirky, yacht-themed décor.

✗ **Restaurant J** – at Hotel J   ≼ 🖼 ⬍ 📷 ⊙ AE ⓪
Ellensviksvägen 1 ✉ *S-131 52* – 𝒞 *(08) 601 30 00* – *www.hotelj.com*
– *Closed 23 December-7 January except 31 January*
Rest – Menu 120/450 SEK – Carte 289/825 SEK
♦ Swedish ♦ Brasserie ♦

Long, narrow restaurant facing the marina; 20min from the city by boat. Large room features maritime décor, an open kitchen and a sizeable fireplace; oversized windows and a terrace provide superb views. Simple global and Swedish cuisine.

AT LILLA ESSINGEN West : 5.5 km by Norr Mälarstrand

✗✗ **Lux Stockholm** (Henrik Norström)   ≼ 🖼 🖼 ⬍ 📷 ⊙ AE ⓪
£3 *Primusgatan 116* ✉ *S-112 67* – 𝒞 *(08) 619 01 90*
– *www.luxstockholm.com*
– *Closed 4 weeks July-August, 2 weeks Christmas-New Year, Saturday lunch, Sunday and Monday*
Rest – *(booking essential)* Menu 975/1250 SEK (dinner) – Carte 380/880 SEK
♦ Innovative ♦ Design ♦ Cosy ♦

Old waterside Electrolux factory built in 1916, with a bright, modern dining room, closely set tables and a large central counter where the chef finishes dishes on view. Contemporary cooking uses well-sourced, seasonal produce and displays some innovative touches. The knowledgeable team explain every dish.
➜ Rainbow salmon with garden fennel, cress capsules and crayfish. Fir tree smoked mallard, pickled currants and black pudding. Preserved plums with plum sorbet, blackcurrants and lemon verbena.

AT BOCKHOLMEN ISLAND Northwest : 7 km by Sveavägen and E18

✗✗ **Bockholmen**   ≼ 🖼 🖼 ⬍ ✿ 🅿 📷 ⊙ AE
Bockholmsvägen ✉ *S-170 78* – Ⓜ *Bergshamra* – 𝒞 *(08) 624 22 00*
– *www.bockholmen.com*
– *Closed Christmas-New Year, midsummer, midweek lunch (except May-September), midweek dinner and Monday in low season and Tuesday-Wednesday January-February*
Rest – *(booking essential)* Menu 365 SEK bi/695 SEK – Carte 115/195 SEK
♦ Swedish ♦ Friendly ♦ Cosy ♦

Endearing 19C former summer house in an idyllic waterside setting, with a lovely terrace, an outside bar and a friendly team. Wide-ranging menu includes a good value 4 course set selection and weekend brunch. Check opening hours carefully.

AT EDSVICKEN Northwest : 8 km by Sveavägen and E 18 towards Norrtälje

✗✗ **Ulriksdals Wärdshus**   ≼ 🖼 🖼 ⬍ ✿ 🅿 📷 ⊙ AE ⓪
(take first junction for Ulriksdals Slott) ✉ *S-170 79* – Ⓜ *Bergshamra*
– 𝒞 *(08) 85 08 15* – *www.ulriksdalswardshus.se*
– *Closed first 2 weeks January and Monday*
Rest – *(booking essential)* Menu 175/495 SEK – Carte 595/715 SEK 🍴
♦ Traditional ♦ Inn ♦

Delightful 19C inn with winter garden décor, charming private rooms, and park and water views. Tasty, well-presented Swedish dishes are served on weekdays; traditional smörgåsbords at weekends. Smart wine cellar and lovely drinks terrace.

SWEDEN - STOCKHOLM

GOTHENBURG
GÖTEBORG

Population: 513 750

Kjell Holmner/Göteborg & Co/www.imagebank.sweden.se

Gothenburg is considered to be one of Sweden's friendliest towns, a throwback to its days as a leading trading centre. This is a compact, pretty city whose roots go back four hundred years. It has trams, broad avenues and canals and its centre is boisterous but never feels tourist heavy or overcrowded. Gothenburgers take life at a more leisurely pace than their Stockholm cousins over on the east coast. The mighty shipyards that once dominated the shoreline are now quiet; go to the centre, though, and you find the good-time ambience of Avenyn, a vivacious thoroughfare full of places in which to shop, eat and drink. But for those still itching for a feel of the heavy industry that once defined the place, there's a Volvo museum sparkling with chrome and shiny steel.

The Old Town is the historic heart of the city: its tight grid of streets has grand façades and a fascinating waterfront. Just west is the Vasastan quarter, full of fine National Romantic buildings. Further west again is Haga, an old working-class district which has been gentrified, its cobbled streets sprawling with trendy cafes and boutiques. Adjacent to Haga is the district of Linné, a vibrant area with its elegantly tall 19th century Dutch-inspired buildings. As this is a maritime town, down along the quayside is as good a place to get your bearings as any.

GOTHENBURG IN...

➡ ONE DAY
The Old Town, Stadsmuseum, The Museum of World Culture.

➡ TWO DAYS
Liseberg amusement park, The Maritiman, Art Museum, a stroll around Linné.

➡ THREE DAYS
A trip on a Paddan boat, a visit to the Opera House.

PRACTICAL INFORMATION

ARRIVAL-DEPARTURE

✈ Landvetter Airport is 25km east of the city. There are regular bus connections to the city centre, including FlyBussarna; payment is by card only and journey time is around 25min.

✈ City Airport is 15km northwest.

GETTING AROUND

The Gothenburg Card gives you unlimited bus, tram and boat travel within the city and is valid for one or two days. It will also guarantee you a sightseeing tour, admission to the Liseberg amusement park, entry to most museums, and discounts in certain shops. Alternatively, buy a 24 or 72 hour credit card style travel pass for unlimited travel on trams, buses and boats. Single tickets are also available. Punts – flat Paddan boats – are a pleasant way to explore this maritime city in summer, gliding past stately canalside buildings.

CALENDAR HIGHLIGHTS

January
International Film Festival.

April
International Science Festival.

June
Match Cup (Sailing),
Symphony Orchestra Summer Concert.

July
Gothia Cup (Youth Football).

August
Jazz Festival, Culture Festival.

September
Art Biennial.

October
Kulturnatta (Culture Night).

December
Liseberg Christmas Market.

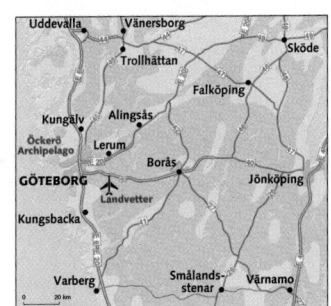

EATING OUT

Gothenburg's oldest food market is called Feskekörka or 'Fish Church'. It does indeed look like a place of worship but its pews are stalls of oysters, prawns and salmon, and where you might expect to find an organ loft, you'll find a restaurant instead. Food – and in particular the piscine variety – is a big reason for visiting Gothenburg. Its restaurants have earned a plethora of Michelin stars, which are dotted all over the compact city. If you're after something a little simpler, head for one of the typical Swedish Konditoris (cafés) – two of the best are Brogyllen and Ahlströms. If you're visiting between December and April, try the traditional cardamom-spiced buns known as 'semla'. The 19C covered food markets, Stora Saluhallen at Kungstorget and Saluhallen Briggen at Nordhemsgatan in Linnestaden, are worth a visit. Also in Kungstorget is the city's most traditional beer hall, Ölhallen 7:an; there are only 6 others in town. Gothenburgers also like the traditional food pairing 'SOS', where herring and cheese are washed down with schnapps.

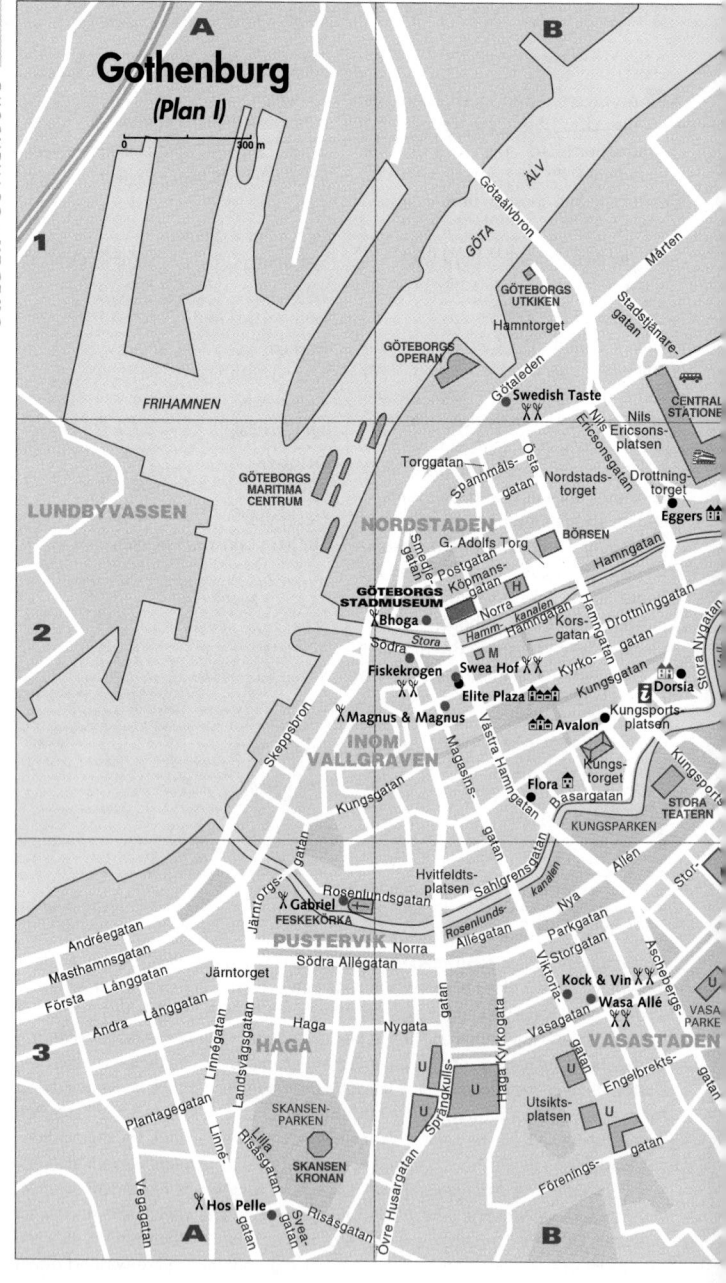

Gothenburg
(Plan I)

0   300 m

A

B

GÖTA ÄLV

GÖTA

Götaälvbron

Mårten

FRIHAMNEN

GÖTEBORGS UTIKEN

Hamntorget

Stadstjänare-gatan

GÖTEBORGS OPERAN

Götaleden

Swedish Taste

Nils Ericssonsgatan

CENTRAL STATIONE

Nils Ericsons-platsen

Torggatan

Spannmåls-gatan

Ota gatan

Nordstads-torget

Drottning-torget

LUNDBYVASSEN

GÖTEBORGS MARITIMA CENTRUM

NORDSTADEN

G. Adolfs Torg

BÖRSEN

Eggers

Smedje-gatan

Postgatan

Köpmans-gatan

Hamngatan

GÖTEBORGS STADMUSEUM

Bhoga

Norra

Hamm kanalen

Stora

Hamngatan

Kors-gatan

Drottninggatan

Stora Nygatan

Södra

Hamngatan

Fiskekrogen

Swea Hof

Elite Plaza

Kyrko-gatan

Kungsgatan

Dorsia

Skeppsbron

Magnus & Magnus

Avalon

Kungsports-platsen

INOM VALLGRAVEN

Madsins-gatan

Västra Hamngatan

Kungs-torget

Kungsgatan

Flora

Basargatan

Kungsports

STORA TEATERN

KUNGSPARKEN

Hvitfeldts-platsen

Sahlgrens-gatan

kanalen

Allén

Stor-

Järntorgs-gatan

Rosenlundsgatan

Gabriel

FESKEKÖRKA

Norra

Rosenlunds-Allégatan

Nya

Parkgatan

Storgatan

Andréegatan

PUSTERVIK

Södra Allégatan

Masthamnsgatan

Järntorget

Kock & Vin

Aschebergs-gatan

Första Långgatan

Wasa Allé

VASA-PARKE

Andra Långgatan

Haga

Nygata

Vasagatan

VASASTADEN

Linnégatan

Landsvägsgatan

HAGA

Haga Kyrkogata

Engelbrekts-gatan

Plantagegatan

SKANSEN-PARKEN

Sprängkulls-gatan

Utsikts-platsen

Linné-

Lilla Risåsgatan

SKANSEN KRONAN

Öfre Husargatan

Förenings-gatan

Vegagatan

Hos Pelle

Svear-gatan

Risåsgatan

A

B

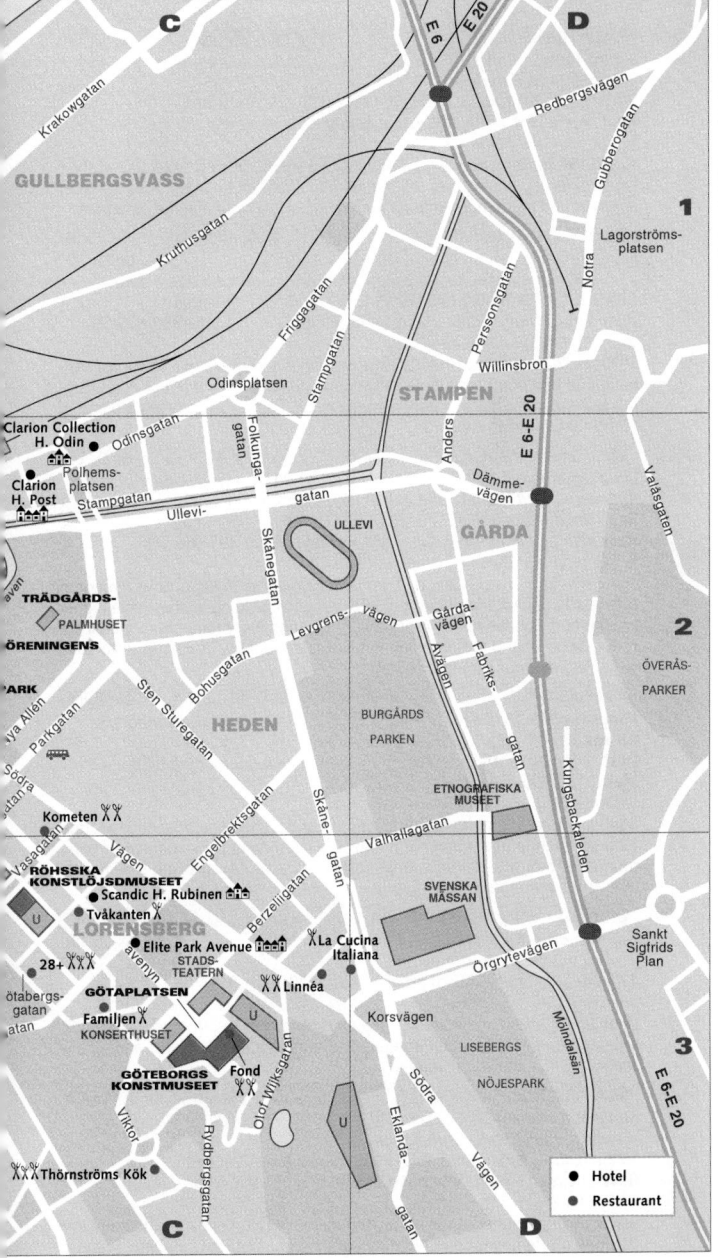

C

D

Krakowgatan

E 6

E 20

Redbergsvägen

Gubberogatan

GULLBERGSVASS

Kruthusgatan

Lagorströms-
platsen

1

Notra

Friggagatan

Stampgatan

Perssonsgatan

Odinsplatsen

Willinsbron

E 6-E 20

STAMPEN

Clarion Collection
H. Odin

Odinsgatan

Folkunga-
gatan

Anders

Dämme-
vägen

Valåsgatan

Clarion
H. Post

Polhems-
platsen

Stampgatan

Ulleví-

gatan

ULLEVI

GÅRDA

TRÄDGÅRDS-

PALMHUSET

Skånegatan

Levgrens-

vägen

Gårda-
vägen

Åvägen

Fabriks-

2

ÖVERÅS-
PARKER

ÖRENINGENS

Bohusgatan

Sten Sturegatan

HEDEN

BURGÅRDS

PARKEN

gatan

Kungsbackaleden

ARK

Nya Allén

Parkgatan

Skåne-

gatan

Valhallagatan

ETNOGRAFISKA
MUSEET

Södra

Engelbrektsgatan

Kometen ✕✕

Vägen

Vasagatan

RÖHSSKA
KONSTLÖJSDMUSEET

Scandic H. Rubinen

SVENSKA
MÄSSAN

U

Tvåkanten ✕

LORENSBERG

Berzeliigatan

Elite Park Avenue

✕ La Cucina
Italiana

Sankt
Sigfrids
Plan

Örgrytevägen

Avenyn

STADS-
TEATERN

28+ ✕✕✕

U

ötabergs-
gatan

GÖTAPLATSEN

✕✕ Linnéa

Mölndalsån

Familjen ✕

KONSERTHUSET

Korsvägen

LISEBERGS

E 6-E 20

3

gatan

GÖTEBORGS
KONSTMUSEET

Fond
✕✕

Olof Wijksgatan

NÖJESPARK

Viktor

Rydbergsgatan

U

Eklanda-

Södra

✕✕✕Thörnströms Kök

gatan

Vägen

● Hotel
● Restaurant

C

D

Elite Plaza 🕭 🕭 🕭 🕭 🕭 🕭 🕭 🕭 🕭

Västra Hamngatan 3 ✉ *S-402 22* – ✆ *(031) 720 40 40* – *www.elite.se*
– Closed 24-26 December **B2**
97 rm ⬚ – ♦1100/2300 SEK ♦♦1400/2500 SEK – 3 suites
Rest *Swea Hof* – see restaurant listing
♦ Luxury ♦ Modern ♦

Grand 19C building near the harbour, with a smart, classical architectural style;
many of its original features still remain. The fifth floor bedrooms are the most
spacious and modern. The fitness room and bar are hidden in the basement.

Elite Park Avenue ⬅ 🕭 🕭 🕭 🕭 🕭 🕭 🕭 🕭 🕭 🕭

Kungsportsavenyn 36-38 ✉ *S-400 15* – ✆ *(031)* 🕭 🕭 🕭
727 1000 – *www.elite.se* – *Closed Christmas, Easter and 22-25 June*
308 rm ⬚ – ♦1050/2150 SEK ♦♦1350/2350 SEK – 9 suites **C3**
Rest *Park Aveny Cafe* – Menu 495 SEK (dinner) – Carte 330/605 SEK
♦ Business ♦ Modern ♦

1950s building with stylish, contemporary inner and smart spa. Spacious, well-
equipped bedrooms with large bathrooms; rooftop suites have balconies. English bar and small Italian eatery-cum-nightclub. Formal bistro offers a blend of
French and Swedish cooking.

Clarion H. Post ⬅ 🕭 🕭 🕭 🕭 🕭 🕭 🕭 rm, 🕭 🕭 🕭 🕭 🕭 🕭 🕭 🕭

Drottningtorget 10 ✉ *411 03* – ✆ *(031) 61 90 00* – *www.clarionpost.se*
495 rm ⬚ – ♦1000/1800 SEK ♦♦1100/3000 SEK – 5 suites **C2**
Rest *Norda Bar & Grill* – Carte 385/515 SEK
Rest *vRÅ* – *(dinner only Tuesday-Thursday)* Menu 395/995 SEK
♦ Historic ♦ Classic ♦

The city's striking neo-Classical Post Office from the 1920s is now a modern
business hotel. Ask for a bedroom in the original building as they have higher
ceilings and wooden floors. Impressive spa; extensive conference facilities and a
cool ground floor bar. Norda Bar and Grill is a slick New York-style restaurant;
vRÅ offers modern Japanese cuisine.

Avalon 🕭 🕭 🕭 🕭 🕭 🕭 🕭 🕭 🕭 🕭 🕭 🕭

Kungstorget 9 ✉ *S-411 17* – ✆ *(031) 751 02 00* – *www.avalonhotel.se*
98 rm ⬚ – ♦1495/2495 SEK ♦♦1695/2695 SEK – 3 suites **B2**
Rest – *(closed Christmas, Easter, midsummer and Sunday lunch)*
Menu 139/495 SEK – Carte 339/715 SEK
♦ Business ♦ Modern ♦

Boutique hotel in a great central location near the shops, harbour and theatres.
Modern, slightly funky bedrooms with the latest mod cons and stylish bathrooms; penthouse suites have small balcony terraces. All-day bistro-style restaurant opens onto the piazza.

Clarion Collection H. Odin without rest 🕭 🕭 🕭 🕭 🕭 🕭

Odinsgatan 6 ✉ *S-411 03* – ✆ *(031) 745 22 00* 🕭 🕭 🕭 🕭
– www.hotelodin.se
171 rm ⬚ – ♦1420/2120 SEK ♦♦1420/2420 SEK – 9 suites **C2**
♦ Business ♦ Modern ♦

Unassuming exterior conceals a light, airy atrium and smart, spacious, Scandic
style apartments with small kitchens and seating areas. Breakfast and all-day
snacks are included in the rate.

Scandic Rubinen 🕭 🕭 🕭 rm, 🕭 🕭 🕭 🕭 🕭 🕭 🕭

Kungsportsavenyn 24 ✉ *S-400 14* – ✆ *(031) 751 54 00*
– www.scandichotels.com/rubinen
191 rm ⬚ – ♦950/2280 SEK ♦♦1250/2580 SEK – 3 suites **C3**
Rest – *(closed 24-26 December)* Menu 105/125 SEK – Carte 305/325 SEK
♦ Business ♦ Modern ♦

Set on the main street, in the heart of town; the red interior paying homage to a
late local resident who collected ruby-coloured objects. Fresh, modern, Scandic-
style bedrooms. Rooftop bar affords great views. Lively Latino restaurant opens
onto the pavement.

Dorsia 🏠 🅰🅲 ⇆ rm, 🛜 🆂🅰 🆅🅸🆂🅰 ⓪ 🅰🅴

Trädgårdsgatan 6 ✉ *411 08 –* ☏ *(031) 790 10 00*
– www.dorsia.se   **B2**
37 rm ⌂ – †1900 SEK ††3100 SEK
Rest – Carte 525/670 SEK

♦ Townhouse ♦ Art Deco ♦ Stylish ♦

Exuberant, eccentric, seductive and possibly a little decadent. This townhouse hotel comes with an evocative Belle Époque style, where art from the owner's own collection, fine fabrics and rich colours add to the joie de vivre. The restaurant is equally vibrant and the atmosphere suitably relaxed.

Eggers 🏠 ⇆ 🛜 🆂🅰 🆅🅸🆂🅰 ⓪ 🅰🅴 ⓪

Drottningtorget ✉ *S-404 24 –* ☏ *(031) 333 44 40*
– www.hoteleggers.se
– Closed 21-25 December   **B2**
69 rm ⌂ – †995/1975 SEK ††1490/2890 SEK
Rest – Carte 318/415 SEK

♦ Traditional ♦ Classic ♦

1859 railway hotel that opened with electricity and telephones in every room. Warm, welcoming interior features original wrought iron, stained glass and period furnishings; some bedrooms have four-posters. Ornate restaurant offers Swedish classics and international favourites.

Novotel Göteborg ⇆ 🐾 ☖ ⇆ 🛜 🆂🅰 🅿 🆅🅸🆂🅰 ⓪ 🅰🅴 ⓪

Klippan 1 (Southwest : 3.5 km by Andréeg taking Kiel-Klippan Ö exit, or boat from Rosenlund) ✉ *SE-414 51 –* ☏ *(031) 720 22 00*
– www.novotel.se
150 rm ⌂ – †990/1850 SEK ††1090/1950 SEK – 1 suite
Rest Carnegie Kaj – Menu 149 SEK (lunch) – Carte 307/545 SEK

♦ Chain hotel ♦ Business ♦ Functional ♦

Converted waterfront brewery, displaying a collection of vintage Porter beers. Clean, bright interior with views of the Göta Älv river. Spacious, Scandic-style bedrooms. Restaurant offers Swedish and international classics.

Flora without rest 🛜 🆅🅸🆂🅰 ⓪ 🅰🅴 ⓪

Grönsakstorget 2 ✉ *411 17 –* ☏ *(031) 13 86 16 – www.hotelflora.se*
– Closed 23 December-13 January   **B2**
65 rm ⌂ – †1150/1595 SEK ††1395/2195 SEK

♦ Family ♦ Functional ♦

There's a funky feel to this nicely run and well-located townhouse, which makes it popular with the fashion industry. The bedrooms are uncluttered and benefit from high ceilings. All-day bar lounge doubles as a breakfast room.

XXX Sjömagasinet (Gustav Trägårdh) ⇆ 🏠 ☖ ⇆ ✿ 🅿

❀ *Klippans Kulturreservat 5, Adolf Edelsvärds gata 5*   🆅🅸🆂🅰 ⓪ 🅰🅴 ⓪
(Southwest : 3.5 km by Andréeg taking Kiel-Klippan exit (Stena Line), or boat from Rosenlund. Also evenings and weekends in summer from Lilla Bommens Hamn) ✉ *S-414 51 –* ☏ *(031) 775 59 20*
– www.sjomagasinet.se
– Closed 23 December-10 January and Sunday
Rest *– (booking essential)* Menu 495 SEK (weekday lunch)/595 SEK
– Carte 545/925 SEK ❀

♦ Swedish ♦ Rustic ♦ Cosy ♦

East India Company warehouse from 1775; now a charming split-level restaurant with a lovely terrace and harbour views. Seafood is the strength, with classic Swedish dishes on the 'Wagner' menu and modern Nordic choices on the 'Trägårdh' menu. Buffet and concise version of the à la carte at lunch.
➔ Shellfish soup with scallops and sweetbread mousse. Fillet of turbot 'Rossini'. Deep fried apple pastry with vanilla ice cream.

XXX
£3 **Thörnströms Kök** (Håkan Thörnström) 🔠 ⅍ ⇔ 𝖵𝖨𝖲𝖠 ◎◎ 🔠 ◎

Teknologgatan 3 ⊠ *S-41132 –* ✆ *(031) 16 20 66*
– www.thornstromskok.com
– Closed 6 July-13 August, 23 December-8 January , Easter and Sunday
Rest *– (dinner only) (booking essential)* Menu 565 SEK   **C3**
– Carte 545/600 SEK ஃ
♦ Classic ♦ Neighbourhood ♦

Set in a quiet residential area, an elegant restaurant with a stunning wine cave.
Good choice of menus, including 3 tasting options. Classically based cooking
follows the Scandic penchant for freshness, simplicity and fullness of flavour.
Smart, knowledgeable team.
➜ Seared scallops with Jerusalem artichoke, pickled roe, dill jelly and
browned butter. Ling with mussels, chard, fennel, and potato garlic purée.
Dark chocolate parfait with blueberry sorbet.

XXX
£3 **28+** 🔠 ⅍ ⇔ 𝖵𝖨𝖲𝖠 ◎◎ 🔠 ◎

Götabergsgatan 28 ⊠ *S-411 34 –* ✆ *(031) 20 21 61 – www.28plus.se*
– Closed 1 July-22 August, 23-26 December, 6-8 January and Sunday
Rest *– (dinner only)* Menu 875 SEK *–* Carte 650/680 SEK ஃ   **C3**
♦ Modern ♦ Formal ♦

This has been a Gothenburg institution for over 25 years. The classical cooking
skilfully blends French and Swedish influences and relies on top ingredients;
there's also an impressive cheese selection. An outstanding wine list is overseen
by a knowledgeable sommelier. Service is very formal.
➜ Pan-fried king scallops with green pea risotto and lentils. Chervil baked
brill, asparagus and wild garlic. Wild strawberry mousse and sorbet, tapioca
and pain d'épice.

XXX
£3 **Kock & Vin** 🔠 ⅍ 𝖵𝖨𝖲𝖠 ◎◎ 🔠 ◎

Viktoriagatan 12 ⊠ *S-411 25 –* ✆ *(031) 701 79 79 – www.kockvin.se*
– Closed 1 July-5 August, Christmas and Sunday-Tuesday   **B3**
Rest *– (dinner only) (booking advisable)* Menu 610/960 SEK
– Carte 575/645 SEK ஃ
♦ Innovative ♦ Friendly ♦ Elegant ♦

Elegant modern restaurant with ornate 19C ceiling, well-spaced tables and a
bright, airy feel. Basement bar serves light plates and fine cheeses; dining
room focuses on creative, seasonal, Nordic dishes. Preparation is precise and
presentation, pleasing. Friendly, clued-up service and good wines by the glass.
➜ Crab with baked Jerusalem artichoke. Pan-fried bycatch, smoked and
salted herring flavoured turnip purée and chicken broth. Celeriac ice
cream and infused pear.

XX
£3 **Fond** (Stefan Karlsson) 🔠 ⅍ 𝖵𝖨𝖲𝖠 ◎◎ 🔠 ◎

Götaplatsen ⊠ *S 412 56 –* ✆ *(031) 81 25 80 – www.fondrestaurang.com*
– Closed 8 weeks summer, 2 weeks Christmas, Sunday and bank holidays
Rest (dinner only and lunch Thursday-Friday)   **C3**
– Menu 795 SEK *–* Carte 505/790 SEK ஃ
♦ Modern ♦ Trendy ♦

Warmly run, modern restaurant with floor-to-ceiling windows looking down
Avenyn. Chef-owner's cooking moves with the seasons, offers clearly defined
flavours, and makes good use of salting and curing. The 'Sampler' menu is the
best way to experience the kitchen's skill; lunch is a simpler affair.
➜ Marinated scallops and shellfish with creamed turnip. Cod with anchovy
salted root vegetables and oyster sauce. Lingonberries, pear and spicy
bread with chocolate and sour cream.

XX **Fiskekrogen** 🔠 ⅍ ⇔ 𝖵𝖨𝖲𝖠 ◎◎ 🔠 ◎

Lilla Torget 1 ⊠ *S-411 18 –* ✆ *(031) 10 10 05 – www.fiskekrogen.se*
– Closed 23 December-9 January, Easter and Sunday   **B2**
Rest *–* Menu 645 SEK *–* Carte 580/935 SEK ஃ
♦ Fish and seafood ♦ Brasserie ♦

Once a 1920s Grand Café, now a real city institution. Impressive room with
smart columns, wood panelling and a central bar. Quality seafood dishes and
extensive buffet lunch. Formal service.

XX Linnéa ✍ VISA ❶❸ AE ①

Södra Vägen 32 ✉ S-412 54 – ☏ (031) 16 11 83
– www.linneaartrestaurant.se
– Closed July, Christmas, New Year and Sunday **C3**
Rest – *(dinner only)* Menu 615 SEK – Carte 585/629 SEK ⅏
♦ Innovative ♦ Design ♦
Striking 'Art Restaurant' and colourful bar displaying modern glass sculptures and installations, all of which are for sale. Adventurous cooking, with set menus and wine pairings available.

XX Wasa Allé VISA ❶❸ AE ①

Vasagatan 24 ✉ 400 16 – ☏ (031) 13 13 70 – www.wasaalle.se
– Closed July-mid August, Sunday, Saturday lunch and Monday dinner
Rest – Menu 335/745 SEK – Carte 425/535 SEK **B3**
♦ Modern ♦ Elegant ♦
Contemporary restaurant with a pleasant bar, occupying an appealing corner spot on a tree-lined avenue. Traditional buffet lunches; more modern dinner menus rely on indigenous ingredients.

XX Swedish Taste ✿ VISA ❶❸ AE ①

Sankt Eriksgatan 6 ✉ SE-411 05 – ☏ (031) 13 27 80
– www.swedishtaste.com
– Closed 4 weeks July-August and Sunday **B1**
Rest – Menu 330/635 SEK – Carte 380/635 SEK
♦ Modern ♦ Fashionable ♦
3-storey venture consisting of a restaurant, deli, café and cookery school. Traditional lunch menu; more elaborate, contemporary offerings at dinner. Top produce and authentic Swedish flavours.

XX Swea Hof – at Elite Plaza Hotel AC VISA ❶❸ AE ①

Västra Hamngatan 3 ✉ S-404 22 – ☏ (031) 720 40 40 – www.sweahof.se
– Closed 23-26 December, Saturday and Sunday lunch **B2**
Rest – Menu 595 SEK – Carte 595/845 SEK
♦ Modern ♦ Formal ♦
Striking hotel restaurant with metal framework and glass roof. Concise business menu at lunch; greater choice at dinner. Fresh, clean cooking combines French and modern Scandinavian influences.

XX Kometen VISA ❶❸ AE ①

Vasagatan 58 ✉ 411 37 – ☏ (031) 137988 – www.restaurangkometen.se
– Closed Christmas **C2**
Rest – *(booking essential)* Menu 295/495 SEK – Carte 265/695 SEK
♦ Scandinavian ♦ Family ♦
Rustic, traditional cooking is celebrated here at the city's oldest restaurant, which opened in 1934 and is now part-owned by celebrated chef Leif Mannerström. It has a clubby feel and the regulars all have their favourite dishes.

X Bhoga VISA ❶❸

Norra Hamngatan 10 ✉ 411 14 – ☏ (031) 13 80 18 – www.bhoga.se
– Closed first week January, Sunday and Monday **B2**
Rest – *(dinner only)* Menu 495/695 SEK
♦ Innovative ♦ Bistro ♦ Minimalist ♦
Two well-travelled young chefs opened this simple, bright little restaurant in 2012 to showcase their considerable talents. The best seasonal ingredients are used in innovative and imaginative ways but dishes never feel overly contrived. The service team are charming and the cocktails are great too.

X Magnus & Magnus VISA ❶❸ AE

Magasinsgatan 8 ✉ 411 18 – ☏ (031) 13 30 00 – www.magnusmagnus.se
– Closed 24-25 December, 1 January and Sunday **B2**
Rest – *(dinner only)* Menu 395/695 SEK
♦ Innovative ♦ Intimate ♦ Neighbourhood ♦
There's a homespun feel to the decoration and an intimacy to the atmosphere. Most diners plump for the 4 course menu; the kitchen uses sound techniques and dishes can be quite elaborate. The service team are bright and well-informed.

Hos Pelle
`⇘ VISA ⓪ AE ⓪`

Djupedalsgatan 2 ⊠ S-413 07 – ℰ (031) 12 10 31 – www.hospelle.com
– Closed Christmas and Sunday A3
Rest – Menu 425 SEK (dinner) – Carte 235/465 SEK
♦ Traditional ♦ Neighbourhood ♦

Long-standing neighbourhood restaurant offering wholesome, traditional cooking. Eat in the wine bar or one of two cosy, rustic dining rooms. Simple blackboard lunch; concise set dinner option.

La Cucina Italiana
`🍴 ⇘ VISA ⓪ AE ⓪`

Skånegatan 33 ⊠ S-412 52 – ℰ (031) 16 63 07 – www.lacucinaitaliana.nu
– Closed Christmas, Easter and Sunday C3
Rest – (dinner only) (booking essential) Menu 499/899 SEK
♦ Italian ♦ Friendly ♦

Enthusiastically run restaurant consisting of just 6 intimate tables. Choose between a 4 or 7 course surprise tasting menu. The chef-owner regularly travels back to his homeland to source produce.

Tvåkanten
`🍴 ⇘ ⇄ VISA ⓪ AE ⓪`

Kungsportsavenyn 27 ⊠ S-411 36 – ℰ (031) 18 21 15 – www.tvakanten.se
– Closed Christmas and Easter C3
Rest – Menu 295/495 SEK – Carte 295/630 SEK 🏵
♦ Traditional ♦ Brasserie ♦

In a prime corner position on one of the most famous streets. Busy bar leads into a warm, cosy cellar-style dining room. Menus range from brunch and all-day snacks to a more ambitious à la carte. Classical cooking; great wine list.

Familjen
`🍴 AK ⇘ VISA ⓪ AE ⓪`

Arkivgatan 7 ⊠ 411 34 – ℰ (031) 20 79 79 – www.restaurangfamiljen.se
– Closed Christmas and Sunday C3
Rest – (dinner only) (booking essential) Menu 335/445 SEK – Carte 309/540 SEK 🏵
♦ Scandinavian ♦ Retro ♦ Design ♦

A funky eatery divided into two parts: a bar with an open-plan kitchen and bench seating, and a bright red room with a characterful cellar and a glass wine cave. Good value daily 3 course set menu and tasting plate selection. Large terrace and an appealing wine list.

Gabriel
`VISA ⓪ AE ⓪`

Feskekôrka ⊠ S-411 20 – ℰ (031) 13 90 51 – www.restauranggabriel.se
– Closed Christmas, Sunday and Monday A3
Rest – (lunch only) (booking advisable) Carte 335/445 SEK
♦ Fish and seafood ♦ Minimalist ♦

Casual first floor restaurant located in the famous 'Fish Church' market and boasting an excellent selection of fresh seafood from local Scandic waters: try the tasty mussels and fried herring.

ENVIRONS OF GOTHENBURG

AT ERIKSBERG West : 6 km by Götaälvbron and Lundbyleden, or boat from Rosenlund

Quality Hotel 11
`⇐ 🕙 & rm, AK ⇘ 🛜 🕉 P VISA ⓪ AE ⓪`

Maskingatan 11 ⊠ S-417 64 – ℰ (031) 779 11 11 – www.hotel11.se
– Closed 23-27 December
259 rm ⊡ – †820/2120 SEK ††920/2920 SEK
Rest Kök & Bar 67 – Menu 79/159 SEK – Carte 277/457 SEK
♦ Business ♦ Functional ♦

Striking former shipbuilding warehouse by the river. Its greatest strength is its huge meeting and events capacity. Good-sized, functional bedrooms; the 8th floor rooms boast city views from furnished balconies. Split-level lounge-bar offers a traditional menu.

Villan without rest   ⟨ 🛜 **P** 𝖵𝖨𝖲𝖠 ⊙⊙ 𝖠𝖤 ①

Sjöportsgatan 2 ⊠ S-417 64 – ℰ (31) 725 77 77 – www.hotelvillan.com
26 rm ⌂ – 📍1100/1700 SEK 📍📍1400/2500 SEK
♦ Traditional ♦ Modern ♦

Characterful Swedish house; once home to a shipbuilding manager. Stylish interior with smart, clean lines. Contemporary bedrooms boast good mod cons – No.31 has a sauna and TV in the bathroom. Breakfast at River Café.

XX   **River Café**   ⟨ 🛜 𝖠𝖢 ↯ 𝖵𝖨𝖲𝖠 ⊙⊙ 𝖠𝖤 ①

Dockepiren ⊠ S-417 64 – ℰ (31) 51 00 00 – www.rivercafe.se
– Closed 22 December-25 January Monday lunch and Sunday
Rest – *(booking advisable)* Menu 375/565 SEK – Carte 486/671 SEK
♦ Modern ♦ Friendly ♦

Delightfully set overlooking the city and the harbour. Elegant first-floor restaurant serves unfussy set lunch and a seasonal, à la carte of fresh, hearty, Scandic dishes at dinner. The simpler ground floor bistro opens onto the pier.

AT LANDVETTER AIRPORT   East : 30 km by Rd 40

Landvetter Airport Hotel   🛜 𝖿𝖺 🛜 🛒 𝖠𝖢 ↯ 🛜 𝖺 **P**

Flygets Hotellväg ⊠ S-438 13 – ℰ (031) 97 75 50   𝖵𝖨𝖲𝖠 ⊙⊙ 𝖠𝖤 ①
– www.landvetterairporthotel.com
133 rm ⌂ – 📍1095/1995 SEK 📍📍1295/2095 SEK – 1 suite
Rest – Menu 102/425 SEK – Carte 355/555 SEK
♦ Business ♦ Modern ♦

Located just minutes from the airport terminal but in a pleasant, semi-rural setting. Light, open interior has a fresh Scandic style and a calm air. Warm, welcoming bedrooms come with interesting art, work desks and baths. Informal restaurant offers a mix of Swedish and global dishes; lunch is buffet style.

SWITZERLAND
SUISSE, SCHWEIZ, SVIZZERA

→ **AREA:**
41 284 km²
(15 940 sq mi).

→ **CAPITAL:**
Bern (Berne).

→ **POPULATION:**
8 000 001.
Density = 193 per km².

→ **CURRENCY:**
Swiss Franc (CHF).

→ **GOVERNMENT:**
Federation of 26 cantons with
2 assemblies (National Council
and Council of State) forming the
Federal Assembly.

→ **LANGUAGES:**
German (64% of population),
French (20%) and Italian (7%),
are spoken in all administrative
departments, shops, hotels and
restaurants.

→ **PUBLIC HOLIDAYS:**
New Year's Day (1 Jan); Ascension
Day (May); Swiss National Day
(1 Aug); Christmas Day (25 Dec).
All other holidays are decided upon
by each canton, the most popular
being: St Berchtold's Day (2 Jan);
Good Friday (Friday before Easter);
Easter Monday (late Mar/Apr); Whit
Monday (late May/June); Corpus
Christi (late May/June); Assumption
of the Virgin Mary (15 Aug);
All Saints' Day (1 Nov); Immaculate
Conception (8 Dec); St Stephen's
Day (26 Dec).

→ **LOCAL TIME:**
GMT+1 hour in winter and GMT
+2 hours in summer.

→ **CLIMATE**
Temperate continental, varies with
altitude – most of the country has
cold winters and warm summers
(Bern: January 0°C; July 19°C).

→ **EMERGENCY**
Police ☎ **117**; Medical Assistance
☎ **144**; Fire Brigade ☎ **118**.
Anglo-Phone 24hr helpline
☎ **0900 576 444**.
(Dialling **112** within any EU country
will redirect your call and contact
the emergency services.)

→ **ELECTRICITY:**
230 volts AC, 50Hz; 2 round pin
sockets.

→ **FORMALITIES:**
Travellers from the European Union
(EU), Iceland and the main countries
of North and South America need
a national identity card or passport
(America: passport required) to
visit Switzerland for less than
three months (tourism or business
purpose). For visitors from other
countries a visa may be required, in
addition to a passport, especially
for those wishing to stay for longer
than three months. We advise you
to check with your embassy before
travelling.

BERN
BERNE

Population: 125 681

N. Parneix/Fotolia.com

To look at Bern, you'd never believe it to be a capital city. Small and beautifully proportioned, it sits sedately on a spur at a point where the River Aare curves gracefully back on itself. The little city is the best preserved medieval centre north of the Alps – a fact recognised by UNESCO when it awarded Bern World Heritage status – and the layout of the streets has barely changed since the Duke of Zahringen chose the superbly defended site to found the city over 800 years ago. Most of the buildings date from between the 14 and 16C – when Bern was at the height of its power – and the cluster of cobbled lanes, surrounded by ornate sandstone arcaded buildings and numerous fountains and wells, give it the feel of a delightfully overgrown village. (Albert Einstein felt so secure here that while ostensibly employed as a clerk in the Bern patent office he managed to find the time to work out his Theory of Relativity.)

BERN IN...

→ **ONE DAY**
River walk, Old Town (cathedral, clock Tower, arcades), Museum of Fine Arts, cellar fringe theatre.

→ **TWO DAYS**
Zentrum Paul Klee, Einstein's house, Stadttheater.

→ **THREE DAYS**
Bern Museum of History, Swiss Alpine Museum, Rose Garden.

The Old Town stretches eastwards over a narrow peninsula, and is surrounded by the arcing River Aare. The eastern limit of the Old Town is the Nydeggbrücke bridge, while the western end is marked out by the Käfigturm tower, once a city gate and prison. On the southern side of the Aare lies the small Kirchenfeld quarter, which houses some impressive museums, while the capital's famous brown bears are back over the river via the Nydeggbrücke.

ARRIVAL-DEPARTURE

 Bern Belp International Airport is 9km southeast of the city. The shuttle bus leaves every 30min and takes about 20min.

GETTING AROUND

The Bern Card is well worth investing in. It gives unlimited travel, free admission to museums and gardens, and various reductions around the city. It's available from the Tourist Office, museums and hotels, and is valid for 24hr, 48hr or 72hr.

As Bern is small enough to walk around, it requires no more than a super-efficient bus and tram network. A short cable-railway links the Marzili quarter to the Bundeshaus. You can buy your ticket at the bus or tram stop.

EATING OUT

Bern is a great place to sit and enjoy a meal. Pride of place must go to the good range of alfresco venues in the squares of the old town – popular spots to enjoy coffee and cake. Hiding away in the arcades are many delightful dining choices; some of the best for location alone are in vaulted cellars that breathe historic ambience. If you want to feel what a real Swiss restaurant is like, head for a traditional rustic eatery complete with cow-bells and sample the local dishes like the Berner Platte – a heaving plate of hot and cold meats, served with beans and sauerkraut –

CALENDAR HIGHLIGHTS

February
Carnival

March
Museums Night.

May
International Jazz Festival, Bern Grand Prix (Run).

June
Berner Tanztage (dance festival).

July
Gurtenfestival (rock music).

July-August
Altstadtsommer (series of concerts in the old town).

October
Tanz In. Bern.

November
Onion Market.

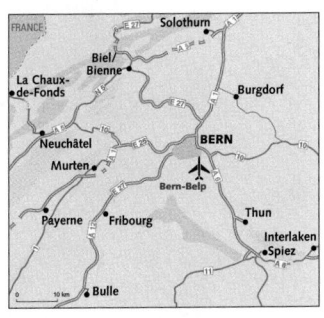

or treberwurst, a sausage poached with fermented grape skins. There's no shortage of international restaurants either, and along with Germany, France and Italy also have their country's cuisine well represented here – it's not difficult to go from rösti to risotto. And, of course, there's always cheese – this is the birthplace of raclette - and tempting chocolates waiting in the wings. A fifteen percent service charge is always added but it's customary to round the bill up.

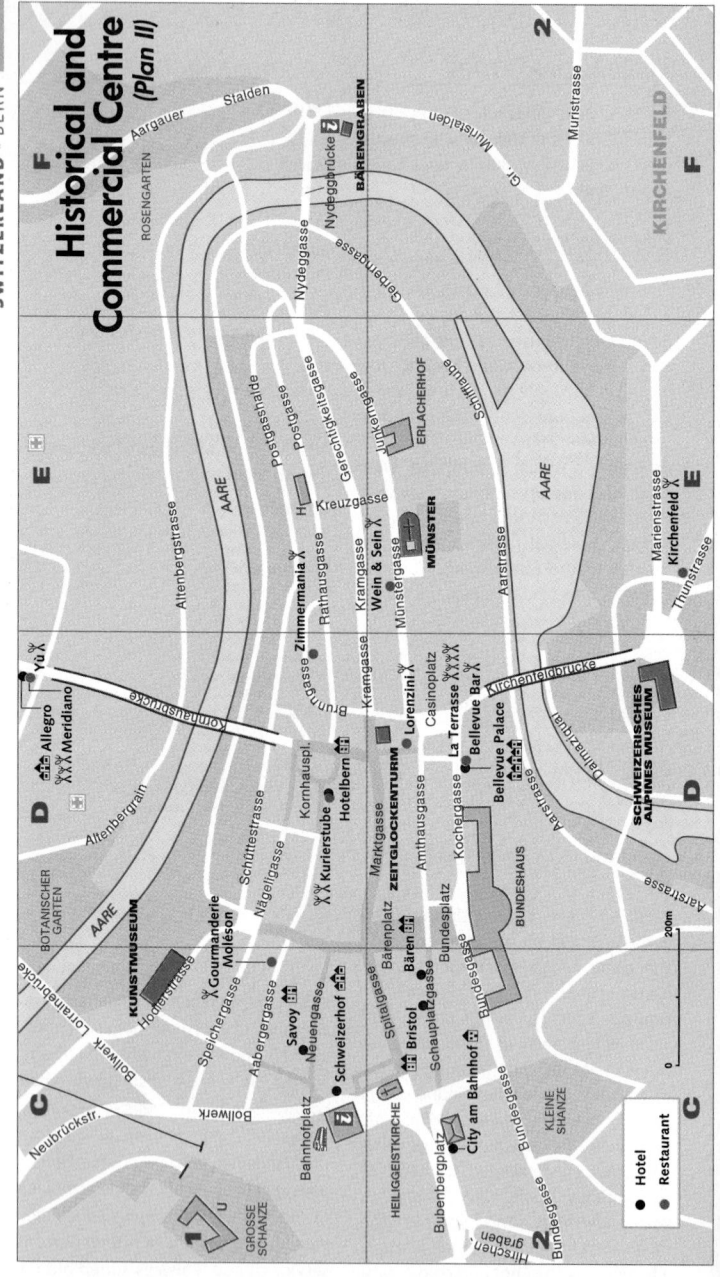

Historical and Commercial Centre
(Plan II)

Bellevue Palace   ≼ Ƭₐ ⋔ & 🅰🄲 🛜 🦶 🆅🅸🆂🅰 ⑳ 🅰🅴 ⓪

Kochergasse 3 ⊠ 3000 – ℰ 031 320 45 45
– www.bellevue-palace.ch   **D2**
128 rm – †399/507 CHF ††529/629 CHF, � 38 CHF – 24 suites
Rest *La Terrasse* Rest *Bellevue Bar* – see restaurant listing
♦ Grand Luxury ♦ Classic ♦
This exclusive hotel established in 1913 and sited in the heart of Bern offers first-class guestrooms and suites and elegant conference facilities in a truly unique atmosphere. Modern gym with sauna. The comfortable Bellevue Bar serves international cuisine.

Schweizerhof   Ƭₐ ⋔ & 🅰🄲 🛜 🦶 🆅🅸🆂🅰 ⑳ 🅰🅴 ⓪

Bahnhofplatz 11 ⊠ 3001 – ℰ 031 326 80 80
– www.schweizerhof-bern.ch   **C1**
99 rm – †490/580 CHF ††590/790 CHF, ⊻ 30 CHF – 5 suites
Rest *Jack's Brasserie* – Menu 80/105 CHF – Carte 66/110 CHF
♦ Business ♦ Historic ♦ Modern ♦
Behind the beautifully restored historic façade lies a happy marriage of modern and classic chic that looks beautiful and provides all the latest technology for business guests. Those of you in search of charm will love Jack's Brasserie.

Allegro   ≼ 🛜 Ƭₐ ⋔ & 🅰🄲 🛜 🦶 🚗 🆅🅸🆂🅰 ⑳ 🅰🅴 ⓪

Kornhausstr. 3 ⊠ 3000 – ℰ 031 339 55 00 – www.kursaal-bern.ch
171 rm – †260/360 CHF ††320/420 CHF, ⊻ 26 CHF – 2 suites   **D1**
Rest *Meridiano* ❀
Rest *Yù* – see restaurant listing
Rest *Giardino* – ℰ 031 339 51 80 – Menu 27 CHF (lunch)/48 CHF
– Carte 60/87 CHF
♦ Business ♦ Modern ♦
This lifestyle hotel is ideal for conferences and events, as well as individual guests. Modern rooms in different categories, plus a beautiful penthouse floor with its own lounge. One of the restaurants, Il Giardino, serves Italian food.

Hotelbern   🛜 & 🛜 🦶 🆅🅸🆂🅰 ⑳

Zeughausgasse 9 ⊠ 3011 – ℰ 031 329 22 22 – www.hotelbern.ch
95 rm – †190/270 CHF ††200/350 CHF, ⊻ 18 CHF   **D1**
Rest *Kurierstube* – see restaurant listing
Rest *7-Stube* – Carte 37/81 CHF
♦ Business ♦ Modern ♦
Located in a striking townhouse in the centre of Bern, this business hotel offers colourful, contemporary guestrooms and meeting rooms complete with the latest facilities. A high-quality, elegant restaurant. Rustic-style restaurant.

Savoy *without rest*   🅰🄲 🛜 🆅🅸🆂🅰 ⑳ 🅰🅴 ⓪

Neuengasse 26 ⊠ 3011 – ℰ 031 311 44 05 – www.hotel-savoy-bern.ch
54 rm ⊻ – †235/275 CHF ††330/370 CHF   **C1**
♦ Business ♦ Classic ♦
This hotel offers high-quality rooms with the latest technology and an attractive breakfast room with a generous buffet. Central location conveniently close to the railway station.

Bristol *without rest*   Ƭₐ ⋔ 🅰🄲 🛜 🆅🅸🆂🅰 ⑳ 🅰🅴 ⓪

Schauplatzgasse 10 ⊠ 3011 – ℰ 031 311 01 01 – www.bristolbern.ch
92 rm ⊻ – †200/300 CHF ††275/370 CHF   **C2**
♦ Business ♦ Modern ♦
This townhouse hotel offers contemporary rooms and a small sauna (additional charge payable) which is shared with the adjacent Hotel Bären.

Bären without rest 🕭 🗚 🛜 🆅🆂🅰 🆇 🅰🅴 🅾

Schauplatzgasse 4 ✉ 3011 – 𝒞 031 311 33 67 – www.baerenbern.ch
57 rm ⚏ – †200/245 CHF ††275/330 CHF   **C2**
♦ Business ♦ Modern ♦

Just a stone's throw from the Bundesplatz, this hotel located in a well-maintained townhouse offers individually furnished guestrooms in a contemporary style. A small sauna is available for an additional charge.

City am Bahnhof without rest 🛜 🆅🆂🅰 🆇 🅰🅴 🅾

Bubenbergplatz 7 ✉ 3011 – 𝒞 031 311 53 77 – www.fassbindhotels.com
58 rm – †160/265 CHF ††200/310 CHF, ⌁ 20 CHF   **C2**
♦ Business ♦ Functional ♦

Conveniently located close to the pedestrian zone and opposite the railway station, this hotel offers well-equipped rooms.

XXXX La Terrasse – Hotel Bellevue Palace ← 🏠 🆅🆂🅰 🆇 🅰🅴 🅾

Kochergasse 3 ✉ 3001 – 𝒞 031 320 45 45 – www.bellevue-palace.ch
Rest – Menu 78 CHF (lunch)/155 CHF – Carte 87/154 CHF 🍸   **D2**
♦ Creative ♦ Classic ♦

Ambitious, contemporary seasonal cuisine with traditional roots is served in this tastefully decorated setting. The terrace affords magnificent views over the Aare.

XXX Meridiano – Hotel Allegro ← 🏠 🗚 ⇩ 🅿 🆅🆂🅰 🆇 🅰🅴 🅾

🕸
Kornhausstr. 3 ✉ 3013 – 𝒞 031 339 52 45 – www.kursaal-bern.ch – Closed 1-14 January, 31 March-8 April, 7-30 July and Saturday lunch, Sunday-Monday
Rest – Menu 135/179 CHF – Carte 120/134 CHF   **D1**
♦ Modern ♦ Trendy ♦

Meridiano is stylish and understated with a touch of elegance. It offers a magnificent view over Bern, which is no less impressive from the covered terrace. Its diners universally praise Markus Arnold's fine, modern cuisine.
➜ Königsmakrele[2], Nashi, Yuzu, Amarant. Entenleber aus Gramat, Granny-Smith Apfel und Erdnuss. Steirisches Reh[2], Seeländer Randen, Himbeeren.

XX Kurierstube – Hotelbern ⅃ 🆅🆂🅰 🆇

Zeughausgasse 9 ✉ 3011 – 𝒞 031 329 22 22 – www.hotelbern.ch
– Closed Sunday-Monday   **D1**
Rest – Carte 55/98 CHF
♦ French classic ♦ Elegant ♦

You have to walk through the '7-Stube' to reach this elegant, modern restaurant. Red upholstered chairs and curtains and interesting old photographs add a few tasteful highlights to the smart dining room.

X Kirchenfeld 🏠 ⇩ 🆅🆂🅰 🆇 🅰🅴 🅾

🕸
Thunstr. 5 ✉ 3005 – 𝒞 031 351 02 78 – www.kirchenfeld.ch
– Closed Sunday-Monday   **E2**
Rest – (booking advisable) Menu 39 CHF (lunch)/68 CHF – Carte 50/81 CHF
♦ Modern ♦ Brasserie ♦

Eating in this loud and lively restaurant is great fun! Try the flavoursome zander fish served on Mediterranean couscous and one of the sweets, which includes lemon tart and chocolate cake, displayed on the dessert trolley. At lunchtimes the restaurant is full of business people who swear by the daily set menu.

X Lorenzini 🏠 ⇩ 🆅🆂🅰 🆇 🅰🅴 🅾

Hotelgasse 10 ✉ 3011 – 𝒞 031 318 50 67 – www.lorenzini.ch
Rest – Carte 43/87 CHF   **D2**
♦ Italian ♦ Friendly ♦

This attractive Italian restaurant located in the pedestrian zone is tastefully decorated with original paintings. It boasts a formal restaurant on the first floor and a bar, bistro and attractive interior courtyard at ground level.

X **Zimmermania** *VISA* **⊕⊙**

Brunngasse 19 ⊠ 3011 – ℰ 031 311 15 42 – www.zimmermania.ch
– Closed 7 July-6 August, Sunday-Monday and Bank Holidays **D1**
Rest *– (July-September: Saturday lunch)* Menu 64 CHF – Carte 38/91 CHF
♦ Traditional ♦ Traditional ♦
The atmosphere in this cosy, traditionally run restaurant located in a narrow alleyway in the old town is lively and informal.

X **Gourmanderie Moléson** *🍴 ✿ VISA ⊕⊙ ①*

Aarbergergasse 24 ⊠ 3011 – ℰ 031 311 44 63 – www.moleson-bern.ch
– Closed Christmas-New Year and Saturday lunch, Sunday **C1**
Rest – Menu 38 CHF (lunch)/83 CHF – Carte 57/93 CHF
♦ Traditional ♦ Brasserie ♦
Established in 1865, the Moléson is a lively restaurant located in the centre of Bern. It serves a range of traditional-style dishes from Alsatian flammekueche to multi-course meals.

X **Yù** – Hotel Allegro *⇐ ৬ ⎌ P ▯ VISA ⊕⊙ AE ①*

Kornhausstr. 3 ⊠ 3000 – ℰ 031 339 52 50 – www.kursaal-bern.ch
– Closed July and Sunday-Monday **D1**
Rest *– (dinner only)* Menu 42 CHF – Carte 46/72 CHF
♦ Chinese ♦ Fashionable ♦
This fifth-floor restaurant open to the hotel's atrium is one of the most fashionable addresses in town. It exudes stylish Asian cool and serves modern Chinese cuisine.

X **Bellevue Bar** – Hotel Bellevue Palace *৬ VISA ⊕⊙ AE ①*

Kochergasse 3 ⊠ 3000 – ℰ 031 320 45 45 – www.bellevue-palace.ch
Rest – Carte 54/114 CHF **D2**
♦ International ♦ Cosy ♦
The sedate charm of this long established grand hotel also extends into the restaurant. Diners, many of whom have travelled from far and wide to get here, can choose from an international menu.

ENVIRONS OF BERN *Plan I*

🏠 **Innere Enge** *🌸 🍴 ৬ 📞 🎿 P VISA ⊕⊙ AE ①*

Engestr. 54 ⊠ 3012 – ℰ 031 309 61 11 – www.innere-enge.ch
26 rm – ♥255/275 CHF ♥♥330/370 CHF **A1**
Rest *Josephine* – Menu 54 CHF (lunch)/92 CHF – Carte 50/100 CHF
♦ Business ♦ Classic ♦
Passionate about jazz, your hosts have created this unique hotel-cum-jazz venue. Many of the rooms are named after famous musicians and decorated with original artefacts. The basement houses a jazz club. Josephine's Brasserie and the historic Park Pavilion offer views over the city.

🏠 **Sternen** *৬ 🛜 🎿 P 🔥 VISA ⊕⊙ AE ①*

Thunstr. 80 – ℰ 031 950 71 11 – www.sternenmuri.ch
– Closed 22 December-6 January, 22 July-4 August **B2**
44 rm ☐ – ♥215/350 CHF ♥♥290/435 CHF
Rest *Sternen* – see restaurant listing
♦ Traditional ♦ Functional ♦
This recently extended hotel offers contemporary rooms decorated in shades of yellow, green and blue in the annexe and more traditional rooms, some with exposed beams, in the main building. Good transport connections into the city. Both the Läubli restaurant and residents' dining room serve contemporary cuisine. Attractive private dining rooms are also available.

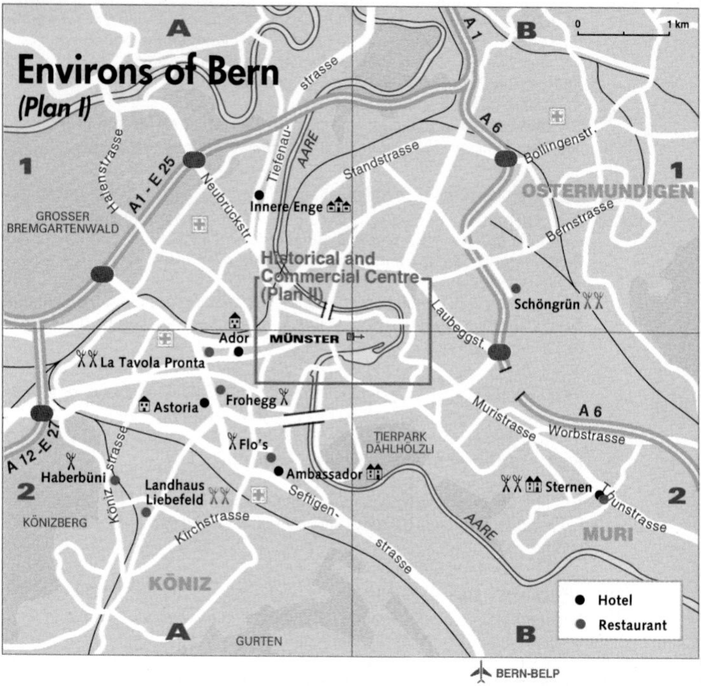

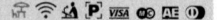

Environs of Bern
(Plan I)

(map of the Environs of Bern showing roads A1-E25, A12-E27, A6, A1, streets including Halenstrasse, Neubrückstr., Tiefenau, Standstrasse, Bollingenstr., Bernstrasse, Laubeggst., Muristrasse, Worbstrasse, Dunstrasse, Könizstrasse, Sefigen-strasse, Kirchstrasse, and areas GROSSER BREMGARTENWALD, OSTERMUNDIGEN, MÜNSTER, TIERPARK DAHLHÖLZLI, KÖNIZBERG, KÖNIZ, MURI, GURTEN. Marked locations: Innere/Enge, Schöngrün, Ador, La Tavola Pronta, Astoria, Frohegg, Flo's, Haberbüni, Ambassador, Landhaus Liebefeld, Sternen. Historical and Commercial Centre (Plan II))

Legend:
- ● Hotel
- ● Restaurant

✈ BERN-BELP

Ambassador

⟨ icons ⟩

Seftigenstr. 99 ✉ *3007 –* ☎ *031 370 99 99*
– www.fassbindhotels.com   A2
97 rm – †210/355 CHF ††255/395 CHF, ⌣ 24 CHF
Rest – Carte 33/85 CHF
Rest Taishi – (closed mid July-mid August and Saturday lunch, Sunday-Monday) Menu 49/95 CHF – Carte 32/93 CHF
♦ Business ♦ Contemporary ♦
This business hotel enjoys good transport links on the edge of the city. It boasts modern, functionally designed bedrooms with good facilities and free underground parking. Japanese cuisine in the Taishi, and international dishes in the light and airy conservatory.

Astoria

⟨ icons ⟩

Zieglerstr. 66 ✉ *3007 –* ☎ *031 378 66 66*
– www.astoria-bern.ch
– Closed 23 December-2 January   A2
62 rm ⌣ – †140/190 CHF ††190/220 CHF
Rest – (closed 23 July-5 August, Saturday-Sunday and Bank Holidays)
Carte 33/57 CHF
♦ Townhouse ♦ Business ♦ Contemporary ♦
Contemporary, functional rooms combine with a location on the edge of the city centre and good transport links to make this hotel ideal for business travellers or visitors on a short city break. Pleasant breakfast room with a small terrace. Bistro-style restaurant offering predominantly Mediterranean fare.

Ador without rest   ♿ 🛜 🛄 🚗 VISA ⓿ AE ⓞ
Laupenstr. 15 ✉ 3001 – ☏ 031 388 01 11 – www.hotelador.ch
– Closed 21 December-3 January   **A2**
59 rm ☕ – ♦155 CHF ♦♦215 CHF
♦ Business ♦ Modern ♦
This hotel located close to the railway station offers small rooms equipped with the latest technology making it ideal for the business traveller.

Schöngrün (Werner Rothen)   🛜 AC ⇔ VISA ⓿ AE ⓞ
Monument im Fruchtland 1 (near Paul Klee Centre) – ☏ 031 359 02 90
– www.restaurants-schoengruen.ch
– closed Monday-Tuesday   **B1**
Rest – *(booking advisable)* Menu 64 CHF (lunch)/180 CHF – Carte 109/132 CHF
♦ International ♦ Fashionable ♦
The light, airy and minimalist glass extension provides a perfect contrast to the original historic villa at Schöngrün. This striking ensemble is not far from the Paul Klee Centre. Enjoy the atmosphere from your smart red dining chair and watch as creative chef Werner Rothen plies his trade in the open kitchen.
➔ Entenleber gebraten, Soja, Hutlattich-Honig, Melone, Sesamcracker. Rotbarbe "petit bateau", Sommer, Yuzu. Hereford Rind, Karotte, Vanille, Maldon Pfeffer, Frühkartoffel.

Landhaus Liebefeld with rm   🛜 ♿ 🛜 ⇔ P VISA ⓿ AE ⓞ
Schwarzenburgstr. 134 – ☏ 031 971 07 58 – www.landhaus-liebefeld.ch
– Closed Sunday   **A2**
6 rm ☕ – ♦178/350 CHF ♦♦285/450 CHF
Rest – *(booking advisable)* Menu 60 CHF (lunch)/133 CHF
– Carte 55/98 CHF ✦
Rest *Gaststube* – *(closed Sunday)* Menu 60 CHF – Carte 48/74 CHF
♦ Traditional ♦ Elegant ♦
Friendly, well-trained staff serve contemporary cuisine in this smart former sheriff's residence. The elegant restaurant boasts a charming garden terrace. Good value classics and seasonal dishes in the bar parlour. The attractive rooms in this hotel are individually furnished and decorated.

La Tavola Pronta   🛜 VISA ⓿ AE ⓞ
Laupenstr. 57 ✉ 3008 – ☏ 031 382 66 33 – www.latavolapronta.ch
– Closed 3 weeks July-August and Saturday lunch, Sunday-Monday
Rest – *(booking advisable)* Menu 58 CHF (lunch)/98 CHF   **A2**
♦ Italian ♦ Cosy ♦
A pleasant little basement restaurant with modern decor where chef Beat Thomi creates flavoursome Piedmontese food in a number of set menus.

Sternen – Hotel Sternen   🛜 ♿ P VISA ⓿ AE ⓞ
Thunstr. 80 – ☏ 031 950 71 11 – www.sternenmuri.ch
– Closed 22 December-6 January and 20 July-4 August   **B2**
Rest – Carte 22/103 CHF
♦ International ♦ Cosy ♦
In the Sternen, guests can take their pick from a number of small, attractive dining rooms – 170 years old with original features to match. On a fun note, to order simply tick the relevant box on the menu and hand it to the waiter.

Flo's   VISA ⓿
Weissenbühlweg 40 ✉ 3007 – ☏ 031 372 05 55 – www.flos-restaurant.ch
– Closed 22 December-20 January, 24 March-7 April, mid June-mid August, end September-mid October and Sunday-Wednesday   **A2**
Rest – *(dinner only) (booking essential)* Menu 65/95 CHF
– Carte 54/79 CHF
♦ Modern ♦ Fashionable ♦
Run by the dedicated Manz siblings, the atmosphere in this modern restaurant is lively and the service very friendly. Watch delicious international dishes being prepared in the open-view kitchen. The number nine tram stops right at the door.

Frohegg ⛺ ✿ 𝚟𝚒𝚜𝚊 ⊙⊙ AE ⓪

Belpstr. 51 ✉ *3007 – ✆ 031 382 25 24 – www.frohegg.ch*
– Closed Sunday and Bank Holidays   **A2**
Rest *– (booking advisable)* Menu 45 CHF (lunch)/69 CHF – Carte 41/78 CHF
♦ Traditional ♦ Cosy ♦
This cosy restaurant located in a 1898 townhouse and serving seasonal cuisine
has been privately run for more than 20 years. It has a lovely winter garden and
wisteria-covered terrace.

Haberbüni ⛺ 𝙿 𝚟𝚒𝚜𝚊 ⊙⊙ AE ⓪

Könizstr. 175 – ✆ 031 972 56 55 – www.haberbueni.ch
– Closed Saturday lunch, Sunday   **A2**
Rest *– (booking advisable)* Menu 61 CHF (lunch)/85 CHF
– Carte 56/89 CHF 🍴
♦ International ♦ Rustic ♦ Cosy ♦
This warm and welcoming restaurant set in the loft of a large renovated farm-
house or Büni offers ambitious contemporary cuisine and a fine selection of
wines. Shorter midday menu and good business lunch options.

GENEVA
GENEVE

Population: 192 385

Kheng Guan Toh/Fotolia.com

In just about every detail except efficiency, Geneva exudes a distinctly Latin feel. It boasts a proud cosmopolitanism, courtesy of a whole swathe of international organisations (dealing with just about every human concern), and of the fact that roughly one in three residents is non-Swiss. Its renowned savoir-vivre challenges that of swishy Zurich, and along with its manicured city parks, it boasts the world's tallest fountain and the world's longest bench. It enjoys cultural ties with Paris and is often called 'the twenty-first arrondissement' – it's also almost entirely surrounded by France.

The River Rhône snakes through the centre, dividing the city into the southern left bank - the old town - and the northern right bank - the 'international quarter' (home to the largest UN office outside New York). The east is strung around the sparkling shores of Europe's largest alpine lake, while the Jura Mountains dominate the right bank, and the Alps form a backdrop to the left bank. Geneva is renowned for its orderliness: the Reformation was born here under the austere preachings of Calvin, and the city has provided sanctuary for religious dissidents, revolutionaries and elopers for at least five centuries. Nowadays, new arrivals tend to be of a more conservative persuasion, as they go their elegant way balancing international affairs alongside la belle vie.

GENEVA IN...

→ **ONE DAY**
St Peter's Cathedral, Maison Tavel, Jet d'Eau, Reformation Wall.

→ **TWO DAYS**
MAMCO (or Art & History Museum), a lakeside stroll, a trip to Carouge.

→ **THREE DAYS**
A day in Paquis, including time relaxing at the Bains des Paquis.

PRACTICAL INFORMATION

ARRIVAL-DEPARTURE

✈ Geneva International Airport is 4km northwest of the city. Trains depart every 15min and take 6min. Bus 10 runs every 10min.

GETTING AROUND

Geneva is served by an efficient public transport network which runs like clockwork. There are various timed cards depending on how much travelling you intend to do: for one hour, one day, or 9am-midnight. A useful alternative: if you're making several trips, pick up a 48hr or 72hr Geneva Transport Card from the tourist office for unlimited use of the city's trams, trains, buses and boats. It also offers free admission to many top museums and attractions, plus reductions in some restaurants and shops. The city encourages cycling and from May to October bikes can be borrowed for free. More information from Geneva Tourism on Rue du Mont-Blanc.

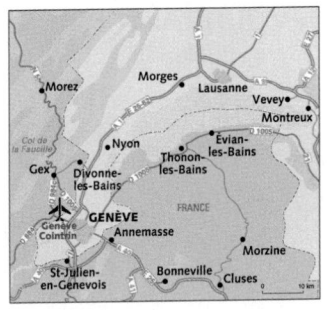

CALENDAR HIGHLIGHTS

February
Winter Carnival.

April
International Exhibition of Inventions.

June
Bol d'Or Regatta, Fête de la Musique.

August
Fêtes de Genève.

October
Flamenco Festival.

December
L'Escalade Procession.

EATING OUT

With the number of international organisations that have set up camp here, this is a place that takes a lot of feeding, so you'll find over 1,000 dining establishments in and around the city. If you're looking for elegance, head to a restaurant overlooking the lake; if your tastes are for home-cooked Sardinian fare, make tracks for the charming Italianate suburb of Carouge; and if you fancy something with an international accent, trendy Paquis has it all at a fair price and on a truly global scale, from Mexican to Moroccan and Jordanian to Japanese. The old town, packed with delightful brasseries and alpine-style chalets, is the place for Swiss staples: you can't go wrong here if you're after a fondue, rustic longeole (pork sausage with cumin and fennel) or a hearty papet vaudois (cream and leek casserole); for a bit of extra atmosphere, head downstairs to a candlelit, vaulted cellar. Although restaurants include a fifteen per cent service charge, it's customary to either round up the bill or give the waiter a five to ten per cent tip.

805

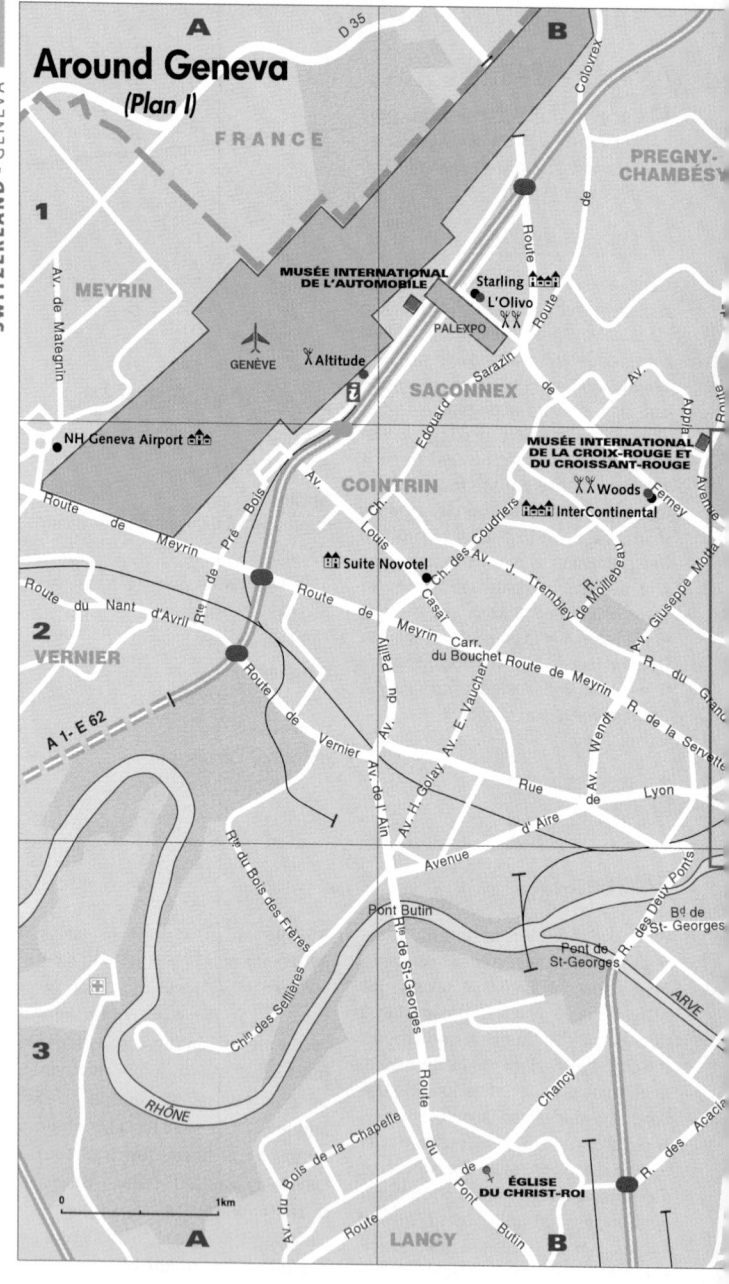

Around Geneva
(Plan I)

FRANCE

MUSÉE INTERNATIONAL DE L'AUTOMOBILE

Av. de Malagnin

MEYRIN

GENÈVE

Altitude

NH Geneva Airport

Route de Meyrin

Route du Nant d'Avril

VERNIER

A 1 - E 62

Rue du Bois des Frères

RHÔNE

Chin des Sellières

Av. du Bois de la Chapelle

Pont Butin

Rte de St-Georges

Route du Pont

Route Butin

LANCY

Starling

L'Olivo

PALEXPO

SACONNEX

Edouard Sarazin

MUSÉE INTERNATIONAL DE LA CROIX-ROUGE ET DU CROISSANT-ROUGE

Woods

InterContinental

COINTRIN

Ch. Louis

Ch. des Coudriers

Suite Novotel

Av. J. Trembley

Route de Casaï

Meyrin

Carr. du Bouchet Route de Meyrin

Av. du Pailly

Av. H. Golay

Av. E. Vaucher

R. Wendt

Rue de

R. de la Servette

Av. Giuseppe Motta

R. du Grand

Lyon

d'Aire

Avenue

Pont de St-Georges

Bd des Deux Ponts

Bd de St-Georges

ARVE

Chancy

R. des Acacia

ÉGLISE DU CHRIST-ROI

PREGNY-CHAMBÉSY

Colovrex

Route de

Appia

Ferney

Avenue

0   1km

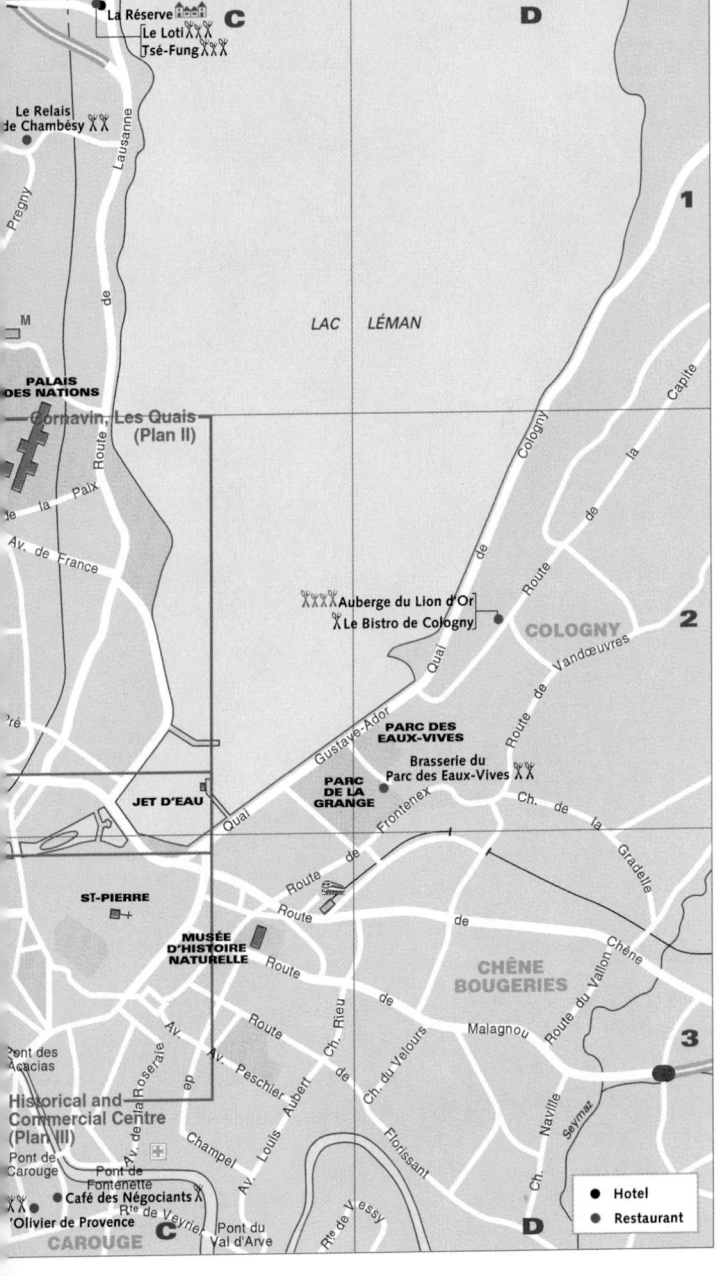

La Réserve
Le Loti
Tsé-Fung

Le Relais
de Chambésy

Lausanne

de

Pregny

M

PALAIS
DES NATIONS

Cornavin, Les Quais
(Plan II)

la Paix

de la

Av. de France

Pré

JET D'EAU

Quai

LAC LÉMAN

Cologny

de

la

Capite

1

Route

Auberge du Lion d'Or
Le Bistro de Cologny

COLOGNY

2

Route de Vandœuvres

Gustave-Ador

PARC DES
EAUX-VIVES

PARC
DE LA
GRANGE

Brasserie du
Parc des Eaux-Vives

de Frontenex

Ch. de

la Gradelle

ST-PIERRE

MUSÉE
D'HISTOIRE
NATURELLE

Route

Route

Route

de

de

Ch. Rieu

du Velours

CHÊNE
BOUGERIES

Malagnou

Route du Vallon

Chêne

3

Pont des
Acacias

Historical and
Commercial Centre
(Plan III)

Pont de
Carouge

Pont de
Fontenette

Café des Négociants

Olivier de Provence

CAROUGE

Av. de la Roseraie

Av. Peschier

Champel

Av. Louis-Aubert

de

Rte de Veyrier

Pont du
Val d'Arve

Florissant

Rte de Vessy

Naville

Seymaz

Ch.

D

C

D

● Hotel
● Restaurant

807

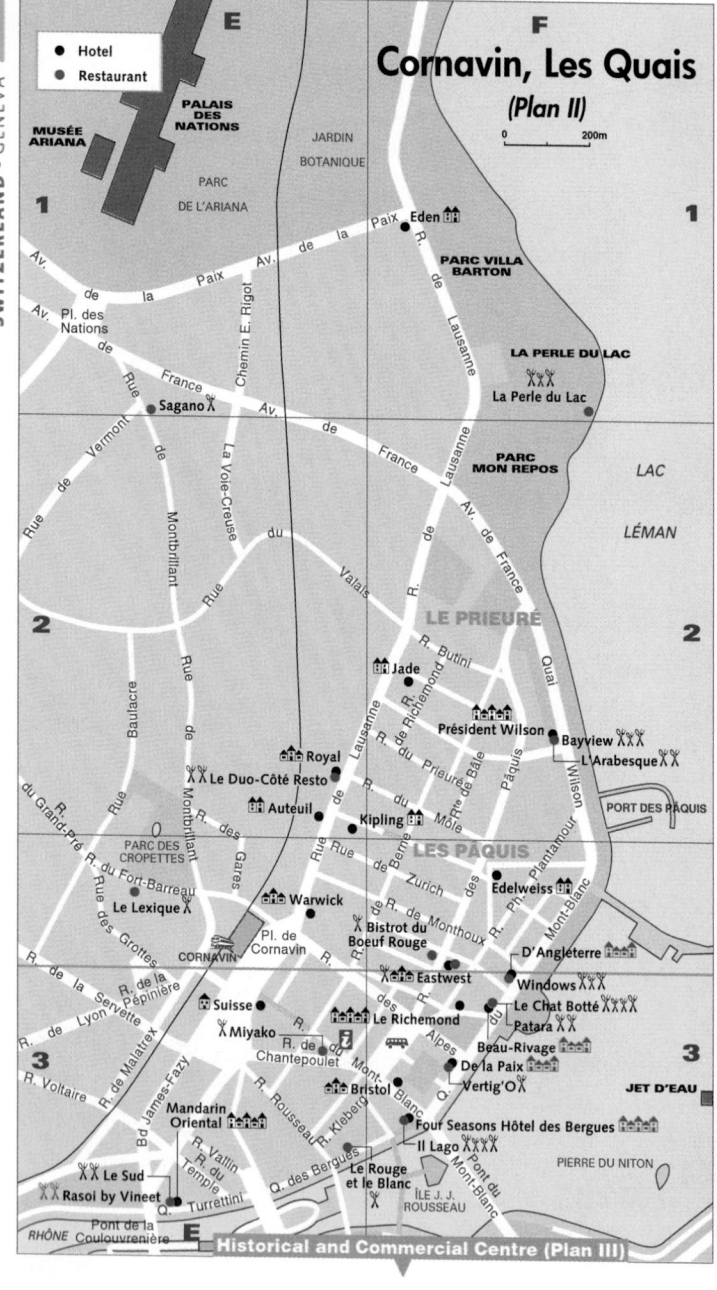

SWITZERLAND - GENEVA

Cornavin, Les Quais
(Plan II)

- ● Hotel
- ● Restaurant

0   200m

MUSÉE ARIANA

PALAIS DES NATIONS

JARDIN BOTANIQUE

PARC DE L'ARIANA

PARC VILLA BARTON

Eden

LA PERLE DU LAC

La Perle du Lac

Av. de la Paix

R. de Lausanne

Av. de la Paix

Pl. des Nations

Chemin E. Rigot

Rue de France

Av. de France

PARC MON REPOS

LAC

LÉMAN

Sagano

Rue de Vermont

Rue de Montbrillant

La Voie-Creuse

R. du Valais

LE PRIEURÉ

R. Butini

Jade

R. de Richemond

R. du Prieuré

Président Wilson

Bayview

L'Arabesque

Quai Wilson

Royal

Le Duo-Côté Resto

Auteuil

Kipling

R. de la Môle

R. de Bâle

Rue de Lausanne

R. de Berne

Paquis

PORT DES PAQUIS

Rue du Grand-Pré

R. du Fort-Barreau

R. de la Servette

Rue des Gares

PARC DES CROPETTES

Le Lexique

Warwick

Pl. de Cornavin

R. de Zurich

LES PAQUIS

R. de Monthoux

Edelweiss

Ph. Plantamour

Mont-Blanc

CORNAVIN

Bistrot du Boeuf Rouge

D'Angleterre

Eastwest

Windows

Le Chat Botté

Suisse

Miyako

R. de Chantepoulet

Le Richemond

Patara

Beau-Rivage

R. des Alpes

De la Paix

Vertig'O

JET D'EAU

R. de Lyon

R. Voltaire

R. de Malatrex

Bd James-Fazy

R. Rousseau

Bristol

Mont Blanc

R. Kléber

Mandarin Oriental

Four Seasons Hôtel des Bergues

Il Lago

PIERRE DU NITON

Le Sud

Rasoi by Vineet

R. du Temple

R. Vallin

Turrettini

Q. des Bergues

Le Rouge et le Blanc

Pont du Mont-Blanc

ÎLE J. J. ROUSSEAU

RHÔNE

Pont de la Coulouvrenière

Historical and Commercial Centre (Plan III)

Mandarin Oriental

Quai Turrettini 1 ✉ 1201 – ✆ 022 909 00 00 – www.mandarinoriental.com/geneva **E3**

182 rm – 755/1470 CHF 1040/1880 CHF, ☕ 49 CHF – 22 suites

Rest *Rasoi by Vineet* ✿ **Rest *Le Sud*** – see restaurant listing

♦ Grand Luxury ♦ Art Deco ♦

Fine moiré fabrics, precious woods and marble panels set the tone in this luxury Art Deco hotel on the banks of the River Rhône. The suites on the seventh floor have terraces with fine views over the city. The last word in understated chic.

Four Seasons Hôtel des Bergues

Quai des Bergues 33 ✉ 1201 – ✆ 022 908 70 00 – www.fourseasons.com/geneva **F3**

115 rm – 725/975 CHF 775/1135 CHF, ☕ 55 CHF – 22 suites

Rest *Il Lago* – see restaurant listing

♦ Palace ♦ Stylish ♦

With a lovely location at the point where the River Rhône rises from the clear waters of Lake Geneva, this was the first of the great Geneva hotels (1834). It is the very essence of the grand hotel with excellent service and a splendid decor (period furniture, marble, fine fabrics, etc). All in all a superb luxury hotel.

Président Wilson

rest,

Quai Wilson 47 ✉ 1211 – ✆ 022 906 66 66 – www.hotelpwilson.com **F2**

180 rm – 720/890 CHF 720/890 CHF, ☕ 47 CHF – 36 suites

Rest *Bayview*

Rest *L'Arabesque* – see restaurant listing

Rest *Poolgarden Terrasse* – *✆ 022 906 64 52 (closed October-May)*

Menu 59 CHF (weekday lunch) – Carte 95/149 CHF

♦ Grand Luxury ♦ Stylish ♦

A large, modern building on the waterfront, the Président Wilson offers every conceivable comfort. This includes wonderful architectural spaces, beautiful materials, a panoramic pool and a range of restaurants. From the upper floors on the Lake Geneva side, the city pales into insignificance before the wonderful green or snow covered scenery beyond.

Le Richemond

Rue Adhémar - Fabri 8 ✉ 1201 – ✆ 022 715 70 00 – www.lerichemond.com **F3**

109 rm – 470/1015 CHF 650/1650 CHF, ☕ 50 CHF – 10 suites

Rest *Le Jardin* – *✆ 022 715 71 00* – Menu 55/98 CHF – Carte 90/142 CHF

♦ Grand Luxury ♦ Modern ♦

Opened in 1863, Le Richemond provides the perfect combination of late-19C European style and the international taste of the modern day. Its original rotunda shaped lobby and wrought iron balconies look out over the city. This contrasts with the luxuriously remodelled areas that are full of refined understatement.

Beau-Rivage

Quai du Mont-Blanc 13 ✉ 1201 – ✆ 022 716 66 66 – www.beau-rivage.ch

90 rm – 850/1300 CHF 850/1300 CHF, ☕ 47 CHF – 16 suites **F3**

Rest *Le Chat Botté* ✿

Rest *Patara* – see restaurant listing

♦ Grand Luxury ♦ Stylish ♦

A truly grand hotel established in the mid-19C. The Beau-Rivage entered into the annals of history in 1898 when Empress Elisabeth of Austria passed away in one of its rooms. Its illustrious past is ever present – though never overbearing – in the timeless beauty of its columns and pillars and its marble and stucco work. An elegant refuge from the modern world.

D'Angleterre

≤ ⅃⅝ 🏢 AC 🛜 🛁 VISA ⑩ AE ①

Quai du Mont-Blanc 17 ✉ *1201* – ☏ *022 906 55 55*
– www.hoteldangleterre.ch
45 rm – †720/1100 CHF ††720/1100 CHF, ⍩ 37 CHF
Rest *Windows* – see restaurant listing

F3

♦ Luxury ♦ Classic ♦

Is it the stone façade reminiscent of Haussmann's Paris that gives the Hotel d'Angleterre its very particular character? Or perhaps the muted London club style of its lounges, or even the carefully chosen decor (classic, Venetian, 'design', etc.) in each of its individually furnished rooms? Whatever the answer, this hotel is without a doubt the epitome of elegance.

De la Paix

≤ ⅃⅝ AC 🛜 🛁 VISA ⑩ AE ①

Quai du Mont-Blanc 11 ✉ *1211* – ☏ *022 909 60 00*
– www.concorde-hotels.com/hoteldelapaix
84 rm – †675/1100 CHF ††720/1100 CHF, ⍩ 43 CHF – 2 suites
Rest *Vertig'O* ⁕ – see restaurant listing

F3

♦ Luxury ♦ Classic ♦

The decorative themes of this hotel, based on drops of water and rose petals, are in perfect harmony with its environment. These themes are evident in all the rooms, whether they face the lake or the garden. It has a tranquil ambience with the sense of service that you would expect from an establishment founded in 1865.

InterContinental

≤ 🕮 ⅃⅝ ⑩ 🏢 ⅄ ⅀ AC rm, 🛜 🛁 P 🚗

Chemin du Petit-Saconnex 7 ✉ *1209*
– ☏ 022 919 39 39 – www.intercontinental-geneve.ch
333 rm – †320/780 CHF ††320/780 CHF, ⍩ 46 CHF – 56 suites
Rest *Woods* – see restaurant listing
Rest *Poolside* – ☏ *022 919 33 63 (closed mid September-mid May)*
Carte 61/117 CHF

VISA ⑩ AE ①

B2

♦ Chain hotel ♦ Design ♦

Situated behind the United Nations not far from Geneva's old quarter, this large international hotel is ideal for business travellers. High quality facilities, including two restaurants, one of which is alongside the swimming pool.

Bristol

⅃⅝ 🏢 AC 🛜 🛁 VISA ⑩ AE ①

Rue du Mont-Blanc 10 ✉ *1201* – ☏ *022 716 57 00* – *www.bristol.ch*
100 rm – †295/800 CHF ††295/800 CHF, ⍩ 38 CHF – 1 suite
Rest – *(closed Saturday-Sunday)* Menu 55 CHF (lunch)/125 CHF
– Carte 91/114 CHF

F3

♦ Business ♦ Classic ♦

An eminently bourgeois-style hotel with extremely comfortable rooms, which are classic yet unfussy in style. Situated in the city centre, this hotel is perfect after a day's work or shopping. There is a chic, hushed ambience in the restaurant, which offers a simpler menu at weekends.

Royal

🕮 ⅃⅝ 🏢 ⅄ AC 🛜 🛁 🚗 VISA ⑩ AE ①

Rue de Lausanne 41 ✉ *1201* – ☏ *022 906 14 14* – *www.manotel.com*
202 rm – †260/615 CHF ††260/615 CHF, ⍩ 30 CHF – 6 suites

E2

Rest *Le Duo - Côté Resto* – see restaurant listing
Rest *Le Duo - Côté Bistro* – Carte 35/90 CHF

♦ Business ♦ Classic ♦

A certain distinction emanates from this neo-Gothic style hotel, whose lounges and cosy guestrooms evoke the atmosphere of a private house. The hotel restaurant, Le Duo, offers two dining options: fine dining at Côté Resto and international cuisine at Côté Bistro.

Eastwest

🛴 🦮 🗚 🛜 🚿 💳 🎫 🅰🅴 🅾

Rue des Pâquis 6 ☒ *1201 –* ℰ *022 708 17 17 – www.eastwesthotel.ch*
41 rm – †313/435 CHF ††365/557 CHF, ☲ 35 CHF – 2 suites   **F3**
Rest *Eastwest* – see restaurant listing
♦ Townhouse ♦ Modern ♦

This pleasant, impeccable hotel is firmly up to date in style with its contemporary furniture, dark tones, occasional splash of colour and open-plan bathrooms. Extremely central location not far from the banks of the river.

Warwick

🗚 🛜 🚿 💳 🎫 🅰🅴 🅾

Rue de Lausanne 14 ☒ *1201 –* ℰ *022 716 80 00*
– www.warwickgeneva.com   **E3**
167 rm – †200/700 CHF †† 200/700 CHF, ☲ 29 CHF – 2 suites
Rest *Teseo –* ℰ *022 716 82 84 –* Menu 31 CHF (lunch)/49 CHF
– Carte 58/89 CHF
♦ Business ♦ Functional ♦

Situated just opposite the railway station, the Warwick couldn't be more convenient for train travellers. However, its location isn't the only attraction of this hotel as it boasts comfortable, contemporary-style rooms decorated in shades of pearl grey, brown and bronze.

Auteuil without rest

🛴 🗚 🛜 🚿 💳 🎫 🅰🅴 🅾

Rue de Lausanne 33 ☒ *1201 –* ℰ *022 544 22 22 – www.manotel.com*
104 rm – †240/560 CHF ††240/560 CHF, ☲ 28 CHF   **E2**
♦ Business ♦ Classic ♦

This carefully maintained hotel is an excellent example of its period. It has a simple yet elegant decor based on a skilful combination of materials and colours. Highly attractive.

Kipling without rest

🗚 🛜 🚿 🅿 🚿 💳 🎫 🅰🅴 🅾

Rue de la Navigation 27 ☒ *1201 –* ℰ *022 544 40 40 – www.manotel.com*
62 rm – †220/430 CHF ††220/430 CHF, ☲ 18 CHF   **E2**
♦ Business ♦ Modern ♦

Named after the famous wayfaring novelist, this hotel has a hint of far-off lands in its decor. The colonial style dominates, evoking the exotic Far East or the charm of the Far South. Original and attractive.

Jade without rest

🗚 🛜 💳 🎫 🅰🅴 🅾

Rue Rothschild 55 ☒ *1202 –* ℰ *022 544 38 38 – www.manotel.com*
47 rm – †220/430 CHF ††220/430 CHF, ☲ 18 CHF   **F2**
♦ Business ♦ Modern ♦

This hotel is inspired by the ideas of the famous Chinese philosopher Feng Shui and focuses on the circulation of energy. It is decorated with ethnic objects and has a tranquil, Zen-like ambience. An excellent place to rest both body and mind.

Edelweiss

🗚 🛜 💳 🎫 🅰🅴 🅾

Place de la Navigation 2 ☒ *1201 –* ℰ *022 544 51 51 – www.manotel.com*
42 rm – †220/430 CHF ††220/430 CHF, ☲ 18 CHF   **F3**
Rest – (closed 2-13 January) (dinner only) Menu 59 CHF – Carte 40/79 CHF
♦ Business ♦ Cosy ♦ Alpine ♦

Named after the famous Swiss flower (known as the immortal flower of the snow), this hotel has the typical ambience of a welcoming Swiss chalet. Light wood dominates in the guestrooms, while the restaurant boasts a real ski resort atmosphere, with its live music (every night) and cheese specialities on the menu.

Eden

🗚 🛜 💳 🎫 🅰🅴 🅾

Rue de Lausanne 135 ☒ *1202 –* ℰ *022 716 37 00 – www.eden.ch*
54 rm ☲ – †190/290 CHF ††245/345 CHF   **F1**
Rest – (closed 21 December-6 January, 26 July-18 August and Saturday-Sunday) Menu 33 CHF – Carte 44/61 CHF
♦ Business ♦ Classic ♦

This hotel dating from the 1930s was built at the same time as the nearby United Nations. Many UN employees stay here, although guests from elsewhere also appreciate its functional, well-maintained and comfortable rooms.

Suisse without rest 🔠 📶 📷 ⦿ 🅰🅴

Place de Cornavin 10 ⊠ 1201 – ℰ 022 732 66 30 – www.hotel-suisse.ch
62 rm ⊑ – †205/245 CHF ††275/305 CHF   E3
♦ Business ♦ Functional ♦
Simply cross the square in front of the railway station to get to this hotel. Each floor has a different identity with 'provincial', contemporary or classic-style guestrooms (those on the sixth floor boast a small balcony).

XXXX   **Le Chat Botté** – Hôtel Beau Rivage   ≤ 🔠 📷 📷 ⦿ 🅰🅾
😴   *Quai du Mont-Blanc 13 ⊠ 1201 – ℰ 022 716 69 20 – www.beau-rivage.ch*
       – Closed 29 March-7 April and Saturday lunch, Sunday   F3
       Rest – *(booking advisable)* Menu 70 CHF (lunch)/220 CHF
       – Carte 128/198 CHF ⅜
       ♦ French classic ♦ Elegant ♦
Foie gras from the Landes, duckling from the Dombes, and sole from the Île d'Yeu all feature on the menu of this restaurant, which includes the best French produce and a selection of superb wines. The skills of the chef perfectly illustrate the motto of the Puss in Boots fairytale (Le Chat Botté in French): "Work and expertise are worth far more than acquired goods". Impeccable service, an intimate atmosphere and a magnificent terrace overlooking Lake Geneva.
➔ Langoustine du Cap en kadaïf, vinaigrette aux agrumes, chiffonnade de basilic. Grenouille de Vallorbe en gigotin et tempura, mousseline de pousses d'épinard, crème d'ail. Foie gras de canard des Landes troussé et poêlé en tranche épaisse, olives noires confites.

XXXX   **Il Lago** – Four Seasons Hôtel des Bergues   🔠 ♿ 📷 📷 ⦿ 🅰🅾
       Quai des Bergues 33 ⊠ 1201 – ℰ 022 908 71 10
       – www.fourseasons.com/geneva   F3
       Rest – *(booking essential)* Menu 78 CHF (lunch)/130 CHF – Carte 105/163 CHF ⅜
       ♦ Mediterranean ♦ Classic ♦
An extremely chic Italian restaurant with a superb decor of pilasters and painted scenes on the walls. The fine Italian cuisine includes specialities such as beef carpaccio with black truffles and crayfish lasagne.

XXX   **Bayview** – Hôtel Président Wilson   ≤ 🛋 ♿ 📷 📷 ⦿ 🅰🅾
       Quai Wilson 47 ⊠ 1201 – ℰ 022 906 65 52 – www.hotelpwilson.com
       – Closed 2 July-2 September and Sunday   F2
       Rest – Menu 95/145 CHF – Carte 121/177 CHF ⅜
       ♦ Mediterranean ♦ Design ♦ Elegant ♦
This restaurant boasts large bay windows overlooking the lake and a sleek, sober and chic decor. It serves highly contemporary cuisine, including dishes such as supreme of Bresse chicken with lemon, almonds and green pepper, and crayfish feuilleté with glazed mushrooms.

XXX   **Windows** – Hôtel D'Angleterre   ≤ 📷 📷 ⦿ 🅰🅾
       Quai du Mont-Blanc 17 ⊠ 1201 – ℰ 022 906 55 55
       – www.hoteldangleterre.ch – Closed Sunday   F3
       Rest – Menu 52 CHF (lunch)/195 CHF – Carte 106/152 CHF
       ♦ International ♦ Brasserie ♦
Part of the Hotel d'Angleterre, this aptly named restaurant offers superb views of Lake Geneva, the Jet d'Eau and the surrounding mountains. The fine cuisine influenced by various regions is full of flavour and is by no means eclipsed by the Alps in the distance.

XXX   **La Perle du Lac**   ≤ 🕭 🔠 📷 ⇔ 🅿 📷 ⦿ 🅰🅾
       Rue de Lausanne 126 ⊠ 1202 – ℰ 022 909 10 20 – www.laperledulac.ch
       – Closed 22-26 December and Monday   F1
       Rest – Menu 62 CHF (lunch)/110 CHF – Carte 83/118 CHF
       ♦ Traditional ♦ Classic ♦
Situated in Mon-Repos park, this 100 year-old pavilion boasts a large terrace overlooking the lake. Timeless surroundings in which to enjoy classic cuisine (cod with Earl Grey tea, lamb in an almond crust etc) with background piano music in the evening.

XX
ⵊ **Rasoi by Vineet** – Hôtel Mandarin Oriental
Quai Turrettini 1 ✉ 1201 – 𝒞 022 909 00 06
– *www.rasoi.ch*
– *Closed Saturday lunch and Sunday-Monday* E3
Rest – *(booking advisable)* Menu 65 CHF (lunch)/130 CHF
– Carte 107/163 CHF
♦ Indian ♦ Design ♦ Fashionable ♦
Enjoy the fragrances and colours of Indian cuisine in an elegant and refined contemporary setting. A delightful dining experience in a chic restaurant worthy of a 21C maharaja!
➜ Tikka de saumon fumé au Tandoor. Turbot aux épices noires rôti en croûte de sésame. Cheese-cake au safran et Gulab jamun, kulfi aux mûres.

XX **Le Duo - Côté Resto** – Hôtel Royal
Rue de Lausanne 41 ✉ 1201 – 𝒞 022 906 14 14
– *www.manotel.com/royal*
– *Closed 2 weeks Christmas-New Year, 3 weeks August and Saturday-Sunday*
Rest – Menu 45 CHF (lunch)/125 CHF – Carte 71/104 CHF E2
♦ French ♦ Elegant ♦ Classic ♦
This restaurant is perfect for a romantic dinner with its intimate atmosphere. It offers ingredients of excellent origin and inventive, carefully prepared dishes such as, saddle of lamb in a herb crust and aubergine with pesto. Good selection of wines by the glass.

XX **L'Arabesque** – Hôtel Président Wilson
Quai Wilson 47 ✉ 1211 – 𝒞 022 906 67 63 – www.hotelpwilson.com
Rest – Carte 61/96 CHF F2
♦ International ♦ Elegant ♦
This restaurant has some of the magical ambience of the Orient with its gold mosaics, white leather, black lacquer and atmospheric lighting. The exotic Eastern feel is echoed in the cuisine, which focuses on Lebanese specialities such as chickpea purée and baklava.

XX **Le Sud** – Hôtel Mandarin Oriental
Quai Turrettini 1 ✉ 1201 – 𝒞 022 909 00 05
– *www.mandarinoriental.com/geneva* E3
Rest – Menu 54 CHF (weekday lunch) – Carte 67/120 CHF
♦ Mediterranean ♦ Mediterranean ♦
This chic brasserie run by Paul Bocuse overlooks the river and is part of the Mandarin Oriental hotel. The menu features cuisine from all over the Mediterranean, with specialities such as Lebanese mezze, Greek salad, Andalusian gaspacho and fish soup from Marseille.

XX **Patara** – Hôtel Beau-Rivage
Quai du Mont-Blanc 13 ✉ 1201 – 𝒞 022 731 55 66
– *www.patara-geneva.ch* F3
Rest – Menu 95 CHF (lunch)/125 CHF – Carte 75/113 CHF
♦ Asian ♦ Exotic ♦
Thai specialities served in one of the most beautiful luxury hotels in Geneva. Stylised gold motifs on the walls evoke the exotic ambience of Thailand, while the delicious specialities on the menu add to the sense of discovery.

XX **Woods** – Hôtel InterContinental
Chemin du Petit-Saconnex 7 ✉ 1209 – 𝒞 022 919 33 33
– *www.intercontinental-geneva.ch* B2
Rest – Menu 59 CHF – Carte 68/123 CHF
♦ Modern ♦ Brasserie ♦
This attractive, contemporary-style restaurant is in the Intercontinental Hotel. It boasts an attractive wood decor and serves cuisine that is full of flavour.

Vertig'O – Hôtel de la Paix   ≤ 🅰🅲 🆅🅸🆂🅰 ⓒⓞ 🅰🅴 ⓞ

Quai du Mont-Blanc 11 ⊠ 1211 – ℰ 022 909 60 73
– www.concorde-hotels.com/vertigo
– Closed end December-early, 2 weeks April, 4 weeks July-August and Sunday-
Monday   **F3**
Rest – *(bookings advisable at dinner)* Menu 65 CHF (lunch)/170 CHF
– Carte 126/149 CHF
♦ French modern ♦ Fashionable ♦
Despite its name, you will experience no Hitchcock-like fear in this restaurant,
where the cuisine is the only thing likely to raise your heartbeat. The dishes
are beautifully presented and deceptively simple, allowing the flavour of the
ingredients to shine through. Trendy decor.
➜ Légumes de Provence en vinaigrette d'agrumes et piment d'Espelette.
Aiguillette de Saint-Pierre de Guilvinec en barigoule d'artichauts et chèvre
frais. Craquelin aux abricots du Valais et amandes de Provence.

Eastwest – Hôtel Eastwest   🏠 🅰🅲 ⇔ 🆅🅸🆂🅰 ⓒⓞ 🅰🅴 ⓞ

Rue des Pâquis 6 ⊠ 1201 – ℰ 022 708 17 07 – www.eastwesthotel.ch
Rest – *(booking advisable)* Carte 55/92 CHF   **F3**
♦ Modern ♦ Design ♦ Cosy ♦
An attractive Japanese influenced decor and inviting patio contribute to the
simple elegance of this restaurant. Provençal vegetables and beef tartare fea-
ture on the menu alongside teriyaki sauce and Thai basil.

Le Lexique   🅰🅲 🆅🅸🆂🅰 ⓒⓞ 🅰🅴 ⓞ

Rue de la Faucille 14 ⊠ 1201 – ℰ 022 733 31 31 – www.lelexique.ch
– Closed 22 December-7 January, 27 July-19 August and Saturday lunch,
Sunday-Monday   **E3**
Rest – *(booking advisable)* Menu 68 CHF – Carte 75/87 CHF
♦ French ♦ Simple ♦ Fashionable ♦
Enjoy a wide selection of flavours in this pleasant restaurant near the railway
station. The focus is on fresh, seasonal produce and excellent value for money,
making this a highly enjoyable dining experience!

Miyako   ⇔ 🆅🅸🆂🅰 ⓒⓞ 🅰🅴 ⓞ

Rue Chantepoulet 11 ⊠ 1201 – ℰ 022 738 01 20 – www.miyako.ch
– Closed Sunday   **E3**
Rest – Menu 34 CHF (lunch)/105 CHF – Carte 61/99 CHF
♦ Asian ♦ Simple ♦
This aptly named restaurant (Miyako is the Japanese for heart) plunges you into
the heart of Japan. It has tatami flooring, teppanyaki cuisine, fresh fish and
attentive service. Arigato!

Sagano   🏠 🅰🅲 ⇔ 🆅🅸🆂🅰 ⓒⓞ 🅰🅴

Rue de Montbrillant 86 ⊠ 1202 – ℰ 022 733 11 50
– Closed Saturday lunch and Sunday   **E1**
Rest – *(booking advisable)* Menu 40 CHF (lunch)/90 CHF – Carte 38/93 CHF
⅛
♦ Asian ♦ Exotic ♦
Often busy with Japanese regulars, Sagano is also popular with non-Japanese
guests who are drawn by the attentive service, minimalist decor (tatami flooring
and low tables) and excellent Japanese cuisine.

Bistrot du Boeuf Rouge   🆅🅸🆂🅰 ⓒⓞ 🅰🅴

Rue Dr. Alfred-Vincent 17 ⊠ 1201 – ℰ 022 732 75 37
– www.boeufrouge.ch
– Closed 22 December-2 January, 13 July-11 August and Saturday-Sunday
Rest – *(booking advisable)* Menu 38 CHF (lunch)/54 CHF   **F3**
– Carte 52/81 CHF
♦ Traditional ♦ Brasserie ♦
Run by the Farina family for over 20 years, this restaurant serves simple, rustic,
yet fresh and tasty cuisine. Dishes include duckling terrine, fera fish from Lake
Geneva in a tarragon sauce, and raspberry tart. Attractive, Parisian bistro-style
decor.

✗ **Le Rouge et le Blanc**

Quai des Bergues 27 ⊠ 1201 – ℰ 022 731 15 50 – www.lerougeblanc.ch
– Closed 23 December-2 January and Saturday lunch, Sunday **E3**
Rest – *(booking advisable)* Menu 45 CHF (lunch)/95 CHF – Carte 67/98 CHF
♦ Modern ♦ Wine bar ♦

This restaurant with its relaxed, convivial atmosphere is a pleasant place for an enjoyable dinner. It offers simple, traditional cuisine and beef specialities served every evening (for two or three people). Well-stocked wine cellar.

LEFT BANK
Plan III

 Swissôtel Métropole

Quai Général-Guisan 34 ⊠ 1204 – ℰ 022 318 32 00
– www.swissotel.com/geneva **H1**
127 rm – ♦510/650 CHF ♦♦510/650 CHF, ☲ 42 CHF – 5 suites
Rest *Le Grand Quai* – ℰ 022 318 34 63 – Carte 81/124 CHF
♦ Luxury ♦ Classic ♦

Situated in the corner of Lake Geneva opposite the Jardin Anglais, this elonga-ted neo-Classical building (1854) evokes the splendid past of this historic diplo-matic capital. A true luxury hotel with a long tradition, the Swissôtel Métropole offers extremely comfortable rooms in a classic or contemporary style.

 Les Armures

Rue du Puits-Saint-Pierre 1 ⊠ 1204 – ℰ 022 310 91 72
– www.hotel-les-armures.ch **H2**
32 rm ☲ – ♦465/555 CHF ♦♦725/760 CHF   **Rest** – Carte 54/95 CHF
♦ Traditional ♦ Historic ♦ Modern ♦

Situated in the heart of the old town, this 17C residence has a certain charm. It has old stone walls and wooden beams, as well as some superb painted ceil-ings. It is also intimate, romantic and resolutely contemporary in style. Offering a completely different atmosphere, the restaurant is an authentic tavern serving raclettes and fondues.

 De la Cigogne

Place Longemalle 17 ⊠ 1204 – ℰ 022 818 40 40
– www.relaischateaux.com/cigogne **H1**
52 rm ☲ – ♦510 CHF ♦♦620 CHF – 6 suites
Rest *De la Cigogne* – see restaurant listing
♦ Traditional ♦ Historic ♦

A cosy, luxurious hotel decorated with pretty prints, antique furniture, paintings and carpets, all of which create a chic, delicate and classic ambience. The sense of comfort and well-being makes it very difficult to leave.

 Tiffany

Rue de l'Arquebuse 20 ⊠ 1204 – ℰ 022 708 16 16 – www.tiffanyhotel.ch
– Closed Easter **G2**
65 rm – ♦234/360 CHF ♦♦287/520 CHF, ☲ 28 CHF
Rest – Carte 48/92 CHF
♦ Traditional ♦ Classic ♦

This small, stylish Belle Époque hotel is situated on the edge of the old town. It offers Art Nouveau decor in its lobby and restaurant and Art Deco furnishings in its guestrooms. Pleasant ambience and friendly welcome.

La Cour des Augustins *without rest*

Rue Jean-Violette 15 ⊠ 1205 – ℰ 022 322 21 00
– www.lacourdesaugustins.com **G3**
40 rm – ♦295/450 CHF ♦♦345/550 CHF, ☲ 24 CHF – 8 suites
♦ Historic ♦ Business ♦ Design ♦

This hotel proves that history and up-to-date fashion can go hand in hand! Dating from 1850, the hotel is ideal for a city break in Geneva with its young, ultra-contemporary feel and designer-style decor. Some of the rooms have kit-chenettes.

SWITZERLAND - GENEVA

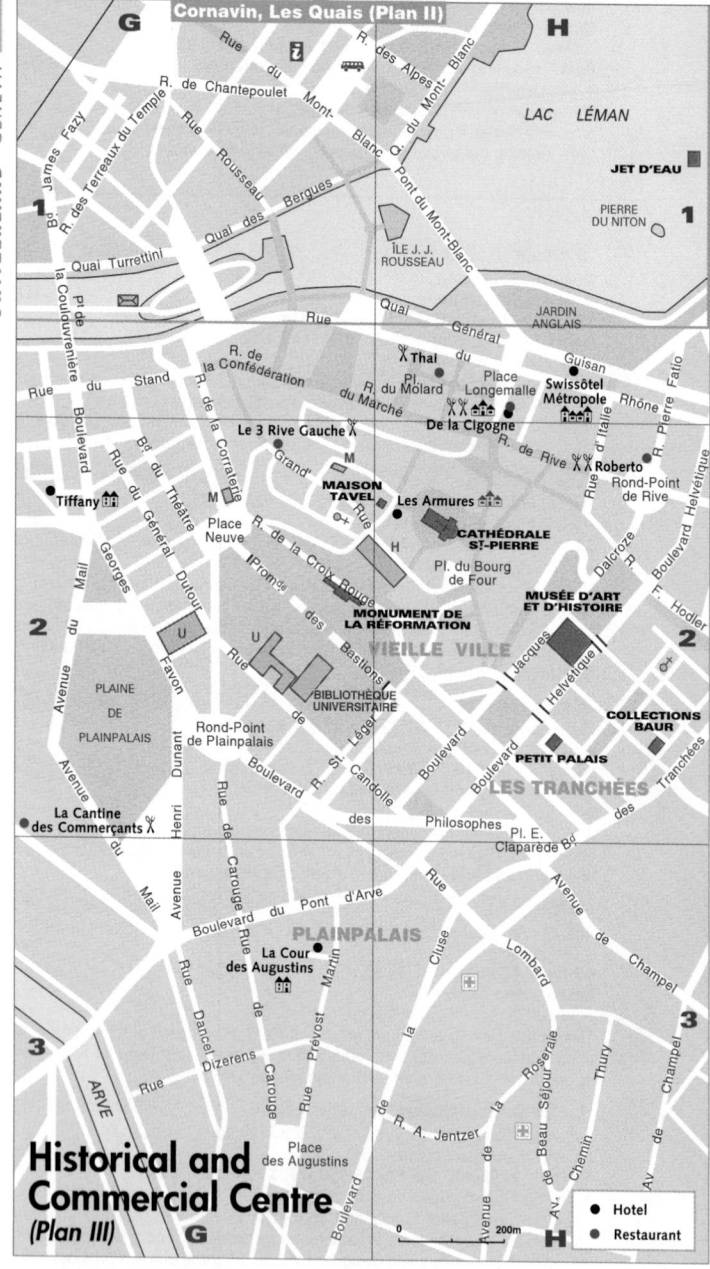

Cornavin, Les Quais (Plan II)

G   **H**

R. des Alpes

Rue du Mont-

R. de Chantepoulet

Bd James Fazy

R. des Terreaux du Temple

Rue Rousseau

Q. du Mont-Blanc

Pont du Mont-Blanc

Quai des Bergues

LAC LÉMAN

JET D'EAU

PIERRE DU NITON

1   **1**

Quai Turrettini

Rue de la Coulouvrenière

ÎLE J. J. ROUSSEAU

Quai Général du

JARDIN ANGLAIS

Rue du Stand

R. de la Confédération

Boulevard du

Rue de la Corraterie

R. du Marché

Pl. du Molard

Thal

Place Longemalle

Guisan

Swissôtel Métropole

Rhône

R. Pierre Fatio

Le 3 Rive Gauche

Grand

De la Cigogne

R. de Rive

Roberto

Rue d'Italie

Rond-Point de Rive

Tiffany

Bd du Théâtre

M

M

MAISON TAVEL

Les Armures

R. de la Croix Rouge

Boulevard Helvétique

Place Neuve

H

CATHÉDRALE ST-PIERRE

Pl. du Bourg de Four

Rue Georges Favon

Prom.

des

MONUMENT DE LA RÉFORMATION

MUSÉE D'ART ET D'HISTOIRE

F. Hodler

Dalcroze

2   **2**

Avenue du Mail

U

U

Rue de

Bastions

VIEILLE VILLE

Jacques

Rue Helvétique

COLLECTIONS BAUR

PLAINE DE PLAINPALAIS

BIBLIOTHÈQUE UNIVERSITAIRE

Rond-Point de Plainpalais

R. St-Léger

Boulevard

St-Candolle

PETIT PALAIS

LES TRANCHÉES

des Tranchées

La Cantine des Commerçants

Rue Henri

Boulevard

des Philosophes

Pl. E. Claparède Bd

Avenue du Mail

Rue de Carouge

Boulevard du Pont d'Arve

PLAINPALAIS

Rue de la Cluse

Avenue de Champel

Rue Martin

La Cour des Augustins

Rue Lombard

Avenue de Beau Séjour

Chemin Thury

AV. de Champel

3   **3**

ARVE

Rue Dizerens

Rue Dancet

Rue de Carouge

Rue Prévost Martin

Bd de R. A. Jentzer

Avenue de la Roseraie

Place des Augustins

Historical and Commercial Centre
(Plan III)

G   **H**

0   200m

● Hotel

● Restaurant

XX **Roberto**   ⌂ AK ⇄ VISA ⦿ AE

Rue Pierre-Fatio 10 ✉ *1204 –* ℰ *022 311 80 33*
– *www.restaurantroberto.ch*
– *Closed Saturday dinner-Sunday and Bank Holidays*   **H2**
Rest – *(booking advisable)* Menu 96/118 CHF
– Carte 82/120 CHF
♦ Italian ♦ Classic ♦

This restaurant is a real mecca for Italian cuisine in Geneva. Diners return time
and time again to taste the fresh, homemade pasta and Mediterranean produce
and to enjoy the classic ambience presided over by a real 'famiglia italiana'!

XX **Brasserie du Parc des Eaux-Vives**   ⟨ ⌂ & ⇄ P

Quai Gustave-Ador 82 ✉ *1211 –* ℰ *022 849 75 75*   VISA ⦿ AE ⓪
– *www.parcdeseauxvives.ch*   **D2**
Rest – Menu 49 CHF (lunch)/89 CHF – Carte 70/97 CHF
♦ Modern ♦ Trendy ♦

Situated in the Parc des Eaux-Vives, this beautiful classic-style building is fronted
by a long green lawn running down to the lake. The menu features fera fish
from the lake, as well as Swiss lamb roasted with oriental herbs. Grilled dishes
are served on the terrace on summer evenings (Tuesday to Saturday).

XX **De la Cigogne** – Hôtel De la Cigogne   AK ⇄ VISA ⦿ AE ⓪

Place Longemalle 17 ✉ *1204 –* ℰ *022 818 40 40*
– *www.relaischateaux.com/cigogne*
– *Closed Christmas-New Year, 20 July-25 August and Sunday lunch*
Rest – Menu 65/125 CHF – Carte 79/108 CHF   **H1**
♦ French classic ♦ Brasserie ♦

This restaurant is sure to please with its intimate atmosphere that is typical of
certain hotel restaurants. The classic cuisine includes dishes such as tomato
and caper tart and crayfish tails with rocket.

X **Le 3 Rive Gauche**   ⌂ VISA ⦿
☺
Grand Rue 3 ✉ *1204 –* ℰ *022 810 29 29 – www.le3rg.com*
– *Closed 21 December-5 January, 27 July-4 August and Saturday-Sunday*
Rest – Carte 63/90 CHF   **G2**
♦ International ♦ Brasserie ♦

This restaurant in the old town has an attractive menu. It features Simmental
beef tartare flavoured with basil and olive oil, grilled slipper lobster in a lobster
sauce, and vegetables in a mango sweet and sour sauce.

X **La Cantine des Commerçants**   ⌂ VISA ⦿ AE ⓪

Avenue Ste Clotilde 18 ✉ *1205 –* ℰ *022 328 16 70*
– *www.lacantine.ch*
– *Closed 23 December-3 January and Sunday-Monday*   **G2**
Rest – Menu 30 CHF (lunch)/75 CHF – Carte 55/74 CHF
♦ International ♦ Design ♦ Fashionable ♦

A neo-bistro in the old abattoir district with white and anise coloured walls,
retro decor and a long bar with seating. The menu features contemporary favourites such as risotto, grilled fish, steak and kidneys.

X **Thai**   ⌂ AK VISA ⦿ AE ⓪

Rue Neuve-du-Molard 3 ✉ *1204 –* ℰ *022 310 12 54*
– *www.thai-geneve.com*
– *Closed Christmas-early January and Sunday*   **H1**
Rest – Menu 37 CHF (lunch)/98 CHF – Carte 51/93 CHF
♦ Asian ♦ Fashionable ♦ Design ♦

The decor at this restaurant is a liberal, highly contemporary interpretation of
Thai style. The same successful blend of the modern and traditional is evident
on the menu, which features innovative and creative Thai cuisine.

SWITZERLAND - GENEVA

SWITZERLAND - GENEVA

La Réserve 🏖️ ≼ 🚗 🐕 🍴 🕤 ⚙️ 🏠 🍸 🏊 ⚒ ☕ rm, 🄰 rm, 🛜
Route de Lausanne 301 – 𝒞 022 959 59 59 🅱️ 📶 🚗 🎫 💳 🅰️ 🅾️
– www.lareserve.ch **C1**
102 rm – 🛏️420/995 CHF 🛏️🛏️480/995 CHF, ⚏ 45 CHF – 17 suites
Rest *Le Loti*
Rest *Tsé-Fung* – see restaurant listing
Rest *Le Lodge* – 𝒞 022 959 59 24 (closed October-April) Carte 68/167 CHF
♦ Grand Luxury ♦ Design ♦
This luxury hotel is a true sanctuary of beauty! Designer Jacques Garcia has used fine materials and dark colours to create guestrooms with an exotic atmosphere and a style that brings to mind an African lodge. Superb spa, access to the lake, boat available for guests – everything seems possible here. Three restaurants offering a vast selection of flavours.

Starling 🍴 🏠 ⚙️ ☕ 🄰 🛜 🅱️ 📶 🚗 💳 🎫 🅰️ 🅾️
Route François-Peyrot 34 – 𝒞 022 747 02 02 – www.shgeneva.com
496 rm – 🛏️200/420 CHF 🛏️🛏️230/460 CHF, ⚏ 39 CHF **B1**
Rest *L'Olivo* – see restaurant listing
Rest *Starling Café* – 𝒞 022 747 02 47 (closed Saturday-Sunday) (lunch only) Carte 49/101 CHF
♦ Business ♦ Contemporary ♦
Situated near the airport and Palexpo, this hotel is worthy of the A380, with almost 500 rooms used mainly by business travellers and conference guests. Despite its size, the hotel is anything but impersonal, with an attentive staff and numerous leisure facilities (fitness room, well-being centre restaurants etc.).

NH Geneva Airport 🏠 ☕ rm, 🄰 🛜 📶 🚗 💳 🎫 🅾️
Avenue de Mategnin 21 – 𝒞 022 989 00 00 – www.nh-hotels.com
190 rm – 🛏️160/360 CHF 🛏️🛏️180/400 CHF, ⚏ 31 CHF **A2**
Rest *Le Pavillon* – Carte 35/74 CHF
♦ Chain hotel ♦ Design ♦
Situated near the runways, this typical modern hotel is designed to appeal to an international clientele. Although similar to hotels elsewhere in the world, the hotel has plenty of style and offers a good level of comfort.

Suite Novotel 🚗 ☕ 🄰 🛜 🅱️ 🚗 💳 🎫 🅰️ 🅾️
Avenue Louis-Casaï 28 – 𝒞 022 710 46 46 – www.accorhotels.com
86 rm – 🛏️170/215 CHF 🛏️🛏️170/215 CHF, ⚏ 11 CHF **B2**
Rest *Swiss Bistro* – (closed Saturday-Sunday) Carte 28/56 CHF
♦ Chain hotel ♦ Functional ♦
A good value hotel on the airport road, the Suite Novotel offers large, well equipped and impeccably kept guestrooms. If possible, opt for one of the quieter rooms facing onto the interior courtyard.

Auberge du Lion d'Or (Thomas Byrne et Gilles Dupont) ≼
𝕏𝕏𝕏𝕏 *Place Pierre-Gautier 5 – 𝒞 022 736 44 32* 🚗 ☕ 🄰 🅱️ 💳 🎫 🅾️
✿ *– www.liondor.ch*
– Closed 21 December-14 January and Saturday-Sunday **D2**
Rest – Menu 78 CHF (lunch)/220 CHF – Carte 150/178 CHF 🦪
Rest *Le Bistro de Cologny* – see restaurant listing
♦ Modern ♦ Elegant ♦
Two heads are often better than one and the two chefs at this restaurant certainly combine their talents to good effect. They offer an excellent choice of produce, original food combinations and cuisine that is full of flavour. Not to mention a romantic view of the lake. A good dining option!
➔ Ris de veau doré à la poêle, asperges de Provence, émulsion de pommes de terre et muscade. Turbotin de pleine mer, cocotte de petits-pois févettes et carottes nouvelles. Jolies cerises noires au naturel, croustillant royal, glace à l'Amaretto.

XXXX
£3 £3
Domaine de Châteauvieux (Philippe Chevrier) with rm
Chemin de Châteauvieux 16 ← 🚗 🏠 Ⓐ rm, 🛜 ♻ Ⓟ 𝑉𝐼𝑆𝐴 ⓒⓞ Ⓐ𝐸
(Satigny, West: 10 km) – ✆ 022 753 15 11 – www.chateauvieux.ch
– Closed 2 weeks Christmas-New Year, 1 week Easter, 2 weeks July-August and Sunday-Monday
13 rm – 🛉220/350 CHF 🛉🛉250/400 CHF, ⌷ 20 CHF
Rest – *(booking advisable)* Menu 96 CHF (lunch)/290 CHF
– Carte 210/229 CHF 🕸
♦ Creative ♦ Luxury ♦
This picturesque restaurant (once a farm) lies off the beaten track on the out-skirts of Geneva and is surrounded by vineyards. Chef Philippe Chevrier demonstrates his technical and artistic skills through creative dishes that are full of natural flavours. Delightful guestrooms for an overnight stay.
➜ Le bavarois d'asperges vertes, œuf de poule poché et jambonnettes de grenouilles, émulsion au lard sèchè du Valais. Le pavé de thon rouge grillé, artichauts Barigoule et nage de tomates séchées aux olives Taggiache. Le biscuit aux pistaches de Sicile et cerises bigarreaux à l'infusion de thé vert.

XXX
£3 £3
Le Floris (Claude Legras) ← 🏠 ♿ Ⓟ 𝑉𝐼𝑆𝐴 ⓒⓞ Ⓐ𝐸 ①
Route d'Hermance 287 (Anières, North-East: 12 km) – ✆ 022 751 20 20
– www.lefloris.com
– Closed 23 December-7 January and Sunday-Monday
Rest – *(booking advisable)* Menu 72 CHF (lunch)/240 CHF
– Carte 128/206 CHF
Rest *Le Café de Floris* 🍴 – see restaurant listing
♦ Modern ♦ Elegant ♦ Mediterranean ♦
Le Floris serves beautifully presented food that is typical of chef Claude Legras. It is clever, creative and prepared with a light hand and a real feel for flavour. The magnificent view over Lake Geneva from the terrace provides the finishing touch.
➜ Bonbon de foie gras. Agneau de la Ferme Gavillet au thym frais. Loup cuit dans l'argile des potiers.

XXX
Le Loti – Hôtel La Réserve ← 🚗 ⌷ 🍴 Ⓐ Ⓟ 𝑉𝐼𝑆𝐴 ⓒⓞ Ⓐ𝐸 ①
Route de Lausanne 301 – ✆ 022 959 59 79 – www.lareserve.ch
Rest – Menu 75 CHF – Carte 82/160 CHF 🕸 **C1**
♦ International ♦ Elegant ♦
Named after the travel writer Pierre Loti, this restaurant with its warm tones and exotic influences, evokes a fascination with other lands. The menu features dishes such as truffle risotto, veal chops, rum baba and chocolate fondant.

XXX
Tsé-Fung – Hôtel La Réserve ← 🏠 ⌷ 🍴 ♿ Ⓐ Ⓟ 𝑉𝐼𝑆𝐴 ⓒⓞ Ⓐ𝐸 ①
Route de Lausanne 301 – ✆ 022 959 58 88 – www.lareserve.ch
Rest – Menu 90/160 CHF – Carte 72/175 CHF 🕸 **C1**
♦ Chinese ♦ Exotic ♦
The La Réserve hotel's restaurants feature cuisine from around the world. At the elegant and original Tsé-Fung, enjoy dim sum, grilled ravioli and an extensive choice of classic Chinese specialities.

XX
£3
Le Cigalon (Jean-Marc Bessire) 🏠 Ⓟ 𝑉𝐼𝑆𝐴 ⓒⓞ Ⓐ𝐸
Route d'Ambilly 39 (South-East: 5 km by Route de Chêne D3)
– ✆ 022 349 97 33 – www.le-cigalon.ch
– Closed 23 December-8 January, 28 March-9 April, 28 July-19 August and Sunday-Monday
Rest – Menu 54 CHF (lunch)/145 CHF – Carte 86/118 CHF
♦ Fish and seafood ♦ Family ♦
This restaurant's speciality is fish – whatever the day's catch brings in. It is just a stone's throw from the French border but is just as close in spirit to the coasts of Brittany and the Mediterranean. Modern interior.
➜ Les ormeaux de Bretagne dorés à la plancha aux saveurs marines. St. Pierre rôti sur un risotto à l'encre de seiche. Les langoustines sautées aux épices thaïlandais.

(vertical, right margin) SWITZERLAND - GENEVA

XX **Le Relais de Chambésy**   🏠 **P** 🆅🆂🅰 🆎

Place de Chambésy 8 – ℰ 022 758 11 05 – www.relaisdechambesy.ch
– Closed Saturday-Sunday   **C1**
Rest – Menu 52/92 CHF – Carte 66/99 CHF
♦ French classic ♦ Rustic ♦

Situated in a quiet village, this old coaching inn continues its tradition of hospitality on the outskirts of Geneva. Classic French cuisine, as well as an attractive terrace surrounded by greenery.

XX **L'Olivo** – Hôtel Starling   🏠 🅰 🆔 **P** 🆅🆂🅰 🆎 ⓘ

Route François-Peyrot 34 – ℰ 022 747 04 00 – www.shgeneva.com
– Closed 19 December-13 January   **B1**
Rest – Menu 43 CHF (lunch) – Carte 67/112 CHF
♦ Italian ♦ Mediterranean ♦

A pleasant restaurant near the airport with a large terrace shaded by olive trees. The flavours of Italy dominate the menu, which features specialities such as pasta, risotto, gnocchi with sweet chestnuts, and veal escalopes in a Milanese sauce.

XX **L'Olivier de Provence**   🏠 🅰 🆂🅰 🆎

Rue Jacques-Dalphin 13 ✉ 1227 – ℰ 022 342 04 50
– www.olivierdeprovence.ch
– Closed 22 December-6 January, 22 July-4 August and Sunday   **C3**
Rest – Menu 50 CHF (weekday lunch)/110 CHF – Carte 77/110 CHF
Rest *Bistro* – Menu 35/93 CHF
♦ Mediterranean ♦ Friendly ♦

This well-named restaurant has a real Provençal flavour. It offers dishes such as fish soup, olive oil focaccia and rouille sauce, sea bass baked with herbs, and beefsteak with tomato sauce. Traditional decor of stone walls, wooden beams and a fireplace. Good value for money at the Bistro, which serves simpler cuisine. Note that the menu offers the choice of three à la carte dishes.

X **Café des Négociants**   🏠 🅰 ⇔ 🆂🅰 🆎

Rue de la Filature 29 – ℰ 022 300 31 30 – www.negociants.ch
– Closed 23 December-3 January and Saturday-Sunday   **C3**
Rest – *(booking advisable)* Menu 29 CHF (lunch)/64 CHF
– Carte 61/98 CHF 🍷
♦ French ♦ Brasserie ♦

This retro-style bistro offers all the pleasures of flavoursome, seasonal cuisine and a wine cellar of gargantuan proportions accompanied by excellent advice. A combination that has more than proved its worth: the restaurant is often fully booked.

X **Altitude**   🅰 ⇔ 🆂🅰 🆎 ⓘ

Route de l'Aéroport 13 – ℰ 022 817 46 09 – www.altitude-geneva.ch
Rest – Menu 55/65 CHF (lunch) – Carte 78/102 CHF   **A1**
♦ International ♦ Fashionable ♦

This restaurant occupies the third floor of the airport (follow signs from the check-in desks). Contemporary decor and international cuisine (buffets on some weekends) with a view of the runways and the Alps. A good place for a meal before catching your flight.

X **Le Café de Floris** – Restaurant Le Floris   ⇐ 🏠 **P** 🆂🅰 🆎 ⓘ

Route d'Hermance 287 (Anières, North-East: 12 km) – ℰ 022 751 20 20
– www.lefloris.com
– Closed 23 December-7 January and Sunday-Monday
Rest – *(booking advisable)* Menu 53 CHF – Carte 64/89 CHF
♦ Traditional ♦ Rustic ♦

This bistro alternative to the Floris has something for every taste. It serves a range of classic and contemporary dishes including Andalusian gazpacho, micuit swordfish with chanterelle mushrooms, pan-fried calves' kidneys and lamb fajitas.

✕ **Le Bistro de Cologny** – Restaurant Auberge du Lion d'Or ⪡
Place Pierre-Gautier 5 – ℰ 022 736 44 32   🌂 ⅖ 🆎 **P** 🆅🆂🅰 ⊙⊙ 🆎 ⓪
– www.liondor.ch
– Closed 21 December-7 January and Saturday-Sunday   **D2**
Rest – Menu 51 CHF (lunch)/82 CHF – Carte 71/85 CHF
♦ Traditional ♦ Bistro ♦
An annexe to the gourmet Lion d'Or restaurant, Le Bistro is much more than an add-on. It serves delicious dishes, which proves that the chef here certainly knows how to cook! Informal atmosphere and superb views from the terrace.

ZURICH
ZÜRICH

Population: 385 468

Mirubi/Fotolia.com

Zurich has a lot of things going for it. A lot of history (2,000 years' worth), a lot of water (two rivers and a huge lake), a lot of beauty and, let's face it, a lot of wealth. It's an important financial and commercial centre, and has a well-earned reputation for good living and a rich cultural life. The place strikes a nice balance – it's large enough to boast some world-class facilities but small enough to hold onto its charm and old-world ambience. The window-shopping here sets it apart from many other European cities – from tiny boutiques and specialist emporiums to a shopping boulevard that's famed across the globe. Although it's not Switzerland's political capital, it's the spiritual one because of its pulsing arts scene: for those who might think the Swiss a bit staid, think again – this is where the nihilistic, anti-art Dada movement began. The attractive Lake Zurich flows northwards into the city, which forms a pleasingly symmetrical arc around it. From the lake, the river Limmat bisects Zurich: on its west bank lies the Old Town, the medieval hub, where the stylishly vibrant Bahnhofstrasse shopping street follows the line of the old city walls. Across the Limmat on the east side is the magnificent twin-towered Grossmünster, while just beyond is the charmingly historic district of Niederdorf and way down south, is the city's largest green space, the Zürichhorn Park.

ZURICH IN...

→ **ONE DAY**
Old Town, Bahnhofstrasse, Zurich West, Grossmünster.

→ **TWO DAYS**
Watch chessplayers on Lindenhof, see Chagall's windows at Fraumünster, Kunsthaus, Cabaret Voltaire, Café Odeon.

→ **THREE DAYS**
Utoquai, Zürichhorn Park, night at the Opera House.

PRACTICAL INFORMATION

ARRIVAL-DEPARTURE

✈ Zurich International Airport (Kloten) is 10km north of the city. Zürich Hauptbahnhof is the main railway station. Trains run every 10-15min and take 10min.

GETTING AROUND

The public transport system runs like clockwork. The city operates an efficient system on bus, tram, metro, train and boat. You can buy a single ticket, a day ticket or a 9 o'clock Pass. Tickets are available from ticket machines and tourist offices. Remember to validate your ticket at the ticket machine or special orange-coloured machine before boarding. The Zurichcard grants unlimited travel on all public transport (including river and lake boats). It also gives admission to more than forty museums and art collections. The card can be purchased for 24 or 72 hours. Cycling is encouraged here; hire bikes for free from beside the main railway station by leaving ID and a deposit.

CALENDAR HIGHLIGHTS

February
Art On Ice, Carnival Procession concluding with the Guggen Monster Concert.

June and July
Zurich Festival.

August
Theatre Spectacle.

September
Weltklasse (Athletics).

October
Zurich International Art Fair.

December
Silvesterlauf (Festive race through the Old Town).

EATING OUT

Zurich stands out in Switzerland (along with Geneva) for its top-class restaurants serving international cuisine. Zurich, though, takes the prize when it comes to trendy, cutting-edge places to dine, whether restaurant or bar, whether along the lakeside or in the converted loft of an old factory. In the middle of the day, most locals go for the cheaper daily lunchtime menus, saving themselves for the glories of the evening. The city is host to many traditional, longstanding Italian restaurants, but if you want to try something 'totally Zurcher', you can't do any better than tackle geschnetzeltes with rösti: sliced veal fried in butter, simmered with onions and mushrooms, with a dash of white wine and cream, served with hashed brown potatoes. A good place for simple restaurants and bars is Niederdorf, while Zurich West is coming on strong with its twenty-first century zeitgeist diners. It's customary to round up a small bill or leave up to ten percent on a larger one.

823

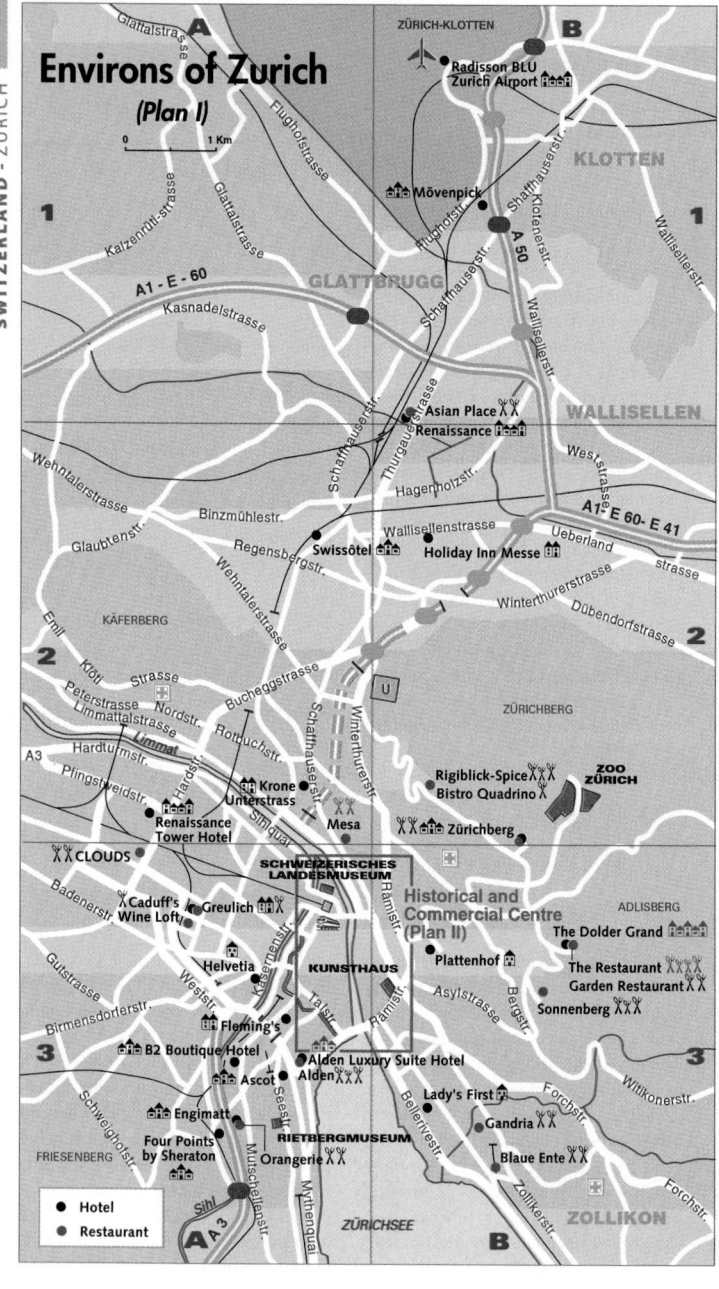

Environs of Zurich
(Plan I)

0   1 Km

ZÜRICH-KLOTTEN

Radisson BLU
Zurich Airport

KLOTTEN

Glattalstrasse

Flughofstrasse

Kalzenrüti-strasse

Glattalstrasse

Schaffhauserstr.

Klotenerstr.

Wallisellerstr.

Mövenpick

A 50

A1 - E - 60

Flughofstr.

Kasnadelstrasse

GLATTBRUGG

Schaffhauserstr.

Wehntalerstrasse

Schaffhauserstr.

Thurgauerstrasse

Asian Place
Renaissance

WALLISELLEN

Weststrasse

Glaubtenstr.

Binzmühlestr.

Regensbergstr.

Hagenholzstr.

A1 E 60- E 41

Wallisellenstrasse

Ueberland strasse

Swissôtel

Holiday Inn Messe

Wehntalerstrasse

Bucheggstrasse

Winterthurerstrasse

Dübendorfstrasse

KÄFERBERG

Emil

Klöti

Strasse

Nordstr.

Peterstrasse

Limmattalstrasse

Rotbuchstr.

Schaffhauserstr.

Winterthurstr.

U

ZÜRICHBERG

A3

Hardturmstr.

Limmat

Hardstr.

Pfingstweidstr.

Krone
Unterstrass

Rigiblick-Spice
Bistro Quadrino

ZOO
ZÜRICH

Sihlquai

Renaissance
Tower Hotel

Mesa

Zürichberg

CLOUDS

SCHWEIZERISCHES
LANDESMUSEUM

Caduff's
Wine Loft

Greulich

Historical and
Commercial Centre
(Plan II)

ADLISBERG

The Dolder Grand

Badenerstr.

Helvetia

KUNSTHAUS

Ramistr.

Plattenhof

The Restaurant
Garden Restaurant

Gutstrasse

Kasernenstr.

Talstr.

Rämistr.

Asylstrasse

Bergstr.

Sonnenberg

Fleming's

Westst.

Weststr.

Birmensdorferstr.

B2 Boutique Hotel

Ascot

Seestr.

Alden Luxury Suite Hotel
Alden

Bellerivestr.

Lady's First

Forchstr.

Wittikonerstr.

Schweighofstr.

Engimatt

Four Points
by Sheraton

FRIESENBERG

Orangerie

Sihl

RIETBERGMUSEUM

Mühlebachstr.

Mythenquai

Gandria

Blaue Ente

Zollikerstr.

Forchstr.

ZOLLIKON

● Hotel
● Restaurant

A 3

ZÜRICHSEE

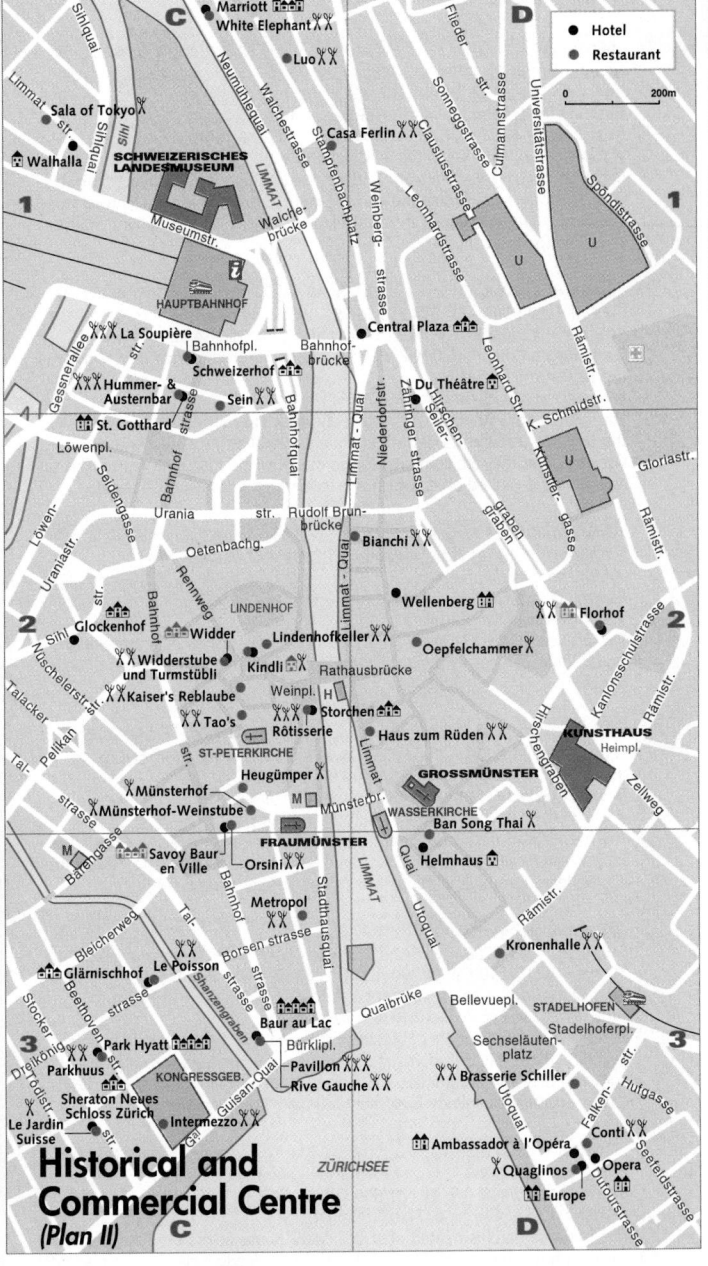

Historical and Commercial Centre
(Plan II)

Legend:
- ● Hotel
- ● Restaurant

0 ─── 200m

Map labels:
- Marriott
- White Elephant
- Luo
- Sala of Tokyo
- Walhalla
- Casa Ferlin
- SCHWEIZERISCHES LANDESMUSEUM
- Museumstr.
- Walchebrücke
- HAUPTBAHNHOF
- La Soupière
- Bahnhofpl.
- Central Plaza
- Hummer- & Austernbar
- Schweizerhof
- Sein
- St. Gotthard
- Löwenpl.
- Du Théâtre
- Bahnhofquai
- Urania
- Rudolf Brun-brücke
- Oetenbachg.
- Bianchi
- Glockenhof
- LINDENHOF
- Widder
- Wellenberg
- Florhof
- Widderstube und Turmstübli
- Lindenhofkeller
- Oepfelchammer
- Kindli
- Kaiser's Reblaube
- Weinpl.
- Rathausbrücke
- Tao's
- Rôtisserie
- Storchen
- KUNSTHAUS
- ST-PETERKIRCHE
- Haus zum Rüden
- GROSSMÜNSTER
- Heugümper
- Münsterhof
- Münsterhof-Weinstube
- WASSERKIRCHE
- Ban Song Thai
- Savoy Baur en Ville
- FRAUMÜNSTER
- Orsini
- Helmhaus
- Metropol
- Stadthausquai
- Le Poisson
- Kronenhalle
- Glärnischhof
- STADELHOFEN
- Baur au Lac
- Bürklipl.
- Park Hyatt
- Parkhuus
- Pavillon
- Rive Gauche
- Brasserie Schiller
- Sheraton Neues Schloss Zürich
- Intermezzo
- Conti
- Le Jardin Suisse
- KONGRESSGEB.
- Ambassador à l'Opéra
- Quaglinos
- Opera
- Europe
- ZÜRICHSEE
- ZÜRICHSEE

Street names:
- Sihlquai, Limmat, Sihlstr., Neumühlequai, Walchestrasse, Stampfenbachplatz, Weinberg-strasse, Leonhardstrasse, Clausiusstrasse, Sonneggstrasse, Culmannstrasse, Universitätstrasse, Spöndistrasse, Rämistr., Gessneralle, Bahnhofstrasse, Bahnhofbrücke, Niederdorfstrasse, Zähringer-strasse, Leonhard Str., K. Schmidstr., Gloriastr., Rämistr., Seidengasse, Bahnhof str., Uraniastr., Rennweg, Weinpl., Limmat-Quai, Hirschen-graben, Künstler-gasse, Kanonnsschulstrasse, Nüschelerstr., Sihl, Talacker, Tal-Pelikan strasse, Bärengasse, Bleicherweg, Beethoven strasse, Stockerstr., Dreikönig-str., Todistr., Gen. Guisan-Quai, Schanzengraben, Borsen strasse, Tal-strasse, Bahnhof str., Quaibrüke, Uhlquai, Limmat-Quai, Uloquai, Bellevuepl., Sechseläuten-platz, Stadelhoferstr., Hufgasse, Falken-str., Seefeldstrasse, Dufourstrasse, Zeltweg, Heimpl.

Marriott ⪕ ♨ ℅ 🛗 rest, 🄰🄲 🛜 🛁 🍽 🆚 🆔 🄰🄴 🆔

Neumühlequai 42 ✉ *8006 – 𝒞 044 360 70 70 – www.zurichmarriott.com*
264 rm – †430 CHF ††455 CHF, ⊑ 39 CHF – 9 suites   **C1**
Rest *White Elephant* – see restaurant listing
Rest *Echo* – 𝒞 *044 360 70 00 (dinner only)* Carte 58/94 CHF
♦ Chain hotel ♦ Classic ♦ Modern ♦
High-rise building with its own underground garage located directly by the
river. The rooms vary in size and are modern in terms of style and technical facilities. Enjoy Thai specialities in the sleek and modern White Elephant. Sunday
brunch in the Echo.

Central Plaza 🍽 ♨ ℅ 🄰🄲 rm, 🛜 🛁 🍽 🆚 🆔 🄰🄴 🆔

Central 1 ✉ *8001 – 𝒞 044 256 56 56 – www.central.ch*   **D1**
105 rm – †200/395 CHF ††220/420 CHF, ⊑ 18 CHF – 4 suites
Rest *King's Cave* – 𝒞 *044 256 55 55 (closed Saturday lunch and Sunday
lunch)* Carte 51/86 CHF
♦ Business ♦ Modern ♦
This 1883 hotel with its classic façade and spacious lobby is located opposite
the railway station and beside the Limmat. Although most of the rooms are
not very large, they are comfortable and modern. Find the King's Cave grill restaurant in the vaulted cellar, which was formerly part of the UBS Treasury.

Wellenberg without rest 🛜 🆚 🆔 🄰🄴 🆔

Niederdorfstr. 10 (at Hirschenplatz) ✉ *8001 – 𝒞 043 888 44 44*
– www.hotel-wellenberg.ch   **D2**
45 rm ⊑ – †220/390 CHF ††260/480 CHF
♦ Business ♦ Modern ♦
The location in the old town is ideal for a city break. Most of the rooms are spacious, some particularly stylish. Fitness park close by. Beauty centre directly
opposite.

Ambassador à l'Opéra 🄰🄲 🛜 🆚 🆔 🄰🄴 🆔

Falkenstr. 6 ✉ *8008 – 𝒞 044 258 98 98 – www.ambassadorhotel.ch*
45 rm – †275/540 CHF ††395/650 CHF, ⊑ 28 CHF   **D3**
Rest *A l'Opera* – Menu 68 CHF (lunch)/82 CHF – Carte 51/98 CHF
♦ Townhouse ♦ Cosy ♦ Contemporary ♦
This former patrician's house is right next to the opera house. As an extra in the
rooms: electrically adjustable beds and espresso machines. The restaurant
l'Opera features murals with operatic scenes. The speciality is fish.

Europe 🄰🄲 🛜 🍽 🆚 🆔 🄰🄴 🆔

Dufourstr. 4 ✉ *8008 – 𝒞 043 456 86 86 – www.hoteleurope-zuerich.ch*
39 rm – †210/290 CHF ††290/400 CHF, ⊑ 25 CHF – 2 suites   **D3**
Rest *Quaglinos* – see restaurant listing
♦ Historic ♦ Townhouse ♦ Cosy ♦
Hotel directly by the opera house. In keeping with the flair of the old buildings
(erected 1898-1900) the rooms are harmoniously appointed with high quality
and classically stylish furniture and fabrics. Three of the rooms have a 1950s
charm. Brasserie Quaglinos: lively, authentic with French cuisine.

Opera without rest 🄰🄲 🛜 🆚 🆔 🄰🄴 🆔

Dufourstr. 5 ✉ *8008 – 𝒞 044 258 99 99 – www.operahotel.ch*
58 rm – †260/470 CHF ††370/600 CHF, ⊑ 26 CHF   **D3**
♦ Business ♦ Cosy ♦ Contemporary ♦
This business hotel is named after the opera house across the road. Tasteful
lobby with tea-making facilities and friendly staff. Modern classic rooms, some
with a balcony.

SWITZERLAND - ZURICH

Florhof

🛜 VISA ⓸ AE ⓪

Florhofgasse 4 ⊠ *8001 – ℰ 044 250 26 26 – www.florhof.ch*
– Closed 22-30 December　　　　　　　　　　　　　　　**D2**
35 rm ⌂ – †245/310 CHF ††370/395 CHF
Rest *Florhof* – see restaurant listing
♦ Traditional ♦ Personalised ♦

It is only a few minutes walk from this decorative patrician's house dating from 1576 to the pedestrian zone. The rooms have country house furniture and appealing details, such as beautiful fabrics and wallpaper. Afternoon tea in the lounge. Two pretty terraces in the Florhof garden – one for relaxing and the other forming part of the cosy and elegant restaurant.

Helmhaus without rest

AC 🛜 VISA ⓸ AE ⓪

Schifflände 30 ⊠ *8001 – ℰ 044 266 95 95 – www.helmhaus.ch*
24 rm ⌂ – †225/320 CHF ††310/470 CHF　　　　　　**D3**
♦ Townhouse ♦ Cosy ♦ Contemporary ♦

This carefully run hotel is in the city centre near the lake. It will impress with its cosy, good value and up-to-date furnishings. There is a friendly and modern breakfast room.

Du Théâtre without rest

🕭 🛜 VISA ⓸ AE ⓪

Seilergraben 69 ⊠ *8001 – ℰ 044 267 26 70 – www.hotel-du-theatre.ch*
50 rm – †130/310 CHF ††190/340 CHF, ⌂ 20 CHF　　**D1**
♦ Townhouse ♦ Modern ♦

Today home cinema and radio plays replace the former theatre. Attic rooms with air-conditioning. La Suite Lounge has a roof terrace for breakfast and international dishes. Only a few minutes walk from the main station.

Conti

VISA ⓸ AE ⓪

Dufourstr. 1 ⊠ *8008 – ℰ 044 251 06 66 – www.bindella.ch*
– Closed 4 weeks mid July-mid August　　　　　　　　**D3**
Rest – Carte 68/111 CHF
♦ Italian ♦ Formal ♦

This restaurant is immediately next to the opera. Find an interior of classical dignity with a lovely high stucco ceiling, an exhibition of paintings, and Italian cuisine.

Haus zum Rüden

🕭 AC 🔄 VISA ⓸ AE ⓪

Limmatquai 42 (1st floor) ⊠ *8001 – ℰ 044 261 95 66*
– www.hauszumrueden.ch
– Closed Saturday-Sunday　　　　　　　　　　　　　**D2**
Rest – Carte 74/131 CHF
♦ French classic ♦ Formal ♦

This restaurant is housed in a large property dating back to 1348 in the middle of the old town. The Gothic Room is spanned by an 11m wide wooden wagon ceiling. Classic cuisine. The small Rüden Bar has a terrace.

Bianchi

🛜 AC VISA ⓸ AE ⓪

Limmatquai 82 ⊠ *8001 – ℰ 044 262 98 44 – www.ristorante-bianchi.ch*
Rest – Carte 51/121 CHF　　　　　　　　　　　　　**D2**
♦ Fish and seafood ♦ Fashionable ♦

This bright, modern restaurant is located in a quiet spot on the banks of the River Limmat. It serves Mediterranean cuisine and diners are invited to take their pick from the fish and seafood on offer at the generous buffet.

Kronenhalle

AC 🔄 VISA ⓸ AE ⓪

Rämistr. 4 ⊠ *8001 – ℰ 044 262 99 00 – www.kronenhalle.com*
Rest – (booking advisable) Carte 59/248 CHF　　　　**D3**
♦ Traditional ♦ Formal ♦

This building, constructed in 1862, is a Zurich institution located on Bellevue Square. Be sure to take a look at the art collection put together over a period of decades. The atmosphere is traditional, as is the cooking.

SWITZERLAND - ZURICH

XX **White Elephant** – Hotel Marriott   ⇐ & AC VISA ⊕ AE ①
Neumühlequai 42 ⊠ 8001 – ℰ 044 360 73 22 – www.zurichmarriott.com
– Closed Saturday lunch, Sunday lunch   **C1**
Rest – Carte 65/112 CHF
◆ Asian ◆ Fashionable ◆
Right in the heart of the city, visitors will really get their money's worth in this restaurant. It serves Southeast Asian cuisine with a focus on Thailand.

XX **Florhof** – Hotel Florhof   ⛩ VISA ⊕ AE ①
Florhofgasse 4 ⊠ 8001 – ℰ 044 250 26 26 – www.florhof.ch
– Closed 22 December-7 January, 21 April-6 May and Saturday lunch, Sunday-Monday, Bank Holidays   **D2**
Rest – Menu 47 CHF (lunch)/112 CHF – Carte 79/120 CHF ⅋
◆ French classic ◆ Intimate ◆
The pretty, intimate decor of this restaurant with its romantic garden may well inspire guests to decorate their own homes in a similar fashion.

XX **Brasserie Schiller**   ⛩ & VISA ⊕ AE ①
Goethestr. 10 ⊠ 8001 – ℰ 044 222 20 30 – www.brasserie-schiller.ch
Rest – Menu 40/70 CHF – Carte 60/97 CHF   **D3**
◆ French classic ◆ Brasserie ◆
This lovely historic building used to be the offices of the Zurich newspaper, the Neue Zürcher Zeitung. Nowadays, the modern brasserie serves classic cuisine including an opera menu available until 11pm. Sunday brunch.

XX **Casa Ferlin**   AC VISA ⊕ AE ①
Stampfenbachstr. 38 ⊠ 8006 – ℰ 044 362 35 09 – www.casaferlin.ch
– Closed mid July – mid August and Saturday - Sunday   **C1**
Rest – *(booking advisable)* Menu 56 CHF (lunch)/135 CHF
– Carte 77/131 CHF
◆ Italian ◆ Family ◆ Traditional ◆
A traditional, family-run establishment with a classic, countrified atmosphere. The restaurant was first opened in 1907 and offers Italian cooking.

XX **Luo** – Hotel Continental   AC VISA ⊕ AE ①
Stampfenbachstr. 60 ⊠ 8006 – ℰ 043 810 00 65
– Closed Saturday lunch, Sunday   **C1**
Rest – Carte 46/92 CHF
◆ Chinese ◆ Friendly ◆
Brick walls and a beautiful wooden ceiling give this restaurant a cared for, rustic feel. Delicious Chinese cuisine is on offer.

X **Oepfelchammer**   ⛩ VISA ⊕ AE ①
Rindermarkt 12 (1st floor) ⊠ 8001 – ℰ 044 251 23 36
– www.oepfelchammer.ch
– Closed 23 December-3 January, 29 March-1 April, 14 July-12 August, Sunday-Monday and Bank Holidays   **D2**
Rest – Carte 61/77 CHF
◆ Traditional ◆ Rustic ◆
The poet Gottfried Keller was a regular of the original wine bar. The restaurant serves modern and traditional cuisine in this 19C building.

X **Ban Song Thai**   AC VISA ⊕ AE
Kirchgasse 6 ⊠ 8001 – ℰ 044 252 33 31 – www.bansongthai.ch
– Closed 22 December-1 January, 22 July-12 August   **D3**
Rest – *(booking advisable)* Menu 29 CHF (lunch)/65 CHF – Carte 45/80 CHF
◆ Asian ◆ Friendly ◆
This restaurant is located near the Kunsthaus and Grossmünster. It offers authentic Thai cuisine made from fresh products - as a lunchtime buffet or from a more extensive evening menu.

SWITZERLAND - ZURICH

Quaglinos – Hotel Europe `VISA` `⑩⑩` `AE` `①`

Dufourstr. 4 ✉ *8008 –* ℰ *043 456 86 76 – www.hoteleurope-zuerich.ch*
Rest – Carte 52/101 CHF   **D3**
♦ French classic ♦ Brasserie ♦

A lively and authentic Quaglinos brasserie based on the tried and tested bistro formula. It offers typical French savoir vivre and, of course, classic French cuisine including duck foie gras and 'Café de Paris' entrecote.

LEFT BANK OF THE RIVER LIMMAT   *Plan II*

Baur au Lac `🚗` `ⅼ₅` `⅙` `AC` `🛜` `𝚊̂` `☕` `VISA` `⑩⑩` `AE` `①`

Talstr. 1 ✉ *8001 –* ℰ *044 220 50 20 – www.bauraulac.ch*   **C3**
120 rm – ♥540 CHF ♥♥870 CHF – 46 CHF – 18 suites
Rest *Pavillon* **Rest** *Rive Gauche* – see restaurant listing
♦ Grand Luxury ♦ Elegant ♦ Personalised ♦

Magnificent 19C architecture with luxurious facilities, conscientious management (the second generation of managers from the same family) and plentiful and attentive staff. Some very lovely newer rooms. A terrace leads to the pretty garden.

Park Hyatt `ⅼ₅` `🎬` `⅙` `AC` `🛜` `𝚊̂` `☕` `VISA` `⑩⑩` `AE` `①`

Beethoven Str. 21 ✉ *8002 –* ℰ *043 883 12 34 – www.zurich.park.hyatt.ch*
142 rm – ♥490/1050 CHF ♥♥640/1200 CHF, ☷ 38 CHF   **C3**
– 4 suites
Rest *Parkhuus* – see restaurant listing
♦ Grand Luxury ♦ Modern ♦ Elegant ♦

The Park Hyatt has a large, elegant hall and a lobby area with an entrance to the striking Onyx Bar. It features stylish and modern rooms with lots of space, and a tasteful little spa. The elegant Parkhuus has a show kitchen and a glazed wine cellar on two floors.

Savoy Baur en Ville `⅙` `AC` `🛜` `𝚊̂` `☕` `VISA` `⑩⑩` `AE` `①`

Poststr. 12 (at Paradeplatz) ✉ *8001 –* ℰ *044 215 25 25*
– www.savoy-zuerich.ch   **C2**
104 rm ☷ – ♥400/530 CHF ♥♥690/820 CHF – 9 suites
Rest *Orsini* – see restaurant listing
Rest *Baur* – *(closed Saturday-Sunday)* Menu 74 CHF – Carte 100/154 CHF
♦ Grand Luxury ♦ Classic ♦

The building of this wonderful hotel in 1838 laid the foundations of a long and lasting hotel tradition. Offering first class service in a made-to-measure interior, the upmarket restaurant features unusual Brazilian rock crystal chandeliers and fine table settings. Live piano music in the bar.

Widder `ⅼ₅` `AC` `🛜` `𝚊̂` `☕` `VISA` `⑩⑩` `AE` `①`

Rennweg 7 ✉ *8001 –* ℰ *044 224 25 26 – www.widderhotel.ch*
49 rm – ♥570/620 CHF ♥♥770/970 CHF, ☷ 48 CHF – 7 suites   **C2**
Rest *Widderstube und Turmstübli* – see restaurant listing
♦ Luxury ♦ Design ♦ Historic ♦

Swiss architect Tilla Theus has successfully combined old and new in these nine beautifully restored townhouses in the old city. Historic detail is combined with some lovely one-off decorative pieces. The service is excellent and the Wirtschaft zur Schtund serves tasty Flammkuchen.

Storchen `⇐` `⅙` `AC` `🛜` `𝚊̂` `☕` `VISA` `⑩⑩` `AE` `①`

Weinplatz 2 (access via Storchengasse 16) ✉ *8001 –* ℰ *044 227 27 27*
– www.storchen.ch   **C2**
67 rm ☷ – ♥430/560 CHF ♥♥600/760 CHF – 1 suite
Rest *Rôtisserie* – see restaurant listing
♦ Traditional ♦ Classic ♦

Right on the banks of the River Limmat, this is one of the oldest hotels in the city. Tasteful toile de Jouy fabrics adorn the elegant guestrooms, while the Storchen suite has a roof terrace and lake view. The restaurant's balcony terrace and the 'Barchetta' café in Weinplatz are wonderful. Sunday brunch.

Schweizerhof

🏧 📶 🦽 🗺 💳 🅱 AE ⓘ

Bahnhofplatz 7 ✉ *8021 –* ☎ *044 218 88 88 – www.hotelschweizerhof.com*
112 rm 🖵 – 🛏 440/510 CHF 🛏🛏 580/790 CHF – 2 suites   **C1**
Rest *La Soupière* – see restaurant listing
◆ Luxury ◆ Classic ◆

Established in the 19C, this city hotel with its imposing façade stands at the entrance to the pedestrian zone and is just a few steps from the railway station. It
offers excellent service with lots of extras and some particularly comfortable
junior suites. Snacks in the Café Gourmet.

Glockenhof

📶 🦽 🏧 📶 🦽 🗺 🅱 AE ⓘ

Sihlstr. 31 ✉ *8022 –* ☎ *044 225 91 91 – www.glockenhof.ch*   **C2**
91 rm 🖵 – 🛏 330/480 CHF 🛏🛏 440/600 CHF – 2 suites
Rest – Carte 42/104 CHF
◆ Business ◆ Stylish ◆

The rooms in this historic hotel in the centre of Zürich are decorated to a high
standard, often using local materials. The quietest are those facing the idyllic
interior courtyard and pretty, plant-decked terrace where you can also eat.
Other dining options are the informal Glogge Egge serving daily specials and
the modern Conrad which offers classic French cuisine.

Four Points by Sheraton

📶 🦽 🏧 📶 🦽 🚗 🗺 🅱 AE ⓘ

Kalandergasse 1 (Sihlcity) ✉ *8045 –* ☎ *044 554 00 00*
– www.fourpointssihlcity.com   **A3**
132 rm – 🛏 220/330 CHF 🛏🛏 220/330 CHF, 🖵 30 CHF – 4 suites
Rest *Rampe Süd* – *(closed Sunday dinner and Bank Holidays)*
Carte 38/99 CHF
◆ Chain hotel ◆ Design ◆

This hotel has a clean-cut style and the latest technology. The Asia Spa on the
top floor is available for use for an additional fee. International food is served in
the trendy restaurant. Guests can enjoy shopping opportunities galore at the
Sihlcity 'Urban Entertainment Centre'.

Sheraton Neues Schloss Zürich

🏧 📶 🦽 🗺 🅱 AE ⓘ

Stockerstr. 17 ✉ *8002 –* ☎ *044 286 94 00*
– www.sheraton.com/neuesschloss   **C3**
60 rm – 🛏 339/539 CHF 🛏🛏 339/539 CHF, 🖵 39 CHF – 1 suite
Rest *Le Jardin Suisse* – see restaurant listing
◆ Business ◆ Classic ◆

Just a stone's throw from Lake Zurich, this hotel features straight lines and
bright, warm natural tones. The walls of the property are adorned with paintings by Swiss artist Thomas Irniger.

Glärnischhof

📶 🏧 📶 🦽 🅿 🗺 🅱 AE ⓘ

Claridenstr. 30 ✉ *8022 –* ☎ *044 286 22 22 – www.hotelglaernischhof.ch*
62 rm 🖵 – 🛏 370/420 CHF 🛏🛏 400/470 CHF   **C3**
Rest *Le Poisson* – see restaurant listing
Rest *Vivace* – Menu 30 CHF – Carte 33/70 CHF
◆ Business ◆ Classic ◆

This business hotel in the banking quarter offers functional, contemporary
rooms, junior suites and free Wi-Fi. There are also Relax rooms with iPod stations
and Nespresso machines. Vivace serves pasta, risotto dishes (including half portions) and Flammkuchen.

St. Gotthard

📶 🎶 🏧 📶 🦽 🗺 🅱 AE ⓘ

Bahnhofstr. 87 ✉ *8021 –* ☎ *044 227 77 00 – www.hotelstgotthard.ch*
142 rm 🖵 – 🛏 275/343 CHF 🛏🛏 308/431 CHF – 9 suites   **C1**
Rest *Hummer- & Austernbar* – see restaurant listing
Rest *Lobbybar-Bistro* – ☎ *044 211 76 25* – Carte 61/94 CHF
◆ Traditional ◆ Classic ◆

Providing traditional hospitality since 1889, the St Gotthard's guestrooms offer
modern elegance in a classical setting. A great location just a stone's throw from
the main station. The Manzoni Bar serves excellent coffee.

Kindli
🛈   📶 VISA 🅾️ AE ⓪

Pfalzgasse 1 ✉ *8001* – ☎ *043 888 76 76* – *www.kindli.ch*   **C2**
21 rm ⌂ – 🛉170/360 CHF 🛉🛉220/440 CHF
Rest *Kindli* – see restaurant listing

◆ **Traditional** ◆ **Cosy** ◆ **Personalised** ◆

For over 500 years pilgrims visited this site, now guests looking for some individuality have taken their place. Although the three single rooms in the eaves don't have en-suites, they do enjoy a lovely view over Zürich. If you want to stay a little longer, try one of the excellent little apartments.

Walhalla *without rest*
📶 ♿ VISA 🅾️ AE ⓪

Limmatstr. 5 ✉ *8005* – ☎ *044 446 54 00* – *www.walhalla-hotel.ch*
48 rm ⌂ – 🛉175/210 CHF 🛉🛉235/300 CHF   **C1**

◆ **Business** ◆ **Functional** ◆

With the railway station just over the road this hotel is convenient for business travellers and tourists visiting the town. Hop onto tram no. 4 and be in the old quarter in a flash. Bike rental 50m away.

Pavillon – Hotel Baur au Lac
♿ AC 🅿️ VISA 🅾️ AE ⓪

Talstr. 1 ✉ *8001* – ☎ *044 220 50 22* – *www.aupavillon.ch*
– *Closed Saturday lunch, Sunday*   **C3**
Rest – Carte 91/190 CHF 🍴

◆ **French classic** ◆ **Elegant** ◆ **Friendly** ◆

Star architect Pierre-Yves Rochon designed the spatial concept of this elegant restaurant. The almost 360° glazed rotunda with its country views is wonderful. Good classic cuisine prepared by Laurent Eperon, with dishes that include roast sea bass with Périgord truffles.

La Soupière – Hotel Schweizerhof
♿ AC VISA 🅾️ AE ⓪

Bahnhofplatz 7 ✉ *8021* – ☎ *044 218 88 40* – *www.hotelschweizerhof.com*
– *Closed Saturday lunch, Sunday*   **C1**
Rest – Carte 87/118 CHF

◆ **Modern** ◆ **Elegant** ◆

An elegant address on the first floor. Warm colours, carefully selected furniture and elegant details set the tone. Serves seasonal, modern cuisine.

Rôtisserie – Hotel Storchen
← 🍴 VISA 🅾️ AE ⓪

Weinplatz 2 (access via Storchengasse 16) ✉ *8001* – ☎ *044 227 21 13*
– *www.storchen.ch*   **C2**
Rest – Carte 65/118 CHF

◆ **French classic** ◆ **Classic** ◆

Take a seat in the tasteful restaurant and marvel first at the wonderful painted ceiling. Then look out of the window (if you aren't already on the terrace) at the wonderful views of the River Limmat and the Great Minister.

Hummer- & Austernbar – Hotel St. Gotthard
AC

Bahnhofstr. 87 ✉ *8021* – ☎ *044 211 76 21*   VISA 🅾️ AE ⓪
– *www.hummerbar.ch*
– *Closed Saturday lunch, Sunday*   **C1**
Rest – Menu 59 CHF (lunch)/145 CHF – Carte 93/205 CHF

◆ **French classic** ◆ **Elegant** ◆

A real Zürich institution that first opened its doors in 1935. The elegant interior and signed postcards from celebrities bear witness to the cult status of this restaurant. Serves largely seafood.

Parkhuus – Hotel Park Hyatt
🍴 ♿ AC VISA 🅾️ AE ⓪

Beethoven Str. 21 ✉ *8002* – ☎ *043 883 10 75* – *www.zurich.park.hyatt.ch*
– *Closed Saturday lunch, Sunday*   **C3**
Rest – Menu 59 CHF (lunch) – Carte 48/189 CHF

◆ **Modern** ◆ **Fashionable** ◆

In keeping with the rest of the hotel, the restaurant is modern and international. It has a large show kitchen producing creative, contemporary cuisine, as well as an impressive glazed wine shop accessed via a spiral staircase.

SWITZERLAND - ZURICH

XX ★ **Sein** (Martin Surbeck)
Schützengasse 5 ⊠ 8001 – 𝒞 044 221 10 65 – www.zuerichsein.ch
– Closed 22 December-6 January, 23 March-8 April, 13 July-5 August and
Saturday-Sunday, December: Saturday lunch, Sunday   **C1**
Rest – Menu 79 CHF (lunch)/160 CHF – Carte 94/144 CHF
◆ French classic ◆ Fashionable ◆
After a little shopping in the famous Bahnhofstrasse, stop off for some creative cuisine by Martin Surbeck and his partner Patricia Lackner. The menu includes vegetarian options. If you fancy something lighter, try the tasty 'Seinigkeiten' nibbles on offer in the Tapas Bar.
➔ Wachtel-Erbsenrisotto mit roh marinierter Entenleber - und jungen Zwiebeln. Störcarpaccio auf Kartoffelstock - mit Kaviar und Sauerrahmsauce. Mariniertes Kalbsfleisch auf Kartoffelstock und Salat - mit einem Ragout vom Kalbsende.

XX **Lindenhofkeller**
Pfalzgasse 4 ⊠ 8001 – 𝒞 044 211 70 71 – www.lindenhofkeller.ch
– Closed 1 week December, during Easter, during Whitsun, 3 weeks July-August
and Sunday, January-October: Saturday-Sunday   **C2**
Rest – Menu 69 CHF (lunch)/135 CHF – Carte 63/126 CHF ♫
◆ French classic ◆ Elegant ◆ Romantic ◆
With its homely romantic touch, this elegant cellar restaurant with wine lounge fits harmoniously into the contemplative old town scene. Classic cooking with modern elements.

XX **Intermezzo**
Beethovenstr. 2 (at Kongresshaus) ⊠ 8002 – 𝒞 044 206 36 42
– www.kongresshaus.ch
– Closed 15 July-13 August, Saturday-Sunday and Bank Holidays
Rest – Carte 82/105 CHF   **C3**
◆ Modern ◆ Formal ◆
Dine in contemporary style at this bright, elegant restaurant in the lakeside Congress Centre. Friendly, attentive service at well-presented tables.

XX **Metropol**
Fraumünsterstr. 12 ⊠ 8001 – 𝒞 044 200 59 00
– www.metropol-restaurant.ch   **C3**
Rest – Carte 70/162 CHF
◆ International ◆ Fashionable ◆ Minimalist ◆
This restaurant is housed in an impressive, neo-Baroque banking building. It has a strong East Asian influence, serving sushi, sashimi and even Japanese-style bento box business lunches. Minimalist interior by Iria Degen.

XX **Tao's**
Augustinergasse 3 ⊠ 8001 – 𝒞 044 448 11 22 – www.taos-lounge.ch
– Closed Sunday   **C2**
Rest – Carte 63/109 CHF
◆ Creative ◆ Exotic ◆ Elegant ◆
A touch of the exotic in the middle of Zurich! Elegant upstairs, a little more informal on the ground floor. Smokers can use Tao's Lounge Bar that offers a Euro-Asian menu. Grilled meats.

XX **Kaiser's Reblaube**
Glockengasse 7 ⊠ 8001 – 𝒞 044 221 21 20 – www.kaisers-reblaube.ch
– Closed mid July-mid August and Saturday lunch, Sunday, April-September:
Saturday lunch, Sunday, Monday dinner   **C2**
Rest – (booking advisable) Menu 58 CHF (lunch)/135 CHF
– Carte 70/102 CHF
◆ International ◆ Rustic ◆ Cosy ◆
Enjoy modern cooking with a traditional influence in this house that was built in 1260 along a small, narrow alley. Comfortable little restaurant on the first-floor and a wine bar on the ground floor.

SWITZERLAND - ZURICH

❕❕ **Rive Gauche** – Hotel Baur au Lac   🏠 AC P VISA ⊕ AE ⓪

Talstr. 1 ✉ *8001 – ℰ 044 220 50 60 – www.agauche.ch*
– Closed mid July-mid August, Sunday and Bank Holidays   **C3**
Rest – Carte 65/131 CHF
♦ International ♦ Trendy ♦
One of the places to be seen in the city centre. The great cosmopolitan interior attracts a trendy young and young at heart crowd to eat and drink (grilled meats) but also to see and be seen.

❕❕ **Widderstube und Turmstübli** – Hotel Widder   🏠

Rennweg 7 ✉ *8001 – ℰ 044 224 25 26*   VISA ⊕ AE ⓪
– www.widderhotel.ch
– Closed Sunday   **C2**
Rest – Menu 39 CHF (lunch)/145 CHF – Carte 99/128 CHF 🍴
♦ Modern ♦ Elegant ♦
Choose between the smart, elegant atmosphere of the Widder restaurant or the more relaxed Turmstübli (smokers welcome!) with its upholstered leather benches. Seasonal, modern cuisine.

❕❕ **Le Poisson** – Hotel Glärnischhof   AC P VISA ⊕ AE ⓪

Claridenstr. 30 ✉ *8022 – ℰ 044 286 22 22 – www.hotelglaernischhof.ch*
– Closed 27 December-6 January, Saturday-Sunday and Bank Holidays
Rest – Menu 79/140 CHF – Carte 85/126 CHF   **C3**
♦ Fish and seafood ♦ Friendly ♦
As the name implies, the specialities on offer in this restaurant come from the water. Enjoy friendly service at your beautifully laid table.

❕❕ **Orsini** – Hotel Savoy Baur en Ville   ♿ AC VISA ⊕ AE ⓪

Poststr. 12 (at Paradeplatz) ✉ *8001 – ℰ 044 215 25 25*
– www.savoy-zuerich.ch   **C3**
Rest – (booking advisable) Menu 72 CHF – Carte 92/146 CHF
♦ Italian ♦ Elegant ♦
This elegant restaurant has been serving classic Italian cuisine for over 30 years. The sumptuous poppy design on the carpet, repeated in the filigree motif in the oil paintings on the walls, adds a special touch.

❕ **Münsterhof** (Tobias Buholzer)   AC VISA ⊕ AE ⓪
☘

Münsterhof 6 (1st floor) ✉ *8001 – ℰ 044 262 33 00*
– www.muensterhof.com
– Closed 1-7 January, 1 July-31 August and Saturday lunch, Sunday-Monday
Rest – (booking advisable) Menu 85 CHF (lunch)/180 CHF   **C2**
– Carte 98/139 CHF
Rest *Münsterhof-Weinstube* – see restaurant listing
♦ French classic ♦ Rustic ♦ Friendly ♦
This restaurant is a real success story. On one hand, a great combination of gourmet cuisine upstairs and wine bar downstairs; on the other, an excellent chef in the shape of Tobias Buholzer. The unbeatable location and charming interior provide the icing on the cake.
➜ Pulpo - mit Tahiti-Vanille als Cannelloni, Erbsen und Sauce von schwarzem Knoblauch. Luma Pork - Schnitzel und Knusperli mit Morcheln, Spargel-Croûton-Rolle. Challon Ente - am Stück gebraten, für zwei Personen, in zwei Service.

❕ **Heugümper**   🏠 ♿ AC ⇄ VISA ⊕ AE ⓪

Waaggasse 4 ✉ *8001 – ℰ 044 211 16 60*
– www.restaurantheuguemper.ch
– Closed Christmas-early January, 22 July-12 August   **C2**
Rest – Carte 62/105 CHF
♦ Euro-asiatic ♦ Fashionable ♦ Bistro ♦
This venerable townhouse in the heart of Zurich serves international cuisine with a Southeast Asian flair. Small lunch menu. Smart modern bistro on the ground floor and an elegant restaurant upstairs.

✗ **Le Jardin Suisse** – Hotel Sheraton Neues Schloss Zürich 🛜 AK

Stockerstr. 17 ✉ *8002* – ☎ *044 286 94 00* VISA ◕◕ AE ◑
– *www.sheraton.com/neuesschloss* – *Closed Saturday-Sunday*

Rest – Carte 51/105 CHF C3

♦ Regional/country ♦ Bistro ♦

A hint of bistro-style pervades this restaurant with its striking exposed stone wall. It offers traditional Swiss specialities that you can enjoy on the terrace (in summer) that skirts round the building.

✗ **Kindli** – Hotel Kindli 🛜 VISA ◕◕ AE ◑

Pfalzgasse 1 ✉ *8001* – ☎ *043 888 76 78* – *www.kindli.ch*
– *Closed Sunday and Bank Holidays* C2

Rest – Carte 62/96 CHF

♦ French classic ♦ Bistro ♦

The restaurant's charming character comes in part from its wonderful old wood panelling and the bistro-style, communal arrangement of its beautifully laid tables.

✗ **Sala of Tokyo** 🛜 AK ⇧ VISA ◕◕ AE ◑

Limmatstr. 29 ✉ *8005* – ☎ *044 271 52 90* – *www.sala-of-tokyo.ch* – *Closed 24 December-9 January, 21 July-11 August and Saturday lunch, Sunday-Monday*

Rest – Menu 72/180 CHF – Carte 53/193 CHF C1

♦ Asian ♦ Friendly ♦ Exotic ♦

This restaurant has been serving authentic Japanese cuisine for over 30 years. In the air-conditioned Sankaiyaki Room meat is grilled at your table in traditional-style. And of course there is a sushi bar.

✗ **Münsterhof-Weinstube** – Restaurant Münsterhof AK

Münsterhof 6 ✉ *8001* – ☎ *044 262 33 00* VISA ◕◕ AE ◑
– *www.muensterhof.com*
– *Closed 1-7 January and Saturday lunch, Sunday-Monday* C2

Rest – Menu 78 CHF – Carte 45/96 CHF

♦ International ♦ Wine bar ♦

The Weinstube on the ground floor attracts diners in search of something a little simpler but not at the expense of quality. The chef is the same as in the gourmet restaurant. Here he serves up dishes such as homemade ravioli, as well as more hearty fare.

NEAR THE AIRPORT *Plan I*

🏠🏠🏠 **Radisson BLU Zurich Airport** ≤ ⅃♨ 🏛 & AK 🛜 ⅙

(directly access to the terminals) ✉ *8058* VISA ◕◕ AE ◑
– ☎ *044 800 40 40* – *www.zurich.radissonblu.com* B1

330 rm – †215/495 CHF ††215/495 CHF, ⊡ 37 CHF – 7 suites

Rest *Angels' Wine Tower Grill* – *(closed Sunday-Monday) (dinner only)*
Carte 65/142 CHF

Rest *filini* – ☎ *044 800 42 20* – Carte 57/110 CHF

♦ Business ♦ Conference hotel ♦ Modern ♦

This is the closest hotel to the airport and it has a 16m-high Wine Tower rising from the imposing atrium lobby. During dinner, marvel as the 'Wine Angels' perform their artistic show at the Angels restaurant (as well as during brunch on Sundays). The Filini restaurant serves Italian specialities.

🏠🏠🏠 **Renaissance** ⅃♨ 🏛 🖾 & AK 🛜 ⅙ 🚗 VISA ◕◕ AE ◑

Thurgauerstr. 101 (Glattpark) – ☎ *044 874 50 00* – *www.renaissancezurich.com*

204 rm – †355 CHF ††355 CHF, ⊡ 37 CHF – 7 suites B1

Rest *Asian Place* – see restaurant listing

Rest *Brasserie und Terrace* – ☎ *044 874 57 21* – Carte 45/81 CHF

♦ Business ♦ Chain hotel ♦ Classic ♦

A koi carp tank adorns the foot of the spiral staircase in the middle of the hotel lobby! Facilities include a large public gym. The Asian Place restaurant serves food ranging from Japanese to Indonesian. The brasserie serves a lunch buffet only with brunch on Sundays. Evening meals are available on the adjoining terrace at 'Next2', which also has a bar.

Mövenpick 🈔 ☕ ⓵ ✆ ⓺ 🅿 VISA ⓸ AE ⓸

Walter Mittelholzerstr. 8 – ✆ *044 808 88 88*
– *www.moevenpick-hotels.com/zuerich-airport* **B1**
333 rm – 🛈245/385 CHF 🛈🛈245/385 CHF, ☟ 33 CHF – 10 suites
Rest – Carte 48/88 CHF
Rest *Le Chalet* – ✆ *044 808 85 55 (closed Saturday lunch)* Menu 75 CHF
– Carte 59/103 CHF
Rest *Dim Sum* – ✆ *044 808 84 44 (closed Saturday lunch, Sunday)* Menu
59/75 CHF – Carte 34/81 CHF
♦ Chain hotel ♦ Modern ♦
This hotel has an ideal location close to the motorway and airport. Clear lines
and cosy colours extend from the lobby through to the guestrooms. The
Appenzeller Stube offers traditional Swiss culinary style while Chinese food is
available in Dim Sum. The hotel restaurant serves brunch on Sundays.

 Swissôtel ⓵ 🈔 ⓵ ⓺ 🗔 ⓸ 🄰 ✆ ⓺ VISA ⓸ AE ⓸

Schulstr. 44 (at Marktplatz) – ✆ *044 317 31 11* – *www.swissotel.com/zurich*
347 rm – 🛈250/580 CHF 🛈🛈250/580 CHF, ☟ 35 CHF – 11 sui- **A2**
tes
Rest *Le muh* – ✆ *044 317 33 91* – Carte 44/89 CHF
♦ Business ♦ Chain hotel ♦ Contemporary ♦
This high-rise hotel is located in the Marktplatz in the centre of Zürich. It boasts
an indoor swimming pool on the 32nd floor with views over the whole city and
a 19-room convention centre. The Le Muh restaurant is divided into two parts:
one casual, the other more elegant.

 Holiday Inn Messe 🈔 🈔 ⓸ 🄰 ⓵ ⓺ VISA ⓸ AE ⓸

Wallisellenstr. 48 – ✆ *044 316 11 00* – *www.holidayinn.com/zurichmesse*
164 rm – 🛈149/349 CHF 🛈🛈149/349 CHF, ☟ 28 CHF **B2**
Rest – Carte 42/73 CHF
♦ Business ♦ Modern ♦ Functional ♦
This hotel stands out chiefly for its convenient location opposite the conference
centre. The spacious rooms are functionally equipped. The 'Bits & Bites' brasserie serves Swiss and international cuisine.

XX **Asian Place** – Hotel Renaissance 🄰 ⓸ VISA ⓸ AE ⓸

Thurgauerstr. 101 (Glattpark) – ✆ *044 874 57 21*
– *www.renaissancezurich.com*
– *Closed 2 weeks mid July and Saturday lunch, Sunday* **B1**
Rest – Menu 39/79 CHF – Carte 48/74 CHF
♦ Asian ♦ Elegant ♦
Asian Place takes you on a tour through the cuisines of Southeast Asia in an elegant decor characterised by its classy, yellow-buttoned leather sofas. The attentive, traditionally clad front of house team serves specialities from Japan, Thailand and China.

ENVIRONS OF ZURICH *Plan I*

 The Dolder Grand ⓺ ⓵ 🈔 🈔 ⓸ ⓵ 🗔 XX ⓸ 🄰 ⓵ ⓺ ⓺

Kurhausstr. 65 ✉ *8032* – ✆ *044 456 60 00* VISA ⓸ AE ⓸
– *www.thedoldergrand.com* **B3**
173 rm – 🛈540/970 CHF 🛈🛈590/1070 CHF, ☟ 32 CHF – 11 suites
Rest *The Restaurant* ❀❀ **Rest** *Garden Restaurant* – see restaurant listing
♦ Grand Luxury ♦ Modern ♦ Historic ♦
The embodiment of exclusivity. Emanating from the 'Curhaus' of 1899 and committed to this tradition just as much as to the requirements of today. The crème
de la crème is the 400m² Maestro suite high above Zurich. There are 4000m² of
various spa facilities in purist style. Panoramic view from the terrace of the Garden Restaurant. Brunch is served on Sundays.

Renaissance Tower Hotel

Turbinenstr. 20 ✉ *8005* – ☏ *044 630 30 30*
– *www.renaissancezurichtower.com*

A2

300 rm – ✚195/565 CHF ✚✚195/565 CHF, ⌷ 25 CHF – 13 suites
Rest *Equinox* – Menu 30 CHF (lunch) – Carte 58/107 CHF

♦ Luxury ♦ Business ♦ Modern ♦

The reception area with its smart minimalist design in light and dark contrasting tones sets the "urban lifestyle" tone which continues throughout the hotel in the rooms, the restaurant and the lobby bar. The Executive Club Lounge and 24hr health club and fitness suite on the top floor offer magnificent views.

Alden Luxury Suite Hotel

Splügenstr. 2 ✉ *8002* – ☏ *044 289 99 99* – *www.alden.ch*

A3

22 suites ⌷ – ✚600/1800 CHF ✚✚600/1800 CHF
Rest *Alden* – see restaurant listing

♦ Luxury ♦ Design ♦

A great little hotel housed in a magnificent listed building dating back to 1895 with individual, exquisitely designed guestrooms. Non-alcoholic drinks from the mini-bar are included in the price. Two loft suites with a roof terrace.

Zürichberg

Orellistr. 21 ✉ *8044* – ☏ *044 268 35 35* – *www.zuerichberg.ch*

B2

66 rm ⌷ – ✚290/590 CHF ✚✚320/590 CHF
Rest *Zürichberg* – see restaurant listing

♦ Traditional ♦ Design ♦

On the outside the classical assembly rooms (1900) contrast with the timber-clad elliptical annexe. On the inside find chic clean-lined design, art and comfort. Enjoy the peace and the view of the city, lake and region from the restaurant terrace. Brunch is served on Sundays.

B2 Boutique Hotel without rest

Brandschenkenstr. 152 ✉ *8002* – ☏ *044 567 67 67*
– *www.b2boutiquehotels.com*

A3

60 rm ⌷ – ✚350 CHF ✚✚400 CHF – 1 suite

♦ Historic ♦ Design ♦

Housed in a listed brewery building constructed in 1866, this strikingly chic hotel will appeal predominantly to younger guests and architecture enthusiasts. The Bibliothek bar (over 30 000 books) serves Spanischbrödlis (hazelnut and carrot pastries) dubbed 'SWaPPa's' or Swiss tapas. The thermal bath and spa are particularly impressive (additional charge).

Ascot

Tessinerplatz 9 ✉ *8002* – ☏ *044 208 14 14* – *www.ascot.ch*

A3

74 rm ⌷ – ✚195/550 CHF ✚✚250/640 CHF
Rest – (closed Saturday-Sunday) Carte 68/128 CHF

♦ Traditional ♦ Classic ♦

The rooms in this hotel in the business district offer modern style and technology. They are all equipped with tea/coffee machines and some have balconies. The restaurant, very "British" with its leather upholstery, mahogany and chequered carpet, serves steaks and seafood. Its speciality is classic roast beef carved from the trolley.

Engimatt

Engimattstr. 14 ✉ *8002* – ☏ *044 284 16 16* – *www.engimatt.ch*

A3

84 rm ⌷ – ✚250/340 CHF ✚✚310/470 CHF – 2 suites
Rest *Orangerie* – see restaurant listing

♦ Business ♦ Personalised ♦

Despite its location close to the city centre this hotel is a green oasis in the district of Enge. A dedicated, family-run hotel with individual guestrooms in cosy colours and each with its own balcony. The restaurant is located in an airy conservatory overlooking the garden.

🏨 Greulich   🕭 🤶 🏠 🅿 🎫 ⦿ ⑩

Herman-Greulich-Str. 56 ⊠ *8004* – 🕿 *043 243 42 43* – *www.greulich.ch*
– Closed 22 December-2 January   **A3**
28 rm – 🛆200/275 CHF 🛆🛆240/315 CHF, ☕ 26 CHF – 5 suites
Rest *Greulich* – see restaurant listing
◆ Business ◆ Modern ◆

Smart, bright and minimalist, the rooms (which include some junior suites) are accessible from the interior courtyard with its birch trees, sound sculpture and herb garden. Enjoy an organic breakfast in the morning or a slice of cake on the pavement café in the afternoon. The restaurant menu is also served on the courtyard terrace.

🏨 Krone Unterstrass   🕭 rm, 🗚 rm, 🤶 🏠 🅿 🎫 ⦿ ⑩

Schaffhauserstr. 1 ⊠ *8006* – 🕿 *044 360 56 56* – *www.hotel-krone.ch*
76 rm – 🛆185/210 CHF 🛆🛆260/450 CHF, ☕ 19 CHF   **A2**
Rest – Carte 57/93 CHF
◆ Business ◆ Contemporary ◆

Hotel above the city centre. Technically well-equipped rooms, the newer ones in the town house have a small kitchen and face the courtyard. Simple daytime restaurant or more refined restaurant with fireplace and bar. Good parking facilities in the nearby public car park.

🏠 Lady's First *without rest*   🕭 🕭 🤶 🎫 ⦿ ⑩

Mainaustr. 24 ⊠ *8008* – 🕿 *044 380 80 10* – *www.ladysfirst.ch*
– Closed 23 December-4 January   **B3**
28 rm ☕ – 🛆230/325 CHF 🛆🛆290/395 CHF
◆ Family ◆ Modern ◆

An individual establishment designed by women. Old building charm meets modern design. For women only: sauna area with roof terrace and massage facilities. Men are also welcome as hotel guests.

🏠 Plattenhof   🤶 🕭 🤶 🎫 ⦿ ⑩

Plattenstr. 26 ⊠ *8032* – 🕿 *044 251 19 10* – *www.plattenhof.ch*
37 rm ☕ – 🛆190/375 CHF 🛆🛆205/395 CHF   **B3**
Rest *Sento* – 🕿 *044 251 16 15 (closed Christmas-early January and Satur-day-Sunday, Bank Holidays)* Carte 52/74 CHF
◆ Business ◆ Design ◆ Minimalist ◆

This hotel is in a residential quarter on the edge of the city centre. Find distinctly personal service and functional rooms in a modern, plain, designer style. Sento has a bistro atmosphere and serves Italian cuisine.

🏠 Fleming's   🗚 🤶 🎫 ⦿ ⑩

Brandschenkestr. 10 ⊠ *8001* – 🕿 *044 563 00 00*
– www.flemings-hotels.com   **A3**
28 rm ☕ – 🛆236/481 CHF 🛆🛆292/537 CHF   **Rest** – Carte 41/60 CHF
◆ Business ◆ Modern ◆

This hotel, close to the stock exchange, contains modern, functional, good value rooms. The granite-glass baths integrated into the space are remarkable. Wi-fi at no extra cost.

🏠 Helvetia   🤶 🎫 ⦿ ⑩

Stauffacherquai 1 ⊠ *8004* – 🕿 *044 297 99 99* – *www.hotel-helvetia.ch*
16 rm – 🛆220/280 CHF 🛆🛆250/350 CHF, ☕ 10 CHF   **A3**
Rest – Carte 49/104 CHF
◆ Townhouse ◆ Cosy ◆ Contemporary ◆

Your host at the Helvetia is relaxed and friendly, just like his hotel where you will quickly feel at home. The rooms are charming with their mix of Art Nouveau and modern touches, as is the restaurant with its stylish upmarket decor and Swiss/French brasserie-style cuisine.

XXXX
ξ3 ξ3

The Restaurant – Hotel The Dolder Grand ⟨ 🛱 ὕ 🖾

Kurhausstr. 65 ⊠ *8032* – ℰ *044 456 60 00* 🚾 ⦿ 🖾 ⓞ
– *www.thedoldergrand.com*
– *Closed 19-28 February, 21 July-13 August and Saturday lunch, Sunday-Monday*   **B3**
Rest – *(booking advisable)* Menu 158/233 CHF – Carte 164/226 CHF
♦ Creative ♦ Fashionable ♦ Classic ♦

Heiko Nieder not only combines textures and flavours with great feeling, he also arranges every dish with such lavish flamboyance that every plate that leaves the kitchen is a masterpiece in its own right. As for the setting, the lovely old coffered ceiling sits comfortably alongside the smart modern wine cabinets. The terrace offers views of both lake and city.

→ Entenmastleber mit Randen, Himbeeren und Verveine. Spargel mit Kaviar, Ei und Brunnenkresse. Dessert von Heidelbeeren, Sellerie, Gurke und Ingwer.

XXX
ξ3

Rigiblick - Spice with rm ⟨ 🛱 ὕ rest. 🛜 🕾 🚾 ⦿ 🖾 ⓞ

Germaniastr. 99 ⊠ *8044* – ℰ *043 255 15 70* – *www.restaurantrigiblick.ch*
– *Closed 23-30 December and Sunday-Monday*   **B2**
7 rm – ♥490/900 CHF ♥♥490/900 CHF
Rest – *(booking advisable)* Menu 66 CHF (lunch)/195 CHF 🍴
Rest *Bistro Quadrino*🍴 – see restaurant listing
♦ Creative ♦ Formal ♦

Creative cuisine lives on at this restaurant under the new young head chef Dennis Puchert. He offers a nine-course menu (you can opt for fewer) in the evenings and a simpler selection at genuinely reasonable prices at lunchtimes. Try a table on the terrace with its impressive view of Zürich. If you want to stay overnight there are a number of ultra-modern junior suites.

→ Thunfisch, Rande, Sauerrahm. Ente, Müsli, Pfifferlinge. Pflaume, Reis, Ingwer.

XXX

Sonnenberg ⟨ 🛱 ὕ 🖾 ⇄ 🅿 🚾 ⦿ 🖾 ⓞ

Hitzigweg 15 ⊠ *8032* – ℰ *044 266 97 97* – *www.sonnenberg-zh.ch*
Rest – *(booking advisable)* Menu 50 CHF – Carte 58/131 CHF   **B3**
🍴
♦ French classic ♦ Formal ♦

A bright, elegant restaurant with attentive table service and an impressive view over Zürich and the lake. The house specialities are veal and beef dishes.

XXX

Alden – Alden Luxury Suite Hotel 🛱 ὕ 🖾 🅿 🚾 ⦿ 🖾 ⓞ

Splügenstr. 2 ⊠ *8002* – ℰ *044 289 99 99* – *www.alden.ch*   **A3**
Rest – Menu 60 CHF (lunch) – Carte 73/124 CHF
♦ Mediterranean ♦ Cosy ♦

The interior of the restaurant is characterised by pure, clean lines. One of the rooms has a wonderful stucco ceiling you shouldn't miss. Classically based Mediterranean cuisine with a contemporary twist.

XX
ξ3

CLOUDS ⟨ ὕ 🖾 ⇄ 🚾 ⦿ 🖾

Maagplatz 5 (at Prime Tower, 35th floor) ⊠ *8005* – ℰ *044 404 30 00*
– *www.clouds.ch*
– *Closed Saturday lunch*   **A3**
Rest – *(booking essential)* Carte 87/127 CHF
♦ Mediterranean ♦ Elegant ♦

At Clouds the term 'high end' takes on a double meaning. Firstly, because this latest Zürich gastro-hotspot sits a cool 126m above the ground, and secondly, thanks to David Martínez Salvany's high quality, modern, Mediterranean-style cuisine. The lively bistro serves everything from breakfast to tapas.

→ Mediterrane Fischsuppe Clouds. Lammrücken & orientalisches Ragout aus der Schulter mit Gewürz-Cous-Cous. Himbeerschokoladenschnitte mit Joghurteis.

XX **Mesa** 🛜 ᕹ 📶 VISA ⓪ AE

Weinbergstr. 75 ✉ *8006 –* ✆ *043 321 75 75*
– www.mesa-restaurant.ch
– Closed Christmas-mid January, 3 weeks July-August and Saturday lunch,
Sunday-Monday   A2
Rest *– (booking advisable)* Menu 55 CHF (lunch)/225 CHF
♦ Modern ♦ Minimalist ♦
Where quality, craft and sensitivity come together, even the most unlikely combinations are apt to produce harmonious results. Mesa's lunchtime offerings are less expensive than its evening menu, so there is really no excuse for not sampling Marcus G. Lindner's excellent contemporary cuisine!

XX **Garden Restaurant** – Hotel The Dolder Grand ᕻ 🛜 ᕹ 📶

Kurhausstr. 65 ✉ *8032 –* ✆ *044 456 60 00*   VISA ⓪ AE ⓪
– www.thedoldergrand.com   A3
Rest *–* Menu 60/120 CHF *–* Carte 82/130 CHF
♦ International ♦ Fashionable ♦
The international and Mediterranean style cuisine and fantastic panoramic terrace are strong arguments for trying this restaurant. It also has a modern design and exclusive service. Brunch served on Sundays.

XX **Gandria** 🛜 VISA ⓪ AE

Rudolfstr. 6 ✉ *8008 –* ✆ *044 422 72 42*
– www.restaurant-gandria.ch
– Closed Christmas-7 January, 5-26 May, 15-22 September and Saturday lunch,
Sunday, January-October: Saturday-Sunday   B3
Rest *–* Carte 63/105 CHF
♦ Mediterranean ♦ Family ♦ Cosy ♦
The Draxlers serve Mediterranean food in this comfortable restaurant close to Lake Zurich. Gernot is at the helm in the kitchen and Regula deals with front of house. A very popular lunchtime haunt.

XX **Zürichberg** – Hotel Zürichberg ᕻ 🛜 ᕹ VISA ⓪ AE ⓪

Orellistr. 21 ✉ *8044 –* ✆ *044 268 35 35 – www.zuerichberg.ch*
Rest *–* Menu 45 CHF (lunch) *–* Carte 53/100 CHF   B2
♦ Modern ♦ Design ♦
An interesting restaurant in an exposed position dominated by strong design features. Diners have a front row view as the chefs set about their work in the exemplary show kitchen. Brunch on Sundays.

XX **Blaue Ente** 🛜 ⇆ VISA ⓪ AE ⓪
🦢
Seefeldstr. 223 ✉ *8008 –* ✆ *044 388 68 40*
– www.blaue-ente.ch
– Closed 1 week end December, 2 weeks February, 2 weeks July-August and
Sunday   B3
Rest *– (booking advisable)* Menu 65/98 CHF
– Carte 57/107 CHF
♦ Modern ♦ Trendy ♦ Friendly ♦
Historical building on the outside, trendy and lively atmosphere inside. Find very friendly and accommodating service. The tasty food ranges from brasserie-style to classic French dishes. The old machinery is a real eye-catcher. Pleasant courtyard.

XX **Orangerie** – Hotel Engimatt 🛜 🍽 ᕹ VISA ⓪ AE ⓪

Engimattstr. 14 ✉ *8002 –* ✆ *044 284 16 16 – www.engimatt.ch*
Rest *–* Menu 53 CHF *–* Carte 39/80 CHF   A3
♦ Traditional ♦ Friendly ♦
In winter and summer alike eating at the Orangerie is like sitting out under a beautiful open sky. The restaurant consists of an elegant, light and airy conservatory, as well as a beautifully appointed terrace. Traditional cuisine.

✗
☺

Bistro Quadrino – Restaurant Rigiblick   ← 🛋 ⚹ 𝗩𝗜𝗦𝗔 ⓒⓓ 𝗔𝗘 ⓘ

Germaniastr. 99 ✉ *8044 –* ☏ *043 255 15 70 – www.restaurantrigiblick.ch*
– Closed 23-30 December and Monday   **B2**
Rest – Menu 58/68 CHF – Carte 48/88 CHF
♦ International ♦ Bistro ♦ Fashionable ♦

The atmosphere at Bistro Quadrino is pleasantly informal and its prices fair.
Snacks including flammekueche are available all day in addition to the delicious
menu, which includes rump steak with herb butter and baked potatoes. Lounge
area, bar food and walk-in wine cabinet.

✗

Caduff's Wine Loft   🛋 𝗩𝗜𝗦𝗔 ⓒⓓ 𝗔𝗘 ⓘ

Kanzleistr. 126 ✉ *8004 –* ☏ *044 240 22 55 – www.wineloft.ch*
– Closed 24 December-3 January, Saturday and Sunday   **A3**
Rest – *(booking advisable)* Carte 46/113 CHF 🍷
♦ Modern ♦ Trendy ♦

This fashionable venue has a modern loft atmosphere. As well as the delicious
fresh cooking made from quality products, there is an impressive wine selection, with over 2,000 labels on offer.

✗

Greulich – Hotel Greulich   🛋 ⚹ 𝗣 𝗩𝗜𝗦𝗔 ⓒⓓ 𝗔𝗘 ⓘ

Herman-Greulich-Str. 56 ✉ *8004 –* ☏ *043 243 42 43 – www.greulich.ch*
– Closed 22 December-2 January and Saturday lunch, Sunday lunch
Rest – *(booking advisable)* Menu 44 CHF (lunch)/74 CHF   **A3**
– Carte 32/68 CHF
♦ Modern ♦ Trendy ♦

Greulich offers contemporary cuisine with seasonal and Mediterranean influences. It is served in the form of 'small plates', which you can combine as the fancy
takes you. Reduced menu at lunchtimes. Various vegetarian options. Lovely
interior courtyard terrace.

→ **AREA:**
244 157 km² (94 269 sq mi).

→ **POPULATION:**
63 100 000 inhabitants.
Density = 258 per km².

→ **CAPITAL:** London.

→ **CURRENCY:**
Pound Sterling (£).

→ **GOVERNMENT:**
Constitutional parliamentary
monarchy (since 1707). Member
of European Union since 1973.

→ **LANGUAGE:** English.

→ **PUBLIC HOLIDAYS:**
New Year's Day (1 Jan); Good Friday
(late Mar/Apr); Easter Monday
(late Mar/Apr); Early May Bank
Holiday (first Mon in May); Spring
Bank Holiday (last Mon in May);
Summer Bank Holiday (last Mon
in Aug); Christmas Day (25 Dec);
Boxing Day (26 Dec).

→ **LOCAL TIME:**
GMT in winter and GMT
+1 hour in summer.

→ **CLIMATE:**
Temperate maritime with cool
winters and mild summers
(London: January 3°C; July
17°C), rainfall evenly distributed
throughout the year.

→ **EMERGENCY:**
Police, Medical Assistance, Fire
Brigade ✆ **999** – also used for
Mountain, Cave, Coastguard and
Sea Rescue. (Dialling **112** within
any EU country will redirect your
call and contact the emergency
services.)

Glasgow

Edinburgh

Birmingham

LONDON

→ **ELECTRICITY:**
230 volts AC, 50Hz; 3 flat pin
sockets.

→ **FORMALITIES:**
Travellers from the European
Union (EU), Switzerland, Iceland,
the main countries of North
and South America and some
Commonwealth countries need
a national identity card or passport
(except for Irish nationals; America:
passport required) to visit the
United Kingdom for less than
three months (tourism or business
purpose).
For visitors from other countries
a visa may be required, in addition
to a passport, especially for those
wishing to stay for longer than
three months. We advise you to
check with your embassy before
travelling.

LONDON

LONDON

Population: 8 174 100

Marc Pinter/Fotolia.com

The term 'world city' could have been invented for London. Time zones radiate from Greenwich, global finances zap round the Square Mile and its international restaurants are the equal of anywhere on earth. A stunning diversity of population is testament to the city's famed tolerance; different lifestyles and languages are as much a part of the London scene as cockneys and black cabs. London grew over time in a pretty haphazard way, swallowing up surrounding villages, but retaining an enviable acreage of green 'lungs': a comforting 30 per cent of London's area is made up of open space.

The drama of the city is reflected in its history. From Roman settlement to banking centre to capital of a 19C empire, the city's pulse has never missed a beat; it's no surprise that a dazzling array of theatres, restaurants, museums, markets and art galleries populate its streets. London's piecemeal character has endowed it with distinctly different areas, often breathing down each other's necks. North of Piccadilly lie the playgrounds of Soho and Mayfair, while south is the gentleman's clubland of St James's. On the other side of town are Clerkenwell and Southwark, artisan areas that have been scrubbed down and freshened up. The cool sophistication of Kensington and Knightsbridge is to the west, while a more touristy aesthetic is found in the heaving piazza zone of Covent Garden.

LONDON IN...

→ **ONE DAY**
British Museum, Tower of London, St Paul's Cathedral, Tate Modern.

→ **TWO / THREE DAYS**
National Gallery, London Eye, Natural History Museum, a walk along the Southbank.

→ **THREE DAYS**
Science Museum, Victoria and Albert Museum, National Portrait Gallery.

PRACTICAL INFORMATION

ARRIVAL-DEPARTURE

✈ Heathrow Airport (20mi west). Heathrow Express to Paddington takes 15 min; or take the Piccadilly Line.

✈ Gatwick Airport (28mi south). Gatwick Express to Victoria Station takes 30 min.

✈ Stansted Airport (34mi northeast).

✈ Luton Airport (35mi north).

✈ London City Airport (10mi east).

GETTING AROUND

If you're in London for any period it's worth investing in an Oyster Card, much beloved by locals: these are smartcards with electronically stored pre-pay credit, and they offer good savings on fares. The Underground, known colloquially as the Tube, has 270 stations across the capital and beyond; get yourself a tube map – it's invaluable and also a design classic. Buses can often be the quickest way to travel short distances, especially during the day; or else register and then pick up a 'Boris Bike' from the various points around the city.

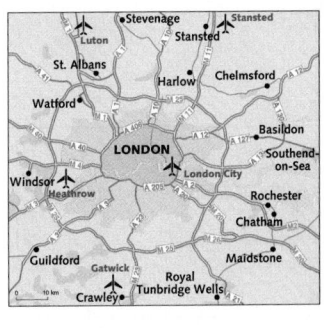

CALENDAR HIGHLIGHTS

February
London Fashion Week.

April
The Boat Race, London Marathon.

May
Chelsea Flower Show.

June
Wimbledon, Trooping the Colour.

August
Notting Hill Carnival.

October
London Film Festival.

November
Lord Mayor's Show.

December
Ice Rinks open across London.

EATING OUT

London is one of the food capitals of the world, where you can eat everything from Turkish to Thai and Polish to Peruvian. Those wishing to sample classic British dishes also have more choice these days as more and more chefs are rediscovering home-grown ingredients, regional classics and traditional recipes. Eating in the capital can be pricey, so check out good value pre- and post-theatre menus, or try lunch at one of the many eateries that drop their prices, but not their standards, in the middle of the day. "Would I were in an alehouse in London! I would give all my fame for a pot of ale and safety", says Shakespeare's Henry V. Samuel Johnson agreed, waxing lyrical upon the happiness produced by a good tavern or inn. Pubs are often open these days from 11am to 11pm (and beyond), so this particular love now knows no bounds, and any tourist is welcome to come along and enjoy the romance. It's not just the cooking that has improved in pubs but wine too; woe betide any establishment in this city that can't distinguish its Gamay from its Grenache.

HOTELS - ALPHABETICAL LIST

UNITED KINGDOM – LONDON

RESTAURANTS - ALPHABETICAL LIST

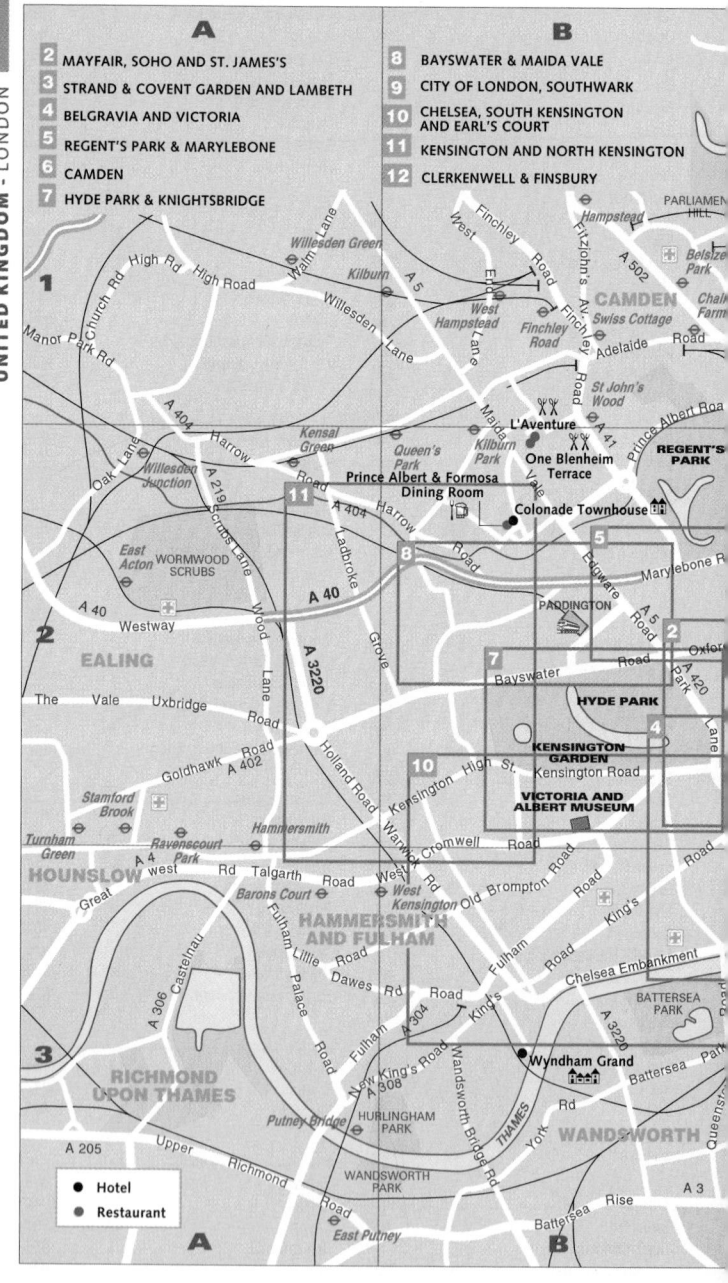

2 MAYFAIR, SOHO AND ST. JAMES'S

3 STRAND & COVENT GARDEN AND LAMBETH

4 BELGRAVIA AND VICTORIA

5 REGENT'S PARK & MARYLEBONE

6 CAMDEN

7 HYDE PARK & KNIGHTSBRIDGE

8 BAYSWATER & MAIDA VALE

9 CITY OF LONDON, SOUTHWARK

10 CHELSEA, SOUTH KENSINGTON AND EARL'S COURT

11 KENSINGTON AND NORTH KENSINGTON

12 CLERKENWELL & FINSBURY

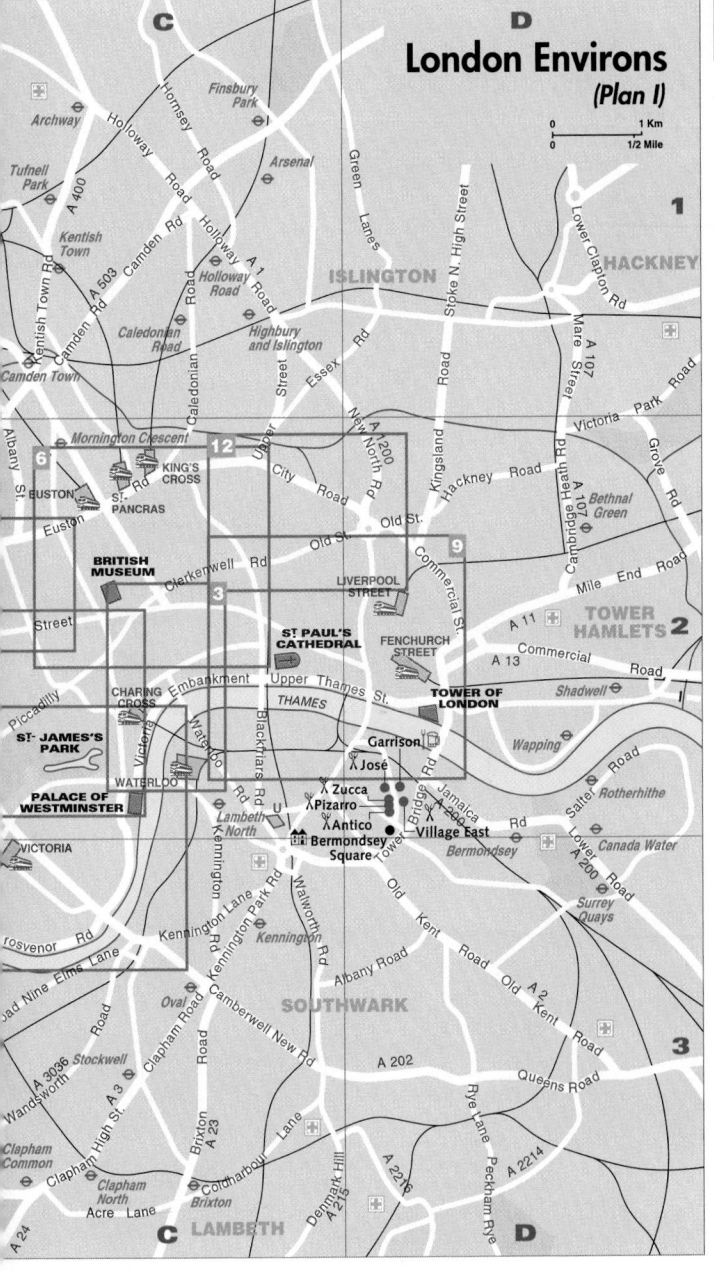

London Environs
(Plan I)

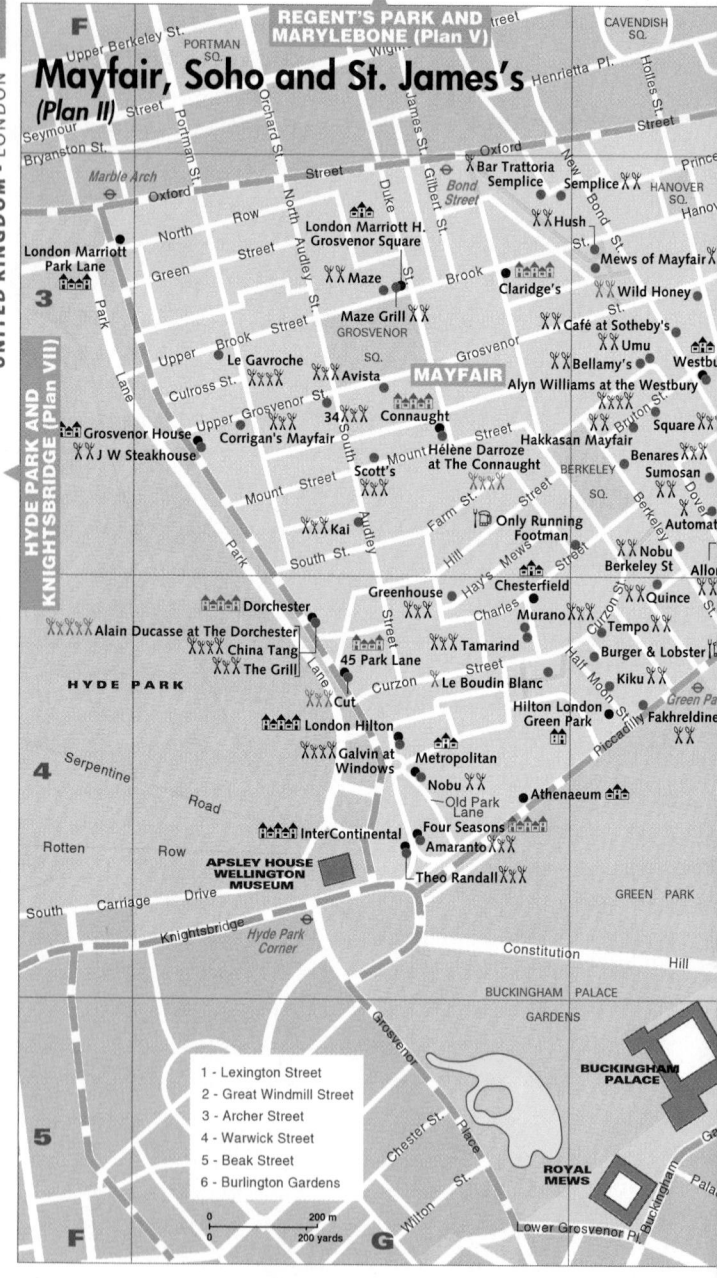

REGENT'S PARK AND MARYLEBONE (Plan V)

Mayfair, Soho and St. James's
(Plan II)

CAVENDISH SQ.

Upper Berkeley St.
Seymour Street
Bryanston St.
PORTMAN SQ.
Wigm Street
James's St.
Henrietta Pl.
HOLLES St.
Street
Prince
HANOVER SQ.
Hanov

Marble Arch
Oxford Street
Oxford Street
Duke St.
Gilbert St.
Bond Street
New Bond St.

Bar Trattoria Semplice
Semplice ✗✗
Hush ✗✗

London Marriott Park Lane
North Row
Green Street
North Audley St.
Brook Street
London Marriott H. Grosvenor Square
Maze ✗✗
Mews of Mayfair ✗
Claridge's
Wild Honey ✗✗

Park Lane
Upper Brook Street
Culross St.
Le Gavroche ✗✗✗✗
Avista ✗✗✗
Maze Grill ✗✗
GROSVENOR SQ.
Grosvenor Street
Café at Sotheby's ✗✗
Umu ✗✗
Bellamy's ✗✗
Westbu
Alyn Williams at the Westbury

Grosvenor House
J W Steakhouse ✗✗
Upper Grosvenor St.
34 ✗✗✗
Corrigan's Mayfair ✗✗✗
Connaught
MAYFAIR
Square ✗✗
Bruton St.
Hakkasan Mayfair
Benares ✗✗✗
Sumosan

Mount Street
Scott's ✗✗✗
Kai ✗✗✗
Farm Street
Hélène Darroze at The Connaught
BERKELEY SQ.
Dove St.
Automat
South St.
South Audley St.
Hill Street
Only Running Footman
Hay's Mews
Chesterfield
Berkeley St.
Nobu Berkeley St
Allo

HYDE PARK
Dorchester
Alain Ducasse at The Dorchester ✗✗✗✗✗
China Tang ✗✗✗
The Grill ✗✗✗
Greenhouse ✗✗✗
Charles Street
Murano ✗✗✗
Quince ✗✗
Tempo ✗✗
Park Lane
45 Park Lane
Tamarind ✗✗✗
Curzon Street
Burger & Lobster ✗
Cut ✗✗✗
Le Boudin Blanc ✗✗✗
Kiku ✗✗
London Hilton
Hilton London Green Park
Green Pa
Fakhreldine ✗✗
Piccadilly

Serpentine
Galvin at Windows ✗✗✗✗
Metropolitan
Nobu ✗✗
Old Park Lane
Athenaeum
Rotten Row
InterContinental
Four Seasons
Amaranto ✗✗✗
Theo Randall ✗✗✗

South Carriage Drive
Knightsbridge
APSLEY HOUSE WELLINGTON MUSEUM
Hyde Park Corner
Constitution Hill
GREEN PARK

BUCKINGHAM PALACE GARDENS

Grosvenor Place
Chester St.
Wilton St.
BUCKINGHAM PALACE
ROYAL MEWS
Lower Grosvenor Pl.

1 - Lexington Street
2 - Great Windmill Street
3 - Archer Street
4 - Warwick Street
5 - Beak Street
6 - Burlington Gardens

0   200 m
0   200 yards

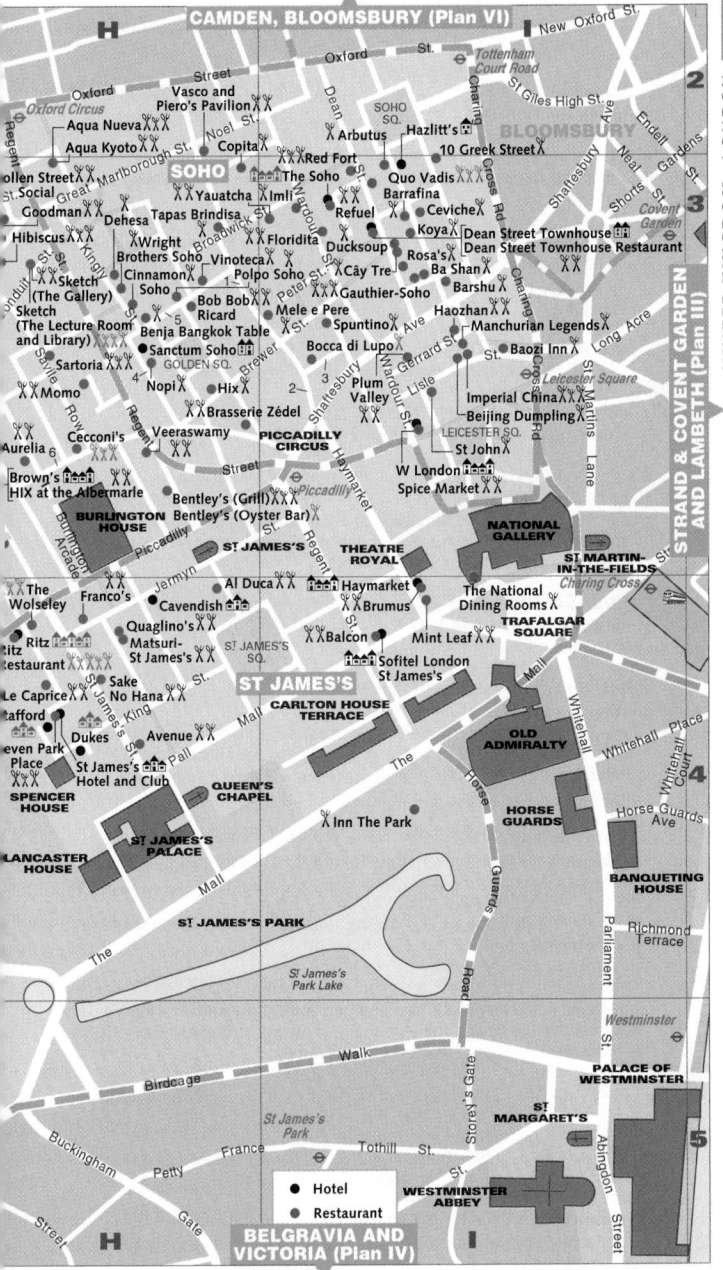

CAMDEN, BLOOMSBURY (Plan VI)

New Oxford St.

Oxford St.

Tottenham
Court Road

St Giles High St.

Endell

Oxford
Oxford Circus

Street

Vasco and
Piero's Pavilion

Noel St.

Dean

St.

Charing

Cross

Rd.

SOHO
SQ.

Hazlitt's

BLOOMSBURY

Aqua Nueva

Copita

Arbutus

10 Greek Street

Shaftesbury

Shorts

Neal

Covent
Garden

Aqua Kyoto

ollen Street

St. Social

Great Marlborough St.

SOHO

Broadwick

The Soho

Red Fort

Imli

Quo Vadis

Barrafina

Gardens

Goodman

Dehesa Tapas Brindisa

Refuel

Ceviche

Koya

Dean Street Townhouse

Long Acre

Hibiscus

Wright
Brothers Soho

Floridita

Ducksoup

Cây Tre

Rosa's

Dean Street Townhouse Restaurant

Cinnamon
Soho

Vinoteca

Polpo Soho

Gauthier-Soho

Ba Shan

Barshu

Sketch
(The Gallery)

King

Bob Bob
Ricard

Mele e Pere

Spuntino

Haozhan

Manchurian Legends

Kingly St.

Peter St.

Gerrard St.

St.

Baozi Inn

Sketch
(The Lecture Room
and Library)

Benja Bangkok Table

Brewer

Bocca di Lupo

Lisle

Leicester Square

St. Martins

Sartoria

Sanctum Soho

GOLDEN SQ.

St.

Plum
Valley

Imperial China

Lane

Momo

Nopi

Hix

Shaftesbury

Windmill St.

Beijing Dumpling

Aurelia

Cecconi's

Brasserie Zédel

LEICESTER SQ.

St John

Veeraswamy

PICCADILLY
CIRCUS

Haymarket

Regent

W London

Spice Market

Brown's

Street

Piccadilly

NATIONAL
GALLERY

HIX at the Albemarle

Bentley's (Grill)

Bentley's (Oyster Bar)

ST MARTIN-
IN-THE-FIELDS

BURLINGTON
HOUSE

Piccadilly

ST JAMES'S

THEATRE
ROYAL

Haymarket

Charing Cross

Burlington
Arcade

Jermyn

Al Duca

The National
Dining Rooms

The
Wolseley

Franco's

Cavendish

Brumus

TRAFALGAR
SQUARE

Ritz

Ritz
Restaurant

Quaglino's

Matsuri-
St James's

Balcon

Mint Leaf

Le Caprice

Sake
No Hana

ST JAMES'S
SQ.

Sofitel London
St James's

tafford

Stafford

St. James's

King

ST JAMES'S

even Park
Place

Dukes

Avenue

Mall

Pall

CARLTON HOUSE
TERRACE

OLD
ADMIRALTY

Whitehall

Whitehall Place

SPENCER
HOUSE

St James's
Hotel and Club

QUEEN'S
CHAPEL

The

Horse

Whitehall
Court

LANCASTER
HOUSE

ST JAMES'S
PALACE

Guards

HORSE
GUARDS

Horse Guards
Ave.

BANQUETING
HOUSE

The

ST JAMES'S PARK

Mall

Guards

Richmond
Terrace

St James's
Park Lake

Road

Parliament

Westminster
St.

PALACE OF
WESTMINSTER

Walk

Birdcage

Storel's Gate

St James's
Park

France

Tothill

St.

ST
MARGARET'S

Abingdon

The

Buckingham

Petty

Gate

France

Tothill St.

Storel's St.

Hotel

Restaurant

WESTMINSTER
ABBEY

Street

BELGRAVIA AND
VICTORIA (Plan IV)

MAYFAIR

Dorchester   🛵 💷 ᴋ 🅰ᴄ 🛜 🧖 🚗 ⱽⁱˢᵃ 💳 🅰ᴇ ⓪

Park Ln. ⊠ W1K 1QA – Ⓜ Hyde Park Corner – ℰ (020) 76298888
– www.thedorchester.com   **G4**
200 rm – 🛉£ 282/618 🛉🛉£ 318/834, � £ 26 – 50 suites
Rest Alain Ducasse at The Dorchester ❀❀❀ **Rest China Tang Rest
The Grill** – see restaurant listing
◆ Grand Luxury ◆ Classic ◆ Stylish ◆
Luxury hotel on a grand scale offering every possible facility. Striking marbled
and pillared promenade provides one of the best backdrops to afternoon tea.
Impressive spa and bedrooms quintessentially English in style. Exemplary levels
of service.

Claridge's   🛵 ᴋ rm, 🅰ᴄ 🛜 🧖 ⱽⁱˢᵃ 💳 🅰ᴇ ⓪

Brook St ⊠ W1K 4HR – Ⓜ Bond Street – ℰ (020) 76298860
– www.claridges.co.uk   **G3**
143 rm – 🛉£ 792/936 🛉🛉£ 792/936, � £ 32 – 60 suites
Rest Gordon Ramsay at Claridge's – ℰ (020) 74990099 (booking essential) Menu £ 30/80 ⬚
◆ Grand Luxury ◆ Classic ◆ Historic ◆
Rightly celebrated for its art deco and one of London's finest hotels. Exceptio-
nally well-appointed and sumptuous bedrooms, all with butler service. Magnificent Foyer for afternoon tea. Grand, handsome restaurant with a menu that is
classically based but with modern touches.

Four Seasons   🛵 💷 🧖 ᴋ 🅰ᴄ 🛜 🧖 🚗 ⱽⁱˢᵃ 💳 🅰ᴇ ⓪

Hamilton Pl, Park Ln ⊠ W1J 7DR – Ⓜ Hyde Park Corner – ℰ (020)
7499 0888 – www.fourseasons.com/london/   **G4**
148 rm – 🛉£ 594/750 🛉🛉£ 594/750, � £ 30 – 45 suites
Rest Amaranto – see restaurant listing
◆ Grand Luxury ◆ Modern ◆ Design ◆
Reopened in 2011 after a huge refurbishment project and has raised the bar for
luxury hotels. Striking lobby sets the scene; sumptuous bedrooms have a rich,
contemporary look and boast every conceivable comfort. Great views from the
stunning roof-top spa.

Connaught   🛵 💷 ▦ 🅰ᴄ 🛜 🧖 ⱽⁱˢᵃ 💳 🅰ᴇ ⓪

Carlos Pl. ⊠ W1K 2AL – Ⓜ Bond Street – ℰ (020) 74997070
– www.the-connaught.co.uk   **G3**
95 rm – 🛉£ 888 🛉🛉£ 888/936, � £ 30 – 26 suites
Rest Hélène Darroze at The Connaught ❀❀ – see restaurant listing
Rest Espelette – ℰ (020) 31477100 – Carte £ 41/86
◆ Grand Luxury ◆ Classic ◆ Historic ◆
One of London's most famous hotels; restored and renovated but still retaining
an elegant British feel. All the luxurious bedrooms come with large marble bathrooms and butler service. There's a choice of two stylish bars and Espelette is an
all-day venue for classic French and British dishes.

InterContinental   ≼ 🛵 💷 🧖 ᴋ rm, 🅰ᴄ 🛜 🧖 🚗 ⱽⁱˢᵃ 💳 🅰ᴇ ⓪

1 Hamilton Pl, Park Ln ⊠ W1J 7QY – Ⓜ Hyde Park Corner – ℰ (020)
74093131 – www.london.intercontinental.com   **G4**
399 rm – 🛉£ 359/790 🛉🛉£ 359/790, � £ 20 – 48 suites
Rest Theo Randall – see restaurant listing
Rest Cookbook Café – Carte £ 30/52
◆ Business ◆ Luxury ◆ Modern ◆
International hotel whose position facing the park is an impressive feature. Everything leads off from the large, open-plan lobby. English-style bedrooms with
hi-tech equipment; luxurious suites. Casual, family-friendly Cookbook Café.

London Hilton

22 Park Ln. ✉ *W1K 1BE* – Ⓜ *Hyde Park Corner*
– ✆ *(020) 74938000*
– *www.hilton.co.uk/londonparklane* G4
397 rm – †£ 263/719 ††£ 263/719, ☕ £ 20 – 56 suites
Rest *Galvin at Windows* ✿ – see restaurant listing
Rest *Podium* – ✆ *(020) 72084022* – Menu £ 23 – Carte £ 34/69
Rest *Trader Vic's* – ✆ *(020) 7208 4113 (closed 25-26 December)*
(dinner only) Carte £ 33/61
♦ Business ♦ Classic ♦ Functional ♦
Rooms at this 28 storey hotel, which celebrates 50 years in 2013, now have a sharp, contemporary edge; the suites remain more traditional. For Polynesian food and a Mai Tai, head to the iconic brand that is Trader's Vic's; for casual, all-day dining, try Podium.

Grosvenor House

Park Ln ✉ *W1K 7TN* – Ⓜ *Marble Arch* – ✆ *(020) 74996363*
– *www.londongrosvenorhouse.co.uk* G3
442 rm – †£ 286/418 ††£ 286/418, ☕ £ 30 – 52 suites
Rest *JW Steakhouse* – see restaurant listing
♦ Business ♦ Classic ♦ Functional ♦
A large, landmark property occupying a commanding position by Hyde Park. Uniform, comfortable but well proportioned bedrooms in classic Marriott styling. Busy banqueting department boasts the largest ballroom in Europe.

45 Park Lane

45 Park Ln ✉ *W1K 1PN* – Ⓜ *Hyde Park Corner* – ✆ *(020) 7493 4545*
– *www.45parklane.com* G4
35 rm – †£ 474/834 ††£ 474/834, ☕ £ 30 – 10 suites
Rest *Cut* – see restaurant listing
♦ Luxury ♦ Townhouse ♦ Stylish ♦
It was the original site of the Playboy Club and has been a car showroom but now 45 Park Lane has been reborn as The Dorchester's sister hotel. The bedrooms, all with views over Hyde Park, are wonderfully sensual and the marble bathrooms are beautiful.

Westbury

Bond St ✉ *W1S 2YF* – Ⓜ *Bond Street* – ✆ *(020) 76297755*
– *www.westburymayfair.com* H3
233 rm – †£ 275/469 ††£ 275/469, ☕ £ 26 – 13 suites
Rest *Alyn Williams at the Westbury* ✿ – see restaurant listing
Rest *Tsukiji* – *(booking advisable)* Menu £ 17 (lunch)
– Carte £ 14/55
♦ Business ♦ Luxury ♦ Modern ♦
Now as stylish as when it opened in the 1950s. Smart, comfortable bedrooms with terrific art deco inspired suites. Elegant, iconic Polo bar and bright, fresh sushi bar. All the designer brands outside the front door.

Brown's

Albemarle St ✉ *W1S 4BP* – Ⓜ *Green Park* – ✆ *(020) 7493 6020*
– *www.roccofortehotels.com* H3
105 rm – †£ 318/1080 ††£ 318/1080, ☕ £ 30 – 12 suites
Rest *HIX at The Albemarle* – see restaurant listing
♦ Luxury ♦ Stylish ♦
Opened in 1837 by James Brown, Lord Byron's butler. This urbane and very British hotel with an illustrious past offers a swish bar with Terence Donovan prints, bedrooms in neutral hues and a classic English sitting room for afternoon tea.

London Marriott H. Park Lane

140 Park Ln ✉ *W1K 7AA* – Ⓜ *Marble Arch* – ☎ *(020) 74937000* – *www.londonmarriottparklane.co.uk* **F3**

144 rm – †£ 299/1020 ††£ 299/1020, ☕ £ 23 – 9 suites

Rest *140 Park Lane* – Menu £ 15 – Carte £ 28/59

♦ Luxury ♦ Design ♦ Functional ♦

Usefully located international hotel, close to the park and shops of Oxford Street. Basement health club has Park Lane's only pool. Smart, generously sized bedrooms are well-equipped; the attractive restaurant overlooks Marble Arch.

Metropolitan

Old Park Ln ✉ *W1K 1LB* – Ⓜ *Hyde Park Corner* – ☎ *(020) 74471000* – *www.metropolitan.como.bz* **G4**

144 rm – †£ 299/479 ††£ 335/515, ☕ £ 22 – 3 suites

Rest *Nobu* ✿ – see restaurant listing

♦ Business ♦ Modern ♦ Minimalist ♦

Minimalist interior and a voguish reputation have made this hotel and its Met Bar the favoured choice of pop stars and celebrities. Sleek design and fashionably attired staff set it apart.

Athenaeum

116 Piccadilly ✉ *W1J 7BJ* – Ⓜ *Hyde Park Corner* – ☎ *(020) 7499 3464* – *www.athenaeumhotel.com* **G4**

153 rm – †£ 390/480 ††£ 390/480, ☕ £ 27.50 – 11 suites

Rest *Athenaeum* – Menu £ 20/30 – Carte £ 35/58

♦ Luxury ♦ Classic ♦ Modern ♦

Refurbished 1920s building opposite the park; its stylish bedrooms come in cool pastel shades and have floor to ceiling windows. Bright restaurant and a bar offering over 270 different whiskies. The hotel also organises events for kids.

Chesterfield

35 Charles St ✉ *W1J 5EB* – Ⓜ *Green Park* – ☎ *(020) 74912622* – *www.chesterfieldmayfair.com* **G4**

103 rm – †£ 192/360 ††£ 216/504, ☕ £ 23 – 4 suites

Rest – Menu £ 22/26 – Carte £ 37/66

♦ Townhouse ♦ Classic ♦ Personalised ♦

An assuredly English feel to this Georgian house. Discreet lobby leads to a clubby bar and wood panelled library. Individually decorated bedrooms, with some antique pieces. Intimate and pretty restaurant.

London Marriott H. Grosvenor Square

Grosvenor Sq. ✉ *W1K 6JP* – Ⓜ *Bond Street* – ☎ *(020) 74931232* – *www.marriottgrosvenorsquare.com* **G3**

226 rm – 11 suites

Rest *Maze Grill* – see restaurant listing

♦ Business ♦ Functional ♦ Modern ♦

A well-appointed international group hotel that benefits from an excellent location in the heart of Mayfair. Many of the bedrooms specifically equipped for the business traveller.

Hilton London Green Park

Half Moon St ✉ *W1J 7BN* – Ⓜ *Green Park* – ☎ *(020) 76297522* – *www.hilton.co.uk/greenpark* **H4**

162 rm – †£ 191/407 ††£ 203/599, ☕ £ 20.95 **Rest** – Carte £ 28/37

♦ Business ♦ Functional ♦ Cosy ♦

A row of sympathetically adjoined townhouses in the heart of Mayfair, dating from the 1730s. Bedrooms vary in size and shape; those on the first and fifth floors have been refurbished in a bright, contemporary style. Modern menu served in airy restaurant.

XXXXX **Alain Ducasse at The Dorchester** – Dorchester Hotel 🖩

✿✿✿ *Park Ln ⊠ W1K 1QA – ⓜ Hyde Park Corner* ⇄ 🚾 🅾 🆎 ⓞ
– ✆ *(020) 76298866 – www.alainducasse-dorchester.com – Closed*
13 August-5 September, 26-30 December, Saturday lunch, Sunday and Monday
Rest – Menu £ 55/85 ⅋ G4
♦ French ♦ Elegant ♦ Luxury ♦

Luxury and extravagance are the hallmarks of Alain Ducasse's London outpost.
The dining room is elegant without being staid; food is modern and refined yet
satisfying and balanced. Service is formal, thoughtful and well-organised.
→ Sauté of lobster, truffled chicken quenelles and pasta. Fillet of beef Rossini with Périgueux sauce. 'Baba like in Monte-Carlo'.

XXXX **Sketch (The Lecture Room & Library)** 🕅 🖩 🚾 🅾 🆎

✿✿ *9 Conduit St (1st floor) ⊠ W1S 2XG – ⓜ Oxford Circus – ✆ (020)*
76594500 – www.sketch.uk.com
– *Closed last 2 weeks August, Saturday lunch, Sunday and Monday*
Rest – *(booking essential)* Menu £ 35 (lunch) – Carte £ 70/129 ⅋ H3
♦ French ♦ Luxury ♦ Elegant ♦

Pierre Gagnaire's London operation is within a striking 18C townhouse which is
full of colour, energy and vitality. The sophisticated French cooking is ambitious
and elaborate in conception and execution; dishes arrive artfully presented.
→ 'Perfume of the Earth'. Saddle of Quercy Lamb. Pierre Gagnaire's 'Grand
Dessert'.

XXXX **Hélène Darroze at The Connaught** – Connaught Hotel 🕅

✿✿ *Carlos Pl. ⊠ W1K 2AL – ⓜ Bond Street* ⇄ 🚾 🅾 🆎 ⓞ
– ✆ *(020) 31477200 – www.the-connaught.co.uk*
– *Closed Sunday and Monday* G3
Rest – *(booking essential)* Menu £ 35/80 ⅋
♦ French ♦ Luxury ♦ Elegant ♦

Landes and the SW of France inform Hélène Darroze's exquisite cooking, although international influences also play a part. The dining room is elegant and
comfortable, with original mahogany wood panelling. Service is courteous and
professional.
→ Duck foie gras with mild spices and dried fruit chutney. Line-caught sea
bass with celeriac purée and salmis sauce. Exotic fruits with bourbon vanilla
and mascarpone cream.

XXXX **Le Gavroche** (Michel Roux Jnr) 🖩 🚾 🅾 🆎 ⓞ

✿✿ *43 Upper Brook St ⊠ W1K 7QR – ⓜ Marble Arch – ✆ (020) 74080881*
– *www.le-gavroche.co.uk*
– *Closed Christmas-New Year, Saturday lunch, Sunday and bank holidays*
Rest – *(booking essential)* Menu £ 52 (lunch)/110 G3
– Carte £ 62/148 ⅋
♦ French ♦ Formal ♦ Luxury ♦

Classical, rich and indulgent French cuisine is the draw at Michel Roux's renowned London institution. The large, smart basement room has a clubby, masculine feel; service is formal and structured but also has charm.
→ Soufflé Suissesse. Râble de lapin et galette au parmesan. Palet au chocolat amer et praliné croustillant.

XXXX **Square** (Philip Howard) 🕅 🖩 ⇄ 🚾 🅾 🆎

✿✿ *6-10 Bruton St. ⊠ W1J 6PU – ⓜ Green Park – ✆ (020) 74957100*
– *www.squarerestaurant.com – Closed 24-26 December and Sunday lunch*
Rest – Menu £ 35/80 ⅋ H3
♦ French ♦ Formal ♦ Classic ♦

Confident and accomplished kitchen which understands the importance of
sound techniques, prime ingredients and clarity of flavour. The room is comfortable and the buoyant atmosphere prevents things becoming too formal. Good
cheeseboard and wine list, which is rooted in the Old World.
→ Lasagne of crab with shellfish cappuccino and champagne foam.
Assiette of Pyrenean lamb with ewe's curd ravioli and pine nuts. Crème
caramel with candied fruit and blood orange brioche roulade.

XXXX
ॐ

Galvin at Windows – London Hilton Hotel   ≤ AC VISA ◑◐ AE ①

22 Park Ln (28th floor) ⊠ W1K 1BE
– Ⓜ Hyde Park Corner – ℰ (020) 72084021
– www.galvinatwindows.com
– Closed 25 December, Saturday lunch and Sunday dinner   **G4**
Rest – Menu £ 29/65
✦ French ✦ Formal ✦ Romantic ✦

Spectacular views from the 28th floor of the Hilton are not the only draw. The room is contemporary and cleverly laid out; service is attentive and efficient; cooking is confident and detailed and dishes balanced and satisfying.
→ Cured salmon, Cornish crab, avocado purée and fennel. Saddle of venison with watercress, red cabbage and pancetta. Tarte Tatin, vanilla ice cream and caramel sauce.

XXXX
ॐ

Alyn Williams at the Westbury – Westbury Hotel   ⑰ AC

Bond St ⊠ W1S 2YF – Ⓜ Bond Street   ⇔ VISA ◑◐ AE ①
– ℰ (020) 7078 9579 – www.westburymayfair.com
– Closed Saturday lunch and Sunday   **H3**
Rest – Menu £ 24/45 ⅏
✦ Modern ✦ Design ✦ Elegant ✦

Confident, cheery service ensures the atmosphere never strays into terminal seriousness; rosewood panelling and a striking wine display add warmth. The cooking is creative and even playful but however elaborately constructed the dish, the combinations of flavours and textures always work.
→ Veal sweetbreads with artichokes, celery and sherry. Cotswold chicken with girolles, smoked egg and charred leek. 'Walnut whip'.

XXXX

China Tang – Dorchester Hotel   AC ⇔ VISA ◑◐ AE ①

Park Ln ⊠ W1K 1QA – Ⓜ Hyde Park Corner – ℰ (020) 76299988
– www.thedorchester.com
– Closed 24-25 December   **G4**
Rest – Menu £ 23 (lunch) – Carte £ 26/79
✦ Chinese ✦ Fashionable ✦ Elegant ✦

Sir David Tang's atmospheric, art deco-inspired Chinese restaurant, downstairs at The Dorchester, is always abuzz with activity. Be sure to see the terrific bar, before sharing the traditional Cantonese specialities.

XXX

Cecconi's   🍴 AC VISA ◑◐ AE ①

5a Burlington Gdns ⊠ W1S 3EP
– Ⓜ Green Park – ℰ (020) 74341500
– www.cecconis.com   **H3**
Rest – (booking essential) Carte £ 30/44
✦ Italian ✦ Fashionable ✦ Formal ✦

Branches of this fashionable restaurant are now opening up around the world. Regulars pop in for a bite at the bar; the restaurant prepares the classic dishes with care. Open from breakfast onwards; popular for weekend brunches.

XXX

Cut – 45 Park Lane Hotel   AC VISA ◑◐ AE ①

45 Park Ln ⊠ W1K 1PN
– Ⓜ Hyde Park Corner – ℰ (020) 7493 4554
– www.45parklane.com   **G4**
Rest – (booking essential) Menu £ 55 (weekday lunch)
– Carte £ 40/119
✦ Meats and grills ✦ Design ✦ Formal ✦

The first European venture from Wolfgang Puck, the US-based Austrian celebrity chef, is this very slick, stylish and sexy room where glamorous people come to eat meat. The not-inexpensive steaks are cooked over hardwood and charcoal and finished off in a broiler.

XXX · ⇔⇔   **Hibiscus** (Claude Bosi)   AC ⇦ VISA ⊙⊙ AE

29 Maddox St ⊠ W1S 2PA – Ⓜ Oxford Circus – ℰ (020) 76292999
– www.hibiscusrestaurant.co.uk
– Closed 23 December-3 January, Sunday and bank holidays   **H3**
Rest – Menu £ 35/80

♦ Innovative ♦ Elegant ♦ Formal ♦

The immaculately dressed room provides a discreet backdrop to Claude Bosi's
creative cooking. Choose 3, 6 or 9 courses and create your own menu from
about 20 ingredients— or just let the kitchen decide. The food is inventive but
not overly intricate and everything on the plate has a reason for being there.
→ Ravioli of white onion and lime, broad bean and mint purée. Roast suckling
pig, carrot and orange purée, and cumin. Chocolate tart with basil ice cream.

XXX · ⇔   **Benares** (Atul Kochhar)   ⑩ AC ⇦ VISA ⊙⊙ AE

12a Berkeley Square House ⊠ W1J 6BS – Ⓜ Green Park
– ℰ (020) 76298886 – www.benaresrestaurant.com
– Closed 24- 26 December and 1 January   **H3**
Rest – Menu £ 32 (lunch)/85 – Carte £ 50/90

♦ Indian ♦ Formal ♦ Intimate ♦

Modern techniques are used to add contemporary touches to the classical base;
the inventive Indian food here continues to evolve. The smart first-floor surroundings match the food in their sophistication. Popular and smart Chef's Table.
→ Fennel lamb chop, chicken and king prawn platter. Seared duck breast,
Goan style spiced savoy cabbage. Star anise apple tart with fennel, vanilla
ice cream and salted butter caramel.

XXX · ⇔   **Murano** (Angela Hartnett)   AC VISA ⊙⊙ AE

20 Queen St ⊠ W1J 5PP – Ⓜ Green Park – ℰ (020) 74951127
– www.angela-hartnett.com – Closed Christmas and Sunday
Rest – Menu £ 25/85   **G4**

♦ Italian ♦ Fashionable ♦ Elegant ♦

Angela Hartnett's Italian influenced cooking exhibits an appealing lightness of
touch, with assured combinations of flavours, borne out of confidence in the
ingredients. This is a stylish and elegant room with an appealingly fresh feel.
→ Octopus with apple purée, white bean and clam ragout. John Dory,
hand-rolled macaroni and morels. Lemon parfait, sesame meringue and
thyme crumble.

XXX · ⇔   **Greenhouse**   ⑩ AC ⇦ VISA ⊙⊙ AE

27a Hay's Mews ⊠ W1J 5NY – Ⓜ Hyde Park Corner – ℰ (020) 74993331
– www.greenhouserestaurant.co.uk
– Closed Saturday lunch, Sunday and bank holidays   **G4**
Rest – Menu £ 29/75 – Carte £ 87/106 ⚬

♦ Innovative ♦ Fashionable ♦ Neighbourhood ♦

Chef Arnaud Bignon's cooking is confident, balanced and innovative and uses
the best from Europe's larder; his dishes exude an exhilarating freshness. The
breadth and depth of the wine list is astounding. This is a discreet, sleek and
contemporary restaurant with well-judged service.
→ Smoked potato with oysters and shallots. Cod with quinoa, lemongrass,
shiitake and coriander. Lemon 'textures'.

XXX · ⇔   **Tamarind**   ⑩ AC VISA ⊙⊙ AE ⓪

20 Queen St. ⊠ W1J 5PR – Ⓜ Green Park – ℰ (020) 76293561
– www.tamarindrestaurant.com
– Closed 25-26 December, 1 January and Saturday lunch   **G4**
Rest – Menu £ 19/68 – Carte £ 30/54

♦ Indian ♦ Formal ♦ Exotic ♦

Makes the best use of its basement location through smoked mirrors, gilded
columns and a somewhat exclusive feel. The appealing and enjoyable Indian
food is mostly traditionally based; kebabs and curries are the specialities, complemented by carefully judged vegetable dishes.
→ Mushrooms with pickled onions in a curry leaf dressing. Tandoor grilled
lamb chops with papaya, chilli and garlic. Stewed pears with fennel and
ginger ice cream.

UNITED KINGDOM - LONDON

XXX **Kai** 🔟 AC ⇔ VISA ⬤⬤ AE ⑪
❀

65 South Audley St ⊠ W1K 2QU – ⓜ Hyde Park Corner – ℰ (020)
74938988 – www.kaimayfair.co.uk
– Closed 25-26 December and 1 January   G3
Rest – (booking essential) Menu £ 27 (lunch) – Carte £ 39/90 ⬚⬚
♦ Chinese ♦ Intimate ♦ Formal ♦
Carefully prepared Chinese food, from a menu that mixes the classics with more
innovative dishes; flavours are authentic and assured. Its smart surroundings
are spread over two floors - ask for the ground floor; sweet natured service.
→ Scallop with spicy XO sauce, lotus root crisp and stir-fried vegetables.
Spiced pork belly in ginger, rice wine, cinnamon and soy. Mango mousse
with dragonfruit, agar and coconut jelly.

XXX **34** AC VISA ⬤⬤ AE ⑪

34 Grosvenor Sq (entrance on South Audley St) ⊠ W1K 2HD
– ⓜ Marble Arch – ℰ (020) 3350 3434 – www.34-restaurant.co.uk/
– Closed 25 December   G3
Rest – Carte £ 29/61
♦ Meats and grills ♦ Brasserie ♦ Fashionable ♦
A wonderful mix of art deco style and Edwardian warmth makes it feel like a
glamorous brasserie. Parrilla grill used for beef— a mix of Scottish dry-aged,
US prime, organic Argentinian and Australian Wagyu— as well as fish and
game.

XXX **HIX at The Albemarle** – Brown's Hotel 🔟 AC VISA ⬤⬤ AE ⑪

Albemarle St ⊠ W1S 4BP – ⓜ Green Park – ℰ (020) 75184004
– www.roccofortecollection.com   H3
Rest – Menu £ 33 – Carte £ 30/61
♦ British traditional ♦ Formal ♦ Intimate ♦
This wood-panelled dining room is lightened with the work of current British
artists. Mark Hix's well-sourced menu of British classics will appeal to the hun-
ter-gatherer in every man.

XXX **The Grill** – Dorchester Hotel AC VISA ⬤⬤ AE ⑪

Park Ln. ⊠ W1K 1QA – ⓜ Hyde Park Corner – ℰ (020) 76298888
– www.thedorchester.com   G4
Rest – Menu £ 27/35 – Carte £ 48/91
♦ British traditional ♦ Formal ♦ Romantic ♦
A bastion of Britishness, where timeless classics are served alongside more
modern creations. The extravagantly kitted out room, bedecked in acres of tar-
tans, is even more memorable.

XXX **Theo Randall** – Intercontinental Hotel AC ⇔ 🔟 VISA ⬤⬤ AE ⑪

1 Hamilton Pl, Park Ln ⊠ W1J 7QY – ⓜ Hyde Park Corner – ℰ (020)
73188747 – www.theorandall.com
– Closed 25-26 December, 1 January, Saturday lunch, Sunday and bank
holidays   G4
Rest – Menu £ 27/60 – Carte £ 45/76
♦ Italian ♦ Fashionable ♦ Design ♦
Expect simple, flavoursome and seasonal Italian dishes from the former head
chef of the River Café. The pleasingly rustic nature of the food is somewhat at
odds with the formal service and the corporate feel of the dining room.

XXX **Amaranto** – Four Seasons Hotel 🏠 AC VISA ⬤⬤ AE ⑪

Hamilton Pl, Park Ln ⊠ W1J 7DR – ⓜ Hyde Park Corner – ℰ (020)
7499 0888 – www.fourseasons.com/london/   G4
Rest – Menu £ 22 (lunch) – Carte £ 32/55
♦ Italian ♦ Trendy ♦ Fashionable ♦
It's all about flexibility as the Italian influenced menu is served in the stylish bar
or comfortable lounge, on the great terrace or in the restaurant decorated in
the vivid colours of the amaranth plant.

XXX **Scott's**   🕙 AC ⇔ VISA ⊕⊕ AE ⓪
20 Mount St ⊠ W1K 2HE – Ⓜ *Bond Street* – ℰ *(020) 74957309*
– www.scotts-restaurant.com
– Closed 25-26 December   **G3**
Rest – Carte £ 35/66
♦ **Fish and seafood** ♦ **Fashionable** ♦ **Formal** ♦
Stylish yet traditional and one of London's most fashionable addresses,
so getting a table can be tricky. Oak panelling is juxtaposed with vibrant artwork
from young British artists. Enticing choice of top quality fish and shellfish.

XXX **Corrigan's Mayfair**   🕙 AC ⇔ VISA ⊕⊕ AE ⓪
28 Upper Grosvenor St. ⊠ W1K 7EH – Ⓜ *Marble Arch* – ℰ *(020)*
74999943 – www.corrigansmayfair.com
– Closed 25-26 December, 1 January and Saturday lunch   **G3**
Rest – Menu £ 27 (lunch) – Carte £ 39/78
♦ **British modern** ♦ **Elegant** ♦
Richard Corrigan's flagship celebrates British and Irish cooking, with game a
speciality. The room is comfortable, clubby and quite glamorous and feels as
though it has been around for years.

XXX **Bentley's (Grill)**   AC ⇔ VISA ⊕⊕ AE ⓪
11-15 Swallow St. ⊠ W1B 4DG – Ⓜ *Piccadilly Circus* – ℰ *(020) 77344756*
– www.bentleys.org
– Closed 25-26 December and 1 January   **H3**
Rest – Menu £ 25 (weekdays) – Carte £ 37/67
♦ **British traditional** ♦ **Elegant** ♦ **Fashionable** ♦
Entrance into striking bar; panelled staircase to richly decorated restaurant.
Carefully sourced seafood or meat dishes enhanced by clean, crisp cooking.
Unruffled service.

XXX **Sartoria**   AC ⇔ 🐶 VISA ⊕⊕ AE
20 Savile Row ⊠ W1S 3PR – Ⓜ *Green Park* – ℰ *(020) 75347000*
– www.sartoria-restaurant.co.uk
– Closed 25 December, Saturday lunch, Sunday and bank holidays
Rest – Menu £ 26 – Carte £ 23/64   **H3**
♦ **Italian** ♦ **Formal** ♦ **Elegant** ♦
In the street renowned for English tailoring, a coolly sophisticated and stylish
restaurant to suit those looking for classic Italian cooking with some modern
touches thrown in. It also comes with confident service.

XXX **Avista**   AC ⇔ 🐶 VISA ⊕⊕ AE ⓪
Millennium Mayfair Hotel, 39 Grosvenor Sq ⊠ W1K 2HP – Ⓜ *Bond Street*
– ℰ *(020) 75963399* – www.avistarestaurant.com
– Closed Saturday lunch and Sunday   **G3**
Rest – Carte £ 25/57
♦ **Italian** ♦ **Luxury** ♦
A large room, softened by neutral shades, within the Millennium Hotel. The
menu traverses Italy and the cooking marries the rustic with the more refined.
Pasta dishes are a highlight.

XX **Wild Honey**   AC 🐶 VISA ⊕⊕ AE
🕸 12 St George St. ⊠ W1S 2FB – Ⓜ *Oxford Circus* – ℰ *(020) 7758 9160*
– www.wildhoneyrestaurant.co.uk
– Closed 25-26 December and 1 January   **H3**
Rest – Menu £ 22 (weekday lunch) – Carte £ 38/45
♦ **Modern** ♦ **Design** ♦ **Friendly** ♦
Skilled kitchen uses seasonal ingredients at their peak to create dishes full of
flavour and free from ostentation. Attractive oak-panelled room; ask for one of
the booths. Personable and unobtrusive service adds to the relaxed feel.
➜ Crab with sweet Italian leaves and avocado. Bouillabaisse 'traditional
Marseille style'. Wild honey ice cream with crushed honeycomb.

XX ❁
Semplice (Marco Torri)   AC ⇆ VISA ●● AE
9-10 Blenheim St ⊠ W1S 1LJ – Ⓜ Bond Street – ℰ (020) 74951509
– www.ristorantesemplice.com
– Closed 2 weeks Christmas, Easter, Sunday and bank holidays   G3
Rest – (booking essential at dinner) Menu £ 28 (lunch) – Carte £ 33/63 ♨
♦ Italian ♦ Fashionable ♦ Neighbourhood ♦

Plenty of regulars are always in evidence in this comfortable and stylish restaurant, decorated with ebony, leather and gold. The enthusiasm of the young owners is palpable; the kitchen uses produce from small, specialist suppliers in unfussy, flavoursome, Italian dishes.
➜ Risotto Milanese with saffron and bone marrow. Rabbit with glazed carrots and artichoke sauce. Tiramisu with Giovanni Erbisti coffee and ice cream.

XX ❁
Hakkasan Mayfair   Ⓥ AC VISA ●● AE
17 Bruton St ⊠ W1J 6QB – Ⓜ Green Park – ℰ (020) 79071888
– www.hakkasan.com
– Closed 25 December   H3
Rest – (booking essential) Menu £ 50 – Carte £ 32/96
♦ Chinese ♦ Minimalist ♦ Trendy ♦

Less a copy, more a sister to the original; a sister who's just as fun but lives in a nicer part of town. This one has a funky, more casual ground floor to go with the downstairs dining room. You can expect the same extensive choice of top quality, modern Cantonese cuisine; dim sum is a highlight.
➜ Crispy duck salad. Roasted silver cod with champagne and Chinese honey. Jivara hazelnut bombe and hot chocolate sauce.

XX ❁
Nobu Berkeley St   Ⓥ AC VISA ●● AE
15 Berkeley St. ⊠ W1J 8DY – Ⓜ Green Park – ℰ (020) 72909222
– www.noburestaurants.com/berkeley
– Closed 25-26 December, Saturday and Sunday lunch and bank holiday
Mondays   H3
Rest – (booking essential) Menu £ 27/90 – Carte £ 34/73
♦ Japanese ♦ Fashionable ♦

Offers all the innovative Nobu favourites, along with specialities from the wood oven. Large, lively but smoothly run first floor operation with plenty of glamour; ground floor destination bar. Helpful, well-informed service.
➜ Tuna sashimi salad with Matsuhisa dressing. Black cod with miso. Chocolate bento box with green tea ice cream.

XX ❁
Umu   AC VISA ●● AE
14-16 Bruton Pl. ⊠ W1J 6LX – Ⓜ Bond Street – ℰ (020) 74998881
– www.umurestaurant.com
– Closed Saturday lunch, Sunday and bank holidays   H3
Rest – Menu £ 25 (lunch) – Carte £ 32/119 ♨
♦ Japanese ♦ Fashionable ♦ Design ♦

Stylish, discreet interior using natural materials, with central sushi bar. Extensive choice of Japanese dishes; choose one of the seasonal kaiseki menus for the full experience. Over 160 different labels of sake.
➜ 'Fuwa-fuwa' foie gras and dashi soufflé. Grade 6 Wagyu, hoba leaf and seasonal vegetables. Wild berry and black sesame panna cotta.

XX ❁
Nobu – Metropolitan Hotel   ≤ AC ⇆ VISA ●● AE ⓪
19 Old Park Ln ⊠ W1Y 1LB – Ⓜ Hyde Park Corner – ℰ (020) 74474747
– www.noburestaurants.com
– Closed 25-26 December   G4
Rest – (booking essential) Menu £ 60/95 – Carte £ 37/68
♦ Japanese ♦ Fashionable ♦ Minimalist ♦

Its celebrity clientele ensure this remains one of London's more glamorous spots. Staff are fully conversant in the innovative menu that adds South American influences to Japanese cooking. Has spawned many imitators around the world.
➜ Yellowtail jalapeño. Black cod with miso. Chocolate bento box with green tea ice cream.

XX
&

Maze `AC` `⇄` `VISA` `●●` `AE`

10-13 Grosvenor Sq ⊠ W1K 6JP – **Ⓜ** *Bond Street –* ℰ *(020) 71070000*
– www.gordonramsay.com/maze G3
Rest – Menu £ 25/70 – Carte £ 27/41 ⁂

◆ Innovative ◆ Fashionable ◆ Design ◆

Choose a variety of small but expertly formed dishes at this sleek and stylish David
Rockwell designed restaurant from the Gordon Ramsay stable. The cooking is
contemporary and nicely balanced; four dishes per person should suffice.

→ Lobster, langoustine and salmon dumpling with aromatic broth. Braised
featherblade beef, pomme purée and togarashi spice. Frozen yoghurt and
granola sandwich, daiquiri sorbet.

XX
&

Pollen Street Social (Jason Atherton) `AC` `⇄` `VISA` `●●` `AE`

8-10 Pollen St ⊠ W1S 1NQ – **Ⓜ** *Oxford Circus –* ℰ *(020) 7290 7600*
– www.pollenstreetsocial.com
– Closed Christmas, Sunday and bank holidays H3
Rest – *(booking essential)* Menu £ 26 (lunch) – Carte £ 42/60

◆ Innovative ◆ Fashionable ◆ Elegant ◆

Jason Atherton's cooking marries innovation and imagination with skilful technique and an innate understanding of good ingredients. Dishes are elaborately
constructed but there are never too many flavours. The room is smoothly run
but not overly formal. Try their terrific version of a negroni.

→ 'Full English breakfast'. Roasted sea bass, celeriac and truffle sauce. Peanut butter parfait, cherry jam, creamed rice puffs.

XX

Bellamy's `AC` `VISA` `●●` `AE`

18 Bruton Pl. ⊠ W1J 6LY – **Ⓜ** *Bond Street –* ℰ *(020) 74912727*
– www.bellamysrestaurant.co.uk
– Closed Saturday lunch, Sunday and bank holidays H3
Rest – Menu £ 25/30 – Carte £ 32/53

◆ French ◆ Brasserie ◆ Family ◆

French deli/brasserie tucked down a smart mews. Go past the caviar and cheeses into the restaurant proper for a very traditional, but well-executed, range of
Gallic classics.

XX

Maze Grill – London Marriott Hotel Grosvenor Square `AC`

10-13 Grosvenor Sq. ⊠ W1K 6JP – **Ⓜ** *Bond Street* `VISA` `●●` `AE`
– ℰ *(020) 74952211 – www.gordonramsay.com* G3
Rest – Menu £ 21/24 – Carte £ 24/111

◆ Meats and grills ◆ Retro ◆ Fashionable ◆

An addendum to Maze, with a menu specialising in steaks, from Hereford grass-
fed to Wagyu 9th grade; all appealingly served on wooden boards. Individually
priced side dishes and sauces can push the bill up.

XX

Aurelia `AC` `VISA` `●●` `AE`

13-14 Cork St ⊠ W1S 3NS – **Ⓜ** *Green Park –* ℰ *(020) 7409 1370*
– www.aurelialondon.co.uk
– Closed Sunday H3
Rest – Carte £ 26/93

◆ Mediterranean ◆ Fashionable ◆ Neighbourhood ◆

The Roman road that stretched from Rome through southern France and into
Spain provides the culinary inspiration. Highlights are meats cooked on the
rotisserie. The atmosphere and the aromas are more enticing downstairs.

XX

Quince `AC` `⇄` `VISA` `●●` `AE`

Stratton St ⊠ W1J 8LT – **Ⓜ** *Green Park –* ℰ *(020) 7915 3892*
– www.quincelondon.com – Closed Saturday lunch H4
Rest – Menu £ 20/25 – Carte £ 28/40

◆ Turkish ◆ Intimate ◆ Fashionable ◆

TV chef Silvena Rowe presents her inimitable Eastern Mediterranean cooking.
Her personality is evident throughout, from personal references on the menu
– "a homage to my grandfather Mehmed" – to the colourful, Ottoman-influen-
ced decoration.

XX **Alloro**   🖂 ⇔ 𝘝𝘐𝘚𝘈 ⑳ 𝘈𝘌 ①

19-20 Dover St ⊠ W1S 4LU – ⓜ Green Park – ℰ (020) 74954768
– www.atozrestaurants.com/alloro
– Closed 25 December, Saturday lunch and Sunday   H3
Rest – (booking essential) Menu £ 35/45
♦ Italian ♦ Fashionable ♦ Elegant ♦
Confidently run and smartly dressed Italian with an appealing menu of easy-to-
eat dishes; breads and pasta are made in-house. Great atmosphere, especially at
busy lunchtimes. Boisterous adjacent baretto.

XX **Goodman**   🖂 ⑳ 𝘈𝘌

26 Maddox St ⊠ W1S 1QH – ⓜ Oxford Circus – ℰ (020) 7499 3776
– www.goodmanrestaurants.com
– Closed Sunday and bank holidays   H3
Rest – (booking essential) Carte £ 25/68
♦ Meats and grills ♦ Brasserie ♦
A worthy attempt at recreating a New York steakhouse; all leather and wood
and macho swagger. Beef is dry or wet aged in-house and comes with a choice
of four sauces; rib-eye the speciality.

XX **Hush**   ⌂ 🖂 ⇔ 𝘝𝘐𝘚𝘈 ⑳ 𝘈𝘌

8 Lancashire Ct., Brook St. ⊠ W1S 1EY – ⓜ Bond Street – ℰ (020)
76591500 – www.hush.co.uk
– Closed Easter, 25-26 December, 1 January and Sunday   H3
Rest – (booking essential) Carte £ 25/54
♦ Modern ♦ Fashionable ♦ Bistro ♦
Appealing and all-purpose European brasserie-style menu served in a busy
room with smart destination bar upstairs and plenty of private dining. Tucked
away in a charming courtyard, with a pleasant summer terrace.

XX **Fakhreldine**   ≼ 🖂 𝘝𝘐𝘚𝘈 ⑳ 𝘈𝘌

85 Piccadilly ⊠ W1J 7NB – ⓜ Green Park – ℰ (020) 74933424
– www.fakhreldine.co.uk   H4
Rest – Menu £ 14/47 – Carte £ 29/41
♦ Lebanese ♦ Fashionable ♦ Exotic ♦
Share some authentic meze then go for one of the succulent lamb dishes at this
sophisticated and long-standing first floor Lebanese restaurant with a hint of
exoticism. Ask for a window table for a view over Green Park.

XX **Tempo**   🖂 ⇔ 𝘝𝘐𝘚𝘈 ⑳ 𝘈𝘌

54 Curzon St. ⊠ W1J 8PG – ⓜ Green Park – ℰ (020) 76292742
– www.tempomayfair.co.uk
– Closed 25-27 December, Saturday lunch, Sunday and bank holidays
Rest – Menu £ 22/25 – Carte £ 30/47   H4
♦ Italian ♦ Neighbourhood ♦ Fashionable ♦
The presence of Henry Togna, the affable and urbane owner, adds to the convi-
viality of this sweet Italian restaurant. The cicchetti, or small plates, are well
worth ordering, as is the homemade pasta and the breads are good too.

XX **Sumosan**   🖂 𝘝𝘐𝘚𝘈 ⑳ 𝘈𝘌 ①

26 Albemarle St. ⊠ W1S 4HY – ⓜ Green Park – ℰ (020) 74955999
– www.sumosan.com
– Closed lunch Saturday-Sunday and bank holidays   H3
Rest – Menu £ 25 (weekday lunch) – Carte £ 19/103
♦ Japanese ♦ Fashionable ♦ Design ♦
Attracts a young and prosperous crowd with its cocktail list, modern interpreta-
tions of Japanese flavours and stylish surroundings. The skilled kitchen deftly
executes a wide-ranging menu.

XX **Mews of Mayfair** ♻ VISA ◐ AE ⓪

10-11 Lancashire Ct, Brook St (1st floor) ⊠ *W1S 1EY –* Ⓜ *Bond Street*
– ℰ (020) 75189388 – www.mewsofmayfair.com
– Closed 25 December H3
Rest – Menu £ 19 – Carte £ 26/48
♦ Modern ♦ Friendly ♦ Formal ♦
This pretty restaurant, bright in summer and warm in winter, is on the first floor
of a mews house, once used as storage rooms for Savile Row. Seasonal menus
offer something for everyone.

XX **Sketch (The Gallery)** AC VISA ◐ AE

9 Conduit St ⊠ *W1S 2XG –* Ⓜ *Oxford Circus – ℰ (020) 76594500*
– www.sketch.uk.com
– Closed 25-26 December, Sunday and bank holidays H3
Rest – *(dinner only) (booking essential)* Carte £ 30/67
♦ Modern ♦ Trendy ♦ Intimate ♦
Martin Creed was the artist charged with changing the look of The Gallery and
he's made it a vibrant, witty and provocative space. The menus have also been
updated and are a mix of original dishes and updated brasserie classics.

XX **JW Steakhouse** – Grosvenor House Hotel AC ♻ VISA ◐ AE

Park Ln ⊠ *W1K 7TN –* Ⓜ *Marble Arch – ℰ (020) 73998460*
– www.londongrosvenorhouse.co.uk G3
Rest – Carte £ 23/92
♦ Meats and grills ♦ Brasserie ♦ Family ♦
It's all about beer, bourbon and beef here – things couldn't get more macho if
they handed out hunting rifles and Stetsons. Along with great steaks (cooked at
650°C) are American classics like short ribs and crab cakes.

XX **Momo** ☂ AC VISA ◐ AE

25 Heddon St. ⊠ *W1B 4BH –* Ⓜ *Oxford Circus – ℰ (020) 743 44040*
– www.momoresto.com
– Closed 25 December, 1 January and Sunday lunch H3
Rest – Menu £ 20 (lunch) – Carte £ 32/49
♦ Moroccan ♦ Exotic ♦ Intimate ♦
Lanterns, rugs, trinkets and music contribute to the authentic Moroccan atmo-
sphere; come in a group to better appreciate it. The more traditional dishes are
the kitchen's strength.

XX **Veeraswamy** AC ♻ ☵ VISA ◐ AE ⓪

Victory House, 99 Regent St (entrance on Swallow St.) ⊠ *W1B 4RS*
– Ⓜ *Piccadilly Circus – ℰ (020) 77341401 – www.realindianfood.com*
Rest – Menu £ 18/24 – Carte £ 35/56 H3
♦ Indian ♦ Design ♦ Fashionable ♦
May have opened back in 1926 but feels fresh and is awash with vibrant colours
and always full of bustle. Skilled kitchen cleverly mixes the traditional with more
contemporary creations.

XX **Cafe at Sotheby's** VISA ◐ AE ⓪

34-35 New Bond St. ⊠ *W1A 2AA –* Ⓜ *Bond Street – ℰ (020) 72935077*
– www.sothebys.com/cafe
*– Closed 3 weeks August, Christmas and New Year, Saturday, Sunday and bank
holidays* H3
Rest – *(lunch only) (booking essential)* Carte £ 26/37
♦ Modern ♦ Intimate ♦ Fashionable ♦
Occupying a cosy space just off the foyer of the famous auction house. The
appealing lunch menu changes weekly; the lobster sandwich is a perennial
favourite. Service is discreet.

XX **Kiku** AC VISA ◐ AE ①

17 Half Moon St. ✉ *W1J 7BE* – ⓜ *Green Park* – ℰ *(020) 74994208*
– www.kikurestaurant.co.uk
– Closed 25-27 December, 1 January, Sunday and lunch on bank holidays
Rest – Menu £ 22/25 – Carte £ 20/83 **H4**
♦ Japanese ♦ Neighbourhood ♦ Formal ♦
Bright and fresh feel thanks to minimalistic décor of stone and natural wood. A plethora of menus, a fierce adherence to seasonality and an authentic emphasis on presentation.

X **Bentley's (Oyster Bar)** 🍴 AC VISA ◐ AE ①

11-15 Swallow St ✉ *W1B 4DG* – ⓜ *Piccadilly Circus* – ℰ *(020) 77344756*
– www.bentleys.org – Closed 25-26 December and 1 January
Rest – Menu £ 25 (lunch) – Carte £ 37/60 **H3**
♦ Fish and seafood ♦ Bistro ♦ Fashionable ♦
Sit at the counter to watch white-jacketed staff open oysters by the bucket load. Interesting seafood menus feature tasty fish pies; lots of daily specials on blackboard.

X **Le Boudin Blanc** 🍴 ⇔ 🏧 VISA ◐ AE

5 Trebeck St ✉ *W1J 7LT* – ⓜ *Green Park* – ℰ *(020) 74993292*
– www.boudinblanc.co.uk – Closed 24-26 December **G4**
Rest – Menu £ 15/45 – Carte £ 27/55
♦ French ♦ Rustic ♦ Neighbourhood ♦
Appealing, lively French bistro in Shepherd Market, spread over two floors. Satisfying French classics and country cooking is the draw, along with authentic Gallic service. Good value lunch menu.

X **Bar Trattoria Semplice** 🍴 AC VISA ◐ AE

22 Woodstock St. ✉ *W1C 2AR* – ⓜ *Bond Street* – ℰ *(020) 74918638*
– www.bartrattoriasemplice.com **G3**
Rest – Menu £ 20/25 – Carte £ 27/42
♦ Italian ♦ Neighbourhood ♦ Friendly ♦
It's all about recognisable Italian dishes and simple preparation at this everyday alternative to Semplice a few doors down. It's the sort of place to pop into for a plate of pasta and a glass of wine at the bar.

X **Automat** AC VISA ◐ AE

33 Dover St. ✉ *W1S 4NF* – ⓜ *Green Park* – ℰ *(020) 74993033*
– www.automat-london.com
– Closed 25 December and 1 January **H3**
Rest – Carte £ 27/47
♦ North-American ♦ Intimate ♦ Family ♦
In contrast to Mayfair's inherent Britishness is this buzzy NYC style brasserie. Stick to the classics – crab cakes, burgers and cheesecakes and don't get palmed off with a table in the first section.

🍴 **Only Running Footman** ⇔ VISA ◐ AE

5 Charles St ✉ *W1J 5DF* – ⓜ *Green Park.* – ℰ *(020) 74992988*
– www.therunningfootmanmayfair.com **H3**
Rest – Menu £ 30/40 – Carte £ 22/39
♦ British traditional ♦ Pub ♦ Formal ♦
Busy ground floor bar with its appealing menu of pub classics doesn't take bookings. By contrast, upstairs is formal and its menu more European and ambitious but simpler dishes still the best.

🍴 **Burger & Lobster** AC VISA ◐ AE

29 Clarges St ✉ *W1J 7EF* – ⓜ *Green Park.* – ℰ *(020) 7409 1699*
– www.burgerandlobster.com **H4**
Rest – *(bookings not accepted)* Menu £ 24
♦ Meats and grills ♦ Pub ♦ Rustic ♦
Choose a burger, a lobster or a lobster roll, with chips, salad and sauces, and mousse for dessert – an ingeniously simple idea. The lobsters are Canadian and the burgers 10oz. It's a well organised bunfight in an old pub.

SOHO

Soho

4 Richmond Mews ⊠ W1D 3DH – ⓜ Tottenham Court Road – ℰ (020) 75593000 – www.sohohotel.com
I3

85 rm – †£ 354 ††£ 402, ⌷ £ 20 – 2 suites
Rest Refuel – see restaurant listing
♦ Luxury ♦ Stylish ♦
Stylish and fashionable hotel that mirrors the vibrancy of the neighbourhood. Boasts two screening rooms, a comfortable drawing room and up-to-the-minute bedrooms; some vivid, others more muted but all with hi-tech extras.

W London

10 Wardour St ⊠ W1D 6QF – ⓜ Leicester Square – ℰ (020) 77581000
– www.wlondon.co.uk
I3

177 rm – †£ 335/503 ††£ 335/503, ⌷ £ 27 – 15 suites
Rest Spice Market – see restaurant listing
♦ Chain hotel ♦ Design ♦ Stylish ♦
Achingly trendy hotel, opened in 2011. A DJ in the lobby lounge, low slung tables in the bar and slick, über cool bedrooms in categories called 'Fantastic' or 'Spectacular'. Anyone over 40 will be lost.

Sanctum Soho

20 Warwick St. ⊠ W1B 5NF – ⓜ Piccadilly Circus – ℰ (020) 72926100
– www.sanctumsoho.com
H3

30 rm – †£ 216/240 ††£ 216/240, ⌷ £ 15
Rest No. 20 – (closed Sunday dinner) Menu £ 19 – Carte £ 20/60
♦ Modern ♦ Design ♦
Plenty of glitz and bling at this funky, self-styled rock 'n' roll hotel, with some innovative touches such as TVs behind mirrors. Rooftop lounge and hot tub. Relaxed and comfortable dining with plenty of classic dishes.

Dean Street Townhouse

69-71 Dean St. ⊠ W1D 3SE – ⓜ Tottenham Court Road – ℰ (020) 74341775 – www.deanstreettownhouse.com
I3

39 rm – †£ 312/528 ††£ 312/528, ⌷ £ 12
Rest Dean Street Townhouse Restaurant – see restaurant listing
♦ Townhouse ♦ Classic ♦
In the heart of Soho where bedrooms range from tiny to bigger; the latter have roll-top baths in the room. All are well designed and come with a good range of extras. Cosy ground floor lounge.

Hazlitt's

6 Frith St ⊠ W1D 3JA – ⓜ Tottenham Court Road – ℰ (020) 74341771
– www.hazlittshotel.com
I3

27 rm – †£ 198/222 ††£ 227/282, ⌷ £ 12 – 3 suites
Rest – (room service only)
♦ Townhouse ♦ Traditional ♦ Historic ♦
Three adjoining early 18C townhouses and former home of the eponymous essayist. Idiosyncratic bedrooms, many with antique furniture and Victorian baths; ask for one of the newer ones.

Quo Vadis

26-29 Dean St ⊠ W1D 3LL – ⓜ Tottenham Court Road – ℰ (020) 74379585 – www.quovadissoho.co.uk
– Closed Sunday and bank holidays
I3

Rest – Menu £ 20 – Carte £ 26/40
♦ British modern ♦ Fashionable ♦
A stylish, elegant Soho institution dating from the 1920s and now owned by the Hart Brothers. First order some great 'bites' then choose from a menu of satisfying British dishes that includes a daily pie and braised dish along with grilled meats and assorted seafood.

XXX **Gauthier - Soho**   🕯 🖭 ⇪ 🕸 💳 ⓜ 🖭

21 Romilly St ⊠ W1D 5AF – ⓜ *Leicester Square –* ℰ *(020) 74943111*
– www.gauthiersoho.co.uk
– Closed Saturday lunch, Sunday and bank holidays   I3
Rest – Menu £ 25/40
♦ French ♦ Intimate ♦ Neighbourhood ♦
Tucked away from the mischief of Soho is this charming Georgian townhouse,
with dining spread over three floors. Alex Gauthier offers assorted menus of his
classically based cooking, with vegetarians particularly well looked after.

XXX **Aqua Nueva**   🖭 ⇪ 🕸 💳 ⓜ 🖭

240 Regent St. (entrance on Argyll St.) ⊠ W1B 3BR – ⓜ *Oxford Circus*
– ℰ *(020) 7478 0540 – www.aqua-london.com*
– Closed 25 December and 1 January   H3
Rest – Menu £ 23 (weekday lunch) – Carte £ 22/60
♦ Spanish ♦ Design ♦ Fashionable ♦
Large operation on the 5th floor of a former department store. Choose between
the elegant main dining room or the more buzzy but equally stylish tapas bar.
Spanish food interpreted in a modern style.

XXX **Red Fort**   🖭 🕸 💳 ⓜ 🖭

77 Dean St. ⊠ W1D 3SH – ⓜ *Tottenham Court Road –* ℰ *(020) 74372525*
– www.redfort.co.uk
– Closed 25 December, lunch Saturday, Sunday and bank holidays
Rest – *(bookings advisable at dinner)* Menu £ 14/49 – Carte   I3
£ 21/53
♦ Indian ♦ Fashionable ♦
A feature in Soho since 1983 but the last makeover gave it a stylish, contemporary look. Balanced Indian cooking uses much UK produce such as Herdwick
lamb; look out for more unusual choices like rabbit.

XXX **Imperial China**   🖭 ⇪ 💳 ⓜ 🖭 ⓞ

White Bear Yard, 25a Lisle St ⊠ WC2H 7BA – ⓜ *Leicester Square*
– ℰ *(020) 7734 3388 – www.imperial-china.co.uk*
– Closed 24-25 December   I3
Rest – *(booking advisable)* Menu £ 18/35 – Carte £ 14/77
♦ Chinese ♦ Elegant ♦
Sharp service and comfortable surroundings are not the only things that set this
restaurant apart: the Cantonese cooking exudes freshness and vitality, whether
that's the steamed dumplings or the XO minced pork with fine beans.

XX **Yauatcha**   🖭 💳 ⓜ 🖭
🕸

15 Broadwick St ⊠ W1F 0DL – ⓜ *Tottenham Court Road –* ℰ *(020)*
74948888 – www.yauatcha.com
– Closed 24-25 December and lunch 26 December and 1 January
Rest – Menu £ 29/55 – Carte £ 23/48   I3
♦ Chinese ♦ Design ♦ Trendy ♦
Refined, delicate and delicious dim sum; ideal for sharing in a group. Stylish sur-
roundings spread over two floors: the lighter, brighter ground floor or the dar-
ker, more atmospheric basement. Afternoon teas also a speciality.
➔ Scallop shui mai with tobiko caviar. Dover sole with shiitake and soya.
Raspberry delice.

XX **Brasserie Zédel**   🖭 💳 ⓜ 🖭 ⓞ
🕸

20 Sherwood St ⊠ W1F 7ED – ⓜ *Piccadilly Circus –* ℰ *(020) 7734 4888*
– www.brasseriezedel.com
– Closed 25 December   I3
Rest – *(booking advisable)* Menu £ 12/20 – Carte £ 16/29
♦ French ♦ Brasserie ♦
A grand French brasserie, which is all about inclusivity and accessibility, in a
bustling subterranean space restored to its original art deco glory. Expect a
roll-call of classic French dishes and some very competitive prices.

XX **Dean Street Townhouse Restaurant** 🍽 🎐 AC
69-71 Dean St. ⊠ *W1D 3SE* — VISA ⦿ AE ⦿
– **M** *Tottenham Court Road* – 𝒞 *(020) 74341775*
– *www.deanstreettownhouse.com* I3
Rest – *(booking essential)* Menu £ 20 *(early dinner)* – Carte £ 27/50
♦ British modern ♦ Brasserie ♦ Elegant ♦
Georgian house now home to a fashionable and very busy bar and restaurant;
the Parlour is the less hectic area. Appealingly classic British food includes some
retro dishes and satisfying puddings.

XX **Aqua Kyoto** AC ⟷ 🔄 VISA ⦿ AE
240 Regent St. (entrance on Argyll St.) ⊠ *W1F 7EB* – **M** *Oxford Circus*
– 𝒞 *(020) 7478 0540* – *www.aqua-london.com*
– *Closed 25 December and 1 January* H3
Rest – Menu £ 20 *(weekday lunch)* – Carte £ 23/61
♦ Japanese ♦ Trendy ♦
The more boisterous of the two large restaurants on the 5th floor of Aqua Lon-
don, along with a busy bar. Ideally suited to larger groups, as the contemporary
Japanese food is designed for sharing.

XX **Bob Bob Ricard** AC VISA ⦿ AE ⦿
1 Upper James St ⊠ *W1F 9DF* – **M** *Oxford Circus* – 𝒞 *(020) 31451000*
– *www.bobbobricard.com*
– *Closed 25-26 December, 1 January, Sunday and Monday* H3
Rest – Carte £ 23/95
♦ British traditional ♦ Retro ♦
Enigmatically decorated and flamboyant grand café, with a menu that offers
everything from caviar and jelly, to beef Wellington or a bowl of cornflakes.
Open from early to very late.

XX **Spice Market** – W London Hotel AC ⟷ VISA ⦿ AE ⦿
10 Wardour St ⊠ *W1D 6QF* – **M** *Leicester Square* – 𝒞 *(020) 77581082*
– *www.spicemarketlondon.co.uk* I3
Rest – Carte £ 32/46
♦ Asian ♦ Fashionable ♦ Exotic ♦
Over two floors and as strikingly decorated and as fun as Jean-Georges Vonge-
richten's original in Manhattan's Meatpacking district. Influences from across
Asia in dishes designed for sharing; curries a highlight.

XX **Floridita** AC ⟷ VISA ⦿ AE
100 Wardour St. ⊠ *W1F 0TN* – **M** *Tottenham Court Road* – 𝒞 *(020)*
73144000 – *www.floriditalondon.com*
– *Closed Sunday, Monday and bank holidays* I3
Rest – *(dinner only and lunch in December for groups of 12 or more)*
Menu £ 28 *(weekdays)* – Carte £ 23/54
♦ Other world kitchens ♦ Musical ♦ Exotic ♦
Mediterranean tapas on the ground floor; the huge downstairs for live music,
dancing and Latin American specialities, from Cuban spice to Argentinean
beef. Great cocktails and a party atmosphere.

XX **Vasco and Piero's Pavilion** AC ⟷ 🔄 VISA ⦿ AE
15 Poland St ⊠ *W1F 8QE* – **M** *Oxford Circus* – 𝒞 *(020) 74378774*
– *www.vascosfood.com*
– *Closed Saturday lunch, Sunday and bank holidays* H2
Rest – *(booking essential at lunch)* Menu £ 15/20 – Carte £ 27/44
♦ Italian ♦ Friendly ♦
Celebrated forty years in 2011; its longevity down to its twice-daily changing
menu and the simple but effective Umbrian-influenced cooking. The bright
room attracts a high proportion of regulars.

UNITED KINGDOM - LONDON

XX

Plum Valley
⟳ VISA ◉◎ AE

20 Gerrard St. ⊠ *W1D 6JQ –* Ⓜ *Leicester Square –* 𝒞 *(020) 74944366*
– Closed 23-24 December   13
Rest – Menu £ 38 – Carte £ 19/37
◆ Chinese ◆ Design ◆

Its striking black façade make this modern Chinese restaurant easy to spot in
Chinatown. Mostly Cantonese cooking, with occasional forays into Vietnam
and Thailand; dim sum is the strength.

XX

Haozhan
AC VISA ◉◎ AE

8 Gerrard St ⊠ *W1D 5PJ –* Ⓜ *Leicester Square –* 𝒞 *(020) 74343838*
– www.haozhan.co.uk
– Closed 24-25December   13
Rest – Menu £ 15/48 – Carte £ 20/78
◆ Chinese ◆ Design ◆

Interesting fusion-style dishes, with mostly Cantonese but other Asian influences too. Specialities like jasmine ribs or wasabi prawns reveal a freshness that
marks this place out from the plethora of Chinatown mediocrity.

XX

Refuel – Soho Hotel
AC VISA ◉◎ AE ⓪

4 Richmond Mews ⊠ *W1D 3DH –* Ⓜ *Tottenham Court Road –* 𝒞 *(020)*
75593007 – www.sohohotel.com   13
Rest – Carte £ 26/50
◆ Modern ◆ Fashionable ◆ Brasserie ◆

At the heart of the cool Soho hotel is their aptly named bar and restaurant. With
a menu to suit all moods and wallets, from Dover sole to burgers, and a cocktail
list to lift all spirits, it's a fun and bustling spot.

X
✿

Arbutus
AC ☞ VISA ◉◎ AE

63-64 Frith St. ⊠ *W1D 3JW –* Ⓜ *Tottenham Court Road –* 𝒞 *(020)*
77344545 – www.arbutusrestaurant.co.uk
– Closed 25-26 December and 1 January   13
Rest – *(booking advisable)* Menu £ 19 (lunch) – Carte £ 29/40 ⅋
◆ Modern ◆ Bistro ◆

It takes a lot of work and experience to make it all look so easy. Bubbly and
enthusiastic service; relaxed, sociable surroundings and bistro-style dishes
packed with flavour from a highly skilled kitchen. Terrific, affordable wine list.
➔ Squid and mackerel burger. Saddle of rabbit, shoulder cottage pie. Classic English custard tart, golden sultanas.

X
✿

St John with rm
AC ☞ 📺 VISA ◉◎ AE ⓪

1 Leicester St ⊠ *WC2H 7BL –* Ⓜ *Leicester Square –* 𝒞 *(020) 3301 8069*
– www.stjohnhotellondon.com   13
15 rm – †£ 150/340 ††£ 230/520, � £ 15
Rest – *(booking advisable)* Menu £ 23 (lunch and early dinner) – Carte
£ 22/52
◆ British traditional ◆ Minimalist ◆

There's a Nordic lucidity to the bedrooms but it is the restaurant that's the heart
of the hotel. It follows the Clerkenwell original with its terse menu descriptions,
fiercely seasonal, no-nonsense "nose to tail" British cooking, municipal-white
surroundings and clued-up staff.
➔ Salt hake and tartare sauce. Ox cheek, celeriac and pickled walnuts.
Rhubarb and sherry trifle.

X
☺

Bocca di Lupo
AC ⟳ VISA ◉◎ AE ⓪

12 Archer St ⊠ *WID 7BB –* Ⓜ *Piccadilly Circus –* 𝒞 *(020) 77342223*
– www.boccadilupo.com
– Closed 24 December-3 January   13
Rest – *(booking essential)* Carte £ 21/35
◆ Italian ◆ Tapas bar ◆

Atmosphere, food and service are all best when sitting at the marble counter,
watching the chefs at work. Specialities from across Italy come in large or small
sizes and are full of flavour and vitality. Try also their Gelato shop opposite.

Copita
`AC` `VISA` `OO` `AE` `O`

27 d'Arblay St ⊠ W1F 8EP – Ⓜ Oxford Circus – ℰ (020) 7436 9448
– www.barrica.co.uk
– Closed bank holidays H3
Rest – *(bookings not accepted)* Carte £ 11/21

♦ **Mediterranean** ♦ **Tapas bar** ♦

Perch on one of the high stools or stay standing and get stuck into the daily menu of small, colourful and tasty dishes. Staff add to the atmosphere and everything on the Spanish wine list comes by the glass or copita.

Benja Bangkok Table
`AC` `VISA` `OO` `AE` `O`

17 Beak St. ⊠ W1F 9RW – Ⓜ Oxford Circus – ℰ (020) 72870555
– www.benja-bangkoktable.com H3
Rest – Menu £ 10/20 – Carte £ 18/26

♦ **Thai** ♦ **Intimate** ♦ **Exotic** ♦

The last makeover left this Thai restaurant on the edge of Soho with a simpler look that is more typical of a Bangkok eatery. The colourful mix of dishes is authentic and the set menus represent excellent value.

Polpo Soho
`AC` `⇔` `VISA` `OO` `AE`

41 Beak St. ⊠ W1F 9SB – Ⓜ Oxford Circus – ℰ (020) 77344479
– www.polpo.co.uk
– Closed 25 December-1 January, Sunday and dinner bank holidays
Rest – *(bookings not taken at dinner)* Carte £ 17/28 H3

♦ **Italian** ♦ **Tapas bar** ♦

A fun and lively Venetian bacaro, with a stripped-down, faux-industrial look. The small plates, from arancini and prosciutto to fritto misto and Cotechino sausage, are so well priced that waiting for a table is worth it.

Barrafina
`AC` `VISA` `OO` `AE`

54 Frith St. ⊠ W1D 3SL – Ⓜ Tottenham Court Road – ℰ (020) 78138016
– www.barrafina.co.uk
– Closed 24 December and 1 January I3
Rest – *(bookings not accepted)* Carte £ 20/30

♦ **Spanish** ♦ **Tapas bar** ♦ **Fashionable** ♦

Centred around a counter with seating for 20; come here if you want authentic Spanish tapas served in a buzzy atmosphere. Seafood is a speciality and the Jabugo ham a must.

Nopi
`AC` `VISA` `OO` `AE`

21-22 Warwick St. ⊠ W1B 5NE – Ⓜ Piccadilly Circus – ℰ (020) 74949584
– www.nopi-restaurant.com
– Closed 25-26 December, 1 January and Sunday dinner H3
Rest – Carte £ 27/47

♦ **Mediterranean** ♦ **Design** ♦

The bright, clean look of Yotam Ottolenghi's restaurant matches the fresh, invigorating food. The sharing plates take in the Mediterranean, Middle East and Asia and the veg dishes stand out.

Dehesa
`🍴` `AC` `⇔` `VISA` `OO` `AE`

25 Ganton St ⊠ W1F 9BP – Ⓜ Oxford Circus – ℰ (020) 74944170
– www.dehesa.co.uk
– Closed Sunday dinner H3
Rest – Carte £ 22/34 ᵇᵇ

♦ **Mediterranean** ♦ **Tapas bar** ♦

Repeats the success of its sister restaurant, Salt Yard, by offering tasty, good value Spanish and Italian tapas. Unhurried atmosphere in appealing corner location. Terrific drinks list too.

Mele e Pere

AC VISA AE

46 Brewer St ⊠ *W1F 9TF* – Ⓜ *Piccadilly Circus* – ℰ *(020) 7096 2096*
– *www.meleepere.co.uk*
– *Closed 25-26 December, 1 January and Sunday*   I3
Rest – Menu £ 13/18 – Carte £ 18/39
♦ Italian ♦ Friendly ♦ Neighbourhood ♦

Head downstairs – the 'apples and pears'? – to a vaulted, if somewhat hard-edged room with an appealing Vermouth bar. The owner-chef has worked in some decent London kitchens but hails from Verona so expect gutsy Italian dishes.

Wright Brothers Soho

AC VISA AE

13 Kingly St. ⊠ *W1B 5PW* – Ⓜ *Oxford Circus* – ℰ *(020) 74343611*
– *www.thewrightbrothers.co.uk*
– *Closed 25-27 December and bank holidays*   H3
Rest – Menu £ 17/19 – Carte £ 23/54
♦ Fish and seafood ♦ Neighbourhood ♦

Bigger than the original in Borough Market, this branch is spread over three levels but the best spot is at the counter on the lower floor. Oysters a speciality but all seafood is handled deftly.

Hix

AC VISA AE

66-70 Brewer St. ⊠ *WIF 9UP* – Ⓜ *Piccadilly Circus* – ℰ *(020) 72923518*
– *www.hixsoho.co.uk*
– *Closed 25-26 December*   H3
Rest – Menu £ 18 (lunch) – Carte £ 26/61
♦ British traditional ♦ Fashionable ♦

The exterior hints at exclusivity but the enormous interior is fun and sociable and comes decorated with the works of eminent British artists. Expect classic British dishes and ingredients.

Tapas Brindisa

VISA AE

46 Broadwick St. ⊠ *W1F 7AF* – Ⓜ *Oxford Circus* – ℰ *(020) 75341690*
– *www.brindisa.com*
– *Closed dinner 24-27 December*   H3
Rest – *(bookings not accepted at dinner)* Carte £ 19/43
♦ Spanish ♦ Tapas bar ♦

Sister to the original Tapas Brindisa in Borough Market. Expect the same quality of tapas from these importers of Spanish produce and the same bustling atmosphere. Service is obliging but bookings are not taken.

Cinnamon Soho

AC VISA AE

5 Kingly St ⊠ *W1B 5PF* – Ⓜ *Oxford Circus* – ℰ *(020) 7437 1664*
– *www.cinnamonsoho.com*   H3
Rest – Menu £ 18/24 – Carte £ 17/29
♦ Indian ♦ Friendly ♦ Trendy ♦

This Cinnamon outpost is altogether more fun than its two older siblings. It blends Indian flavours with traditional British dishes, so you can order Rogan Josh shepherd's pie, curried Cullen Skink or Cumbrian lamb biryani.

10 Greek Street

AC VISA AE

10 Greek St ⊠ *W1D 4DH* – Ⓜ *Tottenham Court Road* – ℰ *(020) 77344677* – *www.10greekstreet.com*
– *Closed Christmas, Easter and Sunday*   I2
Rest – Carte £ 19/34
♦ Modern ♦ Bistro ♦ Neighbourhood ♦

With just 28 seats and a dozen at the counter, the challenge is getting a table at this modishly sparse-looking bistro (no bookings taken at dinner). The chef-owner's blackboard menu comes with Anglo, Med and Middle Eastern elements.

Barshu

☒ AC ⇄ VISA ☎ AE

28 Frith St. ☒ *W1D 5LF –* Ⓜ *Leicester Square –* ☎ *(020) 72878822*
– www.bar-shu.co.uk
– Closed 24-25 December

I3

Rest *– (booking advisable)* Carte £ 20/50
♦ Chinese ♦ Exotic ♦

The fiery and authentic flavours of China's Sichuan Province are the draw here; help is at hand as the menu has pictures. It's decorated with carved wood and lanterns; downstairs is better for groups.

Vinoteca

☒ AC VISA ☎ AE

53-55 Beak St ☒ *W1F 9SH –* Ⓜ *Oxford Circus –* ☎ *(020) 3544 7411*
– www.vinoteca.co.uk
– Closed 24-26 December, 31 December and 1 January.

H3

Rest *– (booking advisable)* Carte £ 20/33 ☝
♦ Modern ♦ Wine bar ♦ Bistro ♦

The terrific wine list mixes the classic with the esoteric and emerging markets are also covered. The food isn't forgotten – cured meats and cheeses are a highlight and European dishes like bavette and risotto also hit the spot.

Spuntino

☒ AC VISA ☎ AE

61 Rupert St. ☒ *W1D 7PW –* Ⓜ *Piccadilly Circus*
– www.spuntino.co.uk
– Closed 24-26 December

I3

Rest *– (bookings not accepted)* Carte £ 15/25
♦ North-American ♦ Rustic ♦

Influenced by Downtown New York, with its no-booking policy and industrial look. Sit at the counter and order classics like Mac 'n' cheese or mini burgers. The staff, who look like they could also fix your car, really add to the fun.

Ba Shan

☒ AC ⇄ VISA ☎ AE

24 Romilly St. ☒ *W1D 5AH –* Ⓜ *Leicester Square*
– ☎ *(020) 72873266*
– Closed 24-25 December

I3

Rest *– (booking advisable)* Carte £ 19/45
♦ Chinese ♦ Cosy ♦

3-4 tables in each of the five rooms. Open all day, serving a mix of 'snack' and 'home-style' dishes, some with Sichuan leanings, others from northern areas and Henan province.

Imli

☒ AC VISA ☎ AE ①

167-169 Wardour St ☒ *W1F 8WR –* Ⓜ *Tottenham Court Road*
– ☎ *(020) 72874243 – www.imli.co.uk*
– Closed 25-26 December and 1 January

I3

Rest *–* Menu £ 20 *(dinner) –* Carte £ 20/26
♦ Indian ♦ Bistro ♦

Diffusion line from the people behind Tamarind restaurant, where good value, fresh and tasty Indian tapas-style dishes prove a popular currency. The long, spacious interior is a busy, buzzy place.

Cây Tre

☒ AC VISA ☎ AE

42-43 Dean St ☒ *W1D 4PZ –* Ⓜ *Tottenham Court Road*
– ☎ *(020) 77396686 – www.caytresoho.co.uk*

I3

Rest *– (booking advisable)* Menu £ 23/29 *–* Carte £ 17/28
♦ Vietnamese ♦ Minimalist ♦

Bright, sleek and bustling surroundings where Vietnamese standouts include Cha La Lot (spicy ground pork wrapped in betel leaves), slow-cooked Mekong catfish with a well-judged sweet and spicy sauce, and 6 versions of Pho (noodle soup).

UNITED KINGDOM - LONDON

Ducksoup

<small>AC VISA ⦾ AE ①</small>

41 Dean St ⊠ *W1D 4PY –* Ⓜ *Leicester Square –* ✆ *(020) 7287 4599*
– www.ducksoupsoho.co.uk
– Closed bank holidays and Sunday dinner   13
Rest – Carte £ 22/31

♦ Modern ♦ Trendy ♦ Neighbourhood ♦

It's compact, with bar seating; decoratively it's knowingly underwhelming; and the menu is handwritten each day – yes, every 'on-trend' box is ticked here. Dishes are all about the produce and are confidently unadorned.

Baozi Inn

<small>⌷</small>

25 Newport Court ⊠ *WC2H 7JS –* Ⓜ *Leicester Square*
– ✆ *(020) 72876877*
– Closed 24-25 December   13
Rest – *(bookings not accepted)* Carte approx. £ 16

♦ Chinese ♦ Exotic ♦

Baozi, or steamed filled buns, are a good way to start, followed by some fiery Sichuan specialities. Simple, honest and friendly restaurant, just off the main strip of Chinatown.

Beijing Dumpling

<small>AC VISA ⦾ AE ①</small>

23 Lisle St. ⊠ *WC2H 7BA –* Ⓜ *Leicester Square*
– ✆ *(0207) 2876888*
– Closed 24-25 December   13
Rest – Menu £ 15/20 – Carte £ 10/39

♦ Chinese ♦ Rustic ♦

This relaxed little place serves freshly prepared dumplings of both Beijing and Shanghai styles. Although the range is not as comprehensive as the name suggests, they do stand out, especially varieties of the famed Siu Lung Bao.

Ceviche

<small>AC VISA ⦾ AE ①</small>

17 Frith St ⊠ *W1D 4RG –* Ⓜ *Tottenham Court Road –* ✆ *(020) 72922040*
– www.cevicheuk.com   13
Rest – Carte £ 13/26

♦ Other world kitchens ♦ Friendly ♦ Fashionable ♦

Based on a Lima Pisco bar, Ceviche is as loud as it is fun. First try the deliriously addictive drinks based on the Peruvian spirit Pisco, and then share some thinly sliced sea bass or octopus, along with anticuchos skewers.

Manchurian Legends

<small>AC ⇔ VISA ⦾</small>

16 Lisle St ⊠ *WC2H 7BE –* Ⓜ *Leicester Square –* ✆ *(020) 72876606*
– www.manchurianlegends.com
– Closed Christmas   13
Rest – Carte £ 20/30

♦ Chinese ♦ Simple ♦ Friendly ♦

Try specialities from a less familiar region of China: Dongbei, the 'north east'. As winters here are long, stews and bbq are popular, as are pickled ingredients and chilli heat. Further warmth comes from the sweet natured staff.

Koya

<small>AC VISA ⦾ AE ①</small>

49 Frith St ⊠ *W1D 4SG –* Ⓜ *Tottenham Court Road –* ✆ *(020) 74344463*
– www.koya.co.uk
– Closed Christmas   13
Rest – *(bookings not accepted)* Carte £ 12/27

♦ Japanese ♦ Neighbourhood ♦

Come for authentic udon noodles, made with wheat kneaded by foot, at this sweetly run, simply adorned place. The dashi base stock is freshly made every day. Be respectful by slurping with abandon.

Rosa's

48 Dean St ✉ W1D 5BF – Ⓜ Leicester Square – ☎ (020) 7494 1638 – www.rosaslondon.com
– Closed Easter and Christmas I3
Rest – *(booking advisable)* Carte £ 18/30
◆ Thai ◆ Simple ◆ Friendly ◆
The worn-in, pared down look of this authentic Thai café adds to its intimate feel. Signature dishes include warm minced chicken salad and a sweet pumpkin red curry. Tom Yam soup comes with lovely balance of sweet, sour and spice.

St James's

Ritz

150 Piccadilly ✉ W1J 9BR – Ⓜ Green Park – ☎ (020) 74938181 – www.theritzlondon.com H4
113 rm – †£ 282/768 ††£ 282/768, ☕ £ 28 – 21 suites
Rest *Ritz Restaurant* – see restaurant listing
◆ Grand Luxury ◆ Classic ◆ Stylish ◆
World famous hotel, opened in 1906 as a fine example of Louis XVI architecture and decoration. Elegant Palm Court famed for its afternoon tea. Many of the lavishly appointed and luxurious rooms and suites overlook the park.

Haymarket

1 Suffolk Pl. ✉ SW1Y 4HX – Ⓜ Piccadilly Circus – ☎ (020) 74704000 – www.haymarkethotel.com I4
47 rm – †£ 318 ††£ 372, ☕ £ 20 – 3 suites
Rest *Brumus* – see restaurant listing
◆ Luxury ◆ Stylish ◆
Smart, spacious hotel in John Nash Regency building, with stylish blend of modern and antique furnishings. Large, comfortable bedrooms in soothing colours. Impressive basement pool often used in photo-shoots.

Sofitel London St James

6 Waterloo Pl. ✉ SW1Y 4AN – Ⓜ Piccadilly Circus – ☎ (020) 77472200 – www.sofitelstjames.com I4
183 rm – †£ 576/1305 ††£ 655/1317, ☕ £ 27 – 8 suites
Rest *Balcon* – see restaurant listing
◆ Luxury ◆ Elegant ◆
Great location for this international hotel in a Grade II former bank. The triple-glazed bedrooms are immaculately kept; the spa is one of the best around. The bar is inspired by Coco Chanel; the lounge by an English rose garden.

Dukes

35 St James's Pl. ✉ SW1A 1NY – Ⓜ Green Park – ☎ (020) 74914840 – www.dukeshotel.com H4
84 rm – †£ 270/444 ††£ 270/444, ☕ £ 24 – 6 suites
Rest *Thirty Six by Nigel Mendham* – Menu £ 28 (lunch) – Carte £ 60/75
◆ Traditional ◆ Luxury ◆ Classic ◆
The wonderfully located Dukes has been steadily updating its image over the last few years, despite being over a century old. Bedrooms are now fresh and uncluttered and the atmosphere less starchy. The basement restaurant offers a modern menu, with dishes that are original in look and elaborate in construction.

Stafford

16-18 St James's Pl. ✉ SW1A 1NJ – Ⓜ Green Park – ☎ (020) 7493 0111 – www.kempinski.com/london H4
105 rm – †£ 260/360 ††£ 400/600, ☕ £ 25 – 8 suites
Rest *The Lyttelton* – Menu £ 28 (lunch) – Carte £ 37/74
◆ Townhouse ◆ Stylish ◆
Currently being refurbished, the bedrooms of this 'country house in the city' are divided between the main house, converted 18C stables and more modern mews. Legendary American bar a feature; British food served in the restaurant.

St James's Hotel and Club   ⓢ 🅐🅒 🛜 🛁 🆚🅘🆂🅐 ⓿ 🅐🅔 ⓪

7-8 Park Pl. ⌗ *SW1A 1LS* – ⓜ *Green Park* – ☏ *(020) 73161600*
– www.stjameshotelandclub.com

H4

55 rm – †£ 300/474 ††£ 300/474, ⌷ £ 22 – 10 suites
Rest *Seven Park Place* ❀ – see restaurant listing
♦ Business ♦ Modern ♦

1890s house in cul-de-sac, formerly a private club, reopened as a hotel in 2008. Modern, boutique–style interior with over 200 mostly German works of art from the '30s and '40s. Fine finish to compact, but well-equipped bedrooms.

Cavendish   ≼ ᇂ rm, 🅐🅒 🛜 🛁 🖧 🆚🅘🆂🅐 ⓿ 🅐🅔 ⓪

81 Jermyn St ⌗ *SW1Y 6JF* – ⓜ *Piccadilly Circus* – ☏ *(020) 7930 2111*
– www.thecavendishlondon.com

H4

228 rm – †£ 179/288 ††£ 179/288, ⌷ £ 23 – 2 suites
Rest – *(closed 25 December, lunch Saturday-Sunday and bank holidays)*
Menu £ 16/20 – Carte £ 27/38
♦ Business ♦ Design ♦

There's been a hotel on this site since the 18C; this one was built in the '60s but is smart and contemporary inside. Great location, bistro-style dining with British menu and good views across London from the top 5 floors; a parking space for every room too!

Ritz Restaurant – Ritz Hotel   🛜 🅐🅒 🕙 🆚🅘🆂🅐 ⓿ 🅐🅔 ⓪

150 Piccadilly ⌗ *W1J 9BR* – ⓜ *Green Park* – ☏ *(020) 74938181*
– www.theritzlondon.com

H4

Rest – Menu £ 45/50 – Carte £ 73/95
♦ British traditional ♦ Elegant ♦ Formal ♦

Grand and lavish restaurant, with Louis XVI decoration, trompe l'oeil and ornate gilding. Delightful terrace over Green Park. Structured, formal service. Classic, traditional dishes are the highlight of the menu. Jacket and tie required.

Seven Park Place – St James's Hotel and Club   🅐🅒 ⇔

❀

7-8 Park Pl ⌗ *SW1A 1LS* – ⓜ *Green Park* – ☏ *(020)*   🆚🅘🆂🅐 ⓿ 🅐🅔 ⓪
73161614 – www.stjameshotelandclub.com

– Closed Sunday and Monday

H4

Rest – *(booking essential)* Menu £ 25/69
♦ Modern ♦ Cosy ♦ Fashionable ♦

Small restaurant concealed somewhat within St James's Hotel and divided between two rooms; ask for the gilded back room. The accomplished food has a French base, displays confidence and clarity and uses quality British ingredients.
➜ Tortellini of lobster with lobster butter sauce. Saddle of lamb with garlic purée and rosemary jus. Dark chocolate mousse cake with raspberries.

The Wolseley   🕙 🅐🅒 ⇔ 🆚🅘🆂🅐 ⓿ 🅐🅔

160 Piccadilly ⌗ *W1J 9EB* – ⓜ *Green Park* – ☏ *(020) 74996996*
– www.thewolseley.com

– Closed 25 December, dinner 24 and 31 December and August bank holiday
Rest – *(booking essential)* Carte £ 24/58   **H4**
♦ Modern ♦ Fashionable ♦

Feels like a grand European coffee house, with pillars and high vaulted ceiling. Appealing menus range from caviar to a hot dog. Open from breakfast and boasts a celebrity following.

Balcon – Sofitel London St James Hotel   🅐🅒 🆚🅘🆂🅐 ⓿ 🅐🅔 ⓪

8 Pall Mall. ⌗ *SW1Y 5NG* – ⓜ *Piccadilly Circus* – ☏ *(020) 79682900*
– www.thebalconlondon.com

I4

Rest – Menu £ 15/30 – Carte £ 21/49
♦ French ♦ Brasserie ♦

A former banking hall with vast chandeliers and a grand brasserie look. It's open from breakfast onwards and the menu features French classics like snails and cassoulet; try the charcuterie from Wales and France.

XX **Matsuri**   AC ⇄ 🈷 VISA ⓪ AE ①

15 Bury St. ⊠ SW1Y 6AL – Ⓜ *Green Park –* ☏ *(020) 78391101*
– www.matsuri-restaurant.com
– Closed 25 December   **H4**
Rest – Menu £ 35 (dinner) – Carte £ 18/119
♦ Japanese ♦ Friendly ♦
Sweet natured service at this longstanding, traditional Japanese stalwart. Teppan-yaki is their speciality, with Scottish beef the highlight; sushi counter also available. Good value lunch menus and bento boxes.

XX **Le Caprice**   !ⓥ AC 🈷 VISA ⓪ AE

Arlington House, Arlington St. ⊠ SW1A 1RJ – Ⓜ *Green Park –* ☏ *(020) 76292239 – www.le-caprice.co.uk*
– Closed 25-26 December   **H4**
Rest – Menu £ 22 – Carte £ 29/46
♦ Modern ♦ Fashionable ♦
For over 30 years Le Caprice's effortlessly sophisticated atmosphere and surroundings have attracted a confident and urbane clientele. Perennials on their catch-all menu include their famous burger and rich salmon fishcake.

XX **Sake No Hana**   AC VISA ⓪ AE ①

23 St James's St ⊠ SW1A 1HA – Ⓜ *Green Park –* ☏ *(020) 79258988*
– www.sakenohana.com
– Closed Sunday   **H4**
Rest – Carte £ 31/75
♦ Japanese ♦ Design ♦
Ground floor sushi bar; first floor restaurant reached by elevator, where cedar wood goes some way to disguising an ugly, if iconic, '60s building. The Japanese menu has been simplified somewhat; service can also be a little lacklustre.

XX **Franco's**   AC 🈷 VISA ⓪ AE

61 Jermyn St ⊠ SW1Y 6LX – Ⓜ *Green Park –* ☏ *(020) 74992211*
– www.francoslondon.com
– Closed Sunday and bank holidays   **H4**
Rest – *(booking essential)* Menu £ 20/26 – Carte £ 29/59
♦ Italian ♦ Formal ♦
Open from breakfast until late, with café at the front leading into smart, clubby restaurant. Menu covers all parts of Italy and includes popular grill section and plenty of classics.

XX **Avenue**   AC ⇄ 🈷 VISA ⓪ AE

7-9 St James's St. ⊠ SW1A 1EE – Ⓜ *Green Park –* ☏ *(020) 73212111*
– www.avenue-restaurant.co.uk
– Closed Saturday lunch, Sunday dinner and bank Holidays   **H4**
Rest – Menu £ 24 (lunch) – Carte dinner £ 25/48
♦ Modern ♦ Elegant ♦
Large canvases have made this large room more colourful and there's greater warmth from the service too. The menu roams predatorily around the globe and dishes display a greater degree of depth than one expects.

XX **Mint Leaf**   AC 🈷 VISA ⓪ AE

Suffolk Pl. ⊠ SW1Y 4HX – Ⓜ *Piccadilly Circus –* ☏ *(020) 79309020*
– www.mintleafrestaurant.com
– Closed lunch Saturday and Sunday   **I4**
Rest – Menu £ 14/20 – Carte £ 28/49
♦ Indian ♦ Design ♦ Fashionable ♦
Cavernous and moodily lit basement restaurant incorporating trendy bar with lounge music and extensive cocktail list. Contemporary Indian cooking with curries the highlight.

XX **Al Duca**   🎴 🍷 VISA 🔴 AE

4-5 Duke of York St ⊠ SW1Y 6LA – Ⓜ *Piccadilly Circus* – ✆ *(020)*
78393090 – www.alduca-restaurant.co.uk
– *Closed Easter, 25 December, Sunday and bank holidays*   **H4**
Rest – Menu £ 20/28
♦ Italian ♦ Friendly ♦
Cooking which focuses on flavour continues to draw in the regulars at this
warm and spirited Italian restaurant. Prices are keen when one considers the
central location and service is brisk and confident.

XX **Quaglino's**   🎴 ⇔ 🍷 VISA 🔴 AE ⓪

16 Bury St ⊠ *SW1Y 6AJ* – Ⓜ *Green Park* – ✆ *(020) 79306767*
– www.quaglinos.co.uk
– Closed 24-27 December and Sunday   **H4**
Rest – Menu £ 20 (lunch) – Carte £ 30/55
♦ Modern ♦ Design ♦
It may be synonymous with the early '90s but the old girl can still shake it on a
weekend for those wanting a fun night out with a bit of glitz. The kitchen deli-
vers on brasserie classics like pork belly and duck confit.

XX **Brumus** – Haymarket Hotel   🎴 🍷 VISA 🔴 AE ⓪

1 Suffolk Pl ⊠ *SW1Y 4HX* – Ⓜ *Piccadilly Circus* – ✆ *(020) 74704000*
– www.haymarkethotel.com   **I4**
Rest – Menu £ 20 – Carte £ 25/50
♦ Modern ♦ Fashionable ♦ Romantic ♦
Ideally positioned for pre or post theatre dining, when a good value menu is
offered. Energetic room, with busy bar attached, and an unthreatening menu
of Mediterranean favourites.

X **Inn the Park**   ≤ 🛋 VISA 🔴 AE

St James's Park ⊠ *SW1A 2BJ* – Ⓜ *Charing Cross* – ✆ *(020) 74519999*
– www.innthepark.com
– Closed 25 December   **I4**
Rest – *(booking essential at dinner)* Carte £ 25/35
♦ British modern ♦ Design ♦
Oliver Peyton's eco-friendly restaurant in the middle of the park, with a terrific
terrace. British menu uses many small suppliers. Cooking is straightforward and
wholesome.

X **Portrait**   ≤ 🎴 VISA 🔴 AE

National Portrait Gallery, (3rd floor), St Martin's Pl. ⊠ *WC2H 0HE*
– Ⓜ *Charing Cross* – ✆ *(020) 73122490 – www.searcys.co.uk*
– Closed 24-26 December   Plan III **I3**
Rest – *(lunch only and dinner Thursday-Saturday) (booking essential)*
Menu £ 18/35
♦ Modern ♦ Design ♦
On the top floor of National Portrait Gallery with rooftop local landmark views: a
charming spot for lunch. Modern British/European dishes; weekend brunch.

X **The National Dining Rooms**   🎴 VISA 🔴 ⓪

Sainsbury Wing, The National Gallery, Trafalgar Sq ⊠ *WC2N 5DN*
– Ⓜ *Charing Cross* – ✆ *(020) 7747 2525 – www.peytonandbyrne.co.uk*
– Closed 24-26 December   **I4**
Rest – *(lunch only and Friday dinner)* Carte £ 26/40
♦ British modern ♦ Design ♦
Set on the East Wing's first floor, you can tuck into cakes in the bakery or grab a
prime corner table in the restaurant for great views and proudly seasonal British
menus.

STRAND AND COVENT GARDEN

Savoy　　　🛝 🔲 ♿ AC 📶 🛁 🚗 VISA 🅿️ AE ⓪

Strand ✉ *WC2R 0EU* – Ⓜ *Charing Cross* – ℰ *(020) 78364343*
– www.fairmont.com/savoy　　　　　　　　　　　　　　　　**J3**
221 rm – †£ 678 ††£ 750, ⌑ £ 30 – 30 suites
Rest *Savoy Grill* **Rest** *River Restaurant* – see restaurant listing
♦ Grand Luxury ♦ Stylish ♦
The grande dame of London hotels dazzles once again! Reopened in 2010 following a 3 year restoration, its luxurious bedrooms and stunning suites come in an Edwardian or art deco style. Thames Foyer is the hotel's heart; choose the famous American Bar or new Beaufort Bar.

One Aldwych　　　🛝 🐾 🔲 ♿ rm, AC 📶 🛁 🅿️ VISA ⓪ AE ⓪

1 Aldwych ✉ *WC2B 4RH* – Ⓜ *Temple* – ℰ *(020) 73001000*
– www.onealdwych.com　　　　　　　　　　　　　　　　**J3**
93 rm – †£ 288/498 ††£ 288/498, ⌑ £ 26 – 12 suites
Rest *Axis* – see restaurant listing
Rest *Indigo* – ℰ *(020) 7300400* – Menu £ 22 (early dinner)
– Carte £ 30/55
♦ Grand Luxury ♦ Modern ♦ Stylish ♦
Former 19C bank, now a stylish hotel with lots of artwork; the lobby changes its look seasonally and doubles as a bar. Stylish, contemporary bedrooms with the latest mod cons; the deluxe rooms and suites are particularly desirable. Impressive leisure facilities. Light, accessible menu at Indigo.

Waldorf Hilton　　　🛝 🐾 🔲 ♿ rm, AC 📶 🛁 VISA ⓪ AE ⓪

Aldwych ✉ *WC2B 4DD* – Ⓜ *Temple* – ℰ *(020) 7836 2400*
– www.hilton.co.uk/waldorf　　　　　　　　　　　　　　　**J3**
292 rm – †£ 215/455 ††£ 215/455, ⌑ £ 22 – 6 suites
Rest *Homage* – *(Closed lunch Saturday and Sunday)* Menu £ 20/28
– Carte dinner £ 31/94
♦ Historic ♦ Elegant ♦
Impressive curved and columned façade: an Edwardian landmark in a great location. Popular for afternoon tea; relaxed brasserie style dining. On-going refurbishment of bedrooms.

St Martins Lane　　　🛝 AC 📶 🛁 🚗 VISA ⓪ AE ⓪

45 St Martin's Ln ✉ *WC2N 3HX*
– Ⓜ *Charing Cross* – ℰ *(020) 73005500*　　　　　　　　**I3**
– www.stmartinslane.com
202 rm – †£ 294/438 ††£ 318/462, ⌑ £ 25 – 2 suites
Rest *Asia de Cuba* – see restaurant listing
♦ Luxury ♦ Design ♦
The unmistakable hand of Philippe Starck is evident at this most contemporary of hotels. Unique and stylish, from the starkly modern lobby to the state-of-the-art bedrooms, which come in a blizzard of white.

Savoy Grill – *Savoy Hotel*　　　AC ↔ 🍽 VISA ⓪ AE

Strand ✉ *WC2R 0EU* – Ⓜ *Charing Cross* – ℰ *(020) 7592 1600*
– www.gordonramsay.com/thesavoygrill　　　　　　　　　　**J3**
Rest – Menu £ 26 (weekday lunch) – Carte £ 30/102
♦ British traditional ♦ Elegant ♦
Archives were explored, designers briefed and much money spent, with the result that The Savoy Grill has returned to the traditions that made it famous. As befits the name, it is the charcoal grilling of meats that takes centre stage.

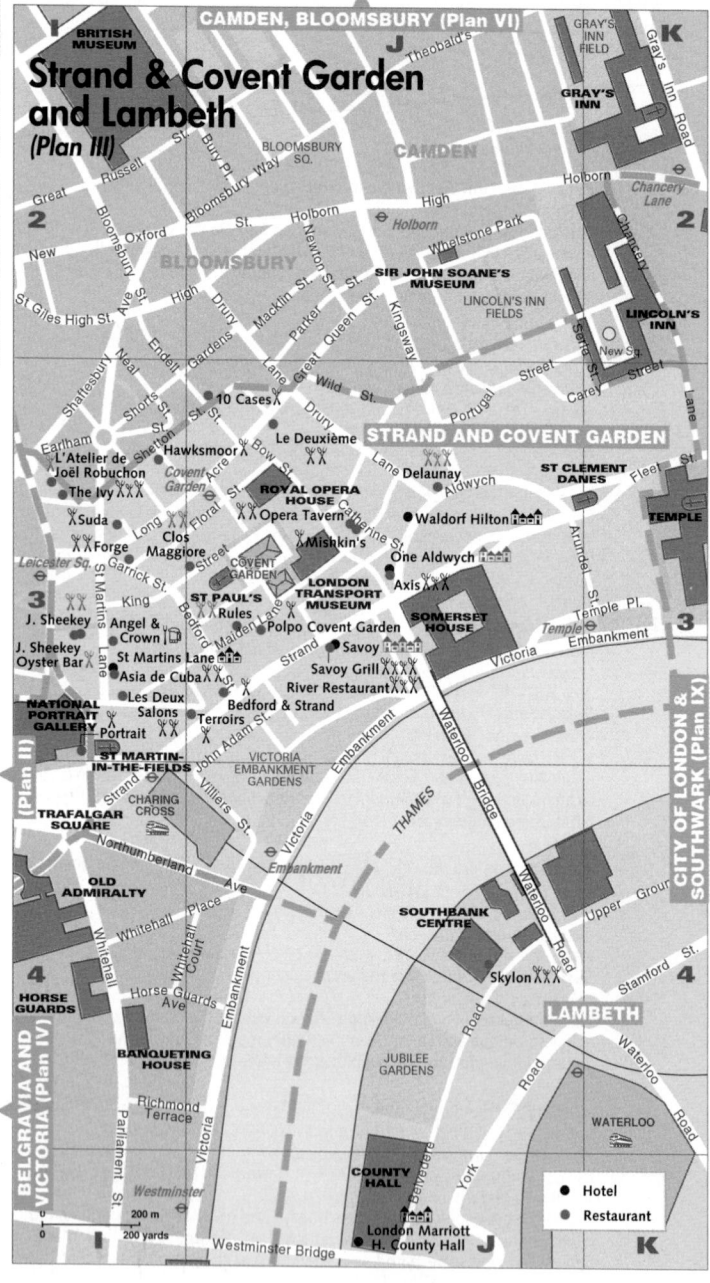

Strand & Covent Garden and Lambeth
(Plan III)

CAMDEN, BLOOMSBURY (Plan VI)

BRITISH MUSEUM

GRAY'S INN FIELD

GRAY'S INN

Theobald's

Russell

Bury Pl.

BLOOMSBURY SQ.

CAMDEN

Holborn

Chancery Lane

Great

Oxford St.

Holborn

High

Holborn

Whetstone Park

New

BLOOMSBURY

Newton St.

SIR JOHN SOANE'S MUSEUM

LINCOLN'S INN FIELDS

LINCOLN'S INN

St Giles High St.

Shaftesbury

Drury

Macklin St.

Parker

Great Queen

Kingsway

New Sq.

Serle St.

Portugal

Carey

Endell

Gardens

Lane

St.

Wild St.

Street

STRAND AND COVENT GARDEN

Fleet St.

Earlham

Shorts

10 Cases

Bow St.

Lane

ST CLEMENT DANES

L'Atelier de Joël Robuchon

Hawksmoor

Le Deuxième

Delaunay

Aldwych

TEMPLE

The Ivy

Covent Garden

Floral

ROYAL OPERA HOUSE

Catherine St.

Waldorf Hilton

Arundel St.

Suda

Clos Maggiore

Opera Tavern

One Aldwych

Temple Pl.

Forge

Garrick St.

COVENT GARDEN

Mishkin's

LONDON TRANSPORT MUSEUM

Axis

SOMERSET HOUSE

Temple

Leicester Sq.

King

ST PAUL'S

Rules

SOMERSET HOUSE

Embankment

J. Sheekey

Angel & Crown

Bedford

Maiden

Polpo Covent Garden

Strand

Savoy

Victoria

J. Sheekey Oyster Bar

St Martins Lane

Savoy Grill

River Restaurant

NATIONAL PORTRAIT GALLERY

Asia de Cuba

Les Deux Salons

Bedford & Strand

Terroirs

Portrait

John Adam St.

VICTORIA EMBANKMENT GARDENS

Embankment

Waterloo

CITY OF LONDON & SOUTHWARK (Plan IX)

ST MARTIN-IN-THE-FIELDS

TRAFALGAR SQUARE

Strand

CHARING CROSS

Villiers St.

Victoria

THAMES

Northumberland Ave.

Embankment

Waterloo Bridge

OLD ADMIRALTY

Whitehall

Whitehall Place

SOUTHBANK CENTRE

Upper Groun

Stamford St.

HORSE GUARDS

Whitehall Court

Horse Guards Ave.

Skylon

Waterloo Road

LAMBETH

BANQUETING HOUSE

Richmond Terrace

JUBILEE GARDENS

Road

WATERLOO

Parliament St.

Victoria

WATERLOO Road

Westminster

COUNTY HALL

York

Road

London Marriott H. County Hall

| ● | Hotel |
| ● | Restaurant |

200 m
200 yards

Westminster Bridge

880

XXX **Delaunay**   AC ⇔ VISA ⓒ AE ⓞ
55 Aldwych ⊠ WC2B 4BB – Ⓜ Temple – ℰ (020) 74998558
– www.thedelaunay.com
– Closed dinner 24 December, 25 December and August bank holiday
Rest *– (booking essential) Carte £ 18/50*   **J3**
♦ Modern ♦ Elegant ♦ Fashionable ♦
The Delaunay was inspired by the grand cafés of Europe but, despite sharing the same buzz and celebrity clientele as its sibling The Wolseley, is not just a mere replica. The all-day menu is more mittel-European, with great schnitzels and wieners.

XXX **The Ivy**   AC ⇔ ⓒ VISA ⓒ AE ⓞ
1-5 West St ⊠ WC2H 9NQ – Ⓜ Leicester Square – ℰ (020) 78364751
– www.the-ivy.co.uk
– Closed 25-26 December   **I3**
Rest *– Menu £ 22 – Carte £ 38/50*
♦ British traditional ♦ Fashionable ♦
One of the original celebrity hang-out restaurants; still pulling them in. Appealing menu, from shepherd's pie to fishcakes and nursery puddings. Staff go about their business with alacrity.

XXX **Axis** *– One Aldwych Hotel*   AC ⇔ ⓒ VISA ⓒ AE ⓞ
1 Aldwych ⊠ WC2B 4RH – Ⓜ Temple – ℰ (020) 73001300
– www.onealdwych.com
– Closed Sunday and Monday   **J3**
Rest *– Menu £ 20 (lunch and early dinner) – Carte £ 34/39*
♦ Modern ♦ Design ♦
A spiral marble staircase leading down to this impressively high-ceilinged restaurant adds to the expectation. The menu is a combination of British classics and lighter European choices.

XXX **River Restaurant** *– Savoy Hotel*   ≤ AC VISA ⓒ AE ⓞ
Strand ⊠ WC2R 0EU – Ⓜ Charing Cross – ℰ (020) 78364343
– www.fairmont.com/savoy   **J3**
Rest *– Menu £ 28 – Carte £ 40/71*
♦ Modern ♦ Formal ♦ Luxury ♦
Homage is paid at this iconic and rejuvenated restaurant to Auguste Escoffier, the legendary chef hired by Richard D'Oyly Carte when he opened the hotel in 1889, in a menu offered alongside more contemporary French creations.

XX **Opera Tavern**   AC VISA ⓒ AE
ⓐ *23 Catherine St. ⊠ WC2B 5JS – Ⓜ Covent Garden – ℰ (020) 7836 3680*
– www.operatavern.co.uk
– Closed 24-26 and 31 December, 1-2 January and Sunday dinner
Rest *– Menu £ 35/40 – Carte £ 11/36 ⅋*   **J3**
♦ Mediterranean ♦ Tapas bar ♦ Wine bar ♦
Shares the same appealing concept of small plates of Spanish and Italian delicacies as its sisters, Salt Yard and Dehesa. All done in a smartly converted old boozer which dates from 1879; ground floor bar and upstairs dining room.

XX **J. Sheekey**   Ⓥ AC ⓒ VISA ⓒ AE
28-34 St Martin's Ct. ⊠ WC2 4AL – Ⓜ Leicester Square – ℰ (020) 72402565 – www.j-sheekey.co.uk
– Closed 25-26 December   **I3**
Rest *– (booking essential) Carte £ 31/75*
♦ Fish and seafood ♦ Fashionable ♦
Festooned with photographs of actors and linked to the theatrical world since opening in 1890. Wood panels and alcove tables add famed intimacy. Accomplished seafood cooking.

UNITED KINGDOM - LONDON

UNITED KINGDOM - LONDON

XX **Rules** [AC] [♿] [🐕] [VISA] [●●] [AE]
35 Maiden Ln ⊠ *WC2E 7LB* – **Ⓜ** *Leicester Square* – ℰ *(020) 78365314*
– www.rules.co.uk
– Closed 25-26 December   J3
Rest – *(booking essential)* Carte £ 35/56
♦ British traditional ♦ Formal ♦
London's oldest restaurant boasts a fine collection of antique cartoons, drawings and paintings. Tradition continues in the menu, specialising in game from its own estate.

XX **Clos Maggiore** [AC] [♿] [🐕] [VISA] [●●] [AE] [①]
33 King St ⊠ *WC2E 8JD* – **Ⓜ** *Leicester Square* – ℰ *(020) 73799696*
– www.closmaggiore.com
– Closed 24-25 December   J3
Rest – Menu £ 16/23 – Carte £ 32/44 ⅜
♦ French ♦ Formal ♦
One of London's most romantic restaurants – but be sure to ask for the enchanting conservatory with its retractable roof. The sophisticated French cooking is joined by a wine list of great depth. Good value and very popular pre/post theatre menus.

XX **Les Deux Salons** [AC] [♿] [🐕] [VISA] [●●] [AE]
40-42 William IV St ⊠ *WC2N 4DD* – **Ⓜ** *Charing Cross* – ℰ *(020) 74202050*
– www.lesdeuxsalons.co.uk
– Closed 25-26 December and 1 January   I3
Rest – Menu £ 18 (weekday lunch) – Carte £ 25/51 ⅜
♦ French ♦ Brasserie ♦
Authentic Parisian brasserie complete with smoked mirrors, globe lights and striking mosaic floor. Ground floor is the better salon for atmosphere. Appealing menu mixes French classics, chargrilled meats and the odd British interloper.

XX **Forge** [AC] [🐕] [VISA] [●●] [AE]
14 Garrick St ⊠ *WC2E 9BJ* – **Ⓜ** *Leicester Square* – ℰ *(020) 73791432*
– www.theforgerestaurant.co.uk
– Closed 2 days Easter and 24-26 December   I3
Rest – Menu £ 15/30 – Carte £ 24/48
♦ Modern ♦ Trendy ♦
Décor mixes the old with the new; the front area is more intimate, the back more fun. Extensive menu offers something for everyone, from pasta to Dover sole, tournedos Rossini to a hamburger.

XX **Le Deuxième** [AC] [🐕] [VISA] [●●] [AE]
65a Long Acre ⊠ *WC2E 9JH* – **Ⓜ** *Covent Garden* – ℰ *(020) 73790033*
– www.ledeuxieme.com
– Closed 24-25 December   J3
Rest – Menu £ 17 (lunch) – Carte £ 31/38
♦ Modern ♦ Brasserie ♦
Caters well for theatregoers: opens early, closes late. Buzzy eatery, simply decorated in white with subtle lighting. International menu but emphasis within Europe.

XX **Asia de Cuba** – St Martins Lane Hotel [AC] [VISA] [●●] [AE] [①]
45 St Martin's Ln ⊠ *WC2N 3HX* – **Ⓜ** *Charing Cross* – ℰ *(020) 73005500*
– www.morganshotelgroup.com   I3
Rest – Menu £ 19/25 – Carte £ 41/66
♦ Asian ♦ Fashionable ♦
The striking Philippe Starck designed room and the Asian and Cuban inspired cooking appeal to a young, hip crowd. Sharing is the key and that should also include the bill.

L'Atelier de Joël Robuchon   [AC] [🍴] [VISA] [●●] [AE]

❄️ ❄️ *13-15 West St.* ✉️ *WC2H 9NE* – Ⓜ *Leicester Square* – ✆ *(020) 70108600*
– *www.joelrobuchon.co.uk*
– *Closed 25-26 December,1 January, Sunday and August bank holiday Monday*
Rest – Menu £ 28/125 – Carte £ 35/69   I3

♦ French ♦ Fashionable ♦

Wonderfully precise, creative and occasionally playful cooking; dishes may look delicate but pack a punch. Ground floor Atelier with counter seating and chefs on view. More structured La Cuisine. Cool top floor bar.

→ Green asparagus cappuccino with golden croutons. Quail stuffed with foie gras and truffle mashed potatoes. Creamy Manjari chocolate, bitter chocolate sorbet and Oreo cookie.

Terroirs   [VISA] [●●] [AE] [①]

🍴 *5 William IV St* ✉️ *WC2N 4DW* – Ⓜ *Charing Cross* – ✆ *(020) 70360660*
– *www.terroirswinebar.com*
– *Closed 25-26 December, 1 January, Sunday and bank holidays*
Rest – Carte £ 25/37 🕸️   J3

♦ French ♦ Bistro ♦

Eat in the ground floor bistro/wine bar or from a slighly different menu two floors below at 'Downstairs at Terroirs'. Flavoursome French cooking, with extra Italian and Spanish influences. Thoughtfully compiled wine list.

Polpo Covent Garden   [AC] [VISA] [●●] [AE]

🍴 *6 Maiden Ln.* ✉️ *WC2E 7NA* – Ⓜ *Leicester Square* – ✆ *(202) 7836 8448*
– *www.polpo.co.uk*
– *Closed 24-26 December*   J3
Rest – *(bookings not taken at dinner)* Carte £ 12/30

♦ Italian ♦ Tapas bar ♦ Trendy ♦

First Soho, now Covent Garden gets a fun Venetian bacaro. The small plates are surprisingly filling, with delights such as pizzette of white anchovy vying with fennel and almond salad, fritto misto competing with spaghettini and meatballs.

J. Sheekey Oyster Bar   [🍴] [VISA] [●●] [AE] [①]

🍴 *33-34 St Martin's Ct.* ✉️ *WC2 4AL* – Ⓜ *Leicester Square* – ✆ *(020) 72402565* – *www.j-sheekey.co.uk*
– *Closed 25-26 December and 1 January*   I3
Rest – Carte £ 32/72

♦ Fish and seafood ♦ Intimate ♦

An addendum to J.Sheekey restaurant. Sit at the bar to watch the chefs prepare the same quality seafood as next door but at slightly lower prices; fish pie and fruits de mer are the popular choices. Open all day.

Hawksmoor   [AC] [⇔] [🍴] [VISA] [●●] [AE]

🍴 *11 Langley St* ✉️ *WC2H 9JG* – Ⓜ *Covent Garden* – ✆ *(020) 7420 9390*
– *www.thehawksmoor.com*
– *Closed 24-26 and 31 December, 1-2 January and Sunday dinner*
Rest – Menu £ 22/25 – Carte £ 39/62 🕸️   I3

♦ Meats and grills ♦ Bistro ♦ Brasserie ♦

Steaks from Longhorn cattle lovingly reared in North Yorkshire and dry-aged for at least 35 days are the stars of the show. Atmospheric, bustling basement restaurant in former brewery cellars.

Bedford & Strand   [VISA] [●●] [AE] [①]

🍴 *1a Bedford St* ✉️ *WC2E 9HH* – Ⓜ *Charing Cross* – ✆ *(020) 78363033*
– *www.bedford-strand.com*
– *Closed 24 December-2 January, Sunday and bank holidays*   J3
Rest – *(booking essential)* Menu £ 18 – Carte £ 19/38

♦ British traditional ♦ Wine bar ♦

They call themselves a 'wine room and bistro' which neatly sums up both the philosophy and the style of the place – interesting wines, reassuringly familiar food and relaxed basement surroundings.

UNITED KINGDOM - LONDON

✗ Suda   🕅 ⛱ 🅰🅲 🆅🅸🆂🅰 ⊙⊙ 🅰🅴

23 Slingsby Pl, St Martin's Courtyard ⊠ *WC2E 9AB* – Ⓜ *Covent Garden*
– ℰ *(020) 72408010* – *www.suda-thai.com*   I3
Rest – Carte £ 15/22
♦ Thai ♦ Friendly ♦

This shiny Thai restaurant in a new development may look like a branded chain restaurant but the quality of its food far exceeds one's expectations. Come in a group, sit upstairs, order cocktails and share plenty of dishes.

✗ 10 Cases   ⇔ 🆅🅸🆂🅰 ⊙⊙ 🅰🅴

16 Endell St ⊠ *WC2H 9BD* – Ⓜ *Covent Garden* – ℰ *(020) 7836 6801*
– *www.the10cases.co.uk*
– *Closed Easter, Christmas-New Year and bank holidays*   J3
Rest – *(booking essential)* Carte £ 24/33
♦ French ♦ Bistro ♦ Intimate ♦

Cosy and inviting little bistrot offering an unpretentious daily menu of 3 starters, 3 main courses and 3 desserts, along with a very reasonably priced wine list of 10 reds and 10 whites available by the glass, carafe or bottle.

✗ Mishkin's   🅰🅲 🆅🅸🆂🅰 ⊙⊙ 🅰🅴

25 Catherine St ⊠ *WC2B 5JS* – Ⓜ *Covent Garden* – ℰ *(020) 72402078*
– *www.mishkins.co.uk*
– *Closed 24-26 and 31 December-2 January*   J3
Rest – Carte £ 16/25
♦ North-American ♦ Retro ♦

The Jewish-American deli, but with cocktails, was the inspiration behind this fun spot from the Polpo people. Lox beigel, chopped liver and salt beef sit alongside nibbles like cod cheek popcorn; the Reuben sandwich hits the spot.

🍴 Angel & Crown   🅰🅲 🆅🅸🆂🅰 ⊙⊙ 🅰🅴 ⓪

58 St Martin's Ln ⊠ *WC2N 4EA* – Ⓜ *Leicester Square.* – ℰ *(020) 77485244*
– *www.theangelandcrown.com*
– *Closed 25 December*   I3
Rest – Carte £ 23/34
♦ British traditional ♦ Pub ♦ Neighbourhood ♦

Tourist spots and good food are rarely seen together but the gastropub revolution is now creeping into the West End. Enjoy British classics like venison pie or wild boar sausages in the upstairs dining room of this handsome Victorian pub.

LAMBETH

🏨 London Marriott H. County Hall   ≤ 🎰 ⊛ 🛠 🔲 ♿

Westminster Bridge Rd ⊠ *SE1 7PB*   rm, 🅰🅲 🤶 ⚿ 🆅🅸🆂🅰 ⊙⊙ 🅰🅴 ⓪
– Ⓜ *Westminster* – ℰ *(020) 79285200* – *www.marriottcountyhall.com*
195 rm – ♦£ 228/414 ♦♦£ 240/426, ⊒ £ 21 – 5 suites
Rest *Gillray's* – Carte £ 32/72   J5
♦ Luxury ♦ Classic ♦

Occupying the historic County Hall building. Many of the spacious and comfortable bedrooms enjoy river and Parliament outlooks. Impressive leisure facilities. World famous views too from Gillray's, which specialises in steaks.

✗✗✗ Skylon   ≤ 🅰🅲 🆅🅸🆂🅰 ⊙⊙ 🅰🅴 ⓪

1 Southbank Centre, Belvedere Rd ⊠ *SE1 8XX* – Ⓜ *Waterloo* – ℰ *(020)*
76547800 – *www.skylon-restaurant.co.uk*
– *Closed 25 December and Sunday dinner*   J4
Rest – Menu £ 29/45 ℬ
♦ Modern ♦ Design ♦

Ask for a window table here at the Royal Festival Hall. Informal grill-style operation on one side, a more formal and expensive restaurant on the other, with a busy cocktail bar in the middle.

BELGRAVIA

UNITED KINGDOM - LONDON

Berkeley

Wilton Pl. ⊠ SW1X 7RL – Ⓜ *Knightsbridge* – ℰ (020) 72356000
– www.the-berkeley.co.uk   **G4**
189 rm – ♦£ 310/660 ♦♦£ 378/900, ⊊ £ 29 – 25 suites
Rest *Marcus Wareing at The Berkeley* ✿✿ **Rest *Koffmann's*** – see restaurant listing
♦ Grand Luxury ♦ Stylish ♦
Discreet and rejuvenated hotel with rooftop pool and opulently decorated bedrooms. Relax in the gilded and panelled Caramel Room or have a drink in the cool Blue Bar.

Lanesborough

Hyde Park Corner ⊠ SW1X 7TA – Ⓜ *Hyde Park Corner* – ℰ (020)
72595599 – www.lanesborough.com   **G4**
83 rm – ♦£ 474/546 ♦♦£ 630, ⊊ £ 35 – 10 suites
Rest *Apsleys* ✿ – see restaurant listing
♦ Grand Luxury ♦ Classic ♦ Historic ♦
Converted in the 1990s from 18C St George's Hospital. Butler service offered. Regency-era inspired decoration; lavishly appointed rooms with impressive technological extras.

Halkin without rest

5 Halkin St ⊠ SW1X 7DJ – Ⓜ *Hyde Park Corner* – ℰ (020) 73331000
– www.halkin.como.bz   **G5**
35 rm – ♦£ 336/552 ♦♦£ 336/552, ⊊ £ 30 – 6 suites
♦ Luxury ♦ Stylish ♦
Opened in 1991 as London's first boutique hotel and still looking sharp today. Thoughtfully conceived bedrooms with silk walls and marbled bathrooms; everything at the touch of a button. Abundant Armani-clad staff. Small, discreet bar.

Belgraves without rest

20 Chesham Pl ⊠ SW1X 8HQ – Ⓜ *Knightsbridge* – ℰ (020) 7858 0100
– www.thompsonhotels.com   **G5**
85 rm – ♦£ 299/599 ♦♦£ 299/599, ⊊ £ 20
♦ Business ♦ Townhouse ♦ Modern ♦
US group Thompson's first UK venture opened in 2012; an elegant, stylish boutique-style hotel with a hint of bohemia and in a great location. Uncluttered, decent sized bedrooms with oak flooring and lovely marble bathrooms.

Jumeirah Lowndes

21 Lowndes St ⊠ SW1X 9ES – Ⓜ *Knightsbridge* – ℰ (020) 78231234
– www.jumeirah.com   **F5**
87 rm – ♦£ 240/762 ♦♦£ 240/762, ⊊ £ 20 – 14 suites
Rest *Lowndes Bar & Kitchen* – Menu £ 17 (lunch) – Carte £ 27/50
♦ Business ♦ Modern ♦ Contemporary ♦
Compact yet friendly modern corporate hotel within this exclusive residential area. Good levels of personal service offered. Close to the famous shops of Knightsbridge. Modern restaurant opens onto street terrace.

Marcus Wareing at The Berkeley – Berkeley Hotel

Wilton Pl. ⊠ SW1X 7RL – Ⓜ *Knightsbridge*
– ℰ (020) 72351200 – www.marcus-wareing.com
– Closed 1 January and Sunday   **G4**
Rest – Menu £ 38 (weekday lunch)/80
♦ French ♦ Formal ♦
Marcus Wareing's cooking is creative, sophisticated and backed by sound classical techniques. The restaurant is sumptuously appointed; service is smooth and well-organised but has personality. The chef's table is one of the best in town.
→ Mackerel, scallop, pine nut and yuzu. Suckling lamb with beans, oregano and Flower Marie. Horlicks, honey, whisky.

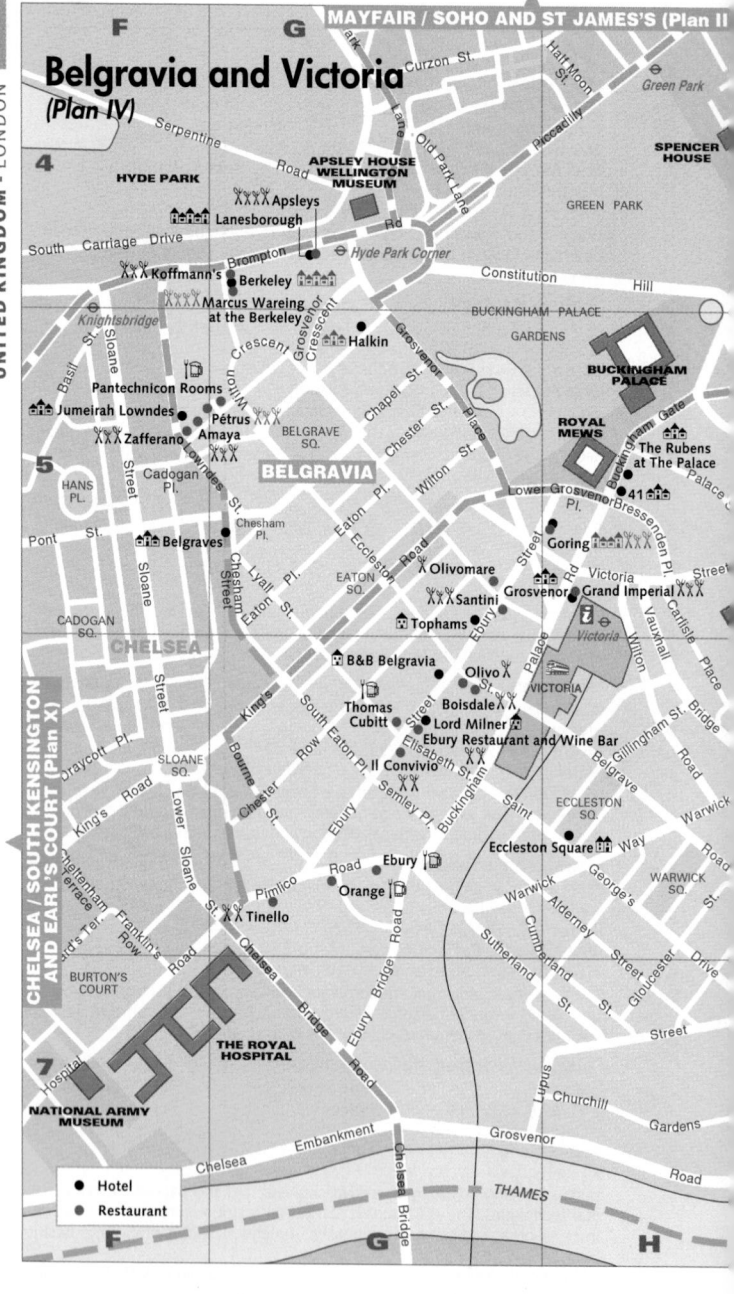

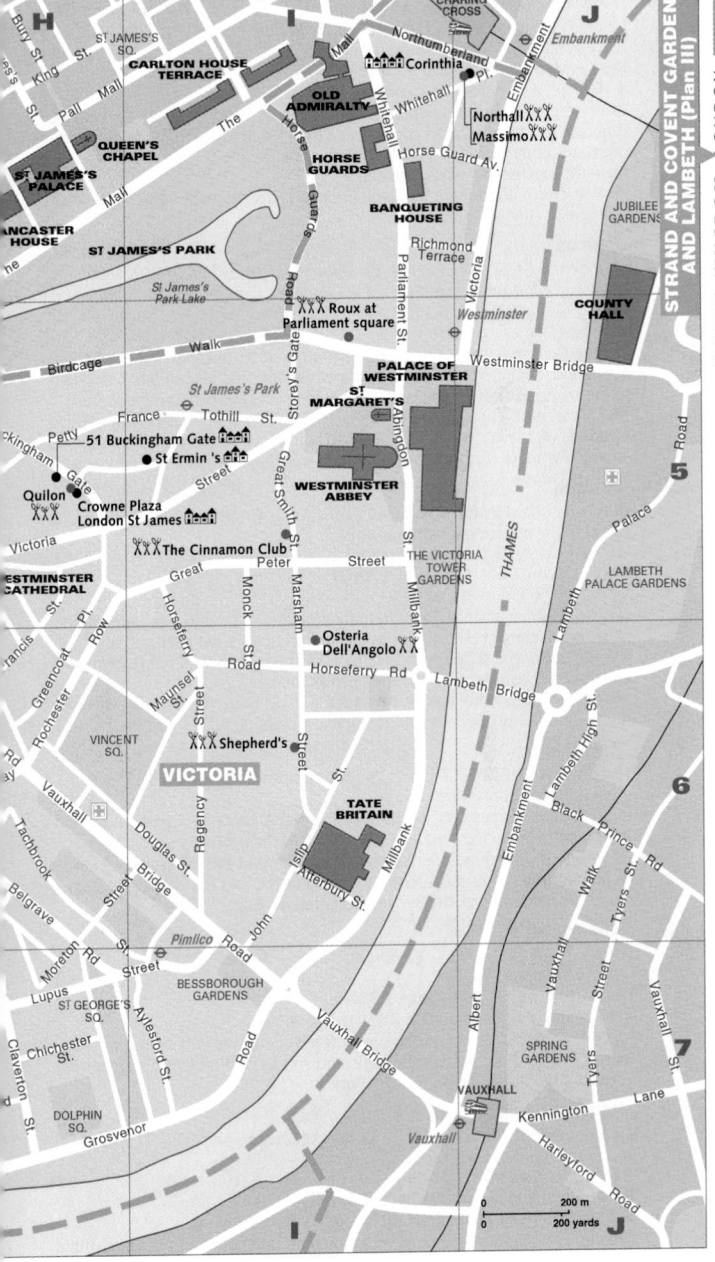

CHARING
CROSS

CARLTON HOUSE
TERRACE

Corinthia

ST JAMES'S
SQ.

Pall Mall

QUEEN'S
CHAPEL

OLD
ADMIRALTY

Northumberland

Northall
Massimo

ST JAMES'S
PALACE

ANCASTER
HOUSE

The Mall

HORSE
GUARDS

Whitehall

Horse Guard Av.

BANQUETING
HOUSE

Embankment

JUBILEE
GARDENS

ST JAMES'S PARK

St James's
Park Lake

Richmond
Terrace

Parliament St.

Victoria

Westminster

COUNTY
HALL

Birdcage

Walk

Roux at
Parliament square

Westminster Bridge

Storey's Gate

St James's Park

France

Tothill

St.

PALACE OF
WESTMINSTER

ST
MARGARET'S

Abingdon

THAMES

51 Buckingham Gate
St Ermin's

Great Smith St.

WESTMINSTER
ABBEY

Palace

Quilon
Crowne Plaza
London St James

Gate

Victoria

The Cinnamon Club

Peter

Street

THE VICTORIA
TOWER
GARDENS

Lambeth

LAMBETH
PALACE GARDENS

WESTMINSTER
CATHEDRAL

Great

Monck

Marsham

St.

Millbank

Francis

St.

Greencoat

Pl.

Horseferry

Row

Rochester

St.

Osteria
Dell'Angolo

Road

Lambeth Bridge

Horseferry Rd

Mainsel St.

Street

Street

Lambeth High St.

Black

Prince

Rd

Embankment

VINCENT
SQ.

Shepherd's

Street

VICTORIA

Regency

St.

TATE
BRITAIN

Millbank

Vauxhall

Walk

Tyers

St.

Vauxhall

St.

Belgrave

Tachbrook

Vauxhall

Douglas St.

Bridge

Atterbury St.

Moreton Rd

St. GEORGE'S
SQ.

Lupus

Street

Pimlico

Road

John

Street

BESSBOROUGH
GARDENS

Chichester
St.

Aylesford St.

Vauxhall Bridge

Albert

SPRING
GARDENS

Tyers

Street

Vauxhall

St.

Claverton

St.

DOLPHIN
SQ.

Grosvenor

Road

VAUXHALL

Vauxhall

Kennington

Lane

Harleyford

Road

0   200 m
0   200 yards

XXXX
🕸

Apsleys – Lanesborough Hotel   🔼 ⇔ P VISA ⬤⬤ AE ⓪

Hyde Park Corner ⊠ SW1X 7TA – Ⓜ Hyde Park Corner – ✆ (020)
73337254 – www.apsleysrestaurant.com   **G4**
Rest – Menu £ 35 (lunch) – Carte £ 59/81

♦ Italian ♦ Elegant ♦ Luxury ♦

Under the guidance of celebrated chef Heinz Beck from Rome's La Pergola.
Exquisite and precise Italian cooking, in a grand, eye-catching but far from inti-
midating room, designed by Adam Tihany. The serving team are polished and
the atmosphere reassuringly upbeat.
→ Fish crudo. Carbonara fagotelli. Chocolate soufflé with vanilla and raspberry.

XXX
🕸

Pétrus   🎲 🔼 ⇔ VISA ⬤⬤ AE

1 Kinnerton St ⊠ SW1X 8EA – Ⓜ Knightsbridge – ✆ (020) 75921609
– www.gordonramsay.com/petrus – Closed 25 December and Sunday
Rest – Menu £ 30/75 ⅏   **G5**

♦ Modern ♦ Elegant ♦

Elegant Gordon Ramsay restaurant, opened in 2010, in stylish tones of silver,
oyster and – as a nod to the name – claret. Experienced team bring personality
to the service. Elaborate French-based cooking uses top quality ingredients.
→ Fricassée of langoustines, snails, crispy chicken wing and parsley cream.
Roasted veal fillet with tongue, crispy anchovies, baby artichokes and
lemon thyme jus. Chocolate sphere with milk ice cream and honeycomb.

XXX
🕸

Amaya   🎲 🔼 ⇔ VISA ⬤⬤ AE ⓪

Halkin Arcade, 19 Motcomb St ⊠ SW1X 8JT – Ⓜ Knightsbridge – ✆ (020)
78231166 – www.realindianfood.com
– Closed dinner 25 December   **F5**
Rest – Menu £ 20/70 – Carte £ 35/69

♦ Indian ♦ Fashionable ♦

Order a selection of small dishes from the tawa griddle, tandoor or Sigri grill and
finish with a curry or biryani. Dishes like lamb chops are aromatic and satisfying
and the cooking is skilled and consistent. The busy restaurant is suitably bright
and colourful; ask for a table by the open kitchen.
→ King scallops with light herb sauce. Crispy baby chicken, green chilli,
thyme and lemon. Saffron and rose panna cotta.

XXX

Zafferano   🔼 ⇔ VISA ⬤⬤ AE ⓪

15 Lowndes St ⊠ SW1X 9EY – Ⓜ Knightsbridge – ✆ (020) 72355800
– www.zafferanorestaurant.co.uk   **F5**
Rest – (booking essential) Menu £ 26 (weekday lunch) – Carte £ 29/56 ⅏

♦ Italian ♦ Fashionable ♦ Neighbourhood ♦

Be sure to sit in the more atmospheric main room of this longstanding Italian
restaurant. The menu sticks to the tried-and-tested and the cooking is reassuringly familiar to its well-dressed local clientele.

XXX

Koffmann's – Berkeley Hotel   🔼 VISA ⬤⬤ AE ⓪

Wilton Pl. ⊠ SW1X 7RL – Ⓜ Knightsbridge – ✆ (020) 72351010
– www.the-berkeley.co.uk   **G4**
Rest – Menu £ 22/26 – Carte £ 39/90

♦ French ♦ Design ♦ Fashionable ♦

Pierre Koffmann, one of London's most fêted chefs, was enticed out of retire-
ment to open this smart, comfortable and spacious restaurant. Expect plenty
of gutsy flavours true to his Gascon roots.

🍴

Pantechnicon   🖾 ⇔ VISA ⬤⬤ AE

10 Motcomb St ⊠ SW1X 8LA – Ⓜ Knightsbridge. – ✆ (020) 77306074
– www.thepantechnicon.com
– Closed 25 December-1 January   **G5**
Rest – (booking advisable) Carte £ 27/55

♦ British modern ♦ Pub ♦ Neighbourhood ♦

Urbane, enthusiastically run pub with a busy ground floor and altogether more
formal upstairs dining room. Traditional dishes are given a modern twist; oysters
and Scottish steaks are perennials.

VICTORIA

Corinthia
Whitehall Pl. ⊠ *SW1A 2BD –* Ⓜ *Embankment –* ℰ *(020) 7930 8181*
– www.corinthia.com/london   **J4**
271 rm – †£ 347/1020 ††£ 347/1020, ☲ £ 26 – 23 suites
Rest *Northall* **Rest** *Massimo* – see restaurant listing
♦ Grand Luxury ♦ Stylish ♦
London's latest grand hotel opened in 2011; its restored Victorian splendour
cannot fail to impress. Tasteful, immaculately finished bedrooms are some of
the largest in town; suites come with butlers. The stunning spa is over four
floors.

Goring
15 Beeston Pl, Grosvenor Gdns ⊠ *SW1W 0JW –* Ⓜ *Victoria –* ℰ *(020)*
73969000 – www.thegoring.com   **H5**
62 rm – †£ 528 ††£ 606, ☲ £ 30 – 7 suites
Rest *Goring* – see restaurant listing
♦ Traditional ♦ Luxury ♦ Classic ♦
Celebrated its centenary in 2010; this very English hotel is still owned, invested
in and run by the Goring family who built it – the fourth generation now at the
helm. Many of the attractive rooms overlook a peaceful garden.

Crowne Plaza London - St James
45 Buckingham Gate ⊠ *SW1E 6AF*
– Ⓜ *St James's Park –* ℰ *(020) 78346655 – www.london.crowneplaza.com*
323 rm – †£ 142/546 ††£ 390/546, ☲ £ 23 – 19 suites   **H5**
Rest *Quilon* ❀ – see restaurant listing
♦ Luxury ♦ Classic ♦
Built in 1897 as serviced accommodation for visiting aristocrats. Behind the
impressive Edwardian façade lies an equally elegant interior. Quietest rooms
overlook courtyard.

51 Buckingham Gate without rest
51 Buckingham Gate ⊠ *SW1E 6AF –* Ⓜ *St James's Park –* ℰ *(020)*
77697766 – www.51-buckinghamgate.com   **H5**
86 suites – ††£ 306/666, ☲ £ 19
♦ Luxury ♦ Classic ♦
In the courtyard of the Crowne Plaza but offering greater levels of comfort and
service. Contemporary in style, suites range from one to nine bedrooms. Butler service available. Restaurants located in adjacent hotel.

St Ermin's
2 Caxton St. ⊠ *SW1H 0QW –* Ⓜ *St James's Park –* ℰ *(020) 7222 7888*
– www.sterminshotel.co.uk   **J5**
290 rm – †£ 474 ††£ 474, ☲ £ 24 – 41 suites
Rest *Caxton Grill* – *(closed lunch Saturday-Sunday)* Menu £ 23 (dinner)
– Carte £ 28/48
♦ Business ♦ Functional ♦
Built as an apartment block in 1897 but it has spent most of its life as a hotel and
has been a favoured spot for many a politician. A comprehensive 2011 refurbishment restored many of its original features; the public areas are the
strength. The restaurant specialises in meat cooked on the Josper grill.

41 without rest
41 Buckingham Palace Rd. ⊠ *SW1W 0PS –* Ⓜ *Victoria –* ℰ *(020)*
73000041 – www.41hotel.com   **H5**
29 rm – †£ 299 ††£ 443, ☲ £ 25 – 1 suite
♦ Luxury ♦ Classic ♦
Smart and discreet addendum to The Rubens hotel next door. Attractively
decorated and quiet lounge where breakfast is served; comfortable bedrooms
boast fireplaces and plenty of extras.

The Rubens at The Palace

39 Buckingham Palace Rd ✉ SW1W 0PS – Ⓜ Victoria – ☎ (020) 78346600 – www.rubenshotel.com **H5**

160 rm – †£ 179/311 ††£ 191/269, ☕ £ 20 – 1 suite

Rest *Old Masters* – *(closed lunch Saturday and Sunday)* Menu £ 30

Rest *Library* – *(dinner only)* Menu £ 40 – Carte £ 40/62

Rest *bbar* – *☎ (020) 79587000 (closed Saturday, Sunday and bank holidays)* Menu £ 17 – Carte £ 23/50

♦ Traditional ♦ Classic ♦

Discreet, comfortable hotel in great location for visitors to London. Constant reinvestment ensures bright and contemporary bedrooms. Old Masters for grills. Fine dining in cosy Library. Casual dining in bbar.

Grosvenor

101 Buckingham Palace Rd ✉ SW1W 0SJ – Ⓜ Victoria – ☎ (0871) 376 9038 – www.guoman.com **H5**

345 rm – †£ 120/240 ††£ 144/360, ☕ £ 22 – 2 suites

Rest *Grand Imperial* – see restaurant listing

Rest *Brasserie* – Menu £ 17 – Carte £ 22/41

♦ Historic ♦ Business ♦ Functional ♦

Grand old lady returned to her original 1862 splendour after a major refurbishment. Impressive lobby, contemporary bedrooms and a stylish bar with views across Victoria Station concourse. Classic menu in the brasserie.

Eccleston Square

37 Eccleston Sq ✉ SW1V 1PB – Ⓜ Victoria – ☎ (020) 3489 1001 – www.ecclestonsquarehotel.com **H6**

39 rm – †£ 234/282 ††£ 270/354, ☕ £ 15

Rest *Bistrot on the Square* – Menu £ 20/25

♦ Townhouse ♦ Stylish ♦ Contemporary ♦

Former down-at-heel hotel in a smart square; reborn as a slick townhouse. Bedrooms are decorated to a high standard and come full of assorted electronic gadgetry. Varied international menu in Bistrot; afternoon tea a feature.

Tophams without rest

24-32 Ebury St ✉ SW1W 0LU – Ⓜ Victoria – ☎ (020) 77303313 – www.tophamshotel.com **G5**

50 rm – †£ 180/225 ††£ 195/275, ☕ £ 15

♦ Townhouse ♦ Personalised ♦

A row of five pretty terraced houses, in a good spot for tourists. Neat bedrooms with large bathrooms and good mod cons; 301 is a family room spread over two floors. Comfortable breakfast room.

B + B Belgravia without rest

64-66 Ebury St ✉ SW1W 9QD – Ⓜ Victoria – ☎ (0207) 2598570 – www.bb-belgravia.com **G6**

17 rm ☕ – †£ 99 ††£ 140/150

♦ Townhouse ♦ Personalised ♦

Two houses, three floors, and, considering the location, representing good value accommodation. Sleek, clean-lined bedrooms. Breakfast overlooking little garden terrace.

Lord Milner without rest

111 Ebury St ✉ SW1W 9QU – Ⓜ Victoria – ☎ (020) 78819880 – www.lordmilner.com **G6**

10 rm – †£ 156 ††£ 192/216 – 1 suite

♦ Townhouse ♦ Classic ♦

A four storey terraced house, with individually decorated bedrooms, three with four-poster beds and all with marble bathrooms. Garden Suite the best room, with its own patio. No public areas.

XXX
☀

Quilon – Crowne Plaza London - St James Hotel   Ⓐⓒ ⟷
41 Buckingham Gate ✉ *SW1E 6AF*   VISA ⓪⓪ ⒜Ⓔ ⓪
– Ⓜ *St James's Park* – ℰ *(020) 78211899 – www.quilon.co.uk*
– *Closed 25 December*   **H5**
Rest – Menu £ 24/43 – Carte £ 28/53
♦ **Indian** ♦ **Design** ♦ **Intimate** ♦
An extensive 2012 makeover left this longstanding restaurant looking slick and contemporary. The elegant surroundings provide the perfect backdrop to chef Sriram Aylur's accomplished and light style of cooking which focuses on India's southwest coast and mixes the modern with the traditional.
➜ Char-grilled scallops with mango and chilli relish. Venison coconut fry. Hot vermicelli kheer with rose ice cream.

XXX

Grand Imperial – Grosvenor Hotel   Ⓐⓒ ⟷ VISA ⓪⓪ ⒜Ⓔ
101 Buckingham Palace Rd ✉ *SW1W OSJ* – Ⓜ *Victoria* – ℰ *(020)*
7821 8898 – www.grandimperiallondon.com   **H5**
Rest – Menu £ 17 – Carte £ 22/41
♦ **Chinese** ♦ **Elegant** ♦
Grand it most certainly is, as this elegant restaurant is in the Grosvenor hotel's former ballroom. It specialises in Cantonese cuisine, particularly the version found in Hong Kong; steaming and frying are used to great effect.

XXX

Roux at Parliament Square   Ⓐⓒ ⟷ VISA ⓪⓪ ⒜Ⓔ
RICS, Parliament Sq. ✉ *SW1P 3AD* – Ⓜ *Westminster* – ℰ *(020) 73343737*
– *www.rouxatparliamentsquare.co.uk*
– *Closed 23 December-4 January, Saturday, Sunday and bank holidays*
Rest – Menu £ 25 (lunch) – Carte £ 36/56   **I5**
♦ **French** ♦ **Elegant** ♦
Light floods through the Georgian windows of this comfortable Westminster restaurant, popular with MPs and surveyors. French base to the food, which is intricate but also light and contemporary.

XXX

The Cinnamon Club   Ⓐⓒ ⟷ 🐾 VISA ⓪⓪ ⒜Ⓔ ⓪
30-32 Great Smith St ✉ *SW1P 3BU* – Ⓜ *St James's Park* – ℰ *(020)*
72222555 – www.cinnamonclub.com
– *Closed 26 December, 1 January and Sunday*   **I5**
Rest – Menu £ 22/24 – Carte £ 28/74
♦ **Indian** ♦ **Elegant** ♦
A plethora of menus is offered at this formally run, busy Indian restaurant housed within the former Westminster Library. Attractively presented, modern food; the tandoori dishes stand out. Buzzy atmosphere; funky basement bar.

XXX

Santini   🍴 Ⓐⓒ 🐾 VISA ⓪⓪ ⒜Ⓔ
29 Ebury St ✉ *SW1W ONZ* – Ⓜ *Victoria* – ℰ *(020) 77304094*
– *www.santinirestaurant.com*
– *Closed Easter, 24-26 December, 1 January and lunch Saturday-Sunday*
Rest – Carte £ 30/66   **G5**
♦ **Italian** ♦ **Fashionable** ♦
Smart, crisp and cool Italian restaurant, with a large, impressive terrace and old-school service. Menu has subtle Venetian accent but is not inexpensive; pastas and desserts are good.

XXX

Shepherd's   Ⓐⓒ ⟷ VISA ⓪⓪ ⒜Ⓔ ⓪
Marsham Ct., Marsham St. ✉ *SW1P 4LA* – Ⓜ *Pimlico* – ℰ *(020) 78349552*
– *www.langansrestaurants.co.uk*
– *Closed Saturday, Sunday and bank holidays*   **I6**
Rest – *(booking essential)* Carte £ 26/37
♦ **British traditional** ♦ **Formal** ♦
A thoroughly British and enjoyably old-school restaurant where the menu reads like a UKIP manifesto; game and traditional puddings are a highlight. Popular with those from Westminster – the booths offer a degree of privacy.

UNITED KINGDOM - LONDON

XXX **Goring** – Goring Hotel   🚄 AC VISA ⦿ AE ⓪
15 Beeston Pl, Grosvenor Gdns ⊠ *SW1W 0JW* – Ⓜ *Victoria* – ℰ *(020)*
73969000 – *www.thegoring.com*
– Closed Saturday lunch   **H5**
Rest – Menu £ 38/50 🏵
♦ British traditional ♦ Elegant ♦
Like the hotel in which it is found, The Goring dining room is a paean to Britishness and ideal for those who still like things done 'properly'. The classics are all
here, from jugged hare to beef Wellington; served by a smart team in urbane
surroundings.

XXX **Northall** – Corinthia Hotel   AC VISA ⦿ AE ⓪
Whitehall Pl. ⊠ *SW1A 2BD* – Ⓜ *Embankment* – ℰ *(020) 7321 3100*
– www.thenorthall.co.uk   **J4**
Rest – Menu £ 25/35 – Carte £ 27/70
♦ British modern ♦ Bistro ♦
The menu champions British produce and producers. You have a choice of two
rooms, linked by a display of meats and cheeses: a modern bistro-style room or
a more formal dining room set over two levels.

XXX **Massimo** – Corinthia Hotel   AC ⟺ 🕃 VISA ⦿ AE ⓪
10 Northumberland Ave. ⊠ *WC2N 5AE* – Ⓜ *Embankment* – ℰ *(020)*
79980555 – *www.massimo-restaurant.co.uk*
– Closed Sunday   **J4**
Rest – Menu £ 25 – Carte £ 30/69
♦ Italian ♦ Elegant ♦ Fashionable ♦
Opulent, visually impressive room with an oyster bar on one side. On offer are
traditional dishes true to the regions; fish and seafood dishes stand out. Impressive private dining room comes with its own chef.

XX **Il Convivio**   AC ⟺ VISA ⦿ AE
143 Ebury St ⊠ *SW1W 9QN* – Ⓜ *Sloane Square* – ℰ *(020) 77304099*
– www.ilconvivio.co.uk
– Closed Christmas-New Year, Easter, bank holidays and Sunday
Rest – Menu £ 20/24 – Carte £ 29/51   **G6**
♦ Italian ♦ Intimate ♦
Handsome Georgian house, with a retractable roof and Dante's poetry embos-
sed on the walls. All pasta is made on the top floor of the house. Dishes are artfully presented and flavoursome.

XX **Tinello**   VISA ⦿ AE
87 Pimlico Rd ⊠ *SW1W 8PH* – Ⓜ *Sloane Square* – ℰ *(020) 77303663*
– www.tinello.co.uk
– Closed Sunday   **G6**
Rest – *(booking essential at dinner)* Carte £ 29/44
♦ Italian ♦ Design ♦ Friendly ♦
Sleekly designed Italian restaurant run by two brothers, both alumni of Locanda
Locatelli. Their native Tuscany informs the cooking; the antipasti and 'small eats'
sections are very appealing.

XX **Boisdale**   🏠 AC ⟺ VISA ⦿ AE ⓪
15 Eccleston St ⊠ *SW1W 9LX* – Ⓜ *Victoria* – ℰ *(020) 7730 6922*
– www.boisdale.co.uk
– Closed Christmas, Saturday lunch and Sunday   **G6**
Rest – Menu £ 20 – Carte £ 28/80
♦ Regional ♦ Cosy ♦
A proudly Scottish restaurant with acres of tartan and a charmingly higgledy-
piggledy layout. Stand-outs are the smoked salmon and the 28-day aged Aber-
deenshire cuts of beef. Live nightly jazz.

XX **The Ebury Restaurant and Wine Bar** [AC] [VISA] [OO] [AE]

139 Ebury St. ⊠ *SW1W 9QU* – Ⓜ *Victoria* – ℰ *(020) 7730 5447*
– www.eburyrestaurant.co.uk
– Closed Christmas-New Year G6
Rest – Menu £ 19 (lunch and early dinner) – Carte £ 26/46
♦ **Modern** ♦ **Neighbourhood** ♦
Going strong for over 50 years and as likeable as ever. Some imaginative touches but generally quite classic cooking. Dairy and gluten free menus offered, along with a keenly-priced wine list.

XX **Osteria Dell' Angolo** [AC] [⇔] [VISA] [OO] [AE] [O]

47 Marsham St. ⊠ *SW1P 3DR* – Ⓜ *St James's Park* – ℰ *(020) 32681077*
– www.osteriadellangolo.co.uk
– Closed Easter, 18 August-1 September, 23-26 December-1-7 January, Saturday lunch, Sunday and bank holidays I6
Rest – Menu £ 17 (lunch) – Carte £ 31/42
♦ **Italian** ♦ **Neighbourhood** ♦
At lunch this Italian opposite the Home Office is full of bustle and men in suits; at dinner it's a relaxed neighbourhood spot. Staff are personable and the menu is approachable; homemade pasta and seafood dishes are good.

X **Olivo** [AC] [VISA] [OO] [AE]

21 Eccleston St ⊠ *SW1W 9LX* – Ⓜ *Victoria* – ℰ *(020) 77302505*
– www.olivorestaurants.com
– Closed lunch Saturday-Sunday and bank holidays G6
Rest – (booking essential) Menu £ 24 (lunch) – Carte £ 28/44
♦ **Italian** ♦ **Neighbourhood** ♦ **Bistro** ♦
Carefully prepared, authentic Sardinian specialities are the highlight at this popular Italian restaurant. Simply decorated in blues and yellows, with an atmosphere of bonhomie.

X **Olivomare** [☆] [AC] [VISA] [OO] [AE]

10 Lower Belgrave St ⊠ *SW1W 0LJ* – Ⓜ *Victoria* – ℰ *(020) 77309022*
– www.olivorestaurants.com
– Closed bank holidays G5
Rest – Carte £ 31/42
♦ **Fish and seafood** ♦ **Design** ♦ **Neighbourhood** ♦
Expect understated and stylish piscatorial decoration and seafood with a Sardinian base. Fortnightly changing menu, with high quality produce, much of which is available in the deli next door.

🍴 **Ebury** [AC] [VISA] [OO] [AE]

11 Pimlico Rd ⊠ *SW1W 8NA* – Ⓜ *Sloane Square.* – ℰ *(020) 77306784*
– www.theebury.co.uk
– Closed 23-28 December and bank holidays G6
Rest – Carte £ 22/40
♦ **Modern** ♦ **Pub** ♦
Smart and stylish room, with an appealing menu ranging from burgers to black bream. Low-slung tables around popular central bar; efficient service. Upstairs is used for private parties.

🍴 **Thomas Cubitt** [VISA] [OO] [AE]

44 Elizabeth St ⊠ *SW1W 9PA* – Ⓜ *Sloane Square.* – ℰ *(020) 77306060*
– www.thethomascubitt.co.uk
– Closed Christmas and New Year G6
Rest – (booking essential) Menu £ 18 (weekday lunch) – Carte £ 32/45
♦ **Modern** ♦ **Pub** ♦
A pub of two halves: choose the busy ground floor bar with its accessible menu or upstairs for more ambitious, quite elaborate cooking with courteous service and a less frenetic environment.

UNITED KINGDOM - LONDON

Orange with rm   🛜 VISA ◉◉ AE
37 Pimlico Rd ⊠ SW1W 8NE – Ⓜ *Sloane Square. – ℰ (020) 78819844*
– www.theorange.co.uk   **G6**
4 rm – 🛇£ 195/225 🛇🛇£ 195/225, �£ 7   **Rest** – Carte £ 23/47
♦ **Modern** ♦ **Friendly** ♦ **Family** ♦

A family-friendly pub with a laid-back atmosphere and a slight colonial feel.
Enjoy pizza from the wood-fired oven in the bar or rustic European cooking in
the upstairs dining room. Bedrooms are named after local streets.

REGENT'S PARK & MARYLEBONE   *Plan V*

 The Landmark London   🛜 ◉ 🛍 ▢ ⴲ AK 🛜 🏋 🚐
222 Marylebone Rd ⊠ NW1 6JQ – Ⓜ *Edgware Road*   VISA ◉◉ AE
– ℰ (020) 76318000 – www.landmarklondon.co.uk   **F1**
291 rm – 🛇£ 215/780 🛇🛇£ 215/780, ⊂ £ 29 – 9 suites
Rest *Winter Garden* – see restaurant listing
♦ **Business** ♦ **Classic** ♦

Imposing Victorian Gothic building with a vast glass-enclosed atrium, overlooked by many of the modern, well-equipped bedrooms. Choice of relaxed wood
panelled cellar bar or more sophisticated Mirror bar.

 Langham   🛜 ◉ 🛍 ⴲ AK 🏋 VISA ◉◉ AE ◉
1c Portland Pl., Regent St. ⊠ W1B 1JA – Ⓜ *Oxford Circus – ℰ (020)*
76361000 – www.langhamhotels.com   **H2**
355 rm – 🛇£ 258/1056 🛇🛇£ 258/1056, ⊂ £ 30 – 21 suites
Rest *Roux at the Landau* – see restaurant listing
♦ **Luxury** ♦ **Stylish** ♦

Was one of Europe's first purpose-built grand hotels when it opened in 1865.
Now back to its best, with its famous Palm Court for afternoon tea, the stylish
Artesian bar and bedrooms that are not without personality and elegance.

 Hyatt Regency London-The Churchill   🛜 🛍 ✕ ⴲ
30 Portman Sq ⊠ W1H 7BH   rm, AK 🛜 🏋 VISA ◉◉ ◉
– Ⓜ *Marble Arch – ℰ (020) 74865800 – www.london.churchill.hyatt.com*
387 rm – 🛇£ 240/600 🛇🛇£ 240/600, ⊂ £ 27.50 – 47 suites   **G2**
Rest *The Montagu* – ℰ (020) 72992037 – Menu £ 25/27 – Carte £ 30/55
♦ **Luxury** ♦ **Modern** ♦

Smart well-located property whose best bedrooms overlook the attractive
square opposite. Elegant marbled lobby with plenty of staff. Well-appointed
and refurbished bedrooms have the international traveller in mind. A British
menu and afternoon tea served in The Montagu.

 Sanderson   🛜 ◉ AK 🛜 VISA ◉◉ AE ◉
50 Berners St ⊠ W1T 3NG – Ⓜ *Oxford Circus – ℰ (020) 73001400*
– www.morganshotelgroup.com   **H2**
150 rm – 🛇£ 318/474 🛇🛇£ 342/486, ⊂ £ 25
Rest *Suka* – see restaurant listing
♦ **Luxury** ♦ **Minimalist** ♦

Designed by Philippe Starck and still attracting a suitably fashionable crowd.
Purple Bar dark and moody; Long Bar bright and stylish. Pure white bedrooms
with idiosyncratic design touches such as a framed picture...on the ceiling.

Arch   🛜 ⴲ rm, AK 🛜 🏋 VISA ◉◉ AE
50 Great Cumberland Pl ⊠ W1H 7FD – Ⓜ *Marble Arch – ℰ (020)*
77244700 – www.thearchlondon.com   **F2**
80 rm – 🛇£ 246/360 🛇🛇£ 246/360, ⊂ £ 22 – 2 suites
Rest *Hunter 486* – ℰ (020) 207 724 0486 – Menu £ 15 (lunch) – Carte
£ 22/58
♦ **Traditional** ♦ **Stylish** ♦

Fashioned out of a row of seven terrace houses and two mews cottages. Plenty
of extras and thoughtful touches are found in the comfortable bedrooms. Interesting pieces of art throughout. Casual restaurant doubles as a bar.

Montcalm 🛗 🚫 🛜 ⓖ rm, 🅰🅲 🛜 🧖 🆅🅸🆂🅰 🆎 🅰🅴 ⓞ

34-40 Great Cumberland Pl. ✉ *W1H 7TW* – Ⓜ *Marble Arch* – ✆ *(020)*
74024288 – *www.montalm.co.uk*   **F2**
126 rm – 🛏£ 420 🛏🛏£ 420/1020, ⊆ £ 20 – 17 suites
Rest *Grill at the Montcalm* – Menu £ 20
 ◆ Business ◆ Stylish ◆
Named after an 18C French general, The Montcalm forms part of a crescent of
townhouses with a Georgian façade. A top-to-toe refurbishment has created
smart and contemporary bedrooms in lively colours. Seasonal British dishes served in Grill at the Montcalm.

Durrants 🅰🅲 rest, 🛜 🧖 🆅🅸🆂🅰 🆎 🅰🅴

26-32 George St ✉ *W1H 5BJ* – Ⓜ *Bond Street* – ✆ *(020) 79358131*
– *www.durrantshotel.co.uk*   **G2**
89 rm – 🛏£ 155/185 🛏🛏£ 240/340, ⊆ £ 23 – 3 suites
Rest – *(closed dinner 25 December)* Menu £ 20/33 – Carte £ 32/51
 ◆ Traditional ◆ Classic ◆
Traditional, privately owned hotel with friendly, long-standing staff. Bedrooms
are now brighter in style but still retain a certain English character. Clubby
dining room for mix of British classics and lighter, European dishes.

Dorset Square 🚘 🅰🅲 🛜 🆅🅸🆂🅰 🆎 🅰🅴 ⓞ

39-40 Dorset Sq ✉ *NW1 6QN* – Ⓜ *Marylebone* – ✆ *(020) 77237874*
– *www.dorsetsquarehotel.co.uk*   **F1**
38 rm – 🛏£ 180/234 🛏🛏£ 282/396, ⊆ £ 16.50
Rest *Potting Shed* – Carte £ 22/34
 ◆ Townhouse ◆ Contemporary ◆
Having reacquired this Regency townhouse, Firmdale refurbished it fully before
reopening it in 2012. It has a contemporary yet intimate feel and visiting MCC
members will appreciate the cricketing theme, which even extends to the cocktails in the sweet, Mediterranean-style basement restaurant.

Mandeville ⓖ rm, 🅰🅲 🛜 🧖 🆅🅸🆂🅰 🆎 🅰🅴 ⓞ

Mandeville Pl ✉ *W1U 2BE* – Ⓜ *Bond Street* – ✆ *(020) 79355599*
– *www.mandeville.co.uk*   **G2**
140 rm – 🛏£ 198/383 🛏🛏£ 234/407, ⊆ £ 22.50 – 2 suites
Rest *Reform Social & Grill* – Menu £ 35/55 – Carte £ 25/39
 ◆ Chain hotel ◆ Design ◆
Usefully located hotel with marbled reception leading into a very colourful and
comfortable bar. Stylish rooms have flatscreen TVs and make good use of the
space available. Modern British cuisine served in bright restaurant.

No. Ten Manchester Street ⓖ rm, 🅰🅲 🛜 🆅🅸🆂🅰 🆎 🅰🅴 ⓞ

✉ *W1U 4DG* – Ⓜ *Baker Street* – ✆ *(020) 73175900*
– *www.tenmanchesterstreethotel.com*   **G2**
45 rm – 🛏£ 167/360 🛏🛏£ 179/480, ⊆ £ 10 – 9 suites
Rest – Menu £ 15 – Carte £ 26/43
 ◆ Townhouse ◆ Modern ◆
Converted Edwardian house in an appealing, central location. Discreet entrance
leads into stylish little lounge; semi-enclosed cigar bar also a feature. Neat and
well-kept bedrooms.

Sumner *without rest* ⓖ 🅰🅲 🛜 🆅🅸🆂🅰 🆎 🅰🅴

54 Upper Berkeley St ✉ *W1H 7QR* – Ⓜ *Marble Arch* – ✆ *(020) 77232244*
– *www.thesumner.com*   **F2**
19 rm ⊆ – 🛏£ 150/222 🛏🛏£ 150/222
 ◆ Townhouse ◆ Personalised ◆
Two Georgian terrace houses in central location. Comfy, stylish sitting room;
basement breakfast room. Largest bedrooms, 101 and 201, benefit from
having full-length windows.

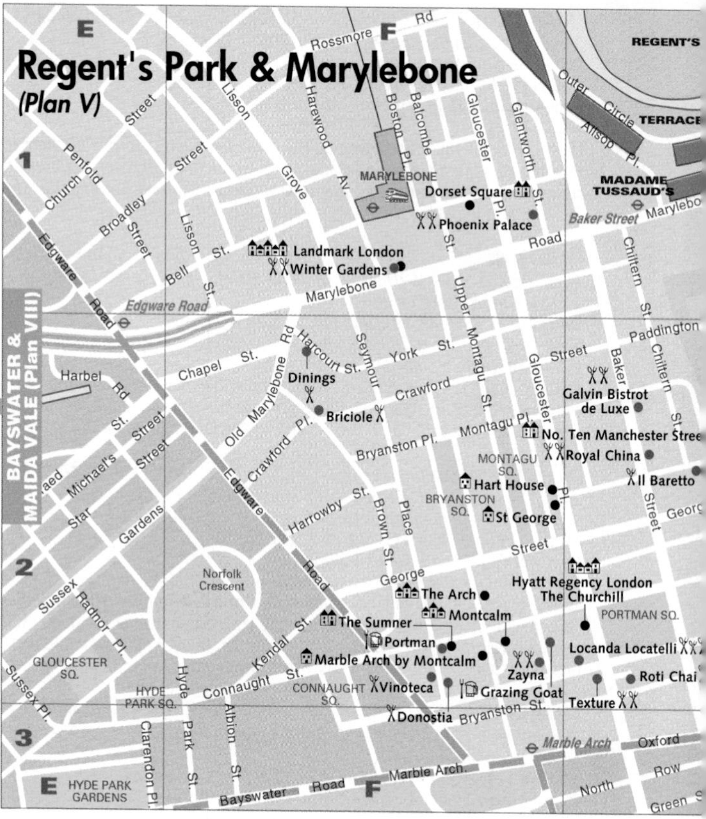

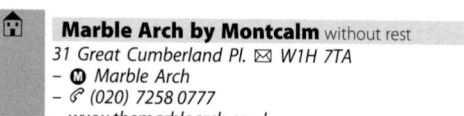

Marble Arch by Montcalm without rest   AC 🛜 VISA ⓸ AE ①

31 Great Cumberland Pl. ⌗ W1H 7TA
- Ⓜ *Marble Arch*
- 🕾 *(020) 7258 0777*
- *www.themarblearch.co.uk*   **F2**

42 rm – ♦£ 202/360 ♦♦£ 260/432, ⌷ £ 20

♦ Townhouse ♦ Stylish ♦

Bedrooms at this 5-storey Georgian townhouse come with the same high standards of stylish, contemporary design as its parent hotel opposite, the Montcalm, but are just a little more compact.

Hart House without rest   🛜 VISA ⓸

51 Gloucester Pl ⌗ W1U 8JF
- Ⓜ *Marble Arch* – 🕾 *(020) 79352288*
- *www.harthouse.co.uk*   **F2**

15 rm ⌷ – ♦£ 95/130 ♦♦£ 135/175

♦ Townhouse ♦ Classic ♦

Within an attractive Georgian terrace and run by the same family for over 35 years. Warm and welcoming service; well-kept, competitively priced bedrooms over three floors.

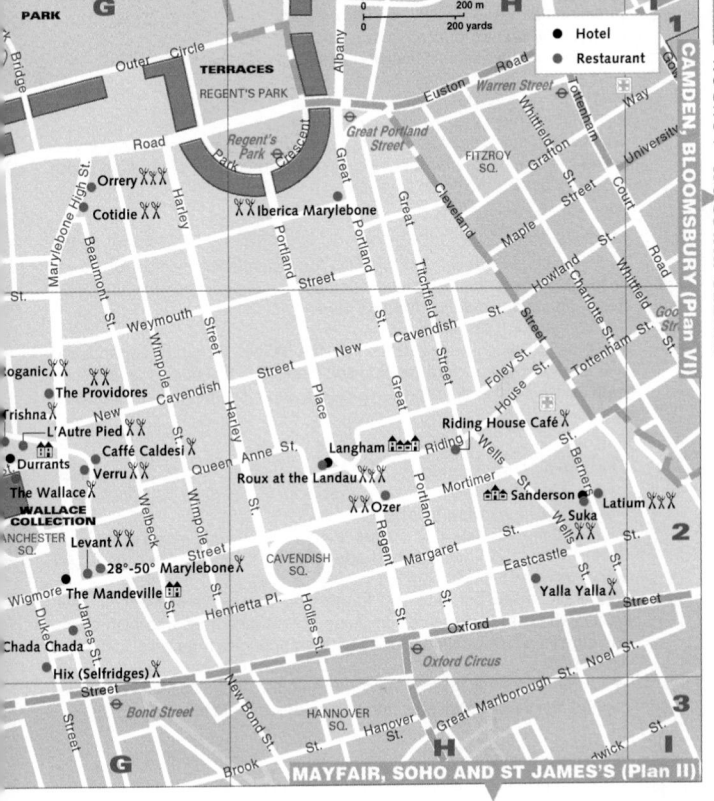

XXX ❋
Locanda Locatelli

AK VISA OO AE

8 Seymour St. ✉ W1H 7JZ – Ⓜ Marble Arch – ℰ (020) 79359088
– www.locandalocatelli.com – Closed 25-26 December and 1 January
Rest – Carte £ 29/62 🕭

G2

♦ Italian ♦ Fashionable ♦

Giorgio Locatelli's slick and dapper-looking Italian comes with a celebrity following and a sophisticated atmosphere. Plenty of appealing dishes on the extensive menu, with cooking that is confident, balanced and expertly rendered; pastas and desserts are the stand-out courses.
➔ Pan-fried scallops with celeriac purée and saffron vinaigrette. Roast rabbit leg, polenta and Parma ham. Tasting of Amedei chocolate.

XXX
Roux at the Landau – Langham Hotel

AK ⟐ VISA OO AE Ⓞ

1c Portland Pl., Regent St. ✉ W1B 1JA – Ⓜ Oxford Circus
– ℰ (020) 79650165 – www.rouxatthelandau.com
– Closed Saturday lunch and Sunday

H2

Rest – Menu £ 40 (lunch and early dinner) – Carte £ 40/78

♦ French ♦ Formal ♦

Grand, oval-shaped hotel restaurant run under the aegis of the Roux organisation. Classical, French-influenced cooking is the order of the day, but a lighter
style of cuisine using the occasional twist is also emerging.

897

XXX **Latium**   AC VISA ⓒⓞ AE

21 Berners St. ⊠ W1T 3LP – ⓜ Oxford Circus – 𝒞 (020) 73239123
– www.latiumrestaurant.com
– Closed 25-26 December, 1 January, Saturday lunch, Sunday and bank
holidays   H2
Rest – Menu £ 23/34
♦ Italian ♦ Neighbourhood ♦
Bright and contemporary surroundings but with warm and welcoming service.
Owner-chef from Lazio but dishes come from across Italy, often using British
produce. Ravioli is the house speciality.

XXX **Orrery**   🛋 AC ⇔ VISA ⓒⓞ AE

55 Marylebone High St ⊠ W1U 5RB – ⓜ Regent's Park – 𝒞 (020)
7616 8000 – www.orrery-restaurant.co.uk   G1
Rest – (booking essential) Menu £ 25/48
♦ Modern ♦ Formal ♦
These are actually converted stables from the 19C but, such is the elegance and
style of the building, you'd never know. Featured is elaborate, modern European cooking; dishes are strong on presentation and come with the occasional
twist.

XX **Texture** (Agnar Sverrisson)   🕙 AC ⇔ VISA ⓒⓞ AE
❀
34 Portman St. ⊠ W1H 7BY – ⓜ Marble Arch – 𝒞 (020) 72240028
– www.texture-restaurant.co.uk
– Closed Christmas-New Year, 2 weeks August, Sunday and Monday
Rest – Menu £ 20 (lunch)/79 – Carte £ 51/71 ⅜   G2
♦ Innovative ♦ Design ♦
Technically skilled but light and invigorating cooking from Icelandic chef-
owner, who uses ingredients from home. Bright restaurant with high ceiling
and popular adjoining champagne bar. Pleasant service from keen staff, ready
with a smile.
→ Graflax and smoked salmon with horseradish. Lightly salted cod, barley
risotto and prawns. Skyr with rhubarb, muesli and ginger.

XX **L'Autre Pied**   🕙 AC VISA ⓒⓞ AE
❀
5-7 Blandford St. ⊠ W1U 3DB – ⓜ Bond Street – 𝒞 (020) 74869696
– www.lautrepied.co.uk
– Closed 4 days Christmas, 1 January and Sunday dinner   G2
Rest – Menu £ 19/68 – Carte £ 34/58
♦ Modern ♦ Design ♦
Chef Andy McFadden's dishes are elaborate yet easy to eat and provide pleasing contrasts in textures; venison dishes are a particular speciality. This more
relaxed sibling to Pied à Terre has a buoyant atmosphere; ask for a table by
the window to better enjoy the local 'village' feel.
→ Ceviche of scallops, black quinoa and dill oil. Suckling pig, purple carrot
and sea buckthorn purée. Bitter sweet chocolate crème, whisky and
espresso granité.

XX **Galvin Bistrot de Luxe**   AC 🅿 VISA ⓒⓞ AE

66 Baker St. ⊠ W1U 7DJ – ⓜ Baker Street
– 𝒞 (020) 79354007
– www.galvinrestaurants.com
– Closed 25-26 December, 1 January and dinner 24 December   G2
Rest – Menu £ 20/22 – Carte £ 31/50
♦ French ♦ Bistro ♦
Firmly established modern Gallic bistro with ceiling fans, globe lights and wood
panelled walls. Satisfying and precisely cooked classic French dishes from the
Galvin brothers.

XX **Cotidie** 🟥 *VISA* 🟠 AE

50 Marylebone High St ✉ *W1U 5HN* – ⓜ *Baker Street* – ℰ *(020)*
7258 9878 – www.cotidierestaurant.com
– Closed Christmas **G1**
Rest – Menu £ 25 (lunch) – Carte £ 35/55
♦ Italian ♦ Elegant ♦
The name of Bruno Barbieri's slick and elegant restaurant means 'everyday'
- this refers to the oft changing menu rather than the sophisticated, imaginative
Italian food influenced by all regions of Italy.

XX **Zayna** 🟥 *VISA* 🟠 AE

25 New Quebec St. ✉ *W1H 7SF* – ⓜ *Marble Arch* – ℰ *(020) 77232229*
– www.zaynarestaurant.co.uk **F2**
Rest – Menu £ 10/25 – Carte £ 18/34
♦ Indian ♦ Elegant ♦ Intimate ♦
Enthusiastically run, elegant restaurant spread over two floors, with keen owner.
Interesting north Indian and Pakistani delicacies; kitchen only uses halal meat
and free-range chicken.

XX **Ozer** 🟥 🐶 *VISA* 🟠 AE

5 Langham Pl., Regent. St. ✉ *W1B 3DG* – ⓜ *Oxford Circus* – ℰ *(020)*
73230505 – www.ozer.co.uk **H2**
Rest – Carte £ 18/44
♦ Turkish ♦ Brasserie ♦
Come in a group of friends to best appreciate the large bar, the excitable atmosphere and the sharing of healthy food. Go for the authentic specialities such as
borek, kofte and the extensive choice of chargrilled meats.

XX **Royal China** 🟥 *VISA* 🟠 AE

24-26 Baker St ✉ *W1U 7AB* – ⓜ *Baker Street* – ℰ *(020) 74874688*
– www.royalchinagroup.co.uk **G2**
Rest – Menu £ 30/40
♦ Chinese ♦ Exotic ♦
Barbeque meats, assorted soups and stir-fries attract plenty of large groups to
this smart and always bustling Cantonese restaurant. Over 40 different types of
dim sum served during the day.

XX **Verru** *VISA* 🟠 AE

69 Marylebone Ln ✉ *W1U 2PH* – ⓜ *Bond Street* – ℰ *(020) 7935 0858*
– www.verru.co.uk **G2**
Rest – Menu £ 15 – Carte £ 28/35
♦ Modern ♦ Intimate ♦
Chef-owner is Estonian so his cooking not only displays a Baltic boldness of flavour but also makes good use of northern European influences. The restaurant
is tiny and tucked away but warmly run and smartly dressed.

XX **Roganic** 🟥 *VISA* 🟠 AE ⓞ

19 Blandford St ✉ *W1U 3DH* – ⓜ *Baker Street* – ℰ *(020) 7486 0380*
– www.roganic.co.uk
– Closed 25-26 December, Sunday and Monday **G2**
Rest – *(booking advisable)* Menu £ 29/80
♦ Innovative ♦ Minimalist ♦
Simon Rogan of L'Enclume in the Lake District created this "extended pop-up
restaurant" by taking on the last 2 years of an existing lease. From the tasting
menus come dishes of invention and originality, using produce from their own
farm.

XX **Suka** – Sanderson Hotel 🟥 *VISA* 🟠 AE ⓞ

50 Berners St ✉ *W1T 3NG* – ⓜ *Oxford Circus* – ℰ *(020) 73005588*
– www.morganshotelgroup.com **H2**
Rest – Menu £ 23/50
♦ Asian influences ♦ Fashionable ♦
Have cocktails in the Sanderson's trendy Long Bar then climb onto one of the
high stools here at Suka. Be prepared to share, from a menu that mixes street
food with more sophisticated Malaysian offerings.

XX **L'Aventure** 🛐 _VISA_ ◎◎ _AE_

3 Blenheim Terr ⊠ _NW8 0EH –_ Ⓜ _St John's Wood –_ 𝒞 _(020) 76246232_
– www.laventure.co.uk
– Closed 19-31 August, first week January, Saturday lunch, Sunday and bank
holidays _Plan I_ **B2**
Rest – Menu £ 19/31
♦ French ♦ Neighbourhood ♦ Romantic ♦
Behind the pretty tree-lined entrance you'll find a charming neighbourhood res-
taurant. Relaxed atmosphere and service by personable owner. Authentic
French cuisine.

XX **Winter Garden** – The Landmark London Hotel _AC_ _VISA_ ◎◎ _AE_

222 Marylebone Rd ⊠ _NW1 6JQ –_ Ⓜ _Edgware Road –_ 𝒞 _(020) 76318000_
– www.landmarklondon.co.uk **F1**
Rest – Menu £ 27 (lunch) – Carte £ 34/55
♦ Mediterranean ♦ Friendly ♦
Dining options north of Marylebone Road can be limited, so the Winter Garden,
housed in the vast atrium of the Landmark, is a useful spot for a business lunch.
The kitchen has a lightness of touch and the confidence not to overcrowd a
plate.

XX **The Providores** _AC_ _VISA_ ◎◎ _AE_

109 Marylebone High St. ⊠ _W1U 4RX –_ Ⓜ _Bond Street –_ 𝒞 _(020)_
79356175 – www.theprovidores.co.uk
– Closed 24 December-4 January **G2**
Rest – Carte £ 47/67
♦ Innovative ♦ Trendy ♦
Packed ground floor for tapas; upstairs for innovative fusion cooking, with spi-
ces and ingredients from around the world, including Australasia. Starter-sized
dishes at dinner allow for greater choice.

XX **Iberica Marylebone** _AC_ ⇄ _VISA_ ◎◎ _AE_

195 Great Portland St ⊠ _W1W 5PS –_ Ⓜ _Great Portland Street –_ 𝒞 _(020)_
76368650 – www.ibericalondon.co.uk
– Closed 1 January, Sunday dinner and bank holidays **H1**
Rest – Carte £ 30/75
♦ Spanish ♦ Trendy ♦
Some prefer the intimacy of upstairs, others the bustle of the ground floor with
its bar and deli. Along with an impressive array of Iberico hams are colourful
dishes to share such as glossy black rice with cuttlefish and prawns.

XX **One Blenheim Terrace** 🛐 _AC_ _VISA_ ◎◎ _AE_

1 Blenheim Terrace ⊠ _NW8 0EH –_ Ⓜ _St John's Wood –_ 𝒞 _(020) 73721722_
– www.oneblenheimterrace.co.uk
– Closed Monday _Plan I_ **B2**
Rest – Carte £ 26/41
♦ Innovative ♦ Neighbourhood ♦
The young chef owner offers something a little different: some dishes are re-
interpretations of '60s and '70s classics, but owe more to modern cooking tech-
niques than nostalgia. The bright room comes with a popular terrace.

XX **Phoenix Palace** ぐ _AC_ ⇄ _VISA_ ◎◎ _AE_

5 Glentworth St. ⊠ _NW1 5PG –_ Ⓜ _Baker Street –_ 𝒞 _(020) 74863515_
– www.phoenixpalace.co.uk
– Closed 25 December **F1**
Rest – (bookings advisable at dinner) Carte £ 26/50
♦ Chinese ♦ Family ♦
The menu may be disconcertingly long at this vast but well-organised Chinese
restaurant but the cooking is good, particularly the Cantonese specialities like
roast pork belly or fish maw with conpoy and winter melon.

XX **Levant** 🔳 VISA 🆗 AE

Jason Ct., 76 Wigmore St. ⊠ *W1U 2SJ –* Ⓜ *Bond Street –* ℰ *(020) 72241111 – www.levant.co.uk*
– Closed 25-26 December **G2**
Rest – Carte £ 25/35
♦ Lebanese ♦ Exotic ♦

Belly dancing, lanterns and a low-slung bar all add up to an exotic dining experience. The Lebanese food is satisfying and authentic, carefully prepared and ideal for sharing in groups.

X **Trishna** (Karam Sethi) 🔳 ⇔ VISA 🆗 AE
✿

15-17 Blandford St. ⊠ *W1U 3DG –* Ⓜ *Baker Street –* ℰ *(020) 79355624*
– www.trishnalondon.com
– Closed 25-28 December and 1-3 January **G2**
Rest – Menu £ 19 (lunch) – Carte £ 20/37
♦ Indian ♦ Neighbourhood ♦ Simple ♦

The coast of southwest India provides many influences at this understated, double-fronted, modern Indian restaurant. The food is balanced, satisfactory and executed with care; be sure to order the wondrously rich Dorset brown crab.
→ Char-grilled tiger prawns with mustard and garlic. Fish tikka with dill raita. Mango kheer and pistachio.

X **The Wallace** VISA 🆗

Hertford House, Manchester Sq ⊠ *W1U 3BN –* Ⓜ *Bond Street –* ℰ *(020) 75639505 – www.thewallacerestaurant.com*
– Closed 24-26 December **G2**
Rest – *(lunch only and dinner Friday-Saturday)* Menu £ 26 – Carte £ 28/40
♦ French ♦ Friendly ♦

Large glass-roofed courtyard on the ground floor of Hertford House, home to the splendid Wallace Collection. French-influenced menu, with fruits de mer section; terrines are the house speciality.

X **Caffé Caldesi** 🔳 VISA 🆗 AE

118 Marylebone Ln. (1st floor) ⊠ *W1U 2QF –* Ⓜ *Bond Street –* ℰ *(020) 74870754 – www.caldesi.com* **G2**
Rest – Menu £ 14/20 – Carte £ 20/44
♦ Italian ♦ Neighbourhood ♦

Head upstairs at this converted corner pub for generously proportioned, big flavoured classics from across Italy. Stay on the ground floor for a simpler and more accessibly priced menu.

X **Roti Chai** 🔳 VISA 🆗 AE ①

3 Portman Mews South ⊠ *W1H 6HS –* Ⓜ *Marble Arch –* ℰ *(020) 74080101 – www.rotichai.com* **G2**
Rest – Menu £ 25/35 – Carte £ 18/31
♦ Indian ♦ Trendy ♦

Representing the new wave of modern, casual Indian restaurants, in appropriately vivid colours. The ground floor is for quick and easy pan-Indian street food; downstairs is swankier and offers a contemporary update of Indian home cooking.

X **Hix (Selfridges)** 🍴 🔳 VISA 🆗 AE

Mezzanine Fl, Selfridges, 400 Oxford St ⊠ *W1A 1AB –* Ⓜ *Bond Street*
– ℰ (020) 74995400 – www.hixatselfridges.co.uk
– Closed 25 December and Sunday dinner **G2**
Rest – Menu £ 18 (lunch) – Carte £ 19/94
♦ Modern ♦ Brasserie ♦

On the mezzanine floor of the famous store; open from breakfast onwards, with a popular champagne bar to refuel shoppers. Menu is lighter and more European than at the other Hix restaurants.

Il Baretto

AC VISA ◉◉ AE

43 Blandford St. ⊠ *W1U 7HF –* Ⓜ *Baker Street –* ✆ *(020) 74867340*
– www.ilbaretto.co.uk
– Closed 25-26 December, lunch 31 December and 1 January

G2

Rest – Carte £ 20/58

♦ Italian ♦ Neighbourhood ♦

The wood-fired oven is the star of the show at this neighbourhood Italian. Extensive and variably priced menu has something for everyone. The basement room has a lively atmosphere, with frantic service to match.

28°-50° Marylebone

AC ☕ VISA ◉◉ AE

15-17 Marylebone Ln. ⊠ *W1U 2NE –* Ⓜ *Bond Street –* ✆ *(020) 74867922*
– www.2850.co.uk
– Closed 25 December

G2

Rest – Menu £ 19 (lunch and early dinner) – Carte £ 21/30 ⅋

♦ Modern ♦ Wine bar ♦ Neighbourhood ♦

This second wine bar from the owners of Texture restaurant offers a great choice of wines by the glass and a terrific Collectors' List. Most plump for the grilled meats from the coal burning oven. Service is as bright as the room.

Riding House Café

AC ⇔ VISA ◉◉ AE

43-51 Great Titchfield St ⊠ *W1W 7PQ –* Ⓜ *Oxford Circus –* ✆ *(020) 79270840 – www.ridinghousecafe.co.uk*
– Closed 25-26 December

H2

Rest – Carte £ 19/35

♦ Modern ♦ Rustic ♦ Fashionable ♦

It's less a café, more a large, quirkily designed, all-day New York style brasserie and cocktail bar. The 'small plates' have more zing than the main courses. The unbookable side of the restaurant is the more fun part.

Briciole

AC VISA ◉◉ AE ◉

20 Homer St ⊠ *W1H 4NA –* Ⓜ *Edgware Road –* ✆ *(020) 77230040*
– www.briciole.co.uk
– Closed 25-26 December

F2

Rest – Carte £ 11/25

♦ Italian ♦ Neighbourhood ♦

Maurizio Morelli opened this fun, all-day Italian as a less expensive and more relaxed alternative to his Latium restaurant. It offers a pleasant local feel and faux-rustic surroundings. Try the homemade sausages and meatballs.

Donostia

◉◉ AE ◉

10 Seymour Pl ⊠ *W1H 7ND –* Ⓜ *Marble Arch –* ✆ *(020) 3620 1845*
– www.donostia.co.uk
– Closed Christmas, Sunday dinner and Monday

F2

Rest – Carte £ 13/30

♦ Basque ♦ Tapas bar ♦

The two young owners were inspired by the food of San Sebastiàn to open this pintxos and tapas bar. Sit at the counter for Basque classics like cod with pil-pil sauce, chorizo from the native pig Kintoa and slow-cooked pig's cheeks.

Vinoteca

AC VISA ◉◉ AE

15 Seymour Pl. ⊠ *W1H 5BD –* Ⓜ *Marble Arch –* ✆ *(020) 7724 7288*
– www.vinoteca.co.uk
– Closed 24-26, 31 December, 1 January, bank holiday Mondays and Sunday dinner

F2

Rest – (booking advisable) Carte £ 22/33 ⅋

♦ Modern ♦ Minimalist ♦

Follows the formula of the original: great fun, great wines, gutsy and wholesome food, enthusiastic staff and almost certainly a wait for a table. Influences from sunnier parts of Europe, along with some British dishes.

UNITED KINGDOM - LONDON

X **Yalla Yalla**

12 Winsley St. ⊠ W1W 8HQ – Ⓜ Oxford Circus – 𝒞 (020) 7637 4748
– www.yalla-yalla.co.uk
– Closed 25-26 December, 1 January and Sunday   **H2**
Rest – Carte £ 19/26

♦ Lebanese ♦ Rustic ♦

Queues form for the Beirut street food which includes zesty mezze and succulent charcoal-grilled lamb dishes. Desserts come from the enticing pastry corner and wines from the Bekaa Valley. Takeaway also available.

X **Dinings**

22 Harcourt St. ⊠ W1H 4HH – Ⓜ Edgware Road – 𝒞 (020) 77230666
– www.dinings.co.uk
– Closed Christmas, Saturday lunch and Sunday   **F2**
Rest – (booking essential) Menu £ 13 (weekday lunch) – Carte £ 18/57

♦ Japanese ♦ Cosy ♦ Minimalist ♦

It's hard not to be charmed by this sweet little Japanese place, with its ground floor counter and basement tables. Its strengths lie with the more creative, contemporary dishes; sharing is recommended but prices can be steep.

X **Chada Chada**

16-17 Picton Pl. ⊠ W1U 1BP – Ⓜ Bond Street – 𝒞 (020) 79358212
– www.chadathai.com
– Closed 25 December and lunch Sunday-Monday   **G2**
Rest – Carte £ 17/36

♦ Thai ♦ Minimalist ♦

Authentic and fragrant Thai cooking; the good value menu offers some interesting departures from the norm. Service is eager to please in the compact and cosy rooms.

🛏️ **Grazing Goat** with rm

6 New Quebec St ⊠ W1H 7RQ – Ⓜ Marble Arch. – 𝒞 (020) 7724 7243
– www.thegrazinggoat.co.uk   **F2**
8 rm – †£ 234/270 ††£ 234/270, ⌑ £ 7
Rest – (booking essential at dinner) Carte £ 27/46

♦ British traditional ♦ Pub ♦ Fashionable ♦

A smart city facsimile of a country pub; it's first-come-first-served in the bar but you can book in the upstairs dining room. Proper pub classics such as pies and Castle of Mey steaks are on offer. Bedrooms with Nordic style bathrooms.

🛏️ **Portman**

51 Upper Berkeley St ⊠ W1H 7QW – Ⓜ Marble Arch. – 𝒞 (020) 7723 8996
– www.theportmanmarylebone.com   **F2**
Rest – Menu £ 15 (weekday lunch) – Carte £ 23/32

♦ Modern ♦ Pub ♦ Friendly ♦

The condemned on their way to Tyburn Tree gallows would take their last drink here. Now it's an urbane pub with a formal upstairs dining room. The ground floor is more fun for enjoying the down-to-earth menu.

CAMDEN   *Plan VI*

BLOOMSBURY

🏛️ **Covent Garden**

10 Monmouth St. ⊠ WC2H 9HB – Ⓜ Covent Garden – 𝒞 (020) 78061000
– www.firmdalehotels.com   **I3**
56 rm – †£ 312 ††£ 384, ⌑ £ 20 – 2 suites
Rest Brasserie Max – see restaurant listing

♦ Luxury ♦ Stylish ♦ Personalised ♦

Popular with those of a theatrical bent. Boldly designed, stylish bedrooms, with technology discreetly concealed. Boasts a very comfortable first floor oak-panelled drawing room with its own honesty bar.

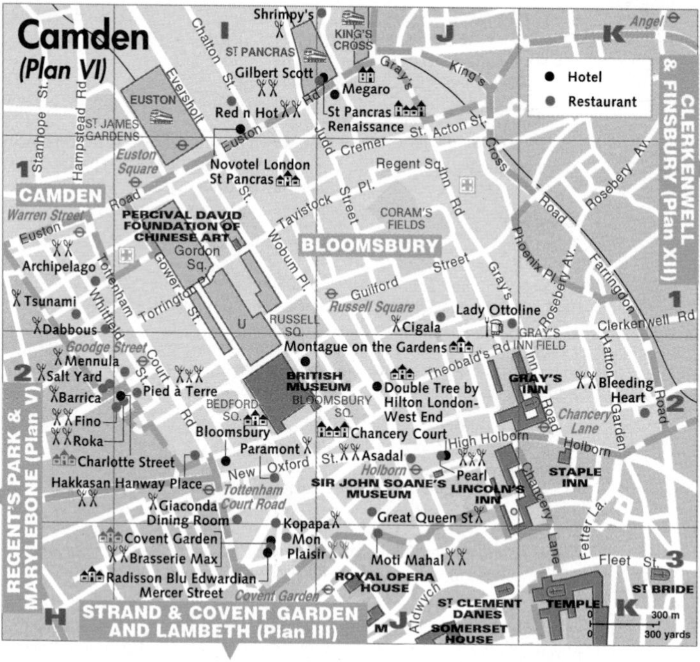

Charlotte Street

15 Charlotte St ⊠ *W1T 1RJ* – Ⓜ *Goodge Street* – ✆ *(020) 78062000*
– *www.charlottestreethotel.co.uk* I2

48 rm – †£ 300 ††£ 372, ☕ £ 20 – 4 suites

Rest *Oscar* – ✆ *(020) 79074005* – Carte £ 30/60

♦ Luxury ♦ Stylish ♦ Design ♦

Stylish interior designed with a charming, understated English feel. Impeccably kept and individually decorated bedrooms. Popular in-house screening room. Colourful restaurant whose terrace spills onto Charlotte Street; grilled meats a highlight.

Montague on the Gardens

15 Montague St. ⊠ *WC1B 5BJ* – Ⓜ *Holborn*
– ✆ *(020) 76371001* – *www.montaguehotel.com* I2

94 rm – †£ 216/300 ††£ 252/300, ☕ £ 20 – 6 suites

Rest *Blue Door Bistro* – Menu £ 25 – Carte £ 24/51

♦ Family ♦ Classic ♦

A traditional but elegant British feel to this period townhouse; its clubby bar and conservatory overlook a secluded garden. Individually decorated bedrooms. Bistro divided between two small, pretty rooms.

Radisson Blu Edwardian Mercer Street

20 Mercer St ⊠ *WC2H 9HD* – Ⓜ *Covent Garden*
– ✆ *(020) 7836 4300* – *www.radissonblu-edwardian.com* I3

137 rm – †£ 234 ††£ 234/318, ☕ £ 23

Rest *The Dial* – Menu £ 25 – Carte £ 23/47

♦ Townhouse ♦ Modern ♦

Radisson Edwardian spent considerable funds transforming their former Mountbatten hotel. The bedrooms come with a contemporary look and relaxed restaurant blends in nicely with the theatreland neighbourhood.

UNITED KINGDOM - LONDON

Bloomsbury

&. rm, AC 🛜 🛋 VISA 🕼 AE ①

16-22 Gt Russell St ✉ *WC1B 3NN* – Ⓜ *Tottenham Court Road*
– ℰ *(020) 73471000*
– *www.doylecollection.com/bloomsbury*　　　　　　I2
153 rm – ♥£ 222/354 ♥♥£ 318/540, � £ 21
Rest *Landseer* – Menu £ 24 (early dinner)
– Carte £ 30/52
♦ Business ♦ Historic ♦ Classic ♦
Neo-Georgian building by Edward Lutyens, built for the YMCA in 1929. Now boasts a smart, comfortable interior, from the lobby to the bedrooms. Restaurant with largely British menu.

DoubleTree by Hilton London - West End

🛗 &.

92 Southampton Row ✉ *WC1B 4BH*　　rm, AC 🛜 🛋 VISA 🕼 ①
– Ⓜ *Russell Square* – ℰ *(020) 7242 2828*
– *www.dtlondonwestend.com*　　　　　　J2
207 rm – ♥£ 132/528 ♥♥£ 132/540, ⊆ £ 18 – 8 suites
Rest *DoubleTree by Hilton London - West End* – (closed Sunday dinner) (dinner only) Menu £ 17/25 – Carte £ 28/38
♦ Business ♦ Contemporary ♦ Functional ♦
Now a corporate-minded hotel with a contemporary feel – the stained glass windows and original staircase are the only clues to the early 1900s origins of the building. Basement restaurant with a wide ranging menu including grills; or order snacks in the brighter bar just off the foyer.

Pied à Terre

🕼 Ⓥ AC ⇄ VISA 🕼 AE
❀

34 Charlotte St ✉ *W1T 2NH* – Ⓜ *Goodge Street* – ℰ *(020) 76361178*
– *www.pied-a-terre.co.uk*
– *Closed last week December-3 January, Saturday lunch, Sunday and bank holidays*　　　　　　I2
Rest – (booking essential) Menu £ 28/75 🍃
♦ Innovative ♦ Elegant ♦ Intimate ♦
Pied à Terre celebrated its 21st birthday in 2012 and is in rude health. Marcus Eaves has settled in well as head chef; his dishes display more of his personality by being bolder in flavour and are imaginative without over-complication.
→ Lobster with suckling pig belly and peanut dressing. Veal with tarragon brioche, morels and parmesan. Tart of Earl Grey tea, milk and vanilla gel, bergamot ice cream and candied orange.

Hakkasan Hanway Place

AC VISA 🕼 AE
❀

8 Hanway Pl. ✉ *W1T 1HD* – Ⓜ *Tottenham Court Road* – ℰ *(020) 79277000* – *www.hakkasan.com*
– *Closed 24-25 December*　　　　　　I2
Rest – Carte £ 50/82
♦ Chinese ♦ Trendy ♦
Cool and seductive subterranean restaurant, with an air of exclusivity. Innovation and originality have been added to the Cantonese base to create dishes with zip and depth. Lunchtime dim sum is a highlight.
→ Peking duck with Royal Beluga caviar. Roasted silver cod. Jivara hazelnut bomb.

Mon Plaisir

🕼 VISA 🕼 AE

19-21 Monmouth St. ✉ *WC2H 9DD* – Ⓜ *Covent Garden* – ℰ *(020) 78367243* – *www.monplaisir.co.uk*
– *Closed Christmas-New Year, Sunday and bank holidays*　　　　　　I3
Rest – Menu £ 13/24 – Carte £ 29/48
♦ French ♦ Family ♦
This proud French institution opened in the 1940s. Enjoy satisfyingly authentic classics in any of the four contrasting rooms, full of Gallic charm; the bar was salvaged from a Lyonnais brothel.

UNITED KINGDOM - LONDON

XX **Roka**   AC VISA ◐◑ AE ◑

37 Charlotte St ⊠ W1T 1RR – Ⓜ Goodge Street – ℰ (020) 75806464
– www.rokarestaurant.com
– Closed 25 December   I2
Rest – Menu £ 50 – Carte £ 18/89
♦ Japanese ♦ Fashionable ♦ Design ♦
Bright, atmospheric interior of teak and oak; bustling and trendy feel. Contemporary touches added to Japanese dishes; try specialities from the on-view Robata grill. Capable and chatty service.

XX **Fino**   AC VISA AE ◑

33 Charlotte St (entrance on Rathbone St.) ⊠ W1T 1RR
– Ⓜ Goodge Street – ℰ (020) 7813 8010 – www.finorestaurant.com
– Closed Saturday lunch, Sunday and bank holidays   I2
Rest – Carte £ 16/44
♦ Spanish ♦ Fashionable ♦
Seafood is handled especially well in this lively, quite smart and smoothly run basement tapas restaurant. Sensibly divided menu, with dishes designed for sharing. Youthful, helpful service.

XX **Archipelago**   AC VISA ◐◑ AE ◑

110 Whitfield St. ⊠ W1T 5ED – Ⓜ Goodge Street – ℰ (020) 73833346
– www.archipelago-restaurant.co.uk
– Closed 24-27 December, Saturday lunch, Sunday and bank holidays
Rest – Menu £ 26/33 – Carte £ 27/38   H1
♦ Innovative ♦ Exotic ♦
Eccentrically decorated in the style of an overflowing bazaar. There's an Asian influence to the equally exotic and highly unusual menu which could include crocodile, zebra and wildebeest.

XX **Brasserie Max** - Covent Garden Hotel   AC VISA ◐◑ AE ◑

10 Monmouth St. ⊠ WC2H 9HB – Ⓜ Covent Garden – ℰ (020) 78061007
– www.firmdalehotels.com   I3
Rest – (booking essential) Menu £ 25 – Carte £ 28/60
♦ Modern ♦ Fashionable ♦ Brasserie ♦
It's not just shoppers and theatregoers who appreciate this stylish brasserie. Its international menu, grilled specialities, Sunday brunches and afternoon teas have widespread appeal.

X **Dabbous** (Ollie Dabbous)   AC VISA ◐◑ AE ◑
❀
39 Whitfield St ⊠ W1T 2SF – Ⓜ Goodge Street – ℰ (020) 7323 1544
– www.dabbous.co.uk
– Closed 23 December-15 January, 29 March-2 April, two weeks August, Sunday
and Monday   H1
Rest – (booking essential) Menu £ 24/49 – Carte £ 22/30
♦ Modern ♦ Design ♦ Neighbourhood ♦
One of the hottest tickets in town – the kitchen adopts the 'less is more' approach; the food comes with elegantly restrained finesse and a bewitching purity. Most have the 7-course menu with its stimulating and sublime combinations of ingredients. The ersatz industrial room has a simple elegance.
➔ Mixed alliums in a chilled pine infusion. Barbecued Iberico pork, savoury acorn praline and homemade vinegar. Chocolate ganache, basil moss and sheep's milk ice cream.

X **Mennula**   AC ✢ VISA ◐◑ AE ◑

10 Charlotte St ⊠ W1T 2LT – Ⓜ Goodge Street – ℰ (020) 7636 2833
– www.mennula.com
– Closed 25-26 December, 1 January, lunch Saturday-Sunday and bank
holidays   I2
Rest – (bookings advisable at dinner) Menu £ 18 – Carte £ 28/42
♦ Italian ♦ Intimate ♦
Sicilian specialities provide the highlights at this enthusiastically run Italian restaurant, whose name means 'almond'. Compact but bright, crisply decorated room; ask for one of the booths.

UNITED KINGDOM - LONDON

Paramount
≤ AC ⇔ VISA ◯◯ AE

Centre Point (31st floor) 101-103 New Oxford St. ✉ *WC1A 1DD*
– 🚇 Tottenham Court Road – ℰ (020) 74202900
– www.paramount.uk.net
– Closed 25-26 December and Sunday dinner   I2
Rest – Menu £ 24 (lunch and early dinner) – Carte £ 32/51
♦ Modern ♦ Minimalist ♦
Worth the palaver of getting into this Grade II listed building: the views are ter-
rific and this is a fun, keenly run restaurant. Ambitious and quite elaborate coo-
king; champagne bar one floor up.

Kopapa
🍴 AC 🍷 VISA ◯◯ AE

32-34 Monmouth St ✉ *WC2H 9HA –* 🚇 *Covent Garden – ℰ (020)*
7240 6076 – www.kopapa.co.uk
– Closed 25 December   I3
Rest – *(booking advisable)* Menu £ 25/37 – Carte £ 24/39
♦ Asian influences ♦ Bistro ♦ Individual ♦
Kopapa, a Maori word for a gathering, is Peter Gordon's just-drop-in-anytime
place. It's cramped but fun, with breakfast morphing into all-day dining. It's the
'fusion'-inspired tapas that will give your taste buds the best workout.

Giaconda Dining Room
AC VISA ◯◯ AE

9 Denmark St. ✉ *WC2H 8LS –* 🚇 *Tottenham Court Road – ℰ (020)*
72403334 – www.giacondadining.com
– Closed 3 weeks August, 2 weeks Easter, 2 weeks Christmas-New Year,
Saturday lunch, Sunday, Monday and bank holidays   I2
Rest – *(booking essential)* Carte £ 24/35
♦ Modern ♦ Cosy ♦ Neighbourhood ♦
Aussie owners run a small, fun and very busy place in an unpromising location.
The very well priced menu offers an appealing mix of gutsy, confident, no-non-
sense food, with French and Italian influences.

Salt Yard
AC VISA ◯◯ AE ◯

54 Goodge St. ✉ *W1T 4NA –* 🚇 *Goodge Street – ℰ (020) 76370657*
– www.saltyard.co.uk
– Closed 24 December-4 January, Saturday lunch and Sunday   H2
Rest – Carte £ 14/24 🍷
♦ Mediterranean ♦ Tapas bar ♦ Intimate ♦
Ground floor bar and buzzy basement restaurant specialising in good value pla-
tes of tasty Italian and Spanish dishes, ideal for sharing; charcuterie a specia-
lity. Super wine list.

Cigala
🍴 AC ⇔ VISA ◯◯ AE ◯

54 Lamb's Conduit St. ✉ *WC1N 3LW –* 🚇 *Russell Square – ℰ (020)*
74051717 – www.cigala.co.uk
– Closed bank holidays   J1
Rest – *(booking essential)* Menu £ 18 (lunch) – Carte £ 23/39 🍷
♦ Spanish ♦ Neighbourhood ♦ Friendly ♦
Relaxed surroundings and an accessible menu allow this Spanish restaurant to
appeal to a wide audience. Try the grilled black pudding, hams from the open
kitchen counter and homemade chorizo, or share a paella.

Tsunami
AC VISA ◯◯ AE

93 Charlotte St. ✉ *W1T 4PY –* 🚇 *Goodge Street – ℰ (020) 76370050*
– www.tsunamirestaurant.co.uk
– Closed Saturday lunch and Sunday   H1
Rest – Menu £ 15 (weekday lunch) – Carte £ 14/47
♦ Japanese ♦ Cosy ♦ Trendy ♦
Sister to the original in Clapham. Sweet, pretty place, with lacquered walls, floral
motif and moody lighting. Contemporary Japanese cuisine is carefully prepared
and sensibly priced.

Barrica 🍴 🛱 AC VISA ⊕ AE ⊕

62 Goodge St ⊠ W1T 4NE – Ⓜ Goodge Street – ℰ (020) 7436 9448
– www.barrica.co.uk
– Closed 25-26 December, 1 January, Sunday and bank holidays
Rest – (booking essential) Carte £ 18/20   **H2**
♦ Spanish ♦ Tapas bar ♦ Friendly ♦
Lively, noisy and warmly decorated tapas bar. Authentic dishes come with
plenty of flavour and are complemented by a thoughtfully compiled Spanish
wine list. Busy front bar.

Lady Ottoline 🛱 VISA ⊕ AE

11a Northington St ⊠ WC1N 2JF – Ⓜ Chancery Lane. – ℰ (020)
78310008 – www.theladyottoline.com
– Closed 24-26 December and bank holidays   **J1**
Rest – Menu £ 14 (weekdays) – Carte £ 21/33
♦ British traditional ♦ Cosy ♦ Neighbourhood ♦
Sister to Princess of Shoreditch, this large red-bricked Victorian pub is largely
unchanged from when it was called The Kings Arms. Enjoy the same gutsy coo-
king in the busy bar or the Queen Anne style upstairs dining room.

EUSTON

Novotel London St. Pancras 🛗 🐾 ⅙ rm, AC 🛜 🏋

100-110 Euston Rd ⊠ NW1 2AJ – Ⓜ Euston
– ℰ (020) 76669000 – www.novotel.com   VISA ⊕ AE ⊕   **I0**
310 rm – ♦£ 250/500 ♦♦£ 250/500, � £ 20 – 2 suites
Rest – (bar lunch Saturday, Sunday and bank holidays) Menu £ 19/23
– Carte £ 30/48
♦ Business ♦ Modern ♦
Halfway between Euston and King's Cross, this hotel has good-sized bedrooms
for London and those on the higher floors enjoy views over the city. Good busi-
ness amenities. International menu and buffet breakfast.

Red N Hot ⇕ VISA ⊕ AE

37 Chalton St ⊠ NW1 1JD – Ⓜ Euston – ℰ (020) 7388 0808
– www.rednhotgroup.com – Closed 25 December   **I0**
Rest – Menu £ 20/23 – Carte £ 16/25
♦ Chinese ♦ Fashionable ♦ Family ♦
The clue is in the name! The fiery pepper dominates the extensive selection of
Sichuan specialities that make good use of freshwater fish and poultry. Simpler
lunchtime menu includes hotpots.

HATTON GARDEN

Bleeding Heart 🛱 ⇕ VISA ⊕ AE ⊕

Bleeding Heart Yard (off Greville St.) ⊠ EC1N 8SJ – Ⓜ Farringdon
– ℰ (020) 72428238 – www.bleedingheart.co.uk – Closed 24 December-
1 January, Saturday, Sunday and bank holidays   **K2**
Rest – (booking essential) Menu £ 25 (weekday lunch) – Carte £ 27/50 🍷
♦ French ♦ Romantic ♦ Formal ♦
Dickensian yard plays host to this atmospheric, candlelit restaurant; popular
with those from The City. Classic French cuisine is the draw, with service that's
formal but has personality. Wines from owners' New Zealand estate.

HOLBORN

Chancery Court 🛗 🐾 🐾 ⅙ AC 🛜 🏋 VISA ⊕ AE ⊕

252 High Holborn ⊠ WC1V 7EN – Ⓜ Holborn – ℰ (020) 78299888
– www.chancerycourt.com   **J2**
354 rm – ♦£ 240/756 ♦♦£ 240/756, ⊑ £ 26 – 2 suites
Rest Pearl – see restaurant listing
♦ Business ♦ Historic ♦ Functional ♦
Striking former Pearl Assurance HQ, built in 1914, now an imposing place to
stay. Impressive marbled lobby and grand central courtyard. Decent
sized bedrooms with comprehensive modern facilities.

XXX **Pearl** – Chancery Court Hotel   `AC` ⇔ `VISA` ◉◉ `AE` ⓪
252 High Holborn ✉ *WC1V 7EN* – Ⓜ *Holborn* – ✆ *(020) 78297000*
– www.pearl-restaurant.com
– Closed 2 weeks August, Sunday, lunch Saturday and bank holidays
Rest – Menu £ 22/25 – Carte £ 48/63 ⌘   **J2**
♦ French ♦ Elegant ♦ Fashionable ♦
Impressive former banking hall, with walls clad in Italian marble and Corinthian columns. Waiters provide efficient service at well-spaced tables; cooking shows originality.

XX **Asadal**   `AC` ⇔ ◉◉ `AE`
227 High Holborn ✉ *WC1V 7DA* – Ⓜ *Holborn* – ✆ *(020) 7430 9006*
– www.asadal.co.uk
– Closed 25-26 December, 1 January and Sunday lunch   **J2**
Rest – Carte £ 20/30
♦ Korean ♦ Friendly ♦
Sharing is the key in this busy basement, where you'll be oblivious to its unprepossessing location. Hotpots, dumplings and barbeques are the highlights from the easy-to-follow menu. Staff cope well with the evening rush.

XX **Moti Mahal**   `AC` ⇔ `VISA` ◉◉ `AE`
45 Great Queen St. ✉ *WC2B 5AA* – Ⓜ *Holborn* – ✆ *(020) 72409329*
– www.motimahal-uk.com
– Closed Christmas, Sunday and lunch Saturday and bank holidays
Rest – Menu £ 15/49 – Carte £ 24/46   **J3**
♦ Indian ♦ Intimate ♦ Fashionable ♦
Restaurant is split between a bright, busy ground floor and more intimate basement. Specialities follow the Grand Trunk Road, stretching from Bengal to the North West and the Pakistan border.

X **Great Queen Street**   `VISA` ◉◉
32 Great Queen St ✉ *WC2B 5AA* – Ⓜ *Holborn* – ✆ *(020) 72420622*
– Closed Christmas-New Year, Sunday dinner and bank holidays   **J2**
Rest – *(booking essential)* Carte £ 18/33
♦ British modern ♦ Rustic ♦ Neighbourhood ♦
The menu is a model of British understatement and is dictated by the seasons; the cooking, confident and satisfying with laudable prices and generous portions. Lively atmosphere and enthusiastic service.

St Pancras

St Pancras Renaissance   📶 `Fó` ◉ 🐾 ▢ ⅆ rm, `AC` 📶 🏋
Euston Rd ✉ *NW1 2AR* – Ⓜ *King's Cross St Pancras*   `VISA` ◉◉ `AE`
– ✆ (020) 7841 3540 – www.stpancrasrenaissance.co.uk   **I0**
207 rm – ♦£ 228/1200 ♦♦£ 228/1200, ⌑ £ 26 – 38 suites
Rest *Gilbert Scott* – see restaurant listing
Rest *Booking Office* – ✆ *(020) 7841 3566* – Carte £ 28/45
♦ Business ♦ Historic ♦ Functional ♦
This Gothic jewel, built in 1873 as the Midland Grand hotel and now finally restored, reopened in 2011 under the Marriott brand. Former taxi rank now the spacious lobby and all-day dining is in the old Booking Office. Corridors and staircases evoke the past; bedrooms are a little more functional.

Megaro   ⅆ rm, `AC` 📶 `VISA` ◉◉ `AE` ⓪
23-27 Euston Rd ((entrance on Belgrove St)) ✉ *NW1 2SD*
– Ⓜ King's Cross St Pancras – ✆ (020) 7843 2222
– www.hotelmegaro.co.uk   **J0**
49 rm – ♦£ 160/200 ♦♦£ 160/200, ⌑ £ 15
Rest *Karpo* – ✆ *(020) 7843 2221* – Carte £ 21/47
♦ Townhouse ♦ Contemporary ♦ Personalised ♦
Contemporary hotel fashioned out of a converted bank. The rooms are unfussy and the bathrooms smart. Daily 'absinthe hour' in the basement bar; simple seasonal modern European menu. Pastries for breakfast from their on-site bakery.

XX **Gilbert Scott** – St Pancras Renaissance Hotel 🏧 ⟷ 𝗩𝗜𝗦𝗔 ⓞⓞ 🅰🅴

Euston Rd ⊠ *NW1 2AR –* Ⓜ *King's Cross St Pancras –* ℰ *(020) 7278 3888*
– www.thegilbertscott.co.uk I0
Rest – Menu £ 22 (weekdays) – Carte £ 29/42

♦ British traditional ♦ Brasserie ♦

Run under the aegis of Marcus Wareing and named after the architect of this
Gothic masterpiece, the restaurant has the look of a Grand Salon but the buzz
of a brasserie. It celebrates the UK's many regional and historic specialities.

X **Shrimpy's** 🍴 🏧 𝗩𝗜𝗦𝗔 ⓞⓞ 🅰🅴 ⓞ

The King's Cross Filling Station, Goods Way ⊠ *N1C 4UR*
– Ⓜ *King's Cross St. Pancras –* ℰ *(020) 88806111*
– www.shrimpys.co.uk
– Closed 24 and 26 December J0
Rest – (booking essential) Carte £ 28/46

♦ Other world kitchens ♦ Fashionable ♦ Bistro ♦

Proof that London's restaurant scene is fast moving, thrilling, witty and epheme-
ral. An old petrol station; no signs; great cocktails; touches of irony; art; lots of
deep-frying; soft shell crab burgers; Latin flavours.

HYDE PARK – KNIGHTSBRIDGE *Plan VII*

🏨 **Mandarin Oriental Hyde Park** ≤ ℒⓢ 🏊 🛋 🕭 🏧 🛜 🏋

66 Knightsbridge ⊠ *SW1X 7LA –* Ⓜ *Knightsbridge –* 𝗩𝗜𝗦𝗔 ⓞⓞ 🅰🅴 ⓞ
– ℰ (020) 72352000 – www.mandarinoriental.com/london F4
173 rm – ♦£ 354/900 ♦♦£ 354/900, ⊇ £ 32 – 25 suites
Rest *Dinner by Heston Blumenthal* ✿
Rest *Bar Boulud* – see restaurant listing

♦ Grand Luxury ♦ Classic ♦

Built in 1889 this classic international hotel, with its striking façade, remains one
of London's grandest. Many of the luxurious bedrooms, which have a charming
English country feel, enjoy views of Hyde Park. Standards of service are extremely high.

🏨 **Bulgari** ℒⓢ 🏊 🖥 🛋 rm, 🏧 🛜 🏋 𝗩𝗜𝗦𝗔 ⓞⓞ 🅰🅴 ⓞ

171 Knightsbridge ⊠ *SW7 1DW –* Ⓜ *Knightsbridge –* ℰ *(020) 71511010*
– www.bulgarihotels.com F4
78 rm – ♦£ 612/828 ♦♦£ 612/828, ⊇ £ 32 – 7 suites
Rest *Il Ristorante* – Menu £ 30 (lunch) – Carte £ 45/76

♦ Luxury ♦ Stylish ♦ Design ♦

Impeccably tailored hotel, opened in 2012, makes stunning use of materials like
silver, mahogany, silk and marble. Luxurious bedrooms with sensual curves,
sumptuous bathrooms and a great spa – and there is substance behind the
style. Down a sweeping staircase to the sleek Italian restaurant.

XXX **Dinner by Heston Blumenthal** – Mandarin Oriental Hyde Park Hotel
✿ *66 Knightsbridge* ⊠ *SW1X 7LA* 🏧 ⟷ 𝗩𝗜𝗦𝗔 ⓞⓞ 🅰🅴
– Ⓜ *Knightsbridge –* ℰ *(020) 7201 3833*
– www.dinnerbyheston.com F4
Rest – Menu £ 32 (weekday lunch) – Carte £ 50/65 ❀

♦ British modern ♦ Design ♦ Fashionable ♦

Don't come expecting 'molecular gastronomy' – this is all about respect for, and
a wonderful renewal of, British food, with just a little playfulness thrown in. Each
one of the meticulously crafted and deceptively simple looking dishes comes
with a date relating to its historical provenance.
➜ Mandarin meat fruit. Spiced pigeon with ale and artichokes. Tipsy cake
with spit-roast pineapple.

XX **Bar Boulud** – Mandarin Oriental Hyde Park Hotel   AC ⇔ 🕿
66 Knightsbridge ✉ SW1X 7LA – Ⓜ Knightsbridge   VISA ◐ AE ①
– ℰ (020) 72013899 – www.barboulud.com   **F4**
Rest – Menu £ 23 – Carte £ 26/54
♦ French ♦ Brasserie ♦ Fashionable ♦
Daniel Boulud's London outpost is fashionable, fun and frantic. His hometown is Lyon but he built his considerable reputation in New York, so charcuterie, sausages and burgers are the highlights.

XX **Zuma**   AC VISA ◐ AE ①
5 Raphael St ✉ SW7 1DL – Ⓜ Knightsbridge – ℰ (020) 75841010
– www.zumarestaurant.com
– Closed Christmas   **F5**
Rest – Carte £ 20/96
♦ Japanese ♦ Fashionable ♦
Now a global brand but this was the original. The glamorous clientele come for the striking surroundings, bustling atmosphere and easy-to-share food. Head for the more modern dishes and those cooked on the robata grill.

XX **Mr Chow**   AC VISA ◐ AE ①
151 Knightsbridge ✉ SW1X 7PA – Ⓜ Knightsbridge – ℰ (020) 75897347
– www.mrchow.com
– Closed 1 January, 24-26 December, Easter Monday dinner and Monday lunch
Rest – Menu £ 25 (lunch) – Carte £ 38/63   **F4**
♦ Chinese ♦ Friendly ♦
Long-standing Chinese restaurant, opened in 1968. Smart clientele, stylish and comfortable surroundings and prompt service from Italian waiters. Carefully prepared and satisfying food.

X **Chabrot**   AC VISA ◐ AE ①
9 Knightsbridge Grn ✉ SW1X 7QL – Ⓜ Knightsbridge – ℰ (020) 72252238
– www.chabrot.co.uk
– Closed 25 December and 1 January   **F5**
Rest – Menu £ 23 (dinner) – Carte £ 27/57 🍷
♦ French ♦ Bistro ♦ Retro ♦
In 2011 Thierry Laborde, formerly of Le Gavroche, got together with three friends to open this fervently French and atmospheric bistro. The kitchen looks to France's SW and Basque country for most of its influences.

BAYSWATER – MAIDA VALE   *Plan VIII*

🏨🏨🏨 **Lancaster London**   ⇐ ᴴ AC 🛜 🏋 P VISA ◐ AE ①
Lancaster Ter. ✉ W2 2TY – Ⓜ Lancaster Gate – ℰ (020) 72626737
– www.lancasterlondon.com   **E3**
394 rm – ⸰£ 143/719 ⸰⸰£ 143/719, ☲ £ 15.50 – 22 suites
Rest *Nipa* – see restaurant listing
Rest *Island* – ℰ (020) 75516070 – Menu £ 13 (lunch and early dinner)
– Carte £ 17/32
♦ Business ♦ Classic ♦
The former Royal Lancaster is an imposing 1960s hotel overlooking Hyde Park. Known for its extensive conference suites. Bedrooms are bright and well-equipped. Island has an accessible, Med-influenced menu, with steaks a highlight.

🏨 **Hotel Indigo London - Paddington**   ⌂ ᵢ6 ᴴ rm, AC 🛜
16 London St ✉ W2 1HL – Ⓜ Paddington   VISA ◐ AE ①
– ℰ (020) 7706 4444 – www.hotelindigo.com   **E2**
64 rm – ⸰£ 192 ⸰⸰£ 216/360, ☲ £ 15
Rest *London Street Brasserie* – Menu £ 14 (lunch and early dinner)
– Carte £ 19/27
♦ Business ♦ Chain hotel ♦ Modern ♦
You'll find a smart, modern, corporate townhouse behind the imposing period façade. Bright bedrooms come with a feature wall depicting scenes of the local area. All-day menu of steaks, pasta and brasserie classics.

Hyde Park & Knightsbridge
(Plan VII)

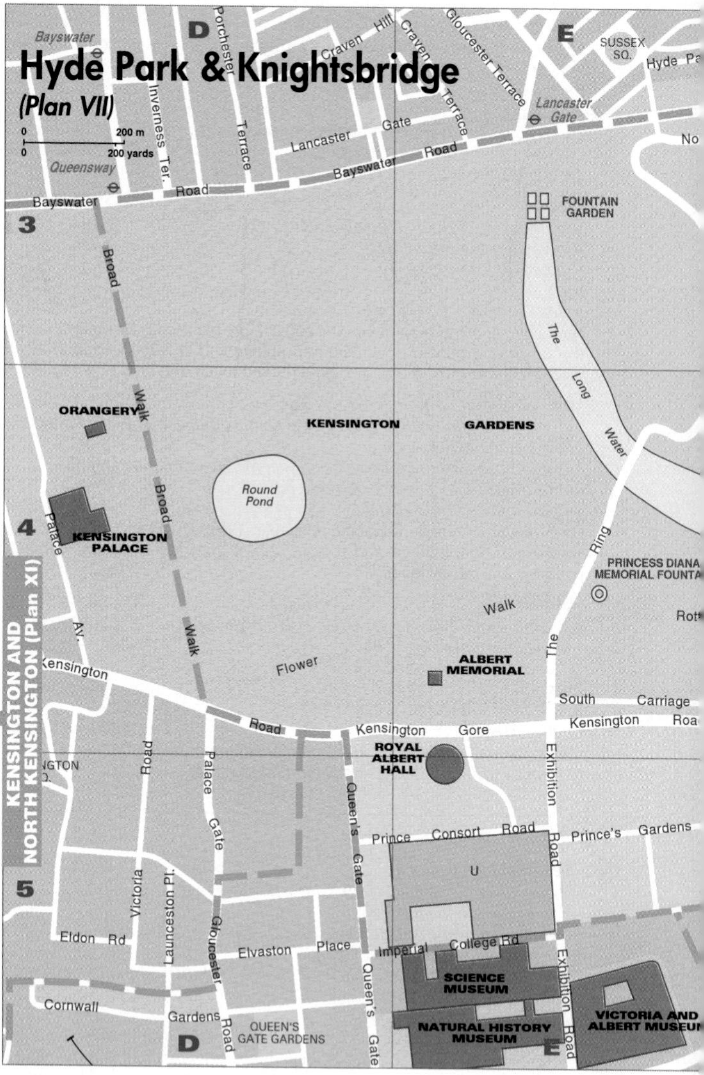

0 ———— 200 m
0 ———— 200 yards

KENSINGTON AND NORTH KENSINGTON (Plan XI)

D | **E**

SUSSEX SQ.

Hyde Pa

Bayswater

Porchester

Craven Hill

Craven

Gloucester Terrace

Inverness Ter.

Lancaster Gate

Lancaster Gate

Queensway

Bayswater Road

Bayswater

Broad Walk

3

No

FOUNTAIN GARDEN

The Long Water

ORANGERY

KENSINGTON **GARDENS**

Round Pond

4

Palace

KENSINGTON PALACE

Broad Walk

Ring

PRINCESS DIANA MEMORIAL FOUNTA

Rot

Kensington Av.

Flower Walk

Walk

ALBERT MEMORIAL

The

South Carriage

Kensington Gore

Kensington Road

South Kensington Roa

ROYAL ALBERT HALL

Exhibition

5

Victoria

Launceston Pl.

Palace Gate

Gloucester

Queen's Gate

Prince Consort Road

Prince's Gardens

U

Prince's

Road

Eldon Rd

Elvaston Place

Imperial College Rd

Exhibition

SCIENCE MUSEUM

Cornwall

Gardens

QUEEN'S GATE GARDENS

Queen's Gate

NATURAL HISTORY MUSEUM

VICTORIA AND ALBERT MUSEUM

D | **E**

Colonnade without rest   AC 🛜 VISA ⊕ AE ①

2 Warrington Cres ⊠ W9 1ER – Ⓜ Warwick Avenue – ℰ (020) 72861052
– www.theetoncollection.co.uk   Plan I **B2**

43 rm – �$\dagger$£ 125/295 �$\dagger\dagger$£ 138/335, ☲ £ 15.50

♦ Townhouse ♦ Classic ♦

Former hospital in quiet yet easily accessible location. Bedrooms range in size according to grade; all are comfortable and classically furnished with good amenities. Lower floor bar.

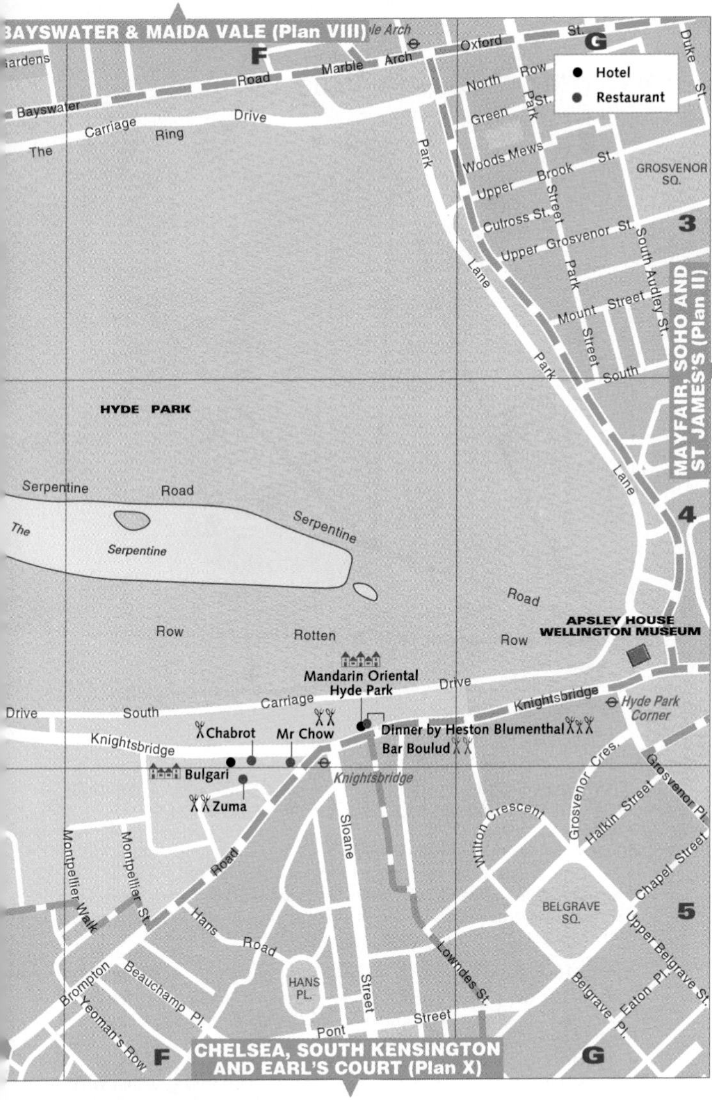
BAYSWATER & MAIDA VALE (Plan VIII)
MAYFAIR, SOHO AND ST JAMES'S (Plan II)
CHELSEA, SOUTH KENSINGTON AND EARL'S COURT (Plan X)
F
G
3
4
5
● Hotel
● Restaurant
HYDE PARK
Bayswater Road
Marble Arch
Oxford St.
North Row
Green St.
Park St.
Woods Mews
Upper Brook St.
Culross St.
Upper Grosvenor St.
Park Street
Mount Street
South Audley St.
South St.
Duke St.
GROSVENOR SQ.
Park Lane
The Ring
Carriage Drive
Serpentine Road
The Serpentine
Serpentine Road
Rotten Row
APSLEY HOUSE WELLINGTON MUSEUM
Mandarin Oriental Hyde Park
South Carriage Drive
Knightsbridge
Hyde Park Corner
Chabrot
Mr Chow
Dinner by Heston Blumenthal
Bar Boulud
Bulgari
Zuma
Knightsbridge
Brompton Road
Montpellier Walk
Montpellier St.
Hans Road
HANS PL.
Sloane Street
Lowndes St.
Pont Street
Beauchamp Pl.
Yeoman's Row
Wilton Crescent
Grosvenor Cres.
Halkin Street
Grosvenor Pl.
Chapel Street
BELGRAVE SQ.
Upper Belgrave St.
Belgrave Pl.
Eaton Pl.

🏘	**Royal Park** without rest ❄ 📶 🅿 VISA ⊙ AE
	3 Westbourne Terr ✉ W2 3UL – Ⓜ Lancaster Gate – ✆ (020) 74796600 – www.theroyalpark.com **E2/3**
	45 rm – 🚹£ 202/286 🚹🚹£ 202/286, ☕ £ 17 – 3 suites
	◆ Townhouse ◆ Cosy ◆ Stylish ◆
	Three attractive 19C townhouses set back from the road, in a pleasant location near Hyde Park. Quiet lounges with period furnishings. Breakfast served in the well-appointed bedrooms.

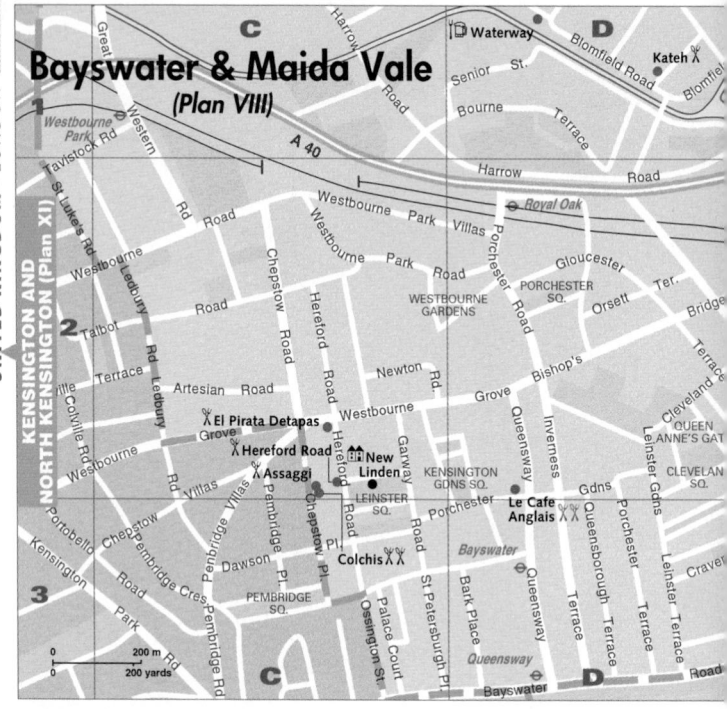

New Linden without rest

🏠 📶 VISA 🞄🞄 AE

59 Leinster Sq. ✉ W2 4PS – Ⓜ Bayswater – ℰ (020) 72214321
– www.newlinden.com
50 rm ⌂ – ♦£ 89/160 ♦♦£ 115/250

C2

♦ Family ♦ Functional ♦ Modern ♦

Smart four-storey white stucco façade. Basement breakfast room opens onto
summer courtyard. Bedrooms are its strength: flat screen TVs and wooden
floors; two split-level family rooms.

Le Café Anglais

XX

AC VISA 🞄🞄 AE

8 Porchester Gdns ✉ W2 4BD – Ⓜ Bayswater – ℰ (020) 72211415
– www.lecafeanglais.co.uk – Closed 25-26 December and 1 January
Rest – Menu £ 23/27 – Carte £ 31/48

D2

♦ Modern ♦ Elegant ♦ Brasserie ♦

Big, bustling and contemporary brasserie with art deco styling, within White-
ley's shopping centre. Large, appealing selection of classic brasserie food; the
rotisserie is the centrepiece. More casual oyster bar by entrance.

Angelus

XX

AC ⇔ VISA 🞄🞄 AE

4 Bathurst St. ✉ W2 2SD – Ⓜ Lancaster Gate – ℰ (020) 74020083
– www.angelusrestaurant.co.uk – Closed 24 December-2 January
Rest – Menu £ 20 (lunch) – Carte £ 40/56

E3

♦ French ♦ Brasserie ♦

Hospitable owner has created an attractive French brasserie within a 19C former pub, with a warm and inclusive feel. Satisfying and honest French cooking
uses seasonal British ingredients.

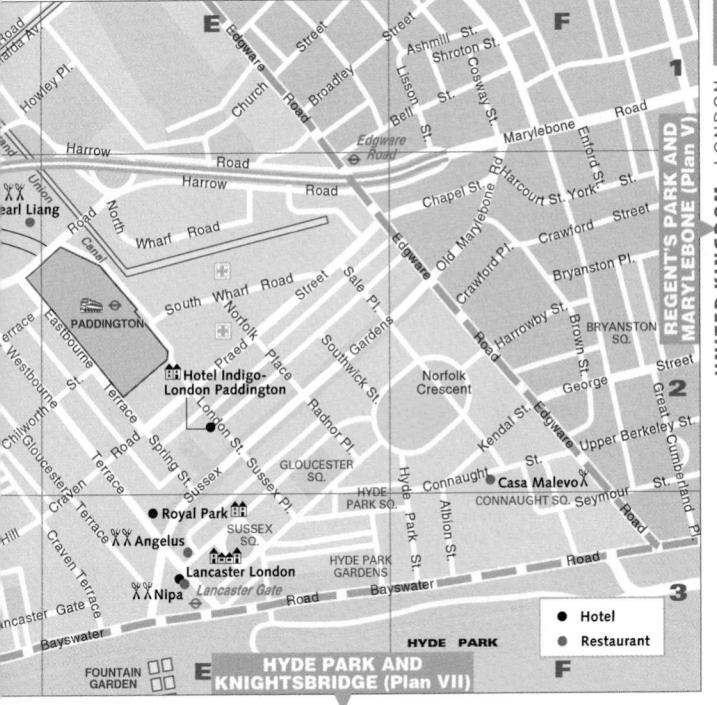

XX **Nipa** – Lancaster London Hotel   AC P VISA ©© AE ①

Lancaster Terr ⊠ *W2 2TY* – Ⓜ *Lancaster Gate* – ℰ *(020) 75516039*
– www.niparestaurant.co.uk
– Closed Christmas-NewYear, Saturday lunch and Sunday   **E3**
Rest – Menu £ 13/29 – Carte £ 23/32

♦ Thai ♦ Exotic ♦

On the 1st floor and overlooking Hyde Park. Authentic and ornately decorated
restaurant offers subtly spiced Thai cuisine. Keen to please staff in traditional silk
costumes.

XX **Pearl Liang**   AC ⇔ VISA ©© AE

8 Sheldon Sq., Paddington Central ⊠ *W2 6EZ* – Ⓜ *Paddington* – ℰ *(020)*
72897000 – *www.pearlliang.co.uk* – *Closed 24 and 25 December*
Rest – Menu £ 25/38 – Carte £ 12/53   **D2**

♦ Chinese ♦ Minimalist ♦

Spacious, business-orientated Chinese restaurant within a corporate development. Extensive choice from a variety of set menus; try the more unusual dishes
like jellyfish or pig's trotter.

XX **Colchis**   🐧 AC VISA ©© AE

39 Chepstow Pl. ⊠ *W2 4TS* – Ⓜ *Bayswater* – ℰ *(020) 72217620*
– www.colchisrestaurant.co.uk – *Closed Christmas-New Year and Monday*
Rest – Carte £ 21/35   **C2**

♦ Other world kitchens ♦ Neighbourhood ♦ Friendly ♦

Hearty Georgian cooking, with its Med and Middle Eastern influences, is celebrated at this former pub. Start with khachapuri (leavened bread with cheese)
or lobio mchadit (red kidney bean stew) and then share shashlyk (kebabs).

915

Hereford Road ⛄ AC VISA ◉◉ AE

3 Hereford Rd. ✉ *W2 4AB* – **Ⓜ** *Bayswater* – ✆ *(020) 77271144*
– www.herefordroad.org
– Closed 24 December-3 January and 27-29 August **C2**
Rest *– (booking essential)* Menu £ 16 (weekday lunch) – Carte £ 20/29
♦ British modern ♦ Neighbourhood ♦
Converted butcher's shop specialising in tasty British dishes without
frills, using first-rate, seasonal ingredients; offal a highlight. Booths for six people
are the prized seats. Friendly and relaxed feel.

Assaggi AC VISA ◉◉

39 Chepstow Pl, (1st Floor) ✉ *W2 4TS* – **Ⓜ** *Bayswater* – ✆ *(020) 77925501*
– Closed 2 weeks Christmas, Sunday and bank holidays **C2**
Rest *– (booking essential)* Carte £ 41/54
♦ Italian ♦ Rustic ♦ Friendly ♦
The pared-down simplicity to this room works well; regulars are given fulsome
welcomes and the atmosphere is great. Cooking puts the focus on the quality of
the ingredients and the wine list is exclusively Italian.

Casa Malevo AC ⇔ VISA ◉◉ AE

23 Connaught St ✉ *W2 2AY* – **Ⓜ** *Marble Arch* – ✆ *(020) 74021988*
– www.casamalevo.com **F2**
Rest *–* Menu £ 15 (weekday lunch) – Carte £ 19/41
♦ Argentinian ♦ Neighbourhood ♦
Carnivores will be in clover at this friendly Argentinian restaurant, with its bare
brick walls and intimate lighting. Most come for the grilled Argentine beef,
accompanied by a bottle of Malbec.

El Pirata De Tapas AC VISA ◉◉ AE

115 Westbourne Grove ✉ *W2 4UP* – **Ⓜ** *Bayswater* – ✆ *(020) 77275000*
– www.elpiratadetapas.co.uk
– Closed 24-26 December, 26-27 August and 1 January **C2**
Rest *–* Menu £ 10/25 – Carte £ 19/25
♦ Spanish ♦ Tapas bar ♦
Contemporary yet warm Spanish restaurant with a genuine neighbourhood
feel. Authentic flavours from a well-priced and appealing selection of tapas,
ideal for sharing with friends.

Kateh ⛄ AC VISA ◉◉ AE

5 Warwick Pl ✉ *W9 2PX* – **Ⓜ** *Warwick Avenue* – ✆ *(020) 7289 3393*
– www.kateh.net **D1**
Rest *– (dinner only and lunch Friday-Sunday) (booking essential)*
Carte £ 20/27
♦ Other world kitchens ♦ Neighbourhood ♦ Intimate ♦
Booking is imperative if you want to join the locals who have already discovered
what a little jewel they have in the form of this buzzy, busy Persian restaurant.
Authentic stews, expert chargrilling and lovely pastries and teas.

Prince Alfred & Formosa Dining Room AC ⇔

5A Formosa St ✉ *W9 1EE* – **Ⓜ** *Warwick Avenue.* VISA ◉◉ AE
– ✆ (020) 72863287 – www.theprincealfred.com *Plan I* **B2**
Rest *–* Menu £ 12/16 – Carte £ 24/47
♦ Modern ♦ Pub ♦ Neighbourhood ♦
Characterful and classic Victorian pub, with a large, more modern dining room
in side extension. Open kitchen and a mix of British specialities and European
classics. Friendly service.

Waterway ⟨ ⛄ AC P VISA ◉◉ AE ◉

54 Formosa St ✉ *W9 2JU* – **Ⓜ** *Warwick Avenue.* – ✆ *(020) 72663557*
– www.thewaterway.co.uk **D1**
Rest *–* Carte £ 23/34
♦ Modern ♦ Pub ♦
Terrific decked terrace by the canal its most appealing feature. Contemporary
interior with busy cocktail bar; menu in separate dining room mixes the classics
with more ambitious dishes.

CITY OF LONDON

Andaz Liverpool Street   *Ĺǎ ⅋ rm, ⒶⒸ ⎙ ⅍ ⓋⓈⒶ ⬤⬤ ⒶⒺ ⓪*
40 Liverpool St. ⊠ EC2M 7QN – Ⓜ Liverpool Street – ℰ (020) 79611234
– www.andazdining.com   **M2**
264 rm – ⚈£ 105/330 ⚈⚈£ 135/360, ⚍ £ 24 – 3 suites
Rest *1901*
Rest *Catch* – see restaurant listing
Rest *Miyako* – ℰ (020) 76187100 (Closed Christmas, Saturday lunch and
Sunday) (booking essential) Carte £ 22/46
♦ Business ♦ Design ♦
A contemporary and stylish interior hides behind the classic Victorian
façade. Bright and spacious bedrooms with state-of-the-art facilities. Various
dining options include Miyako, a compact Japanese restaurant, and a traditional
pub.

Threadneedles   *⅋ ⒶⒸ ⎙ ⅍ ⓋⓈⒶ ⬤⬤ ⒶⒺ ⓪*
5 Threadneedle St. ⊠ EC2R 8AY – Ⓜ Bank – ℰ (020) 7657 8088
– www.theetoncollection.co.uk   **M3**
73 rm – ⚈£ 150/630 ⚈⚈£ 125/630, ⚍ £ 25 – 1 suite
Rest *Bonds* – see restaurant listing
♦ Business ♦ Modern ♦
A converted bank, dating from 1856, with a stunning stained-glass cupola in the
lounge. Bedrooms are very stylish and individual, featuring Egyptian cotton
sheets and thoughtful extras.

Apex Temple Court   *Ĺǎ ⅋ rm, ⒶⒸ ⎙ ⓋⓈⒶ ⬤⬤ ⒶⒺ ⓪*
1-2 Serjeant's Inn, Fleet St ⊠ EC4Y 1LL – Ⓜ Blackfriars – ℰ (020)
3004 4141 – www.apexhotels.co.uk   **K3**
184 rm – ⚈£ 156/348 ⚈⚈£ 156/492, ⚍ £ 20
Rest *Chambers* – Menu £ 20 – Carte £ 22/38
♦ Business ♦ Chain hotel ♦ Contemporary ♦
Former law firm office transformed into a smart, up-to-date hotel. Decently
sized bedrooms: even standard rooms have a seating area and large bathrooms. Chambers is a contemporary brasserie with adjoining busy cocktail bar.

Montcalm London City at The Brewery   *⅋ ⒶⒸ ⎙ ⅍*
52 Chiswell St ⊠ EC1Y 4SD – Ⓜ Barbican   *ⓋⓈⒶ ⬤⬤ ⒶⒺ ⓪*
– ℰ (020) 7614 0100 – www.themontcalmlondoncity.co.uk   **M2**
217 rm – ⚈£ 200/300 ⚈⚈£ 200/300, ⚍ £ 25 – 18 suites
Rest *Chiswell Street Dining Rooms* – see restaurant listing
♦ Business ♦ Stylish ♦
The majority of the contemporary rooms are in the original part of the Whitbread Brewery, built in 1752; ask for a quieter room overlooking the courtyard,
or one of the 25 found in one of the 4 restored Georgian townhouses across the
road.

Hotel Indigo London - Tower Hill   *⅋ rm, ⒶⒸ ⎙ ⓋⓈⒶ ⬤⬤ ⒶⒺ*
142 Minories ⊠ EC3N 1LS – Ⓜ Aldgate – ℰ (020) 7265 1014
– www.hotelindigo.com/lontowerhill   **N3**
46 rm – ⚈£ 119/395 ⚈⚈£ 119/395, ⚍ £ 17   **Rest** – Carte £ 22/35
♦ Business ♦ Modern ♦ Design ♦
Quieter than its city location would suggest, this business hotel comes with
funky modern bedrooms equipped with iPod docks and coffee machines.
Tower Bridge and Tower Hill suites have skyline views. Popular menu in Square
Mile brasserie.

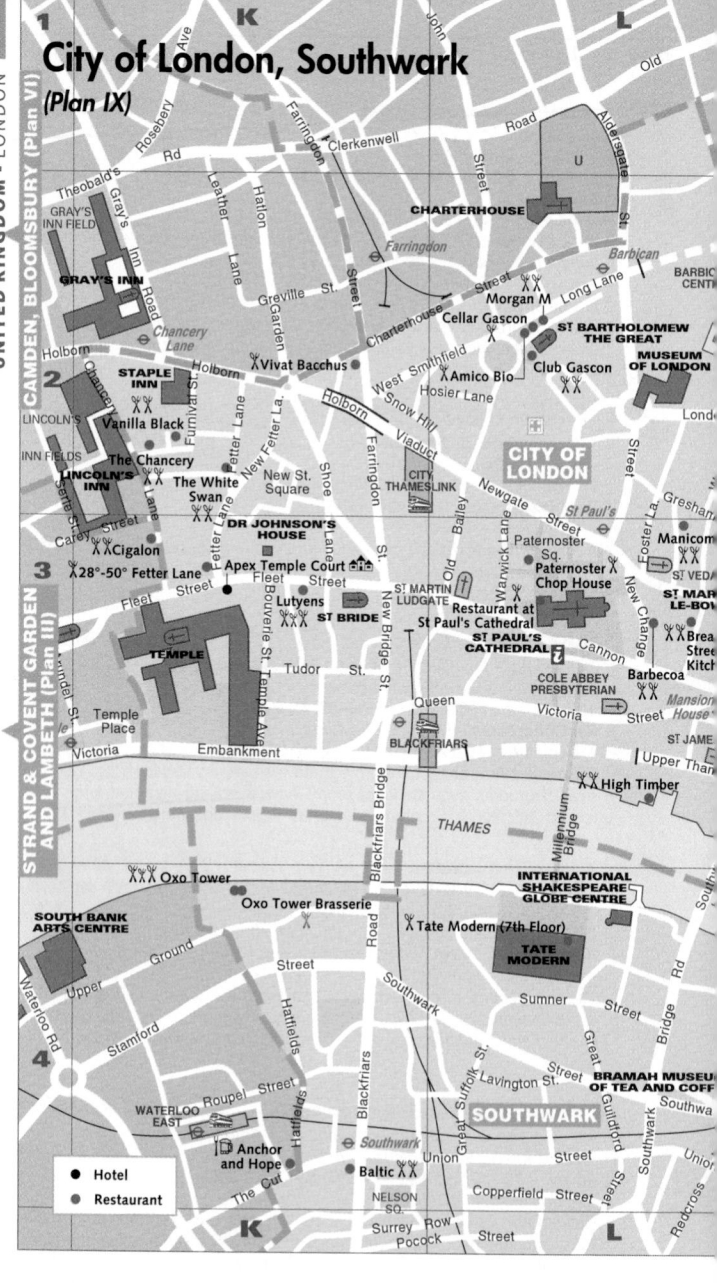

City of London, Southwark
(Plan IX)

UNITED KINGDOM - LONDON

CAMDEN, BLOOMSBURY (Plan VI)

STRAND & COVENT GARDEN AND LAMBETH (Plan III)

1

K

John

Rosebery Ave

Old

Road

Aldersgate

Clerkenwell

Farringdon

U

Theobald's Rd

Leather Lane

Hatton

CHARTERHOUSE

Barbican

GRAY'S INN FIELD

Gray's Inn Road

GRAY'S INN

Greville St.

Garden

Long Lane

BARBIC CENTF

Farringdon

Charterhouse Street

Morgan M ✗✗

Cellar Gascon

St BARTHOLOMEW THE GREAT

MUSEUM OF LONDON

Holborn

STAPLE INN

Holborn

✗Vivat Bacchus

West Smithfield

Amico Bio ✗

Club Gascon ✗✗

Lond

2

LINCOLN'S

Furnival St.

Hosier Lane

Snow Hill

Holborn Viaduct

Farringdon

CITY OF LONDON

London

Vanilla Black

New Fetter La.

New St. Square

Shoe Lane

CITY THAMESLINK

Bailey

Newgate Street

St Paul's

Gresham

INN FIELDS

LINCOLN'S INN

The White Swan ✗✗

The Chancery ✗✗

Carey Street

DR JOHNSON'S HOUSE

Warwick Lane

St Paul's

Foster St.

Manicom

St VEDA

Serle St.

Chancery Lane

✗✗ Cigalon

Fetter Lane

Fleet Street

Apex Temple Court 🏨

New Change

St MAR LE-BOV

3

✗28°-50° Fetter Lane

Bouverie St.

Fleet Street

Lutyens ✗✗✗

St BRIDE

St MARTIN LUDGATE

New Bridge St.

Restaurant at St Paul's Cathedral

Paternoster Sq.

Paternoster ✗ Chop House

Cannon

✗✗ Brea Street Kitch

TEMPLE

Tudor St.

St PAUL'S CATHEDRAL

COLE ABBEY PRESBYTERIAN

Barbecoa ✗✗

Temple Place

Queen

Victoria Street

Mansion House

Victoria

Embankment

BLACKFRIARS

St JAME

Upper Thar

High Timber ✗✗

Blackfriars Bridge

THAMES

Millennium Bridge

4

✗✗✗ Oxo Tower

Oxo Tower Brasserie ✗

INTERNATIONAL SHAKESPEARE GLOBE CENTRE

South

SOUTH BANK ARTS CENTRE

Ground

Street

Tate Modern (7th Floor) ✗

TATE MODERN

Rd

Upper

Stamford

Hatfields

Southwark

Sumner

Street

Bridge

Blackfriars

Road

Great Suffolk St.

Lavington St.

Street

BRAMAH MUSEU OF TEA AND COFF

WATERLOO EAST

Roupel Street

SOUTHWARK

Guildford

Southwark

Union

Anchor and Hope ●

The Cut

Baltic ✗✗

Southwark

Street

Copperfield Street

Street

Redcross

NELSON SQ.

Surrey Row

Pocock Street

● Hotel

● Restaurant

K

L

918

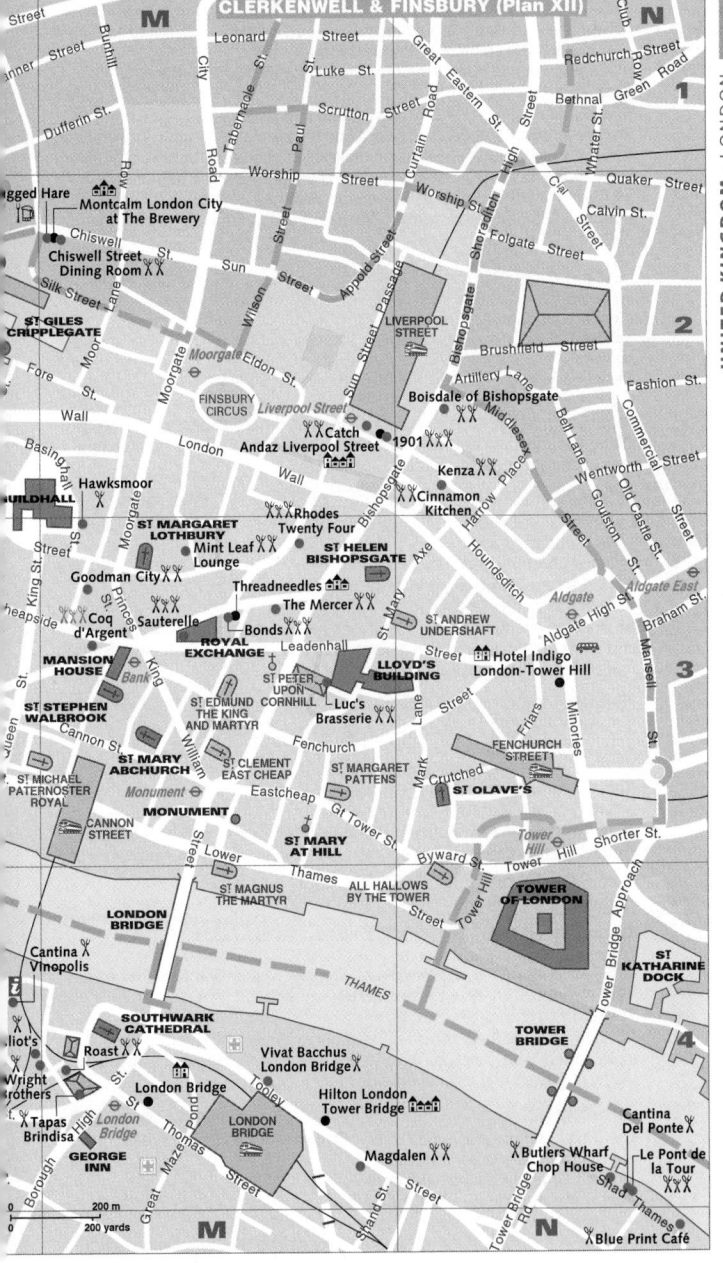

UNITED KINGDOM - LONDON

XXX ✿
Rhodes Twenty Four   ◁ AC ⇄ VISA ⬤ AE ⓪

Tower 42, (24th floor) 25 Old Broad St ✉ EC2N 1HQ – ⓜ Liverpool Street
– ☏ (020) 78777703 – www.rhodes24.co.uk
– Closed Christmas-New Year, Saturday, Sunday and bank holidays
Rest – Carte £ 38/64   M3
♦ **British modern** ♦ **Formal** ♦ **Intimate** ♦

Prepare for security checks at Tower 42 before taking the lift up to its 24th floor; the views will be worth it. The unmistakeable signature of Gary Rhodes is writ large on the menu: seasonal dishes of a pleasingly British persuasion.
→ Glazed lobster omelette thermidor. Steamed mutton and onion suet pudding with buttered carrots. Rhodes Twenty Four signature pudding plate.

XXX
Coq d'Argent   ◁ 🍴 AC 🐾 VISA ⬤ AE ⓪

1 Poultry ✉ EC2R 8EJ – ⓜ Bank – ☏ (020) 73955000
– www.coqdargent.co.uk
– Closed 25-27 December, 1 January, Saturday lunch, Sunday dinner and bank holidays   M3
Rest – (booking essential) Menu £ 28 – Carte £ 34/58
♦ **French** ♦ **Design** ♦

Resembling the bow of a ship; with a busy bar, terrace and formal garden providing commanding views over the Square Mile. Slick, well-run, modern restaurant; appealing shellfish counter.

XXX
1901 – Andaz Liverpool Street Hotel   AC ⇄ VISA ⬤ AE ⓪

Liverpool St. ✉ EC2M 7QN – ⓜ Liverpool Street – ☏ (020) 76187000
– www.andaz.com
– Closed Christmas, Saturday lunch and Sunday   M2
Rest – Menu £ 25 (lunch) – Carte £ 34/51
♦ **French** ♦ **Elegant** ♦

An impressive and imposing room, with an eye-catching cupola, cocktail bar and cheese and wine room. Kitchen makes proud use of British ingredients in refined and skilled cooking.

XXX
Bonds – Threadneedles Hotel   AC ⇄ VISA ⬤ AE ⓪

5 Threadneedle St. ✉ EC2R 8AY – ⓜ Bank – ☏ (020) 76578088
– www.bonds-restaurant.com
– Closed Saturday, Sunday and bank holidays   M3
Rest – Menu £ 24 (lunch) – Carte £ 29/55
♦ **Modern** ♦ **Retro** ♦ **Luxury** ♦

Former banking hall from the 1850s, with pillars, marble and panelling. Experienced kitchen produces dishes with bold flavours; fish from Newhaven and slow-cooked meats the specialities.

XXX
Lutyens   AC ⇄ VISA ⬤ AE

85 Fleet St. ✉ EC4Y 1AE – ⓜ St Paul's – ☏ (020) 7583 8385
– www.lutyens-restaurant.com
– Closed 1 week Christmas-New Year, Saturday, Sunday and bank holidays
Rest – Menu £ 26/22 – Carte £ 28/61   K3
♦ **Modern** ♦ **Fashionable** ♦

The unmistakable hand of Sir Terence Conran: timeless and understated good looks mixed with functionality and an appealing Anglo-French menu with plenty of classics that include fruits de mer.

XXX
Sauterelle   🛇 AC ⇄ VISA ⬤ AE ⓪

The Royal Exchange ✉ EC3V 3LR – ⓜ Bank – ☏ (020) 76182483
– www.sauterelle-restaurant.co.uk
– Closed Saturday, Sunday and bank holidays,   M3
Rest – Menu £ 20/35 – Carte £ 33/55
♦ **French** ♦ **Design** ♦

Impressive location on the mezzanine floor of The Royal Exchange; ask for a table looking down over the Grand Café. A largely French-inspired contemporary menu makes good use of luxury ingredients.

MICHELIN Maps & Guides
Make the most of your journey!

WHERE TO GO?

WHERE TO SLEEP?

WHERE TO EAT?

WHAT TO VISIT?

AT WHAT PRICE?

http://travel.michelin.co.uk
www.ViaMichelin.com
www.travel.ViaMichelin.com

Make the most of your visit
with MICHELIN Green Guides!

Club Gascon (Pascal Aussignac) 🕏 🗚 🆚 ⓒⓔ AE

57 West Smithfield ⊠ EC1A 9DS – Ⓜ Barbican – ℰ (020) 77960600
– www.clubgascon.com
– Closed Christmas - New Year, Saturday lunch, Sunday and bank holidays
Rest – *(booking essential)* Menu £ 25/65 – Carte £ 40/50 ☕   **L2**
◆ French ◆ Intimate ◆ Elegant ◆
The gastronomy of Gascony and France's southwest are the starting points but
the assured and intensely flavoured cooking also pushes at the boundaries.
Marble and huge floral displays create suitably atmospheric surroundings.
→ Braised snails with tulip and wild fennel infusion. Langoustine and squid
with saffron pearls and pig's trotter. Turrón and foie gras macaroon.

Bread Street Kitchen 🗚 🆚 ⓒⓔ AE ⓞ

10 Bread St ⊠ EC4M 9AJ – Ⓜ St Paul's – ℰ (020) 3030 4050
– www.breadstreetkitchen.com
– Closed 25 December   **L3**
Rest – *(booking advisable)* Carte £ 27/59
◆ Modern ◆ Trendy ◆ Brasserie ◆
Gordon Ramsay's take on NY loft-style dining comes with a large bar, thumping
music, an open kitchen and enough zinc ducting to kit out a small industrial
estate. For the food, think modern bistro dishes with an element of refinement.

The Chancery 🗚 ⇄ 🆚 ⓒⓔ AE ⓞ

9 Cursitor St ⊠ EC4A 1LL – Ⓜ Chancery Lane – ℰ (020) 78314000
– www.thechancery.co.uk
– Closed 24 December-4 January, Saturday lunch and Sunday   **K2**
Rest – Menu £ 35
◆ Modern ◆ Formal ◆ Neighbourhood ◆
An elegant restaurant that's so close to the law courts you'll assume your fellow
diners are barristers, jurors, or the recently acquitted. The menu is appealing
concise; dishes come with a classical backbone and bold flavours.

Mint Leaf Lounge 🗚 🆚 ⓒⓔ AE

12 Angel Ct., Lothbury ⊠ EC2R 7HB – Ⓜ Bank – ℰ (020) 76000992
– www.mintleaflounge.com
– Closed 22 December-3 January, Saturday lunch and Sunday   **M3**
Rest – Menu £ 18 (lunch) – Carte £ 29/51
◆ Indian ◆ Design ◆ Fashionable ◆
Sister branch to the original in St James's. Slick and stylish, with busy bar. Well-
paced service of carefully prepared contemporary Indian food, with many of the
influences from the south.

Vanilla Black 🕏 🗚 🆚 ⓒⓔ AE

17-18 Tooks Ct. ⊠ EC4A 1LB – Ⓜ Chancery Lane – ℰ (020) 72422622
– www.vanillablack.co.uk
– Closed 2 weeks Christmas-New Year, Saturday lunch and Sunday
Rest – Menu £ 19/35   **K2**
◆ Vegetarian ◆ Minimalist ◆
Proving that vegetarian food can be flavoursome and satisfying, with a menu
that is varied and imaginative. This is a well-run, friendly restaurant with under-
stated décor, run by a husband and wife team.

Cinnamon Kitchen 🍴 🗚 ⇄ 🆚 ⓒⓔ AE ⓞ

9 Devonshire Sq ⊠ EC2M 4YL – Ⓜ Liverpool Street – ℰ (020) 72222555
– www.cinnamonclub.com
– Closed Sunday and bank holidays   **N2**
Rest – Menu £ 15/75 – Carte £ 20/44
◆ Indian ◆ Friendly ◆ Wine bar ◆
Sister to The Cinnamon Club. Contemporary Indian cooking, with punchy fla-
vours and arresting presentation. Sprightly service in large, modern surroun-
dings. Watch the action from the Tandoor Bar.

UNITED KINGDOM - LONDON

XX **Kenza** 🔲 ⇔ 𝚟𝚒𝚜𝚊 ⬤ 🄰🄴 ⓘ

10 Devonshire Sq. ✉ *EC2M 4YP –* Ⓜ *Liverpool Street –* ✆ *(020) 79295533*
– www.kenza-restaurant.com
– Closed Saturday lunch, Sunday and bank holidays   **N2**
Rest – Menu £ 21 (lunch) – Carte £ 15/30
♦ Lebanese ♦ Exotic ♦ Romantic ♦
Exotic basement restaurant, with lamps, carvings, pumping music and nightly belly dancing. Lebanese and Moroccan cooking are the menu influences and the food is authentic and accurate.

XX **Cigalon** 🔲 ⇔ 𝚟𝚒𝚜𝚊 ⬤ 🄰🄴

115 Chancery Ln ✉ *WC2A 1PP –* Ⓜ *Chancery Lane –* ✆ *(020) 7242 8373*
– www.cigalon.co.uk
– Closed 24 December-2 January, Saturday, Sunday and bank holidays
Rest – Menu £ 20/25 – Carte £ 21/43   **K3**
♦ French ♦ Intimate ♦ Formal ♦
Pays homage to the food and wine of Provence, in an appropriately bright space that was a once an auction house. All the classics are here, from bouillabaisse to pieds et paquets. Busy bar in the cellar.

XX **The Mercer** 🔲 ⇔ 𝚟𝚒𝚜𝚊 ⬤ 🄰🄴

34 Threadneedle St ✉ *EC2R 8AY –* Ⓜ *Bank –* ✆ *(020) 76280001*
– www.themercer.co.uk
– Closed 25 December, Saturday, Sunday and bank holidays   **M3**
Rest – Menu £ 39/49 – Carte £ 26/40 𝄞
♦ Modern ♦ Brasserie ♦
Converted bank, with airy feel thanks to high ceilings and large windows. Brasserie-style menu with appealing mix of classics and comfort food. Huge choice of wines available by glass or carafe.

XX **Boisdale of Bishopsgate** 🔲 𝚟𝚒𝚜𝚊 ⬤ 🄰🄴

Swedeland Crt., 202 Bishopsgate ✉ *EC2M 4NR –* Ⓜ *Liverpool Street*
– ✆ *(020) 72831763 – www.boisdale.com*
– Closed Christmas, bank holidays, Saturday and Sunday
Rest – Menu £ 20 – Carte £ 25/74   **N2**
♦ Regional ♦ Intimate ♦ Cosy ♦
It's champagne and oysters on the ground floor and Scottish hospitality in the characterful vaulted cellar below. Enjoy smoked salmon, roast haggis and 28-day dry aged cuts of beef, along with live jazz most nights.

XX **The White Swan** 🔲 𝚟𝚒𝚜𝚊 ⬤ 🄰🄴

108 Fetter Ln ✉ *EC4A 1ES –* Ⓜ *Chancery Lane –* ✆ *(020) 72429696*
– www.thewhiteswanlondon.com
– Closed 25-26 December, Saturday, Sunday and bank holidays
Rest – Menu £ 16/36 – Carte £ 26/39   **K2**
♦ Modern ♦ Pub ♦ Neighbourhood ♦
Smart dining room above pub just off Fleet Street: mirrored ceilings, colourful paintings on walls. Modern, daily changing menus are good value for the heart of London.

XX **Manicomio** 🔲 𝚟𝚒𝚜𝚊 ⬤ 🄰🄴

6 Gutter Ln. ✉ *EC2V 8AS –* Ⓜ *St Paul's –* ✆ *(020) 77265010*
– www.manicomio.co.uk
– Closed 1 week Christmas, Saturday, Sunday and bank holidays
Rest – Carte £ 27/51   **L3**
♦ Italian ♦ Brasserie ♦
Second branch to follow the first in Chelsea. Regional Italian fare, with top-notch ingredients. Bright and fresh first floor restaurant, with deli-café on the ground floor and bar on top floor.

XX **Luc's Brasserie** VISA ⦿ AE

17-22 Leadenhall Mkt ✉ *EC3V 1LR –* Ⓜ *Bank –* ✆ *(020) 76210666*
– www.lucsbrasserie.com
– Closed 24 December-2 January, Saturday, Sunday and bank holidays
Rest *– (lunch only and dinner Tuesday-Thursday) (booking* **M3**
essential at lunch) Menu £ 18 – Carte £ 25/64
♦ French ♦ Brasserie ♦
Looks down on the Victorian splendour of Leadenhall Market. First appeared in
1890 but re-invigorated this century. The menu is a paean to all things French
and every classic dish is there.

XX **Barbecoa** AC VISA ⦿ AE

20 New Change Passage ✉ *EC4M 9AG –* Ⓜ *St Paul's –* ✆ *(020) 3005 8555*
– www.barbecoa.com
– Closed 25-26 December **L2**
Rest *– (booking essential) Carte £ 30/95*
♦ Meats and grills ♦ Design ♦ Brasserie ♦
Set up by American chef Adam Perry Lane, in collaboration with our own Jamie
Oliver, to show us what barbecuing is all about. The prime meats, butchered in-
house, are just great; go for the pulled pork shoulder with cornbread on the
side.

XX **High Timber** ⟨ 🏠 AC ⟺ VISA ⦿ AE ⓪

8 High Timber St. ✉ *EC4V 3PA –* Ⓜ *Mansion House –* ✆ *(020) 72481777*
– www.hightimber.com – Closed 25-30 December, 1-4 January, Saturday
dinner, Sunday and bank holidays **L3**
Rest *– Menu £ 17 (lunch) – Carte £ 26/55*
♦ Modern ♦ Rustic ♦
Rustic look to the room, despite being in a modern block, offering river views.
Great wine cellar, with large choice from South Africa, the owners' homeland.
Cumbrian steaks the speciality.

XX **Goodman City** AC ⟺ VISA ⦿ AE

11 Old Jewry ✉ *EC2R 8DU –* Ⓜ *Bank –* ✆ *(020) 7600 8220*
– www.goodmanrestaurants.com
– Closed Saturday, Sunday and bank holidays **M3**
Rest *– Menu £ 22 (lunch) – Carte £ 28/77*
♦ Meats and grills ♦ Design ♦ Bistro ♦
Steaks, cut to order, are the stars of the show at this sister to the Mayfair original.
Choose corn-fed, wet-matured USDA beef or Scottish and Irish grass-fed; plenty
of side dishes available too.

XX **Chiswell Street Dining Rooms** – Montcalm London City

56 Chiswell St ✉ *EC1Y 4SA –* Ⓜ *Barbican* AC VISA ⦿ AE
– ✆ *(020) 7614 0177 – www.chiswellstreetdining.com* **M2**
Rest *– Carte £ 30/52*
♦ British modern ♦ Wine bar ♦ Brasserie ♦
The Martin brothers used their Botanist restaurant as the model for this corner
of the old Whitbread Brewery. The cocktail bar comes alive at night. Makes
good use of British produce, especially fish from nearby Billingsgate.

XX **Catch** – Andaz Liverpool Street Hotel AC VISA ⦿ AE ⓪

40 Liverpool St. ✉ *EC2M 7QN –* Ⓜ *Liverpool Street –* ✆ *(020) 76187200*
– www.andazdining.com
– Closed Christmas, Easter, Saturday and Sunday **M2**
Rest *– Menu £ 25 – Carte £ 36/49*
♦ Fish and seafood ♦ Brasserie ♦ Cosy ♦
Catch has been fashioned out of a cordoned off corner of the Andaz hotel's
ground floor, in what was the original hotel entrance. The best dishes are the
simplest, like home-cured salmon, Dover sole and the excellent oysters.

UNITED KINGDOM - LONDON

UNITED KINGDOM - LONDON

Morgan M
　　🍴🍴　　　　　　　　　　　　　🎐⁉️ 🅥 💳 ⊕ Æ

50 Long Ln ✉ *EC1A 9EJ –* Ⓜ *Barbican – ℰ (020) 7609 3560*
– www.morganm.com
– Closed 24-30 December, Saturday lunch and Sunday　　　　　　　**L2**
Rest – Menu £ 26 (lunch and early dinner) – Carte £ 41/51
♦ French ♦ Intimate ♦ Romantic ♦
Morgan Meunier, a proud Frenchman from the Champagne region, moved here late 2011 from his long-standing Islington locale. His bold cooking and formal restaurant keep things in a classical vein; popular vegetarian menu.

Amico Bio
　　🍴　　　　　　　　　　　　　　　🅥 🄰🄲 💳 ⊕ Æ

44 Cloth Fair ✉ *EC1A 7JQ –* Ⓜ *Barbican – ℰ (0207) 6007778*
– www.amicobio.co.uk
– Closed 25 December, Saturday lunch, Sunday and bank holidays
Rest – Menu £ 18 – Carte approx. £ 22　　　　　　　　　**L2**
♦ Vegetarian ♦ Friendly ♦ Neighbourhood ♦
Simple little place owned by an experienced chef and his cousin; the organic produce comes from the family farm in Capua and the combination of flavours remain true to their upbringing in Campania.

Vivat Bacchus
　　🍴　　　　　　　　　　　　　　　🄰🄲 ⇔ 💳 ⊕ Æ

47 Farringdon St ✉ *EC4A 4LL –* Ⓜ *Farringdon – ℰ (020) 73532648*
– www.vivatbacchus.co.uk
– Closed Christmas and New Year, Saturday, Sunday and bank holidays
Rest – Menu £ 15/19 – Carte £ 22/50 ⅋　　　　　　　**K2**
♦ Other world kitchens ♦ Wine bar ♦ Friendly ♦
Wine is the star at this bustling City spot: from 4 cellars come 500 labels and 15,000 bottles. The menu complements the wine: steaks, charcuterie, sharing platters and South African specialities feature along with great cheese.

Hawksmoor
　　🍴　　　　　　　　　　　　　　　🄰🄲 ⇔ 💳 ⊕ Æ

10-12 Basinghall St ✉ *EC2V 5BQ –* Ⓜ *Bank – ℰ (020) 7397 8120*
– www.thehawksmoor.com
– Closed 22 December-2 January, Saturday, Sunday and bank holidays
Rest – (booking essential) Carte £ 39/62 ⅋　　　　　　**M3**
♦ Meats and grills ♦ Traditional ♦ Brasserie ♦
Fast and furious, busy and boisterous, this handsome room is the backdrop for another testosterone filled celebration of the serious business of beef eating. Nicely aged and rested Longhorn steaks take centre-stage.

Paternoster Chop House
　　🍴　　　　　　　　　　　　　　🌤 🄰🄲 💳 ⊕ Æ

Warwick Ct., Paternoster Sq. ✉ *EC4M 7DX –* Ⓜ *St Paul's – ℰ (020) 70299400 – www.paternosterchophouse.co.uk*
– Closed 22 December-2 January, Saturday, Sunday dinner and bank holidays
Rest – Menu £ 23 – Carte £ 30/49　　　　　　　　　　**L3**
♦ British traditional ♦ Brasserie ♦ Trendy ♦
Appropriately British menu in a restaurant lying in the shadow of St Paul's Cathedral. Large, open room with full-length windows; busy bar attached. Kitchen uses thoughtfully sourced produce.

Cellar Gascon
　　🍴　　　　　　　　　　　　　　　　🄰🄲 💳 ⊕ Æ

59 West Smithfield ✉ *EC1A 9DS –* Ⓜ *Barbican – ℰ (020) 7600 7561*
– www.cellargascon.com
– Closed Christmas-New Year, Saturday, Sunday and bank holidays
Rest – (booking essential at lunch) Menu £ 13 (lunch)　　　　**L2**
– Carte £ 18/26 ⅋
♦ French ♦ Tapas bar ♦
It's not unlike a smart tapas bar and the monthly changing menu has plenty of treats: pâtés, rillettes, hams, cheeses and even some salads for the virtuous; but the Toulouse sausages and the Gascony pie stand out.

28°-50° Fetter Lane

140 Fetter Ln ✉ EC4A 1BT – Ⓜ Temple – ✆ (020) 72428877
– www.2850.co.uk
– Closed Saturday, Sunday and bank holidays **K3**
Rest – Menu £ 16 (lunch) – Carte £ 27/35
♦ French ♦ Wine bar ♦ Simple ♦
From the owners of Texture comes this cellar wine bar and informal restaurant. The terrific wine list is thoughtfully compiled and the grills, cheeses, charcuterie and European dishes are designed to allow the wines to shine.

Restaurant at St Paul's Cathedral

St Paul's Churchyard ✉ EC4M 8AD – Ⓜ St Paul's – ✆ (020) 72482469
– www.restaurantatstpauls.co.uk
– Closed Easter and 25 December **L3**
Rest – *(lunch only) (booking advisable)* Menu £ 26 – Carte approx. £ 29
♦ British modern ♦ Bistro ♦
Tucked away in a corner of the crypt of Sir Christopher Wren's 17C masterpiece. The kitchen prepares everything from scratch and celebrates all things British, including drinks.

Jugged Hare

42 Chiswell St ✉ EC1Y 4SA – Ⓜ Barbican. – ✆ (020) 7614 0134
– www.thejuggedhare.com **M2**
Rest – *(booking advisable)* Carte £ 23/51
♦ British traditional ♦ Pub ♦ Trendy ♦
Vegetarians may feel ill at ease – and not just because of the taxidermy. The atmospheric dining room, with its open kitchen down one side, specialises in stout British dishes, with meats from the rotisserie a highlight.

Bermondsey

Hilton London Tower Bridge

rm,
5 More London, Tooley St ✉ SE1 2BY
– Ⓜ London Bridge – ✆ (020) 30024300 – www.towerbridge.hilton.com
245 rm – †£ 155/479 ††£ 155/838, ☕ £ 25 **M4**
Rest – Carte £ 27/48
♦ Business ♦ Modern ♦
Usefully located new-style Hilton hotel with boldly decorated open-plan lobby. Contemporary bedrooms boast well-designed features; 4 floors of executive rooms. Dine on classics and comfort food in restaurant with outdoor seating.

Bermondsey Square

rm,
Bermondsey Sq, Tower Bridge Rd ✉ SE1 3UN – Ⓜ London Bridge
– ✆ (020) 7378 2450 – www.bermondseysquarehotel.co.uk *Plan I* **D2**
80 rm – †£ 99/199 ††£ 99/199, ☕ £ 9
Rest *Gregg's Table* – Menu £ 10 – Carte £ 22/35
♦ Business ♦ Modern ♦
Opened in 2009 in a hip, regenerated square. Cleverly designed hotel, with subtle '60s influences and fun feel. Well-equipped bedrooms, including four loft suites. Open-plan Gregg's Table restaurant.

London Bridge

rm,
8-18 London Bridge St ✉ SE1 9SG – Ⓜ London Bridge – ✆ (020) 78552200 – www.londonbridgehotel.com **M4**
138 rm – †£ 309 ††£ 309, ☕ £ 17 – 3 suites
Rest *Londinium* – *(closed Sunday lunch) (dinner only)* Carte £ 28/43
♦ Business ♦ Classic ♦
In one of the oldest parts of London, independently owned with an ornate façade dating from 1915. Modern interior with classically decorated bedrooms and an impressive gym. Londinium for brasserie dining.

XXX **Le Pont de la Tour** ⟨ 🐟 ⇄ *VISA* ⊕ *AE* ⊕

36d Shad Thames, Butlers Wharf ⊠ *SE1 2YE* – ⓜ *London Bridge*
– ℰ *(020) 74038403* – www.lepontdelatour.co.uk   **N4**
Rest – Menu £ 18/45 🏶
♦ **French ♦ Elegant ♦**
Providing, since 1991, seasonal French cooking, an urbane atmosphere and a
wonderful riverside location, with views of Tower Bridge. Simpler dishes served
in the livelier cocktail bar and grill.

XX **Magdalen** *AC* *VISA* ⊕ *AE*

152 Tooley St. ⊠ *SE1 2TU* – ⓜ *London Bridge* – ℰ *(020) 74031342*
– www.magdalenrestaurant.co.uk
– *Closed bank holidays, Sunday and lunch Saturday*   **M4**
Rest – Menu £ 16 (weekday lunch) – Carte £ 27/40
♦ **British modern ♦ Neighbourhood ♦**
The clever sourcing and confident British cooking will leave you satisfied. Add
genial service, an affordable lunch menu and a food-friendly wine list and you
have the favourite restaurant of many.

X **Zucca** *AC* ⇄ *VISA* ⊕ *AE*
🍸

184 Bermondsey St ⊠ *SE1 3TQ* – ⓜ *Borough* – ℰ *(020) 73786809*
– www.zuccalondon.com
– *Closed 24 December-10 January, Easter, Sunday dinner and Monday*
Rest – *(booking essential at dinner)* Carte £ 18/27 🏶   *Plan I* **D2**
♦ **Italian ♦ Friendly ♦**
Bright and buzzy modern room, where the informed Italian cooking is driven by
the fresh ingredients, the prices are more than generous and the service is
sweet and responsive. The appealing antipasti is great for sharing.

X **Blueprint Café** ⟨ *VISA* ⊕ *AE* ⊕

Design Museum, Shad Thames, Butlers Wharf ⊠ *SE1 2YD*
– ⓜ *London Bridge* – ℰ *(020) 73787031* – www.blueprintcafe.co.uk
– *Closed Sunday dinner except mid-June-August*   **N5**
Rest – Menu £ 13/23 – Carte £ 23/40
♦ **Modern ♦ Brasserie ♦**
Large retractable windows make the most of the river views from this bright
restaurant above the Design Museum. The first change of head chef in 16
years was seamless: the cooking remains light, seasonally pertinent and easy
to eat.

X **Village East** *AC* ⇄ *VISA* ⊕ *AE*

171-173 Bermondsey St ⊠ *SE1 3UW* – ⓜ *London Bridge* – ℰ *(0207)*
3576082 – www.villageeast.co.uk
– *Closed 25-26 December*   *Plan I* **D2**
Rest – Carte £ 23/50
♦ **Modern ♦ Trendy ♦ Neighbourhood ♦**
In a glass-fronted block sandwiched by Georgian townhouses, this trendy res-
taurant has two loud, buzzy bars and dining areas serving ample portions of
modern British fare.

X **Cantina Del Ponte** ⟨ 🐟 *VISA* ⊕ *AE*

36c Shad Thames, Butlers Wharf ⊠ *SE1 2YE* – ⓜ *London Bridge*
– ℰ *(020) 74035403* – www.cantina.co.uk
– *Closed 25-27 December*   **N4**
Rest – Menu £ 15/19 – Carte £ 19/35
♦ **Italian ♦ Rustic ♦**
This Italian stalwart offers an appealing mix of classic dishes and reliable favouri-
tes from a sensibly priced menu, in pleasant faux-rustic surroundings. Its plea-
sant terrace takes advantage of its riverside setting.

Butlers Wharf Chop House ⟨ 🕊 VISA ⓒ AE ⓪

36e Shad Thames, Butlers Wharf ⊠ *SE1 2YE –* Ⓜ *London Bridge*
– 𝒞 (020) 7403 3403 – www.chophouse-restaurant.co.uk   **N4**
Rest – Carte £ 25/55
♦ British traditional ♦ Design ♦
Grab a table on the terrace in summer and dine in the shadow of Tower Bridge.
Rustic feel to the interior; noisy and fun. The menu focuses on traditional Eng-
lish ingredients and dishes; grilled meats a speciality.

Vivat Bacchus London Bridge   VISA ⓒ AE

4 Hays Ln ⊠ *SE1 2HB –* Ⓜ *London Bridge – 𝒞 (0207) 2340891*
– www.vivatbacchus.co.uk
– Closed Christmas and New Year, Saturday lunch, Sunday and bank holidays
Rest – Menu £ 15/19 – Carte £ 22/50 ❀   **M4**
♦ Other world kitchens ♦ Wine bar ♦ Friendly ♦
South African element to both the menu and the very impressive wine list.
Same menu of steaks, charcuterie and assorted sharing plates served in
the ground floor wine bar and the basement restaurant, with its great cheese
room.

Pizarro   AC ⇄ VISA ⓒ AE

171-173 Bermondsey St ⊠ *SE1 3UW –* Ⓜ *Borough – 𝒞 (020) 73789455*
– www.josepizarro.com
– Closed 24-28 December   *Plan I* **D2**
Rest – (bookings not taken at dinner and weekend lunch) Carte £ 23/30
♦ Mediterranean ♦ Neighbourhood ♦
José Pizarro has a refreshingly simple way of naming his establishments: after
José, his tapas bar, comes Pizarro, a larger restaurant a few doors down. Go for
the small plates, like prawns with piquillo peppers and jamón.

Antico   AC VISA ⓒ AE

214 Bermondsey St ⊠ *SE1 3TQ –* Ⓜ *London Bridge – 𝒞 (020) 7407 4682*
– www.antico-london.co.uk
– Closed Sunday dinner and Monday   *Plan I* **D2**
Rest – Menu £ 15/18 – Carte £ 20/41
♦ Italian ♦ Neighbourhood ♦
Once an antique warehouse – hence the name – Antico is fun, bright and
breezy, with honest and straightforward Italian food; the homemade pasta is
good. Check out the seasonal ragu, risotto and sorbet on the blackboard.

José   AC VISA ⓒ AE

104 Bermondsey St ⊠ *SE1 3UB –* Ⓜ *London Bridge – 𝒞 (020) 7403 4902*
– www.josepizarro.com
– Closed Christmas and Sunday dinner   *Plan I* **D2**
Rest – (bookings not accepted) Carte approx. £ 25
♦ Spanish ♦ Minimalist ♦ Tapas bar ♦
Standing up while eating tapas feels so right, especially at this small, fun bar
that packs 'em in like boquerones. Five dishes each should suffice; go for the
daily fish dishes from the blackboard. There's a great list of sherries too.

Garrison   AC ⇄ VISA ⓒ AE

99-101 Bermondsey St ⊠ *SE1 3XB –* Ⓜ *London Bridge. – 𝒞 (020)*
70899355 – www.thegarrison.co.uk
– Closed 25-27 December   *Plan I* **D2**
Rest – (booking essential at dinner) Carte £ 20/34
♦ Mediterranean ♦ Pub ♦
Known for its charming vintage look, booths and sweet-natured service, The
Garrison boasts a warm, relaxed vibe. Open from breakfast until dinner, when
a Mediterranean-led menu pulls in the crowd.

SOUTHWARK

XXX Oxo Tower ≤ ☆ AK VISA ☯ AE ①

Oxo Tower Wharf (8th floor), Barge House St ⊠ *SE1 9PH –* Ⓜ *Southwark*
– ℰ *(020) 78033888 – www.harveynichols.com*
– Closed 25 December, dinner 24 December and lunch 26 December
Rest – Carte £ 44/67 ⅏   K4
Rest *Oxo Tower Brasserie* – see restaurant listing
♦ Modern ♦ Minimalist ♦
Top of a converted iconic factory, providing stunning views of the Thames and
beyond. Stylish, minimalist interior with huge windows. Expect quite ambi-
tious, mostly European, cuisine.

XX Roast AK ☯ VISA ☯ AE

The Floral Hall, Borough Mkt ⊠ *SE1 1TL –* Ⓜ *London Bridge –* ℰ *(0845)*
347300 – www.roast-restaurant.com
– Closed 25-26 December and 1 January   M4
Rest – *(booking essential)* Carte £ 34/60
♦ British modern ♦ Fashionable ♦
Set into the roof of Borough Market's Floral Hall. Extensive cocktail list in bar;
split-level restaurant has views to St Paul's. Robust English cooking uses market
produce.

XX Baltic ⇔ VISA ☯ AE ①

74 Blackfriars Rd ⊠ *SE1 8HA –* Ⓜ *Southwark –* ℰ *(020) 79281111*
– www.balticrestaurant.co.uk
– Closed 24-27 December and 1 January   K4
Rest – *(bookings advisable at dinner)* Menu £ 15/39 – Carte £ 23/34
♦ Other world kitchens ♦ Brasserie ♦
Enjoy big portions of authentic and hearty east European food, served in a
Grade II listed 18C former coach house. The restaurant, which has been going
for over a decade, also has some interesting vodkas; live jazz on Sundays.

X Oxo Tower Brasserie ≤ ☆ AK VISA ☯ AE ①

Oxo Tower Wharf (8th floor), Barge House St ⊠ *SE1 9PH –* Ⓜ *Southwark*
– ℰ *(020) 78033888 – www.harveynichols.com*
– Closed 24 December dinner and 25 December
Rest – Carte £ 34/57   K4
♦ Modern ♦ Design ♦
Less formal but more fun than the next-door restaurant. Open-plan kitchen pro-
duces modern, colourful and easy-to-eat dishes with influences from the Med.
Great views too from the bar.

X Cantina Vinopolis AK VISA ☯ AE

No.1 Bank End ⊠ *SE1 9BU –* Ⓜ *London Bridge –* ℰ *(020) 79408333*
– www.cantinavinopolis.com
– Closed bank holidays   L4
Rest – Menu £ 26 *(weekdays)* – Carte £ 27/62 ⅏
♦ Mediterranean ♦ Rustic ♦
Beneath vast Victorian arches and next to their wine museum sits this bustling
restaurant, popular with larger parties. Impressive wine choice and carefully pre-
pared food with a Mediterranean slant.

X Tate Modern (Restaurant) ≤ VISA ☯ AE

Tate Modern (7th floor), Bankside ⊠ *SE1 9TG –* Ⓜ *Southwark –* ℰ *(020)*
7887 8888 – www.tate.org.uk
– Closed 24-26 December   L4
Rest – *(lunch only and dinner Friday-Saturday)* Carte £ 24/37
♦ British modern ♦ Friendly ♦
7th floor restaurant with floor to ceiling windows on two sides and large mural.
Appealing mix of light and zesty dishes, with seasonal produce. Good choice of
wines and non-alcoholic drinks.

UNITED KINGDOM - LONDON

Elliot's
✗ ☺   VISA ⓄⓄ AE

12 Stoney St., Borough Market ⊠ *SE1 9AD –* Ⓜ *London Bridge – 𝒞 (020) 74077436 – www.elliotscafe.com*
– Closed 25-26 December   **M4**
Rest *– (booking advisable)* Carte £ 19/46
♦ Modern ♦ Rustic ♦ Friendly ♦
Open from breakfast onwards, this busy and unpretentious café sources most of its ingredients from Borough Market, in which it stands. The appealing menu is concise and the cooking is earthy, pleasingly uncomplicated and very satisfying.

Tapas Brindisa
✗   Ⓥ VISA ⓄⓄ AE

18-20 Southwark St, Borough Market ⊠ *SE1 1TJ –* Ⓜ *London Bridge – 𝒞 (020) 73578880 – www.tapasbrindisa.com*   **M4**
Rest *– (bookings not accepted)* Carte £ 16/31
♦ Spanish ♦ Tapas bar ♦
A blueprint for many of the tapas bars that subsequently sprung up over London. It has an infectious energy and the well-priced, robust dishes include Galician-style hake and black rice with squid; do try the hand-carved Ibérico hams.

Wright Brothers
✗   VISA ⓄⓄ AE

11 Stoney St., Borough Market ⊠ *SE1 9AD –* Ⓜ *London Bridge – 𝒞 (020) 74039554 – www.thewrightbrothers.co.uk*
– Closed bank holiday Mondays   **L4**
Rest *– (booking advisable)* Carte £ 26/41
♦ Fish and seafood ♦ Wine bar ♦
Originally an oyster wholesaler; now offers a wide range of oysters along with porter, as well as fruits de mer, daily specials and assorted pies. It fills quickly and an air of contentment reigns.

Anchor & Hope
🍴 ☺   🍽 VISA ⓄⓄ

36 The Cut ⊠ *SE1 8LP –* Ⓜ *Southwark. – 𝒞 (020) 79289898*
– Closed Christmas-New Year, Sunday dinner, Monday lunch and bank holidays
Rest *– (bookings not accepted)* Carte £ 19/34   **K4**
♦ British modern ♦ Pub ♦
As popular as ever thanks to its congenial feel and lived-in looks but mostly because of the appealingly seasonal menu and the gutsy, bold cooking that delivers on flavour. No reservations so be prepared to wait at the bar.

CHELSEA – SOUTH KENSINGTON – EARL'S COURT   Plan X

CHELSEA

Jumeirah Carlton Tower
🏨🏨🏨🏨   ≤ 🚗 🛁 ⊛ 🏊 ▦ 🍽 ⅙ 🎁 🏋 🚘 VISA ⓄⓄ AE Ⓞ

Cadogan Place ⊠ *SW1X 9PY –* Ⓜ *Knightsbridge – 𝒞 (020) 72351234 – www.jumeirahcarltontower.com*   **F5**
186 rm – ♦£ 786/846 ♦♦£ 846/1122, � £ 38 – 30 suites
Rest Rib Room – see restaurant listing
♦ Grand Luxury ♦ Modern ♦ Elegant ♦
Imposing international hotel overlooking a leafy square and just yards from all the swanky boutiques. Well-equipped rooftop health club has great views. Generously proportioned bedrooms boast every conceivable facility.

Wyndham Grand
🏨🏨🏨   ≤ 🍽 🛁 ⊛ 🏊 ▦ & rm, 🅰 🎁 🏋 🚘 VISA ⓄⓄ AE

Chelsea Harbour ⊠ *SW10 0XG – 𝒞 (020) 78233000 – www.wyndhamgrandlondon.co.uk*   *Plan I* **B3**
158 rm ⊠ – ♦£ 228/516 ♦♦£ 228/516
Rest Chelsea Riverside Brasserie – Menu £ 16 – Carte £ 29/53
♦ Luxury ♦ Modern ♦ Contemporary ♦
Modern hotel within an exclusive marina and retail development. Many of the spacious and well-appointed rooms have balconies and views across the Thames. Bright restaurant with wide-ranging menu overlooks the harbour.

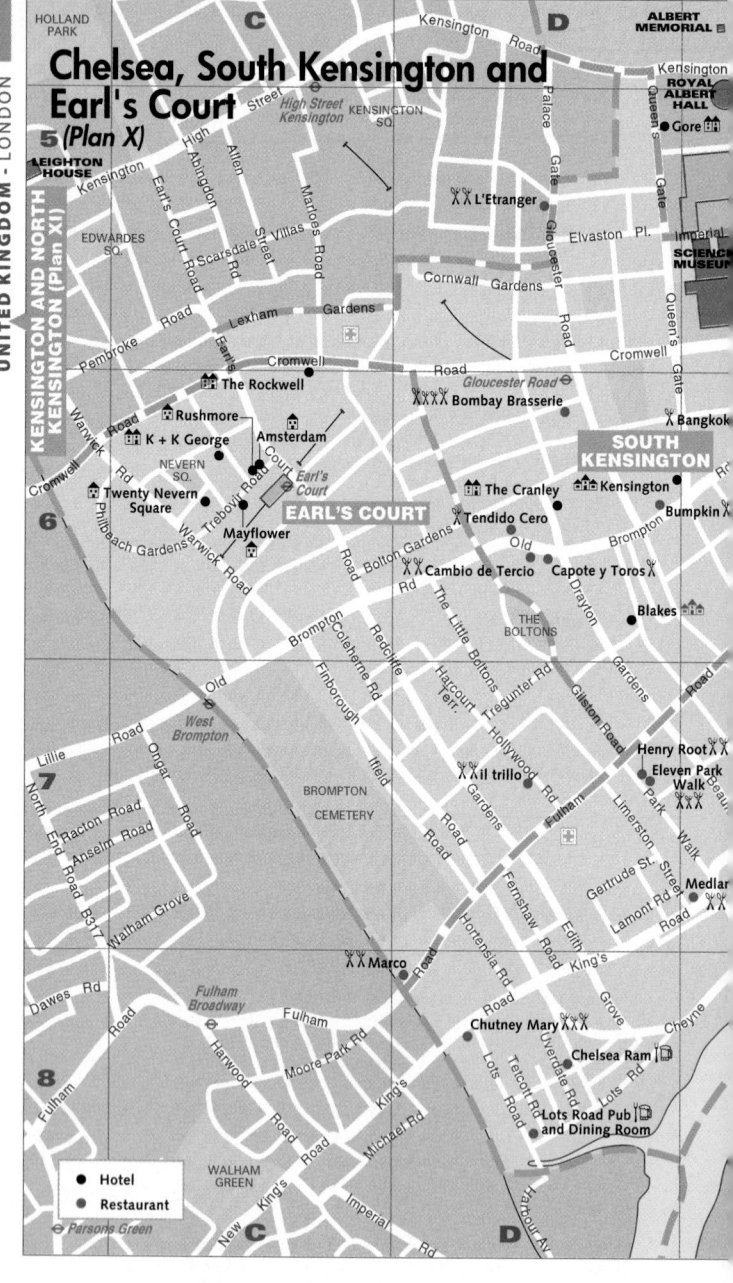

HOLLAND PARK

C

D

Kensington Road

Kensington

High Street Kensington

KENSINGTON SQ.

Chelsea, South Kensington and Earl's Court
(Plan X)

5

LEIGHTON HOUSE

Kensington ROYAL ALBERT HALL

Kensington

Palace Gate

Gore

Queen's Gate

EDWARDES SQ.

Earl's Court Road

Abingdon

High

Allen Street

Marloes Road

Scarsdale Villas

L'Etranger

Gloucester Road

Elvaston Pl.

Cornwall Gardens

Imperial SCIENCE MUSEUM

Pembroke Road

Warwick Road

Lexham Gardens

Earl's

Cromwell Road

Queen's Gate

Gardens

Cromwell

The Rockwell

Rushmore

K + K George

Road

Amsterdam Court

Trebovir Road

Earl's Court

Road

Gloucester Road ⊖

Bombay Brasserie

Bangkok

SOUTH KENSINGTON

Cromwell Rd

Philbeach Gardens

NEVERN SQ.

Twenty Nevern Square

Warwick Road

Mayflower

EARL'S COURT

Bolton Gardens

Road

The Cranley

Kensington

Tendido Cero

Old

Bumpkin

Brompton

6

Cambio de Tercio

Rd

The Little Boltons

Capote y Toros

Drayton

Blakes

Old

West Brompton

Brompton Coleherne Rd

Redcliffe

Finborough

THE BOLTONS

Harcourt Terr

Tregunter Rd

Gilston Road

Gardens

Road

Lillie Road

Olympia Road

Racton Road

Anselm Road

North End Road B317

Warwick

BROMPTON CEMETERY

Ifield

Road

Hollywood Rd

il trillo

Fulham

Road

Gardens

Henry Root

Eleven Park Walk

Fernshaw Road

Edith

Limerston St.

Park Walk

Beau

7

Walham Grove

Gertrude St.

Lamont Rd

King's

Medlar

Dawes Rd

Fulham

Road

Harwood

Fulham Broadway

Road

Moore Park Rd

Hortensia Rd

Marco

Road

King's

Chutney Mary

Uverdale Rd

Grove

Cheyne

Chelsea Ram

8

WALHAM GREEN

King's

Road

Michael Rd

Imperial

Lots

Road

Telcott Rd

Lots Road Pub and Dining Room

⊖ Parsons Green

New King's

Rd

Harbour

C

D

Ave

● Hotel
● Restaurant

930

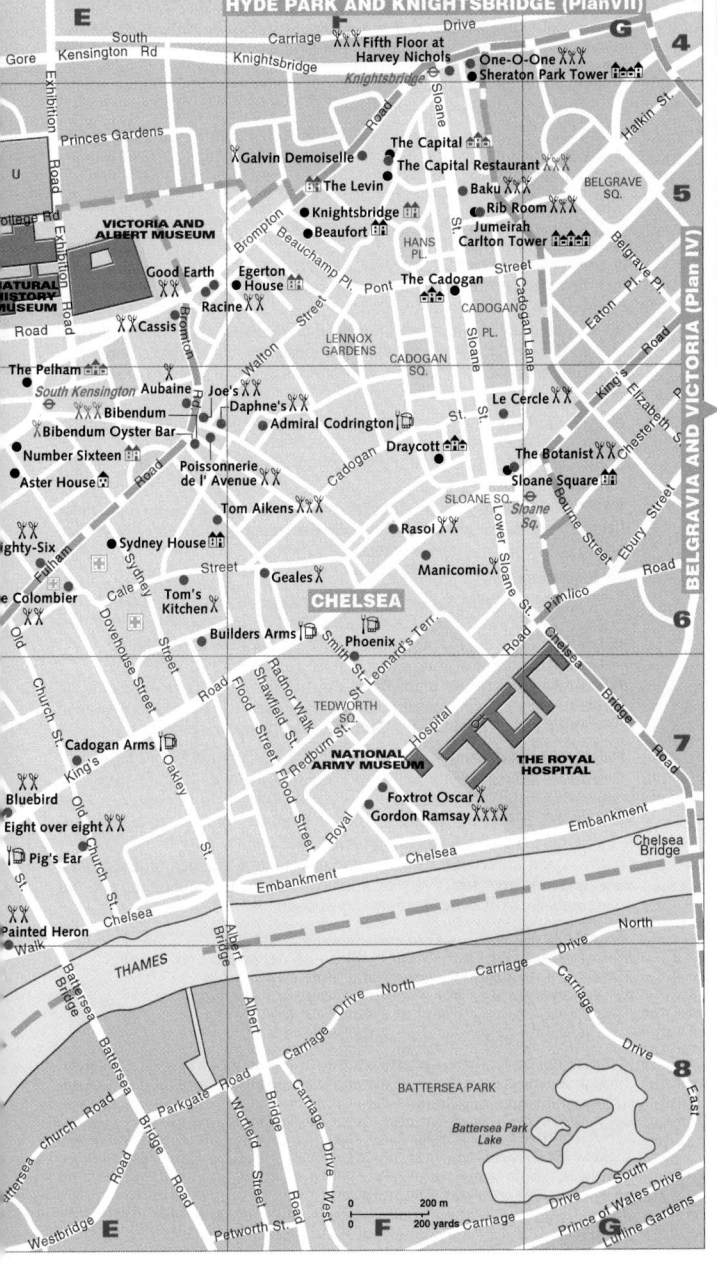

UNITED KINGDOM - LONDON

BELGRAVIA AND VICTORIA (Plan IV)

Gore
South Kensington Rd
Exhibition Road
Princes Gardens
Carriage Drive
Knightsbridge
Knightsbridge Road
Sloane Street

XXX Fifth Floor at Harvey Nichols
One-O-One XXX
Sheraton Park Tower

The Capital
Galvin Demoiselle
The Capital Restaurant XXX
The Levin
Baku XXX
Knightsbridge
Rib Room XXX
Beaufort
Jumeirah Carlton Tower

BELGRAVE SQ.
Halkin St.
Belgrave Pl.
Eaton Pl.

VICTORIA AND ALBERT MUSEUM
NATURAL HISTORY MUSEUM
Road

Good Earth
Egerton House
Cassis
Racine XX
Beauchamp Pl.
HANS PL.
Pont Street
The Cadogan
CADOGAN PL.
Cadogan Lane
CADOGAN SQ.
Sloane St.

The Pelham
South Kensington
Aubaine
Joe's XX
Le Cercle XX
Bibendum
Daphne's XX
Admiral Codrington
Draycott
The Botanist XX
Sloane Square
Bibendum Oyster Bar
Number Sixteen
Aster House
Poissonnerie de l' Avenue XX
SLOANE SQ.
Sloane Sq.
Bourne Street
Ebury Street

Tom Aikens XXX
Rasol XX
ghty-Six
Fulham
Sydney House
Street
Geales X
Manicomio X
Pimlico Road

e Colombier
Cale Street
Tom's Kitchen
CHELSEA
Lower Sloane St.
Builders Arms
Phoenix

Cadogan Arms
King's
Radnor Walk
Shawfield St.
St Leonard's Terr.
TEDWORTH SQ.

Bluebird
Eight over eight XX
Pig's Ear
Oakley St.
Flood Street
Royal Hospital Road
NATIONAL ARMY MUSEUM
THE ROYAL HOSPITAL
Chelsea Bridge Road

Foxtrot Oscar X
Gordon Ramsay XXXX
Embankment
Chelsea Bridge

Painted Heron
Walk
Chelsea
Embankment
THAMES
Albert Bridge
Carriage Drive North
North

Battersea Bridge
attersea church Road
Westbridge
Parkgate Road
Woofield Street
Albert Bridge Road
Petworth St.
Carriage Drive West
BATTERSEA PARK
Battersea Park Lake
Carriage
Prince of Wales Drive
Lurline Gardens

0   200 m
0   200 yards

UNITED KINGDOM - LONDON

Sheraton Park Tower

101 Knightsbridge ⊠ SW1X 7RN – Ⓜ Knightsbridge – ℰ (020) 72358050
– www.sheratonparktower.com   **F4**
258 rm – †£ 250/670, ††£ 250/670, ⌷ £ 27 – 22 suites
Rest One-O-One – see restaurant listing
♦ Luxury ♦ Business ♦ Modern ♦

Built in the 1970s in a unique cylindrical shape. The well-equipped bedrooms
are all identical in size. Top floor executive rooms come with commanding
views of Hyde Park and the city.

The Capital

22-24 Basil St. ⊠ SW3 1AT – Ⓜ Knightsbridge – ℰ (020) 75895171
– www.capitalhotel.co.uk   **F5**
49 rm – †£ 240/318 ††£ 300/600, ⌷ £ 20 – 1 suite
Rest The Capital Restaurant – see restaurant listing
♦ Luxury ♦ Traditional ♦ Classic ♦

This fine, thoroughly British hotel has been under the same private ownership
for over 40 years. Known for its discreet atmosphere, conscientious and attentive service and immaculately kept bedrooms courtesy of different designers.

Draycott

26 Cadogan Gdns ⊠ SW3 2RP – Ⓜ Sloane Square – ℰ (020) 77306466
– www.draycotthotel.com   **F6**
35 rm – †£ 145/285 ††£ 345/399, ⌷ £ 22   **Rest** – (room service only)
♦ Townhouse ♦ Stylish ♦

Charming 19C house with elegant sitting room overlooking tranquil garden for
afternoon tea. Bedrooms are individually decorated in a country house style
and are named after writers or actors.

The Cadogan

75 Sloane St ⊠ SW1X 9SG – Ⓜ Knightsbridge – ℰ (020) 72357141
64 rm – †£ 162/342 ††£ 210/402, ⌷ £ 25   **F5**
Rest Great Taste at the Cadogan – (closed Sunday dinner) Menu £ 28
♦ Luxury ♦ Cosy ♦

An Edwardian townhouse, made famous by two former residents – Oscar Wilde
and Lillie Langtry. Quiet drawing room for afternoon tea; bedrooms are varied
and comfortable. Seasonal British produce championed in restaurant.

Knightsbridge

10 Beaufort Gdns ⊠ SW3 1PT – Ⓜ Knightsbridge – ℰ (020) 75846300
– www.knightsbridgehotel.com   **F5**
44 rm – †£ 195 †††£ 235/285, ⌷ £ 20   **Rest** – (room service only)
♦ Luxury ♦ Townhouse ♦ Stylish ♦

Charming and attractively furnished townhouse in a Victorian terrace, with a
very stylish, discreet feel. Every bedroom is immaculately appointed and has
an individuality of its own; fine detailing throughout.

Egerton House

17-19 Egerton Terr ⊠ SW3 2BX – Ⓜ South Kensington – ℰ (020)
75892412 – www.egertonhousehotel.com   **F5**
27 rm – †£ 276/432 ††£ 276/432, ⌷ £ 29 – 1 suite
Rest – (room service only)
♦ Townhouse ♦ Classic ♦ Cosy ♦

Compact but comfortable townhouse in a very good location, well-maintained
throughout and owned by the Red Carnation group. High levels of personal service make the hotel stand out.

The Levin without rest

28 Basil St. ⊠ SW3 1AS – Ⓜ Knightsbridge – ℰ (020) 75896286
– www.thelevinhotel.co.uk   **F5**
12 rm ⌷ – †£ 282/360 ††£ 282/600
♦ Townhouse ♦ Classic ♦ Stylish ♦

A discreet townhouse and sister to The Capital next door. Impressive façade, contemporary interior and comfortable bedrooms in subtle art deco style, with marvellous champagne mini bars. Simple dishes served all day down at Le Metro.

UNITED KINGDOM - LONDON

Beaufort   AC rm, 🛜 VISA ⊙⊙ AE ①
33 Beaufort Gdns ✉ *SW3 1PP –* Ⓜ *Knightsbridge –* ☏ *(020) 75845252*
– www.thebeaufort.co.uk   **F5**
29 rm – †£ 156/216 ††£ 216/300, � £ 15
Rest – *(room service only)*
♦ Traditional ♦ Classic ♦ Personalised ♦
A vast collection of English floral watercolours adorn this 19C townhouse, set in a useful location. Modern and co-ordinated rooms. Tariff includes all drinks and afternoon tea.

Sydney House *without rest*   AC 🛜 VISA ⊙⊙ AE ①
9-11 Sydney St. ✉ *SW3 6PU –* Ⓜ *South Kensington –* ☏ *(020) 73767711*
– www.sydneyhousechelsea.com
– Closed 25-26 December   **E6**
21 rm – †£ 125/255 ††£ 155/285, ⊡ £ 15
♦ Townhouse ♦ Modern ♦ Cosy ♦
Stylish and compact Georgian townhouse made brighter through plenty of mirrors and light wood. Thoughtfully designed bedrooms; Room 43 has its own terrace. Part of the Abode group.

The Sloane Square   ⅄ AC 🛜 ⅄ VISA ⊙⊙
7-12 Sloane Sq. ✉ *SW1W 8EG –* Ⓜ *Sloane Square –* ☏ *(020) 78969988*
– www.sloanesquarehotel.co.uk   **F6**
102 rm – †£ 120/228 ††£ 165/425, ⊡ £ 16
Rest *Chelsea Brasserie* – *see restaurant listing*
♦ Business ♦ Modern ♦
Well-placed, red-brick hotel boasting bright, contemporary décor. Stylish, co-ordinated bedrooms, with laptops; library of DVDs and games available. Rooms at the back are slightly quieter.

Gordon Ramsay   I♡ AC VISA ⊙⊙ AE
ꝗꝗꝗ *68-69 Royal Hospital Rd.* ✉ *SW3 4HP –* Ⓜ *Sloane Square*
– ☏ *(020) 73524441*
– www.gordonramsay.com
– Closed Christmas, Saturday and Sunday   **F7**
Rest – *(booking essential)* Menu £ 45/95 ❀
♦ French ♦ Formal ♦
Attention to detail ensures that Gordon Ramsay's flagship restaurant still provides the consummate dining experience. Composed, reassuring and discreet service adds to the calmness of the room; Clare Smyth's cooking is elegant, a little more daring than before and supremely skilled.
→ Poached Scottish lobster tail with lardo di colonnata and vegetables à la grecque. Suckling pig, crispy belly, roasted loin, sausage, chou farci and braised leg. Lemonade parfait with honey, bergamot and sheep's milk yoghurt sorbet.

Tom Aikens   I♡ AC ⇔ VISA ⊙⊙ AE
ꝗ *43 Elystan St.* ✉ *SW3 3NT –* Ⓜ *South Kensington –* ☏ *(020) 75842003*
– www.tomaikens.co.uk
– Closed Christmas, Saturday lunch, Sunday and bank holidays   **F6**
Rest – Menu £ 29/50 ❀
♦ Modern ♦ Rustic ♦ Design ♦
The look is now much edgier, with oak tables, atmospheric lighting and food–related aphorisms stencilled on the walls. The kitchen follows the culinary zeitgeist by looking to Scandinavia; each striking-looking dish is focused around one main ingredient and presented on a variety of plates and bowls.
→ Salt-fried duck egg with dandelion and sour onions. Braised short rib of beef, bone marrow and herb purée. Coffee crème and sponge with espresso syrup.

XxX **Bibendum** ⏱ⓥ 🄰🄲 🆅🅸🅂🄰 ⓪🄰 🄰🄴
Michelin House, 81 Fulham Rd. ✉ *SW3 6RD*
– Ⓜ *South Kensington* – ✆ *(020) 75815817*
– *www.bibendum.co.uk*
– *Closed 24-26 December and 1 January*   **E6**
Rest – Menu £ 27/30 – Carte £ 36/66 🕸
♦ French ♦ Design ♦ Fashionable ♦
Has maintained a loyal following for over 20 years, with its French food that comes with a British accent. Located on the 1st floor of a London landmark – Michelin's former HQ, dating from 1911.

XxX **The Capital Restaurant** – The Capital Hotel   🄲 ⇕
22-24 Basil St. ✉ *SW3 1AT* – Ⓜ *Knightsbridge*   🆅🅸🅂🄰 ⓪🄰 🄰🄴 Ⓞ
– ✆ *(020) 75911202* – *www.capitalhotel.co.uk*   **F5**
Rest – *(booking essential)* Menu £ 25 (lunch)/75 – Carte £ 44/58 🕸
♦ French ♦ Formal ♦
Elegant surroundings, formal service and elaborately presented, classic cuisine have featured at the family-owned Capital for many years. It is also known for its superlative wine list.

XxX **Fifth Floor at Harvey Nichols**   🄲 🕸 ⓪🄰 🄰🄴
109-125 Knightsbridge ✉ *SW1X 7RJ*
– Ⓜ *Knightsbridge* – ✆ *(020) 7235 5250*
– *www.harveynichols.com*
– *Closed Christmas and Sunday dinner*   **F4**
Rest – Menu £ 25 – Carte £ 35/48 🕸
♦ Modern ♦ Fashionable ♦ Intimate ♦
If the revamped food hall hasn't left you sated then try the stylish restaurant on the same floor here at Harvey 'Nics'. It's busy with shoppers at lunch but is more intimate at dinner. The food is light and unfussy.

XxX **Rib Room** – Jumeirah Carlton Tower Hotel   ⇕ 🆅🅸🅂🄰 ⓪🄰 Ⓞ
Cadogan Place ✉ *SW1X 9PY* – Ⓜ *Knightsbridge* – ✆ *(020) 7858 7250*
– *www.theribroom.co.uk*   **F5**
Rest – Menu £ 30/55 – Carte £ 48/71
♦ Meats and grills ♦ Elegant ♦ Intimate ♦
Rib of Aberdeen Angus, steaks and other classic British dishes attract a prosperous, international crowd; few of whom appear to have a beef with the prices at this swish veteran.

XxX **Chutney Mary**   ⓥ 🄲 ⇕ 🆅🅸🅂🄰 ⓪🄰 Ⓞ
535 King's Rd. ✉ *SW10 0SZ* – Ⓜ *Fulham Broadway* – ✆ *(020) 73513113*
– *www.realindianfood.com*
– *Closed dinner 25 December*   **D8**
Rest – *(dinner only and lunch Saturday-Sunday)* Menu £ 20/45
– Carte £ 33/53
♦ Indian ♦ Exotic ♦
Since 1990 it has offered a side order of sophistication along with regional specialities from across India. Wine pairings and cocktails also set it apart. The conservatory is slightly less hectic and away from the larger groups.

XxX **One-O-One** – Sheraton Park Tower Hotel   🄲 🆅🅸🅂🄰 ⓪🄰 🄰🄴 Ⓞ
101 Knightsbridge ✉ *SW1X 7RN* – Ⓜ *Knightsbridge* – ✆ *(020) 72907101*
– *www.oneoonerestaurant.com*   **F4**
Rest – Menu £ 22 (lunch) – Carte £ 48/77
♦ Fish and seafood ♦ Formal ♦
Smart ground floor restaurant; lacking a little in atmosphere but the seafood is good. Much of the produce from Brittany and Norway; don't miss the King crab legs. Small tasting plates also offered.

XXX **Eleven Park Walk** 🅰🅒 ⇄ 🆅🆂🅰 ⊙⊙ 🅰🅴

11 Park Walk ✉ *SW10 0AJ –* Ⓜ *South Kensington –* ☎ *(020) 7352 3449*
– www.11parkwalk.co.uk
– Closed 25 December **D7**
Rest – Carte £ 29/64
♦ Italian ♦ Elegant ♦
What was 'Aubergine' is now a sophisticated Italian; its menu traverses the country but it is the Sardinian specialities that shine. It attracts an equally smart set who appreciate the polished service.

XXX **Baku** 🅰🅒 ⇄ 🆅🆂🅰 ⊙⊙ 🅰🅴 ⊙

164 Sloane St (1st Floor) ✉ *SW1X 9QB –* Ⓜ *Knightsbridge –* ☎ *(020)*
7235 5399 – www.bakulondon.com **F5**
Rest – Carte £ 29/56
♦ Other world kitchens ♦ Exotic ♦ Individual ♦
Named after the capital city, Baku offers diners the chance to try subtly lightened Azerbaijani cuisine in fairly opulent surroundings. Kebabs, tandir dishes, soups and plenty of sturgeon from the Caspian Sea feature.

XX **Rasoi** (Vineet Bhatia) 🆔Ⓥ 🅰🅒 ⇄ 🆅🆂🅰 ⊙⊙ 🅰🅴 ⊙
✿
10 Lincoln St ✉ *SW3 2TS –* Ⓜ *Sloane Square –* ☎ *(020) 72251881*
– www.rasoirestaurant.co.uk
– Closed 25-26 December and Saturday lunch **F6**
Rest – Menu £ 27/59
♦ Indian ♦ Intimate ♦
With outposts in Geneva, Mauritius and Dubai, Vineet Bhatia proves that Indian food is as open to innovation and interpretation as any other cuisine. His exotically decorated dining room sits within an archetypal Chelsea townhouse.
➜ Scallop and prawn brochette. Smoked herb-crusted rack of lamb. Rose petal mousse.

XX **Medlar** (Joe Mercer Nairne) 🍴 🅰🅒 ⇄ 🆅🆂🅰 ⊙⊙ 🅰🅴 ⊙
✿
438 King's Rd ✉ *SW10 0LJ –* Ⓜ *South Kensington –* ☎ *(020) 73491900*
– www.medlarrestaurant.co.uk **E7**
Rest – Menu £ 26/40 ⅋
♦ Modern ♦ Neighbourhood ♦ Fashionable ♦
The two young owners, both alumni of Chez Bruce, have created a charming and successful local restaurant. David and his team provide warm, knowledgeable but unobtrusive service; while Joe produces easy-to-eat dishes with a French base and a light touch, where the component flavours marry perfectly.
➜ Crab ravioli with samphire and brown shrimps. Under blade fillet, bone marrow, triple-cooked chips and béarnaise. Vanilla cheesecake with poached rhubarb and hazelnut crumble.

XX **Le Colombier** ⇄ 🆅🆂🅰 ⊙⊙ 🅰🅴

145 Dovehouse St. ✉ *SW3 6LB –* Ⓜ *South Kensington –* ☎ *(020)*
73511155 – www.le-colombier-restaurant.co.uk **E6**
Rest – Menu £ 20 (lunch) – Carte £ 32/60
♦ French ♦ Neighbourhood ♦
Proudly Gallic corner restaurant in an affluent residential area. Attractive enclosed terrace. Bright and cheerful surroundings and service; traditional French cooking.

XX **Racine** 🅰🅒 🍴 🆅🆂🅰 ⊙⊙ 🅰🅴

239 Brompton Rd ✉ *SW3 2EP –* Ⓜ *South Kensington –* ☎ *(020) 75844477*
– www.racine-restaurant.com
– Closed Christmas **E5**
Rest – Menu £ 16 (lunch and early dinner) – Carte £ 30/51
♦ French ♦ Brasserie ♦
An authentic feel to this French brasserie, with dark leather seats, wood floors and mirrors. The menu provides a roll-call of classic regional specialities, from steak tartare to fruits de mer.

XX **Daphne's**   AK ⇔ *VISA* ⊙⊙ AE ⊙

112 Draycott Ave. ⊠ *SW3 3AE –* Ⓜ *South Kensington –* ℰ *(020) 75894257*
– www.daphnes-restaurant.co.uk
– Closed 25-26 December   E6
Rest *– (booking essential)* Carte £ 29/49
♦ Italian ♦ Fashionable ♦

Established over 40 years ago and a Chelsea institution with a 'celebrity' following. Reliable formula of tried-and-tested Italian classics in a room with a
warm, Tuscan feel.

XX **Poissonnerie de l'Avenue**   AK ⇔ *VISA* ⊙⊙ AE ⊙

82 Sloane Ave. ⊠ *SW3 3DZ –* Ⓜ *South Kensington –* ℰ *(020) 75892457*
– www.poissonneriedelavenue.com
– Closed Easter and 25-26 December   E6
Rest *–* Menu £ 30 (lunch) *–* Carte £ 31/66
♦ Fish and seafood ♦ Formal ♦

A smart, personally run, wood-panelled Chelsea institution since 1946. Its extensive choice of carefully prepared, traditional seafood dishes attracts a smart and
loyal following.

XX **Eight over Eight**   AK ⇔ *VISA* ⊙⊙ AE ⊙

392 King's Rd ⊠ *SW3 5UZ –* Ⓜ *South Kensington –* ℰ *(020) 73499934*
– www.rickerrestaurants.com
– Closed 24-27 December   E7
Rest *–* Carte £ 19/54
♦ Asian ♦ Fashionable ♦

Reopened after a fire, with a slightly plusher feel; still as popular as ever with the
fashionable crowds. Influences stretch across South East Asia and dishes are
designed for sharing.

XX **Bluebird**   AK ⇔ ▨ *VISA* ⊙⊙ AE

350 King's Rd. ⊠ *SW3 5UU –* Ⓜ *South Kensington –* ℰ *(020) 75591000*
– www.bluebird-restaurant.co.uk   E7
Rest *–* Menu £ 25 *–* Carte £ 26/47
♦ British modern ♦ Design ♦

Former industrial space incorporates everything from a wine store to a private
members club. Large, buzzy restaurant champions British produce in an appealing menu that has something for everyone.

XX **Le Cercle**   AK *VISA* ⊙⊙ AE

1 Wilbraham Pl. ⊠ *SW1X 9AE –* Ⓜ *Sloane Square –* ℰ *(020) 79019999*
– www.lecercle.co.uk
– Closed Christmas and New Year, Sunday, Monday and bank holidays
Rest *–* Menu £ 19/35 *–* Carte £ 24/38   F6
♦ French ♦ Fashionable ♦

Deep basement location made into a fashionable spot, with drapes and high
ceilings; comes alive more at dinner. Order three or four small plates of the delicate French cooking per person.

XX **Painted Heron**   🎋 AK *VISA* ⊙⊙ AE

112 Cheyne Walk ⊠ *SW10 0DJ –* Ⓜ *Gloucester Road –* ℰ *(020) 73515232*
– www.thepaintedheron.com
– Closed 24-25 December   E7/8
Rest *–* Menu £ 20/45 *–* Carte £ 25/38
♦ Indian ♦ Formal ♦ Neighbourhood ♦

Well-supported locally and quite formally run Indian restaurant. Nooks and
crannies create an intimate atmosphere. Fish and game dishes are the highlight
of the contemporary Indian cooking.

UNITED KINGDOM - LONDON

XX **Eighty-Six** [AC] [VISA] [⦶] [AE] [①]

86 Fulham Rd, (1st Floor) ⊠ *SW3 6HR –* Ⓜ *South Kensington –* ℰ *(020) 7052 9620 – www.86restaurant.co.uk*
– Closed 24-29 December and Sunday **E6**
Rest *– (dinner only)* Menu £ 21 – Carte £ 33/55
♦ Modern ♦ Design ♦ Trendy ♦
A mix of baroque, rococo and bling are used to create a gilded jewel for young movers and shakers. The menu roams around Europe but the best dishes are the simpler ones that use British ingredients.

XX **il trillo** [AC] [VISA] [⦶] [①]

4 Hollywood Rd ⊠ *SW10 9HY –* Ⓜ *Earl's Court –* ℰ *(020) 3602 1759*
– www.iltrillo.net
– Closed 2 weeks August, 2 weeks Christmas and Monday **D7**
Rest *– (dinner only and lunch Saturday-Sunday)* Carte £ 29/57
♦ Italian ♦ Friendly ♦ Neighbourhood ♦
The Bertuccelli family have been making wine and running a restaurant in the Tuscan Hills for over 30 years. Two of the brothers now run this smart local which showcases the produce and wine from their region. Delightful courtyard.

XX **Marco** [AC] [VISA] [⦶] [AE]

Stamford Bridge, Fulham Rd. ⊠ *SW6 1HS –* Ⓜ *Fulham Broadway*
– ℰ *(020) 79152929 – www.marcorestaurant.org*
– Closed Christmas, Easter, Sunday and Monday **D8**
Rest *– (dinner only) (booking advisable)* Carte £ 32/52
♦ French ♦ Brasserie ♦
Marco Pierre White's brasserie at Chelsea Football Club offers an appealing range of classics, from British favourites to satisfying French and Italian fare; puddings are a highlight. Comfortable and well-run room.

XX **Good Earth** [AC] [VISA] [⦶] [AE]

233 Brompton Rd. ⊠ *SW3 2EP –* Ⓜ *Knightsbridge –* ℰ *(020) 75843658*
– www.goodearthgroup.co.uk
– Closed 23-31 December **E5**
Rest – Carte £ 21/48
♦ Chinese ♦ Formal ♦
The basement is busier and more popular than the ground floor. Extensive menu makes good use of quality ingredients and offers appealing choice between classic and more unusual dishes.

XX **The Botanist** [AC] [VISA] [⦶] [AE]

7 Sloane Sq ⊠ *SW1W 8EE –* Ⓜ *Sloane Square –* ℰ *(020) 77300077*
– www.thebotanistonsloanesquare.com
– Closed 25-26 December **F6**
Rest – Carte £ 29/53
♦ Modern ♦ Wine bar ♦ Neighbourhood ♦
Pass through the busy bar to get to the stylish and comfortable restaurant with its warm and vibrant atmosphere. Appealing and accessible menu delivers unfussy and satisfying dishes.

XX **Chelsea Brasserie** – The Sloane Square Hotel [AC] [⦶] [VISA] [⦶]

7-12 Sloane Sq. ⊠ *SW1W 8EG –* Ⓜ *Sloane Square –* ℰ *(020) 78969988*
– www.sloanesquarehotel.co.uk
– Closed Sunday dinner **F6**
Rest – Menu £ 24/28 – Carte £ 31/54
♦ French ♦ Brasserie ♦
Smartly decorated brasserie, with exposed brick, mirrors and tiles; it also has a lively bar attached. Cooking has a strong French base. Good value theatre menu and appropriately brisk service.

XX **Joe's** `AC` `VISA` `CO` `AE`

126 Draycott Ave ⊠ *SW3 3AH* – Ⓜ *South Kensington* – ℰ *(020) 72252217*
– www.joseph.co.uk
– Closed 24-26 December, Easter Sunday and dinner Sunday-Monday
Rest – Menu £ 20 (lunch) – Carte £ 23/34   **E6**
♦ Modern ♦ Fashionable ♦ Design ♦
Back in the '80s when the only thing bigger than the hair was the shoulder pads, Joe's was the place to be seen. It's now fashionable once again and its appealing, fortnightly changing menu comes with Mediterranean overtones.

X **Bibendum Oyster Bar** `VISA` `CO` `AE`

Michelin House, 81 Fulham Rd. ⊠ *SW3 6RD* – Ⓜ *South Kensington*
– ℰ (020) 75891480 – www.bibendum.co.uk
– Closed 24-26 December and 1 January
Rest – (bookings not accepted) Carte £ 21/64   **E6**
♦ Fish and seafood ♦ Rustic ♦
Oysters, potted shrimps and fruits de mer are the highlights at this continental-style café, with its mosaic floor and colourful ceramic tiles. Wine list includes 460ml pots.

X **Foxtrot Oscar** `AC` `VISA` `CO` `AE`

79 Royal Hospital Rd. ⊠ *SW3 4HN* – Ⓜ *Sloane Square* – ℰ *(020) 73524448 – www.gordonramsay.com/foxtrotoscar*
– Closed 25 December   **F7**
Rest – (booking essential) Menu £ 18/25 – Carte £ 23/53
♦ British traditional ♦ Cosy ♦ Neighbourhood ♦
Gordon Ramsay's least known restaurant has a relaxed, local feel, with celebrity photographs adorning its burgundy walls. Bistro cooking, with the Foxtrot Burger a highlight.

X **Henry Root** `AC` `VISA` `CO` `AE`

9 Park Walk ⊠ *SW10 0AJ* – ⓂSouth Kensington – ℰ *(020) 7352 7040*
– www.thehenryroot.com
– Closed 25-27 December   **D7**
Rest – (booking advisable) Carte £ 21/42 🏵
♦ French ♦ Neighbourhood ♦ Intimate ♦
William Donaldson satirised many of the good and the great of his day through the letters of his alter ego, Henry Root. His name lives on in this cheery local spot, with its appealing menu that includes small plates and charcuterie.

X **Manicomio** `AC` `VISA` `CO` `AE` `O`

85 Duke of York Sq., King's Rd. ⊠ *SW3 4LY* – ⓂSloane Square – ℰ *(020) 77303366 – www.manicomio.co.uk*
– Closed 1 January, 24-26 and 31 December   **F6**
Rest – Carte £ 30/44
♦ Italian ♦ Rustic ♦ Neighbourhood ♦
Modern, busy Italian, popular with shoppers and visitors to the Saatchi Gallery; the simplest dishes are the best ones. The terrific terrace fills quickly. Next door is their café and deli.

X **Tom's Kitchen** `VISA` `CO` `AE`

27 Cale St. ⊠ *SW3 3QP* – ⓂSouth Kensington – ℰ *(020) 73490202*
– www.tomskitchen.co.uk   **E6**
Rest – Carte £ 29/62
♦ French ♦ Neighbourhood ♦
A converted pub, whose white tiles and mirrors help to give it an industrial feel. Appealing and wholesome dishes come in man-sized portions. The eponymous Tom is Tom Aikens.

✗ **Galvin Demoiselle**   AC VISA ⓒⓞ AE ⓞ

Ground Floor Food Hall, Harrods, 87-135 Brompton Rd ⊠ SW1X 7XL
– ⓜ Knightsbridge – ℰ (020) 7730 1234 – www.galvinrestaurants.com
– Closed 25 December and Sunday dinner   **F5**
Rest – *(bookings not accepted)* Carte £ 31/36
♦ French ♦ Simple ♦ Friendly ♦
The Galvin brothers' café overlooks Harrods food hall. The light, French-accented menu is ideal for the busy shopper. You'll find a different soup each day, salads, charcuterie, cocottes and their popular baked lobster fishcake.

✗ **Geales**   AC ⇔ VISA ⓒⓞ AE

1 Cale St. ⊠ SW3 3QT – ⓜ South Kensington – ℰ (020) 79650555
– www.geales.com
– Closed 25-26 December, 1-2 January and Monday   **F6**
Rest – Menu £ 10 – Carte £ 21/39
♦ Fish and seafood ♦ Friendly ♦ Neighbourhood ♦
Fish and chips are the main draw at this cosy, warmly run and sweetly decorated spot. Other choices can include fish pie and soft shell crab tempura, along with wholesome, homemade puddings.

🍴 **Admiral Codrington**   🏠 AC ⇔ VISA ⓒⓞ AE ⓞ

17 Mossop St ⊠ SW3 2LY – ⓜ South Kensington. – ℰ (020) 75810005
– www.theadmiralcodrington.com
– Closed 24-26 December   **F6**
Rest – Carte £ 22/43
♦ Modern ♦ Pub ♦
Busy front bar and a separate, rather smart restaurant with a retractable roof. Head for the more familiar dishes from the monthly-changing menu. Beef is big here and is aged in-house; burgers are very popular. A Chelsea institution.

🍴 **Chelsea Ram**   AC ⇔ VISA ⓒⓞ AE ⓞ

32 Burnaby St ⊠ SW10 0PL – ⓜ Fulham Broadway. – ℰ (020) 73514008
– www.geronimo-inns.co.uk/thechelsearam
– Closed 25 December   **D8**
Rest – Menu £ 25/30 – Carte £ 19/33
♦ British modern ♦ Pub ♦
A warm, welcoming and relaxed pub surrounded by residential streets, with a loyal local following. Expect proper 'pub grub' where the portions are generous and the prices fair.

🍴 **Cadogan Arms**   AC VISA ⓒⓞ AE

298 King's Rd ⊠ SW3 5UG – ⓜ South Kensington. – ℰ (020) 73526500
– www.thecadoganarmschelsea.com
– Closed 25-26 December   **E7**
Rest – *(bookings advisable at dinner)* Carte £ 25/36
♦ British traditional ♦ Pub ♦ Friendly ♦
A Victorian corner pub, owned by the Martin brothers, and just as welcoming to drinkers as to diners. The best dishes are the filling, blokey and meaty ones. Original tiling and panelling add to the warmth; pool tables upstairs.

🍴 **Builders Arms**   AC VISA ⓒⓞ AE

13 Britten St ⊠ SW3 3TY – ⓜ South Kensington. – ℰ (020) 73499040
– www.geronimo-inns.co.uk
– Closed 25-26 December   **E6**
Rest – *(bookings not accepted)* Carte £ 21/41
♦ British traditional ♦ Pub ♦ Trendy ♦
Smart looking and busy pub for the Chelsea set; drinkers are welcomed as much as diners. Cooking reveals the effort put into sourcing decent ingredients; rib of beef for two is a favourite. Thoughtfully compiled wine list.

Pig's Ear   VISA ◐◉ AE ⓪

35 Old Church St ⊠ SW3 5BS – Ⓜ *South Kensington. –* ℰ *(020) 73522908*
– www.thepigsear.info   **E7**
Rest – Carte £ 29/45
♦ British traditional ♦ Pub ♦

Honest pub, with rough-and-ready ground floor bar for lunch; more intimate, wood-panelled upstairs dining room for dinner. Robust, confident and satisfying cooking with a classical bent.

Phoenix   ⓢ AC VISA ◐◉ AE

23 Smith St ⊠ SW3 4EE – Ⓜ *Sloane Square. –* ℰ *(020) 77309182*
– www.geronimo-inns.co.uk/thepheonix
– Closed 25 December   **F6/7**
Rest – Menu £ 18/28 – Carte £ 23/36
♦ Modern ♦ Pub ♦

Friendly, conscientiously run Chelsea local, where satisfying and carefully prepared pub classics are served in the roomy, civilised bar or in the warm, comfortable dining room at the back.

Lots Road Pub & Dining Room   AC VISA ◐◉ AE ⓪

114 Lots Rd ⊠ SW10 0RJ – Ⓜ *Fulham Broadway. –* ℰ *(020) 73526645*
– www.lotsroadpub.com   **D8**
Rest – Carte £ 21/31
♦ British traditional ♦ Pub ♦

Lively semicircular shaped pub, close to Chelsea Harbour. Hearty and satisfying classics, from mussels to Perthshire côte de boeuf and a tart of the day. Staff keep things bright and cheery.

SOUTH KENSINGTON

The Pelham without rest   ⅃⅄ AC VISA ◐◉ AE

15 Cromwell Pl ⊠ SW7 2LA – Ⓜ *South Kensington –* ℰ *(020) 7589 8288*
– www.thepelhamhotel.co.uk   **E6**
51 rm – ♥£ 228/276 ♥♥£ 288/354, ⌲ £ 18 – 1 suite
♦ Luxury ♦ Stylish ♦

Immaculately kept hotel, with willing staff and a discreet atmosphere. Decoratively it's a mix of English country house and city townhouse, with a panelled sitting room and library with honesty bar. Sweet and intimate basement restaurant with European menu.

Blakes   ⓢ ⅃⅄ AC rest, ⟫ VISA ◐◉ AE ⓪

33 Roland Gdns ⊠ SW7 3PF – Ⓜ *Gloucester Road –* ℰ *(020) 73706701*
– www.blakeshotels.com   **D6**
33 rm – ♥£ 209/309 ♥♥£ 249/369, ⌲ £ 22.50 – 8 suites
Rest – Menu £ 23 (lunch) – Carte £ 38/62
♦ Luxury ♦ Design ♦

Behind the Victorian façade lies one of London's first 'boutique' hotels. Dramatic, bold and eclectic décor, with oriental influences and antiques from around the globe. Fashionable restaurant with bamboo and black walls.

Kensington   ⅃⅄ ৬ rm, AC ⟫ ⅏ VISA ◐◉ AE

109-113 Queen's Gate ⊠ SW7 5LR – Ⓜ *South Kensington –* ℰ *(020)*
75896300 – www.doylecollection.com   **E6**
147 rm – ♥£ 174/402 ♥♥£ 198/426, ⌲ £ 20 – 2 suites
Rest *Aubrey* – Menu £ 20/23 – Carte £ 33/54
♦ Business ♦ Contemporary ♦ Stylish ♦

Grand façade to this well-placed, modern corporate hotel fashioned out of several townhouses. Appealing superior rooms and top floor studios; the single rooms are quite compact. Attractive drawing room with fireplace; restaurant with masculine feel and modern menus; afternoon tea also popular.

Number Sixteen   🚗 AC rm, 🛜 VISA ⬤ AE ⓪

16 Sumner Pl. ⬚ *SW7 3EG –* ⓜ *South Kensington –* ✆ *(020) 75895232*
– www.numbersixteenhotel.co.uk   **E6**
41 rm – ♦£ 168 ♦♦£ 222, ⊑ £ 20
Rest *– (room service only)*
♦ Townhouse ♦ Luxury ♦ Stylish ♦
Enticingly refurbished 19C townhouses in smart area. Discreet entrance, comfy sitting room and charming breakfast terrace. Bedrooms in English country house style.

The Cranley   AC 🛜 VISA ⬤ AE

10 Bina Gdns ⬚ *SW5 0LA –* ⓜ *Gloucester Road –* ✆ *(020) 7373 0123*
– www.cranleyhotel.com   **D6**
38 rm – ♦£ 198/318 ♦♦£ 198/414, ⊑ £ 17.75 – 1 suite
Rest *– (room service only)*
♦ Townhouse ♦ Stylish ♦
Delightful Regency townhouse combines charm and period details with modern comforts and technology. Individually styled bedrooms; some with four-posters. Breakfast served in bedrooms.

The Rockwell   🏠 AC 🛜 VISA ⬤ AE

181-183 Cromwell Rd. ⬚ *SW5 0SF –* ⓜ *Earl's Court –* ✆ *(020) 72442000*
– www.therockwell.com   **C5/6**
40 rm – ♦£ 110/150 ♦♦£ 160/250, ⊑ £ 10
Rest – Carte £ 27/42
♦ Townhouse ♦ Design ♦
Two Victorian houses with open, modern lobby and secluded, south-facing garden terrace. Bedrooms come in bold, warm colours; 'Garden Rooms' have their own patios. Small dining room offers easy menu of modern European staples.

The Gore   AC 🛜 🏋 VISA ⬤ AE ⓪

190 Queen's Gate ⬚ *SW7 5EX –* ⓜ *Gloucester Road –* ✆ *(020) 75846601*
– www.gorehotel.com   **D5**
50 rm – ♦£ 204/360 ♦♦£ 204/360, ⊑ £ 15
Rest *Bistro 190 – (booking essential)* Menu £ 20/24 – Carte £ 26/42
♦ Traditional ♦ Classic ♦ Historic ♦
Idiosyncratic, hip Victorian house close to the Royal Albert Hall, whose charming lobby is covered with pictures and prints. Individually styled bedrooms have plenty of character and fun bathrooms. Bright and casual bistro.

Aster House *without rest*   🚗 AC 🛜 VISA ⬤

3 Sumner Pl. ⬚ *SW7 3EE –* ⓜ *South Kensington –* ✆ *(020) 75815888*
– www.asterhouse.com   **E6**
13 rm ⊑ *–* ♦£ 108/150 ♦♦£ 162/324
♦ Townhouse ♦ Cosy ♦
End of terrace Victorian house with a pretty little rear garden and first floor conservatory. Ground floor rooms available. Useful location for visiting many tourist attractions.

XXXX   Bombay Brasserie   🍴 AC VISA ⬤ AE ⓪

Courtfield Rd. ⬚ *SW7 4QH –* ⓜ *Gloucester Road –* ✆ *(020) 73704040*
– www.bombaybrasserielondon.com
– Closed 25-26 December   **D6**
Rest *– (bookings advisable at dinner)* Menu £ 43/48 – Carte £ 29/47
♦ Indian ♦ Exotic ♦ Formal ♦
Plush new look for this well-run, well-known and comfortable Indian restaurant; very smart bar and conservatory with a show kitchen. More creative dishes now sit alongside the more traditional.

UNITED KINGDOM - LONDON

✕✕ Cassis

AC VISA ●● AE ①

232-236 Brompton Rd. ⊠ *SW3 2BB –* Ⓜ *South Kensington*
– ℰ (020) 75811101 – www.cassisbistro.co.uk
– Closed 25 December   **E5**

Rest – Menu £ 21/55 – Carte £ 30/68 ❦

◆ French ◆ Design ◆ Fashionable ◆

The colours and aromas of southern France come to South Ken at this crisply stylish Provençal 'bistro'. Start with some 'petites bouchées' such as classic barbajuans or pissaladière; follow up with authentic bouillabaisse or daube of beef.

✕✕ L'Etranger

AC ⇔ VISA ●● AE ①

36 Gloucester Rd. ⊠ *SW7 4QT –* Ⓜ *Gloucester Road – ℰ (020) 75841118*
– www.etranger.co.uk   **D5**

Rest – *(booking essential)* Menu £ 25 (lunch)
– Carte £ 31/57 ❦

◆ Innovative ◆ Neighbourhood ◆ Romantic ◆

Eclectic menu mixes French dishes with techniques and flavours from Japanese cooking. Impressive wine and sake lists. Moody and atmospheric room; ask for a corner table.

✕✕ Cambio de Tercio

I♡ AC ⇔ VISA ●● AE ①

163 Old Brompton Rd. ⊠ *SW5 0LJ –* Ⓜ *Gloucester Road*
– ℰ (020) 72448970 – www.cambiodetercio.co.uk
– Closed 25 December   **D6**

Rest – Menu £ 40 – Carte £ 18/54 ❦

◆ Spanish ◆ Cosy ◆

Good ingredients and authentic Spanish flavours; desserts are more contemporary. Choose tapas or regular menu. Service improves the more you visit. Owner also has tapas bar across the road.

✕ Bumpkin

AC ⇔ VISA ●● AE

102 Old Brompton Rd ⊠ *SW7 3RD –* Ⓜ *Gloucester Road*
– ℰ (020) 73410802 – www.bumpkinuk.com   **D6**

Rest – Carte £ 30/37

◆ British traditional ◆ Neighbourhood ◆

Sister to the Notting Hill original with the same pub-like informality and friendly service. The kitchen champions British seasonal produce; the simpler dishes are the best ones.

✕ Aubaine

AC VISA ●● AE

260-262 Brompton Rd. ⊠ *SW3 2AS –* Ⓜ *South Kensington*
– ℰ (020) 70520100 – www.aubaine.co.uk   **E6**

Rest – Carte £ 22/52

◆ French ◆ Neighbourhood ◆ Brasserie ◆

'Boulangerie, patisserie, restaurant'. Pass the bakery aromas to an all-day eatery with 'distressed' country feel. Well-judged menus range from croque monsieur to coq au vin.

✕ Bangkok

AC VISA ●●

9 Bute St ⊠ *SW7 3EY –* Ⓜ *South Kensington – ℰ (020) 75848529*
– www.bangkokrestaurant.co.uk
– Closed 24 December-2 January and Sunday   **E6**

Rest – Carte £ 23/33

◆ Thai ◆ Neighbourhood ◆

For over 40 years Bangkok has been providing fresh, authentic and traditional Thai food for its many regulars. The surroundings are pleasantly modest, the prices down-to-earth and the atmosphere warm.

X **Tendido Cero** [AC] [VISA] [✦✦] [AE] [①]

174 Old Brompton Rd. ⊠ *SW5 0BA –* Ⓜ *Gloucester Road –* ℰ *(020) 73703685 – www.cambiodetercio.co.uk*
– Closed 25 December **D6**
Rest – Menu £ 30 – Carte £ 10/48
♦ **Spanish** ♦ **Tapas bar** ♦ **Neighbourhood** ♦

Highlights at this busy tapas bar include Galician octopus, white bean stew with chorizo and pork cheeks with potato purée. There are also some unusual dishes, like the mini 'hamburger' made with sardines.

X **Capote y Toros** [AC] [VISA] [✦✦] [AE] [①]

157 Old Brompton Road ⊠ *SW5 0LJ –* Ⓜ *Gloucester Road –* ℰ *(020) 73730567 – www.cambiodetercio.co.uk*
– Closed Sunday and Monday **D6**
Rest – *(dinner only)* Carte £ 14/51 ⌚
♦ **Spanish** ♦ **Tapas bar** ♦ **Cosy** ♦

Expect to queue at this compact and vividly coloured spot which celebrates sherry, tapas, ham...and bullfighting. Sherry is the star; those as yet unmoved by this most underappreciated of wines will be dazzled by the huge variety.

EARL'S COURT

 K + K George 🚗 [⌚] [AC] 📶 [♨] [P] [VISA] [✦✦] [AE] [①]

1-15 Templeton Pl ⊠ *SW5 9NB –* Ⓜ *Earl's Court –* ℰ *(020) 75988700*
– www.kkhotels.com **C6**
154 rm ⌑ – �$£ 130/220 �$�$£ 150/240
Rest – Carte £ 20/32
♦ **Business** ♦ **Modern** ♦

Five converted 19C houses overlooking large rear garden. Scandinavian-style rooms with low beds, white walls and light wood furniture. Breakfast room has the garden view. Informal dining in the bar.

 Twenty Nevern Square without rest 📶 [P] [VISA] [✦✦] [AE]

20 Nevern Sq. ⊠ *SW5 9PD –* Ⓜ *Earl's Court –* ℰ *(020) 75659555*
– www.twentynevernsquare.co.uk **C6**
20 rm ⌑ – �$£ 84/360 �$�$£ 96/480
♦ **Townhouse** ♦ **Functional** ♦

In an attractive Victorian garden square, an individually designed, privately owned townhouse. Original pieces of furniture and some bedrooms with their own terrace.

 Mayflower without rest 📶 [VISA] [✦✦] [AE]

26-28 Trebovir Rd. ⊠ *SW5 9NJ –* Ⓜ *Earl's Court –* ℰ *(020) 73700991*
– www.mayflowerhotel.co.uk **C6**
43 rm ⌑ – �$£ 109/149 �$�$£ 149/299 – 4 suites
♦ **Modern** ♦ **Functional** ♦

Conveniently placed, friendly establishment with a secluded rear breakfast terrace and basement breakfast room. Individually styled bedrooms with Asian influence.

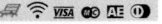 **Amsterdam** without rest 🚗 📶 [VISA] [✦✦] [AE] [①]

7-9 Trebovir Rd. ⊠ *SW5 9LS –* Ⓜ *Earl's Court –* ℰ *(020) 7370 2814*
– www.amsterdam-hotel.com **C6**
19 rm – �$£ 86/99 �$�$£ 108/120, ⌑ £ 3 – 8 suites
♦ **Townhouse** ♦ **Cosy** ♦

Basement breakfast room and a small secluded garden. The brightly decorated bedrooms are light and airy. Some have smart wood floors; some boast their own balcony.

Rushmore without rest 🛜 VISA ⦿ AE ⓘ

11 Trebovir Rd. ⊠ SW5 9LS – Ⓜ Earl's Court – 𝒞 (020) 73703839
– www.rushmore-hotel.co.uk **C6**
22 rm � – †£ 89/119 ††£ 99/149

♦ Townhouse ♦ Retro ♦

Behind its Victorian façade lies a hotel popular with tourists. Individually decorated bedrooms in a variety of shapes and sizes. Piazza-style conservatory breakfast room.

KENSINGTON – NORTH KENSINGTON – NOTTING HILL*Plan XI*

KENSINGTON

Royal Garden ⩽ ㄥ𝑓 ㉙ & rm, AC 🛜 🏊 P̄ VISA ⦿ AE ⓘ

2-24 Kensington High St. ⊠ W8 4PT – Ⓜ High Street Kensington
– 𝒞 (020) 79378000 – www.royalgardenhotel.co.uk **D4**
377 rm – †£ 430/527 ††£ 430/755, � £ 24 – 17 suites
Rest Min Jiang – see restaurant listing
Rest Park Terrace – 𝒞 (020) 73610602 – Menu £ 16/35

♦ Business ♦ Functional ♦

A tall, modern hotel with many of its rooms enjoying enviable views over the adjacent Kensington Gardens. All the modern amenities and services, with well-drilled staff. Bright, spacious Park Terrace offers British, Asian and modern European cuisine.

The Milestone ㄥ𝑓 ㉙ AC 🛜 ⦿ AE ⓘ

1-2 Kensington Ct. ⊠ W8 5DL – Ⓜ High Street Kensington – 𝒞 (020)
79171000 – www.milestonehotel.com **D4**
56 rm – †£ 444/600 ††£ 444/600, � £ 25 – 6 suites
Rest Cheneston's – (bookings essential for non-residents) Menu £ 25
(lunch) – Carte £ 51/68 ⦙

♦ Luxury ♦ Personalised ♦

Elegant and enthusiastically run hotel with decorative Victorian façade and a very British feel. Charming oak-panelled sitting room is popular for afternoon tea; snug bar in former stables. Meticulously decorated bedrooms offer period detail. Ambitious cooking in discreet Cheneston's restaurant.

Baglioni ㄥ𝑓 ㉙ AC 🛜 🏊 VISA ⦿ AE ⓘ

60 Hyde Park Gate ⊠ SW7 5BB – Ⓜ High Street Kensington – 𝒞 (020)
73685700 – www.baglionihotels.com **D4**
52 rm – †£ 324/522 ††£ 324/522, � £ 29 – 15 suites
Rest Brunello – see restaurant listing

♦ Luxury ♦ Stylish ♦

Opposite Kensington Palace and no escaping the fact that this is an Italian owned hotel. The interior is bold and ornate and there's a trendy basement bar. Stylish bedrooms have a masculine feel and boast impressive facilities.

XXX 🛈♡ AC ⇕ VISA ⦿ AE ⓘ
❀ Launceston Place

1a Launceston Pl. ⊠ W8 5RL – Ⓜ Gloucester Road – 𝒞 (020) 7937 6912
– www.launcestonplace-restaurant.co.uk
– Closed 24-30 December, Monday lunch and dinner bank holiday Mondays
Rest – (bookings advisable at dinner) Menu £ 23/46 **D5**

♦ Modern ♦ Neighbourhood ♦

Longstanding intimate neighbourhood restaurant; divided into various areas, where everyone has their favourite spot. The style of food is refined without being dainty and, like most of its customers, sophisticated without being showy. ➜ Scallop with glazed pork belly, apple and celeriac. Lamb with curried cauliflower, peas and broad beans. Baked English custard, poached rhubarb and apple ice cream.

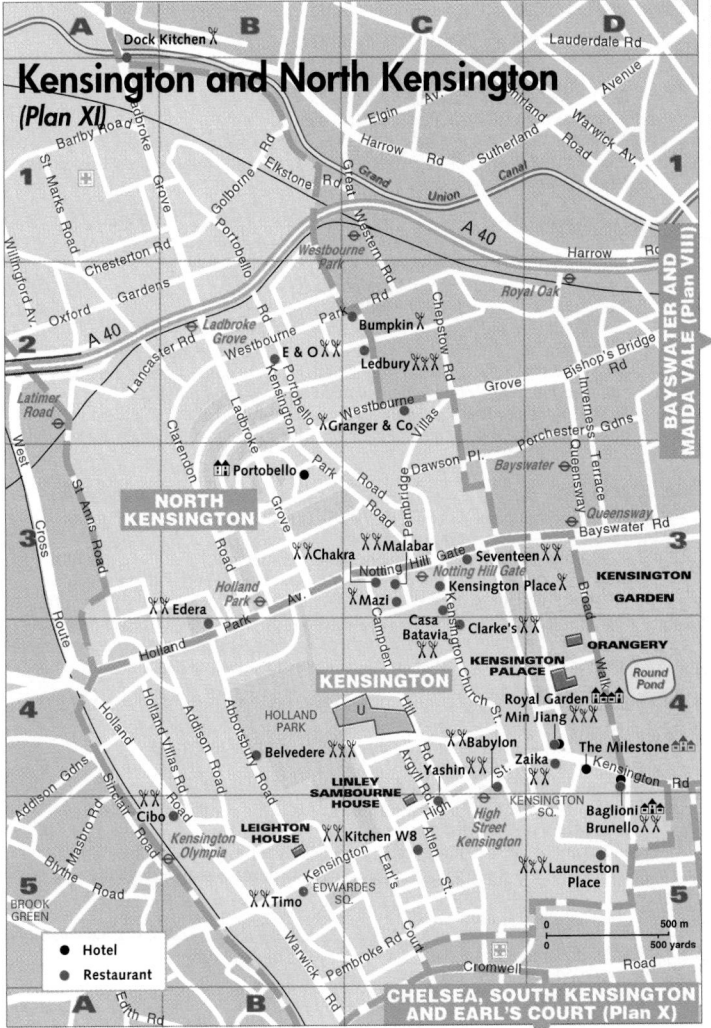

BAYSWATER AND MAIDA VALE (Plan VIII)

Kensington and North Kensington
(Plan XI)

CHELSEA, SOUTH KENSINGTON AND EARL'S COURT (Plan X)

- ● Hotel
- ● Restaurant

XXX **Min Jiang** – Royal Garden Hotel ≤ AC ⇔ VISA ●● AE ①

(10th Floor), 2-24 Kensington High St ⊠ *W8 4PT*
– Ⓜ *High Street Kensington –* ℰ *(020) 73611988 – www.minjiang.co.uk*
Rest – Menu £ 40/45 – Carte £ 23/88 **D4**

♦ Chinese ♦ Elegant ♦ Design ♦

The cooking at this stylish 10th floor Chinese restaurant covers all provinces, but
Cantonese and Sichuan dominate. Wood-fired Beijing duck is a speciality. The
room's good looks compete with the great views of Kensington Gardens.

XXX **Belvedere** 🛗 AC ⇌ ⭐ VISA ⓪ AE

Holland House, off Abbotsbury Rd. ⊠ *W8 6LU* – Ⓜ *Holland Park*
– 𝒞 *(020) 76021238 – www.belvedererestaurant.co.uk*
– Closed 26 December, 1 January and Sunday dinner   **B4**
Rest – Menu £ 20 (weekday lunch)/28 – Carte £ 32/48
♦ Modern ♦ Romantic ♦ Elegant ♦
Former 19C orangery in a delightful position in the middle of the park. On two
floors with a bar and balcony terrace and decorated with huge vases of flowers.
Modern take on classic dishes.

XX **Kitchen W8** AC VISA ⓪ AE
🌼
11-13 Abingdon Rd ⊠ *W8 6AH* – Ⓜ *High Street Kensington –* 𝒞 *(020)*
79370120 – www.kitchenw8.com
– Closed 25-26 December and bank holidays   **C5**
Rest – Menu £ 18/30 – Carte £ 35/55
♦ Modern ♦ Neighbourhood ♦
Smart, comfortable restaurant which is not as casual as its name implies, but
which does have a pleasant, neighbourhood feel. Skilled kitchen produces
balanced dishes free of showiness, with the emphasis on flavour.
➜ Grilled white asparagus with thinly sliced veal, egg and truffle. Cod with
brown shrimps and pickled cauliflower. Hazelnut ice cream with banana
and lime caramel.

XX **Chakra** AC VISA ⓪ AE ⓪

157-159 Notting Hill Gate ⊠ *W11 3LF* – Ⓜ *Notting Hill Gate –* 𝒞 *(020)*
7229 2115 – www.chakralondon.com
– Closed 25-26 December, 1 January and Easter Monday   **C3**
Rest – *(booking advisable)* Menu £ 30 (weekday dinner) – Carte £ 16/43
♦ Indian ♦ Elegant ♦ Exotic ♦
The influences come from the Royal kitchens of the Maharajahs, particularly
those from the North Western province of Lucknow. The spicing is more subtle
than usual, the aroma fresher and the presentation more striking.

XX **Babylon** ≤ AC ⇌ VISA ⓪ AE

The Roof Gardens, 99 Kensington High St ((entrance on Derry St))
⊠ *W8 5SA* – Ⓜ *High Street Kensington –* 𝒞 *(020) 73683993*
– www.roofgardens.virgin.com
– Closed 24-30 December, 1-2 January and Sunday dinner   **C4**
Rest – Menu £ 20/47 – Carte £ 34/57
♦ Modern ♦ Fashionable ♦
Found on the 7th floor and affording great views of the city skyline and an ama-
zing 1.5 acres of rooftop garden. Stylish modern décor in keeping with the con-
temporary, British cooking.

XX **Brunello** – Baglioni Hotel AC VISA ⓪ AE ⓪

60 Hyde Park Gate ⊠ *SW7 5BB* – Ⓜ *High Street Kensington –* 𝒞 *(020)*
73685900 – www.baglionihotels.com   **D4**
Rest – Menu £ 26/30 – Carte £ 42/74
♦ Italian ♦ Trendy ♦
The Baglioni Hotel's ground floor bar, lounge and restaurant all merge into one
in a heady mix of black, gold, velvet and glass. The menu traverses all parts of
Italy and uses prime ingredients.

XX **Clarke's** AC VISA ⓪ AE ⓪

124 Kensington Church St ⊠ *W8 4BH* – Ⓜ *Notting Hill Gate –* 𝒞 *(020)*
72219225 – www.sallyclarke.com
– Closed Christmas-New Year, Sunday dinner and bank holidays   **C4**
Rest – *(booking advisable)* Carte £ 34/43
♦ Modern ♦ Neighbourhood ♦
Forever popular restaurant, serving a choice of dishes boasting trademark fresh,
seasonal ingredients and Sally Clarke's famed lightness of touch. Has enjoyed a
loyal local following for over 25 years.

XX

Yashin

$\boxed{AC}$ $\boxed{VISA}$ $\boxed{OO}$ $\boxed{AE}$

1A Argyll Rd. ⊠ *W8 7DB –* **M** *High Street Kensington –* ☏ *(020) 79381536*
– www.yashinsushi.com
– Closed first Monday in month, Christmas-New Year   **C5**
Rest *– (booking essential)* Carte £ 38/83
♦ Japanese ♦ Design ♦ Fashionable ♦

Ask for a counter seat to watch the chefs prepare the sushi; choose 8, 11 or 15 pieces, to be served together. The quality of fish is clear; tiny garnishes and the odd bit of searing add originality.

XX

Casa Batavia

$\boxed{AC}$ $\boxed{⇔}$ $\boxed{VISA}$ $\boxed{OO}$

135 Kensington Church St ⊠ *W8 7LP –* **M** *Notting Hill Gate –* ☏ *(020) 7221 7348 – www.casabatavia.com*
– Closed 25 December, Easter Sunday and lunch Saturday   **C4**
Rest *– (booking advisable)* Menu £ 19 *(weekday lunch)* – Carte £ 24/36
♦ Italian ♦ Neighbourhood ♦ Intimate ♦

Intimate restaurant opened in 2011 by an experienced restaurateur and a chef from Turin. The refined cooking of Piedmont is the main influence; look out for ricotta crostino, potted rabbit with hazelnuts and, of course, panna cotta.

XX

Zaika

$\boxed{AC}$ $\boxed{VISA}$ $\boxed{OO}$ $\boxed{AE}$

1 Kensington High St. ⊠ *W8 5NP –* **M** *High Street Kensington –* ☏ *(020) 77956533 – www.zaika-restaurant.co.uk*
– Closed 25-26 December, 1-2 January and Monday lunch   **D4**
Rest *–* Menu £ 23/62 – Carte £ 31/49
♦ Indian ♦ Exotic ♦

The smell of incense is one clue that the days of this being a bank are long gone; bright colours offset the high ceiling and wood panelling. The cooking is original and sophisticated but at times the spicing can lack a degree of subtlety.

XX

Timo

$\boxed{AC}$ $\boxed{VISA}$ $\boxed{OO}$ $\boxed{AE}$

343 Kensington High St. ⊠ *W8 6NW –* **M** *High Street Kensington*
– ☏ *(020) 76033888 – www.timorestaurant.net*
– Closed Christmas, bank holidays and Sunday   **B5**
Rest *– (booking advisable)* Menu £ 12/19 – Carte £ 30/42
♦ Italian ♦ Neighbourhood ♦ Design ♦

Comfortable and comforting neighbourhood Italian restaurant, with careful and reliable cooking. Service is smart and conscientious, under the watchful eye of the owner.

XX

Seventeen

$\boxed{AC}$ $\boxed{⇔}$ $\boxed{VISA}$ $\boxed{OO}$

17 Notting Hill Gate ⊠ *W11 3JQ –* **M** *Notting Hill Gate –* ☏ *(020) 79850006 – www.seventeen-london.co.uk*   **C3**
Rest *–* Menu £ 21/36 – Carte £ 17/41
♦ Chinese ♦ Design ♦ Intimate ♦

Stylishly kitted out, intimate and moodily lit Chinese restaurant on two floors. The kitchen, behind an eye-catching glass wall, specialises in authentic Sichuan and Shanghainese delicacies.

XX

Cibo

$\boxed{VISA}$ $\boxed{OO}$ $\boxed{AE}$

3 Russell Gdns ⊠ *W14 8EZ –* **M** *Kensington Olympia –* ☏ *(020) 73716271*
– www.ciborestaurant.net
– Closed 1 week Christmas, Easter and bank holidays   **B5**
Rest *–* Menu £ 20/35 – Carte £ 26/44
♦ Italian ♦ Neighbourhood ♦

Long-standing neighbourhood Italian with local following. More space at the back of the room. Robust, satisfying cooking; the huge grilled shellfish and sea-food platter a speciality.

XX · **Malabar**   `AC` `VISA` `◯◯` `AE`

27 Uxbridge St. ✉ *W8 7TQ –* Ⓜ *Notting Hill Gate –* ☏ *(020) 77278800*
– www.malabar-restaurant.co.uk
– Closed 1 week Christmas   **C3**
Rest *– (buffet lunch Sunday)* Menu £ 18/25 – Carte £ 14/31

♦ Indian ♦ Neighbourhood ♦

Opened in 1983 in a residential Notting Hill street, but keeps up its appearance, remaining fresh and good-looking. Balanced menu of carefully prepared and sensibly priced Indian dishes.

X · **Kensington Place**   `AC` `⇄` `VISA` `◯◯` `AE`

201-209 Kensington Church St. ✉ *W8 7LX –* Ⓜ *Notting Hill Gate*
– ☏ *(020) 77273184 – www.kensingtonplace-restaurant.co.uk*
– Closed Sunday dinner and Monday lunch   **C3**
Rest *–* Menu £ 17 *(weekday dinner)* – Carte £ 20/57

♦ Modern ♦ Neighbourhood ♦ Brasserie ♦

Opened in 1987 as a big, boisterous, brasserie; these days a little less noisy but it remains well run. Competitively priced set menu offers a wide choice of modern European dishes.

X · **Mazi**   `❄` `VISA` `◯◯` `AE`

12-14 Hillgate Rd ✉ *W8 7SR –* Ⓜ *Notting Hill Gate –* ☏ *(020) 72293794*
– www.mazi.co.uk
– Closed 24-30 December   **C3**
Rest *–* Menu £ 22 *(lunch)* – Carte £ 29/43

♦ Greek ♦ Friendly ♦

It's all about sharing at this simple, bright Greek restaurant where traditional recipes are given a modern twist to create vibrant, colourful and fresh tasting dishes. The garden terrace at the back is a charming spot in summer.

NORTH KENSINGTON

🛏 · **The Portobello** without rest   `⊘` `VISA` `◯◯` `AE`

22 Stanley Gdns. ✉ *W11 2NG –* Ⓜ *Notting Hill Gate –* ☏ *(020) 77272777*
– www.portobellohotel.co.uk
– Closed 24-29 December   **B3**
21 rm ⌴ *–* ♦£ 174/234 ♦♦£ 252/378

♦ Townhouse ♦ Personalised ♦ Classic ♦

An attractive Victorian townhouse in an elegant terrace. Original and theatrical décor. Circular beds, half-testers, Victorian baths: no two bedrooms are the same.

XXX · **Ledbury** (Brett Graham)   `⊘` `AC` `VISA` `◯◯` `AE`
✿✿

127 Ledbury Rd. ✉ *W11 2AQ –* Ⓜ *Notting Hill Gate –* ☏ *(020) 7792 9090*
– www.theledbury.com
– Closed 25-26 December, August bank holiday and Monday lunch
Rest *–* Menu £ 30/80 ⅜   **C2**

♦ Modern ♦ Neighbourhood ♦ Fashionable ♦

Elegant, understated surroundings with professional, well-organised service but it still has a neighbourhood feel. Highly skilled kitchen with an inherent understanding of flavour; great ingredients, especially game in season.
➜ Buffalo milk curd with Saint-Nectaire and truffle toast. Breast and confit legs of grouse with foie gras and cherries. Parfait of dried flowers, wild strawberries and vanilla tapioca.

XX · **Edera**   `AC` `⇄` `VISA` `◯◯` `AE`

148 Holland Park Ave. ✉ *W11 4UE –* Ⓜ *Holland Park –* ☏ *(020) 72216090*
– www.edera.co.uk   **B4**
Rest *–* Carte £ 28/53

♦ Italian ♦ Neighbourhood ♦

Warm and comfortable neighbourhood restaurant with plenty of local regulars and efficient, well-marshalled service. Robust cooking has a subtle Sardinian accent and comes in generous portions.

XX **E&O** ⓐ ⟷ VISA ◉ AE ⓪

14 Blenheim Cres. ✉ *W11 1NN* – ⓜ *Ladbroke Grove* – ✆ *(020) 72295454*
– www.rickerrestaurants.com
– Closed 26-27 August, 25-26 December and 1 January   **B2**
Rest – Menu £ 20/59 – Carte £ 18/57

♦ Asian ♦ Trendy ♦

Mean, moody and cool and that's just the customers. Sophisticated, chic and noisy, thanks to contented groups of diners. Menus scour the Far East, with dishes designed for sharing.

X **Dock Kitchen** VISA ◉ AE ⓪

Portobello Dock, 342-344 Ladbroke Grove ✉ *W10 5BU*
– ⓜ *Ladbroke Grove* – ✆ *(020) 8962 1610 – www.dockkitchen.co.uk*
– Closed 24 December-5 January and Sunday dinner   **A1**
Rest – Menu £ 15 (lunch)/55 – Carte £ 26/41

♦ Mediterranean ♦ Design ♦ Trendy ♦

What started as a 'pop-up' became a permanent feature in this open-plan former Victorian goods yard. The chef's peregrinations inform his cooking, which relies on simple, natural flavours.

X **Bumpkin** ⓐ ⟷ VISA ◉ AE

209 Westbourne Park Rd ✉ *W11 1EA* – ⓜ *Westbourne Park* – ✆ *(020)*
72439818 – www.bumpkinuk.com   **C2**
Rest – Carte £ 23/39

♦ British traditional ♦ Bistro ♦ Neighbourhood ♦

Converted pea-green pub with casual, clubby feel and wholesome philosophy of cooking seasonal, carefully sourced and organic food. The same modern, Mediterranean-influenced menu is served on both floors.

X **Granger & Co** VISA ◉ AE

175 Westbourne Grove ✉ *W11 2SB* – ⓜ *Bayswater* – ✆ *(020) 7229 9111*
– www.grangerandco.com
– Closed 25-26 December and 1 January   **C2**
Rest – *(bookings not accepted)* Carte £ 16/36

♦ Modern ♦ Friendly ♦ Simple ♦

When Bill Granger moved from sunny Sydney to cool Notting Hill he opened a local restaurant too. He's brought with him that delightful 'matey' service that only Aussies do, his breakfast time ricotta hotcakes and a fresh, zesty menu.

CLERKENWELL - FINSBURY

Clerkenwell

🏨 **Malmaison** 📶 ⓓ rm, ⓐ 🛜 🛁 VISA ◉ AE ⓪

18-21 Charterhouse Sq ✉ *EC1M 6AH* – ⓜ *Barbican* – ✆ *(020) 7012 3700*
– www.malmaison.com   **L2**
97 rm – ♦£ 135/305 ♦♦£ 155/550, ⌷ £ 18.95
Rest *Brasserie* – *(closed Saturday lunch)* Carte £ 27/68

♦ Townhouse ♦ Modern ♦

Striking early 20C red-brick building overlooking pleasant square. Stylish, comfy public areas. Bedrooms in vivid, bold colours, with plenty of extra touches. Modern brasserie employing meats from Smithfield.

🏠 **The Rookery** *without rest* ⓐ 🛜 VISA ◉ AE ⓪

12 Peters Ln, Cowcross St ✉ *EC1M 6DS* – ⓜ *Barbican* – ✆ *(020)*
73360931 – www.rookeryhotel.com
– Closed 24-26 December   **L2**
32 rm – ♦£ 210/282 ♦♦£ 282/472, ⌷ £ 12 – 1 suite

♦ Townhouse ♦ Modern ♦

A row of charmingly restored 18C houses. Wood panelling, stone-flagged flooring, open fires and antique furniture. Highly individual bedrooms, with Victorian bathrooms.

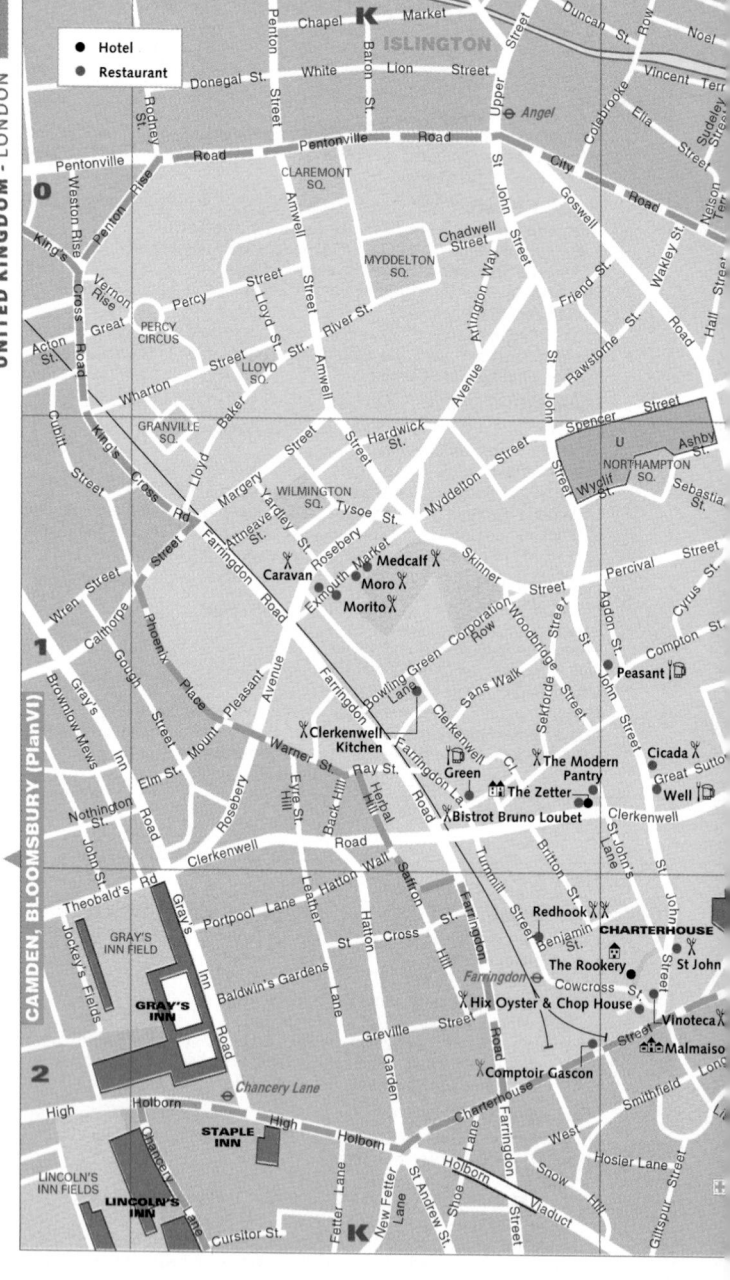

● Hotel
● Restaurant

ISLINGTON

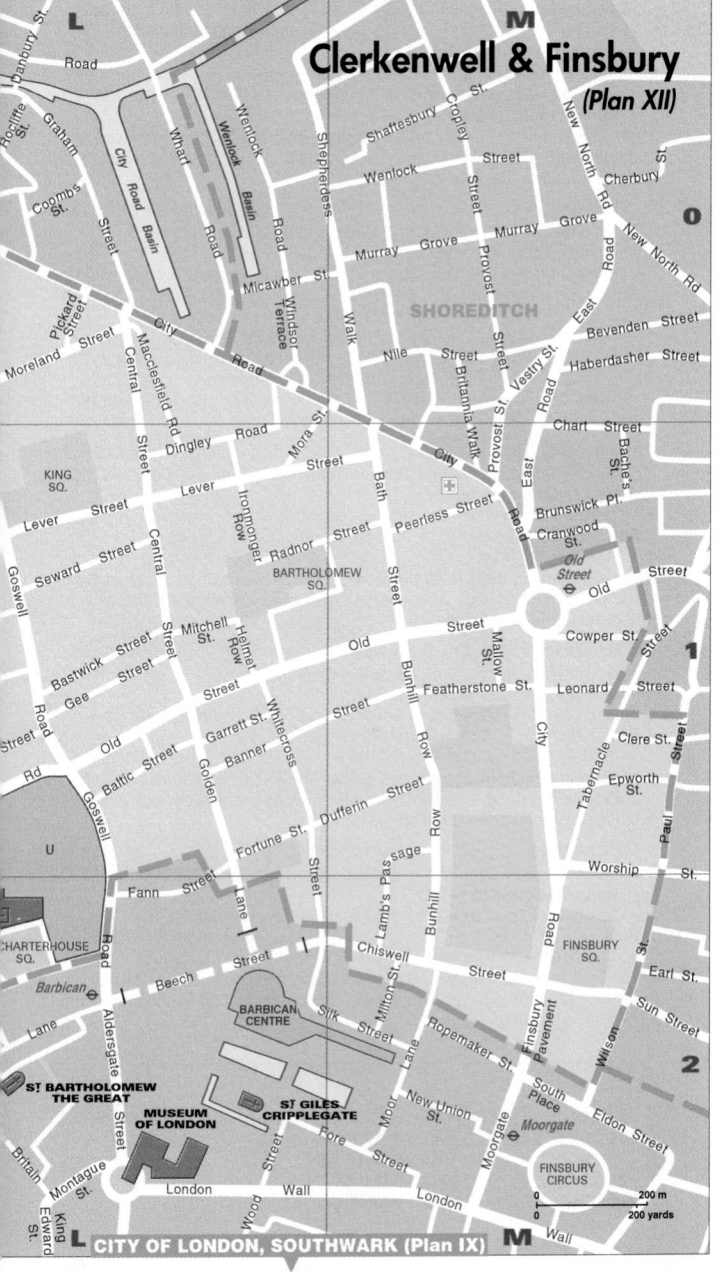

Clerkenwell & Finsbury
(Plan XII)

SHOREDITCH

KING SQ.

BARTHOLOMEW SQ.

CHARTERHOUSE SQ.

Barbican

BARBICAN CENTRE

St BARTHOLOMEW THE GREAT

MUSEUM OF LONDON

St GILES CRIPPLEGATE

FINSBURY SQ.

FINSBURY CIRCUS

Moorgate

London Wall

CITY OF LONDON, SOUTHWARK (Plan IX)

UNITED KINGDOM - LONDON

XX Redhook   AC ⇄ VISA ⊕ AE

89 Turnmill St ⊠ EC1M 5QU – Ⓜ Farringdon – ℰ (020) 70656800
– www.redhooklondon.com
– Closed Easter, 25 December, Saturday lunch and Sunday   **K2**
Rest *– (bookings advisable at dinner)* Menu £ 18 (lunch) – Carte £ 28/44
♦ Meats and grills ♦ Design ♦

Brooklyn comes to Clerkenwell in the shape of this American-style restaurant specialising in seafood and steaks. Bare brick walls, booths and a faux industrial aesthetic add to the New York feel.

X St John   AC ⇄ VISA ⊕ AE ⓪
❀

26 St John St ⊠ EC1M 4AY – Ⓜ Farringdon – ℰ (020) 33018069
– www.stjohnrestaurant.com
– Closed Christmas-New Year, Saturday lunch, Sunday dinner and bank holidays
Rest *– (booking essential)* Carte £ 25/43   **L2**
♦ British traditional ♦ Minimalist ♦ Brasserie ♦

'Nose to tail eating' is how they describe their cooking at this busy, bright, converted 19C smokehouse. Strong on offal, game and unusual cuts; gloriously British, highly seasonal, appealingly simple and very satisfying.
➜ Roast bone marrow and parsley salad. Roast Middle White loin and braised fennel. Eccles cake and Lancashire cheese.

X Comptoir Gascon   AC VISA ⊕ AE
☻

61-63 Charterhouse St. ⊠ EC1M 6HJ – Ⓜ Farringdon – ℰ (020) 7608 0851
– www.comptoirgascon.com
– Closed Christmas-New Year, Sunday, Monday and bank holidays
Rest *– (booking essential)* Menu £ 15 (lunch) – Carte £ 17/29   **K2**
♦ French ♦ Bistro ♦

Buzzy restaurant; sister to Club Gascon. Rustic and satisfying specialities from the SW of France include wine, cheese, bread and especially duck. Further produce on display to take home.

X Hix Oyster and Chop House   🛏 VISA ⊕ AE

36-37 Greenhill Rents ⊠ EC1M 6BN – Ⓜ Farringdon – ℰ (020) 70171930
– www.hixoysterandchophouse.co.uk
– Closed 25-29 December, bank holidays, Saturday lunch and Sunday dinner
Rest *– Menu £ 18 (lunch and early dinner) – Carte £ 27/59*   **L2**
♦ British traditional ♦ Simple ♦

Appropriately utilitarian surroundings put the focus on seasonal and often underused British ingredients. Cooking is satisfying and unfussy, with plenty of oysters and aged beef served on the bone.

X Vinoteca   VISA ⊕ AE

7 St John St. ⊠ EC1M 4AA – Ⓜ Farringdon – ℰ (020) 72538786
– www.vinoteca.co.uk
– Closed 25-26 December, 1 January, bank holidays and Sunday
Rest *– Carte £ 18/31* 🍴   **L2**
♦ Modern ♦ Wine bar ♦

This cosy and passionately run 'bar and wine shop' is always busy and full of life. Thrilling wine list is constantly evolving; the classic and vibrant dishes are the ideal accompaniment.

Finsbury

🏠 Zetter   ♿ AC 🛜 🛁 VISA ⊕ AE

St John's Sq., 86-88 Clerkenwell Rd. ⊠ EC1M 5RJ – Ⓜ Farringdon
– ℰ (020) 7324 4444 – www.thezetter.com   **K1**
72 rm – ♥£ 222 ♥♥£ 222, � £ 14
Rest *Bistrot Bruno Loubet* – see restaurant listing
♦ Townhouse ♦ Modern ♦

A trendy and discreet converted 19C warehouse with well-equipped bedrooms that come with pleasant touches, such as Penguin paperbacks. The more idiosyncratic Zetter Townhouse across the square is used as an overflow.

✕ **Bistrot Bruno Loubet** – Zetter Hotel   🛜 AC VISA ☺☺ AE

St John's Sq., 86-88 Clerkenwell Rd. ✉ *EC1M 5RJ* – Ⓜ *Farringdon*
– ✆ *(020) 7324 4444* – *www.thezetter.com*   **K1**
Rest – *(closed 23-27 December to non-residents) (booking advisable)*
Carte £ 29/36
♦ French ♦ Fashionable ♦
Having made his name in the early '90s, Bruno Loubet's London return was
much anticipated. His flavoursome regional French cooking proves a good fit
for this busy, bright restaurant at the Zetter hotel.

✕ **Moro**   🛜 AC VISA ☺☺ AE

34-36 Exmouth Mkt ✉ *EC1R 4QE* – Ⓜ *Farringdon* – ✆ *(020) 78338336*
– *www.moro.co.uk*
– *Closed 24 December-3 January, bank holidays and Sunday dinner*
Rest – *(booking essential)* Carte £ 28/37 🍸   **K1**
♦ Mediterranean ♦ Friendly ♦
A feature of Exmouth Market for over 15 years and still one of its busiest restau-
rants. Daily changing menu is an appealing and eclectic mix of Mediterranean,
Moroccan and Spanish. Friendly T-shirted staff and a fun atmosphere.

✕ **Medcalf**   🛜 ⇔ VISA ☺☺
😊

40 Exmouth Mkt. ✉ *EC1R 4QE* – Ⓜ *Farringdon* – ✆ *(020) 78333533*
– *www.medcalfbar.co.uk*
– *Closed 31 December-3 January, Sunday dinner and bank holidays*
Rest – *(booking essential)* Carte £ 25/30   **K1**
♦ British traditional ♦ Rustic ♦
Bustling, no-frills former butcher's shop with lively atmosphere. Satisfying
robust cooking, with the emphasis on seasonal, British ingredients. Good
range of beer and wine by the glass.

✕ **Cicada**   🛜 ⇔ VISA ☺☺ AE ①

132-134 St John St ✉ *EC1V 4JT* – Ⓜ *Farringdon* – ✆ *(020) 76081550*
– *www.rickerrestaurants.com*
– *Closed 25 December, 1 January, Saturday lunch and Sunday*   **L1**
Rest – Carte £ 20/36
♦ Asian ♦ Trendy ♦
Set in a culinary hotbed, this buzzy restaurant and vibrant bar is spacious, lively
and popular for its south east Asian dishes. You can even just pop in for one
course and a beer.

✕ **The Modern Pantry**   🛜 AC ⇔ VISA ☺☺ AE

47-48 St John's Sq. ✉ *EC1V 4JJ* – Ⓜ *Farringdon* – ✆ *(020) 75539210*
– *www.themodernpantry.co.uk*
– *Closed 25-26 December and 1 January*   **K1**
Rest – *(booking advisable)* Menu £ 20 (lunch) – Carte £ 28/41
♦ Other world kitchens ♦ Design ♦
Fusion cooking that uses complementary flavours to create vibrant, zesty
dishes. The simple, crisp ground floor of this Georgian building has the buzz;
upstairs is more intimate. Clued-up service.

✕ **Morito**   VISA ☺☺ AE ①
😊

32 Exmouth Mkt ✉ *EC1R 4QE* – Ⓜ *Farringdon* – ✆ *(020) 72787007*
– *www.morito.co.uk*
– *Closed 24 December-3 January and bank holidays*   **K1**
Rest – *(bookings not accepted)* Carte approx. £ 25
♦ Spanish ♦ Intimate ♦ Tapas bar ♦
From the owners of next door Moro comes this authentic and appealingly
down to earth little tapas bar. Seven or eight dishes between two should suffice
but over-ordering is easy and won't break the bank.

Caravan
VISA *Φ* *AE* *①*

11-13 Exmouth Market ✉ *EC1R 4QD –* ⓜ *Farringdon –* ☏ *(020) 78338115*
– www.caravanonexmouth.co.uk
– Closed Christmas-New Year and Sunday dinner   **K1**
Rest *– (booking advisable)* Carte £ 22/31 ♦
♦ Other world kitchens ♦ Trendy ♦
A discernible Antipodean vibe pervades this casual eatery, from the laid-back charm of the service to the kitchen's confident combining of unusual flavours. Cooking is influenced by owner's travels – hence the name.

Clerkenwell Kitchen
VISA *Φ*

27-31 Clerkenwell Cl ✉ *EC1R 0AT –* ⓜ *Farringdon –* ☏ *(020) 71019959*
– www.theclerkenwellkitchen.co.uk
– Closed Christmas-New Year, Saturday, Sunday and bank holidays
Rest *– (lunch only) (booking advisable)* Carte £ 17/23   **K1**
♦ Modern ♦ Friendly ♦
The owner of this simple, friendly, tucked away eatery worked with Hugh Fearnley-Whittingstall and is committed to sustainability. Daily changing, well-sourced produce; fresh, flavoursome cooking.

Green
AC *VISA* *Φ* *①*

29 Clerkenwell Gn ✉ *EC1R 0DU –* ⓜ *Farringdon. –* ☏ *(020) 74908010*
– www.thegreenec1.co.uk
– Closed 25-30 December   **K1**
Rest *–* Carte £ 19/30
♦ British traditional ♦ Pub ♦
The building dates from 1580 and became a tavern in 1720. Appetising and imaginative bar snacks on the ground floor; intimate upstairs dining room for fresh, seasonal and unfussy cooking.

Peasant
VISA *Φ* *AE*

240 St John St ✉ *EC1V 4PH –* ⓜ *Farringdon. –* ☏ *(020) 73367726*
– www.thepeasant.co.uk
– Closed 25 December-1 January and bank holidays except Good Friday
Rest *– (booking essential)* Menu £ 28/35 – Carte £ 25/36   **L1**
♦ British modern ♦ Pub ♦
This handsome Victorian pub was at the vanguard of the gastropub movement. Share a cheeseboard or meze in the bar or book in the upstairs restaurant for more sophisticated yet equally gutsy cooking.

Well
VISA *Φ* *AE*

180 St John St ✉ *EC1V 4JY –* ⓜ *Farringdon. –* ☏ *(020) 72519363*
– www.downthewell.com
– Closed 25-26 December   **L1**
Rest *–* Carte £ 24/36
♦ British modern ♦ Pub ♦ Neighbourhood ♦
Compact pub with sliding glass doors and popular pavement benches. Modern dishes range from potted shrimps to foie gras and chicken liver parfait. Classic puddings; splendid cheeses.

LONDON HEATHROW AIRPORT

Hilton London Heathrow Airport Terminal 5
🏋 I♨

Poyle Rd, Colnbrook (West :   *📶 🐾 ⅙ rm, AC 📶 ⅙ P VISA Φ AE*
2.5 mi by A 3113) ✉ *SL3 0FF –* ☏ *(01753) 686860*
– www.hilton.com/heathrowterminal5
347 rm *–* ♦£ 119/263 ♦♦£ 119/287, ⌷ £ 21 *– 3 suites*
Rest *Mr Todiwala's Kitchen* – see restaurant listing
Rest *Gallery* – Carte £ 23/69
♦ Chain hotel ♦ Business ♦ Functional ♦
A feeling of light and space pervades this modern, corporate hotel. Soundproofed rooms are fitted to a good standard; the spa offers wide-ranging treatments. Open-plan Gallery for British comfort food.

Sofitel
🖿 🕲 🛖 ⅇ 🖳 ⬙ 🛋 **P** VISA ⓿ 🅰🅴 🅾

Terminal 5, Heathrow Airport ✉ *TW6 2GD* – Ⓜ *Heathrow Terminal 5*
– ℰ *(020) 87577777 – www.sofitel.com*
578 rm – †£ 119/359 ††£ 119/2710, ⬚ £ 17 – 27 suites
Rest *La Belle Époque* – *(closed Christmas, Sunday and bank holidays)*
Menu £ 25/45 – Carte £ 35/55
Rest *Vivre* – *(dinner only)* Menu £ 25 – Carte £ 27/46
♦ Chain hotel ♦ Functional ♦
Smart and well-run contemporary hotel, opened in 2008. Designed around a
series of atriums, with direct access to T5. Crisply decorated, comfortable
bedrooms with luxurious bathrooms. Choice of restaurant: international or clas-
sical French cuisine.

Hilton London Heathrow Airport
🖿 🛖 🔲 ⅇ rm, 🖳 ⬙
🛋 **P** VISA ⓿ 🅰🅴

Terminal 4 ✉ *TW6 3AF*
– Ⓜ *Heathrow Terminal 4* – ℰ *(020) 87597755*
– *www.hilton.co.uk/heathrow*
355 rm ⬚ – †£ 197/329 ††£ 251/395 – 5 suites
Rest *Zen Oriental* – see restaurant listing
Rest *Aromi* – *(closed lunch Saturday, Sunday and bank holidays)*
Menu £ 21/29 – Carte £ 29/54
♦ Chain hotel ♦ Business ♦ Functional ♦
Group hotel with a striking modern exterior and linked to Terminal 4 by a
covered walkway. Good-sized bedrooms, with contemporary styled suites.
Casual dining in Aromi which occupies part of the vast atrium.

London Heathrow Marriott
🖿 🛖 🔲 ⅇ rm, 🖳 ⬙ 🛋 **P**
VISA ⓿ 🅰🅴 🅾

Bath Rd., Hayes ✉ *UB3 5AN*
– Ⓜ *Heathrow Terminal 1,2,3* – ℰ *(020) 89901100*
– *www.londonheathrowmarriott.co.uk*
391 rm – †£ 149/198 ††£ 149/198, ⬚ £ 18 – 2 suites
Rest *Tuscany* – Bath Rd, Hayes *(dinner only)* Menu £ 27/39 – Carte £ 29/51
Rest *Allie's grille* – Menu £ 29 – Carte £ 29/46
♦ Chain hotel ♦ Business ♦ Functional ♦
Built at the end of 20C, this modern, comfortable hotel is centred around a large
atrium, with comprehensive business facilities: there is an exclusive Executive
floor. Italian cuisine in bright and convivial Tuscany. Grill favourites in Allie's.

𝕏𝕏 Mr Todiwala's Kitchen – Hilton London Heathrow Airport Terminal 5 Hotel
🖳 **P** VISA ⓿ 🅰🅴 🅾

Poyle Rd, Colnbrook (West : 2.5 mi by A 3113)
✉ *SL3 0FF* – ℰ *(01753) 766482 – www.hilton.com/heathrowterminal5*
– *Closed Sunday*
Rest – *(dinner only)* Menu £ 25 – Carte £ 28/49
♦ Indian ♦ Individual ♦ Design ♦
Secreted within the Hilton is Cyrus Todiwala's appealingly stylish, fresh-looking
restaurant. The choice ranges from street food to tandoor dishes, Goan classics
to Parsee specialities; order the 'Kitchen menu' for the full experience.

𝕏 Zen Oriental – Hilton London Heathrow Airport Hotel
🖳 **P**
VISA ⓿ 🅰🅴 🅾

Terminal 4 ✉ *TW6 3AF* – Ⓜ *Heathrow Terminal 4*
– ℰ *(020) 85649609 – www.hilton.co.uk/heathrow*
– *Closed 25-26 December*
Rest – Menu £ 34/47 – Carte £ 27/50
♦ Asian ♦ Fashionable ♦
With its appealing menu of classics and capable service, Zen Oriental has long
been a favourite at the Hilton. Popular for business lunches; the atmosphere is
more relaxed at dinner.

BIRMINGHAM
BIRMINGHAM

Population: 1 073 000

J. Lorieau/Loop Images/Photononstop

It's hard to visualise Birmingham as an insignificant market town, but England's second city was just such a place throughout much of its history. Then came the boom times of the Industrial Revolution; the town fattening up on the back of the local iron and coal trades. In many people's minds that legacy lives on, the city seen as a rather dour place with shoddy Victorian housing, but 21C Brum has swept away much of its factory grime and polished up its civic face. Its first 'makeover' was nearly a century ago, when the mayor, Joseph Chamberlain, enlarged the city's boundaries to make it the second largest in the country.

Today it's feeling the benefits of a second modernist surge – a multi-million pound regeneration, typified by shopping arcades and appealing squares; it now boasts more canal miles than Venice and more trees than inhabitants. It's pretty much in the centre of England, surrounded by Stratford-on-Avon in the south and Bridgnorth and Ironbridge in the west, with Wolverhampton and Coventry in its hinterland. Former resident JRR Tolkien would be lost nowadays, with the undulating contours of the flyovers, the self-important muscle of the sporting, conference and exhibition centres – the NIA, the ICC and the NEC – and the trendy makeover of the Bullring and the Gas Street Basin. Perhaps he would feel more at home in the elegant Jewellery Quarter further north.

BIRMINGHAM IN...

→ **ONE DAY**
The Rag, The Bullring, Birmingham Museum.

→ **TWO DAYS**
Brindleyplace, a trip on the water-bus to The Mailbox, a cycle ride along the canals.

→ **THREE DAYS**
Take the Shakespeare Express to Stratford, Aston Hall.

PRACTICAL INFORMATION

ARRIVAL-DEPARTURE

✈ Birmingham International Airport is 8 miles east of the city. There's a free AirRail connection to Birmingham International Station every 2min. From there, frequent trains to New St Station take 20min.

GETTING AROUND

There is no central bus station – instead, buses depart from various points all over the city; maps are available from tourist offices, libraries and Travel West Midlands. For a single ticket, be sure to have the correct fare ready to pay the driver, as they don't give change. Birmingham New Street Railway Station, located within the Palisades shopping centre, provides train links all over the country, while Birmingham Snow Hill and Moor Street run mainly local services. The Midland Metro light railway links Snow Hill Station with Wolverhampton.

CALENDAR HIGHLIGHTS

March
St Patrick's Day Parade, Crufts Dog Show.

April
St George's Day Celebration.

May/June
Birmingham Pride.

August
Birmingham International Carnival (Biannual).

September
Artsfest.

November
The Motor Show.

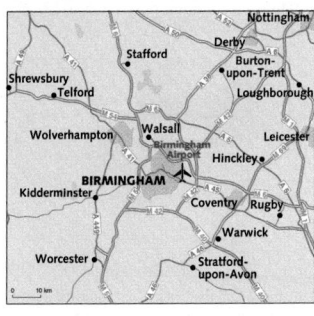

EATING OUT

To the southwest of the city is Cadbury World, the UK's only purpose-built visitor centre devoted entirely to chocolate. It's located in the evocative sounding Bourneville area and staff are on hand to tell visitors the history of chocolate and how it's made, but, let's face it, most people go along to get a face full of the stuff in fresh liquid form straight from the vat. More conventionally, many people who come to Birmingham make for the now legendary area of Sparkbrook, Balsall Heath and Moseley, to the south of the centre. In itself that may not sound too funky, but over the last 30 years it's become the area known as the Balti Triangle. The balti was 'officially' discovered in Birmingham in 1976, a full-on dish of aromatic spices, fresh herbs and rich curries, and The Triangle now boasts over 50 establishments dedicated to the dish. For those after something a little more subtle, the city offers a growing number of lively and fashionable restaurants, offering assured and contemporary cuisine.

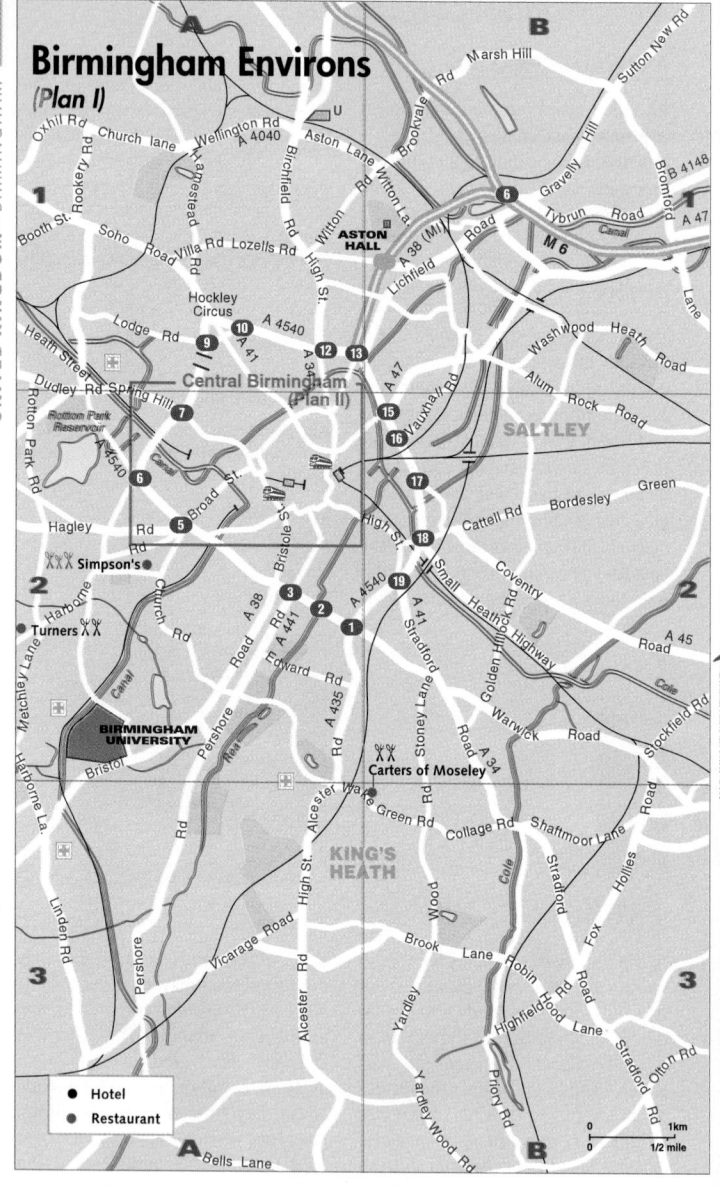

Birmingham Environs
(Plan I)

Hyatt Regency ⟨ᴋ️ 🌐 ⚙ ☒ ⅖ rm, ᴀᴄ 🛰 ᴦ️ 𝘝𝘐𝘚𝘈 ⓿ 🄰

2 Bridge St ✉ *B1 2JZ – 𝒞 (0121) 6431234*
– www.birmingham.regency.hyatt.com **D2**
315 rm – ♦️£ 99/219 ♦♦£ 99/219, ⊑ £ 18 – 4 suites
Rest *Aria* – Menu £ 15/20 – Carte £ 25/38
♦ Business ♦ Luxury ♦ Contemporary ♦
An eye-catching, mirror-fronted, tower block hotel in a prime city centre location with a covered link to the International Convention Centre. Spacious bedrooms have floor to ceiling windows and an excellent level of facilities. Aria restaurant, in the atrium, offers modern European menus.

 Malmaison ᴋ️ 🌐 ⚙ ⅖ rm, ᴀᴄ 🛰 ᴦ️ 𝘝𝘐𝘚𝘈 ⓿ ⓞ

Mailbox, 1 Wharfside St ✉ *B1 1RD – 𝒞 (0121) 2465000*
– www.malmaison.com **E2**
184 rm – ♦️£ 79/225 ♦♦£ 79/250, ⊑ £ 14 – 1 suite
Rest *Brasserie* – Menu £ 13 – Carte £ 19/45
♦ Business ♦ Chain hotel ♦ Modern ♦
One of the few new-build Malmaisons, set next to designer clothes and homeware shops on the site of the old Royal Mail sorting office. Spacious, stylish, contemporary bedrooms; the Penny Black suite has a mini-cinema. Small spa offers good range of treatments. Bustling brasserie serves rustic British menu.

 Hotel Du Vin ᴋ️ 🌐 ⚙ ⅖ rm, ᴀᴄ 🛰 ᴦ️ 🅿 𝘝𝘐𝘚𝘈 ⓿ ⓞ

25 Church St ✉ *B3 2NR – 𝒞 (0121) 2000600 – www.hotelduvin.com*
66 rm ⊑ – ♦️£ 125/165 ♦♦£ 125/165 **E2**
Rest *Bistro* – Menu £ 15 (weekday lunch) – Carte £ 21/44 ✦
♦ Business ♦ Townhouse ♦ Design ♦
Characterful former eye hospital with a relaxed, boutique style. Richly hued bedrooms are named after wine companies and estates; one suite boasts an 8 foot bed, 2 roll-top baths and a gym. Small cellar bar/pub and comfy Bubble Bar for champagne. Classical bistro with a lively buzz and a French bistro menu.

 Hotel La Tour 🛰 ᴋ️ ⅖ rm, ᴀᴄ 🛰 ᴦ️ 𝘝𝘐𝘚𝘈 ⓿ ⓞ

Albert St ✉ *B5 5JE – 𝒞 (0121) 718 8000 – www.hotel-latour.co.uk*
174 rm – ♦️£ 85/250 ♦♦£ 85/250, ⊑ £ 16 **F2**
Rest *Aalto* – Menu £ 13 (lunch) – Carte £ 23/37
♦ Business ♦ Modern ♦ Design ♦
Striking, modern building with a stylish lobby featuring state-of-the-art self check-in terminals. Bedrooms are ideal for business travellers, with media hubs, a TV recording facility and smart, shower-only bathrooms. Extensive meeting facilities and a small gym. Chic café, bar and modern brasserie.

 Hotel Indigo ⟨ 🛰 ᴋ️ 🌐 ⚙ ⅖ rm, ᴀᴄ 🛰 🅿 𝘝𝘐𝘚𝘈 ⓿ 🄰

The Cube ✉ *B1 1PR – 𝒞 (0121) 6432010 – www.hotelindigobirmingham.com*
52 rm ⊑ – ♦️£ 99/249 ♦♦£ 109/259 **E3**
Rest *Marco Pierre White Steakhouse Bar & Grill* – Menu £ 20
– Carte £ 25/45
♦ Business ♦ Design ♦ Stylish ♦
Stylish, modern hotel on the top two floors of the eye-catching 'Cube'. Appealingly styled guest areas and bedrooms decorated in one of four bright colours. Smart steakhouse serving classic dishes, with a champagne bar, terrace and great views from every table.

Hilton Garden Inn Birmingham 🛰 ᴋ️ ⅖ rm, ᴀᴄ 🛰 ᴦ️

1 Brunswick Sq, Brindleyplace ✉ *B1 2HW* 𝘝𝘐𝘚𝘈 ⓿ 🄰 ⓞ
– 𝒞 (0121) 6431003 – www.birminghambrindleyplace.hgi.com
238 rm ⊑ – ♦️£ 89/235 ♦♦£ 99/245 **D2**
Rest *City Café* – 𝒞 (0121) 6336300 (dinner only) Menu £ 20 – Carte £ 26/42
♦ Business ♦ Chain hotel ♦ Stylish ♦
Stylish, modern business hotel in the heart of the lively Brindley Place development. Brightly coloured reception and small, contemporary bar. Well-kept, well-equipped bedrooms; facilities include Apple iMac computers. Popular City Café opens onto a terrace.

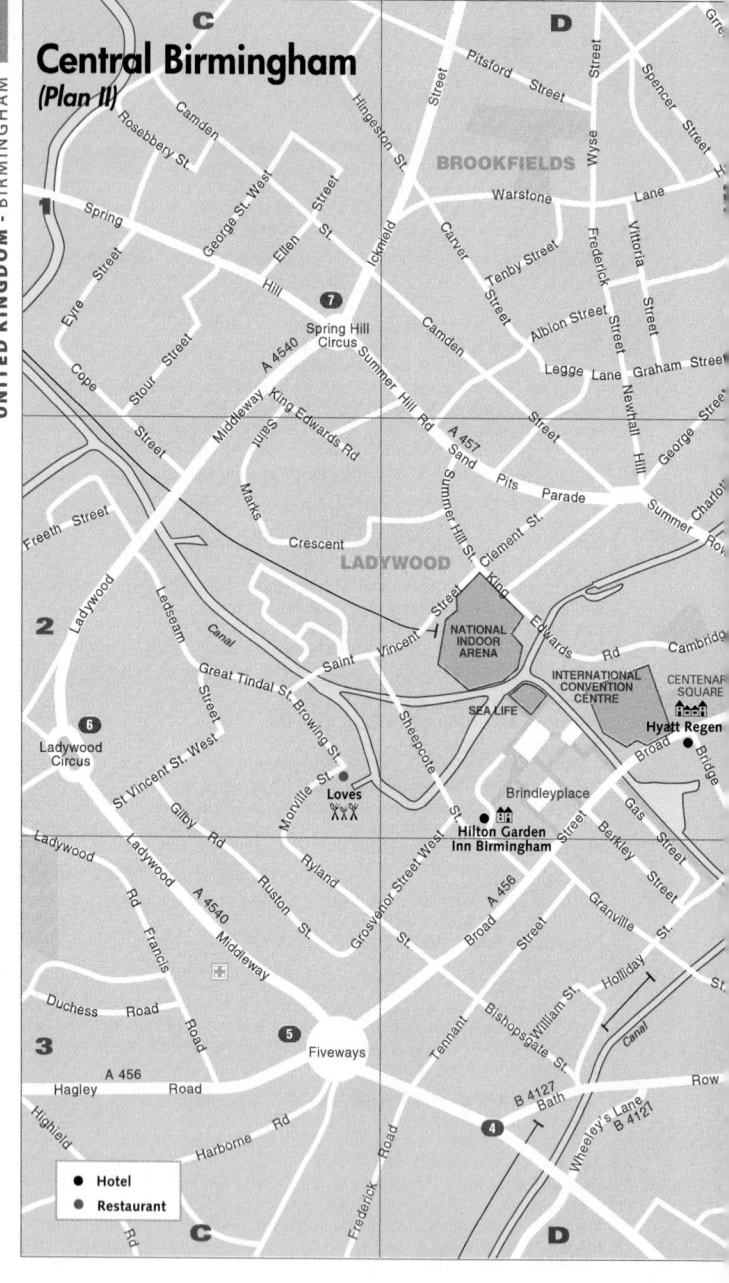

Central Birmingham
(Plan II)

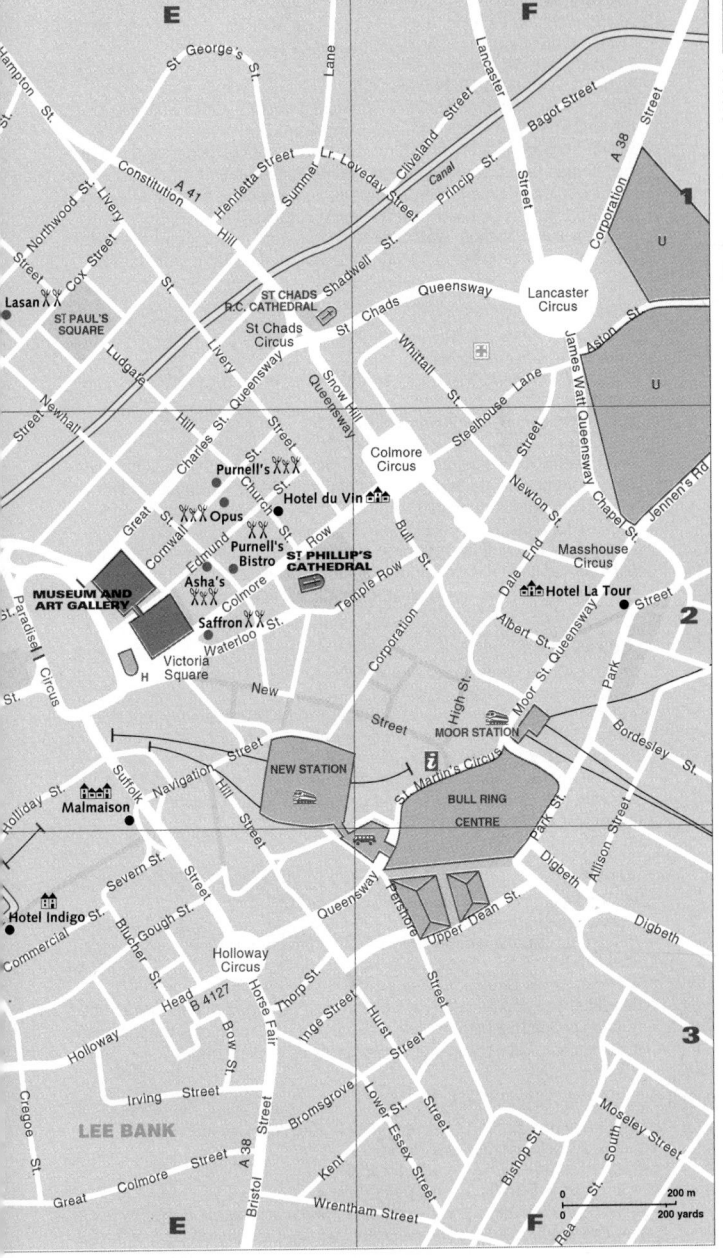

E

F

St. George's St.

Lane

Lr. Loveday Street

Cleveland Street

Lancaster Street

Bagot Street

Street

Corporation

A 38

Street

1

U

Summer

Henrietta Street

Principe St.

Canal

Hampton St.

Constitution Hill

A 41

Shadwell St.

Lasan ✕✕

ST PAUL'S SQUARE

Northwood St.

Cox Street

Livery

Street

Newhall

Street

Ludgate

ST CHADS R.C. CATHEDRAL

St Chads Circus

St. Queensway

Snow Hill Queensway

St Chads

Queensway

Whittall St.

Steelhouse Lane

Lancaster Circus

James Watt Queensway

Aston St.

Jennen's Rd.

U

Charles St.

Purnell's ✕✕✕

Church Street

Colmore Circus

Newton St.

Masshouse Circus

Great Charles St.

Cornwall

Opus ✕✕✕

Edmund

Purnell's Bistro ✕✕

St. Paul's Cathedral

Hotel du Vin

Row

Bull St.

Dale End

Hotel La Tour

Street

2

MUSEUM AND ART GALLERY

Asha's ✕✕✕

Colmore

Saffron ✕✕

Waterloo

St.

Temple Row

Corporation

Albert St.

Moor St. Queensway

Park

Paradise Circus

St.

Victoria Square

H

New

Street

Moor St.

MOOR STATION

Bordesley St.

Holliday St.

Suffolk

Navigation

Street

Hill

Street

NEW STATION

St. Martin's Circus

ℹ️

High St.

BULL RING CENTRE

Park St.

Digbeth

Allison Street

Malmaison

Severn St.

Blucher St.

Gough St.

Queensway

Pershore

Upper Dean St.

Digbeth

Hotel Indigo St.

Commercial

Holloway Circus

Holloway

Head

B 4127

Horse Fair

Thorp St.

Inge Street

Hurst Street

Street

3

Irving Street

Bow St.

Bromsgrove St.

Lower Essex Street

Bishop St.

Moseley Street

LEE BANK

Cregoe St.

Great Colmore Street

A 38

Bristol Street

Kent St.

Wrentham Street

South St.

Rea St.

0   200 m
0   200 yards

E

F

XXX   **Simpsons** (Andreas Antona) with rm   🚗 🛋 AC rest, ♿ **P.**
❀   20 Highfield Rd, Edgbaston ⊠ B15 3DU – ℰ (0121)   VISA ◉◉ AE
       4543434 – www.simpsonsrestaurant.co.uk
       – Closed 25-26 December and bank holidays   Plan I **A2**
       4 rm ⌂ – †£ 160/225 ††£ 160/225
       Rest – (closed Sunday dinner) Menu £ 38 (lunch) – Carte £ 41/54 ⅋
       ♦ Modern ♦ Fashionable ♦ Formal ♦
       Smart Georgian mansion with stylish lounges, pleasant garden terrace and sum-
       mer house. Tables are well-spaced; service is formal and efficient. Classical
       menu displays Mediterranean influences, contemporary twists and excellent
       produce. Spacious bedrooms boast French country styling.
       ➜ Citrus cured salmon, wasabi peas and sesame tacos. Rump of Wiltshire
       lamb, crispy sweetbreads and white asparagus. Raspberry sablé breton.

XXX   **Purnell's** (Glynn Purnell)   AC ♿ VISA ◉◉ AE
❀   55 Cornwall St ⊠ B3 2DH – ℰ (0121) 2129799
       – www.purnellsrestaurant.com
       – Closed 1-14 August, 1 week Easter, 1 week Christmas, Saturday lunch, Sunday
       and Monday   **E2**
       Rest – Menu £ 27 (weekday lunch)/50
       ♦ Modern ♦ Design ♦ Fashionable ♦
       Smart, keenly run restaurant with a loyal local following; its sleek, simply deco-
       rated room proudly displaying photos of Birmingham. Cooking is modern and
       refined with carefully prepared, flavourful dishes served by professional, friendly
       staff. Ask for a seat in the main body of the room.
       ➜ Poached egg yolk with smoked haddock, curry oil and cornflakes. Lamb
       with braised fennel, basil emulsion and pickled cucumber. Burnt English
       egg surprise with warm seasonal fruits and quince sorbet.

XXX   **Loves**   ♿ VISA ◉◉
       The Glasshouse, Browning St ⊠ B16 8FL – ℰ (0121) 4545151
       – www.loves-restaurant.co.uk
       – Closed 2 weeks August, 1 week January, 1 week Easter, Sunday and Monday
       Rest – (dinner only and lunch Friday-Saturday) Menu £ 25/42   **C2**
       ♦ Innovative ♦ Design ♦ Elegant ♦
       Situated on the ground floor of an apartment block on the canal basin, with
       spacious, contemporary interior and smartly laid tables. Cooking uses modern
       techniques and presentation.

XXX   **Opus**   AC ♿ VISA ◉◉ AE
       54 Cornwall St ⊠ B3 2DE – ℰ (0121) 200 2323
       – www.opusrestaurant.co.uk
       – Closed 24 December-6 January, Saturday lunch, Sunday and bank holidays
       Rest – Menu £ 25 – Carte £ 27/46   **E2**
       ♦ Modern ♦ Design ♦ Formal ♦
       Very large and popular restaurant with floor to ceiling windows; enjoy an aperi-
       tif in the cocktail bar before dining in the stylish main room or at the chef's table
       in the kitchen. Daily changing menu of modern brasserie dishes.

XXX   **Asha's**   AC ♿ VISA ◉◉ AE
       12-22 Newhall St ⊠ B3 3LX – ℰ (0121) 2002767 – www.ashasuk.co.uk
       – Closed lunch Saturday and Sunday   **E2**
       Rest – Menu £ 25/45 – Carte £ 18/56
       ♦ Indian ♦ Exotic ♦ Fashionable ♦
       A stylish, passionately run Indian restaurant with exotic décor; owned by renow-
       ned artiste/gourmet Asha Bhosle. Extensive menus cover most parts of the Sub-
       continent, with everything cooked to order. Watch the tandoor chef while you
       wait.

UNITED KINGDOM - BIRMINGHAM

XX ✦✦
Turners (Richard Turner)   AC VISA ⦿⦿
69 High St, Harborne ⊠ B17 9NS – ℰ (0121) 4264440
– www.turnersofharborne.com
– Closed Sunday and Monday   *Plan I* **A2**
Rest – *(booking essential)* Menu £ 22 (weekdays)/60
♦ Modern ♦ Neighbourhood ♦ Formal ♦
Busy neighbourhood restaurant in a suburban parade; smartly decorated with etched mirrors, velvet chairs and 8 neatly set tables. Visually impressive, confidently crafted, flavoursome dishes use top quality ingredients. Only 8 course tasting menus are offered Saturday night. Structured, knowledgeable service.
→ Duck liver with sweet and sour pineapple, coconut and pain d'épice. New season lamb with caramelised sweetbreads and goat's cheese tortellini. Crème brûlée with strawberry, honeycomb, basil and white balsamic.

XX
Carters of Moseley   AC VISA ⦿⦿ AE
2c St Mary's Row, Wake Green Rd ⊠ B13 9EZ – ℰ (0121) 449 8885
– www.cartersofmoseley.co.uk
– Closed 13-26 August, 26-30 December, Sunday dinner and Monday
Rest – *(booking advisable)* Carte £ 30/42   *Plan I* **B3**
♦ British modern ♦ Neighbourhood ♦ Friendly ♦
Stylish neighbourhood restaurant with dark banquette seating, black ash tables and a large wine wall. Modern European cooking features tried-and-tested combinations given a personal twist. Afternoon tea – on Saturdays – is done very well.

XX
Purnell's Bistro   AC VISA ⦿⦿ AE
Ground Floor, Newhall House, 11 Newhall St ⊠ B3 3NY – ℰ (0121) 200 1588 – www.purnellsbistro-gingers.com
– Closed 25-31 December, Sunday and Monday   **E2**
Rest – Menu £ 17 (weekday lunch) – Carte £ 27/38
♦ Modern ♦ Trendy ♦ Fashionable ♦
Glynn Purnell's newest venture is just around the corner from his eponymous restaurant. This simply styled, low-ceilinged restaurant has a lively front bar and offers clever, modern cooking with original combinations. Friendly service.

XX
Saffron   AC 😷 VISA ⦿⦿ AE
126 Colmore Row ⊠ B3 3AP – ℰ (0121) 2120599
– www.saffronbirmingham.co.uk
– Closed Saturday lunch and Sunday   **E2**
Rest – Menu £ 10 (weekday lunch)/45 – Carte £ 24/34
♦ Indian ♦ Elegant ♦ Fashionable ♦
Smart, modern Indian restaurant in the city centre; ask for a table on the raised area overlooking the street. Refined, flavoursome, authentic Indian food: try the more unusual dishes, like the duck or venison.

XX
Lasan   AC VISA ⦿⦿ AE
3-4 Dakota Buildings, James St, St Pauls Sq ⊠ B3 1SD – ℰ (0121) 2123664 – www.lasangroup.com
– Closed 25 December and Saturday lunch   **E1**
Rest – Carte £ 26/55
♦ Indian ♦ Design ♦ Fashionable ♦
Smart, professionally run restaurant on the ground floor of a converted warehouse in the Jewellery Quarter. Authentic Indian cooking has a refined edge; try the unusual beef dishes. Efficient, friendly service.

EDINBURGH
EDINBURGH

Population: 495 360

Doug Pearson/Agency Jon Arnold Images/Age Fotostock

The beautiful Scottish capital is laid out on seven, formerly volcanic, hills – a contrast to the modern city, which is elegant, cool and sophisticated. It's essentially two cities in one: the medieval Old Town, huddled around and beneath the crags and battlements of the castle, and the smart Georgian terraces of the New Town, overseen by the 18C architect Robert Adam. You could also say there's now a third element to the equation: the revamped port of Leith, just two miles away.

This is a city that's been attracting tourists since the 19C; and since 1999 it's been the home of the Scottish Parliament, adding a new dimension to its worldwide reputation. It accepts its plaudits with the same ease that it accepts an extra half million visitors at the height of summer, and its status as a UNESCO World Heritage site confirms it as a city that knows how to be both ancient and modern. In the middle is the castle, to the south is the old town and to the north is the new town. There's a natural boundary to the north at the Firth of Forth, while to the south lie the rolling Pentland Hills. Unless you've had a few too many drams, it's just about impossible to get lost here, as prominent landmarks like the Castle, Arthur's Seat and Calton Hill access all areas. Bisecting the town is Princes Street, one side of which invites you to shop, the other, to sit and relax in your own space.

EDINBURGH IN...

➜ ONE DAY
Calton Hill, Royal Mile, Edinburgh Castle, New Town café, Old Town pub.

➜ TWO DAYS
Water of Leith, Scottish National Gallery of Modern Art, Leith.

➜ THREE DAYS
Arthur's Seat, National Museum of Scotland, Holyrood Park, Pentland Hills.

PRACTICAL INFORMATION

ARRIVAL-DEPARTURE

✈ Edinburgh International Airport is 8 miles west of the city centre. There is an Airlink Bus Service to Waverley Bridge every 10min.

GETTING AROUND

There's no underground or tram system, so it might be wise to invest in a Daysaver ticket for the buses; you'll have the freedom of Edinburgh for 24 hours. There are plenty of guided options for looking around: choose from an open-top bus, a walking or cycling tour, or even a ghost tour of the old town. All bus tours leave from Waverley Bridge and the hop-on, hop-off nature of the ticket will last 24 hours. A great way of gaining access to many of Edinburgh's top sights is by getting an Edinburgh Pass; it gives you free entry to over 30 of the city's attractions and includes many great offers.

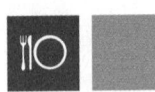

CALENDAR HIGHLIGHTS

March-April
Ceilidh Culture Festival (art, dance and storytelling).

July
Jazz and Blues Festival.

August
Edinburgh Festival Fringe (shows, exhibitions, comedy), International Book Festival.

August-September
International Festival (dance, music, theatre), Edinburgh Art Festival.

December
Markets and funfairs, Four-day Hogmanay celebration (torchlight procession, carnival and street party).

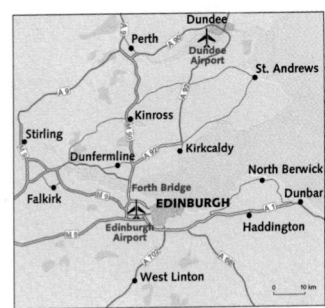

EATING OUT

Edinburgh enjoys a varied and interesting restaurant culture so, whatever the occasion, you should find somewhere that fits the bill. The city is said to have more restaurants per head than anywhere in the UK and they vary from lavish establishments in grand hotels to cosy little bistros; you can dine with ghosts in a basement eatery or admire the city from a rooftop table. Scotland's great larder provides much of the produce, and cooking styles range from the innovative and contemporary to the simple and traditional. There are also some good pubs to explore in the old town, and drinking dens also abound in Cowgate and Grassmarket. Further away, in West End, you'll find enticing late-night bars, while the stylish variety, serving cocktails, are more in order in the George Street area of the new town. If you'd rather drink something a little more special then try the 19C Cadenhead's on the Royal Mile – it's the place to go for whiskies and it sells a mindboggling range of rare distillations. The peaty flavoured Laphroaig is a highly recommended dram.

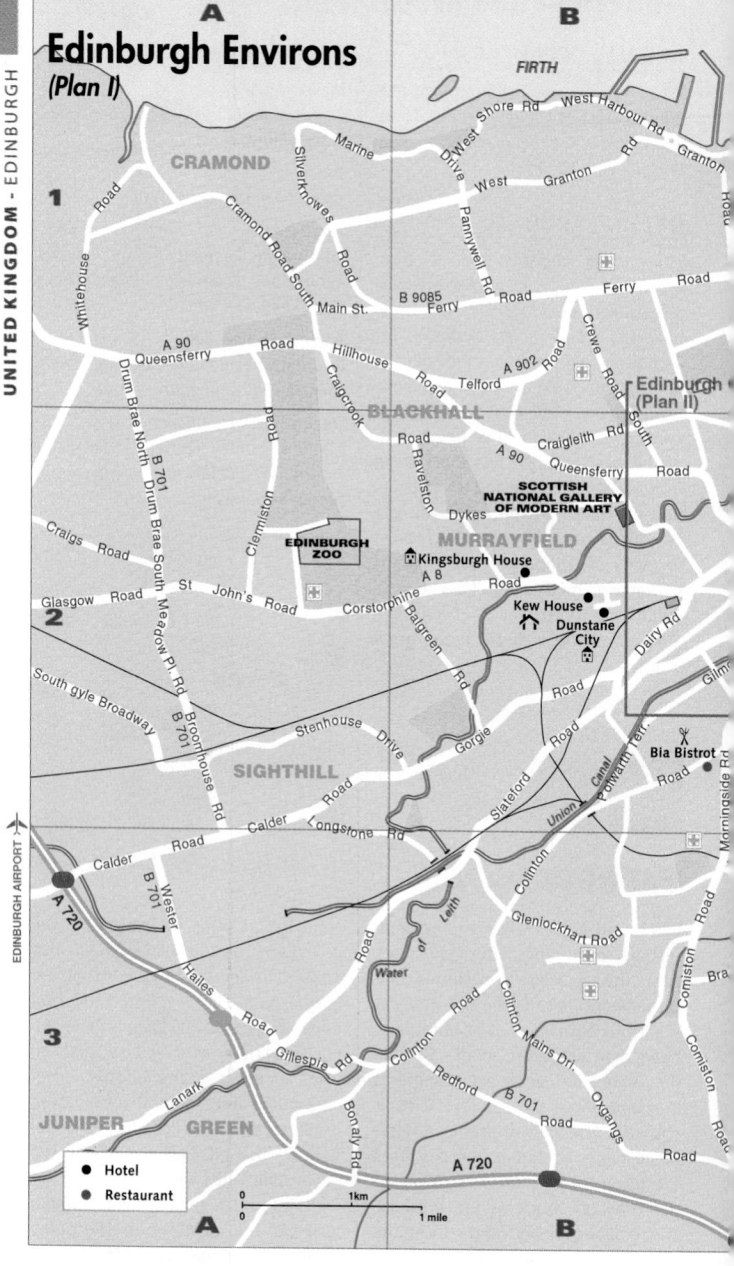

Edinburgh Environs
(Plan I)

FIRTH

CRAMOND

West Shore Rd

West Harbour Rd

Granton Rd

Marine Drive

West Granton Road

West Pannywell Rd

Road

Silverknowes Road

Cramond Road South

Whitehouse Road

B 9085 Main St. Ferry Road

Ferry Road

Crewe Road South

A 90 Queensferry Road

Hillhouse Road

Telford Road

A 902

Edinburgh (Plan II)

Drum Brae North

Drum Brae South

B 701

Craigcrook Road

BLACKHALL

Craigleith Rd

A 90

Clermiston Road

Ravelston Dykes

Queensferry Road

SCOTTISH NATIONAL GALLERY OF MODERN ART

Craigs Road

Glasgow Road

St John's Road

EDINBURGH ZOO

MURRAYFIELD

🏠 Kingsburgh House

A 8 Road

Corstorphine

Balgreen Rd

Kew House ♟

Dunstane City 🏠

Dairy Rd

Glim

South gyle Broadway

Broomhouse Rd

B 701

Stenhouse Drive

Gorgie Road

Road

Polwarth Terr

Canal

🍴 Bia Bistrot

Morningside Rd

SIGHTHILL

Calder Road

Longstone Rd

Slateford Road

Union

Colinton Road

Road

EDINBURGH AIRPORT ✈

A 720

B 701 Wester

Hailes Road

Calder Road

Water of Leith

Glenlockhart Road

Gillespie Rd

Colinton Road

Colinton Mains Dri.

Comiston Road

Bra

JUNIPER GREEN

Lanark Road

Bonaly Rd.

Redford Road

B 701

Oxgangs Road

Comiston Road

A 720

Legend
- ● Hotel
- ● Restaurant

0 ___ 1km
0 ___ 1 mile

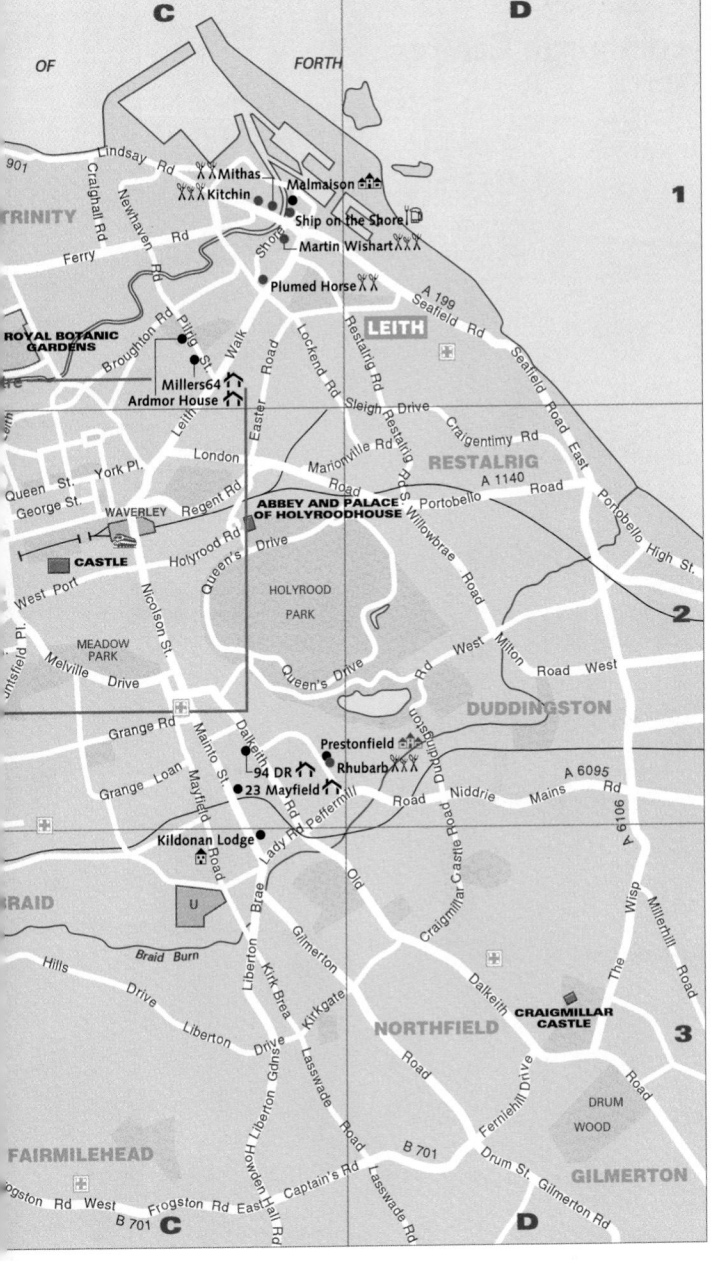

OF FORTH

Lindsay Rd.

Mithas

Kitchin

Malmaison

Ship on the Shore

Martin Wishart

Plumed Horse

LEITH

A 199 Seafield Rd.

Seafield Road East

Portobello High St.

TRINITY

Ferry Rd.

ROYAL BOTANIC GARDENS

Millers64

Ardmor House

Broughton Rd.

Pilrig St.

Leith Walk

Easter Road

Lockend Rd.

Restalrig Rd.

Sleigh Drive

Restalrig Rd.

Craigentimy Rd.

Marionville Rd.

RESTALRIG

A 1140

London

Queen St.

York Pl.

George St.

WAVERLEY

Regent Rd.

ABBEY AND PALACE OF HOLYROODHOUSE

Portobello

Road

Willowbrae Road

CASTLE

West Port

Nicolson St.

Holyrood Rd.

Queen's Drive

HOLYROOD PARK

Road West Milton Road West

MEADOW PARK

Melville Drive

Queen's Drive

DUDDINGSTON

Grange Rd.

Mansio St.

Dalkeith Rd.

Prestonfield

Rhubarb

A 6095

Grange Loan

Mayfield Road

94 DR

23 Mayfield

Duddingston Road

Niddrie Mains Rd.

A 6106

Kildonan Lodge

Lady Rd.

Peffermill

Old

Craigmillar Castle Road

BRAID

U

Braid Burn

Liberton Brae

Gilmerton Road

Kirk Brae

Kirkgate

Dalkeith

NORTHFIELD

Fernliehill Drive

CRAIGMILLAR CASTLE

The Wisp

Millerhill Road

Hills

Drive

Liberton

Liberton Drive

Lasswade Road

Road

DRUM WOOD

Road

GILMERTON

FAIRMILEHEAD

rogston Rd West

Frogston Rd East

Howden Hall Rd.

Liberton Gdns.

Captain's Rd.

Lasswade Rd.

B 701

Drum St.

Gilmerton Rd.

B 701

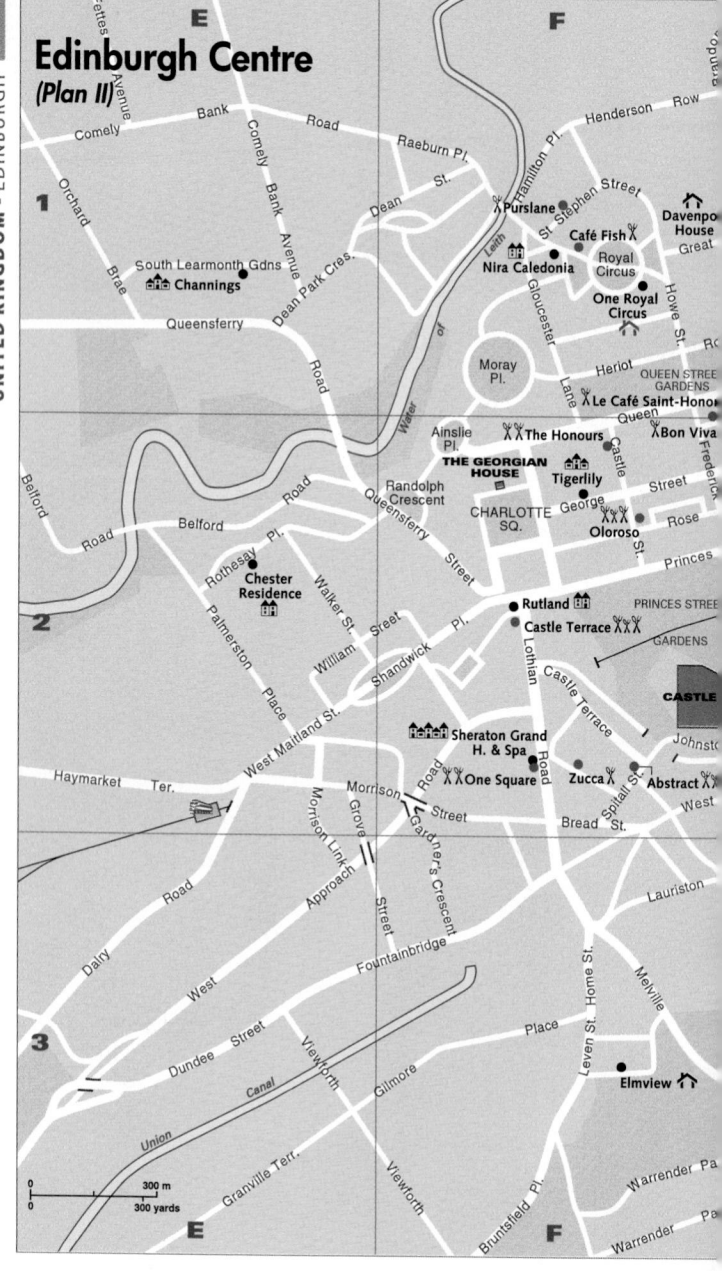

Edinburgh Centre
(Plan II)

E

F

1

Fettes Avenue

Comely Bank

Bank Road

Comely Bank Avenue

Raeburn Pl.

Henderson Row

Orchard Brae

South Learmonth Gdns
Channings

Dean Park Cres.

Dean St.

Leith

Hamilton Pl.

St. Stephen Street

Purslane

Café Fish

Nira Caledonia

Davenpo
House

Great

Royal
Circus

One Royal
Circus

Howe St.

Ro

Queensferry

Gloucester Lane

Moray Pl.

Heriot

QUEEN STREE
GARDENS

Belford Road

Water of Leith

Ainslie Pl.

Randolph Crescent

THE GEORGIAN
HOUSE

CHARLOTTE
SQ.

Queensferry Street

Queen

Le Café Saint-Hono

Castle

The Honours

Bon Viva

Frederick

2

Belford Road

Rothesay Pl.

Chester
Residence

Walker St.

Palmerston Place

William Street

Shandwick Pl.

Tigerlily

George Street

Oloroso

Rose St.

Rutland

Castle Terrace

Lothian Road

Princes

PRINCES STREE

GARDENS

CASTLE

Haymarket Ter.

West Maitland St.

Morrison Grove

Gardner's Crescent

Morrison Street

Lindach Street

Approach

Sheraton Grand
H. & Spa

One Square

Zucca

Castle Terrace

Johnsto

Bread St.

Spittal St.

Abstract

West

3

Dalry Road

West

Dundee Street

Canal

Viewforth

Gilmore

Fountainbridge

Laurison

Leven St.

Home St.

Melville

Place

Elmview

Union

Granville Terr.

Viewforth

Warrender Pa

Bruntsfield Pl.

Warrender Pa

0 — 300 m
0 — 300 yards

E

F

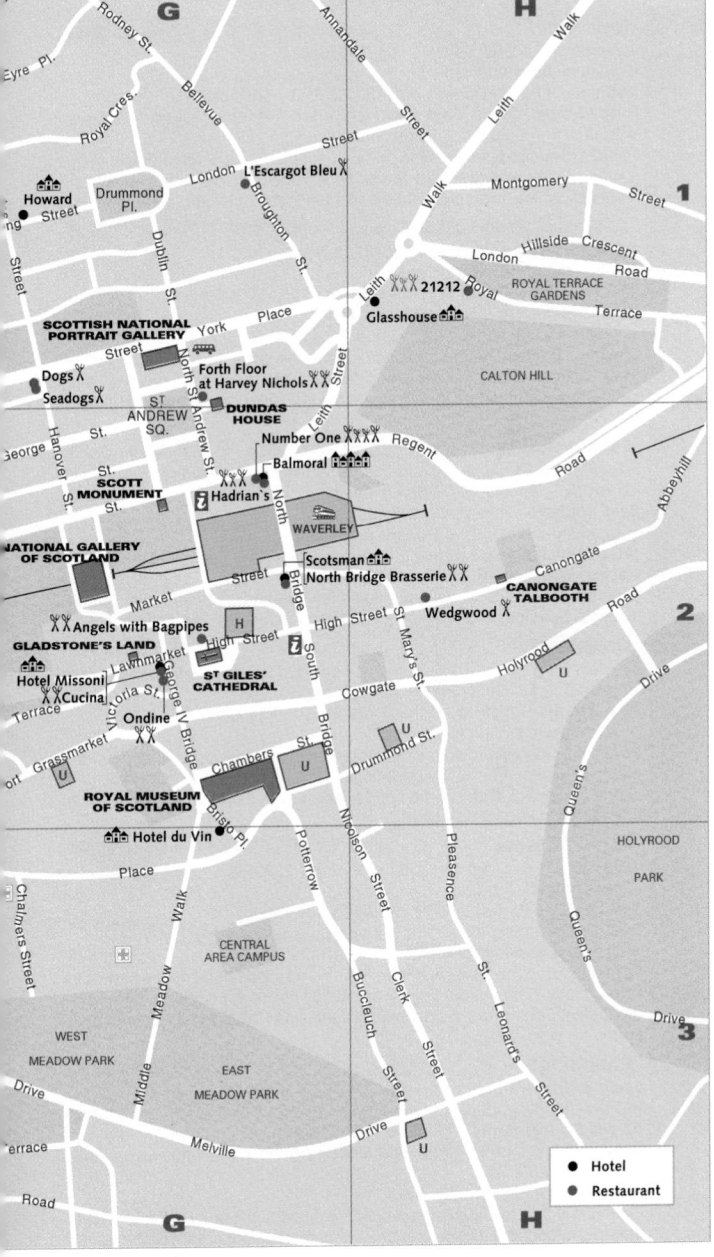

Legend:
● Hotel
● Restaurant

UNITED KINGDOM - EDINBURGH

Balmoral

1 Princes St ⊠ EH2 2EQ – ℰ (0131) 5562414
– www.thebalmoralhotel.com
G2
168 rm – †£ 160/455 ††£ 160/455, ☲ £ 23 – 20 suites
Rest *Number One* ❀ **Rest** *Hadrian's* – see restaurant listing
♦ Luxury ♦ Classic ♦ Stylish ♦
Deluxe Edwardian hotel boasting classically styled bedrooms with rich fabrics and a subtle contemporary edge. Have traditional afternoon tea to the accompaniment of live harp music or try out the cocktails in the bar. Highly detailed service.

Sheraton Grand H. & Spa

1 Festival Sq ⊠ EH3 9SR – ℰ (0131) 2299131
– www.sheratonedinburgh.co.uk
F2
258 rm – †£ 130/450 ††£ 150/450, ☲ £ 20 – 11 suites
Rest *One Square* – see restaurant listing
♦ Grand Luxury ♦ Business ♦ Modern ♦
Spacious, modern hotel which has undergone a top-to-toe refurbishment. Sleek, stylish bedrooms boast strong comforts, the latest mod cons and smart bathrooms with mood lighting. An impressive four-storey glass cube houses the stunning spa.

Prestonfield

Priestfield Rd ⊠ EH16 5UT – ℰ (0131) 2257800 – www.prestonfield.com
18 rm ☲ – †£ 295 ††£ 295 – 5 suites
Plan I **C2**
Rest *Rhubarb* – see restaurant listing
♦ Luxury ♦ Stylish ♦ Personalised ♦
17C country house in a pleasant rural spot, with a dimly lit, opulent interior displaying warm colours, fine furnishings and old tapestries – one of the most romantic hotels around. Various elegant lounges and a whisky room. Unique, luxurious bedrooms boast a high level of modern facilities. Excellent service.

Howard

34 Great King St ⊠ EH3 6QH – ℰ (0131) 5573500 – www.thehoward.com
17 rm ☲ – †£ 120/210 ††£ 160/480 – 1 suite
G1
Rest *Atholl* – (booking essential) Menu £ 32/65 – Carte £ 33/47
♦ Townhouse ♦ Classic ♦
Series of 3 Georgian townhouses displaying characterful original features and plenty of charm. Comfy period lounges. Spacious, luxurious bedrooms with classic furnishings and a contemporary edge; each room is assigned a butler. Fine dining in elegant restaurant.

Hotel Missoni

1 George IV Bridge ⊠ EH1 1AD – ℰ (0131) 2206666
– www.hotelmissoni.com
G2
129 rm ☲ – †£ 160/360 ††£ 170/370 – 7 suites
Rest *Cucina* – see restaurant listing
♦ Luxury ♦ Design ♦ Personalised ♦
Striking, modern hotel; the first from this Milan fashion house, whose trademark stripes feature throughout. Funky bar; boldly coloured bedrooms with clever design features, complimentary mini bar and smart, black mosaic floored bathrooms.

Channings

12-16 South Learmonth Gdns ⊠ EH4 1EZ – ℰ (0131) 315 2226
– www.channings.co.uk
E1
38 rm ☲ – †£ 85/145 ††£ 120/240 – 3 suites
Rest – (closed Sunday dinner and Monday) (dinner only and lunch Friday-Sunday) Menu £ 26
♦ Townhouse ♦ Stylish ♦
Cosy Edwardian townhouse, tastefully furnished and run by a friendly team. Individually appointed bedrooms: the newer rooms are spacious, contemporary and themed after Shackleton, who lived in one of the four houses that now make up the hotel. Formal basement restaurant serves Gallic dishes.

Scotsman

20 North Bridge ✉ *EH3 1TR – ✆ (0131) 5565565*
– www.thescotsmanhotel.co.uk **G2**
67 rm – ♦£ 125/375 ♦♦£ 155/375, ☕ £ 17 – 2 suites
Rest *North Bridge Brasserie* – see restaurant listing
♦ Luxury ♦ Business ♦ Classic ♦
Characterful Victorian hotel set within the old 'Scotsman' newspaper offices. Lovely period guest areas with wood panelling, stained glass and marble staircase. Good business facilities and large leisure club. Traditionally styled bedrooms.

Hotel du Vin

11 Bristo Pl ✉ *EH1 1EZ – ✆ (0131) 2474900*
– www.hotelduvin.com/edinburgh **G3**
47 rm ☕ – ♦£ 109/170 ♦♦£ 119/180
Rest *Bistro* – Carte £ 25/38
♦ Luxury ♦ Design ♦ Personalised ♦
Boutique hotel featuring unique modern murals and dark wood, wine-themed bedrooms; located close to the Royal Mile. Guest areas include a whisky snug offering 300 spirits and a mezzanine bar with a wine tasting room and glass-fronted cellars. The classical bistro offers traditional European-based cooking.

Tigerlily

125 George St ✉ *EH2 4JN – ✆ (0131) 2255005*
– www.tigerlilyedinburgh.co.uk – Closed 25 December **F2**
33 rm ☕ – ♦£ 125/195 ♦♦£ 135/225
Rest – Menu £ 23/38 – Carte £ 23/44
♦ Townhouse ♦ Design ♦ Stylish ♦
Classic Georgian townhouse concealing a funky, boutique interior. Large, individually designed bedrooms are luxurious, boasting seductive lighting, quality furnishings and superb wet rooms. Busy open-plan bar and dining room have similarly stylish, modern décor.

Glasshouse without rest

2 Greenside Pl ✉ *EH1 3AA – ✆ (0131) 5258200*
– www.theetoncollection.co.uk – Closed 24-26 December **H1**
65 rm – ♦£ 115/475 ♦♦£ 115/475, ☕ £ 19
♦ Business ♦ Modern ♦ Stylish ♦
Contemporary glass hotel with 150 year old church façade and impressive two acre roof garden. Stylish bedrooms have floor to ceiling windows and some also boast balconies. Honesty bar and 3 course room service.

Nira Caledonia

6-10 Gloucester Pl ✉ *EH3 6EF – ✆ (0131) 2252720*
– www.niracaledonia.com **F1**
28 rm – ♦£ 99/190 ♦♦£ 135/250, ☕ £ 12.50
Rest – *(closed Sunday) (dinner only)* Carte £ 23/34
♦ Townhouse ♦ Stylish ♦
Luxurious adjoining townhouses with romantic interiors and stunningly restored staircases. Decorated in gold, black and silver colour schemes, bedrooms boast top class furnishings and jacuzzis. Sleek, modern dining room – set in the original house – offers simple, Scottish-based menu.

Rutland

1-3 Rutland St ✉ *EH1 2AE – ✆ (0131) 2293402*
– www.therutlandhotel.com
– Closed 24-25 December **F2**
12 rm – ♦£ 140/315 ♦♦£ 140/315, ☕ £ 10 – 1 suite
Rest – Menu £ 13 (lunch) – Carte £ 26/52
♦ Townhouse ♦ Design ♦ Modern ♦
Boutique hotel with commanding position at top of Princes Street. Stylish, modern bedrooms have bold décor, flat screen TVs and large, slate-floored shower rooms; ask for one with a castle view. Contemporary restaurant uses plenty of Scottish produce in its classic dishes.

Chester Residence without rest

9 Rothesay Pl ⊠ EH3 7SL – 𝒞 (0131) 226 2075
– www.chester-residence.com

E2

23 suites – ♛♛£ 135/550, ⌂ £ 9

♦ Townhouse ♦ Stylish ♦

Collection of townhouses boasting one or two bedroomed suites. State-of-the-art facilities include video entry and sound systems wired throughout. Fully equipped kitchens: the owners provide breakfast items or deliver a continental option.

Dunstane City without rest

5 Hampton Terr, Haymarket ⊠ EH12 5JD – 𝒞 (0131) 3376169
– www.dunstanehotels.co.uk

Plan I **B2**

16 rm ⌂ – ♛£ 89/169 ♛♛£ 109/199 – 1 suite

♦ Townhouse ♦ Stylish ♦

Victorian house with modern feature wallpapers, black granite tiled floors and large chandeliers in guest areas. Stylish, wood-furnished bedrooms offer good facilities; some boast jacuzzis.

Kingsburgh House without rest

2 Corstorphine Rd ⊠ EH12 6HN – 𝒞 (0131) 3131679
– www.thekingsburgh.co.uk

Plan I **B2**

6 rm ⌂ – ♛£ 89/145 ♛♛£ 89/145

♦ Townhouse ♦ Personalised ♦

Attractive Victorian villa with hands-on owners. Comfy lounge and formally laid breakfast room; ornate coving features throughout. Warm, classically styled bedrooms feature antiques, modern facilities and good extras; some are four-posters.

Kildonan Lodge

27 Craigmillar Pk. ⊠ EH16 5PE – 𝒞 (0131) 6672793
– www.kildonanlodgehotel.co.uk
– Closed 25-26 December

Plan I **C3**

12 rm ⌂ – ♛£ 79/240 ♛♛£ 89/240

Rest – *(closed Sunday) (dinner only) (booking essential)* Menu £ 15/35
– Carte £ 19/28

♦ Townhouse ♦ Classic ♦

Well-managed detached Victorian house on main road into city. Spacious and traditionally furnished, with cosy fire-lit drawing room and comfy bedrooms; some with four-posters and jacuzzis. Classical dining, with plenty of Scottish produce.

One Royal Circus without rest

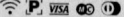

1 Royal Circus ⊠ EH3 6TL – 𝒞 (0131) 625 6669 – www.oneroyalcircus.com

5 rm ⌂ – ♛£ 129/199 ♛♛£ 138/258

F1

♦ Townhouse ♦ Design ♦

Stunning Georgian house at the end of a crescent; designed by William Playfair in 1823. Spacious interior with billiard room and 2 lounges boasting ornate plasterwork, a grand piano and bar. Stylish, understated bedrooms; marble bathrooms.

94 DR without rest

94 Dalkeith Rd ⊠ EH16 5AF – 𝒞 (0131) 6629265 – www.94dr.com
– Closed 4-18 January and 25-26 December

C2

6 rm ⌂ – ♛£ 90/110 ♛♛£ 100/125

♦ Townhouse ♦ Stylish ♦

Victorian terraced house on the main road into the city. Brightly tiled hallway leads to retro-style lounge with honesty bar. Lovely breakfast conservatory opens onto a decked terrace. Stylish, well-equipped bedrooms boast Scottish touches.

UNITED KINGDOM - EDINBURGH

⌂ **23 Mayfield** without rest

23 Mayfield Gdns ⊠ *EH9 2BX* – ℰ *(0131) 667 5806*
– www.23mayfield.co.uk

C2

9 rm 🖵 – ♦£ 80/95 ♦♦£ 100/170

♦ Traditional ♦ Classic ♦

Lovingly restored Victorian house with a very welcoming, helpful owner and an outdoor hot-tub. Spacious lounge has an honesty bar and a collection of old and rare books. Sumptuous bedrooms come with coordinated soft furnishings, some mahogany features and luxurious bathrooms. Extravagant breakfast choices.

⌂ **Millers64** without rest

64 Pilrig St ⊠ *EH6 5AS* – ℰ *(0131) 454 3666* – *www.millers64.co.uk*

3 rm 🖵 – ♦£ 85/95 ♦♦£ 95/150

Plan I **C1**

♦ Townhouse ♦ Stylish ♦

Modernised Victorian house in a renovated terrace, in an up and coming part of town. Smart, spacious bedrooms are all suites and boast good quality linen and extras. Communal breakfasts include a hot special and homemade pastries.

⌂ **Kew House** without rest

1 Kew Terr, Murrayfield ⊠ *EH12 5JE* – ℰ *(0131) 3130700*
– www.kewhouse.com
– Closed January and 25-26 December

Plan I **B2**

7 rm 🖵 – ♦£ 79/96 ♦♦£ 90/185

♦ Townhouse ♦ Personalised ♦

Personally run stone-built house, close to Murrayfield Stadium. Larger than it looks from the outside. Neat lounge and wood-furnished breakfast room. Immaculately kept bedrooms are up-to-date, of a decent size and come with good extras.

⌂ **Elmview** without rest

15 Glengyle Terr ⊠ *EH3 9LN* – ℰ *(0131) 2281973* – *www.elmview.co.uk*
– 1 May-20 November

F3

5 rm 🖵 – ♦£ 70/115 ♦♦£ 95/140

♦ Townhouse ♦ Modern ♦

Occupies the basement of a Victorian house in pretty terrace overlooking The Meadows. Bedrooms are spotlessly kept and very large, with modern bathrooms. Owners are very welcoming.

⌂ **Ardmor House** without rest

74 Pilrig St ⊠ *EH6 5AS* – ℰ *(0131) 554 4944* – *www.ardmorhouse.com*

5 rm 🖵 – ♦£ 65/90 ♦♦£ 85/170

Plan I **C1**

♦ Townhouse ♦ Personalised ♦

Comfortable, laid-back guesthouse on a quiet residential street. Bedrooms range in size and boast bright, fresh décor, original plaster ceilings and granite fireplaces. Homemade bread, preserves and cakes at breakfast. Good local knowledge.

XXXX ❀ **Number One** – Balmoral Hotel

1 Princes St ⊠ *EH2 2EQ* – ℰ *(0131) 5576727*
– www.restaurantnumberone.com
– Closed 2 weeks mid January

G2

Rest – *(dinner only)* Menu £ 64 ఴ

♦ Modern ♦ Formal ♦ Intimate ♦

A stylish, long-standing restaurant located in the basement of a grand Edwardian hotel. The formal dining room feels luxurious and intimate, with plush banquettes and lacquered red walls hung with modern art. Intricate, modern, visually impressive cooking uses prime Scottish produce. Attentive service.

→ Scallops with pig cheek, sauerkraut and apple. Roe deer with skirlie, hogweed and baby beetroot. Banana soufflé with malt ice cream.

XXX ⇧ **21212** (Paul Kitching) with rm 　　　　AC 📶 ⇄ VISA ◉ AE

☒ *EH7 5AB* – ☎ *(0845) 2221212* – *www.21212restaurant.co.uk*
– *Closed 10 days January and 10 days summer*　　　　　　　**H1**
4 rm ☲ – �£ 195/325 ♚♚£ 195/325
Rest – *(closed Sunday and Monday)* Menu £ 28/68
♦ Innovative ♦ Elegant ♦ Design ♦

Smart Georgian townhouse with high-ceilinged dining room, contemporary décor and an open kitchen. The restaurant's name reflects the number of dishes per course; skilful and innovative cooking offers some quirky combinations. Opulent 1st floor sitting room and luxurious bedrooms.
→ Slow-cooked nugget of smoked salmon with spicy jumbo prawns. Fillet of pork, Cumberland sausage and smoked bacon. Strawberry and white chocolate rice pudding with cherry purée.

XXX ⇧ **Castle Terrace** (Dominic Jack)　　　　　AC VISA ◉ AE

33-35 Castle Terr ☒ *EH1 2EL* – ☎ *(0131) 2291222*
– *www.castleterracerestaurant.com*
– *Closed Christmas, New Year, Sunday and Monday*　　　**F2**
Rest – Menu £ 24/70 – Carte £ 45/57
♦ Modern ♦ Design ♦ Elegant ♦

Set in the shadows of the castle, an understatedly stylish restaurant with gilded ceiling and attractive bar-lounge. Refined cooking showcases seasonal, local produce in an assured, unfussy manner, following a 'nature to plate' philosophy.
→ Ceviche of halibut served sushi style. Seared hampe of Scotch beef with crispy ox tongue pastilla. Rhubarb and star anise bavarois, black sesame seed caramel and warm rhubarb soup.

XXX **Hadrian's** – Balmoral Hotel　　　　　　AC VISA ◉ AE ⓞ

2 North Bridge ☒ *EH1 1TR* – ☎ *(0131) 5575000*
– *www.roccofortehotels.com*　　　　　　　　　　　**G2**
Rest – Menu £ 20 – Carte £ 27/49
♦ French classic ♦ Brasserie ♦ Fashionable ♦

Delightful restaurant where a light, bright interior offsets dark floors and brown leather chairs. Brasserie classics display plenty of Scottish produce; excellent value 3 course set menu.

XXX **Rhubarb** – Prestonfield Hotel　　　　🚗 🐾 AC P VISA ◉ AE ⓞ

Priestfield Rd ☒ *EH16 5UT* – ☎ *(0131) 2251333* – *www.prestonfield.com*
Rest – Menu £ 17/33 – Carte £ 35/68　　　　　*Plan I* **C2**
♦ Modern ♦ Elegant ♦ Formal ♦

Richly decorated dining room set within a romantic 17C country house; so named as this was the first place in Scotland where rhubarb was grown. Concise menu of both classic and modern dishes.

XX **The Honours**　　　　　　　　AC 🍽 VISA ◉ AE

58A North Castle St ☒ *EH2 3LU* – ☎ *(0131) 220 2513*
– *www.thehonours.co.uk*
– *Closed 1-3 January, Sunday dinner and Monday*　　　**F2**
Rest – Menu £ 18/20 – Carte £ 24/54
♦ Modern ♦ Brasserie ♦ Fashionable ♦

Owned by a well-established chef; a bustling brasserie with a smart, stylish interior and pleasingly informal atmosphere. Menus take their influences from throughout Europe but have a French leaning and always offer some Scottish dishes.

XX **Ondine**　　　　　　　　　　AC ⇄ VISA ◉ AE

2 George IV Bridge (first floor) ☒ *EH1 1AD* – ☎ *(0131) 2261888*
– *www.ondinerestaurant.co.uk*
– *Closed 1 week early January and 24-26 December*　　**G2**
Rest – Menu £ 17 (lunch and early dinner) – Carte £ 30/45
♦ Fish and seafood ♦ Design ♦ Friendly ♦

Smart, lively restaurant dominated by granite-topped bar and crustacean counter. Classic menus showcase prime Scottish seafood. Straightforward, tasty cooking. Well-structured service.

XX **Forth Floor at Harvey Nichols**   ⇐ 🛋 AC VISA ◎ AE ①
30-34 St Andrew Sq ⊠ EH2 2AD – ℰ (0131) 5248350
– www.harveynichols.com
– Closed 1 January, 25 December, Sunday and Monday dinner   **G1**
Rest – Menu £ 24 – Carte £ 34/48
♦ Modern ♦ Fashionable ♦
Wonderful skyline views from huge room-length window; great sunsets. Bar divides it into formal area with pricier modern European menu, and more casual brasserie; good Scottish ingredients.

XX **North Bridge Brasserie** – Scotsman Hotel   VISA ◎ AE
20 North Bridge ⊠ EH1 1TR – ℰ (0131) 6222900
– www.northbridgebrasserie.com   **G2**
Rest – Menu £ 13 (dinner) – Carte £ 22/56
♦ Regional ♦ Brasserie ♦ Fashionable ♦
Stylish brasserie in a characterful Victorian hotel; once home to 'The Scotsman' newspaper. Beautiful room with ornate ceiling, dark wood panelling and minstrels' gallery. Scottish cuisine.

XX **One Square** – Sheraton Grand Hotel & Spa   🛋 AC ⇔ P
1 Festival Sq ⊠ EH3 9SR – ℰ (0131) 2216422   VISA ◎ AE
– www.onesquareedinburgh.co.uk   **F2**
Rest – Carte £ 22/47
♦ Traditional ♦ Classic ♦ Brasserie ♦
So named because it covers one side of the square, this smart hotel restaurant offers casual all-day dining and views towards Edinburgh Castle. An all-encompassing menu offers dishes ranging from a club sandwich to a modern take on haggis.

XX **Cucina** – Hotel Missoni   AC VISA ◎ AE ①
1 George IV Bridge ⊠ EH1 1AD – ℰ (0131) 2206666
– www.hotelmissoni.com   **G2**
Rest – Menu £ 15 (lunch) – Carte £ 20/46
♦ Italian ♦ Design ♦ Fashionable ♦
Stylish mezzanine restaurant with buzzy atmosphere, set amongst the trademark stripes of this fashion house hotel. Classic Italian dishes served on boldly patterned china; some sharing plates.

XX **Angels with Bagpipes**   🛋 VISA ◎ AE
343 High St., Royal Mile ⊠ EH1 1PW – ℰ (0131) 220 1111
– www.angelswithbagpipes.co.uk
– Closed 24-26 December   **G2**
Rest – Menu £ 12 (lunch) – Carte £ 25/40
♦ Modern ♦ Bistro ♦
Small, split-level restaurant, just across from St Giles Cathedral on the Royal Mile. Simple interior; some tables overlook a rear courtyard. Seasonal menus change every six weeks, offering a mix of unfussy classics and more modern dishes.

X **Dogs**   VISA ◎ AE
⊛ *110 Hanover St ⊠ EH2 1DR – ℰ (0131) 2201208*
– www.thedogsonline.co.uk
– Closed 1 January and 25 December   **G1**
Rest – Carte £ 15/24
♦ British traditional ♦ Bistro ♦ Rustic ♦
Simple eatery set on the first floor of a classic Georgian mid-terraced property; the original opening in the 'Dogs' group. Two high-ceilinged, shabby chic dining rooms and appealing bar area. Robust, good value comfort food is crafted from fresh, local, seasonal produce.

✗ **Café St Honoré** *VISA* **◑◐** **AE**

34 North West Thistle Street Ln. ✉ *EH2 1EA* – ✆ *(0131) 2262211*
– *www.cafesthonore.com*
– *Closed 1 January and 24-26 December* **G2**
Rest – *(booking essential)* Menu £ 16/25 – Carte £ 28/42
♦ French classic ♦ Bistro ♦
Long-standing classical French bistro, hidden away down a side street. Simple interior crammed full of mirrors and bric-a-brac. Affordable daily menu with Gallic touch. Friendly service.

✗ **Cafe Fish** ⌂ *VISA* **◑◐** **AE** **①**

15 North West Circus Pl ✉ *EH3 6SX* – ✆ *(0131) 2254431*
– *www.cafefish.net*
– *Closed 25 December* **F1**
Rest – Menu £ 23 (dinner) – Carte £ 21/31
♦ Fish and seafood ♦ Brasserie ♦ Friendly ♦
Family-run restaurant in a delightfully converted 1930s bank with high ceilings, a fine parquet floor, an open kitchen and a pleasant, west-facing decked area. Daily changing menu of excellent quality, sustainable Scottish seafood.

✗ **L'Escargot Bleu** *VISA* **◑◐** **①**

56-56a Broughton St ✉ *EH1 3SA* – ✆ *(0131) 5571600*
– *www.lescargotbleu.co.uk*
– *Closed 25-26 December, 1-2 January and Sunday in winter* **G1**
Rest – Menu £ 13 – Carte £ 25/41
♦ French classic ♦ Bistro ♦ Neighbourhood ♦
Authentic French bistro with basement épicerie; sit in the front room, with its large windows, gingham tablecloths and buzzy atmosphere. Keenly priced menus offer classic French dishes.

✗ **Bon Vivant** *VISA* **◑◐** **AE**

55 Thistle St ✉ *EH2 1DY* – ✆ *(0131) 225 3275*
– *www.bonvivantedinburgh.co.uk*
– *Closed 25-26 December and 1 January* **F1/2**
Rest – Carte approx. £ 28 ⌘
♦ British traditional ♦ Neighbourhood ♦ Individual ♦
Relaxed eatery in the city backstreets, with a darkly lit interior, tightly packed tables and a cheery, welcoming team. A large blackboard announces the twice daily menu; choose four £ 1 bite-sized starters, then an interesting main dish.

✗ **Zucca** ⌂ *AC* ☺ *VISA* **◑◐** **AE** **①**

15-17 Grindlay St ✉ *EH3 9AX* – ✆ *(0131) 2219323*
– *www.zuccarestaurant.co.uk*
– *Closed 1 January, 25-26 December, Sunday and Monday* **F2**
Rest – *(booking essential)* Menu £ 10/18 – Carte £ 18/32
♦ Italian ♦ Friendly ♦
Friendly, well-run restaurant adjacent to Lyceum Theatre. Head upstairs for classic Italian dishes and all-Italian wine list, with great value pre-theatre menus. Book or come after 8pm.

✗ **Purslane** *VISA* **◑◐** **AE** **①**

33a St Stephen St ✉ *EH3 5AH* – ✆ *(0131) 226 3500*
– *www.purslanerestaurant.co.uk*
– *Closed 25-26 December, 1 January and Monday* **F1**
Rest – *(booking essential)* Menu £ 26 (dinner) – Carte £ 21/24
♦ Traditional ♦ Neighbourhood ♦ Rustic ♦
Set in a residential area in the basement of a Georgian house; an intimate restaurant of just 9 tightly packed tables, with wallpaper featuring a pine tree motif. The chef prepares modern dishes using well-practiced techniques.

※ **Bia Bistrot**   🍴 🆚 ⭘ 🅰🅴

19 Colinton Rd ⊠ *EH10 5DP –* ✆ *(0131) 4528453*
– www.biabistrot.co.uk
– Closed first week January, third week July, Sunday and Monday
Rest – Menu £ 11 (lunch and early dinner) – Carte £ 17/30   *Plan I* **B2**
♦ French classic ♦ Neighbourhood ♦ Bistro ♦
Good value neighbourhood bistro with buzzy vibe and shabby chic style.
Unfussy, flavoursome dishes range in influence due to the friendly owners'
Irish-Scottish and French-Spanish heritages.

※ **Wedgwood**   🆚 ⭘ 🅰🅴

267 Canongate ⊠ *EH8 8BQ –* ✆ *(0131) 5588737*
– www.wedgwoodtherestaurant.co.uk
– Closed 2-24 January and 25-26 December   **H2**
Rest – Menu £ 10 (lunch) – Carte £ 27/48
♦ French classic ♦ Friendly ♦
Popular, atmospheric, split-level bistro with bold white and crimson décor, hid-
den away at bottom of Royal Mile. Personally run, with friendly staff. Well-pre-
sented, seasonal dishes.

LEITH   *Plan I*

🏨 **Malmaison**   🍴 🛁 ও rm, 🆔 rest, 🛜 ⚓ 🅿 🆚 ⭘ 🅰🅴 ⓪

1 Tower Pl ⊠ *EH6 7DB –* ✆ *(0131) 468 5000*
– www.malmaison.com   **C1**
100 rm – †£ 89/175 ††£ 89/265, �£ 10
Rest *Brasserie* – ✆ *(0131) 554 6767* – Menu £ 14 (lunch) – Carte £ 21/57
♦ Business ♦ Stylish ♦ Personalised ♦
Impressive former seamens' mission, set on the quayside; the first of the Malmaison hotels. Mix of bold stripes and black and white décor. Intimate bar and
comfortable, well-equipped bedrooms; one with a four-poster and tartan roll-
top bath.

🍴🍴🍴 **Martin Wishart**   🆔 🆚 ⭘ 🅰🅴
❀

54 The Shore ⊠ *EH6 6RA –* ✆ *(0131) 5533557*
– www.martin-wishart.co.uk
– Closed 1-18 January, 25-26 December, Sunday and Monday   **C1**
Rest – (booking essential) Menu £ 29/70
♦ Innovative ♦ Formal ♦ Elegant ♦
Elegant, modern restaurant with stylish décor, immaculately set tables and attentive, professional service. Appealing à la carte and 2 tasting menus: 1 meat-based
and 1 vegetarian. Fine ingredients are used in well-judged, flavourful combinations; dishes have a classic base and elaborate, original touches.
➔ Baked scallops, halibut skirt and langoustine tails. Loin of roe deer and
braised rose veal cheek with cinnamon. Chocolate cremeux with Yorkshire
rhubarb and fromage blanc mousse.

🍴🍴🍴 **Kitchin** (Tom Kitchin)   🍴 🆔 🆚 ⭘ 🅰🅴
❀

78 Commercial Quay ⊠ *EH6 6LX –* ✆ *(0131) 5551755*
– www.thekitchin.com
– Closed Christmas, New Year, Sunday and Monday   **C1**
Rest – (booking essential) Menu £ 27/70 – Carte £ 57/67
♦ Modern ♦ Design ♦ Fashionable ♦
Converted dockside warehouse overlooking the quay. Expect refreshingly
honest, very flavoursome and unfussy cooking from menus offering considerable choice. Seasonality, freshness and provenance are at the heart of the
chef's philosophy.
➔ Cuttlefish and squid ink pasta with surf clams and broad beans. Turbot
roasted on the bone, braised Swiss chard, lemon and olives. Warm chocolate financier, coffee sabayon and coffee ice cream.

UNITED KINGDOM - EDINBURGH

%% **Plumed Horse**   ⇔ 𝓥𝓘𝓢𝓐 ⓪ ⒜⒠

50-54 Henderson St ✉ EH6 6DE – ℰ (0131) 5545556
– www.plumedhorse.co.uk
– Closed 2 weeks summer, 1 week Easter, Christmas, Sunday and Monday
Rest – Menu £ 27/65   **C1**
♦ Modern ♦ Neighbourhood ♦
Personally run restaurant with ornate ceiling, vivid paintings, an intimate feel
and formal service. Well-crafted, classical cooking with strong, bold flavours
and good use of Scottish ingredients.

%% **Mithas**   🏧 ⇔ 𝓥𝓘𝓢𝓐 ⓪ ⒜⒠

7 Dock Pl ✉ EH6 6LU – ℰ (0131) 554 0008 – www.mithas.co.uk
Rest – Carte £ 22/43   **C1**
♦ Indian ♦ Elegant ♦ Intimate ♦
Smart, 3-roomed Indian restaurant with booth seating. Large selection of
menus centre on kebabs and griddled dishes but there are also many vegetarian options; the set menus offer the best value. Vibrant, tasty cooking. Attentive
staff.

🏠 **Ship on the Shore**   🍴 𝓥𝓘𝓢𝓐 ⓪ ⒜⒠

24-26 The Shore ✉ EH6 6QN – ℰ (0131) 5550409
– www.theshipontheshore.co.uk
– Closed 24-26 December   **C1**
Rest – Carte £ 30/37
♦ Fish and seafood ♦ Pub ♦
Smart period building on the quayside, modelled on the Royal Yacht Britannia
and filled with nautical memorabilia. Seafood menu offers fresh, simply prepa-
red, classical dishes; try the Arbroath smokies or smoked salmon for breakfast.

GLASGOW

GLASGOW

Population: 598 830

Vidler Steve/Prisma/Age Fotostock

The Clyde played a pivotal role in the original growth of Glasgow: in the 18C as a source of trade with the Americas, and in the 19C as a centre of the world's major shipbuilding industries. During this period many of the imposing buildings on show today were constructed; a testament to the city's wealth. This all changed post-World War II, however, as Glasgow's industry fell into tatters and it gained a troubled, poverty-stricken reputation. But Glasgow is also one of the greatest urban success stories: the 1990 City of Culture award turned its image upside down and since then it has grown immensely as an arts, business and retail centre, and tourists have discovered for themselves its grand Victorian façade and eye-catching riverside milieu.

Cocooned within the curving arm of the M8 motorway, the centre is arranged in a neat grid system – and is home to Glasgow's main cultural venues. The 'Merchant City', just to the east, was the original medieval centre but is now a thriving arts quarter, while the West End – a bohemian district filled with cafés, bars and restaurants – has practically reinvented itself as a town in its own right; it's also where you'll find the Kelvingrove Art Gallery and Museum. Cross the Clyde, to the south, and amongst the sprawling suburbs you come across gems like The Burrell Collection and Charles Rennie Mackintosh's House for an Art Lover.

GLASGOW IN...

→ **ONE DAY**
Kelvingrove Art Gallery, Sauchiehall Street, Glasgow School of Art, West End.

→ **TWO DAYS**
Glasgow Green, Provand's Lordship, Necropolis, Science Centre, trip on the Clyde.

→ **THREE DAYS**
Train journey to the Clyde Valley, Pollok Country Park.

PRACTICAL INFORMATION

ARRIVAL-DEPARTURE

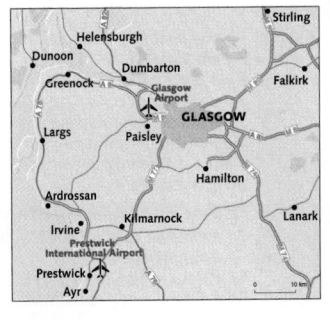

Glasgow International Airport is 8 miles west of the city. The Glasgow Shuttle runs every 10min and takes 25min. The Air Link bus runs every 30min.

GETTING AROUND

Glasgow has a circular underground system covering the centre and west of the city – to go right round it only takes 24 minutes. You can buy single or return fares or 20 multi-journey tickets, as well as day passes (the Discovery ticket) and seven-day passes. A good idea on the buses is to buy a FirstDay ticket from your driver; this will let you hop on or off buses right through until midnight. Black cabs are easy to hail all over the city.

CALENDAR HIGHLIGHTS

January
Celtic Connections.

March
Comedy Festival.

June
West End Festival, International Jazz Festival.

July
Merchant City Festival.

August
World Pipe Band Championships.

November
Whisky Live.

EATING OUT

The dreaded legend of the deep-fried Mars bar did no favours for the reputation of the Scottish diet. Don't mention it in Glasgow, though, because in the last decade the place has undergone a gourmet revolution, and these days you can enjoy good food in restaurants from all areas of the world. There are now many establishments specialising in modern Scottish cooking and fish menus have come of age. If you go to the trendy West End or Merchant City quarters you'll find bistros and brasseries that wouldn't be out of place in France or Italy. Glasgow makes the most of the glorious natural larder on its doorstep: spring lamb from the Borders, Perthshire venison, fresh fish and shellfish from the Western Highlands and Aberdeen Angus beef. It's also always had a lot of respect for its liquid refreshment: if you fancy a beer, you can't go far wrong with a pint of Deuchar's, the award-winning 'Bitter & Twisted' or a Dark Island 'imported' from the Orkneys; the locals have taken to real ale from the Scottish regions in a big way.

GLASGOW - UNITED KINGDOM

Blythswood Square

11 Blythswood Sq ⊠ G2 4AD – ℰ (0141) 2488888
– www.blythswoodsquare.com **D2**
99 rm ☲ – †£ 120/200 ††£ 160/260 – 1 suite
Rest Blythswood Square – see restaurant listing
♦ Historic ♦ Townhouse ♦ Design ♦
Stunning property on delightful Georgian square; formerly the Scottish RAC HQ.
Modern décor contrasts with original fittings. Dark, moody bedrooms and
marble bathrooms; Penthouse Suite displays a bed adapted from a snooker
table. Smart spa.

Hotel du Vin at One Devonshire Gardens

1 Devonshire Gdns ⊠ G12 0UX – ℰ (0141) 3392001
– www.hotelduvin.com *Plan I* **A1**
45 rm ☲ – †£ 125/215 ††£ 135/225 – 4 suites
Rest Bistro – see restaurant listing
♦ Townhouse ♦ Stylish ♦ Elegant ♦
Collection of adjoining 19C townhouses boasting original stained glass, wood
panelling and a labyrinth of corridors. Furnished in dark, moody shades but
with a modern, country house air. Stylish bedrooms; one with a small gym and
sauna.

Radisson Blu Glasgow

301 Argyle St. ⊠ G2 8DL – ℰ (0141) 2043333
– www.radissonblu.co.uk/hotel-glasgow **D2**
246 rm ☲ – †£ 95/205 ††£ 105/215 – 1 suite
Rest Collage – (closed Sunday lunch) Menu £ 18 – Carte £ 27/50
♦ Business ♦ Modern ♦
Stylish, modern, commercial hotel with impressive open-plan interior; set in
central location close to the station. Three styles of bedroom – all offering
good levels of comfort. Spacious dining room with central buffet area and all-
encompassing menu.

Malmaison

278 West George St ⊠ G2 4LL – ℰ (0141) 5721000
– www.malmaison.com **C2**
68 rm – †£ 99/175 ††£ 99/175, ☲ £ 15 – 4 suites
Rest Brasserie – Menu £ 18 (weekday lunch) – Carte £ 28/44
♦ Historic ♦ Stylish ♦
Impressive-looking, former Masonic chapel with moody, masculine décor. Stylish, boldly coloured bedrooms offer good facilities. Named after Billy Connolly,
the Big Yin Suite has a roll-top bath in the room. Chic, glass-roofed champagne
bar.

Grand Central

99 Gordon St ⊠ G1 3SF – ℰ (0141) 2403700
– www.grandcentralhotel.com **D2**
183 rm – †£ 89/269 ††£ 99/279, ☲ £ 17 – 3 suites
Rest Tempus – (dinner only) Carte £ 19/68
♦ Historic ♦ Functional ♦
Renowned hotel built into the main station; the first TV signal broadcast from
London was to this hotel. Smart bedrooms aimed at corporate market. Original
plasterwork in ballroom; marble floors in champagne bar. Contemporary restaurant boasts Murano chandeliers.

Abode Glasgow without rest

129 Bath St ⊠ G2 2SZ – ℰ (0141) 2216789 – www.abodehotels.co.uk
59 rm ☲ – †£ 160 ††£ 170/190 **D2**
♦ Business ♦ Stylish ♦
20C former offices for the education authority. Original brass lift runs up the
centre of a spiral staircase. Small art exhibition; pictures of city landmarks on
every headboard – the best room boasts wood panelling and a feature fireplace.